Random House
Encyclopedic Dictionary
of Classical Music

Random House
Encyclopedic Dictionary
of Classical Music

Edited by
David Cummings

Random House

Library of Congress Cataloging-in-Publication Data

The Random House encyclopedic dictionary of classical music / edited
    by David Cummings.
            p.   cm.
        Originally published: Oxford : Helicon Pub., 1995.
        Discography: p.
        ISBN 0–679–45851–4
            1. Music—Dictionaries.   I. Cummings, David, 1942–
    ML 100.R29   1997
    781.6′8′03—dc21   96–39723
                                                                          CIP
                                                                          MN

Random House Web address http://www.randomhouse.com/
9 8 7 6 5 4 3 2 1
First US Edition
0–679–45851–4
New York   Toronto   London   Sydney   Auckland

Contents

Consultant Editor
Tallis Barker

Editorial Director
Michael Upshall

Managing Editor
Sheila Dallas

Editor
Jane Anson

Assistant Editor
John Clark

Screen Editors
Helen Maxey
Louise Richmond

Systems Administrator
Lorraine Cotterell

Picture Researchers
Elisabeth Agate
Jan Croot

Art and Design Manager
Terence Caven

Production
Tony Ballsdon

Text, page and jacket design
Curtis Garratt Ltd

Quotations compiled by
Anthony Burton

Picture acknowledgements
We are grateful to Zoë Dominic, EMI, Hulton-Deutsch, Image Select, Mansell Collection, Mirror Syndication International, and PolyGram for kind permission to reproduce illustrations.

This book was first published in 1947, under the editorship of Eric Blom, as the *Everyman Dictionary of Music*. Blom revised the Dictionary in 1954 and in the same year was responsible for the nine-volume fifth edition of the *Grove Dictionary*. After Blom's death in 1959, the *Everyman* was revised in 1962 and 1971 by Sir Jack Westrup, Professor of Music at Oxford University. In my own 1988 revision (as the *New Everyman*) I compiled about 1,500 new entries and revised at least 1,000 others.

Now, in this major revision, there has been an addition of 1,500 entries (much of the new material concerned in some way with 20th-century music), expansion of biographies of major composers from earlier times, inclusion of additional works, revision of many existing entries, and updating of musical terms and forms.

The new title of *Encyclopedic Dictionary* reflects not only a significant expansion of the existing text, but also the addition of several important features, most of which appear for the first time in a book of this kind. To the already substantial coverage of opera have been added, in display boxes, detailed plot summaries of 100 of the most frequently performed operas. Hundreds of less-well-known operas now have brief plot summaries, and I am indebted to Tallis Barker for many of these. A further feature starting with the title 'A selection of . . .' lists a choice of works in chronological order for each of 100 composers. The selection is intended as a suggested listening programme to give the reader a representative sample of that composer's range of output. Recordings for the works can be found at the back of the book. Interesting additional biographical information appears in feature boxes for 50 major composers.

To lighten the lexicographical load, there are 200 illustrations, a 'personal choice' from many of today's personalities in the world of classical music, and 400 quotations. Most of the quotations are linked specifically to a nearby entry, either by or relating to the person concerned; all are about music. The *Encyclopedic Dictionary* closes with a list of operatic roles and a chronology that covers every year from 1594.

Arrangement of entries

Entries are ordered alphabetically, as if there were no spaces between words.

Cross-references

These are shown by the symbol ◊ immediately preceding the reference. Cross-referencing is selective; a cross-reference is shown when another entry contains material that is relevant to the subject matter of the first entry, where the reader may not otherwise think of looking.

Works

The A-Z entries for major composers group works in appropriately named paragraphs according to output, e.g. operas, church music, masses, cantatas and oratorios, symphonies, concertos, string quartets, instrumental, and so on. A similar order is usually followed in the single-paragraph listings for lesser composers. However, the order for both lesser composers and for major modern composers is sometimes chronological, particularly if the output of the latter is difficult to define by genre.

Abbreviations

To avoid interrupting the flow of text for the reader, abbreviations have been kept to a minimum. Those that have been retained include some which are widely accepted such as those for American states, music catalogue conventions, standard abbreviations, and a handful of commonly used terms such as: frequently repeated information (e.g. 'first performed' and 'first performance' are written as 'fp', 'orchestra', 'orchestrated', 'orchestration' are written as 'orch.'); and names of well-known organizations (e.g. 'Guildhall School of Music and Drama, London' appears as 'GSM', 'University of California at Los Angeles' as 'UCLA').

*   *   *   *   *

As before I am indebted to fellow lexicographers with whom I have worked: Nicolas Slonimsky and Dennis McIntire (*Baker's Biographical Dictionary of Musicians*), Michael Kennedy (*Oxford Dictionary of Music*), Stanley Sadie (*Grove Concise Dictionary of Music* and *New Grove Dictionary of Opera*) and Karl-Josef Kutsch (*Grosses Sängerlexikon*). Also acknowledged are advice and example from Norman Lebrecht and Desmond Shawe-Taylor, and input from David Fallows as a consultant musicologist on early music and technical aspects generally. And, finally, I am indebted to Tallis Barker for his help and advice from a musicological perspective.

David Cummings

abbr.	abbreviated, abbreviation		**LA**	Louisiana
accomp.	accompanied, accompaniment, accompany		**Lat.**	Latin
AK	Alaska		**lit.**	literally, literary
AL	Alabama		**Litt.D.**	Doctor of Letters
anon.	anonymous		**LPO**	London Philharmonic Orchestra
AR	Arkansas		**LSO**	London Symphony Orchestra
attrib.	attributed		**M.Mus.**	Master of Music
AZ	Arizona		**MA**	Massachusetts
b	born		**MD**	Maryland
B.Mus.	Bachelor of Music		**ME**	Maine
bap.	baptized		**Met.**	Metropolitan Opera House
BBC	British Broadcasting Corporation		**MI**	Michigan
BC	Before Christ		**MIT**	Massachusetts Institute of Technology
BNOC	British National Opera Company		**MN**	Minnesota
BWV	Bach-Werke-Verzeichnis		**MO**	Missouri
c.	century		**MS**	Mississippi
c.	*circa*		**MS**	manuscript
CA	California		**MT**	Montana
CB	Companion of the Order of the Bath		**Mus.B.**	Bachelor of Music
CBE	Commander of the Order of the British Empire		**Mus.D.**	Doctor of Music
CBS	Columbia Broadcasting System		**N**	North
CBSO	City of Birmingham Symphony Orchestra		**NBC**	National Broadcasting Company
cf.	confer (compare)		**NC**	North Carolina
CG	Royal Opera House, Covent Garden, London		**ND**	North Dakota
CO	Colorado		**NDR**	Norddeutscher Rundfunk (North German Radio)
Co.	Company, County		**NE**	Nebraska
CT	Connecticut		**NH**	New Hampshire
D	Deutsch catalogue no. (Schubert's works)		**NJ**	New Jersey
d	died		**NM**	New Mexico
DBE	Dame Commander of the Order of the British Empire		**no.**	number
			NSW	New South Wales
DC	District of Columbia		**NV**	Nevada
DE	Delaware		**NY**	New York
E	East		**NZ**	New Zealand
e.g.	for example		**OH**	Ohio
ENO	English National Opera		**OK**	Oklahoma
EOG	English Opera Group		**op.**	opus
etc.	*et cetera*		**OR**	Oregon
Fest.	Festival		**orch.**	orchestra, orchestrated, orchestration
FL	Florida		**PA**	Pennsylvania
fl.	*floruit* (he/she flourished)		**PO**	Philharmonic Orchestra
fp	first performance, first performed		**pseud.**	pseudonym
GA	Georgia		**pub.**	publication, published, publisher, ...
GSM	Guildhall School of Music and Drama, London		**RAM**	Royal Academy of Music, London
GTO	Glyndebourne Touring Opera		**RCM**	Royal College of Music, London
HI	Hawaii		**RI**	Rhode Island
i.e.	*id est* (that is)		**RLPO**	Royal Liverpool Philharmonic Orchestra
IA	Iowa		**RMA**	Royal Musical Association
ID	Idaho		**RMCM**	Royal Manchester College of Music
IL	Illinois		**RNCM**	Royal Northern College of Music, Manchester
IN	Indiana		**RPO**	Royal Philharmonic Orchestra
IRCAM	Institut de recherche et de co-ordination ...		**S**	South
ISCM	International Society for Contemporary Music		**SC**	South Carolina
K	Kochel catalogue no. (Mozart's works)		**SD**	South Dakota
KS	Kansas		**SO**	Symphony Orchestra
KY	Kentucky			

SW	Sadler's Wells Theatre, London		**VA**	Virginia
symph.	symphonic, symphony		**VT**	Vermont
TCM	Trinity College of Music, London		**W**	West
TN	Tennessee		**WA**	Washington
trans.	translated, translation, translator		**WI**	Wisconsin
TV	television		**WNO**	Welsh National Opera
TX	Texas		**WoO**	*Werk ohne Opuszahl* (work without opus no.)
UCLA	University of California at Los Angeles		**WV**	West Virginia
US(A)	United States (of America)		**WY**	Wyoming
UT	Utah		**Z**	Zimmerman catalogue no. (Purcell's works)

A

A the 6th note, or submediant, of the scale of C major. The note, to which an orchestra tunes, is established by international agreement at a pitch of 440 cycles a second although 415 cycles is often now used for Baroque music.

The note in the treble clef.

Aaron (Aron), Pietro (b Florence, *c* 1480; d Bergamo, *c* 1550), Italian monk and contrapuntist. Wrote on history and science of music; his *Toscanello* 1523, gives advice on musical practice. Worked in Imola and Venice, entered monastery of San Leonardo, Bergamo, 1536.

Aavik, Juhan (b Reval, 29 Jan 1884; d Stockholm, 26 Nov 1982), Estonian conductor and composer. Studied at the St Petersburg Conservatory and became a conductor at Wanemuine in 1911, later director of the Dorpat Conservatory and choral conductor at Reval. Settled in Sweden in 1944.

Works include cantata *Homeland*, unaccompanied choruses; piano sonata in C minor; songs; two symphonies, cello concerto (1949); Requiem (1959).

Abaco, Evaristo, and *Joseph dall'*. ◊Dall'Abaco.

a battuta Italian = 'at the beat, with the beat'; a direction indicating that after a free passage the strict time is to be resumed.

Abbà-Cornaglia, Pietro (b Alessandria, Piedmont, 20 Mar 1851; d Alessandria, 2 May 1894), Italian composer. Studied at the Milan Conservatory and later became a teacher and music historian.

Works include operas *Isabella Spinola* (Milan, 1877), *Maria di Warden*, *Una partita di scacchi* (Pavia, 1892); Requiem; chamber music.

Abbado, Claudio (b Milan, 26 Jun 1933), Italian conductor. He studied with Hans Swarowsky and won the 1958 Koussevitzky competition, Tanglewood; conducted NY PO in 1963. Wider recognition came in 1965, when he made his British debut (Hallé Orchestra), and appeared at Salzburg, Vienna and Milan. He first conducted at La Scala in 1967, became music director 1971 and brought the co. to CG, London, in 1976: his debut at CG had been in 1968 (*Don Carlos*). He took the LSO to Salzburg in 1973 and was music director 1983–88; often heard in modern music and has given works by Nono, Ligeti and Stockhausen (series of concerts with the LSO, 1985, *Mahler, Vienna and the 20th Century*). In 1986 he left his post at La Scala and became director of the Vienna Opera; became music director of the Berlin Philharmonic 1989 and resigned his Vienna post 1991 (opera repertory has included works by Rossini, Mozart, Schubert and Mussorgsky). Founded Gustav Mahler Youth Orchestra 1986, artistic director Salzburg Festival, 1994.

Abbado, Marcello (b Milan, 7 Oct 1926), Italian composer and pianist, brother of Claudio Abbado. He studied with Ghedini at the Milan Conservatory, and since 1951 has held teaching posts in Venice, Piacenza, Pesaro and Milan; director of the Milan Conservatory 1972.

Works include *Ciapo*, cantata (1945); *Costruziono* for five small

Abbado *The conductor Claudio Abbado in rehearsal. Although his off-stage personality is somewhat reserved, his performances are highly charged through his attention to clarity, detail and the immediate emotional needs of the music. He is also known for maintaining a scholarly attitude to the score.*

orchestras (1964), concerto for violin, piano and two chamber orchestras (1967), three string quartets (1947, 1953, 1969), concerto for piano, quartet and orchestra (1969).

Abbatini, Antonio Maria (b Tiferno, now Città di Castello, *c* 1610; d Tiferno, 1679), Italian composer and church musician. Held various posts at churches in Rome.

Works include three operas (including the comic *Dal male il bene* 1653), Masses, motets, psalms, madrigals.

abbellimenti Italian = lit. 'embellishments'; ornaments, especially florid passages introduced into vocal music.

Abbey, John (b Whilton, Northamptonshire, 22 Dec 1785; d Versailles, 19 Feb 1859), English organ builder. Worked in Paris from 1826 and built many organs in France and S America.

Abbott, Emma (b Chicago, 9 Dec 1850; d Salt Lake City, 5 Jan 1891), American soprano. Studied with Achille Errani in NY, later in Milan and Paris, with Mathilde Marchesi and others. She first appeared at

CG 1876 as Donizetti's Marie; New York, Academy of Music 1877, same role. Formed an operatic co. in America, managed by Eugene Wetherall, whom she had married in 1875. Her best role was Marguerite.

Abe, Komei (b Hiroshima, 1 Sept 1911), Japanese composer and conductor. Studied in Tokyo and with Joseph Rosenstock in Germany. Professor of composition at Kyoto University 1969–74. Music is in a diatonic style.

Works include two symphonies (1957, 1960), 11 string quartets (1935–82), serenade, (1963), sinfonietta (1965), cello concerto (1942), piano concerto (1945) and piano sextet (1964).

Abegg Variations Schumann's op. 1, for piano, a set of variations on a theme constructed on the notes A B♭ E G G and bearing the dedication 'à Mlle Pauline, Comtesse d'Abegg', who did not exist, though there was a family of that name. The existence of Meta Abegg has yet to be proved. The work was composed in 1830 and pub. in 1832.

Abeille, Johann Christian Ludwig (b Bayreuth, 20 Feb 1761; d Stuttgart, 2 Mar 1838), German composer, pianist and organist. In the service of the Duke of Württemberg in Stuttgart.

Works include *Singspiele*, songs and keyboard music.

Abel, Carl Friedrich (b Cöthen, 22 Dec 1723; d London, 20 Jun 1787), German composer and harpsichord and viola da gamba player. Worked under Hasse at Dresden 1743–58. From 1759 resident in London, where he was appointed chamber musician to Queen Charlotte. Abel was joint promoter with Johann Christian Bach of the Bach-Abel Concerts (1765–81). Wrote a large quantity of instrumental music, of which the works for viola da gamba are perhaps the most notable. His 40 symphonies and overtures are notable for their advanced harmonic style.

Abel, Christian Ferdinand (b Hanover, c 1683; d Cöthen, 1737), German cellist and viola da gamba player, father of Carl Friedrich Abel. Served at Cöthen under J S Bach, whose unaccompanied cello suites were probably written for him.

Abélard, Pierre (b Pallet near Nantes, 1079; d Saint-Marcel near Châlon-sur-Saône, 21 Apr 1142), French scholar and musician. Composed songs for his beloved, Héloïse, Latin Lamentations, etc. He was castrated after secretly marrying Héloïse in 1118.

Abell, John (b Aberdeenshire, 1653; d Cambridge, 1724), Scottish counter-tenor and lutenist. Possibly a boy chorister at the Chapel Royal in London, of which he became a Gentleman in 1679. Married Frances Knollys, sister of the Earl of Banbury, travelled much abroad, was intendant at Kassel, 1698–99, and returned to England as a stage singer. Pub. some collections of songs.

Abencérages, Les, ou L'Étendard de Grenade, *The Abencerrages, or The Standard of Granada*, opera by Cherubini (libretto by V J E de Jouy, based on a novel by Jean-Pierre de Florian), produced Paris, Opéra, 6 Apr 1813. The story deals with Moorish adventures in Spain.

Abendmusik(en), German, = 'evening music(s)'; evening performances of music of a semi-sacred character established by Tunder at Lübeck in the 1640s and becoming so famous there that they were imitated by other N German towns, especially Hamburg. They were held mainly during Advent.

Abendroth, Hermann (b Frankfurt, 19 Jan 1883; d Jena, 29 May 1956), German conductor. Studied with Mottl at Munich and conducted the Lubeck Opera 1907–11; music director of the Gurzenich Orchestra 1918–34; guest conductor of the LSO 1927–37. Conductor of the Leipzig Gewandhaus Orchestra during the Nazi regime; held posts in East Berlin and Leipzig after World War II; led *Meistersinger* at Bayreuth 1943–44 (CD issued 1994).

Abert, Hermann (b Stuttgart, 25 March 1871; d Stuttgart, 13 Aug 1927), German musicologist of Czech descent. Professor of music at Leipzig University in succession to Riemann from 1920 and at Berlin from 1923. Wrote many historical works, including a greatly enlarged edition of Jahn's *Mozart*.

Abgesang German = 'after-song'; ◊bar.

Abondante, Giulio, Italian 16th-c. lutenist and composer. Pub. several books of music for lute; pieces include galliards, pavans and fantasies.

Abos, Girolamo (b Valetta, 16 Nov 1715; d Naples, Oct 1760), Maltese

(?) composer, especially of Italian opera and church music; several of his operas were also produced in London.

Abraham, Gerald (b Newport, Isle of Wight, 9 Mar 1904; d Midhurst, 18 Mar 1988), English musicologist, specialist in Russian music. Professor of music at Liverpool University 1947–62; Assistant Controller, Music, BBC, 1962–67. Editor of vols. iv, viii and ix of the *New Oxford History of Music* and co-editor of volume iii; wrote *Concise Oxford History of Music*, 1979. CBE, 1974.

Abraham and Isaac Canticle II by Britten for alto, tenor and piano. Composed 1952 for Ferrier and Pears and performed by them Nottingham, 21 Jan 1952.

Sacred ballad for baritone and chamber orchestra by Stravinsky (Hebrew text); composed 1962–64, fp Jerusalem 23 Aug 1964.

Abramsky, Alexander (b Moscow, 22 Jan 1898; d Moscow, 29 Aug 1985), Russian composer. Studied at the Moscow Conservatory. He turned to Soviet ideology by writing an opera on the subject of life on a collective farm (*Laylikhon and Anarkhon*, 1943). Other works include piano concerto (1941) and cantata, *Land of the Silent Lake* (1971).

Ábrányi, Emil (b Budapest, 22 Sept 1882; d Budapest, 11 Feb 1970), Hungarian conductor and composer. Conductor of the Opera at Budapest from 1911. His operas, produced there, include *Monna Vanna* (after Maeterlinck), *Paolo and Francesca* (after Dante, 1912), and *Don Quixote* (after Cervantes, 1917).

Ábrányi, Kornél (b Szentgyörgy-Ábrány, 15 Oct 1822; d Budapest, 20 Dec 1903), Hungarian critic, father of Emil Ábrányi. Part-founder of the music paper *Zenészeti Lapok*, 1860, and professor at Budapest Academy of Music from 1875. Wrote the libretto for his son's *Monna Vanna*.

Abravanel, Maurice (b Thessaloniki, 6 Jan 1903; d Salt Lake City, 22 Sept 1993), Greek-born American conductor. He studied at Lausanne University and with Weill in Berlin. He was in Paris during the 1930s, and moved to NY in 1936; gave *Samson et Dalila*, *Lakmé* and *Lohengrin* at the Met., and then worked on Broadway. He conducted several theatre works by Weill, including the premiere of *Knickerbocker Holiday* (1938), and in 1947 became conductor of the Utah SO. Well known in music by Mahler, Vaughan Williams and Mozart. Retired 1979.

Abreise, Die opera by d'Albert (libretto by F von Sporck, based on a play by August von Steigentesch), produced Frankfurt, 20 Oct 1898). The plot concerns a husband's early return from a journey to test his wife's fidelity.

Absil, Jean (b Péruwelz, Hainault, 23 Oct 1893; d Brussels, 2 Feb 1974), Belgian composer. Studied at the Brussels Conservatory, where he became professor in 1931, after being appointed director of Etterbeek Music Academy in 1923. Among his influences were Hindemith, Milhaud and Bartók.

Works include opera *Peau d'âne* (1937); ballet *Le Miracle de Pan*; radio opera *Ulysse et les Sirennes*; five symphonies (1920–70); four string quartets (1929–41); three string trios and other chamber music.

absolute music broadly speaking, any music not set to words and not based on any kind of literary, pictorial, descriptive or other extramusical subject or idea.

absolute pitch those who can identify by ear any note heard without reference to music are said to possess the faculty of absolute pitch.

Abstrakte Oper no. 1 opera by Blacher (libretto by Werner Egk), fp Frankfurt (concert), 28 Jun 1953; produced Mannheim, 17 Oct 1953. Text consists largely of nonsense words.

Abt, Franz (b Eilenburg, 22 Dec 1819; d Wiesbaden, 31 Mar 1885), German composer and conductor. Studied at St Thomas's and University, Leipzig; later conducted at Bernburg, Zurich and Brunswick. Wrote an enormous number of songs and part-songs.

Abu Hassan Singspiel in one act by Weber (libretto by F C Hiemer), produced Munich, 4 Jun 1811. Abu and his wife attempt to feign death in order to gain a fortune.

Abyngdon, Henry (b c 1418; d c 1497), English musician. In the service of the Duke of Gloucester, 1445; appointed succentor of Wells Cathedral, 1447; Master of the Children of the Chapel Royal, 1456;

was the first to receive a music degree at Cambridge (B. Mus., 1463); master of St Catherine's Hospital, Bristol, 1478, in which year he was succeeded by Gilbert Banastre at the Chapel Royal.

Academic Festival Overture, *Akademische Fest-Ouvertüre*, Brahms's op. 80, composed 1880 and fp at Breslau, 4 Jan 1881, in acknowledgment of the honorary degree of doctor of philosophy, conferred on him by Breslau University in 1879. The thematic material is taken from German students' songs. The *Tragic Overture* was written as a companion-piece.

Academie or Akademie 18th-c. German term for a concert.

Académie de Musique the official title of the Paris Opéra, though never actually called so after 1671. It was first so styled in letters-patent granted by Louis XIV, 28 Jun 1669. It became the Académie des Opera [*sic*] in 1671 and the Académie Royale de Musique in 1672 until the Revolution more than a c. later; after that, at various times, according to the political situation: Théâtre de l'Opéra, Opéra National, Théâtre des Arts, Théâtre de la République et des Arts, Théâtre Impérial de l'Opéra, Théâtre de la Nation, Académie Nationale de Musique, Théâtre National de l'Opéra.

Academy of St Martin-in-the-Fields chamber orchestra founded 1958 by (Sir) Neville Marriner. At first based in London church; director, from 1978, Iona Brown.

Acante et Céphise *pastorale-héroïque* by Rameau (libretto by Marmontel), produced Paris, Opéra, 18 Nov 1751. Lovers are granted telepathic powers as protection against an evil bass.

a cappella Italian also ◊alla cappella (lit. 'at or in the chapel'); a term used now only to designate unaccompanied music for a vocal ensemble.

Accademia, Italian, = 'academy' from Plato's *Academia*; an Italian society for the encouragement and furtherance of science and/or the arts. An 'Accademia di Platone' was founded, on Plato's model, at the Medici court of Florence in 1470. The earliest academy of any importance devoted primarily to music was the 'Accademia Filarmonica' of Verona (1543); later ones included the 'Accademia di Santa Cecilia' at Rome (1584) and the 'Accademia Filarmonica' at Bologna (1666). In France the movement began with the foundation of the 'Académie de poésie et de musique' by Baïf and Thibaut at Paris in 1570, with the aim of promoting the ideals of *musique mesurée*.

Accardo, Salvatore (b Turin, 26 Sept 1941), Italian violinist and conductor. First winner Paganini Competition 1958; has given many performances of the Paganini concertos, including the first in modern times of the E minor concerto (*c* 1815). Works have been written for him by Piston, Donatoni and Xenakis; he has conducted at the Rossini Opera Festival, Pesaro.

accelerando Italian = 'accelerating; quickening the pace'.

accents the metrical or rhythmic stresses of music. Normally the main accent is on the first beat after the bar-line, and in any music divided into bars of more than three beats there is usually a secondary accent, less strongly stressed. But accents are frequently displaced by being marked on a weak beat, transferred by syncopation or omitted on the main beat by the replacement of a rest for a note or chord. Strong accents are marked by the sign > or by the abbreviations *sf* (*sforzando*) or *fz* (*forzando*).

acciaccatura Italian from *acciaccare* = 'to crush'; term now generally used for the short appoggiatura. In old keyboard music it is an ornament consisting of a discordant note struck together with that immediately above, but at once released while the principal note is held on.

An acciaccatura in Bach's Partita No. 3.

accidentals the signs by which notes are chromatically altered by being raised or lowered by a semitone or whole tone. The ♯ (sharp) raises and the ♭ (flat) lowers the note by a semitone: the × (double sharp) raises and the 𝄫 (double flat) lowers it by a whole tone; the ♮ (natural) contradicts a ♯ or ♭ in the key signature or restores a note previously sharpened or flattened to its original position.

It is typical of the muddle-headed nature of musical notation that this term, with its implications of error, should be applied to notes that the composer is particularly anxious should not *be misread.*
Antony Hopkins on accidentals,
Downbeat Music Guide, 1977

---

accompagnato ◊recitativo accompagnato.

accompanied recitative ◊recitativo accompagnato.

accompaniment the instrumental part or parts forming a background to the melodic line of a solo voice or instrument, generally played by a keyboard instrument or by the orchestra. The accompaniment may also be improvised or edited by the setting out of additional parts where the composer's harmony has been left incomplete or indicated only by a figured bass.

Accompaniment to a Film Scene, *Begleitungsmusik zu einer Lichtspielszene*, orchestral work by Schoenberg, op. 34. Composed 1929–30; fp Berlin, 6 Nov 1930, conductor Klemperer. The three movements are for imaginary scenes. (Title *Begleitmusik* etc. is incorrect.)

accordatura Italian the notes to which a string instrument is tuned.

accordion an instrument producing its sound by means of tuned reeds through which wind is driven by pleated bellows opened and closed by the player's hands. The reeds speak when opened by the pressing of buttons and sometimes by the playing of one hand on a keyboard similar to that of the piano.

Achille Italian opera by Paer (libretto by G di Gamera), produced Vienna, Kärntnertortheater, 6 Jun 1801; Achilles and Agamemnon are allies in war but rivals during the siege of Troy. Contains a funeral march said to have been admired by Beethoven.

Achille et Polyxène opera by Lully and Colasse (libretto by J G de Campistron), produced Paris, Opéra, 7 Nov 1687. Left unfinished at Lully's death and completed by his pupil Colasse.

Achille in Sciro, *Achilles in Scyros*, opera by Caldara (libretto by Metastasio), produced Vienna, Burgtheater, 13 Feb 1739. Achilles delayed by love on his way to Troy.

Also settings by Jommelli (Vienna, 1749), Hasse (Naples, 1759), Naumann (Palermo, 1767), Paisiello (St Petersburg, 1778), Pugnani (Turin, 1785).

Achron, Joseph (b Losdseje, Poland, 13 May 1886; d Los Angeles, 29 Apr 1943), Polish-born American violinist and composer. Studied at the St Petersburg Conservatory 1898–1904 with Liadov and Auer; taught at the Kharkov Conservatory 1913–16; emigrated to USA 1925. Worked in Hollywood from 1934, after teaching at the Westchester Conservatory. Later music was influenced by atonality and includes three violin concertos (1925, 1933, 1937, the third was commissioned by Heifetz), *statuettes* for piano 1929, *Sabbath* (1930) and piano concerto (1941).

Achucarro, Joaquin (b Bilbao, 1 Nov 1936), Spanish pianist. He studied with Gieseking and Magaloff. Won Liverpool International Piano Competition 1959; London debut same year.

Acide festa teatrale by Haydn (librettist G A Migliavacca), produced Eisenstadt, 11 Nov 1763. Only fragments survive.

Aci, Galatea e Polifemo Italian serenata by Handel, composed Naples, 1708.

Acis and Galatea masque for soloists, chorus and orchestra by Handel (libretto by John Gay, with additions by Hughes, Pope and Dryden), composed *c* 1718, performed Cannons, near Edgware; first public performance London, King's Theatre, 10 Jun 1732. A composite, bilingual version of this and Handel's Italian serenata (1708) received several performances in 1732. Galatea transforms Acis into a fountain, after he has been killed by the jealous Polyphemus.

Acis et Galatée, *Acis and Galatea*, opera by Lully (libretto by J G de Campistron), produced at Anet at an entertainment given for the Dauphin by the Duke of Vendôme, 6 Sept 1686, fp Paris, 17 Sept 1686.

Ackté, Aïno (b Helsinki, 23 Apr 1876; d Nummela, 8 Aug 1944), Finnish soprano. Debut Paris, 1897, as Marguerite; Met. 1904, same role. First Salome in Britain (CG 1910, conductor Beecham). She wrote the libretto for Merikanto's *Juha*.

acoustics the physical science of all matters pertaining to sound, especially the generation and reception of sound-waves; also, more loosely, the properties of sound-transmission in the interior of buildings.

action the mechanism intervening between the player and an instrument, especially in stringed keyboard instruments, organs and harps (in the last case pedals only).

action musicale French a term used by d'Indy for some of his operas, evidently on the model of Wagner's 'Handlung für Musik'.

act tune a term used in 17th-c. England for a musical intermezzo or entr'acte performance between the acts of a play.

Actus Tragicus name often given to Bach's church cantata no. 106, *Gottes Zeit ist die allerbeste Zeit*. Composed *c* 1707 for a funeral.

adagietto Italian = lit. 'a little adagio'; a tempo direction indicating a pace slightly quicker than *adagio*. Best-known example is the fourth movement of Mahler's 5th symphony.

adagio Italian *ad agio* = 'at ease, comfortably, at a slow pace'; the word is also used as a noun for a slow piece or movement.

Adam, Adolphe (Charles) (b Paris, 24 Jul 1803; d Paris, 3 May 1856), French composer, best known today for the ballet *Giselle*. Allowed to study at the Paris Conservatory only as an amateur. Wrote about 20 vaudeville pieces for three Paris theatres, 1824–29, then wrote an operetta, *Pierre et Catherine*, at the Opéra-Comique in 1829 and his first opera, *Danilowa*, in 1830. Wrote about 80 works for the stage and in 1847 started a new operatic venture, Théâtre National. Member of the Institut, 1844, and professor of composition at the Conservatory, 1849.

Works include operas *Le Châlet* (1834), *Le Postillon de Lonjumeau* (1836), *La Poupée de Nuremberg, Si j'étais roi* (1852), *Falstaff* (1856), *Richard en Palestine* (after Scott), etc.; ballets *Faust* (1833), *Giselle* (1841).

Adam, Claus (b Central Sumatra, 5 Nov 1917; d New York, 4 July 1983), American cellist and composer. Studied at the Salzburg Mozarteum and with Feuermann in New York; studied composition with Stefan Wolpe. He was a founding member of the New Music Quartet 1948–55, and was cellist of the Juilliard Quartet until 1974, giving many premieres of American works, and music by the Second Viennese School. He was composer-in-residence at the American Academy in Rome 1976, and the following year his Variations for Orchestra were performed in NY; he wrote a cello concerto for Stephen Kates 1973.

Adam, Theo (b Dresden, 1 Aug 1926), German bass-baritone and producer. Debut Dresden 1949. Berlin and Bayreuth from 1952; CG 1967 (Wotan), NY Met. 1969 (Sachs). Sang title roles in Cerha's *Baal*, Salzburg 1981 and Berio's *Un re in ascolto*, Salzburg 1984. Other roles included Wozzeck, Ochs and Don Giovanni. Produced Graun's *Cesare e Cleopatra* for the 250th anniversary of the Berlin Staatsoper, 1992.

Adamberger, Valentin (b Munich, 6 Jul 1743; d Vienna, 24 Aug 1804), German tenor. Studied and sang in Italy, appeared in London in 1777 and went to Vienna, becoming a member of the German opera in 1780 and of the Imperial Chapel in 1789. Sang Belmonte in the fp of Mozart's *Entführung*.

Adam de la Halle see ◊La Halle.

Adams, Byron (b Atlanta, 9 Mar 1955), American composer and conductor. Studied at UCLA and Cornell University (lectured at the latter 1985–87). Teacher at University of California at Riverside from 1987.

Works include quintet for piano and strings (1979), concert for trumpet and strings (1983), violin concerto (1984), *Missa Brevis* (1988), *Three Epitaphs* (1988).

Adams, Charles (b Charlestown, MA, 9 Feb 1843; d Charlestown, 4 Jul 1900), American tenor. He sang in Haydn's *Creation* at Boston, in 1856. Between 1867 and 1876 first tenor at the Opera in Vienna; made his first real success in USA in 1877 (first US Rienzi, Academy of Music, 1878).

Adams, John (b Worcester, MA, 15 Feb 1947), American composer and conductor. Studied at Harvard under Kirchner and Del Tredici. Head of composition, San Francisco Conservatory, 1971–81. Composer-in-residence with the San Francisco SO. A leading member of the minimalist school of composers, his best-known piece is *Grand Pianola Music*, for two pianos, two sopranos and mezzo (fp 1982).

Works include operas *Nixon in China* (1987) and *The Death of Klinghoffer* (1991); *Common Tones in Simple Time* for orchestra (1979); *Harmonium* for chorus and orchestra (texts by Donne and Dickinson, 1981); *Shaker Loops* for strings (1978); *Bridge of Dreams* for orchestra (1982–83); *Tromba lontana* (1986); *Short Ride in a Fast Machine*, for orchestra (1986); *Fearful Symmetries* for orchestra (1988); *The Wound Dresser* for baritone and orchestra (1989); *Eros Piano* for piano and orchestra (1989); violin concerto (1993); *I was Looking at the Ceiling and then I Saw the Sky* (1995).

What steals the show is a stunning array of vivid backcloths painted by 26 of California's finest graffiti artists.

Richard Morrison in *The Times* on *I was Looking at the Ceiling and then I Saw the Sky* by John Adams

---

Adams, Suzanne (b Cambridge, MA, 28 Nov 1872; d London, 5 Feb 1953), American soprano. Debut Paris, Opéra, 1895, Juliette; CG 1898 in same role. Created Hero in Stanford's *Much Ado about Nothing*, CG 1901. She married the cellist Leo Stern.

Adam und Eva opera by Theile (libretto by C Richter), produced Hamburg, at the opening of the first established German opera house, Theater beim Gänsemarkt, 12 Jan 1678.

Adam Zero ballet by Bliss (scenario by M Benthall, choreography by Robert Helpmann), produced London, CG, 8 Apr 1946.

added sixth a term invented by Rameau (*sixte ajoutée*) to describe the addition of a 6th from the bass to a subdominant chord when it is followed by the tonic chord.

An added sixth in the key of C major.

Addinsell, Richard (b Oxford, 13 Jan 1904; d London, 14 Nov 1977), English composer. He gained brief fame for his Rakhmaninov rip-off, the *Warsaw* concerto. Studied law at Hertford College, Oxford, but became interested in theatre music and studied at the RCM in London. In 1929–32 he studied abroad, mainly in Berlin and Vienna; in 1933 he visited the USA and wrote film music in Hollywood.

Works include much incidental music for films, theatre (including plays by Clemence Dane) and radio. His greatest success was music for the film *Dangerous Moonlight*, which included the *Warsaw* concerto for piano and orchestra. He also composed light music and songs for theatre revues.

Addison, John (b London, *c* 1766; d London, 30 Jan 1844), English double bass player and composer. His wife (born Willems) sang at Vauxhall Gardens in London; then both went to Liverpool and Dublin, returning to London in 1796 and proceeding to Bath, Dublin and Manchester. From 1805, when he wrote music for Skeffington's *Sleeping Beauty*, he had a number of stage successes in London.

additional accompaniments additional orchestral parts added to old oratorios and other works left by the composers in an incomplete state; to be played originally by the continuo player at the organ or harpsichord. The most familiar examples are Mozart's additional accompaniments for Handel's *Messiah*.

Adelaide song by Beethoven to words by Friedrich von Matthisson, composed 1795–96 and dedicated to the poet.

'Adélaïde' Concerto a violin concerto edited by Marius Casadesus in the early 1930s from a sketch supposedly written by Mozart and dedicated to Princess Adélaïde of France in 1766. It was in fact composed by Casadesus.

Adelson e Salvini opera by Bellini (his first) with libretto by A L Tottola. Produced Naples, San Sebastiano Conservatory, early 1825; revised 1826 with recitative replacing dialogue. Salvini, infatuated by Adelson's fiancée Nelly, recovers his senses after believing he has killed her.

Adeney, Richard (b London, 25 Jan 1920), English flautist. First concert 1938, *St Matthew Passion* under Vaughan Williams. Principal flautist LPO 1941–50 and 1960–69; has played with the Melos Ensemble and the English Chamber Orchestra; often heard as soloist.

Adieux, l'absence et le retour, Les, *Farewell, Absence and Return*, title given by Beethoven's pub. for his piano sonata in E♭ major, op. 81a, composed in 1809–10 and dedicated to the Archduke Rudolph to commemorate his absence from Vienna during the occupation by the French.

Adler, Guido (b Eibenschütz, Moravia, 1 Nov 1855; d Vienna, 15 Feb 1941), Czech-German musicologist and editor. Studied in Vienna; appointed professor of musicology at Prague University, 1885, and professor in Vienna, 1898, in succession to Hanslick. Wrote many books on music inc. studies of Wagner (1904) and Mahler (1916) and edited *Handbuch der Musikgeschichte*, 1924.

Adler, Kurt (b Neuhaus, Bohemia, 1 Mar 1907; d Butler, NJ, 21 Sept 1977), American pianist and conductor. He studied at Vienna; worked at the Berlin Staatsoper 1927–29 and at the German Opera, Prague, 1929–32. He conducted at the Kiev Opera and with the Stalingrad PO after the Nazis came to power; in 1938 moved to the USA. Worked first as a pianist and conductor at the NY Met. 1951–73 (debut with *Die Zauberflöte*). Edited various vocal editions.

Adler, Kurt Herbert (b Vienna, 2 Apr 1905; d Ross, CA, 9 Feb 1988), Austrian-born American conductor and manager. He studied in Vienna and conducted there until leaving for the USA in 1938; Chicago Opera 1938–43, then engaged by the San Francisco Opera. He became general director in 1956 and did much to raise standards of opera performance on the West Coast.

Adler, Larry (Lawrence) (b Baltimore, 10 Feb 1914), American harmonica virtuoso, settled in UK since 1949. Won a competition aged 13, and has since travelled widely, including command performances before King George VI, King Gustav of Sweden, Presidents Roosevelt and Truman. Learned to read music in 1940 and studied with Toch. Many composers have written for him, including Milhaud and Vaughan Williams.

Adler, Peter Hermann (b Jablonec, 2 Dec 1899; d Ridgefield, CT, 2 Oct 1990), Czech-born American conductor. He studied in Prague with Zemlinsky and conducted in Brno, Bremen and Kiev; left for USA in 1938. He assisted Fritz Busch in founding the New Opera Company NY (1941) and from 1949 was director NBC television opera; founded NET opera 1969 and gave the first US performance of Janáček's *From the House of the Dead*. Music director Baltimore SO 1959–67.

Adler, Samuel (b Mannheim, 4 Mar 1928), German-born American composer. He moved to the USA aged 11 and studied with Piston and Thompson at Harvard and with Copland and Koussevitzky at Tanglewood. Professor of composition at Eastman School, Rochester, from 1966.

Works include operas *The Outcasts of Poker Flat* (1962) and *The Wrestler* (1972); *The Disappointment*, reconstruction of an American ballad opera of 1767; six symphonies (1953–83); organ concerto (1970); concerto for orchestra (1977), flute concerto (1977); seven string quartets (1945–81); four violin sonatas (1948–65); *From out of Bondage*, cantata (1969); *The Vision of Isaiah* for bass, chorus and orchestra (1963); piano concerto (1983).

Adlgasser, Anton Cajetan (b Inzel, Bavaria, 1 Oct 1729; d Salzburg, 22 Dec 1777), German organist and composer. A pupil of Eberlin in Salzburg, he was first organist of the cathedral there from 1750. His church music was highly valued by Mozart. Wrote oratorio, *Christus am Ölberg*, performed Salzburg 1754. With Michael Haydn and Mozart he shared in the oratorio *Die Schuldigkeit des ertsen Gebotes* (1767).

ad lib abbr. of Latin *ad libitum* = 'at pleasure'; a direction indicating that a passage may be played freely according to the performer's fancy. The term also applies to an instrumental part that may be added or omitted in the performance of a work.

Adlung, Jakob (b Bindersleben near Erfurt, 14 Jan 1699; d Erfurt, 5 Jul 1762), German organist and scholar. Organist in Erfurt from 1727, and professor at the *Gymnasium* there from 1741. Author of important music treatises.

Admeto rè di Tessaglia, *Admetus, King of Thessaly*), opera by Handel (librettist N F Haym or P A Rolli), produced London, King's Theatre, Haymarket, 31 Jan 1727. Alcestis promises to sacrifice herself to save Admetus; a vehicle for the rival sopranos Cuzzoni and Faustina Bordoni.

Adni, Daniel (b Haifa, 6 Dec 1951), Israeli pianist. Debut Haifa 1963; studied with Perlemuter in Paris and Anda in Zurich. London debut 1970; tours of Europe and USA in Romantic repertory.

Adolfati, Andrea (b Venice, c 1721; d Genoa, 28 Oct 1760), Italian composer. Pupil of Galuppi at Venice. Held church posts there and wrote several operas, including *Artaserse*, *Arianna*, *Adriano in Siria* and *La clemenza di Tito*.

Adorno, Theodor Wiesengrund (b Frankfurt, 11 Sept 1903; d Geneva, 6 Aug 1969), German writer on music. Studied with Sekles in Frankfurt and Alban Berg in Vienna. Music critic in Frankfurt and taught at the university. Emigrated to USA in 1934, working in connection with radio research at Princeton (1938–41). In 1950 returned to Frankfurt and became professor at the university. His writings, which have influenced the younger generation of composers, include *Philosophie der neuen Musik* (1949), and *Klangfiguren* (1959). He was a champion of Schoenberg and was consulted by Thomas Mann for the novel *Dr Faustus*.

Adrastus (b Philippi, Macedonia, ?), Greek 4th-c.BC philosopher. Pupil of Aristotle; wrote a treatise on acoustics, *Harmonicon biblia tria*.

Adriaensen, Emmanuel (b Antwerp, c 1554; d Antwerp, buried 27 Feb 1604), 16th-c. lutenist. Pub. books of lute pieces. Also known as Hadrianus.

Adriana Lecouvreur opera by Cilea (libretto by A Colautti, based on the play *Adrienne Lecouvreur* by Scribe and E Legouvé), produced Milan, Teatro Lirico, 6 Nov 1902. Adriana meets a violent death from poisoned violets, given by a rival in love.

Adriano in Siria, *Hadrian in Syria*, opera by Pergolesi (libretto by Metastasio), produced Naples, Teatro San Bartolommeo, with the intermezzi *Livietta e Tracollo*, 25 Oct 1734. Also settings by Caldara (Vienna, 1732), Galuppi (Turin, 1740), Hasse (Dresden, 1752), J C Bach (London, 1765), Holzbauer (Mannheim, 1768), Anfossi (Padua, 1777), Cherubini (Livorno, 1782), Mayr (Venice, 1798).

Adson, John (d London, c 1640), English musician and composer. He was a member of Charles I's household and pub. *Courtly Masquing Ayres* for various instruments in 1611.

a due Italian = 'in two parts'; generally written '*a* 2'. The term is also used in the opposite sense in orchestral scores where pairs of instruments are to play in unison.

Aegyptische Helena, Strauss, ◊Ägyptische Helena.

Aenéas ballet with chorus by Roussel. Composed 1935, fp Brussels 31 Jul 1935.

Aeneas i Carthago opera by J M Kraus (libretto by J H Kellgren), produced Stockholm, 18 Nov 1799; revived in concert form, Stockholm and NY 1980.

aeolian mode the scale represented by the white keys of the piano beginning on the note A. ◊Ionian mode.

aeoliophone ◊wind machine.

aerophor (or *aerophon*) a German instrument invented by Bernhard Samuel and patented in 1911, with the aid of which wind instruments can sustain notes indefinitely. R Strauss used it in the *Alpensinfonie* and *Festliches Praeludium*.

Aeschylus 525–456BC Greek dramatist, ◊Halévy (*Prometheus*), Hauer (ditto), Honegger (*Prometheus* and *Les Suppliantes*), Meyerbeer (*Eumenides*), Milhaud (*Agamemnon, Choéphares* and *Eumenides*), Oresteia (Taneiev), Parry (H) (*Agamemnon*), Pizzetti (ditto), Prométhée (Fauré), Prometheus (Orff), Schillings (*Orestes*).

Agnus Dei, Latin, = 'Lamb of God'; the fifth and last item of the Ordinary of the ◊Mass. Originally a part of the Litany, it was first introduced into the Roman Mass towards the end of the 7th c. It is not present in the Ambrosian rite. Its text is tripartite in structure, and its music in its simplest form consists of three statements of the same melody.

More complex plainsong settings exist and in the later Middle Ages numerous additional melodies were written. The Agnus Dei is naturally included in polyphonic settings of the Mass Ordinary, and in later settings of the same series of texts.

1 A - gnus De - i, qui tol - lis pec - ca - ta mun-di: 1 mi - se - re - re no - bis
2   2
3   3 do -na no - bis pa - cem

A plainsong setting of the Agnus Dei.

aetherophone, from Greek, an electrophonic instrument invented by Lev Theremin of Leningrad in 1924, producing notes from the air, the pitch of which was determined by movements of the hand but could not be definitely fixed according to the normal chromatic scale, the transitions between the notes producing a sliding wail like that of a siren. But ◊theremin.

Affektenlehre German 'doctrine of affections'; 18th-c. aesthetic theory, associated particularly with J J Quantz and C P E Bach, according to which music should be directly expressive of particular emotions. ◊Empfindsamer Stil.

affettuoso Italian = 'affectionate, feeling' (adv. *affettuosamente*).

Affré, Agustarello (b St Chinian, 23 Oct 1858; d Cagnes-sur-Mer, 27 Dec 1931), French tenor. He was discovered by the director of the Paris Opéra, Pierre Gailhard, and made his debut in 1890, as Edgardo; remained at the Opéra until 1911, singing in the fp of Massenet's *Le Mage* and the first local performance of *Pagliacci*. At CG he sang Faust and Samson; appeared in San Francisco, New Orleans and Havana, 1911–13, often as Gounod's Roméo, and sang for French troops World War I.

affrettando Italian = 'urging, hastening'; the term is often used to indicate emotional pressure as well as increase in speed.

Afranio Albonese (b Pavia, *c* 1480; d Ferrara, *c* 1560), Italian priest. Canon at Ferrara, inventor of the phagotus.

Africaine, L', *The African Girl*, (original title *Vasco da Gama*), opera by Meyerbeer (libretto by Scribe), produced Paris, Opéra, 28 Apr 1865, after Meyerbeer's death. After sailing away from his native Portugal, explorer Vasco is rescued by tropic queen Sélika, whom he marries according to local custom. She later kills herself when he is seen with former love Inés.

Agazzari, Agostino (b Siena, 2 Dec 1578; d Siena, ? 10 Apr 1640), Italian composer. Held various church posts in Rome, but returned to Siena in 1630 as *maestro di cappella* of the cathedral. Wrote an early treatise on ◊thorough-bass, *Del sonare sopra 'l basso* (1607).

Works include pastoral *Eumelio*, madrigals, Masses and other church music, and two books on music.

Age of Anxiety, The second symphony by Leonard Bernstein (after the poem by W H Auden), fp Boston, 8 April 1949, cond. Koussevitzky.

Age of Gold, The, *Zoloty vek*, ballet by Shostakovich, op. 22. Prod. Leningrad, 26 Oct 1930; choreography by E Kaplan and V Vaynonen; concerns activities of a Stalinist football team.

agitato Italian = 'agitated, precipitate, restless'.

Agnelli, Salvatore (b Palermo, 1817; d Marseilles, 1874), Italian composer. Pupil of Donizetti and Zingarelli at Naples. He worked at Marseilles and Paris in later life.

Works include operas, including *Léonore de Médicis* (1855), ballets, church music, etc.

Agnes von Hohenstaufen opera by Spontini (libretto by E Raupach), produced Berlin, Opera, 12 Jun 1829. Heinrich rescues Agnes from the evil King Philip of France; revived Florence 1954.

agogic accent an accent which lends a note prominence by means of increased length rather than greater volume or higher pitch.

Agon, Greek = contest, ballet for 12 dancers by Stravinsky; composed 1953–57 fp (concert) LA, 17 Jun 1957; produced NY, 1 Dec 1957, choreographer Balanchine. Stravinsky's first music in serial idiom.

Agostini, Paolo (b Valerano, *c* 1583; d Rome, 3 Oct 1629), Italian composer. Pupil and son-in-law of B Nanini in Rome. After various posts in Rome, he became master of the Vatican chapel in 1627. Wrote Masses and other church music.

Agostini, Pietro Simone (b Forli, *c* 1635;; d Parma, 1 Oct 1680), Italian composer. *Maestro di cappella* to the Duke of Parma. Wrote five operas, including *Il ratto delle Sabine*, oratorios, church music. He fled his home town on suspicion of murder and was banned from Genoa after becoming involved with a nun.

Agrell, Johan Joachim (b Löth, 1 Feb 1701; d Nuremberg, 19 Jan 1765), Swedish composer. Studied at Linköping and Uppsala, was appointed court musician at Kassel in 1723 and music director at Nuremberg in 1746. Works include harpsichord concertos, sonatas, etc.

Agricola, Alexander (Alexander Ackerman) (b ? 1446; d near Valladolid, late Aug 1506), Flemish composer. His epitaph (printed by Rhaw in 1538) states that he died at the age of 60, the date of death being established by his disappearance from the court rolls of Philip the Handsome, Duke of Austria (Philip I of Spain from 1504). He served at the court of Galeazzo Maria Sforza, Duke of Milan, during the early 1470s, as well as with Lorenzo the Magnificent in Florence. After a brief period at Mantua he returned to the Low Countries, his name appearing in the Accounts of Cambrai Cathedral for 1475–76. After a second visit to Italy he entered in 1500 the service of Philip, whom he accomp. on journeys to Paris and Spain. During his second visit to Spain Philip died of fever, Agricola apparently dying at the same time.

Works include eight Masses, two Credos, 25 motets and 93 secular pieces. He is one of the most florid continental composers of the late 15th c., writing in a contrapuntal and decorative style.

Agricola, Johann Friedrich (b Dobitz, Saxony, 4 Jan 1720; d Berlin, 2 Dec 1774), German composer. Studied with Bach at Leipzig, afterwards with Hasse at Dresden and Quantz and Graun in Berlin. Director of the Hofkapelle there from 1759 to his death. Married the singer Benedetta Molteni in 1751.

Works include operas, psalms, hymns and other church music. Italian secular cantatas.

Agricola, Martin (Martin Sore) (b Schwiebus, 6 Jan 1486; d Magdeburg, 10 Jun 1556), German theorist and composer. His most important treatise was a work on musical instruments, *Musica instrumentalis deudsch* (1528, based on Virdung's *Musica getutscht* of 1511, but in verse), and he contributed three pieces to Georg Rhaw's *Newe deudsche geistliche Gesenge* (1544).

Agrippina opera by Handel (libretto by V Grimani), produced Venice, Teatro San Giovanni Crisostomo, 26 Dec 1709. Wife of Roman emperor has Poppea as a rival in the promotion of her son, Nero.

Aguiar, Alexandra de (b Oporto; d near Talavéra, 12 Dec 1605), Portuguese lutenist and poet. In the service of King Sebastian and later of Philip II of Spain.

Works include Lamentations for Holy Week.

Aguiarl (*Agujari*), Lucrezia (b Ferrara, 1743; d Parma, 18 May 1783), Italian soprano. Made her first appearance at Florence in 1764. In a letter of 24 Mar 1770 Mozart wrote down a remarkably high and florid passage he heard her sing. She married the composer and conductor Giuseppe Colla in 1780; from 1769 had sung in several fps of Colla's operas. Known as 'La Bastardella'.

Aguilera de Heredia, Sebastián (b Huesca, Aragon, c 1565; d Saragossa, 16 Dec 1627), Spanish organist and composer. From 1603 he was for many years organist at the old cathedral of Saragossa.

Works include Magnificats and other church music.

The opera contains absolutely nothing thrilling or electrifying, and if it were not for the magnificent scenery, the audience would not sit through it to the end: it will fill the theatre a few more times and then gather dust in the archives.

Letter to Verdi from **Bertani**, writing about *Aida*, May 1872

Ägyptische Helena, Die, *The Egyptian Helen*, opera by R Strauss (libretto by H von Hofmannsthal), produced Dresden, 6 Jun 1928. Errant Helen is forgiven by cuckolded husband.

Ahle, Johann Georg (b Mühlhausen, Thuringia, bap. 12 Jun 1651; d Mühlhausen, 2 Dec 1706), German composer. Organist at the church of St Blasius, Mühlhausen. Like his father (Johann Rudolf, 1625–73) he wrote hymn tunes.

Ahlersmeyer, Mathieu (b Cologne, 29 Jun 1896; d Garmisch, 23 Jul 1979), German baritone. Debut Mönchengladbach 1929, as Wolfram. Appeared at the Kroll Opera, Berlin, under Klemperer, 1930–31 and in 1934 joined the Dresden Staatsoper: sang there in the fp of *Die schweigsame Frau* (1935) and Joseph Haas's *Die Hochzeit des Jobs* (1944). At the Berlin Staatsoper he created Egk's Peer Gynt (1938) in a production admired by Hitler, and at the 1947 Salzburg Festival co-created the title role in Einem's *Dantons Tod*. He sang with the Hamburg Staatsoper 1945–73 and in 1952 appeared with the company at the Edinburgh Festival as Matthias Grunewald, in the British stage premiere of Hindemith's *Mathis der Maler*.

Ahna, Pauline de (b Ingolstadt, 4 Feb 1863; d Garmisch, 13 May 1950), German soprano. She studied at Munich. Debut Weimar 1890, as Pamina; later roles there included Eva, Elsa and Donna Elvira. She sang at Karlsruhe 1890–91 as Agathe, Leonore and Donna Anna. In 1894 she created Freihild in Strauss's *Guntram*; she married the composer the same year. He dedicated several sets of songs to her, including four Lieder op. 27, and portrayed her in *Ein Heldenleben*, the *Symphonia domestica* and *Intermezzo*. Bayreuth 1891, Elisabeth.

Aho, Kalevi (b Forssa, 9 Mar 1949), Finnish composer. Studied with Rautavaara in Helsinki and Boris Blacher in Berlin. Music has developed from Russian symphonic influences, through atonality to post-modernism.

Works include opera *Insect Life* (1985–87), seven symphonies (1969–88), concertos for violin, cello and piano (1981–89), three string quartets, oboe quintet (1973), solo violin sonata (1973) and accordion sonata (1984).

Ahronovich, Yury (b Leningrad, 13 May 1932), Russian-born Israeli conductor. Moscow Radio SO 1964–72; left Russia 1972 and settled in Israel. Has conducted in Cologne from 1973. CG debut 1974 (*Boris Godunov*); chief conductor of the Gurzenich Orchestra, Cologne 1975–86; Stockholm Philharmonic 1982–87.

Aiblinger, Johann Kaspar (b Wasserburg, Bavaria, 23 Feb 1779; d Munich, 6 May 1867), German composer and conductor. Music

director of the Munich opera, 1819–23, but as a composer devoted mainly to church music.

Aich, Arnt von (Arnt of Aachen) (b ? 1474; d Cologne, c 1530), German music publisher. His *Liederbuch* (Cologne, c 1510) contained 75 four-part songs, sacred and secular, and is possibly the first printed edition of its kind.

Aichinger, Gregor (b Regensburg, c 1564; d Augsburg, 21 Jan 1628), German priest and musician. Organist to the Fugger family at Augsburg, pub. books of sacred music at Venice in 1590 and 1603 and visited Rome for further music study in 1599.

Aida opera by Verdi (libretto by A Ghislanzoni, based on a scenario by F A F Mariette and outlined in French by C Du Locle), produced Cairo, 24 Dec 1871; fp in Italy, Milan, La Scala, 8 Feb 1872. Love triangle among (and eventually under) the pyramids.

Aiglon, L', *The Eaglet*, opera by Honegger and Ibert (libretto by H Cain, based on Rostand's play), produced Monte Carlo, 11 Mar 1937.

Ainsley, John Mark (b Crewe, 9 Jul 1963), English tenor. Studied at Oxford and sang with such early music ensembles as the Taverner Consort and London Baroque; concerts of Handel, Mozart and Stravinsky under Gardiner, Menuhin and Tate; US debut in the B minor Mass (NY, with Hogwood); opera debut in A Scarlatti's *Gli equivici nel sembianti*, Innsbruck; ENO debut 1989, in Monteverdi's *Ulisse*; Mozart roles include Ferrando (GTO 1991), Idamante (WNO, 1991) and Don Ottavio (Glyndebourne, 1994).

Airborne Symphony choral work by Marc Blitzstein in praise of the US Air Force Corps, in which the composer served during World War II; fp NY, 23 Mar 1946.

Aitken, Robert (b Kentville, Nova Scotia, 28 Aug 1939), Canadian flautist and composer. He has played the flute in several Canadian orchestras. and has organized new music concerts in Toronto.

Works include concerto for 12 solo instruments (1964), *Spectra* for four chamber groups (1969), *Spiral* for orchestra with amplified woodwind instruments (1975); *Folia* for woodwind quintet (1980), *Monody* for chorus (1983).

Ajmone-Marsan, Guido (b Turin, 24 Mar 1947), Italian-born American conductor. Studied at the Eastman School, Rochester, and in Salzburg, Venice and Rome. Winner of the Solti Competition 1973 and principal conductor of the Orchestra of Illinois, Chicago, 1982–87; Music Director of Essen Opera 1986–90. Other engage-

THE OPERA

Aida

A four-act opera by Giuseppe Verdi, a story of triumph and tragedy set in Egypt at the time of the Pharaohs. It was first performed in Cairo in 1871, and has been a favourite ever since.

I. The Ethiopian army is threatening Thebes, and Radames (tenor) has been chosen to lead the Egyptian army. Radames is in love with Aida (soprano), Ethiopian slave of Amneris (mezzo-soprano), daughter of the king of Egypt. Radames's armour is blessed in a ceremony at the temple.

II. Having been tricked into confessing her love for Radames, Aida is told by Amneris that she too loves him. The return of the conquering Egyptian army is celebrated in a triumphal scene, which includes the famous Grand March. Radames has the prisoners released but Amonasro (baritone), Aida's father and the King of Ethiopia, remains captive and unknown to the Egyptians. Aida recognizes her father but they must guard their secret. The King offers Amneris to Radames in marriage.

III. Radames is held as a traitor, after Amonasro tells Aida to discover from him the army's plan of attack.

IV. Radames will not give up Aida for Amneris, and he is buried alive. As Amneris prays for peace in vain for her lost love Radames, he discovers Aida in the tomb with him and they sing a final duet before dying together.

THE OPERA

ments at the NY Met., CG, NY City Opera (*Carmen*, 1992) and with the LSO and the Chicago SO.

Ajo nell'imbarazzo, L', *The Tutor in a Fix*, opera by Donizetti (libretto by J Ferretti), produced Rome, Teatro Valle, 4 Feb 1824.

Akeroyde, Samuel (b Yorkshire), English 17th-c. composer. Musician in Ordinary to James II in 1687 and later to William and Mary. Contributed many songs to various collections and to the third part of Durfey's *Don Quixote* in 1696, the music to the first two of which had been written by Purcell the year before his death.

Akhnaten opera by Philip Glass (libretto by the composer with S Goldman, R Israel and R Riddell), produced Stuttgart, 24 Mar 1984. The story is based on the hermaphrodite, monotheist Pharaoh of the 18th dynasty.

Akimenko, Feodor Stepanovich (b Kharkov, 20 Feb 1876; d Paris, 3 Jan 1945), Russian composer. Pupil of Balakirev and Rimsky-Korsakov in St Petersburg. Taught in the court choir, where he had been a chorister, but lived in France 1903–06 and settled there after the Russian Revolution. He was Stravinsky's first composition teacher.

Works include opera, *The Queen of the Alps* (1914); orchestral and chamber music; sonatas; numerous piano works include *Sonate fantastique*.

Akutagawa, Yasushi (b Tokyo, 12 Jul 1925; d Tokyo, 31 Jan 1989), Japanese composer. He was active in Tokyo as a conductor and in promoting new music.

Works include the opera *L'Orphée in Hiroshima* (1967), four ballets, including *Paradise Lost* (1951); *Ostinato Sinfonica* (1967); *Rhapsody* for orchestra (1971).

al Italian masc. = 'at the, to the'; the word is used in various combinations with nouns, as below.

Eugen d'Albert's first *concerto will be played on the* second *of March by his* third *wife.*

Advert quoted in **Milinowski**, *Teresa Carreño 'By the Grace of God'*, 1940

Alagna, Roberto (b Clichy-sur-Bois, 7 Jun 1963), French tenor of Sicilian parentage. Studied in France and Italy; sang Alfredo with GTO at Glyndebourne 1988. Rodolfo, London, CG 1990, returning 1994–95 as Gounod's Roméo, and Don Carlos; Monte Carlo 1992, as Roberto Devereux. Other roles include Faust (Boito and Gounod), Duke of Mantua (Vienna, 1995) and Edgardo. Has also appeared at La Scala, and in Chicago and NY. One of the most promising lyric tenors of his generation.

Alain, Jehan (Ariste) (b St Germain-en-Laye, 3 Feb 1911; d Saumur, 20 Jun 1940), French composer. Studied at the Paris Conservatory: organ with Dupré and composition with Dukas and Roger-Ducasse. He became a church organist in Paris in 1935, but served in World War II and was killed in action.

Works include numerous choral compositions, mainly sacred; three dances for orchestra; chamber music; piano and organ works; songs.

Alain, Marie-Claire (b St Germain-en-Laye, 10 Aug 1926), French organist, sister of Jehan Alain. She studied with Duruflé and Dupré; Paris debut 1950. She has toured in Europe and USA; noted in Bach and the music of her brother.

à la manière de ... French = 'in the manner of ...'; two sets of piano pieces by Casella and Ravel imitating the styles of Wagner, Fauré, Brahms, Debussy, R Strauss, Franck, Borodin, d'Indy, Chabrier and Ravel. Only the Borodin and Chabrier pieces are by Ravel.

alba type of troubadour-trouvère song, in which the singer watches for daybreak on behalf of two lovers (e.g. *Reis glorios*, by ◊Guiraut de Bornelh). As used by the Minnesinger it was called *Tagelied*.

Albanese, Licia (b Bari, 22 Jul 1913), American soprano of Italian origin. Studied in Milan and made her first stage appearance at the Teatro Lirico there in 1934, as Madam Butterfly, followed in the same year by an appearance at La Scala. From 1940 she was a member of the NY Met. She was chosen by Toscanini for his recorded broadcasts

of *La Bohème* and *La Traviata*. Her other roles included Donna Anna, Manon and Aida.

Albani (originally Lajeunesse), (Marie Louise Cécile) Emma (b Chambly near Montreal, 1 Nov 1847; d London, 3 Apr 1930), Canadian soprano. Studied with Duprez in Paris and Lamperti at Milan. Debut at Messina, 1870, and in London at CG, 1872, both as Amina; she was the first London Elsa (1875) and Elisabeth (1876), and was often heard in oratorio. Lived in London, but toured widely. DBE, 1925.

Albéniz, Isaac (Manuel Francisco) (b Camprodón, Catalonia, 29 May 1860; d Camboles-Bains, Pyrenees, 18 May 1909), Spanish composer. He made his appearance as an infant prodigy both as pianist and composer at Barcelona, a *pasodoble*, written at the age of seven, being played by a military band there. Later he appeared in Paris as a child-pupil of Marmontel and afterwards studied at the Madrid Conservatory, where he received a grant from the king to enable him to go to Brussels. There he studied composition with Gevaert and piano with Brassin, and later went to Liszt at Weimar for piano and to Jadassohn and Reinecke at Leipzig for composition. After touring successfully, he settled as a piano teacher first at Barcelona and then at Madrid, from c 1880, but left before long and spent the rest of his life mainly in London and Paris. He had married in 1883. In London he produced operas and began a trilogy on Arthurian legends to a libretto by Francis Money-Coutts (Lord Latymer), who financed him, but he did not progress far. His best-known work, the suite of piano pieces *Iberia* (1906–08) helped to establish a distinctive national flavour, based on folk idioms; also notable for its virtuosity and effects intended to simulate the guitar and castanets.

Works include operas *The Magic Opal* (London, 1893), *Henry Clifford* (Barcelona, 1895), *Pepita Jiménez, San Antonio de la Florida*, *Merlin* (unfinished first part of Arthurian cycle); zarzuelas *Cuanto más viejo, Los Catalanes en Grecia*; contribution to Millöcker's operetta *Der arme Jonathan* for the London production 1893, *Catalonia*, orchestrated with the aid of Dukas; c 250 piano pieces, including *Catalonia, La Vega, Navarra, Azulejos* and the cycle of 12 entitled *Iberia*; 13 songs.

Albergati, Pirro Capacelli, Count (b Bologna, 20 Sept 1663; d Bologna, 22 Jun 1735), nobleman and amateur composer.

Works include operas *Gli amici* (Bologna, 1699), *Il principe selvaggio* (Bologna, 1712); oratorios *Giobbe, L'innocenza di Santa Eufemia, Il convito di Baldassare*; church music, compositions for various instruments.

Albert, Eugen (Eugène Francis Charles) d' (b Glasgow, 10 Apr 1864; d Riga, 3 Mar 1932), French-English (later Germanized) composer and pianist, son of C L N d'Albert. Although born in Scotland, he came from Newcastle upon Tyne, and after being well taught by his father as a very precociously gifted child, he went as Newcastle scholar to the Nat. Training School in London (later the RCM). He appeared with great success as pianist, notably in Bach, Liszt and Beethoven, and later went to Vienna for further study under Richter, finishing with a course under Liszt. In 1892 he married Teresa Carreño, but they were divorced in 1895 (d'Albert married six times). In 1907 he succeeded Joachim as director of the Hochschule für Musik in Berlin. During World War I he repudiated his British birth, declaring himself to be entirely German. Of his 20 operas, only *Tiefland* (1903) has had any real success. The rest of his considerable output has largely fallen into neglect.

Works include operas *Der Rubin* (after Hebbel) (Karlsruhe, 1893), *Ghismonda, Gernot, Die Abreise* (Frankfurt, 1898), *Kain, Der Improvisator, Tiefland, Flauto solo, Tragaldabas (Der geborgte Ehemann)*, *Izeÿl* (Hamburg, 1909), *Die verschenkte Frau, Liebesketten* (Vienna, 1912), *Die toten Augen* (Dresden, 1916), *Der Stier von Olivera* (Leipzig, 1918), *Revolutionshochzeit, Scirocco, Mareika von Nymwegen, Der Golem, Die schwarze Orchidee* (Leipzig, 1928), *Die Witwe von Ephesus, Mister Wu* (unfinished, completed by Blech); *Der Mensch und das Leben*, choral work in six parts; symphony in F; overtures *Esther* and *Hyperion*; two string quartets; piano suite and sonata.

Albert, Heinrich (b Lobenstein, Saxony, 8 Jul 1604; d Königsberg, 6 Oct 1651), German poet, organist and composer. Studied music at Dresden with Schütz, who was his uncle. His parents, however, compelled him to read law at Leipzig University; but in 1626 he set out for Königsberg, was taken prisoner by the Swedes, and at last reached that city in 1628, resuming music studies with Stobäus. In 1631 he was appointed organist at the Old Church there, and became member of the Königsberg school of poets.

Works include Te Deum, many hymns to words of his own, secular songs.

Albert, Stephen (b New York, 6 Feb 1941; d Truro, Cape Cod, MA, 27 Dec 1992), American composer. Studied with Milhaud, Roy Harris and Rochberg. Won Pulitzer Prize 1985 with symphony after Joyce, *Riverrun*. Music embraces a variety of styles, including electronic. A second symphony was posthumously premiered by the NY PO in 1995.

Works include *Supernatural Songs* for soprano and chamber orchestra (1963); *Imitations* for string quartet (1964); *Winter Songs* for tenor and orchestra (1965); *Bacchae* for narrator, chorus and orchestra (1968); *Cathedral Music* (1972); *Voices Within* for orchestra (1975); *Winterfire* for seven players (1979); *Into Eclipse* for tenor and orchestra (1981); *Riverrun* (1984); *Flower on the Mountain* for soprano and chamber orchestra (1985); *Processionals* for orchestra (1987); violin concerto (1988); cello concerto (1990); *Distant Hills Coming Nigh* for soprano, baritone and chamber ensemble (1991); *Wind Canticle* for clarinet and ensemble (1992).

Albert Herring opera by Britten (libretto by E Crozier, based on Maupassant's story *Le Rosier de Madame Husson*), produced Glyndebourne, 20 Jun 1947. Much gaiety at a village fête.

Alberti, Domenico (b Venice, *c* 1710; d Rome, 14 Oct 1746), Italian singer, harpsichordist and composer, pupil of Lotti. The characteristic left-hand accomp. figuration in his keyboard music has given his name to the 'Alberti bass'.

Alberti, Gaspare (b Padua, *c* 1480; d Bergamo, *c* 1560), Italian composer, singer at S Maria Maggiore, Bergamo, from 1508. He was one of the earliest exponents of *cori spezzati*.

Works include five Masses, three Passions and other church music.

Alberti, Giuseppe Matteo (b Bologna 1685; d Bologna, 20 Sept 1751), Italian violinist and composer. Wrote mainly for strings, including concertos influenced by Vivaldi, which were popular in England.

Alberti, Innocenzo di (b Tarvisio, *c* 1535; d 15 Jun 1615), Italian composer. In the service of Alfonso, Duke of Ferrara. In 1568 he dedicated a book of 46 madrigals to Henry, Earl of Arundel.

Works include madrigals, penitential psalms, secular songs.

Alberti bass a conventional broken-chord accomp. common in 18th-c. keyboard music, taking its name from Domenico Alberti, who made much use of it. Many familiar examples of the device can be found in the works of Haydn, Mozart and Beethoven.

Albertus, Magister, Parisian composer of early 12th c. A *Benedicamus Domino* trope, *Congaudeant catholici*, is ascribed to him in the Codex

WNO and Scottish Opera, and at CG. ENO productions have been *Billy Budd*, *Beatrice and Benedict*, *Peter Grimes* and *Lohengrin* (1988–93). British fp of Massenet's *Chérubin* at CG, 1994.

Albicastro, Enrico (Italian from Hainz Weissenburg), Swiss 17th-c. composer and violinist. He was a captain of the Swiss horse, serving in the Spanish war in the Netherlands as a mercenary. Works included eight op. nos. of solo and trio sonatas and one of concertos.

Albinoni, Tommaso (b Venice, 8 Jun 1671; d Venice, 17 Jan 1751), Italian violinist and composer, famous for an adagio which he did not write. Wrote operas and instrumental music; his concertos were among the first to be in three movements, and the oboe concertos op. 7 were the first pub. in Italy. Bach used some of his themes.

Works include 55 operas, including *Radamisto* (Venice, 1698), *Griselda* (Florence, 1703), *Pimpinone* (Venice, 1708) and *L'impresario delle Canarie* (Venice, 1725); nine op. nos. for instrumental chamber combinations, including five sets of 12 concertos, 30 other concertos, 42 trio sonatas and 29 violin sonatas.

Albion and Albanius opera by Grabu (libretto by Dryden), produced London, Duke's Theatre, 3 Jun 1685. An allegory of the Restoration of Charles II.

Alboni, Marietta (b Città di Castello, 6 Mar 1823; d Ville d'Avray, 23 Jun 1894), Italian contralto. Pupil of Rossini; first appearance Bologna, 1842, in Pacini's *Saffo*. Sang with much success in Paris and London, where she was heard as Arsace, Urbain, Cherubino, Zerlina and Fides.

alborada Spanish, from *alba* = 'dawn' = 'morning song', in the same sense that a serenade is an evening song; *cf.* French *aubade*. Originally the alborada was a popular instrumental piece of NW Spain, usually played on bagpipes.

Alborada del gracioso, *The Jester's Morning Song*, a piano piece by Ravel, No. 4 of the set entitled *Miroirs*, composed 1905. Version for orchestra performed Paris, 17 May 1919.

Albrecht, Gerd (b Essen, 19 Jul 1935), German conductor. Study at Hamburg was followed by conducting posts at the opera houses of Mainz, Lübeck and Kassel (1963–72). Appeared as guest conductor with the Berlin PO and gave the 1967 fp of Henze's *Telemanniana* with the orchestra. Principal conductor Berlin, Deutsche Opera, 1972–79 (fp Fortner's *Elisabeth Tudor*, 1972). He has worked with the Zurich Tonhalle orchestra from 1975; fp Henze's *Barcarola*, 1980. At the 1982 Munich Festival he gave *Moses und Aron* and in 1986 *Der fliegende Holländer* at CG and the fp of Reimann's *Troades* at Munich. Chief conductor of the Hamburg Opera from 1988, Czech Philharmonic 1992–95. Premiered Schnittke's *Historia von Dr Johann Fausten*, Hamburg 1995.

Albrechtsberger, Johann Georg (b Klosterneuburg near Vienna, 3 Feb 1736; d Vienna, 7 Mar 1809), Austrian theorist, composer and teacher. Court organist in Vienna and *Kapellmeister* of St Stephen's Cathedral. Renowned as a contrapuntist, he was for a short time Beethoven's teacher. Prolific composer of church music and instrumental music, much of it in a contrapuntal style.

Alberti bass as used in the opening of Mozart's Sonata in C major, K.545.

Calixtinus of Compostela (*c* 1125), and is the earliest known three-part composition.

Albery, Tim (b Harpenden, 4 Jun 1952), English stage director. Directed Racine and Shakespeare in London. Opera debut with *The Turn of the Screw*, Batignano 1983. *Midsummer Marriage* (1985) and *Don Giovanni* for Opera North; *The Trojans* 1986–90 at Leeds, for

Albrici, Bartolomeo (b Rome, *c* 1640; d London, after 1687), Italian 17th-c. organist. In the service of Queen Christina of Sweden, organist at Dresden until 1663, in the service of Charles II from 1664 and James II from 1685. Also active as a private teacher in London.

Albrici, Vincenzo (b Rome, 26 Jun 1631; d Prague, 8 Aug 1696), Italian composer and organist, brother of Bartolomeo Albrici. Pupil of

Carissimi. Director of the Queen of Sweden's Italian musicians, 1652–53; *Kapellmeister* at Dresden from 1654; in the service of Charles II in London, 1664–67; returned to Dresden, 1667; organist of St Thomas's, Leipzig, 1681–82; finally *Kapellmeister* at Prague, St Augustin.

Works include Masses, psalms, concertos and madrigals.

Albright, William (b Gary, IN, 20 Oct 1944), American composer, pianist and organist. Studied at the Juilliard School and in Paris with Messiaen. Teacher of composition at Michigan University and director of electronic music studio there.

Works include multimedia and stage pieces (*Cross of Gold* 1975), orchestral music (*Bacchanal* 1981), chamber music and pieces for organ and piano, with jazz ensemble.

Albumblatt German = 'album leaf, page'; the title often given to a short piece, usually for piano, suggesting that the piece is one of many, forming a gathered album of unrelated pieces. Examples are by Schumann and Wagner.

Alceste ◊Alkestis.

Opera by Gluck (libretto by R Calzabigi after Euripides), Italian version produced Vienna, Burgtheater, 26 Dec 1767. French version, revised by the composer (libretto by C L G L du Roullet after Calzabigi), produced Paris, Opéra, 23 Apr 1776. Alceste and husband Admète are saved from Hades by Hercules, as Alceste prepares to sacrifice herself for dying Admète.

Opera by Schweitzer (libretto by Wieland), produced Weimar, at court, 28 May 1773. The first German opera in the manner of Metastasio.

Opera by Strungk (libretto by P Thiemich, based on Aurelio Aureli's *Antigona delusa da Alceste*), produced Leipzig, 18 May 1693. Written for the opening of the Leipzig opera house.

Incidental music by Handel (later used for *The Choice of Hercules*) to a play by Tobias Smollett, composed for a production in London, CG, in 1750, which did not take place.

Alceste ou Le Triomphe d'Alcide opera by Lully (libretto by Quinault), produced Paris, Opéra, 19 Jan 1674.

Alchemist, The incidental music by Handel, partly adapted from *Rodrigo*, for a revival of Ben Jonson's play, produced London, Drury Lane Theatre, 7 Mar 1732.

Alchymist, Der opera by Spohr (libretto by K Pfeiffer, based on W A Irving's story *The Student of Salamanca*), produced Kassel, 28 Jul 1830. The alchemist Tarnow refuses to let his daughter Louise marry until he has discovered the philosopher's stone. He releases her after her lover impersonates the devil, demanding a young woman as payment.

Alcidor opera by Spontini (libretto by G M Théaulon de Lambert),

THE OPERA

Alceste

A three-act opera written in 1767 by Christoph Gluck, set in Thessaly after the Trojan War and based on Euripides' play of the same name.

I. As the people pray for the recovery of their sick king Admète (tenor), his wife Alceste (soprano) offers sacrifice to Apollo. When the oracle declares that Admète will certainly die unless a sacrifice is made, Alceste decides she would rather sacrifice herself than let Admète die.

II. On recovering from his illness, Admète learns of his wife's promise to the gods and decides to die with her; Alceste remains determined in her vow.

III. Hercules (baritone) resolves to save Alceste; she is driven back from the mouth of Hades, because it is still daylight, and she is joined by her husband. But because only one of the couple may enter Hades, they decide that both of them will have to die. Hercules appears once more, and admiring them as a model of married constancy and love decides that they both should live.

THE OPERA

produced Berlin, 23 May 1825. Designated a 'Zauber-Oper mit Ballet', it begins with a chorus of gnomes accompanied by anvils (anticipating Wagner's *Rheingold*).

Alcina opera by Handel (libretto by A Marchi), produced London, CG, 16 Apr 1735. Sorceress Alcina loses her magic powers on enchanted island, as Bradamante comes in search of the bewitched Ruggiero.

Alcione opera by Marais (libretto by A H de la Motte), produced Paris, Opéra, 18 Feb 1706. Neptune rescues young lovers after shipwreck.

Alcock, John (b London, 11 Apr 1715; d Lichfield, 23 Feb 1806), English organist and composer. Organist at various parish churches in London and Warwicks., and for a time at Lichfield Cathedral. D. Mus. Oxford, 1761.

Works include an opera, anthem with orchestra *We will rejoice*, and other church music, glees and catches, harpsichord suites (1741) and six concertos (1750).

Alcuin (b ?York, c 753; d Tours, 19 May 804), poet, statesman, musician and adviser to Charlemagne. He may also have written about music.

Alda, Frances (b Christchurch, 31 May 1883; d Venice, 18 Sept 1952), New Zealand soprano. Stage debut Melbourne; sang Manon at the Paris Opéra-Comique, 1904. In Dec 1908 she sang Gilda at the NY Met., opposite Caruso; she appeared in NY until Dec 1929, as Mimi, Butterfly and Manon Lescaut, and in the fps of operas by Victor Herbert and Walter Damrosch. She married the manager of the Met., Gatti-Casazza, and was admired by Toscanini: at La Scala in 1908 she appeared under him as the first local Louise.

Aldeburgh Festival annual festival held at Aldeburgh, Suffolk, since 1948. Content of programmes has largely reflected tastes of co-founders, Benjamin Britten and Peter Pears, although visiting foreign composers have included Henze, Lutosławski and Takemitsu. The Maltings concert hall, Snape, and nearby Orford Parish Church have seen many Britten premieres, e.g. the church parables, the third string quartet and *Phaedra*. Artistic directors since Britten's death have included Rostropovich and Murray Perahia. A feature of recent festivals has been the posthumous fp of works by Britten which were withdrawn by the composer and subsequently 'lost'.

Alden, David (b New York, 16 Sept 1949), American stage director. He staged the premieres of operas by Pasatieri and Conrad Susa; in 1980 he produced *Wozzeck* at the Met. and for Scottish Opera. A punk *Rake's Progress* in Amsterdam was followed by *Mazeppa* with chain-saws for ENO; other London stagings have been *Simon Boccanegra* (1987) and *Un Ballo in Maschera* (1989). He staged the fp of Bolcom's *Casino Paradise* at Philadelphia in 1990 and *Faust* for the New Israeli Opera (1994). His twin brother Christopher is also a director: *Cav and Pag* at Tel Aviv, 1995.

Aldenhoff, Bernd (b Duisburg, 14 Jun 1908; d Munich, 8 Oct 1959), German tenor. After engagements at Cologne, Darmstadt and Erfurt he sang at Düsseldorf 1938–44; Dresden 1944–52, as Herod, Max and Walther; Bayreuth 1951–52 and 1957, as Siegfried; NY Met., 1954–55, debut as Tannhäuser, and appeared as guest at La Scala, Paris and Zurich; sang in the *Ring* cycles conducted by Furtwängler in Milan.

Aldrich, Richard (b Providence, RI, 31 Jul 1862; d Rome, 2 Jun 1937), American music critic. After various activities he became music editor of the *New York Times*. His works included two Wagnerian guide-books.

aleatory, from Latin *alea*, 'a die', plur. *aleae*, 'dice', a term applied to music in which the details of performance or the actual notes are left wholly or in part to the players or singers. Most strictly the word is used for works such as Stockhausen's *Klavierstück XI*, in which the choice is between specific alternatives.

Aleko opera by Rakhmaninov (libretto by V I Nemirovich-Danchenko, based on Pushkin's poem *The Gypsies*), produced Moscow, 9 May 1893. Zemfira is killed by Aleko after she tries to join the gypsies.

Alembert, Jean Le Rond d' (b Paris, 16 Nov 1717; d Paris, 29 Oct 1783), French author, philosopher and mathematician. His books included many studies of musical subjects, including acoustics, opera, the theories of Rameau, etc., and he contributed music articles to the *Encyclopédie*. One of the adherents of Gluck against Piccinni.

Aler, John (b Baltimore, 4 Oct 1949), American tenor. Studied at the Juilliard School and made his debut there in 1977, as Ernesto; his European debut was at Brussels 1979 (Belmonte) and he has since appeared at the Vienna Staatsoper, Glyndebourne and CG (both as Ferrando, 1979 and 1986) and the Salzburg Festival (Don Ottavio, 1988). Recordings include Handel's *Semele* and *Messiah*, *Così fan Tutte* and *Carmina Burana*.

Alessandri, Felice (b Rome, 24 Nov 1747; d Casalbino, 15 Aug 1798), Italian conductor and composer. Studied at Naples and first worked at Turin and Paris; produced his first opera at Venice in 1767 and went to London the following year, and in 1786 to St Petersburg in search of a court appointment, which he failed to secure. From 1789 to 1792 he was second *Kapellmeister* at the Berlin Opera.

Works include *c* 35 operas, including *Ezio* (Verona, 1767), *Alcina* (Turin, 1775), *Artaserse* (Naples, 1783) *Il ritorno d'Ulisse* (Potsdam, 1790), *Armida* (Padua, 1794), an oratorio, several symphonies, sonatas.

Alessandro opera by Handel (libretto by P A Rolli), produced London, King's Theatre, Haymarket, 5 May 1726. Alexander the Great in trouble with rival sopranos.

Alessandro della Viola ◊Merlo.

Alessandro nell'Indie, *Alexander in India*, ◊Cleofide and ◊Poro.

Opera by Johann Christian Bach (libretto by Metastasio), produced Naples, Teatro San Carlo, 20 Jan 1762. Defeated by Alexander the Great, Indian King Porus resolves to rescue Queen Cleophis.

The first setting was by Vinci (Rome, 1729); others by Galuppi (Mantua, 1738), Pérez (Genoa, 1745), Sacchini (Venice, 1763) and Piccinni (Naples, 1774).

Alessandro Stradella opera by Flotow (libretto, in German, by F W Riese, pseud. 'W Friedrich'), produced Hamburg, 30 Dec 1844. It deals with doubtful incidents in the scandalous life of Stradella, and is based on a play with music, some by Flotow, by P A A P de Forges and P Dupert. Stradella deflects would-be assassins by singing to them of mercy and kindness.

Alessandro vincitor di se stesso, *Alexander, Victor over himself*, opera by Cavalli (libretto by F Sbarra), produced Venice, Teatro Santi Giovanni e Paolo, probably 20 Jan 1651.

Alexander, Carlos (b Utica, NY, 15 Oct 1915), American bass-baritone. He studied in Berlin and with Friedrich Schorr in New York. Debut St Louis 1941, as Masetto. He sang widely in N and S America in the 1940s and in Germany from 1955. In 1961 he sang Mandryka at Florence and was Gregor Mittenhoffer in the British fp of Henze's *Elegy for Young Lovers*, at Glyndebourne. Bayreuth 1963–64, as Beckmesser. At the Stuttgart Staatsoper he took part in the 1968 fp of Orff's *Prometheus*. He taught at the Salzburg Mozarteum.

Alexander, John (b Meridian, MS, 21 Oct 1923; d Meridian, 8 Dec 1990), American tenor. Debut Cincinnati 1952, Faust. NY City 1957, Alfredo: Met. 1961, Ferrando. He sang Rodolfo and Korngold's Paul in Vienna and in 1970 was Pollione at CG. In 1973, at the Boston Opera, he took the title role in the first complete stage performance of Verdi's *Don Carlos*. He was Idreno in the Sutherland recording of *Semiramide*. Other roles included Bacchus, Walther, and Percy.

Alexander, Roberta (b Lynchburg, VA, 3 Mar 1949), American soprano. Studied in the Hague and appeared with Netherlands Opera in the posthumous premiere of Ullmann's *Emperor of Atlantis* (1975). She made US operatic debut as Pamina at Houston, 1980, and has returned since 1983 at the Met., as Zerlina, Bess, Jenůfa and Mimi; she sang Mimi at CG in 1984 and Jenůfa at Glyndebourne 1989. Other roles include Handel's Cleopatra and Mozart's Electra, Vitellia and Elvira.

Alexander Balus oratorio by Handel (libretto by T Morell), produced London, CG, 23 Mar 1748.

Alexander Nevsky film music by Prokofiev, composed 1938. Later arranged as Cantata, op. 78, for mezzo, chorus and orchestra fp Moscow, 17 May 1939.

Alexander's Feast Dryden's ode set to music by Handel (words arranged and added to by Newburgh Hamilton), produced London, CG, 19 Feb 1736.

Alexandrov, Anatol Nicolaievich (b Plakhino, 25 May 1888; d Moscow, 16 Apr 1982), Russian composer. Studied under Taneiev and at the Moscow Conservatory, later composition under Vassilenko and Ilyinski. Professor at Moscow Conservatory.

Works include operas *Two Worlds, The Forty-First, Bela* (Moscow, 1946), *The Wild Girl* (1957); incidental music for Maeterlinck's *Ariane et Barbe-bleue*, Scribe's *Adrienne Lecouvreur*, etc.; music for film *Thirteen*; overture on popular Russian themes and two suites for orchestra; four string quartets (1921–53); 14 piano sonatas, piano pieces; *Three Goblets*, for baritone and orchestra; songs, folksong arrs.

Alexeev, Dmitri (b Moscow, 10 Aug 1947), Russian pianist. He studied at the Moscow Conservatory and in 1975 became the first Russian to win the Leeds International Competition. London debut 1975, and has appeared with all the leading British orchestras. US debut 1976, with Giulini and the Chicago SO; Carnegie Hall, NY, 1978. Well known in recital and has recorded works by Chopin, Brahms and Prokofiev. Appeared with the Concertgebouw Orchestra and the Berlin PO in 1986.

Aleyn *(Alanus)*, John, English 14th–15th-c. composer whose identity is uncertain, possibly a canon of Windsor who died in 1373 or a minor canon of St Paul's who died in 1437. A motet praising the skill of English musicians in MS 1047 of the Musée Condé, Chantilly, is ascribed to Johannes Alanus, while a *Gloria* in the Old Hall MS is ascribed to Aleyn. A Jean Alain was one of John of Gaunt's musicians in 1396, together with three French minstrels.

Alfano, Franco (b Posillipo, near Naples, 8 Mar 1875; d San Remo, 27 Oct 1954), Italian composer. He is best known for his completion of *Turandot*. Studied first at the Naples Conservatory and afterwards at that of Leipzig, under Jadassohn. He had some piano pieces pub. in Germany before the end of the c. and in 1896 wrote his first opera, *Miranda*, on a subject from Fogazzaro. The ballet *Napoli*, produced Paris 1900, was his first big success, and was followed by the still greater success of his third opera, *Risurrezione*, produced 1904, a work in the *verismo* tradition. His first symphony was performed at San Remo in 1910. In 1919 he was appointed director of the Liceo Musicale Rossini at Bologna and in 1923 of the Conservatory at Turin. His most successful work was the colourful opera *La leggenda di Sakuntala* (1921). After Puccini's death in 1924 he completed the unfinished *Turandot*, finishing the final scenes from Puccini's sketches; his work was not heard complete until 1982.

Works include operas *Miranda, La fonte di Enschir* (Breslau, 1898) *Risurrezione* (based on Tolstoy) (Turin, 1904), *Il principe Zilah, L'ombra di Don Giovanni* (Naples, 1930), *Sakuntala* (after Kalidasa), *L'ultimo Lord, Cyrano de Bergerac* (Rome, 1936) (after

---

All music which depicts nothing is nothing but noise.
Jean Le Rond d'Alembert, quoted in Mellers,
François Couperin, 1950

Rostand), *Il dottor Antonio*; ballet *Napoli*; two symphonies, *Suite romantica* for orchestra; piano tet, three string quartets; sonata for cello and piano; songs included three settings of Tagore and a cycle *Dormiveglia*.

al fine Italian = 'to the end'; the term is used in cases where an earlier portion of a composition is to be repeated (*da capo*) and indicates that it is to be played over again to the end, not to some earlier place, which would otherwise be marked with a special sign, the appropriate direction being then *al segno*.

Alfonso und Estrella opera by Schubert (libretto by F von Schober), composed 1821–22, but never performed in Schubert's lifetime; produced by Liszt at Weimar, 24 Jun 1854, with an overture by Anton Rubinstein. Schubert's original version was premiered at Graz, 28 Sept 1991. Alfonso gains the throne, marrying Estrella, the daughter of his father's enemy.

Alfonso X, King of Castile and Leon, 1221–84, known as *El Sabio* (the Wise). He assembled a collection of 400 songs in Galician-

Portuguese, known as the *Cantigas de Santa Maria*. He founded a chair of music at Salamanca University, 1254.

Alford, John, English 16th-c. lutenist. He lived in London and in 1568 pub. a trans. of Adrien Le Roy's book on the lute, *A Briefe and Easye Instruction to learne ... the Lute*.

Alfred masque by Arne (words by J Thomson and D Mallet), performed at Cliveden, Bucks., the residence of Frederick, Prince of Wales, 1 Aug 1740. It contains 'Rule, Britannia'.

Opera by Dvořák, his first (libretto by K T Korner). Composed 1870; produced Olomouc, 10 Dec 1938. King Alfred defeats the Danes and frees his bride.

Alfred, König der Angelsachsen, *Alfred, King of the Anglo-Saxons*, incidental music by Haydn for a drama by J W Cowmeadow. Perf. Eisenstadt, Sept 1796.

Alfvén, Hugo (b Stockholm, 1 May 1872; d Uppsala, 8 May 1960), Swedish violinist and composer. Studied under Lindegren at the Stockholm Conservatory, and began his career as violinist in the court orchestra. From 1910 to 1939 he was music director at the University of Uppsala. His music is programmatic and in a light vein.

Works include five symphonies, two symphonic poems and Swedish rhapsody *Midsommarvaka* (1903) and two others for orchestra; *Sten Sture* for chorus and orchestra; *The Bells* for solo voice and orchestra; a cantata; two marches; pieces for piano and for violin; songs.

Algarotti, Francesco, Count (b Venice, 11 Dec 1712; d Pisa, 3 May 1764), Italian scholar. His libretto *Iphigénie en Aulide* influenced the text set by Gluck. Among many learned works he wrote a treatise on the reform of opera, *Saggio sopra l'opera in musica*, criticizing the practices of opera seria, pub. 1755.

Algarotti, Giovanni Francesco (b Novara, *c* 1536; d 8 May 1596), Italian composer. Pub. books of madrigals at Venice in 1567 and 1569.

Then comes the part to be sung, but the multitude of fiddles etc., that accompany it in general produce no better an effect than to astonish the faculty of hearing and to drown the voice of the singer.

Francesco Algarotti on opera,
Saggio sopra l'opera in musica, 1755

Alghisi, Paris Francesco (b Brescia, 19 Jun 1666; d Brescia, 29 Mar 1743), Italian composer. Studied under Polarolo and was engaged for some time at the Polish court. Two operas were produced at Venice: *Amor di Curzio per la patria*, 1690, and *Il trionfo della continenza*, 1691. He also wrote several oratorios and other works.

Ali Baba, ou Les Quarante Voleurs, *Ali Baba, or The Forty Thieves*, opera by Cherubini (libretto by Scribe and A H J Mélesville), produced Paris, Opéra, 22 Jul 1833. A new version of *Koukourgi*, composed 1793, but not performed.

Alina, Regina di Golconda opera by Donizetti (libretto by F Romani), produced Genoa, 12 May 1828. Courted by a tenor, Alina is eventually reunited with her lost husband.

aliquot parts, from Latin *aliquot* = 'some', parts contained by the whole, integral factors: in music the parts of a fundamental note vibrating separately as overtones.

aliquot scaling, aliquot strings additional strings, vibrating with those struck by the hammers, introduced into the upper registers of Blüthner's pianos, evidently on the old principle of the sympathetic strings in bowed string instruments.

Alkan, Charles-Valentin (actually Morhange) (b Paris, 30 Nov 1813; d Paris, 29 Mar 1888), French pianist and composer. He is alleged to have met his death under a collapsing bookcase. He was so precocious as a player that he was admitted to the Paris Conservatory at the age of six. After a visit to London in 1833, he settled in Paris as teacher of the piano. In his works he cultivated an advanced, immensely difficult and often very modern technique.

Works include Two piano concertos; piano trio; piano sonatas, numerous piano studies (including one for the right hand and one for the left), character pieces; four op. nos, of pieces for pedal piano.

Alkestis opera by Boughton (libretto taken from Gilbert Murray's English trans. of the tragedy by Euripides), produced Glastonbury, 26 Aug 1922.

Opera by Wellesz (libretto by H von Hofmannsthal, after Euripides), produced Mannheim, 20 Mar 1924.

alla Italian fem. = 'at the, in the manner of', = French *à la*; the word is used in various ways in combination with nouns, e.g. *alla marcia* = 'march-like', *alla francese* = 'in the French manner', etc. (also abbr. *all'* with nouns beginning with a vowel).

alla breve Italian = 'with the breve' (as unit of the beat, instead of the semibreve); a term used for a tempo direction indicating that the time is twice as fast as the note-values would suggest, though not necessarily a rapid tempo. The normal *alla breve* time-signature is ¢.

allargando Italian = 'becoming broader, slowing down'.

Allegranti, Maddalena (b Venice, 1754; d ?Ireland, *c* 1802), Italian soprano. Made her first appearance in Venice in 1770. Appeared in operas by Gassmann, Sacchini and Salieri in Italy and Germany before her 1781 London debut, in Anfossi's *I Viaggiatori Felici*.

allegretto Italian dim. of *allegro* = 'a little fast', i.e. not as fast as *allegro*, although in certain cases, especially in France *c* 1800, faster than *allegro*.

Allegri, Domenico (b Rome, 1585; d Rome, 5 Sept 1629), Italian composer. *Maestro di cappella* at Santa Maria Maggiore in Rome, 1610–29. Works include motets and music for voices and strings.

Allegri, Gregorio (b Rome, 1582; d Rome, 7 Feb 1652), Italian priest and composer. Pupil of the Nanini brothers in Rome, where he sang tenor in the Papal Chapel from 1629. His famous *Miserere* is still sung there; Mozart, as a boy of 14, wrote it down from memory after hearing it in Rome. Allegri also wrote Magnificats, five a capella masses, motets and other church music.

Allegri Quartet British string quartet founded in 1953 with Eli Goren as leader. Since 1983 members have been Peter Carter and David Roth (violins), Roger Tapping (viola) and Bruno Schrecker (cello). Has given performances of quartets by Maconchy, LeFanu, Goehr, Britten and Bridge.

allegro Italian = lit. 'cheerful, sprightly'; in music the term, although originally doubtless describing the character of a piece, now indicates merely speed: a fast but not very fast pace.

Allegro Barbaro work for solo piano by Bartók, composed 1911 but not performed until 27 Feb 1921, in Budapest.

Allegro, il Penseroso ed il Moderato, L', *The Cheerful, the Thoughtful and the Moderate Man*, oratorio by Handel (libretto Parts i and ii by Milton, Part iii by Charles Jennens), produced London, Lincoln's Inn Fields Theatre, 27 Feb 1740.

Alleluia the third chant of the Proper of the Mass, sung immediately after the Gradual. The word is Hebrew (= 'praise ye Jehova'), and was sung in many contexts in Jewish life, but especially in connection with the singing of the Psalms. It was taken over unchanged by the Christian Church and sung both alone and as an addition to chants of various kinds, especially during the Easter season. As a Mass-chant of the Roman rite it was originally sung alone, at first during Easter-tide only and, after the time of Gregory I, during the whole year except from Septuagesima to Easter. At some time before 750 one or more verses were added, in which form it became a responsorial chant, the choir singing the alleluia at the beginning and end, and the soloists the verse or verses in between.

The alleluia of the Ambrosian chant, possibly retaining more of its original oriental characteristics, is even more florid in character.

Allemande French = 'German'; (1) A dance in moderate 4–4 time, divided into two sections, each repeated, and usually beginning with a short upbeat. It occurs in most classical suites, where it takes first place unless they open with a prelude. (2) = Deutscher Tanz.

Allen, Henry Robinson (b Cork, 1809; d London, 27 Nov 1876), Irish baritone. He first became known in London in 1842 when he sang Damon in a performance of *Acis and Galatea* at Drury Lane and made

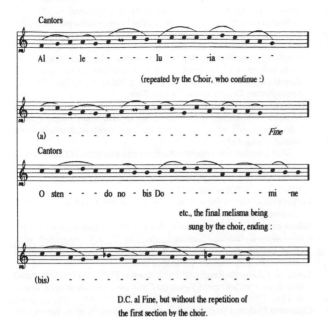

D.C. al Fine, but without the repetition of the first section by the choir.

Alleluia. The exact form as sung since the Middle Ages may be illustrated from the alleluia for the First Sunday of Advent.

a great reputation as an operatic artist, but retired early to devote himself to teaching and the composition of songs, including 'When we two parted'.

Allen, Perceval (b Ripley, 1880; d London, Dec 1955), English soprano. She studied with William Shakespeare and sang in concert with the LSO, 1905. Successful in oratorio and appeared at CG 1908–10, as Brünnhilde, under Richter, and as Lia in a stage version of Debussy's *L'Enfant prodigue* (1910). Toured in N America with the Quinlan co. and was heard in Chicago, Philadelphia and Boston as Brünnhilde, Brangaene, Erda, and Rebecca in Sullivan's *Ivanhoe*.

Allen, Thomas (b Seaham Harbour, Co. Durham, 10 Sept 1944), English baritone. Opera debut 1969, with WNO. CG from 1971, Glyndebourne from 1973. Noted as Papageno, Pelléas and Don Giovanni; also concert singer. In 1985 he sang Ulysses in the Salzburg fp of Monteverdi's *Il ritorno di Ulisse*, arranged by Henze. At the London Coliseum in 1986 he was Faust in the first British stage performance of Busoni's opera. Sang Mozart's Count at LA 1990, Salzburg 1994; Forester and Beckmesser in new productions of *The Cunning Little Vixen* and *Meistersinger* at CG.

Allende, Pedro Humberto (b Santiago, 29 Jun 1885; d Santiago, 17 Aug 1959), Chilean composer and educationist. Studied at the National Conservatory of Chile.

Works included *Tres Tonadas, Escenas campesinas chilenas* (1913) and *La voz de la calles* (1921) for orchestra; concertos for cello (1915), violin (1942), piano (1945).

Allin, Norman (b Ashton-under-Lyme, 19 Nov 1884; d London, 27 Oct 1973), English bass. He studied at the RMCM and from 1916 sang with the Beecham co. as Dosifey, Méphistophélès and Marke; CG 1919–20, as Konchak and Gurnemanz. BNOC 1922–29, as leading bass and director, and sang Bartolo in the 1934 production of *Figaro* which inaugurated the Glyndebourne Fest. Professor RAM, 1935–60. CBE, 1958.

Allison (*Alison, Alyson*), Richard, English 16th–17th-c. composer. He first appeared as a contributor to East's *Whole Book of Psalms* in 1592 and pub. a collection of church melodies set for voices and instruments, *The Psalmes of David in Meter*, in 1599. Other works include lute music and 24 songs for voices and instruments, *An Howres Recreation* ..., pub. 1606.

all' ottava Italian = 'at the octave'; a direction that a passage, so far as it is marked by a dotted line over it, is to be played an octave higher than it is written; it is usually represented by the symbol 8*va*. If the dotted line is below, it means an octave lower.

Almahide opera by ? Giovanni Bononcini (libretto by ?, after Dryden's *Almanzor and Almahide*), produced London, Queen's Theatre, Haymarket, 10 Jan 1710. According to Burney, the first opera performed in England wholly in Italian.

Almeida, Fernando de (b Lisbon, *c* 1600; d Thomar, 21 Mar 1660), Portuguese monk and composer. Pupil of Lobo; entered the monastery of Thomar in 1638; wrote Masses and other church music.

Almeida, Francisco Antonio de (b *c* 1702; d Lisbon, 1755), Portuguese 18th-c. composer. Probably studied in Rome and was the first Portuguese to write Italian operas, including *La Spinalba* (1739) and *La pazienza di Socrate* (1733).

almérie a kind of lute invented in the 18th c. by Jean Lemaire, on whose own name it is an anagram.

Almira opera by Handel (libretto by F C Feustking), produced Hamburg, Theater beim Gänse-markt, 8 Jan 1705. Handel's first opera; Almira loves Fernando but must marry Osman.

Alpaerts, Flor (b Antwerp, 12 Sept 1876; d Antwerp, 5 Oct 1954), Belgian conductor and composer. Studied with Benoit and Blockx at the Antwerp Conservatory, in 1903 became professor there and in 1934–41 was its director. In 1919 he also became conductor of the Antwerp Zoo Orchestra and in 1922–23 he directed the Royal Flemish Opera.

Works include opera *Shylock* (after Shakespeare); incidental music for plays; church music, *Spring* symphony, symphonic poem *Psyche* and other orchestral works; violin concerto; chamber music; piano works; songs.

Alpensinfonie, Eine, *An Alpine Symphony*, symphony by R Strauss, op. 64, fp Berlin 28 Oct 1915.

al rovescio Italian = 'backwards'; ◊Cancrizans.

Also sprach Zarathustra, *Thus spake Zoroaster*, symphonic poem by R Strauss, op. 30, based on Nietzsche, composed 1896, fp Frankfurt, 27 Nov 1896.

Altenberglieder five songs for voice and orchestra to picture-postcard texts by 'Peter Altenberg' (i.e. Richard Englander, 1862–1919), by Berg. At the fp in Vienna of two of the songs, 1913, a riot caused the concert to be abandoned. First complete performance Rome, 24 Jan 1953, conductor Horenstein.

Allen *Thomas Allen as Papageno in* Die Zauberflöte/The Magic Flute *at Covent Garden with Stuart Burrows as Tamino, and the Three Ladies. Well suited to comedy, his dramatic talent is equally successful in serious roles.*

alternatim Latin a manner of performance in which singers or players are heard in alternation, e.g. between two sides of a choir, between choir and organ, etc. It can also be applied to alternation between music styles, e.g. plainsong and polyphony.

alternativo Italian a contrasting section, much the same as the trio in a minuet or scherzo, but often in a piece of a different character, and there may be more than one alternativo in a single piece. Familiar examples appear in Schumann.

Althouse, Paul (b Reading, PA, 2 Dec 1889; d New York, 6 Feb 1954), American tenor. Debut NY, with Philadelphia co., 1911 (Faust); Met. from 1913, as Dmitri and in the fp of works by Herbert, Giordano, de Koven and Cadman. Appeared in Europe from 1929 and after study at Bayreuth sang Tristan at the 1935 Salzburg Festival; returned to the Met. 1934 and sang Tristan and Siegmund, opposite Flagstad. Among his pupils were Richard Tucker and Leopold Simoneau.

Altmeyer, Jeannine (b Pasadena, 4 May 1948), American soprano of German-Italian parentage. She studied with Lotte Lehmann and in Salzburg. NY Met. 1971, Chicago 1972. Salzburg and Zurich from 1973. Sang Sieglinde at Bayreuth, 1979, and Brünnhilde in first compact disc recording of *The Ring* (conductor Janowski). She sang Isolde at Bayreuth in 1986, Leonore at La Scala. Noted for her highly spirited interpretations.

Altnikol, Johann Christoph (b Berna, Silesia, Oct 1719; d Naumburg, buried 25 Jul 1759), German harpsichordist, organist and composer. Pupil of Bach in Leipzig from 1744. Appointed organist at Nieder-wiesa near Greifenberg early in 1748, and later the same year at Naumburg. Married Bach's daughter Elisabetha Juliane Frederica (1726–81) in 1749. Known primarily as a copyist of Bach's music.

alto Italian = 'high'; (1) properly an extension of the highest male-voice register, produced by falsetto, used in Anglican church choirs and in male-voice quartets and choral societies, particularly in glees and part-songs. (2) = contralto. (3) (French) = viola. (4) as a prefix to an instrument = a size larger than the soprano, e.g. alto saxophone.

alto clef the C clef so used as to indicate that middle C stands on the central line of the stave; not now used in vocal music, but still in use for the viola.

The alto clef.

Alto Rhapsody, Brahms, ◊Rhapsodie.

Alva, Luigi (Luis) (b Lima, 10 Apr 1927), Peruvian tenor. Began his career with Radio Lima and in 1953 went to Italy, singing at La Scala in 1954. He specialized in operatic lyric roles, and sang at most of the great opera-houses and festivals. CG from 1960; NY Met. debut 1964, as Fenton. Other roles included Alfredo, Almaviva and Ferrando. Retired from singing 1989.

Alvary, Max (b Düsseldorf, 3 May 1856; d Gross-Tabarz, Thuringia, 7 Nov 1898), German tenor. Debut Weimar, 1879. NY Met. 1885, as Don José; first US Loge, Siegfried and Adolar. Sang in CG *Ring* under Mahler, 1892, as Siegfried. Other roles included Max, Tristan and Spontini's Cortez.

Alwin, Karl (b Königsberg, 15 Apr 1891; d Mexico City, 15 Oct 1945), German conductor, pianist and composer. He studied at Berlin with Humperdinck; conducted opera at Halle, Düsseldorf and Hamburg 1913–20, and worked at the Vienna Staatsoper 1920–38: during this period he was married to Elisabeth Schumann. Appeared widely as guest, and at CG in 1924 gave the first local performance of *Ariadne auf Naxos*, revised version, with Schumann and Lotte Lehmann. Conductor, National Opera, Mexico City, from 1941.

Alwyn, William (b Northampton, 7 Nov 1905; d Southwold, 11 Sept 1985), English composer. Entered the RAM in London as a student for flute, piano and composition, studying the last under McEwen and obtaining the Costa Scholarship. He played the flute in the LSO and his first work for orchestra (*Five Preludes*) was given at a 1927 Prom concert. Wrote music for wartime films and documentaries. Professor of composition RAM 1926–56. CBE 1978. His music from 1939 was neo-classical in spirit; it later became more subjective.

Works include opera, *Miss Julie* (1961–76), music for films, *Our Country, The Lost Illusion*, and many others; five preludes, concerto grosso, overture to a masque, and five symphonies for orchestra (1949–73); piano concerto, violin concerto, *Pastoral Fantasia* for viola and strings; two string quartets, Rhapsody for piano quartet; Sonata-Impromptu for violin and viola, sonatina for viola and piano; piano pieces; Divertimento for solo flute.

Alyabyev, Alexander Alexandrovich (b Tobolsk, 15 Aug 1787; d Moscow, 6 Mar 1851), Russian composer. He was an army officer who fought as a hussar against Napoleon; cultivated music as an amateur from 1823.

Works include two operas after Shakespeare: *Burya* (*The Tempest*, 1835) and *The Enchanted Night* (*A Midsummer Night's Dream*, 1839). His song *The Nightingale* was used by Patti and Viardot for the letter scene in *Il Barbiere di Siviglia*.

Alypios 4th-c. Greek theorist to whom our knowledge of ancient Greek notation is due.

Alzira opera by Verdi (libretto by S Cammarano, based on Voltaire's play *Alzire*), produced Naples, Teatro San Carlo, 12 Aug 1845. Inca chief Zamoro stabs Gusmano, governor of Peru, as the Spaniard attempts to wed Zamoro's intended bride.

Amadei, Filippo (b Reggio, *c* 1670; d after 1729), Italian cellist and composer. His first opera, *Teodosio il giovane*, was produced in Rome in 1711.

Amadeus Quartet British string quartet; members from its foundation in 1948 were Norbert Brainin and Sigmund Nissel (violins), Peter Schidlof (viola) and Martin Lovett (cello). Gave fp of Britten's third quartet in 1975 but mostly associated with the Classical repertory. Brainin, OBE, 1960; other members, 1973. The quartet was disbanded in 1987 on the death of Peter Schidlof.

Amadigi di Gaula, *Amadis of Gaul*, opera by Handel (libretto adapted from A H de la Motte's *Amadis de Grèce*, set by Destouches, 1699), produced London, King's Theatre, Haymarket, 25 May 1715. Amadigi and Oriana are united when the interfering infatuated sorceress Melissa abandons her deceptions.

Amadis opera by Lully (libretto by Quinault, based on the old Iberian romance *Amadis de Gaula*), produced Paris, Opéra, 18 Jan 1684. Amadis in adventures to win the doubting heart of Oriane.

Opera by Massenet (libretto by J Claretie), composed *c* 1895 and performed posthumously in Monte Carlo, 1 Apr 1922.

Amadori, Giuseppe (b *c* 1670; d after 1730), Italian composer. *Maestro di cappella* in Rome, where his oratorio, *Il martirio di Sant' Adriano*, was produced in 1702. He also wrote Masses and other church music.

Amahl and the Night Visitors opera in one act by Menotti (libretto by the composer, after Bosch's painting *The Adoration of the Magi*), produced on NBC Television 24 Dec 1951. It is the first opera especially written for TV.

Amar, Licco (b Budapest, 4 Dec 1891; d Freiburg i/B, 19 Jul 1959), Hungarian violinist. He was leader of the Berlin Philharmonic 1915–20 and in 1921 formed the Amar string quartet, with Hindemith as violist: gave frequent fps of modern works, including Hindemith's string quartets nos. 2, 3 and 4.

Amara, Lucine (b Hartford, CT, 1 Mar 1927), American soprano. Her career began in CA and she made her NY Met. debut in Nov 1950, on the opening night of Rudolf Bing's regime; later sang there as Aida, Mimi, Donna Anna and Eurydice. Glyndebourne 1955–58, as Ariadne and Donna Elvira. She recorded Musetta with Beecham and Elsa with Leinsdorf.

Amarus lyric cantata by Janáček for soprano, tenor, baritone, chorus and orchestra; composed *c* 1897, revised 1901 and 1906. First performed Kroměříž, 2 Dec 1900.

Amat, Juan Carlos (b Monistrol near Barcelona, *c* 1572; d Monistrol, 10 Feb 1642), Spanish scientist and author. He wrote *Guitarra española* ..., the earliest known treatise on the subject, pub. probably 1586.

Amati Italian 16th–17th-c. family of violin makers at Cremona:
Andrea Amati (b before 1511; d Cremona, before 1580).
Antonio Amati (b 1550; d 1638).

Girolamo (or Geronimo) Amati (b 1561; d 1630).

Nicolo Amati (b 3 Dec 1596; d 12 Apr 1684).

Girolamo Amati (b 26 Feb 1649; d 21 Feb 1740).

Andrea Amati and his two sons developed many of the features we see today in the violin, viola and cello; Nicolo (son of Girolamo) created the wider violin type known as the 'Grand Amati'.

Amato, Pasquale (b Naples, 21 Mar 1878; d Jackson Heights, Long Island, NY, 12 Aug 1942), Italian baritone. Made his first appearance in England in 1904 as Amonasro at CG and later had much success in opera in USA. He sang at the NY Met. 1908–21 and created Jack Rance in *La Fanciulla del West*, 1910. Other roles included Valentin, Escamillo, Kurwenal and Amfortas.

Ambache, Diana (b Kent, 6 Jun 1948), English pianist and conductor. Studied at RAM and made debut at Purcell Room, London, 1979. Founded and directed Mozart Chamber Orchestra 1977–83, Ambache Chamber Orchestra 1984. Many tours of Europe, Africa and the Far East in concertos by Mozart, Tailleferre, Dussek, Kozeluch and M Haydn. In 1995 she initiated the three-year concert series Women of Note with the premiere of Clara Schumann's F minor Concertsatz (1847).

Ambiela, Miguel (b Saragossa, 29 Sept 1666; d Toledo, 29 Mar 1733), Spanish priest and composer. Music director of the new cathedral at Saragossa, 1700–07, and *maestro de capilla* at Toledo, 1710–33. Works include Masses, *Stabat Mater* and other church music.

Ambleto, *Hamlet*, opera by Gasparini (libretto by A Zeno and P Pariati), produced Venice, Teatro San Cassiano, Carnival 1705.

Opera by D Scarlatti (libretto ditto), produced Rome, Teatro Capranica, Carnival 1715.

Ambros, August Wilhelm (b Vysoké Myto, 17 Nov 1816; d Vienna, 28 Jun 1876), Czech (Germanized) musicologist. Studied at Prague University. His life's work was a history of music which at his death reached only the fourth volume and the early 17th c. He also composed a Czech opera, *Bratislav and Jitka*, overtures to Shakespeare's *Othello* and Calderón's *Mágico prodigioso*, etc.

Ambrosian Chant the music of the Milanese rite associated with St Ambrose (340–397), Bishop of Milan from 374. The music as we now have it is mostly preserved in late medieval MSS and probably differs considerably from that heard in Ambrosian times; nor can any of the extant tunes to the few authentic hymns of St Ambrose be definitely considered to be of the same date. The rite itself belongs to the Gallican family, containing oriental features not preserved in that of Rome; while the chant, even in its present form, shows Eastern influences to a greater degree than 'Gregorian' Chant.

Ameling, Elly (b Rotterdam, 8 Feb 1934), Dutch soprano. She sang in Amsterdam from 1961; London debut 1966. Sang with Netherlands Opera in 1973 but has most often been heard in Lieder and oratorio. She took part in the 1959 fp of Martin's *Mystère de la Nativité* and has been heard in the cantatas and Passions of Bach, songs by Satie and Schubert and concert music by Mahler and Mendelssohn.

amener, French, probably from *mener* = 'to lead', a French dance of the 17th c. in triple time and moderate pace, with characteristic six-bar phrases. It occurs in French instrumental suites and thence passed to some extent into German and Italian music.

America epic rhapsody by Bloch in three movements (1. 1620; 2. 1861–65; 3. 1926), composed 1926–27. First performed 20 Dec 1928 and then on 21 Dec 1928 simultaneously in seven American cities. It won the prize offered by *Musical America* for the best American symphonic work.

American musical terminology the main differences from British usage are nearly all direct translations from German. Whole note, half note, quarter note, etc. (for semibreve, minim, crotchet, etc.); concert master for leader, and so on. The most potentially confusing is the word 'tone' meaning British 'pitch': hence Americans tend to use 'tone row' for British 'note row', 'neighbor tone' for 'auxiliary note', 'whole step' and 'half step' for British 'tone' and 'semitone'. Other details in which usage tends to cross the Atlantic in both directions include 'flutist' (flautist), and 'measure' (bar).

American organ an instrument similar to the harmonium, differing

from the latter in some details, particularly in sucking in the wind through its reeds instead of expelling it. Its principle was discovered by a workman attached to Jacob Alexandre (1804–1876), an instrument maker in Paris, but he took it to America and the first important instruments of the kind were made by Mason & Hamlin of Boston c 1860.

Amériques work for orchestra by Varèse; instruments include sleighbells, steamboat whistle and hand siren as used by NY Fire Dept; composed 1918–22, fp Philadelphia, 9 Apr 1926, conductor Stokowski.

Amfiparnaso, L', *The Amphi-Parnassus*, madrigal opera by Orazio Vecchi, produced Modena, 1594, and published Venice, 1597, described as a *commedia harmonica*. It consists of three acts and a prologue, and the characters are the stock figures of the *commedia dell' arte*, but the musical setting of their speech is in the form of madrigals for mixed voices. It has been supposed that the action was produced in dumb-show while the madrigals were sung behind the scenes, but a passage in the text which says that 'the spectacle is to enter by the ear, not by the eye' gives good reason to doubt this. The same subject was treated earlier in a smaller form by Lassus.

Amico Fritz, L' opera by Mascagni (libretto by P Suardon, based on Erckmann-Chatrian's novel *L'Ami Fritz*), produced Rome, Teatro Costanzi, 31 Oct 1891. Bachelor Fritz falls for Suzel after encouragement from the matchmaker Rabbi David.

Amid Nature, or *In Nature's Realm*, concert overture by Dvořák, op. 91, composed 1891 and forming, with *Carnival* and *Othello*, a cycle with thematic connections, originally called *Nature, Life and Love*.

Amirov, Fikret Dzhamll (b Kirovabad, 22 Nov 1922; d Baku, 20 Feb 1984), Azerbaijani composer. His music is influenced by local folk tunes.

Works include opera *Sevil* (1953); double concerto for violin, piano and orchestra (1948); *The Pledge of the Korean Guerrilla Fighter* for voice and orchestra (1951); piano concerto (1957).

Amleto, *Hamlet*, opera by Faccio (libretto by Boito, after Shakespeare), produced Genoa, Teatro Carlo Felice, 30 May 1865.

Opera by Mercadante (libretto by Romani, after Shakespeare), produced Milan, La Scala, 26 Dec 1822.

The most perfect technique is that which is not noticed at all.

Pablo Casals, quoted in Julian Lloyd Webber, *The Song of the Birds*, 1985

Ammerbach (*Amerbach*), Elias Nikolaus (b Naumberg, c 1530; d Leipzig, buried 29 Jan 1597), German organist and composer. Was organist of St Thomas, Leipzig, from 1560 and pub. two books of music in organ tablature containing important explanations of ornaments and modes of performance.

Amner, John (b Ely, bap. 24 Aug 1579; d Ely, buried 28 Jul 1641), English organist and composer. He became organist and choirmaster at Ely Cathedral in 1610; wrote services, anthems and *Sacred Hymns*.

Amon, Johann Andreas (b Bamberg, 1763; d Wallerstein, Bavaria, 29 Mar 1825), German horn player, composer and conductor. Toured in France and Germany and had composition lessons from Sacchini in Paris in 1781; became music director at Heilbronn in 1789 and *Kapellmeister* to the Prince of Oettingen-Wallerstein in 1817.

Works include two *Singspiele*, Masses, symphonies, chamber music.

Amor brujo, El, *Love, the Magician*, ballet by Falla, composed 1913–14, fp Madrid, Teatro de Lara, 15 Apr 1915.

Amor coniugale, L' opera by Mayr (librettist G Rossi, after Bouilly), produced Padua, 26 Jul 1805 (four months before *Fidelio*, which is based on the same source). Condensed into one act, Leonore/Fidelio becomes Zeliska/Malvino, Pizarro is Moroski, and Rocco is Peters.

Amore dei tre re, L', *The love of the Three Kings*, opera by Montemezzi (libretto by S Benelli, from his play of the same title), produced Milan, La Scala, 10 Apr 1913. The king strangles his daughter-in-law and spreads poison on her lips; her lover and husband also die after kissing her.

Amorevoli, Angelo (b Venice, 16 Sept 1716; d Dresden, 15 Nov 1798), Italian tenor. He sang in Italy 1730–41, in operas by ◊Porpora, Hasse, Leo and G Scarlatti. Spent most of his time at the court of Dresden in operas by ◊Hasse, 1745–64, and sang in London 1741–43.

amoroso Italian = 'amorous'; a direction indicating an emotional and tender manner of performance.

Amour médecin, L' comédie-ballet by Lully (libretto by Molière), produced Versailles, 16 Sept 1665.

Amours d'Antoine et de Cléopâtre, Les, *The Loves of Antony and Cleopatra*, ballet by R Kreutzer (choreography by J P Aumer, based on Shakespeare), produced Paris, Opéra, 8 Mar 1808.

Amram, David (b Philadelphia, 17 Nov 1930), American composer and horn player. Studied at the Manhattan School of Music and with Charles Mills. Has written incidental music for Shakespeare's plays, films and jazz bands. Commission from the Library of Congress, 1995.

Works include operas *The Final Ingredient* (ABC TV, 1965), *Twelfth Night* (1968); *Shakespearean Concerto* (1960), *King Lear Variations* for wind, percussion and piano (1967), concertos for horn, jazz quintet, bassoon and violin (1968–80); string quartet (1961), sonata for solo violin (1964), wind quintet (1968); cantatas *The American Bell*, *A Year in our Land* and *Let us Remember* (1962–65).

Most people use music as a couch ... But serious music was never meant to be used as a soporific.
Aaron Copland, *New York Times*, 1949

Amy, Gilbert (b Paris, 29 Aug 1936), French composer of advanced tendencies. Studied with Milhaud, Messiaen and Boulez. Dir. of the Concerts du Domaine Musical, specializing in new music. His compositions show influences of oriental music, total serialism and also aleatory techniques.

Works include *Messe* for soloists, chorus and orchestra (1983); *Mouvements* for chamber orchestra (1958), *Adagio et Stretto* for orchestra (1978); *Alpha-Beth* for six wind instruments (1964), *Cycles* for percussion; *Epigrammes* for piano; *Chant pour orchestre* (1980); *La Variation ajoutée* for tape and instruments (1986); *Ecrits sur toile* for reciter and ensemble (1983); *Orchestral* (1987); *Choros* for male vocalists, chorus and orchestra (1989); *Obliques* I–III for piano (1987–89); *Mémoire* for cello and piano (1989).

Ana, Francesco d' (b ? Venice, *c* 1460; d Venice, *c* 1503), Italian composer. At St Mark's, Venice, 1490; composed *frottole*, Lamentations, etc.

Anacréon *acte de ballet* by Rameau (libretto by P-J Bernard), produced Fontainebleau, 23 Oct 1754; revised and produced Paris, Opéra, 10 Oct 1758.

Anacréon, ou L'Amour fugitif, *opera-ballet* by Cherubini (libretto by R Mendouze), produced Paris, Opéra, 4 Oct 1803. Poet Anacréon in love with protégée Chloë.

anacrusis in prosody, an unstressed syllable at the beginning of a verse or line; in music the literary term is borrowed as a synonym for upbeat.

Anakreontika Greek songs for mezzo and instrumental ensemble by Peter Maxwell Davies; fp London, 17 Sept 1976.

analysis as recently as the 1950s, the analysis of music was widely understood to denote any kind of description with some technical component. But for more than a century there has been a growing academic discipline which attempts to explain musical phenomena by means as rigorous and logical as possible, to approach formal models of how music works, or to break down the organism of musical structures into smaller components. Pure musical analysis often eschews value judgment, which is more the province of the critic or aesthetician. ◊Keller, Meyer (L), Nattiez, Reti, Schenker.

Ančerl, Karel (b Tučapy, Bohemia, 11 Apr 1908; d Toronto, 3 Jul 1973), Czech conductor. Studied with Křička and Alois Hába at the Prague Conservatory (1925–29). Assistant to Scherchen in Berlin (1929–31). His public career began in 1931 as a theatre conductor and with Czech radio. Conductor at ISCM festivals, 1933–37. Imprisoned in World War II, he resumed his career in 1945, becoming professor at the Academy of Musical Arts in Prague (1950). Conductor Czech PO 1950–68; music director Toronto SO from 1969.

Anchieta, Juan de (b Azpeitia near San Sebastián, 1462; d Azpeitia, 30 Jul 1523), Spanish composer. He became a court musician in 1489 and a canon of Granada ten years later. From 1500 he was rector of the parish church in his native place. Wrote motets, Magnificats and secular songs.

Ancona, Mario (b Livorno, 28 Feb 1860; d Florence, 23 Feb 1931), Italian baritone. Debut Trieste 1890, as Scindia in Massenet's *Roi de Lahore*. In 1893 he was Tonio in the first local performances of *Pagliacci* at CG and the NY Met. He sang Le Cid at La Scala in 1890 and Bellini's Riccardo at the opening night of the Manhattan Opera House, NY, 1906. Other roles included Don Giovanni, Amonasro, Iago, Sachs and Escamillo.

Anda, Géza (b Budapest, 19 Nov 1921; d Zurich, 14 Jun 1976), Hungarian pianist and conductor. Studied at the Royal Music Academy in Budapest with Dohnányi, winning the Liszt Prize. Left Hungary in World War II and lived in Switzerland. He was best known as an exponent of Brahms, Liszt, Bartók and Mozart, all of whose piano concertos he recorded.

andamento Italian a fugue subject of more than usual length and often in two contrasted sections.

andante Italian = 'going'; a tempo direction indicating a 'walking pace', i.e. a moderate tempo.

andantino Italian, diminutive of *andante* originally intended to indicate a slower pace than *andante*, i.e. a diminutive of 'walking'; but since *andante* is now taken to mean a slow pace, the diminutive suggests an only moderately slow, i.e. slightly quicker tempo.

Anday, Rosette (b Budapest, 22 Dec 1903; d Vienna, 28 Sept 1977), Hungarian-born mezzo. She studied violin with Jenö Hubay at Budapest and made her stage debut there in 1920; sang at the Vienna Staatsoper 1921–61, and was popular there and at Salzburg as Carmen, Orpheus, Dorabella, Clytemnestra and Weber's Fatima. At Salzburg in 1947 she sang in the fp of Einem's *Dantons Tod*. She appeared as a guest in London and in N and S America.

Anders, Peter (b Essen, 1 Jul 1908; d Hamburg, 10 Sept 1954), German tenor. Made his debut in Berlin in 1931 in *La Belle Hélène*, and from 1936 to 1948 sang at the Berlin Staatsoper. British debut in 1950 at the Edinburgh Fest., as Bacchus. CG 1951 as Walther. Other roles included Tamino, Lohengrin and Florestan. He was killed in a car crash.

Anderson, Beth (b Lexington, KY, 3 Jan 1950), American composer and performance artist. She has consulted such composers as Cage, Larry Austin and Terry Riley, but is an autodidact. Her compositions involve freedom of improvisation and employ a wide range of resources.

Works include opera *Queen Christina* (1973) and text-sound piece *Riot Rot* (1984); oratorio *Joan* (1974), music theatre *Soap Tuning* (1976) and *Elizabeth Rex* (1983); *Revel* for orchestra (1985); *Music for Charlemagne Palestine* (1973); *Rosemary Swale* for string quartet (1986).

Anderson, Emily (b Galway, Ireland, 17 Mar 1891; d London, 26 Oct 1962), English musicologist. Although employed in the Foreign Office, she edited and trans. the complete letters of Mozart and his family (two vols., 1938) and those of Beethoven (three vols., 1962).

Anderson, June (b Boston, 30 Dec 1952), American soprano. Debut NY City Opera 1978, Queen of Night; other NY roles including Lucia, Cleopatra and Olympia. European debut 1982, Rome, as Semiramide. In 1985–86 she sang Amina at La Scala and Isabelle in *Robert le Diable* at the Paris Opéra. Her spectacular coloratura was much applauded in a concert performance of *Semiramide* at CG. Other roles include Gilda, Violetta, Rossini's Desdemona and Bellini's Elvira. Met. debut 1989, Gilda.

Anderson, Laurie (b Chicago, 5 Jun 1947), American composer and performance artist. She trained as a violinist and minimalist painter and in 1974 began making her own instruments, including a violin with an internal speaker. She has appeared widely in Europe and the USA, notably in multi-media, cyber-punk shows which employ a voice-activated synthesizer; contact microphones have turned her body into a percussion set. In 1973 she staged the 12-hour audio-visual show *The Life and Times of Josef Stalin* (Brooklyn Academy). She gave a one-woman show in London, 1994.

Works include *Americans on the Move* (1979, developed into *United States Live*, 1983); *New York Social Life*; *Time to Go* (portraying a museum attendant at closing time); *Empty Places* (1989); the autobiographical *Stories from the Nerve Bible* (1993); album *Bright Red* (1994).

Anderson, Marian (b Philadelphia, 17 Feb 1899; d Portland, OR, 8 Apr 1993), American contralto. Won competition to appear with NY PO in 1925; studied in Europe 1933–35. Heard largely in concert repertory but in 1955 became first black singer to appear at NY Met. (Ulrica).

An die ferne Geliebte, *To the Distant Beloved*, song cycle by Beethoven (six songs), op. 98, to poems by A Jeitteles, composed 1816. It is the first German set of songs intended to form a connected cycle.

André, Johann (b Offenbach, 28 Mar 1741; d Offenbach, 18 Jun 1799), German music publisher and composer. Produced his first successful *Singspiel* in 1773 and set Goethe's *Erwin und Elmire* in 1775. Established his publishing firm in 1774. His opera *Belmont und Constanze* of 1781 preceded Mozart's *Entführung*, on the same subject.

André, Johann Anton (b Offenbach, 6 Oct 1775; d Offenbach, 6 Apr 1842), German music publisher, violinist, pianist and composer, son of Johann André. He followed his father in business, acquired Mozart's MSS from Constanze in 1799 and with Senefelder applied the principle of lithography to music publishing.

André, Martin (b West Wickham, 10 Dec 1960), English conductor. Studied at the RCM and Cambridge and made his debut in 1982 with his own edition of Purcell's *King Arthur*. For WNO he has conducted *Aïda*, *Jenůfa* and *Ernani*, and has appeared with Vancouver Opera from 1987, with *The Cunning Little Vixen Ariadne* and *Traviata*. London concert debut 1987, with the ECO, and for ENO has led *The Love for Three Oranges* (1990) and the premiere of John Buller's *The Bacchae*. Conductor of English Touring Opera from 1993.

André, Maurice (b Alès near Nîmes, 24 May 1933), French trumpeter. Debut 1954; has won competitions in Geneva and Munich. Best known in Baroque and contemporary music.

Andrea Chénier opera by Giordano (libretto by L Illica), produced Milan, La Scala, 28 Mar 1896. Chénier and Madeleine guillotined after the Revolution, after Chénier has been denounced by Gérard, a rival in love.

Andreae, Volkmar (b Berne, 5 Jul 1879; d Zurich, 18 Jun 1962), Swiss composer and conductor. Studied at Berne and Cologne, in 1900 became assistant conductor at the Munich Opera, in 1902 choral conductor at Zurich and Winterthur, later conductor of the Zurich symphony concerts. From 1914 to 1916 he lectured at Zurich University and from 1914 to 1939 was director of the Zurich Conservatory.

Works include operas *Ratcliff* (based on Heine's tragedy, produced Duisburg, 1914) and *Abenteuer des Casanova* (produced Dresden, 1924); two symphonies; several concertos; choral works; chamber music.

Andreozzi, Gaetano (b Naples, 1763; d Paris, 21 Dec 1826), Italian composer. Pupil and relation of Jommelli; wrote 45 operas, including *L'Olimpiade* (Pisa, 1782), *Giovanna d'Arco* (Vicenza, 1789) and *Piramo e Tisbe* (1803), three oratorios, chamber music and songs.

Andrésen, Ivar (b Oslo, 27 Jul 1896; d Stockholm, 24 Nov 1940), Norwegian bass. Debut Stockholm, 1919. Dresden and Berlin 1925–36; Bayreuth 1927–36 as Gurnemanz, King Marke and Pogner. Glyndebourne 1935 as Sarastro and Osmin.

Andricu, Michel (b Bucharest, 3 Jan 1895; d Bucharest, 4 Feb 1974), Romanian composer. Studied at the Bucharest Conservatory and later became professor at the Royal Academy there, gaining the Enescu

---

THE OPERA

Andrea Chénier

A four-act opera of 1896 by Umberto Giordano, set in Revolutionary France.

I. The poet Andrea Chénier (tenor) arrives with other guests at the house of aristocratic Madeleine de Coigny (soprano), who is in love with Chénier. Coigny's servant Carlo Gérard (baritone) also secretly loves Madeleine, but when he and a gang of peasants interrupt the party he is dismissed.

II. Chénier is advised to leave Paris in the wake of the Revolution but he will not go until he learns the identity of the woman who has tried to protect him. Chénier is seen talking to Madeleine and is challenged by Gérard, who is now a member of the government; Gérard is wounded but will not identify Chénier.

III. When Chénier is arrested a year later, Madeleine offers herself to Gérard if he will save him, but the tribunal condemns Chénier to death.

IV. Chénier composes a final poem as Madeleine bribes his gaoler to be admitted as a prisoner. The lovers sing a final duet as they are led away to the guillotine, and Gérard is left alone and lamenting.

THE OPERA

Prize for composition in 1924. From 1926 to 1959 he was professor at the Bucharest Conservatory.

Works include ballet *Taina*; 11 symphonies (1944–70), 13 sinfoniettas (1945–73); nine orchestral suites (1924–58); serenade; three *Tableaux symphoniques*; *Suite pittoresque*; *Suite brève*; *Poem*, etc., for orchestra; string quartet (1931); *Novellettes* for piano quintet and other chamber music; sonatina; *Suite lyrique* and other piano works.

Andriessen, Hendrik (b Haarlem, 17 Sept 1892; d Heemstede, 12 Apr 1981), Dutch organist and composer. Studied under Zweers at the Amsterdam Conservatory. Later became director of the Utrecht Conservatory and choirmaster at the Roman Catholic cathedral there.

Works include operas *Philomela* (1950) and *The Mirror from Venice* (1964); eight Masses and *Te Deum*; four symphonies (1930–54), variations for orchestra; songs for voice and orchestra; chamber music; cello and piano sonata; organ works.

Andriessen, Louis (b Utrecht, 6 Jun 1939), Dutch composer, son of Hendrik Andriesson. He studied with his father and with Berio, in Milan. Cage, Ives and Stravinsky are among the composers to whom he owes allegiance. In more recent years he has preferred the simplicities of minimalism.

Works include *Anachronie*, in memory of Ives, for orchestra (1966); *Reconstructie*, anti-imperialist theatre piece (1969); *What it's Like* for electronics and 52 strings (1970); *Uproar* for 16 wind, six percussion and electronics (1970); *The Nine Symphonies of Beethoven* for ensemble and ice-cream bell (1970); *Il Principe*, after Machiavelli (1974); *Orpheus*, theatre piece (1977); *Matthew Passion* (1977); *George Sand*, theatre piece (1980); *Velocity* for orchestra (1983); *De Materie* theatre piece (1985–88); *Dances* for soprano and chamber orchestra (1991); *Facing Death* for four amplified strings (1991); *M is for Man, Music, Mozart* (TV show for the bicentenary); *Rosa* ('a horse drama', with Peter Greenaway, 1994).

Andriessen, Willem (b Haarlem, 25 Oct 1887; d Amsterdam, 29 Mar 1964), Dutch pianist and composer. Studied at the Amsterdam Conservatory, of which he became director in 1937 in succession to Dresden, after teaching at The Hague and Rotterdam.

Works include Mass for solo voices, chorus and orchestra; scherzo for orchestra (1912); piano concerto (1908); piano sonata.

Andrieu, F, late 14th-c. composer. He set a double *ballade* by Eustace Deschamps on the death of Machaut.

Andromaque, *Andromache*, opera by Grétry (libretto by L G Pitra, based on Racine's tragedy), produced Paris, Opéra, 6 Jun 1780.

Anerio, Felice (b Rome, *c* 1560; d Rome, 27 Sept 1614), Italian composer. Chorister in the Papal Chapel as a boy, later *maestro* *di cappella* at the English College in Rome, which he left for the service of Cardinal Aldobrandini. Appointed composer to the Papal Chapel on the death of Palestrina in 1594. He was commissioned to reform the Roman Gradual in 1611.

Works include masses, motets, hymns and other church music; madrigals, canzonets.

Anerio, Giovanni Francesco (b Rome, *c* 1567; d Graz, buried 12 Jun 1630), Italian composer, brother of Felice Anerio. He was *maestro di cappella* at the cathedral of Verona in 1609, and 1613–20 was music instructor at the Seminario Romano and *maestro di cappella* of the church of the Madonna de' Monti in Rome. In the service of Sigismund III of Poland 1624–28.

Works include Masses, Requiem, Te Deum and other church music; his secular music, including madrigals and canzonettas, is more progressive than that of many of his contemporaries.

Anet, Jean-Jacques-Baptiste (b Paris, 2 Jan 1676; d Lunéville, 14 Aug 1755), French violinist and composer. He travelled in France and Italy, studying with Corelli in Rome, and made a great reputation in Paris 1701–35, at the Concert Spirituel with the Violons du Roy. He retired to the court of the ex-king of Poland, Stanislas Leszcsinski, at Lunéville in 1738. Wrote sonatas and other works for his instrument.

Anfossi, Pasquale (b Taggia, near Naples, 25 Apr 1727; d Rome, Feb 1797), Italian composer. Pupil of Piccinni at Naples. Wrote operas from 1763, but had his first real success with *L'incognita perseguitata* (Rome, 1773). Later produced operas in Paris, London (a music director of the King's Theatre 1782–86), Berlin and Prague. In 1762 he became *maestro di cappella* of St John Lateran in Rome. Mozart wrote insertion arias for two of his operas.

Works include operas *Armida* (Turin, 1770), *L'incognita perseguitata*, *La finta giardiniera*, *Il geloso in cimento*, *L'avaro* (Venice, 1775), *Gengis-Kan* (Turin, 1777), *La vera costanza*, *Il curioso indiscreto*, *I viaggiatori felici* (Venice, 1780), *Le gelosie fortunate*, church music.

Don't spoke! Don't spoke! If you didn't like it, you went!

Ernest Ansermet to orchestra, quoted in Culshaw, *Putting the Record Straight*, 1981

Angel, Marie (b Pinnaroo, 3 Jun 1953), Australian soprano. She sang Handel's Galatea on her London debut (1980) and was a member of Opera Factory, London 1982–92, appearing as Mozart's Fiordiligi, Countess and Donna Anna, Poppea, and Polly in *Punch and Judy*; US appearances in Glass's *Akhnaten* at Houston and NY (1984). Created roles in Birtwistle's *The Mask of Orpheus* (ENO, 1986) and *Gawain* (CG, 1991). She married the director of Opera Factory, David ◊Freeman.

Angeles, Victoria de los, ◊Los Angeles.

Angélique opera in one act by Ibert (libretto by Nino), produced Paris, Théâtre Fémina, 28 Jan 1927.

Angiolina, ossia Il matrimonio per susurro, *Angiolina, or The Marriage by Noise*, opera by Salieri (libretto by C P Defranceschi, based on Ben Jonson's *Epicoene*), produced Vienna, Kärntnertortheater, 22 Oct 1800. ◊Schweigsame Frau (Strauss).

anglaise French a dance-form similar to that of the country dance, which in France became the *contredanse* in the 18th c., when the name of anglaise was sometimes given to it instead to show its English origin unmistakably.

Anglebert, Jean Henri d' (b Paris, 1635; d Paris, 23 Apr 1691), French harpsichordist and composer. Pupil of Chambonnières. Became organist to the Duke of Orleans in 1661 and chamber musician to Louis XIV in 1664. He wrote harpsichord and organ pieces and arranged many instrumental pieces from Lully's operas for harpsichord.

Anglican Chant ◊Chant.

ängstlich German = 'anxiously, apprehensively'. Beethoven used the term as a direction for the singing of the recitative in the 'Agnus Dei' section of his *Missa solemnis*.

Aniara opera by Blomdahl (libretto by E Lindegren, after H Martinson's epic poem 'Revue about men in time and space'), produced Stockholm, 31 May 1959. The action is set on board a space-ship.

Anima del filosofo ossia Orfeo ed Euridice, *The Philosopher's Stone, or Orpheus and Eurydice*, Haydn's last opera; composed 1791 in London but not performed. First known production Florence, 10 Jun 1951, conductor E Kleiber, with Callas and Christoff.

animato Italian = 'animated'; a direction originally intended to suggest a spirited performance but later generally the quickening of a passage.

Animuccia, Giovanni (b Florence, *c* 1500; d Rome, 25 Mar 1571), Italian composer. Studied under Goudimel in Rome; *maestro di cappella* at the Vatican from 1555 until his death. A friend of St Philip Neri, for whom he composed a series of *Laude*. He also wrote Masses, other church music in a simplified style, and madrigals.

Animuccia, Paolo (b Florence, *c* 1500; d ? Urbino, *c* 1570), Italian composer, brother of Giovanni Animuccia. *Maestro di cappella* at St John Lateran in Rome 1550–52 before Lassus. Wrote madrigals and church music.

Anna Amalia, Princess of Prussia (b Berlin, 9 Nov 1723; d Berlin, 30 Mar 1787), sister of Frederick the Great and amateur musician. With her *Kapellmeister* Kirnberger she was a champion of the works of Bach and Handel in Berlin, and collected a valuable library of early music. She was also a composer and wrote *Der Tod Jesu*.

Anna Bolena, *Anne Boleyn*, opera by Donizetti (libretto by F Romani), produced Milan, Teatro Carcano, 26 Dec 1830. Anna goes to the block, accompanied by 'Home, Sweet Home'.

Anna Karenina opera by Hubay (libretto, in Hungarian, by S Góth, based on Tolstoy's novel), produced Budapest, 10 Nov 1923.

Opera by Iain Hamilton (libretto by composer) produced London, Coliseum, 7 May 1981.

Années de pèlerinage four sets of piano pieces by Liszt, mainly recording his travels in Switzerland and Italy – *1re Année: En Suisse*, composed 1835–36, pub. 1855: 1. *Chapelle de Guillaume Tell*. 2. *Au Lac de Wallenstadt*. 3. *Pastorale*. 4. *Au Bord d'une source*. 5. *Orage*. 6. *Vallée d'Obermann* (inspired by Senancour's *Obermann*; the valley is an imaginary or unidentified one in the canton of Valais). 7. *Eglogue*. 8. *Le Mal du pays*. 9. *Les Cloches de Genève*. (Nos. 1, 2, 4, 6 and 9 originally formed part of an *Album d'un voyageur* for piano pub. in 1836: they were revised for the pub. of the *Années de pèlerinage* in 1855. – *2me Année: En Italie*, composed 1838–39, pub. 1846: 1. *Sposalizio* (after Raphael's picture in the Brera at Milan). 2. *Il pensieroso* (after Michelangelo's statue of Giuliano dei Medici in the Medici mausoleum at San Lorenzo, Florence). 3. *Canzonetta del Salvator Rosa*. 4. *Sonetto No. 47 del Petrarca*. 5. *Sonetto No. 104 del Petrarca*. 6. *Sonetto No. 123 del Petrarca* (Nos. 4–6 are transcriptions of settings of these Petrarch sonnets for voice and piano). 7. *Après une lecture du Dante: Fantasia quasi Sonata* ('Dante Sonata'). –*3me Année*, composed 1872–77, pub. 1883: 1. *Angelus: Prière aux anges gardiens*. 2. *Aux Cyprès de la Villa d'Este*. 3. ditto: *Thrénodie*. 4. *Les Jeux d'eau de la Villa d'Este*. 5. *Sunt lacrymae rerum en mode hongrois*. 6. *Marche funèbre* (in memory of the Emperor Maximilian I of Mexico, d 19 Jun 1867). 7. *Sursum corda*. —Supplement to Vol. II: *Venezia e Napoli*, composed 1859, pub. 1861: 1. *Gondoliera* (on a canzona by Cavaliere Peruchini). 2. *Canzone* (on the gondolier's song in Rossini's *Otello*). 3. *Tarantella* (on some canzoni by Guillaume Louis Cottrau). (This set is partly a revision of an earlier one of the same title composed in 1840, but not pub.)

Annibale, II Padovano (b Padua, 1527; d Graz, Mar 1575), Italian contrapuntist and composer. Organist at St Mark's, Venice, 1552–66, and then *maestro di cappella* to the Archduke Carl at Graz. Wrote church and organ music, madrigals.

Annibali, Domenico (b Macerata, *c* 1705; d ? Rome, 1779 or later), Italian male soprano. He first appeared at Rome in 1725 and later went to Dresden, where he remained till 1764, singing the soprano lead in many of Hasse's operas. He sang for Handel in London in 1736–37, including the fps of *Arminio*, *Giustino* and *Berenice*.

Ansermet, Ernest (b Vevey, 11 Nov 1883; d Geneva, 20 Feb 1969), Swiss conductor. Originally a professor of mathematics, 1906–10, he studied music with Bloch, Mottl and Nikisch. From 1915 to 1923 he was associated with Diaghilev's ballet company. In 1918 he founded the Orchestre de la Suisse Romande, which he conducted until 1967. He published a book criticizing certain aspects of modern, especially serial, music in 1961. Ansermet was well known for his accurate and well-balanced performances of Stravinsky's earlier music and gave the fps of *The Soldier's Tale* (1918), *Pulcinella* (1920) and *Renard* (1922).

Ansseau, Fernand (b Boussu-Bois, 6 Mar 1890; d Brussels, 1 May 1972), Belgian tenor. Debut Brussels 1913 in *Hérodiade*; successful in Belgium until 1939 as Masaniello, Tannhäuser, Alvaro and in Puccini. CG debut 1919, as Massenet's Des Grieux. In Paris he was heard as Lohengrin and Gluck's Orpheus and Admète. Chicago 1923–28.

anticipation the occurrence of a note or notes from a chord before the rest of the chord is sounded.

An example of 'anticipation' from Beethoven's Piano Sonata, Op. 27, No.2

Antico, Andrea de (b Montona, *c* 1480; d after 1539), Italian composer and music publisher who worked mainly in Rome and then Venice during the first half of the 16th c. His most important pub. was

An answer as found in the top voice of Bach's Fugue in C major, Well-tempered Clavier, Book 1, no. 1.

answer in fugue, the second entry of the subject, brought in while the first entry continues with a counterpoint to it.

Antar a programme symphony by Rimsky-Korsakov, op. 9, based on Senkovsky's oriental story of that name, composed 1868 as '2nd Symphony', revised 1875, fp St Petersburg, Russian Music Society, Jan 1876, republished 1903 as 'symphonic suite'. The titles of the movements are I. Introduction; II. 'Joy of Revenge'; III. 'Joy of Power'; IV. 'Joy of Love'.

Antechrist work for chamber ensemble by Peter Maxwell Davies; composed 1967, fp London, 30 May 1967.

Antegnati, Costanzo (b Brescia, 9 Dec 1549; d Brescia, 14 Nov 1624), Italian composer and member of a family of organ-builders famous in N Italy from 1470 to 1642. They built about 400 organs, including instruments used by Frescobaldi, the Gabrielis and other Renaissance composers. He wrote Masses, motets and madrigals, and organ and other instrumental music.

Antheil, George (b Trenton, NJ, 8 Jul 1900; d New York, 12 Feb 1959), American composer. Studied with Bloch, later in Europe. His music of the 1920s is aggressively 'modern' (the *Ballet mécanique* of 1924 includes eight pianos, aeroplane propellers, motor horns, anvils, etc.) but his later work is much more restrained and classical in character. In 1939 he became associated with the film industry in Hollywood.

Works include operas *Transatlantic* (Frankfurt, 1930), *Helen Retires* (New York, 1934) and *Volpone* (LA, 1953); ballets *Ballet mécanique* and *Dreams*; six symphonies (1920–50), *Zingaresca*, *Capriccio* and *Archipelago* for orchestra (1935); three string quartets; two violin and piano sonatas.

anthem a composition for church choir, with or without solo voices and accomp., sung in the course of Morning or Evening Service in the Anglican Church. There are two kinds: the full anthem is a species sung by the choir throughout, the verse anthem is written for solo voices, with or without sections for the choir.

Anthonello da Caserta ◊Caserta

Anthony, Cristofferus, 15th-c. composer, probably English, of a Magnificat and other pieces from the Trent Codices.

probably *Frottole intabulate da sonar organi* (Rome, 1517), the first-known printed edition of keyboard music in Italy.

Antifone work for orchestra by Henze; composed 1960, fp Berlin, 20 Jan 1962, conductor Karajan.

Antigonae play with music by Orff (text by Hölderlin, after Sophocles), produced Salzburg, 9 Aug 1949.

Antigone incidental music to Sophocles' tragedy by Mendelssohn, produced at the New Palace, Potsdam, 28 Oct 1841, and repeated at the Berlin Opera, 13 Apr 1842. Daughter of Oedipus atttempts to bury her brother, against the wishes of King Creon.

Opera by Honegger (libretto by Cocteau, after Sophocles), produced Brussels, Théâtre de la Monnaie, 28 Dec 1927.

Opera by Zingarelli (libretto by J F Marmontel), produced Paris, Opéra, 30 Apr 1790.

Antigono opera by Gluck (libretto by Metastasio), produced Rome, Teatro Argentina, 9 Feb 1756. Antigonus, king of Macedonia, is rivalled in love by his son.

Opera by Hasse (libretto ditto), produced Hubertusburg near Dresden, 10 Oct 1743.

Antinori, Luigi (b Bologna, *c* 1697), Italian tenor. First appeared in London 1725 and sang in the fps of Handel's *Scipione* and *Alessandro*. Later sang in Venice, Genoa and Florence in operas by Porpora, Pergolesi and A Scarlatti.

There let the pealing Organ blow/To the full-voic'd Quire below/In Service high, with anthems cleer/As may with sweetnes, through mine ear/Dissolve me into extasies,/And bring all Heav'n before mine eyes.
John Milton, *Il Penseroso, c* 1631

---

antiphon, Greek, = 'answering sound'; in Gregorian chant, a refrain sung before and after a psalm, and originally between verses as well. Its name probably derives from its use in connection with antiphonal, or alternative, choir singing. The earliest antiphons are often merely a single verse of the psalm itself, which in that case is not necessarily repeated.

The tone of the psalm always corresponds numerically to the mode of the antiphon, while its ending is chosen to link up with the beginning of the antiphonorary. The bulk of the repertory consists of biblical texts set to non-psalmodic melodies. A basic repertory of nearly 50 themes in the eight modes is used for many thousands of texts. Their structure is often quite regular, and they may even have been sung metrically.

The Introit and Communion of the Mass are antiphons originally sung with a complete psalm. The final stage in its history occurs when the antiphon becomes an independent piece in its own right (e.g. votive and processional antiphons). Originally they were borrowed from antiphons to psalms, but later they were newly composed and often achieved considerable complexity.

Antiquis, Giovanni de, Italian 16th-c. composer. Music director at the church of San Niccolo at Bari; edited two books of *Villanelle alla napolitana* by musicians of Bari, including himself, pub. at Venice, 1574.

An ear for music is a very different thing from a taste for music. I have no ear whatever, I could not sing an air to save my life; but I have the intensest delight in music, and can detect good from bad.
Samuel Taylor Coleridge, *Table Talk*, 1830

Antonacci, Anna Caterina (b Ferrara, 5 Apr 1961), Italian soprano. Studied at Bologna and sang Rosina at Arezzo, 1986. Elizabeth I in *Maria Stuarda* at Bari (1989) and Adalgisa and Fiordiligi elsewhere in Italy. Other Rossini roles include Dorliska, Semiramide, Ermione in the UK fp of the opera (1992) and Elcia in the CG premiere of *Mosè in Egitto* (1994). She sang Ermione at Glyndebourne, 1995. One of the most promising singers of her generation.

Antoni, Antonio d' (b Palermo, 25 Jun 1801; d Trieste, 18 Aug 1859), Italian conductor and composer. Produced a Mass at the age of 12 and became conductor at the Palermo Theatre in 1817; settled at Trieste and founded the Società Filarmonica there, 1829.

Works include operas *Un duello* (Palermo, 1817), *Amina* (Trieste, 1825) and *Amazilda e Zamoro* (Florence, 1826).

Antonio e Cleopatra opera by Malipiero (libretto by composer, based on Shakespeare), produced Florence, Teatro Comunale, 4 May 1938.

Antony and Cleopatra opera by Barber (libretto by composer, after Shakespeare), performed on opening night of NY Met. in Lincoln Center, 16 Sept 1966; revised and produced at Juilliard School, NY, 6 Feb 1975.

anvil an orchestral percussion instrument imitating the sound of a blacksmith's anvil, but constructed of small steel bars struck by a mallet of wood or metal. It can be so made as to produce notes of definite pitch, as in *Rheingold*, but is usually indeterminate in sound.

aolian harp an instrument played by no human performer, but by currents of air blown across its strings when it is hung up in the open. It was first recorded in the 17th c., but the principle dates back to antiquity.

Apel, Nikolaus (b Königshofen, *c* 1475; d Leipzig, 1537), compiler of a large MS in choirbook form (Leipzig, University Bibliothek 1494) containing sacred and secular music of the late 15th and early 16th c. It has been pub. in full by Rudolf Gerber (*Das Erbe deutscher Musik*, xxxii–xxxiv).

Apel, Willi (b Konitz, 10 Oct 1893; d Bloomington, 14 Mar 1988), German, later American, musicologist. Studied mathematics at Bonn, Munich and Berlin Universities, and also piano under Edwin Fischer, Martienssen and others. Settled in the USA in 1936. Taught at the Longy School of Music, Cambridge, MA, 1936–43, and Harvard University, 1938–42. Professor at IN University, 1950–63. His pubs. include *The Notation of Polyphonic Music* (fifth edition 1961),

Harvard Dictionary of Music (revised edition, 1969), *Gregorian Chant* (1958) and *A History of Keyboard Music* (1972). Joint edition (with A T Davison) of *Historical Anthology of Music* (2 vols., 1946 and 1960).

aperto Italian = lit. 'open, frank, straightforward'. Mozart used the adj. in conjunction with *allegro* in some early works, e.g. the A major violin concerto, K219. The meaning is not clear, but may be taken to suggest an energetic delivery strictly in time.

a piacere Italian = 'at pleasure'; a direction indicating that a passage may be played or sung in any way the performer desires, especially in regard to tempo.

Apiarius, Matthias (b Berchingen, *c* 1500; d Berne, 1554), German music publisher. He worked in partnership with Peter Schöffer in Strasbourg, 1543–47, and independently in Berne, 1537–54.

Aplvor, Denis (b Collinstown, Ireland, 14 Apr 1916), Irish composer of Welsh origin. Was chorister at Hereford Cathedral, later at Christ Church, Oxford, and studied composition with Patrick Hadley and Rawsthorne; later influences have included serialism.

Works include operas *She Stoops to Conquer* (libretto by composer after Goldsmith) (1947), *Yerma* (1959), *Ubu Roi* (1966); *The Hollow Men* (T S Eliot) for baritone, chorus and orchestra (1939); piano concerto; two symphonies, two violin concertos; clarinet concertante (1981); Chaucer songs with string quartet (1936), sonata for clarinet, piano and percussion, violin and piano sonata; clarinet quintet (1981); wind quintet (1981); songs with words by F García Lorca and others.

Apollo e Dafne Italian cantata by Handel, for soprano, baritone and chamber ensemble; composed *c* 1708.

Apollo et Hyacinthus Latin intermezzo by Mozart K38 (libretto by Rufinus Widl), produced Salzburg University, 13 May 1767. Hyacinthus murdered by jealous Zephyrus but Apollo transforms him into a flower.

Apollo Musagetes, *Apollo, Leader of the Muses*, ballet for string orchestra by Stravinsky; composed 1927–28, produced Washington DC, 27 Apr 1928 (choreography A Bolm).

apollonicon a large organ playable both by hand and mechanically by barrels, built by Flight & Robson in London and exhibited by them in 1817.

Apostel, Hans Erich (b Karlsruhe, 22 Jan 1901; d Vienna, 30 Nov 1972), Austrian composer of German birth. Entered Karlsruhe Conservatory in 1916. He later studied with Schoenberg and Berg in Vienna, where he lived from 1921. In 1937 his *Requiem* won the Hertzka Prize.

Works include *Requiem* (text by Rilke) for eight-part chorus and orchestra; *Variations on a theme of Haydn* for orchestra (1949); piano concerto; two string quartets; songs with piano or orchestra on texts by Trakl and Hölderlin.

Apostles, The oratorio by Elgar, op. 49 (libretto compiled from the Bible by the composer), Part I of a trilogy of which II is *The Kingdom* and III was never completed. First performed Birmingham Festival, 14 Oct 1903.

Appalachia variations for orchestra with chorus by Delius, composed 1902, fp Elberfeld, 15 Oct 1904, first London performance 22 Nov 1907. The title is the old American Indian name for N America; the theme is an African-American folksong.

Appalachian Spring ballet by Copland (choreographer Martha Graham), produced WA DC, 30 Oct 1944. Orchestral suite from ballet performed NY, 4 Oct 1945, conductor Rodzinski.

Appassionata, Italian, = 'impassioned'; the name commonly used for Beethoven's F minor piano sonata of 1804–05, op. 57, but not authorized by himself.

Appenzeller, Benedictus (b *c* 1485; d after 1558), Flemish 16th-c. composer. Pupil of Josquin des Prés. In the service of Mary of Hungary, dowager regent of the Netherlands.

Works include *chansons*, church music, a *Nenia* on the death of Josquin, etc.

Applausus Latin allegorical oratorio by Haydn for soloists, chorus and orchestra performed Zwettl, 17 Apr 1768.

Appleby, Thomas (b ? Lincoln, 1488; d Lincoln, c 1562), English organist and composer. Appointed organist of Lincoln Cathedral in 1538, the next year organist at Magdalen College, Oxford, but returned to Lincoln in 1541; was succeeded by Byrd there in 1563. Wrote church music.

appoggiatura Italian, from *appoggiare* = 'to lean'; a note of varying length, dissonant with the harmony against which it is heard but resolving on to a note consonant with the harmony.

Where the appoggiatura is short it may in certain contexts occur before the beat. In much Baroque music, especially in recitatives, the appoggiatura is understood without being written, i.e. where a phrase ends with two notes on the same pitch, the first of them should often be sung on the pitch of the preceding note (if it is a 4th higher), or performed a note higher (or sometimes lower than written).

Various symbols have been used in the past to indicate an appoggiatura, the commonest of which is a note in smaller type (above); an approximation of how these are played is shown below.

Apprenti sorcier, L', *The Sorcerer's Apprentice*, scherzo for orchestra by Dukas on Goethe's ballad *Der Zauberlehrling*; fp Paris, Société Nationale de Musique, 18 May 1897.

ap Rhys, Philip, ◊Rhys, Philip ap.

Arabella opera by R Strauss (libretto by H von Hofmannsthal, based on his story *Lucidor*), produced Dresden, 1 Jul 1933. Hofmannsthal's last libretto for Strauss.

Arabesk, An work by Delius for baritone, chorus and orchestra (text by J P Jacobsen); composed 1911 and performed Newport, 1920. First London performance 18 Oct 1929.

Arabeske, (German) Arabesque (French), originally a term applied to ornamentation in Arabic or Moorish architecture; used by some composers (e.g. Schumann, Debussy) for pieces probably meant to be regarded as decorative rather than emotionally expressive.

Aragall, Giacomo (b Barcelona, 6 Jun 1939), Spanish tenor. Debut 1963, Venice, as Gaston in first modern performance of Verdi's *Jérusalem*; sang Romeo in Bellini's *I Capuleti*, La Scala 1966. CG 1966 and NY Met. 1968, both as Duke of Mantua. Other roles included Alfredo, Cavaradossi and Roland in *Esclarmonde*. Sang Don Carlos at Orange, 1990.

Aragonaise French a Spanish dance of Aragon, i.e. the *Jota aragonesa*.

Araia (*Araja*), Francesco (b Naples, 25 Jun 1709; d Bologna, c 1770), Italian composer. He produced his first opera in 1729. From 1735 he was for 24 years opera director to the Russian court in St Petersburg, where he produced several of his own works, e.g. *Il finto Nino* (1737), *Artaserse* (1738), *Scipione* (1745), *Mitridate* (1747) and *Bellerofonte* (1750). Another was *Cephalus and Procris* (1755), the first opera given in Russia known to have been sung in Russian and not in Italian.

Araiza, Francisco (b Mexico City, 4 Oct 1950), Mexican tenor. He sang in concert and oratorio from 1968 and in 1973 was heard as Massenet's Des Grieux and Rodolfo in Mexico City. His European debut was in Karlsruhe, 1974, and he has since appeared in Munich, Salzburg, Aix, London and Vienna; successful in operas by Mozart, Massenet and Donizetti and as Gounod's Faust; US debut 1983, in *Cenerentola* at San Francisco. Sang Lohengrin at Venice, 1990.

Aranaz, Pedro (b Tudela, bap. 2 May 1740; d Cuença, 24 Sept 1820), Spanish priest and composer. Appointed *maestro de capilla* at Saragossa Cathedral in 1766, having been a choir-boy there. After a year at Zamora he went to Cuença Cathedral in 1769.

Works include church music with orchestral accomp., secular songs (*tonadillas* and *villancicos*).

Arányi, d', Jelly (b Budapest, 30 May 1893; d Florence, 30 Mar 1966), Hungarian violinist. Debut Vienna 1909; became British citizen and gave the local premieres in London of both Bartók's violin sonatas, with the composer (1922, 1923). Ravel's *Tzigane* and Vaughan Williams's *Concerto Accademico* are dedicated to her. Gave first British performance of the Schumann concerto (1938), after claiming that the composer had appeared to her in a dream with his neglected MS. Many concerts with her sister Adila Fachiri.

Arbeau, Thoinot (anagram on real name of Jehan Tabourot) (b Dijon, 17 Mar 1520; d Langres, 23 Jul 1595), French priest and author. Wrote a book on dancing, *Orchésographie*, pub. 1589, containing a large number of dance tunes current in 16th-c. France.

Arbore di Diana, L', *Diana's Tree*, opera by Martín y Soler (libretto by da Ponte), produced Vienna, Burgtheater, 1 Oct 1787. Magic apple tree pleases the virtuous but the guilty are pelted.

Arbre enchanté, L', ou Le Tuteur dupé, *The Enchanted Tree, or The Tutor Duped*, comic opera by Gluck (libretto by P L Moline, after J J Vadé), produced Vienna, Schönbrunn Palace, at court, 3 Oct 1759.

Arcadelt, Jacob (b c 1505; d ? Paris, 14 Oct 1568), Flemish composer. Became a singer at the court of the Medici at Florence before 1539, in which year he was appointed singing-master to the boys at St Peter's in Rome, entering the college of papal singers the following year. Many of his madrigals were pub. in his lifetime and stressed clarity of texture.

Works include Masses, motets, madrigals, etc. (The *Ave Maria* attributed to him is a spurious adaptation of his three-part chanson *Nous voyons que les hommes font tous vertu d'aimer*.)

Arcadia in Brenta, L' opera by Galuppi (libretto by Goldoni), produced Venice, Teatro Sant' Angelo, 14 May 1749. The first comic opera by Galuppi written in collaboration with Goldoni. Fabrizio welcomes guests to his new villa by the river Brenta.

Arcana work for large orchestra by Varèse; composed 1925–27, fp Philadelphia, 8 Apr 1927, conductor Stokowski.

'Archduke' Trio the name sometimes given to Beethoven's piano trio in B♭ major, op. 97, composed in 1811 and dedicated to the Archduke Rudolph of Austria.

archlute a large lute of the theorbo type with two sets of strings, the pegs of which were set at different distances in the double neck; the longer bass strings had no fingerboard and could therefore not be altered in pitch during performance. *See illustration on page 22.*

arco Italian = 'bow'; a direction (sometimes *col arco*) in music for bowed string instruments, indicating that the bow is to be resumed after a passage of plucked notes.

——— THE OPERA ———

Arabella

A three-act opera by Richard Strauss, first produced in Dresden in 1933. The opera is set in Vienna at carnival time in about 1860.

I. The impoverished Count Waldner (bass) wishes to find a rich husband for his daughter Arabella (soprano), and is relieved when Mandryka (baritone), son of an old friend, arrives as a suitor. Arabella's sister Zdenka (soprano) is being brought up as a boy because Waldner cannot afford two debutantes, and to complicate matters Zdenka is in love with Matteo, another of Arabella's suitors.

II. Arabella rejects her other suitors in favour of Mandryka. But he becomes suspicious when he sees Zdenka give Matteo the key to her room, ostensibly from Arabella.

III. About to leave the hotel after his rendezvous, Matteo is amazed to see Arabella enter, fully dressed. Mandryka arrives with Arabella's parents and their suspicions seem confirmed when they find Matteo and Arabella together. Zdenka now appears and explains that it was she who spent the night with Matteo; he is now happy to accept the situation. Offering Mandryka a glass of water, a symbol of her purity, Arabella embraces her husband-to-be.

archlute *The archlute was invented 1594 by Alessandro Piccini, who called the instrument an arcileuto. In the latter half of the 17th century the archlute became increasingly popular as a continuo instrument in preference to the theorbo.*

Arden muss sterben, *Arden must die*, opera by A Goehr (libretto by E Fried, after the anon. Elizabethan play *Arden of Faversham*), produced Hamburg, 5 Mar 1967.

Arditti Quartet British string quartet founded in 1974; members are Irvine Arditti and David Alberman (violins), Garth Knox (viola) and Rohan de Saram (cello). Performances in Britain and all over Europe of contemporary works, including quartets by Boulez, Carter, Ferneyhough, Ligeti and Henze; novel techniques include amplification with raad instruments. Complete quartets of Schoenberg issued on CD 1994.

Arensky, Anton Stepanovich (b Novgorod, 12 Jul 1861; d Terioki, Finland, 25 Feb 1906), Russian composer. Pupil of Rimsky-Korsakov for a time, but belonged to the eclectic rather than the nationalist school. Appointed professor at the Moscow Conservatory in 1882.

Works include operas *A Dream on the Volga* (on Ostrovsky's *Voyevoda*) (1891), *Raphael* (1894), *Nal and Damayanti*; ballet, *Egyptian Nights* (1908); incidental music for Shakespeare's *Tempest*; two symphonies (1883 and 1889); piano concerto; chamber music, including piano trio in D minor; numerous piano pieces; choruses, songs, church music.

Argenta, Nancy (b Nelson, British Columbia, 17 Jan 1957), Canadian soprano. Studied with Peter Pears and Gerard Souzay and made concert appearances in Europe and the USA, notably Scarlatti's *La Giuditta* in Italy. Opera debut Aix Festival 1983, in *Hippolyte et Aricie*, returning 1990 for *The Fairy Queen*; Lyon Opera as Susanna and Asteria in Handel's *Tamerlano*, Poppea in London and Roseanne

in Handel's *Floridante* at Toronto. Recordings include sacred music by Bach, Handel and Mozart.

Argento, Dominick (b York, PA, 27 Oct 1927), American composer. He studied with Hovhaness and Hanson at the Eastman School and with Dallapiccola in Italy. His music is in an agreeably tonal idiom.

Works include operas *Sicilian Limes* (1954), *The Boor* (1957), *Christopher Sly* (1963), *The Masque of Angels* (1964), *The Shoemaker's Holiday* (1967), *The Voyage of Edgar Allan Poe* (1976), *Miss Havisham's Fire* (1978), *Casanova's Homecoming* (1985), *The Aspern Papers* (1988), *The Dream of Valentino* (1993); oratorio *Jonah and the Whale* (1973); *A Ring of Time*, for orchestra (1972); choral music and song-cycles, including *Six Elizabethan Songs* for voice and ensemble (1958); *In Praise of Music* (1977); *Five Variations* for orchestra (1982); *Casa Guidi*, five songs for mezzo and orchestra (1983); *Le Tombeau d'Edgar Poe* 91985); *Capriccio: Rossini in Paris*, for clarinet and orchestra (1985).

Argerich, Martha (b Buenos Aires, 5 Jun 1941), Argentine pianist. Studied with Magaloff and Gulda; first prize Chopin Int. Competition Warsaw, 1965. London debut 1964. Admired in Romantic repertory and in partnership with violinist Gidon Kremer.

aria Italian = 'air'; a vocal piece, especially in opera or oratorio, formally more highly organized than a song: in the late 17th and early 18th c. as a rule in three sections, the third being a repetition of the first and the second a contrasting strain (*da capo aria*); later often various modifications of the instrumental sonata form. In the late 18th c. arias were conventionally classified as follows:

aria all' unisono, an aria in which the voice and instrumental parts have the tune in octave unison, without harmony, at any rate so far as the composer's writing went, though chords may have been added by the *continuo* player at the harpsichord.

aria cantabile, an aria with a slow, sustained melody.

aria concertata, an aria making a feature of an elaborate instrumental solo part in the accompaniment.

aria d'agilità = *aria di bravura*.

aria d'imitazione, an aria in which either the voice or some instruments, or both, gave a more-or-less realistic imitation of some other musical or non-musical sounds.

aria di bravura, an aria containing a more than usual amount of brilliant and difficult passages.

aria di mezzo carattere, an aria 'of indeterminate character' which could be almost anything that could not be classified under any other species, but had as a rule an elaborate accompaniment.

aria di portamento, an aria requiring a slow and full-toned delivery and laying great stress on the display of a beautiful voice at the expense of the accompaniment.

aria parlante, an aria of a declamatory kind, intended less to display the voice than the singer's verbal eloquence and dramatic expression.

aria senza accompagnamento, a wholly unaccompanied aria, which was rarely used.

◊parable aria.

Ariadne opera in one act by Martinů (libretto by composer after G Neveux), produced Gelsenkirchen, 2 Mar 1961.

Counterpoint can be the nastiest thing in music.
Claude Debussy, in a letter to Vasnier, 1885

Ariadne auf Naxos play with music (melodrama) by G Benda (text by J C Brandes), produced Gotha, 27 Jan 1775.

Opera by R Strauss (libretto by H von Hofmannsthal), originally a one-act opera played after a shortened version of Molière's *Le Bourgeois gentilhomme*, with incidental music by Strauss, produced Stuttgart, 25 Oct 1912; second version, with a new operatic first act, produced Vienna, Opera, 4 Oct 1916. Ariadne longs for death but gets the tenor instead.

Ariane et Barbe-bleue, *Ariane and Bluebeard*, opera by Dukas (libretto Maeterlinck's play with slight alterations), produced Paris, Opéra-Comique, 10 May 1907. Ariane releases Bluebeard's previous five wives from his castle.

Ariane, ou Le Mariage de Bacchus opera by Grabu (libretto by P Perrin, previously set by Cambert), produced London, Drury Lane Theatre, 30 Mar 1674.

Arianna opera by Marcello (libretto V Cassani), composed 1727, never performed in Marcello's lifetime; edited by O Chilesotti, 1885, produced Venice, Liceo Benedetto Marcello, 27 Apr 1913.

Opera by Handel (*Arianna in Creta*, libretto adapted from P Pariati's *Arianna e Teseo*), produced London, King's Theatre, Haymarket, 26 Jan 1734. Theseus and the Minotaur complicated by love sub-plot.

Arianna a Naxos, *Ariadne on Naxos*, cantata by Haydn for soprano and keyboard; composed 1790.

Arianna e Teseo, *Ariadne and Theseus*, opera by Porpora (libretto by P Pariati), produced Vienna, 1 Oct 1714.

Arianna, L' opera by Monteverdi (libretto by O Rinuccini), produced Mantua, at the ducal court, for the wedding of the Hereditary Prince Francesco Gonzaga with Margherita, Princess of Savoy, 28 May 1608. Most of the music is lost; only the *Lamento d'Arianna* (Ariadne's Lament) survives.

Aribo Scholasticus Flemish 11th-c. monk and music theorist. His treatise *De Musica* is important in the development of modal theory in the West, with its emphasis on melodic formulae as well as scales in the definition of mode.

arietta Italian = 'little air'; a shorter and simpler kind of aria, usually of a lighter character.

ariette French = 'little aria or air'; now the same as an *arietta*, but in early 18th-c. French opera an elaborate aria (sometimes with Italian words) and in late 18th-c. *opéra comique* a song introduced into a scene in dialogue. ◊Debussy (*Ariettes oubliées*).

Ariodant opera by Méhul (libretto by F-B Hoffman, after Ariosto's poem *Orlando Furioso* (1516), produced Paris, Théâtre Favart, 11 Oct 1799. Othon attempts to make Ina leave her lover Ariodant.

Ariodante opera by Handel (libretto by A Salvi, based on Ariosto's *Orlando furioso*), produced London, CG, 8 Jan 1735. Lovers Ginevra and Ariodante threatened by the evil Polinesso, who would have Ginevra for himself.

Ariosi work by Henze for soprano, violin and orchestra, to poems by Tasso; composed for Wolfgang Schneiderhan and Irmgard Seefried and performed by them Edinburgh, 23 Aug 1964.

arioso Italian = 'song-like'; a vocal or instrumental piece or passage of a declamatory or recitative character, to be sung or played in a melodic manner.

Ariosti, Attilo (b Bologna, 5 Nov 1666; d England, ? 1729), Italian composer. Prod. his first opera at Venice in 1696. Court composer in Berlin, 1697–1703. Later visited Vienna, London and Bologna; wrote six operas for the Royal Academy of Music, London.

Works include operas *La più gloriosa fatica d'Ercole* (Vienna, 1703), *Amor tra nemici, La fede ne' tradimenti* (Berlin, 1701), *Coriolano* (London, 1723), *Vespasiano* (London, 1724), *Artaserse, Dario, Lucio Vero*, etc.; oratorio *Nabucodonosor*, Passion oratorio and others, cantatas; lessons for viola d'amore.

Ariosto, Lodovico (1474–1533), Italian poet. ◊Ariodant (*Orlando furioso*, Méhul), Handel (◊Ariodante, ◊Orlando), ◊Holmès (*Orlando furioso*), Roussel (*Enchantements d'Alcine, Les*), Vivaldi (◊Orlando furioso).

Aristoxenus of Tarentum Greek philosopher of 4th c.BC. His treatise on *Harmonics* (i.e. acoustics and music theory) has the merit of being based on the music practice of his day rather than being purely speculative.

Arkhipova, Irina (b Moscow, 2 Dec 1925), Russian mezzo. Moscow, Bolshoi, debut 1956 as Carmen; has sung Eboli and Amneris there. La Scala, 1965, with Bolshoi co. as Marfa and Marina. CG 1975, Azucena; returned as Ulrica, 1988. Countess in *The Queen of Spades* at the Met., 1992; other roles included Charlotte and Prokofiev's Helen.

Arlecchino opera in one act by Busoni (libretto by the composer), produced Zurich, 11 May 1917. Adventures of Harlequin in Commedia dell'arte setting.

Argerich *Pianist Martha Argerich. She applies her formidable technique most brilliantly in the more difficult works by 19th-century composers, especially Chopin and Liszt, and in works by 20th-century composers. After several years out of the limelight she has made a successful comeback.*

Arlesiana, L', *The Girl from Arles*, opera by Ciléa (libretto by L Marenco, based on Alphonse Daudet's play, *L'Arlésienne*), produced Milan, Teatro Lirico, 27 Nov 1897.

Arlésienne, L', *The Girl from Arles*, incidental music by Bizet for Daudet's play, produced Paris, 1 Oct 1872. Bizet afterwards extracted an orchestral suite from it. (The second suite was arranged by Guiraud.)

Arme Heinrich, Der, *Poor Heinrich*, opera by Pfitzner (libretto by J Grun), produced Mainz, 2 Apr 1895. Pfitzner's first opera. Singer and Knight can only be saved by the sacrifice of a virgin.

Armenian Chant the music of the Church in Armenia from its establishment in 303. It pursued an independent path after the separation from the Greek Church in 536. Its original, alphabetical notation was replaced in the 12th c. by a neumatic system (in which the only MSS have survived), which cannot now be deciphered. The Church's

---

THE OPERA

Ariadne auf Naxos

A one-act opera by Richard Strauss, first performed in its original form in 1912. The Prologue is set in Vienna in the 18th century. In the house of a nouveau riche, a young Composer (soprano) is in despair because he has been told that, as part of the evening's entertainment, his opera seria must be performed simultaneously with a Commedia dell'arte farce – because the following fireworks display must not be delayed. Zerbinetta (soprano), leader of the other group, tries to amuse the Composer, but he declares his faith in the power of music. The action of the Opera takes place on the Greek island of Naxos. Surrounded by attendant nymphs, the recently abandoned Ariadne (soprano) longs for release in death. Zerbinetta sings of a more light-hearted response to love. Bacchus (tenor) now arrives and at first mistakes Ariadne for the sorceress Circe; Ariadne, in turn, greets him as Death. Eventually Bacchus leaves for Olympus with Ariadne, who is happy to accept him as her new love (justifying, in Zerbinetta's mind, her much more light-hearted attitude to love).

THE OPERA

collection of hymns (the *Sharakan*) is arranged according to the eight modes or *echoi*, apparently defined by melodic formulae rather than by scale.

Armida opera by Haydn (libretto by J Durandi), produced Eszterháza, 26 Feb 1784. Sorceress Armida attempts to seduce crusader knight Rinaldo.

Opera by Rossini (libretto by G Schmidt, after Tasso), produced Naples, Teatro San Carlo, 11 Nov 1817.

Opera by Dvořák (libretto by J Vrchlický, based on his Czech trans. of Tasso), produced Prague, Czech Theatre, 25 Mar 1904.

Also settings by Traetta (Vienna, 1761), Anfossi (Turin, 1770), Salieri (Vienna, 1771), and Sacchini (Milan, 1772).

Armida abbandonata Italian cantata by Handel for soprano, two violins and continuo; composed 1707.

Armide opera by Gluck (libretto by Quinault, based on Tasso's *Gerusalemme liberata*), produced Paris, Opéra, 23 Sept 1777. Armide's intended victim is Renaud, but he escapes her traps.

Opera by Lully (libretto by Quinault), produced Paris, Opéra, 15 Feb 1686.

Arminio opera by Handel (libretto by A Salvi), produced London, CG, 12 Jan 1737. Rebel chieftain Arminius defeats the Romans in spite of a love sub-plot.

Two operas by Hasse: I. (libretto by G C Pasquini), produced Dresden, at court, 7 Oct 1745; II. (libretto by Salvi), produced Milan, 28 Aug 1730.

Opera by A Scarlatti (libretto by Salvi), produced Villa Medici, Pratolino, Sept 1703.

armonica an instrument also called *glass harmonica*, the notes of which are produced by friction on a series of tuned glasses, either with the fingers or mechanically.

Armstrong, Karan (b Horne, MT, 14 Dec 1941), American soprano. Sang in USA from 1969 before European debut in Strasbourg, 1976, as Salome; Bayreuth 1979, Elsa. In 1981 sang Lulu at CG in first British performance of three-act version of Berg's opera; in the same year she created the title role in Giuseppe Sinopoli's opera *Lou Salomé*, at Munich. LA 1990–92, as Alice Ford, Fidelio and Emilia Marty. Often appears in the productions of her husband, Götz Friedrich.

Armstrong, Richard (b Leicester, 1 Jul 1943), English conductor. Studied Cambridge; CG staff 1966–68, assistant conductor WNO 1968–73, music director 1973–86; conducted several Janáček productions. CG debut 1982 (*Billy Budd*); in 1986 he led WNO in *The Ring* at CG. Music director of Scottish Opera from 1993; CBE 1992.

Armstrong, Sheila (b Ashington, 13 Aug 1942), English soprano. Opera debut SW 1965; Glyndebourne 1966, CG 1973. Roles included Pamina, Zerlina, Despina and Fiorilla. Also heard in concert.

Arne, Michael (b London, *c* 1741; d London, 14 Jan 1786), English singer and composer, illegitimate (?) son of Thomas Augustine Arne. He made his first appearance as a singer in 1750, and a collection of songs, *The Flow'ret*, was pub. the same year. In 1761 he produced his first opera, *Edgar and Emmeline*. He also collaborated with other composers in the production of works for the stage, e.g. *A Midsummer Night's Dream* (with Burney and others, 1763) and *Almena* (with Battishill, 1764). He married the singer Elizabeth Wright on 5 Nov 1766, and the next year wrote the music for Garrick's *Cymon*, his most successful work. In 1771–72 he toured Germany, where he conducted the first German performance of *Messiah*. He was also interested in alchemy; his search for the 'philosophers' stone' twice ruined him. He is still known today for the song 'The lass with a delicate air'.

Arne, Susanna Maria (b London, Feb 1714; d London, 30 Jan 1766), English singer and actress, sister of Thomas Augustine Arne. First appeared on the London stage in 1732. Married Theophilus Cibber in 1734, and sang under her married name. Best known in Handel's *Messiah* and *Samson*.

Arne, Thomas Augustine (b London, bap. 28 May 1710; d London, 5 Mar 1778), English composer. He was educated at Eton and intended for the law, but practised secretly on a muffled harpsichord and learnt the violin from Festing, until his father at length allowed him to make

music his career. He also taught his sister Susanna singing, and she appeared in his first opera, a setting of Addison's *Rosamond*, in 1733. Many successful works for the stage followed, including *Alfred*, containing 'Rule, Britannia', which was produced at the residence of Frederick, Prince of Wales, at Cliveden in 1740. He married the singer Cecilia Young in 1736. In 1742–44 he and his wife worked successfully in Dublin, which they twice revisited in the 1750s. In 1745 Arne was appointed composer to Vauxhall Gardens. D. Mus. Oxford, 1759. In 1760, after a quarrel with Garrick, he gave up his post as composer to Drury Lane Theatre and went over to Covent Garden, where in 1762 he produced his opera *Artaxerxes*, trans. by himself from Metastasio and composed in the Italian manner. Two years later he set the same librettist's *Olimpiade* in the original language. This was a failure, but was followed by the successful *Shakespeare Ode* (1769) and masque *The Fairy Prince* (1771).

Works include OPERAS AND PLAYS WITH MUSIC: *Rosamond* (1733), *The Opera of Operas, or Tom Thumb the Great* (adapted from Fielding), *Love and Glory, The Fall of Phaeton* (1736), *An Hospital for Fools, The Blind Beggar of Bethnal Green* (1741), *Eliza, Britannia* (1755), *The Temple of Dullness, King Pepin's Campaign, Harlequin's Incendiary* or *Columbine, The Triumph of Peace* (1748), *Henry and Emma* (after M Prior), *Don Saverio, The Prophetess, Thomas and Sally* (1760), *Artaxerxes* (1762), *Love in a Village, The Birth of Hercules, The Guardian Outwitted, L'Olimpiade* (1765), *The Ladies' Frolic, The Fairy Prince, Squire Badger* (later *The Sot*), The Cooper (1772), *The Rose, Achilles in Petticoats, May Day, Phoebe at Court*.

MASQUES: *Dido and Aeneas, Comus* (Milton adapted by Dalton), *The Judgment of Paris, Alfred* (1770).

INCIDENTAL MUSIC to Aaron Hill's *Zara*, Shakespeare's *As You Like It* (1740), *Twelfth Night, The Merchant of Venice, The Tempest, Romeo and Juliet* (1750), *Cymbeline*, Mason's *Elfrida* and *Caractacus*.

ORATORIOS: *The Death of Abel* and *Judith* (1761).

Ode on Cheerfulness, Ode to Shakespeare; *c* 25 books of songs; Masses and motets; eight overtures for orchestra; six concertos for keyboard (organ or harpsichord); seven sonatas for two violins and bass; eight harpsichord sonatas.

Arne had kept bad company: he had written for vulgar singers and hearers too long to be able to comport himself properly at the opera-house, in the first circle of taste and fashion.

Charles Burney, on Thomas Arne in
A General History of Music, 1776–89

Arnell, Richard (Anthony Sayer) (b London, 15 Sept 1917), English composer. Studied with John Ireland at the RCM in London and took the Farra Prize in 1938. From 1939 to 1947 he lived in NY, where he was consultant to the BBC's N American service.

Works include operas *Love in Transit* (1958), *The Petrified Princess* (1959); ballets *Punch and the Child, Harlequin in April* and *The Great Detective* (after Conan Doyle) (1953); film music; symphonies, symphonic poem *Lord Byron* and other orchestral music; violin concerto; five string quartets; piano and organ music.

Arnold, Denis (Midgley) (b Sheffield, 15 Dec 1926; d Budapest, 28 Apr 1986), English critic, teacher and musicologist. Studied at Sheffield University and taught at Hull and Nottingham Universities 1964–75; professor of music at Oxford from 1975. He was a specialist in Renaissance and Baroque music. Author of book on Monteverdi; editor, *New Oxford Companion to Music* (1983).

Arnold, Malcolm (Henry) (b Northampton, 21 Oct 1921), English composer, formerly trumpeter. Studied at the RCM in London with a scholarship, 1938–41, then joined the LPO, becoming first trumpet in 1942. In 1945 he became second trumpet of the BBC SO; he rejoined the LPO later as principal (1946–48). He later took up the career of a full-time composer, writing much orchestral and film music in an agreeably diatonic style. Hon. D. Mus., Exeter, 1969; CBE 1970; knighted 1992.

Works include ballets *Homage to the Queen* (1953), *Rinaldo and Armida* (1955) and *Solitaire*; more than 80 film scores, including *The Bridge on the River Kwai*; incidental music for Shakespeare's *Tempest*; overture *Beckus the Dandipratt* for orchestra; symphony for strings; nine symphonies (1951–87); concertos for horn, clarinet (2), flute (2), oboe, piano duet and mouth organ; concertos for trumpet, recorder and cello (1988–89); two string quartets (1951, 1975); violin and piano sonata, viola and piano sonata; piano works.

Arnold, Samuel (b London, 10 Aug 1740; d London, 22 Oct 1802), English composer. Chorister at the Chapel Royal under Gates and Nares; was engaged by Beard as composer to Covent Garden Theatre in 1765, where he produced the pasticcio *The Maid of the Mill* that year. Edited a collection of *Cathedral Music* and the works of Handel. D. Mus., Oxford, 1773, and organist of the Chapel Royal, 1783. Founder of the Glee Club with Callcott in 1787. Organist of Westminster Abbey, 1793.

Works include operas and plays with music *The Maid of the Mill* (1765), *The Portrait* (1770), *The Castle of Andalusia*, *Gretna Green*, *Peeping Tom of Coventry* (1784), *Inkle and Yarica*, *The Enraged Musician* (on Hogarth's picture), *The Surrender of Calais* (1791), *Harlequin, Dr. Faustus* (1766), *The Mountaineers*, *The Shipwreck*, *Obi, or Three-fingered Jack* and many others; oratorios *Elisha, The Cure of Saul*, *The Resurrection* (1770), *The Prodigal Son* (1773); church music; overture for orchestra; odes for chorus; harpsichord music; songs.

Arnould, Madeleine Sophie (b Paris, 13 Feb 1740; d Paris, 22 Oct 1802), French soprano and actress. She made her debut in 1757. Sang Iphigenia in the fp of Gluck's *Iphigénie en Aulide* in Paris, 1774, and Eurydice in the French version of his *Orfeo* the same year.

Aroldo opera by Verdi (libretto by Piave), produced Rimini, Teatro Nuovo, 16 Aug 1857. A revision of *Stiffelio* (1850).

Aronowitz, Cecil (b King William's Town, 4 Mar 1916; d Ipswich, 7 Sept 1978), South African-born British viola player. He studied at the RCM and played violin in various London orchestras until World War II. From 1949 he was principal viola successively of the Goldsbrough Orchestra (later English Chamber Orchestra), London Mozart Players and EOG: Britten's church parables at Aldeburgh. He was a founder member of the Melos Ensemble, in 1950, and was often heard in string quintets with the Amadeus Quartet. Professor, RCM, 1948–75.

arpeggio Italian *arpeggiare* = 'to play, to harp'; the notes of a chord played in rapid succession, either in regular time (as in instrumental and vocal exercises) or freely as an interpretation of the arpeggio sign.

The arpeggio sign indicates that the notes should be rolled upwards, starting from the lowest note.

arpeggione a six-stringed instrument invented by G Staufer of Vienna in 1823; a hybrid between a cello and a guitar, played with a bow and with a fretted fingerboard. Schubert wrote a sonata for it in 1824.

arpicordo Italian = 'harpsichord'; another and much rarer name for the harpsichord.

Arquimbau, Domingo (b c 1758; d Seville, 26 Jan 1829), Spanish composer. Music director of Seville Cathedral, 1795–1829. Wrote a Mass, motets and sacred *villancicos*.

arrangement an adaptation of a melody or musical work for some other medium than that originally intended. In some music of the 17th c. and earlier, it can involve merely the spelling out of one of the possible versions implied in a relatively unspecific musical text. ◊realization.

Arrau, Claudio (b Chillán, 6 Feb 1903; d Murzzuschlag, Austria, 9 Jun 1991), Chilean pianist. First played in public aged five, and in 1910 was sent to study in Berlin, where he settled from 1925 to 1940. From 1941 he lived in the USA. London debut 1922; still active until shortly before his death; admired for his sensitive and powerful interpretations of the Romantic masterworks.

Arriaga y Balzola, Juan Crisóstomo Antonio (b Bilbao, 27 Jan 1806; d Paris, 17 Jan 1826), Spanish violinist and composer. Played and composed as a child and was sent to the Paris Conservatory in 1821. His early death cut short a remarkable career.

Works include *Los esclavos felices/The Happy Slaves*, 1820, symphony in D and three string quartets.

Arrieta y Corera, (Pascual Juan) Emilio (b Puente la Reina, Navarre, 21 Oct 1823; d Madrid, 11 Feb 1894), Spanish composer. Studied under Vaccai at the Milan Conservatory and produced his first opera there in 1845, returning to Spain the following year. Professor of composition at the Madrid Conservatory from 1857 and director from 1868.

Works include Italian operas *Ildegonda* (Milan, 1825), *La conquista di Granada* (1850; revised as *Isabella la Católica*, 1855); zarzuelas *El dómino azul*, *El grumete*, *La Estrella de Madrid*, *Marina* and c 50 others.

Arrigoni, Carlo (b Florence, 5 Dec 1697; d Florence, 19 Aug 1744), Italian lutenist and composer. Gave concerts with Sammartini in London 1732–33, and pub. *10 Cantate da camera* there in 1732.

Arroyo, Martina (b Harlem, NY, 2 Feb 1936), American soprano. Debut New York, Carnegie Hall, 1958, and sang in Europe 1963–65 before Aida at New York Met. 1965; later sang other Verdi roles, and Elsa and Donna Anna. CG from 1968. Concert performances in Varèse and Dallapiccola; she gave the fp of Stockhausen's *Momente* (Cologne, 1962).

ars antiqua Latin = 'the old art'; music of the late 12th and 13th c., before the introduction of the *ars nova* in the 14th c. A term originally used by 14th-c. writers of the music immediately preceding their own time.

ars nova, Latin, = 'the new art'; the title of a treatise (c 1322) by Philippe de Vitry. It described a new and wider range of note-values which can be seen as the main difference between 14th-c. music and that of the 13th c. Hence the word is often used as a descriptive term for all 14th-c. music, though stricter usage confines it to French music of that c. (for the Italian repertory ◊Trecento); the most literal usage restricts it to French works of the first few decades of the c. (for the slightly later repertory, ◊ars subtilior).

ars subtilior, Latin, = 'the more refined art'; a term found in the writings of Philipottus de Caserta to describe a late 14th-c. style of great notational and rhythmic complexity. Certain works by composers such as Philipottus, Senleches, Ciconia and Asproys include cross-rhythms of a baffling complexity that has no parallels until the 20th c.

Artamene opera by Albinoni (libretto by B Vitturi), produced Venice, Teatro di Sant' Angelo, 26 Dec 1740.

Opera by Gluck (libretto ditto), produced London, King's Theatre, Haymarket, 4 Mar 1746. The second of Gluck's two operas for London; he performed an aria from it before Burney in 1770.

Artaria Viennese firm of music pubs., founded in Mainz, 1765; moved to Vienna, 1766; closed in 1858. Prominent in the pub. of works by Haydn, Mozart and Beethoven.

Artaserse, *Artaxerxes*, opera by Abos (libretto by Metastasio), produced Venice, Teatro di San Giovanni Grisostomo, Carnival 1746. Attempt by Artabano to poison Artaserse is prevented by his own son.

Opera by Gluck (libretto ditto), produced Milan, Teatro Regio Ducal, 26 Dec 1741. Gluck's first opera. Other settings by Hasse (Venice, 1730); Graun (Berlin, 1743); and Jommelli (Rome, 1749).

Artaxerxes opera by Arne (libretto by composer, trans. from Metastasio's *Artaserse*), produced London, CG, 2 Feb 1762. Revived London, 16 Mar 1995, in an edition by Peter Holman.

Arteaga, Esteban (b Moraleja (Segovia), 26 Dec 1747; d Paris, 30 Feb 1799), Spanish scholar. He was a Jesuit priest, but after the suppression of the Order went to Italy, where he worked for many years with Padre Martini in Bologna. Five treatises on music survive, the most important of them being that on opera, *Rivoluzioni del teatro musicale italiano*, pub. 1733–38.

Art of Fugue, The ◊Kunst der Fuge.

Arts Florissants, Les French ensemble founded 1979 by William ◊Christie, which specializes in music by Lully, Rameau and M A Charpentier. They gave Purcell's *King Arthur* at CG, 1995.

It pleases me, at my age, to see a new method of composing, though it would please me much more if I saw that these passages were founded upon some reason which could satisfy the intellect.

Giovanni Artusi, *L'Artusi, overo delle Imperfettioni della musica moderna*, 1600

Artusi, Giovanni Maria (b *c* 1540; d Bologna, 18 Aug 1613), Italian composer and theorist. His four-part canzonets appeared in 1598, and his *L'Arte del Contrapunto* in 1586–89. Apart from his polemical works against Zarlino, Galilei and Bottrigari, his *L'Artusi, overo delle Imperfettioni della musica moderna* (1600) singles out nine as yet unpublished madrigals by Monteverdi for special attack, to which the composer replied in the preface to his fifth book of madrigals (1605). Here he promised a treatise, never completed, to be entitled *Seconda Prattica overo delle perfettioni della moderna musica*, in contradistinction to the 'Prima prattica' of the conservatives. The controversy was continued in two more works by Artusi, pub. under a pseud.

Ashkenazy *The pianist and conductor Vladimir Ashkenazy. He began his career as a pianist, taking lessons from the age of six. A champion of Russian composers including Rakhmaninov and Prokofiev, his wide-ranging gifts of intellect, expression and technique are evident in the varying demands of the music.*

(1606 and 1608), and by Monteverdi's brother Giulio Cesare in the preface to the *Scherzi musicali* of 1607.

Arundell, Dennis (b London, 22 Jul 1898; d London, 10 Dec 1988), English actor, producer and composer. Educated at Cambridge, he produced many operas and music plays, trans. several Italian and French librettos and wrote a book on Purcell (1927). In Cambridge and London he produced the *Fairy Queen*, *Semele*, *Katya Kabanová* and *The Soldier's Tale*. He taught at the RNCM until 1974.

Ascanio opera by Saint-Saëns (libretto by G Gallet, after P Meurice), produced Paris, Opéra, 21 Mar 1890. Character from Berlioz' opera *Benvenuto Cellini* resurfaces in episode from Cellini's life at court of Francis I at Fontainebleau.

Ascanio in Alba opera by Mozart (libretto by G Parini), produced Milan, Teatro Regio Ducal, 17 Oct 1771. Venus orders grandson Ascanius to marry the nymph Silvia.

Ascension, L' work for orchestra in four movements by Messiaen; composed 1933, version for organ 1934. Orchestral version performed Paris, Feb 1935.

Ashkenazy, Vladimir (b Gorky, 6 Jul 1937), Russian-born pianist and conductor. Toured US 1958; joint winner Tchaikovsky Competition, Moscow, 1963; moved to Britain 1963 and became Icelandic citizen 1972. World tours in Romantic repertory; principal conductor Philharmonia Orchestra from 1981. He succeeded André Previn as music director of the RPO in 1986, visited Russia with the orchestra as conductor and pianist 1989; resigned 1995. Principal conductor of the Berlin Radio SO, 1989.

Ashley, Robert (b Ann Arbour, MI, 28 Mar 1930), American composer. Studied with Ross Lee Finney and Roberto Gerhard at the University of Michigan and later influenced by Gordon Mumma and John Cage. With Mumma he co-founded the ONCE Festival for Experimental Music, 1961–68. Also involved with the Sonic Arts Union, for the use of electronic music.

Works include TV and video operas *In Memoriam ... Kit Carson* (1963), *That Morning Thing* (1967), *Music with Roots in Aether* (1976), *Perfect Lives* (1980), *The Lessons* (1981), *Atalanta, Acts of God* (1982), *Atalanta strategy* (1984), *Foreign Experiences* (1984), *El Aficionado* (1987), *My Brother Called* (1989); electronic music theatre *Night Train* (1966), *The Wolfman Motorcity Revue* (1968), *What She thinks* (1976), *Title Withdrawn* (1976); film music, chamber pieces and electronic works.

Ashwell, Thomas (Ashewell, Hashewell) (b *c* 1478; d after 1513), English composer. In 1508 he was *informator choristarum*, Lincoln Cathedral, and in 1513 held the equivalent post in Durham. His surviving works include four Masses, two (*God save King Harry* and *Sancte Cuthberte*) in a fragmentary state and two (*Ave Maria* and *Jesu Christe*) complete.

Asioli, Bonifazio (b Correggio, 30 Aug 1769; d Correggio, 18 May 1832), Italian music scholar and composer. Worked in his native town at the beginning and end of his career, but in between was at Turin, Venice, Milan and Paris. Wrote much church, stage, vocal and instrumental music and several theoretical treatises.

Askenase, Stefan (b Lwów, 10 Jul 1896; d Cologne, 18 Oct 1985), Polish-born Belgian pianist. He studied at Vienna with Emil von Sauer; debut 1919. He toured widely in Europe and S America and was best known in Chopin. Belgian citizen from 1950; taught at Brussels Conservatory 1954–61.

Asola, Giammateo (b Verona, *c* 1532; d Venice, 1 Oct 1609), Italian priest and composer. *Maestro di cappella* successively at Treviso (1577) and Vicenza (1578). Wrote church music (including 12 books of masses), madrigals.

Aspelmayr, Franz (b Vienna, bap. 2 Apr 1728; d Vienna, 29 Jul 1786), Austrian composer attached to the Viennese court.

Works include melodrama *Pygmalion* (after Rousseau, 1776), *Singspiele*, ballets, including *Agamemnon vengé* (1771), *Acis et Galathée* (1773), *Ifigenie* (1773), symphonies, chamber music.

Aspern Papers, The opera in two acts by Dominick Argento (libretto by the composer, after Henry James); produced Dallas, 19 Nov 1988.

Asproys (*Hasprois*), Johannes, French composer, one of the singers of the anti-pope at Avignon in 1394. Some of his *chansons* are in an early 15th-c. MS now at Oxford, Bodleian Library, Canonici misc. 213.

Asrael symphony by Josef Suk (his second); written in memory of his wife and of Dvořák, his father-in-law. First performed Prague, 3 Feb 1907.

Assafiev, Boris Vladimirovich (b St Petersburg, 29 Jul 1884; d Moscow, 27 Jan 1949), Russian composer and critic. Studied philosophy at St Petersburg University and music at the Conservatory, where he later became professor. Author of numerous books on composers, including Glinka, Tchaikovsky, Skriabin and Stravinsky, on Russian and Czech music etc., written under the name of Igor Glebov.

Works include OPERAS (nine) including *Cinderella* (1906), *The Treasurer's Wife* (after Lermontov), *The Storm* (after Ostrovsky), *A Feast in Time of Plague* (Pushkin) (1940), *The Bronze Horseman* (Pushkin).

BALLETS (27) including *Solveig* (based on Grieg) (1918), *The Fountain of Bakhchisserai* (after Pushkin), *Lost Illusions* (after Balzac) (1935), *The Beauty is Happy* (after Gorky's story *Makar Chudra*), *Christmas Eve* (after Gogol).

INCIDENTAL MUSIC to Shakespeare's *Macbeth*, *Merchant of Venice* and *Othello*, Tirso de Molina's *Seducer of Seville* (*Don Juan*), Sophocles' *Oedipus Rex*, Schiller's *Fiesco* and *Don Carlos*.

ORCHESTRAL AND CHAMBER: four symphonies (1938–42), sinfonietta for orchestra, Suvarov Suite for wind insts.; piano concerto; string quartet; viola solo sonata, sonata for trumpet and piano; six Arias for cello and piano; piano works; choruses; songs.

assai Italian = 'much, very'.

Assassinio nella cattedrale, L', *Murder in the Cathedral*, opera by Pizzetti (libretto by composer after T S Eliot's dramatic poem), produced Milan, La Scala, 1 Mar 1958. Archbishop Beckett murdered at Canterbury.

Assmayr, Ignaz (b Salzburg, 11 Feb 1790; d Vienna, 31 Aug 1862), Austrian organist and composer. Held several organist's posts at Salzburg and Vienna, was conductor of the Vienna Music Society and wrote oratorios and much church and other music.

Astaritta, Gennaro (b Naples, *c* 1745; d after 1803), Italian composer of *c* 40 operas, 1765–93, including the popular *Circe ed Ulisse*, and *L'isola disabitata* (Florence, 1773), *Armida* (Venice, 1777), *Rinaldo d'Asti* (St Petersburg, 1796).

Aston, Hugh (b *c* 1480; d Nov 1558), English composer. He took the B.Mus. at Oxford, 1510, and was *magister choristarum* at Newarke College, Leicester, 1525–48. His works include six votive antiphons and two Masses, a 'Hornepype' for keyboard, and possibly other keyboard music also. There are works on a ground bass of his by Whytbroke (for viols) and Byrd (for keyboard).

Astorga, Emanuele (Gioacchino Cesare Rincón) d' (b Augusta, Sicily, 20 Mar 1680; d Lisbon or Madrid, ? 1757), Italian nobleman and composer of Spanish descent. His opera, *Dafni*, was produced in Genoa and Barcelona in 1709. His most famous work is a *Stabat Mater* (*c* 1707). He also wrote a number of chamber cantatas in the manner of A Scarlatti. From *c* 1721 he seems to have lived mainly in Spain and Portugal.

Astuzie femminili, Le, *Women's Wiles*, opera by Cimarosa (libretto by G Palomba), produced Naples, Teatro del Fondo, 16 Aug 1794. Orphan Bellina wishes to marry Filandro, but there is competition from Don Lasagna.

Atalanta opera by Handel (libretto adapted from *La caccia in Etolia* by B Valeriani), produced London, CG, 12 May 1736. The nymph Atalanta is united with the shepherd king Meleager, in spite of her initial preference for the hunt and life in the woods.

Atem gibt das Leben, *Breathing gives Life*, work for chorus by Stockhausen; performed Hamburg, 16 May 1975.

a tempo Italian = 'in time'; a direction indicating a return to the principal pace of a composition after a temporary alteration.

Athalia oratorio by Handel (words by S Humphreys), produced Oxford, 10 Jul 1733.

Athalie incidental music for Racine's tragedy by Mendelssohn, op. 74;

choruses composed 1843, overture 1844–45, produced Charlottenburg, 1 Dec 1845.

The choruses were also set by Moreau (Saint-Cyr, 5 Jan 1691), Gossec (1785), Vogler (1786), J A P Schulz (1786) and Boieldieu (1836).

Atherton, David (b Blackpool, 3 Jan 1944), English conductor. Conducted opera at Cambridge, and *Il Trovatore* at CG in 1967; 1976 fp of Henze's *We Come to the River*. In 1968 gave first performance of Birtwistle's *Punch and Judy* (Aldeburgh) and became the youngest conductor ever at Promenade Concerts. Also founded London Sinfonietta in 1968 and gave frequent performances of modern music. Music director San Diego SO 1981–87. Resident conductor at CG 1968–80; principal guest conductor BBC SO 1985–90; Hong Kong Philharmonic 1989. Conducted *Il barbiere di Siviglia* at the NY Met., 1995.

Atlantida, L' scenic oratorio by Falla (text by composer, after J Verdaguer); sketched 1926–46 and completed by E Halffter; produced Milan, La Scala, 18 Jun 1962. Spanish saga, from the flooding of Atlantis to Columbus and the New World.

Atmosphères work for orchestra by Ligeti; fp Donaueschingen, 22 Oct 1961, conductor Rosbaud.

We can no longer tolerate this fetishism of tonality, which has been a burden on entire generations of musicians.

Arthur Honegger, *I am a Composer*, 1951

---

atonality the lack of a tonal centre. In its broadest sense it can be used for passages of free-flowing chromaticism which lose touch with tonality, as occasionally encountered in the music of Liszt and Wagner. More specifically it concerns the conscious attempt to compose without any tonal reference. A highly ordered kind of atonality is ◊Serialism, devised by Schoenberg after working with free atonality.

attacca Italian imper. = 'attack, begin'; a direction placed at the end of a movement indicating that the next movement is to be started without a pause.

attacco Italian = 'attack'; a short musical figure or phrase treated by imitation.

Attaingnant, Pierre (d Paris, 1552), French 16th-c. music printer. He pub. many important music books between 1525 and his death, and his widow (born Pigouchet), whose father he had succeeded, continued after 1553.

Atterberg, Kurt (Magnus) (b Göteborg, 12 Dec 1887; d Stockholm, 15 Feb 1974), Swedish composer and conductor. First trained as a civil engineer, he studied music at the RAM in Stockholm under Hallén, and later at Munich, Berlin and Stuttgart. Music critic of *Stockholms Tidningen* from 1919. He composed in an undemanding style, and conducted much in Europe.

Works include five operas; pantomime-ballets; incidental music for plays; Requiem (1914), *Järnbäraland* (*The Land of Iron-Carriers*), for chorus and orchestra (1919); nine symphonies (one in memory of Schubert), nine suites, *Swedish Rhapsody*, symphonic poem *Le Fleuve, Rondeau rétrospectif* and *The Song* for orchestra; symphonic poem for baritone and orchestra; concertos for violin, cello, piano and horn; three string quartets; cello and piano sonata.

Attey, John (d Ross, Herefordshire, 1640), English composer. His volume of 'Ayres' (1622) marks the virtual end of the lute-song in England.

At the Boar's Head opera by Holst (libretto by composer, drawn from Shakespeare's *Henry IV*), produced Manchester, 3 Apr 1925.

Attila opera by Verdi (libretto by T Solera), produced Venice, Teatro La Fenice, 17 Mar 1846. Odabella avenges herself on Attila after her father has been murdered.

Attwood, Thomas (b London, bap. 23 Nov 1765; d London, 24 Mar 1838), English organist and composer. He was a chorister at the

An example of expressionist atonal music in which the composer avoids any clear key; from Schoenberg's 3 Piano Pieces, op.11 (1909).

Chapel Royal; later studied in Naples and Vienna, where he was a pupil of Mozart 1785–87. Organist of St Paul's Cathedral and composer to the Chapel Royal from 1796 to his death. One of the original members of the Philharmonic Society in 1813, and a professor at the RAM on its foundation in 1823. He was also a friend of Mendelssohn, whose three Preludes and Fugues for organ, op. 37, were dedicated to him.

Works include over 30 dramatic compositions; coronation anthems for George IV and William IV, service settings, anthems and other church music; songs, etc. His harmony and counterpoint exercises for Mozart also survive, with Mozart's corrections.

Atys opera by Lully (libretto by Quinault), produced at Saint-Germain, 10 Jan 1676 and fp Paris, Apr 1676. Atys stabs himself for love and is transformed into a pine tree by Cybele.

Opera by Piccinni (libretto ditto, altered by J F Marmontel), produced Paris, Opéra, 22 Feb 1780.

Atzmon, Moshe (b Budapest, 30 Jul 1931), Israeli conductor. Won Liverpool Int. Competition 1964; conducted in Sydney and Hamburg 1969–76. Opera debut Berlin, 1969. Principal conductor Basle SO from 1972. Director of the Dortmund Opera, 1991.

aubade French from *aube* = 'dawn' = 'morning song', in the same sense that a serenade is an evening song; cf. Spanish *alborada*.

Choreographic concerto by Poulenc, for piano and 18 instruments; fp Paris, 18 Jun 1929.

Auber, Daniel François Esprit (b Caen, 29 Jan 1782; d Paris, 12 May 1871), French composer. He began to compose early, but went to London as a young man to follow a commercial career. He attracted attention with his songs, however, and on his return to Paris in 1804 wrote cello concertos for the cellist Lamarre and a violin concerto for Mazas. In 1805 he appeared with a comic opera, *L'Erreur d'un moment*, the libretto of which had previously been set by Dezède, but he did not produce an opera in public until 1813 (*Le Séjour militaire*) and had no real success until 1820 (*La Bergère châtelaine*). *La muette*

de Portici (1828) was a precursor of French Grand Opera. He wrote a *Manon Lescaut* 37 years before Puccini. In 1842 he became director of the Paris Conservatory and in 1857 of the Imperial chapel.

Works include nearly 50 operas, e.g. *Emma* (1821), *Leicester, Le Maçon, La Muette de Portici* (*Masaniello*) (1828), *La Fiancée, Fra Diavolo* (1830), *Le Dieu et la Bayadère, Le Philtre, Le Serment, Gustave III, Le Cheval de bronze* (two versions, 1835 and 1857), *Actéon, L'Ambassadrice, Le Domino noir* (1837), *Les Diamants de la couronne, La Part du diable, Haydée* (1847), *Marco Spada* (with a later ballet version), *Jenny Bell, Manon Lescaut* (1856), *La Circassienne*.

Wagner is Berlioz without the melody.

Daniel Auber, *Le Ménestrel*, 1863

Aubert, Jacques (b Paris, 30 Sept 1689; d Belleville, 17 or 18 May 1753), French violinist and composer. Pupil of Senaillé; member of the king's 24 violins from 1727 and of the Paris Opéra orchestra from 1728. Wrote numerous violin concertos, concert suites and other instrumental works.

Aubert, Louis (b Paris, 15 May 1720; d Paris, after 1783), French violinist and composer, son of Jacques Aubert. He was violinist and second conductor at the Paris Opéra, 1731–74. Wrote sonatas and other works for his instrument.

Aubin, Tony (Louis Alexandre) (b Paris, 8 Dec 1907; d Paris, 21 Sept 1981), French composer. Studied at the Paris Conservatory, where Dukas was his composition master. Took the Prix de Rome in 1930. In 1939 he was appointed head of the music department of the Paris-Mondial radio station and in 1946 professor at the Paris Conservatory.

Works include suite *Cressida* for solo voices, chorus and orchestra (1935); cantata *Actéon* (1930); *Symphonie romantique* and *Le Sommeil d'Iskander* for orchestra; string quartet; sonata and *Prélude, Récitatif et Final* for piano; six Verlaine songs.

Aubry, Pierre (b Paris, 14 Feb 1874; d Dieppe, 31 Aug 1910), French musicologist and orientalist. Lectured on music history at the École des Hautes Études Sociales in Paris; did important research on French medieval music.

Aucassin et Nicolette a 13th-c. French narrative in prose and verse. Its verse sections show a technique similar to that employed in the *chanson de geste*, in that each pair of lines is sung to the same tune constantly repeated, each section being rounded off by a single line sung to a different tune. Its alternation between prose and verse, however, classifies it as a *chante-fable*.

Aucassin et Nicolette, ou Les Mœurs du bon vieux temps, opera by Grétry (libretto by J M Sedaine, based on the French 13th-c. tale), produced Versailles, at court, 30 Dec 1779, first Paris performance, Comédie- Italienne, 3 Jan 1780.

Audefroi le Bastart (*fl.* 1190–1230), French poet and musician now known from ten courtly *chansons* and six *chansons de toile*.

Auden, W(ystan) H(ugh) (1907–1973), English-born American poet and librettist. From 1935 collaborated with Britten on *Paul Bunyan*, *Ode to St Cecilia* and *Our Hunting Fathers*. Close relationship with Chester Kallman from 1948, providing the librettos for Stravinsky's *Rake's Progress* (1953), Henze's *Elegy for Young Lovers* (1961) and *The Bassarids* (1966). Their work has been judged theatrically effective, but also at times seems contrived and even camp (e.g. the intermezzo in *The Bassarids*).

The writer must be convinced that opera offers possibilities that are excluded from drama, and that these very possibilities are worth more than everything of which drama is capable.

W H Auden, quoted in Henze, *Music and Politics*, 1982

Audran, Edmond (b Lyons, 12 Apr 1840; d Tierceville, 17 Aug 1901), French composer. Studied at Niedermeyer's school in Paris and first made his mark as a church organist and composer at Marseilles and Paris, producing a Mass, but later with operettas, the first of which, *L'Ours et le Pacha*, was produced at Marseilles in 1862. His first production in Paris (1879) was *Les Noces d'Olivette*. Others included *La Mascotte* (1880), *Gillette de Narbonne* (based on Boccaccio) (1882), *La Cigale et la Fourmi* (based on La Fontaine) (1886), *La Poupée*, *Monsieur Lohengrin*.

Auer, Leopold (b Veszprém, 7 Jun 1845; d Loschwitz, 15 Jul 1930), Hungarian violinist. Pupil of Dont in Vienna and Joachim at Hanover. Professor at the St Petersburg Conservatory from 1868. He declined the dedication of Tchaikovsky's violin concerto but after revision of the solo part played it in the year of Tchaikovsky's death. Went to USA after the Russian Revolution. Heifetz and Mischa Elman were among his pupils.

Aufforderung zum Tanz, *Invitation to the Dance*, a piano piece by Weber, op. 65, which he calls a *rondeau brillant*, in waltz form with a slow introduction and epilogue, composed in 1819. Usually heard today in orchestral version by Berlioz.

Aufgesang German = 'fore-song'; ♭bar.

Aufstieg und Fall der Stadt Mahagonny, *Rise and Fall of the City of Mahogany*, opera by Weill (libretto by Brecht), produced Leipzig, 9 Mar 1930. Jenny and Jim make out in the fat city but Jim can't pay the whisky bill.

Auftakt German = 'upbeat'.

Auftrittslied German = 'entry song'; a song or air in a musical play or opera, especially a German *Singspiel*, by which a character introduces and describes himself to the audience, either directly or by addressing another character or characters; e.g. Papageno's first song in Mozart's *Die Zauberflöte*.

Augenarzt, Der, *The Oculist*, opera by Gyrowetz (libretto by J E Veith), produced Vienna, Kärntnertortheater, 1 Oct 1811. Dr Berg restores sight to Wilhelmine, who turns out to be his long-lost sister.

Augenlicht, Das work for chorus and orchestra by Webern (text by H

Jone); composed 1935, fp London, 17 Jun 1938, conductor Scherchen.

Auger, Arleen (b Los Angeles, 13 Sept 1939; d Leusden, Netherlands, 10 Jun 1993), American soprano. Studied in Long Beach and Chicago. Opera debut as the Queen of Night at the Vienna Staatsoper, 1967 (repeated at the NY City Opera, 1969). Many successful concerts, notably in Baroque music; recorded Bach cantatas with Helmuth Rilling. NY Met. debut 1978, as Marzelline; she made London appearances (1985, 1988) as Alcina and Poppea, both recorded.

augmentation the enlargement of a musical figure or phrase by lengthening, usually doubling, the note-values.

augmented said of intervals normally 'perfect' (4th, 5ths, octaves) or 'major' (2nds, 3rds, 6ths, 7ths) which have been made wider by a semitone.

Perfect 4th   Augmented 4th

Major 6th   Augmented 6th

Perfect and augmented intervals.

augmented 6th chords a group of chords that stand as the springboard for much of the more colourful harmonic style of the 19th c. They depend for their effect on the interval of an augmented 6th between the flattened 6th degree and the sharpened 4th degree of the diatonic scale. Almost invariably their logical progression is to the dominant (V) or to a second inversion triad on the dominant (I⁶4) which in turn leads to the dominant.

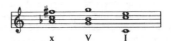

1. Italian

2. German

3. French

4. 'Tristan 6th'.

The earliest augmented 6th chord, occasionally found even in the 17th c., is the Italian 6th, a three-note chord (in C major).

Since the structure of the German 6th (in equal temperament) is identical with that of the dominant 7th, it is extremely useful for modulation to distant keys.

The famous opening chord of Wagner's Tristan und Isolde may be interpreted as an augmented 6th like the French 6th but with the 3rd flattened, thus sometimes called the 'Tristan 6th' (here transposed from A minor to C minor for comparison).

Of the four-note forms, the 'German 6th' first became a firm favourite at the end of the 18th c. and was used with particular force by Beethoven. Less common is the 'French 6th', with its two middle notes a major 2nd apart. Finally, it may be noted that from the middle of the 19th c. many other variants of the principle appear.

Auletta, Pietro (b Sant, Angelo a Scala near Avellino, 1698; d Naples, Sept 1771), Italian composer. He made his debut as an opera composer at Naples in 1725 with *Il trionfo d'amore*, in which year he also received the title of *maestro di cappella* to the Prince of Belvedere. Several comic and then some serious operas followed. His most popular work, *Orazio* (1737), eventually became debased into a pasticcio by the addition of music by other composers, and was pub. in Paris as *Il maestro di musica* in 1753 under the name of Pergolesi.

aulos an ancient Greek double-reed instrument, the equivalent of the Latin *tibia* and akin to the modern oboe. The double aulos often seen in pictures and sculpture would have enabled the melody to be accompanied by a drone.

Aureliano in Palmira opera by Rossini (libretto by F Romani), produced Milan, La Scala, 26 Dec 1813. The overture was afterwards used for *Elisabetta regina d'Inghilterra*, and later for *Il barbiere di Siviglia*. Other parts of the music also appear in the latter work. Roman emperor Aurelianus allows Arsace and Zenobia to marry.

Auric, Georges (b Lodève, Hérault, 15 Feb 1899; d Paris, 23 Jul 1983), French composer. Studied at the Paris Conservatory and the Schola Cantorum. Member of the group 'Les Six' and influenced by Satie and later by Stravinsky.

Works include comic opera *Sous le masque* (libretto by L Laloy) (1907), ballets *Les Noces de Gamache* (from *Don Quixote*), *Les Matelots*, *La Pastorale*, *La Concurrence*, *Les Imaginaires*; incidental music to *Les Fâcheux* (Molière), *The Birds* (Aristophanes) (1928), *Volpone* (Ben Jonson) (1927), *Le Mariage de Figaro* (Beaumarchais), *Le 14 Juillet* (Rolland) (1931), with nine others; film music *À nous la liberté* (René Clair), *Caesar and Cleopatra* (after Bernard Shaw); symphony, suite, overture, *Fox-trot* and *Nocturne* for orchestra; piano concerto; piano sonata and sonatina, *Three Pastorales* for piano; *Chandelles romaines* for piano duet; trio for oboe, clarinet and bassoon; violin and piano sonata; several song cycles.

Aus Italien, *from Italy*, symphony by R Strauss, op. 16, composed 1885–86 during and after a visit to Italy Mar 1887. The four movements are entitled *On the Campagna, The Ruins of Rome, On the Shore of Sorrento* and *Neapolitan Folk Life*, and the last contains a quotation of Denza's *Funiculì funiculà*, which Strauss took for a folksong.

Aus meinem Leben, *From my Life*, subtitle of Smetana's string quartet in E minor (1876). Slow movement depicts Smetana's love of his wife, and a sustained high note on the violin in the finale suggests his tinnitus.

Austin, Frederic (b London, 30 Mar 1872; d London, 10 Apr 1952), English baritone and composer. Began his career as organist and music teacher at Liverpool, but appeared as a singer in 1902 and in opera at CG, London, in 1908. Artistic director of the BNOC from 1924. He arranged *The Beggar's Opera* for the revival at the Lyric Theatre, Hammersmith, London, in 1920, and the sequel, *Polly*, for that at the Kingsway Theatre, in 1922. Stage works include a setting of Congreve's *The Way of the World*.

Austin, Larry (b Duncan, OK, 12 Sept 1930), American composer. Studied in California with Milhaud and Seymour Shifrin and has taught at the University of South Florida and North Texas State University (from 1978). His works employ a full range of electronic effects and are cast for a variety of theatrical media.

Works include *Improvisations*, for orchestra and jazz soloists, (1961); theatre pieces *The Maze* (1967), *Agape* (1970), *Walter* (1971); *Plastic Surgery* for tape and film (1970); *Phantasmagoria*, after Ives' unfinished *Universe* symphony (1982); *Sinfonia Concertante: A Mozartean Episode* (1986); *Concertante Cybernetica* (1987).

Austral (real name **Wilson**), Florence (b Melbourne, 26 Apr 1894; d Newcastle, NSW, 16 May 1968), Australian soprano. Entered Melbourne Conservatory in 1914 and in 1918 studied in NY. She made her debut at CG in 1922 as Brünnhilde. She was known as a leading Wagner singer, touring both Europe and America.

Auxcousteaux, Artus (or Arthur) (d 1656), French singer and composer. He was a singer in Louis XIII's chapel *c* 1613–27 and (?) at Noyon; later music master at the cathedral of Saint-Quentin and singer in the Sainte-Chapelle in Paris, becoming chaplain, precentor and canon at later dates.

Works include Masses, Magnificats, *Noëls* and other church music.

The composer is culpable who, for the sake of a low and trifling imitation, deserts the beauties of expression.
Charles Avison, *An Essay on Musical Expression*, 1752

Avison, Charles (b Newcastle upon Tyne, bap. 16 Feb 1709; d Newcastle upon Tyne, 10 May 1770), English organist and composer. A pupil of Geminiani and organist at St Nicholas' Church, Newcastle 1736–70. He is chiefly remembered for his treatise *An Essay on Musical Expression* (1752), but also wrote a quantity of instrumental music, including 48 concertos for chamber orchestra and (with John Garth) edited Marcello's Psalms in 1757. He is recognized as the foremost English concerto composer of his time.

Avolio (*Avoglio*), Signora, Italian 18th-c. soprano, who sang in the fps of *Messiah* (1742), *Samson* (1743) and *Semele* (1744).

Avondano, Pedro Antonio (b Lisbon, bap. 16 Apr 1714; d Lisbon,

---

Emanuel Ax – pianist

1 Tchaikovsky: *Eugene Onegin*
When I was four I went to a couple of rehearsals of *Eugene Onegin* – and to this day it's my favourite opera, and opera is my favourite music. The music is so direct and frank and beautiful; it's Tchaikovsky at his most inspiring.

2 Brahms: Piano Concerto in B flat
At 17 or 18 I fell in love with this concerto. It drove me bananas. I literally wore out two records; I had it on all the time, every day for months.

3 Haydn: String Quartets
Apart from Brahms, Haydn is probably my favourite composer of the old dead guys. Haydn is more direct than Mozart, and slightly more inventive in terms of harmony and structure, but he's less complicated than Mozart. There's an incredible visceral excitement, an athletic quality to the music of, for example, the string quartets and some piano sonatas, which you don't usually get in classical music except in middle-period Beethoven.

4 Schoenberg: Piano works
I'm a great fan of Schoenberg. There are great parallels between Brahms and Schoenberg. Somebody once suggested that if you were to take a late Brahms piece, one of the Intermezzi or the Fourth Symphony, and leave off the harmonic undertones, you would get a tortured tune like a Schoenberg tone row.

1782), Portuguese composer and violinist of Italian descent.

Works include comic opera *Il mondo della luna* (1765); sacred dramas *Il voto di Jefte* and *Adamo ed Eva* (1772); *Sinfonia* for strings; ? church music and harpsichord pieces destroyed in the Lisbon earthquake of 1755.

Ax, Emanuel (b Lwów, 8 Jun 1949), Polish-born American pianist. Studied Warsaw and in NY; debut there 1973. Won the first Rubinstein Competition, Israel, 1974. London from 1977. Admired in Romantic music, also plays Bartók and Schoenberg. Plays in trio with Yo-Yo Ma and Young Uck Kim. Played Mozart's D minor concerto at the London Proms, 1994.

Axman, Emil (b Rataje, Moravia, 3 Jun 1887; d Prague, 25 Jan 1949), Czech composer. Studied at Prague University and was a composition student of Novák.

Works include melodrama *Just Once*; cantatas and other choral works; six symphonies, symphonic poem *Sorrow and Hope*; suite, sinfonietta, suite *From the Beskides*, Moravian dances for orchestra; violin concerto; four string quartets (1924–46), piano trio, violin and piano sonata, cello and piano sonata; three piano sonatas, sonatina and other piano works.

Axur, Salieri, ◊Tarare.

Aylward, Theodore (b *c* 1730; d London, 27 Feb 1801), English organist and composer. Organist at several London churches. D. Mus. Oxford; appointed professor of music at Gresham College, London, 1771.

Works include incidental music for Shakespeare's *Cymbeline* and *Midsummer Night's Dream* (with M Arne, Battishill and Burney) (1765); lessons for organ; canzonets for two voices; glees, catches and songs.

ayre, Old English, a 16th-17th-c. song with predominantly melodic, as distinct from harmonic or contrapuntal, interest.

Ayrton, Edmund (b Ripon, bap. 19 Nov 1734; d London, 22 May 1808), English organist and composer. Studied with Nares at York Minster, became organist and choirmaster at Southwell Minster in 1754, vicar choral at St Paul's Cathedral in London, 1767, and lay clerk at Westminster Abbey in 1780, also Master of the Children at the Chapel Royal. D. Mus., Cambridge, 1784. Composed services and anthems.

His son William (1771–1858) was a founder of the Philharmonic Society and as director at the King's Theatre staged the first *Don Giovanni* in Britain (1817).

azione sacra Italian = 'sacred action'; a 17th–18th-c. term for a sacred drama with music or acted oratorio, e.g. Mozart's *La Betulia Liberata*.

azione teatrale Italian = 'theatrical action'; a 17th-c. term for an opera or musical festival play.

Azzaiolo , Filippo, Italian 16th-c. composer of *villotte*, popular madrigal-like partsongs. Byrd wrote a keyboard piece on the bass of his popular *Chi passa*.

B

B the seventh note, or leading note, of the scale of C major. In Germany B = B♭, and B♮ is represented by H.

Baal opera by Friedrich Cerha (libretto by the composer after Brecht), produced Salzburg, 7 Aug 1981. The poet Baal as a victim of society.

Baal Shem Three Pictures of Chassidic Life, for violin and piano, by Bloch (1923). Version for violin and orchestra, 1939; fp NY, 19 Oct 1941, with Szigeti.

Baaren, Kees van (b Enschede, 22 Oct 1906; d Oegstgeest, 2 Sept 1970), Dutch composer. Studied with Pijper. He was a leading Dutch exponent of serial music, exploiting both tonal and 12-note varieties of this kind of composition, and also very active as a teacher. From 1957 he was director of the Royal Conservatory in The Hague.

Works include *The Hollow Men* (words by T S Eliot), cantata for chorus and orchestra (1948); *Variazioni per Orchestra* (1959); a string quartet and a wind quintet (*Sovraposizione I and II*) (1963).

Babbitt, Milton (b Philadelphia, 10 May 1916), American composer. Studied at universities of New York and Princeton, and also privately with Sessions. In 1938 he was appointed to the music faculty at Princeton, where from 1943 to 1945 he also taught mathematics. His early work is much influenced by Webern, and later he turned to integral serialism and electronic music.

Works include *Composition for 12 Instruments* (1948); *Composition for four Instruments, Composition for Viola and Piano; Composition for Synthesizer* (1961); *Vision and Prayer* (words by Dylan Thomas) with electronic tape accomp.; *Du*, a song cycle; various electronic and film scores; an opera, *Kräfte* (1975); *A Solo Requiem* for soprano and two pianos (1977); *Dual* for cello and piano (1980); *Elizabethan Sextette* for six voices (1981); Piano Concerto (1985); *Transfigured Notes* for strings (1986); *Beaten Paths* for marimba (1988); *The Crowded Air* for 11 instruments (1988); *Consortini* for five instruments (1989).

Babell, William (b c 1690; d London, 23 Sept 1723), English harpsichordist, violinist and composer. Member of the royal band in London and for some years organist at All Hallows Church.

Works include chamber music; harpsichord pieces, airs from operas arranged by Handel for harpsichord.

Babin, Victor (b Moscow, 13 Dec 1908; d Cleveland, 1 Mar 1972), American pianist and composer of Russian birth. He studied with Schnabel and Schreker in Berlin and in 1933 married his piano duettist partner, Vitya Vronsky; moved to the USA 1937. He was director of the Cleveland Inst. of Music from 1961 and composed two concertos for two pianos and orchestra, which he gave with his wife.

Babi-Yar sub-title of symphony no. 13 in B♭ minor, for bass, male chorus and orchestra by Shostakovich (text by Yevtushenko). Composed 1961, fp Moscow, 18 Dec 1962. Babi-Yar is site of World War II massacre of Russian Jews by the Germans.

Baccaloni, Salvatore (b Rome, 14 Apr 1900; d New York, 31 Dec 1969), Italian bass. Sang as a boy in the choir of the Sistine Chapel. Studied with Kaschmann. As an adult made his first appearance in opera in Rome in 1922 as Rossini's Bartolo. A member of the opera co. at La Scala, Milan, from 1927. He sang also at CG, Glyndebourne and the NY Met. (1940–62). He specialized in *buffo* roles, such as Dulcamara, Don Pasquale and Leporello.

Bacchus et Ariane ballet in two acts by Roussel, scenario by A Hermant; produced Paris, Opéra, 22 May 1931. Suite no. 1 for orchestra, performed Paris, 2 Apr 1933, conductor Munch; Suite no. 2 performed Paris, 2 Feb 1934, conductor Monteux.

Baccusi, Ippolito (b Mantua, c 1550; d Verona, 1609), Italian composer. He was influenced by Venetian contemporaries such as Gabrieli.

Works include madrigals, Masses, motets, psalms and Magnificats.

Bacewicz, Grazyna (b Łódz, 5 Feb 1909; d Warsaw, 17 Jan 1969), Polish composer and violinist. She studied composition at the Warsaw Conservatory under Sikorski and later in Paris with Nadia Boulanger. Taught at Łódz Conservatory 1934–35, returning to Paris 1945. Her fourth string quartet won first prize at the International Competition, Liège, in 1951. Although most of her work has been described as 'neo-classical', her later music also uses avant-garde techniques.

Works include four symphonies (1945–53); seven violin concertos (1937–65); cello concerto; piano concerto; concerto for string orchestra; seven string quartets; two piano quintets; six violin sonatas and various violin pieces.

B.A.C.H. a musical theme formed of the notes B♭, A, C, B♮ in German nomenclature and used by various composers as a reference to Bach, who was himself the first to use it. Here are some examples:

Albrechtsberger, Fugue for keyboard.

Bach, one of the subjects of the final fugue (unfinished) in *Die Kunst der Fugue* (four organ fugues are probably spurious).

Bach, J C, Fugue for clavier or organ.

Busoni, *Fantasia contrappuntistica* for piano and for two pianos.

Casella, *Ricercari sul nome di Bach* for piano.

Eisler, Trio on a 12-note row.

Honegger, *Prélude, ariso et Fughette* for piano.

d'Indy, *Beuron* in *Tableaux de voyage* for piano.

Karg-Elert, *Basso ostinato* in organ pieces *Sempre semplice*, op. 143; Passacaglia and Fugue, op. 150 for organ: Sonata, B♭ minor, op. 46, for Kunstharmonium.

Koechlin, *Offrande musicale* for organ (later orchestra).

Liszt, Fantasy and Fugue for organ.

Nielsen (R), Ricercare, Chorale and Toccata for piano.

Piston, Chromatic Study for organ.

Reger, Fantasy and Fugue for organ.

Rimsky-Korsakov, Fugue in *Chopsticks* Variations for piano by various composers; six variations for piano, op. 10.

Schoenberg, Variations for orchestra, op. 31.

Schumann, Six Fugues for organ or pedal piano.

Bach German 16th–18th-c. family of musicians:

1. Veit Bach (b ? Pressburg; d Wechmar near Gotha, before 1577); a baker by trade, and played the cittern.

2. Hans Bach (b *c* 1550; d Wechmar, 1626), son of 1; a carpet-weaver, known as *Der Spielmann*.

3. Lips (Philippus) Bach (b Wechmar; d ? Wechmar, 10 Oct 1620), grandson of 1.

4. Johannes Bach (b Wechmar, 26 Nov 1604; d Erfurt, buried 13 May 1673), son of 2; town musician in Erfurt.

5. Christoph Bach (b Wechmar, 19 Apr 1613; d Arnstadt, 12 Sept 1661), brother of 4; town musician in Erfurt and Arnstadt.

6. Heinrich Bach (b Wechmar, 16 Sept 1615; d Arnstadt, 10 Jul 1692), brother of 5; composed vocal concertos and organ preludes.

7. Johann Christian Bach (b Erfurt, bap. 17 Aug 1640; d Erfurt, buried 1 Jul 1682), son of 4; town musician in Eisenach.

8. Georg Christoph Bach (b Erfurt, 6 Sept 1642; d Schweinfurt, 24 Apr 1697), son of 5; wrote vocal concertos.

9. Johann Christoph ♭Bach (b Arnstadt, bap. 8 Dec 1642; d Eisenach, 31 Mar 1703), son of 6.

10. Johann Aegidius Bach (b Erfurt, 9 Feb 1645; d Erfurt, buried 22 Nov 1716), son of 4, brother of 7; succeeded Pachelbel in Erfurt.

11. Johann Christoph Bach (b Erfurt, 22 Feb 1645; d Arnstadt, 25 Aug 1693) son of 5; town violinist in Arnstadt.

12. Johann Ambrosius ♭Bach (b Erfurt, 22 Feb 1645; d Eisenach, 20 Feb 1695), son of 5, twin brother of 11, father of 25.

13. Johann Michael ♭Bach (b Arnstadt, bap. 9 Aug 1648; d Gehren, 17 May 1694), son of 6, father of 23.

14. Johann Günther Bach (b Arnstadt, bap. 17 Jul 1653; d Arnstadt, 8 Apr 1683), son of 6; violin maker in Arnstadt.

15. Johann Nikolaus Bach (b Eisenach, 10 Oct 1669; d Jena, 4 Nov 1753), son of 9.

16. Johann Christoph ♭Bach (b Erfurt, 16 Jun 1671; d Ohrdruf, 22 Feb 1721), son of 12, brother of 25.

17. Johann Christoph Bach (b Eisenach, bap. 29 Aug 1676; d? London, 1740), son of 9; travelled to Hamburg and London.

18. Johann Bernhard Bach. (b Erfurt, bap. 25 Nov 1676; d Eisenach, 11 Jun 1749), son of 10.

19. Johann Ludwig Bach (b Thal near Eisenach, 4 Feb 1677; d Meiningen, buried 1 May 1731), great-grandson of 4.

20. Johann Jakob Bach (b Eisenach, 9 Feb 1682; d Stockholm, 16 Apr 1722), son of 12, brother of 25; chamber musician at Stockholm, he was the subject of J S Bach's 'Capriccio on the Departure of a Beloved Brother'.

21. Johann Friedrich B. (b Eisenach, *c* 1682; d Mühlhausen, buried 8 Feb 1730), brother of 17; organist at Mühlhausen, after J S Bach.

22. Johann Ernst Bach (b Arnstadt, 5 Aug 1683; d Arnstadt, 21 Mar 1739), son of 11; organist at Arnstadt.

23. Maria Barbara Bach (b Gehren, 20 Oct 1684; d Cöthen, Jul 1720), daughter of 13, first wife of 25.

24. Johann Christoph Bach (b Erfurt, bap. 17 Aug 1685; d Erfurt, buried 15 May 1740), son of 10; director of town music in Erfurt.

25. Johann Sebastian ♭Bach (b Eisenach, 21 Mar 1685; d Leipzig, 28 Jul 1750), son of 12, husband of 23 and 28.

26. Johann Michael Bach (b Eisenach, bap. 1 Aug 1685; d ?), brother of 18; organ builder in Stockholm.

27. Johann Lorenz Bach (b Schweinfurt, 10 Sept 1695; d Lahm, 14 Dec 1773), grandson of 8; pupil of J S Bach at Weimar and kantor in Lahm.

28. Anna Magdalena Bach (born Wilcke) (b 22 Sept 1701; d 27 Feb 1760), second wife of 25.

29. Johann Elias Bach (b Schweinfurt, 12 Feb 1705; d Schweinfurt, 30 Nov 1755), grandson of 8, brother of 27; secretary and tutor in J S Bach's family.

30. Samuel Anton Bach (b Meiningen, 26 Apr 1713; d Meiningen, 1781), son of 21; court organist at Meiningen.

Musician children of Johann Sebastian Bach (25) by 23:

31. Wilhelm Friedemann ♭Bach (b Weimar, 22 Nov 1710; d Berlin, 1 July 1784).

32. Carl Philipp Emanuel ♭Bach (b Weimar, 8 Mar 1714; d Hamburg, 14 Dec 1788).

33. Johann Gottfried Bernhard Bach (b Weimar, 11 May 1715; d Jena, 27 May 1739); organist at Mühausen.

Musician children of Johann Sebastian Bach (25) by 28:

34. Johann Christoph Friedrich ♭Bach (b Leipzig, 21 Jun 1732; d Bückeburg, 26 Jan 1795).

35. Johann Christian ♭Bach (b Leipzig, 5 Sept 1735; d London, 1 Jan 1782).

Bach, Carl Philipp Emanuel (b Weimar, 8 Mar 1714; d Hamburg, 14 Dec 1788), German harpsichordist and composer, second son of J S and Maria Barbara Bach. Educated at St Thomas's School, Leipzig, and at the universities of Leipzig (1731–34) and Frankfurt an der Oder (1734–38), where he studied law. His musical training, according to himself, he received entirely from his father. He was connected with the household of the Crown Prince of Prussia from 1738, and in 1740, on the latter's accession as King Frederick II, he was appointed harpsichordist to the court at Berlin and Potsdam. In 1744 he married Johanna Maria Dannemann, and in 1747 his father visited him at court. His most important works at this time were keyboard pieces, which contributed much to the development of a more homophonic style and modern formal procedures. His treatise on keyboard playing (*Versuch über die wahre Art das Clavier zu spielen*, 1753 and 1762) is a valuable guide to contemporary practice. Bach found Berlin restricting, partly because his duties involved only harpsichord playing, partly because of the stiff-necked conservatism of the king, and in 1768 he moved to Hamburg as municipal director of music at the five principal churches. Burney visited him there in 1772, and commented on his remarkable improvising. In Hamburg Bach had wider scope, directing concerts, etc., with great success, and there he wrote most of his music for large forces, e.g. oratorios.

Works include oratorios *Die Israeliten in der Wüste* (1769) and *Die Auferstehung und Himmelfahrt Jesu* (1780); Magnificat (1749), *Heilig (Sanctus)* for double choir, Passions and other church music; 19 symphonies; 50 keyboard concertos; *c* 200 keyboard pieces (sonatas, fantasias, rondos, etc.), odes, songs, etc.

Bach is the father, we are the children.
Joseph Haydn on C P E Bach, in *Bodley Head History of Music*, 1974

Bach, Jan (b Forrest, IL, 11 Dec 1937), American composer. Studied with Copland and Donald Martino and has taught at Northern Illinois University from 1966. Works are based on traditional means.

Works include operas *The System* (1974) and *The Student from Salamanca* (1980); piano concerto (1975); *The Happy Prince* for narrator, violin and orchestra (1978); horn concerto (1983); harp concerto (1986); chamber and vocal music.

Bach, Johann Ambrosius (b Erfurt, 22 Feb 1645; d Eisenach, 20 Feb 1695), German organist and composer. Born as the twin of Johann Christoph Bach and taught by his father Christoph Bach. He became town musician at Erfurt in 1667, marrying Elisabeth Lämmerhirt there on 8 Apr 1668. In 1671 he was appointed town musician at Eisenach. His wife died on 3 May 1694 and he married Barbara Margaretha Keul on 27 Nov but died himself three months later.

Bach, Johann (John) Christian (b Leipzig, 5 Sept 1735; d London, 1 Jan 1782), German clavier player and composer, youngest son of J S and Anna Magdalena Bach. Pupil of his father and, after the latter's death in 1750, of his brother Carl Philipp Emanuel in Berlin. In 1756 he went to Italy, studying under Padre Martini in Bologna; embraced Roman Catholicism, wrote much Latin church music, and in 1760 was appointed organist of Milan Cathedral. His first opera, *Artaserse*, was produced at Turin in 1760. Two years later he went to London, where he remained for the rest of his life. In 1763 he produced his first opera for London, *Orione*, and was appointed music master to Queen Charlotte. In 1764 he founded with C F Abel a series of subscription concerts which continued till 1781, and in the same year befriended the young Mozart on his visit to London; Mozart's later music was much influenced by Bach and at the older composer's death he quoted

Bach *J S Bach (1685–1750) represented in his later years in a painting by Gemäide von Elias Gottlieb Haussmann (1746). The seminal figure of the Baroque period, Bach's greatest legacy was his extensive oeuvre of sacred and keyboard works; as a composer for the organ he is unrivalled.*

one of his themes in the slow movement of the piano concerto K414. Bach visited Mannheim in 1772 and 1776, and Paris in 1778, where his last opera was produced in 1779. His popularity in London declined in his last years and he died in obscurity.

Works include operas *Artaserse* (1760), *Catone in Utica* (1761), *Alessandro nell' Indie* (all Metastasio), *Orione ossia Diana vendicata, Zanaida* (1763), *Adriano in Siria* (1765), *Carattaco* (1767), *Temistocle* (1772), *Lucio Silla* (1774), *La Clemenza di Scipione* (1778), *Amadis de Gaule*; oratorio *Gioas rè di Giuda*; church music; over 90 symphonies and similar works for orchestra; *c* 40 concertos and over 30 sonatas for clavier; chamber music; English and Italian cantatas, arias, songs; serenata *Endimione* (after Metastasio), performed King's Theatre, London, 6 Apr 1772.

Bach, Johann Christoph (b Arnstadt, bap. 8 Dec 1642; d Eisenach, 31 Mar 1703), German organist and composer. Became organist at Eisenach in 1665 and remained there to the end of his life. Composed motets, church cantatas, chorale preludes for organ and harpsichord music.

Bach, Johann Christoph (b Erfurt, 16 Jun 1671; d Ohrdruf, 22 Feb 1721), German organist. Pupil of Pachelbel at Erfurt. In Oct 1694 he married Dorothea von Hof, and the next year he took his young brother Johann Sebastian into his house after their parents' death.

Bach, Johann Christoph Friedrich (b Leipzig, 21 Jun 1732; d Bückeburg, 26 Jan 1795), German composer, son of J S and Anna Magdalena Bach. Educated at St Thomas's School and Leipzig University, where he studied law. Received his music training from his father, and in 1750 was appointed chamber musician to Count

Wilhelm of Schaumburg-Lippe in Bückeburg, where he remained for the rest of his life, becoming *Konzertmeister* in 1759. He married the court singer Elisabeth Münchhausen in 1755. In 1778 he visited his brother Johann Christian in London.

Among his most notable works are the oratorios on words by Johann Gottfried Herder (attached to the court at Bückeburg 1771–74), *Die Kindheit Jesu* and *Die Auferweckung Lazarus*; a third oratorio and an opera, *Brutus*, both on words by the same poet, are lost. Other works include Passion oratorio *Der Tod Jesu* (words by Ramler); cantatas (some with Herder); 20 symphonies; keyboard concertos and sonatas; chamber music.

Bach, Johann Michael (b Arnstadt, bap. 9 Aug 1648; d Gehren, 17 May 1694), German organist, instrument maker and composer. Organist and parish clerk at Gehren from 1673. Composed motets, sacred arias, etc.

Bach, Johann Sebastian (b Eisenach, 21 Mar 1685; d Leipzig, 28 Jul 1750), German organist and composer. Although not always appreciated by his contemporaries, Bach's place in music history was aptly summed up by his first major biographer: 'He is the river, to which all other composers are tributaries'. After his father's death in 1695 he was a pupil of his brother Johann Christoph in Ohrdruf. At 15 he became a chorister in Lüneburg, where he may have had organ lessons from Böhm. Appointed violinist in the court orchestra of the Duke of Weimar in 1703, but left the same year to become organist in Arnstadt, from where in 1705 he took leave to travel to Lübeck, to hear Buxtehude play. In 1707 moved to Mühlhausen, where he married his cousin Maria Barbara Bach; among their seven children were Wilhelm Friedemann and Carl Philipp Emanuel. A year later returned to Weimar as court organist, remaining there for nine years. During this time he wrote such famous cantatas as *Christ lag in Todesbanden*, *Weinen, Klagen, Sorgen, Zagen*, and *Ich hatte viel Bekümmernis*.

In 1717 appointed *Kapellmeister* to the court of Prince Leopold of Anhalt-Cöthen. His wife died in 1720, and he married Anna Magdalena Wilcke in 1721, fathering 13 more children. At Cöthen Bach had little opportunity for church music and there he wrote mainly instrumental works, including such masterpieces as the Brandenburg Concertos, Orchestral Suites, and works for solo cello and violin. In these works instrumental music seems for the first time to emerge from private use into the public domain.

In 1723 he returned to church work when he succeeded Kühnau as Cantor of St Thomas's in Leipzig, where he remained for the rest of his life and wrote some of his greatest compositions, including the

Johann Sebastian Bach *A biographical note*
In the last decade of his life, Bach's official duties at Leipzig started to diminish. He had given up the regular quota of cantatas which he had been required to produce for church services, and he was thankful to leave many of his teaching duties to others. Highly impatient with any musical weakness he found, he always had problems of discipline with the youngsters of St Thomas's choir school. In his own youth he had studied long hours, often working throughout the night by flickering candlelight. This regime gradually weakened his sight so that by 1750 he was faced with having an operation or going blind. A well-known English eye surgeon, John Taylor, was performing public operations in Leipzig and Bach was persuaded to visit him. Two operations in early April were at first advertised as a success, but his whole system was soon overwhelmed by the medicines administered to him. A sudden improvement occurred ten days before his death and for a few hours he regained his sight. But a stroke was followed by a fever, and he died on 28 July 'as the unfortunate result of a badly-performed eye operation', according to an obituary published in Leipzig.

B minor Mass, St Matthew Passion and Goldberg Variations. In 1747, with his eldest son, Wilhelm Friedemann, he visited the court of Frederick the Great at Potsdam, where his second son, Carl Philipp Emanuel, was court harpsichordist. Two years later his eyesight failed; an operation in 1750 was unsuccessful, and he spent his last months totally blind.

Although Bach is not credited with revolutionizing musical forms he invested contemporary models with a unique brand of creative polyphony and intense spirituality: all his works were dedicated 'To the Greater Glory of God'.

Works include CHURCH CANTATAS: 200 are extant. Among those most frequently performed are no. 1 *Wie schön leuchtet der Morgenstern* (1725), no. 4 *Christ lag in Todesbanden* (1708), no. 6 *Bleib bei uns, denn es will Abend werden* (1725), no. 8 *Liebster Gott, wann werd ich sterben?* (1724), no. 11 *Lobet Gott in seinen Reichen (Ascension Oratorio*, 1735), no. 12 *Weinen, Klagen, Sorgen, Zagen* (1714), no. 20 *O Ewigkeit, du Donnerwort* (1724), no. 21 *Ich hatte viel Bekümmernis* (c 1714), no. 29 *Wir danken dir, Gott* (1731), no. 34 *O ewiges Feuer, O Ursprung der Liebe* (c 1740), no. 36 *Schwingt freudig euch empor* (1731), no. 51 *Jauchzet Gott in allen Landen* (1730), no. 55 *Ich armer Mensch, ich Sündenknecht* (1726), no. 56 *Ich will den Kreuzstab gerne tragen* (1726), no. 57 *Selig ist der Mann* (1725), no. 61 *Nun komm der Heiden Heiland* (1714), no. 63 *Christen, ätzet diesen Tag* (c 1716), no. 68 *Also hat Gott die Welt geliebt* (1725), no. 76 *Die Himmel erzählen die Ehre Gottes*, no. 80 *Ein feste Burg ist unser Gott* (1724), no. 82 *Ich habe genug* (1727), no. 106 *Gottes Zeit ist die allerbeste Zeit* (c. 1707), no. 132 *Bereitet die Wege, bereitet die Bahn* (1715), no 140 *Wachet auf, ruft uns die Stimme* (1731), no. 147 *Herz und Mund und Tat und Leben* (1723), no. 152 *Tritt auf die Glaubensbahn* (1714), no. 158 *Der Friede sei mit dir*, no. 169 *Gott soll allein mein Herze haben* (1726), no. 191 *Gloria in excelsis Deo* (c. 1740).

SECULAR CANTATAS: no. 201 *Der Streit zwischen Phoebus und Pan* (1729), no. 202 *Weichet nur, betrübte Schatten* (c 1720), no. 208 *Was mir behagt ist nur die muntre Jagd* (1713), no. 209 *Non sa che sia dolore*, no. 211 *Schweigt stille, plaudert nicht* (*Coffee Cantata*, 1734), no. 213 *Hercules auf dem Scheidewege* (1733: most of the music later adapted for use in the *Christmas Oratorio*).

OTHER CHURCH MUSIC: Mass in B minor, BWV 232, assembled c 1748 from music previously composed by Bach; four *Missae breves*, in F, A, G minor and G (late 1730s); five settings of the *Sanctus*; Magnificat in E♭ BWV 243 (1723, including four Christmas texts; revised c 1730, in D, without Christmas texts); *St Matthew Passion* (11 Apr 1727 or 15 Apr 1729); *St John Passion* (7 Apr 1724, later revised); *Christmas Oratorio* BWV 248, six cantatas for Christmas to Epiphany (performed 1734–35); six motets BWV 225–30, *Singet dem Herrn ein neues Lied, Der Geist hilft unser Schwachheit auf, Jesu, meine Freude, Fürchte dich nicht, Komm, Jesu, komm! Lobet den Herrn*; *Easter Oratorio* (1 Apr 1725) BWV 249.

For the glory of the most high God alone/And for my neighbour to learn from.

Johann Sebastian Bach, epigraph to
The Little Organ Book, 1717

ORGAN: 19 preludes and fugues, including E♭, ('St Anne') (1739) and E minor ('Wedge') (c 1730) BWV 548; six trio sonatas BWV 525–530, E♭, C minor, D minor, E minor, C and G; Toccata and Fugue in D minor ('Dorian') BWV 538 and D minor BWV 565 (now doubtful); Fantasia and Fugue in C minor BWV 562 and G minor BWV 542; Toccata, Adagio and Fugue in C BWV 564; six concertos BWV 592–597, all transcriptions from other composers, including Vivaldi; four duets BWV 802–805; four fantasias, in B minor, G and C(2); *Pastorale* in F BWV 590 (c 1710); 134 chorale preludes BWV 599–768, some of the best known being *Allein Gott in der Höh' sei Ehr* BWV 711, *An Wasserflüssen Babylon* BWV 653, *Ein feste Burg* BWV 720, *In dulci jubilo* BWV 729, *Jesu, meine Freude* BWV 713,

A Selection of
J S Bach

Partita in D minor for solo violin	1720
Brandenburg Concerto no. 1	1721
Magnificat in D	1723
St Matthew Passion	1727

Orchestral Suite no. 3	1729
Cantata no. 140	1731
Christmas Oratorio	1734
Goldberg Variations	1741–2
Mass in B minor	c 1748
The Art of Fugue	1750

Komm Gott Schöpfer BWV 667, *Liebster Jesu, Wir sind hier* BWV 706, *Vom Himmel hoch* BWV 700, *Wachet auf* BWV 645; three Chorale partitas BWV 766–768.

OTHER KEYBOARD: The Well-tempered Clavier, Books 1 (1722) and 2 (c 1740), 24 preludes and fugues in each, BWV 846–893; 16 concertos BWV 972–987 (Weimar, 1708–17), all arrangements of works by other composers; Capriccio in B♭, on the departure of a beloved brother BWV 992; Chromatic Fantasia and Fugue in D minor BWV 903 (1720); six English Suites BWV 806–811 in A, A minor, G minor, F, E minor and D minor; six French Suites BWV 812–817 in D minor, C minor, B minor, E♭, G and E; *Goldberg Variations* BWV 988; 15 Inventions BWV 772–786; 15 Sinfonias BWV 787–801; *Italian Concerto* BWV 971; six partitas BWV 825–830, in B♭, C minor, A minor, D, G and E minor; seven toccatas BWV 910–916, in F♯ minor, C minor, D, D minor, E minor, G minor and G, nine fugues, three on themes by Albinoni.

I have always kept one end in view, namely, with all good will to conduct a well regulated church music to the honour of God.

Johann Sebastian Bach, in a letter to
Mülhausen Council, 1708

CHAMBER: three Partitas for solo violin, in B minor, D minor and E, and three Sonatas for solo violin, in G minor, A minor and C BWV 1001–1006 (Cöthen, c 1720); six Sonatas for violin and harpsichord in B minor, A, E, C minor, F minor and G BWV 1014–1019; six Suites for solo cello, in G, D minor, C, E♭, C minor and D BWV 1007–1012 (c 1720); three Sonatas for viola da gamba and clavier, in G, D and G minor BWV 1027–1029 (c 1720); Partita in A minor for solo flute BWV 1013 (early 1720s); *The Musical Offering* BWV 1079 (1747) for flute, violin and continuo; *The Art of Fugue* BWV 1080 (c 1745–50), for keyboard.

ORCHESTRAL: concertos, six Brandenburg, in F, F, G, G, D and B♭ BWV 1046–1051 (1721), for violin in A minor and E, for two violins in D minor, for flute, violin and harpsichord in A minor, seven for harpsichord and strings BWV 1052–1058, three for two harpsichords, two for three and one for four; four orchestral suites in C, B minor, D and D BWV 1066–1069; concerto in D minor for violin, oboe and strings is a reconstruction from the C minor concerto for two harpsichords.

Bach, Wilhelm Friedemann (b Weimar, 22 Nov 1710; d Berlin, 1 Jul 1784), German organist and composer, eldest son of J S and Maria Barbara Bach. Educated at St Thomas's School and Leipzig University; received his musical training from his father. Appointed organist of St Sophia's, Dresden, in 1723, and in 1746 succeeded Zachau as organist of St Mary's, Halle. Married Dorothea Elisabeth Georgi in 1751. He resigned his post in Halle in 1764, and never held another permanent position, living an unsettled life and attempting to support his family mainly by teaching. In 1770 he moved to Brunswick, and in 1774 finally to Berlin. There his remarkable organ playing could still arouse astonishment, but his last years were spent in increasing poverty.

Works include cantatas and other church music; nine symphonies; keyboard concertos; nine sonatas, 12 fantasias, and other works for keyboard; organ music.

Bachauer, Gina (b Athens, 21 May 1913; d Athens, 22 Aug 1976), Greek pianist of Austrian parentage. Won Medal of Honour at an international competition in Vienna, 1933, and from 1933 to 1935 took occasional lessons with Rakhmaninov. Made her professional debut in Athens in 1935; London debut 1947, NY 1950. A piano competition taking place in Utah is named after her.

Bachianas Brasileiras nine pieces for various instrumental combinations by Villa-Lobos, in which Brazilian rhythms are treated in the spirit of Bach's counterpoint (1930–44).

Bachmann, Hermann (b Kottbus, 7 Oct 1864; d Berlin, 5 Jul 1937), German baritone. He sang at Halle 1890–94 and Nuremberg 1894–97. From 1897 he was a leading member of the Berlin Hofoper; worked also as a producer from 1910 and taught singing after his retirement in 1917. He appeared as Kothner at the 1892 Bayreuth Festival and sang Wotan in the *Ring* cycles conducted by Felix Mottl in 1896. Recorded Escamillo in 1909.

Bachofen, Johann Caspar (b Zurich, 26 Dec 1695; d Zurich, 23 Jun 1755), Swiss composer. Cantor of the grammar school in Zurich, 1720, and of the *Grossmünster*, 1742. He compiled and partly composed several books of hymns and sacred songs, collected in *Musikalisches Hallejulah* (1727), and in 1759 wrote a setting of the Passion oratorio by Brockes.

Bachrich, Sigismund (b Zsambokreth, 23 Jan 1841; d Vienna, 16 Jul 1913), Hungarian violinist and composer. Studied at the Vienna Conservatory Played and conducted in Vienna and Paris, became professor at the Vienna Conservatory and played viola in the Philharmonic and Opera Orchestras and with the Rosé quartet.

Works include operas *Muzzedin* (1883) and *Heini von Steier* (1884), operetta *Der Fuchs-Major*; ballet *Sakuntala* (after Kalidasa), etc.

'Bach' Trumpet a special brass wind instrument of the trumpet type invented by Kosleck of Berlin and improved by Walter Morrow of London, so devised as to be capable of playing the high clarino parts in the works of Bach and his contemporaries and forerunners; first heard at Eisenach in 1884.

Bäck, Sven-Erik (b Stockholm, 16 Sept 1919; d Stockholm, 10 Jan 1994), Swedish composer and violinist. Studied composition with Rosenberg at the Stockholm Conservatory 1940–44, and later at the Schola Cantorum, Basel. His early music favoured neo-classicism, but he later worked in the 12-note style and in the electronic medium.

Works include *Ett Spel om Maria*; a scenic oratorio; violin concerto; two string quartets; string quintet; songs and piano music.

backfall = ◊appoggiatura (taken from the note above).

Backhaus, Wilhelm (b Leipzig, 26 Mar 1884; d Villach, 5 Jul 1969), German pianist. Studied at the Leipzig Conservatory under A Reckendorf until 1899, and then with d'Albert in Frankfurt. In 1905 he taught at the RMCM, winning the Rubinstein Prize in the same year. He then began his professional concert career. Backhaus excelled in the standard repertory, especially the sonatas of Beethoven.

Bacon, Ernst (b Chicago, 26 May 1898; d Orinda, CA, 16 Mar 1990), American pianist, conductor and composer. Studied music at Chicago and in Vienna, later in the USA with Bloch and Eugene Goossens. In 1925 he was appointed piano professor at the Eastman School of Music, Rochester, NY; in 1945 director of the music school of the University of Syracuse, NY.

Works include musical comedy *Take your Choice*; musical play *A Tree on the Plains*; cantatas *Ecclesiastes* and *From Emily's Diary* (Emily Dickinson); *Dr. Franklin*, musical play (1976); three symphonies (1932, 1937, 1961), two suites and other orchestral music; settings of Dickinson and Whitman.

Bacquier, Gabriel (b Béziers, 17 May 1924), French baritone. Debut Nice, 1950. Brussels from 1953, Paris from 1956. Glyndebourne 1962, CG 1964, both as Mozart's Count. Other roles include Scarpia, Don Giovanni and Falstaff; he sang Massenet's Sancho Panza at Florence and Monte Carlo, 1992.

Badia, Carlo Agostino (b Venice, 1672; d Vienna, 23 Sept 1738), Italian composer. He was court composer at Innsbruck from 1691, and from 1694 worked at the Hapsburg Court in Vienna, writing operas and oratorios for Leopold I and Joseph I (*Bacco, vincitore dell'India*, 1697).

badinerie French = lit. 'teasing, frivolity, playfulness'; a title given, sometimes as *badinage*, by French and German composers of the 18th c. to light, playful pieces in quick 2–4 time (e.g. final movement of Bach's B minor Orchestral Suite for flute and strings).

Badings, Henk (Hendrik Herman) (b Bandoeng, Java, 17 Jan 1907; d Maarheeze, 26 Jun 1987), Dutch composer. Originally a mining engineer, but studied music with Pijper and in 1935 abandoned science entirely for music. Professor at the Music Lyceum, Amsterdam, and the Rotterdam Conservatory. Director of the Royal Conservatory at The Hague, 1941.

Works include opera *The Night Watch* (after Rembrandt) (1942); ballets and incidental music for plays, including the electronic ballet *Kain* (1956); a cantata; 14 symphonies (1932–68); symphonic variations; *Heroic Overture*; violin concerto, cello concerto, concerto for two violins and orchestra; recitations with orchestra; four string quartets; violin and cello sonatas; piano pieces. From 1956 he composed electronic music, including two operas (*Salto mortale*, 1959).

Badini, Ernesto (b San Colombano, 14 Sept 1876; d Milan, 6 Jul 1937), Italian baritone. Debut 1895, Rossini's Figaro. He sang under Toscanini at La Scala and took part there in the fps of Giordano's *La cena delle beffe* (1924) and Wolf-Ferrari's *Sly* (1927); he had created Gianni Schicchi there in 1922 and repeated the role at CG, 1924. At the Teatro Costanzi, Rome, he sang in the 1921 fp of Mascagni's *Il piccolo Marat*. Other roles included Beckmesser, Ford, Colline and Malatesta.

Badura-Skoda, Paul (b Vienna, 6 Oct 1927), Austrian pianist. He studied with Edwin Fischer in Vienna, and made his debut there in 1948; NY debut 1953. He has pub. books on the piano music of Mozart and Beethoven, and excels as a performer of these composers as well as of Schubert. With his wife Eva (b 1929) he co-wrote *Mozart-Interpretation* (1957).

bagatelle French = 'trifle'; a short piece, generally of a light or humorous character. Beethoven pub. three sets of Bagatelles: 7, op. 33, composed 1782–1802; 11, op. 119, composed 1821; 6, op. 126, composed 1824.

bagpipe an instrument producing its sound by wind stored up in a bag filled by the player through a mouthpiece; the melody is fingered on a pipe attached to that bag, called the chaunter, while a drone-bass is sounded continually by two or three additional pipes giving out fixed notes. In some types the wind is supplied by bellows.

Bahr-Mildenburg, Anna (b Vienna, 29 Nov 1872; d Vienna, 27 Jan 1947), Austrian mezzo and soprano. Made her first appearance at Hamburg in 1895 as Brünnhilde, under Mahler, with whom she had an affair. She became a noted Wagner and Strauss singer and sang in London between 1906 and 1913; first Clytemnestra in London, 1910. Bayreuth 1897–1914, as Kundry and Ortrud (as well as acting as assistant to Cosima Wagner). Other roles inc. Reiza, Waltraute, Norma, Adriano, Amneris and Isolde.

Bailey, Norman (b Birmingham, 23 Mar 1933), English baritone. Debut Vienna, 1959, and sang in Germany during the 1960s (Hans Sachs in

Bremerhaven, 1967) before Sachs with the SW Co. in 1968; also sang this role in his debuts at Bayreuth (1969) and NY Met. (1976). Specialist in Wagner repertory and sang in fp of Goehr's *Behold the Sun* (Duisburg, 1985). He appeared with Opera North as Oroveso in *Norma*, 1993.

Baillie, Alexander (b Stockport, 6 Jan 1956), English cellist. Studied with Jacqueline ◊Du Pré and Andre Navarra. Gave many concerts in Europe and N America, including Penderecki's Second Concerto in Canada; other modern repertory includes the premieres of works by Takemitsu (*Orion and Pleiades*), Schnittke (Sonata), Colin Matthews (Concerto) and Lutoslawski (*Grave*). Also plays Henze's *Sieben Liebeslieder* and the Delius Concerto. US concert debut 1993 with the Boston Philharmonic. Recordings include works by Tippett, Elgar, Bridge and Britten.

Baillie, Isobel (b Hawick, 9 Mar 1895; d Manchester, 24 Sept 1983), Scottish soprano. Debut Manchester, 1921. Sang in Lieder and oratorio in England and USA (1,000 performances of *Messiah*). One of 16 singers in Vaughan Williams's *Serenade to Music*, 1938. DBE 1978; autobiography, *Never Sing Louder than Lovely* (1982).

Baillot, Pierre (Marie François de Sales) (b Passy, near Paris, 1 Oct 1771; d Paris, 15 Sept 1842), French violinist. Studied in Rome and later under Catel, Cherubini and Reicha in Paris; joined Napoleon's private band, 1802, and began to give chamber concerts in 1814. Was professor at the Conservatory and wrote works for his instrument and chamber music. Wrote a violin method (1803) and *L'art du violon* (1834).

Bainbridge, Simon (b London, 30 Aug 1952), English composer and conductor. He studied at the RCM and has taught there. Has conducted the BBC SO and the Scottish Sinfonia.

Works include *Music to Oedipus Rex* (1969); *Heterophony* for orchestra (1970); *Spirogyra* for chamber orchestra (1970); wind quintet (1971); string quartet; viola concerto (1977); *Landscape and Magic Words* for soprano and chamber ensemble (1981); *A cappella* for six voices (1985); *Metamorphosis* for ensemble (1988); *Cantus contra cantum* (1989); Double Concerto for oboe and clarinet (1990); *Caliban Fragments* for mezzo and ensemble (1991); Clarinet quintet (1993).

Bainton, Edgar L(eslie) (b London, 14 Feb 1880; d Sydney, 8 Dec 1956), English composer and teacher. Studied at the RCM in London and in 1901 was appointed professor of piano and composition at the Conservatory of Newcastle upon Tyne, of which he became principal in 1912. In 1934 he went to Australia as director of the State Conservatory at Sydney (1934–47). He wrote operas and orchestral and chamber music.

Baird, Julianne (b Statesville, NC, 10 Dec 1952), American soprano. Studied at the Eastman School and with Nikolaus Harnoncourt. Sang in NY with the Waverley Consort and made her stage debut in Handel's *Il Pastor Fido*, 1980. Her clear, bright voice and agile coloratura are suited to the early music repertory: operas by Gluck, Purcell, Gagliano and Charpentier in LA, Washington and Santa Fe; *Dido and Aeneas* in London, 1992. Recordings include sacred music by Bach, Clérambault, Handel and Pergolesi.

Baird, Tadeusz (b Grodzisk Masowiecki, 26 Jul 1928; d Warsaw, 2 Sept 1981), Polish composer. Studied at Łódz Conservatory. Imprisoned in World War II. His music is influenced by serialism, especially by Berg.

Works include opera *Jutro* (*Tomorrow*, after Conrad) (1966); three symphonies; *Cassation for Orchestra*; *Four Essays for Orchestra*; *Expressions* for violin and orchestra (1959); piano concerto; other orchestral music; *Goethe Letters*, for baritone, chorus and orchestra (1970).

Bairstow, Edward C(uthbert) (b Huddersfield, 22 Aug 1874; d York, 1 May 1946), English organist, conductor and composer. After various organist's posts he took the D.Mus. at Durham in 1901 and became organist and choirmaster at York Minster in 1913. Edited *The English Psalter* and wrote *The Evolution of Musical Form* and (with Plunket Greene) *Singing Learnt from Speech*. Professor of music at Durham University, 1929–46. Knighted 1932.

Works include services, anthems; organ music; variations for two pianos.

Baiser de la fée, Le (Stravinsky). ◊Fairy's Kiss

Bakchantinnen, Die, *The Bacchantes*, opera by Wellesz (libretto by the composer) based on Euripides; produced Vienna Staatsoper, 20 Jan 1931. Dionysus versus Pentheus in ancient Greece.

Bakels, Kees (b Netherlands, 14 Jan 1945), Dutch conductor. After study with Franco Ferrara and Kyril Kondrashin, he held posts with the Amsterdam Philharmonic and the Netherlands Chamber Orchestra. Guest with most regional orchestras in the UK and has appeared in San Diego, Florida, Oregon and Calgary. Opera engagements include *Oberto* and *Butterfly* in San Diego, *Così*, *Figaro* and *Die Zauberflöte* in Vancouver and *Aida* and *Fidelio* with ENO, London.

Baker, Gregg (b Chicago, 7 Dec 1955), American baritone. After experience on Broadway he sang Crown in the Met. premiere of *Porgy and Bess* (1985); has returned to NY as Escamillo; further appearances as Crown at Glyndebourne (1986) and CG. Other roles include Ford, Count Almaviva and Marcello; *Carmen Jones* in London, 1991.

Singing Lieder is like putting a piece of music under a microscope.

Janet Baker, *Opera News*, July 1977

Baker, Janet (b York, 23 Mar 1933), English mezzo. Opera debut 1959, Oxford. Sang with Handel Opera Society and EOG and in Birmingham before international career; she sang in Handel's *Tamerlano* (1962), *Orlando* (1966) and *Admeto* (1968). CG and USA from 1966. Roles include Ariodante, Rameau's Aricie, Dorabella, and Berlioz's Dido. At Glyndebourne from 1970 she sang in Raymond Leppard's editions of Baroque operas, appearing as Cavalli's Callisto and Monteverdi's Penelope and Poppea. Retired from opera 1982, singing Mary Stuart and Gluck's Alceste in London and Orpheus at Glyndebourne. Sang Bach, Britten and Mahler in concert. DBE 1976.

Baker *Janet Baker has been successful in all areas of the vocal repertory. She first made her mark in opera, notably at the Bath and Wexford Festivals and with the Handel Opera Society (from 1959). She is considered to be one of the greatest oratorio mezzo of her generation.*

Baker, Theodore (b NY, 3 June 1851; d Dresden, 13 Oct 1934), American writer on music. He took his PhD at Leipzig with the first major study of American Indian music. Became literary editor of G Schirmer Inc., NY, 1892 and published *A Dictionary of Musical Terms* (1895). His *Biographical Dictionary of Musicians* was issued 1900 and remains the leading US music reference book (fifth and sixth editions by Nicolas Slonimsky, 1978; seventh and eighth by Slonimsky and Dennis McIntire, 1984 and 1992).

Bakfark, Balint Valentin (b Brasso [Kronstadt], 1507; d Padua, 22 Aug 1576), Hungarian, later Polish, lutenist and composer also known by double name of Greff-Bakfark. He went into royal service, learnt the lute, later lived in France, Vienna and Padua, and in 1549–66 was at the Polish court. He was a great virtuoso, as is reflected by the technical difficulty of his extant works. He pub. a lute book with Moderne of Lyons in 1552 and a second with Andreae of Kraków in 1565.

Baklanov, Georgy (b Riga, 4 Jan 1881; d Basel, 6 Dec 1938), Russian baritone. He sang Amonasro and Rubinstein's Demon at Kiev in 1903. Bolshoi and St Petersburg 1905–09, in operas by Rakhmaninov. He appeared widely in Europe until World War I: CG (1910 as Rigoletto and Scarpia), at Berlin (1911) and at Monte Carlo in the 1914 fp of Ponchielli's *I Mori di Valenzia*. Boston 1911–14; Chicago 1917–26 in operas by Février and Rimsky-Korsakov and as Méphistophélès, Prince Igor, Ruslan and Scarpia.

Balakirev, Mily Alexeievich (b Nizhny-Novgorod, 2 Jan 1837; d St Petersburg, 29 May 1910), Russian composer. He formed an important link between Glinka's brightly-coloured idiom and the 'Mighty Handful' of composers. He was taught music by his mother, but learnt most of what he knew as a youth in the house of Ulibishev, on whose estate he was able to use the music library and gain experience with the private orchestra. At 18 he went to St Petersburg, full of enthusiasm for national music, and won the approval of Glinka. In 1861 he began to form the group of nationalist musicians of which he became

the leader, although he was not the oldest. Cui became his first disciple; Mussorgsky, Rimsky-Korsakov and Borodin followed later, and he even influenced Tchaikovsky to some extent at first. In 1862 he helped to establish the Free School of Music with the choral conductor Lomakin, and in connection with it conducted progressive symphonic concerts.

In 1871 he had a grave nervous breakdown and withdrew from public life, feeling that he had been defeated by the 'official' musicians, but his own tyrannical nature alienated everyone; he was forced to become a minor railway official to earn a modest living and he turned to religious mysticism. Not until 1876 did he begin to take some interest in composition again, and only in 1883, when he was appointed director of the Imperial Chapel, did he fully emerge once more. He retired in 1895 with a pension and took up composition anew, but again lived in seclusion and was almost wholly forgotten by his former friends.

Works include incidental music for Shakespeare's *King Lear* (1860); two symphonies, symphonic poems *Russia* and *Tamara*, overtures on a Spanish march, on three Russian themes, to *King Lear* and on Czech themes; piano concerto (finished by Liapunov); many piano works, including sonata in B♭ minor, *Islamey* fantasy (1869), scherzos, mazurkas, nocturnes, waltzes, etc.; 43 songs; two books of folk-songs; six anthems for unaccompanied chorus; cantata for the unveiling of the Glinka monument.

In time he will be a second Glinka.
Mikhail Glinka on Mily Balakirev, quoted in
Garden, *Balakirev*, 1967

---

balalaika a Russian instrument similar to the guitar, but as a rule with a triangular body. It is made in various sizes, so that bands of instruments ranging from treble to bass can be organized.

Balanchine, George (b St Petersburg, 22 Jan 1904; d New York, 30 Apr 1983), Russian-American choreographer. He won fame for his elegant stagings of Stravinsky's later ballets. After leaving Russia in 1924 he was engaged by Diaghilev as choreographer for the Ballets Russes; worked on the first Paris performance of *Apollo Musagetes* and was later choreographer for Stravinsky's *Orpheus*, *Jeu de Cartes* and *Agon*. From 1948 was artistic director of NY City Ballet.

Balassa, Sandor (b Budapest, 20 Jan 1935), Hungarian composer. He studied in Budapest and is music director of Hungarian Radio.

Works include violin concerto (1964); septet for brass; *The Golden Age*, cantata (1965); *Xenia*, nonet (1970); *Iris* for orchestra; opera *Beyond the Threshold* (1976); *Calls and Cries* for orchestra (1982); *Three Fantasies* for orchestra (1984); *The Third Planet*, opera-oratorio (1987).

Balbi, Lodovico (b Venice, 1545; d Venice, Dec 1604), Italian monk, singer and composer. Pupil of Porta; singer at St Mark's, Venice, c 1570; later at Verona Cathedral. Afterwards worked at Venice and Padua, and retired to the Minorite monastery at Venice.

Works include Masses, motets and other church music; madrigals.

Baldassari, Benedetto, Italian 18th-c. tenor. Appeared in London, 1719–22, and took part in the fps of Handel's *Radamisto* and *Floridante*.

Baldwin, John (b before 1560; d London, 28 Aug 1615), English singer and composer. At various times singer in St George's Chapel, Windsor, and a gentleman of the Chapel Royal in London. He copied out much music, especially into a book for his own use, which preserves many valuable works and includes instrumental pieces and sacred and secular works for several voices. He also completed the Sextus part-book of the Forrest-Heyther collection of Tudor Masses, and wrote out *My Ladye Nevells Booke*, a beautifully copied anthology of keyboard music by Byrd, dated 1591.

Balfe, Michael (William) (b Dublin, 15 May 1808; d Rowney Abbey, Herts., 20 Oct 1870), Irish composer and singer. Son of a dancing-master, who removed to Wexford in 1810. On the death of his father in 1823, he was sent to London as a pupil of C E Horn; there he appeared as a violinist and played in the orchestra at Drury Lane Theatre. Next

Balakirev *The composer Balakirev (1836–1910) as drawn by Leon Bakst. Balakirev's tyrannical character earned him many enemies, especially amongst his musical opponents who followed the traditional German school of composition. His works are reminiscent of Glinka, with whom he helped to establish a Russian national style.*

he studied composition with C F Horn and appeared as a singer in Weber's *Freischütz* at Norwich. In 1825 Count Mazzara became his patron and took him to Italy, where he introduced him to Cherubini. He then went to Paris, met Rossini, and in 1827 appeared as Figaro in *Barbiere* at the Théâtre Italien.

Three years later he sang at Palermo and produced his first opera there, *I rivali di se stessi*. At Milan he sang with Malibran and at Bergamo he met the Hungarian singer Lina Rosa, whom he married. Early in 1833 he returned to London and appeared in concerts. His first English opera, *The Siege of Rochelle*, was produced at Drury Lane in 1835 and the next year Malibran sang in *The Maid of Artois*. In 1842 he went to live in Paris for some years and worked there with great success, though in 1843 he returned for a time to produce *The Bohemian Girl* in London, for which he is most famous today. Triumphant visits to Berlin in 1849 and St Petersburg in 1852 followed, and in 1854 he produced *Pittore e Duca* at Trieste. That year he finally returned to England, having bought property in Hertfordshire, where he took to farming.

Works include 29 operas, among which are *Un avvertimento ai gelosi* (Pavia, 1830), *The Siege of Rochelle* (1835), *The Maid of Artois*, *Joan of Arc* (1837), *Falstaff* (1838), *Le Puits d'amour*, *The Bohemian Girl*, *Les Quatre Fils Aymon* (Paris, 1844), *The Bondman*, *The Maid of Honour*, *The Sicilian Bride*, *The Rose of Castile*, *Satanella* (1858), *The Armourer of Nantes* (1863), *Il Talismano*; operetta *The Sleeping Queen*; ballet *La Pérouse*; three cantatas, including *Mazeppa*; many songs, etc.

Ballabene, Gregorio (b Rome, 1720; d Rome, *c* 1803), Italian composer. One of the latest adherents of the *stile antico*, he wrote unaccompanied church music, often of considerable complexity, including a 48-part Mass.

ballabile Italian = 'in a dancing manner' (accent on second syllable); a term applicable to any piece in the form or character of a dance.

ballad a narrative song either traditional or written in traditional style. Applied in the late 19th and early 20th c. to a sentimental, drawing-room song.

I knew a very wise man, so much of Sir Christopher's sentiment, that he believed if a man were permitted to make all the ballads, he need not care who should make the laws of a nation.

Andrew Fletcher of Saltoun to the Marquis of Montrose on ballads, 1703

---

ballade, French, (1) a form of medieval French verse, often set to music by trouvères and 14th-c. composers, in which each stanza is in AAB form with a refrain line at the end. (2) In the 19th and 20th c. an instrumental piece, often of a lyrical and romantic character.

Ballad of Baby Doe, The opera in two acts by Douglas Moore (libretto by J Latouche), produced Central City, CO, 7 Jul 1956. Baby Doe and Tabor in trouble with their silver mine.

Ballad of Blanik, The, *Balada blanická*, symphonic poem by Janáček after a poem by J Vrchický; performed Brno, 21 Mar 1920.

ballad opera an English light operatic entertainment, the fashion for which was set by John Gay's *The Beggar's Opera* in 1728 and continuing its vogue until the 1760s. The most distinctive feature of its music is that it consists mainly of short songs interspersed with dialogue and that they are not specially composed for the piece, but chosen from popular songs of the day.

Ballard French 16th–18th-c. family of music printers. The founders were Robert Ballard (*c* 1525–1588) and Adrien Le Roy, who became music printers to Henry II in 1553, issuing *chanson* collections. The brothers Pierre and Robert ii (*c* 1575–1650) continued the business, while Pierre's son Robert iii (*c* 1610–1673) published orchestral scores; his son Christophe (1641–1715) published works by Campra, Charpentier, the Couperins and Lully. The firm declined from 1722, when Rameau's *Traité* was published.

Ballard, Louis (b Miami, OK, 8 Jul 1931), American Indian composer. He studied at Oklahoma University and had private lessons with Milhaud and Carlos Surinach. He was program director of Indian Affairs at Washington DC 1971–79, and has published *Music of North American Indians* 1975. His works are indebted to the rhythms and tunes of his native music.

Works include ballets: *Koshare* (1966) and *The Four Moons* (1967); *Incident at Wounded Knee* for orchestra (1974); *Ritmo Indio* for woodwind quintet and Sioux flute (1968); *Xactce'oyan/Companion of Talking God* for orchestra (1982); *Fantasy Aborigine* for orchestra (1984).

ballata Italian a 14th-c. verse form, often set to music, in which the refrain precedes and follows each stanza. The term implies an association with dancing.

ballet, ◊ballett, a stage entertainment consisting entirely of dance choreographed to instrumental music composed specifically for the work, although vocal features have been introduced by some modern musicians and were a feature in French ballet of the 18th c., where the term was often short for *opéra-ballet* and the ballet proper was called *ballet-pantomime*.

Ballet comique de la royne stage entertainment performed in Paris, 15 Oct 1581, at the marriage of the Duc de Joyeux and Mlle de Vaudemont, under the supervision of Balthasar de Beaujoyeulx. The verse was by the Sieur de la Chesnaye, the scenery by Patin, and the music by the bass singer Lambert de Beaulieu, Jacques Salmon and others. It is in effect the first of the *ballets de cour*.

ballet de cour, French, = 'court ballet'; a 16th–17th-c. French stage entertainment with music developing from the older tourneys and masquerades, containing vocal and dance movements specially composed. Guédron and Boësset were its chief exponents. The species developed later into the *opéra-ballet* and the opera.

ballet-pantomime ◊ballet.

ballett, or ballet, a type of 16th–17th-c. composed for several voices, resembling a madrigal, but in a lighter, more dance-like style.

balletti, Italian, pieces of music intended for dancing, especially on the stage.

Balling, Michael (b Heidingsfeld, 27 Aug 1866; d Darmstadt, 1 Sept 1925), German conductor. Associated with the Wagner festivals at Bayreuth (1904–25, *Parsifal*, *Tristan*, *Ring*) and conductor of the Hallé Orchestra, Manchester, 1912–14; Darmstadt from 1919. He produced an incomplete edition of Wagner's music (1912–29).

ballo Italian = 'dance'; usually used in combination, e.g. *tempo di ballo*.

Ballo delle Ingrate, Il ballet-opera in one act by Monteverdi (libretto by O Rinuccini), produced Mantua, 1608. The work was pub. in *Madrigali guerrieri et amorosi*, 1638. The '*Ingrate*' of the title are ladies who have declined the attentions of their suitors. The ungrateful spirits are summoned from Hades and perform a melancholy dance.

Ballo in maschera, Un, *A Masked Ball*, opera by Verdi (libretto by A Somma, based on Scribe's *Gustave III* set by Auber), produced Rome, Teatro Apollo, 17 Feb 1859. King Gustav stabbed by jealous husband of Amelia.

Balsam, Artur (b Warsaw, 8 Feb 1906; d NY, 1 Sept 1994), Polish-born American pianist. He studied at the Łódz Conservatory and in Berlin; settled in US 1933. Active in chamber music and as soloist in standard repertory; he pub. cadenzas for Mozart's piano concertos.

Baltimore Symphony Orchestra founded 1914 and conducted until 1930 by Gustav Strube. A summer series is held at Oregon Ridge Park and the Joseph Meyerhoff Symphony Hall was opened 1982. Sergio Commisiona was music director 1970–84, David Zinman from 1985.

Baltsa, Agnes (b Lefkas, 19 Nov 1944), Greek mezzo. Debut Frankfurt, 1968, Cherubino; Octavian in Vienna, 1970. La Scala and CG from 1976; Romeo in Bellini's *I Capuleti* at CG 1984. Other roles include Berlioz's Dido, Dorabella and Carmen. Her vivid stage personality has also been admired as Azucena and as Cenerentola and Dalila (CG 1990–91).

Baltzar, Thomas (b Lübeck, *c* 1630; d London, buried 27 Jul 1663),

────── THE OPERA ──────

Un Ballo in Maschera

A three-act opera by Giuseppe Verdi, first performed in 1859. Set originally in 18th-century Stockholm, the location was changed to the unlikely one of 17th-century Boston.

I. Riccardo (tenor), Governor of Boston, receives news of a plot against his life. His Chief Justice arrives with an expulsion order for Ulrica (mezzo-soprano), a popular fortune teller, accused of witchcraft. Amelia (soprano), arrives at Ulrica's hovel, in search of a cure for her love for Riccardo; when he arrives he is told that he will die at the hand of a friend. The first to take his hand is Renato (baritone), his secretary and husband of Amelia.

II. Gathering curative herbs at night, a veiled Amelia is discovered by Riccardo and they declare their love. When conspirators arrive with Renato he allows the lovers to escape, unaware at first that Amelia is involved.

III. Convinced of his wife's adultery, Renato draws the lot with the conspirators which decides Riccardo's assassin. Stabbed at a masked ball, Riccardo forgives Renato and declares Amelia's innocence.

(The original version of the opera was banned by the Naples censor because it portrayed the historical assassination of King Gustav IV of Sweden; it is this version which is sometimes returned to in performances today, with Riccardo as Gustavus, Ulrica as Mlle. Arvidson and Renato as Anckarstroem.)

────── THE OPERA ──────

German or Swedish violinist. In the service of Queen Christina of Sweden 1653–55 and violinist to Charles II from 1661, helping to develop the technique of English musicians.

Bamert, Matthias (b Ersigen, 5 Jul 1942), Swiss conductor and composer. Studied in Paris with Boulez and worked with the Cleveland Orchestra and the American SO. Music director of the Basel Radio SO 1977–83, principal guest with the Scottish National Orchestra from 1985. He has also led the Ulster Orchestra (Sibelius and Saariaho), BBC SO (fp of Martin Butler's *O Rio!*, 1991), National Youth Orchestra at the 1993 London Proms (*Gawain's Journey* by Birtwistle), and London Mozart Players from 1993.

Bampton, Rose (b Lakewood, OH, 28 Nov 1908), American soprano, originally mezzo. Sang Laura at the NY Met. in 1932 and made her soprano debut in 1937 as Leonora in *Trovatore*. Admired as Donna Anna and Alceste, and from the 1940s as Sieglinde, Kundry and Strauss's Daphne. CG 1937, as Amneris. Taught at Juilliard School from 1974.

Banchieri, Adriano (b Bologna, 3 Sept 1568; d Bologna, 1634), Italian organist, theorist and composer. A pupil of Gioseffo Guami, he was a Benedictine monk. In 1596 he became organist at the monastery of San Michele in Bosco (Monte Oliveto) near Bologna, to which he returned in 1609, remaining there until shortly before his death; from 1600 to 1604 he was organist at Santa Maria in Regola at Imola. He helped to found the Accademia dei Floridi at Bologna in 1615, and wrote theoretical works, especially on figured bass (*L'organo suonarino*, 1605). *Cartella musicale* of 1614 advises on vocal ornamentation. His sequence of madrigals *La pazzia senile* (1595) has been described as the first comic opera.

Works include Masses; sacred symphonies and concertos; comic intermezzi for the stage; organ works.

banda Italian = 'band'; a military band, in particular a band used on the stage or behind the scene in an opera, e.g. in Verdi's *Macbeth*.

bandurria Spanish = pandora; a string instrument of the cittern type, with six double strings which are plucked with the fingers or with a plectrum.

Banestre, Gilbert (b c 1445; d London, Aug 1487), English composer. Master of the Children in the Chapel Royal in succession to Abyngdon, 1478; wrote sacred and secular vocal music.

Banister, John (b London, c 1625; d London, 3 Oct 1679), English violinist and concert promoter. Lived in London; sent to France by Charles II in 1661. Leader of the King's violins 1662–67. Composed music for Dryden's *Tempest* (1667), Davenant's *Circe* and Wycherley's *Gentleman Dancing-Master* and contributed songs to various collections.

Banister, John (b London; d London, ? 1725), English violinist and teacher of his instrument, son of John Banister. Wrote for the stage.

banjo an American string instrument of the guitar type with a hollow body covered with stretched parchment and five strings, which are plucked with the fingers; the neck is fretted. The five-stringed instrument is now the normal type but previously there were up to nine strings.

Bánk-Bán opera by Erkel (libretto by B Egressy, based on a play by József Katona), produced Budapest, 9 Mar 1861. Bánk-Bán defends his wife in 12th-c. Hungary, but both are dead at the end.

Bänkelsänger German = 'a singer of ballads', especially at fairs, a chapman singing the songs he sold.

Banks, Don (b Melbourne, 25 Oct 1923; d Sydney, 5 Sept 1980), Australian composer. Studied at Melbourne Conservatory and later (1950) with Seiber in London and Dallapiccola in Florence (1953). Settled in London.

Works include horn concerto (1960); divertimento for flute and string trio; duo for violin and cello; violin sonata; three studies for cello and piano; Three Episodes for flute and piano; film music.

Banti (born *Giorgi*), Brigitta (b Crema, c 1757; d Bologna, 18 Feb 1806), Italian soprano. She sang in the streets of Venice and the cafés of Paris at first, but was engaged for the Paris Opéra in 1776 and had much success in London from 1779 to 1802 in operas by Paisiello, Zingarelli and Anfossi. Da Ponte described her as ignorant and insolent.

Bantock, Granville (b London, 7 Aug 1868; d London, 16 Oct 1946), English composer, mainly known today for his colourful *Pierrot of the Minute* overture; the massive setting of *Omar Khayyám* is well worth reviving. Son of a doctor; educated for the civil service, but entered the RAM in 1889, where some of his earliest works were performed, and Lago produced the opera *Cædmar* at the Olympic Theatre in 1892. After some experience in theatrical conducting he gave a concert of modern English music in 1896. The next year he was appointed conductor at the Tower, New Brighton, where he introduced much contemporary music. In Feb 1900 he gave a concert of new English music at Antwerp and in Sept was appointed principal of the Birmingham and Midland Inst. School of Music. He remained in Birmingham until 1933, and became professor of music at the University in 1908, succeeding Elgar. Knighted 1930.

Works include STAGE: operas *Cædmar* (1892), *Pearl of Iran* (1894), *The Seal Woman* (1924); five ballets; incidental music for Sophocles' *Electra* (1909), Shakespeare's *Macbeth* (1926), Wilde's *Salome*, etc.

ORCHESTRAL: *Processional* and *Jaga-Naut* (from 24 projected symphonic poems from Southey's *Curse of Kehama*), *Helena* variations, comedy overtures *The Pierrot of the Minute* (after Ernest Dowson) (1908) and *Circus Life*, orchestral ballad *The Sea Reivers*, *Overture to a Greek Tragedy*, symphonic poem *Dante and Beatrice*, *Fifine at the Fair* (after Browning) (1901), overture to *The Frogs* (Aristophanes), *Hebridean Symphony* (1915), *A Pagan Symphony* (1926), serenade *From the Far West*, *Scenes from the Scottish Highlands*, *The Land of Gael* for string orchestra; *Elegiac Poem*, *Sapphic Poem*, *Dramatic Poem* for cello and orchestra (1914).

CHORUS AND ORCHESTRAL (with or without solo voices): *The Fire-Worshippers* (1892), *The Time-Spirit*, *Sea Wanderers* (1906), *Christ in the Wilderness*, *Omar Khayyám* (setting of FitzGerald's translation in three parts, 1909), *Gethsemane*, *The Great God Pan*, *Song of Songs*, oratorio *The Pilgrim's Progress* (Bunyan) (1928).

UNACCOMPANIED CHORUS: choral symphony *Atlanta in Calydon* (Swinburne) (1911), and *Vanity of Vanities* (Ecclesiastes), suite *A Pageant of Human Life* (1913) and many smaller works and part-songs.

SONGS: including cycles *Songs of the East* (six vols), *Songs of the*

Seraglio, Six Jester Songs, Five Ghazals of Hafiz, Ferishtah's Fancies (Browning), *Sappho, Songs from the Chinese Poets* (eight sets).

CHAMBER: Viola sonata (1919), three cello sonatas (1924, 1940, 1945), three violin sonatas (1929, 1932, 1940).

bar, English, (1) originally the line drawn through the music stave or staves to indicate the metrical divisions of a composition, now called 'bar-line' in Britain. (2) The space between two bar-lines, called 'measure' in the USA.

Bar, German, a medieval German musical form (*Barform*) of song, used by the Minnesinger and Meistersinger. Each stanza consists of two similar phrases or periods (*Stollen*, together called the *Aufgesang*), followed by a different but relevant one (*Abgesang*), corresponding to the formula AAB.

Bär, Olaf (b Dresden, 19 Dec 1957), German baritone. He joined the Dresden Staatsoper 1985 and sang Harlequin in *Ariadne* at CG the same year. He made his US debut 1987, as Christus in the *St Matthew Passion* with the Chicago SO; he sang at Glyndebourne in 1987 and 1991, as the Count in *Capriccio* and Don Giovanni. He is also noted as a fine Lieder singer.

Barab, Seymour (b Chicago, 9 Jan 1921), American composer and cellist. After study with Gregor Piatigorsky he played in the symphony orchestras of Cleveland, Portland and San Francisco, 1940–60. He helped found the Composers' Quartet and the New York Pro Musica. He has composed since the 1950s and is best known for his many short operas: *Chanticleer* (after Chaucer, 1957), *A Game of Chance* (1957), *Little Red Riding Hood* (1962), *The Makers of Illusion* (1985).

Barabas, Sari (b Budapest, 14 Mar 1918), Hungarian soprano. Debut Budapest, 1939, as Gilda. She remained in Hungary during World War II and sang at Munich from 1949; appeared as guest in Vienna, France and Italy. Glyndebourne, 1953–57, as Constanze, Adèle (also recorded) and Zerbinetta. She was heard in San Francisco as the Queen of Night (1950).

Barati, George (b Gyor, 3 Apr 1913), Hungarian-born US cellist, conductor and composer. After studying in Budapest he emigrated to the USA 1939, playing in the Westminster String Quartet and teaching at Princeton 1939–43. He was music director of the Honolulu SO and Opera 1950–68, and from 1989 was director of the Barati Ensemble; as a conductor he has appeared with at least 80 orchestras. His music is influenced by Hungarian traditions and his experiences of the Pacific.

Works include opera *Noelani* (1968); ballet *The Love of Don Perlimlin* (1947); Concertos for winds (1952), cello (1953), piano (1973) and guitar (1976) and violin (1986); symphony (1963); *Branches of Time* for two pianos and orchestra (1981); two string quartets (1944, 196??); piano pieces and songs.

Barbaia, Domenico (old spelling Barbaja) (b Milan, ? 1778; d Posillipo near Naples, 19 Oct 1841), Italian impresario. He was first a waiter, then a circus proprietor, and finally the most popular of operatic managers. In 1821–28, coming from the Teatro San Carlo at Naples, he managed the Kärntnertortheater and the Theater an der Wien in Vienna, introducing Rossini and Bellini and commissioning *Euryanthe* from Weber.

Barbé, Anton (d Antwerp, 2 Dec 1564), Flemish composer and first of a line of Antwerp musicians. From 1527 to 1562 he was *Kapellmeister* at Antwerp Cathedral. He pub. Masses, motets and *chansons*, and contributed a Dutch song to Susato's *Het ierste musyck boexken* (1551).

Barbe-bleue, *Bluebeard*, operetta by Offenbach (libretto by H Meilhac and L Halévy), produced Paris, Théâtre des Variétés, 5 Feb 1866. Satirical version of the original 'Bluebeard' story.

Barbella, Emanuele (b Naples, 14 Apr 1718; d Naples, 1 Jan 1777), Italian violinist and composer. He studied at Naples and wrote sonatas and duets for violin, trio sonatas, and also an opera in collaboration with Logroscino, *Elmira generosa* (Naples, 1753).

Barber, Robert, English 16th-c. composer. *Informator choristarum*, Winchester College, 1541–42. A *Dum transisset sabbatum* is in the Gyffard part-books.

Barber, Samuel (b West Chester, PA, 9 Mar 1910; d New York, 23 Jan 1981), American composer. He entered the Curtis Institute of Music in 1924, winning a prize with a violin sonata in 1928. In the following years he won several more prizes, including the American Prix de Rome, 1935. He is best known for his Adagio for strings, a re-scoring of the slow movement of his String Quartet (1936). Barber's music is characterized by late-romantic harmonic influences, as well as more dissonant effects on occasion. In 1964 he was commissioned to write an opera for the opening of the new NY Met. house, and *Antony and Cleopatra* was the result. Owing to an over-elaborate staging the opera was a failure at its premiere, although it has had some success in a revised version (1974).

Works include operas, *Vanessa* (1958), *A Hand of Bridge* and *Antony and Cleopatra* (after Shakespeare) (1966, revised 1974); two symphonies (1936 and 1944), Two Essays, overture to Sheridan's *School for Scandal*, music for a scene from Shelley for orchestra; Adagio for strings (from string quartet of 1936); violin concerto (1940), cello concerto (1945), piano concerto (1962), *Capricorn Concerto* for flute, oboe, trumpet and strings; string quartet, cello and piano sonata, violin and piano sonata, piano sonata, *Excursions* for piano

VOCAL: *Dover Beach* (Matthew Arnold) for baritone and string quartet (1933); works for unaccompanied chorus to words by Helen Waddell, Emily Dickinson, James Stephens and Stephen Spender; song cycle from James Joyce's *Chamber Music* and songs to words by James Stephens, A E Housman, Gerard Manley Hopkins and Yeats.

Most composers bore me because most composers are boring.

Samuel Barber, quoted in Ewen,
American Composers, 1982

Barberiis, Melchiore de, Italian 16th-c. lutenist. He lived at Padua and pub. several books of pieces in lute tablature (including arrangements of Josquin), 1546–49.

Barber of Baghdad, The (Cornelius). ◊Barbier von Bagdad.

Barber of Seville, The (Paisiello, Rossini). ◊Barbiere di Siviglia.

Barbier, Jules, Michel ◊Carré.

Barbiere di Siviglia, Il, ossia La precauzione inutile, *The Barber of Seville, or Vain Precaution*, (original title *Almaviva, ossia L'inutile precauzione*) opera by Rossini (libretto by C Sterbini, based on Beaumarchais' *Le Barbier de Séville*), produced Rome, Teatro Argentina, 20 Feb 1816. Rosina and Almaviva battle it out with Bartolo.

Barbiere di Siviglia, Il, ovvero La precauzione inutile, *The Barber of Seville, or Vain Precaution*, opera by Paisiello (libretto by G Petrosellini, based on Beaumarchais' *Le Barbier de Séville*), produced St Petersburg, Hermitage, at court, 26 Sept 1782.

Barbieri, Fedora (b Trieste, 4 Jun 1920), Italian mezzo. Debut Florence, 1940, and in 1953 sang there in the fp of the revision of Prokofiev's *War and Peace*. NY Met. 1950–75, debut as Eboli. CG 1950–58 as Mistress Quickly, Azucena and Amneris. Also sang Carmen and Orpheus.

Barbieri-Nini, Marianna (b Florence, 18 Feb 1818; d Florence, 27 Nov 1887), Italian soprano. Debut La Scala, 1840, in *Belisario*; not successful until she masked her ugly face. She appeared widely in Italy as Lucrezia Borgia, Anna Bolena and Semiramide; created Verdi's Lady Macbeth and roles in *I due Foscari* and *Il Corsaro*.

Barbier von Bagdad, Der, *The Barber of Baghdad*, opera by Cornelius (libretto by composer), produced Weimar, 15 Dec 1858. Nureddin is helped by Abul Hassan in meeting Margiana.

Barbireau, Jacob (b 1455–56; d Antwerp, 8 Aug 1491), Flemish composer. He was also a singer at 's-Hertogenbosch and Antwerp. Two Masses and various other works by him survive.

Barbirolli, John (b London, 2 Dec 1899; d London, 29 Jul 1970), English conductor. He studied at Trinity College, London (1911–12) and the RAM (1912–17). He made his debut as a cellist, aged 11, and

THE OPERA

Il Barbiere di Siviglia

A two-act opera by Gioachino Rossini set, not surprisingly, in Seville. Despite a disastrous first performance in Rome in 1816, the opera has become one of Rossini's best known and best loved.

I. In disguise as Lindoro, a poor student, Count Almaviva (tenor) serenades Rosina (mezzo-soprano), the ward of the aged Doctor Bartolo (bass). The barber Figaro (baritone) pledges his support for Almaviva, who now enters Bartolo's house by pretending to be a drunken soldier with a billeting order. Almaviva assures the eager Rosina that he is in fact Lindoro, but Bartolo and Don Basilio (bass), Rosina's music teacher, are suspicious and Almaviva is placed under temporary arrest.

II. Almaviva enters the house disguised as a music teacher and gives Rosina her lesson. The still suspicious Bartolo sends Basilio for a notary to expedite his intended marriage to Rosina; he tries to convince her that Lindoro does not really love her. The returning Almaviva reveals his identity and is united with Rosina once more. They cannot escape from the house but when the notary arrives he is bribed into marrying them; Bartolo is then obliged to accept the fait accompli.

THE OPERA

joined the Queen's Hall Orchestra in that capacity in 1915. Achieved recognition as a conductor in 1926, later succeeding Toscanini as chief conductor of the NY PO in 1937. He returned to England in 1943, where he took over the Hallé Orchestra. In 1949 he was knighted and in 1950 received the Royal Philharmonic Society's gold medal. With the Hallé he gave the fps of Vaughan Williams' seventh and eighth symphonies. Guest conductor Berlin PO, Boston SO and Chicago SO. He married the oboist Evelyn Rothwell (1939). Barbi-

Barbirolli *The conductor John Barbirolli (1899–1970) in rehearsal. An exponent of Romantic music, he passionately supported works by the pastoral English composers of his period: Elgar, Delius, Vaughan Williams. He is best remembered for his fine recordings of English music.*

rolli excelled in the Romantic repertory, especially the symphonies of Elgar, Sibelius and Mahler. He conducted Gluck's *Orfeo* and *Tristan* at CG (1953–54); recorded *Otello* and *Butterfly*.

Three farts and a raspberry, orchestrated.
Sir John Barbirolli on 'modern music', quoted in Kennedy, *Barbirolli, Conductor Laureate*, 1971

Barcarola work for orchestra by Henze; it depicts a journey across the river Styx and quotes the Eton Boating Song. Fp Zurich, 22 Apr 1980, conductor Albrecht.

barcarolle, French, from Italian *barcaruola*, a boating-song, especially of the type sung by the gondoliers at Venice. A piece or song in that style, generally in 6–8 time and a moderate tempo with a swaying rhythm.

Barcroft, George (b and d Ely), English 16th–17th-c. organist and composer. Studied at Cambridge and was minor canon and organist at Ely Cathedral, 1579–1610. Composed church music.

Bardi, Giovanni, Count of Vernio (b Florence, 5 Feb 1534; d Rome, Sept 1612), Italian nobleman and amateur musician. He was a patron of the *camerata* at Florence. Works by Caccini, Galilei, Peri and others were performed at his house. He wrote madrigals himself.

Barenboim, Daniel (b Buenos Aires, 15 Nov 1942), Israeli pianist and conductor. Debut as soloist Paris, 1955. Has worked as conductor-soloist in England and USA. London from 1956, NY from 1957. He was music director Orchestre de Paris 1975–88 and made a series of Berlioz recordings. Opera debut Edinburgh, 1973, with *Don Giovanni*, and conducted *Tristan* at Bayreuth in 1981. Also active in chamber music with Zukerman, Perlman and, before her illness, his wife, Jacqueline ◊Du Pré. As a pianist he is particularly well known in the sonatas of Beethoven. On 31 Jul 1986 he gave a Liszt concert at the Bayreuth Festspielhaus, to mark the centenary of Liszt's death. In the late 1980s, due to political reasons, Barenboim was forced to give up his directorship of the Bastille opera in Paris before conducting a single note. He conducted the *Ring* at Bayreuth 1988–93. Music director of the Chicago SO from 1991, Berlin Staatsoper 1992 (debut with *Parsifal*). He has gained recognition with a conducting style which owes much to the long paragraphs of Furtwängler.

Bärenhäuter, Der, *The bear skinner*, opera by Siegfried Wagner (libretto by composer) produced Munich, 21 Jan 1899.

Barham, Edmund (b Beckenham, 22 Mar 1950), English tenor. He sang at Munich and Wuppertal, after study in London. ENO from 1985, as Turiddu, Pinkerton, Alfredo, Cavaradossi and Don Carlos. Other roles include Manrico (Opera North), Otello (Victoria State Opera) and Don José (Bregenz Festival).

bariolage French the alteration on a string instrument of the same note on an open string and a stopped string. Also the playing of high notes on a string instrument in high positions on the lower strings to obtain a different tone-colour or to facilitate the performance of rapid high passages without changing to lower positions.

baritone, from Greek, *barutonos* = deep-sounding; (1) A male voice midway between tenor and bass.

The approximate range of a baritone voice.

(2) A brass instrument of the saxhorn family, of the same pitch as the euphonium but with a smaller bore and only three valves.

(3) Applied to instruments of moderately low compass, e.g. baritone oboe, baritone saxophone.

Barkin, Elaine (b New York, 15 Dec 1932), American composer and writer on music. She studied with Leo Kraft, Irving Fine and Boris Blacher; edited the journal *Perspectives of New Music* 1963–85, and is on the faculty of UCLA. Her music is infuenced by serialism, graphic notation and interactive performance techniques.

Works include string quartet (1969); *Inward and Outward Bound* for 13 instruments (1974); *Ebb Tide* for two vibraphones (1977); *De Amore*, chamber opera (1980); *Quilt Piece*, graphic score (1983); *Women's Voices* for four female reciters, tape and slides (1983); *Encore* for gamelan ensemble (1989).

Barlow, David (b Rothwell, Northamptonshire, 20 May 1927; d Newcastle upon Tyne 9 Jun 1975), English composer. He studied with Gordon Jacob at the RCM and with Boulanger in France. His early music is Romantic in style but from 1963 he adopted serial technique.

Works include church operas *David and Bathsheba* and *Judas Iscariot* (1969 and 1975); two symphonies (1950 and 1959), variations for cello and orchestra (1969), Sinfonietta concertante for clarinet and orchestra (1972); *The Lambton Worm* for narrator and orchestra (1969); string trio, string quartet (1969), brass quintet (1972); *Passion Music* for organ.

Barlow, Samuel (b New York, 1 Jun 1892; d Wyndmoor, PA, 19 Sept 1982), American composer. He studied at Harvard and in Paris and Rome, becoming active on behalf of liberal causes. His opera *Mon ami Pierrot* (1935) is based on the life of Lully and was the first by a US composer to be given at the Paris Opéra Comique. Other operas were *Amanda* (1936) and *Eugénie*. His symphonic concerto *Babar* (1935) uses slide projections but this, a piano concerto (1931), and *Biedermeier Waltzes* (1935) are in a conservative idiom.

Barlow, Stephen (b Seven Kings, 30 Jun 1954), English conductor. After study at the Guildhall School he conducted for the Glyndebourne Tour and Festival, leading *Schweigsame Frau*, *Rosenkavalier* and *Così fan Tutte*; Scottish Opera from 1983 and Opera 80 from its inception, becoming music director 1987. For ENO he has led the *Dutchman*, *Carmen* and *Entführung*; at CG *Turandot* and *Die Zauberflöte* (1989 and 1991). He has also conducted opera in San Francisco (*Capriccio*, 1990), Vancouver and Melbourne, and has led symphony concerts throughout Europe and N America.

Barlow, Wayne (Brewster) (b Elyria, OH, 6 Sept 1912), American composer. Studied with Howard Hanson at the Eastman School and with Schoenberg at the University of Southern CA in 1935. Director of the electronic music studio at Eastman 1968–78.

Works include *Zion in Exile*, cantata (1937), *Three Moods for Dancing*, ballet (1940), *Nocturne* for 18 instruments (1946), piano quintet (1951), *Images* for harp and orchestra (1961), *Vistas* for orchestra (1963), *Moonflight*, for tape (1970), *Soundprints in Concrete* (1972), *Voices of Faith*, cantata (1976), *Divertissement* for flute and chamber orchestra (1980); *Frontiers* for band (1982); *Sonatine for Four* (1984).

Bärmann, Heinrich Joseph (b Potsdam, 14 Feb 1784; d Munich, 11 Jun 1847), German clarinettist. He was a member of the court orchestra at Munich. Weber wrote several works for him.

Barnard, John (b ? 1591), English 17th-c. musician. Minor canon at St Paul's Cathedral in London; pub. the first printed collection of English cathedral music in 1641.

Barnby, Joseph (b York, 12 Aug 1838; d London, 28 Jan 1896), English conductor, organist and composer. Held various organist's posts in London; precentor at Eton College 1875–92, then principal of GSM. Distinguished as a choral conductor, he gave oratorios by Bach and Dvořák and the first English performance of *Parsifal* (concert, 1884). Knighted 1892.

Barnett, John (b Bedford, 15 Jul 1802; d near Cheltenham, 16 Apr 1890), English composer of German descent (original name Beer: Meyerbeer's family). Was a stage singer as a child and studied with C E Horn. In 1825 he composed his first stage piece, which was followed by a large number of others, including *The Mountain Sylph*, produced 25 Aug 1834.

His nephew John Francis (1837–1916) wrote choral works on *The Ancient Mariner* (1867) and *The Eve of St Agnes* (1913), and completed Schubert's sketches for a symphony in E (1883).

Baron, Ernst Gottlieb (b Breslau, 17 Feb 1696; d Berlin, 12 Apr 1760), German author, lutenist and composer, pupil of Weiss. Travelled widely as a lutenist, wrote several theoretical works on the lute, and composed for his instrument.

Baroni Italian 17th-c. family of singers and lutenists:

1. Andreana Baroni Andreana ◊Basile.

2. Leonora Baroni (b Mantua, Dec 1611; d Rome, 6 Apr 1670), daughter of 1. Also played viola da gamba and composed. Milton met her in Rome in 1638 and wrote three poems on her and her mother.

Baroque the music of the years *c* 1600–1750, most easily described as the generations whose compositions were based on continuo practice. Before the late 19th c. the term was one of denigration and practically confined to art history; but soon after the art-historian Heinrich Wölfflin demonstrated positive uses for the word (1888) it was adopted also for its current musical use.

Barraqué, Jean (b Paris, 17 Jan 1928; d Paris, 17 Aug 1973), French composer. He studied with Jean Langlais and Messiaen, later working in the experimental laboratories of the Radiodiffusion Française in Paris. His disciplined technique was well suited to serialism, which formed a cornerstone of his composition.

Works include *Séquence* for soprano and chamber ensemble, (after Nietzsche) (1955); *Le Temps restitué* for voices and orchestra (1957); *Au delà du hasard* (based on Hermann Broch) for voices and instrumental groups (1959), *Chant après chant* for percussion; (1966); piano sonata; *La mort de Virgile*, incomplete dramatic cycle.

Today, conducting is a question of ego: a lot of people believe they are actually playing the music.
Daniel Barenboim, quoted in Jacobson, *Reverberations*, 1975

Barraud, Henry (b Bordeaux, 23 Apr 1900), French composer. Studied first at Bordeaux and later at the Paris Conservatory with Caussade, Dukas and Aubert. He was expelled from the conservatory as a bad influence, but later in life turned to religion and Dante. In 1937 he was in charge of the music at the Paris World Fair; he then joined the radio service, where he rose to the post of head of the national programme in 1948.

Works include operas *La Farce de Maître Pathelin* (1938), *Numance* and *Lavinia* (1959); ballets *La Kermesse* (1943) and *L'Astrologue dans le puits*; film and radio music; oratorio *Les Mystères des Saints Innocents* (1947), cantatas and other choral works, including *La Divine Comédie*, after Dante, for five solo voices and orchestra (1972); three symphonies; piano concerto; woodwind trio, string trio, string quartet (1940), violin and piano sonata; piano music; songs.

barré French = lit. 'barred'; a chord on string instruments with fretted fingerboards, particularly the guitar, is said to be played barré when a finger is laid horizontally across the whole fingerboard, thus raising all the strings in pitch by the same interval's distance from the fundamental tuning.

Barré, Antonio (d ? diocese of Langres), French 16th-c. singer, music printer and composer. He sang as an alto in the choir of St Peter's in Rome in the middle of the century. Wrote madrigals and pub. them, with those of many other composers, in seven books printed by his own press, first in Rome and after 1564 at Milan.

barrel organ a popular mechanical instrument producing music by the mere turning of a handle, but sometimes actuated by clockwork. A cylinder (barrel) moves tongue-shaped keys by means of pins or studs arranged in such an order that its turning produces an ordered piece of music. The keys control pipes similar to those of the organ, but restricted to a single range of tone-colour and limited in compass. Barrel organs were formerly used to play mechanically a number of hymn tunes in small village churches that could not maintain an organ and organist. The barrel organ is often wrongly called ◊hurdy-gurdy, which is a totally different instrument.

Barrett, John (b *c* 1674; d London, ? Dec 1719), English organist, teacher and composer. He wrote incidental music for plays, and many popular songs.

Barrientos, Maria (b Barcelona, 10 Mar 1883; d Ciboure, 8 Aug 1946), Spanish soprano, the foremost coloratura singer of her time. Debut Barcelona, 1898, as Meyerbeer's Ines. She sang in Italy and Germany

------- **THE OPERA** -------

The Bartered Bride

A three-act opera by Bedřich Smetana, set in a Bohemian village. Initially a failure even in its fifth version of 1870, the opera eventually succeeded, achieving 100 performances in Prague during its first 12 years.

I. The parents of Mařenka (soprano) wish her to marry someone wealthier than her true love Jeník (tenor). The marriage broker Kecal (bass) has found the 'right' person in Vašek (tenor), younger and dim-witted son of Tobias Micha, a rich landlord.

II. Mařenka convinces Vašek he would be better off with someone prettier. In return for 300 crowns Jeník signs a document renouncing Mařenka, but he stipulates that her husband must be the son of Tobias.

III. Vašek meanwhile falls for Esmeralda, a dancer with a travelling circus, and hearing of Jeník's action the disillusioned Mařenka agrees to do as her parents wish. Tobias arrives and recognizes Jeník as his long-lost eldest son; Jeník can now marry Mařenka and keep his undertaking and Kecal's money.

------- **THE OPERA** -------

from 1899; among her best roles were Meyerbeer's Marguerite de Valois and Dinorah (La Scala, 1904), Rosina and Lakmé. NY Met. debut 1916, as Lucia; appeared as Norina opposite Caruso and was the Queen of Shemakha in the first local performance of *The Golden Cockerel* (1918). She was well known as Amina and Bellini's Elvira and sang Stravinsky's Nightingale at Monte Carlo (1929).

Barry, Gerald (b 28 Apr 1952), Irish composer. His major influences are the composers with whom he has studied: Peter Schat in the Netherlands, Stockhausen and Kagel in Germany, and Cerha in Austria. His *Cheveaux-de-frises* caused a stir at the 1988 London Proms.

Works include operas *The Intelligence Park* (1987) and *The Triumph of Beauty and Deceit* (1993); piano concerto (1977); *Handel's Favourite Song* for clarinet and ensemble (1981); *Cork* for string quartet (1985); *Sur les pointes* for chamber ensemble (1985); *What the Frog Said* for soprano, bass and ensemble (1985); *Cheveaux-de-frises* for orchestra (1988); *Reflections on Guinness* (1988); Sextet (1992); *Hard D* for orchestra (1992).

Barshai, Rudolf (b Labinskaya, 28 Sept 1924), Russian violist and conductor. He founded the Moscow Chamber Orchestra in 1956 and conducted it until he left Russia for Israel in 1976. Principal conductor Bournemouth SO 1983–88; music director of the Vancouver SO 1985–88. His transcriptions include Prokofiev's *Visions Fugitives*, for chamber orchestra, and Shostakovich's string quartet no. 8, for string orchestra.

Barstow, Josephine (b Sheffield, 27 Sept 1940), English soprano. London debut 1967, SW; from 1969 at CG, where she took part in the fps of Tippett's *The Knot Garden* and *The Ice Break*, and Henze's *We Come to the River*. She sang Autonoe in the first British stage performance of *The Bassarids*, at the Coliseum; other roles there have included Salome, Emilia Marty and Prokofiev's Natasha. NY Met. debut 1977, as Musetta. Bayreuth 1983, Gutrune. In 1986 she created Benigna in Penderecki's *Die schwarze Maske*, at Salzburg, and returned as Verdi's Amelia, 1989. CBE 1985.

Bartered Bride, The, *Prodaná Nevěsta*, opera by Smetana (libretto by K Sabina), produced, first version, Prague, Czech Theatre, 30 May 1866); revised version, 29 Jan 1869; final version (with recitatives), 25 Sept 1870. Mařenka and Jeník wish to marry, but must first overcome a previously arranged marriage and each other's subterfuges.

Barth, Hans (b Leipzig, 25 Jun 1897; d Jacksonville, FL, 9 Dec 1956), German pianist and composer who emigrated to the USA in 1907. A meeting with Busoni encouraged him to experiment with new scales, and in 1928 he invented a ¼-tone piano, for which he composed a number of works. He also composed ¼-tone chamber and instrumental music, as well as more conventional pieces.

Barthélémon, François Hippolyte (b Bordeaux, 27 Jul 1741; d London, 20 Jul 1808), French violinist and composer, an exponent of the 'galant' style. Settled in London, 1765. A year later he produced *Pelopida*, the first of several successful dramatic works, and married the singer Mary Young, daughter of Charles Young and niece of Mrs Arne and Mrs Lampe. Composed stage pieces for Garrick and visited France, Germany and Italy with his wife, who sang there. A friend of Haydn during the latter's visits to London, he is said to have suggested the subject of *The Creation*.

Works include the stage works *Pelopida* (1766), *The Judgement of Paris* (1768), *The Maid of the Oaks* (1774), *Belphegor* (1778); oratorio *Jefte in Masfa*; symphonies; concertos, sonatas, duets for violin.

Bartlet, John, English 16th–17th-c. lutenist and composer. Probably in the service of Lord Hertford. Pub. a *Booke of Ayres* for voices and instruments in 1606.

Bartók, Béla (b Nagyszentmiklós, 25 Mar 1881; d New York, 26 Sept 1945), Hungarian composer and pianist; one of the greatest figures of the 20th c. His father was a director of agriculture; his mother, a schoolteacher, was a musician and taught him from an early age. He appeared in public as a pianist at the age of ten. Studied under László Erkel at Porzsony (now Bratislava) until 1899 and then the piano under István Thomán and composition under Koessler at the Budapest Conservatory.

Under the influence of Strauss, he wrote the symphonic poem

Bartók *The composer Béla Bartók (1881–1945). As one of the first ethnomusicologists he drew upon the music of his native Hungary for inspiration; his knowledge of Bach is also evident in his own often complex contrapuntal procedures. Bartók's music, often very dissonant, is nevertheless highly individual.*

Kossuth (1903), conducted by Richter at Manchester in 1904. His first string quartet (1908) begins with echoes of late Beethoven but soon settles into a characteristic national idiom. About 1905 he began to collect folk tunes, often with Zoltán Kodály, and they discovered that the true Magyar music differed greatly from that of the Hungarian gypsies so far regarded as the only Hungarian folk music. He was appointed professor of piano at Budapest Conservatory in 1907. The powerful opera *Bluebeard's Castle* was composed 1911 but not performed until 1918. After the war of 1914–18 he began to be known in Europe and America, and in 1922 was made an honorary member of the ISCM. Some of his most demanding music was written in the years 1917–34: *The Miraculous Mandarin*, his first two piano concertos, string quartets nos. 2–5 and *Cantata Profana*. The lurid *Mandarin* ballet was written under the influence of Stravinsky and the expressionist Schoenberg; it was banned after a single performance in Cologne.

Increasing political isolation in his homeland (Hungary turned fascist before Germany) encouraged Bartók to pursue a career abroad. The first two piano concertos were premiered by him in Frankfurt, and exploit a full range of percussive effects; Bartók's own keyboard style was not appreciated by all; Percy Scholes reported that he had a touch 'like a paving stone'. Both concertos and the fourth and fifth quartets to some extent employ palindrome patterns, which with their formal repetition help to give coherence to chromatically complex music. A more easily accessible idiom, with longer melodic lines and less astringent harmony, was in evidence by 1938, with the *Music for Strings, Percussion and Celesta* and the second violin concerto. The sixth quartet (1939) was the last music he wrote in Budapest, and seems to find the composer in mourning for the world he was about to leave behind; each movement begins with a long, melancholy viola solo.

In 1940 emigrated to the USA where he taught briefly at Columbia University and Harvard. He was already suffering from leukaemia and was not in demand as a pianist or, initially, as a composer. A 1943 commission from the Koussevitzky Foundation, for the *Concerto for Orchestra*, helped to alleviate his financial hardship. The third piano concerto was written when Bartók was mortally ill; the central adagio religioso pays direct tribute to Beethoven's Song of Thanksgiving from the A minor quartet, although Bartók must have known that in his case there was to be no recovery from illness.

Bartók was one of the foremost composers of the 20th c. Much influenced by Hungarian folk music, he incorporated its rhythms and

---

Bartók   *A biographical note*

Bartók is now so much an established 'Classical' composer that it is difficult to understand the hostility his music once aroused. He visited London in 1922 to perform his First Violin Sonata with Jelly d'Aranyi. Ernest Newman, the leading critic of the day was not impressed: 'The bulk of the Bartók Violin Sonata seems to me the last word (for the present) in ugliness and incoherence. It was as if two people were improvising against each other.' The following year the same performers gave Bartók's Second Sonata. Percy Scholes, later editor of the *Oxford Companion to Music*, was discomforted: 'I suffered more than upon any occasion in my life apart from an incident or two connected with "painless dentistry". To begin with there was Mr. Bartók's piano touch. But "touch", with its implication of light-fingered ease, is a misnomer, unless it be qualified in some such way as that of Ethel Smyth in discussing her dear old teacher Herzogenberg – "He had a touch like a paving stone." ' Perhaps not surprisingly, London critics are now more circumspect in discussing modern music.

---

melodic characteristics into complex, subtle and effective forms. Bartók's orchestral music has become relatively popular, although his genius is more fully revealed in his innovative approach to the keyboard and especially the string quartets, which are widely regarded as the best since Beethoven.

Works include STAGE: *Duke Bluebeard's Castle*, one-act opera (1911), produced Budapest, 1918, conductor Tango; *The Wooden Prince*, one-act ballet (1914–17; produced Budapest, 1917, conductor Tango; *The Miraculous Mandarin*, one-act pantomime (1918–23), produced Cologne, 1926.

A genuine peasant melody of our land is a musical example of perfected art.
Béla Bartók, quoted in Machlis, *Introduction to Contemporary Music*, 1963

ORCHESTRAL: *Kossuth*, symphonic poem (1903), Rhapsody, piano and orchestra, op. 1 (1904), Scherzo (Burlesque), piano and orchestra (1904), Suite no. 1, op. 3 (1905, revised 1920), Suite no. 2, op. 4 (1905–07), violin concerto no. 1 (1907–08, fp Basel, 1958), *Two Portraits* (1907–11), *Two Pictures* (1910), *Four Pieces* op. 12 (1912–21), *The Wooden Prince*, suite from ballet (fp Budapest, 1931), *Romanian Folkdances* (1917), *The Miraculous Mandarin*, suite from pantomime (fp Budapest 1928), *Dance Suite* (1923), piano concerto no. 1 (1926, fp Frankfurt, 1927, with composer, conductor Furtwängler), two Rhapsodies for violin and orchestra (1928), piano concerto no. 2 (1930–31, fp Frankfurt, 1933, with composer, conductor Rosbaud), *Transylvanian Dances* (1931), *Hungarian Sketches* (1933), *Hungarian Peasant Songs* (1933), *Music for Strings, Percussion and Celesta* (1936, fp Basel, 1937, conductor Sacher), violin concerto no. 2 (1937–38, fp Amsterdam, 1939, with Székely, conductor Mengelberg), *Divertimento* for strings (1939, fp Basel, 1940, conductor Sacher), two-piano concerto (1940, fp London, 1942, with Kentner and Kabós, conductor Boult), *Concerto for Orchestra* (1943–44, fp Boston, 1944, conductor Koussevitzky), piano concerto no. 3 (1945, fp Philadelphia, 1946, conductor Ormandy), viola concerto (completed by T Serly, 1945).

VOCAL: *Three Village Scenes* for female voices and orchestra (1926), *Cantata Profana* for tenor, baritone, chorus and orchestra (1930), *Five Hungarian Folk Songs* for low voice and orchestra (1933); choruses on Hungarian and Slovak folksongs; many solo songs, most based on Hungarian folksongs.

CHAMBER: piano quintet (1903–04), six string quartets (1908, 1917, 1927, 1928, 1934, 1939), two piano and violin sonatas (1921, 1922),

A Selection of

Bartók

Duke Bluebeard's Castle 1911
The Miraculous Mandarin...........................1918–23
Piano Concerto no. 2 1930–1
String Quartet no. 5 1934

Music for Strings, Percussion and Celesta 1936
Sonata for 2 pianos and 2 percussion.....................1937
Violin Concerto no. 2 1937–8
Divertimento for strings..........................1939
Concerto for Orchestra............1943–4
Piano Concerto no. 3 1945

two Rhapsodies for violin and piano (1928, also in version with orchestra), Rhapsody for cello and piano (1928), 44 Duos for two violins (1931), sonata for two pianos and two percussion (1937, version with orchestra 1940), *Contrasts* for violin, clarinet and piano (1938), sonata for solo violin (1944).

PIANO: *14 Bagatelles*, op. 6 (1908), *85 Pieces for Children* (1909, revised 1945), *Allegro barbaro* (1911), Sonatina (1915, orchestrated as *Transylvanian Dances*), Suite, op. 14 (1916), *15 Hungarian Peasant Songs* (1914–18), sonata (1926), *Out of Doors* (1926), *Mikrokosmos*, 153 'progressive pieces' in six vols (1926, 1932–39); editions of keyboard music by B Marcello, M Rossi, Frescobaldi, Zipoli and Bach.

Bartoletti, Bruno (b Sesto Fiorentino, 10 Jun 1926), Italian conductor and flautist. He made his debut with *Rigoletto* at Florence (1953) and was music director of the Rome opera 1965–73, Maggio Musicale Orchestra 1957–64; US debut with the Lyric Opera of Chicago 1965 and has been artistic director there from 1975 (Maggio Musicale Opera 1986–91). Has given the premieres of operas by Malipiero, Mortari and Ginastera, and has recorded Verdi and Puccini (video of *Tosca*, 1976).

Bartoli, Cecilia (b Rome, 4 Jun 1966), Italian mezzo-soprano. She sang in concert before her stage debut at Verona, 1987; from 1988 she has been heard in Italy and Germany as Rossini's Rosina, Lucilla (*La scala di seta*) and Isolier; much admired also as Mozart's Cherubino, Despina (Salzburg, 1993) and Cecilio (*Lucio Silla*): US debut 1993, as Rosina at Houston. Her secure technique and attractive personality are also valued in concert.

Bartoš, Jan Zdeněk (b Dvůr Králiové nad-Labem, 4 Jun 1908; d Prague, 1 Jun 1981), Czech composer and violinist. He played the violin in orchestras and as a soloist pre-war; taught at the Prague Conservatory from 1958.

Works include operas *Ripar's Wife* (1949) and *The Accursed Castle* (1949); three ballets; seven cantatas; seven symphonies (1949–78), two viola concertos, violin concerto (1970); 11 string quartets (1940–73).

Bartoli *Italian mezzo Cecilia Bartoli. Since her debut in 1987 she has already recorded several roles to great critical acclaim (Rosina, Cherubino, Dorabella, Ravel's* Concepcion*). Her voice is particularly well-suited to Rossini's works.*

Bary, Alfred von (b Valetta, Malta, 18 Jan 1873; d Munich, 9 Sept 1926), German tenor. He studied medicine and became a neurologist at the University of Leipzig; after being discovered by Nikisch, he made his debut at Dresden in 1903 as Lohengrin. The next year he sang Siegmund at Bayreuth; he returned there until 1914 as Parsifal, Tristan and Siegfried. Dresden until 1912, then six years at Munich.

baryton string instrument of the bass viol type with sympathetic strings which can be plucked by the hand. It was cultivated mainly in Germany and Austria. Haydn's patron, Prince Nikolaus Esterházy, played it and Haydn wrote nearly 200 works for it.

Bashmet, Yuri (b Rostov, 24 Jan 1953), Russian violist and conductor. He won the Munich International Viola Competition 1976 and formed Moscow Soloists 1986, touring with them as soloist and conductor throughout Europe (UK debut tour 1988); he premiered the Schnittke concerto 1986 and has performed the Bartók and Walton concertos in London. Chamber recitalist with Richter, Natalia Gutman and the Borodin Quartet.

Basile, Andreana (b Posillipo near Naples, *c* 1580; d Rome, *c* 1640), Italian singer and instrumentalist. Her career began in Rome and Naples; engaged for the Mantuan court in 1610 and sang there until 1624. Much admired by Monteverdi, she sang in several of his operas and became one of the first prima donnas. She sang widely in Italy after breaking with the Duke of Mantua, and from 1634 lived in Rome, where she played the guitar in musical soirées.

Basili (or *Basily*), Francesco (b Loreto, 31 Jan 1767; d Rome, 25 Mar 1850), Italian singer and composer. Became director of the Milan Conservatory in 1827. *Maestro di cappella* at St Peter's in Rome from 1837.

Works include operas *La locandiera* (1789), *Achille nell' assedio di Troia*, *Ritorno d'Ulisse* (1798), *Antigona* (1799), *Achille, L'orfana egiziana* (1818); oratorio *Sansone* (1824); Requiem for Jannaconi; several settings of *Miserere*; symphony.

Basilius, Der königliche Schäfer, oder Basilius in Arcadien, (*The Royal Shepherd, or Basil in Arcady*), opera by Keiser (libretto by F C Bressand), produced Brunswick, ? 1693. The first of more than 100 operas by Keiser.

Basiola, Mario (b Annico, near Cremona, 12 Jul 1892; d Annico, 3 Jan 1965), Italian baritone. After his 1918 debut he sang at Barcelona and Florence; 1923–25 with the San Carlo, Naples co. in N America NY Met., 1925–31 (debut as Amonasro). In 1930 he took part in the local fp of Rimsky-Korsakov's *Sadko*, conducted by Serafin. Returned to Italy 1933 and joined La Scala co.; CG, 1939, as Iago and Scarpia. He toured Australia in 1946 and remained there until 1951 as a teacher.

Basiron, Philippe (Baziron, Philippon) (b ? Bourges, *c* 1450; d Bourges, 1491), French composer of Masses, motets and *chansons*.

bass (1) the lowest adult male voice.

The approximate range of a bass voice.

(2) Abbr. for ◊double bass.

(3) Applied to instruments of a low compass, e.g. bass trumpet.

(4) The lowest part of a vocal or instrumental ensemble, often used as an abbr. for *basso continuo*.

Bassani, Giovanni Battista (b Padua, *c* 1647; d Bergamo, 1 Oct 1716), Italian violinist and composer of the generation between Monteverdi and Vivaldi. He was organist at Ferrara from 1667 and was later in charge of the cathedral music at Bologna; he returned to Ferrara as *maestro di cappella* in 1683. He composed 12 oratorios, produced nine operas and brought out a large amount of church and instrumental music.

Bassano, Giovanni (b *c* 1558; d Venice, ? 1617), Venetian composer and cornet player who led the instrumental ensemble at St Mark's, Venice. He wrote instrumental music including ornamented transcriptions of vocal works by Gabrieli, Marenzio, etc.

Bassarids, The one-act opera with intermezzo by Henze (libretto by W H Auden and C Kallman after *The Bacchae* of Euripides), produced Salzburg, 6 Aug 1966; first British stage performance London, Coliseum, 10 Oct 1974, conductor Henze. Pentheus, in attempting to establish monotheism, incurs the wrath of Dionysus and his followers, who eventually kill him.

bass chantante French = 'singing-bass'; a bass voice especially suited to melodic delivery and lyrical parts.

bass clarinet a clarinet with a range an octave lower than the ordinary instrument.

bass clef the F clef on the fourth line of the stave, indicating on the piano the F below middle C.

The bass clef.

bass drum the largest of the drums not producing notes of definite pitch. It is usually placed upright and struck sideways, producing a dull thud. It is used both in the orchestra and in military bands, and in the latter it is played in conjunction with the cymbals, one of which is placed on it while the other is held in the player's hand not used to hold the drumstick.

bass drum

basse-contre French low bass, whether a voice, an instrument or an organ stop.

basse danse French dance of the 15th–16th c. So called because the feet were kept low, not thrown up in the air as in some other dances.

basset horn an alto instrument of the clarinet family, with an extra key controlling notes below the normal range of instruments of this family. Mozart frequently wrote for it.

Bassett, Leslie (b Hanford, CA, 22 Jan 1923), American composer. He studied with Ross Lee Finney, Nadia Boulanger and Mario Davidovsky (electronic music); from 1952 he has taught at the University of Michigan, as professor since 1977. His works are clearly constructed and are informed with a strong spiritual content.

Works include variations for orchestra (Pulitzer Prize winner 1966); *Echoes from an Invisible World*, for the Bicentennial, 1976; concerto for two pianos and orchestra (1976); trombone concerto (1983); *From a Source Evolving* for orchestra (1986); four string quartets (1951, 1957, 1962, 1978); Sextet (1979); *Duo-Inventions* for two cellos (1988); wind band music (Concerto grosso, 1982); choral works, songs, keyboard and electronic music.

bass flute a flute with a range a fourth lower than that of the ordinary instrument. It is a transposing instrument in G.

Bassi, Carolina Manna (b Naples, 10 Jan 1781; d Cremona, 12 Dec 1862), Italian contralto. She sang at the Teatro San Carlo, Naples, from 1789. At Turin she sang in the fp of Meyerbeer's *Semiramide* (1819); in the following two seasons she was heard at La Scala in the fps of *Margherita d'Anjou* and *L'esule di Granata*. Also successful in operas by Rossini, Pacini and Mercadante.

Bassi, Luigi (b Pesaro, 5 Sept 1766; d Dresden, 13 Sept 1825), Italian baritone. He appeared in soprano parts at the age of 13 and went to Prague 1784, where he made a great reputation, singing Count Almaviva in the first Prague production of *Le Nozze di Figaro* (1786). He was Mozart's first Don Giovanni there in 1787. He later sang in Leipzig, Vienna and Dresden; other Mozart roles included Guglielmo and Masetto.

basso cantante Italian = 'singing-bass'; a bass voice especially suited to melodic delivery and lyrical parts.

basso continuo Italian = 'continuous bass'; ◊continuo and ◊thorough-bass.

bassoon a double-reed instrument dating from the 16th c.

The normal compass of a bassoon, though a few higher notes are possible.

It is a bass instrument without proper bass strength, oddly weak in sound, bleating, burlesque.
Thomas Mann on the bassoon, *Doctor Faustus*, 1947

basso ostinato Italian, = lit. 'obstinate bass' = ground bass, a bass part in a composition continually tracing the same melodic outline.

bass trumpet a trumpet invented by Wagner, with a written compass an octave below that of the normal orchestral instrument.

bass viol ◊viola da gamba.

Bastardella, La the nickname given to the singer Lucrezia ◊Aguiari, who was the illegitimate daughter of an Italian nobleman.

Bastianini, Ettore (b Siena, 24 Sept 1922; d Sirmione, 25 Jan 1967), Italian baritone. Debut, as a bass, Ravenna, 1945. Debut as baritone 1951, Germont. NY Met. 1953–66; in 1953 sang Andrei in the fp of the revision of Prokofiev's *War and Peace*. La Scala from 1954. CG 1962. Other roles included Onegin, Renato and Posa.

Bastien und Bastienne Singspiel by Mozart, K50 (libretto by F W Weiskern and A Schachtner, based on Favart's parody of Rousseau's *Le Devin du Village*), produced Vienna, at the house of Anton Mesmer (the hypnotist) Sept 1768. Bastienne seeks the advice of a magician to win back the heart of inattentive Bastien.

Bastin, Jules (b Pont, 18 Aug 1933), Belgian bass. Théâtre de la Monnaie, Brussels, from 1960. Has sung in London, Chicago and NY, largely in French repertory, e.g. *Le Prophète*, *Pelléas et Mélisande*, *Benvenuto Cellini*. He sang the Banker in the fp of the three-act version of Berg's *Lulu*, Paris, 1979. Other roles include Osmin, Varlaam, Bartolo, Ochs and the Grand Inquisitor.

Bataille, Gabriel (b ? Brie, 1575; d Paris, 17 Dec 1630), French lutenist and composer. He contributed music to ballets danced at the court of Louis XIII. Between 1608 and 1623 he pub. many lute pieces and songs.

Bates, Joah (b Halifax, bap. 8 Mar 1740; d London, 8 Jun 1799), English organist, scholar and conductor. He conducted the Concert of Ancient Music in London from its foundation in 1776 until 1793, and led the Westminster Abbey Handel concerts of 1784.

Bates, William, English 18th-c. composer. He worked in London, where he produced several stage pieces and wrote songs for the pleasure gardens, glees, catches, etc.

Bateson, Thomas (b Cheshire, c 1570; d Dublin, Mar 1630), English organist and composer. Probably organist at Chester Cathedral until 1609, when he became vicar-choral and organist at Christ Church Cathedral, Dublin. Two books of madrigals by him were pub. 1604 and 1618.

Bathe, William (b Ireland, 2 Apr 1564; d Madrid, 17 Jun 1614), Irish priest and music scholar. In state service at first, he went to Spain and became a Jesuit priest in 1599. He wrote *Briefe Introductions*

bassoon

to the True Art of Musick and the Skill of Song, also *Janua linguarum*.

baton, French, the stick used by the conductor in orchestral and choral performances. It originated from a roll of music used in the 15th c. and passed through a phase of a heavy stick beaten on the floor in the 17th c. (Lully died after striking himself on the foot with his baton; later conductors have favoured a lighter stick.)

Battaglia di Legnano, La, *The Battle of Legnano*, opera by Verdi (libretto by S Cammarano), produced Rome, Teatro Argentina, 27 Jan 1849. Rolando and Arrigo battle against the Germans, but Rolando must also fight when he discovers his wife Lida loves Arrigo. Later, the mortally wounded Arrigo proclaims Lida's innocence and the three are reconciled.

battement, French, see ◊mordent.

Batten, Adrian (b Salisbury, bap. 1 Mar 1591; d London, 1637), English organist and composer. He was a chorister at Winchester Cathedral as a boy. In 1614 he came to London as vicar-choral at Westminster Abbey and in 1626 became organist at St Paul's Cathedral. He was probably the copyist of the Batten Organbook.

Works include 11 services, *c* 50 anthems and other church music.

batterie French an 18th-c. term for rapid broken accompaniment figures. Also a collective term for the group of percussion instruments in the orchestra.

Battishill, Jonathan (b London, May 1738; d London, 10 Dec 1801), English harpsichordist, organist and composer. Chorister at St Paul's Cathedral. About 1762 became harpsichordist to Covent Garden Theatre, where he produced in 1764 the opera *Almena*, written jointly with M Arne. About the same time he became organist of three city churches, and began to write church music. His best-known pieces are the anthems *Call to remembrance* and *O Lord, look down from heaven*. Other works include music for the stage, glees, catches, songs, etc.

Battistini, Mattia (b Rome, 27 Feb 1856; d Colle Baccaro, near Rieti, 7 Nov 1928), Italian baritone. He made his first appearance in opera in Rome, 1878, in *La Favorita*. London, 1883–1906, as Rigoletto, Valentin, Don Giovanni, Amonasro and Onegin. Sang in Russia 1888–1914 (Ruslan and Demon). Other roles included Wolfram, Iago and Boccanegra. The leading Italian baritone of his time.

Battle, Kathleen (b Portsmouth, OH, 13 Aug 1948), American soprano. She studied at the University of Cincinnati and appeared with the NY PO and LA SO from 1972. NY Met. debut 1978. At the 1979 Glyndebourne Festival she was heard as Nerina in Haydn's *La fedeltà premiata*. In 1985 her agile coloratura as Zerbinetta was much acclaimed at CG; she returned as Norina in 1990. A keen-spirited performer who is much admired by audiences.

Battle of Prague, The a descriptive piano piece with violin, cello and drum *ad lib* by Franz Koczwara, composed 1788, of no musical value, but very popular in the early 19th c.

Battle of Vittoria, The Beethoven's 'Battle Symphony', op. 91, originally entitled *Wellingtons Sieg oder die Schlacht bei Vittoria*, fp 8 Dec 1813. An extravagantly descriptive piece, originally intended for a mechanical instrument, it contains quotations from national songs, including *Rule, Britannia*.

Batton, Désiré (Alexandre) (b Paris, 2 Jan 1798; d Versailles, 15 Oct 1855), French composer. He studied at the Paris Conservatory and gained the Prix de Rome in 1817; went to Rome and travelled after producing his first comic opera, *La Fenêtre secrète*, in 1818.

Works include operas *Ethelwina* (1827), *Le Prisonnier d'état*, *Le Champ du drap d'or* (1828); church music; symphonies.

battuta Italian = 'beat'; often used loosely in the plural (e.g. *ritmo di 3 battute*) to indicate a change in the metrical scheme of bars – not beats – grouped in unexpected numbers.

Baudo, Serge (b Marseilles, 16 Jul 1927), French conductor. Debut 1950, with the Concerts Lamoureux. Paris Opéra from 1962 and opera at La Scala and NY Met. Chief conductor Orchestre de Paris 1967–69. He gave the fps of Messiaen's *Et exspecto resurrectionem mortuorum* (Chartres, 1965) and *La Transfiguration* (Lisbon, 1969).

Battle *Soprano Kathleen Battle in a particularly glamorous pose. Since giving up her initial plans to study mathematics she has charmed audiences upon the stage, in concert halls, and even at St Peter's, Rome, where she sang for the Pope.*

He conducted *Hoffmann* and *Samson et Dalila* at the NY Met., 1970–71. Founded the Berlioz Festival, Lyon, 1979.

Baudrier, Yves (b Paris, 11 Feb 1906; d Paris, 9 Nov 1988), French composer. Originally a law student, he formed the group of La Jeune France with Jolivet, Leseur and Messiaen in 1936.

Works include *Agnus Dei* for soprano, chorus and orchestra; symphonies, symphonic poem *Le Grand Voilier* (1939); string quartet (1944); piano pieces.

Bauer, Marion (b Walla Walla, WA, 15 Aug 1887; d South Hadley, MA, 9 Aug 1955), American composer and teacher. She studied with Boulanger in Paris and taught at New York University 1926–51. Her works are often in smaller forms and are neo-classical in spirit.

Works include piano pieces *New Hampshire Woods* (1921), *Sun Splendour* (1926, also for orchestra) and *Dance Sonata* (1932); string quartet (1928); viola sonata (1936); oboe sonata (1940); piano concerto 'American Youth' (1943); *China* for chorus and orchestra (1945). Her books include *20th-Century Music* (1933) and *How Opera Grew* (1955).

Bauermeister, Mathilde (b Hamburg, 1849; d Herne Bay, 15 Oct 1926), German-born soprano. After study at the RAM she sang in Dublin, 1866. London, CG, 1868–1905 (debut as Siebel). She made many tours of the USA, from 1879, and sang at the NY Met, 1891–1906 (debut as Thomas's Gertrude). Other roles included Marguerite de Valois and Elvira.

Bauldeweyn, Noel (d c 1530), Flemish composer. *Maître de chapelle* of Notre Dame at Antwerp, 1513–18. Composed sacred and secular music including the Mass *Da Pacem* formerly thought to be by Josquin.

Baum, Kurt (b Prague, 15 Mar 1908; d New York, 27 Dec 1989), Czech tenor. Debut Zurich 1933, in the fp of Zemlinsky's *Der Kreidekreis*. He sang at the German Theatre, Prague, 1934–39 and appeared as Radames at Chicago in 1939. NY Met, 1941–67, often in operas by Wagner. He sang Rossini's Arnold at the 1952 Florence Festival, and the following year was heard as Radames at CG.

Baumgartner, Rudolf (b Zurich, 14 Sept 1917), Swiss violinist and conductor. He studied with Schneiderhan, with whom he founded the Lucerne Festival Strings in 1956; he has toured worldwide with the orchestra as conductor and has arranged for it Bach's *Musical Offering* and *Art of Fugue*. Artistic director Lucerne Festival 1968–80.

Bavarian Highlands, Scenes from the six Choral Songs with piano, op. 27, by Elgar; composed 1895, fp Worcester, 21 Apr 1896. Version with orchestra 1896. Nos. 1, 3 and 6 were arranged for orchestra alone as *Three Bavarian Dances*, performed Crystal Palace, 23 Oct 1897, conductor August Manns.

Bavichi, John (b Boston, 25 Apr 1922), American composer. He studied with Walter Piston at Harvard and after war service was active in Boston as a conductor and teacher (Arlington Philharmonic, 1968–82). His music often employs classical forms.

Works include concertante for oboe, bassoon and strings (1961); string quartet (1961); music for chamber orchestra (1981); *There is Sweet Music Here* for soprano and orchestra (1985); *Triptych* for horns (1987).

Bawden, Rupert (b London, 1958), English composer. He studied with Robin Holloway at Cambridge and has played the violin and viola in the London Sinfonietta; debut as conductor at the Aldeburgh Festival, 1986.

Works include *The Angel and the Ship of Death* for 13 players (1983, rev. 1987); *Sunless* for ensemble (1984); *Seven Songs from the House of Sand* for brass quintet (1985); *Le Livre de Fauvel* for soprano, mezzo, and 18 players (1986); *Dramatic Cantata on the Legend of Apollo and Daphne* for violin, cello and 13 players (1989); *Ultimo Scena* for chamber ensemble (1989); ballet commission from the Munich Biennale (1990).

Bax, Arnold (Edward Trevor) (b London, 8 Nov 1883; d Cork, 3 Oct 1953), English composer. Entered the RAM in 1900, studying piano with Matthay and composition with F Corder. Stayed frequently in Ireland and travelled in Russia. He never held any official music position until he was appointed Master of the King's Music in 1942. Knighted 1937. He is best known for the vivid and evocative tone

poems *Tintagel* and *November Woods*, reflecting his interest in Celtic legend and landscape, although his colourful symphonies are now also returning to favour. He had a long, illicit relationship with the pianist Harriet ◊Cohen.

Works include DRAMATIC: ballet *The Truth about the Russian Dancers* (J M Barrie) (1920); film music for *Malta G C* (documentary) and *Oliver Twist* (after Dickens).

CHORAL: includes *Enchanted Summer* (1910), *Fatherland* (1907), *I sing of a Maiden, Mater ora Filium, St Patrick's Breastplate, This Worldes Joie* (1922), *To the Name above every Name*; *Te Deum* and Nunc Dimittis for chorus and organ.

ORCHESTRAL: seven symphonies (1922–39), *Sinfonietta*, symphonic poems *November Woods* (1917), *The Garden of Fand, The Happy Forest, Tintagel* (1919); overture *Work in Progress, Overture to a Picaresque Comedy* (1930), *Legend, Two Northern Ballads* and other orchestral works; concertos for violin and orchestra (1938), and for cello and orchestra (1949), symphonic variations and *Winter Legends* for piano and orchestra.

CHAMBER MUSIC: includes nonet, octet, quintets for piano and strings, oboe and strings, strings and harp, strings, three string quartets (1916–36), piano quartet, trios for violin, viola and piano, violin, cello and piano, and flute, viola and harp; three sonatas for violin and piano, sonata for viola and piano, sonata for cello and piano, sonata for clarinet and piano; four piano sonatas (1910–32) and numerous piano pieces; sonata and five other works for two pianos; many songs and a number of folksong arrangements.

One should try everything once, except incest and folk-dancing.

Sir Arnold Bax, *Farewell, my Youth*, 1943

Baxevanos, Peter (b Salonika, 29 Sept 1908; d Vienna, 24 Jun 1982), Greek tenor. Debut 1934 in Wolf-Ferrari's *Sly*, at the Vienna Volksoper. He sang at Zurich until 1938 and was Alwa in the fp of Berg's *Lulu* (1937) and the Kardinal in the fp of Hindemith's *Mathis der Maler* (1938); returned to the Volksoper during World War II and from 1945 appeared at the Staatsoper, Vienna, and in Italy as Manrico, Cavaradossi, Don Carlos, Don José and Florestan.

Bayer, Joseph (b Vienna, 6 Mar 1852; d Vienna, 12 Mar 1913), Austrian conductor and composer. He studied at the Vienna Conservatory, played the violin at the Court Opera and from 1885 was director of the ballet music there.

Works include operettas *Der Chevalier von San Marco, Mr Menelaus, Fräulein Hexe, Der Polizeichef* and others; ballets *Die Puppenfee* (1888) and many others, etc.

Bayreuth the small town in Bavaria where Wagner built the festival theatre for the performance of his works, opened in 1876 with the first production of the *Ring*. The theatre then closed until 1882, when it re-opened with the first production of *Parsifal*. Cosima Wagner was director 1883–1908, her son Siegfried 1908–30. Wieland and Wolfgang Wagner, the composer's grandsons, were directors 1951–66; they revolutionized the way in which the operas were presented; realism was replaced by abstraction. Wieland's 1951 production of *Parsifal* was well received, but later stagings have provoked controversy; the Chéreau production of the *Ring* (1976) was much discussed, but Peter Hall (1983) attempted some return to realism. Harry Kupfer in 1988 reduced the *Ring* to zaniness and controversy. Wieland Wagner has been artistic director from 1966.

Bazelon, Irwin (Allen) (b Evanston, IL, 4 Jun 1922; d New York, 2 Aug 1995), American composer. Studied with Hindemith, Milhaud and Bloch. Experienced in film music and incidental music.

Works include seven symphonies (1963–80), *Chamber Symphony* for seven instruments (1957), *Symphonie Concertante* (1963), *Early American Suite* (1970), *Excursions* for orchestra (1966); *Spirits of the Night* for orchestra (1976), *Sound Dreams* for six instruments (1977), *Spires* for trumpet and orchestra (1981), *Trajectories* for piano and orchestra (1984); *Motivations* for trombone and orchestra (1985);

Bayreuth *The Festspielhaus at Bayreuth (Germany). With the financial support of 'Mad King Ludwig' (Ludwig II of Bavaria) Wagner built his theatre specifically with the monumental needs of the* Ring *in mind. Bayreuth is also home to the pre-Wagnerian Markgräfliches Opernhaus of 1748.*

Legends and Love Letters for soprano and chamber orchestra (1987); *Fourscore 2* for percussion quartet and orchestra (1988); two string quartets, three piano sonatas.

BBC ◊British Broadcasting Corporation.

Beach (born *Cheney*), Amy Marcy (b Henniker, New Hampshire, 5 Sept 1867; d New York, 27 Dec 1944), American pianist and composer, also known as Mrs Henry Beach. She was one of the leading international composers of her day, influenced by Brahms, Debussy, and her American contemporaries writing in a romantic vein.

Works include Mass in E; *Christ in the Universe* for chorus and orchestra (1931); *Gaelic Symphony* (1896, the first symphonic work by an American woman); piano concerto; string quartet, piano trio; numerous songs.

beak flute = German *Schnabelflöte* = ◊recorder.

Beamish, Sally (b London, 26 Aug 1956), English composer and viola player. She studied at RNCM and with L Berkeley. She played viola in various London ensembles. In 1989 she became resident in Scotland, co-founding the Chamber Group of Scotland.

Works include music theatre *Ease* (1993); symphony (1992); *Tam Lin* oboe concerto (1992); Concerto Grosso for strings (1993); viola concerto (1995); *Magnificat* for soprano, mezzo, and ensemble (1992); chamber music.

Bearbeitung German = 'arrangement'; particularly the adaptation of a work for a different performing medium.

Beard, John (b London, *c* 1717; d Hampton, 5 Feb 1791), English tenor. Chorister of the Chapel Royal under Gates, he later sang in the fps of many of Handel's oratorios. The tenor parts in *Israel in Egypt*, *Messiah*, *Samson*, *Judas Maccabeus* and *Jephtha* were composed for him; also created roles in *Ariodante*, *Alcina*, *Atalanta*, *Berenice* and *Semele*.

Bear, The nickname (*L'Ours*) of the first of Haydn's 'Paris' symphonies, no. 82 in C, composed 1786.

Opera by Walton (libretto by P Dehn and the composer, based on Chekhov), produced Aldeburgh, 3 Jun 1967. Widow Popova falls for husband's creditor.

beat (1) the unit of measurement in music, indicated in choral and orchestral music by the conductor. It is not necessarily synonymous with accent. (2) An Old English name for a variety of ornaments.

What the English like is something they can beat time to, something that hits them straight on the drum of the ear.
Handel, quoted in Schmid, *C W von Gluck*, 1854

Béatitudes, Les oratorio by Franck for solo voices, chorus and orchestra (words from the Bible), composed 1869–79, fp privately by Franck's pupils at his house, 20 Feb 1879 (piano accompaniment), and in public only after his death, Dijon, 15 Jun 1891.

Beatrice di Tenda opera by Bellini (libretto by F Romani), produced Venice, Teatro La Fenice, 16 Mar 1833. Beatrice is married to greedy Duke Filippo but loves Orombello. She is executed on account of infidelity and treason by the Duke, who loves only the power acquired through her lands and her lady-in-waiting, Agnese.

Béatrice et Bénédict, *Beatrice and Benedick*, opera by Berlioz (libretto by composer, based on Shakespeare's *Much Ado about Nothing*), produced Baden-Baden, 9 Aug 1862. Shakespeare stripped to essentials.

Beatrix Cenci opera in two acts by Ginastera (libretto by W Shand and A Girri after Shelley's *The Cenci*, 1819, and Stendhal's *Chroniques Italiennes*, 1837), produced Washington DC, 10 Sept 1971. Beatrix is executed after killing her incestuous father.

beats in acoustics, the clashing of soundwaves of slightly different frequencies produced, for example, by two piano strings for the same note not perfectly in tune with each other, or certain organ stops using two pipes for each note purposely kept slightly out of tune to produce that wavering effect. Sensitive ears perceive beats as slight periodical swellings of the tone on sustained notes, and piano tuners rely on beats to tell them whether the strings of any one note are in tune or not.

Beaujoyeulx, Balthasar de (Baldassare da Belgioioso, Baltazarini) (b before 1535; d *c* 1587), Italian violinist, sent to France *c* 1555 with a large band of string players by the Maréchal de Brissac to form the

⸻ THE OPERA ⸻

Béatrice et Bénédict

A two-act opera of 1862 by Hector Berlioz, based on William Shakespeare's *Much Ado About Nothing*, set in Messina, Sicily, in 1700.

I. Hero (soprano) anticipates the return of Claudio (baritone) from the war but her cousin Béatrice (soprano) is engaged in a 'Merry war' with Bénédict (tenor). Bénédict overhears an arranged conversation and is tricked into thinking that Béatrice does indeed love him. She, meanwhile, gains a similar impression, thanks to a plot by Hero and her attendant Ursula (mezzo-soprano).

II. During the wedding banquet of Hero and Claudio, Béatrice acknowledges her love for Bénédict; the two continue to bicker but when a second marriage contract is produced they agree to sign it – without too much reluctance.

⸻ THE OPERA ⸻

orchestra of Catherine de' Medici. He supervised the performance of the *Ballet comique de la royne*.

Beaulieu, Eustorg de (b Beaulieu-sur-Menoire, 1495–1500; d Basel, 8 Jan 1552), French poet and musician. He wrote a few *chansons*, but is better known for his verse, including a collection of early Protestant song texts.

Beaumarchais, Pierre Augustin Caron de (1732–1799), French author and musician. He sang and played the flute and harp, teaching the latter to the daughters of Louis XV. His comedy *Le Barbier de Séville* was at first to be a comic opera with music arranged by Beaumarchais from Spanish songs and dances.

His great trilogy of pre-revolutionary plays is perfectly structured for musical adaptation. *Le Barbier de Séville* (1775) was set by Paisiello in 1782 and performed all over Europe before Rossini's version of 1816. *La Folle Journée, ou Le Mariage de Figaro* (1784) had socially subversive implications that are still present in Mozart's setting (1786). *La Mère Coupable* (1792) forms the basis of John Corigliano's *The Ghosts of Versailles*, successfully performed at the NY Met. in 1991 and featuring Beaumarchais himself as a kindly spirit who attempts to change history by writing a play that will save Marie Antoinette from the guillotine.

If a thing isn't worth saying, you sing it.
Beaumarchais, *Barber of Seville*, Act 1, Scene 2

Beaux Arts Trio American piano trio, founded at the Berkshire Music Festival, Tanglewood, in 1955. Members until 1987: Menahem Pressler (piano), Isadore Cohen (violin) and Bernard Greenhouse (cello). Has toured widely in the Classical repertory. Peter Wiley cellist from 1987.

Bebung German = 'trembling'; an effect of tone-vibration obtainable on the clavichord by moving the finger up and down on the key, thereby varying the tension of the string.

Bechi, Gino (b Florence, 16 Oct 1913; d Florence, 2 Feb 1993), Italian baritone. Debut Empoli, 1936, as Germont. He sang at Rome and La Scala from 1937 and created roles in operas by ◊Rocca and ◊Alfano; appeared as guest throughout Europe and S America and was admired as Nabucco, Amonasro, Gérard and Hamlet. London, 1950 and 1958, as Iago, Falstaff and William Tell. He sang in Chicago and San

Beaux Arts Trio *The Beaux Arts Trio, the current members of whom are Menahem Pressler (piano), Ida Kavafian (violin), and Peter Wiley (cello), has endured since its debut at Tanglewood, which followed its formation in 1955. The Trio has recorded and performed extensively to critical and popular acclaim.*

Francisco (1952) and appeared in films of *Aida*, *Ballo in Maschera* and *Cavalleria Rusticana*. Taught in Florence from 1965.

Becht, Hermann (b Karlsruhe, 19 Mar 1939), German bass-baritone. After engagements in Brunswick and Wiesbaden he sang at the Deutsche Oper, Düsseldorf, from 1974. He is today's leading interpreter of Alberich and has sung the role in London, NY and at

---

Sally Beamish – composer / violist

1. Rakhmaninov: *Suite no. 2 for two pianos*
   I remember hearing this when I was a piano Junior Exhibitioner at Trinity College. I think it was the overt Romanticism that enchanted me – the heart-on-the-sleeve harmonic progressions and effortless concerted strength of two pianos together. I have loved Rakhmaninov ever since.

2. Dvořák: 'New World' Symphony
   When I later began to play the violin and viola in youth orchestras and chamber groups, I really discovered music for the first time. Dvořák's 'New World' Symphony was a revelation to me – I found an old record at home and wore it out.

3. Józef Wieniawski: Violin Concerto no. 2
   At 18 I went to the Royal Northern College of Music to study violin with Bronislav Gimpel. I had a recording of this music, played by Gimpel, which would bring tears to my eyes. I wrote a little sonata for him which echoes the shapes of those wonderful, long Wieniawski lines – it's the first piece I still acknowledge, and in a way it was the sheer joy of Gimpel's performing that put the ingredient of communication into my motivation to compose.

4. Puccini: *La Bohème*
   It was also at college that I discovered opera. There was a student performance of *La Bohème*, and I thought it was the most marvellous thing I'd ever heard. I was playing in the orchestra, but I went to every piano rehearsal I could to see how it was to be staged.

5. Britten: *Les Illuminations*
   I think this was the piece that grabbed my attention most at college. During the rehearsals I became increasingly fascinated. It seemed so simple and yet so compelling. I took it apart and analysed it to try and see how it was made, but I still couldn't explain the magic of it.

6. Boulez: *Le Marteau sans maître*
   Playing *Le Marteau sans maître* was a formative experience. I went into deep shock when I first saw the viola part, and subsequently went through various degrees of anger and despair. But by the first performance I was beginning to get a certain satisfaction from nailing those elusive top notes, and as performances progressed I grew to admire and even to love the piece. It was a baptism by fire.

Bayreuth (from 1979). Other roles include Mandryka, Kurwenal, Amfortas, Falstaff and Pfitzner's Borromeo.

Beck, Conrad (b Lohn, Schaffenhausen, 16 Jun 1901; d Basel, 31 Oct 1989), Swiss composer. After studying engineering, he became a student at the Zurich Conservatory under Andreae and others; later in Berlin and Paris, where he lived 1923–32 and was closely in touch with Roussel and Honegger. Awarded important prizes for composition in 1954, 1956 and 1964.

Works include opera *La Grande Ourse* (1936); incidental music for Goethe's *Pandora* (1945) and other plays; oratorios *Angelus Silesius* and *Der Tod zu Basel*; Requiem; *Der Tod des Oedipus* for chorus and orchestra; *Lyric Cantata* (Rilke) for female voices and orchestra; chamber cantata (sonnets by Louise Labé); five symphonies (1925–30), *Sinfonietta*, *Innominata* and *Ostinato* for orchestra, concerto for string quartet and orchestra, *Konzertmusik* for oboe and strings, concerto, concertino and rhapsody for piano and orchestra, cello concerto; five string quartets (1922–52).

Beck, Franz (b Mannheim, 20 Feb 1734; d Bordeaux, 31 Dec 1809), German violinist and composer. A member of the Mannheim school of symphonists and a pupil of Johann Stamitz. He is said to have fled from Mannheim as the result of a duel; went to Italy and later settled in France.

Works include the operas *La belle jardinière* (Bordeaux, 1767) and *Pandore* (Paris, 1789); *c* 30 symphonies, *Stabat Mater*, keyboard music.

Becker, John (b Henderson, KY, 22 Jan 1886; d Wilmete, IL, 21 Jan 1961), American composer. After studying at the Cincinnati Conservatory, he taught at Notre Dame 1917–27. From 1930 he was associated with Ruggles, Riegger, Cowell, and other avant garde US composers. His series of *Soundscapes* create novel effects of instrumentation, while his theatre pieces anticipate later mixed-media works.

Works include stage: *A Marriage with Space* (1935), *Nostalgic Songs of Earth* (1938), *Rain Down Death* (1939), *When the Willow Nods* (1940) and *Faust: a Television Opera* (1951); seven symphonies (1912–54); two piano concertos and concertos for viola (1937) and violin (1948); *Moments from the Passion* (1945); film music and songs.

Beddoe, Dan (b Ameraman, 16 Mar 1863; d New York, 26 Dec 1937), Welsh-born tenor. He emigrated to the USA after winning an Eisteddfod prize in 1882. Studied at Pittsburgh and New York, concert debut 1903. He sang the title role in a concert performance of *Parsifal* conducted by Walter Damrosch (1904), and until 1934 was highly successful in Cincinnati and NY in oratorios by Mendelssohn and Handel; admired by Caruso for his *messa-di-voce* technique. He sang at Crystal Palace in a 1911 performance of *Messiah* which celebrated the coronation of George V.

Bedford, David (b London, 4 Aug 1937), English composer. He studied at the RAM with Berkeley and in Venice with Nono.

Works include the school operas *The Rime of the Ancient Mariner* (1976) and *The Ragnarok* (1983); *The Camlann Game* (1987), *The Return of Odysseus* (1988) and *Anna* (1993); symphony for 12 players, *Sun Paints Rainbows on the Vast Waves* for orchestra (1982); *Star Clusters, Nebulae and Places in Devon* for chorus and brass (1971); *Seascapes* (1986), *The Transfiguration* (1988), *Frameworks* (1990) and *Plymouth Town* (1992), all for orchestra; *Toccata for Tristan* for brass (1989); *Allison's Concerto* for trumpet and strings (1993); *I am going home with thee* for six women's voices and strings (1993); many pieces for instrumental ensemble and voices and instruments, many of which reflect the fact that he is a teacher and a one-time member of the pop music group *The Whole World*.

Bedford, Steuart (b London, 31 Jun 1939), English conductor. He studied at the RAM. Debut SW, 1967, with the English Opera Group; toured with the group in Europe and the USA. 1975–80, artistic co-director of the English Music Theatre (formerly EOG). Conducted fps of Britten's *Death in Venice* (1973) and *Phaedra* (1976), both at Aldeburgh. Arranged suite from *Death in Venice* (1984).

Bedyngham, John (d London, *c* 1460), English composer. Wrote

Masses, motets and *chansons*, possibly including *O rosa bella*, often ascribed to Dunstable. His music was widely known on the Continent; one of his two Mass cycles is derived from a ballade by Binchois.

There are two golden rules for an orchestra: start together and finish together. The public doesn't give a damn what goes on in between.
Thomas Beecham, in *Beecham Stories*, 1978

Beecham, Thomas (b St Helens, Lancs., 29 Apr 1879; d London, 8 Mar 1961), English conductor, the first of his kind to gain an international reputation. He was educated at Rossall School and Wadham College, Oxford. After conducting the Hallé Orchestra at a concert at St Helens in 1899 he studied composition with Charles Wood, intending to be a composer, but turned his attention to conducting and first appeared in London in 1905. From that time he rapidly became one of the most original and versatile English conductors. From 1909 up to the 1914–18 war, and also during the war, he was responsible for introducing a number of unfamiliar operas to the public, including Strauss's *Feuersnot*, *Ariadne auf Naxos* and *Rosenkavalier* (all first British performances). He made his US debut 1928, with the NY PO, and conducted the Seattle SO 1941–43; Met. Opera 1942–44 in French works, *The Golden Cockerel, Tristan,* and *Falstaff.* In 1929 he gave a festival of Delius' music in London, and in 1932 founded the LPO. During the 1939–45 war he was active as a conductor in Australia, Canada and USA. He founded the RPO in 1947. While excelling in Mozart, he was also passionately interested in the works of Romantic composers, particularly Delius: he conducted the fp of

Beethoven *Ludwig van Beethoven (1770–1827) as drawn in a period sketch by Johann Peter Lyser. The composer is depicted rambling in the street, oblivious to the outside world. Most of his contemporaries tolerated his dishevelled appearance and unsophisticated manners, believing them to be symptoms of his genius.*

the opera *Irmelin* (Oxford, 1953). He was knighted in 1914 and succeeded to his father's baronetcy in 1916. Much of Beecham's renowned and caustic wit is contained in his autobiography, *A Mingled Chime* (1943).

Beeson, Jack (Hamilton) (b Muncie, IN, 15 Jul 1921), American composer. He studied with Howard Hanson at Rochester and with Bartók in NY, 1945, and was professor at Columbia University 1965–88.

Works include operas: *Jonah* (1950), *Hello, Out There* (1954), *The Sweet Bye and Bye* (1957), *Lizzie Borden* (1965), *Dr Heidegger's Fountain of Youth* (after Hawthorne, 1978); also symphony in A (1959), *Transformations* for orchestra (1959), five piano sonatas, TV opera *My Heart's in the Highlands* (after Sorayan, 1970).

Bee's Wedding, The the English nickname of Mendelssohn's *Song without Words* in C major op. 67 no. 4, the German being *Spinnerlied* 'spinning-song'.

Beeth, Lola (b Kraków, 23 Nov 1860; d Bérlin, 18 Mar 1940), German soprano. She studied with Pauline Viardot and Desirée Artôt. Debut Berlin, Hofoper, 1882, as Elsa; remained until 1888 and then sang at the Vienna Hofoper until 1895. She appeared at the NY Met. 1895–96 (debut as Meyerbeer's Valentine). After guest appearances at CG, St Petersburg and Monte Carlo she returned to Vienna, 1898–1901, and often sang under Mahler.

Prince, what you are, you are by the accident of your birth; what I am, I am of myself.
    Beethoven, in a letter to Prince Lichnowsky, 1806

Beethoven, Ludwig van (b Bonn, bap. 17 Dec 1770; d Vienna, 26 Mar 1827), German composer of Flemish descent. He was the son and grandson of musicians in the service of the Elector of Cologne in Bonn. Became pupil of C G Neefe in 1781. In 1783 was harpsichordist in the court orchestra, and the same year pub. three piano sonatas. Second organist at court 1784, and 1789 also viola player. A visit to Vienna in 1787 to study with Mozart was cut short after only a few weeks by his mother's fatal illness, and he continued as a court musician in Bonn, meeting Count Waldstein in 1788. In 1792 he returned to Vienna to be a pupil of Haydn, whom he had met in Bonn. He remained in Vienna for the rest of his life, scarcely leaving the city or its suburbs. From 1793 to 1796 he lived in the house of Prince Lichnowsky, establishing himself in the musical life of Vienna. Tuition with Haydn was not a success (the impatient younger composer could not get on with his master, although his early music is full

A Selection of

Beethoven

Septet	1800
Symphony no. 3 (*Eroica*)	1803
Fidelio	1805
Symphony no. 6	1808
Piano Concerto no. 5 (*Emperor*)	1809
Symphony no. 7	1812
Symphony no. 9 (*Choral*)	1817–24
Mass in D (*Missa Solemnis*)	1819–22
Variations on a Waltz by Diabelli	1819–23
String Quartet in A minor	1825

of Haydn's influence) and he took lessons from Schenk, Albrechtsberger and Salieri. In 1795 he pub. his op. 1, three piano trios, and made his first public appearance in Vienna as a pianist and composer. He lived by playing and teaching, and later increasingly by the publication of his works.

The set of six string quartets op. 18 (1798–1800) are classical in form but are strongly expressive in content: the slow movement of the first work was said by Beethoven to portray the tomb scene in *Romeo and Juliet*. The first symphony (1800) was easily understood in the context of recent works by Haydn and Mozart. The deafness which had threatened from as early as *c* 1795 increased, and his despair gave rise to the suicidal 'Heiligenstadt Testament' in 1802; Beethoven's musical response was the radiant and untroubled second symphony. His third symphony (*Eroica*) was dedicated to Napoleon, but Beethoven changed the dedication when Napoleon proclaimed himself Emperor. The symphony was highly influential in driving music towards the Romantic style asserted later in the century; symphonic form was also hugely extended.

He conducted his only opera in 1805 (*Fidelio*, revised 1806 and 1814); the difficulties faced by Beethoven in reaching a final version are typical of his painstaking working methods. The way in which *Fidelio* develops from old-fashioned Singspiel in the first scene to a totally convincing drama sums up Beethoven's compositional process: from humble beginnings he gradually asserts his creative spirit. *Fidelio* was also a celebration of married love, something Beethoven strove for but never found; he was not assisted by his uncouth and eccentric personal habits.

He refused to accept regular employment under the old system of patronage, but received support from the aristocracy: in 1808, for instance, three noblemen, the Archduke Rudolph, Prince Kinsky and Prince Lobkowitz, agreed to pay him an unconditional annuity; the fifth symphony dates from the same year, and seems to proclaim the individual's sense of worth and identity. By 1806 he was forced to abandon public performance altogether. More time was now available for composition: there followed the fourth piano concerto, the Rasumovsky quartets, the violin concerto, *Pastoral*, seventh and eighth symphonies and the *Emperor* concerto. By turns lyrical, expansive, serene and dynamic, the music of this middle period gained Beethoven further public recognition as the leading composer of the day.

In 1815, after his brother's death, he temporarily became guardian to his nephew Karl, a task he took seriously and which caused him

---

Beethoven   *A biographical note*

Living alone and frequently changing his lodgings, Beethoven often neglected his appearance. Untidy clothes, together with a habit of humming loudly to himself in the street, made his nephew Karl embarrassed to be seen with him. Staying once in the Viennese suburb of Wiener Neustadt he got up early and dressed quickly, including his familiar moleskin trousers which were rather the worse for wear. He soon got lost in unfamiliar surroundings and was spotted by several local residents staring in at their windows. Arrested by a constable, Beethoven was quick to proclaim his identity. 'Impossible', came the reply, 'Beethoven doesn't look like a tramp'. The local Police Commissioner was told about the derelict with no means of identification and ordered that he be locked up until morning. By midnight the Commissioner was woken to be told that the prisoner was insisting that the music director of Neustadt be called to identify him. 'That is Beethoven', proclaimed the director as soon as he arrived at the prison. He took the composer into his house for the night and the next day he returned to Vienna in the Commissioner's coach.

constant worry. The last five great piano works (four sonatas and the Diabelli Variations) were initiated in 1818 by the Hammerklavier sonata; these works pressed instrumental technique to new limits but at the same time combine intellectual depth with expressive power in a unique way, not achieved by any other composer. By 1819 Beethoven was totally deaf, and communication with him was possible only in writing. He had begun work on the Choral symphony in 1817 and this was followed by the Missa Solemnis (1819–22) and the last five quartets (1822–26). The Mass and quartets together feature the most profound and sublimely concentrated thought in all music. He never recovered from an infection caught in 1826, and his death the following year was due to dropsy.

Although contemporary audiences found his visionary late music difficult, Beethoven's reputation was well established throughout Europe. He was aware of the problems his music had created for listeners and performers alike (part of the slow movement of the Choral Symphony had to be cut at its premiere), but as Ben Jonson said of Shakespeare 'He was not of this age but for all time'.

Works include STAGE: opera, Fidelio, (1805, revised 1806 and 1814), incidental music for Egmont (Goethe, 1810), The Ruins of Athens (A von Kotzebue, 1812), King Stephen (Kotzebue, 1812), The Creatures of Prometheus, overture, introduction and 16 nos. for a ballet produced at the Burgtheater, Vienna, 1801.

CHORAL WITH ORCHESTRA: Cantata on the Death of the Emperor Joseph II (1790), oratorio Christus am Ölberge, op. 85 (1803), Mass in C, op. 86 (1807), Choral Fantasia, for piano, chorus and orchestra, op. 80 (1808), Mass in D, (Missa Solemnis), op. 123 (1819–22).

SYMPHONIES: no. 1 in C, op. 21 (1800), no. 2 in D, op. 36 (1802), no. 3 in Eb (Eroica), op. 55 (1803), no. 4 in Bb, op. 60 (1806), no. 5 in C minor, op. 67 (1808), no. 6 in F, (Pastoral), op. 68 (1808), no. 7 in A, op. 92 (1812), no. 8 in F, op. 93 (1812), no. 9 in D minor (Choral), op. 125 (1817–24); 'Battle Symphony', op. 91 (1813).

CONCERTOS: piano, no. 1 in C, op. 15 (1795), no. 2 in Bb, op. 19 (before 1793, revised 1794–95, 1798), no. 3 in C minor, op. 37 (?1800), no. 4 in G, op. 58 (1806), no. 5 in Eb, (Emperor), op. 73 (1809); violin concerto, op. 61 (1806), triple concerto for piano, violin and cello, op. 56 (1804); two Romances for violin and orchestra (1798 and 1802).

OVERTURES: Leonora 1–3, for the first and second versions of Fidelio (1805, 1806), Coriolan, op. 62 (1807), Namensfeier/Nameday, op. 115 (1815), Die Weihe des Hauses/The Consecration of the House, op. 124 (1822).

CHAMBER: Octet for wind instruments op. 103 (1792); Sextet in Eb for two horns and strings (1795); Variations for cello and piano on a theme of Handel (1796) and on themes from Die Zauberflöte (1796 and 1801); Trio in Bb for clarinet, cello and piano op. 11 (1797); Variations for piano trio on Ich bin der Schneider Kakadu op. 121a (1798); Sonata for horn and piano op. 17 (1800); Serenade for flute, violin and viola in D, op. 25 (1800); Septet in Eb op. 20 (1800); two quintets, for piano and wind in Eb (1796), for strings in C, op. 29 (1801); 16 string quartets, op. 18 nos. 1–6, in F, G, D, C minor, A and Bb (1798–1800), op. 59 nos. 1–3, Rasumovsky, in F, E minor and C (1806), op. 74 in Eb Harp, (1809), op. 95 in F minor (1810), op. 127 in Eb (1825), op. 130 in Bb (1826; present rondo finale replaces original Grosse Fuge, op. 133), op. 131 in C#minor (1826), op. 132 in A minor (1825), op. 135 in F (1826); five string trios: op. 3 in Eb (c 1794), op. 8, ('Serenade') in D (1797), op. 9 nos. 1–3, in G, D and C minor (1798); six piano trios: op. 1 nos. 1–3, in Eb, G and C minor (1794), op. 70 nos. 1 and 2, in D (Ghost), and Eb (1808), op. 97 in Bb, (Archduke) (1811); ten violin sonatas: op. 12 nos. 1–3, in D, A and Eb (1798), op. 23 in A minor (1800), op. 24 in F, (Spring) (1801), op. 30 nos. 1–3, in A, C minor and G (1802), op. 47 in A, (Kreutzer) (1803), op. 96 in G (1812); five cello sonatas, op. 5 nos. 1 and 2, in F and G minor (1796), op. 69 in A (1808), op. 102 nos. 1 and 2, in C and D (1815).

Arrangements include: string quintets op. 4 (1795, from Octet op. 103) and op 104 (1817, from piano trio op. 1 no. 3); Serenade for cello and piano op. 64 (c 1796, from Trio op. 3); Quintet for piano and

strings op. 16 (1801, from work for piano and wind); Piano trio op. 38 (1803, from second symphony).

PIANO: 32 sonatas, op. 2 nos. 1–3, in F minor, A and C (1795), op. 7 in Eb (1796), op. 10 nos. 1–3, in C minor, F and D (1798), op. 13 in C minor (Pathétique) (1799), op. 14 nos. 1 and 2 in E and G (1799), op. 22 in Bb (1800), op. 26 in Ab (1801), op. 27 nos. 1 and 2, in Eb and C# minor (Moonlight) (1801), op. 28 in D (Pastoral) (1801), op. 31 nos. 1–3, in G, D minor and Eb (1802), op. 49 nos. 1 and 2, in G minor and G (1802), op. 53 in C (Waldstein) (1804), op. 54 in F (1804), op. 57 in F minor (Appassionata) (1805), op. 78 in F#(1809), op. 79 in G (1809), op. 81a in Eb (Les Adieux) (1801), op. 90 in E minor (1814), op. 101 in A (1816), op. 106 in Bb (Hammerklavier) (1818), op. 109 in E (1820), op. 110 in Ab (1821), op. 111 in C minor (1822); Sonata in D for piano – four hands op. 6 (1797); three sets of bagatelles, op. 33 (1782–1802), op. 119 (1821), op. 126 (1824), 15 Variations and Fugue on a theme from Prometheus, (Eroica Variations) in Eb (1802), 32 variations in C minor (1807), six variations in D, op. 76 (1810), Fantasie in G minor, op. 77 (1810); 33 Variations on a Waltz by Diabelli, op. 120 (1819–23); Rondo a capriccio in G 'Rage over a lost Groschen', op. 129 (1826); Grosse Fuge op. 133 arranged for piano – four hands, op. 134 (1826).

SOLO VOICE: Scena and aria Ah! Perfido! for soprano and orchestra (1796), Adelaide for tenor and piano (1795–96), Six Gellert Songs op. 48 (1802); An die ferne Geliebte for tenor and piano (1816), 37 Scottish songs with piano trio accompaniment (1815–16).

Beffroy de Reigny, Louis Abel (b Lâon, 6 Nov 1757; d Paris, 17 Dec 1811), French playwright and composer. Known as 'Cousin Jacques', under which name he wrote satirical operettas popular during the Revolution, including Nicodème dans la lune, Nicodème aux enfers and La Petite Nanette.

Beggar's Opera, The ballad opera, produced London, Theatre in Lincoln's Inn Fields, 29 Jan 1728, consisting of a play by John Gay interspersed with songs. The music, popular tunes of the day but for the most part not folksongs, was arranged by John Christopher Pepusch, who also composed the overture. There have been several modern realizations, including one by Britten (1948).

Beginning of a Romance, The, Počátek románu, opera in one act by Janáček (libretto by J Tichý, after a story by G Preissová), composed 1891, produced Brno, 10 Feb 1894. Tonek romances the village beauty, Poluška.

Beglarian, Grant (b Tiblisi, 1 Dec 1927), Russian-born American composer. He was influenced by Copland and Finney. Emigrated to USA in 1947 and studied with Ross Lee Finney at the University of Michigan. He taught at the University of Southern California, LA, 1969–82.

Works include string quartet (1948), Symphony in Two Movements (1950), Divertimento for orchestra (1957), woodwind quintet (1966), Diversions for viola, cello and orchestra (1972), Sinfonia for strings (1974); To Manitou for soprano and orchestra (1976), Partita for Orchestra (1986).

There is no musical rule that I have not willingly sacrificed to dramatic effect.

Christoph Willibald Gluck,
Preface to Alceste, 1767

Begleitungsmusik (Schoenberg). ◊Accompaniment to a Film Scene.

Begnis, Giuseppe de (b Lugo, 1793; d New York, Aug 1849), Italian bass. He was a choirboy at Lugo, and made his first operatic appearance at Modena in 1813; created Dandini in La Cenerentola, Rome 1817, and went to Paris and London with his wife, 1819 and 1822; sang there in operas by Rossini, Mayr and Pacini (◊Ronzi de Begnis).

Behrens, Hildegard (b Varel, Oldenburg, 9 Feb 1937), German soprano. Debut Düsseldorf, 1971; repertory at this time included Fiordiligi, Marie and Katya Kabanová. CG 1976, Leonore; Salzburg 1977, Salome. A successful Brünnhilde at Bayreuth, 1983, and Isolde in the Bernstein recording of Tristan und Isolde. Other roles include

Tosca, Eva, Elsa and Agathe; Elektra at the NY Met., 1992.

Behrman, David (b 16 Aug 1937), Austrian-born American composer of electronic music. He studied at Harvard and with Pousseur and Stockhausen in Europe. He worked with John Cage and David Tudor in the 1970s, notably for the Merce Cunningham Dance Company.
Works include *Pools of Phase-locked Loops* (1972); *Cloud Music* (1979); *Indoor Geyser* (1981); *Orchestral Construction Set* (1984); *Inter-species Smalltalk* (1984); *Installation for La Villett* (1985); many albums of experimental music for CBS.

Being Beauteous cantata by Henze for soprano, harp and four cellos (text from Rimbaud), performed Berlin, 12 Apr 1964.

Beinum, Eduard van (b Arnhem, 3 Sept 1901; d Amsterdam, 13 Apr 1959), Dutch conductor. He studied with his brother and composition with Sem Dresden. After a post in Haarlem (1926) he became second conductor of the Concertgebouw Orchestra of Amsterdam (1931–38), an associate to Mengelberg in 1938 and his successor in 1945. He was best known in Beethoven and contemporary Dutch music. He toured Europe and America, and in 1956 became conductor of the LA PO, but resigned and returned to Europe, where he died.

Beirer, Hans (b Vienna, 23 Jun 1911; d Vienna, 24 Jun 1993), Austrian tenor. Debut Linz 1936. He sang at the Berlin Städtischen Oper, 1945–58 and later with the Stuttgart Co. He sang at Bayreuth from 1958 as Parsifal, Tristan and Tannhäuser. He sang Siegfried at the Paris Opéra in 1955 and was often heard at the Vienna Staatsoper: fps of Einem's *Der Besuch der alten Dame* (1971) and *Kabale und Liebe* (1976). Sang Aegisthus in film version of *Elektra*, 1981.

Bekker, Paul (b Berlin, 11 Sept 1882; d New York, 7 Mar 1937), German writer on music. He studied in Berlin and was at first a violinist in the Philharmonic Orchestra there. In 1906 he began to devote himself to music journalism and became critic to several papers; he was later operatic manager at Kassel and Wiesbaden. The Nazi regime drove him to the USA. He wrote on Beethoven, Wagner, Mahler, opera and modern composers, and was a champion of Mahler, Schoenberg, Schreker and Hindemith.

beklemmt German = 'oppressed'; a term used by Beethoven in the Cavatina of the string quartet op. 130.

Belaiev, Mitrofan Petrovich (b St Petersburg, 22 Feb 1836; d St Petersburg, 10 Jan 1904), Russian timber merchant and music amateur. He founded a publishing firm for the propagation of Russian music in 1885, publishing music by Rimsky-Korsakov, Borodin, Mussorgsky and others.

bel canto Italian = lit. 'beautiful song'; singing in the traditional Italian manner, with beautiful tone, perfect phrasing, clean articulation, etc. The art of bel canto culminated in Italy in the 19th c.

Beldemandis, Prosdocimus de (b Padua, *c* 1375; d Padua, 1428), Italian music scholar. Wrote treatises on music, published between 1404 and 1413, and was professor of mathematics and astronomy at Padua in 1422.

Belfagor opera by Respighi (libretto by C Guastalla, based on a comedy by E L Morselli), produced Milan, La Scala, 26 Apr 1923. Candida is made to marry Belfagor, the Devil in disguise.

Belhomme, Hypolite (b Paris, 1854; d Nice, 16 Jan 1923), French bass. Debut Paris, Opéra-Comique, 1879, and sang there until 1916; appeared there in the fps of *Les Contes d'Hoffmann* (1881) and *Louise* (1913). He sang also at Marseilles and Brussels. Other roles included Pistol, Kecal and Benoit.

Belisario opera by Donizetti (libretto by S Cammarano), produced Venice, Teatro La Fenice, 4 Feb 1836. A Roman general blinded and exiled after being accused of his son's murder.

Belkin, Boris (b Sverdlovssk, 26 Jan 1948), Russian violinist. After making his first public appearance at the age of six, he later studied at the Moscow Conservatory and emigrated to Israel 1974. He made his western debut under Mehta, gave further concerts with the Berlin and Los Angeles POs and the Cleveland Orchestra, and played with the London and Royal POs 1987–89. Recordings include concertos by Paganini, Prokofiev, Sibelius and Shostakovich.

Bell, Joshua (b Bloomington, IN, 9 Dec 1967), American violinist. He studied with Josef Gingold and appeared with the Philadelphia Orchestra 1982, aged 14, and has since played with all the major orchestras of Europe and the USA, notably in works by Beethoven, Lalo, Tchaikovsky and Wieniawski. He made his London debut 1987 and premiered the concerto by Nicholas Maw in 1993.

'Bell Anthem' the name once given to Purcell's anthem *Rejoice in the Lord alway*, composed *c* 1682–85. The instrumental introduction contains descending scales resembling the ringing of church bells.

Belle Hélène, La, *The Fair Helen*, operetta by Offenbach (libretto by H Meilhac and L Halévy), produced Paris, Théâtre des Variétés, 17 Dec 1864. A satirical version of the myth.

Bellérophon opera by Lully (libretto by T Corneille with (?) B de Fontenelle and Boileau), produced Paris, Opéra, 31 Jan 1679. Bellérophon threatened by monster Chimaera after he rejects the wife of King Proteus.

Belletti, Giovanni Battista (b Sarzana, 17 Feb 1813; d Sarzana, 27 Dec 1890), Italian baritone. Studied at Bologna and made his debut at Stockholm in 1834 as Rossini's Figaro under the patronage of the sculptor Byström, and then sang with Jenny Lind, London, Her Majesty's Theatre, 1848, in the first local performance of *Attila*, *L'Elisir d'Amore* and *Don Pasquale*.

Bell'haver, Vincenzo (d Venice, ? Sept 1587), Italian composer. From 30 Dec 1586 he was second organist of St Mark's Venice, in succession to Andrea Gabrielli. His works include Magnificats, motets and madrigals.

Belli, Domenico (d Florence, buried 5 May 1627), Italian 16th–17th-c. composer. Probably in the service of the Duke of Parma; he taught at the church of San Lorenzo at Florence, 1610–13. Pub. a book of airs for one and two voices with chitarrone accompaniment, and another of five interludes for Tasso's *Aminta*, called *Orfeo dolente*.

Belli, Girolamo (b Argenta near Ferrara, 1552; d ? Argenta, *c* 1620), Italian composer. Pupil of Luzzaschi; singer at the Gonzaga court at Mantua; in Rome in 1582. Pub. several books of madrigals (six surviving) as well as Masses, psalms and *Sacrae cantiones*.

Belli, Giulio (b Longiano, *c* 1560; d ? Imola, *c* 1621), Italian monk and composer. Held various church appointments at Imola, Venice, Montagnana, Osimo, Forli and Padua. He returned to Imola in 1611. Wrote madrigals and other secular vocal works at first, but (?) only church

Bell *Violinist Joshua Bell has performed with all the major American orchestras in addition to making tours of Europe. He has recorded several 19th-century concertos and has partnered pianist Jean-Yves Thibaudet and the Takacs Quartet in chamber music.*

music later, including numerous Masses, motets and psalms (influenced by Palestrina).

Bellincioni, Gemma (b Como, 18 Aug 1864; d Naples, 23 Apr 1950), Italian soprano. Made her first appearance at Naples in 1879 and sang with great success in Italy and on tour in Europe. In 1895 she first visited England, as Santuzza and Carmen, and in 1899 S America. Other roles included Fedora, Tosca and Salome. A strong stage presence made her a favourite in *verismo* roles.

Carve in your head by letters of brass: An Opera must draw tears, cause horror, bring death, by means of song.

Vincenzo Bellini, in a letter, 1834

Bellini, Vincenzo (b Catania, Sicily, 3 Nov 1801; d Puteaux near Paris, 23 Sept 1835), Italian composer. He was a master of melody and dramatic meaning, bringing Italian opera forward from the roulades of Rossini to the genuine emotion of Donizetti and Verdi.

His father, an organist, was enabled with the help of a Sicilian nobleman to send him to study with Zingarelli at the Naples Conservatory, where he met Donizetti and Mercadante. In 1825 his first opera (*Adelson e Salvini*) was produced, while he was still a student, and attracted the attention of Barbaia, who commissioned him to write a second (*Bianca e Gernando*), which he produced at the Teatro San Carlo in 1826. Its success induced Barbaia to ask for another opera (*Il pirata*) for the La Scala at Milan; this was produced there in 1827 with Rubini in the cast. It was also successfully performed in Paris, and three other operas followed, at Milan, Parma and Venice, before he attained full maturity in *La sonnambula*, brought out at Milan in 1831, with Maria Malibran as the sleepwalking heroine. *Norma* followed in Dec of the same year, with Pasta in the title role. This opera marks the culmination of Bellini's style, with its long and elegiac melodic line and superbly crafted dramatic tension. At first scornful of Bellini (why have Romeo sung by a mezzo?), Berlioz came to admire him, and Wagner too learned from the example in terms of musical and dramatic cohesion.

In 1833 Bellini went to London and Paris, where Rossini advised him to write a work for the Théâtre Italien. This was *I puritani*, produced there in 1835, with Giulia Grisi, Rubini, Tamburini and Lablache in the cast. It was brought to London the same year for Grisi's benefit performance. Bellini went to stay with an English friend at Puteaux, at whose house he was taken ill and died. In the

Bellini *The composer Vincenzo Bellini (1801–1835). Famous for his long phrases, Bellini's melodies are also closely bound to the text. Since a period of neglect earlier this century, his operas have regained popularity thanks largely to singers such as Maria Callas.*

years preceding World War II, Bellini's operas fell into neglect but since then singers, including Callas, Sutherland, and Caballé, have helped to restore their beauties to the public.

Works include operas *Adelson e Salvini*, *Bianca e Gernando*, *Il pirata*, *La straniera* (1829), *Zaira*, *I Capuleti e i Montecchi* (1830, based on Shakespeare's sources for *Romeo and Juliet*), *La sonnambula*, *Norma*, *Beatrice di Tenda* (1833), *I puritani* (1835); church music, songs; symphonies.

Belloc, Teresa Giorgi (b San Benigno near Turin, 2 Jul 1784; d San Giorgio Cavanese, 13 May 1855), Italian soprano of French descent. Made her first appearances at the Teatro Regio, Turin, in 1801 in operas by Pacini and Mayr. Later heard in Rossini roles, including Tancredi and Isabella.

Bells of Zlonice, The symphony no. 1 in C minor by Dvořák; composed 1865 as op. 3 but lost until 1923. Fp Prague, 4 Oct 1936.

Bells, The poem for orchestra, chorus and soloists by Rakhmaninov, op. 35 (text by Edgar Allan Poe, trans. by K Balmont); composed 1913, fp St Petersburg, 30 Nov 1913. Revived 1936 and performed Sheffield, 21 Oct 1936, conductor Henry Wood.

Bellugi, Piero (b Florence, 14 July 1924), Italian conductor. He studied in Europe and at Tanglewood, MA. He was music director of the Oakland and Portland SOs (1955–61), and permanent conductor of the RAI Orchestra at Turin. Guest at La Scala from 1961 (debut with Handel's *Xerxes*) and in Vienna, Rome, Paris and Berlin. Concert repertory includes Mahler and Schoenberg.

belly the surface of string instruments, also sometimes the sound-board of the piano.

Belohlávek, Jiří (b Prague, 24 Feb 1946), Czech conductor. He studied in Prague with Celibidache and was conductor of the Brno State PO 1971–77; chief conductor of the Prague SO 1977–90, principal of the Czech Philharmonic 1990–92; principal guest conductor, BBC SO 1995–. Guest with the Berlin and New York Philharmonics, Vienna SO and City of Birmingham SO; music by Mahler and Zemlinsky with the BBC PO at the 1993 Prom Concerts, London.

A Selection of

Bellini

Oboe Concerto	c 1825
Il pirata	1827
Zaira	1829
I Capuleti e i Montecchi	1830
La sonnambula	1831
Norma	1831
Beatrice di Tenda	1833
I puritani	1835

Belshazzar oratorio by Handel (words by Charles Jennens), produced London, King's Theatre, Haymarket, 27 Mar 1745.

Belshazzar's Feast cantata by William Walton (words from the Bible arranged by O Sitwell), produced Leeds Festival, 8 Oct 1931.

Incidental music by Sibelius for a play by H Procopé, fp Helsinki, 7 Nov 1906. Orchestral Suite op. 51 in four movements fp Helsinki, 25 Sept 1907.

Bemberg, Herman (b Paris, 29 Mar 1859; d Berne, 21 Jul 1931), French composer. Pupil of Dubois and Massenet at the Paris Conservatory.

Works include operas *Le Baiser de Suzon* (1888) and *Elaine* (CG, 1892); cantata *La Mort de Jeanne d'Arc*; recitation with accompaniment *La Ballade du désespéré*; many songs including *Aime-moi* and *Chant hindou*.

bémol French, *bemolle* Italian = 'flat'; the sign ♭.

Beňačková, Gabriela (b Bratislava, 25 Mar 1947), Czech soprano. Opera debut Prague, 1970, as Prokofiev's Natasha. She has sung Jenůfa and other roles by Janáček in Prague and Vienna. Tatyana in Moscow and at CG (debut 1979). In 1984 she was acclaimed as Smetana's Libuse, at the National Theatre, Prague. Her Marguerite, in a production of *Faust* at the Vienna Staatsoper by Ken Russell, was well received. Other roles include Desdemona, Fidelio (Salzburg, 1990) and Katya Kabanova (NY Met., 1991).

Benda Bohemian family of musicians:

1. Franz (František) Benda (b Staré Benátky, bap. 22 Nov 1709; d Nowawes near Potsdam, 7 Mar 1786), violinist and composer. After being a chorister in Prague he travelled widely in his youth until in 1733 he joined the service of the Crown Prince of Prussia. He succeeded J G Graun as *Konzertmeister* to the same patron, now Frederick II, in 1771. His works include trio sonatas; concertos; sonatas, studies, etc., for violin. His daughter Juliane married Reichardt.

2. Georg Anton (Jiří Antonín) Benda (b Staré Benátky, bap. 30 Jun 1722; d Köstritz, 6 Nov 1795), harpsichordist, oboist and composer. Entered the service of Frederick II of Prussia in 1742, appointed *Kapellmeister* to the Duke of Gotha 1750. He retired in 1778. His most influential works were the melodramas (spoken words to instrumental music) *Ariadne auf Naxos* (1775), *Medea* and *Pygmalion* (1779). Other works include *Singspiele*: *Der Dorfjahrmarkt*, *Romeo und Julia* (1776), *Walder*, *Der Holzhauer* (1778); symphonies; concertos; keyboard music.

3. Friedrich Wilhelm Heinrich Benda (b Potsdam, 15 Jul 1745; d Potsdam, 19 Jun 1814), violinist and composer, son of 1. In the service of the Prussian court, 1765–1810, and wrote *Singspiele*, including *Orpheus* (1785) and *Alceste* (1786), concertos, sonatas.

4. Friedrich Ludwig Benda (b Gotha, bap. 4 Sept 1752; d Königsberg, 20 or 27 Mar 1792), violinist and composer. Director of music in Hamburg 1780–82, *Konzertmeister* at Königsberg from 1789. His works include the opera *Der Barbier von Seville* (based on Beaumarchais, 1776) and two others; oratorio; cantatas; instrumental music.

Bender, Paul (b Driedorf, Westerwald, 28 Jul 1875; d Munich, 25 Nov 1947), German bass. From 1903 he made a great reputation at the Munich Opera; first visited London in 1914, as Amfortas in the first stage performance of *Parsifal* in Britain, and again from 1924 onwards. Afterwards he became a leading bass at the Met. Opera in NY, where he sang Hagen, Ochs and Osmin, but he returned to Munich to teach at the State School of Music.

Bendl, Karel (b Prague, 16 Apr 1838; d Prague, 20 Sept 1897), Bohemian composer and conductor. After various posts in foreign countries as a conductor he worked in Prague from 1865 to 1878 and from 1881. He gave much encouragement to Dvořák. His works, partly in a traditional style and partly influenced by Smetana, include 11 operas, choral and orchestral works, and church and chamber music.

Benedetti, Michele (b Loreto, 17 Oct 1778), Italian bass. Debut Naples, 1811, in Spontini's *La Vestale*. He often sang in the fps of Rossini's operas for Naples and created Moses (1818); also appeared in *Otello*, *Armida*, *Ermione La donna del lago* and *Zelmira*.

Benedicite work by Vaughan Williams for soprano, chorus and orchestra; composed 1929, fp Dorking, 2 May 1930, conductor Vaughan Williams.

Benedict, Julius (b Stuttgart, 27 Nov 1804; d London, 5 Jun 1885), German-born English conductor and composer. He was a pupil of Hummel and Weber, and met Beethoven with the latter in Vienna in 1823, when he was appointed conductor at the Kärntnertortheater. Next he went to Naples, where he produced his first Italian opera in 1829. In 1835 he went to Paris and to London, where he remained for the rest of his life. He conducted a great deal in London, both opera and concerts, and was conductor of the Norwich Festival, 1845–78, and of the Liverpool Philharmonic Soc., 1876–80. Knighted 1871.

Works include operas *Giacinta ed Ernesto*, *I Portoghesi in Goa* (1830), *Un anno ed un giorno* (1836), *The Gypsy's Warning*, *The Brides of Venice* (1844), *The Crusaders*, *The Lily of Killarney*, *The Bride of Song* (1864); two symphonies; two piano concertos; five cantatas, etc.

Benelli, Antonio Peregrino (b Forli, 5 Sept 1771; d Börnichen, Saxony, 16 Aug 1830), Italian tenor and composer. He was a pupil of Mattei in Bologna, and first appeared as a singer in 1790 in Naples, where his opera *Partenope* was produced in 1798. Other works include church music and a treatise on singing.

Benet, John, English 15th-c. composer. Wrote Masses and other church music. He was a contemporary of Dunstable, to whom one of his Mass cycles is ascribed.

Benevoli, Orazio (b Rome, 19 Apr 1605; d Rome, 17 June 1672), Italian composer. Held appointments at the churches of San Luigi de' Francesi and Santa Maria Maggiore in Rome, the former with an interruption 1644–46, when he was at the Austrian court in Vienna. In 1646 he became *maestro di cappella* at the Vatican.

Works include Masses, motets and other church music, much of it for several choirs in a large number of parts. The celebrated 53-part *Missa salisburgensis* formerly attributed to him, is probably by Biber.

Bells are profane, a tune may be religious.
Ben Jonson, *The Alchemist*, 1610

Beni Mora Oriental Suite in E minor, op. 29 no. 1 for orchestra by Holst. Composed 1910 after a visit to Algeria: last of three movements is titled 'In the Street of the Ouled Naïls'; fp London, 1 May 1912, conductor Holst.

Benjamin, Arthur (b Sydney, 18 Sept 1893; d London, 9 Apr 1960), Australian pianist and composer. The influence of Latin American dance rhythms remained important throughout his life. He was educated at Brisbane and studied at the RCM in London, where he later became professor. After fighting in the 1914–18 war, he returned to Australia to teach piano at the Sydney Conservatory 1919–20, but having developed as a composer, settled in London. From 1930 to 1936 he lived in Vancouver.

Works include operas *The Devil take her* (1931), *Prima Donna* (1933), *A Tale of Two Cities* (after Dickens) (1950), *Tartuffe*; film music including *An Ideal Husband* (after Oscar Wilde); symphonic suite *Light Music* and *Overture to an Italian Comedy* for orchestra; *Romantic Fantasy* for violin, viola and orchestra, violin concerto (1932), concertino for piano and orchestra, chamber music, songs.

Benjamin, George (b London, 31 Jan 1960), English composer and pianist. He studied with Messiaen and Yvonne Loriod in Paris from 1974, Paris Conservatory 1977, and with Alexander Goehr at Cambridge. With *Ringed by the Flat Horizon* (1980) he became the youngest composer ever to have a work performed at the Prom concerts. At the 1983 Aldeburgh Festival he gave the fp of Britten's *Sonatina Romantica* (1940). Returning to France 1984–87 he availed himself of the electronic music studios at IRCAM.

Works include *At First Light*, for chamber orchestra (1982); *A Mind of Winter*, for soprano and ensemble; violin sonata (1977), octet (1978), duo for cello and piano (1980); *Meditations on Haydn's Name*, for piano (1982); *Antara* for orchestra with electronics

(1985–87), *Jubilation* for orchestra and groups of children (1985), *Cascade* for orchestra (1990), *Upon Silence* for mezzo and five viols (1990); *Helix* (1992) and *Sudden Time* for orchestra (1993).

Bennet, John (b ? Lancashire), English 16th–17th-c. composer. Pub. a book of madrigals in 1599 and contributed others to collections, including *The Triumphes of Oriana*.

Bennett, Richard Rodney (b Broadstairs, Kent, 29 Mar 1936), English composer and pianist. Studied at the RAM with Lennox Berkeley and Howard Ferguson, and in Paris with Boulez. Influenced by Bartók, he has also used serial techniques but also writes in a lighter vein.

Works include operas *The Ledge* (1961), *The Mines of Sulphur* (1963), *A Penny for a Song* (1966), *Victory* (after Conrad) (1970); ballet *Isadora* (1981); symphonies; *Aubade* for orchestra; piano concerto (1968), oboe concerto, *Anniversaries* for orchestra (1982); *Love Songs* for tenor and orchestra (texts by e e cummings) (1985); four string quartets (1952–64); *Calendar* for chamber ensemble; three symphonies (1965, 1967, 1987); Sinfonietta (1984), *Dream Dancing* (1986) and *Celebration* (1992) for orchestra; *Memento* for flute and strings (1983); concertos for harpsichord (1980), clarinet (1987), saxophone (for Stan Getz, 1990) and for trumpet and wind band (1993); vocal music, and film, radio and television music.

Bennett, Robert Russell (b Kansas City, 15 Jun 1894; d New York, 17 Aug 1981), American pianist, conductor, composer and orchestrator. Studied with his parents and later with Nadia Boulanger in Paris. He played in his father's orchestra as a youth and earned a living as an arranger and orchestrator, becoming one of the most successful in the business; he offered to re-write Stravinsky's *Scènes de ballet* but the Russian declined the honour.

Works include opera *Maria Malibran* (1935); ballet-operetta *Endymion* (1927); film music *Sights and Sounds; Abraham Lincoln Symphony* (1931), *Charlestown Rhapsody* (1926), etc for orchestra; March for two pianos and orchestra; orchestrations *Show Boat* (1927), *Oklahoma!* (1943), *South Pacific* (1949), *My Fair Lady* (1956), *The Sound of Music* (1959).

Bennett, William Sterndale (b Sheffield, 13 Apr 1816; d London, 1 Feb 1875), English pianist and composer. Chorister at King's College, Cambridge, and student at the RAM in London. He then went to Leipzig, where he made friends with Mendelssohn. Schumann dedicated his *Études symphoniques* for piano to him. He conducted the first English performance of Bach's *St Matthew Passion*, 1854. Professor of music at Cambridge University, 1856–75. Principal of the RAM, 1866–75. Knighted 1871.

Works include incidental music to Sophocles' *Ajax* (1872); cantata *The May Queen* (1858), odes for the International Exhibition (Tennyson) and the Cambridge Installation of a Chancellor (Kingsley); anthems; six symphonies (1832–64), overtures *The Naiads* and *The Wood-Nymphs*, fantasy-overture on Moore's *Paradise and the Peri*; five piano concertos (1832–38); piano pieces, songs.

Benoît, Camille (b Roanne, Loire, 7 Dec 1851; d Paris, 1 Jul 1923), French writer on music and composer. A pupil of Franck and disciple of Wagner; he arranged Berlioz's *Roméo et Juliette* for piano duet. He was on the staff of the Louvre museum and was curator from 1895.

Works include opera *Cléopâtre* (1889); symphonic poem *Merlin l'enchanteur*; *Eleison* for solo voices, chorus and orchestra; Epithalamium for Anatole France's *Noces corinthiennes*.

Benoit, Peter (Léonard Léopold) (b Harlebeke, 17 Aug 1834; d Antwerp, 8 Mar 1901), Belgian composer. Pupil of Fétis at the Brussels Conservatory. He became conductor at a Flemish theatre and was keenly interested in Flemish national music as distinct from that influenced by French composers. He travelled in Germany and visited Paris, but tended more and more towards an indigenous type of music. His first opera was produced 1857.

Works include French opera *Le Roi des aulnes* (on Goethe's *Erl King*) (1859); Flemish operas *The Mountain Village*, *Isa*, *Pompeja*; incidental music to Flemish plays; Te Deum, *Messe solennelle*, Requiem; oratorios *Lucifer* (1865) and *The Scheldt* (1868); *Petite Cantate de Noël* and many Flemish cantatas, etc.

Bentzon, Nils Viggo (b Copenhagen, 24 Aug 1919), Danish composer.

Studied piano with his mother and composition with Jeppesen.

Works include four operas, including *Faust III* (after Goethe, Kafka and Joyce, 1964); 15 symphonies (1942–80); eight piano concertos, four violin concertos, much chamber music, including chamber concerto, for 11 instruments, a chamber symphony, nine string quartets (1940–76), sonata for solo cello; 11 piano sonatas, *Propostae Novae* for two pianos; vocal music, including *Bonjour Max Ernst*, cantata for chorus and orchestra (1961).

Benucci, Francesco (b Florence, c 1745; d Florence, 5 Apr 1824), Italian bass. He was engaged for Vienna in 1783, and was Mozart's original Figaro there in 1786; also sang in operas by Salieri, Paisiello, Cimarosa and Galuppi.

Benvenuto Cellini opera by Berlioz (libretto by L de Wailly and A Barbier, based on Cellini's autobiography), produced Paris, Opéra, 10 Sept 1838. Boastful sculptor beats Pope's deadline.

Berberian, Cathy (b Attleboro, MA, 4 Jul 1925; d Rome, 6 Mar 1983), American soprano of Armenian parentage. She achieved first success in 1958 with a performance of *Fontana Mix* by John Cage; soon became associated with avant garde music requiring unconventional vocal gymnastics; sang in many performances of works by Berio, to whom she was married 1950–66. In 1983 she sang her own version of the *Internationale* for Italian TV to mark the centenary of the death of Karl Marx; her own works include *Stripsody* and *Morsicath(h)y*.

berceuse French = 'cradle song'; although strictly speaking a song, a berceuse may just as well be an instrumental piece.

Berceuse élégiaque piano piece by Busoni, composed 1909 and added to the *Elegien* of 1907; orchestral version of 1909 is subtitled *Des Mannes Wiegenlied am Sarge seine Mutter/The man's lullaby at his mother's coffin*: Busoni's mother died on 3 Oct 1909. Fp conducted by Mahler at his last concert, NY, 21 Feb 1911.

Berchem, Jachet de (b Berchem, c 1505; d ? Ferrara, c 1565), Flemish composer, not to be confused with Jachet of Mantua. Probably organist to the ducal court at Ferrara in 1555. He wrote church music, madrigals for four and five voices, French *chansons*, etc. He is credited with being the first with a madrigal cycle, his *Capriccio* is a setting of stories from Ariosto's *Orlando furioso*.

Berenice opera by Handel (libretto by A Salvi), produced London, CG, 18 May 1737. Egyptian queen in love problems before marriage to Alexander; a complex plot involving politics, jealousy, and anger resolves happily in the end.

Opera by Perti (libretto ditto), produced Villa Pratolino near Florence, Sept 1709.

Berenice, che fai? Italian cantata by Haydn for soprano and orchestra (text from Metastasio's *Antigono*), composed May 1795.

THE OPERA

Benvenuto Cellini

A two-act opera by Hector Berlioz, first performed in 1838. Based on the autobiography of Cellini, it is set in Rome in 1532.

I. Cellini (tenor) has been commissioned by the Pope to cast a bronze statue of Perseus. In love with Teresa (soprano), daughter of the Papal Treasurer Balducci (bass), Cellini plans to elope with her during the Carnival. The plan is overheard by Fieramosca (baritone), a sculptor who also loves Teresa. Cellini and his apprentice Ascanio (mezzo-soprano) attend the Carnival disguised as monks and in the confusion of an attempted abduction of Teresa by followers of Fieramosca, Pompeo (baritone) is stabbed by Cellini.

II. Cardinal Salviati tells Cellini that his life will be forfeit for his crimes (abduction and murder) if the Pope's statue is not completed by midnight. To make Cellini's task impossible, Fieramosca engineers a strike of foundry workers, but Cellini throws into the crucible all the precious metal in his studio. The statue is cast just in time to earn a Papal pardon.

Berenstadt, Gaetano, Italian 17th–18th-c. bass singer of German descent. The first record of his appearing in London dates from 1717. He sang in the fps of Handel's *Ottone, Flavio* and *Giulio Cesare*.

Berezovsky, Maximus Sosnovich (b Glukhov, 27 Oct 1745; d St Petersburg, 2 Apr 1777), Russian composer. He was a pupil at the academy in Kiev, later a singer in the service of the court. In 1765 went to Italy to study under Martini. On his return to Russia, unable to secure an appointment, he finally cut his throat. His most important contribution was to church music; he also wrote an opera, *Demofoonte* (1773, the first by a Russian to be given in Italy) and other works.

Berezovsky, Nikolai (b St Petersburg, 17 May 1900; d New York, 27 Aug 1953), Russian (Americanized) violinist and composer who wrote the children's opera *Babar the Elephant*. He learnt music in the Imperial Chapel at St Petersburg, became a violinist in the opera orchestras at Saratov and Moscow and conductor at the School of Modern Art there; but emigrated to USA in 1922, where he continued his studies, played in the NYSO, became a member of the Coolidge quartet and appeared as concert and broadcasting conductor.

Works include four symphonies (1931–43), *Sinfonietta* and *Hebrew Suite* for orchestra; waltzes for string orchestra; violin concerto (1931), Fantasy for two pianos and orchestra; *Concerto lirico* for cello and orchestra, *Toccata, Variations and Finale* for string quartet and orchestra; cantata *Gilgamesh* (1947); string quartet, two woodwind quintets, sextet for clarinet, piano and strings, suite for seven brass instruments.

Berg, Alban (b Vienna, 9 Feb 1885; d Vienna, 24 Dec 1935), Austrian composer. Self-taught from the age of 15, he was a pupil of Schoenberg 1904–10. Schoenberg's influence on him was profound and Berg continued a devoted admirer to the end. The nature of this influence may be measured as Berg passes from the extended tonality of his early works to atonality and, later, serialism. His use of serial technique is distinctive in that he does not avoid tonal references (e.g. the violin concerto). Accordingly, he remains the most accessible member of the Second Viennese School. He was also a gifted writer. In 1911 he married Helene Nahowski. His first major work, the string quartet op. 3, dates from the same year.

His music was known only to a small circle until the 1925 production of *Wozzeck*. The Chamber Concerto and Lyric Suite, which followed shortly after, incorporate complex formal patterns,

Berg *The composer Alban Berg (1885–1935). Regarded as the most 'human' of the Second Viennese School composers, Berg adapted the normally strict 12-note procedures to suit his own needs. In the* Lyric Suite *and other works he enciphered his initials and showed an obsession with numbers.*

numerical puzzles and autobiographical allusions. He was a friend of Alma Mahler and the death of her daughter, Manon, occasioned his last completed work, the violin concerto. Dedicated 'To the Memory of an Angel', Berg wrote the concerto as a Requiem for Manon, yet in its poignant lyricism, quoting the Bach chorale *Es ist Genug/It is enough*, it is the composer's own last testament. His second opera, *Lulu*, was begun in 1929 but left unfinished after his death and not performed in the full, three-act version until 1979.

Works include OPERAS: *Wozzeck* (after Büchner) (1917–22; produced Berlin, 1925) and *Lulu* (after Wedekind) (1929–35; two acts produced Zurich, 1937, act 3 realized by F Cerha, performed Paris, 1979).

SONGS, AND VOICE WITH ORCHESTRA: 70 early Lieder, to texts by Ibsen, Altenberg, Rückert, Heine, Rilke and others; *Seven Early Songs* for voice and piano (1905–08, orchestral version 1928); *Four Songs* op. 2 (1909–10); *Five Altenberglieder* for voice and orchestra (1912, fp Rome, 1953); *Three Fragments from Wozzeck*, op. 7 (fp Frankfurt, 1924, conductor Scherchen); *Der Wein*, concert aria to text by Baudelaire (1929); *Lulu-Symphonie* for soprano and orchestra (1934).

ORCHESTRAL: *Three Pieces*, op. 6 (1914–15, revised 1929; fp Oldenburg, 1930); *Three Movements from the Lyric Suite*, arranged for string orchestra (1929; fp Berlin, 1929); Chamber Concerto for piano, violin and 13 wind instruments (1923–24; fp Berlin, 1927); violin concerto (1935; fp Barcelona 1936).

CHAMBER: piano sonata op. 1 (1907–08); Variations on an original theme for piano (1908); string quartet op. 3 (1910); *Four Pieces* for clarinet and piano (1913); *Lyric Suite* for string quartet (1925–26; fp Vienna, 1927, performed with vocal finale NY, 1979); adagio from Chamber Concerto arranged for violin, clarinet and piano (1935).

Berg
A biographical note

With *Wozzeck* Berg achieved the greatest public success of the Second Viennese School. While visiting Prague a few months before the premiere of the opera, he fell in love with the wife of his host, Hanna Fuchs-Robettin, sister of the novelist Franz Werfel. Although their relationship apparently remained platonic, Berg's feelings for Hanna were a constant creative stimulus in the last decade of his life. The six movements of the Lyric Suite for string quartet make great play with what he regarded as his own fateful number (23), interwoven with the numeral 10, designated as Hanna's number. The original last movement of the quartet contained a setting for mezzo-soprano of *De Profundis clamavi*, from Baudelaire's *Fleurs du Mal*. Berg's widow Helene had suppressed the setting, not wishing her husband's love for Hanna to be revealed, and it was not performed until 1979. In the same year the complete 3-act version of Berg's *Lulu* was premiered in Paris. Helene had imposed a ban on the completion of the third act when she realized that the fatal, alluring Lulu was in some respects a portrait of Hanna. The premiere of the opera's first two acts had taken place 18 months after Berg's death in 1935; in spite of an official death date of 24 December, Berg's relatives insisted that he expired on the feared and fated 23rd hour of the 23rd day.

A Selection of

Berg

7 Early Songs	1905–8
String Quartet op. 3	1910
Altenberglieder	1912
Three Orchestral Pieces	1914–15
Wozzeck	1917–22
Chamber Concerto	1923–4
Lyric Suite for string quartet	1925
Der Wein	1929
Lulu	1929–35
Violin Concerto	1935

Berg, (Carl) Natanael (b Stockholm, 9 Feb 1879; d Stockholm, 14 Oct 1957), Swedish composer. Studied at the Stockholm Conservatory and in Paris and Vienna.

Works include operas *Leila* (after Byron's *Giaour*) (1910), *Engelbrekt* (1928), *Judith* (after Hebbel's drama) (1935), *Birgitta*, *Genoveva* (1946); five symphonies; symphonic poems; violin concerto; piano concerto; two string quartets, piano quintet.

When I compose I always feel I am like Beethoven; only afterwards do I become aware that at best I am only Bizet.

Berg, in Adorno, *Alban Berg*, 1968

---

bergamasca an Italian dance from Bergamo at least as old as the 16th c., called bergomask by Shakespeare.

Berganza, Teresa (b Madrid, 16 Mar 1935), Spanish mezzo. Debut Aix 1957, as Dorabella. Glyndebourne 1958, Cherubino; CG 1960, Rosina, and 1976 with co. of La Scala as Cenerentola. US debut 1958, Dallas; NY Met. from 1967. Edinburgh 1977 as Carmen. Other roles include Isabella, Octavia and Cesti's Orontea; sang Carmen in Paris, 1989, and in Madrid, 1991. Also successful in song recitals.

Berger, Arthur (b New York, 15 May 1912), American composer. Studied with Piston at Harvard University, with Pirro at the Sorbonne in Paris, also with Pierre Lalo and Paul Valéry there, and composition with Nadia Boulanger; later influences included Babbitt and Webern. He became music editor of the NY *Sun*.

Works include *Slow Dance* for strings; serenade for chamber orchestra (1944); three pieces for string quartet, wind quartet, two movements for violin and cello; ballet *Entertainment Piece* and other works for piano; *Words for Music Perhaps* (Yeats) and other songs, etc.

Berger, Erna (b Dresden, 19 Oct 1900; d Essen, 14 Jun 1990), German soprano. Salzburg 1932–54 as Blonde and Zerlina. CG 1934–51 as Queen of Night, Constanze, Sophie, Gilda. NY Met. 1949–51. Sang Lieder until 1968, after retiring from the stage in 1955.

Berger, Rudolf (b Brno, 17 Apr 1874; d New York, 27 Feb 1915), Czech baritone, later tenor. Debut Brno, 1896. He sang at the Berlin Hofoper from 1898 and appeared at Bayreuth 1901–08 as Amfortas, Klingsor and Gunther. After singing at CG, Vienna and Paris he made his NY Met. debut in 1914, as Siegmund. Jochanaan was among his 96 baritone roles, and he had 18 tenor roles.

Berger, Theodor (b Traismauer, 18 May 1905; d Vienna, 21 Aug 1992), Austrian composer. He studied at the Vienna Academy, and was much influenced by his teachers, Korngold and Franz Schmidt.

Works include *Malincolia* for strings (1938), *Homerische Symphonie* (1948), *La Parola* for orchestra (1955), *Symphonischer Triglyph*, on themes by Schubert (1957), *Divertimento* for chorus, wind and percussion (1968), violin concerto (1963); two string quartets (1930–31).

Berghaus, Ruth (b Dresden, 2 Jul 1927; d Berlin, 25 Jan 1996), German stage director. She married Paul Dessau and directed his *Verurteilung des Lukullus* at the Berlin Staatsoper, 1960. Director of the Berliner Ensemble 1971–77 and producer at the Frankfurt Opera from 1980 (*Parsifal*, *Les Troyens* and the *Ring*, 1982–87). She was noted for iconoclastic ideas.

Bergknappen, Die, *The Miners*, one-act Singspiel by Umlauf (libretto by P Weidmann), produced Vienna, Burgtheater, on the opening of its career as a national German opera, 17 Feb 1778. Old Walcher competes with young Fritz for the affections of Sophie; Walcher yields after Fritz rescues him in a mine.

Berglund, Joel (b Torsåker, 4 Jun 1903; d Stockholm, 21 Jan 1985), Swedish baritone. Debut Stockholm, 1929. Bayreuth 1942, Dutchman. NY Met. 1946, Sachs. Other Wagner roles in Europe and N and S America were Wotan, Kurwenal and Gurnemanz. Also sang Boccanegra, Philip II and Scarpia. Directed Stockholm Opera, 1949–52.

Berglund, Paavo (b Helsinki, 14 Apr 1929), Finnish conductor. After an early career as a violinist, co-founded the Helsinki Chamber Orchestra in 1953; principal conductor Helsinki Radio SO from 1962, Helsinki PO 1975–79. Has conducted the Bournemouth SO from 1964, music director 1972–79; associated with revival of Sibelius's early *Kullervo* Symphony. Principal guest conductor Scottish National Orchestra from 1981. Recordings include symphonies by Shostakovich.

Bergmann, Carl (b Ebersbach, Saxony, 12 Apr 1821; d New York, 10 Aug 1876), German cellist and conductor. Went to USA in 1850 and did much to establish orchestral music there. He was conductor of the NY Philharmonic Society 1866–76.

Bergonzi Italian family of violin makers who worked in Cremona:

1. Carlo Bergonzi (b ? Cremona, *c* 1683; d Cremona, 1747). He began to work independently about 1716 and created his best instruments in the 1730s, rivalling Guarnieri and Stradivari.

2. Michelangelo Bergonzi (b ? Cremona, 1722; d ? Cremona, after 1758), son of 1.

Bergonzi, Carlo (b Parma, 13 Jul 1924), Italian tenor. Debut 1948 as Rossini's Figaro (a baritone role); tenor debut Bari, 1951, as Chénier. La Scala, Milan, from 1953. US debut 1955, Chicago; NY Met. 1956, Radames. CG from 1962 as Alvaro, Manrico, Riccardo, Cavaradossi. His voice was beautiful and melodious, and he was noted for his tasteful interpretations. He retired 1992.

Bergsma, William (b Oakland, CA, 1 Apr 1921; d Seattle, 18 Mar 1994), American composer. He studied at Stanford University and the Eastman School of Music under Hanson and Bernard Rogers, and after winning many awards became teacher of composition at the Juilliard School NY.

Works include opera *The Wife of Martin Guerre* (1956); ballets *Paul Bunyan* (1938) and *Gold and the Señor Commandante* (1941); choral symphony; choral works; symphony for chamber orchestra; four string quartets (1942–70); songs.

Berio, Luciano (b Oneglia, 24 Oct 1925), Italian composer. He studied with Ghedini in Milan and with Dallapiccola in USA. He is one of the most active composers of electronic music and has worked with Boulez at IRCAM. He has also employed graphic notation; many of his works leave the performer a wide range of choices. He has been particularly concerned to explore the possibilities of language as developed in musical performance. He was at Darmstadt 1954–59 and was on the faculty at Juilliard, NY, 1965–72. He often wrote for his wife, the soprano Cathy Berberian.

Works include DRAMATIC: *Allez-Hop*, mimed story (Venice, 1959, revised 1968), *Passaggio*, messa in scena (Milan, 1963), *Laborin-*

tus II (Paris, 1970), *Opera* (Santa Fe, 1970, revised 1979), *Recital I (for Cathy)* (Lisbon, 1972), *I trionfi del Petraca*, ballet (Florence, 1974), *Linea*, ballet (Grenoble, 1974), *La Vera Storia*, opera (Milan, 1982), *Un Re in Ascolto*, opera (Salzburg, 1984), *Naturale*, ballet (1986).

ORCHESTRAL: *Variazioni* (1954), *Nones* (1954), *Divertimento* (with Maderna) (1958), *Chemins I–IV*, after *Sequenze* for instruments (1965–75), *Tempi concertati* (1959), *Bewegung* (1971), Concerto for two pianos and orchestra (1973), *Still* (1973), *Eindrücke* (1974), *Points on the curve to find ...* for piano and 20 instruments (1974), *Après visage* for orchestra and tape (1974), *Il ritorno degli Snovidenia* for cello and orchestra (1977), piano concerto (1977), *Entrata* (1980), *Accordo* for four wind bands (1981), *Corale* for violin and orchestra (1982), *Voci* for viola and orchestra (1984), *Requies* (1984), *Formazione* (1986), *Concerto II (Echoing Curves)* for piano and ensemble (1988), *Festum* (1989), *Schubert/Berio: Rendering* (1989).

VOCAL: *Quattro canzoni populari* (1947), *Opus Number Zoo* for speaker and wind quintet (1952, revised 1970), *Chamber Music* (texts by Joyce) (1953), *Circles* for female voice, harp and two percussion (texts by e e cummings) (1960), *Epifanie* for female voice and orchestra (texts by Proust, Joyce, Brecht, etc.) (1961), *Sinfonia* for eight solo voices and orchestra (material from Mahler, Wagner, Strauss and Ravel is used in collage fashion) (1968–69), *Ora* (text after Virgil) (1971), *Bewegung II* for baritone and orchestra (1971), *Cries of London*, for eight solo voices (1973–75), *11 Folk Songs* for mezzo and orchestra (1975), *Calmo (in memoriam Bruno Maderna)* for soprano and ensemble (1974), *Coro* for 40 voices and orchestra (1976), *Duo* for baritone, two violins, chorus & orchestra (1982), *Ofanim* for children's and women's voices and Real Time Computer Music (1988).

CHAMBER AND INSTRUMENTAL: suite for piano (1948), string quartet (1956), *Serenata* for flute and 14 instruments (1957), *Différences* for ensemble (1959), *Sincronie* for string quartet (1964), *Wasserklavier* for piano (1964), *Erdenklavier* (1970), *Sequenze* (I–XI) for solo flute, harp, voice, piano, trombone, viola, oboe, violin, clarinet, trumpet and guitar (1958–85), *Duette per due violini* (1979–82), *Riccorenze*, wind quintet (1987), string quartet (1986–90), *Psy* for double bass (1989).

ELECTRONIC: *Mutazioni* (1955), *Perspectives* (1957), *Thema (Omaggio a Joyce)* (1958), *Momenti* (1960), *Visage* (1961), *Chants parallèles* (1975).

Bériot, Charles (Auguste) de (b Louvain, 20 Feb 1802; d Brussels, 8 Apr 1870), Belgian violinist and composer. Played in public at the age of nine, but ten years later went to Paris to perfect himself under Viotti and Baillot. He had a brilliant success in Paris and was appointed chamber musician to the king. In 1826 he visited London for the first time. He travelled much in the company of Malibran, whom he married after her divorce from her first husband; but after her early death in 1836 he retired to Brussels until 1840, when he travelled again and married Marie Huber in Vienna. Professor of violin at the Brussels Conservatory 1843–52.

Works include ten violin concertos, variations and studies for violin, piano trios.

Berkeley, Lennox (Randall Francis) (b Oxford, 12 May 1903; d London, 26 Dec 1989), English composer. Started to study music in 1926 after leaving Merton College, Oxford, when he went to Paris until 1933 as a pupil of Nadia Boulanger. Works of his were heard at the ISCM festivals at Barcelona and London, 1936 and 1938, and at the Leeds and Worcester festivals, 1937–38. Hon.D.Mus., Oxford, 1970. Knighted 1974.

Works include operas *Nelson* (1954), *A Dinner Engagement* and *Ruth* (1956); ballet *The Judgment of Paris* (1938); incidental music for Shakespeare's *Tempest*; music for film *Hotel Reserve*; oratorio *Jonah* (1935); psalm *Domini est terra* for chorus and orchestra; *Missa brevis*; four symphonies (1940–78); *Nocturne* and divertimento for orchestra; piano concerto (1947), violin concerto; three string quartets (1935–70); two violin and piano sonatas, sonata and pieces for piano; *Polka* for two pianos.

A Selection of

Berio

Opus Number Zoo	1952
Circles	1960
Wasserklavier	1964
Sequenza V	1966

Sinfonia	1968–9
Laborintus II	1970
Eindrücke	1974
11 Folk Songs	1975
Coro	1976
Formazioni	1986

Berkeley, Michael (b London, 29 May 1948), English composer, son of Lennox Berkeley. He studied at the RAM with his father, and with Richard Rodney Bennett. In 1982 his oratorio *Or shall we Die?* was performed in London: it contains a vivid protest at the threat of nuclear war. Composer-in-residence, London College of Music, 1987–88.

Works include opera *Baa-baa Black Sheep* (after Kipling, 1993); *Meditations*, for strings (1976), oboe concerto (1977), *Fantasia Concertante*, for chamber orchestra; symphonies *Uprising* (1980), *Gregorian Variations*, for orchestra (1982), cello concerto (1982); *Elegy* for flute and strings (1993); *The Wild Winds*, for soprano and chamber orchestra (1978), *At the Round Earth's Imagin'd Corners* (text by Donne) for soloists, chorus and organ (1980); string trio (1978), violin sonata, string quartet (1981), clarinet quintet (1983).

Berlijn, Anton (b Amsterdam, 2 May 1817; d Amsterdam, 18 Jan 1870), Dutch composer. He wrote nine operas, including *Die Bergknappen* (1841) and *Proserpina*, seven ballets, oratorio *Moses*, and symphonies.

Berlin (born *Israel Baline*), Irving (b Tyu-men, 11 May 1888; d New York, 22 Sept 1989), American songwriter of Russian origin. He had no formal musical training but became one of the most successful composers of popular songs.

Works include songs for plays, films and revues, including *Music Box Revues*, *Annie Get Your Gun* (1946) and *Call Me Madam* (1950); popular songs, e.g. *Alexander's Ragtime Band*, *God Bless America*, *White Christmas*, *Easter Parade* and *Always*.

Irving just loves hits. He has no sophistication about it – he just loves hits.

Oscar Hammerstein II, quoted in Freedland, *Irving Berlin*, 1974

Berlin Philharmonic Orchestra German orchestra founded 1882. Early conductors were Franz Wüllner, Karl Klindworth, Hans von Bülow and Richard Strauss. Later conductors have included Arthur Nikisch, 1895–1922, Wilhelm Furtwängler, 1922–45 and Sergiu Celibidache, 1945–51. Herbert von Karajan was principal conductor 1954–89, Claudio Abbado from 1989. A new Philharmonic Hall was opened in 1963 with a performance of the *Choral* symphony.

Berlioz *The composer Hector Berlioz (1803–1869). At a time in France when literature was considered the greatest art form, Berlioz achieved more than any other composer in placing music on a par with it. He prepared the way for the later Romantics in France and abroad, including Liszt (who settled in Paris) and Wagner.*

Berlioz, (Louis-)Hector (b Côte-Saint-André, Isère, 11 Dec 1803; d Paris, 8 Mar 1869), French composer, whose fanciful and extravagant life is reflected in his music. He was the son of a doctor who taught him the flute, but wished him to study medicine. As a boy he also learnt the guitar and picked up theoretical knowledge from books. Sent to the École de Médecine in Paris, 1821, he found the studies so distasteful that he decided to give them up for music. His parents made great difficulties, but Lesueur accepted him as a pupil in 1823, when he at once set to work on an opera and an oratorio, a Mass following the next year; this work was lost for many years and was given its first modern performance in 1993. He entered the Conservatory 1826, but failed several times to gain the Prix de Rome, obtaining it at last in 1830 with the cantata *La mort de Sardanapale*. In the meantime he had fallen in love with the Irish actress Harriet Smithson and expressed his feelings for her in the *Symphonie fantastique*. Berlioz was in love with the character of Ophelia, as played by Harriet, rather than the actress herself; he was to be obsessed and inspired by Shakespeare all his life. On the point of going to Rome, he became engaged to the pianist, Marie Moke, who during his absence married Camille Pleyel.

He wrote much in Rome, notably the overtures *King Lear* and *Rob Roy*, and returned to Paris in 1832, this time meeting Harriet and

marrying her in Oct 1833. To add to his income he became a music critic, writing witty and brilliant dissections of the idiocies of Parisian musical life. In 1838 Paganini sent him 20,000 francs to enable him to devote all his time to composition; the Paganini-inspired *Harold en Italie* had been written in 1834 and was followed by *Romeo et Juliette* and *Benvenuto Cellini*. He separated from Harriet in 1842 and started a liaison with the singer Marie Recio. He travelled much with her during the next few years, to Germany, Vienna, Prague, Budapest, Russia and London. His brilliant légende dramatique *La Damnation de Faust* was premiered in 1846 and the massive Te Deum in 1855, but Berlioz continued to suffer throughout his life from lack of public recognition, particularly in his own country. After Harriet's death he married Marie in 1854; meanwhile he had resumed his journalistic work. He composed his masterpiece, the vast opera *Les Troyens*, in the late 1850s. The practicalities of staging such a work in the Paris of his time were forgotten as he entered the world of Virgil's epic poem. Marie died in 1862 and he suffered much ill health during the 1860s and was greatly depressed by the death of his son Louis in 1867. After another visit to Russia he had a bad fall at Nice, where he had gone for his health in 1868, and he grew gradually more infirm. He wrote seven books, including *Traité de l'instrumentation* and *Mémoires*.

For many years Berlioz's reputation rested on his *Symphonie Fantastique*. It was not until the 1960s when the operas and other large-scale works were widely performed, that his true genius was fully revealed; romantic feeling and vivid imagination were sustained over huge timespans.

Works include OPERAS: *Benvenuto Cellini* (1834–37), *Les Troyens* (two parts) (1856–58) and *Béatrice et Bénédict* (after Shakespeare's *Much Ado about Nothing*) (1860–62).

ORCHESTRAL: The programme symphonies, *Symphonie fantastique* (1830), *Harold en Italie* (with solo viola) (1834), *Roméo et Juliette* (with voices) (1839) and *Symphonie funèbre et triomphale* (for military band, strings and chorus) (1840), five concert overtures, *Waverley* (1828), *King Lear* (1831), *Rob Roy* (1831), *Carnaval Romain* (1844), *Le Corsaire* (1844); two marches for orchestra.

CHORAL AND SONGS: Mass (1824), *Messe des morts* (Requiem, 1837), *La Damnation de Faust* (1846), Te Deum (1849) and *L'Enfance du Christ* (1850–54); six smaller vocal works with orchestra or piano, including *La mort de Cléopâtre* (1829), *La captive* (1832), *Zaïdel* (1845) and *La mort d'Ophélie* (1847); 28 songs including the cycle *Nuits d'été*; *Lélio, ou Le Retour à la vie*, a lyric monodrama intended as a sequel to the *Symphonie fantastique* (1832).

Berman, Lazar (b Leningrad, 26 Feb 1930), Russian pianist. He studied

A Selection of
Berlioz

Symphonie fantastique	1830
Harold en Italie	1834
Benvenuto Cellini	1834–7
Messe des morts	1837

Roméo et Juliette	1839
Nuits d'été	1841
La damnation de Faust	1846
L'enfance du Christ	1850–54
Les Troyens	1856–8
Béatrice et Bénédict	1860–2

with Richter at the Moscow Conservatory and made his debut in 1940; continued at the Conservatory until 1957. London debut 1958, NY 1976, followed by US tour. Much praised in Liszt, Schumann, Tchaikovsky and Skriabin.

Bermudo, Juan (b Ecija near Seville, *c* 1510; d Andalusia, *c* 1565), Spanish 16th-c. friar and music theorist. Friend of Morales. He wrote three music treatises, pub. 1549–55, including the *Declaración*, (1555), with the first organ music printed locally.

Bernac (real name *Bertin*), Pierre (b Paris, 12 Jan 1899; d Villeneuve-lès-Avignon, 17 Oct 1979), French baritone. From 1936 he special-ized in recitals, frequently in association with Poulenc, many of whose songs he introduced (*Chansons gaillardes*, 1926).

Bernacchi, Antonio (b Bologna, 23 Jun 1685; d Bologna, 13 Mar 1756), Italian castrato and teacher. First heard in London in 1716; in the season 1729–30 he sang in the fps. of Handel's *Lotario* and *Partenope*.

Bernardi, Steffano (b Verona, *c* 1585; d ? Salzburg, 1636), Italian priest and composer. Chaplain at Verona Cathedral, studied in Rome later and became *maestro di cappella* of the church of the Madonna dei Monti. In 1611 he became *maestro di cappella* at Verona Cathedral, and in 1622 went into the service of the Archduke Karl Josef, Bishop of Breslau, and soon afterwards to Salzburg Cathedral, which he helped to consecrate in 1628. He wrote a Te Deum for 12 choirs (now lost), and many Masses, motets, psalms, madrigals and instrumental works. His *Salmi concertati* deploy voices in dif-ferent groups, as in the music of Schütz and Gabrieli.

Bernasconi, Andrea (b Marseilles, 1706; d Munich, Jan 1784), Italian composer. *Kapellmeister* in Munich from 1755. He was stepfather of Antonio ◊Bernasconi, who was his pupil.

Works include 25 operas, most to texts by Metastasio, one oratorio and a large quantity of church music.

Bernasconi, Antonia (b Stuttgart, 1741; d ? Vienna, 1803), German soprano, step-daughter of Andrea ◊Bernasconi. She sang the title role in the first production of Gluck's *Alceste* (Vienna, 1767), also Aspasia in Mozart's *Mitridate* (Milan, 1770).

Berners, Lord (Sir Gerald Hugh Tyrwhitt-Wilson) (b Arley Park near Bridgnorth, 18 Sept 1883; d Faringdon House, Berks, 19 Apr 1950), English composer, painter and author. In the diplomatic service at first, he studied music at Dresden and Vienna, and also sought the advice of Stravinsky and Casella. His operatic setting of Mérimée's comedy *Le Carrosse du Saint-Sacrement* was produced in Paris in 1924, and the ballet *The Triumph of Neptune* in London in 1926; another, with words by Gertrude Stein, *The Wedding Bouquet*, at SW in 1937 with settings designed by himself. He was famed for such

Bernstein *The conductor, composer and pianist Leonard Bernstein (1918–1990). He was renowned for his energetic and even flamboyant conducting style, which drew the best performances out of many an orchestra. His 'rediscovery' of Mahler is largely responsible for the composer's current popularity.*

eccentricities as dyeing the pigeons on his lawns different colours to match his moods.

Works include opera *Le Carrosse du Saint-Sacrement*; ballets *The Triumph of Neptune*, *Luna Park* (1930), *The Wedding Bouquet* (words by Gertrude Stein), *Cupid and Psyche* (1939); three pieces (*Chinoiserie*, *Valse sentimentale*, *Kasatchok*), *Fantaisie espagnole* (1920) and *Fugue* for orchestra (1928); *Variations*, *Adagio and Hornpipe* for string orchestra; *Le Poisson d'or*, *Trois Petites Marches funèbres* and *Fragments psychologiques* for piano; *Valses bour-geoises* for piano duet; songs including three sets in the German, French and English manners.

Bernier, Nicolas (b Mantes, 5 or 6 Jun 1665; d Paris, 6 Jul 1734), French composer. Studied in Rome. *Maître de chapelle* at Chartres and at the church of Saint-Germain-l'Auxerrois in Paris; then music master at the Sainte Chapelle there, 1704–26.

Works include eight books of cantatas, three of motets, church music.

He uses music as an accompaniment to his conducting.

Oscar Levant, on Bernstein in *The Memoirs of an Amnesiac*, 1965

Bernstein, Leonard (b Lawrence, MA, 25 Aug 1918; d New York, 14 Oct 1990), American conductor, composer, pianist, teacher and writer on music, of Russian parentage. He studied at Harvard 1935–39, and with Fritz Reiner and Randall Thompson at Curtis Institute from 1939; assistant to Koussevitzky at Tanglewood 1940–43. In Nov 1943 he deputized for Bruno Walter at a NY PO concert, achieving instant recognition; became sole conductor of the orchestra 1958, conductor laureate for life 1969. Many guest appear-ances with Vienna SO, LSO and Israel PO. With the Boston SO he gave the 1949 fp of Messiaen's ◊*Turangalíla-symphonie*, and at the

A Selection of

Bernstein

Symphony no. 1 (*Jeremiah*)	1944
On the Town	1944
Prelude, Fugue and Riffs	1949
Symphony no. 2 (*The Age of Anxiety*)	1949

Serenade	1954
Candide	1956
West Side Story	1957
Chichester Psalms	1967
Mass	1971
Songfest	1977

Vienna Staatsoper gave *Falstaff* and his own opera *A Quiet Place* (1986). In the concert hall he gave highly charged performances of music by Mahler (all of whose symphonies he recorded), Shostakovich, Beethoven (Choral Symphony in Berlin, 1989), and his own works. As a pianist he was heard in the Mozart concertos, directing from the keyboard, and as accompanist to leading singers. At Tanglewood and Brandeis University he was an inspirational teacher; on television and through his books he influenced several generations of young people. Particularly in his theatre pieces, Bernstein attempted to reconcile the distinctions between 'serious' and popular music. A chance to reassess his orchestral music came in 1986, with a series of concerts in London: the *Serenade* and *The Age of Anxiety* were well received. His status as a composer is sometimes controversial, but in his best works he captures perfectly the energy, self-awareness and sense of freedom which characterize the American spirit. Through his many recordings, Bernstein's stature as a performing musician, a supreme communicator, is beyond dispute.

Works include THEATRE PIECES: *Fancy Free*, ballet (1944), *On the Town*, musical comedy (1944), *Candide*, musical after Voltaire (1956, revised 1982), *Facsimile*, ballet (1946), *Trouble in Tahiti*, one-act opera (1952, revised as *A Quiet Place*, 1983), *Wonderful Town*, musical comedy (1952), *West Side Story* (1957, also filmed), *Mass*, for chorus, boys' chorus, orchestra and dancers (1971), *Dybbuk*, ballet (1974).

WORKS WITH ORCHESTRA: symphony no. 1, *Jeremiah* (1944), symphony no. 2, with piano, *The Age of Anxiety* (1949), *Prelude, Fugue and Riffs* for clarinet and jazz ensemble (1949), *Serenade* for violin, strings and percussion, after Plato's *Symposium* (1954), symphony no. 3, *Kaddish* for narrator, chorus and orchestra (1963), *Chichester Psalms* for chorus and orchestra (1965), *Songfest*, 12 pieces for six singers and orchestra (1977), *Divertimento* for flute, strings and percussion, in memory of Israeli war dead (1981), *Jubilee Games* (1985); Concerto for orchestra (1988); chamber music and songs, including cycle for soprano *I Hate Music* (1943) and three groups of *Anniversaries* for piano (1943, 1948, 1954).

Béroff, Michel (b Epinal, 9 May 1950), French pianist. He studied at the Paris Conservatory with Yvonne Loriod, the wife of Messiaen; has given many performances of Messiaen's music, notably the massive *Vingt regards sur L'Enfant Jésus*. Also heard in Bartók, Debussy, Prokofiev and Mozart; Bartók's second concerto at the Barbican Hall, London, 1995.

Berry, Walter (b Vienna, 8 Apr 1929) Austrian bass-baritone.

Studied in Vienna. Vienna Staatsoper from 1950 as Mozart's Figaro, Leporello, Wozzeck and Ochs. Salzburg from 1952 as Masetto and in the fps of operas by Liebermann, Egk and Von Einem. NY Met. since 1966 (debut as Barak). CG from 1976. Married to the mezzo Christa Ludwig 1957–70. Returned to CG 1986 (Waldner in *Arabella*).

Bertali, Antonio (b Verona, Mar 1605; d Vienna, 17 Apr 1669), Italian violinist and composer. Played in the court chapel in Vienna from 1637 and became *Kapellmeister* in 1649. His opera *L'inganno d'amore* was produced at the Diet of Regensburg in 1653.

Works include several operas, e.g. *Niobe* and *Theti* (both Mantua, 1652); equestrian ballet; two oratorios; Masses and other church music.

Berté, Heinrich (b Galgócz, 8 May 1857; d Vienna, 23 Aug 1924), Austro-Hungarian composer, best-known for his saccharine version of the life of Schubert, *Lilac Time*.

Works include operettas *Die Schneeflocke* (Prague, 1896), *Die Millionenbraut* (Munich, 1905), *Der Märchenprinz*, *Das Dreimäderlhaus* (*Lilac Time*, on music by Schubert, 1916) and others; ballets *Das Märchenbuch*, *Amor auf Reisen* (Vienna, 1895) and others.

Bertheaume, Isidore (b Paris, *c* 1752; d St Petersburg, 20 Mar 1802), French violinist and composer. Appeared at the Concert Spirituel in Paris, 1761, and became conductor in 1783, but left at the Revolution, going first to Eutin and then to St Petersburg, where he joined the Imperial band.

Works include two symphonies; violin concerto and several for two violins; sonatas for piano with violin accompaniment.

Bertini, Gary (b Brichevo, Bessarabia, 1 May 1927), Russian-born Israeli conductor and composer. He studied in Tel Aviv, Milan and Paris; founded Israel Chamber Orchestra 1965, guest conductor with the Israel PO. Scottish National Orchestra from 1970, Detroit SO 1981–83. Chief conductor Cologne Radio SO from 1983; music director of New Israeli opera from 1994, opening with *Boris Godunov*. He has conducted the premieres of four operas by Joseph Tal: *Ashmedai* (Hamburg, 1970), *Masada 967* (Jerusalem, 1973), *Die Versuchung* (Munich, 1977) and *Joseph* (Tel Aviv, 1995).

Works include concerto for horn, string and timpani (1952), solo violin sonata (1953), ballet *The Unfound Door* (1962).

The baton makes no sound.

Trad.

Bertolli, Francesca (Rome–Bologna, 9 Jan 1763), Italian 18th-c. contralto. First heard in London in 1729, she sang in the first production of Handel's *Partenope*, *Ezio*, *Sosarme*, *Orlando* and *Berenice*, as well as in operas by Porpora.

Berton, Henri-Montan (b Paris, 17 Sept 1767; d Paris, 22 Apr 1844), French violinist and composer, son of Pierre-Montan ◊Berton. Violinist at the Paris Opéra from 1782, professor at the Conservatory from 1795 and conductor at the Opéra-Comique from 1807. The first of his 48 operas was produced 1787; collaborated with Kreutzer, Boieldieu and Cherubini in his later works.

Works include operas *Les Promesses de mariage*, *Les Rigueurs du cloître* (1790), *Ponce de Léon* (1797), *Montano et Stéphanie*, *Le Délire*, *Le Grand Deuil*, *Le Concert intérrompu* (1802), *Aline, Reine de Golconde* (1803), *Les Maris garçons*, *Virginie*; oratorios *Absalon* (1786), etc.; ballets; cantatas; instrumental music; also theoretical works.

Berton, Pierre-Montan (b Maubert-Fontaines, 7 Jan 1727; d Paris, 14 May 1780), French composer and conductor, father of Henri-Montan ◊Berton. Appointed conductor at the Paris Opéra 1759 and of the Concert spirituel 1773. He brought Gluck and Piccinni to Paris and gave operas by Lully, Rameau, and Campra in updated versions.

Bertoni, Ferdinando Giuseppe (b Salò, Lake Garda, 15 Aug 1725; d Desenzano, Lake Garda, 1 Dec 1813), Italian composer. Pupil of Martini at Bologna. Organist at St Mark's, Venice, from 1752 and choirmaster at the Conservatorio dei Mendicanti from 1757, writing many works for the female musicians there. He produced his first opera at Florence, 1745. In 1776 produced his *Orfeo*, on the libretto by Calzabigi already set by Gluck in 1762; it contains many echoes of Gluck's music. He visited London to produce operas in 1778–80 and 1781–83. In 1785 he succeeded Galuppi as *maestro di cappella* at St Mark's, Venice.

Works include operas *Cajetto* (1746), *Orazio Curiazo*, *Tancredi* (1766), *Orfeo ed Euridice*, *Quinto Fabio* (1778) and over 40 others; oratorios and Latin cantatas; string quartets; keyboard music.

Bertram, Theodor (b Stuttgart, 2 Feb 1869; d Bayreuth, 24 Nov 1907), German baritone. Debut Ulm, 1889. Bayreuth 1892–1906; first Dutchman there, 1901; NY Met. 1900, same role. Munich 1893–1900 and CG 1900–07 as Wotan, Amfortas and Pizarro. He committed suicide after the death of his wife.

Bertrand, Antoine de (b Fontanges, *c* 1535; d Toulouse, *c* 1581), French composer. In some of his settings of Ronsard's *Amours* he experimented with quarter-tones. Altogether he published three vols of *chansons*, and a volume of *Airs spirituels* appeared posthumously in 1582.

He, Sire, who hearing a sweet concord of instruments or the sweetness of a natural voice feels no pleasure, is not moved and does not shiver from head to foot, as if sweetly enraptured and is not, as it were transported out of himself, gives a sign that he has a twisted, profligate and depraved soul.

Antoine de Bertrand, *Premiere Livre des Amours*, 1576

Berutti, Arturo (b San Juan, 27 Mar 1862; d Buenos Aires, 3 Jan 1938), Argentine composer. Studied at the Leipzig Conservatory and in Paris and Milan, settling at Buenos Aires in 1896.

Works include operas *Vendetta* (1892), *Evangelina* (1893), *Taras Bulba* (after Gogol) (1895), *Pampa* (1892), *Yupanki, Khrysé, Horrida nox* (1908) and *Los heroes*.

Berwald, Franz Adolf (b Stockholm, 23 Jul 1796; d Stockholm, 3 Apr 1868), Swedish violinist and composer. He composed several works before studying in Berlin. He twice visited Vienna, where he had more success than at home. His septet of 1828 was influenced by Spohr and Beethoven; in 1847 Jenny Lind sang in his opera *A Rustic Betrothal* in Sweden. Later stage works were less successful and *The Queen of Golconda* (1864) was not premiered until 1968. He settled at Stockholm in 1849 as director of music at the university and court *kapellmästare*. His best-known music is in the four symphonies of the 1840s: the titles *Capricieuse* and *Singulière* suggest their originality.

Works include operas *Leonida* (1829), *The Traitor, Estrella di Soria* (1848, revised 1862), *The Queen of Golconda* (1864, performed 1968); operettas *I Enter a Convent, The Milliner, A Rustic Betrothal in Sweden* (1847); incidental music to plays.

Four symphonies, no. 1 *Sérieuse* (1842), no. 2 *Capricieuse* (1842), no. 3 *Singulière* (1845), no. 4 (1845); violin concerto (1820), piano concerto (1855); orchestral works include *Recollections of the Norwegian Alps*; Septet (1828); three string quartets, two piano quintets and other chamber music; songs.

Besanzoni, Gabriella (b Rome, 20 Sept 1888; d Rome, 8 Jul 1962), Italian mezzo. She sang Ulrica at Rome in 1913 and appeared at Buenos Aires from 1918. NY Met. 1919–20 as Amneris and Isabella. She appeared in Havana, with Caruso, and sang Orfeo and Carmen at La Scala, under Toscanini, 1923–32; guest at the Berlin Staatsoper. Other roles included Mignon, Adalgisa and Cenerentola.

Besard (Besardus), Jean-Baptiste (b Besançon, *o* 1567; d ? Augsburg, after 1617), French lutenist and composer. Studied law at the University of Dôle, then the lute with Lorenzini in Rome. Later lived at Cologne and Augsburg. Pub. theoretical works and collections of lute music including his own. His *Thesaurus harmonicus* of 1603 contains more than 400 pieces by various composers and includes a manual on lute playing.

Besseler, Heinrich (b Hörde, near Dortmund, 2 Apr 1900; d Leipzig, 25 Jul 1969), German musicologist. Studied at Freiburg i/B, Vienna and Göttingen, where later he became lecturer at the university. Professor at Jena, 1949, and at Leipzig from 1956. Wrote on medieval and Renaissance music, notably in *Die Musik des Mittelalters und der Renaissance* (1951).

Best, W(illiam) T(homas) (b Carlisle, 13 Aug 1826; d Liverpool, 10 May 1897), English organist. Studied at Liverpool and lived most of his life there as organist at St George's Hall, where he gave recitals that made him famous all over the world in the music of Bach. He made many organ arrangements of famous works.

Besuch der Alten Dame, Der, *The Visit of the Old Lady*, opera by Gottfried von Einem (libretto by F Dürrenmatt after his own drama), produced Vienna, Staatsoper, 23 May 1971. Long-jilted lady pays people of her home town for killing her lover.

Betrothal in a Monastery, The, *Obrucheniye monastïre*, opera by Prokofiev (libretto by the composer and M Mendelssohn, after Sheridan's play *The Duenna*); composed 1940–41, fp Leningrad, Kirov Theatre, 3 Nov 1946. After initial opposition from their father, Louisa and Ferdinando are allowed to choose their partners in marriage.

Bettoni, Vincenzo (b Melegnano, 1 Jul 1881; d Melegnano, 4 Nov 1954), Italian bass. After his 1902 debut he sang at La Scala from 1905 and at Buenos Aires from 1910. Gurnemanz in the first Spanish performance of *Parsifal* (Barcelona, 1914). In 1926 he began a series of Rossini performances, with Conchita Supervia. Don Alfonso in the first season at Glyndebourne, 1934, and the following year was heard at CG as Basilio, Don Magnifico and Mustafà.

Betulia Liberata, La, *Betulia Liberated*, oratorio in two acts by Mozart to a text by Metastasio, based on the story of Judith and Holofernes. The work was commissioned by a Paduan nobleman, Giuseppe Ximenes, Prince of Aragon, and composed 1771 in Italy and Salzburg but not performed in Mozart's lifetime. First British performance London, 6 Nov 1968, by Opera Viva. Metastasio's text was first set by Reutter (performed Vienna, 8 Apr 1734). Later settings by Jommelli (Venice, 1734), Holzbauer (Mannheim, 1760), Gassmann (Vienna, 1772) and Schuster (Dresden, 1796).

Betz, Franz (b Mainz, 19 Mar 1835; d Berlin, 11 Aug 1900), German baritone. Made his first appearance at Hanover in 1856, as Heinrich in *Lohengrin*, was Wagner's first Hans Sachs at Munich in 1868, and the first Wotan at Bayreuth. Other roles included Amonasro, Falstaff, Don Giovanni, Marke and Wolfram. He sang at the Royal Opera, Berlin, 1859–97 (Valentin, Pizarro and Telramund).

Bevin, Elway (b *c* 1554; d Bristol, buried 19 Oct 1638), English organist and composer of Welsh descent. Possibly a pupil of Tallis, vicar-choral at Wells Cathedral, 1575–84, and organist at Bristol Cathedral after that. He wrote a *Briefe and Short Instruction in the Art of Musicke* (1631), Composed services, anthems and other church music, keyboard pieces, etc.

Bevis of Hampton or **Beves of Hamtoun** Anglo-Norman 13th-c. romance. ◊Buovo d'Antona (Traetta).

Bialas, Günter (b Bielschowitz, Silesia, 19 Jul 1907; d Glonn, 8 July 1995), German composer. He studied in Berlin, 1927–33, and taught in Breslau, Weimar and Munich. His music shows a wide range of influences, including neo-classicism, twelve-tone technique and medieval polyphony.

Works include three operas, *Hero und Leander* (1966), *Die Geschichte von Aucassin und Nicolette* (1969), *Der gestiefelte Kater* (1974); viola concerto (1940), violin concerto (1949), cello concerto (1962), *Sinfonia piccola*; sacred and secular choral music; three string quartets (1936, 1949, 1969); *Erwartung*, for organ (1972).

Bianca e Falliero, ossia Il consiglio di tre, ... or *The Council of Three*, opera by Rossini (libretto by F Romani, from Manzoni's tragedy *Il conte di Carmagnola*), produced Milan, La Scala, 26 Dec 1819. Bianca loves Falliero but is told to marry Capiello. Falliero is accused of treachery by the Council but is absolved in time to marry Bianca.

Bianca e Fernando opera by Bellini (libretto by D Gilardoni), produced Naples, Teatro San Carlo, 30 May 1826. Bellini's first opera heard in public. Fernando rescues father and sister Bianca from ducal usurper, Filippo.

Bianca und Giuseppe, oder Die Franzosen vor Nizza, ... *or The French before Nice*, opera by J F Kittl (libretto by Wagner), produced Prague, 19 Feb 1848. Wagner had written the libretto for himself in 1836; it is based on a novel by Heinrich König.

Bianchi, Francesco (b Cremona, *c* 1752; d London, 27 Nov 1810), Italian composer, *Maestro al cembalo* at the Comédie Italienne in Paris 1775, where he worked under Piccinni and produced two operas. In 1778 went to Florence, and in 1783 was appointed second *maestro di cappella* at Milan Cathedral. His most successful opera, *La villanella rapita*, was produced the same year in Venice. In 1795 he went to London as composer to the King's Theatre, and three years later to Dublin. He wrote popular opéras-comiques in Paris, 1802–07, but returned to London, where he remained until his death by suicide.

Works include 60 operas, oratorios, church music, trio sonatas.

Biber, Heinrich Ignaz Franz von (b Wartenberg, Bohemia, 12 Aug 1644; d Salzburg, 3 May 1704), Bohemian violinist and composer. He was high steward and conductor at the archbishop's court at Salzburg. His brilliant violin technique is best heard in the solo sonatas with continuo of 1681 and the *Mystery* or *Rosary* sonatas of 1676. Spatial effects are created in the *Vesperae* (1693), the *Missa Sancti Henrici* (1701) and Mass in F minor.

Works include opera *Chi la dura, la vince* (1687), church music, several sets of violin sonatas, *Battalia* with violin, *Nightwatchman's Serenade*, partitas for three instruments; vespers for voices, strings and trombones, and possibly the 53-part *Missa salisburgensis*, performed in Salzburg Cathedral in 1682 and formerly attributed to Benevoli.

Biches, Les, *The Hinds*, ballet in one act with chorus by Poulenc; composed 1923, produced Monte Carlo, 6 Jan 1924, with choreography by Nijinska. Orchestral Suite in five movements (1939–40).

Bierey, Gottlob Benedikt (b Dresden, 25 Jul 1772; d Breslau, 5 May 1840), German composer. Succeeded Weber as conductor at the opera of Breslau in 1808. He wrote numerous operas, operettas and popular Singspiels, including *Rosette, das Schweizer Hirtenmädchen* (Leipzig, 1806), and *Wladimir, Fürst von Novgorod* (Vienna, 1807).

Biggs, E Power (b Westcliff, Essex, 29 Mar 1906; d Boston, MA, 10 Mar 1977), English-born American organist. Studied at the RAM and moved to the USA in 1930. Gave weekly broadcasts in Baroque repertory (1942–58) and commissioned works from Howard Hanson, Roy Harris and Walter Piston.

Only Berlioz can recall Beethoven.
Niccolo Paganini, quoted in *Berlioz Mémoires*, 1870

Bihari, János (b Nagyabony, bap. 21 Oct 1764; d Pest, 26 Apr 1827), Hungarian violinist and composer. He came from a gypsy family. He learnt the violin early and acquired great virtuosity. After his marriage to a daughter of Banyák, a cimbalom player, he soon took up the leadership of his father-in-law's band. It travelled throughout Hungary and repeatedly visited Vienna. As a composer Bihari cultivated the *verbunkos* style with great success; he is also linked with the Rakoczi march, later adapted by Liszt and Berlioz.

Billings, William (b Boston, MA, 7 Oct 1746; d Boston, 26 Sept 1800), American tanner and amateur composer. Wrote many hymn tunes and patriotic songs, collected in *The New-England Psalm-singer* (1770) and *The Singing Master's Assistant* (1778); his most popular tunes include 'Lebanon', 'Chester' and 'Amherst'.

Billington (born *Weichsel*), Elizabeth (b London, *c* 1765; d near Venice, 25 Aug 1818), English soprano, daughter of Carl Weichsel, a German oboist who settled in London. She was a pupil of J C Bach, and first appeared as a child pianist in 1774. She married the double-bass player James Billington in 1783. Made her debut as a singer in

---

THE OPERA

Billy Budd

A two-act opera by Benjamin Britten, with a plot from an unfinished story by Herman Melville. First produced (with an all-male cast) in London in 1951, the action is set on board HMS *Indomitable* in 1797, during the Napoleonic Wars.

I. Able Seaman Billy Budd (baritone) is press-ganged into service on the man-o'-war from his merchant ship. The master-at-arms Claggart (bass) is at first friendly but then becomes suspicious that the good-natured Billy is in fact inciting mutiny. Billy is involved in a fight with Squeak (tenor) and knocks him down. Although the stammering Billy is blameless, Claggart develops a hatred for him; he conspires with the Novice (tenor) to tempt Billy to mutiny with the offer of money.

II. Claggart tells Captain Vere (tenor) that Billy has offered gold to the Novice to join a mutiny. When Billy is brought to Vere's cabin and the charge is repeated, he lashes out unthinkingly and strikes Claggart dead. Billy is condemned by a court martial although he calls on Vere to save him. Alone in chains, Billy sings of a far-shining sail, and as he is about to be hanged from the yardarm he blesses Vere. In an epilogue, Vere laments that he could have saved Billy.

THE OPERA

Dublin, and subsequently sang with great success in London, Paris and Naples. After her return to London in 1801 she continued to be in great demand until her retirement in 1811.

Billy Budd opera by Britten (libretto by E M Forster and E Crozier, on Herman Melville's story), produced London, CG 1 Dec 1951. Revised 1960 and heard on BBC, 13 Nov 1960; produced CG, 9 Jan 1964. Accused of mutiny, Billy kills master-at-arms Claggart and is hanged by Captain Vere.

Billy the Kid ballet by Copland, produced NY, 24 May 1939.

Bilson, Malcolm (b Los Angeles, 24 Oct 1935), American pianist. After study in Paris and Vienna he taught at Cornell University from 1968. Many concerts in the USA and Europe in 18th-c. music using period instruments (director of series On Original Instruments at Merkin Hall, NY). Plays Chopin and Schumann on 1825 Alois Graf piano; Mozart concertos with John Eliot Gardiner (also recorded), Frans Brueggen and Nicholas McGegan; co-founder of the Amadè Trio, 1974.

binary a song or piece in two distinct sections is said to be in binary form. The sections are dependent on each other because the first does not close in the work's tonic key, and the second does not open in it, so that each by itself would fail to give any impression of completeness. They are also usually based on the same or similar thematic material —alike, but not identical. The dances in Bach's suites are examples of binary form.

Binchois, Gilles de Bins (b ? Mons, *c* 1400; d Soignies, 20 Sept 1460), Franco-Flemish composer. Chaplain to Philip, Duke of Burgundy, from *c* 1430 until 1453, when he became provost of Saint-Vincent, Soignies. He composed Mass-movements, Magnificats and other liturgical works in a severely functional style; but his most characteristic works are his *chansons*, mostly in three parts and in the form of *rondeaux* or *ballades*; they are written in a more pleasing and graceful style than his sacred music.

Bindernagel, Gertrud (b Magdeburg 11 Jan 1894; d Berlin, 3 Nov 1932), German soprano. After engagements at Magdeburg, Breslau and Regensburg she sang in Berlin from 1920, chiefly in the Wagner repertory; appeared as guest in Barcelona, Munich and Hamburg. After a performance of *Siegfried* she was shot by her jealous husband, a banker, and died of her wounds shortly after.

Binet, Jean (b Geneva, 17 Oct 1893; d Trélex-sur-Nyon, Switzerland, 24 Feb 1960), Swiss composer. Studied at the Jaques-Dalcroze Institute at Geneva and with Barblan, Templeton Strong, Bloch and

Birtwistle *A scene from the ENO production of* The Mask of Orpheus *(1986). Although still labelled a member of the 'Manchester School', which includes composers Maxwell Davies, Goehr and others, Harrison Birtwistle has diverged from the current idiom of his contemporaries by maintaining a fiercely radical and independent style.*

others. Lived in the USA and Brussels for a time. Several of his works were premiered by Ernest Ansermet.

Works include three psalms for chorus and orchestra, *Cantate de Noël* for chorus and organ; ballets *L'Ile enchantée* and *Le Printemps* (1950); suites on Swiss and English themes and dances for orchestra; concertino for chamber orchestra; string quartet (1927) and other chamber music, songs, part-songs.

Bing, Rudolf (b Vienna, 9 Jan 1902), Austrian-born manager, naturalized British subject 1946. Held appointments in Darmstadt and Berlin, 1928–33, until moving with Carl Ebert to Glyndebourne; manager there 1935–49. He helped found the Edinburgh Festival and was director 1947–49. General manager NY Met. 1950–72. His experiences with prima donnas (male and female) are detailed in two vols. of autobiography: *5,000 Nights at the Opera* (1972) and *A Knight at the Opera* (1981). Knighted 1971.

Bingham, Judith (b Nottingham, 21 Jun 1952), English composer. Studied at the RAM, London, and with Hans Keller; appearances as a singer with the Taverner Consort and Combattimento.

Works include *A Divine Image*, for harpsichord (1976); songs for mezzo, baritone and choruses (*A Hymn before Sunrise in the Vale of Chamonix*, 1982), Mass setting and *A Winter Walk at Noon* (1984); *Chartres* for orchestra (1987), *The Uttermost* for tenor, chorus and orchestra (1992).

Binkerd, Gordon (b Lynch, NE, 22 May 1916), American composer. After study at the Eastman School and Harvard he was professor at the University of Illinois 1947–71. His music is tonally chromatic and contrapuntal in scope and includes four symphonies (1955, 1957, 1961, 1963), two string quartets (1956, 1961); string trio (1979), four piano sonatas (1955–83) and choruses.

Bioni, Antonio (b Venice, 1698; d after 1739), Italian composer. Pupil of Porta. Produced his first opera at Chioggia in 1721; worked at Breslau and Prague, 1726–34.

Works include *c* 25 operas, e.g. *Climene, Issipile*; serenata *La pace fra la virtù e la bellezza* (Metastasio); also church music.

Birthday Odes works for soli, chorus and orchestra written by English composers from the Restoration onwards to commemorate royal birthdays. Purcell wrote six for Queen Mary, consort of William III, as follows: 1. *Now does the glorious day appear* (1689), 2. *Arise my Muse* (1690), 3. *Welcome, welcome, glorious morn* (1691), 4. *Love's goddess sure was blind* (1692), 5. *Celebrate this festival* (1693), 6. *Come ye sons of art away* (1694).

Birtwistle, Harrison (b Accrington, 15 Jul 1934), English composer. Studied at the RMCM and later at the RAM, London. Knighted 1988. As a composer he has often combined violent sonorities with an interest in medieval music. The issue of large-scale form was resolved in more recent years by the evolution of a more organic technique, in which the problems of a work find their solution in the musical material itself rather than relying on pre-existent formal models. He has made some use of electronics; the tape for *The Mask of Orpheus* was prepared at IRCAM. The successful opera *Gawain* was described as 'Birtwistle's *Parsifal*', and was followed by *The Second Mrs Kong*, in which the composer returned to Orphic myth.

STAGE: *Punch and Judy*, opera in one act (1968), *Monodrama* for soprano, speaker and instrumental ensemble (1967), *Down by the Greenwood Side*, dramatic pastoral (1969), incidental music for National Theatre production of *Hamlet* (1975) and *The Oresteia* (1981), *Frames, Pulses and Interruptions*, ballet (1977), *Bow Down*, music-theatre (1977), *The Mask of Orpheus*, opera (1973–75,

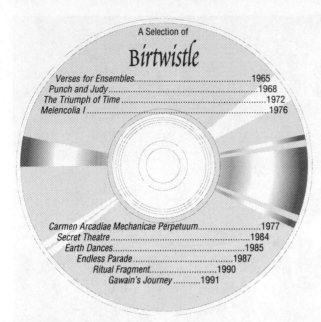

1981–84; produced 1986), *Yan Tan Tethera*, TV opera (1986), *Gawain* (1991), *The Second Mrs Kong* (1994).

ORCHESTRAL: *Chorales* (1960–63), *Three Movements with Fanfares* (1964), *Nomos* (1968), *An Imaginary Landscape* (1971), *The Triumph of Time* (1972), *Grimethorpe Aria* for brass band (1973), *Melencolia 1* (1976), *Silbury Air* for small orchestra (1977), *Still Movement* for 13 solo strings (1984), *Earth Dances* (1985), *Endless Parade* for trumpet and strings (1987), *Ritual Fragment* (1990), *Gawain's Journey* (1991), *Antiphonies* for piano and orchestra (1993), *The Cry of Anubis* (1995), *Panic* for saxophone, drums and orchestra (1995).

VOCAL: *Monody for Corpus Christi* for soprano and ensemble (1959), *Narration: a Description of the Passing Year* for chorus (1963), *Entr'actes and Sappho Fragments* for soprano and ensemble (1964), *Carmen paschale* for chorus and organ (1965), *Ring a Dumb Clarion* for soprano, clarinet and percussion (1965), *Cantata* for soprano and ensemble (1969), *Nenia on the Death of Orpheus* for soprano and ensemble (1970), *The Fields of Sorrow* for two sopranos, chorus and ensemble (1971–72), *Meridian* for mezzo, chorus and ensemble (1970–71), *Epilogue: Full Fathom Five* for baritone and ensemble (1972), ... *agm* ..... for 16 solo voices and three instrumental ensembles (1979), *On the Sheer Threshold of the Night* for four solo voices and 12-part chorus (1980), *Songs by Myself* for soprano and ensemble (1984), *Words Overheard* for soprano, flute, oboe and strings (1985), *Four Songs of Autumn* for soprano and string quartet (1987); *An die Musik* (1988), *White and Light* (1989) and *Four Poems by Jaan Kaplinski* (1991), all for soprano and ensemble.

INSTRUMENTAL: *Refrains and Choruses* for wind quintet (1957), *The World is Discovered* for chamber ensemble (1960), *Tragoedia* for ensemble (1965), *Verses for Ensembles* (1969), *Ut heremita solus*, arrangement of Ockeghem (1969), *Hoquetus David*, arrangement of Machaut (1969), *Medusa* for ensemble (1970, revised 1980), *Chronometer* for eight-track tape (1971), *Chorales from a Toyshop* (1967–74), *Carmen Arcadiae Mechanicae Perpetuum* for ensemble (1977), *For O for O, the Hobby Horse is Forgot* for six percussion (1976), clarinet quintet (1980), *Pulse sampler* for oboe and claves (1981), *Duets for Storab* for two flutes (1983), *Secret Theatre* for string quartet and ensemble (1984), string quartet (1993).

Bishop (born *Riviere*), Anna (b London, 9 Jan 1810; d New York 18 Mar 1884), English soprano. Taught singing by her father and piano by Moscheles, also studied at the RAM, where she met Bishop, whom she married in 1831. She made her debut that year, but in 1839 went on a tour with Robert Bochsa, harpist, bigamist and forger, and soon afterwards eloped with him, never to return to her husband and three children.

Bishop, Henry (Rowley) (b London, 18 Nov 1786; d London, 30 Apr 1855), English conductor and composer. Studied under Bianchi and produced *Angelina* (composed with Lanza) at Margate in 1804 and the ballet *Tamerlan et Bajazet* at the King's Theatre in London, 1806. From that time on he brought out one or more stage pieces almost each year until 1840. In 1813 he was one of the founders of the Philharmonic Society and became one of its conductors. Knighted in 1842; D. Mus. at Oxford in 1853. Professor of music at Oxford, 1848. He was twice married to singers: Sarah Lyon on 30 Apr 1809 and Anna Riviere on 9 Jul 1831.

Works include over 100 pieces for the stage, e.g. *The Corsair*, *The Circassian Bride* (1809), *Guy Mannering* (after Scott) (1816), *The Burgomaster of Saardam*, *The Heart of Midlothian* (after Scott) (1819), *Montrose* (after Scott), *The Law of Java*, *Maid Marian*, *Clari*, *Cortez*, *Faustus* (1825), *Aladdin*, *The Fortunate Isles* (1840); incidental music for three tragedies, for adaptations of Scott, Byron and Shakespeare; oratorio *The Fallen Angel*; cantata *The Seventh Day*; three vols of national melodies with words by Moore and other collections of arrangements.

Bispham, David (Scull) (b Philadelphia, 5 Jan 1857; d New York, 2 Oct 1921), American baritone. Studied with Vannuccini and Lamperti at Milan and with W Shakespeare in London, where he made his first concert appearance in 1890, and his debut on the stage in 1891; in 1892 he sang Kurwenal, under Mahler. Five years later he appeared in NY, at the Met, and sang the Wagner baritone roles, as well as Masetto, Escamillo, Iago and Falstaff.

bisser French verb from *bis* = twice = to encore.

As a musician I tell you that if you were to suppress adultery, fanaticism, crime, evil, the supernatural, there would no longer be the means for writing one note.

Georges Bizet, in a letter to Edmond Galabert, October 1866

---

bitonality the writing of music in two keys at once, e.g. the fanfare in Stravinsky's *Petrushka*, played simultaneously in C major and F♯ major.

F major and F♯ minor appear simultaneously in Ravel's bitonal passage from L'Enfant et les sortilèges.

Bittner, Julius (b Vienna, 9 Apr 1874; d Vienna, 10 Jan 1939), Austrian composer. A lawyer at first, then studied music with Josef Labor and Bruno Walter.

Works include operas *Die rote Gred* (1907), *Der Musikant* (1909), *Der Bergsee* (1910), *Der Abenteurer*, *Das höllische Gold*, *Die Kohlhaymerin*, *Das Rosengärtlein* (1922), *Mondnacht* (1928), *Das Veilchen*; ballets *Der Markt der Liebe*, *Die Todes-Tarantella*; *Missa Austriaca* for solo voices, chorus and orchestra; chamber music, piano pieces; songs.

Bizet, Georges (actually Alexandre César Léopold) (b Paris, 25 Oct 1838; d Bougival near Paris, 3 Jun 1875), French composer. His father, a teacher of singing, gave him his first instruction in music and at the age of nine, being exceptionally gifted, he was admitted to the Paris Conservatory, studying piano under Marmontel, organ under Benoist and composition under Zimmermann. In 1853, when Zimmermann died, he became a pupil of Halévy, having already taken a first prize for piano. He wrote his Symphony in C in 1855; it is the least known of his earlier works and one of the finest of all pieces written by an adolescent. The score lay unconsidered and was not performed until 1935, under Weingartner. Bizet is clearly influenced by Gounod but far transcends his model. In 1857 he won the Prix de Rome, but before he went to Rome he had already gained a prize in a competition for an operetta, *Le Docteur Miracle*, sponsored by Offenbach. He tied with Lecocq, whose setting was produced alternately with his own at the Théâtre des Bouffes-Parisiens.

He wrote several works in Rome and on his return to Paris in 1860 he set out to capture the operatic stage; but although the Opéra-Comique accepted his one-act opera, *La Guzla de l'Émir*, he withdrew it, destroying it later. The Théâtre Lyrique produced his next work, *Les Pêcheurs de perles*, in 1863; *Ivan le Terrible*, written in 1865, said to have been burnt by him, was recovered in 1944 and performed in Germany, at Mühringen Castle, Württemberg. In 1869 Pasdeloup for the first time gave him the chance to appear with an orchestral work, *Souvenirs de Rome*, performed 28 Feb, which he later entitled *Roma*. The same year he married Geneviève Halévy, his former master's daughter.

In 1872 he was commissioned to write incidental music for Daudet's play, *L'Arlésienne*, produced at the Vaudeville on 1 Oct. In 1874 Pasdeloup produced his overture *Patrie* (unconnected with Sardou's play), but he had set to work before that on *Carmen*, which was produced at the Opéra-Comique, with spoken dialogue, on 3 Mar 1875 and received 37 performances; but just after the 33rd perform-

Bizet *The composer Georges Bizet (1838–1875) as portrayed in a chromolithograph published in London 1912. Often criticized for being cynical and complacent in his private life, his letters reveal a caring man, especially with regard to his mentally unstable wife and mother-in-law.*

ance Bizet died, before the work had won through prejudice to a decided success. In a sense, Bizet's reputation has become hostage to his best-loved work; the passion and melody of *Carmen* should not obscure the same qualities to be found in the Symphony in C, *Les Pêcheurs de perles* and even *La Jolie Fille de Perth*.

A Selection of

Bizet

Bizet   *A biographical note*

Bizet's music seems to us today to be such an antithesis of Wagnerian gloom and doom that the initial reception of his greatest opera is difficult to credit. A French reviewer of *Carmen* opined that Bizet belonged to the school of Wagner, in that melody seemed obsolete and voices strangled by the orchestra. A London critic detected the 'forbidding and alluring' world of *Tannhäuser*, while the *New York Times* found that Don José was the only character in the opera of any interest. It was left to the philosopher Nietzsche to praise Bizet's melodic and harmonic richness, contrasting him favourably with his former friend Wagner. The social niceties of Bizet's time made it difficult for Parisian audiences to accept such features as Carmen's open sexuality, and the fact that at the opera's conclusion she is killed on stage – convention then demanded that such action take place out of sight. The premiere production was nevertheless a success, surviving the shock of Bizet's death on the night of the 33rd performance. A bout of rheumatism had followed a swim in the Seine, and he then suffered two heart attacks.

Works include OPERAS: *Don Procopio* (1859), *Les Pêcheurs de perles* (1863), *La Jolie Fille de Perth* (after Scott) (1866), *Djamileh, Carmen* (after Mérimee) (1874); operetta *Le Docteur Miracle*; incidental music to Daudet's *L'Arlésienne* (1872); cantatas *David* and *Clovis et Clotilde*; completion of Halévy's opera *Noë*.

ORCHESTRAL: symphony in C major (1855), suite *Roma* (1868), overture *Patrie, Petite Suite (Jeux d'enfants)* and *Marche funèbre* for orchestra; *Vasco de Gama*, symphonic ode with chorus.

PIANO AND SOLO VOCAL: *Chasse fantastique, Chants du Rhin, Trois Esquisses, Marine, Premier Nocturne, Variations chromatiques* for piano; *Jeux d'enfants* suite for piano duet; *Chanson du rouet* for vocal solo and chorus, *Le Golfe de Bahia* for solo voices and chorus; *Saint Jean de Pathmos* for unaccompanied male chorus, four vocal duets; a number of songs including *Feuilles d'album*.

Bjoner, Ingrid (b Kraakstad, 8 Nov 1927), Norwegian soprano. She sang Third Norn and Gutrune in a concert performance of *Götterdämmerung* for Oslo Radio in 1956, later issued as the opera's first recording. Stage debut Donna Anna, 1957. Munich from 1960 as Strauss's Empress and Daphne; Isolde in the centenary production of the opera's 1865 premiere there. NY Met. debut 1961, Elsa. CG from 1967 as Senta, Sieglinde and Leonore; sang Isolde at Bayreuth 1986, the Dyer's Wife at Munich 1988 and Senta at Oslo 1989. A successful recitalist in the songs of Grieg.

Björling, Jussi (actually Johan) (Jonaton) (b Stors Tuna, Kopparbergslän, 5 Feb 1911; d Stockholm, 9 Sept 1960), Swedish tenor. Studied with his father at the Stockholm Conservatory, and at the Royal Opera School in Stockholm. First appeared as Don Ottavio in *Don Giovanni*, Stockholm, 1930. He sang at CG in 1939 as Manrico; NY Met. from 1938 as Rodolfo, Faust, Verdi's Riccardo and Cavaradossi. One of the finest lyric tenors of his time.

Björling, Sigurd (b Stockholm, 2 Nov 1907; d Helsingborg, 8 Apr 1983), Swedish baritone. He studied with John Forsell at the Stockholm Conservatory; debut 1934. US debut San Francisco 1950, Kurwenal; NY Met. 1952, Telramund. CG 1951, Amfortas. Bayreuth 1952 as Wotan; sang this role until 1973 in Stockholm. Other roles included Balstrode and Hindemith's Mathis.

Blacher, Boris (b Niu-chang, China, 19 Jan 1903; d Berlin, 30 Jan 1975), German composer. Studied in Berlin and began his career under great difficulties during the Nazi regime, but later became very successful as a composer of the avant garde, developing a system of variable metres following arithmetical progressions, upon which many of his works are based. In 1953 he became director of the Berlin Hochschule für Musik.

Works include operas *Fürstin Tarakanova* (1940), *Preussisches Märchen* (1949), *Abstrakte Oper no.1* (1953), *200,000 Taler* (1969), *Das Geheimnis* (1975), chamber operas *Romeo und Julia* (1943, after Shakespeare) *Die Flut* (1946), *Die Nachtschwalbe* (1948); several ballets including *Harlekinade* (1939), *Lysistrate* (1950), *Hamlet* (1949), *Der Mohr von Venedig* (1955); scenic oratorio *Der Grossinquisitor* (after Dostoevsky (1947).

Symphony, symphonic poem *Hamlet* (after Shakespeare), variations on theme by Paganini and other orchestral works; two piano concertos, viola concerto; five string quartets (1930–67) and other chamber music, piano music, songs.

Blachut, Beno (b Ostrava-Vitkovice, 14 Jun 1913; d Prague, 10 Jan 1985), Czech tenor. Debut Olomouc, 1939, Jeník. Prague National Theatre from 1941; British debut with the co. Edinburgh Festival, 1970, as Matej Brouček in the British premiere of Janáček's *The Excursions of Mr Brouček*. Other roles included Lača, Dalibor and the Prince in *Rusalka*. He sang in Vienna as a guest.

Black, Andrew (b Glasgow, 15 Jan 1859; d Sydney, NSW, 15 Sept 1920), Scottish baritone. At first an organist, but studied singing in London and Milan. Appeared in Scotland with success and first sang in London in 1887. Best known in oratorios, e.g. *The Spectre's Bride* (Dvořák), *Elijah* and *The Apostles*.

'Black Key' Study Chopin's piano Study in G♭ major, op. 10 no. 5, written *c* 1831–32 and pub. in 1833. So called because the right hand plays only on the black keys throughout.

Black Knight, The cantata for chorus and orchestra by Elgar, op. 25, a setting of Longfellow's translation of Uhland's ballad *Der schwarze Ritter*, fp Worcester Festival, 1893.

Blackwood, Easley (b Indianapolis, 21 Apr 1933), American composer and pianist. His teachers included Hindemith, Nadia Boulanger and Olivier Messiaen. Concert and solo recitals in music by Ives and Schoenberg; professor at Chicago University from 1968. His technique is highly complex, both rhythmically and harmonically.

Works include five symphonies (1955, 1960, 19964, 1973, 1978); clarinet concerto (1964); concerto for flute and strings (1968); piano concerto (1970); two string quartets (1957, 1959); 12 *Microtonal Etudes* for synthesizer (1982).

bladder pipe an early bagpipe with an animal's bladder used for the bag.

Blades, James (b Peterborough, 9 Sept 1901), English timpanist and percussionist. Employed in dance bands and playing film music in the 1930s. He joined the LSO in 1960 and has been a member of the English Chamber Orchestra and Melos Ensemble; with the EOG for their production of Britten's three church parables. Professor RAM from 1960, OBE 1972.

B-la-F Quartet a string quartet on the name of Belaiev by Rimsky-Korsakov, Liadov, Borodin and Glazunov, performed on M P Belaiev's 50th birthday, 22 Feb 1886. It is constructed on the notes B♭, A, F.

Blake, David (Leonard) (b London, 2 Sept 1936), English composer. He studied at Cambridge, and with Hanns Eisler in Berlin; has taught at York University from 1964. He has used serial technique, and has been influenced by the music of the Far East.

Works include the operas *Toussaint L'Ouverture* (1974–76, revised 1982) and *The Plumber's Gift* (1985–88); chamber symphony (1966), two violin concertos (1976 and 1983); three choruses to poems by Frost (1964), *Lumina*, cantata for soprano, baritone, chorus and orchestra, to text by Pound (1969), *From the Mattress Grave*, 12 Heine poems for soprano and 11 instruments (1978); three string quartets (1962, 1973, 1982), Nonet for wind (1971), Capriccio, for wind, strings and piano (1980); *The Spear* for mezzo, speaker and ensemble (1982), *Rise, Dove* for baritone and orchestra (1982), *Scherzi ed Intermezzi* for orchestra (1984), *Seasonal Variants* for seven players (1985), *Pastoral Paraphrase* for baritone and orchestra (1986), cello concerto (1989–93).

Blake, Rockwell (b Plattsburgh, NY, 10 Jan 1951), American tenor. He made his debut at Washington DC, 1976, as Lindoro, and became widely admired for his robust and forthright style in other Rossini roles: NY City Opera 1977 in *Le Comte Ory*, Met. debut 1981, as Lindoro (other Met. roles include Almaviva, Don Ottavio, and Arturo in *I Puritani*. He has also sung James I in *La donna del lago* at La Scala and Mozart's Ferrando at Dallas.

Blake, William (1757–1827), English poet and artist. ◊Bolcom (*Songs of Innocence and Experience*), ◊Britten (*Songs and Proverbs*), ◊Connolly (*The Marriage of Heaven and Hell*), A ◊Goehr (*Five poems and an Epigram*), ◊Job (Vaughan Williams), ◊Parry (*Jerusalem*), ◊Tippett (*Song of Liberty*).

Blamont, François Colin de (b Versailles, 22 Nov 1690; d Versailles, 14 Feb 1760), French composer. Pupil of his father, who was in the royal band, and later of Lalande. He became in 1719 superintendent of the royal music and, after Lalande's death in 1726, master of the chamber music.

Works include stage pieces (mostly ballets and ballet-operas) *Les Festes grecques et romaines* (1723), *Le Retour des dieux sur la terre* (for the marriage of Louis XV, 1725), *Le Caprice d'Érato* (1730), *Endymion* (1731), *Les Caractères de l'Amour, Les Amours du printemps, Jupiter vainqueur des Titans* (1745), *Les Festes de Thétis* (1750); cantata *Circé* and three books of *Cantates françaises* for solo voice; motets with orchestral accompaniment.

Blanc, Ernest (b Sanary-sur-Mer, 1 Nov 1923), French baritone. Debut Marseilles, 1950; Paris Opéra from 1954. Well known as Scarpia and Rigoletto and in Wagner roles: Bayreuth 1958–59, as Telramund. At Glyndebourne in 1960 as Don Giovanni and Bellini's Riccardo, opposite Sutherland. Guest at Milan, Vienna and in Chicago and San Francisco. Widely known in recordings of *Faust, Carmen, Hoffmann* and *Les Pêcheurs de perles*.

Blanchard, Henri Louis (b Bordeaux, 9 Apr. 1791; d Paris, 18 Dec 1858), French violinist, composer, music critic and playwright. Studied violin under R Kreutzer and composition under Méhul and others. Was conductor and theatre director in Paris. Wrote three operas, including *Diane de Vernon* (after Scott's *Rob Roy*) (1831), chamber music and airs for vaudevilles.

Bland (born *Romanzini*), Maria Theresa (b 1769; d London, 15 Jan 1838), English ballad singer of Italian extraction. Sang with great success, especially at Vauxhall and other London pleasure gardens as well as in opera at Drury Lane. She married Bland, a brother of Mrs Jordan, the actress.

Blangini, (Giuseppe Marco Maria) Felice (b Turin, 18 Nov 1781; d Paris, 18 Dec 1841), Italian tenor and composer. Sang at Turin Cathedral as a child and learnt music there. In 1799 he went to Paris, where he finished an opera left incomplete by P A D Della Maria and produced one of his own. In 1809 he was called to Kassel as music director to King Jérôme; but he returned to Paris in 1814 and two years later became professor of singing at the Conservatory.

Works include over 30 operas, e.g. *La Fausse Duègne* (finished by him), *Chimère et réalité* (1803), *Nephtali, ou Les Ammonites* (1806), *Encore un tour de Caliphe, Inez de Castro* (1810), *Les Fêtes lacédémoniennes* (1807), *Le Sacrifice d'Abraham* (1810); contributed to *La Marquise de Brinvilliers*; cantata *Die letzten Augenblicke Werthers* (after Goethe); 174 songs.

Blaník (Smetana). ◊Má Vlast.

Blankenburg, Quirjin Gerbrandt van (b Gouda, 1654; d The Hague, 12 May 1739), Dutch organist and composer. Studied philosophy and medicine at Leyden, was organist there and later at The Hague. Wrote theoretical books, pub. harpsichord and organ accompaniments to psalms and hymns and, in honour of the betrothal of the Prince of Orange in 1677, wrote pieces in two parts to be sung normally or upside down, forwards or backwards.

Blankenheim, Toni (b Cologne, 12 Dec 1921), German baritone. He studied with Res Fischer. Debut Frankfurt, 1947, as Mozart's Figaro. From 1950 he was principal baritone at the Hamburg Staatsoper; sang Berg's Wozzeck and Dr Schön with the co. at SW, London, in 1962. Bayreuth 1954–60 as Donner, Klingsor, Beckmesser and Kothner. He has appeared widely in Europe, in Mexico and San Francisco and at the NY Met.

Blas de Castro, Juan (b Aragon, *c* 1560; d Madrid, 6 Aug 1631), Spanish composer. In the 1590s he was private musician to the Duke of Alba at Salamanca and in 1605 musician and usher to Philip III. Lope de Vega and Tirso de Molina mentioned him in their works. Only 20 songs for three and four voices survive.

Blass, Robert (b New York, 27 Oct 1867; d Berlin, 3 Dec 1930), American bass of German parentage. Debut Weimar, 1892, as King Henry; sang widely as guest including CG 1899 and appeared at Bayreuth in 1901 as Gurnemanz and Hagen, under Muck and Richter. NY Met. 1900–10 (debut as the Landgrave). Gurnemanz at Amsterdam, in the local fp of *Parsifal* (1905).

Blavet, Michel (b Besançon, 13 Mar 1700; d Paris, 28 Oct 1768), French flautist and composer. Works include *opéra comique Le Jaloux corrigé* (1752), ballets, sonatas and duets for flute. As a soloist, performed at the Concert Spirituel, in the Musique du Roi and at the Opéra.

Blech German = 'brass'; an abbr. often used in scores for *Blechinstrumente*.

Blech, Harry (b London, 2 Mar 1910), English conductor and violinist. He studied in London and Manchester. Played with the BBC SO before World War II and was a founder member of the Blech quartet, 1933–50. Founded the London Mozart Players 1949 and was music director until 1984. Many recordings of Mozart and other composers of 18th-c. Vienna. CBE 1984.

Blech, Leo (b Aachen, 21 Apr 1871; d Berlin, 24 Aug 1958), German conductor and composer. Pupil of Bargiel and Humperdinck,

conductor in his native town, 1892–98; later at Prague and in 1906–37 conductor of the Berlin Opera. Often conducted Wagner and took part in the 1920s revival of interest in Verdi's operas.

Works include operas *Aglaja* (1893), *Cherubina* (1894), *Versiegelt* (Hamburg, 1908), *Das war ich* (Dresden, 1902), *Aschenbrödel, Alpenkönig und Menschenfeind* (after Raimund) (1903); three symphonies; poems; choral works with orchestra.

Blegen, Judith (b Missoula, MT, 27 Apr 1941), American soprano. Opera debut Nuremberg, 1963; Mélisande at Spoleto in 1964. Vienna, Staatsoper, 1969, as Rosina; NY Met. from 1970 as Papagena, Zerlina and Sophie. In the 1969 Santa Fe US premiere of Menotti's *Help! Help! the Globoniks!* she sang the role of Emily and played the violin. CG debut 1975, Despina.

Blessed Damozel, The (Debussy). ◊Damoiselle élue

Blind Man's Buff masque by Peter Maxwell Davies for high voice, mezzo, mime and stage band (text by Davies from Büchner's *Leonce und Lena*, et al), fp London, 29 May 1972, conductor Boulez.

blind octaves a trick of piano writing: figures in octaves rapidly alternating between the two hands where the thumbs trace a continuous melodic line while the outer notes fly off at broken intervals.

Sir Arthur Bliss, Master of the Queen's Music, once described the BBC's pop programme as 'aural hashish', but it's not that good.

Richard Neville, *Playpower*, 1970

Bliss, Arthur (Drummond) (b London, 2 Aug 1891; d London, 27 Mar 1975), English composer. Educated at Rugby and Pembroke College, Cambridge, where he studied music under C Wood. Entered the RCM in London, 1913, studying with Stanford, Vaughan Williams and Holst, but joined the army in 1914, serving all through the war until 1918. Professor of composition at RCM in 1921, but took wholly to composing the next year, never holding any official post until he was appointed music director of the BBC in 1941, an appointment he resigned to Hely-Hutchinson in 1945. He was knighted 1950 and succeeded Bax as Master of the Queen's Music 1953. His early music was miniaturist in scope but he later embraced larger forms. With some success, Bliss sought to evoke comparisons with Elgar in *A Colour Symphony, Introduction and Allegro* and violin concerto.

DRAMATIC: operas, *The Olympians* (libretto by J B Priestley) (1949), and *Tobias and the Angel* (C Hassall) (1960); ballets, *Checkmate, Miracle in the Gorbals* and *Adam Zero*; incidental music for Shakespeare's *Tempest*; film music for *Things to Come* (H G Wells), *Conquest of the Air, Caesar and Cleopatra* (G B Shaw).

ORCHESTRAL: *A Colour Symphony* (1922), *Introduction and Allegro* (1926), *Hymn to Apollo, Meditations on a Theme by John Blow* (1955); concertos for piano and two pianos; march *Phoenix* for the liberation of France; *Music for Strings*.

VOCAL: *Morning Heroes* for orator, chorus and orchestra (1930), *Pastoral* for mezzo, chorus, flute, strings and drums, cantata *Mary of Magdala* for contralto, bass, chorus and orchestra, *Serenade* for baritone and orchestra (1929), concerto for piano, tenor and chamber orchestra, *Rout* for voice and chamber orchestra *Madam Noy* for voice and six instruments; several song cycles with various instruments or piano, including *Five American Songs* (Edna St Vincent Millay).

CHAMBER: *Conversations* for flute, oboe, violin, viola and cello; two string quartets (1941, 1950), oboe quintet, clarinet quintet; sonatas for violin and piano and viola and piano.

Blitheman, John (b *c* 1525; d London, 23 May 1591), English organist and composer. Gentleman of the Chapel Royal from before Dec 1558 until his death. He was a famous organist and a teacher of Bull. Works include motets and six *In Nomines* for virginal.

Blitzstein, Marc (b Philadelphia, 2 Mar 1905; d Fort-de-France, Martinique, 22 Jan 1964), American pianist and composer. Appeared as solo pianist at the age of 15; studied composition with Scalero in NY, Nadia Boulanger in Paris and Schoenberg in Vienna; also piano with

Siloti in USA. His first great success was the light opera *The Cradle Will Rock*, produced in NY 1937 with piano accompaniment directed by Orson Welles, after a full performance was banned by the authorities. He was a political radical and was killed after an argument with American sailors.

Works include operas *Triple Sec* (1929), *Parabola and Circula* (1929), *The Harpies*, *The Cradle Will Rock* (1937); ballet *Cain*; incidental music for Shakespeare's *Julius Caesar*; film music for *Surf and Seaweed*, *The Spanish Earth*, *No for an Answer* (1941), *Chesapeake Bay Retriever*; choral opera *The Condemned*; radio song-play *I've got the Tune*, Children's Cantata; *The Airborne* for orchestra, chorus and narrator (1946); *Romantic Piece*, *Jigsaw* ballet suite, and variations for orchestra; piano concerto (1931), string quartet and serenade for string quartet; piano sonata and *Percussion Music* for piano (1929).

Preposterous ass, that never read so far/To know the cause why music was ordain'd!/Was it not to refresh the mind of man/After his studies or his usual pain.
Shakespeare, *The Taming of the Shrew*,
Act 3, Scene 1, line 9

Bloch, Ernest (b Geneva, 24 Jul 1880; d Portland, OR, 15 Jul 1959), Swiss (Americanized) composer. His music always recalls his spiritual heritage. Pupil of Jaques-Dalcroze at first, then of Ysaÿe and Rasse at the Brussels Conservatory, and later at the Hoch Conservatory at Frankfurt where Iwan Knorr was his composition master. His last teacher was Thuille at Munich, and he then went to live in Paris, where he began the opera *Macbeth* on a French libretto by Edmond Fleg, having already written several important works. It was produced in Paris in 1910, but he had in the meantime returned to Switzerland to conduct subscription concerts at Lausanne and Neuchâtel. From 1911 to 1915 he was professor of music aesthetics at the Geneva Conservatory. In 1917 he went to the USA and settled in NY as professor at the David Mannes School of Music. A second opera *Jézabel*, begun there in 1918, was unfinished.

From 1920 to 1925 Bloch was director of the Cleveland Inst. of Music. In 1930 he retired to Switzerland to live quietly in remote places. Some interest was shown in his work in England and a good deal in Italy, where his *Sacred Service* was produced (at Turin) and *Macbeth* was revived in an Italian translation at Naples, 5 Mar 1938. But the anti-Semitic movement encouraged by the Fascists put an end to this appreciation. As a US citizen he could no longer remain absent from the USA without losing his adopted nationality, and he returned there at the end of 1938.

Bloch's powerful opera *Macbeth* is worth revival and his most characteristic and better-known later music is found in *Schelomo*, the Concerto Grosso and the violin concerto.

Works include opera *Macbeth* (1904–09), *Sacred Service* (*Avodath Hakodesh*) for baritone solo, chorus and orchestra.

ORCHESTRAL: *Israel* symphony for five voices and orchestra; symphony in C♭ minor (1901), symphonic poems *Hiver – Printemps*, *Trois Poèmes juifs* for orchestra, *America*, epic rhapsody for orchestra (1926); *Helvetia*, symphonic fresco (1928), *Evocations*, symphonic suite (1938), suite: *Overture, Passacaglia and Finale*; violin concerto (1938); *Concerto symphonique* for piano and orchestra, *Schelomo* for cello and orchestra (1916), *Concerto grosso* for piano and strings, *Voice in the Wilderness* for cello and orchestra (1926), *Four Episodes* for chamber orchestra (1926).

CHAMBER: five string quartets (1916–56); two violin and piano sonatas, viola and piano suite, piano quintet, *Three Nocturnes* for piano trio; *In the Mountains*, *Night*, *Three Landscapes* and *Recueillement* (prelude) for string quartet.

VOCAL AND INSTRUMENTAL: *Poèmes d'automme* and three Psalms for voice and orchestra; *Enfantines*, *5 Sketches in Sepia*, *In the Night*, *Nirvana*, *Poems of the Sea* and sonata for piano; *Baal Shem* (three

pieces), *Melody, Exotic Night* and *Abodah* for violin and piano; *From Jewish Life* (three pieces) and *Méditation hébraïque* for cello and piano, song cycle *Historiettes au crépuscule* (1903) and other songs.

Blockflöte, German, = lit. 'block flute'; actually fipple flute = ◊recorder.

block harmony a term used for a type of harmonic accompaniment, in which all the notes except the melody move together simultaneously in 'block' chords, without being made to depart from one another by means of figuration or counterpoint.

Blockx, Jan (b Antwerp, 25 Jan 1851; d Antwerp, 26 May 1912), Belgian composer. Learnt music as a choirboy and went to the Antwerp School of Music, later to the Leipzig Conservatory. In 1886 he became professor and in 1901 director of the Antwerp Conservatory, succeeding Benoit, whom he followed as a Flemish music nationalist. Most of his operas and all his cantatas for solo voices, chorus and orchestra are set to Flemish words.

Works include operas *Jets vergeten* (1877), *Maître Martin* (1892), *Herbergprinses* (1896), *Thyl Uilenspiegel* (1900), *De Bruid der Zee*, *De Kapel* (1903), *Baldie*; ballet *Milenka* (1887); cantatas *Op den Stroom*, *Een Droom van 't Paradijs*, *Vredezang*, *Klokke Roeland*, *De Scheldezang*; overture *Rubens*; Romance for violin and orchestra.

Blodek, Vilém (b Prague, 3 Oct 1834; d Prague, 1 May 1874), Czech flautist, teacher and composer. Produced the national opera *In the Well* at Prague in 1867, but his second opera, *Zitek*, remained unfinished at his death; it was completed by F X Vana, and performed in Prague on the centenary of Blodek's birth.

Blom, Eric (Walter) (b Berne, 20 Aug 1888; d London, 11 Apr 1959), English critic, of Danish origin. He was educated privately and first became known in England as assistant to Rosa Newmarch in providing programme notes for the Promenade concerts in 1919. He was London music critic of the *Manchester Guardian* from 1923 to 1931, music critic of the *Birmingham Post* from 1931, and music critic of the *Observer* from 1949 to 1953. He also edited *Music & Letters* from 1937 to 1950 and 1954 to 1959. His books included *The Limitations of Music*, *Mozart*, *Beethoven's Sonatas Discussed*, *Music in England* and the first editions of this dictionary. He also translated several foreign books and edited the fifth edition of *Grove's Dictionary of Music and Musicians* (1954). He was made CBE and Hon. D.Litt. of Birmingham University in 1955. Blom was the last of the inspired 'amateur' lexicographers; the growth of musicology in all its aspects over the last 40 years has made his single-handed perfectionism impossible to achieve.

Blomdahl, Karl-Birger (b Växjö, 19 Oct 1916; d Växjö, 14 Jun 1968), Swedish composer. Studied at Stockholm under various masters, including Rosenberg and Wöldike. In 1960 he was appointed professor at the Stockholm Conservatory.

Works include opera *Aniara* (a spaceship drama) (1957–59); incidental music; three symphonies (1943, 1947, 1950), symphonic dances, concert overture, *Concerto grosso* for orchestra; violin concerto (1946), viola concerto, chamber concerto for piano, wind and percussion; two string quartets, string trio, woodwind trio, suites for cello and piano and bassoon and piano; piano pieces; trios for women's voices.

Blomstedt, Herbert (b Springfield, MA, 11 Jul 1927), US-born Swedish conductor. Studied in Stockholm and conducted the Oslo PO 1962–68, Danish Radio SO 1967–77, concerts with the Dresden Staatskapelle 1975–85, Swedish Radio SO 1977–82. Music Director of the San Francisco SO 1985–95. Best known for his performances of Sibelius and Nielsen.

Blondel de Nesle, *fl.* 1180–1200, French trouvère whose surviving songs (over 20) are exceptionally widely represented in the surviving sources and often formed the basis for later adaptations. The legend that he was associated with King Richard the Lionheart and was instrumental in rescuing him from prison has contributed to Blondel's subsequent fame.

Bloomfield, Theodore (b Cleveland, 14 Jun 1923), American conductor. Studied with Monteux at Juilliard and made debut with NY Little SO, 1945. Worked in Cleveland 1946–52 and was music director of

Blomstedt *US-born Swedish conductor Herbert Blomstedt typifies a post-war generation of conductors which earns the respect of orchestras by quietly crafted musicianship. The old methods of ruling by tyranny and tantrums are rejected in favour of professional courtesy and the exploration of new repertory.*

the Portland SO 1955–59, Rochester PO 1959–63. European posts at the Hamburg Opera 1964–66, Frankfurt-am-Main (music director 1966–68) and Berlin (chief conductor of Berlin SO 1975–82).

Blow, John (b Newark, bap. 23 Feb 1649; d London, 1 Oct 1708), English organist and composer, the major contemporary of Purcell. He became one of the children in the Chapel Royal in London as soon as it was re-established after the Restoration (1660) and was taught by H Cooke. He wrote three anthems in 1663 and took a share with Humfrey and Turner in the 'Club Anthem' *c* 1664. About the same time he set Herrick's 'Go, perjur'd man' in the style of Carissimi at Charles II's request. Hingston and C Gibbons also had a share in Blow's musical education. In 1668 he became organist at Westminster Abbey in succession to Albert Bryne; in Mar 1674 he was sworn a Gentleman of the Chapel Royal and the following Jul he became Master of the Children following Humfrey. In November he married Elizabeth Braddock. D.Mus. at Canterbury, 1677. In 1679 he was followed in the Westminster organist's post by Purcell, returning as organist after Purcell's death in 1695. In 1687 he succeeded Wise as almoner and choirmaster at St Paul's Cathedral (as yet unfinished). James II appointed him a member of the royal band and confirmed a previous appointment as Composer in Ordinary. Towards the end of the century he bought a property at Hampton, but still retained a house at Westminster, where he died.

Works include *c* 12 services; over 100 English anthems, nine Latin anthems; masque *Venus and Adonis* (*c* 1685); Act Songs for Oxford University; at least 16 Welcome Songs, five for St Cecilia's Day, odes on the death of Queen Mary (1695) and of Purcell (1696); three coronation anthems for James II, one for William and Mary; anthem for the opening service at St Paul's Cathedral (1697); sonata for two violins and bass; harpsichord lessons, suites and pieces; some organ pieces; song collection *Amphion Anglicus*, songs and catches, etc.

Bluebeard ◊Ariane et Barbe-bleue; ◊Barbe-bleue; ◊Ritter Blaubart.

Bluebeard's Castle (Bartók). ◊Duke Bluebeard's Castle.

blue notes a device in blues, the playing of certain notes, especially the third and seventh of the scale, deliberately out of tune, between major and minor.

blues song (lament) from black American jazz, usually in a repeating harmonic pattern of 12 bars with flattened thirds and sevenths (◊'blue

notes'). Ravel (sonata for violin and piano), Copland and Tippet have drawn on blues style.

Blume, Friedrich (b Schlüchtern, Hesse, 5 Jan 1893; d Schlüchtern, 22 Nov 1975), German musicologist. Studied at Munich, Leipzig and Berlin. He was a prisoner in England for three years during the 1914–18 war. After teaching in Berlin from 1921 he became professor at Kiel University from 1934 to 1958. He was editor-in-chief of the complete works of M Praetorius and the series *Das Chorwerk*, and was editor of the encyclopedia *Die Musik in Geschichte und Gegenwart*. His books include a history of Protestant church music.

Blumenfeld, Harold (b Seattle, 15 Oct 1923), American composer. Studied composition at Harvard and with Hindemith at Yale; conducting with Bernstein. Directed the Opera Theater of St Louis 1962–66 and the Washington University Opera Studio 1960–71, presenting works outside the standard repertory.

Works include operas *Amphitryon* (1962), *Fritzi* (1979), *4-Score: An Opera of Opposites* (1985) and *Season in Hell: A Life of Rimbaud* (1991); *Eroscapes* for soprano and ensemble (1971); *Song of Innocence* for soloists, chorus and orchestra (1973); *Voyages*, cantata after Hart Crane (1977); *La Face cendrée*, cantata after Rimbaud (1981); *Orchestral Evocations of Rimbaud* (1988).

Blumine original second movement of Mahler's first symphony, in D, and heard in the work's fp, Budapest, 20 Nov 1889. The movement was discarded in 1894 and not performed again until 18 Jun 1976 at Aldeburgh, conductor Britten.

Blüthner, Julius Ferdinand (b Falkenhain, 11 Mar 1824; d Leipzig, 13 Apr 1910), German piano manufacturer. Founded his firm at Leipzig in 1853.

Bluthochzeit opera by Fortner (libretto by E Beck after Lorca's *Bodas de Sangre*), composed for the opening of the new opera house, Cologne, and performed there 8 Jun 1957. Bride runs away with former fiancé on wedding day; bridegroom follows and both men are killed in the ensuing fight.

Opera by Szokolay (*Vérnász*, same source), produced Budapest, 30 Oct 1964.

B Minor Mass Bach's great setting of the Latin text begins in B minor, but as a whole centres on D major. The work was not composed in one piece, however, but in four sections, some of them intended for separate performance. The *Kyrie* and *Gloria* (constituting in themselves a complete Lutheran short Mass) were written in 1733, and used to support Bach's application for the title of Court Composer to the Elector of Saxony; the *Symbolum Nicenum* (Creed) *c* 1748; *Sanctus* 1724; finally, the movements from *Osanna* to *Dona nobis pacem c* 1748. Several of the movements were adapted from earlier works, viz. church cantatas Nos. 11, 12, 29, 46, 120 and 171 and the secular cantata *Preise dein Glücke*.

Boccherini, Luigi (b Lucca, 19 Feb 1743; d Madrid, 28 May 1805), Italian cellist and composer. He was the most important Italian representative of the Viennese Classical style, writing in his own distinctive manner. Pupil of his father, a double-bass player, who sent him to Rome for further study in 1757. On his return to Lucca in 1761 he played cello in the theatre orchestra. With the violinist Manfredi he travelled widely on concert tours in Austria and France. Particularly successful in Paris (1767–68), he pub. there his first chamber music. In 1769 he went to Madrid and settled there, being first in the service of the Infante Don Luis until 1785, when the latter died. In 1787 Boccherini was appointed court composer to Frederick William II of Prussia, who had the exclusive right to his works, but he seems to have maintained his residence in Madrid. After the king's death in 1797 he was apparently without a permanent post, for he spent his last years in increasing poverty, largely owing to inconsiderate treatment by his publishers.

Works include oratorios *Giuseppe riconosciuto* and *Gioas, rè di Giuda* (*c* 1765); *Stabat Mater* (1781), Mass (1800), cantatas, motets, etc.; zarzuela *La Clementina* (1780); concert arias, etc.; 26 symphonies; 11 cello concertos (including a pastiche by Grützmacher) and one each for flute, violin and harpsichord; 91 string quartets, 48 string trios, 125 string quintets, 12 piano quintets, 18 quintets for wind and strings, 16 sextets, two octets; 27 violin sonatas, six cello sonatas.

Bochsa, Robert Nicolas Charles (b Montmédi, 9 Aug 1789; d Sydney, NSW, 6 Jan 1856), French harpist, conductor and composer. Began as a composer of opera, oratorio and ballet at Lyons and Bordeaux; entered the Paris Conservatory in 1806; made a great name as harpist and opera composer, but fled to England in 1817 when exposed as a forger. Although condemned, he was able to live in London, where he made the harp extremely popular and became professor of the instrument on the foundation of the RAM, but in 1827 had to leave owing to scandals, including bigamy. In 1839 he ran away with Bishop's wife, Anna Riviere. They went on a world tour together, during which he died.

Works include opera *Trajan* (Lyon, 1805) and eight others; a ballet; oratorio *Le Déluge universel* (1806; performed CG, 22 Feb 1822); Requiems for Louis XVI, which contains anticipations of Berlioz's *Symphonie funèbre et triomphale*); many pieces for harp.

Bockelmann, Rudolf (August Louis Wilhelm) (b Bodenteich near Lüneburg, 2 Apr 1890; d Dresden, 10 Oct 1958), German bass-baritone. He studied with Oscar Lassner and first appeared in *Lohengrin* at Leipzig, 1921; sang there in title role of Krenek's *Das Leben des Orest*, 1930. He sang regularly at Bayreuth 1928–42, as Gunther, Kurwenal, Sachs and the Dutchman, and frequently in London (CG 1929–38). After the 1939–45 war he settled as a teacher in Hamburg.

Bockshorn, Samuel (Friedrich) (Capricornus) (b Žeržice near Mlada Boleslav, 21 Dec 1628; d Stuttgart, 10 Nov 1665), Bohemian composer. Music director at Pressburg, Nuremberg and Stuttgart.

Works include dramatic cantata *Raptus Proserpinae* (1662); sacred and secular works for voices and instruments; vocal table music, songs.

Bockstriller German = 'goat's trill'; a kind of vocal shake considered of no artistic value, produced by a rapid, bleating repetition of a single note. Wagner asks for this kind of shake from the tailors' chorus in the third act of *Die Meistersinger*.

Bodanzky, Artur (b Vienna, 16 Dec 1877; d New York, 23 Nov 1939), Austrian conductor. Studied at the Vienna Conservatory and after some minor appointments became assistant conductor to Mahler at the Imperial Opera. After several engagements at German opera houses, he became conductor of the German operas at the NY Met, 1915, leading drastically cut versions of Wagner and operas by Weber, Mozart and Beethoven with his own additions. He conducted the Society of the Friends of Music from 1921. At CG in 1914 he conducted the first British stage performance of *Parsifal*.

Bode, Hannelore (b Berlin-Zehlendorf, 2 Aug 1941), German soprano. Debut Bonn, 1964. She sang in Basel 1967–68, then joined the Deutsche Oper, Düsseldorf; Wagner roles, e.g. Eva and Elisabeth. She sang Eva at Bayreuth 1973–74 and in 1975 recorded the role with Solti.

Bodenschatz, Erhard (b Lichtenberg, 1576; d Gross-Osterhausen, 1636), German theologian and musician. He edited various collections of sacred music, notably the *Florilegium Portense*, pub. in two parts (1603 and 1621).

Boehm, Theobald (b Munich, 9 Apr 1794; d Munich, 25 Nov 1881), German flautist and inventor. He wrote music for his instrument and made important changes in its fingering and mechanism.

Boëllmann, Léon (b Ensisheim, 25 Sept 1862; d Paris, 11 Oct 1897), French (Alsatian) organist and composer. Pupil of Gigout at Niedermeyer's school in Paris, later organist at the church of Saint-Vincent-de-Paul there.

Works include symphony in F major; *Fantaisie dialoguée* for organ and orchestra, *Variations symphoniques* for cello and orchestra (1893); piano quartet, piano trio; cello and piano sonata; church music, organ works include two suites (first *Gothique*, 1895).

Boëly, Alexandre (Pierre François) (b Versailles, 19 Apr 1785; d Paris, 27 Dec 1858), French pianist, organist and composer. Organist at the church of Saint-Germain-l'Auxerrois, 1840–51, where he cultivated Bach's organ music.

Works include chamber music (five string trios, four string quartets); organ works; violin and piano sonatas; numerous piano works include sonatas, caprices, studies, preludes and fugues.

Boesmans, Philippe (b Tongeren, 17 May 1936), Belgian composer. Studied with Pousseur at Liège and has worked with him at the electronic music studios there from 1971. His music has also been influenced by the French and Italian avant garde.

Works include operas *La Passion de Gilles* (1983) and *Reigen*, after Schnitzler's play (1993); *Impromptu* for 23 instruments (1965); symphony for piano (1966); *Verticales* for orchestra (1969); *Intervalles* for orchestra (1973); *Multiples* for two pianos and orchestra (1974); *Attitudes* for soprano and ensemble (1977); piano and violin concertos (1978, 1979); *Conversions* for orchestra (1980); *Ricercar* for organ (1983); realization of Monteverdi's *Poppea* with an array of modern instruments (1989).

Boësset French 16th–17th-c. family of musicians:

1. Antoine Boësset, Sieur de Villedieu (b Blois, *c.* 1586; d Paris, 8 Dec 1643). Became Master of the King's Music to Louis XIII through his marriage to Guédron's daughter and held other important posts at court. Wrote 24 ballets and pub. nine books of *Airs de cour* in four and five parts (Paris 1617–42); also wrote Masses and motets.

2. Jean-Baptiste Boësset, Seigneur de Dehault (b Paris, 1614; d Paris, 1685), son of 1). Succeeded his father in 1644. Wrote opera *La Mort d'Adonis*, with words by Perrin, and ballets *Ballet du Temps* (1654), *Triomphe de Baccus* (*c* 1666) and *Alcidiane*; also vocal chamber music.

3. Claude Jean-Baptiste Boësset, Seigneur de Launay (b July 1664; d Paris, *c* 1701), son of 2). Held some of his father's posts and titles from 1686, but was replaced by 1696 by Lully's son Jean-Baptiste and by Colasse. He wrote *Fruits d'automne*.

There is nothing, I think, in which the power of art is shown so much as in playing on the fiddle.

Dr Samuel Johnson, quoted in Boswell,
Life of Johnson, 1791

Boethius, Anicius Manlius Severinus (b Rome, *c* 480; d 524), Roman consul, senator and philosopher. His most important work is the *De consolatione philosophiae* (some verses from which were set to music in Carolingian times), but he is also, in his *De institutione musica*, the interpreter of ancient musical theory to the Western world. In spite of some misconceptions and the irrelevancy of much of the Greek system, his work remained the fundamental basis of almost all medieval and Renaissance musical theory.

Boettcher, Wilfried (b Bremen, 11 Aug 1929; d Aug 1994), German conductor and cellist. After studying in Hamburg and with Pierre Fournier in Paris, he founded the Vienna Soloists 1959. Conductor of the Hamburg SO 1967–71 and guest conductor with other leading orchestras in Europe and the USA. Principal guest conductor of the Northern Sinfonia, Newcastle, from 1986. Opera engagements in Berlin, Vienna (State Opera) and Italy.

Bogatirev, Anatoly Vassilevich (b Vitebsk, 13 Aug 1913), Russian composer. Studied at the Minsk Conservatory under Zolotarev. Later studied folksong and became deputy director of the Conservatory at Minsk.

Works include operas *The Two Foscari* (after Byron) and *In the Thick Woods of Polesye* (1939); incidental music for Romashev's *Stars Cannot be Dimmed*; *The Tale of a Bear* for solo voices, chorus and orchestra, cantata *To the People of Leningrad*; string quartet, piano trio; *Manfred* suite (after Byron) and variations for piano; choruses, songs, folksong arrangements. In 1957 he made a performing version from the sketches of Tchaikovsky's seventh symphony.

Bohème, La, *Bohemian Life*, opera by Leoncavallo (libretto by composer, based on Murger's novel *Scènes de la vie de Bohème*), produced Venice, Teatro La Fenice, 6 May 1897. Composed at the same time as Puccini's work.

──── THE OPERA ────
La Bohème

A four-act opera by Giacomo Puccini, set in the Latin Quarter of
Paris in about 1830. The first performance in 1896 was a comparative failure, but this opera about a tragic love affair soon became an
established favourite.

I. The impoverished poet Rodolfo (tenor) and the painter Marcello
(baritone) are joined in their garret by two other 'Bohemian'
students, the musician Schaunard (baritone) and philosopher Colline (bass). After his friends go out to the café, Rodolfo answers the
door to his neighbour Mimi (soprano), who asks for a light for her
candle. Mimi and Rodolfo soon fall in love.

II. At the café, Rodolfo introduces Mimi to his friends while
Marcello's old flame Musetta (soprano) shows off her elderly
admirer Alcindoro (bass); Alcindoro is left to pay the bill after
everyone leaves.

III. Already ill from consumption, Mimi seeks Marcello's advice
after a quarrel with Rodolfo; the couple agree to part in the spring.

IV. The four Bohemian students meet in their garret and Musetta
arrives to say that Mimi wishes to return to be with Rodolfo.
Marcello leaves to buy medicine, but before he can return, Mimi
dies; Rodolfo collapses heartbroken over her body.

──── THE OPERA ────

Opera by Puccini (libretto by G Giacosa and L Illica, based on
Murger), produced Turin, Teatro Regio, 1 Feb 1896. Rodolfo and
Mimi face love and death in Paris.

Bohemian Girl, The opera by Balfe (libretto by A Bunn, based on a
ballet-pantomime, *La Gypsy*, by J H V de Saint-Georges), produced
London, Drury Lane Theatre, 27 Nov 1843.

Böhm, Georg (b Hohenkirchen near Ohrdruf, 2 Sept 1661; d Lüneburg,
18 May 1733), German composer. Organist at Hamburg before 1698,
then at St John's Church, Lüneburg. As composer and organist an
important forerunner of Bach; his works include a Passion, songs,
organ and harpsichord music.

Böhm, Karl (b Graz, 28 Aug 1894; d Salzburg, 14 Aug 1981), Austrian
conductor. Studied music and law in Vienna. He held posts in many of
the chief European opera houses, including Dresden (1934–43) and
Vienna (1943–45, 1954–56). Böhm was especially well known for
his performances of Mozart and of R Strauss, the fps of whose
Schweigsame Frau (1935) and *Daphne* (1938) he conducted, both in
Dresden; CG debut with the co. in 1936. NY Met. 1957–74, Bayreuth
1962–70, notably in the *Ring* (issued on CD 1994). He was a regular
conductor of the Vienna PO.

Böhme, Kurt (b Dresden, 5 May 1908; d Munich, 20 Dec 1989),
German bass. Dresden 1930–50, where he took part in the fp of *Die
schweigsame Frau*; sang with the co. CG in 1936 as the Commendatore. Bayreuth 1952–67, Pogner and Klingsor. At Salzburg he
created roles in operas by ◊Liebermann and Egk (*Irische Legende*,
1955). NY Met. debut 1954, as Pogner. Sang Hunding, Hagen and
Ochs – his best role – at CG 1956–70.

Bohnen, Michael (b Cologne, 2 May 1887; d Berlin, 26 Apr 1965),
German bass-baritone. Made his debut in Düsseldorf in 1910 as
Kaspar and then sang at the Berlin Hofoper from 1913 to 1921. From
1922 to 1932 he sang at the NY Met. (US premiere of Krenek's *Jonny
spielt auf*, 1929); in Berlin again from 1933–45. Other roles included
Hunding, Daland, Ochs and Sarastro.

Boieldieu, François Adrien (b Rouen, 16 Dec 1775; d Jarcy 8 Oct 1834),
French composer. Studied under Broche, the organist of Rouen
Cathedral, and in 1793 brought out his first opera, *La Fille coupable*,
there, with a libretto by his father, who was secretary to the archbishop. He also wrote many songs at that time, some of which were
pub. in Paris. Having failed to establish a school of music at Rouen on
the model of the Paris Conservatory, he left for the capital, where in
1797 he produced his first opera away from home, *La Famille suisse*,

which was so successful that he brought out four more within two
years. He also became piano professor at the Conservatory in 1798.
Being reproached by Cherubini for having attained too easy a success
on very slender gifts, he placed himself under that master for a course
in counterpoint. In 1802 he married the dancer Clotilde Mafleuray,
with disastrous results, and in 1803 he left for St Petersburg as
conductor of the Imperial Opera. There he wrote nine operas between
1804 and 1810. He returned to Paris in 1811 and had a greater success
than before because there was less competition and he did better
work.

He collaborated by turns with Cherubini, Catel, Isouard,
R Kreutzer, Hérold, Berton, Paer and Auber, also with some of these
and Batton, Blangini and Carafa in *La Marquise de Brinvilliers* of
1831; but his best works are among those he did alone. In *La Dame
blanche*, to match the libretto from Scott, he used some Scottish
folksongs. Soon after he began to suffer from tuberculosis contracted
in Russia, and his fortune declined until he was granted a state
pension. In 1827 he was married for the second time, to the singer
Jenny Philis-Bertin, with whom he had long been living and by whom
in 1815 he had a son, Adrien Louis Victor, who also became a
composer. Boieldieu lived at Geneva for a time not long before his
death.

Works include operas *Le Calife de Bagdad* (1800), *Ma Tante
Aurore* (1803), *Aline, Reine de Golconde* (1804), *La Jeune Femme
colère*, *Télémaque* (1807), *Rien de trop*, *Jean de Paris* (1812), *La Fête
du village voisin*, *Le Petit Chaperon rouge*, *La Dame blanche* (1825),
Les Deux Nuits and others; incidental music for Racine's *Athalie*;
piano concerto (1792), harp concerto (1801), piano trio and other
chamber music; duets for violin and piano and harp and piano, six
piano sonatas.

Boismortier, Joseph Bodin de (b Thionville, 23 Dec 1689; d Roissy-
en-Brie, 28 Oct 1755), French composer. Wrote three opera-ballets,
Les voyages de L'Amour (1736), *Don Quichote* (1743), *Daphnis et
Chloé* (1747); eight cantatas, in two books (1724 and 1737), over 50
instrumental works including many for musette and vielle. He is
reputed to have written the first French concerto (1729).

Boito, Arrigo (b Padua, 24 Feb 1842; d Milan, 10 Jun 1918), Italian poet
and composer. Studied at the Milan Conservatory and produced his
Faust opera, *Mefistofele*, at La Scala there in 1868. Wrote libretti for
several composers as well as for himself, including those of Verdi's
Otello and *Falstaff*. His *Nerone* was not produced until after his death.
He also wrote the opera *Ero e Leandro*, but destroyed the music (the
libretto was set by Bottesini and later by Mancinelli) and he wrote a
libretto on *Hamlet* for Faccio. Boito is most often heard today as
Verdi's late librettist, although his own opera *Mefistofele* is one of the
finest musical settings of the Faust legend.

Bokor, Margit (b Losoncz, 1905; d New York, 9 Nov 1949), Hungarian
soprano. Debut Budapest, 1928. She sang Leonora (*Trovatore*) in
Berlin, 1930, and created Zdenka in *Arabella* at Dresden in 1933. The
following year she was heard as Octavian at Salzburg. After singing at
the Vienna Staatsoper 1935–38, she moved to the USA; appeared at
Chicago, Philadelphia and NY Met.

Bolcom, William (Elden) (b Seattle, 26 May 1938), American composer and pianist. Studied at Stanford University and the Paris
Conservatory; has taught at University of Michigan from 1973. As a
pianist he has been heard in popular early American music, often with
his wife, the mezzo Joan Morris. Works have been influenced by
techniques of collage and microtonal electronics: theatre pieces
Dynamite Tonite (1963), *Greatshot* (1969), *Theatre of the Absurd*
(1970), *The Beggar's Opera* (adaptation of Gay, 1978) and
McTeague (1992); *Oracles*, symphony (1964), piano concerto
(1976), symphony for chamber orchestra (1979), violin concerto
(1983); octet for wind, strings and piano (1962), *Session*, works for
various instrumental groups, with drum play (1965–67), 14 piano
rags (1967–70), piano quartet (1976), brass quintet (1980); *Songs of
Innocence and Experience*, 48 Blake settings for solo voices and
choruses (1958–81; version with orchestra performed Stuttgart
1984); Concertante for viola, cello and orchestra (1985), clarinet

concerto (1989), *Spring Concerto* for oboe and chamber orchestra (1989), *Fantasy Suite* for piano (1989).

bolero a Spanish dance in 3–4 with a characteristic rhythm that usually has a triplet on the second half of the first beat.

Bolero an orchestral work by Ravel, commissioned as a ballet by Ida Rubinstein and first performed by her in Paris, 22 Nov 1928. It consists entirely of a single theme of Spanish character, repeated over and over again with different orchestration and in a gradual taut *crescendo*.

Bolet, Jorge (b Havana, 15 Nov 1914; d Mountain View, CA, 16 Oct 1990), Cuban-born American pianist. Studied at the Curtis Institute from 1926 and from 1932 with Leopold Godowsky and Moriz Rosenthal, both virtuosos at the turn of the century. He made his European debut at Amsterdam, 1935, US debut Philadelphia 1937. He directed *The Mikado* in Tokyo whilst on US army service and found post-war fame as a brilliant interpreter of Liszt (he played the piano for the soundtrack of the Dirk Bogarde film of the composer's life, *Song Without End* (1960)).

When God saw that men were rather indolent ... he blended melody with prophecy in order that, delighted by the modulation of the chant, all might with great eagerness give forth sacred hymns to Him.

St John Chrysostom, (*c* 345–407),
Patrologia Graeca

Bologna, Jacopo da (Jacobus de Bononia), (*fl.* 1340–60), Italian composer, second only to Landini in stature. He belongs to the earliest generation of *trecento* composers: all his known works are madrigals, and nearly all are for two voices. There is also a short treatise, *L'arte del biscanto misurato*.

Bolton, Ivor (b Lancashire, 17 May 1958), English conductor. He studied at Oxford and the RCM and was music director of Glyndebourne Touring Opera 1982–92; operas include *Zauberflöte*, *Rake's Progress* and *La Bohème* (*Orfeo* at the Festival). Founded St James Baroque Players 1983 and directs annual Festival of Baroque Music. Music director of English Touring Opera 1990–93, with *Don Giovanni*, *Lucia di Lammermoor* and *Così fan Tutte*; ENO debut 1992, *Xerxes*; *Poppea* at Bologna 1993. Regular concerts with the London Mozart Players and the ECO, chief conductor of the Scottish Chamber Orchestra from 1994.

Bolt, The ballet in three acts by Shostakovich (scenario by V Smirnov), performed Leningrad, 8 Apr 1931. Ballet suite (no. 5) op. 27a, performed 1933.

Bomarzo opera by Ginastera (libretto by M M Láinez, set in 16th-c. Italy), performed Washington DC, 19 May 1967; banned in Ginastera's own country, Argentina, owing to alleged obscenities in the ballet — Duke Francesco drinks a poisoned potion, believing it will bring immortality; as he dies, flashbacks of his tormented past and unfulfilled sexuality appear before him. Cantata *Bomarzo*, for baritone, speaker, chorus and orchestra, performed Washington, 1 Nov 1964.

bombard the bass instrument of the shawm family, a double-reed wind instrument preceding the oboe, the bombard thus being a forerunner of the bassoon.

bombardon, French, a brass instrument of the tuba variety, derived from bombard (or German *Pommer*), previously applied to various instruments of the oboe and bassoon family. The bombardon takes the lowest bass parts in military and brass bands. ♭saxhorn.

Bomtempo, João Domingos (b Lisbon, 28 Dec 1775; d Lisbon, 18 Aug 1842), Portuguese composer. Settled in Paris 1802, but returned to Lisbon 1815, founded a Philharmonic Society there 1820 and became director of the Conservatory 1833.

Works include Italian opera *Alessandro in Efeso*; Mass for the promulgation of the Portuguese Constitution (1821), Requiems for

Maria I, Pedro IV and Camões; two symphonies; four piano concertos; piano quintet; variations on a fandango and on *God Save the King* for piano.

Bona, Valerio (b Brescia, 1560; d Verona, after 1619), Italian composer and Franciscan friar. *Maestro di cappella* at various churches, including Vercelli, Milan, Brescia and Verona.

Works include Masses, motets and other church music; madrigals and canzonets.

Bonci, Alessandro (b Cesena near Rimini, 10 Feb 1870; d Viserba, 9 Aug 1940), Italian tenor. He studied with Delle Sedie in Paris. Debut Parma, 1896, Fenton; then sang Bellini's Arturo and Elvino at La Scala. He was considered a rival to Caruso and sang Rodolfo at CG in 1900. US debut 1906, as Arturo at the Manhattan Opera House; NY Met. 1907–10, debut as the Duke of Mantua. Sang at Chicago and Rome before his retirement in 1925. Other roles included Alfredo, Riccardo and Faust.

Bond, Victoria (b Los Angeles, 6 May 1945), American composer and conductor. Studied at UCLA and Juilliard, making her debut at Alice Tully Hall, 1973; has also conducted the New Amsterdam SO, RTE Orchestra of Dublin and Shanghai SO (1993). Has written ballets *Equinox* (1977) and *Great Galloping Gottschalk* (1986); opera *Gulliver* (1988) and monodrama *Molly Manybloom* (1991); Sonata for Orchestra (1972); Saxophone Concerto (1993); chamber and vocal music.

Bondeville, Emmanuel (b Rouen, 29 Oct 1898; d Paris, 26 Nov 1987), French composer. He wrote locally successful operas based on famous texts. He was director of the Paris Opéra-Comique 1948–51 and of the Opéra 1951–59.

Works include *L'École des maris* (1935, after Molière, *Madame Bovary* (1951) and *Antoine et Cléopâtre* (1974, after Hugo and Shakespeare).

Bonelli, Richard (b Port Byron, NY, 6 Feb 1887; d LA, 7 Jun 1980), American baritone. He studied with Jean de Reszke and made his NY debut (as Richard Bunn) in 1915, as Valentin. After appearances at La Scala and the Paris Opéra he sang at Chicago 1925–45 and at the NY Met. 1932–45; debut, Germont. Other roles included Amonasro, Posa and Wolfram.

Boni, Guillaume (b Saint-Fleur; d after 1594), French 16th-c. composer. *Maître de chapelle* at the church of Saint-Étienne at Toulouse. Composed two books of sonnets by Ronsard, one of quatrains by Pibrac, *Psalmi Davidici*, etc.

Bonini, Severo (b Florence, 23 Dec 1582; d Florence, 5 Dec 1663), Italian composer. Organist at Forli. Set Rinuccini's *Lamento d'Arianna* in recitative style (1613), and wrote madrigals and spiritual canzonets for a single voice with continuo accompaniment. His *Discorsi e Regole* (*c* 1650) contains important information on early opera.

Boninsegna, Celestina (b Reggio Emilia, 26 Feb 1877; d Milan, 14 Feb 1947), Italian soprano. Debut Reggio Emilia, 1892, as Norina. At the Teatro Costanzi, Rome, she took part in the shared fp of Mascagni's *Le Maschere* (1901), and in 1904 sang Aida at CG. NY Met. debut 1906 as Aida, opposite Caruso. Was heard in London as Amelia and the *Trovatore* Leonora, and appeared as guest at Boston, Barcelona and St Petersburg.

Bonne Chanson, La cycle of nine songs by Fauré, set to poems from Verlaine's volume of that name, composed 1891–92, fp Paris, 20 Apr 1895.

Symphonic poem by Loeffler, on the same source; composed 1901, fp Boston, 11 Apr 1902.

Bonney, Barbara (b Montclair, NJ, Apr 1956), American soprano. Studied in Salzburg and made debut as Anna in *The Merry Wives of Windsor* (Darmstadt, 1979). Her bright, clear voice and attractive stage presence have been admired in such roles as Mozart's Cherubino and Pamina (La Scala, 1985), Gretel, Gilda and Manon. CG and Met. debuts as Sophie (1984, 1991); concerts include Monteverdi's *Vespers*, *Messiah*, and Mozart's *Coronation Mass*.

Bonno, Giuseppe (b Vienna, 29 Jan 1711; d Vienna, 15 Apr 1788), Austrian composer of Italian extraction. Studied in Naples 1726–37.

In 1739 appointed composer to the Austrian court, and in 1774 succeeded Gassmann as *Kapellmeister*.

Works include over 20 operas including *Trajano* (1736), *Il natale di Giove* (1740), *Il re pastore* (1751); three oratorios including *Il Giuseppe riconosciuto* (1774); Masses, Requiems and other church music.

Bononcini (or Buononcini) Italian 17th–18th-c., family of musicians: 1. Giovanni Maria Bononcini, (b Montecorone near Modena, bap. 23 Sept 1642; d 18 Nov 1678), pupil of Bendinelli, *maestro di cappella* of Modena Cathedral. He wrote a treatise, *Musico prattico*, also cantatas, sonatas, suites, etc.

2. Giovanni Bononcini, (b Modena, 18 Jul 1670; d Vienna, 9 Jul 1747), son of 1. Pupil of Colonna and of his father; *maestro de cappella* at San Giovanni in Monte at Modena. He produced his first opera in Rome in 1692. Lived in Vienna, 1698–1711, in Italy 1711–20, in London, 1720–32 (where he had more success than Handel), later in France and Vienna. Wrote operas *Tullo Ostilio* (1694), *Il trionfo di Camilla* (1696), *Xerse, Endimione* (1706), *Astarto* (1715), *Crispo, Erminia* (1719), *Farnace, Calfurnia* (1724), *Astianatte, Griselda* (1733) and many others, including an act in *Muzio Scevola* with Handel and Amadei; seven oratorios; funeral anthem for Marlborough; music for the Peace of Aix-la-Chapelle; Masses, Te Deum, psalms, *Laudate pueri*; chamber cantatas and duets.

3. Antonio Maria Bononcini, (b Modena, 18 Jun 1677; d Modena, 8 Jul 1726), brother of 2. Became *maestro di cappella* to the Duke of Modena in 1721. Wrote about 20 operas, oratorios, etc.

Bonporti, Francesco Antonio (b Trent, bap. 11 Jun 1672; d Padua, 19 Dec 1749), Italian composer. Trained for the priesthood in Rome from 1691 and studied music with Pitoni and Corelli. On his ordination he returned to Trent, and spent the next 40 years in hope of a canonry. He retired disappointed to Padua in 1740.

Works include motets; trio sonatas; concertos; 'Inventions' for solo violin, which may have influenced Bach's works in the same form.

Bontempi, Giovanni Andrea (b Perugia, *c* 1624; d near Perugia, 1 Jul 1705), Italian castrato, theorist and composer. He took the name of a patron, Cesare Bontempi, and sang in St Mark's, Venice, from 1643. At the end of the 1640s he went to Dresden, where he became assistant conductor to Schütz in 1666, but devoted himself to science and architecture the next year. He returned to Italy in 1669 and after another visit to Dresden in 1671 settled down in his birthplace. He wrote three theoretical books.

Works include Italian operas *Paride* (1662), *Dafne* (1671) and *Jupiter and Io* (1673).

Bonynge, Richard, Joan ◊Sutherland.

Boosey & Hawkes London music publishers and instrument makers. Boosey founded 1816 as British agents for Rossini, Hummel, Mercadante etc; manufactured wind instruments from *c* 1850. Hawkes founded 1865, handling brass and military band music. Amalgamation in 1930. Catalogue includes many 20th-c. composers, e.g. Strauss, Prokofiev, Stravinsky, Bartók, Mahler and Britten (1938–63). Contemporary composers include Carter, Bernstein, Reich, Copland, Kurtág, Robin Holloway and Maxwell Davies.

Bordes, Charles (b La Roche-Corbon near Vouvray, 12 May 1863; d Toulon, 8 Nov 1909), French pianist, composer and scholar. Pupil of Marmontel for piano and of Franck for composition. As *maître de chapelle* first at Nogent-sur-Marne and from 1890 at the church of Saint-Gervais in Paris, he devoted himself to research into old polyphonic music and gave performances with the Chanteurs de Saint-Gervais conducted by him. In 1889–90 he explored Basque folk music and in 1894 was one of the founders of the Schola Cantorum.

Works include unfinished opera *Les Trois Vagues* (1892–98), motets, choruses.

Bordoni, Faustina (b Venice, 1700; d Venice, 4 Nov 1781), Italian mezzo, pupil of Gasparini. First appeared in Venice 1716. For two seasons, 1726–28, she sang for Handel in London, creating roles in *Admeto, Riccardo Primo, Siroe* and *Tolomeo*. Her rivalry with Cuzzoni at this time was satirized in *The Beggar's Opera*; the two sopranos traded punches on stage in 1727. Married the composer Hasse in 1731 and sang at Dresden in at least 15 of her husband's operas.

bore the width of the tubing of wind instruments, which affects the character of their tone.

Boréades, Les tragédie-lyrique in five acts by Rameau (libretto by L de Cahusac), written for the court of Louis XV, 1763, but not performed. First full performance (concert) Paris, 16 Sept 1964; first stage performance Aix-en-Provence, 21 Jul 1982. Queen Alphise wants to wed Abaris, but must marry a descendant of Boreas, God of the North Wind. After she gives up the throne and suffers the wrath of Boreas, Abaris is revealed to be related to the god, and the couple marry.

boree one of the old English names for the ◊bourrée, others being borea, bore and borry.

Boretz, Benjamin (b New York, 3 Oct 1934), American composer and editor. Studied in NY with Foss, Milhaud and Sessions. Has taught at Bard College from 1973 and was co-founder and editor of *Perspectives of New Music*, 1961–84.

Works include string quartet (1958); *Group Variations I* for orchestra (1967) and *II* for computer (1971); *Liebeslied* for piano (1974); *Language, as a Music* for speaker, piano and tape (1980); other pieces involving sound on tape.

Borg, Kim (b Helsinki, 7 Aug 1919), Finnish bass. Concert debut 1947, opera debut Aarhus 1951, Glyndebourne 1956 as Don Giovanni; returned in 1959, Pizarro, and 1968, Gremin. NY Met. debut 1959, Almaviva. He has sung Boris at the Bolshoi, and other roles include Marke, Pimen, Berg's Schigolch and Nielsen's Saul.

Borgatti, Giuseppe (b Cento, 17 Mar 1871; d Reno, Lago Maggiore, 18 Oct 1950), Italian tenor. Debut Castelfranco, 1892, Faust. After singing at Madrid and St Petersburg he created Andrea Chénier at La Scala, in 1896; sang Tristan and Siegfried there, under Toscanini (1899–1900) and until 1914 was admired for his forceful interpretations of Wagnerian and verismo roles: Walther, Parsifal, Lohengrin, Des Grieux and Cavaradossi.

Borgioli, Dino (b Florence, 15 Feb 1891; d Florence, 12 Sept 1960), Italian tenor. Debut Milan, 1914, as Bellini's Arturo; sang at La Scala from 1918. Much applauded in England and appeared at CG 1925–39 as Edgardo, Almaviva, the Duke of Mantua and Don Ramiro. Glyndebourne 1937–39, as Ernesto and Ottavio. NY Met. debut 1934, as Rodolfo. Retired 1946 and taught in London.

Borgomastro di Saardam, Il, *The Burgomaster of Saardam*, comic opera by Donizetti (libretto by D Gilardoni, based on a French play by A H J Mélesville, J T Merle and E C de Boirie), produced Naples, Teatro del Fondo, 19 Aug 1827. The subject is that of Lortzing's *Zar und Zimmermann*.

Bori, Lucrezia (b Gandia, 24 Dec 1887; d New York, 14 May 1960), Spanish soprano. Debut Rome, 1908, Micaela. Paris 1910 as Manon Lescaut with the NY Met. co. on tour, and repeated the role in her NY debut; sang there until 1936. In 1911 she was Octavian in the first Italian *Rosenkavalier*. Other roles included Mimi, Norina, Juliette.

Boris Godunov opera by Mussorgsky (libretto by composer, based on Pushkin's drama and N M Karamazin's *History of the Russian Empire*), composed 1868–69; enlarged and revised 1871–72; this later version cut and produced St Petersburg, Imperial Opera, 8 Feb 1874, the original having been rejected in 1870. Rimsky-Korsakov's edition produced St Petersburg, Imperial Opera, 10 Dec 1896. Further revised by Rimsky-Korsakov, 1908. The original produced Leningrad, 16 Feb 1928. Boris becomes tsar after having the heir to the throne murdered, but his guilt drives him insane and he eventually collapses and dies.

Borkh, Inge (b Mannheim, 26 May 1917), German soprano. She sang in Switzerland 1940–51; Bayreuth 1952 as Freia and Sieglinde. US debut San Francisco, 1953. NY Met. debut 1958, as Salome; repeated the role at CG 1959 and sang the Dyer's Wife there in 1976. Other roles: Eglantine, Leonore, Elektra, Lady Macbeth.

THE OPERA

Boris Godunov

A four-act opera by Modest Mussorgsky, who wrote the text about the fabled Russian tsar (based on the tragedy by Aleksander Pushkin). The original version was rejected by the St Petersburg Opera in 1870, and the revised version was not performed until 1874. Even this had to be withdrawn, and the opera was not revived (after further changes by Rimsky-Korsakov) until 1896 – 15 years after Mussorgsky's death. The action is set in Russia and Poland, between 1598 and 1605.

Prologue. A group of peasants pray for guidance and Boris (bass) is crowned Tsar in the Kremlin Square.

I. Learning from the monk Pimen (bass) that Boris has murdered Dimitri, the heir to the throne, the novice Grigory (tenor) vows vengeance and decides to pose as Dimitri. On his way to gain support from Catholic Poland, Grigory escapes capture at the border.

II. Boris expresses remorse for his crimes and when Shuisky (tenor) tells him of Grigory's plot he is terrified that Dimitri has survived.

III. At Sandormierz in Poland Princess Marina (mezzo-soprano) is persuaded by the Jesuit Rangoni (bass) to seduce Grigory; Marina will become Tsarina and Russia will return to Catholicism.

IV. Haunted by hallucinations of Dimitri, Boris falls into a state of delirium; he blesses his son Feodor (soprano) before he dies. Accompanied by mercenaries, Jesuits and a growing band of peasants, Grigory is acclaimed as the new Tsar. A Holy Fool (tenor) is left to lament the sorry fate of Mother Russia.

THE OPERA

Borodin, Alexander Porphyrevich (b St Petersburg, 12 Sept 1833; d St Petersburg, 27 Feb 1887), Russian composer and chemist. Illegitimate son of Prince Gedeanov, who registered him as the son of one of his serfs. He tried to compose at the age of nine and was given music lessons. In his studies at the Academy of Medicine he distinguished himself especially in chemistry, and while studying in Germany he met the pianist Ekaterina Protopopova, whom he married in 1863. The preceding year, having so far been self-taught in composition, he began to take lessons from Balakirev, who conducted his first symphony in 1869. He lectured on chemistry at the School of Medicine for Women from 1872 to his death and wrote important treatises on his subject. In spite of being best known for such 'highlights' as the Nocturne Polovtsian Dances and even *Kismet*, Borodin's music repays much closer attention; his best work is highly charged and colourful, without being lurid or melancholy in the manner of some of his contemporaries.

Works include opera *Prince Igor* (unfinished) (1869–87); three symphonies (third unfinished); *In the Steppes of Central Asia* for orchestra (1880); two string quartets (1874–79, 1881); *Serenata alla spagnuola* for string quartet; *Serenade de quatre galants à une dame* for male-voice quartet; *Petite Suite* for piano; songs.

Music is a pastime, a relaxation from more serious occupations.
Alexander Borodin, in a letter to Krylov, 1867

Borodina, Olga (b Minsk, 29 Jul 1963), Russian mezzo-soprano. She has been a member of the Kirov Opera at St Petersburg from 1987, singing there and on tour to Europe and the USA as Olga, Marina and Marfa. Paris Opéra debut 1992, as Marina; CG 1992–94, as Dalila, Marguerite in *La Damnation de Faust* and Cenerentola. NY Met. 1992, as Marina, with the Kirov. Also admired as a concert artist (Tchaikovsky recital at the Wigmore Hall, London, 1994).

Borodin String Quartet Russian ensemble founded 1946. Since 1974 the members have been Mikhail Kopelman (b 1948) and Andrei

Abramenclov (b 1935), Dmitri Shebalin (b 1930) and Valentin Berlinsky (b 1925). Renowned for their technical skill and interpretive insight, they are today's leading string quartet from E Europe. Recorded the Shostakovich quartets 1985 and gave the complete cycle in London 1986.

Borosini, Francesco (b Modena, *c* 1690), Italian tenor. He sang at the imperial court, Vienna, 1712–31, in oratorios by Caldara and operas by Fux, and went to London in 1724, singing in Handel's and Ariosti's operas in 1724–25; he created Grimoaldo in *Rodelinda* (1725).

Børresen, Hakon (Axel Einar) (b Copenhagen, 2 Jun 1876; d Copenhagen, 6 Oct 1954), Danish composer. Pupil of Svendsen, he took a composition prize in 1901. Later he held many important administrative posts in the musical life of Copenhagen.

Works include operas *The Royal Guest* (1919) and *Kaddara* (1921); ballet *Tycho Brahe's Dream* (1924); incidental music for plays; several symphonies and other orchestral works; chamber music including two string quartets (1913, 1939), songs.

borry English corruption of the French ♭bourrée found in 17th-c. music, e.g. Purcell.

Bortkievich, Sergei Eduardovich (b Kharkov, 28 Feb 1877; d Vienna, 25 Oct 1952), Russian composer. Studied law at St Petersburg and composition under Liadov, later at Leipzig. Lived in Berlin until 1914, when he joined the Russian army, and at Constantinople after World War I. From 1922 till his death he lived in Vienna. He wrote a book about Tchaikovsky and Nadezhda von Meck (1938).

Works include opera *Acrobats* (1938); two symphonies; symphonic poem *Othello*; four piano concertos (one for the left hand), two violin concertos, cello concerto; piano sonatas and pieces; songs.

Bortniansky, Dimitri Stepanovich (b Glukhov, Ukraine, 1752; d St Petersburg, 10 Oct 1825), Russian composer. Studied at Moscow and in St Petersburg under Galuppi, whom he followed to Italy in 1768 with a grant from Catherine II. Further studies at Bologna, Rome and Naples. He wrote motets and operas at Venice in 1776 and at Modena in 1778. In 1779 he returned to Russia and became director of the

Borodin *The composer Alexander Borodin (1833–1887). Until long after his death Borodin's fame rested on the merits of his slender repertory, which consists of only around 20 works. Since the turn of the century Soviet researchers have uncovered another 20 or so.*

Imperial church choir, which he reformed and turned into the Imperial Chapel 1796.

Works include operas *Le Faucon* (1786), *Le Fils rival* (1787), *Creonte* and *Quinto Fabio* (1778); 35 sacred concertos, ten concertos for double choir, Mass, chants.

Börtz, Daniel (b Hässleholm, 8 Aug 1943), Swedish composer. Studied with Rosenberg and Blomdahl; electronic music at Utrecht. His opera *Backanterna* (after Euripides) was premiered 1991 at the Stockholm Opera, directed by Ingmar Bergman. He has also written two church operas, *Landscape with a River* (chamber opera after Hesse, 1974), three string quartets (1966, 1971, 1987); *Josep K* for soloists, chorus and orchestra (1969); eight symphonies (1973–88); two concerti grossi (1978, 1981); violin concerto (1985); oboe concerto (1986); *Parados* for orchestra (1987).

Borwick, Leonard (b London, 26 Feb 1868; d Le Mans, 17 Sept 1925), English pianist. Pupil of Clara Schumann in 1883–89 at Frankfurt, where he made his first appearance, playing in London for the first time in 1890, at a Philharmonic Society concert. He also appeared in Vienna, frequently played with the most eminent artists in chamber music at the London St James's Hall, and gave many recitals with Plunket Greene.

Boschi, Giuseppe (b ? Viterbo), Italian 17th–18th-c. bass. Sang in Venice 1707–14. He first appeared in London in 1710 and subsequently sang in many of Handel's operas; created Argante in *Rinaldo*, 1711, and was engaged at the Royal Academy 1720–28, appearing in 13 operas by Handel.

Böse, Hans-Jurgen von (b Munich, 24 Dec 1953), German composer. Studied in Frankfurt and is best known for his stage compositions: operas *Blutbund* (1974), *Das Diplom* (1974), *Die Leiden des jungen Werthers*, after Goethe (1986), *Chimare* (1986), *63: Dream Palace* (1990, introducing some popular music elements) and *Slaughterhouse Five* (1995); ballets *Die Nacht aus Blei* (1981) and *Werther Szenen* (1989); other pieces include Symphony (1976), Variations for strings (1990), *Sappho-Gesänge* for mezzo and ensemble (1983), oboe concerto (1987), three string quartets (1973, 1977, 1987).

Bösendorfer, Ignaz (b Vienna, 28 Jul 1796; d Vienna, 14 Apr 1859), Austrian piano manufacturer. Founded his firm in Vienna in 1828 and was succeeded in it by his son Ludwig (1835–1919) in 1859. ◊pianola.

Boskovsky, Willi (b Vienna, 16 Jun 1909; d Visp, Switzerland, 21 Apr 1991), Austrian violinist and conductor. Vienna PO 1933–71; co-leader from 1939 and formed the Vienna Octet 1948. From 1954 to

Borodina Russian mezzo-soprano Olga Borodina. Although her coloratura is widely admired in the Russian repertory, she is also successful in such roles as Carmen (at St Petersburg and elsewhere), Rosina and Angelina in La Cenerentola, *which she sang for the first time on stage at Covent Garden in 1994.*

1979 he conducted the New Year's Day concerts in Vienna.

Bossi, (Marco) Enrico (b Salò, 25 Apr 1861; d at sea, 20 Feb 1925), Italian organist and composer. Studied at the Liceo Musicale of Bologna and at the Milan Conservatory. After various organist's and teaching appointments, he became director of the principal music schools at Venice, Bologna and Rome in succession. Meanwhile he had become very famous as a concert organist, and it was while returning from a tour in USA that he died.

Works include operas *Paquita* (1881), *Il veggente* (1890) and *L'angelo della notte*; oratorios *Il Paradiso perduto* (after Milton) and *Giovanna d'Arco* (1914); Masses, motets and sacred cantatas; secular choral works with orchestra or organ including *Il cieco*, *Inno di gloria* and *Cantico dei cantici* (1900); orchestral works; concerto for organ and orchestra; chamber music, 50 organ works including suite *Res severa magnum gaudium*; piano pieces; songs.

Bossi, Renzo (b Como, 9 Apr 1883; d Milan, 2 Apr 1965), Italian composer, son of Enrico Bossi. Studied under his father at the Liceo Benedetto Marcello in Venice and took a composition prize in 1902, when he went to Leipzig, where he continued studying piano, organ and conducting, the last under Nikisch. He was conductor at several German opera houses before he went to Milan as assistant conductor at La Scala. Professor of composition at Parma from 1913 and Milan from 1916.

Works include operas *Rosa rossa* (after Oscar Wilde) (Parma, 1940), *Passa la ronda!* (Milan, 1919), *La notte del mille*, *Volpino il calderaio* (after Shakespeare's *Taming of the Shrew*) (Milan, 1925) and *Proserpina*; symphonies, *Sinfoniale*, *Fantasia sinfonica* and

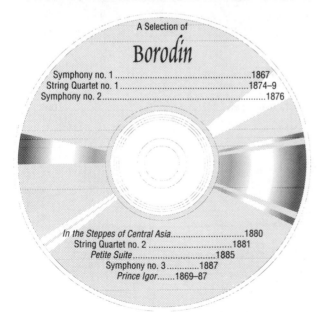

A Selection of
Borodin

Symphony no. 1 1867
String Quartet no. 1 1874–9
Symphony no. 2 1876

In the Steppes of Central Asia 1880
String Quartet no. 2 1881
Petite Suite 1885
Symphony no. 3 1887
Prince Igor 1869–87

Bianco e nero for orchestra; violin concerto; chamber music.

Boston Symphony Orchestra American orchestra founded 1881 by Henry Lee Higginson (1834–1919). Sir George Henschel was conductor 1881–84 and his successors have included Arthur Nikisch (1889–93), Emil Paur (1893–98), Karl Muck (1906–08 and 1912–18), Pierre Monteux (1919–24), Serge Koussevitsky (1924–49), Charles Munch (1949–62), Erich Leinsdorf (1962–69), William Steinberg (1969–72); Seiji Ozawa from 1973. Colin Davis was principal guest conductor 1972–83.

Bott, Catherine (b Leamington Spa, 11 Sept 1952), English soprano. Many concerts with Philip Pickett and the New London Consort: tours of Europe, Latin America and Russia; Medieval Christmas Extravaganza in London; Medici Wedding Celebrations 1539 at the 1990 Proms. Noted for her expressive singing of composers such as Rossi, Monteverdi (recordings of *Vespers* and *Orfeo*), Cavalieri and Carissimi.

Bottesini, Giovanni (b Crema, 22 Dec 1821; d Parma, 7 Jul 1889), Italian double bass player, conductor and composer. Was engaged at Havana, Paris, Palermo, Barcelona and Cairo. As a virtuoso of his instrument he was compared with Paganini.

Works include operas *Marion Delorme* (after Victor Hugo) (Palermo, 1862), *Ali Baba* (London, 1871) and *Ero e Leandro* (Turin, 1879); double bass concertos with orchestra; much music for double bass and piano.

Bottrigari (Bottrigaro), Ercole (b Bologna, 24 Aug 1531; d San Alberto near Bologna, 30 Sept 1612), Italian theorist. His *Il Desiderio* (1594) deals with the problems of combining instruments of different families. From 1600 to 1604 he was involved in a controversy with Artusi.

Boucher, Alexandre (Jean) (b Paris, 11 Apr 1778; d Paris 29 Dec 1861), French violinist. He appeared in public at the age of six, was court violinist at Madrid 1787–1805, and toured Europe 1820–44 with sensational success; notorious for his tastelessness, he was described as a charlatan by Spohr.

Boucourechliev, André (b Sofia, 28 Jul 1925), French composer and musicologist of Bulgarian birth. Studied in Sofia, Paris and Darmstadt. Has worked as music critic and written books on Schumann, Chopin and Beethoven. His works are influenced by Boulez and include the series *Archipel* (from 1967) which allows the performer a wide range of interpretative choices. Other works: *Texte I* and *II* for tape (1959–60), *Grodek* for soprano and ensemble (text by Trakl, 1963), *Musiques Nocturnes* for clarinet, harp and piano (1966), *Ombres* for 11 strings (based on themes from Beethoven's late quartets; fp Brussels 1970, conductor Boulez), *Amers* for orchestra (1973), piano concerto (1976).

Boughton, Rutland (b Aylesbury, 23 Jan 1878; d London, 25 Jan 1960), English composer. Studied at the RCM in London under Stanford and Walford Davies. But he left very soon, and produced some early orchestral works, conducting for a time at the Haymarket Theatre. Idolizing Wagner, he determined to found an English centre of opera on the same lines as Bayreuth and began in a very modest way at Glastonbury with a series of music dramas on the Arthurian legends; in Aug 1914 first producing *The Immortal Hour*. A special theatre was to be built at Glastonbury, but the project had to be abandoned. In 1922 *The Immortal Hour* had a long run in London, and *Alkestis* was produced there by the BNOC in 1924.

Works include music dramas *The Birth of Arthur* (1908–09), *The Immortal Hour* (1914), *Bethlehem* (1913), *The Round Table*, *Alkestis* (1922), *The Queen of Cornwall* (1924), *The Lily Maid* (1934); ballets *Choral Dances*, *Snow White*, *The Moon Maiden*; dramatic scene *Agincourt* from Shakespeare's *Henry V*; works for chorus and orchestra *The Skeleton in Armour* (Longfellow), *The Invincible Armada* (Schiller), *Midnight* (E Carpenter), *Song of Liberty*; unaccompanied choral music, two string quartets.

Bouhy, Jacques (Joseph André) (b Pepinster, 18 Jun 1848; d Paris, 29 Jan 1929), Belgian baritone. Studied at Liège and Paris, where he made his first appearance at the Opéra in 1871 as Méphistophélès. Director of NY Conservatory, 1885–89. Lived and taught in Paris

from 1907. The first Escamillo in Bizet's *Carmen* and sang in the fps of operas by Massé, Massenet and Salvayre.

Bouilly, Jean-Nicolas (1763–1842), French writer. Administrator of a department near Tours during the Terror. Wrote libretti for a number of operas (◊rescue opera) for various composers, including Cherubini and Gaveaux. The libretto of Beethoven's *Fidelio* is based on his book for Gaveaux's *Léonore*.

Boulanger, Lili (Juliette Marie Olga) (b Paris, 21 Aug 1893; d Mézy, Seine-et-Oise, 15 Mar 1918), French composer. Pupil of her sister Nadia at first, then at the Paris Conservatory. Gained the Prix de Rome in 1913 (the first woman ever to do so), but suffered much ill health.

Works include incidental music for Maeterlinck's *La Princesse Maleine* (1918); two poems for orchestra; cantata *Faust et Hélène* (after Goethe) (1913); psalms with orchestra.

Boulanger, Nadia (Juliette) (b Paris, 16 Sept 1887; d Paris, 22 Oct 1979), French composer and teacher, sister of Lili Boulanger. Student at the Paris Conservatory, where she taught later, as well as at the École Normale de Musique and the American Conservatory at Fontainebleau. She went to USA after the outbreak of war in 1939, returning in 1946. Many distinguished composers were her pupils including L Berkeley, Copland, Françaix and Piston. Hon. D.Mus., Oxford, 1968.

Works include incidental music to d'Annunzio's *La città morta* (with Pugno) (1911); cantata *La Sirène* (1908); orchestral works; instrumental pieces, songs.

Boulevard Solitude opera by Henze (libretto by the composer and G Weil), produced Hanover, 17 Feb 1952. A modern version of the Manon story. Lovers Manon and Armand are forced apart by poverty when she must take a rich admirer to support herself and her brother.

Boulez, Pierre (b Montbrison, 26 Mar 1925), French composer and conductor. After abandoning studies in mathematics, he studied with Messiaen at the Paris Conservatory, and later took a course in serial technique with Leibowitz (1946). In 1946 he worked for the Renaud-Barrault theatre co. and in 1953–54 founded the 'Domaine Musical' with Barrault, which specialized in new music. As a composer he belongs to the avant garde, writing in a style which has its roots in Debussy and Webern and also in the ideas of James Joyce and Mallarmé. He is one of the pioneers of integral serialism, but later introduced freer elements into his music. Boulez is also a leading conductor of advanced new music. He was principal conductor of the BBC SO 1971–75; NY PO 1971–77, giving notable performances of works by Berg, Bartók, Stravinsky and members of the Second

A Selection of

Boulez

Piano Sonata no. 1	1946
Le Visage nuptial	1946
Piano Sonata no. 2	1948
Le Soleil des eaux	1948

Le Marteau sans maître	1952–7
Improvisation sur Mallarmé I	1957
Pli selon pli	1958–62
Figures-Doubles-Prismes	1963–6
cummings ist der dichter	1970
Rituel in memoriam Bruno Maderna	1974–5

Boulez *Composer and conductor Pierre Boulez. Working first as a mathematician and then as a composer, Boulez has been at the leading edge of musical developments since World War II. His uncompromising brand of modernism has ignored current populist trends. Since the 1960s he has also been influential as a conductor of 20th-century music.*

Viennese School (including Schoenberg's *Moses und Aron* in London, 1974, also recorded). He conducted *Parsifal* at Bayreuth in 1966, and *The Ring* in 1976; gave first complete performance of *Lulu*, Paris 1979. From 1977 he directed research instrumentation for techniques of modern music, Paris (◊IRCAM).

Works include ORCHESTRAL: *Poésie pour pouvoir* for orchestra and electronic tape (after Michaux, 1958); *Figures-Doubles-Prismes* for orchestra (1963–66); *... explosante fixe ...* (1971–73); *Rituel in memoriam Bruno Maderna* (1974–75); *Répons* for 24 players, six instrumental soloists, computerized electronics (1981).

VOCAL: *Le visage nuptial* (1946); *Le Soleil des eaux* for solo voices, chorus and orchestra (after Char); *Le Marteau sans maître* for alto and six instruments (after Char) (1952–57); *Pli selon pli* for soprano and orchestra (after Mallarmé, 1958–62); *e e cummings ist der dichter* for 16 solo voices and 24 instruments (1970; revised 1986).

INSTRUMENTAL: flute sonatine; three piano sonatas (1946, 1948, 1957); *Structures* I, II for two pianos (1952, 1961); *Livre* for string quartet (1948, revised for string orchestra 1968); *Eclat* for 15 instruments (1965, expanded as *Eclat/Multiples* for 27 instruments, 1966); *Domaines* for clarinet and 21 instruments (1961–68); *Dérive* for small ensemble (1984); *Dérive II* for 11 instruments (1988); *Messageesquisse* for cello.

Webern sounding like Debussy.
Heinrich Strobel on *Le Marteau sans maître*, by Boulez in *Modern French Music*, 1971

Boult, Adrian Cedric (b Chester, 8 Apr 1889; d London, 22 Feb 1983), English conductor. Educated at Westminster School and Christ Church, Oxford, where he received a D.Mus. He then went to Leipzig to study conducting with Nikish (1912–13), also taking lessons from Reger. In 1914 he joined CG, making his debut as an orchestral

conductor in 1918. Boult taught at the RCM in 1919 and was conductor of the CBSO, 1924–30. Later became conductor of the BBC SO and gave the first British (concert) performance of *Wozzeck* (1934) and Busoni's *Doktor Faust* (1937). He left the BBC in 1950 and became conductor of the LPO, 1951–57. Boult was best known for his performance of the standard repertory, although he helped to further the cause of modern (especially English) music; he gave the fps of Vaughan Williams' *Pastoral*, fourth and sixth symphonies. Author of useful books on conducting. Retired 1979. Knighted 1937; CH 1969.

Bourdin, Roger (b Paris, 14 Jun 1900; d Paris, 14 Sept 1973), French baritone. Debut Paris, Opéra-Comique, 1922, as Massenet's Lescaut; sang there for more than 30 years, appearing in the fps of operas by Pierné (*Sophie Arnould*), Ibert, Bondeville (*Madame Bovary*) and Milhaud (*Bolivar*). He sang as guest at the Paris Opéra and was Pelléas at CG in 1930. Sang further in operas by Rameau and Reynaldo Hahn.

Bourgault-Ducoudray, Louis (Albert) (b Nantes, 2 Feb 1840; d Vernouillet, 4 Jul 1910), French composer. A lawyer at first, he entered the Paris Conservatory late and took a composition prize in 1862. In 1869 he founded a choral society in Paris with which he gave performances of unfamiliar works. Collected and pub. Greek and Breton folksongs. Lectured on history of music at the Conservatory from 1878.

Works include operas *L'Atelier de Prague* (1858), *Michel Colomb* (1887), *Bretagne*, *Thamara* (1891), *Myrdhin* (1905); satiric play *La Conjuration des fleurs*; *Stabat Mater*, *Symphonie religieuse* for unaccompanied chorus; *Fantaisie en Ut mineur*, *Carnaval d'Athènes*, *Rapsodie cambodgienne*, *L'Enterrement d'Ophélie* (after Shakespeare) for orchestra.

Bourgeois, Derek (David) (b Kingston upon Thames, 16 Oct 1941), English composer. He studied at Cambridge, and with Howells at the RCM; lecturer at Bristol University from 1971.

Works include two symphonies (1960, 1968), variations on a theme of Mozart, for double bass and orchestra (1967), symphonic fantasy *The Astronauts* (1969); *Jabberwocky-Extravaganza*, for baritone, chorus and orchestra (1963); string quartet (1962), two brass quintets (1965, 1972).

Bourgeois, Loys (b Paris, c 1510; d Paris, c 1561), French musician. A Protestant, he went to Geneva to join Calvin's church, taking the place of Franc, who had gone to Lausanne, and working with Guillaume Fabri. He contributed to the Genevan Psalter by selecting and harmonizing tunes. He also composed secular *chansons*.

Bourgeois, Thomas-Louis (b Fontaine-l'Évêque, Hainaut, 24 Oct 1676; d Paris, c 1750), French countertenor and composer. Choirmaster at Strasbourg 1703, alto at the Paris Opéra 1706–11, when he left to devote himself to composition. Appointed *maître de chapelle* at Toul c 1716.

Works include opera-ballets, solo cantatas, motet *Beatus vir*, etc.

Bourgeois gentilhomme, Le, *The Bourgeois as Gentleman*, comedy-ballet by Molière with music by Lully, produced Chambord, 14 Oct 1670.

Incidental music by R Strauss to a shortened version of Molière's comedy translated by H von Hofmannsthal, preceding the one-act opera *Ariadne auf Naxos*, produced Stuttgart, 25 Oct 1912. Strauss afterwards dropped it for a new operatic first act and made a concert suite for orchestra of the incidental music, adding a minuet by Lully (fp Vienna, 31 Jan 1920, conductor Strauss).

bourrée, French, a French dance in quick 2–2 time beginning with an upbeat (in 17th-c. England 'borry').

boutade French = 'whim, frolic'; an 18th-c. dance, or sometimes a whole ballet, in a style described by the title; also sometimes an instrumental piece of the same character.

Boutique fantasque, La, *The Fantastic Toyshop*, ballet by Respighi, arranged from music by Rossini (choreographed by Leonid Fedorovich Massin), produced London, Alhambra Theatre, 5 June 1919. The music consists mainly of small pieces written by Rossini in his retirement for the amusement of his friends.

The opening of Bach's famous Bourrée from his Cello Suite no. 3.

Boutmy Flemish family of musicians.

1. Josse Boutmy (b Ghent, 1 Feb 1697; d Brussels, 27 Nov 1779), organist, harpsichordist and composer. Went to Brussels early, entered the service of Prince Thurn and Taxis in 1736, taught at court and was appointed organist of the royal chapel in 1744. Works include a cantata and three books of harpsichord pieces.

2. Guillaume Boutmy (b Brussels, 15 Jun 1723; d Brussels, 22 Jan 1791), composer, son of 1. Also served Prince Thurn and Taxis from 1752 and in 1760 was appointed keeper of keyboard instruments at court. Composed sonatas for harpsichord.

3. Jean-Joseph Boutmy (b Brussels, 29 Apr 1725; d Cleves, 1782), harpsichordist, organist and composer, brother of 2. Went to Ghent early, taught the harpsichord there and in 1757 was appointed organist at St Baafs. In 1764 he settled at The Hague and after 1775 at Cleves. Works include six *Divertissements* for harpsichord with violin *ad lib*, and concertos for harpsichord and orchestra.

4. Laurent-François Boutmy (b Brussels, 19 Jun 1756; d Brussels, 3 Nov 1838), harpsichordist, organist and composer, brother of 3. Deputized for his ageing father, but failed to succeed him and in 1779 settled at Rotterdam. In 1789 he went to France, but soon after returned to Brussels after taking refuge in London from the French occupation. Works include various piano pieces, some with violin or flute, vocal works with various accompaniments.

Bovy, Vina (b Ghent, 22 May 1900; d Ghent, 16 May 1983), Belgian soprano. Debut Ghent, 1917, in *Hansel and Gretel*. She sang at the Théâtre de la Monnaie, Brussels, and in S America, as Thaïs, Ophelia and Juliette. NY Met. debut 1936, as Violetta; also sang Gilda, Lakmé and Manon in NY. She sang in Paris during World War II and was director of Ghent Opera 1947–56, adding Elsa, Desdemona and Pamina to her repertory.

bow the stick with horsehair stretched along it with which instruments of the viol and violin family are played. ◊tourte.

Bowen, (Edwin) York (b London, 22 Feb 1884; d London, 23 Nov 1961), English pianist, violinist, horn player and composer. Studied at the RAM in London.

Works include three symphonies, *Symphonic Fantasia* for orchestra; three piano concertos (1904, 1906, 1908), violin and viola concertos; sonata for viola and piano; numerous piano works.

bowing the art of using a bow, or the marking of scores and parts with indications about how to bow. The main signs are ⊓ for a down-bow (that is, starting at the frog and drawing the hand away from the instrument) and V for its opposite, the up-bow. A slur in string-writing is normally an indication to take several notes under a single bow.

Bowles, Paul (Frederic) (b New York, 30 Dec 1910), American composer. Pupil of Aaron Copland, Virgil Thomson and Nadia Boulanger. He lived by turns in Spain, Mexico, Guatemala and N Africa, but later returned to the USA. In 1949 he published a novel, *The Sheltering Sky*, which established him as a writer.

Works include operas *Denmark Vesey* (1938) and *The Wind Remains* (1941–43).

Bowman, James (Thomas) (b Oxford, 6 Nov 1941), English countertenor. Stage debut London, 1967, as Britten's Oberon; the Voice of Apollo in *Death in Venice* (Aldeburgh, 1973) was written for him. Glyndebourne 1970–74 as Endimione in the Cavalli-Leppard *Calisto*. He sang the Priest Confessor and God the Father in the fp of Maxwell Davies's *Taverner*, CG 1972, and co-created the role of Astron in Tippett's *The Ice Break*, 1977. Handel repertory includes

Giulio Cesare, Tamerlano, Xerxes and Scipione; sang Oberon at Aix-en-Provence (1992), Barak in Handel's *Deborah* at the 1993 London Proms.

Boyarina Vera Sheloga (Rimsky-Korsakov.) ◊Pskovitianka.

Boyce, William (b London, Sept 1711; d London, 7 Feb 1779), English organist and composer. Chorister at St Paul's Cathedral and a pupil of Greene, whom he succeeded as Master of the King's Music in 1755. Meanwhile he held various organ posts in London, was appointed composer to the Chapel Royal in 1736, and conductor of the Three Choirs Festival the following year. From 1758 he was organist of the Chapel Royal. Deafness forced him to give up much of his work during his later years. In recent years his music has been revived. Although his dance movements and fugues show much individuality, based on an idiom bequeathed by Handel, his numerous court odes are more easily forgotten.

Works include stage entertainments *The Chaplet* (1749) and *The Shepherd's Lottery* (1751); masque *Peleus and Thetis* (1740) and Dryden's *Secular Masque* (*c* 1746); incidental music for Shakespeare's *Tempest*, *Cymbeline* (1746) and *Romeo and Juliet* (1750); pantomime *Harlequin's Invasion* (with M Arne and Aylward, and containing the song *Heart of Oak*); service settings and anthems; cantatas and odes.

20 symphonies and overtures; 12 trio sonatas; keyboard music;

Boyce *The composer and organist William Boyce (1711–1779). The leading English composer of the late Baroque, Boyce contributed equally to music for the church and for the theatre. His style is reminiscent of Handel, though it shows stronger English characteristics than those of his predecessor.*

songs, etc. He also completed a notable collection of earlier church music begun by Greene (pub. under the title *Cathedral Music* in three vols., 1760–73).

Boyd, Anne (b Sydney, 18 Apr 1946), Australian composer. Studied with Peter Sculthorpe at Sydney and with Bernard Rands in York. Head of the music department at Hong Kong University from 1980. Her music reflects oriental influences and includes some small-scale theatre pieces: *As Far as Crawls the Toad* (1970), *The Rose Garden* (1971), *The Death of Captain Cook* (oratorio, 1978); *The Little Mermaid* (1978) and *The Beginning of the Day* (1980), children's operas; *Black Sun* for orchestra (1989); flute concerto (1992); *Grathawai* for orchestra (1993); three string quartets (1968, 1973, 1991); *Wind across Bamboo* wind quintet (1984); choral and solo vocal music.

Boyhood's End cantata for tenor and piano by Tippett (text by W H Hudson), composed 1943 and performed London, 5 Jun 1943.

Boykan, Martin (b New York, 12 Apr 1931), American composer and pianist. Studied with Walter Piston and Hindemith and has taught at Brandeis University from 1957. As a recitalist he performs serial music and works by avant-garde Americans.

Works include four string quartets (1949, 1967, 1974, 1984); quintet for flute, piano and strings (1953); Chamber Concerto (1970); symphony (1989); *Voyages* for soprano and piano (1992); cello sonata (1992); *Impromptu* for violin (1993).

Bozay, Attila (b Balatonfőzfő, 11 Aug 1939), Hungarian composer. He studied in Budapest at the Bartók Conservatory and with Ferenc Farkas. His music is influenced by serial technique and by Hungarian folksongs.

Works include the operas *Queen Kungisz* (1969) and *Hamlet* (1984); *Pezzo concertato* for viola and orchestra, *Pezzo sinfonico* for orchestra (1967); *Trapeze and Bars*, cantata (1966); two string quartets (1964, 1971), *Formations* for solo cello (1969).

brace a bracket connecting a number of simultaneously played staves, e.g. the two staves in piano and harp music, or a greater number of staves in a score.

Brack, Georg (Jörg), German 16th-c. composer. His part-songs were pub. in collections printed by Schöffer (1513), Arnt von Aich (1519) and others.

Brade, William (b *c* 1560; d Hamburg, 26 Feb 1630), English violist and composer. Worked by turns at the court of Christian IV of Denmark, in the service of the Margraves of Brandenburg and the Duke of Schleswig-Gottorp, and at Halle, Berlin and Hamburg. Pub.

A Selection of

Brahms

Piano Concerto no. 1................................1854–8
String Sextet op. 18 1860
Piano Quintet..1864
A German Requiem 1868

Symphony no. 1 1855–76
Symphony no. 2 1877
Violin Concerto................................1878
Piano Concerto no. 2 1878–81
Violin Sonata no. 1 1879
Symphony no. 4 1884–5

instrumental music in several parts, including pavans, galliards and other dances, *canzone*, concertos and fancies in six books at Hamburg, Lübeck, Antwerp and Berlin, 1609–21.

Braham (real name *Abraham*), John (b London, 20 Mar 1774; d London, 17 Feb 1856), English tenor and composer. Debut as a treble at CG in 1787. When his voice broke he taught the piano, but reappeared at Rauzzini's concerts at Bath in 1794 and in London in 1796. In 1798–1801 he appeared in Paris, Italy and Germany. He then became attached to CG for many years and often interpolated his own songs, which became very popular, in operas. He also contributed to operas produced at the Lyceum and Drury Lane Theatres, including one on Shakespeare's *Taming of the Shrew*. Towards the end of his career he was the first Huon in Weber's *Oberon* (1826).

Brahms, Johannes (b Hamburg, 7 May 1833; d Vienna, 3 Apr 1897), German composer. Son of a double bass player, from whom he learnt the rudiments of music as a child. Although intended for an orchestral player, he made such progress on the piano that his parents decided to make a prodigy performer of him when about 11; but his teachers wisely opposed this. He soon afterwards began to compose, but had to play in sailors' taverns and dancing-saloons at night to supplement his parents' earnings. He gave two concerts in 1848–49, but did not free himself from the drudgery of playing and teaching until he went on a concert tour with Reményi in 1853, when he met Joachim, Liszt and other musicians of importance, particularly Robert and Clara Schumann, who took much interest in him. In 1857–60 he was intermittently engaged at the court of Lippe-Detmold, travelled as pianist and worked at Hamburg, conducting a ladies' choir there. At Hanover in 1859 he premiered his first piano concerto, which, although one of the great masterpieces of the genre, was not well received by audience and critics alike, probably as a result of inadequate rehearsal time.

He first visited Vienna in 1862 and settled there for good the following year. Entirely devoted to composition from 1864, except for some concert tours, on which he played mainly his own works. At Bremen in 1868 he conducted the premiere of his most profound vocal work, *Ein Deutsches Requiem*; one month later he added the movement *Ihr habt nun Traurigkeit* (Though ye now be sorrowful) in memory of his mother. His success as a composer was firmly established during the 1860s, and he became known abroad; but he did not complete his first symphony until 1876. It had taken him 15 years to complete and was written in Beethoven's shadow, but after its premiere Brahms was established as the foremost composer of instrumental music of his time. The symphony was soon followed by a more

Brahms   *A biographical note*

Brahms was 20 years old and in need of recognition when he first visited Robert and Clara Schumann at their home in Düsseldorf. Now near the end of his career, Schumann wrote enthusiastically about Brahms in his journal the *Neue Zeitschrift für Musik*. Only six months later the nervously-disordered Schumann threw himself into the Rhine and shortly after was confined to an asylum. Clara was left with her concert career and seven children to support, but Brahms was eager to help. His own career was interrupted as he took lodgings nearby and helped Clara all he could in her daily chores, including childminding and household accounts. Brahms developed a deep attachment for Clara and was able to declare his love for her after Schumann's death in 1856. The precise nature of Brahms's relationship with Clara is now difficult to determine. With Clara 14 years his senior, there may have been some element of mother-fixation in his feeling for her. There is no doubt that the strength of their relationship had some influence on the fact that he never married. In 1869 he fell in love with Clara's daughter Julie. At first in despair when she rejected him, his feelings are expressed in the grief and eventual consolation of the Alto Rhapsody.

Brahms *The composer Brahms (1833–1897), as pictured in 1860. During this early period he fell in love with Clara Schumann, who, along with husband Robert, gave him the encouragement and support needed to help launch his career. He became the greatest Romantic composer still to adhere to traditional formal models.*

relaxed work in D major. He wrote much during summer holidays in Austria, Germany and Switzerland, but hardly visited other countries except Italy. In 1877 he refused the Cambridge Mus.D. because he did not wish to go to receive it in person, but he accepted the Ph.D. from Breslau in 1879. In 1881 he was the soloist in the premiere of his second piano concerto. The later years were uneventful except for the growing importance of his work. In 1896 he began to suffer seriously from cancer of the liver, the disease from which he died. Brahms was the great compositional conservative of the 19th c. Musicians tended to be classified either as supporters of Brahms or of Wagner, the great innovator of the same period. However, what Brahms lacked in formal invention he more than compensated for in profundity and the perfection of contemporary models.

Works include CHORUS AND ORCHESTRAL: *Ein Deutsches Requiem* (texts from Luther's translation of the Bible), with baritone and soprano soloists (1857–68), *Rinaldo*, for tenor, male chorus and orchestra (1863–68), *Rhapsody* for contralto, male chorus and orchestra (1869), *Schicksalslied* (1871), *Gesang der Parzen* (1882). SYMPHONIES: no. 1 in C minor, op. 68 (1855–76), no. 2 in D, op. 73 (1877), no. 3 in F, op. 90 (1883), no. 4 in E minor, op. 98 (1884–85). CONCERTOS: two for piano, no. 1 in D minor, op. 15 (1854–58), no. 2 in Bb, op. 83 (1878–81); violin in D, op. 77 (1878); violin and cello in A minor, op. 102 (1887).

OTHER ORCHESTRAL: two Serenades, no. 1 in D, op. 11 (1858), no. 2 in A, op. 16 (1859), *Variations on a theme by Haydn* in Bb, op. 56a (1873), *Academic Festival Overture* (1880), *Tragic Overture* (1880). CHAMBER: two string sextets, op. 18 in Bb (1860), op. 36 in G (1865); three string quartets, op. 51 nos. 1–2, in C minor and A minor (1859–73), op. 67 in Bb (1875); two string quintets, op. 88 in F (1882), op. 111 in G (1890); three piano quartets, op. 25 in G minor (1861), op. 26 in A (1861), op. 60 (1855–75); piano quintet op. 34 in F minor (1864); clarinet quintet op. 115 in B minor (1891); three piano trios, op. 8 in B (1854, revised 1890), op. 87 in C (1880–82), op. 101 in C minor (1886); horn trio op. 40 in Eb (1865); two cello sonatas, op.

38 in E minor (1862–65), op. 99 in F (1886); three violin sonatas, op. 78 in G (1879), op. 100 in A (1886), op. 108 in D minor (1886–88); trio for clarinet, cello, piano op. 114 in A minor (1891); two sonatas for viola or clarinet op. 120 in F minor and Eb (1894).

SOLO PIANO: includes three sonatas, op. 1–3, in C, F# minor, F minor (1852–53); Variations on themes by Schumann (op. 9, 1854), Handel (op. 24, 1861), Paganini (op. 35, 1863) and Haydn (version for two pianos of work for orchestra, 1873); rhapsodies, intermezzos etc. ORGAN: includes 11 chorale preludes op. 122 (1896).

VOCAL: numerous part-songs, including *Zigeunerlieder* for four voices and piano op. 103 (1887); the song cycles *Die Schöne Magelone* op. 33 (15 Romances to poems by L Tieck) and *Vier ernste Gesänge* for low voice and piano op. 121 (texts from the New Testament); more than 200 Lieder, composed 1852–86 to texts by Heyse, Möricke, Rückert and Brentano, among others.

Brain, Aubrey (Harold) (b London, 12 Jul 1893; d London, 20 Sept 1955), English horn player. He studied at the RCM; played for Beecham's touring opera co. from 1913, principal, BBC SO 1930–45. The foremost teacher of his instrument (RAM from 1923). His brother *Alfred* (1885–1966), also a horn player, was principal of Wood's Queen's Hall Orchestra; from 1923 principal of the NY SO, then joined the LA PO.

Brain, Dennis (b London, 17 May 1921; d Hatfield, 1 Sept 1957), English horn player, son of Aubrey Brain. Studied under his father, played in orchestras, formed a wind chamber-music group and became the most brilliant soloist on his instrument; Britten's *Serenade* and Hindemith's concerto were written for him. He was killed in a car accident on his way home from the Edinburgh Festival.

Braithwaite, Nicholas (b London, 26 Aug 1939), English conductor. Studied with Swarowsky in Vienna and made debut with WNO 1966, *Don Pasquale*; assistant conductor with the Bournemouth SO 1967–70 and at SW 1971–74 (British premiere of *The Devils of Loudun*, 1973). Led *Tannhäuser* at CG 1973 and was principal conductor of Gothenburg Opera 1981–84, Manchester Camerata 1984–91; also active in Australia. His father, Warwick Braithwaite (1896–1971), was music director of BBC Wales 1924–32 and conducted opera in England and Australia until 1968.

Brambilla, Marietta (b Cassano d'Adda, 6 Jun 1807; d Milan, 6 Nov 1875), Italian contralto. Debut London, 1827, as Rossini's Arsace; successful in such travesti roles as Adriano in *Il crociato* and Zingarelli's Romeo. For Donizetti she created roles in *Lucrezia Borgia* (Milan, 1833) and *Linda di Chamounix* (Vienna, 1842).

Brambilla, Teresa (b Cassano d'Adda, 23 Oct 1813; d Milan, 15 Jul 1895), Italian soprano, sister of Marietta Brambilla. Debut Milan, 1831. She created Gilda at the Teatro Fenice, Venice, in 1851. Her other Verdi roles were Abigaille, Elvira and Luisa Miller.

Bramston, Richard (b c 1485; d Wells, 1554), English composer. He was instructor of the choristers and organist at Wells Cathedral, 1507–31, though apparently *in absentia* from 1508. An antiphon, *Mariae virginis fecunda viscera*, survives.

It is a verbosity which outfaces its commonplaceness by dint of sheer magnitude.
>   **George Bernard Shaw** on Brahms's music,
>   *The Star*, 1892

Branchu, Alexandrine Caroline (b Cap Français, 2 Nov 1780; d Passy, 14 Oct 1850), French soprano. Debut Paris, 1799; sang at the Opéra 1801–26 and took part in the fps of Cherubini's *Anacréon* (1803) and *Les Abencérages* (1813). Highly regarded in operas by Gluck and as Piccinni's Didon.

Brand, Max (b Lwów, 26 Apr 1896; d Langenzersdorf near Vienna, 5 Apr 1980), Austrian-Polish composer. Studied in Vienna under Schreker and Hába. Settled in USA 1940. His opera (fp 1929) is one of the outstanding works of the 'machinist' period of the 1920s; it was banned by the Nazis and not heard again complete until produced by the BBC, 1986. He also experimented with electronic music and wrote *The Astronauts, an Epic in Electronics* (1962). Returned to Austria in 1975.

Works include opera *Maschinist Hopkins*; scenic oratorio *The Gate* (1944); symphonic poems, chamber music.

Brandenburg Concertos a series of six orchestral concertos by J S Bach, dedicated 1721 to the Margrave Christian Ludwig of Brandenburg: I, F, for three oboes, two horns, bassoon, *violino piccolo*, strings and continuo; II, F, for recorder, oboe, trumpet, violin, strings and continuo; III, G, for three violins, three violas, three cellos, bass and continuo; IV, G, for two recorders, violin, strings and continuo; V, D, for flute, violin, harpsichord, strings and continuo; VI, B♭, for two violas, two bass viols, cello, bass and continuo.

Brandenburgers in Bohemia, The, *Braniboři v Čechách*, opera by Smetana (libretto by K Sabina), produced Prague, Czech Theatre, 5 Jan 1866. Brandenburgers invade Bohemia, and are thrown out.

Brandt, Marianne (b Vienna, 12 Sept 1842; d Vienna, 9 Jul 1921), Austrian mezzo. Debut Olomouc, 1867, as Rachel; Berlin 1868–82, as Azucena and Amneris CG 1872, Leonore, and sang Brangaene in the first London performance of *Tristan und Isolde*, Drury Lane 1882, under Richter. In 1876 she was Waltraute in the premiere of *Götterdämmerung*, at Bayreuth, and returned there in 1882 as Kundry. NY Met. 1884–88 as Ortrud, Fides and Eglantine.

Brandts-Buys, Jan (b Zutphen, 12 Sept 1868; d Salzburg, 8 Dec 1933), Dutch composer. He won a state prize as a youth and studied at Frankfurt. Most of his operatic successes were produced in Germany and Austria.

Works include operas *Das Veilchenfest* (Berlin, 1909), *Le Carillon*, *Die Schneider von Schoenau* (Dresden, 1916), *Der Eroberer* (Dresden, 1918), *Mi-carême*, *Der Mann im Mond* (1922), *Traumland*, *Ulysses*; *Oberon Romancero* for orchestra; three piano concertos; suite for strings, harp and horn; string quartets; quintet for flute and strings; piano trios; piano works; songs.

branle a French dance in 2–2 or 3–2 time dating from the 15th c. and cultivated until the 18th, called brawl in England.

Brannigan, Owen (b Annitsford, Northumberland, 10 Mar 1908; d Newcastle, 9 May 1973), English bass. Studied at the GSM 1934–42, winning the GSM Gold Medal in 1942. From 1940 to 1947 he was principal bass at SW, and from 1947 to 1949 he sang at Glyndebourne. He also sang at CG, London and at many important festivals; took part in the fps of Britten's *Peter Grimes*, *Rape of Lucretia*, *Albert Herring* and *A Midsummer Night's Dream* (Bottom).

Brant, Henry Dreyfus (b Montreal, 15 Sept 1913), American composer, flautist and organist. Studied at McGill University and Juilliard; also with Wallingford Riegger and Rubin Goldmark. Worked as orchestrator for various bands in 1930s, taught in NY 1945–54; moved to Santa Barbara, CA, in 1982. Much influenced by Ives and as a composer and performer has explored spatial effects: music emanates from various parts of the concert stage and auditorium.

Works include ballet *The Great American Goof* (1946), *Millenium I–IV* for brass instruments (1950–64), *Behold the Earth*, *Requiem Cantata* (1951), *Feuerwerk*, for fireworks, speaker and instruments (1961), *Solomon's Gardens* for seven voices, chorus, 24 handbells and three instruments (1974), *Antiphony I* for five orchestral groups and five conductors (1953; pre-dating Stockhausen's *Gruppen* by four years), *Grand Universal Circus* (1956), *Violin Concerto with Lights* (1961), *Verticals Ascending* for two separate groups (1968), *Immortal Combat* for two bands (1972), *An American Requiem* (1974), *Homage to Ives* for baritone and three orchestral groups (1975), *Antiphonal Responses* (1978), *Horizontals Extending* (1982); spatial works *Meteor Farm* (1982), *Brant an de Amstel* (1984), *Northern Lights over the Twin Cities* (1985), *An Era Any Time of Year* (1987), *Ghost Nets* (1988) and *Prisons of the Mind*, 'Spatial Symphony' (1990).

Brant, Jobst vom (b Waldersdorf, 28 Oct 1517; d Brand, 22 Jan 1570), German composer. He contributed songs to various collections and also wrote psalms and German songs for several voices.

Branzell, Karin (b Stockholm, 24 Sept 1891; d Altadena, CA, 15 Dec 1974), Swedish mezzo. Debut Stockholm, 1912, in D'Albert's *Izeÿl*;

Berlin 1918–23. NY Met. 1924–44 and in 1951 as Fricka and Brangaene. CG 1935–38, under Beecham. Other roles included Strauss's Nurse and Clytemnestra and Janáček's Kostelnička.

Braslau, Sophie (b New York, 16 Aug 1892; d New York, 22 Dec 1935), American contralto. She studied with Marcella Sembrich. NY Met. 1914–20, as Carmen, Marina and in the fp of Giordano's *Mme Sans-Gêne* (1915). She toured as a concert singer in the US and Europe from 1920.

Brassart, Johannes (de Leodio), Flemish 15th-c. singer and composer. Master of the Imperial Chapel Choir, 1433–43, apparently then moving to Liège and Tongeren. Wrote sacred music and motets.

Braun, Carl (b Meisenheim, 2 Jun 1886; d Hamburg, 24 Apr 1960), German bass. He sang at Wiesbaden, Vienna and the Städtische Oper Berlin 1906–14. He was successful at the NY Met. from 1912 but was rejected as an enemy alien in 1917. At Bayreuth he had one of the longest careers of all singers who have appeared there: 1906–31, as Gurnemanz, Hagen, Wotan, Pogner and Hunding. He worked as a producer in Berlin during the 1930s and was a concert agent from 1937.

Braun, Victor (b Windsor, Ontario, 4 Aug 1935), Canadian baritone. Debut 1961, Escamillo; European debut Frankfurt, 1963. He sang Hamlet in the first CG performance of Searle's opera and other roles have included Don Giovanni, Almaviva, Germont, Posa and Onegin. Sang at Florence from 1987 as Sachs, and Debussy's Golaud; Santa Fe 1990, in the US premiere of *Judith* by S Matthus.

Braunfels, Walter (b Frankfurt, 19 Dec 1882; d Cologne, 19 Mar 1954), German pianist and composer. Studied at the Hoch Conservatory at Frankfurt, later in Vienna and Munich.

Works include operas *Prinzessin Brambilla* (after a story by E T A Hoffmann) (1906–08), *Till Eulenspiegel* (1913), *Die Vögel* (1913–19), *Don Gil von den grünen Hosen* (1921–23), *Der gläserne Berg* (1928), *Galatea*; incidental music to Shakespeare's *Twelfth Night* and *Macbeth*; Mass, Te Deum; orchestral variations and other works; piano music; songs, etc. He wrote operas in a light, post-Wagnerian idiom.

Brautwahl, Die, *The Choice of a Bride*, opera by Busoni (libretto by composer based on a story by E T A Hoffmann), produced Hamburg, 13 Apr 1912. Orchestral suite in five movements performed Berlin, 2 Jan 1913. Albertine has two men over 300 years old among her suitors; she marries her favourite, the young painter Edmund, after he passes a test.

bravura Italian = lit. 'courage, bravery, swagger'; the term refers to passages in a composition or feats in a performance calling for virtuosity.

break the change in tone-quality between different registers of voices and of wind instruments, a natural defect which may be more or less successfully corrected by technical means.

breaking the 17th-c. practice of varying a theme by dividing it into figurations of smaller note-values, as in divisions (variations). Breaking the ground was the same process if the theme was on a ground-bass.

Bream, Julian (Alexander) (b London, 15 Jul 1933), English guitarist and lutenist. He studied guitar with his father, also going to the RCM in London, where he studied piano and cello as well. He was encouraged by Segovia, whose protégé he became. A brilliant performer on many plucked instruments, Bream performs much modern music; Henze has composed *Royal Winter Music* (two sonatas after Shakespeare) for him.

Brecht, Bertolt (1898–1956), German poet and playwright. He was associated with Kurt ◊Weill from 1928 and is credited with the text of the ◊*Dreigroschenoper*; most of it is now known to be by Elisabeth Hauptmann, one of several female collaborators whom Brecht exploited. He had more say in Weill's *Happy End* (1929), ◊*Aufstieg und Fall der Stadt Mahagonny* (1930) and *Der Jasager*. From 1948 Brecht's Berliner Ensemble encouraged social realism and theatrical innovation, spawning a whole generation of original stage producers. ◊*Lehrstück*.

Brehm, Alvin (b New York, 8 Feb 1925), American composer, conductor and double-bass player. He studied at Juilliard with Wallingford Riegger. As a soloist he performed with such groups as the Contemporary Chamber Ensemble (1969–73), the Group for Contemporary Music (1971–73) and the Chamber Music Society of Lincoln Center (1984–89); he has also led modern music as a conductor, from 1947.

Works include Concertina for violin and strings (1975), piano concerto (1977), Sextet for piano and wind quintet (1984), tuba concerto (1982).

Brehme, Hans (b Potsdam, 10 Mar 1904; d Stuttgart, 10 Nov 1957), German composer. Pupil of Robert Kahn in Berlin, he first attracted attention at the Bremen music festival.

Works include three operas *Triptychon* (variations on a theme by Handel) (1936) and *Concerto sinfonico* (1930) for orchestra; piano concerto; partita for string quartet, etc.

Breitengraser, Wilhelm (b Nuremberg, *c* 1495; d Nuremberg, 23 Dec 1542), German composer. He wrote German part-songs and Masses.

Breitkopf & Härtel publishing firm at Leipzig, founded 1719 by Bernhard Christoph Breitkopf (1695–1777); he and his successors issued editions of music from Bach to Brahms, but rejected Wagner's *Ring*. A West German branch was established at Wiesbaden in 1945, becoming independent 1947.

Brema (born *Minny Fehrmann*), Marie (b Liverpool, 28 Feb 1856; d Manchester, 22 Mar 1925), English mezzo of German-American descent. First appearance in London, 1891. Sang at CG as Siebel and Stanford's Beatrice (1901). Bayreuth 1894–97, as Kundry, Ortrud and Fricka. NY Met. 1895 as Brangaene. In 1902 she was the first French Brünnhilde (*Götterdämmerung*), conductor Cortot. Professor RMCM 1913–25.

Brendel, Alfred (b Wiesenberg, 5 Jan 1931), Austrian pianist. Studied with Steuermann and Edwin Fischer; debut Graz, 1948. He played with the Vienna PO at Salzburg in 1960; gave all the Beethoven sonatas for piano in London 1962 and 1994–95; he settled there in 1974. US debut 1963. Has played Bartók and Schoenberg but is heard most often in Liszt and the Viennese classics: he eschews Beethoven's own cadenzas for his concertos. Beethoven sonata series in London, 1994–95.

Brendel *The pianist Alfred Brendel. Although an eccentric, who wears sticking plaster on his finger tips while performing, Brendel's interpretations of the Classical repertory are unsurpassed for their well-balanced phrasing and dignity. His recording of the Liszt sonata is also highly regarded.*

Brendel, Wolfgang (b Munich, 20 Oct 1947), German baritone. From 1971 he has been successful at Munich as Papageno, Wolfram, Germont and Pelléas. NY Met. debut 1975, as Mozart's Count. CG 1985, as Luna. Other roles include Verdi's Miller (Chicago, 1983), Marcello and Mandryka; he sang Renato in *Ballo in Maschera* at Munich, 1994.

Brenet, Michel (pseudonym of Marie Bobillier) (b Lunéville, 12 Apr 1858; d Paris, 4 Nov 1918), French musicologist. Wrote studies of Ockeghem, Palestrina, Handel, Haydn, Grétry and Berlioz.

Brent, Charlotte (b London, *c* 1735; d London, 10 Apr 1802), English soprano. Pupil of Arne, in whose opera *Eliza* she made her first appearance, at Dublin in 1755. London from 1757; sang there in Arne's *Judith* (1761) and *Artaxerxes* (1762).

Bretón, Tomás (b Salamanca, 29 Dec 1850; d Madrid, 2 Dec 1923), Spanish composer. Director of Madrid Conservatory from 1901.

Works include operas *Guzman el Bueno* (1875), *Garin, Raquel* (1900), *Farinelli, El certamen de Cremona, Tabaré* and *Don Gil* (1914); zarzuelas *Los amantes de Teruel, La Dolores, La verbena de la paloma* (1894) and *c* 30 others; oratorio *Apocalipsia* (1882); *Las escenas andalazas, Salamanca, En la Alhambra* for orchestra; violin concerto; three string quartets, piano quintet, sextet for wind, piano trio.

Brett, Charles (b Maidenhead, 27 Oct 1941), English countertenor. He has sung with leading early and Baroque ensembles, under Hogwood, Harnoncourt and John Eliot Gardiner; has toured the USA and Europe with Bach's *St John Passion* and Handel's *Israel in Egypt*. Opera debut Graz 1984 in Fux's *Angelica vincitrice di Alcina*. Founder and director of the Amaryllis Consort; other concerts with Le Grande Ecurie et la Chambre du Roi, under Malgoire.

Breuer, Hans (b Cologne, 27 Apr 1868; d Vienna, 11 Oct 1929), German tenor. He sang every year at Bayreuth 1896–1914, usually as Mime and David. NY Met. debut 1900, as Erik. Member of the Vienna Hofoper 1900–29 and took part in the 1919 fp of *Die Frau ohne Schatten*. He sang at Salzburg from 1910 as Monostatos and Mozart's Basilio; later a producer there.

Bréval, Lucienne (real name Berthe Agnès Lisette Schilling) (b Berlin, 4 Nov 1869; d Neuilly-sur-Seine, 15 Aug 1935), French soprano of Swiss descent. Studied at the Conservatories of Geneva and Paris. Made her first appearance at the Paris Opéra in 1892, as Selika, and remained there for nearly 30 years. She was the first *Walküre* Brünnhilde, Eva and Kundry at the Opéra; created Fauré's Pénélope (Monte Carlo, 1913). In 1906 she sang Armide in the first London performance of Gluck's opera.

breve, Latin *brevis*, = 'short'; a square note equalling two semibreves in value: ◻. So called because it was originally a short note having one half or one third of the value of a long (Latin *longa*).

Bréville, Pierre (Onfroy) de (b Bar-le-Duc, 21 Feb 1861; d Paris, 24 Sept 1949), French composer. Intended for the diplomatic service, he was allowed to study with Dubois at the Paris Conservatory. He decided to devote himself to composition and became a pupil of Franck. Later became professor at the Schola Cantorum, a music critic and member of the committee of the Société Nationale de Musique.

Works include opera *Éros vainqueur* (1905); incidental music for Maeterlinck's *Sept Princesses* and overture for his *La Princesse Maleine*; Mass and motets; *La Cloche fêlée* (after Baudelaire) for orchestra; two violin and piano sonatas.

Brewer, Bruce (b San Antonio, 12 Oct 1944), American tenor. He studied at Texas University, Austin, and with Richard Bonynge. His career began in concert. Stage debut San Antonio, 1970, as Ottavio; later sang at Boston and San Francisco. He appeared at Düsseldorf and Berlin, and at the Aix Festival was heard in Campra; developed into a Baroque specialist and has sung roles in Rameau's *Les Indes Galantes* and *Zoroastre*. He sang Truffaldino in *Turandot* by Busoni at Lyons, 1992.

Brian, Havergal (b Dresden, Staffs., 29 Jan 1876; d Shoreham, 28 Nov 1972), English composer. Mainly self-taught as a composer, he became an organist and music teacher in Staffordshire and wrote criticism at Manchester from 1905. Later he moved to London, where he made a precarious living under great difficulties. Some of his early music was conducted by Wood and by Beecham, although he did not hear any of his 32 symphonies performed until 1954 at the age of 78 (BBC, no. 8). The largest symphony, no. 1 *The Gothic*, was composed 1919–27 but not performed until 1961. Despite the meagre prospects of hearing his own works performed during the early years — most of his 32 symphonies are still unpublished — Brian continued to compose.

Works include operas *The Tigers* (1916–29; fp BBC, 1983), *Turandot* (1950), *The Cenci* (1952), *Faust* (1956), *Agamemnon* (1957); 32 symphonies (1919–68); three *English Suites*, *Hero and Leander*, overtures *For Valour* (Whitman) and *Dr Merryheart*, *Festal Dance*, *Fantastic Variations on Old Rhymes*, symphonic poem *In Memoriam* for orchestra; *By the Waters of Babylon*, *The Vision of Cleopatra* and a setting from Shelley's *Prometheus* for chorus and orchestra (1937–44); Heine's *Pilgrimage to Kevlaar* for chorus and orchestra; songs; part-songs.

Bride of Messina, The, *Nevěsta Messinská*, opera by Fibich (libretto by O Hostinský, based on Schiller's drama *Die Braut von Messina*), produced Prague, Czech Theatre, 28 Mar 1884.

bridge the support over which the strings are stretched and kept away from the belly of string instruments.

Bridge, Frank (b Brighton, 26 Feb 1879; d Eastbourne, 10 Jan 1941), English composer. Student at the RCM, where Stanford was his composition master. He also learnt the violin, viola and conducting. Later played viola in various quartets and gained varied experience as operatic and concert conductor. Won Cobbett Prizes for chamber music in 1905–15 and honourable mention for the E minor string quartet at Bologna in 1906. He won acclaim for such accessible works as *The Sea* (1910), *Lament* for strings (1915) and *There is a Willow* (1928). However, starting with the Piano Sonata (1924), his music explores dissonance to a greater degree, including bitonality. His third and fourth string quartets (1927, 1937) show an advanced harmonic idiom, not far removed from the music of Berg. He was well known as a teacher; one of his pupils was Britten, whose *Variations on a theme of Frank Bridge* (1937) are based on a theme from his master's Idyll no. 2 for string quartet (1906).

Works include opera *The Christmas Rose*, (1918–29; produced London, 1932); symphonic poem *Isabella* (1907), suite *The Sea* (1911), rhapsody *Enter Spring* (1927), tone-poem *Summer* for orchestra; Lament for strings; *There is a willow grows aslant a brook* (on a passage in *Hamlet*); *Phantasm* for piano and orchestra, (1931), *Oration* for cello and orchestra (1930), *Rebus* overture (1940) and *Allegro moderato* for strings (1941). Four string quartets (1901–37), two piano trios, Fantasy quartet and several smaller pieces for string quartet, piano quintet, Fantasy Trio and quartet for piano and strings, string sextet, Rhapsody for two violins and viola, *Divertimenti* for wind instruments, violin and piano sonata, cello and piano sonata; numerous piano works including sonata, four *Characteristic Pieces*, suite *A Fairy Tale*, three Improvisations for the left hand; violin, viola, cello and organ pieces; choruses; songs.

bridge passage a transitional passage in a composition, e.g. the transition between first and second subjects in a sonata-form movement.

Bridgetower, George (Augustus Polgreen) (b Biala, Poland, 11 Oct 1778; d London, 28 Feb 1860), violinist, son of an African father and Polish mother. Met Beethoven in Vienna and Teplice and played the 'Kreutzer' sonata with him at its fp on 17 May 1803.

Briegel, Wolfgang Carl (b Nuremberg, May 1626; d Darmstadt, 19 Nov 1712), German composer. Organist at Schweinfurt and Gotha; from 1671 to his death music director at Darmstadt. Wrote operas and ballets, sacred works for several voices including seven cantatas, *Evangelische Gespräch* and *Evangelischer Blumengarten* (1660–81), pieces for three and four instruments, convivial and funeral songs for several voices, hymns.

Brigg Fair, i.e. the fair at Brigg, Lincs., rhapsody for orchestra by Delius on a Lincolnshire folksong, actually a set of variations, or a kind of passacaglia, composed 1907, performed Basel, 1907; first English performance Liverpool, 18 Jan 1908.

Brilioth, Helge (b Växjo, 7 May 1931), Swedish tenor, formerly baritone. Debut Drottningholm, 1958, as Paisiello's Bartolo and sang further baritone roles in W Germany before tenor debut Stockholm, 1965, as Don José. He has sung Siegmund at Bayreuth and Siegfried at Salzburg; these roles and Tristan and Parsifal at CG from 1970. NY Met. 1970, Parsifal; Glyndebourne 1971, Bacchus.

brillant French, *brillante* Italian = 'brilliant', used either as an adj. in titles or as a direction showing how a particular passage is to be performed.

Brimley, John, English 16th-c. composer. He was a cantor at Durham Cathedral 1536–37, and remained there as organist and choirmaster under the New Foundation until *c* 1576. Some English church music has survived.

brindisi Italian = 'a toast'; drinking of someone's health, a drinking song, especially in opera, e.g. in Donizetti's *Lucrezia Borgia*, Verdi's *Macbeth*, *Traviata* and *Otello* or Mascagni's *Cavalleria rusticana*.

brio Italian = 'spirit, fire, brilliance'; the word is often used in the direction *con* ('with') *brio*.

brisé French = 'broken'; an arpeggio in keyboard or harp music; détaché bowing in string music.

Britain, Radie (b Silverton, TX, 17 Mar 1903; d Palm Desert, CA, 23 May 1994), American composer. Studied in Chicago and with Marcel Dupré in Paris; piano with Leopold Godowsky. Taught privately in Hollywood. Much of her music is evocative of her native southwest scenery, including the orchestral pieces *Heroic Poem* (1929), *Light* (1935), *Ononaga Sketches* (1939), *Serenata sorrentina* (1946), *Cactus Rhapsody* (1953), *Cosmic Mist*, symphony (1962), *Brothers of the Clouds*, for male voices and orchestra (1962); chamber and vocal.

British Broadcasting Corporation founded as the British Broadcasting Company Ltd in 1922 and incorporated under a Royal Charter in 1927, when it took its present name. Now always known by its abbreviation, BBC.

British Broadcasting Corporation Symphony Orchestra, BBC SO, chief orchestra of the BBC, founded in 1930 with Adrian Boult as principal conductor. Since 1950 conductors have been Malcolm Sargent (until 1957), Rudolf Schwarz (1957–62), Antal Dorati (1962–66), Colin Davis (1967–71), Pierre Boulez (1971–75), Rudolf Kempe (1975–76), Gennadi Rozhdestvensky (1978–81). John Pritchard 1981–89, Andrew Davies from 1989. Unlike the other London orchestras, the BBC SO is not dependent on box-office receipts: a much more adventurous repertory of works is therefore given, with many fps of British works. In recent years, the period with Boulez as principal conductor was of particular importance: many performances of works by Schoenberg, Stravinsky, Bartók, Berg and Boulez himself. Regional BBC orchestras are based in Manchester (BBC Philharmonic), Glasgow (Scottish) and Cardiff (BBC National Orchestra of Wales).

There are many dangers which hedge around the unfortunate composer: pressure groups which demand true proletarian music; snobs who demand the latest avant garde tricks; critics who are already trying to document today for tomorrow, to be the first to find the correct pigeonhole definition.

Benjamin Britten, *On Receiving the First Aspen Award*, 1964

Britten, (Edward) Benjamin (b Lowestoft, 22 Nov 1913; d Aldeburgh, 4 Dec 1976), English composer, conductor and pianist. Educated at Gresham's School, Holt; studied piano with Harold Samuel, composition with Frank Bridge; later, with a scholarship, at the RCM, London, under Benjamin and Ireland. He was represented at the ISCM festivals of 1934, 1936 and 1938. During the early war years he was in the USA. His talent showed itself early, and his first

Britten *The composer Benjamin Britten (1913–1976) pictured with his lifelong companion, the tenor Peter Pears. An essentially vocal composer, Britten left his mark on all such genres, especially opera: he is sometimes considered the greatest composer for the stage in the 20th century.*

international success was the *Variations on a theme of Frank Bridge*, played at the Salzburg Festival of 1937. This was followed by a number of works which established him as the leading English composer of the day, especially the stark *Sinfonia da Requiem* (1940) and the *Serenade* (1943). In 1945 his second opera, *Peter Grimes*, established him as a dramatist; it was succeeded by further operas, including the chamber opera *The Turn of the Screw* (1954). Much of Britten's music is inspired by words, as shown by the many song cycles, the *Spring Symphony* (1949) and the *Nocturne* (1958); most of his tenor songs and roles were written for his companion Peter Pears (1910–1986). Close artistic association with Shostakovich and Rostropovich from 1960. The *War Requiem* (1961) combines the liturgical text with poems by Wilfred Owen and was composed to mark the consecration of the new Coventry Cathedral (1962). Britten was an admired conductor and accompanist, often heard in partnership with Pears. OM 1965, life peer 1976. He was a founder of the Aldeburgh Festival, 1948.

By intellectual conviction and personal disposition Britten was an outsider; the themes of lost innocence, persecution and isolation are constantly repeated in his music, especially the operas. Once treated with caution by both conservatives and the avant garde, he has now reached a wider acceptance.

Works include STAGE: operas *Paul Bunyan* (W H Auden, 1941, revised 1974), *Peter Grimes* (M Slater, after Crabbe, 1945), *The Rape of Lucretia* (R Duncan, 1946), *Albert Herring* (E Crozier, after Maupassant, 1947), *The Little Sweep* (Crozier, on Blake's poem *The Chimney Sweep*, 1949), *Billy Budd* (E M Forster and Crozier, after Melville, 1951, revised 1960), *Gloriana* (W Plomer, 1953), *The Turn of the Screw* (M Piper, after James, 1954), *A Midsummer Night's*

Dream (Shakespeare, 1960), *Owen Wingrave* (Piper, after James, 1971) and *Death in Venice* (Piper, after Mann, 1973); *Noye's Fludde* (children's opera, 1957); church parables *Curlew River* (1964), *The Burning Fiery Furnace* (1966) and *The Prodigal Son* (1968); ballet *The Prince of the Pagodas* (1957).

INCIDENTAL MUSIC: including Webster's *Duchess of Malfi*, Priestley's *Johnson over Jordan*, Auden and Isherwood's *Ascent of F.6* and *On the Frontier*, Duncan's *This Way to the Tomb*.

CHORAL: including *A Boy was Born* (1933, revised 1955), *Friday Afternoons* for children's voices (1933–35), *Te Deum* (1935), *Ballad of Heroes* (1939), *AMDG*, Four prayers and holy songs of G M Hopkins (1939), *Hymn to St Cecilia* (Auden, 1942), *A Ceremony of Carols* (1942), cantatas *Rejoice in the Lamb* (C Smart, 1943) and *Saint Nicolas* (Crozier, 1948), *Spring Symphony* (1949), *Cantata Academica* (1959), *War Requiem* (1961), *Cantata Misericordium* (1963).

ORCHESTRAL: including *Variations on a theme of Frank Bridge* for strings (1937), *Young Apollo* for piano and strings (1939), *Sinfonia da Requiem* (1940), Prelude and Fugue for strings (1943), *The Young Person's Guide to the Orchestra* (1946), concertos for piano and for violin (1938–39), *Diversions for piano* (left hand) and orchestra (1940, revised 1954), *Scottish Ballad* for two pianos and orchestra (1941), *Four Sea Interludes from Peter Grimes* (1946), cello symphony (1963), overture *The Building of the House*, Suite on English Folk Tunes (1974).

VOICE AND ORCHESTRA: *Quatre chansons françaises* (1928), *Our Hunting Fathers* (Auden) for high voice and orchestra (1936), *Les Illuminations* (A Rimbaud, 1939) for high voice and strings, *Serenade* (various poets) for tenor, horn and strings, *Nocturne* (various poets, 1958), *Phaedra* for mezzo and orchestra (1975).

CHAMBER AND INSTRUMENTAL: including four string quartets (1931 revised 1974; nos. 1–3, 1941, 1945, 1975); Quartettino (1930), Phantasy String Quintet (1932), Phantasy Oboe Quintet (1932); Suite for violin and piano (1935); Three Divertimenti for string quartet (1936), Temporal Variations for oboe and piano (1936); cello sonata, three suites for solo cello; *Lacrymae* on song by Dowland for viola and piano (also with strings); *Six Metamorphoses after Ovid* for solo oboe; *Holiday Diary* and *Sonatina Romantica* for piano; *Prelude and Fugue on a theme of Vittoria* for organ (1946); *Gemini Variations* for flute, violin and piano four hands (1965).

SONG CYCLES: *On this Island* (Auden, 1937), *Seven Sonnets of Michelangelo* (1940), *The Holy Sonnets of John Donne* (1945),

A Selection of
Britten

Sinfonia da Requiem	1940
Serenade	1943
Peter Grimes	1945
Billy Budd	1951
Gloriana	1953
The Turn of the Screw	1954
A Midsummer Night's Dream	1960
War Requiem	1961
Cello Symphony	1963
Death in Venice	1973

Britten   *A biographical note*

The performance of Britten's music is so often associated with his own centre at Aldeburgh that it is easy to forget that London performances have also been crucial. Many early supporters saw a portent in the BBC studio premiere of the cantata *A Boy was Born*, given on the day that Elgar died in 1934. After the 1938 Promenade Concert premiere of the Piano Concerto, a hiatus in home-based Britten performances was caused by his absence in America. The commission he received there for an opera bore fruit in *Peter Grimes*, premiered at Sadler's Wells one month after the end of the war in Europe. Considerable opposition to the pacifist composer and his live-in leading tenor came from artists whose friends and relatives had fought in the war. He enjoyed an easier ride with the production of *Billy Budd* at Covent Garden in 1951, although Britten had to conduct the premiere himself after the originally designated conductor, Josef Krips, pulled out. In 1953, Coronation year was celebrated at Covent Garden with the premiere of *Gloriana*, an account of the last years of Queen Elizabeth I. The largely unmusical audience was nonplussed about the work as a whole, and the young Queen was deemed to have been affronted when her illustrious ancestor was discovered by the Earl of Essex without her wig. It was not until more than 40 years later that the true merits of *Gloriana* were revealed at Covent Garden, in a guest production by Opera North.

A Charm of Lullabies (various poets, 1947), *Winter Words* (Hardy, 1953), *6 Hölderlin-Fragmente* (1958), *Songs and Proverbs of William Blake* (1965), *The Poet's Echo* (Pushkin, 1965), Five Canticles (1947–74).

Britton, Thomas (b Rushden, near Higham Ferrers, 14 Jan 1644; d London, 27 Sept 1714), English coal dealer and music amateur. Began very poorly as a hawker, but acquired much knowledge in music and science and established weekly concerts in a room over his shop in London which soon had a great following.

Brixi, Franz Xaver (b Prague, 2 Jan 1732; d Prague, Oct 14 1771), Bohemian organist and composer. After various church posts he became *Kapellmeister* of Prague Cathedral in 1756.

Works include largely church music; 105 Masses, including *Missa Pastoralis* (Christmas Mass); 263 offertories, hymns and motets; 11 Requiems; 24 Vespers; Litanies, etc.; also organ pieces (including three concertos), a sinfonia, etc.

Broadwood British family of piano manufacturers and music editors:

1. John Broadwood (b Cockburnspath, Oct 1732; d London, 1812), married Barbara, daughter of Burkat ◊Shudi, in 1769, and was sole proprietor of Shudi & Broadwood from 1782. By 1781 he had built the first Broadwood grand piano, developed from Zampe's square pianos.

2. James Shudi Broadwood (b London, 20 Dec 1772; d London, 8 Aug 1851), son of 1, was taken into partnership in 1795, when the firm became John Broadwood & Son.

3. Thomas Broadwood, brother of 2, was taken into partnership in 1807 and the name became John Broadwood & Sons. 2,500 pianos were manufactured per year by the middle of the century, but the firm declined towards the 1880s.

Brockes (Barthold) Heinrich (1680–1747), German poet. ◊Handel (Passion), ◊Telemann (ditto). Part of his Passion oratorio libretto was used by Bach in the *St John Passion*.

Brockway, Howard (b Brooklyn, 22 Nov 1870; d New York, 20 Feb 1951), American pianist and composer. Studied in NY and Berlin, taught privately in NY from 1895 and in 1903 joined the Peabody Conservatory at Baltimore. Returning to NY in 1910 he taught composition there privately and at the David Mannes Music School. Works include symphony in D major, Ballad, Scherzino, *Sylvan*

Suite for orchestra (1901); *Cavatina and Romanza* for violin and orchestra, suite in E minor for cello and orchestra; violin and piano sonata in G minor; piano pieces.

Brodsky, Adolf (b Taganrog, 21 Mar 1851; d Manchester, 22 Jan 1929), Russian violinist. Pupil of Hellmesberger in Vienna; successively conductor at Kiev, professor at the Leipzig Conservatory, leader of the Hallé Orchestra in Manchester and principal of the RMCM 1895–1929. In 1881 he gave the fp of Tchaikovsky's violin concerto in Vienna, conductor Richter. He was the leader of a string quartet bearing his name. *See illustration on page 90.*

Brodsky String Quartet ensemble founded by former members of the RMCM and named after Adolf ◊Brodsky. They have presented classical and modern repertory: music by Crumb (*Black Angels*), Shostakovich, and Schoenberg. Members are Michael Thomas and Ian Belton (violins), Paul Cassidy (viola), Jacqueline Thomas (cello).

broken consort term in use in England *c* 1600 for an ensemble that performed well-known music with many embellishments or divisions. Also used to refer to ensembles in which different families of instruments were used together.

Broman, Sten (b Uppsala, 25 Mar 1902; d Lund, 29 Oct 1983), Swedish composer, viola player and critic. Studied in Prague, Stockholm, Fribourg (Switzerland) and Berlin, and in 1927 took a degree in music history at Lund University. He became music critic to the *Sydsvenska Dagbladet*. His music progressed from Hindemith to the avant-garde.

Works include incidental music to Aristophanes' *Lysistrata*; fantasy for chorus and orchestra; nine symphonies (1962–77); *Academy Festival Overture*, Chorale Fantasy and concerto for orchestra; prelude, *Gothic Suite* and Litany for string orchestra; suite for viola and strings; three string quartets, keyboard music.

Bronfman, Yefim (b Tashkent, 10 Apr 1958), Russian-born pianist. Studied at Juilliard and with Rudolf Serkin before debut with Israel PO, 1974. Appearances with the NY and LA POs, Chicago and San Francisco SOs; Berlin Philharmonic and other major European orchestras. Recordings include works by Brahms, Prokofiev and Mussorgsky.

Brook, Barry S(helley) (b New York, 1 Nov 1918), American musicologist. Took his PhD in Paris (1959) and has taught there and in the USA (Juilliard from 1977). He has coordinated international bibliographical projects and is the joint editor of the complete works of Pergolesi (1986–). He has also issued *The Symphony, 1720–1840* and *French Opera in the 17th and 18th Centuries*.

Brossard, Sébastien de (b Dompierre, bap. 12 Sept 1655; d Meaux, 10 Aug 1730), French composer. Studied philosophy and theology at Caen and was self-taught in music. He lived there until 1683, when he went to Paris and worked at Notre-Dame, later at Strasbourg. In 1687 he became *maître de chapelle* at the cathedral there and in 1698 music director at Meaux Cathedral. Although he was a prolific composer he is more famous for his dictionary of music (1703, the first in France).

Professional musicians we speak of as vulgar people, and indeed we think it not manly to perform music, except when drunk or for fun.

Aristotle, *Politics, c* 320 BC

Brott, Alexander (b Montreal, 17 Mar 1915), Canadian composer, conductor and violinist. Studied at Juilliard and McGill University, Montreal; taught at Montreal from 1939 and founded chamber orchestra, giving fps of Canadian works. He has made many arrangements of German Classical repertory.

Brott, Boris (b Montreal, 14 Mar 1944), Canadian conductor, son of Alexander Brott. Conducted regional orchestras in N America and Britain (BBC Welsh SO and Northern Sinfonia). Widely active as a music educator.

Brouwenstijn, Gré (Gerda Demphina) (b Den Helder, 26 Aug 1915), Dutch soprano. Studied under various teachers from childhood, becoming a leading singer at the Amsterdam opera. She later sang all over Europe, both in lyric and dramatic roles. CG 1951, Aida;

Brodsky *The violinist Adolf Brodsky and his wife, together with his family visiting Grieg and Nina Hagerup in 1906. Although he retired as a soloist in 1921, Brodsky made a special appearance playing Elgar's concerto for the composer's 70th birthday.*

Elisabeth de Valois 1958. Bayreuth 1954–56 as Elisabeth, Gutrune, Eva and Sieglinde. Glyndebourne 1959–63, as Leonore.

Brown, Christopher (b Tunbridge Wells, 17 Jun 1943), English composer. Studied with Lennox Berkeley and Boris Blacher. Much of his music has a spiritual content: cantata *David* (1970), organ concerto (1979), Magnificat (1980), *The Vision of Saul* (1983), *Landscapes* for soprano, chorus and orchestra (1987).

Brown, Earle (b Lunenburg, MA, 26 Dec 1926), American composer of the *avant-garde*. Much influenced by the ideas of John Cage, and also by the visual arts (Calder, Pollock), he developed a method of notating controlled improvisation by graphical means.

Works include *Available Forms I*; Available Forms II for 98 players and two conductors (1961–62); two octets for eight magnetic tapes; *Light Music* for electric lights, electronic equipment and instruments; *Sign Sounds* for chamber ensemble (1972), *Windsor Jambs* for soprano and orchestra (1979); *Folio II* for instruments (1981); *Sounder Rounds* for orchestra (1982); *Tracer* for ensemble and tape (1984).

Brown, Howard Mayer (b Los Angeles, 13 Apr 1930; d Venice, 21 Feb 1993), American musicologist. Studied at Harvard and was professor at University of Chicago from 1967. Writings include *Music in the French Secular Theater, 1400–1550* (1963), *Music in the Renaissance* (1976), and *Major Unpublished Works in a Central Baroque and Early Classical Tradition* (1977–; planned in 60 volumes). Founded Collegium Musicum at Chicago, for the performance of medieval and Renaissance music.

Brown, Iona (b Salisbury, 7 Jan 1941), English violinist and conductor. She studied with Hugh Maguire and Henryk Szeryng. Philharmonia Orchestra 1963–66. Joined Academy of St Martin-in-the-Fields 1964; director from 1978. Artistic director Norwegian Chamber Orchestra from 1981, Los Angeles CO from 1987.

Browne, John (*fl. c* 1490), English composer who contributed more pieces than anyone else to the Eton Choirbook and now seems the major English composer of his generation.

browning an English form of *fancy* for viols, similar to the 'In Nomine', but based on a folk-tune instead of a plainsong theme.

Browning, John (b Denver, 22 May 1933), American pianist. Studied at Juilliard and made debut in Denver, 1943. After winning 1955 Leventritt Award he played the Paganini Variations with the NY PO. Premiered the concerto by Samuel Barber (1962) and has a repertory of 43 concertos, from Beethoven to Prokofiev.

Brownlee, John (Donald Mackenzie) (b Geelong, 7 Jan 1900; d New York, 10 Jan 1969), Australian baritone. Educated at Geelong College, he was persuaded by Melba to take up singing seriously. He made his debut at her farewell concert in 1926 as Marcello, and in 1927 joined the Paris Opéra; sang there until 1936; Glyndebourne 1935–47 as Alfonso, Don Giovanni and Mozart's Count; NY Met. 1937–56, debut role Rigoletto. In 1956 he became director of the Manhattan School of Music.

Bruce, (Frank) Neely (b Memphis, 21 Jan 1944), American composer and pianist. Studied at the University of Illinois and has taught at the Wesleyan University from 1974. Founded the American Music/Theater Group 1977 and has also given premieres as a solo pianist. His music has progressed from serialism to native American influences: chamber operas *Pyramus and Thisbe* (1965), *The Trials of Psyche* (1971) and *Americana* (1978–83); concerto for percussion and orchestra (1967), violin concerto (1974), *Orion Rising* for orchestra (1988); *Eight Ghosts* for four singers and electronics; keyboard music and songs; chamber pieces with voice.

Bruch, Max (b Cologne, 6 Jan 1838; d Friedenau near Berlin, 2 Oct 1920), German composer. Learnt music as a child from his mother, a singer; later, with a scholarship, from Hiller, Reinecke and Breuning.

Iona Brown – violinist / conductor

1 Bach: Mass in B minor
   If you asked me the composer I could least do without, it
   would be Bach without a shadow of a doubt. My father
   would play from the 48 Preludes and Fugues every day. 'I
   think I can feel a Bach fugue coming on', he would say. We
   all groaned, but now he is gone, I long for someone to turn a
   beautiful fugue. The B minor mass was a piece he often
   conducted. I can't remember when I first heard it, it always
   seems to have been there.

2 Sibelius: Violin Concerto (Neveu/Philharmonia)
   This was the first recording I was given. The intensity of that
   piece and her playing are so extreme. I had wild dreams,
   aged eight, of being in that orchestra (I was, eventually).

3 Vivaldi: *The Four Seasons*
   I first heard the *Four Seasons* in Rome, played by I Musici.
   It made a tremendous impact: I was 19 and had never heard
   such music. Over twenty years I've played that piece to

more people than any other, but a masterpiece like that never
dies on you. It's exquisite.

4 Mozart: *Sinfonia concertante*
   Mozart is the composer who has shaped my career most,
   after Vivaldi. I first played the *Sinfonia concertante* with my
   sister when we were children. It towers above the violin
   concertos: it is one of Mozart's masterpieces.

5 Vaughan Williams: *The Lark Ascending*
   This is very much a piece after my own heart. I was brought
   up in the country and I live there now. I need the certainties
   of rural life, the changing seasons, and the sound of larks.

6 Brahms: Horn Trio
   This is a very important family piece in my life. My mother,
   father and their friend Maurice Handford played it in the
   '40s. My brothers, Tim and Ian, and I played it, and still do.
   It's an intellectual piece, but so poignant.

He visited Leipzig, Munich and other musical centres to gain further experience and in 1863 produced his opera *Loreley* at Mannheim, having obtained permission from Geibel to use the libretto originally written for Mendelssohn. After two appointments at Koblenz and Sondershausen, he lived first in Berlin and then at Bonn, wholly devoted to composition. From 1880 to 1883 he was conductor of the Liverpool Philharmonic Society, and in 1881 he married the singer Clara Tuczek. From 1883 to 1890 he conducted at Breslau and in 1891 he became professor of composition at the Hochschule in Berlin, retiring to Friedenau in 1910. Until recently only the popular G minor violin concerto has allowed Bruch to emerge from the shadow of Brahms; revivals of such works as the oratorio *Odyssey*, the opera *Loreley* and chamber music such as the Septet have allowed a more balanced view of the composer.

Works include operas *Scherz, List und Rache* (Goethe) (Cologne, 1858), *Die Loreley* (Mannheim, 1863) and *Hermione* (after Shakespeare's *Winter's Tale*) (Berlin 1872); works for solo voices, chorus and orchestra: *Frithjof Scenen* (after Tegnér, 1864), *Schön Ellen, Odysseus* (after Homer, 1872), *Das Lied von der Glocke* (Schiller, 1879), *Achilleus* (after Homer), *Das Feuerkreuz* (after Scott's *Lay of the Last Minstrel*), *Moses, Gustav Adolf Damajanti, Die Macht des Gesangs* (Schiller, 1912).

ORCHESTRAL AND CHAMBER: three symphonies; three violin concertos (1868, 1878, 1891), *Scottish Fantasia* for violin, harp and orchestra (1880); *Kol Nidrei* (1881) and *Ave Maria* for cello and orchestra; Marfa's scene from Schiller's *Demetrius* for mezzo and orchestra (1906); Septet (1849), two string quartets, piano trio; string quintet in A minor (1919), many choruses; instrumental pieces; piano music; songs.

Bruck, Arnold van (b Bruges, ? 1500; d Linz, 6 Feb 1554), Netherlands composer. First *Kapellmeister* to the emperor and dean of the Abbey of Laibach. Wrote motets and other church music, sacred and secular songs, especially German songs.

Bruckner, Anton (b Ansfelden, 4 Sept 1824; d Vienna, 11 Oct 1896), Austrian composer and organist. The son of a country schoolmaster, he was intended for the same calling and received little musical education. On the early death of his father in 1837 he was taken in as a choirboy by the monastery of St Florian. There he learnt the organ and was appointed organist in 1845. By this time he had begun to compose, notably the Requiem in D minor, but was dissatisfied with his poor technique and went to study counterpoint with Sechter in Vienna, 1855. Cathedral organist at Linz, 1855–68, where he wrote

much in his spare time, including the first recognized symphony (*Linz*), and became an ardent Wagnerian on visiting Munich for the production of *Tristan* in 1865. The early progress of his work was hindered by his identification, in the minds of influential critics, with the music of Wagner; a more apposite comparison, perhaps, is with Beethoven, particularly the Ninth Symphony. Bruckner's music typically is imbued with a similar kind of spirituality; this is illustrated by the abundance of early religious works, and the late Te Deum. In addition, Bruckner's orchestra tended not to be as massive as Wagner's.

He was appointed professor at the Vienna Conservatory in 1868, when his first symphony received its fp at Linz, and remained in the capital for the rest of his life, but visited Nancy, Paris and London as organ virtuoso in 1869 and 1871. His third symphony, strongly influenced by Wagner, had its fp at Vienna in 1873 but was a failure.

Bruckner   *A biographical note*

Bruckner was probably the most naive and unworldly of all the major composers. Son of a poverty-stricken schoolmaster, his early ambition was no higher than to be a primary school teacher. An apparent lack of confidence in his ability also became evident late in his life when he allowed friends to alter and 'improve' his symphonies. He gained early organist's appointments at St Florian and then Linz, where he heard *Tannhäuser*, and was immediately converted to Wagner's sound world (although he never really understood what Wagner was trying to achieve as a dramatist). A meeting with Wagner in 1865 cemented his allegiance, but made difficult his acceptance in a hostile Vienna. His early symphonies were labelled unperformable by the Vienna Philharmonic, and the 1877 premiere of the Third symphony was a disaster. Bruckner provoked hilarity among the musicians by trying to tip the great conductor Hans Richter on one occasion. Not even the Emperor Joseph escaped Bruckner's naivety; the critic Hanslick having written of the hideous length and nightmarish hangover style of the Eighth symphony, Bruckner asked the Emperor at an investiture 'Please would your Majesty ask Mr Hanslick to be not quite so critical?'

Bruckner *The composer Anton Bruckner (1824–1896). The symphonic repertory formed the backbone of his oeuvre, consisting of monumental sculptures of sound in terms of the overall scale of his works and the slow-moving harmony which typically drives them forward.*

Wide success came after the fp of the seventh symphony (1884). He was pensioned in 1891 and received an honorary doctor's degree from the university of Vienna.

Bruckner's symphonies went through several editions and revisions, first through well-meaning cuts and alterations made by Franz Schalk and the composer himself. The later editions by Robert Haas, succeeded by Leopold Novak, attempt to return to Bruckner's original thoughts.

Works include SYMPHONIES: F minor (1863), D minor ('no. 0', *c* 1863–64, revised 1869), no. 1 in C minor (1865, revised 1868–84), no. 2 in C minor (1871, revised 1873–77), no. 3 in D minor (1873, revised 1874–77), no. 4 in E♭ ('Romantic'; 1874, new scherzo 1878, new finale 1880), no. 5 in B♭ (1875–76), no. 6 in A (1879–81), no. 7 in E (1881–83), no. 8 in C minor (1884–87 and 1889–90), no. 9 in D minor (1891–94).

CHORAL: Mass no. 1 in D minor (1864, revised 1876–82), no. 2 in E minor with wind accompaniment (1866, revised 1869–82), no. 3 in F minor (1867, revised 1876–93); also Mass in F (1844), Requiem in D minor (1849), *Missa Solemnis* in B♭ (1852), Te Deum in C for soloists, chorus and orchestra (1881–84), five Psalm settings (1852–92), many motets.

INSTRUMENTAL: string quartet in C minor (1862), string quintet in F (1879); organ music, piano pieces and songs.

Brudieu, Jean (or *Juan* or *Joan*) (b near Limoges, *c* 1520; d Urgell, Catalonia, 1591), French (Hispanicized) singer and composer. He visited Urgell in the Pyrenees to sing there at Christmas 1538 and remained there as choirmaster until the 1570s, when he was at the church of Santa Maria del Mar at Barcelona, where he pub. a book of madrigals in 1585. He had returned to Urgell in 1579. Composed church music as well as madrigals, including a *Missa defunctorum* (Requiem).

Brüggen, Frans (b Amsterdam, 30 Oct 1934), Dutch conductor, former flautist and recorder player. He studied in Amsterdam and soon became the foremost recorder player of his time; also influential as a teacher. As a conductor, he favours original instruments, and has recorded much Baroque music. He has conducted avant-garde ensembles; from 1985 conducting symphonic music, notably with the Orchestra of the Eighteenth Century (Haydn's London Symphony and Beethoven's Ninth at the London Proms, 1993).

Bruhns, Nicolaus (b Schwabstedt, Slesvig, Advent 1665; d Husum, 29 Mar 1697), German organist, string player and composer. First employed in Copenhagen, then town organist at Husum, Slesvig-Holstein. Wrote cantatas, motets with orchestra and organ music. His elaborate preludes and fugues and sacred concertos form an important link between Buxtehude and Bach.

Brulé, Gace, French 12th-c. trouvère. 90 songs are attributed to him, but only some 30 are accepted as authentic.

Brüll, Ignaz (b Prossnitz, Moravia, 7 Nov 1846; d Vienna, 17 Sept 1907), Austrian pianist and composer. Studied in Vienna, where his family settled when he was three, played there, toured, and produced a number of compositions. Later he taught the piano.

Works include operas *Die Bettler von Samarkand* (1864), *Das goldene Kreuz* (1875), *Der Landfriede* (1877), *Bianca, Königin Mariette* (1883), *Gloria, Das steinerne Herz, Gringoire, Schach dem König* (1893), *Der Husar*; ballet *Champagnermärchen* (1896); symphony; overture to Shakespeare's *Macbeth*, serenade for orchestra; two piano concertos; violin concerto; piano trio and other chamber music; sonata for two pianos; piano music; songs.

> *When God finally calls me and asks 'What have you done with the talent I gave you, my lad?', I will present to him the score of my Te Deum and I hope he will judge me mercifully.*
>
> **Anton Bruckner**, quoted in Sutton, *Introduction to the Te Deum*, 1993

Brumel, Antoine (b *c* 1460; d *c* 1515), French composer. Singer at Chartres Cathedral in 1483, canon at Laon in 1497, and from 1498 to 1501 choirmaster at Notre-Dame in Paris. Went to the court of the Duke of Ferrara in 1506, where he may have died. He is regarded as one of Josquin's most important contemporaries and wrote 15 surviving masses, including *Et ecce terrae motus* for 12 voices, and *L'homme armé* and *Missa pro defunctis*, both for 4 voices. He also

A Selection of
Bruckner

Mass no.1 in D minor.................................1864
Symphony no. 2...1871
Symphony no. 3....................................1873
Symphony no. 4..1874

Symphony no. 5.................................1875–6
String Quintet...1879
Symphony no. 7.................................1881–3
Te Deum...............................1881–4
Symphony no. 8.................1884–7
Symphony no. 9.........1891–4

wrote sequences, antiphons, motets, chansons and instrumental music based on popular melodies of the day.

Bruna-Rasa, Lina (b Milan, 24 Sept 1907; d Milan, Oct 1984), Italian soprano. Debut La Scala, 1926, as Boito's Elena, under Toscanini; the following year took part in the fp of Wolf-Ferrari's *Sly*. Remained in Milan until 1940 as Venus, Loreley and Santuzza, and sang in the 1935 fp of Mascagni's *Nerone*. Appeared widely in Europe as Amelia, Tosca and Gioconda.

Bruneau, (Louis Charles Bonaventure) Alfred (b Paris, 3 Mar 1857; d Paris, 15 Jun 1934), French composer and critic. Son of a painter; learnt music including cello from his parents, who played violin and piano, and took a cello prize at the Paris Conservatory as a pupil of Franchomme. Afterwards studied composition with Massenet and played in Pasdeloup's orchestra. In 1887 he produced his first opera; the next two were based on works by Zola, who himself wrote the libretti for the next three stage works. The first of these, however, failed in 1897 because Bruneau and Zola were ardent supporters of Dreyfus. After Zola's death Bruneau wrote his own libretti, some still based on Zola's work. He wrote in a style indebted to Wagner, yet softened by the gentler lyricism of the French tradition, somewhat reminiscent of Gounod and Massenet.

Works include operas *Kérim* (1887), *Le Rêve* and *L'Attaque du moulin* (after Zola, 1893), *Messidor*, *L'Ouragan* (1901) and *L'Enfant-troi* (libretti by Zola), *Lazare*, *Naïs Micoulin* and *Les Quatre Journées* (after Zola), *Le Tambour*, *Le Roi Candaule*, *Angélo, tyran de Padoue* (1928), *Virginie*; ballets *Les Bacchantes* (after Euripides, 1931) and *Le Jardin de Paradis*; incidental music to his adaptation of Zola's *La Faute de l'Abbé Mouret*; Requiem (1895), choral symphony *Léda*, *La Belle au bois dormant* and *Penthésilée*; cantata *Geneviève de Paris*; *Ouverture héroïque* for orchestra; vocal duets; songs *Chansons à danser* and two books of *Lieds de France* (all words by Catulle Mendès).

Brunelle, Philip (b Faribault, MN, 1 Jul 1943), American conductor. He was music director of the Minnesota Opera 1968–85 and has directed the Plymouth Music Series from 1969. Conducted the Minnesota Orchestra 1963–68 and has guested throughout the USA and Europe; opera at Drottningholm (*Soliman II* by Kraus), Aldeburgh (first recording of *Paul Bunyan* by Britten), San Francisco, Washington DC and Houston.

Brunelli, Antonio (b Bagnorea near Orvieto, c 1575; d Pisa, by 1630), Italian organist, music scholar and composer. Worked at Florence, both at churches and at the Tuscan court. Wrote two learned theoretical books, including *Regole utilissime* (1606), and collaborated with Peri on *Ballo della Cortesia* (1614).

Works include Masses, Requiems, sacred songs, psalms; a ballet; canzonets, madrigals.

brunette French = lit. 'a dark-haired girl'; a light love-song of a type current in 17th–18th-c. France, originally so called because of the association of the words with dark girls.

Brunetti, Gaetano (b ? Fano, 1744; d near Madrid, 16 Dec 1798), Italian violinist and composer. Pupil of Nardini in Florence. Spent most of his life in Spain, in the service of the court and of the Duke of Alba, and there worked with Boccherini, performing music by Haydn.

Works include symphonies, serenades, sextets, quintets, trio sonatas, violin duets.

Brunetti, Giovanni Gualberto (b Pistoia, 24 Apr 1706; d Pisa, 20 May 1787), Italian composer. Succeeded Clari as *maestro di cappella* of Pisa Cathedral in 1754.

Works include seven operas including *Temistocle* (Lucca, 1776); Masses and other church music.

Bruscantini, Sesto (b Porto Civitanova, 10 Dec 1919), Italian bass-baritone. Having originally studied law, he turned to singing and made his debut at La Scala, Milan, in 1949 in *Il Matrimonio segreto*. He was principally known as a *buffo* singer: Glyndebourne 1951–61 as Alfonso, Guglielmo, Dandini, both Figaros and Leporello. From 1962 sang Verdi. Macerata Festival 1990, as Don Alfonso in *Così fan Tutte*.

Bruson, Renato (b Este near Padua, 13 Jan 1936), Italian baritone.

Debut Spoleto, 1961, Luna; NY Met. 1969 as Donizetti's Enrico. British debut Edinburgh, 1972, as Ezio in *Attila*; CG 1976, Renato. In 1982 sang Falstaff under Giulini at San Francisco; later at CG. Sang at Carnegie Hall 1990, as Montfort in *Les Vêpres Siciliennes*.

Brussilovsky, Evgeny (b Rostov-on-Don, 12 Nov 1905; d Moscow, 9 May 1981), Russian composer. Having lost both his parents he joined the army at 16, but was released in 1922 in order to develop his talent at the Moscow Conservatory. He was expelled in 1924 for non-attendance, due to serious illness, but although very poor, managed to go to Leningrad and induced Steinberg to teach him at the conservatory there. In 1933 he was commissioned to do research in Kazakh folk music and went to live at Alma-Ata, the capital of Kazakhstan. There he wrote operas in the national idiom.

Works include operas *Kiz-Ji-Bek* (1934), *Er-Targhin* (1937) and *Jalbir*; eight symphonies (1931–72); instrumental pieces; piano pieces; songs.

Brustad, Bjarne (b Oslo, 4 Mar 1895; d Oslo, 22 May 1978), Norwegian violinist, violist and composer. Studied at the Oslo Conservatory, later under Carl Flesch, and became active as violinist and conductor in Oslo.

Works include symphonic poem *Atlantis* (1945), suite for orchestra, nine symphonies (1948–73); *Nature morte* for string orchestra; four violin concertos (1922–61), *Rhapsody* for violin and orchestra, concertino for violin and chamber orchestra; three string quartets, suite for unaccompanied violin, suite for viola and piano; violin, viola and piano pieces.

Bruzdowicz, Joanna (b Warsaw, 19 May 1943), Polish composer. Studied with K Sikorski and with Messiaen and Schaeffer in Paris. Has founded electronic music studios in Paris and Brussels; teacher at UCLA and Yale.

Works include musical dramas *The Penal Colony* (Tours, 1972), *The Trojan Women* (Paris, 1973), *The Gates of Paradise* (Warsaw, 1989), *Tides and Waves* (Barcelona, 1992), *Maison neuve* (Montreal, 1992); symphony (1974); concerto for piano (1974), violin (1975), double bass (1982); cantatas, chamber and instrumental music.

I consider music a very innocent diversion, and perfectly compatible with the profession of a clergyman.

Jane Austen, *Pride and Prejudice*, 1813

Bryars, (Richard) Gavin (b Goole, 16 Jan 1943), English composer. Studied music privately and has been professor of music at De Montford University from 1985. Earlier compositions were influenced by the ideas of Satie and Cage, later turned to Greek myth for inspiration: *The Sinking of the Titanic* (1969), *My First Homage* (1978), *The English Mail-Coach* (1980) and *Homage to Vivier* (1985) for small ensemble; opera *Medea*, (1984, after Euripides); *Pico's Flight* for orchestra (1986); two string quartets (1985, 1990); *Cadman Requiem* (1989); *The Black River* for soprano and organ (1991); *The Green Ray* for saxophone and orchestra (1991).

Brydon, Roderick (b Edinburgh, 1939), Scottish conductor. Studied in Siena and Vienna and was artistic director of the Scottish Chamber Orchestra 1974–83. Conducted *A Midsummer Night's Dream* at Edinburgh 1983 and at CG 1984. Former music director of Lucerne Opera (*Carmen*, *Don Giovanni*) and director of the Berne Opera 1988–90 (*Capriccio* and *Peter Grimes*). US debut with *Albert Herring* at Los Angeles, 1992; has also led Rossini's *Otello* in Venice, *Alcina* at Karlsruhe and *The Rake's Progress* at the Geneva Opera. Concerts in Munich and Paris.

Brygeman, William (d Bristol, 1524), English 16th-c. composer. Singer at Eton, 1503–04; later at All Saints' Bristol. A fragmentary *Salve Regina* is in the Eton Choirbook.

Brymer, Jack (b South Shields, 27 Jan 1915), English clarinettist. Principal clarinet RPO 1947–63; for most of this time under Beecham. BBC SO 1963–72, then principal clarinet LSO; also active as broadcaster, soloist and chamber-music player.

Bryne, Albert (or Albertus Bryan) (b ? London c 1621; d London, 1671), English organist and composer. Organist of St Paul's Cathedral in London from 1638 and again after the Restoration. After the fire of London in 1666 he became organist of Westminster Abbey, a post in which he was succeeded by Blow in 1668. Wrote services, anthems, dance suites for harpsichord, etc.

Bryn-Julson, Phyllis (b Bowdon, ND, 5 Feb 1945), American soprano of Norwegian parentage. She studied at Tanglewood and made her debut with the Boston SO in 1966 (Berg's *Lulu-Symphonie*). NY PO 1973, under Boulez; British debut London, 1975, in his *Pli selon pli*. In 1976 she sang Malinche in the first US performance of *Montezuma* by Sessions. Noted for her performance of Schoenberg's *Pierrot lunaire*, and in contemporary music.

Bucci, Mark (b New York, 26 Feb 1924), American composer. Studied at Juilliard and with Aaron Copland. He composes in an energetic, diatonic style and has written the operas *The Boor* (1949, after Chekhov), *The Dress* (1953), *Sweet Betsy from Pike* (1953), *Tale for a Deaf Ear* (1957), *The Hero* (1965) and *Midas* (1981); musicals, including *The Caucasian Chalk Circle* (1948), *The Adamses* (1956) and *The Second Coming* (1976).

buccina the Roman bugle horn, used in the army for signalling.

Bucenus, Paulus (b Holstein; *fl.* 1567–84), German composer. He worked as a church musician at Riga, where he may have died.

Works include a *St Matthew Passion* (1578), Masses, motets, *Sacrae Cantiones*.

Buchanan, Isobel (b Glasgow, 15 Mar 1954), Scottish soprano. She studied in Scotland and sang with Australian Opera from 1976; debut as Pamina. She repeated the role at Glyndebourne in 1978 and the same year was successful as Micaela, at the Vienna Staatsoper. She has sung Zerlina and Adina at Chicago and has appeared with the Chicago SO. CG debut 1979. Other roles include Susanna, Fiordiligi and Donna Elvira. Sang Dorabella at Glyndebourne 1987, then heard only in concert.

Buchardo, Carlos López (b Buenos Aires, 12 Oct 1881; d Buenos Aires, 21 Apr 1948), Argentine composer. Studied in Buenos Aires and with Roussel in Paris. On returning to Argentina he became director of the National Conservatory at Buenos Aires.

Works include opera *El sueño* de Alma (1914), *Escenas argentinas* for orchestra (1920); piano pieces; songs.

Buch der hängenden Gärten, Das, *The Book of the Hanging Gardens*, 15 songs for soprano and piano by Schoenberg, op. 15 (texts by Stefan George), composed 1908–09, performed Vienna, 14 Jan 1910.

Buch mit sieben Siegeln, Das, *The Book with Seven Seals*, oratorio by Franz Schmidt (text from the Apocalypse); composed 1935–37, performed Vienna, 15 Jun 1938.

Büchner, Georg (1813–37), German poet and playwright. ◊Blind Man's Buff (P M Davies), ◊Dantons Tod (Einem), ◊Müller-Hartmann (*Leonce und Lena*), ◊Syberg (ditto), ◊Wagner-Régeny (*Günstling*), ◊Weismann (*Leonce und Lena*), ◊Wozzeck (A Berg and M Gurlitt).

Buchner, Johann (Hans von Constantz) (b Ravensburg, Württemberg, 26 Oct 1483; d ? Konstanz, 1538), German composer. Probably a pupil of Hofhaimer. Worked at Konstanz Cathedral, but left in 1526, because of its growing Protestantism, for Überlingen. Wrote sacred and secular songs, organ pieces, etc. His *Fundamentum* is a didactic work incorporating organ music for the liturgical year.

Buckley, Richard (Edward) (b New York, 1 Sept 1953), American conductor. After study in Aspen and at the Salzburg Mozarteum he worked for the Washington Opera Society 1973–74, and was associate conductor of the Seattle SO 1974–84. Music director Oakland SO 1983–86 and led Sallinen's *The King Goes Forth to France*, Santa Fe 1986. Has also conducted Hoffmann in LA, *Aida* in Chicago and Rossini's *Il Viaggio a Reims* for St Louis Opera. CG debut 1992, *L'Elisir d'Amore*.

Budapest String Quartet Hungarian ensemble founded 1917 by players from the Budapest Opera. From 1936 until it disbanded in 1967 its members were Russian and Ukrainian: Joseph Roisman and Jac Gorodetzky (violins), Boris Kroyt (viola) and Mischa Schneider (cello). They were quartet-in-residence at the Library of Congress, Washington, 1938–62, and were highly regarded for their performances of Beethoven; joined by Milton Katims, then Walter Trampler, in the Mozart quintets.

Budavari Te Deum work by Kodály for soloists, chorus and orchestra, performed Budapest Cathedral, 11 Sept 1936.

Budden, Julian (Medforth) (b Hoylake, 9 Apr 1924), English musicologist and radio producer. He studied at Oxford and the RCM. Joined the BBC 1951 and was Chief Producer, Opera 1970–76; External Services Music Organizer 1976–83. Author of *The Operas of Verdi* (three vols, 1973, 1978, 1981) and *Verdi* (1985). An internationally recognized authority on 19th-c. Italian opera.

Buffalo Philharmonic Orchestra US orchestra in NY state, incorporated 1937 with Franco Autori as conductor. Kleinhans Music Hall was opened 1940 and Josef Krips was director 1953–65; modern repertory was favoured by Lukas Foss (1963–70). Michael Tilson Thomas was director 1971–78, Semyon Bychkov 1985–89, succeeded by Maximiano Valdes.

buffo Italian = 'comic', also 'comedian'; in music a singer of comic parts, used especially as adj.; *tenore buffo, basso buffo*.

bugle a treble brass instrument with a wide conical bore, used mainly in the armed forces. Having no valves it can produce only the natural harmonics. ◊key bugle.

Every word we speak, every pulsation of our veins, is related by musical rhythms to the powers of harmony.
Isodor of Seville, *Etymologiae*, 622–633

Bühnenweihfestspiel, German, from *Bühne*, = 'stage', *Weihe* = 'consecration', *Fest* = 'festival', *Spiel* = 'play'; the description given by Wagner to *Parsifal*, which he did not wish to call an 'opera' or a 'music drama'.

Bukofzer, Manfred (b Oldenburg, 27 Mar 1910; d Oakland, CA, 7 Dec 1955), German-American musicologist. Studied at Heidelberg, Berlin and Basel, and went to USA in 1939, where after various appointments he became professor at University of California, Berkeley. He specialized in medieval, particularly English, music and edited the complete works of Dunstable. His most important book is *Studies in Medieval and Renaissance Music* (1950).

Bull, John (b c 1562; d Antwerp, 12–13 Mar 1628), English composer and keyboard virtuoso. He was a choirboy in the Chapel Royal in London under Blitheman and became organist of Hereford Cathedral in 1582. On Blitheman's death in 1591 he became organist of the Chapel Royal. Mus.D., Cambridge, before 1592, and Oxford that year. In 1596 appointed first professor of music at Gresham College. In 1601 he travelled abroad, Thomas Byrd, son of William Byrd, acting as his deputy at Gresham College. Married Elizabeth Walter in 1607 and gave up his professorship, which could be held only by single men. In 1613 he left England, apparently to escape punishment for adultery, and became organist at the archducal chapel in Brussels. In 1617 he was appointed organist at Antwerp Cathedral, where he remained to his death. Much of his technically brilliant music for the virginals is in the collection *Parenthia* (1613).

Works include anthems, including the 'Star' anthem *Almighty Lord*; secular vocal works for several voices; canons; a laud for the Blessed Virgin in Flemish; numerous organ and virginal pieces; some works for viols, etc.

Bull, Ole (Borneman) (b Bergen, 5 Feb 1810; d Lysø near Bergen, 17 Aug 1880), Norwegian violinist and composer. He was largely self-taught, since his father insisted on his studying theology. In 1829 he visited Spohr at Kassel and in 1832 first made his mark as a public player in Paris. He married a Frenchwoman there, appeared with Chopin and Ernst, and visited Italy with great success. Went to England first in 1836 and to USA in 1843. Founded the Norse Theatre at Bergen in 1850. In 1870 he was married a second time, to an American. Wrote two concertos and many other works for the violin.

Buller, John (b London, 7 Feb 1927), English composer. From 1959 he studied with Anthony Milner and in the 1970s produced a series of works based on James Joyce's *Finnegans Wake*. The opera *Bakxai* (after Euripides) was premiered by ENO 1992.

Works include *The Cave* for flute, clarinet, trombone, cello and tape (1970), two *Night Pieces* from *Finnegan's Wake* for soprano, clarinet, flute, piano and cello (1971), *Finnegan's Floras* for chorus, percussion and piano (1972), *Le Terrazze* for 14 instruments and tape (1974), *Familiar*, string quartet (1974), *The Theatre of Memory* for orchestra (1981), *Towards Aquarius* for ensemble (1983), *Kommos* for chorus, soloists and electronics (1981), *Of Three Shakespeare Sonnets* for mezzo and ensemble (1983), *Bakxai* opera (1992), *Bacchae Metres* for orchestra (1993), *Mr Purcell's Maggot* (1994).

Bülow, Hans (Guido) Von (b Dresden, 8 Jan 1830; d Cairo, 12 Feb 1894), German pianist and conductor, first husband of Cosima Wagner (born Liszt). Studied law at Leipzig University and piano with Wieck there. At first exclusively a Wagnerian as a conductor and gave the fps of *Tristan und Isolde* (1865) and *Die Meistersinger* (1868), but after his wife went to live with Wagner became more enthusiastic about Brahms without abandoning Wagner; conducted the fp of Brahms's fourth symphony (1885). Made many tours both as conductor and pianist; as a soloist he gave the first performance of Tchaikovsky's first piano concerto (Boston, 1875).

Bumbry, Grace (b St Louis, MS, 4 Jan 1937), American mezzo and soprano. Debut Paris, Opéra, as Amneris; in 1961 became the first black singer to appear at Bayreuth (as Venus). CG 1963 and NY Met. 1965, both as Eboli. Her Lady Macbeth at Salzburg, 1964, was her first soprano role. Other roles include Santuzza, Tosca, Carmen, Jenůfa and Dukas' Ariane. Her Salome at CG (1970) was a convincing visual and vocal display. She sang Cassandra in *Les Troyens* at the opening of the Opéra Bastille, Paris, 1990; Baba the Turk in *The Rake's Progress* at Salzburg, 1994.

Bungert, August (b Mühlheim an der Ruhr, 14 Mar 1845; d Leutesdorf, 26 Oct 1915), German composer. Studied at Cologne Conservatory and in Paris. Produced his first (comic) opera at Leipzig in 1884. His ambition was to build a special theatre for the production of his tetralogy on the model of Bayreuth.

Works include operas *Die Studenten von Salamanka* (Leipzig, 1884), tetralogy *Homerische Welt* (*Kirke, Nausicaa, Odysseus Heimkehr, Odysseus Tod*, produced Dresden 1898–1903), 'mystery' *Warum? Woher? Wohin?*; incidental music to Goethe's *Faust*; symphony *Zeppelins erste grosse Fahrt*; *Tasso, Hohes Lied der Liebe, Auf der Wartburg* for orchestra; piano quartet: piano pieces; songs.

Buona figliuola, La, *The Good Girl*, also *La Cecchina*, opera by Piccinni (libretto by Goldoni, based on Richardson's *Pamela*), produced Rome, Teatro delle Dame, 6 Feb 1760. Marchese della Conchiglia loves Cecchina, but his sister opposes their marriage because Cecchina is of a lower social class. Problems are resolved when the humble maid is revealed to be the daughter of a baron.

Buonamente, Giovanni Battista (b Mantua; d Assisi, 29 Aug 1642), Italian violinist and composer. Imperial court musician from 1622; *maestro di cappella* at the Franciscan monastery of Assisi from 1633. Wrote sonatas for two violins and bass, music for mixed teams of instruments, etc.

Buovo d'Antona, *Bevis of Hampton*, opera by Traetta (libretto by Goldoni, based on the Anglo-Norman 13th-c. romance), produced Venice, Teatro San Moisè, 27 Dec 1758. Revived Venice 1993, in edition by Alan Curtis. Knight Buovo returns from exile to unite with Druisina and drive out evil Duke Maccabuono.

Burbero di buon cuore, Il, *The Good-hearted Grumbler*, opera by ◊Martín y Soler (libretto by Lorenzo da Ponte, based on Goldoni's French comedy *Le Bourru bienfaisant*), produced Vienna, Burgtheater, 4 Jan 1786. Mozart wrote two extra arias for it when it was revived, Vienna, 9 Nov 1789, and Haydn an additional duet for its production in London, 1794. Bachelor Ferramondo in complication with bankrupt nephew and comely niece.

Burchuladze, Paata (b Tblisi, 12 Feb 1951), Russian bass. Debut Tblisi 1975, as Gounod's Mephistopheles. After study in Italy made British debut 1983, in *The Dream of Gerontius* at the Lichfield

Festival. CG debut 1984, as Ramfis in *Aida*, returning as Khan Konchak in *Prince Igor* and Boris Godunov (1990–91; Salzburg 1987, as the Commendatore; NY Met. 1989 as Rossini's Basilio. Sang Boris at the opening of the new Israeli Opera, Tel Aviv 1994.

Burck, Joachim à (Joachim Moller von Burck) (b Burg, 1546; d Mühlhausen, 24 May 1610), German organist and composer. Organist at various towns in Thuringia.

Works include four Passions, psalms; odes, songs.

burden in old vocal music the refrain sung at the end of each verse; in English medieval carols, the refrain or chorus.

Burg, Robert (b Prague, 29 Mar 1890; d Dresden, 9 Feb 1946), German baritone. After engagements in Prague and Augsburg he joined the Hofoper, Dresden in 1916 and remained until 1944; took part in the Verdi renaissance and created Busoni's Doktor Faust (1925) and Hindemith's Cardillac (1926), both under Fritz Busch. Bayreuth 1933–42, as Kothner, Alberich and Klingsor. Also sang at Munich, Vienna, Berlin and Budapest.

Burgess, Sally (b Durban, 9 Oct 1953), South African-born British mezzo-soprano. Studied at the RCM and joined ENO 1977, at first as soprano (Mimi, Pamina and Martinů's Juliette) then as mezzo from 1981: Charlotte, Octavian and Nefertiti in *Akhnaten* by Philip Glass (1985). Has also sung Carmen and Amneris for Opera North and Fricka and Annius for Scottish Opera; her vivid stage presence also makes her a favourite in such items as the Paul McCartney/Carl Davis *Liverpool Oratorio* and *Show Boat*.

Burgon, Geoffrey (b Hambledon, 16 Jul 1941), English composer. He studied with Peter Wishart and Lennox Berkeley at the GSM. His music shows a range of influences, including jazz and medieval French music. He is best known for his themes for successful TV series, e.g. *Brideshead Revisited*.

Works include opera *Hard Times* (1991, after Dickens); ballets *The Golden Fish* (1964), *Ophelia* (1964), *Persephone* (1979) and *The Trial of Prometheus* (1988); *Brideshead Variations* and *The World Again*, for orchestra (1981 and 1983); *Think on Dredful Domesday* (1969), *Magnificat* (1970), *Veni Spiritus, Orpheus* and *Revelations*, all for soloists, chorus and orchestra (1979–84); *Songs of the Creation* for chorus and organ (1989), *A Vision* for tenor and strings (1991); other works for chorus, and for voice and piano or chamber ensemble.

Burgstaller, Alois (b Holzkirchen, 21 Sept 1871; d Gmund, 19 Apr 1945), German tenor. He made his Bayreuth debut in 1894 and in 1903 sang Siegmund at the NY Met; later the same year was Parsifal in the first staged US performance of the opera: in spite of a ban on performance outside Bayreuth he continued to sing there until 1909.

Burian, Emil František (b Plzeň, 11 Apr 1904; d Prague, 9 Aug 1959), Czech singer, actor, author, stage manager and composer. Studied at the Prague Conservatory, joined the Dada Theatre in Prague and was director of the dramatic studio of the Brno National Theatre in 1929–30; also founded a voice band, which sang to given rhythms without definite pitch, accompanied by percussion.

Works include operas *Alladine and Palomides* (after Maeterlinck, 1923), *Before Sunrise* (1924), *Bubu de Montparnasse, Mr Ipokras, Fear*; ballets *The Bassoon and the Flute* (1925), *Manège, Autobus*; choruses; chamber music, songs.

Burian, Karel (b Rousínov, near Rakovník, 12 Jan 1870; d Senomaty, 25 Sept 1924), Czech tenor, uncle of Emil Burian. Debut Brno, 1891, Jeník. He sang Parsifal at Bayreuth in 1908 and in 1905 created Herod, in Dresden. CG from 1904 as Tristan and Lohengrin. NY Met. 1903, as Tannhäuser, and sang there until 1913. Other roles included Manrico and Cavaradossi.

Burkhard, Willy (b Evilard-sur-Bienne, 17 Apr 1900; d Zurich, 18 Jun 1955), Swiss composer. Studied at the Berne School of Music, at Leipzig with Karg-Elert and Teichmüller and at Munich with Courvoisier, later in Paris. Became piano professor at the Berne Conservatory and conducted choirs and an amateur orchestra. Settled at Davos in 1937 to devote himself entirely to composition.

Works include opera *Die schwarze Spinne* (after Gotthelf, 1948); oratorios *Musikalische Uebung* (Luther, 1934) and *Das Gesicht Jesajas* (1933–35) Te Deum, choral suite *Neue Kraft*, festival cantata

Le Cantique de notre terre, cantata *Das Jahr* and others, Psalm xciii for chorus and organ; *Christi Leidensverkündung* for tenor, chorus and organ; two symphonies, *Ulenspiegel* variations for orchestra; Fantasy, Little Serenade and concerto for string orchestra; two violin concertos, organ concerto (1945); two string quartets, piano trio, two trio sonatas; Variations and Fantasy for organ; numerous song-cycles, including *Frage*, two on poems by Rilke, one on poems by Morgenstern.

burla Italian = 'jest, trick, practical joke'; in music a humorous piece, rather more boisterous than a scherzo.

Burleigh, Cecil (b Wyoming, NY, 17 Apr 1885; d Madison, WI, 28 Jul 1980), American violinist and composer. Studied in USA, Berlin and finally at Chicago. After touring frequently and teaching in various places, he settled down as violin professor at Wisconsin University.

Works include symphonic poem *Evangeline* (1918), *Mountain Pictures*, etc. for orchestra; three violin concertos; two violin and piano sonatas (*The Ascension* and *From the Life of St Paul*); numerous violin pieces.

Burleigh, Henry T(hacker) (b Erie, PA, 2 Dec 1866; d Stamford, CT, 12 Apr 1949), black American singer and composer. Pupil of Dvořák at the National Conservatory in NY, where he introduced African-American tunes to his teacher.

Works include arrangements of African-American spirituals, songs, etc.

burlesca Italian ◊burla.

burlesque another name sometimes used for the ◊burletta in England.

burletta Italian = 'a little joke'; a form of light comic opera or operetta in 18th-and 19th-c. England.

Burmeister, Joachim (b Lüneburg, 1564; d Rostock, 5 Mar 1629), German music theorist. In treatises pub. 1599, 1601 and 1606 he codified as *figurae* the various technical and expressive devices used by 16th-c. composers.

Music is an innocent luxury, unnecessary, indeed, to our existence, but a great improvement and gratification of the sense of hearing.

Charles Burney, *A General History of Music*,
1776–89

Burney, Charles (b Shrewsbury, 7 Apr 1726; d Chelsea, 12 Apr 1814), English organist, music historian and composer. Pupil of Arne, held organ posts in London (1749–51) and King's Lynn (1751–60). D.Mus., Oxford, 1769. Travelled extensively on the Continent 1770–72, collecting material for his four-volume *General History of Music* (pub. 1776–89). He also pub. those parts of his travel diaries relating to music. His daughter was the novelist Fanny Burney, and his friends included Dr Johnson, Reynolds, Garrick, etc. On his travels he made the acquaintance of many of the leading musicians of his day and recorded his findings in *The Present State of Music in France and Italy* (1771); Germany and the Netherlands, 1773. His works included an English version of Rousseau's *Le Devin du Village* under the title *The Cunning Man*, songs for a revival of *A Midsummer Night's Dream* (with M Arne, Aylward and Battishill) and a quantity of instrumental music.

Burning Fiery Furnace, The church parable by Britten (libretto by W Plomer), produced Orford Church, Suffolk, 9 Jun 1966. In honour of visiting Israelites, Babylonian King Nebuchadnezzar organizes a feast, but throws the guests into a furnace when they do not worship his idols. Saved by an angel, they do not burn.

Burrell, Diana (b Norwich, 25 Oct 1948), English composer. Studied at Cambridge and has played the viola in various orchestras. Her music is skilfully crafted and includes the opera *Albatross* (1987); *Landscape* (1988), *Scene with Birds* (1989) and *Resurrection* (1993) for orchestra; choral works *Missa Sancta Endeliente* (1980), *Creator of the Stars of Night* (1989), *You Spotted Snakes* (1991) and *Night Songs* (1991); Concertante (1985) and *Archangel* (1987) for ensemble; wind quintet (1990); *Arched Form with Bella* for organ (1990);

Sequence for cello and tape (1993); *Anima* for strings (1993); viola concerto (1994); *Gulls and Angels* for string quartet (1994).

Burrowes, Norma (b Bangor, Co. Down, 24 Apr 1944), Irish soprano. She appeared in operas by Monteverdi and Puccini while at the RAM and from 1970 sang at Glyndebourne, CG and the ENO: roles included Zerlina, Susanna and Fiorilla; Janáček's Vixen at Glyndebourne, 1975. From 1979 she sang Blondchen, Oscar and Sophie at the NY Met. Retired 1982.

Burrows, Stuart (b Pontypridd, 7 Feb 1933), Welsh tenor. Opera debut with the WNO in 1963 as Verdi's Ismael; CG from 1967 as Beppe, Fenton and Elvino; US debut San Francisco, 1967, as Tamino; NY Met. 1971, Don Ottavio; CG 1989, Mozart's Tito. Other roles include Faust, Lensky, Ernesto and Rodolfo.

Burt, Francis (b London, 28 Apr 1926), English composer. He studied at the RAM and with Blacher in Berlin. Resident in Vienna from 1957; professor of composition at Hochschule für Musik from 1973.

Works include operas *Volpone* (1960) and *Barnstaple, or Someone in the Attic* (1969); ballet *The Golem* (1962); *Iambics* (1953), *Espressione orchestrale* (1959) *Fantasmagoria* (1963) and *Morgana* (1986) for orchestra; *Und Gott der Herr sprach*, for soloists, chorus and orchestra (1983); string quartet (1953); *Echoes* for flute and ensemble (1989).

Burton, Avery (b c 1470; d c 1543), English composer. On 29 Nov 1494 he was paid 20 shillings by Henry VII for composing a Mass; in 1509 he became a Gentleman of the Chapel Royal. On 20 Jun 1513 he went to France with the Chapel Royal, a Te Deum of his being sung after Mass at Tournai on 17 Sept; in Jun 1520 he was present at the Field of the Cloth of Gold. His name disappears from the records of the Chapel Royal after 1542. He is known as the composer of a Mass, *Ut re mi fa sol la*, in the Forrest-Heyther part-books (this is probably not the Mass of 1494) and of a Te Deum for organ.

Burton, John (b Yorkshire, 1730; d Naples ? 3 Sept 1782), English harpsichordist, pianist, organist and composer. Pupil of Keeble. Became a very famous player and had a great success in Germany in 1754, where he became acquainted with the newly designed forte-pianos. Composed sonatas for all his instruments, one keyboard concerto survives.

Burton, Stephen (Douglas) (b Whittier, CA, 24 Feb 1943), American composer. Studied in Vienna and Salzburg and with Henze. Teacher at George Mason University, VA, from 1974. His music is eclectic in spirit.

Works include operas *An American Triptych* (three one-act operas after Craine, Hawthorne and Melville, 1974), *The Duchess of Malfi* (after Webster, 1978) and *Aimée* (1983); *Stravinskiana* for flute and orchestra (1972), Variations on a Theme of Mahler, for chamber orchestra (1982); violin concerto (1983); chamber and vocal music.

Busby, Thomas (b London, Dec 1755; d London, 28 May 1838), English organist and composer. Sang at Vauxhall as a boy with great success, later became a pupil of Battishill. Worked at a music dictionary with Arnold, was appointed church organist at St Mary's, Newington, Surrey, c 1780. Mus.D. at Cambridge 1801. Wrote several books on music, including a history (1825).

Works include incidental music for Cumberland's *Joanna of Montfaucon* (an English version of Kotzebue's *Johanna von Montfaucon*), Holcroft's *Tale of Mystery*, Anna Maria Porter's *Fair Fugitives* and Lewis's *Rugantino*; oratorios *The Prophecy* (from Pope's *Messiah*; c 1784, performed Haymarket, 1799) and *Britannia*; settings of odes by Pope and Gay.

Busch, Adolf (b Siegen, Westphalia, 8 Aug 1891; d Guilford, VT, 9 Jun 1952), German violinist and composer. Studied at Cologne Conservatory and composition with Hugo Grüters at Bonn. In 1918 he became violin professor at the Berlin Hochschule für Musik. In 1919 he formed a string quartet with which he toured all over the world, notably in music by Beethoven, and he was also famous as an interpreter of violin and piano sonatas with Rudolf Serkin. In 1933 he renounced German citizenship as a protest against Nazi rule; moved to USA in 1939 and founded Marlboro School of Music, VT, 1950.

Works include choral, orchestral and much chamber music.

Busch, Fritz (b Siegen, Westphalia, 13 Mar 1890; d London, 14 Sept 1951), German conductor, brother of Adolf Busch. Studied at the Cologne Conservatory and after gaining experience at various German theatres and with orchestras, he became conductor of the Stuttgart Opera 1918 and music director of the Dresden Staatsoper 1922. He conducted there the fps of Strauss's *Intermezzo* (1924) and *Die Ägyptische Helena* (1928), Busoni's *Doktor Faust* (1925) and Hindemith's *Cardillac* (1926). Like his brother he renounced German citizenship; went to Buenos Aires 1933, conducted the Glyndebourne Opera from 1934 to his death, giving the first performances there of *Figaro*, *Così fan Tutte*, *Don Giovanni*, *Macbeth*, and *Idomeneo* (British premiere). He lived in Copenhagen as conductor of the State Radio.

Busch String Quartet German ensemble formed 1919. From 1921–30 members were Adolf Busch and Gösta Andreasson (violins), Karl Doctor (viola), Paul Grümmer (cello). In 1930 Grümmer was replaced by Hermann Busch. Toured widely in standard repertory, particularly admired in Beethoven. Moved to USA 1939, disbanded 1952.

Busenello, Gian Francesco (b Venice, 24 Sept 1598; d Legnaro near Padua, 27 Oct 1659), Italian librettist and poet who is best known for his libretto for Monteverdi's *L'Incoronazione di Poppea* (1642); also libretti for Cavalli's *Gli amori d'Apollo e di Dafne* (1640), *Didone* (1641), and *Statira* (1655).

Bush, Alan (Dudley) (b London, 22 Dec 1900; d Radlett, 31 Oct 1995), English composer and teacher. Studied at the RAM in London and Berlin University, later with John Ireland. He also studied the piano with Schnabel. He became professor at the RAM, conductor of the London Labour Choral Union and in 1936 chairman of the Workers' Music Association.

Works include operas *The Press-Gang* (1946), *Wat Tyler* (1948–51), *The Spell Unbound* (1953), *Men of Blackmoor* (1955), *The Sugar Reapers* (1966) and *Joe Hill: the Man who Never Died* (1970); incidental music for Shakespeare's *Macbeth*, Sean O'Casey's *The Star Turns Red* and Patrick Hamilton's *The Duke in Darkness*; choral work *The Winter Journey* (Randall Swingler) and others; symphony no. 2 'Nottingham' (1949), no. 3 *Byron* (1960), no. 4 *Lascaux* (1983) and other orchestral music; piano concerto with chorus (Swingler), violin concerto, *Concert Suite* for cello and orchestra (1952); string quartet, piano quartet, *Dialectic* for string quartet (1929); instrumental pieces with piano; piano and organ music, including 24 preludes for piano (1977).

until 1482, when (?) he became music director at the church of Saint-Sauveur at Bruges.

Works include two Masses, Magnificat, hymns, 61 songs for three or four voices; motets, including *Fortunata desperata*, used later by Josquin.

Busoni, Ferruccio (Dante Michelangiolo Benvenuto) (b Empoli, 1 Apr 1866; d Berlin, 27 Jul 1924), German-Italian composer and pianist. Appeared as pianist in public at the age of seven; studied at Graz and Leipzig. Taught at the Helsinki Conservatory in 1889; taught at Moscow in 1890 (where he married the Swede Gerda Sjöstrand) and in America (at Boston), 1891–94; his *Indian Fantasy* and *Indian Diary* reflect a personal and musical sympathy for native Americans. Settled in Berlin for good in 1894, but travelled widely as a pianist and during World War I lived first at Bologna as director of the Conservatory and then at Zurich. At Bologna he hoped to influence Italian music, and to prove that he was himself an Italian composer, but was disappointed. He rejected Wagnerian music-drama, and sought to re-establish links with great composers of the past, notably Bach and Mozart, and the *commedia dell'arte*. His opera *Doktor Faust* was completed by Jarnach and first performed in 1925; missing sketches were located 1974 and were used for a new edition by Antony Beaumont, performed Bologna 1985 and London, Coliseum, 1986. His ideas on aesthetics, especially his *Sketch of a New Aesthetic of Music* (1907), were attacked by conservatives such as Pfitzner.

Busoni is sometimes regarded as a composer with a formidable intellect whose works rarely live up to their composer's ambition; he was admired alike by Mahler and Schoenberg (one premiered his *Berceuse élégiaque* and the other arranged it) but it may be his Italianate pieces which are the most readily accessible.

Works include STAGE: operas *Sigune, oder Das vergessene Dorf* (1889), *Die Brautwahl* (1908–11; produced Hamburg, 1912), *Arlecchino* and *Turandot* (1916–17; produced in double bill, Zurich, 1917), *Doktor Faust* (1916–24; posthumously produced Dresden, 1925); incidental music to *Turandot* (produced Berlin, 1911).

ORCHESTRAL: *Symphonische Suite* (1883), *Konzertstück* for piano and orchestra (1890), *Konzert-Fantasie* for piano and orchestra (1889; revised as *Symphonisches Tongedicht*, 1892), Suite no. 2 for orchestra, *Geharnischte* (1895, revised 1903), violin concerto (1897), *Lustpielouvertüre* (1897, revised 1904), piano concerto, with male chorus in finale (1903–04), *Turandot*, suite (1904), *Berceuse élégiaque* (1909), *Nocturne symphonique* (1912), *Indianische Fantasie* for piano and orchestra (1913), *Die Brautwahl*, suite (1912), *Rondò*

Bush, Geoffrey (b London, 23 Mar 1920), English composer. Became a choirboy at Salisbury Cathedral in 1928, went to Lancing College in 1933 and later to Balliol College, Oxford, where he gained the Nettleship Scholarship. B.Mus., Oxford, 1940, D.Mus. 1946. His studies were interrupted by war service at a hostel for abnormal evacuee children. He is mainly self-taught in composition, but had much valuable advice from his masters at Salisbury and Lancing, also from John Ireland and others later.

Works include five operas including *Spanish Rivals* (1948); *Twelfth Night*, entertainment for chorus and orchestra; overtures *In Praise of Salisbury* and *The Rehearsal* for orchestra, Divertimento for string orchestra, two symphonies (1954, 1957); concerto for piano and strings, *Sinfonietta concertante* for cello and chamber orchestra, oboe concerto, rhapsody for clarinet and string quartet; sonatas for violin and piano and trumpet and piano; two piano sonatinas; *Portraits* and *La Belle Dame sans merci* (Keats) for unaccompanied chorus; songs.

Busnois, Antoine (b c 1430; d Bruges, 6 Nov 1492), French composer. Pupil of Ockeghem and later in the service of the Burgundian court

A Selection of

Busoni

Violin Sonata no. 1	1890
Violin Concerto	1897
Violin Sonata no. 2	1898
Piano Concerto	1903–4

Fantasia contrappuntistica	1910
Arlecchino	1916–17
Turandot	1916–17
Doktor Faust	1916–24
Divertimento	1920
Tanzwalzer	1920

arlecchinesco (1915), *Indianisches Tagebuch*, book two, 'Gesang vom Reigen der Geister' (1915), *Concertino* for clarinet and orchestra (1918), *Sarabande und Cortège*, studies for *Doktor Faust* (1919), *Divertimento* for flute and orchestra (1920), *Tanzwalzer* (1920), *Romanza e scherzoso* for piano and orchestra (1921).

VOCAL: Mass (1879), *Le quattro stagioni* for male chorus and orchestra (1882), *Il sabato del villaggio* for soloists, chorus and orchestra (1883), *Unter den Linden* for soprano and orchestra (1893), *Zigeunerlied* and *Schlechter Trost* for baritone and orchestra, texts by Goethe (1923), Lieder.

CHAMBER: *Serenata* for cello and piano (1882), two string quartets (1881, 1887), two violin sonatas (1890, 1898), *Kleine Suite* for cello and piano (1886).

PIANO: *Suite campestra* (1878), *Una festa di villaggio* (1882), 24 preludes (1879–81), six études (1883), *Macchiette medioevali* (1883), *Elegien*, seven pieces (1907), *Indianisches Tagebuch*, book one (1915), *Fantasia contrappuntistica* (1910, as *Grosse Fuge*; revised 1910 and 1912; version for two pianos 1921), six sonatinas (1910–20), *Duettino concertante* on finale of Mozart's concerto K459 for two pianos. Also editions and arrangements of Bach for piano, including D minor Chaconne, and a concert version of Schoenberg's op. 11 no. 2 piano piece.

Busser, (Paul) Henri (b Toulouse, 16 Jan 1872; d Paris, 30 Dec 1973), French conductor and composer. Pupil of Guiraud at the Paris Conservatory. Gained the Prix de Rome in 1893. Successively organist at Saint-Cloud, conductor of the choral class at the Conservatory and director of Niedermeyer's school. Appointed professor of composition at the conservatory in 1921. He conducted Debussy's *Pelléas* at its first production (1902) and made an orchestral version of *Printemps*.

Works include operas *Daphnis et Chloé* (1897), *Colomba* (after Mérimée), *Les Noces corinthiennes* (1922), *La Pie borgne*, *Le Carrosse du Saint-Sacrement* (Mérimée) (1948); Masses and motets; *Hercule au jardin des Hespérides*, *Suite funambulesque* and other orchestral works; choruses, songs.

Bussotti, Sylvano (b Florence, 1 Oct 1931), Italian composer. Studied music in Florence and painting in Paris. After producing some early works in a relatively traditional style, he turned to a graphical manner of composing which is influenced by Cage and attempts to suggest the type of improvisation required.

Works include operas *Lorenzaccio* (1972), *Nottetempo* (1976), *La Racine* (1980), *L'Ispirazione* (1988) and *Fedra* (1988); *Torso* for voice and orchestra; *Fragmentations* for harp; *Five piano pieces for David Tudor* (1959); *Pour clavier* for piano; *Pearson Piece* for baritone and piano; cantata *Memoria* (1962); Requiem (1969); *Opus Cygne* for flute and orchestra (1979).

Bustini, Alessandro (b Rome, 24 Dec 1876; d Rome, 23 Jun 1970), Italian composer. Studied at the Accademia di Santa Cecilia in Rome, where he later became professor.

Works include operas *Maria Dulcis* (based on a story in Berlioz's *Soirées de l'orchestre*) (Rome, 1902), *La città quadrata* and *L'incantesimo di Calandrino*; funeral Mass for Victor Emmanuel II; two symphonies (1899, 1909), symphonic poem *Le tentazioni*; two string quartets; sonatas for violin and piano and viola and piano, piano pieces.

Buths, Julius (b Wiesbaden, 7 May 1851; d Düsseldorf, 12 Mar 1920), German pianist and conductor. Worked at Düsseldorf from 1890, director of the conservatory there and conductor of the Lower Rhine Festival, where he introduced Elgar's *Dream of Gerontius* in 1901.

Butler, Martin (b Romsey, Hants, 1 Mar 1960), English composer. Studied at the RCM and Princeton and has attended Berio's electronic music studio in Florence. His music admits a variety of influences, including jazz.

Works include *From an Antique Land* for ensemble (1982); *The Flight of Coll* for orchestra (1983); string quartet (1984); *Dance Fragments* for ensemble (1984); *Cavalcade* for orchestra (1985); *The Sirens' Song*, opera (1986); *Tin Pan Ballet* (1986); *Night Machines* for tape (1987); *To See the Beauties of the Earth* for chorus (1987);

Songs and Dances from a Haunted Place for string quartet (1988); *Fixed Doubles* (1989) and *O Rio!* (1990) for orchestra; *Jazz Machines* for ensemble (1990); wind quintet (1991); opera *Craig's Progress* (1994).

Butler, Samuel (b Langar near Bingham, Nottinghamshire, 4 Dec 1835; d London, 18 Jun 1902), English author, critic, biologist, painter and amateur composer. He was a passionate admirer of Handel and wrote two cantatas, *Narcissus* and *Ulysses* (1897), in imitation of Handel's oratorio style. *Narcissus*, a dramatic cantata on the Stock Exchange, was revived London, 1985.

Butt, Clara (b Steyning, Sussex, 1 Feb 1872; d North Stoke, Oxon, 23 Jan 1936), English contralto. Studied at RCM in London and in Paris. Made her first concert and stage appearance in 1892 as Orpheus. A great voice made her very popular, and having placed it at the disposal of war charities, she received the DBE in 1920. Elgar's *Sea Pictures* (Norwich, 1899) was composed for her, and she premiered the work dressed as a mermaid.

Butterfly (Puccini). ◊Madama Butterfly.

'Butterfly', (or *'Butterfly's Wing'*) Study, a nickname sometimes given to Chopin's piano Study in G♭ major op. 25 no. 9.

Butterley, Nigel (Henry) (b Sydney, 13 May 1935), Australian composer. Studied at New South Wales Conservatory and with Priaulx Rainier in London. His music has progressed from a style influenced by Bartók, Hindemith and Shostakovich to the avant garde.

Works include opera *Lawrence Hargrave Flying Alone* (1988); *Meditations of Thomas Traherne* for orchestra (1968), violin concerto (1970), symphony (1980), *From Sorrowing Earth* for orchestra (1990); three string quartets (1965, 1974, 1979) and clarinet trio (1979).

Butterworth, Arthur (b Manchester, 4 Aug 1923), English composer and conductor who has drawn primarily on local pastoral traditions, although he has also considered 12-note composition. Conductor of the Huddersfield PO from 1964.

Works include three symphonies (1957, 1965, 1975) and an arrangement of Elgar's Introduction and Allegro for brass band (1976).

Butterworth, George (Sainton Kaye) (b London, 12 Jul 1885; d Pozières, 5 Aug 1916), English composer. Educated at Eton and Oxford, studied music briefly at the RCM in London. He collected folksongs, cultivated folk dancing and composition, but enlisted on the outbreak of war and was killed in action. He suggested the idea for Vaughan Williams's *London Symphony* (1911–13) and the work is dedicated to his memory.

Works include Rhapsody *A Shropshire Lad* (1912) and Idyll *The Banks of Green Willow* (1913) for orchestra; two song cycles on Housman's *Shropshire Lad*; Sussex folksongs arranged; carols set for chorus; a few other choral pieces and songs.

Butting, Max (b Berlin, 6 Oct 1888; d East Berlin, 13 Jul 1976), German composer. Studied at Munich. He followed the contrapuntal example of Reger in his music.

Works include unfinished Mass; ten symphonies (1923–63), chamber symphony; cello concerto; ten string quartets (1914–71) and other chamber music; songs with small orchestra, etc.

Buttsett, Johann Heinrich (b Bindersleben near Erfurt, 25 Apr 1666; d Erfurt, 1 Dec 1727), German organist and composer. Pupil of Pachelbel. Organist of two Erfurt churches from 1684 and of the cathedral from 1691. Works include Masses and a volume of keyboard music, *Musikalische Clavierkunst*.

Buus, Jachet (Jacques) (b ? Ghent, *c* 1500; d Vienna, Aug 1565), Flemish organist and composer. First pub. some work in France, but went to Italy and in 1541 became organist at St Mark's in Venice, succeeding Baldassare da Imola. He went to Vienna on leave in 1550, but never returned and became organist at the court of Ferdinand I.

Works include motets, madrigals; French *chansons; ricercari* for organ.

Buxheimer Orgelbuch large German MS of keyboard music (not all of it necessarily for organ) dateable *c* 1470. It contains mostly ornamented arrangements of sacred and secular vocal works; also several versions of the *Fundamentum organisandi* by Paumann and some liturgical organ music. The upper part is written on a staff of (usually) seven lines, the lower part(s) in letters. In some pieces the use of pedals is indicated.

Buxtehude, Dietrich (b ? Oldesloe, *c* 1637; d Lübeck, 9 May 1707), German or Danish composer and organist. Settled in Denmark and from 1668 organist of St Mary's Church, Lübeck. From 1673 he gave pre-Christmas *Abendmusiken* ('evening concerts') at which his vivid and vocally elaborate cantatas were performed, e.g. *Das neugeborne Kindelein*. His vocal sacred concertos to Latin texts are in a style recalling Venetian models. He was the greatest organ composer of the period preceding Bach (Bach is alleged to have walked 200 miles to hear him play).

Works include concerted works for chorus and orchestra (*Abendmusiken*); church cantatas, all with German texts, except sequence of seven, *Membra Jesu nostri*, 1680; sonatas for strings; organ music, including chorale preludes; suites for harpsichord.

buysine, or *buzine*, in the early Middle Ages a large horn. From the 13th c. a long trumpet, Saracen in origin, which survived till the 16th c. as a ceremonial instrument.

By an Overgrown Path, *Po zarostlém chodnič́ka*, work for piano in ten movements by Janáček (1901–11). The movements are titled: 1. Our evenings; 2. A blown-away leaf; 3. Come along with us; 4. The Virgin of Frýdek; 5. They chattered like swallows; 6. One cannot tell; 7. Good night; 8. In anguish; 9. In tears; 10. The little owl continues screeching.

Bychkov, Semyon (b Leningrad (St Petersburg), 30 Nov 1952), Russian conductor. Studied in Leningrad and New York and was director of Mannes College of Music Orchestra 1976–80; Grand Rapids SO 1980–85; Buffalo PO 1985–89; music director of the Orchestre de Paris 1989, bringing it to the London Proms 1991. Led *Eugene Onegin* in Paris 1992 and was named principal guest conductor of the St Petersburg PO the same year. His brother, Jakov ◊Kreizberg is also a conductor.

Bylsma, Anner (b The Hague, 17 Feb 1934), Dutch cellist. Was principal of the Concertgebouw Orchestra 1962–68 and has toured the world as a concert soloist and recitalist; best known for his performances of Baroque music using original instruments (Bach Suites for solo cello, and trios with Frans Brueggen and Gustav Leonhardt). Teaching posts have included Erasmus Scholar at Harvard (1982).

List to that sweet recorder;/How daintily this Byrd his notes doth vary,/As if he were the Nightingale's own brother.

Anon, 1612

Byrd, William (b ? Lincoln, 1543; d Stondon Massey, Essex, 4 Jul 1623), English composer. After studying under Tallis as one of the children of the Chapel Royal in London, he was appointed organist of Lincoln Cathedral in 1563, at an unusually early age. He married Juliana Birley there, 14 Sept 1568, and on 22 Feb 1569 was elected a Gentleman of the Chapel Royal, but continued his duties at Lincoln until 1572, when he became organist of the Chapel Royal jointly with Tallis. In 1575 Queen Elizabeth granted the two an exclusive licence for printing and selling music and they dedicated to her their *Cantiones sacrae* pub. that year. Byrd married a second time about 1587. In 1593 he bought Stondon Place near Stapleford-Abbott, Essex, where he remained for the rest of his life, as far as his duties in town would let him. He was frequently involved in litigation and was several times prosecuted for recusancy as a Roman Catholic, but remained in favour with the queen.

Byrd's popular reputation rests with his three great Masses, in 3, 4 and 5 parts, in which his contrapuntal mastery is most fully displayed. Other aspects of his genius are found in the ornate *Cantiones Sacrae* and the large body of consort songs and instrumental music.

Works include three Masses; 17 Latin motets in the *Cantiones*

sacrae by Tallis and Byrd; 61 Latin motets in two books of *Cantiones sacrae*; 99 Latin motets in two books of *Gradualia*; *c* 50 motets in MS; four Anglican services; *c* 61 anthems; some misc. English church music; *Psalmes, Sonets and Songs* (18 nos.); *Songs of Sundrie Natures* (47 nos.); *Psalmes, Songs and Sonnets* (32 nos.); four separate madrigals (others are in those three books); consort songs, canons; rounds; fantasies for strings, seven In Nomines for strings, ten pieces for strings on plainsong tunes, some misc. music for strings; *c* 100 virginal pieces, among them fantasias, preludes, grounds, variations, pavans and galliards and other dances.

Byron, George Gordon, Lord (1788–1824), English poet. Overwhelmed by the extravagant emotion of his poetry, and intrigued by an unbuttoned lifestyle that did not stop at incest, the literati of Europe were bowled over by Byron. Composers too were not immune, and the literature-obsessed Berlioz was inspired by *Childe Harold's Pilgrimage* (1812) and *The Corsair* (1814) to write *Harold en Italie* (1834) and the *Corsaire* overture (1831). Similarly moved, Verdi wrote his opera *Il Corsaro* in 1848. The lonely, half-crazed figure of Manfred (1817) found a fellow sufferer in Tchaikovsky; his Symphony of 1885 is one of his most colourful works, while Eugene Onegin (1879) is Byron himself to the last sneer. Schumann wrote incidental music to Byron's play in 1852 and he, Wolf, Mendelssohn, and even Busoni set individual poems. One of the most compelling of all Byron settings is Schoenberg's *Ode to Napoleon* for reciter, string quartet and piano (1942), which plays on the inevitable comparison between Bonaparte and Hitler.

Byttering, *fl. c* 1410; his name formerly misread as Gyttering, English composer represented in the Old Hall MS.

Byzantine Chant the name given to the Christian chant of the Greek-speaking Orthodox Church. In 330 Constantine the Great made Byzantium (henceforth Constantinople) capital of the Roman Empire; but only in 527, with the coronation of Justinian I as Emperor, did Byzantine liturgy, art and music gain supremacy throughout the Empire. Other important dates are 726–843 (the iconoclastic age), 1054 (the final break from Roman Catholicism), and 1453 (the sack of Constantinople by the Turks). During the course of the 11th c. the introduction of new hymns was forbidden, and the power of the Byzantine Empire was broken with the establishment of the Latin Empire (1204–61). However, the restoration of the Eastern Empire in 1261 led to a renaissance which lasted for a century, followed by a gradual deterioration until the end of the Empire.

Byzantine music and liturgy were dominated by its hymns, which adorned the Offices rather than the Mass. The *troparion*

A Selection of

Byrd

The Great Service	1580s
Fantasias	1580s
Motets	1590s
My Lady Nevells Booke	1591

Mass for Three Voices	1593
Mass for Four Voices	1593
Mass for Five Voices	1595
Gradualia	1605–7

(later *sticheron*) was an intercalation between the verses of a psalm. The *kontakion* was a sermon in verse, sung after the reading of the Gospel at the Morning Office. At the end of the 7th c. it was replaced by the *kanon*, consisting of nine odes of nine stanzas each: each ode had its own melody. Finally acclamations to the Emperor were sung throughout the period; unlike music actually sung in church, these were accompanied by instruments, especially the organ.

Byzantine music, notated in neumes, is based on a system of eight modes (*echoi*), defined by characteristic melodic formulas as well as by tonality. Like the verse itself it is Semitic in origin. The comparative simplicity of earlier and middle Byzantine music gave way, at the end of the period, to a highly embellished style in which the balance between verse and music tended to be destroyed.

C

C the keynote, or tonic, of the scale of C major.

cabaletta, Italian, corruption from *cavatinetta*, diminutive of ◊*cavatina*, the quick and usually brilliant final section of an aria consisting of more than one movement.

Caballé, Montserrat (b Barcelona, 12 Apr 1933), Spanish soprano. Debut Basel, 1956. La Scala, Milan, from 1960 as Norma and Maria Stuarda. NY debut (concert) 1965, as Lucrezia Borgia; Met. later that year as Marguerite. Glyndebourne 1965 as the Marschallin; CG debut 1972, Violetta. Other roles include Imogene and Elisabeth de Valois. In a concert performance of Salieri's *Les Danaïdes*, Perugia 1983, she sang Hypermestra, and at CG in 1992 she sang Mme Cortese in Rossini's *Il Viaggio a Reims*. She is noted for her fine technique.

Cabanilles, Juan (Bautista José) (b Algemesí Valencia, bap. 6 Sept 1644; d Valencia, 29 Apr 1712), Spanish organist and composer. In 1665 he was appointed organist of Valencia Cathedral, a post he held till his death. He was regarded as one of the great organ composers of his time, writing mostly tientos, pieces similar to the ricecare.

Cabel, Marie-Josephe (b Liège, 31 Jan 1827; d Maisons-Laffitte, 23 May 1885), Belgian soprano. Debut Paris, Opéra-Comique, 1849. She sang in Brussels from 1850 and visited London with the co. of the Paris Théâtre-Lyrique, as Donizetti's Marie; returned to the Opéra-Comique and created there leading roles in Meyerbeer's *Dinorah* and Thomas' *Mignon*. She was also heard in operas by Halévy and Auber.

Cabezón, Antonio de (b Castrillo de Matajudios, near Burgos, 1510; d Madrid, 26 Mar 1566), Spanish organist and composer. Although blind from early childhood he studied with Tomás Gómez at Palencia and became chamber organist and harpsichordist to Charles V, remaining at court under Philip II, and accompanying him to England on his marriage to Mary I. Composed organ, vihuela and other music.

Cabezón, Hernando de (b Madrid, bap. 7 Sept 1541; d Valladolid, 1 Oct 1602), Spanish organist and composer, son of Antonio de ◊Cabezón. Studied under his father, whom he succeeded at court and whose works he edited in 1578. Wrote organ music.

There is still much good music to be written in C major.

Arnold Schoenberg, quoted in Reich, *Schoenberg*, 1971

Cabo, Francisco Javier (b Nájara, Valencia, 1768; d Valencia, 21 Nov 1832), Spanish organist and composer. After some minor posts he was appointed cantor at Valencia Cathedral in 1810, first organist in 1816 and *maestro de capilla* in 1830, succeeding Andrevi.

Works include church music, vocal music, with organ or orchestra, organ pieces.

cabrette, French, dialect for *chevrette*, = 'she-kid'; a variety of ◊musette from the Auvergnat region in France.

caccia Italian = 'hunt'; a 14th-c. Italian composition in which two voices, with or without a supporting instrument, sang in canon. The texts, though always lively, were not confined to hunting. The corresponding form in France was called ◊*chace*.

Caccini, Francesca (b Florence, 18 Sept 1587; d Florence, *c* 1640), Italian singer and composer. Pupil of her father, Giulio ◊Caccini.

Works include opera *La liberazione di Ruggiero* (1625); ballets *Il ballo delle zigane* (1615) and *Rinaldo innamorato* (after Tasso); sacred and secular cantatas for one and two voices, etc.

Caccini, Giulio (b Rome, *c* 1545; d Florence, buried 10 Dec 1618), Italian singer, lutenist and composer, father of Francesca ◊Caccini. He entered the service of the Medici at Florence in 1564. Visited Paris with his daughter 1604–05. He wrote short vocal pieces in recitative style and sang them to the theorbo, which led to larger essays of the kind, set to scenes by Count Bardi, and eventually to Rinuccini's libretto for the opera *Euridice*, first set by Peri and immediately afterwards by Caccini in 1602.

Works include operas *Euridice* and *Il rapimento di Cefalo* (both 1602); *Nuove musiche* containing madrigals and arias for voice and continuo.

Cachemaille, Gilles (b Orbe, 25 Nov 1951), Swiss bass-baritone. Studied at Lausanne and sang in concert from 1978 (Aix and Salzburg Festivals, Tokyo and Buenos Aires). Opera debut in the stage premiere of *Les Boréades* by Rameau, Lyon, 1982. Mozart roles include Guglielmo at Lausanne, Figaro, Papageno, and Leporello at Houston, Hamburg and Vienna. 1994 Glyndebourne Festival, as Don Giovanni.

cachucha, Spanish, an Andalusian dance in quick, energetic 3–4 time.

Cadéac, Pierre, 16th-c. French composer. He was master of the choirboys at Auch (near Toulouse) in 1556. He composed Masses, motets and *chansons*, including perhaps the *Je suis désheritée* ascribed to him by Attaingnant in 1539 (but to 'Lupus' by the same pub. in 1533). This famous piece was used as the basis of numerous Masses in the 16th c., including one by Palestrina.

cadence, from Latin *cado* = 'I fall', (1) the fall of a melody to its final note. (2) The harmonization of such a fall.

cadence-phrase the final group in the exposition of a sonata movement, leading to the close in a key other than the tonic.

cadenza Italian = 'cadence'; originally the cadenza was simply a cadence; but the custom gradually established itself of creating a feeling of suspense between the chords of a cadence by interpolating brilliant passages of greater or lesser extent and at the same time giving the performer a chance to display technical gifts and inventiveness in improvisation. Cadenzas in concertos are now rarely improvised, but supplied either by the composer or another musician.

Cadi dupé, Le, *The Cadi Duped*, opera by Gluck (libretto by P R Lemonnier), produced Vienna, Burgtheater, Dec 1761. The judge wants to divorce his wife Fatima, taking young Zelmira instead. She refuses him, so he takes revenge by engaging her to an apparently destitute man, who turns out to be her lover, Nouradin.

Cadman, Charles Wakefield (b Johnstown, PA, 24 Dec 1881; d LA, 30 Dec 1946), American composer. Studied at Pittsburgh and became

Cadence, from Latin cado = *'I fall'*
Traditional forms are, in the key of
C major:

(a) perfect (US authentic*): dominant*
to tonic:

(a)

(b) plagal: subdominant to tonic:

(b)

(c) imperfect: tonic to dominant:

(c)

(d) deceptive (or interrupted*): dominant*
to a chord other than the tonic (usually
the submediant or subdominant):

(d)

(e) the so-called Phrygian cadence, where
the fall is in the lowest part (this derives
its name from the Phrygian mode):

(e)

Apart from these traditional forms any harmonic progression which
suggests finality, if only temporarily, is technically a cadence.

organist, chorus conductor and critic there. He explored American Indian music and used it in some of his works. After a visit to Europe in 1910 he became organist at Denver and later settled at LA.

Works include operas *The Garden of Mystery* (1925), *The Land of Misty Water* (1909–12), *The Garden of Death, Shanewis/The Robin Woman* (1918), *A Witch of Salem* (1926), *The Willow Tree*; cantatas for mixed and male voices; *Thunder-bird* suite (1914), *Oriental Rhapsody, Dark Dancers of the Mardi Gras* for orchestra; *American Suite* and *To a Vanishing Race* for string orchestra; string quartet (1917), piano trio; violin and piano sonata, sonata and suite *Omar Khayyám* for piano; songs.

Cadmus et Hermione opera by Lully (libretto by Quinault), produced Paris, Opéra, 27 Apr 1673. Cadmus loves Hermione, but Mars has promised her to the giant Draco. Cadmus proves his bravery by killing a dragon. After complications introduced by the gods, all ends happily.

Caduff, Sylvia (b Chur, 7 Jan 1937), Swiss conductor. Studied in Berlin with Karajan, and in Lucerne. Won the Mitropoulos Competition 1966 and was assistant to Bernstein at the NY PO 1966–67. Guest with the Berlin, Munich and Royal Philharmonics, and first woman to hold a musical directorship in Europe (Solingen, 1977–86).

Caduta de' giganti, La, *The Fall of the Giants*, opera by Gluck (libretto by F Vanneschi), produced London, King's Theatre, Haymarket, 7 Jan 1746.

Cafaro, Pasquale (b San Pietro in Galantina, near Lecce, *c* 1715; d Naples, 23 or 25 Oct 1787), Italian composer. Pupil of Leo in

Naples, appointed director of the Conservatoria della Pietà in 1759, and supernumerary *maestro di cappella* to the court in 1770.

Works include operas *Ipermestra* (1751), *La Disfatta di Dario* (1756), etc.; oratorios *Il Figlio prodigo, Il trionfo di Davidde* (1746), etc.; *Stabat Mater*, Masses, motets and other church music.

Caffarelli (real name *Gaetano Majorano*) (b Bitonoto, 12 Apr 1710; d Naples, 31 Jan 1783), Italian castrato alto. Pupil of Porpora, made his operatic debut in Rome, 1726, in Sarro's *Valdemaro*. Sang for Handel in London, 1738, creating the title roles in *Faramondo* and *Serse*.

Try as we might to make a silence, we cannot.
John Cage, *Silence*, 1961

Cage, John (b Los Angeles, 5 Sept 1912; d New York, 12 Aug 1992), American composer. Studied piano in LA and Paris and composition with, among others, Cowell, Schoenberg and Varèse. Cage was the most prominent pioneer and exponent of such 'experimental' concepts as indeterminacy, chance, silence, etc., his ideas having had a very considerable influence in both America and Europe. He developed the 'prepared piano', in which different objects are inserted between the strings, altering the tone and the sound produced. Influenced by oriental ideas, he attempted to relegate the supremacy of the composer: *4' 33"* is performed in total silence. Cage also explored electronic music. Among his published writings, ideas and lectures on music is the collection *Silence* (1961).

Works include STAGE: *Europeras I–IV* (1987–91), ballet *The Seasons* (1947).

ORCHESTRAL: Concerto for prepared piano and chamber orchestra (1951); *Atlas Eclipticalis* (1962); *Cheap Imitation* (1972); *Etcetera* (1973); Quartet I–VIII for varied instrumental groups (1976); Quartet for concert band and 12 amplified voices (1978); 30 pieces for five orchestras (1981); *Etcetera*, two/four orchestras (1986).

PERCUSSION AND ELECTRONICS: *Construction I in Metal* for percussion sextet (1939); *Imaginary Landscape I* for turntables, frequency recordings, muted piano and cymbal (1939); *Living Room Music* for percussion quartet, (1940); *Construction II* and *III* and *Imaginary Landscape II* and *III*, all for percussion ensemble (1940–42; *Imaginary Landscape IV* (March no. 2) for 12 radios, 24 players and conductor (1951); *Imaginary Landscape V* for tape (1952); *Fontana Mix* for tape or other instruments (1958); *But what about the noise of crumpling paper ...* for percussion ensemble (1986).

CHAMBER: string quartet (1950); *4' 33"* (silent, 1952); Variations I–VI for any number of players, *ad libitum* (1958–66); *HPSCHD* for seven harpsichords, or tape machines; *Cheap Imitation* for violin (1977); *Freeman Etudes and Chorals* for violin (1977–78); *Postcard from Heaven* for 1–20 harpsichords; 30 pieces for string quartet (1984); *13 Harmonies* for violin and keyboard (1986).

PIANO AND PREPARED PIANO: *Metamorphosis* (1938); *Bacchanale* (1940); *In the Name of the Holocaust* (1942); *And the Earth shall Bear Again* (1942); *Amores* (1943); *Totem Ancestor* (1943); *A Valentine out of Season* (1944); *Sonatas and Interludes* (1946–48); *Music of Changes* (1951); *Water Music* (1952); *Etudes Australes* (1974–75); *ASLAP* (1985); *One* (1988); *Swinging* (1989).

VOCAL: five songs for contralto and piano (1938) and *Forever and Sunsmell* for voice and percussion duo (1942, to texts by e e cummings); *The Wonderful Widow of 18 Springs* for voice and closed piano (1942, Joyce); *Experiences 2* for solo voice (1948); *Song Books, Solos for Voice 3–92* (1970); *Hymns and Variations for 12 amplified voices* (1978); *Litany for the Whale* for two voices (1980); *Roaratorio*, an Irish Circus on *Finnegans Wake* for eight Irish musicians (1980); *Four Solos for Voices* (1988).

Cagnoni, Antonio (b Godiasco, Voghera, 8 Feb 1828; d Bergamo, 30 Apr 1896), Italian composer. Studied at the Milan Conservatory 1842–47. *Maestro di cappella* at Vigevano, 1856–63, then at Novara Cathedral, and from 1887 at the church of Santa Maria Maggiore at Bergamo.

Works include operas *Don Bucefalo* (1847), *Il testamento di*

Figaro, *Amori e trappole* (1850), *Giralda, La valle d'Andorra, Il vecchio della Montagna* (1860), *La tombola, Un capriccio di donna, Papa Martin, Francesca da Rimini* (after Dante) (1878), etc.; motets and other church music.

Cahier, Mme Charles (b Nashville, 6 Jan 1870; d Manhattan Beach, CA, 15 Apr 1951), American contralto. Studied with Jean de Reszke in Paris. Debut Nice, 1904; from 1906 she sang Carmen and other roles under Mahler at the Vienna Hofoper: took part in the 1911 fp of *Das Lied von der Erde*, under Walter. NY Met. 1911–13, as Azucena, Amneris and Fricka. She taught in Sweden, Salzburg and NY.

Cahill, Teresa (b Maidenhead, 30 Jul 1944), English soprano. Studied at the GSM. Debut 1967, Rosina with Phoenix Opera. From 1970 she has sung at Glyndebourne and CG, and later with WNO and Scottish Opera. In 1977 she was heard as Alice Ford at Glyndebourne, and in 1990 she sang Strauss's Daphne for Chelsea Opera. She has recorded roles in *Calisto, Cendrillon, Figaro* and *Rosenkavalier* (Sophie).

Caimo, Giuseppe (b Milan, *c* 1545; d Milan, 1584), Italian composer. Organist of Milan Cathedral, 1580 until his death. He wrote canzonets and madrigals, some of the latter employing the extremes of chromaticism favoured by Gesualdo.

Caix d'Hervelois, Louis de (b *c* 1670–80; d *c* 1760), French composer and bass viol player, one of the foremost virtuosi of his day. Wrote many pieces for bass viol, duets for viols and flute sonatas.

calando Italian = 'lowering, decreasing, calming down'; a direction similar to *diminuendo* and *rallentando*, capable of expressing both at once, i.e. weakening in tone as well as slowing down.

calata, Italian, an Italian lute dance of the early 16th c., similar to the French *basse danse*. It was written in duple time, but had a triple rhythm of three-bar groups.

Caldara, Antonio (b Venice, 1670; d Vienna, 28 Dec 1736), Italian composer. Pupil of Legrenzi at Venice. After travelling much and working in Rome and Madrid, he settled in Vienna as vice-conductor under Fux in 1716, writing music for court celebrations there and in Salzburg. He was the first to set many of the libretti of Metastasio.

Works include about 100 operas and other stage works, e.g. *Ifigenia in Aulide* (1718), *Lucio Papirio, Gianguir* (1724), *Don Chisciotte* (1727), *La pazienza di Socrate con due moglie* (with Reutter, 1731), *Il Demetrio, Sancio Panza, Achille in Sciro* (1736); church music, oratorios, cantatas, madrigals, canons, trio sonatas, quartets, septet.

Caldwell, Sarah (b Maryville, MO, 6 Mar 1924), American conductor and producer. She staged her first opera while a student at Tanglewood; founded Boston Opera Co. 1957 and has given first US performance of *War and Peace, Moses und Aron* and the original versions of *Boris Godunov* and *Don Carlos*. In 1976 she became the first woman conductor at the NY Met. (*La Traviata*). First US performance *The Ice Break* (1979).

caledonica an alto bassoon invented by the Scottish bandmaster Meik, *c* 1820. It was played with a clarinet reed mouthpiece.

Calife de Bagdad, Le opera by Boieldieu (libretto by C G de Saint-Just), produced Paris, Opéra-Comique, 16 Sept 1800. Isaoun loves Zétulbe, but wants her to love him for himself, not his riches. He courts her in disguise and wins her heart.

calinda, or calenda, an African-American dance introduced into the West Indies and later cultivated in the southern USA, originally an African ritual dance accompanied by drums, which remained a feature of its music. Delius makes use of it in *Koanga*.

Calisto, La opera by Cavalli (libretto by G Faustini, after Ovid's *Metamorphoses*), produced Venice, Teatro Sant' Apollinare, 1651; known today in a free realization by Raymond Leppard (Glyndebourne, 26 May 1970), and in editions by Paul Daniel and René Jacobs. Jupiter assumes the identity of Diana in order to seduce soprano Callisto.

Callas (real name *Kalogeropoulos*), Maria (b New York, 3 Dec 1923; d Paris, 16 Sept 1977), American-born soprano of Greek descent. Aged 13, she went to Greece and studied at the Athens Conservatory, returning to NY in 1945. Italian debut, Verona, 1947, as Gioconda. In 1949 she married the Italian industrialist G B Meneghini. Sang at La Scala 1950–58, under de Sabata, Giulini, Bernstein, Karajan. CG 1952–53, 1957–59. US debut, Chicago, 1954; NY Met. debut (Norma) 1956. She was highly versatile, and despite being remembered for heavy Romantic roles, she concentrated on earlier Italian operas in later years, including Cherubini's *Médée*, Spontini's *La Vestale* and Donizetti's *Anna Bolena*. Although critics noted her technical inconsistency, her emotionally-charged performances and dramatic presence were without equal. Other roles included Verdi's Aida, Violetta, Lady Macbeth and Leonora (*Il Trovatore*), Bellini's Amina, Imogene and Elvira, and Lucia di Lammermoor. Last appearance in opera, CG, 5 Jul 1965, as Tosca.

Callcott, John Wall (b London, 20 Nov 1766; d Bristol, 15 May 1821), English organist and composer. Son of a bricklayer, he had no regular music teaching, but picked up much knowledge from Arnold and Cooke. Having obtained a deputy organist's post, he found time to compose and in 1785 gained three of the four prizes offered by the Catch Club. Two years later he took part in founding the Glee Club. When Haydn came to England he studied instrumental writing under him, but he continued to write glees and catches with great success. D. Mus., Oxford, 1800. In 1809 he went insane, and died having reached letter P of a music dictionary, feeling unable to proceed further.

Works include setting of Joseph Warton's *Ode to Fancy* (1785); anthem for Arnold's funeral; scena on the death of Nelson; a book of psalms edited with Arnold, with some new tunes; numerous glees, catches and canons.

She shone all too brief a while in the world of opera, like a vivid flame attracting the attention of the whole world, and she had a strange magic that was all her own.

Tito Gobbi on Maria Callas, *My Life*, 1980

Callino casturame, ? corruption from Irish 'Cailín ó chois tSiúire mé', = 'I am a girl from beside the [river] Suir'; a tune mentioned in Shakespeare's *Henry V* (IV. iv) and set by 16th-c. composers including Byrd.

Calm Sea and Prosperous Voyage (Beethoven and Mendelssohn.) ◊Meeresstille.

Calvé, Emma (Rose Emma Calvet) (b Décazeville, 15 Aug 1858; d Millau, 6 Jan 1942), French soprano. First appeared in Brussels in 1881, as Marguerite, and appeared in Paris in 1884. La Scala, Milan, from 1887, as Thomas's Ophelia and in operas by Samara and Mascagni. Famous as an interpreter of the role of Carmen. She created roles in Massenet's *La navarraise* (1894) and *Sapho* (1897).

Calvisius, Seth (b Gorsleben, Thuringia, 21 Feb 1556; d Leipzig, 24 Nov 1615), German scholar and musician. Cantor of St Thomas's School and music director of its church from 1594, and thus a predecessor of Bach. Wrote several learned books on music, compiled collections of vocal music and composed motets, hymns, etc.

Calvocoressi, M(ichael) D(imitri) (b Marseilles, 2 Oct 1877; d London, 1 Feb 1944), English music critic of Greek descent. Studied in Paris, particularly music and languages, lectured there on music at the École des Hautes Études Sociales, 1905–14, and then settled in London, becoming naturalized. His books include studies of music criticism, Mussorgsky, etc.

Calzabigi, Raniero da (b Livorno, 23 Dec 1714; d Naples, Jul 1795), Italian literary critic and author. Lived in Paris and Vienna for a time. His first libretti were in the dry, formal style of Metastasio. From 1762 he collaborated with Gluck in the more dramatically convincing 'reform' operas: ◊Orfeo ed Euridice (1762), *Alceste* (1767) and *Paride ed Elena* (1770). He returned to Italy in the 1770s; his last work, set by Paisiello, returns to his earlier manner.

Cambert, Robert (b Paris, *c* 1628; d London, *c* Feb 1677), French composer. Studied harpsichord with Chambonnières, was organist at the church of Saint-Honoré in Paris and superintendent of the queen's music. He was ousted by Lully and sent to live in London in 1673. His

Pomone (1671) was the first French opera to be staged in public. Most of his music is lost.

Works include comedy with music *La Muette ingrate* (1658); a pastoral performed at Issy and another, *Les Peines et les plaisirs de l'amour* (1671); operas *Ariane, ou Le Mariage de Bacchus, Pomone* (1674); a trio for Brécourt's *Jaloux invisible; airs à boire*.

Cambiale di matrimonio, La, *The Marriage Contract*, opera by Rossini (libretto by G Rossi, based on a comedy by C Federici), produced Venice, Teatro San Moisè, 3 Nov 1810. Rossini's first opera to be performed. Tobias Mill is keen to sell off his daughter Fanny, but young Milfort intervenes.

Cambini, Giovanni Giuseppe (b Livorno, 13 Feb 1746; d ? Paris, 1825), Italian violinist and composer. Pupil of Martini at Bologna. In 1770 he settled in Paris, where at first he had great success both as a composer and conductor. Later his fortunes declined, and he died in poverty.

Works include 19 operas, e.g. *Alcide* (1782), ballets, an oratorio, 60 symphonies, 144 quartets and quintets; church music.

Music, which doth not only make sweet the minds of men, but also many times wild beasts tame; and whoso savoreth it not, a man may assuredly think him not to be well in his wits.

Baldassare Castiglioni, *Il Cortegiano*, 1528

Cambreling, Sylvain (b Amiens, 2 Jul 1948), French conductor. Studied at the Paris Conservatory and was principal guest with the Ensemble Intercontemporain, 1976–81. Made Glyndebourne and London (ENO) debuts 1981, with *Il Barbiere di Siviglia* and *Louise*; La Scala debut 1984 (*Lucio Silla*), NY Met. 1985 (Gounod's *Romeo*) and Salzburg 1986 (Debussy's *Le Martyre*). Music director at Brussels 1981–92, with *Lohengrin* and *Simon Boccanegra*, Frankfurt Opera from 1993 (*Wozzeck, From the House of the Dead* and *Elektra*). Conducted *The Rake's Progress* at Salzburg, 1994.

Camden, Archie (Archibald) (b Newark, 9 Mar 1888; d Wheathampstead, Herts., 16 Feb 1979), English bassoonist. He became a principal with the Hallé Orchestra in 1914, after study in Manchester, and joined the BBC SO in 1933; remained until 1946 and after a season with the RPO became a freelance. Well known as a soloist and an influential teacher (professor at RMCM 1914–33, later at RCM).

Camden Festival annual music festival held in the London area of St Pancras 1954–87. Productions included the British premieres of operas by Haydn (*Orfeo, Il mondo della luna* and *L'infidelta delusa*), Verdi (*Un giorno di regno* and *Il Corsaro*), Donizetti (*Maria Stuarda*), Mozart (*Lucio Silla*), and *Eritrea* by Cavalli. Also concert performances of Strauss's *Friedenstag* (1985), J C Bach's *Adriano in Siria* (1982) and three works by Weill (1986–87).

camera, concerto da (or *camera, sonata de*) Italian = 'chamber concerto or sonata'; a secular work written for performance at home or at concerts, as distinct from a concerto or sonata *da chiesa* = for the church.

camerata Italian = 'society'; a group of intellectuals meeting for cultural exchanges, in particular one at Florence under Count Giovanni de' Bardi in *c* 1573–87 and strongly influenced by Girolamo Mei's research into ancient Greek music. The earliest operas seem to have emerged from their deliberations.

cameriera Italian = 'chambermaid'; a term used in Italian opera, especially of the 17th and 18th c., in the same way as *servetta/servant-girl* for soubrette parts.

Cameron, Basil (b Reading, 18 Aug 1884; d Leominster, 26 Jun 1975), English conductor. He studied in Berlin 1902–06, and as a conductor in Torquay adopted, but only up to the war, the name Basil Hindenburg in an attempt to negate the usual prejudice against conductors with English names. Engaged with seaside orchestras 1912–30, then conducted orchestras in San Francisco and Seattle before returning to Britain in 1938. He assisted Wood, then Boult, with the Prom

Concerts from 1940; in Sept 1945 he conducted the first European performance of Schoenberg's piano concerto.

Cammarano, Salvatore (b Naples, 19 Mar 1801; d Naples, 17 Jul 1852), Italian librettist. He wrote various stage pieces before the libretto for Donizetti's *Lucia di Lammermoor* in 1835; other libretti for him included *Roberto Devereux, Belisario* and *Poliuto*. His first libretto for Verdi was *Alzira*, in 1841; later *La battaglia di Legnano, Luisa Miller* and most of *Il Trovatore*. Also wrote the libretti for Pacini's *Saffo* and Mercadante's *La Vestale* and *Medea*.

Campagnoli, Bartolomeo (b Cento di Ferrara, 10 Sept 1751; d Neustrelitz, 7 Nov 1827), Italian violinist and composer. Pupil of Nardini; worked in Italy, Germany and Paris; wrote concertos, sonatas, duets, etc. for violin; flute music; caprices for viola, etc.; also an important work on violin playing, *Metodo per violino*.

Campana Sommersa, La, *The Sunken Bell*, opera by Respighi (libretto by C Guastalla, after G Hauptmann's *Die versunkene Glocke*); 1923–27, fp Hamburg, 24 Nov 1928. Bell-maker Enrico falls for the elf Rautendelein, and deserts his wife. At the news of his wife's suicide he rejects Rautendelein, but dies because he cannot live without her.

Campanella, La the third of Liszt's *Études d'exécution transcendante d'après Paganini* for piano, composed 1838, already used by him 1831–32 for the *Grande Fantaisie de bravoure sur la Clochette*. The theme is that of the finale of Paganini's violin concerto in B minor, op. 7, a rondo in which harmonics are combined with a bell.

Campanini, Cleofonte (b Parma, 1 Sept 1860; d Chicago, 19 Dec 1919), Italian conductor. Made his first appearance at Parma in 1883 and the same year went to the USA, where he spent most of his life, apart from visits to Italy, England and S America. Conductor Manhattan Opera NY, 1906–09; Chicago Opera Co., 1910–19. Married Eva Tetrazzini, the sister of Luisa ◊Tetrazzini. He conducted the premieres of *Adriana Lecouvreur* (1902) and *Madama Butterfly* (1904).

Campanini, Italo (b Parma, 30 Jun 1845; d Corcagno near Parma, 22 Nov 1896), Italian tenor, brother of Cleofonte ◊Campanini. Debut Parma 1863, as Gennaro; London debut 1872, same role. He was the first Italian Lohengrin (Bologna, 1871) and the first Don José in London and NY (1878). He sang Gounod's Faust in the inaugural performance at the NY Met. (1883) and was heard also in the *Faust* settings by Boito and Berlioz.

Campenhout, François van (b Brussels, 5 Feb 1779; d Brussels, 24 Apr 1848), Belgian tenor and composer. Sang in Belgium, Holland and France until 1827. During the 1830 revolution he wrote the Belgian national anthem, *La Brabançonne*.

Works include operas *Grotius, Le Passepartout, L'Heureux Mensonge*; church music; choruses; songs.

Campian, Thomas, ◊Campion.

Campiello, Il, *The Square*, opera by Wolf-Ferrari (libretto by M Ghisalberti, after Goldoni), produced Milan, La Scala, 12 Feb 1936. A slice of working-class Venetian life.

Campioli (real name *Antonio Gualandi*) (b Germany), 18th-c. Italian castrato alto. Made his operatic debut in Berlin, 1708, and sang in Handel's operas in London, 1731–32; he sang Argone in the fp of *Sosarme* (1732).

Campion (or Campian), Thomas (b London, bap. 12 Feb 1567; d London, buried 1 Mar 1620), English physician, poet and composer. Was sent to Cambridge in 1581 and being a lawyer at first entered Gray's Inn in 1586; (?) took part in the siege of Rouen in 1591 and soon afterwards practised medicine in London. He pub. a first collection of airs to the lute with Rosseter in 1601 and four more followed between *c* 1613 and 1617, all the words of the songs being his own. In 1613 he pub. a book on counterpoint, and wrote the poetry for *Songs of Mourning* on the death of Prince Henry, set by Coprario. He also pub. poems and a book on poetry. His poem *Neptune's Empire* was set for chorus and orchestra by Ernest Walker. Poems set as songs by W Busch.

Works include five books of airs to the lute (over 100) and three separate earlier songs; songs for the production of four masques, 1607–13, including *The Mask of Flowers*.

Campioni, Carlo Antonio (b Lunéville, 16 Nov 1720; d Florence, 12 Apr 1788), Italian composer. In the service of the Grand Duke of Tuscany at Florence and the King of Sardinia.

Works include Requiem and other church music, trio sonatas, duets for two violins and for violin and cello; keyboard music.

Camporese, Violante (b Rome, 1785; d Rome, 1839), Italian soprano. She sang at La Scala 1817–30, in the fps of operas by Morlacchi, Gyrowetz and Rossini (*Bianca e Falliero*, 1819). At the King's Theatre, London, she was heard as Susanna, Donna Anna and Dorabella and in the first local performance of Rossini's *La gazza ladra*, *Mosè* and *Otello*. Retired 1829.

Campra, André (b Aix-en-Provence, bap. 4 Dec 1660; d Versailles, 29 Jun 1744), French composer of Italian descent. He held various provincial organist's posts and settled in Paris in 1694, when he was appointed music director at Notre-Dame, where his motets soon attracted large congregations; but he became equally famous as a stage composer. After many years of neglect, his works are now being revived and recorded.

Works include operas and opera-ballets *L'Europe galante* (1697), *Le Carnaval de Venise* (1699), *Hésione, Tancrède, Iphigénie en Tauride* (with Desmarets, 1704), *Alcine, Hippodamie* (1708), *Les Festes vénitiennes, Idoménée* (1712), *Le Jaloux trompé, Achille et Déidamie* (1735), etc.; pasticcios *Fragments de Lully* and *Télémaque* (the latter with pieces by Charpentier, Colasse, Desmarets, Marais and Rebel senior); entertainments *Amaryllis, Les Festes de Corinthe, Le Génie de la Bourgogne, Les Noces de Vénus* (1740), etc.; a Mass, cantatas, motets and. psalms.

canary, English, (also canarie or canaries), a dance in quick triple time with a dotted rhythm, possibly originating from the Canary Islands.

cancan a lively dance of a risqué nature fashionable in Paris from *c* the middle of the 19th c. It is in very animated 2–4 time.

cancel American = natural, ♮.

canción Spanish = 'song'.

cancionero Spanish = a song-book.

cancrizans from Latin *cancer* = 'crab' = 'crab-wise'; a term used for the device of repeating a musical phrase or theme backwards, note for note. 'Canon cancrizans' is a canon in which one part or more proceed normally while another one or more go backwards. In serial music the reversed form of the series is sometimes called cancrizans instead of the more usual *retrograde*.

Candeille, Amélie-Julie (b Paris, 31 Jul 1767; d Paris, 4 Feb 1834), French actress, singer, pianist and composer. Made her debut as a singer at the Paris Opéra in 1782, but left to become an actress. Ten years later she sang in her first opera, for which she had written both words and music.

Works include operas *La Belle Fermière* (1792), *Bathilde ou le Duc* and *Ida ou l'Orpheline* (1807); chamber music; piano music; songs.

Candeille, Pierre Joseph (b Estaires, 8 Dec 1744; d Chantilly, 24 Apr 1827), French singer and composer, father of Amélie-Julie. Wrote operas, including *Castor et Pollux* (revision of Rameau, 1791); ballets, pantomime, incidental music.

Candide comic operetta by Bernstein (libretto by L Hellman, after Voltaire), produced Boston, 29 Oct 1956; revised 1973 and produced NY, City Opera, 13 Oct 1982. In spite of all the evidence to the contrary, Candide (tenor) believes everything in life is for the best. He eventually decides, after many adventures, that his philosophy was mistaken, and resolves to build a new life.

Caniglia, Maria (b Naples, 5 May 1905; d Rome, 16 Apr 1979), Italian soprano. Debut Turin, 1930, Chrysothemis. La Scala 1930–51; appeared with the co. at CG in 1950. NY Met. 1938 as Aida. Other Verdi roles included all three Leonoras, Amelia and Alice Ford. Also sang Tosca, Fedora and Respighi's Lucrezia.

Canis, Corneille (Cornelis de Hond) (b ? Antwerp; d Prague, 15 Feb 1561), Flemish composer. Choirmaster of Charles V's imperial chapel in the Netherlands from 1548, later chaplain to the Emperor Ferdinand in Prague. Wrote church music, *chansons*, etc.

Cannabich, (Johann) Christian (b Mannheim, bap. 28 Dec 1731; d Frankfurt, 20 Jan 1798), German violinist, conductor and composer. Pupil of Stamitz in Mannheim and Jommelli in Rome, became *Konzertmeister* of the Mannheim orchestra in 1758 and director of instrumental music in 1774. From 1778 he worked in Munich. His conducting was admired by Mozart, who taught his daughter Rosa Cannabich in 1777 and wrote a piano sonata for her.

Works include operas, ballets, e.g. *Renaud et Armide* (1768), symphonies, chamber music.

Cannon, Philip (b Paris, 21 Dec 1929), English composer. Studied with Imogen Holst and later at the RCM with Gordon Jacob (composition) and Pierre Tas (violin). This was followed by some study with Hindemith. After a period of lecturing at Sydney University he returned to the RCM in 1952.

Works include three operas; string quartet (1964) and other chamber music, vocal and choral music including *Lord of Light*, oratorio for soloists, chorus and orchestra (1980), piano compositions; two symphonies, including *Son of Man*, for Britain's entry to the EC.

canon Greek *kanón* = 'rule'; a polyphonic composition, or section of a composition, in which one part is imitated by one or more others which enter successively, so that the entries overlap. *See illustration on page 106.*

cantabile Italian = 'song-like, songful, singable'; the direction is usually placed against phrases in instrumental rather than vocal music where the composer desires an expressive delivery.

cantata Italian = 'a sung piece'; The definition has become narrowed in modern times to short vocal works, sacred or secular, and for single voices or chorus, with instrumental accompaniment.

Work by Stravinsky for soprano, tenor, female chorus and instrumentation ensemble (seven texts from anonymous English lyrics, including *Tomorrow shall be my dancing day* and *Westron wind*); composed 1951–52, fp LA, 11 Nov 1952.

Cantata Academica work by Britten for soloists, chorus and orchestra, composed 1959 on Latin texts, for the 500th anniversary of Basel University; fp Basel, 1 Jul 1960.

Cantata Misericordium work by Britten for tenor, baritone, small chorus and chamber orchestra (text by P Wilkinson), composed for the centenary of the International Red Cross, fp Geneva, 15 Sept 1963, conductor Ansermet.

Cantata on the death of the Emperor Joseph II work by Beethoven for soloists, chorus and orchestra (text by SA Averdonk). The cantata was commissioned from Beethoven in Bonn after the death of the Emperor on 20 Feb 1790, but was not performed. The MS was probably seen by Haydn, on his return from his first visit to England, and led to his offering Beethoven lessons in Vienna. Not performed until 1884, the cantata contains an anticipation of a theme from the last scene of *Fidelio*.

Cantata Profana, *A kilenc csodaszarvas/The Nine Enchanted Stags*, work by Bartók for tenor, baritone, chorus and orchestra, composed 1930, fp in BBC concert, 25 May 1934.

Cantelli, Guido (b Novara, 27 Apr 1920; d Paris, 24 Nov 1956), Italian conductor. Studied at the Milan Conservatory and, after escaping from a German prison camp and a Fascist prison hospital in the war, began to conduct concerts with the Scala orchestra in Milan. He then quickly made his way in Italy and abroad as a conductor whose gifts were second only to Toscanini's. He conducted the NBC SO from 1949 and the Philharmonia, London, from 1951. He was killed in an air accident.

Canteloube (de Malaret), (Marie) Joseph (b Annonay, Ardèche, 21 Oct 1879; d Paris, 4 Nov 1957), French composer. Studied with d'Indy at the Schola Cantorum in Paris. In 1900 he began to collect and study French folksong, particularly of Auvergne, of which he pub. several collections. Lecturer on French music and folksong from 1923. He is best known for his folksong arrangements *Chants d'Auvergne* (four vols., pub. 1923–30).

Works include operas *Le Mas* (1910–13) and *Vercingetorix* (produced 1933); symphonic poems *Vers la princesse lointaine* and

(a) 'standard'

(b) by inversion

(c) by diminution

If the imitation is exact the canon is termed 'strict'; if it is modified by the addition or omission of accidentals it is 'free as to intervals'. A canon may proceed (1) by inversion, with one part going up where the other goes down and vice versa *(illustration (b)); (2) by augmentation, with one part in notes twice or more the length of the other (illustration (c)); (3) by diminution, with one part in notes half or less the length of the other; (4) by retrograde motion (*canon cancrizans*), with one part going backwards while the other goes forward. Various combinations of these forms are also possible. A canon may be accompanied by one or more independent parts. Two or more canons can occur simultaneously.*

Lauriers; *Pièces françaises* for piano and orchestra; *Poème* for violin and orchestra; *Dans la montagne* for violin and piano; songs with orchestra and with piano; many folksong arrangements.

canticle a category of sacred song, usually Biblical, used in Christian church services; including the Te Deum, Benedictus, Magnificat, Nunc Dimittis.

Canticles series of five works by Britten: no. 1 *My beloved is mine* (text by F Quarles), for high voice and piano, fp Aldeburgh, 1 Nov 1947; no. 2 *Abraham and Isaac* (text from Chester miracle play), for alto, tenor and piano, fp Nottingham, 21 Jan 1952; no. 3 *Still falls the rain* (text by E Sitwell), for tenor, horn and piano, fp London, 28 Jan 1955; no. 4 *The Journey of the Magi* (text by T S Eliot), for countertenor, tenor, baritone and piano, fp Aldeburgh, 26 Jun 1971; no. 5 *The Death of Narcissus* (text by Eliot), for tenor and harpsichord, fp Schloss Elmau, 15 Jan 1975.

Canticum Sacrum (ad honorem Sancti Marci nominis) work by Stravinsky, in honour of St Mark's, Venice, for tenor, baritone, chorus and orchestra; composed 1955, fp Venice, 13 Sept 1956.

Canti di Prigionia, *Songs of Captivity*, work by Dallapiccola for chorus, two pianos, two harps and percussion (texts by Mary Stuart, Boethius and Savanarola); composed 1938–41 in protest against Italian fascism, fp Rome, 11 Dec 1941.

cantigas Spanish = 'canticles'; Spanish sacred songs for single voice of the 13th c., mostly in honour of the Virgin Mary, allied in form to the French *virelai* and the Italian *lauda*.

cantilena Italian = a sustained, flowing melodic line, especially when sung *legato* or played in the manner of such singing.

cantillation chanting in unison in the Jewish synagogue service.

cantino Italian the E string of the violin.

cantiones sacrae Latin = 'sacred songs'; a title often given to collections of Latin motets in the 16th and 17th c.

canto Italian = 'song'; in instrumental as much as in vocal music, usually the part of a composition which has the chief melody. The direction *marcato il canto* indicates that such a melody is to be emphasized.

canto carnascialesco Italian = 'carnival song'; a Florentine part-song of the 15th–16th c. with secular, often ribald, words, sung in carnival processions.

canto fermo Italian ▷cantus firmus.

cantor Latin = 'singer'; a church singer, especially the leader or director of a choir in a Lutheran church (e.g. Bach at Leipzig) or in a synagogue.

cantoris in English cathedrals and in churches where the choir is divided, the cantoris side is that on the north of the chancel, near the stall of the cantor or precentor, the other being the *decani* side.

cantus firmus Latin = lit. 'fixed song'; a pre-existing melody chosen by a composer to envelop in contrapuntal parts of his own, either for exercise or for the production of a composition. Although the term dates back to the Middle Ages, it has been used constantly ever since where appropriate.

Canyons aux étoiles, Des, *From the Canyons to the Stars*, work by Messiaen for piano, horn and orchestra, composed 1970–74, fp NY, 20 Nov 1974.

canzona, canzone Italian = 'song, ballad'; (1) a part-song in the style of a madrigal but lighter in character and less elaborately polyphonic. (2) An instrumental piece in a polyphonic style, originally *canzone francese*.

canzonet from Italian *canzonetta* = 'little song'; light songs written in England round about 1600, either for several voices with or without instruments or for a single voice with lute accompaniment. Later simply a song in England, e.g. Haydn's English Canzonets.

canzonetta Italian = 'little song'; often synonymous with ◊canzona in 16th–17th-c. Italy; later a light song or short and simple air in an opera, etc.

canzoniere Italian = a songbook.

Cape, Safford (b Denver, 28 Jun 1906; d Uccele, 26 Mar 1973), American conductor and musicologist. Studied in Belgium, and at Brussels in 1933 founded the Pro Musica Antiqua, for the performance of medieval and Renaissance music. Many tours in Europe and the Americas, and recordings for the Anthologie Sonore and History of European Music in Sound. Established European Seminar on Early Music at Bruges and Lisbon (1961).

Capecchi, Renato (b Cairo, 6 Nov 1923), Italian baritone. Debut Reggio Emilia, 1949, Amonasro. NY Met. 1951 as Germont. CG 1962 and 1973 as Melitone and Rossini's Bartolo. Recent roles include Dandini, Gianni Schicchi, Don Giovanni and Mozart's Figaro. Glyndebourne 1977 and 1980, Falstaff. Recent roles include Fallito in Gassman's *L'Opera Seria* (1994).

Capella, Martianus (b ?Madaura, N Africa), 4th–5th-c. philosopher. His *De musica* is the ninth and last book of his *De nuptiis Mercurii et Philologiae*. His treatise, deriving in part from Varro and Quintilian, had considerable influence on later medieval theorists.

Capirola, Vincenzo (b Brescia, 1474; d after 1548), Italian lutenist and composer. His collection of lute music (*c* 1517) is among the most important early MSS of the repertory.

The English may not like music, but they absolutely love the noise it makes.
Sir Thomas Beecham, *New York Herald Tribune*, 1961

Caplet, André (b Le Havre, 23 Nov 1878; d Paris, 22 Apr 1925), French conductor and composer, much influenced by Debussy, who allowed him to orchestrate a part of *Le Martyre de Saint Sebastien*, which Caplet premiered in 1911.

Works include symphonic study *Le Masque de la Mort rouge* (after Poe, 1909); *Epiphanie* for cello and orchestra (1923); Mass for unaccompanied voices; *Le Miroir de Jésus* for voices, string quintet and harp (1924); *Le Pie Jésus* for voice and organ; *Suite persane* for ten wind instruments; *Conte fantastique* (after Poe) for harp and string quartet (an arrangement of *Le Masque de la Mort rouge*); *Sonata de chiesa* for violin and organ; children's suite for piano duet; song cycles *Prières, La Croix douloureuse, 3 Fables de La Fontaine, Cinq Ballades françaises*. He orchestrated Debussy's *Children's Corner* and conducted the fp of *Le Martyre de Saint Sébastien* (1911).

Capoul, Victor (b Toulouse, 27 Feb 1839; d Pujaudran-du-Gers, 18 Feb 1924), French tenor. Debut Paris, Opéra-Comique, 1861, in Adam's *Le Chalet*. In 1871 he sang for the first time in London and NY; CG from 1875, Met. from 1883. Among his best roles were Wilhelm Meister, Otello, Meyerbeer's Robert and Gounod's Roméo. Stage manager, Paris Opéra, from 1897.

Cappuccilli, Piero (b Trieste, 9 Nov 1929), Italian baritone. Debut Milan, 1957; La Scala from 1964. NY Met. debut 1960 as Germont. CG from 1967 as Renato, Iago and Boccanegra; sang Posa at Salzburg in 1975. Chicago from 1969. Sang Boccanegra at Barcelona, 1990.

──────── THE OPERA ────────
Capriccio

A one-act opera by Richard Strauss, first produced during World War II at Munich (1942). The action – really a dramatized conversation – takes place in a chateau near Paris in 1775. The Countess Madeleine (soprano) listens to a string sextet composed for her by one of her admirers, the musician Flamand (tenor). Flamand's rival is the poet Olivier (baritone), who hopes to press his suit with a play performed for the Countess's birthday. The rivalry of the two men is mirrored in the different claims of their arts – music and drama. The impresario La Roche (bass) urges the practical requirements of theatrical performance. The Countess's brother (baritone), in love with the actress Clairon (soprano), takes up the suggestion of La Roche that Flamand and Olivier should write an opera based on the recent artistic arguments and including the characters present at the chateau. After the guests depart the Countess muses in the moonlight on the claims of her admirers, both of whom she is due to meet – and decide between – in the morning. We are never told whom she chooses.

──────── THE OPERA ────────

capriccio Italian = 'whim'; a name given to various types of composition at different times in the 17th and 18th c. to animated pieces in a fugal style, but not strictly fugues in form; by Bach to a harpsichord piece in several movements on the departure of his brother Johann Jakob; *c* from the middle of the 18th c. to studies for the violin (e.g. Paganini's); later still to fantasies for piano on well-known themes; last of all to short pieces in a humorous or whimsical manner.

Capriccio opera by R Strauss (libretto by C Krauss and the composer), produced Munich, Staatsoper, 28 Oct 1942. An elegant 'conversation piece' in which composer Flamand and poet Olivier compete for the affections of Countess Madeleine; a deconstructionist opera about opera.

Work by Janáček in four movements for piano left hand and orchestra; composed 1926, fp Prague, 2 Mar 1928.

Work by Stravinsky for piano and orchestra; composed 1929, fp Paris, 6 Dec 1929, conductor Ansermet.

Capriccio espagnol, *Spanish Caprice*, orchestral work by Rimsky-Korsakov, written as a display piece for the St Petersburg Orchestra, finished 4 Aug and performed St Petersburg, 17 Dec 1887. It contains brilliant solo parts for most of the principal instruments and for the brass in groups. It was originally intended to be for violin and orchestra, a companion-piece to Rimsky-Korsakov's *Russian Fantasy*.

Capriccio italien, *Italian Caprice*, orchestral work by Tchaikovsky, composed during a visit to Rome in 1880 and first performed Moscow, 18 Dec 1880.

Caprichos, Los fantasia for orchestra by Henze; composed 1963, fp Duisburg, 6 Apr 1967.

Caproli (or Caprioli), Carlo (b Rome, *c* 1615; d Rome, *c* 1693), Italian violinist and composer. Was brought to Paris by Cardinal Mazarin and produced the opera *Le nozze di Peleo e Teti* there in 1654. He wrote the oratorio *Davidde prevaricante* in 1683.

Capuana, Franco (b Fano, 29 Sept 1894; d Naples, 10 Dec 1969), Italian conductor. His early career was at Naples and Brescia; conductor at La Scala 1937–40, with fps of works by Refice and Bianchi, and took the co. to CG in 1946 (music director La Scala, 1949–52). He was noted for his wide repertory and gave first local performance of operas by Janáček and Hindemith, revivals of Verdi and Bellini and works by Strauss and Wagner. He died while conducting Rossini's *Mosè*.

Capuleti e i Montecchi, I, *The Capulets and Montagues*, opera by Bellini (libretto by F Romani, based on Shakespeare's sources for *Romeo and Juliet*), produced Venice, Teatro La Fenice, 11 Mar 1830. Juliet romanced by a mezzo Romeo. Bellini's example persuaded Berlioz to set the play as an extended symphony with voices.

Cara, Marchetto (b Verona, *c* 1470; d ? Mantua, after 1525), Italian lutenist and composer. In service at the ducal court of Mantua, 1495–1525. Wrote *frottole* and other songs.

Caractacus cantata for solo voices, chorus and orchestra by Elgar, op. 35 (libretto by H A Acworth), composed in 1898 and produced Leeds Festival, 5 Oct 1898. Ancient Briton battles the Romans.

Music by Arne for a dramatic poem by W Mason (pub. 1759), performed London CG, 6 Dec 1776.

Carafa (di Colobrano), Michele Enrico (b Naples, 17 Nov 1787; d Paris, 26 Jul 1872), Italian composer. On the failure of his first opera he enlisted in the bodyguard of Murat, then king of Naples, took part in the Russian campaign in 1812 and was decorated by Napoleon, after whose fall he returned to music. He produced operas not only in Italy but in Vienna and Paris, where he settled in 1827 and became very popular. Professor of composition at the Paris Conservatory, 1840–58.

Works include *c* 35 operas, e.g. *Il fantasma* (1805), *Il vascello d'occidente*, *Gabriella di Vergy* (1816), *Ifigenia*, *Berenice*, *Le Solitaire*, *La Violette* (1828), *La Fiancée de Lammermoor* and *Elisabetta in Derbyshire* (after Scott, 1818), *Masaniello* (competing with Auber's *Muette de Portici*, 1827), *La Prison d'Édimbourg* (after Scott's *Heart of Midlothian*), *Jeanne d'Arc* (after Schiller, 1821).

Carattaco opera by J C Bach (libretto by G G Bottarelli), performed London, King's Theatre, 14 Feb 1767.

Cardew, Cornelius (b Winchcombe, Gloucestershire, 7 May 1936; d London, 13 Dec 1981), English composer and pianist. Studied at the RAM with, among others, Howard Ferguson (composition). In 1958 he went to Cologne to study electronic music, also working with Stockhausen until 1960. Cardew belonged at one time to the *avant-garde* school, whose ideas are much influenced by Cage, but later espoused Marxist principles and pub. a book, *Stockhausen Serves Imperialism* (1974). He led the Scratch Orchestra from 1969. His works have been widely performed in Europe.

Works include *Octet 1959*; 193-page graphic score *Treatise* (1967); *The Great Learning* (1970); *Autumn 60* for orchestra; *A Bun* for orchestra; *The East is Red* for violin and piano (1972) *The Old and the New*, for soprano, chorus and orchestra (1973); piano music.

> *I feel that Elgar's music is usually either opening or closing something institutional.*
>
> **Neville Cardus**, *Radio Times*, 1931

Cardillac opera by Hindemith (libretto by F Lion, based on E T A Hoffmann's story *Das Fräulein von Scudéri*), produced Dresden, 9 Nov 1926; revised version produced Zurich, 20 Jun 1952. Goldsmith Cardillac murders his clients to recover his handywork. After stabbing his daughter's fiancé, Cardillac reveals he is a murderer and a mob kills him.

Cardoso, Manuel (b Fronteira near Portalegre, bap. 11 Dec 1566; d Lisbon, 24 Nov 1650), Portuguese monk, organist and composer. Studied at the seminary of Evora and became choirmaster of the cathedral there. Joined the Carmelite monastery at Lisbon in 1588 and became its music director.

Works include Masses, motets, Magnificats and other church music.

Cardus, (John Frederick) Neville (b Manchester, 3 Apr 1888; d London, 28 Feb 1975), English critic. Began to write for the *Daily Citizen* at Manchester in 1913 and in 1917 joined the *Manchester Guardian* as assistant critic to Samuel Langford, whom he succeeded in 1927. He wrote on cricket as well as music, but not on the latter in London until 1931, edited Langford's writings and pub. a book on *Ten Composers* as well as several on cricket. In 1939–47 he lived in Australia. In 1948 he settled in London. Knighted 1967.

Carestini, Giovanni (b Ancona, *c* 1705; d *c* 1760), Italian castrato alto. First appeared in Rome, 1721, and sang in Handel's operas in London, 1733–35, creating roles in *Arianna in Creta*, *Ariodante* and *Alcina*.

Carewe, John (b Derby, 24 Jan 1933), English conductor. Studied with Boulez and Messiaen and founded New Music Ensemble 1957: fps of

Davies and Birtwistle with performances of Stockhausen and Boulez. Conducted the Fires of London 1980–84; fp of Carter's oboe concerto (Zurich, 1988). Chief conductor of Chemnitz Opera and Robert Schumann PO from 1993.

Carey, Henry (b ? Yorkshire *c* 1689; d London, 5 Oct 1743), English poet, composer and dramatist. Pupil of Roseingrave and Geminiani. Wrote libretti for Lampe's operas *The Dragon of Wantley*, *Margery* and *Amelia*.

Works include cantatas and songs to his own words; ballad operas *The Contrivances* (1729), *A Wonder, or the Honest Yorkshireman* (1735), *Nancy, or the Parting Lovers* (1739), etc.; songs for Vanbrugh and Cibber's *The Provok'd Husband*.

carillon a set of bells hung in a church steeple or specially built tower, controlled by a keyboard below and played like an organ on manuals and pedals. Carillons are found particularly in the Netherlands.

Carissimi, Giacomo (b Marino near Rome, bap. 18 Apr 1605; d Rome, 12 Jan 1674), Italian composer. *Maestro di cappella* at Assisi in 1628–29; then went to Rome, where he held a similar post at the church of Sant' Apollinare attached to the German College. He cultivated the oratorio and cantata in their early stages.

Works include Masses, motets; *Lauda Sion* and *Nisi Dominus* for eight voices; oratorios *History of Job*, *Baltazar*, *Abraham and Isaac*, *Jephtha*, (*c* 1650), *The Last Judgment*, *Jonah*; sacred cantatas; vocal duets.

Carl Rosa Opera Company, The Royal founded by Carl ◊Rosa in 1873 for the performance of opera in English.

Carlton, Nicholas (II) (b *c* 1570; d Boeley, Worcs., 1630), English composer and friend of Thomas Tomkins. A few keyboard works survive, one of which is an *In nomine* for keyboard duet (four hands at one keyboard).

Carlton, Richard (b *c* 1558; d *c* 1638), English composer. Educated at Cambridge; became vicar at St Stephen's Church, Norwich, and minor canon at the cathedral. Pub. a book of madrigals in 1601 and contributed to *The Triumphes of Oriana*.

Carlyle, Joan (b Wirral, 6 Apr 1931), English soprano. Debut CG 1955, as Frasquita; remained until 1969 as Pamina, Sophie, Arabella, Desdemona and Tippett's Jenifer. Glyndebourne 1965, Mozart's Countess. She appeared as guest at Munich and Vienna and recorded Nedda with Karajan.

Carmen opera by Bizet (libretto by H Meilhac and L Halévy), based on the story by Mérimée), produced Paris, Opéra-Comique, 3 Mar 1875. Don José caught between gypsy Carmen and original love Micaela. Obsessed by Carmen, who soon rejects him, José turns to crime, eventually killing her outside a bullring.

Carmen, Johannes (*fl*. Paris, *c* 1400–20), French composer later praised by Martin le Franc. Of his compositions only three motets survive.

Carmina Burana a 13th-c. collection of Latin poems and other material, of Bavarian origin. Some of the poems have been provided with music, but the notation is in neumes which cannot be read except by comparing them with other MSS.

A setting of the poems by Carl Orff for chorus, orchestra and soloists (1937), fp 8 Jun 1937, Frankfurt. See also ◊Catulli Carmina and ◊Trionfo di Afrodite.

Carmirelli, Pina (b Varzi, 23 Jan 1914; d Carpena, 27 Feb 1993), Italian violinist and teacher. Studied in Milan and in Rome, where she later taught. Gave concerts from 1937 and founded the Boccherini Quintet 1949 and the Carmirelli Quartet 1954; many performances of Boccherini, and made an edition of his works. Joined pianist Sergio Lorenzi in duo and played the Beethoven sonatas with Rudolf Serkin in NY, 1970.

Carnaval, *Carnival*, suite of piano pieces on the notes A S (German Es = E♭; also As = A♭) C H (German = B♮) by Schumann, op. 9, the letters representing the only musical ones in Schumann's surname and the town of Asch in Bohemia, the home of Ernestine von Fricken, with whom he was in love in 1834–35, when he wrote the work. She is alluded to in the piece entitled *Estrella*; other persons referred to are Clara Wieck in *Chiarina*, Chopin and Paganini under their own

——— THE OPERA ———
Carmen

A four-act opera by Georges Bizet set in Seville in about 1820. First produced in Paris in 1875, the opera was initially slated by most critics.

I. Micaela (soprano) comes in search of corporal Don José (tenor). He is provocatively thrown a flower by Carmen (mezzo-soprano), the most flirtatious of the girl workers leaving a cigarette factory after work. Carmen is arrested after wounding another girl in a fight, but Don José, already infatuated, allows her to escape.

II. Carmen dances with Frasquita (soprano) and Mercedes (soprano) at the inn of Lillas Pastia. Carmen and the bullfighter Escamillo (baritone) are attracted to each other but Carmen waits for Don José (who has been released from a short prison sentence), and then encourages him to desert. When Don José threatens his captain Zuniga (bass), who has come to court Carmen, he is obliged to desert and join Carmen and her gypsy band of smugglers.

III. Tiring of Don José, Carmen scorns him but still helps to break up a fight between him and Escamillo. Micaela then brings news to Don José of his dying mother, and he leaves with her.

IV. Carmen and Don José meet outside the bull ring in Seville. When she refuses to return to him he stabs her, and she dies as the crowd in the ring acclaim their hero Escamillo.

——— THE OPERA ———

names, and Schumann himself in his two different imaginary characters of *Florestan* and *Eusebius*.

Ballet on Schumann's music, orchestrated by Glazunov and others (choreographed by Fokin), produced Paris, Opéra, 4 Jun 1910.

Carnaval des animaux, Le, *The Carnival of the Animals*, suite ('grand zoological fantasy') by Saint-Saëns for chamber orchestra with two pianos, privately performed and not intended by the composer to be published. It contains a number of humorous musical allusions.

Carnaval romain, Le, *The Roman Carnival*, concert overture by Berlioz, op. 9, written in 1843 on material from the opera *Benvenuto Cellini* of 1834–38, fp Paris, 3 Feb 1844.

Carnegie Hall New York's principal concert hall, built 1891 and endowed by Andrew Carnegie (1835–1919). Home to leading orchestras until 1962 and after opening of Lincoln Center threatened with demolition. Refurbished 1986 and again thriving.

Carner, Mosco (b Vienna, 15 Nov 1904; d Stratton, near Bude, Cornwall, 3 Aug 1985), English critic and writer of Austrian origin. Studied at the New Vienna Conservatory and musicology at the university under Adler, taking a Ph.D. degree there in 1928. He then became opera conductor in Vienna, Troppau and Danzig until 1933, when he settled in London, later becoming naturalized. He worked as critic and music correspondent to foreign journals and pub. books, including *A Study of 20th-c. Harmony*, *Of Men and Music*, *Puccini, a Critical Biography*, *Alban Berg*, chapters on Schubert, Dvořák, etc.

Carnicer, Ramón (b Tárrega, near Lérida, 24 Oct 1789; d Madrid, 17 Mar 1855), Spanish composer. Choirboy at Urgel Cathedral, later went to Barcelona and in 1808 fled to Minorca when Spain was invaded by France. Later managed the Italian opera at Barcelona and wrote Italian works for it, into which he introduced Spanish songs. In 1827 he was called by royal command to directed the opera at Madrid.

Works include operas *Adele di Lusignano* (1819), *Elena e Constantino*, *Don Giovanni Tenorio, ossia Il convitato di pietra* (1822), *Elena e Malvina*, *Cristoforo Colombo* (1831), *Eufemio di Messina*, *Ismalia* (1838); *Missa solemnis*, two Requiems; symphonies.

Carnival (1) Concert overture by Dvořák, op. 92, composed 1891 and forming, with *Amid Nature* and *Othello*, a cycle with thematic connections originally called *Nature, Life and Love*.

(2) Suite by Schumann, ◊Carnaval.

carol originally a round dance from France (*carole*), in which the participants sang a burden (formally a separate refrain) while dancing in a circle, alternating with stanzas sung by the leader while they remained still. In 15th-c. England it lost its original dance associations and became a polyphonic form, still characterized by the alternation of stanzas and burden, but frequently with a sacred text. It was only after the Reformation that the word lost its specifically formal connotation and became primarily a Christmas song, though even today common usage admits the possibility of secular carols and carols celebrating seasons other than Christmas.

Caron, Firminius (*fl.* 1450–80), ? Flemish composer, much praised by writers of the time. Five Masses and nearly 20 *chansons* survive. He may have had some connection with the Burgundian court, although it has proved impossible to identify him firmly with any surviving documentation.

Caron (born *Meuniez*), Rosa-Lucile (b Monerville, Seine-et-Oise, 17 Nov 1857; d Paris, 9 Apr 1930), French soprano. Studied at the Paris Conservatory where she became professor of singing in 1902. Made her first stage appearance at Brussels in 1884 as Alice in *Robert le Diable*. Other roles included Sieglinde, Desdemona, Leonore and Reyer's *Salammbô*, which she created (1890).

Caroso, Fabritio (b c 1530; d after 1605), Italian dancing master. Wrote two important treatises on dancing, *Il Ballarino* (1581) and *Nobiltà di Dame* (1600), both of which contain much music.

Caroubel, Pierre-Francisque (b Cremona; d Paris, summer 1611), French violinist and composer in the service of Henri III of Anjou from 1576. He wrote and harmonized numerous dance-tunes, including 78 from *Terpsichore musarum* by Michael Praetorius (1612).

Carpani, Giuseppe (Antonio) (b Villalbese near Como, 28 Jan 1752; d Vienna, 22 Jan 1825), Italian poet and writer on music. Settled in Vienna. Friend and biographer of Haydn. His book on the composer was plagiarized by Stendhal.

Carpenter, John Alden (b Park Ridge, Ill., 28 Feb 1876; d Chicago, 26 Apr 1951), American composer. Learnt music privately and studied with Paine while a student at Harvard University, and (briefly) with Elgar in Rome in 1906, later at Chicago with Bernhard Ziehn. Although a businessman, he composed much in a varied style. *Skyscrapers* features red traffic lights operated by a keyboard.

Works include ballets *Krazy-Kat* (produced 1921), *Skyscrapers* and *The Birthday of the Infanta* (after Wilde, 1919); *Song of Faith* for chorus and orchestra; symphonies, *Adventures in a Perambulator* (1915) and *Sea Drift* (after Whitman) for orchestra; concertino for piano and orchestra, violin concerto; string quartet (1927), piano quintet; many songs including *Gitanjali* cycle (Tagore).

Carr, Benjamin (b London, 12 Sept 1768; d Philadelphia, 24 May 1831), American composer and publisher. He wrote the first extant US opera. Arriving in Philadelphia in 1793, he founded a music publishing business there, becoming known as the Father of Philadelphia Music. He was co-founder of the Musical Fund Society in 1820; active also in NY and Baltimore as a publisher, concert promoter and organist. He was the first to publish *Yankee Doodle* in America and his ballad opera *The Archers, or Mountaineers of Switzerland* (NY, 1796) is the first US opera of which music parts survive.

Carré work by Stockhausen for four orchestras, four choruses, with four conductors, fp Hamburg, 28 Oct 1960.

Carré (born *Marthe Giraud*), Marguerite (b Cauborg, 16 Aug 1880; d Paris, 26 Dec 1947), French soprano. She sang at Nantes in 1899 and from 1902 appeared at the Paris Opéra-Comique. She created roles in operas by Charpentier, Leroux and Rabaud and was successful as Pamina, Butterfly, Manon and Mélisande but was alleged by the press to owe her career to her husband, Albert Carré, the director of the Opéra-Comique. They were divorced in 1924 but remarried on her retirement.

Carré, Michel (b Paris, 1819; d Argenteuil, 27 Jun 1872), French librettist. Collaborated with Jules Barbier (1822–1901) in texts for most French opera composers of their time; Shakespeare, Goethe, Molière and Corneille were raided to provide material to suit the bourgeois tastes of contemporary audiences. ◊Contes d'Hoffmann

Carreras *The tenor José Carreras is one of the most popular lyric tenors of his generation. The sweet tone of his voice is best suited to the lighter roles across his diverse repertory, ranging from Verdi to Bernstein's* West Side Story. *He made a courageous return after battling against leukaemia.*

(Offenbach), ◊Françoise de Rimini, ◊Hamlet and ◊Mignon (Thomas), ◊Médecin malgré lui, ◊Mireille, ◊Reine de Saba and ◊Roméo et Juliette (Gounod), ◊Pardon de Ploëmerl (Meyerbeer), ◊Pêcheurs de Perles (Bizet).

Carreras, José (b Barcelona, 5 Dec 1946), Spanish tenor. Early roles included Verdi's Ismaele and Donizetti's Gennaro; London debut (concert) 1971 as Leicester in *Maria Stuarda*. NY debut with the City Opera as Pinkerton in 1972; Met. as Cavaradossi, 1974. CG since 1974 as Alfredo, Nemorino and Oronte in *I Lombardi*; in 1984 he sang Andrea Chénier there. Returned after illness 1987 and sang Verdi's Stiffelio at CG, 1993.

Carrillo, Julián (b San Luis Potosí, 28 Jan 1875; d Mexico City, 9 Sept 1965), Mexican composer. Studied at the National Conservatory at Mexico City, gained a violin prize and made further studies at Leipzig and Ghent Conservatories. Returning to Mexico in 1905, he was active as a violinist and conductor as well as composer. He experimented in his later works with music using small fractional divisions of the scale.

Works include operas *Ossian* (1902), *Mexico in 1810* (1909) and *Xulitl* (1920, revised 1947); two Masses, Requiem; six symphonies, (1901–48), three suites, overture *8 de Septiembre*, symphonic poem *Xochimilco* for orchestra; fantasy for piano and orchestra, concerto for flute, violin and cello; four string quartets, piano quintet, string sextet; four violin and piano sonatas; 40 works in fractional scales, including *Ave Maria* for chorus, *Fantasía Sonido 13* for chamber orchestra, *Preludio a Cristobál Colón* for soprano and ensemble.

Carron, Arthur (b Swindon, 12 Dec 1900; d Swindon, 10 May 1967), English tenor. Debut London, 1929; sang with SW until 1935 as Tannhäuser, Manrico and Otello. NY Met. 1936–46, as Siegmund, Tristan and Canio. He had appeared at CG in the 1930s and returned 1946–52. Sang widely as guest in N and S America.

Carrosse du Saint-Sacrement, Le, *The Coach of the Holy Sacrament*, opera by Lord Berners (libretto from Mérimée's play), produced Paris, Théâtre des Champs-Élysées, 24 Apr 1924. Viceroy of Peru lends his mistress his new carriage.

Carse, Adam (b Newcastle upon Tyne, 19 May 1878; d Gt Missenden, 2 Nov 1958), English music scholar and composer. Studied in Germany and at the RAM. Assistant music master at Winchester College, 1909–22 and professor at the RAM from 1923. He made a special study of instruments and the orchestra, and left a collection of early wind instruments to the Horniman Museum.

Carter, Charles Thomas (b Dublin, *c* 1735; d London, 12 Oct 1804), Irish composer. Choirboy at Christ Church Cathedral, Dublin, and organist at St Werburgh's Church there, 1751–69. He became very popular as a song-writer and settled in London in 1770. Produced a comic opera, *Just in Time*, in 1792 and wrote lighter stage pieces, etc.

Carter, Elliott (b New York, 11 Dec 1908), American composer. Educated at Harvard University, where he studied music with Piston; later a pupil of Nadia Boulanger in Paris. From 1960 to 1962 he was professor of composition at Yale University and in 1960 was awarded the Pulitzer Prize. Teacher at Juilliard from 1972. His music is many-layered and of extreme rhythmic complexity, sometimes recalling Charles Ives, with cross-rhythms and different rhythms played simultaneously. His concept of metrical modulation allows different instruments or groups to remain synchronized while playing at changing speeds (String quartet no.1, Double Concerto). Featured composer, Warsaw Autumn Festival 1986.

Works include STAGE: opera *Tom and Lily* (1934), ballets *Pocahontas* (1939) and *The Minotaur* (1947).

ORCHESTRAL: horn concerto (1937), *Prelude, Fanfare and Polka* (1938), symphony no. 1 (1942, fp 1944), *Holiday Overture* (1944, fp 1948), *Variations* (1953–55, fp 1956), *Double Concerto* for piano, harpsichord and two chamber orchestras (1961), piano concerto (1965, fp 1967), *Concerto for Orchestra* (1969, fp 1970), *A Symphony of Three Orchestras* (1976, fp 1977), *Penthode* for chamber orchestra (1985), *Fanfare* (1986), *Three Occasions* (1986–89), oboe concerto (1987), violin concerto (1990), *Partita* (1993), *Gra* (1993), *Adagio Tenebroso* (1995).

CHORAL: *Tarantella* (1936), *To Music* (1937), *Heart not so Heavy as Mine* (1938), *The Defence of Corinth* (1941), *The Harmony of Morning* (1944), *Musicians Wrestle Everywhere* (1945), *Emblems* (1947).

SOLO VOCAL: *Warble for Lilac Time* for soprano and instruments (after Whitman, 1943, fp 1946), *A Mirror on Which to Dwell* for

A Selection of

Elliott Carter

String Quartet no. 1	1951
Variations for orchestra	1953–5
String Quartet no. 2	1959
Piano Concerto	1965

Concerto for Orchestra	1969
String Quartet no. 3	1971
Brass Quintet	1974
String Quartet no. 4	1986
Three Occasions	1986–9
Violin Concerto	1990

soprano and nine players (six settings of Elizabeth Bishop, 1975), *Syringa*, cantata for mezzo, bass and 11 instruments (1978), *In Sleep, in Thunder*, song cycle for tenor and 14 players (texts by Robert Lowell, 1981), *Of Challenge and of Love*, song cycle for soprano and piano (1995).

INSTRUMENTAL: flute sonata (1934), *Canonic Suite* for four saxophones (1939, revised for four clarinets 1956), *Pastorale* for ensemble (1940), piano sonata (1946), woodwind quintet (1948), cello sonata (1948), *Eight Etudes and a Fantasy* for woodwind quintet (1950), five string quartets (1951, 1959, 1971, 1986, 1995), sonata for, flute, oboe, cello and harpsichord (1952), duo for violin and piano (1974), brass quintet (1974), *Night Fantasies* for piano (1980), *Triple Duo* for paired instruments: flute/clarinet, violin/cello, piano/percussion (1982), *Changes* for guitar (1983), *Esprit rude/Esprit doux* for flute and clarinet (60th birthday tribute to Pierre Boulez, 1985), *Enchanted Preludes* for flute and cello (1988), *Con leggerezza pensosa* for clarinet, violin and cello (1990), quintet for piano and wind (1992), *Trilogy* for oboe and harp (1992).

Cartier, Antoine (*fl.* Paris, 1552–88), French composer, organist of Saint-Séverin, Paris, 1570–88. His surviving works consist entirely of *chansons* for three and four voices.

Cartier, Jean-Baptiste (b Avignon, 28 May 1765; d Paris, 1841), French violinist and composer. Pupil of Viotti; held posts at court before and after the Revolution, during which he played in the Opéra orchestra. Composed two operas, two symphonies, violin music and other works.

Caruso, Enrico (b Naples, 27 Feb 1873; d Naples, 2 Aug 1921), Italian tenor. Made his debut at Naples in 1894 and began to become famous when he sang in the production of Giordano's *Fedora* at Milan in 1898. He first sang in London, with Melba, in 1902 as the Duke of Mantua, and at the NY Met. from 1903 until 1920; sang Johnson in fp of *La Fanciulla del West*, NY Met, 1910. He appeared at the Met. more than 600 times; among his most popular roles in NY were Radames, Canio, Enzo, Rodolfo, Cavaradossi, Samson, Don José, Faust and Pinkerton. Through his many recordings became one of the most highly-paid opera singers of all time.

Caruso, Luigi (b Naples, 25 Sept 1754; d Perugia, 1822), Italian composer. Pupil of Sala at Naples. *Maestro di cappella* at Perugia Cathedral from 1790.

Works include more than 60 operas, Masses, oratorios, cantatas, etc.

Carvalho, João de Sousa (b Estremoz, 22 Feb 1745; d Alentejo, 1798), Portuguese composer. Studied at Naples; taught at Lisbon on his return.

Works include 15 Italian operas, e.g. *Perseo* (1779), *Testoride Argonauta* (1780), *Penelope* (1782), *L'Endimione* (1783); Masses and other church music with orchestra; harpsichord sonatas.

Carvalho, Marie (Caroline Félix Miolan-) (b Marseilles, 31 Dec 1827; d Puys, 10 Jul 1895), French soprano. Studied under her father and at the Paris Conservatory; debut in 1849 as Lucia di Lammermoor and was engaged by the Opéra-Comique in 1850. At the Théâtre-Lyrique she created Gounod's Marguerite, Baucis, Juliette (aged 40 and weighing 170 lbs) and Mireille. She married in 1853 Léon Carvalho (1825–97), who later became manager of that theatre.

Carver, Robert (b *c* 1490; d after 1546), Scottish monk and composer. Canon of Scone Abbey. He was influenced by such major Flemish contemporaries as Josquin and Heinrich Isaac.

Works include Masses (one in ten parts), motets (one in 19 parts) and other church music.

Cary, Annie Louise (b Wayne, ME, 22 Oct 1841; d Norwalk, CT, 3 Apr

Caruso *The tenor Enrico Caruso (1873–1921). After overcoming difficulties with his technique (caused by a lack of training), Caruso became the greatest tenor of his day, arguably of the century. His fame has endured through his numerous early recordings.*

1921), American contralto. Studied at Milan and later with Pauline Viardot. Made her debut in Copenhagen, 1869, as Azucena. Made her first appearance in London (CG 1870) as Maffio Orsini in *Lucrezia Borgia*. She was the first US Amneris, 1873, and sang Ortrud there in 1877.

Cary, Tristram (Ogilvie) (b Oxford, 14 May 1925), English composer. He has been a pioneer in the performance of electronic music in Britain and has experimented with the concept of environmental sound; he founded his own electronic studio and was an influential teacher at the RCM. Dean at Adelaide University from 1982. Works include the cantata *Peccata mundi* (Cheltenham, 1972) and stage and film music.

Caryll, Ivan (actually Felix Tilkin) (b Liège, 12 May 1861; d New York, 29 Nov 1921), Belgian-American composer. Studied at the Liège Conservatory.

Works include operettas *The Duchess of Dantzic* (1903), *The Earl and the Girl*, *Our Miss Gibbs*.

Casadesus, Jean-Claude (b Paris, 7 Dec 1935), French conductor. Studied with Boulez and Pierre Dervaux and was conductor at the Paris Opéra 1969–71; Lille National Orchestra from 1976 (*Revolution Revisited* series at South Bank, London, 1989). Conducted the Philharmonia in the World Piano Competition, London 1994.

Casadesus, Robert (Marcel) (b Paris, 7 Apr 1899; d Paris, 19 Sept 1972), French pianist and composer. As a boy he showed precocious ability. He studied at the Paris Conservatory, where he won prizes in 1913, 1919, 1921. He began his career as a concert pianist in 1922, and on the outbreak of World War II went to the USA, where he taught and lectured at Princeton University. From 1935 he was professor at the American Conservatory at Fontainebleau, of which he became director in 1945. He composed much for the piano, and was also a noted exponent of French piano music. He was often heard in Mozart's concertos. His uncles Henri (1879–1947) and Marius (1892–1981) issued faked 'classical' compositions, notably the *Adelaide* concerto, still sometimes accepted as Mozart's.

Casali, Giovanni Battista (b Rome, *c* 1715; d Rome, 6 Jul 1792), Italian composer. *Maestro di cappella* of St John Lateran, 1759–92. Wrote

Accademia di Santa Cecilia. In 1924 he founded, with d'Annunzio and Malipiero, an association for the propagation of modern Italian music. His own work moved from the influence of Debussy and Mahler through atonality and towards neo-classicism.

Works include operas *La donna serpente* (after Gozzi, 1928–31), *La favola d'Orfeo* (1932), *Il deserto tentato*; ballets *Il convento veneziano* and *La giara* (after Pirandello); three symphonies, suite *Italia, Elegia eroica, Pagine di guerra, Introduzione, aria e toccata* (1933), *concerto* for orchestra; *A notte alta, Partita* and *Scarlattiana* for piano and orchestra; concerto for violin, cello, organ and orchestra; *Notte di maggio* for voice and orchestra (1914); concerto and five pieces for string quartet and other chamber music; cello and piano sonata; many piano works including sonatina and *Sinfonia, arioso e toccata*; two suites for piano duet; numerous songs.

Caserta, Anthonello (Marotus) da (b ? Caserta, *c* 1365; d ? Naples, after 1410), Italian composer. His works include eight French songs, several in the most complex three-voice style of the Ars Subtilior, and eight simpler Italian songs, mostly in two voices.

Caserta, Philipottus da (b ? Caserta, *c* 1350; d after 1390), Italian composer and theorist. Composed works for the Papal Court of Clement VII (1378–94) and for the Milanese court of Bernabò Visconti (1354–85) and probably taught Ciconia. Works include one Credo, six French ballades (several in the most complex Ars Subtilior style), three treatises on music.

Casken, John (b Barnsley, 15 Jul 1949), English composer. He studied at Birmingham University with John Joubert and Peter Dickinson. His work has been influenced by Polish music and serialism; lecturer, Durham University from 1981. Featured composer at Bath Festival 1980.

Works include opera *Golem* (1990); piano concerto (1980), *Masque* for oboe, two horns and strings (1982); *Erin* for double bass and small orchestra (1983), *Orion over Farne* (1984), *Maharal Dreaming* (1989), cello concerto (1991), *Darting the Skiff* for strings (1993); *Kagura* for 13 wind instruments (1973), *Amarantos* for nine players (1978), *Fonteyn Fanfares* for 12 brass instruments; string quartet (1982); *Ligatura* for organ; *Clarion Sea* for brass quintet (1985), piano quintet (1990).

Cassadó, Gaspar (b Barcelona, 30 Sept 1897; d Madrid, 24 Dec 1966), Spanish cellist, son of the composer Joaquín Cassadó. He made his first public appearance aged nine, and later studied with, among others, Casals. He joined Menuhin and Kentner in piano trios. He was also a composer, mostly for strings and piano.

Cassandra opera by Gnecchi (libretto by L Illica), produced Bologna, Teatro Comunale, 5 Dec 1905. In 1909 the Italian critic Giovanni Tebaldini created a sensation by pointing out that Strauss's *Elektra*, which did not appear until that year, contained passages strikingly resembling Gnecchi's music.

Casals *The cellist Pablo Casals (1876–1973) was one of the greatest musicians of his instrument this century. He favoured simplicity over tasteless virtuosity and constantly strove for artistic truth. He was also an influential pedagogue and an accomplished pianist.*

much church music; also operas, e.g. *Candaspe* and *Antigona*; oratorios, e.g. *Santa Firmina, La Benedizione di Giacobb.*

Casals, Pablo (Pau) (b Vendrell, 29 Dec 1876; d Rio Piedras, Puerto Rico, 22 Oct 1973), Catalan cellist, conductor and composer. He studied at the Madrid Conservatory and first appeared as a soloist in Paris 1898. In 1905 he joined the piano trio founded by Cortot and recorded the major trios of Schubert, Beethoven and Mendelssohn. In the early years of the century he did much to establish the solo suites of Bach in the cellist's repertory. In 1919 he founded the Orquestra Pau Casals in Barcelona. He formed a liaison with one of his pupils, the cellist Guilhermina Suggia, and toured with her. After the Spanish Civil War he left Catalonia and made his home at Prades, in the Pyrenees, where he held an annual festival from 1950. He settled in Puerto Rico in 1956.

Works include oratorio *El Pessebre* (1943–60); church music; orchestral works; works for cello and piano, violin and piano.

Casanova, André (b Paris, 12 Oct 1919), French composer. Studied the 12-note technique with Leibowitz. Works include trio for flute, viola and horn, piano pieces, songs.

Case, Anna (b Clinton, NJ, 29 Oct 1888; d New York, 7 Jan 1984), American soprano. NY Met. from 1909 as Aida and Carmen; Feodor and Sophie in the first US performance of *Boris Godunov* and *Rosenkavalier* (both 1913).

Casella, Alfredo (b Turin, 25 Jul 1883; d Rome, 5 Mar 1947), Italian composer. Was sent to the Paris Conservatory in 1896 to study piano under Diémer and composition under Fauré. He lived there until the 1914–18 war, when he went to Rome and taught piano at the

The cello is like a beautiful woman who has not grown older, but younger with time, more slender, more supple, more graceful.

Pablo Casals, in *Time*, 1957

cassation an 18th-c. term, similar to divertimento and serenade, for a work in several movements suitable for open-air performance. The origin of the word is uncertain.

Casse-Noisette (Tchaikovsky) ♭Nutcracker.

Cassilly, Richard (b WA, DC, 14 Dec 1927), American tenor. He sang on Broadway in Menotti's *The Saint of Bleecker Street* before his NY, City Opera, debut as Tchaikovsky's Vakula; Chicago 1959 as Laca, which he repeated on his CG debut in 1968. Other roles there were Florestan, Tannhäuser, Siegmund and Otello. Vienna, Munich and La Scala debuts 1970; NY Met. 1973 as Radames. In 1974 he sang Aaron in a London concert performance of Schoenberg's *Moses und Aron*. Sang Tannhäuser at Chicago, 1988.

Cassiodorus, Flavius Magnus Aurelius (b *c* 487; d *c* 580), Roman senator, ecclesiastical historian and theologian. He wrote no specifically musical work, but the music theory contained in his *Institutiones* (*c* 560), deriving largely from Aristoxenus, caused him to be regarded, with Boethius and Isidore of Seville, as one of the three founders of medieval music theory.

Castagna, Bruna (b Bari, 15 Oct 1905; d Pinamar, Argentina, 10 Jul 1983), Italian contralto. Debut Mantua, 1925; sang at La Scala 1925–34, under Serafin and Toscanini, as Isabella, Adalgisa and Laura. NY Met. 1936–45 (debut as Amneris). Well known as Carmen in Australia, Chicago and Spain.

castanets, from Spanish *castañetas*, a percussion instrument, doubtless originally made of chestnut wood (*castaña*), held between the fingers and made to strike against each other by motions of the hand. So used mainly by Spanish dancers, but a simplified form is made for use in orchestras and bands.

Castelmary, Armand (b Toulouse, 16 Aug 1834; d New York, 10 Feb 1897), French bass. He sang at the Paris Opéra from 1863 and took part in the fps. of *L'Africaine* and *Don Carlos*. CG 1889–96. NY Met. debut 1893, as Vulcan in Gounod's *Philémon*. Often heard as Méphistophélès. As Sir Tristan he died on stage at the Met. at the end of the first act of *Martha*. He was married to Marie Sass (Elisabeth in the fp of *Don Carlos*).

Castelnuovo-Tedesco, Mario (b Florence, 3 Apr 1895; d Hollywood, 16 Mar 1969), Italian composer. Studied at the Istituto Musicale Cherubini at Florence and later with Pizzetti. At the age of 15 he wrote *Cielo di settembre* for piano (later orchestra) and in 1925 he gained a prize for his opera *La Mandragola* (after Machiavelli). He settled in USA in 1939, at first at Larchmont, NY, and then at LA.

Works include OPERAS *La Mandragola* (1926), *Bacco in Toscana*, *Aucassin et Nicolette* (1938), *The Merchant of Venice*, *All's Well that Ends Well* (both after Shakespeare, 1959, 1961), *The Importance of being Earnest* (after Wilde, 1962).

ORCHESTRAL: seven Shakespearian concert overtures, *The Taming of the Shrew*, *The Merchant of Venice*, *Twelfth Night*, *Julius Caesar*, *A Winter's Tale*, *A Midsummer Night's Dream*, *King John*; two piano concertos (1928, 1939), *Concerto italiano*, symphonic variations and *The Prophets* for violin and orchestra, concerto for cello and orchestra, concerto for guitar and orchestra.

CHAMBER AND INSTRUMENTAL: concertino for harp and seven instruments; three string quartets (1929, 1948, 1964); piano trio; *Sonata quasi una fantasia* and suite on themes by Donizetti for violin and piano, cello and piano sonata; six illustrations for Voltaire's *Candide* and other piano pieces.

VOCAL: settings of all the songs in Shakespeare's plays (in English) for voice and piano, *Sonnets from the Portuguese* (Elizabeth Barrett Browning) and other songs.

Castiglioni, Niccolo (b Milan, 17 Jul 1932), Italian composer and pianist. Studied with Ghedini at the Milan Conservatory. He has also pursued a career as a concert pianist. His music is eclectic in style, influenced by Debussy, Messiaen, Webern and Cage, and remarkable for its frequently delicate textures.

Works include *Impromptus I–IV* for orchestra; *Rondels* for orchestra; *Movimento continuato* for piano and small ensemble (1959), *Gymel* for flute and piano; *Inizio di movimento* for piano; *A Solemn Music I* for soprano and chamber orchestra (after Milton, 1963); *Sinfonia* (1969).

Castil-Blaze, François Henri Joseph Blaze (b Cavaillon, 1 Dec 1784; d Paris, 11 Dec 1857), French critic, composer, translator of opera libretti and author of books on music. Critic of the *Journal des Débats* before Berlioz. He produced operas by Mozart, Weber and Rossini, in his own French versions, in the 1820s.

Works include three operas, church music and chamber music.

Castileti, Johann (Jean Guyot) (b Châtelet, near Liège, 1512; d Liège, 11 Mar 1588), Flemish composer. He wrote Masses, motets and *chansons*, and added a further six voices to Josquin's six-part motet *Benedicta es caelorum regina*.

Castillo, Bernardo Clavijo del (b *c* 1549; d Madrid, 1 Feb 1626),

Spanish organist and composer. Wrote motets and organ music.

Castore e Polluce, *Castor and Pollux*, opera by Vogler (libretto based on one by C I Frugoni), produced Munich, 12 Jan 1787. Weber wrote variations for piano on an air from it, op. 5.

Castor et Pollux opera by Rameau (libretto by P J J Bernard), produced Paris, Opéra, 24 Oct 1737; revised version produced Jun 1754. Based on the Greek myth; Pollux to the rescue of twin brother Castor, with help from Jupiter.

castrati, Italian, male singers of the 17th and 18th c., mainly but not exclusively in Italy, who were castrated in boyhood to prevent the breaking of their voices and to supply male sopranos and contraltos to the churches and theatres of the time. They made their greatest and most sensational successes on the operatic stage. The last famous castrato was Velluti (1780–1861).

Castro, Jean de (b Liège, *c* 1540; d 1600), South Netherlands composer of Portuguese descent. Worked at Antwerp, Vienna, Cologne, etc. Wrote Masses, motets, madrigals, *chansons*.

Castro, Juan (José) (b Avellaneda, Buenos Aires, 7 Mar 1895; d Buenos Aires, 5 Sept 1968), Argentine conductor and composer. Studied in Buenos Aires and with d'Indy in Paris. On his return he formed a quintet with himself as violinist and his brother as cellist, and in 1928 a chamber orchestra. In 1930–43 he was conductor at the Teatro Colón.

Works include opera, *Prosperina y el extranjero* (produced La Scala, 1952); ballet *Mekhano*; three symphonies, *Sinfonia Argentina* and *Sinfonia Biblica*, symphonic poems *Dans le Jardin des morts*, *A una madre* and *La Chellah*, etc. for orchestra; *Suite brève* for chamber orchestra; piano concerto; songs.

Castrucci, Pietro (b Rome, 1679; d Dublin, 29 Feb 1752), Italian violinist, conductor and composer, brother of Prospero ◊Castrucci. Studied with Corelli in Rome and went to England with Lord Burlington 1715. He became leader in Handel's opera orchestra, but was replaced by Festing in 1737. In 1750 he settled in Dublin. He played an instrument of his own invention, the ◊violetta marina, in Handel's *Orlando*.

Works include 12 *Concerti grossi* and three books of violin sonatas.

Castrucci, Prospero (Rome–? London, 1760), Italian violinist, brother of Pietro ◊Castrucci. Probably also studied with Corelli and went to England with his brother or later. He is supposedly the original of Hogarth's 'Enraged Musician'. In 1739 he pub. six violin sonatas.

Catalani, Alfredo (b Lucca, 19 Jun 1854; d Milan, 7 Aug 1893), Italian composer. Studied first with his father, an organist, and produced a Mass at the age of 14. Went to the Paris Conservatory 1871 and then taught at the Milan Conservatory.

Works include operas *La Falce* (1875), *Elda* (1880), *Dejanice* (1883), *Edmea*, *Loreley* (1890) and *La Wally* (1892); Mass; symphonic poem *Ero e Leandro*, etc.

---

*The voice, to be sure, is neither man's or woman's;
but it is more melodious than either, and it warbled so
divinely, that, while I listened, I really thought myself
in paradise.*

Tobias Smollett, about castrati in
Humphrey Clinker, 1771

Catalani, Angelica (b Sinigaglia, 10 May 1780; d Paris, 12 Jun 1849), Italian soprano. First appearance, Teatro La Fenice, Venice, 1795, in Mayr's *Lodoìska*. Went to Portugal 1804, to London 1806 and sang until 1813 in operas by Portugal, Nasolini, Paisiello and Piccinni. She was the first London Susanna (1812). Was manager of the Italian Opera in Paris, 1814–17, after which she resumed her career as a singer.

Catalogue d'oiseaux piano work by Messiaen in seven books based on his notations of birdsong, composed 1956–58, fp Paris, 15 Apr 1959.

catch a part-song, in vogue in England from the early 17th to the 19th c., in which the voices follow each other in the manner of a canon or round, with the difference in the most characteristic examples that the words, thus mixed up, acquire new and ludicrous meanings, often of an indecent nature in the 17th c.

Catch Club a society named The Noblemen and Gentlemen's Catch Club, founded in London in 1761 for sociable gatherings and the singing of catches.

Catel, Charles Simon (b L'Aigle, Orne, 10 Jun 1773; d Paris, 29 Nov 1830), French composer. Pupil of Sacchini and Gossec in Paris. After working as teacher, he became chief musician with Gossec of the Garde Nationale, for which he wrote much military music, and accompanist at the Opéra in 1790. Appointed professor of harmony at the Conservatory on its foundation in 1795, and pub. a treatise on the subject in 1802.

Works include operas *Sémiramis* (1802), *L'Auberge de Bagnières* (1807), *Les Bayadères* (1810), *Wallace, ou le ménestral ecossais* (1817) etc.; *De Profundis*, *Hymn of Victory*; symphony for wind instruments; choral pieces; chamber music; songs.

Caterina Cornaro opera by Donizetti (libretto by G Sacchero), produced Naples, Teatro San Carlo, 12 Jan 1844; revived in 1972 with a concert performance in London and a production in Naples. Venetian Caterina loves Gerardo but has been sworn to Lusignano, King of Cyprus. The competing wooers are reconciled when Lusignano saves Gerardo's life.

catgut strings a term used to distinguish such strings from those made of metal or artificial material. Although still often so called, such strings are not made of the bowels of cats but of sheep.

What can be more strange than that the rubbing of a little Hair and Cat-gut together, shou'd make such a mighty alteration in a Man that sits at a distance?
Jeremy Collier, *An Essay of Musick*, 1702

---

catline, also catling, catlin, catleen, in the 16th c., a kind of roped and polished gut string, particularly for low pitches on viols and lutes; by the late 18th c. it could refer to any high gut string.

Catone in Utica opera by Vinci (libretto by Metastasio), produced Rome, Teatro delle Dame, 19 Jan 1728. Marcia, daughter of Cato (ruler of Utica) secretly loves Caesar, but Cato wants her to marry Arbace. When Caesar's armies overrun the Uticans and Cato commits suicide, Marcia is sworn to hatred against Caesar.

Also versions by Hasse (Turin, 1731), Vivaldi (Verona, 1737), J C Bach (Naples, 1761), and Paisiello, (Naples, 1789).

'Cat's Fugue, The' popular name for D Scarlatti's G minor harpsichord sonata (no. 30 in Kirkpatrick's list). Its bizarre subject has been taken to represent a cat picking its way along a keyboard. Experiment suggests that no cat would hit upon this particular succession of intervals.

Catterall, Arthur (b Preston, Lancs., 25 May 1883; d London, 28 Nov 1943), English violinist. Studied in Manchester, became a member of the Queen's Hall Orchestra in London in 1909, later of the Hallé Orchestra in Manchester and in 1929 of the BBC SO, which he left in 1936. He founded a string quartet in 1910.

Catulli Carmina scenic cantata by Orff (text from poems by Catullus), the second of three works together called *Trionfi* (other two are *Carmina Burana* and *Trionfo di Afrodite*), produced Leipzig, 6 Nov 1943.

Caturla, Alejandro García (b Remedios, 7 Mar 1906; d Remedios, 12 Nov 1940), Cuban composer. Studied at Havana and with Nadia Boulanger in Paris. He married a black woman and was much influenced by Afro-Cuban folk music. He was a lawyer, then later a judge, and was shot dead by a criminal.

Works include three *Danzas cubanas*, symphonic poem *Yamba-O*, *La Rumba* for orchestra; *Bembé* suite for 14 instruments, *Primera Suite cubana* for six wind instruments and piano, sonata and prelude for piano; songs.

Caurroy, (François) Eustache du Sieur de Saint-Frémin (b Gerberoy, near Beauvais, bap. 4 Feb 1549; d Paris, 7 Aug 1609), French composer. Went to Paris *c* 1569 as a singer in a royal chapel, where he became master of the children in 1583. He became a canon in the Sainte-Chapelle and the title of Surintendant de la Musique du Roy was created for him in 1599.

Works include Requiem, motets, psalms, noëls, two books of *Preces ecclesiasticae*; instrumental fantasies on sacred and secular tunes, etc.

Causton, Thomas (b *c* 1520; d London, 28 Oct 1569), English composer. Gentleman of the Chapel Royal in London. Wrote services, anthems, psalms, and contributed to Day's *Certaine Notes* and *Whole Psalmes*, 1563.

Cavaccio, Giovanni (b Bergamo, *c* 1556; d Bergamo, 11 Aug 1626), Italian composer. *Maestro di cappella* at Bergamo Cathedral in 1583 and later at the church of Santa Maria Maggiore there. Wrote a Requiem, Magnificats, psalms, madrigals, in the Venetian style, and contributed psalms to a collection dedicated to Palestrina.

Cavalieri, Catharina (b Währing near Vienna, 19 Feb 1760; d Vienna, 30 Jun 1801), Austrian soprano. Pupil and mistress of Salieri in Vienna, where she made her operatic debut in 1775 in Anfossi's *La finta giardiniera*. Mozart wrote for her the role of Constanze in *Die Entführung*, specially designing the virtuoso part, as he wrote to his father, for her 'flexible gullet'. She sang Donna Elvira in the first Viennese production of *Don Giovanni* (1788).

Cavalieri, Emilio de' (b Rome, *c* 1550; d Rome, 11 Mar 1602), Italian composer. He was long in the service of Ferdinando de' Medici at Florence. In 1589 he oversaw the production of a lavish series of *intermedi*, to celebrate the marriage of Ferdinando to Christine of Lorraine. He was in close touch with the *Camerata*, and with them worked towards the evolution of opera; in 1600 Cavalieri produced *Euridice*, text by Rinuccini, music by Caccini and Peri, the first opera of which the music is extant. His own works were still dramatic pieces to be performed in concert form. They include the following, all set to words by L Guidiccioni: *Il satiro*, *La disperazione di Fileno* and *Il giuoco della cieca* (all lost), and *La rappresentatione di Anima, et di Corpo*, an allegory produced 1600 and the first play set throughout to music.

Cavalieri, Lina (b Viterbo, 25 Dec 1874; d Florence, 7 Feb 1944), Italian soprano. Born of humble parents, she first sang in cafés, but later studied seriously and made her first appearance in opera at Lisbon in 1901 as Mimi. First visited England in 1908, when she sang Fedora, Manon Lescaut and Tosca, but her greatest successes were in USA. She was killed in an air raid, while attempting to retrieve the jewellery given to her by many titled admirers.

Cavalleria rusticana, *Rustic Chivalry*, opera by Mascagni (libretto by G Menasci and G Targioni-Tozzetti, based on G Verga's play), produced Rome, Teatro Costanzi, 17 May 1890. Turiddu loves Lola,

———— THE OPERA ————

Cavalleria Rusticana

A one-act opera by Pietro Mascagni. It had already won an opera competition when it was first produced in Rome in 1890. The dramatic action takes place at Easter time in a village in Sicily in 1880. Santuzza (soprano) is in despair because she is pregnant by Turiddu (tenor), who has deserted her for his former sweetheart, Lola (mezzo-soprano). Turiddu is deaf to Santuzza's pleas and she is driven to telling the drover Alfio (baritone), husband of Lola, of all that has happened. Alfio swears vengeance for his betrayal. An Intermezzo is played, with an empty stage, between scenes. As the villagers emerge from church, Alfio challenges Turiddu to a duel. Bidding farewell to his mother and entrusting Santuzza to her care, Turiddu runs off to fight; soon the shout goes up that he has been killed.

now married to Alfio. Former love Santuzza tells Alfio of the infidelity; Alfio challenges Turiddu to a duel and kills him.

Cavalli (originally Caletti-Bruni), (Pietro) Francesco (b Crema, 14 Feb 1602; d Venice, 14 Jan 1676), Italian composer. Became a singer under Monteverdi at St Mark's, Venice, in 1617, second organist of that church in 1640, first organist in 1665 and *maestro di cappella* in 1668. His first opera was produced 1639, and in 1660 he was called to Paris to perform his *Serse* at Louis XIV's marriage. He wrote operas for the five theatres of Venice. In recent years his operas have been heard in free adaptations by Raymond ◊Leppard and in more faithful renderings by conductors such as Jane Glover and René Jacobs.

Works include operas *Le nozze di Teti e di Peleo* (1639), *Gli amori di Apollo e di Dafne* (1640), *La Didone*, *L'Egisto* (1643), *Ormindo* (1644), *Calisto* (1651), *Eritrea* (1652), *Erismena* (1656), *Il Giasone*, *L'Oristeo*, *Serse*, *Il Ciro*, *L'Hipermestra*, *Ercole amante* (1662), *Scipione affricano*, *Mutio Scevola*, *Il Coriolano* and about 20 others; *Vespers of the Annunciation* (1675), *Messa concertata*, motets, psalms, antiphons, Requiem (1676).

Cazden, Norman (b New York, 23 Sept 1914; d Bangor, ME, 18 Aug 1980), American composer. Studied at Juilliard and with Walter Piston at Harvard. Worked as pianist with dance groups and collected folk music.

Works include *The Lonely Ones*, ballet (1944), symphony (1948), *Songs from the Catskills*, for band (1950), viola concerto (1972); wind quintet (1966) and other chamber music; songs.

Cazzati, Maurizio (b Guastalla, *c* 1620; d Mantua, 1677), Italian organist and composer. Held successive posts at Mantua, Ferrara, Bergamo and Bologna. Composed secular vocal and instrumental music as well as works for the church.

C clef the clef, derived from an ornamental letter C, which indicates that the line on which it is placed represents middle C. Only two C clefs are in use today: the alto, for the viola, and the tenor, for the tenor trombone and the upper register of the bassoon, cello and double bass.

Soprano   Mezzo-soprano   Alto   Tenor

All five C clefs were formerly used; the baritone F clef is often substituted for the last.

cavata Italian = lit. 'a thing carved or engraved' (e.g. an epitaph), in music, a short arioso following a recitative, especially in the early 18th c.

cavatina Italian possibly from *cavata* in the 18th c. a song in an opera less elaborate than an aria. Now normally used of a short, sustained piece or air.

Cavazzoni, Girolamo (b *c* 1525; d after 1577), Italian organist and composer. He was organist of the ducal church of Santa Barbara, Mantua, from 1565 until at least 1577. His two books of organ music (1543 and before 1549) contain *ricercari*, *chanson* arrangements (*canzoni*), hymns, Magnificats and Masses.

Cavazzoni, Marco Antonio (b Bologna, *c* 1490; d Venice, *c* 1560), Italian composer, father of Girolamo ◊Cavazzoni. The two *ricercari* from his *Recerchari*, *Motetti*, *Canzoni* for organ (Venice, 1523) are toccata-like pieces designed as preludes to the two motet arrangements; the *Canzoni* are arrangements of French *chansons* and the forerunners of the Italian instrumental *canzona*.

It was a pity I wrote Cavalleria *first: I was crowned before I was king.*

Pietro Mascagni, quoted in Carner,
Giacomo Puccini, 1974

Cavendish, Michael (b ? Cavendish Overhall, Suffolk, *c* 1565; d London, *c* 5 Jul 1628), English composer. Belonging to a noble family, he seems to have held no appointments. He contributed to East's *Whole Booke of Psalmes* in 1592 and pub. a volume of his own compositions, dedicated to Lady Arabella Stuart, his second cousin, in 1598, containing 20 airs to the lute, or with three other voices, and eight madrigals. He also contributed a madrigal to *The Triumphes of Oriana*.

Cavos, Catterino (b Venice, 1775; d St Petersburg, 10 May 1840), Italian composer. Assisted his father, who was conductor at the Teatro La Fenice, later conducted at Padua and taught at Venice. In 1800 he went to Russia with Astaritta's opera co., and in 1803 became director of the Italian and Russian operas there, for which he had to write works in both languages, as well as some in French. His Russian opera, *Ivan Susanin*, produced 1815, was very successful; conducted the premiere of Glinka's *A Life for the Tsar*, 1836.

cebell a dance occurring in English 17th-c. music, similar to the ◊gavotte.

Cebotari, Maria (b Kishinev, 10 Feb 1910; d Vienna, 9 Jun 1949), Russian-born Austrian soprano. Debut Dresden, 1931, Mimi; created Aminta in *Die schweigsame Frau* (1935) and visited CG with Dresden co. in 1936. She returned to London in 1947 with the Vienna Opera and on both occasions was heard in operas by Strauss and Mozart. Also active in Salzburg, she created roles in operas by ◊Sutermeister and ◊Einem. Best known as Donna Anna, Salome, Arabella and Susanna.

Ceccato, Aldo (b Milan, 18 Feb 1934), Italian conductor. Studied in Milan and made his debut there in 1964, with *Don Giovanni*. US debut with the Chicago Opera 1969 and was music director of the Detroit SO 1973–77. Led Rossini's *L'equivico stravagante* at the 1968 Wexford Festival, *Traviata* at CG 1970 and *Ariadne* at Glyndebourne, 1971. Posts with the Hamburg State PO 1975–83, Bergen SO from 1985. *Maria Stuarda* at Bergamo, 1989.

Cecilia, Saint the patron saint of music and the blind. A member of the early Christian church, she is said to have suffered martyrdom under Marcus Aurelius with her husband and other friends whom she had converted to Christianity, and to have praised God by vocal and instrumental music. Her festival is 22 Nov.

cédez French imperative = lit. 'cede, give, surrender' = 'hold back'; a direction used by Debussy and some other French composers to indicate a *ritenuto*.

celesta a keyboard instrument brought out by Mustel of Paris in the 1880s. The tone is produced by hammers struck upon steel plates.

Celestina, La opera by Pedrell (libretto based on an anonymous 15th–16th-c. Spanish dialogue novel, *La comedia de Calisto y Melibia*, sometimes attributed to Fernando de Rojas), not produced.

Celibidache, Sergiu (b Rome, 28 Jun 1912; d Paris, 14 Aug 1996), Romanian conductor. He studied musicology and conducting in Berlin, 1939–45, becoming resident conductor of the Berlin PO in 1948. In 1948 he shared the orchestra with Furtwängler on a tour of the USA. He was a guest conductor with the LSO from 1977, and chief conductor of the Munich PO from 1979. He also composed four symphonies and a Requiem. Joined Curtis Institute of Music, Philadelphia, in 1985.

cello, Italian diminutive ending, the now accepted name of the ◊violoncello.

cellone Italian = lit. 'big cello'; a modern cello of large size made by Stelzner of Dresden, capable of being played seated and intended to supply a double bass instrument for chamber music. It has four strings tuned in perfect fifths two octaves below the violin.

Cello Symphony work by Britten for cello and orchestra, op. 68, composed 1963 and performed Moscow, 12 Mar 1964 by Rostropovich.

Celos aun del ayre matan, *Jealousy, even of the air, is deadly*, opera on the subject of Cephalus and Procris by Juan Hidalgo (libretto by Calderón), produced Madrid, Buen Retiro, 5 Dec 1660. The first Spanish opera.

cembalist harpsichord player. ◊maestro al cembalo.

cembalo Italian abbr. for *clavicembalo*, accent on first syllable = harpsichord; also used to designate a thorough-bass *continuo* part.

Cendrillon, *Cinderella*, opera by Isouard (libretto by C G Étienne, after Perrault), produced Paris, Opéra-Comique, 22 Feb 1810. Opera by Massenet (libretto by H Cain, after Perrault), produced Paris, Opéra-Comique, 24 May 1899. Prominence given to Cinderella's father, the hen-pecked Pandolphe.

Cenerentola, *Cinderella*, opera by Wolf-Ferrari (libretto by M Pezzè-Pescolato, after Perrault), produced Venice, Teatro La Fenice, 22 Feb 1900.

Cenerentola, La, ossia La bontà in trionfo, *Cinderella, or The Triumph of Goodness*, opera by Rossini (libretto by J Ferretti, based on Etienne's text for Steibelt's opera), produced Rome, Teatro Valle, 25 Jan 1817. Fairy tale with a Freudian sub-text substitutes bracelet for slipper.

cent in acoustics, unit by which musical intervals are measured, a cent being a hundredth part of a semitone in an equal-tempered scale.

Céphale et Procris opera by Grétry (libretto by Marmontel), produced Versailles, at court, 30 Dec 1773; first Paris performance, Opéra, 2 May 1775. Cephalus tests his wife's fidelity by courting her in disguise.

Ce qu'on entend sur la montagne, *What is heard on the Mountain*, symphonic poem by Liszt, based on a poem by Victor Hugo; composed 1848–49, fp Weimar, Feb 1850.

Ceremony of Carols, A 11 settings by Britten for treble voices and harp; composed 1942, fp Norwich, 5 Dec 1942.

⸺ THE OPERA ⸺
La Cenerentola

A two-act opera version of the Cinderella story by Gioachino Rossini, first performed in 1817.

I. Angelina (soprano), known as Cenerentola (Cinderella), lives in the house of her step-father Don Magnifico (bass) with his two very plain daughters, Clorinda (soprano) and Thisbe (mezzo-soprano). Angelina is mistreated and humiliated by all in the house. Prince Ramiro (tenor) has exchanged identities with his valet Dandini (baritone) and arrives at the house to escort the 'ugly sisters' to a ball at his palace. He falls instantly in love with Angelina, but is told that she is only the servant. The Prince's tutor Alidoro (bass) helps Angelina to attend the ball.

II. Angelina gives Ramiro a silver bracelet by which she can be identified. Angelina returns to Don Magnifico's house as a storm gathers. Alidoro makes sure that the Prince's coach breaks down outside the door. When he seeks refuge from the storm he is united with Angelina, whom he marries.

⸺ THE OPERA ⸺

Cererols, Joan (b Martorell, Catalonia, 9 Sept 1618; d Montserrat, 28 Aug 1676), Spanish composer. He joined the monastery at Montserrat as a choirboy, became a novice in 1636 and remained to his death a director of music; a versatile musician as well as composer. His works are often for double chorus and include a *Missa de batalla*, for 12 voices, two Requiems, a Magnificat and the antiphon *Alma redemptoris mater*.

Cerha, Friedrich (b Vienna, 17 Feb 1926), Austrian composer and violinist. He studied musicology at Vienna University and also composition with Alfred Uhl. In 1958, with Kurt Schwertsik, he founded *Die Reihe*, an organization devoted to the performance of new music. He became director of the electronic studios of the Vienna Music Academy, 1960. His completion of Act 3 of *Lulu* from Berg's short score was performed Paris, 1979.

Works include *Espressioni Fondamentali* for orchestra; *Relazioni Fragile* for harpsichord and chamber orchestra; *Intersecazioni* for violin and orchestra; *Spiegel I–VII* (1960–68); concerto for violin, cello and orchestra (1975); *Baal*, opera (1974–79; fp Salzburg, 1981); *Baal-Gesänge* for baritone and orchestra (1982); concerto for flute, bassoon and orchestra (1982); *Requiem für Hollensteiner* (1983); *Keintate* for voice and 11 instruments (1983); *Der Rattenfänger*, opera (1987).

Cernohorský, Bohuslav Matěj (b Nymburk, Bohemia, ? 16 Feb 1684; d Graz, ? 1 Jul 1742), Bohemian composer, theorist and friar. Held church apointments at Padua and Assisi, where Tartini was his pupil. From 1739 he was director of music at St James's Church in Prague. He was a highly valued composer of church and organ music, but most of his works were destroyed by fire in 1754.

Certon, Pierre (b? Melun; d Paris, 23 Feb 1572), French composer. He was in the Sainte-Chapelle in Paris, 1532, and became choirmaster there before 1542 and chaplain in 1548. As a canon of Notre-Dame at Melun he founded an annual service there.

Works include Masses, *c* 50 motets, psalms, canticles, *c* 200 *chansons*.

High up it sounds nasal, low down it growls.
Antonín Dvořák on the cello, quoted in Michael Stegemann, *Introduction to Dvořák Cello Concerto*, 1918

Cervetto, Giacobbe Basevi (b Italy, *c* 1682; d London, 14 Jan 1783), Italian cellist and composer. Settled in London *c* 1738 and played in the orchestra at Drury Lane, where he was later theatre manager. Wrote sonatas, etc. for his instrument, chamber music.

Cervetto, James (b London, 1747 or 1749; d London, 5 Feb 1837), English cellist and composer of Italian descent, son and pupil of Giacobbe Basevi ◊Cervetto. Composed music for his instrument.

Cesaris, Johannes (*fl. c* 1385–*c* 1420), French organist and composer. Mentioned (with Carmen and Tapissier) by Martin le Franc in his poem *Le Champion des dames* (1441–42) as having 'astonished all Paris' in the recent past. One motet and several *chansons* survive.

Cesti, (Pietro) Antonio (b Arezzo, bap. 5 Aug 1623; d Florence, 14 Oct 1669), Italian composer. After serving as a choirboy at Arezzo he became a Minorite friar in 1637. He was a pupil of Carissimi in Rome, and in 1645 was appointed *maestro di cappella* at Volterra Cathedral. In 1653, having previously become a priest, he entered the service of the court at Innsbruck and remained there, with a brief interval as tenor in the papal chapel, for 13 years. From 1666 to 1669 he was vice-*Kapellmeister* in Vienna, where his spectacular opera *Il pomo d'oro* was performed in 1667; it is reputed to have been the most elaborate and expensive production ever staged.

Works include operas *L'Orontea* (1649), *Il Cesare amante* (1651), *Alessandro il vincitor di se stesso*, *L'Argia*, *La Dori* (1657), *Tito*, *Nettuno e Fiora festeggianti* (1666), *Il pomo d'oro*, *Semiramide*, *Le disgrazie d'Amore* (1667); motets; cantatas.

Chabrier, (Alexis) Emmanuel (b Ambert, Puy-de-Dôme, 18 Jan 1841; d Paris, (13 Sept 1894), French composer. Studied law and was employed at the Ministry of the Interior, but cultivated music as a gifted amateur. Having produced two operettas in 1877 and 1879, he devoted himself entirely to composition. After the production of *Le Roi malgré lui*, the run of which was interrupted by the fire of 25 May 1887 at the Opéra-Comique, he came under the influence of Wagner.

Works include operas *Le Roi malgré lui*, *Gwendoline* (1885) and *Briséis* (unfinished, one act performed Paris, 1897); operettas *L'Étoile* and *Une Éducation manquée* (1879); rhapsody *España* (1883) and *Joyeuse Marche* for orchestra; *La Sulamite* for mezzo, chorus and orchestra; ten *Pièces pittoresques*, *Habanera* and *Bourrée fantasque*, etc. for piano; three *Valses romantiques* for two pianos; songs.

chace Old French = *chasse* = 'chase, hunt'; a 14th-c. term for ◊canon, because the parts 'chase' each other.

chaconne, French, originally a dance, probably of Spanish provenance. Now a composition, generally in 3–4 time, on an unvarying ground-bass which goes on throughout the piece and over which, at each reappearance, the upper parts are freely varied in different ways. This definition applies even to Bach's chaconne for unaccompanied violin, since the bass is always implied even when not actually heard.

chacony English = ◊chaconne.

Chadwick, George (Whitefield) (b Lowell, MA, 13 Nov 1854; d Boston, 4 Apr 1931), American composer. Studied at Boston, Leipzig and Munich, in the last place under Rheinberger. Returned to America in 1880, became organist at Boston, then professor at the New England Conservatory and its director in 1897.

Works include operas *Tabasco* (1894), *Judith*, *The Padrone* (1912), etc.; works for chorus and orchestra *The Viking's Last Voyage*, *The Song of the Viking*, *Lovely Rosabelle*, *The Lily Nymph*, *Phoenix expirans*, etc.; three symphonies (1882–94), symphonic poems *Cleopatra*, *Aphrodite*, *Angel of Death*, *Tam o'Shanter* (after Burns), overtures *Rip van Winkle*, *Thalia*, *Melpomene*, *Adonis* (after Shelley), *Euterpe*, etc., *Symphonic Sketches*, *Sinfonietta*, *Suite symphonique*; five string quartets (1878–98) piano quintet.; songs with orchestra and with piano; piano and organ works; church music, part-songs.

Chagrin, Francis (b Bucharest, 15 Nov 1905; d London, 10 Nov 1972), Anglo-Romanian composer. Studied at Zurich, Bucharest and, with Dukas and Nadia Boulanger, in Paris; later with Seiber in London, where he joined the French section of the BBC Overseas Service in 1941. In 1943 he founded the Committee for the Promotion of New Music.

Works include incidental music for Shaw's *Heartbreak House* and Gozzi's *Re cervo*; music for films and broadcasts; Prelude and Fugue and suites for orchestra; two symphonies; piano concerto; chamber music; piano pieces; over 100 songs.

You listen to four sensible persons conversing, you profit from their discourse, and you get to know the peculiar properties of their several instruments.
Johann Wolfgang von Goethe on chamber music, quoted in Barzun, *Pleasures of Music*, 1977

Chailly, Luciano (b Ferrara, 19 Jan 1920), Italian composer. He studied in Bologna and Milan and with Hindemith at Salzburg. Artistic director La Scala, Milan, 1968–71; Milan Conservatory from 1969. His style is neo-classical, with some serial and electronic effects.

Works include operas *Il canto del cigno* (Bologna, 1957), *Una demanda di matrimonio* (after Chekhov; Milan, 1957), *Procedura penale* (Como, 1959; English translation by A Jacobs as 'Trial by Tea-Party'), *Il Mantello*, 'surrealist opera' (Florence, 1960), *L'Idiota* (after Dostoievsky, Rome, 1970).

Chailly, Riccardo (b Milan, 20 Feb 1953), Italian conductor, son of Luciano ◊Chailly. He studied in Milan and Sienna and became assistant conductor at La Scala in 1972 and in 1974 gave *Butterfly* in Chicago. With Henze founded the music school in Montepulciano. In

Chailly *The conductor Riccardo Chailly, son of the composer Luciano Chailly. His conducting style is visually impressive and his interpretations are noted for their attention to details and dynamics.*

1978 he conducted *I Masnadieri* at La Scala and *Don Pasquale* at CG; NY Met. debut 1982 with *Les Contes d'Hoffmann* and in the same year was appointed chief conductor of RIAS (West Berlin Radio Orchestra), and principal guest conductor of the LPO. Director of the Concertgebouw Orchestra from 1986.

chalumeau a single-reed wind instrument, the forerunner of the clarinet. Also the name for the lowest register of the clarinet.

Chamberlain, Houston Stewart (b Portsmouth, 9 Sept 1855; d Bayreuth, 9 Jan 1927), English-born German writer. He wrote mainly on Wagner. Educated at Cheltenham and in Switzerland. Married Wagner's daughter Eva in 1908 and became a naturalized German. Great champion of Wagner and propagandist of Pan-German and proto-fascist theories.

chamber music properly music played in a private room, consisting of works assigning individual parts to a few players (more rarely singers). From the 19th c. more and more 'chamber music' was composed for performance in large concert halls and therefore carries the title only by virtue of its small ensemble and solo allocation. See also ◊string quartet *et seq*.

chamber opera a type of opera written for few singers without chorus and a small orchestra often consisting entirely of solo instruments. Well-known examples are Strauss's *Ariadne auf Naxos* (1916) and Britten's *The Turn of the Screw* (1954).

chamber orchestra a small orchestra designed for the performance of table music, serenades, etc. in domestic surroundings or small concert halls.

chamber organ a small organ with one or two manuals, suitable for playing figured-bass accompaniments or 18th-c. solo concertos.

chamber pitch ◊Kammerton.

Chamber Symphony title given by Schoenberg to his op. 9 (1906) for 15 solo instruments and arranged by him for orchestra 1922 and 1935. A second work with the same title was begun 1906 and completed 1939.

Chambonnières, Jacques Champion, Sieur de (b Paris, *c* 1602; d Paris, 1672), French harpsichordist and composer. In the service of Louis XIII and XIV, also for a time in Sweden. He taught several of the later harpsichordists, including Couperin and d'Anglebert, and pub. two

Chamber Symphony *A page from the manuscript of Arnold Schoenberg's Kammersymphonie. The two systems (divided in the middle of the page by a short double line) demonstrate the composer's orchestrational skills. The different motives are distributed varyingly amongst the instruments.*

books of harpsichord pieces, illustrating an important stage in the evolution of explicitly noted ornamentation.

Chaminade, Cécile (Louise Stéphanie) (b Paris, 8 Aug 1857; d Monte Carlo, 18 Apr 1944), French pianist and composer. Studied with various masters, including Godard for composition. Began to compose at the age of eight, and at 18 gave her first concert. Toured widely in France and England.

Works include comic opera *La Sévillane*; ballet *Callirhoë* (1888); *Symphonie lyrique* for chorus and orchestra; suites for orchestra; *Concertstück* for piano and orchestra (1896); two piano trios; numerous light piano pieces; songs.

Champein, Stanislas (b Marseilles, 19 Nov 1753; d Paris, 19 Sept 1830), French composer. Went to Paris *c* 1775 and produced a comic opera in 1780, which was followed by some 50 other works for the stage, including (?) a setting of a French prose translation of Sophocles' *Electra*, rehearsed at the Opéra, but prohibited.

Works include operas *La Mélomanie* (1781), *Le Nouveau Don Quichotte* (1789), etc.; Masses and other church music, etc.

Chance, Michael (b Penn, 7 Mar 1955), English countertenor. After study at Cambridge he sang with the Monteverdi Choir in NY and at the Aix-en-Provence Festival (*Messiah*). Opera roles include Apollo in Cavalli's *Giasone* (Buxton, 1983), Andronico in Handel's *Tamerlano* at Lyon, Julius Caesar for Scottish Opera. He sang Apollo in *Death in Venice* at Glyndebourne, 1988, and returned 1994–95 as Orpheus in the premiere production of Birtwistle's *The Second Mrs Kong*.

Chandos Anthems 12 anthems by Handel, composed *c* 1717–20 for the Earl of Carnarvon, later Duke of Chandos, for performance in his private chapel at Canons near Edgware.

Chang, Sarah (b Philadelphia, 10 Dec 1980), US-born Korean violinist. Studied at Juilliard with Dorothy DeLay and made debut aged eight

with the NY PO. Further appearances with the LA PO, Chicago SO, LSO and Leipzig Gewandhaus Orchestra. Her youthful virtuosity is admired in concertos by Saint-Saëns, Paganini and Tchaikovsky.

chanson French = 'song'; in a special technical sense the *chanson* is an old French part-song cultivated in France before and during the period when the madrigal occupied the composers of the Netherlands, Italy and England. Though it is often polyphonic in construction, many examples approximate more closely to the lighter type of canzonet. Many such *chansons* were arranged for solo voice and lute.

chanson de geste French = 'song of deeds', epic or heroic song; 11th–13th-c. verse chronicle recited to music by Jongleurs. The subject-matter might be secular or religious. In form it consisted of verse-paragraphs (*laisses*) of unequal length, the music being the same for each line of verse except the last.

chanson de toile French = 'cloth song'; a French medieval song which tells its story or performs its actions with reference to a female, not a male, character. Hence the name, which doubtless referred to spinning or weaving.

Chansons de Bilitis, Trois songs for voice and piano by Debussy (texts by P Louÿs) composed 1892, fp Paris, 17 Mar 1897 (version with orchestra performed Paris, 20 Feb 1926). Incidental music for two flutes, two harps and celesta, composed 1900, fp Paris, 7 Feb 1901; arranged by Boulez with the addition of a reciter, performed London, 23 Mar 1965.

Chansons madécasses three songs by Ravel for voice, flute, cello and piano (texts by E Parny), composed 1925–26, fp Paris, 13 Jun 1926.

Chant in Catholic church music the singing of psalms, canticles, Masses, etc. in plainsong to Latin words; in Anglican church music the singing of the psalms to harmonized and measured tunes, the rhythm of which may, however, be modified or obscured by the necessity to fit longer or shorter psalm verses.

Chant du Rossignol, Le symphonic poem in three movements by Stravinsky, based on music from his opera *The Nightingale*, arranged 1917, fp Geneva, 6 Dec 1919, conductor Ansermet; ballet version performed Paris, Opéra, 2 Feb 1920.

chanterelle French = lit. 'the singing one'; the E string of the violin or (less often) the highest string of any stringed instrument.

chant-fable French = 'song-fable'; a 13th-c. narrative interspersed with songs.

Chapel Royal the English court chapel, including not only the building but the whole institution, including the composers, organists, and singers themselves, dating back to the 12th c. at the latest. It achieved prominence during the reigns of Henry V and VI; later members included Byrd, Purcell and Handel.

Music that fancy employs/In rapture of innocent flame,/We offer with lute and with voice/To Cecilia's bright name.

Christopher Fishburn, text for Purcell's *Ode for St Cecilia's Day*, 1683

Chapí y Lorente, Ruperto (b Villena near Alicante, 27 Mar 1851; d Madrid, 25 Mar 1909), Spanish composer. Studied at the Madrid Conservatory and in 1872 was given a musical post in the artillery. Lived in Rome for a time from 1873.

Works include operas *Margarita la Tornera* (1909), *La serenata*, *Roger de Flor*, *Circe* and four others, 155 zarzuelas; oratorio *Los Angeles*, *Veni Creator* for double chorus and orchestra; symphony in D minor, Moorish fantasy *La corte de Granada*, legend *Los gnomos de la Alhambra* and other orchestral works; *Jota* for violin and orchestra; four string quartets, piano trio; piano pieces; songs.

Chaplet, The musical stage entertainment by Boyce (libretto by M Mendez), produced London, Drury Lane Theatre, 2 Dec 1749.

Charakterstück German = 'character or characteristic piece'; a short instrumental piece outlining some definite mood, human character or literary conception.

Charpentier, Gustave (b Dieuze, Meurthe, 25 Jun 1860; d Paris, 18 Feb 1956), French composer. Went into business at Tourcoing at the age of 15, but studied music at the Lille and Paris Conservatories, gaining at the latter the Prix de Rome as a pupil of Massenet in 1887. In 1902 he founded the Conservatoire de Mimi Pinson, providing free instruction in music for working-class girls.

Works include operas *Louise* (produced 1900) and *Julien* (1913); cantata *Didon* (1887); symphonic drama for solo voices, chorus and orchestra, *La Vie du poète* (afterwards used in *Julien*); orchestral suite *Impressions d'Italie* (1889); *Fête du couronnement de la Muse* (later used in *Louise*); *Impressions fausses* (Verlaine) and *Sérénade à Watteau* for voice and orchestra (1896); *Poèmes chantés* and five poems from Baudelaire's *Fleurs du mal* for voice and piano.

Charpentier, Marc-Antoine (b Paris, c 1645; d Paris, 24 Feb 1704), French composer. Pupil of Carissimi in Rome. On his return he became domestic musician to Mlle de Guise and composer to the Comédie-Française, where he worked with Molière and continued after Molière's death. In 1679 he was appointed church composer to the Dauphin; later music master to a Jesuit college and composition teacher to the Duke of Orleans. In 1698 he became *maître de chapelle* at the Sainte-Chapelle. He was long known only through a Te Deum and Christmas *Messe de minuit*, but Charpentier's stage works have been successfully revived in recent years. William ♭Christie and his Arts Florissants have revealed the drama, colour and variety of such operas as *Médée* and *David et Jonathas*.

Works include operas *Les Amours d'Acis et Galatée* (1678), *La Descente d'Orphée aux enfers*, *Endimion*, *Médée* (1693), *David et Jonathas* (1688), c 12 others; incidental music for Molière's *La Comtesse d'Escarbagnas* and *Le Malade imaginaire* (1674), for P Corneille's *Polyeucte* and *Andromède*, T Corneille's *La Pierre philosophale*, T Corneille and Visé's *Circé* and *L'Inconnu* and Visé's *Les Amours de Vénus et d'Adonis*; ballets, etc.; c ten Masses, Requiem, motets, psalms and other church music (some with orchestra) including four settings of the Te Deum; *Histoires sacrées*, *Tragédies spirituelles*; vocal chamber music, *Airs sérieux et à boire*; instrumental pieces.

Charton-Demeur (born *Charton*), Anne Arsène (b Saujon, 5 Mar 1824; d Paris, 30 Nov 1892), French soprano. Made her debut at Bordeaux in 1842 as Lucia. She sang the part of Dido in Berlioz's *Les Troyens à Carthage* in 1863; sang Béatrice in 1862. Other roles included Cassandre and Amina.

Chartreuse de Parme, La, *The Carthusian Monastery of Parma*, opera by Sauguet (libretto by A Lunel, based on Stendhal's novel), produced Paris, Opéra, 16 Mar 1939.

Chase, Gilbert (b Havana, 4 Sept 1906; d Chapel Hill, NC, 22 Feb 1992), American music critic. Studied in NY and Paris, where he lived in 1929–35 as music critic to the *Daily Mail*. In 1936 he settled in NY. He made a special study of Spanish music and wrote *The Music of Spain* (1941, revised 1959); *America's Music* (1955, revised 1966). Visiting professor at University of Texas at Austin, 1975–79.

Chasse, La, *The Hunt*, nickname of Haydn's symphony no. 73, in D major, composed in 1781; also of his string quartet in B♭ major, op. 1 no. 1, written c 1755.

Chasseur maudit, Le, *The Accursed Huntsman*, symphonic poem by Franck, based on a ballad by Bürger, composed 1882. Fp Paris, Société Nationale, 31 Mar 1883.

Chausson, Ernest (b Paris, 20 Jan 1855; d Limay, 10 Jun 1899), French composer. Pupil of Massenet at the Paris Conservatory, then of Franck. He never held an official appointment, but helped to found the Société Nationale de Musique and was its secretary 1889–99. His early music was influenced by Massenet and Wagner but he later turned to 18th-c. French musical models. He was a pioneer of cyclic form, and the first person to die in a cycling accident.

Works include operas *Le Roi Arthus* (1886–95), *La Légende de Sainte Cécile* (1891), etc.; incidental music to Shakespeare's *Tempest*; symphony in B♭ major (1890), symphonic poem *Viviane*; *Poème de l'amour et de la mer* for voice and orchestra (1882–90); string quartet (unfinished), concerto for violin and piano with string quartet

A Selection of
Marc-Antoine Charpentier

Le Malade imaginaire 1674
Anthems for Advent 1680s

Port Royal Mass and Magnificat 1680s
Actéon 1683–5
David et Jonathas 1688
Office de Ténèbres .... c 1690
Marian Devotions 1690s
Médée 1693

(1891), piano trio, piano quartet, *Chanson perpétuelle* for voice, string quartet and piano; piano and organ pieces; 10 op. nos. of songs.

Chávez, Carlos (b Mexico City, 13 Jun 1899; d Mexico City, 2 Aug 1978), Mexican composer. He was taught music as a child by his brother and two casual teachers, but later went to Europe and NY to gain experience. In 1928 he founded a Mexican symphony orchestra, of which he later became conductor, and the same year he became director of the National Conservatory. A post in the Department of Fine Arts enabled him to do still more for the country's musical reorganization, and he did much to explore Mexican folk music.

Works include opera *Panfilo and Lauretta* (1953, produced NY, 1957), ballets *El fuego nuevo*, *Los cuatro soles* and *H P*; *Sinfonía de Antigona*, *Sinfonía proletaria* and *Sinfonía India* for orchestra; concertos for harp and for piano and orchestra; *Energía* for instrumental ensemble *El sol* for chorus and orchestra; three string quartets (1921, 1932, 1944); sonata for four horns; piano pieces.

Checkmate ballet by Bliss (choreographed by N de Valois), produced by Sadler's Wells Ballet, Paris, Théâtre des Champs-Élysées, 15 Jun 1937; first London performance SW, 5 Oct 1937.

chef d'attaque French the leader of an orchestra, so called because great importance was always attached in France to unanimity of bowing and attack in orchestral string playing.

chekker a 14th–16th-c. keyboard instrument used in England, France and Spain, in which latter countries it was called *échiquier* and *exaquir* (and similar names). Its German name is properly *Schachtbrett*, from the old Flemish word *Schacht* (spring or quill), and has nothing to do with the modern *Schachbrett* (chessboard). The instrument is clearly a forerunner of the harpsichord or clavichord.

Chelard, Hippolyte (André Jean Baptiste) (b Paris, 1 Feb 1789; d Weimar, 12 Feb 1861), French conductor and composer. Studied at the Paris Conservatory, violin under R Kreutzer and composition under Gossec, Méhul and Cherubini. Gained the Prix de Rome in 1811, studied church music in Rome under Baini and Zingarelli, afterwards opera with Paisiello and Fioravanti at Naples, where he produced an Italian comic opera in 1815. In 1816 he became violinist at the Paris Opéra, where he produced *Macbeth* in 1827. After the 1830 Revolution he settled at Munich and remained in Germany to the end of his life. In 1832 and 1833 he conducted German opera in London, with Schröder-Devrient and Haitzinger as the chief singers. From 1835 to 1840 he was employed as conductor at Augsburg, finally becoming court music director at Weimar.

Cherubini *The composer Luigi Cherubini (1760–1842), depicted here receiving divine inspiration from one of the Muses, painted by J A D Ingres (1842). Beethoven considered Cherubini his greatest contemporary. Although his reputation has declined this century, he greatly influenced a generation of Romantic composers.*

Works include operas *La casa da vendere* (1815), *Macbeth* (in French), libretto by R de l'Isle (1827), *La Table et le logement* (later German version *Der Student*), *Mittenacht, Die Hermannsschlacht* (1835).

Chéreau, Patrice (b Lezigen, Maine-et-Loire, 2 Nov 1944), French stage director. Directed theatre in Lyon and Paris from 1966, then *L'Italiana in Algeri* at Spoleto (1969) and *Hoffmann* in Paris (1974). Staged a radical *Ring des Nibelungen* at Bayreuth (1976), which was unpopular at first but later won acceptance. Premiere of the three-act version of *Lulu* at the Paris Opéra (1979), *Wozzeck* at the Théâtre du Châtelet (1992); Mozart's *Lucio Silla* at La Scala (1984) and *Don Giovanni* at the 1994 Salzburg Festival, after which he turned to film.

Cherkassky, Shura (b Odessa, 7 Oct 1911), American pianist of Russian birth. He studied first with his mother and later with Josef Hofmann. As a child prodigy, he played before President Hoover in the USA in 1923. First European tour 1945; played the Gershwin concerto at the 1993 London Proms.

Chernov, Vladimir (b Moscow, 22 Sept 1953), Russian baritone. Studied in Moscow and at La Scala. Career with the Kirov Opera, St Petersburg from 1983, as Germont, Figaro and Valentine. US debut at Boston 1988, as Marcello, Posa in *Don Carlos* at LA 1990, NY Met. 1992. Scottish Opera and CG, London 1990, as Don Carlo in *La Forza del Destino*, and Rossini's Figaro. One of the most highly valued baritones of his generation. Sang Stankar in the Met. premiere production of Verdi's *Stiffelio*.

Chérubin opera (comédie chantée) in three acts by Massenet (libretto by F de Croisset and H Cain, after the play by Croisset), produced Monte Carlo, 14 Feb 1904; not produced in the USA until 1989 (Santa Fe) and England 1993 (CG). Seventeen-year-old Chérubin is spoiled for choice but settles for Nina.

Cherubini, Luigi (Carlo Zanobi Salvatore Maria) (b Florence, 8 or 14 Sept 1760; d Paris, 15 Mar 1842), Italian composer. Studied first under his father, a musician at the Teatro della Pergola at Florence, then under various minor masters. At the age of 16 he had written an oratorio, Masses, etc. About 1778, with a grant from the Grand Duke, he went to study with Sarti at Venice and in 1780 he produced his first opera, *Quinto Fabio*. In 1785 and 1786 he produced *La finta principessa* and *Giulio Sabino* in London and was appointed composer to the King, but left for Paris in the latter year. After a brief return to Italy he settled in Paris for good in 1788 and produced his first French opera, *Démophon*, there, to a libretto by Marmontel. He soon became very busy conducting and writing operas, but was not very successful. In 1795 he married Cécile Tourette. In 1806 he produced *Faniska* in Vienna, where it had been specially commissioned, and met Beethoven, who admired his work and whose *Fidelio* was influenced by it. On his return to France he lived retired and embittered at the Prince de Chimay's country residence and there wrote church music as well as more operas. In 1816 he and Lesueur became attached to the royal chapel with large salaries and in 1822 he became director of the Conservatory, where he often confronted the precocious Berlioz. He has sometimes been held as a model of pedantry but his operas are dramatically varied and highly influential; Beethoven admired Cherubini's stage and sacred music.

Works include operas *Armida abbandonata* (1782), *Alessandro nell' Indie, Demetrio, Ifigenia in Aulide, Lodoïska* (French), *Médée* (1797), *Les Deux Journées/The Water Carrier* (1800), *Anacréon, ou L'Amour fugitif* (1803), *Faniska, Pimmalione, Les Abencérages* (1813), *Bayard à Mézières, Ali Baba, ou Les Quarante Voleurs* (1833); ballet-pantomime *Achille à Scyros*; ten Masses and two coronation Masses, two Requiems (one for male voices) and other choral works; symphony in D major and overture for orchestra; six string quartets (1834–37), string quintet; songs.

chest of viols a set of (usually six) viols of various sizes in a cupboard or chest, an article of furniture which was often found in households of well-to-do English families of the 16th and 17th c.

chest voice one of the so-called 'registers' in singing, used or said to be used for the lower notes of the singer's range, and so called because its resonance gives the sensation of being lodged in the chest, not in the head, as in the case of the Head Voice.

Chevillard, (Paul Alexandre) Camille (b Paris, 14 Oct 1859; d Chatou, 30 May 1923), French conductor and composer. Pupil of Chabrier and son-in-law of Lamoureux, whose concerts he conducted after Lamoureux's retirement.

Works include incidental music for E Schuré's play *La Roussalka* (1903), *Ballade symphonique*, symphony poem *Le Chêne et le*

> *My dear general, you are certainly an excellent soldier; but, in regard to music, you must excuse me if I don't think it necessary to adapt my compositions to your comprehension.*
> **Luigi Cherubini** to Napoleon, quoted in Bellasis, *Cherubini*, 1874

Roseau and *Fantaisie symphonique* for orchestra; string quartet, piano quintet, quartet and trio (1882–84); sonatas for violin and piano and cello and piano; variations and *Étude chromatique* for piano; violin and cello pieces.

Chevreuille, Raymond (b Watermael, 17 Nov 1901; d Montignies-le-Tilleul, 9 May 1976), Belgian composer. Mainly self-taught, although he took some courses at the Brussels Conservatory. His works are in a harmonically advanced idiom.

Works include chamber opera *Atta Troll* (1952), three ballets; symphony with vocal quartet, *Évasions* for soprano and chamber orchestra, *Saisons* for baritone and chamber orchestra; concerto for three woodwind instruments, cello concerto; six string quartets (1930–45).

Chezy (born **von Klencke**), Wilhelmine (or **Helmina**) von (1783–1856), German dramatist and novelist. Wrote the libretto of Weber's *Euryanthe* and Schubert's *Rosamunde*.

Chiara, Maria (b Oderzo near Venice, 24 Nov 1939), Italian soprano.

Debut Venice, 1965, as Desdemona. She sang Liù at Verona in 1969, with Domingo, and repeated the role on her CG debut (1973, returned for Desdemona, 1978). In 1970 she appeared at Munich and Vienna. NY Met. debut 1977, Traviata. She opened the 1985–86 season at La Scala, as Aida. Other roles include Maria Stuarda, Anna Bolena, Elisabeth de Valois and Amelia Boccanegra. Sang the *Trovatore* Leonora at Turin, 1991.

chiavette Italian = lit. 'little keys' (actually little clefs); clefs other than those normal in 16th- and early 17th-c. vocal music, used either to avoid leger-lines or to indicate transposition, e.g. the tenor clef might be used for a bass part, the treble clef for a soprano part, and so on.

Chicago Opera Company US opera co., first founded 1910 as the Chicago Grand Opera Company, with Campanini as director; Mary Garden was artistic director 1921–22, when Prokofiev led the premiere of *The Love for Three Oranges*. Civic Opera Company established 1922–32, with new house 1929. Visiting companies only 1932–54, then Carol Fox (1926–81) founded the present Lyric Opera of Chicago, 1954. Ardis Krainik is the general director and Bruno Bartoletti was artistic director from 1975.

Chicago Symphony Orchestra American orchestra founded 1891 by Theodore Thomas; conducted by Thomas until 1905 and by Frederick Stock until 1942. Other conductors include Rafael Kubelik 1950–53, Fritz Reiner 1953–63, Jean Martinon 1963–69; Georg Solti 1969–91; Daniel Barenboim from 1991.

Chihara, Paul (b Seattle, 9 Jul 1938), American composer. Studied with Boulanger in Paris and Pepping in Berlin. Taught at UCLA 1966–74. Composer-in-residence with the San Francisco Ballet from 1980. His music has employed serial and aleatory techniques.

Works include viola concerto (1963); srting quartet (1965); *Magnificat* (1966); *Redwood* for viola and percussion (1967); *Rain Music*, tape collage (1968); *Forest Music* for orchestra, *Ceremony* series for various instrumental groups (I–V, 1971–75); *Missa Carminum* (1976); symphony (1982); *Sequoia* for string quartet and tape (1984); ballets *Mistletoe Bride* (1978) and *The Tempest* (1980).

Child, William (b Bristol, *c* 1606; d Windsor, 23 Mar 1697), English composer and organist. Educated at Bristol Cathedral and appointed one of the organists at St George's Chapel, Windsor, in 1632. At the Restoration he received a court appointment and in 1663 he took the Mus.D. degree at Oxford.

Works include *c* 25 services, *c* 50 anthems, motet *O bone Jesu*, 20 psalms for three voices with *continuo*, chants, Magnificat, 'in Gamut', Te Deum and Jubilate and other church music; secular vocal pieces, catches and ayres; two suites of dances for viols.

Childhood of Christ (Berlioz). ◊Enfance du Christ.

Child of our Time, A oratorio by Tippett for soloists, chorus and orchestra composed 1939–41, inspired by persecution of Jews following assassination of a Nazi envoy in Paris. Tippett's own text includes African-American spirituals; fp London, 19 Mar 1944.

Children's Corner a set of piano pieces, with English titles, by Debussy, composed 1906–08, dedicated to his daughter Claude-Emma Debussy (Chouchou): 1. *Doctor Gradus ad Parnassum*; 2. *Jimbo's Lullaby*; 3. *Serenade for the Doll*; 4. *The Snow is Dancing*; 5. *The Little Shepherd*; 6. *Golliwogg's Cake-Walk*. Fp Paris, 18 Dec 1908; orchestral version by André Caplet performed NY, 1910.

Childs, Barney (b Spokane, WA, 13 Feb 1926), American composer. Studied at Oxford and Stanford Universities, and with Carter and Copland. Professor of composition at the University of Redlands, CA, 1976–92. His music belongs to the avant garde, and allows the performer a large degree of freedom through improvisation and 'self-generating structures'.

Works include two symphonies (1954, 1956); eight string quartets (1951–74); two violin sonatas (1950, 1956); *Interbalances*, six pieces for various groups (1941–64); *When Lilacs Last in the Dooryard Bloom'd* (after Whitman, for soloists, chorus and band, 1971); *Couriers of the Crimson Dawn*, for any instruments (1977); *13 Classic Studies for the Contrabass* (1981); *Sunshine Lunch and Like Matters* for bass clarinet and ensemble (1984); horn octet (1984); concerto for timpani and orchestra (1989).

Chilingirian Quartet string quartet formed 1971, with Levon Chilingirian (born Nicosia, 1948) as leader. They were coached by Siegmund Nissel and Hans Keller and were Resident at Liverpool University 1973–76, Sussex 1978–93. NY debut 1977, with regular tours of the USA and Europe. Repertory includes works by Bartók, Korngold, Berwald and Debussy, in addition to the Viennese classics.

Chinese block, or *temple block*, a percussion instrument in the shape of a hollow wooden box on which a dry, rapping sound is produced.

Chinese pavilion an instrument shaped like a tree or pagoda and hung with brass plates and small bells, shaken to make a jingling noise and used in military bands, especially in the 18th c. It was popularly called 'Jingling Johnny' or 'Turkish Crescent'.

chiroplast Logier's apparatus invented in the early years of the 19th c. to facilitate piano practice by mechanically making the hands flexible.

Chisholm, Erik (b Glasgow, 4 Jan 1904; d Cape Town, 8 Jun 1965), Scottish pianist, organist, conductor and composer. Studied composition under Tovey and in 1934 took the Mus.D. degree at Edinburgh University. After touring in Canada he returned to Glasgow as organist and conductor, founded a society for the propagation of modern music in 1930 and became conductor of the Glasgow Grand Opera Co., with which he gave interesting performances, particularly of Berlioz's operas (e.g. *Les Troyens*, 1935). In 1947 he became principal of the Cape Town School of Music.

Works include opera *Isle of Youth* (libretto by composer, 1941); ballets *The Forsaken Mermaid* (1942) and *The Pied Piper of Hamelin*; two symphonies, etc.

chitarrone Italian = lit. 'big guitar' (from *chitarra*); a very large double-necked lute or theorbo, used as a bass to the lute family in Italy in the 17th c.

Chlubna, Osvald (b Brno, 22 Jul 1893; d Brno, 30 Oct 1971), Czech composer. Pupil of Janáček and later professor at the Brno Conservatory. He scored the last act of Janáček's *Sarka* (staged 1925) and gave an upbeat ending to *From the House of the Dead* (1930).

Works include operas *Catullus's Vengeance* (1917), *Alladine and Palomides* (after Maeterlinck) (1922), *Nura* and *The Day of Beginning*; cantatas *Lord's Prayer*, *Minstrel's Child* and others; *Symphony of Life and Love*, symphonic poems *Dreams*, *Before I go dumb*, *Two Fairy Tales*, *Song of my Longing*; overture *Fairy Land*, two suites for orchestra; *Sinfonietta* for chamber orchestra; five string quartets, piano music, songs.

An opera may be allowed to be extravagantly lavish in its decorations, as its only design is to gratify the senses, and keep up an indolent attention in the audience.

Joseph Addison, *The Spectator*, 1711

Chmura, Gabriel (b Wroclaw, 7 May 1946), Polish-born conductor. He emigrated to Israel 1955 and studied in Vienna, winning the 1971 Karajan Competition in Berlin. Music director in Aachen 1974–82 and Bochum SO from 1982; US debut 1980, with the NY PO; has also guested with the Berlin PO, LSO, and Vienna SO. Opera performances in Paris and Munich; *Werther* at Parma, 1990. Music director of the National Arts Centre Orchestra at Ottawa, 1987–90.

choirbook a large book in which the parts of a polyphonic composition, though written out separately, were collected together on the open page so that they could be read simultaneously by all the performers. (If a piece was too long for one 'opening' the parts were copied so that the turn came simultaneously in all of them.) The format was first employed in motet MSS of the 13th c. (superseding score arrangement) to save space), was common in England in the 15th and early 16th c. (◊Eton Choirbook), and was also used for chamber music and lute songs in England in the later 16th and early 17th c., the parts now being arranged so that the book could be placed flat on a table and the performers seated around it.

Chopin *The composer Frédéric Chopin (1810–1849) as depicted on a cigarette card of 1912. He died of lung disease (tuberculosis) at an early age, but he nevertheless left behind a large quantity of quintessentially romantic music, written mostly for piano solo.*

choir organ formerly often a small instrument set apart from the principal organ in a church and used separately to accompany the choir. It is now the name given to the lowest manual of an organ with three or more manuals, of which it forms an integral part.

Chopin, Frédéric (François) (originally *Fryderyk Franciszek*) (b Zelazowa Wola, ? 1 Mar 1810; d Paris, 17 Oct 1849), Polish composer of French descent. The family moved to Warsaw later in 1810, Chopin's father becoming professor of French there. Chopin took piano lessons at the age of six, played at a musical evening at seven and in public at eight; took composition lessons with Elsner from 1822, made great progress in composition and improvisation, and first pub. a work, a Polonaise in G minor, at the age of seven. Left Warsaw Conservatory 1827 and played in Vienna in 1829. On his return he fell in love with the singer Konstancia Gladkowska, who appeared at the third of his public concerts in 1830; but he left Poland that year, playing in Vienna and Munich and visiting Stuttgart, where he heard of the taking of Warsaw by the Russians. Went to Paris in Oct 1831 and decided to remain there. He appeared frequently in public and gave private lessons, especially in French and Polish aristocratic circles.

He met Maria Wodzińska at Dresden in 1835 and Marienbad in 1836, fell in love with and became secretly engaged to her, but the engagement was broken off by her family. In 1838 he visited George Sand at Nohant, where she held house-parties in the summer, and an intimacy developed between them. She took him to Majorca in Nov for his health, but the stay, until Feb 1839, was spoilt by bad weather and primitive living conditions. Most summers were spent at Nohant until 1847, when a family quarrel between G Sand and her children led to one with Chopin and they parted. He suffered from tuberculosis of the throat and gave his last public concert in Feb 1848, but continued to teach and play at private houses. His pupil Jane Stirling took him to Scotland in Aug 1848 for a rest at the country house of her brother-in-law, Lord Torphichen. He afterwards played at Manchester, Glasgow, Edinburgh, and returned to London in Nov. In Jan 1849 he was back in Paris in a critical state of health and finance, but was supported by wealthy friends until his death.

Chopin's music, written almost exclusively for solo piano, was the most important of the 19th c. (along with Liszt's) in the development and perfection of a Romantic style. It is entirely original, with an apparent melodic simplicity that usually masks a variety of more complex undercurrents of harmony and rhythm.

Works include two concertos in E minor and F minor (1829–30); four other works with orchestra including *Andante Spianato* (1834); 50 Mazurkas in 13 sets (1830–49), 27 Studies, 26 Preludes (24 in all keys), op. 28 (1836–39), 19 Nocturnes, 14 Waltzes (1827–41), 16 Polonaises, four Ballades in G minor, F, A♭, F minor (1831–42), four Impromptus, four Scherzos in B minor, B♭ minor, C♯ minor, E (1831–39), three Rondos, three sonatas in C minor (1828), B♭ minor (1839), B minor (1844), *Barcarolle* in F♯, *Berceuse*, *Bolero*, Fantasy in F minor, *Tarantella* and other misc. piano pieces; piano trio (1829); cello and piano sonata (1832).

Chopsticks a childish little waltz played on the piano by children with the forefingers of each hand, to which the name refers by analogy with the two sticks with which the Chinese eat their food.

'Chopsticks' Variations a set of variations for piano (three hands, the second player playing a variant in 2–4 time of the above with one hand) by Borodin, Cui, Liadov and Rimsky-Korsakov, written before 1880, when a second edition appeared and Liszt contributed a new variation of his own.

Choral (German), chorale (English), Lutheran hymn. The German word was originally used to mean the choral parts of Latin chant, and by extension plainsong in general, a meaning which it still bears today. At the Reformation it took on the secondary meaning of the monophonic congregational singing of the Lutheran liturgy, many of the melodies being adaptations from the plainsong itself; hence the term *Choralbearbeitung/chorale arrangement* to denote any kind of setting of such melodies. The English word is simply an adaptation of the German in its Lutheran sense, the final 'e' being added to make the pronunciation clear and to avoid confusion with the adj. 'choral'.

chorale ◊choral.

chorale cantata term used for a form of church cantata, especially by Bach, which draws on the text and, usually, music of a Lutheran hymn. The chorale words and melody may (rarely) be present in each movement of the cantata (e.g. in *Christ lag in Todesbanden*), or some verses may be replaced by free paraphrases of the text or completely new material set as recitatives, arias, etc. Treatment varies from the simple harmonizations found as the last movement of many cantatas to the complexity of the massive fantasia-like chorus which opens *Ein' feste Burg*.

A Selection of

Chopin

Piano Concerto no. 2	1829–30
Piano Concerto no. 1	1830
Waltzes	1827–41
Nocturnes	1830–46
Mazurkas	1830–49
Ballades	1831–42
Études op. 25	1832–6
24 *Preludes* op. 28	1836–9
Piano Sonata op. 35	1839
Piano Sonata op. 58	1844

chorale fantasy a type of organ composition in which a hymn-tune is freely treated.

choral prelude a type of organ piece for church use e.g. by Bach; introducing the tune of the hymn about to be sung by the congregation and artistically elaborating it by contrapuntal treatment or by the provision of an original accompaniment.

'Choral Symphony' popular name for Beethoven's ninth symphony in D minor, op. 125, on account of its last movement, a setting of Schiller's ode *An die Freude/To Joy* for solo quartet, chorus and orchestra. Composed *c* 1817–24, fp Vienna, 7 May 1824.

chord the sounding together of three or more notes.

chording a term used to designate either the spacing of the notes in a chord in composition or the performance of them strictly in tune in relation to each other.

choreography the invention, design and stage management of the dancing in a ballet.

Chorley, Henry F(othergill) (b Blackley Hurst, Lancs., 15 Dec 1808; d London, 16 Feb 1872), English music critic, librettist and author, contributed to the *Athenaeum* from 1830.

Choron, Alexandre (Étienne) (b Caen, 21 Oct 1771; d Paris, 29 Jun 1834), French music scholar and composer. Among his books are a music encyclopaedia and treatises on music study, part-writing, plainsong, etc.

Works include a Mass, a *Stabat Mater*, psalms, hymns, etc.

Chorton German = lit. 'choir-pitch'; the pitch to which church organs in Germany were tuned in the 17th-18th c. It was higher, usually by a whole tone, than *Kammerton* ('chamber-pitch'), and it is for this reason that Bach transposed the woodwind parts in his cantatas up, or alternatively transposed the organ parts down. The strings, could, as necessary, play at either pitch.

Chorzempa, Daniel (Walter) (b Minneapolis, 7 Dec 1944), American organist, pianist and composer. Studied in Minneapolis and Cologne and played the organ in the UK from 1969; piano debut at Oxford (1970) with the Diabelli Variations. Many tours as organist in the music of Liszt and Reubke. Has composed at the electronic music studios, Cologne, from 1970.

Chout, *The Buffoon*, ballet in six scenes, op. 21, by Prokofiev (scenario by the composer, from a story by A Afansyev), composed 1915, revised 1920; produced Paris, Ballets Russes, 17 May 1921. Symphonic Suite from the ballet arranged 1920, fp Brussels, 15 Jan 1924.

Chou Wen-chung (b Chefoo, 28 July 1923), Chinese-born American composer. Studied in USA from 1946, at first with Slonimsky and Luening. Lessons with Varèse 1949–54 and completed his *Nocturnal*; editions of *Ameriques* (1972) and *Octandre* (1980). Professor at Columbia University from 1972. His music reflects oriental and avant-garde influences.

Works include *Landscapes* for orchestra (1949); *Metaphors* for wind orchestra (1961); *Pien* for piano, percussion and wind (1966); *Beijing in the Mist* for chamber ensemble (1986); *Echoes from the Gorge* for percussion quartet (1989); *Windswept Peaks* for violin, cello, clarinet and piano (1990; choral and piano works, film music.

I'm a revolutionary, money means nothing to me.
Frédéric Chopin, quoted in Hedley, *Chopin*, 1947

Christelflein, Das opera by Pfitzner (libretto by I von Stach and the composer), produced Munich, 11 Dec 1906, conductor Mottl. Dying girl gets her Christmas tree before elf takes her to heaven.

Christie, William (b Buffalo, NY, 19 Dec 1944), American conductor and harpsichordist. Studied with Igor Kipnis and Ralph Kirkpatrick, and moved to Paris 1971, becoming a member of the Five Centuries Ensemble and founding Les Arts Florissants, 1979. Many performances in Europe and the USA with Baroque opera: *Atys* by Lully in Paris and NY, *Les Indes Galantes* and *Pygmalion* by Rameau, Rossi's *Orfeo* in Vienna, *Alcina* in Paris and Geneva, 1990. London debut 1990 with Charpentier's *Actéon*, and *Dido and Aeneas*; returned

---

Chopin   *A biographical note*

Chopin had premiered both his piano concertos by the time he first arrived in Paris, in September 1831. He wrote to a friend: 'One finds here in Paris magnificent riches, filthy streets, the most virtuous people and the most depraved ... one may dress like a derelict and still be accepted by the best society.' Chopin himself was fastidious about his appearance, spending much of his considerable income on clothes, including the white gloves that became his trademark. A certain refinement of manner and an admired, ethereal musical profile led to him being dubbed by the critics 'The Ariel of the piano'. His technique was not suited to large concert halls, and he gained his success at the salons of the nobility, at which he also met leading painters and writers of the day. One such was the novelist George Sand, an early feminist whose real name was Aurore Dupin. Chopin soon formed an unlikely liaison with her, becoming the passive partner to the trouser-wearing, cigar-chewing writer; not surprisingly, Liszt's comment on their relationship was 'Poor Frédéric'. Early in their relationship, Sand confided in a friend that Chopin was a reluctant lover; Sand's novel *Lucrezia Floriani* portrays Chopin as a milksop. Nevertheless, they did not part until 1847, by which time Chopin was mortally ill with tuberculosis.

1992, with *The Fairy Queen*. Conducted *King Arthur* at CG 1995. Professor at the Paris Conservatory from 1982.

Christmas Concerto Corelli's Concerto grosso, op. 6. no. 8.

Christmas Eve, *Notch Pered Rozhdestvom*, opera by Rimsky-Korsakov (libretto by the composer, based on Gogol's story), produced St Petersburg, 10 Dec 1895.
◊Vakula the Smith.

Christmas Oratorio a series of six cantatas by Bach (1734) designed for separate performance between Christmas and Epiphany. Not originally intended for performance as one composite work.

Christmas Symphony (Haydn) ◊Lamentatione.

Christoff, Boris (b Sofia, 18 May, 1914; d Rome, 28 Jun 1993), Bulgarian bass-baritone. Initially a law student, he later studied singing in Rome and Salzburg, making his debut in Rome in 1946 as Colline; sang Boris at CG in 1949 and Philip II in 1958. US debut San Francisco, 1956. Other roles included Marke, Gurnemanz, Ivan Susanin, Fiesco and Haydn's Pluto (Florence, 1951). He excelled in the Russian repertory (especially *Boris Godunov*) and also gave numerous recitals.

Christophe Colomb opera by Milhaud (libretto by P Claudel), produced in Germany, Berlin, Staatsoper, 5 May 1930, conductor Kleiber. The work makes use of film. In the final scene, Queen Isabella rides to heaven on a mule provided by Columbus.

Christophers, Harry (b Goudhurst, Kent, 26 Dec 1953), English conductor and choral director. Studied at Oxford and founded choral group The Sixteen, 1977; many tours of Europe, the Far East and N and S America in the *Messiah*, Bach's Passions and *Christmas Oratorio*. Led The Sixteen in the premiere of Birtwistle's *Gawain* (CG, 1991) and made world tour with *Messiah*, 1992. Recordings include Taverner *Festal Mass* series, Monteverdi *Vespers*, Byrd Mass in four parts, *The Fairy Queen* and *Alexander's Feast* by Handel.

Christophorus, oder Die Vision einer Oper opera by Schreker (libretto by the composer), composed 1925–29 but the original production was banned by the Nazis; fp Freiburg i/B, 1 Oct 1978. Student attempts to write an opera based on the life of St Christopher, but the characters of the legend become confused with his own friends.

Christus oratorio by Liszt (words from the Bible and the Roman Catholic liturgy), composed 1855–66, fp. Weimar, 29 May 1873.

Oratorio by Mendelssohn (words by Chevalier Bunsen), began 1844, resumed 1847, but left unfinished.

Christus am Oelberg, *Christ at the Mount of Olives*, oratorio by Beethoven, op. 85 (libretto by F X Huber), produced Vienna, 5 Apr 1803.

chromatic, from Greek *chrōmatikos*, = 'coloured'; the chromatic scale is one proceeding entirely by semitones, i.e. taking in all the notes available in normal western music. Chromatic harmony consists of chords using notes not included in the scale of the prevailing key and thus, in notation, involving the use of many accidentals.

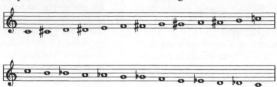

An ascending and descending chromatic scale beginning on C.

Chromatic Fantasy and Fugue a keyboard work in D minor by Bach, written *c* 1720, revised *c* 1730. The adj. refers to the harmonies of the fantasy and the subject of the fugue.

chromatic harp a French type of harp which, instead of being tuned to the scale of C♭ major, like the normal harp, where each string can be raised in pitch by a semitone or a whole tone with the aid of pedals, has strings for all the notes of the chromatic scale. They are not all strung parallel, but slightly crossed, so that except where they actually intersect they stand away from each other in two ranges, one representing the diatonic scale of C major, the other the sharps or flats, like the white and black notes on the piano.

chromaticism composition with extensive use of non-diatonic notes, that is, pitches that are not part of the prevailing major or minor scale. This is obviously a relative term, but it is most often applied to music of the 19th c. and later, and especially that which verges on atonality.

chromatic madrigal (1) A madrigal making free use of chromatic harmony.

(2) In 16th-c. Italy *a madrigale cromatico* was one using black notes as the basis of measurement and hence moving at a brisk speed.

Chronochromie, *Time-colour*, work for orchestra in seven sections by Messiaen; composed 1960, fp Donaueschingen, 16 Oct 1960, conductor Rosbaud.

Chrysander, (Karl Franz) Friedrich (b Lübtheen, Mecklenburg, 8 Jul 1826; d Bergedorf near Hamburg, 3 Sept 1901), German music scholar and editor. Lived in England for some time, researching material for his great biography of Handel, pub. 1858–67, never completed. He also edited Handel's complete works. Other works of his on old music are valuable, but he was violently opposed to all 'modern', i.e. post-Handelian, music.

At the rehearsals of the opera he will never disclose his intention to any of the actors, wisely reflecting that they desire to do everything in their own way.
Benedetto Marcello, *The Theatre à la Mode*, 1720

Chung, Kyung-Wha (b Seoul, 26 Mar 1948), Korean violinist. She went to the USA in 1961 and in 1967 shared first prize in the Leventritt Competition; 1968 soloist with the NY PO. 1970 European debut with the LSO. Appearances at Salzburg, Vienna and Edinburgh Festivals. Concerto recordings of Beethoven, Stravinsky, Bartók and Tchaikovsky. Her sister, *Myung-Wha* (b Seoul, 19 Mar 1944), is a cellist who made her orchestral debut in 1957 and studied at Juilliard. Many concerts and chamber music tours of Europe and the USA from 1971, including recitals with the Chung Trio.

Chung, Myung-Whun (b Seoul, 22 Jan 1953), Korean-born US conductor. Studied at Juilliard and was associate conductor of the LA Philharmonic 1978–81. Europe from 1981, with the Berlin, Munich and Israel POs and the major London orchestras. Music Director of the Saarland Radio SO 1984–90; guest in the USA with Boston SO,

NY PO and Cleveland and Chicago Orchestras. NY Met. debut 1986, *Simon Boccanegra*, and has led *Boris Godunov, Idomeneo* and *The Invisible City of Kitezh* at Florence. Music Director of the Opéra Bastille, Paris 1990, opening the new house with *Les Troyens*, but left in controversial circumstances, 1994. Conducted the premiere of Messiaen's *Concert à quatre* 1994. Formerly a concert pianist and has played in a trio with his sisters Kyung-Wha ◊Chung and Myung-Wha Chung.

Chute de la Maison Usher, La, *The Fall of the House of Usher*, opera by Debussy (libretto by himself, based on E A Poe's story), worked at between 1908 and 1918, but never completed. Realizations of Debussy's fragments were performed at Yale University and Frankfurt, 1977.

Ciampi, Vincenzo Legrenzio (b Piacenza, 1719; d Venice, 30 Mar 1762), Italian composer. Pupil of Durante. He was resident in London 1748–60, and from the latter year to his death *maestro di cappella* at the Ospizio degli Incurabili in Venice.

Works include 22 operas, e.g. *Bertoldo, Bertoldino e Cacasenno* (1748) and *Il negligente* (1749); four oratorios; church music; chamber music.

Cibber Susanna Maria ◊Arne.

Ciccimarra, Giuseppe (b Altamura, 22 May 1790; d Venice, 5 Dec 1836), Italian tenor. He was highly regarded as a Rossini singer at Naples; created Iago (1818) and took part in the fps of *Armida, Mosè, Ermione* and *Maometto II*. He taught in Vienna after his retirement from the stage.

Chung *Pianist and conductor Myung-Whun Chung. In addition to his career as a soloist, he has also collaborated with his sisters Kyung-Wha (violin) and Myung-Wha (cello) in chamber music and Beethoven's Triple Concerto.*

Ciconia, Johannes (b Liège, ? *c* 1370; d Padua, Jun–Jul 1412), Liègeois composer and theorist. His only clearly documented activity is as choirmaster at Padua Cathedral from *c* 1401, though some believe that he was born *c* 1335 and was active earlier in Avignon. Perhaps the most important and influential composer of his generation. Works include Mass movements, motets and secular works in both French and Italian. There is also a treatise, *Nova musica*.

Cid, Der opera by Cornelius (libretto by composer, based on Corneille's drama), produced Weimar, 21 May 1865.

Cid, Le opera by Massenet (libretto by A P d'Ennery, L Gallet and E Blau, based on Corneille's drama), produced Paris, Opéra, 30 Nov 1885. Chimène loves Rodrigue; when Rodrigue's father is appointed guardian to the king's son, Chimène's father insults Rodrigue, who then kills him in a duel. Chimène seeks revenge against Rodrigue, but forgives him after he has saved Spain in battle.

Ciesinski, Katherine (b Newark, 13 Oct 1950), American mezzo-soprano, sister of Kristine ◊Ciesinski. Studied at the Curtis Institute and sang in Europe from 1976. US debut at Santa Fe 1979, as Geschwitz in the US fp of the three-act version of *Lulu*; sang in the fp of Argento's *The Aspern Papers* at Houston and made Met. debut, as Nicklausse, 1988. Other roles include Cassandre for Scottish Opera (also at CG), Judith, Brangaene, Laura, and Leonore in the French version of *La Favorite*. She is a versatile singing actress.

Ciesinski, Kristine (b Wilmington, 5 Jul 1952), American soprano, sister of Katherine ◊Ciesinski. Studied in Boston and made concert debut at NY 1977, in *Messiah*. Sang at the Salzburg Landestheater 1979–81, Bremen 1985–88. Sang Donna Anna with Scottish Opera 1985, Cassandre in *Les Troyens* for Opera North and WNO, 1986–87. ENO debut 1989, in Weill's *Street Scene*. Guest in N America and Europe as Lady Macbeth, Salome, Aida, Judith, Fidelio, and Berg's Marie. An exciting performer with a wide repertory.

Cifra, Antonio (b near Terracina; d Loretto, 2 Oct 1629), Italian composer. Pupil of G B Nanini in Rome. He was *maestro di cappella* of the German College there in 1609, at Loreto from 1609 to 1622 and at the church of St John Lateran, Rome, from 1622 to 1625, returning to Loreto in 1626.
Works include Masses, motets, psalms, madrigals.

Cigna, Gina (b Paris, 6 Feb 1900), Italian soprano. Debut La Scala, 1927, as Freia; remained until World War II as Abigaille, Gioconda and Turandot. CG 1933–39. NY Met. debut 1936, as Aida. She appeared as guest in Chicago and San Francisco.

Cikker, Ján (b Banská Bystrica, 29 Jul 1911; d Bratislava, 21 Dec 1989), Slovak composer. Studied composition with J Kricka and Novák. He became professor at Bratislava Conservatory in 1951. His chief interest was in theatre composition, writing in an atonal, though romantically inclined, idiom.
Works include operas *Beg Bajazid* (1954), *Resurrection* (after Tolstoy, 1962), *Mr Scrooge* (after Dickens, 1963), *Coriolanus* (after Shakespeare, 1974); *The Sentence: Earthquake in Chile* (1979), *The Siege of Bystrica* (1983) and *From the Life of the Insects* (1987).

Cilea, Francesco (b Palmi, Calabria, 26 Jul 1866; d Varazze, 20 Nov 1950), Italian composer. Studied at Naples and while still at the Conservatory produced his first opera there in 1889. The pub. Sonzogno then commissioned a second, produced at Florence in 1892. Professor at the Reale Istituto Musicale at Florence, 1896–1904.
Works include operas *Gina* (1889), *La Tilda*, *L'Arlesiana* (after Daudet), *Adriana Lecouvreur* (after Scribe, 1902), *Gloria*; cello and piano sonata; numerous piano works.

Cillario, Carlo Felice (b San Rafael, 7 Feb 1915), Argentine conductor. Studied in Bologna and founded a chamber orchestra there 1946. Chicago Opera and Glyndebourne debuts 1961, with *Forza del Destino* and *L'elisir d'amore*. Conducted *Tosca* at CG 1964 and *La sonnambula* at the Met., 1972. Royal Opera Stockholm from 1980, Drottningholm 1982 (*Il fanatico Burlato* by Cimarosa). Principal guest and music consultant to Australian Opera from 1988.

Cimador(o), Giovanni Battista (b Venice, 1761; d Bath, 27 Feb 1805), Italian composer. Successfully produced dramatic works *Ati e Cibeli* (1789), *Il ratto di Proserpina* (Venice, 1791) and 'scena lyrica'

Pimmalione in Italy, but settled in London 1791. Other works include concerto for double bass; vocal pieces.

Cimarosa, Domenico (b Dec Aversa near Naples, 17 Dec 1749; d Venice, 11 Jan 1801), Italian composer. Studied at Naples, among his masters being Sacchini and Piccinni, and produced his first opera there in 1772. Later lived in Rome and Naples by turns, became famous with several operas, travelled much and in 1787 went to the court of Catherine II at St Petersburg. In 1791 the Emperor Leopold II invited him to Vienna, to succeed Salieri as court *Kapellmeister*. There he produced his most successful opera, *Il matrimonio segreto*, in 1792, which was encored in its entirety at its premiere. His engagement in Vienna ended the same year, when, on the death of Leopold, Salieri was re-appointed, Cimarosa returned to Naples, becoming *maestro di cappella* to the king. He was imprisoned because of his involvement in the Neapolitan rising of 1799. On his release he set out for St Petersburg, but died at Venice on the way, allegedly by poison.
Works include over 60 operas, e.g. *Le stravaganze del conte*, *L'Italiana in Londra* (1779), *Il pittore parigino*, *La ballerina amante* (1782), *L'Olimpiade*, *Artaserse* (1784), *L'impresario in augustie*, *Cleopatra* (1789), *Idalide*, *Il matrimonio segreto*, *Le astuzie femminili* (1794), *Il marito disperato*, *L'impegno superato*, *Gli Orazi ed i Curiazi*, *Penelope* (1795), *Achille all' assedio di Troia*; Masses, oratorios, cantatas.

> *Swans sing before they die – 'twere no bad thing/Did certain persons die before they sing.*
> **Samuel Taylor Coleridge**, (1772–1834), epigram on a volunteer singer

Cimarrón, El work by Henze for baritone, flute, guitar and percussion (text from *The Autobiography of a Runaway Slave*, by E Montejo), fp Aldeburgh, 22 Jun 1970.

cimbalom a Hungarian national instrument, descendant of the dulcimer, with strings stretched over a horizontal sound-board which are struck by hammers.

Cincinnati Symphony Orchestra US orchestra, founded 1895 and conducted by Fran van der Stucken 1896–1907. Stokowski was conductor 1909–12, Fritz Reiner 1922–31 and Eugene Goossens 1931–47. First US orchestra to make a world tour (under Max Rudolf, 1967); other directors have been Thomas Schippers (1970–77), Michael Gielen (1980–86) and Jesus Lopez-Cobos from 1986.

Cinderella ◊Cendrillon, ◊Cenerentola.

Cinesi, Le, *The Chinese Ladies*, opera by Caldara (libretto by Metastasio), produced Vienna, at court, Carnival 1735. Four friends while away the time acting out legends.
Opera by Gluck (libretto ditto), produced Schlosshof, near Vienna, at court, 24 Sept 1754.

cinquepace from French *cinq pas* = 'five steps' (also colloqial 'sink-a-pace'); a dance of the 16th c. in quick 3–4 time and requiring movements in groups of five paces. The name was used both for the galliard following the pavan and for the tordion concluding the basse danse. Shakespeare makes a pun on it in *Much Ado about Nothing*.

Cinti-Damoreau, Laure (Cinthie Montalant) (b Paris, 6 Feb 1801; d Paris, 25 Feb 1863), French opera singer. Studied at the Paris Conservatory first appearance at the Théâtre Italien at the age of 14, in *Una Cosa rara*, and at the Opéra in 1826. She remained there until 1835 and sang leading roles in the fps of *Le Siège de Corinthe*, *Moïse*, *Le Comte Ory*, *Guillaume Tell* and *Robert le Diable*.

ciphering the escape of sound from organ pipes by a fault in or damage to the mechanism.

Circe and Penelope two parts of a cyclic opera, *Ulysses*, by Keiser (libretto by F C Bressand), produced Brunswick, Feb 1696.

circular canon a canon whose tune, instead of coming to an end, returns to the beginning and may be repeated *ad infinitum*. The round, e.g. *Three blind mice*, is a familiar example.

Circus Polka work for piano by Stravinsky, to accompany the elephants in the Ringling Bros' circus; scored for wind band by D Raksin, 1942; arranged by the composer for orchestra, fp Cambridge, MA, 13 Jan 1944.

Ciro in Babilonia, o sia La caduta di Baldassarre, *Cyrus in Babylon or The Fall of Belshazzar*, opera by Rossini (libretto by F Aventi), produced Ferrara, 14 Mar 1812. Belshazzar is 'found wanting' Amira, wife of King Cyrus, who has been defeated by the Babylonians. Cyrus faces execution, but his fate improves when his forces counterattack.

citole medieval plucked instrument, probably with wire strings.

cittern, or cithren, cither, cythern, etc, plucked instrument with a flat back, popular in 16th and 17th c., possibly descended from the medieval gittern. The finger-board was fretted and the strings were played with a plectrum. The modern German and Austrian ◊zither derives its name from it, but is a different instrument.

The cittern usually had four pairs of wire strings tuned either

or

City of Birmingham Symphony Orchestra English orchestra, founded 1920 as the City of Birmingham Orchestra, with Appleby Matthews as its first regular conductor. It was re-named 1948 and made continental tours from 1955. Louis Fremaux was conductor 1969–78, Simon Rattle from 1980. Many programmes of modern music, notably 'Towards the Millenium' series.

Cividale del Friuli, Antonio da (Antonius de Civitate Austriae), Italian 14th-15th-c. composer, active at Florence as well as in N Italy. Five motets, three Mass movements, four *chansons* and one *ballata* survive.

Civil, Alan (b Northampton, 13 Jun 1929; d London, 19 Mar 1989), English horn player. He studied with Aubrey Brain, and was principal horn RPO 1952–55, co-principal Philharmonia Orchestra 1955–57, with Dennis Brain (principal 1957–66). In 1966 he became principal horn of the BBC SO and professor at the RCM.

Clapisson, Antoine Louis (b Naples, 15 Sept 1808; d Paris, 19 Mar 1866), French violinist and composer. Violinist at the Paris Opéra, 1832–38, after which he made a great success with songs and comic operas. His collection of early instruments is in the Paris Conservatory.

Works include operas *La Figurante* (1838), *Le Code noir* (1842), *Gibby la Cornemuse, La Promise* (1854), *La Fanchonnette, Madame Grégoire,* etc.

Clapp, Philip Greeley (b Boston, MA, 4 Aug 1888; d Iowa City, 9 Apr 1954), American composer. Graduated at Harvard University and studied with Schillings at Stuttgart, and in London. After several academic appointments he became professor of music at University of Iowa.

Works include cantata *A Chant of Darkness* (H Keller); 12 symphonies (1908–44), piano concerto in B minor, Fantasy on an Old Plainchant for cello and orchestra, *Dramatic Poem* for trombone and orchestra; songs with orchestra; string quartet, etc.

Clarey, Cynthia (b Smithfield, VA, 25 Apr 1949), American mezzo-soprano. Studied at Juilliard and appeared at NY City Opera in *The Voice of Ariadne* by Musgrave; Boston 1979 in the US fp of Tippett's *The Ice Break* (returned 1984 for the premiere of *The Mask of Time.* Glyndebourne 1984–86, as Octavia in *Poppea* and Serena in *Porgy and Bess.* Wexford Festival 1985–87, as Polinesso in *Ariodante* and Thomas' *Mignon.* London concerts 1993–94 in music by Weill and in Berg's *Lulu.*

Clari, Giovanni Carlo Maria (b Pisa, 27 Sept 1677; d Pisa, 16 May 1754), Italian composer. *Maestro di cappella* successively at Pistoia (*c* 1712), Bologna (1720) and Pisa (1736). Five of his vocal duets were used by Handel in *Theodora.*

Works include opera *Il Savio delirante* (1695); 11 oratorios; Masses, *Stabat Mater* and other church music.

The many-keyed clarinet, which can sound so ghostly in the deep chalumean register but higher up can gleam in silvery blossoming harmony.
Thomas Mann, *Doctor Faustus*, 1947

---

clarinet a woodwind instrument with a single reed made in various pitches, the most current being clarinets in A and in B♭ (there is also a smaller clarinet in E♭). It came into use later than the other woodwind instruments still current, and did not establish itself regularly in the orchestra until after the middle of the 18th c.

Other members of the family are the ◊basset horn, the ◊clarinette d'amour, the bass clarinet and the contrabass (or pedal) clarinet (with a compass two octaves below the ordinary clarinet).

clarinette d'amour French = 'love clarinet'; a large clarinet made in continental Europe between late 18th c. and *c* 1820, usually a major third or fourth lower than the clarinet in C.

clarino Italian = 'clarion'; the name given to the trumpet in the 17th and 18th c., also the name of the highest register of the instrument, from C above middle C upwards, which was regularly used for florid passages in the works of Bach and his contemporaries.

As a name for the instrument it = tromba. In the early 18th c. it sometimes = clarinet, for which the normal Italian term was *clarinetto.*

Clark, Graham (b Littleborough, Lancs., 10 Nov 1941), English tenor. Studied in London and sang with Scottish Opera from 1975; ENO from 1976, notably as Ginastera's Bomarzo, Hoffmann, Alexey in *The Gambler* and Mephistopheles in Busoni's *Doktor Faust.* Sang David in *Meistersinger* at Bayreuth, 1981, Mime and Loge from 1988. NY Met. debut 1985 (Števa in *Jenůfa*), returning as Begaerss in John Corigliano's *The Ghosts of Versailles* (1991). Much admired for his character roles.

Clarke, Jeremiah (b ? London, *c* 1673; d London, 1 Dec 1707), English composer. Pupil of Blow at the Chapel Royal, organist at Winchester College, 1692–95, may have assisted Blow at St Paul's Cathedral in London. Sworn Gentleman-extraordinary of the Chapel Royal in 1700 and organist in 1704. His famous 'Trumpet Voluntary' in D was previously ascribed to Purcell. He committed suicide, supposedly after an unhappy love affair.

Works include anthems; odes on the Assumption of the Blessed

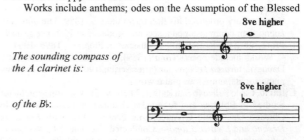

The sounding compass of the A clarinet is:

of the B♭:

of the E♭:

Virgin, in praise of Barbadoes and *O Harmony*; setting of Dryden's *Alexander's Feast* (1697), operas *The Island Princess* (with D Purcell and Leveridge) (1699), *The World in the Moon* (Settle, with D Purcell) (1697); incidental music for Shakespeare's *Titus Andronicus*, Sedley's *Antony and Cleopatra* and other plays; harpsichord music, including *The Prince of Denmark's March* ('Trumpet Voluntary').

Clarke, Rebecca (b Harrow, 27 Aug 1886; d New York, 13 Oct 1979), English viola player and composer. Studied at the RAM in London. In a competition in USA in 1919 for a work for viola and piano she won the prize with a sonata, second only to Ernest Bloch's Suite. She settled in NY in 1944 and married the pianist James ◊Friskin.

Works include Psalm for chorus; piano trio (1921); viola and piano sonata, Rhapsody for cello and piano (1923), duets for viola and cello; songs for voice and violin and for voice and piano; instrumental pieces, etc.

Classical a term commonly used to denote the period of Haydn, Mozart and Beethoven, as opposed to the later Romantic period and earlier Baroque period.

Classical Symphony symphony no. 1 in D, op. 25, by Prokofiev, written in emulation of Haydn, performed Petrograd (St Petersburg), 21 Apr 1918.

Claudel, Paul (1868–1955), French poet and dramatist. ◊Christophe Colomb (Milhaud), ◊Homme et son désir (ditto), ◊Honegger (*Danse des morts*, *Soulier de satin*, three songs), ◊Jeanne d'Arc au bûcher (Honegger), ◊Milhaud (*Protée*, *Annonce faite à Marie*, Aeschylus translations and songs).

Claudine von Villa Bella play for music by Goethe.

Music by Schubert (libretto from Goethe's play); all three acts were composed in 1815 but the MS of Acts 2 and 3 were used as firelighters by the servants of Josef Hüttenbrenner. Overture and Act 1 performed Vienna, Gemeindehaus Wieden, 26 Apr 1913.

clausula an interpolation in regular rhythm into 12th- and 13th-c. ◊organum, without words, but either sung to the syllable of the text immediately preceding it or played by instruments or both together. The lowest (tenor) part, which in the main portions of the music is in very long notes, here moves at a quicker speed, the notes being arranged in a rhythmical pattern. Numerous clausulae were also designed apparently as independent pieces. In later usage the term meant 'cadential formula'.

clavecin French = harpsichord (old spelling sometimes *clavessin*).

clavicembalo Italian = harpsichord. The abbr. *cembalo* is often used.

clavichord a stringed keyboard instrument which differs in its tone-production from the harpsichord. The strings are not plucked, but struck by a tangent which presses against them as long as the key is held down by the finger and produces a very faint note which can, if necessary, be made to vibrate by a gentle shaking of the finger. The pitch of the note is determined by the place at which the string is struck by the tangent, so that the same string can be used for two adjacent notes, which then can never be sounded simultaneously. Such instruments are called 'fretted' clavichords; those which have a separate string for each note are 'fretless'.

clavicytherium, Latin, a harpsichord whose wing-shaped body stood upright instead of being placed horizontally as in the grand piano.

clavier, French and German = keyboard; German also = harpsichord or piano, in English the word may be used to designate any stringed keyboard instrument, especially the harpsichord, clavichord and early piano in cases where it is doubtful which was used in performance or where the choice was at the player's discretion.

Clavierübung German = lit. 'keyboard practice'; a collection of keyboard music by Bach, pub. in four parts: I (1731), six partitas; II (1735), Italian concerto and French overture; III (1739), organ prelude and fugue in Eb major framing 21 chorale preludes on the catechism and four manual *duetti*; IV (1741 or 1742), 'Goldberg' variations.

claviorganum an instrument combining harpsichord and organ mechanisms, dating from the late 16th c. and made in various forms until the 18th.

Clay, Frederic (b Paris, 3 Aug 1838; d Great Marlow, 24 Nov 1889), English composer. Pupil of Molique and of Hauptmann at Leipzig. He began by writing light operas for amateurs, 1859–60, but produced *Court and Cottage* at CG in London in 1862.

Works include light operas *Princess Toto*, *Don Quixote* (1876), *The Merry Duchess* (1883), *The Golden King*, etc.; incidental music for Shakespeare's *Twelfth Night*; cantatas *The Knights of the Cross* and *Lalla Rookh* (Moore), the latter including 'I'll sing thee songs of Araby'; songs 'She wandered down the mountainside', *The Sands of Dee*.

Clayton, Thomas (b ? 1660–70; d ? 1720–30), English composer and adapter. He set Addison's opera libretto of *Rosamond*, which proved a complete failure, in 1707. *Arsinoë*, produced as his own opera in 1705, was a pasticcio of Italian songs. In 1711 he produced a setting of an altered version of Dryden's *Alexander's Feast*.

clef the sign in front of the key and time signatures at the beginning of a composition and repeated on each stave, determining the position of the notes shown on the stave; e.g. the C clef placed on the third line indicates that the note on that line is middle C.

Clemencic, René (b Vienna, 27 Feb 1928), Austrian recorder player, harpsichordist and conductor. Studied in Vienna and founded the Ensemble Musica Antiqua 1958; Clemencic Consort from 1969. Concerts worldwide, and first modern performances of Peri's *Euridice* and Leopold I's *Il luto dell'universo*; sacred music by Josquin, Monteverdi, Dufay, Obrecht and Ockeghem; medieval *Carmina burana* in his own edition.

Clemens non Papa, Clément, Jacques (b *c* 1510–*c* 1515; d ? Dixmuide, *c* 1556), Flemish composer. Worked at Bruges, (?) at Antwerp Cathedral and at the cathedral of 's Hertogenbosch. His nickname was long said to have distinguished him from Pope Clement VII, but it did not appear on pubs. until 14 years after that pope's death.

Works (over 400) including Masses, motets, psalms in Flemish, *chansons*.

Clément, Félix (b Paris, 28 Mar 1867; d Nice, 24 Feb 1928), French tenor. Debut Paris, Opéra-Comique, 1889, in *Mireille*; remained there until 1910 and sang in the fps of operas by Bruneau, Saint-Saëns (*Phryné* and *Hélène*), Godard, Hahn and Erlanger. NY Met. 1909–11. Other roles included Fenton, Pinkerton and Massenet's Des Grieux.

Clement, Franz (Joseph) (b Vienna, 17 Nov 1780; d Vienna, 3 Nov 1842), Austrian violinist. First appeared at the age of seven; leader of the orchestra at the Theater an der Wien in Vienna 1802–11 and 1817–21. Beethoven wrote his violin concerto for him; premiered in 1806. In the same concert he performed variations with his violin turned upside down.

The clavichord gives a fretful waspish kind of sound, not at all suited to tender expression.
John Robison, *Encyclopaedia Britannica*, 1801

Clementi, Aldo (b Catania, 25 May 1925), Italian composer. Studied with Petrassi and Maderna, who influenced him towards 12-note serialism. Works are densely structured and include *Informels* (1961–63; concerto for wind orchestra and two pianos (1967); stage series *Blitz* (1973); *Collage 4* (1979) and *Es* (1981); concerto for piano and 11 instruments (1986).

Clementi, Muzio (b Rome, 23 Jan 1752; d Evesham, 10 Mar 1832), Italian pianist, composer, pub. and piano manufacturer. Showed early promise, and had composed several works by the age of 14, when Peter Beckford took him to England to complete his education. Pub. his first piano sonatas in 1773, and appeared with spectacular success as a virtuoso pianist and composer. He was conductor of the Italian Opera in London 1777–80, after which he toured extensively on the Continent, in 1781 playing before the Viennese court in competition with Mozart (who thought little of him). Back in London, Cramer and John Field were his pupils. He was associated with the pubs. and piano manufacturers Longman & Broderip, upon whose bankruptcy in 1798 he re-established the firm in partnership with Longman. His interest in the co. (trading under a constantly changing variety of names) continued to his death. He was again on tour in Europe 1802–10, taking Field with him to St Petersburg, where the latter remained. In 1807 he met Beethoven in Vienna. From 1810, apart from occasional further travels, he remained in England.

Works include four symphonies; *c* 60 piano sonatas; 100 progressive piano studies entitled *Gradus ad Parnassum*; capriccios and other piano pieces; sonatas for various instruments and piano; chamber music.

Clemenza di Scipione, La, *The Clemency of Scipio*, opera by J C Bach, produced London, King's Theatre, Haymarket, 4 Apr 1778. Scipio holds prisoners after victory at Carthage. Luceius attempts to rescue his love, Arsinda, but is captured. Facing execution, he is saved when Arsinda threatens suicide and Scipio shows mercy.

Clemenza di Tito, La, *The Clemency of Titus*, ◊Tito Vespasiano.

Opera by Gluck (libretto by Metastasio), produced Naples, Teatro San Carlo, 4 Nov 1752.

Opera by Mozart (libretto ditto, altered by Caterino Mazzolà), produced Prague, to celebrate the coronation of the Emperor Leopold II as King of Bohemia, 6 Sept 1791. Titus forgives Vitellia and Sextus for plotting against him.

Cleofide opera by Hasse (libretto by M A Boccardi, based on Metastasio's *Alessandro nell'Indie*), produced Dresden, at court, 13 Sept 1731. Alexander the Great falls for Cleophis but she remains faithful to Porus.

Cleopatra, *Die betrogene Staats-Liebe, oder Die unglückselige Cleopatra, Königin von Egypten*, opera by Mattheson (libretto by F C Feustking), produced Hamburg, Theatre beim Gänsemarkt, 20 Oct 1704. Based on Shakespeare's play and the events described in Plutarch's *Lives*.

Cleopatra e Cesare opera by Graun (libretto by G C Bottarelli, based on Corneille's *La Mort de Pompée*), produced Berlin, Opera, 7 Dec 1742. Written for the inauguration of that theatre. Revived Berlin 1992 (250th anniversary).

Cléopâtre opera by Massenet (libretto by L Payen), produced Monte Carlo, 23 Feb 1914.

Clérambault, Louis Nicolas (b Paris, 19 Dec 1676; d Paris, 26 Oct 1749), French organist and composer. Pupil of André Raison. Organist at various Paris churches. Wrote 25 cantatas and pieces for organ and for harpsichord, solo violin (with continuo) and trio sonatas.

Cleveland Orchestra American orchestra founded 1918 with Nikolay Sokoloff as principal conductor; conductors since 1933 have been Arthur Rodzinski, until 1943; Erich Leinsdorf, 1943–44; George Szell, 1946–70; Lorin Maazel, 1972–82; Christoph von Dohnányi from 1984.

──────── THE OPERA ────────

La Clemenza di Tito

A two-act opera by Mozart, first performed in Prague in 1791. The action is set in Rome in AD 80, at the time of Titus (the Tito of the title).

I. The jealous Vitellia (soprano) schemes with Sesto (mezzo-soprano) to kill Emperor Tito (tenor) and set fire to the Capitol because he has chosen another as his bride. Annio (soprano) wants to marry Servilia (soprano), sister of Sesto, although Tito declares his own interest in Servilia. But Tito renounces Servilia when she confesses that she loves Annio. Learning of Tito's change of heart, Vitellia tries to recall Sesto from his murderous mission, but the Capitol is ablaze as the act ends.

II. Sesto confesses his crime to Annio even though he knows that Tito is still alive, and it turns out that somebody else has been stabbed in mistake for Tito. Following his arrest, Sesto does not wish to incriminate Vitellia. But when she confesses her part in the attempt on his life, Tito pardons both the conspirators.

──────── THE OPERA ────────

Cleveland Quartet US ensemble. Debut concert at the Marlboro Festival 1969, and became Resident at the Cleveland Institute the same year. Eastman School from 1976. Many tours of the USA, Europe and Australasia and was joined by Brendel, Zukerman and Bernard Greenhouse in quintets and sextets. Members were David Wallerstein, Peter Salaff, Atar Arad and Paul Katz. Disbanded 1994.

Cliburn, Van (b Shreveport, LA, 12 Jul 1934), American pianist. In 1954 he graduated from Juilliard, and appeared with the NY PO; in 1958 became the first American to win the International Tchaikovsky Competition, Moscow. Debut as conductor 1964. Established his own piano competition at Fort Worth, TX, in 1962.

Clifford, James (b Oxford, 1622; d London, Sept 1698), English divine and musician. Chorister at Magdalen College, Oxford, 1632–42; appointed minor canon at St Paul's Cathedral in London, 1661. Pub. a collection of the words of *Divine Services and Anthems*, 1663.

Clive (born *Raftor*), Catherine (Kitty) (b London 1711; d Twickenham, 6 Dec 1785), English actress and stage singer in ballad operas. Attached to Drury Lane Theatre in London, 1728–41.

'Clock Symphony' the nickname of Haydn's symphony no. 101, in D major (no. 9 of the 'Salomon' symphonies), written for London in 1794. The name derives from the ticking motion of the accompanying figuration in the slow movement.

Clori, Tirsi e Fileno large-scale Italian cantata for two sopranos, alto and chamber ensemble by Handel; composed 1707. First modern revival, London, 1984.

Club Anthem an anthem composed jointly by Blow, Humfrey and W Turner *c* 1664, when they were choirboys at the Chapel Royal. It is a setting of the words 'I will always give thanks'.

Cluer, John (d London, Oct 1728), English music publisher. Worked in London early in the 18th c. and was succeeded by his widow and later her second husband, Thomas Cobb. He pub. some of Handel's operas, including *Giulio Cesare* and *Admeto*.

Cluytens, André (b Antwerp, 26 Mar 1905; d Paris, 3 Jun 1967), Belgian conductor. Studied piano at Antwerp Conservatory. He first worked for his father as a chorus trainer at the Théâtre Royal in Antwerp, where he later conducted opera. He then held numerous posts in France, including director of the Paris Opéra Comique, 1947–49. In 1955 he conducted *Tannhäuser* at Bayreuth. US debut 1956, with the Vienna PO; Staatsoper from 1959.

Coates, Albert (b St Petersburg, 23 Apr 1882; d Milnerton near Cape Town, 11 Dec 1953), English conductor and composer (mother Russian). Sent to school in England and entered Liverpool University, returned to Russia to enter his father's business, but was sent to the Leipzig Conservatory. Studied conducting with Nikisch and conducted opera at several German theatres before he was engaged at St Petersburg, where he conducted Wagner at the Mariinsky Theatre. He fled to England during the Revolution in 1919 and settled in London for good, conducting *Tristan* and the *Ring* at CG; led the first public performance of *The Planets* (1920).

Works include operas *Assurbanipal*, *Samuel Pepys*, *Pickwick* (CG, 1936), *Gainsborough's Duchess*; symphonic poem *The Eagle*, Russian Suite for orchestra; piano pieces.

Coates, Edith (b Lincoln, 31 May 1908; d Worthing, 7 Jan 1983), English mezzo. Studied TCM and with Dino Borgioli. SW 1931–46, in Rimsky-Korsakov's *Snow Maiden* and *Tsar Saltan*, and as Eboli, Carmen and Amneris. CG debut 1937; last appeared there in 1967. She was successful as Tchaikovsky's Countess and sang in the fps of Britten's *Peter Grimes* (1945) and *Gloriana* (1953).

Coates, Eric (b Hucknall, Nottinghamshire, 27 Aug 1886; d Chichester, 23 Dec 1957), English composer. Studied at the RAM in London and became a viola player in a quartet and in the Queen's Hall Orchestra, but later devoted himself to the composition of light and popular music. He is best known for the signature tune for BBC Radio's 'Desert Island Discs'.

Coates, John (b Girlington, near Bradford, 29 Jun 1865; d Northwood, near London, 16 Aug 1941), English tenor. He was trained for and began to make a career as a baritone, but made his first appearance as a tenor in 1899. He became equally famous in opera and oratorio, and was successful in Elgar's oratorios and as Siegfried, Tristan and Lohengrin. Later in life he was one of the finest song recitalists.

Cobbett, W(alter) W(ilson) (b Blackheath, 11 Jul 1847; d London, 22 Jan 1937), English music amateur and editor. A wealthy business-man, he did much valuable work for chamber music by offering prizes for new works by British composers e.g. Bridge, Bax and Britten, especially one-movement fantasies, and he edited a *Cyclopaedia of Chamber Music* pub. 1929 (revised 1963).

Cobbold, William (b Norwich, 5 Jan 1560; d Beccles, 7 Nov 1639), English organist and composer. Organist at Norwich Cathedral, 1599–1608. He was one of the ten musicians who harmonized the tunes in East's Psalter of 1592 and he contributed a madrigal to *The Triumphes of Oriana* in 1601. Among his other few surviving works are 11 consort songs.

Cocchi, Gioacchino (b ? Naples, *c* 1720; d ? Venice, after 1788), Italian composer. Worked at Naples, Rome and Venice until 1757, when he went to London as composer to the King's Theatre, remaining there till 1773. He was also conductor of Mrs Cornely's subscription concerts.

Works include over 40 operas, e.g. *La Maestra* (1747), *Li Matti per Amore* (1754), *Demetrio re di Siria*.

Coccia, Carlo (b Naples, 14 Apr 1782; d Novara, 13 Apr 1873), Italian composer. Pupil of Paisiello. He produced many operas in Italy between 1807 and 1820, when he went first to Lisbon and then to London. He became conductor of the Opera there, also professor of composition at the RAM, and stayed until 1828, returning in 1833, but eventually settling at Novara as *maestro di cappella* in succession to Mercadante, 1840.

Works include *c* 40 operas, e.g. *Il matrimonio per cambiale* (1807), *Donna Caritea, Maria Stuarda* (1827), *Il lago delle fate*, two cantatas.

Coccia, Maria Rosa (b Rome, 4 Jan 1759; d Rome, Nov 1833), Italian composer. At the age of 16 she passed a severe examination at the Accademia di Santa Cecilia in Rome with brilliant success and an account of it was published. In 1780 another eulogy of her was issued with letters from Martini, Metastasio and Farinelli.

Works include Magnificat for voices and organ, written at 15, *Dixit Dominus* and a cantata, but most are lost.

Cochlaeus, Johannes (Johann Dobnek) (b Wendelstein near Nurem-berg, 10 Jan 1479; d Breslau, 10 Jan 1552), German cleric and music scholar. He was a Roman Catholic and an opponent of Luther, in office at Cologne, Worms, Mainz and Frankfurt. Wrote a treatise on music and wrote odes, etc.

Cockaigne (In London Town) concert overture by Elgar, op. 40, composed 1900, fp London, Philharmonic Society, 20 Jun 1901.

Coclico (Coclicus), Adrianus Petit (b Flanders, 1499 or 1500; d Copenhagen, after Sept 1592), Flemish composer. He became a Protestant and went to Wittenberg in 1545. After various posts in Ger-many he went to the Danish court at Copenhagen. Pub. a treatise en-titled *Compendium musices* and *Consolationes piae* (psalm settings).

coda Italian = 'tail'; the part of a musical composition which forms a peroration, where it can be regarded, from the structural point of view, as a distinct and separate section. It is thus most clearly marked, for example, in sonata form, where it appears as a fourth division after the exposition, development and recapitulation, or in a minuet or scherzo with trio, where it rounds off the movement after the restatement of the first section, usually with material based either on that or on the trio.

codetta Italian = 'little tail'; a small form of ◊coda, not appearing as a rule at the end of a movement, but rather rounding off a section of such a movement, or a theme or group of themes, thus assuming the function of a bridge-passage.

Coelho, Rui (b Alcacer do Sal, 2 Mar 1892; d Lisbon, 5 May 1986), Portuguese composer. Studied at Lisbon and later with Humperdinck, Bruch and Schoenberg in Berlin. Became music critic of the *Diario de Noticias* at Lisbon and in 1924 won a prize with his second opera.

Works include operas *Crisfal* (1919), *Belkiss* (1924), *Inés de Castro* (1925), *Tá-Mar* (1936), *Entre giestas* (1946); symphonic

poems *5 Sinfonias camoneanas, Promenade d'été*, etc.; chamber music; piano; pieces; songs.

Coerne, Louis (Adolphe) (b Newark, NJ, 27 Feb 1870; d Boston, MA, 11 Sept 1922), American conductor and composer. Studied in Europe and at Harvard University. After filling an organist's post at Buffalo and conducting there and at Columbus, he became associate professor at Smith College, Northampton, MA, and also taught at Harvard. Later he held other distinguished teaching posts and visited Germany, where some of his works were performed.

Works include operas *A Woman of Marblehead, Zenobia* (1902, produced Bremen, 1905) and *Sakuntala* (after Kalidasa); incidental music to Euripides' *Trojan Women*; six-part Mass; symphonic poem *Hiawatha* (after Longfellow) and other works for orchestra; violin concerto, string quartet in C minor, three piano trios in canon; songs.

Coffee Cantata name given to J S Bach's secular cantata BWV 211 (*c* 1734–35), *Schweigt stille, plaudert nicht*. The libretto by Picanader deals in a humorous way with the then new vogue for drinking coffee.

Cohen, Harriet (b London, 2 Dec 1895; d London, 13 Nov 1967), English pianist. Studied at the RAM and with T Matthay, making her debut, aged 13, at the Queen's Hall, London. She did much for English music, especially that of Bax (whose mistress she was), and also pub. a book, *Music's Handmaid*, on piano-playing and interpret-ation. In 1937 she was awarded the CBE.

Cohn, Arthur (b Philadelphia, 6 Nov 1910), American composer, conductor and writer. Studied at Juilliard and conducted in Philadel-phia 1942–65. Books include *Twentieth-Century Music in Western Europe* (1961) and *The Encyclopedia of Chamber Music* (1990). He has written six string quartets (1928–45), a flute concerto (1941) and *Kaddisch* for orchestra (1965).

Colas Breugnon opera by Kabalevsky (libretto by V Bragin after R Rolland's novel), produced Leningrad, 22 Feb 1938); revised 1953 and 1969. Carpenter Colas recalls his colourful life, in which he revenges himself on the Duke who has destroyed his creations.

Colasse, Pascal (b Rheims, bap. 22 Jan 1649; d Versailles, 17 Jul 1709), French composer. Studied at the Maîtrise de Saint-Paul and the Collège de Navarre in Paris, and *c* 1677 obtained an appointment at the Opéra from Lully, in whose works he wrote some of the subordi-nate parts. In 1683 he became one of the four superintendents of the royal chapel, each of whom had to direct the music for three months in the year, and two years later he shared with Lalande the appointment of royal chamber musician. *Maître de musique de chambre* from 1696.

Works include operas *Achille et Polyxène* (with Lully, 1687), *Thétis et Pélée* (1689), *Énée et Lavinie* (1690), *Jason, La Naissance de Vénus* (1696), *Polyxène et Pyrrhus*, etc.; motets, *Cantiques spiri-tuels* and other church music.

There is not any Musicke of Instruments whatsoever, comparable to that which is made of the voyces of Men.

William Byrd, *Psalmes, Sonets and Songs*, 1588

Colbran, Isabella (Angela) (b Madrid, 2 Feb 1785; d Bologna, 7 Oct 1845), Spanish soprano. Made her debut in Italy in 1806; married Rossini in 1822; she had already sung in the fps of his *Elisabetta, Otello, Armida, Mosè, La donna del lago, Maometto II and Zelmira*. Also successful in such roles as Spontini's Vestale and Mayr's Medea. She retired after singing Zelmira in London, 1824.

Cole, Vinson (b Kansas City, 21 Nov 1950), American tenor. Studied at Curtis Institute and made debut there 1975, as Werther. European debut 1976, with WNO as Belmonte. Sang with St Louis Opera 1976–80, as Tamino and Comte Ory. Season 1991–92 in Mozart's Requiem under Solti, Edgardo at Detroit and Ferrando at Seattle. NY City Opera from 1981 (debut as Nicolai's Fenton).

Coleman, Charles (d London, before 9 Jul 1664), English composer. Chamber musician to Charles I and after the Civil War music teacher in London. Mus.D., Cambridge, 1651; appointed composer to

Charles II, 1662. With Cooke, Hudson, H Lawes and Locke he contributed music to Davenant's *Siege of Rhodes* (entertainment at Rutland House), 1656.

Coleman, Edward (b London; d Greenwich, 29 Aug 1669), English singer, lutenist and composer, son of Charles ◊Coleman. Both he and his wife sang in *The Siege of Rhodes* in 1656. He became a Gentleman of the Chapel Royal on its re-establishment in 1660 and succeeded Lanier in the royal band in 1662. Composed incidental music to Shirley's *Contention of Ajax and Achilles* in 1653, contributed songs to *Select Musicall Ayres and Dialogues* the same year, and pieces of his appeared in Playford's *Musical Companion* in 1672.

Coleridge-Taylor, Samuel (b London, 15 Aug 1875; d Croydon, 1 Sept 1912), English composer. Son of a black doctor and an English mother. Sang at a church at Croydon as a boy, and entered the RCM as a violin student in 1890, but also studied composition under Stanford. He had works performed while still at college and in 1899 he was represented at the N Staffordshire Festival at Hanley. Appointed conductor of the Handel Society in 1904, and visited USA that year, as well as in 1906 and 1910; but otherwise devoted all his time to composition and private teaching, with some teaching activity at the GSM in the last years of his life.

Works include opera *Thelma* (1907–09); settings for solo voices, chorus and orchestra of portions from Longfellow's *Hiawatha* (three parts, 1898), Coleridge's *Kubla Khan* (1905), Noyes's *A Tale of Old Japan*; *Five Choral Ballads* (Longfellow), *Sea Drift* (Whitman) for chorus; oratorio *The Atonement*; incidental music for Shakespeare's *Othello* and Stephen Phillips's *Herod*, *Ulysses*, *Nero* and *Faust* (after Goethe); symphony in A minor; violin concerto in G minor; nonet for strings and wind, piano quintet, clarinet quintet, string quartet in D minor and other chamber music; piano music, songs.

Coletti, Filippo (b Anagni, 11 May 1811; d Anagni, 13 Jan 1894), Italian baritone. Debut Naples, 1834; sang at the Teatro San Carlo in the fps of *Caterina Cornaro* and *Alzira*. At Her Majesty's, London, he created Francesco in *I Masnadieri* (1847). Well known as Boccanegra and in operas by Pacini and Bellini.

Colgrass, Michael (Charles) (b Chicago, 22 Apr 1932), American composer and percussionist. Studied with Milhaud, Lukas Foss and Ben Weber. Has worked in NY with various theatre ensembles.

Works include *Chamber Music* for four drums and string quartet (1954), *Chant* for chorus and vibraphone (1954), *Divertimento* for eight drums, piano and strings (1960), *Seventeen* for orchestra (1960), *Virgil's Dream*, theatre piece (1967), *The Earth's a Baked Apple* for chorus and orchestra (1969), *Nightingale Inc.*, opera (1971), *Letter from Mozart*, collage for piano and orchestra (1976), *Concertmasters*, concerto for three violins and orchestra (1976), *Theatre of the Universe* for solo voices, chorus and orchestra (1976–77), piano concerto (1982), viola concerto (1984); *Wings of Nagual* for wind ensemble (1985), *The Schubert Birds* for orchestra (1989), *Snow Walker* for organ and orchestra (1990), *Arctic Dreams* for band (1991).

Colla, Giuseppe (b Parma, 4 Aug 1731; d Parma, 16 Mar 1806), Italian composer. *Maestro di musica* to the court at Parma, 1766, and to Ferdinand of Bourbon, 1785. He married the singer Lucrezia Aguiari in 1780.

Works include operas *Adriano in Siria* (1762), *Enea in Cartagine* (1769), *Andromeda* and six others; also church music.

colla parte Italian = 'with the part'; a direction indicating that the accompaniment to a vocal or instrumental solo part is to follow the soloist in a passage performed without strict adherence to the tempo.

Collard, Jean-Philippe (b Mareuil-sur-Ay, 27 Jan 1948), French pianist. Studied at the Paris Conservatory 1959–64, and has appeared worldwide in 19th-c. repertory and Ravel. US debut in concerts with San Francisco SO and and has returned with NY PO and Philadelphia Orchestra 1992–93. Has appeared with all major UK orchestras and played Rakhmaninov's 1st at the 1993 London Proms.

collegium musicum Latin = 'musical fraternity'; an association for the performance of chamber and orchestral music in various German towns in the 18th c. Now used in universities specifically for an ensemble performing early music.

col legno Italian = 'with the wood'; a direction indicating that a passage for a string instrument or a group of such instruments is to be played by striking the strings with the stick of the bow.

Colles, H(enry) C(ope) (b Bridgnorth, 20 Apr 1879; d London, 4 Mar 1943), English music critic and scholar. Educated at Oxford and the RCM in London. Assistant music critic to Fuller Maitland on *The Times* until 1911, when he became chief critic, and lecturer at the RCM from 1919. Pub. various books on music, including *Brahms*, *The Growth of Music*, *Voice and Verse*, etc., the seventh volume of the *Oxford History of Music*, and edited the third and fourth editions of *Grove's Dictionary of Music and Musicians*.

Collier, Marie (b Ballarat, 16 Apr 1927; d London, 8 Dec 1971), Australian soprano. She studied in Melbourne and Milan; CG debut 1956, as Musetta; among her best roles there were Tosca, Manon Lescaut and Jenůfa. She was the first Hecuba in Tippett's *King Priam*, and Katerina Izmaylova in the first stage performance in Britain of Shostakovich's opera (1963). Also admired as Emilia Marty and Katya Kabanová.

Music is nothing else but wild sounds civilised into time and tune.

Thomas Fuller, *Worthies of England: Musicians*, 1662

Collin, Heinrich Joseph von (1771–1811), Austrian poet. His chief connection with music is the drama *Coriolan* for which Beethoven wrote an overture. Stadler wrote incidental music for his tragedy *Polyxena*.

Collingwood, Lawrance (b London, 14 Mar 1887; d Killin, Perthshire, 19 Dec 1982), English conductor and composer. Chorister at Westminster Abbey and organ scholar at Exeter College, Oxford; lived in Russia for a time and worked with Albert Coates at the St Petersburg Opera; married there and returned to England during the Revolution. Principal conductor SW 1931–46. Conducted the British fps of Rimsky-Korsakov's *Snow Maiden* (1933) and *The Tale of Tsar Saltan* (1937).

Works include opera *Macbeth* (1934), symphonic poem for orchestra, two piano sonatas, etc.

Colombe, La, *The Dove*, opera by Gounod (libretto by J Barbier and M Carré, after La Fontaine), produced Baden-Baden, 3 Aug 1860. Sylvie in rivalry with another Florentine lady.

Colonna, Giovanni Paolo (b Bologna, 16 Jun 1637; d Bologna, 29 Nov 1695), Italian composer. Studied in Rome with Carissimi, Abbatini and Benevoli. Became organist of San Petronio at Bologna in 1659 and *maestro di cappella* in 1674.

Works include opera *Amilcare di Cipro* (1692) and other dramatic works; Masses, motets, psalms, litanies; oratorios.

Colonne, Édouard (actually Judas) (b Bordeaux, 23 Jul 1838; d Paris, 28 Mar 1910), French violinist and conductor. Founder of the Concerts Colonne. He was the first to popularize Berlioz and was well known for his performances of Wagner, Tchaikovsky and other composers then unknown in France.

color Latin in medieval music = melodic figuration in general. Also a melodic unit repeated in the context of an ◊isorhythmic structure.

coloratura Italian = lit. 'colouring'; florid singing, especially in soprano parts containing elaborately decorative passages.

colour a word frequently used metaphorically for the different qualities of tone produced by various instruments and combinations of instruments. ◊Tone-colour is now generally current.

colour music composers referring to or using colour (light):

Bantock, *Atalanta in Calydon*, during the performance of which the concert-room is to be lighted in a different colour for each movement.

Bliss, *Colour Symphony*, each movement of which bears the name of a colour as title.

Schoenberg, *Die glückliche Hand*, in which coloured light plays a part, as noted in the score.

Skriabin, *Prometheus*, which contains an optional part for the *tastiera per luce*, designed to throw differently coloured lights.

Combattimento di Tancredi e Clorinda, Il, *The Combat of Tancredi and Clorinda*, dramatic cantata by Monteverdi (text by Tasso, from Canto XII, *Gerusalemme liberata*), performed Venice, Palazzo Mocenigo, 1624. Pub. in Monteverdi's *Madrigali guerrieri e amorosi*, 1638.

combination tones the secondary sounds produced by intervals of two notes struck at the same time. There are two kinds of combination tone. Difference tones, produced by the difference between the two generating notes, which consequently sound below the generators, and summation tones, produced by the sum of these two notes, which sound above. All combination tones are faint, and some are virtually inaudible. Tartini was the first to observe difference tones.

comédie lyrique, French, an 18th-c. French name for comic opera.

Comedy on a Bridge, *Veselohra na moste*, opera for radio in one act by Martinů (libretto by the composer, after V K Klicera), produced Prague Radio, 18 Mar 1937. Bridge connects two feuding villages.

come prima Italian = 'as at first'; a direction indicating that the opening section of a movement is to be played again exactly as before, or that a passage is to be treated in the same manner as before.

Comes, Juan Bautista (b Valencia, *c* 1582; d Valencia, 5 Jan 1643), Spanish composer. *Maestro de capilla* at Lérida at first, later music director at Valencia Cathedral from 1613 and again from 1632 with an appointment at the royal chapel in Madrid and another at the Colegio del Patriarca at Valencia in between.

Works include much church music on a large scale; sacred music with Spanish words, etc.

come sopra Italian = 'as above'; a direction asking the player to repeat the manner of performance of a passage heard earlier.

Come, thou monarch of the vine song by Schubert, from Shakespeare's *Antony and Cleopatra*, translated by F von Mayerhofer as *Trinklied*, 'Bacchus', and composed in Germany in 1826.

Come, ye sons of art, away ode by Purcell for the birthday of Queen Mary II, 1694 (text by ? N Tate).

Comissiona, Sergiu (b Bucharest, 16 Jun 1928), Romanian-born US conductor. Studied with Silvestri and conducted in Romania 1946–59. London debut with the LSO, 1960, and worked in Israel 1960–66; Gothenburg SO 1966–77, Baltimore SO 1969–84. Music director Houston SO 1984–88, NY City Opera 1987–88; Helsinki PO from 1990. CG opera debut 1979 (although he had conducted the CG ballet since 1962) with *Il Barbiere di Siviglia*.

commedia per musica Italian = 'comedy for music'; a Neapolitan term of the 18th c. for comic opera.

common chord the non-technical term for a major or minor ◊triad.

common time a loose but widely current term for 4–4 time, sometimes indicated by C.

Communion the last item of the Proper of the Roman Mass. Originally a psalm with antiphon before and after each verse, only the antiphon is now retained. In general style the Communion resembles the ◊Introit.

compact disc a form of ◊gramophone record in which the music is digitally encoded and read by laser.

compass the range of notes covered by a voice or instrument.

Compenius German family of organ builders who also worked in Denmark:

1. Heinrich Compenius the elder (b *c* 1525; d Nordhausen, 2 May 1611). Theorist and composer.

2. Esaias Compenius (b Eisleben; d Hillerød, 1617), son of 1. Built organ at Frederiksborg Castle (still playable). Co-author with Praetorius of *Organographia*.

3. Heinrich Compenius the younger (b Eisleben; d Halle, 22 Sept 1631), brother of 2. Built organ at Magdeburg Cathedral.

4. Johann Heinrich Compenius (d 1642) nephew of 3. Built organ at St Mauritius, Halle, for Samuel Scheidt.

Compère, Loyset (b Hainaut, *c* 1445; d Saint-Quentin, 16 Aug 1518), French composer. At first a chorister, later a canon and chancellor of Saint-Quentin Cathedral.

Works include Masses, magnificats and other church music; also many secular songs with French and Italian words.

compound intervals any intervals exceeding the compass of an octave, so called, as distinct from simple intervals, because they differ from the latter only in width, not in character; e.g. a major tenth is essentially the same as a major third, etc.

compound time any musical metre in which the beats can be subdivided into three, e.g. 6–8, 9–8, 12–8, where there are respectively two, three and four beats in the bar, each divisible into three quavers. In simple time, on the other hand, the beats are divisible into two.

computers in music among the innumerable contributions of the 'new technology' to music may be mentioned (a) its use for electronic composition and performance, ◊synthesizer; (b) its use for setting music in print; (c) its use for analysing music, particularly style characteristics or details of a particular performance.

Comte Ory, Le, *Count Ory*, opera by Rossini (libretto by Scribe and C G Delestre-Poirson), produced Paris, Opéra, 20 Aug 1828. Young Count Ory and his page Isolier pursue Countess Adèle, dressed first as pilgrims, then as nuns. They must escape before Adèle's husband returns.

Comus masque by Milton, with music by Henry ◊Lawes, produced Ludlow Castle, 29 Sept 1634.

The same with alterations by Dalton and music by Arne, produced London, Drury Lane Theatre, 4 Mar 1738.

con Italian = 'with'; the preposition is often used in directions indicating the manner of performance of a piece or movement, e.g. *con brio* = 'with dash', *con molta espressione* = 'with much expression', etc.

con amore Italian = 'with love, with affection'; indicating an enthusiastic manner of performance.

concento Italian = 'union, agreement'; the playing of the notes of a chord exactly together.

concert originally, as in the English 'consort', the singing or playing together under any conditions; now a public performance of music, except that of an opera or as a rule that given by a single performer, which is more often called a recital.

concertante Italian = 'concertizing' (*concertant*, French); an adj. used to designate instrumental or more rarely vocal parts in a composition which are designed largely for the display of virtuosity. A *sinfonia concertante*, for example, is a work with a prominent and brilliant solo part or several such parts.

concertato Italian = 'concerted'; a work or portion of a composition written for several persons to perform together.

concerted music any music written for several soloists to perform together. Any chamber music or a quartet or other ensemble in an opera or oratorio is concerted music, but the opera or oratorio itself is not, neither is, for example, a symphony or a choral part-song.

Concertgebouw Orchestra Dutch orchestra based in the Concertgebouw, Amsterdam, built in 1888. First conductor Willem Kes. Other conductors have included Willem Mengelberg, 1895–1945, Eduard van Beinum, 1945–59, Bernard Haitink and Eugen Jochum, jointly 1961–64; Haitink 1964–86. Present director is Riccardo ◊Chailly.

concertina an instrument, patented in 1829, similar to the accordion, producing its sound by means of metal reeds set vibrating by wind driven by pleated bellows opened and closed by the player's hands.

concertino Italian = 'little concert or little concerto'; in the former sense the concertino is a group of solo instruments playing alternately with the orchestra (*ripieno*) in a work of the *Concerto grosso* type; in the latter a concertino is a concerto for a solo instrument formally on a smaller scale.

Examples include that by Janáček for piano, clarinet, horn, bassoon, two violins, viola; composed 1925, fp Brno, 16 Feb 1926; also by Stravinsky for string quartet, composed 1920; revised 1952 for 12 instruments, fp LA, 11 Nov 1957.

concertmaster, American, the term used in the USA for the leader of an orchestra, derived from the German *Konzertmeister*.

concerto etymologically the word carries two implications: performing together (in 'concert') and fighting or struggling (from the Latin 'concertare'). So the earliest common uses of the word appear in contexts such as the Ferrarese 'concerto delle donne' of the 16th c., a superbly coordinated madrigal ensemble. Many concertos of the 17th and 18th c. are simply ensemble pieces. From the early 18th c. a concerto increasingly became an ensemble work in which a single performer was given the opportunity to display particular soloistic virtuosity; and from the 19th c. onward, especially with regard to Romantic music, the concerto has characteristically included a component of struggle between soloist and orchestra.

concerto grosso Italian = 'grand or big concert'; an orchestral work of the 17th–18th c. played by an orchestra in which generally a group of solo instruments take a more or less prominent part. The group of soloists was called the *concertino* and the main orchestra (*tutti*) the *ripieno*. Bach's Brandenburg Concertos are works of the concerto grosso type, although nos. 3 and 6 contain no *concertino* parts.

Concert Spirituel a musical institution founded in Paris by A Philidor in 1725 for the production of sacred works, but afterwards widening its scope to include secular music, especially symphonies and concertos. It lasted until 1791, but was later replaced by similar organizations.

Concertstück German, also *Konzertstück* = 'concerto piece'; a title sometimes given to works of the concerto type for solo instrument and orchestra which are not fully developed concertos. *Concertstücke* are often in one movement or in several connected sections. Although German, the title has been used by composers in other countries, e.g. Chaminade and Pierné in France, Cowen in England.

Conchita opera by Zandonai (libretto, in French, by M Vaucaire, translated into Italian by C Zangarini, based on P Louÿs' novel *La Femme et le pantin*), produced Milan, Teatro dal Verme, 14 Oct 1911. The libretto was originally written for Puccini. Mateo teased by lover Conchita until he gets tough.

concord the sounding together of notes in harmony that satisfies the ear as being final in itself and requiring no following chord to give the impression of resolution.

Concord Sonata work for piano by Ives in four movements: *Emerson*, *Hawthorne*, *The Alcotts*, *Thoreau*, after the Concord, MA, group of writers admired by Ives; composed 1909–15, first complete performance NY, 20 Jan 1939, by John Kirkpatrick.

concrete music ◊musique concrète.

conducting groups of more than about six performers have nearly always needed someone to ensure ensemble and consistency of interpretation, and there is iconographic evidence of conductors in Egypt and Sumeria from the third millenium BC, just as there is for medieval chant choirs. With the rise of written polyphony, however, ensembles tended to be small and musical direction normally lay in the hands of a leading performer – in the Baroque era often controlling the ensemble from an organ, harpsichord or (particularly in Classical music) from the violin. Conducting with a baton as an independent activity arose mainly in the 19th c., particularly with Spontini, Spohr and Mendelssohn; and the earliest professional career conductor seems to have been Otto Nicolai (1810–49). But until the 20th c. the most important conductors were usually primarily composers.

Until recent years many conductors were famous (or notorious) for their eccentricities (Beecham and Klemperer) or their dictatorial methods (Toscanini and Karajan). More recently, conductors have tended to cooperate more on terms of mutual respect with their musicians (Haitink, Abbado and Rattle). The waning of the personality cult has also allowed a far wider range of music to be performed, particularly from the pre-Classical era.

conductus a 12th–13th-c. vocal composition originally processional in character and written for one or more voices. The basic melody of a *conductus* was generally a tune specially composed. A *conductus cum cauda* was a polyphonic composition ending with an elaborate tailpiece without words (*cauda*, Latin = 'tail'). In the polyphonic *conductus* the parts normally move in the same rhythm.

Congreve, William (1670–1729), English dramatist and poet. F ◊Austin (*The Way of the World*), J◊Eccles (ditto, *Love for Love*, *Semele* and Ode for St Cecilia's Day), ◊Finger (*Love for Love* and *Mourning Bride*), ◊Judgment of Paris (J Eccles, Finger, D Purcell and Weldon), ◊Philidor (8) (*Ode for St Cecilia's Day*), ◊Purcell (*Double Dealer and Old Bachelor*), ◊Semele (Handel), ◊Wellez (*Incognita*).

Conlon, James (b New York, 18 Mar 1950), American conductor. Studied at Juilliard and led fp of revised version of *Antony and Cleopatra* there, 1975. NY Met. debut 1976 (*Die Zauberflöte*) and led *Macbeth* at Scottish Opera in the same year. *Don Carlos* at CG 1979; chief conductor of the Rotterdam PO 1983–91, Cologne Opera 1989. Chicago Lyric Opera debut 1988 (*Macbeth*), *Oberon* at La Scala, 1993.

You must have the score in your head, not your head in the score.

Hans von Bulow, quoted in Schönberg, *The Great Conductors*, 1987

Connell, Elizabeth (b Port Elizabeth, South Africa, 22 Oct 1946), Irish mezzo, later soprano. Debut as Varvara (*Katya Kabonová*) at Wexford in 1972. She then sang with Australian Opera and appeared as a mezzo with ENO 1975–80, as Eboli and Herodias. CG debut 1976, as Viclinda in *I Lombardi*. She sang Ortrud at Bayreuth in 1980; other mezzo roles include Lady Macbeth, Venus, Kundry and La Vestale. Geneva 1984, Norma. NY Met. debut 1985, as Vitellia. She returned to CG in 1985–86 for the *Trovatore* Leonora and Leonore in *Fidelio*. Sang Isolde in concert, London 1993; Abigaille in *Nabucco* at Geneva, 1995.

Connolly, Justin (Riveagh) (b London, 11 Aug 1933), English composer. He studied at the RCM with Fricker; professor there since 1966. He taught at Yale University in the early 1960s and his music has been influenced by Milton Babbitt and Elliott Carter.

conducting *A cartoon of Hector Berlioz conducting the Société Philharmonique by Gustave Doré, 1850. Despite the comic nature of the drawing, the artist successfully captures the 19th-century heroic ideal of the conductor as the great individual who leads – or even battles – a mass of musicians.*

Works include six sets of *Triads* (trios) for various instrumental ensembles (1964–74), five sets of *Obbligati* for various chamber ensembles (1965–81), *Antiphonies* for 36 instruments (1966), two sets of *Poems of Wallace Stevens* for soprano, clarinet and piano (1967–70), *Rebus* for orchestra (1970), *Diaphony* for organ and orchestra (1977), *Sentences* for chorus, brass and organ (to poems by Thomas Traherne, 1979),) oratorio *The Marriage of Heaven and Hell* (text by Blake); *Chimaera* for dancer, alto, baritone and ensemble (1979), *Fourfold from the Garden Forking Path* for two pianos (1983); *Spelt from Sibyl's Leaves* for six solo voices and ensemble (1989), *Cantata* for soprano and piano (1991), symphony (1991).

Conradi, Johann Georg (d Oettingen, 22 May 1699), German composer. Music director at Ansbach, 1683–86, and director of the Hamburg opera 1690–93. One of the earliest composers of German operas, which include *Die schoene und getreue Ariadne* (1691), *Diogenes Cynicus, Numa Pompilius, Der tapffere Kayser Carolus Magnus* (1692), *Der Verstöhrung Jerusalem, Der wunderbarvergnügte Pygmalion*; sacred music.

Consecration of the House (Beethoven) ◊Weihe des Hauses.

consecutive an adj. used to describe the progression of intervals of the same kind in similar motion.

consequent the second phrase of an antecedent/consequent structure, 'answering' the antecedent phrase. Associated with the 18th-c. Classical style.

Conservatoire National Supérieur de Musique the chief school of music in Paris, opened 1795 with Sarrette as director, having grown out of the École Royale du Chant, established in 1784 under the direction of Gossec. Later directors were Cherubini, Auber, A Thomas, Dubois, Fauré, Rabaud, Delvincourt, M Dupré and Loucheur.

conservatorio, Italian, later Conservatoire (French), Conservatorium (German), Conservatory (English, especially American), a school of music originating in Italy, especially Venice and Naples, an orphanage where children were 'conserved' to become useful citizens and at the same time trained as musicians.

console the part of an organ which is directly under the control of the player's hands and feet.

THE OPERA

Les Contes d'Hoffmann

A three-act opera by Jacques Offenbach, based ultimately on stories by Ernst Hoffmann. Offenbach died during rehearsals for the first performance in early 1881 and the opera was rearranged, being restored to its original version in 1893.

Prologue. In Luther's tavern in Nuremberg, Councillor Lindorf intercepts a note of assignation from the prima donna Stella (soprano) to the poet Hoffmann (tenor), who then arrives and agrees to tell the story of his three lost loves.

I. Hoffmann falls for the mechanical doll Olympia (soprano) after looking through magic spectacles sold to him by Coppelius (bass-baritone). Coppelius destroys the doll when he is swindled by Spalanzani (baritone), her other maker.

II. Hoffmann is in love with the consumptive singer Antonia (soprano), but Dr Miracle (bass-baritone) causes her death by forcing her to perform.

III. The Venetian courtesan Guilietta (mezzo-soprano) is persuaded by the magician Dapertutto to connive in obtaining Hoffmann's shadow, symbol of his soul. Guilietta easily fascinates Hoffmann, who tries to get the key to her room from Schlemil (bass). Hoffmann kills Schlemil in a duel, as Guilietta sails away in a golden gondola with the dwarf Pitichinaccio.

Epilogue. Back in the tavern Hoffmann is now drunk, and when Stella appears she is led away by Lindorf (who has earlier played the roles of Coppelius, Dr Miracle and Dapertutto).

THE OPERA

---

consonance the purely intoned sounding together of notes capable of producing concord.

consort 16th- and 17th-c. English term for ensemble. The earliest uses are specifically associated with groups of diverse instruments, i.e. what is often called a ◊broken consort.

Constant, Marius (b Bucharest, 7 Feb 1925), Romanian-born French composer and conductor. He studied in Paris with Messiaen and Honegger; directed Ballets de Paris 1956–66, music director Ars Nova, an ensemble promoting new music 1963–71. His early works were impressionistic; later turned to serialism. Collaborated with Peter Brook in his reductions of *Carmen* and *Pelléas et Mélisande*.

Works include operas *La Serrure* and *Le Souper* (both 1969), *La Tragédie de Carmen* (1981); ballets *Jouer de flute* (1952), *Haut Voltage* (1956), *Cyrano de Bergerac* (1960), *Paradise Lost* (1967), *Candide* (1970), *Le Jeu de Sainte Agnès* ('ecclesiastical action' for singers, dancers, actor, organ, electric guitar, trombone and percussion; 1974); piano concerto (1954), *Turner*, three essays for orchestra (1961), *Winds* for 13 wind instruments and double bass (1968), *14 Stations* for 92 percussion instruments and ensemble (1970), *103 Regards dans l'eau* for violin and orchestra (1981); *Pelléas and Mélisande Symphony* (1986); *Des droits de l'homme*, oratorio (1989).

Consul, The opera by Menotti (libretto by the composer), produced Philadelphia, 1 Mar 1950. Freedom fighter John Sorel must emigrate to evade the secret police. His wife Magda tries to obtain a visa at the consulate, but fails. John is arrested and Magda commits suicide.

contano Italian = 'they count' (accent on first syllable); a direction in a vocal or instrumental part of a work where the performers have a prolonged rest, warning them to count bars in order to make sure of coming in again at the proper moment.

Conte Caramella, Il opera by Galuppi (libretto by Goldoni, partly based on Addison's comedy *The Drummer, or The Haunted House*), produced Verona, 18 Dec 1749.

Contesa dei numi, La, *The Contest of the Gods*, opera by Gluck (libretto by Metastasio), produced Copenhagen, at court, 9 Apr 1749, to celebrate the birth of Prince Christian, later Christian VII.

Contes d'Hoffmann, Les, *The Tales of Hoffmann*, opera by Offenbach (libretto by J Barbier and M Carré, based on a play of their own and on stories by E T A Hoffmann), produced Paris, Opéra-Comique, 10 Feb 1881, after Offenbach's death. He did not finish it; the scoring is partly by Guiraud. Hoffmann tells of doomed love for Olympia, Antonia and Giulietta.

Conti, Francesco Bartolomeo (b Florence, 20 Jan 1681; d Vienna, 20 Jul 1732), Italian lutenist and composer. Theorbo player to the Austrian court in Vienna, 1701–05 and again from 1708; court composer from 1713.

Works include operas *Alba Cornelia* (1714), *Clotilda, Il trionfo dell' Amore, I satiri in Arcadia, Don Chisciotte in Sierra Morena* (1719), *L'Issipile, Pallade trionfante* (1722), etc., stage serenades; oratorios, cantatas.

Conti, Gioacchino (b Arpino, 28 Feb 1714; d 25 Oct 1761), Italian soprano castrato. A rival of ◊Caffarelli. Sang in Rome from 1730 and at CG 1736–37, in the fps of Handel's *Atalanta, Arminio, Giustino* and *Berenice*. Sang in Italy and Spain until 1755 in operas by Hasse, Jommelli and Galuppi. Praised for his expressive singing in a high range.

continental fingering the fingering of piano music now in universal use, with the fingers marked 1–5 from the thumb. This system has displaced the so-called English fingering, marked + for the thumb and 1–4 for the other fingers, which however was by no means in use throughout the whole history of English keyboard music.

Contino, Giovanni (b Brescia, *c* 1513; d *c* 1574), Italian composer. Active at Trent, perhaps teacher of Marenzio. From 1561 *maestro di cappella* to the Mantuan court. Composed Masses, Lamentations and motets.

continuo Italian = abbr. for *basso continuo*; a practice first written down shortly before 1600 by which the bass line of a work is performed by one or more players who add chords above the line using an established set of principles often notated by ◊**thorough-bass** (also called figured bass). Characteristically the continuo group consisted of a melody instrument or instruments (cello, bass, bassoon, trombone, viola da gamba) and chordal instruments (organ, harpsichord, chitarrone, harp, lute, etc). Much operatic music of the 17th and 18th c., for example, was written purely as a melodic line with continuo: normally the harmonic structure was entirely clear from those two lines, and the function of the continuo players was not only to provide a firm basis against which the melody could be heard and to fill in the chords, but more particularly to provide variety of texture and rhythm. As time progressed the continuo group tended to become smaller: in chamber music from around 1680 it normally comprised only a keyboard instrument and a cello.

contra Latin = 'against'; a prefix used for organ stops denoting that the stop indicated by the word following it sounds an octave lower.

contrabassoon ◊double bassoon.

contrafactum Latin = 'counterfeit'; a vocal composition in which the original words have been replaced by new ones, either secular words substituted for sacred, or vice versa. In the 16th c. the Reformation was responsible for several changes of this kind, especially from Latin to vernacular words in the conversion of plainsong melodies to hymn-tunes.

contralto the lowest woman's voice, frequently abbreviated to *alto*, though this term is also used for the highest (falsetto) male voice and for a low boy's voice.

A contralto is a low woman who sings.

Anon.

---

contrapunctus Latin ◊counterpoint.

contrary motion ◊motion.

contratenor in the 14th and 15th c., a voice in the same range as the tenor but generally moving in far less conjunct fashion.

contredanse, French, ◊country dance.

Convenziene ed inconvenienze teatrali, Il one-act opera (*farsa*) by Donizetti (libretto by the composer), after A S Sografi), performed Naples, Teatro Nuovo, 21 Nov 1827. Sometimes given in modern revivals under the spurious title *Viva la Mama*. A satirical commentary on the 'conveniences' or agreed rules, concerning the rank of contemporary Italian singers.

Converse, Frederick (Shepherd) (b Newton, MA, 5 Jan 1871; d Westwood, MA, 8 Jun 1940), American composer. Although intended for a commercial career, he studied music at Harvard University under Paine. Later he studied piano with Carl Baermann and composition with Chadwick at Boston, and took a finishing course at Munich. After his return to USA he held various teaching posts at Boston and Harvard until 1907. In 1910 his *Pipe of Desire* became the first US opera to be performed at the NY Met. From 1917 to 1919 he served in the army and in 1930 he became Dean of the New England Conservatory, a post which he held until 1938.

Works include operas *The Pipe of Desire* (1905), *The Sacrifice* (1910), *The Immigrants* (1914), and *Sinbad the Sailor*; *Job* for solo voices, chorus and orchestra, *Laudate Dominum* for male voices, brass and organ; five symphonies (1920–40), orchestral tone-poems *Endymion's Narrative* (1901), *The Mystic Trumpeter* (after Whitman, 1905), *Ormazd, Ave atque vale, Song of the Sea, Flivver Ten Million*, romance *The Festival of Pan* for orchestra; *Night and Day* for piano and orchestra (after Whitman); *Hagar in the Desert* for contralto and orchestra, *La Belle Dame sans merci* for baritone and orchestra (Keats, 1902); three string quartets; piano trio; sonata and concerto for violin and piano; piano pieces; songs.

Convitato di pietra, Il, *The Stone Guest*, opera by Fabrizi (*c* 1765–?) (libretto by G B Lorenzi), produced Rome, 1787.

Convitato di pietra, Il, o sio Il dissoluto opera by Righini (libretto by ?), produced Prague, 1776. A setting of the Don Juan legend, produced 11 years before Mozart's.

Conyngham, Barry (b Sydney, 27 Aug 1944), Australian composer.

Studied with Peter Sculthorpe and Takemitsu and has taught at University of Melbourne from 1975; visiting scholar at Minnesota and Pennsylvania State Universities. His music admits oriental and modern French influences.

Works include music theatre pieces *Ned* opera (1975–78), *The Apology of Bony Anderson* (1978), *Fly* opera (1984), *Bennelong* puppet opera (1988); *Crisis: Thoughts in a City* (1968), *Five Windows* (1969); concerto for orchestra (1981), *Vast* I–IV for orchestra (1987); concertos, vocal and chamber music (string quartet, 1979).

Cook, Thomas (Aynsley) (b London, Jul 1831 or 1836; d Liverpool, 16 Feb 1894), English bass. Studied with Staudigl at Munich and sang at various Bavarian theatres before he made his debut in England at Manchester in 1856. Sang at CG until 1866 in works by Balfe (Devilshoof in *The Bohemian Girl*), Wallace and Benedict. The maternal grandfather of E and L Goossens.

Cooke, Arnold (b Gomersal, Yorkshire, 4 Nov 1906), English composer. Educated at Repton School and Caius College, Cambridge, where he took the Mus.B. degree in 1929. From that year to 1932 he was a pupil of Hindemith in Berlin, and in 1933 was appointed professor of harmony and composition at the RMCM. In 1938 he settled in London; appointed professor of composition at TCM, 1947.

Works include operas *Mary Barton* (1949–54), *The Invisible Duke* (1976); cantata *Holderneth* for baritone, chorus and orchestra; six symphonies (1946–84), two clarinet concertos, concert overture for orchestra, Passacaglia, Scherzo and Finale for string orchestra, piano concerto; four Shakespeare sonnets for voice and orchestra; five string quartets (1933–78), and other chamber music.

Cooke, Benjamin (b London, 1734; d London, 14 Sept 1793), English organist and composer. Pupil of Pepusch, whom he succeeded in 1752 as conductor to the Academy of Ancient Music. In 1757 he was appointed choirmaster at Westminster Abbey in succession to Gates. Mus.D., Cambridge, 1775, and Oxford, 1782, when he became organist of St Martin-in-the-Fields, London.

Works include services, anthems (some for special occasions), psalms, chants and hymns; ode for Delap's tragedy *The Captives*; *Ode on the Passions* (Collins), odes for Christmas Day, on Handel, on Chatterton and for the king's recovery, ode *The Syren's Song to Ulysses*; glees, catches and canons; orchestral concertos; organ pieces; harpsichord lessons.

Cooke, Deryck (b Leicester, 14 Sept 1919; d Thornton Heath, 26 Oct 1976), English musicologist. Studied privately and at Cambridge. From 1947 to 1959 he worked for the BBC, devoting much time to writing and broadcasting. His best-known works include the book *The Language of Music* (1959) and his performing version of Mahler's unfinished tenth symphony, heard in London on 13 Aug 1964 (revised 1972).

Cooke, Henry (b ? Lichfield, *c* 1615; d Hampton Court, 13 Jul 1672), English bass and composer. Pupil of the Chapel Royal; was a captain in the Duke of Northumberland's army during the Civil War. Appointed singer and Master of the Children at the Chapel Royal at the Restoration. With Charles Coleman, Hudson, H Lawes and Locke he contributed to Davenant's *Siege of Rhodes* (entertainment at Rutland House), 1656, and sang in it. His daughter married Humfrey.

Works include coronation music, hymn for the installation of Knights of the Garter, anthems, songs for one and more voices, etc.

Cooke, Thomas (Simpson) (Tom) (b Dublin, 1782; d London, 26 Feb 1848), Irish tenor, violinist and composer. Learnt music from his father, Bartlett Cooke, an oboist, played a violin concerto in public at seven, learnt composition from Giordani, was leader of the Crow Street Theatre orchestra at 15 and kept a music shop 1806–12. In 1813 he appeared in London with great success and settled there. For *c* 20 years he not only sang at Drury Lane Theatre, but led the orchestra, played nine different instruments, managed the house and provided music stage pieces for it. He also taught singing with success.

Works include stage pieces *Frederick the Great* (1814), *The Wager, The Brigand, Peter the Great, King Arthur and the Knights of the Round Table* (1834); songs for Shakespeare's *Midsummer Night's Dream*; songs, glees, catches.

Coolidge, Elizabeth Sprague (b Chicago, 30 Oct 1864; d Cambridge, MA, 4 Nov 1953), American music patron. In 1918 she established the Berkshire Festivals of Music and in 1925 created a foundation (named after her) to produce concerts, music festivals, to make awards, etc. She instituted the award of a gold medal (also named after her) for distinguished services to chamber music in 1932. The composers from whom she commissioned works included Schoenberg, Webern, Stravinsky, Bartók, Prokofiev, Malipiero, Casella, Piston and Bridge.

Cooper, Emil (b Kherson, 20 Dec 1877; d New York, 19 Nov 1960), Russian conductor. After study at Odessa and Vienna he conducted in Russia and gave the fp of *The Golden Cockerel* (Moscow, 1909). Later led the first *Ring* and *Meistersinger* by Russian companies. Chicago 1929–36. NY Met. 1944–50 (*Peter Grimes* and *Khovanshchina*), Montreal Opera Guild from 1950.

Cooper, Imogen (b London, 28 Aug 1949), English pianist, daughter of Martin ◊Cooper. Studied with Kathleen Long at the Paris Conservatory, and with Brendel in Paris. London Prom concerts from 1973, USA from 1984 (debut at LA). Noted as a sensitive interpreter of Mozart and Schubert.

Cooper, John, ◊Coperario.

Cooper, Kenneth (b New York, 31 May 1941), American harpsichordist, conductor and musicologist. Studied at Mannes College and Columbia University, returning to Mannes 1975 to teach, as professor of harpsichord. London debut 1965, NY 1973; frequent tours of the USA as a soloist and chamber music performer. Well known in Baroque music and has premiered works by Barab, Busoni and Krenek in addition to many modern revivals. Publications include an edition of Monteverdi's *Tirsi e Clori* (1967) and *Three Centuries of Music in Score*.

Cooper, Martin (Du Pré) (b Winchester, 17 Jan 1910; d Richmond, Surrey, 16 Mar 1986), English writer on music. Father of Imogen ◊Cooper. Educated at Winchester College and Oxford, studied music with Wellesz in Vienna. His work included books on Gluck, Bizet and Beethoven. He was chief music critic of *The Daily Telegraph* 1950–76 and was editor of *The Musical Times* 1953–56.

Coperario, John (b c 1570–80; d ? London, 1626), English lutenist, violist and composer. Studied in Italy and on his return, c 1604, adopted the Italianized name of Coperario or Coprario. He taught the children of James I and was the master of W and H Lawes. Composer-in-ordinary to Charles I, 1625.

Copland *The composer Aaron Copland (1900–1990) in his role as conductor. Perhaps the greatest American composer of the 20th century, Copland represented in music the rustic frontier spirit, in contrast to the style of many serial composers who often dominated the scene in the USA following World War II.*

Works include *The Masque of the Inner Temple and Gray's Inn* (F Beaumont), *The Masque of Flowers*; *Funeral Teares* on the death of the Earl of Devonshire, *Songs of Mourning* on the death of Prince Henry (words by Campion); anthems; works for viols and for viols and organ; fancies for the organ based on Italian madrigals; lute music; songs, etc.

Copland, Aaron (b Brooklyn, NY, 14 Nov 1900; d Westchester, NY, 2 Dec 1990), American composer. Began to learn the piano at the age of 13 and studied theory with Rubin Goldmark; later went to France and became a pupil of Nadia Boulanger at the Fontainebleau School of Music. In 1924 a Guggenheim scholarship enabled him to spend two more years in Europe. He was represented for the first time at an ISCM festival at Frankfurt in 1927 and won a prize in American music with his *Dance Symphony* in 1930. He was first influenced by Stravinsky and Boulanger but later assimilated local American styles, notably in the ballets *Billy the Kid* and *Appalachian Spring*. His chamber music is more introspective and complex in character. He did much propaganda work for American music, and wrote and lectured on music. He also toured widely as a conductor of his own and other American music.

Works include opera *The Tender Land* (1952–54); ballets *Billy the Kid* (1938), *Rodeo*, *Appalachian Spring* (1943–44); school opera *The Second Hurricane*; music for films includes *Of Mice and Men*; orchestral works: three symphonies, (1925, 1933, 1946), *Music for the Theatre*, *Symphonic Ode*, *A Dance Symphony*, *Statements*, *El Salón México* (1933–36), *Music for the Radio*, *An Outdoor Overture*, *Quiet City* (1939), *Letter from Home*, *Danzón Cubano*; *Lincoln Portrait* for orator and orchestra (1942), piano concerto (1926), clarinet concerto (1948), *Connotations* for orchestra (1962), *Inscape* (1967), *Three Latin American Sketches* (1972).

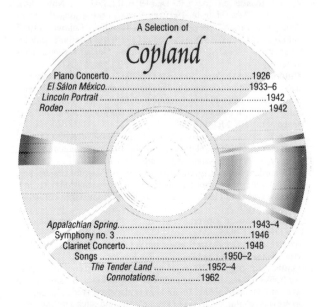

The House on the Hill and *An Immorality* for female chorus; two pieces for string quartet; sextet for clarinet, strings and piano; piano quartet; nonet; violin and piano sonata; piano sonata, piano pieces.

Music that is born complex is not inherently better or worse than music that is born simple.
Aaron Copland, quoted in Jacobson, *Reverberations*,
1975

Coppélia, ou La Fille aux yeux d'émail, *Coppelia, or The Girl with Enamel Eyes*, ballet by Delibes (scenario by C Nuitter and A Saint-Léon; choreographed by L Mérante), produced Paris, Opéra, 25 May 1870.

Coppola, Pier Antonio (b Castrogiovanni, Sicily, 11 Dec 1793; d Catania, 13 Nov 1877), Italian composer. Studied at Naples and produced his first opera, *Il figlio del bandito*, there in 1816. He was at Lisbon in 1839–42 as conductor of the San Carlo Theatre and again 1850–71.

Works include operas *La pazza per amore* (*Eva* in French), 1835), *Gli Illinesi*, *Inés de Castro* (1841), etc.; Masses, litanies and other church music.

Coprario, Giovanni, ◊Coperario.

Coptic Chant the music of the Christian Church in Egypt, which from the middle of the fifth c. has been Monophysite. There was a primitive system of notation by the tenth c., but nothing definite is known about the chant in its original form. It still flourishes today, and is characterized by the use of percussion instruments.

Coq d'or (Rimsky-Korsakov) ◊*Golden Cockerel*.

cor anglais ◊English horn.

cor anglais

Corbett, William (b *c* 1675; d ? London, 7 Mar 1748), English violinist and composer. At various times leader of the orchestra at the King's Theatre, Haymarket, director of Lincoln's Inn Fields Theatre, member of the royal band; lived for some time in Italy, where he toured as a violinist and collected instruments.

Works include incidental music to plays, e.g. Shakespeare's *Henry IV* (1699), orchestral concertos and sonatas for various instruments.

cordatura Italian the notes to which a string instrument is tuned, e.g. G, D, A, E for the violin. Any change in the normal tuning made temporarily is called *scordatura*.

Corder, Frederick (b London, 26 Jan 1852; d London, 21 Aug 1932), English teacher, conductor and composer. Studied at the RAM in London and under F Hiller at Cologne. Professor of composition at RAM from 1888. First English translation of Wagner's *Ring*.

Works include opera *Nordisa* (1887), cantatas *The Bridal of Triermain* (after Scott) and *The Sword of Argantyr* (1889), overture *Prospero* (after Shakespeare's *Tempest*), Elegy for 24 violins and organ; recitations with music; songs, part-songs.

Cordier, Baude (*fl.* 1400 or shortly before), French composer. Recent research makes it seem likely that he was the harpist Baude Fresnel (d 1397–98), though certain features of his style make such an early death-date hard to accept. Of his ten surviving *chansons* two are particularly famous because of their notation: *Belle, bonne*, written out in the form of a heart; and *Tout par compas*, written down in a circle.

Corelli, Arcangelo (b Fusignano, Imola, 17 Feb 1653; d Rome, 8 Jan 1713), Italian composer and violinist. Studied at Bologna, settled in Rome *c* 1685 and pub. his first violin sonatas. He lived at the palace of his patron, Cardinal Pietro Ottoboni. Visited Modena and Naples, conducted at the Roman residence of Queen Christina of Sweden, collected pictures and taught many violin pupils, including Geminiani and Locatelli. His music has been admired for the poise, balance and brilliance of its style.

Works include a set of 12 *Concerti grossi* op. 6, including no. 8 in

Corelli *The composer Arcangelo Corelli (1653–1713) as represented in a mezzotint by I Smith Anglus (after Hugh Howard). Although he was by no means a prolific composer, Corelli's influence spread far and wide as other composers copied his once-original gestures.*

G minor, '*fatto per la notte di nattale*', i.e. Christmas; five sets of chamber sonatas.

Corelli, Franco (b Ancona, 8 Apr 1921), Italian tenor. Debut Spoleto, 1951, Don José; Milan, La Scala, since 1954. CG debut 1957, Cavaradossi; NY Met. 1961, as Manrico. Paris, Opéra, and Vienna Staatsoper since 1970. Much admired as Calaf, Ernani, Radames and Raoul in *Les Huguenots*.

Corena, Fernando (b Geneva, 22 Dec 1916; d Lugano, 26 Nov 1984), Swiss bass. Debut Trieste, 1947, as Varlaam (after minor roles in Geneva pre-war). NY Met. debut 1954, as Leporello. Edinburgh 1955 and 1963 as Falstaff and Don Pasquale. CG 1960 as Rossini's Bartolo. Other roles included Escamillo, Osmin, Dulcamara and Don Alfonso.

Corigliano, John (b New York, 16 Feb 1932), American composer. Studied with Otto Luening at Columbia University and privately with Paul Creston; has taught at Lehmann College, NY, from 1973. His brilliant and romantic extravaganza *The Ghosts of Versailles* was staged at the NY Met. in 1991.

Works include violin sonata (1963), *Elegy* for orchestra (1966), piano concerto (1968), clarinet concerto (1977), *Hallucinations* for orchestra (1981); incidental music for plays by Sophocles, Molière and Sheridan; *Naked Carmen*, arrangement of Bizet for singers, pop and rock groups, synthesizer and instruments; *Echoes of Forgotten Rites* for orchestra (1982); Symphony (1990); opera *The Ghosts of Versailles* (1991).

Coriolan Beethoven's overture, op. 62, to the play of that name by Heinrich von Collin, composed 1807 and produced with the play in March of that year. Apart from its subject the play has no connection with Shakespeare's *Coriolanus*.

Corkine, William (*fl.* 1610–12), English lutenist and composer. Pub. two books of airs to the lute and bass viol, followed by dances and other instrumental pieces; an anthem is also preserved. The second book of airs contains settings of Donne's 'Go and catch a falling star';

Break of Day: ''Tis true, 'tis day'; *The Bait*: 'Come live with me, and be my love'.

Cornago, Johannes (*fl.* 1450–75), Spanish Franciscan friar and composer. He was at the Neapolitan court of Alfonso V and his son Ferrante I. His *Missa de la mapa mundi* has a *cantus firmus* with the text 'Ayo visto lo mappamundo'. His other works include a motet, and secular pieces to Spanish words.

Corneille, Pierre (1608–1684), French poet and dramatist. M-A ◊Charpentier (*Polyeucte* and *Andromède*), ◊Cid (Cornelius and Massenet), ◊Cleopatra e Cesare (Graun), ◊Dukas (*Polyeucte* overture), ◊Flavio (Handel), ◊Lully (Œdipe), ◊Martyrs (Donizetti), ◊Poliuto (Donizetti), ◊Polyeucte (Gounod), ◊Rieti (*Illusion comique*), ◊Roberto Devereux (Mercadante), ◊Sacchini (*Gran Cid*), ◊Tito Vespasiano (Caldara and Hasse), J ◊Wagenaar (*Cid*).

Corneille, Thomas (1625–1709), French poet and dramatist, brother of Pierre ◊Corneille. ◊Bellérophon (Lully), M-A ◊Charpentier (*Pierre philosophale* and two plays with Visé), ◊Médée (M-A Charpentier), ◊Psyché (Lully).

Cornelius, Peter (b Mainz, 24 Dec 1824; d Mainz, 26 Oct 1874), German composer and author. Studied music after failing as an actor, first with Dehn in Berlin, 1845–50, and from 1852 with Liszt at Weimar, where he joined the new German group of musicians and wrote eloquently about them in Schumann's *Neue Zeitschrift*, without however succumbing to Wagnerian influence in his own work. He sought out Wagner in Vienna in 1858 but declined to follow him to Munich in 1865 for the premiere of *Tristan und Isolde*.

Works include operas *Der Barbier von Bagdad* (1855–58), *Der Cid* (1860–62) and *Gunlöd* (unfinished); choral works *Trauerchöre* and *Vätergruft*; duets for soprano and baritone; songs including cycles *Liedercyclus*, *Weihnachtslieder* (1859), *Brautlieder* (1856–58), etc.

Cornelius, Peter (b Labjerggard, 4 Jan 1865; d Snekkersten, 30 Dec 1934), Danish tenor. He sang baritone roles from 1892, debut Copenhagen, as Escamillo. From 1902 he was heard in the Wagner heldentenor roles: Siegfried at Bayreuth, 1906, and in the first English-language *Ring* performed at CG, 1908–09.

Cornelys (born *Imer*), T(h)eresa (b Venice, 1723; d London, 19 Aug 1797), Italian singer, married to the dancer Pompeati, but assumed the name of Cornelys when at Amsterdam. She made her first appearance in London in 1746 as Signora Pompeati, in Gluck's *Caduta de' giganti*, and in 1760 began to give musical entertainments at Carlisle House in Soho Square, continuing until 1771, when she was indicted for keeping it for immoral purposes, just possibly at the instigation of jealous rivals. A talented singer, she died in the Fleet prison, leaving a daughter by Casanova.

Corner, Philip (b New York, 10 Apr 1933), American composer. Studied in Paris with Messiaen and in New York with Luening and Cowell; teacher at Rutgers University from 1972. His works show the influence of Cage, minimalism and Asian music.

Works include theatre music *Carrot Chew Performance* (1963), *Rationalize Outside Sounds* (1966), *Metal Meditations* (1973), *Democracy in Action* (1979); *This is it .... This Time* for orchestra (1959); ensemble works, including *Composition With or Without Beverly* (1962); *Flares*, mixed media (1963); series *'Gamelan'* from 1975; piano music and works in graphic notation.

cornet a brass wind instrument derived from the coiled post-horn and 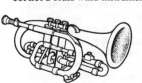 fitted with valves to enable it to produce all the chromatic notes within its compass. It is a regular member of the military band and the treble instrument of the brass band. It is also used in the orchestra as an addition to the trumpets, less often as a substitute. Cornets are usually in A or B♭ and transpose accordingly; a smaller cornet in E♭ is standard in brass bands. To be distinguished from ◊cornett.

cornett wind instrument made of wood or ivory in the shape of a long, thin, slightly tapering tube, either straight or slightly curved, and covered with leather. Cornetts were often used as treble instruments

with sackbuts (trombones), frequently in church. The serpent belongs to the same family.

corno di bassetto, Italian, = ◊basset horn. (In 1888–89 Bernard Shaw wrote music criticism for *The Star* under the pseudonym of C di B).

Cornyshe, William (d ? Hylden, Kent, *c* Oct 1523), English composer. Attached to the courts of Henry VII and Henry VIII, not only as musician, but as actor and producer of interludes and pageants. Gentleman of the Chapel Royal from *c* 1496; succeeded Newark as Master of the Children in 1509. He wrote music for the court banquets and masques and officiated in France at the Field of the Cloth of Gold in 1520.

Works include motets, Magnificats, *Ave Maria*; secular songs, some with satirical words, for instruments and voices, including a setting of (?) Skelton's *Hoyda, Jolly Rutterkin*.

A William Cornyshe senior (d *c* 1502), not to be confused with this composer, was the first recorded master of the choristers at Westminster Abbey (*c* 1480–90).

coronach, Gaelic, = 'crying together'; a funeral cry, or in its more cultivated musical form a dirge.

Coronation Anthems four anthems by Handel, composed for the coronation of George II and performed at the ceremony in Westminster Abbey, 11 Oct 1727. 1. 'Zadok the Priest', 2. 'The King shall rejoice', 3. 'My heart is inditing', 4. 'Let thy hand be strengthened'. A number of other composers, from H Cooke in the 17th c. to Vaughan Williams in the 20th, have written anthems for coronations in England.

'Coronation' Concerto the nickname of Mozart's piano concerto in D, K537 (dated 24 Feb 1788), performed by him at Frankfurt at the coronation festivities for Leopold II, 15 Oct 1790.

'Coronation' Mass Mozart's Mass in C K317 (dated 23 Mar 1779), so called because it is said to have been written to commemorate the crowning in 1751 of a miraculous image of the Virgin Mary.

Coronation Ode work by Elgar in six sections for soloists, chorus and orchestra, op. 44; composed 1901–02, fp Sheffield, 2 Oct 1902. Finale is 'Land of Hope and Glory', based on tune from *Pomp and Circumstance* march no. 1.

Corregidor, Der, *The Mayor*, opera by Wolf (libretto by R Mayreder, based on P A de Alarcón's story *El sombrero de tres picos* = *The Three-cornered Hat*), produced Mannheim, 7 Jun 1896. Frasquita tries to avoid Don Eugenio's amorous advances while her husband Tio Lukas is detained by the Don's men. Incorrectly believing that Frasquita has been unfaithful, Lukas sets out to seduce the Don's wife, Donna Mercedes. After mistaken identities are resolved, Frasquita and Lukas are reunited.

corrente Italian ◊courante.

Corrette, Michel (b Rouen, 1709; d Paris, 22 Jan 1795), French organist, teacher and composer. He held various organist's posts from 1737, and between 1737 and 1784 pub. 17 methods on performing practice; these included *L'école d'orphée* (1738), for violin, *Les amusements du Parnasse* (1749, harpsichord), *Le parfait maître à chanter* (1758), *Les dons d'Apollon* (1762, guitar), *Les délices de la solitude* (1766, cello), *Nouvelle methode pour apprendre la harpe* (1774) and *Le berger galant* (1784, flute).

Works include ballets *Les âges* (1733) and *Le lys* (1752); sacred music, e.g. motets, Te Deum (1752), Laudate Dominum (1766), *Trois leçons de ténèbres* for low voice and organ (1784); secular vocal pieces including ariettes and cantatas; concertos for musette, vielle, flute and violin; sonatas, organ and harpsichord music.

Corri, Domenico (b Rome, 4 Oct 1746; d London, 22 May 1825), Italian conductor, publisher and composer. Pupil of Porpora. Settled at Edinburgh in 1771 as conductor of the Music Society, pub. and singing-master. He failed in business and settled in London *c* 1790, where he set up in partnership with Dussek, who married his daughter Sophia in 1792.

Works include operas *Alessandro nell' Indie* (1774) and *The Travellers* (1806); instrumental sonatas, rondos and other pieces; songs including *Six Canzones dedicated to Scots Ladies*, etc. He also wrote theoretical works, including a music dictionary.

Corri, Sophia, ◊Dussek.

Corsaire, Le overture by Berlioz, op. 21, composed in Italy, 1831, rewritten in Paris, 1844, fp Paris, 19 Jan 1845, as *La Tour de Nice*; final version (*Le Corsaire*) fp Brunswick, 8 Apr 1854.

Corsaro, Il, *The Corsair*, opera by Verdi (libretto by F M Piave, based on Byron's poem), produced Trieste, 25 Oct 1848. The Pasha of Coron captures Corsair Corrado, who falls in love with Gulnara, a slave in the harem. She frees him and kills her master, and together they return to Corrado's home, where they find his betrothed, Medora, dying.

Corsi, Jacopo (b Florence, 17 Jul 1561; d Florence, 29 Dec 1602), Italian nobleman and amateur composer. Took part in the initiation of opera at Florence. Peri's *Dafne* was produced at his house in 1598 and he took some share in its composition.

Corteccia, Francesco di Bernardo (b Florence, 27 Jul 1502; d Florence, 7 Jun 1571), Italian organist and composer. Organist at the church of San Lorenzo from 1531 and *maestro di cappella* from 1539 to Cosimo I de' Medici, for the marriage of whose son Francesco to Joanna of Austria in 1565 he wrote music with Striggio, for Cini's intermezzo *Psiche ed Amore*.

Works include hymns in four parts, canticles and responses, madrigals, pieces for four–eight voices and instruments.

Cortez, Viorica (b Bucium, 26 Dec 1935), Romanian mezzo. After a concert career she sang Dalila at Toulouse in 1965. Her Carmen has been admired at CG (from 1968). NY Met. debut 1971. In 1974 she was heard as Adalgisa at La Scala and as Dulcinea in Massenet's *Don Quichotte* at the Paris Opéra. Other roles include Amneris, Eboli, Charlotte; Ulrica (Genoa, 1992).

Cortot, Alfred (Denis) (b Nyon, Switzerland, 26 Sept 1877; d Lausanne, 15 Jun 1962), French pianist and conductor. He studied at the Paris Conservatory, where he gained the *premier prix* in 1896. After serving as a *répétiteur* at Bayreuth he founded the Société des Festivals Lyriques at Paris and conducted the fp in France of *Götterdämmerung* in 1902. In 1905 he formed a piano trio with Jacques Thibaud and Pablo Casals. From 1907 to 1917 he taught at the Paris Conservatory and in 1918 was joint founder of the École Normale de Musique. In addition to his continuous activity as a pianist and conductor he gave many lectures on piano technique and interpretation and collected a valuable library of rare works. He was charged with Nazi collaboration, 1944.

Cosa rara (Martín y Soler) ◊Una cosa rara.

Così fan tutte, o sia La scuola degli amanti, *All women do it, or The School for Lovers*, opera by Mozart (libretto by L da Ponte), produced Vienna, Burgtheater, 26 Jan 1790. Ferrando and Guglielmo test the fidelity of Dorabella and Fiordiligi by swapping partners and courting them in disguise.

Cossira, Emile (b Orthez, 1854; d Quebec, Feb 1923), French tenor. Debut Paris, Opéra-Comique, 1883; appeared at the Opéra 1888–91 and created Saint-Saëns's Ascanio (1889). At Brussels and Lyons he was the first local Tristan and Walther. CG 1891–1900 as Faust, Don José and Raoul.

Cossotto, Fiorenza (b Crescentino, Vercelli, 22 Apr 1935), Italian mezzo. Debut, Milan, La Scala, in the premiere of Poulenc's *Carmélites* (1957); roles at La Scala have included Azucena, Eboli, Adalgisa and Santuzza. CG since 1959, debut in Cherubini's *Médée*. US debut Chicago, 1964; sang Amneris at NY Met. 1968, and at Buenos Aires 1990.

Cossutta, Carlo (b Trieste, 8 May 1932), Italian tenor. Sang small roles in Buenos Aires from 1956 before creating Ginastera's Don Rodrigo in 1964; CG debut same year, as Duke of Mantua. Other roles in London have included Otello, Manrico, Gabriele Adorno and Don Carlos. He sang Pollione at the NY Met. in 1973 and Radames in Moscow with the La Scala co. on tour in 1974.

Costa, Michael (Michele Andrea Agniello) (b Naples, 4 Feb 1808; d Hove, 29 Apr 1884), Italian (anglicized) conductor and composer of Spanish descent. Studied in Naples and produced his first two operas at the Conservatory there 1826–27, and wrote a Mass, three symphonies and other works. In 1829 he was sent to Birmingham by Zingarelli to conduct a work by that composer at the Festival, but by a mistake was made to sing tenor instead. He then settled in London, wrote many ballets and operas and perfected the orchestra at the Opera; in 1846 he was appointed conductor of the Philharmonic Society and Covent Garden opera, and he became the most important festival conductor. Knighted in 1869.

Works include operas *Il delitto punito*, *Il sospetto funesto*, *Il carcere d'Ildegonda*, *Malvina*, *Malek Adhel* (on M Cottin's novel; for Paris, 1838), *Don Carlos* (London, 1844); ballets *Kenilworth* (after Scott), *Une Heure à Naples*, *Sir Huon*; oratorios *La passione*, *Eli*, *Naaman*; Mass for four voices, *Dixit Dominus*; symphony; vocal quartet *Ecco il fiero istante*.

Costanza e Fortezza, *Constancy and Fortitude*, opera by Fux (libretto by P Pariati), produced Prague, Hradžin Palace, at the coronation of the Emperor Charles VI as king of Bohemia, and birthday of the Empress Elizabeth Christina, 28 Aug 1723. Etruscans in siege of Rome; composed in elaborate style and staged in great splendour.

Costeley (Cauteley), Guillaume (b Fontagnes, Auvergne, c 1531; d Évreux, 28 Jan 1606), French organist and composer. He was organist to Henri II and Charles IV. First president of the St Cecilia society at Évreux established in 1570s. Wrote *chansons* for several voices, instrumental pieces.

Cosyn, Benjamin (b c 1570; d 1652 or later), English organist and composer. Organist at Dulwich College, 1622–24, and afterwards at the Charterhouse. Wrote church music and collected a book of virginal pieces by various composers.

Cotrubas, Ileana (b Galati, 9 Jun 1939), Romanian soprano. Debut as Debussy's Yniold, Bucharest, 1964. She sang in Frankfurt, Brussels and Salzburg before Glyndebourne, in 1969, as Mélisande; Callisto in the first modern performance of Cavalli's opera, 1970. CG debut 1971, as Tatyana; other London roles included Susanna, Violetta, Gilda, Antonia and Micaela. US debut in Chicago, as Mimi, in 1973; NY Met. from 1977. Sang Desdemona at Barcelona 1988 and retired 1989.

Cotton, John (also known as John of Afflighem), English or Flemish 12th-c. music scholar. Author of a Latin treatise on music which seems to have been widely distributed in MS; six copies are preserved in various European libraries.

Couci, Le Chastelain de (Gui II) (d 1203), castellan, 1186–1201, of the Château de Coucy, N of Soissons. He died in the crusade which was to

────────── **THE OPERA** ──────────

Così fan tutte

A two-act opera by Mozart full of disguises and assumed identities. It was first performed in 1790 and is set in Naples in the late 18th century.

I. When the two friends Ferrando (tenor) and Guglielmo (baritone) boast of the fidelity of the two sisters to whom they are engaged, they are challenged by their cynical friend Don Alfonso (bass). The sisters Fiordiligi (soprano) and Dorabella (mezzo-soprano) say a sad goodbye as the men depart, apparently to the army, having bet Don Alfonso that the women will remain faithful in their absence. Don Alfonso persuades the maid Despina (soprano) to introduce the men as they return disguised as Albanians. Guglielmo now courts Dorabella, and Ferrando tries to woo the more reluctant Fiordiligi. When the men are initially rejected, they pretend to take poison but are revived by Despina disguised as a doctor.

II. First Dorabella and then Fiordiligi yield to their new suitors and agree to marry them. When a military march is heard, the Albanians flee the scene of the wedding feast and return almost immediately without their disguises. They are outraged to find a marriage contract, drawn up by Despina in her second disguise as a lawyer, but the girls plead for forgiveness and the deception is revealed to them.

────────── **THE OPERA** ──────────

lead to the establishment of the Latin Empire in Constantinople (◊Byzantine Chant). He was a *trouvère*; 15 of his poems with their music have survived.

Couleurs de la cité céleste work by Messiaen for piano, 13 wind, xylophone, marimba and four percussion; composed 1963, fp Donaueschingen, 17 Oct 1964, conductor Boulez.

Council of Trent an ecclesiastical council held at Trent (Italian Trento, German Trient) in S Tyrol between 1545 and 1563 in three different periods, each including a number of sessions. It was intended to introduce counter-reforms into the Roman Catholic Church to make the Reformation appear superfluous to Catholics who inclined to embrace Protestantism. Musical reforms were not discussed in detail until near the end, especially at the meeting of 11 Nov 1563. They included the abolition of all Sequences except four (*Dies irae*, *Veni Sancte Spiritus*, *Victimae Paschali* and *Lauda Sion*), the expunging of all tunes with impious or lascivious associations used as *cantus firmi*, the simplifying of polyphony to make the words clearly audible (some members advocating the use of plainsong alone), correspondence between the music and the meaning of the words, etc. The opening of a Roman seminary for the training of priests was also decided, and this was opened in 1565 with Palestrina as music master.

counter, verb, to perform improvised variations on a tune in the 16th–17th c.

counterpoint the art of combining two or more independent melodic lines. The general practice of counterpoint as a technique of composition is called polyphony. Double (or invertible) counterpoint is the term used where the top-and-bottom position of two melodies combined in counterpoint can be reversed (illustration).

Continent, where it was used for ballroom dancing and cultivated by composers of distinction, including Mozart and Beethoven.

coup d'archet French = 'stroke of the bow'; the bow attack in string playing.

coup de glotte French = 'stroke of the glottis'; a trick in singing whereby vowel sounds are preceded by a kind of click in the throat produced by a momentary cutting off of the breath-stream. It is effective as an inflection and insisted on as a point of good technique by many singing teachers, while others consider it harmful to the voice.

Many musical compositions, particularly when much of the merit lies in Counterpoint, however they may transport and ravish the ears of you connoisseurs, affect my simple lug no otherwise than merely as melodious din.

Robert Burns in a letter, 1792

Couperin French 17th–18th-c. family of musicians.

1. Louis ◊Couperin (b Chaumes-en-Brie, *c* 1626; d Paris, 29 Aug 1661).

2. François Couperin, Sieur de Crouilly (b Chaumes-en-Brie, *c* 1631; d Paris, *c* 1710), brother of 1. Keyboard player.

3. Charles ◊Couperin (b Chaumes-en-Brie, 9 Apr 1638; d Paris, Jan or Feb 1679), brother of 2. Keyboard player.

4. François ◊Couperin (b Paris, 10 Nov 1668; d Paris, 11 Sept 1733), son of 3.

Inversion

An example by Bach of double counterpoint. The second system reverses the position of each line.

The basic principles of contrapuntal theory have remained more or less the same since the 13th c.: the voices should often proceed by contrary motion, particularly in approaching a cadence; motion in parallel fifths and octaves is unacceptable; motion in parallel thirds and sixths should not last for more than a few notes; dissonances should be carefully prepared though passing notes give life to the structure; and (starting in practice in the 16th c.) each line should have its own independent rhythmic life.

counter subject the name for a theme in a ◊fugue which continues in the first voice at the point where the second voice enters with the subject.

A regular counter subject recurs from time to time in association with the subject in the course of the composition.

countertenor properly a high-pitched type of male voice which is produced naturally in contrast to the *falsetto* of the male alto.

country dance an English dance which became very popular in France in the 18th c. and was called *Contredanse* there, having appeared as *Contredanse anglaise* in a pub. as early as 1699. It spread to other countries, being called *Contratanz* or *Kontretanz* in Germany and Austria. It lost not only its rustic name but also its rustic nature on the

5. Marguerite-Louise Couperin (b Paris, 1676 or 1679; d Versailles, 30 May 1728), daughter of 2. Singer in Paris.

6. Marie-Anne Couperin (b Paris, 11 Nov 1677; d ?), sister of 5.

7. Nicolas Couperin (b Paris, 20 Dec 1680; d Paris, 25 Jul 1748), brother of 6. Organist at St Gervais 1733–48.

8. Marie-Madeleine-(Cécile) Couperin (b Paris, bap. 11 Mar 1690; d Maubuisson, 16 Apr 1742), daughter of 4. Abbey organist.

9. Marguerite-Antoinette Couperin (b Paris, 19 Sept 1705; d Paris, *c* 1778), sister of 8. Court harpsichordist 1729–41.

10. Armand-Louis Couperin (b Paris, 25 Feb 1727; d Paris, 2 Feb 1789), son of 7. Died when run over in the street on his way to church.

11. Pierre-Louis Couperin (b Paris, 14 Mar 1755; d Paris, 10 Oct 1789), son of 10. Died of grief at his father's fate.

Couperin, Charles (b Chaumes-en-Brie, 9 Apr 1638; d Paris, Jan or Feb 1679), French organist and composer. Succeeded his brother Louis as organist at the church of Saint-Gervais in Paris in 1661.

Couperin, François (b Paris, 10 Nov 1668; d Paris, 11 Sept 1733), French composer, harpsichordist and organist, son of Charles ◊Couperin. The greatest member of a large musical family. Learnt music from his father and from Jacques-Denis Thomelin, organist of the

Couperin *The composer François Couperin le Grand (1668–1733). A near contemporary of J S Bach, Couperin was one of the greatest representatives of the French Baroque. One of his most important achievements was the codification of ornaments, especially those for the keyboard.*

king's chapel. Appointed organist at the church of Saint-Gervais in 1685, where he remained until his death. In 1693 he succeeded Thomelin as one of the organists to the king, and in 1717 received the title of Ordinaire de la Musique de la chambre du Roi. He had been connected with the court before and taught the royal children. In wider circles, too, he was famous as a harpsichord teacher and laid down his system in the treatise *L'Art de toucher le clavecin*, pub. in 1716. He married Marie-Anne Ansault *c* 1689, and they had two daughters, the second of whom, Marguerite-Antoinette, became a distinguished harpsichordist.

Works include four books of harpsichord pieces (*c* 230); 42 organ pieces; four *Concerts royaux* for harpsichord, strings and wind instruments; ten chamber concertos *Les Goûtsréünis* (1724); four suites for strings and harpsichord *Les Nations* (1726); chamber sonatas *Le Parnasse, ou l'Apothéose de Corelli* and *L'Apothéose . . . de Lully* (1725); two suites of pieces for viols with figured bass; some misc. chamber works; 12 songs for one, two or three voices; church music, including *Laudate pueri Dominum, Leçons de Ténèbres* (*c* 1715), a number of motets, etc.

Couperin, Louis (b Chaumes-en-Brie, *c* 1626; d Paris, 29 Aug 1661), French composer, harpsichordist and organist, son of Charles Couperin (*c* 1595–1654). He was sponsored by Chambonnières, musician at court, and was active in Paris from at least 1651; in 1653 he became the first of his family to hold the organist's post at St Gervais. He was a treble viol player at court and took part in several ballet performances, including *Psyché* (1656). He is regarded as one of the finest keyboard composers of the 17th c.; among his 215 surviving pieces are allemandes, courantes, sarabandes, chaconnes and pascailles for harpsichord, preludes, fugues and plainsong versets for organ, and fantaisies for chamber ensemble.

coupler an appliance whereby two manuals of an organ or a manual and the pedals can be so connected that while only one is being played the stops controlled by the other are brought into action. Special couplers can also be used to double the notes played automatically an octave above or below.

couplet French lit. a verse or stanza in a poem. In music a strophic song, generally of a light and often of a humorous type, in which the same music recurs for each verse. Also the forerunner of the ♭episode in the ♭rondo form, occurring in the French rondeau as cultivated by Couperin and others, where a main theme returns again and again after statements of various *couplets* between.

courante, French, (1) A dance in 3–2 time popular especially in the 17th c., whose name ('the running one', from *courir* = 'to run') suggests some affinity with the English 'running set'. It has two parts of equal length, each repeated, and its special feature is the rhythmic modification of the last bar of each section, where the notes appear in two groups of three instead of three groups of two, as in the rest of the piece. (2) An Italian dance (*corrente*) in brisk 3–4 or 3–8 time, with running passages.

Examples of both types occur in Bach's suites and partitas.

courses sets of strings in instruments, especially of the lute type, used in pairs and producing the same note, usually in unison, but sometimes in octaves.

Courteville English family of musicians, (?) of French descent:

1. Raphael Courteville (d ? London, 28 Dec 1675), Gentleman of the Chapel Royal under Charles I and again under Charles II after the Restoration.

2. Ralph (or Raphael) Courteville (b ? London; d ? London, *c* 1735), son of 1. Educated in the Chapel Royal. Appointed organist of the church of St James, Westminster, in 1691. He wrote incidental music for Southerne's dramatic version of Aphra Behn's *Oroonoko* and for Part III of Durfey's *Don Quixote*; sonatas for two flutes; hymn-tune *St James*; many songs, influenced by Purcell.

3. Raphael Courteville (b ? London; d London, buried 10 Jun 1772), son of 2, whom (?) he succeeded at St James's Church. He was also active as a composer.

Covent Garden Theatre London theatre. First house opened 7 Dec 1732, burnt down 19 Sept 1808; second opened 18 Sept 1809, burnt down 5 Mar 1856; third opened 15 May 1858. The theatre did not become a regular opera house until 1847, though opera had long been performed in it (e.g. Handel's first season there in 1734 and Weber's *Oberon* in 1826). The first work in 1847 was Rossini's *Semiramide*. It became the Royal Opera in 1892 and ran annual seasons, wholly in Italian at first, but later in French and German also, until 1914, and again between the two World Wars from 1919 to 1939. After being used as a dance hall 1940–45 it re-opened as a national opera house in 1946. At first opera only in English was attempted, but this impractical course was soon abandoned for productions in the original language: a truly international house, under the administration of David Webster, then John Tooley, has therefore been developed. Jeremy Isaacs appointed General Administrator 1987, with effect from 1988 (retiring 1997). Surtitles were introduced and Nicholas Payne became Opera Director 1993.

As hardly anyone has composed more than myself ... I hope that my family will find in my wallet something to make them regret my passing.

François Couperin, Preface to *Pièces de Clavecin*, 1730

Cowell, Henry (Dixon) (b Menlo Park, CA, 11 Mar 1897; d Shady, NY, 10 Dec 1965), American composer and writer on music. Studied in NY, at California University and in Berlin. Toured in Europe and America as a pianist, lectured on music at universities and colleges in USA and contributed to many music papers. As early as 1912–13 he developed a technique using tone-clusters, played by striking the keyboard with the fist, forearm or elbow. He used these devices in, among other works, his piano concerto (1929). He also employed sounds produced by plucking or stroking the strings inside the piano.

With Lev Theremin he invented the rhythmicon, an instrument allowing accurate performance of different, conflicting rhythms.

Works include opera *O'Higgins of Chile* (1949); ballets *The Building of Bamba* (1917) and *Atlantis*; 21 symphonies (1916–65), *Synchrony, Reel, Hornpipe, Sinfonietta, Scherzo*, etc. for orchestra; ten 'tunes', 18 *Hymns and Fuguing Tunes, Exultation* and *Four Continuations* for strings; piano concerto; six string quartets (1915–62); Toccata for soprano (wordless), flute, cello and piano; other chamber music; many piano works.

Cowen, Frederic (Hymen) (b Kingston, Jamaica, 29 Jan 1852; d London, 6 Oct 1935), English composer and conductor. Studied in London, Leipzig and Berlin. Conductor by turns of the London Philharmonic Society, at Liverpool and Manchester. Knighted 1911.

Works include operas *Pauline* (1876), *Thorgrim, Signa* (1893) and *Harold* (1895); operettas and incidental music; oratorios *The Deluge* (1878), *St Ursula, Ruth* (1887), *The Veil*, etc.; cantatas *The Corsair, The Sleeping Beauty, St John's Eve, Ode to the Passions* (Collins), *John Gilpin* (Cowper); jubilee (1897) and coronation (1902) odes; cantatas for female voices, anthems, partsongs.

Six symphonies (1869–98: no. 3 *Scandinavian*, no. 4 *Welsh*, no. 6 *Idyllic*); four concert overtures, *Sinfonietta, Indian Rhapsody* and other works for orchestra; concerto and *Concertstück* for piano and orchestra; string quartet (1866), piano trio; many piano pieces; *c* 300 songs.

Cowie, Edward (b Birmingham, 17 Aug 1943), English composer. He studied with Goehr, Fricker and Lutoslawski and has taught in England, W Germany and Australia: several works based on the Australian criminal Ned Kelly. His interest in painting is reflected in the *Choral Symphony* of 1982, subtitled *Symphonies of Rain, Sea and Speed*.

Works include operas *Commedia* (1978) and *Kelly* (1980–82); *Kate Kelly's Roadshow* for mezzo and ensemble (1982); *Concerto for Orchestra* (1980), two symphonies: (*The American* and *The Australian*, 1980–82), two clarinet concertos (1969, 1975), harp concerto (1982); *Endymion Nocturnes* for tenor and string quartet (1973, revised 1981), *Kelly Choruses* for voices and harp (1981), *Missa Brevis* (Mass for Peace, 1983), *Ancient Voices* for four voices (1983); four string quartets (1973–83), *Kelly Passacaglia* for string quartet (1980).

Cowper, Robert (b *c* 1474; d between 1535 and 1540), English composer. Clerk of King's College, Cambridge, 1493–95. Wrote sacred pieces and carols, especially in *XX songs ix of iii partes and xi of three partes* (1530).

Cox, Jean (b Gadsen, AL, 16 Jan 1922), American tenor. He sang Lensky in Boston in 1951, then moved to Europe; Bayreuth debut 1956, and from 1967 as Lohengrin, Parsifal, and Siegfried. He sang Siegfried at CG in 1975 and returned in 1985 for Bacchus. Chicago from 1964; NY Met. debut 1976, as Walther. Other roles included Janáček's Steva and Strauss's Apollo.

Cox, John (b Bristol, 12 Mar 1935), English stage director. After study at Oxford he was assistant at Glyndebourne; director of productions 1971–81, with Richard Strauss series including *Arabella, Intermezzo* and *Capriccio*. General administrator of Scottish Opera 1981–86, including first local staging of *Lulu*. NY Met. debut 1982, *Il Barbiere di Siviglia*, US premiere of *The Midsummer Marriage* at San Francisco, 1983. Has also staged *Daphne* at Munich and *Il re pastore* at Salzburg. Director of productions at CG from 1988 (*Il Viaggio a Reims* and *Die Frau ohne Schatten*, 1992).

Crabbé, Armand (b Vandergoten, 23 Apr 1883; d Brussels, 24 Jul 1947), Belgian baritone. Debut Brussels, 1904, in *Le Jongleur de Notre Dame*. CG 1906–14, as Valentin, Silvio and Ford. La Scala debut 1914, as Rigoletto; 1929 in the fp of Giordano's *Il re*. Buenos Aires 1916–26, as Rossini's Figaro and Marouf. At Antwerp and Milan he was successful as Beckmesser.

Cradle will Rock, The 'play with music' in ten scenes by Marc Blitzstein. The Federal Theater banned the work because it depicted class warfare in Steeltown, USA. At the fp on 16 Jun 1937 the cast sang from stalls seats, with the composer at a piano. Orson Welles directed.

Craft, Robert (b Kingston, NY, 20 Oct 1923), American conductor and writer on music. He studied at the Juilliard School and from 1948 was closely associated with Stravinsky: Craft was influential in his conversion to serial technique in the early 1950s. He collaborated with Stravinsky in recording his music, and was the first to record the complete works of Webern. At Santa Fe in 1963 he conducted the first US performance of Berg's *Lulu* (two-act version); also recorded much of Schoenberg's music. With Stravinsky he compiled six vols. of 'conversations' (1959–69). Other books include *Stravinsky in Photographs and Documents* (1976).

Craig, Charles (b London, 3 Dec 1919), English tenor. He sang with the CG chorus from 1947 and in 1952 was heard in a London concert with Beecham, (Handel's *Ode for St Cecilia's Day*). CG debut 1959, as Pinkerton; sang in the first London performance of Dvořák's *Russalka*, at SW, the same year. He was successful with the ENO as Otello, at the age of 65. As a guest he appeared at Chicago, Berlin, Paris and Vienna.

Cramer, Johann Baptist (b Mannheim, 24 Feb 1771; d London, 16 Apr 1858), German (anglicized) pianist, conductor and composer. Was taken to London at the age of one, taught by his father and later went to Clementi for piano study; first appeared in public in 1781. In 1824 he established a music publishing business. He lived abroad from 1835 to 1845.

Works include nine piano concertos; two piano quartets and quintets; 124 piano sonatas, two vols. of 42 studies each, 16 later studies, 100 daily exercises, etc.

Cramer, Wilhelm (b Mannheim, bap. 2 Jun 1746; d London, 5 Oct 1799), German violinist, father of Johann Baptist ◊Cramer. Member of the Mannheim Orchestra 1757–72. Settled in London 1772; leader of the royal band and of many important concert organizations. Works include three violin concertos and chamber music.

Crawford (Seeger), Ruth (Porter) (b East Liverpool, OH, 3 Jul 1901; d Chevy Chase, MD, 18 Nov 1953), American composer. She studied at the Chicago Conservatory and with Charles Seeger, whom she later married. Compiled many folksong anthologies, e.g. *American Folk Songs for Children* (1948) and wrote hundreds of her own piano accompaniments. Her own compositions are regarded as anticipating certain later developments in music: they include suite for piano and woodwind quintet (1927), nine piano preludes (1924–28), string quartet (1931), *Risselty, Rosselty* for small orchestra (1941), *2 Ricercari* for voice and piano (1932).

Creation Mass (Haydn.) ◊Schöpfungsmesse.

I was never so devout as when I was at work on The Creation.

Joseph Haydn, quoted in Hughes, *Haydn*, 1970

Creation, The, *Die Schöpfung*, oratorio by Haydn (libretto by Gottfried van Swieten after an English model, now lost, based on Genesis and Milton's *Paradise Lost*), produced Vienna, Schwarzenberg Palace, 29 Apr 1798.

Credo, Latin, = 'I believe'; the third item of the Ordinary of the Mass. Its text dates from the Council of Nicea (325), and its use was ordered in the Mozarabic and Gallican liturgies in 589. It was not introduced into the Roman liturgy until 1071. Later medieval melodies are also known. *See illustration on page 142.*

Créquillon (or Crécquillon), Thomas (b between *c* 1480 and *c* 1500; d ? Béthune, 1557), Flemish composer. Choirmaster in Charles V's imperial chapel in the Netherlands. Wrote Masses, motets, Lamentations, *chansons*.

crescendo Italian = 'growing'; increasing in loudness.

Crescentini, Girolamo (b Urbania near Urbino, 2 Feb 1762; d Naples, 24 Apr 1846), Italian male soprano. Made his first appearance in Rome in 1783; sang in London in 1785–87. In Italy he sang in the fps

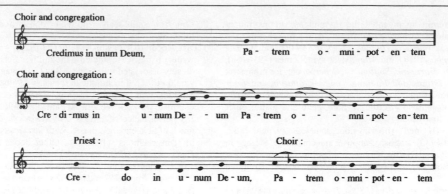

The example shows (i) the Mozarabic, (ii) the Gallican, and (iii) the Roman plainsong variants of the Credo.

of Rispoli's *Ipermestra* (1785), Cimarosa's *Gli Orazi* (1797), Zingarelli's *Meleagro* (1798) and Federici's *Ifigenia* (1809).

Crespin, Régine (b Marseilles, 23 Mar 1927), French soprano. Studied at the Paris Conservatory. After making her debut in the provinces, she appeared at the Paris Opéra in 1950 as Elsa. Bayreuth 1958–61, as Kundry and Sieglinde. Glyndebourne, 1959–60, as the Marschallin, the role of her NY Met. debut, 1962. Retired 1989 after singing the Countess in *The Queen of Spades* at Paris.

Creston (real name *Joseph Guttovegio*), Paul (b New York, 10 Oct 1906; d San Diego, 24 Aug 1985), American composer and teacher of Italian descent. Studied piano and organ, but was self-taught in harmony, theory and composition. He also did research in musicotherapy, aesthetics, acoustics and the history of music. In 1938 he was awarded a Guggenheim Fellowship. His music uses jazzy rhythms and a rich orchestral palette.

Works include six symphonies (1941–82), 15 concertos, including one for two violins, much orchestral music; choral works, many based on texts by Whitman, chamber music, songs.

Cristofori, Bartolommeo di Francesco (b Padua, 4 May 1655; d Florence, 27 Jan 1731), Italian harpsichord maker. Worked first at Padua and then at Florence. Inventor of the piano, the first specimens of which he made in the earliest years of the 18th c. Three of his pianos (1720–26) survive.

criticism, from Greek *kritein*, = 'to judge'; the evaluation and explanation of a work or a performance. In general parlance it concerns musical reporting in newspapers and journals. In more academic terms it follows the usage of, for example, literary criticism, in striving for a reasoned appreciation of a work or repertory taking the broadest possible account of its style, historical context and aesthetic impact.

A review, however favourable, can be ridiculous at the same time if the critic lacks average intelligence, as is not seldom the case.

Franz Schubert, in a letter, 1825

Crivelli, Gaetano (b Brescia, 20 Oct 1768; d Brescia, 10 Jul 1836), Italian tenor. Appeared in Italy at a very early age and first went to Paris in 1811 and London in 1817; appeared in operas by Cimarosa, Paer and Mozart. In 1824 he created Adriano in Meyerbeer's *Il crociato in Egitto*.

Croce, Giovanni (b Chioggia near Venice, *c* 1557; d Venice, 15 May 1609), Italian priest and composer. Pupil of Zarlino, at Venice, where he worked at St Mark's and succeeded Donati as *maestro di cappella* in 1603. Wrote motets, psalms, madrigals, *capricci* for voices.

Croche, Monsieur an imaginary character under whose name Debussy pub. a selection of his critical articles in 1917, the book being entitled *Monsieur Croche, antidilettante*.

Crociato in Egitto, Il, *The Crusader in Egypt*, opera by Meyerbeer (libretto by G Rossi), produced Venice, Teatro La Fenice, 7 Mar

1824. Crusader Armando, disguised as Elmireno, has secretly married the Sultan's daughter, Palmide. In a struggle between Islam and Christianity, Sultan Aladino eventually allows Palmide to accompany Armando to Europe after the crusader saves Aladino's life.

Croesus, *Der hochmütige, gestürzte und wieder erhabne Croesus*, opera by Keiser (libretto by L von Bostel after the Italian of N Minato), produced Hamburg, Theater beim Gänsemarkt, Carnival, 1710. King Croesus battles against King Cyrus and loses. Croesus' mute son, Atis, now able to speak, returns to court and tests the fidelity of Elmira. About to execute Croesus, Cyrus has a change of heart. The happy ending is complete when Atis and Elmira are to marry.

Croft, William (b Nether Ettington, Warwicks, bap. 30 Dec 1678; d Bath, 14 Aug 1727), English organist and composer. Chorister of the Chapel Royal under Blow. Organist of St Anne's, Soho, from 1700 and, with Clarke, of the Chapel Royal from 1704. Master of the Children there and organist of Westminster Abbey from 1708, succeeding Blow. Mus.D. Oxford, 1713. His most famous work is his setting of the Burial Service, which is still in use. Much other church music survives, including two vols. of anthems pub. under the title *Musica Sacra* in 1724. Other works include theatrical pieces, keyboard music.

Croiza, Claire (b Paris, 14 Sept 1882; d Paris, 27 May 1946), French mezzo. Attached to the Opéra-Comique in Paris and appeared from 1906 at the Théâtre de la Monnaie in Brussels, where she sang Erda, Carmen, Berlioz's Dido, Clytemnestra and Charlotte. She was known mainly as a singer of modern French songs. In 1934 she became professor of singing at the Paris Conservatory.

crook a detachable piece of tubing that can be fitted into brass wind instruments, especially horns, to alter the length of the tube and thus change the tuning.

Crosby, John (b New York, 12 Jul 1926), American conductor and administrator. Studied at Yale and Columbia Universities and was coach and conductor at NY City Opera 1951–56. Founded Santa Fe Opera 1956, giving operas by Strauss and many contemporary works. President of the Manhattan School of Music 1976–80.

Crosdill, John (b London, 1755; d Eskrick, Yorkshire, Oct 1825), English cellist. The best English player of his time, attached to the Concert of Ancient Music, the Chapel Royal, etc. Chamber musician to Queen Charlotte.

Cross, Joan (b London, 7 Sept 1900; d Aldeburgh, 12 Dec 1993), English soprano. She sang major roles with SW, London, from 1931 to 1946; created Ellen Orford there in 1945. Other Britten creations were the Female Chorus (1946), Lady Billows (1947), Elizabeth I (1953) and Mrs Grose (1954). She was a founder member of the EOG, 1945, and taught from 1955, especially at the National School of Opera.

Crosse, Gordon (b Bury, 1 Dec 1937), English composer. He studied with Wellesz and Petrassi and has taught at Birmingham and Essex Universities.

Works include operas *Purgatory* (1969), *The Grace of Todd*

(1969), *The Story of Vasco* (1974); ballet *Young Apollo* (1984); two symphonies (1964 and 1976), two violin concertos (1962, 1969), *Dreamsongs* for orchestra (1979), *Array* for trumpet and strings (1986); *Quiet* for wind band (1987); string quartet (1980); piano trio (1986); pieces for children: *Meet my Folks* (Hughes), *Potter Thompson* and *Holly from the Bongs*.

cross-fingering a method of fingering woodwind instruments which omits intermediate holes. It is often necessary for high notes and may also be convenient as an alternative.

Crossley, Paul (b Dewsbury, Yorkshire, 17 May 1944), English pianist and educator. He studied at Oxford and with Messiaen in Paris. London debut 1968. Tippett wrote for him the third sonata (1973). Well known in Romantic and modern music; has played with the London Sinfonietta. In 1986 presented a successful series of TV programmes on 20th-c. classics and played in the British stage fp of Janáček's *Diary of One who Disappeared* (London Coliseum). Joint artistic director of London Sinfonietta from 1988; played with them at the 1993 Proms in Henze's Requiem.

cross-rhythm the device in composition of making the accentuation of a theme or melody conflict with (*a*) the normal strong beats of the bar or (*b*) the accents of another tune combined with it. For example a melodic shape in groups of three crotchets to the bar would be a simple cross-rhythm if it occurred in a piece with the time-signature of 6–8.

Crotch, William (b Norwich, 5 Jul 1775; d Taunton, 29 Dec 1847), English composer. Played the organ in London at the age of four, went to Cambridge at 11 to assist Randall at the organs of Trinity and King's Colleges and produced an oratorio *The Captivity of Judah* there in 1789, having moved the preceding year to Oxford for theological studies. He turned to music finally in 1790 and was appointed organist at Christ Church there. Mus.D., Oxford, 1799, having already succeeded Hayes as professor in 1798. On the establishment of the RAM in London in 1822 he became its first principal.

Works include oratorios *Palestine* (1805–11) and *The Captivity of Judah* (two settings); *Ode to Fancy* (J Warton) and ode for the installation of Lord Grenville as Chancellor of Oxford University, ode for the accession of George IV; funeral anthem for the Duke of York; anthems and chants, motet *Methinks I hear*; glees; concertos and fugues for organ.

crotchet a note or rest taking half the time of a minim and forming the unit of any time-signature of which the lower figure is 4, also that marked C (= 4–4).

Crozier, Eric (b London, 14 Nov 1914; d France, 7 Sept 1994), English librettist and stage director. Studied in London and Paris and produced plays for BBC TV 1936–39. Associated with Britten from 1945 and co-founded with him the English Opera Group (1947) and the Aldeburgh Festival (1948). Librettist of Britten's *Albert Herring* (1946), *Saint Nicolas* (1948), *Let's Make an Opera* (1949) and *Billy Budd* (with E M Forster, 1951). Produced the premiere of *Peter Grimes* (1945) and its US fp (Tanglewood 1946); *The Rape of Lucretia* at Glyndebourne, 1946. Translated operas by Verdi, Mozart and Strauss.

When a singer at a prison concert sang 'Home, Sweet Home', the inmates were so deeply moved that seven of them escaped the same night.
         Slonimsky, *A Thing or Two about Music*, 1948

Crucible, The opera in four acts by Robert Ward (libretto by composer and B Stambler after Arthur Miller's play), produced NY City Opera, 26 Oct 1961. 17th-c. New England witchcraft trial seen as precursor of Cold War anti-communist hysteria.

Crüger, Johann (b Gross-Breese, Prussia, 9 Apr 1598; d Berlin, 23 Feb 1662), German theorist and composer. Cantor at St Nicholas' Church, Berlin, from 1622. Wrote several chorales afterwards used by Bach.

Works include *Praxis pietatis melica* containing hymn-tunes with

Crossley *British pianist Paul Crossley studied in Paris and is an expert interpreter of the French school. He is a champion of new music; Michael Tippett's Third Piano Sonata is dedicated to him.*

bass, *Geistliche Kirchen-Melodien* containing hymn-tunes prescribed by Luther set for four voices with instruments (1649), Magnificats; secular songs.

Crumb, George (Henry) (b Charleston, WV, 24 Oct 1929), American composer. He studied in Berlin with Blacher and at the University of Michigan with Ross Lee Finney. An early influence was Schoenberg, and aleatory techniques have also been employed.

Works include the orchestral pieces *Variazoni* (1959), *Echoes of Time and the River* (1967); *Star-Child* for soprano, children's voices, male speaking choir, bell ringers and orchestra, performed NY, 1977, conductor Boulez), *A Haunted Landscape* for instrumental ensemble (1984); *Night Music* for soprano and ensemble (1963), four books of madrigals for soprano, with various instrumental ensembles (1965–69), *11 Echoes of Autumn* for violin, flute, clarinet, piano (1965), *Ancient Voices of Children* for soprano and ensemble (1970), *Black Angels* for amplified string quartet, *13 Images from the Dark Land* (1970); *Voice of the Whale*, with electronics (1972), *Federico's Little Songs* for soprano, flute and percussion (1986); four books of *Makrokosmos* for amplified piano and percussion (1972–79); *Processional* for piano (1983), *An Idyll for the Misbegotten* for amplified flute and three percussionists (1985), *Zeitgeist* for two amplified pianos (1987).

crumhorn, or cromorne, a woodwind instrument made of wood and bent, played with a double reed enclosed in a cap. It was used in the 16th and 17th c., particularly in Germany and mainly for dance music. It has a nutty, buzzing tone, somewhat reminiscent of a kaazoo.

Crusell, Bernhard Henrik (b Unsikaupunki near Turku, 15 Oct 1775; d Stockholm, 28 Jul 1838), Finnish composer and clarinettist. He was a member of the military band at Svaeborg castle, Finland, before moving to Stockholm in 1791; studied

Cui *The composer César Cui (1835–1918) in a drawing by I Y Ryepin. As a member of the Russian nationalist circle of composers, his contribution was mainly in terms of literary support. His own music lacked the technique required to fulfil his calling.*

there with the Abbé Vogler. In 1798 he went to Berlin and in 1803 studied with Berton and Gossec in Paris. A leading clarinet virtuoso of his day, he also worked at the Stockholm Opera; translated and conducted for the first time in Sweden operas by Beethoven, Rossini, Meyerbeer and Auber.

Works include an opera *The Little Slave Girl* (*Den lilla slavinnan*, 1824); three clarinet concertos (1811, 1818, 1828), Concertante for horn, bassoon, clarinet and orchestra (1816), Concertino for bassoon and orchestra; three quartets for clarinet and strings (1811, 1817, 1823), three clarinet duos (1821), Divertimento for oboe and strings (1823); 37 songs for four-part chorus.

Cruvilli (Crüwell), Johanne (Jeanne) Sophie Charlotte (b Bielefeld, 12 Mar 1826; d Monte Carlo, 6 Nov 1907), German soprano. Made her debut at Venice in 1847 as Odabella in *Attila*; first sang in Paris in 1851 and was engaged for the Opéra in 1854. She sang there in *Les Huguenots*, *La Vestale* and *La juive*; Hélène in the fp of *Les Vêpres Siciliennes*, 1855.

Cruz, Ivo (b Cidade de Corumba, Brazil, 19 May 1901; d Lisbon, 8 Sept 1983), Portuguese conductor and composer. Studied music and law at Lisbon, where later he founded the review *Renascimento musical*, resuming his studies at Munich 1924. On his return he founded a choral society 1930 and a chamber orchestra 1933. Appointed director of the Lisbon Conservatory 1938.

Works include *Nocturnos da Lusitania* and *Motivos lusitanos* (1928) for orchestra, *Vexilla regis* for soprano and orchestra, sonatina for violin and piano, piano music, songs.

crwth, Welsh = crowd, also called crot, crotta, crotte or rotte, an early bowed string instrument, ancestor of the violin family.

Cry work by Giles Swayne for 28 amplified voices, depicting the creation of the world; composed 1978, fp London, 23 Jul 1980.

csárdás, Hungarian, a Hungarian dance consisting of a slow movement called *lassú* and a quick one called *friss*.

Csermák, Antal György (b c 1774; d Veszprém, 25 Oct 1822), Hungarian violinist and composer. He became leader in a Budapest theatre orchestra, visited many noble houses and under the influence of Bihari began to cultivate a national style, especially that of the *Verbunkos*.

Cubana, La, oder Ein leben für die Kunst, *La Cubana, or a Life for the Arts*, vaudeville by Henze (text by M Enzensberger, after M Barnet); composed 1973, fp NY, NET theatre, 4 Mar 1974; stage premiere Munich, Theater am Gärtnerplatz, 28 May 1975.

Cuberli, Leila (b Austin, TX, 29 Sept 1945), American soprano. Studied in Dallas and made opera debut at Budapest (Violetta, 1975). La Scala from 1978 as Mozart's Constanze and Countess and in *Il re pastore* and *Ariodante*. Salzburg debut 1986, Vienna 1988 (*Il Viaggio a Reims*); CG and NY Met. 1990, as Mathilde in *Guillaume Tell* and Semiramide. Also a noted concert artist.

Cuclin, Demetre (b Galatz, 5 Apr 1885; d Bucharest, 7 Feb 1978), Romanian composer. Studied at Bucharest Conservatory and later with Widor at the Conservatory and d'Indy at the Schola Cantorum in Paris. In 1922–30 he taught in NY but returned to Romania to become professor at Bucharest Conservatory.

Works include operas *Soria* (1911), *Agamemnon* (1922), *Trojan and Bellerophon* (1925); overture for chorus and orchestra, sacred and secular choruses; 20 symphonies (1910–72), symphonic scherzo for orchestra; violin concerto; piano trio; violin and piano sonatas, suites for violin and piano and cello and piano; piano pieces; songs.

cue a few notes printed in small music type in instrumental or vocal parts of a musical work, serving as a guide to show where the performer is to come in after a lengthy rest.

Cuenod, Hugues (b Vevey, 26 Jun 1902), Swiss tenor. After a career as a concert singer sang also in opera from 1928. He created Stravinsky's Sellem (Venice, 1951). Glyndebourne 1954–84, in *Figaro, Falstaff, Calisto* and *The Cunning Little Vixen*. Active as a recitalist into his 80s, singing the Emperor in *Turandot* at the NY Met. in 1987.

Cui, César Antonovich (b Wilno, 18 Jan 1835; d Petrograd, 26 Mar 1918), Russian composer and critic of French descent. Educated at the High School of Wilno, where his father, a French officer left behind in the retreat from Moscow in 1812, was professor of French. He had some lessons in music from Moniuszko, but was sent to the School of Military Engineering at St Petersburg in 1850, where he became sub-professor in 1857. He became an authority on fortifications and remained an amateur in music. But he joined Balakirev's circle of Russian nationalist composers and became one of the 'Kutchka' group, though the least exclusively Russian among them. He became a critic in 1864 and did much literary work for the nationalist cause.

Works include operas *The Mandarin's Son* (1859, produced 1878), *The Captive in the Caucasus* (after Pushkin), *William Ratcliff* (after Heine, 1869), *Angelo* (after Hugo), *Le Flibustier* (libretto by J Richepin), *The Saracen* (after Dumas senior, 1889), *A Feast in Time of Plague* (Pushkin, 1900), *Mam'zelle Fifi* (after Maupassant), *Matteo Falcone* (after Mérimée) and *The Captain's Daughter* (1911); works for chorus with and without orchestra; four suites and other works for orchestra; string quartets in C minor (1890) and D (1907); 15 op. nos. of piano pieces, three pieces for two pianos; various instrumental pieces; *c* 25 op. nos. of songs including settings of Pushkin, Lermontov, Nekrassov, Richepin and Mickiewicz.

Cummings, Conrad (b San Francisco, 10 Feb 1948), American composer. Studied at Yale, Stanford and Tanglewood. Has worked at the Columbia-Princeton Electronic Music Center and at IRCAM, Paris. Teacher at the Oberlin Conservatory from 1980. His music draws on Baroque models as well as electronic resources.

Works include operas *Eros and Psyche* (1983), *Cassandra* (1985, revised as a dramatic scene), *Positions* (1956) (1988, after 1950s sex manuals), *Insertions* (1988), *Photo-Op* (1989) and *Tonkin* (after an incident in the Vietnam War, 1993). Other music includes *Subway Songs* for four-track tape (1974), *Movement* for orchestra (1975), *Skin Songs* for soprano and ensemble (1978), *Dinosaur Music* for ten-track tape and 14 loudspeakers (1981), *Music for Starlore* for stereo tape (1982).

cummings, e(dward) e(stlin), (1894–1962) American poet. Richard R ◊Bennett (*Love Songs*), ◊Berio (*Circles*), ◊Boulez (*cummings ist der* *dichter*), ◊Dickinson (songs), D ◊Erb (*Cummings Cycle*), E ◊Harper (*seven poems by e e c*), ◊Smalley (septet for soprano and ensemble).

Cummings, W(illiam) H(ayman) (b Sidbury, 22 Aug 1831; d London, 6 Jun 1915), English organist, tenor and scholar. Sang under Mendelssohn's direction as a boy and later made an edition of 'Hark! the Herald Angels Sing' to music from Mendelssohn's *Festgesang*. Sang in the Bach Passions and conducted the Sacred Harmonic Society; co-founded the Purcell Society and edited three volumes for it; wrote a biography of Purcell, 1881. Also wrote on Blow, Arne and Handel (biography, 1904). Principal of the GSMD 1896–1910.

cummings ist der dichter, *cummings is the poet*, work by Boulez for 16 voices and 24 instruments; composed 1970, fp Stuttgart, 25 Sept 1970; work in progress. Title allegedly arose as the result of a misheard telephone conversation, concerning the name of the poet who provided the work's text (e e cummings).

Cunning Little Vixen, The, *Příhody lišky Bystroušky*, opera by Janáček (libretto by the composer after R Těsnohlídek's verses for a comic strip published serially in a Brno newspaper during 1920). Composed 1921–23, produced Brno, 6 Nov 1924. Vixen is captured, but escapes, marries, and raises a litter. She is shot by a poacher, but her spirit survives in her cubs.

Cupid and Death masque by James Shirley with music by Locke and C Gibbons, performed London, before the Portuguese ambassador, Leicester Fields, 26 Mar 1653.

Curioso indiscreto, Il, *Indiscreet Curiosity*, opera by Anfossi (libretto by ?), produced Rome, Teatro della Dame, Feb 1777. Mozart wrote two extra soprano arias for this when it was produced in Vienna, 30 Jun 1783. Marchese Calandrino tests fidelity of Clorinda, who falls in love with the Contino, the Marchese's friend.

Curlew River church parable in one act by Britten (libretto by W Plomer after the Japanese Noh play *Sumidagawa*), produced Orford Church, Suffolk, 12 Jun 1964. Ferryman conveys Madwoman to her son's grave; during prayer, an angel restores her sanity.

Curran, Alvin (b Providence, RI, 13 Dec 1938), American composer. Studied with Carter at Yale, and at Rome co-founded the group Musica Electronica Viva, 1966; has also given solo performances at festivals of new music, from 1973.

Works include *Songs and Views from the Magnetic Gardens* (1975); *Light Flowers, Dark Flowers* (1977); *The Works* (1980); *Maritime Rites* for foghorns, ships and rowing boats full of singers (1984); *Crystal Psalms*, with six choruses (1988); *Electric Rags I and II* (1985, 1989).

curtain tune an old term sometimes used in the place of 'act tune' for an ◊intermezzo or entr'acte in the incidental music for a play.

curtal(l) the 16th–17th-c. English name for the bassoon and dulcian.

Curtin, Phyllis (b Clarksburg, WA, 3 Dec 1921), American soprano. Studied in Boston and made debut as Lisa with the New England

---

THE OPERA

The Cunning Little Vixen

A three-act opera of 1924 by Leoš Janáček, set in his homeland of Moravia.

I. Sharpears the vixen (soprano) is caught by the Forester (baritone) but escapes in the confusion when she provokes a revolt by the hens against their cock.

II. Sharpears takes over the lair of the badger (bass) while at the inn the Forester and the Schoolmaster (tenor) lament their lost love. Sharpears and the fox Goldenmane (soprano or tenor) are married by the woodpecker.

III. Sharpears is shot and killed by the poacher Harasta (bass). Back at the inn, the Forester misses the vixen, confusing her with his former love. It is springtime in the woods and as he marvels at the renewal of nature the Forester observes a fox cub, so much like its mother Sharpears.

THE OPERA

Opera Theater, 1946. Sang with NY City Opera from 1953 (debut in Von Einem's *Der Prozess*) and NY Met. from 1961 (debut as Fiordiligi). Glyndebourne 1969, as Donna Anna; Geneva 1966, as Rosina in the premiere of Milhaud's *La mère coupable*. Other roles included Eva, Mozart's Countess, and Violetta (all at the Met.), Salome, and Walton's Cressida. Retired 1984 and became active as a teacher.

Curtis, Alan (b Mason, MI, 17 Nov 1934), American conductor, harpsichordist and musicologist. He studied at Michigan and Illinois Universities and with Gustav Leonhardt in Amsterdam. Professor at Berkeley, CA, since 1970. He is an authority on early keyboard music and has edited for recording and produced several 17th-c. operas, e.g. Monteverdi's *Poppea*, Cavalli's *Erismena* and Cesti's *Il Tito* (Innsbruck, 1983).

I cannot conceive of music that expresses absolutely nothing.

Béla Bartók, quoted in Machlis, *Introduction to Contemporary Music*, 1963

Curtis Institute of Music school of music in Philadelphia, founded 1924 by Mrs Mary Louise Bok. Directors have included Josef Hofmann (1926–38), Efrem Zimbalist (1941–68), Rudolf Serkin (1968–76), John de Lancie (1977–85) and Gary Graffman (from 1986).

Curwen English family of music educationists and publishers:

1. John Curwen (b Heckmondwike, Yorkshire, 14 Nov 1816; d Manchester, 26 May 1880), founded the Tonic Sol-fa method of music teaching, established the Tonic Sol-fa Association 1853 and the publishing firm in London in 1863.

2. John Spencer Curwen (b London, 30 Sept 1847; d London, 6 Aug 1916), son of 1. He studied at the RAM under Macfarren, Sullivan and Prout, carried on his father's work and began the competition festival movement in England with the Stratford (E London) Festival in 1882.

3. Annie (Jessy), born Gregg (b Dublin, 1 Sept 1845; d Matlock, 22 Apr 1932), wife of 2. She studied at the Royal Irish Academy of Music, married in 1877 and wrote a number of books on a music-teaching method of her own.

Curzon, Clifford (b London, 18 May 1907; d London, 1 Sept 1982), English pianist. Entered RAM in 1919, winning two scholarships and the Macfarren Gold Medal. He made his debut, aged 16, at the Queen's Hall, London. In 1926 he was appointed professor at the RAM and in 1928 went to Berlin to study with Schnabel for two years. He later studied with Landowska and Nadia Boulanger, resigning his post at the RAM in 1932 to devote himself to concert work. He married in 1931. His great sensitivity and musical intelligence made him one of the finest pianists of the day, especially in the work of Schubert, Brahms and Mozart. Knighted 1977.

Cusins, William (George) (b London, 14 Oct 1833; d Remonchamps, Ardennes, 31 Aug 1893), English pianist, violinist, organist, conductor and composer. Studied under Fétis at the Brussels Conservatory and at the RAM in London. Was active in various musical organizations in London and at court. Knighted 1892.

Works include oratorio *Gideon* (1871); *Royal Wedding Serenata*; overture to Shakespeare's *Love's Labour's Lost* (1875); piano concerto in A minor, etc.

Cutting, Francis (*fl.* 1583–*c* 1603), English lutenist and composer. Virtually nothing is known of his life; he composed much lute music, including 11 pieces in Barley's *A New Booke of Tabliture* (1596).

Cutting, Thomas, English 16th–17th-c. lutenist. In the service of lady Arabella Stuart until 1607, then of Christian IV of Denmark at Copenhagen until 1611, when he returned and entered Prince Henry's private band.

Cuzzoni, Francesca (b Parma, *c* 1700; d Bologna, 1770), Italian soprano. Made her operatic debut in 1716, and sang 1723–28 in Handel's operas in London; created roles in *Ottone, Giulio Cesare, Tamerlano, Rodelinda* and *Alessandro*. Her rivalry with Faustina

◊Bordoni became notorious, and they fought on stage during a performance of Bononcini's *Astianatte* in 1727.

cyclic form the form of a composition in several movements, usually a symphony or chamber work, in which one or more themes appear in at least two movements and lend organic unity to the whole.

cyclic mass a misleading term for a setting of the Ordinary of the Mass in which there is some kind of thematic connection between the movements.

cymbals plate-shaped brass percussion instruments, a pair of which is struck together or one of which is made to sound in various ways by being touched with hard or soft drum-sticks. They have no fixed pitch, but there are ancient cymbals of smaller size which give out definite notes.

Cyrano opera by W Damrosch (libretto by W J Henderson, based on Rostand's play *Cyrano de Bergerac*), produced NY Met. 27 Feb 1913.

Cyrano de Bergerac opera by Alfano (libretto by H Cain, based on Rostand's play), produced in Italian translation, Rome, Teatro Reale, 22 Jan 1936. Cyrano has a nose for amorous trouble, writing love letters for the verbally inept Christian, who loves Roxane.

Cythère assiégée, La, *Cytherea Besieged*, opera by Gluck (libretto by C S Favart, based on Longus's *Daphnis and Chloe*), produced Vienna, Burgtheater, spring 1759. Scythian warriors lay siege to Cytherea but fall for her attendant nymphs.

cymbals *These are the small cymbals which were used by women dancers in Bacchanalian rituals. Cymbals of this type are also seen in paintings of the Middle Ages.*

Czerny *Although most famous today for his virtuosic (if mechanical) études, Carl Czerny (1791–1857) represents more significantly a crucial link in the chain of Romantic pianists. As a teacher he disseminated the ideas of his own mentor, Beethoven, to his pupils, who included Liszt.*

czakan a woodwind instrument, probably originating from Transylvania but very fashionable in Vienna *c* 1830, of the flute type, but made in the shape of a walking-stick and often used as such.

Czech Philharmonic Orchestra Czech ensemble, founded independently 1941 (formerly the orchestra of Prague National Opera) and directed 1919–41 by Vaclav Talich; international recognition gained during these years. Later music directors have included Rafael Kubelik (1941–48), Karel Ancerl (1950–68), Vaclav Neumann (1968–89), Jiri Belohlavek (1990–92) and Gerd Albrecht (from 1992).

Czernohorsky ◊Cernohorský.

> *In each corner of his study was a desk with an unfinished score ... After finishing a page of one score, he passed on to another desk; and by the time he had written a page at the fourth desk, he resumed his labours at desk No. 1.*
>
> **John Ella** on a visit to Czerny, *Musical Sketches*, 1878

Czerny, Carl (b Vienna, 21 Feb 1791; d Vienna, 15 Jul 1857), Austrian pianist, teacher and composer. He was first taught the piano by his father, played brilliantly at the age of ten and became a pupil of Beethoven about that time; he also took advice from Hummel and Clementi. Not liking to appear in public, he took to teaching and soon had an enormous following of pupils, among which he chose only the most gifted. This left him enough leisure for composition, which he cultivated so assiduously as to produce almost 1,000 works.

Works include 24 Masses, four Requiems, 300 graduals and offertories; many symphonies, overtures; concertos; string quartets and trios; choruses; songs and, most numerous of all, masses of piano music, including studies, exercises, preludes and fugues in all the keys and endless arrangements of other composers' works.

Czerwenka, Oscar (b Linz, 5 Jul 1924), Austrian bass. Debut Graz, 1947, in *Der Freischütz*; Vienna Staatsoper since 1951, Salzburg since 1953. Glyndebourne debut 1959, as Ochs; NY Met. 1960, as Rocco. Other roles include Osmin, Kečal and Abu Hassan in *Der Barbier von Bagdad*.

Cziffra, György (b Budapest, 5 Nov 1921; d Morsang-sur-Orge, 15 Jan 1994), Hungarian-born French pianist. He studied at the Liszt Academy, Budapest, with Dohnányi and was a recitalist before war service. He was a political prisoner during the early 1950s and escaped to France 1956. Best known in the music of Liszt, Chopin and Schumann.

Czyż, Henryk (b Grudziadz, 16 Jun 1923), Polish conductor and composer. He held posts with the orchestras of Łódz and Kraków, 1957–68, and in 1966 was in Munster to conduct the fp of Penderecki's *St Luke Passion*. In 1969 he gave the fp, in Hamburg, of Penderecki's opera *The Devils of Loudun*. Led the Düsseldorf orchestra 1971–74 before returning to Łódz until 1980, when he became a professor at the Warsaw Academy. US debut 1973, with the Minnesota Orchestra.

Works include *Etude* for orchestra (1949), Symphonic Variations (1952), and the comic opera *Kynolog w rosterce* (*The Dog-lover's Dilemma*; composed 1964, produced Kraków, 1967).

D

D the second note, or supertonic, of the scale of C major.

d the tonic note in any key in Tonic Sol-fa notation, pronounced 'doh'.

d' French names with the prefix *de* abbr. to *d'* before a vowel appear under the principal surnames: e.g. Vincent d'Indy as 'Indy, Vincent d''.

D, abbr., = *Deutsch*, followed by a number, indicates listing of work by Schubert in the thematic catalogue by O E Deutsch.

Dabadie, Henri-Bernard (b Pau, 19 Jan 1797; d Paris, May 1853), French baritone. In 1819 he made his debut at the Paris Opéra, in Spontini's *La Vestale*, and remained until 1834; created leading roles in Rossini's *Moïse*, *Le Comte Ory* and *Guillaume Tell*. He sang in Italy and created Belcore in *L'elisir d'amore* (Milan, 1832).

da capo Italian = 'from the beginning' a direction indicating that from the point at which it is marked the performer is to turn back to the beginning of the composition.

da capo al fine Italian = 'from the beginning to the end'; as with the simple *da capo*, the performer is asked to go back to the beginning; the composition is not in this case to be repeated as a whole, but only to the point where the word *fine* ('end') appears.

da capo aria a distinctive type of vocal piece for a single voice (though duets and other ensemble pieces may be in the same form) consisting of three sections, the third of which is a repetition of the first, while the middle section is a contrast based sometimes on similar and sometimes on wholly different thematic material. The da capo aria was cultivated in the second half of the 17th and first half of the 18th c. (up to the earlier works of Gluck), notably by A Scarlatti, Handel, Bach, Hasse, Jommelli, etc.

Dafne opera by Schütz (libretto by Martin Opitz, partly translated from Rinuccini), produced Torgau, Hartenfels Castle, at the wedding of Georg, Landgrave of Hesse, and Sophia Eleonora, Princess of Saxony, 23 Apr 1627. The music has not survived.

Dafne, La opera by Gagliano (libretto by O Rinuccini), produced Mantua, at the ducal court, Jan 1608.

Opera by Peri (libretto ditto), produced Florence, Palazzo Corsi, Carnival 1597. The first Italian opera and first opera on record anywhere. After belittling Cupid, Apollo falls victim to the arrows of love, pursuing an unyielding Daphne.

Dagincourt or d'Agincourt, François (b Rouen, 1684; d Rouen, 30 Apr 1758), French organist and composer. Appointed organist to the royal chapel in Paris, 1714. Wrote organ and harpsichord pieces.

Dahl, Ingolf (b Hamburg, 9 Jun 1912; d Frutigen, near Berne, 6 Aug 1970), German-born American composer. After study in Cologne and Zurich he moved to the USA in 1935, teaching at the University of Southern California from 1945. His earlier work was dissonant and expressionistic; later came under Stravinsky's influence.

Works include Concerto for saxophone and wind orchestra (1949), Symphony Concertante for two clarinets and orchestra (1953), *The Tower of St Barbara* for orchestra (1955), piano quartet (his first serial work, 1957), *Elegy Concerto* for violin and orchestra (1963), *Aria Sinfonica* (1965), *Intervals* for strings (1970).

Dahlhaus, Carl (b Hanover, 10 Jun 1928; d Berlin, 13 Mar 1989), German musicologist and editor. His early study, at Göttingen, was in Renaissance music. Later became a leading Wagner scholar, edited complete edition, from 1970; pub. *Wagner's Music Dramas* (1971). From the early 1970s he was editor of the *Riemann Musik-Lexicon* and co-ed of the *Neue Zeitschrift für Musik*.

Dalayrac (originally *d'Alayrac*), Nicholas (b Muret, 8 Jun 1753; d Paris, 26 Nov 1809), French composer. He was first intended for the law, then in 1774 went to Versailles to embark on a military career. But his main interest was music and he took lessons from Langlé. In 1777 he pub. six string quartets, and two small operas were performed privately in 1781. The following year he made his debut with *L'Eclipse totale* at the Théâtre Italien. He changed his name from its aristocratic form during the Revolution. He adapted operatic airs to lyrics with Republican sentiments.

Works include about 60 operas, e.g. *Nina ou la Folle par amour* (1786), *Les Deux petits Savoyards*, *Camille*, *Adolphe et Clara* (1799), *Maison à vendre* etc.; 36 string quartets.

Dalberg, Frederick (b Newcastle on Tyne, 7 Jan 1908; d Cape Town, May 1988), English bass. He studied in Dresden and Leipzig, after a childhood in South Africa, and made his debut in 1931. He sang at Leipzig, Berlin and Vienna, and from 1942 to 1951 at Bayreuth, where Hagen, Pogner and Fafner were his roles. Munich 1948–51 and CG during the 1950s: created Claggart in *Billy Budd* (1951); stage premiere in Britain of *Wozzeck* (1952) and the fp of *Gloriana* (1953); within the space of ten years he had sung for Hitler at Bayreuth and before Queen Elizabeth at CG. Glyndebourne 1952, Banquo. Mannheim from 1957.

Dalby, Martin (b Aberdeen, 25 Apr 1942), Scottish composer. He studied at the RCM with Herbert Howells (composition) and Frederick Riddle (viola). He has been influenced by jazz and by Spanish music; from 1965 has held administrative posts in London and Glasgow.

Works include symphony (1970), *Concerto Martin Pescatore*, for strings (1971), viola concerto (1974), *Nozze di Primavera* for orchestra (1984); *The Keeper of the Pass* for soprano and instruments (1971), *Orpheus* for chorus, narrator and 11 instruments (1972), *Call for the Hazel Tree*, for chorus and electronics (1979); *Yet still she is the Moon*, brass septet (1973), *Aleph* for eight instruments (1975), *Man Walking*, octet for wind and strings (1980); two piano sonatas (1985, 1989).

Dale, Benjamin (b London, 17 Jul 1885; d London, 30 Jul 1943), English composer. Studied at the RAM in London, where he later became professor of composition and warden.

Works include cantata *Before the Paling of the Stars* (1912), and *Song of Praise* for chorus and orchestra (1923); violin and piano sonata.

Dalibor opera by Smetana (libretto in German, by J Wenzig, translated into Czech by E Špindler), produced Prague, Czech Theatre, 16 May 1868. Milada attempts to rescue imprisoned Dalibor, but her plan is betrayed and both die in a final battle.

Dalis, Irene (b San José, CA, 8 Oct 1925), American mezzo. She studied in New York and Milan and with Margarete Klose in Berlin. Debut Oldenburg, 1953; Berlin 1955–60. She sang Eboli at her NY Met. debut in 1957 and first sang at CG in 1958. Bayreuth 1961–63 as Kundry and Ortrud. Much admired as the Nurse in *Die Frau ohne Schatten* (SW 1966, in the opera's first London performance). Founder and executive director of Opera San José from 1984.

Dall' Abaco, Evaristo Felice (b Verona, 12 Jul 1675; d Munich 12 Jul 1742), Italian violinist and composer. Worked at Modena, Munich and Brussels; wrote chiefly string music. Like Torri, he followed the Elector Max Emanuel into exile at Brussels.

Dall' Abaco, Joseph Clemens Ferdinand (b Brussels, bap. 27 Mar 1710; d near Verona, 31 Aug 1805), Italian-German cellist and composer, son of Evaristo Felice ◊Dall' Abaco. Worked at Bonn and played in London, Vienna, etc. Wrote sonatas for his instrument.

Dallam, Thomas (b Lancashire, *c* 1570; d after 1614), English organ builder. Built organs for King's College, Cambridge, and Worcester Cathedral. Travelled to Constantinople in 1599–1600 with a mechanical organ, a present from Queen Elizabeth I to the Sultan.

Robert Dallam (1602–65), Ralph Dallam (d 1673) and George Dallam, also organ builders, were probably members of the same family.

Dallapiccola, Luigi (b Pisino, Istria, 3 Feb 1904; d Florence, 19 Feb 1975), Italian composer. For political reasons his family were moved to Graz in 1917, where his decisive first contacts with music (especially opera) were made. The family returned to Italy in 1921, where Dallapiccola studied at the Florence Conservatory and in 1931 became professor. In 1956 he was appointed professor at Queen's College, NY. Dallapiccola's mature music, while using serial techniques, modified them to allow for a more lyrical style than is usual, not avoiding tonal references, thematic structures and harmonic progressions.

Works include OPERAS: *Volo di notte* (after Saint-Exupéry, 1937–39), *Il Prigionero* (1944–48), *Ulisse* (1960–68); ballet *Marsia* (1942–43).

VOICES AND ORCHESTRAL: *Canti di prigionera* (1941), *Canti di liberazione* (1955), *Parole di San Paolo* (1964), *Dalla mia terra*, *Laudi* (Jacopone da Todi). Two lyrics from the *Kalevala*, three studies, rhapsody, *I cori di Michelangelo Buonarroti il giovane*, *Tre laudi*.

ORCHESTRAL: partita; *Piccolo concerto* for piano and orchestra (1941), *Variations* (1954), *Tartiniana*, divertimento for violin and chamber orchestra (1951), *Piccola musica notturna* (1954; for chamber ensemble 1961), *Dialoghi* for cello and orchestra (1960).

Music for three pianos; *Liriche anacreontiche Roncevals*, cycle of Greek and other songs; *Commiato* for soprano and 15 instruments (1972); *Ciaccona, intermezzo e adagio* for solo cello (1945).

Dalla Rizza, Gilda (b Verona, 2 Oct 1892; d Milan, 4 Jul 1975), Italian soprano. Debut Bologna 1912, as Charlotte. She sang in Buenos Aires from 1915. Puccini wrote Magda for her (*La Rondine*, Monte Carlo, 1917) and she was successful as Lauretta, Suor Angelica and Minnie. At La Scala she sang 1923–39, often under Toscanini; appeared as Salud in the local fp of *La Vida Breve*, 1933. Other roles included Violetta, Arabella and Zandonai's Giulietta (creation, Rome, 1922). CG 1920, in Puccini.

Dallas Symphony Orchestra US ensemble, founded 1911 under Carl Venth but not fully professional until conducted by Antal Dorati, 1945–49. Walter Hendl was conductor 1949–58, Paul Kletski 1958–61, Donald Johanos 1962–70. Eduardo Mata was music director 1977–93, succeeded by Andrew Litton. A new hall was opened 1988.

Dal Monte, Toti (b Mogliano, Veneto, 27 Jun 1893; d Treviso, 26 Jan 1975), Italian soprano. Took up singing after her piano studies had been interrupted by an accident. She made her debut at La Scala, Milan, in 1916, in Zandonai's *Francesca da Rimini*; sang Gilda there in 1921. NY Met. debut 1924, as Lucia; Chicago 1924–28. London, CG, as Lucia and Rosina, in 1926. Other roles included Mimi, Butterfly and Stravinsky's Nightingale.

Dalmorès, Charles (b Nancy, 21 Dec 1871; d LA, 6 Dec 1939), French tenor. Debut Lyons 1899 as Loge, in a concert performance of *Das Rheingold*. Brussels 1900–06, as Siegfried and in other Wagner roles. CG 1904–11; fp of Leoni's *L'Oracolo*, 1905. Bayreuth 1908, Lohengrin. At the Manhattan Opera House, 1906–10 he was admired in Massenet's *Thaïs* and *Grisélidis*. Chicago 1910–18.

dal segno . . . Italian = 'from the sign . . .'; a direction indicating that where a composition is to be performed over again from an earlier point, it is to be resumed, not at the beginning, as in an ordinary *da capo*, but from where a certain sign or 'signal' has been placed by the composer. The sign normally used is 𝄋.

Dalza, Joan Ambrosio (*fl.* 1508), Italian lutenist and composer, active in Milan. In 1508 he composed and arranged a book of lute pieces for Ottaviano Petrucci. Pieces in the collection include 42 dances (in nine suites), ricercares and four arrangements of vocal pieces. Pavans appear here for the first time in print; each is followed by a saltarello and *piva* (a quick dance in triple-time, originally performed to the accompaniment of bagpipes).

Damascene, Alexander (d London, 14 Jul 1719), French composer of Italian descent. Settled in London, composer of William III and Gentleman of the Chapel Royal after Purcell's death in 1695. Contributed songs to several collections.

Dame blanche, La, *The White Lady*, opera by Boieldieu (libretto by Scribe, based on Scott's *Guy Mannering* and *The Monastery*), produced Paris, Opéra-Comique, 10 Dec 1825. It contains some Scottish tunes. At auction George Brown prevents the castle from falling into the wrong hands. With help from orphan Anna, it is revealed that George is actually the missing heir Julien Avenel.

Damett, Thomas (d *c* 1437), English composer. At the Chapel Royal, 1413–31; canon of Windsor, 1431 until his death. Works are included in the Old Hall MS.

Damnation de Faust, La dramatic cantata by Berlioz (words by composer and A Gandonnière, based on Goethe's drama), composed 1846, incorporating the *Huit Scènes de Faust* of 1828; fp Paris, Opéra-Comique, 6 Dec 1846; produced as an opera, Monte Carlo, 18 Feb 1893.

Damoiselle élue, La, *The Blessed Damozel*, cantata for soprano, mezzo and female chorus and orchestra by Debussy, set to French translation by Gabriel Sarrazin of Rossetti's poem in 1887–88. Fp Paris, Salle Erard, 8 Apr 1893.

Dämon, Der, *The Demon*, dance pantomime by Hindemith, scenario by M Krell; composed 1922 and performed Darmstadt, 1 Dec 1923. Concert suite for small orchestra arranged 1923.

damping pedal the so-called 'soft' pedal of the piano, which on a grand piano so shifts the hammers of the instrument that they touch only two strings or a single string for each note, instead of three or two, for which reason its use is often indicated by the words *una corda* (one string). This outdated term should not be confused with the 'damper pedal', which is actually the sustaining pedal, receiving its name from the fact that the dampers are all lifted off the strings.

If a young man at the age of twenty-three can write a symphony like that, in five years he will be ready to commit murder.

Walter Damrosch, after conducting Copland's First Symphony, quoted in Sallas, *Aaron Copland*.

Damrosch, Leopold (b Posen, 22 Oct 1832; d New York, 15 Feb 1885), German, later American, conductor, violinist and composer. Studied medicine in Berlin, but gave it up for music. Appeared as violinist and became leader of the Weimar court orchestra under Liszt. Having conducted at Breslau 1850–71, he went to NY, where he did much to advance orchestral music and opera at the Met. Opera House.

Damrosch, Walter (Johannes) (b Breslau, 30 Jan 1862; d New York, 22 Dec 1950), American conductor and composer, son of Leopold ◊Damrosch. Studied in Germany and settled in USA in 1871; became conductor of the NY Oratorio and Symphonic Societies 1885. Director of the Damrosch Opera Co. 1894–99, giving the first US performance of several operas by Wagner.

Works include operas *The Scarlet Letter* (after Hawthorne, 1896), *Cyrano de Bergerac* (after Rostand, 1913), *The Dove of Peace*, *The Man without a Country* (1937); incidental music to Euripides' *Electra*, *Iphigenia in Aulis* and *Medea*; *Abraham Lincoln's Song* for baritone solo, chorus and orchestra; Te Deum; violin and piano sonata; songs.

Danaïdes, Les opera by Salieri (libretto by F L du Roullet and L T de Tschudy, partly based on and translated from Calzabigi's *Ipermestra* intended for Gluck, composed by Millico), produced Paris, Opéra, 26 Apr 1784. When Danaus orders his fifty daughters to kill their husbands, Hypermestra alone refuses for love of Lyncaeus.

dance since the earliest known manifestations of music are almost all associated with dance, it follows that any serious consideration of the essence of music will take account of its physical aspect. For the earliest surviving written repertories of western music only vocal works survive, though in most cases it is possible to discern a dance background even here. From the 16th c. dance music was increasingly written down; and it has been argued that there is very little in the music of the 17th and 18th c. that is not best understood in terms of its relationship to the dance. Since about 1800, 'art-music' in the western world has increasingly separated itself from the dance. ◊Allemande, ◊Ballata, ◊Ballet, ◊Ballet comique de la royne, ◊Ballet de Cour, ◊Ballett, ◊Bergamasca, ◊Branle, ◊Calinda, ◊Canary, ◊Cancan, ◊Chaconne, ◊Courante, ◊Deutsche Tänze, ◊Ecossaise, ◊Gavotte, ◊Jig, ◊Mazurka, ◊Minuet, ◊Passacaglia, ◊Passamezzo, ◊Passepied, ◊Pavan, ◊Polka, ◊Quadrille, ◊Sarabande, ◊Waltz.

Dance Rhapsody two works for orchestra by Delius: no. 1 composed 1908, fp Hereford Festival 8 Sept 1909, conductor Delius; no. 2 composed 1916, fp London, 23 Oct 1923, conductor Wood.

Dances of Galánta orchestral work by Kodály, composed for the 80th anniversary of the Budapest Philharmonic Society, fp Budapest, 11 Dec 1936.

Dances of Marosszék work for piano by Kodály, composed 1927. Version for orchestra fp Dresden, 28 Nov 1930, conductor F Busch.

Dance Suite work for orchestra in six movements by Bartók, composed 1923 for 50th anniversary of the merging of Pest, Buda and Obuda into Budapest. Fp Budapest, 19 Nov 1925, conductor E Dohnányi. Version for piano 1925.

Danckerts, Ghiselin (b Tholen, Zeeland, *c* 1510; d after Aug 1565), Dutch composer. Singer in the Papal Chapel in Rome, 1538–65. He acted as judge in the dispute between Vicentino and Lusitano. Wrote motets and madrigals.

Without music, life would be a mistake.
Friedrich Nietzsche, *Götzendämmerung*, 1889

Dancla, (Jean Baptiste) Charles (b Bagnères-de-Bigorre, 19 Dec 1817; d Tunis, 10 Nov 1907), French violinist. Pupil of Baillot at the Paris Conservatory, where he later became violin professor. He composed much music including educational works for violin.

Danco, Suzanne (b Brussels, 22 Jan 1911), Belgian soprano. Studied at Brussels Conservatory. In 1936 she won an international singing competition in Venice. Debut Genoa, 1941, as Fiordiligi. London, CG, 1951 as Mimi; Glyndebourne as Donna Elvira same year. Other roles included Ellen Orford and Marie. She was a noted exponent of Ravel and Debussy.

Dandelot, Georges (Edouard) (b Paris, 2 Dec 1895; d St-Georges de Didonne, 17 Aug 1975), French composer. Studied at the Paris Conservatory and in 1919 became professor of composition at the Ecole Normale de Musique there.

Works include oratorio *Pax* (1937); piano concerto; *Trio en forme de suite*, string quartet; waltzes for two pianos; *Bilitis*: 17 songs (Pierre Louÿs).

Dandrieu (or *d'Andrieu*), Jean François (b Paris, 1682; d Paris, 17 Jan 1738), French organist and composer. Became organist of the church

of Saint-Barthélemy in Paris in succession to his uncle, Pierre Dandrieu, and in 1704 of that of Saint-Merry; member of the royal chapel in 1721; wrote a book on harpsichord accompaniment.

Works include a set of symphonies *Les Caractères de la guerre* (1718); trios for two violins and bass; violin sonatas; organ pieces; three vols. of harpsichord pieces.

D'Angeri (originally *von Angermayer*), Anna (b Vienna, 14 Nov 1853; d Trieste, 14 Dec 1907), Austrian soprano. She studied in Vienna and sang at the Hofoper 1878–79; appeared as guest at CG 1874–77 and was the first London Ortrud and Venus (1875, 1876). Success in Wagner did not dissuade Verdi from inviting her to sing Amelia in the revision of *Simon Boccanegra* (1881).

Danican, Michel (b Dauphiné; d Paris, *c* 1659), French oboist in the service of Louis XIII, who bestowed on him the name of Philidor after the great oboist Filidori of Siena. (For all other members of the family ◊Philidor.)

Daniel, John, John ◊Danyel.

Daniel, Paul (b Birmingham, 1 Jul 1958), English conductor. Studied with Franco Ferrara, Boult and Edward Downes. Has led major orchestras in Britain and Europe; US debut 1988, with the London Sinfonietta. Music director of Opera Factory, London, 1987–90, giving works by Birtwistle (*Punch and Judy*), Cavalli, Ligeti and Davies. Work for ENO includes Ligeti's *Le Grand Macabre*, *The Mask of Orpheus*, Glass's *Akhnaten* and the British premiere of Reimann's *Lear* (1989). Music director of Opera North 1990–96, leading the local stage premiere of Verdi's *Jerusalem* and the British premiere of Schreker's *Der ferne Klang* (1992); music director of ENO from 1996.

Daniel-Leseur, Jean-Yves (b Paris, 19 Nov 1908), French organist and composer. Pupil of Tournemire, Caussade and others. In 1938 he became professor of counterpoint at the Schola Cantorum in Paris. He was also appointed organist at the Benedictine abbey, and with Baudrier, Jolivet and Messiaen formed the group known as 'La Jeune France'.

Works include operas *Andrea del Sarto* (1969), *Ondine* (1982) and *La reine morte* (1987); *Suite française* for orchestra (1935); *Passacaille* for piano and orchestra (1937); *Le Voyage d'Automne* for voices and orchestra (1990); *Fantasie Concertante* for cello and orchestra (1993); suite for string trio and piano; three Heine songs for voice and string quartet; *Noëls* and suite *Le Carillon* for piano; *La Vie intérieure* for organ; songs.

Daniel, Play of, *Danielis Ludus*, a medieval liturgical music drama dealing with the story of Daniel in the lions' den. It was written by students of Beauvais between 1227 and 1234 and intended for performance after matins on the feast of the Circumcision (1 Jan).

Daniels, Barbara (b Grenville, OH, 7 May 1946), American soprano. Debut 1973, as Susanna with West Palm Beach Opera. Sang in Austria and Germany from 1974, Rosalinde at CG 1978 (later as Musetta, Donna Elvira and Alice Ford). NY Met. from 1983, as Violetta, Marguerite and Minnie (1991). Sang Handel's Agrippina at Schwetzingen 1985, Jenůfa at Innsbruck 1990.

Danning, Sophus Christian (b Copenhagen, 16 Jun 1867; d Odense, 7 Nov 1925), Danish conductor and composer. Studied in Copenhagen, Sondershausen and Leipzig. Travelled widely, lived for a time in Finland, then taught at Copenhagen and in 1899 went to Norway as theatre conductor at Bergen. In 1907–11 he was conductor at Oslo.

Works include operas *Gustav Adolf*, *Elleskudt* and *Kynthia*; operatta *Columbine*; incidental music to Oehlenschläger's *Aladdin* and other plays; symphonies (including *Dante*) and overtures for orchestra; cantatas; violin concerto; piano pieces; songs.

Dannreuther, Edward (George) (b Strasbourg, 4 Nov 1844; d Hastings, 12 Feb 1905), German–English pianist, teacher and critic. Studied at Leipzig and went to live in London in 1863. Professor at the RAM from 1895 and author of a valuable work on ornamentation.

Danse, La last of three entrées which make up Rameau's opéra-ballet *Les fêtes d'Hébé* (libretto by A G de Montdorge), produced Paris, Opéra, 21 May 1739. Often heard as a separate item.

Danse Sacrée et Danse Profane work by Debussy for harp and strings; composed 1903, fp Paris, 6 Nov 1904.

Danses Concertantes work for chamber orchestra by Stravinsky; composed 1942, in Hollywood, fp LA, 8 Feb 1942.

Dante Alighieri (1265–1321), Italian poet. ◊Dante Sonata, ◊Dante Symphony (Liszt); ◊Francesca da Rimini (operas, Goetz, Nápravník, Rakhmaninov, Zandonai; symphonic fantasy, Tchaikovsky); ◊Françoise de Rimini (opera, A Thomas); ◊Generali (*Francesca da Rimini*); ◊Morlacchi, (*Francesca da Rimini* and *Narration of Ugolino*); ◊Trittico (*Gianni Schicchi*, Puccini); ◊Wolf-Ferrari (*Vita Nuova*).

Dante Sonata a one-movement sonata by Liszt, entitled *Après une lecture du Dante*, in the Italian volume of his *Années de pèlerinage*, composed 1837–39, revised 1849. Liszt called it a *sonata quasi fantasia*.

Dante Symphony a symphony by Liszt based on Dante's *Divina commedia*, composed 1855–56, fp Dresden, 7 Nov 1857. There are two movements, *Inferno* and *Purgatorio*.

Dantons Tod, *Danton's Death*, opera by Einem (libretto by Boris Blacher and composer, based on Georg Büchner's drama), produced Salzburg, 6 Aug 1947. During the French Revolution, the evil Robespierre spreads rumours that Danton is an aristocrat. After the trial Danton is guillotined; Lucile, the wife of his friend Desmoulins (also killed) longs for death.

Danyel (or *Daniel*), John (b Wellow, near Bath, bap. 6 Nov 1564; d ? London, *c* 1630), English lutenist and composer, brother of the poet Samuel Danyel. When his brother died in 1619 he succeeded him as inspector of the Children of the Queen's Revels and later joined the royal company of musicians.

Danza, La opera in one act by Gluck (libretto by Metastasio), performed Vienna, Laxenberg, 5 May 1755.

Danzi, Franz (b Schwetzingen, 15 Jun 1763; d Karlsruhe, 13 Apr 1826), German cellist and composer. Pupil of Vogler; was a member of the court band at Mannheim and from 1778, at Munich. *Kapellmeister* to the court of Württemberg at Stuttgart, and later at Karlsruhe. A minor member of the Mannheim school of symphonists.

Works include operas *Die Mitternachtsstunde* (1788), *Turandot* (after Gozzi, 1817); church music; symphonies, concertos and concertantes; chamber music.

Daphne opera in one act by R Strauss (libretto by Joseph Gregor), produced Dresden, 15 Oct 1938. Daphne spurns Apollo and sprouts into a laurel tree.

Daphnis et Alcimadure pastoral by Mondonville (libretto, in the Languedoc dialect, by the composer), produced Fontainebleau, at court, 4 Nov 1754, first Paris performance, Opéra, 29 Dec 1754.

Daphnis et Chloé ballet by Ravel (scenario after Longus, choreography by Fokin), produced Paris, Théâtre du Chatelet, 8 Jun 1912.

Da Ponte, Lorenzo, Lorenzo da ◊Ponte,

Daquin (or *d'Aquin*), Louis Claude (b Paris, 4 Jul 1694; d Paris, 15 Jun 1772), French organist, harpsichordist and composer. Pupil of Marchand. He played before Louis XIV as a child prodigy at the age of six, and at 12 was appointed organist of Petit St Antoine in Paris. In 1727 he was Rameau's successful rival for the post of organist of St Paul, and in 1739 succeeded Dandrieu at the Chapel Royal.

Works include cantata *La Rose*; harpsichord pieces including *Le Coucou*; *Noëls* for organ or harpsichord.

Darclée, Hariclea (b Braila, 10 Jun 1860; d Bucharest, 10 Jan 1939), Romanian soprano. She studied with Faure in Paris and made her debut there in 1888 as Marguerite. La Scala, 1890, as Chimène in Massenet's *Le Cid*; she created Catalani's Wally at Milan in 1892 and Mascagni's Iris in 1898. The first Tosca, Rome 1900. Other roles included Juliette, Manon Lescaut, Santuzza, Ophelia, Aida and Desdemona.

Dardanus opera by Rameau (libretto by C A L de La Bruère), produced Paris, Opéra, 19 Nov 1739). Iphise loves her father's enemy Dardanus, but Teucer wants his daughter to marry Antenor. Captured by Antenor, Dardanus later escapes and slays an avenging sea monster, saving Antenor. Dardanus and Iphise are united.

Opera by Sacchini (libretto ditto, altered by N F Guillard), pro-

duced Versailles, at court, 18 Sept 1784; first Paris performance, Opéra, 30 Nov 1784.

dargason an English country dance and folksong at least as old as the 16th c. Holst used it in his *St Paul's Suite*.

Dargillières Parisian family of instrument makers, including:

1. Anthoine Dargillières (b *c* 1518; d 1572), 'faiseur d'orgues de la Chapelle du roi'; built various church organs in Paris.

2. Roch Dargillières (b 27 Jan 1559), son of Anthoine; built numerous organs in the Paris neighbourhood, including those at Rouen (St Michael) and Chartres (cathedral).

Dargomizhsky, Alexander Sergeievich (b Troitskoye, Tula district, 14 Feb 1813; d St Petersburg, 17 Jan 1869), Russian composer. Studied music as an amateur at St Petersburg and after retiring from four years' government service in 1835 led the life of a dilettante. In 1833 he met Glinka, who lent him his notes taken during his studies with Dehn in Berlin, and he set to work on his first opera. After the next stage attempt he devoted himself mainly to songs between 1856 and 1860, including many of a satirical nature anticipating those of Mussorgsky. In 1864 he visited western Europe, but was able to gain a hearing only in Belgium, where he performed his orchestral fantasies. On his return he associated himself with Balakirev's nationalist group, without actually joining it. He set Pushkin's *Stone Guest* as an opera word for word; it was orchestrated by Rimsky-Korsakov.

Works include operas *Esmeralda* (after Hugo, 1847), *Rusalka* (after Pushkin, 1856), *Rogdana* (unfinished). *The Stone Guest* (Pushkin, completed by Cui and Rimsky-Korsakov; produced posthumously 1872); ballet *Bacchus' Feast*: a duet for an opera *Mazeppa*; orchestral fantasies *Kazatchok*, *Baba-Yaga* and *Mummers' Dance*; *Tarantelle slave* for piano duet; *c* 90 songs, vocal duets, trios, quartets, choruses.

Darke, Harold (Edwin) (b London, 29 Oct 1888; d Cambridge, 28 Nov 1976), English organist and composer. Studied organ with Parratt and composition with Stanford at the RCM in London. Organist at St Michael's, Cornhill, 1916–66.

Works include *The Kingdom of God* for soprano, chorus and orchestra, *Ring out ye crystal spheres* (Milton) for chorus, organ and orchestra, other choral works include *O Lord Thou art my God*, *Hymn of Heavenly Beauty* (Spenser); church music; organ works; songs.

Darmstadt city in Germany where summer courses in new music have been held since 1946 (annually at first, biennially from 1970). Lecturers have included Varèse, Messiaen, Berio, Henze and Stockhausen. Reached apogee in 1950s with premieres by Cage and others, but still attracts the avant-garde: *4 Darmstadter Aphorismen* by Chris Dench, 1989.

Dart, (Robert) Thurston (b Kingston, Surrey, 3 Sept 1921; d London, 6 Mar 1971), English musicologist and harpsichordist. Studied at the RCM and London University After further studies with C van den Borren in Brussels he became lecturer in music at Cambridge in 1947 and professor in 1962. Professor of Music, London University (King's College) 1964–71. He was an expert continuo player and soloist on the harpsichord; author of *The Interpretation of Music* as well as learned articles.

Daser, Ludwig (b Munich, *c* 1525; d Stuttgart, 27 Mar 1589), German composer. He was *Kapellmeister* to the Bavarian court at Munich, 1552–59, when Lassus succeeded him, and held a similar post at the court of Württemberg at Stuttgart from 1572 to his death. Wrote Masses, motets, a passion, organ music.

Daughter of the Regiment (Donizetti.) La ◊Fille du Régiment.

Dauvergne, Antoine (b Moulins, 3 Oct 1713; d Lyons, 11 Feb 1797), French violinist and composer. Pupil of his father, Jacques Dauvergne; played at Clermont-Ferrand and went to Paris in 1739 as violinist in the court chamber music and in 1744 at the Opéra. In 1762 he became one of the directors of the Concert Spirituel and later manager of the Opéra.

Works include over 20 operas and other stage works, e.g. *Les Amours de Tempé* (1752), *Les Troqueurs* (1753); motets; symphonies, divertimenti; violin sonatas.

Davenant (or *D'Avenant*), William (1606–1668), English poet and playwright. ◊Banister (*Circe*); W ◊Lawes (*Triumph of the Prince d'Amour* and *Unfortunate Lovers*); ◊Locke (*Macbeth*); ◊Pepys ('Beauty retire'); ◊Siege of Rhodes (Locke, H Lawes, H Cooke, Coleman and Hudson).

David opera in five acts and 12 scenes by Milhaud (libretto by A Lunel), written to celebrate the establishment of Jerusalem as the capital of Judea, produced Jerusalem, 1 Jun 1954. Founder of Jerusalem fathers Solomon out of Bathsheba.

If the music doesn't say it, how can words say it for the music?

John Coltrane, quoted in Hentoff, *Jazz is*, 1978

David, Félicien (César) (b Cadenet, Vaucluse, 13 Apr 1810; d Saint-Germain-en-Laye, 29 Aug 1876), French composer. Entered the Paris Conservatory 1830, having been a chorister at Aix Cathedral and afterwards conductor at the theatre. In 1833 he travelled in the near East, returned in 1835, lived near Igny for a time on finding that Paris neglected him, but settled in the capital in 1841 and made a great success with his oriental descriptive symphony *Le Désert* in 1844.

Works include operas *La Perle du Brésil* (1851), *Herculanum* (1859), *Lalla-Roukh* (after Moore, 1862), *Le Saphir* and *La Captive* (withdrawn); oratorio *Moïse au Sinaï*; mystery *Eden*; motets and hymns; descriptive symphony *Le Désert* and *Christophe Colomb*; four symphonies; four string quartets; 24 string quintets, two nonets for wind; *Mélodies orientales* for piano; songs.

David, Ferdinand (b Hamburg, 19 Jun 1810; d Klosters, Switzerland, 18 Jul 1873), German violinist and composer. Studied with Spohr and Hauptmann and made his first appearance at the Leipzig Gewandhaus in 1825, where he became leader under Mendelssohn in 1836; gave the fp of Mendelssohn's violin concerto in 1845. Wrote five concertos and many other works for the violin; chamber music.

David, Johann Nepomuk (b Eferding, 30 Nov 1895; d Stuttgart, 22 Dec 1977), Austrian composer. He was a choirboy at St Florian and studied at the Vienna Academy. He taught composition successively at Leipzig, Salzburg and Stuttgart, and published analytical studies of classical composers.

Works include eight symphonies (1936–65), two partitas for orchestra, two concertos for string orchestra; flute concertos, two violin concertos, *Requiem chorale* for soli, chorus and orchestra; three string quartets, four string trios and other chamber music; three cello sonatas; chorale preludes and other works for organ.

David, Karl Heinrich (b St Gall, 30 Dec 1884; d Nervi, 17 May 1951), Swiss conductor and composer. Studied at the Cologne and Munich Consevatories. Conducted at various theatres, became professor at the Basel Conservatory 1910 and settled at Zurich 1917. Editor of the *Schweizerische Musikzeitung* (1928–41).

Works include operas *Der Sizilianer* (after Molière, 1924), *Traumwandel* (after Turgenev, 1928); choral works and chamber music.

Davidde penitente, *The Penitent David*, cantata by Mozart, K469 (libretto ? by L da Ponte), made up in Mar 1785, mainly from portions of the unfinished C minor Mass, K427, of 1782–83. Only two arias are new.

Davide, Giovanni (b Naples, 15 Sept 1790; d St Petersburg, 1864), Italian tenor and bass, son and pupil of Giacomo ◊Davide. Made his first appearance at Brescia in 1810. He took part in the fps of Rossini's *Il turco in Italia*, *Otello*, *La donna del lago* and *Zelmira*.

Davidov, Karl (b Goldingen, Courland, 15 Mar 1838; d Moscow, 26 Feb 1889), Russian cellist and composer. Made his first appearance at the Leipzig Gewandhaus in 1859 and later became first cellist in its orchestra and professor at the Conservatory. In 1862 he was appointed to a similar post at the St Petersburg Opera and was director of the Conservatory there in 1876–86. Wrote four cello concertos and many other works for his instrument, etc.

Davidovsky, Mario (b Buenos Aires, 4 Mar 1934), American composer. He studied at Buenos Aires and moved to the USA 1958; has worked at the electronic studios of Columbia and Princeton Universi-

ties. Member of Columbia faculty from 1981.

Works include four string quartets (1954, 1958, 1976, 1980), *Planos* for orchestra (1961), two *Studies* for electronics (1961–62), *Contrasts* for strings (1962), *Inflexions* for 14 instruments (1965), *Chacona* for piano trio (1972), *Scenes from Shir Hashirim*, cantata for four voices and chamber ensemble (1976); *Synchronism* series of eight dialogues for electronics (1963–74; no. 6 won the 1971 Pulitzer Prize); Divertimento for cello and orchestra (1984).

Davidsbund German = 'League of David'; an association formed 1834 by Schumann and his friends to combat the musical 'Philistines'.

Davidsbündler, German, the members of the ◊Davidsbund. They appear in the title of Schumann's *Davidsbündlertänze* and in the finale of his *Carnaval* in a 'marche contre les Philistins'.

Davidsbündlertänze, *Dances of the League of David*, a set of 18 piano pieces by Schumann, op. 6, composed in 1837, the title alluding to the ◊Davidsbund.

Davie, Cedric Thorpe (b Blackheath, 30 May 1913; d Dalry, Kirkcudbrightshire, 18 Jan 1983), Scottish composer and organist. Studied at the Scottish National Academy of Music, Glasgow, the RAM in London and later the RCM there, where he was a pupil of R O Morris, Vaughan Williams and Gordon Jacob, gaining the Cobbett and Sullivan Prizes in 1935. He also studied piano with Egon Petri in Germany, and composition with Kodály at Budapest and Kilpinen at Helsinki. Head of music at St Andrews University from 1945.

Works include opera *Gammer Gurton's Needle*, ballad opera *The Forrigan Reel* (James Bridie); concerto for piano and strings; string quartet; violin and piano sonata, sonatinas for cello and piano and flute and piano; eight *Little Songs*.

Davies, (Albert) Meredith (b Birkenhead, 30 Jul 1922), English conductor and organist. Studied at the RCM, graduating in 1938, and then Keble College, Oxford, taking his B.Mus. in 1946. He took the post of organist at St Albans Cathedral in 1947 and Hereford in 1949, also conducting at the Three Choirs Festival. From 1956 to 1959 he was organist of New College, Oxford. He has since conducted frequently in Britain and abroad. Principal, TCL from 1979. CBE 1982.

Davies, Arthur (b Wrexham, 11 Apr 1941), Welsh tenor. After study at the RNCM he sang with WNO from 1972: Nadir, Nero, Lensky, Don José, Rodolfo and Nemorino. London, CG, from 1976, in the fp of *We Come to the River* and as Alfredo, Steva (*Jenůfa*), Pinkerton and Walton's Troilus (1995). Roles with ENO include the Duke of Mantua in Jonathan Miller's 'mafia' production of *Rigoletto*. Other appearances in NY, Chicago and Moscow.

Davies, Ben(jamin) Grey (b Pontardawe, near Swansea, 6 Jan 1858; d Bath, 28 Mar 1943), Welsh tenor. Studied at the RAM in London; made his first concert appearance at Dublin in 1879 and first sang in opera at Birmingham in 1881, in Balfe's *Bohemian Girl*. Successful in oratorio.

Davies, Cecilia (b ? London, *c* 1750; d London, 3 Jul 1836), English soprano. Sang at Dublin in 1763 and first appeared in London in 1767. The following year she went to Paris and Vienna with her sister Marianne (1744–?), a flute, harpsichord and harmonica player, where they had a great success, Hasse writing an ode for them to words specially provided by Metastasio; and in 1771–73 they were in Italy where Cecilia became famous as 'L'Inglesina', and created Sacchini's Armida, Milan, 1772.

Davies, Dennis Russell (b Toledo, 16 Apr 1944), American conductor. He studied at Juilliard and founded the Juilliard Ensemble, with Berio; in 1970 conducted the fp of Berio's *Opera*, at Santa Fe. Music director St Paul Chamber Orchestra 1973–80. Bayreuth debut 1978, *Der fliegende Holländer*; Württemberg Staatsoper, Stuttgart, from 1980. He has conducted the fps of works by Cage, Carter and Feldman, and in 1984 gave in Stuttgart the fp of Bolcom's *Songs of Innocence and Experience*. Opera premieres include Henze's *English Cat* (1983), Glass's *Akhnaten* (1984), Henze's *König Hirsch* (original version, 1985), and Bolcom's *McTeague* (Chicago, 1992).

Davies, Fanny (b Guernsey, 27 Jun 1861; d London, 1 Sept 1934), English pianist. Studied at Leipzig and under Clara Schumann at

Frankfurt, making her first London appearance in 1885; often toured abroad and gave recitals with Casals.

Davies, (Henry) Walford (b Oswestry, 6 Sept 1869; d Wrington, Som., 11 Mar 1941), English organist, educationist and composer. Educated at St George's Chapel, Windsor, under Parratt, and at the RCM in London, where Stanford was his composition master. Held various organist's appointments, took the Cambridge Mus.D. degree in 1898, when he was appointed organist and choirmaster at the Temple Church. Professor of Music at the University of Wales, Aberystwyth, from 1919. Knighted 1922. He resigned from the Temple in 1923 and became organist at St George's, Windsor, in 1927 and Master of the King's Music in succession to Elgar in 1934. He wrote sacred music and pieces for children.

Davies, Peter Maxwell (b Manchester, 8 Sept 1934), English composer. Studied at the RMCM and in 1957 with Petrassi in Rome. From 1959 to 1962 he taught music at Cirencester Grammar School, and in 1962 went to the USA to study with Sessions at Princeton University. His music is strongly influenced by medieval techniques, which he uses in combination with serial devices. Many concerts with his ensemble, The Fires of London, 1970–87; stage works with Fires of London Productions from 1987. Since 1970 he has been based in Orkney. Music director Dartington Summer School, S Devon, 1979–84. CBE 1981. Knighted 1987.

Works include STAGE: *Nocturnal Dances* (1970), *Blind Man's Buff*, masque (1972), *Taverner*, opera (1972), *The Martyrdom of St Magnus*, chamber opera (1977), *The Two Fiddlers*, opera for children (1978), *Le Jongleur de Notre Dame*, masque (1978), *Salome*, ballet (1978), *The Lighthouse*, chamber opera (1980), *Cinderella*, pantomime (1980), *The Rainbow*, for children (1981), *The no. 11 Bus*, for vocal soloists, dancers, mime and ensemble (1984), operas *Resurrection* (1987), *Redemption* (1988), ballet *Caroline Mathilde* (1990), opera *The Doctors of Myddfai* (premiere scheduled for 1996).

The years given for the following works are of fp:

ORCHESTRAL: *St Michael*, Sonata for 17 wind instruments (1957), *Two Fantasias on an In Nomine of John Taverner* (1962, 1964), *Antechrist*, for chamber ensemble (1967), *Stedman Caters* (1968), *Worldes Blis* (1968), *Vesalii Icones* for dancer, cello and ensemble (1969), *Ave Maris Stella*, for chamber ensemble (1975), six symphonies (1976, 1981, 1985, 1989, 1994, 1996), *Image, Reflection, Shadow* (1981), Sinfonia Concertante (1983), Sinfonietta Accademica (1983), violin concerto (1986), trumpet concerto (1988), ten Strathclyde concertos, for oboe (1987), cello (1988), horn and

Davies *The composer Peter Maxwell Davies is probably the foremost British composer of our time. His early avant garde works have given way more recently to an accessible means of expression admired by both critics and the general public. He is active in support of the arts in the face of funding cuts.*

trumpet (1989), clarinet (1990), violin and viola (1991), flute (1991), double bass (1992), bassoon (1993), six wind instruments and strings (1995), concerto for orchestra (1995), *The Beltane Fire* (1995).

VOCAL: *O Magnum Mysterium*, four carols a cappella (1960), *Leopardi Fragments* for soprano, mezzo and instruments (1962), *Veni Sancte Spiritus* for soloists, chorus and orchestra (1964), *The Shepherds' Calendar* for chorus and ensemble (1965), *Revelation and Fall* for soprano and 16 instruments (1968), *Eight Songs for a Mad King* for voice and ensemble (1969), *From Stone to Thorn* for mezzo and instruments (1971), *Hymn to St Magnus* for mezzo and instruments (1972), *Notre Dame des Fleurs* for soloists and ensemble (1973), *Tenebrae super Gesualdo* for mezzo, guitar and ensemble, *Stone Litany* for mezzo and orchestra (1973), *Miss Donnithorne's Maggot* for mezzo and ensemble (1974), *Fiddlers at the Wedding* for mezzo and instruments (1974), *The Blind Fiddler* for soprano and ensemble (1976), *Anakreontika* for mezzo and ensemble (1976), *Westerlings* for chorus a cappella (1977), *Solstice of Light* for tenor, chorus and orchestra (1979), *Black Pentecost* for mezzo, baritone and orchestra (1982), *The Yellow Cake Revue* for singers and piano (1980), *Into the Labyrinth*, cantata (1983), *Winterfold* for mezzo and ensemble (1986); *Apple-Basket, Apple-Blossom* (1990), *Hymn to the Word of God* (1990) and *Corpus Christi, with Cat and Mouse* (1993).

CHAMBER AND INSTRUMENTAL: including Piano sonata (1981), Organ sonata (1982), Sea Eagle, for horn (1982), sonata for violin and cimbalom (1984), guitar sonata (1984), *For Grace of Light* for oboe (1991).

WORKS FOR CHILDREN: including *Kirkwall Shopping Songs* (1979), *Songs of Hoy* (1981), *First Ferry to Hoy* (1985).

Davies, Ryland (b Cwm, Ebbw Vale, 9 Feb 1943), Welsh tenor. He sang Paris in the British premiere of Gluck's *Paride ed Elena* while still at the RMCM (1963). Professor debut as Almaviva with the WNO, 1964. In 1968 he sang Belmonte at Glyndebourne, and at CG in 1969 Hylas in the first complete performance of *Les Troyens* in French. US debut 1970, San Francisco; NY Met. 1975 as Mozart's Ferrando. Other roles include Fenton, Ottavio and Lensky. Glyndebourne 1989–90, as Britten's Lysander and Janáček's Tichon.

Davis, Andrew (b Ashridge, Herts., 2 Feb 1944), English conductor and keyboard player. He studied at Cambridge and in Rome. First came to notice with the BBC SO in the *Glagolitic Mass* of Janáček. Associate

A Selection of

Peter Maxwell Davies

Eight Songs for a Mad King	1969
Stone Litany	1973
Miss Donnithorne's Maggot	1974
The Martyrdom of St Magnus	1977
Solstice of Light	1979
Black Pentecost	1982
An Orkney Wedding with Sunrise	1985
Trumpet Concerto	1988
Symphony no. 4	1989
Strathclyde Concerto no. 5	1991

conductor Philharmonia 1973, and led *Capriccio* at Glyndebourne the same year; has since given *Intermezzo* and *Schweigsame Frau* there. US debut 1974, with the NY PO. Principal conductor Toronto SO from 1975; Royal Liverpool PO as guest conductor 1974–76. Principal conductor BBC SO from 1989, music director Glyndebourne, 1989. Led the UK fps of Tippett's *The Mask of Time* (1986) and *New Year* (1990). Has directed his own edition of *The Art of Fugue* from the harpsichord. CBE 1991.

Davis, Anthony (b Paterson, NJ, 20 Feb 1951), American composer and jazz pianist. Studied at Yale University and has been active in jazz ensembles in the USA and abroad; director of Episteme and co-founder of Advent, 1973. Performances in NY with members of the Advancement of Creative Musicians.

Works include operas *X: the Life and Times of Malcolm X*, premiered at NY City Opera 1986, and *Under the Double Moon*, St Louis 1989; piano concerto *Wayang V* (1985); *Notes from the Underground* for orchestra (1988); violin concerto (1988).

Davis, Colin (b Weybridge, 25 Sept 1927), English conductor. Studied at the RCM. From 1957 to 1959 he was assistant conductor of the BBC Scottish Orchestra, becoming principal conductor at Sadler's Wells in 1961; he was also their music director, 1959–65. US debut with Minneapolis SO, 1960. From 1967 to 1971 he was principal conductor of the BBC SO and music director at Covent Garden 1971–86. Principal guest conductor Boston SO 1972–83. NY Met. debut 1967 (*Peter Grimes*). The first Briton to conduct at Bayreuth (*Tannhäuser*, 1977); Bavarian Radio SO 1983–92; principal conductor London SO from 1995. Admired in Mozart, Berlioz, Stravinsky and Tippett; conducted fps *The Knot Garden* (1970), *The Ice Break* (1977) and *The Mask of Time* (1984). Knighted 1980.

Davison, J(ames) W(illiam) (b London, 5 Oct 1813; d Margate, 24 Mar 1885), English critic attached to *The Times*, 1846–1879. Married the pianist Arabella Godard.

Davy, Gloria (b New York, 29 Mar 1931), American soprano. She studied at Juilliard and was the Countess in the US fp of Strauss's *Capriccio*, 1954. She sang in Europe from 1957 and was the soloist in the fp of Henze's *Nachtstücke und Arien* at Donaueschingen, under Rosbaud. She made her NY Met. and CG debuts as Aida (1958, 1960). Other roles included Purcell's Dido, Gluck's Armide and Santuzza.

Davy, John (b Upton Helions, near Exeter, 23 Dec 1763; d London, 22 Feb 1824), English composer. Pupil of Jackson at Exeter. Played in the CG orchestra in London and wrote music for many plays, including Shakespeare's *Tempest*. His song *The Bay of Biscay* became famous.

Davy, Richard (b *c* 1467; d ? Exeter, *c* 1507), English composer. Educated at Magdalen College, Oxford, where he was organist and choirmaster in 1490–92. Chaplain to Anne Boleyn's grandfather and father 1501–15. Wrote motets, Passion music for Palm Sunday, part-songs, etc.

Dawson, Lynne (b York, 3 Jun 1953), English soprano. Studied at the GSMD and made opera debut as Mozart's Countess for Kent Opera, 1986. Monteverdi's Orfeo at Florence 1987, Pamina for Scottish Opera 1988 and Xiphares in Mozart's *Mitridate*, Paris 1991. Specialist in the Baroque repertory and has sung Angelica in Handel's *Orlando* and Cornelia in Graun's *Cesare e Cleopatra*, Berlin Staatsoper, 1992. Concerts and recordings of *Messiah*, B minor Mass, *The Fairy Queen* and *Dido and Aeneas*.

DC Italian abbr. ◊da capo.

De Amicis, Anna Lucia (b Naples, *c* 1733; d Naples, 1816), Italian soprano. She sang in comic operas on the continent before visiting London and taking part in the fp of J C Bach's *Orione* (King's Theatre, 1763). She then sang in operas by Gluck and Jommelli in Venice and Naples. Highly regarded by Mozart, she sang Giunia in the fp of *Lucio Silla* (Milan, 1772).

Dean, Stafford (b Kingswood, Surrey, 20 Jun 1933), English bass. He studied at the RCM and sang minor roles at SW and Glyndebourne before Leporello at the Coliseum, 1968; repeated the role in San Francisco and Munich. CG debut 1969, Masetto. NY Met. debut, as Mozart's Figaro, 1976. He is also heard in oratorio and the operas of

Monteverdi. CG 1990–92 as Gessler in *Guillaume Tell* and Melisso in *Alcina*.

Dean, Winton (Basil) (b Birkenhead, 18 Mar 1916), English writer on music, son of the producer Basil Dean. Educated at Harrow and King's College, Cambridge; read classics and English, but studied music privately, translated choruses, etc. from Aristophanes' *Frogs* for Walter Leigh and Weber's *Abu Hassan*. His books include *Bizet* (1948, revised 1965), *Handel's Dramatic Oratorios* (1959) and *Handel's Operas, 1704–1726* (1987), *Essays on Opera* (1990).

De Angelis, Nazareno (b Rome, 17 Nov 1881; d Rome, 14 Dec 1962), Italian bass. Debut Aquila 1903, in *Linda di Chamounix*. He appeared at La Scala in 1905 and returned until 1933 as Mosè, Marke, Méphistophélès, Zaccaria and Hunding. At Buenos Aires in 1911 he was the first local Philip II. Other roles included Barnaba, Bartolo and Procida.

'Death and the Maiden' Quartet Schubert's string quartet in D minor D810, begun March 1824, finished or revised Jan 1826 and first performed Vienna, 1 Feb 1826. It is so called because the second movement is a set of variations on the introduction and the second half of his song, *Der Tod und das Mädchen* (D531, 1817, text by M Claudius), which consists of Death's quiet and reassuring answer to the girl's agitated plea to be spared. The work is sometimes heard today in an arrangement for string orchestra by Mahler.

Death and Transfiguration (Strauss.) ◊Tod und Verklärung.

Death in Venice opera by Britten (libretto by Myfanwy Piper, after Thomas Mann), produced Snape, Maltings 16 Jun 1973). Writer Aschenbach, believer in order, is seduced by the passion of Venice; his frustrated love of beauty and of the boy Tadzio destroys his ideals and finally himself.

Death of Klinghoffer, The opera in two acts by John Adams (libretto by Alice Goodman, based on the Palestinian hijacking of the *Achille Lauro*, 1985), produced Brussels, Théâtre de la Monnaie, 19 Mar 1991.

De Bassini, Achille (b Milan, 5 May 1819; d Cavadei Tirreni, 3 Jul 1881), Italian baritone. During the 1830s he was heard in operas by Bellini and Donizetti in the Italian provinces. A favourite baritone of Verdi, he took part in the premieres of *I due Foscari* (1844), *Il Corsaro* (1848), *Luisa Miller* (1849) and *La Forza del Destino* (1862).

De Begnis, Giuseppe, Giuseppe de ◊Begnis.

Debora e Jaele, *Deborah and Jael*, opera by Pizzetti (libretto by composer), produced Milan, Teatro alla Scala, 16 Dec 1922. Loosely based on the Biblical story, Sisera, here the king of Canaa, faces a conflict between love for Jael and duty. Later Jael splits the sleeping Sisera's skull, rather than leave him to a worse death before the victorious Israelites.

Deborah oratorio by Handel (words by S Humphreys), produced London, King's Theatre, Haymarket, 17 Mar 1733.

The colour of my soul is iron-grey and sad bats wheel about the steeple of my dreams.
Claude Debussy, in a letter to Chausson, 1894

Debussy, (Achille) Claude (b Saint-Germain-en-Laye near Paris, 22 Aug 1862; d Paris 25 Mar 1918), French composer. Son of a shopkeeper, took his first piano lessons at the age of seven, and from 1870 was taught for three years by Mme Mauté de Fleurville, a former pupil of Chopin. Entered the Paris Conservatory 1873, studying with Lavignac and Marmontel, later with Emile Durand. At 17 he failed to win a piano prize, but entered a composition class in 1880. For the next two summers became domestic musician to Nadezhda von Meck, Tchaikovsky's former patroness, whose children he taught and who took him to Switzerland and Italy the first time and to Russia the second. Gained first Prix de Rome in 1884 and went to Rome the next year, but left in 1887 before the statutory three years were completed. During these years he began to reject the prevalent Wagnerian currents in music of the day, forging a new path towards impression-

Debussy *The composer Claude Debussy (1862–1918) pictured with his first wife, Rosalie Texier. During the years they spent together (1899–1904)* Pelléas et Mélisande *was produced and Debussy consolidated his reputation as the leading impressionist composer. Following their separation his technique evolved in works such as* La Mer *and* Images.

ism. He began to compose seriously in the new manner for which he became known with a French translation of Rossetti's *Blessed Damozel*, finished 1888. Influenced by Satie in 1891 and performed his first important mature work, the prelude to Mallarmé's poem *L'Après-midi d'un faune*, in 1894. He married a dressmaker, Rosalie (Lili) Texier, in 1899, and in the same year completed his *Nocturnes*, symphonic triptych for orchestra. He became music critic for the *Revue blanche* in 1901; produced his only finished opera, a setting of Maeterlinck's *Pelléas et Mélisande*, 30 Apr 1902. The opera was described by its conductor, André Messager, as opening a window on

the whole world of modern music; clear themes and strong contrasts are replaced by atmospheric depictions of mood. Debussy left his wife in 1904 for Emma Bardac, whom he married after divorcing his first wife in 1905. Growing success, abroad as well as in France during the last ten years, but about 1909 he began to suffer from cancer. Debussy's elusive and colouristic style has profoundly influenced his French successors, notably Messiaen and Boulez.

Works include STAGE: opera *Pelléas et Mélisande* (1902); incidental music to d'Annunzio's *Le Martyre de Saint Sébastien* (1911); ballets *Jeux* (1913) and *Khamma*.

A Selection of

Debussy

String Quartet	1893
Prélude à l'après midi d'un faune	1894
Trois Nocturnes	1899
Pelléas et Mélisande	1902

La Mer	1905
Images for piano	1905, 1907
Préludes	1909–10, 1912–13
Images for orchestra	1912
Jeux	1913
Violin Sonata	1917

Debussy
A biographical note

Entering the Paris Conservatoire at only ten years of age, Debussy was surrounded by some of the most important musicians of the day. The popular opera composer Ambroise Thomas was director of the Conservatoire and Cesar Franck was among his teachers; Eric Satie and Paul Dukas were among his fellow-students. The most successful French composer of the day, Charles Gounod, was influential in his winning the Prix de Rome in 1884. At the Paris Exposition of 1889 Debussy discovered a new musical world in the Javanese gamelan bands. He later wrote of them: 'Their Conservatoire is the rhythm of the sea, the wind rustling the leaves and the myriad sounds of nature'. The gamelan sound was to find its way into such music as *Pagodes*, from *Images* for piano. In common with contemporaries such as Van Gogh, Debussy also came under the spell of Japanese prints; *The Hollow Wave* by Katsushika Hokusai adorned the cover of the orchestral score of *La Mer*. Orientalisms were even detected in Debussy's appearance: an American critic wrote of him 'I see his curious asymmetrical face, the pointed fawn ears, the projecting cheek bones – the man is a wraith from the East.'

VOCAL: cantatas *L'Enfant prodigue* and *La Damoiselle élue*, three *Chansons de France* (Charles d'Orléans) for unaccompanied chorus; songs including sets *Cinq Poèmes de Baudelaire* (1890), *Ariettes oubliées* (Verlaine), two sets of *Fêtes galantes* (Verlaine), *Proses lyriques* (Debussy), *Trois Ballades de Villon*, *Chansons de Bilitis* (Pierre Louÿs) (1898), *Le Promenoir des deux amants* (Tristan Lhermite), *Trois Poèmes de Stéphane Mallarmé*.

ORCHESTRAL: *Printemps*, *Prélude à l'Après-midi d'un faune* (1895) *Trois Nocturnes* (1899), *La Mer* (1905) and *Trois Images* for orchestra (1912); *Fantasie* for piano and orchestra (1889); *Danse sacrée et danse profane* for harp and strings (1904).

CHAMBER AND PIANO: string quartet (1893); sonatas for cello and piano; flute, viola and harp; and violin and piano (1915–17) and some smaller chamber works for saxophone, clarinet and flute; many piano pieces including *Suite bergamasque*, suite *Pour le Piano* (1901), *Trois Estampes* (1903), *Masques*, *L'Île joyeuse* (1904), two sets of three *Images*, suite *Children's Corner*, two sets of 12 *Préludes* (1910, 1913), and 12 *Etudes* (1915); *Petite Suite*, *Marche écossaise*, *Six Epigraphes antiques* (on Pierre Louÿs's *Chansons de Bilitis*), etc. for piano duet; *Lindaraja* and *En blanc et noir* (1915) for two pianos.

decani in English cathedrals and in churches where the choir is divided, the decani side is that on the south of the chancel, near the dean's stall, the other being the *Cantoris* side.

Decius, Nikolaus (b Hof, *c* 1485; d after 1546), German Lutheran pastor and theologian. He wrote the words and composed or adapted the music of three chorales, anticipating even Luther in this field.

Decker, Franz-Paul (b Cologne, 22 Jun 1922), German conductor. Studied with Jarnach in Cologne and was director of Wiesbaden Opera 1950–53; Bochum 1956–64, Rotterdam PO 1962–68. Music director Montreal SO 1967–75, Barcelona SO from 1986. Chief conductor of the New Zealand SO from 1990, principal guest of the Orchestra of the National Arts Centre, Ottawa, 1991.

decrescendo Italian = 'waning, decreasing'; synonym of *diminuendo*, which is now more frequently used.

Dedekind, Constantin Christian (b Reinsdorf, Anhalt-Cöthen, 2 Apr 1628; d Dresden, 2 Sept 1715), German poet and composer. Studied at Dresden and in 1654 became a member of the Saxon court chapel and *Konzertmeister* in 1666. He arranged words for sacred music dramas.

Works include psalms, sacred and secular vocal music, concertos for voices and instruments.

Dedekind, Heinrich (or Enricius) (b Neustadt, Bavaria, Dec 1554; d Luneburg, 30 Nov 1619), German clergyman and composer. Cantor at St John's Church, Lüneburg. Wrote psalms and other sacred vocal works.

Dedekind, Henning (b Neustadt, 30 Dec 1562; d Gebsee, Thuringia, 28 Jul 1626), German composer, brother of Heinrich ◊Dedekind. Held posts as cantor and preacher at Langensalza and Gebsee.

Works include Mass; secular vocal music.

Defesch, William, Willem de ◊Fesch.

DeGaetani, Jan (b Massillon, OH, 10 Jul 1933; d Rochester, NY, 15 Sept 1989), American mezzo. After study at Juilliard she specialized in technically demanding modern works, giving the fps of works by Crumb and Davies (*A Stone Litany*, 1973) and recording *Pierrot lunaire*. Also heard in medieval music. Professor, Eastman School, from 1973.

Deidamia opera by Handel (libretto by P A Rolli), produced London, Theatre Royal, Lincoln's Inn Fields, 10 Jan 1741. Handel's last opera. Achilles dresses up as a girl but Deidamia discovers his secret; when Ulysses makes advances to Deidamia, Achilles reveals himself and joins Ulysses to fight at Troy.

Delacôte, Jacques (b Remiremont, Vosges, 16 Aug 1942), French conductor. He studied at the Vienna Academy, with Swarowsky, and won the 1972 Mitropoulos Competition NY; NY PO from 1973. Has conducted opera at Hamburg, Paris and London (CG) and appeared with the LSO, Cleveland SO and other orchestras. In Mahler, Bruckner and French music. Promenade Concerts, London, 1986. Conducted Massenet's *Le Cid* at Chicago, 1993.

Delage, Maurice (Charles) (b Paris, 13 Nov 1879; d Paris, 19 Sept 1961), French composer. Pupil of Ravel. He travelled to the east and incorporated exotic elements into his music.

Works include overture to a ballet *Les Bâtisseurs de ponts* (after Kipling), symphonic poem *Conté par la mer* and other orchestral works; piano pieces; songs.

Delannoy, Marcel (François Georges) (b Ferté-Alain, 9 Jul 1898; d Nantes, 14 Sept 1962), French composer. A painter and architect at first, he was mainly self-taught in music.

Works include operas *Le Poirier de misère* (1925), *Philippine* (1937), *Fête de la danse*, *Ginevra* (1942); ballet-cantata *Le Fou de la dame*, ballets *La Pantoufle de vair* and *L'Eventail de Jeanne* (with others); incidental music for Aristophanes' *Peace* and other plays; symphonies and *Figures sonores* for orchestra, *Sérénade concertante* for violin and orchestra; string quartets; many songs.

De Lara, Isidore, Isidore ◊Lara.

Delatre, Petit Jean (b ? Liège, *c* 1510; d Utrecht, 31 Aug 1569), Flemish composer of *chansons* and motets. He is not to be confused with the French composer Claude Petit Jehan (d Metz, 1589).

Delibes, (Clément Philibert) Léo (b Saint-Germain-du-Val, 21 Feb 1836; d Paris, 16 Jan 1891), French composer. Studied at the Paris Conservatory, where Adam was his composition master. He became accompanist at the Théâtre Lyrique in 1853 and was organist successively at two churches. Later he became accompanist and chorus master at the Opéra and in 1881 professor of composition at the Conservatory.

Works include operas *Maître Griffard* (1857), *Le Jardinier et son seigneur* (1863), *Le Roi l'a dit* (1873), *Jean de Nivelle*, *Lakmé* (1883), *Kassya* (unfinished); ballets *La Source* (with Minkus), *Coppélia* (on E T A Hoffmann's story *Olympia*), *Sylvia*, *Le Pas des fleurs*; divertissement for Adam's ballet *Le Corsaire*; incidental music for Hugo's *Le Roi s'amuse*; operettas *Deux Sous de charbon* (1856), *Deux Vielles Gardes*, *L'Omelette à la Follembûche* (1859), *Le Serpent à plumes* (1864), *L'Ecossais de Chatou* and others; Mass; cantata *Alger*; dramatic scene *La Mort d'Orphée*; songs; children's choruses.

Delius, Frederick (b Bradford, 29 Jan 1862; d Grez-sur-Loing, 10 Jun 1934), English composer of German descent. His father was a well-to-do businessman and wished him to follow a commercial career; but music was cultivated in the home and although Delius had little systematic teaching until he went to Florida as an orange planter in 1884 and came under the influence of Thomas Ward, organist at Jacksonville, he worked steadily at music by himself. In 1886, after some teaching in USA, he went to the Leipzig Conservatory for a

A Selection of
Delius

Florida	1887
Appalachia	1898–1903
Paris: the Song of a Great City	1899
A Village Romeo and Juliet	1900–1
Sea Drift	1904
A Mass of Life	1904–5
Brigg Fair	1907
On Hearing the First Cuckoo in Spring	1911
Summer Night on the River	1913
Violin Concerto	1915

short time, but found its conservative teaching uncongenial. In 1887 he visited Norway and became friendly with Grieg, who persuaded his father to let him devote himself to composition. From 1889 he lived in France, mainly Paris, and in 1897 he married Jelka Rosen, a German painter of Danish descent, and they settled at Grez-sur-Loing, near Fontainebleau. A concert of his works was given in London in 1899 and he became known here and there in Germany. He had assimilated early influences of Wagner, Grieg and Debussy, and found his own voice in *Koanga, Paris: Song of a Great City*, and *A Village Romeo and Juliet*. From 1907 important fps were given in England: Beecham gave *Paris* (1908) and *A Mass of Life* (1909) and Wood conducted *Sea Drift* in 1908. He contracted syphilis and in 1922 was attacked by paralysis, which gradually increased until four years later he was helpless and totally blind. In 1928 Eric Fenby volunteered to live in his house and act as amanuensis.

Works include OPERAS *Irmelin* (1890–92; produced 1953), *The Magic Fountain* (1893–95; fp BBC 1977), *Koanga* (1896–98; produced 1904), *A Village Romeo and Juliet* (1900–01; produced 1907),

---

What should have been evident at first hearing was the remotely alien sound of it, a note in English music stranger than any heard for over two hundred years.

Sir Thomas Beecham on Delius, *A Mingled Chime*, 1943

Margot-la-Rouge (1902; fp BBC, 1982), *Fennimore and Gerda* (1909–10; produced 1919); incidental music for Heiberg's *Folkeraadet* and Flecker's *Hassan*.

    ORCHESTRAL WORKS: *Florida* suite (1887), *Over the Hills and Far Away*, (c 1895), *Paris* (1899), *Life's Dance* (1819), *Brigg Fair* (1907), *In a Summer Garden*, two *Dance Rhapsodies* (1908, 1916), *On hearing the First Cuckoo in Spring* (1911), *Summer Night on the River* (1913), *North Country Sketches, Eventyr* (after Asbjørnsen's fairy-tales, 1917), *A Song before Sunrise*; concertos for piano, violin, cello and violin and cello (1897, 1915, 1916, 1921).

    CHAMBER MUSIC: string quartet (1916); three violin and piano sonatas; sonata for cello and piano (1916).

    CHORUS AND ORCHESTRA: *Appalachia* (1898–1903), *Sea Drift* (1904), *A Mass of Life* (1904–05), *Songs of Sunset, Arabesk* (1911), *A Song of the High Hills, Requiem* (1914–16).

    OTHER VOCAL: some part-songs, songs with orchestra including cycle from Tennyson's *Maud*, seven Danish songs, Dowson's *Cynara*; c 40 songs with piano.

Della Casa, Lisa (b Burgdorf, Berne, 2 Feb 1919), Swiss soprano. Studied at the Berne Conservatory and in Zurich, beginning her international career at the Salzburg Festival of 1947, as Zdenka; sang Donna Elvira there in 1953. She became known as one of the outstanding Mozart and Strauss singers of her day, also doing much to further the cause of Swiss music; NY Met. debut 1953, as Mozart's Countess. London, CG, 1953 as Arabella. Retired 1974.

Deller, Alfred (b Margate, 31 May 1912; d Bologna, 16 Jul 1979), English counter-tenor. Entirely self-trained, he became a lay clerk at Canterbury Cathedral in 1940 and in 1947 joined the choir of St Paul's Cathedral. He was widely known as a soloist of outstanding musicianship, also frequently singing with the Deller Consort, which he formed in 1948.

Dello Joio, Norman (b New York, 24 Jan 1913), American composer. Studied at the Juilliard Graduate School in NY with Wagenaar, later with Hindemith at Yale School of Music. He joined the teaching staff of Sarah Lawrence College; Boston University 1972–79.

Works include operas *The Ruby* (1953), *The Triumph of St Joan* (1959) and *Blood Moon* (1961); symphonic ballet *On Stage*; *Western Star* for solo voices, narrator, chorus and orchestra; sinfonietta, ballet suite *Duke of Sacramento* (1942), symphonic movement *Silvermine* for orchestra *Colonial Variations* for orchestra (1976), concertos for piano, two pianos, harp and flute; *Variations on a Bach Chorale* for orchestra (1985); Mass (1976); quartet and trio for woodwind, trio for

flute, cello and piano; violin and piano sonata, *Duo concertante* for cello and piano, sonatina for cello solo; suite and *Duo concertante* for two pianos; two sonatas, suite and two preludes for piano.

Del Mar, Norman (René) (b London, 31 Jul 1919; d Bushey, 6 Feb 1994), English conductor and writer on music. Studied at the RCM with R O Morris and Vaughan Williams. In 1944 he founded the Chelsea SO, and in 1947 became conductor of the Croydon SO. In the same year he was appointed assistant to Beecham with the RPO. He was especially noted as a performer of complex modern scores, e.g. Busoni's piano concerto and Mahler's symphonies, and wrote a three-volume study of the music of Richard Strauss. CBE 1975.

His son, Jonathan (b London, 7 Jan 1951) has conducted leading British orchestras.

Delmas, Jean-Francois (b Lyons, 14 Apr 1861; d Saint-Alban de Monthel, 29 Sept 1933), French bass-baritone. At the Paris Opéra he was a leading singer 1886–1927; created Athanael in *Thaïs*, 1894, and was admired in Méhul's *Joseph*, Reyer's *Salammbô* and Dukas' *Ariane et Barbe-Bleue*. He was Hagen and Gurnemanz in the Opéra fps of *Götterdämmerung* and *Parsifal* (1908, 1914).

Del Monaco, Mario (b Florence, 27 Jul 1915; d Mestre, near Venice, 16 Oct 1982), Italian tenor. Studied at the Pesaro Conservatory and made his debut in Milan in 1941 as Pinkerton, but later served in the Italian army during World War II. From 1951 to 1959 he sang with the NY Met. as Des Grieux, Don José, Cavaradossi, Manrico. A dramatic singer, one of his finest roles was that of Verdi's Otello, which he sang in London, CG, in 1962.

Delna, Marie (b Meudon, near Paris, 3 Apr 1875; d Paris, 23 Jul 1932), French contralto. Debut Paris, Opéra-Comique, 1892, as the Berlioz Dido; the following year she was Charlotte in the first French performance of *Werther*. Mistress Quickly, 1894. She sang at the Opéra 1898–1901 and in Milan 1898–1900; engaged by Toscanini for the NY Met. in 1909 but did not repeat her European success. Retired from stage 1922 and gave concerts until 1930.

Delogu, Gaetano (b Messina, 14 Apr 1934), Italian conductor. Studied with Franco Ferrara and directed the regional orchestras of the RAI, Italy; guest with the NY PO and the National SO, Washington, 1968–69. Conductor of the Teatro Massimo, Palermo, 1975–78; music director of the Denver SO 1979–86.

Del Tredici, David (b Cloverdale, CA, 16 Mar 1937), American composer. He studied at Berkeley and with Roger Sessions at Princeton. His early music contains several settings of Joyce: *I Hear an Army*, for soprano and string quartet (1964), *Night Conjure-Verse* for voices and instruments (1965), *Syzygy* for soprano, horn, bells and chamber orchestra (1968).

His recent music been concerned with Lewis Carroll: *Pop-Pourri*, for voices, rock group and orchestra (1968), *The Lobster Quadrille* for soprano, folk music ensemble and orchestra (1969, revised 1974), *Vintage Alice* (1971; same forces), *An Alice Symphony* (1976), *Final Alice*, for orchestra (1976), *Child Alice*, work for soprano and orchestra, and in four parts: *In Memory of a Summer Day, Happy Voices, All in the Golden Afternoon* and *Quaint Events* (1977–81; performed separately in St Louis, San Francisco, Philadelphia and Rotterdam, 1980–83. First complete performance Aspen, 1984); *March to Tonality* for orchestra (1985); *Haddock's Eyes* for soprano and ensemble (1986); *Steps* for orchestra (1990).

De Luca, Giuseppe (b Rome, 25 Dec 1876; d New York, 26 Aug 1950), Italian baritone. Debut Piacenza, 1897 as Valentin; 1902–04 created the baritone leads in *Adriana Lecouvreur*, Giordano's *Siberia*; and *Madama Butterfly*. NY Met. 1915–40; debut as Rossini's Figaro and created Paquiro in *Goyescas* by Granados (1916). London, CG, 1907, 1910 and 1935.

De Lucia, Fernando (b Naples, 11 Oct 1860; d Naples, 21 Feb 1925), Italian tenor. Debut Naples, 1885, as Faust. In 1891 he created the title role in Mascagni's *L'Amico Fritz* and repeated the role on his CG (1892) and NY Met. (1894) debuts; also created roles in Mascagni's *I Rantzau* (1892), *Silvano* (1895) and *Iris* (1898). He sang in London, CG, until 1900: roles included Rodolfo, Turridu, Cavaradossi and Canio.

De Lussan, Zélie, Zélie de ◊Lussan.

De Main, John (b Youngstown, OH, 11 Jan 1944), American conductor. Studied at Juilliard and was assistant conductor of the St Paul Chamber Orchestra 1972–74 and music director of Texas Opera Theater 1974–76; Opera Omaha 1983–91, Houston Grand Opera 1979–93: conducted the premieres of Bernstein's *A Quiet Place* (1983), Adams' *Nixon in China* (1987) and Tippett's *New Year* (1989). Local fp of *A Midsummer Night's Dream* at Houston, 1993.

Demetrio, *Demetrius*, libretto by Metastasio.

Opera by Caldara, produced Vienna, at court, 4 Nov 1731. Further settings by Hasse (1732), Gluck (1742) and Jommelli (1749). Cleomice, new queen of Syria, must choose a husband. She loves Alcestis, a commoner, whom rival Olinto orders to leave the country. When it is revealed that Alcestis is in fact Prince Demetrius, the marriage goes ahead.

Demetrio e Polibio opera by Rossini (libretto by V Vigano-Mombelli). Rossini's first opera, it was written while he was a student at the Bologna Conservatory, from 1806; produced Rome, Teatro Valle, 18 May 1812. Demetrio, king of Syria, finds his long-lost son at the court of King Polibio.

Demidenko, Nikolai (b Aniskino, 1 Jul 1955), Russian pianist. Studied at the Moscow Conservatory and has given concerts in Russia and abroad from 1978; UK debut with the Moscow Radio SO, 1985. Resident in Britain from 1980 and gave series of six concerts at the Wigmore Hall, 1993, recreating 19th-c. recitals by Alkan and Rubinstein. Frequent tours of Japan and concerts with the St Petersburg PO, London PO and Philharmonia. Recordings include Medtner, Bach-Busoni, Chopin and Liszt.

Demofoonte, rè di Tracia, *Demophoon, King of Thrace*, libretto by Metastasio.

Opera by Caldara, produced 4 Nov 1733. Further settings by Gluck (1743), Jommelli, (1743, the first of four), Graun (1746) and Hasse (1748). King Demophoön wants to sacrifice a virgin to appease Apollo, but the intended victim (Dirce) is secretly married to his son, Timanthes. Many twists in the plot, but a happy ending.

Demon, The opera by A Rubinstein (libretto, in Russian, by P A Viskovatov, based on Lermontov's poem), produced St Petersburg, 25 Jan 1875. Revived Wexford, 1994. Demon kills Tamara's lover but she is rescued by an angel.

Démophoon opera by Cherubini (libretto by Marmontel, based on Metastasio's *Demofoonte*), produced Paris, Opéra, 5 Dec 1788. Cherubini's first French opera.

Let me have music dying, and I seek/No more delight.
John Keats, *Endymion*, 1818

Demougeot, Marcelle (b Dijon, 18 Jun 1871; d Paris, 24 Nov 1931), French soprano. Debut Paris, Opéra, 1902, as Donna Elvira; 1909 Fricka in the local fp of *Das Rheingold* and sang in the Monte Carlo premiere of Saint-Saëns's *Déjanire*, 1911. She was successful as Elisabeth, Brünnhilde and Venus; sang Kundry in the Paris fp of *Parsifal*, 1914.

Dempsey, Gregory (b Melbourne, 20 Jul 1931), Australian tenor. He sang in Australia before joining the SW Co., London, in 1962; sang David in *The Mastersingers*, 1968, and Matej Brouček in the first production by a British company of Janáček's *The Excursions of Mr Brouček*; he sang Gregor in *The Makropoulos Case* on his US debut (San Francisco, 1966) and Steva in *Jenůfa* at CG in 1972. Other roles included Mime, Peter Grimes, and Aeneas in *Les Troyens*. His last major role was Bob Boles in *Peter Grimes*, Sydney, 1980.

Demus, Jörg (b St Polten, 2 Dec 1928), Austrian pianist. He studied with Gieseking and Kempff; debut Vienna, 1943, London 1950. Tours worldwide in classical repertory and has accompanied leading singers and instrumentalists: piano duets with Paul Badura-Skoda. Plays from his own collection of historical instruments.

Demuth, Leopold (b Brno, 2 Nov 1861; d Czernowitz, 4 Mar 1910), Austrian baritone. Debut Halle 1889, as Hans Heiling; sang in Leipzig and Hamburg before going to Vienna, under Mahler, in 1898. Sang leading roles and took part in the fp of Goldmark's *Ein Wintermärchen* (based on *A Winter's Tale*, 1908). Bayreuth 1899 as Sachs and Gunther.

Demuth, Norman (b London, 15 Jul 1898; d Chichester, 21 Apr 1968), English composer and author. Educated as a choirboy at St George's Chapel, Windsor, and at Repton School. Studied music at the RCM in London and became professor of composition at the RAM there in 1930. His books include studies of Franck, Ravel and Roussel.

Works include five operas, including *Volpone* (after Jonson) and *The Oresteia* (Aeschylus); five ballets; four symphonies, two piano concertos; three sonatas for violin and piano, string trio, string quartet etc.

De natura sonoris two works by Penderecki: no. 1 for orchestra, fp Royan, France, 7 Apr 1966; no. 2 for wind, percussion and strings, performed New York, 3 Dec 1971.

Dench, Chris (b London, 10 Jun 1953), English composer. Self-taught and resident in Berlin from 1988. A leading member of the avant-garde, with performances of his music by the London Sinfonietta, Ensemble InterContemporain, and the Arditti Quartet. Appearances at Darmstadt, the Venice Biennale and the ISCM World Music Days.

Works include *Helical* for piano (1975), *Caught Breath of Time* for flute (1981), *Enonce* for 15 players (1984), *Strangeness* for string quartet (1985), *4 Darmstadter Aphorismen* (1986–89); *Sulle Scale della Fenice* for flute (1989), *Dark Neumes* for guitar, six brass and amplified ensemble (1989).

Denisov, Edison (b Tomsk, 6 Apr 1929), Russian composer. Studied at Moscow Conservatory with Shebalin and taught there from 1960. An early Soviet exponent of serial and electronic music.

Works include opera *L'ecume des jours* (1981), and ballet *Confession* (after de Musset, 1984), *The Four Girls* opera after Picasso, (1986); concertos for cello (1972), flute (1975), violin (1978), flute and oboe (1978), bassoon and cello (1982), oboe (1986), and clarinet (1989); symphony (1987); string trio (1969), piano trio (1971), clarinet and piano quintets, with strings (1987), Octet (1992), Requiem (1980).

Density 21.5 work for solo flute by Varèse; fp NY, 16 Feb 1936. Title refers to the specific gravity of platinum.

Dent, Edward J(oseph) (b Ribston, Yorks, 16 Jul 1876; d London, 22 Aug 1957), English musicologist and composer. Educated at Eton and Cambridge, Professor of Music there from 1926 to 1941. President of the ISCM from its foundation in 1922 until 1938. A governor of Sadler's Wells Opera, for which he translated many works. His books include works on A Scarlatti, Mozart's operas, English opera, Handel and Busoni, and his compositions include polyphonic motets and a version of *The Beggar's Opera*. He was a member of the editorial board of the *New Oxford History of Music*.

Denza, Luigi (b Castellammare di Stabia, 24 Feb 1846; d London, 26 Jan 1922), Italian singing-teacher and composer. Studied at the Naples Conservatory. Settled in London in 1879, made a success with many of his light songs, especially *Funiculì funiculà*, and was professor of singing at the RAM from 1898.

Works include an opera on Schiller's *Wallenstein*, over 500 songs, etc.

De Priest, James (b Philadelphia, 21 Nov 1936), American conductor. Studied with Persichetti in Philadelphia and conducted there 1959–62. Assistant at the NY PO 1965–66, European debut with the Rotterdam PO 1969. Associate conductor with the National SO, Washington, 1971–75, music director of L'Orchestre Symphonique de Québec, 1976–83. Oregon SO at Portland from 1980, Malmo SO from 1991. Guest conductor in the USA and Europe.

De Reszke, Edouard (b Warsaw, 22 Dec 1853; d Garnek, 25 May 1917), Polish bass. Debut as Amonasro in the French premiere of *Aida* (Paris, 1876). CG 1880–84, as Alvise and Rossini's Basilio. Fiesco in the revival of *Simon Boccanegra*, Milan 1881. He sang Frère Laurent on his NY Met. debut and other roles included Gounod's Méphistophélès, Leporello, and, late in his career, Wagner's Daland, Sachs, Hagen and Wanderer.

De Reszke, Jean (b Warsaw, 14 Jan 1850; d Nice, 3 Apr 1925), Polish tenor; brother of Edouard ◊De Reszke. Debut Venice, 1874, as Alfonso in *La favorite* (a baritone role). Debut as tenor Madrid, 1879, as Meyerbeer's Robert; created the title role in Massenet's *Le Cid*, Paris 1885, and sang Radames at Drury Lane, London, in 1887. CG roles included Meyerbeer's Vasco da Gama and Raoul, Faust and Riccardo. US debut Chicago 1891, as Lohengrin; sang Tristan and Siegfried in NY and retired 1902.

Dering (or *Deering*), Richard (b *c* 1580; d London, buried 22 Mar 1630), English organist and composer. Became a Catholic and went to Brussels in 1617 as organist to the convent of English nuns, but returned to England to become organist to Henrietta Maria on her marriage to Charles I in 1625.

Works include *Cantiones sacrae* for several voices, motets, anthems; canzonets for three and four voices, quodlibets on street cries; fancies and other pieces for viols.

Dérivis, Henri Etienne (b Albi, 2 Aug 1780; d Livry, 1 Feb 1856), French bass. He sang at the Paris Opéra 1803–28 and was well known in operas by Spontini: created leading roles in *La Vestale* (1807), *Fernand Cortez* (1809) and *Olympie* (1819). In 1826 he sang the title role in Rossini's revision of *Maometto II/Le Siège de Corinthe*).

Dérivis, Prosper (b Paris, 28 Oct 1808; d Paris, 11 Feb 1880), French bass, son of the Henri Etienne ◊Dérivis. He sang at the Paris Opéra 1831–41 and created roles in *Les Huguenots* (1836), *Benvenuto Cellini* (1838) and *Les Martyrs* (1840). In 1842 he was in Milan for the fp of *Nabucco* (Zaccaria) and in Vienna for the fp of Donizetti's *Linda di Chamounix*. Retired 1857.

Dermota, Anton (b Kropa; 4 Jun 1910; d Vienna, 22 Jun 1989), Slovenian-born Austrian tenor. He sang Alfredo at the Vienna Staatsoper in 1936 and Florestan at the re-opening of the house in 1955. Best known for his Mozart roles, he sang Ottavio under Furtwängler at Salzburg. Other roles included David and Palestrina.

Dernesch, Helga (b Vienna, 3 Feb 1939), Austrian soprano, later mezzo. Debut Berne, 1961, as Marina. Bayreuth since 1965 as Elisabeth, Eva and Gutrune; Brünnhilde, Leonore and Isolde at Salzburg, from 1969, under Karajan. With Scottish Opera and in London CG, she has sung Leonore, the Marschallin, and Sieglinde. Mezzo roles from 1979, e.g. Fricka and Waltraute; (Adelaide in *Arabella*, CG 1986). She sang Hecuba in the fp of Reimann's *Troades* (Munich 1986). 1991–92 season as Clytemnestra in San Francisco and Paris.

Dervaux, Pierre (b Juvisy-sur-Orge, 3 Jan 1917; d Marseilles, 20 Feb 1992), French conductor. Studied at the Paris Conservatory, making his debut with the Pasdeloup Orchestra 1947. Principal conductor of the Paris Opéra-Comique 1947–53, Paris Opéra 1956–70. Conductor of the Concerts Colonne 1958, Québec SO 1968–71. Director of the Pays de la Loire PO 1971–78, Nice 1979–82. Teacher of conducting at Montreal 1965–72, Ecole Normale de Paris, and the Nice Academy 1971–82.

De Sabata, Victor (b Trieste, 10 Apr 1892; d Santa Margherita Ligure, 11 Dec 1967), Italian conductor and composer. Studied under his father, a chorus master at the Teatro alla Scala, Milan, and at the Conservatory there, with Orefice and others. He became conductor at La Scala and at the Royal Opera in Rome, Monte Carlo from 1918 (fp *L'Enfant et les Sortilèges*, 1925). Visited USA in 1938, conducted at Bayreuth in 1939 (*Tristan*) and became known in London in 1946; with Scala co. 1950 (*Otello* and *Falstaff*).

Works include operas *Lisistrata* (after Aristophanes), *Il macigno*, *Mille e una notte* (1931); incidental music for Shakespeare's *Merchant of Venice*; symphonic poems *Juventus*, *La notte di Platon*, *Gethsemani*, suite for orchestra.

de Saram, Rohan (b Sheffield, 9 Mar 1939), Sri Lankan cellist. Studied with Cassado and Casals. European concerts followed by US debut at Carnegie Hall, 1960. Resident in London from 1972, becoming a teacher at TCL. Often heard in Bach's suites and in music by Xenakis, Pousseur, Dallapiccola and Berio. Cellist of the ◊Arditti Quartet.

descant (1) a melodic line added to an existing melody, hence in general = counterpoint and was so used by older English writers.

Dernesch *Soprano (and later mezzo) Helga Dernesch as the Marschallin with Jules Bastin as Ochs in the 1974 Covent Garden production of* Der Rosenkavalier. *She has a warm and powerful voice, and commands an attractive stage presence.*

(2) The upper part of a polyphonic composition, whether vocal or instrumental; hence descant recorder, viol.

(3) In modern usage the addition of a treble part to a well-known tune, either by a composer or by improvisation: the word faburden (or fauxbourdon) is often used as an equivalent.

Descartes, René (b La Haye, 31 Mar 1596; d Stockholm, 11 Feb 1650), French philosopher. Wrote a book on music, *Compendium musicae* (1618), in which he outlined the relationship between the physical aspect of sound and its perception by the listener.

Deschamps-Jehin, Blanche (b Lyons, 18 Sept 1857; d Paris, Jun 1923), French contralto. In 1879 she sang Mignon at Brussels; created Massenet's Hérodiade there (1881) and Uta in Reyer's *Sigurd*, 1884. In 1885 she was at the Paris Opéra-Comique, in the fp of Massé's *Une Nuit de Cléopâtre*, and remained for the fps of *Le medicin malgré lui* (1886) and *Le Roi d'Ys* (1888). Carmen at CG in 1891, and the first local Dalila and *Walküre* Fricka, at the Paris Opéra, 1892–93.

Déserts work by Varèse for wind instruments, percussion and magnetic tapes *ad lib*; composed 1953–54, fp Paris, 20 Dec 1954, conductor Scherchen. Early use is made here of electronic sound.

Desmarets, Henri (b Paris, Feb 1661; d Lunéville, 7 Sept 1741), French composer. Educated at the court of Louis XIV. At the end of the century he secretly married the daughter of a dignitary at Senlis and fled to Spain, becoming music superintendent to Philip V in 1700. In 1708 he became music director to the Duke of Lorraine at Lunéville.

Works include operas and ballets *Didon* (1693), *Circé, Théagène et Chariclée* (on Heliodorus's *Aethiopica*, 1695), *Les Amours de Momus, Vénus et Adonis, Les Fêtes galantes* (1698), *Iphigénie en Tauride* (with Campra) and *Renaud ou La Suite d'Armide* (1722), motet and Te Deum for the marriage of Princess Elisabeth Thérèse to the King of Sardinia; church music written early in his career under the name of Goupillier.

Désormière, Roger (b Vichy, 13 Sept 1898; d Paris, 25 Oct 1963), French conductor. Studied at the Paris Conservatory and in 1924 became conductor of the Swedish ballet. From 1925 to 1929 he worked with the Ballet Russe and from 1936 to 1944 conducted at the Opéra Comique; he gave *Pelléas et Mélisande* with the co. at CG in 1949. He became seriously ill in 1950 and was forced to give up his career.

Des Prés ◊Josquin.

Desprez ◊Josquin.

Dessau, Paul (b Hamburg, 19 Dec 1894; d East Berlin, 28 Jun 1979), German composer. From 1910 he studied in Berlin at the Klindworth-Scharwenka Conservatory and later in Hamburg, where in 1913 he became a coach at the opera. He conducted all over Germany, but was forced to leave and in 1939 went to NY. He returned to East Germany in 1948.

Works include operas *Das Verhör des Lukullus* (1949; produced 1951), *Puntila* (1959; prod 1966), *Lanzelot* (1969), *Einstein* (1973), *Leonce und Lena* (1979); children's operas *Das Eisenbahnspiel*, *Tadel der Unzuverlässigkeit*; concertino for solo flute, clarinet, horn and violin; a piano sonata; much vocal and orchestral music, film and incidental music.

dessus French = 'top of the viols'; the treble ◊viol.

Destinn (born *Kittl*, later known as *Destinnova*), Emmy (b Prague, 26 Feb 1878; d České Budějovice, 28 Jan 1930), Czech soprano. Made her first appearance in Berlin in 1898 as Santuzza; first visited London (CG) in 1904 as Donna Anna. Later in London as Butterfly and Aida. Created Minnie in *La fanciulla del West*, NY Met. 1910. She wrote poems and novels.

Destouches, André(-Cardinal) (b Paris, bap. 6 Apr 1672; d Paris, 7 Feb 1749), French composer. A sailor at first, and then a musketeer, he studied with Campra and produced his first stage work, *Issé*, in 1697. He held various court appointments and was director of the Opéra in 1728–31.

Works include operas *Amadis de Crèce* (1699) *Marthésie, Omphale, Callirhoé, Télémaque et Calypso* (1714), *Sémiramis* (1718), *Les Stratagèmes de l'Amour*; heroic pastoral *Issé*; comedy-ballet *Le Carnaval et la folie*; ballet *Les Eléments* (with Lalande, 1721), cantatas (*Enone*) and *Sémélé*.

détaché French = 'detached, separated'; a bowing style in string playing. In quick passages the bow changes direction so that each note is clearly separated, but without the sound being perceptibly interrupted, as in *staccato*.

Detroit Symphony Orchestra US ensemble, founded 1914, with Gabrilowitsch as conductor 1918–35. Disbanded 1949, re-formed 1951, with Paul Paray in charge 1952–63, Sixten Ehrling 1963–73, Aldo Ceccato 1973–77. During Antal Dorati's tenure, 1977–81, they made their first European tour; Gary Bertini was music director 1981–83, Gunther Herbig 1984–90, Neeme Järvi from 1990.

Dettingen Te Deum a Te Deum composed by Handel to celebrate the victory of Dettingen won on 26 Jun 1743. fp London, Chapel Royal, 27 Nov 1743.

Deutekom, Cristina (b Amsterdam, 28 Aug 1932), Dutch soprano. Her coloratura was admired in Mozart's Queen of Night at her NY Met. (1967) and CG (1968) debuts. She sang Bellini's Elvira at Buenos Aires in 1972 and returned to the Met. for Verdi's Hélène, in 1974. Other roles included Rossini's Armida, Verdi's Odabella and Giselda and Mozart's Constanze.

Deuteromelia the second part of a collection of canons, rounds and catches pub. by Ravenscroft in London in 1609, the first part being *Pammelia*.

Deutsch, Otto Erich (b Vienna, 5 Sept 1883; d Vienna, 23 Nov 1967), Austrian music biographer and bibliographer. Made a special study of first editions and of Schubert and other composers. After the *Anschluss* he took refuge in England and settled at Cambridge, but returned to Vienna in 1954. His pubs. include the complete Schubert, Handel and Mozart documents, a thematic catalogue of Schubert's works (1951), listing them in chronological order prefixed by 'D', a study of Mozart editions (with C B Oldman), Leopold Mozart's later letters (with B Paumgartner), the Harrow Replicas of various pubs., etc.

Deutsches Requiem (Brahms.) ◊German Requiem.

Deutsche Tänze German = 'German dances'; not an equivalent of the Allemande, but a type of country dance in 3–4 (slow waltz) time, cultivated by Mozart, Beethoven, Schubert and others. The adj. 'Deutsche' was frequently used alone in titles.

Deux Journées, Les, *The Two Days*: better known as *The Water-Carrier*, opera by Cherubini (libretto by J N Bouilly), produced Paris, Théâtre Feydeau, 16 Jan 1800. Fugitive Armand and his wife Constance are helped by water-seller Mikéli. After several incidents Armand must reveal his identity to save Constance, but at that moment news arrives that the ban against the couple has been lifted.

development ◊working-out.

Devienne, François (b Joinville, Haute-Marne, 31 Jan 1759; d Paris, 5 Sept 1803), French flautist, bassoonist, teacher and composer. After study with members of his family, he played the flute and bassoon in various opera orchestras in Paris, from 1779. His wind concertos were performed from 1780, notably at the *Loge Olympique* and Concert Spirituel concerts. The first of his opéras-comiques, *Le mariage clandestin*, was produced at the Theâtre Feydeau in 1790; other works in the genre were *Les visitandines* (1792), *Agnès et Félix* (1795) and *Le valet de deux maîtres* (1799). The Revolutionary opera *Le congrés des rois* was produced at the Opéra-Comique in 1794. An influential method for the one-key flute was pub. in 1794, and the following year he was appointed professor of flute at the newly-founded Paris Conservatory. Devienne died in the mental asylum at Charenton.

Devil and Kate, The, *Cĕrt a Káča*, opera by Dvořák (libretto by A Wenig), produced Prague, Czech Theatre, 23 Nov 1899. Kate is carried off to hell after announcing that she would dance even with the Devil, but her tongue gets her thrown out.

Devils of Loudun, The, *Diably z Loudun*, opera by Penderecki (libretto by composer after John Whiting's play *The Devils*, based on a narrative by Aldous Huxley which describes a case of diabolic possession in a 17th-c. convent of Ursuline nuns; Father Grandier is accused of bewitching them), performed Hamburg, 20 Jun 1969.

The angels were all singing out of tune,/And hoarse with having little else to do.
Lord Byron, *The Vision of Judgement*, 1822

Devil's Opera, The opera by Macfarren (libretto by G Macfarren, the composer's father, a satire on the diabolic elements in works like Weber's *Freischütz*, Meyerbeer's *Robert le Diable*, Marschner's *Vampyr*, etc.), produced London, Lyceum Theatre, 10 Sept 1838.

Devil's Trill (Tartini.) ◊Trillo del Diavolo.

Devil's Wall, *Certova stena*, opera by Smetana (libretto by E Krasno-horska), produced Prague, Czech Theatre, 29 Jan 1882. Smetana's last completed opera. Javek searches for a wife for Vok, but Beneš wants him to stay single and thereby receive Vok's inheritance. The Devil, in league with Beneš, tries to drown Vok in a monastery but the beautiful Hedvika warns Vok. Beneš repents, and Vok marries Hedvika.

Devin du village, Le, *The Village Soothsayer*, opera by Rousseau (libretto by composer), produced Fontainebleau, at court, 18 Oct 1752, with overture and recitatives by Pierre de Jélyotte (1713–87) and Francœur; Paris, Opéra, 1 Mar 1753, with music all by Rousseau. Soothsayer unites discordant couple, Colin and Colette.

Devisenarie German = 'device aria'; a type of aria of the 17th and 18th c. in which the first word or words occur separately in the voice-part, as though the singer were announcing a title, before the first line of the text or more is sung continuously, often after a further instrumental passage.

de Vito, Gioconda (b Martina Franca, 26 Jul 1907; d Rome, 24 Oct 1994), Italian-born British violinist. Studied in Rome and won international competition at Vienna, 1932. Played in public from 1925 and appeared with LSO 1947, with many concerts throughout Europe, Australia and Argentina. Appeared also at the Edinburgh Festival. Gave stylish accounts of the standard repertory and retired 1961. Major recordings issued 1990 as *The Art of Gioconda de Vito*.

Devlin, Michael (b Chicago, 27 Nov 1942), American bass-baritone. Opera debut as Spalanzi in *Hoffmann* at New Orleans, 1963. Sang with NY City Opera 1966–78, debut in Ginastera's *Don Rodrigo*. UK debut at Glyndebourne 1974, as Mozart's Count; London CG from 1977 (Don Giovanni). NY Met. debut 1978, as Escamillo, followed by the *Hoffmann* villains. Santa Fe from 1972, in Reimann's *Melusine* and in Strauss's *Aegyptische Helena* and *Friedenstag*.

de Vol, Luana (b St Bruno, San Francisco, 30 Nov 1942), American soprano. Studied in San Diego and London. Debut San Francisco 1983, as Ariadne. European debut Stuttgart 1983, as Leonore. Berlin, Staatsoper and Detsche Oper from 1986, as Weber's Euryanthe, Agathe, Rezia and Senta. Sang Isolde at St Gallen 1990, Empress in *Die Frau ohne Schatten* at Munich, 1993. One of the most promising dramatic sopranos of her generation.

Devrient, Eduard (Philipp) (b Berlin, 11 Aug 1801; d Karlsruhe, 4 Oct 1877), German baritone and actor. A close friend of Mendelssohn, to whom he devoted a volume of memoirs, and librettist of Marschner's *Hans Heiling* and other operas. He sang in operas by Gluck, Mozart, Spohr and Marschner; on 11 Mar 1829 he was Christus in the historic performance of the *St Matthew Passion* in Berlin, under Mendelssohn.

Dew, John (b Santiago de Cuba, 1 Jun 1944), British stage director. Studied with Felsenstein and Wieland Wagner and directed Mozart and Wagner cycles at Krefeld. Head of production at Bielefeld from 1981, with challenging work on 20th-c. operas: Schreker's *Irrelohe*, Hindemith's *Neues vom Tage* and Brand's *Maschinist Hopkins*. Directed the premiere of Neikrug's *Alamos* at Berlin (Deutsche Oper) 1988, and his updated *Huguenots* was seen at CG 1991. Vienna Staatsoper, 1994, *I Puritani*. Staged the premiere of Schnittke's *Historia von Dr Johann Fausten*, Hamburg 1995.

Diabelli, Anton (b Mattsee near Salzburg, 5 Sept 1781; d Vienna, 8 Apr 1858), Austrian publisher and composer. Educated for the priesthood, but studied music with M Haydn. Went to Vienna as piano and guitar teacher and joined Peter Cappi in his pub. firm in 1818; it became Diabelli & Co in 1824.

Works include operetta *Adam in der Klemme* (Vienna, 1809); Masses; many piano pieces, including the little waltz on which Beethoven wrote the 33 variations op. 120, etc.

'Diabelli' Variations ◊Diabelli and ◊Vaterländischer Künstlerverein.

Diable dans le beffroi, Le, *The Devil in the Belfry*, opera by Debussy (libretto by himself, based on Edgar Allan Poe's story), worked at in 1903 but not completed.

diabolus in musica Latin = 'the devil in music'; a medieval warning against the use of the tritone – the interval of the augmented fourth (e.g. C–F♯ or F–B), which was looked at askance as a melodic progression.

Diaghilev, Sergey Pavlovich (b Government of Novgorod, 31 Mar 1872; d Venice, 19 Aug 1929), Russian impresario. Studied law and music at St Petersburg, founded an art review there in 1899, produced Russian music in Paris from 1907 and in 1909 organized the Russian Ballet there, which first visited London in 1911. He encouraged many composers to write for his company, including Stravinsky, Ravel, Debussy, Prokofiev, R Strauss, de Falla, Poulenc, Milhaud, etc. and was thus directly responsible for some of the most important music of the 20th c. Works written for him by Stravinsky include *The Firebird* (1910), *Petrushka* (1911), *The Rite of Spring* (1913), *Pulcinella* (1920), *Les Noces* (1923) and *Oedipus Rex* (1927).

Dialogues des Carmélites, Les opera by Poulenc (libretto by G Bernanos), produced Milan (La Scala), 26 Jan 1957. During the French Revolution the sisters of the Carmelite order are condemned to death. The opera follows the contrasting Blanche and Constance, who meet the same fate.

Diamond, David (Leo) (b Rochester, New York, 9 Jul 1915), American composer of Austrian descent. Studied at the Eastman School of Music at Rochester and later at Fontainebleau with Nadia Boulanger. After his return to America he was awarded several composition prizes. Juilliard School from 1973.

Works include 11 symphonies (1941–89), sinfonietta, serenade, variations, *Psalm*, *Elegy in Memory of Ravel* and ballet suite *Tom* for orchestra; concerto and *Rounds* for string orchestra (1944); violin concerto (1936–67), *Hommage à Satie* and ballade for chamber orchestra, concertos for piano, cello and violin (2) with chamber orchestra; *A Night Litany* (Ezra Pound) for chorus and three madrigals for unaccompanied chorus (James Joyce) *Choral Symphony: To Music* (1967); *A Secular Cantata* (1976); ten string quartets (1943–76), string trio; sonatina for violin and piano, cello and piano sonata, partita for bassoon and piano; sonata and sonatina for piano; 52 preludes and fugues for piano.

diapason from Greek = 'through all' [the notes], hence 'interval of an octave'; French = 'a tuning-fork' and hence 'pitch'

the normal modern English use of the term designates the foundation stops of the organ which produce the instrument's most distinctive and characteristic tone. There are two kinds of diapason pipes: open and stopped, which may appear in 4-ft, 8-ft, and 16-ft sizes. The open diapason is often called 'principal' on English organs.

diapente, Greek, the interval of the fifth. In old music canons at the fifth were called epidiapente when answered in the fifth above and subdiapente when answered below.

diaphony, or Latin *diaphonia*, in Latin 'dissonance', as distinct from *symphonia* = 'consonance'. Also the name given by some medieval theorists to early ◊organum.

Diary of one who disappeared, *Zápisník zmizelého*, cycle of 22 songs by Janáček for tenor, mezzo, three women's voices and piano; composed 1917–21, performed Brno, 18 Apr 1921.

diastole from Greek = 'distinction, differentiation'; an old term, in use to the middle of the 18th c., for the divisions of music into sections or phrases.

diatonic the diatonic scale is, in a major key, one involving no accidentals (illustration). In a minor key the diatonic scale has three forms, (*a*) melodic, (*b*) harmonic, and (*c*) the less frequently used natural minor. Diatonic harmony is the opposite of chromatic harmony, using the notes proper to the prescribed major or minor scale only, without

Major

Minor (melodic)

Minor (Harmonic)

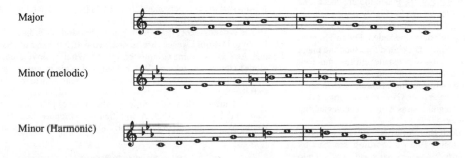

Three commonly used diatonic scales.

deviations to those marked with additional accidentals. Diatonic discords are those that occur in diatonic harmony.

Diaz, Justino (b San Juan, 29 Jan 1939), Puerto Rican bass. NY Met. debut 1963, as Monterone; created Barber's Antony in 1966 and in the same year sang Escamillo at Salzburg, under Karajan. He sang Mahometo II in Rossini's *Assedio di Corinto* at La Scala in 1969. Among his other roles are Attila, Don Giovanni and Procida. CG debut 1976, Escamillo. He sang Iago in the 1986 film version of *Otello*, directed by Zeffirelli. Sang Franchetti's Cristoforo Colombo for Greater Miami Opera, 1992.

Dibdin, Charles (b Southampton, bap. 15 Mar 1745; d London, 25 Jul 1814), English singer, author and composer. Chorister at Winchester Cathedral, went to London at the age of 15. Made his stage debut in 1762, and shortly afterwards was engaged as a singing actor at CG, where his pastoral *The Shepherd's Artifice* was produced in 1764. Over 100 dramatic works followed. In 1778 appointed composer to Covent Garden Theatre, and during the 1780s dabbled in theatrical management with variable success. A projected journey to India came to nothing, but the fundraising travels which were to have financed it provided material for his *Musical Tour* (1788). In 1789 he began his series of 'Table Entertainments', in which he was author, composer, narrator, singer and accompanist. One of the most successful, *The Oddities*, contained the song *Tom Bowling*. Many other sea-songs achieved great popularity. Towards the end of his life a publishing venture made him bankrupt, and he was saved from destitution by a public subscription. He also wrote an account of his professional life and other literary works.

Works include over 100 dramatic pieces, e.g. *Lionel and Clarissa* (1768), *The Padlock, The Ephesian Matron, The Captive, The Ladle* (1773), *The Trip to Portsmouth, The Seraglio* (1776), *Rose and Colin, The Touchstone, The Milkmaid, Tom Thumb, Harvest Home* (1787); over 30 'Table Entertainments' containing innumerable songs.

Dichter, Mischa (b Shanghai, 27 Sept 1945), Chinese-born American pianist of Polish parentage. He was brought up in LA and studied at Juilliard. Silver medal at the 1966 Tchaikovsky Competition; US debut with Boston SO, same year. London debut 1967, with the New Philharmonia. He has often visited Russia and is well known for his poetic interpretations of Chopin, Brahms and Beethoven.

Dichterliebe, *Poet's Love*, song cycle by Schumann, op. 48 (16 poems by Heine), composed 1840.

Dickie, Murray (b Bishopton, Renfrewshire, 3 Apr 1924; d Cape Town, 19 June 1995), Scottish tenor. Debut London 1947, Almaviva. At CG he sang in the fp of Bliss's *Olympians* (1949). Glyndebourne 1950–54, as Pedrillo and Sellem and in the British fp of Busoni's *Arlecchino*. In 1951 he joined the Vienna Staatsoper (buffo roles, and the fp of Martin's *The Tempest*). NY Met. 1962, David and Ottavio. He produced *Eine Nacht in Venedig* London Coliseum 1976.

His son, John Murray (b London, 1953) has sung widely on the Continent in operas by Mozart, Donizetti and Tchaikovsky.

Dickinson, Peter (b Lytham St Annes, 15 Nov 1934), English composer and teacher. He studied at Cambridge and at the Juilliard School, NY; met Cage and Varèse in USA, other influences have been Satie and Stravinsky. Professor at Keele University 1974–84.

Works include *Vitalitas*, ballet (1959), music-theatre piece *The Judas Tree* (1965); *Monologue* for strings (1959), *Transformations, Homage to Satie* for orchestra (1970); piano concerto (1978–84); violin concerto (1986); settings of poems by Auden, Dylan Thomas, Alan Porter, e.e. cummings and Emily Dickinson for voice and piano (1956–71); *Mass of the Apocalypse* for female chorus and four percussion (1984); two string quartets; piano and organ music.

Dido, **Königin von Carthago** opera by Graupner (libretto by Heinrich Hinsch), produced Hamburg, Theater beim Gänsemarkt, spring 1707. Dido is pursued by Numidian King Iarbas, as Aeneas receives sailing orders from Mercury and Venus.

Dido and Aeneas opera by Purcell (libretto by N Tate, after Virgil), produced Chelsea, London, Josias Priest's boarding school ('by young gentlewomen'), Dec 1689. Aeneas sails off while Dido laments.

Didon, *Dido*, opera by Piccinni (libretto by Marmontel), produced Fontainebleau, at court, 16 Oct 1783, first Paris performance, Opéra, 1 Dec 1783.

Didone abbandonata, *Dido Forsaken*, libretto by Metastasio:

Opera by Hasse, produced Hubertusburg, near Dresden, 7 Oct 1742. Further settings by Jommelli (1747) and Traetta (1757).

Didone, La, *Dido*, opera by Cavalli (libretto by G Busenello), produced Venice, Teatro San Cassiano, Carnival 1641. Dido accepts love of Iarbas, as Aeneas departs for Italy.

Didur, Adam (b Wola Sekowa, near Sanok, 24 Dec 1874; d Katowice, 7 Jan 1946), Polish bass. After study in Lwów he made his debut at Rio in 1894, Warsaw Opera 1899–1903. He sang Colline and Leporello at CG in 1905. NY Met. 1908–33; sang in the fps of *La Fanciulla del West* and *Königskinder*, and was the first NY Boris, Gremin and Konchak. Returned to Poland in 1933 and taught at Katowice after the war.

Dienstag aus Licht, *Tuesday from Light*, opera in two acts by Stockhausen, the fourth of a projected seven (libretto by composer), fp Lisbon, 10 May 1992. The day named after Mars depicts philosophical and martial battles between Michael and Lucifer.

Diepenbrock, Alphons (b Amsterdam, 2 Sept 1862; d Amsterdam, 5 Apr 1921), Dutch composer. At first a philologist, self-taught in music.

Works include incidental music for Aristophanes' *The Birds*, Sophocles' *Electra* (1920), Goethe's *Faust*, Vondel's *Gysbrecht van Amstel*; *Stabat Mater*, Te Deum for solo voices, chorus and orchestra, Mass; songs with orchestra; chamber music; songs.

The only perfect English opera ever written.

Gustav Holst, on Purcell's *Dido and Aeneas*, *The Heritage of Music*, 1928

Dieren, Bernard van (b Rotterdam, 27 Dec 1887; d London, 24 Apr 1936), Dutch (anglicized) composer. Educated for science, he had little musical experience, apart from violin playing, before the age of 20, when he began to compose. In 1909 he settled in London as correspondent to foreign papers, after making serious music studies, which he continued in Germany in 1912, when his real creative career began. He also produced a book on the sculptor Epstein and a volume of musical essays, *Down among the Dead Men*.

Works include opera *The Tailor* (R Nichols, 1917); symphony on Chinese poems for solo voices, chorus and orchestra; *Les Propous des beuveurs* (Rabelais) for chorus and orchestra; *Beatrice Cenci*, orchestral epilogue to Shelley's drama (1909), overture *Anjou*; serenade for small orchestra, overture for chamber orchestra; *Diafonia* for 17 instruments and baritone (Shakespeare sonnets, 1916), *Fayre eies* (Spenser) for baritone and chamber orchestra; six string quartets

THE OPERA

Dido and Aeneas

A three-act tragic opera by Henry Purcell, first seen in public in 1700. It is set in Carthage, just after the Trojan War.

I. Dido (soprano) is persuaded by Belinda (soprano) and the court to declare her love for Aeneas (tenor).

II. The Witches meet to plot the defeat of Dido and of Carthage. Out hunting, Dido and Aeneas are entertained with a masque of Diana and Acteon. A storm summoned by the Witches drive Aeneas alone to their cave, where a Witch disguised as the messenger god Mercury (mezzo-soprano) reminds Aeneas of his duty to travel on to Italy.

III. As Aeneas makes ready to leave, the Witches plan to sink his ships and destroy Carthage. A dignified Dido prepares herself for death ('When I am laid in earth') and Cupids hover from the clouds to scatter roses on her tomb.

THE OPERA

(1912–28); three unaccompanied choruses; sonata and three studies for unaccompanied violin, etc.

Dièse (or ***Dièze***) French = sharp; the sign ♯.

Dies irae, *Day of wrath*, the sequence from the Mass for the Dead originally associated with a distinct plainsong theme which has been frequently used or quoted by various composers, e.g.:

Bantock, Witches' Dance in incidental music to *Macbeth*.

Berlioz, Witches' Sabbath in *Fantastic Symphony*, and Requiem.

Dallapiccola, *Canti di prigionia*.

Davies (Maxwell), *St Michael*.

Liszt, *Totentanz* for piano and orchestra.

Miaskovsky, symphony No. 6.

Rakhmaninov, Rhapsody on a Theme by Paganini for piano and orchestra and Symphonic Dances, op. 45.

Respighi, *Impressioni brasiliane*.

Saint-Saëns, *Danse macabre* for orchestra.

Stevenson (Ronald), *Passacaglia on DSCH*.

Tchaikovsky, Theme and Variations in Suite No. 3 for orchestra and song *In Dark Hell*.

Vaughan Williams, *Five Tudor Portraits* for chorus and orchestra (lament for Philip Sparrow).

A recent theory claims the Dies Irae as the 'hidden' theme of Elgar's 'Enigma' Variations.

diesis, Greek, in ancient Greece, either the interval between a fourth and two 'major' tones or a quarter-tone. In modern acoustics (*a*) the great diesis is the difference between four minor thirds and an octave; (*b*) the enharmonic diesis is the difference between an octave and three major thirds.

Dietrich, Albert (Hermann) (b Golk near Meissen, 28 Aug 1829; d Berlin, 20 Nov 1908), German composer and conductor. Court music director at Oldenburg from 1861. Wrote a violin and piano sonata jointly with Schumann and Brahms, 1853.

Works include opera *Robin Hood* (1879); incidental music to Shakespeare's *Cymbeline* (performed London, 1896); symphony in D minor; choral and orchestral works; horn concertos; chamber music.

All the worst things happen in the best works, and the worst music appears to be streaked all through with the most luscious bits.

Bernard van Dieren,
Down Among the Dead Men, 1935

Dietrich, Sixt (b Augsburg, *c* 1491; d St Gall, 21 Oct 1548), German composer. Studied at the Universities of Freiburg i/B and Wittenberg, holding appointments at Strasbourg and Konstanz between. Wrote Magnificats, antiphons and other vocal music.

Dietsch, (Pierre-)Louis(-Philippe) (b Dijon, 17 Mar 1808; d Paris, 20 Feb 1865), French conductor and composer. He composed an unsuccessful opera to the original French libretto of Wagner's *Flying Dutchman, Le Vaisseau fantôme*, produced at the Paris Opéra in 1842. Conducted the disastrous performance of Wagner's *Tannhäuser* in 1861. Works include church and organ music.

Dieupart, Charles (b France; d London, *c* 1740), French violinist, harpsichordist and composer. Settled in London *c* 1700 and was involved in the promotion of Italian opera at Drury Lane. Later abandoned opera, gave concerts and taught the harpsichord. Wrote suites, etc., for harpsichord.

Dillon, James (b Glasgow, 29 Oct 1950), Scottish composer. Studied in London; his music has had Renaissance and non-Western influences and is densely composed. Works featured at Bath, Darmstadt, Warsaw and Paris festivals.

Works include *Babble* for 40 voices (1976), *Cumha* for 12 strings (1978), *Once Upon a Time* for 12 instruments (1980), *Spleen* for piano (1980), *Come Live With Me* for mezzo and four instruments (1981), string quartet (1983), *Le Rivage* for wind quintet (1984), *Windows and Canopies* (1985), *Helle Nacht* for orchestra (1987),

Shrouded Mirrors (1988), *Blitzschlag* (1991), string quartet no.2 (1991), *Viriditas* (1993).

diminished said of intervals normally 'perfect' (fourths, fifth, octaves) or 'minor' (seconds, thirds, sixths, sevenths) which have been made a semitone narrower.

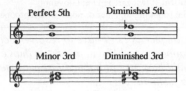

Perfect and diminished intervals.

diminished seventh chord a chord of three superimposed minor thirds.

The example illustrates two of the three possible diminished 7th chords.

diminuendo Italian = 'waning, lessening'; a direction to decrease the sound of a note, chord or phrase, synonymous with *decrescendo* and now more frequently used.

diminution a shortening of a musical figure or phrase by its reduction to smaller note-values.

Dimitrij opera by Dvořák (libretto by M Červinková-Riegerová), produced Prague, Czech Theatre, 8 Oct 1882. The subject is the 'false Dimitri', the pretender who also figures in Mussorgsky's *Boris Godunov*. Having assumed the throne, Tsar Dmitrij marries Marina and then falls in love with Xenie. Jealous, Marina reveals that Dmitrij is in fact the son of a peasant. The opera ends when Prince Šujský shoots him.

Dimitrova, Ghena (b Beglej, 6 May 1941), Bulgarian soprano. Debut at Sofia, 1966, as Abigaille; sang with Bulgarian National Opera until 1970, then in Italy (1975) and at Vienna from 1978. US debut Dallas 1981 as Elvira in *Ernani*, NY Met. 1988 (Turandot). Sang Lady Macbeth at the 1984 Salzburg Festival and made CG debut in the same year (Turandot). Other roles include Aida (Luxor, 1987), Norma (Houston, 1987), and Leonora in *Il Trovatore*.

Di Murska, Ilma (b Zagreb, 4 Jan 1836; d Munich, 14 Jan 1889), Croatian soprano. Debut Florence 1862, as Martha; appeared widely on the continent and sang Lucia, in London in 1865. At Drury Lane in 1870 she was Senta in *Der fliegende Holländer*, the first Wagner production in Britain. Other roles included Amina, Constanze and the Queen of Night.

Dinorah (Meyerbeer.) ◊Pardon de Ploërmel.

Dioclesian (Purcell.) ◊Prophetess.

direct a sign used in plainsong notation and often in early music in staff notation, indicating at the end of the stave the position of the first note at the beginning of the following one.

dirge a funeral composition, usually vocal, performed at a burial or more rarely on a memorial occasion. The word derives from the Latin *Dirige Domine*, the opening words of an antiphon from the Office for the Dead.

Diruta, Agostino (b Perugia; d Rome), Italian 16th-17th-c. organist and composer. Organist at Venice, 1617, Asolo, 1620–22, and Rome, 1630–47.

Works include Masses, motets, psalms, *Sacrae cantiones*, canticles and other vocal music.

Diruta (real name ***Mancini***), Girolamo (b Deruta near Perugia, *c* 1554; d after 1610), Italian Franciscan monk, organist and composer, uncle and master of Agostino ◊Diruta. Pupil of Zarlino, Porta and Merulo. Organist at Chioggia and Gubbio Cathedrals. He was a famous player and wrote a treatise on organ playing, *Il Transilvano*, dedicated to the Prince of Transylvania, Sigismund Bathori. Wrote organ music.

discord the opposite of concord: the sounding together of notes that, according to traditional rules of harmony, do not satisfy the ear as being final in themselves and require a following chord to give the impression of resolution.

disjunct motion ◊motion.

Dissoluto punito, Il (Mozart.) ◊Don Giovanni.

dissonance the sounding together of notes which produces discord.

Every dissonance doesn't have to resolve itself if it doesn't happen to feel like it, any more than every horse should have its tail bobbed just because it's the prevailing fashion.

Charles Ives, quoted in Wooldridge, *Charles Ives*, 1974

Dissonance Quartet string quartet no. 19 in C, K465 by Mozart, composed 1785. The dissonant introduction to the first movement gives the work its name.

Di Stefano, Giuseppe (b near Catania, 24 Jul 1921), Italian tenor. Milan, La Scala from 1947. NY Met. 1948–65, debut as Duke of Mantua. Edinburgh 1957 as Nemorino; CG 1961, as Cavaradossi. Sang in Italian repertory; also Faust, Nadir, Massenet's Des Grieux and Don José. Made an ill-advised concert tour with Callas 1973–74. In his prime, noted for his discretion and vocal elegance.

Distler, Hugo (b Nuremberg, 24 Jun 1908; d Berlin, 1 Nov 1942), German organist and composer. Studied at Leipzig, became organist and cantor at Lübeck in 1921 and professor of composition at the Stuttgart Conservatory in 1937. He committed suicide.

Works include 52 motets entitled *Jahrkreis*, a Passion, oratorio *Nativity*; organ works; harpsichord concerto.

Distratto, Il nickname of Haydn's symphony no. 60 in C major, so called on account of its being an adaptation of the incidental music to *Der Zerstreute* (1775), a German version of Regnard's *Le Distrait*.

dital harp ◊harp lute.

Dittersdorf, Karl Ditters von (originally simply Karl Ditters) (b Vienna, 2 Nov 1739; d Neuhof, Pilgram, Bohemia, 24 Oct 1799), Austrian composer and violinist. Educated in the household of Prince Hildburghausen in Vienna, studied composition with Bonno. Played in the orchestra of the Imperial Opera in Vienna, 1761–63, when he travelled to Italy with Gluck, winning great success as a violinist. In 1765 succeeded Michael Haydn as *Kapellmeister* to the Bishop of Grosswardein, and from 1769 to 1795 served the Prince Bishop of Breslau in the same capacity. But much of his time was spent in Vienna, where his most popular opera, *Doktor und Apotheker*, was produced in 1786. He was ennobled in 1773, henceforth calling himself von Dittersdorf. Kelly's *Reminiscences* contain an account of Dittersdorf playing string quartets with Haydn, Mozart and Vanhal. During his last years he was in the service of Baron Stillfried at Rothlhotta. His autobiography, dictated shortly before his death, was pub. in 1801.

Works include over 40 operas, e.g. *Amore in musica*, *Betrug durch Aberglauben*, *Doktor und Apotheker* (1786), *Hieronimus Knicker* (1789), *Das rothe Kaeppchen*, *Die Hochzeit des Figaro* (after Beaumarchais), etc.; oratorios *Isacco* (1766), *Davidde Penitente* (1771), *Esther*, *Giobbe* (1786); Masses and other church music; over 100 symphonies, including 21 on Ovid's *Metamorphoses*; concertos; divertimenti, chamber music.

Diversions work by Britten for piano, left hand, and orchestra; composed 1940, revised 1954, fp Philadelphia, 16 Jan 1942, Paul Wittgenstein soloist.

divertimento a work for instrumental ensemble in several movements akin to the suite and predominantly light-hearted in character.

divertissement mainly a term connected with ballet, where it means a set of varied dances with no particular plot. In music a suite, particularly of arrangements or pieces based on familiar tunes, an entertaining piece of any kind or a fantasy of a lighter sort, such as Schubert's *Divertissement à la hongroise*. In 18th-c. French usage a dance

interlude, with or without songs, in a play or opera; also sometimes a short play with dances and songs.

Divine Poem, The title of symphony no. 3 in C minor, op. 43 by Skriabin, fp Paris, 29 May 1905, conductor Nikisch. The work's three movements, titled 'Struggles', 'Delights' and 'Divine Play', reflect Skriabin's mystic beliefs.

divisi Italian = 'divided'; a direction found in orchestral scores where string parts are intended to be distributed in such a way as to play in two or more parts within a single group of instruments which would normally play in unison.

divisions a term used in 17th-c. England for variations. It became current because variations then usually consisted of breaking up the melody of the theme into notes of smaller value.

division viol a bass ◊viol of moderate size on which divisions were often played in the 17th c. Simpson, for example, wrote for it.

Dixon, (Charles) Dean (b New York, 10 Jan 1915; d Zug, 4 Nov 1976), American conductor who overcame prejudice to win fame. Studied in NY and made debut there at Town Hall, 1938. Guested with major orchestras, and founded American Youth Orchestra (1944) but was unable to gain a permanent post owing to racism. Music director Gothenburg SO 1953–60, Hesse Radio SO at Frankfurt 1961–74. UK debut with the BBC SO 1963 and led the Sydney SO from 1964. Returned to conduct in the USA from 1970.

Djamileh opera by Bizet (libretto by L Gallet, based on Musset's *Namouna*), produced Paris, Opéra-Comique, 22 May 1872. Haroun changes his mistress every month, but Djamileh, who has fallen in love with him, returns in disguise, winning his heart.

Djinns, Les, *The Genii*, symphonic poem by Franck for piano and orchestra, based on verses from Hugo's *Les Orientales*, composed 1884; fp Paris, 15 Mar 1885.

do the old name for the note C (◊solmization), still used in Latin countries. In Tonic Sol-fa notation the tonic note in any key, represented by the symbol d, pronounced doh.

Dobbs, Mattiwilda (b Atlanta, 11 Jul 1925), American soprano. She studied with Lotte Lehmann and Pierre Bernac. Concert career from 1947; stage debut 1952, with Netherlands Opera. Glyndebourne 1953–61 as Zerbinetta, Constanze and the Queen of Night. CG 1954 as the Queen of Shemakha. NY Met. debut 1956, as Gilda. She sang at Stockholm 1957–73. A secure coloratura technique.

Dobroven, Issay Alexandrovich (b Nizhny-Novgorod, 27 Feb 1891; d Oslo 9 Dec 1953), Russian conductor and composer. Studied with Taneiev and others at the Moscow Conservatory and later took a piano course with Godowsky in Vienna. He became professor at the Moscow Conservatory in 1917 and conductor of the Opera in 1919. Later he conducted Russian opera on tour in Germany and in 1927–28 he was conductor of the Bulgarian State Opera at Sofia. In the 1930s he conducted extensively in the USA and Palestine.

Works include opera *A Thousand and One Nights* (performed Moscow, 1922); incidental music to Verhaeren's *Philip II*; piano concerto, violin concerto; sonata and *Fairy Tales* for violin and piano; sonatas, studies and pieces for piano; songs.

dodecaphony, dodecaphonic, composition making equal use of all twelve notes of the chromatic octave. Normally this term is used only in reference to twelve-note serialism, ◊twelve-note music.

Dodge, Charles (b Ames, IA, 5 Jun 1942), American composer. Studied with Schuller and Luening; computer music at Princeton. Teacher at Brooklyn College from 1980, specialising in electronic music. Music performed at Tanglewood, Warsaw and Stockholm festivals and by the NY and LA POs.

Works include *Changes* (1970), *Earth's Magnetic Field* (1970), *Extensions* (1973), *Palinode* with orchestra (1976), *The Waves* with soprano (1984), *Song Without Words* (1986), *The Voice of Binky* (1989).

Dodgson, Stephen (b London, 17 Mar 1924), English composer and broadcaster. He studied at the RCM; taught there since 1964. Best known for his guitar concertos, he has also written for the clavichord and harpsichord. Other works include piano quartet, Symphony for wind (1974), *Epigrams from a Garden* for mezzo and clarinets

(1977), concertos for bassoon (1969), clarinet (1983) and trombone (1986); string quartet (1986); songs.

Doese, Helena (b Götenburg, 13 Aug 1946), Swedish soprano. Debut Götenburg 1971, as Aida. Berne 1972–75, as Jenůfa, Micaela and Donna Anna. Royal Opera Stockholm from 1975, as Katya Kabanova and Eva. Glyndebourne from 1974, as Mozart's Countess and Fiordiligi. At CG she has been admired since 1974 as Mimi, Gutrune, Agathe and Amelia Boccanegra. US debut San Francisco, 1982. Other roles include Ariadne, the Marschallin, and Elisabeth de Valois. Sang Ariadne at Stuttgart, 1992.

doh the name for the tonic note in any key in Tonic Sol-fa, so pronounced, but in notation represented by the symbol *d*.

Dohnányi, Christoph von (b Berlin, 8 Sept 1929), German-born conductor, grandson of Ernö Dohnányi. He studied in Munich, Florida, and at Tanglewood; held opera posts in Frankfurt, Lübeck and Kassel, 1952–66, and was chief conductor Cologne Radio SO 1964–70. Hamburg Opera 1977–84, music director Cleveland Orchestra from 1984. London debut 1965, with the LPO, and has conducted *Salome* and *Wozzeck* at CG. He gave the fps of Henze's *Der junge Lord* (Berlin, 1965) and *The Bassarids* (Salzburg, 1966); with his wife, the soprano Anja Silja, has given frequent performances of Schoenberg and Berg. New production of the *Ring* at Vienna Staatsoper, 1992–93.

Dohnányi, Ernö (or Ernst von) (b Pozsony = Pressburg, 27 Jul 1877; d New York, 9 Feb 1960), Hungarian pianist and composer. Studied under Carl Forstner, the cathedral organist at his native town, until 1893, when he went to the Hungarian Academy at Budapest, where he studied piano under Stephan Thomán and composition under Koessler. In 1897 he had some lessons from d'Albert and appeared as pianist in Berlin and Vienna. He visited England in 1898 and the USA in 1899, made many tours later, but eventually became better known as a composer. From 1908 to 1915 he was professor of piano at the Hochschule in Berlin and in 1919 became conductor of the Budapest PO and director of the city's conservatory. As a pianist his powers were prodigious, while as a composer he drew upon the classical German tradition, especially Brahms.

Works include operas *Aunt Simona* (Dresden, 1913), *The Tower of Voivod* (Budapest, 1922) and *The Tenor* (1929); ballet *Pierrette's Veil*; symphonies in F minor, D minor and E major, suite in F♯ minor and *Suite en valse* for orchestra; two piano concertos and *Variations on a Nursery Song* for piano and orchestra (1913); two violin concertos, *Concertstück* for cello and orchestra; three string quartets, piano quintet, sextet for violin, viola, cello, clarinet, horn and piano, serenade for string trio; sonatas for violin and piano and cello and piano; 12 op. nos. of piano music, including a passacaglia, four rhapsodies, *Humoresques in form of a Suite*, *Ruralia hungarica*; songs.

Doktor, Paul (b Vienna, 28 Mar 1919; d New York, 21 Jun 1989), American violist. Was a soloist with the Lucerne Orchestra 1939–47 and made US debut 1948. Toured widely and taught at Juilliard from 1971. Premiered concertos by Walter Piston and Quincy Porter.

Doktor Faust opera by Busoni (libretto by composer) based on the Faust legend and Marlowe's *Dr Faustus* (1589); not based on Goethe. Left unfinished at Busoni's death and completed by Jarnach: produced Dresden, 21 May 1925. First produced in Britain, London, Coliseum, 25 Apr 1986; given in a new edition by Antony Beaumont, first heard at Bologna 1985, in which the dying Faust transfers his soul to the corpse of a child.

dolce Italian = 'sweet'; a direction indicating a suave and ingratiating performance, usually but not necessarily in a soft tone.

dolcian an early form of ◊bassoon.

Doles, Johann Friedrich (b Steinbach, Saxe-Meiningen, 23 Apr 1715; d Leipzig, 8 Feb 1797), German organist and composer. Pupil of Bach at Leipzig from 1739. Cantor of St Thomas's School there from 1756 in succession to Harrer. Performed Bach's motet *Singet dem Herrn* for Mozart, when the latter visited Leipzig in 1789.

Works include Passions, Masses, motets, cantatas and other church music.

Dolly suite of six children's pieces for piano duet by Fauré, op. 56,

Dohnányi *The conductor Christoph von Dohnányi is a grandson of the Hungarian composer ErnöDohnányi. He abandoned his studies in law and turned to music, and has been highly successful in Germany and abroad. He is noted for his technique and control of the orchestra.*

composed in 1893, orchestra for a ballet by Rabaud in 1896; first produced Paris, 23 Jan 1913. It is dedicated to the daughter of Mme Emma Bardac, later Debussy's second wife. As in the case of Debussy's *Children's Corner*, the title and two of the sub-titles seem to suggest some English association: 1. *Berceuse*; 2. *Mi-a-ou*; 3. *Le Jardin de Dolly*; 4. *Kitty-Valse*; 5. *Tendresse*; 6. *Le Pas espagnol*.

Dolmetsch, Arnold (b Le Mans, 24 Feb 1858; d Haslemere, 28 Feb 1940), Swiss (anglicized) musicologist, instrument maker and performer on early instruments. He studied violin under Vieuxtemps at Brussels, but turned his interests to early music and instruments. Worked with the piano firm of Chickering at Boston, 1902–09, and then with that of Gaveau in Paris until 1914, when he went to live in England and set up his own workshop for harpsichords, viols, lutes, recorders, etc. at Haslemere, where he arranged periodical festivals of early music and brought up a family to take part in it with various instruments. He edited early music and wrote a book on interpretation. His second son, Carl, (b Fontenay-sous-Bois, France, 23 Aug 1911), was a well-known recorder player.

Domaine Musical founded by Jean-Louis Barrault, Madeleine Renaud and Pierre Boulez in 1954 to promote concerts of new music, with Boulez as music director. The group had as its headquarters the Petit Marigny theatre.

Domaines work by Boulez for solo clarinet and 21 instruments; 1968, fp Brussels, 20 Dec 1968.

Domaninská, Libuše (b Brno, 4 Jul 1924), Czech soprano. She sang at Brno 1945–55, then joined the Prague National Theatre; visited Edinburgh with the Co. in 1964 and sang Milada in the first British performance of Smetana's *Dalibor*. Her best roles were Janáček's Vixen, Jenůfa and Katya Kabanova. She sang at the Vienna Staatsoper 1958–68.

Domestic Symphony (R Strauss.) ◊Symphonia domestica.

Domgraf-Fassbänder, Willi (b Aachen, 19 Feb 1897; d Nuremberg, 13 Feb 1978), German baritone. He studied in Berlin and Milan. Debut Aachen, 1922; sang in Düsseldorf and Stuttgart before joining the Berlin Staatsoper in 1928; successful there in the production of Egk's *Peer Gynt* which was admired by Hitler. Glyndebourne 1934–37 as Figaro, Guglielmo and Papageno. Father of the mezzo, Brigitte ◊Fassbaender.

dominant (1) the fifth note of the major or minor scale above the tonic

Domingo *Placido Domingo is regarded as the greatest lyric-dramatic tenor of our time. His supreme musicianship and versatility is matched by his dramatic conviction. Possessing an exceptionally wide repertory, Domingo has nevertheless been identified especially as Verdi's Otello.*

or keynote, or the fourth below it. In classical harmony the dominant is the most conspicuous note in the scale apart from the tonic.

(2) the name often given to the reciting note of a psalm-tone or mode. ◊modes

Domingo, Placido (b Madrid, 21 Jan 1941), Spanish tenor. He spent his childhood in Mexico and sang in zarzuelas before opera debut as Alfredo in Monterrey, 1961; US debut same year, as Arturo, to Sutherland's Lucia, in Dallas. Israel National Opera 1962–65; NY, City Opera, Pinkerton, 1965. NY Met. from 1968 and London, CG, from 1971; debut as Cavaradossi. Other roles include Don José, Hoffmann, Dick Johnson, Radames, Otello, Samson and Aeneas in *Les Troyens*. He has sung Wagner's Walther on record and Lohengrin NY and Hamburg. Debut as conductor *Attila*, Barcelona, 1973. Autobiography, *My First 40 Years* (1983). In terms of vocal consistency and range of repertory he is without a serious modern rival. Returned to CG 1987, as Otello. Sang Parsifal at the NY Met. 1991, and Siegmund at Vienna Staatsoper, 1992.

Dominguez, Oralia (b San Luis Potosi, 15 Oct 1928), Mexican contralto. Stage debut Mexico City 1950. She sang Cilea's Princesse de Bouillon at La Scala, in 1953. She was Sosostris in the 1955 fp of *The Midsummer Marriage*, at CG, and in the same year sang Mistress Quickly at Glyndebourne; she returned for Rossini's Isabella (1957) and was Arnalta in the Leppard-Monteverdi *Poppea* of 1962. Deutsche Oper, Düsseldorf, from 1960.

Dom Sébastien, Roi de Portugal, *Dom Sebastian, King of Portugal*, opera by Donizetti (libretto by Scribe), produced Paris, Opéra, 13 Nov 1843. Crusade against the Moors led by King of Portugal Dom Sebastian. Although defeated by the Moors, Sebastian is saved by amorous Zayda. Sebastian returns to Spain to find the throne has been usurped by his uncle, who throws the couple into prison; they are shot when they try to escape.

Donath, Helen (b Corpus Christi, 10 Jul 1940), American soprano. She sang in concert from 1958 and made her stage debut at Cologne in 1963; moved to Munich in 1967 and sang Pamina at Salzburg the same year. In 1971 she sang Sophie at San Francisco and the Bolshoi, Moscow. Among her recordings are *Freischütz*, *Dido and Aeneas*, *Palestrina* and operas by Schubert.

Donato (or *Donati*), Baldassare (b ? Venice, *c* 1530; d Venice, 1603),

Italian organist, singer and composer. Appointed to St Mark's at Venice in 1550, he remained there in various capacities all his life, becoming *maestro di cappella* in succession to Zarlino in 1590. He also taught singing at the seminary attached to St Mark's.

Works include motets, psalms; madrigals, *villanelle, canzoni.*

Donatoni, Franco (b Verona, 9 Jun 1927), Italian composer. He studied in Rome with Pizzetti; has been influenced by him, and has used serial and, more recently, aleatory techniques.

Works include Concerto for bassoon and strings (1952), Divertimento for violin and chamber orchestra (1954), *Black and White*, for 37 strings (1964), *Doubles II* for orchestra (1970), *Portrait* for harpsichord and orchestra (1976); four string quartets (1950–63), *Etwas ruhiger in Ausdruck*, for chamber ensemble (1968; title from no. 2 of Schoenberg's piano pieces op. 23); *Spiri* for string quartet and ensemble (1977), *Tema* for woodwind and strings (1981), *Refrain* for eight instruments (1986), *Flag* for 13 instruments (1987), *Chantal* for flute, clarinet, harp and string quartet (1990). Vocal music includes *The Book with Seven Seals*, oratorio for soloists, chorus and orchestra (1951) and *Serenata* for soprano and 16 instruments (1959; text by Dylan Thomas), and *Arias* for soprano and orchestra (1978).

Don Carlos opera by Verdi in five acts (libretto by F M Méry and C Du Locle, based on Schiller's drama), produced Paris, Opéra, 11 Mar 1867. Verdi's second French opera. Revised in four acts, in Italian, and produced Milan, La Scala, 10 Jan 1884. Don Carlos (heir to the throne) and Elisabeth love each other, but she has been promised to Carlos' father, King Philip. After the marriage, the lovers are discovered; Elisabeth withdraws to a monastery, where Carlos meets her. Philip arrives to hand his son over to the Inquisition, but Carlos is taken into the cloister by his grandfather's ghost.

Dönch, Karl (b Hagen, 8 Jan 1915; d Vienna, 16 Sept 1994), German bass-baritone. Debut Gorlitz 1936. Vienna Staatsoper from 1947; often heard as Beckmesser and sang in the fp of Martin's *Tempest*, 1956. He sang at Salzburg from 1951, as Alfonso and Berg's Doctor, and as Leiokritos in the 1954 fp of Liebermann's *Penelope*. NY Met. 1959–67; guest at Milan.

THE OPERA

Don Carlos

A five-act opera about the problems of royalty by Giuseppe Verdi, produced originally in 1867. The action is set in France and Spain in 1568.

I. At the forest of Fontainebleu, Don Carlos (tenor) and Elisabeth de Valois (soprano) declare their love but her father decides she must marry King Philip of Spain, the father of Carlos.

II. At the monastery of San Juste, Carlos's friend Rodrigo (baritone) persuades him to abandon his love and take up instead the cause of Spanish-occupied Flanders. After Carlos once more declares his love for Elisabeth, the suspicious King Philip (bass) orders Rodrigo to keep guard.

III. Carlos keeps an anonymous assignation but mistakes the veiled Princess Eboli (mezzo-soprano) for Elisabeth. As the jealous Eboli – the king's former mistress – plans revenge, Rodrigo tells Carlos to give him any documents concerning the revolt in Flanders. Carlos and Flemish deputies plead their cause at an auto-da-fé (burning of heretics). Rodrigo saves the king after he orders the arrest of Carlos and his son threatens him.

IV. Philip is persuaded by the Grand Inquisitor (bass) to kill Carlos and hand over Rodrigo for arrest. Confessing to Elisabeth that she was the king's mistress, Eboli vows to enter a convent. Rodrigo is shot in his cell but tells Carlos that Elisabeth will be at San Juste the following day.

V. As Carlos and Elisabeth say farewell to each other, Philip and his men enter to seize them. But the figure of the long-dead Emperor Charles V (bass) appears from his tomb to rescue Carlos.

THE OPERA

Don Chisciotte in Sierra Morena, *Don Quixote in the Sierra Morena*, opera by Conti (libretto by Zeno and P Pariati, based on Cervantes), produced Vienna, 11 Feb 1719.

Don Giovanni, *Don Juan*, Opera by Mozart (first title: *Il dissoluto punito, ossia Il Don Giovanni: The Rake Punished, or Don Juan*) (libretto by Lorenzo da Ponte), produced Prague, 29 Oct 1787. In Vienna, with additions, Burgtheater, 7 May 1788. Dangerous Don has a catalogue of conquests, but he can't convince the Commendatore, murdered father of Donna Anna, who returns to drag him down to Hell.

Don Giovanni Tenorio, ossia Il convitato di pietra, *Don Juan Tenorio, or The Stone Guest*, opera by Gazzaniga (libretto by G Bertati, based on Tirso de Molina), produced Venice, Teatro San Moisè, 5 Feb 1787.

Donington, Robert (b Leeds, 4 May 1907; d Firle, Sussex, 20 Jan 1990), English instrumentalist and musicologist. Educated at St Paul's School, London, and Oxford, he studied early instruments and interpretation of music with Dolmetsch at Haslemere. He edited music, wrote learned articles, performed with various teams on early instruments and produced books on instruments and ornaments, including *The Interpretation of Early Music*. He also pub. *Wagner's Ring and its Symbols* (1963) and *The Rise of Opera* (1981). OBE 1979.

Donizetti, Gaetano (Domenico Maria) (b Bergamo, 29 Nov 1797; d Bergamo, 8 Apr 1848), Italian composer. Studied at Bergamo and at the Liceo Filarmonico at Bologna. He entered the army to avoid following his father's trade and while at Venice in 1818 produced his first opera, *Enrico di Borgogna*, there. After that, except in 1821, he produced operas annually until 1844, when *Caterina Cornaro* came out as the last at Naples and his reason began to fail. In 1839–40 and 1843 he visited Paris and produced operas there. He became paralysed in 1845. In his early work he was influenced by the florid vocal style of Rossini, but he later developed the dramatic and lyric aspects of his art. Donizetti's operas first found favour through such great singers as Grisi and Lablache; more recently, such prima donnas as Callas, Sutherland and Caballé have helped find a new audience, in particular for the recently neglected serious works.

Works include more than 70 operas. Among those most frequently heard today are *Zoraida di Granata* (Rome, 1822), *L'ajo nell'imba-*

Donizetti *The composer Gaetano Donizetti (1797–1848). Following the death of Bellini in 1835, Donizetti was the unrivalled leader of Italian opera until Verdi emerged in the 1840s. Donizetti's comedies have endured especially well, thanks largely to their melodic spontaneity and charm.*

razzo (Rome, 1824), *Emilia di Liverpool* (Naples, 1824), *Gabriella di Vergy* (composed 1826, performed Naples, 1869), *Il borgomastro di Saardam* (Naples, 1827), *Le convenienze ed inconvenienze teatrali* (Naples, 1827), *Il Giovedì Grasso* (Naples, 1828), *Alina, regina di Golconda* (1828), *Elisabetta, o Il castello di Kenilworth* (Naples, 1829), *Anna Bolena* (Milan, 1830), *Gianni di Parigi* (Milan, 1831), *Fausta* (Naples, 1832), *Ugo, conte di Parigi* (Milan, 1832), *L'elisir d'amore* (Milan, 1832), *Il furioso all'isola di San Domingo* (Rome, 1833), *Torquato Tasso* (Rome, 1833), *Lucrezia Borgia* (Milan, 1833), *Rosmonda d'Inghilterra* (Florence, 1834), *Maria Stuarda* (Naples, 1834), *Gemma di Vergy* (Milan, 1834), *Marino Faliero* (Paris, 1835), *Lucia di Lammermoor* (Naples, 1835), *Belisario* (Venice, 1836), *Il campanello di notte* (Naples, 1836), *L'assedio di Calais* (1836), *Pia de' Tolomei* (Venice, 1837), *Roberto Devereux* (Naples, 1837), *Maria di Rudenz* (Venice, 1838), *Poliuto* (Naples, 1848; composed 1838 for Naples it was banned and produced in Paris 1840 as *Les Martyrs*), *La fille du régiment* (Paris, 1840), *La favorite* (Paris, 1840), *Maria Padilla* (Milan, 1841), *Linda di Chamounix* (Vienna, 1842), *Caterina Cornaro* (Naples, 1842), *Don Pasquale* (Paris, 1843), *Dom Sébastien* (Paris, 1843). *Le duc d'Albe* was written for Paris in 1840 but not produced. The score was completed by M Salvi and others and produced Rome, Teatro Apollo, 22 Mar 1882.

THE OPERA

Don Giovanni

A two-act opera (*dramma giocoso*) by Mozart dating from 1787. The action takes place in Seville in about 1600.

I. Don Giovanni (baritone) rushes from the house of Donna Anna (soprano), whom he has attempted to seduce. Challenged by Anna's father, the Commendatore (bass), Don Giovanni kills him in a duel. Donna Anna and her betrothed, Don Ottavio (tenor), swear vengeance. Donna Elvira (soprano), an old flame of Don Giovanni, comes in search of him but – aided by his servant Leporello (baritone) – he escapes and pays court instead to the peasant girl Zerlina (soprano). Elvira intervenes and is followed by Ottavio and Donna Anna, who realize the Don's identity only after he has left. Elvira, Anna and Ottavio wear masks to attend Don Giovanni's party; they unmask themselves as he attempts to drag Zerlina away and she resists, but he escapes.

II. Leporello and the Don exchange clothes, and Elvira is tricked by the deception; Leporello abandons his disguise when he encounters a vengeful Zerlina and her betrothed, Masetto (baritone). Leporello and his master meet in a cemetery, and when they are interrupted by the statue of the Commandatore, the Don invites him to supper. The Don clasps the Commandatore's cold hand but refuses to repent his crimes and is dragged down to Hell, to the relief and delight of the other principals.

THE OPERA

While his magical tunes bring joy to the world, while everyone sings them and trills them, he himself sits, a terrible picture of insanity, in a lunatic asylum near Paris.

Heinrich Heine on Donizetti, *Letters on the French Stage*, 1847

Don Juan Symphonic poem by R Strauss, op. 20, based on Lenau's poem, composed 1887–88, fp Weimar, 11 Nov 1889.

Donna del Lago, La, *The Lady of the Lake*, opera by Rossini (libretto by A L Tottola, based on Scott's poem), produced Naples, Teatro San Carlo, 24 Sept 1819. In Scotland King James V loves Ellen, the daughter of rebel Douglas. She in turn loves Malcolm, but must marry Douglas' ally Roderick. After Roderick is killed, James spares the captive Douglas and sanctions marriage between Ellen and Malcolm.

A Selection of

Donizetti

Anna Bolena	1830
L'elisir d'amore	1832
Lucrezia Borgia	1833
Maria Stuarda	1834
Lucia di Lammermoor	1835
La fille du régiment	1840
La favorite	1840
Maria Padilla	1841
Don Pasquale	1843
Poliuto	1848

Donna Diana opera by Reznicek (libretto by composer based on Moreto's comedy), produced Prague, German Theatre, 16 Dec 1894. Haughty Diana is humbled by persistent suitor.

Donna serpente, La, *The Serpent-Woman*, opera by Casella (libretto by C Lodovici, based on Gozzi's comedy), produced Rome, Teatro Reale, 17 Mar 1932. Wagner's *Die Feen* was on the same subject. Fairy Miranda marries Altidor against the wishes of her father, Demogorgòn, who forces her to test most cruelly Altidor's devotion. When eventually he fails the test she is turned into a snake, but thanks to the magic of wizard Geònca and Altidor's bravery, Miranda is restored.

Donne curiose, Le, *The Inquisitive Ladies*, opera by Wolf-Ferrari (libretto by L Sugano, based on Goldoni's comedy), produced Munich, in German, 27 Nov 1903. Gourmet men suspected of infidelities by their inquisitive womenfolk.

Donnerstag aus Licht, *Thursday from Light*, first opera by Stockhausen from projected opera cycle **Licht**. The work is semi-autobiographical: the three acts are titled *Michael's Youth*, *Michael's journey around the earth* (a huge concerto for trumpet and orchestra) and *Michael's homecoming*; composed 1978–81, produced Milan, La Scala, 3 Apr 1981.

Donohoe, Peter (b Manchester, 18 Jun 1953), English pianist. He studied at the RMCM and with Yvonne Loriod in Paris. Debut 1979, Prom Concerts. 1982 joint silver medal winner of Tchaikovsky International Competition, Moscow; frequent visits to Russia since. He plays modern works as well as the Romantic repertory, and in 1983 gave the fp of Dominic Muldowney's piano concerto. Tchaikovsky's 2nd concerto at the 1993 London Proms.

Don Pasquale comic opera by Donizetti (libretto by composer and ?, based on Angelo Anelli's *Ser Marcantonio*, composed by Pavesi in 1810), produced Paris, Théâtre Italien, 3 Jan 1843. Pasquale disapproves of match between nephew Ernesto and Norina, but changes his mind after a mock marriage to 'Sofronia', Norina in disguise.

Don Quichotte opera in five acts by Massenet (libretto by H Cain, based on Cervantes and Jacques Le Lorrain's comedy, *Le Chevalier de la longue figure*), produced Monte Carlo, 19 Feb 1910. Quichotte recovers Dulcinea's necklace from bandits, but she rejects him.

Don Quixote Symphonic poem by R Strauss, op. 35, based on Cervantes, composed 1897, fp Cologne, 8 Mar 1898. The work is described as 'Fantastic Variations on a theme of knightly character' and contains important solo parts for cello (Don Quixote) and viola (Sancho Panza).

Don Quixote, The Comical History of play by Thomas Durfey, based on Cervantes, with music by Purcell and others, composed parts i and ii, 1694, by Purcell and Eccles; part iii, 1695, by Akeroyde, Courteville, Pack, Morgan and D Purcell. i. produced London, Dorset Gardens, May 1694; ii. ditto Jun 1694; iii. London, Drury Lane Theatre, Nov 1695.

Donzelli, Domenico (b Bergamo, 2 Feb 1790; d Bologna, 31 Mar 1873), Italian tenor. Made his first appearance in Italy 1816, and sang in Rossini's *Tancredi*, *Torvaldo e Dorliska* and *Cenerentola*; Paris, 1825, in the fp of *Il viaggio a Reims*. London, Drury Lane, 1829, in Bellini's *Il pirata*, and in 1831 created Pollione in *Norma* (La Scala). Also successful in operas by Donizetti, Auber and Mercadante.

Dooley, William (b Modesto, CA, 9 Sept 1932), American baritone. Studied at the Eastman School and in Munich. Debut Heidelberg 1957 as Posa. Member of the Deutsche Oper Berlin from 1962, notably in the premieres of *Montezuma* by Sessions (1964), Reimann's *Gespenstersonate* (1984), Rihm's *Oedipus* (1987) and *Alamos* by Neikrug (1988). NY Met. from 1964 as Amonasro, Eugene Onegin and Telramund. Salzburg Festival 1966, in the premiere of *The Bassarids* by Henze.

Doppio Concerto work by Henze for oboe, harp and strings, written for Heinz and Ursula Holliger and performed by them Zurich, 2 Dec 1966.

doppio movimento Italian = 'double movement'; a direction indicating that a new tempo is to be exactly twice as fast as the one it displaces.

Doppler Polish-Hungarian family of musicians, including:
1. Albert Franz Doppler (b Lwów, 16 Oct 1821; d Baden near Vienna, 27 Jul 1883), flautist and composer. Taught at Pest and wrote operas, including *Benyovsky* (1847 and *Judith* (1870), 15 ballets, overtures, flute concertos, etc. Chief conductor of the Vienna Court Opera ballet.
2. Karl Doppler (b Lwów, 12 Sept 1825; d Stuttgart, 10 Mar 1900), flautist, conductor and composer, brother of 1. Toured widely and became conductor at the Pest National Theatre. Wrote operas, including *Erzébeth* (1857) with Albert D. and Erkel, ballets, flute music etc.

Dorati, Antal (b Budapest, 9 Apr 1906; d Gerzensee, near Berne, 13 Nov 1988), Hungarian-born American conductor. Studied at the Budapest Academy of Music with Bartók and Kodály. He first conducted at the age of 18. In 1947 he became an American citizen and in 1948 conductor of the Minneapolis SO. From 1963 to 1967 he was chief conductor of the BBC SO; RPO 1975–78, Detroit SO 1977–81). He recorded all the Haydn symphonies and most of the operas. He also composed, and made a number of successful arrangements (e.g. *Graduation Ball*, after J Strauss).

THE OPERA

Don Pasquale

A three-act *opera buffa* by Gaetano Donizetti, first produced in 1843. This tale of deception is set in Rome in the 19th century.

I. The rich and ill-tempered old bachelor Don Pasquale (bass) threatens to disinherit his nephew Ernesto (tenor) if he marries the young widow Norina (soprano). Doctor Malatesta (baritone), a friend of both parties, arranges for his supposed sister 'Sofronia' (Norina in disguise) to marry Don Pasquale.

II. Malatesta informs Ernesto of the plot when he arrives, and when the mock ceremony is over 'Sofronia' abandons her former sweet nature and makes Pasquale despair with her behaviour.

III. Pasquale asks Malatesta to get him out of his misery and they agree to meet the following day with 'Sofronia', when Ernesto is to bring his intended bride Norina. When the deception is revealed, Pasquale is so glad to be out of his 'marriage' that he forgives everyone and agrees to the union of Ernesto and Norina.

THE OPERA

Dorian mode the scale represented by the white keys on the piano beginning on the note D.

'Dorian' Toccata and Fugue organ work in D minor by Bach, so called on account of its notation without key-signature, the B♭ being inserted where necessary as an accidental.

Dori, La, ovvero La schiava fedele, *Doris, or The Faithful Slave*, opera by Cesti (libretto by A Apolloni), produced Innsbruck, Hof-Saales, 1657. Dori, disguised as a man, is sold as a slave to Arsinoe, her sister. Complicated plot ends happily with sisters' marriage to Tolomeo and Oronte.

Dorn, Heinrich (Ludwig Egmont) (b' Königsberg, 14 Nov 1804; d Berlin, 10 Jan 1892), German composer, teacher and conductor. Pupil of Zelter in Berlin, teacher of Schumann at Leipzig, opera conductor at Hamburg and Riga, where he succeeded Wagner in 1839. Finally conductor at the Royal Opera and professor in Berlin.

    Works include operas, e.g. *Die Rolandsknappen* (1826), *Die Nibelungen* (1854), etc.; ballet *Amors Macht*; Requiem; cantatas; orchestral works; piano music; songs.

Dostoievsky, Feodor Mikhailovich (b Moscow, 11 Nov 1821; d St Petersburg, 9 Feb 1881), Russian novelist. R ◊Chailly (*L'Idiota*); ◊From the House of the Dead (Janáček); ◊Gambler (Prokofiev); ◊Grossinquisitor (Blacher); ◊Idiot (Henze); ◊Rebikov (*Christmas Tree*); ◊Ruyneman (*Brothers Karamazov*); ◊Sutermeister (*Raskolnikov*).

Nothing is capable of being well set to music that is not nonsense.

Joseph Addison,
The Spectator, 1711

---

dot (1) above or under a note normally indicates *staccato*. Uses other than this are: (*a*) in 18th-c. violin music a series of dots with a slur indicates notes to be detached without changing the bow; (*b*) in 18th-c. clavichord music a series of dots with a slur above or under a single note indicates repeated pressure on the key; (*c*) in older French music dots above or under a succession of quavers or semi-quavers could mean the observance of equal note-values (*notes égales*), as opposed to the current fashion of lengthening or shortening such notes alternately (*notes inégales*).

    (2) A dot to the right of a note normally lengthens it by half. ◊dotted notes.

dotted notes notes with a dot placed on their right, with the effect of prolonging them by half their original value. A double dot has the effect of adding another half of the smaller value to the original note, which is thus lengthened by three-quarters of its value. Double dots were introduced by Leopold Mozart, before whose time their effect could not be precisely indicated in notation, though it was often produced at will by the interpreter, especially in slow movements written in singly dotted rhythm, such as the slow introductions in Lully's and Handel's overtures.

dot-way a 17th-c. system of notation for recorders, with staves where each line represented a fingerhole, while dots placed over the lines showed which fingers were to be kept down for each note.

Dotzauer, (Justus Johann) Friedrich (b Hildburghausen, 20 Jan 1783; d Dresden, 6 Mar 1860), German cellist. Played first in the court orchestra at Meiningen, then at Leipzig, Berlin and Dresden. Wrote an opera, *Graziosa* (1841), a symphony, chamber music and many cello works.

double French, the old French name for a type of variation that was merely a more highly ornamented version of a theme previously played in plainer notes.

double bar a pair of bar-lines placed very close together and marking off a principal section of a composition, such as the end of the exposition and beginning of the development in a sonata or symphony. It may be preceded or followed by repeat signs, or both, in which case the music before and/or after it must be repeated.

double bass the largest stringed instrument, the bass of the string section in the orchestra and occasionally in chamber music.

double bassoon a ◊bassoon with a range an octave lower than that of the ordinary instrument.

double bass viol ◊violone.

Double Chant a chant in two sections used in the Anglican Church and covering two verses of a psalm.

double concerto a concerto for two solo instruments: e.g. Bach's D minor for two violins, Mozart's E♭ major for two pianos, Brahms's A minor for violin and cello, Elliott Carter's for piano and harpsichord, etc.

double counterpoint ◊counterpoint.

double dots ◊dotted notes.

double flat an accidental, ♭♭, lowering the note before which it stands by a whole tone.

double fugue (1) a fugue on two subjects which appear simultaneously.

    (2) A fugue in which a second subject appears in the course of the composition.

double sharp an accidental, ✕, raising the note before which it stands by a whole tone.

double stopping the production of two notes simultaneously on any string instrument.

doucemelle, French, a keyboard instrument of *c* the 15th c.; a forerunner of the piano. Also = ◊dulcimer.

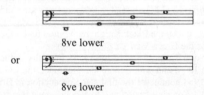

The double bass has four strings, formerly three, tuned.

The first of these is the one in general use. The range can be artificially extended either by tuning down the bottom string or by the addition of a fifth string.

In the latter case the instrument is normally tuned

8ve lower

If the C string is tuned down to B, this will continue the tuning in fourths.

Douglas, Barry (b Belfast, 23 Apr 1960), British pianist. Made his professional debut 1977 and studied at RCM 1978–82. In 1986 became first Westerner since Van Cliburn (1958) to win the Tchaikovsky Competition, Moscow, outright. Played Bethoven's 4th concerto at the 1993 London Proms.

Dowd, Ronald (b Sydney, 23 Feb 1914; d Sydney, 15 Mar 1990), Australian tenor. Sang in Australia from 1948 as Lohengrin, Florestan and Cavarodossi. SW, London, from 1956, as Grimes, Tannhäuser and Idomeneo. Hamburg Staatsoper 1968–69, in the fps of Searle's *Hamlet* and Goehr's *Arden Must Die*. Sang Aeneas in *Les Troyens* for Scottish Opera (1969) and at CG; returned to Australia 1973 and sang Pierre in *War and Peace* at the opening of the Sydney Opera House.

Dowland, John (b ? London, 1563; d London, buried 20 Feb 1626), English lutenist and composer. He entered the service of the English ambassador, Sir Henry Cobham, in Paris in 1580, and was from 1583 in that of his successor, Sir Edward Stafford. He became a Roman Catholic, returned to England soon after and married. In the 1590s he sought a place at Elizabeth's court, but was not admitted, and went to Germany in the service of the Duke of Brunswick, then entered that of the Landgrave of Hesse and travelled to Italy, returning home towards the end of the century and turning to Protestantism again. In Nov 1598 he went to Denmark as court musician to Christian IV, returning in 1601 to buy instruments for the king and living in London again for a time in 1603, finally settling there in 1606 on being dismissed from Copenhagen. He complained of neglect after his successes abroad, but from 1612 to 1618 he was employed at court.

Works include three vols. of songs to the lute (1597–1603); a book of instrumental pavans entitled *Lachrymae*; a book of songs with lutes and viols, *A Pilgrimes Solace*; lute, viol and vocal music contributions to Leighton's *Teares and Lamentacions*, East's Psalter and to a number of foreign collections, including Füllsack's and Fuhrmann's.

Semper Dowland Semper Dolens. (Always Dowland, always sad.)

John Dowland, title of pavan

Dowland, Robert (b ? London, *c* 1591; d London, 1641), English lutenist and composer, son of John ◊Dowland. Appointed lutenist to Charles I on his father's death in 1626. Composed lessons for the lute, etc. and pub. a book of airs by continental composers.

downbeat the downward motion of the conductor's baton indicating the stressed beats of any bar. The corresponding upward motion is called the upbeat.

down bow the movement of the bow in the playing of string instruments in the direction from the heel to the point.

Down by the Greenwood Side dramatic pastoral in one act by Birtwistle (libretto by M Nyman), for soprano, five actors and chamber ensemble; performed Brighton, Pier Pavilion, 8 May 1969. St George is defeated by the Black Knight but revives under the vernal earth magic of the Green Man.

Downes, Edward (b Birmingham, 17 Jun 1924), English conductor. He studied at the RCM and with Scherchen. He joined the CG staff in 1951 and in 1963 conducted the first stage production in Britain of Shostakovich's *Katerina Izmaylova*. In 1967 he gave the first post-war *Ring* cycle by a British conductor; fps of Bennett's *Victory* (1970) and Maxwell Davies's *Taverner* (1972). First complete performances of Wagner's *Die Feen*, *Das Liebesverbot* and *Rienzi* (BBC, 1970s). He gave *War and Peace* on the opening night of the Sydney Opera House (1973) and remained with Australian Opera until 1976. Principal conductor BBC Philharmonic Orchestra 1980–91; principal at CG 1991. Knighted 1991.

Downes, (Edward) Olin (b Evanston, IL, 27 Jan 1886; d New York, 22 Aug 1955), American writer on music and critic. As critic for the *Boston Post* 1906–24 and the *New York Times* 1924–55, he was an advocate of contemporary European masters (*Sibelius the Symphonist*, pub. 1956). He was the mainstay of the Met. broadcast interval quizzes and wrote further *Symphonic Masterpieces* (1935, revised 1972). His son, Edward O Downes (b Boston, 12 Aug 1911) taught at Queens College NY until 1983 and was Met. quizmaster from 1958. Authority on J C Bach and other early classical opera composers.

Draeseke, Felix (August Bernhard) (b Coburg, 7 Oct 1835; d Dresden, 26 Feb 1913), German composer. Studied at the Leipzig Conservatory and with Liszt at Weimar, later taught at Dresden, Lausanne, Munich and Geneva, and finally settled at Dresden in 1876, becoming professor of composition at the Conservatory in 1884.

Works include operas *Gudrun* (1884), *Herrat* and *Merlin* (1903–05); Requiem, trilogy of oratorios *Christus*, Easter scene from Goethe's *Faust* for solo voices, chorus and orchestra (1907); five symphonies, overtures for orchestra, including *Penthesilea* (after Kleist); concerto for piano, violin and cello; three string quartets, string quintet; many piano works including a sonata.

drag a stroke on the side-drum preceded by a group of grace-notes, usually three or four.

Draghi, Antonio (b Rimini, *c* 1634; d Vienna, 16 Jan 1700), Italian composer. Began his career as a singer at Venice. Went to Vienna to take up a court appointment in 1658, and appointed *Hofkapellmeister* in 1682. He was also a librettist for other composers, including Bertali, Ziani and the Emperor Leopold I.

Works include 67 operas, including *Timone misantropo*, after Shakespeare, (1696), 116 smaller stage pieces, *c* 40 oratorios, cantatas, hymns, etc.

Draghi, Giovanni Battista (b *c* 1640; d London, 1708), Italian harpsichordist and composer. Settled in London; music master to the Princesses Mary and Anne and organist to Catherine of Braganza, wife of Charles II. Set Dryden's Ode for St Cecilia's Day, 1687, contributed music to Durfey's *Wonders in the Sun*, 1706, and composed many harpsichord lessons and songs.

Dragonetti, Domenico (b Venice, 10 Apr 1763; d London, 16 Apr 1846), Italian double bass player and composer. He was admitted to the opera orchestras at Venice from the age of 13 and soon began to compose concertos, sonatas and other works for his instrument. His first appearance abroad was in 1794 in London, where he spent most of the rest of his life with the cellist Lindley as partner. He led the double basses in the fp of the Choral Symphony (Vienna, 1824), complaining to Beethoven about the complexity of his part.

drame lyrique a modern French term for a serious opera.

dramma (per musica) Italian = 'drama (for music)'; 18th-c. term for opera; actually plays written especially for the purpose of being set to music.

dramma giocoso Italian = 'jocular drama'; name occasionally used

---

Barry Douglas – pianist

1   Tchaikovsky: Piano Concerto no. 1
When I was about five years old I completely fell in love with this piece. Later, when I arrived at college, it was one of the first concertos I learned. I didn't play it again for years, but then I took it up when I was preparing for the Tchaikovsky Competition, and I played it a lot. So the work has punctuated my life in three places.

2   Rakhmaninov: Piano Concerto no. 3
As a teenager I was in the City of Belfast Youth Orchestra and the conductor asked me to play a piano concerto. The first bassoon lent me a record of Rakhmaninov's Third Piano Concerto and I thought it was amazing, so I studied it and decided to play it. The work showed me the multitude

of things the piano could do: it was orchestral, it was vocal, it was percussive; it was a both a contrapuntal and chordal instrument.

3   Wagner: *Tristan und Isolde* (Vickers/Dernesch/Berlin PO/ Karajan)
When I was at college, I saw Wagner's *Ring* at Covent Garden. I had never been to an event which had made such a deep impression. It led me to study *Tristan und Isolde* and to go to Covent Garden again. And that was the first time I heard Jon Vickers. I'd never heard singing like it. His voice was not necessarily 'beautiful' but always dramatic, with a rare emotional depth.

for *opera buffa* in the later 18th c. Mozart's original designation of *Don Giovanni*.

Drdla, František (b Žďár, Moravia, 28 Nov 1868; d Gastein, 3 Sept 1944), Czech violinist and composer. Studied at the Prague and Vienna Conservatories, played violin in the Vienna Court Opera orchestra and toured Europe as a virtuoso.

    Works include operettas *The Golden Net* (1916) and *The Shop Countess* (1917); many violin pieces; piano pieces; songs, etc.

Dream of Gerontius, The oratorio by Elgar, op. 38 (words selected from Cardinal John Henry Newman's poem), fp Birmingham Festival, 3 Oct 1900.

Dreigroschenoper, Die, *The Threepenny Opera*, operetta by Weill (libretto based on Elisabeth Hauptmann's German version of Gay's *Beggar's Opera*, with some additions by Brecht), produced Berlin, Theater am Schiffbauerdamm, 31 Aug 1928. Mack the Knife escapes the gallows.

Drei Pintos, Die, *The Three Pintos*, unfinished opera by Weber (libretto by T Hell, based on Carl Ludwig Seidel's story *Der Brautkampf*), partly composed 1821; produced in an edition completed by Mahler, Leipzig, 20 Jan 1888. Don Pinto's misadventures on his way to wooing Clarissa. He is impersonated by her true love Don Gomez, who eventually marries her.

Dresden, Sem (b Amsterdam, 20 Apr 1881; d The Hague, 31 Jul 1957), Dutch conductor and composer. Studied under Zweers at the Copenhagen Conservatory and with Pfitzner in Germany. He became a choral conductor, cultivating particularly motets and madrigals in Holland. Director of the Amsterdam Conservatory, 1924–37, and then of that at The Hague, in succession to Wagenaar. He was compelled to withdraw from public life during the German occupation of Holland, but composed much during that period. He wrote a book on *Dutch Music since 1880*.

    Works include opera, *François Villon*, (produced posthumously Amsterdam, 1958); *Chorus tragicus* for chorus and orchestra; variations for orchestra; violin concerto; *Symphonietta* for clarinet and orchestra; string quartet, sextet for strings and piano, three sextets for wind and piano; sonatas for violin and piano, cello and piano and flute and harp; duo for two pianos; piano pieces; songs.

Dressler, Ernst Christoph (b Greussen, Thuringia, 1734; d Kassel, 6 Apr 1779), German composer and singer. Worked as secretary and singer at Bayreuth and Gotha, later *Kapelldirektor* to Prince Fürstenberg at Wetzlar, finally opera singer in Vienna and Kassel. Beethoven's first pub. work was a set of variations (1782) on a march by D.

Dressler, Gallus (b Nebra, 16 Oct 1533; d Zerbst, *c* 1585), German composer. Wrote Lutheran psalms and hymns as well as Latin church music.

Drigo, Riccardo (b Padua, 30 Jun 1846; d Padua, 1 Oct 1930), Italian conductor and composer. He became ballet conductor at the St Petersburg Court Opera.

    Works include ballet *Harlequin's Millions* (1900), many drawing-room pieces, etc.

Driscoll, Loren (b WY, MN, 14 Apr 1928), American tenor. Debut Boston 1954, in *Falstaff*. He sang at the NY City Opera 1958–59 and in 1962 joined the Deutsche Oper, Berlin; well known there as Ottavio, Flamand and Berg's Painter. In 1965 he created Lord Barrat in Henze's *Der Junge Lord* and in 1968 was Eumaus in the fp of Dallapiccola's *Ulisse*. At the 1966 Salzburg Festival he created Dionysus in *The Bassarids*. Glyndebourne 1962, Ferrando. Sang at Rome 1982 in Lortzing's *Undine*.

drone the three lower pipes of the bagpipe, which produce a fixed chord above which the melody is played on the ◊chanter. The name was also given to a bowed instrument with a single string stretched on a stick over a bladder; this was also called bumbass.

drone bass an unvaryingly sustained bass on any composition, resembling the drone of a bagpipe.

Druckman, Jacob (b Philadelphia, 26 Jun 1928; d New Haven, CT, 24 May 1996), American composer. He studied at the Juilliard School and in Paris. He directed electronic music centres at Princeton and Yale Universities. Composer-in-residence, NY PO, from 1982.

Works include violin concerto (1956), *Dark upon the Harp* for mezzo, brass quintet and percussion (1962); *The Sound of Time* for soprano and orchestra (1965); *Animus I–IV* for mezzo, instruments and tape (1966–77), *Windows* for orchestra (1972); *Lamia* for soprano and orchestra (1974); *Chiaroscuro* for orchestra (1976); Viola concerto 1978); *Aureole* for orchestra (1979); *Prism*; three pieces for orchestra after music from operas by M A Charpentier, Cavalli and Cherubini (1980); three string quartets (1948, 1961, 1981); *Athenor* for orchestra (1985).

Drum Mass (Haydn.) ◊Paukenmesse.

'Drum-Roll' Symphony, German *Symphonie mit dem Paukenwirbel*, nickname of Haydn's symphony no. 103 in E♭ major (composed for London, 1795), so called because it opens with a timpani roll.

drums percussion instruments on which the sound is produced by beating a skin stretched tightly over a hollow space left open by a framework of various patterns. ◊bass drum, ◊kettledrums, ◊side drum, ◊snare drum, ◊tabla, ◊tabor, ◊tambourine, ◊tenor drum.

Dryden, John (1631–1700), English poet, dramatist and satirist. ◊Acis and Galatea (Handel); ◊Albion and Albanius (Grabu); ◊Alexander's Feast (Handel); ◊Almahide (G Bononcini); ◊Boyce (*Secular Masque*); J ◊Clarke (*Alexander's Feast*); ◊Clayton (ditto); ◊Cymon (M Arne); G B ◊Draghi (*Ode for St Cecilia's Day*); J ◊Eccles (*Spanish Friar*); ◊Humfrey (*Conquest of Granada* and *Indian Emperor*); ◊Indian Queen and ◊King Arthur (Purcell); ◊Ode for St Cecilia's Day (Handel); ◊Purcell (*Amphitryon, Aureng-Zebe, Cleomenes, Love Triumphant, Spanish Friar, Tyrannic Love* and *Oedipus*); ◊Staggins (*Conquest of Granada* and *Marriage à la Mode*).

Düben German-Swedish family of musicians;

    1. Andreas Düben (b Lützen, 27 May 1558; d Leipzig, 19 Apr 1625), organist at St Thomas's Church, Leipzig.

    2. Andreas Düben (b ? Leipzig, *c* 1597; d Stockholm, 7 Jul 1662), organist and composer, son of 1. Pupil of Sweelinck at Amsterdam, 1614–20, went to Sweden in 1621, became organist at the German church in Stockholm in 1625 and court music director in 1640. Composed dances for viols, etc.

    3. Gustaf Düben (b Stockholm, *c* 1628; d Stockholm, 19 Dec 1690), organist and composer, son of 2. Succeeded his father in both his posts. Built up a large collection of music manuscripts, including works by Buxtehude. Wrote church music, *concerti grossi*, symphonies and dances for strings, etc.

    4. Andreas Düben (b Stockholm, 28 Aug 1673; d Stockholm, 23 Aug 1738), son of 3, whom he succeeded. He left the Düben Collection, including 1500 vocal works, to Uppsala University in 1732.

Dubois, (François Clément) Théodore (b Rosnay, Marne, 24 Aug 1837; d Paris, 11 Jun 1924), French composer. Studied at Rheims and then at the Paris Conservatory, where he took the Prix de Rome in 1861. Returning to Paris in 1866, he was active as organist and teacher, at last succeeding Saint-Saëns as organist at the Madeleine in 1877. From 1896 to 1905 he was director of the Conservatory.

    Works include operas *La Guzla de l'Emir* (1873), *Le Pain bis* (1879), *Aben-Hamet, Xavière* (1895); ballet *La Farandole*; Requiem, *Messe de la Délivrance* and other Masses, motets and other church music; oratorios, *Les Sept Paroles du Christ* and *Paradis perdu*; orchestral works.

Dubourg, Matthew (b London, 1703; d London, 3 Jul 1767), English violinist and composer. Pupil of Geminiani. Lived much of his life in Dublin, where he played in the first performance of *Messiah* in 1742.

Ducis, Benedictus (b near Konstanz, *c* 1490; d Schalckstetten, near Ulm, 1544), German composer and Lutheran pastor. Wrote Lutheran psalms and hymns, Latin church music, and German part-songs.

Due Foscari, I, *The Two Foscari*, opera by Verdi (libretto by F M Piave, based on Byron's drama), produced Rome, Teatro Argentina, 3 Nov 1844. The Doge's son Jacopo has been accused of murder. He is first imprisoned, then exiled, against the pleas of his wife, Lucrezia. It is revealed too late that Jacopo is innocent: he died upon leaving Venice.

Duenna, The, or The Double Elopement opera by Thomas Linley, father and son (libretto by Sheridan), produced London, CG 21 Nov 1775. Sheridan was son-in-law of Linley senior.

Opera by Roberto Gerhard (libretto by composer and C Hassall after Sheridan), fp BBC broadcast 23 Feb 1949; stage premiere Madrid, 21 Jan 1992. Luisa is inclined to Antonio but must marry Isaac Mendoza. After mistaken identities and twists in the plot, the opera ends with a triple wedding: Luisa marries Antonio, Luisa's brother Ferdinand marries Clara, and Isaac Mendoza marries Margaret, Luisa's duenna. ◊*Betrothal in a Monastery*.

Duesing, Dale (b Milwaukee, 26 Sept 1947), American baritone. Studied at Lawrence University and sang in Germany from 1972; San Francisco as Billy Budd and Belcore; Seattle Opera as Onegin and Wolfram. Glyndebourne from 1976, as Olivier in *Capriccio*, Guglielmo, Ottone and Figaro. At the NY Met. (from 1979) he has sung Billy Budd, Pelléas and Papageno. Season 1992 as Nardo in *La finta giardiniera* at Salzburg, and 'I' in the premiere of Schnittke's *Life with an Idiot*, at Amsterdam.

duet a composition in two parts for voices or instruments. A duet may be in two single melodic parts only, or it may be accompanied by instruments in fuller harmony or it may be itself for two harmonic instruments or a single such instrument for two players (e.g. piano duet).

Dufallo, Richard (b Chicago, 30 Jan 1933), American conductor. Studied with Boulez and William Steinberg. Conducted Buffalo PO 1962–67, NY PO on tour of Far East 1967. Director of contemporary music series at Aspen from 1970 and Juilliard 1972–79. European debut Paris 1971 and has led the Concertgebouw, LSO, Chicago SO, and Royal and Berlin Philharmonics. Opera engagements in Cincinatti, for NY City Opera and at the Bath, Edinburgh and Holland festivals.

Dufay, Guillaume (b ? Cambrai, *c* 1400; d Cambrai, 27 Nov 1474), Franco-Flemish composer. After being a chorister at Cambrai Cathedral he travelled much, especially in Italy, and was a member of the Papal choir, 1428–37. From 1439 to 1450 and from 1458 until his death he was resident as a canon of Cambrai, but had strong connections in the court of Burgundy and was at various times resident at the court of Savoy.

His 13 isorhythmic motets including *Nuper rosarum flores* for the dedication of Florence Cathedral (25 Mar 1436). Over 80 songs in French and Italian show an extraordinary range of techniques and musical emotions. His earlier sacred works often show a stark simplicity of style and he may well have been the inventor of ◊fauxbourdon. The Mass *Caput* is now thought to be by an anonymous English composer, not Dufay. But his grandest achievements are in the four cantus firmus Mass cycles of his late years, works that pioneered the four-voice style that was to dominate sacred music for the next century: *Se la face ay pale*, probably for the court of Savoy in the 1450s; *L'homme armé*, perhaps composed for the court of Burgundy; *Ecce ancilla Domini* (? 1463); and *Ave regina caelorum*, probably for the dedication of Cambrai Cathedral on 5 Jul 1472.

THE OPERA

Duke Bluebeard's Castle

A one-act opera by Béla Bartók, first produced in 1918. It is set in legendary times. Judith (mezzo-soprano) enters the dingy castle hall of her new husband, the much-married idealist Bluebeard (bass). Curious about the seven doors that surround them, Judith demands to enter them all. The first two reveal blood-stained instruments of torture and weapons, while the third is Bluebeard's treasury. The fourth door opens to a rose garden but Judith pricks her finger and it bleeds. The fifth door reveals Bluebeard's kingdom but the sixth door opens onto a sea of tears. At the last door, three ghostly figures emerge, all former wives of Bluebeard and dedicated successively to the morning, afternoon and evening. Now that he has met her at night, Judith completes an ethereal quartet, and must join the other wives in their prison.

THE OPERA

Dufranne, Hector (b Mons, 25 Oct 1870; d Paris, 4 May 1951), Belgian bass-baritone. Debut Brussels 1896, Valentin. At the Paris Opéra-Comique he sang in the fp of Massenet's *Grisélidis* and created Debussy's Golaud. Monte Carlo 1907, in the fp of Massenet's *Thérèse*. He sang in NY 1908–10 and in Chicago 1910–22; fp *The Love for Three Oranges*, 1921. Also heard in works by Strauss and Falla (fp *El retablo de Maese Pedro*, Paris 1923).

Dugazon (born *Lefèbvre*), Louise Rosalie (b Berlin, 18 Jun 1755; d Paris, 22 Sept 1821), French mezzo. Trained as a dancer, and made her debut at the age of 12. Her voice was discovered by Grétry, in whose *Sylvain* she first appeared as a singer in 1774. Married the actor Dugazon in 1776. She created about 60 roles in Paris, and sang in operas by Dalayrac, Isouard and Boieldieu.

Dukas, Paul (b Paris, 1 Oct 1865; d Paris, 17 May 1935), French composer. Studied at the Paris Conservatory, among his masters being Dubois and Guiraud. Professor of composition there from 1913 to his death. From 1909 he taught orchestration at the Paris Conservatory and from 1913 composition. In 1926 he also began teaching at the Ecole Normale. His best-known piece is the brilliant orchestral scherzo *L'Apprenti sorcier* (1897), and his opera *Ariane et Barbe-bleue* (1907) is among the finest French operas of its day, premiered four years before Bartók wrote *Duke Bluebeard's Castle*.

Works include opera *Ariane et Barbe-bleue* (Maeterlinck, 1907); ballet *La Péri* (1912); symphony in C major, (1896), overture to Corneille's *Polyeucte*, *L'Apprenti sorcier* (on Goethe's poem *Der Zauberlehrling*); sonata in E♭ minor, *Variations on a theme by Rameau*, *Prélude élégiaque* on the name of Haydn and *La Plainte, au loin, du faune* in memory of Debussy for piano; *Sonnet de Ronsard* and *Vocalise* for voice and piano; *Villanelle* for horn and piano, etc. (including unpublished overtures to Shakespeare's *King Lear* and Goethe's *Götz von Berlichingen*).

Duke Bluebeard's Castle, *A kékszakállú hercegvára*, opera in one act by Bartók (libretto by B Balázs); composed 1911, produced Budapest, 24 May 1918, conductor Tango. Inquisitive bride Judith tours Bluebeard's blood-spattered castle and joins his former wives in eternal gloom.

Dukelsky, Vladimir (b Parfianovka near Pskov, 10 Oct 1903; d Santa Monica, 16 Nov 1969), Russian-American composer. Studied at Moscow and Kiev, Glière being among his teachers. Went to live in Constantinople in 1920 and settled in NY in 1922. Under the infuence of Gershwin he wrote light music under the name of Vernon Duke, but cultivated an advanced modern style under his own name. In 1924 Diaghilev heard his piano concerto and commissioned him to write a work for the Russian Ballet.

Works include operetta *Yvonne* (1926); ballets *Zéphir et Flore* and *Public Gardens*; oratorio *The End of St Petersburg* (1937); four symphonies, *Dédicaces* for soprano, piano and orchestra, piano concerto; string quartet; violin sonata; song cycle *Triolets of the North* (Feodor Sologub); Three Chinese songs and other songs.

dulce melos, Latin, = 'sweet melody'; another name for the ◊chekker.

dulciana an open ◊diapason organ stop of delicate tone. It may embrace 4-ft., 8-ft. or 16ft. pipes.

dulcimer an instrument akin to the ◊psaltery, with a set of strings stretched over a sound-board which are struck by hammers. The Hungarian ◊cimbalom is a descendant of it.

dulcitone a keyboard instrument producing its sound on a set of tuning-forks, similar to the ◊celesta.

Dulichius, Philipp (b Chemnitz, 18 Dec 1562; d Stettin, 24 Mar 1631), German composer. Took the D.Phil. degree at Chemnitz and went to Stettin as music teacher at the Pädagogium in 1587.

Works include sacred and secular compositions for several voices.

Du Mage, Pierre (b Beauvais, bap. 23 Nov 1674; d Laon, 20 Oct 1751), French organist and composer. Pupil of Marchand in Paris, organist of the collegiate church at Saint-Quentin 1703–13. He played at the inauguration of the new organ at Notre-Dame in Paris. Pub. a volume of organ pieces in 1708.

Dumanoir, Guillaume (b Paris, 16 Nov 1615; d Paris, *c* 1697), French violinist and composer. As 'Roi des Violons' he came into conflict with the dancing-masters, whom he wished to compel to contribute to the violinists' guild of Saint-Julien, and being unsuccessful he wrote the abusive pamphlet *Le Mariage de la musique avec la danse* in 1664. He composed dance music which was liked by Louis XIV, who appointed him ballet master of the royal pages.

Dumanoir, Guillaume (Michel) (b Paris; d ? Paris, 1697), French violinist and composer, son of Guillaume ◊Dumanoir, whom he succeeded as head of the Confrérie de Saint-Julien. He renewed his father's quarrel with the dancing masters, resigning in 1685. Before that he had quarrelled with Lully over the privilege of training orchestra musicians and lost a law-suit against him in 1673. Wrote dance music.

Dumbarton Oaks concerto in E♭ for chamber orchestra by Stravinsky; composed 1937–38, performed Washington DC, at Dumbarton Oaks, the private estate of R W Bliss, 8 May 1938. First public performance Paris, 4 Jun 1938.

dumka, Polish, Russian and Czech, a lament, which in music takes the form of a slow piece alternating with more animated sections, as e.g. in Dvořák's *Dumky* Trio.

dumky plur. of ◊dumka.

'Dumky' Trio a piano trio by Dvořák, op. 90, based on music of the type of the above, composed 1891.

Dunhill, Thomas (Frederick) (b London, 1 Feb 1877; d Scunthorpe, Lincs., 13 Mar 1946), English composer. Entered the RCM in 1893, Stanford being his composition master. He was assistant music master at Eton College 1899–1908 and organized concerts for chamber music and for the promotion of British music in London during the early years of the century. Professor of composition at the RCM. His second ballet was produced at Hamburg 1937.

Works include operas *The Enchanted Garden* (1928), *Tantivy Towers* (A P Herbert, 1931) and *Happy Families*; ballets *Dick Whittington* and *Gallimaufry*; symphony in A minor, *Elegiac Variations* in memory of Parry and overture *Maytime* for orchestra; *Triptych* for viola and orchestra; piano quartet, two piano trios, five quintets.

Duni, Egidio Romoaldo (b Matera near Naples, bap. 11 Feb 1708; d Paris, 11 Jun 1775), Italian-French composer. Pupil of Durante in Naples, where he produced his first opera in 1731. Travelled widely, and settled in Paris in 1757, becoming a leading composer of *opéras comiques*.

Works include operas *Nerone* (1735), *Le Caprice amoureux, Le Peintre amoureux de son modèle* (1757), *L'Isle des fous, Le Milicien, Les Deux Chasseurs et la laitière* (1763), *La Fée Urgèle, La Clochette, Les Moissonneurs, Les Sabots* (1768).

Dunn, Mignon (b Memphis, 17 Jun 1931), American mezzo. She sang Carmen at the NY City Opera in 1956 and appeared at the Met. from 1958 as Fricka, Amneris, Venus, Ortrud and Santuzza; Azucena, and Anna in *Les Troyens*, 1973. Düsseldorf from 1965, as Eboli and Dalila. Sang Clytemnestra in *Elektra* at Barcelona, 1990.

Dunstable, John (b c 1390; d ? London, 24 Dec 1453), English mathematician, astrologer, and composer. Possibly connected with St Albans Cathedral, he was certainly in the Duke of Bedford's retinue during the English occupation of Normandy in the 1420s. As the most famous and most prolific English composer of his time he was admired throughout Europe and considered to have had an important influence on the new musical style of Dufay and Binchois.

Works include Mass music, isorhythmic motets, service music and devotional pieces, though the widely admired song *O rosa bella* was probably composed by his younger contemporary Bedyngham.

Duparc, Elizabeth (d 1778), French soprano. She appeared in Italy in her youth, where she was given the nickname of La Francesina, under which name she sang in many of Handel's operas and oratorios in London from 1738; she sang in the fps of *Saul, Israel in Egypt, Imeneo, Deidamia, Semele* and *Belshazzar*.

Duparc, (Marie Eugène) Henri (Fouques-) (b Paris, 21 Jan 1848; d Mont de Marsan, 12 Feb 1933), French composer. Was taught the piano as a child by Franck at the Jesuit College of Vaugirard in Paris, and later became a composition pupil of that master. He never took

any share in official musical life, but continued to compose at intervals until 1885, when he began to suffer from an incurable nervous complaint and retired to Switzerland.

Works include symphonic poem *Lénore* (on Bürger's poem, 1875) and nocturne *Aux Etoiles*; motet *Benedicat vobis Dominus*; 15 songs including *Phydilé, Invitation au voyage, Soupir, La vague et la cloche, Extase, Le manoir de Rosemonde* and *Lamento*; and several afterwards destroyed.

duplet a group of two notes occupying the time of three.

duple time two beats in a bar, e.g. 2–4 or 6–8.

Duport, Jean Louis (b Paris, 4 Oct 1749; d Paris, 7 Sept 1819), French cellist. Made his first appearance at the Concert Spirituel in Paris in 1768. He went to the Prussian court in Berlin at the outbreak of the Revolution and there Beethoven played with him (or with his brother, Jean Pierre ◊Duport) his two cello sonatas, op. 5. He returned to Paris 1806.

Duport, Jean Pierre (b Paris, 27 Nov 1741; d Berlin, 31 Dec 1818), French cellist, brother of Jean Louis ◊Duport. Made his first appearance at the Concert Spirituel in Paris in 1761, visited England in 1769 and Spain in 1771, and in 1773 went to the court of Frederick II of Prussia in Berlin. Mozart wrote piano variations on a minuet of his (K573).

The good composer is slowly discovered; the bad composer is slowly found out.
    Ernest Newman (1868–1959), attr.

Du Pré, Jacqueline (b Oxford, 26 Jan 1945; d London, 19 Oct 1987), English cellist. She studied at the GSM with William Pleeth, and with Rostropovich and Tortelier. Debut recital Wigmore Hall, London, 1961; Elgar cello concerto at RFH, 1962, and on her US debut in NY, Carnegie Hall, in 1965. Married Daniel Barenboim, 1967, and gave orchestral and chamber-music concerts with him. Afflicted with multiple sclerosis from 1973, she taught and gave master classes. She was admired for her spirited interpretations. OBE 1976.

Dupré, Marcel (b Rouen, 3 May 1886; d Meudon, 30 May 1971), French organist and composer. Played Bach from memory at the age of ten, in 1898 was appointed organist of the church of Saint-Vivien at Rouen and produced an oratorio in 1901. After that he studied piano, organ and composition at the Paris Conservatory and gained the Prix de Rome in 1914 as a pupil of Widor. Organist at Notre-Dame 1916–22 during the illness of Vierne. Appointed professor of organ at the Paris Conservatory in 1926 and organist at Saint-Sulpice in 1936, succeeding Widor. From 1954 to 1956 he was director of the Conservatory.

Works include oratorio *Le Songe de Jacob*, motets and *De Profundis*; two symphonies; concerto for organ and orchestra (1934); violin and piano sonata; cello pieces; songs; many organ works including *Symphonie-Passion*, 79 chorales, *Le Chemin de la Croix*.

Duprez, Gilbert (Louis) (b Paris, 6 Dec 1806; d Paris, 23 Sept 1896), French tenor and composer. First appeared at the Théâtre de l'Odéon in Paris, 1825. He sang in the fps of *Benvenuto Cellini*, Donizetti's *Les Martyrs, La favorite* and *Dom Sébastien* and Verdi's *Jérusalem*. Professor at the Conservatory 1842–50.

Du Puy, (Jean Baptiste) Edouard (b Corcelles, Neuchâtel, 1770 or 1; d Stockholm, 3 Apr 1822), Swiss baritone, violinist, pianist and composer. Studied piano with Dussek in Paris and became a member of the orchestra of Prince Henry of Prussia at Rheinsberg in 1785 and leader in 1787. In 1793 he settled at Stockholm, but was expelled in 1799, when he went to sing in opera at Copenhagen and taught singing to the wife of the future Christian VIII, with whom he was exiled for a love affair in 1809. In 1811 he returned to Stockholm and became court conductor and professor.

Works include operas *Ungdom og Galskab* (a Danish version of the libretto of Méhul's *Une Folie*, 1806) and *Felicie* (1821); several ballets; funeral music for Charles XIII, etc.

Dutoit *The conductor Charles Dutoit. An exponent of the greatest 20th-century works, Dutoit is especially famous for his performances of Stravinsky, which remain faithful to the score and are always full of energy. He has built the Montreal Symphony Orchestra into a world-class ensemble.*

dur, German, from Latin *durus*, = 'hard'; the word for major, because *B durum* meant B♮.

Durand (*Duranowski*), Auguste Frédéric (b Warsaw, 1770; d Strasbourg, 1834), Polish-French violinist and composer. He was sent to Paris in 1787 to study under Viotti, travelled much in Germany and Italy, joined the French army and settled at Strasbourg in 1814. Wrote much superficial concert music for his instrument.

Durand, (Marie) Auguste (b Paris, 18 Jul 1830; d Paris, 31 May 1909), French publisher, organist and composer. Studied at the Paris Conservatory; was organist at various churches and was a partner in the pub. firm of Durand & Fils. He wrote drawing-room music for piano, including popular waltzes.

Durante, Francesco (b Fratta Maggiore, near Naples, 31 Mar 1684; d Naples, 30 Sept 1755), Italian composer. Educated at Naples, where he later became *maestro di cappella* at the Conservatorio di S Maria (1742) and S Onofrio (1745). His pupils included Traetta, Paisiello, Sacchini, Pergolesi, Piccinni, etc. Unusually for a Neapolitan composer, he wrote no operas. His works consist largely of church music, also sonatas, toccatas, etc., for harpsichord.

Durastanti, Margherita (b *c* 1685), Italian soprano. Visited London in 1720 and again in 1733, singing in several of Handel's operas. She created Agrippina (Venice, 1709) and in London took part in the fps of *Radamisto*, *Ottone*, *Flavio*, *Giulio Cesare* and *Arianna*.

Durazzo, Count Giacomo (b Genoa, 27 Apr 1717; d Venice, 15 Oct 1794), Italian nobleman. He was director of the Imperial Theatres in Vienna 1754–64. With Gluck he helped to establish opéra-comique in Vienna and played an influential role in the reform of music drama, particularly in connection with Gluck's *Orfeo*.

Durchführung German = lit. 'through-leading'; the German term for the ◊development or working-out section of a movement in sonata form.

durchkomponiert German = lit. 'set throughout'; a song is said in Germany to be *durchkomponiert* if the words are set to music continuously, not strophically with the same music repeated for each verse.

Durey, Louis (b Paris, 27 May 1888; d St Tropez, 3 Jul 1979), French composer. He did not study music until the age of 22, and in 1914 he enlisted on the outbreak of war. In 1916, during leave, he came under the influence of Satie and joined the group of 'Les Six', but was the first to secede from it in 1921, and in 1923 he went to live in seclusion in the S of France, writing very little.

Works include opera on Mérimée's *L'Occasion* (1925); incidental music to Hebbel's *Judith* (1918); three string quartets, piano trio, string trio; song cycles with chamber music or piano.

durezza Italian = 'hardness'; up to the 17th c. the term was used for discord in Italy; it is now used in the direction *con durezza* to indicate that a harsh or unyielding manner of performance is required.

Durfey (*D'Urfey*), Thomas (1653–1723), English playwright and poet. ◊Akeroyde (*Don Quixote*); Ralph ◊Courteville, (ditto); ◊Don Quixote, The Comical History of, (Purcell and others); G B ◊Draghi (*Wonders in the Sun*); J ◊Eccles (*Don Quixote*); ◊Locke (*Fool turned Critic*); D ◊Purcell (*Cynthia and Endymion*); ◊Purcell (*Fool's Preferment*, *Marriage-Hater Matched*, *Richmond Heiress*, *Sir Barnaby Whigg* and *Virtuous Wife*); William ◊Turner (*Fond Husband* and *Madam Fickle*).

Durkó, Zsolt (b Szeged, 10 Apr 1934), Hungarian composer. He studied in Budapest and with Petrassi in Rome. His music breaks away from local influences and favours the avant-garde.

Works include opera *Moses* (produced Budapest 1977); *Organismi* for violin and orchestra (1964), *Dartmouth Concerto* for soprano and orchestra (1966), *Fioriture* for orchestra (1966), *Altimara* for chorus and orchestra (1968), *Funeral Oration*, oratorio (1972), *Turner Illustrations* for orchestra (1976); two string quartets (1966, 1969), *Impromptus in F* for flute and ensemble (1984); wind octet (1988); *Ilmarinen* for chorus (1989).

Durón, Sebastián (b Brihuega, Castile, bap. 19 Apr 1660; d Cambó, Pyrenees, 3 Aug 1716), Spanish composer. Was organist at Las Palmas, Canary Islands, and in 1691 became *maestro de capilla* at the court of Madrid until 1702. Not having supported the Bourbon succession, he seems to have gone into exile. He was an early exponent of Spanish opera.

I believed I could make musical criticism readable even by the deaf.
George Bernard Shaw, *London Music in 1888–9*, 1935

Works include operas and zarzuelas *Muerte en amor es la ausencia*, *Apolo y Dafne*, *Selva encantada de Amor*, *Las nuevas armas de Amor*, *La guerra de los gigantes*, *Salir el amor del mundo*; incidental music for a comedy, *Jupiter*; two ballets.

Dürr, Alfred (b Charlottenburg, Berlin, 3 Mar 1918), German musicologist. He studied at the University of Göttingen. From 1953 he has edited the *Bach-Jahrbuch* and he has been principal contributor to the Bach *Neue Ausgabe* (complete works). Bach's cantatas are at the centre of his research.

Dürr, Walter (b Berlin, 27 Mar 1932), German musicologist. He studied at Tübingen University and has taught there from 1962; from 1965 he has been joint editor of the *Neue Schubert-Ausgabe* at Tübingen. Other fields of study have been Mozart, and the Italian madrigal.

Duruflé, Maurice (b Louviers, Eure, 11 Jan 1902; d Paris, 24 Jun 1986), French organist and composer. Learnt music in the choir school of Rouen Cathedral, 1912–18, and then studied at the Paris Conservatory under Vierne, Tournemire and Dukas. Appointed organist at the church of Saint-Etienne-du-Mont 1929.

Works include Requiem for chorus and orchestra (1947); *Messe cum jubilo* (1966); chorale on *Veni Creator*, suite and many other works for organ; *Prelude, Recitative and Variations* for flute, viola and piano; three dances for orchestra.

Dušek, Jan Ladislav ◊Dussek.

Dušek, Franz (František Xaver) (b Choteborky, 8 Dec 1731; d Prague, 12 Feb 1799), Bohemian pianist and composer. Pupil of Wagenseil in Vienna; taught in Prague, master of many famous pupils. He and his wife were friends of Mozart, who worked on *Don Giovanni* at their home in Prague.

Dušek (born *Hambacher*), Josefa (b Prague, 6 Mar 1754; d Prague, 8 Jan 1824), Bohemian soprano, wife of Franz ◊Dušek. She travelled in Austria and Germany. Mozart wrote the concert aria *Bella mia fiamma* (K528) for her. She gave the fp of Beethoven's *Ah, perfido* (Leipzig, 1796).

Dushkin, Samuel (b Suwalki, 13 Dec 1891; d New York, 24 Jun 1976), Polish-born American violinist. He studied in Paris and with Auer and Kreisler in NY. European tour 1918, US debut 1924. He advised Stravinsky on the composition of the violin concerto and gave fp Berlin, 23 Oct 1931. He gave Stravinsky's *Duo Concertant* with Stravinsky in Berlin on 28 Oct 1932.

Dussek (or *Dušek*, *Dusík*), Jan Ladislav (b Čáslav, 12 Feb 1760; d St Germain-en-Laye, Paris, 20 Mar 1812), Bohemian pianist and composer. Educated at the Jesuit College in Jihlav and Prague University, where he read theology. He had shown early promise, and c 1779 went to the Netherlands, holding organ posts at Malines and Bergen-op-Zoom. He gave up his organist's career c 1782, and won great success in Amsterdam and The Hague as a pianist and composer. Concert tours took him to Hamburg (where he studied with C P E Bach), Berlin and St Petersburg, where he entered the service of Prince Radziwill, spending the next two years on the latter's estate in Lithuania. He played before Marie Antoinette in Paris in 1786, and after a visit to Italy returned there in 1788. At the Revolution he fled to London, where he first appeared at one of Salomon's concerts in 1790. He married the singer and pianist Sophia Corri in 1792, and joined his father-in-law's firm of music publishers. The business failed, and he went to Hamburg to escape his creditors in 1800. More travels followed. He was with Prince Louis Ferdinand of Prussia 1803–06, then in the service of the Prince of Isenburg and, finally, Talleyrand.

Works include incidental music for *The Captive of Spilburg* (London, 1798) and Sheridan's *Pizarro* (both with Kelly); three overtures and serenade for orchestra; Mass (1811); three string quartets, two piano quartets, piano quintet. c 20 piano trios; c 12 sonatas for piano duet, sonata for two pianos; piano music; c 18 concertos, c 32 sonatas, c 25 rondos, c 20 sets of variations, various misc. pieces; c 65 sonatas with violin or flute.

Dutilleux, Henri (b Angers, 22 Jan 1916), French composer. He studied at the Paris Conservatory and won the Prix de Rome in 1938; professor at the Conservatory since 1970. His music is regarded as being in the tradition of Ravel, Debussy and Messiaen.

Works include two symphonies (performed Paris, 1950 and Boston, 1959); ballets *Le Loup* (1953) and *Summer's End* (1981), *La Giole* for voice and orchestra (1944), *Cinq Métaboles* for orchestra, fp Cleveland, 1965), *Tout un monde lointain* for cello and orchestra (1970), *Timbres, espaces, mouvement* for orchestra (fp Washington, 1978), *Ainsi parle la nuit* for string quartet (1976); *L'arbre des songes* for violin and orchestra (1985), *Mystère de l'instant* for 24 strings, cimbalom and percussion (1989), *Le Jeu des contraires* for piano (1989), *Diptyque, Les Citations* for oboe, harpsichord, double bass and percussion (1991).

Dutoit, Charles (b Lausanne, 7 Oct 1936), Swiss conductor. Studied at the Lausanne Conservatory and at Tanglewood. Debut with Berne SO 1964; chief conductor 1966–77. Guest conductor with Suisse Romande and Zurich Tonhalle Orchestras and the RPO, London. Music director Montreal SO from 1977; many performances of Haydn, Stravinsky and Debussy. The second of his three wives was the pianist Martha ◊Argerich. Released recording of *Les Troyens*, 1994.

Duval, Denise (b Paris, 23 Oct 1921), French soprano. Debut Bordeaux 1941, as Lola. At the Paris Opéra-Comique she created Thérèse in Poulenc's *Les Mamelles de Tirésias*, 1947, and in 1959 was Elle in the fp of *La Voix Humaine*; at the Opéra she was Blanche in the first local

Dvořák *The composer Antonin Dvořák (1841–1904) in a portrait with his wife. Dvořák successfully blends the two most important factors influencing music in the 19th century: Romanticism, as expressed formally by composers such as Brahms, and Nationalism, as embodied in the growing prominence of regional folk song.*

performance of the *Carmélites*. Glyndebourne, 1962, Mélisande. Other roles included Massenet's Salomé and Ravel's Concepcion. Retired 1965.

Duval, François (b Paris, c 1673; d Versailles, 27 Jan 1728), French violinist and composer. He was a member of Louis XIV's '24 violons du roi' and wrote violin sonatas in the Italian style and pub. as the first of the kind in 1704. Wrote numerous books of sonatas for violin and bass and two violins and bass.

Dux, Claire (b Witkowicz, 2 Aug 1885; d Chicago, 8 Oct 1967), Polish soprano. Debut Cologne 1906, Pamina. Berlin Hofoper 1909–18, debut as Mimi. At CG in 1913 she sang Eva and was Sophie in the first London performance of *Rosenkavalier* under Beecham. She had two brief marriages and sang in Chicago 1921–24; retired after her third marriage, to a millionaire meat-packer.

Dvořák, Antonín (b Nelahozeves, 8 Sept 1841; d Prague, 1 May 1904), Czech composer. Son of a village innkeeper and butcher. He heard only popular and simple church music as a child, but developed remarkable gifts. He was sent to the organ school at Prague in 1857; began to compose two years later and joined an orchestra as violinist; later played viola in the orchestra at the Czech National Theatre, under Smetana. In 1865 he wrote the song cycle *Cypresses*, inspired by his hopeless love of his pupil, Josefina. In 1873 he married Anna Čermaková, Josefina's sister, and produced his first compositions to receive attention, including the third symphony; earlier works had been under the shadow of Wagner. The next year he received for the first time the Austrian state prize for composition and became a friend of Brahms, who was on the committee and introduced him to his pub., Simrock. The Slavonic Rhapsodies and Dances of 1878 brought an essentially Nationalist character to his music; they were followed by the first of his great String Quartets, the Eb op. 51, and the powerful 6th Symphony: in one work folk elements are most obvious, in the other the presence of Brahms is felt.

He first visited England in 1884 to conduct the *Stabat Mater* in

Dvořák
A biographical note

The early years of Dvořák's marriage were marred by the tragic deaths of his first three children, two from illness and one in an accident. Beginning with the birth of his daughter Otilie in 1878, Dvořák was to have six surviving children and shared with some of them his two principal hobbies. When in Prague he spent much time at the Franz-Josef station, collecting train numbers. While a teacher at the Conservatory, Dvořák would often send out a student for an elusive number. The young Josef Suk, currently courting Otilie and Dvořák's future son-in-law, was sent on such an errand but returned with the number of the coal tender instead of the engine: 'And this is the man who wishes to marry my daughter!' Dvořák lamented. While staying in New York during 1892 he was not allowed to observe from the platforms at Grand Central station. He was able to indulge his other hobby – pigeon fancying – at Central Park Zoo. However, his favourite fantails and pouters were not on view, and American settlers had already exterminated an entire species of the bird – the passenger pigeon.

London. In 1885 he bought the country estate of Vysoká, which remained his home. Hon.Mus.D. at Cambridge in 1891, when he was appointed professor at Prague Conservatory, of which he became director in 1901. In 1892–95 he was director of the new National Conservatory in NY, and spent some holidays at the Czech colony of Spillville, Iowa. The premiere of the *New World Symphony* at Carnegie Hall was one of the greatest successes of Dvořák's career.

In 1896 he paid the last of his many visits to England, where he had produced several works at the music festivals. The mighty and classically modelled 7th symphony was premiered in London in 1885, and the cello concerto followed ten years later; Josefina, his first love, died during the concerto's composition, and in memory of her the slow section of the finale quotes her favourite song from *Cypresses*.

Works include OPERAS: (ten) all except the first produced in Prague: *Alfred* (1870; produced Olomouc, 1938), *King and Coal Burner* (*Král a uhlíř*, 1874), *The Pig-headed Peasants* (*Tvrdé palice*, 1881), *Vanda* (1876), *The Peasant A Rogue* (*Šelma sedlák*, 1878), *Dimitrij* (1882), *The Jacobin* (1889), *The Devil and Kate* (*Čert a Káča*, 1899), *Rusalka* (1901), *Armida* (1904).

ORCHESTRAL: nine symphonies: no. 1 in C minor, *The Bells of Zlonice* (1865); no. 2 in B♭, (1865); no. 3 in E♭, op. 10 (1873); no. 4 in D minor, (1874); no. 5 in F, op. 76 (1875); no. 6 in D, op. 60 (1880); no. 7 in D minor, op. 70 (1885); no. 8 in G, op. 88 (1889); no. 9 in E minor, 'From the New World', op. 95 (1893). five symphonic poems *The Water-Sprite* (1896), *The Noon-day Witch* (1896), *The Golden Spinning-Wheel*, *The Wood-Dove*, *Hero's Song* (1897); seven concert overtures including *Husitská* (1883) and the cycle *Amid Nature*, *Carnival* and *Othello* (1891–92); various orchestral works including Serenade in D minor for wind, cello and bass (1878); *Czech Suite* (1879), three *Slavonic Rhapsodies*, *Scherzo capriccioso* (1883), *Symphonic Variations* (1877); two sets of Slavonic Dances; *Serenade* and *Notturno* for string orchestra; concertos for piano, violin and cello (1876, 1880, 1895); four smaller pieces for solo instruments and orchestra.

CHAMBER MUSIC: 14 string quartets: no. 1 in A, op. 2 (1862), no. 2 in B♭ (*c* 1870), no. 3 in D (*c* 1870), no. 4 in E minor (1870), no. 5 in F minor op. 9 (1873), no. 6 in A minor, op. 12 (1873), no. 7 in A minor op. 16 (1874), no. 8 in E, op. 80 (1876), no. 9 in D minor, op. 34 (1877), no. 10 in E♭, op. 51 (1879), no. 11 in C, op. 61 (1881), no. 12 in F, op. 96 (*American*), no. 13 in G, op. 105 (1895), no. 14 in A♭, op. 106 (1895); two string quintets: in G, op. 77, with double bass (1875), in E♭, op. 97, with viola (1893); string sextet in A, op. 48 (1878); four piano trios; in B♭, op. 21 (1875), in G minor, op. 26 (1876), in F minor, op. 65 (1883), in E minor, 'Dumky', op. 90 (1891);

two piano quartets in D, op. 23 (1875), in E♭, op. 87 (1889); piano quintet in A, op. 81 (1887). *Bagatelles* for two violins, cello and harmonium (1878); *Terzetto* for two violins and viola (1887); sonata (1880), sonatina (1893) and smaller pieces for violin and piano

CHORUS AND ORCHESTRAL: (some with solo voices): *Stabat Mater* (1877), *The Spectre's Bride*, *St Ludmilla* (1886), Psalm cxlix, Mass in D major, Requiem (1890); *The American Flag*, Te Deum; smaller choral works: *The Heirs of the White Mountain*, *Song of the Czechs*, *Hymn of the Czech Peasants*, *Hymnus*, *Festival Song*; several sets of partsongs; four sets of vocal duets; 68 songs.

> *Why on earth didn't I know that one could write a violincello concerto like this? If I had only known, I would have written one long ago.*
> **Johannes Brahms** on Dvořák, quoted in Robertson, *Dvořák*, 1964

PIANO: 14 op. nos. of piano pieces, including Theme and Variations, *Poetic Tone-Pictures*, Suite and *Humoresques*, also some separate piano pieces; six sets of piano duets, including Slavonic Dances, *Legends* and *From the Bohemian Forest*.

Dvořákova, Ludmila (b Kolín, 11 Jul 1923), Czech soprano. Debut Ostrava 1949, Katya Kabanova. Sang in Bratislava, Prague and Vienna before Berlin debut 1960, as Octavian. Bayreuth 1965–71 as Gutrune, Venus, Kundry. London, CG, 1966–71 as Brünnhilde and Isolde. NY Met. debut 1966 as Leonore. Other roles included Ortrud, the Marschallin, Ariadne and Jenůfa. Sang at the Vienna Staatsoper 1964–85.

Dyck, Ernest (Marie-Hubert) van (b Antwerp, 2 Apr 1861; d Berlaer-les-Lierre, 31 Aug 1923), Belgian tenor. After studying law and working as a journalist, he learnt singing and made his debut in Paris in 1883. In 1887 he sang the first of the Wagnerian parts with which he was afterwards chiefly associated, Lohengrin in Paris, and the following year he was first engaged as Parsifal at Bayreuth. He also sang in Wagner's operas in London, Brussels, NY, etc. He created Massenet's Werther (Vienna, 1892). NY Met. debut, 1898, Tannhäuser.

Dygon, John (b ? Canterbury, *c* 1485; d 1541), English cleric and composer. Took the B.Mus. at Oxford in 1512, (?) in 1521 went to Louvain to study with the Spanish humanist Juan Luis Vives, and became a prior at St Austin's Abbey, Canterbury. A motet of his is preserved and a treatise on proportions in Trinity College library, Cambridge.

A Selection of

Dvořák

Symphony no. 5 1875
Serenade for Strings 1879
Symphonic Variations 1877
Symphony no. 6 1880

Symphony no. 7 1885
Piano Quintet 1887
Piano Trio op. 90 1891
Symphony no. 9 1893
String Quartet op. 96 1893
Cello Concerto 1895

Dykes, John Bacchus (b Hull, 10 Mar 1823; d Ticehurst, Sussex, 22 Jan 1876), English church musician. Learnt music from an organist at Hull, graduated at Cambridge, where he studied music under Walmisley, and became curate at Malton, Yorkshire, becoming precentor and minor canon at Durham Cathedral in 1849–62. Wrote services, anthems and especially many hymn-tunes, and took part in the compilation of *Hymns Ancient and Modern*.

dynamics the degrees of loudness and softness in music, and the musical symbols that represent them.

Dyson, George (b Halifax, 28 May 1883; d Winchester, 28 Sept 1964), English composer. Studied at the RCM in London and became music director at Winchester College in 1924, having already held the appointments of music master at Osborne, Marlborough, Rugby and Wellington, serving in the 1914–18 war between. In 1937 he was appointed director of the RCM in succession to Hugh Allen, retiring in 1952. Knighted 1941.

Works include *The Canterbury Pilgrims* (setting of Chaucer's prologue, 1931) and other compositions for solo voices, chorus and orchestra; orchestral, chamber and piano music; songs.

Dzerzhinsky, Ivan (b Tambov, 9 Apr 1909; d Leningrad, 18 Jan 1978), Russian composer. Studied at the Gnessin School of Music at Moscow and at the Leningrad Conservatory.

Works include operas *Quiet Flows the Don*, *Ploughing the Fallows* (both after novels by Mikhail Sholokhov, 1934), *In the Days of Volochaiev*, *The Storm* (after Ostrovsky, 1940), *The Blood of the People*; incidental music for plays; film music: *Spring*, *Poem of the Dnieper* and *Russian Overture* for orchestra; three piano concertos; piano pieces; song cycles.

E

E the third note, or mediant, of the scale of C major.

Eadie, Noel (b Paisley, 10 Dec 1901; d London, 11 Apr 1950), Scottish soprano. Studied piano at first, then singing with Esta d'Argo in London. She first appeared in London, at CG, in 1931, joined the BNOC and after an engagement at the Chicago Opera sang Constanze and the Queen of Night in the Mozart performances at Glyndebourne 1935–36.

Eaglen, Jane (b Lincoln, 4 Apr 1960), English soprano, Studied at RNCM and made her debut with ENO 1984, as Lady Ella in *Patience*; has returned as Eva (1989) and Tosca (1990), the *Trovatore* Leonora, Donna Elvira and Santuzza. CG debut 1986; sang Rossini's Mathilde there 1992. Appearances as Donna Anna and Fiordiligi for Scottish Opera, Verdi's Odabella in Geneva. La Scala, Milan 1994, as Brünnhilde in *Die Walküre*. Eglantine in *Euryanthe* at the QEH, London 1994.

Eagles, Solomon, ◊Eccles.

Eames, Emma (b Shanghai, 13 Aug 1865; d New York, 13 Jun 1952), American soprano. She studied in Paris, and made her debut there in 1889 as Juliette. London, CG, 1891–1901 as Marguerite, Mireille, Elisabeth, Eva and Desdemona. NY Met. 1891–1909 as Donna Anna, Pamina, Santuzza, Tosca and the first Alice Ford in the US. Concert tours only from 1911.

Earth Dances work for orchestra by Birtwistle, fp London, 14 Mar 1986.

ear training the development of the sense of pitch, the ready distinction of intervals, identification of various types of chords, etc.

Easdale, Brian (b Manchester, 10 Aug 1909), English composer. Educated at Westminster Abbey choir-school and the RCM in London.

Works include operas *Rapunzel* (1927), *The Corn King* (1935) and *The Sleeping Children* (1951); incidental music for Eugene O'Neill's *Mourning Becomes Electra*; film music *The Red Shoes*; *Missa Coventrensis*, *Dead March*, *Tone Poem*, *Six Poems* for orchestra; piano concerto (1938); string trio; pieces for two pianos; song cycles.

East, Michael (b London, c 1580; d Lichfield, 1648), English composer. He was apparently in the service of Lady Hatton in London early in the 17th c. and from 1618 organist of Lichfield Cathedral.

Works include Evening Service, anthems; six books of madrigals (some with anthems) and a madrigal contributed to *The Triumphes of Oriana*; music for viols.

East, Thomas (b c 1535; d London, 1608), English publisher and the first major music printer in England. He worked in London and brought out several works by Byrd and the Elizabethan madrigalists; other publications include *Musica Transalpina* (1588, 1597), *The Whole Book of Psalmes* (1592) and *The Triumphs of Oriana* (1601).

Easter music-drama ◊liturgical drama.

Easter Oratorio, *Kommt, eilet und laufet*, work by J S Bach performed as a church cantata 1725 and revised 1732–35 as an oratorio.

Eastman School of Music American conservatory, in Rochester, NY, founded 1912 and taken over 1917 by George Eastman (1854–1932).

It became part of the University of Rochester 1921, with Howard Hanson as director 1924–64; he was succeeded by Walter Hendl, 1964–72, and Robert S Freeman from 1972. The Cleveland Quartet has been quartet-in-residence.

Easton, Florence (b Middlesbrough, 25 Oct 1882; d New York, 13 Aug 1955), English soprano. She was engaged in Berlin and Hamburg 1907–15 and made her NY Met. debut in 1917; created Lauretta in 1918. Sang 35 of her 150 roles in NY, ending with Brünnhilde in 1936. London, CG, 1909 as Butterfly; 1927 and 1932 as Turandot, Brünnhilde and Isolde. Other roles included Carmen, the Marschallin and Tosca.

Eaton, John (b Bryn Mawr, PA, 30 Mar 1935), American composer. Studied with Sessions and Babbitt at Princeton; has taught at Indiana University, from 1970. Works use microtones, serial techniques and synthesizer called syn-ket; operas *Ma Barker* (1957), *Heracles* (1968), *Myshkin* (1973), *The Tempest* (1985), *The Reverend Jim Jones* (1989).

Eben, Petr (b Zamberk, 22 Jan 1929), Czech composer. He studied in Prague and has taught at the university there from 1955. His works reflect an interest in religion and myth.

Works include piano concerto (1961); oratorio *Apologia Sokratus* (1964); *Ubi caritas et amor* for chorus (1965); wind quintet (1965); *Faust* for organ (1980); string quartet (1981); *Curses and Blessings*, ballet (1980); organ concerto (1983); piano trio (1986); *Hommage à Dietrich Buxtehude* for organ (1987); two *Invocations* for trombone and organ (1989).

Eberl, Anton (b Vienna, 13 Jun 1765; d Vienna, 11 Mar 1807), Austrian pianist and composer. Friend and possibly pupil of Mozart, he toured as a pianist in Germany with Mozart's widow and from 1796 to 1800 was *Kapellmeister* in St Petersburg.

Works include operas ◊La Marchande des modes (1787), *Die Königen der schwarzen Inseln* (1801), etc.; melodrama *Pyramus und Thisbe* (1794); symphonies; piano concertos; chamber music; sonatas, variations, etc. for piano; songs. Much of his music was mistakenly ascribed to Mozart.

Eberlin, Johann Ernst (b Jettingen, 27 Mar 1702; d Salzburg, 19 Jun 1762), German organist and composer. Settled in Salzburg in 1724, where he became organist to the court and cathedral in 1729, and *Kapellmeister* in 1749. He was esteemed as a composer of church music.

Works include several operas, to texts by Metastasio, over 50 Masses; 12 Requiems; offertories, etc.; several oratorios; organ music.

Ebert, Carl (b Berlin, 20 Feb 1887; d Los Angeles, 14 May 1980), German opera producer and manager. He produced *Le nozze di Figaro* in Darmstadt (1927) and worked in Berlin before leaving with Fritz Busch in 1933; with Busch founded the Glyndebourne Festival in 1934. He was artistic director there until 1939 and again 1947–59; helped to create new standards in the performance of Mozart's operas. He staged the fp of *The Rake's Progress* (Venice, 1951) and worked again at the Berlin Städtische Oper 1954–61. His son **Peter** (b Frankfurt, 6 Apr 1918) has worked at Glyndebourne and LA and in West Germany. Director of productions, Scottish Opera 1965–75; general administrator 1977–80.

Eberwein, Traugott Maximillian (b Weimar, 27 Oct 1775; d Rudolstadt, 2 Dec 1831), German violinist and composer. Son of a member of the Weimar court band, in which he played as a child. Through Zelter's influence he was much esteemed by Goethe. He went into the service of the Prince of Schwarzburg-Rudolstadt in 1797 and became music director there in 1817.

Works include operas *Claudine von Villa Bella* (1815) and *Der Jahrmarkt von Plundersweilen* (1818) (libretti by Goethe), *Preciosa* (P A Wolff) and eight others; Mass; three cantatas; concertos, *Sinfonia concertante* for wind instruments; vocal quartets; songs.

Ebony Concerto work by Stravinsky for clarinet and orchestra, composed 1945 for Woody Herman and his band and performed by them, NY, 25 Mar 1946.

Blessed Cecilia, appear in visions/To all musicians, appear and inspire:/Translated Daughter, come down and startle/Composing mortals with immortal fire.
W H Auden, 'Song for St Cecilia's Day',
Collected Poems, 1976

Eccard, Johann (b Mühlhausen, Thuringia, 1553; d Berlin, 1611), German composer. Pupil of David Köler in the choir-school attached to the Weimar court chapel, 1567–71, and of Lassus at Munich. In the service successively of Jacob Fugger at Augsburg, at Königsberg, of the Margrave of Brandenburg-Ansbach and of the Elector Joachim Friedrich of Brandenburg in Berlin and his successor, Johann Sigismund. He was a follower of Lassus; his music was still printed 30 years after his death.

Works include motets, chorales (some harmonized, some newly composed by him); sacred songs; secular German songs for several voices, wedding songs, odes, festival songs.

Eccles, Eagles, English family of musicians:
1. Solomon Eccles (b *c* 1618, d London, 2 Jan 1682), descendant of a musical family, teacher of virginals and viols. He embraced Quakerism *c* 1660 and burnt all his music and instruments, but in 1667 pub. a book arguing for and against the moral justification of music. He went to the West Indies with George Fox to establish Quakerism in 1671, was in New England in 1672 and was prosecuted for sedition at Barbados in 1680.
2. Solomon Eccles (b *c* 1645; d Guildford, buried 1 Dec 1710), violinist and composer, (?) son of 1, musician at the courts of James II and William and Mary. Works include music for plays by Aphra Behn and Otway.
3. John Eccles (b London, 1668; d Hampton Wick, 12 Jan 1735), composer, son of 2. Pupil of his father. Began to write music for the theatres *c* 1690. He became a member of the King's Band in 1694 and its Master in 1700 on the death of Staggins, and the same year gained the second prize in a contest for the best composer of Congreve's masque *The Judgment of Paris*, Weldon being first and D Purcell and Finger third and fourth. For about a quarter of a century he lived in retirement at Kingston, devoted mainly to fishing, though he continued to write odes for the royal household. He wrote music for many plays, e.g. *The Spanish Friar* (Dryden), *Love for Love* (Congreve), *Don Quixote* (Durfey, with Purcell), *The Stage Coach* (Farquhar), *Macbeth* (Shakespeare, 1694), *Europe's Revels for the Peace* (1697), *Rinaldo and Armida* (1698), *The Way of the World* and *Semele* (both Congreve), *The Biter* (Rowe); music for Queen Anne's coronation; Congreve's *Ode for St Cecilia's Day* (1701); many songs.
4. Henry Eccles (b London, *c* 1690; d Paris, ? 1742), violinist and composer, son of 2. Member of the King's Band, 1689–1710, but went to Paris, considering himself neglected at home, and joined the royal band there. Wrote sonatas for violin and for viol.

5. Thomas Eccles (b London, *c* 1672; d *c* 1745), violinist, son of 2. Pupil of his brother Henry (4), although highly gifted, secured no appointment, being a wastrel, but made such a living as he could by playing at taverns.

échappée French, short for *note échappée* = 'escaped note'; a progression between two adjacent notes which deviates by at first taking a step in the opposite direction and then taking the second note aimed at by an interval of a third.

An échappée between the notes E and D in the top voice of this example.

Échelle de soie, L', *The Silken Ladder*, opera by Gaveaux (libretto by F A E de Planard), produced Paris, Opéra-Comique, 22 Aug 1808. The original of Rossini's *Scala di seta*.

echo in composition various echo effects have been used in many ways at all times; e.g. Lassus's madrigal *Olà, che buon eco*, the witches' chorus in Purcell's *Dido and Aeneas*, the *Echo* piece in Bach's B minor clavier partita, the *Scène aux champs* in Berlioz's *Fantastic Symphony*, the second act of Humperdinck's *Hänsel und Gretel*, etc.

Écho et Narcisse opera by Gluck (libretto by L T de Tschudy), produced Paris, Opéra, 24 Sept 1779. Écho is in despair when Narcissus prefers his own reflection to her. She dies from grief, but when Narcissus recovers his senses she is restored to life.

Eck, Franz (b Mannheim, 1774; d Strasbourg; 1804), German violinist. Pupil of his brother Johann. Played in the court band at Munich as a youth, then travelled much and took Spohr to Russia with him as his pupil.

Eck, Friedrich Johann (b Schwetzingen, 25 May 1767; d Schwetzingen, 22 Feb 1838), German violinist, conductor and composer, brother of Franz ◊Eck. In the service of the court at Munich from 1778, *Konzertmeister* 1788, later opera conductor there. Left Munich 1800 and settled in France.

Works include six violin concertos, *Concertante* for two violins.

Eckardt, Johann Gottfried (b Augsburg, 21 Jan 1735; d Paris, 24 Jul 1809), German pianist, composer and miniature painter. Settled in Paris, 1758. Wrote sonatas, variations, etc. for piano

Eckert, Carl (Anton Florian) (b Potsdam, 7 Dec 1820; d Berlin, 14 Oct 1879), German pianist, violinist, conductor and composer. Pupil of Mendelssohn at Leipzig. Accompanist at the Théâtre Italien in Paris and to Henriette Sontag in the USA, then conductor at the same theatre in Paris, director of the Court Opera in Vienna, *Kapellmeister* at Stuttgart in succession to Kücken, and successor of Dorn in Berlin.

Works include operas *Das Fischermädchen* (1830), *Wilhelm von Oranien*; oratorios *Ruth* (1833) and *Judith*; church music, symphonies; cello concerto; piano pieces; songs.

Éclat work by Boulez for 15 instruments; fp LA, 26 Mar 1965. Expanded as *Éclat/Multiples* and performed London, 21 Oct 1970; work in progress.

École d'Arcueil a group of French composers gathered round Satie in his later years at his home in the Arcueil suburb of Paris, formed in 1923 and included Henri Cliquet-Pleyel, Roger Désormière, Maxime Jacob, Henri Sauguet and others.

ecossaise French = lit. 'Scottish one'; a dance long supposed to be of Scottish origin but no longer considered so. As a fashionable ballroom dance in the early 19th c. it was in fairly animated 2–4 time, about halfway between the polka and the galop in speed. Among the composers who cultivated it were Beethoven, Schubert and Chopin. The German *Schottisch* (usually written *Schottische* in English) is the same thing.

Écuatorial work by Varèse for bass voice, eight brass, piano, organ, two ondes Martenots and six percussion (text is a Spanish translation of a prayer from the sacred book of the Maya Quiché, the *Popul Vuh*), fp NY, 15 Apr 1934, conductor Nicolas Slonimsky.

Eda-Pierre, Christiane (b Fort-de-France, Martinique, 24 Mar 1932), French soprano. Studied at the Paris Conservatory and made her debut at Nice, 1958, as Bizet's Leila. Sang Lakmé at the Paris Opéra-Comique, 1961 and Fatima in *Les Indes Galantes* at the Opéra, 1962 (other roles there have included Lucia di Lammermoor, Constanze, and the Angel in the 1983 fp of Messiaen's *St François d'Assise*); NY Met. from 1976 as Mozart's Countess (with the Opéra), Gilda and Antonia. Professor at the Paris Conservatory from 1977.

Edelmann, Johann Friedrich (b Strasbourg, 5 May 1749; d Paris, 17 Jul 1794), Alsatian pianist and composer. He became famous in Paris through the patronage of his pupil, Baron Dietrich. He was a friend of Gluck, and Mozart thought well of his piano compositions. He apparently played a discreditable part during the French Revolution, and died on the guillotine.

Works include operas *Ariane dans l'île de Naxos* (1782), *La Bergère des Alpes* (1781) and *Diane et l'Amour* (1802); symphonies; keyboard concertos and sonatas.

Edelmann, Otto (b Vienna, 5 Feb 1917), Austrian bass-baritone. Studied at the Vienna State Academy of Music. His career was interrupted by World War II, but in 1947 he joined the Vienna Staatsoper, and in 1951 sang at Bayreuth, as Sachs; NY Met. 1954, same role. Salzburg 1960 as Ochs. Other roles include Leporello, Amfortas, Gurnemanz and Dulcamara.

Eder, Helmut (b Linz, 26 Dec 1916), Austrian composer. Studied in Stuttgart and with Carl Orff in Munich. Co-founder of electronic music school at Linz Conservatory, 1959, and Professor at the Salzburg Mozarteum from 1967. His music has progressed towards electronics from neo-classicism and serialism.

Works include operas *Oedipus* (1960), *Der Kardinal* (1965), *Der Aufstand* (1975), *Georges Dandin* (1979), *Mozart in New York* (1991); ballets *Moderner Traum* (1957), *Anamorphose* (1963), and *Die Irrfahrten des Odysseus* (1965); five symphonies (1950–80), three violin concertos (1963, 1964, 1982), cello concerto (1981), concertino for classical orchestra (1984); string quartet (1948), clarinet quintet (1982).

Edgar opera by Puccini (libretto by F Fontana, based on Musset's *La Coupe et les lèvres*), produced Milan, La Scala, 21 Apr 1889. Edgar loves Fidelia, but runs away with moorish Tigrana when she is threatened by villagers. Regretting the loss of Fidelia, he decides to join soldiers in battle. Later reunited with Fidelia, who stabs Tigrana.

Edinburgh Festival annual festival of arts held in late summer in the Scottish capital, founded 1947. Directors: Rudolf Bing (1947–49), Ian Hunter (1949–55), Robert Ponsonby (1955–60), Earl of Harewood (1961–65), Peter Diamand (1966–78), John Drummond (1979–83), Frank Dunlop 1984–91, Brian McMaster from 1992. Until 1978 the festival had strong musical emphasis. Many leading orchestras have performed, and visiting opera companies, including Glyndebourne, Hamburg and Prague, have given first British performances of *The Rake's Progress*, *Mathis der Maler* and *The Excursions of Mr Brouček*. The Kirov Co., St Petersburg, visited in 1995.

Edipo Re, *King Oedipus*, opera in one act by Leoncavallo (libretto by G Forzano, after Sophocles), produced Chicago, 13 Dec 1920.

To the devil with all those who have seen in our sublime art nothing but an innocent tickling of the ear.

Georges Bizet, in a letter to Marmontel, 1857

Eduardo e Cristina opera in two acts by Rossini (libretto by G Schmidt, written for Pavesi, altered by A L Tottola and G Bevilacqua-Aldovrandini), produced Venice, Teatro San Benedetto, 24 Apr 1819. Pastiche, assembled from *Ricciardo e Zoraide*, *Ermione* and *Adelaide di Borgogna*.

Éducation manquée operetta in one act by Chabrier (libretto by

E Leterrier and A Vanloo), produced privately Paris, 1 May 1879. Paris, Théâtre des Arts, 9 Jan 1913. Count Gontran is educated in the facts of life.

Edwards, Richard (b near Yeovil, *c* 1522; d London, 31 Oct 1566), English composer. Pupil of the musician, physician and Greek scholar George Etheridge of Thame, entered Corpus Christi College, Oxford in 1540, and transferred to Christ Church on its foundation in 1546. Appointed Master of the Children of the Chapel Royal in London in 1561 and wrote two plays for them. He was also a playwright, producing *Palamon and Arcite* before Queen Elizabeth and also writing *Damon and Pithias*, etc., and a poet, compiling and contributing to a book of verse, *The Paradise of Dainty Devices*.

Works include music to his own *Damon and Pithias*; part-songs *In Going to My Naked Bed* and *O the Silly Man*.

Edwards, Ross (b Sydney, 23 Dec 1943), Australian composer. Studied in Sydney and Adelaide, with Peter Sculthorpe and Maxwell Davies. Lecturer at the NSW conservatory from 1976.

Works include *Quen Quaeritis*, children's nativity play (1967); *Etude* for orchestra (1969); *Mountain Village in a Clearing Mist* for orchestra (1973); string quartet (1982); piano concerto (1982); *Christina's World*, theatre piece (1983); series *Maninya I–V* for chamber ensemble with voices (1981–86); *Reflections* for piano and three percussion (1985); *Flower Songs* for chorus and percussion (1986); *Maninyas* for violins and orchestra (1988); *Varregh* for solo percussion and orchestra (1989).

Edwards, Sian (b West Chiltington, Sussex, 27 Aug 1959), English conductor. Studied with Neeme Järvi and Norman Del Mar, and at the Leningrad Conservatory. Guest conductor with leading British orchestras; opera debut with Scottish Opera 1986 (*Mahagonny*). Glyndebourne debut 1987 (*Traviata*), CG 1988, as the first woman to conduct there (*The Knot Garden*). Led the premiere of Turnage's *Greek* at the Munich Biennale, 1988, and *The Gambler* at ENO, 1990; music director there 1993–96, conducting *Jenůfa* in her first season; *Khovanshchina* in 1994.

Egdon Heath work for orchestra by Holst, after the Dorset landscape described by Hardy in *The Return of the Native* (1878). Commissioned by the NY SO and performed 12 Feb 1928 in NY.

Egge, Klaus (b Gransherad, Telemark, 19 Jul 1906; d Oslo, 7 Mar 1979), Norwegian composer. Studied under Valen and in Germany. He edited *Tonekunst* in 1935–38.

Works include five symphonies (1945–69), three piano concertos, trio for violin, cello and piano, violin and piano sonatas.

Egisto, L', *Aegisthus*, opera by Cavalli (libretto by G Faustini), produced Venice, Teatro San Cassiano, autumn 1643. First modern revival Santa Fe 1974, in a free realization by Raymond Leppard. Egisto and Clemene resolve to find their original lovers after being separated by pirates. They become involved in love triangles which eventually resolve happily.

Egk, Werner (b Auchsesheim, Bavaria, 17 May 1901; d Inning, near Munich, 10 Jul 1983), German composer. Mainly self-taught and spent some time in Italy. He began to compose to broadcasting commissions. Settled near Munich and succeeded Graener as head of the faculty of composition in the Nazi Reichsmusikkammer. From 1936 to 1940 he conducted at the Berlin Staatsoper and from 1950 to 1953 was director of the Hochschule für Musik in Berlin. He wrote music for the opening of the Berlin Olympics (1936).

Works include operas *Columbus* (1932; produced 1942), *Die Zaubergeige* (1935), *Peer Gynt* (1938), *Circe* (1945), *Irische Legende* (after Yeats, 1953), *Der Revisor* (after Gogol, 1957), *Die Verlobung in San Domingo* (1963); ballets *Joan de Zarissa* and *Abraxas* (1948); dance suite *Georgica* for orchestra; violin concerto (*Geigenmusik*, 1936), Französische Suite, after Rameau (1949), *Spiegelzeit* for orchestra (1979).

Egli, Johann Heinrich (b Seegraben near Zürich, 4 Mar 1742; d Zürich, 19 Dec 1810), Swiss composer. Pupil of Pastor Schmiedli at Wetzikon near Zurich and later music teacher at Zurich.

Wrote many songs which he pub. in several books.

Egmont incidental music by Beethoven for Goethe's tragedy of that name, op. 84, written in 1809–10 for a revival at the Burgtheater in Vienna on 15 Jun 1810.

Ehrling, Sixten (b Malmö, 3 Apr 1918), Swedish conductor. He gave his first opera at the Stockholm Opera in 1940 and was music director there 1953–70; conducted the fp of Blomdahl's *Aniara* in 1959 and gave it soon after with the Stockholm co. in Edinburgh and London (CG). 1963–73 music director Detroit SO, and taught at the Juilliard School. Conducted *Simon Boccanegra* and a *Ring* cycle at the NY Met. 1973–77; principal guest conductor, Denver SO 1978–85; artistic adviser for the San Antonio SO 1985–88.

Eichendorff, Joseph von (1788–1857), German poet and novelist. ◊Franz (songs); ◊Lothar (*Freier*); ◊Pfitzner (*Von deutscher Seele*); ◊Schoeck (*Schloss Dürande, Wandersprüche* and songs); ◊Schumann (*Liederkreis*); six songs by ◊Brahms; 16 by ◊Schumann; 28 (including eight early) by H ◊Wolf.

Eighteen-Twelve Overture (Tchaikovsky.) ◊Year 1812.

eighth-note American = quaver.

Eimert, Herbert (b Bad Kreuznach, 8 Apr 1897; d Cologne, 15 Dec 1972), German composer and critic. Studied music and musicology at Cologne Conservatory and University (1927–1933). Worked for German radio and from 1936 to 1945 edited the *Kölnische Zeitung*. In 1951 he founded an electronic studio at the Cologne branch of West German Radio and from 1955 edited *Die Reihe*. He wrote extensively on modern music.

Works include *Glockenspiel* (1953); *Etüden über Tongemische*; *Requiem für Aikichi Kuboyama* (1962); choral and chamber music and electronic pieces.

Eine kleine Nachtmusik (Mozart.) ◊Kleine Nachtmusik.

Einem, Gottfried von (b Berne, 24 Jan 1918; d Obern Dürnbach, 12 July 1996), Austrian composer. His opera *Der Besuch der alten Dame* was based on a stage vehicle for Ingrid Bergman. He worked at the Wagner theatre at Bayreuth (1938) and the Staatsoper in Berlin; studied further in London and Vienna. A plan to become Hindemith's pupil was frustrated by the latter's suspension by the Nazis in 1934, and Einem and his mother were themselves arrested by the Gestapo. After his release he studied with Boris Blacher, with whom he wrote the libretto for his first opera and secured a post at the Dresden Staasoper. In 1948, after the success of *Dantons Tod*, he was invited to help to direct the festival at Salzburg, where he later lived.

Works include operas *Dantons Tod* (on Büchner's drama, 1947), *Der Prozess* (after Kafka, 1953), *Der Besuch der alten Dame* (after Dürrenmatt, 1971); *Kabale und Liebe* (after Schiller, 1976), *Jesu Hochzeit* (1980), *Prinz Chocolat* (1983) and *Tuliphant* (1990); ballet *Prinzessin Turandot* (after Gozzi), *Capriccio* and concerto for orchestra; 'Philadelphia' symphony (1960); piano concerto; *Bruckner Dialog* for orchestra (1971), *Wiener Symphonie* (1976), *Ludi Leopoldini* (1980); piano pieces; Hafiz songs; three string quartets (1975, 1977, 1980); wind quintet (1976).

Einleitung German = 'introduction'.

Einstein, Alfred (b Munich, 30 Dec 1880; d El Cerrito, CA, 13 Feb 1952), German musicologist. Pupil of Sandberger, took his doctor's degree in 1903. Became editor of the *Zeitschrift für Musikwissenschaft* in 1918, and was music critic of the *Berliner Tageblatt* from 1929, in 1933 went into exile from Germany, settling first in London, then at Florence and lastly in Northampton, MA, where he was professor at Smith College. He revised Riemann's *Musiklexicon* (1912, 1922, 1929) and Köchel's Mozart catalogue (1937), and wrote works on German viola da gamba music, on Gluck and Mozart, a short history of music and in particular specialized in the study of the Italian madrigal, on which he wrote a monumental book (1949). He also pub. *Schubert* (1951).

Einstein on the Beach opera by Philip Glass (text by Robert Wilson), produced Avignon, 25 Jul 1976; NY Met. 21 Nov 1976 (at Lincoln Center but not with Met. Co.). Text includes poems by a mentally-impaired man; references are made to Patty Hearst and pop idols David Cassidy and the Beatles. The audience is invited to come and go at will during the 4 ½ hours of performance.

Eisinger, Irene (b Kosel, 8 Dec 1903; d Weston-super-Mare, 8 Apr 1994), German soprano. She studied in Vienna. Debut Basel, 1926. Joined Klemperer at the Kroll Opera, Berlin, and was successful as Susanna (1931); sang at Prague 1933–37 and from 1934 was a leading performer at Glyndebourne: Despina, Papagena, Blondchen, Susanna and Polly Peachum, until 1940. Despina in 1949.

Eisler, Hanns (b Leipzig, 6 Jul 1898; d Berlin, 6 Sept 1962), German composer. Studied with Schoenberg in Vienna and gained a composition prize in 1924. In 1925–33 he taught in Berlin, but emigrated to USA when a price was put on his head for being interested in music for the proletariat and in anti-Nazi activities. He was appointed professor at the New School of Social Research there. He left the USA in 1948, living first in Vienna and then in E Berlin.

Works include operas *Galileo* (1947) and *Johannes Faustus* (1953), didactic plays *Mother* (after Gorky's novel, 1931), *Hangmen Also Die, For Whom the Bell Tolls; The Roundheads and the Pointedheads* and others; *Die Massnahme* (1930), *Lenin-Requiem* (1937), *Solidaritätslied* (1930), *Kinderlieder* (1951) and *Schweyk in Zweiten Weltkrieg* (1957), all to texts by Brecht; music for numerous films; *German Symphony* for solo voices, chorus and orchestra (1935–39), cantatas, choral ballads, proletarian songs, etc.; orchestral suites on Russian and Jewish folksongs; string quartet (1937), nonet (1939), two septets (1941, 1947), piano quintet (1944); chamber cantata *Palmström* for speech-song, flute, clarinet, violin and cello; *Zeitungsausschnitte* for voice and piano; *Ernste Gesänge* for baritone and orchestra (1962).

Eisteddfod, Welsh, plur. Eisteddfodau, = 'a sitting of the learned'; an annual gathering, now taking the form of a mainly music festival, but

---

Mark Elder – conductor

1   Bach: *St Matthew Passion*
    As a chorister at Canterbury Cathedral, I took part in a performance of Bach's *St Matthew Passion*. Singing in a work whose emotional scale was so much beyond what we were used to was an incredibly powerful experience. The thrill of being part of the enormously varied dramatic tapestry and of being moved by the way the music changes from description and narrative to reflection in such a huge, endless span was incredibly exciting. It was a life-changing experience.

2   Strauss: *Ariadne auf Naxos*
    When I first went up to Cambridge, I was invited to play in an undergraduate performance of this lovely opera. I'd

never heard Strauss's ornate, ripe chromatic harmonies before. I was completely captivated by the sound world this composer could muster. The quality of Strauss's ear and his sensitivity to orchestral effects was absolutely thrilling. *Ariadne* is the opera I sing to myself more than any other.

3   Janáček: *Katya Kabanova*
    Like all of Janáček's operas, *Katya* has a blazing quality that really moves an audience. His music screams with compassion and sympathy for the characters. It's to do with the beauty and dramatic power of the music, and also its ability to express character and psychology in the broadest sense. It makes Janáček an extremely important voice in the 20th century.

formerly a triennial assembly of Welsh bards, dating back to the 7th c. at latest.

Eitner, Robert (b Breslau, 22 Oct 1832; d Templin near Berlin, 2 Feb 1905), German musicologist and bibliographer. Founder of the Gesellschaft für Musikforschung in 1868, editor of the *Monatshefte für Musikgeschichte*, compiler of the *Quellen-Lexicon* (a catalogue of the contents of music libraries) and other bibliographical works.

Elder, Mark (b Hexham, 2 Jun 1947), English conductor. He studied at Cambridge and in 1970 was on the staff at Glyndebourne and CG; debut there 1976, *Rigoletto*. ENO, London, from 1974; principal conductor 1979–93 (fp of David Blake's *Toussaint* 1977). In 1980 he became principal guest conductor of the London Mozart Players and in 1981 gave *Die Meistersinger* at Bayreuth. In Apr 1986 he gave the British stage premiere of Busoni's *Dr Faust* (London Coliseum). Music director Rochester PO 1989, principal guest conductor CBSO

A further development of instrumental music seems now to be completely open, since the unreplaceable qualities of instrumental music – especially its changeability in the course of history, its 'aliveness' – are now combined with the achievements in electronic music into a new unity.

Karlheinz Stockhausen, Notes on *Mixtur*, 1964

1992. Conducted *Euryanthe* at the QEH, London, 1994. CBE 1989.

electrochord an electrophonic piano invented by Vierling of Berlin 1929–33, producing its notes by the conversion of electrical waves into audible sounds.

electronde an electrophonic instrument, invented by Martin Taubman of Berlin in 1929, producing notes from the air graded according to the chromatic scale by means of a switch, not indeterminate in pitch like those of the ◊aetherophone or ◊theremin.

electronic music music generated by and composed for electronic means and performed often from a recording, usually a tape (recent examples include Stockhausen's *Donnerstag aus Licht* and Birtwistle's *The Mask of Orpheus* (1986)). If original sounds are not electronic but simply modified by electronic means, it is normally called ◊musique concrète.

electrophone the class of musical instruments that generate their tone by electronic means. ◊instruments, classification of.

elegy, from Greek *elegeia*, in poetry, a piece of sorrowful and usually commemorative character; in music either a vocal setting of such a poem or an instrumental piece suggesting the mood awakened by it.

Elegy for Young Lovers opera by Henze (libretto by W H Auden and Chester Kallman), produced Schwetzingen, Schlosstheater, 20 May 1961; first British production Glyndebourne, 13 Jul 1961. Poet gains inspiration from mountainside death of lovers.

Elektra opera by R Strauss (libretto by H von Hofmannsthal, a much modernized reinterpretation of Sophocles), produced Dresden, Royal

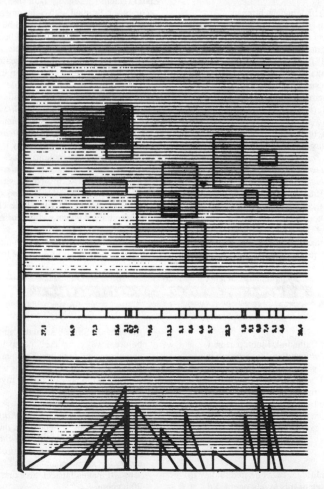

An extract from a score used for the performance of electronic music; from Stockhausen's Studie II.

THE OPERA

Elektra

A one-act opera dating from 1909 by Richard Strauss, based on Sophocles's tragedy of the same name. The scene is set in the palace at Mycenae, following the Trojan War. Elektra (soprano) laments the death of her father Agamemnon, murdered by her mother Clytemnestra on his return from Troy. Her sister Chrysothemis (soprano) will not help Elektra to avenge the murder, so she decides to act alone. Clytemnestra (mezzo-soprano) is gnawed by guilt but is relieved to hear of the reported death of Elektra's absent brother Orestes. Elektra starts to dig for her mother's murder weapon, but is intrigued by the arrival of a stranger. At first, only the palace dogs recognize Orestes but a rapturous Elektra sees him enter the palace to axe Clytemnestra; her lover Aegisthus meets a similar fate. A triumphant Elektra dances herself to exhaustion and collapses in death.

THE OPERA

Opera, 25 Jan 1909. After Clytemnestra kills their father, Elektra and Orestes decide to take revenge.

His Majesty does not know what the Band has just played, but it is never *to be played again.*
George V, after a band performed a selection from *Elektra*, quoted in Reid, *Thomas Beecham*, 1961

Elgar, Edward (William) (b Broadheath near Worcester, 2 Jun 1857; d Worcester, 23 Feb 1934), English composer. Son of a Worcester music dealer and organist at St George's Roman Catholic Church. Self-taught as a composer. Wrote music for a little domestic play, *The Wand of Youth*, at the age of 12. Sent to a solicitor's office at 15, but preferred to help at his father's shop; joined a wind quintet as bassoonist and the Worcester Glee Club, and at 17 became an orchestral violinist. In 1879 he became conductor of the Worcester Glee Club and of the band at the county lunatic asylum, for which he arranged much music. Also played organ at his father's church and became member of Stockley's orchestra at Birmingham, which gave the first public performance of a work of his, the *Sérénade mauresque*. Married Caroline Alice Roberts in 1889 and went to live in London.

In 1890 the Three Choirs Festival (at Worcester that year) for the first time played a work of his, the *Froissart* overture. Elgar reveals here for the first time a characteristic confidence of manner and mastery of orchestration. Choral works, including *King Olaf* and *Caractacus*, were heard at festivals, and the *Enigma* variations for orchestra were conducted by Hans Richter in Jun 1899. A setting of Cardinal Newman's *Dream of Gerontius* was produced at Birmingham Festival, 3 Oct 1900 and, in Germany, at the Lower Rhine Festival, Düsseldorf, in 1901 and 1902. An Elgar Festival at Covent Garden Theatre in London, Mar 1904, brought him greater recognition, and he was knighted on 5 Jul that year. He was professor of Music at Birmingham University, 1905–06.

His first symphony was performed by Richter in Manchester and London (Dec 1908), and its immense success led to 100 further performances throughout Europe. Fritz Kreisler premiered the Violin Concerto Nov 1910. During the war of 1914–18 he wrote much topical music and afterwards the valedictory cello concerto and three chamber works. After the death of his wife in 1920 he wrote only some small pieces and incidental music. At his death he left unfinished a third symphony and an opera, *The Spanish Lady*, based on Ben Jonson's *The Devil is an Ass*.

Works include incidental music for Yeats and George Moore's *Grania and Diarmid* (1901), Algernon Blackwood's *The Starlight Express* (1915) and other plays.

ORCHESTRAL: two symphonies (1908, 1911); concert overtures

A Selection of

Elgar

Enigma Variations	1899
The Dream of Gerontius	1900
Cockaigne Overture	1901
Falstaff	1902–1913

In the South	1904
Introduction and Allegro	1905
Symphony no. 1	1908
Violin Concerto	1910
Symphony no. 2	1911
Cello Concerto	1919

Froissart (1890), *Cockaigne* (1901), *In the South* (1904), *Polonia*; many misc. orchestral works, including two suites from *The Wand of Youth* (1907–08), serenade for strings (1892), *Enigma* variations (1899), *Introduction and Allegro* for strings (1905), symphonic study *Falstaff* (1902–13), *Dream Children* (after Lamb) for small orchestra, *Nursery Suite*; violin concerto (1910), cello concerto (1919).

The trees are singing my music – or have I sung theirs?
Edward Elgar, quoted in Anne Dunkel, *Notes on Elgar's* Cello Concerto, 1993

Elgar
A biographical note

After a long struggle for recognition, Elgar gained major success with the *Enigma Variations* in 1899. The next years saw a succession of triumphs, culminating in the First symphony, premiered under Hans Richter at Queen's Hall in 1908. In just over a year it was performed more than 100 times throughout Europe. Richard Strauss was among those to recognize Elgar as England's leading composer – and not just of his time. The Second symphony was composed in Venice and Tintagel between 1910 and 1911; it conveys to some extent the brilliant warmth and light of Italy and the rugged grandeur of the Cornish coast. The first movement, *Allegro vivace e nobilimente*, is full of restless energy and expresses the contrasts in Elgar's own character, exuberant and out-going but at the same time self-doubting and introspective: 'Rarely, rarely, comest thou O spirit of Delight' is the inscription from Shelley at the beginning of the work. The second movement, *Larghetto*, was dedicated to the memory of the recently deceased King Edward VII, but is in reality a lament for a dear friend who was a patron of music and amateur conductor. It is music that has the power to move and bring solace to all those who suffer from a sense of loss. Elgar's grief becomes universal as the movement unfolds, as though he is lingering over the memory of an England which he knows will soon disappear.

Elgar *The composer Edward Elgar (1857–1934). His works, the greatest expressions of a romantic English composer, range from the dignified and publicly oriented* Pomp and Circumstance *marches and the First Symphony to the intimate and emotive* Dream of Gerontius *and the Cello Concerto.*

VOCAL: cantatas *The Black Knight* (1889–93), *King Olaf, The Banner of St George, Caractacus* (1898), *Coronation Ode* (1902), *The Music Makers* (1902–12); oratorios *The Light of Life, The Dream of Gerontius* (1900), *The Apostles, The Kingdom.*

CHAMBER: string quartet, E minor, piano quintet, A minor (1919), violin and piano sonata, E minor (1918); numerous smaller choral pieces and part-songs; songs for solo voice, including cycle *Sea Pictures* with piano or orchestra (1897–99); *Severn Suite* for brass band, etc.

Elijah, German *Elias*, oratorio by Mendelssohn (words from the Old Testament), produced first in the English version at the Birmingham Festival, 26 Aug 1846; first German performance Hamburg, 7 Oct 1847.

Elisabetta regina d'Inghilterra, *Elizabeth, Queen of England*, opera by Rossini (libretto by G Schmidt), produced Naples, Teatro San Carlo, 4 Oct 1815. The overture was taken from *Aureliano in Palmira* and afterwards used for *Il barbiere di Siviglia*. Elizabeth I imprisons Leicester when he marries Mathilde, daughter of Mary, Queen of Scots. She later releases him and survives an assassination attempt by the treacherous Norfolk.

Elisir d'amore, L', *The Love Potion*, opera by Donizetti (libretto by F Romani, based on Scribe's *Le Philtre*, composed by Auber), produced Milan, Teatro della Canobbiana, 12 May 1832. Simple Nemorino hopes to win landowner Adina with a love potion from the fraud Dulcamara. At first she spurns him, ready to marry Belcore, but then falls genuinely in love with him, without the help of the bogus potion.

Elizalde, Federico (b Manila, 12 Dec 1907; d Manila, 16 Jan 1979), Spanish conductor and composer. Educated at Stanford University, CA, and Cambridge; studied music with Pérez Casas in Madrid, Alfred Hertz and Bloch at San Francisco and E Halffter in Paris.

Works include opera *Paul Gauguin* (1943); overture *La pájara*

pinta; sinfonia concertante for piano and orchestra; violin concerto; music for 15 solo instruments.

Elleviou, Jean (b Rennes, 2 Dec 1769; d Paris, 6 May 1842), French tenor. Debut Paris 1790 in Monsigny's *Le Déserteur*, as a bass. He sang as a tenor at the Comédie Italienne 1797–1801, then moved to the Opéra-Comique, where he was heard as Blondel in Grétry's *Richard Cœur de Lion* and created Méhul's Joseph (1807) and Boieldieu's Jean de Paris (1812). A popular actor and singer, he retired in 1813, when he was refused a massive pay increase by Napoleon.

Ellis, Brent (b Kansas City, MO, 20 Jun 1944), American baritone. Studied in NY and made his debut at Washington DC in the fp of Ginastera's *Bomarzo*. Santa Fe Opera from 1972, notably in the 1982 fp of Rochberg's *The Confidence Man*. NY City Opera debut 1974, as Otho in *Poppea*; Met. from 1979, as Belcore and Rossini's Figaro. Glyndebourne from 1977, as Ford, Marcello, Don Giovanni and Germont. Sang in the fps of Pasatieri's *Washington Square* and *The Seagull*. CG debut 1988, Rigoletto.

Ellis, David (b Liverpool, 10 Mar 1933), English composer. He studied at the RMCM and has worked as an administrator with the BBC since 1964. Head of Music, BBC North, 1978–86; artistic director, Northern Chamber Orchestra, from 1986.

Works include opera, *Crito* (1963); Sinfonietta (1953), violin concerto, piano concerto (1962), *Fanfares and Cadenzas* for orchestra (1968), *February Music* for cello and chamber orchestra (1977), *Circles* (1979); *Suite franglaise* for strings (1987); choral music includes *Sequentia I–V* for soloists, chorus and orchestra (1962–75); string trio (1954), wind quintet (1956); piano sonata (1956); string quartet (1980).

Ellsworth, Warren (b Worcester, MA, 28 Oct 1950; d Houston, 25 Feb 1993), American tenor. Studied at Juilliard and sang first at Houston as a baritone (Malatesta, Almaviva and Escamillo); returned 1979 as a tenor (Pinkerton). WNO debut 1981 as Smetana's Jenik, Parsifal 1983; repeated the role under Goodall at ENO (1986) and at CG under Haitink (1988). Sang Siegmund for WNO at CG 1986 and at the Deutsche Oper Berlin, from 1989, where he also sang Don José, Lohengrin, Max and Samson. US appearances at San Francisco (as Boris in *Katya Kabanova*), LA (Drum Major) and Washington (Nerone). Sang Shostakovich's Sergei for ENO, 1991.

You know, the critics never change; I'm still getting the same notices I used to get as a child. They tell me I play very well for my age.

Mischa Elman, quoted in Antony Hopkins, *Music All Around Me*, 1967

Elman, Mischa (b Talnoye, 20 Jan 1891; d New York, 5 Apr 1967), Russian-born American violinist. Began serious studies at the age of

THE OPERA

L'Elisir d'amore

A two-act opera by Gaetano Donizetti, produced in 1832, and set in a Tuscany village early in the 19th century.

I. Determined to win Adina (soprano), the young Nemorino (tenor) buys a love potion from the quack Dulcamara (bass). Adina is put out by Nemorino's seeming overconfidence and decides to marry Sergeant Belcore (baritone) instead; she refuses Nemorino's request to wait, to give the potion time to take its effect.

II. Hearing that his rich uncle has died, the village girls surround the unsuspecting Nemorino who has joined the army and drunk another bottle of elixir (in reality, red wine). Becoming jealous, Adina realizes that it is he she really loves; she buys him out of the army and, as they marry, Dulcamara cites their union as evidence of the potency of his elixir and continues to do good business.

THE OPERA

six and in 1902 was accepted by Auer for his master class. He made his debut in 1904 in Berlin, later touring Europe and America. London debut 1905 (Glazunov concerto), NY 1908. Martinů wrote his second violin concerto for him and he gave the fp in Boston, 31 Dec 1943.

Elmendorff, Karl (b Düsseldorf, 25 Oct 1891; d Hofheim am Taunus, 21 Oct 1962), German conductor. After studying philology he entered the Cologne Conservatory in 1913. He held various conducting appointments, including Berlin Staatsoper, Munich, Wiesbaden, Kassel, Mannheim and Dresden. From 1927–42 he was a regular guest conductor at Bayreuth (*Tristan, Meistersinger* and *The Ring*).

Elming, Poul (b Aalborg, 1949), Danish tenor. Sang baritone roles with Jutland Opera from 1979, then at Stockholm from 1984 as Posa, Mozart's Count and Eugene Onegin. Re-trained as a tenor and sang Parsifal at Copenhagen 1989 (also at Bayreuth, 1992 and 1994). Siegmund at CG 1991 and 1994; Erik, Max and Lohengrin in Berlin, Vienna and Mannheim.

Eloy, Jean-Claude (b Mont-Saint-Aignan, 15 Jun 1938), French composer. Studied with Milhaud and Boulez; other influences include Varèse, Webern and oriental music. Worked at electronic music studio, Cologne, with Stockhausen.

Works include *Etude III* for orchestra (1962); *Equivalences* for wind and percussion (1963); *Polychronies* for chamber ensemble (1964); *Kamakala* for chorus and three orchestral groups (1971); *Kshara-Akshara* for soprano, chorus and three orchestral groups (1974); *Shanti* for six solo voices and electronics (1972–74); *Fluctuante-Immuable* for orchestra (1977); *Yo-In* (Reverberations) for four tapes and percussion (1980).

El Salón México symphonic sketch by Copland, named after a Mexico City nightclub and including local colour and tunes. Fp Mexico City, 27 Aug 1937, conducted by Carlos Chávez.

Elsner, Ksawéry Jozef (b Grotków, Silesia, 1 Jun 1769; d Warsaw, 18 Apr 1854), Polish composer of Swedish descent. Being intended for medicine, he had little music teaching in his youth, but learnt the violin and some harmony at Breslau and studied more assiduously on going to Vienna. In 1791 he became violinist at the Brno theatre and the next year conductor at Lwów. He went to Warsaw as theatre conductor in 1799, establishing a music society there in 1815 and became the first director of the Conservatory opened in 1821. Among his pupils there was Chopin.

Works include 27 operas (22 in Polish, e.g. *Krol Lokietek* (1818), ballets and melodramas; *Stabat Mater*, church music; 11 symphonies; six string quartets; instrumental pieces.

Elwell, Herbert (b Minneapolis, 10 May 1898; d Cleveland, 17 Apr 1974), American composer. Studied with Bloch in NY and with Boulanger in Paris. Head of composition at the Cleveland Institute 1928–45, teacher at Oberlin Conservatory from 1946.

Works include ballet *The Happy Hypocrite* (1925); *I Was With Him*, cantata (1937); *Introduction and Allegro* for orchestra (1942); *Blue Symphony* for voice and string quartet (1944); *Lincoln: Requiem Aeternam* (1946); two string quartets; piano sonata.

Elwes, Gervase (Cary) (b Northampton, 15 Nov 1866; d near Boston, USA, 12 Jan 1921), English tenor. Studied in Vienna, Munich, Paris and London. In British diplomatic service, 1891–95. Made his first professional appearance in 1903. He sang in *The Dream of Gerontius* in London in 1904, and in 1909 gave the fp of Vaughan William's song cycle *On Wenlock Edge*. He was killed by a train, while on tour in America.

Avoid 'Have you read any good embouchures recently?', as it betrays ignorance.
Antony Hopkins, *Downbeat Music Guide*, 1977

---

embouchure, French, but used in English, the position of the lips on the mouthpiece in wind instrument playing.

Emma di Resburgo, *Emma of Roxburgh*, opera by Meyerbeer (libretto by G Rossi), produced Venice, Teatro San Benedetto, 26 Jun 1819.

Meyerbeer's first major success, but Weber opined that he had imitated Rossini.

Émmanuel, (Marie François) Maurice (b Bar-sur-Aube, 2 May 1861; d Paris 14 Dec 1938), French musicologist and composer. Student at the Paris Conservatory and pupil of Gevaert at Brussels. After various appointments as historian and musician he became professor of music history at the Conservatory in succession to Bourgault-Ducoudray in 1907 and retained the post until 1936. He wrote several learned books on the musical idiom, Greek music, modal accompaniment, Burgundian folksong, etc.

Works include operas *Prométhée enchaîné* (1916–18) and *Salamino* (1921–28, both after Aeschylus); operetta *Pierrot peintre* (1886); incidental music for Plautus's *Amphitryon*; two symphonies, *Suite française, Ouverture pour un conte gai, Zingaresca* for orchestra; three *Odelettes anacréontiques* for voice, flute and piano (1911); violin and piano and cello and piano sonatas; *Sonate bourguignonne* and six sonatinas for piano; *In memoriam matris* and *Musiques* for voice and piano.

'Emperor' Concerto nickname for Beethoven's E♭ major piano concerto, op. 73, used only in Britain and USA, probably invented by J B Cramer. There is nothing to justify it, though it suits the majestic work well enough.

Emperor Jones opera by Gruenberg (libretto by K de Jaffa, based on Eugene O'Neill's play), produced NY, Met, 7 Jan 1933. Escaped convict Brutus Jones rules Caribbean island, exploiting the locals until they rebel against him and he commits suicide.

'Emperor' Quartet ◊Emperor's Hymn.

Emperor's Hymn, The *Gott erhalte Franz den Kaiser* (words by L L Haschka), composed by Haydn and first sung to celebrate the Emperor's birthday, 12 Feb 1797. Also used by Haydn as a theme for variations in the string quartet op. 76 no. 3 (known as the 'Emperor' quartet). Later adopted as the Austrian national anthem. Well-known in England as a hymn-tune.

Empfindsamer Stil German = 'sensitive style'; term applied to music by some German 18th-c. composers, especially C P E Bach, Quantz, etc., who sought to make their music directly expressive of feeling. ◊Affektenlehre.

Encina, Juan del (b near Salamanca, 12 Jul 1468; d León, 1529), Spanish poet, playwright and composer. Studied at Salamanca University, entered the service of the Duke of Alba at Toledo, was appointed archdeacon of Málaga in 1509, went to Rome in 1514 and to the Holy Land in 1519, and became prior of Laón. Produced *Farsa de Placida e Vittoriano* in Rome and composed many songs for his own plays. His poems were pub. at Salamanca, 1496. Over 60 of his songs are contained in a MS at Madrid, the *Cancionero Musical de Palacio*. He cultivated especially the *villancico*, a form resembling the French *virelai*.

Ende einer Welt, Das, *The End of a World*, radio opera in two acts by Henze (libretto by W Hildesheimer), performed Hamburg, 4 Dec 1953; revised for the stage 1964 and produced Frankfurt, 30 Nov 1965.

Enescu, George (b Dorohoiû, 19 Aug 1881; d Paris, 4 May 1955), Romanian violinist and composer. Studied at the Vienna Conservatory 1888–93, and then went to Paris to finish his violin studies with Marsick and composition with Massenet, Gedalge and Fauré. In 1899 he began his career as a virtuoso violinist and teacher of the instrument; Yehudi Menuhin and Arthur Grumiaux were among his pupils.

Works include opera *Œdipe* (after Sophocles, 1921–31; produced 1936); five symphonies (1905, 1912–14, 1916–21, with chorus and piano solo, 1934 and 19441, with tenor and chorus); *Poème roumain/ Romanian Rhapsodies*, suites and intermezzi, etc. for orchestra; string octet (1900), wind dectet (1906), two piano quintets (1894, 1940), two piano quartets (1909, 1943), two string quartets (1920, 1953), two piano trios (1897, 1916); three violin and piano sonatas (1897, 1899, 1926), two cello sonatas (1898, 1935); suites and other works for piano; songs.

Enfance du Christ, L', *The Childhood of Christ*, oratorio by Berlioz, op. 25, for solo voices, chorus and orchestra, composed 1850–54, fp Paris, 10 Dec 1854.

Enfant et les sortilèges, L', *The Child and the Spells*, opera in one act by Ravel (libretto by Colette), produced Monte Carlo, 21 Mar 1925. Spoiled child faces all the animals he has tortured; he redeems himself by tending a wounded squirrel.

Enfant prodigue, L', *The Prodigal Son*, lyric scene by Debussy (libretto by E Guinand), written for the Prix de Rome and pub. 1884; produced as an opera, London, CG, 28 Feb 1910 with Perceval Allen, conducted by Pitt. ◊Prodigal Son.

Engel, Carl (b Paris, 21 Jul 1883; d New York, 6 May 1944), American musicologist. Studied at Strasbourg and Munich and settled in USA 1905. Appointed chief of the music division of the Library of Congress, Washington DC, 1922; succeeded Sonneck as editor of the *Musical Quarterly* 1929. One of the organizers and 1937–38 president of the American Musicological Society. Pub. many articles and books on music, including essay collections *Alle Breve, from Bach to Debussy* (1921) and *Discords Mingled* (1931).

Engel, Karl (b Birsfeld, 1 Jun 1923), Swiss pianist. He studied in Bern and Paris with Bernhard Baumgartner and Cortot. A leading recitalist in the classical repertory since the early 1950s, he has accompanied singers in Lieder, including Dietrich Fischer-Dieskau. Professor at the Hanover Hochschule from 1959.

English Baroque Soloists English ensemble founded 1978 by John Eliot Gardiner; they perform on period instruments or copies and often appear with the Monteverdi Choir: concert performances of *L'Incoronazione di Poppea* and Mozart operas in Europe and London, followed by prize-winning recordings. Other recordings include the Monteverdi *Vespers*, the B minor Mass and the Missa Solemnis.

English Cat, The opera ('a story for singers and instrumentalists') in two acts by Henze (libretto by Edward Bond after Balzac's *Peines de coeur d'une chatte anglaise*), produced Schwetzingen, 2 Jun 1983. All cats: Minette must marry Lord Puff. She is seen with Tom, and is taken to divorce court for adultery. Minette is drowned, Tom is stabbed and 'the lawyers will make a huge profit'.

English Chamber Orchestra orchestra founded 1948 by Arnold Goldsborough, under his own name, to perform Baroque music. Adopted present name in 1960 and has given fps of works by many British composers; since 1960 at the Aldeburgh Festival; (fps *A Midsummer Night's Dream* and Britten's church parables in Suffolk, *Owen Wingrave* on TV, the *Cello Symphony* in Moscow.) No principal conductor until 1985, when Jeffrey ◊Tate was appointed.

English horn, from French *cor anglais*, a term which has not been satisfactorily explained, a woodwind instrument with double reed, belonging to the oboe family, played exactly like that instrument but standing a fifth lower in pitch and written for as a transposing instrument. Its tone is nasal, like that of the oboe, but darker in quality.

English National Opera London opera company, originally known as Sadler's Wells Opera. The Sadler's Wells Theatre was built in the 18th c., when Islington was a village outside London and Sadler's Wells was a watering place and pleasure garden dating back to the end of the 17th c. It was used for plays and pantomime into the 19th c., then became a music hall, and later fell into disuse, but was acquired as a northern branch of the Old Vic Theatre for the alternate production of classical drama and opera, rebuilt and opened 6 Jan 1931. From 1935 plays were confined exclusively to the Old Vic and opera to Sadler's Wells, which became the only permanent repertory opera house in Britain for the production of opera in English. *Peter Grimes* was premiered 1945, and among post-war music directors were Alexander Gibson (1957–59) and Colin Davis (1959–65). In 1968 operas were transferred to the Coliseum, Charles Mackerras was music director 1970–78 and the company became ENO in 1974, continuing with an adventurous repertory despite straitened circumstances (Busoni's *Dr Faust* and Birtwistle's *The Mask of Orpheus*, 1986). Lord ◊Harewood was manager 1972–85, then Peter ◊Jonas until 1993, followed by Dennis Marks. Mark ◊Elder was music director 1979–93, Sian ◊Edwards 1993–96, then Paul Daniel. In 1994 it was

proposed to introduce surtitles, in spite of the fact that operas were still apparently being sung in English.

English Opera Group company founded 1946 by Britten, John Piper and Eric Crozier. Many performances of operas by Britten and other English composers at home and abroad (e.g. Birtwistle, *Punch and Judy*, Aldeburgh 1968). Re-formed 1976 as English Music Theatre, under Colin Graham and Steuart Bedford. Disbanded 1980.

English Suites six keyboard suites by Bach, composed by 1724–25. In what respect they are 'English' has never been fully explained.

Englund, (Sven) Einar (b Ljurgan, 17 Jun 1916), Finnish composer. Studied with Palmgren in Helsinki and Copland at Tanglewood. Teacher at the Sibelius Academy from 1958; influenced by Sibelius and Shostakovich.

Works include seven symphonies (1946–88), cello concerto (1954), two piano concertos (1955, 1974), concerto for 12 cellos (1981), violin concerto (1981), serenade for strings (1983), piano trio (1982), flute concerto (1985), string quartet (1985), suite for cello, *The Last Island* (1986).

enharmonic, adj., in Greek music there were three *genera*: the diatonic, the chromatic and the enharmonic, and the last had divisions into degrees smaller than semitones. In modern usage the word enharmonic is applied to modulations made by means of changes of a note or notes between sharps and flats, e.g. C♯ becoming D♭, E♭ becoming D♯, etc. On the piano or other instrument using the tempered scale these notes actually remain the same, but in string instruments there is, at least to the player's feeling, a minute difference between them.

enigma canon a canon written down in a single part with no indication where the subsequent entries of the other parts are to occur, the performers being left to guess how the music fits by solving a riddle.

enigmatic scale, Verdi's, ◊scala enigmatica.

'Enigma' Variations a set of orchestral variations by Elgar, op. 36, entitled *Variations on an Original Theme*, composed 1898, fp London, 19 Jun 1899, conductor Richter. Each variation is a musical portrait of some person indicated only by initials or by a nickname, all of whom have, however, been identified. The word 'Enigma' appears over the theme. ◊Potter.

Enna, August (b Nakskov, 13 May 1859; d Copenhagen, 3 Aug 1939), Danish composer of Italian descent. The son of a cobbler, he was almost entirely self-taught. The family moved to Copenhagen in 1870. In 1888 Gade helped him to study in Germany for a year. He had already produced an operetta by that time and become a provincial conductor.

THE OPERA

Die Entführung aus dem Serail

A three-act opera by Mozart, first produced in Vienna in 1782 with the composer conducting. The opera is set in Pasha Selim's palace in Turkey, in the 16th century.

I. The Pasha (spoken) has captured Constanze (soprano) and her English servant Blonde (soprano). Also captive is Pedrillo (tenor), servant of the Spanish nobleman Belmonte (tenor), who has come in search of Constanze. The Pasha tries to persuade Constanze of his love but she is engaged to Belmonte, who is now introduced by Pedrillo as an architect.

II. The Pasha's steward Osmin (bass) unsuccessfully courts Blonde and, after Constanze declares her resolve once more, Pedrillo initiates a plan of escape by getting Osmin drunk. Pedrillo and Blonde unite with Belmonte and Constanze in a concluding quartet.

III. Osmin catches the lovers as they prepare to escape. When they are brought before the Pasha it is revealed that Belmonte is the son of the man who sent Pasha into exile. The Pasha generously forgives them all and the four captives are set free.

Works include operas *Heksen/The Witch*, 1892), *Cleopatra*, *Aucassin and Nicolette* (1896), *The Little Match-Seller* and *The Princess on the Pea* (both after Andersen), *Komedianter/The Jesters*, after Hugo), *Gloria Arsena* (after Dumas *père*), *Don Juan Mañara* (1922), etc.; operetta, *A Village Tale*; ballets; choral work *Mother-Love*; two symphonies, Festival Overture, symphonic pictures; violin concerto.

Enoch Arden melodrama for reciter and piano by Strauss, op. 38 (a setting of Tennyson's poem in German translation by A Strodtmann), fp Munich, 24 Mar 1897 (performed in Vienna, 13 Jan 1899, with Zemlinsky at the piano).

En Saga (Sibelius.) ◊Saga, En.

ensalada Spanish = lit. 'salad'; a kind of burlesque madrigal cultivated in Spain in the 16th c., in dramatic form, like Vecchi's *Amfiparnaso*, not intended for stage performance. Also a ◊quodlibet.

ensemble French = 'together'; the word is used in England for concerted singing or playing, especially in critical descriptions of such singing or playing.

Entflieht auf leichten Kähnen double canon for chorus *a cappella* by Webern, op. 2; composed 1908, fp Fürstenfeld, 10 Apr 1927.

Entführung aus dem Serail, Die, *The Elopement from the Harem*, opera by ◊Mozart (libretto by C F Bretzner [*Belmont und Constanze*] altered by G Stephanie, junior), produced Vienna, Burgtheater, 16 Jul 1782. Constanze resists the amorous Pasha Selim, who keeps her locked up. Belmonte (her true lover) and Pedrillo attempt to rescue her but are caught. The Europeans expect execution but are shown mercy by the Pasha.

entr'acte, French, ◊intermezzo.

entrée French = 'entrance, entry'; in the 17th and 18th c. a piece of music in a stately rhythm accompanying the entry of processions, etc. in ballets and other stage pieces; also, more generally, an introduction or prelude to any work, but more especially a ballet or opera where it accompanies the rise of the curtain; an entrée could also be the beginning of each new scene in a ballet.

Entremont, Philippe (b Rheims, 6 Jun 1934), French pianist and conductor. He studied with Marguerite Long and at the Paris Conservatory; has appeared internationally since the early 1950s in a wide repertory (won the Long-Thibaud Competition, Brussels in 1951). US debut, NY, 1953; music director New Orleans PO 1981–84. Vienna Chamber Orchestra 1976–80; New Orleans PO 1980–85.

Entführung *A scene from the Covent Garden production of Mozart's* Entführung aus dem Serail, *with Robert Lloyd (bass) as Osmin. Despite Emperor Joseph II's comment 'too many notes my dear Mozart', the opera was an immediate success and established Mozart's fame outside Austria.*

Music director Denver SO 1987–89, Orchestre Colonne, Paris, from 1988. Conductor of the Netherlands Chamber Orchestra, 1993.

entries the appearances of the subject in the different parts of a fugue.

entry a 17th-18th-c. English term for ◊prelude.

Éolides, Les symphonic poem for orchestra by Franck, on a poem of the same name by Leconte de Lisle; composed 1876, fp Paris, 13 May 1877.

Eötvös, Péter (b Székely-Udvarhely, 2 Jan 1944), Hungarian conductor and composer. He studied at Budapest and Cologne; resident West Germany from 1971. Music director Ensemble Intercontemporain, Paris, 1979–91. In 1981 he gave the fp of Stockhausen's *Donnerstag aus Licht*, at La Scala, and premiered Reich's *Desert Music* 1984. Principal guest conductor BBC SO from 1985; with the orchestra he gave the 1986 fp of Birtwistle's *Earth Dances*.

Works include *Hochzeitmadrigal* for six soloists (1963/1976), and *Chinese Opera* for chamber orchestra (1984).

Epic of Gilgamesh, The oratorio by Martinů for soloists, speaker, chorus and orchestra; composed 1954–55, fp Basel, 24 Jan 1958, conductor Sacher. The work's three sections are titled *Gilgamesh*, *The death of Enkidu* and *Invocation*.

episode an incidental passage in a composition that may be described as a digression from the main theme or themes. It may or may not be derived from the chief thematic material: in a fugue it is often so derived, whereas in a rondo it is as a rule an entirely new idea placed between two recurrences of the subject, but may assume the function of a second subject, as in sonata form.

Epstein, Matthew (b New York, 23 Dec 1947), American administrator and consultant. Studied at Pennsylvania University and joined Columbia Artists Mangagement, NY, 1973. Adviser to Chicago Lyric Opera (1980), Kennedy Center and San Francisco Opera (from 1992). General director WNO 1993–94.

equale Italian, plur. *equali* = 'equals'; a term used for instrumental pieces, especially trombones (e.g. Beethoven's equale), written for a group of similar instruments.

equal temperament the tuning of an instrument, especially the piano or organ, by dividing the octave into 12 semitones all divided by exactly the same ratio of vibrations, as distinct from ◊just intonation, where the intervals vary slightly and the sharps and flats are not precisely the same in pitch.

Equivoci, Gli, *The Doubles*, opera by Storace (libretto by L da Ponte, based on Shakespeare's *Comedy of Errors*), produced Vienna, Burgtheater, 27 Dec 1786). Identical couples cause comic confusion.

Equivoci nel sembiante, Gli, *Dissimilarity in Similarity*, opera by A Scarlatti (libretto by D F Contini), produced Rome, Teatro Capranica, 5 Feb 1679. Scarlatti's first opera. Nymph Lisetta and sister Clori in love with shepherd Eurillo, and with Armindo, disguised as Eurillo.

Érard, Sébastien (b Strasbourg, 5 Apr 1752; d near Passy, 5 Aug 1831), French piano and harp maker, uncle of Pierre Erard, founder of the firm established *c* 1777. He made their first grand piano 1796. He introduced mechanical improvements that enhanced key and pedal action.

Erb, Donald (b Youngstown, OH, 17 Jan 1929), American composer. Early career was as trumpeter in dance bands. Studied at Cleveland Institute and with Boulanger in Paris. Has taught in Cleveland and Bloomington; professor of composition at Southern Methodist University in Dallas from 1981. Works influenced by jazz and neo-classical techniques; also employ electronics: *Symphony of Overtures* (1964), *The Seventh Trumpet*, for orchestra (1969), cello concerto (1975), trumpet concerto (1980); *The Last Quintet* for woodwinds (1982), *Fantasy for Cellist and Friends* (1983); clarinet concerto (1984); concerto for orchestra (1985); concerto for brass and orchestra (1986); *Cummings Cycle* for mixed chorus and orchestra (1963), *New England's Prospect* for choruses and orchestra (1974); electronic music included *The Purple-roofed Ethical Suicide Parlor* (1972) and *Autumnmusic* (1973).

Erb, Karl (b Ravensburg, 13 Jul 1877; d Ravensburg, 13 Jul 1958), German tenor. He was self-taught and after appearances in Stuttgart and Lübeck sang Lohengrin in Munich; created Pfitzner's Palestrina there in 1917. Other roles included Parsifal, Adolar, Pylades, Florestan and Belmonte (London, CG, 1927). From 1930 in Lieder and oratorio; often heard as the Evangelist in Bach's Passions and appears in Thomas Mann's novel *Dr Faustus* (1945) as Erbe, who sings in the fp of Adrian Leverkühn's *Apocalypse* oratorio, under the direction of Otto Klemperer.

Erba, Dionigi, Italian 17th-c. composer. *Maestro di cappella* at the church of San Francesco, Milan, in 1692. Wrote a Magnificat for double choir from which Handel borrowed for *Israel in Egypt*.

Ercole amante, *Hercules as Lover*, opera by Cavalli (libretto by F Buti), produced Paris, Tuileries, 7 Feb 1662. The only opera specially written for Paris by Cavalli. The ballet music was by Lully. The title alludes to the marriage of Louis XIV. Hercules wants Iole, but she hates him for having killed her father, who consented to her marriage with Hercules' son, Hyllus. Hercules imprisons his son and is about to marry Iole when she saves herself by giving him a deadly shirt to wear.

Erdely, Csaba (b Budapest, 15 May 1946), Hungarian viola player and conductor. Studied at the Franz Lizst Academy, Budapest, and was principal of the Philharmonia, London, 1974–78. Member of the Chilingirian Quartet 1981–87 and professor at Indiana University 1987–91; Rice University, Texas, from 1991. Frequent recital and concerto soloist in Europe and the USA: gave the US premiere of the Brahms/Berio viola sonata. Editions include the Bartók concerto, Mozart's Concertante K364 for string sextet and the Brahms op. 78 sonata.

Erede, Alberto (b Genoa, 8 Nov 1909), Italian conductor. He studied in Milan and with Weingartner and Fritz Busch; assistant to Busch at Glyndebourne from 1934 and conducted *Figaro* and *Don Giovanni* 1938–39. Returned 1955 for *Il barbiere di Siviglia*. Gave many performances at the Cambridge Theatre, 1946–48, with the New London Opera Co., and was engaged at the NY Met. 1950–55 (debut with *Traviata*). He conducted opera in Düsseldorf 1958–62 and in 1968 led *Lohengrin* at Bayreuth; *Otello* for Scottish Opera, 1975, *Boccanegra* at Rome, 1988. Many recordings of Italian opera.

Erickson, Robert (b Marquette, MI, 7 MAr 1917), American composer. Studied at the Chicago Conservatory and with Krenek at Hamline. Professor at the University of California, San Diego, from 1967. His music has progressed from serialism, through electronic means, to *musique concrète*.

Works include chamber concerto (1960), concerto for piano and seven instruments (1963), concerto for siren and other flyers, for orchestra (1965), *cardenitas*, for singer, seven musicians and tape (1968), *Pacific Sirens* for instruments and tape (1969), *East of the Beach* for small orchestra (1980), *Auroras* for orchestra (1982), *Sierra* for voice and chamber orchestra (1984), *Solstice* for string quartet (1985).

Erismena opera by Cavalli (libretto by A Aureli), performed Venice, Teatro San Apollinare, 1656. Modern editions by L Salter (BBC, 1967) and A Curtis (1974). Erismena dresses as an Armenian soldier to pursue seducer Idraspe.

Eritrea opera by Cavalli (libretto by G Faustini), performed Venice, Teatro San Apollinare, 1652. An edition by Jane Glover was conducted by her at the Wexford Festival in 1975. Disguised as her dead brother, captured Eritrea falls for Egyptian prince.

Erkel, Ferenc (b Békésgyula, 7 Nov 1810; d Budapest, 15 Jun 1892), Hungarian composer. As a pianist and conductor, he organized musical life at Kolozsvar in his early days. In 1825 he became music director of the Hungarian theatre in Buda, in 1836 assistant conductor of the German theatre in Pest, and in 1838 conductor of the National Theatre. In 1845 he gained the prize in a competition for a Hungarian national anthem. He founded the Budapest Philharmonic Society in 1853 and was director of the Academy of Music 1875–89. His operas were very popular for their patriotic subjects and national music.

Works include operas *Bátori Mária* (1840), *Hunyadi László* (1844), *Bánk Bán* (1861), *Dózsa György, Brankovics György* (1874), *Névtelen Hösök, István Király/King Stephen*); piano music; songs, etc.

Erlanger, Camille (b Paris, 25 May 1863; d Paris, 25 Apr 1919), French composer. Studied at the Paris Conservatory and gained the Prix de Rome in 1888.

Works include operas *Saint Julien l'Hospitalier* (after Flaubert), *Kermaria* (1897), *Le Juif polonais* (after Erckmann-Chatrian, 1900), *Aphrodite* (1906), *Bacchus triomphant* (1909), *La Sorcière, Le Fils de l'étoile* and *La Forfaiture*; cantata *Velléda* (1888); *Sérénade carnavalesque* for orchestra; piano pieces; *Poèmes russes* and other songs.

Erlkönig, *Erl* (real name Alder) *King*, a ballad by Goethe, set by Schubert in 1815 at the age of 18, first sung in public by Johann Michael Vogl, Vienna, 7 Mar 1821, pub. as op. 1 that year.

Ermler, Mark (b Leningrad, 5 May 1932), Russian conductor. Studied in Leningrad and made debut with the Leningrad PO, 1952. Joined Bolshoi Opera, Moscow, 1956, leading *Fidelio, Eugene Onegin* and *Figaro* in his first season. UK debut with Bolshoi Ballet in London, 1974. Opera tours with the Bolshoi to Paris, Tokyo (1970), Milan, New York and Washington (1980), and Berlin. Conducted *Carmen* at CG, London, 1986, returning for *Butterfly, Onegin, Médée* and *Bohème*. Guest with the (former) USSR State SO on tour to Europe, Prokofiev's *War and Peace* for Seattle Opera (1990) and Tchaikovsky's *The Oprichnik* at the 1992 Edinburgh Festival.

Ernani opera by Verdi (libretto by F M Piave, based on Victor Hugo's drama *Hernani*), produced Venice, Teatro La Fenice, 9 Mar 1844. The first of Verdi's operas produced outside Milan. Outlawed Ernani and Don Carlos, King of Spain, both in love with Elvira. Don Carlos becomes Holy Roman Emperor, Ernani marries Elvira, Silva (guardian and former fiancé of Elvira) gets revenge.

Ernst, Heinrich Wilhelm (b Brno, 6 May 1814; d Nice, 8 Oct 1865), Moravian violinist and composer. Pupil of Böhm, Seyfried and Mayseder in Vienna. Lived in Paris from 1832 to 1838.

Works include concertos, fantasies, variations, an *Elégie*, etc. for violin, also, with Heller, *Pensées fugitives* for violin and piano.

Ernster, Deszö (b Pécs, 23 Nov 1898; d Zurich, 15 Feb 1981), Hungarian bass. Debut Düsseldorf 1925; Bayreuth 1931. On tour in US with Salzburg Opera Guild 1938–39; NY Met. debut 1946, as King Marke (until 1963). Hagen at CG, London, 1949 and 1954; Glyndebourne 1952, Alfonso. Salzburg 1953 as the Commendatore, under Furtwängler. At the Kroll Opera, Berlin, he sang in the fp of Hindemith's *Neues vom Tage* (1929, under Klemperer).

'Eroica' Symphony Beethoven's symphony No. 3 in E♭ major, op. 55,

---

THE OPERA

Ernani

A four-act opera by Giuseppe Verdi, produced first in Venice in 1844. It is set in Spain in 1590.

I. The outlawed Don Juan de Aragon (assumed name Ernani, tenor) has sworn to avenge the death of his father at the hands of Don Carlo, King of Castile (baritone). Both men are in love with Elvira (soprano) and hope to abduct her from the castle of elderly Don Ruy Gomez de Silva (bass), to whom she is betrothed. When Ernani is discovered in the compliant Elvira's rooms, Silva challenges him to a duel but Don Carlo allows him to escape.

II. Don Carlo takes Elvira hostage on the day of her wedding to Silva. Laws of hospitality prevent Silva from punishing Ernani, but the younger man says he will take his own life at the sounding of his silver horn (which he gives to Silva) once he has rescued Elvira.

III. At the tomb of Charlemagne at Aix-la-Chapelle, Ernani and other conspirators meet to plot Carlo's death; Carlo emerges from hiding and the traitors are captured. When Elvira intercedes for Ernani, Don Carlo agrees to their marriage.

IV. The horn is sounded during Ernani's wedding celebrations and he must now carry out his pledge; a distraught Elvira cannot prevent him from stabbing himself to death.

THE OPERA

composed 1803–04. It was to have been entitled *Bonaparte*, but on hearing that Napoleon had declared himself Emperor, Beethoven renamed it *Sinfonia Eroica, composta per festeggiare il souvenire di un grand'uomo/Heroic symphony, composed to celebrate the memory of a great man.*

'Eroica' Variations Beethoven's piano variations and fugue, op. 35 (composed 1802), so called because they used the same theme as the finale of the 'Eroica' symphony. The theme, however, was taken from one of Beethoven's dances, and the variations were written before the symphony.

Erös, Peter (b Budapest, 22 Sept 1936), Hungarian conductor. After study at the Franz Liszt Academy and with Zoltan Kodaly, he assisted Fricsay at the Holland Festival, 1958–61. Associate conductor of the Concertgebouw Orchestra 1960–65, music director of Malmo SO 1966–68, San Diego SO 1972–80. Australian Broadcasting Commission 1975–79; Peabody SO, Baltimore, 1982. Music director of the Aalborg SO from 1983.

Ershov, Ivan (b Novocherkassk, 20 Nov 1867; d Tashkent, 21 Nov 1943), Russian tenor. Studied Moscow and St Petersburg; debut 1893, as Faust. Sang at the Maryinsky Theatre 1895–1929 in Russian repertory and as Don José, Otello, Tristan, Siegfried and Lohengrin. Highly praised as an actor. Taught at Leningrad Conservatory 1916–41.

Erwartung monodrama for soprano and orchestra by Schoenberg (libretto by Marie Pappenheim), composed 1909 but first produced Prague, 6 Jun 1924, conductor Zemlinsky, with Marie Gutheil-Schoder. Solitary woman searches through a wood for her lover; she finds his murdered body, which prompts an array of stark emotions.

'You can't brush your teeth to Erwartung.'
Pierre Boulez, quoted in Jacobson, *Reverberations*, 1975

Eschenbach, Christoph (b Breslau, 20 Feb 1940), German pianist and conductor. He studied in Cologne and Hamburg and made his London debut in 1966. Gave the fp of Henze's second piano concerto (Bielefeld, 29 Aug 1968) and in 1969 made his US debut, with the Cleveland Orchestra. Debut as conductor 1973; plays Mozart's piano concertos while conducting from the keyboard. CG debut 1984, *Così fan tutte.* Conductor of the Tonhalle Orchestra, Zurich, 1982–85; music director Houston SO from 1980. Conducted *Parsifal* at Houston, 1992.

Esclarmonde opera by Massenet (libretto by E Blau and L de Gramont), produced Paris, Opéra-Comique, 15 May 1889. Esclarmonde, daughter of the King of Byzantium, uses magic powers to seduce the knight Roland. She is later exorcised and forced to renounce him, but Roland wins her back at a tournament, becoming king.

Escobar, Pedro (b Oporto, *c* 1465; d ? Evora, after 1535), Spanish composer, *maestro de capilla* at Seville early in the 16th c. Composed church music and secular pieces for three and four voices.

Escobedo, Bartolomeo (b Zamora, *c* 1500; d Segovia, 1563), Spanish composer. Entered the Papal Chapel in Rome in 1536, acted as judge in a dispute between Vicentino and Lusitano in 1551. In 1554 he returned to Spain as *maestro de capilla* at Segovia. Wrote Masses, motets, Magnificats, Miserere, etc.

Escribano, Juan (b ? Salamanca *c* 1480; d Spain, Oct 1557), Spanish singer and composer. Sang in the Papal Chapel in Rome, 1507–39. Wrote church music, *chansons* for several voices.

Escudier, Léon (b Castelnaudary, Aude, 17 Sept 1821; d Paris, 22 Jun 1881), and his brother *Marie Escudier*, (b Castelnaudary, Aude, 29 Jun 1819, d Paris, 7 Apr 1880).

French writers on music and publishers, brothers, who did most of their work jointly. It included biographies of singers and of Rossini, and a music dictionary; they founded *La France musicale* (1837). Léon was director of the Théâtre Italien 1874–76.

Esham, Faith (b Vanceburg, KY, 6 Aug 1948), American soprano. Studied at Juilliard and made debut at NY City Opera, 1977, as Cherubino; returned in the soprano roles of Gilda, Manon, Musetta

and Cendrillon. European debut at Nancy 1980 as Nedda; Glyndebourne 1981, Cherubino. Sang Micaela in Francesco Rosi's 1984 film version of *Carmen*, and Marzelline at the NY Met. 1986; Desdemona for WNO, 1990. Other roles include Pamina and Marguerite (City Opera), Zerlina (Washington DC) and Antonia (Las Palmas). Concerts at the Mostly Mozart Festival, NY.

Esmeralda opera by Fabio Campana (1815–82) libretto by G T Cimino, based on Victor Hugo's novel, *Notre-Dame de Paris*), produced St Petersburg, 30 Dec 1869.

Opera by Dargomizhsky (libretto by composer translated from Victor Hugo's libretto based on his *Notre-Dame de Paris*, and written for Louise Angélique Bertin [1805–77] for her opera produced Paris, 1836), produced Moscow, 17 Dec 1847.

España rhapsody for orchestra by Chabrier of Spanish tunes collected by the composer during a visit to Spain in 1882–83; composed 1883, fp Paris, 4 Nov 1883. Waldteufel later made a ballroom waltz of it.

Esplá, Oscar (b Alicante, 5 Aug 1886; d Madrid, 6 Jan 1976), Spanish composer. Studied civil engineering and took the degree of doctor of philosophy, but also worked at music and took a prize for an orchestral suite in Vienna in 1909. Settled at Brussels in 1936.

Works include ballets *El contrabandista* (1928) and *Ciclopes*; symphonic poems *El sueno de Eros* (1904), *La vela de armas de Don Quixote* (1924) and *Los Cumbres, Poema de niños, Ambito de la danza* and *Levantine Suite* for orchestra; quintet; violin and piano sonata; sonata, scherzo and other works for piano.

Esposito, Michele (b Castellamare near Naples, 29 Sept 1855; d Florence, 26 Nov 1929), Italian pianist and composer. Studied at the Naples Conservatory, lived in Paris in 1878–82 and was then appointed professor of piano at Dublin, where in 1899 he established the Dublin Orchestral Society, which he conducted.

Works include operetta *The Postbag* (1902); incidental music for Douglas Hyde's *The Tinker and the Fairy* (1910); cantata *Deirdre*; Irish Symphony, overture to Shakespeare's *Othello*; two string quartets; sonatas for violin and piano and cello and piano.

Esquivel, Juan (b Ciudad-Rodrigo, *c* 1565; d after 1613), Spanish composer. He was *maestro de capilla* at Salamanca Cathedral (1608) and at Ciudad-Rodrigo (1611–13). His Masses and motets were pub. (in two vols.) in 1608, and a volume of misc. sacred works in 1613. An *Officium pro defunctis* survives in MS.

essential discord a chord which is dissonant according to acoustic theory, but whose notes belong to the key in which a composition or passage is written and has become sufficiently current to be introduced without preparation.

Esswood, Paul (b West Bridgford, Nottinghamshire, 6 Feb 1942), English countertenor. He studied at the RCM. Debut 1965 (*Messiah*). Opera debut Berkeley, CA, in Cavalli's *Erismena*, 1968. Has appeared all over Europe in operas by Monteverdi and has recorded many of the church cantatas of Bach. Sang Death in the fp of Penderecki's *Paradise Lost* (Chicago, 1978) and at La Scala 1979; created Glass's Akhnaten at Stuttgart, 1984. Handel's Admeto at Karlsruhe, 1990; Riccardo Primo at CG, 1991.

Estampes, *Engravings*, a set of three piano pieces by Debussy, composed 1903; 1. *Pagodes*, 2. *Soirée dans Grenade*, 3. *Jardins sous la pluie.*

estampida, (Provençal), *estampie* (French), an instrumental dance form of the 13th and 14th c., related to the troubadour/trouvère repertory. Its form consisted of several *puncta* (sections), each played twice, with first-and second-time endings, called *ouvert* and *clos.* Frequently the *ouvert* and *clos* endings, which often comprised the greater part of each *punctum*, were the same throughout the piece, resulting in a great deal of repetition.

Estes, Simon (b Centreville, IA, 2 Mar 1938), American bass-baritone. He studied at Juilliard, NY, and engagements in Berlin and Hamburg soon followed; appeared in the USA from 1966; Met. debut 1976, as Oroveso. Later NY roles have been Boris, Philip II and Amonasro. He sang the Dutchman at the 1978 Bayreuth festival, and returned as Amfortas, but was rejected for the 1983 Solti-Hall *Ring*, allegedly because he is black: sang Wotan with great success in a *Ring* produced

THE OPERA
Eugene Onegin

A three-act opera by Pyotr Tchaikovsky dating from 1879. The action takes place in the country estate of the Larinas near St Petersburg, early in the 19th century.

I. Madame Larina's daughter Tatyana (soprano) falls in love with Onegin (baritone), a friend of Lensky (tenor), fiancé of Tatyana's sister, Olga (mezzo-soprano). Tatyana stays up all night to put all her feelings into a passionate letter to Onegin, but the next morning he coldly rebuffs her.

II. Irritated by gossip about him at Tatyana's birthday party, Onegin dances with Olga and, when Lensky tries to reprove her, she is annoyed and continues flirting with Onegin. The jealous Lensky challenges Onegin to a duel with pistols. Beside an old mill at dawn the next day, Lensky is killed with a single shot.

III. Returning from abroad six years later, Onegin arrives at a ball being given in the St Petersburg house of Prince Gremin (bass), now Tatyana's husband. Seeing Tatyana again, Onegin declares his love for her, but although initially responsive, she recalls her duty and Onegin flees in despair.

THE OPERA

at Berlin, 1984–85; also heard in *Die Walküre* at NY Met, 1986. CG debut 1986, as the Dutchman. Also heard as a concert singer. Sang Porgy at the Met. 1985, and Macbeth for Greater Miami Opera, 1992.

Esther oratorio by Handel. Fp as a masque entitled *Haman and Mordecai* (libretto probably by Pope and Arbuthnot, after Racine), Canons, near Edgware, *c* 1720. Subsequently recast, with additional words by Samuel Humphreys, and performed as an oratorio in London, at first privately to celebrate Handel's birthday and then at King's Theatre, Haymarket, 2 May 1732.

Oratorio by Dittersdorf (libretto by S I Pintus), performed Vienna, 21 Dec 1773. During the interval of a revival of the work, 16 Dec 1785, Mozart's piano concerto no. 22, K482 received its fp.

estinto Italian = 'extinct, dead'; a direction indicating that a passage is to be performed in a toneless manner.

estompé French = lit. 'stumped, shaded off'; damped, muffled, a direction frequently used by Debussy where he asks for a veiled or dull tone.

Es war einmal, *Once upon a time*, opera by Zemlinsky (libretto by Drachmann), produced Vienna, Hofoper, 22 Jan 1900. The opera was conducted by Mahler, who assisted Zemlinsky in revising the work. Princess married to a gypsy fits the wedding dress offered by a mystery prince, her husband in disguise.

Eszterháza castle near Süttör, Hungary, built in 1766 in imitation of Versailles by the Princes Esterházy. The project was started by Paul Anton Esterházy, who engaged Haydn as vice-*Kapellmeister* in 1761, and completed by Nikolaus Esterházy. In 1766 Haydn took charge of the opera house and marionette theatre, as well as the castle's orchestra. He wrote orchestral and instrumental music for his master and supervised frequent opera productions: all his own operas from *Le pescatrici* (1770) to *Armida* (1784) were fp at Esterháza, but works by Anfossi, Salieri, Sacchini and Cimarosa were the staple fare. The musical activities at Esterháza were much reduced in 1790, and Haydn worked in Vienna and London, but between 1796 and 1802 he wrote six great masses for performance at the castle. Beethoven's Mass in C was given its fp there on 13 Sept 1807.

Eternal Gospel, The, *Věčné evangelium*, legend by Janáček for soprano, tenor, chorus and orchestra (text by J Vrchlický), composed 1914, revised 1924. Fp Prague, 5 Feb 1917.

Et exspecto resurrectionem mortuorum work in five sections by Messiaen for 18 woodwind, 16 brass and three percussion, composed 1964 to commemorate the dead of two World Wars. Fp Paris, Sainte-Chapelle, 7 May 1965, conductor Baudo.

Etler, Alvin (b Battle Creek, IA, 19 Feb 1913; d Northampton, MA,

13 Jun 1973), American composer. Studied at the Cleveland Institute and with Hindemith at Yale. Teacher at Smith College 1949–73; from 1968 chairman of Hampshire College electronic music workshop. His music is influenced by serialism and shows concern for textural elements.

Works include two sinfoniettas (1940, 1941), concerto for orchestra (1957), concerto for wind quintet and orchestra (1962), concerto for string quartet and orchestra (1968), concerto for cello and chamber group (1971); concerto for violin and wind quintet (1958); two string quartets (1963, 1965).

Étoile du Nord, L', *The North Star*, opera by Meyerbeer (libretto by Scribe), produced Paris, Opéra-Comique, 16 Feb 1854. Disguised Katherine joins Russian army and warns Tsar Peter of conspiracy.

Étoile, L' opéra bouffe by Chabrier (libretto by E Leterrier and A Vanloo), produced Paris, Théâtre Bouffes-Parisiens, 28 Nov 1877. On the advice of an astrologer, a superstitious king cancels the execution of Lazuli, a pedlar who has insulted him.

Eton Choirbook, (Eton College Library, MS 178), the most important source of English church music of the late 15th c., containing works by John Browne, William Cornyshe, Walter Lambe, Richard Davy, Robert Fayrfax and many others. The repertory reflects the statutes of the college, which prescribed the singing of a polyphonic antiphon to the Virgin every evening (in Lent, the *Salve Regina*). The MS originally contained 67 antiphons to the Virgin and other saints (including 15 settings of the *Salve Regina*), 24 Magnificats, the St Matthew Passion by Davy, and a setting of the Apostles' Creed in the form of a 13-part round by Robert Wylkynson. The settings, except for this last, are for from four to nine voices. About half the original contents are now lost, although some works can be recovered from other sources. The MS is pub. in *Musica Britannica*, vols. x–xii. For the format, ⟩choirbook.

etouffé French = 'stifled, smothered'; a direction to deaden the tone on instruments where it is liable to vibrate after being sounded, as on the harp or the kettledrums.

Ettinger, Max (b Lwów, Poland, 27 Dec 1874; d Basel, 19 Jul 1951), German composer. Studied in Berlin and Munich and lived at both places until 1933, when he went into exile in Italian Switzerland.

Works include operas Clavigo (after Goethe, 1926), Judith (after Hebbel), *Frühlingserwachen* (after Frank Wedekind, 1928), *Juana* (after Georg Kaiser), *Dorlores* (1931); oratorios *Königin Esther*; *Moses, Weisheit des Orients* (from Omar Khayyám) for solo voices, chorus and orchestra; string quartet (1945).

étude French = 'study'; a technical exercise for an instrumental (more rarely a vocal) performer, which may be as much an exercise in expression as in technique.

Études symphoniques a set of 12 concert studies for piano by Schumann, op. 13, at first entitled *Études en forme de variations*, composed 1834. They are variations on a theme by the father of Ernestine von Fricken, with whom Schumann was in love at that time, but they are dedicated to Sterndale Bennett, in whose honour Schumann introduced into the finale a theme from Marschner's *Ivanhoe* opera *Der Templer und die Jüdin*: a song in praise of England. Five further variations are sometimes now given.

etwas German = 'somewhat, rather'. Used in conjunction with an adjective denoting speed or character, eg *etwas langsam*.

Eugene Onegin opera by Tchaikovsky (libretto by composer and K S Shilovsky, based on Pushkin's poem-novel), produced, by students of the Conservatory, Moscow, 29 Mar 1879. First professional performance Moscow, Bolshoi, 23 Jan 1881. Onegin rejects Tatiana's proposal by letter, but realizes too late by Act III that he loves her after all; she is now married to Prince Gremin.

Eulenburg a pub. firm founded in Leipzig in 1874 by Ernst Eulenburg (1847–1926). In 1892 the firm took over the series of miniature scores issued by Albert Payne and extended its scope to cover a wide repertory of oratorios, operas, orchestral works and chamber music. The firm is now owned by Schott.

eunuch flute an early woodwind instrument with a mouthpiece containing a membrane vibrating when the player sang into it. It dates back to the 16th c. at least, but it was never much more than a toy. ◊mirliton.

euphonium, ◊saxhorn., a four-valved brass instrument of the tuba family, used chiefly in military and brass bands.

The compass of the euphonium.

euphony suavity and harmoniousness of sound, the opposite of cacophony.

eurhythmics a system of teaching musical, especially rhythmic, perception by means of bodily movements, invented by ◊Jaques-Dalcroze.

Euridice, L' opera by Caccini (libretto by Ottavio Rinuccini), produced Florence, Palazzo Pitti, 5 Dec 1602. Orfeo's bride, Euridice, dies from a snake bite, but is allowed to return from Hades after divine intervention.

Opera by Peri (libretto ditto), produced Florence, Palazzo Pitti, 6 Oct 1600.

Euripides (*fl. c* 484–406 BC), Greek dramatist. ◊Alkestis (Boughton and Wellesz); ◊Bakchantinnen (Wellesz); ◊Bassarids (Henze); ◊Börtz (*Backanterna*); Buller (*Bakxai*); ◊Coerne (*Trojan Women*); W ◊Damrosch (*Electra, Iphigenia in Aulis, Medea*); ◊Foulds (*Trojan Women*); ◊Ghedini (*Baccanti, Ifigenia in Tauride*); C ◊Gray (*Trojan Women*); ◊Ifigenia in Aulide (Caldara, Cherubini, Graun, Zingarelli); ◊Ifigenia in Tauride (Galuppi, Maio and Traetta); ◊Iphigénie en Aulide (Gluck); ◊Iphigénie en Tauride (Campra, Gluck and Piccinni); ◊Schürmann (*Getreue Alceste*); ◊Senilov (*Hippolytus*); ◊Slonimsky (*Orestes*); ◊Taubert (*Medea*); V ◊Thomson (ditto); ◊Toch (*Bacchantes*); ◊Troades (Reimann); C ◊Wood (*Ion and Iphigenia in Tauris*).

Europe Galante, L' opera-ballet by Campra (libretto by A H de la Motte), produced Paris, Opéra, 24 Oct 1697. The work's four entrées are entitled *La France, L'Espagne, L'Italie, La Turquie*, and depict the amorous inclinations of each country.

Euryanthe opera by Weber (libretto by H von Chézy), produced Vienna, Kärntnertortheater, 25 Oct 1823. Lysiart in league with evil Eglantine to prove Euryanthe, Adolar's bride, unfaithful. They trick her and Lysiart succeeds in winning a bet, thereby ruining Adolar. Later the innocent Euryanthe is vindicated.

Eusebius one of the two imaginary characters, Florestan and Eusebius, used by Schumann as pseudonyms for his critical writings and also introduced into his music (*Carnaval, Davidsbündlertänze*) to personify what he felt to be his dual character as an artist. Florestan represents an impetuous romantic and Eusebius portrays a dreamer.

Euterpe the Muse of lyric poetry in Greek mythology, and since such poetry was sung, also the Muse of music, which had no separate patroness among the nine Muses.

Evans, Anne (b London, 20 Aug 1941), English soprano. Studied at the RCM and in Geneva: small roles at the Grand Théâtre there. She joined ENO in 1968 and sang Mimi, Tosca, Elsa, the Marschallin and Sieglinde at the Coliseum, London. With WNO she has sung Senta, Chrysothemis, the Empress and Donna Anna; her Brünnhilde in the *Ring* (1985) was repeated with great success at CG in 1986 when the co. visited London. At San Francisco she has been heard as Elsa and Elisabeth de Valois. Sang Brünnhilde at Bayreuth 1989–92, Isolde for WNO 1993 (also at CG); NY Met. debut 1992.

Evans, Damon (b Baltimore, 1960), American tenor. Debut in Glass's *Akhnaten* for NY City Opera, 1985. Virginia Opera 1985 in the fp of Musgrave's *Harriet: the Woman Called Moses*. Sang Sportin' Life in *Porgy and Bess* at Glyndebourne 1986, repeated in Boston and Moscow and at CG, London. Concerts include the UK fp of Blitzstein's *Airborne Symphony, A Child of our Time* and Weill's *Lost in the Stars* suite (Carnegie Hall, 1989). Sang Don José in *Carmen Jones*, London 1991.

Evans, Geraint (Llewellyn) (b Pontypridd, Glamorgan, 16 Feb 1922; d Aberystwyth, 19 Sept 1992), Welsh baritone. Studied at the GSM and later in Hamburg, Geneva and in Italy. He made his debut at CG in 1948, and created roles in Britten's *Billy Budd* (1951) and *Gloriana* (1953); later sang all over Europe, including La Scala, Milan, in 1960 and the Vienna Staatsoper in 1961; both debuts as Mozart's Figaro. Glyndebourne 1950–61 as Guglielmo, Masetto, Leporello and Papageno. NY Met. debut 1964, as Falstaff. Last opera performance London CG, 1984, as Dulcamara. Other roles included Beckmesser and Wozzeck. Knighted 1971.

Evans, Nancy (b Liverpool, 19 Mar 1915), English mezzo. Studied in Liverpool and with Maggie Teyte. Sang at CG from 1939; Britten's Lucretia at Glyndebourne, 1946. Created Nancy in *Albert Herring* (1947) and toured widely with English Opera Group in Britten's operas. Premiered *A Charm of Lullabies* (1948). CBE 1991.

Éventail de Jeanne, L', *Joan's Fan*, ballet by Auric, Delannoy, Ferroud, Ibert, Milhaud, Poulenc, Ravel, Roland-Manuel, Roussel and Schmitt (choreography by Alice Bourgat), produced Paris, in private, 16 Jun 1927; Opéra, 4 Mar 1929.

Eventyr, *Once upon a time*, ballad for orchestra by Delius after fairy tales by P C Asbjørnsen (1812–85), composed 1917 and dedicated to Henry Wood, who gave the fp in London, 28 Jun 1919.

Everding, August (b Bottrop, 31 Oct 1928), German director and administrator. Studied in Bonn and Munich; director of the Münchner Kammerspiele 1963–73. Directed the fp of Searle's *Hamlet* at Hamburg, 1968, and was resident at the Staatsoper 1973–77. Intendant at Munich Staatsoper from 1977, producing a *Zauberflöte* which was seen at London, CG, 1979. Bayreuth Festival and NY Met. 1974, *Tristan und Isolde* and *Boris Godunov*. *Ring* cycle at Chicago from 1992.

Everyman incidental music for Hugo von Hofmannsthal's German version of the 15th-c. English morality play, *Jedermann*, by Sibelius, op. 83, composed 1916, fp Helsinki, National Theatre, 5 Nov 1916. Six monologues from Everyman were set by Frank Martin for baritone and piano in 1943; orchestral version 1949.

Évocations three symphonic poems by Roussel, composed 1910–12: 1. *Les Dieux dans l'ombre des cavernes*; 2. *La Ville rose*; 3. *Aux bords du fleuve sacré*; fp Paris, Société Nationale, 18 May 1912.

My idea is that there is music in the air, music all around us, the world is full of it and you simply take as much of it as you require.

Edward Elgar, quoted in Buckley,
Sir Edward Elgar, 1904

Evocations symphonic suite by Bloch, composed 1937; fp San Francisco, 11 Feb 1938. three movements: *Contemplation, Houang/God of War, Renouveau*.

Evstatieva, Stefka (b Rousse, 7 May 1947), Bulgarian soprano. Debut at the Rousse Opera 1972 as Amelia (*Ballo in Maschera*); sang also Aida and Desdemona. Bulgarian National Opera from 1978; Vienna debut as the *Trovatore* Leonora; Paris as Elvira in *Ernani*. Sang Desdemona with CG co. in Manchester 1981, Elisabeth de Valois in London 1983; latter role repeated in NY debut, 1984. Sang Santuzza at Caracalla Festival, Rome, 1993. Also appears in concert.

Ewen, David (b Lwów, Poland, 26 Nov 1907; d Miami, 28 Dec 1985), American writer on music. He moved to the USA in 1912 and studied in NY; University of Miami from 1965. In 50 years he pub. more than 80 music reference books, e.g. *Dictators of the Baton* (1943), *Encyclopedia of the Opera* (1955, revised 1971), *The World of 20th-Century Music* (1968), *Composers Since 1900* (1969), *Musicians Since 1900* (1978) and *American Composers* (1982).

Ewing, Maria (b Detroit, 27 Mar 1950), American soprano. She studied in Cleveland with Eleanor Steber and Jennie Tourel; debut 1973 Ravinia Festival with Chicago SO. In 1976 she sang Cherubino at the NY Met. and Mélisande at La Scala, Milan. Glyndebourne 1978 and 1984–85 as Dorabella, Poppea and Carmen in productions by her then husband, Peter ◊Hall. Sang Salome at LA, 1986 and on CG debut 1988. Carmen at CG 1991; also NY Met. 1994, as Katerina in Shostakovich's *Lady Macbeth*. Also a successful concert artist.

Excursions of Mr Brouček, The, *Výlety pana Broučka*, opera by Janáček (libretto by the composer with F Gellner, V Dyke, F S Procházka and others, after two novels by S Čech), produced Prague, 23 Apr 1920. Not produced in Britain until Edinburgh, 5 Sept 1970, by the Prague National Theatre Co. Part I depicts sausage-eating Brouček amidst aesthetic, vegetarian moon-dwellers; part II concerns the 1420 Czech defence in battle of their Hussite faith. Brouček is almost punished for cowardice but returns to the present.

Expert, Henri (b Bordeaux, 12 May 1863; d Tourrettes-sur-Loup, 18 Aug 1952), French musicologist. Studied, and later taught, at Niedermeyer's school in Paris, and was also a pupil of Franck and Gigout. Professor of music at the École des Hautes Études Sociales and librarian of the Conservatory library. Edited series of early French music, *Les Maîtres musiciens de la renaissance française* and *Monuments de la musique française*, of settings of Ronsard's poetry, early songs, church and harpsichord music.

'**...explosante-fixe...**' work by Boulez for unspecified forces. Given with flute, clarinet and trumpet in London on 17 Jun 1971; with same forces, plus strings and computer-controlled electronics, NY PO, conductor Boulez, on 5 Jan 1973. Further revised under Boulez, with the BBC SO in Rome, on 13 May 1973 '... work in progress ...'.

Not many composers have ideas. Far more of them know how to use strange instruments which do not require ideas.

George Gershwin, *The Composer in the Machine Age*, 1930

---

exposition the first setting forth of thematic material in a composition. In a fugue the exposition is the statement of the subject by its first entry in each voice; in a rondo the statement of the subject up to the first episode; in a sonata-form movement the whole first section up to the point at which the ◊development (or working-out) section begins.

Expressionism a term properly belonging to painting, especially in Austria and Germany in the 1910s, but loosely applied to music aimed at a similar kind of interpretation, not of outward and visible things, but of moods and states of mind. Schoenberg's *Erwartung* (1909) is a familiar example.

expression marks all the indications by which the composer indicates his or her wishes as to the manner of performance of a work, especially from the dynamic point of view (*forte, piano, crescendo, diminuendo*); but they may extend also to matters of speed and rhythm (e.g. *rallentando, rubato, accelerando*, etc.). Expression marks were little used before the 18th c. and hardly at all before the 17th.

extemporization ◊improvisation.

extravaganza, corrupt. from Italian *stravaganza*, a word sometimes used for a composition of a freakish nature, especially for a light and fantastic stage piece with music, e.g. Gilbert and Sullivan's *Trial by Jury*.

Eybler, Joseph Leopold von (b Schwechat near Vienna, 8 Feb 1765; d Vienna, 24 Jul 1846), Austrian composer. Pupil of Albrechtsberger and, after holding various apointments in Vienna, chief *Kapellmeister* to the Austrian court from 1824 to 1833. He attempted to complete Mozart's Requiem (1791) and suffered a stroke while conducting it in 1833.

Works include opera *Das Zauberschwert* and others; oratorio *Die vier letzten Dinge* (1810), Requiem in C minor (1803, for Empress Maria Theresa), cantata *Die Hirten bei der Krippe*, seven Te Deums, 32 Masses, offertories, graduals and other church music; symphonies; chamber music, piano pieces, etc.

Ezio, *Aetius*, libretto by Metastasio, first set by Porpora (Venice, 1728); other settings by Handel (1732); Jommelli (1741); Gluck (1750) and Hasse (1755). General Aetius and Emperor Valentinian both love Fulvia. Maximus, her father, plays them off against each other to try and gain the throne. After much complication, Aetius and Fulvia are united and Maximus is pardoned.

F

F the fourth note, or subdominant, of the scale of C major.

f the subdominant note in any key in Tonic Sol-fa notation, pronounced Fah.

f, abbr., the symbol commonly employed in music to indicate a loud (*forte*) tone. Progressively even louder dynamics are marked *ff*, *fff*, etc.

fa the old name for the note *F* (◊solmization), still used in Latin countries, and in Tonic Sol-fa notation the sub-dominant note in any key represented by the symbol *f*, pronounced fa.

Faber, Heinrich (b Lichtenfels, before 1500; d Olsnitz, 26 Feb 1552), German theorist and composer, author of a *Compendiolum musicae pro incipientibus* (Brunswick, 1548), which ran into numerous editions. There is some church music to Latin and German texts.

fabliau old French = 'fable'; a troubadour ballad with narrative words, distinct from the love songs sung by the troubadours.

Fabri, Annibale Pio (b Bologna, 1697; d Lisbon, 12 Aug 1760), Italian tenor. Pupil of Pistocchi. Sang in Handel's operas in London, 1729–31, and created roles in *Poro* and *Partenope*.

Fabricius, Werner (b Itzehoe, Holstein, 10 Apr 1633; d Leipzig, 9 Jan 1679), German organist and composer. Studied under his father, Albert Fabricius, organist at Flensburg and under Selle and Schiedemann at the Hamburg Gymnasium. After pursuing other studies at Leipzig University, including law, he became music director at St Paul's Church there in 1656 and, in addition, at St Nicolas' Church in 1658. He was also a public notary.

Works include motets, hymn tunes; sacred and secular songs for several voices; suites for viols and other instruments, etc.

Fabrizi, Vincenzo (b Naples, 1764; d after 1812), Italian composer. He had written 14 operas by the time he was 24; many of them were short comic pieces, performed all over Italy. His *Il convitato di pietra (Don Giovanni Tenorio)* was premiered at Rome in the same year as *Don Giovanni* was given in Prague, and rivalled the success of Mozart's work for several years.

faburden English ◊fauxbourdon.

Façade diversion by Walton (poems by Edith Sitwell), privately produced London, Chenil Gallery, Chelsea; first public performance London, Aeolian Hall, 12 Jun 1923. Two concert suites arranged later for enlarged orchestra and for piano duet. Produced as a ballet (choreography by Frederick Ashton), London, Cambridge Theatre, 26 Apr 1931.

Faccio, Franco (b Verona, 8 Mar 1840; d Monza, 21 Jul 1891), Italian conductor and composer. Studied at the Milan Conservatory, produced his first opera there and the second at La Scala in 1863. Appointed professor of harmony at the Conservatory in 1868 and later conductor at the Carcano and Scala theatres. He was Verdi's conductor for *Aida* and *Otello* at Milan, 1872 and 1887. He also conducted the fps of the revised versions of *Simon Boccanegra* (1881) and *Don Carlos* (1884) and the fp of *La Gioconda* (1876).

Works include operas *Le sorelle d'Italia*, *I profughi fiamminghi*, *Amleto* (after Shakespeare's *Hamlet*); symphony in F major.

Fachiri (born *d'Aranyi*), Adila (b Budapest, 26 Feb 1886; d Florence, 15 Dec 1962), Hungarian-born British violinist, a great-niece of Joachim, with whom she studied. She settled in London and appeared frequently as a soloist, often in double concertos with her sister, Jelly d'◊Aranyi; they played the Bach concerto for the last time 1960.

Fackeltanz German = 'torch dance'.

fadinho, (Portuguese *fado*), a type of popular song performed in Portuguese towns, in the streets and cafés, accompanied by the guitar and enlivened by dancing.

Faenza Codex, Faenza, Bib. Comm., MS 117, a large MS of keyboard music from the late 14th or early 15th c., containing ornamented transciptions of French and Italian secular vocal works (including some by Machaut and Landini), and some liturgical organ music. The notation is on two staves with regular barring. In the mid-15th c. parts of the original contents were erased by Bonadies to make room for sacred vocal works by himself and others.

Faggioni, Piero (b Carrera, 12 Aug 1936), Italian stage director. Worked with Luchino Visconti and made solo debut at Venice in 1964, with *La Bohème*. Produced *Alceste* at La Scala 1972 and *La Fanciulla del West* at CG 1977 (returned for *Il Trovatore*, 1989). He staged *Carmen* at the 1977 Edinburgh Festival and *Francesca da Rimini* at the NY Met. 1984. His *Don Quixote* was seen in Paris 1986 and *Boris Godunov* in Florence 1987. He belongs to the Italian realist school of opera producers.

Fago, Nicola (b Taranto, 26 Feb 1677; d Naples, 18 Feb 1745), Italian composer, nicknamed Il Tarantino after his birthplace. Educated at the Conservatorio della Pietà dei Turchini in Naples. *Maestro di cappella* at the Conservatorio di S Onofrio, 1704–08, and at the Conservatorio della Pietà, 1705–40. His works consist mainly of church music but he also wrote four or more operas including *Radamisto* (1707) and *Cassandra* (1711), oratorios, etc.

Fagott German = 'bassoon'.

fagotto Italian = lit. 'fagot or bundle' = bassoon.

Faignient, Noël (b Cambrai), Flemish 16th-c. composer. From 1561 he lived in Antwerp. Wrote *chansons*, madrigals, songs to Dutch texts, and sacred Latin works.

Fairies, The opera by John Christopher Smith (libretto by composer, based on Shakespeare's *A Midsummer Night's Dream*), produced London, Drury Lane, 3 Feb 1755.

Fairy Queen, The semi-opera by Purcell (libretto adapted from Shakespeare's *A Midsummer Night's Dream* ? by Elkanah Settle), produced London, Dorset Gardens Theatre, Apr 1692. The plot broadly follows that of Shakespeare's play, without setting any of the words. Revived by ENO for the Purcell tercentenary, 1995.

Fairy's Kiss, The, *Le Baiser de la fée*, ballet in four scenes by Stravinsky, based on songs and piano pieces by Tchaikovsky, produced Paris, Opéra, 27 Nov 1927, choreographed by Nijinska. Suite for orchestra, Divertimento, 1934.

Fairy Tale, *Pohádka*, work by Janáček for cello and piano, after the tale

fagott *A 16th-century name for a bassoon, the name being derived from the Italian* fagotto *meaning 'bundle'. The appearance of the two tubes bound together is like a bundle of sticks.*

Czar Berendei by V A Zhukovsky, fp Brno, 13 Mar 1910, revised *c* 1923.

Faisst, Immanuel (Gottlob Friedrich) (b Esslingen, near Stuttgart, 13 Oct 1823; d Stuttgart, 5 Jun 1894), German organist and composer. Studied theology at Tübingen University, but gave it up, on Mendelssohn's advice, for music, in which he was self-taught. He travelled as organist and settled at Stuttgart, where he founded an organ school in 1847 and a society for the study of church music and was one of the founders of the Conservatory. He wrote on and edited music.

Works include cantata *Des Sängers Wiederkehr*, choral setting of Schiller's *Die Macht des Gesanges*; double fugue for piano; organ works; vocal quartets.

fa-la a light 16th–17th-c. English composition for several voices of the ◊ballett type. Its name derives from the syllables to which the refrain was sung.

Falcon, (Marie) Cornélie (b Paris, 28 Jan 1812; d Paris, 25 Feb 1897), French soprano. Student at the Paris Conservatory and pupil of Nourrit for operatic acting. First appearance 1832, at the Opéra, as Alice in *Robert le Diable*. She created Rachel in *La juive* (1835) and Valentine in *Les Huguenots* (1836). She gave her name to a particular kind of dramatic voice.

Falcon, Ruth (b Residence, Los Angeles, 2 Nov 1948), American soprano. Studied in New York and made her debut at the City Opera 1974, as Micaela. European debut Berne, 1975, in Mayr's *Medea in Corinto*; Bayerische Staatsoper 1976–80, as Verdi's Leonoras and Mozart's Countess and Elettra. Paris Opéra 1981, as Donna Anna, Vienna Staatsoper 1983, as the *Trovatore* Leonora. She made her CG and NY Met. debuts 1987 and 1989, as the Empress in *Die Frau ohne Schatten*. Other roles include Anna Bolena (Nice, 1985), Norma and Ariadne.

Falconieri, Andrea (b Naples, 1586; d Naples, 29 Jul 1656), Italian composer. Lived successively at Parma, Florence, Rome and Modena, and visited Spain. *Maestro di cappella* at Naples from 1650.

Works include motets, madrigals, instrumental pieces.

fall a ◊cadence (e.g. 'dying fall' in Shakespeare).

Fall, Leo (b Olomouc, 2 Feb 1873; d Vienna, 16 Sept 1925), Austrian composer. Studied at the Vienna Conservatory and became conductor at Berlin, Hamburg and Cologne. Wrote *c* 25 works for the stage, chiefly operettas, including *Die Dollarprinzessin* (1907), *Eternal Waltz*, *Die geschiedene Frau* (*The Girl in the Train*), *Der liebe Augustin* (*Princess Caprice*), *Madame Pompadour*.

The excellence of natural Andalusian melody is revealed by the fact that it is the only music continuously and abundantly used by foreign composers.

Manuel de Falla, *Cante Jondo*, 1922

Falla, Manuel de (b Cádiz, 23 Nov 1876; d Alta Gracia, Argentina, 14 Nov 1946), Spanish composer. Began to study the piano in Madrid at the age of eight and produced a *zarzuela*, *Los amores de Inés*, written with very little tuition in composition in 1902. This had no success, and he studied composition with Pedrell, 1902–04. In 1905 he gained two prizes for piano playing and for his opera *La vida breve*. He lived in Paris 1907–14, becoming friendly with Debussy, Ravel and Dukas, but returned to Spain and settled in Madrid on the outbreak of war. The production of *La vida breve* at Nice and Paris in 1913 and of the ballet *The Three-cornered Hat* in London in 1919 spread his reputation. In 1921 he moved to Granada and became more exclusively a nationalist composer again; but had later works performed in England, Paris and NY. During the Spanish Civil War he settled in South America and remained there.

Works include OPERAS: *La vida breve* (1904–05), *Fuego fatuo* (based on Chopin's music), *El retablo de maese Pedro* (for puppets after Cervantes's *Don Quixote*, 1923), *L'Atlantida* (posthumously completed by Ernesto Halffter, produced La Scala, Milan, 1962); ballets *El amor brujo* (1915); *El sombrero de tres picos/The Three-cornered Hat*, on Alarcón's story).

INSTRUMENTAL AND SOLO VOCAL: *Noches en los jardines de España* for piano and orchestra (1911–15); *Psyché* for mezzo-soprano, flute, violin, viola, cello and harp (1924); concerto for harpsichord, flute, oboe, clarinet, violin and cello (1923–26); four Spanish pieces, *Fantasia baetica* and *Pour le tombeau de Paul Dukas* for piano; *Homenaje: pour le tombeau de Debussy* for guitar; three songs (Gautier), seven popular Spanish songs. *A Cordoba/Góngora*, for voice and harp.

false relations the simultaneous or closely adjacent occurrence in a

A Selection of

Falla

La vida breve	1904–5
Noches en los jardines de España	1911–15
7 Canciones populares españolas	1914–15
El amor brujo	1915
Fantasia Bética	1919
El sombrero de tres picos	1919
El retablo de maese Pedro	1923
Harpsichord Concerto	1923–6
L'Atlántida	1926–46

composition in several parts of two notes a semitone apart, at least one of which is foreign to the key of the passage in question. They often arise as a result of the independent movement of parts. 16th-c. and early 17th-c. composers readily accepted simultaneous false relations and they were still being used by English composers in the latter half of the 17th c., partly as a result of tradition and partly as a means of expression.

falsetto, Italian, the tone-production of male singers resulting in notes above their normal pitch and sounding like those of an unbroken voice. Falsetto is the voice normally cultivated by male countertenors.

falsobordone Italian ◊fauxbourdon.

Falstaff ◊At the Boar's Head; ◊Lustigen Weiber von Windsor; ◊Sir John in Love.

Opera by Verdi (libretto by Boito, based on Shakespeare's *Merry Wives of Windsor* and *King Henry IV*), produced Milan, La Scala, 9 Feb 1893. Falstaff hopes to solve his money problems by seducing Alice Ford and Meg Page; he realizes his folly when he is tipped into the Thames.

Symphonic study by Elgar, op. 68 (based on Shakespeare's *King Henry IV* and references to Falstaff in *King Henry V*), composed 1913, performed Leeds Festival, 2 Oct 1913.

Falstaff, ossia Le tre burle, *Falstaff, or The Three Jests*, opera by Salieri (libretto by C P Defranceschi, after Shakespeare), produced Vienna, Kärntnertortheater, 3 Jan 1799. Beethoven wrote an early set of piano variations on the opera.

Fancelli, Giuseppe (b Florence 24 Nov 1833; d Florence, 23 Dec 1887), Italian tenor. Debut Milan 1860, in *Guillaume Tell*. At CG, 1866–72, Alfredo, Pollione and Elvino. In 1872 he was Radames in the first Italian performance of *Aida*, at La Scala. Other roles included Raoul, Vasco da Gama and Edgardo.

Fanciulla del West, La, *The Girl of the [Golden] West*, opera by Puccini (libretto by G Civinini and C Zangarini, based on David Belasco's play), produced NY Met., 10 Dec 1910. Jack Rance the sheriff and Dick Johnson the bandit compete for Minnie's affections. Realizing that Dick is an outlaw, Jack hunts him down and prepares to lynch him, but Minnie arrives in time to save the day.

fancy the old English term equivalent to the Italian *fantasia*, i.e. a polyphonic composition for a consort of viols or ◊broken consort or

THE OPERA

Falstaff

A three-act opera by Giuseppe Verdi, based on references to Falstaff in William Shakespeare's *Merry Wives of Windsor* and *Henry IV*. The opera was first produced in Milan in 1893 and is set in Windsor, during the reign of Henry IV.

I. At the Garter Inn, the impecunious Sir John Falstaff (baritone), tells his retainers Bardolph (tenor) and Pistol (baritone) that he wishes to seduce the wives of Page and Ford. The retainers refuse to carry Falstaff's love letters and he lectures them on honour. Alice Ford (soprano) and Meg Page (mezzo-soprano) read Falstaff's identical letters; while they plot their response, Nannetta Ford (soprano) steals a kiss from Fenton (tenor).

II. Falstaff is encouraged in his designs on Alice by Mistress Quickly (mezzo-soprano); Ford himself expresses his jealousy. When Falstaff visits Alice, they are interrupted by Meg and he hides in a laundry basket. The house is searched by Ford and the others, and Falstaff is tipped into the Thames.

III. Outside the Garter, a still soaking but unrepentant Falstaff is given another assignation with Alice by Mistress Quickly. At Herne's Oak in Windsor Forest, Nannetta calls on fairy spirits (local people in disguise) to torment Falstaff. In the ensuing melée, Nannetta and Fenton are married, and in a fugal finale, Falstaff finally sees the funny side of life.

THE OPERA

THE OPERA

La Fanciulla del West

A three-act work by Giacomo Puccini, first produced in 1910, which brought the Wild West to the opera stage. It is set in California in about 1850, during the Gold Rush.

I. At the Polka Saloon, sheriff Jack Rance (baritone) proposes to Minnie (soprano), owner of the saloon and guardian of the miners' gold. The bandit Ramerrez arrives, passing himself off as Dick Johnson (tenor). He plans with his gang to steal the gold, but when Minnie shows him where it is hidden he fails to take his opportunity.

II. Alone in her cabin, Minnie and Johnson declare their love. Rance and his deputies arrive with a photograph of Ramerrez, and when Johnson emerges from hiding, Minnie tells him to leave. He is shot and wounded outside and has to return; when Rance comes to claim him, Minnie earns him a reprieve by challenging the sheriff to a game of poker, which she wins by cheating.

III. Ramerrez/Johnson is about to be lynched by the miners but Minnie rescues him wielding a gun, and they ride off together to a new life.

THE OPERA

keyboard instrument. Fancies had no definitely determined form, but always made considerable use of counterpoint and were generally divided into a number of sections, played without a break but not thematically connected.

fandango a Spanish dance in lively triple time, probably South American in origin, with guitar and castanets prominent in the accompaniment. A slower, Basque, form also exists, which was adopted by Gluck in the ballet *Don Juan*, and subsequently by Mozart in *Figaro*.

fanfare a flourish of trumpets, in France also a brass band. Fanfares have also been written for other instruments, though usually wind and mainly brass, or imitated in any medium (e.g. strings in Purcell's *Dido and Aeneas* or piano in Debussy's *Feux d'artifice* prelude). In opera fanfares have frequently served as an excellent scenic effect (e.g. in Beethoven's *Fidelio*, Bizet's *Carmen*, Verdi's *Otello*).

Fantaisie (French), *fantasia* (Italian), *Fantasie* (German) ◊fantasy.

Fantaisies symphoniques title for Martinů's sixth and last symphony; composed 1953 to celebrate the 75th anniversary of the founding of the Boston SO. Fp Boston, 12 Jan 1955, conductor Munch.

Fantasia Concertante on a Theme of Corelli work for strings by Tippett, based on Corelli's Concerto Grosso op. 6 no. 2, composed 1953 for the tercentenary of his birth. Fp Edinburgh, 29 Aug 1953.

Fantasia Contrappuntistica work for piano composed 1910, with sub-title Grosse Fuge, by Busoni. Based on Contrapunctus XVIII of Bach's *The Art of Fugue* and completes the last unfinished fugue, with extra subject of Busoni's own. Two more versions for solo piano by 1912 and version for two pianos 1921, fp Berlin, 16 Nov 1921.

Fantasia on a Theme by Thomas Tallis work for double string orchestra and string quartet by Vaughan Williams, based on no. 3 of nine psalm tunes (1567) by Tallis, fp Gloucester, 6 Sept 1910.

Fantasia on a theme of Handel work by Tippett for piano and orchestra, composed 1939–41. Fp London, 7 Mar 1942. Written while Tippett was in conflict with wartime government as a conscientious objector: just over a year after the fp he spent three months in Wormwood Scrubs prison.

Fantasiestück German = 'fantastic piece'; a short instrumental piece of a free or fantastic character, rather less extended as a rule than a fantasy and keeping to a single movement and mood, whereas the latter is usually in several connected sections.

Fantastic Symphony (Berlioz.) ◊Symphonie fantastique.

fantasy an instrumental composition of a free or fantastic character, in no particular form, usually in a number of linked-up but not thematically connected sections. A fantasy may also be a composition based on a chosen musical theme from another composer's work, a folk-song, a popular tune, an operatic air, etc.

Faramondo opera by Handel (libretto by A Zeno, altered), produced London, King's Theatre, Haymarket, 3 Jan 1738. In medieval France, King Gustaavo plots revenge against Faramondo, the alleged murderer of one of his sons. An unusually convoluted plot also deals with deceptions and love rivalries.

farandole, French, a dance of Provence, probably of Greek origin. It is danced by large groups of people in procession through the streets and accompanied by pipe and tabor. The music is in 6–8 time, so that the example in Bizet's *Arlésienne* music is not traditionally correct, though very evocative.

farce, English and French, from Latin *farcire* = 'to stuff, to lard', in earlier English the verb had the meaning it still has in French of stuffing food with seasoning, and in music it was used for the practice of interpolating words in the *Kyrie eleison*. In 18th-c. opera, a comic scene introduced into a serious work. Hence a complete comic opera so interpolated, or simply a comic opera in one act (Italian *farsa*). The modern sense of the term in English (an absurdly comic play) is derived from this.

Farewell, Absence and Return (Beethoven.) ◊Adieux, l'absence et le retour.

'Farewell' Symphony nickname of Haydn's symphony no. 45 in F♭ minor, composed 1772 as a hint to Prince Esterházy that the orchestra would welcome leave of absence. In the finale the players leave one by one until only two violins remain.

Farinelli (real name *Carlo Broschi*) (b Andria, 24 Jan 1705; d Bologna, 15 Jul 1782), Italian castrato soprano. Pupil of Porpora, in whose *Eumene* he made his debut in Rome in 1721. Sang with great success in many European cities, including Vienna and London. In the service of the European court court 1737–59, singing every night in private for Philip V, then Ferdinand VI. Retired to Bologna.

In the famous air Son qual Nave, *which was composed by his brother, the first note he sang was taken with such delicacy, swelled by minute degrees to such an amazing volume, and afterwards diminished in the same manner to a mere point, that it was applauded for full five minutes.*

Charles Burney on Farinelli, *The Present State of Music in France and Italy*, 1773

Farkas, Ferenc (b Nagykanizsa, 15 Dec 1905), Hungarian composer. Studied at the Budapest Conservatory and with Respighi in Rome. After travelling to enlarge his experience and holding two posts at provincial schools of music, he became professor of composition at the Academy of Dramatic Art in Budapest in 1948.

Works include opera *The Magic Cupboard* (1942); musical plays and operettas; opera *A Gentleman from Venice*, produced Budapest, 1991; ballet *Three Vagabonds*; incidental music (including Shakespeare's *Timon of Athens*, *As You Like It* and *Romeo and Juliet*); cantata *Fountain of St John*; symphonies and other orchestral works, chamber music, piano music, songs.

Farkas, Ödön (b Jászmonostor, 1851; d Kolozsvár, 11 Sept 1912), Hungarian conductor and composer. Studied at the Academy of Music in Budapest and in 1880 became director of the Kolozsvár Conservatory. He had great influence as a teacher.

Works include seven operas, an operetta; church music, choral and orchestral works, five string quartets and other chamber music, piano music, songs.

Farley, Carole (b Le Mars, IA, 29 Nov 1946), American soprano. Studied in Munich and made her debut at NY Town Hall, 1969. Sang Lulu for WNO 1971 (the first production by a British company of Berg's opera), and Offenbach's Hélène for NY City Opera, 1976; Lulu at the Met., 1977. Engagements in Cologne, Lyon and Brussels (fp of *La Passion de Gilles* by Boesmans, 1983). Other roles include

Salome, Berg's Marie (Buenos Aires, 1989) and Violetta. Many concerts with her husband, José ◊Serebrier.

Farmer, John (b *c* 1570), English 16th–17th-c. composer. He was organist of Christ Church Cathedral at Dublin 1595–99, when he went to London. He wrote a treatise on the polyphonic setting of plainsong tunes.

Works include psalm tunes set for four voices contributed to East's Psalter; madrigals; instrumental pieces.

Farnaby, Giles (b *c* 1565; d London, buried 25 Nov 1640), English composer. He lived in London, where he married in 1587, and took the B.Mus. at Oxford in 1592.

Works include 20 canzonets for four and one for eight voices, madrigals, psalm tunes set for four voices in East's Psalter; over 50 virginal pieces.

Farnaby, Richard (b London, *c* 1594; d ?), English composer, son of Giles ◊Farnaby. In 1608 he became apprentice to Sir Nicholas Saunderson of Fillingham, Lincs.; in 1614 he married. 52 keyboard pieces were included in the Fitzwilliam Virginal Book, compiled by Francis Tregian, who died in 1619.

Farncombe, Charles (b London, 29 Jul 1919), English conductor. Studied in London and in 1955 founded the Handel Opera Society; first production *Deidemia*, followed by many important revivals, including *Alcina*, *Semele*, *Rodelinda*, *Serse* and *Ottone*. He took the Society to several European festivals, including Drottningholm, where he was music director 1970–79. Translated many Handel operas and has performed them in a style which attempts to recreate 18th-c. performing practice. Music director London Chamber Opera from 1983, chief guest conductor at Karlsruhe from 1979 (Handel's *Admeto* 1990). Recordings include Handel's *Rodrigo* and Rameau's *Castor et Pollux*.

Farquhar, George (1678–1707), Irish dramatist. J E ◊Eccles (*Stage Coach*); ◊Finger (*Sir Harry Wildair*); ◊Leveridge (*Constant Couple, Recruiting Officer, Love and a Bottle*); D ◊Purcell (*Beaux's Stratagem, Constant Couple, Inconstant*).

Farrant (1), John, English organist and composer. Organist of Ely Cathedral 1567–72, when he married Margaret Andras at Salisbury, where he became lay clerk and choirmaster at the cathedral. In 1587 he was appointed organist but he was expelled in 1592 for an attack made on the dean. He then became organist of Hereford Cathedral, but lost that post too in 1593 because of his ungovernable temper. Wrote church music.

Farrant (2), John (b Salisbury, 28 Sept 1575; d Salisbury, 1618), English organist and composer, son of John ◊Farrant (1). He became a choirboy at the cathedral under his father, and later organist, holding the post in 1598–1606 and 1611–16, probably without any interruption between. Wrote church music.

Farrant, Richard (b *c* 1530; d London, 30 Nov 1580), English organist and composer. Gentleman of the Chapel Royal in London until 1564, when he became organist and choirmaster at St George's Chapel, Windsor. Also wrote music for the Blackfriar's Theatre, London.

Works include Service in A minor (usually sung in G minor), anthems *Call to Remembrance* and *Hide not Thou Thy Face* and other church music, songs for plays produced by him with the choirboys before Queen Elizabeth; keyboard pieces in the Mulliner Book.

Farrar, Geraldine (b Melrose, MA, 28 Feb 1882; d Ridgefield, CT, 11 Mar 1967), American soprano. Studied first in Boston and later in Paris and Berlin, making her debut in 1901. From 1906 to 1922 she sang at the NY Met., creating Puccini's Suor Angelica there in 1918. On retiring from the stage became a concert singer. Her most famous role was that of Madame Butterfly.

Farrell, Eileen (b Willimantic, CT, 13 Feb 1920), American soprano. She sang in concert and on radio from 1942 until her stage debut at Tampa in 1956, as Santuzza: she had already sung Berg's Marie and Cherubini's Medea in NY concert performance. At Chicago she was heard as the *Trovatore* Leonora, in 1958. NY Met. 1960, as Alceste. She also sang Brünnhilde and Isolde, in concert performance under Bernstein.

farsa (or *farsa per musica*) Italian = 'farce' or 'farce for music', an

Italian term of the early 19th c. for a type of comic opera in one act, e.g. Rossini's *La cambiale di matrimonio*.

Farthyng, Thomas (d ? Dec 1520), English 15th–16th-c. composer. At King's College, Cambridge as chorister, 1477–83, and as clerk, 1493–99. At the Chapel Royal, 1511–20. Wrote church music and secular songs.

Farwell, Arthur (b St Paul, 23 Apr 1872; d New York, 20 Jan 1952), American composer and educationist. Studied engineering, but afterwards went to Germany as a pupil of Humperdinck and Pfitzner and to Guilmant in Paris. On returning to the USA in 1899 he began to collect Indian folk music, and became a music lecturer, critic and publisher. Professor in the music department of the Michigan State College, 1927–39.

Works include masque *Caliban* for the Shakespeare tercentenary (1916); symphony, Symbolistic Studies (no. 3 based on Whitman), suite *The Gods of the Mountain* (1928), *Prelude to a Spiritual Drama* and other orchestral works; symphonic song suite *Mountain Song* and other choral works; string quartet, piano quintet; sonatas for violin solo and for violin and piano; violin pieces; piano works.

Fasano, Renato (b Naples, 21 Aug 1902; d Rome, 3 Aug 1979), Italian composer and conductor. He studied in Naples and in 1948 founded the Collegium Musicum Italicum: in 1952 and 1957 this ensemble developed into two groups dedicated to the performance of 18th-c. Italian music: I Virtuosi di Roma and Piccolo Teatro Musicale Italiano. The latter group toured in Europe and the USA with operas by Paisiello, Pergolesi and Galuppi. Fasano was director of the Rome Conservatory 1960–72 and from 1972 was responsible for a complete edition of the sacred works of Vivaldi.

Fasch, Carl Friedrich (Christian) (b Zerbst, 18 Nov 1736; d Berlin, 3 Aug 1800), German harpsichordist and composer. Pupil of his father, Johann Friedrich ◊Fasch, and later of Hertel at Strelitz. Appointed second harpsichordist (with C P E Bach) to the court of Frederick the Great in 1756, but the outbreak of the Seven Years War (1756–63) cost him his position and forced him to live by teaching. Conductor of the court opera in Berlin 1774–76. In 1791 he founded the Berlin *Singakademie*, the choral society which he conducted until his death.

Works include oratorio *Giuseppe riconosciuto* (1774), Mass for 16 voices, cantatas, psalms and other church music; also some instrumental music.

Fasch, Johann Friedrich (b Büttelstedt near Weimar, 15 Apr 1688; d Zerbst, 5 Dec 1758), German organist and composer; father of Carl Friedrich ◊Fasch. Pupil of Kuhnau at St Thomas's School, Leipzig. He founded the 'Collegium musicum' at Leipzig, travelled after 1714, held various posts at Gera, Greitz and in the service of Count Morzin at Lukaveč, Bohemia, and in 1722 was appointed *Kapellmeister* at Zerbst.

Works include four operas e.g. *Die getreue Dido* (1712); Masses, a Requiem, church cantatas, motets, a Passion; about 90 orchestral suites, 60 concertos, trios, sonatas, etc.

Fasolo, Giovanni Battista (b Asti, *c* 1600; d ? Sicily, after 1659), Italian 17th-c. monk, organist and composer. He became a Franciscan *c* 1645 and in 1659 was appointed *maestro di cappella* to the Archbishop of Monreale at Palermo.

Works include *Arie spirituali*, cantatas, ariettas, sacred and secular songs; organ works; guitar pieces.

Fassbaender, Brigitte (b Berlin, 3 Jul 1939), German mezzo and stage director, daughter of Willi Domgraf-Fassbaender. She studied at the Nuremberg Conservatory and made her debut in Munich, 1961, as Nicklaus; other roles have been Sextus, Eboli, Marina and the Countess Geschwitz. Salzburg 1970, Dorabella; Easter Festival 1973, as Fricka. Octavian was the role of her CG (1971) and NY Met. (1974) debuts, and she has been well-known as Carmen and Charlotte. Glyndebourne debut 1990, as Clairon in *Capriccio*. Staged *Der Rosenkavalier* at Munich, 1989, and the British premiere of Schreker's *Der ferne Klang* for Opera North, 1992. Also successful as a concert singer (*Das Lied von der Erde*).

Fassbender, Zdenka (b Tetschen, 12 Dec 1879; d Munich, 14 Mar 1954), Czech soprano. She sang Halévy's Rachel at Karlsruhe in

A Selection of

Fauré

Cantique de Jean Racine	1865
Violin Sonata no. 1	1876
Requiem	1887–90
La Bonne Chanson	1894
Piano Quartet no. 1	1895
Pelléas et Mélisande	1898
Pénélope	1913
Masques et bergamasques	1919
L'Horizon chimérique Chansons	1921

1899. Munich 1906–32, as Elektra, Tosca and the Marschallin; at first with her husband, Felix Mottl. In 1913 she sang Isolde at CG, under Beecham.

Faun and Shepherdess song-suite for mezzo and orchestra by Stravinsky (text by Pushkin); composed 1906, fp St Petersburg, 4 Feb 1908; in the same concert the E♭ symphony, dedicated to Rimsky-Korsakov, was given its fp.

Fauré, Gabriel (Urbain) (b Pamiers near Foix, 12 May 1845; d Paris, 4 Nov 1924), French composer. Studied at Niedermeyer's school of music in Paris, 1854–66, and became church organist at Rennes in the latter year. Returned to Paris in 1870, became organist first at Saint-Sulpice and then at Saint-Honoré, and choirmaster at the Madeleine in 1877, being appointed organist there in 1896, a post he held until 1905, when he became director of the Conservatory, where he had been professor since 1896. He resigned 1920. He had many distinguished composition pupils, including Ravel, Enescu and Koechlin. His early music, notably the song cycle *La Bonne Chanson*, 1st violin sonata and 1st piano quartet, was lyrical and contemplative in nature. His best known work, the *Requiem*, also dates from this period. He adopted a terser, more rigorous style at the turn of the century, with the opera *Prométhée*, and continued in this style with the piano quintets and cello sonatas.

Works include STAGE: music-drama *Prométhée* (1900), opera *Pénélope* (1913); incidental music *Caligula* (Dumas), *Shylock* (*Merchant of Venice*: Shakespeare), *La Voix du bonheur* (G Clemenceau), *Pelléas et Mélisande* (Maeterlinck, 1898).

ORCHESTRAL: *Pavane* (1887), suite *Masques et bergamasques* (1919); symphony (unpublished); *Ballade & Fantaisie* for piano and orchestra; *Romance* for violin and orchestra.

CHAMBER: two piano quintets (D minor, C minor, 1906, 1921), two piano quartets (C minor, G minor, 1879, 1886); string quartet (1924); piano trio (1923); two sonatas for violin and piano (A major, E minor, 1876, 1926), two sonatas for cello and piano; pieces for violin and piano, cello and piano and flute and piano.

VOCAL: *Cantique de Jean Racine* and *Les Djinns* (Hugo) for chorus and orchestra; *La Naissance de Vénus* for solo voices, chorus and orchestra; *Madrigal* for vocal quartet; Requiem for solo voices, chorus and orchestra (1887–90); *Messe basse* for female voices and organ; 11 misc. religious vocal pieces.

SOLO PIANO: 34 op. nos. of piano music, including three *Romances sans paroles*, five Impromptus, 13 Barcarolles, four Valses-caprices, eight Nocturnes, Theme and Variations, eight *Pièces brèves*, nine

Fauré *The composer Gabriel Fauré (1845–1924). The last great romantic French composer, Fauré developed his musical language from a solidly 19th-century idiom to a more progressive style in the 1890s which involved the use of bolder harmonies and an increased sense of counterpoint.*

Preludes; *Dolly*, six pieces for piano duet.

SOLO VOCAL: 96 songs including cycles *Poème d'un jour, Cinq Mélodies de Verlaine, La Bonne Chanson* (1893, Verlaine), *La Chanson d'Ève* (Charles van Lerberghe, 1906–10), *Le Jardin clos* (ditto), *Mirages, L'Horizon chimérique.*

Faure, Jean-Baptiste (b Moulins, 15 Jan 1830; d Paris, 9 Nov 1914), French baritone. Studied at the Paris Conservatory. Made his first

THE OPERA

Faust

A five-act opera by Charles Gounod, based on Goethe's poem about a man who sells his soul to the Devil. First produced in Paris in 1859, it is set in Germany in the 16th century.

I. Faust (tenor) promises Méphistophélès (bass) his soul in return for eternal youth and the love of the beautiful Marguerite (soprano).

II. Departing for the wars, Marguerite's brother Valentine (baritone) entrusts her to the care of Siebel (mezzo-soprano). Marguerite shyly refuses Faust's first approach.

III. Méphistophélès and Faust leave a casket of jewels for Marguerite, and she decks herself with them. Faust returns and is united with Marguerite.

IV. Marguerite is now pregnant, and when Valentine returns with the other soldiers, he challenges Faust to a duel; with the help of Méphistophélès, Faust kills him.

V. On Walpurgis Night in the Harz mountains, a ballet depicts an orgy of famous courtesans. Faust finds Marguerite in prison, awaiting execution for the murder of her baby; she recoils from Faust as if from the devil. As she dies her soul is borne to heaven and Faust kneels in prayer before being carted down to Hell by Méphistophélès.

THE OPERA

appearance at the Opéra-Comique in 1852 and from 1861 was attached for many years to the Opéra, where he created Nelusko in *L'Africaine*, Posa in *Don Carlos* and Thomas' Hamlet. London, CG, 1860–63.

Faust A ◊Adam (ballet); S ◊Arnold (Dr Faustus); ◊Bentzon (*Faust III*); ◊Damnation de Faust (Berlioz); ◊Doktor Faust (Busoni); ◊Goethe, Mefistofele (Boito); ◊Pousseur (*Votre Faust*); H ◊Reutter (*Doktor Faust*); ◊Schnittke (*Historia von D Johann Fausten*)◊Szenen aus Goethes 'Faust' (Schumann).

Episodes from Lenau's *Faust*: two orchestral pieces by Liszt, *Night Procession* and *Dance in the Village Inn* (first *Mephisto Waltz*), composed *c* 1860, fp Weimar, 8 Mar 1861.

Opera by Gounod (libretto by J Barbier and M Carré, based on Goethe's drama), produced Paris, Théâtre Lyrique, 19 Mar 1859.

Opera by Spohr (libretto by J K Bernard, founded on the Faust legend without reference to Goethe's work, not completed at that time), produced Prague, 1 Sept 1816. Revised without spoken dialogue 1852 and produced London, CG, 4 Apr 1852.

Overture by Wagner, not for Goethe's drama, but a kind of symphonic poem on it, composed Paris, 1839–40 after hearing Beethoven's symphony at the Conservatory; fp Dresden, 22 Jul 1844; rewritten 1854–55 and performed at Zurich, 23 Jan 1855.

Fausta, i.e. Empress Fausta, wife of Constantine I, opera by Donizetti (libretto by D Gilardoni), produced Naples, Teatro San Carlo, 12 Jan 1832. Not related to the Faust legend. Fausta, wife of the Emperor Constantine, loves her stepson, Crispo, who loves Beroe. Crispo rejects Fausta, but charges are nonetheless brought against him for supposedly loving the queen. He is condemned to death and Fausta poisons herself.

The artist should love life and show us that it is beautiful; without him, we might doubt it.
Gabriel Fauré, quoted in Mellers, *Studies in Contemporary Music*, 1947

Fausto, *Faust*, opera by Louise Angélique Bertin (1805–1877) (libretto, in Italian, by composer, based on Goethe's drama), produced Paris, Théâtre Italien, 8 Mar 1831. The first *Faust* opera and the only one by a woman. Bertin was the sister of Berlioz's editor of the *Journal des Débats*: Berlioz may have had a hand in the work; at any rate he probably suggested the subject.

Faust-Symphonie, Eine symphony by Liszt, based on Goethe's drama, 'in three character pictures': 1. *Faust*; 2. *Gretchen*; 3. *Mephistopheles*, with final chorus 'Alles Vergängliche ist nur ein Gleichnis'; finished without the chorus, 19 Oct 1854, chorus added 1857 and revised 1880; fp Weimar, Court Theatre, 5 Sept 1857, on the occasion of the unveiling of the Goethe-Schiller monument. The work is dedicated to Berlioz. It was performed at Bayreuth (conductor Barenboim) on the centenary of Liszt's death, 31 Jul 1986.

Fauvel, Roman de a satirical poem written in two parts (1310 and 1314) by Gervais de Bus. One MS (Paris, Bibliothèque) Nationale, fr. 146) incorporates musical interpolations by Chaillou de Pesstain in 1316. The most important of these are 33 motets in two and three parts, but there are numerous other pieces, sacred and secular, polyphonic and monophonic. The collection is important as an anthology of music stretching back over a century (with many pieces newly adapted) and as the earliest source of works by Philippe de Vitry and his generation.

fauxbourdon French, *Faburden* (English), *Falsobordone* (Italian) = lit. 'false bass', name given to a wide variety of technical procedures in the 15th–16th c., usually involving improvisation. As originally used by Dufay and others, the term implied the use of chains of 6–3 chords, the middle part being 'improvised' by doubling the top part a fourth lower throughout; later, different techniques were employed to achieve the same effect. The English used their version of the word for a similar process, the three parts being improvised straight from plainsong (at first in the middle, later in the top part). The fauxbourdon itself (i.e. the lowest part) was also used as the basis of entirely new compositions.

In the later 15th and early 16th c. the use of the term in both France and England was enormously extended to include techniques in which the idea of 6–3 chords was entirely lost. It is to this final stage in its history that the Italian use of the term belongs, meaning initially a kind of fauxbourdon in four parts with the 'true' bass supplied beneath the false one, and ultimately nothing more than simple declamatory composition in note-against-note style.

Favart, Charles Simon (1710–1792), French playwright and librettist. ◊Bastien und Bastienne (Mozart); ◊Cythère assiégée (Gluck); ◊Lottchen am Hofe (J A Hiller); ◊Rosina (Shield); ◊Süssmayr (*Soliman II*).

Favart (born *Duronceray*), Marie Justine Benoîte (b Avignon, 15 Jun 1727; d Paris, 21 Apr 1772), French dancer, actress and singer. After making her debut as a dancer in 1744, she married Charles Simon ◊Favart in 1745 and in 1751 joined the Comédie-Italienne. In 1753 she appeared in her own *Bastien et Bastienne* (the direct model for Mozart's little opera), a parody of Rousseau's *Devin du village* with popular tunes in the style of a ballad opera.

Favero, Mafalda (b Ferrara, 6 Jan 1903; d Milan, 3 Sept 1981), Italian soprano. Debut Cremona 1925, Lola. She sang Liù at Parma in 1927 and in 1929 Eva at La Scala, under Toscanini; returned until 1950 as Manon, Mimi, Thaïs and in the fps of works by Lattuada and Wolf-Ferrari. CG 1937–39, NY Met. 1938. Sang in concert from 1950.

Favola d'Orfeo, La, *The Story of Orpheus*, opera by Monteverdi (libretto by A Striggio), produced Mantua, at the court of the Hereditary Prince Francesco Gonzaga, Carnival 1607. Revived in a version by d'Indy and given in concert performance, Paris, 1904; staged Oxford 1925, under Westrup. Also versions by Malipiero, Orff, Hindemith, Leppard and Harnoncourt.

Opera by Casella (libretto by C Pavolini, after A Ambrogini = Poliziano (1454–1494), produced Venice, Teatro Goldoni, 6 Sept 1932.

favola per musica Italian = 'story for music'; an early Italian term for opera of a legendary or mythological character; actually a story of that kind in dramatic form written for the purpose of being set to music.

Favorite, La opera by Donizetti (libretto, in French, by A Royer and G Vaëz, with Scribe's assistance), produced Paris, Opéra, 2 Dec 1840. Fernand falls in love with King Alphonse's mistress, Léonor, without

──────────── **THE OPERA** ────────────

La Favola d'Orfeo

A five-act opera with prologue by Claudio Monteverdi dating from as long ago as 1607, and set in the fields of Thrace. Prologue. La Musica (soprano) tells of the effect music has on the human spirit.
I. A shepherd tells of the happiness of Orpheus with Eurydice (soprano), and his sentiments are echoed by the lovers.
II. Orpheus (tenor or baritone) recalls the course of his love but is interrupted by the Messenger (soprano or contralto), who brings news of Eurydice's sudden death while gathering flowers. Orpheus resolves to descend into Hades in search of her.
III. Orpheus reaches the river Styx, and with his song lulls to sleep Charon (bass), the reluctant ferryman.
IV. Prosperina (soprano), wife of Pluto, the king of Hades, pleads for Eurydice to be returned to Orpheus. Pluto (bass) agrees, on condition that Orpheus does not look back as he departs his kingdom. The impatient Orpheus, fearing treachery by Pluto, does turn round as he reaches the light and Eurydice is condemned to remain in Hades.
V. Orpheus weeps for his wife as an echo supports his voice. Orpheus's father Apollo (tenor) descends, and as he offers his son immortality with Eurydice they rise to the heavens.

──────────── **THE OPERA** ────────────

knowing her true identity. After their marriage he finds out and feels dishonoured, retreating to a monastery. Later Léonor contracts a fatal illness, and as she dies is reconciled with Fernand.

Fayrfax, Robert (b Deeping Gate, Lincs., 23 Apr 1464; d St Albans, 24 Oct 1521), English composer. Lived for a time (?) at Bayford, Herts., and became organist and choirmaster at St Albans Cathedral before 1502. He took the Mus.D. degree at Oxford in 1504 for his Mass *O quam glorifica*; doctorate of music 1511. On the accession of Henry VIII in 1509 he was a Gentleman of the Chapel Royal, with which he attended at the Field of the Cloth of Gold in 1520.

Works include six cyclic Masses, motets, two Magnificats, *Stabat Mater*; songs for several voices, etc.

Feast at Solhaug, The incidental music for Ibsen's play by H Wolf for a production of a German translation by Emma Klingenfeld, Vienna, 21 Nov 1891.

Fedé, Jehen (b Douai, c 1415; d Paris? 1477), French composer. He was vicar of Douai, 1439–40, a papal singer, 1443–45; at the Sainte Chapelle, 1449; at the court of Charles VII, 1452–53; at St Peter's Rome, 1466; and a member of Louis XI's chapel, 1473–74. He wrote sacred and secular music.

Fedeltà premiata, La dramma pastorale giocoso by Haydn (libretto by G Lorenzi), performed Eszterháza, 25 Feb 1781; successfully revived in recent years at the Camden and Glyndebourne Festivals. The goddess Diana demands a sacrifice of two faithful lovers unless one hero offers to take their place. Fileno and Celia face this danger, but when Fileno offers his life to save Celia's, Diana shows mercy.

Fedora opera by Giordano (libretto by A Colautti, based on Sardou's play), produced Milan, Teatro Lirico, 17 Nov 1898. Fedora's husband, Vladimir, is murdered. After tracking down the killer, Count Loris, Fedora learns that the motive was revenge for an affair Vladimir had had with Loris' wife. The two fall in love, but come to a bad end when Vladimir's father takes revenge.

Fedoseyev, Vladimir (Ivanovich) (b Leningrad, 5 Aug 1932), Russian conductor. Graduated from Moscow Conservatory 1971 and made debut with the Leningrad PO. Principal of Academic Orchestra of Russian Folk Instruments, 1959–74; Moscow Radio SO from 1974: concerts throughout Russia and tours to Europe, including UK. Guest with Vienna and Tokyo POs; *Carmen* at the Vienna Staatsoper 1993. Conducted the Berlioz *Faust* with the Vienna SO at the 1992 Bregenz Festival.

Fedra, *Phaedra*, opera by Pizzetti (libretto G d'Annunzio's tragedy), produced Milan, La Scala, 20 Mar 1915. Phaedra, wife of Theseus, loves her stepson, Hippolytus, who rejects her. She makes Theseus believe Hippolytus has raped her, and Hippolytus is then killed. Phaedra takes poison, but unlike the version in Greek myth, she remains defiant to the end.

Feen, Die, *The Fairies*, opera by Wagner (libretto by composer, based on Gozzi's comedy, *La Donna serpente*), composed 1833, when Wagner was aged 20, and not staged in his lifetime; produced Munich, 29 Jun 1888; rehearsed by Richard Strauss, who was not allowed to conduct the performance. Dramatic ideas from *Die Feen* are developed in Strauss's opera *Die Frau ohne Schatten* (1919). Ada, half fairy, marries King Arindal on the condition that he does not ask about her true identity. He fails, and she is turned to stone, but Arindal restores her and the two leave for fairyland.

Fée Urgèle, La, ou Ce qui plaît aux dames, *The Fairy Urgéle, or What Pleases the Ladies*, opera by Duni (libretto by C S Favart, based on a story by Voltaire, founded on Chaucer's *Tale of the Wife of Bath*), produced Fontainebleau, at court, 26 Oct 1765; fp Paris, Comédie-Italienne, 4 Dec 1765. In 7th-c. France, knight Robert is imprisoned and can be released only when he successfully answers a riddle. To find the answer he agrees to marry the crone La Vieille, who turns out to be his lover, Marton.

Feinhals, Fritz (b Cologne, 14 Dec 1869; d Munich, 30 Aug 1940), German baritone. After engagements in Essen and Mainz he sang at Munich 1898–1927; took part in the fp of Pfitzner's *Palestrina* there, 1917. CG 1898 and 1907; 1908 at the NY Met., in the first US performance of *Tiefland*. He sang in operas by Verdi but was best known as Sachs; also appeared as Telramund, Amfortas and Wotan.

Fel, Marie (b Bordeaux, 24 Oct 1713; d Chaillot near Paris, 2 Feb 1794), French soprano. Made her first appearance at the Paris Opéra and at the Concert spirituel in 1734. She sang in the fps of Rameau's *Castor et Pollux* (both versions), *Les fêtes d'Hébé*, *Dardanus*, *Zaïs*, *Naïs*, *Zoroastre* and *Acante et Céphise*.

Felciano, Richard (b Santa Rosa, 7 Dec 1930), American composer. Studied with Milhaud and Dallapiccola; has worked at University of California at Berkeley.

Works include opera *Sir Gawain and the Green Knight* (1964); *Contractions* for woodwind quintet (1965); *Mutations* for orchestra (1966); *Soundspace for Mozart* for flute and tape (1970); *Galactic Rounds* for orchestra (1972); *In Celebration of Golden Rains* for organ and gamelan (1977); *Salvatore Allende* for ensemble (1983); *Palladio* for violin, piano and percussion (1989).

Feldman, Jill (b Los Angeles, 21 Apr 1952), American soprano. Studied musicology at Santa Barbara and has sung with early music groups in Europe and the USA. US opera debut as Music in Monteverdi's *Orfeo*, 1979; European debut Spoleto 1980, as Clerio in Cavalli's *Erismena*. Concerts with William Christie and Les Arts Florissants, including Charpentier's *Médée* in Paris, 1984. Sang in first modern revival of Marazolli's *La Vita Humana*, Glasgow 1990. Recordings include works by Charpentier, Rameau and Cesti.

Feldman, Morton (b New York, 12 Jan 1926; d Buffalo, NY, 3 Sept 1987), American composer. Studied with Stefan Wolpe and Wallingford Riegger. Influenced by abstract expressionist painting, he introduced the element of chance into his music, indicating often only an approximation of what is to be played.

Works include *Durations I–V* (1960–61); *Extensions I–V* (1951–60); *Vertical Thoughts I–V* (1963); *Two Instruments* for cello and horn; *For Franz Kline* for soprano, violin, cello, horn, chimes and piano; *De Kooning* for piano, cello, violin, horn and percussion (1963); ballet *Ixion*; *The Swallows of Salangan* for chorus and 76 instruments; *The Viola in my Life I–IV* (1970–71); *The Rothko Chapel* for viola, chorus and percussion (1972); *Neither*, monodrama to text by Beckett for soprano and orchestra (1977); series of works with orchestra, featuring cello, string quartet, piano, obeo, flute and violin (1972–79); two string quartets (1979, 1983); Trio (1980); *The Turfan Fragments* for orchestra (1980); *Triadic Memories* for piano (1981); *For John Cage* (1982); *Three Voices* for three sopranos, or voice and tape (1982); violin concerto (1984).

Feldpartie (or *Feldpartita*) German = lit. 'field suite'; an old German term for suites written for wind instruments and played in the open on military occasions.

Fellowes, Edmund H(orace) (b London, 11 Nov 1870; d Windsor, 21 Dec 1951), English clergyman and musicologist. Educated at Winchester College and Oxford. Attached to St George's Chapel, Windsor, as minor canon from 1900. Hon. Mus. D., Dublin, 1917 and Oxford, 1938. Author of books on the English madrigal, Byrd and O Gibbons; editor of *The English Madrigal School*, English lutenist songs, Byrd's works and co-editor of *Tudor Church Music*.

Felsenstein, Walter (b Vienna, 30 May 1901; d Berlin, 8 Oct 1975), Austrian opera producer. He studied in Graz and Vienna; worked in Cologne, Frankfurt and Zurich before moving to the Komische Oper, Berlin, in 1947 as director. Gained wide recognition for his realistic and minutely rehearsed productions of *Carmen*, *The Cunning Little Vixen* and *Otello*. Those who worked with him include Götz Friedrich and Joachim Herz, and others whose work has been driven by a politically-inspired concept.

Felsztynski, Sebastian (b Felsztyn, near Przemysl, *c* 1490; d *c* 1544), Polish composer. Studied at Kraków University. He compiled a hymn-book for Sigismund I in 1522. Wrote church music.

Felton, William (b Drayton, 1715; d Hereford, 6 Dec 1769), English organist and composer. Educated at Manchester and Cambridge, he became a clergyman, vicar-choral and later minor canon at Hereford Cathedral. He became famous as a performer on the organ and harpsichord, for which he wrote concertos and lessons. The celebrated *Felton's Gavotte* was a set of variations in one of the concertos.

feminine cadence a cadence in which the conclusive tonic chord is reached on a weak beat of the baritone.

Fenby, Eric William (b Scarborough, 22 Apr 1906), English composer and writer on music. Became an organist at the age of 12 and studied music with A E Keeton. From 1928–34 he acted voluntarily as amanuensis to Delius, who was living blind and paralysed at Grez-sur-Loing, and helped him to commit *Songs of Farewell*, *A Song of Summer Fantastic Dance-Idyll* and other late works to paper. Professor of harmony at the RAM 1964–77. OBE 1962.

Works include symphonic, overture *Rossini on Ilkla Moor*, etc. He pub. a memoir, *Delius as I knew him*, in 1936 (revised 1981).

I can only say that I am amazed at Mr Fenby's fortitude in enduring, for several years, experiences that nearly drove me insane after only a few days.
Cecil Gray on visiting Delius, *Musical Chairs*, 1948

Fennell, Frederick (b Cleveland, 2 Jul 1914), American conductor. Studied at the Eastman School and conducted the Little Symphony and Symphonic Band, 1939–65. Founded the Eastman Wind Ensemble 1952 and made many successful recordings with it. Conductor-in-residence at University of Miami School of Music, FL, 1965–80; Kosei Wind Orchestra, Tokyo, from 1984.

Fennelly, Brian (b Kingston, NY, 14 Aug 1937), American composer. Studied at Yale University and has been professor at NY University. His music draws on a wide range of sources, and includes *Evanescences* for ensemble (1969); string quartet (1971); *In Wildness is the Preservation of the World*, fantasy for orchestra after Thoreau (1975); series *Tesserae*, for various instrumental groups (1971–81); *Quintuplo* for brass quintet and orchestra (1978); *Scintilla* for cello and orchestra (1981); *Winterkill* for chorus and piano (1981); saxophone concerto (1984); brass quintet (1987); *On Civil Disobedience* (1992–93).

Fennimore und Gerda opera in 11 pictures by Delius (libretto, in German, by composer, based on P Jacobsen's novel *Niels Lyhne*), produced Frankfurt, 21 Oct 1919. Erik and Niels love Fennimore. She marries Erik and thier relationship sours. Later Erik is accidentally killed; the last two pictures concentrate on Niels' romance with Gerda.

Fenton (real name *Beswick*), Lavinia (b London, 1708; d Greenwich, 24 Jan 1760), English soprano and actress. Made her first appearance at the King's Theatre in London in 1726 and was the first Polly in *The Beggar's Opera* in 1728. She retired at the end of the season and became the mistress of the Duke of Bolton, who married her on the death of his wife in 1751.

Feo, Francesco (b Naples, 1691; d Naples, 28 Jan 1761), Italian composer. Pupil of Gizzi and Fago at the Conservatorio della Pietà della Turchini in Naples, and later of Pitoni in Rome. Produced his first opera, *L'amor tirannico*, in Naples, 1713. *Maestro di cappella* of the Conservatorio St Onofrio, 1723–28, and of the Conservatorio dei Poveri, 1739–43. Jommelli and Pergolesi were among his pupils.

Works include operas *Siface* (1723), *Ipermestra*, *Arianna* (1728), *Andromaca* (1730), *Arsace* (1740) and others; Masses and other church music.

Feragut (or *Feraguti*), Beltrame (or Bertrand) (b Avignon, *c* 1385; d *c* 1450 ?), French composer who travelled in France and Italy. His motet *Excelsa civitas Vincencia* was written in honour of a new bishop of Vicenza, Francesco Malipiero, in 1433. A few other sacred works survive.

Feramors opera by A Rubinstein (libretto, in German, by J Rodenberg, based on Moore's *Lalla Rookh*), produced Dresden, 24 Feb 1863. Kashmiri Princess Tulipchuk loves Feramors but must marry the Khan of Bbukhara. The two men turn out to be the same person.

Ferber, Albert (b Lucerne, 29 Mar 1911; d London, 11 Jan 1987), Swiss pianist. He studied with Gieseking and Marguerite Long. Toured

Brian Ferneyhough – composer

1   John Browne: *O Maria Salvatoris mater*
Standing for almost any work from the Eton Choir Book, this is a polyphonically sumptuous work, by turns splendidly monumental and affectingly tender, by a figure considered by many the greatest English composer between Dunstable and Taverner.

2   Tallis: *Spem In Alium*
Massively inventive in the deployment of forty individually-characterized vocal parts; impressive formal treatment of both temporal and spatial dimensions. Unforgettable in live performance.

3   Monteverdi: *Vespers* (1610)
A brilliant kaleidoscope of sacred genres from the beginning of the 17th century, the unity in diversity of this sustained collection never fails to inspire the exuberant *meraviglia* so prized by Italian composers of the period.

4   Schoenberg: String Quartet no. 2 in F♯ minor
One of the truly towering works of our century. Straddles and exemplifies a major fault line separating poignant late tonal expressivity from a radically new, free-floating world – as the text has it: 'air from another planet'. Almost no other work, to my knowledge, reveals its wounds to such transcendent effect.

5   Sibelius: Symphony no. 7 in C
My personal favourite among the composer's symphonies, perhaps because of its successful assimilation of conventional four-movement symphonic form into a single, flowing statement. Sibelius's mastery of temporal architecture makes him a 'composer's composer' par excellence, in spite of the general accessibility of his personal idiom.

6   Varèse: *Octandre*
The first musical experience I ever had which could be termed 'contemporary' in any sense meaningful to me, this artfully-engineered confrontation of the rubble of received convention with imperious innovation consistently succeeds in reminding one that the 'shock of the new' remains an inalienable and irreducible component of certain works of no matter what period.

7   Stockhausen: *Gruppen* for three orchestras
Astonishing fecundity of timbral and textural imagination makes this one of the major milestones of the mid-20th century. I still retain vivid (if incoherent) memories of the first British performance.

---

widely and appeared with most leading orchestras. His repertory was broad, but he often played Fauré, Debussy and Mozart. Resident in England from 1938.

Ferencsik, János (b Budapest, 18 Jan 1907; d Budapest, 12 Jun 1984), Hungarian conductor. He studied in Budapest and in 1953 became music director of the Opera and chief conductor of the Hungarian National PO; in 1963 and 1973 took the Opera Co. to Edinburgh for performances of Bartók's *Duke Bluebeard's Castle*. US debut 1962 and conducted in Vienna, London and Salzburg.

Ferguson, Howard (b Belfast, 21 Oct 1908), Irish composer and pianist. Educated at Westminster School and the RCM in London as a pupil of R O Morris. Professor at RAM 1948–63; made many editions of piano works and was active as an accompanist.

Works include ballet *Chaunteclear* (1948); partita and four *Diversions on Ulster Airs* for orchestra; concerto for piano and strings (1951); octet; two violin and piano sonatas, four pieces for clarinet and piano; sonata and five bagatelles for piano; two ballads for baritone and orchestra; three *Medieval Carols* for voice and piano; *The Dream of the Rood* for soprano or tenor, chorus and orchestra.

fermata Italian = 'pause', indicated by the sign ⌒, prolonging a note or rest beyond its normal length. For very short pauses a square sign was invented by Vincent d'Indy, but this device never found general acceptance.

In *da capo* arias the fermata sign over the final chord of the first section indicates where the aria is to end after the repeat.

In a chorale, or a chorale prelude, it indicates the end of a line.

Fernand Cortez, ou La Conquête de Mexique, *Hernáen Cortés, or The Conquest of Mexico*, opera by Spontini (libretto by J A Esménard and V J E de Jouy, based on a tragedy by Piron), produced Paris, Opéra, 28 Nov 1809. Cortez' brother Alvar is a prisoner of the Aztecs; Cortez' Aztec lover Amazily, seen as a traitor by her own people, offers her life to save Alvar, but Cortez rescues her in the nick of time.

Fernandez, Wilelmina (b Philadelphia, 5 Jan 1949), American soprano. Studied at Juilliard and made her debut at Houston, 1977, as Gershwin's Bess. Toured Europe and the USA in *Porgy and Bess*, Musetta at the Paris Opéra 1979. Appearances at the NY City Opera, Boston, Toulouse and Liège as Aida, Marguerite, Luisa Miller and

Donna Anna. Appeared in the film *Diva* and sang Carmen Jones in London, 1991.

Fernando operetta by Schubert (libretto by A Stadler), composed 1815; never performed in Schubert's lifetime; produced Magdeburg, 18 Aug 1918 (concert performance Vienna, 1905). Fernando rescued from life as a hermit after killing his brother-in-law.

Ferne Klang, Die, *The Distant Sound*, opera by Schreker (libretto by composer) produced Frankfurt, 18 Aug 1912. Young couple Fritz and Greta separate to seek their fortunes: the 'Distant Sound'. Fritz becomes a composer and Greta a courtesan. They meet years later and he dies in her arms.

Ferneyhough, Brian (b Coventry, 16 Jan 1943), English composer. He studied in Birmingham and with Lennox Berkeley at the RAM; further study in Amsterdam and with Klaus Huber in Basel. Since 1971 has taught at the Frankfurt Hochschule and lectured at Darmstadt. His music is of the advanced avant garde, including electronic devices.

Works include *Prometheus* for wind sextet (1967), *Sonatas* for string quartet, *Epicycle* for 20 strings (1969), *Missa Brevis* for 12 voices (1971), *Firecycle Beta* for orchestra with five conductors (1971), *Sieben Sterne* for organ, *Transit* for six voices and chamber orchestra (1975), *La Terre est un Homme* for orchestra (1978), *Funerailles* for strings and harp (two versions), String quartet no. 2 (1980), *Carceri d'Invenzione*, for chamber ensemble (1982), for flute and chamber orchestra (1984), *Études Transcendantals* for voices and ensemble (1984); *Intermedio alla Ciaccona* for violin (1980); *Mnemosyne* for bass flute and tape (1986); third and fourth string quartets (1987, 1990); *Kurze Schatten* for guitar (1983–89); *Trittico per G S* for double bass (1989).

Ferrabosco English family of musicians; later members include:

1. Alfonso Ferrabosco (b ? Greenwich, c 1610; d London, before 1660). Son of Alfonso ◊Ferrabosco (2), junior violist and wind player at court.

2. Henry Ferrabosco (b ? Greenwich, c 1615; d Jamaica, c 1658). Brother of 1; succeeded his father as composer to the King's Music.

3. John Ferrabosco (b ? Greenwich, bap. 9 Oct 1626; d London, buried 15 Oct 1682). Brother of 2; wind player at court; appointed

organist at Ely Cathedral in 1662. Wrote services and anthems.

4. Elizabeth Ferrabosco (b Greenwich, 1640). Singer, daughter of 1.

Ferrabosco (1), Alfonso (b Bologna, bap. 18 Jan 1543; d Bologna, 12 Aug 1588), Italian composer. Settled in London before 1562; left the service of Queen Elizabeth in 1569, after becoming involved in a murder case, and returned to Italy on leave, which he extended until 1572. In 1578 he left England for good and entered the service of the Duke of Savoy at Turin. Many of his works appear in *Musica Transalpina*.

Works include motets, madrigals, etc.

Ferrabosco (2), Alfonso (b Greenwich, *c* 1575; d Greenwich, buried 11 Mar 1628), English composer of Italian descent, son of Alfonso Ferrabosco (1). He was left behind, being probably illegitimate, when his father left England in 1578. Trained in music at Queen Elizabeth's expense, he became one of James I's court musicians; succeeded Coprario as composer to the King's Music in 1626.

Works include songs for masques (Ben Jonson) *The Masque of Blackness*, *Hymenaei*, *The Masque of Beauty*, *The Hue and Cry after Cupid*, *The Masque of Queens*, *Love freed from Ignorance and Folly*; fancies for viols; lessons for lyra viol; ayres with lute and bass viol; contributions to Leighton's *Teares or Lamentacions*.

An instrument to tickle human ears by friction of a horse's tail on the entrails of a cat.

Ambrose Bierce, about the fiddle in *The Devil's Dictionary*, 1911

Ferrabosco, Domenico Maria (b Bologna, 14 Nov 1513; d Bologna, Feb 1574), Italian composer, grandfather of Alfonso ◊Ferrabosco (2). *Maestro di cappella* of the church of San Petronio at Bologna from 1547. Appointed to a similar post at the Vatican basilica in Rome, *c* 1548, was a singer in the Papal Chapel there, 1550–55; sacked for taking a wife.

Works include motets, madrigals.

Ferrani, Cesira (b Turin, 8 May 1863; d Pollone, near Biella, 4 May 1943), Italian soprano. Debut Turin 1887, Gilda. She was well known in operas by Puccini and created Manon Lescaut (1893) and Mimi (1896); sang at La Scala 1894–1911 and as guest in Spain, Russia and Egypt. Successful as Elsa and Elisabeth and chosen by Toscanini to be the first Mélisande in Italy (La Scala 1908).

Ferrarese del Bene, (born Gabrieli), Adrianna (b Ferrara, *c* 1755; d ?Venice, after 1798), Italian soprano. Pupil of the Ospedaletto at Venice, married to one Del Bene and called La Ferrarese. Appeared in London 1785–86 and in Vienna in 1788–91, debut in Martín Soler's *L'arbore di Diana*; later in operas by Salieri, Guglielmi and Paisiello. The first Fiordiligi in Mozart's *Così fan tutte*, 1790. In the 1789 revival of *Figaro* she sang Susanna: Mozart replaced her two arias with K579 and K577.

Ferrari, Benedetto (b Reggio, *c* 1597; d Modena, 22 Oct 1681), Italian theorist, playwright and composer. Lived at Venice, where he began to produce music dramas with words and music of his own in 1637. In 1645 he went to the court of Modena, where he remained until 1662, except for a visit to Vienna 1651–53. He was then dismissed, but appointed again in 1674. The final duet of his opera *Il pastor regio* (Bologna, 1641) may have been used as the duet at the end of Monteverdi's *L'incoronazione di Poppea*.

Works include operas *Armida* (1639), *La ninfa avara* (1641), *Il pastor regio* (1640), *Proserpina rapita* and others; oratorio *Sansone*; three books of *Musiche varie a voce sola*.

Ferrari, Domenico (b Piacenza, *c* 1722; d Paris, 1780), Italian violinist. Pupil of Tartini. Won great acclaim on concert tours as one of the leading players of his time. Worked in Vienna and Stuttgart, and finally settled in Paris. Pub. 36 violin sonatas, trio sonatas.

Ferras, Christian (b Le Touquet, 17 Jun 1933; d Paris, 15 Sept 1982), French violinist. He studied in Nice and Paris; made his debut 1946 and in 1948 won the Marguerite Long-Jacques Thibaud Competition,

Brussels. Many tours of Europe and the USA: often heard in the Berg and Brahms concertos.

Ferreira, Manuel (d ? Madrid, 1797), Spanish composer and conductor. Attached to a Madrid theatre for which he wrote incidental music for plays and light operas which are early examples of *tonadillas*.

Works include opera *El mayor triunfo de la mayor guerra*, numerous light operas, incidental music to plays by ◊Calderón, ◊Moreto, etc., including Antonio de Zamora's Don Juan play.

Ferretti, Giovanni (b *c* 1540; d Loreto, after 1609), Italian composer and priest. He was *maestro di capella* at Ancona Cathedral from 1575; then worked at the Santa Casa in Loreto. Apart from a few sacred works, he specialized in the lighter types of madrigal, publishing five books of *Canzoni alla Napolitana* (1573–1585).

Ferrier, Kathleen (b Higher Walton, Lancs., 22 Apr 1912; d London, 8 Oct 1953), English contralto. Studying the piano at first and taking a diploma for it, she turned to singing in 1940 and sang in factories during World War II. Made her operatic debut in the fp of Britten's *Rape of Lucretia* at Glyndebourne in 1946 and sang Gluck's Orpheus there and in Amsterdam and USA. She toured very extensively, sang at the Edinburgh and Salzburg Festivals, and gave song recitals accompanied by Bruno Walter. The emotional warmth of her voice and personality were admired in *Das Lied von der Erde* and she sang in the first British performance of Mahler's third symphony (London, 1947). Received the CBE and sang in *Orfeo* again at CG on 20 Feb 1953, but was by then so ill with cancer that she had to withdraw.

Fervaal opera by d'Indy (libretto by composer, based on and altered from Tegnér's *Axel*), produced Brussels, Théâtre de la Monnaie, 12 Mar 1897. Fervaal can save his people only if he renounces love, but he falls for Guilhen. Defeated by the Saracens, he carries Guilhen's body away, pledging a new age of Christianity.

Fesca, Friedrich Ernst (b Magdeburg, 15 Feb 1789; d Karlsruhe, 24 May 1826), German violinist and composer ? of Italian descent.

Works include operas *Cantemira* and *Leila*; *De profundis*; three symphonies; 19 string quartets.

Fesch, Willem de (b Alkmaar, 25 Aug 1687; d London, 3 Jan 1761), Dutch violinist and composer. *Maître de chapelle* at Antwerp Cathedral 1725–30, settled in London 1732, where he became known as a violin teacher and composer of oratorios.

Works include operetta *The London 'Prentice*, serenata *Love and Friendship*; oratorios *Judith* (1733) and *Joseph* (1745); sonatas for cello(s) and a large quantity of other chamber music.

Festa, Costanzo (b Piedmont, *c* 1490; d Rome, 10 Apr 1545), Italian composer. He probably studied with Mouton in Paris, then became a member of the Papal choir in Rome, 1517, and later *maestro di cappella* at the Vatican. Composed four Masses, 13 Magnificats, Litanies, 40 motets, Te Deum; madrigals.

festa teatrale, Italian, = 'theatrical feast or festival'; an 18th-c. type of opera of a festive kind, especially one expressly written for an occasion, such as a royal or princely patron's wedding. The subject of the libretto was usually mythological and allegorical. Mozart's *Ascanio in Alba* (1771) is an example.

Festes vénitiennes, Les, *The Venetian Feasts*, opera by Campra (libretto by A Danchet), produced Paris, Opéra, 17 Jun 1710. Revived Aix-en-Provence, 1975. Prologue followed by five (originally three) acts: independent love stories.

Festin de l'araignée, Le, *The Spider's Banquet*, ballet by Roussel (choreography by G de Voisins, based on Henri Fabre's *Souvenirs entomologiques*), produced Paris, Théâtre des Arts, 3 Apr 1913.

Festing, Michael (Christian) (b *c* 1680; d London, 24 Jul 1752), English violinist and composer, ? of German birth or descent. Pupil of Geminiani in London. Made his first appearance there 1724 and became a member of the King's Band in 1735. Music director of the Italian Opera in 1737 and of Ranelagh Gardens from 1742.

Works include Paraphrase of the third chapter of Habakkuk, Milton's *Song on May Morning* (1748), Addison's *Ode for St Cecilia's Day* and other odes, cantatas; symphonies, concertos and sonatas for various instruments; songs.

Festschrift German = 'festival writing(s)'; a volume containing essays written by various authors as a tribute to an eminent colleague or master on some anniversary occasion.

Fêtes de l'Amour et de Bacchus, Les, *The Feasts of Cupid and Bacchus*, pastorale by Lully (libretto by Quinault, with Molière and I de Benserade), produced Paris, Opéra, 15 Nov 1672. A pastiche from his and Molière's *comédies-ballets*.

Fêtes de Thalie, Les, *Thalia's Feasts*, opera-ballet by Mouret (libretto by J de Lafont), produced Paris, Opéra, 19 Aug 1714. Prologue followed by three independent 'entrées' (acts) about love: 'La fille', 'La veuve', 'La femme'.

Fêtes d'Hébé, Les, ou Les Talens lyriques, *Hebe's Feasts, or The Lyrical Gifts*, opera-ballet by Rameau (libretto by A M de Montdorge), produced Paris, Opéra, 21 May 1739. Divinities gather on the banks of the Seine to celebrate gifts to the lyric stage: *La poésie*, *La musique*, *La danse*.

Fétis, François Joseph (b Mons, 25 Mar 1784; d Brussels, 26 Mar 1871), Belgian musicologist. Apppointed professor at the Paris Conservatory, 1821, and librarian, 1827. Director of the Brussels Conservatory from 1833. Author of *a Biographie universelle des musiciens* (1835–44), an *Histoire générale de la musique* (1869–71, unfinished) and many theoretical works. He also wrote several operas. This extraordinarily energetic man must count, among his innumerable other achievements, as the founder of modern musical lexicography and probably the most prolific musicologist ever, though his work is, perhaps understandably, often highly unreliable.

Feuermann, Emanuel (b Kolomyja near Lwów, 22 Nov 1902; d New York, 25 May 1942), Austrian-born American cellist. Made his first appearance in Vienna, 1912, later travelled and studied with Klengel at Leipzig and became professor at the Cologne Conservatory at 16. In 1929–33 professor in Berlin, in succession to Hugo Becker; driven to USA by the Nazi régime; taught at the Curtis Institute from 1941. He played in trios with Huberman and Schnabel, and gave other recitals with Heifetz and Rubinstein. Among his best recordings are *Don Quixote*, the Dvořák concerto, the Brahms double concerto (with Heifetz) and Schubert's B♭ piano trio.

Feuersnot, *Fire Famine*, opera by R Strauss (libretto by Ernst von Wolzogen), produced Dresden, 21 Nov 1901. As revenge against the mocking and chaste Diemut, Konrad casts a spell by which all the town's lights are extinguished until Diemut yields to Konrad's desires.

Févin, Antoine de (b? Arras, *c* 1474; d Blois, *c* 1512), French composer. Wrote nine Masses, 20 motets, Magnificats, Lamentations, etc. He was a follower of Josquin.

Févin, Robert de (b Cambrai), French 15th–16th-c. composer. In the service of the Duke of Savoy early in the 16th c. Wrote Masses, etc.

Février, Henri (b Paris, 2 Oct 1875; d Paris, 8 Jul 1957), French composer. Studied under Massenet and Fauré at the Paris Conservatory.

Works include operas *Monna Vanna* (after Maeterlinck, 1909), *Ghismonda* (1918), *La Damnation de Blanchefleur*, *La Femme nue* (1932), *L'Île désenchantée*, operetta *Sylvette* (with Delmas); comic operas *Le Roi aveugle*, *Agnès dame galante*, *Carmosine* (after Musset); songs etc.

Ffrangcon-Davies, David (Thomas) (b Bethesda, Carnarvon, 11 Dec 1855; d London, 13 Apr 1918), Welsh baritone. Studied at GSM, London, and made his first appearance with the Carl Rosa Opera Co. in 1890, but later became mainly a concert singer. He sang in North America and Berlin 1896–1901. Gave up singing 1907 after a nervous breakdown.

f holes (or *ff holes*) the sound-holes of instruments of the violin family, so called because of their shape.

Fiamma, La, *The Flame*, opera by Respighi (libretto by C Guastalla after H W Jenssen), produced Rome, Teatro Reale, 23 Jan 1934. Silvana, wife of Basilio, falls in love with her stepson, Donello, using magic to seduce him. The two are found together; Basilio drops dead, and Silvana is tried for witchcraft. She realizes the futility of her passion and is condemned to death.

------ **THE OPERA** ------

Fidelio

A two-act opera by Beethoven, the first version of which was performed – with Beethoven conducting – at Vienna in 1805. The action is set at a prison near Seville, Spain, in the 18th century.
I. Leonore (soprano) has disguised herself as a youth called Fidelio and is assistant to the chief jailer Rocco (bass), in the hope of finding her imprisoned husband, Florestan (tenor). Rocco's daughter Marzelline (soprano) is in love with Fidelio, to the irritation of her suitor Jacquino (tenor). The tyrannical prison governor Pizarro (bass-baritone) receives news of an impending inspection and resolves to kill Florestan before he can be discovered. Rocco refuses to help in the murder but agrees to dig the grave. Leonore overhears their plans, and as the prisoners emerge briefly into the sunlight, she searches in vain for her husband.
II. Rocco and Leonore descend to the dungeon where Florestan is in chains. They are joined by Pizarro, who tries to kill Florestan but is prevented by Leonore who brandishes a pistol and at the same time reveals her true identity. When the inspecting Minister Don Fernando (bass) arrives, Pizarro is arrested and the prisoners freed. Leonore is allowed to release Florestan's shackles herself.

------ **THE OPERA** ------

Fibich, Zdeněk (b Šerbořic near Časlav, 21 Dec 1850; d Prague, 15 Oct 1900), Czech composer. Very precociously gifted, he studied at the Leipzig Conservatory under Carl Richter and Jadassohn, also Moscheles for the piano. Later in Paris and Mannheim. After teaching in Poland for a time, he returned to Czechoslovakia in 1874 and conducted at the National Theatre in Prague. He soon retired to devote himself entirely to composition, and wrote over 600 works of various kinds.

Works include operas *Bukovin* (1874), *Blaník* (1881), *The Bride of Messina* (after Schiller, 1884), *The Tempest* (after Shakespeare), *Hedy* (after Byron's *Don Juan*), *Sarka* (1897), *Pad Arkuna*; melodramas *Christmas Eve*, *Eternity*, *The Water-Sprite*, *Queen Emma*, *Haakon* and the trilogy *Hippodamia* (1888–91); incidental music to Vrchlický's comedy *A Night at Karlstein*; three symphonies, overtures, symphonic poems *Othello* and *The Tempest* (both after Shakespeare) and four others; two string quartets (1874, 1879), piano quartet, piano trio, quintet for piano, violin, cello, clarinet and horn; piano sonata, 350 pieces *Moods, Impressions and Memories* for piano; songs, vocal duets.

Fida ninfa, La, *The faithful nymph*, opera by Vivaldi (libretto by S Maffei), produced Verona, Teatro Filarmonico, 6 Jan 1732. Pub. Cremona 1964 in an edition by R Monterosso. Licori is pusued by pirate Oralto but remains true to Osmino.

fiddle a colloquial generic term for instruments of the violin family. More specifically the word is used for chest-held bowed instruments of the Middle Ages, particularly those with a flat back.

Fiddler's Child, The, *Šumařovo dítě*, ballad for orchestra by Janáček, after a poem by S Čech, composed 1912. Fp Prague, 14 Nov 1917.

Fidelio, oder Die eheliche Liebe, *Fidelio, or Wedded Love*, opera by Beethoven (libretto by J Sonnleithner, based on Bouilly's libretto of *Léonore, ou L'Amour conjugal* written for Gaveaux), produced Vienna, Theater an der Wien, 20 Nov 1805, conductor Beethoven, with the overture *Leonora No.2*; revised version, with overture *Leonora No. 3*, same theatre, 29 Mar 1806, conductor Seyfried; overture *Leonora No. 1* written for the fp but abandoned as unsuitable; second revision produced Vienna Kärntnertortheater, 23 May 1814, with *Fidelio* overture in E major. Political prisoner Florestan is rescued by his disguised wife (Leonore/Fidelio) when the evil Pizarro arrives to kill him.

Fiedler, Arthur (b Boston, 17 Dec 1894; d Brookline, MA, 10 Jul 1979), American conductor and violinist. Studied with his father and with Willy Hess in Berlin. Played violin, then viola, in the Boston SO (from 1915) and formed the Boston Sinfonietta 1924. Conducted the Boston 'Pops' concerts from 1930, in a gregarious style that won him national recognition. In 1977 he was given the Medal of Freedom by President Ford.

Field, Helen (b Awyd, N Wales, 14 May 1951), Welsh soprano. She has appeared with WNO since 1977 as Musetta, Poppea, Mimi and Tatyana. Much applauded as Janáček's Vixen and Jenůfa; Desdemona 1986. Mussorgsky's Emma at CG in 1982; appeared with the ENO at the NY Met. as Gilda. Other roles include Pamina, Marenka, Marguerite and Tippett's Jenifer. In 1987 sang title role in first British production of Strauss's *Daphne*. Sang Jo-Ann in the fp of Tippett's *New Year* at Houston (1989) and again at Glyndebourne (1990); created Pearl in Birtwistle's *The Second Mrs Kong* for GTO at Glyndebourne, 1994.

Field, John (b Dublin, 26 Jul 1782; d Moscow, 23 Jan 1837), Irish pianist and composer. Son of a violinist at the Dublin theatre, he was taught music and the piano by his grandfather, an organist. Having moved to Bath and then to London, his father apprenticed him to Clementi, who taught him and at whose piano warehouse he was employed to show off the instruments by improvisation. He made his first public appearance at Giordani's concerts at Dublin in 1792 and in London in 1794. In 1802 Clementi took him to Paris, Germany and Russia leaving him behind at St Petersburg in 1803, where he became a piano teacher. He married Mlle Percheron in 1808. In 1822 he settled down at Moscow, where he had as great a success as he had had in the new capital. He travelled much as a pianist, visited London in 1832, afterwards Paris, Switzerland and Italy. At Naples he was taken ill and lay in hospital for months until a Russian family took him back to Moscow, where he died soon after his return.

Works include seven piano concertos (1799–1822); 17 nocturnes, four sonatas and many rondos, fantasies, variations, etc., for piano; piano quintet and other chamber music; works for piano duet.

Fielding, Henry (1707–54), English novelist and dramatist, author of ballad operas *The Intriguing Chambermaid*, *The Lottery*, *Miss Lucy in Town*, *Don Quixote in England* and others. T A ◊Arne; ◊Monro (*Temple Beau*); ◊Tom Jones (Philidor, 8).

Field Mass work by Martinů for baritone, male chorus and orchestra, composed 1939 in Paris. Fp Prague, 28 Feb 1946, conductor Kubelik.

Fierrabras Spanish *Fierabrás* = *The Braggart*, opera by Schubert (libretto by Kupelwieser, after Calderón, taken from A W von Schlegel's *Spanisches Theater*), composed 1823, but not performed during Schubert's lifetime; produced Karlsruhe, 9 Feb 1897. French Roland loves Moorish Princess Florinda; her brother Fierrabras loves Charlemagne's daughter Emma, who in turn loves Eginhard. Moorish leader Boland imprisons Roland and other knights, but Charlemagne arrives victorious to save the day.

Fiery Angel, The, *Ogenny Angel*, opera in five acts by Prokofiev (libretto by composer after novel by V Bryusov), composed 1919–27. Fp (concert) Paris, 25 Nov 1954; produced Venice, 29 Sept 1955. Themes from the opera are used in Prokofiev's third symphony, in C minor, op. 33; composed 1928, fp Paris, 17 May 1929, conductor Monteux. Renata, possessed by the spirit of her former lover, Heinrich, fails to find release in the passion of admirer Ruprecht. She is ordered to be burned when she enters a convent and involves the nuns in diabolic possession.

fifara Italian 17th-c. name for the transverse flute.

fife a simple form of small transverse flute with finger-holes and without keys, generally used in military bands in connection with drums. The name is now used for a military flute in B♭ with six finger-holes and several keys, used in drum and fife bands.

The vile squealing of the wry-necked fife.
Shakespeare, *The Merchant of Venice*,
Act 2, Scene 5, line 30

Fifine at the Fair orchestral fantasy by Bantock on Robert Browning's poem, composed 1901, fp Birmingham Music Festival 1912.

fifth an interval covering three whole tones and a semitone, in which case it is a perfect fifth, e.g. D–A. If either of these notes is sharpened or flattened, the result is an augmented or a diminished fifth: D♭–A or D–A♯ is an augmented fifth, D♯–A or D–A♭ a diminished fifth.

Figaro (Mozart.) ◊Nozze di Figaro.

Figlia del reggimento ◊Fille du Régiment.

Figner, Medea (b Florence, 4 Apr 1859; d Paris, 8 Jul 1952), Italian-born Russian mezzo, later soprano. Debut Sinaluga 1874, Azucena. She sang widely as a mezzo, often as Carmen, until 1890; CG 1887, as Meyerbeer's Valentine and Leonore in *La favorite*. She married Nikolay Figner in 1899 (divorced 1904) and appeared with him at St Petersburg until 1912. She created Tchaikovsky's Lisa and Iolanta and was admired as Desdemona, Tatyana, Tosca, Elsa and Brünnhilde.

Figner, Nikolay (b near Kazan, 21 Feb 1857; d Kiev, 13 Dec 1918), Russian tenor. Debut Naples 1882, in Gounod's *Philémon*. He sang in Rio and Buenos Aires 1884–86, with performances under Toscanini, and sang Elvino and Ernani at CG in 1887. He then appeared at the Imperial Opera St Petersburg until 1907, as Hermann in the fp of *The Queen of Spades* (1890) and as Lensky, Don José, Werther, Lohengrin and Rubinstein's Nero.

figuration the persistent use of decorative or accompanying figures of similar type throughout a piece of music.

figure a short musical phrase, especially one that assumes a distinctive character in the course of a composition.

figured bass ◊thorough-bass.

figured chorale a hymn-tune setting, especially for organ, in which the plain notes of the melody are surrounded by more rapid patterns of notes, usually all of the same kind of formation.

Figures-Doubles-Prismes work for orchestra by Boulez, fp Strasbourg, 10 Jan 1964; an expansion of *Doubles* for orchestra, fp Paris, 16 Mar 1958.

Filar la voce (or *Filar il tuono*) (Italian), *Filer la voix* (French), *Filer le son* (French) 'spin the voice' (or 'spin the tone'), sustaining the voice in singing on a long-drawn soft note, without *crescendo* or *diminuendo*.

fileuse = 'spinner', from *filer* = to spin, French the name of a special type of instrumental piece with rapid figurations of various kinds suggesting the motion of a spinning-wheel and often, in its melody, a spinning-song. There are familiar examples by Raff and Fauré (in the latter's incidental music for *Pelléas et Mélisande*), and Mendelssohn's Song without Words, op. 67 No. 4, although not so entitled, conforms to the type, being in fact nicknamed *Spinnerlied* in German, though called *The Bee's Wedding* in English. The prototype of the fileuse was vocal, e.g. the spinning-choruses in Haydn's *Seasons* (Winter) and Wagner's *Flying Dutchman*, Schubert's song *Gretchen am Spinnrade*.

Fille du Régiment, La, *The Daughter of the Regiment*, opera by Donizetti (libretto by J H V de Saint-Georges and J F A Bayard), produced Paris, Opéra-Comique, 11 Feb 1840. Donizetti's first French opera. Marie, found as an infant, has been brought up by the regiment. Tonio becomes a soldier in order to marry her. After complications by Marie's newly-discovered relatives, all ends happily.

Filosofo di campagna, Il, *The Country Philosopher*, opera by Galuppi (libretto by Goldoni), produced Venice, Teatro San Samuele, 26 Oct 1754. Eugenia loves Rinaldo but has been promised to Nardo, whom she has not yet met. Eugenia's sister Lesbina impersonates Eugenia and falls in love with Nardo. Complications are followed by marriage.

Filtz, Anton (Antonín Fils) (b Eichstätt, Bavaria, bap. 22 Sept 1733; d Mannheim, buried 14 Mar 1760), German cellist and composer. Entered the orchestra at Mannheim in 1754 and became one of the early symphonists attached to that court. Wrote *c* 40 symphonies, overtures, a Mass, trios.

final the tonic note of the modes on which the scales of the authentic modes begin and end. In the plagal modes the final is on the fourth above the starting-note. ◊modes.

final French = 'finale'.

finale the last movement of any instrumental work in several movements, also the last number in any act of an opera where the music is divided into more or less distinctly separated pieces, provided that this number is on a large scale (e.g. the great ensemble piece at the end of Act II of Mozart's *Figaro* is a finale, but the aria at the end of Act I is not).

Finck, Heinrich (b Bamberg, 1445; d Vienna, 9 Jun 1527), German composer. Educated in the court chapel at Warsaw and at Leipzig University and held apointments at the Polish court *c* 1492–1506; then at the Court of Württemberg at Stuttgart until 1514. Later he lived at the Scottish monastery in Vienna, and worked at Salzburg cathedral.

Works include four Masses, motets, hymns and other church music, sacred and secular songs for several voices, songs to the lute.

Finck, Hermann (b Pirna, Saxony, 21 Mar 1527; d Wittenberg, 29 Dec 1558), German composer and theorist. Studied at the University of Wittenberg, where he taught music from 1554. In 1557 he was appointed organist, but he died the following year at the age of 31. He wrote a theoretical book, *Practica musica* in five vols. Works include motets, sacred songs and wedding songs for several voices.

Fine, Irving (b Boston, 3 Dec 1914; d Boston, 23 Aug 1962), American composer. He studied at Harvard with Walter Piston and in Paris with Boulanger; professor at Harvard and Brandeis Universities. His music has reflected two of the major trends of the 20th c. – neoclassicism and atonality.

Works include *Toccata concertante* (1948), *Partita* for wind quintet, *Alice in Wonderland*, suite for chorus and orchestra (1949), *Mutability*, six songs for mezzo and piano (1952), string quartet (1952), *Serious Song* (1955), *Blue Towers* for orchestra (1959), *Diversions* for orchestra (1958), *Symphony* (1962).

Fine, Vivian (b Chicago, 28 Sept 1913), American composer and pianist. Studied in Chicago 1919–31 and with Roger Sessions 1934–42. Performer of contemporary piano works from 1931 and teacher at Bennington College, Vermont, 1964–87.

Works include ballet *Alcestis* (1960) and chamber opera *The Woman in the Garden* (1978); *A Guide to the Life Expectancy of a Rose*, for soprano, tenor and chamber ensemble (1956); *Paen* for narrator, women's voices and brass ensemble (1969); *Drama for Orchestra* (1982); *Poetic Fires* for piano and orchestra (1984); *After the Tradition* for chamber orchestra (1988).

Fine Arts Quartet American string quartet founded Chicago, 1946, with Leonard Sorkin as leader and George Sopkin as cellist. Quartet-in-residence at the University of Wisconsin from 1963, and has toured throughout the world. Performances in a wide repertory, including works by Babbitt, Husa and Wuorinen.

Fingal's Cave (also called *Hebrides*) concert overture by Mendelssohn, op. 26, composed in recollection of a visit to the Hebrides in 1829, Rome, Dec 1830; revised version, London, summer 1832. (The first score was entitled *Die einsame Insel/The Lonely Island*).

Finger, Gottfried (or Godfrey) (b Olomouc, *c* 1660; d Mannheim, buried 31 Aug 1730), Moravian composer. Nothing is known of his career until he went to London *c* 1685, working under the patronage of James II. He left in 1702, piqued at having gained only the fourth prize after Weldon, Eccles and D Purcell for the composition of Congreve's masque *The Judgment of Paris*, and went into the service of the Queen of Prussia, Sophia Charlotte, in Berlin. Later he lived in the Palatinate and wrote some operas for Neuburg and Heidelberg.

Works include operas *The Virgin Prophetess* (Settle), *Sieg der Schönheit über die Helden* (1706), *L'amicizia in terzo* (in part); masques *The Loves of Mars and Venus* (Motteux, with Eccles) and *The Judgment of Paris* (Congreve, 1701); incidental music (some with D Purcell) for Lee's *Rival Queens, The Wive's Excuse, Love for Love* and *The Mourning Bride* (both Congreve), *Love at a Loss, Love makes a Man* (Cibber), *The Humours of the Age* (Southerne), *Sir Harry Wildair* (Farquhar) and *The Pilgrim* (Vanbrugh); concertos and sonatas for various instruments; pieces for violin and flute (with Banister), etc.

fingerboard the part of the neck of a string instrument to which the strings are pressed by the fingers in order to change their length and thus produce different notes.

fingered tremolo ◊tremolo.

Fingerhut, Margaret (b London, 30 Mar 1955), English pianist. Studied at the RCM and the Peabody Institute, Baltimore. Many tours of Europe and the USA, notably with the London and Royal POs and the LSO. Young Musician of the Year 1981, and further tours to Africa, India and Israel. Recordings include *Winter Legends* by Bax and music by Dukas, Moeran and Falla.

fingering the use of the fingers on any instrument to produce the notes in various ways; also the figures written above the notes indicating which finger is to be used to produce this or that note.

Let a player run up and down with either first, middle, or third finger, aye even with his nose if that would help him, provided everything is done clearly, correctly and gracefully.

Michael Praetorius, about fingering
in *Syntagma Musicum*, 1619

---

finite canon a canon sung through once, without repetition of its phrases.

Finke, Fidelio (b Josefstal, Bohemia, 22 Oct 1891; d Dresden, 12 Jun 1968), German-Czech composer. Studied at the Prague Conservatory with his uncle Romeo Fidelio and with Novák for composition. He taught there from 1915, became inspector of the German music schools in Czechoslovakia in 1920 and director of the German Academy of Music in Prague in 1927.

Works include opera *Die Jacobsfahrt* (1936); *Pan* symphony, overture and other works for orchestra; two string quartets.

Finlandia symphonic poem for orchestra by Sibelius, op. 26, composed in 1899 (revised 1900; fp Helsinki, 2 Jul 1900). It has become a work for national celebrations in Finland, being based on material sounding like Finnish patriotic songs, the whole of which, however, is the composer's own invention, not folk music.

Finney, Ross Lee (b Wells, MN, 23 Dec 1906), American composer. Educated at Carleton College, MN, and studied music at Minnesota University and later in Paris and Vienna with Nadia Boulanger and Alban Berg, also with Sessions at Harvard University. Professor of Music and resident composer at University of Michigan. His compositions have attempted a reconciliation between tonal and serial music.

Works include Overture to a Social Drama for orchestra; four symphonies (1942–72); piano concerto, violin concerto; *John Brown* for tenor, male chorus and chamber orchestra; eight string quartets (1935–60), piano trio; violin and piano sonata; four piano sonatas; eight Poems for soprano, tenor and piano.

Finnie, Linda (b Paisley, 9 May 1952), Scottish mezzo. Studied in Glasgow and made debut with Scottish Opera 1976. WNO from 1979 and with ENO has sung Brangaene, Eboli, Amneris and Ortrud. Has sung in the *Ring* at CG and at Bayreuth (from 1988) and at the Vienna Staatsoper (1994–95). Debuts with Frankfurt and Nice Operas 1987, as Amneris and Waltraute. Concerts include Mahler's 8th (Prom Concerts, 1986) and *Alexander Nevsky*.

Finnissy, Michael (b London, 17 Mar 1946), English composer. He studied at the RCM with Bernard Stevens and Humphrey Searle. Music department London School of Contemporary Dance 1969–74.

Works include operas *The Undivine Comedy* (Paris 1988) and *Thérèse Raquin* (London 1993); *Mysteries*, eight separately performable music theatre pieces with Latin texts from the Bible: 1. *The Parting of Darkness*, 2. *The Earthly Paradise*, 3. *Noah and the Great Flood*, 4. *The Prophecy of Daniel*, 5. *The Parliament of Heaven*, 6. *The Annunciation*, 7. *The Betrayal and Crucifixion*, 8. *The Deliverance of Souls*; *Orfeo* for soloists and instruments (1975), *Mr Punch* for voice and instruments (1977), *Vaudeville* for mezzo, baritone, instruments and percussion (1983); seven piano concertos (two for piano alone), *Offshore* for orchestra, *Pathways of Sun and Stars* for orchestra (1976); *Jeanne d'Arc* for soprano, tenor, cello and small orchestra (1971), *Babylon* for mezzo and ensemble, *Sir Tristan* for soprano and ensemble (1979), *Ngano* for mezzo, tenor, chorus, flute and percussion (1984); string trio (1986); *Red Earth* (1988) and *Eph-phatha* (1989) for orchestra; *Obrecht Motetten* I–IV for various instrumental groups (1989–92); *In stiller Nacht* for violin, cello and piano (1990); *Cambridge Codex* for flute, violin, cello and two bells (1991); *Two Motets* for countertenor and guitar (1992); *Nine Romantics* for piano (1992); string quartet (1986).

Finta giardiniera, La, *The Pretended Garden-Girl*, opera by Anfossi (libretto by R de Calzabigi), produced Rome, Teatro delle Dame, Carnival 1774.

Opera by Mozart (libretto ditto), produced Munich, 13 Jan 1775. Count Belfiore has fled, believing he has killed Countess Violante in a quarrel. However, she seeks him amorously, disguised as Sandrina, a gardener.

Finta semplice, La, *The Pretended Simpleton*, opera by Mozart (libretto by M Coltellini), composed for Vienna, 1768, but not performed there; produced Salzburg, 1 May 1769). Fracasso and Simone marry Giacinta and Ninetta, as Giacinta's brothers fall for the Baroness Rosina, sister of Fracasso.

Finto Stanislao, Il, *The False Stanislas*, opera by Gyrowetz (libretto by F Romani), produced Milan, La Scala, 5 Aug 1818. The libretto was used by Verdi in 1840 for *Un giorno di Regno*.

Finzi, Gerald (b London, 14 Jul 1901; d Oxford, 27 Sept 1956), English composer. Private pupil of Bairstow and R O Morris; professor of composition at the RAM in London, 1930–33, and afterwards went to live in the country to give his whole time to composition. His music owes something to English pastoral traditions, but more to his literary heritage: settings of Milton, Crashaw, Shakespeare and Traherne show a vivid response to verbal imagery.

Works include incidental music for Shakespeare's *Love's Labour's Lost*; festival anthem (Crashaw), *Intimations of Immortality* (Wordsworth, c 1938, revised 1950) and *For St Cecilia* (Edmund Blunden) for chorus and orchestra; three Elegies (Drummond) and seven partsongs (Robert Bridges) for unaccompanied chorus.

New Year Music for orchestra, *Romance* for strings; *Introit* for violin and small orchestra, concerto for clarinet and strings (1949), cantata *Dies Natalis* (Traherne) for high voice and orchestra (1926–39), *Farewell to Arms* (Ralph Knevet and George Peele) for tenor and small orchestra, two Sonnets by Milton for ditto; *Interlude* for oboe and string quartet, Prelude and Fugue for string trio; five Bagatelles for clarinet and piano; Thomas Hardy song cycles *By Footpath and Stile* for baritone and string quartet (1922), *A Young Man's Exhortation* (1926–29), *Earth and Air and Rain* and *Before and After Summer*; five Shakespeare songs, *Let us Garlands Bring*.

Fiocco Italian-Belgian family of musicians.

1. Pietro Antonio Fiocco (b Venice, c 1650, d Brussels, 3 Sept 1714). Conductor and composer; he went to Brussels late in the 17th c. and was appointed conductor of the court band. Composed prologues for several of Lully's operas; Masses, motets; *Sacri concerti*; cantata *Le Retour du printemps*, etc.

2. Jean-Joseph Fiocco (b Brussels, bap. 15 Dec 1686; d Brussels, 30 Mar 1746). Conductor, son of 1; succeeded his father as conductor in 1714.

3. Joseph-Hector Fiocco (b Brussels, 20 Jan 1703; d Brussels, 22 Jun 1741). Conductor, harpsichordist and composer, son of 1; he was conductor at Brussels in 1729, became choirmaster at Antwerp Cathedral in 1731 and at Sainte-Gudule at Brussels in 1737. Wrote harpsichord pieces, church music etc.

Fioravanti, Valentino (b Rome, 11 Sept 1764; d Capua, 16 Jun 1837), Italian composer. Pupil of Sala at one of the Naples Conservatories. Produced his first opera in Rome in 1784. Conductor at Lisbon from 1803 and visited Paris in 1807, returning to Italy to become *maestro di cappella* at St Peter's in Rome.

Works include operas *Le avventure di Bertoldino* (1784), *Le cantatrici villane* (1799), *I virtuosi ambulanti* (1807), *Ogni eccesso è vizioso* and 66 others; church music etc.

Fiorillo, Federigo (b Brunswick, 1 Jun 1755; d after 1823), Italian-German violinist and composer. Pupil of his father. Travelled on concert tours, and in 1782 was appointed *Kapellmeister* in Riga. Visited Paris in 1785, and from 1788 to 1794 lived in London, where he appeared mostly as a viola player.

Works include a large quantity of violin music, including 36 *Caprices* (studies); string quartets, quintets and other chamber music, etc.

Fiorillo, Ignazio (b Naples, 11 May 1715; d Fritzlar, Hesse, Jun 1787), Italian composer, father of Federigo ◊Fiorillo. Pupil of Leo and Durante at Naples. Produced his first opera, *Mandane* at Venice 1736; became court *Kapellmeister* at Brunswick in 1754 and at Kassel in 1762, retiring in 1780.

Works include 21 operas, most to texts by Metastasio; oratorio, *Isacco*; Requiem, three Te Deums; symphonies; sonatas.

fioriture Italian = lit. 'flowerings, flourishes, decorations'; ornamental figures elaborating a plainer melodic passage, either according to the composer's notation or improvised according to the performer's fancy.

fipple flute a generic term for a woodwind instrument held vertically and blown into through a mouthpiece in which the air is diverted by an obstructive block called the 'fipple'. The recorder (German *Blockflöte*) is the chief member of the family.

Firebird, The, *Zhar Ptitsa*, ballet by Stravinsky (choreography by Fokin), produced Paris, Opéra, 25 Jun 1910, conductor Gabriel Pierné.

Firenze, Ghiradello da, ◊Gherardello.

Fires of London, The ensemble founded 1967 by Maxwell Davies and Harrison Birtwistle as the Pierrot Players; based on forces required for Schoenberg's ◊*Pierrot lunaire* (Birtwistle left 1970). Many fps of works by Davies, e.g. *Eight Songs for a Mad King*, *The Martyrdom of St Magnus*, and other composers. Ensemble disbanded 1987; Fires of London Productions formed same year for performance of stage works.

Fire Symphony a nickname of a symphony by Haydn, No. 59, in A major, composed c 1766–68.

Fireworks fantasy for large orchestra by Stravinsky, composed 1908 to celebrate the marriage of Nadezhda Rimsky-Korsakov, his teacher's daughter, to Maximilian Steinberg, St Petersburg 17 Jun 1908. The score was revised for smaller forces and performed 22 Jan 1910.

Fireworks Music Handel's *Music for the Royal Fireworks*, a suite of pieces originally for wind band, was composed for the celebrations of the Peace of Aix-la-Chapelle, fp London, Green Park, 27 Apr 1749.

Firkušný, Rudolf (b Napajedlá, Moravia, 11 Feb 1912; d Staatsburg, NY, 19 Jul 1994), Czech pianist and composer. Studied at Brno Conservatory with Vilem Kurz (piano) and Janáček for composition. Later he studied with Suk and Schnabel. Debut Prague, 1922; England 1933, USA, 1938. Resident in the USA from 1940 and taught at Juilliard. Well known in classics and modern music, especially Janáček, and premiered concertos by Menotti (1945), Hanson (1948) and Martin (1949, 1956). His compositions include a piano concerto and many piano solos.

Firsova, Elena (b Leningrad, 21 Mar 1950), Russian composer. Studied at the Moscow Conservatory, and has learned from Edison Denisov. She is one of several composers who chose to live in the West after the collapse of Communism. Her music is in a variety of instrumental forms, many of them small scale, and was first heard outside the USSR in 1979 (Paris and Venice). British debut 1980, with *Petraca's Sonnets*. Professor and composer-in-residence Keele University 1993.

Works include operas *Feast in Time of Plague* (1972) and *The Nightingale and the Rose* (1991); cello concerto (1973), two violin concertos (1976, 1983), four chamber concertos (1978, 1982, 1985, 1988), concerto for violin and 13 strings (1993); *Chamber Music* (1973), *Stanzas* (1975), *Autumn Music* (1988) and *Cassandra* (1993) for orchestra; four string quartets (1970, 1974, 1980 — in memoriam Igor Stravinsky — and 1989); *Spring Sonata* for flute and piano (1982); *The Night Demons* for cello and piano (1993); *Petraca's*

Sonnets for voice and ensemble (1976) and settings of Pasternak, Mayakovsky, Madelstam and Shakespeare for voice and instruments; *Silentium* for mezzo and string quartet (1991), *Distance* for voice, clarinet and string quartet (1992); *Music for 12* (1986) and *Odyssey* for ensemble (1990); *Before the Thunderstorm* for soprano and ten instruments (1995); piano sonata (1986).

first-movement form the term is sometimes used for 'sonata form', but does not serve well, since there are some first sonata movements in other forms (e.g. variations) while there are any number of slow movements and still more of finales in regular sonata form.

First of May, The symphony no. 3 in E♭, op. 20, by Shostakovich. The finale is a choral tribute to International Workers' Day (text by S Kirsanov) but the fp in Leningrad on 21 Jan 1930 did not gain official approval. Shostakovich met with further trouble in his next work, *Lady Macbeth of the Mtsensk District*, denounced in *Pravda* and by Stalin.

Fischer, Adam (b Budapest, 9 Sept 1949; d Budapest, 20 Apr 1995), Hungarian conductor, brother of Ivan ◊Fischer. Studied with Swarowsky in Vienna and Franco Ferrara in Italy. Won the 1973 Cantelli Competition, Milan, and conducted the Finnish National Opera 1974–77, Kassel Opera 1987–92. Vienna Staatsoper from 1980, with *The Bartered Bride*, *Manon*, *Maria Stuarda* and *Gioconda*. US debut 1984, with the Boston and Chicago SOs; guest with the Cincinnati, Denver, and Detroit Orchestras. CG debut 1988, (*Die Fledermaus*), ENO 1991 (*Bluebeard's Castle*). Has conducted the Austro-Hungarian Haydn Orchestra at the Haydn Festival, Eisenstadt, and in the complete symphonies of Haydn on CD.

Consort not with a female musician lest thou be taken in by her snares.
             Ben Sira, *The Book of Wisdom, c.* 190 BC

Fischer, Annie (b Budapest, 5 Jul 1914; d Budapest, 20 Apr 1995), Hungarian pianist. She studied at the Budapest Academy with Dohnányi and in 1933 won the International Liszt Competition in Budapest. Her concert career had begun in 1928, and after war years spent in Sweden continued to tour worldwide. Well known in Beethoven, Mozart, Brahms and Schubert.

Fischer, Edwin (b Basel, 6 Oct 1886; d Zurich, 24 Jan 1960), Swiss pianist and conductor. Studied at the Basel Conservatory, where he taught for several years. He returned to Switzerland in 1942. In addition to his activities as a soloist he also conducted orchestras in Lübeck, Munich and Berlin. He edited a number of early keyboard works and wrote books on Bach and on Beethoven's piano sonatas. A successful teacher in Lucerne and elsewhere.

Fischer, Emil (b Brunswick, 13 Jun 1838; d Hamburg, 11 Aug 1914), German bass-baritone. Debut Graz 1857 in Boieldieu's *Jean de Paris*. Appeared in various German centres and sang Sachs at CG in 1884. NY Met. debut 23 Nov 1885; remained until 1890, taking part in the first US performance of *Meistersinger*, *Rienzi*, *Euryanthe*, *Tristan und Isolde* and *Der Ring des Nibelungen*.

Fischer, György (b Budapest, 12 Aug 1935), Hungarian-born Austrian conductor and pianist. He studied in Budapest and Salzburg; assistant to Karajan at Vienna and conducted operas by Mozart there. Cologne Opera from 1973; many performances of Mozart, with the producer Jean-Pierre Ponnelle. British debut with WNO 1973, with *Die Zauberflöte*; has returned for *Die Entführung*, *Figaro* and *Così fan Tutte*. London debut 1979, in a concert performance of Mozart's *Mitridate*. English Chamber Orchestra since 1980 and has given concerts widely in Europe and South America. Often heard as an accompanist to leading singers. Formerly married to Lucia Popp. Conducted *Così fan Tutte* for Australian Opera, 1987.

Fischer, Ivan (b Budapest, 20 Jan 1951), Hungarian conductor, brother of Adam ◊Fischer. He studied in Budapest and with Swarowsky; conducted in Italy from 1975 and guest with the BBC SO from 1976. Opera debut Zurich 1977; gave *Agrippina* with Kent Opera in 1982

and was music director 1984–89. *La Clemenza di Tito* with CG Opera at Manchester 1983. Music director Northern Sinfonia 1979–82. In 1983 he took the LSO to the Far East and was guest with the LA SO. Conducted *The Magic Flute* for ENO (1987) and *Don Giovanni* in Vienna (1988).

Fischer, Johann (b Augsburg, 25 Sept 1646; d Schwedt, Pomerania, c 1716), German violinist and composer. Studied with Bockshorn at Stuttgart and went to Paris, where he became copyist to Lully. Later he travelled, worked for a time at Augsburg and Schwerin, in Denmark and Sweden, and finally became *Kapellmeister* to the Margrave of Schwedt.

Works include *Feld und Helden Musik* describing the battle of Hochstadt, table music, overtures, dances and other pieces for violin and for viola, some with *scordatura*.

Fischer, Johann Caspar Ferdinand (b c 1665; d Rastatt, 27 Mar 1746), German composer. Was *Kapellmeister* to the Margrave of Baden in Schlackenwerth (Bohemia) and Rastatt from 1692. His keyboard music includes *Ariadne Musica* (1715), a series of 20 preludes and fugues, each in a different key, and thus a precursor of Bach's *Das Wohltemperierte Clavier*.

Other works include *Musicalisches Blumen-Büschlein* (a collection of keyboard suites in the French style), *Musicalischer Parnassus* (nine suites named after the Muses), *Blumenstrauss* (organ preludes and fugues on the eight modes), *Le Journal de Printemps* (suite for orchestra with trumpets *ad lib*), church music.

Fischer, Johann Christian (b Freiburg i/B, 1733; d London, 29 Apr 1800), German oboist and composer. In the service of the Saxon court at Dresden, 1760–64. Concert tours took him in 1768 to London, where he settled, marrying Gainsborough's daughter in 1780. Played frequently at the concerts promoted by J C Bach and Abel (1768–81), and was a member of the queen's band. He was again on tour on the continent, 1786–90. Mozart, hearing him in Vienna in 1787, thought little of his playing, though he had already (1774) composed piano variations on a minuet by Fischer K179.

Works include ten oboe concertos, divertimenti for two flutes, flute sonatas and quartets, etc.

Fischer, Ludwig (b Mainz, 18 Aug 1745; d Berlin, 10 Jul 1825), German bass, the original Osmin in Mozart's *Die Entführung*. Sang with success in Paris, Prague, Dresden and London (Salomon concerts, 1794 and 1798).

Fischer, Michael Gotthard (b Albach near Erfurt, 3 Jun 1773; d Erfurt, 12 Jan 1829), German organist and composer. Pupil of Kittel at Erfurt and later organist of the Franciscan church there. Wrote organ music, symphonies, string quartets, piano sonatas, songs.

Fischer, Res (b Berlin, 8 Nov 1896; d Stuttgart, 4 Oct 1974), German contralto. She studied in Prague and in Berlin with Lilli Lehmann. Basel 1927–35; Frankfurt 1935–41; Stuttgart from 1941. She was a friend of Carl Orff and created his Antigonae at Salzburg in 1949; returned for the fp of Wagner-Régeny's *Das Bergwerk zu Falun*, 1961. She sang Clytemnestra in a concert performance of *Elektra* in London, 1955. Bayreuth 1959–61.

Fischer-Dieskau, Dietrich (b Berlin, 28 May 1925), German baritone and conductor. Studied in Berlin with Georg Walter and with Weissenborn. Made his debut in 1947 and his first stage appearance in 1948 as Posa, in Berlin. London, 1951, in *A Mass of Life* by Delius. He sang at most of the great opera houses and music centres of the world; CG 1965 as Mandryka, Bayreuth 1954–61 as Wolfram, Kothner and Amfortas; other Wagner roles were Sachs, Kurwenal and the Dutchman. US debut Cincinnati, 1955. Conducting debut 1973. He sang in the fps of Henze's *Elegy for Young Lovers* (1961), Britten's *War Requiem* (1962), Tippett's *The Vision of St Augustine* and Reimann's *Lear* (1978). An equally fine Lieder and opera singer, he was a musician of great intelligence, with a fine voice of remarkable range and flexibility and a perfect technique; highly regarded as Barak, Busoni's Faust, Hindemith's Mathis, Almaviva and Wozzeck.

He published his memoirs in 1987 (*Nachklang/Echoes of a Lifetime*). Last public appearance at Munich, New Year's Eve, 1992. Among his best recordings are Schubert's *Schöne Müllerin* and

Winterreise, Bach's *St Matthew Passion* (under Klemperer), *Tristan und Isolde* (Fürtwangler) and *Tannhäuser* (Bayreuth, 1961).

Fischietti, Domenico (b Naples, *c* 1720; d Salzburg, *c* 1810), Italian composer. Pupil of Durante and Leo in Naples, where he produced his first opera 1742. Worked as conductor in Prague, then became *Kapellmeister* at Dresden 1766–72, and at Salzburg Cathedral 1772–79.

Works include operas *Lo Speziale* (with V Pallavicini, 1754), *Il Signor Dottore*, *Il Mercato di Malmantile*, *La Ritornata di Londra* (all on libretti by Goldoni) and *c* 20 others; church music.

Fišer, Luboš (b Prague, 30 Sept 1935), Czech composer. Studied in Prague, where his two operas, *Lancelot* and *The Good Soldier Schweik*, were produced 1961 and 1962. Emigrated to the USA 1971 and became composer-in-residence with the American Wind Symphony Orchestra at Pittsburgh. His music often returns to myth and religion for inspiration.

Works include ballet *Changing Game* (1972); two symphonies (1956, 1960); *15 Prints after Dürer's Apocalypse*, for orchestra (1965); *Requiem* (1968); *Lament over the Destruction of the City of Ur*, for soloists, narrators, chorus and bells (1969); *Kretzer Etude* for chamber orchestra (1974); *Serenade for Salzburg* (1977); *Albert Einstein* for organ and orchestra (1979); piano concerto (1980); *Centaurs* for orchestra (1983); string quartet (1955), cello sonata (1975), piano trio (1978), and five piano sonatas (1955–78).

There are composers who write difficult music with ease, and others who write a facile music with difficulty.

Georges Auric, quoted in Honegger,
I am a Composer, 1951

Fisher, John (b Glasgow, 1950), Scottish conductor. Studied in Glasgow and worked for Unitel opera films, playing the harpsichord on Harnoncourt's *Mitridate*. Former artistic adviser of the Rossini Festival at Pesaro, and has conducted Netherlands Opera, Cologne Opera, and the Maggio Musicale, Florence. Artistic director of the Teatro La Fenice, Venice, from 1990: *Figaro, Semele, Rinaldo* and *Così fan Tutte*. CG debut 1992, Handel's *Alcina*.

Fisher, John Abraham (b London, 1744; d ? London, May 1806), English violinist and composer. Pupil of Pinto, made his debut as a violinist in 1765. His marriage in 1770 brought him a part-share in Covent Garden Theatre, and over the next ten years he composed many dramatic works. On the death of his wife in 1780 he went on tour on the Continent. Married the singer Nancy Storace in Vienna in 1784, but his ill-treatment of her caused him subsequently to be banished from Austria. Later he spent some years in Dublin.

Works include oratorio *Providence* (1777); incidental music for Shakespeare's *Macbeth*; pantomimes; songs for Vauxhall Gardens, etc.; symphonies, and other instrumental music.

Fisher, Sylvia (b Melbourne, 18 Apr 1910), Australian soprano. She sang in Melbourne from 1932 and appeared as Leonore at CG in 1949; returned until 1958 as Sieglinde, Gutrune, the Marschallin and the Kostelnička in the British fp of *Jenůfa* (1956). She sang Britten roles with the EOG 1963–71; created Mrs Wingrave, on BBC TV, 1971. The title part in *Gloriana* was one of her best roles.

Fistoulari, Anatole (b Kiev, 20 Aug 1907; d London, 21 Aug 1995), Russian-born conductor. Studied with his father and conducted Tchaikovsky's sixth symphony at the age of eight. From 1933 he was in Paris and in 1940 he settled in England. He was principal of the LPO in 1943 and conducted much ballet music.

Fitelberg, Jerzy (b Warsaw, 20 May 1903; d New York, 25 Apr 1951), Polish-born American composer. He played percussion in his father's orchestra as a boy and studied composition at the Warsaw Conservatory and under Schreker in Berlin; settled in Paris in 1933 and in NY in 1940. His fourth string quartet (1937) received an Elizabeth Sprague ◊Coolidge award.

Works include Concert Pieces, *Sinfonietta* (1946), *Polish Pictures, Nocturne* and two suites for orchestra, symphony for strings, piano, harp and percussion, concerto for strings; two piano concertos (1929, 1934), two violin concertos, cello concerto; five string quartets (1926–45), string trio, woodwind quintet; Suite for violin and piano, sonatina for two violins, duo for violin and cello, sonata for cello solo; piano sonata and pieces.

Fitzwilliam, Viscount (Richard Wentworth) (1745–1816), English collector and founder of the Fitzwilliam Museum at Cambridge, which houses his collection of MSS and printed music, among other things left by him, including the old English church music pub. as *Fitzwilliam Music* by Vincent Novello in 1825 and English virginal music edited as the *Fitzwilliam Virginal Book* by J A Fuller-Maitland and W Barclay Squire in 1899.

Fitzwilliam Virginal Book a large MS of keyboard music written between 1609 and 1619 by Francis Tregian while in Fleet Prison, now in the Fitzwilliam Museum, Cambridge. It is an important source of pieces by Byrd, Bull and Giles Farnaby.

Five Movements for String Quartet work by Webern; composed 1909, fp Vienna, 8 Feb 1910. Version for string orchestra 1929, fp Philadelphia, 26 Mar 1930.

Five Orchestral Pieces, *Fünf Orchesterstücke*, work for large orchestra by Schoenberg, op. 16, composed 1909 revised 1922; fp London, 3 Sept 1912, conductor Wood. Schoenberg gave the five pieces the titles *Premonitions, The Past, Chord-Colours, Peripetie, Endless Recitative*.

Schoenberg's pupil, Webern, wrote Five Pieces for orchestra 1911–13, fp Zurich, ISCM concert, 22 Jun 1926 (four of the five pieces last for less than one minute). Webern's five posthumous pieces for orchestra (1913) were performed Cologne, 13 Jan 1969.

'Five, The' ◊Kutchka.

Five Tudor Portraits choral suite by Vaughan Williams on poems by Skelton. 1. Ballad, *The Tunning of Elinor Rumming*; 2. Intermezzo, *My Pretty Bess*; 3. Burlesca, *Epitaph on John Jayberd of Diss*; 4. Romanza, *Jane Scroop: Her Lament for Philip Sparrow*; 5. Scherzo, *Jolly Rutterkin*. For mezzo-soprano, baritone, chorus and orchestra, fp Norwich Festival, 25 Sept 1936.

Flackton, William (b Canterbury, bap. Mar 1709; d Canterbury, 5 Jan 1798), English organist and composer. He was a bookseller, but played the organ and violin, taught and composed harpsichord and string music, including works for viola.

Flagello, Ezio (b New York, 28 Jan 1933), American bass. He studied in NY with Friedrich Schorr. Stage debut Rome 1956, as Dulcamara. NY Met. from 1957; debut as Leporello, created Barber's Enobarbus in the opening production at the new house, Lincoln Center, 1966. From 1968 he sang widely in the US and Europe. His recordings include *I Puritani, Lucrezia Borgia, Ernani, Luisa Miller* and *Alcina*. Sang Sarastro for Pennsylvania Opera Theater, 1991.

Flagello, Nicolas (b New York, 15 Mar 1928; d New Rochelle, NY, 16 Mar 1994), American composer, conductor and pianist. Gave piano recitals from age five and studied in Rome and at the Manhattan School of Music; professor there 1950–77. Conducted at the NY City and Chicago Lyric Operas, and accompanied leading singers on the piano. His Italian origins are reflected in his music.

Works include operas *Mira* (1953), *Rip Van Winkle* (1957), *The Sisters* (1958), *The Judgment of St Francis* (1959), *The Pied Piper of Hamelin* (1970), and *Beyond the Horizon* (1983); two symphonies (1968, 1970), four piano concertos (1950, 1956, 1962, 1975), concerto for saxophone quartet and orchestra (1985); *Passion of Martin Luther King*, oratorio (1968); choruses, songs, and chamber music.

Flagstad, Kirsten (Malfrid) (b Hamar, 12 Jul 1895; d Oslo, 7 Dec 1962), Norwegian soprano. She first appeared in opera at the Oslo National Theatre in 1913, in d'Albert's *Tiefland*, and continued to sing in Scandinavia (including operetta) until 1930. In 1933 she sang for the first time at Bayreuth and in 1934 sang Sieglinde and Gutrune there. For the next 17 years she enjoyed an international reputation as a Wagnerian soprano. NY Met. 1935 as Sieglinde and Isolde; the conductor of *Die Walküre*, Artur Bodansky, is reported to have dropped his baton in astonishment when he first her voice. London, CG, 1936–37 as Isolde, Brünnhilde and Senta; returned 1948–51, to sing Wagner in English. She sang in the fp of Strauss's *Four Last Songs* (London, 1950) and also appeared as Dido in Purcell's *Dido and Aeneas* 1951–53. From 1958–60 she was director of the Norwegian State Opera. The nobility and security of her singing are best displayed in her recording of Isolde (1953).

flam a double stroke, as distinct from a roll, on the ◊side drum.

flat the sign ♭, which lowers a note by a semitone. Also an adj. describing out-of-tune intonation on the flat side.

flautando Italian = 'fluting'; flute-like tone produced on the violin by drawing the bow lightly over the strings near the end of the finger-board.

flautino Italian = 'little flute'; a small recorder, either the descant recorder or the flageolet, also called *flauto piccolo* in the early 18th c. (e.g. in Handel's *Rinaldo*).

flautist the English word for flute-player, derived from Italian *flauto* and *flautista*.

flauto traverso, Italian, the transverse flute distinguished from the recorders and similar flutes played vertically.

Flavio, rè de' Longobardi, *Flavius, King of the Lombards*, opera by Handel (libretto by N F Haym, partly based on Corneille's *Cid*), produced London, King's Theatre, Haymarket, 14 May 1723. Set in a mythical Britain; Guido kills the father of his lover Emilia in a duel; King Flavio restores Guido to her after his execution is threatened.

Flavius Bertaridus, König der Longobarden, *Flavius Bertaridus, King of the Lombards*, opera by Telemann (libretto by C G Wendt), produced Hamburg, Theater beim Gänsemarkt, 23 Nov 1729.

Flecha (1), Mateo (b Prades, Tarragona, 1481; d Poblet, *c* 1553), Spanish monk and composer. Pupil of Juan Castelló at Barcelona, *maestro de capilla* to the Infantas of Castile, the daughters of Charles V. Later became a Carmelite and settled in the monastery of Poblet.

Flecha (2), Mateo (b Prades, 1530; d Solsona, Lérida, 20 Feb 1604), Spanish monk and composer, nephew of Mateo ◊Flecha (2). Pupil of his uncle. In the service of the Emperor Charles V until 1558 and of Philip II, then in Prague in that of the Emperor Maximilian, after whose death in 1576 he remained there until 1599, when he went to the abbey of Solsona as a Franciscan monk. A stage work of his, *El Parnaso*, (?) was performed at Madrid in 1561.

Works by the two Flechas (not always distinguishable) include church music, madrigals, *ensaladas* (burlesque madrigals), etc.

Fledermaus, Die, *The Flittermouse, The Bat*, operetta by J Strauss, junior (libretto by C Haffner and R Genée, based on a French vaudeville, *Le Réveillon*, by H Meilhac and L Halévy, taken from a German comedy, *Das Gefängnis*, by R Benedix), produced Vienna,

THE OPERA
Die Fledermaus

Set in Vienna, 19th century and premiered there in 1874.

I. Rosalinde (soprano) is serenaded by the opera singer Alfred (tenor), who hopes to gain access to Rosalinde once her husband Eisenstein (tenor) has gone to prison for a minor offence he has committed. When Dr. Falke (baritone) arrives, he suggests to Eisenstein that prison can wait and they should go instead to a party given by Prince Orlofsky (mezzo-soprano or tenor). The prison governor Frank (baritone) arrives later and, mistaking Alfred for Eisenstein, takes the singer off to prison.

II. Rosalinde goes to Orlofsky's party masked as a Hungarian countess and is flirted with by her husband, who does not suspect her true identity.

III. Eisenstein arrives at the prison to begin his sentence, and is surprised to find Alfred doing time in his place. He is soon joined by Rosalinde, and the various mistaken identities are sorted out before the final ensemble in praise of champagne.

THE OPERA

THE OPERA
Der Fliegende Holländer

Originally a one-act opera (later made into three acts) by Richard Wagner, who also wrote the libretto. First produced as a complete opera in Dresden in 1843, it is a tale of eternal damnation. The action is set in a fishing village in Norway in 1650.

I. The Dutchman (baritone) has been condemned by an act of blasphemy to sail his ship forever until he achieves salvation with the love of a faithful woman. Once every seven years he may attempt salvation, and storms have now driven him to harbour. When his ship is moored, the Dutchman offers untold wealth to a delighted Daland (bass) in exchange for his daughter.

II. In Daland's house, Senta (soprano) sings the ballad of the legendary Dutchman. When Daland introduces them, they find in each other all that they have been looking for – Senta's suitor Erik (tenor) is soon forgotten.

III. Daland's sailors celebrate, taunting the silent ship of the Dutchman. Erik renews his suit to Senta and, when the Dutchman overhears them, he misunderstands and believes all is lost. He leaves on his ship but Senta jumps from a cliff to join him. The Dutchman is redeemed by her faith, and together they rise towards the heavens.

THE OPERA

Theater an der Wien, 5 Apr 1874. Rosalinde, husband Eisenstein, and lover Alfred mixed up in a practical joke at Prince Orlofsky's ball.

Fleischer, Edytha (b Falkenstein, 5 Apr 1898), German soprano. Debut Berlin 1918, as Constance. Salzburg 1922, as Susanna and Zerlina. She toured America 1922–24 and sang at the NY Met. 1926–36 and in the first US performances of operas by Rossini, Rimsky-Korsakov and Puccini (*La Rondine* 1928). She was well known in concert and appeared at Buenos Aires 1936–49.

Fleischer-Edel, Katharina (b Mülheim, 27 Sept 1873; d Dresden, 18 Jul 1928), German soprano. She sang at Dresden 1894–97 and was then engaged by Pollini for the Hamburg Opera; remained there until 1917, mainly in Wagnerian roles. Bayreuth 1904–08, as Elisabeth, Brangaene, Sieglinde and Elsa. Sang at CG 1905–07 and the NY Met. 1906–07.

Fleisher, Leon (b San Francisco, 23 Jul 1928), American pianist and conductor. He studied with Schnabel and in NY; appeared with NY PO before the war and in 1952 won Queen Elisabeth Competition, Brussels. In the early 1960s lost the use of his right hand; learned the piano left-hand repertory and conducted major orchestras all over the USA. After surgery in 1981 he was able to resume his bimanual career as piano soloist. From 1959 active as teacher, then conductor in Baltimore.

Flem, Paul Le, ◊Le Flem.

Fleming, Renée (b Rochester, NY, 14 Feb 1959), American soprano. Studied in New York and made her debut at the Salzburg Landestheater, 1986, as Mozart's Constance. She is best known as the Countess, which she has sung in Houston, San Francisco and Paris. CG debut 1988, as Glauce in Cherubini's *Médée*, returning as the Comtesse in Rossini's *Il Viaggio a Reims*, 1992. Created Rosina in Corigliano's *The Ghosts of Versailles*, NY Met. 1991, and sang Fiordiligi at Glyndebourne, 1992 (returned 1994, as the Countess). Other roles include Pamina and Tatiana (both at the Met.), Donna Elvira (La Scala), Massenet's Thais (Washington DC), and Rossini's Armida.

Flesch, Carl (b Moson, 9 Oct 1873; d Lucerne, 14 Nov 1944), Austro-Hungarian violinist and teacher. Studied in Vienna and Paris, where he was a pupil of Marsick with Kreisler. Made his first public appearance in Vienna, 1895, toured widely and taught by turns at Bucharest, Amsterdam, Philadelphia and Berlin. In 1934 he settled in London. Wrote books on violin playing and composed violin studies. A bi-annual competition in his name has been held since 1945.

Fleta, Miguel (b Albalate de Cinca, 28 Dec 1893; d La Coruña, 30 May

1938), Spanish tenor. Debut Trieste 1919, as Zandonai's Paolo; Rome 1922, as Romeo in the fp of Zandonai's *Giulietta e Romeo*. He was soon heard in Rome, Vienna and Buenos Aires as Radames, the Duke of Mantua and Don José. NY Met. debut 1923, as Cavaradossi; the following year returned to La Scala and created Calaf there in 1926. He fought for Franco during the Civil War and was sentenced to death by the Communists.

Fleury, Louis (b Lyons, 24 May 1878; d Paris, 11 Jun 1925), French flautist. Studied at the Paris Conservatory. From 1905 until his death he was head of the Société Moderne d'Instruments à Vent. It was for him that Debussy composed *Syrinx*.

flicorno an Italian brass instrument used in military bands, corresponding to the saxhorn and flügelhorn.

Fliegende Holländer, Der, *The Flying Dutchman*, opera by Wagner (libretto by composer, based on Heine's *Memoiren des Herrn von Schnabelewopski*, ? Marryat's novel *The Phantom Ship* and other sources), produced Dresden, 2 Jan 1843. Dutchman condemned by blasphemy to sail his ship forever until redeemed by the love of a faithful woman; Senta is ready to die for him.

Flood, The musical play by Stravinsky (text by Robert Craft from Genesis and the York and Chester miracle plays); composed 1961–62, fp CBS TV, 14 Jun 1962. First stage performance Hamburg, 30 Apr 1963, conductor Craft.

Floquet, Étienne Joseph (b Aix-en-Provence, 23 Nov 1748; d Paris, 10 May 1785), French composer. He received his musical education at the church of Saint-Sauveur at Aix, wrote a motet at the age of ten and went to Paris 1767. In 1774, having come into conflict with Gluck's partisans, he went to Naples, where he studied under Sala, and to Bologna, where he sought further instruction from Martini, but returned to Paris in 1777.

Works include operas *Hellé* (1779), *Le Seigneur Bienfaisant*, *La Nouvelle Omphale* (1782) and *Alceste* (Quinault, 1783); opera-ballets *L'Union de l'Amour et des Arts* and *Azolan*; two Requiems, ode *La Gloire du Seigneur* (J B Rousseau).

Flor, Claus Peter (b Leipzig, 16 Mar 1953), German conductor. Studied at Weimar and with Kurt Masur at Leipzig. Principal conductor of Suhler PO 1981–84 and guest with the Gewandhaus Orchestra and the Dresden Staatskappelle. Music director of the Berlin SO and principal guest with the Philharmonia, London, both 1985. US debut with the Los Angeles PO, 1985. Further concerts with the Boston, Dallas, St Louis and Cincinnati SOs, opera in Berlin (Deutsche Oper and Staatsoper), Dresden and Hamburg.

Florence (actually *Houghton*), Evangeline (b Cambridge, MA, 12 Dec 1873; d London, 1 Nov 1928), American soprano. Made her first appearance at Boston in 1891. Later continued her studies in London and appeared much in England.

Florentinische Tragödie, Eine opera in one act by Zemlinsky (text from the blank-verse drama *A Florentine Tragedy* by Wilde, in German translation by M Meyerfeld); composed 1915–16, produced Stuttgart, 30 Jan 1917, conductor Max von Schillings. Performed in a Hamburg Opera production 1983 at Edinburgh and in 1985 at CG. Jealous husband Simone kills Guido in a duel and is reunited with wife Bianca over the corpse.

Florestan one of the two imaginary characters, Florestan and Eusebius, used by Schumann as pseudonyms for his critical writings and also introduced into his music (*Carnaval, Davidsbündlertänze*) to personify what he felt to be his dual character as an artist, Florestan representing an impetuous romantic and Eusebius portraying a dreamer.

Florida suite for orchestra by Delius, composed 1886–87 and dedicated to the people of Florida (it had been Delius's ambition to become an orange planter). Performed privately in Leipzig 1888; first public performance London, 1 Apr 1937, conductor Beecham. Not pub. until 1963. The four movements are titled *Daybreak, By the River, Sunset* and *At Night*.

Floridante, II opera by Handel (libretto by R A Rolli), produced London, King's Theatre, Haymarket, 9 Dec 1721. Floridante loves Elmira, adopted daughter of usurper King Oronte. Oronte also loves Elmira, and threatens Floridante with death. At the last moment Oronte is overpowered; Floridante and Elmira become king and queen.

Flos Campi, *Flower of the Field*, work by Vaughan Williams in six movements for viola, wordless chorus and small orchestra, fp London 10 Oct 1925, with Lionel Tertis, conductor Wood.

Floss der *Medusa, Das*, *The Raft of the Medusa*, 'popular and military oratorio' by Henze (text by E Schnabel), for soloists, chorus and orchestra, dedicated to the memory of Ché Guevara. The projected fp in Hamburg on 9 Dec 1968 had to be cancelled when members of the chorus, revolting students and the police came into conflict. Fp (concert) Vienna 29 Jan 1971; stage production Nuremberg, 15 Apr 1972. The *Medusa* of the title was a French frigate abandoned at sea in 1816. The officers escaped in lifeboats and cut adrift the entire crew on a single raft.

Flothuis, Marius (b Amsterdam, 30 Oct 1914), Dutch composer. Studied with Hans Brandts-Buys. Artistic director of the Concertgebouw Orchestra 1955–74; professor of musicology at the University of Utrecht from 1974.

Works include concertos for flute, horn, violin, chamber orchestra; *Sinfonietta Concertante* for clarinet, saxophone and chamber orchestra; cello sonata; *Partita* for two violins (1966), *Romeo's Lament* for horn (1975), *Hommage à Mallarmé* for voice, flute, cello and piano (1980), sonata for oboe, horn and harpsichord (1986), *Preludio e Fughetta* for three trumpets (1986).

Flotow, Friedrich von (b Teutendorf, Mecklenburg-Schwerin, 27 Apr 1812; d Darmstadt, 24 Jan 1883), German composer. Son of a nobleman. Went to Paris in 1827 and studied music under Reicha and others. Began to produce operas at aristocratic houses and wrote incidental music for the play *Alessandro Stradella* (enlarged into an opera, 1844) at the Palais-Royal in 1837. Over the next two years he contributed musical numbers to Grisar's operas *Lady Melvill* and *L'Eau Merveilleuse*, and in 1839 he made his first public stage success with *Le Naufrage de la Méduse*. His greatest success came with *Martha*, produced at Vienna in 1884; its blend of German sentiment and Italian ardour made it popular for many years in Europe and at the NY Met. He was intendant of the court theatre at Schwerin in 1856–63. He then returned to Paris, but went to live near Vienna in 1868.

Works include French, German and Italian operas, e.g. *Le Naufrage de la Méduse* (see above, under *Floss der Meduse*; 1839), *L'Esclave de Camoëns* (1843), *Stradella* (1844), *L'Âme en Peine*, *Martha* (1847), *Rübezahl*, *L'Ombre*, *Il Fior d'Harlem*, *Rob Roy* (after Scott); ballets *Lady Henriette* (with Burgmüller and Deldevez, on which *Martha* was based later), *Die Libelle* and *Tannkönig*; incidental music to Shakespeare's *A Winter's Tale* (1859); *Fackeltanz*, overtures, etc. for orchestra; chamber music, songs.

flourish lit., in old English, a fanfare, but in modern music terminology a short figure used as an embellishment rather than as a theme.

The flute is not an instrument that has a good moral effect: it is too exciting.

Aristotle, *Politics, c.* 330 BC

Floyd, Carlisle (b Latta, SC, 11 Jun 1926), American composer. He studied at Syracuse University and privately with Rudolf Firkušný. His first opera, *Susannah*, was produced at University of Houston 1955 and at NY City Opera in 1956; it has since become the most widely produced of all American operas.

Other stage works include *Wuthering Heights* (Santa Fe, 1958), *The Passion of Jonathan Wade* (NY, 1962), *The Sojourner and Mollie Sinclair* (Raleigh, S Carolina, 1963), *Markheim* (New Orleans, 1966), *Of Mice and Men*, after Steinbeck (Seattle, 1970), *Bilby's Doll* (Houston, 1976), *Willie Stark* (Houston, 1981), *All the King's Men* (1981).

Flügel German = lit. 'wing'; the German name for the grand piano, which is wing-shaped.

Flügelhorn German = lit. 'wing horn'; a brass wind instrument akin to the keyed bugle and alto saxhorn, still called by its German name in England though spelt 'flugelhorn' (generally abbr. to 'flugel'). It is made in three pitches, soprano, alto and tenor, and used in military and brass bands. In England only the middle size (in B♭) is used, and normally only in brass bands.

flute a woodwind instrument played horizontally (◊bass flute, ◊piccolo). It is played through an open mouth-hole without reeds and the notes are controlled by keys, many more being obtainable, however, by overblowing and cross-fingering.

In the 17th c. flute normally meant recorder, sometimes called the English flute.

8ve higher

The compass of the flute.

flûte à bec French = 'beak flute' = fipple flute, flageolet, recorder.

flûte douce French = lit. 'sweet flute' = recorder.

flutter-tonguing a special kind of tone production used mainly in playing the flute and clarinet, in which the player rolls an R while playing.

Flying Dutchman ◊*Fliegende Holländer*, ◊*Vaisseau-fantôme*.

Fodor, Eugene (b Turkey Creek, CO, 5 Mar 1950), American violinist. Studied with Ivan Galamian and Josef Gingold; master classes with Heifetz. Won the 1972 Paganini Competition at Genoa and shared second prize at the 1974 Tchaikovsky International, Moscow. Public concerts from age ten, with White House recitals 1984 and 1986. Further appearances with leading orchestras. Among his recordings is the Mendelssohn concerto.

Fodor-Mainvielle, Joséphine (b Paris, 13 Oct 1789; d Saint-Genis, near Lyons, 14 Aug 1870), French soprano, daughter of the violinist and composer Joseph Fodor (1751–1828). First appeared at the Opéra-Comique in Paris, 1814, in operas by Grétry and Berton. In London and Paris she was heard as Rossini's Elisabetta, Rosina and Ninetta (*La gazza ladra*). She retired in 1833.

Foerster, Josef Bohuslav (b Dětenice, 30 Dec 1859; d Nový Vestec near Stará Boleslav, 29 May 1951), Czech composer. Studied at Prague Organ School. Music teacher and critic at Hamburg, 1893–1903, and Vienna, 1903–18. Returned to Prague and was appointed professor at the Conservatory, and director in 1922.

Works include operas *Deborah* (1893), *Eva*, *Jessica* (on Shakespeare's *Merchant of Venice*, 1905), *The Invincibles*, *The Heart*, *The Fool*; incidental music for Vrchlický's *Samson*, Strindberg's *Lucky Peter's Journey*, Schiller's *Maria Stuart* and other plays; *Stabat Mater* and other works for chorus and orchestra, five symphonies (1887–1929), six suites, four symphonic poems and two overtures for orchestra; two violin concertos; five string quartets, three piano trios, quintet for wind instruments; two violin and piano sonatas, cello and piano sonata; works for piano, organ and harmonium; ten recitations with piano accompaniment; songs, part-songs.

Foerstrová-Lautererová, Berta (b Prague, 11 Jan 1869; d Prague, 9 Apr 1936), Czech soprano, wife of Josef Bohuslav ◊Foerster. Debut Prague, 1887 as Agathe; created Julia in Dvořák's *Jacobin* (1889) and was heard as Tchaikovsky's Tatyana. Hamburg from 1893, under Mahler, and in 1900 followed him to the Hofoper, Vienna; roles there included Euryanthe, Nedda, Adalgisa, Mignon, Eva and Sieglinde.

Foggia, Francesco (b Rome *c* 1604; d Rome, 8 Jan 1688), Italian composer. Studied under Cifra, Nanini and Agostini; went into the service of the Elector of Cologne and Bavaria and the Archduke Leopold of Austria in turn and after his return held various church

64

Flute *The flute was described as 'transverse', as in this period drawing, in order to distinguish it from the recorder, which was also known as 'flute'. The instrument pictured is conical, a feature which persisted until the cylindrical design superseded it in the 19th century.*

appointments in Italy including St John Lateran in Rome 1636–61, and Santa Maria Maggiore there from 1677.

Works include Masses, motets and other church music.

Fogliano, Giacomo (b Modena, 1468; d Modena, 10 Apr 1548), Italian composer of madrigals and *frottole*, brother of Ludovico ◊Fogliano. Organist at Modena cathedral from 1489; influenced by Josquin.

Fogliano, Ludovico (b Modena; d after 1538), brother of Giacomo ◊Fogliano. He sang in the papal chapel and was choirmaster at Modena Cathedral. His *Musica Theorica* was pub. 1529, and a single *frottola* was included in Petrucci's ninth book (1508).

Foldes, Andor (b Budapest, 21 Dec 1913; d Herrliberg, Switzerland, 9 Feb 1992), Hungarian-born American pianist and conductor. Studied at Budapest Music Academy with Dohnányi, winning the International Liszt Prize in 1933. He toured Europe until 1939, when he went to the USA, becoming a citizen 1948. He was well known as a performer of Bartók's music and for his playing of the classical repertory. He conducted from 1960.

Foli (*Foley*), Allan James (b Cahir, Tipperary, 7 Aug 1835; d Southport, 20 Oct 1899), Irish bass. Studied at Naples and made his first appearance at Catania in 1862 in Rossini's *Otello*; in London in 1865. He sang Daland in *Der fliegende Holländer*, 1870; the first Wagner opera performed in England. He sang regularly in oratorio as well as in opera.

Folia, La, *The Folly*, term used for melody found in popular dances and songs of the Baroque period. First mentioned by Francisco de Salinas in 1577, the melody was first used as the basis for variations in 1604 and later variations have been by Corelli, Albicastro and Marais (*c* 1700), A Scarlatti and C P E Bach (1778). Liszt uses the theme in his *Rhapsodie Espagnole*, Rakhmaninov in his *Variations on a theme of Corelli*, (dedicated to Fritz Kreisler, fp Montreal, 12 Oct 1931), and Henze in *Aria de la folia española* (1977).

folksong (◊Volkslied), a traditional song of often great but indeterminate antiquity, whose origins and composer are unknown, but which has been preserved by being handed down orally from generation to generation, often in several different versions or corruptions.

Folquet de Marseille (b Marseilles, *c* 1155; d Toulouse, 25 Dec 1231), French troubadour; he was a poet and musician 1179–93. He entered the Church at the end of the 12th c. and died as Bishop of Toulouse; much admired by Dante. 19 poems and 13 tunes of his songs are extant.

Fomin, Evstigney Ipatovich (b St Petersburg, 16 Aug 1761; d St Petersburg, 27 Apr 1800), Russian composer. Studied under Martini at Bologna and later became conductor in St Petersburg. His opera *The Americans* is about the Spanish conquest of the Americas.

Works include melodrama *Orfey i Evridika* (1792) and operas *Boyeslav* (1786), *Orpheus* (1792), *Clorinda and Milo*, *The Americans* (1800), *The Golden Apple*, etc.

Fontaine, Pierre (b ? 1390; d *c* 1450), French singer and composer. Sang in the Papal Chapel in Rome 1420. Wrote *chansons*.

Fontana, Giovanni Battista (b Brescia, ?; d Padua, *c* 1631), Italian violinist and composer. Wrote sonatas for his instrument.

The whole trouble with a folk song is that once you have played it through there is nothing you can do except play it over again and play it rather louder.
Constant Lambert, *Music Ho!*, 1934

Fontanelli, Alfonso Count (b Reggio d'Emilia, 15 Feb 1557; d Rome, 11 Feb 1622), Italian composer. Was in the service of the Duke of Modena at the end of the 16th c. and in 1605 settled in Rome. Wrote madrigals.

Foote, Arthur (William) (b Salem, MA, 5 Mar 1853; d Boston, 8 Apr 1937), American organist and composer. Studied at the New England Conservatory at Boston and later with Paine. For many years held organ appointments at Boston.

Works include cantatas on Longfellow's *The Farewell of Hiawatha* (1885), *The Wreck of the Hesperus* (1887) and *The Skeleton in Armour* (1891); overture *In the Mountains*, prologue to *Francesca da Rimini* and three suites for orchestra; cello concerto; three string quartets (1883–1901), piano quartet, piano quintet, two piano trios; choral works; organ and piano pieces; songs.

Forbes, Elizabeth (b Camberley, 3 Aug 1924), British critic and writer on music. She is well known as a journalist and has contributed to *Opera*, the *Financial Times* (1970–80) and the *Musical Times*. Her publications include *Mario and Grisi* (1985), and many entries on singers for the *New Grove* and *Opera Grove* dictionaries (1980 and 1992). Her translations include operas by Spontini, Meyerbeer and Berwald for Nottingham University and Max Brand's *Maschinist Hopkins* (BBC 1986).

Forbes, Sebastian (b Amersham, 22 May 1941), English composer and organist, son of Watson Forbes, violist. Studied at RAM and King's College, Cambridge; later organist at Trinity.

Works include opera *Tom Cree* (1971); Chaconne and Symphony for orchestra; piano quintet, piano trio, three string quartets, sonata for eight instruments (1978); carols, madrigals and anthems for chorus; solo songs and organ music.

Ford, Bruce (b Lubbock, TX, 15 Aug 1956), American tenor. Studied at Houston and made his debut there 1981, in the premiere of Floyd's *Willie Stark*. Wuppertal Opera 1983–85, as Belmonte, Dardanus in T Gatti's *Scylla*, and Ramiro; Mannheim 1985–87, as Fenton, Ferrando and Tamino. Much admired in such Rossini roles as Argirio

(*Tancredi*, Wexford 1986), Rinaldo (*Armida*), Agorante (*Ricciardo e Zoraide*, Pesaro, 1990). Made his CG debut 1991 as Almaviva; also sang Mitridate there in a new production of Mozart's opera in the same year.

Ford, Thomas (b *c* 1580; d London, buried 17 Nov 1648), English lutenist and composer. He was in the service of Henry, Prince of Wales, in 1611 and appointed one of the musicians to Charles I in 1626.

Works include *Musick of Sundrie Kindes* (1607) with airs to the lute (also to be performed in four vocal parts), catches and rounds; two anthems contributed to Leighton's *Teares and Lamentacions* and others including *Miserere my Maker*, dances for lute.

forefall = ◊appoggiatura ('from below').

Forest English composer, possibly the John Forest who was canon and later dean of Wells, dying there in 1446. His motet *Qualis est dilectus tuus* was included (together with the beginning of *Ascendit Christus*, ascribed to Dunstable in a continental MS), among the latest additions to the Old Hall MS. Other sacred music survives in continental sources.

Forkel, Johann Nikolaus (b Meeder, 22 Feb 1749; d Göttingen, 20 Mar 1818), German organist and music historian. Studied law at Göttingen, where he was director of music at the University from 1779 to his death. Among his many writings his biography of Bach (1802) is most notable – the first biography of Bach and an important contribution to the awakening interest in his music.

forlana (or *furlana*), Italian, an old Italian dance in 6–8 time. A classical example of its use is in Bach's Overture (Suite) in C for orchestra and a modern one in Ravel's *Tombeau de Couperin*.

form the form of a composition is the course it is planned to take from beginning to end in such a way as to unfold itself logically. ◊binary, ◊fugue, ◊rondo, ◊sonata, ◊suite, ◊ternary, ◊variations.

Only when the form grows clear to you, will the spirit become so too.
Robert Schumann, *Advice to Young Musicians*, 1848

Formé, Nicolas (b Paris, 26 Apr 1567; d Paris, 27 May 1638), French composer. He was a clerk and singer in the Sainte-Chapelle in Paris, 1587–92, then became a countertenor in the royal chapel and succeeded Eustache du Caurroy as choirmaster and composer there in 1609. Although almost dismissed from the Sainte-Chapelle for not conforming to the ecclesiastical rules, he returned there in 1626 and, as a favourite musician of Louis XIII, enjoyed special privileges.

Works include Masses, motets, Magnificat and other church music.

Formes, Karl Johann (b Mülheim, 7 Aug 1816; d San Francisco, 15 Dec 1889), German bass. Debut Cologne 1842, Sarastro; created Flotow's Plunkett at Kärntnertortheater, Vienna, 1847. CG 1850–68 as Rocco, Leporello and in operas by Meyerbeer; sang in fp of the revised version of Spohr's *Faust* (1852). He appeared in NY from 1857, later taught at San Francisco.

Forqueray French family of viola da gamba players:
1. Antoine Forqueray (b Paris, Sept 1672; d Mantes, 28 Jun 1745). Pupil of his father; he played before Louis XIV at the age of five. In 1689 he became a royal chamber musician.
2. Jean Baptiste Antoine Forqueray (b Paris, 3 Apr 1699; d Paris, 15 Aug 1782). Son of 1; his father's pupil; in the service of the Prince of Conti.

Forrester, Maureen (b Montreal, 25 Jul 1930), Canadian contralto. Debut (recital) Montreal, 1953. Appeared in Paris 1955 and made NY (Town Hall) debut in 1956. The following year she sang in Mahler's *Resurrection* Symphony, under Bruno Walter, with the NY PO, and in the Verdi *Requiem* in London, under Sargent. Debut in opera Toronto 1961, as Gluck's Orpheus, and other roles included Ulrica, Brangaene, Cornelia in *Giulio Cesare* and La Cieca. In 1975 she made her belated NY Met. debut, as the *Rheingold* Erda. Well-known in *Das Lied von der Erde* and as The Angel in *Gerontius*.

Forrest-Heyther Part-Books a set of six books in the Bodleian Library, Oxford (Music School e. 376–81) containing 18 Masses of the early Tudor period; the books were started at Cardinal College, Oxford, and contain masses by Taverner. They belonged to a William Forrest in 1530 and subsequently to William Heyther, who may have written down the three English anthems which the books also contain. The last part of the sixth book is in the hand of John Baldwin.

Forsell, John (b Stockholm, 6 Nov 1868; d Stockholm, 30 May 1941), Swedish baritone. Debut Stockholm 1896, Rossini's Figaro. In 1909–10 he was heard at the NY Met. as Amfortas, Germont and Telramund. His best role was Don Giovanni, which he sang at CG in 1909 and at Salzburg in 1930. He was director of Stockholm Opera 1924–39. Other roles included Sachs, Beckmesser, Scarpia and Onegin.

Förster, (Emanuel) Aloys (b Niederstein, Silesia, 26 Jan 1748; d Vienna, 12 Nov 1823), German oboist and composer. After two years as a military bandsman, 1766–68, he lived as a freelance teacher and composer, first in Prague, then, from 1779, in Vienna. Author of a treatise on ◊thorough-bass. Beethoven acknowledged his debt to Förster in the composition of string quartets.

Works include 48 string quartets; four string quintets; six piano quartets, and other chamber music; piano concertos, sonatas, variations etc.

Forster, Georg (b Amberg/Oberpfalz, c 1510; d Nuremberg, 12 Nov 1568), German music publisher and composer. He pub. five sets of German songs, the *Frische Teutsche Liedlein*, 1539–56, some of which are by himself; he also composed sacred and Latin works.

forte Italian = lit. 'strong'; loud; generally abbr. by the symbol *f*.

Forte, Allen (b Portland, 23 Dec 1926), American music theorist. He is known for his formulation of set-series, particularly to explain atonal music. His major works are *The Structure of Atonal Music* (1973) and *The Harmonic Organization of The Rite of Spring* (1978).

fortepiano Italian = lit. 'loud-soft'; the early Italian name for the piano, given to the instrument because, unlike the harpsichord, it was capable of having varying intensities of tone production by the player's touch. In current usage it designates such keyboards dating from the mid-19th century and earlier.

Forti, Anton (b Vienna, 8 Jun 1790; d Vienna, 18 Jul 1859), Austrian baritone and tenor. His career began at Eisenstadt and he sang at the Kärntnertortheater, Vienna, 1813–34; often heard in Mozart and created Pizarro in the final version of *Fidelio* (1814) and Weber's Lysiart (1823). Among his tenor roles were Max and Rossini's Otello. Appeared occasionally until 1841; sang also in operas by Isouard and Halévy.

fortissimo Italian superlative = lit. 'strongest'; loudest; abbr. by *ff*.

Fortner, Wolfgang (b Leipzig, 12 Oct 1907; d Heidelberg, 11 Sept 1987), German composer. Studied with Hermann Grabner. From 1931 to 1954 he taught theory and composition at the Evangelical Church Music Institute in Heidelberg, where he founded and conducted a chamber orchestra. In 1954 he became professor of composition at the NW German Music Academy in Detmold, and in 1957 succeeded Genzmer at the Musikhochschule in Freiburg i/B. His music shows the influence of Reger and Hindemith. He also used serial techniques in later years, approaching integral serialism.

Works include *Bluthochzeit* (after Lorca, 1956; revised 1963), *Corinna* (1958), *In seinem Garten liebt Don Pimperlin Belison* (after Lorca, 1962), *Elisabeth Tudor* (1972); ballet *Die Weisse Rose* (after Wilde); *Deutsche Liedmesse, Marianische Antiphonen* for unaccompanied chorus; symphonies, *Sinfonia concertante* for chamber orchestra; concertos for various instruments and small orchestra; four string quartets (1929–75), *Suite* for solo cello (1932), *5 Bagatelles* for wind quintet (1960).

Forty-Eight (Preludes and Fugues) (Bach.) ◊Wohltemperierte Clavier, Das.

Forza del destino, La, *The Force of Destiny*, opera by Verdi (libretto by F M Piave, based on the drama by A P de Saavedra, Duke of Rivas, *Don Alvaro, o La fuerza de sino*), produced St Petersburg, 10 Nov 1862; fp in Italy, Rome, Teatro Apollo, 7 Feb 1863. Leonora and

---

THE OPERA

La Forza del destino

A four-act opera by Giuseppe Verdi, first performed in St Petersburg in 1862. It is set in Spain and Italy in the middle of the 18th century, where monasteries provided sanctuary for people in trouble.

I. Don Alvaro (tenor) is about to elope with Leonora (soprano) when they are discovered by their father, the Marquis of Calatrava (bass). Alvaro throws down his pistol but it accidentally goes off and the Marquis is killed. The dying man curses his daughter.

II. Separated from Alvaro, Leonora disguises herself as a man and finds her brother Don Carlo (baritone) at an inn, determined on killing Alvaro. Arriving later at a monastery, Leonora asks the Padre Guardiano (bass) to allow her sanctuary.

III. Alvaro has become a captain in the Spanish army. He rescues Carlo and, after a further skirmish, Alvaro himself is wounded. His identity is revealed to Carlo who, in turn, declares himself, and challenges Alvaro to a duel. They are separated and Alvaro also joins a monastery.

IV. After searching for five years, Carlo discovers Alvaro but is mortally wounded by him. Leonora is briefly reunited with Alvaro but then goes to her brother's aid. Carlo stabs her and she dies in the belief that she and Alvaro will meet in heaven. Alvaro, the only survivor, finally fulfils his destiny.

THE OPERA

Alvaro elope together, but he accidentally kills her father and the two are separated in their flight. Leonora's brother Carlo searches to find her 'seducer', to avenge the dishonour fallen upon the family. After a series of coincidences, Leonora and Alvaro die together.

Foss (originally *Fuchs*), Lukas (b Berlin, 15 Aug 1922), German-born American composer, conductor and pianist. Studied in Berlin with Julius Goldstein and from 1933 in Paris with Lazare Lévy (piano) and Noel Gallon (composition). In 1937 he went with his parents to the USA, studying at the Curtis Institute in Philadelphia. Later he studied with Hindemith at Yale University; in 1944 he gave the Boston fp of Hindemith's *Four Temperaments* for piano and strings. In 1945 he won a Guggenheim Fellowship and in 1950 a Fulbright Fellowship. He became professor of composition at California University in 1953. He has composed much, in more recent years using an aleatory style. He was appointed conductor of the Buffalo PO in 1964; music director Milwaukee SO 1981–86. Featured composer, Aldeburgh Festival, 1987. His music has progressed from neo-classicism to the avant garde.

Works include operas *The Jumping Frog of Calaveras County* (after Mark Twain, 1950), *Griffelkin* (television opera, 1955), *Introductions and Goodbyes* (libretto by Foss and Menotti); ballet *Gift of the Magi*; cantata *The Prairie* (after Carl Sandberg), oratorio *A Parable of Death* (Rilke, 1952); *Time Cycle* for soprano and ensemble (1960), *American Cantata* for tenor, chorus and orchestra (1976), *Thirteen Ways of Looking at a Blackbird* for soprano, flute, piano and percussion (1978), *Round a Common Centre* for voice and ensemble (1979), *De Profundis* (1983), *With Music Strong* for mixed chorus and ensemble (1988); two piano concertos (1944, 1951); three symphonies (no. 3 *Symphony of Sorrows*, 1988); *Orpheus* for cello, oboe and clarinet; *Solomon Rossi Suite* (1975), *Renaissance Concerto* for flute and orchestra (1986), *American Landscapes*, guitar concerto (1989); three string quartets (1947, 1973, 1975), brass quintet (1978), percussion quartet (1983), horn trio (1984), *Taski* for six instruments (1986), *Central Park Reel* for violin and piano (1989); incidental music to *The Tempest*.

Fossa, Johannes de (b c 1540; d Munich, 1603), German or Flemish composer. He wrote six Masses and other sacred works. He succeeded Lassus as *Kapellmeister* at the Munich court in 1594.

Foster, Lawrence (b Los Angeles, 23 Oct 1941), American conductor.

He studied in LA with Fritz Zweig and was assistant conductor of the LA PO 1965–68. Chief guest conductor RPO 1969–74; Houston SO 1971–78. In 1976 he led the revised version of Walton's *Troilus and Cressida* at CG. Music director Deutsche Oper am Rhein, Düsseldorf-Duisburg, from 1981. He is active on behalf of modern music and has given the fps of works by Birtwistle, Goehr and Crosse. Chief conductor of the Monte Carlo PO and Opera from 1979; music director at Duisburg 1981–88, Lausanne CO 1985–90, Jerusalem SO from 1988.

Foster, Stephen (Collins) (b near Pittsburgh, 4 Jul 1826; d New York, 13 Jan 1864), American composer. Almost wholly self-taught in music; pub. his first song as early as 1842. He wrote *c* 175 popular songs, including *Old Folks at Home, My Old Kentucky Home, Massa's in the Cold, Cold Ground.*

Foulds, John (Herbert) (b Manchester, 2 Nov 1880; d Calcutta, 24 Apr 1939), English composer and conductor. He joined a theatre orchestra in Manchester at the age of 14 and the Hallé Orchestra in 1900. Worked at various opera houses abroad, gave concerts for the forces during the 1914–18 war, and later conducted various music societies in London.

Works include incidental music for Kalidasa's *Sakuntala*, Euripides' *Trojan Women* and several others; *A Vision of Dante* (concert opera 1905–08), *A World Requiem* for solo voices, chorus and orchestra (1919–21); *Epithalamium, Keltic Suite* (1911) and *Suite Fantastique* for orchestra; *Holiday Sketches, Suite Française* and *Gaelic Dream Song* for small orchestra; *Idyll* for string orchestra; *Mood Pictures* for violin and piano; *Variations* and *Essays in the Modes* for piano.

Fountain, Ian (b Welwyn Garden City, 15 Oct 1969), English pianist. Studied at the RNCM and has performed widely in the USA and Europe from 1986. Joint winner of the Rubinstein International Competition at Tel-Aviv, 1989, and made concert debut with the Royal Liverpool PO 1990; London recital debut 1991. US debut at the the Savannah, GA, and has appeared further in Warsaw, Berlin, Madrid and Pasadena.

Fourestier, Louis (Félix André) (b Montpellier, 31 May 1892; d Boulogne-Billancourt, 30 Sept 1976), French conductor and composer. Pupil of Leroux, Gédalge, Vidal and d'Indy at the Paris Conservatory, and a follower of Dukas; took the Prix de Rome in 1925. He conducted much in Paris and also took charge of concerts at Angers, Cannes and Vichy, being appointed conductor of the Paris Opéra in 1938.

Works include cantata *La Mort d'Adonis* (1927), symphonic poem *Polynice* and *À Saint-Valéry* for orchestra; *Orchestique* (Paul Valéry); four poems by Tagore for voice and orchestra; string quartets.

Four Last Songs, *Vier letzte Lieder*, sequence of songs for soprano and orchestra by Strauss, composed 1948; his last work. Fp London, 22 May 1950, with Flagstad and Furtwängler. First three texts are by Hermann Hesse; *Frühling, September, Beim Schlafengehen*. No. 4 by Eichendorff: *Im Abendrot.*

Fournet, Jean (b Rouen, 14 Apr 1914), French conductor. Made his debut at Rouen, 1936, and conducted there until 1944. Music director of the Paris Opéra-Comique 1944–57. Led the first Japanese performance of *Pelléas et Mélisande* at Tokyo (1958) and made his US debut with the Chicago Lyric Opera, 1965. Conducted the Netherlands Radio Orchestra 1961–68, Rotterdam PO 1968–73. NY Met. debut 1987, *Samson et Dalila*; conducted *Dialogues des Carmélites* at Seattle, 1990.

Fournets, René (b Pau, 2 Dec 1858; d Paris, Dec 1926), French bass. Debut Paris, Opéra-Comique, 1884, as Gounod's Frère Laurent. At the Opéra he was successful 1892–99 as Méphistophélès, Wotan, Leporello and the Landgrave. At the Concerts Lamoureux he sang in the 1897 fp of Chabrier's *Briseïs*. He was highly regarded in operas by Massenet.

Fournier, Pierre (b Paris, 24 Jun 1906; d Geneva, 8 Jan 1986), French cellist. Studied at the Paris Conservatory, making his debut in 1925. He toured widely and was professor of cello at the Paris Conservatory

1941–49. Chamber music with Szigeti, Primrose and Badura-Skoda. He gave the fps of concertos by Roussel, Martin and Martinů.

Four Saints in Three Acts opera in four acts by Virgil Thomson (libretto by Gertrude Stein), produced in concert form at Ann Arbor, MI, 20 May 1933 and on the stage at Hartford, CT, 8 Feb 1934. It deals with the deeds of 16th-c. Spanish saints.

Four Sea Interludes concert work by Britten, derived from his opera *Peter Grimes* (fp London, 1945). The four sections are titled *Dawn, Sunday Morning, Moonlight* and *Storm*; fp Cheltenham, 13 Jun 1945.

Four Seasons, The, *Le quattro Stagioni*, four violin concertos by Vivaldi in E, G minor, F and F minor, depicting the seasons. The first four of 12 violin concertos op. 8 pub. 1725 in Amsterdam as 'The contest between harmony and invention'.

Four Serious Songs (Brahms.) ◊Vier ernste Gesänge.

Four Temperaments, The title for symphony no. 2, op. 16, by Nielsen; composed 1901–02, fp Copenhagen, 1 Dec 1902.

Four Temperaments, Theme and Variations, The work for piano and string orchestra by Hindemith. Commissioned by Balanchine and composed 1940; fp (concert) Boston, 3 Sept 1944, Lukas Foss as soloist. Stage production NY, City Ballet, 20 Nov 1946. The four main sections are titled *Melancholy, Sanguine, Phlegmatic* and *Choleric.*

fourth an interval which embraces four degrees of the diatonic scale. If perfect, it covers two tones and a semitone.

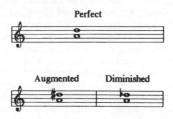

A fourth may be perfect; it can also be augmented or diminished.

Fou Ts'ong (b Shanghai, 10 Mar 1934), Chinese-born British pianist. Studied at Warsaw Conservatory; prize in Chopin Competition 1955. Settled in London from 1958. Widely heard in Debussy and Mozart.

Fowke, Philip (Francis) (b Gerrards Cross, 28 Jun 1950), English pianist. Studied at RAM 1967–74 and has returned there as professor of piano. Debut concert at the Wigmore Hall, London, 1974; US debut 1982. Regular concerts from 1979 with the leading London orchestras, with tours throughout Europe, the Far East and USA. Recordings include concertos by Rakhmaninov, Ravel, Chopin and Tchaikovsky.

Fowler, Jennifer (b Bunbury, W Australia, 14 Apr 1939), Autralian composer. Studied in Perth and at the electronic music studio, Utrecht. Resident in London from 1969.

Works include *Look on this Oedipus* (1973), *Chant with Garlands* (1974) and *Ring out the Changes* for orchestra; *Revelation* for string quintet (1971); *Chimes, Fractured* for ensemble (1970), *The Arrows of St Sebastian* I and II for ensemble (1981); *Line Spun with Stars* for piano trio (1983); *Echoes from an Antique Land* for ensemble (1983); *Threaded Stars* harp solo (1983); *Between Science and the World* for wind quintet (1987); *We Call it to You, Brother* for ensemble (1988); *And Ever Shall Be* for mezzo and ensemble (1989); *Reeds, Reflections* for oboe and string trio (1990).

Fox, Tom (b Cincinnati, 1949), American baritone. Sang first with Texas Opera Theater and Houston Opera, then a member of Cincinnati Opera 1976–80. Frankfurt Opera from 1981 as Orestes, Escamillo, Amonasro and Klingsor; sang in a revival of J C Bach's *Amadis* at Hamburg, 1983. Escamillo for WNO 1985. One of his best roles is Alberich in the *Ring*, which he has sung in Nice, Paris, San Francisco, and New York (Met., 1992). Season 1993–94 as Scarpia at Chicago, Klingsor in Munich and Kurwenal in Brussels.

Fox, Virgil (Keel) (b Princeton, IL, 3 May 1912; d West Palm Beach, 25 Oct 1980), American organist. Gave a public recital in Cincinnati, aged 14, then studied in Baltimore; further study with Marcel Dupré in Paris. Carnegie Hall debut 1931; organist at Riverside Church, NY, 1946–65. He was the first US organist at the Thomaskirche, Leipzig, and also played at Westminster Abbey. He was famed for a highly extrovert style of performance.

Fox Strangways, A(rthur) H(enry) (b Norwich, 14 Sept 1859; d Dinton, near Salisbury, 2 May 1948), English musicologist, critic and editor. Educated at Wellington College and Balliol College, Oxford and studied music in Berlin. After teaching at Dulwich and Wellington Colleges until 1910, and visiting India, on the music of which he wrote a book, *The Music of Hindostan*, he became assistant critic of *The Times* in London in 1911 and chief critic of the *Observer* 1925. Founded *Music & Letters* 1920 and edited it until 1936. He also wrote a biography of Cecil Sharp and translated many songs (some with Steuart ◊Wilson), by Schubert, Brahms, Wolf.

Fra Diavolo, ou L'Hôtellerie de Terracine, *Brother Devil, or the Inn at Terraccina*, opera by Auber (libretto by Scribe), produced Paris, Opéra-Comique, 28 Jan 1830. Lorenzo on the hunt for the bandit Fra Diavolo, who plans to kill Zerlina, Lorenzo's love. He catches the criminal and gets the girl.

Fra due litiganti il terzo gode, *Between Two Litigants the Third Makes Profit*, opera by Sarti (libretto altered from Goldoni's *Le Nozze*), produced Milan, La Scala, 14 Sept 1782. Mozart quotes a tune from it in the second-act finale of *Don Giovanni*: it was first produced in Vienna, 28 May 1783. Set against a background of feuding Count and Countess, steward Masotto wins the heart of serving maid Dorina after out-manoeuvring rivals Titta and Mingone.

Frager, Malcolm (b St Louis, 15 Jan 1935; d Pittsfield, MA, 20 Jun 1991), American pianist. Studied in NY and at Fontainebleau. Recital debut 1941, concerto 1945. Won Leventritt Award 1959, followed by first concert tours of USA and Europe; further tours to the Far East and the former USSR. Repertoire ranged from Haydn and Mozart (played on fortepiano) to Prokofiev and Bartók. Discovered and performed the original version of Tchaikovsky's First Concerto.

Franc, Guillaume Le, ◊Le Franc.

Français, Jean (b Le Mans, 23 May 1912), French composer. Studied under his father, director of the Le Mans Conservatory, and Nadia Boulanger in Paris. His music is noted for its wit and brilliance.

Works include operas *Le Diable boiteux* (1938), *La Main de gloire* (1950), *Paris à nous deux* (1954) *La princesse de Clèves* (1965); ballets *Beach* and *Le Roi nu* (after Hans Andersen); two symphonies (1932, 1953), *Suite concertante*; *L'horloge de flore* for oboe and orchestra (1959); *Divertissement* for string trio and orchestra; piano concerto (1936) and concertino, flute concerto (1966), Fantasy for cello and orchestra.

Concertos for violin (1970, 1979), double bass (1974), bassoon and strings (1979), guitar and strings (1983), trombone and wind (1984), flute and clarinet (1991); Cassazione for three orchestras (1975), *Mozart new-look* for double bass and ten wind instruments (1981), Concerto for 15 soloists and orchestra (1988); *Petit Quatuor* for strings, quintet for flute, harp and strings, two wind quintets (1948, 1987), octet (1972), *Danses Exotiques* for 12 players (1986), *Dixtuor* for wind and string quintet (1986), *Elegie* for wind instruments (1990), Suite for four saxophones (1990); songs and piano music.

Francesca da Rimini ◊Françoise de Rimini; ◊Paolo e Francesca.

Opera by Generali (libretto by P Pola, based on Dante), produced Venice, Teatro La Fenice, 26 Dec 1829.

Opera by Nápravník (libretto by O O Paleček and E P Ponomarev, based on a play by Stephen Phillips, *Paolo and Francesca*, and farther back on Dante), produced St Petersburg, 9 Dec 1902. After a part of Dante's *Inferno*. Francesca must marry the crippled Gianciotto, but she falls in love with his brother, Paolo. After learning of her infidelity, Gianciotto sets a trap and kills the pair.

Opera by Rakhmaninov (libretto taken from scenes of Pushkin's play, with additions by Modest Tchaikovsky, based on Dante), produced Moscow, 24 Jan 1906.

Opera by Zandonai (libretto by T Ricordi, based on d'Annunzio's tragedy, and farther back on Dante), produced Turin, Teatro Regio, 19 Feb 1914.

Symphonic fantasy by Tchaikovsky, op. 32 (based on Dante), composed 1876, fp Moscow, 9 Mar 1877.

Unfinished opera by Goetz, completed by Ernst Frank (libretto by composer), produced Mannheim, 30 Sept 1877.

Francescatti, Zino (b Marseilles, 9 Aug 1902; d La Ciotat, France, 17 Sept 1991), French violinist. Made his debut aged five and played Beethoven's violin concerto aged ten. In 1926 he toured England with Ravel. US debut 1939, NY PO.

Francesco Canova da Milano (b ? Monza, 18 Aug 1497; d Milan 15 Apr 1543), Italian lutenist and composer. Known as 'Il divino', he was the finest composer of lute music before Dowland. In the service first of the Duke of Mantua, *c* 1510, and then of Pope Paul III from 1535. Pub. and contributed to several books of lute pieces.

Franchetti, Alberto (b Turin, 18 Sept 1860; d Viareggio, 4 Aug 1942), Italian composer. Studied first in Italy, then with Draeseke at Dresden and at the Munich Conservatory under Rheinberger. Director of the Cherubini Conservatory, Florence, 1926–28.

Works include operas *Asrael* (1888), *Cristoforo Colombo* (1892), *Fior d'Alpe*, *Signor di Pourceaugnac* (after Molière, 1897), *Germania*, *La figlia di Jorio* (after d'Annunzio), *Notte di leggenda*, *Glauco* and (with Giordano) *Giove a Pompeii* (1921); symphony in E minor.

Franchomme, Auguste (Joseph) (b Lille, 10 Apr 1808; d Paris, 21 Jun 1884), French cellist. Studied at the Paris Conservatory. He played in various theatre orchestras and had much success as solo and quartet player. Professor at the Conservatory from 1846. Chopin, whose friend he was, wrote the Polonaise for cello and piano, op. 3, for him, and Franchomme collaborated with him, as well as with Bertini and Osborne, in duos on operatic airs, Chopin's choice being Meyerbeer's *Robert le Diable*. He was the cellist in Alard's quartet. Chopin's cello sonata is dedicated to him.

Francis of Assisi (1181/2–1226) Italian saint and poet. ◊Liszt (two *Legends*); ◊Nobilissima Visione (Hindemith); ◊St François d'Assise (Messiaen).

Francisque, Antoine (b Saint-Quentin, *c* 1570; d Paris, buried 5 Oct 1604), French lutenist and composer. He lived at Cambrai in 1596 and was married there, but went to Paris not long after, pub. a book of lute pieces, *Le Trésor d'Orphée* (1600), some composed by himself, others arranged from popular dances.

The Choral is not a choral and the Fugue is not a fugue.

Camille Saint-Saëns on César Franck's Prélude, Choral and Fugue, quoted in Demuth's *Vincent d'Indy*, 1951

Franck, César (Auguste) (b Liège, 10 Dec 1822; d Paris, 8 Nov 1890), Belgian composer. Precociously gifted, especially as a pianist, he made a concert tour in Belgium at the age of 11. Sent to Paris in 1835 to study, he entered the Conservatory in 1837. There he won prizes each year until he left in 1842. He returned to Belgium, but settled permanently in Paris in 1844. In 1848 he married a young actress and was appointed organist at the church of Saint-Jean-Saint-François in 1851. In 1853 he became choirmaster and in 1858 organist at Sainte-Clotilde. Appointed professor of the organ at the Conservatory in 1872. He became a chevalier of the Legion of Honour in 1885 and two years later, 30 Jan 1887, a festival of his music was held. Six months before his death he was involved in a street accident. He was a pioneer of cyclic form, and his harmonic style was influenced by his experience as a church organist.

Works include OPERAS: *Le Valet de ferme* (1851–53, unpublished), *Hulda* (1882–85), *Ghisèle*; symphony in D minor (1888); symphonic poems, *Les Éolides* (1876), *Le Chasseur maudit* (after Burger), *Psyché* (with chorus); *Les Djinns* and *Variations symphoniques* for piano and orchestra.

Franck *The composer César Franck (1822–1890) pictured sitting in the middle of a group of musicians and students. Franck held several part-time teaching posts before being appointed professor of organ. His class also assumed the function of composition seminar; d'Indy was amongst his pupils.*

CHAMBER: four piano trios (1834–42), piano quintet (1879), string quartet; sonata for violin and piano (1886).

WORKS FOR CHORUS AND ORCHESTRA: (some with solo voices): *Ruth*, *La Tour de Babel*, *Les Béatitudes* (1870), *Rédemption* (1874), *Rébecca*, Psalm 10l; *Paris*: *chant patriotique* for tenor and orchestra; *Messe solennelle* for bass and organ; Mass for three voices, organ, harp, cello and double bass; three motets, three offertories and other small sacred vocal works.

KEYBOARD AND SONGS: *c* 16 works for piano, including *Prélude, Choral et Fugue* and *Prélude, Aria et Final*; nine works for organ, including six *Pièces pour Grand Orgue*, 44 *Petites Pièces*, three *Pièces pour Grand Orgue*, three *Chorals*; five works for harmonium; songs to poems by Chateaubriand, Hugo, Musset, Dumas senior, Sully-Prudhomme, Joseph Méry, Jean-Pierre de Florian, Jean Reboul, Marceline Desbordes-Valmore.

Franck, Johann Wolfgang (b Unterschwaningen, bap. 17 Jun 1644; d ? London, *c* 1710), German composer. *Kapellmeister* at Ansbach between 1673 and 1679, when he killed a musician of the chapel and wounded his wife from jealousy and fled to Hamburg, where he produced 17 operas 1679–86. After 1690 he lived in London for some years, giving concerts with Robert King, contributed songs to the *Gentleman's Journal* and writing one for Colley Cibber's *Love's Last Shift*, also music for a masque by Motteux added to Shadwell's adaptation of Shakespeare's *Timon of Athens*.

Franck, Melchoir (b Zittau, *c* 1579; d Coburg, 1 Jun 1639), German composer. Worked at Augsburg and briefly at Nuremberg, and in 1603 became *Kapellmeister* to the Duke of Coburg. He was influenced by Hassler and the Venetians.

Works include *Melodiae sacrae* for three to 12 voices, *Paradisus musicus* for four voices, church music, hymn-tunes; songs with instrumental accompaniment; madrigals; instrumental pieces.

Franckenstein, Clemens von (b Wiesentheid, Bavaria, 14 Jul 1875; d Hechendorf, Bavaria, 19 Aug 1942), German composer. Studied in

Franck

A biographical note

Much of Franck's music had to wait until after his death before it became truly popular. Sympathetic interpreters, such as Eugene Ysaye with the Violin Sonata, then spread the gospel. Perhaps no work of Franck gained admiration in stranger circumstances than the String Quartet. In 1916, during the worst days of the World War I, the members of a quartet led by Caston Poulet were approached by a stranger who arranged for a private performance to be given for him. At the appointed time the players assembled in the middle of the night and proceeded to the house of Marcel Proust, where they duly performed the Franck Quartet for the novelist as he reclined among the scattered manuscript pages of *A la recherche du temps perdu*. The strains of the quartet duly found their way into the novel in the form of the Vinteuil septet, and the musicians frequently returned to play the same work. The undemonstrative yearnings of this piece probably suited a man who was protected from the rigours of the world outside his house by a cork-lined room – the passionate F minor declarations of Franck's piano quintet would have been too much for him. The Proustian aesthetic of past experience emerging from the concealed store of the unconscious nevertheless suggests an acute musical sensibility.

Vienna and later at Munich with Thuille and at Frankfurt with Knorr. After a visit to USA he conducted the Moody-Manners Opera Co. in England, 1902–07, then worked at the court theatres of Wiesbaden and Berlin, and in 1912 became general intendant of the Munich court theatres.

Works include operas *Griseldis* (1898), *Rahab* (1911) and *Des Kaisers Dichter* (1920); ballet *Die Biene*; orchestral works: variations on a theme by Meyerbeer, Dance Suite, Serenade, Rhapsody, Praeludium, Symphonic Suite, *Das alte Lied*, four Dances, *Festival Prelude*, chamber music; piano works; songs.

Francœur, François (b Paris, 21 Sept 1698; d Paris, 5 Aug 1787), French violinist and composer. Pupil of his father, Joseph Francœur, he joined the Opéra orchestra at the age of 15 and there met Rebel, with whom he worked for the rest of his life. In 1720 he pub. his first violin sonatas, and in 1723 went with Rebel to Prague for the coronation of Charles VI. After his return to Paris in 1726 he gradually rose to the highest positions in French music: composer to the court 1727; member of the king's band 1730; 1743 Inspector, 1757 Director of the Opéra, 1760 Superintendent of the king's music (the last three jointly with Rebel). His nephew, Louis Joseph Francœur (1738–1804), was also a violinist and composer and for a time Director of the Opéra.

Works include operas, composed jointly with Rebel, beginning with *Pyrame et Thisbé* (1726), ballets, violin sonatas, etc.

Françoise de Rimini, *Francesca da Rimini*, opera by A Thomas (libretto by J Barbier and M Carré, based on Dante), produced Paris, Opéra, 14 Apr 1882.

Franco of Cologne 13th-c. music theorist, author of an *Ars cantus mensurabilis* surviving in seven MSS. It expounds the system of notation in his day, now called 'Franconian'. An anonymous monk of Bury St Edmunds, writing of Parisian music in the 13th c., refers also to a 'Franco primus', apparently a Parisian, who also wrote on the same subject.

Francs-Juges, Les, *The Judges of the Secret Court*, unfinished opera by Berlioz (libretto by H Ferrand), composed 1827–28; fp of the overture Paris, 26 May 1828. The rest discarded or used elsewhere, e.g. in the *Symphonie fantastique*.

Frankel, Benjamin (b London, 31 Jan 1906; d London, 12 Feb 1973), English composer. He studied in Germany and at 17 returned to London and picked up a precarious living as music teacher, café pianist and jazz-band violinist. He managed to attend the GSM in the daytime and gradually improved his living as orchestrator and theatre conductor, finally succeeding as conductor and composer of film music; in his published work he became an early English exponent of serial technique. An opera, *Marching Song* (libretto by H Keller, after J Whiting's play) was unfinished at his death; completed by Buxton Orr and performed on BBC 1983.

Other works include music for many films, *Pezzo sinfonico* for orchestra, *Solemn Speech and Discussion* and *Music for Young Comrades* for string orchestra, *The Aftermath* (Robert Nichols) for tenor, strings, trumpet and drums; eight symphonies (1952–72); violin concerto; five string quartets, *Three Sketches* for string quartet, string trio, trio for clarinet, cello and piano, *Early Morning Pieces* for oboe, clarinet and bassoon; violin and piano sonata, sonatas for unaccompanied violin and viola, *Sonata ebraica* for cello and harp, *Élégie juive* for cello and piano; Passacaglia for two pianos; piano pieces.

Frankl, Peter (b Budapest, 2 Oct 1935), Hungarian-born British pianist. He studied in Budapest; debut there 1950. Won competitions in Paris, Munich and Rio de Janeiro in late 1950s. London debut 1962; British citizen from 1967. Has formed piano trio with György Pauk (violin) and Ralph Kirshbaum (cello). Played with Pauk at the Mozart Festival (London 1991) and with Tamás Vásáry at the 1993 London Proms.

Franklin, David (b London, 17 May 1908; d Evesham, Worcs., 22 Oct 1973), English bass. He sang at Glyndebourne 1936–39 as the Commendatore, Banquo and Sarastro. CG 1947–50 as Rocco, Ochs, Pimen, Pogner, Marke, and Mars in *The Olympians* by Bliss. After a throat operation in 1951 he was unable to sing but took speaking parts

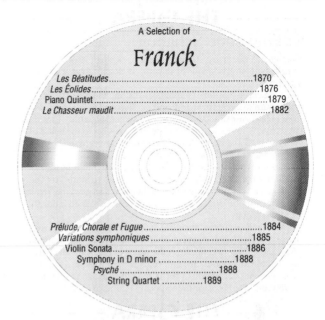

A Selection of

Franck

Les Béatitudes..1870
Les Éolides...1876
Piano Quintet...1879
Le Chasseur maudit..1882

Prélude, Chorale et Fugue.......................................1884
Variations symphoniques 1885
Violin Sonata...1886
Symphony in D minor 1888
Psyché 1888
String Quartet 1889

in *Ariadne auf Naxos* and *Die Entführung* at Glyndebourne, 1953–58.

Frantz, Ferdinand (b Kassel, 8 Feb 1906; d Munich, 26 May 1959), German bass-baritone. Debut Kassel 1927. He sang in Hamburg from 1938, until the opera house was destroyed, and in Munich from 1943; appeared in the major Wagner roles and sang Jupiter with the Munich co. at CG in the only production in Britain to date of Strauss's *Die Liebe der Danae* (1953). NY Met. debut 1949 as the *Walküre* Wotan and recorded the same role with Furtwängler. Often heard as Sachs and recorded role in *Die Meistersinger* with Kempe.

Frantz, Justus (b Hohensalza, 18 May 1944), German pianist. Studied in Hamburg and with Wilhelm Kempff at Positano. Has given concerts from 1960, notably a Mozart concerto series with Karajan and the Berlin PO. US debut 1975, with the NY PO under Bernstein. Worldwide tour 1983 with pianist Christoph Eschenbach. Professor at Hamburg Musikhochschule from 1985; founded and directed the Schleswig-Holstein music festival 1986–94 (Beethoven concertos, 1988). Toured the Mozart concertos throughout Europe, 1987–88.

Franz (originally *Knauth*), Robert (b Halle, 28 Jun 1815; d Halle, 24 Oct 1892), German composer. After much parental opposition he became a pupil of Schneider at Dessau in 1835, and after two years returned home, devoting himself to study and composition without being able to secure a musical post. He became one of the best exponents of German songs, the first of which he pub. in 1843 and which attracted the attention of Schumann, Mendelssohn, Liszt and others. He then became a church organist and choral conductor, also lecturer at Halle University. Much troubled by increasing deafness and a nervous complaint, he had to retire in 1868, but did much work in editing the older choral classics. His output of Lieder, though influenced by Schubert and Schumann, was characterized by its striving toward simplicity and the style of folksong.

Works include more than 350 songs to texts by Burns, Eichendorff, Lenau, Geibel, Heine, Müller and Goethe; church music; part-songs.

Fraschini, Gaetano (b Pavia, 16 Feb 1816; d Naples, 23 May 1887), Italian tenor. Appeared as a church and opera singer at Pavia in 1837 in operas by Donizetti; sang in the fps of six operas by Pacini in Naples. Between 1845 and 1859 created roles in Verdi's *Alzira, Il corsaro, La battaglia di Legnano, Stiffelio* and *Un ballo in maschera*. London debut, 1847.

Fraser, Marjory Kennedy (b Perth, 1 Oct 1857; d Edinburgh, 22 Nov 1930), Scottish singer and folksong collector, daughter of David Kennedy. Studied under her father and Mathilde Marchesi in Paris

THE OPERA

Die Frau ohne Schatten

A three-act opera by Richard Strauss, written 1914–17. The woman without a shadow of the title is a spirit, trying to gain mortality.

I. A messenger (baritone) announces that the Empress (soprano) must return to her spirit world, and her husband will be turned to stone unless she can acquire a shadow – symbol of fertility – within three days. The Nurse (mezzo-soprano) takes her to the house of the dyer Barak (baritone); his wife (soprano) agrees to sell her own shadow and renounce motherhood.

II. Barak's wife is further tempted by the vision of a handsome youth, but the Empress's conscience begins to disturb her. Out hunting, the Emperor is suspicious of his wife's actions, and Barak is on the point of killing his own wife for her declared infidelity when she recants.

III. Although separated from his wife by a thick wall in a cave, Barak declares his continuing love for her. When the Empress enters she refuses to drink from the water of life, which will give her the desired shadow. She still refuses even when her husband turns to stone; her unselfish act is rewarded as she is granted a shadow, and the Emperor miraculously returns to life.

THE OPERA

and began to visit the Hebrides to collect folksongs in 1905. Pub. several collections of these songs and wrote the libretto for Bantock's opera *The Seal Woman*.

Frasi, Giulia, Italian singer. Made her London debut in 1743, the same year sang in *Roxana, or Alexander in India* (an adaptation of Handel's *Alessandro*), and subsequently in several of Handel's oratorios, including *Susanna, Solomon, Theodora* and *Jephtha*.

Frauenliebe und -Leben, (*Woman's Love and Life*), song cycle by Schumann, op. 42 (eight poems by Adelbert von Chamisso), composed 1840.

Frauenlob (Heinrich von Meissen) (b Meissen; d Mainz, 1318), German *Minnesänger*. His songs belong to the end of the tradition of the *Minnesinger*, and in some ways foreshadow those of the *Meistersinger*.

Frau ohne Schatten, Die, *The Woman without a Shadow*, opera by R Strauss (libretto by H von Hofmannsthal), produced Vienna, Opera, 10 Oct 1919. The Empress searches for her shadow, the symbol of fertility, in order to save her husband from being turned to stone. In contrast, Barak's wife is willing to sell her shadow, but is eventually united with her husband, while the Empress gains her own shadow.

FRCO abbr. = Fellow of the Royal College of Organists.

Fredegunda opera by Keiser (libretto by J U König, from the Italian by Francesco Silvani), produced Hamburg, Theater beim Gänsemarkt, Mar 1715.

Frederick II (the Great) (b Berlin, 24 Jan 1712; d Potsdam, 17 Aug 1786), king of Prussia, flautist and composer. Learnt music from Gottlob Hayne, the Berlin Cathedral organist, and in 1728 had flute lessons from Quantz. In 1734 established a private band at his castle at Rheinsberg and on his accession in 1740 a court band at Berlin and Potsdam. Graun, Quantz and C P E Bach were in his service.

Works include part of the opera *Il rè pastore* (Metastasio) and the libretti for several operas by Graun; over 120 instrumental works, many with prominent flute parts.

Fredigundis opera by Franz Schmidt (libretto by B Warden and I M Welleminsky, after F Dahn); composed 1916–21, produced Berlin, 19 Dec 1922. Fredegundis murders the wife of King Chilpenich and becomes queen, but a poison she prepares for a rival is drunk by her husband and daughter.

Fredman, Myer (b Plymouth, 29 Jan 1932), English conductor. Studied at Dartington and the London Opera School. Principal conductor of GTO 1968–74 and conducted operas by Mozart, Verdi, Maw and Von

Einem at the Glyndebourne Festival. Guest conductor with leading UK orchestras and led Cavalli's *L'Ormindo* at Brussels, 1972. Music director of Adelaide Opera from 1975, leading Australian fps of *Death in Venice* and *The Midsummer Marriage*; head of Opera NSW Conservatory at Sydney, 1981–92, with the fp of Nigel Butterley's *Lawrence Hargrave*, 1988. Has recorded symphonies by Bax and Brian.

Freed, Isadore (b Brest-Litovsk, 26 Mar 1900; d Rockville Center, NY, 10 Nov 1960), Russian-born American conductor, pianist and composer. After emigrating to the USA he studied with Josef Hofman and Ernest Bloch, and with d'Indy in Paris. Conducted the Concert Spirituel 1930–33 and returned to the USA to head the music department at Hart College, 1944–60. Wrote ballet *Vibrations* (1928) and opera *The Princess and the Vagabond* (1948), two symphonies (1941, 1951), concertos for violin (1953) and cello (1953), and three string quartets.

Freeman, David (b Sydney, 1 May 1952), Australian stage director. He founded Opera Factory in Sydney, 1973, in Zurich, 1976 (20 Swiss productions) and in London, 1981. Stage fp of Birtwistle's *Yan Tan Tethera* (1986) and *Calisto, Punch and Judy, The Knot Garden* and Reimann's *Ghost Sonata*; Mozart's Da Ponte operas for the bicentenary. For ENO he has directed the local fp of Glass's *Akhnaten* (1985) and the premiere of Birtwistle's *The Mask of Orpheus*; *The Return of Ulysses* 1989. Directed Prokofiev's *The Fiery Angel* for St Petersburg, CG and the NY Met., 1992. His work is noted for its strong sense of theatre; human relationships are shown as paramount.

Freischütz, Der, lit. *The Freeshooter*, opera by Weber (libretto by F Kind, based on a story in Apel and Laun's *Gespensterbuch*), produced Berlin, Schauspielhaus, 18 Jun 1821. Max invokes the 'Black Huntsman' to help win a shooting competition and Agathe. He is banished for his use of the supernatural, but is allowed to return in a year to marry.

Freising, Eberhard von (Eberhardus Frisingensis), 9th-c. author of a short treatise on the measurement of organ pipes.

Freitas, Frederico de (b Lisbon, 15 Nov 1902; d Lisbon, 12 Jan 1980), Portuguese conductor and composer. Studied at the Lisbon Conservatory. He visited Brazil, France, Spain and Holland as conductor and became broadcasting conductor at Lisbon.

Works include opera *Luzdor*; ballets *Ribatejo* and *Nazeré*; cantata *The Seven Words of Our Lady*; symphonic poems *Lenda dos bailarins* and *Suite colonial*; poem on an eclogue by Virgil and prelude on a Lisbon street-cry for string orchestra; *Quarteto Concertante* for two violins, two cellos and string orchestra; sonata for violin and cello; instrumental works; piano pieces; songs.

Freitas Branco, Luiz (b Lisbon, 12 Oct 1890; d Lisbon 27 Nov 1955), Portuguese composer. Studied at Lisbon, with Humperdinck in

THE OPERA

Der Freischütz

A three-act opera by Carl Maria von Weber. A tale of a 'free-shooter' (a huntsman with magic bullets), it is set in Bohemia after the Thirty Years War, and was first produced in 1821.

I. The huntsman Max (tenor) hopes to gain the right to marry Agathe (soprano) by winning a shooting competition. He loses to Caspar (bass), who has sold his soul to the wicked Samiel (spoken). Caspar demonstrates his magic bullets to Max and they agree to mould more bullets at the Wolf's Glen.

II. Calming Agathe's fears, Max departs, but Caspar has already met Samiel at the Glen and they agree on Max as a substitute victim. The magic bullets are duly moulded.

III. Agathe has a vision of herself as a dove felled by Max's bullet. At the shooting contest, Max is commanded to shoot a dove and Agathe rushes to intervene. Although she falls as if dead, it is Caspar who is killed. Max is forgiven after a full confession.

THE OPERA

Berlin, and in Paris. Taught score-reading at the Lisbon Conservatory from 1916 and in 1930 took charge of the master-class in composition.

Works include oratorio, cantata; four symphonies (1924–52), two Portuguese suites for orchestra; violin concerto, Ballad for piano and orchestra; songs with orchestra; string quartet; two violin and piano sonatas, cello and piano sonatas; piano pieces; songs; madrigals to words by Camoens.

Fremaux, Louis (b Aire-sur-Lys, 13 Aug 1921), French conductor. Studied at the Paris Conservatory and was music director of Monte Carlo Orchestra 1955–66; principal of the Rhône-Alpes PO at Lyon 1968–71. City of Birmingham SO 1969–78, notably with concerts of Berlioz and modern music. Chief conductor, then principal guest, of the Sydney SO 1979–85. Appearances throughout Europe and South America, with recordings of music by Rameau, Campra and Berlioz (*Grand Messe des Morts*).

Fremstad, Olive (b Stockholm, 14 Mar 1871; d Irvington, NY, 21 Apr 1951), Swedish-born American soprano. Adopted by an American couple, who took her to Minnesota, she studied piano in Minneapolis and then singing in NY in 1890. In 1893 she studied in Berlin with Lilli Lehmann, making her debut in 1895, in Cologne, as Azucena. She later sang at Bayreuth, Munich, Vienna and London, becoming a leading soprano at the NY Met. from 1903 to 1914, where she was heard as Sieglinde, Kundry, Selika, Carmen, Salome and Armide in the fp of Gluck's opera in the US (1910). Her first Isolde, 1 Jan 1908, was on Mahler's debut as conductor at the Met. An outstanding Wagner singer, she also excelled in Italian opera.

French horn ◊horn.

French overture ◊overture.

French sixth ◊augmented sixth chords.

French Suites six keyboard suites by Bach, composed mainly at Cöthen *c* 1722 and completed by *c* 1724. They differ from the English Suites in having no preludes.

Freni, Mirella (b Modena, 27 Feb 1935), Italian soprano. Debut Modena 1955, Micaela. Glyndebourne 1960–62 as Zerlina, Susanna, Adina. London, CG, since 1961 as Nannetta and Violetta. US debut Chicago 1963 as Marguerite. Sang Mimi at La Scala, Milan in 1963 and on her NY Met. debut in 1965. Toured the US with the Paris Opéra Co. in 1976. Later and heavier roles include Amelia Boccanegra, Elisabeth de Valois (Salzburg, with Karajan), Butterfly and Manon. She returned to CG 1993, as Giordano's Fedora.

Frescobaldi, Girolamo (b Ferrara, Sept 1583; d Rome, 1 Mar 1643), Italian composer and organist. Studied at Ferrara under the cathedral organist Luzzaschi. Visited Brussels, 1607–08. Appointed organist at St Peter's in Rome, 1608; it was reported that 20,000 people came to hear his first recital there. He was given leave of absence from 1628 to 1633, during which time he served as organist to Ferdinand II, Duke of Tuscany; also worked in Brussels, Mantua and Florence. Froberger was among his pupils. A copy of his *Fiori musicali* (1635) was owned by Bach; it contains various pieces for use in the Mass. His most influential music is in his technically advanced keyboard works.

Works include two Masses, a Magnificat, motets and madrigals; *ricercari*, *canzoni*, toccatas, etc. for organ and for harpsichord; fantasies for instruments in four parts; madrigals.

The setting to music of a poem must be an act of love, never a marriage of convenience.

Francis Poulenc, quoted in Bernac,
Francis Poulenc, 1977

Frescoes of Piero della Francesca, The work for orchestra in three movements by Martinů, depicting three of the frescoes by Piero at Arezzo; composed 1955, fp Salzburg, 28 Aug 1956, conductor Kubelik.

frets the small strips of gut, wood or metal fixed on the fingerboard on certain string instruments (including the lute, viols, guitar, mando-line, banjo, ukelele and the Russian balalaika), enabling the player to

Frescobaldi *The composer and organist Girolamo Frescobaldi (1583–1643). Frescobaldi was the most important keyboard composer of the period, his works spanning the stylistic divide between the late Renaissance and the Baroque. He left a huge number of manuscripts for future scholars and musicians.*

play in tune with certainty, the string being stopped by the finger at exactly the right spot, determined by the frets.

Freunde von Salamanka, Die, *The Friends of Salamanca*, operetta by Schubert (libretto by J Mayrhofer), composed 1815, but never performed in Schubert's lifetime; produced with a new libretto by G Ziegler, Halle, 6 May 1928. Don Alonso wins Countess Olivia with the help of his friends.

Frey, Paul (b Heidelberg, Toronto, 1942), Canadian tenor. He played professional ice hockey, then made his debut at Toronto 1978, as Werther. Basel Opera from 1979, in operas by Strauss and Wagner, and as Don José and Peter Grimes. British debut 1986, as Weber's Huon at Edinburgh; Bayreuth and NY Met. debuts 1987, as Lohengrin and Bacchus. Munich Festival 1986–88, as Apollo (*Daphne*) and Midas (*Die Liebe der Danae*). CG and Sydney 1988, as Lohengrin and Walther. Recorded roles include Strauss's Emperor and Bacchus.

Frezzolini, Erminia (b Orvieto, 27 Mar 1818; d Paris, 5 Nov 1884), Italian soprano. Made her first appearance in 1837 at Florence in Bellini's *Beatrice di Tenda*. Sang in Vienna, London, St Petersburg, Madrid, Paris, USA and Milan, where she sang in the fps of Verdi's *I Lombardi* and *Giovanna d'Arco*.

Friberth, Karl (b Wullersdorf, Lower Austria, 6 Jun 1736; d Vienna, 6 Aug 1816), Austrian tenor, author and composer. Studied with Bonno and Gassmann in Vienna and in 1759 joined the Esterházy household under Haydn, for whom he wrote the libretto of *L'incontro improv- viso*. Returned to Vienna as *Kapellmeister* to the Jesuits and Minorites in 1776. Composed mainly church music.

Fricci, Antonietta (b Vienna, 8 Jan 1840; d Turin, 7 Sept 1912), Austrian soprano. Debut Pisa 1858, Violetta. La Scala 1865–73, as Norma, Lady Macbeth and Selika. In Jun 1867 she sang Eboli at CG, in the first British performance of *Don Carlos*.

Frick, Gottlob (b Olbronn, 28 Jul 1906; d Pforzheim, 18 Aug 1994), German bass. Debut Coburg 1934, as Daland. Dresden 1940–50; Munich and Vienna from 1953. Bayreuth 1957–64 as Pogner, Hagen and Hunding. London, CG 1957–67 in productions of *Der Ring des Nibelungen*; from 1963 under Solti, with whom he recorded Hagen in the first stereo issue of *Götterdämmerung*. Gurnemanz at CG in 1971. NY Met. debut 1961 as Fafner; a proposed debut in 1950 was vetoed by Rudolf Bing on account of Frick's Nazi past.

Fricker, Peter Racine (b London, 5 Sept 1920; d Santa Barbara, 1 Feb 1990), English composer, partly of French descent. He studied at the RCM in London and later with Seiber. His wind quintet won the Clements Prize in 1947 and his first symphony won the Koussevitsky Award. Composer-in-residence, University of California at Santa Barbara from 1964. His music avoided local pastoral influences and learned instead from continental neo-classical and serial models.

Works include radio operas *The Death of Vivien* and *My Brother Died* (1954); ballet *Canterbury Prologue* (after Chaucer); oratorio *A Vision of Judgment* (1957–58); *Whispers at the Curtains* for baritone, chorus and orchestra (1984); five symphonies (1948–76); *Prelude, Elegy and Finale* for strings; violin and viola concertos, *Concertante* for three pianos and strings; wind quintet, four string quartets (1947–76); violin and piano sonata; organ sonata.

Fricsay, Ferenc (b Budapest, 9 Aug 1914; d Basel, 20 Feb 1963), Hungarian conductor. He studied with Bartók and Kodály at the Budapest Academy, and was successively conductor at the Szeged Opera 1934–44, the Budapest Opera, 1945, and the Vienna Staatsoper, 1947; at the 1947 Salzburg Festival he conducted the fp of von Einem's *Dantons Tod*. From 1948 to 1952 he was director of the Berlin City Opera, and from 1956 to 1959 of the Munich Staatsoper. He appeared frequently as a guest conductor in England (debut 1950, Edinburgh, with Glyndebourne Opera, in *Figaro*), Italy, Holland and America; and made a large number of recordings.

Friderici, Daniel (b Eichstedt, Querfurt, 1584; d Rostock, 23 Sept 1638), German composer and writer. Cantor at St Mary's Church, Rostock, from 1618 to his death. Pub. Morley's three-part madrigals with German words in 1624.

Works include madrigals, German songs for three–eight voices.

Fried, Miriam (b Satu-Mare, 9 Sept 1946), Romanian-born Israeli violinist. Studied in the USA with Isaac Stern, Josef Gingold and Ivan Galamian. Won the Paganini Competition at Genoa, 1968, and made NY debut the following year. UK debut at the Windsor Festival 1971, under Menuhin. Season 1994–95 with the Chicago and Boston SOs, and Cleveland and Phialdelphia Orchestras. Recordings include the Bach solo works and the Sibelius Concerto.

Friede auf Erden, *Peace on Earth*, work for chorus a cappella by Schoenberg (text by C F Mayer); composed 1907, fp Vienna, 9 Dec 1911, conductor Schreker.

Friedenstag, *Peace Day*, opera by R Strauss (libretto by J Gregor, who first suggested it to Stefan Zweig, based on Calderón's play *La redención de Breda* and Velázquez's picture illustrating that), produced Munich, 24 Jul 1938. Besieged town faces self-destruction rather than defeat. At the last moment a peace is declared and enemies meet as brothers.

Friedlaender, Max (b Brieg, Silesia, 12 Oct 1852; d Eichkamp near Berlin, 2 Oct 1934), German baritone and writer of music. Studied under Garcia in London and Stockhausen at Frankfurt. Taught in Berlin and at Harvard University. Edited songs by Schubert and Schumann and German folksongs and wrote books on German song and Brahms's songs.

Friedrich, Götz (b Naumburg, 4 Aug 1930), German opera producer. He assisted Felsenstein at the Komische Oper, Berlin, and produced *Così fan Tutte* in Weimar in 1958; director of production 1968. Hamburg from 1973, Deutsche Oper Berlin from 1980. Starting with his *Tannhäuser* at Bayreuth in 1972, and continuing with *Der Ring des Nibelungen* at CG, 1974–76, his productions have been seen as reflecting his Marxist beliefs. He is married to the soprano Karan Armstrong (1941–   ) and with her has worked on the British fp of the three-act version of Berg's *Lulu* (CG, 1981) and in 1985 Korngold's *Die tote Stadt* at the Vienna Staatsoper. His staging of the *Ring* 1984–85 was partly realized at CG, 1989–91. US stagings include *Wozzeck* (Houston, 1982), and *Otello* and *Katya Kabanova* at LA, 1986 and 1988.

Friedrichs, Fritz (b Brunswick, 13 Jan 1849; d Königslutter, 15 May 1918), German baritone. After minor roles in Brunswick and elsewhere, from 1869, he moved to Nuremberg in 1883; well known there and at Bremen as a Wagner singer. Bayreuth 1888–1902 as Beckmesser, Alberich and Klingsor. He made guest appearances in Berlin, London and Vienna, and sang at the NY Met. 1899–1900.

Friend, Lionel (b London, 13 Mar 1945), English conductor. Studied at the RCM and London Opera Centre; debut WNO 1969, *La Traviata*. Conducted at WNO 1968–72, Kassel Opera 1972–75. Staff conductor for ENO 1976–89, including the fp of David Blake's *The Plumber's Gift*. Music director of New Sussex Opera from 1989, including a well-received *Tannhäuser*. In 1983 he conducted BBC forces in the fp of the opera *The Tigers* by Havergal Brian, composed 1916–30.

Friml, Rudolf (b Prague, 2 Dec 1879; d Hollywood, 12 Nov 1972), Czech composer and pianist. Studied at the Prague Conservatory with Juranek (piano) and Foerster (composition). Toured for some time as accompanist to Jan Kubelík, remaining in America after a tour in 1906. He appeared as a soloist with many orchestras.

Works include operettas, *The Firefly*, *High Jinks*, *Katinka*, *Rose Marie* (1924), *The Vagabond King* (1925) and many others.

Friskin, James (b Glasgow, 3 Mar 1886; d New York, 16 Mar 1967), Scottish pianist and composer. Studied at the RCM in London. In 1914 he went to NY and became piano professor at the Institute of Musical Art. He married Rebecca ◊Clarke in 1944. He was admired for the intellectual clarity of his interpretations, notably of Beethoven's Diabelli Variations.

Works include two motets on Scottish psalm tunes; suite for orchestra; piano quintet in C minor; phantasy string quartet; cello and piano sonata.

Froberger, Johann Jacob (b Stuttgart, bap. 19 May 1616; d Héricourt near Montbéliard, 7 May 1667), German organist and composer. Studied under his father, who was a singer, and later *Kapellmeister* at Stuttgart. Appointed court organist in Vienna on the accession of the Emperor Ferdinand III in 1637, remaining there until 1657, but spending 1637–41 in Italy as a pupil of Frescobaldi. In 1662 he went to London where he is said to have arrived destitute, having been twice robbed on the way. In later years he lived in the house of Sibylla, Dowager Duchess of Württemberg, at her retreat at Héricourt.

Works include harpsichord suites, many pieces for organ and harpsichord including toccatas, *ricercari* and 30 suites.

'Frog' Quartet the nickname of Haydn's string quartet in D major, op. 50 No. 6, the finale of which is supposed to have a 'croaking' theme.

Fröhlich Austrian family of musicians, four sisters, friends of Schubert:

1. Anna (Nanette) Fröhlich (b Vienna, 19 Nov 1793; d Vienna, 11 Mar 1880). Pianist and soprano; pupil of Hummel, Hauss and Siboni, singing teacher at the Vienna Conservatory 1819–54. She gave the fps of several of Schubert's works.

2. Barbara Fröhlich (b Vienna, 30 Aug 1797; d Vienna, 30 Jun 1879). Contralto and painter; married Ferdinand Bogner, professor of flute at the Vienna Conservatory.

3. Katharina Fröhlich (b Vienna, 10 Jun 1800; d Vienna, 3 Mar 1879). Intimate friend of Grillparzer, who lived in the sisters' house until his death in 1872.

4. Josephine Fröhlich (b Vienna, 12 Dec 1803; d Vienna, 7 May 1878), Soprano; pupil of her sister Anna, made her first appearance in 1821 in *Die Entführung*, later went to Copenhagen to study under Siboni and sang with success in Scandinavia, also, *c* 1829–31, in Italy. Grillparzer wrote texts of *Zögernd leise* (*Ständchen*) and *Mirjams Siegesgesang*, set by Schubert, for her.

Froissart concert overture by Elgar, op. 19, composed 1890 and performed at the Worcester Festival of that year on 9 Sept, conductor Elgar. Title refers to the French historian Jean Froissart (1338–1404). Elgar prefaced the score with a quotation from Keats: 'When chivalry lifted up her lance on high'.

Fromm, Andreas (b Pänitz, Brandenburg, 1621; d Strahov, Prague, 16 Oct 1683), German composer. He was cantor and professor at the Pädagogium of Stettin in the middle of the century.

Works include oratorio (one of the earliest known in German) *Actus Musicus*, *Vom reichen Mann und Lazarus* (1649); *Dialogus Pentecostalis*.

'From My Life' (Smetana.) ◊Aus meinem Leben.

From the House of the Dead, Janáček, ◊House of the Dead, From the.

'From the New World' (Dvořák.) ◊'New World' Symphony.

Frosch German = 'frog'; the heel of the violin bow. The direction 'am Frosch' found in German scores means that a passage is to be bowed near the heel of the bow.

frottola an early 16th-c. Italian song, originating in Milan, for several voices or for solo voice and instruments, forerunner of the madrigal but less polyphonically elaborate.

The term is used in a general sense to cover numerous different forms: *strambotto*, *oda*, *capitolo*, etc., and also in a particular sense, to mean a song in several stanzas with a refrain or burden (*ripresa*) sung complete at the beginning and (usually) curtailed, but often with a musical extension, after each stanza; the same music serves for both refrain and stanza.

Frühbeck de Burgos, Rafael (b Burgos, 15 Sept 1933), Spanish conductor of German parentage. Studied at Madrid and Munich. Madrid National Orchestra 1962–77. Guest conductor Philharmonia Orchestra, London. Düsseldorf SO 1966–71. US debut 1968; Washington SO from 1980. Principal conductor of the Vienna SO from 1991.

Frye, Walter (d ? Canterbury, *c* 1475), 15th-c. English composer. He is believed to have been a choral conductor at Ely Cathedral in the 1440s and later joined the London Guild of Parish Clerks. He wrote three Masses (*Flos Regalis*, *Nobilis et Pulchra* and *Summa Trinitati*), *chansons* and antiphons; his *Ave Regina Caelorum Mater Regis* was copied into 13 continental MSS and is found in three arrangements for keyboard in the ◊*Buxheimer Orgelbuch*.

Fuchs, Eugen (b Nuremberg, 3 Sept 1893; d Berlin, 3 Mar 1971), German baritone. He sang at Nuremberg, 1914–20, and after engagements at Breslau and Freiburg i/B appeared at the Berlin Staatsoper, 1930–60. Guest in London, Rome and Paris and at Bayreuth, 1933–43, was heard as Beckmesser; returned there 1956–60. CG 1937, as Alberich.

Fuchs, Marta (b Stuttgart, 1 Jan 1898; d Stuttgart, 22 Sept 1974), German soprano. Debut Aachen 1928; Dresden from 1930 in mezzo roles. She sang Kundry at Bayreuth, 1933, and returned until 1942 as Isolde and Brünnhilde. London, CG, 1936 with Dresden co. as Donna Anna, Ariadne and the Marschallin.

Fuchs, Robert (b Frauenthal, 15 Feb 1847; d Vienna, 19 Feb 1927), Austrian composer. Professor at the Vienna Conservatory 1875–1912, where Mahler, Wolf, Zemlinsky and Schreker were among his pupils. His serenades are still sometimes performed in Germany.

Works include two operas, *Die Königsbraut* (1889) and *Die Teufelsglocke* (1893); Mass; symphony in C major, five Serenades (four for strings); piano concerto; chamber music.

The exposition of Bach's fugue in A♭ major, Well-tempered Clavier, Book II, no. 17.

Fuenllana, Miguel de (b Navalcarnero, Madrid, *c* 1525; d after 1588), Spanish lutenist and vihuelist. Although blind, he became a great player, and in 1554 he pub. *Orphénica lyra*, a book of music for *vihuela* and similar instruments, including compositions of his own and many arrangements of works by Guerrero, Morales, Arcadelt, Verdelot and others.

fuga = 'flight'; = fugue; in earlier times one of the Italian terms for canon, another being caccia.

fuga ricercata ◊ricercare.

fugato Italian = 'fugued'; a passage written in the manner of a fugue, occurring merely incidentally in a composition; or a piece in fugal style that cannot be considered to be in the form of a fugue.

Fugère, Lucien (b Paris, 22 Jul 1848; d Paris, 15 Jan 1935), French baritone. Having failed as a sculptor and made a living as a commercial traveller, he appeared at the Bata-clan café-concert in Paris in 1870 with Planquette's marching-song *Le Régiment de Sambre-et-Meuse* and made his first stage appearance at the Bouffes-Parisiens in 1874. First sang at the Opéra-Comique in 1877 and continued singing until he was 80. Roles included Papageno, Leporello, Schaunard and Massenet's Don Quichotte.

fughetta Italian = 'little fugue'; unlike a *fugato*, a fughetta is formally a proper fugue, but much more condensed.

fugue a contrapuntal composition in two or more parts, based on a 'subject', short or long, which is introduced successively in imitation at the beginning and recurs in the course of the piece. The second entry of the subject, generally at a level a fifth higher or a fourth lower (but sometimes a fourth higher or a fifth lower), is called the answer. It does not necessarily imitate the subject exactly: it may be modified to preserve the tonality of the piece or to facilitate a third entry. A third entry is often deferred for a few bars, the intervening space being occupied by a codetta.

The answer is accompanied by a counterpoint which, if it also recurs in the course of the piece, is called the countersubject. After all the initial entries of the subject and answer there is generally an episode, derived from the material already heard or completely independent, leading to a further entry of the subject. The remainder of the fugue is made up of an alternation of episodes and entries, which may include treatment of the subject in canon.

A fugue may have more than one subject and more than one countersubject. It may be written for instruments or voices or for both combined and may occur as part of a large-scale work, such as a symphony, opera or oratorio.

Fuhrmann, Georg Leopold, German 16th–17th c. lutenist, engraver and bookseller. Worked at Nuremberg, where in 1615 he pub. a book of lute pieces, *Testudo Gallo-Germanica*, including some by J and R Dowland.

Fujikawa, Mayumi (b Asahigawa City, 27 Jul 1946), Japanese violinist. Studied with Leonid Kogan in Nice and has appeared worldwide from London debut in 1975; concerts with orchestras in Philadelphia, Boston, Pittsburgh and Chicago. Played the Mozart concertos with the Scottish Chamber Orchestra on BBC TV, and the Concertante K364 at the 1991 London Proms.

Fulda, Adam of (b *c* 1445; d Wittenberg, 1505), German monk, theorist and composer. Wrote a tract on music and composed motets, etc.

Fuleihan, Anis (b Kyrenia, Cyprus, 2 Apr 1900; d Stanford, CA, 11 Oct 1970), Cyprus-born American pianist and composer. Educated at the English School in Cyprus and studied music in USA, where he settled in 1915. Toured much in USA and the East, and lived at Cairo for two years. After his return to America in 1928 he conducted and composed.

Works include opera *Vasco* (1958); several ballets; symphonies, suite *Mediterranean* and *Preface to a Child's Story-Book* for orchestra, suite for chamber orchestra; three piano concertos (1936, 1937, 1963), cello concerto, two violin concertos, two symphonies (1936, 1962), concerto for Theremin, Fantasy for viola and orchestra; five string quartets (1940–65), clarinet quintet, horn quintet; sonatas for violin, viola and cello; 11 piano sonatas.

Fulkerson, James (b Streator, IL, 2 Jul 1945), American composer and

trombonist. Graduated from the University of Illinois and became a Fellow at the Center for Creative Performing Arts, Buffalo, 1969–72. Resident at Victorian College of the Arts, Melbourne, 1977–79, and at Dartington Hall, Devon, from 1981. His compositions often display his virtuosity on the trombone: *Co-ordinative Systems* 1–10 (1972–76); *Music for Brass Instruments* 1–6 (1975–78); *Vicarious Thrills* for amplified trombone and pornographic film (1979); symphony (1980); *Force Fields and Spaces* for trombone, tape and dancers (1981); *Rat's Tale* for six dancers, trombone and ensemble (1983).

Fuller, Albert (b Washington DC, 21 Jul 1926), American harpsichordist and conductor. Studied at the Peabody Conservatory and with Ralph Kirkpatrick and Hindemith at Yale. Debut recital in NY 1957, first European tour 1959; most often heard in French Baroque music and the sonatas of Scarlatti. Professor of harpsichord at Juilliard from 1964, president and artistic director of the Asta Magna Foundation (study of Baroque music) 1972–83. Has conducted Rameau's *Dardanus* (1975) and Handel's *Acis and Galatea* (NY, 1978) and *Xerxes* (1985).

Fuller-Maitland, J(ohn) A(lexander) (b London, 7 Apr 1856; d Carnforth, Lancs., 30 Mar 1936), English critic, editor and writer on music. Educated at Westminster School and Cambridge. Studied with Stanford, Dannreuther and Rockstro, became a music critic in London and was from 1889 to 1911 chief critic of *The Times*. Edited early music especially for the harpsichord, including the *Fitzwilliam Virginal Book* with W Barclay Squire, and was editor of the second edition of Grove's Dictionary. Among his books is the fourth volume of the *Oxford History of Music*.

The very people who proclaim intense dislike of fugues are likely to adore Handel's Messiah, *many of whose choruses are fugal.*

Antony Hopkins, *Downbeat Music Guide*, 1977

Füllsack, Zacharias (b *c* 1580; d Lübeck, buried 11 Jan 1621), German lutenist and trombonist. Worked at Hamburg until 1612 and later in the court chapel at Dresden. In 1607, with Christoph Hildebrand, he pub. a book of *Auserlesne Paduanen und Galliarden*, including many pieces by English composers.

Fulton, Thomas (b Memphis, 18 Sept 1949), American conductor. After study with Eugene Ormandy at the Curtis Institute, he worked in Hamburg and San Francisco. Paris Opéra debut 1979 (*Robert le Diable*). NY Met. 1981 (*Manon Lescaut*, followed by *Butterfly*, operas by Verdi, and *Billy Budd*). Conducted *Macbeth* at the Deutsche Oper Berlin (1986) and the French-language *Don Carlos* at Seattle (1993).

functional harmony ◊harmonic analysis.

fundamental bass an imaginary harmonic phenomenon expounded by Rameau. The fundamental bass is the root bass of any chord occurring in a composition, and according to Rameau no composition was aesthetically satisfying unless that bass, either actually present or implied, was in each chord used, proceeding from the one before it to the one after it in accordance with definite rules of musical logic.

funeral march ◊march.

Funeral Ode (Bach.) ◊Trauer-Ode.

furiant, Czech, a lively Czech dance in 3–4 time with a characteristic effect of cross-rhythm, often used in place of a scherzo by Dvořák and other Czech composers of the national school.

Furlanetto, Ferrucio (b Pordenone, Sicily, 16 May 1949), Italian bass. Debut as Sparafucile at Vicenza, 1974. Sang Colline in *La Bohème* at Trieste (1974) and has appeared widley in Italy in operas by Verdi (Banquo at La Scala). US debut as Zaccaria at New Orleans (1978); San Francisco 1979, as Alvise. Sang Melibeo in Haydn's *La fedeltà premiata* at Glyndebourne (1980) and Mozart's Figaro at the 1986 Salzburg Festival. He is best known as Leporello, in *Don Giovanni*, which he has sung at CG (1988), the NY Met., (1990) and at Salzburg under Karajan (also filmed).

furlong an old English name for the ◊forlana.

Furrer, Beat (b Schaffhausen, 1954), Swiss-born composer. Studied with Haubenstock-Ramati. Formed Société de l'art acoustique ensemble.

Works include music drama *Die Blinden* to texts by Rimbaud, Hölderlin and Maeterlinck (Vienna, 1989); *Risonanze* for orchestra in three groups (1988); *Face de la Chaleur* for five instrumental groups (1991); two string quartets.

Fürst, Janos (b Budapest, 1935), Hungarian conductor. Studied at the Liszt Academy, Budapest, and formed the Irish Chamber Orchestra, 1963. London debut 1972 with the RPO. Chief conductor of Malmo Orchestra 1974–78, music director Aalborg SO 1980–83. Conducted the RTE Orchestra, Dublin, 1983–89, with a Mahler series 1988–89. Opera engagements with ENO and Scottish Opera; *Elektra* at Marseilles, 1989. Music director Winterthur Municipal Orchestra, 1990; US debut with the Indianapolis SO, 1990. Recordings include the ballet *Salome*, by Maxwell Davies.

Fürstenau, Anton Bernhard (b Münster, 20 Oct 1792; d Dresden, 18 Nov 1852), German flautist and composer, one of a family of musicians. In the court orchestra at Dresden from 1820. Wrote two methods and many pieces for his instrument. He accompanied Weber to London in 1826.

Fürtwangler was once told in Berlin that the people in the back seats were complaining that they could not hear some of his soft passages. 'It does not matter', he said, 'they do not pay so much.'
Neville Cardus, *Manchester Guardian*, 1935

Furtwängler, Wilhelm (b Berlin, 25 Jan 1886; d Baden-Baden, 30 Nov 1954), German conductor and composer. Studied at Munich with Rheinberger and Schillings, and early began gaining experience as conductor of concerts and opera at Zurich, Munich, Strasbourg (where he was a deputy to Pfitzner) and Lübeck. After an engagement at Mannheim he followed Nikisch at the Leipzig Gewandhaus, and in 1922 he became conductor-in-chief of the Berlin PO. He made his London debut in 1924, NY 1925. Conducted the Vienna PO from 1924 (principal conductor 1927–28 and 1933–54). In 1934 he was obliged to resign his post, when he supported Hindemith against the attacks of Goebbels and other Nazis. He toured infrequently but with great success, including Bayreuth (1931–44) and London (CG,

1935–38, *Tristan* and *The Ring*). He won renown for his measured, spacious recreations of Beethoven, Brahms and Bruckner, but was also active on behalf of modern music: gave the fps of works by Schoenberg (Variations for Orchestra, op. 31), Bartók (1st piano concerto) and Hindemith (*Mathis der Maler* symphony). Furtwängler was also active as a composer, producing three symphonies, a piano concerto, a Te Deum and some chamber music.

Thanks to re-issues of his recordings, many taken from live performances, Furtwängler's reputation remains as high as ever; among his best recordings are the *Ring* from La Scala (1951), *Tristan* (1953), symphonies by Bruckner, Brahms and Beethoven (*Choral* from the 1951 Bayreuth Festival) and *Don Giovanni* from the 1954 Salzburg Festival (also on video, released 1995). His influence on later conductors has been considerable; Reginald Goodall and Daniel Barenboim have been avowed disciples.

Fussell, Charles C(lement) (b Winston-Salem, NC, 14 Feb 1938), American composer and conductor. Studied at the Eastman School and with Blacher in Berlin. Founded the Group for New Music at the University of Massachusetts, 1974, and has taught at Boston University from 1981. His music is largely traditional in scope and content.

Works include opera *Caligula* (1962); three symphonies (1963, 1964–67, 1978–81); *Northern Lights* for chamber orchestra (portraits of Janáček and Munch, 1979); *Virgil Thomson Sleeping* for chamber orchestra (1981); *Cymbeline*, romance for soprano, tenor and ensemble (1983); *A Song of Return* for chorus and orchestra (1989); *Wilde* two monologues for baritone and orchestra (1990); *Last Trombones* for five percussionists, two pianos and six trombones (1990).

Fux, Johann Joseph (b Hirtenfeld, Styria, 1660; d Vienna, 14 Feb 1741), Austrian theorist and composer. Became organist to the Schottenstift in Vienna in 1696, court composer 1698, second *Kapellmeister* at St Stephen's Cathedral 1705 and first in 1712, vice-*Kapellmeister* to the court 1713, *Kapellmeister* 1715. His *Gradus ad Parnassum* (1725) was for many years the standard treatise on counterpoint, and was studied by Haydn and Beethoven among others.

Works include 18 operas, e.g. *Costanza e fortezza* (1723); 11 oratorios including *Gesù Cristo negato da Pietro* (1719); 70 Masses and quantities of other church music; 38 trio sonatas; partitas, etc., for orchestra; keyboard music.

fz, abbr. for Italian *forzando*, a direction which, placed against a note or chord, indicates that it should be strongly accentuated. The more usual word is *sforzando*, marked *sf*.

G

G the fifth note, or dominant, of the scale of C major.

Gabrieli, Andrea (b Venice, c 1533; d Venice, 30 Aug 1585), Italian composer. Apparently a pupil of Lassus in Munich. Became second organist at St Mark's, Venice, in 1566 and in 1584 first organist. He was a famous teacher and had many distinguished pupils, Italian and foreign, including his nephew Giovanni ◊Gabrieli and the Germans Hassler and Aichinger; he visited Graz, Munich and Augsburg. His music makes much use of the spatial effects possible within St Mark's; vocal and instrumental groups are separated in contrasting ensembles.

Works include Masses, motets and other church music with instruments; spiritual songs; madrigals, etc. for several voices; choruses for Sophocles' *Oedipus Tyrannus*; *ricercari* for organ.

Gabrieli, Giovanni (b Venice, c 1555; d Venice, 12 Aug 1612), Italian composer, nephew of Andrea ◊Gabrieli. Pupil of his uncle, musician to the Duke of Bavaria under Lassus 1575–79; became first organist at St Mark's in Venice in 1585 in succession to Andrea Gabrieli, like whom he had many famous Italian and foreign pupils (Schütz 1609–12).

Works include church music for voices and instruments, often laid out antiphonally for choral and orchestral groups; *Sacrae symphoniae* in many vocal and instrumental parts pub. in two vols., 1597 and 1615; instrumental pieces of various kinds; organ music and madrigals.

Gabrieli Quartet British string quartet founded in 1966; members are Kenneth Sillito and Brendan O'Reilly (violins), Ian Jewel (viola) and Keith Harvey (cello). Since 1967 has given a wide repertory of works, including the fps of quartets by Alwyn, Crosse and Alan Bush. Foreign tours from 1975.

Gabrielli, Adriana, ◊Ferrarese del Bene.

Gabrielli, Catterina (b Rome, 12 Nov 1730; d Rome, 16 Feb 1796), Italian soprano. Pupil of Garcia and Porpora, made her first appearance at Vienna in 1755, and sang in Gluck's *Le cinesi*, *La danza* and *Il rè pastore*. From 1759 to 1772 sang in operas by ◊Traetta in Parma and St Petersburg.

Gabrilovich, Ossip Salomonovich (b St Petersburg, 7 Feb 1878; d Detroit, 14 Sept 1936), Russian-born American pianist, conductor and composer. Studied piano with Anton Rubinstein, later at the St Petersburg Conservatory, where Liadov and Glazunov were among his masters, and finished his piano studies with Leschetizky in Vienna, 1894–96, making his first appearance in Berlin in the latter year. He toured much in Europe and USA, married the contralto Clara Clemens, daughter of Mark Twain, in 1908 and settled in NY as an American citizen in 1914. Appointed conductor of the Detroit SO in 1918.

Works include Overture-Rhapsody for orchestra; Elegy for cello and piano; many piano pieces; songs.

Gaburo, Kenneth (b Somerville, NJ, 5 Jul 1926; d Iowa City, 26 Jan 1993), American composer. Studied at the Eastman School and with Petrassi in Rome. Professor at the University of Illinois 1955–68, and

at San Diego 1968–75. Founded and directed the Studio for Cognitive Studies at San Diego 1975–83; his music was concerned with extending verbal limits within composition, and frequently employed electronics: series of *Antiphonies* I–X (1958–89). Other works include operas *The Snow Queen* (1952), *Blur* (1956) and *The Widow* (1961); string quartet (1956); *Shapes and Sounds* for orchestra (1960); *A Dot is no Small Thing*, for orchestra (1984).

Gade, Niels Vilhelm (b Copenhagen, 22 Feb 1817; d Copenhagen, 21 Dec 1890), Danish composer. He is regarded as the most important Danish composer of the 19th c. Pupil of Berggreen, Weyse and others. He learnt various instruments and became a violinist in the royal orchestra; and having gained a composition prize with the *Ossian* overture 1841, was enabled to go to Leipzig for further study with a royal grant. There he came into touch with Mendelssohn, who produced his first symphony in 1843 and engaged him to conduct the Gewandhaus concerts in his absence. He returned to Copenhagen 1848 and worked as organist, conductor and teacher, becoming court music director 1861.

Works include opera *Mariotta* (1849); cantatas *Baldurs Drom* (1858), *Comala*, *Erl King's Daughter*, *Zion*, *The Crusaders*, *Den Bjaergtagne* (1873), *Psyche*, etc.; eight symphonies (1842–71), overtures *Echoes from Ossian*, *In the Highland*, *Hamlet* (after Shakespeare), *Michelangelo*, etc., suite *Holbergiana* for orchestra.

String quartet, quintet, string octet, piano trios and other chamber music; four violin and piano sonatas; instrumental pieces; piano sonata in E minor and pieces for piano solo and duet; songs, part-songs.

Gadski, Johanna (b Anklam, Prussia, 15 Jun 1872; d Berlin, 22 Feb 1932), German soprano. Made her first appearance in Berlin in 1889. US debut with Damrosch Co. in NY, 1895, as Elsa. NY Met. 1900–17, as Brünnhilde, Isolde and in Verdi repertory London, CG, 1898–1901, as Aida and Santuzza.

Gafori, Franchino (b Lodi, 14 Jan 1451; d Milan, 25 Jun 1522), Italian priest, composer and writer on music. *Maestro di cappella* at Monticello and Bergamo, and from 1484 attached to Milan Cathedral. Wrote several theoretical books, including *Theorica musicae* (1492) and *Practica musicae* (1496), and composed Masses and other church music. Leonardo da Vinci was among his friends.

Gage, Irwin (b Cleveland, 4 Sept 1939), American pianist. Studied at the University of Michigan and with Erik Werba in Vienna. He has appeared throughout the USA and at major European festivals as accompanist to leading singers: Hermann Prey, Jessye Norman, Lucia Popp, Dietrich Fischer-Dieskau and Peter Schreier. Teacher at the Zurich Conservatory.

Gagliano (actually *Zenobi*), Giovanni Battista da (b Gagliano near Florence, 20 Dec 1584; d Florence, 8 Jan 1651), Italian composer. Instructor at the church of San Lorenzo at Florence in 1613 in succession to his brother Marco da ◊Gagliano and later musician to the Grand Duke of Tuscany.

Works include motets, psalms and other church music.

Gagliano, Marco da (Zenobi) (b Gagliano near Florence, 1 May 1582; d Florence, 25 Feb 1643), Italian composer, brother of Giovanni Battista da ◊Gagliano. Studied organ and theorbo under Luca Bati at the church of San Lorenzo at Florence, where he became instructor in 1602 and *maestro di cappella* in 1608 and was a priest. In 1607 he founded the Accademia degl' Elevati for the cultivation of music and *c* 1610 became *maestro di cappella* to the Grand Duke of Tuscany. He was also in touch with the ducal family of Gonzaga at Mantua, where his opera *Dafne*, a setting of Rinuccini's libretto, was produced in 1608. Following Monteverdi's epoch-making *Orfeo* by one year, it also developed early operatic form, to include airs and choruses as well as recitative. He also wrote music for the wedding of the duke's son.

Works include operas *Dafne*, *La Flora*, *Il Medoro* (music lost); oratorio *La regina Santa Orsola* (1624, music lost); Masses, Offices for the Dead, *Sacrae cantiones*; madrigals.

gagliarda Italian = ◊galliard.

Gailhard, Pierre (b Toulouse, 1 Aug 1848; d Paris, 12 Oct 1918), French baritone. Studied at the Toulouse and Paris Conservatories and made his first appearance 1867 as Thomas' Falstaff, at the Opéra-Comique. He first appeared in London 1879, and until 1883 his roles included Osmin and Méphistophélès. He was joint manager of the Opéra 1884–91, 1893–99 and 1900–05 and sole manager 1899–1900 and 1905–08. Responsible for several French fps of Wagner's operas.

gaillarde ◊galliard.

galant French and German = 'courtly'; an adj. used to designate a special musical style of the 18th c., especially that of C P E Bach and the Mannheim school. Its main characteristics are elegance, a certain restraint of feeling, formality (often using sonata form), and the abandonment of Baroque counterpoint in favour of a distinct division between melody and accompaniment.

galanteries, French, or *Galanterien* (German) = lit. 'courtesies'; the extra dances or other pieces added to those which were normal in the Baroque suite or partita (◊allemande, ◊courante, ◊sarabande and ◊gigue). The most frequently used galanteries were ◊bourrées, ◊minuets, ◊passepieds, ◊chaconnes and, among pieces other than dances, airs.

Galeffi, Carlo (b Malamocco, near Venice, 4 Jun 1884; d Rome, 22 Sept 1961), Italian baritone. Debut Rome 1903, Enrico. He was soon heard in Naples, as Amonasro and Rigoletto, and sang Posa at La Scala in 1912; remained until 1938, as Nabucco, Germont, Luna, often under Toscanini, and in the fps of Boito's *Nerone* and *L'amore dei tre re*. NY Met. debut 1910, as Germont; the following year took part in the fp of Mascagni's *Isabeau*, at Buenos Aires. Other roles included Amfortas and Boccanegra.

Galilei, Vincenzo (b Santa Maria in Monte near Florence, *c* 1520; d Florence, buried 2 Jul 1591), Italian composer, lutenist and theorist. Studied under Zarlino at Venice. He took part in the discussions which, after his death, helped transform the Florentine *camerata* into opera; he also wrote theoretical books. Galilei upheld Greek drama against the contemporary madrigal, becoming involved in contro-

Pavane

Galliard

This galliard by Byrd opens with a melody related to the pavane also shown here.

Gál, Hans (b Brunn, near Vienna, 5 Aug 1890; d Edinburgh, 3 Oct 1987), Austrian composer and musicologist. Pupil of Mandyczewski in Vienna and lecturer at the University there from 1918; later director of the Music Academy at Mainz. After the *Anschluss* he took refuge at Edinburgh, where he was lecturer at the University 1945–57.

Works include operas *Der Fischer*, *Der Arzt der Sobeide* (1919), *Ruth*, *Die heilige Ente* (1923), *Das Lied der Nacht* (1926), *Die beiden Klaus*, *Der Zauberspiegel*; *Requiem für Mignon* (from Goethe's *Wilhelm Meister*, 1923) for chorus and orchestra, and other choral works; *Sinfonietta*, *Ballet Suite*, *Pickwickian Overture* (after Dickens), etc. for orchestra; serenade for strings; piano concerto, violin concerto; four string quartets (1916–71), five Intermezzi for string quartet, serenade for string trio; piano works.

Galamian, Ivan (Alexander) (b Tabriz, 23 Jan 1903; d New York, 14 Apr 1981), Iranian-born American violinist. Studied in Moscow and Paris and made his debut in Paris, 1924. Taught in Paris until 1939, then moved to New York and from 1946 taught at Juilliard and the Curtis Institute, Philadelphia. Among his most distinguished pupils were Kyung-Wha Chung, Miriam Fried, Jaime Laredo, Pinchas Zukerman and Itzhak Perlman. He wrote on violin technique.

versy with Zarlino. He was the father of the astronomer Galileo Galilei.

Works include cantata *Il Conte Ugolino* from Dante, a setting of the Lamentations of Jeremiah (both lost, and both among the earliest music for a single voice with accompaniment); two books of madrigals; pieces for two viols; a lute book in tablature; *Dialogo della musica antica et della moderna* (1581).

For all the height of excellence of the practical music of the moderns, there is not heard or seen today the slightest sign of its accomplishing what ancient music accomplished.

Vincenzo Galilei, *Dialogo della musica antica e della moderna*, 1581

---

galimat(h)ias French = 'gallimaufry, farrago, gibberish'; in music the term is found in Mozart's *Galimathias musicum* (K32) written by him at The Hague in 1766, at age of ten, for the coming of age of William of Orange. It contains the Dutch national air 'Wilhelmus van Nassouwe'.

Gall, Jeffrey (b Cleveland, 19 Sept 1950), American countertenor. Studied at Princeton and Yale and was a member of the Waverley Consort 1974–78. Debut at the Brooklyn Academy, in Cavalli's *Erismena*, and sang in Europe from 1980 (La Scala, Edinburgh, Venice and Naples). US engagements at Chicago and Santa Fe (1986) and the NY Met. 1988 as Tolomeo in *Giulio Cesare*; returned 1994, in *Death in Venice*; Ruggiero in *Orlando* at San Francisco, 1989; Polinesso in *Ariodante* at Philadelphia. Featured in the title role of the Peter Sellars version of *Giulio Cesare*; has also sung in operas by Jommelli (La Scala), Lully, Cesti and Purcell.

Gall, Yvonne (b Paris, 6 Mar 1885; d Paris, 21 Aug 1972), French soprano. Debut Paris, Opéra, 1908 as Woglinde in *Götterdämmerung*; returned until 1935 and sang at the Opéra-Comique, 1921–34. In 1922 she was Daphné in the fp of Busser's *Les noces corinthiennes*. Chicago from 1918, including Ravel's Concepcion in 1920. CG 1924, as Tosca. Other roles included Rossini's Mathilde and Rameau's Phebé.

Gallenberg, Wenzel (Robert) von, Count (b Vienna, 28 Dec 1783; d Rome, 13 Mar 1839), Austrian composer. Studied with Albrechtsberger and married Countess Giulietta Guicciardi, a pupil of Beethoven.

Works include *c* 50 ballets, e.g. *Wilhelm Tell* (1810), *Jeanne d'Arc* (1821), three overtures, eight pieces for wind band, dances for orchestra and for piano, contributions to periodical publications.

Galli, Antonius (b Vienna, 2 Apr 1565), Flemish 16th-c. composer, active in Bruges, 1544–50. Wrote much church music and a few *chansons*.

Galli, Caterina (b *c* 1723; d London, 1804), Italian mezzo-soprano. Lived in London from *c* 1742, and sang leading parts in several of Handel's oratorios, including *Joshua*, *Susanna*, *Solomon*, *Theodora* and *Jephtha*.

Galli, Filippo (b Rome, 1783; d Paris, 3 Jun 1853), Italian bass, at first a tenor. Made his first appearance as a tenor at Bologna in 1804 and as a bass at Venice in 1812. He created roles in Rossini's *L'inganno felice*, *L'italiana in Algeri*, *Maometto II* and *Semiramide*.

galliard, English, from French *gaillarde* and Italian *gagliarda*, a sprightly dance dating from the early 16th c., originally in 3–2 time but later also in 2–2 time; often used in music as a contrast to the pavan and frequently based on the same musical material.

Galliard, Johann Ernst (John Ernest) (b Celle, *c* 1680; d London, 1749), anglicized oboist and composer of French-German origin. Pupil of J B Farinelli and Steffani, settled in England *c* 1706 as oboist to Prince George of Denmark. Later active as a composer, especially for the theatre, and also translated Tosi's treatise on singing under the title *Observations on the Florid Song* (1742).

Works include operas *Calypso and Telemachus* (1712), *Pan and Syrinx* (1718) and *Oreste e Pilade* (unfinished); several pantomimes and other stage entertainments; choruses for the Earl of Buckingham's *Julius Caesar*; *The Hymn of Adam and Eve* from Milton's *Paradise Lost*; church music; instrumental music, including piece for 24 bassoons and four double basses.

Gallican Chant the Provençal plainsong in use in France until the introduction of the Roman ritual in the 8th c.

Galliculus (? *Hähnel*, *Hähnlein*), Joannes, German 16th-c. theorist and composer, pupil of Isaac. Worked at Leipzig as a teacher, 1520–50; wrote a theoretical work *Isagoge* (later *Libellus*) *de compositione cantus* and composed a Passion according to St Mark, two Magnificats, a psalm, liturgical works for Easter and Christmas.

Galli-Curci, Amelita (b Milan, 18 Nov 1882; d La Jolla, CA, 26 Nov 1963), Italian soprano. Studied piano at Milan Conservatory but mainly self-taught as a singer. She made her debut at Trani in 1906. Joined the Chicago Opera Co. in 1916, when she sang Gilda, and sang subsequently in NY (Met. debut 1921, Violetta). Other US roles included Rosina, Lakmé, Manon, Lucia and Dinorah. Concert tours in England from 1924. She retired through illness in 1930.

Galli-Marié, Marie (Célestine Laurence) (b Paris, Nov 1840; d Vence

near Nice, 22 Sept 1905), French mezzo-soprano. Pupil of her father; made her first appearance at Strasbourg in 1859. She was the first Mignon (A Thomas) and Carmen.

Gallus, Jacobus, ◊Handl.

Gallus, Johannes (Jehan Le Cocq), Franco-Flemish 16th-c. composer, not to be confused with ◊Handl (Jacobus Gallus). Wrote *chansons*.

galop French = 'gallop'; a quick ballroom dance in 2–4 time, a variant of the ◊polka, first appearing under that name in Paris in 1829, but of older German origin, its German name (now *Galopp*) having been *Hopser* 'hopper' or *Rutscher* 'glider'.

galoubet, Provençal, a small wind instrument, the pipe used with the accompanying tabor (French *tambourin*).

Brave Galuppi! that was music! good alike at grave and gay!/I can always leave off talking when I hear a master play.
Robert Browning, *A Toccata of Galuppi's*, 1855

Galuppi, Baldassare (b Burano, near Venice, 18 Oct 1706; d Venice, 3 Jan 1785), Italian composer. Pupil of his father and later, after the failure of his first opera in 1722, of Lotti in Venice. His operatic career proper began in 1728, after which he composed a vast quantity of works. His *opere serie* met with indifferent success, but his comic operas are notable, especially those on libretti by Goldoni, the most famous being *Il filosofo di campagna* (1754). Visited London 1741–43, where he produced several operas. Appointed Second *maestro di cappella* at St Mark's, Venice, 1748; first *maestro* and Director of the Ospitale degl' Incurabili, 1762. Director of Catherine the Great's chapel at St Petersburg 1765–68, writing new operas and Russian sacred music. Thereafter composed few operas and devoted himself chiefly to oratorios for the Incurabili.

Works include operas *Alessandro nell' Indie* (1738), *L'Olympiade*, *L'Arcadia in Brenta* (1749), *Il Conte Caramella*, *Il mondo della luna* (1750), *Il mondo alla roversa*, *La calamità de cuori*, *Il filosofo di campagna*, *Le nozze* (1755), *L'amante di tutte*, *Le tre amanti ridicoli*, *Il Marchese Villano* (1762), *Ifigenia in Tauride* (1768), etc. (over 90 in all); 27 oratorios; church music; instrumental music.

Galway, James (b Belfast, 8 Dec 1939), Irish flautist. He studied in London and with Jean-Pierre Rampal in Paris. Flautist with SW, then BBC SO, from 1960; principal flautist RPO and LSO. Berlin PO

Galway *The flautist James Galway, more than any other musician, has popularized his instrument through a blend of virtuosity and careful choice of popular tunes. He has transcribed for his own performance several works which were originally written for other instruments.*

1969–75, under Karajan. Solo career from 1975; a popular performer on TV with his 18-carat gold flute. He arranged Vivaldi's *Four Seasons* for his instrument and pub. an autobiography in 1979.

gamba, abbr., ◊viola da gamba.

Gamba, Piero (b Rome, 16 Sept 1937), Italian conductor. Conducted Beethoven in Rome aged eight; toured Europe and the Americas and gave a concert of music by Beethoven and Dvořák in London, 1948. Often led the London SO 1959–63 and recorded the Beethoven concertos with Julius Katchen. Music director Winnipeg SO 1970–81, Adelaide SO 1982–87.

Gambill, Robert (b Indianapolis, IA, 31 Mar 1955), American tenor. Studied in Hamburg and made his debut at Geneva in 1977 as the Count of Lerma (*Don Carlos*). Also Milan, 1981, as Michael in the fp of Stockhausen's *Donnerstag aus Licht*. Sang at Frankfurt and Wiesbaden, then Glyndebourne 1982–85, as Rossini's Almaviva and Don Ramiro. Venice 1983 as Mozart's Ferrando, Aix 1984 as Lindoro, and Wagner's Steersman at the NY Met., 1990. Vienna 1988 in a revival of Schubert's *Fierabras*, under Abbado, and David in *Die Meistersinger* at CG, 1990.

Gambler, The, *Igrok*, opera in four acts by Prokofiev (libretto by composer, after the story by Dostoievsky); composed 1915–17, revised 1928, produced Brussels, 29 Apr 1929; planned for performance in St Petersburg, 1917, but cancelled at the outbreak of the Revolution. Orchestral Suite *Portraits*, op. 49, in four movements; fp Paris, 12 Mar 1932. Alexey, in love with Pauline, ruins himself for her sake. He takes to gambling and makes a fortune, but she rejects him.

gamma Greek = letter γ; the name of the lowest note of the musical scale known to medieval theory, G on the bottom line of the bass stave. Where the hexachord was based on it, it received the name of 'gamma-ut' (hence ◊'gamut'), and in France the name of the scale is still *gamme*.

gamut old English term for the scale or key of G, whether major or minor, and hence for a scale or range in general. ◊hexachord, ◊solmization.

The lowest note of the gamut.

gamut-way a 17th-c. term for music written in ordinary notation, as distinct from tablature.

Ganassi, Silvestro di (b Fontego, near Venice, 1492; d Venice), Italian theorist, who pub. tutors for the recorder, including *Opera Intitulata Fontegara* (1535), and the viol (*Regola Rubertina*, 1542).

Ganne, (Gustave) Louis (b Buxière-les-Mines, Allier, 5 Apr 1862; d Paris, 14 Jul 1923), French composer. Pupil of Dubois and Franck. He conducted the Opéra balls in Paris and orchestras at Royan and Monte Carlo, and became very popular as a composer of ballets and operettas.

Works include operettas *Rabelais*, *Les Colles des femmes*, *Les Saltimbanques* (1899) and *Hans le joueur de flûte* (1906); ballet *La Source du Nil* and several others; popular songs including *La Marche Lorraine* and *Le Père la Victoire*; dances *La Tsarine*.

Gänsbacher, Johann (b Sterzing, Tyrol, 8 May 1778; d Vienna, 13 Jul 1844), Austrian composer. Pupil of Vogler and Albrechtsberger. Became *Kapellmeister* of St Stephen's Cathedral in Vienna, 1823.

Works include incidental music to Kotzebue's *Die Kreuzfahrer*; 35 Masses, eight Requiems and other church music; a symphony; piano music, songs.

Ganz, Rudolf (b 24 Feb 1877; d Chicago, 2 Aug 1972), Swiss-born American pianist and conductor. Studied with Busoni in Berlin and made his debut there in 1899, with the Emperor Concerto and Chopin's First. He moved to the USA 1901 and became music director of the St Louis SO 1921–27, director of the Chicago Musical College 1929–54. Conducted the NY PO's Young People's Concerts 1938–49, and in other concerts championed the work of contemporary European composers. Among his own works were a symphony (premiered with the Berlin PO in 1900) and a piano concerto (1941).

gapped scales any scales containing less than seven notes, e.g. the pentatonic scale, which has five.

Garbin, Edoardo (b Padua, 12 Mar 1865; d Brescia, 12 Apr 1943), Italian tenor. Debut Vicenza 1891, as Alvaro. He sang in Milan from 1893; created Fenton, in *Falstaff*, and in 1900 was heard in the fp of Leoncavallo's *Zazà*, under Toscanini. Guest in Vienna, Berlin and Barcelona; CG 1908. Often appeared with his wife, Adelina Stehle, the first Nannetta.

García Spanish family of singers:

1. Manuel (del Popolo Vicente) García (b Seville, 21 Jan 1775; d Paris, 9 Jun 1832), tenor, teacher and composer. Was a chorister at Seville Cathedral and became well known as singer, conductor and composer in his teens. In 1808 he made his first appearance in Paris and in 1811 in Italy. At Naples he composed an opera, *Il Califfo di Bagdad*, not the first of a number of works for the stage. In 1816 he created Almaviva in *Il Barbiere di Siviglia*. He now sang much in Paris and London, in operas by Rossini and Mozart, and in 1825, took the first Italian opera co., including himself, his son (2) and elder daughter (3), to NY, where they performed in *Don Giovanni*. In 1826–28 was in Mexico.

2. Manuel (Patricio Rodríguez) García (b Madrid, 17 Mar 1805; d London, 1 Jul 1906), singing teacher, son of 1. Pupil of his father and of Fétis in music theory. He appeared early in opera, but in 1829 retired to devote himself to teaching only. Appointed professor at the Paris Conservatory 1842 and at the RAM in London in 1848, where he remained to the end of his long life, retiring 1895. He was the inventor of the laryngoscope.

3. Maria Felicità García (b Paris, 24 Mar 1808; d Manchester, 23 Sept 1836), daughter of 1. ◊Malibran.

4. (Michelle Ferdinande) Pauline García (b Paris, 18 Jul 1821; d Paris, 17–18 May 1910), daughter of 1. ◊Viardot-Garcia.

5. Gustave García (b Milan, 1 Feb 1837; d London, 15 Jun 1925), baritone, son of 2. Appeared as an opera singer in London and then sang at Milan, but settled in London as teacher, at the RAM from 1880 and was professor at the RCM from 1883.

Garcia, José Maurício Nunes (b Rio de Janeiro, 20 Sept 1767; d Rio de Janeiro, 23 Mar 1830), Brazilian composer. He directed the Rio Cathedral from 1798 and composed about 20 Masses, the later ones being influenced by Italian opera. His brilliant Requiem of 1816 established his reputation throughout South America.

Gardane, Antonio (b southern France, 1509; d Venice, 28 Oct 1569), Italian music printer, established at Venice from 1538. His sons Cipriano and Annibale continued the business, as well as two other relatives, Angelo and Alessandro Gardane, until 1619.

Gardelli, Lamberto (b Venice, 8 Nov 1915), Italian conductor. He studied in Pesaro and was assistant to Serafin in Rome; debut there 1944, *La Traviata*. Swedish Opera, Stockholm, 1946–55. 1955–61 Danish Radio SO and conducted opera in Budapest and Berlin. Glyndebourne 1964–68, *Macbeth* and *Anna Bolena*. NY Met. 1966, *Andrea Chénier*. Regular at CG since 1969; debut with *Otello*; *Norma* 1980. Bavarian Radio SO from 1983. Budapest Opera 1990–92, *La Forza del Destino* and Rossini's *Moïse*.

Garden, Mary (b Aberdeen, 20 Feb 1877; d Inverurie, 3 Jan 1967), Scottish soprano. Went to America as a child and first studied singing in Chicago. In 1895 she went to Paris, where she continued her studies under various teachers, making her debut in 1900 as Charpentier's Louise. She created the roles of Debussy's Mélisande in 1902 and Massenet's Chérubin in 1905. Other roles included Juliette, Ophelia, Carmen and Salome. In 1910 she joined the Chicago Opera and was its director 1921–22.

Garden of Fand, The symphonic poem by Bax, composed 1913, fp Chicago, 29 Oct 1920. (Fand is a heroine of Irish legend, but in this work the garden of Fand is simply the sea, charged with Irish legendry.)

Gardiner, H(enry) Balfour (b London, 7 Nov 1877; d Salisbury, 28 Jun 1950), English composer. Educated at Charterhouse School and Oxford, and studied music under Knorr at Frankfurt. Became music master at Winchester College for a short time, then devoted himself to

Gardiner *The conductor John Eliot Gardiner has been highly successful in bringing to life on period instruments the vocal compositions, whether well-known or obscure, of past centuries. He has won several awards for his work, which is marked by rhythmic vitality and high scholarly standards.*

composition. Financed and conducted series of concerts at Queen's Hall, 1912–13, including early performances of works by British contemporaries, including the fp of *The Planets*.

Works include *News from Wydah* (Masefield) for chorus and orchestra (1912); symphony in D, *English Dance*, Fantasy and *Shepherd Fennel's Dance* (after Hardy) for orchestra; string quartet, string quintet (1905) and other chamber music; *Noel*, five pieces, etc. for piano; part-songs.

Gardiner, John Eliot (b Fontmell Magna, Dorset, 20 Apr 1943), English conductor. He founded the Monteverdi Choir while still at Cambridge and gave the Monteverdi Vespers in his own edition at the Prom Concerts, London, in 1968; founded Monteverdi Orchestra the same year and later the English Baroque Soloists. He conducted Gluck's *Iphigénie en Tauride* at CG in 1973 and in 1975 gave in London a concert performance of Rameau's opera *Les Boréades*, the MS of which he had discovered in Paris; first stage production Aix, 1982. Artistic director Handel Festival, Göttingen, 1981–90; music director Lyons Opera 1983–88. Salzburg debut 1990, Monteverdi's *Orfeo*. Principal conductor North German Radio Orchestra (Hamburg) from 1991. Founded the Orchestre Révolutionnaire et Romantique (1990) and with it gave the first modern performance of Berlioz's early Mass of 1824 (1993). With the English Baroque Soloists he has toured Europe with the operas of Mozart and Monteverdi's *Poppea*. His conducting is characterized by buoyant rhythms, clarity of line and scrupulous regard for textual accuracy.

Gardiner, William (b Leicester, 15 Mar 1770; d Leicester, 16 Nov 1853), English hosiery manufacturer, music amateur, writer and editor. Admirer of Haydn, to whom he sent six pairs of silk stockings with themes from Haydn's works woven into them. He adapted to English words music by Haydn, Mozart and Beethoven.

Gardner, Jake (b Oneonta, NY, 14 Nov 1947), American baritone. Sang Valentin at Houston 1975 and created James Stewart in Musgrave's *Mary, Queen of Scots* at Edinburgh, 1977. Boston Opera 1979, in the US fp of Tippett's *The Ice Break* and sang Escamillo in Peter Brook's version of *Carmen* throughout Europe and at Lincoln Center, NY. Principal baritone at Cologne Opera from 1989, Glyndebourne debut 1991, as Guglielmo. Weill/Grosz concert at the 1993 London Proms.

Gardner, John (Linton) (b Manchester, 2 Mar 1917), English composer. Educated at Wellington and Oxford, became music master at Repton School in 1939, and after doing war service was appointed coach at CG, London. Chamber music of his was heard in London and Paris in the 1930s, but his first great success was the performance of the first symphony at the Cheltenham Festival of 1951. Taught at Morley College 1952–76. CBE 1976.

Works include operas *The Moon and Sixpence* (after Somerset Maugham, 1957) and *Tobermory* (1977); symphony and Variations on a Waltz by Nielsen for orchestra (1952); piano concerto (1957), *An English Ballad* for orchestra (1969); Mass in C (1965), *Cantata for Easter* (1970); string quartet (1939), oboe quintet; two piano sonatas; *Intermezzo* for organ; songs.

Garland for the Queen a set of songs for mixed voices dedicated to Queen Elizabeth II on her coronation in 1953, with contributions by Bax, Berkeley, Bliss, Finzi, Howells, Ireland, Rawsthorne, Rubbra, Tippett and Vaughan Williams.

Garlandia, Johannes de, 13th-c. scholar and writer on music. Taught at the University of Paris. His two treatises on plainsong and mensural music (*c* 1240), were among the most influential writings of their time.

Garrard, Don (b Vancouver, 31 Jul 1929), Canadian bass. He sang Don Giovanni for Canadian TV and in 1961 was heard at SW, London; roles with the co. (later ENO) have been Silva, Attila, Sarastro and the Wanderer. Glyndebourne from 1965 as Gremin, Trulove and Arkel; CG debut 1970. He has sung widely as guest in North America and Europe. Sang King Mark in *Tristan* at Cape Town, 1992.

Garrett, Lesley (b Thorne, Doncaster, 10 Apr 1955), English soprano. Studied at the RAM and made debut with ENO 1980, as Alice in *Le Comte Ory*. Wexford Festival 1980–81, in Handel's *Orlando* and as Mozart's Zaide. Has sung Zerlina and Despina with GTO and at Glyndebourne (from 1984), Mozart's Servilia at Geneva and a Schoenberg cabaret in Paris. ENO from 1984, as Bella in *The Midsummer Marriage*, Janáček's Vixen and Susanna. Her recordings include *Diva* and *Primadonna*.

Garrigues, Malwina (b Copenhagen, 7 Dec 1825; d Karlsruhe, 8 Feb 1904), German soprano. Was engaged for the Opera at Karlsruhe, where she met the tenor Ludwig Schnorr von Carolsfeld, whom she married. In 1860 they were engaged by the Dresden Court Opera. In 1865 she was Wagner's first Isolde in the Munich production of *Tristan und Isolde*, to the Tristan of her husband, who died the following month.

Garsi, Santino (b 22 Feb 1542; d Parma, ? 17 Jan 1604), Italian composer, lute-player at the court of Parma from 1594 until his death. Wrote dance music for lute.

Gascongne, Matthieu, French 16th-c. composer, priest in the diocese of Cambrai; he is mentioned in a document of 1518. Wrote numerous Masses, including one on de la Rue's *Pourquoi non*, motets and *chansons*.

Gasdia, Cecilia (b Verona, 14 Aug 1960), Italian soprano. Debut Florence, 1982, as Bellini's Giulietta. La Scala from 1982, as Anna Bolena and Elena in *La Donna del lago*; Paris Opéra debut 1983, as Anais in Rossini's *Moïse*. US debut Philadelphia, 1984, as Gilda, NY Met. 1986 as Gounod's Juliette, and Nedda in *Pagliacci* at the 1993 Verona Arena. Other roles include Verdi's Hélène, in *Jerusalem*, Violetta and Mimi. Recordings include Rossini's *Armida* (title role).

One yearns unspeakably for a composer who gives out his pair of honest themes, and then develops them unashamed, and then hangs out a brisk coda to them, and then shuts up.

H L Mencken, *Huneker in Motley,* 1914

Gaspard de la Nuit three poems for piano by Ravel after Aloysius Bertrand; 1908, fp Paris, 9 Jan 1909. The movements are *Ondine, Le Gibet* and *Scarbo*.

Gasparini, Francesco (b Camaiore near Lucca, 5 Mar 1668; d Rome, 22 Mar 1727), Italian composer. Pupil of Corelli and Pasquini; choirmaster at the Ospedale della Pietà, Venice; appointed *maestro di cappella* of St John Lateran, Rome, 1725. Author of *L'armonico pratico al cimbalo* (1708).

Works include 61 operas, e.g. *Il più fedel fra i vassalli, La fede* tradita e vendicata (1704), *Ambleto* (on Shakespeare's *Hamlet*, 1705); oratorios *Mosè liberato dal Nilo*, *La nascita di Cristo* and *Le nozze di Tobia* (1724); church music; cantatas.

Gasparini, Quirino (b Bergamo, 1721; d Turin, 30 Sept 1778), Italian cellist and composer, pupil of Padre Martini in Bologna. Worked at Turin, Brescia, Venice and Bergamo, and was *maestro di cappella* at Turin cathedral from 1760.

Works include operas *Artaserse* (1756) and *Mitridate* (1767), instrumental music, church music.

Gassenhauer German = lit. 'street-beater'; a 16th-c. term for a popular dance, which was very soon used to mean a popular song. It survived till the 20th c. The modern term is *Schlager*.

Gassmann, Florian Leopold (b Brüx, 3 May 1729; d Vienna, 20 Jan 1774), Bohemian composer, pupil of Padre Martini in Bologna. Settled in Vienna as a ballet composer 1763. In 1771 he was instrumental in founding the *Tonkünstlersocietät* (Vienna's first music society). Appointed court *Kapellmeister* in succession to Reutter in 1772. His hilarious *L'opera seria* (1769), a satire on contemporary operatic practices, was revived in Berlin, 1994.

Works include 25 operas, e.g. *Gli uccellatori* (1759), *L'amore artigiano*, *La notte critica* (1768), *La contessina*; oratorio, *La Betulia liberata* (1772); over 50 symphonies; much church music; chamber music.

Gast, Peter (actually ***Johann Heinrich Köselitz***) (b Annaberg, 10 Jan 1854; d Annaberg, 15 Aug 1918), German composer. Studied at the Leipzig Conservatory and later went to Basel as a friend and disciple of Nietzsche, some of whose compositions he revised. Afterwards he lived at Venice and Weimar.

Works include operas *Wilbram* (1879), *Orpheus und Dionysos*, *König Wenzel*, *Die heimliche Ehe* (based on the libretto of Cimarosa's *Matrimonio segreto* and farther back on Colman and Garrick's *Clandestine Marriage*, 1891); festival play *Walpurgis* (1903), *Hosanna* for chorus and orchestra; symphonies, symphonic poem *Helle Nächte* and other orchestral works; string quartet, septet, songs.

'Gastein' Symphony a symphony in C major, supposed to have been written by Schubert during a visit to Gastein in Autumn 1825, of which no trace is left. It has been suggested that it is identical with the Grand Duo for piano duet, op. 140, but recent views identify it as the 'Great' C major symphony. It must therefore have been composed in 1825, not, as previously thought, in 1828.

Gastoldi, Giovanni Giacomo (b Caravaggio, *c* 1550; d 1622), Italian composer. *Maestro di cappella* at the church of Santa Barbara at Mantua from 1592 until 1608; then choirmaster at Milan Cathedral.

Works include a Magnificat and other church music; madrigals; *canzoni* and *balletti* for voices and instruments (those of 1591 influenced Morley and Weelkes).

Gatti, Daniele (b Milan, 1962), Italian conductor. Studied in Milan and made his debut there 1982, with Verdi's *Giovanna d'Arco*; La Scala debut 1988 (*L'Occasione fa il ladro*); Pesaro Festival 1989, with Rossini's *Bianca e Falliero*. US debut Chicago 1991 (*Madama*

Gaultier the name of several French lutenists of the 17th c.:

1. Ennemond Gaultier (b ? Lyons, *c* 1575; d Villette, Dauphiné, 11 Dec 1651), taught Queen Marie de' Medici and Richelieu. Wrote lute pieces.

2. Jacques Gaultier, ? unrelated to 1. Fled to London, *c* 1617 and was attached to the court until 1647. Visited Holland and Spain and composed lute pieces and songs.

3. Denis Gaultier (b ? Marseilles, *c* 1603; d Paris, 1672), nephew or cousin of 1. Wrote a large number of lute pieces.

4. Pierre Gaultier (b Orléans; d after 1638), ? unrelated to 3. He was in Rome in 1638 and pub. lute pieces there.

Gavazzeni, Gianandrea (b Bergamo, 27 Jul 1909; d Milan, 5 Feb 1996), Italian conductor and composer. Studied in Rome and Milan, and later became a composer. Pupil of Pizzetti and Pilati. He has also been active as a conductor and a critic; he conducted *Anna Bolena* at Glyndebourne in 1965. Music director, La Scala, 1965–68. US debut Chicago 1957, *La Bohème*; NY Met. 1976, *Il trovatore*.

Works include opera *Paolo e Virginia* (after Saint-Pierre, 1935); oratorio *Canti per Sant' Alessandro* (1934); choral triptych; Symphonic Prelude, *Three Episodes*, etc. for orchestra; concertos for violin and for cello; chamber music.

Gaveau, Étienne (b Paris, 7 Oct 1872; d Paris, 26 May 1943), French piano manufacturer. Followed his father Joseph Gaveau (1824–1903) and built a factory at Fontenay-sous-Bois in 1896 and a concert hall (Salle Gaveau) in Paris in 1907.

Gaveaux, Pierre (b Béziers, 9 Oct 1760; d Paris, 5 Feb 1825), French composer and tenor. Pupil of Beck at Bordeaux, where he first appeared as an opera singer; he then moved to Paris, where he was well known as a singer from *c* 1790.

Works include operas *Les Deux Suisses* (1792), *La Famille indigente*, *Le Petit Matelot* (1796), *Léonore, ou L'Amour conjugal* (1798, based on the same libretto of Bouilly used by Beethoven for *Fidelio*), *Un Quart-d'heure de silence*, *Le Bouffe et le tailleur*, *Monsieur Deschalumeaux* (1806), *L'Enfant prodigue*; revolutionary hymn *Le Réveil du peuple*; Italian canzonets and French romances for voice and piano.

Gaviniès, Pierre (b Bordeaux, 11 May 1728; d Paris, 8 Sept 1800), French violinist and composer. Made his first appearance in Paris in 1741, at the Concert spirituel, of which he was conductor 1773–77. Professor of violin at the Conservatory from its foundation in 1795.

Works include opera *Le Prétendu* (1760); violin concertos; sonatas for violin and bass, violin and piano, two violins and unaccompanied violin, violin studies *Les Vingt-quatre Matinées*, violin pieces including the *Romance de G*.

gavotte, French, a French dance in moderately animated 2–2 time, generally beginning on the second beat, in two sections, each of which is repeated, the first ending usually in the dominant.

It often occurs in 18th-c. suites, but is not a necessary constituent of them. It may have an alternative or trio section, sometimes in the character of a ♭musette.

The opening of Bach's gavotte from his *French Suite, No. 5.*

Butterfly); CG 1992 (*I Puritani*, returning with the house premiere of Verdi's *Due Foscari*, 1995). Concerts with the LPO, Cleveland Orchestra and Boston and Chicago SOs. Music director of the Royal PO, London, from 1995. Conducted *Butterfly* at the NY Met., 1995.

Gaudentios 2nd-c. AD Greek theorist, the first to formulate a system of eight *tonoi* (modes in the scalic sense) based on the idea of joining the interval of a fourth to that of a fifth with one note common to both.

Gavrilov, Andrei (b Moscow, 21 Sept 1955), Russian pianist. In 1974 he won the Tchaikovsky Competition, Moscow. British debut 1976, and has since appeared with all the leading London orchestras. NY debut Apr 1985. He is widely admired in Bach, Chopin, Prokofiev and Ravel. After defecting from Russia he decided to return in 1986, under an agreement in which he was allowed artistic freedom.

Gawain opera in two acts by Harrison Birtwistle (libretto by D Harsent

Gavrilov *The pianist Andrei Gavrilov. Since winning the 1974 Tchaikovsky Competition he has concentrated on the Romantic repertory, to which his powerful technique is well-suited. He also supports Russian music, playing Skriabin, Prokofiev and Tchaikovsky; he has recorded the Shostakovich violin sonata with Gidon Kremer.*

after the anonymous medieval poem *Sir Gawain and the Green Knight*), produced London, CG, 30 May 1991.

Gawriloff, Saschko (b Leipzig, 20 Oct 1929), German violinist. Studied in Leipzig and Berlin and was leader of major orchestras in Germany, 1945–66. Has appeared throughout Europe and in Japan with modern repertory (Berg Concerto with Boulez); premieres of works by Maderna and Schnittke. Formed a trio with Klaus Storck and Alfons Kontarsky in 1971. Succeeded Max Rostal as teacher at the Cologne Musikhochschule. Recorded the concerto by Ligeti, under Boulez, 1994.

Gay, John (1685–1732), English poet and playwright. ◊Acis and Galatea (Handel); ◊Beggar's Opera, ◊Busby (odes); ◊Dreigroschenoper (Weill); ◊Polly.

Music might tame and civilize wild beasts, but 'tis evident it never yet could tame and civilize musicians.
John Gay, *Polly*, 1729

Gay, Maria (b Barcelona, 13 Jul 1879; d New York, 29 Jul 1943), Spanish mezzo-soprano. Studied sculpture and violin as a girl, but was self-taught in singing. In 1902 Pugno engaged her to sing at his and Ysaÿe's concerts in Brussels and she appeared as Carmen at the Théâtre de la Monnaie at five days' notice. English debut in 1906. In 1913 she married the tenor Giovanni Zenatello. Roles included Carmen, Dalila and Amneris.

Gayarre, Julián (b Valle de Roncal, 9 Jan 1844; d Madrid, 2 Jan 1890), Spanish tenor. Debut Varese 1867, as Nemorino. London, CG, 1877–87 as Fernando in *La Favorite*, Glinka's Sobinin (1887) and Faust. He created Enzo in *La Gioconda* (Milan, 1876) and Marcello in the posthumous 1882 premiere of Donizetti's *Il duca d'Alba* (Rome). Retired 1889.

Gayer, Catherine (b Los Angeles, 11 Feb 1937), American soprano. After study in San Francisco and Berlin her debut was in the fp of Nono's *Intolleranza 60* (Venice 1961). She joined the Deutsche Oper Berlin and in 1968 created Nausikaa in Dallapiccola's *Ulisse*; she was Marie in Zimmermann's *Die Soldaten*, when the co. visited Edinburgh in 1972. At Schwetzingen she was heard in the fp of Reimann's *Melusine* (1971), and she appeared with Scottish Opera. Other roles included Jenifer, Lulu and the Queen of Night (CG 1962). Sang in Joplin's *Treemoniska* at the 1992 Schwetzingen Festival.

Gaztambide y Garbayo, Joaquín (Romualdo) (b Tudela, Navarre, 7 Feb 1822; d Madrid, 18 Mar 1870), Spanish conductor and composer. Studied at Pamplona and the Madrid Conservatory. After a stay in Paris he became a theatre manager and conducted in Madrid.

Works include 44 *zarzuelas*, e.g. *La mensajera*, *El estreno de una artista*, *El valle de Andorra*, *Catalina*, *Los Magyares*, *El juramento*, *La conquista de Madrid*, etc.

Gazza ladra, La, *The Thieving Magpie*, opera by Rossini (libretto by G Gherardini, based on the French melodrama, *La Pie voleuse*, by J-M T B d'Aubigny and L C Caigniez), produced Milan, La Scala, 31 May 1817. Ninetta condemned to death for stealing silverware but released when a magpie is identified as the culprit.

Gazzaniga, Giuseppe (b Verona, 5 Oct 1743; d Crema, 1 Feb 1818), Italian composer, pupil of Porpora and Piccinni in Naples, where his first opera was produced 1768. Later lived chiefly in Venice, until his appointment as *maestro di cappella* at Crema Cathedral in 1791. Of his 44 operas, *Don Giovanni o sia Il convitato di pietra* (1787) was an immediate forerunner of Mozart's opera with the same title (produced later the same year in Prague); it has been revived at Wexford and elsewhere in recent years. Other works include oratorios, a symphony and three piano concertos.

Gazzelloni, Severino (b Roccasecca, Frosinone, 5 Jan 1919; d Cassino, 21 Nov 1992), Italian flautist. He studied in Rome, making his debut there 1945. Often heard in Baroque music. He developed new techniques for his instrument in performances of works by Maderna, Boulez, Berio and Nono.

Gebel, Georg (junior) (b Brieg, 25 Oct 1709; d Rudolstadt, 24 Sept 1755), German organist, harpsichordist and composer, son and pupil of Georg Gebel senior. Appointed second organist of St Mary Magdalen in Breslau in 1729. After apointments in Oels, Warsaw and Dresden, he became *Konzertmeister* to the court in Rudolstadt in 1747, and *Kapellmeister* three years later.

Works include over 12 operas (none extant), and large quantities of cantatas, symphonies, chamber music, keyboard music.

Gebel, Georg (senior) (b Breslau, 1685; d Breslau, c 1750), German organist and composer, pupil of Tiburtius Winckler in Breslau. Appointed organist in Brieg in 1709, but in 1713 returned to Breslau, where he became director of music at St Christoph the following year.

Works include Mass for double chorus; motets; cantatas; Passion oratorio; concertos; organ and harpsichord music.

Gebel, Georg Sigismund (b Breslau, c 1715; d Breslau, 1775), German organist, harpsichordist and composer, brother of Georg Gebel junior. Organist of several churches at Breslau. Composed organ music and cantatas.

Gebrauchsmusik German = lit. 'utility music'; a term for a species of work written for practical use and best translated as 'workaday music'. It was common among German composers in the 1920s and 1930s. Hindemith's pub. works of the kind (several are unpublished) are: *Spielmusik* for strings, flutes and oboes (1927); four three-part *Songs for Singing Groups*; an educational work for concerted violins in first position (1927); *Music to Sing or Play* (five nos. for various vocal or instrumental combinations); *Lesson* for two male voices, narrator, chorus, orchestra, a dancer, clowns and community singing (1929); *Let's Build a Town*, a musical game for children (1930); *Plöner Musiktag* (1932; four nos. for various vocal and instrumental combinations). Some other composers, e.g. Milhaud in France, Copland in USA, and Weill and Orff in Germany, have done similar work.

Geburtstag der Infantin, Der, *The Birthday of the Infanta*, pantomime by Schreker after the story by Wilde; composed 1908, fp Vienna, 27 Jun 1908. Orchestrated in 1923 as a suite for large orchestra and performed Amsterdam, 18 Oct 1923, conductor Mengelberg; new ballet scenario by Schreker, 1926, under title *Spanisches Fest*, performed Berlin 22 Jan 1927, conductor Leo Blech. Wilde's story was set as an opera by Zemlinsky in 1920–21; Der ◊Zwerg.

gedackt sometimes *gedact*, German properly *gedeckt* = 'covered' an adj. used for stopped ◊diapason organ stops producing a muted 8-ft tone.

gedämpft German = lit. 'damped'; = 'muted, muffled' (drums).

Gedda, Nicolai (b Stockholm, 11 Jul 1925), Swedish tenor of Russian parentage. Studied in Stockholm, making his debut there in 1952. In 1953 he sang in Paris and at CG in 1954 as the Duke of Mantua; has returned as Benvenuto Cellini. In 1958 at the NY Met. he created Anatol in Barber's *Vanessa*. Other roles include Tamino, Faust and Palestrina. First London song recital Apr 1986. Sang Christian II in a revival of Naumann's *Gustaf Wasa*, Stockholm 1991.

Geduldige Socrates, Der, *The Patient Socrates*, opera by Telemann (libretto by J U von König, after Minato), produced Hamburg, 28 Jan 1721. Socrates has his patience tried by the squabbling of his two wives.

Geharnischte Suite second suite for orchestra by Busoni; composed 1895, revised 1903, fp Berlin, 1 Dec 1904. (*Geharnischte* = 'armoured man'.)

Geheime Königreich, Das, *The Secret Kingdom*, fairy-tale opera in one act by Krenek (libretto by composer; 1926–27, produced in a triple bill with *Der Diktator* and *Schwergewicht*, Wiesbaden, 6 May 1928. King and queen find the answer in the forest to the riddle 'What contains the whole world in itself?'.

Geheimnis des entwendeten Briefes, Das chamber opera by Blacher (libretto by H Brauer after E A Poe's story *The Mystery of the Purloined Letter*). The fp was planned for 2 Feb 1975 but postponed after Blacher's death on 30 Jan; produced Berlin, 14 Feb 1975.

Geibel, Emanuel von (1815–1884), German poet. ◊Jensen (*Spanisches Liederbuch*); ◊Loreley (Bruch and Mendelssohn); ◊Schumann (*Vom Pagen und der Königstochter*); ◊Spanisches Liederbuch (H Wolf); ◊Volbach (*Vom Pagen und der Königstochter*).

Geige German = 'fiddle', the familiar German name of the ◊violin.

Geiringer, Karl (Johannes) (b Vienna, 26 Apr 1899; d Santa Barbara, 10 Jan 1989), Austrian-born American musicologist. Studied in Berlin and Vienna and was librarian at the Vienna Gesellschaft der Musikfreunde, 1930–38. Resident in the USA from 1940 and professor of music history and theory at Boston University, 1941–62. Professor of music at the University of California, Santa Barbara, 1962–72. He made editions of music by Haydn and published *Haydn: A Creative Life in Music* in 1946 (third edition 1983). Also wrote on Brahms (1935), musical instruments (1943, third edition 1978), and the Bach family (1954).

Geisslerlieder German = 'flagellants' songs'; sacred German monophonic songs of the Middle Ages in the Italian *laude* tradition and particularly cultivated at the time of the Black Death in 1349. The chief MS is the *Chronikon* of Hugo von Reutlingen, which also describes how the singing was accompanied by penitential rites performed by the *Geissler* ('flagellants').

Gellert Lieder six songs by Beethoven for voice and piano to texts by C F Gellert, op. 48; composed *c* 1802. The titles are, 1. *Bitten*; 2. *Die Liebe des Nächsten*; 3. *Vom Tode*; 4. *Die Ehre Gottes aus der Natur*; 5. *Gottes Macht und Vorsehung*; 6. *Busslied*.

Gelmetti, Gianluigi (b Rome, 11 Sept 1945), Italian conductor. Studied in Rome and Vienna. Conducted the RAI SO at Rome 1980–84, Rome Opera 1984–85. Chief conductor of the South German Radio SO 1989, Orchestre Philharmonique of Monte Carlo 1990. Conducted the premiere of Henze's 7th Symphony (1984); *Tosca* at Venice (1989) and *La Gazza Ladra* at Pesaro, 1989. Rossini double bill at the Ravenna Festival and *Tancredi* at Bologna, 1992.

Geminiani, Francesco Saverio (b Lucca, bap. 5 Dec 1687; d Dublin, 17 Sept 1762), Italian violinist and composer, pupil of Corelli in Rome. Went to England 1714, where he had great success as a virtuoso. Apart from periods of residence in Dublin (1733–40 and 1759–62) and Paris, he remained there for the rest of his life. His teaching introduced modern violin technique to England, and his *Art of Playing on the Violin*. (1751) was one of the earliest tutors on violin-playing. He also wrote several other theoretical works.

Works include *concerti grossi*, violin sonatas, cello sonatas, trio sonatas, keyboard pieces.

Gemma di Vergy opera by Donizetti (libretto by E Bidera, based on the elder Dumas's play, *Charles VII chez ses grands vassaux*), produced Milan, La Scala, 26 Dec 1834. Count of Vergy wants to annul marriage with infertile wife Gemma. Her slave Tamas stabs new wife Ida then kills himself; Gemma grieves.

gemshorn a medieval recorder originally made from a chamois horn, and hence an organ stop with soft, nasal tone.

Gencer, Leyla (b Istanbul, 10 Oct 1924), Turkish soprano. She sang Santuzza in Ankara, 1950 and in Naples, 1953, on her Italian debut. Milan, La Scala, since 1956; sang in the fp of Poulenc's *Carmélites*, 1957. US debut San Francisco, 1956. Glyndebourne 1962–65 as Countess Almaviva and Anna Bolena. Maria Stuarda and Rossini's Elisabetta at Edinburgh, 1969 and 1972. A specialist in the less-often heard Italian operas of the 19th c.

Genée, (Franz Friedrich) Richard (b Danzig, 7 Feb 1823; d Baden near Vienna, 15 Jun 1895), German conductor and composer. Studied medicine at first, but took to music and became conductor successively at Reval, Riga, Cologne, Aachen, Düsseldorf, Danzig, Mainz, Schwerin, Amsterdam, Prague and Vienna. He wrote or collaborated in many libretti for operettas by Viennese composers. Librettist of *Die Fledermaus*.

Works include operettas *Der Geiger aus Tirol* (1857), *Der Musikfeind*, *Die Generalprobe*, *Rosita*, *Der schwarze Prinz*, *Am Runenstein* (with Flotow), *Der Seekadett* (1876), *Nanon, Im Wunderland der Pyramiden*, *Die letzten Mohikaner* (after Fenimore Cooper, 1879), *Nisida, Rosina* (1881), *Die Zwillinge* (1885), *Die Piraten, Die Dreizehn*; part-songs including the comic *Italienischer Salat*.

Generalbass German = lit. 'general bass' = ◊thorough-bass.

Generali (real name *Mercandetti*), Pietro (b Masserano, 23 Oct 1773; d Novara, 3 Nov 1832), Italian composer. Studied under Giovanni Masi in Rome and in 1802 produced his first opera there. In 1817–21 he conducted opera at Barcelona, and later became *maestro di cappella* at Novara Cathedral.

Works include *c* 60 operas, e.g. *Gli amanti ridicoli*, *Il Duca Nottolone*, *La villana in cimento*, *Le gelosie di Giorgio*, *Pamela nubile* (after Richardson, *via* Goldoni's comedy, 1804), *La calzolaia*, *Misantropia e pentimento* (after Kotzebue), *Gli effetti della somiglianza*, *Don Chisciotte* (after Cervantes), *Orgoglio ed umiliazione*, *L'idolo cinese*, *Lo sposo in bersaglio*, *Le lagrime di una vedova* (1808), *Adelina* (1810), *La moglie giudice del marito*, *I baccanali di Roma* (1816), *Francesca da Rimini* (after Dante); Masses and other church music; cantata *Roma liberata*.

Genet, Elzéar (Carpentras) (b Carpentras, *c* 1470; d Avignon, 14 Jun 1548), French composer. He was a papal singer to Julius II in 1508 and *maestro di cappella* under Leo X from 1513 to 1521, as well as being at the court of Louis XII some time between those dates. He wrote secular works to both Italian and French texts, and numerous sacred works (Masses, motets, hymns, Magnificats).

Genoveva opera by Schumann (libretto by composer, altered from one by R Reinick based on the dramas of Tieck and Hebbel), produced Leipzig, 25 Jun 1850. Genoveva's husband Siegfried departs for battle and entrusts his castle to Golo, who loves Genoveva. After being rejected, he frames her for adultery and is about to execute her, when Siegfried returns and the couple are reconciled.

Gentle Shepherd, The ballad opera (libretto by Allan Ramsay), produced Edinburgh, Taylor's Hall, 29 Jan 1729. It was first pub. (1725) as a pastoral comedy, and is therefore not, as is sometimes said, the first ballad opera, since *The Beggar's Opera* (1728) was staged earlier. Patie, of noble birth but brought up as a shepherd, wants to marry humble Peggy, but he believes it would be socially impossible. Later it turns out that she too is of noble blood.

Genzmer, Harald (b Blumental, near Bremen, 9 Feb 1909), German composer. Studied first in Marburg and later with Hindemith in Berlin. From 1946 to 1957 he was professor of composition at the Hochschule für Musik in Freiburg i/B, and from 1957 professor at the Munich Hochschule.

Works include cantata *Racine* (1949); Mass in E; symphony no. 1,

Bremen symphony; concertos for piano, cello, oboe, flute (2), trautonium (2); two string quartets; sonatas for violin, flute and other chamber music.

George, Stefan (1868–1933), German poet. A ◊Berg (*Wein*; ◊*Lyric Suite*); ◊Schoenberg (*Buch der hängenden Gärten*); ◊Webern (songs op. 3 and op. 4).

Georgian, Karine (b Moscow, 5 Jan 1944), Russian cellist. Studied with Rostropovich in Moscow and has appeared with such orchestras as the Leningrad and Royal Philharmonics, the Philadelphia and the Berlin PO. US debut with the Chicago SO, 1969. Prom concerts, London, 1985 and 1990. Professor at the Detmold Hochschule from 1984.

Gerber, Ernst Ludwig (b Sondershausen, 29 Sept 1746; d Sondershausen, 30 Jun 1819), German lexicographer and organist. His most important work was the dictionary of musicians, *Historischbiographisches Lexicon der Tonkünstler* (two vols., 1790–92), later much expanded as *Neues historisch-biographisches Lexikon* (four vols., 1812–14).

Gerber, Heinrich Nicolaus (b Wenigen-Ehrich, 6 Sept 1702; d Wenigen, 6 Aug 1775), German organist and composer, father of Ernst Ludwig◊Gerber. Studied at Leipzig University and became a disciple of Bach there. Court organist at Sonderhausen from 1731. Improved and invented instruments, including the *Strohfiedel*.

Works include a hymn-book with figured basses; variations on chorales for organ; music for harpsichord, organ, harp.

Gerbert, Martin (b Horb on Neckar, 12 Aug 1720; d St Blasien, 13 May 1793), German music historian. Entered the Benedictine monastery of St Blasien in 1737, ordained priest 1744, abbot 1764. Pub. a history of church music in 1774 under the title *De cantu et musica sacra*, and a collection of medieval music treatises 1784.

Gergiev, Valery (b Moscow, 2 May 1953), Russian conductor. Studied in Leningrad and assisted Temirkanov at the Kirov Theatre there. Chief conductor Armenian State Orchestra 1981–85, and has guested with Berlin and Dresden POs and L'Orchestre de France. Conducted at the Kirov from 1977 and became artistic director and chief conductor 1988; took the co. to the NY Met. 1992, with *Boris Godunov* and *The Queen of Spades*. Co-productions with CG have involved *Boris* and *The Fiery Angel*; *War and Peace* given in St Petersburg but postponed in London. Led the Kirov in a Rimsky-Korsakov festival at St Petersburg and in a concert of *The Invisible City of Kitezh*, London 1994; staged at Edinburgh Festival, 1995.

Gerhard, Roberto (b Valls, Catalonia, 25 Sept 1896; d Cambridge, 5 Jan 1970), Spanish composer and pianist. Although a choirboy and a tentative pianist and composer from an early age, he began serious music studies late, owing to parental opposition. But after two years' commercial studies in Switzerland, he studied piano with Granados and composition with Pedrell at Barcelona in 1915–22 and then composition with Schoenberg in Vienna 1923–28. In 1929–38 he lived and taught at Barcelona, was in charge of the music department of the Catalan Library, for which he edited music by 18th-c. Catalan composers, translated various music treatises into Spanish and contributed to the literary weekly *Mirador*. Pedrell introduced him as a composer and he began to make his way in Spain and Latin America. After the downfall of the Spanish Republic he emigrated to England and in 1939 settled at Cambridge with a research scholarship from King's College. His achievement was to unite atonal methods with the colours and rhythms of his native Spain; some of his later music, notably the Third Symphony (*Collages*, 1960) allows some avant-garde techniques. His masterpiece, the opera *The Duenna*, was broadcast 1949 but not staged until 1992 (Madrid and Leeds).

Works include opera *The Duenna* (after Sheridan, 1945–47); ballets *Ariel* (1934), *Soirées de Barcelone* (1938), *Don Quixote* (after Cervantes), *Alegrias* (1942) and *Pandora*; oratorio *The Plague* (after Camus, 1964); music for radio plays *Cristobal Colón* and *Adventures of Don Quixote* (Eric Linklater after Cervantes); four symphonies (1952–67, no. 3 *Collages* for orchestra and magnetic tape); concerto for orchestra (1965); *Epithalamion* for orchestra (1966); violin con-

certo (1943); *Cancionero de Pedrell*, *Serranillas* and *Cançons i Arietes* for voice and orchestra.

Hymnody for 11 players (1963); *Concert for eight*; nonet (1956), two string quartets (1955, 1962); piano trio (1918), wind quintet; *Gemini* for violin and piano; cantata for solo voices, chorus and orchestra; song cycle *L'infantament meravellós de Shaharazada* (1917) and other songs; various arrangements of old Spanish music.

Gerhardt, Elena (b Leipzig, 11 Nov 1883; d London, 11 Jan 1961), German mezzo-soprano. Studied at the Leipzig Conservatory with Marie Hedmont, making her debut in 1903. She owed much to the encouragement of Arthur Nikisch, who accompanied her at many of her recitals. She excelled in the interpretation of Lieder. In 1933 she left Germany and settled in London, where she was active in later years as a teacher.

Gerl, Barbara (born Reisinger) (b Vienna or Bratislava, 1770; d Mannheim, 25 May 1806), Austrian singer and actress. She performed as a child in Moravia and Silesia from 1780; sang with Schikaneder's co. from 1789, appearing in operas by Guglielmi and her husband, Franz Xaver Gerl. In 1791 she created Papagena, in *Die Zauberflöte*. After two years in Vienna she moved to Brno, then Mannheim.

Gerl, Franz Xaver (b Andorf, Upper Austria, 30 Nov 1764; d Mannheim, 9 Mar 1827), Austrian bass and composer. He studied with Leopold Mozart in Salzburg and by 1789 was a member of Schikaneder's opera co.; appeared in varied roles, including Figaro and Don Giovanni, and contributed as composer to many Viennese *Singspiele*: *Don Quixotte und Sancho Pansa* (1790), and a series of pieces with the character Anton as hero. In 1791 he created Sarastro, in *Die Zauberflöte*, with his wife Barbara as Papagena.

Gerle, Hans (b Nuremberg, *c* 1500; d Nuremberg, 1570), German 16th-c. lutenist, violist and lute-maker. Son of Conrad Gerle (d 1521), also a lute-maker. He pub. a book on viol and lute playing and two collections of lute pieces in tablature.

German, Edward (originally Edward German Jones) (b Whitchurch, Shropshire, 17 Feb 1862; d London, 11 Nov 1936), English composer. Educated at Chester. On his return home he organized and conducted a band and learnt the violin. Later he studied at Shrewsbury and the RAM in London. He became an orchestral violinist and in 1888 music director of the Globe Theatre, writing incidental music for various productions, including well-received music for Henry Irving's version of *Henry VIII* (1892). In 1901 he completed *The Emerald Isle*, left unfinished by Sullivan. He had his enduring success

A Selection of

Gershwin

Rhapsody in Blue...1924
Piano Concerto 1925
Strike up the Band...1928
An American in Paris 1928

Girl Crazy....................................1930
Variations on 'I Got Rhythm'.......1934
Porgy and Bess.............1935

the following year, with *Merrie England*, often performed by amateur opera companies. Knighted 1928.

Works include light operas *The Rival Poets* (1886, revised 1901), *Merrie England* (1902), *The Princess of Kensington*, *Tom Jones* (after Fielding), *Fallen Fairies* (W S Gilbert); incidental music for Shakespeare's *Richard III*, *Henry VIII*, *Romeo and Juliet*, *As You Like It*, *Much Ado about Nothing*, Anthony Hope's *Nell Gwyn*, etc.; two symphonies, symphonic suite in D minor, symphonic poem *Hamlet*, symphonic suite *The Seasons*, *Welsh Rhapsody*, *Theme and Six Diversions* and other orchestral works; Coronation March and Hymn for George V; chamber music and many songs.

German flute the name for the transverse ♭flute in England in the 18th c.

Germani, Fernando (b Rome, 5 Apr 1906), Italian organist and composer. Pupil of Respighi and others. He taught at the Curtis Institute in Philadelphia, in Siena and at the Rome Conservatory, and was organist at St Peter's, Rome, from 1948. He travelled widely as a soloist and pub. a *Metodo per organo* and began an edition of works by Frescobaldi, as well as pub. organ works of his own.

German Requiem, A work for chorus, soprano and baritone solo and orchestra by Brahms, op. 45, composed 1866–69, fp Leipzig, 18 Feb 1869, conductor Reinecke. The original name, *Ein deutsches Requiem*, means that Brahms did not set the liturgical Latin text, but a choice of his own from Luther's translation of the Bible.

German sixth ♭augmented sixth chords.

Gero, Jhan (*fl.* 1540–55), Franco-Flemish composer. He lived in Venice and was connected with the music printers Gardano and Scotto. Composed motets, madrigals and a highly successful book of duos (1541).

Gershwin, George (b Brooklyn, NY, 26 Sept 1898; d Hollywood, 11 July 1937), American composer and pianist. Wrote a popular song at the age of 14, studied the piano and had lessons in theory from R Goldmark. From 1914 to 1917 he worked as pianist in a music publisher's office and wrote songs and a musical comedy. In 1924 at the invitation of Paul Whiteman, he wrote the *Rhapsody in Blue*. His musical comedies, mostly to lyrics by his brother Ira, were among Broadway's most successful in the 1920s and 1930s, including *Strike up the Band* (1927), *Funny Face* (1927) and *Girl Crazy* (1930).

Although his melodic gift was long recognized, it took many years for his masterpiece, *Porgy and Bess*, to reach a wide audience; it was not staged at the Met. until 1985, and had to wait until 1986 for its premiere by a British company, at Glyndebourne.

Gershwin *The composer and pianist George Gershwin (1898–1937). He occupies a unique position, lying midway between the spheres of classical music and jazz. His compositions helped to legitimize the role of jazz in white-American culture.*

Works include opera *Porgy and Bess* (1935); many musical comedies including *Lady, Be Good* and *Of Thee I Sing*; music for several films; *An American in Paris* (1928) and *Cuban Overture* (1932) for orchestra; *Rhapsody in Blue* (1924) and concerto for piano and orchestra (1925); a large number of popular songs, including *Lady Be Good*, *I Got Rhythm*, *The Man I Love*, *Embraceable You* and *Love Walked In*.

Gershwin   *A biographical note*

Although destined by his father for a career as an accountant, Gershwin soon chose music instead and it was not long before his royalties were calling for accountancy skills. His song *Swanee*, recorded by Al Jolson in 1920, earned $100,000 in its first year alone. His first real fame as a composer came in 1924, with the *Rhapsody in Blue*. The New York concert at which it was given was billed as An Experiment in Modern Music. The Rhapsody was the first important work to combine jazz with symphonic music, and from its stratospheric opening clarinet solo captured the spirit of the hedonistic age. To the English writer Beverly Nichols 'It seemed that the whole of new America was blossoming into beauty before me. The phrases swept up the piano with the stern, unfaltering grace of a skyscraper.' Over the next ten years, the Rhapsody earned a quarter of a million dollars for Gershwin; he and his brother Ira were paid $100,000 in 1930 for the film score *Delicious*. Always eager to improve himself, Gershwin often sought musical advice from 'serious' composers; Schoenberg preferred to keep him as a tennis partner, however. When he approached Ravel for lessons the Frenchman asked him how much he earned in a year. On receiving the reply Ravel said 'In that case you should be giving me lessons.'

I don't think there has been such an inspired melodist on this earth since Tchaikovsky ... but if you want to speak of a composer, *that's another matter.*

                    Leonard Bernstein on Gershwin,
                              The Atlantic Monthly, 1955

Gerster, Etelka (b Kassán, Hungary, 25 Jun 1855; d Pontecchio near Bologna, 20 Aug 1920), Hungarian-German soprano. Studied with Mathilde Marchesi in Vienna and made her first stage appearance at Venice in 1876 as Gilda. London 1877 as Amina, Lucia and Queen of Night. NY from 1878 in *Lohengrin* and *Les Huguenots*. She married the Italian conductor Carlo Gardini.

Gertler, André (b Budapest, 26 Jul 1907), Hungarian, later Belgian, violinist. Studied with Hubay and Kodály. In 1928 he settled in Belgium, and formed his own string quartet in 1931. He was professor at the Hanover Hochschule, 1964–78. He was well known as a performer of 20th-c. music, especially Bartók.

Gervaise, Claude, 16th-c. French musician who composed a considerable amount of dance music for various instruments, and several books of *chansons*, 1541–57.

Gerville-Réache, Jeanne (b Orthez, Pyrenees, 26 Mar 1882; d New York, 5 Jan 1915), French contralto. She sang at the Paris Opéra-Comique, 1899–1903, creating Geneviève. At CG she was heard as Orpheus (1905) and from 1907 appeared with the Manhattan Opera

Company, NY; the first US Clytemnestra, 1910. Until the war she was heard widely in North America as Dalila and Hérodiade.

Gesang der Jünglinge, *The Song of the Youths*, work by Stockhausen for sung and spoken boys' voices, electrically processed and relayed through five loudspeakers; text from the *Book of Daniel*, on three Hebrew youths undergoing ordeal by fire in Babylon. Fp Cologne, 30 May 1956.

Geschöpfe des Prometheus, Die, *The Creatures of Prometheus*, ballet by Beethoven (choreographed by Salvatore Vigano), produced Vienna, Burgtheater, 28 Mar 1801.

Gese (or *Gesius*), Bartholomäus (or *Barthel Göss*) (b Müncheberg near Frankfurt an der Oder 1562; d Frankfurt, Aug 1613), German theologian and composer. Cantor at Frankfurt from 1593.

Works include Masses (one on themes by Lassus), motets, psalms, hymns, sacred songs, etc., all for the Lutheran Church; Passion according to St John; wedding and funeral music.

Gesellschaft der Musikfreunde German = lit. 'Society of the Friends of Music' = Philharmonic Society; a society formed in Vienna in 1812 for the promotion, performance and collection of music.

Gesius ◊Gese.

Gessendorf, Mechthild (b Munich, 1937), German soprano. Studied in Cologne and sang with the Vienna Chamber Opera from 1961. Munich from 1981, as Aida, the Empress and the Marschallin; Salzburg 1981, Amelia Boccanegra. NY Met. debut 1986, as the Marschallin, returning as the Empress and Senta (1990). London CG 1987, as Wagner's Elisabeth. Sieglinde at the Met., 1993.

Gestalt German = 'shape, formation'; a word that has gained currency as a musical term in German-speaking countries, used in music analysis and in philosophical or pseudo-philosophical discussions on music to designate a musical idea as it comes from the composer's mind in what is supposed to be a kind of primeval or pre-existing form.

gestopft German = 'stopped, obstructed'; notes on the horn played with the hand inserted into the bell to produce an altered sound; formerly to obtain extra notes not in the series of natural harmonics, a device made unnecessary by the value horn.

Gesualdo opera by Alfred Schnittke (libretto by Richard Bletschacher), produced Vienna, Staatsoper, 26 May 1995.

Gesualdo, Carlo, Prince of Venosa (b Naples, c 1560; d Gesualdo Avellino, 8 Sept 1613), Italian composer and lutenist. In spite of his position as a member of the nobility, he took his music studies seriously in his youth and became a very accomplished lutenist. He married a noble Neapolitan lady in 1586, but assassinated her with her lover in 1590. In 1594 he went to the court of Ferrara and married Eleonora d'Este there, but returned to his estate at Naples. His work is notable for its expressive power and chromatic harmony. In 1960 Stravinsky orchestrated three of Gesualdo's madrigals, to mark the 400th anniversary of his birth. He is the subject of Alfred Schnittke's second opera, *Gesualdo*.

Works include seven books of madrigals (the last posthumously pub. of pieces composed in 1594); two books of *Sacrae cantiones*, responds for six voices.

Geszty, Sylvia (b Budapest, 28 Feb 1934), Hungarian soprano. Debut, Budapest, 1959; Amor at the Berlin Staatsoper, 1961. She sang the Queen of Night at CG 1966 and repeated the role at Salzburg, 1967. After joining the Hamburg Opera she sang Zerbinetta at Glyndebourne (1971). At Buenos Aires and LA she was heard as Sophie. Other roles included Alcina, Constanze and Olympia. Sang Rosina in Haydn's *La Vera Costanza* (Vienna, Schönbrunn, 1984).

Gevaert, François Auguste (b Huysee near Oudenaarde, 31 Jul 1828; d Brussels, 24 Dec 1908), Belgian music historian, theorist and composer. Studied at Ghent and worked as organist there; later travelled in Spain, Italy and Germany. Director of music at the Paris Opéra, 1867–70; of the Brussels Conservatory from 1871. He wrote several treatises on history, plainsong and theory.

Works include operas *Hugues de Zomerghem* (1848), *La Comédie à la ville*, *Georgette* (1848), *Le Billet de Marguerite*, *Les Lavandières de Santarem* (1855), *Quentin Durward* (after Scott, 1858), *Le Diable au moulin*, *Château Trompette*, *La Poularde de Caux* (1861), *Les Deux Amours*, *Le Capitaine Henriot*; Requiem for male voices and orchestra (1853), Christmas cantata, psalm *Super flumina*, cantatas *De nationale verjaerdag* and *Le Retour de l'armée*; orchestral *Fantasia sobre motivos españoles*.

Gewandhaus German = 'Cloth Hall'; originally the hall of the clothmakers' guild at Leipzig, used for concerts from 1781 and rebuilt especially as a concert hall in 1884. The first concert was conducted by J A Hiller. Mendelssohn was conductor of the Gewandhaus Orchestra 1835–47; Julius Rietz 1854–60; Carl Reinecke 1860–95; Arthur Nikisch 1895–1920; Furtwängler 1922–29; Bruno Walter 1929–33; Franz Konwitschny 1949–62; Kurt Masur from 1970. The hall was destroyed in World War II, on 4 Dec 1943.

Gezeichneten, Die, *The Stigmatized*, opera by Schreker (libretto by composer; composed 1913–15, produced Frankfurt, 25 Apr 1918. Crippled Alviano loves Carlotta, but loses her to the handsome Tamare. Carlotta dies as Alviano kills his rival.

Ghedini, Giorgio Federico (b Cuneo, Piedmont, 11 Jul 1892; d Nervi, 25 Mar 1965), Italian composer. Studied at Turin and Bologna, at first intended to be a conductor, later taught at the conservatories of Turin, Parma and Milan, but eventually devoted himself to composition. He made editions of music by Monteverdi, the Gabrielis and Frescobaldi.

Works include eight operas, including *Le baccanti* (after Euripides, produced Milan, 1948), and *Billy Budd* (after Meville, produced Venice, 1949); incidental music for Euripides' *Iphigenia in Tauris*; two Masses and various choral works; *Partita*, symphonies, *Concerto dell' Albatro* (after Melville's *Moby Dick*) for orchestra; concertos for piano, two pianos, two cellos and violin; concerto for violin and flute with chamber orchestra; wind quintet, piano quartet; two string quartets and other chamber music; violin and piano sonata; piano works; songs.

Gheorghiu, Angela (b Adjud, 7 Sept 1965), Romanian soprano. Graduated from Budapest Academy 1990 and sang Zerlina at CG 1992; has returned to London as Mimi, Liu, Nina in *Chérubin* and Violetta in a new production of *La Traviata* (1994). Vienna Staatsoper and NY Met. debuts as Adina and Mimi. Season 1995 as Gounod's Juliette at Washington DC, and Desdemona at Salzburg. Regarded as the most promising lyric soprano of her generation.

Gherardello da Firenze (b c 1320–25; d Florence, 1362 or 1363), Italian composer of sacred works and madrigals etc., famous especially for his *caccia* (canonic hunting-song) 'Tosto che l'alba del bel giorno appare'.

Gherardeschi, Filippo Maria (b Pistoia, 1738; d Pisa, 1808), Italian composer, pupil of Padre Martini at Bologna, 1756–61. *Maestro di cappella* at the cathedrals of Volterra and Pistoia, and finally, from c 1766 to his death, at S Stefano in Pisa. Also music director to the court of the Grand Duke of Tuscany.

Works include seven operas, church music, keyboard music.

Gheyn, Matthias van den (b Tirlemont, 7 Apr 1721; d Louvain, 22 Jun 1785), Flemish harpsichordist, organist, carilloneur and composer. Son of a bell founder. The family moved to Louvain 1725 and in 1741 Gheyn became organist at the church of Saint-Pierre there, having been (?) a pupil of Déodat Raick. In 1745 he was appointed carilloneur to the city. Wrote organ, harpsichord and carillon music.

Ghiaurov, Nicolai (b Velingrad, 13 Sept 1929), Bulgarian bass. Debut, Sofia 1955, Rossini's Basilio. He sang Gounod's Méphistophélès on his Paris Opéra (1957), Italian (Bologna, 1958) and NY Met. (1965) debuts. London, CG, and Vienna since 1962. His best roles are Boris Godunov, Philip II, Don Giovanni and Massenet's Don Quichotte. Sang Gremin at CG, 1993.

Ghiselin (or *Verbonnet*), Jean (b c 1455; d ? Bergen op Zoom, c 1511), Flemish composer, active especially in Ferrara. Petrucci of Venice pub. several of his works between 1501 and 1507. Composed Masses (volume pub. 1503), motets, songs, etc.

Ghislanzoni, Antonio (b Lecco, 25 Nov 1824; d Caprino Bergamasco, 16 Jul 1893), Italian baritone, novelist, music editor and librettist. He edited the *Gazzetta musicale* of Milan and collaborated on the libretto for Verdi's *Aida*, as well as writing *c* 85 libretti of his own.

Ghiuselev, Nicola (b Pavlikeni, 14 Aug 1936), Bulgarian bass. Studied in Sofia and made debut there 1961, as Timur. NY Met. debut 1965, as Ramphis. London, CG, from 1976, as Pagno in *I Lombardi*, Boris Godunov (1984) and Galitzky in *Prince Igor* (1990). Attila at the Vienna Staatsoper 1990, Rossini's Mustafa at the Deutsche Oper, Berlin, 1992.

Ghosts of Versailles, The opera in two acts by John Corigliano (libretto by W H Hoffmann, after Beaumarchais), produced NY Met., 19 Dec 1991. Beaumarchais himself makes a ghostly appearance, and attempts to rescue Marie Antoinette from the guillotine.

'Ghost' Trio the nickname given to Beethoven's piano trio in D major, op. 70 no. 1, on account of its slow movement in D minor, which has a mysterious, gloomy and haunting theme, accompanied frequently by string tremolos. Sketches for the work appear on the same sheet as sketches for a projected opera on Macbeth.

Ghro (or **Groh**), Johann (b Dresden, *c* 1575; d 1627), German 16th–17th-c. organist and composer. Organist at Meissen 1604–12 and later music director at Wesenstein.

    Works include *intradas*, pavans, galliards etc. for several instruments; sacred music.

Giacobbi, Girolamo (b Bologna, bap. 10 Aug 1567; d Bologna, *c* 1629), Italian composer. *Maestro di cappella* at San Petronio at Bologna.

    Works include operas and intermedi: *Andromeda* (produced Salzburg, 1618; perhaps first opera outside Italy), *L'Aurora ingannata*, *Amor prigioniero*, *La selva dei mirti*, *Il Reno sacrificante*; motets, psalms and other church music.

Giacomelli, Geminiano (b Piacenza, *c* 1692; d Loreto, 25 Jan 1740), Italian composer. Pupil of Capelli at Parma and possibly later of A Scarlatti. *Maestro di cappella* at Parma, 1719–27 and 1732–37; at Piacenza, 1727–32; at Loreto from 1738.

    Works include operas *Ipermestra* (1724), *Cesare in Egitto* (1735) and *c* 16 others; two oratorios, other sacred works; concert arias.

Giannettini, Antonio (b probably Fano, 1648; d Munich, 12 Jul 1721), Italian composer. He sang at St Mark's, Venice, *c* 1674–86, and was *maestro di cappella* at the ducal court of Modena from 1686. Produced his first opera, *Medea in Atene*, at Venice, 1675.

    Works include operas, e.g. *Temistocle* (1683), *Artaserse* (1705), oratorios, cantatas, motets, psalms.

Giannini, Dusolina (b Philadelphia, 19 Dec 1900; d Zurich, 26 Jun 1986), American soprano, sister of Vittorio ◊Giannini. Stage debut Hamburg, 1925, as Aida; CG 1929, same role. Donna Anna at Salzburg under Walter, and Alice Ford under Toscanini. NY Met. 1936–41; NY City Opera 1941–44, as Carmen, Santuzza and Tosca. She sang Carmen at the Vienna Staatsoper in 1950 and retired in 1962.

Giannini, Vittorio (b Philadelphia, 19 Oct 1903; d New York, 28 Nov 1966), American composer, brother of Dusolina ◊Giannini. Studied at Juilliard with Rubin Goldmark and taught there from 1939; Curtis Institute from 1956. His music reflects his Italian ancestry.

    Works include operas *Lucedia* (1934), *The Scarlet Letter* (1938), *Beauty and the Beast* (1938), *The Taming of the Shrew* (1953), *The Harvest* (1961) and *The Servant of Two Masters* (1967); symphony *In Memoriam Theodore Roosevelt* (1935) and four numbered symphonies; three divertimenti; piano concerto (1937), *Stabat Mater* and Requiem (1937); chamber music and songs.

Gianni Schicchi (Puccini.) ◊Trittico.

Giant's Fugue the nickname of Bach's fugal chorale prelude on 'Wir glauben all', in Part III of the *Clavierübung*, so named because of a striding figure in the pedals.

Giardini, Felice de (b Turin, 12 Apr 1716; d Moscow, 8 Jun 1796), Italian violinist and composer. Choirboy at Milan Cathedral and later pupil of Somis at Turin. Played in the opera orchestras at Rome and Naples, in 1748 visited Germany and then settled in London, becoming leader of the Italian opera orchestra at the King's Theatre in 1752, succeeding Festing. He played and taught there until 1784, when he retired to Italy, but he reappeared in London in 1790 and died during a tour of Russia.

    Works include operas *Enea e Lavinia* (1764), *Il rè pastore* (1765)

and others; incidental music for Wm Mason's *Elfrida*; oratorio *Ruth* (with Avison); 12 violin concertos; 21 string quartets, six string quintets, seven sets of string trios; sonatas for violin and piano; violin duets.

Giasone, (Jason), opera by Cavalli (libretto by G A Cicognini), produced Venice, Teatro San Cassiano, probably 5 Jan 1649. After the Greek myth, Jason and the Argonauts. Jason gets the fleece and falls in love with Medea, but in the end returns to his first love, Hypsipyle.

It is proportion that beautifies everything, this whole universe consists of it, and music is measured by it.
                                          Orlando Gibbons,
           The First Set of Madrigals and Motets, 1612

Gibbons English family of musicians:

    1. William Gibbons (b Oxford, *c* 1540; d Cambridge, Oct 1595), singer and/or player. Lived at Cambridge from 1567, but returned to Oxford *c* 1579 and went back to Cambridge *c* 1587.

    2. Edward Gibbons (b Cambridge, Mar 1568; d ? Exeter, *c* 1650), organist and composer, son of 1. Graduated Mus.B. at Cambridge and later (1592) at Oxford. Lay clerk at King's College chapel, Cambridge, and from *c* 1606 held an appointment at Exeter Cathedral. He wrote anthems, Kyrie and Creed; In Nomine in five parts, etc.

    3. Orlando Gibbons (b Oxford, bap. 25 Dec 1583; d Canterbury, 5 Jun 1625), composer and organist, son of 1. Brought up at Cambridge, where he took the Mus.B. in 1606. Was a singer at the Chapel Royal from 1603 and organist from *c* 1615 until his death. Oxford conferred the Mus.D. on him in 1622. Appointed organist at Westminster Abbey in 1623. He died suddenly at Canterbury while waiting to officiate at Charles I's marriage service, for which he had written music. He wrote Anglican church music (five services, *c* 13 full anthems, *c* 25 verse anthems); 20 madrigals; *Cries of London* for voices and strings, 30 fantasies for strings, four *In Nomine* for strings, two pavans and two galliards for strings; 16 keyboard fantasies, six sets of variations for keyboard and other keyboard pieces.

    4. Christopher Gibbons (b London, bap. 22 Aug 1615; d London, 20 Oct 1676), composer and organist, son of 3. Pupil of his father in the Chapel Royal, but (?) was adopted by his uncle Edward Gibbons at Exeter on Orlando's death. Appointed organist at Winchester Cathedral in 1638. In 1646 he married Mary Kercher, who died in 1662, and later Elizabeth Ball. On the Restoration in 1660 he was appointed private organist to Charles II, also organist at the Chapel Royal and Westminster Abbey. D. Mus., Oxford, 1663. He wrote music for Shirley's masque *Cupid and Death* (with Locke, 1659); anthems; many fantasies for strings; motets; organ music.

Gibbs, C(ecil) Armstrong (b Great Baddow, near Chelmsford, 10 Aug 1889; d Chelmsford, 12 May 1960), English composer. Educated at Winchester College and Trinity College, Cambridge, where he studied music with Dent, and later at the RCM in London, where he became a professor of composition.

    Works include incidental music to Maeterlinck's *The Betrothal* (1921); comic opera *The Blue Peter* (A P Herbert, 1923); play with music *Midsummer Madness* (Clifford Bax); Nativity play *The Three Kings*; cantata *The Birth of Christ* (1929), Passion according to St Luke, choral symphony *Odysseus*; *La Belle Dame sans merci* (Keats, 1928), *The Highwayman* (Alfred Noyes) and *Deborah and Barak* for chorus and orchestra; symphony in E major; string quartet in A major; songs.

Gibbs, Joseph (b ? Dedham, 23 Dec 1699; d Ipswich, 12 Dec 1788), English organist and composer. Organist at various Essex churches, finally from 1748 to his death at St Mary-le-Tower in Ipswich. His most important pub. is a set of eight violin sonatas (*c* 1746); six string quartets (*c* 1777) and organ music also survive.

Gibson, Alexander (b Motherwell, 11 Feb 1926; d London, 14 Jan 1995), Scottish conductor. He studied in Scotland and London; spent the 1950s with SW Opera and the BBC Scottish SO. Principal conductor Scottish National Orchestra 1959–84. Co-founded Scottish Opera in 1962; *Les Troyens* (1969) and *Der Ring des Nibelungen* (1971) were notable achievements. US debut with Detroit SO 1970; principal guest conductor Houston SO from 1981. Season 1990 with *Tosca* for Scottish Opera. *Otello* for Kentucky Opera and *Tristan* at the Bruckner Festival, Linz. Knighted 1977.

Gielen, Michael (b Dresden, 20 Jul 1927), Austrian conductor and composer. He studied in Buenos Aires and Vienna; worked at the Staatsoper 1951–60. Principal conductor Stockholm Opera 1961–65; from 1965 in Cologne, where he gave the fp of Zimmermann's opera *Die Soldaten*. Netherlands Opera from 1972. Chief guest conductor BBC SO from 1978; frequent performances of modern music, especially Second Viennese School: he gave a concert performance of Schoenberg's *Moses und Aron* in Salzburg, later issued on record. Music director Cincinnati SO 1980–86. Chief conductor SWF Radio Orchestra from 1986; professor of conducting at the Salzburg Mozarteum, 1987.

Gieseking, Walter (b Lyons, 5 Nov 1895; d London, 26 Oct 1956), German pianist. Studied privately and at the Hanover Conservatory, and first appeared in 1915; London debut 1923. US debut 1926, with Hindemith's op. 36 no. 1. He won great fame by his sensitive performances, especially of Debussy and Mozart.

giga Italian = ◊jig.

Gigault, Nicolas (b ? Paris, *c* 1625; d Paris, 20 Aug 1707), French organist and composer. Organist at various Paris churches from 1646. Pub. two books of organ pieces in 1683 and 1685.

Gigli, Beniamino (b Recanati, 20 Mar 1890; d Rome, 30 Nov 1957), Italian tenor. Of humble parentage, he began to make his way with difficulty, but gained a scholarship to the Rome Liceo Musicale and in 1914 made his first stage appearance as Enzo, at Rovigo. NY Met. debut 1920, as Boito's Faust. London, CG, 1930–46; debut as Andrea Chénier. Other roles included Rodolfo, Nadir, Lionel and Nemorino. A beautiful voice, not always used with taste or discretion. He won worldwide fame and was considered the successor of Caruso.

Gigout, Eugène (b Nancy, 23 Mar 1844; d Paris, 9 Dec 1925), French organist and composer. Studied music at Nancy Cathedral and the École Niedermeyer in Paris. He was a pupil of Saint-Saëns there and often deputized for him as organist at the Madeleine. Married one of Niedermeyer's daughters and became professor at his school. Appointed organist of Saint-Augustin Church in 1863 and travelled much as organ virtuoso. In 1885 he founded an organ school. Organ professor at Paris Conservatory from 1911.

Works include church music; Meditation for violin and orchestra; piano sonata; *c* 50 organ works for concert use and *c* 400 smaller organ pieces with pedals *ad lib*. for the church.

gigue French = ◊jig.

Gilbert, Anthony (b London, 26 Jul 1934), English composer. He studied at Morley College under Anthony Milner and Walter Goehr. Has taught in Manchester and London and has worked as a music editor.

Works include *Sinfonia* for chamber orchestra (1965); *Regions* for two chamber orchestras (1969); *The Scene Machine*, one-act opera produced Kassel 1971; *Cantata* (1972); Symphony (1973); *The Chakravaka Bird*, song drama for radio (1977); *Towards Asavari* for piano and small orchestra (1978); *Vasanta with Dancing* for chamber ensemble (1981); *Beastly Jingles* for soprano and ensemble (1984); *Dream Carousels* for wind orchestra (1988); *Certain Lights Reflecting* for soprano and orchestra (1989); two string quartets (1986–87); *Tree of Singing Names* for chamber orchestra (1989, revised 1993); *Upstream River* for narrator and ensemble (1991).

Gilbert, Henry (Franklin Belknap) (b Somerville, MA, 26 Sept 1868; d Cambridge, MA, 19 May 1928), American composer. Studied at Boston and became a businessman, but later devoted himself to composition. He often used African-American tunes for his thematic material.

Works include ballet *The Dance in Place Congo* (after G W Cable); symphonic prologue to Synge's *Riders to the Sea* (1913); *Salammbô's Invocation to Tanith* (after Flaubert) for soprano and orchestra; *Indian Sketches* and *Hymn to America* for chorus and orchestra;

Americanesque, *Comedy Overture on Negro Themes* (1906), three *American Dances*, *Negro Rhapsody*, *Legend* and *Negro Episode* for orchestra; *The Island of Fay* (after Poe, 1923); *Indian Scenes* and *Negro Dances* for piano; *Pirate Song* (Stevenson) for voice and piano; editor of 100 folksongs.

Gilbert, Kenneth (b Montreal, 16 Dec 1931), Canadian harpsichordist and organist. Studied in Paris with Duruflé and Gustav Leonhardt. Church organist in Montreal 1955–67 and taught at the conservatory there 1957–74. Professor of harpsichord at the Salzburg Mozarteum and Paris Conservatory from 1988. Made London debut 1968 and has given many performances of the Baroque keyboard masters, notably Couperin and Scarlatti, whose works he has edited, respectively, in four vols. (1969–72) and 11 vols. (1971–85). Also plays Bach, Byrd and Froberger.

I only know two tunes. One is 'God Save the Queen'. The other isn't.

W S Gilbert, quoted in Lebrecht, *Discord*, 1982

Gilbert, W(illiam) S(chwenck) (1836–1911), English playwright and librettist. Libretti for operettas with music by Sullivan, ◊Gondoliers, ◊Grand Duke, ◊HMS Pinafore, ◊Iolanthe, ◊Mikado, ◊Patience, ◊Pirates of Penzance, ◊Princess Ida, ◊Ruddigore, ◊Sorcerer, ◊Thespis, ◊Trial by Jury, ◊Utopia Limited, ◊Yeomen of the Guard.

Gilels, Emil (b Odessa, 19 Oct 1916; d Moscow, 14 Oct 1985), Russian pianist. Studied in Odessa and made his debut there 1929. At the age of 16 he won first prize in the Soviet Pianists Competition and in 1936 second prize in the international piano competition in Vienna. In 1938 he won first prize in the Brussels international piano competition and began teaching at Moscow Conservatory. Paris and New York debuts 1955; London 1959. Well known in Russian music and classical repertory.

Giles, Nathaniel (b Worcestershire, *c* 1558; d Windsor, 24 Jan 1634), English organist and composer. Organist of Worcester Cathedral, 1581–85, when he became organist and choirmaster of St George's Chapel, Windsor, and also, in 1596, of the Chapel Royal in London, where he took the official titles of Gentleman and Master of the Children on the death of Hunnis in 1597; collaborated with Ben Jonson at Blackfriars Theatre from 1600. Mus.D., Oxford, 1622.

Works include services, anthems, motets; madrigal *Cease now, vain thoughts*.

Gilly, Dinh (b Algiers, 19 Jul 1877; d London, 19 May 1940), French-Algerian baritone. Pupil of Cotogni. Made his first appearance in London, at CG, in 1911 as Amonasro; also sang Jack Rance and Rigoletto. NY Met. 1909–14 as Luna and Lescaut. Married the contralto Edith Furmedge.

Gilman, Lawrence (b Flushing, NY, 5 Jul 1878; d Franconia, NH, 8 Sept 1939), American critic. Self-taught in music, he wrote for various papers at first and in 1923 became music critic to the *New York Herald-Tribune* in succession to Krehbiel. Wrote books on MacDowell, Wagner, modern music, etc., and was a well-known programme annotator and radio commentator.

Gilmore, Gail (b Washington DC, 21 Sept 1950), American mezzo. Sang in Germany from 1975, then in Vienna and Venice (Kundry in *Parsifal*, 1983). NY City Opera debut 1981, Met. 1986, as Kundry. Verona Arena 1983–86, as Carmen and Ulrica. Sang Wagner's Venus at Lisbon, 1993. Other roles include Cassandre, Dalila and Orpheus.

Gilson, Paul (b Brussels, 15 Jun 1865; d Brussels, 3 Apr 1942), Belgian composer. Pupil of Gevaert and others, he gained the Belgian Prix de Rome in 1889. Appointed professor of harmony at the Conservatory of Brussels in 1899 and of Antwerp in 1904. He was also music critic of *Le Soir*, 1906–14, and then of *Le Midi*.

Works include operas *Prinses Zonneschijn* and *Zeevolk* (1895); ballets *La Captive* and *Daphne*; oratorio *Le Démon* (after Lermontov); *Francesca da Rimini* (after Dante) for solo voices, chorus and orchestra (1892); *La mer* for reciter and orchestra (1892).

Gimenez, Raul (b Santa Fe, 14 Sept 1950), Argentinian tenor. Debut

Buenos Aires 1980, as Ernesto. European debut at Wexford, 1984, in Cimarosa's *Astuzie Femminili*. US debut at Dallas, 1989, as Ernesto. CG, London, from 1990 as Almaviva, Ernesto and Ramiro. Debuts at the Vienna Staatsoper 1990, as Almaviva, and La Scala 1993, as Argirio in *Tancredi*. An outstanding lyric tenor.

Ginastera, Alberto (b Buenos Aires, 11 Apr 1916; d Geneva, 25 Jun 1983), Argentine composer. Studied with Athos Palma at the National Conservatory of Buenos Aires and graduated in 1938. Visited USA, 1945–47. Taught from 1948 in Buenos Aires, where he was director of the Centre for Advanced Musical Studies from 1963. Lived in USA from 1968 and Europe from 1970. Best known for his operas, which renounce his earlier nationalist style for more advanced atonal techniques. After *Bomarzo* was banned in Argentina for alleged obscenities in the ballet, he left Buenos Aires to live abroad.

Works include operas *Don Rodrigo* (1964), *Bomarzo* (1967), *Beatrix Cenci* (1971); ballets *Panambi* (1940) and *Estancia*; psalms for chorus and orchestra; *Variacones concertantes* for orchestra (1953), *Concerto per corde* (1965), *Estudos sinfónicos* (1967), two piano concertos (1961, 1972), violin concerto (1963), two cello concertos (1968, 1980).

Three string quartets (1948, 1953, 1973), three piano sonatas (1952, 1981, 1982), piano quintet (1963), cello sonata (1979).

Cantata *Bomarzo* for narrator, baritone and orchestra (1964).

Gines Pérez, Juan (b Orihuela, Oct 1548; d ? Orihuela, 1612), Spanish composer. He held a church appointment in his native town at the age of 14, in 1581–95 was *maestro di cappella* and director of the choir school at Valencia, and in 1595 returned home as canon at Orihuela Cathedral.

Works include motets, psalms; secular Spanish songs; contributions to the Mystery play performed annually at Elche, near Alicante.

Gingold, Josef (b Brest Litovsk, Belorussia, 28 Oct 1909; d Bloomington, 11 Jan 1995), American violinist and teacher. Moved to NY 1920, making debut 1926. Studied further with Ysaÿe and was leader of the NBC Orchestra under Toscanini, 1937–43; Detroit SO 1943–46, Cleveland Orchestra 1947–60 (also soloist). Taught at Meadowmount School of Music 1955–81, Indiana University from 1960: his pupils included Jaime Laredo, Ulf Hoelscher, Joseph Silverstein and Miriam Fried.

Gintzler, Simon (b c 1500; d after 1550), German composer. His collection of lute music was published in Venice, 1547, and he also contributed to Hans Gerle's *Eyn Newes ... Lautenbuch* (Nuremberg, 1552).

Gioconda, La opera by Ponchielli (libretto by Boito, based on Victor Hugo's *Angelo*), produced Milan, La Scala, 8 Apr 1876. Gioconda loves Enzo, but so does Laura. The evil Barnaba does his best to thwart everyone's happiness, eventually causing Gioconda's suicide.

giocoso Italian = 'playful, joking, humorous'.

Gioielli della Madonna, I, *The Jewels of the Madonna*, opera by Wolf-Ferrari (libretto by E Golisciani and C Zangarini), produced, in German, Berlin, Kurfürsten-Oper, 23 Dec 1911. Gennaro wins Mariella by stealing the jewels of the Madonna, but rival Raffaele intervenes and the lovers kill themselves.

gioioso Italian, formerly *giojoso* = 'joyous, joyful'.

Giordani Italian family of musicians:

1. Carmine Giordani (b Cerreto Sannita, near Benevento, c 1685; d Naples, 1758), singer and composer. Produced an opera, *La vittoria d'amor coniugale* at Naples in 1712. Other works include cantata for soprano, *Versetti* for organ.

2. Giuseppe Giordani (called Giordanello) (b Naples, 9 Dec 1743; d Fermo, 4 Jan 1798), composer, ? son of 1. Studied music at the Conservatory di Loreto at Naples and brought out his first opera there in 1771. He became *maestro di cappella* at Fermo Cathedral in 1791. Works include over 30 operas, e.g. *L'astuto in imbroglio* (1771); *La disfatta di Dario*, etc.; oratorios *La fuga in Egitto* (1775), *La morte d'Abele*, etc. The *canzonetta* 'Caro mio ben' is attributed to him, but many of the works formerly supposed to be his are by Tommaso ◊Giordani.

——————— THE OPERA ———————
La Gioconda

A four-act opera by Amilcare Ponchielli based on a tragedy by Victor Hugo. It was first performed in Milan in 1876, and is set in 17th-century Venice.

I. La Gioconda – The Joyful Girl (soprano) – rejects the advances of the spy Barnaba (baritone). As an act of revenge he accuses her blind mother La Cieca (mezzo-soprano) of witchcraft. Enzo Grimaldi (tenor) intervenes, and gains the further admiration of La Gioconda. In love with her himself, Barnaba offers help to Enzo in his planned elopement with Laura Adorno (mezzo-soprano), wife of Alvise (bass).

II. At first intent on killing her rival, Gioconda assists the lovers when she realizes that Laura has also helped her mother. However, Alvise appears and the escape attempt fails.

III. Alvise orders his wife to drink poison, but Gioconda provides her instead with a sleeping potion. Believing Laura to be dead, Enzo is arrested after an angry declaration. Gioconda offers herself to Barnaba to save Enzo.

IV. Gioconda then contemplates suicide and, as Enzo makes his escape, he ignores her and rushes to Laura. Gioconda stabs herself rather than yield to Barnaba; as she dies, he tells her that he has just killed her mother.

——————— THE OPERA ———————

Giordani, Tommaso (b Naples, c 1730; d Dublin, Feb 1806), Italian composer, unrelated to either Carmine or Giuseppe ◊Giordani. Son of a travelling opera impresario, produced his first opera with his father's co. in London in 1756. Subsequently lived chiefly in London (1768–83, director at King's Theatre, Haymarket) and Dublin, composed a large number of theatrical works for both capitals.

Works include operas *La comediante fatta cantatrice* (1756), *L'eroe cinese* (1766), *Love in Disguise* (1766), *Il padre e il figlio rivali*, *Artaserse*, *Il re pastore* (1778), *Phillis at Court* (also others, c 50 in all; songs for Sheridan's *The Critic*; oratorio, *Isaac*; church music; concertos and sonatas for piano and other instruments; string quartets, trios; songs.

Giordano, Umberto (b Foggia, 28 Aug 1867; d Milan, 12 Nov 1948), Italian composer. Son of an artisan, he was allowed to learn music as best he could, but in the end studied at the Naples Conservatory under Serrao. He attracted the attention of the pub. Sonzogno with the opera *Marina* and soon became very successful with a series of stage works. He is best known for his opera set in the French Revolution, *Andrea Chénier*, although *Fedora* has also found some favour in recent years; both works are effective vehicles for tenors and prima donnas.

Works include operas *Marina* (1889), *Mala vita* (1892), *Regina Diaz* (1894), *Andrea Chénier* (1896), *Fedora* (after Sardou, 1898), *Siberia* (1903), *Marcella*, *Mese Mariano*, *Madame Sans-Gêne* (after Sardou and Moreau, 1915), *Giove a Pompei* (with Franchetti), *La cena delle beffe* (1924), *Il rè*.

Giorgi-Righetti, Geltrude (b Bologna, 1792; d Bologna, 1862), Italian mezzo-soprano. Made her first appearance at Bologna in 1814 and was Rossini's first Rosina in *Il Barbiere di Siviglia* in 1816. She pub. her reminiscences of Rossini in 1823. Retired 1836.

Giorno di regno, Un, ossia Il finto Stanislao, *A Day's Reign, or The False Stanislas*, opera by Verdi (libretto by F Romani, used earlier by Gyrowetz, ◊Finto Stanislao), produced Milan, La Scala, 5 Sept 1840. Verdi's only comic opera except *Falstaff*. Belfiore is disguised as King Stanislaus to protect the sovereign. A comedy in which he prevents his love, the widow Marchesa, from marrying another.

Giornovichi, Giovanni (Mane) (known as Jarnowick) (b Palermo, c 1740; d St Petersburg, 23 Nov 1804), Italian violinist and composer. Possibly a pupil of Lolli, made his first appearance at the Concert Spirituel in Paris, 1770. Having lived in Paris, Berlin, Austria, Russia and Sweden, he went to London in 1791, but left for Hamburg in 1796, whence he went to St Petersburg in 1802. He wrote 17 violin concertos, three string quartets and much music for the violin.

Giovanna d'Arco, *Joan of Arc*, opera by Verdi (libretto by T Solera, based on Schiller's drama *Die Jungfrau von Orleans*), produced Milan, La Scala, 15 Feb 1845. Joan rallies the troops of defeated Charles VII of France. Although denounced as a follower of Satan by her father, Giacomo, she goes on to save the day, but falls in battle.

Giovanna di Guzman (Verdi.) ◊Vêpres siciliennes.

Giovannelli, Ruggiero (b Velletri near Rome, *c* 1560; d Rome, 7 Jan 1625), Italian composer. After holding various church apointments in Rome, he succeeded Palestrina as *maestro di cappella* at St Peter's in 1594 and became a member of the Sistine Chapel in 1599; *maestro di cappella* 1614. At the request of Pope Paul V he contributed to a new edition of the Gradual. He retired in 1624.

Works include Masses, Miserere and other church music; six books of madrigals, one of *canzonette* and *villanelle*, etc.

Giovannini, ? de (d 1782), Italian composer. The customary identification of Giovannini with the Comte de St Germain remains without proof. The only works extant under the name Giovannini are a handful of songs (including 'Willst du dein Herz mir schenken' in Bach's *Anna Magdalena Notebook*) and eight violin sonatas.

Giove in Argo, *Jupiter in Argos*, opera by Lotti (libretto by A M Lucchini), produced Dresden, Redoutensaal, 25 Oct 1717, the new opera house not being ready. The latter was opened with the same work 3 Sept 1719. (An English adaptation of the same libretto, under the title *Jupiter in Argos*, was set by Handel, produced London, King's Theatre, 1 May 1739.)

Gioventù di Enrico V, La, *The Youth of Henry V*, opera by Pacini (libretto by J Ferretti, partly based on Shakespeare's *Henry IV*), produced Rome, Teatro Valle, 26 Dec 1820.

Gipps, Ruth (b Bexhill, 20 Feb 1921), English composer, pianist and oboist. Pupil of her mother, at the Bexhill School of Music and later at the RCM in London. In 1944–45 she was in the CBSO as second oboe and English horn. Professor RCM from 1967. Conducted the London Repertoire Orchestra 1955–86.

Works include ballet *Sea Nymph*; five symphonies (1942–80), other orchestral music, including six concertos, and chamber works.

Giraldoni, Eugenio (b Marseilles, 20 May 1871; d Helsinki, 24 Jun 1924), Italian baritone, son of Leone ◊Giraldoni. Debut Barcelona, 1891, Escamillo. At the Teatro Constanzi, Rome, he created Scarpia (1900); repeated the role at La Scala and was heard there as Onegin and Gérard. NY Met. debut 1904, as Barnaba. Widely known in the Italian repertory and in the role of Boris Godunov.

Giraldoni, Leone (b Paris, 1824; d Moscow, 1 Oct 1897), Italian baritone, father of Eugenio ◊Giraldoni. He sang in Italy from 1847 and in 1857 created Verdi's Simon Boccanegra (Venice). He was Renato in the 1859 fp of *Un Ballo in Maschera* and at the Teatro Apollo, Rome, sang the title role in the fp of Donizetti's posthumously produced *Il duca d'Alba* (1882). Retired 1885.

Girardeau (born ? *Calliari*), Isabella, Italian 17th–18th-c. soprano, French by marriage. Made her first appearance in London in 1710 and created Almirena in Handel's *Rinaldo*.

Giraud, Fiorello (b Parma, 22 Oct 1868; d Parma, 28 Mar 1928), Italian tenor. Debut, Vercelli 1891, as Lohengrin; the following year he was Canio in the fp of *Pagliacci*, at Milan. In 1907 he sang Siegfried under Toscanini, at La Scala, and in 1908 was the first Italian Pelléas. In Barcelona, Lisbon and South America he was well known in Puccini roles.

Girdlestone, C(uthbert) M(orton) (b Bovey-Tracey, 17 Sept 1895; d St Cloud, 10 Dec 1975), English scholar. Educated at the Sorbonne in Paris and Cambridge, where he became lecturer in French. Professor of French at King's College, Newcastle-upon-Tyne, 1926–61. Author of *Mozart et ses concertos pour piano* and *Jean-Philippe Rameau*.

Girelli Aguilar, Antonia Maria, Italian 18th-c. soprano. She sang in the fps of Gluck's *Il trionfo di Clelia* (1763) and *Le feste d'Apollo* (1769). Created Silvia in Mozart's *Ascanio in Alba* at Milan in 1771 and the following year appeared in London, succeeding Grassi at the King's Theatre.

Giselle, ou Les Wilis ballet by Adam (choreography by Jean Coralli, on a story by Heine, adapted by Théophile Gautier), produced Paris, Opéra, 28 Jun 1841.

Gismondi, Celeste (d London, 28 Oct 1735), Italian mezzo-soprano. Made her first appearance in London in 1732 and sang in the fps of *Orlando* and *Deborah*. Later in operas by Porpora. She married an Englishman named Hempson.

gittern the medieval guitar with four strings, played with a plectrum. It survived in England until *c* 1400; the term was then applied to other members of the guitar family in the 16th–17th c.

Giuliani, Mauro (Giuseppe Sergio Pantaleo (b Bisceglie, near Bari, 27 Jul 1781; d Naples, 8 May 1829), Italian guitar virtuoso and composer. Settled in Vienna 1806, and in 1808 gave the fp of the first of his three guitar concertos. He was widely active in Vienna as teacher, performer and composer, writing more than 200 works for his instrument. Often appeared with Spohr, and in 1813 played the cello in the fp of Beethoven's seventh symphony. Returned to Italy in 1819, working in Rome, then Naples. Played the lyre-guitar in his last years.

Giulietta e Romeo, *Juliet and Romeo*, opera by Vaccai (libretto by F Romani, after Shakespeare's sources for Romeo and Juliet), produced Milan, Teatro della Canobbiana, 31 Oct 1825.

Opera by Zandonai (libretto by A Rossato, after Shakespeare), produced Rome, Teatro Costanzi, 14 Feb 1922.

Opera by Zingarelli (libretto by G M Foppa), produced Milan, La Scala, 30 Jan 1796.

Giulini, Carlo Maria (b Barletta, 9 May 1914), Italian conductor. Studied at the Academy of Santa Cecilia in Rome, viola and conducting (Bustini). Later he studied conducting further with Casella and B Molinari. From 1946 to 1951 he worked for Italian Radio, in 1950 becoming conductor of Radio Milan. He made his debut at La Scala, Milan, during the 1951–52 season; principal conductor from 1953. British debut, Edinburgh 1955, with Glyndebourne Opera (*Falstaff*). *Don Carlos* at CG in 1958; after *Traviata* in 1967 gave concerts with Philharmonia, Vienna SO, Chicago SO; principal conductor LA PO 1978–84. Returned to opera 1982, with *Falstaff* in LA and London. A recording of his 1958 CG *Don Carlos*, with Gobbi, Christoff and Vickers, was issued 1994. He is known for the high standards which he has maintained in a limited repertory.

Giulio Cesare opera by Malipiero (libretto by composer, based on Shakespeare's *Julius Caesar*), produced Genoa, Teatro Carlo Felice, 8 Feb 1936.

Giulio Cesare in Egitto, *Julius Caesar in Egypt*, opera by Handel (libretto by N F Haym), produced London, King's Theatre, Hay-

——— THE OPERA ———

Giulio Cesare

A three-act opera by George Frideric Handel, first produced in London in 1724. Handel's Caesar is much younger than his historical counterpart (Julius Caesar was 54 when he met Cleopatra).

I. Giulio Cesare (alto) has defeated Pompey in battle and his severed head is displayed by Achillas (bass), a captain in the Egyptian army. Pompey's son Sesto (soprano) vows to avenge his father's death. Achillas falls for Pompey's widow, Cornelia (contralto), but she is wanted for the harem of Tolomeo, King of Egypt (alto).

II. Caesar and Cleopatra (soprano, sister of Tolomeo) start to get acquainted but news of an assassination attempt against Caesar interrupts them. Achillas hopes to marry Cornelia with false news of the death of Caesar, but Tolomeo intervenes with his own plans for her.

III. The Egyptians defeat the Romans in battle; Caesar swims ashore and the mortally wounded Achillas confesses to Sesto that he killed his father. Sesto kills Tolomeo in a revolt led by Caesar, and Cleopatra is crowned Queen of Egypt.

——— THE OPERA ———

market, 20 Feb 1724. Caesar beats off rivals in love and war to marry Cleopatra.

Giuramento, Il, *The Vow*, opera by Mercadante (libretto by G Rossi, based on victor Hugo's *Angelo*), produced Milan, La Scala, 10 Mar 1837. Manfredo commands Bianca to take poison after her adultery with Viscardo, but envious Elaisa substitutes a sleeping potion.

Giustini, Lodovico (b Pistoia, 12 Dec 1685; d Pistoia, 7 Feb 1743), Italian composer and organist. Pub. in 1732 a book of sonatas, probably the first pub. music specifically written for the piano, as distinct from music for keyboard instruments in general.

Giustinian, Leonardo (b Venice, *c.* 1383; d Venice, 10 Nov 1446), Italian poet. He wrote love poems for musical settings, some of which he provided himself, which were called after him as late as the 16th c. ◊Justiniana.

Giustino opera by Handel (libretto altered by ? from Nicolo Beregani), produced London, CG, 16 Feb 1737. Giustino joins Anastasius in battle against Vitalian. Later Giustino and Vitalian join forces to defeat the usurping Amantius, who has imprisoned Anastasius. The opera concludes with Giustino united with Leocasta, whom he has rescued earlier.

giusto Italian = 'just, strict, suitable'; a direction used, generally as an adj. with *tempo*, to indicate that a movement is to be played without ◊*rubato*.

Gizziello ◊Conti.

Gjevang, Anne (b Oslo, 1948), Norwegian contralto. Studied in Rome and Vienna. Debut Klagenfurt, as Baba the Turk in *The Rake's Progress*. Sang in Germany as Ulrica, Carmen and Orpheus. Bayreuth Festival from 1983, as Erda in the *Ring*. Zurich Opera from 1985, NY Met. 1958; London, CG 1991, as Erda. Concerts include *Messiah* (Chicago, 1984), the *Missa Solemnis* (under Giulini) and *Das Lied von der Erde*. Also admired as a recitalist.

Glagolitic Mass work by Janáček for soloists, chorus, organ and orchestra (text by M Weingart from Ordinary of the Mass in 9th-c. Slavonic). Five main sections are *Gospodi pomiluj*, *Slava*, *Veřuju*, *Svet*, *Agneče Božij*; composed 1926, fp Brno, 5 Dec 1927.

Glanville-Hicks, Peggy (b Melbourne, 29 Dec 1912; d Sydney, 25 Jun 1990), Australian composer. Studied at the Melbourne Conservatory and from the age of 19 under Vaughan Williams, Gordon Jacob and R O Morris at the RCM in London. She gained a scholarship in 1932 and another in 1935, which enabled her to travel and to study further with Wellesz in Vienna and Nadia Boulanger in Paris. In 1938 her choral suite was performed at the ISCM festival in London and in 1939 she

married Stanley Bate, with whom she went to the USA, living in NY until 1958 and Greece from 1959.

Works include operas *Cœdmon* (1934), *The Glittering Gate* (1959), *Nausicaa* (1961), *Sappho* (1963); Sinfonietta, *Prelude* and *Scherzo*, *Span*, *Suite* and *Music for Robots* for orchestra; choral suite (Fletcher) for women's voices, oboe and strings; piano concerto, flute concerto; *Concertino da camera* for flute, clarinet, bassoon and piano; six Housman songs.

Glareanus, Henricus (real name Heinrich Loris) (b Mollis, Glarus, Jun 1488; d Freiburg i/B, 28 Mar 1563), Swiss theorist. Studied music at Berne and Cologne, taught at Basel from 1515 and again from 1522, after holding a professorship in Paris from 1517 on the recommendation of Erasmus of Rotterdam. In 1529 he moved to Germany, settling at Freiburg i/B. He studied the relationship between the Greek and the church modes and wrote treatises, notably *Isagoge in musicen* (1516) and *Dodecachordon* (1547), containing his new theory of 12 church modes.

Philip Glass's Akhnaten/Seems bound to dishearten/As the Pharaoh emotes/On very few notes.
Katie Mallet Parrott, *How to be Tremendously Tuned in to Opera*, 1989

Glasenapp, Carl Friedrich (b Riga, 3 Oct 1847; d Riga, 14 Apr 1915), German biographer. Author of the first large biography of Wagner (1876–77) and of various other unreliable works on him.

Gläser, Franz (b Horní Jiřetín, Obergeorgental, 19 Apr 1798; d Copenhagen, 29 Aug 1861), Bohemian composer. Studied in Prague; appointed conductor at the Leopoldstadt Theatre in Vienna, 1817, at the Josephstadt Theatre, 1822, and at the Theatre an der Wien, 1827. Later in Berlin and Copenhagen. Wrote mainly operas, e.g. *Des Adlers Horst* (1832), *Bryllupet ved Como-Søen* (after Manzoni's *Promessi sposi*, 1849) and two other Danish operas.

Glass, Louis (Christian August) (b Copenhagen, 23 Mar 1864; d Copenhagen, 22 Jan 1936), Danish composer. He studied at the Brussels Conservatory and came under the influence of César Franck. He is best known for his symphonies, some of which have been revived in recent years by Edward Downes: no. 1 (1893), no. 2 (1899), no. 3 *Skovsymfoni/Wood Symphony* (1901), no. 4 (1911), no. 5 *Svastica* (1911), no. 6 *Skjoldungeaet/Birth of the Scyldings* (1926); concertos for oboe, violin and cello; four string quartets (1890–1906); string sextet (1892); piano quintet (1896); cello sonata and two violin sonatas; piano music and songs. Glass was a contemporary of Nielsen but his music more often recalls Austrian models of the same period.

Glass, Philip (b Baltimore, 31 Jan 1937), American composer. He studied at the Juilliard School and with Boulanger in Paris. Under the influence of Indian and N African music has evolved a technique (minimalism) whereby melodic ideas are not developed but juxtaposed in 'timeless' repetitions. He won early fame in NY with the four-hour *Einstein on the Beach*, and this success was consolidated with Gandhi opera *Satyagraha* (1980) and the pharaonic *Akhnaten* (1984). Later works seemed to have lacked fresh musical ideas, but creative renewal came with an opera for Columbus Day, given at the Met. in 1992.

Works include *Einstein on the Beach* (Avignon and NY Met, 1976); *Satyagraha* (Rotterdam, 1980); *The Photographer* (Amsterdam, 1982); *Civil Wars* (1982–84); *Akhnaten* (Stuttgart, 1984); *The Juniper Tree* (Cambridge, MA, 1985, with Robert Moran), *The Fall of the House of Usher* (Cambridge, 1988), *The Making of the Representative for Planet 8* (Houston, 1988), *1,000 Airplanes on the Roof* (Vienna Airport, 1988), *Hydrogen Jukebox* (Charleston, SC, 1990), *The Voyage* (NY Met., 1992); also instrumental ensemble works, including *Music with Changing Parts* (1970), *Music in 12 Parts* (1971–74); violin concerto (1987) and string quartet (1993).

glass harmonica ◊armonica.

Glaz, Herta (b Vienna, 16 Sept 1908), Austrian contralto. Debut, Breslau 1931. She fled Germany in 1933 and toured as a concert

A Selection of
Philip Glass

Einstein on the Beach................1976
Satyagraha 1980
Glassworks 1981
Company for string quartet........1983

Akhnaten 1984
Metamorphosis for piano 1989
Hydrogen Jukebox 1990
Low Symphony 1992

Glass *The composer Philip Glass is prominent among minimalist composers. He reacted against the overly complex and intellectual music prevalent in the 1950s and 1960s through a return to simplicity, carried out most successfully in his several operas which have achieved wide popularity.*

singer before visiting the USA in 1937 (LA, under Klemperer, in *Das Lied von der Erde* and *St Matthew Passion*); she sang at Chicago, 1940–42, and made her NY Met. debut in Dec 1942; often heard there as Octavian. Retired 1962.

Glazunov, Alexander Konstantinovich (b St Petersburg, 10 Aug 1865; d Paris, 21 Mar 1936), Russian composer. After being taught music at home as a child, he studied with Rimsky-Korsakov from 1880 and finished his course in 18 months, having a first symphony ready for performance early in 1882. Belaiev arranged a concert of his works in 1884 and began to pub. them. Visited W Europe, 1884, and his music thereafter reconciled current European musical trends with local influences from Tchaikovsky and Borodin. In 1897 he conducted the premiere of Rakhmaninov's 1st symphony, allegedly while drunk. Appointed director of the St Petersburg Conservatory 1905 and wrote little after that to augment his enormous earlier output. He completed several of Borodin's unfinished works, notably the overture to *Prince Igor*. He left Russia 1928 and settled in Paris.

Works include ballets, *Raymonda* (1897), *Les Ruses d'amour* (1898) and *The Seasons* (1899); incidental music for Romanov's play, *The King of the Jews* (1913); eight symphonies (1881–1906); five concert overtures including two on Greek themes and *Carnival*, symphonic poems *Stenka Razin* (1885), *The Sea*, *The Kremlin* (1890), suite *From the Middle Ages*, two serenades, fantasy *The Forest*, *Introduction and Salome's Dance* (after Oscar Wilde), many misc. orchestral works; violin concerto (1904), two piano concertos, concerto for saxophone.

INSTRUMENTAL AND VOCAL: seven string quartets (1881–1930), string quintet, *Novelettes* and suite for string quartet; many works for piano including two sonatas and Theme and Variations; Fantasy for two pianos; various small instrumental pieces; 21 songs; three cantatas; *Hymn to Pushkin* for female voices.

glee a part-song, usually for male voices, in not less than three parts, much cultivated by English composers in the 18th and early 19th c.

The word is derived from the Anglo-Saxon *gliw* = 'entertainment', particularly musical entertainment. Webbe, Stevens, Callcott, Horsley, Attwood, Battishill, Cooke and others cultivated the glee.

Glee Club a club formed in London in 1783 and existing until 1857, for the performance of glees, madrigals, motets, canons and catches at table after dinner at a member's house or in a tavern or coffee-house.

Gleichnisarie German ◊parable aria.

Glennie, Evelyn (b Aberdeen, 19 Jul 1965), Scottish percussionist. She became profoundly deaf during childhood and entered the RAM 1982. Played first in the National Youth Orchestra of Scotland and made Wigmore Hall debut 1986; US concerts in NY, St Louis and LA. Has played with all major British orchestras and premiered works by John McLeod and James MacMillan, among others. Recordings include Bartók's Sonata for Two Pianos and Percussion, with Georg Solti.

Glière, Reinhold Moritzovich (b Kiev, 11 Jan 1875; d Moscow, 23 Jun 1956), Russian composer of Belgian descent. Learnt the violin as a child, but soon began to compose and was sent to the Kiev School of Music and later to the Moscow Conservatory, where he was a pupil of Arensky, Taneiev and Ippolitov-Ivanov. Taught at the Gnessin School of Music in Moscow and at the Kiev Conservatory, of which he became director 1914, but settled at Moscow 1920 (professor of composition at Conservatory until 1941). He made research into Azerbaijani, Uzbek and Ukrainian folksong and based some of his later works on it. In 1939 he became chairman of the Organizing Committee of USSR composers. Among his pupils was Prokofiev, who said of him 'Glière is fat and middle-aged, rather like a well-fed cat'.

Works include operas *Shakh-Senem* (1926), *Leyli and Mejnun* (1937), *Rachel* (after Maupassant's *Mlle Fifi*), *Ghulsara* (1949); ballet *The Red Poppy*, 1927; incidental music for Sophocles' *Oedipus Rex*, Aristophanes' *Lysistrata*, Beaumarchais's *Marriage of Figaro*, etc.; three symphonies (No. 3, *Ilia Muromets*, 1909–11), three symphonic poems, concert overtures; harp concerto, concerto for soprano and orchestra; fantasy for wind instruments; four string quartets (1900–48); three string sextets, string octet; many instrumental pieces; 18 op. nos. of piano music, 22 op. nos. of songs.

Glinka, Mikhail Ivanovich (b Novospasskoye, Government of Smolensk, 1 Jun 1804; d Berlin, 15 Feb 1857), Russian composer. He is often regarded as the founder of Russian music, exerting a strong influence on two generations of composers, his most notable successes being Mussorgsky, Tchaikovsky and Stravinsky. The son of a wealthy landowner, he was sent to school at St Petersburg, 1817–22. He took some piano lessons from Field and others, also studied violin and theory. At his father's wish he worked in the Ministry of Communications 1824–28, but not being obliged to earn a living and wishing to devote himself to music, he gave it up. He visited Italy, 1830–33, where he had lessons from Basili at Milan, and afterwards Vienna and Berlin, studying under Dehn in the latter city. On his father's death he returned to Russia, settled in St Petersburg and married in 1835. There he worked at *A Life for the Tsar* and succeeded in having it produced 1836; it was an immediate success, wedding nationalist musical elements with a patriotic tale composed at a time of unrest. *Ruslan and Ludmilla* was delayed by domestic troubles and the separation from his wife in 1841. It was produced 1842. In 1844 he visited Paris and Spain, in 1848 Warsaw, and France again 1852–54. It was during a visit to Berlin, 1856–57, that he died.

Works include operas *A Life for the Tsar* (formerly *Ivan Sussanin*) (1836) and *Ruslan and Ludmilla* (1842); incidental music to Count Kukolnik's *Prince Kholmsky*; orchestral works: *Jota aragonesa* (*Capriccio brillante*), *A Night in Madrid* (1851), *Kamarinskaya* (1848), *Valse-Fantaisie*; string quartet in F major; trio for clarinet, bassoon and piano; sextet for piano and strings; *c* 40 piano pieces; Polish hymn and *Memorial Cantata* for chorus; *c* 85 songs; some vocal duets and quartets.

glissando Italian, from French *glisser* = 'to glide, slide'; a direction for rapid scales played on the piano or harp by sliding the fingers over the keys or strings. On the piano only the C major and pentatonic scales can thus be played (on white and black keys respectively), and this applies also to the chromatic harp with its crossed strings, where however a chromatic scale can be played in addition if the strings are touched at the point of intersection. A glissando effect can also be obtained on string instruments by sliding the finger along the string, or by the voice by scooping, but in both cases the direction for this is more properly *portamento*. Trombones can play glissando passages by not interrupting the breath while the slide is brought to another position.

Globokar, Vinko (b Anderny, Meurth-et-Moselle, 7 Jul 1934), Yugoslav composer and trombonist. He studied in Ljubljana and at the Paris Conservatory; later with Leibowitz and Berio. From 1968 he has been professor of trombone at the Cologne Musikhochschule. His avant garde virtuosity encouraged Stockhausen, Kagel and Berio to write works for him. With Heinz Holliger he gave the UK fp of Takemitsu's *Gemeaux*, Edinburgh 1989. Featured composer at Dartington, 1992. His own music includes *Voie* for narrator, chorus and orchestra (1965); *Fluide* for 12 instruments (1967); *Traumdeutung* for four choruses and instruments (1967); *Concerto grosso* for five solo players, orchestra and chorus (1970); *Ausstrahlungen* for soloists and 20 players (1971); *Carrousel* for four voices and 16 instruments (1977); *Discours I–IX* for various instruments (1967–93); *Les Émigrés* (1982–86); *L'Armonia Drammatica* (1986–889); *Labour* (1992); *Blinde Zeit* (1993).

Glock, William (b London, 3 May 1908), English pianist, administrator and music critic. Studied with Boris Ord and Edward Dent at Cambridge in 1926–30 and with Schnabel in Berlin in 1930–33. He joined the *Observer* 1934 and succeeded Fox Strangways as chief music critic 1940, resigning 1945. In 1948 he co-founded a summer school for advanced courses in music which is now held at Dartington Hall, Devon; remained as music director until 1979. He was BBC Controller of Music, 1959–73, and was knighted in 1970. He appointed Boulez as conductor of the BBC SO in 1971; did much to improve the Promenade Concerts. Director of Bath Festival 1976–84.

Glockenspiel German = 'play of bells'; a set of tuned steel bars played either with two hammers held one in

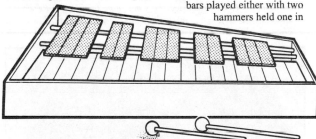

each hand, or with a piano keyboard (e.g. Papageno's bells in Mozart's *Zauberflöte*). In the former case not more than two notes can be struck together.

Glogauer Liederbuch an extensive MS collection in three part-books of Latin pieces, German songs and instrumental pieces, dating from *c* 1480. It was in Berlin until World War II, but is now in Kraków. It is the earliest surviving set of part-books.

Gloria Latin *Gloria in excelsis Deo* = 'Glory to God in the highest'; the second item of the Ordinary of the Mass, following immediately after the Kyrie. Although the Ambrosian Gloria is sung to an even simpler tone, the melody printed with Mass XV of the Vatican edition is probably the oldest.

Gloriana opera by Britten (libretto by William Plomer), produced London, CG, 8 Jun 1953. Robert Devereux, Earl of Essex, and Lord Mountjoy compete for Queen Elizabeth I's attention. Essex is appointed to suppress an Irish rebellion but fails, himself becoming rebellious to the Crown. Reluctantly the Queen has him beheaded.

Glossop, Peter (b Sheffield, 6 Jul 1928), English baritone. He sang with SW, 1953–62, as Onegin, Scarpia and Luna. CG from 1961 as Demetrius, Posa, Iago and Boccanegra. NY Met. debut 1967, as Rigoletto. Other roles included Falstaff, Billy Budd and Renato. His Iago was admired at Salzburg.

Glover, Jane (b Helmsley, Yorkshire, 13 May 1949), English conductor and musicologist. She studied at Oxford, Ph.D. on Cavalli, later issued as a book. Professional debut as conductor Wexford Festival, 1975, with her own edition of Cavalli's *Eritrea*, then in London, 1982. She started her Glyndebourne career as chorus mistress, then as conductor on tour (1982–85); *Don Giovanni* at the Festival, 1982. Artistic director London Mozart Players 1984–92; CG debut 1988, *Die Entführung*; ENO 1989, *Don Giovanni* (*Princess Ida* by Sullivan, 1992); *War Requiem* Proms 1995. Has led the LSO, CBSO, RPO, ECO and Bournemouth Sinfonietta. *See 'personal choice' on page 242.*

Gluck (born *Fiersohn*), Alma (b Bucharest, 11 May 1884; d New York, 27 Oct 1938), Romanian-American soprano. Was taken to USA as a child and worked as a stenographer in NY until her marriage to Bernard Gluck in 1906, when she began to study singing, making her first appearance in 1909 with the Met. Opera Co. as Massenet's Sophie. Other roles included Gluck's Euridice, Marguerite, Venus, Gilda and Mimi. Concert career from 1913. In 1914 she married the violinist Efrem Zimbalist.

In this I have striven to be more painter and poet than musician.

Christoph Willibald von Gluck on *Armide*, quoted in Neumann, *History of Music*, 1886

Gluck, Christoph Willibald (b Erasbach, Upper Palatinate, 2 Jul 1714; d Vienna, 15 Nov 1787), Bohemian-German composer. His series of 'reform' operas moved music away from the formal conventions of the day, in which the interests of singers predominated; in particular, endless recitative was replaced by orchestral accompaniments, which improved dramatic flow.

Son of a forester, he left home in face of parental opposition to music and matriculated at Prague University in 1731. In Vienna *c* 1735 entered the service of Prince Melzi, with whom he went to Italy. Possibly a pupil of Sammartini in Milan, where he made his debut as an opera composer 1741 with *Artaserse* (libretto by Metastasio). A number of operas followed, all in the conventional Italian form. Went to England, perhaps with Prince Lobkowitz, in 1745, possibly visiting Paris on the way. In London, where he met Handel, produced two operas and appeared as a performer on the glass harmonica. In *c* 1747

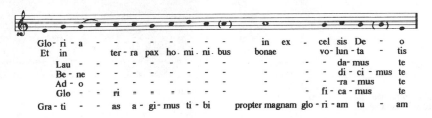

The plainsong melody of the Gloria found in Mass XV of the Vatican edition.

Jane Glover – conductor

1   Mozart: Horn Concertos nos. 1–4
    This was one of the first LPs my father bought, with Dennis
    Brain as soloist. We played it endlessly. It turned out to be
    far more significant than I could ever have realized, because
    in my adult life Mozart has been a lasting passion and I
    conduct those concertos regularly.

2   Handel: *Messiah*
    Messiah comes round to me quite frequently, and every time
    I find it a great alpha-plus piece. Every number is a show-
    stopper; the whole work is uplifting: whether it's a small- or
    large-scale performance, on original instruments or modern,
    it always works.

3   Britten: *War Requiem*
    I conduct Britten's music whenever I can, but I didn't do the
    War Requiem until 1989. It turned out to be an unbelievably
    moving occasion. The line-up of soloists included Heather
    Harper, who'd sung in the first performance of the work, in
    Coventry Cathedral. It was 10 November, the day the Berlin
    Wall came down, and people arrived stunned, having heard
    the news on their car radios. The atmosphere was incredible.

4   Berg: Violin Concerto
    This was a set work for my music A-level. For me it was a
    revelation. It took me into completely new spheres musically
    and confirmed my lasting interest in 20th-century music.

joined the Mingotti touring opera company, of which he subsequently
became *Kapellmeister*, and travelled widely.

Married in 1750, he settled in Vienna two years later, being
connected with the court from 1754, though without official title (only
in 1774 was he appointed court composer). Under the management of
Count Durazzo the Viennese theatre moved away from conventional
opera seria, and Gluck wrote a number of French *opéras-comiques*.
The dramatic ballet *Don Juan*, embodying Noverre's ideas on modern
dance, was produced 1761.

Finally in *Orfeo* (1762) Gluck and his librettist Calzabigi realized
in opera the current demands for greater dramatic truth in the theatre.
The aims of this 'reform' were set out in the prefaces to *Alceste* (1767)
and *Paride ed Elena* (1770). In many ways, e.g. prominent use of
chorus and ballet, these works adopted features of French opera, and
Gluck now turned to Paris, where *Iphigénie en Aulide* was produced
1774, followed by French versions of *Orfeo* and *Alceste* (1774 and
1776) and *Armide* (1777). Gluck was reluctantly involved in a
squabble between his supporters and the partisans of Piccinni, but this
was decisively closed by the triumph of his *Iphigénie en Tauride*
(1779). His last opera for Paris, *Écho et Narcisse*, was unsuccessful,
and he returned to Vienna, remaining there until his death.

Gluck's idea of a drama in which music and stage action are fully
integrated had a profound influence on later composers: Wagner's
concept of the 'total art-work' is an obvious successor. Although
Orfeo ed Euridice has remained popular, the rest of his output is still
relatively neglected. Such works as *La Rencontre imprévue*, *Armide*
and the two *Iphigénie* operas have been successfully recorded but
they await revival by major opera companies.

Apart from a number of symphonies, eight trio sonatas, a setting of
De profundis for chorus and orchestra, and settings of Klopstock's
Odes, Gluck's works are almost entirely for the theatre, viz. opere
serie: *Artaserse* (1741), *Demetrio*, *Demofoonte* (1743), *Il Tigrane*, *La
Sofonisba* (1744), *Ipermestra*, *La caduta de' giganti* (1746), *Arta-
mene*, *Le nozze d'Ercole e d'Ebe*, *Semiramide riconosciuta* (1748),
La Contesa dei numi, *Ezio* (1750), *La clemenza di Tito* (1752), *Le
Cinesi*, *Antigono*, *Il re pastore*, *Il Telemaco*, etc.; French opéras-
comiques: *L'Isle de Merlin* (1758), *La Cythère assiégée*, *L'Arbre
enchanté*, *L'Ivrogne corrigé*, *Le Cadi dupé* (1761), *La Rencontre
imprévue* (1764), etc.; 'reform' operas: *Orfeo*, *Alceste*, *Paride ed
Elena* (1770); French operas for Paris: *Iphigénie en Aulide* (1774),

A Selection of
Gluck

Gluck *The composer Christoph Willibald von Gluck (1714–1787). He
is most famous for his later 'Reform Operas' in which the musical
excesses of the earlier tradition, caused largely by the demands of
prima donnas and the composers who bowed before them, were purged
for the sake of dramatic power.*

Orphée et Euridice and *Alceste* (both French versions of the earlier Italian operas), *Armide* (1777), *Iphigénie en Tauride*, *Écho et Narcisse* (1779); ballets: *Don Juan* (1761), *Semiramide* (1765), etc.

Glückliche Hand, Die, *The Lucky Hand*, opera by Schoenberg (libretto by composer); composed 1913, produced Vienna, Volksoper, 14 Oct 1924. Symbolic drama in which artist/Man is made to face choice between worldly success and spiritual truth.

Glushchenko, Fedor (b Rostov-on-Don, 1944), Russian conductor. Studied in Moscow and Leningrad. Chief conductor of the Karelian Radio SO, Finland, 1971 and former chief of the Ukrainian State SO. Guest throughout Russia, and British debut with the BBC Scottish SO, 1989, returning with the Royal Liverpool PO and the Scottish Chamber Orchestra. Frequent concerts with the BBC PO (Manchester).

Glyndebourne Festival Opera a small private opera house opened by John Christie on his estate of Glyndebourne, Sussex, in 1934, for the performance of opera in beautiful surroundings with an international company of singers. Musical directors have been Fritz Busch (1934–51), Vittorio Gui (1951–60), John Pritchard (1960–77), Bernard Haitink (1977–87 and Andrew Davis from 1989. Gunther Rennert succeeded Carl Ebert as chief producer in 1959 and others have been John Cox (1971–83) and Peter Hall (1984–90). Until World War II the repertory was devoted almost wholly to Mozart, the only exceptions being Verdi's *Macbeth* and Donizetti's *Don Pasquale*. Since 1946 it has been considerably extended to include operas by Britten, Haydn, Henze, Janáček and Stravinsky; Venetian opera by Monteverdi and Cavalli has been given in enterprising editions by Raymond Leppard; also a Strauss series. An earlier Rossini series was recalled with the first UK staging of *Ermione* in 1995. Mozart is still sometimes performed, however, and in 1994 a newly-built auditorium was opened with *Le Nozze di Figaro*, commemorating the first production 60 years earlier.

Glyndebourne Touring Opera British company formed 1968 to make autumn tours to major provincial centres in the Midlands and South of England. Artistic directors have included Nicholas Braithwaite (1977–80), Jane Glover (1982–85), Graeme Jenkins (1986–91) and Ivor Bolton, from 1992. A major feature has been fps given at Glyndebourne in the autumn and repeated at the summer Festival the following season: Osborne's *Electrification of the Soviet Union* 1987–88 and Birtwistle's *The Second Mrs Kong* 1994–95.

Glynne, Howell (b Swansea, 24 Jan 1906; d Toronto, 24 Nov 1969), Welsh bass. He sang with the Carl Rosa Co. in the 1930s in small roles. SW, 1946–64, as Kecal, Bartolo and Fiesco and in the British fp of *I quattro rusteghi*. He sang in the 1949 fp of Bliss's *Olympians*, at CG, and was well-known there in the 1950s as Varlaam and Ochs.

Gnecchi, Vittorio (b Milan, 17 Jul 1876; d Milan, 5 Feb 1954), Italian composer. Studied music at Milan. His first opera, given at Bologna in 1905, was at the centre of great controversy in 1909, when Strauss's *Elektra* appeared and showed striking similarities to Gnecchi's music.

Works include operas *Cassandra* (after Homer's *Iliad*, 1905), and *La Rosiera* (1927); heroic poem for orchestra *Notte nel campo di Holoferne*, etc.

Gnecco, Francesco (b Genoa, c 1769; d Milan, c 1810), Italian composer. Pupil (?) of Mariani and Cimarosa. *Maestro di cappella* at Savona Cathedral.

Works include 26 operas, e.g. *Carolina e Filandro* (1804) and *La prova d'un opera seria* (1803).

Gnessin, Mikhail Fabianovich (b Rostovon-Don, 2 Feb 1883; d Moscow, 5 May 1957), Russian composer and teacher. Studied with Rimsky-Korsakov and Liadov at the St Petersburg Conservatory and in Germany from 1911 to 1914. Settled at Rostov in 1914, at Moscow in 1923 and became professor at the Leningrad Conservatory 1936; pupils included Khachaturian and Khrennikov. His work is influenced by Jewish music.

Works include operas *Youth of Abraham* (1921–23) and *The Maccabees*; incidental music for plays, including Sophocles' *Antigone* and *Oedipus Rex* (1915), Gogol's *The Revisor*, Blok's *The Rose*

and the Cross, etc.; *The Conqueror Worm* (after Poe), 1905–17 for solo voices, chorus and orchestra (1926); *Symphonic Fragment* (after Shelley), *Song of Adonis* and *Fantasia in the Jewish Style* for orchestra; *Requiem* for piano quintet, *Variations on Jewish Themes* and *Azerbaijan Folksongs* for string quartet, sextet *Adygeya*; violin and piano sonata in G minor, *Sonata-Ballade* for cello and piano; songs with orchestra; song cycles to words by Alexander Blok, Sologub, etc.; Jewish folksong arrangements.

I don't particularly like your voice, but when you sing I forget to play.
Orchestral player to Tito Gobbi, from Gobbi, *My Life*, 1979

Gobbi, Tito (b Bassano del Grappa, 24 Oct 1915; d Rome, 5 Mar 1984), Italian baritone. Originally studied law, then sang in Rome with Crimi, making his debut in Rome in 1938. He first appeared at La Scala, Milan, in 1942 as Belcore; Wozzeck same season. London, CG, 1950–74. US debut, San Francisco 1948; NY Met. 1956, as Scarpia. Gobbi had a huge repertory of some 102 roles, and was especially outstanding as a Verdi and Puccini singer. Other roles included Posa, Almaviva, Don Giovanni, Germont and Boccanegra. Active as opera producer in London, Chicago and elsewhere, notably with *Simon Boccanegra*. He was also a fine actor and made many films.

Godard, Benjamin (Louis Paul) (b Paris, 18 Aug 1849; d Cannes, 10 Jan 1895), French composer. Studied violin and composition at the Paris Conservatory. He became a viola player in chamber music. In 1878 he tied with Dubois in gaining the prize in a competition organized by the municipality of Paris with the dramatic symphony *Le Tasse* for solo voices, chorus and orchestra. In 1885 he established a series of 'modern concerts' without success.

Works include operas *Pedro de Zalamea* (1884), *Jocelyn* (1888), *Le Dante* (1890), *La Vivandière*, *Les Guelfes*; incidental music to Shakespeare's *Much Ado about Nothing* and Fabre's *Jeanne d'Arc*; *Scènes poétiques* (1879), dramatic poem *Diane*, *Symphonie-Ballet*, *Symphonie gothique*, *Symphonie orientale* and *Symphonie légendaire* for orchestra; two violin concertos, two piano concertos; three string quartets (1883–93), two piano trios; five violin and piano sonatas; piano pieces; over 100 songs.

Goddard, Arabella (b Saint-Servan, Saint-Malo, 12 Jan 1836; d Boulogne, 6 Apr 1922), English pianist. Pupil of Kalkbrenner in Paris and later of Thalberg in England. Made her first public appearance in London in 1850. She studied the classics with the critic J W Davison, whom she married in 1859.

Godfrey, Dan(iel Eyers) (b London, 20 Jun 1868; d Bournemouth, 20 Jul 1939), English conductor. Son of the bandmaster Daniel Godfrey (1831–1903). Studied at the RCM in London and first conducted a military band and opera, and in 1892 became conductor of a small seaside orchestra at Bournemouth, which in time he raised to a full symphony orchestra; frequent fps of British works. He was knighted in 1922 and retired in 1934.

Godowsky, Leopold (b Wilno, 13 Feb 1870; d New York, 21 Nov 1938), Polish (Americanized) pianist and composer. Very precociously gifted, he appeared in public at the age of nine, made a tour of Poland and Germany, and then entered the Hochschule für Musik in Berlin, studying with Bargiel and Rudorff. He first visited the USA in 1884, where he settled in 1901 and later became director of the Chicago Conservatory. In 1909–14 he taught in Vienna. He made many arrangements for piano and composed studies, concert pieces.

God save the Queen (or **God save the King**) the British national anthem. A tune of possibly remote but uncertain ancestry, appearing in *Harmonia anglicana* in 1744; earliest known performance 1745, when it became very popular as a royalist song attacking the Young Pretender. The tune has been adopted in several other countries.

Goebel, Reinhard (b Siegen, 31 Jul 1952), German conductor and violinist. Studied in Cologne, and with Gustav Leonhardt in Amster-

Reinhard Goebel – baroque violinist

1 Biber: *Harmonia artificiosa*
While studying at the Cologne Conservatory, early music really began to interest me. One time I went to a local record shop and bought a record of Biber's *Harmonia artificiosa* with violinist Marie Leonhardt. That was music which changed my life. The record must have practically worn away: I played it about 20 times a day.

2 Bach: Secular Cantatas
I first heard the Bach cantatas, performed by Elly Ameling on Cologne Radio, when I was about 14. Now, when I travel between Berlin and Cologne by car, I take with me about 20 Bach cantatas and I'm constantly discovering new things: how incredibly artful they are, how Bach managed to set the words to music and the wonderful combination of singers and instruments.

3 Bach: harpsichord concertos
It was listening to an old recording of Bach's harpsichord concertos with Gustav Leonhardt (an oldie but still a goldie) that made me want to go and study with his wife. I can still hear every note, every sound of that recording, including the double and the triple concertos, and I can remember vividly the sound of Marie's violin.

dam. Founded the Musica Antiqua Cologne 1973 and has given many concerts of early music throughout Europe, the Americas and the Far East. York Festival, England, 1989 with music by Legrenzi, Schmelzer and Biber. Recordings include Telemann's *Tafelmusik*.

Goehr, Alexander (b Berlin, 10 Aug 1932), English composer. Studied at the RMCM and at the Paris Conservatory with Messiaen. He writes frequently in a free serial technique. Professor, Leeds University, 1971–76; professor, Cambridge University, from 1976. The opera *Arianna* was premiered at CG, 1995.

Works include STAGE: operas *Arden muss sterben/Arden must Die* (1967), *Behold the Sun* (1985) and *Arianna* (1995); ballet *La Belle dame sans merci* (1958); *Triptych*, music theatre in three parts: *Naboth's Vineyard*, *Shadowplay*, *Sonata about Jerusalem* (1968–70).

CHORAL AND SOLO VOCAL: *The Deluge*, cantata after da Vinci (1958), *Sutter's Gold*, cantata for baritone, chorus and orchestra (1960), five *Poems and an Epigram of William Blake* for chorus and trumpet (1964), *Psalm IV* for soprano, mezzo, women's voices, viola and organ (1976), *Babylon the Great is Fallen* for chorus and orchestra (1979), *Das Gesetz der Quadrille* for baritone and piano, to texts from Kafka (1979), *Behold the Sun*, concert aria from the opera (1981), *Eve Dreams in Paradise* for mezzo, tenor and orchestra (1988), *Sing, Ariel* for mezzo, two sopranos and five instruments (1990), *The Death of Moses* for soloists, chorus and 13 instruments (1992), *Psalm 39* for chorus and wind (1993).

ORCHESTRAL: *Fantasia* (1954), *Hecuba's Lament* (1961), violin concerto (1962), *Little Symphony* (1963), *Little Music for Strings* (1963), *Pastorals* (1965), *Romanza* for cello and orchestra (1968), *Symphony in one movement* (1970), Concerto for 11 instruments (1970), piano concerto (1971), *Chaconne* for 19 wind instruments (1974), *Metamorphosis/Dance* (1974), *Sinfonia* (1980), *Deux Études* (1981), *A musical offering (JSB 1985)*, *Symphony with Chaconne* (1986), *Still Lands* for small orchestra (1990), *Colossus or Panic*, symphonic fragment after Goya (1992).

CHAMBER: piano sonata (1952), *Suite* for ensemble (1961), piano trio (1966), four string quartets. (1957, 1967, 1976, 1990), *Lyric Pieces* for wind septet and double bass (1974), Prelude and fugue for three clarinets (1978), cello sonata (1988).

Goehr, Walter (b Berlin, 28 May 1903; d Sheffield, 4 Dec 1960), German-born British conductor and composer, father of Alexander ◊Goehr. Studied with Schoenberg in Berlin, conducting Radio Orchestra there, 1925–31. Moved to London 1933 and was music director of the Columbia Graphophone Co. until 1939. Conducted, Morley College concerts from 1943. Gave fps of Britten's *Serenade* and Tippett's *A Child of our Time*. Made editions of Monteverdi's *Vespers* of 1610 and *Poppea*.

Works include symphony, radio opera, incidental and chamber music.

Goethe, Johann Wolfgang von (1749–1832), German poet, novelist, dramatist and philosopher. His most significant influence in the world of music has been through his drama ◊*Faust*. Successful settings of other dramas have been made by Beethoven (*Egmont*), Mendelssohn (*Die erste Walpurgisnacht*), Brahms (*Rinaldo*), Thomas (*Mignon*) and Massenet (*Werther*). Much of Goethe's poetry was created with musical setting in mind. Many of Schubert's greatest Lieder are based on Goethe, although the poet failed to recognize his genius, preferring simple strophic settings. Some of Schubert's Goethe Lieder are *An den Mond*, *Erlkönig*, *Der Fischer*, *Ganymed*, *Gretchen am Spinnrade*, *Heidenröslein*, *Kennst du das Land?*, *Der Musensohn*, *Nähe des Geliebten*, *Prometheus*, *Wanderers Nachtlied*. J ◊André (*Erwin und Elmire*); ◊Apprenti sorcier (Dukas); ◊Bentzon (*Faust III*); ◊Blangini (*Die Letzten Augenblicke Werthers*); ◊Brahms (*Gesang der Parzen*, *Rinaldo*); ◊Claudine von Villa Bella (Schubert and Reichardt); ◊Dukas (*Apprenti sorcier* and *Götz von Berlichingen*); ◊Egmont (Beethoven); ◊Erlkönig (Schubert); ◊Gál (*Requiem für Mignon*); C ◊Goldmark (*Götz von Berlichingen* and *Meeresstille und glückliche Fahrt*); E T A ◊Hoffmann (*Scherz, List und Rache*); A ◊Hüttenbrenner (*Erlkönig*); ◊Koechlin (*Nuit de Walpurgis classique*); ◊Krenek (*Triumph der Empfindsamkeit*); C ◊Loewe (*Erlkönig*); ◊Meeresstille (Beethoven and Mendelssohn); ◊Mendelssohn (*Erste Walpurgisnacht*); ◊Mignon (A Thomas); ◊Rhapsodie (Brahms); ◊Rinaldo (Brahms); Anton ◊Rubinstein (*Wilhelm Meister*); ◊Scherz, List und Rache (Bruch); ◊Schoeck (*Erwin und Elmire*, *Dithyrambe* and songs); ◊Schubert (*Claudine von Villa Bella* and 20 Lieder); ◊Schumann (*Requiem für Mignon*); ◊Stiehl (*Jery und Bätely*); ◊Tasso (Liszt); ◊Tomášek (songs); ◊Veilchen (Mozart); ◊Vogler (*Erwin und Elmire*); ◊Webern (two choral songs); ◊Wellesz (*Scherz, List und Rache*); ◊Werther (Massenet); ◊Winter (*Scherz, List und Rache* and *Jery und Bätely*); ◊Zelter (songs); ◊Zumsteeg (*Clavigo*).

Five songs by Brahms, one by Mozart (*Veilchen*), 71 by Schubert, 19 by Schumann, 60 (including nine early) by Wolf.

◊Faust and ◊Faust Symphonie.

'What's the difference between Godowsky and a pianola?' Busoni would ask. Godowsky can play ten times as fast, but the pianola has ten times as much feeling.

Carl Fleisch, *Memoirs*, 1957

Goetz ◊Götz.

Gogol, Nikolai Vassilievich, (1809–1852), Russian novelist. ◊Assafiev (*Christmas Eve*); ◊Berutti (*Taras Bulba*); ◊Christmas Eve (Rimsky-Korsakov); ◊Gnessin (*Revisor*); ◊The Marriage (Mussorgsky and Martinů); ◊May Night (Rimsky-Korsakov); ◊Nose, (Shostakovich); ◊Revisor (Egk); ◊Searle (*Diary of a Madman*); ◊Serov (*Christmas Eve Revels*); ◊Sorotchintsy Fair (Mussorgsky); ◊Taras Bulba (Janáček); ◊Vakula the Smith (Tchaikovsky); K ◊Weis (*Revisor*).

Göhringer, Franzilla, ◊Pixis.

Golani, Rivka (b Tel-Aviv, 22 Mar 1946), Israeli violist. Studied with

Ödön Partos in Tel-Aviv and emigrated to Canada 1974. Performances throughout Europe and the USA with the Bartók concerto, Martinů's Rhapsody and the Elgar cello concerto arranged by Tertis. Almost 200 works have been written for her, including concertos by Robin Holloway and Michael Colgrass, and pieces by Holmboe and Heinz Holliger.

Goldberg, Johann Gottlieb (b Danzig, bap. 14 Mar 1727; d Dresden, buried 15 Apr 1756), German harpsichordist, possibly pupil of W F and J S Bach. The latter allegedly wrote for him (aged only 15) the 'Goldberg Variations', pub. 1741/2.

Goldberg, Reiner (b Grostau, 17 Oct 1939), German tenor. He studied in Dresden and made his debut there in 1966. Joined Dresden Opera in 1973 and visited Tokyo with the Co. in 1980. London, CG, debut 1982 as Walther. Has visited Vienna, Hamburg, Berlin and Leningrad in roles of Bacchus, Max and Siegmund. He sang the title role on the soundtrack of the Syberberg film version of *Parsifal*, while the part was being mimed onscreen by a woman. Sang Walther at CG 1990, Florestan and Tannhäuser at the NY Met., 1992. Recorded Strauss's Guntram 1985.

Goldberg, Szymon (b Wloclawek, 1 Jun 1909; d Oyami-machi, Japan, 19 Jul 1993), Polish-born American violinist and conductor. Studied with Carl Flesch in Berlin and made debut at Warsaw, 1921. Led the Dresden PO 1925–29, Berlin PO (under Fürtwangler) 1929–34. Played in string trio with Hindemith and Feuermann, 1930–34, recording the Beethoven Serenade op. 8. US debut 1938, and moved there post-war; chamber music concerts at Aspen, 1951–65, and solo career from 1955. Conducted Netherlands Chamber Orchestra 1955–78, Manchester Camerata 1977–79. Taught at Juilliard 1978–80, Manhattan School of Music from 1981. Noted for his Mozart concerto performances, and sonatas with Lili Kraus (1935–40).

'Goldberg Variations' monumental set of 30 variations by Bach for two-manual harpsichord, BWV 998. A wide variety of keyboard technique is explored, in particular the canon, which is developed in each third variation.

Golden Age (Shostakovich.) ◊Age of Gold.

Golden Cockerel, The, *Zolotoy Petushok*, an opera by Rimsky-Korsakov (libretto V I Bielsky, based on Pushkin's satirical fairytale), produced Moscow, 7 Oct 1909, after Rimsky-Korsakov's death. It is his last opera. King Dodon's astrologer presents a golden cockerel, which can warn of trouble. The King falls in love with Queen Shemakha, whom the astrologer names as his price for the cockerel. The King refuses and the cockerel kills him.

Goldene Bock, Der chamber opera by Krenek (libretto by composer), produced Hamburg, 16 Jun 1964. Jason time-travels to Route 66 in the USA, and divorces Medea when she serves him soup made from the flesh of a Greek shipping magnate.

Golden Legend, The oratorio by Sullivan (on Longfellow's poem), produced Leeds Festival, 1886; revived at Leeds, 15 Mar 1986, conductor Mackerras.

'Golden Sonata' the nickname given to the ninth (F major) of Purcell's ten *Sonatas of IV Parts* for two violins, cello and continuo, pub. posthumously in 1697.

Goldmark, Karoly (Carl) (b Keszthely, 18 May 1830; d Vienna, 2 Jan 1915), Austro-Hungarian composer. Son of a poor Jewish cantor, who managed to enter him at the Sopron school of music in 1842. He studied violin and made such rapid progress that he was sent to Vienna the next year and entered the conservatory in 1847. During the 1848 Revolution he played at the theatre at Györ in Hungary and was nearly shot as a rebel. In 1850 he returned to Vienna, where he eventually settled as a teacher. His best-known work today is the *Rustic Wedding Symphony*, although he established his reputation with the Wagner-influenced opera *Die Königin von Saba/The Queen of Sheba*.

Works include operas *Die Königin von Saba* (1875), *Merlin* (1886), *Das Heimchen am Herd* (after Dickens's *Cricket on the Hearth*, 1896), *Die Kriegsgefangene*, *Götz von Berlichingen* (after Goethe, 1902), and *Ein Wintermärchen* (after Shakespeare's *Winter's Tale*, 1908); symphonic poem *Rustic Wedding* and two sym-

phonies; two Scherzos for orchestra and overtures *Sakuntala* (after Kalidasa), *Penthesilea* (after Kleist), *Im Frühling*, *Der gefesselte Prometheus*, *Sappho*, *In Italien* and *Aus Jugendtagen*, symphonic poem *Zrinyi*; *Meeresstille und glückliche Fahrt* (Goethe) for male chorus and horns, other choral works; two violin concertos.

String quartet (1860), piano quintet, three piano trios and other chamber music; two suites and sonata for violin and piano, cello and piano sonata; piano pieces; songs.

Goldmark, Rubin (b New York, 15 Aug 1872; d New York, 6 Mar 1936), American composer of Austro-Hungarian descent, nephew of Carl ◊Goldmark. Studied at the Vienna Conservatory and the National Conservatory in NY, where Dvořák was his composition master. He was director of the Colorado College Conservatory 1895–1901, but returned to NY in 1902 and settled as private piano and composition teacher, until in 1924 he was appointed to the Juilliard Graduate School there.

Works include *Hiawatha* (after Longfellow, 1900), *Samson* (1914), *Requiem* (on Lincoln's address at Gettysburg), *Negro Rhapsody* and *The Call of the Plains* for orchestra; string quartet in A major; piano trio in D minor; violin and piano sonata; violin pieces; piano music, songs; choruses, etc.

Goldoni, Carlo (b Venice, 25 Feb 1707; d Paris, 6 or 7 Feb 1793), Italian playwright and librettist. ◊Arcadia in Brenta (Galuppi); ◊Buovo d'Antona (Traetta); ◊Burbero di buon cuore (Martín y Soler); ◊Donne curiose (Wolf-Ferrari); ◊Filosofo di campagna (Galuppi); ◊Fischietti (four operas); ◊Fra due litiganti (Sarti); ◊Generali (*Pamela nubile*, after Richardson); ◊Isola disabitata (G Scarlatti); ◊Lottchen am Hofe (J A Hiller); ◊Malipiero (three operas); ◊Mondo alla roversa (Galuppi); ◊Mondo della luna (ditto and Haydn); ◊Paisiello (*Ciarlone*); ◊Pescatrici (Bertoni and Haydn); ◊Piccinni (*Vittorina*); ◊Quattro rusteghi (Wolf-Ferrari); ◊Scarlatti (6) (*Portentosi effetti*); ◊Speziale (Haydn); ◊Tigrane (Gluck); ◊Usiglio (*Donne curiose*); ◊Vendemmia (Gazzaniga); J ◊Wagenaar (*Philosophical Princess*); E W ◊Wolf (*Dorfdeputierten*).

Mozart should have composed Faust.
Goethe, *Conversations with Eckermann*, 1827

Goldovsky, Boris (b Moscow, 7 Jun 1908), Russian-born American conductor and opera producer. Studied in Moscow, Berlin and Budapest. Moved to the USA 1930 and studied with Reiner at Curtis. Headed the opera department at the New England Conservatory 1942–64, producing a truncated US fp of *Les Troyens* (1955). Led the opera workshop at Tanglewood 1946–62, mounting the US fps of *Idomeneo*, *Peter Grimes* and *Albert Herring*. Directed the Goldovsky Opera Theater and toured with it until 1984. Among his books is *Road to Opera* (1979).

Goldschmidt, Adalbert von (b Vienna, 5 May 1848; d Vienna, 21 Dec 1906), Austrian composer. He devoted himself as an amateur to the composition of large-scale works, the first of which, produced in Berlin in 1876, showed remarkable affinities with Wagner's *Ring*, not heard until later in the year at Bayreuth.

Works include music-dramas *Die sieben Todsünden* (1876), *Helianthus*, *Gaea* (trilogy), opera *Die fromme Helene* (after Wilhelm Busch); symphonic poem; *c* 100 songs, etc.

Goldschmidt, Berthold (b Hamburg, 18 Jan 1903), German-born English conductor and composer. Studied in Berlin, became assistant conductor of the Staatsoper there 1926 and conducted at the Darmstadt Opera in 1927. In 1931–33 he conducted on the Berlin Radio and was artistic adviser to the municipal opera there, but the Nazi régime drove him to England. In 1964 he conducted the fp of Deryck Cooke's performing version of Mahler's tenth symphony. His music was long neglected after he moved to England, but the opera *Beatrice Cenci* was given a London concert premiere 1988 and *Der gewaltige Hahnrei* was revived in Berlin, 1992. His clarinet quintet (1983) was premiered in Pasadena, 1985.

Works include operas *Der gewaltige Hahnrei* (after Crommelynck, produced Mannheim, 1932) and *Beatrice Cenci* (after Shelley, 1949–50); ballet *Chronica*; overture to Shakespeare's *Comedy of Errors*, symphonies and other orchestral works, including *Ciaconna Sinfonica* (1936, premiered in Vienna 1960, performed under Simon Rattle in Berlin 1987 and heard at the 1993 London Proms); violin, cello and harp concertos, chamber music, including four string quartets (1925, 1936, 1989, 1992), clarinet quintet, piano trio (1985), string trio (*Retrospectum*, 1991), *Capriccio* for violin (1992).

Goldschmidt, Otto (b Hamburg, 21 Aug 1829; d London, 24 Feb 1907), German pianist and composer. Studied at the Leipzig Conservatory under Mendelssohn and in 1848 went to Paris intending to study with Chopin. In 1849 he went to London, where he settled in 1858. Accompanist and husband of Jenny Lind. Founder of the Bach Choir.

Works include oratorio *Ruth* (1867), cantata *Music* for soprano and female voices (1898); piano concerto; piano trio; two duets for two pianos; studies and pieces for piano; songs.

Golgotha oratorio by Frank Martin for five soloists, chorus and orchestra (text from the Bible and St Augustine); composed 1945–48, fp Geneva, 29 Apr 1949.

Golschmann, Vladimir (b Paris, 16 Dec 1893; d New York, 1 Mar 1972), French-born American conductor. Studied in Paris and formed the Golschmann concerts there 1919, giving performances of music by Les Six. Conducted Diaghilev's Ballets Russes and worked in the USA from 1923 (principal of the St Louis SO 1931–56, Tulsa SO 1958–61, and Denver SO 1964–70).

Goltermann, Georg (Eduard) (b Hanover, 19 Aug 1824; d Frankfurt, 29 Dec 1898), German cellist, conductor and composer. Studied at Munich and began to tour as a cello virtuoso in 1850. In 1853 he became second and in 1874 first conductor at the Frankfurt theatre. Composed a symphony, a cello concerto and many other cello pieces.

Goltz, Christel (b Dortmund, 8 Jul 1912), German soprano. She studied in Munich and sang Agathe there in 1935. Dresden 1936–50; Berlin, Vienna and Munich from 1947 in Strauss roles, Tosca and Leonore. London, CG, from 1951; in 1952 sang Marie there in the first British stage production of *Wozzeck*. NY Met. debut, Dec 1954, as Salome. Other roles included Isolde, the Dyer's Wife and Orff's Antigonae.

Gombert, Nicolas (b *c* 1495; d ? Tournai, *c* 1556), Flemish composer. Pupil of Josquin des Prés. He was in service at the Emperor Charles V's chapel in Flanders from 1562 and became *maître des enfants* in 1529; later he became a canon at Tournai and in 1537 went to Spain with 20 singers and held a post in the imperial chapel in Madrid; exiled in 1540 for gross indecency with his choirboys. His music was admired for its sombre colours and close-knit textures.

Works include ten Masses, 160 motets, psalms; *c* 80 *chansons*.

Gomes, (Antônio) Carlos (b Campinas, 11 Jul 1836; d Belém, 16 Sept 1896), Brazilian composer of Portuguese descent. Studied with Lauro Rossi in Milan. In 1895 he was appointed director of the Conservatory at Pará, but he was delayed at Lisbon by illness and died soon after his arrival. The once-popular *Il Guarnay*, to a local Indian legend, has been revived in recent years with Placido Domingo.

Works include operas *A noite do castello* (1861), *Joana di Flandres*, *Il Guarany* (1870), *Fosca*, *Salvator Rosa* (1874), *Maria Tudor* (on Victor Hugo's play, 1879), *Lo schiavo*, *Condor* (1891); revues *Se sa minga* and *Nella luna*; ode *Il saluto del Brasil* (Philadelphia Exhibition, 1876) and cantata *Colombo* (Columbus Festival, 1892).

Gomez, Jill (b New Amsterdam, British Guiana, 21 Sept 1942), British soprano. She studied in London; sang Mélisande at Glyndebourne in 1969 and returned as Calisto and Anne Trulove. She created Flora in *The Knot Garden* at CG (1970); other London roles have been Tippett's Jenifer, Tytania and Ilia. With Scottish Opera she has been heard as Pamina, Fiordiligi and Henze's Elizabeth Zimmer. Often heard in concert, and at Lausanne in 1985 sang in Handel's *Belshazzar*. Premiered *Cantiga* by David Matthews, 1988

Gomis, José Melchor (b Onteniente, Valencia, 6 Jan 1791; d Paris, 26 Jul 1836), Spanish composer. Bandmaster at Barcelona, moved to Madrid *c* 1817 and in 1823 went to Paris for political reasons. In

1826–29 he taught singing in London, where he pub. many Spanish songs, and then returned to Paris, where he produced comic operas.

Works include Spanish monodrama *Sensibilidad y prudencia, ó La aldeana*, French comic operas *Le Diable à Séville* (1831), *Le Revenant* (after Scott, 1835), *Le Portefaix* and *Rock le barbu* (1836); *L'inverno* for four voices and orchestra; songs.

Gondoliers, The, or The King of Barataria operetta by Sullivan (libretto by W S Gilbert), produced London, Savoy Theatre, 7 Dec 1889. The baby Prince of Baratavia is brought up by gondoliers. Not knowing the heir's true identity, the Inquisitor later appoints Marco and Giuseppe as rulers, but it is eventually revealed that servant Luiz is the true king.

gong an oriental bronze disc with turned-down rims. It is struck with a mallet covered with various materials according to the quality of sound required. Also called ɔtam-tam.

Gönnenwein, Wolfgang (b Schwabisch-Hall, 29 Jan 1933), German conductor. Studied in Stuttgart and conducted the South German Madrigal Choir there, from 1959; tours throughout Europe and South America. Director of the Cologne Bach Choir 1969–73, and artistic director of the Ludwigsburg Castle Festivals from 1972, leading *Die Zauberflöte*, *Fidelio* and *Der Freischutz*, 1972–89. General director of the Stuttgart State Theatre from 1985. Recordings include the Bach Passions and Magnificat, Haydn's *Creation* and *Seasons*, and the Missa Solemnis.

Gonzaga, Guglielmo (b Mantua, 24 Apr 1538; d Mantua, 14 Aug 1587), Duke of Mantua, he succeeded to the duchy in 1556, became a great patron of music and was himself a composer, publishing anonymously a book of madrigals and one of *Sacrae cantiones*.

Goodall, Reginald (b Lincoln, 13 Jul 1901; d Bridge, near Canterbury, 5 May 1990), English conductor. He studied at the RCM and in Germany. Conducted the fp of *Peter Grimes* at SW, London, in 1945. On staff at CG from 1946, but his gifts were not properly recognized. Major success came with *The Mastersingers* at SW in 1968. His broad tempi and intensity of expression were regarded as belonging to the best traditions of German conductors. *Parsifal* at CG *1971*. The *Ring* at the London Coliseum 1973; *Tristan* with the WNO 1979. Conducted *The Valkyrie* for WNO, 1984, *Parsifal* for ENO, 1986. Also conducted Bruckner's symphonies. Knighted 1985.

Goode, Richard (b New York, 1 Jun 1943), American pianist. Studied at Mannes College and with Rudolf Serkin. NY debut 1962, Europe from 1964 (Spoleto Festival). Many concerts with the NY, LA and Royal Philharmonics, Philadelphia Orchestra, and the Orpheus Chamber Orchestra. Founding member of the Chamber Music Society of Lincoln Center, NY, 1969. Has recorded the complete Beethoven sonatas and Schubert's posthumous works for piano.

Good-Humoured Ladies, The ballet by Tommasini on music by D Scarlatti (choreography by Massin), produced Rome, Teatro Costanzi, 12 Apr 1917.

Goodman, Benny (b Chicago, 30 May 1909; d New York, 16 Jun 1986), American clarinettist, composer and band-leader. He played in various jazz and dance bands from 1921. In 1938 recorded the Mozart quintet with the Budapest Quartet and commissioned Bartók's *Contrasts* (fp 1939). Copland and Hindemith wrote concertos for him (both fps 1950).

Goodman, Roy (b Guildford, 26 Jan 1951), English conductor and violinist. Studied at Cambridge and the RCM. Directed Ensemble of Early Music at the RAM and founded the Brandenburg Consort 1975. Co-director of the Parley of Instruments 1979–86, and principal conductor of the Hanover Band from 1986. Many recordings of Classical and early Romantic music, with frequent tours to the USA. Guest conductor with the German Handel soloists, I Virtuosi di Praga and Gran Canaria PO and Choir; Handel's *Tamerlano* in Paris. Conducted a revival of Arne's *Artaxerxes*, London 1995.

Goossens, Eugene (b London, 26 May 1893; d Hillingdon, 13 Jun 1962), English conductor and composer of Belgian descent, grandson of Eugène Goossens (1845–1906) and son of Eugène Goossens (1867–1958), both conductors of the Carl Rosa Opera Co. After study at Bruges, Liverpool and the RCM, he played violin in the Queen's

Hall Orchestra, 1911–15, and then, until 1920, conducted some of Beecham's operatic productions. After that he formed an orchestra of his own, giving early English performances of works by Stravinsky, and conducting the Russian Ballet. From 1923 he conducted the PO at Rochester, USA. In 1931 he was appointed conductor of the Cincinnati SO and continued to live there until he was appointed conductor of the Sydney Orchestra, and director of the Conservatory there 1947–56. Knighted 1955.

Works include operas *Judith* (1929) and *Don Juan de Mañara* (1937); ballet *L'École en crinoline*; two symphonies (1940, 1944), sinfonietta; *Silence* for chorus and orchestra; Fantasy Concerto for piano and orchestra, oboe concerto (1927), violin concerto; two string quartets (1915, 1940).

Goossens, Léon (b Liverpool, 12 Jun 1897; d Tunbridge Wells, 12 Feb 1988), English oboist, brother of Eugene ◊Goossens. From 1913 he was first oboist of the Queen's Hall Orchestra, afterwards playing with the RPO and with CG Opera. Taught at the RAM and the RCM. Elgar, Vaughan Williams and Gordon Jacob wrote works for him. His sisters **Marie** (1897–1991) and **Sidonie** (1899–) were both harpists: Marie played for the Queen's Hall Orchestra 1920–30, LSO 1940–59 and London Mozart Players from 1972; Sidonie was principal with the BBC SO 1930–80.

Goovaerts, Alphonse (Jean Marie André) (b Antwerp, 25 May 1847; d Brussels, 25 Dec 1922), Belgian composer and writer on music. Studied at the Jesuit College of Antwerp and at the age of 15 was obliged by financial losses to take a commercial career; but he studied music thoroughly by himself and in 1866 obtained a post at the Antwerp town library. In 1869 his *Messe solennelle* was performed. In 1874 he was appointed music secretary to Antwerp Cathedral where he established a special choir, for which he copied a vast quantity of old motets of various schools. He began to write on the reform of church music and in 1898 was appointed keeper of the royal archives in Brussels.

Works include motets, *Petite Messe*, *Messe solennelle* and other church music; songs, part-songs.

gopak (or *hopak*) a Russian folk dance with music of a lively character in quick 2–4 time.

Stuffing birds or playing stringed instruments is an elegant pastime, and a resource to the idle, but it is not education.

Cardinal Newman,
The Idea of a University Defined, 1873

Gorchakova, Galina (b Novkuznetsk, 1 Mar 1962), Russian soprano. Studied at Novosibirsk and sang with Sverdlovsk Opera from 1988, as Tatiana, Butterfly, Tamara in *The Demon*, Katerina in *Lady Macbeth* and Yaroslavna. Has sung in St Petersburg as Lisa (*Queen of Spades*) and the *Trovatore* Leonora; dramatically convincing performances there and at CG and the NY Met. as Renata in *The Fiery Angel*, 1992. Sang with the Kirov Opera as Fevronia in *The Invisible City of Kitezh*, St Petersburg and London, 1994. Sang Butterfly at the Met., 1995.

Gorczycki, Grzegorz (b Bytom, Silesia, c 1664; d Kraków, 30 Apr 1734), Polish composer. *Magister capellae* at Kraków Cathedral from 1698. Wrote motets and other church music.

Górecki, Henryk (b Czernica, 6 Dec 1933), Polish composer. Studied with Szabelski in Katowice. He tended once towards strict serialism, but was also influenced by neo-classicism. He has more recently turned to the simplicities of religious faith. His third symphony, *Sorrowful Songs* has attained wide popularity.

Works include cantata *Epitafium*; *Symphony no. 1* (1959), *No. 2* for soprano, baritone, chorus and orchestra (1972), *No. 3* for soprano and orchestra (1973); *Scontri* for orchestra (1960); *Canticum Graduum* for orchestra (1969); *Old Polish Music* for brass and strings (1969); harpsichord concerto (1980); *Concerto-Cantata* for flute and orchestra (1992); *Epitaph* for mixed chorus and instruments (1956);

Gorchakova *Russian soprano Galina Gorchakova. One of her first operatic experiences was listening to recordings of singers such as Mirella Freni, Renata Tebaldi, and Maria Callas: 'Opera was always a fairy tale for me. It was everything a child's imagination could want.' She memorized many leading roles by the time she was six.*

Genesis III: Monodrama (1963); *Two Sacred Songs* for baritone and orchestra (1971); *Beatus Vir* for baritone, chorus and orchestra (1979); chamber: *Quartettino* for wind (1956); sonata for two violins (1957); series *Genesis I–IV* for various instrumental groups (1962–70); *Aria* for tuba and ensemble (1987); *Already it is Dusk* (string quartet no. 1, 1988); *Quasi una fantasia* for string quartet (1991); *Kleines Requiem für eine Polka*, for piano and 13 instruments (1993).

Goritz, Otto (b Berlin, 8 Jun 1873; d Berlin, 16 Apr 1929), German baritone. Debut Neustrelitz 1895, in *Fra Diavolo*. After engagements at Breslau and Hamburg he sang at the NY Met. 1903–17; appeared in the local fps of *Fledermaus*, *Hansel and Gretel*, *Rosenkavalier* (Ochs, 1911) and in the fp of *Parsifal* outside Bayreuth.

Görner, Johann Gottlieb (b Penig, Saxony, bap. 16 Apr 1697; d Leipzig, 15 Feb 1778), German organist and composer. Educated in Leipzig and held various organ posts there: St Paul (1716), St Nikolai (1721) and St Thomas (1729). In 1723 he founded a Collegium Musicum. Wrote church music.

Gorr, Rita (b Ghent, 18 Feb 1926), Belgian mezzo. Debut, Antwerp 1949 as Fricka; sang this role and Ortrud at Bayreuth 1958–59. She sang Charlotte at her Paris, Opéra-Comique, debut and was also known as Massenet's Hérodiade. Often heard in the Verdi repertory; Amneris was the role of her CG (1959) and NY Met. (1962) debuts. Also a distinguished Eboli, Azucena and Ulrica. Sang in the *Carmélites* and *Salome*, Lyon, 1990.

Gorzanis, Giacomo (b Apulia, c 1525; d ? Trieste, after 1575), Italian composer. He pub. four books of lute music, including numerous dance-suites in two or three movements. One of these, consisting of a *passo e mézzo* and *padovana* (1561), provides an early example of 'sonata' used as a title. He was blind.

Göss, Barthel, Bartholomäus ◊Gese.

Goss, John (b Fareham, Hants., 27 Dec 1800; d London, 10 May 1880), English organist and composer. Studied under his father, organist at Fareham, then under J S Smith at the Chapel Royal in London and finally under Attwood. After holding several organ appointments, he succeeded Attwood as organist of St Paul's Cathedral in 1838 and in 1856 became one of the composers to the Chapel Royal in succession to Knyvett. Knighted 1872 and Mus.D., Cambridge, 1876.

Works include services, anthems, chants, psalms; orchestral pieces; glees; songs.

Gossec, François Joseph (b Vergnies, Hainaut, 17 Jan 1734; d Passy

────── THE OPERA ──────

Götterdämmerung

A three-act music drama that concludes Wagner's monumental *Der Ring des Nibelungen*. It depicts – and its title means – the twilight of the gods.

I. On the Valkyrie rock Three Norns foretell the end of the gods. Emerging from their night together, Siegfried (tenor) gives Brünnhilde (soprano) the Ring before he departs for new adventures. At the Hall of the Gibichungs, Alberich's son Hagen (bass) plots with his half-brother Gunther (baritone) and half-sister Gutrune (soprano). Given a draught of forgetfulness, Siegfried falls in love with Gutrune and, in return for her bridal promise, agrees to fetch Brünnhilde for Gunther. Back at the Valkyrie rock, Brünnhilde's sister Waltraute (mezzo-soprano) fails in her demand for the Ring to be returned to the Rhine-maidens. Siegfried appears disguised as Gunther and drags the Ring from her before leading her away.

II. The Gibichung vassals are summoned by Hagen for a double wedding. When she is led in, Brünnhilde accuses Siegfried of treachery, but he still fails to recognize her. Hagen, Gunther and Brünnhilde plot Siegfried's death.

III. The Rhine-maidens plead with Siegfried for the Ring to be returned. Hagen appears and Siegfried, with his memory restored, recounts his love for Brünnhilde. Speared by Hagen, Siegfried's body is returned to the Gibichung Hall. Gunther is killed by Hagen in a quarrel over the Ring, and Brünnhilde takes it herself before plunging into a funeral pyre. The Rhine overflows, Hagen is drowned, and Valhalla is consumed in flames.

────── THE OPERA ──────

near Paris, 16 Feb 1829), Belgian-French composer. Chorister at Antwerp Cathedral, went to Paris in 1751, where with Rameau's help he obtained a post in La Pouplinière's private orchestra in 1754. Later music director to the Prince of Condé. Founded the Concert des Amateurs in 1770, and in 1773 took over the direction of the Concert Spirituel. On the foundation of the Paris Conservatory in 1795 he became one of its directors and professor of composition. As one of the leading composers of the French Revolution, he wrote many works for public ceremonies, often using vast forces. After 1800 he wrote little.

Works include OPERAS: *Le Tonnelier* (1765), *Le Faux Lord*, *Les Pêcheurs*, *Toinon et Toinette* (1767), *Le Double Déguisement*, *Hilas et Silvie*, *Sabinus* (1773), *Alexis et Daphné*, *Philémon et Baucis* (1775), *La Fête de village*, *Thésée* (1782), *Rosine* (1786), etc.; ballets *Les Scythes enchaînés*, added to Gluck's *Iphigénie en Tauride* (1779), *La Reprise de Toulon*, *Mirsa* and *Callisto*; incidental music for Racine's *Athalie* and Rochefort's *Électre*.

ORATORIOS: *La Nativité* (1774), *Saül* and *L'Arche d'alliance*; *Requiem* (1760), *Dixit Dominus*, *Exaudiat*, *Dernière Messe des vivants*, motets, etc.; funeral music for Mirabeau, *Le Chant du 14 juillet*, *L'Offrande à la liberté*, *Le Triomphe de la République* and other music for the Revolution.

c 50 symphonies (1756–1809), overtures and other orchestral works; 12 string quartets, trios and other chamber music.

Gossett, Philip (b New York, 27 Sept 1941), American musicologist. He studied at Princeton (Ph.D. 1970) and has taught at the University of Chicago since 1968 (professor and chairman of the music department 1978–84). General editor of the critical edition of Verdi's works; joint editor of the Rossini edition from 1979; co-editor with Charles Rosen of *Early Romantic Operas* (NY, 1978–83, in 44 vols.); facsimile edition of *Il Barbiere di Siviglia* (Rome, 1993).

Gosswin, Antonius (b Liège, *c* 1540; d *c* 1597), Flemish composer, a pupil of Lassus in Munich; worked there in 1570s. Wrote German songs, madrigals, motets and seven Masses, four modelled on Lassus.

Gostena, Giovanni Battista dalla (b Genoa, *c* 1540; d Genoa, Dec 1598), Italian composer. Pupil of Philippe de Monte, *maestro di cappella* at Genoa Cathedral from 1584 to 1598, when his nephew, Molinaro, succeeded him.

Works include motets and other church music; four books of madrigals, two of *canzonette*; 25 fantasies for lute.

Gostling, John (b East Malling, Kent, *c* 1650; d London, 17 Jul 1733), English cleric and bass. Became a Gentleman of the Chapel Royal in London, 1679, and later held various clerical posts in and out of the capital. Purcell's anthems afford evidence of his remarkable compass.

Gothic Symphony the first by Havergal Brian, for soloists, children's choruses, brass band and orchestra of 180; last of four movements is a setting of the Te Deum. Composed 1919–27, fp by amateur forces, London, 24 Jun 1961; first professional performance London, 30 Oct 1966, to mark Brian's 90th birthday. Broadcast live to the USA by satellite, 25 May 1980.

Gotovac, Jakov (b Split, 11 Oct 1895; d Zagreb, 16 Oct 1982), Yugoslav conductor and composer. Studied at his home town, at Zagreb and in Vienna. In 1923 he became conductor of the Croatian Opera at Zagreb, also of a Balkan choral society, with which he travelled in Europe.

Works include operas *Morana* (1930) and *Ero the Joker* (1935); incidental music for pastoral play *Dubravka* (1928); choral works; Symphony *Kolo* and *The Ploughers* for orchestra; chamber music; songs.

Götterdämmerung, *Twilight of the Gods*, opera by Wagner (libretto by composer), produced Bayreuth, 17 Aug 1876. Ring des Nibelungen, Der. Following the conclusion of *Siegfried*, this fourth and final opera of the cycle opens with the awakening of Brünnhilde. Siegfried, having inadvertently drunk a magic potion, betrays her to Gunther; Gutrune hopes to acquire Siegfried. Meanwhile Hagen, Alberich's son, has conspired to try to gain power and the Ring. Hagen murders Siegfried, but Brünnhilde takes the Ring, returning it to the Rhine-maidens as Valhalla burns.

Gottschalk, Louis Moreau (b New Orleans, 8 May 1829; d Rio de Janeiro, 18 Dec 1869), American pianist and composer. He studied in Paris and had much success there as a pianist from his debut in 1844; admired by Chopin and Berlioz. He toured throughout Europe and, from 1853, North and South America; died of yellow fever on tour in Brazil. His works are noted for their virtuosic exhibition of various American musical idioms.

Works include *Escenas campestres* for soprano, tenor, baritone and orchestra (1860); two symphonic poems, *La nuit des tropiques* and *Montevideo*; numerous piano pieces including *The Dying Poet* and *Grand Fantasy on the Brazilian National Anthem*.

Götz, Hermann (b Königsberg, 7 Dec 1840; d Hottingen near Zurich, 3 Dec 1876), German composer. At first he studied music only incidentally when a student at Königsberg University, but later went to the Stern Conservatory in Berlin. In 1863 he went to Switzerland as organist at Winterthur and in 1867 he settled at Zurich. From 1870 he devoted himself wholly to composition.

Works include operas *Der Widerspänstigen Zähmung* (on Shakespeare's *Taming of the Shrew*, 1874) and *Francesca da Rimini* (unfinished, produced Mannheim, 1877); *Nänie* (Schiller) and Psalm cxxxvii for solo voices, chorus and orchestra; cantata for male voices and orchestra; symphony in F major, *Spring* overture for orchestra; violin concerto in G major (1868), piano concerto in B♭ major; piano quintet, piano quartet, piano trio; sonata for piano duet; sonatina, *Genrebilder* and other works for piano; songs.

Goudimel, Claude (b Besançon, *c* 1514; d Lyons, 28 Aug 1572), French composer. First appeared as composer in Paris in 1549. About 1557, having become a Huguenot, he went to live at Metz with the Protestant colony there, but about ten years later left for Besançon, and afterwards for Lyons, where he died in the massacre of the Huguenots.

Works include five Masses, three Magnificats, psalms in motet form and other works for the Catholic Church; psalms, including a complete psalter, for the Protestant Church; sacred songs and numerous secular *chansons* for several voices.

Gould, Glenn (b Toronto, 25 Sept 1932; d Toronto, 4 Oct 1982), Canadian pianist. Studied at the Royal Conservatory of Music in Toronto, graduating at the age of 12, the youngest ever to do so. Made his debut in Toronto, aged 14, and his European debut (under Karajan) in 1957. From 1964 confined himself to broadcasts and recordings.

Gould, Morton (b Richmond Hill, NY, 10 Dec 1913; d Orlando, FL, 21 Feb 1996), American composer and conductor. He studied at NY University; later worked as a pianist at Radio City Music Hall and presented music programmes on radio. His works are much indebted to popular idioms:

BALLETS: *Interplay* (1945), *Fall River Legend*, on Lizzie Borden — America's most famous orphan (1947) and *Fiesta* (1957);

FOR ORCHESTRA: *Little Symphony* (1939), four symphonies (1942, 1944, 1947, 1952), three *American Symphonettes* (1922, 1935, 1937), piano concerto (1937), violin concerto (1938), *A Lincoln Legend* (1941), *Spirituals* (1941), viola concerto (1943), *Concerto for Orchestra* (1945), *Dance Variations* for two pianos and orchestra (1953), *Concerto for Tap Dancer* (1953), *Jekyll and Hyde Variations* (1957), *Festive Music* (1965), *Venice* for double orchestra and brass bands (1966), *Vivaldi Gallery* (1967), *Symphony of Spirituals* (1976), *American Ballads* (1976), *Housewarming* (1982), flute concerto (1984), *Chorales and Rags* (1988), *Concerto Grosso* (1988). Music for Broadway shows, films, state occasions (LA Olympics, 1984).

Gounod, Charles (François) (b Paris, 18 Jun 1818; d Saint-Cloud, 18 Oct 1893), French composer. Son of a painter. His mother, a good pianist, taught him music from an early age and he was educated at the Lycée Saint-Louis and in music at the Paris Conservatory, where his masters included Halévy, Paer and Lesueur. He gained the Prix de Rome in 1839 and spent the statutory three years in Rome, studying early Italian church music; his interest in this music culminated in the elaborate *Messe solennelle de Ste Cécile* (1855). After a tour in Austria and Germany he returned to Paris and was appointed organist at the church of the Missions Étrangères. Intending to become a priest, he did not produce any important music until his opera *Sapho* appeared in 1851. In 1852–60 he conducted the united choral societies named Orphéon. His five-act setting of *Faust* for the Paris Opéra (1859) brought his melodic gift before a huge public and Gounod became the most popular opera composer of his time; his success was consolidated by a saccharine but effective version of *Romeo and Juliet* (1867). In 1870–75 he lived in London, where he founded what became the Royal Choral Society.

Gounod *The composer Charles Gounod (1818–1893) in an early photograph. Gounod is remembered today mostly for his vocal works, but in France his influence on younger composers was considerable in a wide range of genres. Saint-Saëns, Bizet and Massenet all owe a debt to him.*

Works include operas *Sapho* (1851), *La Nonne sanglante* (1854), *Le Médecin malgré lui* (on Molière, 1858), *Faust* (after Goethe, 1859), *Philémon et Baucis*, *La Reine de Saba*, *Mireille* (after Mistral), *La Colombe*, *Roméo et Juliette* (after Shakespeare, 1867), *Cinq-Mars* (after Alfred de Vigny), *Polyeucte* (after Corneille, 1878), *Le Tribut de Zamora*; incidental music for Ponsard's *Ulysse*, Legouvé's *Les Deux Reines* and Barbier's *Jeanne d'Arc*; oratorios *La Rédemption*, *Mors et Vita*, *Tobie*; eight cantatas; 16 Masses, Requiem (1895), *Stabat Mater*, Te Deum, *De profundis*, *Ave verum corpus*, *Pater noster*, Magnificat and other sacred vocal pieces; two symphonies (1855–56); some piano compositions including the *Funeral March for a Marionette*; *Méditation sur le premier Prélude de Bach* for soprano, violin piano, and organ; some smaller choral works; many songs.

Musical ideas sprang to my mind like a flight of butterflies, and all I had to do was to stretch out my hand to catch them.

Charles Gounod, quoted in Harding, *Gounod*, 1973

A Selection of

Gounod

Sapho	1851
Symphony no. 1	1855
St Cecilia Mass	1855
Faust	1859
Philémon et Baucis	1860
Mireille	1864
Roméo et Juliette	1867
Mors et Vita	1885
Petite Symphonie	1885
Songs	

Gow Scottish family of musicians:

1. Niel Gow (b Strathbrand, Perthshire, 22 Mar 1727; d Inver near Dunkeld, 1 Mar 1807), violinist. Intended to become a weaver, he made his fame by playing Scottish dance tunes at balls in Scotland and pub. three collections of reels (1784–92).

2. William Gow (b Inver, c 1760; d Edinburgh, 1791), violinist, son of 1. Leader of the Edinburgh Assembly orchestra until his death.

3. Nathaniel Gow (b Inver near Dunkeld, 28 May 1763; d Edinburgh, 19 Jan 1831), trumpeter, violinist and pub., son of 1. At 16, when living at Edinburgh, he was appointed royal trumpeter, learnt the violin from Mackintosh, became leader of the Edinburgh Assembly orchestra on the death of his brother and provided dance music by playing, composing, and after 1796 publishing it. He wrote

songs, pieces descriptive of Edinburgh street cries (including 'Caller Herrin'', at first an instrumental piece and not fitted with words by Lady Nairne until *c* 20 years later).

4. **Neil Gow** (b Edinburgh, *c* 1795; d Edinburgh, 7 Nov 1823), composer, son of 3, He joined his father in the pub. business in 1818. Wrote songs, including 'Flora Macdonald's Lament', 'Cam' ye by Athol', etc.

Goyescas opera by Granados (libretto, in Spanish, by F Periquet y Zuaznabar), produced NY Met, 28 Jan 1916. Much of the material is taken from the piano work below. Pacquito and Fernando duel over Rosario; Fernando dies in her arms.

Two sets of piano pieces by Granados, inspired by etchings of Spanish scenes by Goya, fp Paris, 4 Apr 1914: I. *Los requiebros/The Compliments, Coloquio en la reja/Colloquy at the Grilled Window, El fandango del candil/The Fandango of the Lantern, Quejas, ó La maja y el ruiseñor/Plaints, or The Maja and the Nightingale*; II. *El Amor y la Muerte/Love and Death, Epilogo: la serenata del espectro/ Epilogue: the Spectre's Serenade*. (A *maja* is the feminine counterpart of *majo* = a fop, a dandy). Granados also wrote a separate *escena goyesca* for piano: *El pelele* (a puppet or straw-man tossed in a blanket).

Gozzi, Carlo (1722–1806), Italian dramatist. ◊Chagrin (*Re cervo*); ◊Danzi (*Turandot*); ◊Donna serpente (Casella); ◊Einem (*Turandot*); ◊Feen (Wagner); J P E ◊Hartmann (*Ravnen*); ◊Himmel (*Sylphen*); ◊Jensen (*Turandot*); ◊König Hirsch (Henze); ◊Love for Three Oranges (Prokofiev); ◊Sessions (*Turandot*); ◊Stenhammar (*Turandot*); ◊Turandot (incidental music Weber; operas, Busoni and Puccini).

Graarud, Gunnar (b Holmestrand near Oslo, 1 Jun 1886; d Stuttgart, 6 Dec 1960), Norwegian tenor. He sang at Mannheim, Berlin and Hamburg, 1920–28, and made his Bayreuth debut in 1927, as Tristan; returned for Parsifal, Siegmund and Siegfried. Vienna Staatsoper 1928–37, and appeared as guest in London, Paris and Milan. At Salzburg he was heard in *Elektra* and *Der Corregidor*.

Grabmusik, *Funeral music*, cantata by Mozart for soloists, chorus and small orchestra; composed 1767 (when Mozart was ill), performed Salzburg Cathedral, 7 Apr 1767.

Grabu (or *Grabut, Grebus*), Louis (b *fl* 1665; d 1694), French violinist and composer. Appointed composer to Charles II in 1665 and Master of the King's Music 1666–74.

Works include operas *Ariane, ou le mariage de Bacchus* (1674) and *Albion and Albanius* (libretto by Dryden), 1685.

grace notes (or *graces*) = ◊ornaments.

Gracis, Ettore (b La Spezia, 24 Sept 1915; d Treviso, 12 Apr 1992), Italian conductor. Studied at Venice and conducted at Bergamo 1951–56, leading premieres of operas by Chailly and Testi. Naples Festival from 1961, with revivals of operas by Piccinni, Rossini and Cimarosa, and Mozart's *La finta semplice* and *Zauberflöte*. Maggio Musicale, Florence, 1948–50, and the Teatro de la Fenice, Venice, 1959–71; led fps of works by Malipiero, Sinopoli and Turchi at the Biennale.

Gradual Latin *gradus* = 'a step'; the second item of the Proper of the Mass. It is a responsorial chant following the reading of the epistle.

Gradus ad Parnassum, Latin *Steps to Parnassus*, (I) a treatise on counterpoint by Fux, pub. 1725; (II) a series of 100 instructive and progressive piano pieces by Clementi, pub. in 1817. The first piece in Debussy's *Children's Corner* for piano alludes satirically to Clementi's collection.

Graener, Paul (b Berlin, 11 Jan 1872; d Salzburg, 13 Nov 1944), German composer. He was one of a large number of composers who were successful during the Third Reich. Was a choirboy in Berlin Cathedral and at 16 entered the Veit Conservatory, but soon began to teach himself, leading a wandering life, conducting at various theatres and composing a number of immature works. He was in London as teacher at the RAM and conductor at the Haymarket Theatre, 1896–1908, and was then appointed director of the New Conservatory in Vienna and in 1910 of the Mozarteum at Salzburg. After some years in Munich he succeeded Reger as professor of composition at the

Leipzig Conservatory, but resigned 1924. In 1930 he became director of the Stern Conservatory in Berlin and under the Nazi régime vice-president of the Reichsmusikkammer, being succeeded by Egk in 1941.

Works include operas *Der vierjährige Posten* (Körner, 1918), *Das Narrengericht* (1931), *Don Juans letztes Abenteuer* (1914), *Theophano* (*Byzanz*, 1918), *Schirin und Gertraude, Hanneles Himmelfahrt* (after G Hauptmann, 1927), *Friedemann Bach* (1931), *Der Prinz von Homburg* (after Kleist, 1935); choral works; symphonies (*Schmied Schmerz*), *Romantic Fantasy, Variations on a Russian folksong* and other orchestral works; six string quartets, three piano trios and other chamber music; sonata and suite for violin and piano, suite for cello and piano; piano pieces; over 100 songs.

Graf (or *Graff*), Friedrich Hartmann (b Rudolstadt, 23 Aug 1727; d Augsburg, 19 Aug 1795), German flautist and composer. Travelled widely as a flute virtuoso, and was appointed music director in Augsburg in 1772. Later visited Vienna, and 1783–84 was conductor of the Professional Concerts in London.

Works include oratorios, cantatas, symphonies, concertos, chamber music.

Graf, Hans (b Linz, 15 Feb 1949), Austrian conductor. Studied at Graz and made Vienna Staatsoper debut 1977 (*Petrushka* there, 1981). Munich and Vienna Festivals from 1981, Paris Opéra 1984, with *Die Entführung*. Director of the Mozarteum Orchestra at Salzburg, 1984–92, and has led Wagner's *Ring* there. Guest with the Vienna SO and the Dresden, St Petersburg, Vienna and Liverpool Philharmonics. Conducted *Die Zauberflöte* on tour with the Vienna Staatsoper to Japan (1989) and at the Savonlinna Festival (1992).

Graf, Herbert (b Vienna, 10 Apr 1904; d Geneva, 5 Apr 1973), American stage director. Worked first in Germany, then Salzburg Festival from 1935: staged *Die Entführung* and *Meistersinger* and *Die Zauberflöte* for Toscanini. NY Met. 1935–60, including *Salome, Falstaff, Wozzeck, Don Giovanni* and *Otello*. Head of opera department at Curtis Institute 1949–58, Geneva Opera 1965–73. Staged *Parsifal* at London, CG, 1959.

Graffman, Gary (b New York, 14 Oct 1928), American pianist. Studied at the Curtis Institute and with Serkin and Horowitz. Debut Philadelphia 1947. His international career was interrupted 1979 by a hand injury. Artistic director of Curtis Institute from 1986.

Graham, Colin (b Hove, 22 Sept 1931), English stage director. Studied at RADA and made debut at Aldeburgh 1958, with the premiere of *Noye's Fludde*; staged Britten's three church parables and *Death in Venice* 1973, and wrote the text for his *Golden Vanity* (1970). Director of productions for English Opera Group 1961–75, and has worked with SW/ENO from 1965 (*Gloriana* 1966, *War and Peace* 1972, *The Excursions of Mr Brouček* English stage premiere, 1978). Artistic director of Opera St Louis from 1978, writing the libretti for two operas by Stephen Paulus. Directed the premiere of Corigliano's *The Ghosts of Versailles* (NY Met. 1991) and *Death in Venice* at CG, 1992.

Graham, Susan (b Roswell, NM, 23 Jul 1960), American mezzo. Studied in NY and sang first with St Louis Opera and at Seattle, notably as Massenet's Charlotte. From 1989 sang Mozart's Annius at Chicago and Dorabella at Santa Fe; Carnegie Hall debut in Mahler's *Des Knaben Wunderhorn*. Sang the title role in the first US and UK stagings of Massenet's *Chérubin* (Santa Fe, 1989, CG, 1993). NY Met. from 1991 as Cherubino, and Ascanio in *Les Troyens*. Salzburg from 1993, as Cecilio in *Lucio Silla* and as Meg Page in *Falstaff*. Concerts include *Les Nuits d'été* and Beethoven's Ninth. Sang Dorabella and created Goehr's Arianna at CG, 1995.

Grainger, Percy (Aldridge) (b Melbourne, 8 Jul 1882; d White Plains, NY, 20 Feb 1961), Australian-American pianist and composer. Studied under his mother and Louis Pabst at Melbourne, later in Germany with Kwast, Knorr and Busoni. He lived in London in 1900–14 and became interested in folk music, toured Scandinavia in 1909 and settled in USA in 1914, later becoming naturalized. He made a successful NY debut 1915 and in 1928 married Ella Viola Ström at the Hollywood Bowl; conducting his *To a Nordic Princess* in honour of the occasion. In 1938 he founded a museum at Melbourne, to house his manuscripts and souvenirs; his request for the museum to display his skeleton after his death was declined.

Works include compositions for chorus and orchestra with and without solo voices: *Marching Song of Democracy* (1901–17), *The Bride's Tragedy* (Swinburne, 1908), *Father and Daughter* (Faroe folksong), *Sir Eglamore*, *We have fed our seas* (Kipling, 1900–04), *Tribute to Foster*, *Bridal Song*, etc.; part-songs *Brigg Fair*, *Morning Song of the Jungle* (Kipling), etc.; pieces for small orchestra: *Molly on the Shore* (1907), *Colonial Song*, *Shepherd's Hey* (1913), *Mock Morris*, *Irish Tune from County Derry* (Londonderry Air), clog dance *Handel in the Strand*; suite *In a Nutshell* for two pianos; four Irish dances on themes by Stanford, *Walking Tune*, etc. for piano; songs. He edited and arranged hundreds of British and Scandinavian folksongs.

Salvation Army Booth objected to the devil having all the good tunes. I object to jazz and vaudeville having all the best instruments!

Percy Grainger, preface to *Spoon River*, 1930

Gramm, Donald (b Milwaukee, 26 Feb 1927; d New York, 2 Jan 1983), American bass-baritone. He sang Donizetti's Raimondo in Chicago in 1944. After study in Chicago and Santa Barbara sang Colline at the NY City Opera in 1952; other roles there were Leporello, Falstaff and Ochs. In 1963 he sang Dr Schön at Santa Fe in the first US performance of Berg's *Lulu* (two-act version) and at Boston in 1966 was Moses in the US premiere of *Moses und Aron*; also heard in Schoenberg's oratorio *Die Jakobsleiter*. Glyndebourne 1975–76 as Nick Shadow and Falstaff, 1980 as Ochs.

gramophone, formerly phonograph, an instrument invented in its primitive form by Edison in 1877. The music is now recorded on magnetic tape, afterwards transferred to a disc of vinylite. The sound-waves of the music are reproduced thereon in a continuous groove. In performance the disc revolves, a static needle is brought into contact with the groove, and the 'frozen' sound-waves are released and electronically amplified. From 1958 sounds were directed to the listener with greater realism by means of stereophonic recordings, followed in the 1970s by quadraphonic recordings.

A more recent development is the *compact disc*, on which the musical signal is digitally encoded so that it can be decoded by laser with absolutely no wear to the disc, with complete fidelity and with virtually no danger of destroying the disc through careless handling.

Granados, Enrique (b Lérida, 27 Jul 1867; d at sea, 24 Mar 1916), Spanish composer. Studied composition with Pedrell at Barcelona and piano in Paris. Returning to Spain in 1889, he became a well-known pianist and in 1900 he founded the Sociedad de Conciertos Clásicos in Madrid, which he conducted. After a visit to NY for the production of *Goyescas* in the operatic version in Jan 1916, he went down in the *Sussex*, torpedoed by a German submarine in the English Channel; he had swum to the rescue of his wife, but was weighed down with the gold that the Met. had paid him for *Goyescas*.

Works include operas and zarzuelas *Maria del Carmen* (1898), *Gaziel* (1906), *Goyescas* (based on the piano work), *Petrarca*, *Picarol*, *Follet*, *Liliana*; symphonic poem *La nit del mort*, four suites etc. for orchestra; *Cant de las Estrelles* for chorus, organ and piano; piano trio, *Oriental* for oboe and strings; *Goyescas* (two vols.), ten Spanish Dances, six pieces on Spanish folksongs, *Escenas románticas*, *Escenas poéticas* (1926), *Libro de horas*, Impromptus, children's pieces for piano; songs *Escritas en estilo antiguo* and a collection of *tonadillas*.

gran cassa Italian = lit. 'great case, great box' = ◊bass drum.

grand chœur French = lit. 'great choir' = 'full organ', a direction that the organ is to be used with all the registers.

Grand Duke, The, or The Statutory Duel, operetta by Sullivan (libretto by W S Gilbert), produced London, Savoy Theatre, 7 Mar 1896. Gilbert's last libretto for Sullivan.

Grande-Duchesse de Gérolstein, La operetta by Offenbach (libretto by H Meilhac and L Halévy), produced Paris, Théâtre des Variétés, 12 Apr 1867. Grand-Duchess has an eye for recruit Fritz, promoting him eventually to the rank of general. When he still prefers to marry peasant Wanda, she turns against him. After complications a happy ending.

Grande Messe des Morts, Requiem, work by Berlioz for tenor, chorus and orchestra, (composed 1837; revised 1852 and 1867). Fp Paris, 5 Dec 1837).

Grandi, Alessandro (b Ferrara, *c* 1575; d Bergamo, *c* 1630), Italian composer. Pupil of (?) G. Gabrieli at Venice, *maestro di cappella* of the church of the Santo Spirito at Ferrara, 1610–17, and then at St Mark's, Venice, where he sang under Monteverdi's direction and became his deputy 1620. His church music was in part inspired by the spacious architecture of St Mark's, and many of his motets are in the concertato style. His later motets employ instrumental accompaniments and anticipate the sacred concertos of Schütz and other North European masters. He became choirmaster at the church of Santa Maria Maggiore at Bergamo. He died of the plague.

Works include five Masses, *c* 200 motets, psalms; madrigals; cantatas, arias for solo voice.

Grandi, Margherita (b Hobart, 4 Oct 1894; d Milan, 1972), Australian soprano. She studied with Calvé in Paris and in 1922 created Massenet's Amadis, at Monte Carlo. She sang in Italy from 1932 and was admired as Aida and Monteverdi's Octavia. Glyndebourne 1939, as Lady Macbeth; in 1949 she sang Amelia with the co. at Edinburgh. London 1947–50, as Tosca, Donna Anna and the *Trovatore* Leonora.

grand jeu French = lit. 'great play' = ◊grand chœur; also used for a harmonium stop that brings the whole instrument into play.

Grand Macabre, Le opera by Ligeti (libretto by composer and M Meschke, after M de Ghelderode), produced Stockholm, 12 Apr 1978. London, Coliseum, 2 Dec 1982, with the original roles of Spermando and Clitoria 'translated' by G Skelton as Amando and Miranda. Nekrotzar returns from the grave in an attempt to destroy the world, but is disappointed when a threatening comet passes by harmlessly.

grand piano ◊pianoforte.

Grange, Phillip (b London, 17 Nov 1956), English composer. Studied at York University and with Peter Maxwell Davies. Lecturer in composition at Exeter University from 1989.

Works include piano sonata (1978); *Cimmerian Nocturne* for ensemble (1979); sextet for wind quintet and piano (1980); *The Kingdom of Bones* music theatre (1983); *Variations* (1986); *Concerto for Orchestra* (1988); *Changing Landscapes* (1990). Performances at most major UK festivals, also in Europe and the USA; London Proms, 1983.

Gran Mass, 'Graner Messe', a Mass by Liszt for solo voices, chorus, orchestra and organ, composed 1855 for the inauguration of a church at Gran (Esztergom) in Hungary and performed there 31 Aug 1856.

Grant, Clifford (b Randwick, NSW, 11 Sept 1930), Australian bass. Stage debut Sydney 1952, as Donizetti's Raimondo. He studied with Otakar Kraus in London and was heard with SW/ENO from 1966 as Silva, Seneca, Sarastro and Hagen. US debut San Francisco 1967. Glyndebourne 1972, as Monteverdi's Neptune; CG 1974, Mozart's Bartolo. Other roles include Pogner, Trulove and Philip II. Appeared with Australian Opera 1976–90. He sang Alvise in *Gioconda* for Opera North, 1993.

graphic scores scores by 20th-c. composers which seek to convey musical ideas by means of non-traditional notation. Some scores are intended to symbolize particular sounds or textures, others allow the interpreter more latitude. Examples are by Feldman, Stockhausen, Cage, Ligeti, Bussotti and Cornelius Cardew. Graphic scores have been admired as much for their visual as their musical qualities; they have not been seen (or heard) in recent years. *See illustration on page 252.*

Grassi, Cecilia (b Naples, *c* 1740; d after 1782), Italian soprano. Went to London in 1766, where she married J C Bach, *c* 1776; at the King's Theatre she had sung in his oratorio *Gioas* (1770) and serenata *Endimione* (1772). She was left destitute on the death of her husband.

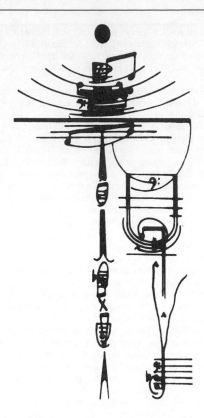

A typically imaginative graphic score from Cardew's Treatise, 1963–67.

Grassini, Josephina (b Varese, 18 Apr 1773; d Milan, 3 Jan 1850), Italian contralto. Studied singing at Milan and made her first appearances there in 1790 in operas by Guglielmi, Paisiello and Sarti. She first sang in Paris in 1800; continued an affair with Napoleon and received a generous salary. London 1804, in operas by Winter (Proserpine to Mrs Billington's Ceres), Nasolini and Fioravanti.

Graun German family of musicians, the most important of whom was Carl Heinrich (3):

1. August Friedrich Graun (b Wahrenbrück, Saxony, 1699; d Merseburg, 5 May 1765), cantor at Merseburg from 1729.

2. Johann Gottlieb Graun (b Wahrenbrück, *c* 1703; d Berlin, 27 Oct 1771), violinist and composer, brother of 1. Pupil of Pisendel and of Tartini; played in the Dresden court orchestra until 1726, when he became orchestra leader at Merseburg. In 1732 he went into the service of the Crown Prince of Prussia at Rheinsberg and followed him to Berlin when he became Frederick II, becoming conductor of the court orchestra. He wrote symphonies; concertos for violin, for harpsichord and for organ; trio sonatas with two flutes; violin sonatas.

3. Carl Heinrich Graun (b Wahrenbrück, 1703 or 1704; d Berlin, 8 Aug 1759), tenor and composer, brother of 2. Chorister at Dresden, went in 1725 to Brunswick, first as a singer, later as composer and vice-*Kapellmeister* (1727). In 1735 he joined his brother (2) at Rheinsberg, and on the accession of Frederick II in 1740 was appointed court *Kapellmeister*, with responsibility for the Berlin opera. His opera *Cleopatra e Cesare* opened the new opera house in 1742 and was revived at the Berlin Staatsoper, 1992. His most famous work is the Passion oratorio to words by Ramler, *Der Tod Jesu* (1755), perhaps the most popular continental oratorio of the 18th c.

He wrote operas *Sancio und Sinilde* (1727), *Iphigenia in Aulis* (1731), *Polidorus, Scipio Africanus, Lo specchio della fedeltà* (1733), *Pharao Tubaetes, Rodelinda, regina de Langobardi* (1741), *Cleopatra e Cesare, Artaserse* (1743), *Demofoonte, Ifigenia in Aulide*

(Italian), *Silla* (1753), *Montezuma* (1755), *Merope*, etc.; several Passion cantatas including *Der Tod Jesu*, Te Deum; funeral music for the Duke of Brunswick and for Frederick William I of Prussia; secular cantatas, songs; harpsichord concertos; trio sonatas.

Graupner, Christoph (b Kirchberg, Saxony, 13 Jan 1683; d Darmstadt, 10 May 1760), German composer. Pupil of Schelle and Kuhnau at St Thomas's, Leipzig, he was harpsichordist at the Hamburg opera under Keiser 1707–09, and there produced his first operas. In 1709 he entered the service of the Landgrave Ernst Ludwig of Hesse-Darmstadt as vice-*Kapellmeister*, becoming *Kapellmeister* in 1712 on the death of Briegel. Elected cantor of St Thomas's, Leipzig, in 1722/23, but he was unable to obtain his release from Darmstadt, so that the post fell to Bach.

Works include operas *Dido* (1707), *Antiochus und Stratonica* (1708), *La costanza vince l'inganno* (1715), etc.; over 1,400 church cantatas; 113 symphonies; 87 overtures; *c* 50 concertos; quantities of chamber music, keyboard music.

grave Italian = 'heavy, serious'; a direction indicating a slow tempo.

gravicembalo Italian = clavicembalo (♭harpsichord), of which it is a perversion.

Gray, Cecil (b Edinburgh, 19 May 1895; d Worthing, 9 Sept 1951), Scottish writer on music and composer. Studied music privately. In 1920 he became joint editor of the *Sackbut* with Philip Heseltine, with whom he also wrote a book on Gesualdo, and whose biography as a composer (Peter Warlock) he pub. Other books are a *History of Music*, essays *Predicaments* and *Contingencies*, and two works on Sibelius.

Works include operas *Deirdre, The Temptation of St Anthony* (after Flaubert) and *The Trojan Women* (after Euripides).

Gray, Linda Esther (b Greenock, 29 May 1948), Scottish soprano. She studied in Scotland and with Eva Turner in London. Debut as Mimi with Glyndebourne Touring co. 1972; debut at Glyndebourne as Mozart's Electra, 1974. Scottish Opera from 1975 as Donna Elvira, Eva, Ariadne and Amelia. ENO debut 1978 as Micaela, later Aida and Tosca. She sang Isolde with WNO in 1979 and Sieglinde on her CG and US (Dallas, 1981) debuts. She suspended her career in 1984.

grazia, con Italian = 'with grace' = *grazioso*.

Graziani, Francesco (b Fermo, 26 Apr 1828; d Fermo, 30 Jun 1901), Italian baritone. Debut Ascoli Piceno 1851, in *Gemma di Vergy*. At CG he was heard 1855–80 as the first local Luna, Germont, Rigoletto and Renato; also admired as Don Giovanni, Nelusko and Thomas' Hamlet. He was Macbeth in Dublin (1859) and on 10 Nov 1862 created Don Carlo in *La forza del destino*, at St Petersburg.

Grazioli, Giovanni Battista (b Bogliaco, Lake Garda, 6 Jul 1746; d Venice, *c* 1820), Italian organist and composer. Pupil of Bertoni, he was appointed second organist of St Mark's, Venice, 1782, first organist 1785.

Works include 12 harpsichord sonatas, six sonatas for violin and harpsichord, church music.

> *Willie Walton, in his symphony particularly, uses pedals so continuously that if it were a bicycle he would have crossed America from the Atlantic to the Pacific.*
>
> **Cecil Gray**, *Notebooks*, (ed. Pauline Gray), 1989

grazioso Italian = 'graceful'; an adj. sometimes used alone to indicate the character of a piece or passage and more often in combination with a tempo indication, e.g. *allegro grazioso, andantino grazioso*, etc.

Great Fugue (Beethoven.) ♭Grosse Fuge.

great organ the principal manual keyboard of the organ.

great staff a theoretical construct to clarify the relationship of the traditional clefs. On an 11-line stave with, for example, the treble clef four lines from the top and the bass clef, four lines from the bottom, the middle line will represent middle C.

Greaves, Thomas (*fl.* 1604), English lutenist and composer. In the service of Sir Henry Pierpont, whose wife was a cousin of Michael

Cavendish. In 1604 he pub. a book of *Songs of Sundrie Kindes* containing seven songs to the lute, four songs for voice and viols and four madrigals.

Greber, Jakob (b Mannheim, buried 5 Jul 1731), German composer. Went to London *c* 1702 with Margherita de l'Épine and stayed there until *c* 1706. In Innsbruck, then Vienna, in the service of the Emperor Charles VI, from *c* 1708, and in the Palatinate (Heidelberg, etc.) 1717–23.

Works include opera *Gli amori d'Ergasto* (1705; *The Temple of Love* attributed to him is by Saggione), shorter stage pieces, serenatas, etc.; cantatas for solo voice and various instruments.

Greco, Gaetano (b Naples, *c* 1657; d Naples, *c* 1728), Italian composer. Possibly pupil of A Scarlatti at Naples. Taught for many years at the Conservatorio dei Poveri di Gesù there. Wrote harpsichord music, *Salve Regina* (1681) etc.

Greef, Arthur de (b Louvain, 10 Oct 1862; d Brussels, 29 Aug 1940), Belgian pianist and composer. Pupil of Brassin at the Brussels Conservatory and of Liszt at Weimar. He began his career about the age of 20 and became piano professor at the Brussels Conservatory in 1887. He toured widely in Europe and frequently visited England.

Works include opera, *De Marketenster* (1879); symphony, *Four Old Flemish Folksongs* for orchestra; Ballad for string orchestra; Concerto & Fantasy for piano and orchestra, *Menuet varié* for piano and strings; *Chants d'amour* for voice and orchestra; sonata for two pianos; piano pieces; songs.

Greek opera in two acts by Mark-Anthony Turnage (libretto by composer and J Moore, after S Berkoff's play), produced Munich, Carl-Orff Saal, 17 Jun 1988. Updated version of Oedipus legend, in troubled urban setting: Eddy kills a café manager and marries his wife, who later turns out to be his mum.

Greek Passion, The opera by Martinů (libretto by composer from the novel by N Kazantzakis); composed 1955–58 in Nice, New York, Pratteln and Rome, produced Zurich, 9 Jun 1961, conductor Sacher. The villagers of Lyeovrissi prepare for their annual Passion play. Manolios, who is to play Christ, fights for some local refugees, but is killed by Panais, who was to play Judas.

Greenawald, Sheri (b Iowa City, 12 Nov 1947), American soprano. Sang at first in NY, then in the premieres of Floyd's *Bilby's Doll* and Pasatieri's *Washington Square* (Houston and Detroit, 1976). Netherlands Opera 1980, as Susanna, and concerts in San Francisco and Rotterdam. Houston 1983, in the premiere of Bernstein's *A Quiet Place*. At Chicago 1991 she sang Pauline in the US fp of Prokofiev's *The Gambler*. Sang Mozart's Countess with WNO, 1995.

Greenberg, Noah (b New York, 9 Apr 1919; d New York 9 Jan 1966), American conductor and music editor. Founded NY Pro Musica Antiqua 1952, for performance of medieval and Renaissance music. Revived medieval dramas *The Play of Daniel* (1958) and *The Play of Herod* (1963). Toured Europe with ensemble 1960 and 1963.

Greene, Maurice (b London, 12 Aug 1696; d London, 1 Dec 1755), English organist and composer. Son of a clergyman, he was a chorister at St Paul's Cathedral, studied the organ there under Richard Brind, and after holding church posts was appointed organist of St Paul's in 1718. On Croft's death in 1727 he became organist and composer of the Chapel Royal, and in 1730 succeeded Tudway as professor at Cambridge University. Appointed Master of the King's Music in 1735. An inheritance in 1750 enabled him to devote time to a collection of English church music, which after his death was completed by Boyce and pub. under the title *Cathedral Music*.

Works include over 100 anthems, the most notable pub. in *Forty Select Anthems* (1743), and other church music; oratorios *The Song of Deborah and Barak* (1732) and *Jephtha* (1737); pastorals *Florimel, or Love's Revenge* (1734), *The Judgment of Hercules* and *Phoebe* (1747); Odes for St Cecilia's Day and other occasions; misc. songs, catches, etc.; overtures; organ voluntaries; harpsichord music.

Greenhouse, Bernard (b Newark, NJ, 3 Jan 1916), American cellist. Studied at Juilliard and with Casals and Emanuel Feuermann. Debut NY 1946 and founder member of Harpsichord Quintet (1947–54); played with the Bach Aria Group 1948–76. Has premiered many US

chamber works, including Carter's cello sonata (1949). Founder member of the Beaux Arts Trio 1955 and made many tours worldwide until 1987. Teacher at the Manhattan School of Music 1950–82, State University of NY 1960–85, State University of New Jersey from 1987.

Grefinger, Wolfgang (b *c* 1475; d after 1525), German organist and composer. He was a pupil of Hofhaimer and was organist of St Stephen's Cathedral, Vienna, early in the 16th c. Wrote Latin church music and secular German songs and edited a hymn book.

greghesca a type of *villanella*, pub. 1564, for three voices to words that are a mixture of Greek and Venetian dialect, written by the Levantine Venetian Antonio Molino. The music was by various Venetian composers.

Gregor, Bohumil (b Prague, 14 Jul 1926), Czech conductor. He studied in Prague and worked at the Ostrava Opera 1958–62, where he gave Janáček's *Katya Kabanová* and *Mr Brouček*. Prague National Theatre from 1962; brought *From the House of the Dead* to the Edinburgh Festival 1964. He has given *The Cunning Little Vixen* all over Europe and conducted *Jenůfa* in San Francisco in 1969. In 1970 returned to Edinburgh with Prague co. to give Janáček's *Makropoulos Case* and *The Cunning Little Vixen*; Prague 1993, with *The Bartered Bride* and *Katya Kabanova*.

Gregorian Chant the official repertory of plainsong traditionally associated with the name of Pope (St) Gregory (*c* 540–604), who is said to have been the first to supervise its organization.

Gregorian tones the chants of the Gregorian psalmody sung in groups corresponding to the eight church modes (four authentic and four plagal).

Greindl, Josef (b Munich, 23 Dec 1912; d Vienna, 16 Apr 1993), German bass. He studied with Bender and Bahr-Mildenburg in Munich. Debut, Krefeld 1936 and sang in Düsseldorf before moving to Berlin during World War II. First sang at Bayreuth in 1943, as Pogner, and returned often up to 1969. His performances of Hagen in *Götterdämmerung* were memorable: the declamatory style which he developed was used also in Berlin 1959, when he gave Schoenberg's Moses at the Deutsche Oper. NY Met. debut, 1952, as Heinrich in *Lohengrin*.

Greiter, Matthias (b Aichach, Bavaria, *c* 1495; d Strasbourg, 20 Dec 1550), German singer, poet and composer. He was a monk and a chorister in Strasbourg Cathedral, but became a Lutheran in 1524. In 1549 returned to the Catholic church. He wrote words and music of hymns and composed German songs for four and five voices.

Grenon, Nicolas (b *c* 1380; d Cambrai, 1456), French composer. First heard of in Paris in 1399; he later worked at Laon and Cambrai cathedrals, at the Burgundian court chapel under John the Fearless, at the papal chapel and finally again at Cambrai where he was for many years Dufay's neighbour and was probably an influence on the younger composer. Wrote sacred Latin music and *chansons*.

Gresham, Thomas (1519–1579), founder of Gresham College in London. Knighted 1559. The College was provided for by his will and among the professorships was one for music, which has continued to the present day. The first professor, appointed 1596, was Bull.

Gresse, André (b Lyons, 23 Mar 1868; d Paris, 1937), French bass. Debut Paris, Opéra-Comique, 1896 as the Commendatore, in a performance with Victor Maurel as Don Giovanni. He followed his father, Leon, as principal bass at the Opéra in 1900; the first local Marke, Titurel and Fasolt, and sang in the 1909 fp of Massenet's *Bacchus*: the following year he created Massenet's Sancho Panza, at Monte Carlo. Retired *c* 1930.

Gretchaninov, Alexander Tikhonovich (b Moscow, 25 Oct 1864; d New York, 3 Jan 1956), Russian composer. Although the son of semi-literate small shopkeepers, he managed to study the piano at the Moscow Conservatory under Safonov, but in 1890 he went to St Petersburg as a composition pupil of Rimsky-Korsakov. He settled in Paris *c* 1925, and later in USA.

Works include operas *Dobrinya Nikitich* and *Sister Beatrice* (after Maeterlinck's play, 1910), incidental music for plays; much music for the Russian Church, including 44 complete liturgies; Catholic church music, including Masses and motets; choral works; five symphonies (1894–1936), Elegy for orchestra; concertos for cello, violin and flute; four string quartets; *Music Pictures* for bass solo, chorus and orchestra.

Gretchen am Spinnrade, *Margaret at the Spinning-Wheel*, Schubert's setting of Gretchen's song in Goethe's *Faust*, Part I, composed 1814 at the age of 17, pub. as op. 2 in 1821.

In general, the sentiment must be in the melody; the spirit, the gestures, the expression must be distributed through the accompaniment.
André Grétry, *Memoires*, 1797

Grétry, André Ernest Modeste (b Liège, 8 Feb 1741; d Montmorency near Paris, 24 Sept 1813), Belgian composer. He is best known through the arrangement of his *Zémire et Azor* made by Beecham. Chorister at St Denis's, Liège, received his initial training from his father (a violinist) and local church musicians. By 1759 he had already composed some symphonies and church music, which won him a scholarship to study in Rome, where he remained until 1765, producing there in 1765 the intermezzo *La vendemmiatrice*. After a time in Geneva he went to Paris in 1767 to make his way as an opera composer. From 1768 he produced a continuous stream of *opéras-comiques*, the most popular being *Richard Cœur-de-Lion* (1784), an early example of a ◊rescue opera. He was made an inspector of the Paris Conservatory on its foundation in 1795, and the same year became one of the original members of the Institut de France. He pub. his memoirs in three vols. 1789–97, and wrote other literary works.

Works include opéras-comiques: *La vendemmiatrice* (1765), *Isabelle et Gertrude*, *Le Huron* (1768), *Lucile*, *Le Tableau parlant* (1769), *Silvain*, *Les Deux Avares*, *L'Amitié à l'épreuve*, *Zémire et Azor* (1771), *L'Ami de la maison*, *Le Magnifique*, *La Rosière de Salency*, *La Fausse Magie* (1775), *Les Mariages samnites* (several versions), *Matroco* (1777), *Le Jugement de Midas*, *Les Fausses Apparences, ou L'Amant jaloux* (1778), *Les Événements imprévus*, *Aucassin et Nicolette* (1779), *Thalie au Nouveau Théâtre*, *Théodore et Paulin* (later *L'Épreuve villageoise*), *Richard Cœur-de-Lion* (1784), *Les Méprises par ressemblance*, *Le Comte d'Albert* (1786), *Le Prisonnier anglais* (later *Clarice et Belton*), *Le Rival confident*, *Raoul Barbebleue* (1789), *Pierre le Grand*, *Guillaume Tell* (1791), *Basile, Les Deux Couvents, Joseph Barra, Callias* (1794), *Lisbeth, Le Barbier du village, Elisca*.

Grieg *The composer Edvard Grieg (1843–1907). Grieg's output consists largely of keyboard and vocal works of a characteristic Norwegian flavour, reflecting the fact that he was a fine pianist and that his wife Nina was a singer (he considered her the greatest interpreter of his songs).*

Produced at the Opéra: *Céphale et Procris* (1773), *Les Trois Âges de l'Opéra* (1778), *Andromaque, La Double Épreuve, ou Colinette à la cour, L'Embarras des richesses* (1782), *La Caravane du Caire, Panurge dans l'île des lanternes* (after Rabelais, 1785), *Amphitryon, Aspasie, Denys le Tyran, La Fête de la Raison, Anacréon chez Polycrate* (1797), *Le Casque et les Colombes* (1801), *Delphis et Mopsa*, etc.

Grétry, Lucile (b Paris, 16 Jul 1772; d Paris, 25 Aug 1790), French composer, daughter of André ◊Grétry. At the age of 13 she composed the opera *Le Mariage d'Antonio* which, scored by her father, was successfully produced in 1786 at the Comédie Italienne, followed by *Toinette et Louis* a year later.

Grieg (originally **Greig**), Edvard (Hagerup) (b Bergen, 15 Jun 1843; d Bergen, 4 Sept 1907), Norwegian composer of Scottish descent. Once dismissed by Debussy as 'a pink bonbon stuffed with snow', Grieg is now returning to critical favour. Son of a merchant. He was taught the piano by his mother from 1849. Ole Bull persuaded his parents to send him to Leipzig for study in 1858, and he entered the Conservatory there. In 1863 he went to live in Copenhagen and studied with Gade. In 1864 he met Rikard Nordaak, who fired his enthusiasm for Norwegian national music, and became engaged to his cousin Nina Hagerup, whom he married in 1867. Settled as teacher and conductor at Christiania in 1867. Two years later, at Copenhagen, he premiered his most enduring work, the Piano Concerto in A minor. In 1874 Ibsen invited him to write incidental music for his *Peer Gynt*, which was produced 24 Feb 1876 and secured his reputation as the leading Scandinavian composer of the day; the work's colourful and evocative vignettes represent Grieg's talent at its best. In 1888–89 he and his wife appeared in London, Paris and Vienna, and in 1894 he was made honorary Mus.D. by Cambridge University and honorary Mus.D. by Oxford University in 1906.

A Selection of

Grieg

Piano Concerto	1868
Sigurd Jorsalfar	1872
Peer Gynt	1874–5

Holberg Suite	1884
Violin Sonata no. 3	1887
Symphonic Dances	1896–7
Lyric Suite	1904
Songs	

Works include incidental music for Ibsen's *Peer Gynt* (1874–75) and Bjørnson's *Sigurd Jorsalfar* (1872); symphony in C minor (1864); concert overture *In Autumn*; *Holberg Suite* for string orchestra (1884); piano concerto in A minor (1868).

WORKS FOR SOLO VOICES, CHORUS AND ORCHESTRA: *Before the Cloister Gate*, *Land-sighting*, *Olaf Trygvason*; *Bergliot* (Bjørnson) for declamation and orchestra; four Psalms for mixed voices unaccompanied; a set of part-songs for male voices; *Den bergtekne* (*The Solitary*) for baritone solo, strings and two horns (1878).

CHAMBER AND SOLO VOCAL: String quartet in G minor (1878); three sonatas for violin and piano; sonata for cello and piano; 24 op. nos. of piano pieces, including ten vols. of *Lyric Pieces*, sonata in E minor, Ballad in variation form, arrangement of Norwegian folk tunes; four for piano duet; old Norwegian melody with variations for two pianos; 143 songs, including *Haugtussa* cycle (Garborg, 1895), settings of Ibsen, Bjørnson.

Grieg (born *Hagerup*), Nina (b Bergen, 24 Nov 1845; d Copenhagen, 9 Dec 1935), Norwegian singer, cousin and wife of Edvard Grieg, most of whose songs she was the first to sing both at home and on their tours abroad.

Griffel, Kay (b Eldora, IA, 26 Dec 1940), American soprano. Studied with Lotte Lehman and made debut in Chicago 1960, as Mercédès in *Carmen*. Appeared in German opera houses and sang at Salzburg 1973, in the fp of Orff's *De Temporum fine Comoedia*. Glyndebourne 1976–77, as Alice Ford; tour of Japan 1977 with the Berlin Staatsoper as the Marschallin and Mozart's Countess. NY Met. from 1982, as Elettra, Rosalinde, Arabella, the Countess and Tatiana. Sang Wagner's Eva at Wellington, 1990.

Griffes, Charles T(omlinson) (b Elmira, New York, 17 Sept 1884; d New York, 8 Apr 1920), American composer. Studied in Berlin with Humperdinck and taught there for a time. Returned to USA in 1907, and became music teacher at a boys' school at Tarrytown, NY, until his early death, brought about by ill-health and overwork.

Works include Japanese mime play *Schojo* (1917); dance drama *The Kairn of Koridwen* (1916); *The Pleasure Dome of Kubla Khan* (after Coleridge) for orchestra (1917); Poem for flute and orchestra; *These things shall be* (J A Symonds) for unison chorus; Sketches on Indian themes for string quartet; piano sonata and pieces; songs.

Griffiths, Paul (b Bridgend, Glamorgan, 24 Nov 1947), English critic and writer on music. He studied at Oxford; critic for various journals from 1971. Chief music critic *The Times* 1982–92; *New Yorker* from 1992. A specialist in 20th-c. music, he had responsibility for this area in the *New Grove Dictionary of Music* (1980), and the *New Oxford Companion to Music* (1983). His own books include studies of Boulez, Davies, Ligeti, Bartók and Messiaen; also *A Concise History of Modern Music* (1978), *A Guide to Electronic Music* (1979), *Modern Music: the Avant Garde since 1945* (1981), *The String Quartet* (1983), *An Encyclopedia of 20th-Century Music* (1986) and *Stravinsky* (1992).

Grigny, Nicolas de (b Rheims, bap. 8 Sept 1672; d Rheims, 30 Nov 1703), French organist and composer. Son of Louis de Grigny (*c* 1646–1709), organist at Notre-Dame of Rheims. Studied under his father and in Paris, was organist of Saint-Denis Abbey, Paris, 1693–95 and then of Rheims Cathedral. Wrote organ music (pub. 1699) which Bach knew and copied in his early years.

Grillparzer, Franz (1791–1872), Austrian poet and dramatist. Friend of Beethoven and Schubert. Wrote funeral oration for the former and sketched inscription for the latter's gravestone.

For works used by composers, see J N ◊Hummel (*Ahnfrau*); C ◊Kreutzer (*Libussa* and *Melusine*); ◊Sappho (Kaun); ◊Schöne Melusine (Mendelssohn and C Kreutzer); ◊Schubert (*Ständchen* and *Mirjams Siegesgesang*); ◊Seyfried (*Ahnfrau* and *König Ottokar*); O ◊Straus (*Traum ein Leben*).

Grisar, Albert (b Antwerp, 26 Dec 1808; d Asnières, 15 Jun 1869), Belgian composer. He was intended for a business career and sent to Liverpool, but ran away to Paris to study music in 1830; became a pupil of Reicha, but was driven to Antwerp by the Revolution; produced *Le Mariage impossible* at Brussels in 1833, returned to

Paris, where he made further operatic successes. Studied with Mercadante at Naples in 1840 and returned to Paris in 1844.

Works include operas *Sarah* (after Scott, 1836), *L'An 1000*, *Lady Melvill* (1838) and *L'Eau merveilleuse* (both with Flotow), *Le Naufrage de la Méduse* (with Flotow and Pilati), *Les Travestissements* (1839), *L'Opéra à la cour* (with Boïeldieu, junior), *Gille Ravisseur* (1848), *Les Porcherons* (1850), *Bonsoir M Pantalon*, *Le Carillonneur de Bruges* (1852), *Les Amours du diable*, *Le Chien du jardinier* (1855), *Voyage autour de ma chambre* (after Xavier de Maistre, 1859), *La Chatte merveilleuse* (1862), *Bégaiements d'amour*, *Douze innocentes* (1865).

Griselda, La opera by A Scarlatti (libretto after A Zeno), produced Rome, Teatro Capranica, Jan 1721. The last of Scarlatti's 69 operas, beginning with *Gli equivoci* (1679). Modern edition by L Salter. King Gualtiero tests his wife, Griselda. She must live as a peasant, is threatened with the loss of her son, and is pursued by Ottone. She remains true and is restored as queen.

Grisélidis opera by Massenet (libretto by A Silvestre and E Morand), produced Paris, Opéra-Comique, 20 Nov 1901. Revived Wexford Festival, 1983. Grisélidis the shepherdess marries the Marquis de Saluces, who has the Devil test her fidelity.

Grisi, Giuditta (b Milan, 28 Jul 1805; d Robecco near Cremona, 1 May 1840), Italian mezzo-soprano. Studied at the Milan Conservatory, and made her debut in Vienna in 1826 (Rossini's *Bianca e Falliero*). In 1830 she created Romeo in Bellini's *I Capuleti*; sang Isoletta in *La Straniera*, Venice, London and Paris, 1832.

I am sure my music has a taste of codfish in it.
Edvard Grieg, speech, 1903

Grisi, Giulia (b Milan, 22 May 1811; d Berlin, 29 Nov 1869), Italian soprano, sister of Giuditta ◊Grisi. Pupil of her sister, Boccabadati, Guglielmi and others. Made her debut in 1828 and was engaged for Milan in 1829; created Adalgisa in *Norma*, 1831. In 1832 she first sang in Paris, as Semiramide, and in 1834 in London, in operas by Rossini, Mozart and Bellini. Other roles included Elvira (*Puritani*), Susanna and Lucrezia Borgia.

Grist, Reri (b New York, 29 Feb 1932), American soprano. She appeared in *West Side Story* on Broadway and sang Blondchen at Santa Fe in 1959; European debut Cologne 1960, as Queen of Night. She sang Despina and Zerbinetta at Glyndebourne in 1962; CG from 1962 as Olympia, Gilda and Susanna. NY Met. debut 1966, as Rosina. Other roles included Mozart's Aminta and Zerlina, Sophie and Adina.

Griswold, Putnam (b Minneapolis, 23 Dec 1875; d New York, 26 Feb 1914), American bass-baritone. Debut CG 1901 in the fp of Stanford's *Much Ado about Nothing*. Toured US 1904–05 as Gurnemanz in an English version of *Parsifal* and sang in Berlin 1906–11; decorated by the Kaiser. NY Met. debut 1911, as Hagen; returned until 1914 as Pogner, Marke and Daland.

Grobe, Donald (b Ottawa, IL, 16 Dec 1929; d Berlin, 1 Mar 1986), American tenor. Debut Chicago 1952, in *Rigoletto*. Sang in NY 1953–56 and moved to Germany 1956; Deutsche Oper, Berlin, from 1960 (fps Henze's *Der junge Lord*, 1965, and Fortner's *Elisabeth Tudor*, 1972). With the Munich Opera he sang Ferrando at Edinburgh in 1965 and visited CG in 1972, as Strauss's Flamand and Henry Morosus. Highly regarded in modern opera, sang Alwa, Tom Rakewell and Aschenbach, and appeared in *Mathis der Maler* and Orff's *Trionfi*.

Grocheio, Johannes de, music theorist of uncertain nationality who worked in Paris *c* 1300. His *De musica* survives in two MSS and is important for the light it throws on the secular music of his day and how it was performed.

Grofé, Ferde (b New York, 27 Mar 1892; d Santa Monica, 3 Apr 1972), American composer and arranger. Worked as an arranger for the Paul Whiteman band and in 1924 arranged Gershwin's *Rhapsody in Blue*. His own music includes *Mississippi Suite*, *Hollywood Suite* and the well-known *Grand Canyon Suite*, premiered under Whiteman, 1931.

Groot, Cor de (b Amsterdam, 7 Jul 1914), Dutch pianist and composer. Studied at the Amsterdam Conservatory and in 1936 won the international piano competition in Vienna. He has toured widely in Europe.

Works include ballet *Vernisage*; two piano concertos, piano concertino, concerto for two pianos, and a number of piano pieces.

grosse caisse French = lit. 'great case or chest' = ◊bass drum.

Grosse Fuge, *Great Fugue*, a work for string quartet by Beethoven, op. 133, in a fugal form 'tantôt libre, tantôt recherchée', written 1825 as the finale of the B♭ major string quartet, op. 130, and first performed with it, Vienna, 21 Mar 1826. Beethoven was persuaded by his publisher that it was too long, difficult and abstruse for that purpose and subsequently wrote the new finale, now part of op. 130. Also version for two pianos, op. 134.

Also title for first version of Busoni's *Fantasia contrappuntistica* (1910).

Grossi, Carlo (b Vicenza, *c* 1634; d Venice, 14 May 1688), Italian singer and composer. Worked as singer and *maestro di cappella* successively at Reggio, Vicenza, Venice and Mantua.

Works include four operas, including *Artaxerse* (1669); Masses and other church music; sacred concertos; sonatas; cantatas; songs; etc.

Grossin (*Grossim*), Estienne, French composer, chaplain at St Merry, Paris, 1418, and *clerc de matines* at Notre Dame, 1421. Wrote church music and *chansons*, including a Mass (without *Agnus*) with a part labelled 'trombetta'.

Grossinquisitor, Der, *The Grand Inquisitor*, oratorio by Blacher (text by L Borchard, from Dostoievsky's *The Brothers Karamazov*); composed 1942, fp Berlin, 14 Oct 1947.

Grossvater-Tanz German = 'grandfather's dance'; believed at one time to be a 17th-c. German dance, with words referring to a grandfather's wooing, sung and danced at weddings and later used as the final dance at balls and therefore called *Kehraus*, 'sweep-out'. Schumann used it both in *Papillons*, op. 2, and *Carnaval*, op. 9, in the latter to stand for the 'Philistines' in the finale. The dance was actually written by Karl Gottlieb Hering (1765–1853).

Grosz, Wilhelm (b Vienna, 11 Aug 1894; d New York, 10 Dec 1939), Austrian composer. Pupil of Adler for theory and Schreker for composition. Conductor at Mannheim Opera 1921, but returned to Vienna 1922 to make a living as pianist and composer; worked with a gramophone company in Berlin from 1928, conducted the Kammerspiele in Vienna, 1933–34, when he became a refugee in London and NY. His music has become associated with Kurt Weill, and a concert of their music was given at the London Proms, 1993.

Works include operas *Sganarell* (1925) and *Achtung, Aufnahme* (1930); play with music *St Peters Regenschirm*; ballets *Der arme Reinhold* (1928) and *Baby in der Bar*; incidental music to Werfel's *Spiegelmensch* and Hauptmann's *Die versunkene Glocke*; music for films and radio; Symphonic Variations, serenade, suite, overture to an opera buffa, etc. for orchestra; Symphonic Dance for piano and orchestra; string quartet; two violin and piano sonatas; three piano sonatas.

ground a composition built on a ground bass, or the bass itself.

ground bass a melodic figure used as a bass in a composition, constantly repeated without change, except sometimes by way of transposition, while the upper structure of the music is developed freely at the composer's will.

Grout, Donald J(ay) (b Rock Rapids, IA, 28 Sept 1902; d Skaneateles, NY, 9 Mar 1987), American musicologist. Studied at Syracuse and Harvard Universities and in Strasbourg and Vienna. Taught at Harvard 1936–42; professor of music Cornell University 1945–70. Early opera, e.g. A Scarlatti, was at the centre of his research. His books include *A Short History of Opera* (1948, revised 1965), *A History of Western Music* (1960, revised 1973, 1980 and, with C V Palisca, 1988), *Mozart in the History of Opera* (1972).

Grove, George (b London, 13 Aug 1820; d London, 28 May 1900), English civil engineer, biblical scholar and writer on music. Secretary to the Crystal Palace co., 1852–1873; first director of RCM 1883–94.

Groves *The conductor Charles Groves. In addition to his secure foundation in the symphonic repertory, Groves could have been considered Beecham's spiritual heir in terms of his affinity for the choral works of Delius, such as* A Mass of Life *and* Sea Drift.

Editor of the first edition of the *Dictionary of Music and Musicians* (1879–89) and author of a book on Beethoven's symphonies. Knighted 1883.

Groves, Charles (b London, 10 Mar 1915; d London, 15 Jan 1995), English conductor. He studied at the RCM and was chorus master at the BBC 1938–42. BBC Northern Orchestra 1944–51; Bournemouth SO 1951–61; Royal Liverpool PO 1963–77 (also brief spells as opera conductor with WNO, 1961–63, and ENO 1978–79). Noted for his solid performances of the standard repertory, and the choral works of Delius and Mahler. Knighted 1973.

Grove's Dictionary of Music and Musicians first edition compiled by George Grove and pub. in four vols. 1879–89; second edition J A Fuller Maitland, 1904–10; third edition H C Colles, 1927; fourth edition H C Colles, 1940; fifth edition Eric Blom, 1954, in nine vols.; sixth as *The New Grove Dictionary of Music and Musicians* editor Stanley Sadie, 1980, in 20 vols. A seventh edition, under Dr Sadie's direction, is promised 1999, in 24 vols.

Grovlez, Gabriel (Marie) (b Lille, 4 Apr 1879; d Paris, 20 Oct 1944), French conductor, pianist and composer. Studied at the Paris Conservatory, later taught piano at the Schola Cantorum and in 1939 became professor of chamber music at the Conservatory. Conducted at Lisbon, Chicago and Paris, from 1914 director at the Opéra.

Works include operas *Cœur de rubis* (1906) and *Psyche*; *conte lyrique*, *Le Marquis de Carabas*; three ballets including *Maïmouna* (1916); symphonic poems *Dans le Jardin*, *Madrigal lyrique*, etc.; cello and piano sonata; pieces for wind instruments; *Almanach aux images*, *Le Royaume puéril*, two Impressions, etc. for piano; three *Ballades françaises* and other songs.

Gruber, H(einz) K(arl) (b Vienna, 3 Jan 1943), Austrian composer. Studied at the Vienna Hochschule and with von Einem. He has played the double bass in various Viennese orchestras; co-founded the avant-garde group MOB art and tone ART.

Works include the melodrama *Die Vertreibung aus dem Paradies* for speakers and six instruments (1966), the spectacle *Gomorrah* (1972), 'pandemonium' *Frankenstein!!* for baritone and orchestra (1977); stage work *Gloria von Jaxtberg* (1993); Concerto for orchestra (1964), *Manhattan Broadcasts* for chamber orchestra, *Arien* for violin and orchestra, *Demilitarized Zones* for brass band (1979),

Rough Music, concerto for percussion and orchestra (1983); two violin concertos (1978, revised 1992, and 1988); cello concerto (1989); Mass for chorus, two trumpets, horn, double bass and percussion (1960), *Reportage aus Gomorrah* for five singers and eight players (1976), *Bring Me the Head of Amadeus*, TV film for the Mozart bicentenary (1991).

Gruberová, Edita (b Bratislava, 23 Dec 1946), Czech soprano. Debut Bratislava 1968, as Rosina. She sang Queen of Night at the Vienna Staatsoper in 1970 and has returned as Lucia, Gilda and Violetta. Salzburg from 1974, often with Karajan. NY Met. debut 1979, as Lucia. In 1984 sang Giulietta in a new production of Bellini's *I Capuleti e i Montecchi*, at CG. At Munich she has sung Massenet's Manon. Season 1992 as Lucia at Munich and Semiramide at Zurich. She is admired for her confident coloratura technique.

Gruenberg, Erich (b Vienna, 12 Oct 1924), Austrian-born British violinist. After study in Vienna he made his solo debut in Jerusalem, 1938. Moved to London 1946; leader, LSO 1962–65, RPO from 1972. Well known as a recitalist, he has partnered Edmund Rubbra, William Pleeth and William Glock; all Beethoven's violin sonatas recorded with David Wilde. He led the London String Quartet and has been heard in works by Messiaen, Goldschmidt, Gerhard and Britten.

Gruenberg, Louis (b Brest-Litovsk, 3 Aug 1884; d LA, 10 Jun 1964), American pianist and composer of Russian descent. He was taken to USA at the age of two. Studied in Berlin and Vienna, piano pupil of Busoni; first appeared as pianist in Berlin in 1912 and then began to travel, but from 1919 remained in USA to devote himself wholly to composition. His most successful work was the opera *The Emperor Jones*, premiered at the Met. 1933, with Lawrence Tibbett in the title role.

  Works include operas *The Bride of the Gods* (1913; libretto by Busoni), *The Dumb Wife*, *Jack and the Beanstalk*, *Emperor Jones* (after Eugene O'Neill, 1931), *Helena of Troy* (1936); children's opera *The Witch of Brocken*; radio opera *Green Mansions* (after W H Hudson); five symphonies, *Hill of Dreams*, *Enchanted Isle*, Serenade for orchestra; violin concerto; *The Daniel Jazz* (V Lindsey), *Animals and Insects* and *The Creation* for voice and chamber orchestra; *Four Indiscretions* for string quartet, two string quartets, two sonatas for violin and piano; piano pieces.

Grumiaux, Arthur (b Villers-Perwin, 21 Mar 1921; d Brussels, 16 Oct 1986), Belgian violinist. He studied in Brussels and with Enescu in Paris. British debut 1945, and performed with great distinction worldwide in classical repertory; formerly with Clara Haskil in sonatas by Mozart and Beethoven. Also played Berg and Bartók. Made a baron by King Baudouin in 1973.

Grümmer, Elisabeth (b Diedenhofen, Alsace-Lorraine, 31 Mar 1911; d Berlin, 6 Nov 1986), German soprano. After three years as an actress she made her singing debut in 1941 as Octavian, in Aachen. Sang in many of the leading European opera houses, including CG 1951 as Eva. Bayreuth 1957–61: Eva, Elsa, Gutrune. NY Met. debut 1967, as Elsa. She was especially well known for her singing of Mozart and R Strauss. Her best roles were Donna Elvira, Pamina, Ilia, the Countess in *Capriccio* and *Figaro* and the Marschallin.

Grünbaum, Therese (b Vienna, 24 Aug 1791; d Berlin, 30 Jan 1876), Austrian soprano. Her father was the popular Viennese theatre composer Wenzel Müller. At Prague she sang in operas by Mozart, from 1807, and was a leading member of the Kärntnertortheater, Vienna, from 1816; created Weber's Eglantine (1823) and often heard in Rossini. Taught in Berlin from 1830.

Grundheber, Franz (b Trier, 27 Sept 1937), German baritone. Studied at Indiana University and in San Diego. Has sung with Hamburg Staatsoper from 1966; many appearances in the USA, and sang Strauss's Mandryka at the Vienna Staatsoper 1983; Salzburg 1985, as Olivier in *Capriccio* (returned 1989, as Orestes). Savonlinna Festival 1989, as Amonasro. Season 1992 as Wozzeck in Paris (Châtelet) and Barak in *Die Frau ohne Schatten* at CG. Recordings include *Arabella* (with Kanawa) and *Wozzeck* (video from Vienna).

Grünewald, Gottfried (b Eywau, Lusatia, 1675; d Darmstadt, 19 Dec 1739), German singer and composer. Sang at Hamburg 1703–04,

where two of his operas *Germanicus* and *Der ungetreue Schäfer Cardillo* were produced. Appointed vice-*Kapellmeister* in Weissenfels 1709, and settled in Darmstadt as vice-*Kapellmeister* under Graupner *c* 1712.

Gruppen work by Stockhausen for three orchestras, placed in different parts of a hall and playing different music; composed 1955–57, fp Cologne, 24 Mar 1959.

gruppo, gruppetto Italian = 'trill, turn'.

Grützmacher, Friedrich (Wilhelm Ludwig) (b Dessau, 1 Mar 1832; d Dresden, 23 Feb 1903), German cellist and composer. Studied at Leipzig, where he became first cellist at the Gewandhaus in 1849 and later teacher at the Conservatory. In 1860 he became chamber virtuoso to the King of Saxony at Dresden. Composed mainly concertos and studies for cello, but also orchestral and chamber works, songs. His edition of the 'Boccherini cello concerto in B♭' is a pasticcio from several works.

GSM abbr. = ◊Guildhall School of Music.

Guadagni, Gaetano (b Lodi or Vicenza, *c* 1725; d Padua, Nov 1792), Italian castrato alto, later soprano. Made his first appearance at Parma in 1747 and went to London in 1748, where he sang in *Messiah*, *Samson* and *Theodora* (fp 1750). Later sang in Dublin, Paris, Lisbon, Italy and Vienna, where he was the first Orpheus in Gluck's *Orfeo* in 1762.

Guami, Francesco (b Lucca, *c* 1544; d Lucca, 30 Jan 1602), Italian composer and organist. Sackbut player at the Munich court, 1568–80; *maestro di cappella* at San Marciliano, Venice, from 1593 and at Lucca from 1598. Wrote madrigals, church music, instrumental music.

Guami, Gioseffo (b Lucca, *c* 1535; d Lucca, 1611), Italian organist and composer, brother of Francesco ◊Guami. Pupil of Willaert at St Mark's, Venice. He was at Munich with his brother, and organist of St Mark's, Venice, from 1588 to 1591; later organist at Lucca Cathedral. Wrote numerous madrigals, church music and instrumental music. Bull wrote a fantasia for keyboard on a theme from his instrumental canzona *La Guamina*. Of his eight sons Domenico (*c* 1580–1631) and Valerio (1587–1649) are known as composers. Vincenzo (d 1615) was for a short time from 1613 organist at the chapel of the Archduke Albert at Antwerp.

Though there seemed no chance of her throwing a whole party into raptures by a prelude on the pianoforte of her own composition, she could listen to other people's performance with very little fatigue.
Jane Austen, *Northanger Abbey*, 1818

Guarneri Italian family of violin makers:

  1. Andrea Guarneri (b *c* 1626; d Cremona, 7 Dec 1698). Pupil of Amati.

  2. Pietro Giovanni Guarneri (b Cremona, 18 Feb 1655; d Mantua, 26 Mar 1720), son of 1. Worked at Mantua.

  3. Giuseppe Giovanni Battista Guarneri (b Cremona, 25 Nov 1666; d Cremona, *c* 1740), son of 1.

  4. Pietro Guarneri (b Cremona, 14 Apr 1695; d Venice, 7 Apr 1762), nephew of 2. Worked at Venice.

  5. Giuseppe Guarneri (b Cremona, 21 Aug 1698; d Cremona, 17 Oct 1744), son of 3. Worked at Cremona and is known as *del Gesù* 'of Jesus' because of the letters I.H.S. ('Jesus Saviour of the World') printed on his labels; the most important violin maker in the family, rivalling Stradivari with instruments showing strength and beauty of tone.

Guarneri Quartet American string quartet formed in Vermont 1964 with the members Arnold Steinhardt and John Dalley (violins), Michael Tree (viola) and David Soyer (cello). First visited Europe 1965 and gave the complete Beethoven quartets in London 1970. Recordings of most classical repertory works (piano quintets with Arthur Rubinstein) and also heard in Bartók.

Guarnieri, (Mozart) Camargo (b Tietê, 1 Feb 1907; d Sao Paolo, 13 Jan 1993), Brazilian composer. Pupil of Koechlin in Paris; often visited the USA where many of his works were performed. Conductor of the Orquestra Sinfônica Municipal, São Paulo, and director of the Conservatory from 1960.

Works include four symphonies; five piano concertos (1936–70), two violin concertos (1940, 1953); chamber music; cello and piano sonata; piano pieces; songs.

Gubaidulina, Sofia (b Chistopol, 24 Oct 1931), Russian composer. Studied at the Moscow Conservatory 1954–59 and later with Shebalin. Co-founded the group Astreya, 1975, for improvisations on folk instruments from Russia and Caucasia. A leading member of the New Music generation of Russian composers, she has often turned to literature and religion for inspiration. Resident in Germany from 1991, the year in which her opera-oratorio-ballet, *Prayer for the Age of Aquarius* was premiered.

Works include ORCHESTRAL: *Fairytale Poem* (1971), *Stufen/Steps* (1972–92), concerto for bassoon and strings (1975), concerto for jazz band and orchestra (1976), *Introitus* concerto for piano and chamber orchestra (1978), *Offertorium* violin concerto (1980–86), *Seven Words* for cello, bayan and strings (1982), *stimmen ... verstummen* symphony in 12 movements (1986), *Answer without Question* collage for three orchestras (1988), *Pro et Contra* for large orchestra (1989), *The Feast in Full Swing* for cello and orchestra (1993).

VOCAL: *Fatseliya* vocal-symphonic cycle for soprano and orchestra (1956), *Night in Memphis* cantata (1968–92), *Rubayat* cantata for baritone and orchestra (1969), *Hour of the Soul* for mezzo and winds (1974), *Laudatio pacis* oratorio (1975), *Perception* for soprano, baritone and seven strings (1985), *Hommage à T S Eliot* for soprano and octet (1987), *Witty Waltzing* for soprano and octet (1989), *Jauchzt vor Gott* for chorus and organ (1989), *Alleluja* for chorus, boy soprano and orchestra (1990), *Aus dem Stundenbuch/From the Book of Hours* for cello, orchestra, male chorus and female speaker (1991), *Prayer for the Age of Aquarius* opera-oratorio-ballet (1991).

CHAMBER: piano quintet (1957), four string quartets (1971, 1987, 1987, 1990), ten preludes for cello (1974), quartet for four flutes (1977), *De Profundis* for bayan (1978), *Garten von freuden und Traurigkeiten* for flute, harp and viola (1988), *Rejoice* sonata for violin and cello (1981), string trio (1988), *Silenzio* five pieces for bayan, violin and cello (1991), *Even and Uneven* for seven percussionists (1991), *The Ropedancer* for violin and piano (1993), *Meditation on the Bach Chorale Vor deinen Thron* for harpsichord and ensemble (1993).

Gudehus, Heinrich (b Altenhagen near Celle, 30 Mar 1845; d Dresden, 9 Oct 1909), German tenor. Studied with Malwina Schnorr von Carolsfeld at Brunswick and Gustav Engel in Berlin; made his debut there in 1871 in Spohr's *Jessonda*; sang Parsifal at Bayreuth in 1882; also sang Walther and Tristan there. First went to London in 1884, when he sang Parsifal in the first (concert) performance of the opera in Britain. NY Met. debut 1890 as Tannhäuser. Retired 1896.

Gueden, Hilde (b Vienna, 15 Sept 1917; d Klosterneuburg, 17 Sept 1988), Austrian soprano. She made her debut in Zurich in 1939. In 1946 she joined the Vienna Staatsoper, becoming an Austrian *Kammersängerin* in 1950 and singing there until 1973. Also sang at Salzburg, London and NY: roles included Zerbinetta, Susanna, Daphne and Anne Trulove.

Guédron, Pierre (b Châteaudun, *c* 1565; d ? Paris, *c* 1621), French singer and composer. He was a chorister in the chapel of the Cardinal de Guise and later of Henri IV. In 1601 he was appointed composer to the king in succession to Claude Le Jeune and held various other posts at court, finishing as Surintendant de la Musique under Louis XIII in 1613. His daughter Jeanne married Boësset, with whom, as well as Bailly, Maudit and Bataille, he collaborated in the composition of court ballets. He also pub. six books of airs with lute accompaniment (*airs de cour*) and contributed others to various collections.

Guerre des Bouffons French = lit. 'War of the Buffoons'; the quarrel that broke out in Paris in 1752 between the adherents of French music, especially opera, and the imported art of the Italians, who produced or revived several examples of *opera buffa* in the French capital that year.

Guerrero, Francisco (b Seville, 4 Oct 1528; d Seville, 8 Nov 1599), Spanish composer. Pupil of his brother Pedro Guerrero and of Fernández de Castilleja at Seville Cathedral, where he was a chorister; he also had some lessons from Morales as a child. Appointed to the cathedral of Jaén in 1546 and after the death of Morales to that of Málaga, though he never resided there, filling posts at Seville Cathedral until he succeeded Castilleja as *maestro de capilla* on 9 Mar 1574. Visited Lisbon, Rome (twice), Venice and the Holy Land.

Works include 18 Masses, *c* 150 liturgical pieces, including motets, psalms, vespers, Magnificats, Te Deum; sacred and secular songs.

Many clerics and monks of the religious order, neglect the psalms, the sacred readings, the nocturnal vigils, and the other works of piety that arouse and lead us on to everlasting glory, while they apply themselves with unceasing and most foolish effort to the science of singing which they can never master.

Guido d'Arezzo, *Prologus antiphonarii sui*, c. 1025

Gueymard, Louis (b Chapponay, 17 Aug 1822; d Paris, Jul 1880), French tenor. He sang at CG in 1854 and at the Paris Opéra 1848–68; created roles in *Les vêpres siciliennes* (1855), *Le Prophète* (1849) and Gounod's *La Reine de Saba* (1862); his wife Pauline (b 1834) appeared with him in Gounod's opera and also created Verdi's Eboli and Thomas' Gertrude (1867–68).

Guglielmi, Pietro Alessandro (b Massa Carrara, 9 Dec 1728; d Rome, 19 Nov 1804), Italian composer. Pupil of Durante in Naples, he produced his first opera there in 1757, and thereafter had great success throughout Italy and abroad. He was in England intermittently 1767–72, and also visited Brunswick and Dresden. In 1793 he was appointed *maestro di cappella* at St Peter's, Rome.

Works include *c* 100 operas, e.g. *Il ratto della sposa* (1765), *La sposa fedele* (1767), *La villanella ingentilita* (1779), *I finti amori*, *La virtuosa di Mergellina* (1785), *L'inganno amoroso*, *La pastorella nobile*, *La bella pescatrice* (1789); oratorios, e.g. *La morte d'Abele*, *La Betulia liberata*, etc.; church music, symphonies; chamber music, keyboard music.

Guglielmi, Pietro Carlo (b ? Naples, *c* 1763; d Naples, 21 Feb 1817), Italian composer, son of Pietro ◊Guglielmi. Studied at the Conservatorio di Santa Maria di Loreto in Naples, producing the first of many successful operas in 1794 in Madrid. Also visited London, Lisbon and Paris.

Works include almost 50 operas, e.g. *Amor tutto vince* (1805), *Guerra aperta* (1807); oratorio *La distruzione di Gerusalemme* (1803).

Guglielmo, Ebreo da Pesaro (b ? Pesaro, *c* 1425; d ? after 1480), Jewish-Italian dancing-master and theorist. He served many European courts. His book, *De pratica seu arte tripudii vulgare opusculum* (*c* 1460), included both tunes and choreography.

Guglielmo Ratcliff, *William Ratcliff*, opera by Mascagni (libretto by composer, based on Heine's tragedy), produced Milan, La Scala, 16 Feb 1895. An earlier work than *Cavalleria rusticana*, although produced later. Mary and Count Douglas are to marry, but Ratcliff wants to kill Douglas to avenge his father, killed by Mary's father. In the end he kills Mary and himself as well.

Gui, Vittorio (b Rome, 14 Sept 1885; d Florence, 16 Oct 1975), Italian conductor and composer. Student at the Liceo di Santa Cecilia in Rome. Appointed conductor at the Teatro Adriano there and later conducted opera at Turin, Naples and Milan. In 1928 he founded the Orchestra Stabile (later Maggio Musicale) festival at Florence, and conducted operas by Spontini, Gluck and Cherubini there. Glyndebourne 1948–64, *Così fan Tutte*, *Macbeth*, *Alceste*, *Figaro*, *Zauberflöte* and *Falstaff*; he was one of the most important conductors in the history of the festival.

Works include opera *La fata Malerba*; symphonic poems; chamber music.

Guidetti, Giovanni (b Bologna, Dec 1530; d Rome, 30 Nov 1592), Italian priest. Pupil of Palestrina, whom he assisted in compiling the revised church services commissioned by Pope Gregory XIII, the *Directorium chori* (pub. 1582), in 1576–81.

Guido d'Arezzo (b Arezzo, *c* 990; d Pomposa, *c* 1050), Italian Benedictine monk and music theorist. Lived in Pomposa and Arezzo and visited Rome. He greatly advanced solmization and mutation by adapting the syllables Ut, Re, Mi, Fa, Sol, La to the hexachord and by demonstrating the hexachordal positions on the fingers by the use of the 'Guidonian hand'. He was once, rather doubtfully, credited with the invention of the music stave, the use of which he certainly encouraged. His chief theoretical work is entitled *Micrologus de musica* (*c* 1026).

Guignon, Jean-Pierre (Giovanni Pietro Ghignone) (b Turin, 10 Feb 1702; d Versailles, 30 Jan 1774), Italian-French violinist and composer, a champion of the Italian style of playing in France. In 1733 appeared at court, and received in 1741 the title of *Roi des violons et des ménétriers*, being the last to hold the position.

Works include sonatas, concertos, etc. for violin, trio sonatas.

Guildhall School of Music and Drama (GSM) a music school established 1880 to serve the City of London; it was housed in a new building in 1887 and in another in 1977. Its principal 1978–88 was John Hosier, Ian Horsbrugh from 1988.

Guilelmus Monachus 15th-c. theorist of uncertain nationality who lived in Italy but may possibly have been English. His treatise *De praeceptis artis musicae* contains references to the English use of 'fauxbourdon' and 'gymel'.

Guillaume Tell, *William Tell*, opera by Grétry (libretto by J M Sedaine), produced Paris, Comédie-Italienne, 9 Apr 1791.

Opera by Rossini (libretto by V J E de Jouy and H L F Bis, based on Schiller's drama), produced Paris, Opéra, 3 Aug 1829. Rossini's last opera. Swiss patriot William Tell would lead the uprising against the Austrians, but he has been imprisoned. Arnold, once in love with Austrian Mathilde, joins the fight after his father is executed. After the storm sunny skies for Switzerland.

Guillemain, (Louis) Gabriel (b Paris, 15 Nov 1705; d Paris, 1 Oct 1770), French violinist and composer. Appointed to the court in Versailles in 1737, composed sonatas for violin and chamber music.

Guilmant, (Félix) Alexandre (b Boulogne-sur-Mer, 12 Mar 1837; d Meudon, 29 Mar 1911), French organist and composer. Pupil of his father, an organist at Boulogne, where he afterwards held several church appointments, studying briefly in Brussels with Lemmens in

---

THE OPERA

Guillaume Tell

Grand Opera in four-acts by Rossini. Set in Switzerland, 1307.
I. The Swiss patriot Tell (baritone) leads resistance against the occupying Austrian Gessler (baritone). Tell rescues Leuthold (baritone), pursued by the Austrians after he has killed one of them for molesting his daughter.
II. Arnold (tenor) and the Austrian Princess Mathilde (soprano) declare their love. Arnold decides to join Tell's cause after he learns that his father has been killed by the Austrians.
III. In the square of Altdorf, Tell alone refuses to defer to Gessler. As punishment, he is condemned to shoot an apple from his son Jemmy's head. Tell succeeds, but reveals that a bolt was reserved for Gessler if he had failed. Tell is arrested and taken to a castle in the Lake of Lucerne.
IV. Arnold gathers his supporters at the edge of the lake and a signal is given for the revolt to begin. Tell finds his way to shore and he shoots Gessler. The Swiss people sing of their deliverance.

THE OPERA

1860 and moving to Paris in 1871, where he was organist at the Trinité Church until 1901. He toured widely with great success and was professor of organ at the Schola Cantorum, which he had helped Bordes and d'Indy to found, and at the Conservatory.

Works include two symphonies for organ and orchestra; eight sonatas and 25 sets of pieces for organ, organ music for church use.

Guiraud, Ernest (b New Orleans, 23 Jun 1837; d Paris, 6 May 1892), French composer. Son of a musician. Studied at the Paris Conservatory and gained the Prix de Rome 1859. He became professor at the Conservatory 1876, following Massé as the head of the advanced composition class in 1880. Debussy was one of his pupils.

Works include operas *Sylvie* (1864), *En Prison* (1869), *Le Kobold* (1870), *Madame Turlupin*, *Piccolino* (1876), *Galante Aventure*, *Le Feu*, *Frédégonde* (unfinished, completed by Saint-Saëns); ballet *Gretna Green* (1873); overture *Arteveld*, *Chasse fantastique* (after Hugo's *Beau Pécopin*), and suite for orchestra; Caprice for violin and orchestra, etc. Recitatives for Bizet's *Carmen* and orchestration of Offenbach's *Contes d'Hoffmann*.

Guirlande, La, ou Les fleurs enchantées acte de ballet by Rameau (libretto by J-F Marmontel), produced Paris, Opéra, 21 Sept 1751. The garlands exchanged by Myrtil and Zélide will only stay fresh as long as they remain faithful.

guitar a string instrument of great antiquity. Its back is flat, its belly has a waist, as though to allow for the playing with a bow, but the strings are plucked with the fingers or a plectrum. The sound-hole in the

The open strings of the modern classical guitar.

sound-board is often very decoratively carved. The finger-board is fretted. The modern classical guitar has six strings, usually tuned E, A, D, G, B, E.

With the guitar, it is of course vital to avoid confusion in anyone's mind about when the soloist should be heard and, conversely, where the orchestra may be given its head.

Stephen Dodgson, *Introduction to his Concerto for Guitar and Chamber Orchestra*, 1959

---

guitar violoncello ◊arpeggione.

Gulbranson, Ellen (b Stockholm, 4 Mar 1863; d Oslo, 2 Jan 1947), Swedish soprano. Concert debut 1886; stage debut Stockholm 1889, as Amneris (mezzo role). She sang Brünnhilde at Bayreuth 1896 and repeated in the role until 1914, gaining a reputation for reliability rather than brilliance; also sang Kundry. She sang in Berlin from 1895, Vienna from 1896. CG 1900 and 1907–08, as Brünnhilde under Richter.

Gulda, Friedrich (b Vienna, 16 May 1930), Austrian pianist. Studied with Bruno Seidlhofer, winning first prize in the Geneva International Pianists' Competition in 1946. Toured Europe in 1947–48, and made his American debut 1950. Outside the classical repertory he is also well known as a jazz pianist; from 1962 has given jazz and improvised music concerts.

Guleghina, Maria (b Odessa, 1959), Russian soprano. Studied in Odessa and sang with Minsk Opera from 1984. La Scala 1987, Amelia in *Ballo in Maschera*. Widely successful in such dramatic roles as Maddalena (NY Met., 1990), Lisa (Kirov Opera and San Francisco), Tosca, Odabella and Santuzza. Resident in Hamburg from 1990.

Gumpeltzhaimer, Adam (b Trostberg, Bavaria, *c* 1559; d Augsburg, 3 Nov 1625), German composer. Studied at the monastery of St Ulric at Augsburg. From 1581 until his death he was cantor at the church of St Anna at Augsburg. He pub. a treatise, *Compendium musicae latinum-germanicum*, in 1591.

Works include psalms, hymns, sacred songs.

Gundry, Inglis (b London, 8 May 1905), English composer. Educated at Oxford, where he read law, but turned to literature, writing poems and a novel, *The Countess's Penny*. Studied at RCM under Vaughan Williams, Gordon Jacob and R O Morris. After war service in the navy became instructor Lieutenant and music adviser to the Admiralty education department, for which he edited a *Naval Song Book*.

Works include operas *Naaman: the Leprosy of War* (1937), *The Return of Odysseus* (after Homer, 1938), *The Sleeping Beauty* and *Partisans* (1946); ballet *Sleep*; Variations on an Indian theme and overture *Per mare, per terram* for orchestra; Comedy Overture for small orchestra; *Sostenuto and Vivace* for strings; Fantasy string quartet; songs.

Gungl, Joseph (b Zsámbék, 1 Dec 1810; d Weimar, 31 Jan 1889), Austro-Hungarian bandmaster and composer. Entered the Austrian army and later made tours with a military band of his own. In 1849 he visited the USA, becoming music director to the King of Prussia on his return and in 1858 to the Austrian Emperor. In 1864 he went to live at Munich and in 1876 at Frankfurt. He wrote hundreds of marches and dances.

Günther von Schwarzburg opera by Holzbauer (libretto by A Klein), produced Mannheim, at court, 5 Jan 1777. Günther battles Karl for control of the Holy Roman Empire, finally being poisoned by Karl's mother; admired by Mozart.

Our sweetest songs are those that tell of saddest thought.

Percy Bysshe Shelley, 'To a Skylark' 1819

Guntram opera by R Strauss (libretto by composer) produced Weimar, 10 May 1894. Strauss's first opera; revised version produced Weimar, 22 Oct 1940. Guntram kills Duke Robert after being attacked by him, but the idealistic minstrel realizes that his deed was caused by love for the Duke's wife, Freihild. Guntram seeks solitude for introspection.

Gura, Eugen (b Pressern near Saatz, 8 Nov 1842; d Aufkirchen, Bavaria, 26 Aug 1906), Bohemian-German baritone. After technical and art studies in Vienna, he studied singing at the Munich Conservatory and made his first stage appearance there in 1865. In 1876 he appeared in the production of Wagner's *Ring* at Bayreuth as Donner and Gunther. Sang Sachs and Marke in the first British productions of *Meistersinger* and *Tristan* (Drury Lane, 1882, conductor Richter).

Guridi, Jesús (b Victoria, 25 Sept 1886; d Madrid, 7 Apr 1961), Spanish composer of Basque descent. Studied at the Schola Cantorum in Paris, also at Liège and Cologne. His music is based on Basque themes.

Works include operas *Mirentxu* (1915) and *Amaya* (1920), zarzuela *El caserío* (1926); orchestra and organ music; church music; four string quartets; settings of Basque folksongs.

Gurlitt, Manfred (b Berlin, 6 Sept 1890; d Tokyo, 29 Apr 1972), German conductor and composer. Studied composition with Kaun and Humperdinck, conducting with Muck and piano with Breithaupt in Berlin. After various operatic appointments he was general music director at Bremen from 1914 and of the Berlin Staatsoper from 1924. Later he appeared as guest opera conductor in Germany and Spain, but his works were banned by the Nazis and he went to live in Japan 1939, forming the Gurlitt Opera Company.

Works include operas *Die Heilige*, *Wozzeck* (after Büchner, 1926), *Soldaten*, *Nana* (after Zola, 1933), *Seguidilla bolero*, *Feliza*; incidental music for two Spanish plays; music for films; *Goya* symphony, *Shakespeare* symphony; cello concerto; chamber concertos for piano and violin; piano quintet in C minor; piano sonata; songs with chamber orchestra.

Gurney, Ivor (Bertie) (b Gloucester, 28 Aug 1890; d Dartford, Kent, 26 Dec 1937), English composer and poet. He was a choirboy at Gloucester Cathedral and later studied at the RCM in London with a scholarship. He suffered much from ill-health and during World War I was badly wounded and shell-shocked. He struggled for a time against poverty, but in 1922 lost his reason; he died of tuberculosis.

Works include *The Apple Orchard* and *Scherzo* for violin and piano; two sets of piano pieces; song cycles *Ludlow and Teme* (A E Housman) and *The Western Playland*, over 200 songs, some to his own poems. Two vols. of poetry, *Savern and Somme* and *War's Embers*.

Gurrelieder, *Songs of Gurra*, work by Schoenberg for five soloists, speaker, four choruses and large orchestra, including iron chains (text a German translation of the Danish poems by J P Jacobsen); composed 1900–11, fp Vienna 23 Feb 1913, conductor Franz Schreker. First US performance Philadelphia, 8 Apr 1932, conductor Stokowski.

Guschlbauer, Theodor (b Vienna, 14 Apr 1939), Austrian conductor. Studied in Vienna and conducted the Baroque Ensemble there, 1961–69. Chief conductor of the Salzburg Landestheater 1966–68, Lyon Opera 1968–75; Linz-Bruckner SO 1975–83. Currently chief conductor of the Strasbourg PO; led *Così fan Tutte* there 1990. Guest appearances at Salzburg, Prague, Aix and Lucerne Festivals; Vienna, Hamburg, Paris, Munich and Geneva Operas. Has recorded much music by Mozart, and Cesti's *Il Pomo d'Oro*.

Gustafson, Nancy (b Evanston, IL, 27 Jun 1956), American soprano. After study in San Francisco she sang there as Freia (debut), Musetta and Antonia. Appeared in Minnesota and Santa Fe before her European debut as Rosalinde at Paris, 1985. Glyndebourne from 1988, as Katya Kabanova, and Lisa in *The Queen of Spades* (1992). Chicago and NY Met. debuts 1989 (as Marguerite and Musetta); La Scala and London, CG, debuts 1990 and 1993, as Eva in *Die Meistersinger*. Other roles include Amelia Boccanegra, Elettra and Violetta.

Gustave III, ou Le Bal masqué, *Gustavus III, or The Masked Ball*, opera by Auber (libretto by Scribe), produced Paris, Opéra, 27 Feb 1833. ◊Ballo in maschera for plot synopsis.

Gutheil-Schoder, Marie (b Weimar, 16 Feb 1874; d Ilmenau, 4 Oct 1935), German soprano. She made her debut in Weimar, where she received coaching from Richard Strauss, and after engagements in Berlin and Leipzig was engaged by Mahler at the Hofoper, Vienna. Early roles, from 1900, were Nedda and Carmen; she was criticized for her small voice but the force of her dramatic characterisations made her a favourite until 1926; she was the first Viennese Elektra and sang Octavian at CG in 1913. She sang the soprano part in the riotous fp of Schoenberg's second string quartet (Vienna, 1908) and was The Woman in the fp of *Erwartung* (Prague, 1924).

Gutiérrez, Antonio Garcia (1812–1884), Spanish dramatist. ◊Simon Boccanegra and ◊Trovatore (Verdi).

Gutman, Natalia (b Moscow, 14 Jun 1942), Russian cellist. Studied in Moscow under Rostropovich. Won awards in Moscow, Munich and Vienna, and has appeared with the Vienna and Berlin POs, Philharmonia London and Concertgebouw Orchestra. Tours of USA with Russsian State SO and of Russia with the BBC SO. Chamber music with Oleg Kagan and Richter; premieres of works by the New Music School of Russian composers, Gubaidulina, Schnittke and Denisov.

Gutmann, Adolph (b Heidelberg, 12 Jan 1819; d Spezia, 27 Oct 1882), German pianist and composer. Pupil and friend of Chopin. Wrote numerous piano works, including ten *Études caractéristiques*.

Guy, Barry (b London, 22 Apr 1947), English composer and double bass player. His early interest was in jazz; later studied at the GSM with Buxton Orr and Patric Standford. After forming the Jazz Composers' Orchestra in 1971 his works have combined improvisatory with more controlled avant garde techniques.

Works include *D* for 15 solo strings (1972); *Anna* for amplified double bass and orchestra (1974); *Statements III* and *IV* for jazz orchestra (1972–75); string quartet *III* (1973); *Songs from Tomorrow* for 13 instruments (1975); *Voyages of the Moon* for double bass and orchestra (1983); *Blitz*, septet (1984); *rondOH!* for piano, violin and double bass (1985); *Video Life* for double bass and electronics (1986); ballet for London Contemporary Dance Theatre; *After the Rain* (1992); *Bird Gong Game* (1992); *Witch Gong Game* (1993); *Portraits* (1993).

Guyon, Jean (b c 1514; d after 1574), French composer, first a choirboy (from 1523) and later canon (from 1545) of Chartres Cathedral. Wrote two Masses, a motet and several *chansons*.

Guy-Ropartz, Joseph Guy Marie Ropartz (b Guingamp, Côtes du Nord, 15 Jun 1864; d Lanloup, 22 Nov 1955), French composer. He first studied law, but went to the Paris Conservatory as a pupil of Dubois, Massenet and Franck. In 1894 he became director of the Nancy Conservatory and in 1919 of that of Strasbourg. Later he retired to Brittany, where he was born.

Works include OPERA: *Le Diable couturier, Marguerite d'Écosse, Le Miracle de Saint-Nicolas* (1905), *Le Pays* (1913); ballet *L'Indiscret*; incidental music for a stage version of Pierre Loti's *Pêcheur d'Islande* and for Sophocles' *Oedipus at Colonus*; *Messe de Sainte-Odile, Messe de Sainte-Anne*, Requiem (1939), Psalm cxxxvi, motets and other church music.

INSTRUMENTAL: five symphonies (1895–1945), *Petite Symphonie, Paysage de Bretagne, Les Landes, Dimanche breton, La Cloche des morts, Concert in D major* and other orchestral works; *Rhapsodie* for violin and orchestra; six string quartets (1893–1951), string trio, piano trio; three violin and piano sonatas, two cello and piano sonatas; songs; organ music.

Gwendoline opera by Chabrier (libretto by C Mendès), produced Brussels, Théâtre de la Monnaie, 10 Apr 1886. Gwendoline, daughter of Saxon leader Armel, is to marry Danish Harald. Armel plans to massacre the Danes during the festivities. Gwendoline tries to warn Harald, but it is too late, then she kills herself.

Gyffard Part-Books a set of four books containing sacred Latin works, written down c 1555 but including works written earlier, such as John Taverner's Mass *The Western Wind*. It once belonged to a Dr Philip Gyffard.

gymel from Latin *gemellum* = 'a twinsong'; vocal music in two parts, both of the same range. A characteristic feature is the use of parallel thirds. The term first occurs in the 15th c., when it usually refers to a divided voice-part in a polyphonic composition, but examples are found as early as the 14th c.

Gymnopédies three pieces for piano by Satie, composed 1888. Nos. 1 and 3 (*Lent et triste, Lent et grave*) were orchestrated by Debussy and performed Paris, 20 Feb 1897.

Gymnopédies refers to Greek dances in honour of Apollo, performed by naked men and boys; Debussy's music has become a popular ballet.

Gyrowetz (*Jírovec*), Adalbert (Vojcěch) (b Budějovice, 20 Feb 1763; d Vienna, 19 Mar 1850), Bohemian composer. Learnt music from his father, a choirmaster; later studied law in Prague, but continued to work at music. As private secretary to Count Franz von Fünfkirchen, he was expected to take part in the domestic music. He then went to Italy for study under Sala at Naples and later visited Paris, where symphonies of his had been performed under the name of Haydn. In 1789 the Revolution drove him to London, where the score of his opera *Semiramis* was burnt in the fire of the Pantheon in 1792. He returned to Vienna soon after, and in 1804 was appointed conductor at the court theatres, where he wrote many works until 1831. He knew Beethoven, and was a pall-bearer at his funeral in 1827.

Works include Italian operas *Federica ed Adolfo* (1812) and *Il finto Stanislao* (1818), German operas *Agnes Sorel* (1806), *Ida die Büssende* (1807), *Der Augenarzt, Robert, oder Die Prüfung* (1815), *Helene, Felix und Adele, Hans Sachs, Die Junggesellen-Wirtschaft, Der Sammtrock, Aladin* (after Oehlenschläger), *Das Ständchen* (1823), etc.; ballet *Die Hochzeit der Thetis* (1816) and others; melodramas *Mirina* and others; comic cantata *Die Dorfschule*; over 60 symphonies, serenades, overtures and other orchestral works; c 60 string quartets, quintets, numerous trios; c 40 violin and piano sonatas; instrumental pieces, dances; songs.

H

H the German symbol for the note B♯.

Haas, Joseph (b Maihingen, Bavaria, 19 Mar 1879; d Munich, 30 Mar 1960), German composer. Pupil of Reger at Munich and then at the Leipzig Conservatory. Teacher of composition at Stuttgart from 1911 and Munich from 1921.

Works include operas *Tobias Wunderlich* (1937) and *Die Hochzeit des Jobs* (1944); choral works; serenade for orchestra; two string quartets, divertimento for string trio, trio for two cellos and piano and other chamber music; sonata and sonatina for violin and piano; many piano works; organ pieces; songs.

Haas, Monique (b Paris, 20 Oct 1906; d Paris, 6 Jun 1987), French pianist. She studied at the Paris Conservatory and privately with Casadesus and Serkin. Debut 1927; many recitals and recordings of Schubert and Mozart, French music and modern classics. Was married to the composer Marcel ◊Mihalovici.

Haas, Robert (Maria) (b Prague, 15 Aug 1886; d Vienna, 4 Oct 1960), Austrian musicologist. Took his Ph.D. at Prague University and became assistant to Adler. Later lecturer at Vienna University and director of the music department of the State Library there. Editor of the original versions of Bruckner's works, 1932–42, succeeded by Leopold Nowak. Author of books on Baroque music, musical performance, Mozart and Bruckner (1934).

Hába, Alois (b Vizovice, Moravia, 21 Jun 1893; d Prague, 18 Nov 1973), Czech composer. Gained a knowledge of folk music before he studied at the Prague Conservatory under Novák; later a pupil of Schreker in Vienna and Berlin. Worked for Universal Edition in Vienna and gained a good knowledge of Schoenberg's music. Appointed professor at the Prague Conservatory 1924. He became interested in the division of the scale into quarter-tones, on which much of his later work is based (from second string quartet, 1920). Later employed sixth-tones (fifth quartet, 1923) and fifth-tones (16th quartet, 1967). Also wrote some 12-tone music (*Fantasia* for nonet, 1932).

Works include opera *Matka/Mother*, produced Munich 1931; Overture and Symphonic Music for orchestra; Fantasy for piano and orchestra; violin concerto; 16 string quartets (1919–67) and other chamber music; piano sonata and other works (some for quarter-tone piano); works for string instruments.

Hába, Karel (b Vizovice, 21 May 1898; d Prague, 21 Nov 1972), Czech violinist and composer, brother of Alois Hába. Studied violin under Karel Hoffmann, composition under Křička, Foerster and Novák, and quarter-tone music with his brother. He played viola in the Czech PO 1929–36 and in 1949 became head of the education section of Czech Radio.

Works include opera *Jánošik* (1934); two symphonies (1947–54); violin and cello concertos; four string quartets (1922–69); septet; piano music; songs.

Habanera a dance, with words to be sung, introduced into Spain from Africa via Cuba. It is in a moderate 2–4 time and has a basic rhythm of four quavers, the first of which is dotted. A famous example is that in the first act of Bizet's *Carmen*.

Habeneck, François Antoine (b Mézières, 22 Jan 1781; d Paris, 8 Feb 1849), French violinist and conductor of German descent. Pupil of Baillot. Founder of the Société des Concerts du Conservatoire in Paris; conductor at the Opéra 1824–47; gave the fps of *Guillaume Tell*, *Les Huguenots*, *La Juive* and *Benvenuto Cellini*. The first conductor to cultivate Beethoven in France.

Habich, Eduard (b Kassel, 3 Sept 1880; d Berlin, 15 Mar 1960), German baritone. Debut Koblenz, 1904. Berlin Staatsoper 1910–30 as Falke and Faninal; Bayreuth 1911–31 as Alberich and Klingsor. From 1924 to 1938 he was heard at CG, London, as Telramund and Beckmesser.

Hacker, Alan (b Dorking, 30 Sept 1938), English clarinettist and conductor. He studied at the RAM; taught there since 1959. Member of the LSO 1959–66; founder member of the Pierrot Players, later Fires of London, giving fps of many works by Peter Maxwell Davies. Founded his own group, Matrix, in 1971 and has given fps of works by Boulez, Blake, Birtwistle and Goehr. He has been involved in 'authentic' performances of classical music, often with early versions of the clarinet. From 1977 he has conducted authentic versions of symphonies by Mozart and Beethoven, and Haydn Masses; first production of Mozart's complete *Finta Giardiniera* (Swedish National Opera, 1987), Keiser's *Claudius* at the Vadstena Academy (1989) and the premiere of Weir's *The Vanishing Bridegroom* (Glasgow, 1990). Stuttgart Opera 1990–92, *Don Giovanni* and Monteverdi's *Ulisse*. *Giulio Cesare* at the 1992 Halle Festival.

Hacomblene (Hacomplaynt), Robert (b London, *c* 1456; d Cambridge, 8 Sept 1528), English composer. He was scholar of Eton, 1469–72, and of King's College, Cambridge, from 1472. He was a Fellow there, 1475–93, and Provost from 1509 until his death. A *Salve Regina* by him is in the Eton Choirbook.

Hadley, Henry (Kimball) (b Somerville, MA, 20 Dec 1871; d New York, 6 Sept 1937), American conductor and composer. Studied with his father, with Chadwick at Boston and Mandyczewski in Vienna. Conducted opera in USA and Germany, and in 1909 became conductor of the symphony orchestra at Seattle; San Francisco 1911–15. From 1920 lived in NY.

Works include operas *Safié* (1909), *Azora, Daughter of Montezuma* (1917), *Bianca, Cleopatra's Night* (1920) and *Mirtil in Arcadia*; *Music, The New Earth* and *Resurgam* for solo voices, chorus and orchestra; five symphonies, overtures *In Bohemia*, *Herod* and to Shakespeare's *Othello*, Symphonic Fantasy, tone-poems *Salome*, *Lucifer* and *The Ocean*.

Hadley, Jerry (b Peoria, 16 Jun 1952), American tenor. Has sung with NY City Opera from 1979, as Arturo, Rodolfo, Pinkerton and Tom Rakewell. European debut as Nemorino at Vienna, 1982; Glyndebourne and CG 1984, as Idamante and Fenton (returned to London 1993, as the Berlioz Faust). NY Met. debut 1987, as Massenet's Des Grieux. Guest at Chicago, Berlin, Munich and Geneva as Tamino, Gounod's Faust and Alfredo. Sang Bernstein's Candide under the composer's direction, London 1989.

Hadley, Patrick (Arthur Sheldon) (b Cambridge, 5 Mar 1899; d King's Lynn, 17 Dec 1973), English composer. Educated at Winchester College and Cambridge University, and studied music at the RCM in London, where in 1925 he joined the teaching staff. Mus. D. Cambridge in 1938, appointed lecturer at the university and Professor of Music in succession to Dent from 1946 to 1962.

Works include incidental music to Sophocles' *Antigone*; symphony for baritone and chorus *The Trees so high* (1931), *La Belle Dame sans merci* (Keats) for tenor, chorus and orchestra, *My Beloved Spake* (Song of Solomon) for chorus and orchestra; cantatas *The Hills* for soprano, tenor, bass, chorus and orchestra (1944), and *Travellers*; *Ephemera* (Yeats) and *Mariana* (Tennyson, 1937) for voice and chamber orchestra; string quartet in C major, fantasy for two violins and piano; songs; part-songs.

Hadow, W(illiam) H(enry) (b Ebrington, Gloucestershire, 27 Dec 1859; d London, 8 Apr 1937), English educationist and music scholar. Educated at Malvern College and Oxford, where later he lectured on music, having studied at Darmstadt and under C H Lloyd. Principal of Armstrong College, Newcastle-upon-Tyne, 1909–19, and Vice-Chancellor of Sheffield University, 1919–30. He edited the *Oxford History of Music* and wrote volume v, *The Viennese Period*; other books include *Studies in Modern Music*, *English Music*, etc. He also composed chamber music and songs. Knighted 1918.

Haebler, Ingrid (b Vienna, 20 Jun 1926), Austrian pianist. She studied in Salzburg and Vienna, and with Marguerite Long in Paris. Debut Salzburg, 1937. She has recorded all the concertos of Mozart and all Schubert's sonatas; has appeared worldwide with this repertory, also Haydn, Schumann and early Beethoven. Frequent concerts with the London Mozart Players. Has taught at the Salzburg Mozarteum since 1969.

Haefliger, Ernst (b Davos, 6 Jul 1919), Swiss tenor. Studied in Zurich and later in Vienna with Patzak and in Prague with Carpi. He made his debut in Salzburg in 1949 and from 1953 sang in Berlin. He appeared in Glyndebourne in 1956 as Belmonte. He was especially noted as a Mozart singer, Evangelist in the Bach Passions and also as a performer of modern music; he created Tiresias in Orff's *Antigonae*, Salzburg, 1949.

Haenchen, Hartmut (b Dresden, 21 Mar 1943), German conductor. Studied in Dresden and conducted the Halle SO 1966–72; Dresden PO 1973–76 and permanent guest conductor of the Dresden Staatsoper. Music director of Netherlands Opera from 1985 with *Die Frau ohne Schatten*, the Berlioz *Faust* and *Samson et Dalila* in 1992. Opera guest in Berlin (Komische Oper), Munich, Warsaw, Geneva and the USA. CG 1991–92, with *Orfeo ed Euridice* and Mozart's *Mitridate*.

Haendel, Ida (b Chełm, Poland, 15 Dec 1924), British violinist. She studied in Warsaw and with Flesch and Enescu. British debut 1937 at a Promenade Concert, under Wood; gave further concerts in London throughout the war, and toured US 1946–47. Has lived in Canada since 1952. A popular performer of the standard repertory. Played Britten's concerto at the 1994 London Proms.

Haessler, Johann Wilhelm (b Erfurt, 29 Mar 1747; d Moscow 29 Mar 1822), German pianist, organist and composer. Pupil of the organist Kittel, a pupil of Bach. Travelled much, establishing concerts at Erfurt in 1780, visited London and St Petersburg 1790–94, when he settled at Moscow.

Works include piano sonatas, *Grande Gigue* in D minor and many other works for piano, organ works; songs.

'Haffner' Serenade Mozart's Serenade in D major, K250, written at Salzburg in Jul 1776 for the marriage of Elisabeth Haffner, daughter of the late Bürgermeister Sigmund Haffner, celebrated on 22 Jul.

'Haffner' Symphony Mozart's symphony in D major K385, composed in Vienna in summer 1782 for the Haffner family, probably on the occasion of the ennoblement of Sigmund Haffner, junior, on 29 Jul 1782.

Hafgren, Lily (b Stockholm, 7 Oct 1884; d Berlin, 27 Feb 1965), Swedish soprano. She began her career as a pianist but was advised to take up singing by Siegfried Wagner: Bayreuth 1908–24 as Freia, Elsa and Eva. She sang further in Mannheim and in Berlin, 1912–20, where she was the first local Empress in *Die Frau ohne Schatten*. She was active in Paris, Milan and Stockholm; retired Dresden 1934. Other roles included Ariadne, Isolde and Brünnhilde.

Hagegård, Håkan (b Karlstad, 25 Nov 1945), Swedish baritone. He studied in Stockholm and with Tito Gobbi and Gerald Moore. Debut Stockholm 1968, as Papageno; later sang role in Bergman's film version of *Die Zauberflöte*. He has appeared at Drottningholm since 1970 and Glyndebourne from 1973 (as the Count in *Figaro* and *Capriccio*, and Guglielmo); made concert tours of the USA in 1975 and 1977: Met. debut in 1979, as Malatesta; CG debut, Wolfram, 1987. Created Beaumarchais in *The Ghosts of Versailles*, NY Met., 1991. He is well known in operas by Mozart, Verdi and Rossini, and often appears in concert.

The greater the works of art confronting the interpreter, the wider becomes the range of possible great performances.

Eric Blom, *Beethoven's Pianoforte Sonatas Discussed*, 1938

Hageman, Richard (b Leeuwarden, 9 Jul 1882; d Beverly Hills, CA, 6 Mar 1966), Dutch-American conductor and composer. Studied at the Amsterdam Conservatory, of which his father was director, and later at the Brussels Conservatory. He was appointed conductor of the Amsterdam Opera and in 1907 settled in USA, where he conducted opera and concerts in various cities. From 1908 to 1922 he conducted at the Met. Opera, NY.

Works include opera *Caponsacchi* (produced Freiburg i/B, 1932); many songs, including *At the Well*.

Hager, Leopold (b Salzburg, 6 Oct 1935), Austrian conductor. Studied at the Salzburg Mozarteum and made his debut at Mainz (1958) with *L'Italiana in Algeri*. Conducted opera in Linz, Cologne and Freiburg i/B, then principal conductor of the Salzburg Mozarteum Orchestra, 1969–81; Salzburg Festival 1971, with a revival of Mozart's *Mitridate*. Conducted *Fidelio* at Vienna 1973, *Le Nozze di Figaro* at the Met. 1976 (returning for *Così fan Tutte*, 1991). Buenos Aires 1977, *Tristan und Isolde*; CG 1978, Figaro. Returned to the Met. 1995, *Don Giovanni*. Has recorded such early Mozart operas as *La Finta semplice*, *Lucio Silla* and *Il re pastore*.

Hagith opera in one act by Szymanowski (libretto by composer after F Dormann); composed 1912–13, while Szymanowski was living in Vienna; produced Warsaw, 13 May 1922. Hagith is stoned to death after she refuses to become a sacrifice for King David.

Hagley, Alison (b London, 9 May 1961), English soprano. Studied at the GSM and sang in Rodelinda at Aldeburgh; Camden Festival 1986, in Mozart's *La finta giardiniera*. Glyndebourne from 1988, as Nannetta, Papagena, and Susanna in *Figaro* at the opening of the new auditorium (1994). ENO 1991–92, Lauretta, Gretel and Nannetta. Sang an appealing Mélisande under Boulez for WNO, 1992.

Hahn, Reynaldo (b Caracas, Venezuela, 9 Aug 1874; d Paris, 28 Jan 1947), French composer and conductor. Was sent to the Paris Conservatory at the age of 11, where he studied under various masters, including Massenet. He was popular in Parisian salons as a performer of his own songs, and was admired by Proust. In 1934 he was appointed music critic of *Le Figaro*, and in 1945 became music director of the Paris Opéra.

Works include operas *L'Ile du rêve* (1898), *La Carmélite* (1902), *La Colombe de Bouddha* (1921), *Nausicaa*, *Le Pauvre d'Assise*, *La Reine de Saba*, *Le Temps d'aimer*, *Brummel* (1931), *Le Marchand de Venise* (after Shakespeare, 1935), many operettas including *Ciboulette*; ballets *La Fête chez Thérèse* (1907) and *Le Dieu bleu* (1912); incidental music for Shakespeare's *Much Ado*, Rostand's *Le Bois sacré*, Sacha Guitry's *Mozart* (1925), etc.; ode *Prométhée* for solo voices, chorus and orchestra; symphonic poem *Nuit d'amour bergamasque*; string quartet and other chamber music; piano pieces; songs

Haimovitz *Cellist Matt Haimovitz has had a successful career since his studies at Juilliard, playing a wide repertory which ranges from the standard concertos of the 18th and 19th centuries to the solo works by Reger, Britten, Crumb and Ligeti.*

including cycles *Chansons grises, Chansons latines, Chansons espagnoles.*

Haimovitz, Matt (b Tel Aviv, 3 Dec 1970), Israeli cellist. Studied at Juilliard and made concert debut with the Israel PO under Mehta, Tel-Aviv 1985. London debut with the ECO under Barenboim (1985), Chicago SO under Levine, 1988; first US recital tour 1990. Berlin Philharmonic debut 1990, tour of Australia 1991 and Dallas SO concert 1992. Recordings include concertos by Lalo, Haydn and Saint-Saëns; also plays modern works by Ligeti and Crumb.

hairpins the colloquial word for *crescendo* and *diminuendo* marks shown by the conventional signs < and >.

Haitink, Bernard (b Amsterdam, 4 Mar 1929), Dutch conductor. Initially an orchestral violinist, in 1955 he became conductor of the Radio Orchestra in Amsterdam. He was guest conductor of the Concertgebouw Orchestra on their American tour of 1961, becoming their permanent conductor when they returned to Holland and subsequently conductor of the LPO 1967–79. Glyndebourne debut 1972 (*Die Entführung*); music director 1977–88 (returned 1994 for *Figaro* at the re-opening of the house. NY Met. debut 1982. Music director CG, London, 1987–97 (*Arabella* there 1986). Led *Ring* cycles 1989–91 and 1994–95, *Prince Igor* 1990, *Katya Kabanova* 1994. He is well known for his balanced and carefully structured performances of the standard classics. Recordings include the complete symphonies of Mahler, Beethoven and Bruckner, *Don Giovanni* from Glyndebourne and a *Ring* cycle. Honorary KBE 1977.

Haitzinger, Anton (b Wilfersdorf, Liechtenstein, 14 Mar 1796; d Karlsruhe, 31 Dec 1869), Austrian tenor. Made his first appearance at the Theater an der Wien in Vienna in 1821; created Adolar in *Euryanthe*, 1823. Sang later in Paris, London and St Petersburg. London, CG, 1833 as Tamino, Max and Florestan.

Hale, Adam de la, ◊La Halle.

Hale, Robert (b Kerrville, TX, 22 Aug 1943), American bass-baritone. Studied with Boris Goldovsky in NY and made debut 1966, as Mozart's Figaro. NY City Opera from 1967, as Don Giovanni, Oroveso and the Father in *Louise*. European debut at Stuttgart 1978 as the Dutchman; CG 1988 as Jochanaan (returned as Orestes, 1990).

Sang Barak in *Die Frau ohne Schatten* at Salzburg, 1992. His Wotan in the *Ring* has been admired at the Vienna Staatsoper (1992–93) and in Paris (Théâtre du Châtelet, 1994). Recordings include *Die Frau ohne Schatten* (video from Salzburg).

Halévy (actually *Lévy*), Jacques François Fromental (Elias) (b Paris, 27 May 1799; d Nice, 17 Mar 1862), French composer. Studied at the Paris Conservatory under Berton and Cherubini from 1809 and, after twice taking a second prize, gained the Prix de Rome in 1819. He continued to study in Italy, and on his return to Paris tried to gain a foothold on the operatic stage, for which he had already written more than one work. He succeeded with *L'Artisan* in 1827, after which he wrote an enormous number of operas. He became professor of harmony and accompaniment at the Conservatory in 1827, of counterpoint and fugue in 1833 and of composition in 1840.

Works include *c* 40 operas, e.g. *La Dilettante d'Avignon, Ludovic* (begun by Hérold), *La Juive* (1835), *L'Éclair, Guido et Ginevra, Le Shérif, Le Guitarréro, La Reine de Chypre, Charles VI* (1843), *Les Mousquetaires de la reine* (1846), *Le Val d'Andorre, La Fée aux roses, La Tempestà* (in Italian, after Shakespeare, 1850), *La Dame de Pique* (after Mérimée), *Le Juif errant* (after Sue), *Jaguarita l'Indienne* (1855), *La Magicienne*, etc.; ballets *Yella, Manon Lescaut* (after Prévost); incidental music to *Prométhée enchaîné* (translated from Aeschylus); cantatas *Les Derniers Moments du Tasse, La Mort d'Adonis* and *Herminie*; funeral march and *De profundis* on the death of the Duc de Berry.

half-close an imperfect cadence, i.e. one in which the dominant chord is preceded by the tonic.

A half-close from C to G major.

Halffter, Cristóbal (b Madrid, 24 Mar 1930), Spanish composer. Nephew of Ernesto and Rodolfo Halffter. Studied with Conrado del Campo and Alexandre Tansman. In 1962 he became professor of composition at Madrid Conservatory. His music tends towards total serialism. Lecturer at the University of Navarra, 1970–78; director of the electronic music studio at Freiburg i/B from 1978.

Works include opera, *Don Quichotte* (produced Düsseldorf, 1970), *Cantata in Expectatione Resurrectionis Domini* (1962); concertino for string orchestra; *Sinfonia* for three instrumental groups (1963); *Cinco microformas* for orchestra; *Dos movimientos* for timpani and string orchestra; cello concerto (1974); violin concerto (1979), two cello concertos (1979, 1985), Sinfonia ricercata for organ and orchestra (1982), flute concerto (1982), concerto for violin, viola and orchestra (1984), piano concerto (1988), *Espejos* for four percussionists and tape (1963); ballet *Saeta; Misa ducal; Tres piezas* for string quartet; *Formantes* for two pianos; *Tres piezas* for solo flute; sonata for solo violin; *Antifona pascual* for soloists, chorus and orchestra, *Dona nobis pacem* for mixed chorus and ensemble (1984).

Halffter, Ernesto (Esriche) (b Madrid, 16 Jan 1905; d Madrid, 5 Jul 1989), Spanish conductor and composer. Conductor of the Orquesta Bética de Cámera. After the Spanish war he settled in Portugal. He completed Falla's cantata *Atlántida* (produced Milan, 1962).

Works include *Dos retratos, Dos bocetos, Rapsodia portuguesa* for orchestra; *Suite ancienne* for wind instruments; two string quartets.

Halffter, Rodolfo (b Madrid, 20 Oct 1900; d Mexico City, 14 Oct 1987), Spanish composer, brother of Ernesto ◊Halffter. He was self-taught in composition and began to write music in 1924. In 1939 he left Spain and settled in Mexico, having fled after the fall of the Republic and lost some of his works in an air-raid during his escape to France on foot. Director of the music department of the National

Institute of Fine Arts, Mexico City, 1959–64.

Works include ballets *Don Lindo de Almeria* (1935, produced 1940) and *The Baker's Morning*; *Obertura concertante* for piano and orchestra, violin concerto (1940); Tripartita (1960) and Alborado (1976) for orchestra; piano pieces.

Halgrimson, Amanda (b Fargo, ND, 28 Nov 1956), American soprano. Has sung at opera houses in 32 American states, notably as Fiordiligi, Norina and Rosalinde. Texas Opera on tour 1987, as Lucia and European debut 1988, as the Queen of Night with Netherlands Opera (repeated for Geneva Opera, 1994). Deutsche Oper Berlin from 1991 with further opera at Houston and Vienna. Sang Mozart's Donna Anna with the CBSO under Simon Rattle, 1993; other concerts with Roger Norrington (Missa Solemnis at Boston, 1993), and G Gelmetti (Beethoven's Ninth). Mozart's Requiem on tour in Europe, 1991.

Halíř, Karel (b Hohenelbe, Bohemia, 1 Feb 1859; d Berlin, 21 Dec 1909), Czech violinist. Studied at the Prague Conservatory, and under Joachim, of whose quartet he became a member, besides leading one of his own.

Halka opera by Moniuszko (libretto, in Polish, by W Wolski, based on a story by K W Wójcicki), concert performance Wilno, 11 Jan 1848; produced Wilno, 28 Feb 1854; revised version Warsaw, 1 Jan 1858. The chief Polish national opera, Wallek-Walewski's opera *Jontek's Revenge* is a sequel to it. Halka commits suicide after she is seduced and abandoned by the nobleman Janusz.

Hall, Henry (b New Windsor, *c* 1655; d Hereford, 30 Mar 1707), English organist and composer. He was a choirboy in the Chapel Royal in London under Cooke. Appointed organist at Exeter Cathedral in 1674 and at Hereford Cathedral in 1688.

Works include Te Deum in E♭ major, Benedicite in C minor, *Cantate Domino* and *Deus misereatur* in B♭ major, anthems and other church music; songs, duets, catches.

Hall, Marie (b Newcastle-upon-Tyne, 8 Apr 1884; d Cheltenham, 11 Nov 1956), English violinist. Taught the harp by her father, she decided to take up the violin and studied with Elgar, Wilhelmj, at the RAM in London and with Ševčik in Prague, where she first appeared in 1902; in Vienna and London in 1903. US debut 1905. In 1921 she gave the fp of Vaughan William's *The Lark Ascending*.

Hall, Peter (b Bury St Edmunds, 22 Nov 1930), English producer and director. First opera production Gardner's *The Moon and Sixpence*, SW 1957. In 1965 he mounted with John Bury at CG, London, the first production in Britain of Schoenberg's *Moses und Aron*. Tippett's *The Knot Garden* (1970) was another successful production, but Hall did not find congenial the working conditions of an international opera house. From 1970 he has worked at Glyndebourne (artistic director 1984–90), mounting well-received productions of Mozart's three Da Ponte operas and Raymond Leppard's editions of operas by Cavalli and Monteverdi (*L'Incoronazione di Poppea*, 1984, with his then wife, Maria Ewing, in the title role). *Simon Boccanegra* (1986), *La Traviata* (1987), *Falstaff* (1988). Premiere of Tippett's *New Year* at Houston, 1989. Productions of *Macbeth* at the NY Met. (1982) and the *Ring* at Bayreuth (1983) have found less favour. Knighted 1977.

Man and boy we have all been going to the Hallé concerts these many years (and man and boy we have all been listening to the same music).

Neville Cardus, *Manchester Guardian*, 1938

Hall, Richard (b York, 16 Sept 1903; d Horsham, 24 May 1982), English composer and teacher. Studied at Cambridge. After early church appointments he was professor of composition RMCM 1938–56; taught Goehr, Maxwell Davies and Birtwistle. Director of music, Dartington Hall 1956–67. His works were influenced by Hindemith: five symphonies (1941–64), two string quartets (1946, 1973).

Halle (or *Hale*), Adam de la, ◊La Halle.

Hallé, Charles (originally Carl Halle) (b Hagen, Westphalia, 11 Apr 1819; d Manchester, 25 Oct 1895), German-English pianist and conductor. Studied first under his father, an organist, then at Darm-

Haitink *The conductor Bernard Haitink divides his time between orchestral and operatic work. In both fields he has been praised for his 'no-nonsense' approach, which seeks to reproduce the composer's intentions without introducing indulgent affectations.*

stadt and Paris, where he had piano lessons from Kalkbrenner. Settled in England 1848 and founded the Hallé concerts at Manchester; first concert 30 Jan 1858. He conducted many concerts and festivals elsewhere in the country as well and frequently appeared as pianist, usually in sonatas by Schubert and Beethoven. His second wife was the violinist Wilma ◊Neruda, whom he married in 1888. First Principal RMCM, 1893. Knighted 1888.

Hallé, Lady, ◊Neruda.

Hallén, (Johan) Andreas (b Göteborg, 22 Dec 1846; d Stockholm, 11 Mar 1925), Swedish conductor, critic and composer. Studied at Leipzig, Munich and Dresden and later worked mainly at Göteborg and Stockholm.

Works include operas *Harold der Wiking* (in German, produced Leipzig, 1881), *Hexfällan* (later revised as *Valborgsmässan* (Stockholm, 1902), and *Valdemarsskatten*; ballads for solo voices, chorus and orchestra; symphonic suite *Gustaf Vasas Saga*, symphonic poems *The Island of the Dead* (after Böcklin's picture 1898; pre-dates work by Rakhmaninov of same title by 11 years), *Sounds of the Spheres*, *Autumn* and *A Summer Saga*, two rhapsodies for orchestra; instrumental pieces; songs.

Hallé Orchestra founded by Charles Hallé at Manchester in 1857. John Barbirolli was chief conductor 1943–70, James Loughran 1971–83. Stanislav Skrowaczewski 1984–92, then Kent Nagano.

Halling a Norwegian dance originating from the Hallingdal between Oslo and Bergen. It is usually in 2–4 time and goes at a moderately quick pace. In its early form, as distinct from that cultivated by Grieg and other composers, its music is played on the Hardanger fiddle.

Hallström, Ivar (b Stockholm, 5 Jun 1826; d Stockholm, 11 Apr 1901), Swedish pianist and composer. Had private music lessons and studied law at Uppsala University. There he met Prince Gustaf, with whom he wrote an opera, which was produced at Stockholm in 1847. After the prince's death he became librarian to Prince Oscar, later Oscar II, and in 1861 he was appointed director of Lindblad's music school, where he had taught the piano.

Works include operas *Hvita frun på Drottningholm* (with Prince Gustaf, 1847), *Den bergtagna* (1874), *Hertig Magnus och sjöjungfrun*, *Vikingarne*, *Nero* (1882), *Liten Karin*; operettas *Den förtrollade katten/The enchanted cat* (1869), *Mjölnarvargen*, *Per Svinaherde*;

Hampson *The baritone Thomas Hampson. In addition to his operatic repertory, which includes Don Giovanni and Rossini's Figaro, Hampson has recorded works of Mahler with Bernstein and Geoffrey Parsons. He is also co-editor of a critical edition of Mahler songs.*

ballets *En dröm*, *Ett aventyr i Skottland*; cantatas; songs.

Hamari, Julia (b Budapest, 21 Nov 1942), Hungarian mezzo. She studied in Budapest and in 1966 sang in the *St Matthew Passion* (Vienna, under Richter) and the *Alto Rhapsody* (Rome, under Gui). She has appeared with Karajan, Solti and Böhm as a concert singer, in works by Bach, Mahler and Handel, and from 1973 in operas by Verdi, Gluck and Mascagni. In 1979 she sang Celia in *La fedeltà premiata*, at Glyndebourne. NY Met. from 1984, as Rosina and Despina. Other roles include Gluck's Orpheus and Handel's Cornelia.

Hambourg, Mark (b Boguchar, 31 May 1879; d Cambridge, 26 Aug 1960), Russian-born English pianist. A pupil of Leschetizky, he first appeared in Moscow in 1888. With his brothers Jan (1882–1947) and Boris (1884–1954) he formed a piano trio, but in later years devoted himself entirely to solo performances. He lived in London for most of his life.

Hambraeus, Bengt (b Stockholm, 29 Jan 1928), Swedish composer and musicologist. Studied musicology at the University of Uppsala from 1947 to 1956, and from 1957 worked for Swedish Radio, at the same time teaching at Uppsala University. He participated in the Darmstadt courses, being chiefly influenced by the work of Webern, Stockhausen and Boulez.

Works include *Rota* for three orchestras, percussion and electronic tape (1964); *Constellation I* for organ; *Constellation II* for recorded tape; *Constellation III* derived from nos I and II; *Doppelrohr II*, an electronic piece; *Introduzione-Sequenze-Coda*; chamber opera *Experiment X* (1971), church opera *Se nännis kan* (1972).

Hamerik (originally *Hammerich*), Asger (b Copenhagen, 8 Apr 1843; d Frederiksborg, 13 Jul 1923), Danish composer of German descent. Pupil of Gade at Copenhagen, later of Bülow in Berlin for piano and of Berlioz in Paris for orchestration. In 1872–98 he was in USA as director of the Conservatory of the Peabody Institute at Baltimore.

Works include operas *Tovelille* (1865), *Hjalmar og Ingeborg*, *La vendetta* (1870) and *Den Rejsende*; Requiem, two choral trilogies; eight symphonies, the last for strings, five Northern Suites and other orchestral works.

Hamerik, Ebbe (b Copenhagen, 5 Sept 1898; d near Copenhagen, 11 Aug 1951), Danish conductor and composer, son of Asger ◊Hamerik. Pupil of his father and Frank van der Stucken. Conductor of the royal theatre at Copenhagen, 1911–22, and of the Musikforeningen there, 1927–30. He then went to live in Austria, but returned home 1934. He was drowned in the Kattegat.

Works include operas *Stepan* (1924), *Leonardo da Vinci* (1939), *Marie Grubbe* (after Jacobsen) and *Rejsekammeraten* (*The Travelling Companion*, after Andersen, 1946); five symphonies (1937–50), *Quasi Passacaglia e Fuga*, Variations on an old Danish folk-tune; two string quartets; suite for contralto and chamber orchestra; piano pieces; organ works; songs.

Hamilton, Iain (Ellis) (b Glasgow, 6 Jun 1922), Scottish pianist and composer. Studied at the RAM in London, where various works of his were introduced, and won the Royal Philharmonic Society prize for his clarinet concerto and the Koussevitsky Award for his second symphony. Professor, Duke University, North Carolina, 1961–81.

Works include operas *Agamemnon* (1969), *The Royal Hunt of the Sun* (1967–69; produced 1977), *The Catiline Conspiracy* (after Jonson, 1974), *Tamburlaine* (1977), *Anna Karenina* (1981), *Lancelot* (1984); *The Tragedy of Macbeth* (1990); *London's Fair* (1992); ballet *Clerk Saunders*; four symphonies (1950–81), two violin concertos (1952, 1971); two piano concertos (1949, 1967). Variations for strings; *Aurora* for orchestra (1975); *Requiem* (1979), Mass in A (1980), *St Mark Passion* (1982); clarinet quintet, string quartet, flute quartet; Variations for solo violin; viola and piano sonata; pieces for wind instruments and piano; piano sonata; violin concerto; octet for strings (1984).

Hamlet ◊Ambleto; ◊Amleto; ◊Shakespeare.

Incidental music for Shakespeare's tragedy by Tchaikovsky, op. 67a, including 16 numbers and an abridged version of the *Hamlet* fantasy-overture, op. 67, fp St Petersburg, 17 Nov 1888; the play fp with Tchaikovsky's music, St Petersburg, 21 Feb 1891.

Hammerklavier, Hammerclavier, German name (lit. 'hammer keyboard instrument'), an alternative to the Italian word *pianoforte*, used to distinguish the piano from the (plucked) harpsichord. Beethoven designated his sonatas opp. 101 and 106 as 'für das Hammerclavier', and the word is now used as a nickname for the latter sonata.

Hammerschmidt, Andreas (b Brüx, 1612; d Zittau, 29 Oct 1675), Bohemian composer. Taken to Freiberg, Saxony, in 1626. Became organist there, 1635, and at Zittau, 1639. Wrote much Lutheran church music, published in 14 collections (1639–71).

Works include sacred concertos and madrigals for several voices, sacred dialogues for two voices, odes, motets and hymns, 17 short Lutheran Masses; thanksgiving for eight voices for the Saxon victory at Liegnitz; dances for viols.

Hammerstein, Oscar (Greeley Glendenning) (II) (b New York, 12 Jul 1895; d Doylestown, PA, 23 Aug 1960), American librettist and producer. He worked on musical shows from 1917, but his first major success came with *Show Boat* in 1927, for Jerome Kern. Worked with Friml, Romberg and Gershwin on further shows and between 1943 and 1959 collaborated with Richard Rogers on *Oklahoma*, *Carousel*, *South Pacific*, *The King and I*, *Flower Drum Song* and *The Sound of Music*. His adaptation of *Carmen* as a musical (*Carmen Jones*) was premiered in 1943. His grandfather *Oscar Hammerstein* (I) (1846–1919) established the Manhattan Opera House 1906, in rivalry with the Metropolitan; US premieres of *Elektra* and *Pelléas et Mélisande* were given but in 1920 he was bought out by the Met. and prevented from mounting opera in New York and other major US cities. A London Opera House, opened at Kingsway in 1911, lasted only two seasons.

Hammond, Joan (b Christchurch, 24 May 1912), New Zealand soprano. Opera debut Sydney 1929. Sang in Vienna 1938 and with the

Thomas Hampson – singer

1   *Lotte Lehmann Farewell Recital Live, Town Hall, 1950* (Lehmann/Paul Ulanowsky)
To have *retired* with this recital can only teach us about an era of great singers gone by!

2   *The Art of Giuseppe de Luca* (de Luca/Metropolitan Opera Orch./Giulio Setti)
This classic collection is probably the greatest testament to the art of bel canto and legato singing available.

3   Schubert: *Songs, Volumes I and II* (Fischer-Dieskau/Gerald Moore)
Fischer-Dieskau's supreme achievements in music and singing culture will take years to digest. This collection serves as one of his many summits of artistry.

4   Wagner: *Act 1 Die Walküre* (Lehmann/Melchior/Emmanuel List/Vienna PO/Walter)
The sheer vocalism and spontaneous music-making create an overwhelming dramatic, musical experience.

5   Verdi: *Simon Boccanegra. Live from the Metropolitan Opera, 1939* (Rethberg/Martinelli/Warren/Metropolitan Opera Orch./Panizza)
An awe-inspiring stage performance of legend-making proportions.

6   Adams: *Harmonielehre, The Chairman Dances,* (etc.) (CBSO/Rattle)
A turning point in the orchestral music-writing and performance of the late 20th century.

7   Mahler: *Nine Symphonies* (NYPO/Bernstein)
A seminal achievement of music-making and historical perspective to one of the greatest composers of the last one hundred years.

8   Beethoven: *Nine Symphonies* (Chamber Orch. of Europe/Harnoncourt)
A singular achievement of modern recorded history. A musical dialogue of composer and musicians that truly illuminates the landscape of the human soul.

Carl Rosa Co., London, during the war as Violetta, Butterfly and Tosca. CG 1948–51, debut as the *Trovatore* Leonora. SW 1951 and 1959 as Elisabeth de Valois and Rusalka. She sang with NY City Opera in 1949 and toured Russia in 1957. Frequent recordings and concerts. Most often heard in Puccini but opera roles also include Tatyana, Desdemona and Aida. DBE 1974.

Hammond organ an electrophonic organ invented by Laurens Hammond of Chicago in 1934, producing its notes by means of electromagnets and offering a choice of tone colours by the selection and combination of the appropriate harmonics.

Hammond-Stroud, Derek (b London, 10 Jan 1929), English baritone. After study with Gerhard Hüsch he made his London debut as Creon in a concert performance of Haydn's *Orfeo* (1955); stage debut 1957, as Publio in *La Clemenza di Tito*. From 1962 he has sung with SW (later ENO) Opera as Bartolo, Melitone, Alberich and Beckmesser. CG from 1971, Glyndebourne from 1973. NY Met. debut 1977, as Faninal. Sang at Munich until 1983, NY Met., 1989. OBE 1987.

Hampe, Michael (b Heidelberg, 3 Jun 1935), German stage director. Studied in Munich and Vienna and worked first at Berne and Zurich (1961–70). Director of the National Theatre Mannheim 1972–75, Cologne from 1975. Salzburg debut 1982, *Così fan Tutte*. London, CG, *Andrea Chénier* (1984), returning for *Il barbiere di Siviglia* (1985) and *La Cenerentola* (1990). Also works in Munich and Vienna.

Hampson, Thomas (b Elkhart, IN, 28 Jun 1955), American baritone. Studied at UCLA and at Santa Barbara. Sang at Dusseldorf from 1981, as Harlequin, the Herald in Lohengrin, Belcore and Nanni in Haydn's *L'infideltà delusa*; Henze's Prinz von Homburg at Darmstadt, 1982. Santa Fe 1983, as Malatesta; NY Met. debut 1986, as Mozart's Count. Has been a member of the Zurich Opera and in season 1989–90 made his Berlin and San Francisco debuts (Don Giovanni and Monteverdi's Ulisse). London, CG, debut as Rossini's Figaro (1993). Many Lieder recitals in Europe and the USA. Mahler concerts under Bernstein in Vienna and the new Met.'s 25th anniversary gala, 1991.

Hampton, John (b *c* 1455; d after 1522), English composer. Master of the choristers at Worcester Priory, 1484–1522. He is represented in the Eton Choirbook.

Hanboys, John, English Franciscan friar and music theorist of the 15th c. His treatise *Summa . . . super musicam* is a commentary on Franco of Cologne.

Handbass! Austrian & South German dialect = 'little hand bass'; Leopold Mozart's name for the ◊violoncello piccolo.

My Lord, I should be sorry if I only entertained them; I wished to make them better.

George Frideric Handel to Lord Kinnol, after a performance of the *Messiah*, quoted in Young, *Handel*, 1947

Handel, George Frideric (originally Georg Friedrich Händel) (b Halle, 23 Feb 1685; d London, 14 Apr 1759), German-English composer. After initial opposition from his father, a barber-surgeon, he studied music with Zachow in Halle, and in 1702 matriculated at the university there to read law, at the same time holding the probationary post of organist at the Domkirche. The next year he left for Hamburg, where he played violin, later harpsichord, at the opera under Keiser, and had the operas *Almira* and *Nero* staged in 1705. Travelled in Italy 1706–09, visiting the principal cities and meeting the leading composers. *Agrippina* was successfully produced at Venice in 1709, and he also made a great reputation as a harpsichordist. Other works composed in Italy include the oratorios *La resurrezione* and *Il trionfo del tempo*, solo canatatas, chamber duets, etc. With the support of Steffani he was appointed to succeed the latter as *Kapellmeister* to the Elector of Hanover in 1710, but left almost immediately on leave of absence for London, where *Rinaldo* was given with great success the next year. Again in London on leave in 1712, he settled there, never returning to his post in Hanover. Between 1712 and 1715 he staged four operas, and in 1713 wrote a *Te Deum* and *Jubilate* to celebrate the Peace of Utrecht, receiving a life pension of £200 from Queen Anne. On her death in 1714 the Elector of Hanover succeeded to the throne as George I, but apparently took a lenient view of his former *Kapellmeister's* truancy, for Handel's pension was soon doubled. In 1716 he composed the *Water Music*, to accompany George I on his journey down the Thames. As music director to the Earl of Carnavon (later Duke of Chandos) 1717–20, he wrote the *Chandos Anthems*, *Acis and Galatea* and the masque *Haman and Mordecai*.

With the founding of the RAM in 1720 began Handel's most prolific period as an opera composer, and over the next 20 years he wrote more than 30 works. Opera in Italian met with limited success ('an exotic and irrational entertainment', in Dr Johnson's words) and

Handel *The composer George Frideric Handel (1685–1759), German by birth and later naturalized British, was almost an exact contemporary of J S Bach. Although both composers wrote many vocal works, Handel wrote for the theatre as well as for the church; his compositions also admit a greater range of influences.*

it is not until recent years that the beauties of *Giulio Cesare, Orlando, Ariodante* and *Alcina* have become appreciated. Handel experienced difficulties with the formation of partisan factions round himself and his rival Bononcini, and were aggravated by internal strife between his two leading ladies, Faustina and Cuzzoni. The popular success of *The Beggar's Opera* in 1728 made matters worse, and in that year the RAM went bankrupt. Handel continued to produce operas, acting as his own impresario in partnership with Heidegger, but rival factions, now of a political nature, again undermined his success, and in the 1730s he increasingly turned to oratorio. *Esther* (a revision of the masque *Haman and Mordecai*), 1732, was followed by *Deborah, Saul* and *Israel in Egypt*. His last opera was produced 1741, after which he devoted his time chiefly to oratorio, *Messiah* being performed in Dublin in 1742. This was the summation of his life's work, composed in a single burst of inspiration but including some elements from earlier music. The success of *Messiah* encouraged him to write 12 more oratorios, some on Old Testament texts (*Samson, Solomon*) others on Classical mythology (*Semele*). He continued to appear in public as conductor and organist, playing concertos between the parts of his oratorios, but his health declined and he spent his last years in blindness. His last major public success came in 1749 with the suite for wind instruments, to accompany the Royal Fireworks in Green Park. The wide recognition gained by Handel in his later years, together with the range and quality of his music, place him with Bach as the greatest composer of his time.

Works include OPERAS: *Almira* (1705), *Nero, Rodrigo* (1707), *Agrippina* (1710), *Rinaldo* (1711), *Il pastor fido, Teseo* (1713), *Silla* (1713), *Amadigi di Gaula* (1715), *Radamisto* (1720), *Muzio Scevola, Floridante* (1721), *Ottone* (1723), *Flavio* (1723), *Giulio Cesare* (1724), *Tamerlano* (1724), *Rodelinda* (1725), *Scipione, Alessandro* (1726), *Admeto* (1727), *Riccardo Primo* (1727), *Siroe* (1728), *Tolomeo* (1728), *Lotario* (1729), *Partenope* (1730), *Poro, Ezio, Sosarme* (1732), *Orlando* (1733), *Arianna* (1734), *Ariodante* (1735), *Alcina* (1735), *Atlanta* (1736), *Arminio* (1737), *Giustino, Berenice* (1737),

Faramondo, Serse (1735), *Imeneo* (1740), *Deidamia* (1741); incidental music to Ben Jonson's *The Alchemist* and Smollett's *Alceste*.

ORATORIOS: *Brockes Passion* (1716) *La resurrezione, Esther* (1732), *Deborah* (1733), *Athalia* (1733), *Saul* (1739), *Israel in Egypt* (1739), *Messiah* (1742), *Samson* (1743), *Joseph and his Brethren* (1744), *Belshazzar* (1745), *Occasional Oratorio, Judas Maccabaeus* (1747), *Joshua, Alexander Balus* (1748), *Susanna* (1749), *Solomon* (1749), *Theodora* (1750), *Jephtha* (1752), *The Triumph of Time and Truth* (1757).

OTHER CHORAL WORKS: *Roman Vespers* (c 1709), *Acis and Galatea* (1718); *Alexander's Feast* (1736), *Ode for St Cecilia's Day* (1739), *L'Allegro, il Penseroso ed il Moderato* (after Milton), *Semele* (1744), *Hercules* (1745), *The Choice of Hercules*; 11 'Chandos' Anthems: *As pants the hart, Have mercy on me, O God, In the Lord I put my trust, I will magnify thee, O my God, Let God arise, My song shall be alway, O be joyful, O come let us sing unto the Lord, O praise the Lord with one consent, O sing unto the Lord* and *The Lord is my light* (1717–18); anthems for the coronation of George III: *Let thy hand be strengthened, My heart is inditing, The king shall rejoice* and *Zadok the priest*; dramatic cantatas: *Il duello amorso* (1708), *Aminta e Fillide* (1708), *Clori, Tirsi e Fileno* (1707), *Apollo e Dafne* (1708) and *Aci, Galatea e Polifermo* (1708); numerous other solo and duo cantatas, including *Diana cacciatrice* (1707), *Il delirio amoroso* (1707), *Armida abandonata* (1707), *La Lucrezia* (1709), *Mi palpita il cor* and *Silete venti* (1729); funeral anthem for Queen Caroline, Utrecht *Te Deum* and *Jubilate*, Dettingen *Te Deum* (1743), and other church music; numerous Italian cantatas, chamber duets etc.

INSTRUMENTAL: sonatas for various instruments and continuo, trio sonatas, etc.; 12 *concerti grossi* for strings, 'oboe concertos', organ concertos, *Water Music* (1717), *Fireworks Music* (1749), etc.; keyboard music, including organ fugues and harpsichord suites.

Handford, Maurice (b Enfield, 11 Nov 1929; d Warminster, 16 Dec 1986), English conductor and horn player. Studied at the RAM. Principal horn, Hallé Orchestra, 1949–61; conducted the orchestra from 1966, notably in complex scores by Messiaen and Lutoslawski, but resigned in 1971. Often heard with regional BBC orchestras and was principal conductor of the Calgary PO 1971–75.

Handel
A biographical note

POP PLAQUE PLAN ROCKS CLASSICISTS. Thus ran a headline in the London *Times* of 16 March 1995. The Handel House trust, headed by Dr Stanley Sadie, had acquired 25 Brook Street, Mayfair, Handel's home for 39 years, and with number 23 next door wished to turn it into a museum devoted to the composer. Problems arose when English Heritage expressed a desire to decorate the front of number 23 with a commemorative plaque dedicated to the rock guitarist Jimi Hendrix, who had lived in the house in 1969. Dr Sadie promptly deemed such a move 'inappropriate', perhaps mindful of the fact that Hendrix had only lived in the house for a few months prior to his squalid death the following year. While Sadie acknowledged Hendrix as 'an important figure in the history of pop music', the star himself was unimpressed with Handel: 'To tell you the God's honest truth, I haven't heard much of the fella's stuff.' Opposition to the plaque for Hendrix shocked a former lover ('Hendrix has sold more records than Handel … he's more relevant to today's society than Handel'), while another acolyte opined that a certain musical elitism was at work. Denying any such motive, Dr Sadie pointed out that his *New Grove Dictionary of American Music* carried a long entry for Hendrix. In a small masterpiece of understatement this volume has the final word on the star: 'He was not gifted with a naturally fine singing voice.'

Handl, Jacob (Latinized Jacobus Gallus) (b Reifnitz, Carniola, ? 31 Jul 1550; d Prague, 18 Jul 1591), Austrian composer. *Kapellmeister* to the Bishop of Olomouc 1579–85 and later cantor in Prague. Wrote 16 Masses, motets, Te Deum and other church music, including cycle of music for the liturgical year.

Handley, Vernon (b Enfield, 11 Nov 1930), English conductor. He studied at Oxford and the GSM. Debut Bournemouth SO 1961; conducted and taught at the RCM, 1966–72. From 1970 he gave concerts with the LSO and LPO; frequent performances of British music with the BBC; Ulster Orchestra 1985–89; Malmö SO 1985–91.

Handt, Herbert (b Philadelphia, 26 May 1926), American tenor, conductor and musicologist. He studied at Juilliard and in Vienna; debut there as singer, 1949. He sang in the 1958 Brussels fp of Menotti's *Maria Golovin* and later appeared in operas by Malipiero, Berg and Britten. Since his conducting debut (Rome 1960) he has led his own instrumental and vocal ensembles in performances of rare and early music. Among his operatic roles have been Don Ottavio, Haydn's Orfeo and Rossini's Otello.

Hann, Georg (b Vienna, 30 Jan 1897; d Munich, 9 Dec 1950), Austrian bass-baritone. After study in Vienna he joined the Munich Opera in 1927; created La Roche there in 1942. At Salzburg (1931–47) his roles were Pizarro, Sarastro and Leporello. London, CG, 1947 with Vienna co. Other roles included Kecal, Falstaff, Ochs and Amfortas.

Hannikainen, Ilmari (b Jävaskylä, 19 Oct 1892; d Helsinki, 25 Jul 1955), Finnish pianist and composer. Studied at the Helsinki Conservatory, also in Vienna, Leningrad, Berlin, Paris, Antwerp and London. With his brothers Arvo and Tauna, a violinist and a cellist, he founded a piano trio and toured Europe widely with them.

Works include opera *Talkootanssit*; piano concerto; piano quartet; piano music, songs.

Hansell, Kathleen (Amy Kuzmick) (b Bridgeport, CN, 21 Sept 1941), American musicologist and organist. Studied at University of Illinois and took her Ph.D. at Berkeley, 1980. Teacher and organist in Illinois and Iowa, from 1967; archivist at the Swedish Music History Archive, Stockholm, from 1982. Publications include *Lucio Silla*, for the Mozart Ausgabe, editions of Berwald and Hindemith and *Zelmira* for *Tutte le opere di G Rossini*. Contributions to *Grove* and other dictionaries.

Hänsel und Gretel opera by Humperdinck (libretto by A Wette, Humperdinck's sister, from a tale by the Brothers Grimm), produced Weimar, 23 Dec 1893. Based on the fairy tale; using her gingerbread

Handley *The conductor Vernon Handley in 1985. Handley has concentrated on the works of British composers, including Bax, Vaughan Williams, Britten, Bridge, Delius and Elgar. He came to prominence in 1970 when he appeared as a last-minute substitute at the Swansea Festival.*

house as bait, the wicked witch preys on hungry children, but Hänsel and Gretel outwit her, saving themselves and all her previous victims. *See opera plot on page 270.*

Hans Heiling opera by Marschner (libretto by E Devrient, originally written for Mendelssohn), produced Berlin, Opera, 24 May 1833. The gnome Heiling gives up his supernatural powers to live above ground with peasant girl Anna, but he returns to the caves after losing her affections.

Hanslick, Eduard (b Prague, 11 Sept 1825; d Baden near Vienna, 6 Aug 1904), Austrian music critic. Wrote for the *Neue freie Presse* in Vienna and was lecturer on music history at the University. A fierce opponent of Wagner's later music and ardent partisan of Brahms, he argued that the true value of music lay within the formal aesthetics of music itself, not in the expression of extra-musical feelings. His books included *Vom Musikalisch-Schönen/Of the Beautiful in Music*. In Wagner's original draft for the libretto of *Die Meistersinger* the role of Beckmesser was given as Hans Lich.

> *The Prelude to* Tristan and Isolde *reminds me of the old Italian painting of a martyr whose intestines are slowly unwound from his body on a reel.*
> **Eduard Hanslick**, *Neue Freie Presse*, 1864–95

Hanson, Howard (b Wahoo, NE, 28 Oct 1896; d Rochester, NY, 26 Feb 1981), American composer of Swedish descent. Studied music in NY and at Evanston University, Illinois. After various appointments, he gained the American Prix de Rome, and after his stay in Italy was director of the Eastman School of Music at Rochester, NY 1924–64.

Works include opera *Merry Mount* (after Hawthorne, 1934); choral work *The Lament for Beowulf*; seven symphonies (1923–77),

A Selection of

Handel

Water Music	1717
Acis and Galatea	1718
Giulio Cesare	1724
Coronation Anthems	1727
Alcina	1735
Saul	1739
Israel in Egypt	1739
Messiah	1742
Semele	1744
Music for the Royal Fireworks	1749

THE OPERA

Hänsel und Gretel

A three-act opera by Engelbert Humperdinck, based on a well-known Grimms' fairy tale. It was first performed in Weimar in 1893.

I. The children Hänsel (mezzo-soprano) and Gretel (soprano) fail to help their mother around the house and, as a punishment, are sent out to gather strawberries in the wood. Their father (baritone) is anxious for their safety because he knows of a child-consuming witch who lurks nearby.

II. The children eat all the strawberries they have collected and fall asleep in the woods, protected by hovering angels.

III. Now hungry again, the children begin eating a house they find, made of marzipan and sweets. Captured by the witch, Hänsel is kept for fattening and Gretel is set to work. She catches the witch unawares and pushes her into the oven; a tasty cake emerges after the house has collapsed.

THE OPERA

symphonic poems *North and West*, *Lux aeterna* and *Pan and the Priest* for orchestra; string quartet (1923), piano quintet, concerto for piano quintet; piano pieces; songs.

Hans Sachs opera by Lortzing (libretto by composer and F Reger, based on a play by J L F Deinhardstein), produced Leipzig, 23 Jun 1840. An earlier opera on the subject of Wagner's *Meistersinger*, which was also used before that by Gyrowetz. Sachs loses bride Kunigunde to Eoban in a rigged singing competition, but the Emperor Maximilian intervenes.

Harawi, chant d'Amour et de Mort song cycle by Messiaen for soprano and piano (text by composer, performed Brussels 1946. The first of a trilogy of works inspired by the Tristan legend: others are the *Turangalîla* symphony (1946–48) and *Cinq Rechants* for chorus *a cappella* (1949).

Harbison, John (b Orange, NJ, 20 Dec 1938), American composer. Studied at Harvard and with Sessions at Princeton. Taught at MIT 1969–82; composer-in-residence Pittsburgh SO 1982–84.

Works include operas *The Winter's Tale* (1979) and *Full Moon in March* (after Yeats, 1979); ballets after Homer *Ulysses' Raft* and *Ulysses' Bow* (1983–84); violin concerto (1980), two symphonies (1981, 1987), concerto for oboe, clarinet, and strings (1985), viola concerto (1990); two string quartets (1985, 1987).

Hardanger fiddle, Norwegian *Hardengerfelen*, a Norwegian violin with four strings and four sympathetic strings used for playing folk dances.

Harding, James (b *c* 1560; buried Isleworth, 28 Jan 1626), English composer and instrumentalist. Wrote two keyboard fancies and instrumental dance music.

Hardy, Thomas, (1840–1928), English novelist and poet. ◊Egdon Heath (Holst); E ◊Harper (*Fanny Robin* and *The Mellstock Quire*); ◊Hoddinott (*Trumpet Major*); ◊Muldowney (*Love music for Bathsheba and Gabriel Oak*); ◊Paulus (*The Woodlanders*); ◊Tess (Erlanger); poems set as songs by, among others, Bax, Britten, Finzi, Holst, Ireland.

Harewood, Earl of (George H H L) (b London, 7 Feb 1923), British administrator, critic and writer. He studied at Cambridge and in 1950 founded *Opera* magazine, which he edited until 1953; held various posts at CG 1951–72 and was managing director of SW (later ENO) Opera 1972–85; at the end of his tenure led the co. on a tour of the USA. Artistic adviser New Philharmonia Orchestra 1966–76. He was editor of the eighth, ninth and tenth editions of *Kobbé's Complete Opera Book* (1953, 1976, 1986). Artistic director of Adelaide Festival, 1988.

Harington, Henry (b Kelston, Som., 29 Sept 1727; d Bath, 15 Jan 1816), English physician and amateur musician. Studied first theology and then medicine at Oxford and settled in practice at Bath. Composed glees, catches, rounds, songs, etc. The popular setting of Ben Jonson's 'Drink to me only with thine eyes' is attributed to him.

Hark, hark, the lark song by Schubert from Shakespeare's *Cymbeline*, translated by A W Schlegel as *Ständchen aus 'Cymbeline'* and composed in Germany, in 1826.

harmonic a prefix denoting organ pipes, producing harmonic notes from pipes of double, triple or quadruple speaking-length. ◊harmonics.

harmonica a modern term for the mouth organ. For the glass harmonica ◊armonica.

> *When Augustus Harris himself went to America, it was to produce Humperdinck's* Hansel and Gretel *... but the opera was a 'frost', and the last touch of humour which nailed its coffin on the first night was a speech from Harris wherein he suggested 'a hope that there was enough artistic spirit in America to appreciate the wonderful work of this great composer, Pumpernickel'.*
>
> **Jimmy Glover**, *Jimmy Glover – His Book*, 1911

harmonic analysis a method of describing the chords and progressions used mainly in music of the 18th and 19th c. The principles rest on the identification of a chord by its root and by the position of the root within the scale. Thus a root-position chord on the tonic is designated as I, its first inversion as Ib (or, using the parlance of ◊thorough bass, I⁶) and its second inversion as Ic (or I⁶⁄₄); further elaborations of the system are all based on figured bass notation. Within diatonic music with straightforward harmonies, the main chords are I, IV and V; II and VI are also common, but III and VII are used more rarely. First inversions are important and used frequently except in structural cadences. Second inversions of triads are normally considered discords and can be used only in particular circumstances.

A further refinement of this system is 'functional harmony', first devised by Heinrich Riemann in his *Vereinfachte Harmonielehre* (1893). Here every chord was described as part of a tonic (I), dominant (V) or subdominant (IV) function. This system, still little practised outside Germany, makes the entire chordal vocabulary of the classical and romantic eras more comprehensible as a logical system; but at the same time many details need to be glossed over and this leads to the use of 'reduction' graphs which describe certain chords as passing chords within a broader progression. Hierarchical reductions of this kind led to the analytical techniques of Heinrich Schenker and his followers.

harmonic bass another name for the acoustic bass organ stop.

harmonic minor the minor scale conforming to the key signature, with the exception of the leading-note, which is raised a semitone.

harmonic rhythm the rhythm of harmonic change. For most tonal music, the variety of harmonic rhythm is of considerable importance to the musical effect. Thus it may be noted, for instance, that in many simple melodies of the classical era the harmonic rhythm speeds up towards the cadence: the faster chord changes at that point help to clarify the end of the phrase. Another example might be the moment

The harmonic minor scale on C.

before the recapitulation in sonata-form movements (sometimes called the 'retransition'): here the harmonic rhythm often slows down to a standstill, normally on the dominant, thus not only increasing the tension but allowing for a sudden change in harmonic rhythm at the moment of recapitulation.

harmonics a commonly used term for (upper) partial tones (overtones) in the notes of a musical instrument. Also a technical term for notes produced by lightly touching (not depressing to the fingerboard) a bowed string at suitable (nodal) points, or similarly by making a hole in an open organ pipe. In acoustics, compound elements of a periodic vibration. The corresponding elements in the vibration of a bell or a drum are 'inharmonic'. ◊harmonic series.

harmonic series the composite series of notes that can be produced by a vibrating substance or air column.

isticated use of suspensions. 17th–18th-c.: incorporation of dominant seventh chord, Neapolitan sixth, diminished chords and certain secondary sevenths. Classical era: augmented sixth chords. Later 19th-c.: chromatically altered chords. From around 1900: a wide variety of practices including whole-tone harmony, chords of superimposed fourths, diatonic harmony within unusual scales, atonal and polytonal harmony.

Harnasie ballet pantomime by Szymanowski (scenario by J Iwaszkiewicz and J M Rytard); composed 1923–31, produced Prague, 11 May 1935.

Harnoncourt, Nikolaus (b Berlin, 6 Dec 1929), Austrian conductor, cellist and musicologist. He studied in Vienna and played with the Vienna SO 1952–69; formed the Vienna Concentus Musicus and from 1957 gave concerts of Baroque music using period instruments; attempted to re-create original performing practice. Recorded the

The harmonic series. Those marked x *are not in tune with the normal scale. The members of the series have a proportional relation to each other. Thus if the lowest note vibrates at 64 cycles per second, the octave above it will be at 128 cps, the G (no. 3) at 172 cps, middle C at 256, and so on.*

Harmonie der Welt, Die, *The Harmony of the World*, opera by ◊Hindemith (libretto by the composer) in five acts, produced Munich, 11 Aug 1957. Symphony from the opera 1951; fp Basel 24 Jan 1952. Based on the life of the astronomer Johannes Kepler (1571–1630), who maintained in *Harmonices mundi* that the planets emit musical sounds in their orbits round the Sun.

Harmoniemesse Mass in B♭ by Haydn, composed 1802 and performed Eisenstadt, 8 Sept 1802. Title derives from prominent use of wind instruments (German *Harmonie* = 'wind band'). Haydn's last Mass.

Harmoniemusik, German, music for a combination of woodwind and brass instruments with or without percussion, i.e. for military band.

Harmonious Blacksmith, The name given to the Air and Variations in Handel's E major harpsichord suite (Book I, no. 5, pub. 1720). Despite the traditional story that Handel composed the piece after hearing a blacksmith singing at his work, the nickname is of 19th-c. origin.

harmonium a keyboard instrument, the sound of which is produced by reeds played by wind coming from bellows worked by the player's feet. It dates from the early 19th c. The American organ is similar to it, except that the wind is sucked into instead of driven out through the reeds.

harmony the musical effect derived from combining different pitches simultaneously. In general parlance this is contrasted with counterpoint, the combination of musical lines, though the one is often difficult to separate from the other. Harmony and counterpoint are perhaps best seen as different aspects of the combination of musical sounds, or even merely as tendencies. The distinction between harmony and counterpoint first became important for Western musical theory in the use of a continuo section playing from thorough bass at a time when written music was otherwise largely imitative polyphony. Harmonic theory as it is understood today goes back to Rameau's recognition of the notion of the root of a chord; and this led to the principle of harmonic analysis in the early 19th c. as a way of describing the vertical component of music in the 18th- and 19th-c. traditions. Yet it is also possible to talk of 'modal harmony', 'atonal harmony' and 'melodic harmony' (i.e. the harmonies implied within a single line).

The main stages in the history of harmony in Western music may be summarized as follows: 12th–13th-c.: open fifth and octaves as the main consonances, with the open fourth gradually losing favour. 14th–16th-c.: elimination of the open fourth as a consonance; increasing use of full triads, though most often in root position and only rarely as a concluding chord; increasingly systematic and soph-

Brandenburg concertos in 1962, gave *Messiah* in London 1966 and recorded Rameau's *Castor et Pollux* and Monteverdi's operas. Harnoncourt's own editions of Monteverdi are a valuable alternative to the free realizations of Raymond Leppard, and his performances of the Bach solo cello suites are in contrast to the subjective approach of Casals and Rostropovich. Conducted *Così fan tutte* for Netherlands Opera (1989), Beethoven symphony series with the Philharmonia, London, 1994 (his debut with a British symphony orchestra).

From harmony, from heav'nly harmony/This universal frame began:/From harmony to harmony/ Through all the compass of the notes it ran./The diapason closing full in Man.
    John Dryden, *A Song for St Cecilia's Day*, 1687

Harnoy, Ofra (b Hadera, 31 Jan 1965), Israeli-born Canadian cellist. Began her studies in Tel-Aviv and moved to Toronto in 1972; debut with the Boyd Neel Orchestra, after further study at the Royal Conservatory of Music. She has played in New York from 1982 and has given performances in the USA of concertos by Bliss and Sullivan, with Sir Charles Mackerras. She gave the fp of a recently-discovered concerto by Offenbach, has recorded works by Haydn and Vivaldi, and given the US fp of Sullivan's concerto (reconstructed by Mackerras).

Harold en Italie a descriptive symphony by Berlioz, op. 16, for solo viola and orchestra, based on Byron's *Childe Harold*, composed 1834, fp Paris, 23 Nov. It was suggested by Paganini, but not played by him.

harp an instrument dating from prehistoric times, so shaped that the strings stretched parallel across its frame are graded in length and thus produce the different notes of a musical scale. Early harps had comparatively few strings and their notes were fixed; the modern concert harp has a range of 6½ octaves and the strings represent the diatonic scale of C♭ major; but each note can be raised individually throughout all the octaves at once by a semitone and by a whole tone at will by means of a set of pedals at the base of the instrument. Thus the harp can be tuned in a moment to any diatonic scale. The chromatic scale is available only on the chromatic harp .

Harper, Edward (b Taunton, 17 Mar 1941), English composer. He studied at Oxford and with Gordon Jacob and at the RCM; lecturer at Edinburgh University from 1964.

Works include piano concerto (1969); *Bartók Games* for orchestra

harp *The illustration shows an instrument of the old style, lacking pedals to operate a device which can change the pitch of the strings. The pedal mechanism had been developed in Germany by 1770.*

(1972); *Ricercari in memoriam Luigi Dallapiccola* for 11 instruments (1975), *Fanny Robin*, opera in one act from an episode in Hardy's *Far from the Madding Crowd*, 1975); *seven poems by e e cummings* for soprano and orchestra (1977); *Chester Mass* for chorus and orchestra (1979); clarinet concerto (1982); *Intrada after Monteverdi* for chamber orchestra (1982); *Hedda Gabler*, opera after Ibsen's play (1985); *The Mellstock Quire* opera after Hardy (1987); *Double Variations* for oboe, bassoon and wind (1989); *In Memoriam* for cello and piano (1990), *The Lamb* for soprano, chorus and orchestra (1990), *Homage to Thomas Hardy* for baritone and chamber orchestra (1990); string quartet (1986).

Harper, Heather (Mary) (b Belfast, 8 May 1930), British soprano. Studied at TCM, London, and privately. First appeared in opera at Oxford 1954; Glyndebourne from 1957, CG from 1962. She sang at Bayreuth (Elsa, 1967–68) and Buenos Aires, 1969–72. Other roles included Britten's Helena and Ellen Oxford, Eva, Arabella and The Woman in *Erwartung* (first London production 1960). Has also made a reputation as a concert singer; sang in the fps of Britten's *War Requiem* (1962) and Tippett's third symphony (1972). Hon. Mus.D., Queen's University, Belfast, 1966. Sang Nadia in *The Ice Break* at the 1990 London Proms.

harp lute an instrument sometimes called dital harp, invented early in the 19th c. It was derived from instruments of the lute type, but had a larger number of strings held by pegs in the harp-shaped head, *c* half of them changeable in pitch by a finger-board, the others remaining open and thus capable of playing only a single fixed note.

'Harp' Quartet the nickname given to Beethoven's string quartet in E♭ major, op. 74, composed 1809, because it contains, in the first movement, several arpeggios divided between the instruments.

harpsicall, harpsicon old English terms, corruptions of ◊harpsichord.

harpsichord a keyboard instrument shaped usually in the wing form of a grand piano and played by means of a similar keyboard, but producing its notes by plucking the strings with plectra, not striking them with hammers. The square-shaped virginal and the spinet are instruments of the same type but smaller. Harpsichords often have two keyboards, each controlling a different set of strings or quills, harder and softer, and there are frequently stops by which yet other ranges of quills can be set into action; but the tone cannot be controlled by the player's fingers.

Harrell, Lynn (b New York, 30 Jan 1944), American cellist. He studied at Juilliard with Leonard Rose; debut Carnegie Hall 1960. Principal, Cleveland Orchestra 1965–71, under Szell; soloist since 1971. British debut 1975, with LSO under Ashkenazy.

Harrhy, Eiddwen (b Trowbridge, 14 Apr 1949), Welsh soprano. She sang Despina at the RMCM, 1970, and appeared professionally from 1974 (Alcina with Handel Opera and in the *Ring* at CG). At the London Coliseum she has sung Adèle (1977) and with Kent Opera, Pamina and the Taurian Iphigénie; she sang Diana in *La Fedeltà premiata* at the 1979 Glyndebourne Festival. Other roles include Donna Anna, Butterfly (Coliseum 1984) and Berg's Marie (WNO 1986). Sang in the fp of Blake's *The Plumber's Gift*, ENO 1989.

Harries, Kathryn (b Hampton Court, 15 Feb 1951), English soprano. Studied at the RCM and made debut at the Festival Hall, 1977. Opera debut as a flower-maiden in *Parsifal* with WNO, 1993 (Sieglinde 1984 and Gutrune 1985). ENO, London, from 1983, as Irene in *Rienzi*, Eva, Katya Kabanova and Donna Anna in *The Stone Guest*. Created Hedda Gabler in Edward Harper's opera for Scottish Opera (1985) and sang Kundry at the NY Met. 1986 (returned as Gutrune, 1989). Sang Dido in *Les Troyens* at Lyon in 1987 and for Scottish Opera 1990 (also at CG, where she had made her debut 1989, in the UK fp of Berlioz's *Un re in ascolto*. Orange Festival 1992, as Carmen.

Harris, Augustus (b Paris, 1852; d Folkestone, 22 Jun 1896), English impresario. Manager at DL 1879–94 (British fps of Meistersinger and Tristan, 1882) and at CG 1888–96 (Ring cycle under Mahler, 1892).

Praise the Lord upon the harp: sing to the harp with a psalm of thanksgiving.

Prayer Book, 1662

Harris (actually Leroy Harris), Roy (b Lincoln Co., OK, 12 Feb 1898; d Santa Monica, CA, 1 Oct 1979), American composer. His father was a farmer who migrated to California during Harris's boyhood, and at 18 Harris had a farm of his own. In 1916 he enlisted to fight in World War I, returning to USA in 1918 and becoming a music student at the University of California, driving a dairy cart to earn a living. Next he studied under Arthur Farwell for two years and produced an Andante for strings for the NY PO in 1926, when he went to Paris for a further two years' study with Nadia Boulanger. He returned to USA in 1929 and later held posts at the Westminster Choir school at Princeton, NJ, Cornell University, Colorado, Logan (UT), Nashville and Pittsburgh. His most successful work was the third symphony, declaring American ruggedness at the onset of war. It was premiered under Koussevitsky at Boston 1939.

Works include 13 symphonies (1934–76), *Farewell to Pioneers* (1936), *Three Symphonic Essays, Memories of a Child's Sunday* and other works for orchestra; *Chorale* and *Prelude and Fugue* for string orchestra; concerto for violin and orchestra, symphony for chorus and orchestra, *Whitman Suite* and *Second Suite* for women's chorus and two pianos, *Song for Occupation, Story of Noah* and *Symphony for Voices* for eight-part unaccompanied chorus.

CHAMBER AND INSTRUMENTAL: three string quartets (1930–39), sextet and quintet for wind and piano, string sextet, piano quintet, piano trio, *Variations on a Theme* for flute and string quartet, *4 Minutes*

20 Seconds for flute and string quartet, concerto for piano clarinet and string quartet; violin and piano sonata; pieces for violin and viola and piano; piano works, including sonatas and *Children's Suite*.

Harrison, Beatrice (b Roorkee, India, 9 Dec 1892; d Smallfield, Sussex, 10 Mar 1965), English cellist. She studied at the RCM and made her 1907 debut with Wood; in 1920 took part with him in the fp of Delius's Double Concerto. With Hamilton Harty she gave the 1918 fp of the Delius cello sonata and in 1923 the first British performance of the concerto, under Goossens. In 1924 she gave the first London performance of Kodály's solo sonata op. 8; recorded the Elgar concerto with the composer.

Harrison, Frank Llewelyn (b Dublin, 29 Sept 1905; d Canterbury, 29 Dec 1987), Irish musicologist and educationist. Studied in Ireland and later under Schrade and Hindemith at Yale University He was music director at Queen's University, Kingston (Canada), 1935–46, and Professor of Music at Colgate University, Hamilton (NY), 1946–47 and at WA University, St Louis, 1947–52. From 1952 to 1970 he was a lecturer in music, subsequently reader, at Oxford University. Professor of Ethnomusicology at Amsterdam University, 1970–80. He specialized in the study of English medieval music, and edited *The Eton Choirbook* (three vols.) and pub. *Music in Medieval Britain* (1958). He was general editor of the series *Early English Church Music*.

Harrison, Julius (b Stourport, Worcs., 26 Mar 1885; d Harpenden, 5 Apr 1963), English conductor and composer. Studied under Bantock at the Midland Institute, Birmingham. Conducted opera under Beecham's management and with the BNOC and from 1930 to 1940 was music director at Hastings.

Works include Mass for solo voices, chorus and orchestra;

Harrell *The cellist Lynn Harrell. His recordings range from the solo cello suites by Bach to accompanied cello sonatas and piano trios by Beethoven (with Ashkenazy and Perlman) to 19th- and 20th-century concertos. He has toured extensively throughout the world.*

Requiem Mass; suite *Worcestershire Pieces* for orchestra; *Troubadour Suite* for strings, harp and two horns; string quartet *Widdicombe Fair* and other chamber music; viola and piano sonata; piano works, instrumental pieces; songs.

Harrison, Lou (b Portland, OR, 14 May 1917), American composer. Studied with Cowell and Schoenberg 1937–40. He then taught at Mills College and at the University of California in 1942. From 1945 to 1948 he was a music critic for the *New York Herald-Tribune*. Taught at San José State University 1967–82, Mills College 1980–85. Harrison has experimented with new sonorities, including novel scales and methods of tuning. He helped promote the music of Varèse, Ruggles and Cowell, and conducted the fp of Ives' third symphony ·(1946). A visit to the Far East in 1961 inspired much music for the gamelan.

Works include opera *Rapunzel* (1959); ballets *Solstice*, *The Perilous Chapel* (1949), *Almanac of the Seasons*, *Johnny Appleseed*, *Changing World* and others; Prelude and Saraband for orchestra, three symphonies, piano concerto (1985); string quartet set (1979), *Ariadne* for flute and percussion (1987); three suites; *Four Strict Songs* for eight baritones and orchestra in pure intonation (1955); *Recording Piece* for percussion; *Simfony I*; violin concerto with percussion orchestra; string trio; suite for cello and harp; piano music.

The harpsichord, however it may sound in a small room – and to my mind it never has a pleasant sound – in a large concert hall sounds just like the ticking of a sewing machine.
Ralph Vaughan Williams, broadcast talk, 1950

Harsányi, Tibor (b Magyarkanizsa, 27 Jun 1898; d Paris, 19 Sept 1954), Hungarian composer. Studied at the Budapest Conservatory under Kodály and later settled in Paris in 1923.

Works include operas *Illusion*, *Les Invités* (1928); ballets *The Last Dream* and *Shota Roustaveli* (1945) (with Honegger and A Tcherepnin); Christmas Cantata for chorus and strings (1939); suite, *Suite hongroise*, *Ouverture symphonique*, *La Joie de vivre* for orchestra;

harpsichord *The harpsichord, or cembalo, was the most important keyboard instrument (excluding the organ) until the fortepiano came to prominence at the end of the 18th century. The illustration, though representing the general features of the harpsichord, lacks the full details of the keyboard and mechanism.*

Concertstück for piano and orchestra, Divertimento No. 1 for two violins and orchestra; *Aria and Rondo* for cello and orchestra, Divertimento No. 2 for trumpet and strings; *The Story of the Little Tailor* for seven instruments and percussion; two string quartets (1918, 1935), piano trio, concertino for piano and string quartets; sonatas for violin and piano and cello and piano; piano pieces; songs.

Harshaw, Margaret (b Narbeth, PA, 12 May 1909), American mezzo, later soprano. She studied at Juilliard, NY, and made her debut at the Met. in 1942; after Senta there in 1950 she sang in the soprano repertory; succeeded Helen Traubel as Isolde, Kundry and Brünnhilde. Glyndebourne 1955 (Donna Anna); CG, London, 1953–60, as Brünnhilde. She left the Met. in 1963 and taught at Bloomington University from 1962. Sang Brünnhilde at Bloomington, 1970.

Hartmann German-Danish family of musicians:

1. Johann Ernst Hartmann (b Glogau, Silesia, 24 Dec 1726; d Copenhagen, 21 Oct 1793), German violinist, conductor and composer. Worked at Breslau and Rudolstadt before he settled in Copenhagen, where he became leader of the royal orchestra in 1768.

Works include opera *The Fishermen*, produced 1780, containing the song *Kong Christian* by D L Rogert, now the Danish national anthem.

2. Johann Peter Emilius H. (b Copenhagen, 14 May 1805; d Copenhagen, 10 Mar 1900), composer, grandson of 1. Succeeded his father as organist of the Garrison Church in Copenhagen in 1824, appointed organist of the cathedral 1843. Professor at Copenhagen Conservatory, he became one of its directors in 1867.

Operas *Ravnen* (1832), *Korsarerne* (1835), *Liden Kirsten* (after Andersen); melodrama *Guldhornene*; incidental music for plays; ballets; two symphonies; sonatas, etc., for piano.

3. Emil Hartmann (b Copenhagen, 21 Feb 1836; d Copenhagen, 18 Jul 1898); organist and composer, son of 2. Pupil of his father and Gade, who was his brother-in-law. Organist at various churches 1861–73 and conductor of the Music Society 1891–92, succeeding Gade. operas *En Nat mellem Fjaeldene* (1863), *Elverpigen* (1867), *Korsikaneren* and *Ragnhild* (1896); ballet *Fjeldstuen*; cantata *Winter and Spring*; seven symphonies, *Northern Folk Dances* and overture *A Northern Campaign*; concertos for violin and for cello; serenade for clarinet, cello and piano-songs.

Hartmann, Karl Amadeus (b Munich, 2 Aug 1905; d Munich, 5 Dec 1963), German composer. Studied with Josef Haas at the Munich Academy and later with Scherchen. Began composing late in life, but destroyed his early works and turned to serialism under the influence of Webern. After World War II he organized the important 'Musica Viva' concerts in Munich to propagate new music. In 1952 he was

elected to the German Academy of Fine Arts and in 1953 became president of the German section of the ISCM.

Works include chamber opera *Des Simplicius Simplicissimus Jugend* (1934–35; produced 1949), eight symphonies (1936–62); concerto for piano, wind and percussion, *Musik der Trauer* for violin and strings (1939); two string quartets.

Hartmann, Rudolf (b Ingolstadt, 11 Oct 1900; d Munich, 26 Aug 1988), German producer and administrator. He produced opera at Nuremberg (1928–34) and the Berlin Staatsoper (1934–38), then became associated with Clemens Krauss and the operas of Strauss at Munich: fps of *Friedenstag* (1938) and *Capriccio* (1942). Produced *The Ring* at CG (1954) and returned for *Arabella* (1965). His work was noted for its discretion and good taste. Wrote book on the production of Strauss's stage works (1980).

Harty, (Herbert) Hamilton (b Hillsborough, Ireland, 4 Dec 1879; d Hove, 19 Feb 1941), Irish conductor and composer. Studied piano, viola and composition under his father and became an organist at the age of 12. Later organist at Belfast and Dublin, where he studied further under Esposito. In 1900 he settled in London as accompanist and composer and married the soprano Agnes ◊Nicholls. He then took to conducting and after much much experience in London was appointed conductor to the Hallé Orchestra at Manchester in 1920; gave the first British performance of Mahler's ninth symphony in 1930. Retired 1933. Knighted and Mus. D. Dublin, 1925.

Works include arrangement of Handel's *Water Music* and *Fireworks Music*, Irish Symphony (1924), *Comedy Overture*, symphonic poem *With the Wild Geese* for orchestra (1910); violin concerto; cantata *The Mystic Trumpeter* (Whitman); *Ode to a Nightingale* (Keats) for soprano and orchestra (1907); many songs.

Harvey, Jonathan (b Sutton Coldfield, 3 May 1939), English composer. He studied at Cambridge and Glasgow Universities; professor at Sussex University from 1980. He has worked with Stockhausen and Babbitt.

Works include symphony (1966); *Persephone Dream* for orchestra (1973), *Smiling Immortal* for chamber orchestra and tape (1977), *Easter Orisons* for strings (1983); *Madonna of Winter and Spring* (1986), *Lightness and Weight* for tuba and orchestra (1986); cello concerto (1990); ten Cantatas for soloists and various instrumental combinations (1965–76), *Hymn* for chorus and orchestra (composed 1979 for the 900th anniversary of Winchester Cathedral), *Passion and Resurrection*, church opera, performed Winchester 1981); opera *Inquest of Love* (1993); chamber and instrumental music including *Mortuos plango, vivos voco* for computer-processed concrete sounds, performed Lille 1980; *Modernsky Music* of 1981, for two oboes, bassoon and harpsichord, derives its title from one of Schoenberg's

Jonathan Harvey - composer

1 Boulez: *Le visage nuptial*
   The warmest work of a master of perfectly-heard complex textures: it inhabits a magical world.

2 Schoenberg: *Pelléas und Mélisande*
   Tonal music at the peak of its expressive intensity just before it collapsed: it's an 'ultimate'.

3 Mozart: *Don Giovanni*
   By a short head this must be the Mozart work that has it all, from wit to spirituality, from light to dark, from warm humanity to psychoanalysis. I always find it mysterious.

4 Skriabin: Sonata no. 10
   Given the sort of performance Ashkenazy can offer, this work seems to live in the air.

5 Webern: *First Cantata*
   This too lives in a floating, timeless, radiant world, its symmetries and harmonies as satisfying as an Alpine landscape.

6 Tristan Murail: *Désintegrations*
   One of the great masterpieces of spectralism, the art that will change music: an exploration of the inner structure of sound.

7 John Chowning: *Stria*
   A pure and beautiful work for tape, soft-edged and serene, composed of constantly shifting sine-tones.

8 Schubert: String Quintet in C major
   Another work on the edge: classical yet with a totally new feeling. I find it infinitely touching.

3 Satires op. 28, in which Stravinsky is mocked as 'Modernsky', for apparently following musical fashion. *Curve with Plateaux* for cello (1982), *Valley of Aosta* for 13 players (1988); *Scena* for violin and ensemble (1992); *Chant* for viola (1992).

Harwood, Basil (b Woodhouse, Olveston, Gloucestershire, 11 Apr 1859; d London, 3 Apr 1949), English organist and composer. Educated at Charterhouse and Oxford, studied music at Bristol, Oxford and the Leipzig Conservatory. Organist first in London, then at Ely Cathedral, 1887–92, and Christ Church, Oxford, 1892–1909, and choragus of the university.

Works include psalms and motets with orchestra; services, anthems and other church music; *Ode on a May Morning* (Milton) for chorus and orchestra (1913), cantata *Love Incarnate*; organ concerto with orchestra; organ works.

Harwood, Elizabeth (b Barton Seagrave, Northants., 27 May 1938; d Ingatestone, Essex, 21 Jun 1990), English soprano. She studied at the RMCM. SW London, from 1961 as Gilda, Zerbinetta, Constanze and Rossini's Adèle. In 1967 she sang for the first time at CG, with Scottish Opera and at the Aix Festival: roles included Tippett's Bella, Fiordiligi (role of NY Met. debut, 1975), and Strauss's Sophie. Salzburg from 1970, as Donna Elvira and Mozart's Countess. In 1980 she sang the Marschallin at Glyndebourne.

Háry János ballad opera by Kodály (libretto by B Paulini and Z Harsányi, based on a poem by János Garay), produced Budapest, 16 Oct 1926. It contains popular Hungarian tunes and begins with an orchestral imitation of a sneeze. Orchestral Suite performed NY, 15 Dec 1927. János tells tall tales about his youth, spent defeating Napoleon, winning the heart of the Emperor's wife. But all along he remained true to his bride back in his native village.

Haskil, Clara (b Bucharest, 7 Jan 1895; d Brussels, 7 Dec 1960), Romanian pianist. Made her debut aged seven in Vienna, then entered the Paris Conservatory, where she studied with Cortot and Fauré and won a prize at the age of 14. She later studied with Busoni on his invitation. She was especially well known as a performer of Mozart and Beethoven; violin sonatas with Arthur Grumiaux.

Hass, Sabine (b Brunswick, 8 Apr 1949), German soprano. Studied in Berlin and Munich and sang at the Stuttgart Opera from 1970. State Operas of Munich and Vienna in 1976, as Senta and Ariadne; Bregenz 1977 as Reiza in *Oberon*. Sang Elsa at La Scala 1983 and returned to Munich 1983 and 1988, as Isabella in Wagner's *Liebesverbot* and as Strauss's Danae. NY Met. 1985–86, as Senta and Elsa. Other roles include Sieglinde (Deutsche Oper Berlin) and Isolde (Basel, 1990).

Hassan, or The Golden Journey to Samarkand incidental music by Delius for the play by James Elroy Flecker; 1920, produced London, His Majesty's, 20 Sept 1923, with ballets arranged by Fokine. Orchestral suite by Eric Fenby, with instruments including camel-bells, performed on BBC, 1 Aug 1933.

Hasse, Faustina, ◊Bordoni.

Hasse, Johann Adolf (b Bergedorf near Hamburg, bap 25 Mar 1699; d Venice, 16 Dec 1783), German composer. Sang tenor at the Hamburg Opera under Keiser, 1718–19, then at Brunswick, 1719–22, where his first opera, *Antioco*, was produced 1721. Went to Italy 1722, and studied with Porpora and A Scarlatti. After many successful operas for Naples, became *maestro di cappella* at the Conservatorio degli Incurabili in Venice in 1727. Married the singer Faustina ◊Bordoni in 1730, and in 1734 went to Dresden as *Kapellmeister* to the Saxon Court, a post he held for 30 years. But he was allowed generous leave of absence, and travelled widely, including a visit to London in 1734, becoming the most successful *opera seria* composer of his generation. In 1764, after the death of the Saxon Elector, he moved to Vienna, then in 1773 to Venice, where he lived for the rest of his life.

Works include operas *Antioco* (1721), *Il Sesostrate* (1726), *Tigrane* (1729), *Artaserse*, *Cleofide* (1731), *Cajo Fabricio* (1732), *Il Demetrio, Siroe, rè di Persia* (1733), *Tito Vespasiano* (1735), *Lucio Papirio* (1742), *Didone abbandonata, Antigono* (1743), *Semiramide riconosciuta* (1744), *Arminio, Leucippo, Demofoonte* (1748), *Attilio Regolo* (1750), *Il Ciro riconosciuto* (1751), *Solimano, Ezio, Olim-*

piade, Alcide al Bivio (1760), *Il trionfo di Clelia* (1762), *Partenope, Piramo e Tisbe* (1768), *Ruggiero* (1771), and many others; oratorios *I Pellegrini al sepolcro, Sant' Elena al calvario* (1746), *La Conversione di Sant' Agostino* (1750); Masses and other church music; concertos for flute, violin, etc.; solo sonatas, trio sonatas, harpsichord pieces.

Hassell, Jon (b Memphis, 22 Mar 1937), American composer and trumpeter. Studied with Stockhausen and Pousseur in Cologne and at the Eastman School. As composer and performer has been involved with minimalism, Balinese music and electronics. Works include *Music for Vibraphones* (1965); *Blackboard Piece with Girls and Loops* (1969); *Goodbye Music* (1969); *Solid State* for two synthesizers (1969); *Superball* (1969); *Landscape Series* (1969–72); *Sulla Strada*, theatre piece after Kerouac's *On the Road* (performed Venice, 1982). Recordings include music from the Far East (*Earthquake Island, Aka-Dhari-Java*).

Hasselmans, Alphonse (Jean) (b Liège, 5 Mar 1845; d Paris, 19 May 1912), Belgian, naturalized French, harpist and composer. Settled early in Paris and became harp professor at the Conservatory in 1884. Appeared frequently as a virtuoso and composer *c* 50 works for the harp, including *Patrouille* and *L'Orientale*.

Hassler, Hans Leo (b Nuremberg, 25 Oct 1564; d Frankfurt, 8 Jun 1612), German organist and composer. Pupil of his father, Isaac Hassler (*c* 1530–91) and, after an appointment at Nuremberg, was sent to Venice for further study under A Gabrieli (the first German to study in Italy). Organist to Octavian Fugger at Augsburg, 1585–1600. Having returned to Nuremberg as organist of the church of Our Lady, he married and went to live at Ulm in 1604, but soon went into the service of the Emperor Rudolph in Prague. In 1608 he became organist to the Elector of Saxony at Dresden, but suffered from tuberculosis and died during a visit with the elector to Frankfurt.

Works include Masses, Magnificats, hymntunes, motets (including two collections *Sacrae cantiones* and *Sacri concentus*), fugal psalms and Christian songs; Italian canzonets for four voices, Italian and German madrigals, *Lustgarten neuer teutscher Gesäng* (32 German songs for four–eight voices, 1601); *ricercari*, toccatas, etc. for organ

Hassler, Jacob (b Nuremberg, bap. 18 Dec 1569; d ?1622), German organist and composer, brother of Hans Leo ◊Hassler. Studied under his father and at Venice, became organist to Christoph Fugger at Augsburg and then to Prince Eitel-Fritz of Hohenzollern at Hechingen, and was in the service of the court in Prague 1602–12.

Works include Masses and other church music. Italian madrigals; organ works.

Hassler, Kaspar (b Nuremberg, bap. 17 Aug 1562; d Nuremberg, Aug 1618), German organist and composer, brother of Hans Leo and Jacob ◊Hassler. Studied under his father and (?) at Venice. Organist at the church of St Laurence at Nuremberg. Edited collections of motets, including some by his brother Hans Leo.

Hatton, John (Liptrott) (b Liverpool, 12 Oct 1808; d Margate, 20 Sept 1886), English composer. He was almost wholly self-taught in music. In 1832 he settled in London, in 1842 became attached to Drury Lane Theatre as composer and in 1844 visited Vienna to produce his opera *Pascal Bruno*. In 1848 he went to the USA and later became music director of the Prince's Theatre, London, where he wrote much incidental music for Kean's productions.

Works include operas *Pascal Bruno* (1844) and *Rose, or Love's Ransom* (1864), operetta *The Queen of the Thames*; incidental music for Shakespeare's *Macbeth, Henry VIII, Richard II, King Lear, The Merchant of Venice* and *Much Ado About Nothing*, Sheridan's *Pizarro*, an adaptation of Goethe's *Faust* and other plays; Mass, two services, eight anthems; oratorio *Hezekiah*; cantata *Robin Hood*; over 150 songs, including *To Anthea* (Herrick); many part-songs.

Haubenstock-Ramati, Roman (b Kraków, 27 Feb 1919; d Vienna, 3 Mar 1993), Polish, later Israeli, composer. Studied composition in Kraków and Lwów from 1937 to 1940. From 1947 to 1950 he was music director of Radio Kraków and then emigrated to Israel, where he became director of the music library in Tel-Aviv. In 1957 he moved to Paris, living also in Vienna, where he worked for Universal Edition. His early works are conservative in idiom, but his mature music used serial and experimental techniques.

Works include opera *Amerika* (after Kafka, 1966); *Ulysses*, ballet (1977), *La Symphonie des timbres* for orchestra; *Vermutungen über ein dunkles Haus* for three orchestras; *Papageno's Pocket-size Concerto* for glockenspiel and orchestra (1955); *Recitativo and Aria* for cembalo and orchestra; *Sequences* for violin and orchestra; *Petite Musique de nuit*, mobile for orchestra (1958); *Blessings* for voice and nine players; *Mobile for Shakespeare* for voice and six players (1960); *Jeux* for six percussion groups; concerto for strings (1977); *Interpolation*, mobile for solo flute; *Ricercari* for string trio.

Hauer, Josef (Matthias) (b Wiener-Neustadt, 19 Mar 1883; d Vienna, 22 Sept 1959), Austrian composer. Pub. a series of pamphlets on composition according to a 12-note system of his own, different from that of Schoenberg, his material being based on groups of notes he called *Tropen*, derived from the combinations of the 12 notes of the chromatic scale allowed by the agreement of their overtones.

Works (all based on this system) include opera *Salammbô* (after Flaubert, 1929; performed Vienna, 1983); play with music, *Die schwarze Spinne* (after Jeremias Gotthelf, 1932; performed Vienna, 1966); Mass for chorus, organ and orchestra; cantata *Wandlungen*; music for Aeschylus's *Prometheus Bound* and tragedies by Sophocles: *Vom Leben*, recitation with singing voices and chamber orchestra for broadcasting. Sinfonietta, eight suites, seven Dance Fantasies (1928), Concert Piece, *Apocalyptic Fantasy* (1913), *Kyrie*, etc. for orchestra; symphony for strings, harmonium and piano; violin concerto, piano concerto; six string quartets (1924–26), quintet for clarinet, violin, viola, cello and piano; many piano pieces including two sets of Studies and pieces on Hölderlin titles; *c* 87 *Zwölftonspiele* for different instruments and instrumental combinations; six song-cycles to poems by Hölderlin and other songs.

Haug, Hans (b Basel, 27 Jul 1900; d Lausanne, 15 Sept 1967), Swiss conductor and composer. Studied at Basel and Munich and became orchestra and chorus conductor of various Swiss towns and professor at the Lausanne Conservatory.

Works include operas *Don Juan in der Fremde* (1930), *Madriso* (1934), *Tartuffe* (after Molière, 1937), *E liederlieg Kleeblatt* (in Swiss dialect), *Ariadne*; Te Deum; oratorio *Michelangelo* (1943); symphonies and other orchestral works; violin concerto, piano concerto; chamber music, including three string quartets; part-songs, arrangements of Swiss folksongs, songs with piano; film and radio music.

Mozart said: 'Papa,' (as he usually called him), 'you have no education for the great world and you speak too few languages.' 'Oh,' replied Haydn, 'my language is understood all over the world.'

Dies, *Biographische Nachrichten von Joseph Haydn*, 1810

Haugland, Aage (b Copenhagen, 1 Feb 1944), Norwegian bass. He sang first at Oslo and Bremen; Stockholm from 1973. In 1975 he was heard as Hunding at CG and as Hagen at the ENO; other London roles have been Varlaam and Ochs. US debut St Louis 1979, as Boris; NY Met. from 1979 as Klingsor, Gremin, Marke, Boris and Khovansky. In 1982 he sang Rocco at Salzburg and the following year Hagen at Bayreuth. Edinburgh Festival 1990, as Marke in *Tristan*. A noted concert artist.

Hauk, Minnie (b New York, 16 Nov 1851; d Triebschen, Lucerne, 6 Feb 1929), American mezzo of German descent. Made her debut at Brooklyn, 1866 and her European debut at CG, London, 1868; first London Carmen, 1878.

Hauptmann, Cornelius (b Stuttgart, 1951), German bass. Studied in Berne and with Dietrich Fischer-Dieskau. Sang at Stuttgart Opera from 1981, and at Heidelberg from 1985, as Masetto, King Philip and Osmin. Karlssruhe from 1987, as Sarastro, and Mozart's Figaro. Sang

in the fp of Henze's *English Cat* (Schwetzingen 1983) and has appeared in John Eliot Gardiner's Mozart opera series in London (also recorded) and the *St Matthew Passion*.

Hauptmann, Moritz (b Dresden, 13 Oct 1792; d Leipzig, 3 Jan 1868), German theorist, writer on music and composer. Studied at Dresden and began to work there, lived in Russia 1815–20, played violin in Spohr's orchestra at Kassel from 1822 and was cantor at St Thomas's Church in Leipzig from 1842 to his death. Wrote on acoustics, harmony, fugue, etc.

Works include opera *Mathilde* (1826); two Masses, motets and psalms; choruses and part-songs; three sonatas for violin and piano, violin duets; songs.

Hausegger, Siegmund von (b Graz, 16 Aug 1872; d Munich, 10 Oct 1948), Austrian conductor and composer. Studied under his father, a Wagnerian critic, and others. After conducting at Graz, he shared the conductorship of the Kaim Orchestra at Munich with Weingartner. Later in charge of concerts at Frankfurt, Glasgow and Edinburgh (Scottish Orchestra) and Hamburg, and at Munich again 1920–38.

Works include opera *Zinnober* (1898), *Barbarossa* and *Natursinfonie*, *Dionysische Phantasie*, *Wieland der Schmied* and *Aufklänge* for orchestra; Mass and Requiem; choral works, part-songs.

Hauser, Franz (b Krasovice, near Prague, 12 Jan 1794; d Freiburg i/B., 14 Aug 1870), Bohemian-German baritone. Pupil of Tomášek and successful opera singer until 1837; sang under Spohr in Kassel and under Weber in Dresden. Roles included Figaro, William Tell and Spohr's Faust. From 1846 to 1864 he was director of the Munich Conservatory. He pub. a singing method in 1866.

Hausmann, Robert (b Rottleberode, Harz, 13 Aug 1852; d Vienna, 18 Jan 1909), German cellist. Studied at the Hochschule für Musik in Berlin and with Piatti in London and Italy. He joined the Joachim quartet in 1879. In 1886 gave the fp of Brahms's F major cello sonata and in 1887 the fp of the Double concerto, with Joachim.

Haussman, Valentin (d *c* 1612), German 16th–17th-c. organist and composer. He was organist and town councillor at Gerbstädt near Merseburg. Edited vocal pieces by Marenzio, Vecchi, Gastoldi and Morley with German words.

Works include German secular songs for four–eight voices, instrumental dances, including *Venusgarten* containing 100 dances, mostly Polish.

Haydn

A biographical note

With the death of Haydn's employer Nicholas Esterhazy in 1790, Haydn was released from regular court service and was free to accept commissions. The London-based German impresario Johann Peter Salomon went to Vienna and invited Haydn to return with him. The terms were far more generous than anything Haydn had earned while in service and he was eager to accept, in spite of the friendly warnings given to him by Mozart. Stopping at Bonn on the way to Calais, Haydn met Beethoven for the first time, and was sufficiently impressed by his Joseph II cantata to offer him lessons on his return. After a journey of 17 days Haydn arrived in London in January 1791. His first concert two months later 'electrified the audience', according to Charles Burney, and 'awakened a frenzy of enthusiasm'. Of the many sights and sounds which impressed Haydn on his two visits to London, none was greater than hearing Handel performed in Westminster Abbey. The memory of the great choruses he heard was still fresh in his mind back in Vienna in 1795, when he was invited by Baron van Swieten to compose an oratorio, *The Creation*, based on Milton's *Paradise Lost*. The first public performance in 1799 was one of Haydn's last great successes, the audience responding as much to the vivid instrumental depiction of primeval chaos as to such choruses as The Heavens are Telling – written perhaps in emulation of the Hallelujah Chorus from *Messiah*.

hautboy from French *hautbois* = lit. 'loud wood'; the old English name for the ♭oboe, sometimes spelt 'hoboy'.

haute-contre, French, alto or high tenor, whether voice or instrument. Hence one of the old names for the alto or tenor viol and the viola.

Hawes, William (b London, 21 Jun 1785; d London, 18 Feb 1846), English musician. He was master of choristers at St Paul's Cathedral and the Chapel Royal but neglected and brutalized his charges. From 1804 he made many adaptations for the stage of operas by Mozart and Weber.

Hawkins, John (b London, 29 Mar 1719; d London, 21 May 1789), English music historian. Devoted at first to architecture and then to law, he gradually became interested in literature and music. Having married a wealthy wife in 1753, he was able to retire and to undertake, in addition to minor works, his *General History of the Science and Practice of Music*, pub. in five vols. in 1776, the same year as the first volume of Burney's similar work. Knighted 1772.

Hawte, William (b Canterbury, *c* 1430; d 2 Jul 1497), English composer. Wrote four settings of the *Benedicamus Domino* (Cambridge, Magdalene College, Pepys MS. 1236) and a processional antiphon, *Stella caeli*.

Haydn, Franz Joseph (b Rohrau, Lower Austria, 31 Mar 1732; d Vienna, 31 May 1809), Austrian composer. Son of a wheelwright, he went at the age of eight as a chorister to St Stephen's Cathedral in Vienna under Georg Reutter (junior). On leaving the choir-school *c* 1749 he lived at first as a freelance, playing violin and organ, teaching, etc. He was for a time pupil-manservant to Porpora, but in composition he was largely self-taught, studying the works of C P E Bach, Fux's *Gradus ad Parnassum*, etc. From these years date his earliest compositions, especially church music, including two Masses. His first string quartets were written *c* 1755 for Baron Fürnberg, through whom he obtained the post of music director to Count Morzin in 1759. The next year he contracted what was to prove an unfortunate marriage, and in 1761 entered the service of the Esterházy family, in 1766 succeeding Franz Gregor Werner as *Kapellmeister*, a post he held for the rest of his life. At Eszterháza, the magnificent palace in the Hungarian marshes, completed in 1766, where the household now spent the greater part of the year, Haydn was responsible for all the musical entertainment, and there wrote the majority of his instrumental music and operas. At first he wrote symphonies and instrumental pieces for the Prince, notably more than 100 baryton trios over ten years. Beginning with with symphony no. 22 ('Philosopher', 1764) and continuing through the 1760s to

Haydn *The composer Joseph Haydn (1732–1809) in an engraving of c. 1792 by Luigi Schiavotti. One of the great composers who defined the universal style of Viennese Classical music, Haydn spent most of his creative life, however, in isolation at the estate of the Esterházy family in Hungary.*

no. 49 ('La Passione'), Haydn gained his maturity as a composer, showing inventiveness in each work. The first truly mature string quartets, the set of six op. 20 (1772) continue this developing mastery and were followed by the quartets op. 33 (1781), which include *The Joke* and *The Bird*; they were claimed to be written 'in a quite new and special manner'. In the set of op. 50 (1787) Haydn repays the debt which Mozart had acknowledged when dedicating his own quartets to the older composer.

Though he was isolated in Eszterháza his fame spread; his works were pub. abroad, and he received invitations to travel, which, however, his duties obliged him to refuse. In 1786 he was commissioned to compose six symphonies for the Concert de la Loge Olympique in Paris; these works are full of splendid invention and brilliant orchestral effects, declaring for the first time Haydn's genius to the world at large. On the death of Prince Nicolaus in 1790 the Esterházy musicians were disbanded and Haydn, though retaining his title and salary, was free to accept an invitation from the violinist and impresario J P Salomon to go to England. His first visit to London, 1791–92, for which he composed an opera (not produced) and six symphonies, was a great success, and was followed by another in 1794–95, for which a further six symphonies were written. The twelve London symphonies confirmed his reputation as the most original composer of the genre during his time. The wit, melodic inventiveness and densely woven developments of these works were matched in the great sets of string quartets between 1791 and 1797 (op. 64, op, 71, op. 74 and op. 76). In 1792 he received the honorary degree of Mus.D. at Oxford. On the accession of Prince Nicolaus II in 1795 the Esterházy music establishment was in part revived; but Haydn's duties were light, chiefly involving the composition of a Mass each year for the princess's name-day, and giving rise to the six great Masses of 1796–1802. Inspired by the works of Handel he had heard in London, he composed *The Creation* (1798) and *The Seasons*

A Selection of

Joseph Haydn

Symphony no. 48 .... *c* 1769
String Quartet op. 20 no. 5 1772
Symphony no. 86 1786
String Quartet op. 64 no. 5 1790

Symphony no. 99 1793
Symphony no. 104 1791–5
String Quartet, op. 76 no. 2 1797
Mass in D minor (*Nelson*) 1798
Die Schöpfung (*The Creation*) 1798
Die Jahreszeiten (*The Seasons*) 1801

(1801). From 1803 he composed little, living in retirement in Vienna.

In spite of huge advances made in the knowledge and performance of Haydn's music in recent years, the sheer range and quantity of his output may be intimidating, so that he still awaits wide recognition. Works (some still unpublished) include:

> *He is the master of us all.*
> **Joseph Haydn** on Handel, quoted in Headington,
> *The Bodley Head History of Music*, 1974

OPERAS: 20 works for the stage, of which seven are lost (all fps at Eszterháza, unless otherwise stated): *Acide*, festa teatrale (Eisenstadt, 1763), *La cantarina*, intermezzo (Eisenstadt, 1766), *Lo speziale*, dramma giocosa (1768), *Le pescatrici*, dramma giocosa (1770), *L'infedeltà delusa*, burletta (1773), *L'incontro improvviso*, dramma giocosa (1775), *Il mondo della luna*, dramma giocosa (1777), *La vera costanza*, dramma giocosa (1779), *L'isola disabitata*, azione teatrale (1779), *La fedeltà premiata*, dramma pastorale giocosa (1781), *Orlando Paladino*, dramma eroicomico (1782), *Armida*, dramma eroico (1784), *L'anima del filosofo* (now known by its alternative title of *Orfeo ed Euridice*. Written for London in 1791 but not performed; first known production Florence, 10 Jun 1951, with Callas and Christoff.) Marionette operas *Philemon und Baucis* (1773), *Hexen-Schabbas* (1773; lost), *Dido* (1776; lost), *Die Feuerbrunst* (1776), *Die Bestrafte Rachbegierde* (1779).

MASSES: 14: *Missa 'Rorate coeli desuper'* (1748), *Missa brevis* in F (1749), *Missa Cellensis*, *Cäcelienmesse* in C (1766), *Missa in honorem BVM*, *Grosse Orgelmesse*, in Eb (1771), *Missa Sancti Nicolai*, in G (1772), *Missa brevis* in Bb, *Kleine Orgelmesse* (1778), *Missa Cellensis*, *Mariazeller Messe* (1782), *Missa Sancti Bernardi* (*Heiligmesse*) Bb (1796), *Missa in tempore belli*, *Paukenmesse*, in C, (Vienna, 26 Dec 1796); Mass in D minor, *Nelson Mass* (Eisenstadt, 23 Sept 1798); Mass in Bb, *Theresienmesse* (1799); Mass in Bb, *Schöpfungsmesse* (Eisenstadt, 13 Sept 1801); Mass in Bb, *Harmonie-messe* (Eisenstadt, 8 Sept 1802). A fragment of the lost Mass *Sunt bona mixta malis*, (*c* 1769) was discovered in Ireland in 1983.

CANTATAS AND ORATORIOS: *Stabat Mater* (1767), *Applausus* (Zwettl, 17 Apr 1768), *Il ritorno di Tobia* (Vienna, 2 Apr 1775), *Die Sieben letzten Worte unseres Erlösers am Kreuze*, *Seven Last Words* (Vienna, 26 Mar 1796), *Die Schöpfung* (*The Creation*), (Vienna, 29 Apr 1798), *Die Jahreszeiten*, *The Seasons* (Vienna, 24 Apr 1801). Also Te Deum in C (1800).

SYMPHONIES: 104: nos 1–5 (1758–60); nos 6–8, *Le Matin*, *Le Midi*, *Le Soir* (1761); nos 9–21 (*c* 1762); no. 22 in Eb, *The Philosopher* (1764); nos 23–25 (1764); no. 26 in D minor, *Lamentatione* (1770); nos 27–29 (1765); no. 30 in C, *Alleluja* (1765); no. 31 in D, *Hornsignal* (1765); nos 32–42 (*c* 1768) no. 43 in Eb, *Mercury* (1772); no. 44 in E minor, *Trauersinfonie* (1772); no. 45 in F♯ minor *Farewell* (1772); no. 46 in B and no. 47 in G (1772); no. 48 in C, *Maria Theresa*, and no. 49 in F minor, *La Passione* (*c*. 1768); nos 50–52 (1773); no. 53 in D, *The Imperial* (1775); nos 54–59 (1774); no. 60 in C, *Il Distratto* (1774); nos 61–72 (*c* 1779); no. 73 in D, *La Chasse* (1782); nos 74–81 (1781–84); nos 82–87 *Paris Symphonies*; no. 82 in C, *The Bear*, no. 83 in G minor, *The Hen*, no. 84 in Eb, no. 85 in Bb, *La Reine*, no. 86 in D, no. 87 in A (1785–86); no. 88 in G, no. 89 in F, no. 90 in C, no. 91 in Eb (1787–8); no. 92 in G, *The Oxford* (1789); nos 93–104 *London Symphonies*: no. 93 in D, no. 94 in G, *The Surprise*, no. 95 in C minor, no. 96 in D, *The Miracle*, no. 97 in C, no. 98 in Db, no. 99 in Eb, no. 100 in G, *The Military*, no. 101 in D, *The Clock*, no. 102 in Bb, no. 103 in Eb, *The Drumroll*, no. 104 in D, *The London* (1791–95).

CONCERTOS: four for violin, in C, D, A, and G (1769–71); two for cello in C and D (1761 and 1783); organ concerto in C (1756); concerto for violin and harpsichord (1766); harpsichord concertos in F, G and D (1771–84); for trumpet in Eb (1796); Sinfonia concertante in Bb for oboe, violin, cello and bassoon (1792); five concertos for lire organizzate (*c* 1786); five concertos for oboe, flute, horn and bassoon are either lost or spurious.

STRING QUARTETS: The usually given number of 83 is incorrect; from this must be subtracted the set of six op. 3, now known to be by Romanus Hoffstetter, and the arrangement of *The Seven Last Words*, hitherto counted as seven separate quartets. Op. 1 nos 1–6 (*c* 1757); op. 2 nos 1, 2, 4 and 6 (*c* 1762); op. 9 nos. 1–6 (*c* 1771); op. 17 nos. 1–6 (*c* 1772), op. 20, nos 1–6, *Sun Quartets*: in Eb, C, G minor, D, F minor, A (1772); op. 33 nos. 1–6, *Russian Quartets*: in B minor, Eb (*The Joke*), C (*The Bird*), Bb, G D (1781); op. 42 in D minor (1785); op. 50 nos 1–6: in Bb, C, Eb, F♯ minor, F and D (*The Frog*) (1787); op. 54 nos 1–3: in G, C and E (1788); op. 55 nos 1–3: in A, F minor and Bb (1790); op. 64 nos 1–6: in C, B minor, Bb, G, D (*The Lark*) and Eb (1791); op. 71 nos 1–3: in Bb, D and Eb (1795); op. 74 nos 1–3: in C, F and G minor (*The Rider*) (1796); op. 76 nos 1–6: in G, D minor (*The Fifths*), C (*The Emperor*), Bb (*The Sunrise*), D, Eb (1797); op. 77 nos 1 and 2: in G and F (1802); op. 103 in D minor (1803).

OTHER INSTRUMENTAL: 32 piano trios, 126 baryton trios and other chamber music; 60 piano sonatas (1760–94), five sets of variations, for piano including F minor (1793); solo songs, part-songs, arrangements of Scottish and Welsh folksongs. 12 Canzonettas to English words for solo voice and piano including *My mother bids me bind my hair*, *Sailor's Song* and *She never told her love* (1794–95); Solo cantatas *Arianna a Naxos* (1789) and *Berenice che fai* (1795).

Haydn, (Johann) Michael (b Rohrau, Lower Austria, 14 Sept 1737; d Salzburg, 10 Aug 1806), Austrian composer, brother of Franz Joseph ◊Haydn. Chorister at St Stephen's Cathedral in Vienna under Reutter from *c* 1745. Appointed *Kapellmeister* to the Archbishop of Grosswardein (Hungary) 1757, and became *Konzertmeister* to the Archbishop of Salzburg in 1762, where he was cathedral organist from 1781. Apart from occasional visits to Vienna, he remained in Salzburg till his death, in 1801 refusing the post of vice-*Kapellmeister* (under his brother Joseph) to Prince Esterházy.

Works include 32 Masses including *Missa Hispanica* (1786), two Requiem Masses, including C minor Requiem, for Archbishop Sigismund, 1771, which influenced Mozart's Requiem, eight German Masses, six *Te Deum* settings, 117 Graduals, 45 Offertories, 27 Holy Week Responsories, etc.; opera *Andromeda e Perseo* (1787), German *Singspiele* and other music for the stage, oratorios; cantatas; 46 symphonies including one with a slow introduction by Mozart (K444: Mozart's '37th' symphony); five concertos; six string quintets; 11 string quartets; keyboard music.

'Haydn' Quartets the familiar name of Mozart's six string quartets dedicated to Haydn: G major, K387 (1782), D minor, K421 (1783), Eb major, K428 (1783), Bb major, K458 (1784), A major, K464 (1785), C major, K465 (1785).

'Haydn' Variations a set of variations by Brahms for orchestra, op. 56a, or for two pianos, op. 56b on a theme called the 'St Anthony Chorale' from a Divertimento for wind instruments, attributed formerly to Haydn, where it is also treated in variation form. Fp of the orchestral version, Vienna, 2 Nov 1873.

Hayes, Catherine (b Limerick, 25 Oct 1825; d London, 11 Aug 1861), Irish soprano. Studied under Antonio Sapio at Dublin, where she made her first appearance in 1840. Later she studied with Garcia in Paris and Ronconi at Milan, where she sang at La Scala in 1845 in *Linda di Chamounix*, after a debut at Marseilles as Bellini's Elvira. After many successes in Italy and Vienna, she first appeared in London in 1849, in operas by Ricci, Mercadante and Rossini.

Hayes, Philip (b Oxford, bap. 17 Apr 1738; d London, 19 Mar 1797), English organist and composer, son of William ◊Hayes. He succeeded his father as professor and organist at Magdalen College; edited many works by earlier composers, particularly Purcell and Boyce, and supervised Haydn's visit to Oxford in 1791. His works show some familiarity with symphonic style and include the oratorios *Prophecy* (1778), *The Judgement of Hermes* (1783), 16 psalms, about 50 anthems, the masque *Telemachus* (1763), 17 Odes including *Ode for St Cecilia's Day* (1779); glees and catches; keyboard concertos and sonatas. His extreme corpulence was responsible for his nickname 'Fill Chaise'.

Hayes, William (b Gloucester, bap. 26 Jan 1708; d Oxford, 27 Jul 1777),

English organist and composer, father of Phillip ◊Hayes. He was organist at Worcester Cathedral from 1731 and organist and master of the choristers at Magdalen College, Oxford, from 1734; professor 1742. He introduced many of Handel's works to Oxford, Bath and Winchester; his own works were indebted to Handel and include oratorios *The Fall of Jericho* and *David* (*c* 1776), 16 psalms, Te Deum in D, 20 anthems, masques *Circe* (1742), and *Peleus and Thetis*; Odes *When the fair consort* (1735), *Where shall the Muse* (1751), *O that some pensive Muse* (Ode to the memory of Handel, *c* 1760), *Ode on the Passions* (*c* 1760) and *Daughters of Beauty* (1773); six cantatas, concertos and trios.

Haym, Nicola Francesco (b Rome, 6 Jul 1678; d London, 11 Aug 1729), Italian cellist, librettist and composer of German descent. Went to London in 1702, and with Dieupart and Clayton was active in establishing Italian opera there. From 1713 wrote several libretti for Handel, including *Teseo*, *Radamisto*, *Giulio Cesare* and *Rodelinda*, also for Bononcini and Ariosti. His own works include a Latin oratorio and a serenata, anthem *The Lord is King*, two sets of trio sonatas.

Hayman, Richard (b Sandia, NM, 29 Jul 1951), American composer. Studied at Columbia University, later learned from Cage and Boulez. Early employment included renovating church organ pipes; also sold earplugs in the subway. In 1975 wrote *Dali*, commissioned by the artist and inscribed on a toothpick. *It is not here* was realized in Morse Code at the Museum of Modern Art, NY, 1974. Later works include *sleep whistle* (1975), which the composer performs while asleep in a store window, and *roll*, executed while lying down in the street and covered by Hindu bells. *Dreamsound* was performed at Berkeley, CA, in 1976.

Haymon, Cynthia (b Jacksonville, FL, 6 Sept 1958), American soprano. Debut season 1985, as Xanthe in the US fp of Strauss's *Liebe der Danae*, at Santa Fe, and title role in the premiere of Musgrave's *Harriet, the Woman Called Moses* (Norfolk, VA). European debut at Glyndebourne 1986, as Gershwin's Bess (repeated at CG, where she has also sung Mimi, and Liu on tour with the company to the Far East). Concerts include *Carmina Burana* (Detroit SO), the Brahms Requiem (under Masur) and Rossini's *Stabat Mater* (Tilson Thomas).

Hayne van Ghizeghem (b *c* 1445; d between 1472 and 1497), Franco-Flemish composer whose life is documented only for his years at the court of Burgundy, 1457–72. His entire surviving output is of French *chansons*, several of which were among the most successful of their age, including '*De tous biens plaine*', '*Allez regretz*' and '*Amours, amours*'.

Hayward, Marjorie (Olive) (b Greenwich, 14 Aug 1885; d London, 10 Jan 1953), English violinist. Studied with Sauret at the RAM and with Ševčik in Prague (1903–06). In 1924 she became violin professor at the RAM. She led the English String Quartet and the Virtuoso Quartet, also played in the English Ensemble Piano Quartet and the Kamaran Trio.

Head, Michael (Dewar) (b Eastbourne, 28 Jan 1900; d Cape Town, 24 Aug 1976), English singer, pianist and composer. Gave up the study of mechanical engineering for music, which he studied at the RAM in London, including composition under Corder. In 1927 he became piano professor there. He gave many song recitals and broadcasts, playing his own accompaniments, and toured widely in the Commonwealth.

Works include Tone Poem and Scherzo for orchestra; *Jabberwocky* (Lewis Carroll) for chorus; piano concerto; *c* 60 songs including cycles *Songs of the Countryside* (W H Davies), *Over the Rim of the Moon*, part-songs.

Heart's Assurance, The song cycle by Tippett for high voice and piano (poems by Sidney Keyes and Alun Lewis); commissioned by Peter Pears and performed by him and Britten in London on 7 May 1951.

Heath, John, English 16th-c. composer. His morning and communion services were printed by John Day (1560), but had already been in use in Edwardian times (*c* 1548). There is also an anthem and a part-song, and a keyboard piece in the Mulliner Book is almost certainly his. He

is not to be confused with his namesake of Rochester (d 1668), possibly his grandson, who wrote English church music.

Hebenstreit, Pantaleon (b Eisleben, 1667; d Dresden, 15 Nov 1750), German dulcimer player. At first a violinist and dancing-master at Leipzig, he made his name as a virtuoso on the dulcimer towards the end of the 17th c. and had such a success in Paris in 1705 that Louis XIV named his instrument after him, and it was long called 'Pantaleon'. In 1714 it was introduced into the court band at Dresden, with him as player.

'Hebrides' Overture (Mendelssohn.) ◊Fingal's Cave.

Heckel, Johann Adam (b Adorf, 14 Jul 1812; d Biebrich, 13 Apr 1877), German instrument-maker and founder (1831) of the family firm at Biebrich. Became the foremost German bassoon-maker, making many improvements to the instrument.

Heckel, Wolff (b Munich, *c* 1515; d *c* 1562), German lutenist and composer. His lutebook (including some pieces for two lutes) was pub. 1556 in Strasbourg.

Heckelclarina the name of a special instrument created by the firm of Heckel at Biberich for the playing of the shepherd's pipe part in Act III of Wagner's *Tristan*.

Heckelphone a double-reed instrument invented by the German instrument maker Wilhelm Heckel (1856–1909) in 1905. The standard type has a compass an octave lower than the oboe. There are also smaller members of the family.

Hedley, Arthur (b Dudley, Northumberland, 12 Nov 1905; d Birmingham, 8 Nov 1969), English writer on music. Studied at Durham University, In 1946 became correspondent of the Chopin Institute at Warsaw. Author of a book on Chopin and many articles. His collection of Chopin MSS and related material is in the Museo de Chopin, Majorca.

Hedmont, Charles (b Ontario, 24 Oct 1857; d London, 25 Apr 1940), Canadian tenor. Sang at Leipzig from 1882 as Max and in operas by Mozart. Sang with the Carl Rosa Co. from 1891 and at CG, in Wagner, from 1895; Loge in the *Ring*, with Clarence Whitehill as Wotan (1908).

Heger, Robert (b Strasbourg, 19 Aug 1886; d Munich, 14 Jan 1978), German conductor and composer. Studied at Zurich and Munich, Schillings being his chief master. He conducted opera in many German cities, also in Vienna and London; conducted the fp of Strauss's *Capriccio* in Britain at CG, 1953.

Works include operas *Ein Fest zu Haderslev*, *Der Bettler Namenlos* (from Homer's *Odyssey*, 1932), *Der verlorene Sohn* (1936), *Lady Hamilton* (1951); melodrama *Die Jüdin von Worms*; *Ein Friedenslied* for solo voices, chorus, orchestra and organ; three symphonies.

I occasionally play works by contemporary composers and for two reasons. First, to discourage the composer from writing any more, and secondly to remind myself how much I appreciate Beethoven.

Jascha Heifetz, *Life*, 1961

Heifetz, Jascha (b Vilna, 2 Feb 1901; d Los Angeles, 10 Dec 1987), Russian-American violinist. First played in public aged five, having learned from his father, and at the age of six played the Mendelssohn concerto. In 1910 he entered the St Petersburg Conservatory, soon becoming a pupil of Auer. In 1912 he played in Berlin to great acclaim. After the Revolution of 1917 he went to America, where his debut recital at Carnegie Hall was a major success. He made tours of England in 1920 and Palestine in 1926. He made important recordings in the 1930s, including trios with Feuermann and Rubinstein. After World War II chamber music came to replace solo concerts and he collaborated in recitals at LA and during the 1960s at Carnegie Hall. His perfect technique made him a respected teacher at UCLA. His complete recordings were issued on CD in 1994.

Heiligmesse *Holy Mass*, *Missa Sancti Bernardi von Offida*, in B♭, composed 1796 by Haydn as a companion to the *Missa in tempore belli/Mass in time of war*.

Heiller, Anton (b Vienna, 15 Sept 1923; d Vienna, 25 Mar 1979), Austrian composer and organist. After studying organ and composition privately, he entered the Vienna Conservatory 1941–42. In 1945 he was appointed professor of organ at the Vienna Academy of Music. In 1952 he won first prize at an international organ competition in Haarlem, Holland.

Works include *Symphonie Nordique*; *Psalmen-Kantate*; *Te Deum*; five Masses; *Tentatio Jesu* for soloists, chorus and two pianos (1952); toccata for two pianos; much organ music.

Heimchen am Herd, Das, *The Cricket on the Hearth*, opera by Goldmark (libretto by A M Willner, based on Dickens's story), produced Vienna, Opera, 21 Mar 1896. May is to marry Tackleton, owner of a doll factory, after her love Edward, a sailor, goes to sea. Edward returns and the two marry.

Heimkehr aus der Fremde, Die, *The Return from Abroad*, better known as *Son and Stranger*), operetta by Mendelssohn (libretto by K Klingemann), produced Leipzig, 10 Apr 1851. Kauz has to leave town in a hurry after he tries to impersonate the son of a magistrate.

Heine, Heinrich (1797–1856), German poet. ◊Brian (*Pilgrimage to Kevlaar*); ◊*Dichterliebe* (Schumann); ◊*Der Fliegende Holländer* (Wagner); ◊*Giselle* (Adam); ◊*Guglielmo Ratcliff* (Mascagni); *Wallfahrt nach Kevlaar* (◊Humperdinck); ◊*Liederkreis* (Schumann); ◊*Schwanengesang* (Schubert); ◊*William Ratcliff* (Cui). Six songs by Brahms, six by Schubert, 39 by Schumann.

Heinichen, Johann David (b Krössuln near Weissenfels, 17 Apr 1683; d Dresden, 16 Jul 1729), German composer and theorist. Pupil of Schelle and Kuhnau in Leipzig, first practised as a lawyer in Weissenfels, but in 1709 returned to Leipzig, as an opera composer. The following year he went to Italy to study, remaining there until 1716. In 1717 he was appointed *Kapellmeister* to the Elector of Saxony in Dresden, where he lived till his death. Wrote two important treatises on figured bass.

Works include operas, numerous Masses, motets and other church works, cantatas, symphonies, orchestral suites, solo and trio sonatas.

Heinlen, Paul (b Nuremberg, 11 Apr 1626; d Nuremberg, 6 Aug 1686), German organist, wind player and composer. Studied with a town musician at Nuremberg and 1646–49 in Italy. Appointed to various Nuremberg churches 1655–58, finishing as organist at St Sebald's Cathedral. Wrote church music and set many sacred poems by contemporary authors.

Heinö, Mikko (b Tampere, 18 May 1958), Finnish composer. Studied in Berlin, and at the Helsinki University, where he taught 1977–85; professor of musicology at University of Turku, from 1985. Works include five piano concertos, horn concerto, concerto for orchestra, *Brass Mass*, *Wind Pictures* for choir and orchestra. Books include *The Twelve Tone Age in Finnish Music* (1986) and *Postmodern Features in New Finnish Music* (1988).

Heinrich, Anthony Philip (b Krásný Búk, 11 Mar 1781; d New York, 3 May 1861), Bohemian-born American composer. His status in the history of American music is suggested by his nickname, 'Father Heinrich'. He emigrated to America 1810, settling first in Philadelphia then moving to Kentucky 1817; at Lexington he conducted a performance of a Beethoven symphony, claimed to be the first such in America. His first compositions date from 1818; they include the locally unprecedented collection of songs and violin and piano pieces titled *The Dawning of Music in Kentucky, or the Pleasures of Harmony in the Solitudes of Nature*. His orchestral music, often for huge forces and developing from models by Haydn and Beethoven, dates from 1831 with *Pushmataha, a venerable Chief of Western Tribe of Indians*; later such works include *The Treaty of William Penn with the Indians* (1834), *The Ornithological Combat of Kings* (1847) and *The Wildwood Troubadour* (1834–53). He visited Europe from 1827 and his *Ornithological* symphony was performed at Graz in 1836. Popular throughout the main US music centres of the time, New York, Boston and Philadelphia, he became known as the 'Beethoven of America'. Heinrich's experiences of the frontier included a deep awareness of American Indian music, and in *The Jubilee* (1841) a work for soloists, chorus and orchestra he depicts the story of the British colonists in America. Other works include *The War of the Elements and the Thundering of Niagra*, for orchestra (c 1845) and *A Chromatic Ramble of the Peregrine Harmonist*, for piano.

Heise, Peter Arnold (b Copenhagen, 11 Feb 1830; d Ny Taarback, 12 Sept 1879), Danish composer. Pupil of Berggreen at Copenhagen and Hauptmann at Leipzig.

Works include *Paschaens Datter* (1869) and *Drot og Marsk* (1878); incidental music for many plays, including Oehlenschläger's *Palnatoke* and Hauch's *Marsk Stig*; *Rusk Cantata* and cantata *Tornerose* (*Sleeping Beauty*); symphony; six string quartets; piano music.

Heldenleben, Ein, *A Hero's Life*, symphonic poem by R Strauss, composed autumn 1898. Fp Frankfurt, 3 Mar 1899. The work is autobiographical.

Helffer, Claude (b Paris, 18 Jun 1922), French pianist. He studied with Casadesus and Leibowitz; debut Paris 1948. He has toured widely since the 1960s and given many performances of works by Amy, Boulez, Ravel and Barraqué. Played under Berio at the 1989 Salzburg Festival. The complete piano works of Schoenberg and the Boulez sonatas are among his recordings.

Heliogabalus Imperator 'allegory for music' by Henze, after M Enzensberger; composed 1971–77, fp Chicago, 16 Nov 1972, conductor Solti.

Hellendaal, Pieter (b Rotterdam, bap. 1 Apr 1721; d Cambridge, 19 Apr 1799), Dutch violinist, composer and organist. After his family moved to Amsterdam during 1737 he studied with Tartini in Italy. He was active as a composer from 1744, and at Leiden between 1749 and 1751 attempted to establish himself as a musician. After moving to London in 1751 he obtained posts in Oxford and King's Lynn, finally moving to Cambridge in 1762; widely respected in East Anglia as musician and composer.

Works include sonatas for violin and basso continuo, concertos for strings (pub. Amsterdam, London and Cambridge), glees, vocal canons and catches (pub. London and Cambridge) and the cantata *Strephon and Myrtilla* (c 1785).

Hell is full of musical amateurs.
George Bernard Shaw, *Man and Superman*, 1902

Heller, Stephen (b Pest, 15 May 1813 or 1814; d Paris, 14 Jan 1888), Hungarian pianist and composer. Studied with Anton Halm in Vienna and made his first public appearance at Pest in his teens and later went on tour in Germany. He lived at Augsburg 1830–38 after a long illness, working quietly at composition, and settled in Paris 1838. He visited England in 1850 and 1862.

Works (nearly all for piano) include four sonatas, a very large number of studies, variations and fantasies on operatic tunes, five Tarantellas, Caprice on Schubert's *Trout*, several sets entitled *Im Walde*, *Promenades d'un solitaire* (after Rousseau's letters on botany), *Blumen-, Frucht- und Dornenstücke* (after Jean Paul, 1853), *Dans le bois*, *Nuits blanches*, etc. With Ernst he wrote violin and piano pieces entitled *Pensées fugitives*.

Helletsgruber, Luise (b Vienna 30 May 1901; d Vienna, 5 Jan 1967), Austrian soprano. She made her debut in Vienna in 1922 and sang there until 1942, often in the operas of Mozart. Salzburg 1928–37 as Cherubino, Donna Elvira, Liù and Zdenka. Glyndebourne 1934–38 as Dorabella, Cherubino and Donna Elvira.

Hellmesberger Austrian family of musicians:

1. Georg Hellmesberger (b Vienna, 24 Apr 1800; d Neuwaldegg, 16 Aug 1873), violinist, conductor and composer. Studied in Vienna and became in 1821 assistant teacher and in 1833 professor of the violin at the Conservatory; Joachim was among his pupils. In 1829 he was appointed conductor of the court Opera. Wrote many works for his instrument.

2. Joseph Hellmesberger (b Vienna, 23 Nov 1828; d Vienna, 24 Oct 1893), violinist and conductor, son and pupil of 1. Appeared as an infant prodigy and was appointed violin professor at the Conservatory in 1851, and conductor of the Gesellschaft concerts. He resigned the

latter post to Herbeck in 1859, but retained that of director of the Conservatory. He also held posts at the Opera and the court concerts, and led a string quartet from 1849 to 1887; gave fps of works by Schubert, Brahms and Bruckner.

3. Georg Hellmesberger (b Vienna, 27 Jan 1830; d Hanover, 12 Nov 1852), violinist and composer, brother of 2. Studied with his father and toured with him and his brother Joseph in Germany and England. In 1850 he was appointed leader of the opera orchestra at Hanover, where he wrote the operas *Die Bürgschaft* (after Schiller, produced Hanover 1851) and *Die beiden Königinnen*.

4. Joseph Hellmesberger (b Vienna, 9 Apr 1855; d Vienna, 26 Apr 1907), violinist and composer, son of 2. Pupil of his father, in whose quartet he played second violin until 1887, when he succeeded him as leader. Solo violinist at the Opera and court chapel and violin professor at the Conservatory from 1878. Appointed court *Kapell-meister* 1890; succeeded Mahler as conductor of VPO in 1901. Works include 22 operettas and six ballets.

Helm, Everett (b Minneapolis, 17 Jul 1913), American composer and writer. Studied at Harvard with Walter Piston, and later with Malipiero and Vaughan Williams. He has appeared widely as teacher and lecturer and has written books on Bartók (1965) and Liszt (1972).

Works include two piano concertos (1951, 1956); *Adam and Eve*, medieval adaptation (1951); *Le Roy fait battre tambour*, ballet (1956); *Sinfonia da camera* (1961); string quartets, woodwind quintet (1967).

Helmholtz, Hermann (Ludwig Ferdinand) von (b Potsdam, 31 Aug 1821; d Berlin, 8 Sept 1894), German scientist. After holding three professorships in physiology he turned to physics, of which he became professor at Berlin University in 1871. He specialized in the musical aspects of acoustics and in 1863 pub. his *Lehre von den Tonempfindungen als physiologische Grundlage für die Theorie der Musik* (translated by A J Ellis as *On the Sensations of Tone*).

Hely-Hutchinson, (Christian) Victor (b Cape Town, 26 Dec 1901; d London, 11 Mar 1947), English pianist and composer. Educated at Eton and Balliol College, Oxford, and became lecturer in music at Cape Town University in 1922. In 1926 he returned to England and joined the staff of the BBC, first in London and then as regional director of music at Birmingham, where he became professor of music at the university in 1934. He resigned in 1944 to take up the appointment of music director of the BBC.

Works include *A Carol Symphony* and variations for orchestra; piano quintet, string quartet; choral works; songs, including settings of Edward Lear; film music.

Heming, Percy (b Bristol, 6 Sept 1883; d London, 11 Jan 1956), English baritone. Studied at the RAM in London and early began to specialize in opera; joined the Beecham Opera Co. in 1915 and sang Amfortas, Scarpia and Ford. BNOC from 1922, SW from 1933. He sang a great variety of parts with great distinction.

hemiolia (or *hemiola*) Greek = lit. 'the proportion 3 : 2'; a simulated change of metre effected by the substitution of three beats where two

would be normal; e.g. by writing three minims instead of two dotted minims in a bar of 6–4, or over two bars of 3–4.

Hemmel, Sigmund (d 1564), German composer. He composed the first complete polyphonic metrical psalter in Germany (pub. Tübingen, 1569). He also wrote German and Latin sacred songs, and a Mass.

Hempel, Frieda (b Leipzig, 26 Jun 1885; d Berlin, 7 Oct 1955), German soprano. Studied at the Conservatories of Leipzig and Berlin, and made her first appearance at the Berlin Royal Opera in 1905 as Nicolai's Frau Fluth. London, CG, 1907; Drury Lane 1914 as Queen of Night and the Marschallin. She won worldwide fame and made her first appearance in NY as Marguerite de Valois, 1912; other roles included Euryanthe, Eva and Violetta. She settled in USA and pursued a concert career.

Hemsley, Thomas (b Coalville, 12 Apr 1927), English baritone. Debut Purcell's Aeneas, London 1951. Glyndebourne 1953–61 as Masetto, the Speaker, Don Fernando and Dr Reischmann in Henze's *Elegy for Young Lovers*. He sang with the EOG from 1955, sang Demetrius (1960) in the first production of *A Midsummer Night's Dream*, and appeared in Aachen, Düsseldorf and Zurich 1953–67. CG debut 1970, as Mangus in the fp of *The Knot Garden*; WNO 1977–85. He was heard in Bayreuth and London as Beckmesser and was a frequent recitalist.

Henderson, Roy (b Edinburgh, 4 Jul 1899), British baritone and teacher. He studied at the RAM and in 1925 was heard as Delius's Zarathustra. Stage debut CG 1928, as Donner. Glyndebourne 1934–39 as Figaro, Guglielmo, Papageno and Masetto. He continued to appear in concert and took part in the fps of Vaughan William's *Dona nobis pacem* (Huddersfield, 1936) and *Five Tudor Portraits* (Norwich, 1936). Kathleen Ferrier was among his pupils.

Henderson, W(illiam) J(ames) (b Newark, NJ, 4 Dec 1855; d New York, 5 Jun 1937), American music critic. After some general journalistic work he became music critic to the *New York Times* in 1887 and the *New York Sun* in 1902. In 1904 he was appointed lecturer at the Institute of Musical Art in NY. His books include studies of the history and practice of singing, aesthetics, the evolution of music, Wagner, early Italian opera, etc. He was a savage opponent of much modern music. He died by suicide.

Hendricks, Barbara (b Stephens, AR, 20 Nov 1948), American soprano. She studied at Juilliard and made her debut in the NY fp of Virgil Thomson's *Lord Byron* (1972). She sang Calisto at Glyndebourne in 1974 and the title role in *The Cunning Little Vixen* at Santa Fe the following year. Further opera engagements in Boston, Berlin and at Orange. CG 1982, as Nannetta. NY Met. debut 1986, as Strauss's Sophie. Sang Manon at Parma, 1991, Micaela at Orange, 1992. Other roles include Susanna, Pamina and Amor.

Henkemans, Hans (b The Hague, 23 Dec 1913), Dutch composer and pianist. Studied piano with Sigtenhorst-Meyer and composition with Pijper. Made his debut, aged 19, in his own piano concerto. He later studied medicine and for some time practised as a psychiatrist, before

Roy Henderson – singer

1   Bach: *St Matthew Passion*
    I consider this his greatest and most moving composition. It was my final concert as a singer.

2   Mozart: *Die Zauberflöte*/The Magic Flute
    Music of great charm and an example of six great arias using only three or four chords with their inversions and an occasional interrupted cadence. The overture is my favourite.

3   Mahler: *Um Mitternacht* (Ferrier/Walther)
    This shows the magnificence of Kathleen Ferrier's voice, and the last verse is most poignant in that respect. As she was my pupil, we studied it together.

4   Elgar: *The Apostles*
    My favourite Elgar work. It has such variety and I am sure has been neglected because it requires six soloists.

5   Vaughan Williams: Symphony no. 1 (*A Sea Symphony*)
    One of my favourite choral works, especially with Vaughan Williams himself conducting.

devoting himself entirely to music. He was a concert pianist until 1969.

Works include symphony; two piano concertos (1923, 1936); concertos for flute, violin, viola, harp; three string quartets; sonatas for cello, violin, two pianos.

Henrici, Christian Friedrich (known as Picander) (b Stolpen, near Dresden, 14 Jan 1700; d Leipzig, 10 May 1764), German poet and cantata librettist. After study in Wittenberg he moved to Leipzig in 1720. He was well known as a playwright and pub. five vols. of poems, under the title *Ernst schertzhafte und satyrische Gedichte*. From 1726 he was involved in a collaboration with Bach which resulted in the texts for the *St Matthew Passion*, *St Mark Passion* and part of the *Christmas Oratorio*. He also furnished libretti for many of Bach's occasional vocal works and some of the church cantatas.

Henry, Pierre (b Paris, 9 Dec 1927), French composer. Studied with Messiaen and Nadia Boulanger. Worked with Pierre Schaeffer at the Groupe de Recherche de Musique Concrète 1950–58. Founded private electro-acoustical studio at Apsome, 1958; collaborations with Schaeffer *Symphonie pour un homme seul* (1950) and opera *Orphée* (1953); also ballets *Haut Voltage* (1956), *Le Voyage* (1962), *Messe pour le temps présent* (1967) and *Nijinsky, clown de Dieu* (1971); *Messe de Liverpool* (1967), *Gymkhana* (1970), *Ceremony* (1970), *Futuriste I* (1975).

Henry IV (b Bolinbroke Castle, 3 Apr 1367; d Westminster, 20 Mar 1413), King of England 1399–1413. He is a less likely candidate than his son Henry V as composer of the pieces ascribed to 'Roy Henry' in the ◊Old Hall MS.

Henry V (b Monmouth, Aug 1387; d Bois de Vincennes, 31 Aug 1422), King of England, 1413–22. ◊Henry IV.

Henry VIII (b Greenwich, 28 Jun 1491; d Windsor, 28 Jan 1547), King of England, 1509–47. He composed or arranged several songs found in an MS (British Museum, Add. 31,922) dating from his reign, and a three-part motet *Quam pulchra es*.

Henry VIII opera by Saint-Saëns (libretto by L Détroyat and P A Silvestre, produced Paris, Opéra, 5 Mar 1883. Henry defies the Pope to marry Anne Boleyn.

Henschel, (Isidor) Georg (later George) (b Breslau, 18 Feb 1850; d Aviemore, Inverness, 10 Sept 1934), German (naturalized British) baritone, conductor, pianist and composer. Appeared as pianist in Berlin in 1862 and at Hirschberg as singer in 1866. After studying in Leipzig, where he sang Hans Sachs in a concert performance, and in Berlin, he appeared at the Lower Rhine Festival in 1874, sang Christus in *St Matthew Passion* under Brahms, 1875, and sang for the first time in England in 1877. He remained there until 1881, when he married the American soprano Lillian Bailey and became conductor of the new Boston SO. In 1884 he settled in London and organized various orchestral and choral concerts, also conducting the Scottish Orchestra 1893–95. His wife died 1901 and he married Amy Louis in 1907. He sang again, in England and on the Continent, often accompanying himself, until he gave his last recital in London in 1914, when he was knighted.

Works include operas *Friedrich der Schöne* and *Nubia* (produced Dresden, 1899); operetta *A Sea Change*; incidental music for Shakespeare's *Hamlet*; English Mass for eight voices, Te Deum, Stabat Mater (1894), Requiem (1901), Psalm cxxx, anthems; Festival March for orchestra; Ballade for violin and orchestra; string quartet in B♭ major; many piano works; numerous songs (some with orchestra).

Henschel, Jane (b Los Angeles, 1949), American mezzo. Studied at UCLA and sang Haydn's Berenice and Monteverdi's Ottavia at the 1977 Aspen Festival. European debut at Aachen (1977) and sang at Wuppertal and Dortmund as Schoeck's Penthesilea, Eboli, Amneris and Brangaene. CG debut as the Nurse in *Die Frau ohne Schatten* (1992) returning as Ulrica, and Fricka in *Die Walküre* (1994). Sang Birtwistle's Judy at Amsterdam (1993) and engaged as Cassandre in *Les Troyens* at La Scala, 1996. Glyndebourne debut 1994, as Baba the Turk, in *The Rake's Progress*.

Hensel, Heinrich (b Neustadt, 29 Oct 1874; d Hamburg, 23 Feb 1935), German tenor. He studied in Vienna and Frankfurt and sang at Freiburg i/B 1897–1900. In Karlsruhe he took part in the 1910 fp of Siegfried Wagner's *Banadietriech*; sang Loge under Wagner at Bayreuth 1911–12. Hamburg Opera 1912–29. New York and Chicago 1911–12 as Siegmund, Siegfried and Lohengrin. CG 1914, as the first stage Parsifal in Britain.

Henselt, Adolf von (b Schwabach, Bavaria, 9 May 1814; d Warmbrunn, Silesia, 10 Oct 1889), German pianist and composer. Pupil of Hummel at Weimar and Sechter in Vienna. He toured Germany 1836 and settled in St Petersburg in 1838. He was appointed court pianist and teacher to the Tsar's children.

Works include piano concerto in F minor, piano trio; much piano solo music, comprising two sets of Studies (e.g. *Si oiseau j'étais*), *Frühlingslied*, *Wiegenlied*, impromptu in C minor, *La Gondola*.

I have taken the decision that in my work I will embody all the difficulties and all the problems of contemporary bourgeois music, and that I will, however, try to transform these into something usable, into something that the masses can understand.

Hans Werner Henze, *Music and Politics*, 1982

Henze, Hans Werner (b Gütersloh, 1 Jul 1926), German composer. Studied with Fortner at Heidelberg and Leibowitz in Paris. He is influenced by Schoenberg, though not strictly a 12-note composer, and has also done much to further the ballet in Germany; in 1950–52 he was ballet adviser to the Wiesbaden Opera. He moved to Italy in 1953, and his music began to show a wider range of influences. From the late 1960s his works reflected current political trends; the opera *We Come to the River* (1976) and the ballet *Orpheus* (1980) were written in collaboration with Edward Bond. In recent years Henze has returned to the musical past, and has become increasingly lyrical and elaborate: his reconstruction of Monteverdi's *Il Ritorno di Ulisse* was staged at Salzburg 1985.

Works include STAGE WORKS: *Das Wundertheater*, opera for actors (Heidelberg, 1949; revised for singers and produced Frankfurt 1965), *Jack Pudding*, ballet (Wiesbaden, 1951), *Die schlafende Prinzessin*, ballet after Tchaikovsky (Essen, 1954), *Ein Landarzt*, radio opera after Kafka (1951; revised for stage 1965), *Boulevard Solitude*, opera after Prévost's novel *Manon Lescaut* (Hanover, 1952), *Der Idiot*, ballet after Dostoievsky (Berlin, 1952), *Das Ende einer Welt*, radio opera (1953; revised for stage 1965), *König Hirsch*, opera after Gozzi (Berlin, 1956; revised as *Il re Cervo* and produced Kassel, 1963), *Maratona*, ballet (Berlin, 1957), *Ondine*, ballet (London, 1958), *Der Prinz von Homburg*, opera after Kleist (Hamburg, 1960), *The Emperor's Nightingale*, pantomime after Andersen (Venice, 1959), *Elegy for Young Lovers*, chamber opera (Schwetzingen and Glyndebourne, 1961), *Der junge Lord*, comic opera (Berlin, 1965), *The Bassarids*, opera seria (Salzburg, 1966), *Moralities*, scenic cantatas after Aesop (Cincinnati, 1968), *La Cubana, oder ein Leben für die Kunst*, vaudeville (produced Munich, 1975), *We Come to the River*, actions for music (London, 1976), *Don Chisciotte*, opera after Paisiello (Montepulciano, 1976), *Orpheus*, ballet by Edward Bond (Stuttgart, 1979), *Pollicino*, fairy-tale opera (Montepulciano, 1980), *The English Cat*, chamber opera (Schwetzingen, 1983), *Il Ritorno di Ulisse in Patria*, realization of Monteverdi (Salzburg, 1985), *Das verratene Meer* opera (Berlin, 1990).

VOCAL MUSIC: *Whispers from Heavenly Death*, cantata after Whitman (1948), five *Neapolitan Songs* for baritone and orchestra (1956), *Nocturnes and Arias* for soprano and orchestra (1957), *Novae de Infinito Laudes*, cantata for soloists, chorus and orchestra, after Giordano Bruno, the early astronomer who was burned at the stake for his beliefs (1962), *Ariosi* for soprano, violin and orchestra after Tasso (1963), *Being Beauteous*, cantata after Rimbaud (1963), *Muses of Sicily*, for chorus, two pianos, wind and percussion (1966), *Versuch über Schweine* (*Essay on Pigs*, 1969), *Das Floss der Medusa*, oratorio to the memory of Ché Guevara (1968), *El Cimarrón*, for baritone and ensemble (1970), *Voices*, for mezzo, tenor and instruments (22 revolutionary texts; 1973), *Jephtha*, realization of Carissimi (1976), *The King of Harlem*, for mezzo and instruments after Lorca (1980), three Auden poems, for voice and piano (1983).

FOR ORCHESTRA: eight symphonies (1947–1993); two violin concertos (1948, 1978), two piano concertos (1950, 1967), *Ode to the West Wind* for cello and orchestra, after Shelley, *Sonata for Strings* (1958), *Three Dithyrambs* for chamber orchestra (1958), *Antifone* (1960), *Los Caprichos* (1963), *Doppio Concerto* for oboe, harp and strings (1966), *Telemanniana* (1967), *Heliogabalus Imperator* (1972), *Tristan* for piano, tape and orchestra (1973), *Aria de la folia española* (1977), *Il Vitalino raddopiato* for violin and chamber orchestra (1977), *Barcarola* (1979), *Orpheus*, scenes from the ballet (1980), *I sentimenti di C P E Bach* for flute, harp and strings (1982), *Le Miracle de la Rose* for clarinet and 13 instruments (1982), *Barcarola* (1983), guitar concerto (1986), *Sieben Liebeslieder* for cello and orchestra (1985), *12 Kleine Elegien* for Renaissance instruments (1986), *Allegro brillante* (1989), *Requiem* (nine spiritual concertos) for piano, trumpet and chamber orchestra (1992).

CHAMBER MUSIC: including five string quartets (1947–77), *Apollo et Hyazinthus* for mezzo and ensemble (1949), Wind quintet (1952), *Concerto per il Marigny* for piano and seven instruments (1956), *Royal Winter Music*, two sonatas for guitar on Shakespearean characters (1975–79), *L'Autumno* for wind quintet (1977), Sonata for viola and piano (1980), *Capriccio* for cello (1983), *Selbst- und Zwiegespräche* for viola, guitar and small organ (1985), Serenade for violin (1986), *Five Night Pieces* for violin and piano (1990).

KEYBOARD: piano sonata (1959), *Lucy Escott Variations* (1963), *Divertimenti* for two pianos (1964), *Euridice* for harpsichord (1990).

Heppner, Ben (b Murrayville, BC, 14 Jan 1956), Canadian tenor. Sang in operas by Mozart and Rossini at Toronto and re-emerged as a dramatic tenor at Melbourne in 1988, as Bacchus. Chicago, the same year, as Wagner's Walther, returning as McTeague in the fp of Bolcom's opera (1992). European debut at Stockholm 1989, as Lohengrin; CG and La Scala 1990, Walther. Sang Strauss's Emperor at Amsterdam, 1991. Recordings include Walther in *Die Meistersinger*, under Sawallisch (1994).

heptachord, from Greek, a scale of seven notes.

Herbeck, Johann (Franz) von (b Vienna, 25 Dec 1831; d Vienna, 28 Oct 1877), Austrian conductor and composer. Lived in Vienna; appointed conductor of the Gesellschaft concerts in 1859 and director of the Court Opera in 1871.

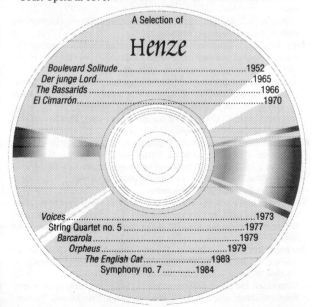

A Selection of

Henze

Boulevard Solitude	1952
Der junge Lord	1965
The Bassarids	1966
El Cimarrón	1970
Voices	1973
String Quartet no. 5	1977
Barcarola	1979
Orpheus	1979
The English Cat	1983
Symphony no. 7	1984

Works include seven Masses; four symphonies, symphonic variations and other orchestral music; three string quartets; songs, part-songs.

Herbert, Victor (b Dublin, 1 Feb 1859; d New York, 26 May 1924), Irish-American cellist, conductor and composer. Studied in Germany and toured Europe; settled in NY in 1886. Director of the Pittsburgh SO 1898–1904. The second of his two cello concertos (1894) inspired Dvořák to write his own cello concerto.

Works include operas *Natoma* (1911) and *Madeleine* (1914), operettas *The Wizard of the Nile* (1895), *Babes in Toyland* (1903) and over 30 others; cantata *The Captive*; symphonic poem *Hero and Leander* and three suites for orchestra; Serenade for strings; songs.

Herbig, Günther (b Ustí-nad-Labem, 30 Nov 1931), Czech-born German conductor. He studied in Weimar and was assistant to Scherchen and Karajan. Held posts in Erfurt, Weimar, Potsdam and East Berlin before becoming music director of Dresden PO 1972. Chief conductor East Berlin SO from 1977; guest conductor Dallas SO 1979–81, and was music director Detroit SO 1984–89; Toronto SO from 1989. Guest conductor BBC Philharmonic from 1980. Well known in Bruckner.

Herbst, Johann Andreas (b Nuremberg, 9 Jun 1588; d Frankfurt 24 Jan 1666), German composer. He was *Kapellmeister* at various places, including Darmstadt, Nuremberg and Frankfurt. Pub. four theoretical works.

Works include German and Latin madrigals; motets; settings of hymn-tunes, etc.

Hercules secular oratorio by Handel (libretto by T Broughton), produced London, King's Theatre, Haymarket, 5 Jan 1745.

Herder, Johann Gottfried von (1744–1803), German philosopher, philologist and author. J C F ◊Bach (*Brutus*, oratorios and cantatas); ◊Jensen (*Stimmen der Völker*); ◊Prometheus (Liszt); ◊Reichardt (*Morning Hymn*).

Herincx, Raimund (b London, 23 Aug 1927), English bass-baritone. Debut WNO 1950, as Mozart's Figaro. London, SW (later ENO) in almost 50 roles from 1953, including Nick Shadow, Germont and Wotan (1974–76). In 1968 he sang King Fisher in a new production of *The Midsummer Marriage*, at CG, and returned for the fps of *The Knot Garden* (1970) and *Taverner* (1972). US debut in Delius's *A Mass of Life* (NY 1966); US opera debut Boston, 1967. In the seasons 1973–74 he sang Pogner and Fafner at Salzburg, under Karajan. NY Met, debut 1977, in *Le Prophète*; sang as the White Abbot in the US fp of *Taverner*, Boston 1986.

Hermann, Roland (b Bochum, 17 Sept 1936), German baritone. Debut Trier, 1967, as Mozart's Figaro; member of Zurich opera from 1968 and guest appearances in Munich, Buenos Aires, Paris and Berlin. Among his best roles are Don Giovanni, Amfortas, Wolfram and Germont. He has a wide repertory and has recorded Busoni's *Doktor Faust*, Schumann's *Genoveva*, Marschner's *Vampyr*, Orff's *Prometheus* and Schoenberg's *Moses und Aron*. Created the Master in Höller's *Meister und Margarita*, Paris 1989.

Hermannus Contractus, Hermann the Cripple (b Sulgen, 18 Jul 1013; d Alleshausen, near Biberach, 24 Sept 1054), German music scholar and composer. Studied in Switzerland at the monastery of Reichenau and became a Benedictine monk. Wrote musical treatises and composed hymns, sequences, etc.

Hermann von Salzburg 14th-c. Austrian monk and composer. He belonged to the tradition of the *Minnesinger* but also wrote a few polyphonic pieces and a love song addressed to a lady acquaintance of the Archbishop of Salzburg.

Hermione opera by Bruch (libretto by E Hopffer, based on Shakespeare's *Winter's Tale*), produced Berlin, Opera, 21 Mar 1872.

Hernried, Robert (b Vienna, 22 Sept 1883; d Detroit, 3 Sept 1951), Austrian-born American scholar and composer. Studied in Vienna and after a career as opera conductor 1908–14 he held various teaching posts and professorships in Germany and the USA, where he emigrated 1934. In 1946 he was appointed professor at Detroit University. He wrote several books and over 300 articles.

Works include operas *Francesca da Rimini* (after Dante) and *The*

Peasant Woman; Mass; over 60 choral works; concert overture for orchestra; chamber music and songs.

Hero and Leander ◊Ero e Leandro.

Herodiade orchestral recitation by Hindemith, after Mallarmé; composed 1944, fp Washington DC, 30 Oct 1944, with the Martha Graham dance group.

Hérodiade, *Herodias*, opera by Massenet (libretto by P Milliet and 'Henri Grémont' (Georges Hartmann), based on a story by Flaubert), produced Brussels, Théâtre de la Monnaie, 19 Dec 1881. Salome, the abandoned daughter of Hérodiade, loves John the Baptist and kills herself rather than yield to Herod.

Hérold, (Louis Joseph) Ferdinand (b Paris, 28 Jan 1791; d Paris, 19 Jan 1833), French composer. Studied under his father, the pianist François Joseph Hérold (1755–1802), and later under Fétis, Louis Adam, Catel and Méhul, and took the Prix de Rome in 1812. In Rome and Naples, where he became pianist to Queen Caroline, he wrote several instrumental works, also a comic opera *La Jeunesse de Henri V*. Returning to Paris in 1816, he collaborated with Boieldieu in *Charles de France* and in 1817 began to produce operas of his own. He was accompanist at the Théâtre Italien 1820–27, when he married Adèle Élise Rollet and became choirmaster at the Opéra. About this time he began to suffer seriously from tuberculosis, from which he died. He is best known today for the ballet *La Fille mal gardée* (1828).

Works include operas *Les Rosières* (1817), *La Clochette* (1817), *Le Premier Venu*, *Les Troqueurs* (1819), *L'Amour platonique*, *L'Auteur mort et vivant* (1820), *Le Muletier* (1823), *Lasthénie*, *Le Lapin blanc*, *Vendôme en Espagne* (with Auber), *Le Roi René* (1824), *Marie*, *L'Illusion*, *Emmeline* (1829), *L'Auberge d'Auray* (with Carafa), *Zampa* (1831), *Le Pré aux Clercs* (1832), *Ludovic* (unfinished, completed by Halévy); ballets *Astolphe et Joconde* (1827), *Le Sonnambule* (1827), *Lydie*, *La Fille mal gardée*, *La Belle au bois dormant* (after Perrault); incidental music for Ozaneaux's *Dernier Jour de Missolonghi*; two symphonies; four piano concertos; cantata *Mlle de la Vallière*, *Hymne sur la Transfiguration*; three string quartets; two sonatas, variations, rondos, etc. for piano.

Heroldt, Johannes (b Jena, *c* 1550; d Weimar, buried 8 Sept 1603), German composer. His works include a setting of the *St Matthew Passion* for six voices, pub. Graz, 1594.

Hero's Life (R Strauss.) ◊Heldenleben.

Herreweghe, Philippe (b Ghent, 2 May 1947), Belgian conductor. Founded the Collegium Vocale of Ghent in 1969, for the performance of early music. Co-founded the Ensemble Vocal La Chapelle Royale (1977) and has collaborated with Ton Koopman, G Leonhardt, N Harnoncourt and the Kuijken brothers in such projects as the *Towards Bach* series, London 1989. Conductor of European Vocal Ensemble 1989 and led *Dido and Aeneas* at Brussels, 1992.

Herrmann, Bernard (b New York, 29 Jan 1911; d Los Angeles, 24 Dec 1975), American composer and conductor. After winning a composition prize at the age of 13, he began studying with Phillip James at NY University and later at the Juilliard Graduate School of Music. He then became a radio conductor with CBS, later living in Hollywood where he composed many film scores, in particular for Hitchcock and Orson Welles.

Works include opera *Wuthering Heights* (1948–50; produced Portland, OR, 1982), cantatas *Moby Dick*, *Johnny Appleseed*; symphonic poem *City of Brass*; *Fiddle Concerto*; symphony; string quartet; film scores including *Citizen Kane*, *Psycho* and *The Birds*. His last film music was for *Taxi Driver* (1976).

Herschel, Friedrich Wilhelm (b Hanover, 15 Nov 1738; d Slough, 25 Aug 1822), English astronomer and musician of German parentage. He played the oboe in the band of the Hanoverian Guards and in 1755 was posted to Durham. For the next 11 years he was active in Newcastle, Halifax and Leeds as an organist, violinist and composer of symphonies. He moved to Bath in 1766 and directed choral concerts. While earning his living as a musician he pursued a private interest in astronomy; his discovery of Uranus (1781) led to his appointment as Astronomer Royal, 1782. He now cultivated music only as an amateur. After his knighthood in 1817 he became in 1821

the first President of the Royal Astronomical Society. Works include 24 symphonies (1760–64), concertos for oboe, organ and violin; six fugues, 24 sonatas and 33 voluntaries for organ.

Such was his ardour for discovery, that in some benefit concerts, which he gave, he had his telescope fixed in the window, and was making his observations between the acts.
William Gardiner on Friedrich Wilhelm Herschel,
Music and Friends, 1838

Hertz, Alfred (b Frankfurt, 15 Jul 1872; d San Francisco, 17 Apr 1942), German-born American conductor. Conducted opera in Germany, then gave fp of *Parsifal* outside Bayreuth, NY Met. 1903; also conducted early US performances of Strauss. San Francisco SO 1915–29. Hollywood Bowl from 1922.

Hertzka, Emil (b Budapest, 3 Aug 1869; d Vienna, 9 May 1932), Hungarian-born Austrian music publisher. Studied chemistry at the University of Vienna, and also music. In 1901 he joined Universal Edition, founded that year, becoming director 1907 until his death. He did great service to modern music, publishing the work of such composers as Bartók, Berg, Krenek, Schoenberg, Webern, Weill and others. He also encouraged many other young composers. ◊Kalmus.

Hervé (real name Florimond Ronger) (b Houdain, Pas de Calais, 30 Jun 1825; d Paris, 3 Nov 1892), French composer. Studied music as a choirboy, then with Elwart and Auber. Organist at various Paris churches, including Saint-Eustache; later theatre manager, operetta singer, librettist, and conductor.

Works include more than 80 operettas, e.g. *Don Quixote et Sancho Pança* (after Cervantes, 1848), *Le Hussard persécuté*, *La Fanfare de Saint-Cloud*, *Les Chevaliers de la Table Ronde* (1866), *L'Œil crevé*, *Chilpéric*, *Le Petit Faust*, *Les Turcs* (parody of Racine's *Bajazet*, 1869), *La Belle Poule*, *Le Nouvel Aladin*, *Frivoli* (1886); ballets *Dilara*, *Sport*, *La Rose d'Amour*, *Cléopâtre*, *Les Bagatelles*; symphony *The Ashanti War* for solo voices and orchestra (1874); many light songs.

Herz, Henri (Heinrich) (b Vienna, 6 Jan 1803; d Paris, 5 Jan 1888), Austrian pianist and composer. Pupil of his father and of Hünten, entered the Paris Conservatory 1816 and settled there, becoming a fashionable teacher. Appointed piano professor at the Conservatory 1842. Toured USA, Mexico and the West Indies 1845–51, making a fortune with which to begin a piano manufacture, and built a concert hall.

Works include eight piano concertos and some 200 works for piano solo: variations, studies, fantasies.

Herz, Joachim (b Dresden, 14 Jun 1924), German producer and administrator. He was assistant to Felsenstein at the Komische Oper, Berlin 1953–56; returned as Intendant, 1976–81. Leipzig Opera 1957–76, and has worked as guest in Moscow, Hamburg and London: *Salome* and *Fidelio* with ENO; *Butterfly* with WNO 1979. His work is marked by strong beliefs in politics and in music theatre; *Parsifal* at the London Coliseum (Mar 1986) had mixed reviews. Director of productions at the Dresden Opera, 1981–90.

Herz, Das, *The Heart*, opera by Pfitzner (libretto by H Mahner-Mons); composed 1930–31, produced Berlin and Munich, 12 Nov 1931. Pfitzner's last opera. Dr Athanasius attempts the diabolic resuscitation of the Duke's dead son, but the price is his wife's heart. He is condemned for sorcery, but atones.

Herzgewächse work by Schoenberg for high soprano, celesta, harmonium and harp, op. 20; composed 1911: Schoenberg's last work before *Pierrot lunaire*. First British performance BBC concert, 1 Dec 1960.

Herzogenberg, Heinrich von (Baron H Peccaduc) (b Graz, 10 Jun 1843; d Wiesbaden, 9 Oct 1900), Austrian composer and conductor. Studied at the Vienna Conservatory and settled at Leipzig 1872. Conducted the Bach society there 1875–85 and then became professor of composition at the Berlin Hochschule für Musik. Husband of Elisabeth von Herzogenberg (1842–92), a fine amateur pianist and pupil of Brahms.

Works include Mass (1895), Requiem (1891), psalms; oratorios *Die Geburt Christi* and *Die Passion*, cantata *Columbus*; three symphonies, no. 1 entitled *Odysseus*; five string quartets (1876–90), two piano trios, two string trios; two violin and piano sonatas, cello and piano sonata; two sets of variations for two pianos, many piano pieces and duets; fantasies for organ; songs, vocal duets, part-songs.

Hesch, Wilhelm (b Týnec nad Labem, 3 Jul 1860; d Vienna, 4 Jan 1908), Czech bass. Debut Brno 1880, as Kecal; sang with Prague National Theatre from 1882 and joined the Hamburg Opera in 1894. Vienna, Hofoper, 1896–1908; often sang under Mahler as Beckmesser, Papageno, Leporello and Rocco.

Heseltine, Philip, ◊Warlock, Peter.

Hess, Myra (b London, 25 Feb 1890; d London, 25 Nov 1965), English pianist. Studied at the RAM with Matthay, making her debut 1907 under Beecham in London. Her success was immediate and she toured widely. In 1941 she received the DBE for her work in organizing the National Gallery wartime concerts. She was especially noted for her playing of Mozart, Beethoven and Schumann, and her own Bach transcriptions.

Hess, Willy (b Mannheim, 14 Jul 1859; d Berlin, 17 Feb 1939), German violinist. Studied with his father, a pupil of Spohr, was taken to USA as a child, played in T Thomas's orchestra there and made his first appearance as a soloist in Holland in 1872. Later studied with Joachim in Berlin, became professor at Rotterdam, leader of the Hallé Orchestra at Manchester, and worked by turns at Cologne, London, Boston and Berlin. Led the Boston SO 1904–10.

Hessenberg, Kurt (b Frankfurt, 17 Aug 1908), German composer. Studied with Günther Raphael at Leipzig and then taught composition there. In 1933 he became professor of composition at the Hoch Conservatory at Frankfurt.

Works include incidental music for Shakespeare's *Tempest*; cantata (Matthias Claudius) and other choral works; three symphonies (1935–54), *Concerto grosso*, etc. for orchestra; harpsichord and piano concertos; five string quartets, piano quartet; two violin sonatas, cello sonata; piano music, songs, etc. His Concerto Grosso and second symphony were premiered by Furtwängler.

heterophony from Greek = 'other sound'; the use of two parts to be simultaneously performed in different versions, one more elaborate than the other.

Heuberger, Richard (Franz Josef) (b Graz, 18 Jun 1850; d Vienna, 28 Oct 1914), Austrian music critic and composer. Studied engineering at first, but at the age of 26 devoted himself to music, becoming a choral conductor in 1878 and a critic in 1881. His best-known work is *Der Opernball/Ball at the Opera House*

Works include operas *Abenteuer einer Neujahrsnacht* (1896), *Manuel Venegas* (1889), *Miriam* (later *Das Maifest* 1894), *Barfüssele*; operettas *Der Opernball* (1898), *Ihre Excellenz*, *Der Sechsuhrzug*, *Das Baby*, *Der Fürst von Düsterstein*, *Don Quixotte* (after Cervantes); ballets *Die Lautenschlägerin* and *Struwwelpeter*.

Heugel, Johannes (Heigel, Hegel, etc.) (b Degendorf, before 1500; d Kassel, c 1585), German composer. He wrote many Latin motets.

Heure espagnole, L', *The Spanish Hour*, opera in one act by Ravel (libretto by Franc-Nohain, based on his own comedy), produced Paris, Opéra-Comique, 19 May 1911. Mule-driver Ramiro and poet Gonzalve keep good time with clockmaker's wife Concepción.

Heward, Leslie (Hays) (b Liversedge, Yorks, 8 Dec 1897; d Birmingham, 3 May 1943), English conductor. In 1924 he went to Cape Town as music director to the South African Broadcasting Corporation and conductor of the Cape Town Orchestra, but returned to England 1927 and rejoined the BNOC. In 1930 he succeeded Boult as conductor of the CBSO and gave frequent performances of Dvořák and Sibelius; premiere of Moeran's Symphony in G minor.

hexachord, from Greek = six strings, a scale of six notes, which Guido d'Arezzo in the 11th c. named Ut, Re, Mi, Fa, Sol, La. There were three hexachords, beginning respectively on G, C and F, and the same names were used for the notes of each. Since the hexachords overlapped, every note after the first three could have two or more names.

The G hexachord was called hard (*durum*), the C natural (*naturale*) and the F soft (*molle*). (*Durum* and *molle* are the origins of the German words for major and minor.) ◊solmization.

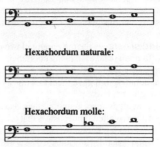

The three hexachords on G, C, and F respectively.

hexachord fantasy a type of composition cultivated particularly by 16th–17th-c. English composers, a piece based on the first six notes of the scale, ascending or descending. The pieces were often entitled 'Ut, re, mi, fa, sol, la'.

Hexameron a collective piano work, pub. in 1837, consisting of bravura variations on the march in Bellini's *Puritani* by Liszt, Thalberg, Pixis, Herz, Czerny and Chopin, with an introduction, finale and connecting passages by Liszt.

hey an old country dance similar to the ◊reel and probably to the ◊canary.

Heyden, Sebald (b Bruck, near Erlangen, 8 Dec 1499; d Nuremberg, 9 Jul 1561), German theologian and music theorist. He is particularly valuable for his explanations of the musical notation of his time.

Heyns, Cornelius, Flemish 15th-c. composer. He was succentor at St Donatian in Bruges in 1452–53 and 1462–65. His Mass *Pour quelque paine* has also been attributed to Ockeghem.

Heyse, Paul (Johann Ludwig) (1830–1914), German poet and novelist. ◊Italienisches Liederbuch (H Wolf); ◊Jensen (*Spanisches Liederbuch*); ◊Spanisches Liederbuch (H Wolf).

Heyther (Heather), William (b Harmondsworth, c 1563; d Jul 1627), English singer, from 1586 to 1615 at Westminster Abbey and from 1615 in the Chapel Royal. He founded the chair of music at Oxford University in Feb 1627 and presented the Music School with instruments and music.

Heywood, John (b ? London, 1497; d ? Mechlin, 1587), English musician. He was 'player of the virginals' to Henry VIII, succentor of St Paul's Cathedral and a friend of Thomas Mulliner. He was also a playwright and may have collaborated with Redford in the production of music plays. After the death of Mary in 1558 he fled to Mechlin on account of his Catholicism.

Hiawatha three cantatas for solo voices, chorus and orchestra by Coleridge-Taylor, a setting of parts of Longfellow's poem: 1. *Hiawatha's Wedding Feast*, 2. *The Death of Minnehaha*, 3. *Hiawatha's Departure*, fp as a whole, London, 22 Mar 1900.

Hickox, Richard (b Stokenchurch, Bucks., 5 Mar 1948), English conductor. He was an organ scholar at Cambridge and studied at the RCM; founded the Richard Hickox Singers, giving concerts with a wide range of repertory. He has worked with the City of London Sinfonia and the Northern Sinfonia (Newcastle). In 1983 became assistant conductor of the San Diego SO and assistant to Abbado at the LSO (associate conductor from 1985). Artistic director of Northern Sinfonia 1982–90. Co-founded Collegium Musicum, 1990 (Baroque concerts and recordings). Performances of *Alcina* and *Poppea* at the City of London Festival 1985 and 1988 (also recorded). Conducted *Troilus and Cressida* at CG, *Russalka* for ENO, 1995. Recorded the Vaughan Williams symphonies with the Bournemouth SO, 1995.

Hidalgo, Elvira de (b Aragón, 27 Dec 1892; d Milan, 21 Jan 1980), Spanish soprano. Debut Naples 1908, NY Met. 1910, as Rosina; sang

Gilda there and at CG in 1924. Taught in Athens from 1932; Maria Callas was among her pupils.

Hidalgo, Juan (d Madrid, 30 Mar 1685), Spanish composer. Harpist in the royal chapel at Madrid. Said to have invented an instrument called the *claviharpa*.

Works include operas *Celos aun del aire matan* (libretto by Calderón, 1660), and *Los celos hacen estrellas* (libretto by Guevara); incidental music to various plays by Calderón including *Ni Amor se libra de Amor*.

hidden fifths, hidden octaves the movement of two parts in the same direction to a fifth or an octave. In many contrapuntal styles this is to be avoided, especially when involving the top or bottom line. Textbooks in formal counterpoint gave them this title as having an effect similar to that of consecutives.

Highland fling a Scottish dance-step, rather than a dance itself, although that is often so called. The music is that of the Strathspey and the step is a kick of the leg backwards and forwards.

Hignard, (Jean Louis) Aristide (b Nantes, 20 May 1822; d Vernon, 20 Mar 1898), French composer. Pupil of Halévy at the Paris Conservatory, where he gained the second Prix de Rome in 1850.

Works include operas *Hamlet* (after Shakespeare; composed 1868 but not produced until 1888, owing to success of Thomas' *Hamlet*), *Le Colin-Maillard*, *Les Compagnons de la Marjolaine* and *L'Auberge des Ardennes* (all on libretti by Jules Verne and Michael Carrol) and eight others; choruses; *Valses concertantes* and *Valses romantiques* for piano duet; songs.

We are no longer the prisoners of the key.
Paul Hindemith, *The Craft of Musical Composition*,
1937

Hildegard, Saint, also known as 'Hildegard of Bingen' (b Böckelheim, 1098; d Rupertsberg, near Bingen, 17 Sept 1179), German abbess and musician. Educated at the Benedictine nunnery of Disisbodenberg, where she became abbess in 1136. She wrote monophonic music for the church which shows some departures from traditional plainsong style. She wrote music to her own poetry from 1140, collected in the 1150s as *Symphonia armonie celestium revelationum* (77 poems based on the liturgical calendar). The morality play *Ordo virtutum* concerns the struggle of virtue against the devil and contains 82 melodies.

Hill, Alfred (b Melbourne, 16 Nov 1870; d Sydney, 30 Oct 1960), Australian composer, conductor and teacher. His early career was in Leipzig; moved to New Zealand 1902 and became influenced by Maori music. Professor, NSW Conservatory, 1915–35.

Works include eight operas, e.g. *Tapu* (1903), *A Moorish Maid* (1905), *Giovanni, the Sculptor* (1914); ten symphonies (1896–1958); 17 string quartets, six sonatas for violin and piano.

Hill, Joseph (1715; d London, 1784), English violin maker. He worked in London. The house of his descendants W E Hill and Sons is now in Great Missenden.

Hillebrecht, Hildegard (b Hanover, 26 Nov 1927), German soprano. Debut Freiburg i/B 1951, as the *Trovatore* Leonora; she sang in Berlin from 1954 and in 1968 took part in the fp of Dallapiccola's *Ulisse* there. Munich from 1961 and Zurich from 1972, as the Marschallin, Ariadne and Leonore. CG 1967 as the Empress. Other roles included Tosca, Donna Anna and the Duchess of Parma in *Doktor Faust*.

Hillemacher, Paul (Joseph Wilhelm) (b Paris, 29 Nov 1852; d Versailles, 13 Aug 1933), and ***Lucien (Joseph Édouard)*** (b Paris, 10 Jun 1860; d Paris, 2 Jun 1909), French composers, brothers who wrote all their works in collaboration. Studied at the Paris Conservatory, where Paul gained the Prix de Rome in 1876 and Lucien in 1880.

Works include operas *Saint-Mégrin* (1886), *La Légende de Sainte Geneviève*, *Une Aventure d'Arlequin* (1888), *Le Régiment qui passe* (1894), *Le Drac*, *Orsola*, *Circé* (1907); mimed dramas *One for Two* and *Fra Angelico*; incidental music for Haraucourt's *Héro et Léandre*

and for George Sand's *Claudie*; symphonic legend *Loreley* and other orchestral works; chamber music, songs, part-songs.

Hiller, Ferdinand (b Frankfurt, 24 Oct 1811; d Cologne, 11 May 1885), German pianist, conductor and composer. Was taught music privately as a child and appeared as pianist at the age of ten. In 1825 he went to Weimar to study under Hummel. After a brief return to Frankfurt he lived in Paris 1828–35, where he taught and gave concerts. He produced his first opera at Milan in 1839 and his first oratorio at Leipzig in 1840, then studied with Baini in Rome, lived at Frankfurt, Leipzig and Dresden, became conductor at Düsseldorf 1847 and at Cologne 1850, where he remained and founded the Conservatory.

Works include operas *Romilda* (1839), *Die Katakomben* (1862), *Der Deserteur* (1865); oratorios *Die Zerstörung Jerusalems* (1840) and *Saul*; cantatas *Nala und Damajanti*, *Prometheus*, *Rebecca* and others, including one from Byron's *Hebrew Melodies*; four symphonies, four overtures (e.g. to Schiller's *Demetrius*) and other orchestral works; two piano concertos (1835, 1861), violin concerto (1875); three string quartets, three piano quartets, five piano trios; violin and cello sonata; sonata, 24 studies, *Modern Suite* and many other works for piano; songs, part-songs.

Hiller, Johann Adam (b Wendisch-Ossig near Görlitz, 25 Dec 1728; d Leipzig, 16 Jun 1804), German composer. Chorister under Homilius in Dresden, studied law at Leipzig University After a short period in the service of Count Brühl, he returned to Leipzig, working as flautist, singer, conductor, etc. In 1763 he founded subscription concerts on the model of the Paris Concert Spirituel, these becoming the Gewandhaus concerts in 1781. He also produced a musical weekly (*Wöchentliche Nachrichten*, 1766–70) and was one of the originators of the German *Singspiel*, of which he wrote many successful examples, 1766–82. Left Leipzig in 1785, but after some short-term posts returned to succeed Doles as municipal music director and Cantor of St Thomas's.

Works include *Singspiele*: *Der Teufel ist los* (after Coffey's *The Devil to Pay*, 1766), *Lisuart und Dariolette*, *Lottchen am Hofe* (1767), *Die Muse*, *Die Liebe auf dem Lande* (1768), *Die Jagd*, *Der Dorfbalbier* (1771), *Der Aerndtekranz*, *Der Krieg* (1772), *Die Jubelhochzeit*, *Das Grab des Mufti*, *Das gerettete Troja*; settings of Gellert's odes and other choral works; cantatas; 100th Psalm; instrumental music; also many theoretical and critical writings on music.

Hiller, Lejaren (b New York, 23 Feb 1924), American composer. Learned from Sessions and Babbitt and co-created the first computer composition (*Illiac Suite*, 1957). Directed the experimental music studio at University of Illinois (1958–68); Professor of music at

---

Hindemith
A biographical note

Hindemith sought to make his music accessible to the masses, but history, in the form of Nazi ideology, was against him. After gaining an early reputation as an iconoclast – the 1929 opera *Neues vom Tage* featured a soprano naked in a bath tub – Hindemith worked towards respectability, notably in his practical and undemanding instrumental music. But Nazi officials had long memories, and after they came to power in 1933 there was a drive to label Hindemith with the standard fatwah of Cultural Bolshevism. Matters came to a head with the 1934 premiere of the symphony *Mathis der Maler*, under Wilhelm Furtwängler. In spite of dealing with an episode from German history in music of impeccable diatonism, increasing pressure was placed on Hindemith and those linked with him. Furtwängler, Hitler's favourite conductor, felt obliged to resign his post – at least for the time being. Minister of Propaganda Josef Goebbels now felt free to attack Hindemith openly: 'Opportunity creates not only thieves but also atonal [sic] musicians, who in their eagerness to make a sensation exhibit naked women in a bathtub in the most disgusting and obscene situations.' Hindemith emigrated to the United States shortly before the outbreak of World War II.

SUNY, Buffalo, from 1968. Works include: two symphonies (1953, 1960), piano concerto (1949), seven string quartets (1949–79), six piano sonatas (1946–72); *Computer Cantata* (1963), seven *Electronic Studies* (1963), *Rage over the Lost Beethoven* (1972); *The Fox Trots Again*, for chamber orchestra (1985). Collaborated with Cage on *HPSCHD* for 1–7 harpsichords and 1–51 tapes (1968).

Hillier, Paul (Douglas) (b Dorchester, 9 Feb 1949), English bass, writer and conductor. Studied at GSMD and was Vicar-Choral at St Paul's Cathedral, 1973–74. Co-founded and directed the Hillier Ensemble 1974–90, for the performance of late medieval and Renaissance music with an ensemble of four male voices. Professor of music at the University of California at Davis, from 1990.

Hilton, John (1) (d Cambridge, Mar 1608), English organist and composer. Appointed organist to Trinity College, Cambridge, in 1594. Composed anthems, madrigals, etc.

Hilton, John (2) (b ? Oxford, 1599; d Westminster, buried 21 Mar 1657), English organist and composer, (?) son of John ◊Hilton (1). Took the Mus. B. degree at Cambridge in 1626 and two years later became organist at St Margaret's Church, Westminster.

Works include services and anthems; madrigals, *Ayres, or Fa La's* for three voices (pub. 1627; the last English madrigal publication); *Elegy on the death of Wm Lawes* for three voices and bass; collection of catches, rounds and canons *Catch that catch can* (1652); songs, fantasies for viols, hymn 'Wilt Thou forgive that sin where I begun' from Donne's *Divine Poems*.

Himmel, Friedrich Heinrich (b Truenbrietzen, Brandenburg, 20 Nov 1765; d Berlin 8 Jun 1814), German harpsichordist, pianist and composer. Read theology at Halle University, but later under the patronage of Frederick William II of Prussia studied music at Dresden under Naumann and in Italy, where he produced two operas. Appointed court *Kapellmeister* in Berlin in 1795, he was still able to travel and visited Russia, Scandinavia, Paris, London and Vienna.

Works include operas *Il primo navigatore* (1794), *La morte di Semiramide* (1795), *Alessandro* (1799), *Vasco da Gama* (1801), *Frohsinn und Schwärmerei*, *Fauchon das Leyermädchen* (1804), *Die Sylphen*, *Der Kobold* (1813), oratorio *Isacco*; funeral cantata for the King of Prussia; Masses, Te Deum, motets, psalms and other church music; instrumental music, songs.

Hindemith, Paul (b Hanau, 16 Nov 1895; d Frankfurt, 28 Dec 1963), German composer. He was taught the violin as a child and entered the Hoch Conservatory at Frankfurt, where he studied under Arnold Mendelssohn and Sekles. Later he played in the Frankfurt Opera orchestra and was leader there 1915–23; in 1921 he founded a string

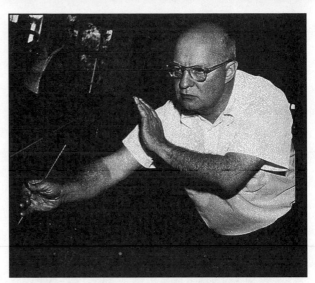

Hindemith *The composer Paul Hindemith (1895–1963) shown here in his role as conductor, rehearsing for a performance of Beethoven's 9th Symphony at Bayreuth in 1953. Hindemith made his mark in all areas: as pedagogue, performer and composer of his own theoretically grounded kind of tonal music.*

quartet with the Turkish violinist Licco Amar (Amar-Hindemith quartet) in which he played viola. The quartet was disbanded 1929, the year in which he premiered Walton's viola concerto in London. Works of his were heard at the Donaueschingen festival in 1921 and at the ISCM festival at Salzburg in 1922. His one-act operas of 1921–22 scandalized audiences and some musicians, and he had an early reputation as an iconoclast. His Kammermusik series, begun in 1922, sought to re-establish the musical values of the Baroque concertos; the opera *Cardillac* (1926) uses neo-classical forms, although its story of a goldsmith who murders his clients to regain his work recalls the savagery of his early pieces for the stage.

From 1927 he taught composition at the Berlin Hochschule für Musik, and his music was conducted by Furtwängler and Klemperer, but the Nazis proscribed his works as degenerate art (◊Neues vom Tage). His opera *Mathis der Maler* was therefore produced in Switzerland, at Zurich, in 1938; a three-movement symphony from the opera was premiered at Berlin in 1934 by Fürtwangler, prompting a temporary break with the Nazi authorities. For some years after 1933 he was at Ankara in an official capacity to reorganize Turkish music education. In 1939 he emigrated to USA, where he taught at Yale University, but in 1946 he returned to Europe and was active for several years as a conductor. In his late, largely orchestral works, Hindemith sought further to establish the values of tonality and Classical restraint. The vision of astronomer Johannes Kepler in his last opera, *Die Harmonie der Welt*, suggests the composer himself striving to hear the sounds emitted by the planets as they circle the sun, oblivious to the harsher musical realities around him.

Works include OPERAS: *Mörder, Hoffnung der Frauen* (Kokoschka, 1921), *Das Nusch-Nuschi* (for Marionettes), *Sancta Susanna* (1922), *Cardillac* (after E T A Hoffmann, 1926), *Hin und Zurück* (1927), *Neues vom Tage* (1929), *Mathis der Maler* (1938), *Harmonie der Welt* (1957), *The Long Christmas Dinner* (1961); ballets *Der Dämon* (1923), *Nobilissima Visione* (1938), *Cupid and Psyche*, *Hérodiade* (after Mallarmé, 1944); incidental music for Christmas play on Immermann's *Tuttifänchen* (1922); *Wir bauen eine Stadt/Let's build a town*, children's opera (1930); realization of Monteverdi's *Orfeo* (1943).

ORCHESTRAL: *Lustige Sinfonietta* (1916), *Kammermusik* nos. 1–7 (1922–27; see separate entry), *Concerto for Orchestra* (1925), *Konzertmusik* nos. 1–3, with viola, with piano, brass and two harps, with

A Selection of

Hindemith

Kammermusik	1922–7
Cardillac	1926
Concert Music for brass and strings	1930
Der Schwandendreher	1935
Mathis der Maler	1938
Nobilissima Visione	1938
The Four Temperaments	1940
Cello Concerto	1940
Symphonic Metamorphosis	1943
Requiem	1946

brass and strings (1930), *Konzertstück* for trautonium and strings (1931), *Philharmonisches Konzert* (1932), *Mathis der Maler*, symphony from the opera (1934), *Der Schwanendreher*, concerto after folksongs, for viola and small orchestra (1935), *Trauermusik* for viola and strings (1936), *Symphonische Tänze* (1937), *Nobilissima Visione*, suite from the ballet (1938), violin concerto (1939), cello concerto (1940), Symphony in E♭ (1940), *Theme and Variations 'The Four Temperaments'* for piano and strings (1940), *Cupid and Psyche*, ballet overture (1943), *Symphonic Metamorphosis on Themes of Carl Maria von Weber* (1943), piano concerto (1943), *Symphonia Serena* (1946), clarinet concerto (1947), horn concerto (1949), Sinfonietta, in E (1950), Symphony in B♭ for concert band (1951), *Die Harmonie der Welt*, symphony from the opera (1951), *Pittsburgh Symphony* (1958), organ concerto (1962).

CHAMBER AND KEYBOARD: six string quartets (1918–45); two string trios (1924, 1933); 16 sonatas for various instruments; some pieces for solo instruments and piano; three sonatas, *1922 Suite, Ludus tonalis*: 12 fugues with prelude and postlude, and some other works for piano; seven waltzes for piano duet (unpublished); sonata for two pianos; three organ sonatas. ◊Gebrauchsmusik.

CHORAL AND SOLO VOCAL: *Die junge Magd*, six songs for mezzo, flute, clarinet and string quartet (texts by Trakl, 1922), *Das Marienleben*, 15 songs for soprano and piano (texts by Rilke, 1922–23; revised 1948; version with orchestra 1938 and 1948), *Die Serenaden*, cantata for soprano, oboe, viola and cello (1924), *Lehrstück*, cantata to texts by Brecht for soloists, chorus and orchestra (1929), *Das Unaufhörliche/The Unending*, oratorio for soloists, chorus and orchestra (1931), Requiem, after Walt Whitman, *When Lilacs Last in the Dooryard Bloom'd* (1946), *Ite, angeli veloces/Go, flights of angels*, cantata to texts by Paul Claudel in three parts: *Triumphgesang Davids, Custos, quid de nocte* and *Cantique de l'esperance* (1953), *Mainzer Umzung* for soloists, chorus and orchestra (1962), Mass for unaccompanied chorus (1963); many other works for chorus, including canons, chansons, motets and madrigals; Lieder and *Nine English Songs* (1942–44; texts by Moore, Thompson, Shelley, Blake, Whitman and Herrick).

Hines, Jerome (b Hollywood, 8 Nov 1921), American bass and composer. Debut 1941 San Francisco, in *Tannhäuser*. Méphistophélès in New Orleans 1944; Boris Godunov at the NY Met. 1954 and sang the role at the Bolshoi, Moscow, 1962. Bayreuth 1958–60 as Gurnemanz, King Marke and the *Walküre* Wotan. Other roles include Sarastro, Don Giovanni, Nick Shadow (Edinburgh, 1953), and Rossini's Basilio. Pub. autobiography 1968 and *Great Singers on Great Singing* 1983. His own opera, *I am the Way*, is based on the life of Christ.

Hingston, John (b ? York, c 1610; d London, buried 17 Dec 1688), English organist, violinist and composer. Pupil of O Gibbons. Musician to Charles I and later to Cromwell, in whose household he was organist at Hampton Court and played on the organ removed from Magdalen College, Oxford. He taught Cromwell's daughters. At the Restoration in 1660 he became violinist in the royal band and keeper of the organs at court, in which he was succeeded by Purcell.

Hin und Zurück, *There and Back*, opera in one act by Hindemith (libretto by M Schiffer after an English revue sketch), produced Baden-Baden, 17 Jul 1927. The plot, concerning a jealous husband, goes into reverse at half way. At the fp the part of the errant, palindromic wife was sung by Otto Klemperer's wife, Johanna.

Hippolyte et Aricie, *Hippolytus and Aricia*, ◊Ippolito ed Aricia.

Opera in five acts by Rameau (libretto by S J de Pellegrin), produced Paris, Opéra, 1 Oct 1733. Hippolytus and Aricia are in love. Believing her husband Theseus to be dead, Phaedra confesses love for her stepson Hippolytus, who rejects her. Theseus returns and condemns his son for what appears to be an attack on Phaedra. Hippolytus is carried off by a sea monster, but survives and is reunited with Aricia.

Hirt auf dem Felsen, Der, *The Shepherd on the Rock*, song by Schubert D965, for piano and soprano with clarinet obbligato (text by W Muller and ? H von Chezy); commissioned by Anna Milder-

Hauptmann (1785–1838), the first Leonore in *Fidelio* (1805). With *Die Taubenpost*, Schubert's last work; composed Oct 1828.

Hislop, Joseph (b Edinburgh, 5 Apr 1884; d Upper Largo, Fife, 6 May 1977), Scottish tenor. Debut Stockholm, 1916, as Faust; repeated the role at CG opposite Shalyapin, and sang there 1920–28 in operas by Verdi and Puccini. US debut Chicago, 1921; Milan, La Scala, 1923 as Edgardo. He sang in Stockholm until 1937 and was well known as Roméo and Des Grieux. Birgit Nilsson and Jussi Björling were among his Stockholm pupils, and he taught in London from 1948 (GSM, SW and CG).

Histoire du soldat, *The Soldier's Tale*, action for a narrator, actors and dancers by Stravinsky (libretto by C F Ramuz), produced Lausanne, 28 Sept 1918, conductor Ansermet.

Histoires Naturelles song cycle by Ravel for voice and piano; composed 1906, fp Paris, 19 Mar 1907. The five animals depicted are *The Peacock, The Cricket, The Swan, The Kingfisher* and *The Guinea-fowl*.

Hitchcock, (Hugh) Wiley (b Detroit, 28 Sept 1932), American musicologist. He studied in Michigan and Paris (with Boulanger) and has been professor of music at Brooklyn College from 1971. His research interests involve American music history and the music of the French Baroque. He was editor for the Americas in the *New Grove Dictionary* and co-editor of the *Grove Dictionary of American Music*. Other publications include *Music in the United States* (1969, 1975, 1988), *Les oeuvres de Marc-Antoine Charpentier* (1982) and editions of Caccini, Leo and Lully.

HMS Pinafore operetta by Sullivan (libretto by W S Gilbert), produced London, Opéra Comique, 25 May 1878. The first work by Gilbert and Sullivan to be a worldwide success.

Hoboken, Anthony van (b Rotterdam, 23 Mar 1887; d Zurich, 1 Nov 1983), Dutch musicologist. He studied in Frankfurt and Vienna and in 1927 founded a MS archive in the National Library in Vienna; an almost complete thematic catalogue of Haydn's works was pub. 1957, 1971. Haydn's works are commonly designated 'Hob.' with roman numeral denoting group classification (e.g. opera, symphony etc.) followed by Arabic numeral for work within group.

Hobrecht, Jacob, ◊Obrecht.

Hochzeit des Camacho, Die, *Camacho's Wedding*, opera by Mendelssohn (libretto by C A L von Lichtenstein, based on Cervantes' *Don Quixote*), produced Berlin, Schauspielhaus, 29 Apr 1827. Quiteria loves Basilio but must marry the rich Camacho. At the wedding Basilio feigns attempted suicide; Camacho allows him to marry Quiteria so that he may die a happy man. The subterfuge is revealed, but Camacho accepts the lovers' union.

hocket a word similar to 'hiccup' and derived from the French equivalent *hoquet*. It is used for a device in medieval vocal and instrumental music, consisting of phrases when broken up by rests, in such a way that when one part is silent another fills the gap. Also a piece written in this style.

Hoddinott, Alun (b Bargoed, Glamorgan, 11 Aug 1929), Welsh composer. He studied at the University College of South Wales, Cardiff, where he was appointed Professor of Music 1968. Artistic director of Cardiff Festival of 20th-Century Music, 1966–89.

Works include operas *The Beach of Falseá* (1974), *Murder, The Magician* (1976), *The Rajah's Diamond* (1979), *The Trumpet Major*, after Hardy (1981); eight symphonies (1954–92), four Sinfoniettas (1968–71), *Variants, Night Music* for orchestra, two clarinet concertos (1954, 1986), oboe concerto, three piano concertos, organ concerto (1967), *Doubles* for oboe, harpsichord and strings (1982), Triple concerto for violin, cello and piano (1986), *Noctis Equi* for cello and orchestra (1989); choral music; clarinet quartet, three string quartets (1966, 1984, 1988), string trio; ten piano sonatas.

Hodgson, Alfreda (b Morecambe, 7 Jun 1940; d Morecambe, 16 Apr 1992), English contralto. Studied in Manchester and sang in concert from 1961, notably in oratorio and in the Passions of Bach. She was much admired in Mahler, singing in the second symphony under Klemperer, the eighth with Colin Davis and *Das Lied von der Erde* with Simon Rattle. Also valued in *Messiah, The Dream of Gerontius* and the *Alto Rhapsody*. US concerts with the Chicago and Pittsburgh SOs and the Cleveland Orchestra.

Hoelscher, Ulf (b Kitzingen, 17 Jan 1942), German violinist. Studied with Josef Gingold and Ivan Galamian. Many tours of Europe, the USA and the Far East, notably with the Dresden Staatskapelle. Has premiered the concertos by David Kirchner (1984) and Franz Hummel (1987), both with the Berlin PO, and Aribert Reimann's concerto for violin and cello (Montreux, 1989). Chamber recitals with Heinrich Schiff, Michel Béroff and Christian Zacharias. Recordings include Shostakovich with Vishnevskaya and Rostropovitch. Professor at the Berlin Hochschule from 1987. Played the Hindemith Concerto in London, 1995.

Hoengen, Elisabeth (b Gevelsberg, 7 Dec 1906), German mezzo. Debut Wuppertal 1933; sang in Düsseldorf and Dresden and, from 1943. Vienna. Roles there included the Nurse in *Die Frau ohne Schatten*. London, CG, 1947 with Vienna Co. as Dorabella and Marcellina. Salzburg 1948–59 in operas by Strauss, Britten and Erbse. NY Met. debut Jun 1952 as Herodias.

Hoesslin, Franz von (b Munich, 31 Dec 1885; d off Site, 28 Sept 1946), German conductor and composer. Pupil of Mottl for conducting and Reger for composition. After engagements at various theatres in Germany and Switzerland he became conductor at the Volksoper in Berlin 1922–23, later conducting at Dessau and Breslau and for six years at Bayreuth (1927–40: *Parsifal* and *The Ring*). He was killed in a plane crash.

Works include orchestral and choral music; chamber music; songs.

Høffding, (Nils) Finn (b Copenhagen, 10 Mar 1899), Danish composer. Pupil of Jeppesen in Copenhagen and J Marx in Vienna. Appointed professor at the Royal Danish Conservatory 1931, where he started the Copenhagen Folk Music School with Jørgen Bentzon. Author of several theoretical books.

Works include operas *The Emperor's New Clothes* (after Andersen, 1928), etc.; four symphonies (one with chorus); two string quartets (1920, 1925), duet for oboe and clarinet; piano pieces; songs.

Höffer, Paul (b Barmen, 21 Dec 1895; d Berlin, 31 Aug 1949), German composer. He was trained as a pianist in the first place, at Cologne, and later studied composition with Schreker in Berlin, where he became professor of piano at the Hochschule für Musik in 1923 and professor of composition in 1930. He was appointed director in 1948, but died of a heart attack.

Works include operas *Borgia* (1931) and *Der falsche Waldemar* (1934), three children's operas; incidental music for Shakespeare's *Coriolanus*, Goethe's *Faust*, etc.; four oratorios including *Der reiche Tag* (1938) and *Von edlen Leben* (1941) and other choral works; symphonies, two serenades, etc. for orchestra; various concertos; three string quartets, clarinet quintet, wind sextet.

Hoffmann, (E)rnst (T)heodor (A)madeus (originally Wilhelm) (b Könisberg, 24 Jan 1776; d Berlin, 25 Jun 1822), German novelist, composer and writer on music. He changed his third name to Amadeus in homage to Mozart. He is the hero of Offenbach's *Tales of Hoffmann*.

Compositions include operas (mostly lost) *Der Renegat* (1803), *Faustine* (1804), *Die lustigen Musikanten* (Brentano, 1805), *Der Kanonikus von Mailand, Liebe und Eifersucht* (after Calderón, 1807), *Der Trank der Unsterblichkeit* (1808), *Das Gespenst* (1809), *Aurora, Undine* (after Fouqué, 1816; vocal score edited by Pfitzner, 1907), *Julius Sabinus* (unfinished); ballet *Harlekin* (unfinished); incidental music to Goethe's *Scherz, List und Rache* and other plays; two Masses; symphonies. For musical works based on his writings ◊Braunfels (*Prinzessin Brambilla*); ◊Brautwahl (Busoni); ◊Cardillac (Hindemith); ◊Contes d'Hoffmann (Offenbach); ◊Delibes (*Coppélia*); ◊Kreisleriana (Schumann); G ◊Malipiero (*Capricci di Callot*); ◊Nutcracker (Tchaikovsky); ◊Offenbach (*Goldsmith of Toledo*).

Hoffman, Grace (b Cleveland, 14 Jan 1921), American mezzo. She studied in NY and Milan; small roles in USA and Europe from 1951. Stuttgart and La Scala, Milan, from 1955. Bayreuth 1957–70 as Brangaene, Waltraute and Fricka. NY Met. debut 1958. London, CG, 1959–71; debut as Eboli. Professor of voice at Stuttgart Hochschule

from 1978. Sang in Zimmermann's *Soldaten* at Strasbourg, 1988.

Hoffmann, Karel (b Smichov, Prague, 12 Dec 1872; d Prague, 30 Mar 1936), Czech violinist. Studied at the Prague Conservatory and founded the Bohemian quartet with Suk, Nedbal and Berger in 1892. Appointed violin professor at the Conservatory in 1922.

Hoffmeister, Franz Anton (b Rothenburg am Neckar, 12 May 1754; d Vienna, 9 Feb 1812), Austrian publisher and composer. He started in Vienna as a law student but in 1783 established his publishing firm; Beethoven and Mozart were among his clients. With Kühnel in Leipzig he established a bureau which became the publishing house C F Peters. The best known of his nine operas was *Der Königssohn aus Ithaka* (Vienna, 1803); also wrote 66 symphonies, about 60 concertos, including 25 for flute; 42 string quartets and 18 string trios. Whether by accident or design, many of his works were ascribed to Haydn.

Hoffmeister Quartet string quartet no. 20, in D major, by Mozart (K499); composed 1786 and pub. by F A ◊Hoffmeister.

When I came hither first, I found, among the English, many good players and no composers: but now, they are all composers and no players.
George Frideric Handel, quoted in Burney,
Commemoration of Handel, 1785

Hoffstetter, Roman (b Laundenbach, 24 Apr 1742; d Mittenburg, 21 May 1815), German composer. He was choral director at the monastery of Amorbach until 1803, writing sacred and orchestral music and string quartets; he is believed to be the composer of the 'Serenade' quartet formerly attributed to Haydn as op. 3 no. 5.

Hofhaimer (Hoffheimer), Paul (b Radstadt, 25 Jan 1459; d Salzburg, 1537), Austrian organist and composer. In the service of the Emperor Maximilian at Innsbruck, 1480–1519, and was organist to the Archbishop of Salzburg from 1522 to his death.

Works include setting of odes by Horace *Harmoniae poeticae* for four voices, German songs for three and four voices, organ music.

Hofmann, Heinrich (Karl Johann) (b Berlin, 13 Jan 1842; d Gross-Tabarz, Thur., 16 Jul 1902), German pianist and composer. Was a chorister at the cathedral in Berlin and studied at Kullak's academy. He taught the piano and played much in public.

Works include operas *Cartouche* (1869), *Der Matador, Armin* (1872), *Aennchen von Tharau* (1878), *Wilhelm von Oranien* (1882), *Donna Diana* (Moreto, 1886), *Hungarian Suite, Fritdjof* symphony (after Tegnér), suite *Im Schlosshof*, scherzo *Irrlichter und Kobolde*, etc. for orchestra; cantatas *Die schöne Melusine* (1876), *Aschenbrödel* (1881), *Editha, Prometheus* (1892), *Waldfräulein, Festgesang*; several works for voices and orchestra; cello concerto; piano quartet, piano trio, string sextet, octet; piano pieces; songs, duets.

Hofmann, Josef (Casimir) (b Kraków, 20 Jan 1876; d Los Angeles, 16 Feb 1957), Polish-American pianist and composer. Studied early with his elder sister and his faher, the pianist and conductor Casimir Hofman, and made his first public appearance at the age of six. At 19 he toured Europe and in 1887 paid his first visit to USA where, after further study with Anton Rubinstein, and success in Europe, he settled in 1898 and became naturalized in 1926. He was best known as a gifted and sensitive interpreter of Chopin and Liszt. His works appeared for a time under the pseudonym of Michel Dvorsky.

Works include symphony in E major, symphonic narrative *The Haunted Castle*; five piano concertos and *Chromaticon*, for piano and orchestra; numerous piano works.

Hofmann, Leopold (b Vienna, 14 Aug 1738; d Vienna, 17 Mar 1793), Austrian composer. *Kapellmeister* at St Stephen's Cathedral in Vienna from 1772. He belongs to the Viennese school of symphonists.

Works include church music, symphonies, concertos.

Hofmann, Ludwig (b Frankfurt, 14 Jan 1895; d Frankfurt, 28 Dec 1963), German bass-baritone. Debut Bamberg 1918. Bayreuth 1928–42 as Gurnemanz, Marke, Hunding, Hagen and Daland. Berlin

Hogwood *The conductor, harpsichordist and musicologist Christopher Hogwood. Hogwood has been crucial since the late 1960s in widening the appeal of early music and 'authentic' performances, thanks largely to his interpretative vitality and insistence on high technical standards.*

1918–35; Vienna 1935–55. Salzburg Festival as Osmin, Mozart's Figaro and Marke. CG and NY Met. 1923–29 in Italian and French repertory.

Hofmann, Peter (b Marienbad, 12 Aug 1944), German tenor. He studied in Karlsruhe; debut Lübeck 1972 as Tamino. In 1976 sang Siegmund in Bayreuth and London, CG, production of the *Ring*. US debut San Francisco 1977, Siegmund; NY Met. 1980, Lohengrin. Has sung Parsifal at CG and Salzburg. Other roles include Max, Tristan, Florestan and Bacchus. Sang Siegmund in the Kupfer production of the *Ring* at Bayreuth, 1988.

Hofmannsthal, Hugo von (b Vienna, 1 Feb 1874; d Rodaun, 15 Jul 1929), Austrian poet and dramatist. ◊Ägyptische Helena (R Strauss); ◊Alkestis (Wellesz); ◊Arabella (R Strauss); ◊Ariadne auf Naxos (ditto); ◊Bourgeois gentilhomme (ditto); ◊Elektra (ditto); ◊Everyman (Sibelius); ◊Frau ohne Schatten (R Strauss); ◊Josephslegende (ditto); F ◊Martin (*Jedermann*); ◊Oedipus und die Sphinx (Varèse); ◊Reuss (*Tor und der Tod*); ◊Rosenkavalier (R Strauss); A ◊Tcherepnin (*Hochzeit der Sobeide*); H ◊Unger (*Tor und der Tod*); ◊Wagner-Régeny (*Bergwerk zu Falun*); ◊Wellesz (*Alkestis, Lied der Welt* and *Leben, Traum und Tod*); ◊Zemlinsky (*Das gläserne Herz*).

Hogwood, Christopher (b Nottingham, 10 Sept 1941), English harpsichordist, musicologist and conductor. He studied at Cambridge and in Prague. Co-founder 1967 with David Munrow of Early Music Consort. Played with Academy of St Martin-in-the-Fields and in 1973 founded Academy of Ancient Music; 'authentic' performances with original instruments, including complete recording of Mozart's symphonies. Toured USA 1974; from 1979 professor-in-residence Sydney University. Has edited works by Purcell, J C Bach and Croft and pub. a book on Handel for the tercentenary year. Music director St Paul's Chamber Orchestra, Minnesota, from 1987; principal guest from 1992.

Hoiby, Lee (b Madison, WI, 17 Feb 1926), American composer. He studied at the Curtis Institute and in Rome and Salzburg. Best known for his operas, influenced by Menotti: *The Scarf* (after Chekhov, produced Spoleto 1958), *Beatrice* (after Maeterlinck, 1959), *Natalia Petrovna* (after Turgenev, 1964), *Summer and Smoke* (after T N

Williams, 1971); also incidental music to Webster's *The Duchess of Malfi* (1957).

Holborne, Anthony (b ? London; d ? 29 Nov 1602), English musician and composer in the service of Queen Elizabeth I. He pub. a volume of music for strings or wind in 1599 and in 1597 *The Cittharn Schoole*, which includes three-part songs by his brother William.

Holbrooke, Joseph (or Josef) (b Croydon, Surrey, 5 Jul 1878; d London, 5 Aug 1958), English composer. Studied at the RAM. After a hard struggle as pianist and conductor he came under the patronage of Lord Howard de Walden, who wrote the libretti for his dramatic trilogy. He engaged in much militant propaganda on behalf of some British composers.

Works include operas *Pierrot and Pierrette* (1909; revised 1924 as *The Stranger*), *The Snob, The Wizard*, and the trilogy *The Cauldron of Annwen* (*The Children of Don, Dylan* and *Bronwen*); ballets *The Red Mask* (after Poe), *The Moth and the Flame, Coromanthe*, etc.; *Dramatic Choral Symphony* and *The Bells* for chorus and orchestra (both after Poe, 1903); symphonic poems *The Raven, Ulalume* and *The Masque of the Red Death* (all after Poe); violin concerto (1917); six string quartets (including *Pickwick Club* after Dickens), piano music and songs.

Hölderlin, Johann Christian Friedrich (1770–1843), German poet. ◊Apostel (songs); ◊Britten (*Hölderlin Fragmente*); Brahms ◊Schicksalslied; R ◊Strauss (three hymns).

Hole, William (d 15 Sept 1624), and Robert. English music engravers and publishers. William produced *Parthenia* for keyboard, the first music ever engraved on copper plates in England, in 1612 or 1613, and Robert produced its successor, *Parthenia In-violata*, in 1614.

Holl, Robert (b Rotterdam, 1947), Dutch bass. Sang with the Munich Opera from 1973 but then gave highly-praised concerts and Lieder recitals, notably in songs by Brahms, Wolf and Schubert (Hohenems Schubertiade and Salzburg Festivals). Concerts with Giulini, Karajan and Bernstein. From 1988 has returned to opera: Schubert's *Fierabras* in Vienna, followed by Rossini's Assur and Strauss's La Roche, Zurich, 1992.

Hollander, Benno (Benoit) (b Amsterdam, 8 Jun 1853; d London, 27 Dec 1942), Dutch (anglicized) violinist and composer. Studied at the Paris Conservatory with Massart, later composition with Saint-Saëns. After a tour in Europe he settled in London in 1876. He played viola in Auer's quartet and led several important orchestras, later formed one of his own.

Works include opera *Mietje*; symphony *Roland*, symphonic poem *Pompeii*, orchestral pieces *Drame* and *Comédie*; two concertos and *Pastoral Fantasy* for violin and orchestra; two string quartets, septet for piano, strings and horns, piano trio, string trio; two violin and piano sonatas; piano sonata.

After he had stalked out of the New York Met. in 1954, someone observed to Rudolf Bing, that Georg Szell was his own worst enemy. 'Not while I'm alive', said Bing.

Martin Mayer, *The Met*, 1983

Hollander, Christian Janszon (b Dordrecht, *c* 1510; d Innsbruck, 1568 or 1569), Flemish singer and composer. Appointed choirmaster at St Walburg's Church at Oudenarde in 1549 and from 1559 was a singer in the Imperial Chapel in Vienna. Innsbruck from 1564.

Works include many motets, sacred songs for several voices, secular German songs.

Hölle, Matthias (b Rottweil am Nekar, 8 Jul 1951), German bass. Member of the Cologne Opera 1976–87; Ludwigsburg Festival 1978, as the Commendatore. Bayreuth Festival from 1981 as Fasolt, Hunding and King Marke. Milan 1981 and 1984, in the premieres of Stockhausen's *Donnerstag* and *Samstag* from *Licht*. NY Met. 1986, in *Fidelio*. Other roles include Henri VIII in *Anna Bolena*, Basilio, and Gremin. CG debut 1994, as Hunding in *Die Walküre*.

Höller, Karl (b Bamberg, 25 Jul 1907), German composer. Studied at

Munich under Josef Haas. Taught at the Musikhochschule in Frankfurt 1937–49, and became President of the Musikhochschule in Munich 1954.

Works include orchestral and solo concertos, symphonic fantasy on a theme by Frescobaldi (1934), *Gregorianische Hymnen*; concertos for organ, violins (2) and cello (2); six string quartets, eight violin sonatas, cello sonatas, piano and organ works.

Höller, York (b Leverkusen, 11 Jan 1944), German composer. He studied at the Cologne Musikhochschule, under Zimmermann and Alfons Kontarsky, and came under the influence of Boulez at Darmstadt; has worked at the electronic studio, Cologne.

Works include operas *Der Meister und Margarita* (1989) and *Caligula* (1992); *Topic* for orchestra (1967), cello sonata (1969), piano concerto (1970), *Horizont*, electronic (1972), *Chroma* for orchestra (1974), *Tangens*, electronic (1973), *Antiphon* for string quartet (1977), *Arcos* for orchestra (1978), *Moments musicaux* for flute and piano (1979), *Mythos* for orchestra (1980), *Traumspiel* for soprano, orchestra and tape (1983), *Improvisation sur le nom de Pierre Boulez* for 17 instruments (1985), *Fanal* for trumpet and orchestra (1990), *Pensées* for piano, orchestra and tape (1991), *Aura* for orchestra (1992), *Pas de deux* for cello and piano (1993).

Holliger, Heinz (b Langenthal, 21 May 1939), Swiss oboist and composer. Studied oboe and piano in Bern and Paris, and composition with Veress in Bern and Boulez in Paris. He has won several prizes for his oboe playing; Henze, Krenek, Berio, Penderecki and Stockhausen have written works for him.

Works include cantata *Himmel und Erde* for tenor and chamber group (1961); *Studie* for soprano, oboe and cello with harpsichord; *Improvisation* for oboe, harp and 12 string instruments (1963); *Pneuma* for 34 wind instruments and percussion (1970), *Come and Go*, chamber opera (1977), *Engführung* for chamber orchestra (1984), *Der ferne Klang* for ensemble (1984), *Tonscherben* for orchestra (1985), *What Where*, chamber opera (1988), *Scardanelli-Zglus* 1–4 (1975–91); sonata for oboe and piano; sonata for oboe solo; string quartet (1975).

Holloway, David (b Grandview, MO, 12 Nov 1942), American baritone. Studied in Rome and made debut in Kansas City 1968, as Belcore. Billy Budd at Chicago (1970), NY City Opera 1972, as Guglielmo; NY Met. from 1973, as Sharpless, Lescaut and Guglielmo. Glyndebourne 1985, as Escamillo. Other roles include Mozart's Count and Papageno, Dandini and Nick Shadow.

Holloway, Robin (b Leamington Spa, 19 Oct 1943), English composer who studied at Cambridge. His music, which shows a textural and harmonic eclecticism, has been influenced by German Romanticism.

Works include opera *Clarissa* (1968–76; fp 1990); *Scenes from Schumann*, seven paraphrases for orchestra (1970) and *Fantasy-Pieces*, on the Heine *Liederkreis* of Schumann, for 13 players (1971). Other works include two Concertos for Orchestra (1969, 1979); *Serenata Notturna* for four horns and orchestra (1982); *Clarissa Symphony*, for soprano, tenor and orchestra (1981); *Serenade in G* (1986); *Inquietus* for chamber orchestra, in memory of Peter Pears (1986); Concerto for clarinet and saxophone (1988), violin concerto

Robin Holloway – composer

1   Bach: *Ich will den Kreutzstub gerne tragen* (Cantata no. 56)
The perfection of German Protestantism in music – joyfully shouldering the burden, voyaging through life in certain hope of a safe haven. I love it especially as sung in the understated non-German manner by Gérard Souzay.

2   Schubert: *Winterreise*
Simply the greatest of all song cycles, a kind of secular counterpart to the Bach cantata, with its weary journey through a frozen world fuelled by illusion and despair rather than by faith and hope. No recording, however distinguished, seems as great as the music.

3   Mozart: Trio in E flat for clarinet, viola, and piano
As Tovey said of (I think) this piece (I'm paraphrasing from memory), the consummate ease of every solution can beguile the delighted listener into believing that there are, for Mozart, no problems.

4   Brahms: Trio in A minor op. 114 for clarinet, cello, and piano
It's moving to see Brahms, after apparently 'retiring', coming to life again in this work, so muscular and virile in its outer movements, so kittenish and teasing in the scherzo, so darkly hermaphroditic in the slow second movement.

5   Bruckner: Symphony no. 9 in D minor
The fact that the master never finished its finale means (for me) that the three complete movements remain uncompromised in exaltation; in the adagio the sublimest strains ever put on paper by mortal man. Again, no performance I've heard seems as great as the composition itself.

6   Schoenberg: *Five Orchestral Pieces* op. 16
Rafael Kubelik's recording of this endlessly fascinating work first showed me, as a schoolboy, how sheerly *beautiful* it can also be, with no sacrifice of expressionistic force.

7   Tchaikovsky: *The Nutcracker* (complete ballet)
This evergreen is the perfect antidote to blue or black moods. It's incredible that Tchaikovsky declared himself dissatisfied with such a cornucopia, which most other composers would give an arm and a leg to have written. I especially like John Lanchbery's complete recording because it sounds so experienced, the speeds just right for dancing.

8   Debussy: *La damoiselle élue*
I love this early flower of Debussy's genius, with its undisguised delight in strains from Wagner, Chabrier, Massenet, as much as anything he achieved later and greater. It needs singing as tender and supple as the Blessed Damozel herself; no subsequent recording displaces the old version by Victoria de los Angeles.

9   Stravinsky: *Agon*
Another wonderful instance of an old composer's self-renewal. Here Stravinsky gathers in such far-flung sources as English Elizabethan virginalists, French Renaissance dance-patterns, Webern, Tchaikovsky, Bach, and probably others too – not with effortful learning, but with wit, brio, and fun.

10 Ligeti: Chamber Concerto
If there is to be a living composer, it has to be Ligeti. This piece shows as well as any the fabulous precision and inventiveness of his ear: textures delicate or violent, mechanistic or fluid, in rapid succession and sometimes simultaneous.

A Selection of

Holst

Beni Mora	1910
The Cloud Messenger	1910
St Paul's Suite	1913
The Planets	1914–16
The Hymn of Jesus	1917
The Perfect Fool	1923
Egdon Heath	1927
Fugal Overture	1929

(1989), *The Spacious Firmament* for chorus and orchestra (1989), *Wagner Nights* for orchestra (1989), *Serenade for Strings* (1990), *Summer Music* and *Winter Music* for ensemble (1991, 1992).

Hollreiser, Heinrich (b Munich, 24 Jun 1913), German conductor. He held posts in Darmstadt and Mannheim before Munich Staatsoper, 1942. Düsseldorf 1945–52; Vienna Staatsoper until 1961. Deutsche Oper Berlin 1961–64. Has given operas by Henze, Britten and Hindemith. Well known in Strauss and has conducted *Tannhäuser* and *Die Meistersinger* at Bayreuth (debut 1973). Guest conductor Cleveland Orchestra from 1978.

Hollywood String Quartet American ensemble founded 1947 with Felix Slatkin as leader. Members were session musicians in Holly-wood's studios and concerts and so were largely restricted to the West Coast; Edinburgh Festival 1957. Their polished recordings of late Beethoven, Brahms and Schubert have been re-issued on CD. Also gave works by Shostakovich, Walton, Schoenberg and Creston. Disbanded 1971.

Holm, Richard (b Stuttgart, 3 Aug 1912; d Munich, 20 Jul 1988), German tenor. In 1948 he joined the Munich Staatsoper and first sang at CG in 1953 as David; also role of NY Met. debut, 1952. A fine Wagner singer, he also excelled in Mozart. Roles included Flamand in first British *Capriccio* (1953), Belmonte, Tamino and Aschenbach.

Holman, Peter (b London, 1946), English harpsichordist, director and writer. Studied at King's College, London, with Thurston Dart. Founded the early music group Ars Nova while still a student; co-founded with Roy Goodman the Parley of Instruments (1979); many performances in the UK and Europe with Renaissance and early Baroque string consort music. Music director of Opera Restor'd from 1985, performing 18th-c. English masques and operas in authentic style. Former professor at the RAM, London, and currently joint artistic director of the Boston Early Music Festival. Publications include *The Violin at the English Court, 1540–1690* (1993) and a book on Purcell for the tercentenary (1995). His edition of Arne's *Artaxerxes* was performed in London under Roy Goodman, 1995.

Holmboe, Vagn (b Horsens, Jutland, 20 Dec 1909), Danish composer. Studied with Jeppesen and Høffding in Copenhagen and Toch in Berlin. With his wife, the Romanian pianist Meta Graf, he explored Romanian folk music.

Works include opera *Fanden og Borgmesteren* (1940); ballet *Den galsindede Tyrk*; 12 symphonies (1935–88); 13 chamber concertos (1939–56), 20 string quartets (1948–75), three violin sonatas.

Holmes, Alfred (b London, 9 Nov 1837; d Paris, 4 Mar 1876), English violinist and composer. With very little regular instruction he became a famous violinist, playing duets with his brother Henry (1839–1905) and later touring widely with him in Europe. He settled in Paris in 1864. He met Spohr in London and Kassel; dedicatee of Spohr's violin duos.

Works include opera *Inez de Castro*: symphony *Jeanne d'Arc, The Youth of Shakespeare, Robin Hood, The Siege of Paris, Charles XII* and *Romeo and Juliet* (after Shakespeare); overtures *The Cid* (after Corneille) and *The Muses*.

Holmès (originally *Holmes*), Augusta (Mary Anne) (b Paris, 16 Dec 1847; d Paris, 28 Jan 1903), Irish naturalized French pianist and composer. Although her parents were against her taking up music, she played the piano and sang as a child prodigy and began to compose under the name of Hermann Zenta. Later studied with Franck.

Works include operas *Héro et Léandre, La Montagne noire* (1895), *Astarté, Lancelot du Lac*; choral works *Les Argonautes* (on Homer's *Iliad*, 1881), psalm *In exitu*, ode *Ludus pro patria* and *Ode triomphale*; symphony on Ariosto's *Orlando furioso, Lutèce* and *Pologne*, symphonic poem *Irlande* (1882); song-cycle *Les Sept Ivresses*.

Holmes, Edward (1797–London, 28 Aug 1859), English author and critic. He wrote *A Ramble among the Musicians of Germany* (1828) and the first English biography of Mozart (1845).

Holmes, Eugène (b Brownsville, TN, 7 Mar 1934), American baritone. Studied at Bloomington and made debut with the Goldovsky Opera in New York, in Ward's *The Crucible* (1963). Sang with the NY City Opera from 1971; Washington DC 1970 (US fp of *Koanga* by Delius) and at Seattle and San Fransisco. Member of the Deutsche Oper am Rhein, Dusseldorf, from 1983, as Nabucco, Amonasro, Macbeth and Boccanegra. Opera and concert tours to Russia and Japan.

Holmes, George (b Lincoln, 1721), English organist and composer. At first organist to Bishop of Durham, he was appointed organist of Lincoln Cathedral in 1704. Wrote anthems, burial sentences for Lincoln Cathedral, Ode for St Cecilia's Day, catches.

Holmes, Ralph (b Penge, 1 Apr 1937; d Beckenham, 4 Sept 1984), English violinist. After study at the RAM and with Enescu in Paris he made his London debut in 1951, with the RPO. US debut Carnegie Hall 1966, under Barbirolli. He was heard in chamber works by Delius, Bartók and Prokofiev and in concertos by Berg, Shostakovich and Schoenberg, as well as the standard repertory. Formed a piano trio in 1972 with Anthony Goldstone and Moray Welsh.

Holoman, D(allas) Kern (b Raleigh, NC, 8 Sept 1947), American musicologist and conductor. Studied in North Carolina and played the bassoon in an orchestra there before becoming the founding director of the Early Music Ensemble, 1973–79. Chairman of the music department at Davis, CA, 1980–88. The music of Berlioz has been at the centre of his research, and he has published on this composer's creative process (1980), a Catalogue (1987) and a biography (1989).

Never compose anything unless the not composing of it becomes a positive nuisance to you.

Gustav Holst in a letter, 1921

Holst, Gustav (Theodore) (b Cheltenham, 21 Sept 1874; d London, 25 May 1934), English composer of Swedish descent. The family had been in England since 1807. His father was a music teacher and his mother a pianist, and he was intended to follow their career; he also had early experience as organist and choral and orchestral conductor in a small way. In 1892 he was sent to the RCM in London, but disliked the keyboard instruments and studied composition under Stanford; he also formed a lifelong friendship with Vaughan Williams, with whom he shared an interest in folk music. Suffering from neuritis, he took up the trombone instead of the piano, and on leaving played in the orchestra of the Carl Rosa Opera Co. and later in the Scottish Orchestra. In 1903 he became music master at a school in south London, in 1905 at St Paul's Girls' School, where he remained to his death, and in 1907 was appointed music director at Morley

Holst *The composer Gustav Holst, pictured sitting at the piano with Eugene Goossens, Oliver Bernard and Percy Pitt (Covent Garden, 1923). Holst required many years to find his true artistic voice:* The Planets *was his first such work on a large scale, written at the age of nearly 40.*

College for Working Men and Women; in 1912 he conducted there the first modern performance of Purcell's *Fairy Queen*. He was also influenced by the early music of Weelkes and Byrd. From 1919 he taught composition at the RCM and 1919–23 at Reading College. Balfour Gardiner had arranged a private performance of *The Planets* in 1918, and with its public premiere the following year, Holst achieved the first real success of his career. In 1923 he conducted at the University of Michigan and his opera *The Perfect Fool* (a satire on Wagnerism) was given at CG. The Choral Symphony after Keats was given at the 1925 Leeds Festival and in 1928 his bleak tone poem after Hardy, *Egdon Heath*, was premiered by the NY SO. The *Choral Fantasia* was first heard in 1931 and the *Brook Green Suite* in 1933.

Works include operas *The Idea* (1898), *The Wandering Scholar*, *Sāvitri* (1908; produced 1916), *The Perfect Fool* (1923), *At the Boar's Head* (on Shakespeare's *Henry IV*, 1925); ballets *The Golden Goose* (1926) and *The Morning of the Year* with chorus and orchestra (1926–27).

CHORAL: Choral hymns from the *Rig Veda* with orchestra (1908–12), two psalms for chorus, strings and organ, *The Hymn of Jesus* for chorus and orchestra (1917), Festival Te Deum, *Ode to Death* (Whitman) for chorus and orchestra, choral symphony (Keats) for soprano, chorus and orchestra (1925), choral fantasy (Bridges) for chorus, organ, strings, brass and percussion; two motets for unaccompanied chorus, *Ave Maria* for female voices, part-songs and arrangements of folksongs for unaccompanied chorus.

ORCHESTRAL: *A Somerset Rhapsody* (1907), *Beni Mora* suite (1910), *The Planets* (1914–16), *Japanese Suite, Fugal Overture, Egdon*

Heath (after Thomas Hardy) for orchestra (1927); *St Paul's* suite for strings; *Fugal Concerto* for flute, oboe and strings, concerto for two violins and orchestra (1929); two suites for military band: *A Moorside Suite* for brass band. Nine hymns from the *Rig Veda* for voice and piano (1908), 12 songs (Humbert Wolfe) for voice and piano, four songs for voice and violin; a few piano pieces.

Holst, Imogen (b Richmond, Surrey, 12 Apr 1907; d Aldeburgh, 9 Mar 1984), English pianist and composer, daughter of Gustav ◊Holst. Studied with her father and at the RCM in London and taught music at several schools, did much work for the English Folk Dance Society and wrote books on Holst, Purcell and Britten.

Works include overture for orchestra, piano pieces, folksong arrangements, string quintet (1981).

Holstein, Franz (Friedrich) von (b Brunswick, 16 Feb 1826; d Leipzig, 22 May 1878), German composer. Although trained for the army, he studied music under Griepenkerl. When he had written two operas *Zwei Nächte in Venedig* and *Waverley* (after Scott), Moritz Hauptmann persuaded him in 1852 to take entirely to music and gave him further instruction.

Works include operas *Der Haideschacht*, *Der Erbe von Morley*, *Die Hochländer* and *Marino Faliero* (after Byron); overtures *Loreley* and *Frau Aventiure*; vocal scene from Schiller's *Braut von Messina* and another, *Beatrice*.

Holt, Simon (b Bolton, 21 Feb 1958), English composer. Studied at the RNCM with Anthony Gilbert and was featured composer at the 1985 Bath Festival. Commissions from the Nash Ensemble and London Sinfonietta. Works include: *Syrensong* (1987), and *Walking with the* *river's roar* (1991) for orchestra; ensemble pieces *Mirrormaze* (1981), *Shadow Realm* (1983), *Burlesca obscura*, clarinet quintet (1985), *Danger of the Disappearance of Things* for string quartet (1989), *Sparrow Flight* (1989) and *Icarus Lamentations* (1992); vocal works with ensemble *Wyrdchanging* (1980), *Canciones* (1986), *Ballad of the Black Sorrow* (1988), *A Song of Crocuses and Lightning* (1989), *Tangara* (1991), *A Knot of Time* (1992); *Lunas Zauberschein* for mezzo and bass flute (1979); piano music.

Holz, Carl (b Vienna, 1798; d Vienna, 9 Nov 1858), Austrian violinist. Lived in Vienna, where he became a member of Schuppanzigh's quartet in 1824 and took part in the fps of Beethoven's last string quartets. A devoted friend of Beethoven.

Holzbauer, Ignaz (b Vienna, 17 Sept 1711; d Mannheim, 7 Apr 1783), Austrian composer. Originally intended for a career in law, he was largely self-taught in music, and visited Italy to complete his studies. Director of the court opera in Vienna intermittently 1742–1750, he was appointed *Kapellmeister* in Stuttgart in 1751, and two years later to the court of the Elector Palatine in Mannheim, where the orchestra under Johann Stamitz was the most famous of the time. During visits to Italy on leave of absence he produced several operas, and in Mannheim produced the German opera *Günther von Schwarzburg*. As a composer of symphonies he belongs to the Mannheim School.

Works include operas *Il figlio delle selve* (1753), *L'isola disabitata* (1754), *Nitetti* (1758), *Alessandro nell' Indie*, *Tancredi*, *Günther von Schwarzburg* (1777), etc.; oratorios *La Passione* (1754), *Isacco* (1757), *La Betulia liberata* (1760), etc.; Masses, motets and other church music; 65 symphonies; concertos, chamber music.

Holzbläser German = lit. 'woodblowers' = woodwind instruments.

Holzblasinstrumente German = 'woodwind instruments'.

Holzmair, Wolfgang (b Vienna, 1952), Austrian baritone. Studied in Vienna and has appeared throughout Germany and Austria as a song recitalist; England from 1990, incuding *Schwanengesang* 1993, with Imogen Cooper. Sang with Bern Opera from 1985, as Valentin, Orpheus and Eugene Onegin (1991). Early music repertory includes Ireo in Cesti's *Semiramide* at Innsbruck (1988) and Peri's Orfeo at Wuppertal. A leading exponent of Mozart's Papageno, which he sang at CG 1993.

Holztrompete German = 'wooden trumpet'; an instrument designed

Holzmair *Austrian baritone Wolfgang Holzmair. His success as a recitalist in Lieder, together with his idiomatic interpretation of Papageno in* The Magic Flute, *has evoked comparisons with Hermann Prey; Holzmair's operatic repertoire is much more varied than his great predecessor, however, including works by Zimmermann and Osborne as well as early music.*

for use in the third act of Wagner's *Tristan*, actually a revival of the cornett, but provided with a valve.

Homer Greek poet. ◊Bruch (*Achilles* and *Odysseus*); Gnecchi (*Cassandra*); ◊Heger (*Bettler Namenlos*); Herzogenberg (*Odysseus* symphony); ◊Holmès (*Argonautes*); ◊Homerische Welt (Bungert); ◊Ritorno di Ulisse (Monteverdi, Henze); ◊Ulisse (Dallapiccola).

Homer, Louise (b Pittsburgh, 30 Apr 1871; d Winter Park, FL, 6 May 1947), American contralto. She studied in Boston and Paris and in 1898 at Vichy was heard as Leonora (*La favorite*). CG 1899–1900 as Lola and Ortrud. NY Met. 1900–29 as Amneris and Azucena and in Wagner; she sang under Toscanini in Gluck's *Orfeo* and *Armide* and was the Witch in the 1910 fp of Humperdinck's *Königskinder*. Also sang in San Francisco and Chicago and was successful as Dalila.

Homerische Welt, *Homeric World*, operatic tetralogy by Bungert (libretto by composer, based on Homer's *Odyssey*):

I. *Kirke/Circe*, produced Dresden, 29 Jan 1898. II. *Nausikaa/Nausicaa*, produced Dresden, 20 Mar 1901. III. *Odysseus Heimkehr/The Return of Ulysses*, produced Dresden, 12 Dec 1896. IV. *Odysseus Tod/The death of Ulysses*, produced Dresden, 30 Oct 1903. Bungert's attempt to create a Wagnerian cycle, but based, like Berlioz's *Troyens* and Taneiev's *Oresteia*, on classical Greek subjects.

Homilius, Gottfried August (b Rosenthal, Saxony, 2 Feb 1714; d Dresden, 2 Jun 1785), German composer and organist. Pupil of Bach at Leipzig, appointed organist of the church of Our Lady, Dresden, 1742, and music director of the three principal churches there, 1755.

Works include many cantatas and motets, *Messiah* (c 1776), a Passion cantata, Christmas oratorio, several settings of the Passions, a book of 167 hymns; six German arias; organ music.

Homme armé, L' French = 'the armed man'; the name of an old French secular song the tune of which was often used by composers of the 15th and 16th c. as *cantus firmus* for their Masses, which were then designated by that name.

Homme et son désir, L', *Man and his Desire*, ballet by Milhaud (words, 'plastic poem', by Paul Claudel, choreographed by Jean Borlin), produced Paris, Théâtre des Champs-Élysées, 6 Jun 1921.

homophonic from Greek = lit. 'alike-sounding'; applied to music in which the individual lines making up the harmony have no independent significance, that is to say, for most purposes chordal.

Honauer, Leontzi (b ? Strasbourg, c 1735; d c 1790), German composer. Settled in Paris c 1760 and pub. three sets of harpsichord

A Selection of

Honegger

Pastoral d'été	1920
Le Roi David	1921
Pacific 231	1923
Symphony no. 1	1930
Les Misérables (film music)	1934
Jeanne d'Arc au bûcher	1938
Symphony no. 2	1941
Symphony no. 3	1946
Symphony no. 4 (*Deliciae Basiliensis*)	1946
Symphony no. 5 (*Di Tre Re*)	1951

sonatas, some movements of which were later arranged as concerto movements in Mozart's K37, 40 and 41.

Honegger, Arthur (b Le Havre, 10 Mar 1892; d Paris, 27 Nov 1955), Swiss composer. Was first taught by the organist R C Martin at his birthplace, then sent to the Zurich Conservatory, 1909–11, and studied at the Paris Conservatory 1911–13. After that he became a private pupil of Widor and d'Indy and in 1914 began to compose. Though always in touch with Switzerland, he belonged mainly to the French school, and he joined the group which *c* 1920 became known as 'Les Six'. He married the composer Andrée Vaurabourg, who was also attached to it, though not as a member.

Works include OPERAS: *Antigone* (after Sophocles, 1927), *L'Aiglon* (with Ibert, 1937) and *Charles le Téméraire* (1944); stage oratorios *Le Roi David* (1921), *Judith, Cris du monde, Jeanne d'Arc au bûcher* (Paul Claudel, 1938) and *Nicolas de Flue*.

BALLETS: *Horace victorieux* (1920), *Sémiramis* (Paul Valéry, 1934), *Amphion* (Valéry, 1931), *Un oiseau bleu s'est envolé* (Sacha Guitry), *Shota Roustaveli* (with A Tcherepnin and Harsányi, 1946).

INCIDENTAL MUSIC for *Le Dit des jeux du monde* (1918), *La Mort de Sainte Alméenne* (Max Jacob), *Saül* (André Gide, 1922), *Fantasio* (Musset), *Phædre* (d'Annunzio, 1926), *Les Suppliantes* (Aeschylus), *La Mandragora* (Machiavelli), *Le Soulier de satin* (Claudel), *Sodôme et Gomorrhe* (Jean Giraudoux, 1943), *Hamlet* (Shakespeare, 1946), *Prométhée* (Aeschylus) *Oedipe-Roi* (Sophocles, 1948).

ORCHESTRAL AND VOCAL WITH ORCHESTRA: radio and film music; *La Danse des morts* (Claudel) for solo voices, chorus and orchestra (on Holbein), prelude to Maeterlinck's *Aglavaine et Sélysette, Chant de joie*, prelude to Shakespeare's *Tempest, Mouvements symphonique*: *Pacific 231, Rugby* and No. 3 (1923–33), five symphonies (1930–51), *Prélude, Arioso et Fugue* on B.A.C.H., suite *Jour de fête suisse, Suite archaïque* for orchestra, *Pastorale d'été* (1920) and *Sérénade à Angélique* for chamber orchestra; concertino for piano and orchestra, cello concerto; Five Poems by Guillaume Apollinaire for voice and orchestra (1910–17).

CHAMBER AND SOLO VOCAL: three string quartets (1916–36) and other chamber music, two violin and piano sonatas, sonatas for viola and piano, cello and piano, clarinet and piano; piano and organ music; songs to poems by Apollinaire, Paul Fort, Jean Cocteau, Claudel, Giraudoux and others.

Hook, James (b Norwich, ? 3 Jun 1746; d Boulogne, 1827), English organist and composer. Studied under Garland, the Norwich Cathedral organist. He made a success in London in early manhood and in 1769 became organist and composer to Marylebone Gardens, and acted in the same posts at Vauxhall 1774–1820. He married Miss Madden *c* 1766 and wrote music for her play, *The Double Disguise*, in 1784. In 1795 and 1797 he did the same for two libretti by his son James (1772–1828), *Jack of Newbury* and *Diamond cut Diamond*, and from 1805 for several works by his second son, Theodore Edward (1788–1841). Of his vast output of songs for Vauxhall, some are still remembered, e.g. 'The Lass of Richmond Hill'.

Works include musical plays *Love and Innocence* (1769), *Country Courtship* (1772), *The Lady of the Manor* (1778), *Too civil by half* (1782), *The Triumph of Beauty, The Peruvian, The Soldier's Return* (1805), *The Siege of St Quintin* (1808), Hannah Moore's *The Search after Happiness*, etc.; odes, cantatas, catches.

Hooper, Edmund (b Halberton, Devon, *c* 1553; d London, 14 Jul 1621), English organist and composer. After being a chorister at Exeter Cathedral he went to London and joined the Westminster Abbey choir, becoming a Gentleman of the Chapel Royal 1604 and organist of the abbey 1606. He contributed harmonizations of hymn tunes to East's and Ravenscroft's Psalters, also two vocal pieces to Leighton's *Teares or Lamentacions* and one to Myriell's *Tristitiae remedium*.

Works include services and anthems; secular music for several voices; virginal music.

hopak ọgopak.

Hopf, Hans (b Nuremberg, 2 Aug 1916; d Munich, 25 Jun 1993), German tenor. Debut 1936, as Pinkerton; sang in Augsburg and Dresden, and in Oslo during the Nazi occupation of Norway. Berlin from 1946; member of Munich Co. from 1949. Bayreuth from 1951 as Walther and Siegfried. London, CG, 1951–53 as Radames. NY Met. debut 1952, Walther. La Scala, Milan, 1963 as Siegfried. Other roles include Strauss's Emperor and Max, Tristan and Otello.

Hopkins, Antony (originally Reynolds) (b London, 21 Mar 1921), English educator, conductor, writer on music and composer. He studied at the RCM with Cyril Smith and Gordon Jacob; successful as writer of incidental music for films, radio and the theatre (music for 15 of Shakespeare's plays). For SW he wrote the opera *Lady Rohesia* (1948) and while music director of Intimate Opera, from 1952, several one-act works. Series of radio broadcasts, *Talking About Music*, 1954–92. Books include *Understanding Music* (1979), *The Nine Symphonies of Beethoven* (1980) and *The Concertgoer's Companion* (two vols. 1984, 1986; reprinted as a single vol. 1994).

Hopkins, Bill (b Presbury, Cheshire, 5 Jun 1943; d Chopwell, near Newcastle, 10 Mar 1981), English composer and writer on music. Studied with Nono (at Dartington), Wellesz and Messiaen. His music was also influenced by Boulez and Barraqué: *Sous-structures*, for piano (1964), *Two Pomes* for soprano and ensemble (after Joyce, 1964), *Musique de l'indifférence*, ballet after Beckett (1965), *Études en série*, piano pieces in three books (1965–72), *En attendant*, for ensemble (1977).

Hopkinson, Francis (b Philadelphia, 21 Sept 1737; d Philadelphia, 9 May 1791), American lawyer, politician and amateur musician, sometimes regarded as the first American composer. Wrote a number of songs, including 'Beneath a weeping willow's shade', and the 'oratorical entertainment' *The Temple of Minerva*. Also developed some mechanical improvements for keyboard instruments.

Horenstein, Jascha (b Kiev, 6 May 1898; d London, 2 Apr 1973), Russian-born conductor. Went with his family to Germany as a child. Studied with Max Bode in Königsberg and with Adolph Busch in Vienna, also studying composition with Schreker in Berlin. He was appointed conductor of the Düsseldorf Opera in 1926 and settled in the USA in 1941; gave the first US performance of Busoni's *Doktor Faust* there in 1964. Well known in Schubert, Bruckner and Mahler and conducted the fps of Berg's Three Movements for strings (Berlin, 1929) and *Altenberg Lieder* (Rome, 1953). Conducted *Parsifal* at CG a few weeks before his death.

I am like a steam engine: I need to be stoked up, it takes me a long time to get ready for genuine work.
Arthur Honegger, *I am a Composer*, 1951

Horigome, Yuzuko (b Tokyo, 1957), Japanese violinist. Won Queen Elizabeth of the Belgians Competition 1980 and made London debut 1983, with the LSO under Abbado. US debut at Tanglewood 1982, with the Boston SO; further concerts with Chicago SO and the Los Angeles PO. Toured Europe and Japan with the Salzburg Camerata 1988. Appeared in the Shostakovich film *Testimony* and has recorded Bach's solo violin works.

Horizon Chimérique, L' song cycle by Fauré, op. 118 (texts by Jean de la Ville de Mirmont); composed 1921, fp Paris, 13 May 1922, with Charles Pinzéra.

horn a brass wind instrument with its tube bent in a circular form. In its early stages it could produce only the natural harmonics and was used mainly for hunting fanfares. When composers began to write for it in the early 18th c. they were still restricted to the natural harmonics; but by the invention of a series of crooks which could be inserted, the length of the tube could be altered and the instrument played in a variety of keys, with additional notes of darker tone quality being produced by inserting the hand into the bell ('handstopping'). It was only by the introduction of valves about the 1830s that the full chromatic scale could be played on a single instrument. However, this came

Antony Hopkins – musician/author

1 Mozart: *The Marriage of Figaro*
   Surely the most perfect opera ever written, in which for the
   first time the stage is taken over by credible human beings
   rather than creatures of myth and legend. The delineation of
   character in music is masterly, the musical invention
   unflagging.

2 Bach: Concerto in D minor for two violins
   Mainly remembered for the wonderfully lyrical slow
   movement, this is a work that reveals Bach's mastery of
   counterpoint, with the two soloists sharing the material so
   that neither dominates; when they combine to create four-
   part harmonies in the third movement Bach provides us with
   one of the most thrilling sounds in music.

3 Beethoven: Piano Concerto no. 4 in G major op. 58
   The magical opening is an unprecedented stroke of
   originality, setting the scene for a movement in which the
   soloist, unable to dominate the orchestra by force, has
   recourse to gentler means. This is movingly demonstrated in
   the slow movement, where the savagery of the unison strings
   is tamed by the serene restraint of the piano part. A witty
   and joyful finale rounds off a perfect work.

4 Beethoven: Piano Sonata in A flat major op. 110
   A wonderfully lyrical and restrained first movement leads to
   a miniature scherzo of concentrated ferocity; the finale
   reveals a profound grief which Beethoven twice tries to
   exorcise by turning to the Classical purity of Fugue, only to
   find salvation in a marvellously Romantic apotheosis. Here a
   conscious rejection of the past leads to a joyous embrace of
   the future.

5 Chopin: Piano Concerto no. 2 in F minor op. 21
   Despite the usual label, this is actually Chopin's first
   concerto, written unbelievably at the age of 19. Sometimes
   criticized for the lack of interest in the orchestral part, it is

notable for a completely original style of writing for the
keyboard and a slow movement which is one of his most
magically beautiful creations.

6 Berlioz: *Symphonie fantastique*
   A stunning *tour de force* of orchestration as well as being
   unprecedented in its structure. Openly reflecting the
   composer's emotional state during his infatuation for the
   Irish actress Harriet Smithson (and in the finale the bitter
   aftermath), it is a unique if occasionally flawed masterpiece.

7 Stravinsky: *Petrushka*
   Without question one of the most vividly descriptive scores
   of all time, full of authentic Russian folk melodies and
   musical portraits that make the characters come to life even
   if one has never seen the ballet.

8 Canteloube (arr.): 'Baïlero' from *Chants d'Auvergne*
   Outrageously over-orchestrated and lush Canteloube's
   arrangement may be, yet this song is hauntingly beautiful
   and never fails to touch the heart.

9 Elgar: Violin Concerto in B minor op. 61
   Richly endowed with memorable themes, splendidly
   orchestrated and superbly written for the violin, this concerto
   is notable for its unique feature – the lengthy cadenza in the
   third movement in which the soloist surveys and reflects
   upon material from the preceding movements.

10 Tippett: Concerto for Double String Orchestra
   One of the most immediately appealing of Tippett's
   compositions. The dancing, almost jazzy rhythms have
   enormous vitality, while the lyrical tunes which emerge from
   time to time go straight to the heart. The main theme of the
   slow movement with its characteristic 'blue' note has the
   simplicity of a folk song and the emotional quality of a
   spiritual.

at the price of the natural horn's purity of tone. The keyed horn fully replaced the natural horn in the late 19th c., largely due to its versatility. In recent years the natural horn has been revived.

The normal compass of the horn. One or two higher and lower notes are possible. The modern keyed horn is built in F and high B♭, with four valves, one of which transposes the instrument from the lower to the higher pitch.

Horn, Charles Edward (b London, 21 Jun 1786; d Boston, MA, 21 Oct 1849), English tenor-baritone singer and composer of German descent. He studied under his father, Karl Friedrich ◊Horn, and had singing lessons from Rauzzini at Bath in 1808, making his first stage appearance in London in 1809. He then began to write theatrical pieces, starting with *The Magic Bride* in 1810. In 1823 he visited Dublin and brought Balfe back with him as a pupil. Having been music director at the Olympic Theatre 1831–32, he went to USA in 1833, became a music teacher and pub. at Boston, where after a brief return to England he settled for good in 1847, becoming conductor of the Handel and Haydn Society.

Works include stage pieces *Lalla Rookh* (after Moore), *The Bee-*

hive (1811), *Rich and Poor*, *Peveril of the Peak* (after Scott), *Honest Frauds* (1830), and many others.

Horn, Karl Friedrich (b Nordhausen, Thuringia, 13 Apr 1762; d Windsor, 5 Aug 1830), German organist and composer, father of C E Horn. Pupil of C G Schröter, settled in England 1782, where under the patronage of Count Bruhl he quickly rose to become music teacher to Queen Charlotte and her daughters. In 1810 he pub. with S Wesley the first English edition of Bach's *Wohltemperierte Clavier*. He was appointed organist of St George's Chapel, Windsor, 1824.

Works include sonatas for piano and flute or violin, divertimenti for piano and violin, divertimenti for military band.

Hornbostel, Erich (Moritz) von (b Vienna, 25 Feb 1877; d Cambridge, 29 Nov 1935), Austrian musicologist. Studied physics and philosophy at Vienna and Heidelberg, and in 1906 became head of the gramophone archives in Berlin for the recording of ethnic music, on which he wrote several learned works. In 1933 he went to NY and the following year to London and Cambridge. He is most famous for his part in the Sachs-Hornbostel classification of musical instruments, still employed by most scholars and museums.

Horne, David (b Stirling, 1970), Scottish pianist and composer. Studied in Edinburgh and at the Curtis Institute (1989), and at Harvard. Has won prizes at Huddersfield Festival, as composer, and BBC Young Musician of the Year (piano section). Solo concerts with the CBSO, London Sinfonietta and Scottish National Orchestra; Prokofiev's Third Concerto at the 1990 Proms. Compositions include string quartet (1988), *Splintered Unisons* and *Towards Dharma* for ensemble (1988–89), *Light Emerging* for orchestra (1989), *Northscape* for chamber orchestra (1992), piano concerto (1992).

Horne, Marilyn (b Bradford, PA, 16 Jan 1934), American mezzo. She studied in California; stage debut Gelsenkirchen, 1957 as Giulietta. US debut, San Francisco, 1960 as Berg's Marie; London, CG, 1964 in same role. In 1962 began stage and concert association with Joan Sutherland; many performances of operas by Rossini and Bellini. NY Met. debut 1970, as Adalgisa; other roles there included Rosina, Carmen, Isabella and Fides. Has sung Rinaldo and Tancredi in Houston, and Malcolm in *La donna del lago* at CG (1985). Her last Rossini role was as Isabella in *L'Italiana in Algeri* at CG, 1993. She has been regarded as one of the most persuasive singers ever to appear in her repertory.

Horneman, Christian (Frederik Emil) (b Copenhagen, 17 Dec 1840; d Copenhagen, 8 Jun 1906), Danish composer. Studied with his father and at the Leipzig Conservatory. On his return to Copenhagen he founded a concert society and in 1880 a music school.

Works include opera *Aladdin* (Oehlenschläger, 1885); overture *A Hero's Life*; piano pieces; songs.

hornpipe an English dance, so called because it was at first accompanied on a pipe of the same name, made from an animal's horn. It did not always have nautical associations and up to the time of Handel, who has such an example in one of his concerti grossi, it was in 3–2 time. The later form is in 2–4.

The horn, the horn, the lusty horn/is not a thing to laugh to scorn.
William Shakespeare, *As You Like It*, Act 4, Scene 2, line 17.

Horn Signal, Symphony with the nickname of Haydn's symphony no. 31 in D major, composed 1765, so called because of the horn fanfares at the beginning and end.

Horowitz, Vladimir (b Kiev, 1 Oct 1904; d New York, 5 Nov 1989), Russian, later American pianist. Studied in Kiev with Felix Blumenfeld and made his debut in Kharkov, aged 17. Later he went to Paris and in 1928 made his American debut under Beecham. In 1933 he married Toscanini's daughter Wanda. From 1938 to 1939 he lived in Switzerland and in 1940 settled in America. He retired from concert life for 12 years, returning in 1965; retired again, but reappeared 1974 and played in Russia 1986. One of the most technically gifted and interpretatively charismatic pianists of his day.

Horsley, Charles Edward (b London, 16 Dec 1822; d New York, 28 Feb 1876), English pianist, organist and composer. Studied under his father, William ◊Horsley, and Moscheles, later with Hauptmann at Cassel and Mendelssohn at Leipzig. In 1845 he returned to London and became organist at St John's Church, Notting Hill, wrote several works for provincial festivals, etc. In 1862 he went to Australia and in the early 1870s to the USA.

Works include oratorios *David* (1850), *Joseph* (1853) and *Gideon* (1860); setting of Milton's *Comus*; Ode *Euterpe* for the opening of Melbourne Town Hall; piano trio.

Horsley, William (b London, 15 Nov 1774; d London, 12 Jun 1858), English organist and composer, father of Charles Edward ◊Horsley. Studied music privately, but had some advice from Callcott. He became organist of Ely Chapel, Holborn, in 1794, assisted Callcott as organist at the Asylum for Female Orphans and succeeded him in 1802. Later he held several other appointments. He was one of the founders of the Philharmonic Society in 1813. His family were close friends of Mendelssohn's.

Works include anthem *When Israel came out of Egypt*, hymn and psalm tunes; three symphonies; many glees.

Horszowski, Mieczyslaw (b Lwów, 23 Jun 1892; d Philadelphia, 22 May 1993), Polish-born American pianist. Debut Warsaw; appeared all over Europe as soloist and settled in NY 1940 (US citizen 1948);

Horowitz *The pianist Vladimir Horowitz (1904–1989) defined for many years the ultimate standard of the virtuoso. His recordings are legendary, spanning nearly three-quarters of a century. In later years he withdrew from the concert hall, making only occasional appearances.*

gave many chamber concerts with Szigeti and Casals and solo recitals of Mozart and Beethoven. He played at Aldeburgh in 1984.

Horvat, Milan (b Pakrac, 28 Jul 1919), Croatian conductor. Studied at Zagreb and was conductor of the Zagreb PO 1946–53 and 1958–69; chief conductor of the RTE SO at Dublin, 1953–58. Principal of Zagreb Opera 1958–65, giving many Yugoslav fps; Austrian Radio SO 1969–75, with many concerts as guest elsewhere in Europe (Salzburg Festival 1970, Penderecki's *St Luke Passion*). Conductor of the Zagreb SO from 1975. Recordings include music by Shostakovich and Hindemith.

Horwood, William (d 1484), English composer. He became master of the choristers at Lincoln Cathedral in 1477. His music, consisting of Latin antiphons and a Magnificat, is included in the Eton Choirbook; a fragmentary *Kyrie* has also survived.

Hothby, John (b *c* 1410; d ? Nov 1487), English Carmelite, music scholar, composer and doctor of theology. Graduated at Oxford and lectured there in 1435. Travelled (?) in Spain, France and Germany, settled *c* 1440 (?) at Florence and also (?) lived at Ferrara. He was called Giovanni Ottobi in Italy and spent *c* 1468–86 at Lucca. He taught there, but was recalled to England by Henry VII. Wrote a number of theoretical treatises. Some sacred and secular compositions were entered in the Faenza Codex .

Hotter, Hans (b Offenbach-am-Main, 19 Jan 1909), German bassbaritone. Initially an organist and choirmaster, studying church music, he later turned to opera. After studying with Roemer, a pupil of De Reszke, he made his debut in 1929 at Troppau; later sang at Breslau, Prague and Hamburg. In 1940 he became a member of the Munich and Vienna operas. London, CG, 1947–67; Bayreuth from 1952. He created roles in Strauss's *Friedenstag* (1938), *Capriccio* (1942) and *Die Liebe der Danae* (1944). Produced the *Ring* at CG, 1962–64. He was one of the leading Wagner singers of his day and also an impressive actor. Both these qualities were seen at their best in his Wotan, which he sang for the last time in Paris, 1972. Other roles included Sachs, the Dutchman, Don Giovanni and Palestrina's Borromeo. Late in his career he sang Berg's Schigolch in Munich, San

Francisco (1989) and Paris (1991). The Speaker in Schoenberg's *Gurrelieder* at the 1994 London Proms.

Hotteterre French 17th and 18th c. family of woodwind instrument makers, performers and composers; developments of the oboe from the shawm, the bassoon from the curtal and the transverse flute from the cylindrical flute are often credited to them. *Jacques Hotteterre* (b Paris, 29 Sept 1674; d Paris, 16 Jul 1763) is the best known of the family; he called himself *Le Romain* after an early visit to Italy. From 1708 at the latest he was a bassoonist in the Grands Hautbois and was a flautist in the service of the king. His book *Principes de la flute traversière* (1707) was the first such treatise to be published; it was followed by *L'art de préluder sur la flute traversière* and *Methode pour la musette* (1737).

Hough, Stephen (b Heswell, Cheshire, 22 Nov 1961), English pianist. Has appeared with leading orchestras in the USA, including the Chicago and Detroit SOs, Cleveland Orchestra and Los Angeles PO; annual concerts at the Hollywood Bowl. All major British orchestras, and London Prom concerts from 1985 (Bartók's Third Concerto, 1993). Recordings include concertos by Brahms and Hummel, and solo pieces by Britten.

House of the Dead, From the, *Z Mrtvého Domu*, opera in three acts by Janáček (libretto by the composer, after Dostoievsky), produced Brno, 12 Apr 1930. Various prisoners in a Siberian gulag recall their earlier lives. The opera is framed by the incarceration and eventual release of the political prisoner, Alexandr.

Housman, A(lfred) E(dward) (1859–1936), English poet and Latin scholar. Poems from *A Shropshire Lad* and *Last Poems* set to music by many composers, including Barber, Butterworth, Gurney, Ireland, Moeran, C W Orr, Somervell and Vaughan Williams.

Houston Grand Opera US opera company founded in Texas 1955 by Walter Herbert; David Gockley general manager from 1972. John De Main has been music director from 1977 and performances from 1987 have been in two auditoria at the Wortham Theater Centre. A notable feature has been productions of modern classics and world premieres: Joplin's *Treemonisha* (1975), three Carlisle Floyd fps, Bernstein's *A Quiet Place* (1983), Glass's *Akhnaten* (1984), *Nixon in China* by Adams (1987), Tippett's *New Year* (1989) and Robert Moran's *Desert of Roses* (1992) and *The Dracula Diary* (1994).

Houston Symphony Orchestra US orchestra founded 1913 with Julian Paul Blitz as conductor; reorganized 1930 and increased in size under Ernst Hoffmann (1936–47). Later conductors have been Efrem Kurtz (1948–54), Beecham (1954–55), Stokowski (1955–60), Barbirolli (1961–67), Previn (1967–69), Lawrence Foster (1971–78); Sergiu Commissiona 1980–88; Christoph Eschenbach from 1988.

Hove, Joachim van den (b Antwerp, 1567; d The Hague, 1620), Flemish lutenist and composer. Pub. a book of songs for two voices and lute, one of songs and dances arranged for lute and one of preludes for lute and viol.

Hovhaness, Alan (b Somerville, MA, 8 Mar 1911), American composer of Armenian descent. Studied piano with Heinrich Gebhard and composition with Converse and Martinů. He is much influenced by Indian and other oriental music. He has composed much, but destroyed a great deal of it in 1940.

Works include ten operas; 63 symphonies (1939–88), *And God Created Whales* (1970) including taped part for humpbacked whale, two *Armenian Rhapsodies* for strings, 23 concertos (1936–80) including *Elibris* for flute and strings; *Lousadzak* for piano and strings; concerto for trumpet and strings; *Sosi* for violin piano, percussion and strings; *Arekeval* for orchestra; concerto for orchestra; *Ad Lyram* for orchestra; chamber music including five string quartets (1936–76).

Howard, Ann (b Norwood, 22 Jul 1936), English mezzo. After 1961 debut at CG, London, she studied further in Paris. From 1964 she has sung widely in Britain and North America as Carmen, Fricka and Azucena and in operettas by J Strauss and Offenbach. Season 1992 as Orlofsky for ENO and the Hostess in *Boris Godunov* for Opera North. Her Witch in *Hansel and Gretel* has been recorded.

Howard, Samuel (1710–London, 13 Jul 1782), English organist and composer. Pupil of Croft at the Chapel Royal and later of Pepusch. Appointed organist at the churches of St Clement Danes and St Bride. Mus.D., Cambridge, in 1769. He assisted Boyce in compiling his *Cathedral Music*.

Works include anthems and other church music; pantomimes, *The Amorous Goddess*, or *Harlequin Married* and *Robin Goodfellow*; cantatas and songs.

Howarth, Elgar (b Cannock, Staffs., 4 Nov 1935), English conductor, trumpeter and composer. He studied at the RMCM and played the trumpet in the Philip Jones brass ensemble and the RPO (1963–68). He has been director of the London Sinfonietta since 1973 and has toured widely, often in modern music; conducted the 1978 Stockholm fp of Ligeti's opera *Le Grand Macabre* and in 1986 the London, Coliseum, fp of Birtwistle's *The Mask of Orpheus*. Conducted the premieres of Birtwistle's *Gawain* at CG, 1991, and the *The Second Mrs Kong* for GTO at Glyndebourne, 1994. He has composed and arranged works for brass band, e.g. Mussorgsky's *Pictures at an Exhibition*.

Howarth, Judith (b Ipswich, 11 Sept 1962), English soprano. Studied at the Royal Scottish Academy and sang Mozart arias with the ECO, 1984, CG from 1985, in Zemlinsky's *Der Zwerg* and as Siebel, Oscar, Elvira in *L'Italiana in Algeri*, Iris in *Semele* and Morgana in *Alcina* (1992). Appearances for Opera North and Scottish Opera, as Susanna and Zerlina. Salzburg Festival 1991, *Der Schauspieldirektor*. US debut Seattle 1989, in concert with Domingo. Sang Walton's Cressida at CG 1995.

Howell, Gwynne (b Gorseinon, 13 Jun 1938), Welsh bass. He studied at the RMCM and sang in operas by Wagner there. London, SW, from 1968; CG from 1970 in operas by Strauss, Puccini, Verdi and Mussorgsky, and in the 1972 fp of Maxwell Davies' *Taverner*. He is well known as a concert singer in Europe and North America (e.g. the *Missa solemnis*) and in Mar 1986 sang Gurnemanz in a new pro-

---

Elgar Howarth – conductor / composer / trumpeter

1 Byrd: Masses
   Brilliantly inventive rhythms and programmatic flair.

2 Debussy: *Preludes*
   Cool, scrupulous.

3 Ives: *Three Places in New England*
   A great, original, daring mind.

4 Beethoven: Symphony no. 5
   Revolution.

5 Dowland: songs
   Elegant melancholy.

6 Ligeti: *Melodien*
   Strange, superbly crafted original music of great beauty.

7 Stravinsky: *Agon*
   The composer's preoccupations in his later years. Poised, witty, entirely personal in its orchestration.

8 Birtwistle: *Secret Theatre*
   A nocturnal dance. His masterpiece for small orchestra.

duction of *Parsifal* at the London Coliseum. NY Met. debut 1985, as Pogner in *Meistersinger*; King Philip in *Don Carlos* for ENO, 1992.

Howells, Anne (b Southport, 12 Jan 1941), English mezzo. She studied at the RMCM and sang Helen there in the first British production of Gluck's *Paride e Helena* (1963). London, CG, from 1967; roles have included Ophelia in Searle's *Hamlet*, Rosina, Cherubino and Siebel. Glyndebourne 1967, as Eribse in the Cavalli-Leppard *L'Ormindo*, and has returned in operas by Maw, Strauss and Monteverdi; in 1974 she was Diana in *Calisto*. NY Met. debut 1975, Dorabella. Season 1992 as Giulietta in *Hoffmann* and Despina at CG.

Howells, Herbert (Norman) (b Lydney, Gloucestershire, 17 Oct 1892; d Oxford, 24 Feb 1983), English composer. Pupil of Herbert Brewer at Gloucester Cathedral and later under Stanford at the RCM in London, where he became professor of composition. Later, having been first sub-organist at Salisbury Cathedral, lived a retired life 1917–20 owing to poor health. Music Director at St Paul's Girls' School from 1936, in succession to Holst. Mus.D., Oxford, 1937. He was Professor of Music at London University 1952–62 and was created CBE 1953. His best-known work is the *Hymnus Paradisi*, written in memory of his son, and in which he escapes the influence of Vaughan Williams and other pastoralists.

Works include ballet *Penguinski*; *Sine Nomine*, *A Kent Yeoman's Song* and *Hymnus Paradisi* for soli, chorus and orchestra (1938); *Procession*, *Pastoral Rhapsody* (1923), *Paradise Rondel*, *Merry-Eye*, *Puck's Minuet*, *King's Herald* for orchestra; Lady Audrey's Suite for string orchestra; *Pageantry* for brass band; two piano concertos (1913, 1924); song cycle *In Green Ways* with orchestra.

CHAMBER: fantasy string quartet, string quartet *In Gloucestershire* (1923), clarinet quintet; three violin and piano sonatas, two organ sonatas; oboe sonata, clarinet sonata; *Lambert's Clavichord* and *Howells' Clavichord* for clavichord; piano pieces; much church music; songs.

Howes, Frank (b Oxford, 2 Apr 1891; d Standlake, Oxfordshire, 28 Sept 1974), English music critic. Educated at St John's College, Oxford. He joined *The Times* as assistant music critic in 1925, became lecturer at the RCM in 1938 and was chief *Times* critic 1943–60. His books include a life of Byrd, studies of Vaughan Williams and Walton, of musical appreciation, psychology, opera, the orchestra and others.

Hoyland, Vic(tor) (b Wombwell, Yorkshire, 11 Dec 1945), English composer. Studied at York University with Bernard Rands and Robert Sherlaw-Johnson. Senior lecturer at Barber Institute, Birmingham, from 1993. Works have been featured at the Bath, Aldeburgh and California Contemporary Music Festivals. Has directed performances of electronic music (Stockhausen's *Momente* in London, 1994). Works include: *Em* for 24 voices (1970); *Ariel* for voice and ensemble (1975), *Serenade* for 14 players (1979); *Xingu*, music theatre (1979); *Michelangiolo* for baritone and ensemble (1981); *Quartet Movement* (1982); quintet for brass (1985); string quartet (1985); *In Transit* for orchestra (1987) *Of Fantasy*, *Of Dreams and Ceremonies* for 13 strings (1989); Trio (1990); piano quartet (1990); Chamber Concerto, with piano (1993).

Hubay, Jenö (originally Eugen Huber) (b Budapest, 15 Sept 1858; d Budapest, 12 Mar 1937), Hungarian violinist and composer. Pupil of his father Karl Huber, he appeared as a prodigy at the age of 11, but later went to study with Joachim in Berlin. He travelled much, edited and completed some of Vieuxtemps' works and became violin professor at the Brussels Conservatory in 1882 and at the Budapest Conservatory in 1886, of which he was director 1919–34.

Works include operas *Alienor* (1891), *A Cremonai Hegedüs* (after Coppée's *Luther de Crémone*, 1894), *A Falu Rossza*, *Karenina Anna* (after Tolstoy, 1915), *Az álarc*, etc.; four symphonies; four violin concertos; *Sonate romantique* for violin and piano; many violin pieces, studies.

Huber, Hans (b Eppenburg, Solothurn, 28 Jun 1852; d Locarno, 25 Dec 1921), Swiss composer. After attending seminary at Solothurn, he studied music under Carl Munzinger there and later at the Leipzig Conservatory. After teaching in Alsace, he settled at Basel 1877. In 1889 he became professor at the Conservatory there and succeeded Selmar Bagge as its director 1896, retiring 1918.

Works include operas *Weltfrühling* (1894), *Kudrun* (1896), *Simplicius* (1912), *Die schöne Bellinde*, *Frutta di mare* (1918); Masses, cantatas, etc.; nine symphonies (No. 2 on pictures by Böcklin) and other orchestral works *Sommernächte*, *Serenade*, *Carneval* and *Römischer Carneval*; four piano concertos, violin concerto; much chamber music; piano music; songs, including Hafiz cycle.

Huber, Klaus (b Berne, 30 Nov 1924), Swiss composer. Studied with Willy Burkhard at the Zurich Conservatory and with Blacher in Berlin. From 1950 he taught violin in Zurich and from 1960 music history at the Lucerne Conservatory. His music combines avant-garde techniques with a strong religious awareness.

Works include cantata for voices and four instruments *Des Engels Anredung an die Seele* (1957); oratorio *Mechthildis* for alto voice and chamber orchestra (1957). *Auf die ruhige Nacht-Zeit* for soprano and chamber group (1958); *Soliloquia* for soloists, chorus and orchestra; *Sonata da chiesa* for violin and organ, *Concerto per la Camerata* (1955), *Tempora*, violin concerto (1970); *Jot, oder Wann kommt der Herr Zürück* opera (1973); *Turnus* for orchestra and tape (1974); *Litania instrumentalis* for orchestra (1975); *Von Zeit zu Zeit*, string quartet (1985); *Protuberanzen* for orchestra (1986); *Spes contra spem* for voice, narrator and orchestra (1988).

Huberman, Bronislaw (b Czestochowa, 19 Dec 1882; d Nant-sur-Corsier, Switzerland, 15 Jun 1947), Polish violinist. Studied at the Warsaw Conservatory, in Paris and Berlin, played in public at the age of seven and later toured the world. With William Steinberg organized the Palestine SO (1936; Israel PO from 1948). Admired for the freedom of his interpretations.

Hucbald (b ? Tournai c 840; d Saint-Amand, 20 Jun 930), French monk and musician. Lived at the monastery of Saint-Amand. Wrote the treatise *De harmonica institutione* (c 880), one of the earliest known writings on Western music theory.

Hudson, George (b c 1615; d Greenwich, Dec 1672), English violinist and composer. Worked in London. Took part, with Coleman, senior, Cooke, H Lawes and Locke, in providing music for Davenant's *Siege of Rhodes* (entertainment at Rutland House) in 1656; member of the King's Band from 1661 and composer to the king.

Hüe, Georges (Adolphe) (b Versailles, 6 May 1858; d Paris 7 Jun 1948), French composer. Studied at the Paris Conservatory, where he obtained the Prix de Rome in 1879. Member of the Académie des Beaux-Arts in 1922 in succession to Saint-Saëns.

Works include operas *Les Pantins*, *Le Roi de Paris* (1901), *Le Miracle*, *Titania* (after Shakespeare, 1903), *Dans l'ombre de la cathédrale* (1921), *Riquet à la Houppe* (after Perrault); ballets *Siang Sin* and *Nimba*, pantomime *Coeur brisé.*; incidental music to Rostand's *Les Romanesques*, Kalidasa's *Sakuntala*, etc.; symphonies, symphonic legend *Rübezahl*, and other orchestral works; songs.

Gentlemen, the difference between what you played tonight and what I wrote would make a new opera.
Arnold Schoenberg, after a performance of *Von Heute auf Morgen*, quoted in Slonimsky, *Music Since 1900*, 1971

Huffstodt, Karen (b Illinois, 31 Dec 1954), American soprano. Sang with NY City Opera from 1982, as Micaela, Violetta and Donna Anna; Santa Fe 1984 and 1989, in the US fps of Henze's *We Come to the River* and Massenet's *Chérubin*. Chicago Lyric Opera as Fiordiligi and Washington DC 1986, in the fp of Menotti's *Goya*, with Domingo. Has sung Mozart roles in Vienna, Munich and Cologne; NY Met. debut 1989, Violetta. Title role in the French version of *Salome* (Lyon 1990) and Odabella in *Attila* at CG, 1991. Opened the season at La Scala as Spontini's *Vestale* (1993) and sang Sieglinde in Paris (Théâtre du Châtelet) 1994.

Huggett, Monica (b London, 16 May 1953), English violinist. Studied with Ton Koopman and co-founded with him the Amsterdam

Baroque Orchestra (leader 1980–87). Many concerts with gut-string instrument, notably with the Hanover Band (also directing) and the Academy of Ancient Music. Beethoven's Concerto with the Orchestra of the Age of Enlightenment, 1991. Recordings with Hausmusik and the Raglan Baroque Players; Beethoven symphonies with the Hanover Band.

Hughes, Anselm (actually Humphrey Vaughan) (b London, 15 Apr 1889; d Nashdom, 8 Sept 1974), English music scholar and Anglican Benedictine, Prior of Nashdom Abbey. Part-editor of the pub. of the Old Hall MS. He was a member of the Editorial Board of the *New Oxford History of Music*, editor of Vol. II and joint editor of Vol. III.

Hughes, Owain Arwel (b Cardiff, 21 Mar 1942), Welsh conductor. Studied at the RCM and with Haitink and Kempe. Music director of the National Eisteddfod of Wales, 1977, associate conductor of the BBC Welsh SO from 1980. Directed the Huddersfield Choral Society 1980–86, founder and director of the Welsh Proms, 1986. Well known in the popular repertory.

His father Arwel (1909–1988) was a conductor in Wales and wrote the opera *Menna* (1951), a symphony and three string quartets.

Hughes, Gervase (b Birmingham, 1 Sept 1905), English composer. He took the B.Mus. at Oxford in 1927 and in 1926 joined the music staff of the BNOC; later conducted at various theatres. In 1933 he left the music profession, but after World War II took to composing again. Wrote books on Sullivan (1960) and Dvořák (1967).

Works include opera *Imogen's Choice*, operettas *Castle Creevy* and *Venetian Fantasy*; symphony in F minor, *Overture for a Musical Comedy* for orchestra; piano music, songs.

Hugh the Drover, or Love in the Stocks opera by Vaughan Williams (libretto by Harold Child), produced London, RCM, 4 Jul 1924. Itinerant Hugh wins Mary in a boxing contest and both are released from the stocks to lead a wandering life.

Hugo, Victor (1802–1885), French poet, novelist and dramatist. Balfe (◊Armourer of Nantes), ◊Liszt (*Ce qu'on entend ...*); ◊Cui (*Angelo*); ◊Dargomizhsky (*Esmeralda* and *Notre-Dame de Paris*); ◊Delibes (*Le Roi s'amuse*); Franck (◊Djinns); Verdi (◊Ernani); Campana, Dargomizhsky (◊Esmeralda); ◊Fauré (songs); Ponchielli (◊Gioconda; Mercadante ◊Giuramento; Donizetti (◊Lucrezia Borgia); Gomes (◊Maria Tudor; Liszt (◊Mazeppa); F Schmidt (◊Notre Dame); ◊Pedrotti (*Marion Delorme*); ◊Ponchielli (ditto); Verdi (◊Rigoletto); Glover, Marchetti and Mendelssohn (◊Ruy Blas); ◊Wagner-Régeny (*Der Günstling*).

Huguenots, Les opera by Meyerbeer (libretto by Scribe and Émile Deschamps), produced Paris, Opéra, 29 Feb 1836. Amorous conflict set against 16th-c. religious massacres.

Huizar, Candelario (b Jérez, 2 Feb 1888; d Mexico City, 3 May 1970), Mexican composer of Indian origin. Studied at the National Conservatory in Mexico, where he later taught.

Works include four symphonies on native tunes (1930–42); string quartet.

Hulda opera by C Franck (libretto by C Grandmougin, based on a play by Bjoĺrnson), not performed in Franck's lifetime; produced Monte Carlo, 8 Mar 1894. In 11th-c. Norway, Hulda seeks revenge on Aslak and his clan, who killed her family. All end up dead.

Hull, Arthur Eaglefield (b Market Harborough, 10 Mar 1876; d Huddersfield, 4 Nov 1928), English writer on music. He was editor of the *Monthly Musical Record* from 1912; an early champion of Skriabin, and in 1924 pub. a *Dictionary of Modern Music and Musicians* (German translation, with many corrections, by Alfred Einstein, 1926). His *Music: Classical, Romantic and Modern* (1927) was exposed by Percy Scholes as consisting of unadorned borrowings from other writers. Such accusations were taken seriously in the 1920s, and Hull felt obliged to throw himself under a train at Huddersfield station. He edited the complete organ works of Bach and Mendelssohn.

Hullah, John (Pyke) (b Worcester, 27 Jun 1812; d London, 21 Feb 1884), English conductor, teacher and composer. Had music lessons from Wm Horsley in London and studied singing at the RAM. In 1836 he became known as the composer of Dickens's opera, *The Village Coquettes*. After a stay in Paris he taught singing in London, especially at a school opened at Exeter Hall in 1841 for the instruction of schoolmasters, In 1847 his friends opened St Martin's Hall for him, and he gave concerts there until 1860, when the hall was burnt down. Later he held a number of music appointments and wrote several books.

Hüllmandel, Nicolas Joseph (b Strasbourg, 23 May 1756; d London, 19 Dec 1823), Alsatian harpsichordist, pianist and composer. Pupil of C P E Bach. He appeared in London 1771 and settled there 1790 after a visit to Italy and residence in Paris. Wrote a treatise on piano playing.

Works include numerous sonatas for harpsichord and later for piano, many with violin accompaniment.

Hume, Tobias (b *c* 1569; d London, 16 Apr 1645), English viola da gamba player and composer. He was an army captain and towards the end of his life a pensioner in the Charterhouse. Wrote dances for viola da gamba, songs to the lute, etc., pub. in *Musicall Humours* and *Poeticall Musicke* (1607).

Humfrey, Pelham (b ? London, 1647; d Windsor, 14 Jul 1674), English composer. Entered the re-established Chapel Royal in London in 1660 under Cooke, joined Blow and Turner in the composition of the so-called 'club anthem' and was sent abroad for study by Charles II in 1664. Returned in 1667 from France and Italy and became a Gentleman of the Chapel Royal, where he succeeded Cooke as Master of the Children in 1672; he died aged only 26.

Works include music to Shakespeare's *Tempest* (1674), Dryden's *Conquest of Granada* and *The Indian Emperor*, Crowne's *History of Charles VIII* and Wycherley's *Love in a Wood*; anthems; odes, sacred songs, airs for one and two voices.

Hummel, Ferdinand (b Berlin, 6 Sept 1855; d Berlin, 24 Apr 1928), German pianist, harpist and composer. After playing piano and harp in public as a child, he studied at Kullak's Conservatory in Berlin and later had a success with realistic operas.

Works include operas *Mara* (1893), *Angla* (1894), *Ein treuer Schelm* (1894), *Assarpai*, *Sophie von Brabant* (1899), *Die Beichte* (1899), *Die Gefilde der Seligen*; incidental music for 14 plays by Wildenbruch and others; symphony, overture; piano concerto, fantasy for harp and orchestra; choral works; chamber music; piano pieces.

Never come near me again! You are a faithless cur, and may the hangman take all faithless curs.
Beethoven in a letter to Johann Hummel, 1799

Hummel, Johan Nepomuka (Johann Nepomuk) (b Pozsony, 14 Nov 1778; d Weimar, 17 1837), Hungarian pianist and composer. Learnt music at first from his father, the conductor Joseph Hummel, who went to Vienna in 1785 as conductor of the Theater auf der Wieden. By that time he was already a brilliant pianist and Mozart took him as a pupil for two years. In 1787 he went to tour in Germany, Holland, Scotland and England and had further lessons from Clementi in London, where he stayed until 1792. In 1793 he was back in Vienna, studying composition with Albrechtsberger, Haydn and Salieri. In 1803 he visited Russia and 1804–11 he was music director to Prince Esterházy. In 1816–19 he held a similar post at the court of Württemberg at Stuttgart and 1819–22 and 1833–37 at that of Weimar, undertaking extensive concert tours in between, spending much time in London. He was a friend of Beethoven and the original dedicatee of Schubert's last three piano sonatas. He married the singer Elisabeth Röckl (1793–1883).

Works include operas *Die Rückfahrt des Kaisers* (1814) and *Mathilde von Guise* (1810); ballets *Hélène et Paris* (1807), *Das belebte Gemälde*, *Sappho*; pantomime *Der Zauberring* (1811), incidental music to Grillparzer's *Die Ahnfrau*; Masses and other church music; seven piano concertos; trumpet concerto (1803), chamber music; sonatas for piano with another instrument; piano sonatas, rondos, variations.

humoresque, French; *Humoreske* (German), a piece (or in Schumann a series of movements) of capricious or fantastic rather than humorous character.

Humperdinck, Engelbert (b Siegburg, 1 Sept 1854; d Neustrelitz, 27 Sept 1921), German composer. Studied under F Hiller at the Cologne Conservatory and later with F Lachner and Rheinberger at Munich. In 1879 he met Wagner in Italy and acted as his assistant at Bayreuth 1880–81. Later he travelled in France, Italy and Spain and taught at the Barcelona Conservatory 1885–87. In 1890–96 he taught at the Hoch Conservatory at Frankfurt and was for a time music critic of the *Frankfurter Zeitung*. His enduring success, *Hänsel und Gretel*, was premiered at Weimar in 1893 under Richard Strauss. In 1900 he became director of the Meisterschule for composition in Berlin.

Works include operas *Hänsel und Gretel* (1893), *Dornröschen* (1902), *Die Heirat wider Willen* (1905), *Königskinder* (1910), *Die Marketenderin*, *Gaudeamus*; play with music *Königskinder* (an earlier version of the opera); spectacular pantomime *The Miracle*; incidental music to Shakespeare's *Merchant of Venice* (1905), *Winter's Tale* (1906), *The Tempest* (1906) and *Twelfth Night*, Maeterlinck's *The Blue Bird* (1912), Aristophanes' *Lysistrata*; choral works *Das Glück von Edenhall* (Uhland), *Die Wallfahrt nach Kevlaar* (Heine); *Humoreske* and *Maurische Rhapsodie* for orchestra; part-songs, songs.

Humphrey, Pelham, ◊Humfrey.

Humphries, John (b c 1707; d c 1740), English composer. Pub. six solos for violin and bass and two sets of concertos. He is possibly identical with J S Humphries, who c 1733 pub. a set of sonatas for two violins.

Hungarian Sketches work for orchestra by Bartók, arranged from piano pieces including *Four Dirges* and *Three Burlesques*, 1931; fp Budapest, 26 Nov 1934. Movements are titled *An evening in the village*, *Bear dance*, *Melody*, *Slightly tipsy*, *Swineherd's Dance*.

Hungarian String Quartet ensemble founded in Budapest 1935, with Sándor Végh and Péter Szervánsky (violins), Dénes Koromzay (viola) and Vilmos Palotai (cello). Zoltán Székely replaced Vegh as leader, who took the part of second violin, and by the time the ensemble was disbanded (1970) Michael Kuttner had become second violinist and Gabor Magyar cellist. Initially resident in Holland, the quartet moved to the USA 1950; Székely's association with Bartók (he premiered the Second Concerto in 1939) lent particular distinction to their concerts and recordings of the six quartets. Also admired for their performances of Beethoven.

Hunnenschlacht, *Battle of the Huns*, symphonic poem by Liszt inspired by Kaulbach's fresco, composed 1857; fp Weimar, 29 Dec 1857.

Hunnis, William (d London, 6 Jun 1597), English composer. Gentleman of the Chapel Royal in the reigns of Edward VI, Mary I and Elizabeth I, though dismissed as a Protestant in Mary's time. He became Master of the Children in 1566.

Works include metrical psalms and other portions of the Bible versified by himself.

Hunt, Arabella (b c 1645; d London, 26 Dec 1705), English singer and lutenist. Music teacher of Princess (later Queen) Anne and a favourite of Queen Mary. Blow and Purcell wrote many songs for her. Congreve wrote an ode on her and Kneller painted her portrait.

Hunter, Rita (b Wallasey, 15 Aug 1933), English soprano. She studied in Liverpool and London. SW chorus from 1954 and Carl Rosa Co., solo roles with SW, from 1959, including Marcellina, Senta and Odabella in *Attila*. Sang Brünnhilde in *Die Walküre* at the London Coliseum 1970, also role of NY Met. debut in 1972. Brünnhilde in *Ring* cycle at Coliseum 1973; other roles have been Norma, Santuzza and Leonora (*Trovatore*). Sang Turandot at the Albert Hall, London, 1990.

'Hunt' Quartet the familiar nickname of Mozart's B♭ major string quartet, K458, because the opening suggests hunting-horns.

Hunyady László opera by Erkel (libretto by B Egressy), produced Budapest, 27 Jan 1844. The chief Hungarian national opera. After surviving one plot against him, politician László is imprisoned by the palatine Gara, the father of László's fiancée Mária, who promises his daughter to the king in exchange for László's death. László survives three blows of the executioner's sword, but the fourth kills him.

Huon de Bordeaux medieval French romance. ◊Oberon (Weber and Wranitzky).

hurdy-gurdy, onomatopoeic, the English name for the medieval *organistrum*. Its strings, usually six, are set vibrating by a wheel turned with a handle. The tune is played on the top string by means of a keyboard, the lower strings remaining unchanged in pitch and thus acting as a drone.

hurdy-gurdy

Hurford, Peter (b Minehead, 22 Nov 1930), English organist and composer. Studied at the RCM and Cambridge University. Concert tours of Europe, the USA, Australasia and Japan from 1958. Master of the Music at St Albans 1958–78, visiting artist-in-residence at the Sydney Opera House, 1979–82. Broadcast series include the Bach chorale preludes, BBC 1994. Recordings include complete organ works of Bach, Couperin, Handel and Hindemith. OBE 1984.

Hurlebusch, Konrad Friedrich (b Brunswick, 1696; d Amsterdam, 17 Dec 1765), German organist and composer, son of Heinrich Hurlebusch. Travelled much as a virtuoso, visiting Italy and Sweden, holding brief offices at Brunswick and Hamburg, and finally settling at Amsterdam.

Works include operas, cantatas, hymns, overtures, harpsichord pieces, songs, etc.

Hurlstone, William (Yeates) (b London, 7 Jan 1876; d London, 30 May 1906), English pianist and composer. Studied at the RCM in London, having already pub. waltzes for piano at the age of nine. Professor of counterpoint at the RCM from 1905 to his early death.

Works include Fantasy-Variations on a Swedish Air and suite *The Magic Mirror* for orchestra (1896); piano concerto (1896); string quartet in E minor, piano and wind quintet, piano quartet, Fantasy string quartet (1906); sonatas for violin and piano, cello and piano, bassoon and piano, suite for clarinet and piano.

Hurford *The organist Peter Hurford is one of the most eminent performers of the instrument today. Since his appointment as Master of Music at St Albans, Hertfordshire, in 1958 he has done much to promote the organ as a concert instrument. He has also been active as an editor of organ music.*

Hurwitz, Emanuel (b London, 7 May 1919), English violinist. Leader of the Goldsborough (later English) Chamber Orchestra 1948–68; Melos Ensemble 1956–72; Aeolian Quartet from 1970. Hurwitz Chamber Orchestra 1968, from 1972 known as the Serenata of London. CBE 1978.

Husa, Karel (b Prague, 7 Aug 1921), Czech-born American composer and conductor. Studied at Prague Conservatory and with Boulanger and Honegger in Paris. Emigrated to USA 1954; professor Cornell University from 1961. He has been influenced by Czech folk music, neo-classicism and serialism.

Works include ORCHESTRAL: Sinfonietta (1947), *Trois Fresques* (1949), Divertimento for strings (1949), Symphony (1954), *Fantasies* (1957), Mosaïques (1961), Concerto for brass quintet and orchestra (1970), trumpet concerto (1974), *Monodrama* (1976), *The Trojan Women*, ballet for orchestra (1981); *Symphonic Suite* (1984), Concerto for Orchestra (1980), concertos for organ, trumpet and cello (1987–88); three string quartets (1948–68); *12 Moravian Songs*; *Variations* for piano quintet (1984).

Hüsch, Gerhard (b Hanover, 2 Feb 1901; d Munich, 21 Nov 1984), German baritone. Made his debut in Osnabrück in 1924 and then sang at the Cologne Opera 1927–30 and in Bayreuth 1930–31 (Wolfram), Berlin from 1930 to 1942, London, CG 1930–38 as Falke and Papageno. In addition to being a fine opera-singer he was also a distinguished Lieder-singer, particularly in Schubert.

Husitská concert overture by Dvořák, op. 67, composed 1883, fp Prague, reopening of the National Theatre, 13 Nov 1883. Based on the 10th-c. St Vaclav chorale and the 15th-c. Hussite hymn.

Huston, Scott (b Tacoma, WA, 10 Oct 1916), American composer. Studied with Howard Hanson at the Eastman School and taught at the Cincinnati Conservatory 1952–88. Works include opera *Blind Girl* (New York 1984), six symphonies (No. 6, *The Human Condition*, 1982), *Sounds of the Courtesans* for voice and ensemble (1985), *The Unpredictable Pendulum of Temperaments*, for dancers and ensemble (1988).

Hutchings, Arthur (James Bramwell) (b Sunbury-on-Thames, 14 Jul 1906; d Colyton, Devon, 13 Nov 1989), English writer on music and composer. Author of books on Schubert, Mozart's piano concertos, Delius and the Baroque concerto. In 1947 he followed Bairstow as Professor of Music at Durham University, becoming professor at Exeter University from 1968 to 1971. Pub. *Mozart: The Man, the Musician* (1976), *Purcell* (1982).

Works include *O quanta qualia, or Heart's Desire* (Abélard) for double chorus, orchestra, brass band and organ; motets and other church music; works for string orchestra.

Hüttenbrenner, Anselm (b Graz, 13 Oct 1794; d Ober-Andritz, near Graz, 5 Jun 1868), Austrian composer. Pupil of Salieri and friend of Schubert, whose unfinished symphony he withheld from the world until 1865.

Works include operas *Die Französische Einquartierung* (1819), *Ödipus auf Kolonos* (Sophocles, 1836), *Armella* and *Lenore*; incidental music for several plays; ten Masses, four Requiems and other church music; eight symphonies; two string quartets; songs including a setting of Goethe's *Erlkönig*.

Huttenlocher, Philippe (b Neuchâtel, 29 Nov 1942), Swiss baritone. Sang with the Ensemble Vocale de Lausanne in Europe and Japan, then Zurich Opera from 1975 as Orfeo and in other Monteverdi operas directed by Jean-Pierre Ponnelle. Baroque repertory in Vienna, Berlin, Milan and Hamburg. London Bach Festival, 1978. Recordings include *Castor et Pollux* and *Les Indes Galantes* by Rameau, Charpentier's *David et Jonathas* and *L'Incoronazione di Poppea* (video).

Huygens, Constantin (b The Hague, 4 Sept 1596; d The Hague, 28 Mar 1687), Dutch official, physicist, poet, writer, linguist and musician. He was military secretary at The Hague from 1625 to his death. He was a lutenist and also played viol and the keyboard instruments, paying three visits to England and others to Germany, Italy and France. He collected a library and wrote on the use of the organ in church and other musical subjects. Composed nearly 900 pieces for

Hvorostovsky *Baritone Dmitri Hvorostovsky has been active as a recitalist and an opera singer. He has performed much Tchaikovsky, Verdi and Rossini. He applies his beautiful, well-trained voice with sophistication.*

lute, theorbo, guitar, etc. One of his sons, Christian (1629–95), was also a musician as well as a mathematician.

Hvorostovsky, Dmitri (b Krasnoyarsk, Siberia, 16 Oct 1962), Russian baritone. Sang with the Kirov Opera 1987 and won the 1989 Cardiff Singer of the World Competition. London debut at the Wigmore Hall 1989 (songs by Tchaikovsky); CG 1982, as Riccardo in *I puritani*. Sang Yeletsky in *The Queen of Spades* at Nice 1989 and Paris (Châtelet) 1992. US debut as Germont at the Chicago Lyric Opera, 1993. Also a distinguished recitalist.

Hyde, Walter (b Birmingham, 6 Feb 1875; d London, 11 Nov 1951), English tenor. While still a student at the RCM he appeared in operas by Weber and Stanford. CG, London, 1908–23; sang Siegmund under Richter, 1908, and Sali in the first London performance of *A Village Romeo and Juliet* (1910). NY Met. debut Mar 1910, as Siegmund. Often sang Mozart with the Beecham Opera Company and the BNOC.

Hygons, Richard (b c 1435; d Wells, 1508), English composer. He was one of the organists at Wells Cathedral, 1461–62, and master of the choristers there, 1479–1508, when he was succeeded by John Clausy. His only complete surviving work, a five-part *Salve regina*, is in the Eton Choirbook.

Music in England was ruined by Hymns Ancient and Modern.

Edward Elgar, quoted in Redwood, *An Elgar Companion*, 1982

---

hymn a metrical song in praise of God. Many medieval hymns survive with plainsong melodies, which traditionally should be sung unaccompanied. The Protestant churches in the 16th c. adopted the practice of harmonizing hymn tunes. ◊choral.

Hymne au Saint Sacrément work for orchestra by Messiaen; composed 1932, fp Paris, 23 Mar 1933. First US performance NY, 13 Mar 1947, conductor Stokowski.

Hymnen, *Anthems*, work for electronic instruments by Stockhausen, which re-processes a selection of the world's national anthems;

composed 1966, fp Cologne, 30 Nov 1967. Also in versions with added soloists and, shorter, with orchestra.

Hymn of Jesus, The work by Holst for three choruses and orchestra, op. 37 (text Holst's translated from the Apocryphal Acts of St John); composed 1917 and dedicated to Vaughan Williams, fp London, 25 Mar 1920.

Hymn of Praise, Lobgesang, Mendelssohn's symphonic cantata, op. 52, in which three movements of a symphony precede the choral portion; produced Leipzig, St Thomas's Church, 25 Jun 1840; in English, Birmingham Festival, 23 Sept 1840.

Hymn of the Nations (Verdi.) ◊Inno delle nazioni.

Hymnus Amoris, *Hymn of Love*, work by Nielsen for soloists, adult and children's choruses and orchestra (text in Danish by A Olrik, in Latin by J L Heiberg); composed 1896, fp Copenhagen, 27 Apr 1897, conductor Nielsen.

Hynninen, Jorma (b Leppevirta, 3 Apr 1941), Finnish baritone and administrator. Sang with the Finnish National Opera from 1969, notably as Topi in the premiere of *The Red Line* by Sallinen (also at CG 1979 and NY Met., 1983). Created title roles in Sallinen's *The King Goes Forth to France* (1984), Rautavaara's *Thomas* (1985) and *Vincent* (1990), and Sallinen's *Kullervo* (Los Angeles, 1992). Edinburgh Festival 1987, as Rigoletto and Merikanto's Juha. Sang at Chicago and San Francisco, 1988–89. Artistic director of Finnish National Opera 1984–90. Recordings include *Winterreise* and songs by Sibelius.

Hyperprism work by Varèse for wind and percussion; fp NY, 4 Mar 1923.

When one integrates in a composition known music with unknown, one can hear especially well how it was integrated ... The more self evident the WHAT, the more attentive the listener becomes to the HOW.
Karlheinz Stockhausen, *Notes to Hymnen*, 1967

Hytner, Nicholas (b Manchester, 7 May 1956), English stage director. Studied at Cambridge and directed *The Turn of the Screw* for Kent Opera, 1979. (King Priam 1983). His innovative productions for ENO have been *Rienzi* (with trenchcoats, 1983), *Xerxes* (with deckchairs, 1985), and *The Force of Destiny* (1992). CG 1987–88, with Sallinen's *The King Goes Forth to France* and *The Knot Garden*. Glyndebourne 1991, *La Clemenza di Tito*. Has also staged *Giulio Cesare* in Paris and *Le Nozze di Figaro* in Geneva. Theatre productions include a controversial *Carousel* for the National Theatre (1992).

I

Iberia four sets of piano pieces by I Albéniz, representing different parts of Spain, composed at various times before 1909; I. *Evocación, El Puerto, Fête-Dieu à Séville*; II. *Triana, Almeria, Rondeña*; III. *El Albaicin, El Polo, Lavapiés*; IV. *Málaga, Jérez, Eritaña*.

Ibéria (Debussy.) ◊Images pour Orchestre.

Ibert, Jacques (François Antoine) (b Paris, 15 Aug 1890; d Paris, 5 Feb 1962), French composer. Studied at the Paris Conservatory and gained the Prix de Rome in 1919. He became director of the French Academy in Rome in 1937 and returned there after World War II. From 1955 to 1957 he was director of the Opéra-Comique in Paris. His music is brittle, witty and allusive.

Works include OPERAS: *Angélique* (1927), *Persée et Andromède* (1929), *On ne saurait penser à tout, Le Roi d'Yvetot* (1930), *Gonzague, L'Aiglon* (after Rostand, with Honegger, 1937), *Le Petit Cardinal* (with Honegger, 1938); radio opera *Barbe-bleue* (1943).

BALLETS: *Les Rencontres* (1925), *Diane de Poitiers* and contributed to *L'Éventail de Jeanne*.

INCIDENTAL MUSIC to Labiche's *Le Chapeau de paille d'Italie* and other plays, also (with six others) for Rolland's *Le 14 Juillet*; film music including *Don Quichotte*; cantata *Le Poète et la Fée*.

ORCHESTRAL: Symphonic poem *La Ballade de la geôle de Reading* (after Wilde, 1922); suites *Escales* (1992) and *Paris, Scherzo féerique, Nationale* (for Paris Exhibition, 1937), Jeux, *Donogoo, Ouverture pour une fête*, Symphonie Concertante for oboe and strings (1949), Symphony no. 2 ('Bostonian', 1955), *Hommage à Mozart* (1956), *Divertissement* for chamber orchestra (1930); concertos for piano, for saxophone and for cello and wind.

CHAMBER: String quartet (1944).

PIANO: including *Pièces romantiques, Noël de Picardie, Le Vent dans les ruines, Matin sur l'eau, Le Petit Âne blanc*, etc.; five pieces for harp; pieces for pipes and piano.

Ice Break, The opera by Tippett (libretto by composer), produced London, CG, 7 Jul 1977, conductor C Davis. Soviet dissident Juri joins his wife Nadia and son Juri in the USA, Nadia dies, father and son fall out, and son is injured in a race riot. Father and son are reconciled in the end.

Ideale, Die, *The Ideals*, symphonic poem by Liszt, based on a poem by Schiller, composed 1857, fp Weimar, 5 Sept 1857 at the unveiling of the Goethe-Schiller monument.

idée fixe Berlioz's term for a theme (e.g. in the *Fantastic Symphony*) which recurs in varying forms in the course of a composition as an allusion to some definite idea.

Idiot, Der ballet-pantomime by Henze (scenario by I Bachmann after Dostoievsky), produced Berlin, 1 Sept 1952.

Idoménée, *Idomeneus*, opera by Campra (libretto by A Danchet), produced Paris, Opéra, 12 Jan 1712.

Idomeneo, rè di Creta, ossia Ilia ed Idamante, *Idomeneus, King of Crete, or Ilia and Idamantes*, opera by Mozart (libretto by G B Varesco, based on the French libretto by A Danchet), produced Munich, 29 Jan 1781. Not given at CG, London, until 1978; NY Met.

1982. Returning Cretan king must sacrifice his son to fulfil his promise to the gods.

Idyll work for string orchestra in seven movements by Janáček; 1878, fp Brno, 15 Dec 1878.

Idyll: Once I passed through a populous city work by Delius for soprano, baritone and orchestra (text from Walt Whitman); composed 1930–32, with re-workings from the then unperformed opera *Margot-la-Rouge*, 1901–02; fp London, 3 Oct 1933, conductor Wood. Delius's last work.

Ifigenia in Aulide, *Iphigenia in Aulis*, opera by Caldara (libretto by A Zeno), produced Vienna, 4 Nov 1718.

Opera by Cherubini (libretto by F Moretti), Turin, Teatro Regio, 12 Jan 1788. Opera by Graun (libretto by L de Villati, after Racine's *Iphigénie en Aulide*), produced Berlin, Royal Opera, 13 Dec 1748. Frederick II of Prussia probably collaborated. Opera by Zingarelli (libretto by F Moretti), produced Milan, La Scala, 27 Jan 1787. (All libretti based ultimately on Euripides.) ◊Iphigénie for plot synopsis.

Ifigenia in Tauride, *Iphigenia in Tauris*, opera by Galuppi (libretto by M Coltellini), produced St Petersburg, at court, 2 May 1768.

Opera by Traetta (libretto by M Coltellini), produced Vienna, Schönbrunn Palace, at court, 4 Oct 1763. (Libretti based on Euripides.) ◊Iphigénie for plot synopsis.

Ifigenia, L' opera by Jommelli (libretto by M Verazi), produced Rome, Teatro Argentina, 9 Feb 1751.

Ileborgh, Adam, 15th-c. German priest and musician. He compiled and owned a collection of keyboard music, now in the Curtis Institute of

——— THE OPERA ———

Idomeneo, rè di Creta

A three-act opera by Mozart set in Sidon, Crete, following the Trojan wars. Its first stage production was in Munich in 1781.

I. Idamante (soprano or tenor) is in love with Ilia (soprano), the captive daughter of King Priam sent to Sidon by Idamante's father, Idomeneo King of Crete (tenor). A sudden storm causes Idomeneo to placate the gods by offering as a sacrifice the first person he meets on landing. When Idamante comes to greet him, the king hurries away.

II. Idomeneo attempts to save his son by ordering him to escort Elettra (soprano), in love with Idamante, to her native Argos. Ilia is naturally unhappy but before Idomeneo can leave, a sea monster appears and threatens the populace; Idomeneo confesses his guilt.

III. Ilia and Idamante renew their love before he goes to kill the monster. The High Priest (tenor) is now reluctant to make the sacrifice, but Idamante does not want his father to break his vow. The Oracle of Neptune (bass) announces that the king must abdicate; Idamante then succeeds him.

——— THE OPERA ———

Music, Philadelphia. It bears the date 1448 and contains early examples of preludes for organ including pedals.

Île de Merlin, L', ou Le Monde renversé, *Merlin's Island or the World Upside-down*, opera by Gluck (libretto by L Anseaume), produced Vienna, Schönbrunn Palace, at court, 3 Oct 1758. Pierrot and Scapin are rewarded with love and happiness on miraculous island, courting Merlin's nieces Argentine and Diamantine.

Illica, Luigi (b Piacenza, 9 May 1857; d Colombarone, 16 Dec 1919), Italian playwright and librettist. The first of his 88 libretti was for Smareglia's *Il vassallo di Szigeth* (produced Vienna, 1889); also collaborated with Catalani, Giordano, Mascagni and D'Erlanger. Best known for libretti for Puccini's *Manon Lescaut*, *La Bohème* (with G Giacosa), *Tosca* and *Madama Butterfly*.

Illuminations, Les song cycle by Britten for high voice and strings (text nine prose poems by A Rimbaud, 1872–73); composed 1938–39, fp London, 30 Jan 1940.

Ilosvay, Maria von (b Budapest, 8 May 1913; d Hamburg, 16 Jun 1987), Hungarian mezzo. She toured North America with the Salzburg Opera Guild 1937–39, as Dorabella; joined Hamburg Opera 1940 and guest in Vienna, Munich and Stuttgart after the war. She took part in the 1949 fp of Orff's *Antigonae*, at Salzburg, and from 1951 was heard as Erda at Bayreuth. CG 1956. Berg's Countess Geschwitz is among her recorded roles.

Images two sets of piano pieces by Debussy: first series composed 1905, *Reflets dans l'eau*, *Hommage à Rameau*, *Mouvement*, fp Paris, 3 Mar 1906; second series, composed 1907, *Cloches à travers les feuilles*, *Et la lune descend sur le temple qui fut*, *Poissons d'or*, fp Paris, 21 Feb 1908.

Images pour Orchestre three symphonic pieces by Debussy: *Gigues* (originally *Gigues tristes*), composed 1906–11; *Rondes de printemps*, composed 1909; *Ibéria* (*Par les rues et par les chemins*, *Les Parfums de la nuit* and *Le Matin d'un jour de fête*), finished 1908. *Ibéria* fp Paris, 20 Feb 1910, conductor Pierné; fp three pieces Paris, 26 Jan 1913, conductor Pierné.

Imai, Nobuko (b Tokyo, 18 Mar 1943), Japanese violist. Studied at Juilliard and was a member of the Vermeer Quartet 1974–79. Solo career from 1979, including concerts with the LSO, Chicago SO, Concertgebouw Orchestra, Boston SO and Stockholm Philharmonic. Festivals include Marlboro, Houston, Aldeburgh and London Proms. Has recorded Tippett's Triple Concerto and *Harold in Italy* with Colin Davis, Brahms sonatas and music by Schubert and Schumann with Roger Vignoles, Schnittke's Concerto and the Mozart Sinfonia Concertante with Iona Brown.

Imbrie, Andrew (Welsh) (b New York, 6 Apr 1921), American composer and pianist. He studied with Sessions and at University of California, at Berkeley; professor there from 1960. Writes in standard forms, with 12-note technique.

Works include three symphonies (1966–70), concertos for violin (1954), cello (1972), piano (1973, 1974) and flute (1977); five string quartets (1942–87), cello sonata (1969); operas *Christmas in Peebles Town* (1964) and *Angle of Repose* (1976); Requiem for soprano, chorus and orchestra (1984).

Imeneo, *Hymeneus*, opera by Handel (libretto adapted from S Stampiglia), composed 1738, produced Lincoln's Inn Fields, London, 22 Nov 1740. Handel's penultimate opera. Athenian Rosmene has promised her hand to Tirinto, but marries Imeneo, who has rescued her from pirates. The moral: gratitude and reason should triumph over the passions.

imitation a device in composition whereby a musical figure is repeated after its first statement, either exactly or with some change, such as displacement to a higher or lower position, augmentation, diminution, rhythmic distortion, elaboration, simplification, etc. Such an imitation may either be deferred until the first statement has been completed or made to overlap with it.

Immortal Hour, The opera by Boughton (libretto by composer, adapted from plays and poems by Fiona Macleod), produced Glastonbury, 26 Aug 1914. King Eochaidh falls in love with fairy princess Etain, who cannot remember her true identity. She is later reclaimed by Midir; the Lord of Shadows mercifully kills Eochaidh so that he will not suffer.

imperfect cadence ◊half-close.

Impériale, L' nickname of Haydn's symphony no. 53 in D major, composed *c* 1775.

Impresario in angustie, L', *The Impressario in Distress*, opera by Cimarosa (libretto by G M Diodati, similar to that of Mozart's *Schauspieldirektor*), produced Naples, Teatro Nuovo, Oct 1786.

Impresario, The (Mozart.) ◊Schauspiel-direktor.

I proclaimed freedom in harmonic impressions long before Debussy, and really do not need French impressionism.
Leoš Janáček in a letter to Jan Mikota, 1926

Impressionism a term properly belonging to painting but transferred, more or less loosely, to composers (especially French) contemporary with the school of impressionist painters. Debussy became known as the leader of the movement although he disapproved of the unofficial title. One of the chief aims of impressionism is to interpret artistically a momentary glimpse of things rather than their permanent state.

Nobuko Imai = violist

1 R Strauss: *Don Quixote*
This piece changed the course of my future. I was on tour in America as a violinist with the Toho School's string orchestra in 1965 when we visited Tanglewood. The Boston SO was playing *Don Quixote*. First came the wonderful cello part and then I heard another incredible sound and discovered, with a shock, that it was a viola. It was in this performance by Joseph de Pasquale that I first glimpsed the instrument's possibilities. I rushed backstage and asked him whether he thought my hands were big enough for the viola. He said yes, and I was so happy I switched immediately.

2 Bartók: Viola Concerto
I have always loved Bartók and his complex rhythms. I feel the music in my blood. I graduated with this piece; it was a great joy for me to create all those colours; it stretched my imagination.

3 Brahms: Clarinet Quintet, op. 115
I think the quartet repertoire is perhaps the most valuable of all chamber music; music is pared down to its four essential voices. Brahms has been overridingly important; he revelled in dark tonalities. But perhaps uniquely beautiful is his clarinet quintet.

4 Hindemith
Paul Hindemith's viola writing changed the status of the instrument for ever. What first struck me was his atmosphere: so heavy, dark and deep. His music can be so touching and sad, but what I value more than anything is his energy: so much music can be lyric, elegant and poetic, but what I seek is that sustained energy and intensity he brings.

impromptu from Latin *in promptu* = 'in readiness'; a piece of music suggesting, or intended to suggest, that it resembles an improvisation.

improvisation performance of music that is not written down or goes beyond the details of the written score. The term inevitably covers a wide range of musical phenomena, since it can involve merely slight deviation of rhythm and articulation from what had been rehearsed; the relatively carefully planned realization of a continuo line or embellishment along accepted lines; the addition of accompaniments or counterpoints in a received style; and many freer kinds of unplanned music. The apparently unfettered improvisation of the church organist or the jazz player is rarely entirely original but rather built upon an assembly and juxtaposition of received formulas.

Improvisation sur Mallarmé two works by Boulez after Stéphane Mallarmé: no. 1 for soprano, harp, tubular bells, vibraphone and four percussion; composed 1957, fp Hamburg, 13 Jan 1958, conductor Rosbaud. Also for soprano and orchestra, fp Donaueschingen, 20 Oct 1962, conductor Boulez. no. 2, same forces as 1.i, with piano; composed 1957, fp 13 Jan 1958.

Inbal, Eliahu (b Jerusalem, 16 Feb 1936), Israeli conductor. Studied at the Paris Conservatory and with Celibidache. Won Cantelli Competition 1963 and made Salzburg debut with the Vienna PO, 1969; opera debut with *Elektra* at Bologna, 1969. Chief conductor Frankfurt Radio SO 1974–90, artistic director La Fenice, Venice, 1983–86 (revivals of Donizetti's *Maria di Rudenz*, and Verdi's *Stiffelio* with its revised version *Aroldo*). Guest conductor in Europe and North America, and led *La forza del destino* at Zurich, 1992. Recordings include the complete Mahler and Bruckner symphonies.

incalzando Italian = 'persuading, urging forward', *i.e.* accelerating the pace.

incidental music songs and instrumental music introduced into spoken drama, either in the form of preludes or interludes or as an essential part of the action, e.g. marches, dances.

Incledon, Charles (Benjamin) (b St Keverne, Cornwall, bap. 5 Feb 1763; d London, 18 Feb 1826), English tenor. Chorister at Exeter Cathedral, he joined the Navy at the age of 16, but on his return to England in 1783 became a professional singer. Made his London debut at Vauxhall Gardens in 1790. In 1800 sang in first British performance *The Creation*, at CG.

Incognita opera by Wellesz (libretto by E Mackenzie, on Congreve's story), produced Oxford, 5 Dec 1951. Amorous intrigues and mistaken identities.

Incontro Improvviso, L', *The Unforeseen Meeting*, opera by Haydn (libretto by K Friberth, translated into Italian from Dancourt's *La Rencontre imprévue*, composed by Gluck), produced Eszterháza, 29 Aug 1775. Prince Ali and Princess Rezia were once lovers, but were captured by pirates and separated. Rezia, now the favourite of the Egyptian sultan, escapes with newly found Ali, thanks to the help of slave Osmin.

Incoronazione di Poppea, L', *The Coronation of Poppaea*, opera by Monteverdi (libretto by Busenello, based on Tacitus), produced Venice, Teatro Saints Giovanni e Paolo, autumn 1643. Modern editions by Westrup (first British production, Oxford 1927), Krenek, d'Indy, Malipiero, Ghedini, Leppard, Norrington, Harnoncourt and Curtis. It was the first opera not to be based on a mythical or religious theme. Poppea defeats her rivals and weds Nero.

Indes galantes, Les, *Love in the Indies*, opera-ballet by Rameau (libretto by L Fuzelier), produced Paris, Opéra, 23 Aug 1735. The four entrées are *Le turc généreux, Les Incas du Pérou, Les fleurs, Les sauvages*. Revived NY, 1961, London, 1972.

India, Sigismondo d' (b Palermo, *c* 1582; d ? Modena, before 1629), Italian composer and singer. Best known as composer of madrigals and regarded as the most important of Monteverdi's contemporaries: collections pub. in Milan and Venice 1609–23. During this time he was director of music to the Duke of Savoy in Turin. In 1625 his sacred drama *Sant' Eustachio* was produced in Cardinal Maurizio's palace, Rome. The following year he moved to Modena. Other important influences on his style came from Marenzio and the chromaticism of Gesualdo.

THE OPERA

L'Incoronazione di Poppea

A three-act opera with Prologue of 1642 by Claudio Monteverdi, set in Rome in AD 65 at the time of the coronation of Poppea.
Prologue. The figures of Fortune, Virtue and Cupid argue their respective merits.
I. The Roman Emperor Nero (soprano) has abandoned his wife Ottavia (soprano) and taken as his mistress the ambitious Poppea (soprano). Ottavia will not be consoled by Seneca (bass), and when the philosopher reproaches Nero, the emperor orders him to commit suicide. Poppea's former lover Ottone (mezzo-soprano) attempts a reconciliation, but when he is rebuffed, he decides to kill her, at the same time turning his attention to the courtier Drusilla (soprano).
II. Encouraged by Ottavia, Ottone disguises himself in Drusilla's clothes and approaches the sleeping Poppea; she is protected by Cupid and Ottone flees.
III. Drusilla is arrested for the attempt on Poppea's life, and she tries to protect Ottone, even when he is ready to confess his guilt. Nero banishes them both, together with the distressed Ottavia, and the coronation of Poppea can proceed.

THE OPERA

Indianische Fantasie work by Busoni for piano and orchestra op. 44, based on American Indian themes (Busoni was professor at New England Conservatory 1891–94); composed 1913, fp Berlin, 12 Mar 1914.

Indian Queen, The play by Dryden and Robert Howard, produced 1664; adapted as a semi-opera with music by Henry and Daniel Purcell, produced London, Drury Lane Theatre, 1695. Mexican Queen Zempoalla fights invading Peruvian forces led by Montezuma. He discovers she has overthrown the legitimate queen, who is revealed to be Montezuma's long-lost mother.

Indy, (Paul Marie Théodore) Vincent d' (b Paris, 27 Mar 1851; d Paris, 2 Dec 1931), French composer. Although born in Paris, he belonged to a noble family of the Ardèche district in the Vivarais. His mother died at his birth and he was brought up by his paternal grandmother, a good musician. At the age of 11 he was sent to Diémer for the piano and Lavignac for theory, and later studied piano under Marmontel. In 1870 he pub. his first works and served in the defence of Paris against the Prussian army. To please his family he studied law, but was determined to be a musician and went for advice to Franck, who offered to teach him. He also joined Colonne's orchestra as timpanist to gain experience. Pasdeloup gave the fp of one of his works, the overture to Schiller's *Piccolomini*, afterwards part of his *Wallenstein* trilogy. Next to Franck he admired Liszt, with whom he spent two months at Weimar in 1873, and Wagner, whose first *Ring* cycle he attended at Bayreuth in 1876. He helped the conductor Lamoureux introduce Wagner's music to Paris (*Lohengrin*, 1887) and revived works by Rameau, Gluck and Monteverdi (*Poppea* in his own edition). In 1894 he joined Charles Bordes, together with Guilmant, in founding the Schola Cantorum; he taught there until his death and had many pupils of the highest distinction. From 1912 he also directed the orchestral class at the Conservatory.

Works include operas *Attendez-moi sous l'orme* (after Regnard, 1882), *Le Chante de la cloche* (1879–83), *Fervaal* (1897), *L'Étranger, La Légende de Saint Christophe* (1908–15), *La Rêve de Cinyras*.

INCIDENTAL MUSIC for Catulle Mendès's *Médée*.

ORCHESTRAL: two symphonies, *Jean Hunyade* and *De bello gallico*, symphonic trilogy *Wallenstein* (after Schiller), symphonic variations *Istar* (1896), *Jour d'été à la montagne* (1905); *Symphonie sur un chant montagnard français* (*Symphonie cévenole*) for piano and orchestra (1886).

CHAMBER: three string quartets (1890, 1897, 1929), string sextet, piano quartet and piano quintet (1888, 1924), trios for piano, clarinet and cello and piano, violin and cello, suite for trumpet, two flutes and string quartet, and some other chamber works; sonatas for violin and piano and cello and piano.

PIANO AND SONGS: 18 op. nos. of piano works, including *Poèmes des montagnes*, *Tableau de voyage*, sonata in E major, *Thème varié*, *Fugue et Chanson*; three organ works; ten songs; 90 *Chansons popularies du Vivarais* arranged 12 French folksongs for unaccompanied chorus; various vocal works with and without orchestra.

Inextinguishable, The, *Det Undslukkelige*, title of Nielsen's fourth symphony; composed 1915–16, fp Copenhagen, 1 Feb 1916, conductor Nielsen.

Infantas, Fernando de las (b Córdoba, 1534; d after 1609), Spanish composer, descendant of the Fernández family of Córdoba, known by that name because one of his ancestors conveyed the infantas Constanza and Isabella to Bayonne, occupied by the English in the 14th c., before their marriage to John of Gaunt and Edmund Langley. His compositions attracted the attention of the Bishop of Cordoba, the Archduke Charles of Austria. He settled in Rome *c* 1559, but took holy orders in 1584 and went to Paris; returned to Spain by 1608.

Works include motets, some for special occasions, such as the death of the Emperor Charles V (1558) and the battle of Lepanto (1571), a setting of Psalm xcix, etc.

To write music is to raise a ladder without a wall to lean it against.

Arthur Honegger, *I am a Composer*, 1951

---

infinite canon a canon contrived to make the end overlap with the beginning, so that it can be repeated to infinity.

Inganno felice, L', *The Happy Deceit*, opera by Rossini (libretto by G M Foppa), produced Venice, Teatro San Moise, 8 Jan 1812. Falsely accused of adultery, abandoned Isabella is reunited with her husband.

Ingegneri, Marc Antonio (b Verona, *c* 1545; d Cremona, 1 Jul 1592), Italian composer. Learnt music from V Ruffo at Verona Cathedral and *c* 1570 became *maestro di cappella* at Cremona Cathedral. Monteverdi was his pupil there.

Works include two books of Masses, three books of motets, one of hymns and eight of madrigals; also 27 responsories for Holy Week (long attributed to Palestrina).

Ingenhoven, Jan (b Breda, 29 May 1876; d Hoenderloo, 20 May 1951), Dutch conductor and composer. He was a choral conductor before he had any systematic musical education, but studied later with Brandts-Buys and with Mottl at Munich, where he conducted both orchestral and choral concerts, as he did later both in Holland and abroad. He also sang tenor and played the piano and clarinet.

Works include three symphonic pieces for orchestra; symphonic fantasy on Nietzsche's *Zarathustras Nachtlied* (1906) and ballad *Klaus Tink* for voice and orchestra; three string quartets (1908–12); violin and piano sonata in C major, cello and piano sonata in G major; choruses and vocal quartets; songs, etc.

Inghelbrecht, D(ésiré-) É(mile) (b Paris, 17 Sept 1880; d Paris, 14 Feb 1965), French conductor and composer. Conducted many concerts of modern music in Paris, also the Swedish Ballet in Paris and London. Conducted at the Paris Opéra 1945–50 and founded the French National Radio Orchestra 1934, conducting it until 1944 and again 1951–58.

Works include operas *La Nuit vénitienne* (after Musset, 1908), and *La Chêne et le tilleul* (1960); two operettas; ballets *El Greco* (1920) and *Le Diable dans le beffroi* (1921); Requiem; *Cantique des créatures de Saint François* for chorus and orchestra; *Sinfonia breve* (1930); string quartet; sonata for flute and harp; quintet for strings and harp; *Suite Petite-Russienne* and other piano works; *La Nursery* for piano duet (three books); songs.

Inghilleri, Giovanni (b Porto Empedocle, 9 Mar 1894; d Milan, 10 Dec 1959), Italian baritone and composer. Debut Milan 1919, as Valentin. He sang at CG 1928–35 and Chicago 1929–30; sang in the fps of Casella's *La Donna Serpente* (Rome 1932) and Malipiero's *Giulio*

Cesare (Genoa 1936). Well known as Gérard, Scarpia, Amonasro and Amfortas. Taught at Pesaro from 1956. The opera *La burla* is among his compositions.

In Nature's Realm (Dvořák.) ◊Amid Nature.

innig German = 'inward, intimate, heartfelt'; a term frequently used by German romantic composers, especially Schumann, where profound feeling is required in performance.

Innocenza giustificata, L', *Innocence Vindicated*, opera by Gluck (libretto by G Durazzo, with words for the airs by Metastasio), produced Vienna, Burgtheater, 8 Dec 1755. Julia's innocence proved by divine intervention.

Inno delle nazioni, Hymn of the Nations, cantata by Verdi written for the International Exhibition in London, but produced at Her Majesty's Theatre, 24 May 1862. It introduced national airs in contrapuntal combination.

in nomine an instrumental piece of the later 16th c. for viols or keyboard, similar to the fancy or fantasia, but based on a plainsong melody used as a *cantus firmus*. The melody is that of 'Gloria tibi Trinitas', an antiphon for Trinity Sunday, which was used by Taverner as the *cantus firmus* of a Mass with the title *Gloria tibi Trinitas*. Part of the *Benedictus* of this Mass, beginning at the words 'In nomine Domini', was arranged as an instrumental piece, and this seems to have suggested to other composers the idea of writing original instrumental pieces on the same *cantus firmus*. The last composer to write *in nomine*s was Purcell.

Inori, *Adorations*, work for soloist(s) and orchestra by Stockhausen, fp Donaueschingen, 20 Oct 1974.

In questa tomba oscura a collective work, of which only Beethoven's song remains known today. In 1808 composers were invited to set this poem by Giuseppe Carpani, probably at the invitation of Countess Rzewuska in Vienna. Among the 63 composers who responded were, apart from Beethoven, Asioli, Cherubini, Czerny, Paer, Reichardt, Righini, Salieri, Tomášek, Weigl and Zingarelli.

Insanguine, Giacomo (b Monopoli, Bari, 22 Mar 1728; d Naples, 1 Feb 1795), Italian composer. Studied at the Conservatorio di Sant' Onofrio at Naples, where he taught from 1767, eventually becoming *maestro di cappella*. Between 1756 and 1782 he produced 21 operas. Other works include Masses and other church music, cantatas, arias.

Institut de recherche et de co-ordination acoustique/musique ◊IRCAM.

instrumentation the art of writing for instruments in a manner suited to their nature, also ◊orchestration.

instruments, classification of among the many possible ways of classifying musical instruments, the one most commonly used by instruments museums is that devised by Curt Sachs and Erich von Hornbostel in 1914 which describes instruments in terms of the vibrating body: *idiophones* (a solid body, as in a wood-block); *membranophones* (a stretched skin, as in a drum); *chordophones* (a string, as in a violin, guitar or piano); and *aerophones* (a hollow body, as in wind instruments). To this more recent studies have inevitably added the *electrophones*, accounting for a wide range of electronic instruments.

intavolatura Italian tablature. In the 16th and 17th c. the term was used for pubs. issued for keyboard instruments and written on two staves, as distinct from instrumental music printed in score or in separate parts.

Intégrales work for small orchestra and percussion by Varèse; composed 1923, fp NY, 1 Mar 1925, conductor Stokowski.

Intendant German the manager or director of an opera-house or other theatre in Germany, especially one attached to a court in former times.

interdominant a useful term to describe temporary dominants in the keys in which episodes may appear in the course of a composition, other than the dominant of the prescribed key. The same as the German *Zwischendominante*.

interlude a piece of music played or (more rarely) sung between two others or forming a bridge between two distinct sections of a large-scale composition; also a musical piece performed between parts of some other performance or function, such as certain liturgical portions of a church service, acts or scenes of a play, dances at a ball or courses of a dinner, etc. Act-tunes (*entr'actes*) in a theatre are, properly speaking, interludes.

intermède French = 'interlude, intermezzo'.

intermedio ◊intermezzo.

intermezzo Italian = 'interlude'; in the 16th c. (*intermedio*) a series of vocal and instrumental pieces interpolated in a festival play or other dramatic entertainment.

In the 18th c. a comic operatic piece, usually in two scenes and for two or three characters, one of whom could be a 'mute', played as an interlude between the acts of a serious opera in Italy, especially Naples. The most famous example is Pergolesi's *La serva padrona*. In general any musical piece played between the parts of a larger work, musical or theatrical. Also a short concert piece, not necessarily designed for any purpose implied by the name, e.g. Brahms's Intermezzi for piano.

Intermezzo opera by R Strauss (libretto by composer) produced Dresden, 4 Nov 1924. The material of the libretto is autobiographical. Composer Robert Storch is in trouble when his wife Christine reads a misdirected love letter.

How could you sing with that dreadful orchestra; they accompanied you half a tone sharp all the evening?
Jules Massenet, to a tenor singing flat, quoted to Isidore de Lara, *Many Tales of Many Cities*, 1928

International Society for Contemporary Music ◊ISCM.

interval the difference between two musical pitches. There are two main ways of measuring intervals: diatonically, that is in terms of the major or minor scale, for which purposes it is normal to include the first and last notes, thus the distance between C and D is called a major second; and acoustically, particularly in terms of a ratio (e.g. 3:2 as the measure of a fifth) or in terms of 'cents', divisions of the semitone into 100 equal parts and the octave into 1,200 equal parts.

In the Mists, *V mlhách*, work by Janáček in four movements for piano; composed 1912.

In the South, Alassio concert overture by Elgar, op. 50, composed during a visit to Italy 1903 and pub. in 1904. Fp London, 16 Mar 1904, conductor Elgar.

Intimate Letters, *Listy důverné*, sub-title of Janáček's second string quartet, composed 1928 and inspired by his unrequited love for Kamilla Stoesslová, 38 years his junior, and to whom he wrote almost daily letters during the last ten years of his life. Fp Brno, 11 Sept 1928; one month after Janáček's death.

intonazione Italian = lit. 'intonation'; a 16th-c. term for a prelude, especially one for organ used in church to precede a service.

intoning in plainsong, the singing of the opening phrase by a singer in authority to ensure that the right melody will be sung and at the proper pitch.

Into the Labyrinth cantata for tenor and orchestra by Maxwell Davies (text by G Mackay Brown), fp Kirkwall, Orkney, 22 Jun 1983.

intrada Italian, now *entrada* = lit. 'entrance, entry' = introduction, prelude.

Introduction and Allegro work for string quartet and string orchestra by Elgar; composed 1904–05, fp London, 8 Mar 1905, conductor Elgar.

Title of Ravel's Septet for harp, string quartet, flute and clarinet; composed 1906, fp Paris, 22 Feb 1907.

Introit Latin *introitus* = 'entrance'; the first item of the Proper of the Mass, accompanying the entry of the ministers. Originally a complete psalm with antiphon before and after each verse, it was reduced in the Middle Ages to its present form of antiphon, psalm-verse, *Gloria Patri* and repeat of antiphon. The antiphon is a freely-composed melody, the psalm being sung to a slightly ornate psalmtone.

Inventions the title given to Bach's two sets of short keyboard pieces written strictly in two and three parts respectively, and probably designed as technical studies. He called the three-part set 'symphonies', but there is no essential difference in character between them and the two-part inventions.

inversion (1) Of a melody. Writing a melody upside-down, i.e. the intervals remain the same but go in the opposite direction.

(2) Of a chord. A three-note chord has two possible inversions. A four-note chord has three possible inversions, and so on.

(3) Of an interval. The inversion of a fifth is a fourth.

(4) Of counterpoint. ◊counterpoint.

A root position triad on C with first and second inversions.

invertible counterpoint ◊counterpoint.

Invisible City of Kitezh, The Legend of the ◊Legend of the Invisible City of Kitezh, The.

Invitation to the Dance (Weber) ◊Aufforderung zum Tanz.

Iolanta opera in one act by Tchaikovsky (libretto by Modest Tchaikovsky, Tchaikovsky's brother, based on Hertz's play *King René's Daughter*), produced St Petersburg, 18 Dec 1892. Blind Iolanta's sight is restored in response to amorous interest from Vaudemont.

Iolanthe, or The Peer and the Peri operetta by Sullivan (libretto by W S Gilbert), produced London, Savoy Theatre, 25 Nov 1882, and NY, Standard Theatre, same date. Phyllis loves Strephon, but his half-fairy parentage and the Lord Chancellor cause problems. Fairy mother Iolanthe intervenes and the couple are united.

Ionian mode one of the two authentic modes recognized by Glareanus in the 16th c., the other being the Aeolian mode. Represented by the white keys of the piano beginning from C, it corresponds exactly to the modern C major scale. ◊modes.

Ionisation work by Varèse for 13 percussion, piano and two sirens; 1931, fp NY 6 Mar 1933, conductor Slonimsky.

Ipermestra, *Hypermnestra*, opera by Gluck (libretto by Metastasio), produced Venice, Teatro San Giovanni Cristostomo, 21 Nov 1744. Warned by an oracle, King Danaus orders his daughter to kill her betrothed, Lynceus, on their wedding night. She cannot do it, and instead separates from him. A happy ending after complications.

Iphigénie en Aulide, *Iphigenia in Aulis*, opera by Gluck (libretto by F L L du Roullet, based on Racine and further back on Euripides), produced Paris, Opéra, 19 Apr 1774. Gluck's first opera for the Paris stage, though not his first French work. Agamemnon must sacrifice his daughter, Iphigénie, in order to gain favourable winds to sail for Troy. At the last moment she is saved by the goddess Diana, who leaves a deer in her place.

Iphigénie en Tauride, *Iphigenia in Tauris*, opera by Desmarets and Campra (libretto by J F Duché and A Danchet), produced Paris, Opéra, 6 May 1704.

Opera by Gluck (libretto by N F Guillard), produced Paris, Opéra, 18 May 1779. Opera by Piccinni (libretto by A C Dubreuil), produced Paris, Opéra, 23 Jan 1781. A sequel to *Iphigénie en Aulide*; Iphigénie has been transported to Tauris from the sacrificial altar by Diana. Orestes, Iphigénie's brother, arrives in the barbaric kingdom to return a statue of Diana to Greece. After being captured, a happy ending. (All libretti based on Euripides.) ◊Ifigenia.

Ippolito ed Aricia, *Hippolytus and Aricia*, opera by Traetta (libretto by C I Frugoni, translated from S J de Pellegrin's libretto for Rameau's *Hippolyte et Aricie*, 1733), produced Parma, 9 May 1759, for plot synopsis.

Ippolitov-Ivanov, Mikhail Mikhailovich (b Gatchina near St Petersburg, 19 Nov 1859; d Moscow, 28 Jan 1935), Russian composer. Studied under Rimsky-Korsakov at the St Petersburg Conservatory. In 1884 he was appointed conductor of the Imperial opera at Tiflis, and in 1893 professor at the Moscow Conservatory, of which he was director 1906–22. He orchestrated the re-discovered St Basil scene from *Boris Godunov* (1925) and added three acts to Mussorgsky's unfinished opera *The Marriage* (1931).

Works include operas *Ruth* (1887), *Azra*, *Assia* (after Turgenev's story, 1900), *Treachery* (1910), *Ole from Norland* (1916), *The Last Barricade*, also completion of Mussorgsky's *Marriage* (1931); *Hymn to Labour* for chorus and orchestra (1934), two symphonies, *Caucasian Sketches* (1894), *Iberia*, *Armenian Rhapsody* (1895), *Mtsyri* (after Lermontov), *From Ossian*, *Episode from Schubert's Life*, *Turkish Fragments* (1930), *Musical Scenes from Uzbekistan*, *The Year 1917*, *Catalonian Suite*, etc. for orchestra.

Two string quartets; *An Evening in Georgia* for harp and wind instruments; violin and piano sonata; piano and other instrumental pieces; cantatas for chorus and piano; 116 songs.

IRCAM, abbr., = Institut de recherche et de co-ordination acoustique/ musique. Electronic studios in Pompidou Centre, Paris. Established 1977 under Pierre Boulez, to explore modern composition techniques. The tape for Harrison Birtwistle's opera *The Mask of Orpheus* (1986) was prepared there.

Ireland, John (b Bowdon, Ches., 13 Aug 1879; d Washington, Sussex, 12 Jun 1962), English composer. Studied at the RCM in London 1893–1901, with Stanford. Apart from organist's appointments, and his later composition professorship at the RCM, he devoted himself entirely to creative work. His pupils included Britten, Moeran and Searle. In 1932 he received the honorary Mus.D. degree from Durham University. His music is small scale, and influenced by Debussy and early Stravinsky.

Works include film music *The Overlanders* (1946–47); *Greater Love Hath no Man*, motet for chorus, orchestra and organ (1912); Morning and Evening Services; *These Things shall be* (John Addington Symonds) for chorus and orchestra (1936–37).

ORCHESTRAL: prelude *The Forgotten Rite* (1913), symphonic rhapsody *Mai-Dun* (1920–21), *A London Overture* (1936), *Epic March* and overture on Petronius' *Satyricon* for orchestra; *Concertino pastorale* for string orchestra (1939); concerto in E♭ and *Legend* for piano and orchestra; *A Downland Suite* for brass band; *Maritime Overture* for military band (1944).

CHAMBER: two string quartets (1895–97), three piano trios; two violin and piano sonatas, cello and piano sonata, fantasy-sonata for clarinet and piano; piano sonata, sonatina; settings of poems by C Rossetti, Housman and Masefield.

Iris opera by Mascagni (libretto by L Illica), produced Rome, Teatro Costanzi, 22 Nov 1898. Abducted by Osaka and Kyoto, Iris is thrown into Kyoto's brothel. She kills herself when her father finds out.

Irische Legende opera by Egk (libretto by composer) after Yeats's drama *The Countess Cathleen*, 1898), produced Salzburg, 17 Aug 1955, conductor Szell; revised 1970. Benevolent Countess sells her soul to rescue famine-stricken people.

Irish Symphony Stanford's third symphony, in F min, op. 28, composed 1887, fp London, 27 Jun.

Irmelin opera in 3 acts by Delius (libretto by composer), produced Oxford, 4 May 1953, conductor Beecham. Composed 1890–92.

Much-courted Irmelin is rescued from her suitors by Nils, a prince brought up as a swineherd.

Irrelohe opera by Schreker (libretto by composer), composed 1919–23, produced Cologne, 27 Mar 1924, conductor Klemperer. Count Henry of Irrelohe rises above the reputation of his rapist father, marrying Eva and defending her against Peter.

Isaac, Henricus (Heinrich) (b Brabant or E Flanders, *c* 1450; d Florence, 26 Mar 1517), Flemish composer. In *c* 1484, when he seems to have been at Innsbruck and in touch with Hofhaimer there, he went *via* Ferrara to Florence as musician to the Medici family. He became organist at the chapel of San Giovanni there, visited Rome in 1489 and married Bartolomea Bello, the daughter of a wealthy butcher. Lorenzo de' Medici having died in 1492 and his successor, Pietro, keeping a less lavish household, Isaac accepted an invitation from the Emperor Maximilian, who visited Pisa in 1496, to join the Imperial court, just then about to be transferred from Augsburg to Vienna; but he seems to have visited Innsbruck again to be formally appointed and possibly in Augsburg too. His duties were not arduous, so that he was able to live by turns in Vienna, Innsbruck, Constance (all connected with the court) and Italy. He also spent much time at the court of Ercole d'Este, Duke of Ferrara, and during his last years he remained at Florence. His wide travel is reflected in the various national influences in his music. He was a major contemporary of Josquin, Obrecht and La Rue.

Works include many Masses, *c* 50 motets, sequences, Lamentation *Oratio Jeremiae*, 58 four-part settings of the offices under the title *Choralis Constantinus*, the first polyphonic cycle of liturgical works for the ecclesiastical year: Webern wrote a dissertation on the *Choralis Constantinus* in 1906; four-part Monodia on the death of Lorenzo de' Medici (words by Poliziano); many German, Italian, French and Latin songs (including 'Innsbruck, ich muss dich lassen', which may not be his own tune), 58 instrumental pieces in three–five parts, 29 domestic pieces in two–five parts.

Isaacs, Jeremy (b Glasgow, 28 Sept 1932), English administrator. Studied at Merton College, Oxford, and worked in television until 1987 (chief executive, Channel Four, 1981–87). General Director of the Royal Opera House, Covent Garden, 1988–97, presiding over the introduction of subtitles and an ambitious rebuilding programme.

Isabeau *leggenda drammatica* by Mascagni (libretto by L Illica), produced Buenos Aires, 2 Jun 1911, conductor Mascagni. Disobedient Isabeau is condemned by her father, King Raimondo, to ride naked before the populace. The townspeople pity her and do not watch. The only exception, Folco (with whom Isabeau falls in love) is killed.

ISCM, abbr., = International Society for Contemporary Music. Annual festival founded at Salzburg in 1922, under presidency of E J Dent. Held at different centre each year.

Isepp, Martin (b Vienna, 30 Sept 1930), Austrian-born English keyboard player and conductor. Studied at Oxford and the RCM and worked for English Opera Group in the 1950s. On music staff at Glyndebourne from 1957 (head of music staff 1978–93), conducting operas by Mozart at the Festival and with GTO). Head of Opera

---

Jeremy Isaacs – general director, Royal Opera House

Now that music is so large a part of my working life, I listen far less to recordings than I used. So it is the old favourites, heard long ago, I still remember. It is always a joy to know they are still in the catalogue, or have been re-issued.

1   Haydn: Mass in D minor (*Nelson*)
     I go for, and still get huge pleasure from, the Haydn Masses, particularly the *Nelson* Mass. Willcocks with the LSO and the Choir of King's College, Cambridge, is the one on my shelf.

2   Schubert: Piano Sonata no. 21 in B flat
     I enjoy Schubert's piano music, and particularly his long, leisurely, loving last sonata.

3   Rossini: *Le Comte Ory*
     I could happily hear this again and again. I love the Glyndebourne records of the performances I first heard as a student at the Edinburgh Festival. Gui conducts. The music fizzes, delectably, still.

Training at Juilliard 1973–77, head of music studies at the National Opera Studio from 1978. Has accompanied such singers as Janet Baker, Söderström and Schwarzkopf in recital; director at the William Walton Foundation on Ischia, 1992.

Isidor of Seville (b Carthage, *c* 560; d Seville, 4 Apr 636), philosopher and theologian. He was Archbishop of Seville from 599. His contribution to music theory is contained in book III of his *Etymologiae* (largely a summary of Cassiodorus), and he deals with practical matters of church music in *De Ecclesiasticis Officiis*.

Isis opera by Lully (libretto by Quinault), produced Saint-Germain, 5 Jan 1677 and first performed Paris, Apr 1677.

Isle of the Dead, The symphonic poem by Rakhmaninov, after a painting by A Böcklin; composed 1907, fp Moscow, 1 May 1909.

Isola disabitata, L', *The Desert Island*, Opera by Haydn (libretto by Metastasio), produced Eszterháza, 6 Dec 1779. Shipwrecked sisters Constanza anad Silvia are rescued by husband Germando and lover Enrico. Also settings by G Scarlatti (Venice, 1751) and Traetta (Bologna, 1768).

isometric from Greek = 'equally metrical'; a manner of writing vocal music in several parts mainly in block chords, i.e. in the same rhythm.

isorhythmic from Greek = 'equally rhythmic'; a modern term for a method of construction used by composers for polyphonic music in the 14th and 15th c. One or more of the parts were arranged in a rhythmic pattern several bars long, which was repeated throughout the piece, sometimes with changes of tempo (indicated by the use of smaller note-values, or different mensuration signs).

Isouard, Nicolò (also known as Nicolò di Malta, or just Nicolò (b Valletta, Malta, 6 Dec 1775; d Paris, 23 Mar 1818), Maltese composer of French descent. Educated at a military academy in Paris, he had to leave France at the Revolution, and after a time in Malta studied music in Palermo and in Naples under Sala and Guglielmi. Made his debut as an opera composer in Florence with *L'avviso ai maritati* in 1794. The following year he was appointed organist to the Order of St John of Malta in Valetta, and later became *maestro di cappella* there. Leaving Malta in 1799 he settled in Paris, where he produced many operas and also appeared as a pianist.

Works include over 40 operas, e.g. *L'avviso ai maritati*, *Artaserse* (1794), *Le Tonnelier* (1801), *Michel-Ange* (1802), *Cendrillon* (1810), *Le Billet de loterie* (1811), *Joconde, Jeannot et Colin, Aladin ou La Lampe merveilleuse* (1822), etc.; Masses, motets, cantatas and other vocal works.

Israel in Egypt oratorio by Handel (words from the Bible and the Prayer Book version of the psalms), composed 1738, performed London, King's Theatre, Haymarket, 4 Apr 1739.

'Israel' Symphony a symphony by Bloch, composed 1912–16, fp NY, 3 May 1916.

Issé opera by Destouches (libretto by A H de la Motte), produced Fontainebleau, at court, 7 Oct 1679; first Paris performance, Opéra, 30 Dec 1697. Apollo woos Issé, disguised as shepherd Philemon.

Isserlis, Steven (b London, 9 Dec 1958), English cellist. Studied at the International Cello Centre (1969–76) and Oberlin College, Ohio (1976–78). Debut at Wigmore Hall, London, 1977, and has appeared with leading orchestras in Britain, Europe and North America. Notable recordings include Tavener's *The Protecting Veil*, the Britten Symphony, Bloch's *Schelomo*, *Don Quixote* and the Elgar concerto.

-issimo Italian superlative ending denoting an extreme quality, e.g. *pianissimo* = softest; *fortissimo* = loudest, etc.

Istar symphonic variations by d'Indy, op. 42, fp Brussels, 10 Jan 1897. The work is based on the Babylonian legend of Ishtar's descent into limbo and illustrates her disrobing at the seven stations of her progress by the devices of presenting the variations first, in diminishing complexity, and stating the theme only at the end, in bare octave unison.

Istel, Edgar (b Mainz, 23 Feb 1880; d Miami, FL, 17 Dec 1948), German musicologist. Studied at Munich, composition with Volbach and Thuille and musicology with Sandberger. He lived and taught there until 1913, when he went to Berlin as lecturer on music. In 1920 he was in Madrid and later went to the USA. His books include works on Wagner, Cornelius, Paganini and especially on various aspects of opera.

istesso tempo, l' Italian from *lo stesso tempo* = 'the same pace'; a direction given where a change is indicated in the time-signature, but the composer wishes the music to continue at the same pace or beat in the new rhythm. The change is thus merely one of metre, not of movement.

Istomin, Eugene (b New York, 26 Nov 1925), American pianist. He studied at the Curtis Institute, Philadelphia, with Serkin. Debut with NY PO 1943. Chamber music at the Casals Prades Festival from 1950; married Casals's widow in 1975. Trios with Isaac Stern and Leonard Rose from 1961.

Steven Isserlis – cellist

Any list of a few favourite works has to be arbitrary, so I thought that I would narrow down the field a bit by choosing only works that I feel have been somewhat neglected. They are (in no particular order):

1 Schumann: Variations in E flat for piano, op. post.
Schumann seems to me to be the most underrated of all great composers; his late music is consistently under-valued, and is scarcely ever performed. These variations were the last thing he wrote before being taken to the asylum at Endenich in 1854; based on a theme he believed to have been dictated to him by angels, these simple, touching variations sound to me like a sublime farewell to life.

2 Fauré: *Maria, Mater gratiae*, op. 47, no. 2; *Ave Verum*, op. 65, no. 1; *Tantum Ergo*, op. 65, no. 2
I once came across an intriguing-looking record of short Fauré works sung by the Chorale Gabriel Fauré. It immediately became one of my all-time favourite recordings, largely because of these three pieces, which are imbued with Fauré's uniquely radiant sense of beauty.

3 Dvořák: *Romantic Pieces* for violin and piano, op. 75
I am amazed that these pieces are not the standard fare of violin recitals. They are Dvořák at his most intimate; the last piece in particular is sheer magic.

4 Haydn: *The Seasons*
I have only heard this large-scale choral work once (when Roger Norrington conducted it at the 1993 Proms); it was a revelation to hear this masterpiece, fully the equal of its more famous sibling *The Creation*. Haydn is so incredibly original, and life and vitality seem to burst out of every note of this work.

5 Rakhmaninov: *The Isle of the Dead*
This is the work that silences any snobs who claim not to like Rakhmaninov's music (which usually means that they've only heard a couple of his works!). Particularly in the recording Rakhmaninov himself conducted with the Philadelphia Orchestra, this tone-poem oozes dark, savage power – it's glorious!

Italiana in Algeri, L', *The Italian Girl in Algiers*, opera by Rossini (libretto by A Anelli), produced Venice, Teatro San Benedetto, 22 May 1813. Captured Isabella outwits amorous Mustafà and is reunited with Lindoro.

Italian Concerto a harpsichord work in three movements by Bach, pub. (together with the 'French Overture') in the second part of the *Clavierübung* in 1735. The two manuals of the harpsichord are used to reproduce the contrast between *concertino* and *ripieno* characteristic of the *concerto grosso*.

Italian in Londra, L', *The Italian Girl in London*, opera by Cimarosa (libretto by G Petrosellini), produced Rome, Teatro Valle, 28 Dec 1778. Livia arrives in London to search for her lover Arespingh, who has abandoned her. Arespingh is torn between his arranged marriage and Livia, whom he still loves. In the end he chooses Livia.

Italian overture ◊overture.

Italian sixth ◊augmented sixth chords.

'Italian' Symphony Mendelssohn's fourth symphony, op. 90, in A major and minor, begun in Italy, 1831 and finished in Berlin, 31 Mar 1833; London, 13 May 1833, conducted by the composer.

Italienisches Liederbuch, *Italian Song Book*, H Wolf's settings of Italian poems in German translated by Paul Heyse, composed (22 nos.) 1890–91 and (24 nos.) 1896.

Iturbi, José (b Valencia, 28 Nov 1895; d Hollywood, 28 Jun 1980), Spanish pianist and conductor. Studied as a child in Barcelona, and afterwards played in cafés to earn money. Later he studied in Paris at the Conservatory and graduated in 1912. He began teaching at the Geneva Conservatory in 1919 and in 1923 began his career as a concert pianist. Conducted Rochester PO 1936–44.

Ivanhoe opera by Sullivan (libretto by J R Sturgis, based on Scott's novel), produced London, Royal English Opera House (now Palace Theatre), 31 Jan 1891. Rowena and Rebecca compete for errant knight Ivanhoe.

Ivan le Terrible opera by Bizet (libretto by A Leroy and H Trianon, first offered to Gounod and abandoned by him), composed in 1865 and accepted for production by the Théâtre Lyrique in Paris, but withdrawn by the composer. The fp (concert) took place at Mühringen (Württemberg) in 1946. First stage performance Bordeaux, 12 Oct 1951. Tsar Ivan defeats assassination attempt and marries Princess Marie.

Ivanov, Mikhail Mikhailovich (b Moscow, 23 Sept 1849; d Rome, 20 Oct 1927), Russian composer and critic. Studied with Tchaikovsky and others at the Moscow Conservatory, lived mainly in Rome 1870–76 and then became music critic to the *Novoie Vremya*.

Works include operas *Potemkin's Feast* (1902), *Zabava Putiatishna* (1899), *The Proud Woman* and *Woe to the Wise*; ballet *The Vestal Virgin* (1888); Requiem; symphony, symphonic prologue *Savonarola*, *Suite champêtre* for orchestra; piano pieces; songs.

THE OPERA

L'Italiana in Algeri

A two-act opera by Gioachino Rossini, first performed in 1813. The plot concerns a ruler who has tired of his wife.

I. Mustafà, the Bey of Algiers (bass), no longer loves his wife Elvira (soprano), and wishes to marry her off to an Italian slave, Lindoro (tenor). An Italian ship is wrecked offshore and Isabella (mezzo-soprano), the Italian Girl of the opera's title, arrives with Taddeo, an elderly 'uncle'. Isabella is in search of her lover Lindoro, and persuades the admiring Mustafà to give him to her as a slave.

II. His love for Isabella has made Mustafà unusually docile, but his plans to be alone with her come to nothing. Lindoro convinces him that Isabella will be ready for marriage when he becomes a member of the 'Pappataci' (those who eat and stay silent). The Italians pretend that the arrival of a ship is part of the initiation ceremony, and they make good their escape.

THE OPERA

Ivanov, Nikolay (b Poltava, 22 Oct 1810; d Bologna, 19 Jul 1880), Russian tenor. He visited Italy with Glinka in 1830 and made his debut at Naples in 1832, as Donizetti's Percy; repeated the role on his London debut, 1833, and returned until 1837. Often heard in Rossini's operas and in 1843 at Palermo was Riccardo in the fp of Pacini's *Maria Tudor*; Vienna 1844, as Roberto Devereux. Other roles included Ernani, Arnold and Gianetto.

Ivan Susanin opera by Cavos (libretto by Prince A A Shakhovskoy), produced St Petersburg, 31 Oct 1815. The subject is that on which Glinka's *Life for the Tsar* was based in 1836.

The title given to Glinka's *Life for the Tsar* in Soviet Russia.

Ivan the Terrible (Rimsky-Korsakov.) ◊Pskovitianka.

Ive (or *Ives*), Simon (b Ware, 1600; d London, 1 Jul 1662), English singer, organist and composer. Vicar-choral at St Paul's Cathedral in London; singing-master during the Commonwealth, returned to St Paul's in 1661. In 1633 he took part with W Lawes in the composition of Shirley's masque *The Triumph of Peace*. Other works include elegy on the death of W Lawes, catches and rounds; fancies and other instrumental works, etc.

These prefatory essays were written by the composer for those who can't stand his music – and the music for those who can't stand his essays; to those who can't stand either, the whole is respectfully dedicated.

Charles Ives, *Essays before a Sonata*, 1920

Ives, Charles (Edward) (b Danbury, CT, 20 Oct 1874; d New York, 19 May 1954), American composer. Pupil of H Parker and D Buck at Yale University, where he wrote his first symphony (1895–98). He was already impatient with tradition and from an early age he was interested by disparate sounds occurring simultaneously; the occasion when he heard two bands playing different tunes made a lasting impression. He moved to NY in 1898, working as an insurance agent and setting up his own agency in 1907. A second symphony (1900–02) was written in his spare time, and the Third (1904–11) impressed Mahler, then conductor at the Met. Much of his music was written from 1910, but by 1918 his health was suffering. He gradually retired from business and took to revising earlier works, rather than writing new ones. The huge *Concord* sonata was published 1919, but not performed (by John Kirkpatrick) until 1939. The work was greeted with acclaim, in spite of its complexities. His orchestral music

A Selection of

Ives

Symphony no. 1	1896–8
Symphony no. 2	1897–1901
String Quartet no. 1	1898
Symphony no. 3	1901–4

Three Places in New England	1903–14
New England Holidays	1904–13
The Unanswered Question	1908
Symphony no. 4	1910–16
Violin Sonata no. 4	1915
Piano Sonata no. 2 (*Concord*)	1909–15

was taken up first by Eugene Goossens (NY, 1927) then by Nicolas Slonimsky. The Third Symphony was permiered at NY under Lou Harrison in 1946 but the Fourth was not given until 11 years after Ives' death, under Stokowski. Leonard Bernstein was also a successful champion of the symphonies.

Much of Ives' music is in a polytonal idiom, and it employs on occasion microtones. In addition, he experimented with conflicting rhythms, dissonant harmony and counterpoint, chord clusters and the spatial presentation of music. He also made frequent use of hymn and folk tunes. Ives is now recognized as the most important founder of modern American music.

Works include ORCHESTRAL: four symphonies: no. 1 in D minor (1896–98), no. 2 (1897–1901, fp NY, 22 Feb 1951), no. 3 (1901–04, for chamber orchestra, *The Camp Meeting*; fp NY, 5 Apr 1946), no. 4 (1910–16, fp NY, 26 Apr 1965 conductor Stokowski); *New England Holidays* (*Washington's Birthday, Decoration Day, Fourth of July, Thanksgiving*; 1904–13); *Three Places in New England* (Orchestral Set no. 1: *The St Gaudens in Boston Common, Putnam's Camp, Redding, Connecticut* and *The Housatonic* at Stockridge; 1903–14, fp NY 1931 conductor Slonimsky); Orchestral Set no. 2: *An Elegy to our Forefathers, The Rockstrewn Hills Join in the People's Outdoor Meeting* and *From Hanover Square North at the end of a Tragic Day*; 1909–15); *Central Park in the Dark* (1898–1907, fp NY, 11 May 1947); *The Unanswered Question* (1908); Theater Orchestra Set: *In the Cage, In the Inn, In the Night* (1904–11); *Tone Roads*, two pieces for chamber orchestra (1911, 1915); *Robert Browning Overture* (1908–12); Orchestral Set no. 3 (1919–27).

CHORAL: *The Circus Band* for bass, chorus and orchestra (1894); *The Celestial Country*, cantata (1899); *General William Booth Enters into Heaven* for bass, chorus and orchestra (1914); *Lincoln the Great Commoner* for chorus and orchestra (1912); eight Psalm settings (1897–1901); *Three Harvest Home Chorales* for chorus, brass, double bass and organ (1898–1912).

CHAMBER: string quartet no. 1 (*A Revival Service*, 1898; first public performance NY, 1957), no. 2 (1907–13); piano trio (1904–13); four sonatas for violin and piano (1902–15); *From the Steeples and the Mountains* for brass quintet (1901); *Adagio Sostenuto* for horn, flute, strings and piano (1910).

PIANO AND SONGS: Piano sonata no. 1 (1909), no. 2 (*Concord, Massachusetts, 1840–1860: Emerson, Hawthorne, The Alcots, Thoreau*; 1909–15, fp NY 1939); 22 Studies for piano; organ music; 114 songs (1884–1921).

Ivogün, Maria (b Budapest, 18 Nov 1891; d Beatenberg, 2 Oct 1987), Hungarian soprano. She studied in Munich; debut there 1913, Mimi; created Ighino in Pfitzner's *Palestrina*, 1917. London, CG, 1924–27 as Zerbinetta, Gilda, Constanze. Left Munich 1925 and sang in Berlin until 1934. Other roles included Queen of Night and Norina. Married to Karl Erb 1921–32; and to Michael Raucheisen, her accompanist, from 1933.

A base barreltone voice.

James Joyce, *Ulysses*, 1922

Ivrea Codex a large collection of 14th-c. music, and an important source of music by Philippe de Vitry and Machaut. It is housed in the cathedral of the city of Ivrea.

Ivrogne corrigé, L', *The Reformed Drunkard*, opera by Gluck (libretto by L Anseaume on a fable by La Fontaine), produced Vienna, Burgtheater, Apr 1760. Drunkard Mathurin is reformed by a chorus of demons in disguise. In the process he allows his niece to marry the man of her choice.

Izzo d'Amico, Fiamma (b Rome, 1964), Italian soprano. Studied at the Rome Conservatory and made her debut at Treviso 1984, as Mimi; Bologna 1985, Violetta. Discovered by Karajan and sang Élisabeth de Valois at the 1986 Salzburg Festival (returned as Micaela). US debut with Pavarotti at Philadelphia 1986, as Mimi. Further appearances at the NY Met. and CG; Verdi Requiem at Salzburg.

J

Jaches de Wert ◊Wert.

Jachet da Mantova (Jaquet ?) (b Vitré; d Mantua, 1559), Flemish singer and composer. Attached to San Pietro Cathedral at Mantua 1527–58. Wrote Masses, Magnificats, motets, psalms, hymns, etc.

jack the mechanism in the virginal, harpsichord and similar instruments by which the strings are plucked. In a piano the jack accommodates the fall of the hammer from the string.

Jackson, Francis (b Malton, Yorkshire, 2 Oct 1917), English organist and composer. He studied at Durham University and with Edward Bairstow; succeeded him as organist at York Minster in 1946. He is well known as a recitalist, most often heard in Vierne and Franck. His own works include a *Te Deum* and *Jubilate* (1964), Symphony in D minor for orchestra, and *Sonata giocosa* for organ (1972). OBE 1978.

Jackson, William (b Exeter, 29 May 1730; d Exeter, 5 Jul 1803), English organist and composer. Learnt music as a choirboy in Exeter Cathedral, then studied in London, became music teacher at Exeter and from 1777 held various appointments at the cathedral there.

Works include operas *The Lord of the Manor* (1780), and *The Metamorphosis* (1783); a stage piece *Lycidas* (based on Milton, 1767), Te Deum, services, anthems and other church music; setting of Pope's ode *The Dying Christian*; various vocal pieces and songs; harpsichord sonatas.

Jacob, Gordon (Percival Septimus) (b London, 5 Jul 1895; d Saffron Walden, 8 Jun 1984), English composer and conductor. Studied under Stanford and C Wood at the RCM, where later he became professor of orchestration. D.Mus., London, 1935.

Works include ballets *The Jew in the Bush* and *Uncle Remus* (after J C Harris); music for films; sinfonietta (1942), variations on an air by Purcell and on an original theme for orchestra, *Passacaglia on a Well-known Theme* ('Oranges and Lemons') for orchestra (1931); two symphonies (1929, 1944) and *Denbigh* suite for strings, Divertimento for small orchestra; concertos for piano, violin, viola, oboe, bassoon and horn; clarinet concerto (1980); suite for military band; quartets for oboe and strings and clarinet and strings and other chamber music; instrumental pieces.

Jacobi, Frederick (b San Francisco, 4 May 1891; d New York, 24 Oct 1952), American conductor and composer. Pupil of Bloch and others in USA and of Juon in Berlin. Assistant conductor at NY Met., 1913–17, later studied music of the Pueblo Indians in Mexico and Arizona. Professor of composition in NY from 1924. Taught at Juilliard, 1936–50.

Works include opera *The Prodigal Son* (1944); two symphonies (1924, 1948), *Indian Dances*, *The Eve of St Agnes* (after Keats), etc. for orchestra; concertos for piano, violin and cello; concerto for piano and strings; Sabbath Evening Service (1931); *Two Assyrian Prayers* and *The Poet in the Desert* for voice and orchestra; three string quartets (1924–45), piano quintet *Hagiographia*, scherzo for wind instruments.

Jacobin, The opera by Dvořák (libretto by M Cervinková-Riegrová); composed 1887–88, produced Prague, 12 Feb 1889; revised 1897.

Bohuš returns to father's favour after false accusations by cousin Adolf.

Jacobs, Arthur (b Manchester, 14 Jun 1922), English critic, translator and editor. Music critic for various newspapers from 1947; 1960–71 deputy editor *Opera* magazine. Lecturer at RAM from 1964, Huddersfield Polytechnic 1979–85. Has translated 20 opera libretti and pub. *A New Dictionary of Music* (four editions 1958–78), *Short History of Western Music* and two vols. on Sullivan (1951, 1984), *Penguin Book of Musical Performers* (1990) and *Henry J Wood, Maker of the Proms* (1994). His work is notable for its concision.

Jacobs, René (b Ghent, 30 Oct 1946), Belgian countertenor, conductor and editor. Studied at the University of Ghent and made debut in Cavalli's *Erismena* at Amsterdam 1974, under Alan Curtis; has also appeared in ensembles directed by Gustav Leonhardt, N Harnoncourt and S Kuijken. Has directed his own ensemble, Collegium Vocale, from the 1970s, in operas by Cesti (*L'orontea*), Cavalli (*Giasone*), Charpentier (*David et Jonathas*) and Monteverdi (*Poppea* at Montpellier, 1989). Conducted Graun's *Cesare e Cleopatra* at Versailles and Conti's *Don Chisciotte* at Innsbruck, both 1992. Salzburg Festival debut 1993, with Monteverdi's *Orfeo* in his own edition. Recordings as singer include Handel's *Alessandro*, *Admeto*, and *Tamerlano*; as director, *Giasone*, and Handel's *Flavio* and *Giulio Cesare*. A leading figure in the revival of interest in early opera.

Jacobsen, Jens Peter (1847–1885), Danish poet and novelist. ◊Fennimore und Gerda (Delius); ◊Gurrelieder (Schoenberg); E ◊Hamerik (*Marie Grubbe*).

Jacques, Reginald (b Ashby de la Zouch, 13 Jan 1894; d Stowmarket, 2 Jun 1969), English organist and conductor. He studied at Oxford and held various posts there before founding the Bach Choir, London, in 1931; conductor until 1960. Founded Jacques Orchestra 1936 and gave many wartime concerts. Well-known for performances of the Bach Passions with traditional forces and style. CBE 1954.

Jacquet, Élizabeth, ◊La Guerre.

Jadin, Louis Emmanuel (b Versailles, 21 Sept 1768; d Paris, 11 Apr 1853), French composer, son of the violinist and composer Jean Jadin. Worked as accompanist at the Théâtre de Monsieur in Paris from 1789 and became piano professor at the Conservatory 1802.

Works include opera *Joconde* (1790) and c 40 others; vocal and instrumental works for the Revolution festivals; *La Bataille d'Austerlitz* for orchestra; chamber music; works for one and two pianos.

Jadlowker, Hermann (b Riga, 5 Jul 1877; d Tel Aviv, 13 May 1953), Latvian tenor. Studied in Vienna and made his debut at Cologne in 1899, as Nicolai's Fenton. He sang in Berlin 1907–12. NY Met. debut 1910, as Faust; sang in the fp of *Königskinder* the same year. In 1912 he created Bacchus, in *Ariadne auf Naxos* (Stuttgart). Retired 1929. Other roles included Parsifal, Tannhäuser, Florestan and Don Carlos.

Jaffe, Monte (b Philadelphia, 5 Jun 1940), American baritone. Studied at Curtis and sang at Krefeld, Germany as Wotan, Dr Schön, Reimann's Lear and in Cerha's Baal; Komische Oper Berlin 1985, in the fp of *Judith* by Matthus. Has sung with the NY Met. in *Death in*

Arthur Jacobs – music critic / biographer

1   Britten: *Spring Symphony*
A great renewal of the human spirit without calling on worn-out religion, and with the most inventive re-hearing of supposedly commonplace chords.

2   Gluck: *Orphée et Euridice*
The myth celebrating the power of music unforgettably dramatized by means of music itself – especially in Act 2 at the gates of Hades.

3   Handel: *Acis and Galatea*
The supreme musical genius, freeing himself from both oratorio and *opera seria*, sculpts a perfect English opera almost without knowing it.

4   Mendelssohn: *A Midsummer Night's Dream* – overture
To have composed this at the age of 17, a work at the very summit of romantic imagination, makes Mendelssohn a more remarkable prodigy than Mozart.

5   Sullivan: *Iolanthe*
Writing the first new work for London's newly built Savoy Theatre, Sullivan surpassed himself in the vigour and delicacy of his response to W S Gilbert's text.

6   Tchaikovsky: *Romeo and Juliet* – overture-fantasia
Originality, both of musical ideas and of orchestration, achieves a popular appeal which may be backed by the most discriminating appreciation.

Venice, as Lear for ENO and Bartók's Bluebeard for Scottish Opera; ENO 1991 as Timon of Athens in the fp of the opera by Stephen Oliver. Other roles include the *Walküre* Wotan at Turin, Barak, Klingsor, Scarpia, and Konchak in *Prince Igor*.

Jagd, Die, *The Hunt*, opera by J A Hiller (libretto by C F Weisse, based on J M Sedaine's libretto for Monsigny's *Le Roi et le fermier*), produced Weimar, 29 Jan 1770. Röschen loves Töffel, but can only marry after her brother, Christal, has married his fiancée, who has been kidnapped by the evil Count. She escapes, and the King arrives to bless the two marriages.

Jagel, Frederick (b Brooklyn, 10 Jun 1897; d San Francisco, 5 Jul 1982), American tenor. He studied in NY and Milan; debut Livorno 1924, as Rodolfo. After appearing widely in Italy he sang at the NY Met. from 1927 (debut as Radames). San Francisco from 1931, Buenos Aires 1939–41. He sang the title role in the first professional US performance of *Peter Grimes*.

Jahn, Otto (b Kiel, 16 Jun 1813; d Göttingen, 9 Sept 1869), German philologist, archaeologist and writer on art and music. Studied at Kiel, Leipzig and Berlin, became professor at Greifswald and later at Bonn. His numerous writings on music include the first large-scale work written on Mozart (first edition, four vols, Leipzig, 1856–59; sixth edition, by A A Abert, 1955). He discovered the copy of a sinfonia concertante for four wind instruments and orchestra; this has frequently been given as Mozart's concerto K297b, although many regard the attribution as doubtful.

Jakobsleiter, Die, *Jacob's Ladder*, oratorio by Schoenberg; composed 1917–22, unfinished. Scoring completed by Winfried Zillig, fp Vienna 16 Jun 1961, conductor Kubelik.

jaleo a Spanish dance in moderate 3–8 time, accompanied by castanets.

James, Philip (b Jersey City, NJ, 17 May 1890; d Southampton, Long Island, 1 Nov 1975), American conductor, organist, teacher and composer. Studied in NY and became professor at Columbia and NY Universities.
Works include *Missa imaginum*, *Stabat Mater* and other choral works; three symphonies, including *Sea Symphony* for baritone and orchestra (1928), overtures on French Noëls and *Bret Harte*, Welsh rhapsody *Gwallia, Station WGZBX*, for orchestra (1932); suite for string orchestra; piano quartet, woodwind quintet, string quartet (1924).

Janáček, Leoš (b Hukvaldy, Moravia, 3 Jul 1854; d Morava-Ostrava, 12 Aug 1928), Czech composer. Son of a poor schoolmaster; became a choirboy at the monastery of the Austin Friars at Brno; later earned his living as music teacher and went to the Organ School in Prague for study. Conducted various choral societies, made some desultory studies at Leipzig and Vienna, and in 1881 returned to Brno to found an organ school there. He had meanwhile become involved with Moravian folk music, collecting, harmonising and performing folksongs; their influence is heard in his first mature work, the opera

Jenůfa, started in 1894 and staged at Brno in 1904. Although a success, wider recognition did not come until the opera's production in Prague (1916), followed by a production in Germany. The last ten years of Janáček's life saw a great burst of creative activity, with the composition of many new works that are full of exuberance, expressive power and characteristic jagged rhythms. The opera *The Excursions of Mr Brouček* was premiered in Prague, 1920, and the following year the rhapsody after Gogol, *Taras Bulba*, was given in Brno. Much of his astonishing later music, in particular the opera *Katya Kabanova* and the second string quartet ('Intimate Letters') was inspired by his unrequited love for Kamilla Stoesslova, to whom he wrote constant letters in the last decade of his life. Many scenes in his operas, as well as the song cycle *Diary of a Young Man Who Disappeared*, seem to have an epistolary basis; they are often brief vignettes in which the characters communicate with one another in a confiding, confessional manner.

He made close studies of folksong and speech, which he applied to his vocal music; speech rhythms were particularly important to

Janáček   *A biographical note*

Janáček's career achieved a remarkable revival with the 1916 production of *Jenůfa*, but it was his friendship with Kamila Stösslova which inspired a great increase in creative activity in his last years. Kamila was 38 years Janáček's junior and the wife of a Pisek-based antique dealer. In a totally unrequited relationship, Janáček sent her almost daily love letters and in his last year kept a Kamila diary. His first Kamila-inspired work was *The Diary of a Young Man who Disappeared* (1917–19), a song cycle which tells of a young man's decision to leave his wife for a gypsy girl. Further emotional sublimation came with the operas *Kata Kabanova* (a young wife's doomed affair with her lover) and *The Cunning Little Vixen* (fulfilment and domesticity with countless offspring). *The Makropoulos Case*, featuring an emotionally cold, 337-year-old Emilia Marty, has been seen as an ironic reversal of the Janáček–Kamila relationship. Both Janáček's string quartets are intense expressions of erotic yearning and unfulfilled love. No. 1, 'The Kreutzer Sonata', is based on Tolstoy's tale of jealousy and marital desolation, while No. 2, 'Intimate Letters', premiered posthumously, sadly rehearses the feelings of his one-sided correspondence before ending in despairing triumph. Before he could hear his second quartet, Janáček visited his country retreat with Kamila and her young son. While out searching for the boy when he got lost, Janáček caught a chill and died of the pneumonia that soon developed.

Janáček in the portrayal of a person's mood. His vocal music often reflects this, and moves fluently between neutral speech-dominated patterns and moments of intense emotion and expressive power. Although he was not an orthodox religious believer, Janáček's music suggests an articulate pantheism, with a profound sympathy for the human condition and an ecstatic celebration of the natural world and the part of a creator in it.

Works include OPERAS: *The Beginning of a Novel* (1894), *Osud/Fate* (1903–07; produced 1958), *Jenůfa/Her foster-daughter* 1904), *The Excursions of Mr Brouček* (after Čech, 1920), *Káta Kabanová* (1921), *The Cunning Little Vixen* (1924), *Šárka* (1925), *The Makropoulos Case* (on a play by Čapek, 1926), *From the House of the Dead* (after Dostoievsky, 1930).

VOCAL: *Amarus* (1897–1906), *The Eternal Gospel* (1914) and *Glagolitic Mass* for solo voices, chorus and orchestra (1926), *The Wandering Madman* (Tagore) for soprano and male-voice chorus, numerous choral works, many for male voices.

ORCHESTRAL: *Šumařovo Dítě*, rhapsody *Taras Bulba* (on Gogol, 1918), *The Ballad of Blanik*, Sinfonietta for orchestra (1926); concertino for piano and chamber orchestra (1925), *Capriccio* for piano left hand and ensemble (1926).

CHAMBER: two string quartets (one on Tolstoy's *Kreutzer Sonata*, 1923, no. 2 *Intimate Letters*, 1928), wind sextet *Mládí* (*Youth*), suite for two violins, viola, cello and double bass; violin and piano sonata, *Fairy Tale* for cello and piano; piano sonata (1905), *By an Overgrown Path* (1901–08), variations, etc.; organ works; *The Diary of a Young Man who Disappeared* (1921) for voices and piano, Moravian folksongs for voice and piano.

I do not play about with empty melodies. I dip them in life and nature.
Leoš Janáček in a letter to K E Sokol, 1924

Janáček *The composer Leoš Janáček (1854–1928). Although born before many later Romantic composers such as Mahler and Wolf, Janáček's musical style often looks beyond the 19th century, especially in terms of his dissonant harmonic conception. Even in his seventies he kept abreast of current compositional trends.*

Janiewicz, Felix (b Vilna, 1762; d Edinburgh, 21 May 1848), Polish violinist. Studied in Vienna, where he met Haydn and Mozart and in Italy. Appeared in Paris and London (Haydn's concerts, 1794). Settled first in Liverpool, then in Edinburgh (1815).

Janigro, Antonio (b Milan, 21 Jan 1918; d Milan, 1 May 1989), Italian cellist and conductor. He studied in Milan and with Casals. Debut as cellist 1934, as conductor 1948; founded I Solisti di Zagreb 1954 and gave frequent performances of Baroque repertory with them until

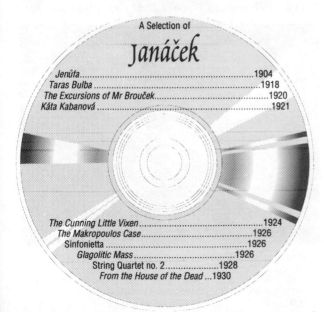

A Selection of

Janáček

1967. Formed trio with Jean Fournier and Paul Badura-Skoda. Professor of cello at Düsseldorf Conservatory 1964; conductor Saar Radio Orchestra from 1968.

Janis, Byron (b McKeesport, PA, 24 Mar 1928), American pianist. Studied in New York and with Horowitz. Debut with Pittsburgh SO 1994, with Rakhmaninov's Second Concerto. Carnegie Hall debut 1948, European debut with Concertgebouw Orchestra 1952; tours of Russia 1960 and 1962. Career interrupted by arthritis in both hands during the 1960s but resumed 1972; discovered MSS of two Chopin waltzes in Paris, 1967. Appearances with Boston SO and Philadelphia Orchestra. Also plays Liszt, Gottschalk and Prokofiev.

Janissaries Turkish infantry which formed a bodyguard for the sultan. Their music made use of special percussion instruments including the Turkish crescent or jingling johnny, imitated by western composers, as in Haydn's 'Military' Symphony (no. 100) and Mozart's *Entführung*. Brahms playfully called the third movement of his fourth symphony 'janissaries' music'.

Janků, Hana (b Brno, 25 Oct 1940), Czech soprano. Debut Brno 1959; later sang at Prague. Wider recognition came in 1967, with Turandot at La Scala and Vienna. Deutsche Oper Berlin from 1970 as the *Trovatore* Leonora, Gioconda, Ariadne and Elisabeth. CG 1973, as Tosca. Other roles included Lady Macbeth and Smetana's Milada.

Jannacom, Giuseppe (b Rome, 1741; d Rome, 16 Mar 1816), Italian composer. Studied in Rome, where in 1811 he became *maestro di cappella* at St Peter's in succession to Zingarelli.

Works include 30 Masses, 42 psalms, motets and other church music, some for several antiphonal choirs.

Jannequin, Clément (b Châtellerault, *c* 1485; d Paris, 1558), French composer. Pupil (?) of Josquin des Prés. He may have become a Huguenot in the course of his long life.

Works include Masses on his own songs *La Bataille* and *L'Aveugle Dieu*, motet *Congregati sunt*, *Proverbes de Salomon*, *Psaumes de*

David (both to French rhymed versions); *280 chansons* for four voices, many of which contain imitative and descriptive passages, e.g. *Le chant des oiseaux*..

Janowitz, Gundula (b Berlin, 8 Feb 1937), German soprano. A protégée of Karajan, she sang Pamina, Mimi, and the Empress at Vienna in the early 1960s; Countess in *Figaro* and Fiordiligi at Salzburg and Sieglinde at the NY Met. in 1967, when Karajan gave *Die Walküre* there. London, CG, 1976 (Donna Anna). Other roles included Agathe, Elisabeth, Eva and Arabella. Returned to CG 1987, Ariadne. Director of the Graz Opera, 1990–91.

Janowski, Marek (b Warsaw, 18 Feb 1939), Polish conductor. He studied in Cologne and Vienna. Conducted opera in Hamburg, Munich and Berlin before becoming music director at Freiburg i/B, then Dortmund, 1973–79. London debut 1969, SW Theatre, Henze's *Der Junge Lord* with Cologne Opera; Royal Liverpool PO 1983–86. US from 1980 (Chicago, *Lohengrin*); NY Met. 1984, *Arabella*. With Dresden forces made the first compact disc recording of Wagner's *Ring*; conducted *Meistersinger* in Paris (Châtelet) 1990.

Jansons, Mariss (b Riga, 14 Jan 1943), Latvian conductor. Studied in Leningrad, Vienna and Salzburg; won second prize in Karajan Competition, 1971. Assistant conductor of the Leningrad PO, then principal of the Oslo PO from 1979, with tours to Japan, the USA and Edinburgh Festival. Gave complete Tchaikovsky symphonies with the BBC Welsh SO and in season 1987–88 made debuts with the Montreal SO, Los Angeles PO and Berlin Philharmonic. Salzburg Festival debut 1990, London Proms 1993 (both with Oslo SO). Recordings include music by Tchaikovsky, Svendsen and Shostakovich.

Janssen, Herbert (b Cologne, 22 Sept 1892; d New York, 3 Jun 1965), German baritone. He studied in Berlin and made his debut in the first local production of Schreker's *Der Schatzgräber*; remained at the Staatsoper until 1938 in Wagner and Verdi repertory London, CG, 1926–39. Bayreuth 1930–37 as Wolfram, Amfortas, and Gunther. Met. co. debut on tour in Philadelphia, 1939, as the Wanderer; also heard as Sachs in USA.

Japanische Festmusik work for orchestra by Strauss, op. 84; composed for the 2,600th anniversary of the Japanese Empire; fp Tokyo, 11 Dec 1940; less than a year before Pearl Harbor. See also ◊Sinfonia da Requiem.

Japart, Johannes, 15th–16th-c. composer, many of whose *chansons* were printed by Petrucci in Venice. He was a singer at the Ferrara court.

Jaques-Dalcroze, Émile (b Vienna, 6 Jul 1865; d Geneva, 1 Jul 1950), Swiss teacher and composer. Studied with Delibes in Paris, with Bruckner and Fuchs in Vienna and at the Geneva Conservatory, where in 1892 he became professor of harmony. There he invented a system of teaching music by co-ordination with bodily movement, known as Eurhythmics. In 1910 he founded an institute for this purpose at Hellerau near Dresden.

Works include operas *Le Violon maudit* (1893), *Janie* (1894), *Sancho Panza* (after Cervantes, 1897), *Le Bonhomme Jadis* (1906), *Les Jumeaux de Bergame*, *La Fille au vautour* (after W von Hillern's *Die Geier-Wally*), festival play *La Fête de la jeunesse et de la joie* (1932); choral works *La Veillée*, *Festival vaudois*; suite for orchestra; two violin concertos (1902, 1911); three string quartets; piano music and songs.

Jarnach, Philipp (b Noisy, France, 26 Jul 1892; d Bornsen, near Bergedorf, 17 Dec 1982), Franco-Spanish composer. Studied piano with Risler and composition with Lavignac in Paris, went to Switzerland in 1914 and taught counterpoint at the Zurich Conservatory 1918–1921, when he settled in Berlin and continued to study with Busoni, whose unfinished ópera *Doktor Faust* he completed from the material then available; further sketches were completed by Antony Beaumont for performance in 1985.

Works include prelude to *Prometheus*, suite *Winterbilder* (1915), *Prologue to a Tournament*, *Sinfonia brevis*, *Morgenklangspiel* (1925), Prelude No. 1, *Musik mit Mozart* for orchestra (1935), string quartet and quintet (1916, 1920); violin and piano sonata, two sonatas

for unaccompanied violin; *Konzertstück* for organ; sonatina and other works for piano; songs with orchestra and with piano.

Järnefelt, Armas (b Viborg, 14 Aug 1869; d Stockholm, 23 Jun 1958), Finnish conductor and composer. Studied at Helsinki, Berlin and Paris, conducted at various German theatres and 1898–1903 at Helsinki. Appointed conductor of the Opera there 1903 and at Stockholm 1907–32. He often conducted Sibelius and gave the first Swedish performances of works by Mahler and Schoenberg.

Works include incidental music to *The Promised Land*; choral works; orchestral music including *Praeludium* and *Berceuse* for small orchestra; songs.

Järvi, Neeme (b Tallinn, 7 Jun 1937), Estonian conductor. Studied with Mravinsky at Leningrad Conservatory; conducted widely in Estonia and Russia. Emigrated to USA 1980 and was guest conductor with leading orchestras; NY Met. from 1979, with *Eugene Onegin* and *Samson et Dalila*. Principal guest conductor CBSO 1981–84. Music director Scottish National Orchestra 1984–88. Music director Detroit SO from 1990. Recordings include complete symphonies of Berwald, Gade, Prokofiev, Shostakovich and Skriabin.

Harmony and rhythmic complexity vary from period to period, but a powerful melodic line, some true blues feeling, some swing – they are always there: they hold jazz together.

Wynton Marsalis, notes on *Resolution to Swing*, 1993

---

jazz American dance music of the 20th c. that developed out of ragtime and relying for its effects mainly on syncopations, rhythmic displacement of accents, certain jazz harmonies and inprovisation; and on a special combination of instruments, including plucked string instruments and saxophones, often made to play in an unconventional manner, e.g. *pizzicato* double bass, muted brass, etc. Jazz has influenced certain composers, e.g. Stravinsky in *Ragtime* and *Ebony Concerto*, Milhaud in *La Création du monde* and *Le Bœuf sur le toit*, Krenek in *Jonny spielt auf*, Gershwin in the *Rhapsody in Blue*, Copland in the ballet *Billy the Kid*, Blitzstein in his operas, etc., Hindemith in *Kammermusik no. 1*, Lambert in *The Rio Grande*. Jazz was an important element in German opera of the inter-war years: Brand's *Maschinst Hopkins*, and Weill's *Mahagonny* and *Die Dreigroschenoper*.

Jean de Paris opera by Boieldieu (libretto by C G de Saint-Just),

Järvi *Conductor Neeme Järvi in action with the Gothenburg Symphony Orchestra. He conducted a wide repertory of operas during his tenure as music director of the Estonian Opera Theatre, and has made many recordings of concert works. His interpretations favour a rich, lyrical style.*

produced Paris, Opéra-Comique, 4 Apr 1812. The King has chosen the Princess of Navarre as a bride for the Dauphin. Disguised as simple Jean, the Dauphin meets her and falls in love.

Jeanne d'Arc au bûcher, *Joan of Arc at the Stake*, dramatic oratorio by Honegger (libretto by Paul Claudel), produced Basel, 12 May 1938.

Jedlička, Rudolf (b Skalice, 22 Jan 1920), Czech baritone and administrator. Studied in Vienna and Prague and made debut at Dresden 1944, as Marcello. Sang in opera at Prague from 1945 and produced at Usti-nad-Labem 1945–49. Guest singer with the Berlin Staatsoper from 1958, and in Vienna, Russia and Germany as Don Giovanni, Posa and Rossini's Figaro. Visited Edinburgh 1964 and 1970 with the Prague National Opera in the UK fps of Janáček's *From the House of the Dead* and *The Excursions of Mr Brouček*. Director of the National Theatre at Prague from 1989.

Jeffreys, George (b c 1610; d Weldon, Northants., 1 Jul 1685), English composer. Steward to Lord Hatton of Kirby, Northamptonshire, member of the Chapel Royal, organist to Charles I at Oxford in 1643 during the Civil War.

Works include services, anthems, over 120 motets, sacred solos and duets, carols; music for masques and plays; secular songs, duets, etc.; fancies for strings and virginals.

Jeffries, Matthew, English 16th–17th-c. composer. Vicar-choral at Wells Cathedral. Composed services, anthems, etc.

Jélyotte, Pierre de (b Lasseube, Basses-Pyrénées, 13 Apr 1713; d Estos, Basses-Pyrénées, 11 Sept 1787), French tenor, guitarist and composer. Originally intended for the priesthood, he made his operatic debut in Paris in 1733. He created roles in the revised version of Rameau's *Castor et Pollux* (1754) and in *Zaïs* (1748). He was also guitar teacher to the king, and as a composer produced the opera-ballet *Zelisca* (1746).

Jemnitz, Alexander (b Budapest, 9 Aug 1890; d Balatonfüred, 8 Aug 1963), Hungarian composer and critic. Studied at the Budapest Conservatory, then with Reger at Leipzig and lastly with Schoenberg in Berlin, where he also taught. Later he returned to Budapest.

Works include ballet *Divertimento* (1947); Prelude and Fugue, seven *Miniatures* for orchestra (1947); choral music; string quartet, two string trios (1924, 1927), trios for various other instruments, Partita for two violins, three violin and piano sonatas, sonata for viola and cello.

'Jena' Symphony a symphony in C major discovered at Jena in 1909 and attributed to Beethoven because it bears the inscription 'par L van Beethoven' in an unidentifiable hand; it is now known to be by Friedrich Witt (1771–1837). Edited by Fritz Stein and first performed by him, Jena, 17 Jan 1910.

Jenkins, Graeme (James Ewers) (b London 1958), English conductor. Studied at Cambridge and the RCM. Led Verdi's *Stiffelio* while a student (1981) and *The Beggar's Opera* for Kent Opera, 1982 (returned for *Figaro* and *Entführung*). Conducted Cesti's *La Dori* at the Spitalfields Festival and was artistic director of GTO 1986–91 (*Simon Boccanegra*, and operas by Britten). Glyndebourne debut 1987 (*Carmen*), European debut 1987 (*Hänsel und Gretel* at Geneva); ENO 1988 *Così fan tutte* (returned for the fp of *Timon of Athens* by Oliver, 1991). Concerts with the Hallé Orchestra, BBC PO and SO, Royal Philharmonic and Scottish Chamber Orchestra. Music director of Dallas Opera from 1994.

Jenkins, John (b Maidstone, 1592; d Kimberley, Norfolk, 27 Oct 1678), English composer, lutenist and string player. He lived under the patronage of the gentry and nobility, especially Sir Hamon L'Estrange in Norfolk and Lord North, whose sons, including Roger, he taught music. His last patron was Sir Philip Wodehouse at Kimberley.

Works include fancies and consorts for viols and violins with organ anthems and psalms; Elegy on the death of W Lawes, *Theophila, or Love's Sacrifice* (Benlowes), *A Divine Poem* for voices; rounds, songs.

Jenkins, Newell (b New Haven, 8 Feb 1915), American conductor and scholar. Studied in Dresden and with Carl Orff in Munich. Debut with *Dido and Aeneas* at Freiburg i/B, 1935. Founded Yale Opera Group 1940 and conducted Bologna Chamber Orchestra 1948–53. Music director of the Clarion Music Society, NY, from 1957, giving performances of J M Kraus, Steffani, Monteverdi and Cavalli. Lecturer at University of California at Irvine, 1971–79. Recordings of operas by Mayr and Rossini, Kraus's Funeral Ode and Cherubini's Mass in D Minor.

Jensen, Adolph (b Königsberg, 12 Jan 1837; d Baden-Baden, 23 Jan 1879), German pianist and composer, grandson of the organist and

---

Graeme Jenkins – conductor

1   Tchaikovsky: *Eugene Onegin* (Vishnevskaya/Atlantov/ Mazurok/Orch. & Chorus of the Bolshoi Theatre/ Rostropovich)

Without doubt the best Onegin on disc at present, from the heart-rending string opening, through a passionate Tatiana Letter Scene, with extraordinary orchestral accompaniment, the recording echoes the torment in the composer's own life at the time of composition.

2   Britten: *Peter Grimes* (Pears/Cross/BBC Theatre Chorus/ CG/Goodall)

Pears always said this 1948 recording surpassed the composer's own one. Here Grimes is in fresher voice, just listen to the repeated 'now, now' in the Great Bar aria and apart from being a mere three years away from the premiere, everything is much more poignantly sung and played, there is a real rawness and a vindictiveness present. The famous sea interludes are wonderfully gripping, perhaps Goodall's finest recording?

3   Strauss: *Capriccio* (Janowitz/Fischer-Dieskau/Bayerische Rundfunk Orch./Böhm)

One of the greatest operatic recordings of all time conducted by Strauss's favoured successor. Just listening to the Moonlight interlude and Janowitz's indecision in the closing scene together will melt even the toughest hearted.

4   Beethoven: Symphony no. 6 (*Pastoral*) (Chamber Orch. of Europe/Harnoncourt)

A new look at the *Pastoral* in the hands of one of the most thought-provoking conductors working today; in my opinion a perfect blend of traditional with a more Classical approach, the open-valve trumpets giving an added tension to the orchestral palate. The second movement is simply wonderful.

5   Elgar: Symphony no. 1 (Philharmonia/Barbirolli)

This 1962 recording embodies an optimism and a delight in just being English, every phrase is given that unique Elgarian shape, lingeringly when needed, but without ever losing the great St Pancras station style architecture that Beecham considered (but often cut) in this magnificent work. Listening to it again makes one want to put the Great back into Britain!

THE OPERA

Jenůfa

A three-act opera by Leoš Janáček, who also wrote the text. It is a dramatic tale of complicated family relationships set in Moravia in 1900, and was first performed in Brno in 1904.

I. At Grandmother Buryjovka's mill, Jenůfa (soprano) awaits the arrival of Števa Buryja (tenor). She is pregnant by him, and he hopes he can avoid conscription so that they can marry. He is drunk when he arrives, and the Kostelnička (soprano), Jenůfa's stepmother, forbids an immediate marriage. When Števa leaves, his half-brother Laca Klemeň (tenor) makes advances to Jenůfa. When he is rejected he slashes her face.

II. Disgraced by the birth of Jenůfa's son, the Kostelnička demands that Števa marry her; but he is engaged to Karolka (mezzo-soprano). When Laca appears, ready to marry Jenůfa, the Kostelnička encourages him by saying that the child is dead; she goes out to drown the baby before Jenůfa awakes.

III. As the two couples are about to be married, news is brought that a baby's body has been found. Jenůfa recognizes the baby as her own and, when the Kostelnička admits her guilt, Jenůfa forgives her. Laca is now offered his freedom but he remains true to his love for Jenůfa.

THE OPERA

composer Wilhelm Jensen (professor of music at Königsberg University; d 1842). He studied under various masters, visited Russia and Copenhagen, where he made friends with Gade, was back at Königsberg 1860–66, taught the piano in Berlin for the next two years and then lived at Dresden, Graz and elsewhere for his health.

Works include opera *Die Erbin von Montfort* (adapted to a new libretto based on Gozzi's *Turandot* by Kienzl after his death, 1858–65); cantatas *Jephthas Tochter* (1864), *Der Gang der Jünger nach Emmaus* (1865), *Donald Caird* (Scott, 1875), and *Adonisfeier*; concert overture and *Geistliches Tonstück* for orchestra; *c* 25 op. nos. of piano music and settings of Heyse and Geibel (*Spanisches Liederbuch*) and Herder.

Jenůfa opera by Janáček (libretto by composer after G Preissova; known in Czech as *Jeji Pastorkyna – Her Foster-daughter*); composed 1894–1903, produced Brno, 21 Jan 1904. Revised 1906–16 and performed Prague 26 May 1916 with some re-orchestration by the conductor, Karel Kovařovic (1862–1920). Jenůfa is to marry Števa, but she is disfigured by Števa's half-brother Laca, who later wins her love. Her step-mother the Kostelnička hides her while she bears Števa's child. After Števa rejects Jenůfa the Kostelnička drowns the baby, but later must pay the price.

Jephtas Gelübde, *Jephtha's Vow*, opera by Meyerbeer (libretto by A Schreiber), produced Munich, 23 Dec 1812. Meyerbeer's first opera.

Jephte oratorio by Carissimi; composed by 1650 and pub. in several modern editions; realized by Henze and performed London, 14 Jul 1976.

Jephté, *Jephtha*, opera by Montéclair (libretto by S J de Pellegrin), produced Paris, Opéra, 28 Feb 1732. After making a vow to the gods, Israelite general Jephtha must sacrifice his daughter Iphthé for success on the battlefield.

Jephtha oratorio by Handel (libretto by T Morell), produced London, CG, 26 Feb 1752.

Jeremiáš, Jaroslav (b Písek, 14 Aug 1889; d Budějovice, 16 Jan 1919), Czech composer and pianist. Pupil of Novák and others at the Prague Conservatory.

Works include opera *The Old King* (1919), choral and chamber music.

Jerger, Alfred (b Brno, 9 Jun 1889; d Vienna, 18 Nov 1976), Austrian bass-baritone. He began his career as conductor and actor; began singing 1915 and after two years at Munich joined Vienna Staatsoper in 1920; remained until 1964 in 146 roles, including Don Giovanni,

Sachs, Scarpia and Almaviva. In 1924 he created The Man in Schoenberg's *Die glückliche Hand*, at the Vienna Volksoper, and in 1933 was the first Mandryka in *Arabella* (Dresden), his role in London, CG, debut (1934). After the war he worked as producer and teacher in Vienna.

Jeritza (real name *Jedlitzka*), Maria (b Brno, 6 Oct 1887; d Orange, NJ, 10 Jul 1982), Czech soprano. Studied in Brno and first appeared in the chorus of the Brno Opera. She made her debut as a soloist at Olmütz in 1910 and was a member of the Vienna Staatsoper from 1913 to 1932; she created the title role in both versions of *Ariadne* and was the first Empress in *Die Frau ohne Schatten* (1919). She also sang at the NY Met. 1921–32 as Jenůfa, Tosca, Turandot and Marietta in *Die tote Stadt*.

Jérusalem the title of the French version of Verdi's opera *I Lombardi alla prima crociata*.

Jerusalem, Siegfried (b Oberhausen, 17 Apr 1940), German tenor. His career began as a bassoonist; opera roles at Stuttgart from 1975. Bayreuth debut 1977 and in recent years has sung Lohengrin, Siegmund, Parsifal and Walther there. Berlin, Deutsche Oper, 1977–80; has sung widely in Europe and North America as Max, Florestan, Idomeneo and Lensky. In March 1986 he sang Parsifal at the London Coliseum and Erik at CG. Season 1992 as Parsifal at the NY Met., and Siegfried at Bayreuth.

Jessonda opera by Spohr (libretto by E H Gehe, based on Lemierre's tragedy *La Veuve de Malabar*), produced Kassel, 28 Jul 1823. Portuguese general Tristan discovers his long-lost love Jessonda is to be immolated, but has sworn not to interfere in local ceremonies. He is free to rescue her, and does so, after the Indians break a cease-fire.

Jesus and the Traders (Jezus es a kufarok), motet by Kodály for mixed voices a cappella, composed 1934.

jeté French = 'thrown'; a style of bowing on string instruments. The upper part of the bow is made to fall lightly on the string so that it rebounds several times during the downward motion and repeats notes in a rapid *staccato*.

Jeu de Cartes, *Card Game*, ballet in three deals by Stravinsky; composed 1936 in Paris, produced NY Met. 27 Apr 1937, with choreography by Balanchine.

Jeune France, La a group of young French composers formed in 1936 by Baudrier, Jolivet, Lesur and Messiaen.

Jeune Henri, Le, *The Young Henry*, opera by Méhul (libretto by J N Bouilly, originally intended for Grétry and called *La Jeunesse de Henri IV*), produced Paris, Opéra-Comique, 1 May 1797. The overture called *La Chasse du jeune Henri* was known as a concert piece long after the opera was forgotten. The worthy deeds of Henry, who kills a wolf and wins a race, magnanimously giving up his prize.

Jeux ballet by Debussy (choreography by Nizhinsky), composed 1912 and produced Paris, Théâtre du Châtelet, 13 May 1913.

Jeux d'enfants suite for piano duet by Bizet, op. 22, composed 1871; *Petite Suite* for orchestra arranged from five pieces of it, 1872, fp Paris, 2 Mar 1873.

Jewels of the Madonna (Wolf-Ferrari.) ◊Gioielli della Madonna.

Jew's harp an ancient instrument consisting of a metal frame held between the player's teeth and a vibrating metal tongue set in motion by the fingers and emitting a note which can be varied by changes in the cavity of the mouth.

jig an old dance in binary form in some kind of animated duple time, usually 6–8 or 12–8; the Italian *giga* and French *gigue*. It was the fourth of the dances regularly found in the classical suite. The second half was often built on an inversion of the theme of the first.

Jirák, Karel Boleslav (b Prague, 28 Jan 1891; d Chicago, 30 Jan 1972), Czech composer and conductor. Studied with Novák in Prague and was later influenced by J B Foerster. Professor of composition at Prague Conservatory from 1920 and head of music at Czech Radio 1930–1945. Professor at Roosevelt College, Chicago, from 1949.

Works include opera *Apollonius of Tyana* (later called *Woman and the God*, 1928); six symphonies (1915–68); piano concerto; seven string quartets (1915–60), string sextet; sonatas for violin and piano, viola and piano and cello and piano; song-cycles *Tragi-Comedy*

(Heine), *Meditations*, *Brief Happiness*, *Three Songs of Home*, *Evening and the Soul*; *Suite in the Old Style* for piano.

Jo, Sumi (b Seoul, 22 Nov 1962), Korean soprano. Studied in Seoul and Rome; debut Trieste 1986, as Gilda. Sang in France and was discovered by Karajan, singing Barbarina and Oscar at Salzburg, 1989–90. Munich from 1988, Vienna from 1989. NY Met. debut 1988, and Fra Diavalo at La Scala (1992); her coloratura has been admired as the Queen of Night at Chicago (1990), and elsewhere. Other roles include Matilde in Rossini's *Elisabetta* (Naples) and Thetis in Jommelli's *Fetonte* at La Scala.

Joachim, Joseph (b Kittsee, near Pozsony, 28 Jun 1831; d Berlin, 15 Aug 1907), Hungarian (Germanized) violinist, composer and conductor. Made his first appearance at the age of seven. Studied at the Vienna Conservatory and in Leipzig, where he came under the influence of Mendelssohn; played under him at the Gewandhaus concerts (1843) and the following year played the Beethoven concerto in London. Leader of the orchestra at Weimar, 1849–53, and at Hanover, 1853–68. Appointed director of the Berlin Hochschule für Musik, 1868. Founded the Joachim quartet, 1869. He visited England every year from 1862 and in 1877 conducted the first British performance of Brahms' first symphony; took part in the fp of the Double Concerto, 1887. He was the dedicatee of Dvořák's concerto, but refused to play it.

Works include overtures for orchestra to Shakespeare's *Hamlet* and *Henry IV*, in commemoration of Kleist and on two comedies by Gozzi; three violin concertos (including 'Hungarian'), variations for violin and orchestra.

Joan of Arc ◊Giovanna d'Arco; ◊Jeanne d'Arc au bûcher; ◊Maid of Orleans.

Job masque for dancing by Vaughan Williams (choreography by Ninette de Valois, settings by Gwendolen Raverat, based on Blake's illustrations to the Book of Job), produced London, Cambridge Theatre, 5 Jul 1931.

Oratorio by Parry (words from the Book of Job), produced Gloucester Festival, 1892.

Jochum, Eugen (b Babenhausen, 1 Nov 1902; d Munich, 26 Mar 1987), German conductor. Studied piano and organ at Augsburg Conservatory (1914–22) and composition at the Munich Academy of Music (1922–24). After some time as a *répétiteur* in Munich and Kiel, he conducted at Mannheim and Duisburg, becoming music director of the Hamburg Staatsoper 1934–45. From 1949 he was conductor of the Munich Radio Orchestra. US debut, with Concertgebouw Orchestra, 1961. He conducted Bartók and Stravinsky during World War II in Hamburg and was well known in Bach and Bruckner.

Johannes de Grocheo ◊Grocheio.

Johannesen, Grant (b Salt Lake City, 30 Jul 1921), American pianist. Studied with Robert Casadesus and Egon Petri; debut at Times Hall, NY, 1944, with the New York PO; tour of Europe with the orchestra, 1956–57; USSR and Europe with the Cleveland Orchestra, and solo tour of Russia 1970. Music director of the Cleveland Institute 1974–84. Recordings include Fauré's complete piano music.

Johannsson, Kristjan (b Akureyi Du, 1950), Icelandic tenor. Studied with Tagliavini and made debut at Reykjavik 1981, as Rodolfo. Sang Pinkerton at Spoleto (1983) and Faust at the Chicago Lyric Opera, 1991. Has also appeared at the NY Met., Vienna Staatsoper, and La Scala, Milan, as Radames, Cavaradossi and Dick Johnson. Calaf and Turiddu at the Verona Arena (1991–93) and Manrico at Genoa, 1991. Sang Verdi's Renato at the Munich Staatsoper, 1994 and at CG, 1995.

Johansson, Eva (b Copenhagen, 25 Feb 1958), Danish soprano. Studied at Juilliard and Copenhagen, and sang at the Royal Opera there 1982–88 as Mozart's Countess, Tatiana and Pamina. Berg's Marie at the Paris Opéra 1986, Gutrune and Freia in the *Ring* at Berlin and Bayreuth, 1988 (returned as Elsa, 1990). Vienna Staatsoper 1989, as Fiordiligi and CG debut 1992, Donna Anna.

Johns, William (b Tulsa, OK, 2 Oct 1936), American tenor. Debut at Lake George 1967, as Rodolfo. European debut with the Bremen Opera, then WNO 1970–72, as Radames and Calaf. Has sung further at Dallas, Hamburg, Houston, Vienna and the NY Met. CG debut

1987, as Bacchus; Philadelphia 1988, as Florestan. Sang Tristan at San Francisco, 1991. Other roles include Siegfried, Lohengrin, Tannhäuser and Strauss's Emperor.

Johnson, Edward, English 16th–17th-c. composer ? in the service of Lord Hertford at Elvetham, where (?) he contributed music to an entertainment given to Queen Elizabeth I in 1591. Mus.B., Cambridge, 1594. He contributed to East's psalter and the *Triumphes of Oriana*.

Works include madrigals, viol music, virginal pieces.

Johnson, Edward (b Guelph, Ontario, 22 Aug 1878; d Toronto, 20 Apr 1959), Canadian tenor. He studied in NY and Florence. Debut Padua 1912, as Chénier. At La Scala he was the first Parsifal in Italy, in 1914, and the following year sang there in the fp of Pizzetti's *Fedra*; returned 1918 for the fp of Montemezzi's *La Nave*. CG 1923, as Faust. Chicago 1919–22; NY Met. 1922–35, in the fps of works by Howard Hanson and Deems Taylor. Other roles included Siegfried, Tannhäuser and Pelléas. Manager, Met., 1935–50.

Music-making as a means of getting money is hell.
Gustav Holst, quoted in Imogen Holst, *Holst*, 1974

Johnson, Emma (b Barnet, 20 May 1966), English clarinettist. Studied at Cambridge and was BBC TV Young Musician of the Year 1984. Debut at the Barbican Hall, London 1985 and has appeared since with all leading UK orchestras; Vienna debut 1985, Tokyo 1990, New York 1992. Recordings include concertos by Crusell, Spohr, Finzi and Mozart.

Johnson, Graham (Rhodes) (b Bulawayo, 10 Jul 1950), Rhodesian-born English pianist. Studied at the RAM and the GSM; London debut 1972. Accompanied leading singers in recital and has been artistic director of the Songmakers' Almanac from 1976; thematically-linked recitals with a small group of singers. Has recorded all Schubert's Lieder with Fischer-Dieskau, Lucia Popp, Peter Schreier and others.

Johnson, John (b *c* 1540; d London, 1595), English lutenist and composer. Attached to Queen Elizabeth's court and (?) to the household of Sir Thomas Kitson at Hengrave Hall, Suffolk, and in London, 1572–74. Took part in Leicester's entertainments at Kenilworth Castle in 1575. Wrote lute solos and duets.

Johnson, Robert (b Duns, *c* 1500; d 1554), Scottish priest and composer. Fled to England as a heretic and settled at Windsor, where he may have been chaplain to Anne Boleyn. Wrote Latin motets, English services and prayers, in nomines for instruments, songs.

Johnson, Robert (b *c* 1583; d London, 1633), English lutenist and composer, son of John Johnson. Was taught music at the expense of Sir George Carey, husband of Sir Thomas Kitson's granddaughter, in whose household he was brought up, and was appointed lutenist to James I in 1604; taught Prince Henry and remained in his post under Charles I.

Works include songs for several voices; songs to the lute; catches; pieces for viols; also songs in Shakespeare's *Tempest*, in Fletcher's *Valentinian* and *The Mad Lover*.

Johnson, Robert Sherlaw (b Sunderland, 21 May 1932), English composer and pianist. He studied at Durham University, the RAM and in Paris (authority on Messiaen). Has taught at Leeds and York Universities and, from 1970, Oxford.

Works include opera *The Lambton Worm* (produced Oxford, 1978); *Carmen Vernalia* for soprano and chamber orchestra (1972); *Where the Wild things Are* for soprano and tape (1974); *Festival Mass of the Resurrection* for chorus and orchestra (1974); *Anglorum Feriae* for soprano, tenor, chorus and orchestra (1977); *Veritas veritatis* for six voices (1980); piano concerto (1983); three piano sonatas; two string quartets (1966, 1969).

Joio, Norman dello, ◊Dello Joio.

Jolas, Betsy (b Paris, 5 Aug 1926), French-born American composer. Studied at Bennington College, 1940–46, the Paris Conservatory with Milhaud and Messiaen; taught at the Conservatory from 1974 and has taught widely in the USA.

Graham Johnson – pianist

1. Mozart: String Quintet in C (Amadeus String Quartet/Aronowitz)
Writing for strings simply does not get better than this – a flawless and haunting work less known than the Schubert String Quintet in the same key, but equally rewarding.

2. Schubert: *Winterreise* (Pears/Britten)
It was thanks to this great song cycle, and working with these performers, that I knew I had to be an accompanist: what a joy to be able to work with these 24 songs as well as the hundreds of other Schubert Lieder! This profound music of deceptive simplicity – a cornerstone of the song repetoire and of early Romanticism.

3. Schubert: Piano Sonata in D major (Curzon)
An enchanting and daring performance (what rubato, what articulation!) of a great work. Thank heavens the Schubert sonatas are no longer neglected by great pianists.

4. Brahms: Piano Quintet (Guarneri Quartet/Rubinstein)
Benjamin Britten (who is well known to have disliked Brahms's music) adored this work. It is the writing of a young master full of passion and drama – and what marvellous tunes!

5. Wolf: Goethe Lieder (Schwarzkopf/Gerald Moore)
A great composer setting the words of the greatest of German poets and performed by a great soprano and the father of the modern art of piano accompaniment. Wolf's Lieder are second only to Schubert's; because he only wrote songs it is all too easy to underestimate his importance.

6. Chabrier: *Le roi malgré lui* (conducted by Dutoit)
Anything that Chabrier wrote fills me with delight. This opera, neglected because of its nonsensical libretto, is full of ravishing music sumptuously orchestrated.

7. Ravel: *Schéhérazade* (Crespin/conducted by Ansermet)
The classic performance of the most sensual of orchestral song cycles. Crespin's voice is full of the perfumed languor of the orient yet remains perfectly controlled to obey the subtly understated demands of Ravel's score.

8. Poulenc: *Mélodies* (Bernac/Poulenc)
Poulenc's songs – hauntingly sad and grave as well as frivolous and openly entertaining – are one of the glories of the vocal repertoire. No one has equalled the authority and expressive range of the baritone for whom so many of them were written.

9. Britten: *Billy Budd* (conducted by Britten)
Not nearly as popular as *Peter Grimes*, this opera contains some of the very best Britten (as well as the most accessible) with marvellous sea shanties and battle scenes. It is a stirring tale with disturbing psychological and musical depths.

10. Anything (almost) sung by Maria Callas – Bellini, Donizetti, Rossini, Verdi or Puccini.
The element of personal tragedy in Callas's life and career pairs her with the greatest of jazz singers, Billie Holiday. Both were artists of rare genius, whose musical insight made them full creative partners of their chosen composers.

Works include operas *Le pavillon au bord de la rivière* (1975), *Le cyclope* (1986) and *Schliemann* (1989); *Musique d'hiver* for organ and small orchestra (1971), *Trois Recontres* for string trio and orchestra (1973) and *Stances* for piano and orchestra (1978); *D'un opéra de voyage* (1967), *États* (1969), *How Now* (1973) and *Préludes-Fanfares-Interludes-Sonneries* (1983) for ensemble; two string quartets (1973, 1989), string trio (1990), keyboard music and songs.

Jolie Fille de Perth, La, *The Fair Maid of Perth*, opera by Bizet (libretto by J H V de Saint-Georges and J Adenis, based on Scott's novel), produced Paris, Théâtre Lyrique, 26 Dec 1867. Catherine and Smith are united, despite competition from the Duke of Rothsay and a case of mistaken identity.

Jolivet, André (b Paris, 8 Aug 1905; d Paris, 20 Dec 1974), French composer. Pupil of Le Flem and Varèse. He formed the group 'La Jeune France' with Baudrier, Lesur and Messiaen in 1936.

Works include opera *Dolorès* (1947); two ballets; oratorio *La Vérité de Jeanne* (1956); three symphonies (1953, 1959, 1964); concertos for trumpet (2), flute, piano, harp, bassoon and Ondes Martenot; string quartet; sonata and suite *Mana* for piano, songs.

Joll, Philip (b Merthyr Tydfil, 14 Mar 1954), Welsh baritone. Studied at the RNCM and with Hotter and Goodall. WNO from 1979, as Orestes, Amfortas, Kurwenas, Barak and Wotan (also at CG, 1986). CG debut 1982, in Salome; NY Met. debut 1987, as Donner in *Das Rheingold*. Sang Wagner's Dutchman at the 1988–89 Bregenz Festival; Verdi's Francesco Foscari at the 1993 Edinburgh Festival.

Jommelli, Niccolò (b Aversa near Naples, 10 Sept 1714; d Naples, 25 Aug 1774), Italian composer. Pupil of Durante, Feo and Leo in Naples, made his debut as an opera composer there in 1737, and soon became famous throughout Italy and in Vienna. *Kapellmeister* to the Duke of Württemberg at Stuttgart 1753–69, he then returned to

Naples, but was unable to recapture his old success in Italy; he had developed the dry conventions of the Metastasian *opera seria*, but the Neapolitans were turning their attentions to comic opera.

Works include over 50 extant operas, e.g. *Ricimero* (1740), *Ezio* (three settings: 1741, 1748, 1758), *Semiramide* (1741), *Sofonisba* (1746), *Artaserse* (1749), *Ifigenia in Aulide* (1751), *Talestri*, *Attilio Regolo* (1753), *Fetonte*, *La clemenza di Tito* (two settings: 1753, 1765), *Pelope*, *Il matrimonio per concorso*, *La schiava liberata*, *Armida* (1770), *Ifigenia in Tauride* (1771); oratorios *Isacco*, *Betulia liberata* (1743), *Santa Elena al Calvario*, etc.; Passion oratorio, *Miserere*, Masses and other church music; cantatas; symphonies and other instrumental music.

Jonas, Peter (b London, 14 Oct 1946), English administrator. Studied at the RCM and RNCM (1968–71). Artistic administrator of the Chicago SO (1976–85); general director of ENO 1985–93, presiding over many thought-provoking productions. Intendant of the Bavarian State Opera at Munich, from 1993. CBE 1992.

Joncières, Victorin de (actually Félix Ludger Rossignol) (b Paris, 12 Apr 1839; d Paris, 26 Oct 1903), French composer. Began by studying painting, but set a friend's adaptation of Molière's *Le Sicilien* as a comic opera with such success that he entered the Conservatory. He left again after a disagreement about Wagner, whom he admired, and studied privately. In 1871 he became music critic to *La Liberté*.

Works include operas *Sardanapale* (1867), *Le Dernier Jour de Pompéi* (after Bulwer-Lytton, 1869), *Dimitri*, *La Reine Berthe* (1878), *Le Chevalier Jean* (1885), *Lancelot*, incidental music to Shakespeare's *Hamlet*; *La Mer*, symphonic ode for mezzo, chorus and orchestra (1881); suite for orchestra *Les Nubiennes*, *Sérénade hongroise*, overture, marches and other orchestral music; violin concerto.

Jones, Daniel (b Pembroke, 7 Dec 1912; d Swansea, 23 Apr 1993),

Peter Jonas – director, Bavarian State Opera

1   Verdi: *Quattro Pezzi Sacri* (Philharmonia/Giulini)
    If I had to choose one 'Desert Island' piece it would be this.
    The universality of Verdi's late work, its beauty and love for
    God and Life makes it indispensable and, for me, a musical
    reference point.

2   Bach: English Suite no. 2 in A minor (Pogorelich)
    A work which never pales in its freshness and recorded here
    by a master of technique whose rhythmic intensity and
    dynamic sense of momentum release emotion with respect
    for the composition's structure.

3   Handel: *Giulio Cesare* (Radio tape, BRF: Murray/Robson/
    Bayerische Staatsoper/Bolton, or commercial recording:
    Concerto Köln/Jacobs)
    Handel was, arguably, the greatest of musical dramatists and
    Giulio Cesare one of his greatest works. The two arias of
    Cesare, 'Va Tacito' and 'Aure deh, per pieta', are pinnacles
    of the composer's achievement.

4   Dowland: *First booke of Songs 1597* (The Consort of Music/
    Rooley)
    Exemplary matching of music and text – a composer whose
    creative fire is ignited by poetic inspiration.

5   Schumann: Fantasiestücke, op. 12 – *Des Abends*
    (Rubinstein)
    The essence of Romanticism played by one of the great
    Romantic piano interpreters.

6   Mozart: String Quintet in G minor (Heifetz/Israel Baker/
    Primrose/Virginia Majewski/Piatigorsky)
    The greatest performance of this 'Everest' of chamber
    music.

7   Mendelssohn: Piano Trio in D minor, op. 49 (Rubinstein/
    Heifetz/Piatigorsky)
    A great but underestimated work which never fails to uplift
    the soul, in a historic performance of grandeur, nobility, and,
    at the same time, intimacy.

8   Tippett: *Midsummer Marriage* – Act 1, Scene 3, 'I don't
    know who they really are …'
    Mark's monologue has a tumescent quality which, for me,
    makes it a highlight of this great, visionary and very moving
    opera of our century.

9   Elgar: *The Dream of Gerontius* – 'Sanctus fortis, Sanctus
    Deus' (Nash/Huddersfield Choral Society/RLPO/Sargent)
    Elgar wrote, at the end of his full score of this work, 'This is
    the best of me'. There is nothing more to be said.

10 Humperdinck: *Hänsel und Gretel* – 'Abends will ich
    schlafen gehen' (Popp/Fassbaender/Vienna PO/Solti)
    A prelude to dreams, whether passing or eternal, and a
    musical moment close to my heart.

Welsh composer. Studied at University College, Swansea, where he read English, and later at the RAM in London. He studied conducting with Sir Henry Wood and composition with Harry Farjeon. He began composing at a very early age and later produced a large quantity of music, including 12 symphonies. OBE 1968.

Works include operas *The Knife* (1963) and *Orestes* (1967); incidental music for *Under Milk Wood* (Dylan Thomas); twelve symphonies (1944–90); symphonic poems *Cystuddiau Branwen*, *Cloud Messenger*; concertino for piano and orchestra; eight string quartets, string quintet, five string trios, violin sonata, cello sonata, piano sonata, sonata for kettle-drums, wind septet, wind nonet.

Jones, Della (b Neath, 13 Apr 1946), Welsh mezzo. Studied at the RCM and Geneva; debut at the Opéra there 1970, as Fyodor in *Boris Godunov*. Has sung with SW/ENO from 1973 in *The Devils of Loudun* (debut) and as Rossini's Rosina and Ninetta, Sextus in *Julius Caesar* and Dolly in the fp of Hamilton's *Anna Karenina* (1981). CG debut 1983, in *L'Enfant et les Sortilèges*, returning as the Marchesa Melibea in *Il Viaggio a Reims*, 1992. US debut 1986, as Ruggiero in *Alcina* at Los Angeles. Roles with WNO include Dido in *Les Troyens*, Brangaena (1993) and Ariodante (1994).

Jones, Edward (b Llanderfel, Merioneth, bap. 29 Mar 1752; d London, 18 Apr 1824), Welsh harpist and song collector. Taught the harp by his father, he went to London in 1775 and was appointed bard to the Prince of Wales in 1783. Pub. several collections of Welsh and other national airs.

Jones, Gwyneth (b Pontnewydd, 7 Nov 1936), Welsh soprano. Studied at the RCM and in Siena. Debut Zurich, 1962, Gluck's Orpheus. Sang Lady Macbeth with WNO 1963; Fidelio and the *Trovatore* Leonora, CG, 1964. First Wagner role in London was Sieglinde, 1965, and following year she made her Bayreuth debut; Brünnhilde in the centenary *Ring* 1976. Vienna since 1966; NY Met. 1972. In Nov 1985 she sang both the Empress and the Dyer's Wife in a performance of *Die Frau ohne Schatten* at the Zurich Opera. In 1986 she returned to

CG, as Salome. Sang Brünnhilde at CG 1991, NY Met. 1993. Other roles include Isolde, the Marschallin (Salzburg, 1979), Aida, Desdemona, Donna Anna, Tosca, Elisabeth de Valois and Strauss's Helena. CBE 1976; DBE 1986.

Jones, John (b London, 1728; d London, 17 Feb 1796), English organist and composer. Appointed organist of the Middle Temple in 1749, of Charterhouse, succeeding Pepusch, in 1753 and of St Paul's Cathedral in 1755. Wrote chants, harpsichord lessons, etc.

Jones, Parry (b Blaina, Mon., 14 Feb 1891; d London, 26 Dec 1963), Welsh tenor. After a tour of the US he sang with the Carl Rosa co. 1919–22; CG debut with the co. 1921, as Turiddu. BNOC 1922–29. He was the Kardinal in the first British performance of *Mathis der Maler* (concert, 1939) and Mephistopheles in a concert performance of Busoni's *Doktor Faust* (under Boult, 1937). He took part in the first concert and stage performances of *Wozzeck* in England (1934, 1952). Other roles included Walther, Parsifal and Lohengrin.

---

*What I'd like best of all, time and again, would be to
set myself to music.*

Richard Strauss,
in a letter to von Hofmannsthal, 1927

Jones, Philip (Mark) (b Bath, 12 Mar 1928), English trumpet player and administrator. Studied at RCM and was principal with leading London orchestras, 1948–71. Founder and director of the Philip Jones Brass Ensemble, 1951–86. Head of wind and percussion at RNCM 1975–77, GSM 1983–88. Principal of TCL 1989–94. CBE 1986.

Jones, Richard (b London, 7 Jun 1953), English stage director. Studied in Hull and London; debut with Scottish Opera 1982, Argento's *A Water Bird Talk*. Battignano Festival 1984–85, with operas by Mozart, Salieri and Paisiello; *Mignon* at the 1986 Wexford Festival, *Manon* and *Carmen* for Opera North 1987. *The Love for Three*

Oranges and the fp of *The Plumber's Gift* by David Blake at ENO (1989). Has also worked at Scottish Opera (*Macbeth* and *Die Walküre*), Bregenz (*Mazeppa*) and Munich (*Giulio Cesare*, dominated by a dinosaur). A stimulating *Ring* cycle for CG (1994–95) began with latex-rubber Rhinemaidens in *Das Rheingold* and continued with a gym-slip Brünnhilde in *Die Walküre*.

Jones, Robert (b *c* 1485; d *c* 1536), English composer. He was a Gentleman of the Chapel Royal from 1513. He composed a song, 'Who shall have my fair lady', a Mass, *Spes nostra*, and a Magnificat.

Jones, Robert (b *c* 1570; d *c* 1617), English lutenist and composer. He worked for several patrons and took the B.Mus. degree at Oxford in 1597. In 1610, with Rosseter and others, he obtained a patent to train children for the queen's revels, and in 1615 they were allowed to erect a theatre in Blackfriars, but its opening was subsequently prohibited.

Works include madrigals, five books of *Songs and Ayres* to the lute, anthems.

Jongen, Joseph (b Liège, 14 Dec 1873; d Sart-lez-Spa near Liège, 12 Jul 1953), Belgian composer. Studied at the Liège Conservatory. Gained a prize from the Académie Royale in 1893 and the Belgian Prix de Rome in 1897. After teaching for a short time at the Liège Conservatory, he went to Rome and later travelled in Germany and France, taking up a professorship at Liège in 1903. In 1914–18 he was in England as a war refugee, but returned to Liège until 1920, when he became professor at the Brussels Conservatory, of which he was later appointed director.

Works include ballet *S'Arka*; symphony (1910), *Fantaisie sur deux Noëls wallons* (1902), symphonic poem *Lalla Rookh* (after Thomas Moore, 1904), *Impressions d'Ardennes* (1913), *Tableaux pittoresques* (1917), *Passecaille et Gigue* for orchestra (1930); *Pièce symphonique* for piano and wind orchestra, violin concerto, harp concerto (1944), suite for viola and orchestra, *Symphonie concertante* for organ and orchestra (1926), concerto for wind quintet (1923); three string quartets (1894, 1916, 1921), two serenades for string quartet, piano trio; two violin and piano sonatas, cello sonata; *Sonata eroica* for organ; songs.

jongleur French = 'juggler'; a medieval wandering minstrel, one of whose accomplishments was juggling, but who also sang and played.

Jongleur de Notre Dame, Le, *Our Lady's Juggler*, opera by Massenet (libretto by M Léna on a story by Anatole France in *L'Étui de nacre*, based on a medieval miracle play), produced Monte Carlo, 18 Feb 1902. Juggler Jean, having given up street performances, enters a monastery. As a tribute, he performs before a statue of the Virgin, and expires amidst a sacred halo.

Jonny spielt auf, *Johnny strikes up*, opera by Krenek (libretto by composer), produced Leipzig, Munich, Opera, 10 Feb 1927. Composer Max woos prima donna Anita, but she is more interested in the violinist, Daniello. Max finds new inspiration from life, and is reunited with Anita.

Jonson, Ben(jamin) (1573–1637), English poet and dramatist. Handel (◊Alchemist); Salieri (◊Angiolina); ◊Auric (*Volpone*); ◊Ferrabosco (masques); ◊Harington ('Drink to me only'); ◊Lanier (*Lovers made Men* and *Vision of Delight*); ◊Lothar (*Lord Spleen*); Bliss (◊Pastoral); R Strauss (◊Schweigsame Frau), Elgar (◊Spanish Lady); ◊Vaughan Williams (*Pan's Anniversary*).

Joplin, Scott (b near Marshall, TX, 24 Nov 1868; d New York, 1 Apr 1917), American composer and pianist. First came to attention as a pianist at brothels in St Louis and Chicago. Achieved fame with *Maple Leaf Rag* (1899) and was considered the leading exponent of 'classic rag', in which the standard syncopated rhythm was treated with some sophistication. Published *The Entertainer* 1902 and formed the Scott Joplin Opera Company 1903, for the performance of his opera *A Guest of Honour* (music lost). *Treemonisha*, an opera about a black baby girl found under a tree by a woman called Monisha, was completed 1911 and performed in concert 1915. Joplin's last years were ruined by syphilis. His posthumous fame was initiated with a revival of *Treemonisha* at Atlanta (1972) and continued in 1974, when *The Entertainer* was one of the best-selling discs. Joplin was awarded a posthumous Pulitzer Prize in 1976.

Jorda, Enrique (b San Sebastian, 24 Mar 1911), Spanish-born American conductor. Studied at Madrid and conducted the SO there 1940–45; Cape Town SO 1948–54, San Francisco SO 1954–63 (including the 1962 fp of Roy Harris's 8th symphony). Conducted the Antwerp PO 1970–75 and the Euskadi SO 1982–84.

Jordan, Armin (b Lucerne, 9 Apr 1932), Swiss conductor. Studied at Lausanne and was chief conductor of the Bienne Opera 1961–66; Zurich Opera 1963–71, Basel Opera from 1971. Music director Lausanne CO 1973–85, Orchestre de la Suisse Romande from 1985. Conducted, and played Amfortas in a film version of *Parsifal*, directed by Syberberg.

The Most High has a decided taste for vocal music, provided it be lugubrious and gloomy enough.
Voltaire, *Dictionnaire Philosophique*, 1764

Jordan, Irene (b Birmingham, AL, 25 Apr 1919), American soprano. Studied in New York and made debut at the Met. 1946, as Mallika in *Lakmé*. Re-trained as soprano and sang Donna Anna at Chicago, 1954. Sang at the NY City Opera from 1957 and returned to the Met. the same year as the Queen of Night. Also sang as Aida, Lady Macbeth, Butterfly and Euryanthe.

Jörn, Karl (b Riga, 5 Jan 1873; d Denver, 19 Dec 1947), Latvian-born American tenor. Debut Freiburg i/B 1896, as Lionel; sang at Hamburg 1899–1902 and Berlin from 1902; first local Parsifal, 1914. CG 1905–08. He sang at the NY Met. 1908–14 and attempted to retire in 1916. After a business disaster he toured with Johanna Gadski and the German Opera co. 1928–31; particularly successful as Parsifal. Other roles included Faust and Don José. Taught in NY from 1932.

Joseph opera by Méhul (libretto by A Duval), produced Paris, Opéra-Comique, 17 Feb 1807. Weber wrote piano variations, Op. 28, on a romance from it. Joseph, sold into slavery by his brothers, is successful in Egypt. He later meets them and tests their remorse.

Joseph and his Brethren oratorio by Handel (libretto by J Miller), performed London, CG, 2 Mar 1744. Blind Jacob is reunited with his long-lost son.

Josephs, Wilfred (b Newcastle, 24 Jul 1927), English composer. He studied at the GSM and in Paris. His *Requiem* of 1963 won first prize in a La Scala competition.

Other works include opera *Rebecca* (after Hollywood rather than du Maurier; produced Leeds 1983); dramatic works for children and for TV; ballets *The Magic Being* (1961), *La Répétition de Phèdre* (1965), *Equus* (1978) and *Cyrano de Bergerac* (1985); ten symphonies (1955–85); two piano concertos, violin concerto, clarinet concerto (1975), concerto for viola and chamber orchestra (1983); *Mortales* for soloists, chorus and orchestra (texts by Blake, Shelley, Nashe and Luther; fp Cincinnati, 1970); four string quartets (1954–81), octet (1964), two violin sonatas, piano trio (1974).

Josephslegende ballet in one act by Strauss (scenario by H Kessler and Hugo von Hofmannsthal); composed 1912–14, produced Paris, Opéra, 14 Feb 1914, Ballet Russe.

Joshua oratorio by Handel (libretto by T Morell), performed London, CG, 23 Mar 1748.

Josquin Desprez, or des Pres (b NE France, perhaps *c* 1440; d Condé, 27 Aug 1521), French composer. By 1459 he was apparently a singer at Milan Cathedral, remaining there for nearly 20 years, also working at the court of René of Anjou and in the Papal Chapel (1486–94). In the years *c* 1500 he was briefly at the French royal court, then at Ferrara (1503–04) before becoming provost at Condé, where he seems to have spent the rest of his life. The story of his life is currently much disputed because so many of the documents refer simply to 'Josquin', which was a very common name at the time.

His reputation throughout the 16th c. as the purest and most accomplished composer of his time is partly endorsed (though also confused) by the enormous number of spurious works ascribed to him in the MSS — more than double the number that are accepted as authentic by scholars today. His 18 authentic complete Mass cycles

A Selection of

Josquin Desprez

Missa Ave Maris Stella
Missa L'Homme armé sexti toni
Missa Pange Lingua

Missa Hercule dux Ferrarie
Motets
Missa L'Homme armé super voces
musicales
Deploration
Missa La sol fa re mi

include examples of the canonic, *cantus firmus*, paraphrase and so-called 'parody' types; the most famous in his own time was the Mass *De beata virgine*, whereas today the Mass *Pange lingua* is perhaps best known. His numerous motets and psalm-settings (63 seem certain to be his) are remarkable for their careful adherence to the spirit of the words. His shorter secular works (over 50) are mostly from the years after 1500 and many of them treat received semi-popular songs in the most elaborate polyphonic texture, though *Mille regretz* and his lament for Ockeghem, *Nymphes des bois*, make their impact through superficially simpler means.

Josten, Werner (b Elberfeld, 12 Jun 1885; d New York, 6 Feb 1963), German-born American composer and conductor. Studied in Munich, Geneva (with Jaques-Dalcroze) and Paris. In 1918 he became assistant conductor at the Munich Opera, but in 1920 emigrated to USA. Appointed professor at Smith College, Northampton, MA, in 1923; conducted the first US performance of *L'Incoronazione di Poppea* (1926); also led *Orfeo* (1929) and the US premieres of Handel's *Giulio Cesare* (1927), *Rodelinda* (1931) and *Serse* (1928). In 1938 he gave the first modern revival of Fux's *Costanza e fortezza* (1723).

Works include ballets *Batouala* (1931), *Joseph and his Brethren* (1936), *Endymion* (1933); *Crucifixion* for bass solo and chorus, *Hymnus to the Quene of Paradys* for contralto solo, women's chorus, strings and organ, *Ode for St Cecilia's Day* for solo voices, chorus and orchestra (1925); symphony in F major, serenade, symphonic movement *Jungle* (on Henri Rousseau's picture 'Forêt exotique', 1929), etc. for orchestra; symphony and two *Concerti sacri* for strings and piano.

jota Spanish dance, especially of Aragon and Navarre. It dates from the 12th c. and is said to derive its name from the Moor Aben Jot. It is in quick 3–4 time. The music is played on instruments of the guitar type and often accompanied by castanets and other percussion.

Joubert, John (b Cape Town, 20 Mar 1927), South African composer. Studied at Cape Town University and the RAM in London. Lecturer at Hull University, 1950–62, at Birmingham University, 1962–86.

Works include operas *Antigone* (1954), *In the drought* (1956), *Silas Marner* (1961), *Under Western Eyes* (1968); cantatas *The Leaves of Life* and *Urbs beata*; three motets; symphonic prelude, two symphonies (1956, 1971), *In Memoriam, 1820* for orchestra; violin concerto (1954), piano concerto; two string quartets (1950, 1977) and other chamber music; choral works; songs.

Jour de Fête a collective work for string quartet: 1. *Les Chanteurs de*

Noël (Glazunov); 2. *Glorification* (Liadov); 3. *Chœur dansé russe* (Rimsky-Korsakov).

Journet, Marcel (b Grasse, 25 Jul 1867; d Vittel, 5 Sept 1933), French bass. Studied at the Paris Conservatory and made his first appearance at Béziers in 1891 in *La favorite*. He sang in Brussels 1894–1900 and at CG, London, 1897–1928. Paris, Opéra, 1908–31 as Dosifey, Sachs, Wotan and Gurnemanz. NY Met. debut 1900, as Ramfis.

Joyce, Eileen (b Zeehan, Tasmania, 21 Nov 1912; d Limpsfield, Surrey, 25 Mar 1991), Australian pianist. Studied at Leipzig (master classes with Schnabel) and made London debut 1930. Played Busoni's *Indian Fantasy* at the 1934 Proms, under Wood, and championed concertos by Ireland and Shostakovich. Also performed as harpsichordist with George Malcolm and Thurston Dart.

Joyce Book a collection of settings of poems by James Joyce by George Antheil, Arnold Bax, Arthur Bliss, Edgardo Carducci, Bernard van Dieren, Eugene Goossens, Herbert Howells, Herbert Hughes, John Ireland, E J Moeran, C W Orr, Albert Roussel and Roger Sessions, edited by Herbert Hughes, pub. 1932. Other composers who have set works by Joyce include Berio (*Chamber Music* 1902 and *Ulysses* 1922); Matyas Seiber (*Ulysses Cantata*); Bridge, Barber, del Tredici and Szymanowski (*Chamber Music*); Dallapiccola (*Portrait of the Artist as a Young Man*, in *Requiescant*) and John Cage, parts of *Finnegans Wake* in *The Wonderful Widow of Eighteen Springs* for mezzo and closed piano (1942), and *Roaratorio* 'an Irish circus' (1979).

Jubel-Ouvertüre, *Jubilee Overture*, a concert overture by Weber, op. 59, composed 1818 as a companion-piece to the *Jubel-Cantate* for the 50th anniversary of the accession of the King of Saxony, Frederick Augustus, and performed Dresden, 20 Sept. It concludes with the tune of 'God save the King'.

Juch, Emma (b Vienna, 4 Jul 1863; d New York, 6 Mar 1939), American soprano. Stage debut London 1881, in Mignon; sang in US with Mapelson's co. from 1881. Toured with American Opera co. 1884–89 and formed her own co. which toured widely in Central and North America until 1894. Well known as Senta and the Queen of Night.

Judas Maccabaeus oratorio by Handel (libretto by T Morell), composed 9 Jul–11 Aug 1746, produced London, CG, 1 Apr 1747.

Judd, James (b Hertford, 30 Oct 1949), English conductor. Studied at the TCL and worked at the London Opera Centre and with the Cleveland Orchestra. Associate conductor of the European Community Youth Orchestra 1978; co-founder and conductor of the Chamber Orchestra of Europe from 1987. Led *Cenerentola* at Glyndebourne 1985, *Trovatore*, *Figaro* and *Rigoletto* for ENO. US opera debut with *Don Giovanni* at Miami 1988; artistic director of Greater Miami Opera from 1993. Has guested with the Vienna and Prague SOs and the Berlin PO; recent tours with the LSO, ECO and the Royal Philharmonic.

Judenkünig, Hans (b *c* 1450; d ? Vienna, 4 Mar 1526), German or Austrian lutenist. Lived in Vienna and wrote and arranged pieces for his instrument.

Judgment of Paris, The masque by Congreve, for the composition of which a prize was advertised in the *London Gazette* in 1700, the first four prizes being won by Weldon, Eccles, D Purcell and Finger in 1701. Eccles's setting produced London, Dorset Gardens Theatre, 21 Mar and Finger's 27 Mar 1701. The libretto was later set by G Sammartini, produced Cliveden, Bucks., 1 Aug 1740, and by Arne, produced Drury Lane, London, 12 Mar 1742.

Judith opera by Natanael Berg (1879–1957), (libretto in Swedish, by composer, based on Hebbel's drama), produced Stockholm, 22 Feb 1936. Biblical blood-letting, as Holofernes is decapitated.

Oratorio by Arne (libretto by I Bickerstaffe), performed London, Drury Lane Theatre, 27 Feb 1761. Oratorio by Parry (libretto from the Bible), performed Birmingham Festival, 1888. Play with music by Honegger (libretto by R Morax), produced Mézières, open-air Théâtre du Jorat, 13 Jun 1925; operatic version, Monte Carlo, 13 Feb 1926.

Juditha triumphans devicta Holofernes barbarie oratorio by

Vivaldi (text by J Cassetti), performed Venice 1716. Sometimes given in modern revivals as a stage work, e.g. Camden Festival, London, 1984.

Juha opera in three acts by Merikanto (libretto by Aino Ackté), composed 1920–22; produced Lahti, Music College, 28 Oct 1963. Juha drowns himself when the truth of his wife's infidelity is revealed.

Juilliard Quartet American string quartet founded 1946 by William Schuman, then president of the Juilliard School, NY, with Robert Mann as leader. Other members are Earl Carlyss, Samuel Rhodes and Joel Krosnick. Many tours in US and Europe with quartets by Mozart and Beethoven; fps of Carter's quartets nos. 2 and 3, and works by Sessions and Piston. Made the first recording of the quartets of Schoenberg. In residence, Library of Congress, Washington DC, since 1962. Regular visits to England and the Continent in the standard repertory.

Juive, La, *The Jewess*, opera by Halévy (libretto by Scribe), produced Paris, Opéra, 23 Feb 1835. Prince Leopold, posing as a Jew, woos Rachel, the apparent daughter of Jewish goldsmith Eléazar. When Rachel discovers the deception, and that Leopold is married, she denounces him. All three face trial for inter-racial love, and Rachel and Eléazar are executed.

Julie opera by Dezède (libretto by J M B de Monvel), produced Paris, Comédie-Italienne, 28 Sept 1772. Mozart wrote piano variations K264) on the air 'Lison dormait' in 1778.

I am ... terrified at the thought that so much hideous and bad music will be put on records forever.
Sir Arthur Sullivan, Edison recording, 1888

Julien, ou La Vie du poète, *Julian, or The Poet's Life*, opera by G Charpentier, sequel to *Louise* (libretto by composer), produced Paris, Opéra-Comique, 4 Jun 1913. Julien's artistic fantasies and peregrinations.

Julietta, or The Key to Dreams lyric opera by Martinů (libretto by composer) after the play by G Neveux); composed 1936–37, produced Prague, National Theatre, 16 Mar 1938. Michel and Julietta meet and part in a disturbing dream-world where reality and fantasy mingle.

Julius Caesar (Handel and Malipiero.) ◊Giulio Cesare.

Jullien, (Jean Lucien) Adolphe (b Paris, 1 Jun 1845; d Chaintreauville, 30 Aug 1932), French critic. Studied law at first, and music with a retired professor of the Conservatory. He began to write for the music papers and to champion Berlioz, Wagner, Schumann and modern music. Appointed music critic to *Le Français* 1872 and the *Journal des Débats* 1873. His books include studies of 18th-c. opera, Berlioz, Wagner, Goethe and music, etc.

Jullien (originally *Julien*), Louis Antoine (b Sisteron, 23 Apr 1812; d Paris, 14 Mar 1860), French conductor. Son of a bandmaster, he studied unsuccessfully at the Paris Conservatory, became a conductor of dance music and compiler of quadrilles on popular operas.

June, Ava (b London, 23 Jul 1931), English soprano. She sang with SW/ENO from 1957 as Mozart's Countess and Donna Anna, the Marschallin and Sieglinde. CG from 1958. US debut San Francisco 1974, as Ellen Orford. Other roles included Leonore, Katya Kabanova and Donizetti's Elizabeth I. She later became a singing teacher.

Jung, Manfred (b Oberhausen, 9 Jul 1945), German tenor. He studied in Essen and was a member of Bayreuth chorus before Dortmund debut, 1974. Sang the *Götterdämmerung* Siegfried at Bayreuth, 1977, and in the TV version of the Chéreau-Boulez *Ring* cycle; same role in Solti-Hall Bayreuth *Ring*, 1983. NY Met. debut 1981; Tristan and Parsifal at Salzburg Easter Festival, 1980. Sang Mime at the 1994 Bayreuth Festival.

Junge Lord, Der, *The Young Lord*, opera by Henze (libretto by Ingeborg Bachmann, after Wilhelm Hauff), produced Berlin, Deutsche Oper, 7 Apr 1965. Milord Edgar, a simian in disguise, makes a monkey of German townspeople.

Junge Magd, Die, *The Young Girl*, six songs for alto, flute, clarinet and string quartet by Hindemith (texts by George Trakl); fp Donaueschingen, 31 Jul 1922.

Jungfernquartette German = 'maiden quartets'; another nickname for Haydn's six string quartets, op. 33, also known as 'Russian quartets' and more generally as 'Gli Scherzi'.

Jungfrun i Tornet, *The Maiden in the Tower*, opera in one act by Sibelius (libretto by Hertzberg); composed 1896 for Robert Kajanus's Helsinki Orchestra and orchestra school, fp 7 Nov 1896. Imprisoned maiden is released to lover.

Jungwirth, Manfred (b St Polten, 4 Jun 1919), Austrian bass. Debut Bucharest 1942, as Méphistophélès. From 1948 he sang widely in Austria and Germany; member Frankfurt Opera from 1960. His best role is Ochs; Glyndebourne 1965, later recorded under Solti. CG debut 1981, as Waldner in *Arabella*; Dallas 1982, as Ochs. He was also been heard in operas by Wagner and Lortzing.

Juon, Paul (b Moscow, 6 Mar 1872; d Vevey, Switzerland, 21 Aug 1940), Russian composer. Studied with Taneiev and Arensky in Moscow and with Bargiel in Berlin, where he settled and was later appointed professor at the Hochschule für Musik by Joachim.

Works include ballet *Psyche*; symphony in A, serenade and other works for orchestra; three violin concertos (1909, 1913, 1931), *Épisodes concertantes* for violin, cello and piano and orchestra; chamber symphony, five pieces for string orchestra; three string quartets (1898, 1904, 1920), sextet for piano and strings, two piano quintets (1906, 1909), two piano quartets (1908, 1912), piano trios (1901, 1915), Divertimento for wind and piano, ditto for clarinet and two violas; instrumental pieces; *Satyrs and Nymphs*, *Preludes* and *Capriccios*, etc. for piano.

'Jupiter' Symphony nickname (not the composer's own) given to Mozart's last symphony, K551 in C major, finished 10 Aug 1788.

Jürgens, Jürgen (b Frankfurt, 5 Oct 1925; d Hamburg, 4 Aug 1994), German conductor. Studied in Frankfurt and directed the Hamburg Monteverdi Choir from 1955; tours of Europe and the USA with music by Josquin, Gagliano, Ockeghem and Henze. Music director at Hamburg University from 1966, professor 1977. Recordings include Monteverdi's Vespers and *Orfeo*, Schütz's *St Luke Passion* and *Seven Last Words*, Gagliano's *La Dafne*.

Jurinac, Sena (b Travnik, 24 Oct 1921), Yugoslav soprano. Studied singing in Zagreb, making her debut there 1942. From 1944 she was a member of the Vienna Staatsoper. She also sang at Glyndebourne (from 1949) and CG (debut 1947), and was especially noted for her singing of Mozart and R Strauss, e.g. Cherubino, Donna Anna, Donna Elvira, Octavian and the Marschallin.

justiniana a type of 16th-c. *villanella* for three voices, the words of which satirized the Venetian patricians. There is no connection between this and the *villanella* set to poetry of the type originated by L Giustinian.

just intonation singing or instrumental playing in what is said to be the pure natural scale, not that artificially fixed on keyboard instruments by equal temperament.

K

K, (abbr.) = Köchel, the thematic catalogue of Mozart's works edited by Ludwig von ◊Köchel. Mozart's works are identified by the letter K followed by catalogue numbers instead of by opus numbers.

Kabaivanska, Raina (b Burgas, 15 Dec 1934), Bulgarian soprano, well known in Italian opera. Appeared in Bellini's *Beatrice di Tenda* at La Scala in 1961 and in the following year sang for the first time at CG, London, and the NY Met. In 1973 she sang Hélène in Maria Callas's production of *Les Vêpres siciliennes* in Turin. Other roles include Nedda, Imogene, Desdemona, Elisabeth de Valois, Lisa, Liù, Tosca and Madama Butterfly. Sang the *Trovatore* Leonora at Genoa, 1991.

Kabale und Liebe opera by Einem (libretto by composer after Schiller's tragedy, 1784), fp Vienna, Staatsoper, 17 Dec 1976. ◊Luisa Miller.

Kabalevsky, Dmitri Borisovich (b St Petersburg, 30 Dec 1904; d Moscow, 16 Feb 1987), Russian composer. Entered the Skriabin School of Music at Moscow when the family settled there in 1918, studying piano and becoming a composition pupil of Vassilenko and Catoire, afterwards of Miaskovsky. Later became professor of composition there.

Works include operas *The Golden Spikes*, *Colas Breugnon* (after Romain Rolland's 1938 novel), *Before Moscow* (1943), and *Nikita Vershinin* (1955); incidental music for Shakespeare's *Measure for Measure*, Sheridan's *School for Scandal* and an adaptation of Flaubert's *Madame Bovary*; film music *Poem of Struggle*, *Our Great Fatherland* and *People's Avengers* for chorus and orchestra; four symphonies (no. 3 *Requiem for Lenin*); three piano concertos (1931–53); violin concerto, two cello concertos; two string quartets (1928, 1945); three sonatas, two sonatinas and other piano music; Requiem; songs.

Kabeláč, Miloslav (b Prague, 1 Aug 1908; d Prague, 17 Sept 1979), Czech composer. Studied composition at the Prague Conservatory 1928–31 with K B Jirák and later also the piano at the Master School. In 1932 he joined the staff of Czech Radio.

Works include eight symphonies (1941–70); cantatas *Mystery of Time*, *Do not retreat*; two overtures; wind sextet; suite for saxophone and piano; violin and piano pieces; choral music.

Kabós, Ilona (b Budapest, 7 Dec 1893; d London, 28 May 1973), Hungarian-born British pianist. She studied with Leo Weiner and Kodály and began her career during World War I. She was a champion of contemporary music and gave fps of works by Dallapiccola and Chávez. With her husband, Louis Kentner, she gave the fp of Bartók's concerto for two pianos and orchestra (London, 1942). Highly regarded as a teacher, among her pupils were Peter Frankl and John Ogdon. In the last ten years of her life she taught at the Juilliard School, NY, and the Dartington Summer School.

Kadosa, Pál (b Leva, (now Levice), Czechoslovakia, 6 Sept 1903; d Budapest, 30 Mar 1983), Hungarian composer and pianist. He studied with Kodály at the Budapest Academy and taught piano at Fodor Conservatory 1927–43. Professor, Budapest Academy, from 1945. Influenced by Bartók.

Works include opera *The Adventure of Huszt* (1951); five cantatas (1939–50); eight symphonies (1941–68); four piano concertos (1931–66); two violin concertos (1931, 1941); concerto for string quartet and chamber orchestra (1936); three string quartets (1934–57); two string trios (1930, 1955); two piano sonatas (1926–60).

Kagel, Mauricio (b Buenos Aires, 24 Dec 1931), Argentine composer of advanced tendencies. Studied in Buenos Aires, settling in Cologne 1957. He has evolved a very complex style, employing serial and aleatory techniques, permutations of different languages, light effects and aural distortions.

Works include *Anagrama* for four soloists, speaking chorus and chamber ensemble (1958); *Sur scène*, theatrical piece in one act for speaker, mime, singer and three instruments (1962); *The Women*, dramatic scene for three female voices, three actresses, a dancer, chorus of women, and electronic tapes; *Match* for three players; *Diaphony* for chorus, orchestra and two projectors (1964); *Transición I* for electronic sounds; *Transición II* for piano, percussion and two tapes; *Hetrophonie* for an orchestra of solo instruments; string sextet; *Ludwig Van*, film score (1970); *Staatstheater*, 'ballet for nondancers', with instruments including chamber pot (1971); opera, *Die Erschöpfung der Welt* (produced Stuttgart, 8 Feb 1980), *Sankt—Bach—Passion* (1985); piano trio (1985); *A Letter* for mezzo and orchestra (1986); *Dance School* ballet (1988); *Quodlibet* for women's voices and orchestra (1988); third string quartet (1988); *Fragende Ode* (1989).

Kahane, Jeffrey (Alan) (b Los Angeles, 12 Sept 1956), American pianist. Studied in San Francisco and at Juilliard. Debut at San Francisco 1973, runner-up in 1977 Clara Haskil Competition. Won the 1983 Rubinstein International Competition. NY debut 1983, London 1985; played in Bernstein's *The Age of Anxiety* at the 1991 Prom concerts. Frequent concerts with the NY and LA POs, Pittsburgh Orchestra and San Francisco SO. Quintets with the Tokyo String quartet.

Kajanus, Robert (b Helsinki, 2 Dec 1856; d Helsinki, 6 Jul 1933), Finnish conductor and composer. Studied at the Helsinki and Leipzig Conservatories, also composition with Svendsen in Paris. Founded the orchestra of the Helsinki Philharmonic Society in 1882, with which later he paid several important visits to foreign countries, giving many early performances of Sibelius. Director of music at Helsinki University, 1897–1926.

Works include symphony *Aino* (on an incident from the *Kalevala*), etc.

Kalabis, Viktor (b Cereveny Kostelec, 27 Feb 1923), Czech composer. Studied at the Prague Academy and Charles University. Manager of the music department at Prague Radio, 1953–72.

Works include five symphonies (1956, 1961, 1971, 1972, 1976); Concerto for Orchestra (1966), and nine instrumental concertos; two nonets, two wind quintets, seven string quartets; sonatas for violin, cello, clarinet and trombone (1967–82); ballet on *Alice in Wonder-*

land, Two Worlds (1980); Incantations for 13 wind instruments (1988).

Kalbeck, Max (b Breslau, 4 Jan 1850; d Vienna, 4 May 1921), German critic and writer on music. Worked in Vienna. Translated opera libretti and wrote the first full Brahms biography.

Kalcher, Johann Nepomuk (b Freising, Bavaria, 15 May 1764; d Munich, 2 Dec 1827), German organist and composer. Studied at Munich, where he became court organist in 1798. Weber was one of his pupils. Wrote Masses, symphonies, organ music, songs.

Kalenberg, Josef (b Cologne, 7 Jan 1886; d Vienna, 8 Nov 1962), German tenor. Debut Cologne 1911, as Turiddu. He sang at Krefeld, Barmen and Düsseldorf 1912–25 and returned to Cologne 1925. In 1927 he sang Parsifal at the Vienna Staatsoper and returned there until 1942. Salzburg 1928–36; Tristan 1935. Retired 1949.

Kalevala, The Finish national epic. ◊Dallapiccola (two lyrics); ◊Kajanus (*Aino*); Sibelius and Sallinen (◊*Kullervo*); A ◊Merikanto (*Abduction of Kylliki*); Sibelius (◊*Lemminkainen's Return* and three other Legends, ◊*Pohjola's Daughter*, ◊*Swan of Tuonela* and ◊*Tapiola*.

Kalichstein, Joseph (b Tel-Aviv, 15 Jan 1946), Israeli pianist. He studied at the Juilliard School and in 1967 won the Leventritt Competition. Has appeared all over the USA; among his recordings are the Mendelssohn concertos, with Previn. Also noted as interpreter of Brahms, Prokofiev, Chopin and Bartók.

Kalinnikov, Vassily Sergeyevich (b Voina, 13 Jan 1866; d Yalta, 11 Jan 1901), Russian composer. He was educated at a seminary, where he conducted the choir. In 1884 went to Moscow and, in spite of great poverty, obtained a musical education at the Philharmonic Society Music School. After conducting Italian opera for the 1893–94 season, he was found to suffer from consumption and lived mainly in the Crimea, devoted to composition.

Works include incidental music to Alexey Tolstoy's *Tsar Boris* (1899); cantatas *St John Chrysostom* and *Russalka*; two symphonies, suite, two Intermezzi and two sketches for orchestra; string quartets; piano pieces; songs.

Kalisch, Alfred (b London, 13 Mar 1863; d London, 17 May 1933), English critic of German descent. Educated at Oxford for law, but became a music journalist in 1894. Translator of R Strauss's operas.

Kalisch, Paul (b Berlin, 6 Nov 1855; d St Lorenz am Modensee, 27 Jan 1946), German tenor. His early career was in Italy, and after a year in Munich he sang with the Berlin Opera from 1884 to 1887. In 1888 he married the soprano Lilli Lehmann and from the following year appeared with her in many productions at the Metropolitan. He was well known as Pollione, Florestan, Don Ottavio and Manrico and he was successful in such lighter Wagnerian roles as Tannhäuser and Siegmund.

Kalkbrenner, Friedrich (Wilhelm Michael) (b on a journey between Kassel and Berlin, Nov 1785; d Enghien-les-Bains, 10 Jun 1849), German pianist, teacher and composer. Studied under his father, Christian Kalkbrenner (1755–1806) and at the Paris Conservatory. Made his first public appearance in Vienna in 1803, returning to Paris in 1806. Lived in London as teacher and performer 1814–23 and then settled in Paris as a member of the piano firm of Pleyel, but continued to teach and perform.

Works include four piano concertos (1823–35), concerto for two pianos; piano septet, sextet and quintet; piano school with studies appended, sonatas, variations and numerous other works for piano.

Kallir, Lillian (b Prague, 6 May 1931), Czech pianist. Studied at the Mannes College of Music, NY, and appeared with the New York PO 1948; recital debut 1949. Many concert tours in Europe and the USA; recent concerts at the Norfolk, Grant Park and Tanglewood Festivals. Chamber music with the Juilliard, Tokyo and Emerson Quartets; European concerts with Berlin PO, at the Festival Hall and the Concertgebouw Orchestra. Teacher at Mannes College from 1975.

Kalliwoda, Johan Vaclav (b Prague, 21 Feb 1801; d Karlsruhe, 3 Dec 1866), Bohemian violinist and composer. Studied at the Prague Conservatory 1811–17 and played in the orchestra 1817–22. He then became music director to Prince Fürstenberg at Donaueschingen until his retirement in 1866.

Works include opera *Blanka*; seven symphonies (1826–43); concertinos for violin, for clarinet and other instruments; three string quartets; violin duets, violin pieces.

Kálmán, Emmerich (b Siófok, 24 Oct 1882; d Paris, 30 Oct 1953), Hungarian composer. He studied in Budapest. In 1908 he had great success with the operetta *Tatárjárás* (given in NY and elsewhere as *The Gay Hussar*); lived in Vienna until 1938 and among other works produced *Der gute Kamerad* (1911), *Der Zigeunerprimas* (1912), *Die Csárdásfürstin* (1915), *Die Faschingsfee* (1917), *Gräfin Mariza* (1924), *Die Zirkusprinzessin* (1924) and *Der Teufelsreiter*. He moved to Paris in 1939, then to NY and Hollywood.

Kálmán, Oszkár (b Kis-Szent-Péter, 18 Jun 1887; d Budapest, 18 Sept 1971), Hungarian bass. He sang at the Budapest Opera from 1913 and in 1918 sang Bluebeard in the fp of Bartók's opera. He joined Otto Klemperer at the Kroll Opera, Berlin, in 1927 and took part in the first German performance of Stravinsky's *Oedipus Rex*. In 1929 he sang in the fp of Hindemith's *Lehrstück* (Baden-Baden). He was successful all over Europe until 1939 and was noted in Hungary as an interpreter of Kodály's songs.

Kalmus, Alfred (b Vienna, 16 May 1889; d London, 25 Sept 1972), Austrian-born English music publisher. He studied with Guido Adler and joined Universal Edition in 1909; helped further the careers of Bartók, Janáček and composers of the Second Viennese School. He moved to London in 1936 and founded the local branch of Universal; continued his services for modern music after the war and pub. leading continental composers, e.g. Stockhausen and Boulez, and such home-grown talent as Birtwistle and David Bedford.

Kalomiris, Manolis (b Smyrna, 26 Dec 1883; d Athens, 3 Apr 1962), Greek composer. Studied in Athens, Constantinople and Vienna. He taught at Kharkov 1906–10 and then settled in Athens as professor at the Conservatory. From 1919 he was director of the Hellenic Conservatory there but in 1926 he founded the National Conservatory and became its director.

Works include operas *The Master Builder* (after N Kazantzakis, 1915), *The Mother's Ring* (after J Kambyssis, 1917), *Anatoli* and *The Haunted Waters* (after Yeats, 1950–52); incidental music; two symphonies, symphonic poems, etc., for orchestra; chamber music; piano works; songs.

Kalter, Sabine (b Jaroslaw, 28 Mar 1889; d London, 1 Sept 1957), Hungarian mezzo. Debut Vienna 1911 and sang in Hamburg 1915–35; admired for her interpretations of roles by Wagner, Meyerbeer, Verdi and Gluck. She was obliged to leave Germany in 1935 and until the war was successful at CG, as Ortrud, Brangaene and Fricka. At the Kroll Opera, Berlin, she took part in the 1929 fp of Hindemith's *Neues vom Tage*, under Klemperer. Other roles included Herodias and Lady Macbeth.

Kamarinskaya fantasy for orchestra on two Russian themes by Glinka, composed 1848 and known only in an edition revised by Rimsky-Korsakov and Glazunov.

Kamensky, Alexander (b Geneva, 12 Dec 1900; d Leningrad, 7 Nov 1952), Russian pianist. He graduated from the Petrograd Conservatory in 1923 and became widely known in Russia before the war. During the two-year siege of Leningrad by the Germans he gave nearly 500 recitals, often in conditions of extreme danger and hardship; featured works by Schoenberg and Stravinsky as well as Soviet composers.

Kamieński, Maciej (b Sopron, 13 Oct 1734; d Warsaw, 25 Jan 1821), Hungarian-Polish composer. Studied in Vienna and settled at Warsaw c 1760. He produced the first Polish opera there on 11 May 1778.

Works include opera *Happiness in Unhappiness* and five others in Polish and two in German; church music, cantata for the unveiling of the Sobjeski monument.

Kamionsky, Oscar (b Kiev, 1869; d Yalta, 15 Aug 1917), Russian baritone. He studied at St Petersburg and made his debut in Naples, 1891. From 1893 until his retirement in 1915 his career was in Russia; many appearances at Kharkov, Kiev, Tiblisi, St Petersburg and the Zimin theatre, Moscow, as Onegin, Mazeppa, Renato and the Figaro of Mozart and Rossini. Recorded from 1901 in French and Italian repertory.

Kammel, Antonin (b Bělec, bap. 21 Apr 1730; d ? London by 1787), Czech-born violinist and composer. He studied at Prague University and in Italy, and by 1764 he was established in London; mentioned by Leopold Mozart in his travel notes. He appeared in the Bach-Abel concerts and was probably a royal chamber musician. He was successful as a composer and nearly all his works feature the violin.

Kammermusik German = ◊chamber music.

Kammermusik, *Chamber Music*, seven works by Hindemith composed 1921–27; no. 1 for small orchestra, fp Donaueschingen, 31 Jul 1922, conductor Scherchen; no. 2 for piano and 12 instruments, fp Frankfurt 31 Oct 1924, conductor Clemens Krauss; no. 3 for cello and ten instruments, fp Bochum, 30 Apr 1925, conductor Hindemith; no. 4 for violin and chamber orchestra, fp Dessau, 25 Sept 1925; no. 5 for viola and chamber orchestra, fp Berlin, 3 Nov 1927, conductor Klemperer; no. 6 for viola d'amore and chamber orchestra, fp Cologne, 29 Mar 1928; no. 7 for organ and chamber orchestra, fp Frankfurt, 8 Jan 1928. also ◊Neo-classicism.

Kammerton, German, = lit. 'chamber-pitch'; the pitch to which orchestral instruments in Germany were tuned in the 17th–18th c. It was lower, by a whole tone or more, than the *Chorton* (choir-pitch) used for church organs, and it was for this reason that Bach, in his Leipzig cantatas, transposed the organ parts down a tone in order to make them agree with the orchestra. The transposition applied only to the organ parts: the orchestral parts could be used as they stood.

Kamu, Okko (b Helsinki, 7 Mar 1946), Finnish conductor and violinist. Debut as a violinist before his teens and was leader of Finnish National Opera Orchestra 1966–68; won first Karajan International Competition 1969. London debut 1970; chief conductor Helsinki PO 1979–90; principal of the Sjaelland (Denmark) SO from 1988. Led the premiere of Sallinen's *The Red Line* (1978) and its fp at the NY Met. (1983). In 1987 at CG he conducted the British fp of Sallinen's *The King goes forth to France*.

K. Anh, abbr., = Köchel Anhang, ◊Köchel's appendix to his catalogue in which works are given the suffix K. Anh. followed by the number.

Kapell, William (b New York, 20 Sept 1922; d King's Mount., CA, 29 Oct 1953), American pianist. He studied at Philadelphia and at the Juilliard school; debut 1941, widely known as champion of the Khachaturian concerto, had a reputation for virtuosity rather than musicianship. Killed in Californian aircrash on returning from tour of Australia.

Kapelle German = 'chapel'; originally the music establishment of a king's or prince's chapel; later by transference, an orchestra.

Kapellmeister German originally choirmaster, later also conductor.

The term Kapellmeistermusik came to have derogatory implications since the music written by a sort of musical equivalent to the Civil Service tended to lack inspiration.
Antony Hopkins, *Downbeat Music Guide*, 1977

Kapellmeistermusik German = 'conductor's music'; a contemptuous term for a musical work which betrays creative weakness and has no merit but that of a knowledge of rules and glib craftsmanship.

Kaplan, Mark (b Boston, 30 Dec 1953), American violinist. Studied at Juilliard and won the 1973 Leventritt Competition; concerts followed with the Cleveland Orchestra, LA PO and Baltimore SO. European debut 1980, with the Berlin PO under Tennstedt. Gave European fp of Neikrug's Concerto with the Hallé Orchestra, 1986. Plays in piano trio with David Golub and Colin Carr.

Kapp, Julius (b Steinbach, Baden, 1 Oct 1883; d Hinang bei Alstädten-im-Allgau, 18 Mar 1962), German writer on music. Studied chemistry and then became a literary editor. In 1921 he edited the paper of the Berlin Staatsoper and in 1923 he became dramatic director there and adapted a number of works for its stage. He edited Wagner's letters

and his books include studies of Liszt, Wagner, Berlioz, Weber, Meyerbeer, and R Strauss. His book *Wagner und die Frauen* (1912) was reprinted 15 times by 1929.

Kappel, Gertrude (b Halle, 1 Sept 1884; d Munich, 3 Apr 1971), German soprano. She sang at Hanover 1903–24 and between 1912 and 1926 appeared in major roles by Wagner and Strauss at CG. A member of the NY Met. 1928–36, roles included Brünnhilde, Isolde and Elektra; retired shortly before World War II.

Kapsberger, Johann Hieronymus (b Venice, *c* 1575; d Rome, *c* 1651), German lutenist and composer. Lived in Venice and pub. three books of music for chitarrone in tablature. He also wrote vocal *villanelle* with that instrument, motets, an epithalamium and an apotheosis of Ignatius Loyola.

Karajan, Herbert von (b Salzburg, 5 Apr 1908; d Anif, near Salzburg, 16 Jul 1989), Austrian conductor. Studied at Salzburg Mozarteum and in Vienna. Made his debut at the Salzburg Landestheater in 1927 with *Fidelio*; moved to Ulm in 1928, remaining there until 1933. He continued to work under the Nazi régime and was a member of the party. From 1934 to 1938 he was at Aachen, and at the Berlin Staatsoper 1938–42, making his name with *Tristan*. After Furtwängler's death in 1954 he took over the Berlin PO and in 1956 became director of the Vienna Staatsoper, resigning in 1964. Conducted, and recorded with, the Philharmonia Orchestra, London, 1948–60. Founded Salzburg Easter Festival 1967, and took its production of *Die Walküre* to the NY Met. in 1967. One of the best-known conductors of his day, Karajan was especially noted for his performances of Beethoven, Wagner, Bruckner and R Strauss. In later years he added Mahler and the Second Viennese School to his repertory. At Salzburg he produced operas by Wagner, Mussorgsky and Verdi. It has been fashionable to praise Karajan for no more than the technical polish of his performances; his recorded legacy (e.g. *Tristan* and the Brahms symphonies) shows that he was also capable of an intensity that was under perfect control.

Karel, Rudolf (b Pizeň [Pilsen], 9 Nov 1880; d Terezín, 6 Mar 1945), Czech composer. Studied composition under Dvořák at the Prague Conservatory. In 1914, on holiday in Russia, he was interned as an Austrian subject, then taught at Taganrog and Rostov-on-Don, fled to Siberia and eventually escaped to Czechoslovakia, where he became professor at the Prague Conservatory. He died tragically in a concentration camp.

Works include operas *Ilsa's Heart* (1909) and *Godmother's Death* (1932); incidental music to Knud Hamsun's *The Game of Life*; *Awakening*, symphony for solo voices, chorus and orchestra; two symphonies, *Renaissance* and *Spring*, symphonic poems *The Ideals* and *Demon*, suite, fantasy, Slavonic dances, etc. for orchestra; violin concerto, three string quartets (1902–36).

Karelia incidental music in nine movements by Sibelius; composed 1893, fp Viipuri, 13 Nov 1893. Suite for orchestra in three movements op. 11, 1893.

Karetnikov, Nikolay (b Moscow, 28 Jun 1930; d Moscow 10 Oct 1994), Russian composer. Studied with Shebalin at the Moscow Conservatory. From the time of his Fourth Symphony (1963) he was obliged to compose and publish in secrecy, owing to his political dissent. His opera *Til'Ulenshpigel* was written and recorded over five years with the co-operation of friends; dubbed the first samizdat opera and premiered at Bielefeld 1993. Other works include *The Mystery of Apostle Paul*, opera oratorio (1972–87), Chamber suite *From Shalom-Aleham* (1986), quintet for piano and strings (1990) and *Six Spiritual Songs* (1992)

Karg-Elert, (real name Karg), Sigfrid (b Oberndorf-am-Neckar, 21 Nov 1877; d Leipzig, 9 Apr 1933), German organist, pianist and composer. Studied at the Leipzig Conservatory and became professor at those of Magdeburg and Leipzig; was a brilliant pianist, but was persuaded by Grieg to devote himself to composition.

Works include a symphony, two piano concertos (1901, 1913); string quartet; violin and piano sonatas; sonata and other works for piano; over 100 songs; pieces for harmonium and many organ works, including 66 chorale improvisations (1908–10), 24 preludes and postludes, Sonatina, passacaglia, fantasy and fugue in D major, *Chaconne*, *Fugue-Trilogy and Chorale*, ten characteristic pieces, three symphonic chorales, seven *Pastels from Lake Constance* (1919), six *Cathedral Windows* (1923), 54 variation-studies *Homage to Handel*.

Karlowicz, Miecyslaw (b Wiszezwo, 11 Dec 1876; d Zakopane, 8 Feb 1909), Polish composer. The son of a noble family, he travelled much as a child and learnt the violin in Prague, Dresden and Heidelberg, and soon played chamber music with his parents, a cellist and a pianist. Later studied at Warsaw, where his composition teacher was Noskowski, and afterwards with Urban in Berlin; also conducting with Nikisch at Leipzig. Settled at Zakopane in the Tatra mountains in 1908 and was killed by an avalanche there.

Works include incidental music to *Biala Golabka*; symphony in E minor, symphonic poems *Returning Waves* (1907), *The Sad Story* (*Preludes to Eternity*), *Stanislas and Anna Oswiecim* (1912), *An Episode of the Masquerade*, serenade (1897), *Lithuanian Rhapsody* for orchestra; violin concerto (1902); songs.

Karl V opera by Krenek (libretto by composer), produced Prague, German Opera, 15 Jun 1938; revised version, Vienna, 1984. Reminiscences of Emperor Charles V, presented as an anti-Nazi parable, but not appreciated by Viennese authorities, and cancelled in rehearsal, 1934.

Karr, Gary (b Los Angeles, 20 Nov 1941), American double-bass player. His career began in 1962 with appearances with the NY PO and as a solo recitalist; he toured Europe in 1964 and in 1967 was the soloist in the fp of Henze's Concerto for double bass and orchestra, a work which he also commissioned.

Kars, Jean-Rodolphe (b Calcutta, 15 Mar 1947), Austrian pianist. He studied at the Paris Conservatoire and in 1968 won the Messiaen Competition at Royan; has since become renowned for his interpretations of the French composer's works, in particular the massive *Vingt regards sur l'enfant Jésus*. Also noted for his performances of Debussy and Ravel.

Kaschmann, Giuseppe (b Lussimpiccolo, Istria, 14 Jul 1847; d Rome, 7 Feb 1925), Italian baritone. He studied at Padua and Udine and sang in the performance of Zajc's *Mislav* which opened the Zagreb Opera, 1870. Turin 1876, as Donizetti's Alphonse; La Scala from 1878. He sang Enrico (*Lucia*) in the inaugural season at the NY Met. and returned 1896 for Telramund. Bayreuth 1892–94, as Wolfram and Amfortas. Towards the end of his career sang *buffo* roles in operas by Rossini, Donizetti and Cimarosa.

THE OPERA

Káta Kabanová

A three-act opera by Leoš Janáček, first performed in Brno in 1921, in which a thunderstorm plays a leading part. This grim story of a young wife's extramarital affair is set in Kalinov in the late 19th century.

I. Boris (tenor) tells his friend Kudryash (tenor) of his love for Káta (soprano). Káta's husband Tichon Kabanov (tenor) is dominated by his mother Kabanicha (contralto), who is jealous of the attention Tichon gives Káta. In conversation with the foundling girl Varvara (soprano), Káta tells of her guilty love for Boris. As Tichon departs on a journey, his mother demands that he warns Káta not to take a lover in his absence.

II. After further nagging from Kabanicha, Káta joins Boris in the garden, where the lovers Kudryash and Varvara have already met. Káta returns Boris's love.

III. Distressed at the imminent return of her husband, Káta interprets a thunderstorm as divine punishment for her adultery. She confesses to the people assembled and, after a brief farewell to Boris, throws herself into the River Volga. Her body is recovered and displayed before Kabanicha.

THE OPERA

Kashchei the Immortal, *Kashchei Bessmertny*, opera by Rimsky-Korsakov (libretto by composer), produced Moscow, 25 Dec 1902. Kashchei is the wizard of Russian fairy lore who appears also in Stravinsky's *Firebird* ballet.

Kashperov, Vladimir Nikitich (b Simbirsk, 6 Sept 1826; d Romantsevo, 8 Jul 1894), Russian composer. Studied with Henselt in St Petersburg and later in Berlin and Italy. Professor of singing at the Moscow Conservatory 1866–72.

Works include operas *The Gypsies*, *Mary Tudor* (after Hugo, Milan, 1859), *Rienzi* (after Bulwer-Lytton, Florence, 1863), *Consuelo* (after George Sand, Venice, 1865), *The Storm* (after Ostrovsky, Moscow, 1867), *Taras Bulba* (after Gogol, Moscow, 1893).

Kašlik, Václav (b Poličná, 28 Sept 1917; d Prague, 4 Jun 1989), Czech composer, conductor and producer. Worked in Prague and Brno theatres during World War II. Co-founded Prague Grand Opera of May 5 in 1945, which became National Theatre 1945. Produced operas by Janáček and Martinů (fp of *Mirandolina*, 1959) and with designer Josef ◊Svoboda collaborated in Prague and elsewhere with productions that used advanced techniques of lighting and film projection (fp of Nono's *Intolleranza 60*, Venice 1961, and *Pelléas et Mélisande* at CG, 1969).

Kasprzyk, Jacek (b Biala, 10 Aug 1952), Polish conductor. Studied at Warsaw and made his debut at the Opera there, 1975. Principal conductor of the Polish National Radio SO, 1976–82. Resident in England from 1982, leading the Philharmonia, the Hallé Orchestra and regional BBC orchestras; guest with the Berlin PO, Bavarian Radio SO and San Diego SO. *Die Zauberflöte* at Stockholm, *Fliegende Holländer* for Opera North and *Barber of Seville* for ENO (1992).

Kastner, Jean Georges (Johann Georg) (b Strasbourg, 9 Mar 1810; d Paris, 19 Dec 1867), Alsatian composer and theorist. Studied theology at home, but produced an opera *Die Königin der Sarmaten* and was sent by the Strasbourg town council to study with Berton and Reicha at the Paris Conservatory. He wrote a treatise on orchestration, a manual on military music, and methods for various instruments.

Works include operas, cantatas and songs.

Kastorsky, Vladimir (b Bloshiye Soly, 14 Mar 1871; d Leningrad, 2 Jul 1948), Russian bass. He started his career as a chorister. Debut Maryinsky Theatre St Petersburg, in Serov's *Rodneda*; remained until 1930 as Gremin, Dargomyzhky's Miller, Hagen, Wotan and Marke. Visited Paris 1908 and sang Pimen in the production of *Boris Godunov* mounted by Diaghilev.

Káta Kabanová opera by Janáček (libretto by V Červinka, based on Ostrovsky's play *Groza*), produced Brno, 23 Nov 1921. Adulterous Káta is driven to suicide in the Volga.

Katchen, Julius (b Long Branch, NJ, 15 Aug 1926; d Paris, 29 Apr 1969), American pianist. Studied in New York with David Saperton, making his debut in 1937. He toured widely; well-known interpreter of Beethoven, Brahms and Schumann.

Katerina Izmailova (Shostakovich.) ◊Lady Macbeth of the Mtsensk District.

Katims, Milton (b New York, 24 Jun 1909), American violist and conductor. He worked for a NY radio station, after studying at Columbia University, and in 1943 joined the NBC SO, under Toscanini. He remained there until 1954, when he became conductor of the Seattle SO; was well known as a performer of chamber music, in particular as additional violist with the Budapest quartet.

Katin, Peter (b London, 14 Nov 1930), British-born Canadian pianist. He studied at the RAM and made his debut 1948; has toured worldwide, specializing in Romantic repertory. Noted interpreter of Chopin, on whom he has written a book.

Katz, Mindru (b Bucharest, 3 Apr 1925; d Istanbul, 30 Jan 1978), Romanian-born Israeli pianist. From 1947 to 1957 his career was restricted to eastern Europe, then toured in the West, making his British debut in 1958. The following year he became an Israeli citizen and in 1962 joined the music staff at Tel Aviv University. Died during a recital.

Kauer, Ferdinand (b Dyjákovičky, Moravia, 18 Jan 1751; d Vienna,

13 Apr 1831), Austrian composer. Studied at Znaim and Vienna, where he was appointed leader and second conductor at the Leopold-stadt Theatre, for which he wrote music for *c* 100 pantomimes, farces, etc. as well as operettas and operas.

Works include operas *Das Donauweibchen* (1798), *Das Wald-weibchen*; oratorio *Die Sündflut*; trio *Nelsons grosse See-Schlacht*.

Kaufmann, Julie (b Iowa, 25 May 1950), American soprano. Sang widely in Germany, after study at Hamburg, and appeared at Munich 1983, as Despina (member of the Bavarian State Opera from 1984). CG debut 1984, Zerlina, Salzburg Festival 1987, Blondchen. Sang in *Carmina Burana* at the 1990 Munich Festival, Zdenka in *Arabella* at La Scala, 1992.

Kaun, Hugo (b Berlin, 21 Mar 1863; d Berlin, 2 Apr 1932), German composer. He had written over 150 works before he was 16 and studied with Kiel at the Berlin Academy of Arts. In 1884 he went to USA as a pianist, but had to give up that career owing to an injury; in 1887 settled in Milwaukee, but returned to Berlin in 1901, teaching composition first at the Academy and from 1922 at the Klindworth-Scharwenka Conservatory.

Works include operas *Der Pietist*, *Sappho* (1917), *Der Fremde* (1920) and *Menandra* (1925); several choral works; three symphonies, *Minnehaha und Hiawatha* (after Longfellow), symphonic prologue *Marie Magdalene*, humoresque *Falstaff* (after Shakespeare) and other orchestral works; four string quartets, piano quintet, two piano trios, octet; violin and piano sonata.

Kavrakos, Dimitri (b Athens, 26 Feb 1946), Greek bass-baritone. Sang at Athens Opera 1970–78, debut as Zaccaria. NY Met. debut 1979, as Verdi's Grand Inquisitor; has returned as Silva, Walter in *Ernani* and Gounod's Capulet. Chicago opera in *Aida*, *Fidelio* and *Lakmé*. UK debut at Glyndebourne 1982, as the Commendatore; CG 1984, as Pimen in *Boris Godunov*, returned as Douglas in *La donna del lago* and Enrico in *Anna Bolena* (1988). Sang Rossini's Moise at Tel-Aviv, 1993. Other roles include Alvise in *La Gioconda* (San Francisco) and Tchaikovsky's Gremin (Chicago).

Kay, Ulysses Simpson (b Tuscon, 7 Jan 1917; d Englewood, NJ, 20 May 1995), American composer. He studied with Howard Hanson at the Eastman School and with Hindemith at Tanglewood. Professor, Lehman College, NY, 1968–88.

Works include operas *The Boor* (after Chekhov; composed 1955, produced 1968), *The Juggler of our Lady* (composed 1956, produced 1962), *The Capitoline Venus* (1971), *Jubilee* (1976); Suite for Strings (1949), *Song of Jeremiah*, cantata (1954), Serenade for Orchestra (1954), Fantasy Variations for orchestra (1963), *Scherzi musicali* for chamber orchestra (1971); two string quartets (1953, 1956), piano quintet (1949); choral pieces and songs.

Keats, Donald (Howard) (b New York, 27 May 1929), American composer. Studied at Yale and Columbia Universities until 1953. Professor of music at the University of Denver, from 1975. His music is basically tonal, and includes setting of Eliot (*The Hollow Men*), Cummings (*Anyone Loved in a Pretty How Town*) and Yeats (*A Love Triptych*). Other works include two symphonies (no. 2 Elegiac, 19960), two string quartets (1951, 1965), piano sonata (1966) and *Musica Instrumentalis* for nine instruments (1980).

Kee, Piet (b Zaandam, 30 Aug 1927), Dutch organist and composer. He has toured widely, with a largely Dutch and German repertory, and has also recorded extensively; well known for his improvisations, and as a teacher.

Keeble, John (b Chichester, *c* 1711; d London, 24 Dec 1786), English organist and composer. He studied at Chichester Cathedral and in London, under Pepusch. In 1737 he became organist at St George's, Hanover Square, and was later organist at Ranelagh Gardens. Works include sets of voluntaries and psalm interludes.

Keene, Christopher (b Berkeley, CA, 21 Dec 1946; d New York, 8 Oct 1995), American conductor. He conducted operas by Britten and Henze while at the University of California and later assisted Kurt Adler in San Francisco and Menotti at Spoleto; principal conductor NY City Opera 1970–86, general director from 1989; gave first NY stage performance of *Moses und Aron*, 1990. At Stuttgart in 1990 he

led the Philip Glass trilogy, *Akhnaten*, *Satyagraha* and *Einstein on the Beach*. NY City Opera 1990–92, with the local stage premieres of *From the House of the Dead* and Busoni's *Doktor Faust*. At the NY Met. from 1971, debut with *Cavalleria Rusticana*; gave the 1971 premiere of Menotti's opera *The Most Important Man*.

Keenlyside, Simon (b London, 3 Aug 1959), English baritone. Studied at the RNCM and won the Richard Tauber Competition in 1986. Sang at first in concert then appeared with Scottish Opera as Papageno, Billy Budd and Guglielmo. Season 1995 as Thomas' Hamlet at Geneva, Mozart's Count at CG. He is a fluent interpreter of Schubert Lieder.

Keilberth, Joseph (b Karlsruhe, 19 Apr 1908; d Munich, 21 Jul 1968), German conductor. From 1935 to 1940 he conducted at the Karlsruhe Staatsoper and from 1940 to 1945 was conductor of the Berlin PO. He conducted at Dresden 1945–51 and at Bayreuth 1952–56 (*The Ring*, *Fliegende Holländer* and *Lohengrin*). He was best known as a conductor of R Strauss's operas (*Rosenkavalier* at Edinburgh, 1952). He died while conducting *Tristan und Isolde*. Among his recordings are operas by Hindemith and Pfitzner.

Keiser, Reinhard (b Teuchern, near Weissenfels, Saxony, bap. 12 Jan 1674; d Hamburg, 12 Sept 1739), German composer. A pupil of Schelle at St Thomas's School, Leipzig, worked at Brunswick from 1692 under Kusser, whom he succeeded as chief composer to the Hamburg Opera in 1695. There he composed over 100 operas, making Hamburg the most distinguished operatic centre in Germany. Appointed *Kapellmeister* to the Danish Court in Copenhagen in 1723, returned to Hamburg as Cantor of the cathedral, 1728.

Works include operas *Basilius*, *Circe* (1702), *Penelope* (1702), *Der geliebte Adonis*, *Augustus*, *Orpheus* (1702), *La forza della virtù*, *Stoertebecker und Joedge Michaels*, *Die verdammt Statt-Sucht* (1703), *Nebucadnezar* (1704), *Octavia*, *Masagniello furioso* (1706), *Desiderius* (1709), *Croesus* (1710), *Fredegunda* (1715), *Die gross-müthige Tomyris* (1717), *Ulysses*, *Der lächerliche Printz Jodelet* (1726), etc.; Passion oratorios *Der für die Sünde der Welt gemartete und sterbende Heiland Jesus* (text by Brockes, 1712), *Der blutige und sterbende Jesus* (Hunold, 1704); cantatas; motets; instrumental music.

Kelemen, Milko (b Podravska, Slatina, 30 Mar 1924), Croatian composer. Studied at the Zagreb Conservatory with Sulek. His mature style employes serial and aleatory techniques.

Works include operas *König Ubu* (1965), *State of Siege* (after Camus' *The Plague*, 1970) and *Apocalyptica* ballet-opera (1979); *Koncertantne Improvizacije* for string (1955); *Concerto giocoso* for chamber orchestra; concertos for violin and bassoon; concertino for double bass and strings; *Symphonic Music 57*; *Abecedarium* for strings (1973); *Mageia* for orchestra (1979); *Dramatico* for cello and orchestra (1985); *Fantasmas* for viola and orchestra (1986); *Memoirs* for string trio (1987); *Sonnets* for string quartet (1988); nonet (1988); *Games* song cycle; piano sonata.

A kind of musical Malcolm Sargent.
Thomas Beecham on Herbert von Karajan, quoted in Atkins and Newman, *Beecham Stories*, 1978

Kelemen, Zoltán (b Budapest, 12 Mar 1926; d Zurich, 9 May 1979), Hungarian bass. After study in Budapest and Rome his early career was in West German opera houses; sang Alberich in the *Ring* at Bayreuth in 1964 and later repeated the role under Karajan at the Salzburg Easter Festival and at CG (1970) and the NY Met. Well known as Klingsor, also admired in such *buffo* roles as Falstaff, Leporello, Osmin and Ochs.

Kell, Reginald (b York, 8 Jun 1906; d Frankfort, KY, 5 Aug 1981), English clarinettist. After study at the RAM he was principal clarinettist under Beecham with the LPO at CG, joined the Philharmonia on its foundation in 1945, and from 1948 his career was largely in the USA. He pub. a clarinet method in 1968.

Keller, Gottfried (1819–1890), Swiss poet and novelist. ◊Kleider machen Leute (Zemlinsky); ◊Romeo und Julia auf dem Dorfe (Delius); ◊Schoeck (*Gesangfest im Frübling, Lebending begraben, Gaselen, Unter Sternen, Sommernacht* and songs); ◊Vrieslander (songs). Six of his poems were set by Hugo Wolf.

Keller, Hans (b Vienna, 11 Mar 1919; d London, 6 Nov 1985), Austrian-born British journalist and critic. After studying in Vienna he fled to England in 1938; played the violin and viola in various ensembles and in 1959 joined the BBC. He had much influence on broadcasting policy, and in his programmes of functional analysis sought to elucidate structure and ideas by musical example, rather than verbal explanation. An apparent mastery of his adopted language led to a prolific career as a journalist; natives were sometimes bemused by a certain subjectivity and love of paradox. He wrote the libretto for Benjamin Frankel's opera *Marching Song* (BBC 1983). Author of *The Great Haydn Quartets* (1986).

Kelley, Edgar Stillman (b Sparta, WI, 14 Apr 1857; d New York, 12 Nov 1944), American composer and writer on music. Studied at Chicago and Stuttgart, and on his return to USA became organist and critic in California, where he also made a study of Chinese music. He then taught at Yale University, in Berlin and, from 1910, at the Cincinnati Conservatory.

Works include operetta *Puritania* (1892); incidental music for Shakespeare's *Macbeth*; orchestral suite on Chinese themes, *Aladdin, Gulliver* symphony (after Swift), *New England Symphony*, suite *Alice in Wonderland* (after Lewis Carroll, 1913); cantata *Pilgrim's Progress* (after Bunyan, 1918), *Wedding Ode* for tenor, male chorus and orchestra; *My Captain* (Whitman) and *The Sleeper* (Poe) for chorus; variations for string quartet, string quartet, piano quintet; piano pieces; songs.

Kellner, Johann Peter (b Gräfenroda, Thuringia, 28 Sept 1705; d Gräfenroda, 17 Apr 1772), German organist and composer. Appointed Cantor at Frankenhain in 1725, he returned in a smiliar capacity to his home town in 1728, a post which he held till his death. He knew Bach and Handel.

Works include cantatas, an oratorio, organ and harpsichord music.

Kellogg, Clara Louise (b Sumterville, SC, 9 Jul 1842; d New Hartford, CT, 13 May 1916), American soprano. Studied in NY and made her debut there in 1861, as Gilda; sang Marguerite in NY and London (debut 1867).

Kelly, Bryan (b Oxford, 3 Jan 1934), English composer who studied with Gordon Jacob and Herbert Howells; has written extensively for brass band and for educational use. Professor of composition at RCM 1962–84, then moved to Italy.

Works include *The Tempest* Suite, for strings (1967); *Edinburgh Dances* and Concertante Music, for brass band (1973); *Stabat Mater*, for soloists and orchestra (1970); *Latin Magnificat*, for chorus and wind instruments (1979); two symphonies (1982, 1986); *The Spider Monkey Uncle King*, opera pantomime (1971); *Herod, do your worst*, nativity opera (1968).

Education in music is most sovereign, because more than anything else rhythm and harmony find their way to the inmost soul.

Plato (427–347 BC), *The Republic*

Kelly, Michael (b Dublin, 25 Dec 1762; d Margate, 9 Oct 1826), Irish tenor, actor and composer. Pupil of M Arne and others, went to Naples 1779 to study with Fenaroli and Aprile, and there made his operatic debut 1781. At the Court Opera in Vienna, 1784–87, he was the first Basilio and Curzio in Mozart's *Figaro* (1786). Returned to London 1787, and two years later produced the first of over 60 theatrical compositions. His entertaining *Reminiscences* (pub. 1826), though not fully reliable, contain valuable information on his contemporaries, especially Mozart.

Works include dramatic works *A Friend in Need* (1797), *The Castle Spectre, Blue Beard* (1798), *Pizarro* (Sheridan, 1799), *The*

Gipsy Prince (1801), *Love laughs at Locksmiths* (1803), *Cinderella, Polly* (1813).

Kelterborn, Rudolf (b Basel, 3 Sept 1931), Swiss composer. Studied with J Handschin and Willy Burkhard, Blacher and Fortner. In 1960 he became an instructor at the Detmold Music Academy; director of the Basel Academy from 1983. In his music he tends towards integral serialism.

Works include operas *Die Errettung Thebens* (1963), *Kaiser Jovian* (1967), *Ein Engel kommt nach Babylon* (1977); *Der Kirschgarten* (after Chekhov, 1984); *Julia* (1991); *Metamorphosen* for orchestra (1960); concertino for violin and chamber orchestra; concertino for piano and chamber orchestra; suite for woodwind, percussion and strings; sonata for 16 solo strings (1955).

Cantata Profana for baritone, chorus and 13 instruments (1960); cantata *Ewige Wiederkehr* for mezzo, flute and string trio (1960); cello concerto (1962); chamber music for various instrumental groups including five string quartets (1954–70), *5 Fantasien* for flute, cello and harpsichord; *7 Bagatellen* for wind quintet; *Metamorphosen* for piano; *Meditation* for six wind instruments.

Kelway, Joseph (b ? Chichester, c 1702; d London, May 1782), English organist and harpsichordist. Pupil of Geminiani, he was organist of St Michael's Cornhill, London, 1730–36, then of St Martin-in-the-Fields. Made a great reputation as a player, was teacher to Queen Charlotte, and often deputized for Handel at the organ. Wrote harpsichord music.

Kelway, Thomas (b Chichester, c 1695; d Chichester, 21 May 1744), English organist and composer, elder brother of Joseph ◊Kelway. Chorister at Chichester Cathedral under John Reading, whom he succeeded as organist in 1733. Composed church music.

Kemble, Adelaide (b London, 1814; d Warsash House, Hants., 4 Aug 1879), English soprano, daughter of the actor Charles Kemble. She first appeared in London and at the York Festival in 1835, then went to Germany and Italy for further study, last with Pasta. In 1839 she appeared as Norma in Venice, toured widely in Italy and returned to London for an appearance in the same part in 1841. Also sang in operas by Mozart, Rossini and Cimarosa.

Kemp, Barbara (b Kochem, 12 Dec 1881; d Berlin, 17 Apr 1959), German soprano and producer. She sang in Berlin 1913–32 and assumed Wagnerian roles at the NY Met. and at Bayreuth (1914–27); married the composer Max von Schillings in 1923 and later the same year sang the title part of the first Met. performance of his *Mona Lisa*; also sang Elsa, Isolde and Kundry there. She produced *Mona Lisa* in Berlin shortly before World War II.

Kempe, Rudolf (b Nieder-Poyritz, near Dresden, 14 June 1910; d Zurich, 12 May 1976), German conductor. Studied oboe, becoming first oboe in the Leipzig Gewandhaus Orchestra in 1929. Began conducting 1936 and 1949–52 was music director of the Dresden Staatsoper and 1952–54 of the Munich Staatsoper. From 1954 to 1956 he conducted at the NY Met. (*Tannhäuser, Tristan, Meistersinger* and *Der Rosenkavalier*). He conducted at many of the great opera houses of the world, including many appearances at CG (1953–74), and was music director of the RPO 1961–75. Conducted the *Ring* at Bayreuth 1960–63, and was musical director of the Zurich Tonhalle Orchestra 1965–72, Munich PO from 1967. Well known in performances of Strauss and Wagner, where his interpretations were noted for balance and clarity.

Kempen, Paul van (b Zoeterwoude, 16 May 1893; d Hilversum, 8 Dec 1955), Dutch conductor and violinist. His career began in 1910 as a violinist in the Concertgebouw Orchestra, under Mengelberg; he became chief conductor of the Dresden PO in 1934 and remained in Germany during World War II, a fact which did not endear him to his Dutch colleagues. He was nevertheless chief conductor of Hilversum Radio from 1949.

Kempff, Wilhelm (b Jüterborg, 25 Nov 1895; d Positano, 23 May 1991), German pianist and composer. Studied piano with H Barth and composition with R Kahn. After winning both the Mendelssohn Prizes in 1917, he became a concert pianist. From 1924 to 1929 he was head of the Hochschule für Musik in Stuttgart. London debut 1951,

NY 1964. He was best known as one of the finest and most thoughtful interpreters of the classical piano repertory, especially the music of Beethoven.

His compositions include the operas *König Midas* (1930) and *Die Familie Gozzi* (1934); symphonies and ballets; concertos for piano and violin; string quartets; and many pieces for solo piano and organ.

Kendale, Richard (d 1431), English grammarian and music theorist. A short musical treatise by him is included in the MS written down by John Wylde, precentor of Waltham Holy Cross Abbey, *c* 1460 (British Museum, Lans. 763).

Kennedy, Michael (b Manchester, 19 Feb 1926), English critic and writer on music. He joined the northern edition of *Daily Telegraph* in 1941; editor 1960–86. Active as music critic since 1950. His books include histories of the Hallé Orchestra (1960 and 1983) and studies of Vaughan Williams (1964), Elgar (1968), Barbirolli (1971), Mahler (1974), Strauss (1976), Britten (1981) and Boult (1987). Edited *Concise Oxford Dictionary of Music* (1980; revised as *Oxford Dictionary of Music*, 1985 and 1994).

Kennedy, Nigel (b Brighton, 28 Dec 1956), English violinist. He studied at the Yehudi Menuhin school and in NY; debut 1977. He was in the first rank of his generation of violinists, and became particularly associated with the Elgar and the Mendelssohn concertos. He affected a populist image and manner, issuing a chart-topping recording of *The Four Seasons*. He has joined Stephan Grappelli in jazz concerts; appeared with the Berlin PO in 1980 and toured the US 1985; returned 1987, with BBC SO. In 1991 at the Festival Hall he played the Berg Concerto, dressed in a Dracula outfit; in recent years he has made informal music-making the focus of his endeavours.

Kenny, Yvonne (b Sydney, 25 Nov 1950), Australian soprano. Debut London 1975, as Donizetti's Rosamunda d'Inghilterra (concert performance). CG debut 1976, in the fp of Henze's *We Come to the River*; other London roles have been Ilia, Oscar, Pamina and Micaela. ENO 1977, Sophie. Victoria State Opera, Melbourne, since 1978 as Mélisande, Adèle and Gilda. She sang Ilia at Glyndebourne in 1985. Many concert engagements in Europe. Season 1992–93 with Handel's *Alcina* at CG and *Deborah* at the London Proms.

Kentner, Louis (b Karwin, Silesia, 19 Jul 1905; d London, 22 Sept 1987), Hungarian-born pianist, British citizen since 1946. He studied in Budapest and made his debut in 1920; closely identified with the music of Bartók, giving the fp in Hungary of the second piano concerto and taking part in the world premiere of the concerto for two pianos and orchestra (London, 1942). With Yehudi Menuhin, his brother-in-law, gave the fp of Walton's violin sonata.

Kent Opera English opera company founded in 1969 by Norman Platt and Roger Norrington (music director until 1984). Gave revivals of early works, including Handel's *Atlanta* (1970) and *Agrippina* (1982); Monteverdi series in editions by Norrington, 1974–78. *King Priam* (1984) and the fp of Weir's *A Night at the Chinese Opera* (1987). Disbanded by Arts Council 1989 but re-formed 1994 and gave performances of Britten's *Prodigal Son* in 1995.

Kepler, Johannes (b Weil der Stadt, 27 Dec 1571; d Regensburg, 15 Nov 1630), German philosopher, astronomer and writer on music. He was an early supporter of the Copernican view of the solar system, which placed the Sun at its centre, and was the first to propose that the orbits of the planets are eliptical. His *Harmonices Mundi* (1619) elaborates various music theories; book five elaborates on the ancient Greek doctrine of Pythagoras that the planets emit musical sounds in their orbits round the sun. Kepler's theories form the basis of ◊Hindemith's opera *Die ◊Harmonie der Welt* (1957).

Kerl (or Keril), Johann Caspar (b Adorf, Saxony, 9 Apr 1627; d Munich, 13 Feb 1693), German organist and composer. Settled early in Vienna as a pupil of Valentini; then studied in Rome under Carissimi and probably the organ under Frescobaldi. In the service of the Elector of Bavaria in Munich, 1656–74. Again went to Vienna, as private teacher, and was appointed court organist there 1677, but returned to Munich 1684.

Works include operas *Oronte*, *Erinto*, *Le pretensioni del sole* (1667), *I colori geniali*; Masses, motets and other church music;

sonatas for two violins and bass; toccatas, *ricercari* and other works for organ.

Kerle, Jacob van (b Ypres, *c* 1531; d Prague, 7 Jan 1591), Flemish composer. He spent some time in Italy, partly in Rome in the service of Otto von Truchsess, Cardinal-Archbishop of Augsburg, in whose service he was 1562–75, and with whom he was also at Augsburg at times, and with whom he (?) attended the Council of Trent 1562–63. Later he became canon of Cambrai, but was often in Vienna and Prague attending on the Emperor Rudolf.

Works include *Preces*, commissioned by the Cardinal of Augsburg in 1562, Masses, motets, Te Deums, Magnificats, hymns, *Sacrae cantiones*.

I am trying to do something for the future of American music, which today has no class whatsoever and is mere barbaric mouthing.

Jerome Kern, quoted in *New York Times*, 1920

Kerman, Joseph (Wilfred) (b London, 3 Apr 1924), American music scholar and critic. Studied London, NY and Princeton. Professor at University of California from 1960; Oxford 1971–74. He is an authority on William Byrd. Books include *Opera as Drama* (1956), *The Beethoven Quartets* (1967) and *Musicology* (1985).

Kern, Adele (b Munich, 25 Nov 1901; d Munich, 6 May 1980), German soprano. Debut in Munich and appeared there for almost 20 years, as well as Vienna and Salzburg and at CG, London (1931–34); sang regularly under Clemens Krauss and was admired in Strauss (Sophie and Zerbinetta) and Mozart (Susanna and Despina).

Kern, Jerome (David) (b New York, 27 Jan 1885; d New York, 11 Nov 1945), American composer. Pupil of Paolo Gallico and Alexander Lambert in NY. He turned to the composition of musical comedy and other light music. His most successful musical was *Show Boat*, including the number 'Ol' Man River'. He moved to Hollywood 1939 and wrote songs for the movies, including the Academy Award-winning 'The Last Time I Saw Paris', from the film *Lady be Good* (1941).

Works include musical comedies *Sunny* (1925), *Show Boat* (1927), *Music in the Air* (1932), *Roberta* (1933) and others; film music.

Kern, Patricia (b Swansea, 4 Jul 1927), Welsh mezzo who first sang with the WNO; joined SW, London, in 1959. She has been much admired in operas by Rossini and Mozart; in 1966 took part in the premiere of *The Violins of St Jacques*, by Malcolm Williamson. She has sung widely in North America.

Kerns, Robert (b Detroit, 8 Jun 1933; d Vienna, 15 Feb 1989), American baritone. He appeared with the NY City Opera in 1959 but then sang in Europe; sang in Berlin and Vienna and at the Aix-en-Provence and Salzburg Festivals. At CG (debut 1964) he performed Mozart's Guglielmo many times and was also heard as Billy Budd, Count Almaviva and Rossini's Figaro. He was a permanent guest at the Deutsche Oper, Berlin from 1973; successful as Germont, Posa, Amfortas, Wolfram, Onegin and Scarpia.

Kertész, István (b Budapest, 28 Dec 1929; d Kfar Saba, Israel, 16 Apr 1973), Hungarian conductor. Kodály was among his teachers and after experience at the Budapest Opera he left Hungary at the 1956 uprising. He was musical director of the Cologne Opera from 1964 until his death and brought the company to London in 1969. His British debut was with the Royal Liverpool PO in 1960, principal conductor LSO 1965–68. Led *Un Ballo in maschera* at CG, 1966. Noted for his interpretations of Mozart and Dvořák; also heard in Britten, Prokofiev, Bartók, Stravinsky and Henze. He drowned while swimming near Tel-Aviv.

Ketting, Piet (b Haarlem, 29 Nov 1905; d Rotterdam, 25 May 1984), Dutch pianist and composer. Studied with Pijper and later became professor at the Rotterdam Conservatory.

Works include two symphonies (1929, 1970); choral music, three string quartets (1927–28), trio for flute, clarinet and bassoon and other chamber music, sonatas for flute, bass clarinet and piano and flute,

kettledrums

oboe and piano, partita for two flutes; four sonatinas, fugue, etc., for piano; songs, including Shakespeare sonnets.

kettledrums drums with a single head of skin stretched over a cauldron-shaped hemisphere. They produce notes of definite pitch which can be altered by the turning of screws at the rim of the 'kettle', thus tightening or relaxing the skin. A mechanical device now widely used enables the player to increase or relax the tension by means of a pedal. The modern orchestra has at least three kettledrums of different sizes, and more may be demanded by the composer, in which case one player may not be sufficient. A variety of sticks covered with different materials can be used to produce a harder or softer impact.

Keuchenthal, Johannes (b Ellrich am Harz, *c* 1522; d St Andreasberg, 1583), German clergyman and musician. Pub. *Kirchengesang, lateinisch und deutsch*, a collection of music for the Lutheran Church, including a setting of the Passion, at Wittenberg in 1573.

Keuris, Tristan (b Amersfoort, 3 Oct 1946), Dutch composer. Studied at Utrecht with Ton de Leeuw (1963–69). Currently head of composition at the Sweelinck Conservatory, and lectures in America, Norway and Berlin.

Works include quintet for orchestra (1967); *Choral Music* (1969); *Soundings* for orchestra (1970); alto saxophone concerto (1971); *Sinfonia* (1975); *Serenade* (1976); piano concerto (1980); *Movements* for orchestra (1982); two string quartets (1982, 1985); violin concerto (1984); *Symphonic Transformations* (Houston SO commission, 1987); *To Brooklyn Bridge* for 24 voices and ensemble (1988); *Five Pieces* for brass quintet (1988); *Catena: Refrains and Variations* for 31 wind instruments, percussion and celesta (1989); organ concerto (1993).

key (1) The levers by means of which notes are produced on keyboard instruments by being pressed down or struck. Also those on wind instruments stopping the note-holes which cannot be reached directly by the fingers.

(2) The tonality of a piece of music which is based on a particular major or minor scale and accepts harmonic relationships deriving from the notes of those scales. The first note of the scale (or ◊tonic) gives its name to the key, e.g. key of D major, key of E♭ minor.

Lose no opportunity to hear artistic singing; in so doing, the keyboard player will learn to think in terms of song.

C P E Bach, *Essay on the True Art of Playing Keyboard Instruments*, 1753

---

keyboard the array of levers on instruments of the piano type and on the organ, also on such instruments as the hurdy-gurdy and the accordion, by means of which the fingers, and on the organ also the feet, control the sound.

key bugle, also Kent bugle, an instrument invented in the early 19th c.; a bugle with side-holes covered with keys similar to those used on woodwind instruments.

keynote the ◊tonic: the note on which the scale begins and ends, which determines the key of a piece of music in major or minor and after which that key is named.

key relationships these may be close or remote, based largely on the similarity of key signatures, e.g. in the key of C major the relation of the tonic chord (C) with the dominant (G) is close.

The relation of C minor with E♭ major (its relative major) is also close, whereas the relation of C major with E♭ major is less close. Transference from one key to another may be abrupt or may be effected by modulation.

Tonic/dominant and relative major/minor relationships are close; C major and E♭ major are not closely related.

key signature the sharps and flats which occur in the key of a given composition, written at the beginning of each stave.

Keys with five–seven sharps or flats overlap enharmonically; in the tempered scale of the piano they are identical as follows: B major and G♯ minor = C♭ major and A♭ minor; F♯ major and D♯ minor = G♭ major and E♭ minor; C♯ major and A♯ minor = D♭ major and B♭ minor.

Khachaturian, Aram Ilich (b Tbilisi, 6 Jun 1903; d Moscow 1 May 1978), Russian composer. His father, a poor workman, was able to send him to Moscow only after the Revolution; he entered the Gnessin School of Music there and studied under that master in 1923; in 1929 he went to the Moscow Conservatory as a pupil of Vassilenko and afterwards of Miaskovsky. Studied the folksongs of Russian Armenia and other southern regions, which influenced his compositions. He was successful with a pre-war symphony and piano concerto, but was denounced in the composers' purge of 1948 and as a result turned to patriotic film and ballet music; his *Sword Dance* from the film *Spartacus* (1954) has been popular TV theme music.

Works include ballets *Happiness* (1939), *Gayaneh* (1942) and *Spartacus* (1954), incidental music for Shakespeare's *Macbeth*, Lope de Vega's *Widow of Valencia*, Pogodin's *Kremlin Chimes*, Kron's *Deep Drilling*, Lermontov's *Masquerade*, etc.; film music *Song of Stalin* for chorus and orchestra; three symphonies (1932–47), *Dance Suite* and *Solemn Overture*, 'To the End of the War' for orchestra; marches and pieces on Uzbek and Armenian themes for wind band; concertos for piano, violin, cello and violin and cello.; string quartet (1932), trio for clarinet, violin and piano; sonata and pieces for violin and piano; piano music, part-songs; songs for the Russian army.

Khaikin, Boris Emmanuilovich (b Minsk, 26 Oct 1904; d Moscow, 10 May 1978), Russian conductor. Graduated from the Moscow Conservatory in 1928 and conducted opera at the Stanislavsky theatre; moved to Leningrad in 1936 and gave the fps of Prokofiev's *The Duenna* (1946) and *The Story of a Real Man* (1948). He made guest appearances conducting opera in Florence and Leipzig and in 1966 took the Leningrad PO to Italy. Kiril Kondrashin was among his pupils.

Khamma ballet-pantomime in two scenes by Debussy (scenario W L Courtney and M Allan), composed in short score 1911–12, orchestrated by Koechlin 1912–13; fp (concert) Paris, 15 Nov 1924, conductor Pierné. First stage performance Paris, Opéra-Comique, 26 Mar 1947.

Kharitonov, Dimitri (b Kùioyshev, 18 Oct 1958), Russian baritone. Studied in Leningrad and Odessa (1976–84). Sang at the Bolshoi

Maj. Min.

C A

G E

D B

A F♯

E C♯

B G♯

F♯ D♯

C♯ A♯

C♭ A♭

G♭ E♭

D♭ B♭

A♭ F

E♭ C

B♭ G

F D

The complete series of key signatures in order of increasing complexity by sharps, returning towards C major through the flat keys.

Opera 1985–88 as Mazeppa, Eugene Onegin and Luna. UK debut as Jochanaan in *Salome* at the Edinburgh Festival; settled in England from 1989. US debut at Chicago 1990, as Sonora in *La Fanciulla del West*; San Francisco then Los Angeles from 1991, as Escamillo,

THE OPERA

Khovanshchina

A five-act opera about religious zeal by Modest Mussorgsky, set in Russia at the time of the accession of Peter the Great in 1682. It was unfinished at the time of Mussorgsky's death, and was completed by Rimsky-Korsakov. The opera was first performed in St Petersburg in 1886.

I. Prince Ivan Khovansky (bass), leader of the Streltsy guards, is plotting against the state while his son Andrei (tenor) pursues Emma (soprano), who is rescued by Marfa (mezzo-soprano), a former lover of Andrei. Marfa's fellow Old Believer, Dosifei (bass), foretells troubled times.

II. Prince Golitsin (tenor), representing the new ideas of Tsar Peter, meets Khovansky and Marfa, and news is brought that the Khovanskys have been proclaimed traitors.

III. Marfa sings of her former love for Andrei while the boisterous Streltsy gather; Khovansky advises them to disperse and avoid the tsar's troops.

IV. Khovansky is assassinated by Shaklovity. Andrei and Marfa quarrel, and Andrei's Streltsy arrive with blocks for their own execution. But they are pardoned by Tsar Peter.

V. The Old Believers would rather die than compromise their ultra-orthodox religious ideals under the tsar. Dosifei, Marfa and Andrei gather in a forest clearing; when the chapel there is ablaze, they walk into the flames.

THE OPERA

Andrei in *War and Peace*, Enrico (*Lucia*), Gerard and Renato (*Ballo*). Glyndebourne debut 1992, as Yeletsky in *The Queen of Spades*.

Khoklov, Pavel (b Spassky, Tambov, 2 Aug 1854; d Moscow, 20 Sept 1919), Russian baritone. He studied in Moscow and made his debut there in 1879; two years later he sang the title part in the first professional performance of Tchaikovsky's *Eugene Onegin*. He was closely identified with this role, as well as Rubinstein's Demon, and also appeared in operas by Verdi, Wagner and Meyerbeer; a noted Boris Godunov and Prince Igor.

khorovod, Russian, a type of ancient Russian folksong sung in chorus of two or more parts in a primitive kind of counterpoint. It was sung mainly at religious and family festivals and on seasonal occasions.

Khovanshchina unfinished opera by Mussorgsky (libretto by composer and V V Stassov), produced as completed and scored by Rimsky-Korsakov after Mussorgsky's death, St Petersburg, 21 Feb 1886. Shostakovich also added to Rimsky-Korsakov's work. The plot is based on historical events surrounding the opponents of Tsar Peter the Great: Prince Khovansky, head of the militia, the Regent Sofia as represented by the actions of Prince Golitsin, the 'Old Believers' as personified by Marfa. All come to an unhappy end.

Khrennikov, Tikhon Nikolaievich (b Elets, 10 Jun 1913), Russian composer. He was taught music at home, but entered the Gnessin School of Music at Moscow in 1929 and the Conservatory in 1932 as a pupil of Shebalin. Secretary, Union of Soviet Composers, from 1948; Hero of Socialist Labour 1973. He played a prominent part in the Stalinist-inspired denunciations of Prokofiev and Shostakovich; renewed his attacks with the emergence of the New Music generation of composers, Schnittke and Sofia Gubaidulina.

Works include operas *The Brothers* (*In the Storm*, 1939); *Mother* (after Gogol, 1957); incidental music for Shakespeare's *Much Ado about Nothing*, an adaptation of Cervantes' *Don Quixote*, etc., film music for *The Pigs and the Shepherd*; three symphonies (1955–73); three piano concertos (1933–82); piano pieces; songs to words by Pushkin and Burns; war songs.

Kielflügel, German, = lit. 'quill-wing' = harpsichord, so named from the quills that pluck the strings and the wing shape of the instrument's body.

Kienlen, Johann Christoph (b Ulm, bap. 14 Dec 1783; d Dessau, 7 Dec

1829), German composer. He appeared as singer and pianist at the age of seven and was later sent to Paris to study with Cherubini. After being music director at Ulm he went to Vienna in 1811, where he taught, and in 1823 he became singing-master to the Berlin opera.

Works include operas, e.g. *Claudine von Villa Bella* (Goethe, 1810); a symphony; additions to E T A Hoffmann's incidental music for Goethe's *Scherz, List und Rache*; two piano sonatas; many songs.

Kienzl, Wilhelm (b Waizenkirchen, Styria, 17 Jan 1857; d Vienna, 19 Oct 1941), Austrian composer. His father, a lawyer, became mayor of Graz in 1861 and the family settled there. He studied there under W Mayer, who also taught Weingartner and Busoni, later went to Prague and Vienna for further study. Jensen and Liszt encouraged him to compose and he came into close touch with Wagner at Bayreuth for a time. He was an opera conductor at Amsterdam, Krefeld, Hamburg and Munich (till 1893).

Works include operas *Urvasi* (1886), *Heilmar der Narr* (1892), *Der Evangelimann* (1895), *Don Quixote, In Knecht Rupprechts Werkstatt* (1907), *Der Kuhreigen* (1911), *Das Testament* (1916), *Hassan der Schwärmer* (1925), *Sanctissimum*; orchestral, choral and chamber works; *Dichterreise* and many other piano works; *Tanzbilder* for piano duet; over 100 songs; etc. He adapted Jensen's opera *Die Erbin von Montfort* to a new libretto based on Gozzi's *Turandot*.

Kiepura, Jan (b Sosnowiec, 16 May 1902; d Harrison, NY, 15 Aug 1966), Polish tenor. He studied in Warsaw and Milan and came to wider notice in Vienna (1926, Cavaradossi); he appeared there until the war and sang major roles in operas by Bizet, Massenet and Puccini in Europe and the USA. Sang at the Met. 1938–42, debut as Rodolfo, but after his marriage to the Hungarian soprano and film star Martha Eggerth turned increasingly to films as a career outlet.

Kilpinen, Yrjö (b Helsinki, 4 Feb 1892; d Helsinki, 2 Mar 1959), Finnish composer. Had a few lessons in theory at the Helsinki Conservatory and in Berlin and Vienna, but was otherwise self-taught. In receipt of a small government grant, he devoted himself entirely to composition.

Works include cello sonata, viola da gamba sonata; piano sonatas; over 500 songs on Finnish, Swedish and German poems.

Kim, Earl (b Dinuba, CA, 6 Jan 1920), American composer. Studied at UCLA with Schoenberg (1939) and with Bloch and Sessions at Berkeley. In its precision and rhythmic subtlety his music reflects his Korean origins. Professor of music at Harvard, 1967–90.

Works include opera *Footfalls*, 1981; *Dialogues* for piano and orchestra (1959); violin concerto (1979); 12 caprices for violin (1980); *Now and Then* for soprano, flute, viola and harp (1981); *Where Grief Slumbers* for soprano, harp and strings (1982); *The 11th Dream* for soprano, baritone, piano, violin and cello (1989); *Three Poems in French* for soprano and string quartet (1989); *Some thoughts on Keats and Coleridge* for chorus (1990).

Kim, Young Uck (b Seoul, 1 Sept 1947), Korean violinist. Studied at Curtis Institute, Philadelphia, made debut there 1963. Many concerts in Europe and USA with Vienna and Berlin POs, LSO, NY and LA POs. Season 1992 with US and European fps of commissioned concerto by Gunther Schuller; also plays Berg, Prokofiev and Stravinsky. Piano trio recitals with Yo-Yo Ma and Emanuel Ax.

Kindermann, Johann Erasmus (b Nuremberg, 29 Mar 1616; d Nuremberg, 14 Apr 1655), German composer and organist. He studied with J Staden and in common with other German composers of his time probably visited Venice, where he would have met Frescobaldi and Cavalli. Organist, Egidienkirche Nuremberg, from 1640.

Vocal works including *Cantiones Jesu Christi* (1639), *Friedens Clag* (1640), *Concentus Salomonis* (1642), *Opitianischer Orpheus* (1642), *Musica catechetica* (1643), *Gottliche Liebesflamme* (1651) and nine cantatas. Instrumental works include *Harmonia organica* (1645), 27 Canzoni, nine sonatas and 30 suite movements.

Kinderscenen, *Scenes from childhood*, 13 piano pieces by Schumann, op. 15; composed 1838.

Kindertotenlieder, *Songs of Dead Children*, cycle of five songs by Mahler, with orchestra or piano, to poems by Rückert; composed 1902, fp Vienna, 29 Jan 1905, conductor Mahler.

King, Charles (b Bury St Edmunds, 1687; d London, 17 Mar 1748), English singer, organist and composer. Chorister under Blow at St Paul's Cathedral, where he succeeded his father-in-law Clarke as Almoner and Master of the Children in 1708. Wrote church music.

King, James (b Dodge City, 22 May 1925), American tenor, formerly baritone. He was engaged in Berlin from 1962 and in that year appeared at the Salzburg Festival in Gluck's *Iphigénie en Aulide*; Bayreuth Festival from 1965 and NY Met. from 1966 (debut as Florestan), specialising in Strauss and Wagner, e.g. the Emperor and Siegmund; sang Bacchus at CG in 1985, Florestan 1986. Sang Lohengrin at Nice 1990, Aegisthus in *Elektra* at the Met., 1992.

King, Matthew (Peter) (b London, 1773; d London, Jan 1823), English composer. Studied under C F Horn.

Works include many stage pieces (some with Braham, Kelly and others); oratorio *The Intercession*; four sets of piano sonatas; solo cantatas, glees, songs.

You can't teach a young musician to compose any more than you can teach a delicate plant to grow, but you can guide him a little by putting a stick in here and a stick in there.

Frederick Delius, quoted in Fenby,
Delius as I Knew Him, 1936

King, Robert, English 17th–18th-c. composer. He joined the royal band in 1680 on the death of Banister, received a licence to give concerts in 1689 and took the Mus.B. at Cambridge in 1696.

Works include incidental music for Crowne's *Sir Courtly Nice* and many other plays; Shadwell's Ode on St Cecilia's Day, Motteux's Ode for John Cecil, Earl of Exeter; many songs for one and more voices.

King, Robert (John Stephen) (b Wimbourne, 27 Jun 1960), English conductor and harpsichordist. Studied at St John's College, Cambridge, and founded the King's Consort 1979; many performances throughout Europe in the Baroque and English Restoration repertory. Music director of the European Baroque Orchestra from 1986, National Youth Music Theatre, 1987. With the King's Consort he inaugurated the Purcell tercentenary year (1995) with a concert at Banqueting House, Whitehall.

King, Thea (b Hitchin, 16 Dec 1925), English clarinettist. She studied at the RCM and from 1956–64 was principal clarinettist of the London Mozart Players; moved to the English Chamber Orchestra in 1964 and until 1968 was a member of the all-female Portia ensemble. She has given the fps of works by Howells, Ireland, Searle and Rawsthorne, and has been associated with the modern revival of interest in the music of the 19th-c. Finnish clarinettist and composer Bernhard Crusell.

King, William (b Winchester, 1624; d Oxford, 17 Nov 1680), English organist and composer, son of George King, organist of Winchester Cathedral (d 1665). He went to Oxford as a clerk of Magdalen College in 1648, took the BA there in 1649, became a chaplain at the college in 1652, went to All Souls' College as probationer-fellow in 1654 and became organist of New College in 1664.

Works include a service, a litany, anthems; songs to a thorough-bass for theorbo, harpsichord or bass viol to poems by Cowley, etc.

King and Charcoal-Burner, *Král a Uhlíř*, opera by Dvořák (libretto by B Guldener), produced Prague, Czech Theatre, 24 Nov 1874. Dvořák's first opera to be produced. King Matyáš, lost in the forest, talks to Liduška, daughter of charcoal burner Matěj. Young Jeník becomes jealous and embarks on a glorious military career before he is united with her.

King Arthur, or The British Worthy semi-opera by Purcell (libretto by Dryden), produced London, Dorset Gardens Theatre, 1691. Arthur and Merlin fight Saxon leader Oswald to establish a united Britain and rescue the beloved Emmeline.

King Charles II opera by Macfarren (libretto by M D Ryan, based on a

THE OPERA

King Priam

A dramatic three-act opera by Michael Tippett, who also wrote the text, based on Homer's *Iliad*. First performed in 1962, it is set in ancient Troy.

I. When it was prophesied that his baby son Paris would eventually cause his death, Priam (baritone) had ordered the child to be killed. Years later, out hunting with his eldest son Hector (baritone), Priam is relieved to find Paris still alive. He is taken back to Troy and, after a visit to Greek Sparta, Paris returns with Helen (mezzo-soprano), wife of Menelaus. Hermes (tenor) sets up the Judgment of Paris, and Helen is chosen.

II. The Greeks have surrounded Troy but their chief warrior, Achilles (tenor), sulks in his tent. A victory by the Trojans is weakened by continual quarrelling between Hector and Paris. Hector kills Petroclus (baritone), friend of Achilles.

III. When Hector is killed in turn by Achilles, Priam brings the body of Petroclus in exchange for that of his son. Returning to his altar, the still-grieving Priam is killed by the son of Achilles.

THE OPERA

play by J H Payne), produced London, Princess's Theatre, 27 Oct 1849.

King Christian II incidental music by Sibelius for a play by A Paul; composed 1898, fp Helsinki, 28 Feb 1898, conductor Sibelius. Suite for orchestra in six movements, 1898. First British performance London, 26 Oct 1901, conductor Wood.

Kingdom, The oratorio by Elgar, op. 51 (libretto compiled from the Bible by the composer), Part II of a trilogy of which I is *The Apostles* and III was never completed. Fp Birmingham Festival, 3 Oct 1906.

King Goes Forth to France, the, *Kuningas lahtee Ranskaan*, opera in three acts by Aulis Sallinen (libretto by P Haavikko), produced Savonlinna Festival, 7 Jul 1984. Also staged at Santa Fe (1986) and CG (1987). A future prince seizes power from the prime minister, and facing a new ice age leads an army south into France.

King Lear ◊Re Lear. Verdi worked at the Shakespearean subject for many years, but never brought the opera anywhere near completion, and his sketches were destroyed after his death, at his own wish.

Incidental music for Shakespeare's tragedy by J André, produced Berlin, 30 Nov 1778. Incidental music by Balakirev, produced St Petersburg, 1861. Overture by Berlioz, op. 4, composed in Italy, 1831, fp Paris, 9 Nov 1834. Opera by Frazzi (1922–28, produced Florence, 1939). For opera by Reimann see ◊Lear.

'King of Prussia' Quartets (Mozart.) ◊'Prussian' Quartets.

King Olaf cantata for solo voices, chorus and orchestra by Elgar, op. 30, set to words by Longfellow altered by H A Acworth, produced at the N Staffordshire Festival, Hanley, 30 Oct 1896.

King Priam opera in three acts by Tippett (libretto by composer), produced by the company of the Royal Opera, CG, at Coventry, 29 May 1962. Judgement of Paris followed by the destruction of Troy.

King Roger opera by Szymanowski (libretto by composer and J Iwaszkiewicz), produced Warsaw, 19 Jun 1926. Queen Roxane and her husband Roger are converted by a wandering shepherd-prophet, Dionysus in disguise.

King Stephen (Beethoven.) ◊König Stephan.

Kinkeldey, Otto (b New York, 27 Nov 1878; d Orange, NJ, 19 Sept 1966), American musicologist. After a general academic education in NY and Berlin, he studied music with MacDowell 1900–02 while he was a schoolmaster and chapel organist. After further studies at the university and academy for church music in Berlin, he became organ teacher at a similar institution at Breslau, and later lecturer and professor of musicology. Returning to USA 1914 he was alternately chief of the music division of the NY Public Library and professor at Cornell University. He wrote a dissertation on 16th-c. keyboard

music and many valuable contributions to periodicals, early music, etc.

Kinsky, Georg (b Marienwerder, Prussia, 29 Sept 1882; d Berlin, 7 Apr 1951), German music scholar and editor. Self-taught in music, he worked at first at the Prussian State Library in Berlin and then became curator until 1927 of the Heyer Museum of musical instruments, of which he compiled a valuable catalogue. From 1921 he was also active at the Cologne Conservatory, from which he retired 1932. His books include a *History of Music in Pictures*, works on instruments and a catalogue of Beethoven's works.

Kipnis, Alexander (b Zhitomir, 13 Feb 1891; d Westport, CT, 14 May 1978), Russian bass. Studied conducting at the Warsaw Conservatory, and later singing in Berlin, making his debut 1915. From 1918 to 1925 he sang in Berlin, in Chicago 1923–32 and at the NY Met. 1940–46; heard there as Gurnemanz, Pogner, Marke, Boris, Ochs and Philip II. In 1931 became an American citizen. One of the finest singers of his time.

Kipnis, Igor (b Berlin, 27 Sept 1930), American harpsichordist, son of Alexander ◊Kipnis. After an early career as a critic and as director of a NY radio station he made his public debut as a harpsichordist in 1962; appeared with the NY PO in 1975 and has toured all over the world. His large repertory includes contemporary American works by Rorem, Kolb, Rochberg and others, and he has taught Baroque performing practice.

Kirbye, George (b ? Suffolk, c 1565; d Bury St Edmunds, buried 6 Oct 1634), English composer. He first appeared as the most copious contributor, except Farmer, to East's Psalter. In 1598 he married Anne Saxye, and he seems to have lived at that time at Rushbrooke near Bury St Edmunds as domestic musician at the residence of Sir Robert Jermyn, to whose daughters he dedicated his book of 24 madrigals in 1597. In 1601 he contributed a madrigal to *The Triumphes of Oriana*.

Works include motets, a hymn; madrigals; pavan for viols.

Kircher, Athanasius (b Geisa near Fulda, 2 May 1601; d Rome, 27 Nov 1680), German mathematician, philosopher and music scholar. He was professor at the Jesuit College of Würzburg, but was driven from Germany by the 30 Years War in 1633, going to Avignon, Vienna and in 1637 to Rome, where he settled for the rest of his life. His chief musical-literary work is *Musurgia universalis* (1650).

Kirchgassner, Marianne (b Bruchsal, 5 Jun 1769; d Schaffhausen, 9 Dec 1808), German glass harmonica player, blind from infancy. On her first concert tour she was heard by Mozart, then only months before his death, and he composed three works for her instrument. She continued performing until her death, which is alleged to have been caused by the unique vibrations set up by the glass harmonica.

Kirchhoff, Walter (b Berlin, 17 Mar 1879; d Wiesbaden, 26 Mar 1951), German tenor. He studied at Berlin; debut there 1906, as Faust. He remained at the Hofoper until 1920, often in Wagner. Bayreuth 1911–14, as Walther, Siegfried and Parsifal. CG 1913, 1924. NY Met. 1926–31; 1929 as Max in the US fp of Křenek's *Jonny spielt auf*. Guest at Paris, Rio and Buenos Aires.

Kirchner, Leon (b Brooklyn, 24 Jan 1919), American composer, pianist and conductor. He studied with Ernest Bloch in San Francisco and Roger Sessions in NY. Professor at Harvard University from 1961. Early influences were Bartók and Stravinsky; then followed Schoenberg, but in a non-doctrinaire way.

Works include opera *Lily* (after Bellow's *Henderson, the Rain King*, 1977); *Toccata* for strings, wind and percussion (1956), two piano concertos (1956, 1963), *Music for Orchestra* (1969); three string quartets (no. 3 with electronics, 1948, 1958, 1967), piano trio (1954), *Lily* for chamber ensemble and voice (from the opera, 1973); *The Times are Nightfall* for soprano and piano (1943), *Dawn* for chorus and organ (1946), *Of Obedience and the Runner* for soprano and piano (after Whitman, 1950), *Words from Wordsworth* for chorus (1966), *Music for 12* (1985).

Kirkby, Emma (b Camberley, 26 Feb 1949), English soprano. Studied Classics at Oxford before her London debut in 1974; with her pure, vibrato-free voice she has become a specialist in early music, appear-

Igor Kipnis – harpsichordist

1 Wagner: *Die Walküre*, Act 3 – *Wotans Abschied* (A. Kipnis/Berlin State Opera Orch./Blech)
Though my father often sang the part of Wotan in his earlier days, especially in Chicago in the 1920s, he was far better known for his *Parsifal* Gurnemanz or King Mark in *Tristan*. Working on his forthcoming biography has given me new insights into his career and personality, but this early electrical recording of 1926 has always touched me for its warmth and strength.

2 Brahms: 'Sandmänchen' (A. Kipnis/Ernst Victor Wolff)
My father's 1939 recording, contained in a Volume 2 selection of Brahms songs, has always seemed to me a perfect example of the greatest tenderness and intimacy.

3 Mussorgsky: *Boris Godunov* (A. Kipnis/Metropolitan Opera Orch./Szell)
I was fortunate enough to have attended this 1943 broadcast performance of Mussorgsky's opera, a rehearing of which never fails to stir me with its dramatic power.

4 Verdi: *Otello* (NBC Symphony/Toscanini)
As a confirmed though not uncritical Toscanini-ite, I recall this performance as a teenager when it was first broadcast in 1947; the work still strikes me as Verdi's greatest, the interpretation unforgettable.

5 Rakhmaninov: Concerto no. 3 in D minor (Horowitz/RCA Victor Symphony Orch./Fritz Reiner or Horowitz/LSO/Coates)
Historical recordings are still my great passion, perhaps none so much as the earlier Horowitz performances with which I grew up, including the 1930 Rakhmaninov cut version with Albert Coates, but I also could not do without the 1951 Reiner version with its electrifying displays of digital velocity.

6 Wagner: *Siegfried*, Act 1 – 'Forging Song' (Melchior/LSO/Coates)
A colleague of my father, the matchless Melchior was often criticized for cavalier fidelity to the musical text when he was in his heyday, but could one possibly imagine a more exciting, stentorian *heldentenor* voice than his, especially in this hair-raising excerpt?

7 Chopin: Mazurkas (complete) (Karen Kuschner or Rubinstein)
My grandfather, a Polish pianist/teacher/composer, is responsible for my love of Chopin; I grew up with Rubinstein's spontaneous first integral recorded performance of the Mazurkas but adore this young American pianist's quite recent traversal just as much.

8 Grainger: *Scotch Strathspey and Reel* (Hopkins/Sydney SO)
Grainger's polyphonic variation technique was a relatively late attraction for me (his free-wheeling romantic approach as a pianist was a far earlier enthusiasm), but I have never been able to hear this scintillating melange of folk ditties without a broad smile breaking out.

9 Ravel: *L'Enfant et les sortilèges* (Ernest Bour/Orch. National de la Radiodiffusion Française)
This almost fairy-tale opera is, I believe, Ravel's greatest work for its gentle moralizing, sly humour, exquisite tenderness, and unparalleled orchestral imagination.

10 Beethoven: Piano Sonata, op. 13 (*Pathétique*) (I. Kipnis)
Modesty should by all rights prevent me from listing one of my own performances, but, perhaps because of both the realistic sound and some intriguing aspects of late 18th-century performance practice, I believe I can take some pride in this recent recording of relatively early Beethoven on an original (1793) instrument.

---

ing with the Academy of Ancient Music, the Consort of Musicke and similar ensembles. Her US debut was in 1978; three tours of the Middle East with the lutenist Anthony Rooley. Formerly married to Andrew Parrott, with whom she has sung in the B minor Mass and the Monteverdi ◊ Vespers. Sang Dorinda in Handel's *Orlando* at the 1989 London Proms. Recordings include Florentine *Intermedi*, *Venus and Adonis* by Blow, *Dido and Aeneas* and Pergolesi's Stabat Mater.

My head was filled with tunes of all kinds and since for a long while I couldn't whistle, I had to hum or sing instead.

Emma Kirkby, *A Portrait*, 1964

Kirkby-Lunn, Louise (b Manchester, 8 Nov 1873; d London, 17 Feb 1930), English mezzo-soprano. After study in Manchester and at the RCM she made her debut at the College in the first British performance of Schumann's only opera, *Genoveva*. She had several seasons at CG, London, both before and after World War I, and sang at the NY Met. 1902–08; was well known in operas by Wagner and Verdi; in 1910 appeared in NY in one of the last concerts conducted by Mahler (Elgar's *Sea Pictures*).

Kirkpatrick, John (b New York, 18 Mar 1905; d Ithaca, NY, 8 Nov 1991), American pianist and scholar. He studied at Princeton and with Nadia Boulanger in Paris; performed works by many modern American composers, in particular Charles Ives. In 1939 he gave the

fp in NY of the Concord Sonata, vital in the wider recognition of the music of Ives; his work as a scholar also contributed here.

Kirkpatrick, Ralph (b Leominster, MA, 10 Jun 1911; d Guilford, CT, 13 Apr 1984), American harpsichordist and musicologist. Studied piano at home and theory at Harvard, later with Nadia Boulanger in Paris. In Paris he took harpsichord lessons with Landowska, also working with Arnold Dolmetsch in Haslemere. He received a Guggenheim Fellowship in 1937 and toured Europe studying early MSS, etc. In 1940 he was appointed to Yale University. He pub. a number of scholarly editions, including Bach's *Goldberg Variations* and an important book on D Scarlatti (1953) which gives definitive listings for all the sonatas given 'Kk' nos.

Kirnberger, Johann Philipp (b Saalfeld, Thuringia, 24 Apr 1721; d Berlin, 27 Jul 1783), German theorist and composer. Pupil of Bach in Leipzig, 1739–41, after various posts he entered the service of Frederick the Great as a violinist in 1751. Appointed *Kapellmeister* and teacher of composition to Princess Amalia of Prussia in 1758, he increasingly abandoned performance and composition to devote his time to theoretical writings. Among many treatises the most important is *Die Kunst des reinen Satzes*, in which he promoted the conservative musical values of J S Bach.

Compositions include cantatas, motets and instrumental music.

Kirshbaum, Ralph (b Denton, TX, 4 Mar 1946), American cellist and conductor. Debut as soloist with the Dallas SO aged 13. He won the 1970 International Tchaikovsky Competition in Moscow and in the following year settled in London; has appeared all over the world as a

Ralph Kirshbaum – cellist

1 Bruch: *Kol Nidrei*
The very first impression I have of music creating an impact on me is in the realm of religious music. Primarily this was from the Jewish congregation we belonged to in Texas, and more specifically, this piece by Bruch, which I first played at the age of nine. I still get chills when I play it and I hear those opening chords. I have always felt most moved by the purity and simplicity of that opening.

2 Bach: Cello Suites
I also remember hearing from an early age at Easter the oratorios of Bach: again the purity of harmonic sound and also of form moved me quite profoundly. Since then, the music of Bach has always had a very special place in my heart. I find in the cello suites those same qualities of form and harmony. That's why for me the heart of all the suites is the sarabande, which is maybe the purest distillation of those elements.

3 Elgar: Cello Concerto
It has always been performances, rather than recordings, that have crystallized my image of a piece of music. I count myself very fortunate to have been present when Jacqueline du Pré came to the States and played the Elgar Cello Concerto for the first time there, in Carnegie Hall. I didn't know her name and I didn't know the Elgar Cello Concerto at that point either. I was totally mesmerized. That remains for me one of the performances that I remember most vividly, that you could count on the fingers on one hand in a lifetime of concerts.

4 Chopin: Piano Sonata no. 2 in B flat minor (*Funeral March*)
Another instance like that of hearing Jacqueline du Pré play Elgar's Cello Concerto was hearing Horowitz play Chopin's 'Funeral March'. There is that very brief, frenetic last movement after the drawn intensity of the third – the line of intensity he drew from the beginning of the sonata to the end was phenomenal.

---

soloist and plays in a piano trio with György Pauk and Peter Frankl.

Kirsten, Dorothy (b Montclair, NJ, 6 Jul 1915; d Los Angeles, 18 Nov 1992), American soprano. After appearances in Chicago and San Francisco she sang Mimi at the NY Met. in 1945; remained there on a regular basis until 1956 and gave a farewell performance there in 1975. She was admired in operas by Puccini, Gounod and Charpentier; sang in the first US performance of Walton's *Troilus and Cressida* (1955) and Poulenc's *Carmélites* (1957) – both in San Francisco.

Kissin, Evgeny (b Moscow, 10 Oct 1971), Russian pianist. Studied at the Ghessin Institute, Moscow from 1977 and played Beethoven sonatas in concert aged seven. Moscow PO concert debut 1983, with both Chopin concertos. Discovered by Karajan and played the Tchaikovsky First Concerto with the Berlin PO, 1987. British debut 1987, at the Lichfield Festival; London 1988, with the LSO. US debut with the New York PO under Mehta, 1990; Carnegie Hall recital with works by Prokofiev, Chopin, Schumann and Liszt. Further concerts with the Boston SO, Philadelphia Orchestra and Chicago SO. Salzburg debut recital 1993, returning 1994 with all-Chopin programme.

Kiss, The, *Hubička*, opera by Smetana (libretto by E Krásnohorská, based on a story by K Svetlá), produced Prague, 7 Nov 1876. Vendulka declines a kiss from widower Lukaš, for fear of offending the spirit of his dead wife. The pair are later united.

kit a diminutive violin, formerly used by dancing-masters, who on account of its small size and narrow shape were able to carry it in the long pockets of their tail-coats. Its French name is therefore *pochette* and its German *Taschengeige*.

kithara a plucked string instrument of ancient Greece. ◊lyre.

Kittel, Hermine (b Vienna, 2 Dec 1879; d Vienna, 7 Apr 1948), Austrian contralto. Debut Lwów 1897; studied further with Materna and sang in Vienna 1901–36, at first under Mahler (later appeared often as soloist in *Das Lied von der Erde*). Bayreuth 1908, Erda. Salzburg 1922–25 as Mozart's Marcellina.

Kittel, Kaspar (b Lauenstein, 1603; d Dresden, 9 Oct 1639), German lutenist, organist and composer. Studied under Schütz and 1624–28 in Italy at the expense of the Elector of Saxony. He taught theorbo at Dresden from 1630 and two years later became inspector of instruments. He wrote arias and cantatas in the style of Caccini.

Kittl, Johann Friedrich (b Vorlík, Bohemia, 8 May 1806; d Lissa, Poland, 20 Jul 1868), Bohemian composer. Pupil of Tomašek in Prague, where he gave a first concert in 1836. In 1843 he succeeded Dionys Weber as director of the Prague Conservatory.

Works include operas *Bianca und Giuseppe, oder Die Franzosen vor Nizza* (libretto by Wagner, originally written for himself, 1848), *Die Waldblume* (1852), and *Die Bilderstürmer* (1854); *Jagdsymphonie* for orchestra.

Kiurina, Berta (b Linz, 18 Feb 1882; d Vienna, 3 May 1933), Austrian soprano. Debut Linz 1904; Vienna Hofoper 1905–27, as Liù,

---

Evgeny Kissin – pianist

1 Berlioz: *Symphonie fantastique*
When I was very young we had a record of this music at home and I liked very much to listen to it: I think it was conducted by Gennady Rozhdestvensky. I haven't listened to it for a long time, but I remember it very well, and I still love the piece.

2 Chopin: Piano concertos nos. 1 and 2
Chopin has always been very important to me, extremely close to my heart. In fact I started with him when I played both his concertos in the Great Hall of the Moscow Conservatoire when I was 12.

3 Bach
What appeals to me about Bach's music is its universality. It is a beginning, and there is absolutely everything in it, like Pushkin in Russian poetry.

4 Prokofiev: Sonatas nos. 2, 4, 6 and 8
I love Prokofiev, and these sonatas are my favourites.

5 Scott Joplin: piano works
I like Scott Joplin's music very much; it has great character and a sense of humour. I play this music at home, and it's refreshing.

Desdemona, Nedda, Eva and Pfitzner's Ighino. Salzburg 1906 as Cherubino, under Mahler. Guest in Brno, Budapest and Buenos Aires and was admired in Schoenberg's *Gurrelieder*.

Kjerulf, Halfdan (b Christiania, 17 Sept 1815; d Grefsen, near Christiania, 11 Aug 1868), Norwegian composer. At his father's desire he studied law at Christiania University, but on the death of his father in 1840 he decided to devote himself to music. He taught, and pub. some songs, even before he had done much in the way of theoretical study. About 1850 he received a government grant to study at Leipzig for a year, and on his return he tried to establish classical subscription concerts, with little success. He became a friend of Björnson, who wrote many poems especially for him to set.

Works include choruses and quartets for male voices; piano pieces; over 100 songs.

Kk, abbr., Ralph ◊Kirkpatrick.

Klafsky, Katharina (b Szt János, 19 Sept 1855; d Hamburg, 22 Sept 1896), Hungarian mezzo, later soprano. Appeared in Leipzig, as Venus and Brangaene, and after performing with Angelo Neumann's touring co. was engaged at Hamburg; added roles in operas by Weber and Mozart to her repertory and in 1892 visited London with the Hamburg Co., under the direction of Mahler, sang Leonore, Agathe and Isolde at Drury Lane in 1894. She had a brief career in the USA.

Klagende Lied, Das, *The Song of Lamentation*, cantata by Mahler (text by composer) for soloists chorus and orchestra; first version 1880 in three parts: *Waldmärchen*, *Der Spielmann*, *Hochzeitstück*. Revised 1888 with part one omitted, fp Vienna, 17 Feb 1901, conductor Mahler; fp original version Vienna, 8 Apr 1935, conductor Arnold Rosé.

Klas, Eri (b Tallinn, 7 Jun 1939), Estonian conductor. Studied at the Tallinn Conservatory and conducted *West Side Story* at Tallinn Opera 1964 (director there 1975, having conducted at the Bolshoi from 1972). Music director Royal Opera Stockholm 1985–89 (*Don Giovanni* 1988). Chief conductor Aarhus SO 1990; guest from 1990 with Cleveland Orchestra, LA PO, and Dallas, Detroit and Baltimore SOs. Hamburg 1989, with the fp of Schnittke's ballet, *Peer Gynt*.

Klaviatur, German, = keyboard.

Klavier, German, = pianoforte (but ◊clavier).

Klavierübung (J S Bach.) ◊Clavierübung.

Klebe, Giselher (b Mannheim, 28 Jun 1925), German composer. Studied at the Berlin Conservatory with Kurt von Wohlfurt and later with Josef Rufer and Blacher. From 1946 to 1949 he worked for Berlin Radio. His music follows the traditions of Schoenberg and Webern.

Works include operas *Die Räuben* (after Schiller, 1957), *Die tödlichen Wünsche* (1959), *Alkmene* (1961), *Figaro lässt sich scheiden* (1963), *Jacobowsky und der Oberst* (1965), *Ein wahrer Held* (after Synge, 1975), *Das Mädchen aus Domrémy* (1976), *Des Rendez-vous* (1977), *Der jüngste Tag* (1980) and *Die Fastnachtsbeichte* (1983); *Con moto* for orchestra, five symphonies (1951–77), *Divertissement joyeux* for chamber orchestra, *Zwitschermaschine* for orchestra (after Paul Klee); concerto for violin, cello and orchestra(1954); concertos for cello, organ, clarinet and harpsichord (1957, 1980, 1985, 1988); ballet *Pas de trois*; *Geschichte der lustigen Musikanten* for tenor, chorus and five instruments; wind quintet, two sonatas for solo violin, viola sonata, three string quartets (1949, 1963, 1981); double bass sonata (1971).

Kleber, Leonhard (b ? Göppingen, *c* 1495; d Pforzheim, 4 Mar 1556), German composer and organist. He compiled a tablature, dated 1524, containing music by himself and others and arrangements by himself of vocal music.

Klee, Bernhard (b Schleiz, 19 Apr 1936), German conductor. Studied at the Cologne Conservatory and was assistant to Sawalisch at the opera house there; debut with *Die Zauberflöte*, 1960. Worked at opera houses in Salzburg, Oberhausen and Hanover, then music director at Lübeck, 1966–73. UK debut at Edinburgh 1969 (*Fliegende Holländer* with Hamburg Opera); CG 1972 (*Così fan Tutte*), US debut 1974, with the NY PO (later guest in San Francisco, Detroit, Chicago and Washington). Led *Figaro* at Salzburg (1976) and was chief conductor of the Hanover Radio SO 1976–79, and from 1991. Music director of

the Düsseldorf SO 1977–87 and chief guest with the BBC PO 1985–89 (Bruckner's Ninth at the 1991 Proms, London).

Kleiber, Carlos (b Berlin, 3 Jul 1930), German-born Argentine conductor, the son of Erich ◊Kleiber. He studied in Argentina and was advised against a career in music by his father; after early experience in Munich, Berlin and Zurich he was engaged at Stuttgart in 1966. Wider recognition came in 1974, when he conducted *Der Rosenkavalier* at CG, London, and *Tristan und Isolde* at Bayreuth. US debut San Francisco, 1977, *Otello*. He became an Austrian citizen in 1980. Conducted the Berlin PO 1982 and made NY Met. debut 1988, with *La bohème*. Recordings include *Der Freischütz* and *Tristan und Isolde*, with the Dresden Staatskapelle.

When there is no trouble in a theatre, I make it!
Erich Kleiber, quoted in Harewood,
The Tongs and the Bones, 1981

Kleiber, Erich (b Vienna, 5 Aug 1890; d Zurich, 27 Jan 1956), Austrian conductor. He became music director of the Staatsoper Berlin, 1923, (debut in *Fidelio*) after apprentice years in Darmstadt and Düsseldorf. He gave several important premieres, in particular that of *Wozzeck* (1925), of which he also conducted the first British stage performance (1952). He made his London concert debut in 1935, with the LSO, and in 1938 gave *Der Rosenkavalier* at CG; NY debut 1930. Differences with the Nazis over artistic policy obliged him to resign his Berlin post, and from 1937 to 1949 he was active in Buenos Aires, becoming an Argentine citizen in 1938. He returned to Europe in 1948, conducting the LPO, and in Florence, 1951, gave the first known performance of Haydn's last opera, *Orfeo ed Euridice*, with Maria Callas.

Kleider Machen Leute opera by Zemlinsky (libretto by L Feld after G Keller), produced Vienna, Volksoper, 2 Dec 1910). Nettchen and other villagers assume that travelling tailor Strapinski is a count. Nettchen falls in love with him, but her feelings remain unchanged after his lowly origins are revealed.

Klein, Peter (b Zündorf, 25 Jan 1907; d Vienna, 4 Oct 1992), German tenor. His early career was in Düsseldorf and Zurich, and from 1934 he was much admired in Hamburg and Vienna in such character roles as Mozart's Basilio, Monostatos and Pedrillo and Wagner's Mime; appeared as Mime at CG, London, until 1960. He sang the baritone role of Beckmesser at the Vienna Staatsoper in 1965.

Kleine Nachtmusik, Eine, German, = 'Little Serenade'; Mozart's own title for his serenade in G major for strings, K525, finished 10 Aug 1787.

Kleinknecht German family of musicians:

1. Johannes Kleinknecht (b Ulm, bap. 7 Dec 1676; and Ulm, buried 4 Jun 1751), violinist and organist. Studied in Venice, second organist of Ulm Cathedral from 1712.

2. Johann Wolfgang Kleinknecht (b Ulm 17 Apr 1715; d Ansbach, 20 Feb 1786), violinist and composer, son of 1. Entered the service of the court at Stuttgart in 1733, from 1738 to his death *Konzertmeister* at Bayreuth.

3. Jakob Friedrich Kleinknecht (b Ulm, bap. 8 Jun 1722; d Ansbach, 11 Aug 1794), flautist, violinist and composer, brother of 2. Entered the service of the court at Bayreuth in 1743, and rose to *Kapellmeister*.

Works include *Sinfonia concertata*, flute sonatas, trio sonatas.

4. Johann Stephan Kleinknecht (b Ulm, 17 Sept 1731; d Ansbach, after 1791), flautist, brother of 3. Toured as a flute virtuoso, entered the service of the court at Bayreuth in 1754.

Kleist, (Bernd) Heinrich (Wilhelm) von (1777–1811), German poet, novelist and dramatist. ◊Draeseke (*Penthesilea* overture); C ◊Goldmark (ditto); ◊Graener (*Prinz von Homburg*); ◊Joachim (commemoration overture); ◊Marschner (*Prinz von Homburg*); ◊Penthesilea (Schoeck); ◊Pfitzner (*Käthchen von Heilbronn*); ◊Prinz von Homburg (Henze); ◊Wagner-Régeny (*Zerbrochene Krug*); H ◊Wolf (*Penthesilea*).

Klemperer, Otto (b Breslau, 14 May 1885; d Zurich, 6 Jul 1973),

German conductor. He studied in Frankfurt, with James Kwast and Ivan Knorr, and in Berlin with Pfitzner. Debut Berlin 1906, *Orpheus in the Underworld*. On Mahler's recommendation was appointed to the German Theatre, Prague, in 1907; moved to Hamburg 1910 but was obliged to leave in 1912, following a scandalous liaison with the recently-married Elisabeth Schumann. After appointments in Barmen and Strasbourg, where he was Pfitzner's deputy, he became music director of the Cologne Opera in 1917; gave there the first German performance of *Káta Kabanová* and the fps of Zemlinsky's *Der Zwerg* and Schreker's *Irrelohe*. In 1927 was appointed director of the Kroll Opera, Berlin, with a brief to perform new works, and repertory pieces in an enlightened manner. Few major premieres were given by Klemperer in Berlin, but he led the first German performance of *Oedipus Rex*; *Erwartung* and *From the House of the Dead* were given by his deputies, Zemlinsky and Fritz Zweig.

After the 1931 closure of the Kroll, Klemperer moved to the State Opera, Berlin, and emigrated to the USA in 1933. His debut there had been in 1926, and until the war he led the orchestras of Philadelphia and NY; with the LA PO gave the 1938 fp of Schoenberg's arrangement of the Brahms G minor piano quartet. Illness restricted his wartime activity, but he worked at the Budapest Opera 1947–50. He conducted the Philharmonia, London, the following year; conductor for life 1964, when Walter Legge attempted to disband the orchestra. A manic-depressive all his life, Klemperer's earlier conducting style had been aggressive and hard-driven; in his London years he won renown for his massive, monumental performances of Mahler and the Viennese classics. In the early 1960s he led new productions of *Fidelio*, *Die Zauberflöte* and *Lohengrin* at CG. Retired to Switzerland in 1972. Among his compositions are six symphonies (from 1960) and nine string quartets.

Klenau, Paul von (b Copenhagen, 11 Feb 1883; d Copenhagen, 31 Aug 1946), Danish conductor and composer of German descent. Studied violin and composition, the latter with Malling, at Copenhagen, and after 1902 with Bruch in Berlin and Thuille in Munich. When appointed operatic conductor at Stuttgart in 1908 he studied further with Schillings. In 1914 he returned home and established the Philharmonic Society, at which he introduced many modern orchestral works; he also conducted orchestral and choral concerts in Vienna.

Works include operas *Sulamith* (1913), *Kjartan and Gudrun* (revised as *Gudrun in Iceland*, 1918), *The School for Scandal* (after Sheridan, 1927), *Michael Kohlhaas* (after Kleist), *Rembrandt van Rijn* (1937); ballet *Lille Ida's blomster* (after Andersen); seven symphonies (1908–41), three orchestral fantasies on Dante's *Inferno*, *Bank-Holiday Souvenir of Hampstead Heath* for orchestra; oratorio *Job*, *The Song of the Love and Death of Cornet Christof Rilke* for baritone solo, chorus and orchestra (1915); *Dialogues with Death* for contralto and orchestra, *Ebbe Skammalsen* for baritone and orchestra; string quartet in E minor; piano pieces.

Klengel, August (Alexander) (b Dresden, 29 Jun 1783; d Dresden, 22 Nov 1852), German organist and composer. Pupil of Clementi, with whom he travelled from 1803 onwards. He visited Russia, Paris and London, and in 1816 was appointed court organist at Dresden.

Works include two piano concertos; piano quintet; much piano music, including especially canons and fugues, etc.

Klengel, Julius (b Leipzig, 24 Sept 1859; d Leipzig, 27 Oct 1933), German cellist and composer. Studied cello with Emil Hegar and composition with Jadassohn, joined the Leipzig Gewandhaus orchestra at the age of 15, began to travel as virtuoso in 1875 and in 1881 became leading cellist in the orchestra and professor of cello at the Conservatory.

Works include four cello concertos, double concertos for violin and cello and two cellos, *Hymnus* for 12 cellos; *Caprice in form of a Chaconne* for cello solo, many cello pieces and studies.

Klenovsky, Nikolai Semenovich (b Odessa, 1853; d Petrograd, 6 Jul 1915), Russian composer and conductor. Studied at the Moscow Conservatory, Tchaikovsky being among his teachers; conducted the fp of the latter's *Eugene Onegin*; later conductor of the university orchestra and assistant conductor at the Imperial Opera. Collected and edited folksongs with Melgunov. Appointed director of the school of music at Tiflis, 1893, and assistant director of the Imperial Chapel at St Petersburg, 1902.

Works include several ballets; incidental music to Shakespeare's *Antony and Cleopatra* and other plays; *Georgian Liturgy* for uaccompanied chorus; cantatas.

Klenovsky, Paul, a name invented by Sir Henry Wood to shoulder his orchestral arrangement of Bach's D minor Toccata and Fugue.

Kletzki, Paul (b Łódz, 21 Mar 1900; d Liverpool, 5 Mar 1973), Polish conductor. Studied the violin and played in the Łódz PO. Later (1921–33) he studied and conducted in Berlin. From 1935 to 1938 he taught composition in Milan, while continuing as a conductor. Between 1958 and 1961 he was conductor of the Dallas SO. Suisse Romande Orchestra 1967–69.

Klien, Walter (b Graz, 27 Nov 1928; d Vienna, 9 Feb 1991), Austrian pianist who first appeared in public in 1951; American debut 1969. He recorded most of the piano music of Brahms, Schubert and Mozart and appeared as an accompanist to instrumentalists and singers.

Klimov, Valery (b Kiev, 16 Oct 1931), Russian violinist. Studied at Odessa and with David Oistrakh in Moscow. Debut with the Moscow PO 1957, winner of the Tchaikovsky Competition 1958. British debut 1967 at the Festival Hall. Concerts worldwide with leading conductors; plays concertos by Schnittke, Hindemith and Prokoviev in addition to the standard repertoire.

Klindworth, Karl (b Hanover, 25 Sept 1830; d Stolpe, 27 Jul 1916), German pianist and conductor. Pupil of Liszt; arranger of music for his instrument, including vocal scores of Wagner's works. He lived in London as pianist, conductor and teacher 1854–68, then became piano professor at the Moscow Conservatory, but returned to Germany in 1884 and opened a school of music in Berlin, 1893. His adopted daughter Winifred Williams (1897–1980) married Siegfried Wagner.

Klingsor, Tristan (Léon Leclère) (1874–1966), French poet. ◊Shéhérazade (Ravel).

Klobucar, Berislav (b Zagreb, 28 Aug 1924), Croatian conductor. Studied with Clemens Krauss at Salzburg and conducted at the Zagreb Opera (1943–51). Vienna Staatsoper from 1953, Bayreuth 1968–69 (*Die Meistersinger* and *Lohengrin*). NY Met. 1968, with *Der fliegende Holländer* and *Die Walküre*. Music director at Graz 1960–71, Royal Opera, Stockholm 1972–81. Principal conductor of Nice Opera 1983–89. Guest in Italy, France and elsewhere.

Klopstock, Friedrich (1724–1803), German poet. C P E ◊Bach (*Morgengesang am Schöpfungstage*); ◊Gluck (odes); ◊Lesueur (*Mort d'Adam*); ◊Meyerbeer (sacred cantatas); ◊Resurrection Symphony (Mahler); C ◊Schröter (songs); ◊Schwenke (odes); ◊Spohr (*Vater unser*); ◊Stadler (*Frühlingsfeier*); ◊Wolfram (*Grosse Hallelujah*). 13 songs by Schubert.

Klose, Margarete (b Berlin, 6 Aug 1902; d Berlin, 14 Dec 1968), German mezzo. Stage debut Ulm, 1927. Berlin 1929–56. Bayreuth 1936–42 as Fricka, Waltraute, Ortrud and Brangaene. London, CG, 1935–37. Other roles included Carmen, Adriano, the Kostelnička and Orpheus.

Kluge, Die, *The Clever Girl*, opera by Orff (libretto by composer, after Grimm), produced Frankfurt, 20 Feb 1943.

Kmentt, Waldemar (b Vienna, 2 Feb 1929), Austrian tenor. Debut Vienna 1950, in the Choral Symphony; opera debut at the Volksoper, as the Prince in *The Love for Three Oranges* (1951). Vienna Staatsoper from 1952, as Strauss's Emperor and Jacquino at the re-opening of the opera house in 1955. Salzburg Festival from 1955, as Mozart's Idamante, Ferrando and Tamino and in the fp of Cerha's *Baal* (1981).

Knaben Wunderhorn, Des, *The Youth's Magic Horn*, German anthology of old folk poetry. ◊Mahler (songs, nine with piano, 13 with orchestra); ◊Vrieslander (songs). The 13 *Knaben Wunderhorn* songs which Mahler scored for voice and orchestra, in 1900, are: 1) *Der Schildwache Nachtlied*; 2) *Verlor'ne Muh*; 3) *Trost im Unglück*; 4) *Wer hat dies Liedlein erdacht?*; 5) *Das irdische Leben*; 6) *Des Antonius von Padua Fischpredigt*; 7) *Rheinlegendchen*; 8) *Lied des Verfolgten in Turm*; 9) *Wo die schönen Trompeten blasen*; 10) *Lob* *des hohen Verstandes*; 11) *Es sungen drei Engel*; 12) *Urlicht*; 13) *Das himmlische Leben*.

Knappertsbusch, Hans (b Elberfeld, 12 Mar 1888; d Munich, 26 Oct 1965), German conductor. Studied at the Cologne Conservatory with Steinbach and Lohse (1909–12) and then took various positions as an opera conductor. In 1922 he became conductor at the Munich Staatsoper, where he remained until 1938, in which year he became director of the Vienna Staatsoper. In 1937 he made his Salzburg opera debut *Der Rosenkavalier*) and conducted his only opera in London (*Salome*, CG). Guest conductor VPO 1947–64. He was best known for his performances of Wagner, especially *Parsifal*, which he conducted at Bayreuth from 1951.

Knecht, Justin Heinrich (b Biberach, 30 Sept 1752; d Biberach, 1 Dec 1817), German organist and composer. Worked as organist and conductor in Biberach from 1771, and was vice-*Kapellmeister* in Stuttgart, 1806–08.

Works include a symphony entitled *Le Portrait musical de la nature* (*c* 1784) which has a programme similar to that of Beethoven's 'Pastoral' Symphony.

Kniegeige German = 'knee fiddle' = viola da gamba.

Knight, Gillian (b Redditch, 1 Nov 1939), English mezzo. Studied at RAM and sang with D'oyly Carte Opera 1959–64. SW/ENO from 1968, as Ragonde in *Le Comte Ory*, Juno (*Semele*) and Carmen. CG from 1970 as Erda, Herodias and Carmen, and in the fps of *Taverner* (1972) and *We Come to the River* (1976). Grimgerde in *Die Walküre*, 1994. US debut 1979, as Olga at Tanglewood; WNO 1979, as the nurse in *The Woman without a Shadow*.

Kniplová Naděžda (b Ostrava, 18 Apr 1932), Czech soprano. After study in Prague she sang in Brno; roles there included Libuše, the Kostelnička, Emilia Marty, Renata and Katerina Izmaylova. From 1965 she sang in Prague and in W Europe and the USA. Other roles include Aida, Tosca, Senta; Brünnhilde in a complete recording of Wagner's *Ring*.

Knöfel, Johann (b Lauban, Silesia, *c* 1530; d ? Prague, after 1592), German composer. He wrote church music and a collection, *Newe Teutsche Liedlein*, 1581.

Knorr, Iwan (b Mewe, W Prussia, 3 Jan 1853; d Frankfurt, 22 Jan 1916), German composer and teacher. Studied at the Leipzig Conservatory after having lived in small Russian towns 1857–68. He returned to Russia and became professor at Kharkov in 1874, but settled at Frankfurt in 1883, where he became director of the Hoch Conservatory 1908. He had a number of English pupils, including C Scott and H Balfour Gardiner.

Works include operas *Dunja* (1904), *Die Hochzeit* (1907) and *Durchs Fenster* (1908); symphonic fantasy for orchestra; piano quartets, variations on a theme by Schumann for piano trio; *Ukrainian Love-Songs* for vocal quartet and piano; piano works for two and four hands; songs.

knot the ornamental fretwork sound-hole of many flat-bellied string instruments and keyboard instruments, more generally called rose.

Knote, Heinrich (b Munich, 26 Nov 1870; d Garmisch, 15 Jan 1953), German tenor. Debut Munich 1892 in Lortzing's *Waffenschmied*; Lohengrin there in 1900. London, CG, 1901–13 as Siegfried, Walther and Tristan. NY Met. 1904–08 in Wagner repertory and as Manrico. Other roles included Rienzi and Goldmark's Assad.

Knot Garden, The opera by Tippett (libretto by composer), produced London, CG, 2 Dec 1970, conductor C Davis. Under the auspices of psychoanalyst Mangus, Faber and Thea overcome marital difficulties; gay couple Mel and Dov separate when Mel's lust is directed towards Thea's sister, Denise.

Knüpfer, Paul (b Halle, 21 Jun 1866; d Berlin, 4 Nov 1920), German bass. Studied at the Conservatory of Sondershausen and made his first stage appearance there in 1885. He sang at Bayreuth 1901–12 as Gurnemanz, Daland, Marke and Pogner, London from 1909 (first British Ochs), and was leading bass at the Berlin Opera, 1898–1920.

Knussen, Oliver (b Glasgow, 12 Jun 1952), English composer and conductor. He studied in US with Gunter Schuller. An eclectic and prolific composer, his works included the operas *Where the Wild*

Things Are and *Higglety Pigglety Pop* (1979–84; produced at Glyndebourne); three symphonies (1966–79); Concerto for Orchestra (1970); *Coursing* for chamber orchestra (1979); *Chiara* for orchestra (1986); *Hums and Songs of Winnie-the-Pooh* for soprano and ensemble (1970–83), *Trumpets*, for soprano and three clarinets (1975); *Late Poems and an Epigram of Rainer Maria Rilke* for soprano (1988), *Whitman Settings* for soprano and orchestra (1991); *Sonya's Lullaby* for piano (1978); *Variations* for piano (1989); *Songs Without Voices* for eight instruments (1992).

Knyvett English family of musicians:

1. Charles Knyvett (b ? London, 22 Feb 1752; and London, 19 Jan 1822), alto and organist. Appointed Gentleman of the Chapel Royal, 1786, and one of the organists, 1796. Established the Vocal Concerts with Samuel Harrison in 1791.

2. Charles Knyvett (b London, 1773; and London, 2 Nov 1859), organist, teacher and composer, son of 1. Pupil of Samuel Webbe. Appointed organist of St George's, Hanover Square, 1802, and pub. a *Selection of Psalm Tunes*, 1823.

3. William Knyvett (b London, 21 Apr 1779; and Ryde, 17 Nov 1856), alto and composer, brother of 2. Appointed Gentleman of the Chapel Royal, 1797, and composer to it in succession to Arnold, 1802. He sang and conducted much at concerts and festivals, and composed anthems, glees, songs.

4. Deborah Knyvett (born Travis; b Shaw nr Oldham; and London, 10 Feb 1876), singer, wife of 3. Studied under Greatorex and made her first appearance in 1815.

Koanga opera by Delius (libretto by C F Keary, based on G W Cable's novel *The Grandissimes*), produced Elberfeld, in Germany, 30 Mar 1904. Uncle Joe tells the story of Koanga, a slave-prince who falls in love with slave-girl Palmyra. Plantation owner Perez prevents the wedding. Koanga kills him and is himself captured and killed. Palmyra commits suicide.

Kobbé, Gustav (b New York, 4 Mar 1857; d Long Island, 27 Jul 1918), American writer on music. He studied at Wiesbaden and NY; visited 1882 Bayreuth Festival and pub. a two-volume biography of Wagner (1890). Also wrote *Loves of the Great Composers* (1905) and *Wagner and his Isolde* (1906). His *Complete Opera Book*, containing detailed synopses, was pub. 1919. Many reprints; ninth edition Lord Harewood, 1976, tenth edition 1986. Kobbé was killed in his yacht by a navy seaplane.

Koch, Erland von (b Stockholm, 26 Apr 1910), Swedish composer. Studied at the Stockholm Conservatory and later in London, Paris and Dresden.

Works include four symphonies (1938–53); symphonic poem *A Tale from the Wilderness*, *Symphonic Episode*, *Symphonic Dance*; three piano concertos (1936–72); violin concerto; suite for chamber orchestra; six string quartets (1934–63), string trio; violin and piano sonata; piano works; songs.

Köchel, Ludwig (Alois Friedrich) von, Ritter (b Stein, near Krems, 14 Jan 1800; d Vienna, 3 Jun 1877), Austrian naturalist and music bibliographer. He lived at Salzburg in 1850–63 for the purpose of compiling his thematic catalogue of Mozart's works, pub. in 1862 (sixth edition 1964).

Kocis, Zoltan (b Budapest, 30 May 1952), Hungarian pianist and composer. Studied in Budapest 1964–73 and made debut in 1970. Toured the USA 1971 and made London and Salzburg debuts 1972. Most often heard in Bach and Bartók (second concerto in London, 1988). Compositions include *Memento (Chernobyl '86)* for orchestra.

Koczwara ◊Kotzwara.

Kodály, Zoltán (b Kecskemét, 16 Dec 1882; d Budapest, 6 Mar 1967), Hungarian composer. Learnt the violin in his childhood, sang in a cathedral choir and tried to compose without systematic instruction. In 1900, after living in small provincial towns, he entered the University of Budapest to study science, but also became a pupil at the Conservatory. Studied Hungarian folksong and in 1906 wrote his university thesis on it; in the same year his *Summer Evening* was premiered in Budapest. He collected folksongs in collaboration with

Bartók, 1907–14. Appointed professor at the Conservatory and deputy director in 1919. His music was performed at the ISCM festivals from their inception in 1923. Beatrice Harrison gave London performances in 1924 of his finest chamber work, the sonata for solo cello, and further recognition on the international stage came with the premieres of the *Háry János* suite (1927) and the *Dances from Maurosszek* (1930). The popular *Psalmus Hungaricus* was performed in London and New York from 1927; Henry Wood programmed *Summer Evening* and *Dances from Galanta* at the London Prom concerts in 1930 and 1931. The *Variations on a Hungarian Folksong* (Peacock) was composed for the Concertgebouw Orchestra in 1939 and the *Concert for Orchestra* for the Chicago SO (1941). His final work for orchestra was the symphony in C 'In memoriam Arturo Toscanini', premiered at Lucerne under Ferenc Fricsay in 1961. In 1945 he became president of the newly founded Hungarian Arts Council, and in 1967 was awarded the Gold Medal of the Royal Philharmonic Society. Hon.D.Mus., Oxford, 1960.

Works include plays with music *Háry János* (1926) and *Székely Fonó* (1932).

ORCHESTRAL: *Summer Evening* (1906), *Ballet Music* and *Suite*, for *Háry János* (1925–27), *Theatre Overture*, *Dances of Galánta* (1933), *Marosszék Dances* (1930), *Variations on a Hungarian Folksong, The Peacock* (1939), Concerto for orchestra (1940), Symphony in C (1930s–61).

CHAMBER AND VOCAL: two string quartets (1909, 1918); duo for violin and cello (1914), serenade for two violins and viola; sonatas for cello solo (1915) and for cello and piano (1909); *Meditation on a motif by Debussy, Valsette*, nine pieces (op. 3), seven pieces (op. 11) for piano; 21 songs, *Enekszó* (16 songs on folk words); 57 folksong arrangements; 21 works for chorus with and without orchestra, including *Psalmus Hungaricus, Jesus and the Traders, Budavari Te Deum* (1936), *Bicinia Hungarica* (60 children's songs), *Missa brevis*.

There must be a strenuous attempt to replace music that comes from the fingers and the mechanical playing of instruments with music that comes from the soul and based on singing.
Zoltán Kodály, *Fifty-five Two-part Exercises*, 1954

Koechlin, Charles (b Paris, 27 Nov 1867; d Canadel, Var, 31 Dec 1950), French composer. Studied at the Paris Conservatory, finally under Fauré. He never appeared as an executive musician or held any official appointment, but devoted himself largely to composition and the writing of some theoretical books as well as studies of Debussy and Fauré. Other influences on his music were Ravel, Poulenc and Stravinsky.

Works include ballet *La Divine Vesprée* (1918); incidental music to Rolland's *14 Juillet* (with six others, 1936); two symphonies, orchestral cycles *La Forêt* and *Les Saisons, Seven Stars Symphony* (on film stars including Garbo, Dietrich and Chaplin)), *Les Bandar-Log* (after Kipling, 1939–40), and other orchestral works: *En Mer la nuit, Études antiques, Nuit de Walpurgis classique* (after Goethe), *Rapsodie sur des chansons françaises, Les Heures persanes, La Course de printemps* (after Kipling's *Jungle Book*, 1925–27); three *Chorals* for organ and orchestra, *Ballade* for piano and orchestra.

CHAMBER MUSIC: three string quartets, piano quintet, trio for flute, clarinet and bassoon, pieces for piano, violin and horn, suite for piano, viola and flute; sonatas for violin, viola, cello, flute, oboe, clarinet, bassoon and born, all with piano, sonata for two flutes; sonatinas, *Esquisses, Pastorales, Petites Pièces*, etc. for piano, suites and *Sonatines françaises* for piano duet and two pianos; choruses, songs.

Koffler, Józef (b Stryj, 28 Nov 1896; d Wieliczka, near Kraków, during a roundup of Jews, 1943), Polish composer. Studied composition with Grädener and musicology with Adler in Vienna, where he came under the influence of Schoenberg and began to cultivate the 12-note system; was the first Polish composer to do so. Later he became professor at the Lwów State Conservatory.

Works include ballet *Alles durch M.O.W.*; three symphonies (no. 3 performed London, 1938) and *Polish Suite* for orchestra, 15 variations for string orchestra; string quartet, string trio (performed Oxford, 1931), cantata *Die Liebe* for voices, viola, cello and clarinet; piano music, 40 *Polish Folksongs, Musique de ballet, Musique quasi una sonata*, sonatina, etc.; four poems for voice and piano.

Kogan, Leonid (b Dniepropetrovsk, 14 Nov 1924; d Mytishcha, 17 Dec 1982), Russian violinist. Studied first with his father and later with Abram Yampolsky at the Moscow Conservatory, graduating in 1948 and becoming a teacher there. In 1951 he won first prize at the international competition in Brussels. He was married to the sister of Emil Gilels, Elisabeth.

Kokkonen, Joonas (b Iisalmi, 13 Nov 1921), Finnish composer. He studied with Palmgren and Hannikainen at the Sibelius Academy, Helsinki; professor of composition there 1959–63. His early work was neo-classical in spirit; later influences have been Bach, Sibelius and Bartók.

Works include opera *Viimeiset Kiusauset/The Last Temptations*, produced Helsinki 1975, London 1979); five symphonies (1960–82), *Music for Strings* (1957), cello concerto (1969); *Missa a capella* (1963), Requiem (1983); piano trio (1948), three string quartets (1959, 1966, 1976), *Sinfonia da camera* for 12 strings (1962), ... *durch einen spiegel* for 12 strings and harpsichord (1977), *Improvvisazione* for violin and piano (1982), *Il Paesaggio* for chamber orchestra (1987).

Kokoschka, Oskar (1886–1980), German poet, playwright and painter. Hindemith (◊*Mörder, Hoffnung der Frauen*); Křenek (◊*Orpheus und Eurydike*).

Kolb, Barbara (b Hartford, 10 Feb 1939), American composer. Studied at Hartt College and with Foss and Schuller at the Berkshire Music Center. She has taught theory and composition in NY and has directed the Third Street Music School Settlement from 1979. Residency at IRCAM, Paris, 1983–84.

Works include *Trobar clus* for 13 instruments (1970); *Soundings for 11 instruments and tape* (1972); *Frailties* for tenor, tape and orchestra (1971); *Musique pour un vernissage* for ensemble (1977); *The Point that Divides the Wind* for organ and four percussionists (1981); *Millefoglie* for chamber orchestra (1988); *The Enchanted Loom* for orchestra (1989); *Voyants* for piano and chamber orchestra (1991); *Clouds* for organ, piano and tape (1992); *All in Good Time* for orchestra (1993).

Kolb, Carlmann (b Kösslarn, Lower Bavaria, bap. 29 Jan 1703;

A Selection of
Kodály

Summer Evening	1839
Duo for violin and cello	1914
Sonata for solo cello	1915
String Quartet no. 2	1918
Psalmus Hungaricus	1923
Háry János Suite	1927
Marrosszék Dances	1930
Dances of Galánta	1933
Variations on a Hungarian Folk Song	1938–9
Concerto for Orchestra	1940

d Munich, 15 Jan 1765), German priest, organist and composer. In 1729 was ordained priest and became organist of Ansbach Abbey, but later spent much of his time as music tutor to a noble hosuehold in Munich. Composed organ music for liturgical use.

kolenda, Polish, a type of Polish folksong (carol) sung at Christmas, some specimens dating back to the 13th c.

Köler, David (b Zwickau, *c* 1532; d Zwickau, 25 Jul 1565), German composer. After working at Altenburg and Güstrow in Mecklenburg, he was recalled to Zwickau to become cantor at St Mary's Church.

Works include ten psalms for four–six voices, Mass on a motet by Josquin des Prés, sacred songs.

There was a review by Irving Kolodin which noted that Korngold's Violin Concerto had more corn than gold.

Nicolas Slonimsky,
A Thing or Two About Music, 1948

Kolisch, Rudolf (b Klamm, Austria, 20 Jul 1896; d Watertown, MA, 1 Aug 1978), Austrian violinist. Studied at the Music Academy and the University in Vienna, graduating in 1913. He also studied the violin with Ševcik and composed with Schoenberg, who was his brother-in-law from 1924. In 1922 he founded the Kolisch quartet, who were especially well known for their performances of modern music; gave the fps of Berg's *Lyric Suite* (1927) and the last two string quartets of Schoenberg and Bartók. Disbanded 1941. In 1944 Kolisch became leader of the Pro Arte quartet. He taught at the University of Wisconsin until 1967.

Kollmann, August Friedrich Christoph (b Engelbostel, Hanover, 21 Mar 1756; d London, 19 Apr 1829), German organist, theorist and composer. Held a post at Lüne, near Lüneburg, but in 1782 went to London, where he was appointed sacristan and cantor of the German Chapel, St James's. Wrote many theoretical works, and also composed a piano concerto, chamber music.

Kollo, René (b Berlin, 20 Nov 1937), German tenor. Studied in Berlin, opera debut Brunswick, 1965. Bayreuth since 1969 as Lohengrin, Walther and Parsifal; Siegfried in the centenary *Ring*, 1976. London, CG, 1976 as Siegmund. He sang Walther at Salzburg in 1974 and Lohengrin on his NY Met. debut in 1976. Sang Siegfried at San Francisco 1990, Tannhäuser at the Deutsche Oper Berlin, 1995.

Kol Nidre, *All Vows*, work for cello and orchestra by Bruch, composed 1881. Also version for cello and piano.

Work by Schoenberg for speaker (rabbi), chorus and orchestra, op. 39; composed autumn 1938, fp LA, 4 Oct 1938, conductor Schoenberg.

kolo a Siberian dance in quick 2–4 time. The 15th of Dvorák's *Slavonic Dances* for piano duet is a kolo.

Koltai, Ralph (b Berlin, 31 Jul 1924), German-born English stage designer. Designed for the New Opera Company, London, including Schoenberg's *Erwartung* (1960) and Henze's *Boulevard Solitude* (1962). Work with SW/ENO has included *From the House of the Dead* (1965) and a *Ring* cycle (1970–73) wth striking use of bleak materials. CG 1972 and 1977, with the fps of *Taverner* and *The Ice Break*; Tippett's *Midsummer Marriage* for WNO, 1978, *Tristan und Isolde* for Scottish Opera (1973), *Tannhäuser* at Sydney and Geneva (1974 and 1986).

Kondracki, Michal (b Poltava, 4 Oct 1902), Polish composer. Studied with Szymanowski at Warsaw and with Dukas and Nadia Boulanger in Paris, returning to Poland in 1931.

Works include opera *Popieliny* (1934); ballet *Legend of Kraków* (1937); *Cantata ecclesiastica* and humorous cantata *Krasula*; orchestral works *Little Mountain Symphony*, symphonic action *Metropolis* (1929), toccata and fugue, symphonic picture *Soldiers march past*, *Match*, partita for small orchestra, nocturne for chamber orchestra; piano concerto.

Kondrashin, Kiril (b Moscow, 6 Mar 1914; d Amsterdam, 7 Mar 1981), Russian conductor. He conducted opera in Leningrad and

Moscow 1936–56 and was principal conductor Moscow PO 1960–75; assistant conductor Concertgebouw Orchestra from 1975. He recorded the Shostakovich symphony and gave the fps of no. 13 (1962) and the second violin concerto (1967). Conducted at Hollywood Bowl one month before his death.

Konetzni, Anny (b Ungarisch-Weisskirchen, 12 Feb 1902; d Vienna, 6 Sept 1969), Austrian soprano. She studied in Berlin and sang Adriano in Vienna in 1927. Berlin 1931–34; Hélène in the German fp of *Les vêpres Siciliennes*. She appeared at CG and at the NY Met. in the 1930s, and in 1935 sang Isolde at Salzburg. Other roles included Ortrud, Elektra, the Marschallin and Brünnhilde (CG 1951).

Konetzni, Hilde (b Vienna, 21 Mar 1905; d Vienna, 20 Apr 1980), Austrian soprano, sister of Anny ◊Konetzni. She studied in Prague and Vienna and sang in both centres in the 1930s. She sang Mařenka, Donna Elvira and Elisabeth at CG 1938–39, and after the war Leonore, Sieglinde and Gutrune. Sang at Salzburg from 1936 and in the USA 1937–39. Taught in Vienna from 1954.

König Hirsch, *The Stag King*, opera by Henze (libretto by H von Cramer after Gozzi's *Re Cervo*, 1762), produced Berlin, 23 Sept 1956. Revised as *Il Re Cervo* 1962 and produced Kassel, 10 Mar 1963. First staging of complete score in original version at Stuttgart, 5 May 1985. King Leandro assumes the shape of a stag and his treacherous chancellor, Tartaglia, magically transforms himself to the King's appearance, and orders a stag hunt. Tartaglia is killed by the assassin Coltellino, who, under contract from Tartaglia himself, believes him to be the King. All rejoice.

Königin von Saba, Die, *The Queen of Sheba*, opera by C Goldmark (libretto by S H Mosenthal), produced Vienna, Opera, 10 Mar 1875. King Solomon's diplomat Assad forsakes his fiancée Sulamith for a secret affair with the Queen of Sheba. Assad blasphemes publicly, placing the Queen above the gods; he is banished to the desert, where he is reconciled with Sulamith and dies.

Königskinder, *King's Children*, opera by Humperdinck (libretto by E Rosmer), produced as a play with accompanying music, Munich, 23 Jan 1897; the operatic version produced NY Met. 28 Dec 1910. Goose-girl escapes from the witch and is united with the King's son, but both are rejected by the townspeople, and die after eating the witch's poisoned bread.

Königsperger, Marianus (b Roding, Bavaria, 4 Dec 1708; d Prüfening, near Regensburg, 9 Oct 1769), German priest, organist and composer. He was educated and took his vows at the Benedictine abbey of Prüfening, where he was organist and choirmaster all his life.

Works include Masses, offertories, Litanies, etc.; symphonies and sonatas for various instruments with organ preludes, fugues and other works for organ.

König Stephan incidental music by Beethoven, op. 117, for Kotzebue's play written for the opening of the new theatre at Pest and performed there 9 Feb 1812.

Kontakte work by Stockhausen for piano, percussion and four-track tape (1959–60, fp Cologne, 11 Jun 1960).

Kontarsky, Aloys (b Iserlohn, 14 May 1931), German pianist. He studied at Cologne and Hamburg. Formed duo with his brother *Alfons* (b Iserlohn, 9 Oct 1932) in 1955 and gave many performances of modern works, including fps of duos by Berio, Bussotti, Kagel and B Zimmermann. In 1966 he gave the fp of Stockhausen's *Klavierstücke I–XI*. Has taught at Darmstadt from 1960.

Kontrapunkte work by Stockhausen for six wind instruments, piano, harp, violin and cello (1952–53, fp Cologne, 26 May 1953).

Konwitschny, Franz (b Fulnek, 14 Aug 1901; d Belgrade, 28 Jul 1962), German conductor. Studied in Leipzig and Brünn, playing violin and viola in various orchestras. His conducting career began at Stuttgart in 1926. He later conducted in many of the leading German opera houses and in 1959 conducted the *Ring* at Covent Garden. Chief conductor Leipzig Gewandhaus Orchestra from 1949.

Konya, Sandor (b Sarkad, 23 Sept 1923), Hungarian tenor. Debut Bielefeld, 1951, as Turiddu. Berlin Stadttheater, from 1955; created Leandro in Henze's *König Hirsch*, 1956. Bayreuth from 1958 as Lohengrin and Walther. San Francisco 1960–65; NY Met. 1961–74

Ton Koopman – harpsichordist

1   Bach: Mass in B minor – 'Agnus Dei' (sung by Alfred
    Deller)
    The most moving singing of baroque music I ever heard.

2   Paganini/Liszt: *La Campanella* (*The Art of Paderewski*,
    vol. 2)
    The way the piano was played in the past, happily available
    again on CD; you wish every modern pianist played like
    this.

3   Mozart: Songs (Schlick/Tini Mathot)
    As natural as music-making was when Mozart was alive.

4   *Vor-Bachisches Archiv* (Musica Antiqua Köln/Reinhard
    Göbel)
    Very personal but effective native way of performing Bach's
    predecessors.

5   Bach: *Die Kunst der Fuge* (Hesperion XX/Jordi Savall)
    Although I am convinced that Bach's *Art of Fugue* was
    written for harpsichord(s), Jordi Savall is such a great
    musician that he almost proves the contrary.

6   Bach: *Goldberg Variations* (Leonhardt or Kempff)
    Both different but genuine interpretations.

7   Schubert: Symphony no. 5 in B flat major (Royal
    Concertgebouw Orch./Harnoncourt)
    As nobody else, Harnoncourt can make a 'normal'
    symphony orchestra play and interpret a well-known work
    like this with such an 'authentic' sound.

8   Satie (played by Rienbert de Leeuw)
    If only all minor composers had such great defenders of their
    music.

---

as Lohengrin, Radames, Calaf, Pinkerton, Walther and Cavaradossi; 212 performances in 21 roles. London, CG, from 1963. Other roles included Rodolfo, Max and Parsifal.

Konzertmeister German = 'concert master'; the leader of an orchestra.

Konzertstück ◊Concertstück.

Koopman, Ton (b Zwolle, 2 Oct 1944), Dutch harpsichordist, organist and conductor. Studied in Amsterdam with Leonhardt. He has conducted Musica Antiqua and formed the Amsterdam Baroque Orchestra 1977; annual tours to Europe, Japan and the USA. Westminster Abbey concert 1989, to celebrate the tercentenary of William and Mary of Orange; Purcell's *King Arthur* at the Concertgebouw. Recordings include complete harpsichord works of Sweelinck and the Bach Orchestral Suites.

Korchmaryov, Klementy Arkadievich (b Verkhni Udinsk, 3 Jul 1899; d Moscow, 7 Apr 1958), Russian composer. Pupil of Malishevsky at the Odessa Conservatory.

Works include operas *Ivan the Soldier* and *Ten Days that Shook the World*; ballet *The Serf Ballerina* (1927); incidental music for plays; vocal symphony on his second opera; two piano sonatas.

Kord, Kazimierz (b Pogorze, 18 Nov 1930), Polish conductor. He studied at Leningrad and Kraków; Kraków Opera from 1962, Polish Radio Orchestra 1968–73. NY Met. 1972 (*Queen of Spades*), and has conducted opera in San Francisco and London (*Eugene Onegin* at CG, 1976); guest conductor with the Chicago SO and Cleveland Orchestra, and from 1977 artistic director National PO, Warsaw. Principal guest conductor Cincinnati SO 1980–82.

Korn, Peter (Jona) (b Berlin, 30 Mar 1920), German-born American composer and conductor. After studies with Rubbra in London, he moved to the USA in 1941, continuing his studies with Toch and Schoenberg. Founded and conducted the Los Angeles New Orchestra, 1948–56; director of the Strauss Conservatory at Munich from 1967.

Works include opera *Heidi* in Frankfurt (1963, fp 1978); three symphonies (1946, 1952, 1956), violin concerto (1965), *Beckmesser* variations for orchestra (1977), trumpet concerto (1979); two string quartets (1950, 1963), wind quintet (1964), piano trio (1975), octet (1976), duo for viola and piano (1978).

Korngold, Erich (Wolfgang (b Brno, 29 May 1897; d Hollywood, 29 Nov 1957), Austrian composer. Son of Julius ◊Korngold (1860–1945), music critic of the *Neue Freie Presse* in Vienna, thanks to whose influence he had his pantomime *Der Schneemann* (orchestrated by Zemlinsky) produced at the Court Opera at the age of 13. He studied with Fuchs, Grädener and Zemlinsky. Appointed conductor at the Hamburg Opera, 1919, and professor at the Vienna State Acad-

emy, 1927. After the *Anschluss* he emigrated to USA. Collaborated with Max Reinhardt at his Theatre School at Hollywood; successful as a writer of film music, without needing to alter his earlier style.

Works include operas *Der Ring des Polycrates*, *Violanta* (1916), *Die tote Stadt* (1920), *Das Wunder der Heliane* (1927), *Die Katrin* (1939); ballet-pantomime *Der Schneemann* (1910); incidental music to Shakespeare's *Much Ado about Nothing* (1919); film music *Sea Hawk*, *The Adventures of Robin Hood*, etc.

Symphonietta, symphony-overture, overture to a play; piano concerto for the left hand (1923); violin concerto (1946); string quartet, piano trio, piano quintet, sextet; violin and piano sonata; three piano sonatas and pieces; songs.

Košler, Zdènek (b Prague, 25 Mar 1928; d Prague, 2 July 1995), Czech conductor. Studied at Prague and made his debut at the National Theatre there 1951, *Il Barbiere di Siviglia*. Won the 1963 Mitropoulos Competition and was assistant to Bernstein at the New York PO, 1963–64. Artistic director of the Olomouc and Ostrava Operas, 1958–66. Vienna Staatsoper debut 1965, *Salome*. Music director of the Komische Oper Berlin, 1966–68; conducted the Czech PO 1971–80 and at the Prague National Theatre 1980–85, returning 1989–90. Conducted Martinů's *Greek Passion* in Paris, 1990.

Kossuth symphonic poem in ten tableaux by Bartók; composed 1903, fp Budapest, 13 Jan 1904.

Kostelanetz, André (b St Petersburg, 22 Dec 1901; d Port-au-Prince, Haiti, 13 Jan 1980), Russian-born American conductor. After study in Petrograd he emigrated to the USA; worked for CBS from 1930 as conductor and arranger. His versions of the popular classics, in the manner of film music, found favour in his adopted homeland; more serious work was commissioned from Schuman, Walton and Copland (Lincoln Portrait). He married Lily Pons in 1938.

koto Japanese musical instrument; a long zither of ancient Chinese origin, having 13 silk strings supported by movable bridges. It rest on the floor and the strings are plucked with ivory finger plectra, producing a brittle sound.

Kotter, Johannes (b Strasbourg, c 1480; d Berne, 1541), German organist and composer, a pupil of Hofhaimer. He compiled a tablature in the form of an instruction book in organ playing and composition. He worked in Fribourg (Switzerland) but was tortured and then dismissed because he was a Protestant.

Kotzebue, August (Friedrich Ferdinand) von (1761–1819), German playwright. ◊Generali (*Misantropia e pentimento*); Beethoven (◊*König Stephan*); ◊Lortzing (◊*Wildschütz*); ◊Reichardt (*Kreuzfahrer*); P ◊Ritter (*Eremit auf Formentara*); Beethoven (◊*Ruins of Athens*); ◊Salieri (*Hussiten vor Naumburg*); ◊Süssmayr (*Wildfang*); Schubert (◊*Teufels Lustschloss*); ◊Wranitzky (music for plays).

Kotzwara (Koczwara), Franz (František) (b Prague, 1730; d London, 2 Sept 1791), Bohemian composer. Settled in London in the 1780s, visited Ireland in 1788 and played in the King's Theatre Orchestra in London, 1790. He accidentally hanged himself while entertaining a prostitute.

Works include *The Battle of Prague* for piano with violin, cello and drums *ad lib*.

Koussevitzky, Sergey (b Tver, 26 Jul 1874; d Boston, MA, 4 Jun 1951), Russian-born American conductor. Studied in Moscow and became a double bass player in the Imperial Orchestra, later specialized as a soloist on the instrument and toured Europe. He then formed an orchestra of his own and took to conducting. In 1924 he was appointed conductor of the Boston SO; in 1931 he commissioned Stravinsky's *Symphony of Psalms* and in 1943 Bartók's Concerto for orchestra. Other works he premiered include the Mussorgsky/Ravel *Pictures* (1922), Prokofiev's first violin concerto and second symphony (1923, 1925) and Bernstein's second symphony (1949). The Koussevitsky Music Foundation, set up as a memorial to his wife, commissioned *Peter Grimes* (1945), among other works.

Ven my stick touches the air, you play.
Sergey Koussevitsky, quoted in Gattey,
Peacocks on the Podium, 1982

Kout, Jiri (b Novedvory, 26 Dec 1937), Czech conductor. Studied in Prague and conducted at the National Opera there; principal of the Deutsche Oper am Rhein, Düsseldorf, 1978–84; *Der Rosenkavalier* at Munich, 1985, debut with the Berlin PO 1987. Resident conductor at the Deutsche Oper, Berlin, leading *Lady Macbeth*, *Tristan*, *Mathis der Maler* and *Tannhäuser* (1992). Los Angeles from 1988, with *Káta Kabanova*, *Boris Godunov* and *Parsifal*; NY Met. debut 1991, *Der Rosenkavalier*. CG debut 1993, *Jenůfa*.

Kovacevich (formerly Bishop-Kovacevich), Stephen (b Los Angeles, 17 Oct 1940), American pianist and conductor of Yugoslav parentage. Debut San Francisco, 1951. Moved to London 1959 (studied with Myra Hess) and made British debut with Beethoven's Diabelli Variations; gave fp of R R Bennett's concerto, Birmingham, 1968. Often heard in Bartók, Mozart and Schubert. Conducted the LA PO at the Hollywood Bowl (1990) and in England has led the CBSO, BBC PO, RLPO and Chamber Orchestra of Europe. Annual appearances at the Aspen Festival, Colorado. Recordings include the Brahms concertos (LPO/Sawallisch) and the late Schubert and Beethoven sonatas.

Kovacic, Ernst (b Kapfenburg, 12 Apr 1943), Austrian violinist. Studied at the Vienna Academy and has premiered works by such local composers as Gruber, Helmut Eder and Kurt Schwerstik; also performs British concertos by Holloway, Osborne and Thomas Wilson (1993 Proms). Has guested throughout Europe and the USA; Salzburg 1979, in the fp of Cerha's concerto for violin and cello (also plays Tippett's triple concerto). Liverpool 1989, in the UK fp of Janáček's reconstructed violin concerto.

Kovařovic, Karel (b Prague, 9 Dec 1862; d Prague, 6 Dec 1920), Czech conductor and composer. Studied clarinet and harp at the Prague Conservatory, became an orchestral harpist in 1885 and then studied composition with Fibich. He toured as accompanist with the violinist Ondříček. Conductor at Brno and Plzeň, 1885–88, in 1895 conducted at the Ethnographic Exhibition in Prague, and 1900–20 chief conductor at the National Opera there. In 1916 he conducted Janáček's *Jenůfa*, with his own revisions.

Works include operas *The Peasants' Charter*, *At the Old Bleaching-House* (1901), comic operas *The Bridegrooms* (1884), *The Way through the Window* (1886), *The Night of Simon and Jude* (1892); ballets *Hashish* (1884) and *A Tale of Luck Found*; incidental music to Tyl's *Wood Nymph*, Čech's *The Excursions of Mr Brouček* and other plays; symphonic poem *The Rape of Persephone*, dramatic overture in C minor; piano concerto in F minor; three string quartets; choral pieces, songs.

Koven, (Henry Louis) Reginald de (b Middletown, CT, 3 Apr 1859; d Chicago, 16 Jan 1920), American composer. Graduated at Oxford in 1879 and then studied music on the Continent. He was music critic for several American papers.

Works include operas *The Begum*, *Robin Hood* (*Maid Marian*) and *Rob Roy* (both after Scott), *The Canterbury Pilgrims* (after Chaucer), *Rip van Winkle* (after Washington Irving), many operettas and ballets; orchestral works; piano sonata and pieces; *c* 400 songs, etc.

Kowalski, Jochen (b Wachow, Brandenburg, 30 Jan 1954), German countertenor. Studied in Berlin and made debut at Halle 1982, in Handel's *Mucio Scevola*. Komische Oper Berlin from 1983 and visiting CG 1989, as Orpheus; returned to London as Orlofsky, and Farnace in *Mitridate* (1990–91). Paris Opéra 1987, as Ptolemeo in *Giulio Cesare*; Salzburg Festival 1993, as Ottone in *L'Incoronazione di Poppea*.

Kozeluch (Kotzeluch, Koželuh), Leopold (b Welwarn 26 Jun 1747; d Vienna, 7 May 1818), Bohemian composer. Pupil of his cousin Johann Anton Kozeluch (1738–1814), studied law at Prague University, but devoted himself entirely to composition from 1771. Went to Vienna in 1778 and succeeded Mozart as Imperial composer in 1792.

Works include operas *Didone abbandonata*, *Judith*, *Deborah*, etc.; oratorio *Moisè in Egitto* (1787); 24 ballets and three pantomimes; 11 symphonies; 22 piano concertos and several for other instruments; six string quartets, 63 trios,; piano sonatas, folksong arrangements.

Kozub, Ernst (b Duisburg 1925; d Frankfurt, 27 Dec 1971), German tenor. Debut Berlin, Komische Oper, 1950, in *Czar und Zimmermann*. Frankfurt 1954–62. Hamburg from 1962; sang Hoffmann, Radames and Don José and was the Emperor in the first London performance of *Die Frau ohne Schatten* (SW, 1966). Milan 1963, as Siegmund and Siegfried.

Kraemer, Nicholas (b Edinburgh, 7 Mar 1945), Scottish conductor and harpsichordist. Was soloist with the Academy of St-Martin-in-the-Fields and in English Baroque Soloists. Founded the Raglan Baroque players 1978, and has been artistic director of the London Bach Orchestra from 1985. Operas by Handel in Amsterdam and Geneva, Rinaldo in Lisbon. Also conducts the Manchester Camerata (Mozart's Requiem), Prague and Polish chamber orchestras and the Northern Sinfonia. ENO debut 1992, *The Magic Flute*; Marseille 1993, with *Poppea*.

Kraft, Anton (b Rokitzan, near Plzeń, 30 Dec 1749; d Vienna, 28 Aug 1820), Bohemian cellist and composer. Originally intended for a career in law, he was engaged by Prince Esterházy as principal cellist in 1778, remaining till 1790 and receiving tuition in composition from Haydn. Subsequently in the service of Prince Grassalkovich and (from 1795) Prince Lobkowitz. Beethoven's Triple Concerto was composed for him, and he played in the fp of the seventh symphony (1813).

Works include concertos, sonatas, etc. for cello, duets for two cellos, etc. Haydn's D major cello concerto was once ascribed to Kraft.

Kraft, Nicolaus (b Eszterháza, 14 Dec 1778; d Stuttgart, 18 May 1853), Bohemian cellist and composer, son of Anton ◊Kraft. Pupil of his father, with whom he travelled. Settled in Vienna, 1790, and became chamber musician to Prince Lobkowitz in 1796; played in the Schuppanzigh Quartet from the same time. In 1801 he had further lessons with Duport in Berlin. In 1809 he became a member of the Vienna Court Orchestra, and in 1814 went to Stuttgart as a member first of the Court Opera and then of the Court Chapel.

Works include four cello concertos; *Scène pastorale* for cello and orchestra; fantasy for cello and string quartet; duets and divertissements for two cellos.

Kraft, William (b Chicago, 6 Sept 1923), American composer and timpanist. Studied at UCLA, then at Columbia 1949–52, with Henry Brant and Otto Luening. Founded and directed the Los Angeles percussion Ensemble, giving US fps of Stockhausen's *Zyklus* and Boulez's *Le Marteau sans Maître*. Principal with the LA PO 1955–81 and composer-in-residence 1981–85.

Works include *Concerto Grosso* (1961); Concerto for four

percussion and orchestra (1966); *Triangles* for percussion and ten instruments (1969); piano concerto (1973); timpani concerto (1983); *Weavings* for string quartet and percussion (1984); *Contextures II* for soprano, tenor and chamber orchestra (1984); *A Kennedy Portrait* for narrator and orchestra (1988); horn concerto (1988).

Krainev, Vladimir (Vsevolodovich) (b Krasnoyarsk, 1 Apr 1944), Russian pianist. Graduated the Moscow Conservatory 1967 and has given many concert tours of the USA, England, France, Germany and eastern Europe. Most often heard in Brahms, Prokofiev, Beethoven and Bartók. Was runner-up in the first Leeds International Competition (1963) and won the 1970 Tchaikovsky International Competition.

Krainik, Ardis (b Manitowoc, WI, 8 Mar 1929), American director and administrator. Studied at Northwestern University and sang sub-principal roles with the Chicago Lyric Opera 1954–59; became artistic administrator 1975, general director 1981. Has presided over recent productions of *Alceste* with Jessye Norman (1990), a *Ring* cycle conducted by Zubin Mehta, the first major US staging of Prokofiev's *The Gambler* (1991) and the premiere of Bolcom's *McTeague* (1992).

Krakowiak a Polish dance from the region of Kraków, sometimes introduced into ballets and ballrooms in the 19th c. under the name of *Cracovienne*. In its original form it was danced by all the assembled couples and sometimes words were sung to it. It is in quick 2–4 time. The best-known example is Chopin's concert rondo op. 14 (1828).

Krämerspiegel, *The Shopkeeper's Mirror*, cycle of 12 songs for voice and piano by Richard Strauss (texts by A Kerr); composed 1918 and includes ironic references to German publishers: no. 2 *Einst kam der Bock als Bote*, refers to Berlin pub. firm, Bote und Bock. Fp Berlin, 1 Nov 1926.

Krasner, Louis (b Cherkassy, 21 Jun 1903; d Brookline, MA, 4 May 1995), Russian-born American violinist. As a small child he was taken to the USA, studying at the New England Conservatory, and graduating in 1923. He then studied abroad, where his teachers included Flesch, Lucien Capet and Ševčik. After a period as leader of the Minneapolis SO, he became professor at Syracuse University He commissioned Berg's violin concerto, giving its fp (Barcelona, 1936) and also gave the fp of Schoenberg's violin concerto (Philadelphia, 1940).

Krásová, Marta (b Protivin, 16 Mar 1901; d Vráž, 20 Feb 1970), Czech mezzo. Debut Bratislava 1924, as Julia in Dvořák's *Jacobin*; joined the Prague Opera 1927 and sang there until 1966 as the Kostelnička, Eboli, Amneris and Carmen. She appeared as guest in Germany and France; sang Wagner in North America 1937–39. Edinburgh 1964, with Prague Co.

Kraus, Alfredo (b Las Palmas, 24 Sept 1927), Spanish tenor. Debut Cairo, 1956, as Duke of Mantua. La Scala, Milan, and CG from 1959. US debut Chicago 1962; NY Met. from 1966. Roles include Faust, Nemorino, Werther, Arturo and Don Ottavio. Returned to CG 1991–92, as Hoffmann and Nemorino.

Kraus, Ernst (b Erlangen, 8 Jun 1863; d Waldstadt, 6 Sept 1941), German tenor. Debut Mannheim 1893, as Tamino. He sang at Bayreuth 1899–1909 as Siegfried, Walther and Erik. NY Met. debut 1903, as Siegmund. In 1910 he was the first London Herod (*Salome*), under Beecham.

Kraus, Felix von (b Vienna, 3 Oct 1870; d Munich, 30 Oct 1937), Austrian bass. His early career was in concert. In 1899 he sang Hagen at Bayreuth; appeared there until 1909 as Gurnemanz, the Landgrave and Marke: London, CG, 1907. Taught in Munich 1908–25.

Kraus, Joseph Martin (b Miltenberg, near Mainz, 20 Jun 1756; d Stockholm, 15 Dec 1792), German-born Swedish composer. Studied law and philosophy at Mainz, Erfurt and Göttingen, also composed with Vogler. He went to Stockholm and remained there as theatre conductor, becoming music director in 1781. In 1782–87 he travelled widely with a grant from the King of Sweden. In 1788 he succeeded Uttini as *Kapellmeister*. His operas have recently been revived at the Drottningholm Theare, near Stockholm (*Proserpina*, 1981).

Works include operas *Soliman II*, *Aeneas at Carthage* (produced 1799), *Proserpina* (1781), church music; *Funeral Cantata for Gustavas III* (1792); symphonies and overtures; string quartets.

Kraus, Lili (b Budapest, 4 Mar 1903; d Asheville, NC, 6 Nov 1986), Hungarian pianist. Studied at the Budapest Academy under Kodály and Bartók. She taught in Vienna during the 1920s, after study with Schnabel, then toured widely in the classical repertory; continued her career in 1948 after wartime internment by the Japanese. She taught at Austin University, TX, from 1967 and retired in 1983. Also heard in recital with the violinist Szymon Goldberg.

Kraus, Otakar (b Prague, 10 Dec 1909; d London, 28 Jul 1980), Czech, later English baritone. Studied in Prague and later in Milan with Fernando Carpi, making his debut in Brno in 1935. He went to England in World War II, joining the EOG in 1946. He sang in the fps of Britten's *Rape of Lucretia*, Walton's *Troilus and Cressida* and Tippett's *Midsummer Marriage*, and also created the role of Nick Shadow in Stravinsky's *Rake's Progress* in 1951. A fine Wagner singer, he was especially noted for his Alberich.

Krause, Tom (b Helsinki, 5 Jul 1934), Finnish baritone. Debut Berlin 1958 as Escamillo. Hamburg from 1962; in 1964 created Jason in Krenek's *Der goldene Bock* and in 1968 the title role in Searle's *Hamlet*. He sang the Count in *Capriccio* on his Glyndebourne debut, in 1963, and Almaviva at the NY Met. in 1967. The following year he sang Don Giovanni at Salzburg. Other roles include Malatesta, Germont and Guglielmo. Salzburg Festival 1992, as Frère Bernard in Messiaen's *St François d'Assise*.

Krauss, Clemens (b Vienna, 31 Mar 1893; d Mexico City, 16 May 1954), Austrian conductor. Studied with Grädener and Heuberger at the Vienna Conservatory and from 1912 conducted at various provincial opera houses in Germany and Austria. In 1922 he became conductor at the Vienna Staatsoper and in 1924 Opera intendant and conductor of the Museum concerts at Frankfurt. In 1929–34 he was director of the Vienna and in 1934–36 of the Berlin Staatsoper, after which he directed the Opera at Munich. He was closely associated with Richard Strauss as conductor and in the case of *Capriccio*, as joint librettist; conducted the fps of *Arabella*, *Friedenstag* and *Die Liebe der Danae*. He married the singer Viorica Ursuleac (1894–1985).

Krauss, (Marie) Gabrielle (b Vienna, 24 Mar 1842; d Paris, 6 Jan 1906), Austrian soprano. Studied at the Vienna Conservatory and with Mathilde Marchesi; after singing at concerts she made her stage debut at the Vienna Opera in 1859 as Rossini's Mathilde, and in Paris, at the Théâtre des Italiens, in 1867; in 1875–88 she was a member of the Opéra almost continuously. Other roles included Norma, Lucia, Gilda, Elsa and Donna Anna.

Krebs, Helmut (b Dortmund, 8 Oct 1913), German tenor. His career began as a concert singer; stage debut Berlin (1938): from 1947 engaged at the Städtische Oper there. In 1953 he sang Belmonte and Idamante at Glyndebourne and the following year was Aron in the fp (concert) of Schoenberg's *Moses und Aron*, at Hamburg. Made guest appearances in Milan, London, Vienna and Munich and was well known in the passions and oratorios of Bach. Returned to the Deutsche Oper Berlin 1988, in *From the House of the Dead*. He recorded Stravinsky's Oedipus and Monteverdi's Orfeo.

Krebs, Johann Ludwig (b Buttelstedt, Thuringia, 10 Oct 1713; d Altenburg, 1 Jan 1780), German organist, harpsichordist and composer. Pupil of Bach at Leipzig from 1726, organist at Zwickau, Zeitz and Altenburg.

Works include Magnificat, settings of the Sanctus; trios; sonatas, suites, fugues, choruses, with variations, etc., for clavier; flute sonatas, organ music.

Krebs, Johann Tobias (b Heichelheim, 7 Jul 1690; d Buttstädt, 11 Feb 1762), German organist and composer, father of Johann Ludwig ◊Krebs. Pupil of Walther, later of Bach, appointed organist at Buttstädt in 1721. Composed organ music.

Krehbiel, Henry (Edward) (b Ann Arbor, MI, 10 Mar 1854; d New York, 20 Mar 1923), American music critic and author. After studying law at Cincinnati, he became music critic to the *Cincinnati Gazette*, 1874, and to the *NY Tribune*, 1880. He edited Thayer's life of

Beethoven, collected and wrote on African-American folksongs and wrote many books including studies of opera, of Wagner and of American musical life.

Kreidekreis, Der, *The Chalk Circle*, opera by Zemlinsky (libretto by composer after Klabund); 1932, produced Zurich, 14 Oct 1933. Zemlinsky's last completed opera. Prostitute Haitang becomes Empress of China after Prince Pao reveals he is the father of her child.

Kreisler, Fritz (b Vienna, 2 Feb 1875; d New York, 29 Jan 1962), Austrian-born American violinist and composer. Appeared as an infant prodigy at the age of seven. Studied at the Vienna Conservatory under Hellmesberger and J Auber, and at the Paris Conservatory under Massart and Delibes, winning the gold medal at the age of 12. After touring in USA in 1889 he returned to Austria to study medicine. After his military service and a period of intense study he reappeared as a soloist in Berlin in 1899 and again toured in USA. After three months' service in the Austrian army in 1914 he was discharged on account of wounds and returned to the USA, where he eventually made his home. He made frequent tours in Europe and gave the fp of Elgar's violin concerto (10 Nov 1910). He was best known for his broad-toned and emotionally committed performances of the Brahms and Beethoven concertos. His compositions include a string quartet and an operetta (*Apple Blossoms*, 1919), and a number of violin solos, some of which he at first tried to present as the work of 18th-c. composers.

Kreisler plays as the thrush sings in Thomas Hardy's poem, hardly conscious of his own lovely significance.

Neville Cardus, *The Delights of Music*, 1966

Kreisleriana a cycle of piano pieces by Schumann, op. 16, composed in 1838 and dedicated to Chopin. The title is borrowed from the musician Kreisler in E T A Hoffmann's stories *Fantasiestücke in Callots Manier*.

Kreissle von Hellborn, Heinrich (b Vienna, 19 Jan 1822; d Vienna, 6 Apr 1869), Austrian lawyer and state official, first biographer of Schubert, on whom he published *F Schubert: eine biographische Skizze*, 1861, and *Franz Schubert*, 1865.

Kreizberg, Jakov (b Leningrad, 24 Oct 1959), Russian-born conductor, brother of Semyon Bychkov. Studied first in Leningrad then moved to the USA and studied under Leinsdorf, Ozawa and Bernstein in Tanglewood. Won Stokowski Competition, NY 1986, and was music director at Krefeld Opera from 1988. Komische Oper Berlin 1992, with a revival of Goldschmidt's *Der gewaltige Hahnrei* (music director from 1994). Glyndebourne debut 1992 (*Jenůfa*), ENO 1994 (*Der Rosenkavalier*). Further operas in Lyon, Michigan and Toronto. Bournemouth SO from 1995.

Krejčí, Iša (b Prague, 10 Jul 1904; d Prague, 6 Mar 1968), Czech composer. Pupil of Novák and Jirák. After working for some time at Bratislava he returned to Prague and joined the radio service.

Works include opera *Confusion at Ephesus* (on Shakespeare's *Comedy of Errors*, 1946), operatic scene *Antigone* (after Sophocles, 1934), sinfonietta for orchestra; *Little Ballet* for chamber orchestra; string quartet in D major, nonet, trios for oboe, clarinet and bassoon and clarinet, double bass and piano; sonatina for clarinet and piano; songs.

Kremer, Gidon (b Riga, Latvia, 27 Feb 1947), Russian violinist. He studied with D Oistrakh at the Moscow Conservatory and won the 1970 Tchaikovsky Competition: international career in standard concertos and modern works. Often performs works by Schnittke. At London in May 1986 he played Bernstein's *Serenade*. Duo recitals with pianist Martha Argerich (Franck, Schumann, Bartók and Beethoven). Has played the Berg concerto under C Davis and gave Gubaidulina's *Offertorium* at the 1991 Prom concerts, London.

Kremer, Martin (b Geisenheim, 23 Mar 1898; d Prien, 19 Feb 1971), German tenor. He studied with Giuseppe Borgatti in Milan; Kassel 1924–27. At the Dresden Staatsoper he created three roles by Richard

Strauss: Matteo (*Arabella*, 1933), Henry (*Die schweigsame Frau*, 1935) and Leukippos (*Daphne*, 1938). Visited London with the Dresden co. 1936 and sang in Oslo during the German occupation. Well known as David.

Krenek, Ernst (b Vienna, 23 Aug 1900; d Palm Springs, CA, 23 Dec 1991), Austrian-born American composer. Pupil of Schreker in Vienna and Berlin. In the 1920s he appeared at several of the smaller festivals in Germany and 1925–27 was conductor at the operas of Kassel, Wiesbaden and other smaller towns in order to gain experience in operatic stagecraft. His first wife was Anna Mahler, the composer's daughter. After the success of the jazz-inspired *Jonny spielt auf* first produced at Leipzig in 1927, he later worked in 12-note music as a disciple of Schoenberg. In 1933, when the Nazi régime gained the upper hand, he settled in Vienna and worked on behalf of progressive Austrian composers, but was opposed by the Fascist party and his 12-tone opera *Karl V* was banned at the Vienna Staatsoper. He left Austria for the USA in 1937, where he later became Dean of the School of Fine Arts and director of the Music Dept. at Hamline University, St Paul, 1942–47; he lived in California from 1948. His book, *Über neue Musik*, is a defence of the 12-note system. Amends for his former hostile treatment in Vienna were made with the 1990 fp of his 1930 musical satire *Kehraus um St Stephan*. (A revision of *Karl V* had been given at Vienna in 1984.) Beleated recognition in his homeland was also shown with the 1988 Salzburg Festival premiere of his 1935 oratorio *Symeon der Stylit*.

Works include OPERAS: *Zwingburg* (1924) *Der Sprung über den Schatten* (1924), *Orpheus und Eurydike* (1926), *Jonny spielt auf* (1927), *Leben des Orest* (1930), *Karl V* (1938), *Tarquin* (1941), *Ausgerechnet und Verspielt* (1962), *Der goldene Bock* (1964), *Sardakai* (1970), also three one-act operas: *Der Diktator, Das geheime Königreich* and *Schwergewicht* (1928).

BALLETS: *Mammon, Der vertauschte Cupido* (after Rameau, 1925); incidental music to Shakespeare's *Midsummer Night's Dream*, Goethe's *Triumph der Empfindsamkeit* and Calderón's *La vida es sueño*.

CHORAL MUSIC: *The Seasons* (1925); *Symeon der Stylit* (1935, fp Salzburg, 1988); *Lamentatio Jeremiae Prophetae* (1941); *The Santa Fe Timetable* (1945); *Six Motets* after Kafka (1959); *German Proper for the Mass of Trinity Sunday* (1967); *Opus sine nomine*, oratorio (1989).

ORCHESTRAL: five symphonies (1921–50) and *Little Symphony*, two *Concerti grossi*, variations on *I wonder where I wander* for orchestra; *Symphonic Elegy* for strings, on the death of Webern (1946); four piano concertos (1923–50), two violin concertos (1924, 1954), cello concerto; theme and 13 variations for orchestra (1931), concerto for organ and strings (1979).

CHAMBER AND SOLO VOCAL: eight string quartets (1921–52); violin and piano sonata, sonata for solo viola; six piano sonatas; 25 songs, song cycles *Reisebuch aus den österreichischen Alpen, Fiedellieder, Gesänge des späten Jahres*.

EDITIONS: Monteverdi's *Poppea* (Vienna, 1937) and performing versions of the first and third movements of Mahler's tenth symphony (1924).

Krenn, Fritz (b Vienna, 11 Dec 1887; d Vienna, 17 Jul 1964), Austrian bass-baritone. He sang at the Vienna Volksoper in 1917 and at the Staatsoper 1919–50, with intervals. At the Kroll Opera, Berlin, he sang in the fp of Hindemith's *Neues vom Tage* (under Klemperer, 1929). At Salzburg he was heard as Ochs (1936) and repeated the role on his 1951 NY Met. debut.

Krenn, Werner (b Vienna, 21 Sept 1942), Austrian tenor. After an early career as a bassoonist he sang in *The Fairy Queen*, at Berlin in 1966. The following year he was heard in the Missa Solemnis at Salzburg, the first of many concerts under Karajan. Aix 1969, Ottavio. He recorded roles in operas by Berg and Shostakovich but was best known in Mozart: as Titus and in *Il rè Pastore, Ascanio in Alba* and *Idomeneo*.

Krenz, Jan (b Wioclawek, 14 Jul 1926), Polish conductor and composer. He studied in Łódz and worked at Poznán in orchestra and opera repertory from 1948. Chief conductor Polish Radio Orchestra from 1953; worldwide tours. Artistic director Warsaw Opera 1967–73. Music director, Bonn Opera 1979–83. Has conducted in England since 1961 (BBC SO). Works include *Nocturnes* for orchestra, *Capriccio* for 24 instruments, *Antisymphony* (1962). He made orchestral transcriptions of Bartók's *Mikrokosmos* and Szymonowski's *Myths*.

Kreusser, Georg Anton (b Heidingsfeld, 27 Oct 1746; d Aschaffenburg, 1 Nov 1810), German violinist and composer. Studied in France and Italy; entered the service of the court at Mainz in 1773, appointed *Konzertmeister* 1774.

Works include Passion oratorio *Der Tod Jesu* (Ramler, 1783); symphonies; chamber music.

Kreutzer, Conradin (b Messkirch, Baden, 22 Nov 1780; d Riga, 14 Dec 1849), German conductor and composer. He first learnt music as a choirboy, went to Freiburg i/B to study law, but gave it up for music, travelled in Switzerland as pianist and singer and in 1804 went to Vienna to study composition with Albrechtsberger. After conducting at the court of Stuttgart and Donaueschingen, he returned to Vienna and became conductor at the Kärntnertortheater for three periods between 1822 and 1840 and of the Josefstadttheater in 1833–40. Later he worked at Cologne and Paris, and again in Vienna.

Works include operas *Conradin von Schwaben* (1812), *Die Alpenhütte* (1815), *Libussa* (libretto by Grillparzer, 1822), *Melusine* (libretto ditto, 1833), *Das Nachtlager von Granada* (1834), *Cordelia* and *c* 25 others; incidental music to plays including Raimund's *Der Verschwender*; oratorio *Sending Moses* (1814); church music; chamber music; piano works; male-voice part-songs and songs.

Kreutzer, Rodolphe (b Versailles, 16 Nov 1766; d Geneva, 6 Jan 1831), French violinist and composer. He was taught mainly by his father and at the age of 16 was appointed by Marie Antoinette first violin in the royal chapel, where he learnt much from hearing Mestrino and Viotti. Later he became leader at the Théâtre Italien, where he began to write operas of his own. He toured much and became violin professor at the Paris Conservatory 1795. In 1798 he went to Vienna in the suite of Bernadotte and made friends with Beethoven. He often played violin duets with Rode, on whose departure to Russia in 1801 Kreutzer became leader at the Opéra, and later he held court appointments under both Napoleon I and Louis XVIII. He compiled a *Méthode de violon* with Baillot.

Works include operas *Jeanne d'Arc à Orléans* (1790), *Paul et Virginie* (after Saint-Pierre), *Lodoïska* (1791), *Imogène, ou La Gageure indiscrète* (after Boccaccio, 1796), *Astyanax, Aristippe* (1808), *La Mort d'Abel* (1810), *Mathilde* and many others; ballets *Paul et Virginie*, *Le Carnaval de Venise*, *Clari* and others; 19 violin concertos (1783–1810), four *Symphonies concertantes*; 15 string quartets; 15 trios; sonatas, caprices, studies, airs with variations for violin.

'Kreutzer' Sonata the nickname of Beethoven's A-major violin and piano sonata, op. 47, composed in 1803 and dedicated to R Kreutzer. The work is the subject of Tolstoy's novel *The Kreutzer Sonata*, in which it has a disastrous effect on the morals of the characters. Beethoven and George Bridgetower gave the fp on 17 May 1803.

Sub-title of Janáček's first string quartet, composed 1923–24, based on lost piano trio of 1908–09. Fp Prague, 17 Sept 1924.

Křička, Jaroslav (b Kelc, Moravia, 27 Aug 1882; d Prague, 23 Jan 1969), Czech composer. Studied at the Prague Conservatory, 1902–05, and came under the influence of Novák, enlarged his experience in Berlin, and then went to Russia, teaching at the music school of Ekaterinoslav. On his return to Prague in 1909 he became conductor of the Glagol choral society. Director of the Prague Conservatory, 1942–45.

Works include operas *Hypolita* (after one of Maurice Hewlett's *Little Novels of Italy*, 1916) and *The Gentleman in White* (after Wilde's *Canterville Ghost*, 1929); several operas for children; choral works *The Temptation in the Wilderness* (1922) and many others with and without orchestra; symphony in D minor, symphonic poems *Faith*, overture to Maeterlinck's *Blue Bird* (1911), *Polonaise* and

Elegy on the Death of Rimsky-Korsakov, *Children's Suite* for small orchestra (1907), *Nostalgia* for string orchestra; three string quartets (1907–39), violin and piano sonata; piano music and songs.

Krieger, (Johann) Philipp (b Nuremberg, 25 Feb 1649; d Weissenfels, 6 Feb 1725), German organist and composer, brother of Johann ◊Krieger. Travelled in Italy and studied under Rosenmüller at Venice; entered the service of the Duke of Saxe-Weissenfels, was chamber musician and organist at Halle from 1677 and music director at Weissenfels from 1712.

Works include opera *Der grossmütige Scipio* (1690) and others; plays with music; church music; arias for one–four voices with instruments; sonatas for violin and viola da gamba; *Partien* for wind instruments.

Krieger, Adam (b Driesen, Prussia, 7 Jan 1634; d Dresden, 30 Jun 1666), German organist, composer and poet. Pupil of Scheidt, organist of St Nicholas's Church at Leipzig and afterwards court organist at Dresden.

Works include cantatas and funeral songs, arias for voice and bass, songs for one–five voices and instruments, etc.

Krieger, Johann (b Nuremberg, 28 Dec 1651; d Zittau, 18 Jul 1735), German organist and composer. Pupil of his brother, Philipp ◊Krieger; court organist at Bayreuth, 1671–77, and later organist and town music director at Zittau.

Works include plays with music; sacred and secular songs for several voices with instruments; organ works; six partitas, preludes & fugues, for clavier.

Kringelborn, Solveig (b Oslo, 1965), Norwegian soprano. Studied in Stockholm and sang at the Royal Opera there as Susanna and Papagena. Oslo Opera 1990–91, as Mimi, Jenůfa and Micaela. Sang Mozart's Countess at LA (1993), Fiordiligi at Salzburg (1995) and Ilia at Geneva (1991). Premiere of Lutoslawski's *Chantefleurs et Chantefables* at the 1991 London Proms. Mahler's 4th at the 1994 Liverpool Cathedral Festival; Mozart's Countess, Salzburg 1995.

Krips, Josef (b Vienna, 8 Apr 1902; d Geneva, 13 Oct 1974), Austrian conductor. Studied in Vienna with Mandyczewski and Weingartner and became a violinist in the Volksoper there. In 1924 he began his career as a conductor and from 1926 to 1933 was general music director at Karlsruhe. In 1933 he became a conductor at the Vienna Staatsoper and in 1935 professor at the Vienna Academy of Music. Salzburg Festival debut 1935, *Der Rosenkavalier*; returned 1946, *Don Giovanni*. During World War II he lost these positions, but rejoined the Vienna Staatsoper in 1945; he took the company to CG in 1947, conducting Mozart's three Da Ponte operas; returned with the CG company 1963, *Don Giovanni*. From 1950 to 1954 he was conductor at the LSO; San Francisco SO 1963–70, NY Met. from 1967 (*Zauberflöte*).

Krombholc, Jaroslav (b Prague, 30 Jan 1918; d Prague, 16 Jul 1983), Czech conductor. Debut 1940, Prague National Theatre; chief conductor there 1968–75. 1973–78 conductor Prague Radio SO. Gave Czech opera widely in Europe, including the British fp of Janáček's *Excursions of Mr Brouček* (Edinburgh, 1970); ENO, London, 1978 (*Don Giovanni*).

Krommer, Franz (originally Kramář, František Vincenc) (b Kamenice, 27 Nov 1759; d Vienna, 8 Jan 1831), Moravian violinist, organist and composer. Having been an organist 1776–84, he went to Hungary and later became music director to Prince Grassalkovich in Vienna. In 1818 he succeeded Kozeluch as court music director.

Works include two Masses; music for wind band; symphonies; 69 string quartets and quintets.

Kronos Quartet American string quartet founded 1973 by leader David Harrington in Seattle and re-formed 1978 in San Francisco. NY debut 1984, with regular tours of Europe. Has given more than 400 fps of works by Cage, Riley, Reich, Carter, Rihm, Gubaidulina and Feldman among others. Also plays rock transcriptions in a virtuosic style. Further recent tours to Africa, South America and the Far East.

Krull, Annie (b Rostock, 12 Jan 1876; d Schwerin, 14 Jun 1947), German soprano. She sang at Dresden 1901–10 and created Strauss's

Diemut (*Feuersnot*), 1901, and Elektra (1909); Elektra under Beecham at CG, 1910. Later sang at Mannheim and Weimar as Elisabeth and Sieglinde.

Krumpholz, Johann Baptist (b Zlonice near Prague, 3 May 1742; d Paris, 19 Feb 1790), Bohemian-French harpist and composer. He grew up in Paris, travelled as a virtuoso, and was in the service of Prince Esterházy, 1773–76, receiving tuition in composition from Haydn. After further travels he settled in Paris, and was responsible for some notable improvements to his instrument. On the desertion of his wife with J L Dussek he drowned himself in the Seine.

Works include eight concertos, 32 sonatas for harp; two symphonies for harp and small orchestra; harp duets.

Krumpholz, Wenzel (b c 1750; d Vienna, 2 May 1817), Bohemian-French violinist, mandolin player and composer, brother of Johann Baptist ◊Krumpholz. He was a member of Prince Esterházy's orchestra under Haydn, and in 1796 entered the service of the court in Vienna. He was friendly with Beethoven, who wrote a mandolin sonata for him. Wrote violin music.

To my knowledge I am the only composer of my generation who has thoroughly and consistently practiced what is called 'serialism', and I have been blamed (a) for doing it at all, (b) for doing it too late, and (c) for still being at it.

Ernst Krenek, *Horizons Circled*, 1974

Kruszelnicka, Salomea (b Bilavyntsy, 23 Sept 1873; d Lwów, 16 Nov 1952), Russian soprano. Debut Lwów 1892; sang the *Forza* Leonora at Trieste in 1897 and Butterfly at Brescia in 1904. La Scala from 1907 as Isolde, Salome and Elektra and in the fps of Cilea's *Gloria* and Pizzetti's *Fedra* (1915). Buenos Aires 1906–13, Palermo 1911, as the *Götterdämmerung* Brünnhilde. Last stage appearance Naples 1920; concert tour USA 1927, for Ukranian emigrés.

Kubelík, Jan (b Michle, near Prague, 5 Jul 1880; d Prague, 5 Dec 1940), Czech violinist. He was taught by his father, a gardener and good music amateur, and made his first public appearance in Prague in 1888. In 1892 he entered the Conservatory as a pupil of Ševčik and began his real career with a concert in Vienna, 1898. London debut 1900; US from 1902. Retired 1940. Among his compositions are six violin concertos.

Kubelík, Rafael (b Bychory, near Kolín, 29 Jun 1914; d Kastanienbaum, Switzerland, 11 Aug 1996), Czech conductor and composer, son of Jan ◊Kubelík. Studied at the Prague Conservatory, making his debut with the Czech SO in 1934. From 1939 to 1941 he was conductor of the National Theatre in Brno and from 1942 to 1948 of the Czech PO. Between 1948 and 1950 he was much in England and in 1950 was appointed principal conductor of the Chicago SO. He returned to Europe in 1953 and became music director at CG, London (1955–58); conducted the first British *Jenůfa* there in 1956 and the first complete *Troyens* (1957). In 1961 he became conductor of the Bavarian Radio SO and in Vienna gave the fp of Schoenberg's oratorio *Die Jakobsleiter*. NY Met. debut 1973 (*Les Troyens*). Returned to Czechoslovakia 1990, after its liberation from Russia, and conducted Smetana's *Ma Vlást* to wide acclaim. His works include the operas *Veronika* (1947) and *Cornelia Faroli* (on the life of Titian, 1972), a choral symphony, concertos for violin and cello, a Requiem and some chamber music.

Kubik, Gail (b Coffeyville, OK, 5 Sept 1914; d Covina, CA, 20 Jul 1984), American violinist and composer. Studied at the Eastman School of Music, Rochester, NY, and gained several composition prizes.

Works include ballet *Frankie and Johnnie* for dance band and folksinger (1946); *In Praise of Johnny Appleseed* (Vachel Lindsay) for baritone, chorus and orchestra; three symphonies (1949–57); suite for orchestra; two violin concertos, *American Caprice* for piano and 32 instruments; two *Sketches* for string quartet, piano trio, wind quintet, *Trivialities* for flute, horn and string quartet.

Kuebler, David (b Detroit, 23 Jul 1947), American tenor. Sang with Santa Fe Opera from 1972; Berne 1974, as Tamino. Mozart and bel canto roles with Cologne Opera; Ferrando at Glyndebourne, 1976 (returned as Flamand and Matteo, 1987–90). NY Met. from 1979. Bayreuth 1980–82, as the Steersman. Bregenz Festival 1992, as the Berlioz Faust.

Kugelmann, Hans (b ? Augsburg, c 1495; d Königsberg, summer 1542), German trumpeter and composer. He was trumpeter in the service of the Emperor Maximilian at Innsbruck in 1519 and afterwards at the ducal court of Königsberg, where he became music director. In 1540 he pub. a Lutheran service book, containing a Mass, a Magnificat and hymns, some composed by himself.

Kuhlau, (Daniel) Frederik (Rudolph) (b Ülzen, Hanover, 11 Sept 1786; d Copenhagen, 12 Mar 1832), Danish composer of German origin. A child of poor parents, he picked up musical knowledge at Brunswick and Hamburg. During the French occupation he went to Denmark to escape conscription and became flautist in the court orchestra at Copenhagen. In 1825 he visited Vienna and met Beethoven, who composed a punning canon on his name.

Works include operas *Røverborgen* (1814), *Trylleharpen* (1817); *Lulu* (1824) and several others; incidental music for Heiberg's *Elverhøj* (1828); piano works; flute pieces.

Kuhlmann, Kathleen (b San Francisco, 7 Dec 1950), American mezzo. She studied in Chicago and first sang at the Lyric Opera there in 1979. In 1980 she sang Meg Page at La Scala, Milan, and in 1982 Charlotte and Rosina in Cologne and Ino and Juno in *Semele* at CG. The following year sang Cenerentola at Glyndebourne and in 1985 Penelope in the fp of Henze's reconstruction of Monteverdi's *Il Ritorno di Ulisse*, at Salzburg. Returned to CG in 1986 as Rosina, 1991–92 as Carmen, and Bradamante in *Alcina*. San Francisco 1992, in Rossini's *Ermione*.

Kuhn, Gustav (b Turrach, near Salzburg, 28 Aug 1947), Austrian conductor. Studied with Swarowsky and Karajan in Vienna, Turkish State Opera 1970–73, debut with *Fidelio*. Principal at the Netherlands Opera 1974–75, Dortmund 1975–77. Vienna Staatsoper from 1977, debut with Elektra. Glyndebourne 1980 (*Die Entführung*), CG 1981 (*Don Giovanni*). Music director at Bern Opera 1979–83, Bonn Opera 1982–85; US debut Chicago, 1981. Artistic director of Rome Opera 1986, and revived Rossini's *Ermione* at Pesaro, 1987. Conducted *Don Carlos* at the Verona Arena, 1992.

Kuhnau, Johann (b Geising, Saxony, 6 Apr 1660; d Leipzig, 5 Jun 1722), German organist, harpsichordist, composer and writer on music. Cantor at Zittau, went to Leipzig in 1682; became organist at St.Thomas's Church in 1684, music director of the university and the churches of St Nicholas and St Thomas in 1700, and cantor of St Thomas's in 1701, in which post he preceded Bach. His biblical sonatas for harpsichord are early examples of programme music.

Other works include motets on hymn-tunes and other church music; partitas and other pieces for harpsichord, including seven sonatas entitled *Frische Clavier-Früchte*, and the six sonatas *Biblische Historien* (1700).

Kühnel, August (b Delmenhorst, 3 Aug 1645; d c 1700), German viola da gamba player and composer. He was in the court chapel of Zeitz, 1661–81, visited France in 1665 to study the players there, played at various German courts on his return, visited London in 1685 and was subsequently *Kapellmeister* at the court of Kassel. He wrote sonatas for his instrument.

Kuijken, Sigiswald (b Dilbeck, near Brussels, 16 Feb 1944), Belgian conductor and violinist. He studied at the Brussels Conservatory; has taught Baroque violin at Hague Conservatory since 1971. Co-founder of La Petite Bande, 1971; performances of Handel, Rameau, Haydn and Bach. His ensemble The Age of Enlightenment gave its first London concert in 1986. He co-directed the 'Towards Bach' series at the South Bank, London, 1989, and conducted Haydn's *L'Infideltà delusa* at Antwerp, 1990. Founded the Kuijken string quartet, 1986.

His brothers are **Wieland Kuijken** (1938–), a cellist and viola da gamba player, and **Barthold Kuijken** (1949–) a flautist and recorder player.

Kulenkampff, Georg (b Bremen, 23 Jul 1898; d Schaffhausen, 4 Oct 1948), German violinist. He studied in Berlin and taught there from 1923. Leader Bremen PO 1916, followed by a distinguished career as a soloist. He recorded the Beethoven concerto, and partnered Georg Solti in recordings of the sonatas. His memoirs were published posthumously.

Kulka, Janos (b Budapest, 11 Dec 1929), Hungarian conductor. Conducted at the Budapest Opera 1953–56. Bavarian State Opera 1957–59, principal at the Hamburg Opera 1961–64. Music director at Wuppertal 1964–75; chief conductor at Stuttgart State Oprea from 1976; Nordwestdeutsche Philharmonie, 1976–87. US debut Boston, 1969. Premieres include Boehmer's *Doktor Faust* (Paris Opéra, 1985).

Kullak, Theodor (b Krotoschin, Posen, 12 Sept 1818; d Berlin, 1 Mar 1882), German pianist and composer. He was intended for a career in law and at some time studied medicine, but in 1842 decided definitely in favour of music and went to Vienna to finish his piano studies with Czerny. In 1846 he became court pianist to the King of Prussia and settled in Berlin, founding a Conservatory with Stern and Marx there, 1850, and one of his own in 1855.

Works include piano concerto in C minor; piano trio; duets for piano and violin; a vast number of piano pieces, studies.

Kullervo symphonic poem by Sibelius for soloists, chorus and orchestra, based on legends from the *Kalevala*. Withdrawn after its fp in Helsinki on 28 Apr 1892 and not heard again until after Sibelius' death in 1957.

Opera in two acts by Sallinen (libretto by composer, after A Kivi), produced Los Angeles, Music Center, 25 Feb 1992. Raised in violence and alienation, Kullervo commits violence on all around him, before his own suicide.

Kullman, Charles (b New Haven, CT, 13 Jan 1903; d New Haven, 8 Feb 1983), American tenor. He studied in NY and in 1931 sang Pinkerton under Klemperer at the Kroll Opera, Berlin; Staatsoper 1932–35; London, CG, 1934–38. Salzburg 1934–36 as Ferrando, Belmonte and Walther. NY Met. 1935–60 as Faust, Fenton, Tamino, Tannhäuser and Parsifal. Took part in Walter's 1936 recording of *Das Lied von der Erde*.

Kunst der Fuge, Die, *The Art of Fugue*, Bach's last work, left unfinished at his death in 1750. A series of examples of the art of fugal and canonic writing, all based on the same theme. ◊Per Arsin et Thesin.

Kunz, Erich (b Vienna, 20 May 1909; d Vienna, 8 Sept 1995), Austrian bass-baritone. Studied in Vienna and made his debut in 1933 in Breslau. He sang in the Glyndebourne chorus in 1935, returned 1948 as Guglielmo. Salzburg Festival from 1942 (debut as Mozart's Figaro). Vienna from 1940; sang Beckmesser at Bayreuth in 1943. CG debut 1947, as Leporello with Vienna State Co.; NY Met. debut 1952, as Leporello. He was one of the finest *buffo* baritones of the day, Mozart's Figaro and Papageno being among his most famous roles.

Kunzen, Friedrich Ludwig Aemilius (b Lübeck, 24 Sept 1761; d Copenhagen, 28 Jan 1817), German conductor and composer. Pupil of his father, Adolph Karl Kunzen (1720–81). Having given up legal studies, he went to the Copenhagen Opera, where he produced his first work. After a period in Berlin, where he edited a music journal with Reichardt, he went as conductor to Frankfurt, 1792, and Prague, 1794, producing his only German opera at the former city. He returned to Copenhagen 1795 as director of the Opera.

Works include operas *Holger Danske* (1789), *Ossians Harfe*, *Hemmeligheden* (1796), *Dragedukken* (1797), *Erik Ejegod* (1798), *Min Bedstemoder, Kærlighed paa Landet, Stormen* (on *The Tempest*).

Kupfer, Harry (b Berlin, 12 Aug 1935), German stage director. Debut with *Russalka* at Halle, 1958. Worked at various East German opera houses 1958–70, then directed *Die Frau ohne Schatten* at the Berlin Staatsoper, 1971. Chief producer at the Dresden State Opera 1971–81, Komische Oper, Berlin from 1981 (revival of Goldschmidt's *Der gewaltige Hahnrei*, 1992). Bayreuth Festival 1978, *Der fliegende Holländer; Ring* 1988, with laser-directed perspectives). *Elektra* for WNO 1978, *Pelléas et Mélisande* at ENO 1981. Komische

Oper *Orfeo* seen at CG 1989 and returned to stage Gluck's opera 1991 (*La Damnation de Faust*, 1993). Staged and co-wrote the libretto for Penderecki's *Die schwarze Maske*, Salzburg 1986. He is at the forefront of technology; his *Parsifal* at the Berlin Staatsoper (1992) replaced the Flowermaidens with TV monitors.

Kupferman, Meyer (b New York, 3 Jul 1926), American composer and clarinettist. Debut as soloist NY 1946. Teacher at Sarah Lawrence College from 1951. Music derives from jazz, electronics and serialism.

Works include six operas, including *In a Garden* (1949) and *Doctor Faustus Lights the Lights* (1953), both after Gertrude Stein; two piano concertos (1948, 1978); 11 symphonies (1950–83); concerto for cello and jazz band (1962); violin and clarinet concertos (1976, 1984); *Savage Landscape* for orchestra (1989); five string quartets; *Sound Phantoms*, ten pieces for chamber ensemble, no. 10 1981; *Top Brass Five* for five trumpets (1989); *Wicked Combinations*, song cycle for mezzo and piano (1989); *A Crucible for the Moon* for soprano, alto saxophone and percussion orchestra (1986).

Kupper, Annelies (b Glatz, 21 Aug 1906; d Munich, 8 Dec 1987), German soprano. Debut Breslau 1935. Hamburg 1940–46. Bayreuth 1944, Eva. Munich 1946–61. Sang in *The Rape of Lucretia* at Salzburg in 1950 and in 1952 the title role in the first official production of Strauss's *Die Liebe der Danae*. Other roles included Elsa, Senta and Chrysothemis (CG 1953).

Kurt, Melanie (b Vienna, 8 Jan 1880; d New York, 11 Mar 1941), Austrian soprano. Debut Lübeck, 1902, Leonore. Sang in Brunswick and Berlin 1905–14. CG 1910–14 as Brünnhilde, and Kundry in the first London stage performance of *Parsifal*. NY Met. 1915–17 as Isolde, Pamina and Gluck's Taurean Iphigénie.

Kurtág, György (b Lugoj, Rumania, 19 Feb 1926), Hungarian composer. He studied in Budapest and Paris; early influences were Bartók and Kodály, later employed a post-Webern serial technique, in which mosaics of sound are used to build a larger compositional picture.

Works include string quartet (1959); eight Duets for violin and cimbalom (1961); *In Memory of a Winter Sunset*, for soprano, violin and cimbalom (1969), string quintet (1971); *Splinters*, for solo cimbalom (1975); *Homage to Luigi Nono*, for chamber ensemble (1980); *Messages of the Late Miss R V Troussova* for soprano and chamber ensemble (1980); *Scenes from a Novel* for soprano and ensemble (1981); *Attila-Jószef Fragments* for soprano (1981); *Kafka Fragmente* for soprano and violin (1986); *Requiem for the Beloved* for soprano and piano (1987); *Officium Breve* for string quartet (1989); Double concerto for piano, cello and two chamber ensembles (1990); *Samuel Beckett: What is the Word* for alto voices and ensemble.

Kurtz, Efrem (b St Petersburg, 1 Nov 1900; d 27 Jun 1995), Russian-born American conductor. Led the Berlin PO from 1921, Stuttgart PO 1924–33 (also conducted ballet). US orchestras from 1933; Kansas City PO 1943–48, Houston SO 1948–54. Guest conductor in Russia, 1966.

Kurz, Selma (b Bielitz, Silesia, 15 Oct 1874; d Vienna, 10 May 1933), Austrian coloratura soprano. Studied with Pless, making her debut at the Frankfurt opera. In 1899 Mahler engaged her at the Vienna Hofoper and she remained with that co. until 1926; her roles included Tosca, Eva, Sieglinde, Oscar and Violetta. She first sang in London in 1904 as Gilda. In 1916 she sang Zerbinetta in the revision of *Ariadne auf Naxos*.

Kurzwellen, *Shortwaves*, work by Stockhausen for electronics and four short-wave radios; fp Bremen, 5 May 1968. Developed as *Beethausen, opus 1970, von Stockhoven*.

Kusche, Benno (b Freiburg i/B, 30 Jan 1916), German bass-baritone. Debut Koblenz, 1938, as Renato. Sang in Augsburg during war, Munich from 1946; London, CG, 1953 as La Roche in the first British performance of *Capriccio*. He sang Beckmesser on his NY Met. debut, in 1971.

Kusnetzova, Maria (b Odessa, 1880; d Paris, 26 Apr 1966), Russian soprano and dancer. St Petersburg, Maryinsky Theatre, 1905–13 as Tatyana, Oxana, Juliette; created Rimsky-Korsakov's Fevronia (*Kitezh*, 1907). London, CG, 1909–10 as Mimi and Marguerite.

Danced Potiphar's Wife in the fp of Strauss's ballet *Josephslegende*, Paris 1914.

Kusser (or Cousser), Johann Sigismund (b Pressburg = Pozsony, 13 Feb 1660; d Dublin, Nov 1727), German conductor and composer. Pupil of Lully in Paris, where he lived 1674–82. He was one of the directors of the Hamburg Opera 1694–96, and *Kapellmeister* at Stuttgart 1700–04. He went to London 1705, and later to Dublin, where he became director of music to the viceroy.

Works include operas *Erindo* (1694), *Porus, Pyramus and Thisbe* (1694), *Scipio Africanus*, *Jason and Ariadne* (1692); serenade for the king's birthday; ode on the death of Arabella Hunt; suites (with overtures) for strings; collection of opera overtures and airs.

kutchka, Russian, = 'handful'; short for *mogutchaya kutchka* = 'the mighty handful'; the group of five Russian composers who under the leadership of Balakirev began a conscious campaign in favour of nationalist music based on folk music; as opposed to the more Western-oriented composers also active in Russia at the time. The other members of the group were Borodin, Cui, Mussorgsky and Rimsky-Korsakov.

tra; cantata for baritone solo, chorus and orchestra; six string quartets, piano quintet, piano trio; two violin and piano sonatas, cello and piano sonata; piano sonata and pieces; songs, etc.

Kwella, Patrizia (b Mansfield, 26 Apr 1953), British soprano of Polish-Italian parentage. She studied at the RCM and appeared with John Eliot Gardiner at the 1979 Promenade concerts; later sang with Richard Hickox, Christopher Hogwood and Trevor Pinnock. Much valued for her Handel (as Esther and in *Alcina*, *L'Allegro* and *La Resurrezione*), Bach (B minor Mass) and Monteverdi (*Orfeo*). US debut San Diego 1983. At the 1985 Aldeburgh Festival she sang in the fp of *Night's Mask*, by Colin Matthews, Handel's *Alcina* at the 1985 Spitalfields and Cheltenham Festivals.

Kynaston, Nicolas (b Morebath, Devon, 10 Dec 1941), English organist. He studied with Fernando Germani and Ralph Downes; Westminster Cathedral 1960–71. Solo debut London 1966; toured USA 1974. Well-known interpreter of Franck, Messiaen and Reger.

Kyrie, Greek, *Kyrie eleison*, = 'Lord, have mercy'; the first item of the Ordinary of the Mass. Originally it was not part of the Mass but of

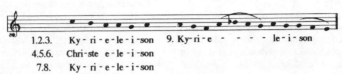

1.2.3.   Ky - ri - e - le - i - son   9. Ky - ri - e - - - - le - i - son
4.5.6.   Chri - ste - e - le - i - son
7.8.   Ky - ri - e - le - i - son

A kyrie in which the plainsong melody is varied only on the ninth and final time.

Kvapil, Jaroslav (b Fryšták, Moravia, 21 Apr 1892; d Brno, 18 Feb 1958), Czech composer. Studied with Janáček at Brno and was later appointed professor of organ and counterpoint at the Organ School there. In 1911–13 he continued studying at the Leipzig Conservatory, and on his return to Brno became professor of piano and composition at the Conservatory and conductor of the Philharmonic Society.

Works include four symphonies, variations and fugue for orches-

various Litanies, at the head of which it still stands. In the Mass it has a nine-fold structure, and the simplest melodic form consisted of eight repetitions of a simple melody followed by a quite different melody for the ninth clause.

This melody closely resembles that still used for the Litany Kyries for Rogationtide and Holy Saturday. Other musical forms in common use were: *aaa bbb aaa'*; *aaa bbb ccc'*; and *aba cdc efe'* (a stroke represents an extended form of the phrase concerned).

L

l the submediant note in any key in Tonic Sol-fa notation, pronounced Lah.

La the old name for the note A (◊solmization), still used in Latin countries, and in Tonic Sol-fa notation the submediant note in any key, represented by the symbol **l**, pronounced Lah.

La Barbara, Joan (b Philadelphia, 8 Jun 1947), American composer and vocal performer. Vocal studies with Phyllis Curtin at Tanglewood and in New York. Composition at NY University. Vocalist with Steve Reich and Musicians 1971–74, and worked with Philip Glass 1973–76; performances involve novel techniques of sound production, rather than singing as such; fps of works by Cage, Morton Feldman and her husband, Morton Subotnick.

Works include *Hear What I Feel* for amplified voice (1974), *Space Testing* for acoustic voice (1976), *Chandra* for amplified solo voice, men's voices and chamber orchestra (1978), *Winds of the Canyon* for voice and tape (1982), *The Solar Wind I-III* for voice(s) and ensembles (1983–84), *Loose Tongues* for eight amplified solo voices and tape (1985), *Urban Tropics*, sound portrait (1988), *Conversations* for low voice (1988), *In the Dreamtime*, self-portrait sound collage (1990), *Awakenings*, for chamber ensemble (1991), *Klangbild Köln/Sound Portrait of Cologne* (1991).

Labbette, Dora (b Purley, 4 Mar 1898; d Purley, 3 Sept 1984), English soprano. She studied at the GSM and from 1917 her career was in oratorios and song recitals. Opera debut Oxford, 1934, as Telaire in Rameau's *Castor et Pollux*. Mimi was the role of her first and last appearances in London (CG, 1935, and SW, 1943). She sang Mimi, Desdemona and Mignon in Germany and France in the late 1930s. Other roles included Marguerite, Mélisande and Delius's Vreli. She was persuaded by Beecham to adopt the stage name Lisa Perli (Purley = *Perli*).

Labèque, Katia and Marielle (b Hendaye, 3 Mar 1950 and 6 Mar 1952 respectively), French piano duo. Studied at the Paris Conservatory. Well-known performers of the standard repertory and works by Boulez, Lutosławski and Messiaen. Also heard in jazz.

Labia, Maria (b Verona, 14 Feb 1880; d Malcesine del Garda, 11 Feb 1953), Italian soprano. She sang in Milan and Stockholm before joining the Komische Opera Berlin in 1906; debut as Tosca and distinguished as Mimi, Thaïs, and Carmen. Manhattan Opera 1908–10. She sang Salome at La Scala in 1913 and was the first European Giorgetta (Rome, 1919). Retired 1936; taught in Warsaw and Italy from 1930. Her sister *Fausta* (1870–1935) was heard in Italy and Spain 1892–1912 as Eva, Sieglinde and Brünnhilde.

Labinsky, Andrey (b Kharkov, 26 Jul 1871; d Moscow, 8 Aug 1941), Russian tenor. He sang at the Maryinsky Theatre St Petersburg 1897–1911; created Vsevold in Rimsky-Korsakov's *Kitezh* (1907) and was admired as Lohengrin, Sinodal in *The Demon* and Don José. Bolshoi 1912–24; taught in Moscow from 1920.

Lablache, Luigi (b Naples, 6 Dec 1794; d Naples, 23 Jan 1858), Italian bass, of French descent. Made his debut at the Teatro San Carlo, Naples in 1812; sang Dandini at La Scala in 1817. Paris from 1830 and created there Lord Walton in *I Puritani* (1835) and Don Pasquale (1843). London 1830–55 as Leporello, Pollione and Bartolo. At Vienna in 1827 he sang in Mozart's Requiem, for Beethoven's funeral service.

La Borde, Jean Benjamin de (b Paris, 5 Sept 1734; d Paris, 22 Jul 1794), French author and composer. Pupil of Rameau for composition, chamberlain to Louis XV. He died on the scaffold during the Revolution.

Works include 32 operas, e.g. *Le Chat perdu et retrouvé* (1769), songs with violin and bass, songs with piano. He wrote books including an *Essai sur la musique ancienne et moderne* (1780).

Labroca, Mario (b Rome, 22 Nov 1896; d Rome, 1 Jul 1973), Italian critic and composer. Pupil of Respighi and Malipiero. Critic of *Il Lavoro fascista* and *L'Idea nazionale*, superintendent of the Teatro Vitorio Emanuele at Florence and organizer of the *Maggio musicale*.

Works include *Stabat Mater* (1935), *Il lamento dei mariti e delle mogli* for six voices and small orchestra; symphony for piano and small orchestra; three string quartets, piano trio; sonata for violin and piano, suite for violin and piano; pieces; songs.

Labuński, Feliks Roderyk (b Ksawerynówo, 27 Dec 1892; d Cincin-

Labèque *The pianists Katia and Marielle Labèque are known for their collaboration as a duo team. They are admired for their vivacious performances of modern music and gave a performance of Poulenc's concerto for two pianos at the 1995 London Proms.*

nati, 28 Apr 1979), Polish, later American, composer. Studied at Warsaw and with Dukas and Nadia Boulanger in Paris. He founded a society of Polish musicians there and later went to live in the USA.

Works include symphony and *Pastoral Triptych* for orchestra (1931); concertino for piano and orchestra; string quartet; divertimento for flute and piano; *Olympic Hymn* for chorus and orchestra; *The Birds* for voice and orchestra (1934), Polish Cantata, for solo voices and chorus (1932); piano pieces; songs.

Lächerliche Prinz Jodelet, Der, *The Ridiculous Prince Jodelet*, opera by Keiser (libretto by J P Praetorius, based on P Scarron's comedy, *Jodelet, ou Le Maître valet*), produced Hamburg, Theater beim Gänsemarkt, 1726.

Lachner German family of musicians, three brothers:

1. Franz Lachner (b Rain, 2 Apr 1803; d Munich, 20 Jan 1890), conductor and composer. Pupil of his father, Theodor Lachner, and later of Stadler and Sechter in Vienna, where he became a friend of Schubert. Appointed assistant conductor at the Kärntnertortheater there, 1826, and succeeded Weigl as chief conductor 1827. In 1834 he went to Mannheim as opera conductor and in 1836 to Munich as court music director. He worked in Munich until 1864, when Wagner, his personal and musical enemy, moved to the city.

Works include operas *Die Bürgschaft* (on Schiller's poem, 1828), *Alidia* (1839), *Catarina Cornaro* (1841) and *Benvenuto Cellini* (1849); oratorios *Moses* and *Die vier Menschcenalter* (1829); Requiem, three Masses; cantatas and other choral works; eight symphonies; harp and bassoon concertos; six string quartets, nonet for wind instruments, trios and other chamber music, piano pieces; songs.

2. Ignaz Lachner (b Rain, 11 Sept 1807; d Hanover, 24 Feb 1895), conductor and composer. Studied under his father and at Augsburg, joined his brother Franz in Vienna, 1824, became assistant conductor at the Kärntnertortheater there, 1825, appointed court music director at Stuttgart, 1831, and at Munich, 1842, jointly with Franz. Later he filled various posts at Hamburg, Stockholm and Frankfurt. operas *Der Geisterturm* (1837), *Die Regenbrüder* (1839) and *Loreley* (1846); ballets and melodramas; Masses; symphonies; string quartets; piano music; songs.

3. Vincenz Lachner (b Rain, 19 Jul 1811; d Karlsruhe, 22 Jan 1893), conductor and composer. Studied with his father and at Augsburg. He became organist in Vienna, 1834, and was court music director at Mannheim, 1836–73. He retired to Karlsruhe, where he taught at the Conservatory. incidental music to Schiller's adaptation of Gozzi's *Turandot*; part-songs, songs.

Lachrimae John Dowland's collection of 21 dances for five bowed instruments with lute (London, 1604). Its opening pavan, *Lachrimae antiquae*, is a version of his song *Flow my teares* (first pub. 1600), though in its original form it was probably a pavan for solo lute. In the early 17th c. the piece appeared in many other arrangements for different ensembles and by different hands, usually with the title *Lachrimae*.

Lachrymae work for viola and piano by Britten, '*Reflections on a song of John Dowland*'; composed 1950, fp Aldeburgh, 20 Jun 1950. Arranged for viola and string orchestra 1976, fp Recklinghausen, 3 May 1977.

Lacy, Michael Rophino (b Bilbao, 19 Jul 1795; d London, 20 Sept 1867), Irish violinist. Learnt music as a child in Spain, was sent to school at Bordeaux, 1802, and in 1803 went to Paris to finish his training with R Kreutzer. He first appeared in Paris, 1804, and London, 1805. He played with success for many years there as well as at Liverpool, Edinburgh, Glasgow, Dublin, etc., and made a number of tasteless adaptations of operas and oratorios by various composers. He was an early Handel scholar and collaborated with Schoelcher.

Lady Macbeth of the Mtsensk District, *Lady Macbeth Mtsenskago Uyezda*, opera by Shostakovich (libretto by A Preis and composer, based on a novel by N S Leskov), produced Moscow, 22 Jan 1934. Very successful at first, but afterwards discountenanced as decadent by the Soviet government. Revised as *Katerina Izmailova* and produced 1963. Tormented by her father-in-law Boris, Katerina Izmay-

lova has an affair with Sergei while her ineffectual husband, Zinovy, is away. Boris discovers Sergei and brutally whips him, but Katerina has her revenge by poisoning Boris. Suspicious, Zinovy returns and beats her, but Sergei intervenes and kills him. The police are informed and the couple are led away. In a group of convicts, Sergei flirts with a young prisoner to provoke Katerina. She throws her rival off a bridge, and jumps into the rapids herself.

Lady of the Lake, The songs by Schubert set to German translations from Scott's poem by P A Storck 1825 and pub. 1826 as op. 52.1. Ellen's first song, 'Soldier, rest!'; 2. Ellen's second song, 'Huntsman, rest!'; 3. Ellen's third song, 'Ave Maria'; 4. Norman's song, 'The heath this night'; 5. Lay of the Imprisoned Huntsman, 'My hawk is tired'. Op. 52 contains two more poems from Scott's work, *Boating Song* for male chorus and *Coronach* for female chorus.

Laffitte, Léon (b Saint-Genies, 28 Jan 1875; d Paris, Sept 1938), French tenor. Debut Paris, Opéra, 1898 as David; sang Mime there in the first French performance of *Siegfried*, 1908. Brussels 1899–1914; was heard there and at CG in 1906 as Jean in *Le Jongleur de Notre Dame*. Buenos Aires 1916; returned Paris 1923, as Samson and the Berlioz Faust.

Lafont, Charles Philippe (b Paris, 1 Dec 1781; d near Tarbes, 23 Aug 1839), French violinist, singer and composer. He was at first taught by his mother, a sister of the violinist Berthaume, and he travelled to Germany with his uncle as a child, playing there with success. Later he studied with R Kreutzer in Paris, appeared as a ballad singer at the Théâtre Feydeau, completed his violin studies with Rode and went on tour in 1801–08. In 1808–15 he was solo violinist to the Tsar in St Petersburg, and then received a similar appointment from Louis XVIII. In 1831–39 he made long tours with Herz, cut short by a carriage accident that caused his death.

Works include two operas; seven violin concertos; duets for violin and piano written with Kalkbrenner, Herz and others; more than 200 songs.

La Grotte, Nicolas de (b *c* 1530; d *c* 1600), French composer and keyboard-player. He pub. settings of Ronsard in 1569 and examples of *musique mesurée à l'antique*. In 1583 he pub. with Le Jeune pieces for the *Balet comique de la Royne*.

La Guerre (born *Jacquet*), Elisabeth Claude de (b Paris, ? 1664; d Paris, 27 Jun 1729), French harpsichordist and composer. A pupil of her father, she showed early promise and attracted the patronage of Louis XIV and later Mme de Montespan. She married the composer Marin La Guerre in 1687.

Works include opera *Céphale et Procris* (1694); cantatas; *Te Deum* and other church music; violin sonatas, trio sonatas, harpsichord music.

La Guerre, Michel de (b Paris, *c* 1605; d Paris, buried 13 Nov 1679), French organist and composer, father-in-law of Élisabeth de ◊La Guerre. Organist of the Sainte-Chapelle in Paris, 1633–79. His two sons, Jérôme (*c* 1654–?) and Marin (1658–1704) were both organists and composers; the latter married Élisabeth Jacquet.

Works include opera *Le Triomphe de l'Amour sur des bergers et bergères*; airs de cour.

Lah the name for the submediant note in any key in Tonic Sol-fa, so pronounced, but in notation represented by the symbol *l*.

La Halle (or *La Hale*), Adam de (b ? Arras, *c* 1230; d Naples, before 1288), French poet and composer. He was educated for the priesthood, but fell in love and married a young girl, whom he left to retire to Douai in 1263 (?) to rejoin the Church. In 1282 he went to Naples with the Comte d'Artois.

Works include stage pieces *Le Jeu d'Adam, ou de la feuillée* and *Le Jeu de Robin et de Marion* (1285); motets; *chansons*.

La Hèle (or *Helle*), Georges de (b Antwerp, 1547; d Madrid, 27 Aug 1586), Flemish composer. Chorister at the royal chapel in Madrid in his youth. Choirmaster at Tournai Cathedral in 1578, but probably back in Spain by 1580. He obtained two prizes at the Puy de Musique at Évreux in 1576.

Works (some destroyed in a fire at Madrid in 1734) include Masses, motets; *chansons*.

lai, French, later English *lay*, a medieval lyrical poem in pairs of stanzas in different metrical forms; also the music set to such poems.

Laidlaw, Robena Anna (b Bretton, Yorkshire, 30 Apr 1819; d London, 29 May 1901), English pianist. Pupil of Herz and L Berger. Played with much success on the Continent. Appointed court pianist to the Queen of Hanover, 1840. Schumann dedicated his *Fantasiestücke*, op. 12, to her.

Lajtha, László (b Budapest, 30 Jun 1892; d Budapest, 16 Feb 1963), Hungarian folksong expert and composer. Studied at the Music High School at Budapest, specialized in folk music and joined the folklore department of the National Museum in 1913. Professor at the Budapest Conservatory, 1919–49.

Works include three ballets including *Lysistrata* (1933) and *Capriccio* (1944); two Masses and other choral works; ten symphonies (1936–61); violin concerto; ten string quartets and other chamber music; sonatas for violin, cello and piano, etc.

Lakes, Gary (b Dallas, 26 Sept 1950), American tenor. Studied at Seattle and made debut with Dallas Opera 1981, as Wagner's Froh. Sang Florestan in Mexico City, 1983. NY Met. from 1986, as the High Priest in *Idomeneo*, Tannhäuser, Siegmund, Strauss's Emperor and Aeneas in *Les Troyens*. Season 1991–92 as Lohengrin at Buenos Aires and in *Das Lied von der Erde* at the London Proms. Montpellier Festival 1993, as Rienzi. Recordings include *Die Walküre*, under Levine, and *Les Troyens* conducted by Dutoit.

Lakmé opera by Delibes (libretto by E Gondinet and P Gille), produced Paris, Opéra-Comique, 14 Apr 1883. Brahmin priest Nilakantha opposes an affair between his daughter Lakmé and English officer Gerald. After being stabbed, Gerald is nursed by Lakmé, who poisons herself when she realizes that Gerald must return to his duties.

Lalande, Michel-Richard de (b Paris, 15 Dec 1657; d Versailles, 18 Jun 1726), French organist and composer. He learnt music as a chorister at the church of Saint-Germain-l'Auxerrois in Paris and taught himself the violin, bass viol and harpsichord. On being refused admission to Lully's orchestra, he took to the organ and secured organist's appointments at three churches. He failed to obtain the post of court organist, but was given charge of the princesses' musical education and in 1683 was appointed one of the superintendents of the royal chapel. He became master of the royal chapel in 1704. In 1684 he married the court singer Anne Rebel, who died in 1722, and in 1723 he married again, Mlle de Cury, daughter of one of the court surgeons.

Works include ballets and opera-ballets *Ballet de la jeunesse* (1686), *Le Palais de Flore* (1689), *Adonis* (1696), *Myrtil et Mélicerte* (1698), *Les Fées* (1699), *L'Amour fléchi par la Constance, L'Hymen champêtre* (1700), *Ballet de la Paix, Les Folies de Cardenio* (from Cervantes's *Don Quixote*, 1720), *Ballet de l'inconnu, Les Éléments* (with Destouches, 1725), *L'Amour berger, Églogue, ou Pastorale en musique, Les Fontaines de Versailles*; 70 motets with orchestral accompaniment; cantata *Le Concert d'Esculape*; Trois Leçons des Ténèbres, Miserere for solo voice; music for the royal table, including *Sinfonias pour les soupers du Roi*.

Lallouette, Jean François (b Paris, 1651; d Paris, 31 Aug 1728), French violinist and composer. He studied violin with Guy Leclerc and composition with Lully. From 1668 to 1677 he was violinist and conductor at the Opéra, but Lully dismissed him for claiming collaboration in his *Isis*, which may have been true, for he was said to have often assisted Lully. In 1693 he became *maître de chapelle* at Rouen Cathedral, in 1695 at Notre-Dame at Versailles, and in 1700 at Notre Dame in Paris.

Works include dramatic interludes and ballets; Masses, motets, Misereres.

Lalo, (Victor Antoine) Édouard (b Lille, 27 Jan 1823; d Paris, 22 Apr 1892), French composer of Spanish descent. He first studied violin and cello at the Lille Conservatory and then violin at that of Paris, taking composition lessons privately at the same time. In 1855 he became viola in the Armingaud-Jacquard quartet. He wrote little until 1865, the year of his marriage to Mlle Bernier de Maligny, who sang his songs in public. Gradually his success grew both in the opera-house and the concert-room. His most popular works during his

lifetime were the opera *Le Roi d'Ys* and the ballet *Namouna*; he is best known today for the five-movement *Symphonie espagnole* for violin and orchestra, and the cello concerto.

Works include operas *Fiesque* (after Schiller, composed 1866–67), *Le Roi d'Ys* (1888), *La Jacquerie* (unfinished, completed by Coquard, performed 1895); pantomime with choruses *Néron*; ballet *Namouna* (1882); symphony in G minor (1886), *Divertissement, Rhapsodie norvégienne* and scherzo for orchestra, two aubades for small orchestra, concerto, *Symphonie espagnole* (1874), *Fantaisie norvégienne* (1878), *Romance-Sérénade* (1879) and *Concerto russe* (1879) for violin and orchestra, concertos for piano and for cello.

String quartet (later revised as No. 2), three piano trios; violin and piano sonata and a number of pieces, cello and piano sonata and pieces; *La Mère et l'enfant* for piano duet; over 30 songs and two vocal duets; church music.

Lambe, Walter (b Salisbury, *c* 1452; d *c* 1500), English composer. He was King's Scholar at Eton in 1467 (aged 15), and clerk at St George's, Windsor, from 1479 to 1499 or later, acting as master of the choristers (at first jointly with William Edmunds), 1480–84. His known music was all included in the Eton Choirbook: it consists of a Magnificat and five votive antiphons (a sixth can be completed from another MS; another is partially lost and four more completely so.)

In addition to its intrinsic interest as a new craft, writing for films will have the salutary effect of keeping composers in touch with a large audience and its human reactions.

Constant Lambert, *Essay*, 1936

Lambert, Constant (b London, 23 Aug 1905; d London, 21 Aug 1951), English composer, conductor and critic. Son of the painter George Washington Lambert. Studied at the RCM in London. Diaghilev commissioned the ballet *Romeo and Juliet* from him when he was still a student and produced it at Monte Carlo in 1926. He began to make his mark as a conductor of ballet with the Camargo Society and later engaged to conduct ballet at SW Theatre, with which he appeared in Paris in 1937, having already conducted at the ISCM Festival at Amsterdam, 1933. He also became a concert conductor, was for a time music critic to the *Referee* and pub. a book of criticism, *Music Ho!*. Such works as *Horoscope* and *The Rio Grande* react against contemporary English pastoralism and look to jazz and early Stravinsky for inspiration.

Works include ballets *Romeo and Juliet* (Monte Carlo, 1926), *Pomona* (Buenos Aires, 1927), *Horoscope* (London, 1938); incidental music for Shakespeare's *Hamlet*; music for films *Merchant Seamen* and *Anna Karenina* (after Tolstoy); *Summer's Last Will and Testament* (Nash), masque for baritone solo, chorus and orchestra (1932–35); *The Rio Grande* for piano, orchestra and chorus (1927); dirge in Shakespeare's *Cymbeline* for voices and orchestra; *Music for Orchestra, Aubade héroïque* for small orchestra; concerto for piano and chamber orchestra; piano sonata; four poems by Li-Po for voice and piano.

Lambert, Michel (b Champigny-sur-Veude, *c* 1610; d Paris, 29 Jun 1696), French lutenist, singer and composer. He was master of the royal chamber music and in 1663 became master of the children in the royal chapel. Lully married his daughter Madeleine. He wrote songs to the lute.

Lambertini, Giovanni Tomaso (b Bologna), Italian 16th–17th c. priest and composer. Singer at San Petronio at Bologna, 1548–73. From 1573 active in Rome.

Works include penitential psalms and other church music; madrigals, *villotte*.

Lamentatione name (apparently authentic) given to Haydn's symphony no. 26 in D minor, composed *c* 1768, on account of the use it makes of a chant associated with the Lamentations of Jeremiah.

Lamentations the Lamentations of Jeremiah used in the Roman Catholic service at matins in Holy Week; originally sung in plainsong and still surviving in that form, but from the early 16th c. also used in polyphonic settings.

Lamento Italian = 'lament'; a plaintive aria in early 17th-c. Italian opera conventionally placed before the tragic culmination of the plot. The best known example is the *Lamento d'Arianna*, the only surviving fragment from Monteverdi's *Arianna*.

Lammers, Gerda (b Berlin, 25 Sept 1915), German soprano. After study in Berlin sang until 1955 in Lieder and concert; her stage debut, at Bayreuth, was followed by an engagement at Kassel (1955–70); debut as Marie, other roles included Senta, Alceste, Isolde and Brünnhilde. London, CG, 1957, as Elektra; Kundry 1959. NY Met. debut Mar 1962, as Elektra. She also sang Medea and Purcell's Dido and recorded Hindemith's song cycle *Das Marienleben*.

Lamond, Frederic (b Glasgow, 28 Jan 1868; d Stirling, 21 Feb 1948), Scottish pianist. Studied piano, organ and violin at home and after becoming a church organist went to the Raff Conservatory at Frankfurt in 1882. Although he wished to become a composer, he studied piano further with Bülow and Liszt, making his debut in Berlin in 1885. In Britain he first played in 1886, at Glasgow and London. He toured widely, but mainly in Germany, and from 1904, when he married the actress Irene Triesch, he had his home in Berlin. It was not until World War II that he settled in London.

Lamoureux, Charles (b Bordeaux, 28 Sept 1834; d Paris, 21 Dec 1899), French violinist and conductor. Studied violin and theory at the Paris Conservatory, joined a theatre orchestra, then played at the Opéra, in 1860 helped to found a chamber music society for the introduction of new works, conducted choral works by Bach, Handel and others in the 1870s, became conductor at the Opéra and in 1881 founded the Concerts Lamoureux, at which he made a great deal of orchestral music, including Wagner, known to a wide public. Toured Russia 1893; regular concerts in London from 1896.

Lampe, Johann Friedrich (John Frederick) (b Saxony, 1703; d Edinburgh, 25 Jul 1751), German bassoonist and composer. Went to England from Brunswick about 1725 and settled in London, but went to Dublin in 1748 and to Edinburgh in 1750. Married Isabella Young, sister of T A Arne's wife.

Works include comic operas *The Dragon of Wantley* (1757) and *Margery, or A Worse Plague than the Dragon* (1738; libretti by Carey), mock opera *Pyramus and Thisbe* (from Shakespeare's *Midsummer Night's Dream*, 1745), masque *The Sham Conjurer* (1741); music for Carey's *Amelia*; *c* ten other stage works; cantata to celebrate the suppression of the Stuart rebellion; songs.

Lampugnani, Giovanni Battista (b Milan, 1706; d Milan, 1786), Italian composer. Studied in Naples, and made his debut as an opera composer there in 1732. Successful throughout Italy, he went to London in 1743 to take over from Galuppi the opera at the King's Theatre, but later returned to Milan, where he wrote his five comic operas (1758–69). From 1779 he was *maestro al cembalo* at the Teatro alla Scala.

Works include *c* 30 operas, e.g. *Semiramide* (1741), *Rossane*, *Tigrane* (1747), *Artaserse*, *Siroe* (1755), *L'amor contadino* (1760), etc.; also trio sonatas, church music.

Lancelot and Elaine symphonic poem no. 2 by MacDowell, op. 25, based on the Arthurian legend, composed 1888.

Lancie, John de (b Berkeley, CA, 26 Jul 1921), American oboist and administrator. Studied at Curtis from 1935, and was a member of the Pittsburgh SO 1940–42. Met Richard Strauss at Garmisch while on military service and requested an oboe concerto from him. Principal of the Pittsburgh SO 1954–74 and taught at Curtis during same period (director 1977–85). Commissioned and gave the fps of Françaix's *L'horloge de Flore* (1961) and the concerto by Benjamin Lees (1963). Director of the New World School of Music from 1987.

Landarzt, Ein, *A Country Doctor*, radio opera by Henze after the story by Kafka; broadcast Hamburg, 29 Nov 1951; revised for Dietrich Fischer-Dieskau as a monodrama, 1964; fp Berlin, 12 Oct 1965. Radio opera revised for stage 1964, fp Frankfurt, 30 Nov 1965. Doctor's macabre night-call to village boy.

Landi, Stefano (b Rome, *c* 1586; d Rome, 28 Oct 1639), Italian singer

and composer. He was *maestro di cappella* at Padua about 1620 and in Rome from 1624, and sang alto in the Papal Chapel from 1630. His sacred opera *Il Sant' Alessio* has been successfully revived at Rome and Innsbruck (1981) and at LA (1988).

Works include operas *La morte d'Orfeo* (1619) and *Il Sant' Alessio* (1631); Masses and psalms; madrigals and cantatas; arias for one voice.

Landini (or *Landino*), Francesco (b Fiesole, *c* 1325; d Florence, 2 Sept 1397), Italian organist, lutenist, composer and poet. Although blind from early childhood, he perfected himself on various instruments, in particular the portative organ, and became organist of the church of San Lorenzo at Florence (1369–96). He is one of the chief exponents of the Italian *ars nova*.

Works include madrigals, *ballate*, etc.

Landini Sixth a cadence in music of the 14th and 15th c. named after Francesco Landini, of whose vocal works it is a feature. The idiom is

The landini sixth in C major.

not confined to Italian music nor is there any evidence to suggest that Landini invented it.

Ländler an Austrian country dance having the character of a slow waltz. Mozart, Beethoven and Schubert left many examples.

Landon, H(oward) C(handler) Robbins (b Boston, MA, 6 Mar 1926), American musicologist. He studied at Swarthmore College and Boston University. Since 1947 he has lived in Europe. He has devoted himself particularly to the study of late 18th-c. music and has pub. a number of articles and books, including *The Symphonies of Joseph Haydn* (1955), *The Collected Correspondence and London Notebooks of Joseph Haydn* and *Haydn: Chronicle and Works*, five vols. (1976–80), as well as editions of numerous works by Haydn, including several operas and the complete symphonies; *Haydn: His Life and Music* (1988). He has pub. books on Beethoven (1970) and Mozart as a Mason (1983), and also in 1983 edited recently discovered material for Handel's Roman Vespers. *Mozart's Last Year* (1988); *Mozart: The Golden Years* (1989), *Mozart and Vienna* (1991), *Vivaldi, Voice of the Baroque* (1993).

You play Bach your way and I'll play him his way.
Wanda Landowska, attr.

Landowska, Wanda (b Warsaw, 5 Jul 1877; d Lakeville, CT, 16 Aug 1959), Polish harpsichordist, pianist and music research scholar. She toured widely and settled in France, where in 1927 she opened a school for the study of early music at Saint-Leu-la-Forêt, near Paris. From 1941 she lived in the USA. She wrote books and articles on aspects of early music. Falla's harpsichord concerto (1923–26) and Poulenc's *Concert Champêtre* (1927–28) were composed for her. She gave the first public performance of the Goldberg Variations (1933) and recorded the Well-Tempered Clavier (1949–56).

Lane, Gloria (b Trenton, 6 Jun 1930), American mezzo. Debut Philadelphia 1950, in the fp of Menotti's *The Consul*; 1954 on Broadway in the fp of *The Saint of Bleecker Street*. Glyndebourne 1958–63 as Baba the Turk and Dorabella; returned 1972 for Ariadne and Lady Macbeth. CG 1960, Carmen. Guest at Vienna, Paris and Florence; Santuzza at NY City Opera, 1971.

Lang, Paul Henry (b Budapest, 28 Aug 1901; d Lakeville, CT, 21 Sept 1991), Hungarian-born American musicologist. In 1924 he went to the University of Paris and four years later to the USA. He became professor of musicology at Columbia University in NY in 1939. In 1945 he became editor of the *Musical Quarterly*. Among his writings are *Music in Western Civilization* (1941) and *George Frideric Handel* (1966).

H C Robbins Landon - musicologist

1. Gabrieli: *A Venetian Coronation* (Gabrieli Consort/McCreesh)
A splendid evocation of a grand ceremony in St Mark's.

2. Monteverdi: *Vespro Della Beata Vergine* (English Baroque Soloists/Gardiner)
One of the greatest rediscoveries of the 20th century, it is staggering that this masterpiece could have languished over 300 years in shameful obscurity.

3. Bach: *Christmas Oratorio* (Monteverdi Choir/Gardiner)
When I was young there was no recording of this great compilation. Although perhaps not the equal of that other great choral compilation – the Mass in B minor – this is nonetheless splendid, affirmative music by the greatest Baroque composer of them all.

4. Handel: *Israel in Egypt* (Monteverdi Choir/Gardiner)
This is arguably Handel's greatest oratorio, full of sublime music (for instance, 'Sing ye to the Lord' at the end), and as always I prefer Gardiner to the other CDs.

5. Haydn: *La fedeltà premiata* (Soloists include Cotrubas, von Stade, Valentini, Alva/Dorati)
The Haydn opera series conducted by Dorati was one of the great events of LP and even more when they were brilliantly transferred to CD. In my opinion, this is the greatest of them all, and the performance is superb.

6. Haydn: *Missa Sancti Bernardi de Offida* (Tölzer Knabenchor/Tafelmusik/Weil)
One of Haydn's most moving and inward-looking late masses in an exemplary performance by one of Haydn's great interpreters.

7. Mozart: Music to *Thamos, König in Aegypten* (Royal Concertgebouw Orch./Harnoncourt or Monteverdi Choir/Gardiner)
Another 20th-century discovery, this magnificent incidental music is prophetically moving – a foretaste of *Idomeneo* and *Die Zauberflöte*; both performances are brilliant.

8. Mozart: *La clemenza di Tito* (Krenn/Bergenza/Popp/Vienna State Opera/Kertész)
A classic, this magnificent recording did much to re-establish this long-neglected masterpiece.

9. Bruckner: Symphony no. 8 in C minor (Vienna PO/Karajan)
This was the work with which Karajan established himself after being de-Nazified at an historic concert in the autumn of 1947 with this orchestra. Of the several fine recordings Karajan made of this symphony, this is perhaps the finest. I consider this to be the greatest symphonic work after Beethoven.

10. Berlioz: *Les Troyens* (CG/Colin Davis)
Another great gramophone classic, this recording will in my opinion go down as one of the 20th century's greatest contributions to the LP (or now, CD).

11. Wagner: *Tristan und Isolde* (Vienna PO/Furtwängler)
This desperately moving and magnificent recording will also, in my opinion, go down as a gramophone classic. It was one of Walter Legge's many triumphs as a producer.

Langbein, Brenton (b Gawler, 21 Jan 1928; d Zurich, 6 Jun 1993), Australian conductor. Trained as violinist and played with the Sydney SO 1947–51. Formed trio with Maureen Jones and Barry Tuckwell and premiered the *Trio* by Don Banks at the 1962 Edinburgh Festival. Toured throughout Australia and Europe as conductor and co-founded Opera Factory at Zurich, 1973; London appearances with the group in *Acis and Galatea* (1980), Gluck's conflated *Iphigenias* (1987) and Kelterborn's *Julia* (1991).

Langdon, Michael (b Wolverhampton, 12 Nov 1920; d Hove, 12 March 1991), English bass. He studied in Geneva and London. From 1951 leading roles at CG and took part in the fps of *Billy Budd* (1951), *Gloriana* (1953), *The Midsummer Marriage* (1955), and Henze's *We Come to the River* (1976). Retired 1977 and became director of National Opera Studio 1978–86. Best known as Ochs; other roles included Hagen, Hunding, Rocco and Varlaam.

Langlais, Jean (b La Fontenelle, Ille-et-Vilaine, 15 Feb 1907; d Paris, 8 May 1991), French organist and composer. He was educated at an institute for the blind and studied organ under André Marchal, also blind, later with Dupré at the Paris Conservatory, where he also studied composition with Dukas. He held several organist's appointments at Paris churches, lastly at Sainte-Clotilde, and taught organ and composition at the Institut des Jeunes Aveugles. His best-known works are for organ, but he also wrote many others.

Langridge, Philip (b Hawkhurst, Kent, 16 Dec 1939), English tenor. He studied at the RAM and began his career as a violinist. An unusually wide repertory, and has been heard in operas by Handel, Rameau and Monteverdi as well as in performances of contemporary Music; recorded Schoenberg's Aron, with Solti, and in 1986 co-created the title role in Birtwistle's opera *The Mask of Orpheus*, at the London Coliseum. NY Met. debut 1985 (as Ferrando), Salzburg 1987, as Schoenberg's Aron (returned as Idomeneo, 1990 and Monteverdi's Nero, 1993). Sang Pelegrin in the UK fp of Tippett's *New Year*, Glyndebourne 1990. CBE 1994.

Lanier (or *Laniere*), Nicholas (b London, bap. 10 Sept 1588; d London, buried 24 Feb 1666), English painter, flautist, singer and composer of French descent (? Lanière). He was probably a pupil of his father, John Lanier (or Lanyer), a sackbut player. In 1613, with Coperario and others, he composed a masque for the marriage of the Earl of Somerset and in 1617 he not only set Ben Jonson's *Lovers made Men*, but sang in it and painted the scenery. In 1625 he was sent to Italy to collect pictures for the royal collection. Appointed Master of the King's Music in 1626. Lived in the Netherlands during the Commonwealth, but resumed his post at the Restoration. Several other members of the family were musicians in the royal service.

Works include masques, e.g. *Lovers made Men* (1617) and *The Vision of Delight* (Jonson, 1617); cantata *Hero and Leander*, New Year's songs; vocal dialogues, songs.

Lankester, Michael (b London, 12 Nov 1944), English conductor. Studied at the RCM and conducted the ECO, 1967. Music director of the National Theatre (1969–75) and conducted opera at the RCM, 1969–80. Made orchestral suite of Britten's ballet *The Prince of the Pagodas* and gave fp 1979. Worked with the Pittsburgh SO from 1980, conductor-in-residence 1984–88; music director of the Hartford SO from 1986.

Lanner, Joseph (Franz Karl) (b Vienna, 12 Apr 1801; d Oberdöbling, near Vienna, 14 Apr 1843), Austrian violinist and composer. Son of a

Larrocha *Pianist Alicia de Larrocha has built her repertory upon the works of Mozart and the composers of her native Spain. Although her small hands put her at a disadvantage when playing large Romantic works, her dextrous technique is admirably suited to 18th-century music.*

glove-maker. He taught himself the violin. Anxious to conduct an orchestra, he began by getting together a string quartet, in which J Strauss, senior, played viola. They played at various taverns selections from favourite operas arranged by him. He soon turned to the composition of country dances and waltzes, in which he was to be Strauss's greatest rival. He was engaged to conduct the orchestra at dances, visited provincial cities with his own band and finally conducted the court balls in turn with Strauss.

Works include over 200 waltzes, country dances, quadrilles, polkas, galops, marches.

Lantins, Arnold de (d Rome, 1432), early 15th-c. Flemish composer from the diocese of Liège. He was in Venice in 1428 and was included (with Dufay) in a list of papal singers in 1431. He composed *chansons*, motets and a Mass, *Verbum incarnatum*.

Lantins, Hugo de, Flemish composer, possibly brother of Arnold de ◊Lantins. Like Arnold he visited Italy, and in 1420 wrote an epithalamium for Cleofe Malatesta di Pesaro. Two of his five motets connect him with Venice (1423) and Bari respectively. He also wrote numerous *chansons*.

Laparra, Raoul (b Bordeaux, 13 May 1876; d Suresnes, 4 Apr 1943), French composer. Studied at the Paris Conservatory. His *Habanera* was given at CG 1910, NY Met. 1924. He was killed in an Allied air raid near Paris.

Works include operas *Peau d'âne* (1899), *La Habanera* (1908), *La Jota* (1899), *Le Joueur de viole*, *Las Toreras* (1929), *L'Illustre Fregona*; *Un Dimanche basque* for piano and orchestra; string quartet; songs.

Lapicida, Erasmus (b 1445–50; d Vienna, 19 Nov 1547), German composer. Towards the end of his life he is found in the Imperial court, described as being 'in extreme old age'. He wrote church music, a *frottola* (the latter and much of the former pub. by Petrucci) and German songs.

La Pouplinière (or *Poupelinière*), Alexandre Jean Joseph le Riche de (b Chinon, 26 Jul 1693; d Paris, 5 Dec 1762), French music patron. He was farmer-general of taxes and amassed a huge fortune. He kept a private orchestra, had Rameau living in his house for several years

and studied under him, and patronized a number of other composers and performers, including Mondonville.

Lara (actually *Cohen*), Isidore de (b London, 9 Aug 1858; d Paris, 2 Aug 1935), English composer. Studied composition with Mazzucato and singing with Lamperti at the Milan Conservatory, later went to Lalo in Paris. He returned to London and became well known in wealthy drawing-rooms as a song composer and performer. Later he came under the patronage of the Princess of Monaco, which enabled him to have his operas staged in the grand manner.

Works include operas *The Light of Asia* (1892), *Amy Robsart* (after Scott's *Kenilworth*, 1893), *Moïna* (1897), *Messaline* (1899), *Soléa*, *Sanga, Naïl, Les Trois Masques* (1912), *The Three Musketeers* (after Dumas, 1921), and others; cantata *The Light of Asia* (first version of the opera); many songs.

Laredo, Jaime (b Cochabamba, 7 Jun 1941), Bolivian-born American violinist. Studied in San Francisco and at Curtis with Ivan Galamian. Debut San Francisco 1952 and won the Queen Elisabeth of the Belgians Competition, 1959. New York (Carnegie Hall) debut 1961, London (Albert Hall) 1961. Has appeared at the Tanglewood and Edinburgh Festivals and given concerts as soloist/director with St Paul's and Scottish Chamber Orchestras. Premiered Ned Rorem's concerto (1985); formed piano trio with Joseph Kalichstein and Sharon Robinson, 1980.

largamente Italian = 'broadly, spaciously'; an indication that a movement or phrase is to be played in a broad manner.

large the largest note-value in the medieval system of measured notation. It was known in Latin as *duplex longa* or *maxima*, and was divisible into two longs.

larghetto Italian = lit. little *largo* a tempo indication for a slow movement, less slow than a *largo*.

largo Italian = 'large, broad, wide, spacious'; a tempo indication for a slow movement denoting a broad style as much as a slow pace. ◊larghetto.

'Largo' the popular name for the aria 'Ombra mai fù/Shade never was') from Handel's opera *Serse* (*Xerxes*), more generally known as an instrumental piece pub. in all kinds of arrangements. The familiar title is not even the original tempo indication, which is *Larghetto*.

Lark Ascending, The romance for violin and orchestra by Vaughan Williams, composed 1914, fp London, Queen's Hall, 14 Jun 1921, conductor Boult.

'Lark' Quartet a nickname sometimes given to Haydn's string quartet in D, op. 64 No. 5, on account of the exposed high first-violin passage at the opening.

Larmore, Jennifer (b Atlanta, 21 Jun 1958), American mezzo-soprano. Studied at Westminster College, Princeton, and in New York. European debut 1986, as Mozart's Sesto at Nice. She is best known for her vivacious performances of Rossini's Rosina, which she has sung in Paris, Rome, London (CG) and elsewhere; other Rossini roles include Isabella and Adèle in Turin and Milan, and Arsace in a recording of *Semiramide*. Sang Dorabella at the 1993 Salzburg Festival and made her Wigmore Hall (London) debut March 1993. Other roles include Monteverdi's Ottavia, Bellini's Romeo, Donna Elvira, and Jane Seymour in *Anna Bolena*.

Larrivée, Henri (b Lyons, 9 Jan 1737; d Paris, 7 Aug 1802), French baritone. He sang at the Paris Opéra from 1755, at first in operas by Rameau; became closely associated with Gluck and took part in the fps of the two *Iphigénie* operas as well as *Armide* and the revised *Alceste*. Was also heard in operas by Philidor, Gossec (*Sabinus*, 1773), Piccinni and Grétry (*Andromaque*, 1780). In 1784 he created Danaus in Salieri's *Les Danaïdes*.

Larrocha, Alicia de (b Barcelona, 23 May 1923), Spanish pianist. Concert debut with Madrid SO in 1935. London debut 1953; US debut, with San Francisco SO, 1955. Formed duo with cellist Gaspar Cassado in 1956. Well known in performances of Falla, Granados and Albeniz; also plays Mozart.

Larsen, Jens Peter (b Copenhagen, 14 Jun 1902; d Copenhagen, 22 Aug 1988), Danish musicologist. Studied at Copenhagen University and taught there from 1928, becoming professor in 1945. Organist at

Vangede Church, 1930–45. Editor of several works by Haydn and other composers, and author of *Die Haydn-Überlieferung*, *Die Haydn Kataloge* and *Handel's 'Messiah'*. Wrote entry for Haydn in the *New Grove Dictionary* (1980).

Larsen, Libby (b Wilmington, OE, 24 Dec 1950), American composer. Studied at the University of Minnesota with Dominick Argonto. Artistic director of the Hot Notes Series, from 1993; performances with synthesized sound.

Works include operas *Tumbledown Dick* (1980), *Frankenstein, the Modern Prometheus* (1990) and *Mrs Dalloway* (1993); *Symphony: Water Music* (1985); *Coming Forth into Day* oratorio (1985); *Sonnets from the Portuguese*, song cycle for soprano and chamber ensemble (1989); Piano concerto: 'Since Armstrong' (1990); *Ghosts of an Old Ceremony*, dance (1991); Third Symphony 'Lyric' (1991); *Marimba* concerto (1992); *Quartet: Schoenberg, Schenker and Schillinger*, for string quartet (1991); *Mary Cassat*, for mezzo, trombone and orchestra (1994).

Larsen-Todsen, Nanny (b Hagby, 2 Aug 1884; d Stockholm, 26 May 1982), Swedish soprano. Debut Stockholm 1906, as Agathe; regular in Sweden until 1923, when she sang Isolde at La Scala, Milan. NY Met. debut 1925 as the *Götterdämmerung* Brünnhilde; also sang Kundry, Leonore, Rachel and Gioconda. Bayreuth 1927–31. Other roles included Donna Anna, Tosca, Reiza and Aida.

Larson, Sophia (b Linz, 1954), Austrian soprano. Studied at the Salzburg Mozarteum and made debut at St Gallen 1976, as Amelia Boccanegra. Sang at Ulm and Bremen, 1979–83, then guested at Hamburg, Stuttgart and Rome (roles have included Mozart's Ilia and Fiordiligi, Leonore and Káta Kabanová). Bologna 1985, as the Duchess of Parma in the fp of the fully revised version of Busoni's *Doktor Faust*. Bayreuth Festival from 1984, as Gutrune and Sieglinde. Holland Festival 1992, as Els in *Der Schatzgräber* by Schreker.

Larsson, Lars-Erik (b Akarp near Lund, 15 May 1908; d Helsingborg, 27 Dec 1986), Swedish conductor and composer. Studied at the RAM at Stockholm, and later in Leipzig and Vienna, where he was a pupil of Berg. Conductor for Swedish radio 1937–54; professor of composition, Stockholm Conservatory, 1947–59; director of music, Uppsala University, 1961–66.

Works include opera *The Princess of Cyprus* (1937); incidental music to Shakespeare's *Winter's Tale*; three symphonies (1927–45), two concert overtures, lyric suite for orchestra; sinfonietta for strings (1932), divertimento for chamber orchestra; saxophone concerto.

La Rue, Jan (b Kisaran, Sumatra, 31 Jul 1918), Indonesian-born American musicologist. He studied at Harvard and Princeton; NY University from 1957. He has written particularly about style analysis and 18th-c. music, with a special emphasis on objectively verifiable conclusions.

La Rue, Pierre de (b ? Tournai, *c* 1460; d Courtrai, 20 Nov 1518), Flemish composer. Pupil of Ockeghem, in the service by turns of the court of Burgundy, Charles V and Margaret of Austria when governor of the Netherlands. He was appointed prebendary of Courtrai and later of Namur. Regarded as the equal of his contemporaries, Isaac, Obrecht and Brumel.

Works include 31 Masses, Requiem, 38 motets; *chansons*.

Laruette, Jean Louis (b Toulouse, 27 Mar 1731; d Toulouse, 10 Jan 1792), French actor, singer and composer. He appeared at the Opéra-Comique and the Comédie-Italienne in Paris.

Works include operas *Cendrillon* (1759), *L'Ivrogne corrigé* (after La Fontaine) and eight others, operettas.

LaSalle Quartet American string quartet founded 1949 at the Juilliard School, NY; members are Walter Levine and Henry Meyer (violins), Peter Kamnitzer (viola), Lee Fiser (cello). European debut 1954. Much valued for performances and recordings of works by the Second Viennese School and quartets by Apostel, Ligeti, Lutosławski, Penderecki and Kagel. Disbanded 1988.

La Scala ◊Scala Theatre.

Laserna, Blas (b Corella, Navarre, bap. 4 Feb 1751; d Madrid, 8 Aug 1816), Spanish composer. He became official composer to several Madrid theatres in 1779.

A Selection of
Lassus
Misa Bell'Amfitrit'altera
Lagrime di San Pietro
Chansons
Prophetiae Sibyllarum

Missa Qual donna attende a gloriosa fama
Missa Osculetur me
Lamentations of Jeremiah à 5
Psalmi Davidis poenitentiales
Missa Pro defunctis – 4vv
Missa Pro defunctis – 5vv

Works include numerous *tonadillas*, comic opera *La gitanilla por amor* (1791); incidental music for plays by Calderón, Lope de Vega, Moreto, Ramón de la Cruz's *El café de Barcelona* (1788) and others, lyric scene *Idomeneo* (1792), etc.

Las Huelgas Codex an important MS, *c* 1325, containing monophonic and polyphonic music, the latter included *conductus*, motets and settings of the Mass Ordinary. It is housed in the monastery of Las Huelgas near Burgos in N Spain.

Lassalle, Jean Louis (b Lyons, 14 Dec 1847; d Paris, 7 Sept 1909), French baritone. He was intended to follow his father in the business of a silk merchant, but went to Paris, first to study painting and then singing at the Conservatory and privately. He made his debut at Liège in 1868 in *Les Huguenots*, Paris, Opéra, from 1872 as William Tell and in operas by Reyer and Saint-Saëns. London, CG, 1879–93 as Sachs, the Dutchman and Telramund. NY Met. from 1892 (debut as Nelusko).

Lassen, Eduard (b Copenhagen, 13 Apr 1830; d Weimar, 15 Jan 1904), Danish-born conductor and composer. Was taken to Brussels at the age of two, later studied at the Conservatory there, and took the Belgian Prix de Rome in 1851. Unable to get his first opera staged at Brussels, he took it to Liszt at Weimar, who produced it in 1857. He was music director there from 1858 and conductor of the opera from 1860. He conducted the fp of Saint-Saëns's *Samson et Dalila* (1877).

Works include operas *Landgraf Ludwigs Brautfahrt* (1857), *Frauenlob* (1860), *Le Captif*; including music to Sophocles' *Oedipus*, Goethe's *Faust* and *Pandora*, Calderón's *Circe*, Hebbel's *Nibelungen* (1876; the year of the first production of *The Ring*, at Bayreuth); festival cantata, Te Deum; *Biblische Bilder* for voices and orchestra; two symphonies, *Beethoven* and *Festival* overtures.

A child, I sang the treble *part,/A youth, the* counter *claim'd my art;/A man, the* tenor *was my place,/But now I'm station'd in the* bass.
Epitaph on Orlando di Lasso's monument

Lassus, Orlande de (Orlando di Lasso) (b Mons, probably 1532; d Munich, 14 Jun 1594), Flemish composer. He seems to have gone to Italy as a boy, and he travelled there and served in various noble households, in Sicily, Naples and Milan. In 1553–54 he was choirmaster at St John Lateran in Rome, after which he returned home and settled for two years at Antwerp, where in 1555–56 he began to pub.

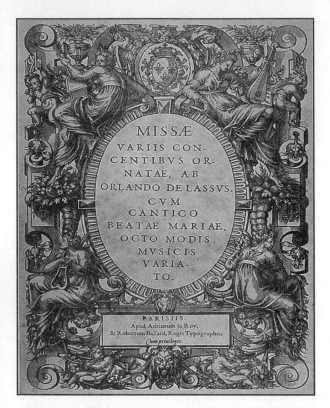

Lassus *The title page of the* Missae variis concentibus ornatae *by Orlando de Lassus, published by Adrian Le Roy and Robert Ballard in Paris, 1577. Lassus (1532–1594) has been compared to Palestrina for his supreme mastery of technique and conservative musical inclinations.*

his first works. In 1556 he went to Munich and entered the service of the Duke of Bavaria. There he married Regina Weckinger in 1558, and in 1563 became chief *Kapellmeister* in succession to Daser. Visit to Venice, 1567, to find musicians for Munich, and to Ferrara. In 1570 he was ennobled by the Emperor Maximilian. After a visit to Paris in 1571 Charles IX offered him a post as chamber musician, but he returned to Munich after the king's death in 1574. That year he went to Rome to present Pope Gregory XIII with a volume of Masses and received the order of the Golden Spur. In spite of an offer from Dresden, he remained attached to the Bavarian court to the end. His Latin motets were collected and pub. in 1604 by his sons Ferdinand and Rudolph under the title *Magnum opus musicum*. The abundance, variety and polyphonic ingenuity of his music places him as one of the greatest composers of the Renaissance.

Works include more than 2,000 compositions: about 60 Masses, four Passions, 101 Magnificats, Requiem, about 500 motets, *Sacrae cantiones*, psalms (including seven penitential psalms); madrigals, Italian *canzoni*, French *chansons*, German songs for several voices.

Last Judgment, The the English title of Spohr's oratorio *Die letzten Dinge*, produced Kassel, 25 Mar 1826.

László, Magda (b Marosvásárehely, *c* 1920), Hungarian soprano. She studied in Budapest and sang there during the war as Elisabeth and Maria Boccanegra. Created The Mother in the first production of Dallapiccola's *Il Prigionero* (Florence, 1950). She sang Alceste at Glyndebourne in 1953; returned in 1954 for Dorabella and 1962 as Poppea in the fp of the Leppard version of Monteverdi's opera. Other roles include Marie, Senta, Norma. Created Walton's Cressida (CG 1954).

Latham-Koenig, Jan (b London, 15 Dec 1953), English conductor. Studied at the RCM and founded the Koenig Ensemble 1976; pianist until 1981. Conducted Mahler symphonies at Montepulciano (1981–86) and *Giulio Cesare* at Stockholm, 1985. ENO and Wexford debuts 1987, with *Tosca* and *La Straniera*. Premieres of Bussotti's *L'ispirazione* and *Fedra*, at Florence and Rome, 1988. Montpellier Festival from 1990, with Graun's *Montezuma*, Magnard's *Berenice* and Sacchini's *Oedipe a Colone*. Recordings include several stage works by Weill.

Latilla, Gaetano (b Bari, 12 Jan 1711; d Naples, 15 Jan 1788), Italian composer. Chorister at Bari Cathedral, he studied with Prota and Feo at the Conservatorio di Sant'Onofrio in Naples, where his firt opera was produced in 1732. Appointed vice-*maestro di cappella* at Santa Maria Maggiore, Rome, in 1738, he returned to Naples in 1741 for health reasons. Later choirmaster at the Conservatorio della Pietà in Venice (1756) and vice-*maestro di cappella* at St Mark's (1762). Retired to Naples 1772.

Works include *c* 50 operas, e.g. *Li marite a forza* (1732), *Gismondo* (1737), *Madame Ciana, Romolo* (1739), *Siroe* (1740), etc.; oratorio *Omnipotenza e misericordia divina*; church music; instrumental music.

Latrobe, Christian Ignatius (b Fulneck, Leeds, 12 Feb 1757; d Fairfield, near Liverpool, 6 May 1836), English clergyman and composer. Studied at the college of the Moravian Brethren at Niesky in Upper Lusatia and in 1795 became secretary of the English branch. Dedicated three sonatas to Haydn, with whom he made friends during the latter's visits to England. Edited Moravian hymn-tunes and six vols of German and Italian church music.

Works include *Dies irae* (1823), Te Deum, Miserere (1814), anthems and other church music; instrumental sonatas; airs to poems by Cowper and Hannah More, etc.

Laubenthal, Horst (b Eisfeld, Thuringia, 8 Mar 1939), German tenor. Born Neumann, he adopted the name of his teacher, Rudolf Laubenthal. Debut Würzburg 1967, as Ottavio. Stuttgart Staatsoper from 1968; Deutsche Oper Berlin from 1973. He sang Belmonte at Glyndebourne in 1972. Guest at Aix, Salzburg and Munich as Lensky, Tamino, Palestrina and Florestan. Well known in sacred music by Bach.

Laubenthal, Rudolf (b Düsseldorf, 18 Mar 1886; d Pöcking, Starnbergsee, 2 Oct 1971), German tenor. He studied in Berlin, debut there in 1913; remained until 1923, when he sang Walther at the NY Met. Appeared until 1933 in Wagner roles and was the first US Steva (1924), Menelaos (1928) and Babinski (1931). London, CG, 1926–30. Guest in Chicago and Vienna.

Lauda Sion a sequence sung at Mass on the Feast of Corpus Christ in the Roman Church, words by St Thomas Aquinas, *c* 1264.

Cantata by Mendelssohn written for a festival at Liège and performed there on 11 Jun 1846.

Laudi spirituali Italian sacred songs of the 13th c. and later, with words in the vernacular, at first for single voice and later in parts. Their centre of origin was Florence.

Laudon Symphony nickname of Haydn's symphony no. 69 in C, composed *c* 1778 and dedicated to Field-Marshal Baron Gideon Ernst von Loudon.

Laurence, Elizabeth (b Harrogate, 22 Nov 1949), English mezzosoprano. Studied at RCM, London, and sang in Boulez's *Le marteau sans maître* at Vienna 1983, under the composer. Has specialized in contemporary repertory and sang in the fps of Osborne's *Electrification of the Soviet Union* and *Terrible Mouth* (Glyndebourne 1987 and London 1992), Höller's *Der Meister und Margarita* (Paris 1989) and Birtwistle's *Gawain* (CG 1991). Also admired as Bartók's Judith (BBC TV), Wagner's Erda and Fricka and in the fp of *Le Visage Nuptial* by Boulez (1988, revised version).

Lauri-Volpi, Giacomo (b Rome, 11 Dec 1892; d Valencia, 17 Mar 1979), Italian tenor. He studied in Rome. Debut Viterbo 1919, as Arturo. Sang at La Scala from 1922, at first under Toscanini; active in

Italy until 1965. NY Met. debut 1923 as Duke of Mantua; sang until 1934 in Italian repertory, including the first US Calaf (1926). London, CG, 1925 and 1936 as Chénier, Radames and Cavaradossi. Other roles included Nerone, Arnold, Des Grieux, Raoul and Manrico.

Lavallée, Calixa (b Verchères, Quebec, 28 Dec 1842; d Boston, MA, 21 Jan 1891), Canadian pianist and composer. Studied at the Paris Conservatory and later toured as pianist in North America.

Works include opera *The Widow* (1882); symphony; two string quartets; national air 'O Canada'.

Lavignac, (Alexandre Jean) Albert (b Paris, 21 Jan 1846; d Paris, 28 May 1916), French musicologist. Studied at the Paris Conservatory, where he became professor in 1882. Founder and first editor of the *Encyclopédie de la musique* (1913–16); also wrote many technical treatises and a study of Wagner.

lavolta, or Italian *volta* or French *volte*, an old dance in 3–2 time, probably of Italian origin, since the jump that was a feature of it retained the Italian word *volta*.

Lavotta, János (b Pusztafödémes, 5 Jul 1764; d Tállya, 11 Aug 1820), Hungarian violinist and composer. He was of noble birth, but left home on his father's remarriage and became a professional musician, at the same time following a legal career. He became very fashionable in Vienna and Budapest, conducted at various theatres, but took to drink and ended in decay. As a composer he was one of the outstanding exponents of ◊verbunkos music.

Lawes, Henry (b Dinton, Wiltshire, 5 Jan 1596; d London, 21 Oct 1662), English composer. Pupil of Coperario, appointed gentleman of the Chapel Royal in 1626. Having supplied music for Thomas Carew's masque *Coelum Britannicum*, produced at court, 18 Feb 1634, he was commissioned by the Earl of Bridgewater to set Milton's *Comus* for performance at Ludlow Castle, 29 Sept 1634. He was the subject of a sonnet by Milton, 1646. He was re-appointed to the court service on the Restoration in 1660 and wrote a coronation anthem for Charles II.

Works include opera *The Siege of Rhodes* (with Locke, Cooke, Colman and Hudson); masques (as above); coronation anthem *Zadok the Priest*, anthems, psalm-tunes; elegy on the death of his brother William; songs in plays by William Cartwright, Christmas songs in Herrick's *Hesperides*; airs, dialogues and songs for one and more voices.

Lawes, William (b Salisbury, bap. 1 May 1602; d Chester, 24 Sept 1645), English composer, brother of Henry ◊Lawes. Studied with Coperario and became a musician at Charles I's court. He joined the Royalist army during the Civil War and was killed by a shot during the siege of Chester.

Works include music for Shirley's masque *The Triumph of Peace* (with Ive, 1634) and Davenant's *The Triumph of the Prince d'Amour* and *The Unfortunate Lovers* (1638); anthems and psalms; music for consorts of viols; airs for violin and bass; catches and canons; airs and dialogues for one and more voices.

Lawrence, Marjorie (b Dean's Marsh, Victoria, 17 Feb 1907; d Little Rock, AR, 13 Jan 1979), Australian soprano. She studied in Paris. Debut Monte Carlo 1932, as Elisabeth. Paris, Opéra, 1933–36 as Ortrud, Brünnhilde, Massenet's Salomé, Reyer's Brunehild, Donna Anna and Brangaene. NY Met. debut 18 Dec 1935 as the *Walküre* Brünnhilde; also sang Salome, Thaïs and Tosca. Stricken by polio in 1941 but sang in opera until 1943, with limited stage movement. Retired 1953. Autobiography, *Interrupted Melody*, 1949.

Lawton, Jeffrey (b Oldham, 1939), English tenor. Studied at the RMCM and sang Alvaro and Otello in Manchester 1974–75. WNO from 1981, as Florestan, Huon, Laca and Aeneas in *Les Troyens*; his Siegfried and Tristan (1986 and 1993) were also admired at Covent Garden. Sang Otello in Paris and Brussels (1987), Siegmund and Siegfried at Cologne, 1988–89. ENO 1989 as Edmund in Reimann's *Lear*. Opera North 1992, as Shuisky.

Layolle, François de (Francesco dell' Aiolle) (b Florence, 4 Mar 1492; d Lyons, c 1540), French organist and composer. He was Benvenuto Cellini's music teacher; worked at church of SS Annunziate,

Florence, until 1518. His son Aleman Layolle afterwards taught Cellini's daughter and became organist at Lyon by 1521.

Works include Masses, motets; *canzoni*, madrigals.

Lazarev, Alexander (b Moscow, 5 July 1945), Russian conductor. Studied in Moscow and conducted at the Bolshoi there from 1973; chief conductor and artistic director from 1987. Contemporary music concerts from 1978 and has guested with the Berlin, Dresden and Munich Philharmonics. UK debut 1987, with the Royal Liverpool PO. Led the Bolshoi company at Glasgow and Edinburgh 1990, with *Mlada*, Tchaikovsky's *Maid of Orleans* and Prokofiev's *The Duenna*. Metropolitan Opera with the Bolshoi 1991, principal guest of the BBC SO from 1992.

Lazaro, Hippolito (b Barcelona, 13 Aug 1887; d Madrid, 14 May 1974), Spanish tenor. Debut Barcelona 1909; sang in the fp of Mascagni's *Parisina* (Milan, 1913), and at Rome in 1921 created the title role in *Piccolo Marat*. NY Met. debut 1918, as the Duke of Mantua; also successful as Arturo. Returned to La Scala 1924 (fp Giordano's *La cena della beffe*).

Lazzari, Sylvio (b Bozen, 30 Dec 1857; d Paris, 18 Jun 1944), Austro-Italian composer, later belonging to the French school and naturalized French. Studied at Innsbruck, Munich and the Paris Conservatory, where Franck was one of his teachers.

Works include operas *Amor* (Prague, 1898), *La Lépreuse* (Paris, 1912), *Le Sautériot* (Chicago, 1918), *Melaenis, La Tour de feu* (Paris, 1928); incidental music for Goethe's *Faust*; symphony in E♭ major, orchestral suite in F major, and chamber music.

Thou'rt all so fit, that some have pass'd their votes
Thy notes beget the words, not words thy notes.
T Norton, *Commendatory Verses on Henry Lawes*, 1653

Lazzari, Virgilio (b Assisi, 20 Apr 1887; d Castel Gandolfo, 4 Oct 1953), Italian, later American, bass. Opera debut Rome 1914. US debut St Louis 1916, as Ramfis; Chicago 1918–36 and NY Met. 1933–50 (debut as Pedro, in *L'Africaine*). He sang Pistol and Leporello at Salzburg 1934–39. CG 1939. Sang Montemezzi's Archibaldo at Genoa in the year of his death.

leader the usual English name for the principal first violin in an orchestra or of a string quartet or other chamber music team.

In America, especially in journalism, the conductor is often called 'leader'; the usual US term for the leading first orchestral violin is Concertmaster, from German *Konzertmeister*.

leading motif ◊Leitmotiv.

leading-note the seventh note of a major or ascending minor scale 'leading' to the tonic by a semitonal step.

Lear opera by Reimann (libretto by C Henneberg after Shakespeare), produced Munich, 9 Jul 1978. King Lear disowns faithful daughter Cordelia after she is unable to express her love for him, dividing his kingdom between treacherous daughters Goneril and Regan instead. Lear becomes insane and all end up dead.

Lear, Evelyn (b Brooklyn, 8 Jan 1926), American soprano. She studied at Juilliard and in Berlin; debut there as the Composer, 1958. Created Klebe's Alkmene, Berlin 1961, and in 1962 sang the first of many performances of Berg's Lulu (London, SW, 1966; also recorded, under Böhm). She created Lavinia in Levy's *Mourning Becomes Elektra*, on her NY Met. debut (1967) and sang there until 1985 in operas by Mozart, Puccini, Strauss and Verdi; often with her husband Thomas Stewart, whom she married 1955. Sang the Marschallin at NY Met. Oct 1985. Sang in Bernstein's *On the Town*, London 1992.

Lebel, Firmin (b Noyon; d Rome, 18 Nov 1573), French cleric and musician. Worked in the diocese of Noyon, but in 1540 succeeded Mallapert as *maestro di cappella* at Santa Maria Maggiore in Rome and later occupied a similar post at San Luigi dei Francesi, eventually becoming, in 1561, a singer in the Papal choir.

Leben des Orest, *The Life of Orestes*, opera by Křenek (libretto by composer), produced Leipzig, 19 Jan 1930. Orestes travels from early matricide to eventual forgiveness.

Lebrun (born *Danzi*), Franziska (b Mannheim, bap. 24 Mar 1756; d Berlin, 14 May 1791), German soprano and composer of Italian descent, daughter of a cellist at the court of Mannheim, sister of Franz Danzi and wife of Ludwig Lebrun. She made her first appearance 1772 in Sacchini's *La contadina in corte*, was engaged by the court opera Mannheim, where she sang in the fp of Holzbauer's *Gunther von Schwarzburg*. Composed sonatas. Sang in the first production at La Scala, (Salieri's *Europa riconsciuta*, 1778), and in England. She was an exact contemporary of Mozart.

Lebrun, Jean (b Lyons, 6 Apr 1759; d Paris, 1809), French horn player. Pupil of Punto in Paris. Played in the Paris Opéra orchestra, 1786–92, and later worked in London and Berlin. He is said to have invented the mute for the horn.

Lebrun, Louis (Sébastien) (b Paris, 10 Dec 1764; d Paris, 27 Jun 1829), French tenor and composer. He sang at the Paris Opéra and Opéra-Comique and was Napoleon's *maître de chapelle*.

Works include operas *Marcelin* (1800), *Le Rossignol* (1816) and many others; a Te Deum, etc.

Lebrun, Ludwig (August) (b Mannheim, bap. 2 May 1752; d Berlin, 16 Dec 1790), German oboist and composer of French descent. He was oboist at the Mannheim court, which he followed to Munich in 1778, and toured all over Europe with his wife, Francesca.

Works include seven oboe concertos; 12 trios with oboe parts.

Lechner, Leonhard (b Etsch valley, *c* 1553; d Stuttgart, 9 Sept 1606), Austrian composer. Pupil of Lassus in the court chapel at Munich, became a schoolmaster at Nuremberg in 1570 and in 1579 began to pub. a revised edition of Lassus's works. In 1584–85 he was music director to Count Eitel Friedrich of Hohenzollern at Hechingen and in 1595 took a similar post at the court of Württemberg at Stuttgart.

Works include Masses, motets, Magnificat, psalms, introits, wedding motet for the Elector Johann Georg I of Saxony; sacred and 160 secular German songs for two–five voices in seven pub. books; St John Passion (1594).

Leclair, Jean-Marie (b Lyons, 10 May 1697; d Paris, 22 Oct 1764), French composer and violinist. Began his career as a dancer, and in 1722 was ballet master in Turin, but while there turned to the violin, studying with Somis. In 1728 he settled in Paris, having great success as a player and composer. Member of the royal orchestra 1734–36, he then went to Holland, returning to Paris after various travels in 1743. For a time in the service of Don Philip of Spain at Chambéry, he joined the orchestra of the Duke of Gramont in 1748. He met his death at the hand of an unknown murderer. He is best known for his Italian-influenced instrumental pieces, although the opera *Scylla et Glaucus* has been successfully performed (1979) and recorded.

Works include opera *Scylla et Glaucus* (1746; concert performance London, 1979); ballets and 'divertissements'; 12 violin concertos; 48 violin sonatas; violin duets; trio sonatas.

Lecocq, (Alexandre) Charles (b Paris, 3 Jun 1832; d Paris, 24 Oct 1918), French composer. Studied at the Paris Conservatory, 1849–54, and produced his first operetta, *Le Docteur Miracle*, in 1857, having tied with Bizet in a competition organized by Offenbach. He did not make a great success until he produced *Fleur de thé* in 1868 and until then supplemented his income by teaching and organ playing. After that he made a fortune with his many operettas.

Works include opera *Plutus* (1886); operettas *Les Cent Vierges*, *La Fille de Madame Angot* (1872), *Giroflé-Giroflà* (1874), *La Petite Mariée* (1875), *Le Petit Duc* (1878), *Camargo* (1878), *Ninette*, *Barbe-bleue* and about 40 others; orchestral works; violin and piano sonata; sacred songs for women's voices *La Chapelle au couvent*; instrumental pieces; piano works; songs.

Leçons des Ténèbres, French, settings of the Lamentations of Jeremiah for performance at matins on the last three days of Holy Week. ◊Lamentations.

Ledger, Philip (b Bexhill, 12 Dec 1937), English conductor, keyboard player and editor. He studied at Cambridge and has held posts there and at the University of East Anglia. Active at Aldeburgh Festival since 1968 and has been accompanist to leading singers. As a conductor he has given Purcell's *King Arthur* with the EOG in Britain and abroad. His recordings of Bach and Handel have a sure sense of period style. Principal of Royal Scottish Academy of Music and Drama from 1982.

Leduc, Simon (b Paris, *c* 1748; d Paris, Jan 1777), French composer and publisher. A pupil of Gaviniès, he was joint director (with the latter and Gossec) of the Concert Spirituel from 1773. As a publisher he issued from 1767 works by himself and other composers.

Works include three violin concertos; three symphonies and two *symphonies concertantes*; violin sonatas and duets; trio sonatas.

Lee, Nathaniel (b ? 1653; d 1692), English playwright. ◊Finger (*Rival Queens*, with D Purcell); ◊Purcell (*Oedipus*, *Massacre of Paris*, *Sophonisba* and *Theodosius*); ◊Stagins (*Gloriana*).

Leech, Richard (b Binghampton, CA, 1956), American tenor. Sang widely in the USA from 1980; NY City Opera debut 1988 (Duke of Mantua), NY Met. 1990 (Faust). Sang Raoul in *Les Huguenots* at the Berlin Deutsche Oper (1987) and at CG (1992). Other roles include Rodolfo (Chicago 1987 and La Scala 1991), Donizetti's Edgardo and Nemorino, and Pinkerton (Washington DC, and Florence).

Leeds Musical Festival a triennial music festival established at Leeds, on the opening of the new town hall, in 1858. Many performances of choral music including fps of works by Elgar (*Caractacus* and *Falstaff*), Vaughan Williams (*Sea Symphony*), Holst (*Choral Symphony*) and Walton's *Belshazzar's Feast*. John ◊Warrack.

Lees, Benjamin (b Harbin, Manchuria, 8 Jan 1924), Russian-born American composer, taken to the USA as a child. He studied piano in San Francisco and Los Angeles. After serving in the US Army 1942–45, he studied at UCLA, theory, harmony and composition with Halsey Stevens, Ingolf Dahl and Ernst Kanitz, also taking private lessons from George Antheil. In 1955 he won a Guggenheim Fellowship and in 1956 a Fulbright Fellowship.

Works include operas *The Oracle* (1955) and *The Gilded Cage* (1971); five symphonies (1953–86; no. 3 for string quartet and orchestra); concertos for violin, oboe and piano (2); *Profile* for orchestra, concerto for orchestra, *Declamations* for string orchestra and piano; *Visions of Poets*, a dramatic cantata (1961); concerto for brass and orchestra (1983); *Portrait of Rodin* for orchestra (1984),

Philip Ledger – conductor / organist

1   Bach: Mass in B minor – 'Sanctus'
    It offers complete and indisputable reassurance that, despite the muddles in our lives, everything is all right.

2   Schubert: Piano Quintet (*Trout*)
    The first movement is like champagne and never fails to elevate my spirits.

3   Mozart: Symphony no. 41 in C (*Jupiter*)
    The finale has a quite extraordinary combination of exuberance and elegance.

4   Delius: 'On hearing the first cuckoo in Spring'
    Based on a Norwegian folksong, but wonderfully evocative of the English countryside.

5   Fauré: Requiem – 'In Paradisium'
    This piece has an ethereal, other-worldly quality and, for me, is associated with the Chapel of King's College, Cambridge, where for many years I was Director of Music.

horn concerto (1992); four string quartets (1951, 1955, 1982, 1989), three violin sonatas (1953, 1972, 1991), cello sonata (1981), piano trio (1983); four piano sonatas (1949, 1950, 1956, 1963), violin sonata; piano music.

Leeuw, Ton de (b Rotterdam, 16 Nov 1926), Dutch composer. Studied composition in Paris with Messiaen and Thomas de Hartmann. He became interested in musical folklore and in 1961 toured India to collect material. His chief interest is in experimental music, and he has been influenced by *musique concrète* as well as serialism.

Works include TV opera *Alceste* (1963), opera *De Droom/The Dream*, 1965): oratorio *Job* (1956); two symphonies, *Ombres* for orchestra and percussion, concertos for piano and string orchestra; *Spatial Music I–IV*, *Litany of Our Time* (1965–68), *Resonances* for orchestra (1985), concerto for guitar and strings (1989); two string quartets (1958, 1964); *Apparences I* for cello (1987); choral and piano music; electronic pieces.

LeFanu, Nicola (b Wickham Bishops, Essex, 28 Apr 1947), English composer, daughter of Elizabeth Maconchy. She studied at Oxford and with Wellesz and Petrassi. Lecturer, Morley College 1970–75, King's College, London, from 1977.

Works include operas *Dawnpath* (1977), *Blood Wedding* (1992) and *Wild Man* (1995), ballet *The Last Laugh* for soprano, tape and chamber orchestra (1972); *Preludio* for strings (1967; revised 1976), *The Hidden Landscape* for orchestra (1973), *Columbia Fall* for percussion, harp and strings (1975), *Farne* for orchestra (1979); *Variations* for piano and orchestra (1982); concerto for alto saxophone and orchestra (1989); *The Valleys shall Sing* for chorus and wind (1973), *For we are the Stars* for 16 voices (1978), *Like a Wave of the Sea* for chorus and ensemble of early instruments (1981), *Stranded on my Heart* for tenor, chorus and strings (1984); *The Silver Strand* for chorus (1989); Clarinet quintet (1971), *Collana* for six instruments (1976), *Deva* for cello and seven instruments (1979); *Invisible Places* clarinet quintet (1986); *Nocturne* for cello and piano (1988).

Leffler-Burckhard, Martha (b Berlin, 16 Jun 1865; d Wiesbaden, 14 May 1954), German soprano. She studied with Viardot in Paris. Debut Strasbourg 1888; sang in Breslau, Cologne and Bremen 1889–97, Wiesbaden 1900–12 and at the Hofoper Berlin 1913–18. Bayreuth 1906–08 as Kundry, Sieglinde and Ortrud. CG 1903 and 1907 as Brünnhilde, Leonore and Isolde. NY Met. 1908.

Le Flem, Paul (b Lézardrieux, Côtes-du-Nord, 18 Mar 1881; d Trégastel, Côtes-du-Nord, 31 Jul 1984), French composer and critic. Pupil of d'Indy and Roussel, among others, later professor at the Schola Cantorum, chorus master at the Opéra-Comique, conductor of the Chanteurs de Saint-Gervais and critic for *Comoedia*.

Works include operas *Le Rossignol de Saint-Malo* (1942) and *Dahut*; choreographic drama on Shakespeare's *Macbeth*; cantata *Aucassin et Nicolette*; four symphonies (1908–78), *Triptyque symphonique* for orchestra; fantasy for piano and orchestra; chamber music; violin and piano sonata; piano works; choral music.

Le Franc, Guillaume (b Rouen; d Lausanne, Jun 1570), French composer. Fled to Switzerland as a Protestant, settled at Geneva in 1541 and established a school of music, becoming master of the children and singer at the cathedral the next year, and edited Calvin's Genevan Psalter, in which Bourgeois and Marot also had a hand; but in 1545 he left for the cathedral of Lausanne. In 1565 he issued a new Psalter there with some tunes of his own.

legato Italian = 'bound, tied'; in music the word is used to designate a sustained manner of singing or playing, one note leading smoothly to the next; the opposite of *staccato*.

Legende von der heiligen Elizabeth, Die, *The Legend of St Elizabeth of Hungary*, oratorio by Liszt (words by Otto Roquette), fp in Hungary, Budapest, 15 Aug 1865; first produced as an opera, Weimar, 23 Oct 1881.

Legend of Joseph, The (Strauss.) ◊Josephslegende.

Music with dinner is an insult both to the cook and the violinist.

G K Chesterton, quoted in *New York Times*, 1967

Legend of the Invisible City of Kitezh and the Maiden Fevronia, *Skazhanie o nevidimom gradie Kitezh i dieve Fevronie*, opera by Rimsky-Korsakov (libretto by V I Bielsky), produced St Petersburg, 20 Feb 1907. Revived St Petersburg and London, 1994. A golden mist magically hides the city of Kitezh from the invading Tatars. Fevronia, captured by the barbarians, escapes to her slain groom, Prince Vsevolod, in eternal life in the Invisible City.

Legend of Tsar Saltan, The, *Skazka o Tsarie Saltanie*, opera by Rimsky-Korsakov (libretto by V I Bielsky, after Pushkin), produced Moscow, 3 Nov 1900. Prince Guidon transforms himself into a tree to rescue his mother and return her to the Tsar.

leger lines the short strokes drawn through or between those notes which go above or below the stave in musical notation.

Legge, Walter (b London, 1 Jun 1906; d St Jean, Cap Ferrat, 22 Mar 1979), English administrator and writer. Engaged 1927 by HMV record co. as a writer and formed subscription societies for recording of then neglected music such as Haydn's quartets and Wolf's Lieder. After a war spent in troop entertainment he was not reluctant to engage artists who had been tainted with Nazism: many major recordings including opera sets conducted by Karajan, Knappertsbusch and Furtwängler and a *Rosenkavalier* with his wife, Elisabeth Schwarzkopf. Founded Philharmonia Orchestra, London, 1945 and helped set new standards in orchestral performance. He attempted to

---

Nicola LeFanu – composer

1   Mozart: *Nozze di Figaro/Marriage of Figaro*(Berganza/ Blegen/Harper/Geraint Evans/Fischer-Dieskau/English Chamber Orch./Barenboim)
A happy reminder of my first Figaros in the 1960s, when I got to know the opera both as a student sitting in the slips, and as the director of a youth production.

2   Janáček: *Káta Kabanová* (Söderström/Vienna Staatsoper/ Vienna PO/Mackerras)
The 'double' love duet in Act 2 (two pairs of such different lovers) is one of the most moving of Janáček's scenes.

3   Maconchy: *My Dark Heart* (Manning/Odaline de la Martinez/Lontano)
Among my favourite works by my mother, Elizabeth Maconchy, is this haunting setting of three of Petrarch's sonnets in memory of Laura, in the Anglo-Irish version of Synge.

4   Lumsdaine: *Aria for Edward John Eyre* (Manning/Guy/ Howarth/Gemini)
A musical journey following Eyre's epic exploration of Australia; hearing the première of this marvellous work in 1972 was one of the turning points of my career.

5   Gilbert: *Nine or Ten Osannas* (Music Projects London/ Richard Bernas)
The exuberant invention of this chamber work by Anthony Gilbert never ceases to delight me.

disband the orchestra in 1964 but it was immediately re-formed as the New Philharmonia Orchestra with Otto Klemperer as conductor for life.

Leggenda di Sakuntala, La opera by Alfano (libretto by composer, based on Kalldasa's play), produced Bologna, Teatro Comunale, 10 Dec 1921. The MS was destroyed during World War II. Alfano reconstructed the opera for production in 1952, as *Sakuntala*. Sakuntala expires after meeting lover king, but their child becomes a world hero.

Legrant, Guillaume, Franco-Flemish composer. Between 1419 and 1421 he was a member of the papal chapel. He wrote three *chansons*, a florid organ piece without title, and a very chromatic *Gloria-Credo* pair.

Legrenzi, Giovanni (b Clusone near Bergamo, bap. 12 Aug 1626; d Venice, 27 May 1690), Italian composer. Organist at his birthplace, then *Maestro di cappella* at Ferrara. In 1672 he became director of the Conservatorio dei Mendicanti at Venice and in 1685 *maestro di cappella* of St Mark's there.

Works include operas *Achille in Sciro* (1663), *Eteocle e Polinice* (1675), *La divisione del mondo*, *Germanico sul Reno* (1676), *Totila*, *I due Cesari* (1683), *Il Giustino*, *Pertinace* (1684), and *c* ten others; Masses, motets, psalms and other church music; orchestral works; church sonatas.

Legros, Joseph (b Monampteuil, near Laon, 7 Sept 1739; d La Rochelle, 20 Dec 1793), French tenor and concert manager. Made his operatic debut in 1764 in Paris and sang in Rameau's *Castor et Pollux*, *Zoroastre*, *Hippolyte et Aricie* and *Dardanus*. Later became Gluck's principal tenor; he was the first tenor Orphée and created roles in *Alceste* and both *Iphigénie* operas. He was forced by corpulence to abandon the stage in 1783, and turned to concert management.

There is nothing to it. You have only to hit the right notes at the right time and the instrument plays itself.
J S Bach on playing the organ, quoted in Geiringer, *The Bach Family*, 1954

Lehár, Ferencz (Franz) (b Komárom, 30 Apr 1870; d Ischl, 24 Oct 1948), Hungarian composer. Studied at the Prague Conservatory and became a military bandmaster. Later he devoted himself entirely to the successful composition of operettas. During his last years he lived in retirement at Ischl.

Works include opera *Kukuška* (later called *Tajana*, 1896), operettas *The Merry Widow* (1905), *The Count of Luxembourg* (1909), *Gypsy Love* (1910), *The Three Graces*, *Pompadour*, *Springtime*, *Frasquita* (1922), *Clo Clo*, *The Blue Mazurka*, *Frederica* (1928), *The Land of Smiles* (1929) and many others; symphonic poem *Fieber*, three comedy scenes for orchestra.

Lehmann, Lilli (b Würzburg, 24 Nov 1848; d Berlin, 17 May 1929), German soprano. Studied under her mother, the singer and harpist Marie Loew, appeared at Prague in 1865 in *Die Zauberflöte*. At an early age, was engaged at Danzig in 1868, at Leipzig in 1869, and made her first appearance in Berlin in 1870. In 1876 she sang minor roles in the first production of the *Ring*, at Bayreuth, and in 1880 first visited London, returned 1884, CG, as Isolde and Elisabeth. NY Met. 1885–99 as Carmen, Brünnhilde, Venus and Marguerite. She was successful in more than 150 roles.

Lehmann, Liza (Elizabetta Nina Mary Frederika) (b London, 11 Jul 1862; d Pinner, Middlesex, 19 Sept 1918), English singer and composer. Studied first with her mother, Amelia Chambers, an accomplished amateur composer and later at Rome, Wiesbaden and at home with MacCunn, also singing with Randegger. In 1885 she made her first appearance as a singer at St James's Hall, where she sang for the last time in 1894, when she married Herbert Bedford. The composer David Bedford is her grandson.

Works include light opera *The Vicar of Wakefield* (after Goldsmith, 1906), musical comedy *Sergeant Brue* (L Housman); incidental music for *Everyman* and other plays; ballads for voice and

orchestra; song cycles *In a Persian Garden* (Omar Khayyám), *In Memoriam* (Tennyson).

Lehmann, Lotte (b Perleberg, 27 Feb 1888; d Santa Barbara, 26 Aug 1976), German soprano. Studied in Berlin with Erna Tiedke, Eva Reinhold and Mathilde Mallinger, making her debut in Hamburg in a small role. She soon established herself and in 1914 was engaged at the Vienna Staatsoper, where R Strauss selected her to sing the Composer in *Ariadne auf Naxos* and Octavian in *Der Rosenkavalier*. Later she also sang the Marschallin in the latter opera, one of her greatest roles; she created the Dyer's Wife in *Die Frau ohne Schatten* (1919) and Christine in *Intermezzo* (1924). She was a great Wagner singer and made her American debut in the role of Sieglinde in *Die Walküre*, London, CG, 1924–38 as Donna Elvira, Leonore, Elsa, Eva and Desdemona; much valued for the warmth of personality revealed in her interpretations. In 1938 she settled in the USA, living mostly in California. She pub. a novel, an autobiography, and other writings on music.

Lehnhoff, Nikolaus (b Hanover, 20 May 1939), German stage director and designer. Trained at the Deutsche Oper Berlin, Bayreuth and the NY Met. Debut as director with *Die Frau ohne Schatten* at the Paris Opéra (1972), *Elektra* at Chicago, 1975. The *Ring* at San Francisco (1983–85) and Munich (1987). NY Met. debut 1989, *Salome*. At Glyndebourne has staged Janáček's *Káta Kabanova* (1988), *Jenůfa* (1989) and *The Makropoulos Case* (1995). Salzburg Festival 1990, *Idomeneo*.

Lehrstück German = 'didactic piece, educational play'; a small form of music drama cultivated in Germany in the 1920s–1930s by Eisler, Hindemith, Weill and other composers, the chief literary exponent being Bertolt Brecht. It was cultivated mainly by the working classes in Germany at first, though later the influence spread to other European countries and to the USA. The Lehrstück makes use of historical material and dialectical discussion for the purpose of enlightening the masses, and it was for a time a counteragent to the Nazi movement until its exponents were forced to emigrate.

The fp of Hindemith's *Lehrstück*, for soloists, chorus and orchestra (texts by Brecht) was at Baden-Baden, 28 Jul 1929.

Leibowitz, René (b Warsaw, 17 Feb 1913; d Paris, 29 Aug 1972), French-Polish composer. Settled in Paris in 1926 and in 1930–33 studied in Germany and Austria with Schoenberg and Webern. He destroyed all his works written up to 1937, including six string quartets and devoted himself entirely to 12-note music. He conducted works of that school in the USA in 1947–48. He was known as a leading teacher of 12-note composition and published *Schoenberg et son école* and *Introduction à la musique de douze sons*.

Works include music drama *La Nuit close* (1949); four unaccompanied choruses; symphonies and variations for orchestra; chamber symphony for 12 instruments, chamber concerto for violin, piano and 17 instruments, *Tourist Death* for soprano and chamber orchestra (1943), *L'Explication des métaphores* for speaker, two pianos, harp and percussion; string quartet, ten canons for oboe, clarinet and bassoon, wind quintet; violin and piano sonata; sontata and pieces for piano; songs.

Leicester, ou Le Château de Kenilworth opera by Auber (libretto by Scribe and A H Mélesville, based on Scott's *Kenilworth*), produced Paris, Opéra-Comique, 25 Jan 1823. Leicester's friendship with Elizabeth I makes his wife superfluous.

Leich German = 'lay'; a medieval type of German song similar to the French *lai*.

Leichtentritt, Hugo (b Pleszow, Posen, 1 Jan 1874; d Cambridge, MA, 13 Nov 1951), German musicologist. Studied with Paine at Harvard University and later at the Hochschule für Musik in Berlin, where he became professor at the Klindworth-Scharwenka Conservatory. In 1933 he left Germany as a refugee from the Nazi régime and returned to USA to join the staff of Harvard University. His books include studies of Keiser, Handel, Chopin, Busoni and the motet.

Leider, Frida (b Berlin, 18 Apr 1888; d Berlin, 4 Jun 1975), German soprano. Debut Halle 1915, as Elisabeth. Berlin, Staatsoper, 1923–40 as Dido in *Les Troyens*, Donna Anna and Leonore. London, CG,

1924–38 as the Marschallin, Armide, Senta, Venus and the *Trovatore* Leonora. Bayreuth 1928–38 as Brünnhilde, Kundry and Isolde; NY Met. 1933–34, same roles. Also sang in Chicago (debut 1928), Buenos Aires, Paris and Milan.

Leiferkus, Sergei (b Leningrad, 4 Apr 1946), Russian baritone. Studied in Leningrad and joined the Kirov Opera 1977, as Andrei in *War and Peace*. Wexford Festival 1982–86, in Massenet's *Grisélidis* and *Le Jongleur de Notre Dame*, *Hans Heiling* and *Königskinder*. Scottish Opera from 1985 as Don Giovanni and Onegin. Has sung at CG from 1987 as Eugene Onegin and Tomsky (with the Kirov), Count Luna, Prince Igor, and Ruprecht in *The Fiery Angel* (1992). US debut 1987 in Shostakovich's 13th symphony, with the Boston SO; opera debut as Telramund at San Francisco, 1990. Glyndebourne debut 1989, as Mandryka; NY Met. as Iago, 1994.

Leigh, Walter (b London, 22 Jun 1905; d near Tobruk, Libya, 12 Jun 1942), English composer. Studied at Cambridge and with Hindemith in Berlin. In 1932 a work of his was performed at the ISCM festival in Vienna. He joined up during World War II and was killed in action.

Works include comic operas *The Pride of the Regiment*, *Jolly Roger* (1933); pantomime *Aladdin* (1931); revues *Nine Sharp* and *Little Revue*, 1939; incidental music to Aristophanes' *Frogs*, Shakespeare's *Midsummer Night's Dream*; overture *Agincourt, Music for String Orchestra*, *Three Pieces for Amateur Orchestra*; concertino for harpsichord and strings; three movements for string quartet (1929), trio for flute, oboe and piano and sonatina for viola and piano; songs.

Leighton, Kenneth (b Wakefield, 2 Oct 1929; d Edinburgh, 25 Aug 1988), English composer. Studied at Queen's College, Oxford and with Petrassi in Rome. He won several prizes for composition. Lecturer at Edinburgh University, 1956–68, and at Oxford University, 1968–70. Professor at Edinburgh University from 1970.

Works include opera *Columba* (1980); concerto for strings; two symphonies (1964, 1974); three piano concertos (1951–69), violin concerto, cello concerto; string quartet, two violin sonatas; three piano sonatas; Fantasy-Octet, 'Homage to Percy Grainger' (1982); choral works.

Leighton, William (b ? Plash, Shropshire, c 1565; d London, buried 31 Jul 1622), gentleman pensioner under Elizabeth and James I. He pub. in 1614 a collection of airs for voices and instruments entitled *The Teares or Lamentacions of a Sorrowfull Soule* with contributions by Bull, Byrd, Coperario, Dowland, A· Ferrabosco (junior), Ford, O Gibbons, Giles, Hooper, Robert Johnson, Robert Jones, Kindersley, Leighton, T Lupo, John Milton (senior), Peerson, Pilkington, John Ward, Weelkes and Wilbye.

Leinsdorf, Erich (b Vienna, 4 Feb 1912; d Zurich, 11 Sept 1993), Austrian, later American, conductor. Studied with Paul Emerich and Hedwig Kammer-Rosenthal at the Vienna Gymnasium. In 1934 he became assistant to Bruno Walter and Toscanini at the Salzburg Festival and later appeared as a conductor in Italy, France and Belgium. In 1938 he was engaged as an assistant conductor at the NY Met, debut with *Die Walküre*, becoming chief conductor 1939–43. He served in the US Army from 1944 and returned to the Met. 1958–62. Music director Boston SO 1962–69. 1977–80 principal conductor West Berlin Radio SO.

Leipzig Gewandhaus Orchestra ◊Gewandhaus.

Leitmotiv (plural *Leitmotive*) German = lit. 'leading motif'; a short theme associated with a personage, object or idea in an opera or other work, quoted at appropriate moments or worked up symphonically. Its chief exponent is Wagner, but it was not his invention, for it occurs in earlier compositions. ◊*idée fixe*.

Leitner, Ferdinand (b Berlin, 4 Mar 1912), German conductor. He studied in Berlin with Schreker, Schnabel and Muck; conducted in Berlin, Hamburg and Munich before moving to Stuttgart. He was music director until 1969 and led many productions of Wieland Wagner; also gave fps of Orff's *Oedipus der Tyrann* (1959) and *Prometheus* (1968). US debut at Chicago 1969 (*Don Giovanni*). He was at Zurich Opera 1969–84 and was principal conductor of the Hague PO 1976–80. Well known conductor of Bruckner and Mozart

and gave operas by Berg and Busoni (the only recording of *Doktor Faust*). Conducted Mozart's C-minor Mass at Salzburg, 1985, *Tannhäuser* at Chicago (1988) and *Ariadne auf Naxos* for RAI at Turin, 1989.

Le Jeune, Claude (or Claudin) (b Valenciennes, c 1530; d Paris, buried 26 Sept 1600), Franco-Flemish composer. Worked most of his life in Paris. Having turned Huguenot, he tried to escape from Paris during the siege of 1588, and his MSS were saved from seizure by the Catholic soldiers by his colleague Mauduit, himself a Catholic. Later Le Jeune became chamber musician to the king. Like Baïf and Mauduit, he was an exponent of *musique mesurée*.

Works include motets, psalms set to rhymed versions in measured music and also to tunes in the Genevan Psalter set for three voices; *chansons*, madrigals; instrumental fantasies, etc.

Lekeu, Guillaume (b Heusy, near Verviers, 20 Jan 1870; d Angers, 21 Jan 1894), Belgian composer. Studied with Franck and d'Indy in Paris. In 1891 he obtained the second Belgian Prix de Rome with the lyric scene *Andromède*.

Works include symphonic study on Shakespeare's *Hamlet* (1887), *Fantasie sur deux airs populaires angevins* for orchestra; Adagio for string quartet and orchestra; Introduction and Adagio for brass; *Chant lyrique* for chorus and orchestra; piano quartet (completed by d'Indy), piano trio; violin and piano sonata (1891), cello and piano sonata (completed by D'Indy); three piano pieces; *Trois Poèmes* for voice and piano.

Lélio, ou Le Retour à la Vie, *Lélio, or The Return to Life*, 'lyric monodrama' by Berlioz for an actor, solo voices, chorus, piano and orchestra, op. 14bis, composed in 1831 as a sequel to the *Symphonie fantastique* and first performed with the latter, Paris Conservatory, 9 Dec 1832.

Le Maistre, Matthieu (b Roclenge-sur-Geer, near Liège, c 1505; d Dresden, 1577), Flemish composer. He succeeded Walther as *Kapellmeister* to the Saxon court at Dresden in 1554, a post from which he retired with a pension in 1568.

Works include Masses, motets; Latin and German sacred songs, setting of the Lutheran catechism in Latin; German secular songs, etc.

Lemare, Edwin (Henry) (b Ventnor, Isle of Wight, 9 Sept 1865; d LA, 24 Sept 1934), English organist and composer. Studied at the RAM in London and after various church apointments became organist of St Margaret's, Westminster. In 1900 he toured in the USA, having by that time become a very successful concert organist. He was attached to the Carnegie Institute at Pittsburg 1902–15, was municipal organist at San Francisco, 1917–21, and at Portland, ME, from 1921.

Works include two symphonies for organ and a vast amount of other concert music for his instrument.

Lemeshev, Sergey (b Knyazevo, 10 Jul 1902; d Moscow, 26 Jun 1977), Russian tenor. He studied with Stanislavsky; debut Sverdlovsk 1926. Bolshoi, Moscow, from 1931 as Lensky, Faust, Roméo and Alamaviva and in operas by Glinka, Rimsky-Korsakov and Nápravník. Retired 1961. Made some films, and directed opera from 1951.

Lemmens, Jaak Nikolaas (b Zoerle-Parwijs, Westerloo, 3 Jan 1823; d Linterpoort, near Malines, 30 Jan 1881), Belgian organist, pianist and composer. Studied at the Brussels Conservatory and with Hesse at Breslau. In 1849 he became organ professor at the Brussels Conservatory, but after 1857, when he married Hellen Sherrington, he lived much in England.

Works include sonata, offertories and other concert music for organ, a treatise for accompaniment of plainsong, etc.

Lemmens-Sherrington (born *Sherrington*), Hellen (b Preston, 4 Oct 1834; d Brussels, 9 May 1906), English soprano, wife of Jaak ◊Lemmens. Studied with Verhulst at Rotterdam and at the Brussels Conservatory, and made her debut in London in 1856.

Lemminkäinen's Return symphonic legend by Sibelius, op. 22, one of four on subjects from the *Kalevala*, composed 1893–95, fp Helsinki, 13 Apr 1896. The other three are *The Swan of Tuonela*, *Lemminkainen and the Maidens of Saari*, *Lemminkainen in Tuonela*.

Lemnitz, Tiana (b Metz, 26 Oct 1897; d Berlin, 5 Feb 1994), German soprano. Studied in Metz and then at the Hoch Conservatory in

Frankfurt. She made her debut in 1921 and sang at Aachen 1922–29. From 1929 to 1933 she was the leading soprano at Hanover and 1934–57 at the Berlin Staatsoper; roles there included Mimi, Aida, Desdemona, Sieglinde and Jenůfa. She sang at CG in 1936 and 1938, as Eva, Octavian and Pamina.

Lemoyne, Jean Baptiste (b Eymet, Périgord, 3 Apr 1751; d Paris, 30 Dec 1796), French composer and conductor. Having conducted in the provinces, he went to Berlin to study with Graun, Kirnberger and Schulz, and was there appointed second *Kapellmeister* by Frederick the Great. But after visiting Warsaw he returned to France and produced in 1782 the opera *Électre* in the style of Gluck, whose pupil he claimed to be. When Gluck denied this, he joined the partisans of Piccinni.

Works include operas *Électre* (after Sophocles, 1782), *Phèdre* (after Racine, 1786), *Les Prétendus* (1789), *Nephté*, etc.; ballets.

Lenér Quartet Hungarian ensemble founded 1918 with Janö Lenér and Joseph Smilovits (violins), Sandor Roth (viola), Imre Hartmann (cello). Many concerts in London 1922–39; most often heard in performances of Beethoven quartets, which they recorded complete. NY from 1929. Largely avoided modern repertory.

'Leningrad' Symphony Shostakovich's seventh symphony, op. 60, awarded the Stalin prize 1942 and first performed in Kuibishev, by the evacuated Bolshoi Theatre Orchestra of Moscow, 5 Mar 1942. The Nazi march in the first movement is parodied by Bartók in his Concerto for Orchestra (1944).

lento Italian = 'slow'.

Lenton, John (1656–London, c 1719), English violinist and composer. He was a musician at court under Charles II, William and Mary and Anne, pub. an instruction book for the violin containing airs of his own, revised the tunes for Durfey's *Wit and Mirth* and contributed songs for various collections.

Works include incidental music for Shakespeare's *Othello* (1697), Otway's *Venice Preserved* (1707), Rowe's *Tamerlane* and *The Fair Penitent* and other plays.

Lenya, Lotte (b Vienna, 18 Oct 1898; d New York, 27 Nov 1981), Austrian-born American actress. After study in Zurich moved to Berlin and married Kurt Weill there 1926. Sang in *Mahagonny* at Baden-Baden 1927, and created Jenny in *Die Dreigroschenoper* 1928; Weill had to compromise on the range of her part, owing to her vocal limitations: her success here and in 1950s revivals of Weill's German works was as much due to her histrionic talents.

Leo, Leonardo (Lionardo Oronzo Salvatore de) (b San Vito degli Schiavi, near Brindisi, 5 Aug 1694; d Naples, 31 Oct 1744), Italian composer. Pupil of Provenzale and Fago in Naples at the Conservatorio della Pietà dei Turchini, 1709–13, where his first oratorio was performed 1712. Appointed supernumerary organist to the court in 1713, he rose to become royal *maestro di cappella* just before his death. As a teacher at the Conservatorio della Pietà (from 1715, *maestro* 1741) and the Conservatorio S Onofrio (from 1725, *maestro* 1739) he included among his pupils Piccinni and Jommelli.

Works include operas *Sofonisba* (1718), *Lucio Papirio*, *Caio Gracco* (1720), *La 'mpeca scoperta* (in Neapolitan dialect, 1723), *Timocrate*, *Il trionfo di Camilla*, *La semmeglianza di chi l'ha fatta*, *Il Cid*, *Catone in Utica* (1729), *La clemenza di Tito* (1735), *Demofoonte*, *Farnace* (1736), *Siface*, *Ciro riconosciuto*, *L'amico traditore*, *La simpatia del sangue*, *L'Olimpiade* (1737), *Vologeso*, *Amor vuol sofferenza* (*La finta Frascatana*, 1739), *Achille in Sciro* (1740), *Scipione nelle Spagne* (1740), *Il fantastico* (*Il nuovo Don Chisciotte*), after Cervantes, 1743) and c 40 others; oratorios *Il trionfo della castità di S Alessio* (1713), *Dalla morte alla vita* (1722), *La morte di Abele*, *S Elena al Calvario* (1734), *S Francesco di Paolo nel deserto* and others; Masses, motets, psalms and other church music; concerto for four violins, six cello concertos; harpsichord pieces.

Leoncavallo, Ruggiero (b Naples, 23 Apr 1857; d Montecatini, near Florence, 9 Aug 1919), Italian composer. Studied piano privately at first and then entered the Naples Conservatory, which he left in 1876 with a master diploma. He went to Bologna to attend Carducci's lectures in literature. There he was on the point of producing his first

opera, *Chatterton*, but was swindled and found himself penniless. He made a precarious living by giving lessons and playing the piano at cafés, but later managed to travel widely as café pianist. He then began a trilogy on the Italian Renaissance, *Crepusculum*, with *I Medici*, but never produced the planned two following works, *Savonarola* and *Cesare Borgia*. In the meantime he made an enormous success with *Pagliacci* at Milan in 1892 and soon all over Italy. *La Bohème* at Venice in 1897 suffered from the appearance of Puccini's work on the same subject, and in spite of a commission for a German opera for Berlin, *Der Roland von Berlin*, in 1904, he never repeated his *Pagliacci* success. He wrote all his own libretti and some for other composers.

Works include operas *Chatterton* (after Alfred de Vigny, composed 1876, produced 1896), *I Medici*, *Pagliacci* (1892), *La Bohème* (after Murger, 1897), *Zaza*, *Der Roland von Berlin* (after Willibald Alexis, 1904), *Maia* (1910), *Gli zingari*, *Goffredo Mameli*, *Edipo rè* (after Sophocles, 1920), *Tormenta* (unfinished); operettas *A chi la giarettiera* (1919), *Il primo bacio*, *Malbruk* (1910), *La reginetta delle rose* (1912), *Are you there?* (1913), *La candidata* and *Prestami tua moglie*; ballet *La vita d'una marionetta*; symphonic poem *Serafita* (after Balzac's novel).

Leonhardt, Gustav (b 's Graveland, 30 May 1928), Dutch harpsichordist and conductor. He studied in Basel; debut Vienna 1950 in a solo performer of *The Art of Fugue*. Founded the Leonhardt Consort, 1955. Frequent tours of Europe and USA in wide range of early keyboard music; has conducted Baroque opera and choral music. Appeared as J S Bach in the film *The Chronicles of Anna Magdalena Bach* (1967) and conducted Monteverdi's *Poppea* at Amsterdam, 1972. He has edited most of Sweelinck's keyboard works and two performances of the *Goldberg Variations* by Bach are among his recordings.

Leoni, Leone (b Verona, c 1560; d Vicenza, 24 Jun 1627), Italian composer. *Maestro di cappella* of Vicenza Cathedral from 1588.

Works include Masses, motets (some in many parts with instruments), *Sacrae cantiones*, psalms, Magnificats and other church music, sacred and secular madrigals.

Leoninus, Leonius, now sometimes called Léonin (d Paris, c 1201), French poet, theologian and composer. First documented in 1179, he was active mainly at Notre-Dame, Paris, for which he is said to have composed the *Magnus liber organi* containing at least 42 settings of music for the Mass and Office in two voices. This formed the basis of the great Notre-Dame repertory later elaborated by Perotinus and others.

Leonora, ossia L'amore conjugale, *Leonora, or Wedded Love*, opera by Paer (libretto by ? G Cinti, based on Bouilly's libretto for Gaveaux), produced Dresden, 3 Oct 1804. Beethoven's ◊*Fidelio* for plot synopsis.

Leonora Overtures (Beethoven.) ◊Fidelio.

Léonore, ou L'Amour conjugal, *Leonora, or Wedded Love*, opera by Gaveaux (libretto by J N Bouilly, based on a real event), produced Paris, Théâtre Feydeau, 19 Feb 1798. A forerunner and model of Beethoven's ◊*Fidelio*.

Leonova, Daria (Mikhailovna) (b Vyshny-Volotchok, 21 Mar 1829; d St Petersburg, 6 Feb 1896), Russian contralto. Pupil of Glinka; made her first appearance at St Petersburg in his *Life for the Tsar* in 1852. She created roles in Dargomizhsky's *Russalka* and *Boris Godunov*; helped Mussorgsky towards the end of his life by engaging him as pianist on a tour in southern Russia and at her singing-school at St Petersburg.

Leopold I (b Vienna, 9 Jun 1640; d Vienna, 5 May 1705), Holy Roman Emperor. Composed an opera, *Apollo deluso*, to a libretto by his court musician Antonio Draghi, 1669, and contributed to numerous other operas by the same composer. His oratorios include *Il sagrifizio d'Abramo* (1660), *Il figliuol prodigo* (1663), *Il lutto dell'universo* (1668).

Leopolita, Martinus (Marcin Lwowczyk) (b Lwów, c 1540; d Lwów, 1589), Polish composer. Member of the College of Roratists and court composer at Kraków from 1560.

Works include Masses (e.g. *Missa Paschalis*), motets; secular songs for several voices, etc.

L'Épine, (Francesca) Margherita de (b *c* 1683; d London, 8 Aug 1746), French soprano. She settled in England 1692, and married Pepusch in 1718; sang in many masques and cantatas by him.

Leppard, Raymond (b London, 11 Aug 1927), English conductor, harpsichordist and editor. He studied at Cambridge. Debut as conductor London, 1952; regular conductor of English Chamber Orchestra since 1960, BBC Northern SO 1973–80. He gave *Solomon* at CG in 1959 and in 1964 Monteverdi's *L'incoronazione di Poppea* at Glyndebourne. This was the first of several realizations of Venetian opera, all of which have attracted negative scholarly comment for making too many transpositions, having too much music from other sources and instrumental parts realized in too lavish a manner. However, Leppard's versions of Monteverdi, and Cavalli's *L'Ormindo*, *La Calisto*, *L'Egisto* and *Orione*, have been popular with the public. He has also realized Monteverdi's *Ballo delle ingrate* (1958) and Cavalli's Messa Concertata. US concert debut at NY, 1969, opera at Santa Fe, 1974 (*Egisto*); NY Met. 1978, *Billy Budd*. He has been based in the USA since 1976: principal guest conductor St Louis SO from 1984; Indianapolis SO from 1986. CBE 1983.

Le Roux, François (b Rennes, 30 Oct 1955), French baritone. Studied at the Paris Opéra Studio and sang with Opéra Lyon 1980–85, as Mozart's Don Giovanni, Papageno and Count. He is particularly associated with the role of Pelléas, recording it with Abbado and singing it in Paris (1985), La Scala (1986), Vienna (1988) and at CG (1993). Glyndebourne debut 1987, as Ramiro in *L'Heure Espagnole*. CG from 1988, as Lescaut in *Manon*, Papageno, Malatesta, and the title role in the premiere of Birtwistle's *Gawain* (1991).

Leroux, Xavier (Henri Napoléon) (b Velletri, 11 Oct 1863; d Paris, 2 Feb 1919), Italian-born French composer. Studied at the Paris Conservatory, among his masters being Massenet, and gained the Prix de Rome in 1885. He became harmony professor there in 1896 and edited the periodical *Musica*.

Works include operas *Évangeline* (1885), *Astarté*, *La Reine Fiammette* (after Catulle Mendès, 1903), *William Ratcliff* (after Heine, 1906), *Théodora*, *Le Chemineau* (1907), *Le Carillonneur* (1913), *La Fille de Figaro* (1914), *Les Cadeaux de Noël*, 1814, *Nausithoé*, *La Plus Forte*, *L'Ingénu*; incidental music to Sardou and Moreau's *Cléopâtre* (1890), Aeschylus's *The Persians* and Richepin's *Xantho chez les courtisanes*; cantatas *Endymion* (1885) and *Vénus et Adonis* (1897); overture *Harald*; Mass with orchestra; motets; numerous songs.

Le Roy, Adrien (b Montreuil-sur-mer, *c* 1520; d Paris, 1598), French singer, lutenist, publisher and composer. He worked in Paris and associated himself with Robert Ballard (1) in 1552, having married his sister the preceding year. Lassus visited him in 1571 and he pub. some works of his. He pub. an instruction book for the lute and another for the cittern.

Leschetizky, Theodor (b Łańcut, Poland, 22 Jun 1830; d Dresden, 14 Nov 1915), Polish-Austrian pianist, teacher and composer. Pupil of Czerny and Sechter in Vienna. He was piano professor at St Petersburg Conservatory, 1852–78, and then settled in Vienna as an independent teacher of many famous pupils, including Paderewski.

Works include opera *Die erste Falte* (produced Prague 1867); many piano pieces.

L'Escurel, Jehannot de (d probably 1303), French composer. His 34 secular works, all but one of which are monophonic, are included in the same MS as the *Roman de ◊Fauvel*.

Lessel, Franz (Franciszek) (b Pulawy, *c* 1780; d Piotrków, 26 Dec 1838), Polish-Austrian composer. Studied medicine in Vienna, but became a pupil of Haydn, whom he looked after until his death. He then returned to Poland and lived with Prince Czartoryski's family until they were driven away by the Revolution. The rest of his life was unsettled.

Works include three Masses, Requiem and other church music; five symphonies; piano concerto; chamber music; piano sonatas and fantasies, etc.

lesson a 17th–18th-c. term for a keyboard piece, generally of an instructive character.

Lesueur, Jean François (b Drucat-Plessiel, near Abbeville, 15 Feb 1760; d Paris, 6 Oct 1837), French composer. He first learnt music as a choirboy at Abbeville, then held church appointments at Amiens and Paris. After 1781 he became *maître de chapelle* successively at Dijon Cathedral, Le Mans, Tours, Saints Innocents, Paris, 1784, and Notre-Dame, Paris, 1786. He was allowed to use a full orchestra at Mass and to open the proceedings with an overture. This aroused a controversy which led to his resignation, and he spent 1788–92 in the country, devoted to the composition of operas. In 1793 he was appointed professor at the school of the National Guard and in 1795 one of the inspectors at the newly opened Conservatory. In 1804 he succeeded Paisiello as *maître de chapelle* to Napoleon, after whose fall he was appointed superintendent and composer to the chapel of Louis XVIII. In 1818 he became professor of composition at the Conservatory, where his pupils included Berlioz and Gounod.

Works include operas *Télémaque* (1796), *La Caverne* (1793), *Paulin et Virginie* (after Saint-Pierre, 1794), *Ossian, ou Les Bardes* (1804), *Le Triomphe de Trajan* (with Persuis, 1807), *La Mort d'Adam* (after Klopstock, 1809), and some others; Mass and Te Deum for Napoleon's coronation, three Solemn Masses, *Stabat Mater*, motets, psalms and other church music; oratorios *Messe de Noël*, *Debora*, *Rachel*, *Ruth et Noémi*, *Ruth et Boaz*; cantatas.

A psalm brings a tear even from a heart of stone.
St Basil (330–378), *Homily on the First Psalm*

Le Sure, François (b Paris, 23 May 1923), French musicologist and librarian. He worked at the Bibliothèque Nationale, Paris 1950–87, and taught at the École des Hautes-Études. His interests include bibliography, the sociology of music and 16th-c. French music.

Letters, Music based on composers have sometimes amused themselves by turning names or other words into notes representing in musical nomenclature the letters of which they are formed, or as many as can be thus used. In English the letters A to G can be thus represented; in German H (= B♮) and S (Es = E♭) can be added, and in French and Italian the syllables Do, Re, Mi, Fa, Sol, La, Si may be used. In France a system was devised for the works on the names of Fauré and Haydn listed below, whereby the notes A to G were followed by further octaves named from H onwards. Here are some examples:

Abegg (supposed friends of Schumann's): Schumann, *Variations on the Name of Abegg* for piano, op. 1. Asch (the birthplace of Ernestine von Fricken): Schumann, *Carnaval* for piano op. 9. Bach. ◊B.A.C.H., *also* Faber *below*. Bamberg (the maiden name of Cui's wife): Cui, scherzo for piano duet (on B.A.B.E.G. and C.C. = César Cui). Belaiev: Borodin, Glazunov, Liadov and Rimsky-Korsakov, string quartet on 'B-la-F'. Faber: canon in seven parts by Bach, dated 1 Mar 1749, sung over a ground or *Pes* on the notes F. A. B(♭). E. and marked 'F A B E Repetatur', thus forming the name Faber, which may be a Latin form of some German surname derived from some kind of manual labour. The canon also bears an inscription in Latin containing the following acrostics on the names of Faber and Bach: 'Fidelis Amici Beatum Esse Recordari' and 'Bonae Artis Cultorem Habeas'. ◊B.A.C.H. Fauré: pieces by Aubert, Enescu, Koechlin, Ladmirault, Ravel, Roger-Ducasse and Schmitt contributed to a Fauré number of the *Revue musicale* in 1924. Gade: Schumann's piano piece so entitled in *Album für die Jugend*. Rheinberger, fughetta for organ. Gedge: Elgar, allegretto for violin and piano on G.E.D.G.E., dedicated to the Misses Gedge. Haydn: Ravel, *Menuet sur le nom d'Haydn* for piano. Sacha: Glazunov, *Suite sur le thème du nom diminutif russe* for piano, op. 2. Schumann (letters S.C.H.A. only): *Carnaval* (inversion of the letters A.S.C.H.).

Leutgeb (or *Leitgeb*), Ignaz (b ? Salzburg, *c* 1745; d Vienna, 27 Feb 1811), Austrian horn-player. He was first horn in the orchestra of the Archbishop of Salzburg, then settled in Vienna as a cheese merchant.

Levine *Conductor James Levine. Beginning his career as a pianist, Levine soon turned to conducting. He has worked extensively in the field of opera, and has forged a long-standing relationship with the Metropolitan Opera as musical and artistic director.*

Mozart wrote three of his four horn concertos and the horn quintet for him.

Levasseur, Nicolas (Prosper) (b Bresles, Oise, 9 Mar 1791; d Paris, 6 Dec 1871), French bass. Studied at the Paris Conservatory and made his first stage appearance in 1813 in Grétry's *La caravane du Caire*; created roles in Rossini's *Moïse*, Meyerbeer's *Margherita d'Anjou*, *Robert le diable*, *Les Huguenots* and *Le Prophète* and Donizetti's *La favorite*.

Levasseur, Rosalie (Marie Claude Josephe) (b Valenciennes, 8 Oct 1749; d Neuwied-on-Rhine, 6 May 1826), French soprano. Sang at the Paris Opéra from 1766 (debut in Campra's *L'Europe galante*), and in the 1770s had great success in Gluck's Paris operas; created the title roles in *Armide*, *Alceste*, *Iphigénie en Tauride*.

Leveridge, Richard (b London, c 1670; d London, 22 Mar 1758), English bass and composer. He appeared as a singer mainly in pantomimes etc., but also in Italian opera, his career extending from 1695 to 1751. As a composer he is remembered for his songs.

Works include incidental music for Shakespeare's *Macbeth* (1702), Farquhar's *The Recruiting Officer*, *Love and a Bottle* and (with D Purcell) *The Constant Couple*, Vanbrugh's *Aesop* and other plays; masque *Pyramus and Thisbe* (after Shakespeare, 1716); songs, e.g. 'The Roast Beef of Old England'.

Levi, Hermann (b Giessen, 7 Nov 1839; d Munich, 13 May 1900), German conductor. Studied with V Lachner at Munich and at the Leipzig Conservatory. After various appointments he became director of the Munich court theatre, 1872–96 (gave his own editions of Mozart's operas). Conducted the fp of Wagner's *Parsifal* at Bayreuth. At first, Wagner objected that a Jew should conduct what was essentially a Christian opera, but nevertheless accepted him as 'the ideal Parsifal conductor'. He continued at Bayreuth until 1894, and conducted at Wagner's funeral.

Levin, Robert D (b Brooklyn, 13 Oct 1947), American pianist and musicologist. Studied with Nadia Boulanger (1960–64) and graduated from Harvard 1968. Solo and chamber concerts throughout the USA, Europe and Japan from 1970; pianist with the New York Philomusica from 1971. Mozart has been at the centre of his research and he has published completions of various works, including a four

wind concertante with conjectural orchestration but retaining the wind parts of the concerto known as K297b (with clarinet replaced by original flute). Has also completed the D minor Requiem. Recordings with Malcolm Bilson and Melvyn Tan.

Levine, James (b Cincinnati, 23 Jun 1943), American conductor. He studied at the Juilliard School and was assistant conductor to George Szell in Cleveland 1964–70. British debut with WNO 1970, with *Aida*, and in 1971 conducted *Tosca* at the NY Met; music director from 1975, giving the house fps of *Lulu* (1971), *Idomeneo* (1982), and *Porgy and Bess*; led the premiere of *The Ghosts of Versailles* (1991). He has conducted at Salzburg from 1976, (notably *Moses und Aron*), and in 1982 gave *Parsifal* at Bayreuth; returned 1994, with the *Ring*. Often heard conducting Mahler's symphonies.

Levy, Marvin David (b Passic, NJ, 2 Aug 1932), American composer. He studied at NY and Columbia Universities; worked as music critic in 1950s.

Works include operas *Sobota Komachi* (1957), *The Tower* (1957), *Escorial* (1958), *Mourning Becomes Elektra* (produced NY Met. 1967), *The Balcony* (1978); string quartet (1955); Christmas Oratorio, *For the Time Being* (1959); Symphony (1960); *Sacred Service* (1964); piano concerto (1970).

Lewenthal, Raymond (b San Antonio, 29 Aug 1926; d Hudson, NY, 21 Nov 1988), American pianist and editor. Well known in performances of Thalberg, Henselt and Liszt and edited a collection of piano works by Alkan.

Lewis, Anthony (Carey) (b Bermuda, 2 Mar 1915; d Haslemere, 5 Jun 1983), English musicologist, conductor and composer. Educated at Wellington College and Cambridge, he studied music at the latter, at the RCM in London and with Nadia Boulanger in Paris. He was on the music staff of the BBC 1935–47 (except during his war service 1939–45), organizing various series of music including finally the music on the Third Programme (Radio Three). From 1947 to 1968 he was Professor of Music at Birmingham University and in 1968 was appointed principal of the RAM in London; remained until 1982. He edited and conducted operas by Purcell, Rameau and Handel. Knighted 1972.

Works include *Choral Overture* for unaccompanied voices; *Elegy and Capriccio* for trumpet and orchestra; horn concerto.

Lewis, Henry (b Los Angeles, 16 Oct 1932), American conductor. Studied at UCLA and played the double bass with the Los Angeles PO from 1948. Conducted the US 7th Army SO overseas 1955–57. Founded Los Angeles Philharmonic Orchestra and toured with it to Europe 1963. Music director of the New Jersey SO 1968–76. NY Met. debut 1972 with *La Bohème* (first black conductor there) and has returned for *Carmen*, *Ballo*, *Le prophète* and Gounod's *Roméo*. Scottish Opera 1978 with *Simon Boccanegra*; Hamburg Opera from 1983, *Les Troyens*, *Semiramide* and *Turandot*. Chief conductor of the Dutch Radio SO from 1989.

Lewis, Keith (b Methven, 6 Oct 1950), New Zealand tenor. Studied at London Opera Centre and sang Don Ottavio with GTO 1977 (Glyndebourne 1978). CG 1978–79, in *I Capuleti* and the fp of Taverner's *Thérèse*. Glyndebourne from 1978, as Mozart's Ferrando, Belmonte, Ottavio and Idomeneo; Tamino and Rossini's Almaviva with ENO, from 1982; US debut San Francisco, 1984; Oedipus Rex in Philadelphia and New York, 1993. Salzburg Festival 1989, as the Berlioz Faust, with the Chicago SO.

Lewis, Richard (b Manchester, 10 May 1914; d Eastbourne, 13 Nov 1990), English tenor. Studied privately with T W Evans at the RMCM and later at the RAM with Norman Allin. He made his debut in the Glyndebourne chorus in 1947. In the same year he also sang at CG, London, as Peter Grimes; created Walton's Troilus and Tippett's Mark there, and sang Aron in the first British performance of Schoenberg's *Moses und Aron* (1965). Also heard in concert (Elgar and Mahler) and sang in the fp of Stravinsky's *Canticum Sacrum* (Venice 1956).

Ley, Henry G(eorge) (b Chagford, Devon, 30 Dec 1887; d near Ottery St Mary, 24 Aug 1962), English organist and conductor. Studied at Keble College, Oxford, and was appointed organist at Christ Church

Cathedral there in 1909. Later taught organ at the RCM in London.
Works include church music; variations on a theme by Handel for orchestra; chamber music; organ music; songs.

Lhérie, Paul (b Paris, 8 Oct 1844; d Paris, 17 Oct 1937), French tenor, later baritone. He sang at the Paris Opéra-Comique from 1866 and in 1875 created Don José there. By 1884 he had changed to a baritone and sang Posa at La Scala, in Verdi's revision of *Don Carlos*. CG 1887, as Rigoletto and Luna. Retired 1894.

L'Héritier, Jean (b *c* 1480; d after 1552), French composer. Pupil of Josquin Desprez. Wrote Masses, motets, etc. He was in Rome in the 1520s and was music director to the Cardinal de Vermont at Avignon 1540–41.

Lhévinne, Josef (b Orel, 13 Dec 1874; d New York, 2 Dec 1944), Russian pianist. After some study at home he entered the Moscow Conservatory and studied with Safonov, playing Beethoven's fifth piano concerto at the age of 15. He graduated in 1891 and in 1895 won the Rubinstein Prize. From 1900 to 1902 he taught at the Tiflis Conservatory and 1902–06 at the Conservatory in Moscow. He made many tours and from 1907 to 1919 lived mostly in Berlin. He went to the USA 1919 and taught at the Juilliard Graduate School. He had an impeccable technique and a profound understanding of music. His wife *Rosina* (1880–1976), gave piano recitals until the mid-1960s and taught at Juilliard from 1922.

L'Homme armé ◊Homme armé.

Liadov, Anatol (Constantinovich) (b St Petersburg, 10 May 1855; d Novgorod, 28 Aug 1914), Russian composer. Studied under his father and later with Rimsky-Korsakov at the St Petersburg Conservatory, where he became a teacher in 1878. The Imperial Geographical Society commissioned him, with Balakirev and Liapunov, to collect folksongs in various parts of the country. His gift was essentially reclusive and small-scale; Stravinsky described his relief at not getting the commission for *The Rite of Spring* from Diaghilev.

Works include symphonic poems *Baba Yaga* (1904), *The Enchanted Lake* (1909), *Kikimora* (1909), two orchestral scherzos, *The Inn-Muzurka*, *Polonaise in Memory of Pushkin for orchestra*; choral settings from Schiller's *Bride of Messina* and Maeterlinck's *Sœur Béatrice*, three choral works for female voices; *c* 40 op. nos. of piano pieces, including *Birulki/Spillikins*), ballads *From Days of Old*, *Marionettes*, *Musical Snuff-Box*, variations on a theme by Glinka and on a Polish song, *From the Book of Revelation*, studies, preludes, mazurkas, etc.; songs, folksong settings (1903).

Liapunov, Sergey Mikhailovich (b Yaroslavl, 30 Nov 1859; d Paris, 8 Nov 1924), Russian pianist and composer. Studied at Nizhny-Novgorod and at the Moscow Conservatory. In 1893 the Imperial Geographical Society commissioned him, with Balakirev and Liadov, to collect folksongs. From 1891 to 1902 he was assistant director of the Imperial Chapel, and from 1910 professor at the St Petersburg Conservatory. He took refuge in Paris from the Revolution.

Works include two symphonies (1887, 1910–17), *Ballad, Solemn Overture*, Poloniase and symphonic poem *Hashish* for orchestra; two piano concertos (1890, 1909), rhapsody on Ukrainian themes for piano and orchestra (1908); numerous piano pieces, including suite *Christmas Songs*, etc.; folksong settings.

Liberati, Antimo (b Foligno, 3 Apr 1617; d Rome, 24 Feb 1692), Italian singer, organist and composer. Pupil of Allegri and Benevoli in Rome, where in 1661 he became a singer in the Papal Chapel (and later *maestro di cappella*) and organist at two churches. He wrote a letter giving particulars for Palestrina's biography and another defending a passage in Corelli.

Works include oratorios, madrigals, arias.

Liberté '14 tableaux inspirés par l'histoire du peuple de France', music by Delannoy, Honegger, Ibert, Lazarus, Milhaud, Roland-Manuel, Rosenthal, Tailleferre and others, produced Paris, Théâtre des Champs-Élysées, May 1937.

libretto Italian = 'booklet'; the text of an opera or other vocal work in dramatic form.

Libuše opera by Smetana (libretto in German, by J Wenzig, Czech translation by E Spindler), produced Prague, Czech Theatre, 11 Jun 1881. Libuše, new queen of Bohemia, must choose a husband to help her rule after her quarreling brothers Chrudos and Šťáhlov refuse to obey her authority. Peasant Přemysl is the lucky man.

licenza (plural *licenze*) Italian = 'licence, freedom, liberty', e.g. the direction *con alcune licenze* = 'with some freedom' (in form, style or performance); up to the 18th c., a cadenza or ornament inserted at the performer's discretion and not written down by the composer; also, in 17th-c. opera, especially in Vienna, a musical epilogue to a stage performance with special reference to the occasion (royal birthday, wedding, etc.).

It all depends on a good libretto. A libretto, a libretto and the opera is made!

Giuseppe Verdi in a letter, 1865

Licette, Miriam (b Chester, 9 Sept 1892; d Twyford, 11 Aug 1969), English soprano. She studied in Milan and Paris. Debut Rome 1911, Butterfly. Joined Beecham's co. 1915 and sang at CG 1919–29. Other roles included Eva, Eurydice (with Clara Butt), Juliette, Pamina, Gutrune and Desdemona.

Lichnovsky, (Prince) Karl (b Vienna, 21 Jun 1761; d Vienna, 15 Mar 1814), Polish aristocrat, resident in Vienna. After early patronage of Mozart he was introduced to Beethoven by Haydn. Beethoven's early chamber works were played at his house before publication, notably the string quartets op. 18, with the Schuppanzigh quartet.

Licht, (Light), cycle of seven projected operas by Stockhausen, one for each day of the week. ◊Dienstag, ◊Donnerstag, ◊Montag, ◊Samstag.

Lickl, Johann Georg (b Korneuburg, 11 Apr 1769; d Pécs, 12 May 1843), Austrian composer. He wrote several musical plays for Schikaneder's theatre.

Works include plays with music; Masses, motets; chamber music, etc.

Lidarti, Christian Joseph (b Vienna, 23 Feb 1730; d Pisa, after 1793), Austro-Italian composer. Pupil of his uncle, Bonno, in Vienna and later of Jommelli in Italy. In the service of the Cavalieri di S Stefano in Pisa, 1757–84.

Works include trio sonatas, catches and glees.

Lidholm, Ingvar (b Jönköping, 24 Feb 1921), Swedish composer. Studied at the Stockholm Conservatory with, among others, Hilding Rosenberg and Tor Mann. Later he studied in Italy and France, and also with Seiber. From 1947 to 1956 he was conductor of the Örebro SO.

Works include opera *The Dutchman* (after Strindberg, 1967), concerto for string orchestra, *Toccata e canto* for chamber orchestra (1944), *Ritornell* for orchestra (1956); concertino for flute, cor anglais, oboe and bassoon; *Greetings from an Old World* for orchestra (1976); *Kontakion* for orchestra (1978); *De Profundis* for chorus; *Cantata* for baritone and orchestra; string quartet, four pieces for cello and piano, sonata for solo flute.

Lidl, Andreas (b Vienna, *c* 1740; d London, *c* 1789), Austrian baryton virtuoso and composer. He increased the strings on his instrument, travelled much on the Continent and first appeared in London in 1778.

Works include chamber music; pieces for the baryton.

Lie, Sigurd (b Drammen, 23 May 1871; d Vestre Aker, 30 Sept 1904), Norwegian conductor, violinist and composer. Studied at the Leipzig Conservatory and in 1894 became a choral and theatre conductor at Bergen. After further study in Berlin he became choral conductor at Christiania.

Works include symphony in A minor (1903), *Orientalisk Suite* (1899), *Marche symphonique* for orchestra; cantatas and other choral works; piano quintet; songs.

Liebe der Danae, Die, *Danae's Love*, opera by R Strauss (libretto by Josef Gregor), intended for production at the Salzburg Festival and given public dress rehearsal on 16 Aug 1944. Production postponed owing to war; produced there 14 Aug 1952. (The title was originally *Der Kuss der Danae/Danae's Kiss*). Danae, who spurns all men, is pursued by King Midas and Jupiter, favouring the 'golden touch' of

Midas. She then falls genuinely in love with him, and continues to love him after vengeful Jupiter makes him destitute.

Liebe im Narrenhaus, Die, *Love in the Madhouse*, opera by Dittersdorf (libretto by G Stephanie, junior), produced Vienna, Kärntnertortheater, 12 Apr 1787. Constanze has been promised to lunatic asylum director Bast, so her lover Albert feigns insanity. When Albert inherits a fortune the lovers are allowed to marry.

Liebermann, Rolf (b Zurich, 14 Sept 1910), Swiss composer and administrator. Studied conducting with Scherchen and composition with Vladimir Vogel at Zurich, and was later appointed to the staff of Radio-Zurich. Director of Hamburg Opera, 1959–73, presiding over fps of operas by Searle (*Hamlet*), Goehr (*Arden Must Die*), Křenek, Penderecki and others. Intendant, Paris Opéra 1973–80. Some of his work is based on the 12-note system. In 1987 his first opera for 30 years was produced in Geneva.

Works include operas *Leonore 40/45* (1952), *Penelope* (1954), *School for Wives* (after Molière 1957), *La forêt* (1987); incidental music; film music; cantata *Streitlied zwischen Leben und Tod*; polyphonic studies and folksong suite for orchestra; concerto for jazz band and orchestra; solo cantatas *Une des fins du monde* (Giraudoux), *Chinesische Liebeslieder* (Klabund) and *Chinesisches Lied* (ditto), piano sonata.

Lieberson, Peter (b New York, 25 Oct 1946), American composer. Studied in New York, with Babbitt, Wuorinen and Martino. Studied Buddhism 1976–81 and was inspired to write his piano concerto of 1983. Other works, in a serial idiom, include *Tashi Quartet* (1979); *Lalita (Chamber Variations)* for ten instruments 1984; *Drala* for orchestra (1986); *Gesar Legend* for orchestra (1988); *Raising the Gaze* for seven instruments (1988); *Wind Messengers* for 13 instruments (1990).

Liebert, Reginaldus, early 15th-c. French composer. He probably succeeded Grenon at Cambrai in 1424. His main work is a complete Mass (Ordinary and Proper) of the Blessed Virgin Mary for three voices. A Gautier Liebert, composer of three *rondeaux*, was a papal singer in 1428.

Liebeslieder, *Love Songs*, a set of waltzes by Brahms for piano duet with solo vocal quartet *ad lib.*, op. 52, composed 1869. There is a second set of *Neue Liebeslieder*, op. 65, written in 1874.

Liebesverbot, Das, oder Die Novize von Palermo, *The Love-Ban, or The Novice of Palermo*, opera by Wagner (libretto by composer, based on Shakespeare's *Measure for Measure*), produced Magdeburg, 29 Mar 1836. Viceroy Friedrich outlaws pleasure but desires Isabella. Friedrich having imprisoned her brother Claudio, Isabella is willing to sacrifice herself for Claudio's agreed release, but she sends Friedrich's wife to the rendezvous. Friedrich's hypocrisy is exposed; a happy ending.

Lied German = 'song'.

Lieder eines fahrenden Gesellen, Songs of a Wayfarer, song-cycle by Mahler for low voice and piano (texts by Mahler); composed 1884, orchestrated *c* 1895 and performed in this version Berlin, 16 Mar 1896, conductor Mahler. Titles of songs are 1. *Wenn mein Schatz Hochzeit macht/When my sweetheart gets married*, 2. *Ging heut' Morgen übers Feld/I walked this morning through the fields*: thematically related to the first movement of the contemporary first symphony; 3. *Ich hab ein glühend Messer in der Brust/I have a burning knife in my breast*; 4. *Die zwei blauen Augen/The two blue eyes*. Also heard in version with chamber ensemble by Schoenberg.

Liederkreis, German, title used for two sets of songs by Schumann: nine Heine settings op. 24 and 12 Eichendorff settings op. 39 (both 1840). ◊song cycle.

Lieder ohne Worte 36 piano pieces by Mendelssohn in the form and character of songs exploiting the principle of accompanying melody rather than polyphonic textures. Vol. I, op. 19, nos. 1–6 (1830–32); II, op. 30, 7–12 (1833–7); III, op. 38, 13–18 (1836–37); IV, op. 53, 19–24 (1841); V. op. 62, 25–30 (1842–43); VI, op. 67, 31–6 (1843–45). The only titles which are Mendelssohn's own are those of the three *Venezianische Gondellieder* (*Venetian Barcarolles*), nos. 6, 12, and 29, the *Duetto*, no. 18, and the *Volkslied*, no. 23.

Liederspiel German = lit. 'song-play'; a play with songs similar to the *Singspiel*. The term was first used by Reichardt in 1800. It may also mean 'song cycle', e.g. Schumann's *Spanisches Liederspiel*.

Liedertafel German = lit. 'song-table' or 'singing-table'; a male-voice choral association doubtless deriving its name from early gatherings seated round a table drinking and singing.

Lied von der Erde, Das, *The Song of the Earth*, symphony for mezzo, tenor and orchestra by Mahler (so called by the composer, but not numbered among his other symphonies). The words are from Hans Bethge's anthology of German translations of Chinese poetry, *Die chinesische Flöte*: 1. (Li-Tai-Po). *Das Trinklied vom Jammer der Erde/The Drinking-Song of Earth's Misery*; 2. (Tchang-Tsi) *Der Einsame im Herbst/The Lonely One in Autumn*; 3. (Li-Tai-Po) *Von der Jugend/Of Youth*: 4. (ditto) *Von der Schönheit/Of Beauty*; 5. (ditto) *Der Trunkene im Frühling/The Drunkard in Spring*; 6. (Mong-Kao-Yen and Wang-We) *Der Abschied/The Farewell*). Composed 1908; fp Munich, 20 Nov 1911, after Mahler's death.

Lieutenant Kijé symphonic suite by Prokofiev, arranged in 1934 from film music composed 1933. The five movements are *Birth of Kijé*, *Romance*, *Wedding*, *Troika*, *Burial*; fp Paris, 20 Feb 1937, conductor Prokofiev.

Life for the Tsar, A, *Zhizn za Tsaria*; now *Ivan Susanin*, opera by Glinka (libretto by C F Rosen), produced St Petersburg, 9 Dec 1836. Ivan Susanin delays the wedding of his daughter Antonida to Bogden Sobinin because of invading Poles who are hunting down the Tsar. Knowing where the Tsar is hiding, Susanin deliberately leads the Poles astray, knowing that he will be killed when the deception is discovered. Susanin willingly sacrifices his life for the Tsar; his bravery is praised by all.

Ligabue, Ilva (b Reggio Emilia, 23 May 1932), Italian soprano. She studied in Milan; debut at La Scala in Wolf-Ferrari's *I quattro Rusteghi*. Glyndebourne 1958–61 as Alice Ford, Fiordiligi and Donna Elvira. In 1961 she sang Bellini's Beatrice at La Scala, Milan, and Margherita in Boito's *Mefistofele* at the Lyric Theatre, Chicago; NY debut (in concert) 1963. She appeared as guest in Vienna, Dallas and Buenos Aires.

ligature(s) a group of two or more notes in medieval and Renaissance music. Also the various signs, originating in plainsong notation, by which such groups are indicated.

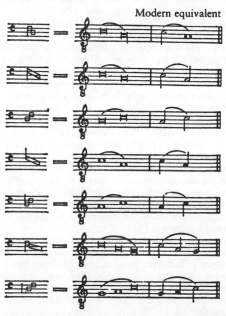

Various ligatures (left), with literal and modern representations (right).

Ligendza, Catarina (b Stockholm, 18 Oct 1937), Swedish soprano. Debut Linz, 1963, as Mozart's Countess. After singing in Germany she was heard as Arabella at La Scala, Milan, in 1970; sang Leonore at the NY Met. the following year, also Brünnhilde at Bayreuth; Isolde there 1974–77. Salzburg Easter Festival from 1969. Bayreuth Festival 1986–87, as Elsa and Isolde. Retired 1988.

Ligeti, Andras (b Budapest, 1953), Hungarian conductor. Studied violin at the Budapest Academy and was leader of the Hungarian State Opera House Orchestra, 1976–80. Solo concerts in Europe and Canada then associate conductor with the Budapest SO, from 1985 (tours of Britain and the USA). British debut with the BBC SO, 1989; BBC PO 1991 (*Bluebeard's Castle* and Mahler's 5th symphony).

Ligeti, György (b Dicsöszentmarton, Transylvania, 28 May 1923), Hungarian composer. Studied composition with Sándor Veress and Ferenc Farkas at the Budapest Music Academy (1945–49), becoming an instructor there 1950–56. In 1956 he went to the Studio for Electronic Music at Cologne, and in 1959 was appointed instructor at the International Courses for New Music at Darmstadt. In 1961 he was visiting professor of composition at the Stockholm Music Academy, and eventually settled in Vienna. His mature music is experimental in nature, featuring complex textures which Ligeti called 'micropolyphony', in which the individuality of a large number of separate parts is subsumed, giving the impression of a slowly changing single mass.

    Works include opera *Le Grand Macabre* (produced Stockholm 1978); *Artikulation* for electronic sounds (1958); *Apparitions* for orchestra (1959); *Atmosphères* for large orchestra (1961); *Poème symphonique* for 100 metronomes; *Aventures* for soprano, alto and baritone with seven instruments (1962); *Nouvelles Aventures* for soprano and seven instruments; Requiem for soloists, chorus and orchestra (1965; Kyrie used in film *2001*); *Lux aeterna* for 16 solo voices; cello concerto (1967); *Ramifications* for string orchestra (1969); Chamber Concerto for 13 instruments (1970); *San Francisco Polyphony* for orchestra (1974); Trio for violin, horn and piano (1982), *3 Phantasien* and *Hungarian Studies*, both for 16 voices (1983); *Etudes* for piano (1985); Piano concerto (1985–88); *Nonsense Madrigals* for six voices (1988); violin concerto (1990); *L'escalier du diable* for piano (1993).

Lighthouse, The chamber opera in one act by Peter Maxwell Davies (text by composer, based on 1900 disappearance of three Outer Hebridean lighthouse keepers); composed 1979, fp Edinburgh, 2 Sept 1980.

A Selection of
Ligeti

String Quartet no. 1	1954
Atmosphères	1961
Cello Concerto	1966
Ten Pieces for Wind Quintet	1968
Ramifications	1969
Chamber Concerto	1970
Melodien	1971
Concerto for flute and oboe	1972
Le Grand Macabre	1978
Piano Concerto	1983

Light of Life, The, *Lux Christi*, oratorio by Elgar for soloists, chorus and orchestra, op. 29 (text by E Capel-Dure from the Scriptures); composed 1896, fp Worcester, 10 Sept 1896, conductor Elgar.

Lill, John (b London, 17 Mar 1944), English pianist. He studied at the RCM and with Wilhelm Kempff. London debut (Festival Hall) 1963. In 1970 won the Tchaikovsky Competition Moscow. NY (Carnegie Hall) from 1969. OBE 1978. A powerful performer in 19th-c. music, especially Beethoven.

Lilliburlero a satirical song sung in Ireland after the appointment of General Talbot to the lord-lieutenancy in 1687. It is not likely that the earlier attribution of the tune to Purcell is justified: it was probably a popular melody merely arranged by him, much as *The Prince of Denmark's March* was arranged by J Clarke.

Lima, Jeronymo Francisco de (b Lisbon, 30 Sept 1743; d Lisbon, 19 Feb 1822), Portuguese composer and organist. He was elected to the Brotherhood of St Cecilia, visited Italy and in 1798 became conductor of the Royal Opera at Lisbon.

    Works include opera *Le nozze d'Ercole e d'Ebe* (1785) and five others (all Italian); church music; cantatas.

Lima, Luis (b Cordoba, 12 Sept 1948), Argentine tenor. Debut Lisbon 1974 as Turiddu. He sang Edgardo at La Scala in 1977 and at the Vienna Staatsoper in 1981. In 1978 he was heard as Pinkerton at Verona and as Alfredo at the NY Met. At CG he has been admired as Nemorino and Don Carlos, both in 1985 (returned 1991 as Don José; Don Carlos at San Francisco (1992) and Cilea's Maurizio at the Met., 1994.

Limburgia, Johannes de, late 14th-and early 15th-c. composer from N France. He worked at churches in Liège, 1408–19, and in Italy from *c* 1430. His 50 or so compositions (all church music) include a complete Mass (three and four voices) and 16 motets.

Lin, Cho-Liang (b Taiwan, 21 Jan 1960), Chinese-born American violinist. Studied at Juilliard with Dorothy DeLay and made US and British debuts 1976 (Philadelphia Orchestra under Ormandy and LSO under Previn). Many concerts in Europe, the USA and the Far East, with recordings of concertos by Mendelssohn, Mozart, Sibelius and Nielsen.

Lincke, Josef (b Trachenberg, Prussian Silesia, 8 Jun 1783; d Vienna, 26 Mar 1837), German cellist and composer. He settled in Vienna in 1808, becoming a member of Rasumovsky's quartet and later first cellist at the Vienna opera. Beethoven wrote the two sonatas op. 102 for him. He wrote concertos, variations, etc. for the cello.

Lincoln Portrait, A work by Copland for orchestra and a speaker, who declaims portions of Lincoln's speeches, fp by Cincinnati SO, 14 May 1942.

Lind, Eva (b Innsbruck, 14 Jun 1965), Austrian soprano. Debut Innsbruck 1983, in *Parsifal*. Sang Lucia at Basel 1985, and the Queen of Night at Paris, 1987. Vienna Staatsoper from 1986, as Lucia, the Queen of Night and Strauss's Sophie. Glyndebourne 1988, as Nannetta. Sang Gounod's Juliet at Zurich 1990, Weber's Aennchen at Bonn, 1993. Recordings include *Fledermaus* (Domingo), *Die Zauberflöte* (Marriner) and *Hoffmann* (Tate).

The London hangman went one night to the pit of Her Majesty's Theatre to hear Jenny Lind, and on seeing the Swedish nightingale, exclaimed, breathless with admiration and excitement, 'What a throat to scrag!'

    Edwards, *History of Opera*, 1862

Lind, Jenny (b Stockholm, 6 Oct 1820; d Wynd's Point, Malvern Wells, 2 Nov 1887), Swedish soprano. She was called 'The Swedish Nightingale'. First appeared at Stockholm, 1838, when she sang Agathe, Pamina and Euryanthe; studied with Garcia in Paris; sang much in Germany; went to England 1847 and settled in London permanently; her roles there included Alice in *Robert le diable*, Amina, Marie, Susanna and Amalia in the fp of Verdi's *I Masnadieri* (1847). Distinguished in opera in her early years, but afterwards mainly as a concert singer. She made many extensive tours. Married Otto Goldschmidt in 1852.

Linda di Chamounix opera by Donizetti (libretto by G Rossi, after a vaudeville, *La Grâce de Dieu*), produced Vienna, Kärntnertortheater, 19 May 1842. Poor Linda loves the viscount Carlo, who has disguised himself as a destitute painter. She follows him to Paris and learns his true identity, but goes mad upon learning of his supposed marriage to another woman. Carlo reassures her and Linda recovers.

Lindberg, Christian (b Stockholm, 1958), Swedish trombonist. Studied in Stockholm, London and Los Angeles, 1978–83. Solo career in Europe and the USA with Baroque music, and modern works by Schnittke (concerto and *Dialogue*), Takemitsu (Concerto and *Gemeaux*), Xenakis and Pärt. Premiere of the concerto by Ellen Zwilich at Carnegie Hall, 1993. Tours to Australia, the Far East and Europe (Nash Ensemble in London). Played the Concerto by Xenakis (*Troorkh*) at Glasgow, 1994.

Lindberg, Oskar Fredrik (b Gagnef, 23 Feb 1887; d Stockholm, 10 Apr 1955), Swedish organist and composer. Studied at the Stockholm Conservatory and at Sonderhausen. In 1906 he was appointed organist at a Stockholm church and in 1919 professor at the Conservatory. Works include Requiem (1922) and cantata for solo voices, chorus and orchestra; symphony in F major (1912); *Three Pictures from Dalarne*, three overtures, symphonic poems *Wilderness*, *Flor and Blancheflor* and *From the Great Forests*, suite *Travel Memories* for orchestra; piano pieces; songs with orchestra and with piano.

Lindblad, Adolf Fredrik (b Skänninge near Stockholm, 1 Feb 1801; d Linköping, 23 Aug 1878), Swedish composer and singing-teacher. Studied with Zelter in Berlin and in 1827 settled at Stockholm as teacher of singing. Jenny Lind was among his pupils. Works include opera *Frondörerna* (1835); two symphonies; seven string quartets; duo for violin and piano; vocal duets, trios and quartets; numerous songs.

Lindblad, Otto Jonas (b Karlstorp, 31 Mar 1809; d Ny Mellby, 24 Jan 1864), Swedish composer. Learnt the organ while studying theology, which he afterwards abandoned in order to study music, mainly by himself, though he had a few lessons at Copenhagen. Having learnt the violin he joined a touring opera company, took part in a music festival at Hamburg in 1841 and founded a students' choral society at Lund. Works include numerous choruses, vocal quartets, trios and duets, songs.

Lindenstrand, Sylvia (b Stockholm, 24 Jun 1942), Swedish mezzo-soprano. Studied in Stockholm and made debut there 1962, as Olga; further appearances at the Royal Opera as Marina, Dorabella, Cherubino, Octavian, Cenerentola and Brangaene. Tchaikovsky's Maid of Orleans 1986 and Dionysus in the 1991 premiere of Backanterna by Daniel Börtz. Guest at Copenhagen and the Bolshoi; Glyndebourne 1975 and 1979, as Dorabella (also televised) and Amaranta in Haydn's *Fedeltà premiata*. Sang Zerlina at Aix (1976) and Idamantae at Drottningholm.

Lindholm, Berit (b Stockholm, 18 Oct 1934), Swedish soprano. Debut Stockholm, 1963, as Mozart's Countess. She sang Chrysothemis at CG in 1966; later heard there as Isolde and Brünnhilde. Bayreuth from 1967 (debut as Venus). US debut San Francisco, 1972; NY Met. 1975, as the *Walküre* Brünnhilde. Other roles include Élisabeth, Tosca, Leonore and Cassandre in the Colin Davis recording of *Les Troyens*. Sang Divina in the fp of Goehr's *Behold the Sun* (Duisburg, 1985).

Lindley, Robert (b Rotherham, 4 Mar 1776; d London, 13 Jun 1855), English cellist and composer. Learnt violin and cello from his father, then studied cello under Cervetto, played at the Brighton theatre, and in 1794–1851 was principal cellist at the Opera in London. He wrote concertos and other works for cello.

Lindner, Friedrich (b Liegnitz, Silesia, c 1540; d Nuremberg, buried 15 Sept 1597), German composer and editor. He was choirboy in the electoral chapel at Dresden and later studied at Leipzig University, became musician to the Margrave of Brandenburg and in 1574 cantor at St Giles' Church at Nuremberg. He edited several books of Italian church music and madrigals, and composed two Passions.

Lindpaintner, Peter Joseph von (b Koblenz, 9 Dec 1791; d Nonnenhorn, Lake Constance, 21 Aug 1856), German composer and conductor. Studied at Augsburg and (?) with Winter at Munich, where in 1812 he became conductor at a minor theatre. In 1819 he went to Stuttgart as court *Kapellmeister*. In 1853–54 he visited London to conduct the New Philharmonic concerts. Works include operas *Der Bergkönig* (1825), *Der Vampyr* (1828), *Die Genueserin* (1839), *Lichtenstein* (1846) and 24 others; ballet *Joko* and two others; incidental music to Goethe's *Faust; Stabat Mater*, six Masses; oratorios *Abraham* and others; cantatas *The Widow of Nain*, Schiller's *Lied von der Glocke*; symphonies and overtures; concertos; chamber music; over 50 songs.

Lindsay String Quartet British ensemble founded in 1966. Members are Peter Cropper and Ronald Birks (violins), Robin Ireland (who replaced Roger Bigley in 1985, viola) and Bernard Gregor-Smith (cello). Their many recordings including complete cycles of quartets by Bartók and Beethoven. In 1979 they gave the fp of Tippett's fourth quartet at the Bath Festival. Haydn series in Sheffield and at the Wigmore Hall, London, 1987. Quartet in residence at the University of Manchester.

linear counterpoint a term for a kind of counterpoint in 20th-c. music which regards the individuality of melodic lines as more important than the harmony they produce in combination.

Linley English family of musicians:

1. Thomas Linley (b Badminton, 17 Jan 1733; d London, 19 Nov 1795) singing-master and composer. Studied with Thomas Chilcot, organist of Bath Abbey, and with Paradisi in London; settled at Bath as singing-teacher and concert promoter. From 1774 he managed the oratorios at Drury Lane Theatre in London jointly with Stanley and from 1786 with Arnold. Sheridan having become his son-in-law in 1773, he and his son Thomas (3) wrote music for Sheridan's play *The Duenna* in 1775. In 1776 he moved to London and bought Garrick's share in Drury Lane Theatre, where he managed the music and wrote music for various pieces.

Works include opera *The Royal Merchant* (1767); music for Sheridan's *Duenna* (1781) and *School for Scandal* (the song 'Here's to the maiden'), *The Carnival of Venice* (1781), *The Gentle Shepherd*, *Robinson Crusoe* (pantomime by Sheridan, after Defoe), *The Triumph of Mirth, The Spanish Rivals* (1784), *The Strangers at Home* (1785), *Love in the East* (1788), and other plays; adaptations from Grétry: *Zelmire and Azor* and *Richard Cœur de Lion*; accompaniments for *The Beggar's Opera*; music for Sheridan's monody on the death of Garrick; six elegies for three voices; 12 ballads; cantatas, madrigals.

2. Elizabeth Ann Linley (b Bath, 5 Sept 1754; d Bristol, 28 Jun 1792), soprano, daughter of 1. Pupil of her father, she first sang in his concerts in Bath. Made her London debut in 1770 but after her marriage to Sheridan in 1773 retired from singing. Her portrait was painted by Gainsborough and Reynolds.

3. Thomas Linley junior (b Bath, 5 May 1756; d Grimsthorpe, Lincs., 5 Aug 1778), violinist and composer, brother of 2. Pupil of his father and of Boyce, later of Nardini in Florence, where he struck up a friendship with the young Mozart in 1770. On his return to England he played in his father's concerts, and collaborated with him in the composition of *The Duenna* in 1775. He was drowned in a boating accident. opera *The Cadi of Bagdad* (1778); music for Shakespeare's *The Tempest* (1777) and Sheridan's *The Duenna* (with his father); oratorio *The Song of Moses* (1777); *Ode on the Witches and Fairies of Shakespeare*; anthem 'Let God arise'; violin concerto, several elegies.

4. Mary Linley (b Bath, 4 Jan 1758; d Clifton, Bristol, 27 Jul 1787), singer, sister of 3. Pupil of her father, sang at festivals, oratorios, etc., but retired on her marriage to Richard Rickell, commissioner of stamps and dramatist (wrote *The Carnival of Venice* for his father-in-law and altered Ramsay's *Gentle Shepherd* for him).

5. William Linley (b Bath, Feb 1771; d London, 6 May 1835), government official and composer. Pupil of his father and Abel, he held official posts in India, but in between was Sheridan's partner in

the management of the Drury Lane Theatre, for which he composed some unsuccessful works. Settled in London in 1806 as writer and composer. pantomimes, etc. *Harlequin Captive*, *The Honey Moon*, *The Pavilion*; songs to Shakespeare's plays; glees.

'Linz' Symphony Mozart's symphony in C major, K425, composed at the house of Count Thun at Linz, where Mozart and his wife stayed on their return from Salzburg to Vienna, and performed there 4 Nov 1783.

Lioncourt, Guy de (b Caen, 1 Dec 1885; d Paris, 24 Dec 1961), French musicologist and composer. Studied under d'Indy at the Schola Cantorum in Paris and later taught there. In 1918 he gained a prize with a musical fairy-tale, *La Belle au bois dormant* (after Perrault).

Works include opera *Jean de la lune*, liturgical drama *Le Mystère d'Emmanuel* (1924); church music; cantata *Hyalis le petit faune* (Samain, 1909–11) and sacred cantatas; chamber music, etc.

Lipatti, Dinu (b Bucharest, 19 Mar 1917; d Geneva, 2 Dec 1950), Romanian pianist and composer. Studied at the Bucharest Conservatory and with Cortot, Dukas and Nadia Boulanger in Paris. He had a very brilliant career which was cut short by illness. Much admired in Bach, Chopin and Mozart.

Lipinski, Karol Józef (b Radzyń, 30 Oct 1790; d Urlow, near Lwów, 16 Dec 1861), Polish violinist and composer. Travelled widely and became leader of the court orchestra at Dresden, 1839. Edited a collection of Polish and Ruthenian folksongs with the poet Zalewski. Schumann's *Carnaval* was dedicated to him.

Works include opera *The Siren of the Dnieper* (1814); *Polonaise guerrière* for orchestra; four violin concertos; string trio; violin pieces, etc.

Lipkin, Malcolm (b Liverpool, 2 May 1932), English composer and pianist. Studied at the RCM and with Seiber. Lecturer, Kent University from 1975.

Works include three symphonies (1958–82), piano concerto (1957), concerto for flute and strings (1974); obo concerto (1989); string quartet, five piano sonatas (no. 5, 1986).

Lipovšek, Marjana (b Ljubliana, 3 Dec 1946), Slovenian mezzo-soprano. Studied in Graz and sang at the Staatsoper, Vienna in 1979, and at the Bavarian State Opera from 1983, as Konchakovna (*Prince Igor*) and Fricka. Created Emilie in the 1981 fp of Cerha's *Baal* at Salzburg and has returned as Rosa Sacchi in the fp of Penderecki's *Die schwarze maske* (1986) and as the Nurse in *Die Frau ohne Schatten* (1992). Bregenz Festival from 1988, as Dalila and Carmen. London debut 1988 (*Das Lied von der Erde*); CG 1990, as Clytem-

nestra, under Solti. NY Met. debut 1990, as Fricka. Also a recitalist at Salzburg, Hohenems and the Wigmore Hall.

Lipp, Maria Magdalena (d 1827), Austrian singer. Married Michael Haydn at Salzburg in 1768.

Lipton, Martha (b New York, 6 Apr 1916), American mezzo-soprano. Studied at Juilliard and sang in concert from 1940. NY City Opera 1941, as Tchaikovsky's Pauline; Met. from 1944, as Siebel, Amneris, Maddalena and Hansel (almost 300 performances in all). Sang at Carnegie Hall 1952 in Wolf's *Der Corregidor* and at Chicago 1956, as Herodias. Many concert appearances.

lira, Italian, a generic name given to various early bowed string instruments, such as the ◊rebab, or rebec, and the ◊crwth in earlier times.

lira da braccio Italian = lit. 'arm lyre'; a bowed string instrument current in the 16th and early 17th c. It had seven strings, two or more of which served as drones. As the name implies, it was played on the arm.

lira da gamba Italian = lit. 'leg lyre'; a larger version of the *lira da braccio*, played between the legs. The number of strings, including drones, varied from 11 to 15.

lira organizzata ◊vielle organisée.

Lisley, John, English 16th-17th-c. composer. One of the contributors to the madrigal collection *The Triumphes of Oriana* 1601; nothing is otherwise known about him.

Lissenko, Nikolai Vitalievich (b Grilky, Government of Poltava, 22 Mar 1842; d Kiev, 6 Nov 1912), Russian composer. Studied natural science, but while making researches in ethnography he became interested in Ukrainian folksong, specimens of which he began to collect. He then studied at the Leipzig Conservatory and later with Rimsky-Korsakov at St Petersburg. He settled at Kiev.

Works include operas *Taras Bulba* (after Gogol, produced 1903), *Sappho*, *The Aeneid* (after Virgil) and others; operettas; cantatas and other choral works; *Ukrainian Rhapsody* for violin and piano; piano pieces; songs, settings of Ukrainian folksongs.

List, Emmanuel (b Vienna, 22 Mar 1888; d Vienna, 21 Jun 1967), Austrian bass. He sang as a chorister and in vaudeville before Vienna Volksoper debut, 1922, as Gounod's Méphistophélès, Berlin Staatsoper 1923–33. CG from 1925 as Pogner, Marke and Ochs. NY Met. debut 1933 as the Landgrave; sang Gurnemanz, Hunding and Hagen at Bayreuth same year. Salzburg 1931–35 as Osmin, the Commendatore and Rocco. Lived in Vienna from 1952.

List, Eugene (b Philadelphia, 6 Jul 1918; d New York, 28 Feb 1985), American pianist. Studied in Philadelphia, debut there 1934. Toured widely as sergeant in US army. Eastman School 1964–75. Often heard in Gottschalk .

A Selection of
Liszt

> *The prodigy, the itinerant virtuoso, and the man of fashion ruined the composer before he had even started.*
>
> **Johannes Brahms** on Franz Liszt, quoted in Gall, *Johannes Brahms*, 1961

Liszt, Ferencz (more commonly *Franz*) (b Raiding, Hungary, 22 Oct 1811; d Bayreuth, 31 Jul 1886), Hungarian pianist and composer. His father, a steward of the Esterházy family's property, was Hungarian, his mother Austrian. At the age of nine he gave a concert at Sopron and in 1823 he had advanced so amazingly that his father took him to Vienna and Paris, where he had an immense success. In Vienna he studied briefly with Salieri and Czerny. In 1824–25 he paid two visits to England and another in 1827. At 14 he attracted attention as a composer as well, producing his opera *Don Sanche* in Paris. His father died 1827 and he was taken to Paris by his paternal grandmother, who looked after his education there. He remained there, and after a period of religious mysticism under the influence of Lamennais achieved great success and fame as a pianist, his flamboyant stage manner having almost as much to do with his success as his dazzling technique. He began a love affair with the Comtesse d'Agoult in 1833. They went to live at Geneva in 1835, where a daughter,

Liszt *The composer and pianist Franz Liszt (1811–1886). He was the leading virtuoso pianist of the 19th century, and perhaps of all time. In later years he retired from the concert platform, turning increasingly to composition and religion.*

Blandine, was born, followed by another, Cosima (later Wagner's second wife) at Como in 1837. A son, Daniel, was born in Rome, 1839.

He travelled widely as pianist and made much money. In 1840 he collected funds for the Beethoven memorial at Bonn, and he often played for charitable purposes organized on a large scale. In 1840–41 he paid further visits to England, playing before Queen Victoria, and in 1842–44 he toured in Russia, Turkey, Denmark, etc. After a break with the countess in the latter year, he went to Spain and Portugal in 1845; two years later, at Kiev, he met princess Caroline Sayn-Wittgenstein, the wife of a wealthy Russian landowner, who fell violently in love with him and in 1848 left with him for Weimar, where he was engaged as conductor and music director to the grand-ducal court for certain periods of the year. He produced many new operas there, including Wagner's *Lohengrin* (1850) and Berlioz's *Béatrice et Bénédict* (1862), and settled down to write various works, some on a very large scale, having previously confined himself almost exclusively to piano music. His piano sonata of 1853, followed by the *Faust* and *Dante* symphonies, were revolutionary for their extension of sonata form in a cyclic process extending for several movements, and for their use of limited motifs that become transformed as a means of development. The music of this period had a profound influence on his contemporaries: Wagner was moved by the opening theme of the *Faust* symphony to accompany Sieglinde's solo scene at the end of *Die Walküre* act II, while traces of the *Dante* symphony survive in *Parsifal*. Until recently, Liszt's posthumous reputation has not been high; his lurid lifestyle has distracted attention from his music. Frequent modern performances of the symphonies and symphonic poems, as well as the work of such pianists as Leslie Howard, Alfred Brendel and Mikhail Rudy, has revealed a more thoughtful and serious composer. He retired to Rome in 1861, and in 1865 took minor orders. He continued, however, to visit Weimar and also Budapest as a teacher. In his last years he often visited his daughter at Bayreuth, and irritated Wagner with his new-found religious fervour.

Works include a vast number of piano compositions, including three vols. of *Années de pèlerinage* (1866–77), 12 *Études d'exécution transcendante* (1851), two *Légendes* (*Saint François d'Assise prédicant aux oiseaux* and *Saint François de Paule marchant sur les flots*), *Liebsträume* (three nocturnes, originally songs), sonata in B minor (1853), 20 Hungarian Rhapsodies; innumerable transcriptions for piano including 50 operatic pieces and fantasies of themes from operas by Bellini, Meyerbeer, Verdi and Wagner, *c* 40 works by various composers (Beethoven's symphonies, Berlioz's *Symphonie fantastique*, six caprices by Paganini, nine waltzes by Schubert [*Soirées de Vienne*], etc., *c* 150 songs including many by Schubert).

ORCHESTRAL: *Faust* and *Dante* symphonies (1854–57 and 1856); 13 symphonic poems for orchestra; *Ce qu'on entend sur la montagne* (1849, orchestrated by Raff, revised 1850–54); *Tasso: lamento e trionfo* (1849, orchestrated by Conradi, revised 1850–54); *Les Préludes* (1848); *Orpheus* (1854); *Prometheus* (1850, orchestrated by Raff, revised 1855); *Mazeppa* (1851, orchestrated with Raff); *Festklänge* (1853); *Héroïde funèbre* (1850, orchestrated by Raff, revised 1854); *Hungaria* (1854); *Hamlet* (1858); *Hunnenschlacht* (1857); *Die Ideale* (1857); *Von der Wiege bis zum Grabe* (1882). Other orchestral works include two Episodes from Lenau's *Faust*; two piano concertos in E♭ (1849, revised 1853, 1856) and A (1839, revised 1849–61), Hungarian fantasy, *Malédiction*, *Totentanz* and fantasy on Beethoven's *Ruins of Athens* for piano and orchestra.

VOCAL AND ORGAN: oratorios *St Elizabeth* (1857–62) and *Christus* (1862–67); *Gran Mass* for solo voices, chorus and orchestra, Hungarian Coronation Mass (1867), and two other Masses, three psalms and a number of other choral works; 55 songs; six recitations with piano; fugue on B.A.C.H., fantasy (1885) and fugue on *Ad nos, ad salutarem undam* and a few other organ works.

Litaniae Lauretanae Latin = 'Litanies of Loreto'; a litany sung in honour of the Virgin Mary in the Roman church, dating probably from the 13th c. It has its own plainsong melody, but has also been set by composers, including Palestrina, Lassus and Mozart.

litany a supplicatory chant consisting of a series of petitions with an infrequently changing response to each. The best-known litanies in the Roman Church are the Litany of the Saints, sung on Holy Saturday and during Rogationtide, and the 13th-c. ◊*Litaniae Lauretanae*. The reformed churches have also adopted the litany, excluding references to the saints, as in Cranmer's litany, still used in the Anglican Church.

Literes, Antonio (b Artá, Majorca, ?18 Jun 1673; d Madrid, 18 Jan 1747), Spanish bass viol player and composer (often confused with

---

Liszt

A biographical note

In 1842 Liszt was appointed court conductor at Weimar, but continued his career as an international virtuoso, earning a following dubbed 'Lisztomania' by the poet Heine. While on a tour of Russia in 1847, he met Princess Carolyne Sayn-Wittgenstein. When he returned to her in the autumn, he decided to give up his concert career and live with her in Weimar. Liszt and Carolyne set up an artists' centre at Villa Altenberg, but after she was condemned by the Tsar for leaving her husband she was not welcome in court. The Weimar years were the most successful of Liszt's career, conducting the premiere of *Lohengrin* in 1850 and composing the piano sonata and *Faust* and *Dante* symphonies later in the decade. Musical gatherings at Villa Altenberg featured concerts on Beethoven's Broadwood piano and a spinet that once belonged to Mozart. The occasional infatuation apart, Liszt remained dedicated to Carolyne, but he was still capable of inspiring devotion in others. A maid of honour at the Weimar court had around her for a time the aura of stale tobacco smoke; only reluctantly did she reveal that she had picked up a cigar stump discarded by Liszt in the street, and had worn it next to her bosom enshrined in a locket decorated with the initials F L.

his son, also called Antonio, who was a well-known organist). Member of the royal band in Madrid from 1693.

Works include operas *Júpiter y Danae*, *Los Elementos*, *Dido y Eneas*; zarzuela *Coronis*; 14 psalm settings; eight Magnificat settings.

Litolff, Henry (Charles) (b London, 7 Aug 1818; d Bois-les-Combes, near Paris, 5 Aug 1891), Anglo-Alsatian composer, pianist and publisher. His father was Alsatian, his mother English. As a boy of 13 he became a pupil of Moscheles for piano, made his first appearance in 1832 and at 17 left for France, having married against his parents' wish. He travelled widely as concert pianist until 1851, when he acquired a music pub. business at Brunswick, marrying as his second wife the widow of the former owner. But he soon left his adopted son Theodor Litolff in charge and settled in Paris, where later he married again, a Comtesse de la Rochefoucauld. He produced his best opera at Brussels in 1886.

Works include operas *Les Templiers* (1886) and *Héloïse et Abelard* (1872); oratorios *Ruth and Boaz*; five piano concertos including no. 4 (1852) with the popular Scherzo, violin concerto; overture *Robespierre* and others; chamber music; piano works.

Little, Tasmin (b London, 1965), English violinist. Studied at the Menuhin School and the GSMD. Has appeared with all the leading British orchestras and with the Gewandhaus Orchestra, the Royal Danish SO and the Berlin SO. Often heard in the concertos of Delius, Elgar, Dvořák and Sibelius. Premiered the concerto by Robert Saxton (Leeds 1989) and gave the reconstructed Janáček Concerto at the 1990 London Proms. Also a recitalist; she is especially valued for her performances of Beethoven's Kreutzer Sonata.

Little, Vera (b Memphis, 10 Dec 1928), American mezzo. Debut NY City Opera 1950, as Preziosilla. She sang in Europe from 1951 and was heard in Berlin in 1958 as Carmen; sang at the Deutsche Oper from 1959 and in 1965 created Begonia in Henze's *Der junge Lord*; the following year she created Beroe in *The Bassarids*, at Salzburg. Guest in Milan and Genoa and was heard in concert music by Bach and Mozart. Recorded Gaea in Strauss's *Daphne*.

'Little Russian' Symphony Tchaikovsky's second symphony in C minor, op. 17, also called *Ukrainian* symphony, composed 1872, performed Moscow, 18 Feb 1873.

Little Slave Girl, The, *Den lilla slavinnan*, opera by Crusell (libretto by composer), produced Stockholm, 18 Feb 1824.

Litton, Andrew (b New York, 16 May 1959), American conductor. After graduation from Juilliard worked as assistant conductor at La Scala. London debut at the 1982 Proms with the BBC SO. Assistant

with the National SO, Washington SO, 1982–86, principal of the Bournemouth SO 1988–94. Conducted *Eugene Onegin* at the NY Met. (1989) and the house premiere of *Porgy and Bess* at CG, 1992. Music director of the Dallas SO from 1994.

Liturgical Drama a medieval church representation of Bible and other stories. It originated, probably in France, in a 10th-c. trope to the Introit for Easter Day, which takes the form of a dialogue for the Angel and the Marys at the sepulchre. In the second half of the century it was transferred to Matins. The music was originally an extension of plainsong but in course of time came to consist of original compositions. Later subjects treated include the Walk to Emmaus, the Nativity, Epiphany, the Massacre of the Innocents, Old Testament stories and the lives of the saints. The texts were generally in Latin but sometimes also in the vernacular.

Choristers bellow the tenor, as it were oxen; bark a counterpoint as it were a kennel of dogs; roar out a treble, as it were a sort of bulls; grunt out a bass, as it were a number of hogs.

William Prynne, *Histriomastix*, 1632

---

lituus, Latin, the Roman cavalry trumpet. In the 18th-c. the word was occasionally used to mean 'horn'.

Litvinne (actually *Litvinova*), Félia (b St Petersburg, 1861; d Paris, 12 Oct 1936), Russian soprano. Studied with Maurel and others in Paris and made her first appearance there in 1880. She was particularly successful in Wagnerian roles; sang Isolde and Brünnhilde in Paris, London, Brussels. Other roles included Aida, Donna Anna, Alceste and Selika.

Liuzzi, Fernando (b Senigallia, 19 Dec 1884; d Florence, 6 Oct 1940), Italian musicologist and composer. Studied with Fano and later with Reger and Mottl and Munich. He became professor of harmony at the Conservatories of Parma and of Florence successively, and professor of music history at Rome University 1927–28. He edited Italian *laudi*, arranged performances of Vecchi's *Amfiparnaso* (Florence, 1938) and of Sophocles' *Oedipus Rex* with A Gabrieli's music (Rome, 1937). Wrote books on the *laudi*, on Italian musicians in France and a volume of critical studies *Estetica della musica*, also numerous learned articles.

Livietta e Tracollo intermezzo by Pergolesi (libretto by T Mariani), produced Naples, Teatro San Bartolommeo, between the acts of

---

≋≋≋ *Tasmin Little – violinist* ≋≋≋

1   Rakhmaninov: Symphony no. 3 (RLPO/Mackerras)
Mackerras unerringly gives this symphony the shape and long line necessary to maintain the interest and excitement throughout – the recorded sound is superb and the RLPO are at their very best.

2   Ravel: *Daphnis et Chloé* (Montreal SO/Dutoit)
Everything about this performance feels right – the tempi are so natural, the technical expertise of the orchestra is in abundance and Ravel's lush orchestration is so beautifully cáptured on this disc. An absolute 'must' for any record collection!

3   Strauss: *Four Last Songs* (Jessye Norman/Gewandhaus Orch./Masur)
Another desert island disc for me! Jessye Norman's richly powerful sonorities give the feeling of enormous breadth and her range of expression brings out the poetry in this wondrous composition, written at the end of Strauss's life.

4   Puccini: *La Bohème* (Los Angeles/Björling/RCA Victor Orch. & Chorus/Beecham)
A classic performance which after nearly forty years still captures the sparkling orchestration, wit and poignancy of Puccini's score. The soloists are beautifully matched and Beecham's understanding of this work is second to none.

5   Delius: *Paris* (RLPO/Mackerras)
One of Delius's most exciting and dynamic compositions, given the vitality and subtlety it deserves in this superb performance.

6   Chopin: Ballade no. 4 (Donohoe)
Donohoe's commitment, style, and precision are what puts this performance in a class of its own – this is arguably Chopin's greatest solo piano piece and it receives a truly romantic reading without cloying sentimentality.

7   Prokofiev: *Romeo and Juliet* (Gewandhaus Orch./Masur)
This is one of Prokofiev's most powerful compositions and is given a weighty and moving performance by Masur and the Gewandhaus.

Lloyd Webber *The composer Andrew Lloyd Webber has had unparalleled success with his many musical hits, including* Cats *and* Starlight Express. *Although his more recent* Requiem *does not compare favourably with Mozart's, he can take consolation in the fact that he will not, unlike Mozart, die a pauper.*

Pergolesi's serious opera *Adriano in Siria*, 25 Oct 1734. Livietta encourages petty thief and trickster Tracallo to reform.

Livre pour quatuor work in six movements for string quartet by Boulez; composed 1948–49, performed Donaueschingen and Darmstadt 1955–62. Revised as *Livre pour cordes*, for string orchestra and performed Brighton, 8 Dec 1969, conductor Boulez.

Ljunberg, Göta (b Sundsvall, 4 Oct 1893; d Lidingo, near Stockholm, 30 Jun 1955), Swedish soprano. Debut Stockholm 1918, as Gutrune; sang Elsa the same season. She returned to Stockholm until 1937. CG 1924–29; created the title role in Goossens' *Judith* (1929) and also sang Sieglinde. Salzburg 1928–33. NY Met. 1931–35, as Isolde and Brünnhilde and in the fp of Hanson's *Merry Mount* (1933). Particularly convincing as Salome.

Lloyd, Charles Harford (b Thornbury, Gloucestershire, 16 Oct 1849; d Slough, 16 Oct 1919), English organist and composer. Educated at Oxford; D. Mus. there in 1892. Appointed organist at Gloucester Cathedral, 1876, and Christ Church, Oxford, 1882; precentor at Eton College, 1892–1914, then organist at Chapel Royal, London.

Works include services and anthems; motet *The Souls of the Righteous* (1901); cantatas *Hero and Leander* (1884), *Song of Balder*, *Andromeda*, *The Longbeards' Saga* (1887), *A Song of Judgment* (1891), *Sir Ogie and Lady Elsie* (1894); incidental music to Euripides' *Alcestis* (1887); sonata, concerto, and other works for organ; madrigals and part-songs.

Lloyd, Edward (b London, 7 Mar 1845; d Worthing, 31 Mar 1927), English tenor. Choirboy at Westminster Abbey in London until 1860 and one of the Gentlemen of the Chapel Royal from 1869. First important public appearance at Gloucester Festival, 1871, when he sang in Bach's *St Matthew Passion*; sang in fp of Elgar's *King Olaf*, 1896, and was the first Gerontius, 1900.

At every one of those concerts in England you will find rows of weary people who are there, not because they really like classical music, but because they think they ought to like it.
George Bernard Shaw, *Man and Superman*, 1902

Lloyd, George (b St Ives, Cornwall, 28 Jun 1913), English composer. Studied violin with Albert Sammons and composition with Harry Farjeon. His father wrote the libretti for his three operas, the first of which was produced at Penzance in 1934 and the second at CG in 1938. He was severely wounded in World War II. OBE 1970.

Works include operas *Iernin* (1934), *The Serf* (1938) and *John Socman* (1951); 12 symphonies (1932–88); four piano concertos; two violin concertos; *Symphonic Mass* for chorus and orchestra (1992).

Lloyd (also *Floyd*), John (b c 1475; d London, 3 Apr 1523), English composer. He sang at the funeral of Prince Henry in 1511 and was present at the Field of the Cloth of Gold in 1520. He composed a Mass *O quam suavis*, preceded by an antiphon, *Ave regina*, bearing the inscription 'Hoc fecit iohannes maris' (*mare* = 'sea' = 'flood' = Floyd or Lloyd).

Lloyd, Jonathan (b London, 30 Sept 1948), English composer. Studied with Roxburgh 1965–69 at the RCM and worked with Tristram Cary at the electronic studio there. Later study with Pousseur and Ligeti.

Robert Lloyd – singer

1 Beethoven: Piano Concerto no. 4
It overwhelms me every time I hear it. Could this be the greatest music ever written?

2 Bach: *Ich habe genug* (Cantata no. 82)
Such melodies! Such heart-breaking oboe!

3 Wagner: *Parsifal* – Good Friday music
It provokes in me an extraordinary sensation of spiritual cartharsis.

4 Berlioz: *Benvenuto Cellini* – overture (conducted by Colin Davis)
I love the abandoned and unpredictable quality of this music. I relish the strange compatibility between composer and conductor.

5 Verdi: Requiem – 'Dies Irae'
Spectacular realization of the words. Verdi for me is the ultimate in vocal music.

6 Shostakovitch: Symphony no. 5 in D minor
This music is for me the quintessence of a musical culture I have spent much of my life with and seems to speak with the voice of a sad and wonderful people.

7 Mozart: *Nozze di Figaro/Marriage of Figaro* – aria 'Dove sono'
How does one choose from Mozart? I can never believe anyone dare sing this music, it is so ravishing.

8 The Welsh folk song 'Ddoi di dai' sung by unaccompanied soprano.
The perfect example of the rich eloquence of simplicity.

Has worked as street musician and was composer-in-residence at Dartington College 1978–79.

Works include *Cantique* for small orchestra (1968), *Everthing Returns* for soprano and orchestra (1978), *Toward the Whitening Dawn* for chorus and chamber orchestra (1980), *Fantasy* for violin and orchestra (1980), *If I Could Turn You On* for soprano and chamber orchestra (1981), *Rhapsody* for cello and orchestra (1982), viola concerto (1980); *Wa Wa Mozart* for piano and orchestra (1991); *There* for guitar and strings (1991); *Tolerance* for orchestra (1993); five symphonies (1983–89); *Three Dances*, *Waiting for Gozo* and *Won't it Ever be Morning*, for ensemble (1980–82); *John's Journal* for saxophone and piano (1980), two string quintets (1982), *Almeida Dances* for clarinet, piano and string quartet (1986); Mass for six voices (1983); *Revelation* for eight voices (1990).

Lloyd, Robert (b Southend, 2 Mar 1940), English bass. Debut London 1969, in the first version of *Fidelio*. SW 1969–72; CG from 1972 as Banquo, Sarastro, Fiesco, Boris and Philip II in the French version of *Don Carlos*. Has sung as guest in Aix, Paris, Boston, San Francisco and Milan. Also heard in Lieder (especially *Winterreise*) and oratorio. Appeared as Gurnemanz in the Syberberg film version of *Parsifal*. Sang this role at CG in 1988; returned in the UK fp of Massenet's *Chérubin* and as Frère Laurent in *Roméo et Juliette* (1994). Sang Boris at the Kirov Opera 1990 and Vienna Staatsoper, 1991.

Lloyd-Jones, David (b London, 19 Nov 1934), English conductor and editor. He studied at Oxford and with Iain Hamilton. Guest conductor with the BBC Welsh SO from 1963. Opera conductor from 1967 and has given the first British stage performances of Haydn's *La fedeltà premiata* and Prokofiev's *War and Peace*; has made an edition of *Boris Godunov* which returns to Mussorgsky's full score, and given the opera with Scottish Opera and ENO and at CG. Music director ENO North, Leeds, from 1977; in 1983 conducted the fp of Josephs' *Rebecca*. Gave the UK fps of Křenek's *Jonny spielt auf* and Strauss's *Daphne* (Leeds, 1984 and 1987).

Lloyd Webber, Andrew (b London, 22 Mar 1948), English composer. He studied at Oxford and in 1965 formed a partnership with Tim Rice as librettist. Their first musical success was *Joseph and the Amazing Technicolor Dreamcoat* (staged 1972). This was followed by *Jesus Christ Superstar* and *Evita* (1976). *Cats* (after T S Eliot, 1981), *Song and Dance* (1983) and *Starlight Express* (1984) were all popular successes. More lofty ambition was shown with *The Phantom of the Opera* (1986), while *Aspects of Love* (1989) and *Sunset Boulevard* (1993) returned to earlier territory. A *Requiem* (1984) was not regarded as making a significant contribution to the liturgical music of the 20th c.

Lloyd Webber, Julian (b London, 14 Apr 1951), English cellist, brother of Andrew ◊Lloyd Webber. He studied at the RCM and with Pierre Fournier. London debut, QE Hall, 1971; soloist with leading orchestras; NY debut 1980. In 1981 he gave the fp of a concerto written for him by Rodrigo. Professor at GSM since 1978. He has made two dozen world premiere recordings, including works by Britten, Holst, Sullivan, Vaughan Williams and Arnold.

Lloyd Webber *The cellist Julian Lloyd Webber. He has made the first recordings of certain works by the British composers Arnold, Britten, Holst and Vaughan Williams. He is also admired for his persuasive performances of the Dvořák and Elgar concertos.*

Lobe, Johann Christian (b Weimar, 30 May 1797; d Leipzig, 27 Jul 1881), German flautist, composer and writer on music. Studied at the expense of the Grand Duchess of Weimar, Maria Pavlovna, appeared as flute soloist at Leipzig in 1811, and then joined the court orchestra at Weimar, where his five operas were produced. He left in 1842 and four years later became editor of the *Allgemeine Musikalische Zeitung* at Leipzig; he also pub. several books on music.

Works include operas *Wittekind* (1819), *Die Flibustier* (1829), *Die Fürstin von Granada* (1833), *Der rote Domino* (1835) and *König und Pächter* (1844); two symphonies, overtures; piano quartets.

Lobgesang ◊Hymn of Praise.

Lobkowitz (Prince) Joseph Franz Maximilian (b Roudnice nad Labem, 7 Dec 1772; d Třeboň, 15 Dec 1816), Bohemian aristocrat and patron of music, resident in Vienna; he had sole direction of the Viennese theatres from 1807. Commissioned Haydn's string quartets

---

Julian Lloyd Webber — cellist

1   Elgar: Symphony no. 1 (Philharmonia/Barbirolli)
    Beecham famously compared this symphony (slightly disparagingly) to St Pancras station. However, both the symphony and the station have emerged unscathed. A towering 20th-century symphony.

2   Shostakovich: Cello Concerto no. 1 in E flat, op. 107 (Rostropovitch/Philadelphia Orch./Ormandy)
    A superb 20th-century cello concerto, dedicated to the great Rostropovich and a fitting tribute to his peerless talents.

3   Gavin Bryars: *The Green Ray*
    One of the most imaginative and original scores of the last few years.

4   Mozart: String Quartet in G minor, K516 (Griller Quartet/Primrose)
    A masterpiece, superbly performed by the legendary Griller Quartet and the renowned William Primrose.

5   William Lloyd Webber: *Aurora* (London PO/Maazel)
    Obviously an intensely personal evocation of the Goddess of the Dawn, *Aurora* is the essence of my father's music.

op. 77 and was a co-sponsor of *The Creation* and *The Seasons*. The Eroica Symphony was first performed in his house and Beethoven dedicated the quartets op. 18 and fifth and sixth symphony, the Triple Concerto, the string quartet op. 74 and *An die ferne Geliebte* to him.

Lobo, Alonso (b Osuna, *c* 1555; d Seville, 5 Apr 1617), Spanish composer. He was a choirboy at Seville Cathedral and assistant to the *maestro di capilla* from 1591; principal post there from 1604. Palestrina, Victoria and Guerrero were among his models.

Works include *Liber primus missarum* (1602), containing six Masses and seven motets; Credo romano, three passions, Lamentations, psalms, hymns.

Lobo (also called *Lopez* or *Lupus*), Duarte (b Alcáçovas, bap. 19 Sept 1565; d Lisbon, 24 Sept 1646), Portuguese composer. Studied under Mendes at Evora and later became choirmaster there. Afterwards he went to Lisbon with an appointment to the Royal Hospital and became *maestro di cappella* at the cathedral *c* 1590. Widely known as a polyphonist.

Works include Masses, offices for the dead, canticles, motets and much other church music.

Locatelli, Pietro (b Bergamo, 3 Sept 1695; d Amsterdam, 30 Mar 1764), Italian violinist and composer. Pupil of Corelli in Rome. Travelled widely as a virtuoso and settled down at Amsterdam, where he established public concerts.

Works include a set of 12 concerti grossi, op. 1, and solo concertos; sonatas; studies, caprices, etc. for violin.

Lochamer Liederbuch (also *Locheimer Liederbuch*) a German 15th-c. songbook, now in Berlin. It contains 44 German and three Latin songs, mostly monophonic and all anonymous. It dates *c* 1455–65. Also bound with the book is a copy of Paumann's *Fundamentum Organisandi*.

Locke (or *Lock*), Matthew (b Exeter, *c* 1622; d London, Aug 1677), English composer. He was a choirboy at Exeter Cathedral under Edward Gibbons. He visited the Netherlands in 1648, and having returned to London collaborated in Shirley's masque *Cupid and Death* performed before the Portuguese ambassador in 1653. In 1656 he wrote the *Little Consort* for viols in three parts for William Wake's pupils and the same year he was one of the composers who took part in the setting of Davenant's *Siege of Rhodes*. He was Composer in Ordinary to the King and for Charles II's coronation in 1661 he wrote instrumental music for the procession. In 1663, having turned Roman Catholic, he became organist to Queen Catherine. He was a vigorous and acrimonious defender of 'modern music', writing in 1666 a pamphlet defending his church music and in 1672 opening a controversy with Thomas Salmon. Purcell wrote an elegy on his death.

Works include operas, Davenant's *The Siege of Rhodes* (with Coleman, Cooke, Hudson and H Lawes, 1656), *Psyche* (with G B Draghi); masque, Shirley's *Cupid and Death* (with C Gibbons, 1653); incidental music to Stapylton's *The Stepmother*, (?) Shakespeare's *Macbeth* altered by Davenant and containing material from Middleton's *The Witch*, and for Shadwell's version of Shakespeare's *Tempest* (1674), song in Durfey's *The Fool turned Critic*; Kyrie, Credo, anthems, Latin hymns; consorts for viols in three and four parts; songs in three parts, duets; songs for one voice with accompaniment.

To be a composer and not a musician is a tragedy; it is to have genius and not talent.

Nadia Boulanger, quoted in Kendall, *The Tender Tyrant: Nadia Boulanger*, 1976

Lockhart, James (b Edinburgh, 16 Oct 1930), Scottish conductor and pianist. He worked as an organist in Edinburgh and London, then assistant conductor in German opera houses and at CG, London; regular conductor there 1962–68 and in 1967 gave the fp at Aldeburgh of Walton's *The Bear*. Music director WNO 1968–73 (Berg's *Lulu*, 1971). Director, Kassel Opera 1972–80; Koblenz Opera from 1981. Conducted ENO in *War and Peace* at the NY Met. (1984) and was director of opera at RCM 1986–93; London Schools' Vocal Faculty,

from 1993. He often performed in partnership with the soprano Margaret Price.

Lockspeiser, Edward (b London, 21 May 1905; d London, 3 Feb 1973), English critic. Studied with Nadia Boulanger in Paris and at the RCM in London. Author of *Debussy: His Life and Mind* (two vols., 1962–65) and many other books.

loco Italian, sometimes *al loco* = 'to the place' = 'place'; a direction indicating that a passage is to be played in the normal position indicated by the written notes, often given for greater safety after a passage shown to be played an octave higher or lower.

Loder, Edward (James) (b Bath, 1813; d London, 5 Apr 1865), English composer. He first learnt music from his father, John David Loder (1788–1846), a violinist and music pub., and in 1826–28 studied with F Ries at Frankfurt. After a second period of study there he settled in London and was induced by Arnold to set an opera, *Nourjahad*, for the New England Opera House, under which name the Lyceum Theatre opened with it in 1834. He was theatre conductor in London and later in Manchester. About 1856 began to suffer from a disease of the brain.

Works include operas and plays with music, *Nourjahad* (1834), *The Dice of Death* (1835), *Francis I* (a concoction from his songs), *The Foresters* (1838), *The Deerstalkers* (1841), *The Night Dancers* (1846), *Robin Goodfellow* (1848), *The Sultana, The Young Guard, Raymond and Agnes*, etc.; masque *The Island of Calypso* (1852); string quartets; numerous songs, including *12 Sacred Songs*, and *The Brooklet* (a translation of Wilhelm Müller's *Wohin* set by Schubert in *Die schöne Müllerin*).

Loder, Kate (Fanny) (b Bath, 21 Aug 1825; d Headley, Surrey, 30 Aug 1904), English pianist and composer, cousin of Edward ◊Loder. Studied at the RAM in London, where she later became professor of harmony; made her first appearance in 1844, when she played Medelssohn's G minor concerto. The fp in England of Brahms's Requiem took place at her house on 7 Jul 1871, the accompaniment being played on the piano by herself and C Potter.

Works include opera *L'elisir d'amore*, etc.

Lodoïska opera by Cherubini (libretto by C F Fillette-Loraux), produced Paris, Théâtre Feydau, 18 Jul 1791. Evil Count Dourlinski imprisons Lodoïska in order to force her to agree to marry him. Count Floreski rescues her with the help of some Tatar warriors.

Opera by R Kreutzer (libretto by J C B Dejaure), produced Paris, Comédie-Italienne, 1 Aug 1791.

Lodoiska opera by Mayr (libretto by F Gonella), produced Venice, Teatro Le Fenice, 26 Jan 1796. Plot similar to ◊*Lodoïska*, but Lodoiska is imprisoned by a Count Boleslao and rescued by a Lovinski.

Lodoletta opera by Mascagni (libretto by G Forzano, after Ouida), produced Rome, Teatro Costanzi, 30 Apr 1917. Dutch flower-seller follows poet to Paris but dies of cold when she gets there.

Loeffler, Charles Martin (Tornow) (b Mulhouse, 30 Jan 1861; d Medfield, MA, 19 May 1935), Alsatian-American composer. Before Alsace was lost to France in the 1870–71 war, Loeffler, whose father was an agricultural chemist and an author who wrote under the name of 'Tornow', was taken to Smela, near Kiev, and it was there that he was first given violin lessons. The family later moved to Debreczin in Hungary and about 1873 to Switzerland. There he decided to become a violinist and went to Berlin to study with Rappoldi, Kiel, Bargiel and lastly Joachim. Later he had a period of study with Massart and Guiraud in Paris, joined the Pasdeloup Orchestra and that of a wealthy amateur, where he remained until 1881. That year he went to the USA, played in Damrosch's orchestra, in quartets and with touring companies. In 1882 he joined the Boston SO, where he remained, sharing the first desk with the leader, until 1903. In 1887 he became a naturalized American.

Works include psalm *By the waters of Babylon* for women's voices and instruments, *Beat! Beat! Beat! Drums!* (from Whitman's *Drum Taps*, 1917) for male voices and orchestra, *Evocation* for women's voices and orchestra; chamber music.

Lœillet, Jean-Baptiste (b Ghent, bap. 18 Nov 1680; d London, 19 Jul 1730), Flemish flautist, oboist and composer. He made an early success as a performer, went to Paris in 1702 and to London in 1705, where he joined the orchestra of the King's Theatre in the Haymarket. He retired 1710 and made a living by teaching and giving concerts in his house in Hart Street (now Floral Street), Covent Garden.

Works include sonatas for one, two and three flutes, for oboe or violin.

Loeschhorn, Albert (b Berlin, 27 Jun 1819; d Berlin, 4 Jun 1905), German pianist, teacher and composer. Studied in Berlin, where he taught from 1851 and became professor in 1858.

Works include quartets; sonatas and especially studies and other instructive works for piano, etc.

Loewe ◊Löwe.

Loewe, Frederick (Fritz) (b Berlin, 10 Jun 1901; d Palm Springs, 14 Feb 1988), German-born American composer. Studied with Busoni and d'Albert in Berlin and emigrated to USA 1924. Worked on Broadway from the 1930s and began a collaboration with lyricist Alan J Lerner in 1942; their biggest successes were *Brigadoon* (1947), *My Fair Lady* (1956) and *Camelot* (1960). Wrote music for the Lesley Caron vehicle, *Gigi*, in 1958.

Loewe, (Johann) Carl (Gottfried) (b Löbejün, near Halle, 30 Nov 1796; d Kiel, 20 Apr 1869), German composer. He was a choirboy at Cöthen, and in 1809 went to the grammar-school at Halle. Encouraged by Jérôme Bonaparte, then king of Westphalia, he devoted himself to composition, to further studies, to the learning of French and Italian and later, at Halle University, the study of theology. The flight of Jérôme in 1813 deprived him of his income, but he managed to make a living and in 1820 became professor and cantor at Stettin, and in 1821 music director and organist. He visited Vienna in 1844, London in 1847, Sweden and Norway in 1851 and France in 1857. In 1864 he suffered from a six weeks' coma and was asked to resign in 1866, when he went to live at Kiel. He died there after a similar attack.

Works include operas *Die Alpenhütte* (1816), *Rudolf der Deutsche* (1825), *Malekadhel* (after Scott's *The Talisman*, 1832), *Neckerein* (1833), *Die drei Wünsche* (1834), *Emmy* (after Scott's *Kenilworth*, 1842); oratorios *Die Zerstörung Jerusalems* (1829), *Palestrina* (1841), *Hiob*, *Die Auferweckung des Lazarus* (1863) and 12 others; symphonic; concertos; piano solos and duets; numerous songs and ballads, including Goethe's *Erlkönig*, Fontane's German versions of *Archibald Douglas*, *Tom the Rhymer*.

Loewe, Sophie (b Oldenburg, 24 Mar 1815; d Budapest, 28 Nov 1866), German soprano. She sang in Vienna from 1832 and at La Scala in 1841 created Donizetti's Maria Padilla; sang in London the same year. At the Teatro Fenice, Venice, she created Verdi's Elvira (1844) and Odabella (1846).

Loewenberg, Alfred (b Berlin, 14 May 1902; d London, 29 Dec 1949), English music bibliographer of German origin. Studied at Jena University and graduated there in 1925. The Nazi régime drove him from Germany in 1934, and he settled in London, where he compiled *Annals of Opera 1597–1940*, containing details of c 4,000 operas in chronological order (pub. 1943; third edition 1978, editor Harold Rosenthal).

Loewenstern, Matthaeus (Apelles) von (b Neustadt, Silesia, 20 Apr 1594; d Bernstadt, near Breslau, 16 Apr 1648), German poet and composer. Studied (?) at the University of Frankfurt o/O. Having been schoolmaster and cantor at Leobschütz, he entered the service of the Duke of Oels-Bernstadt.

Works include choruses for Opitz's tragedy *Judith*; Latin and German motets; sacred concertos; book of 30 sacred songs to words of his own entitled *Frühlings-Mayen*.

Logier, Johann Bernhard (b Kassel, 9 Feb 1777; d Dublin, 27 Jul 1846), German musician of French descent. Pupil of his father. He settled in England as a boy after his parents' death and soon went to Ireland, settling finally at Dublin in 1809 as bandmaster and music dealer. He invented the chiroplast, an appliance used in learning the piano, spent three years in Berlin, returned to Dublin, and composed and arranged piano music. In 1809 he produced an ode on the 50th year of George III's reign.

Logroscino, Nicola (b Bitonto, bap. 22 Oct 1698; d ? Palermo, after 1765), Italian composer. Pupil at the Conservatorio di Santa Maria de Loreto, 1714–27, he held an organ post in Conza, 1728–31. He was chiefly a composer of *opera buffa*, though his first known opera was not written till 1738. From 1747 taught counterpoint at the Conservatory in Palermo.

Works include operas *Inganno per inganno* (1738), *L'Inganno felice* (1739), *Ciommetella correvata* (1744), *Il Governadore* (1747), *Giunio Bruto* (1748), *Leandro*, *Li zite*, *Don Paduano*, *La Griselda* (1752), *Le finte magie* (1756) and many others; oratorio *La spedizione di Giosué* (1763); two settings of the *Stabat Mater*; church music.

Lohengrin opera by Wagner (libretto by composer), produced Weimar, Court Theatre, by Liszt, 28 Aug 1850. Elsa marries knight Lohengrin but loses him after asking his name and dies of grief when he leaves her.

Lohet, Simon (b Liège, c 1550; d Stuttgart, Jul 1611), German organist and composer. Appointed organist to the court of Württemberg at Stuttgart in 1571.

Works include pieces in fugal style, *canzoni* and hymn-tune fantasies for organ, etc.

Lolli, Antonio (b Bergamo, c 1725; d Palermo, 10 Aug 1802), Italian violinist and composer. In the service of the court of Württemberg at Stuttgart, 1758–74, and of Catherine II of Russia in St Petersburg, 1774–83, he nevertheless spent most of his time as a touring virtuoso. Of his many works for violin (concertos, sonatas, etc.), probably only the solo parts are by Lolli.

Lombard, Alain (b Paris, 4 Oct 1940), French conductor. Studied at the Paris Conservatory and made debut with the Pasdeloup Orchestra 1961 (appeared with the orchestra as violinist in 1951). Worked with Lyon Opera 1961–65 and led Massenet's *Hérodiade* in concert at NY, 1963; NY Met. 1966, *Faust*. Conducted the New York PO at Salzburg 1966 and was music director of the Miami PO 1966–74; Strasbourg PO 1972–83; Opéra du Rhin at Strasbourg 1974–80. Conducted opera in Paris 1981–86 and worked in Bordeaux from 1988 (*Die Zauberflöte* there 1992).

Lombardi alla prima crociata, I, *The Lombards at the First Crusade*, opera by Verdi (libretto by T Solera, founded on a romance by T Grossi), produced Milan, La Scala, 11 Feb 1843. Taken prisoner by the Muslims, Griselda falls in love with her captor Oronte. They resolve to run away together, but he dies in battle, and she returns to the victorious Christians.

─── THE OPERA ───

Lohengrin

An epic three-act opera by Richard Wagner, first performed in 1850 (although not seen by Wagner until 11 years later). The action takes place in Antwerp, early in the 10th century.

I. Frederick of Telramund (baritone) accuses his ward Elsa (soprano) of having killed her brother Gottfried to obtain the throne of Brabant. Elsa's reply is a vision of a knight who will defend her. The call for a champion is answered by the knight Lohengrin (tenor), appearing in a boat drawn by a swan. He agrees to champion Elsa on condition that she will never ask his name or origin. Telramund is duly defeated, but Lohengrin spares his life.

II. The banned Telramund and his wife Ortrud (mezzo-soprano) recriminate gloomily when Elsa appears; Ortrud gains her trust but, as the marriage procession gathers at the cathedral steps, Ortrud accuses Lohengrin of sorcery. Telramund joins in and Elsa tries to ignore them.

III. In her bridal chamber with Lohengrin, Elsa grows increasingly agitated and demands to know his name. Telramund breaks in but is killed by Lohengrin with a single blow. At the banks of the River Scheldt, Lohengrin reveals his name to all, and declares that he is a knight of the Holy Grail. When he greets the swan, it is revealed as Gottfried, Elsa's lost brother. A dove of the Grail bears Lohengrin's boat away.

London (real name **Burnstein**), George (b Montreal, 5 May 1919; d Armonk, NY, 24 Mar 1985), Canadian bass-baritone and opera producer. Studied in LA with Richard Lert and made his debut in 1941, in Coates's *Gainsborough's Duchess*. Later he studied in NY and toured the USA. He was engaged to sing at the Vienna Staatsoper in 1949 as Amonasro and in 1951 sang at the NY Met. Appeared there until 1966 as Boris, Mandryka, Don Giovanni, Almaviva and Escamillo. Bayreuth 1951–64 as Amfortas and the Dutchman. Produced *The Ring* in Seattle, 1973–75.

London College of Music Founded 1887, mainly for part-time students. Now caters for *c* 300 full-time students. Director is John McCabe. Michael Berkeley composer-in-residence 1987–88.

London Mozart Players chamber orchestra founded by Harry Blech in 1949 from his London Wind Players. Many tours throughout Europe and has given frequent premieres, in addition to 18th-c. repertory. Blech was succeeded as artistic director by Jane Glover in 1984; Matthias Bamert from 1993.

London Philharmonic Orchestra founded in 1932 by Sir Thomas Beecham and associated with the Royal Philharmonic Society for its concerts in London, also with the Covent Garden Opera. During World War II it became a self-governing company. Principal conductors have been Adrian Boult (1951–57), William Steinberg (1958–62), John Pritchard (1962–71), Bernard Haitink (1967–79), Georg Solti (1979–83), Klaus Tennstedt 1983–87. Glyndebourne Opera orchestra since 1964.

London Sinfonietta English chamber orchestra founded 1968, with David Atherton as music director. Later conductors have included Elgar Howarth, Simon Rattle and Lothar Zagrosek. Berio, Birtwistle, Boulez, Henze and Ligeti have led the orchestra in performances of their own music. Joined forces in 1984 with Opera Factory; works by Tippett, Cavalli and Nigel Osborne have been given. Elgar Howarth and Simon Rattle have been frequent conductors. Paul Crossley joint artistic director 1988–94; Markus Stenz principal conductor from 1994.

London Symphony ◊Haydn's symphony no. 104, in D major (no. 12 of the 'Salomon' symphony), written for performance in London in 1795.

London Symphony, A the second symphony by Vaughan Williams, composed 1912, fp London, 27 Mar 1914; revised version London, Queen's Hall, 4 May 1920.

London Symphony Orchestra founded in 1904 from the bulk of players of the first Queen's Hall Orchestra, who left Henry J Wood, since he insisted on abolishing the system of sending deputies to rehearsals and concerts. Recent conductors have been Josef Krips (1950–54), Pierre Monteux (1961–64), Istvan Kertesz (1965–68), André Previn (1968–79), Claudio Abbado 1979–87, Michael Tilson Thomas (1988–95), Colin Davis from 1995.

long the name of a note-value in old mensural notation, half the value of the large and equal to either two or three breves.

Long, Marguerite (b Nîmes, 13 Nov 1874; d Paris, 13 Feb 1966), French pianist and teacher. She studied at the Paris Conservatory and taught there 1906–40. Formed own school 1920 and in 1920 began a partnership with the violinist Jacques Thibaud; a competition was established in their name. A champion of French music, Long gave the fps of Ravel's piano concerto (1932) and *Le Tombeau de Couperin* (1919).

Long Christmas Dinner, The, *Der Lange Weihnachtsmal*, opera in one act by Hindemith (libretto by Thornton Wilder), produced Mannheim, 17 Dec 1961; first produced in English, Juilliard School, NY, 1963. Ninety Christmas dinners over the four generations of a family.

Longo, Alessandro (b Amantea, 30 Dec 1864; d Naples, 3 Nov 1945), Italian pianist and editor. He became professor of piano at the Naples Conservatory, but later moved to Bologna, where he founded the Cercolo Scarlatti and the Società del Quartetto. He edited the journal *L'arte pianistica* and brought out editions of early Italian keyboard music including the sonatas of D Scarlatti in 11 vols. His system of numbering the sonatas was in use until superseded by that of Ralph ◊Kirkpatrick.

Longueval, Antoine de, N French 15th-c. composer about whom very little is known. He wrote three motets, a *chanson*, and a Passion, formerly attributed to Obrecht, based on all four gospels.

Loosemore, George (b Cambridge; d ? Cambridge, *c* 1682), English organist and composer. Studied under his father, Henry Loosemore, as a chorister at King's College Chapel, Cambridge, and in 1660 became organist of Trinity College there.
Works include anthems, etc.

Loosemore, Henry (b Devon; d Cambridge, 1670), English organist and composer, father of George ◊Loosemore. He learnt music as a choirboy at Cambridge and became organist of King's College Chapel there in 1627.
Works include Service in D minor, anthems, two Latin litanies; a piece for three viols and organ, etc.

Lopardo, Frank (b New York, 1958), American tenor. Made his debut at St Louis in 1984, as Tamino. International career from 1985, with appearances at Aix, La Scala and Amsterdam. Glyndebourne and the Vienna Staatsoper 1987, as Ferrando, and Belfiore in *Il Viaggio a Reims*. Chicago and CG 1989, as Rossini's Almaviva and Lindoro (*L'Italiana in Algeri*); returned to London 1994, as Alfredo. Season 1991/92, as Lindoro and Don Ottavio. Recordings include Ferrando in *Così fan tutte*, conducted by Solti.

Lopatnikov, Nikolai Lvovich (b Reval, 16 Mar 1903; d Pittsburgh, 7 Oct 1976), Estonian-born American pianist and composer. Studied at the St Petersburg Conservatory, left for Finland during the 1917 Revolution and in 1920 settled in Germany, studying piano with Willi Rehberg and composition with Toch in Berlin. In 1933 he returned to Finland and sought the advice of Sibelius. Settled in USA in 1939 and became an American citizen in 1944. Appointed professor of composition at Carnegie Institute of Technology, Pittsburgh, 1945.
Works include opera *Danton* (after Rolland's play, 1930–32); four symphonies (1928–71), variations, concertino and *Intro. and Scherzo* for orchestra; two piano concertos (1921, 1930), concerto for two pianos, violin concerto; three string quartets (1920, 1924, 1955); violin and piano sonata (with side-drum *ad lib.*), three pieces for violin and piano; cello sonata.

Lopez-Cobos, Jesus (b Toro, 25 Feb 1940), Spanish conductor. Studied with Franco Perrera and Hans Swarowsky in Europe, and at Juilliard. Season 1969 conducted at the Prague Spring Festival and *Die Zauberflöte* at Venice. Gave *Lucia di Lammermoor* at San Francisco 1972 (US debut). CG debut 1975 (*Carmen*), NY Met. 1978, *Adriana Lecouvreur*. Music director at the Deutsche Oper Berlin 1981–90, leading the company in Japan's first *Ring* cycle, 1987. Principal guest conductor of the LPO 1982–86, and artistic director of the Spanish National Orchestra, 1984–89. Music director of the Cincinatti SO from 1986; Lausanne Chamber Orchestra from 1990, led the ensemble in *Cosi fan tutte* at Mezières, 1993.

López de Velasco, Sebastián (b Segovia; d ? Madrid, *c* 1650), Spanish composer. He may have been a pupil of Victoria, whose post as *maestro de capilla* he was given later by the Infanta Juana at the convent of the Descalzas Reales in Madrid.
Works include Masses, motets, psalms, Magnificats and other church music.

Loqueville, Richard de (d Cambrai, 1418), French composer. He was in the service of Duke Robert of Bavaria in 1410 and *maître de chant* at Cambrai Cathedral from 1413 until his death. He wrote church music and *chansons* in the Burgundian style of his day. He probably taught Dufay.

Loreley ◊Lurline.
Opera by Bruch (libretto by E Geibel, originally written for Mendelssohn), produced Mannheim, 14 Jun 1863. Leonore falls in love with Count Otto, unaware of his imminent marriage to Countess Bertha. When she discovers the deception she sells her soul in exchange for beauty. Otto then rejects Bertha in favour of Leonore, but Bertha dies of grief, Otto then commits suicide, and evil spirits claim Leonore. Unfinished opera by Mendelssohn (libretto by E Geibel). Only the first-act finale, an *Ave Maria* and a chorus of vintners exist.

Lorengar, Pilar (b Saragossa, 12 Oct 1921; d Berlin, 2 June 1996), Spanish soprano. After early performances in concert her career in opera started in 1955: Cherubino at Aix and Violetta at CG. Glyndebourne 1956–60 as Pamina and Mozart's Countess. NY Met. debut 1966, as Donna Elvira. Other roles included Donna Anna, Fiordiligi, Eurydice, Eva, Mélisande and Regina in *Mathis der Maler*. Sang Meyerbeer's Valentine at the Deutsche Oper Berlin, 1987; Lyon 1989 as Maddalena in *Andrea Chénier*. Retired 1991.

Lorenz, Alfred (Ottokar) (b Vienna, 11 Jul 1868; d Munich, 20 Nov 1939), Austrian conductor and writer on music. After various other appointments he became conductor at Coburg-Gotha in 1898; but he retired, took a degree in 1922, became lecturer at Munich University, 1923, and professor 1926. He edited Wagner's literary works and Weber's early operas, and wrote several books on the form of Wagner's music dramas, on the history of western music and on A Scarlatti's early operas.

Lorenz, Max (b Düsseldorf, 10 May 1901; d Vienna, 12 Jan 1975), German tenor. He studied in Berlin and sang at the Staatsoper 1929–44. Vienna 1929–54 in Wagner repertory and as Otello and Bacchus. NY Met. debut 1931, as Walther; sang there until 1950. Bayreuth 1933–54 as Siegfried, Parsifal, Lohengrin and Tristan. At Salzburg he sang in the fps of von Einem's *Der Prozess* (1953) and Liebermann's *Penelope* (1954).

Lorenzani, Paolo (b Rome 1640; d Rome, 28 Nov 1713), Italian composer. Pupil of Benevoli in Rome. In 1675 he went to Sicily and became *maestro di cappella* at the cathedral of Messina. In 1678 the French viceroy, Marshal de Vivonne, induced him to go to Paris. From 1679 to 1683 he was one of the superintendents of the queen's music. After her death he became *maître de chapelle* at the Theatine monastery, where he wrote motets. His opera *Orontée* was produced at Chantilly in 1688 by order of the Prince de Condé. He returned to Rome as *maestro di cappella* of the Papal chapel in 1694.

Works include operas *Nicandro e Fileno* (1681) and *Orontée* (1688); motets and Magnificats; cantatas; Italian and French airs.

Loriod, Yvonne (b Houilles, Seine-et-Oise, 20 Jan 1924), French pianist. She studied with Messiaen and later became his second wife; closely associated with his music since the fp of *Visions de l'Amen* in 1943. US debut Boston 1949, in the fp of the *Turangalîla* symphony, under Bernstein. Has also played Boulez, Schoenberg, Bartók and Barraqué.

Loris, Heinrich, ◊Glareanus.

Lortzing, (Gustav) Albert (b Berlin, 23 Oct 1801; d Berlin, 21 Jan 1851), German composer, singer, conductor and librettist. He had some lessons with Rungenhagen in Berlin as a child, but his parents being wandering actors, he had to obtain his general and music education as best he could. He learnt the piano, violin and cello and studied such theoretical works as he could pick up. He married in 1823 and found it very difficult to make a living in a travelling opera co. His first stage work, *Ali Pascha von Janina*, was produced at Münster in 1828 and repeated at Cologne, Detmold and Osnabrück. In 1833–34 he was able to lead a more settled life, being engaged as tenor and actor at the Leipzig municipal theatre. The first two comic operas he wrote there were very successful, and so was his adaptation from Kotzebue, *Der Wildschütz*, in 1842, when he gave up acting. Two short terms as conductor at Leipzig and Vienna were unsuccessful. He had a large family by this time and fell upon more and more difficult times. The conductorship at a suburban theatre in Berlin in 1850 merely humiliated him without doing much to relieve the situation. Although not well known outside Germany, such operas as *Undine* and *Der Wildschütz* occupy in his homeland a similar position enjoyed by the works of Gilbert and Sullivan in England.

Works include operas *Die beiden Schützen* (1837), *Zar und Zimmermann* (1837), *Hans Sachs* (1840), *Casanova*, *Der Wildschütz* (after Kotzebue, 1842), *Undine* (after de La Motte Fouqué, 1845, *Der Waffenschmied* (1846), *Zum Grossadmiral, Rolandsknappen* (1849), *Regina* and others; operettas *Ali Pascha von Janina* (1824), *Die Opernprobe oder Die vornehmen Dilettanten* (1851); oratorio *Die Himmelfahrt Christi* (1828); incidental music for plays including

Goethe's *Faust*, Grabbe's *Don Juan und Faust* (1829), Scribe's *Yelva*; plays with music *Der Pole und sein Kind* (1832), *Der Weihnachtsabend* (1832), *Szenen aus Mozarts Leben* (with music adapted from Mozart, 1832); part-songs, songs.

Los Angeles, Victoria de (real name Victoria Gomez Cima) (b Barcelona, 1 Nov 1923), Spanish soprano. She made her debut in Madrid in 1944 and in 1947 won an international contest at Geneva. In 1949 she toured Europe and South America and appeared at the Salzburg Festival in 1950. London, CG, 1950–61 as Mimi, Eva, Elsa, Santuzza, Butterfly and Manon. Ny Met. 1951–61 as Marguerite and Desdemona. La Scala 1950–56 as Ariadne, Donna Anna, Agathe and Rosina. In 1979 she sang Carmen at the NY City Opera. Wigmore Hall recitals, 1990.

Los Angeles Philharmonic Orchestra founded 1919 and conducted until 1928 by Walter Henry Rothwell. Arthur Rodzinski was principal conductor 1929–33, Otto Klemperer 1933–43 (fp of the Brahms/Schoenberg piano quartet, 1938); Alfred Wallenstein 1943–56, Eduard Van Beinum 1956–58, Zubin Mehta 1962–77 (concerts in Dorothy Chandler Pavilion of Los Angeles Music Center from 1964); Carlo Maria Giulini 1978–84, André Previn 1986–89, and Esa-Pekka Salonen from 1992. Summer concerts in Hollywood Bowl.

To know whether you are enjoying a piece of music or not you must see whether you find yourself looking at the advertisement of Pears' soap at the end of the programme.

Samuel Butler, *Note-Books*, 1912

Lotario opera by Handel (libretto by ?, based on Antonio Salvi's *Adelaide*, not, as Burney says, on Matteo Noris's *Berengario*), produced London, King's Theatre, Haymarket, 2 Dec 1729. Strife in 10th-c. Italy as Queen Adelaide's husband is killed by Berengario, who wants her to marry his son Idelberto. Held prisoner, she appeals to King Lotario of Germany, who defeats Berengario and rescues Adelaide.

Lothar, Mark (b Berlin, 23 May 1902; d Munich, 7 Apr 1985), German composer. He studied at the Berlin Musikhochschule with Schreker (composition), Juon (harmony) and Krasselt (conducting). Later he had lessons with Wolf-Ferrari and others. After appointments as director of music at two Berlin theatres, he was in charge of the music at the Bavarian Staatstheater in Munich 1945–55.

Works include operas *Tyll* (1928), *Lord Spleen* (after Ben Jonson's *Epicoene*, 1930), *Münchhausen* (1933) and *Schneider Wibbol* (Berlin, 1938), *Rappelkopf* (Munich, 1958), *Der Widerspenstige Heilige* (Munich, 1968); incidental music for Eichendorff's *Die Freier* and other plays; *Narrenmesse* for male chorus; *Orchesterstücke* and suite for orchestra; serenade for chamber orchestra; music for film and radio; piano trio; piano pieces; songs.

Lott, Felicity (b Cheltenham, 8 Apr 1947), English soprano. She studied at the RAM and in 1975 sang Pamina with ENO. Anne Trulove at Glyndebourne in 1977, and has sung Christine in *Intermezzo*, the Countess in *Capriccio*, Octavian and Arabella there. In 1984 she sang with the Chicago SO. Other roles include Mozart's Countess (at Chicago and CG) the Marschallin (NY Met., 1990). Sang Eva in *Die Meistersinger* at CG (1990) and Strauss's Countess at Vienna, 1993. She has often been heard in concert with the Songmakers' Almanac, a group which includes readings in its recitals. She sang at the Royal Wedding of 1986.

Lotti, Antonio (b ? Venice, *c* 1667; d Venice, 5 Jan 1740), Italian composer. Pupil of his father and of Legrenzi in Venice. Appointed singer at St Mark's 1687, and rose to become second organist (1692), first organist (1704), finally *maestro di cappella* (1736). Produced his first opera, *Il trionfo dell' innocenza* in Venice in 1692 (*Giustino*, 1683, commonly ascribed to him, is by Legrenzi). Visited Dresden 1717–19 as an opera composer, but after his return to Italy devoted himself entirely to church music.

Works include operas *Porsenna* (1713), *Irene Augusta* (1713),

Polidoro (1714), *Alessandro Severo, Constantino* (for Vienna, 1716, with Fux and Caldara), *Giove in Argo* (1717), *Ascanio, Teofane* (1719), etc.; oratorios *Il voto crudele* (1712), *L'umiltà coronata in Esther* (1714), *Gioa, Giuditta*; Masses, Requiems, Misereres, motets and other church music.

Loughran, James (b Glasgow, 30 Jun 1931), Scottish conductor. He was an assistant conductor at opera houses in Bonn, Amsterdam and Milan before he became associate of the Bournemouth SO in 1962. CG debut 1964 (*Aida*). Principal conductor BBC Scottish SO 1965–71, Hallé Orchestra 1971–83. Bamberg SO 1978–83. US debut with the New York PO, 1972.

Louise opera by G Charpentier (libretto by composer, produced Paris, Opéra-Comique, 2 Feb 1900. Louise joins lover Julien against her parents' wishes.

Louis Ferdinand of Prussia, Prince (b Friedrichsfelde, near Berlin, 18 Nov 1772; d Saalfeld 13 Oct 1806), German amateur composer and pianist. Beethoven praised his playing and dedicated to him the C minor piano concerto. From 1804 Dussek was in his service as his companion and teacher. He fell in the battle of Saalfeld. Wrote piano trios, piano quartets and quintets and other chamber music; piano pieces.

loure, French, originally a special type of bagpipe, found especially in Normandy; later the name of a dance in fairly slow 6–4 time.

Lourié, Arthur (Vincent) (b St Petersburg, 14 May 1892; d Princeton, 13 Oct 1966), Russian-born American composer of French descent. Studied for a short time at the St Petersburg Conservatory, but was self-taught later. Appointed director of the music section of the Ministry of Public Instruction in 1918, but left in 1921. He settled in France and in 1941 in the USA.

Works include operas *A Feast in Time of Plague* (after Pushkin, 1935), and *The Blackamoor of Peter the Great* (1961); ballet *Le Masque de neige* and others; two symphonies; *Sonate liturgique* for orchestra, piano and chorus; *Ave Maria, Salve Regina* and other church music; *Regina coeli* for contralto, oboe and trumpet (1915), *Improperium* for baritone, four violins and double bass (1923); *Canzona di Dante* for chorus and strings; Japanese Suite for voice and orchestra; three string quartets; sonata for violin and double bass; three piano sonatinas; song-cycles *Elysium* (Pushkin, 1918) and *Alphabet* (A Tolstoy).

Love for Three Oranges, The, *Liubov k trem Apelsinam*, opera by Prokofiev (libretto by composer, based on Gozzi's comedy *Fiaba dell' amore delle tre melarancie*), produced in French translation, Chicago, Auditorium, 30 Dec 1921. The March from it has become popular. In an imaginary realm the Prince's melancholy is cured by the jester Truffaldino. Enraged, Fata Morgana (who was plotting against the prince) casts a spell by which the Prince becomes obsessed by three oranges. But the oranges contain princesses, one of whom the Prince marries.

Love in a Village opera by Arne (libretto by I Bickerstaffe), produced London, CG, 8 Dec 1762. Partly a ballad opera and pasticcio, Arne having introduced popular songs and airs by Handel, Galuppi, Geminiani and others.

Lowe, Edward (b Salisbury, c 1610; d Oxford, 11 Jul 1682), English organist and composer. Chorister at Salisbury Cathedral; became organist of Christ Church, Oxford, about 1630. Appointed one of the organists at the Chapel Royal in London, 1660. Wrote on the performance of cathedral music and composed anthems.

Löwe, Ferdinand (b Vienna, 19 Feb 1865; d Vienna, 6 Jan 1925), Austrian conductor. Studied at the Vienna Conservatory and taught there, 1884–97. From 1896 to 1898 he conducted the Wiener Singakademie, and from 1900 to 1904 the Gesellschaft concerts. He held further posts in Munich, Budapest and Berlin and was director of the Vienna Academy of Music from 1919 to 1922. He championed the symphonies of Bruckner, in spurious editions.

Löwe, Johann Jakob (b Vienna, bap. 31 Jul 1629; d Lüneburg, Sept 1703), German organist and composer. Pupil of Schütz at Dresden; held appointments at Wolfenbüttel from 1655 and Zeitz from 1663, appointed organist of St Nicholas's Church, Lüneburg in 1682.

Works include operas *Amelinde, Andromeda* and *Orpheus aus Thracien*; ballets; symphonies.

Lowe, Thomas (d London, 1 Mar 1783), English tenor. Made his first stage appearance at Drury Lane Theatre, London, in 1740. He sang in many Handel oratorios, including the fps of *Samson, Joshua, Alexander Balus, Susanna, Solomon* and *Theodora*.

Lowinsky, Edward (E)lias (b Stuttgart, 12 Jan 1908; d Chicago, 12 Oct 1985), German-born American musicologist. He studied in Stuttgart and Heidelberg. US citizen from 1947. Taught at Queens College, NY (1947–56), Berkeley (1956–61) and at University of Chicago. He was editor of the series Monuments of Renaissance Music (1964–77). Josquin, Lassus, Willaert and Gombert featured in his research.

Last year, I gave several lectures on 'Intelligence and Musicality in Animals'. Today, I shall speak to you about 'Intelligence and Musicality in Critics'. The subject is very similar.

Erik Satie, *In Praise of Critics*, 1918

Lualdi, Adriano (b Larino, 22 Mar 1885; d Milan, 8 Jan 1971), Italian composer and music critic. Studied with Wolf-Ferrari at Venice, became critic to the *Secolo* at Milan and in 1936 to the *Giornale d'Italia* in Rome. He later became director of the Naples Conservatory. He was a political conservative and supporter of Mussolini.

Works include operas *Le Nozze di Haura* (1908; staged 1943), *La figlia del rè* (1922), *Le furie del Arlecchino* (1915), *Il diavolo nel campanile* (after Poe, 1925), *La Granceola* (1932); ballet *Lumawig e la Saetia*; choral pieces; *La leggenda del vecchio marinaio, Suite adriatica*, colonial rhapsody *Africa*, three folk-tunes *Samnium* for orchestra; *Sire Halewyn* for soprano and orchestra; *La rosa di Saron* for tenor and orchestra; string quartet in E major; violin and piano sonata; passacaglia for organ; songs, etc.

Lubbock, John (b Much Hadham, Herts., 18 Mar 1945), English conductor and choirmaster. Studied at the RAM, founding the Camden Chamber Orchestra there 1967, becoming the Orchestra of St John's Smith Square, 1972; many concerts in Westminster and on tour in the UK and to Europe, the USA and Canada. Guest with the CBSO, LPO (debut 1987), LSO, London Mozart Players and the Stuttgart SO. Conducted Berio's *Sinfonia* at the Barbican Hall (1985), *The Dream of Gerontius* at Wexford, 1992.

Lübeck, Vincenz (b Padingbüttel, Hanover, Sept 1654; d Hamburg, 9 Feb 1740), German organist and composer. Organist at Stade until 1702, when he was appointed organist at St Nicholas's Church at Hamburg.

Works include cantatas, chorale-preludes and other organ music.

Lubin, Germaine (b Paris, 1 Feb 1890; d Paris, 27 Oct 1979), French soprano. She studied at the Paris Conservatory and with Lilli Lehmann. Paris, Opéra, 1914–44 in Wagner repertory and as Octavian, Elektra, Donna Anna, Thaïs and in the fps of works by d'Indy, Sauguet and Milhaud. London, CG, 1937 as Alceste and Dukas' Ariane. Bayreuth 1938–39 as Kundry and Isolde.

Lubotsky, Mark Davidovich (b Leningrad, 18 May 1931), Russian violinist. Studied at Moscow Conservatory and with D Oistrakh. He has toured widely from the early 1960s; GB debut 1970 with Britten's concerto, at the Promenade Concerts. Professor at the Hamburg Hochschule from 1986.

Lucas, Leighton (b London, 5 Jan 1903; d London, 1 Nov 1982), English composer and conductor. He studied music by himself while engaged in the career of a dancer and at 19 became a theatre conductor. He served in the RAF during World War II.

Works include ballets *Orpheus* and *The Horses* (1946), masques (tragic) *The Wolf's Bride* and (Japanese) *Kanawa, the Incantation*; film music for *Target for To-night*; *Missa pro defunctis* for solo voices, chorus and orchestra (1934); *Masque of the Sea* for chorus and orchestra; passacaglia, chaconne and Litany for orchestra; sonnets for piano and orchestra; *La Goya*, two dance impressions for chamber

───── THE OPERA ─────

Lucia di Lammermoor

A dramatic three-act opera by Gaetano Donizetti, set in Scotland in the late 16th century (as is Scott's novel *The Bride of Lammermoor*, on which the opera is based). It was first produced in Naples in 1835.

I. Lucy Ashton (soprano) loves Sir Edgar Ravenswood (tenor), an enemy of her family. But her brother, Lord Henry Ashton (baritone), wishes her to marry Arthur Blacklaw (tenor). When Lucia and Edgar meet, he wishes to be reconciled with the Ashtons.

II. Henry attempts to discourage Lucy by showing her a letter, allegedly from Edgar to another woman. Lucy then agrees to marry Arthur but Edgar bursts in on the wedding ceremony and curses Lucy.

III. Edgar accepts Henry's challenge to a duel, but at the castle Lucy has gone mad and killed Arthur. She enacts a wedding ceremony with the absent Edgar, wearing her bloodstained nightgown. Arriving at the place appointed for the duel, Edgar hears the bell announcing Lucy's death and, in his grief, throws himself on his sword.

In Italian versions of the opera, the forenames of the principal characters are usually given as Lucia, Edgardo, Enrico and Arturo.

───── THE OPERA ─────

orchestra; partita for piano and chamber orchestra, *Eurhythmy* for violin and strings, four divertissements for violin and chamber orchestra, piano trio in F major; songs.

Lucca, Pauline (b Vienna, 25 Apr 1841; d Vienna, 28 Feb 1908), Austrian soprano of Italian origin. Studied in Vienna, joined the Opera chorus and made her first stage appearance at Olomouc in 1859 as Elvira in *Ernani*. In 1863 she first visited London; appeared until 1882 as Valentine, Marguerite, Selika, Cherubino, Elisabeth de Valois and Carmen. She was a member of the Vienna Opera from 1874 to 1889; sang La Gioconda and Boito's Margherita.

Luchetti, Veriano (b Viterbo, 12 Mar 1939), Italian tenor. After study in Milan and Rome made debut at Wexford as Alfredo, 1965. Many appearances in Europe and the USA: sang in *L'Africaine* and Spontini's *Agnes von Hohenstaufen* at Florence (1971 and 1974), Foresto in *Attila* at La Scala (1975) and Cherubini's Jason at Aix (1976). London, CG, 1973–76, as Rodolfo, Pinkerton and Gabriele Adorno (with company of La Scala). Sang Foresto at the Vienna Staatsoper 1988, Radames at Turin, 1990. Often heard in the Verdi Requiem (CG, 1976).

Lucia di Lammermoor opera by Donizetti (libretto by S Cammarano, based on Scott's *Bride of Lammermoor*), produced Naples, Teatro San Carlo, 26 Sept 1835. Lucia loves the family enemy Edgardo, but her brother Enrico forces her to marry Arturo. When Edgardo finds out, Lucia goes mad and kills Arturo. Edgardo commits suicide from grief.

Lucier, Alvin (b Nashua, NH, 14 May 1931), American composer. Studied at Yale University 1950–54, Brandeis 1958–60; choral director there 1962–70. Founded Sonic Arts Union 1966 (with Gordon Mumma and Robert Ashley), for the performance of electronic music. Professor at Wesleyan University, 1970–84. His *Music for Solo Performer* (1965) uses amplified brain signals in harmony with percussion instruments.

Works include *Vespers* (1969); *The Queen of the South* with closed circuit TV system (1972); *Bird and Person Dying* (1975); *Shape of Sounds from the Board* for piano (1979); , sound installation (1983); *Serenade* for 13 winds and pure wave oscillator (1985); *Music for Men, Women and Reflecting Walls* (1986); *Salmon River Valley Songs* (1986); *Fidelio-trio* (1988); *Navigations* for string quartet (1991).

Lucio Silla opera by J C Bach (libretto by G de Gamerra, with alterations by Metastasio), produced Mannheim, at court, 4 Nov 1774.

Opera by Mozart (libretto ditto), produced Milan, Teatro Regio Ducal, 26 Dec 1772. Banished Cecilio returns to Rome to try to rescue fiancée Giunia from the dictator Sulla. Cecilio, after failing in an assassination attempt, is condemned to die by Sulla, but the dictator shows compassion when Giunia declares her love.

Lucrezia Borgia opera by Donizetti (libretto by F Romani, based on Victor Hugo's tragedy), produced Milan, La Scala, 26 Dec 1833. Gennaro, unknowingly the son of Lucrezia Borgia, defaces her family crest with his friends. To avenge her honour, Lucrezia intends to poison his friends, but not Gennaro himself, who she knows is her son. The plot misfires and he dies as well.

Ludford, Nicholas (b c 1485; d London, c 1557), English composer. He was for long active at the Royal Chapel of St Stephen, Westminster. He wrote seven festal Masses, motets, a Magnificat, and a set of seven Masses for the daily Mass of Our Lady which is unique. A John Ludford, composer of a Mass *Dame sans per*, belonged to the previous generation; nothing is known of his life.

Ludikar, Pavel (b Prague, 3 Mar 1882; d Vienna, 19 Feb 1970), Czech bass-baritone. Debut Prague 1904, as Sarastro; sang in Vienna and Dresden and at Rome in 1911 was the first Italian Ochs. Boston 1913–14 and appeared frequently at Buenos Aires. NY Met. 1926–32, in *La Rondine* and *Luisa Miller* and as Rossini's Figaro. Director, Prague Opera, from 1935 and in 1938 created there the title role in Křenek's *Karl V*, under Karl Rankl.

Ludovic opera by Hérold, left unfinished and completed by Halévy (libretto by J H V de Saint-Georges), produced Paris, Opéra-Comique, 16 May 1833. Chopin wrote piano variations on an air from it, op. 12.

Ludwig, Christa (b Berlin, 16 Mar 1924), German mezzo. Studied with her mother and with Felice Hüni-Mihaček, making her debut in 1946. After appearing in a number of German opera houses she sang at the Salzburg Festival in 1954 as Cherubino, and was engaged by the Vienna Staatsoper in 1955. She was married to the baritone Walter Berry 1957–70. NY Met. from 1959 as the Dyer's Wife, Dido in *Les Troyens* and Leonore. London, CG, 1968 and 1976 as Amneris and Carmen. Other roles included Eboli, Lady Macbeth, Octavian, the Marschallin, Dorabella and Brangaene. She was a frequent recitalist at Salzburg and elsewhere (Wigmore Hall, London, 1993). Last appearance as Clytemnestra in *Elektra* at the Vienna Staatsoper, 14 Dec 1994. Much admired in Mahler and for the vocal warmth and dramatic strength of her stage performances. One of the great voices of the century; some of her best recordings are *Der Rosenkavalier* (under Bernstein), *Così fan tutte* (Böhm), *Das Lied von der Erde* (Klemperer) and *Norma* (as Adalgisa).

Ludwig, Friedrich (b Potsdam, 8 May 1872; d Göttingen, 3 Oct 1930), German musicologist. Studied at Marburg and Strasbourg Universities He became a lecturer at Strasbourg in 1905 and professor at Göttingen in 1911, where he was later appointed Rector. His comprehensive studies of 13th- and 14th-c. music remain indispensable.

Ludwig, Leopold (b Ustrava-Witkowitz, 12 Jan 1908; d Lüneburg, 24 Apr 1979), Austrian conductor. After appointments in Czechoslovakia and Germany he worked in Vienna and Berlin 1939–50. Hamburg 1951–70; led the fps of Krenek's *Pallas Athene weint* (1955) and Henze's *Der Prinz von Homburg* (1960). In 1952 he took the Hamburg Co. to Edinburgh for the British premiere of *Mathis der Maler*, and in 1962 to London for the first *Lulu* in Britain. He conducted *Der Rosenkavalier* at Glyndebourne in 1959 and *Parsifal* at the NY Met. in 1970.

Ludwig, Walther (b Bad Oeynhausen, 17 Mar 1902; d Lahr, 15 May 1981), German tenor. He studied medicine and started his stage career in 1928. Schwerin 1929–32, and in 1931 created there the title role in Graener's *Wilhelm Friedemann Bach*. Städtische Oper, Berlin, 1932–45, in the lyric repertory. Glyndebourne 1935, as Belmonte and Tamino; also highly praised at Salzburg as a Mozart singer. Many concert tours in Europe and South America. Retired 1962 and resumed his medical career.

THE OPERA

Luisa Miller

A three-act opera by Giuseppe Verdi, written in 1849. This tragic tale is set in the Tyrol, early in the 18th century.

I. Rodolfo (tenor), son of the wicked Count Walter (bass), is in love with Luisa (soprano), although he is expected to marry Federica (mezzo-soprano). Walter has Luisa and her father arrested, but releases them when Rodolfo threatens to reveal his disreputable past.

II. To save her father, Luisa is made to write to Wurm (bass), in service with Walter, that it is him she loves and not Rodolfo. Wurm and Walter further compel her to tell Federica the same lie. Rodolfo challenges Wurm to a duel, but is persuaded by his father to marry Federica.

III. Miller is released on the day of the marriage and when Rodolfo questions Luisa, she confirms her letter. Rodolfo offers her a poisoned drink which he has just taken himself. Luisa reveals the truth before she dies and Rodolfo kills Wurm before he too falls dead.

THE OPERA

Ludwig II, King of Bavaria, Richard ◊Wagner.

Luening, Otto (b Milwaukee, 15 Jun 1900), American composer, conductor, flautist and educator. Studied at Munich and conducted opera there and in Zurich 1917–20; also conducted opera in the US (Chicago and Eastman School) and gave the fps of Menotti's *The Medium* and Thomson's *The Mother of us All* (NY, 1946–47). A pioneer of electronic music; co-director Columbia-Princeton Electronic Music Center from 1959. Taught at Juilliard 1971–73.

　　Works include opera *Evangeline* (1928–33, produced NY 1948); flute concertino (1923), *Kentucky Concerto* (1951), *Wisconsin Symphony* (1975); *Potawatomi Legends* for chamber orchestra (1980), *Symphonic Fantasias* I–IX (1924–88); three string quartets (1919–28); many chamber suites and sonatas for violin, flute and cello; *Green Mountain Evening* for six instruments (1988); electronic music, including *Rhapsodic Variations*, with Ussachevsky (1954).

Lugg (or *Lugge*), John (b *c* 1587; d Exeter, after 1647), English organist and composer. He was vicar-choral and organist at Exeter.

　　Works include services, anthems, motets; organ voluntaries; canons; jig for harpsichord, etc.

Lugg (or *Lugge*), Robert (b Exeter, 6 Nov 1620), English organist and composer, son of John ◊Lugg. B.Mus. Oxford, 1638, and organist at St John's College. He became a Roman Catholic and went abroad.

　　Works include services, anthems.

Luigini, Alexandre (Clément Léon Joseph) (b Lyons, 9 Mar 1850; d Paris 29 Jul 1906), French violinist, conductor and composer. Studied at the Paris Conservatory, became leader at the Grand Théâtre of Lyons in 1869 and conductor in 1877. In 1897 he became conductor of the Opéra-Comique in Paris.

　　Works include operas *Faublas* (after Louvet de Couvray, produced 1881) and *Les Caprices de Margot* (produced 1877); ballets; cantata *Gloria victis*; *Ballet égyptien* (1875), *Ballet russe*, *Carnaval turc* and other light works for orchestra.

Luisa Miller opera by Verdi (libretto by S Cammarano, based on Schiller's drama *Kabale und Liebe*), produced Naples, Teatro San Carlo, 8 Dec 1849. Luisa loves Rodolfo, but is forced to declare love for Wurm in exchange for the release of her father, Miller, who has been imprisoned by Count Walther. Feeling betrayed, Rodolfo poisons Luisa and himself before learning the truth.

Lukomska, Halina (b Suchedniów, 29 May 1929), Polish soprano. From 1960 has been heard most often in technically demanding music: Webern, Lutosławski, Serocki and *Pli selon pli* by Boulez.

Lully, Jean Baptiste (originally Giovanni Battista Lulli) (b Florence, 28 Nov 1632; d Paris, 22 Mar 1687), Italian-French composer. Son of a miller, he had little education and learnt guitar and violin without much guidance. At first joined strolling players, but in 1646 was discovered by the Chevalier de Guise and taken to France, where he entered the household of Mlle de Montpensier, the king's cousin, as a scullion; but when she found that he was musical she made him a personal servant and leader of her string band. In 1652 he passed into the service of Louis XIV, who was then 14. Lully became ballet dancer, violinist in the king's '24 violins' and composer. In 1658 he began to compose ballets of his own, having contributed to some since 1653, in which the king himself danced. In 1661 he became a naturalized Frenchman and Composer to the King's Chamber Music and in 1662 Music Master to the Royal Family; continued to enjoy royal protection, in spite of his open activity as a pederast — at that time punishable by death.

　　His first opera, *Cadmus et Hermione*, appeared in 1673, when he obtained a royal patent granting him the monopoly of operatic production and annulling a previous patent given to Perrin and Cambert. The Académie Royale de Musique, as the Opéra was first called, was opened 1672 with a pasticcio from earlier works of his, *Les Festes de l'Amour et de Bacchus*. Most of his operas were written in collaboration with Philippe Quinault, and most of the ballets with Molière. His last complete opera was *Acis et Galatée* in 1686; by this time he had transformed French operatic style, developing the formal French overture and introducing a declaimed accompanied recitative, which replaced the former recitative with harpsichord accompaniment. In 1687 he injured his foot with the staff with which he conducted a Te Deum to celebrate the king's recovery and died of blood poisoning. The opera *Achille et Polyxène*, left unfinished by him, was completed by Colasse.

　　Works include OPERAS: *Cadmus et Hermione* (1673), *Alceste* (1674), *Thésée* (1675), *Atys*, *Isis* (1677), *Psyché* (1678), *Bellérophon* (1679), *Proserpine*, *Persée*, *Phaéton* (1683), *Amadis de Gaule* (1684), *Roland*, *Armide et Renaud* (1686), *Acis et Galatée* (1686), *Achille et Polyxène* (Act I only by Lully; produced 1687).

Lully *The composer Jean Baptiste Lully (1632–1687). He dominated and defined the scene in French music during the early Baroque period. He was instrumental in modernizing violin-bowing technique and was one of the first recognized conductors who used a large staff for a baton.*

COMEDY-BALLETS (all with Molière): *Les Fâcheux, La Mariage forcé, L'Amour médicin* (1665), *La Princesse d'Elide* (1664), *Le Sicilien, Georges Dandin, Monsieur de Pourceaugnac* (1669), *Les Amants magnifiques* (1670), *Le Bourgeois Gentilhomme* (1670).

PASTORALS AND DIVERTISSEMENTS: *Les Plaisirs de l'île enchantée* (1664), *La Pastorale comique* (1667), *L'Églogue de Versailles* (or *La Grotte de Versailles*, words by Quinault, 1668), *L'Idylle sur la paix* (or *Idylle des Sceaux*, words by Racine, 1685).

BALLETS: (some possibly by Boësset and others) *Ballet d'Alcidiane* (1658), *Ballet de la raillerie* (1659), *Ballet de Xerxès* (for Cavalli's opera, 1660), *Ballet de l'impatience* (1661), *Ballet des saisons, Ballet de l'Ercole amante* (1662), *Ballet des arts* (1663), *Ballet des noces de village, Ballet des amours déguisés* (1664), *La Naissance de Vénus* (1665), *Ballet des gardes, Le Triomphe de Bacchus dans les Indes* (1666), *Ballet des Muses* (1666), *Le Carnaval ou Mascarade de Versailles, Ballet de Flore* (1669), *Ballet des ballets* (1671), *Le Triomphe de l'Amour* (1681), *Le Temple de la paix* (1685). Incidental music to Corneille's *Œdipe*; church music, Miserere, *Plaude laetare*, Te Deum, *De profundis, Dies irae* and Benedictus, five *Grands Motets*, 12 *Petits Motets*, motets for double chorus; dances for various instruments. *Suites de trompettes, Suites de symphonies et trios.*

Lulu unfinished opera by Berg (libretto by composer), based on Frank Wedekind's plays *Erdgeist* and *Die Büchse der Pandora*), Acts 1 and 2 and a fragment of 3 produced Zurich, 2 Jun 1937. Third act realized by Friedrich Cerha; first complete performance Paris, 24 Feb 1979, conductor Boulez. Femme fatale leaves a trail of corpses but is killed by Jack the Ripper.

He merits with good reason the title of Prince of French Musicians, being regarded as the inventor of this beautiful and great French music.
Titon du Tillet on Jean Baptiste Lully, quoted in Mellers, *François Couperin*, 1950

Lumbye Danish family of musicians:

1. Hans Christian Lumbye (b Copenhagen, 2 May 1810; d Copenhagen, 20 Mar 1874), conductor and composer. Conducted a light orchestra at the Tivoli in Copenhagen from 1848 and wrote much dance and other light music for it.

2. Carl Christian Lumbye (b Copenhagen, 9 Jul 1841; d Copenhagen, 10 Aug 1911), conductor and composer, son of 1. He suc-

A Selection of

Lully

Le Bourgeois Gentilhomme 1670
Alceste 1674
Atys 1676
Te Deum 1677

Phaéton 1683
Armide 1686
Harpsichord works

THE OPERA

Lulu

An unfinished three-act opera by Alban Berg, set in Prague and London in about 1930. It was first produced in Zurich in 1937, two years after Berg's death.

I. A circus ringmaster (bass) presents his show to the audience, bringing forth Lulu (soprano) as one of the acts. The Painter (tenor) chases Lulu round his studio and, when her elderly husband bursts in, he collapses and dies of a heart attack. The Painter marries Lulu, but when Dr Schön (baritone) tells him of his own affair with her, he commits suicide with a razor. Schön gets engaged to another girl, but Lulu makes him break it off by threatening to run away with an African prince (tenor).

II. Now married to Lulu, Schön overhears his son Alwa (tenor) declare his love for her. Schön urges Lulu to shoot herself, but instead she kills him. A film shows Lulu's conviction for murder, but the lesbian Countess Geschwitz (mezzo-soprano) helps her to escape from prison.

III. Anxious not to be sold to an Egyptian as a prostitute, Lulu runs from a Paris casino. Escaping to London with Alwa, Geschwitz and the senile Schigolch (bass), she entertains Jack the Ripper as one of her clients. But instead of becoming one of Lulu's victims, he murders her first, then disposes of Geschwitz.

THE OPERA

ceeded his father in 1865 and also wrote dances, marches, etc.

3. Georg August Lumbye (b Copenhagen, 26 Aug 1843; d Oringe, 29 Oct 1922), conductor and composer, brother of 2. Wrote chiefly for the stage, including the opera *The Witch's Flute.*

Lumsdaine, David (b Sydney, 31 Oct 1931), Australian-born British composer. Educated in Sydney, moved to London in 1952 and studied with Seiber at the RAM. Lecturer at Durham University from 1970; founded electronic studio there.

Works include *Episodes* (1969) and *Shoalhaven* (1982) for orchestra, *Mandala* II and III for chamber orchestra; *Mandala V* (1988) for orchestra; *Easter Fresco* for soprano and ensemble (1966); *Aria for Edward John Eyre* (1972); *Round Dance* for sitar, tabla, flute , cello and piano (1989); *Mandala IV* for string quartet (1983).

Lupi, Johannes (Jean Leleu) (b Cambrai, *c* 1506; d Cambrai, 20 Dec 1539), French composer. He was associated with Cambrai Cathedral from 1526, first as singer then as choirmaster. He wrote church music and *chansons*.

A different Johannes Lupi was organist at Nivelles in 1502, possibly the composer of a lament on the death of Ockeghem (1495); the name is also found in the records of Antwerp Cathedral in 1548. It is often impossible to be certain to which of these composers to assign various works. Lupus Hellinck (*c* 1496–1541) is again a distinct composer, as is the slightly younger Didier Lupi of Lyon.

Lupo, Thomas (d London, Jan 1628), English composer and player of stringed instruments. His father Joseph (b ? Milan; d London, 1616), his uncle Ambrose (b ? Milan; d London, 10 Feb 1591) and his son Theophilus (*fl.* 1628–42) are also known as composers, but Thomas is distinguished by his pavans and fantasies for viol consort, particularly in five and six voices.

Lupu, Radu (b Galati, 30 Nov 1945), Romanian pianist. He studied at the Moscow Conservatory; won the Van Cliburn Competition in 1966 and the Leeds International in 1969. London debut 1969; US 1972, with the Cleveland SO; Salzburg Festival debut 1979, with the Vienna PO under Muti. Premiered André Tchaikowsky's concerto, London 1975. He has played in the 19th-c. repertory with all the leading orchestras, and with the violinist Szymon Goldberg has given the Mozart sonatas. *See illustration on page 384.*

Luria, Juan (b Warsaw, 20 Dec 1862; d Auschwitz, 1942), Polish baritone. Debut Stuttgart 1885; sang widely in Germany, often in Wagner. NY Met. 1890–91. At La Scala he was the first local Wotan

Lupu *The pianist Radu Lupu is a soloist with the world's leading orchestras. He concentrates on the standard 18th- and 19th- century repertory, and has recorded the complete set of Beethoven concertos with Zubin Mehta and the Israel Philharmonic. He makes frequent tours of Britain.*

(1893) and at Elberfeld he took part in the fp of Pfitzner's *Die Rose vom Liebesgarten* (1901). He taught in Berlin from 1914 and with the rise of the Nazis fled, as a Jew, to Holland. Although in his 80th year he was arrested and transported to Auschwitz.

Luscinius (real name *Nachtgall* or *Nachtigall*), Othmar (b Strasbourg, *c* 1478; d Freiburg i/B, 5 Sept 1537), German organist and composer. Pupil of Hofhaimer. He was organist at Strasbourg, but left for Freiburg i/B in 1523, owing to the Reformation, and settled at a Carthusian monastery. He wrote musical treatises and composed organ music.

lusingando or lusinghiero Italian = 'wheedling, coaxing'; a direction to perform a piece or passage in a charming, alluring manner.

Lusitano, Vicente (b ? Olivença; d after 1553), Portuguese theorist and composer. He was known as Vicente de Olivença in Portugal, but was called Lusitano ('the Portuguese') in Rome, where he settled about 1550. In 1551 he had a dispute with Vicentino, which was settled in his favour, with Danckerts and Escobedo as judges. He pub. a treatise on *cantus firmus* in 1553.

Works include motets *Epigrammata*, etc.

He capers nimbly in a lady's chamber/To the lascivious pleasing of a lute.
William Shakespeare, *Richard III*,
Act 1, Scene 1, line 12

Lussan, Zélie de (b Brooklyn, NY, 21 Dec 1861; d London, 18 Dec 1949), American mezzo of French origin. After some parental opposition, she was trained by her mother and made her stage debut at Boston in 1886. In 1888 she went to London and sang Carmen at CG, which became her great part. She also sang soprano parts and commanded French, Italian and English with equal ease; other roles included Mignon, Zerlina and Cherubino. She appeared all over the world, but on her marriage in 1907 retired and settled in London.

Lustigen Weiber von Windsor, Die, *The Merry Wives of Windsor*, comic opera by Nicolai (libretto by S H Mosenthal, after Shakespeare), produced Berlin, Opera, 9 Mar 1849. German version of Falstaff's amorous adventures.

Lustige Witwe, Die, *The Merry Widow*, operetta by Lehár (libretto by V Léon and L Stein), produced Vienna, Theater an der Wien, 30 Dec

1905. Baron Zeta wants Count Danilo to marry the widow Hanna Glawari for her money, but the two fall geuinely in love, although they hide their feelings at first. All ends well.

lute a plucked string instrument with a pear-shaped body. Its origin is eastern. It gained currency in Europe in medieval times and was still very popular in the 17th c., but declined in the 18th. In the 16th c. there were five pairs of strings, two to each note, and one single string. Other tunings were adopted in the 17th c. Music for the lute is played from a tablature of letters or figures.

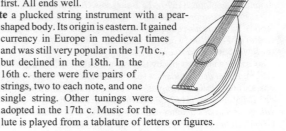

The open strings typical of the lute during the 16th century.

lute-harpsichord an instrument made for Bach in 1740, called *Lautenclavicymbel*, with gut strings and a keyboard.

lutenist a lute-player, also a singer to the lute and often a composer for the instrument.

Luther, Martin (b Eisleben, 10 Nov 1483; d Eisleben, 18 Feb 1546), German reformer and amateur musician. The musically relevant facts of his biography are that his reforms of the church service, begun in 1522, included the much greater scope given to singing by the congregation and the consequent necessity to sing in the vernacular, instead of in Latin. He arranged a German Mass in 1524 and he had the assistance of Walter and of Conrad Rupff, music director to the Elector of Saxony, in compiling a German hymn-book, with tones selected by him, some adapted from Latin and earlier German hymns and some possibly invented by himself.

For literary works set by other composers ◊Burkhard (*Musikalische Uebung*); S ◊Otto (hymn 'Ein' feste Burg'); J ◊Walther (sacred songs).

luthier, French, originally a lute-maker, later, by transference, a maker of string instruments in general.

Lutosławski, Witold (b Warsaw, 25 Jan 1913; d Warsaw, 7 Feb 1994), Polish composer. Studied at the Warsaw Conservatory with Maliszewski (theory and composition) and Lefeld (piano), graduating in 1937. At the same time he studied mathematics at Warsaw University. His earlier music is influenced by Bartók and Stravinsky, and also by Polish folk music, partly as a result of official Communist constraints, but later he adopted a more advanced, aleatory technique.

Works include ORCHESTRAL: four symphonies (1941–92), *Symphonic Variations* (1938), *Concerto for Orchestra* (1954), *Venetian Games* for small orchestra (1961), *Musique funèbre* for strings (in memory of Bartók), five *Dance Preludes* for clarinet, strings, harp and percussion; cello concerto (1970), *Preludes and fugues* for 13 strings (1971), *Mi Parti* for orchestra (1976), Concerto for oboe, harp and chamber orchestra (1982), *Chain I* for chamber orchestra (1983), *Chain II* for violin and orchestra (1984), *Chain III* (1986), piano concerto (1988), Slides for 11 soloists (1988), Interludium for chamber orchestra (1989).

VOCAL: *Trois Poèmes d'Henri Michaux* for wind instruments, two pianos, percussion and 20-part chorus; *Silesian Tryptych* for soprano and orchestra (1951), *Paroles tissées* for voice and orchestra (1965), *Les espaces du sommeil* for baritone and orchestra (1975), *Chantefables et Chantefleurs* for soprano and orchestra (1990).

CHAMBER: string quartet (1964); *Grave* for cello and piano (1981), Partita for violin and piano (1984, version with orchestra, 1988), *Variations* on a theme of Paganini for two pianos.

Lutyens, Elisabeth (b London, 9 Jul 1906; d Hampstead, 14 Apr 1983), English composer. Daughter of the architect Sir Edwin Lutyens. Studied viola and composition at the RCM in London, the latter with Harold Darke, and later with Caussade in Paris. She married the BBC conductor Edward Clark. Her later work was generally, though not

A Selection of

Lutosławski

Variations on a theme of Paganini	1941
Symphony no. 1	1947
Musique funèbre	1958
String Quartet	1964

Livre pour Orchestre	1968
Cello Concerto	1970
Preludes and Fugues	1971
Symphony no. 3	1983
Chain II for violin and orch.	1985
Piano Concerto	1988

invariably, written in 12-note technique. In a lecture at Dartington in the 1950s she coined the term 'Cowpat Music' to describe the work of such composers as Vaughan Williams, Delius and Holst, who turned to pictorial pastoralism in their music; in her own music Lutyens resolutely avoided ruminant obstructions.

Works include operas *Infidelio* (1956, produced 1973) and *Time Off? Not a Ghost of a Chance* (produced 1972); ballet *The Birthday of the Infanta* (after Oscar Wilde, 1932); chamber cantata *Winter the Huntsman* (Osbert Sitwell), *Bienfaits de la lune* (Baudelaire) and other choral works; three symphonic preludes, *Petite Suite*, *Divertissement* and other orchestral works; viola concerto, *Lyric Piece* for violin and orchestra; six chamber concertos (1939–48).

12 string quartets (1938–82), string trio, *Suite gauloise* for wind octet; *Aptote* for solo violin, sonata for solo viola; piano music, suite for organ; *O saisons, o châteaux* (Rimbaud, 1946), and other works for voice and chamber ensemble, including *And Suddenly it's Evening* for tenor and 11 instruments (1967), *Essence of our Happiness* for tenor and ensemble (1968), *Vision of Youth* (1970), *Dirge for the Proud World* (1971), *The Tears of Night* (1971), *Elegy for the Flowers* (1978), two *Cantatas* (1979), *Echoes* (1979), *Fleur du Silence* for tenor and ensemble (1980), *Mine Eyes, My Bread, My Spede* for tenor and string quartet (1980); songs.

That the singing of spiritual songs is a good thing and one pleasing to God is, I believe, not hidden from any Christian.

Martin Luther, Foreword to *Wittemberg Gesangbuch*, 1524

Luxon, Benjamin (b Redruth, 24 Mar 1937), English baritone. He studied at the GSM and in 1971 created Britten's Owen Wingrave on TV. Glyndebourne from 1972 as Ulisse, Almaviva, Janáček's Forester and Don Giovanni. At CG his roles have included the Jester and Death in the fp of *Taverner* (1972), Eugene Onegin, and Diomed in the revised version of *Troilus and Cressida*. Other roles include Posa, Papageno, Eisenstein and Wolfram. Often heard in Lieder. Sang Falstaff at LA, 1990, and for ENO 1992.

Luyton, Karel (b Antwerp, c 1556; d Prague, Aug 1620), Flemish organist and composer. He was in the service of the Emperor Maximilian II at Prague in 1576, when that monarch died, and was appointed

Luzzaschi *The title page to a set of madrigals by Luzzasco Luzzaschi (c.1545–1607), published by Simone Verovio in Rome, 1601. He was important as a monodist (in which only one melodic line is present), working during an era which was still dominated by polyphonists.*

to the Emperor Rudolf II in the same capacity. He was court composer in succession to Monte from 1603.

Works include Masses, motets, Lamentations, *Sacrae cantiones*; Italian madrigals; *Fuga suavissima* and *Ricercare* for organ.

Luzzaschi, Luzzasco (b Ferrara ? 1545; d Ferrara, 10 Sept 1607), Italian organist and composer. Pupil of Rore at Ferrara and by 1576 organist and *maestro di cappella* to Duke Alfonso II. Among his organ pupils was Frescobaldi.

Works include motets, *Sacrae cantiones*; madrigals; organ music, etc. His *Madrigali per cantare et sonare* (1601) are for three voices and have keyboard accompaniments.

Lvov, Alexis Feodorovich (b Reval, 5 Jun 1798; d Romanovo, near Kovno, 28 Dec 1870), Russian composer. Studied with his father, Feodor Lvov, an authority on church music and folksong, who succeeded Bortniansky as director of the Imperial Chapel in 1825. His son, who rose to high rank in the army and became adjutant to Nicholas I, succeeded him there 1837–61. He was a good violinist and founded a string quartet at St Petersburg. He became deaf and retired in 1867.

Works include operas *Bianca e Gualtiero* (1844), *Undine* (after Fouqué, 1847) and *The Bailiff* (1854), much church music; violin concerto; fantasy *The Duel* for violin and cello; Russian Imperial hymn 'God save the Tsar' (1833), quoted by Tchaikovsky in his *1812* overture.

Lyadov, Anatol, Anatol ◊Liadov.

Lydian Mode one of the old ecclesiastical modes with semitones between the fourth and fifth and seventh and eighth notes of the scale, represented by the scale beginning on F on the white notes of the piano keyboard.

Dame Moura Lympany – pianist

1   Ravel: *Daphnis et Chloé*
    I think this is such sensuous music – it 'sends' me each time
    I hear it.

2   Fauré: *Chanson d'Amore* (de los Angeles)
    It doesn't matter what Victoria de los Angeles sings – she
    always moves me.

3   Widor: Organ Symphony no. 5 – Toccata
    I love to hear the Toccata at the end of a marriage ceremony
    – it's so happy and optimistic.

4   Chopin: Preludes (Cortot)
    Cortot is so moving.

5   Beethoven: Concerto no. 5 in E flat (*Emperor*) (Schnabel)
    Whatever Schnabel plays he 'speaks'.

6   Moszkowski (Horowitz)
    Just stunning!

Lympany, Moura (b Saltash, 18 Aug 1916), English pianist. Studied at the RCM; debut 1928, Harrogate. Often heard in performances of Russian music and has toured widely with concertos by Delius, Rawsthorne and Ireland. Played Mendelssohn at the 1991 Prom concerts, London. CBE 1979. DBE 1992.

lyra (l) = ◊lira.
(2), a percussion instrument with tuned steel bars or plates which are played with hammers, similar to the Stahlspiel, used in English military bands and made for them in the shape of a lyre.

Each musician performs his part as freely as if he were the only player: the rhythmic values serve only as a guide.
Witold Lutosławski, instruction to musicians playing
Jeux Venitiens, 1961

---

lyra viol a small bass viol, tuned in various ways and played from a tablature. It was in use in England *c* 1650–1700; also variously called 'lero viol', 'leero viol' or 'viol lyra way'.

lyre the most important instrument of ancient Greece, of eastern origin. The number of strings varied. They were stretched on a framework with a hollow sound-box at the bottom and plucked, like those of a harp, with both hands, but only the left used the finger-tips, while the right played with a plectrum. The large instrument of the type was called kithara, a name from which the modern word 'guitar' derives.

lyre-guitar or Apollo lyre, a string instrument produced in France near the end of the 18th c., built to suggest the shape of the ancient Greek lyre, but with a fretted fingerboard. It had six strings.

Lyric Suite work for string quartet in six movements by Berg; composed 1925–26, fp Vienna 8 Jan 1927. Movements 2, 3 and 4 were arranged for string orchestra and performed Berlin, 31 Jan 1929, conductor Horenstein. Berg quotes from *Tristan* and Zemlinksy's *Lyric Symphony* and bases the work's note-row on the name of Hanna Robettin-Fuchs, with whom he had an affair. An alternative vocal finale, with text a translation by Stefan George of Baudelaire, was performed NY, 1 Nov 1979.

Lyrische Symphonie, *Lyric Symphony*, work by Zemlinsky in seven movements for soprano, baritone and orchestra (text by Tagore in a German translation by the composer); composed 1922–23, fp Prague, 4 Jun 1924, conductor Zemlinsky (two days later Zemlinsky conducted the fp of Schoenberg's *Erwartung*). The format of the Lyric Symphony is modelled on *Das Lied von der Erde*, although the content is Zemlinsky's own.

Lyubimov, Yuri (Betrovich) (b Yaroslavl, 30 Sept 1917), Russian-born Israeli stage director. Artistic director of the Taganka Theatre at Moscow, 1964–84. Has staged *The Queen of Spades* at the Paris Opéra, *Don Giovanni* in Budapest, *Khovanshchina* at La Scala, *Rigoletto* in Florence and *Tristan* at Bologna. Mussorgsky's *Salambo* in Paris and Naples, 1986. London, CG, 1986 and 1988, with *Jenůfa* and *Das Rheingold*, both with a strong sense of theatre and vivid stage pictures. Season 1991 with *The Love for Three Oranges* at Munich.

lyzarden or lyzardyne the old English name for the bass cornett or corno torto, the predecessor of the serpent, which came into use in the 17th c. Also sometimes called lizard or lysard.

M

M' for names with this prefix ◊Mac. . . .

m The mediant note in any key in Tonic Sol-fa notation, pronounced Me.

Ma, Yo Yo (b Paris, 7 Oct 1955), American cellist of Chinese parentage. He studied at Juilliard with Leonard Rose. Many appearances with leading orchestras and plays in trio with Emanuel Ax and Young Uck Kim. Played all Bach's solo suites in a single evening at Barbican Hall, London, 1995.

Maag, Peter (b St Gallen, 10 May 1919), Swiss conductor. Studied piano and theory with Marek and conducting with Franz von Hoesslins and Ansermet. After a number of lesser posts became first conductor of Düsseldorf Opera, 1952–54, and then music director of Bonn Opera, specializing in the performance of lesser-known works. US debut 1959, Cincinnati SO; NY Met. 1972 (*Don Giovanni*).

Maas, Joseph (b Dartford, 30 Jan 1847; d London, 16 Jan 1886), English tenor. He was a choirboy at Rochester Cathedral, and after working as a clerk in Chatham dockyard he went to Milan in 1869 to study singing under San Giovanni. He first appeared at a concert in London, taking Sims Reeves's place, in 1871, and on the stage in 1872. His roles included Rienzi, Radames, Des Grieux and Lohengrin.

Maazel, Lorin (b Neuilly, France, 6 Mar 1930), American conductor and violinist. Brought to USA as a child, and soon displayed great musical ability, conducting NY PO aged nine. At 15 formed his own string quartet and also appeared as violin soloist. He became a member of the Pittsburgh SO and its conductor in 1949. He has since appeared with all the great European orchestras, including the Vienna PO, and also at Salzburg, Bayreuth (*Lohengrin* and the *Ring*; 1960, 1968) and La Scala, Milan. He was music director of the Deutsche Oper Berlin and chief conductor of the Berlin Radio SO 1965–71 and from 1971 associate conductor of the New Philharmonia Orchestra; principal guest conductor from 1976. Music director Cleveland Orchestra 1972–82. Director, Vienna Opera 1982–84; CG 1978, *Luisa Miller*. Music director Pittsburgh SO from 1986.

Mabellini, Teodulo (b Pistoia, 2 Apr 1817; d Florence, 10 Mar 1897), Italian conductor and composer. Studied at the Istituto Reale Musicale at Florence and produced his first opera there at the age of 19. After further study with Mercadante at Novara, he settled at Florence, became conductor of the Società Filarmonica in 1843 and of the Teatro della Pergola in 1848. In 1860–87 he was professor at the Istituto.

Works include operas *Matilda a Toledo* (1836), *Rolla* (1840), *Ginevra degli Almieri* (1841), *Il conte di Lavagna*, *I Veneziani a Constantinopoli* (1844), *Maria di Francia* (1846), *Il venturiero*, *Baldassare* (1852), and *Fiammetta* (1857); oratorios *Eudossio e Paolo* (1845) and *L'ultimo giorno di Gerusalemme* (1857); cantatas *La caccia* (1839), *Il ritorno* (1846), *Elegiaca*, *Rafaelle Sanzio* and *Lo spirito di Dante* (performed 1865); much church music.

Macal, Zdenek (b Brno, 8 Jan 1936), Czech-born American conductor. Studied at Brno and conducted the Moravian PO 1963–67. Debut with the Czech PO 1966, at the Prague Spring Festival; tours throughout Europe. UK debut 1969, with the Bournemouth SO. Music director of the Cologne Radio SO 1970–74, US debut with the Chicago SO, 1972. Music director of the Milwaukee SO from 1986 and principal of the San Antonio SO 1988–92. Artistic director of the New Jersey SO from 1993. Conducted *Prince Igor* at Grant Park, Chicago, 1990.

Macbeth incidental music by (?) Locke for Davenant's version of Shakespeare's play, produced London, Dorset Gardens Theatre, summer 1674. There were later productions with music by D Purcell, Eccles, Leveridge, etc.

Opera by Bloch (libretto by E Fleg, after Shakespeare), produced Paris, Opéra-Comique, 30 Nov 1910.

Opera by Collingwood (libretto by composer, chosen from Shakespeare), produced London, SW, 12 Apr 1934.

Opera by Verdi (libretto by F M Piave and A Maffei, after Shakespeare), produced Florence, Teatro della Pergola, 14 Mar 1847; revised version (French libretto by C Nuitter and A Beaumont) produced Paris, Théâtre Lyrique, 21 Apr 1865. Lady Macbeth takes centre stage in Italian version.

Overture by Spohr, op. 75. Symphonic poem by R Strauss, op. 23, composed 1886–87, revised 1890, fp Weimar, 13 Sept 1890.

MacCunn, Hamish (b Greenock, 22 Mar 1868; d London, 2 Aug 1916), Scottish composer and conductor. Studied with Parry and Stanford at the RCM in London and had an overture *Cior Mhor* performed at the

---

THE OPERA

Macbeth

The first of Verdi's works to be based on Shakespeare, this four-act opera, based on Shakespeare's play, is set in 11th-century Scotland. It received its first performance in 1847 but was later revised by Verdi.

I. Macbeth (baritone) is greeted by a chorus of witches as the future Thane of Cawdor and King of Scotland; his companion Banquo (bass) is to be the father of kings. After Cawdor's execution for treachery, Macbeth duly gains his title. As King Duncan arrives at their castle, Lady Macbeth persuades her husband that the crown can be his. Led by the vision of a dagger, Macbeth murders the king.

II. Now King of Scotland, Macbeth orders the death of Banquo and his son Fleance, to negate the prophecy of the witches. Fleance escapes the assassins, and at his banquet, Macbeth is haunted by the image of Banquo.

III. Revisiting the witches, Macbeth is told he need fear no man born of woman; he is safe until Birnam Wood comes to Dunsinane.

IV. The guilt-ridden Lady Macbeth walks in her sleep. News of her suicide is brought to Macbeth at Dunsinane as English soldiers, under Duncan's son Malcolm (tenor), approach carrying tree branches. The caesarean-born Macduff (tenor) kills Macbeth.

THE OPERA

Crystal Palace at the age of 17. He married a daughter of the painter John Pettie in 1889 and soon afterwards conducted the Carl Rosa Opera Co. for some time, also German's light operas at the Savoy Theatre.

Works include operas *Jeanie Deans* (after Scott, 1894), *Diarmid* (1897) and *Breast of Light* (unfinished), light operas *The Golden Girl* (1905) and *Prue*; music for *The Masque of War and Peace* and *Pageant of Darkness and Light*; cantatas *The Moss Rose* (1885), *Lord Ullin's Daughter* (Thomas Campbell, 1888), *The Lay of the Last Minstrel* (after Scott), *Bonny Kilmeny* (James Hogg), *The Cameronian's Dream* (James Hyslop, 1890), *Queen Hynde of Caledon* (Hogg), *The Death of Parcy Reed*, *The Wreck of the Hesperus* (Longfellow, 1905), and others; Psalm 8 for chorus and organ; overture *The Land of the Mountain and the Flood*; ballads *The Ship o' the Fiend* and *The Dowie Dens o' Yarrow*, three descriptive pieces *Highland Memories* for orchestra; three Romantic pieces for cello and piano (1914).

Here tottered, tipsy e'er the day begun/That prince of bad composers H MacCunn.

Constant Lambert, quoted in Motion, *The Lamberts*, 1986

MacDowell, Edward (Alexander) (b New York, 18 Dec 1860; d New York, 23 Jan 1908), American composer and pianist. Learnt the piano at home at first, was taken to the Paris Conservatory in 1876, where he studied piano under Marmontel and theory under Savard; afterwards worked with Louis Ehlert at Wiesbaden, 1878, and entered the Frankfurt Conservatory in 1879, where Raff taught him composition. In 1881 he became piano professor at the Darmstadt Conservatory, and the next year played his first piano concerto at Zurich at Liszt's invitation. Returned to USA in 1884 and married Marian Nevins, who had been his pupil at Frankfurt, 21 Jul. After another period at Frankfurt and Wiesbaden, he went home for good and settled at Boston in 1888, making his first public appearance in USA there, 19 Nov. In 1896 he was appointed head of the new music department at Columbia University in NY and became honorary Mus. D. at Princeton University. Resigned in 1904, but continued to teach and compose. In 1904 he began to suffer from mental illness which afflicted him until his death.

Works include symphonic poems *Hamlet and Ophelia* (after Shakespeare, 1885), *Lancelot and Elaine*, *Lamia* (after Keats, 1889); two suites (no. 2 *Indian*) for orchestra; two piano concertos (1882, 1889); six orchestral works; 26 op. nos. of piano solos, including four sonatas, two *Modern Suites*, 24 studies, *Woodland Sketches*, *Sea Pieces*, *Fireside Tales*, *New England Idylls*, also two books of technical exercises; two sets of pieces for piano duet; 42 songs; 26 part-songs.

Mace, Thomas (b Cambridge *c* 1613; d ? Cambridge, *c* 1709), English writer on music. Clerk of Trinity College, Cambridge; pub. *Musick's Monument* in 1676. He invented a 'table organ' for use with a consort of viols and in 1672 a lute with 50 strings which he called the 'Dyphone', designed to serve him when he was becoming deaf. His compositions included an anthem 'I heard a voice'.

Macfarren, George (Alexander) (b London, 2 Mar 1813; d London, 31 Oct 1887), English composer and educationist. Pupil of C Lucas from 1827, entered the RAM in 1829, of which he became a professor in 1834 and principal in 1876. In 1845 he married the German contralto and translator Natalia Andrae (1828–1916). He edited works by Purcell and Handel. In the 1870s his eyesight began to fail and he eventually became blind, but he continued to work at composition and to teach. Knighted 1883.

Works include operas *The Devil's Opera* (1838), *The Adventures of Don Quixote* (after Cervantes, 1846), *King Charles II* (1849), *Robin Hood* (1860), *Jessy Lea* (1863), *She Stoops to Conquer* (after Goldsmith, 1864), *The Soldier's Legacy*, *Helvellyn*; masque *Freya's Gift*; oratorios *St John the Baptist* (1873), *The Resurrection* (1876),

Joseph (1877), *King David*; cantatas *Emblematical Tribute on the Queen's Marriage* (1840), *The Sleeper Awakened*, *Lenora*, *May Day*, *Christmas*, *The Lady of the Lake* (after Scott, 1876); much church music; symphony in F minor and seven others (1831–74), overtures, to Shakespeare's *Hamlet*, *Romeo and Juliet* and *The Merchant of Venice*, Schiller's *Don Carlos* (1842), overture *Chevy Chase* and other orchestral works; violin concerto; five string quartets and other chamber music; sonatas for various instruments.

MacGregor, Joanna (b London, 16 Jul 1959), English pianist and composer. Studied at Cambridge with Hugh Wood, at the RAM and with Van Cliburn in Texas. London debut 1985 and has since appeared with all the leading British orchestras. Gave the fp of Wood's Concerto at the 1991 London Proms and returned 1993 for Messiaen's *Turangalîla-Symphonie*. Premiere of Birtwistle's *Antiphonies*, under Boulez, 1993. Other modern repertory by Berio, Xenakis, Ligeti and Takemitsu. Founded the Contemporary Music platform in London, 1991–93. Composer of music for theatre, radio and TV.

Machaut (or *Machault*), Guillaume de (b at or near Rheims, ? 13 Apr 1300; d Rheims, 1377), French composer and poet. He became secretary, *c* 1323, to John of Luxemburg, King of Bohemia, and went with him to Poland, Lithuania and Italy. On the king's death in 1346 Machaut went into the service of his daughter, the Duchess of Normandy, and on her death in 1349 into that of Charles, King of Navarre; later into that of the Dauphin (afterwards Charles V) and his brother Jean, Duc de Berry. He became canon of Rheims Cathedral in 1333. An exponent of the *ars nova* in France. His rhythmic style and progressive use of polyphony has influenced many later composers (such as Birtwistle, *Machaut à ma manière*).

Works include Mass for four voices, *La Messe de Nostre Dame*; the earliest complete polyphonic mass setting by a single composer. Motets, vocal ballades and *rondeaux*, *chansons balladées*, *lais*, etc.

Machover, Tod (b New York, 24 Nov 1953), American composer and cellist. Studied with Dallapiccola in Florence and with Carter at Juilliard. Director of musical research at IRCAM, Paris, 1980–85; experimental media facility at MIT from 1986.

Works include concerto for amplified guitar and ensemble (1978), *Nature's Breach* (1985), and *Descres* (1985–89), computer-generated opera *Valis* (fp Paris, 2 Dec 1987) and *Epithalamion* (1990) for vocal soloists, 25 players and live and recorded electronics.

Macintyre, Margaret (b India, *c* 1865; d London, April 1943), English soprano. London, CG, 1888–97 as Donna Elvira, the Countess and Elisabeth. She created Rebecca in Sullivan's *Ivanhoe* (1891) and sang Sieglinde at La Scala.

Mackenzie, Alexander (Campbell) (b Edinburgh, 22 Aug 1847; d London, 28 Apr 1935), Scottish composer. Studied in Germany and at the RAM in London, of which, after 14 years as violinist and teacher at Edinburgh and some years at Florence, he became principal in 1888. Knighted 1895.

Works include operas *Colomba* (1883), *The Troubadour* (1886), *The Cricket on the Hearth* (after Dickens, 1914) and *The Eve of St John* (1924); incidental music for *Marmion* and *Ravenswood* (plays based on Scott), Shakespeare's *Coriolanus*, Byron's *Manfred* and Barrie's *The Little Minister*.

Oratorios *The Rose of Sharon* (1884), *Bethlehem* (1894), *The Temptation* (after Milton, 1914); cantatas *The Bride*, *Jason*, *The Story of Sayid*, *The Witch's Daughter*, *The Sun-God's Return*; *The Cottar's Saturday Night* (Burns) for chorus and orchestra (1888). Suite, Scottish Rhapsody, Canadian Rhapsody, ballad *La Belle Dame sans merci* (after Keats, 1883), *Tam o' Shanter* (after Burns), overtures *Cervantes* (1877), *Twelfth Night* (Shakespeare), *Britannia* and *Youth*, *Sport and Loyalty* for orchestra; concerto, Scottish Concerto (1897), suite and *Pibroch* suite for violin and orchestra; string quartet (1875); piano quartet, piano trio; violin and piano pieces; organ and piano music; songs; part-songs.

Mackerras, Charles (b Schenactady, NY, 17 Nov 1925), American-born Australian conductor and editor. Taken to Sydney aged two. Studied at Sydney Conservatory and then became first oboe of Sydney SO and began his career as a conductor. Went to England in

Mackerras *The conductor Charles Mackerras. Important as an operatic interpreter, Mackerras has played a leading role in bringing to light lesser known works. He has played a vital part in the performance of Janáček's music and has performed a series of his operas in Prague.*

1946 and from 1947 to 1948 studied with V Talich in Prague. On his return to England he was engaged by SW Opera and has since conducted throughout the world with considerable success; gave the first UK performance of an opera by Janáček (*Káta Kabanová*) at SW 1951, and helped to initiate 'authentic' styles of interpretation with a highly ornamented *Figaro* (1965). NY Met. debut 1972 (*Orfeo ed Euridice*), Glyndebourne 1990 (*Falstaff*). Principal conductor of SW Opera, 1970–80; Sydney SO from 1982. Best known for his performances of Janáček's operas, and has given works by Gluck, Sullivan, Handel, Mozart and J C Bach. Knighted 1979. Music director, WNO, from 1986–91.

Mackintosh, Robert (b Tullymet, Perthshire, 1745; d London, Feb 1807), Scottish violinist and composer. Settled at Edinburgh as violin teacher and concert organizer, but went to live in London in 1803. He wrote and arranged reels, strathspeys, minuets, gavottes, etc.

MacMillan, Ernest (b Mimico, Ontario, 18 Aug 1893; d Toronto, 6 May 1973), Canadian conductor, organist and composer. Organist from 1903; conductor, Toronto SO 1931–56. Conducted annual performances of *Messiah* and the *St Matthew Passion*, and many fps of Canadian works.

MacMillan, James (b Kilwinning, Ayrshire, 1959), Scottish composer. Studied at Edinburgh University and at Durham with John Casken. Composer-in-residence at Maxwell Davies's Magnus Festival, 1989. Teacher at the Royal Scottish Academy from 1990. In works such as *The Confessions of Isobel Gowdie* (London Proms, 1990), he has forsaken modern orthodoxies for a more popular approach. Other music includes chamber opera *Tourist Variations* (1991) and opera *Inès de Castro* (1993); music theatre *Busqueda* (1988) and *Visiatio Sepulchri* (1993); *Into the Ferment* for ensemble and orchestra (1988), *Tryst* for orchestra (1989), *The Berserking*, piano concerto (1990), *Sinfonietta* (1991), *Veni, Veni Emmanuel*, percussion concerto for Evelyn Glennie (1992), *Epiclesis*, trumpet concerto (1993), *VS* for orchestra (1993); *Tuireadh (Requiem)* for clarinet and string quartet (1991), *Scots Song* for soprano and chamber quintet (1991); Music for band, choral pieces and piano music.

MacNeil, Cornell (b Minneapolis, 24 Sept 1922), American baritone.

Became well known after appearing in Menotti's *The Consul* (1950) and joined NY City Opera Co. Sang also in Europe, appearing at La Scala, Milan, in 1959, as Carlo in *Ernani*. NY Met. debut 1959, as Rigoletto, and returned until 1987 as Amonasro, Iago, Scarpia, Nabucco and Luna; 450 performances. CG debut 1967, Macbeth.

Maconchy, Elizabeth (b Broxbourne, Herts., 19 Mar 1907; d Norwich, 11 Nov 1994), English composer of Irish descent. Studied composition under Vaughan Williams and piano under Arthur Alexander at the RCM in London; later in Prague. Several of her works were performed at the ISCM festivals abroad and were successful in Belgium and E Europe. She married William LeFanu, who translated poems by Anacreon for her. Their daughter is the composer Nicola ◊LeFanu. CBE 1977, DBE 1987.

Works include operas *The Sofa* (1957), *The Departure* (1961) and *The Three Strangers* (1967): performed as trilogy Middlesbrough 1977. Ballets *Great Agrippa* (from Hofmann's *Shock-headed Peter*) and *The Little Red Shoes* (after Andersen); two motets for double chorus (Donne); *The Leaden Echo and the Golden Echo* (Gerard Manley Hopkins) for chorus and chamber orchestra (1978).

Symphony and suites for orchestra *The Land* (on a poem by V Sackville-West) and *Puck*; piano concerto (1930), violin concerto (1963), concertino for clarinet; *Samson at the Gates of Gaza* for voice and orchestra; Sinfonietta (1976), *Little Symphony* (1981), *Music for Strings* (1983); 13 string quartets (1933–85), string trio, *Prelude Interlude* and *Fugue* for two violins; song-cycle *The Garland* (Anacreon).

Macque, Giovanni de (b Valenciennes, *c* 1551; d Naples, Sept 1614), Flemish composer. Pupil of Philippe de Monte. He went to Italy, living in Rome 1576–82, and at Naples from 1586, where he was choirmaster of the royal chapel from 1594. Wrote 14 vols of madrigals and *madrigaletti*. Other works include motets, and keyboard music.

Madama Butterfly opera by Puccini (libretto by Giacosa and L Illica, based on David Belasco's dramatic version of a story by John Luther Long), produced Milan, La Scala, 17 Feb 1904. US naval officer Pinkerton marries Madam Butterfly while visiting Japan. After fathering a son, he abandons her for an American wife. Honour requires Butterfly's suicide.

Madame Sans-Gêne opera by Giordano (libretto by R Simoni after the play by Sardou and Moreau), produced NY Met. 25 Jan 1915, conductor Toscanini. Laundress Caterina marries Sergeant Lefèbvre and becomes Duchess of Danzig after promotion following the French Revolution. Chastised for her common behaviour, Caterina is

---

THE OPERA

Madama Butterfly

A three-act opera by Giacomo Puccini, possibly based on a real happening. It was a fiasco when first performed (as a two-act opera) in early 1904, and the work was reorganized into three acts. It is set in Nagasaki, Japan, early in the 20th century.

I. The American naval officer, Pinkerton (tenor) ignores the warnings of the American consul Sharpless (baritone) and marries the underage geisha Cio-Cio-San, Madam Butterfly (soprano).

II. With her son 'Trouble', the deserted Butterfly awaits Pinkerton's return, one fine day. Sharpless cannot bring himself to tell her that Pinkerton has taken an American wife. Butterfly and her servant Suzuki (mezzo-soprano) see Pinkerton's ship enter harbour and prepare for his arrival by showering the house with petals.

III. Pinkerton cannot face Butterfly as he approaches her house with his wife Kate (mezzo-soprano). Butterfly tells Kate that Pinkerton may have their child if he comes for him himself. Dishonoured by her experience, Butterfly stabs herself with her father's sword. Pinkerton arrives to lament over her body.

summoned before Napoleon, a former washing customer, who forgives her.

Maddalena opera in one act by Prokofiev (libretto by composer after M Lieven); 1911–13, fp BBC, 25 Mar 1979: orchestrated by E Downes and conducted by him. Maddalena's husband Genaro and lover Stenio kill each other in a struggle.

Maddalena, James (b Lynne, MA, 1954), American baritone. Studied at the New England Conservatory and made debut with the Boston Pops Orchestra, 1974. Associated with director Peter Sellars from 1981, notably as Don Giovanni, in Handel's *Orlando* (1982), *Così fan tutte* (1984), Haydn's *Armida* and *Giulio Cesare* (1985). Sang in the fps of two operas by John Adams: title role in *Nixon in China* (Houston, 1987) and the Captain in *The Death of Klinghoffer* (Brussels). Further Sellars productions of *Figaro* (as the Count) and *Die Zauberflöte* (as Papageno, Glyndebourne 1990). Created Merlin in the premiere of Tippett's *New Year* at Houston, 1989.

Madeira, Jean (b Centralia, IL, 14 Nov 1918; d Providence, 10 Jul 1972), American mezzo. Studied at the Juilliard School and sang small roles at the NY Met. from 1948. Carmen in Vienna in 1955 and appeared at Bayreuth and CG as Erda. The following year she sang Clytemnestra at Salzburg and returned to the Met., as Carmen. In 1968 she created Circe in Dallapiccola's *Ulisse* at the Deutsche Oper, Berlin.

We no longer regard Machaut as as 'isolated naturalist' but as the consummation of a school which had existed for three hundred years.
Emil Naumann, *The History of Music*, 1886

Maderna, Bruno (b Venice, 21 Apr 1920; d Darmstadt, 13 Nov 1973), Italian composer and conductor. Studied violin and piano, and composition with Bustini at Academy of St Cecilia in Rome, and then took composition and conducting lessons with Malipiero and Scherchen. He then conducted throughout Europe, specializing in modern music. Co-founder with Berio of the electronic music studio of Italian Radio at Milan (1954). He visited the USA 1965, with Nono's *Intolleranza* at Boston and concerts in NY and Chicago. His music progressed from the example of Stravinsky, through advanced serialism (1950s), to the electronic (the composite theatre piece *Hyperion*, staged 1964).

Works include *Hyperion*, composite theatre work (performed Venice 1964); concertos for piano, two pianos, flute, oboe; *Introduzione e Passacaglia* for orchestra (1947); *Musica su due Dimensioni* for flute, percussion and electronic tape (1952–58); instrumental works include *Composizione in tre tempi, Improvisizione I, II, Serenata I, II* for 11 and 13 instruments (1946–57); *Studi per il Processo di Franz Kafka* for speaker, soprano and chamber orchestra (1949); electronic music including *Notturno, Syntaxis, Continuo, Dimensioni*.

Madetoja, Leevi (Antti) (b Uleaaborg, 17 Feb 1887; d Helsinki, 6 Oct 1947), Finnish conductor, critic and composer. Studied at the Conservatory of his native town and later with Järnefelt and Sibelius at Helsinki; afterwards with d'Indy in Paris and Fuchs in Vienna. In 1912–14 he conducted the Helsinki orchestra, afterwards that of Viborg; became music critic at Helsinki in 1916 and teacher at the Conservatory, and in 1926 at the university.

Works include operas *Pohjalaisia* (1924) and *Juha* (1935); ballets; three symphonies (1916, 1918, 1926), symphonic poems and overtures; *Stabat Mater*; eight cantatas; piano trio; violin and piano sonata; *Lyric Suite* for cello and piano; piano pieces; songs.

Madonna of Winter and Spring work for orchestra and electronics by Jonathan Harvey; fp London, 27 Aug 1986, conductor Peter Eötvös.

madrigal a composition for several voices cultivated in the 16th c. and continuing until the early 17th. Among its special features were a richly polyphonic style and its association with poetry of high value. The texts were secular, except where they were otherwise designated (e.g. *madrigali spirituali*), and the music showed a tendency to keep a definite melody in the top part; indeed madrigals were often sung by a single voice, the lower parts being played by instruments; and sometimes the whole performance was instrumental. The madrigal was cultivated particularly by Italian, Flemish and English composers. In the 14th c. the word was used for a poetic form and its music.

madrigal comedy, ◊Amfiparnaso, a sequence of madrigals in a quasi-dramatic form. The most famous but not the earliest example is Orazio Vecchi's *L'Amfiparnaso*, and similar works of his are *La selva di varie ricreazioni/The Forest of Multifarious Delights*, *Il convito musicale/The Musical Banquet* and *Le veglie di Siena/The Vigils of Siena*. A similar work, Simone Balsamino's *Novellette*, based on Tasso's *Aminta*, appeared the same year as *L'Amfiparnaso* (1594), but there were earlier ones, notably Striggio's *Il cicalamento delle donne al bucato/The Cackling of Women at the Wash*, and later Vecchi was imitated by Banchieri and others.

Maessins, Pieter (b Ghent, c 1505; d Vienna, probably Oct 1563), Flemish composer. Chief *Kapellmeister* in Vienna, 1546–60. Composed Latin motets.

maestoso Italian = lit. 'majestic' = stately, dignified.

maestro Italian = 'master', a title given by Italians to a distinguished musician, whether composer, performer or teacher.

maestro al cembalo Italian = lit. 'master at the harpsichord'; in the late 17th and 18th c. the harpsichord player who not only played continuo in the orchestra but also acted as assistant to the conductor and helped to coach singers.

maestro de capilla Spanish = ◊maestro di cappella.

maestro di cappella, Italian, director of music in a cathedral, a royal or princely chapel, or any similar musical establishment.

Magalhães, Filippe (b Azeitão, near Lisbon, c 1571; d Lisbon, 17 Dec 1652), Portuguese composer. Pupil of Mendes at Evora. *Maestro de capilla* of the Misericordia at Lisbon and from 1614 of the royal chapel there under the Spanish king, Philip III.

Works include Masses, canticles to the Blessed Virgin, chants.

Magaloff, Nikita (b St Petersburg, 8 Feb 1912; d Vevey, 26 Dec 1994), Russian-born Swiss pianist. Studied piano with I Philipp at the Paris Conservatory, and composition with Prokofiev. Began his career as accompanist to Szigeti, later turning to solo concert performances. In 1949 he succeed Lipatti as professor of piano at the Geneva Conservatory. Well known in Ravel, Prokofiev and Stravinsky.

Magelone Romances a cycle of 15 songs by Brahms, settings of poems from Ludwig Tieck's *Die schöne Magelone/Story of the Fair Magelone*, op. 33, composed 1861–66.

maggiore Italian = 'major'; the word is sometimes explicitly stated at a point in a composition where the major key returns after a prolonged section in minor, especially in variations, to prevent the performer from overlooking the change of key.

Magic Flute (Mozart). ◊Zauberflöte.

Magic Fountain, The opera by Delius (libretto by composer and J Bell); composed 1894–95, fp BBC broadcast, 20 Nov 1977, conductor Del Mar. Explorer Solano seeks a magic fountain with native Indian lover Watawa as a guide. Although she has sworn revenge on white men, she falls in love with him, but both die when they drink the fountain's poisonous water.

magic opera a species of opera not unlike the English pantomime, popular particularly on the Viennese stage at the end of the 18th and opening of the 19th c., where it was called *Zauberoper*. It consisted of dialogue and musical numbers, had a fairy-tale subject with incidents of low comedy, and contained numerous scenic effects. The outstanding example is Mozart's *Zauberflöte*; others are Müller's *Zauberzither*, Wranitzky's *Oberon*, Süssmayr's *Spiegel von Arkadien*, Schubert's *Zauberharfe*; the work nearest to it in character in the English language is Weber's *Oberon*.

Magini-Coletti, Antonio (b Iesi, near Ancona, 1855; d Rome, 7 Jul 1912), Italian baritone. He sang in Italy from 1880; at La Scala he took part in the fps of Puccini's *Edgar* (1889) and Mascagni's *Le Maschere* (1901). NY Met. from 1891 as Nevers and Amonasro, with the De Reszkes, Nordica and Lilli Lehmann. He appeared as guest at CG and Monte Carlo.

Magnard, (Lucien Denis Gabriel) Albéric (b Paris, 9 Jun 1865; d Baron, Oise, 3 Sept 1914), French composer. Studied at the Paris Conservatory and in 1888 became a private pupil of d'Indy. As the son of Francis Magnard, editor of *Le Figaro*, he was comfortably off and never held any official posts. He retired to Baron to devote himself to composition, pub. his works himself and never took any trouble to have them performed, though some were brought out by enthusiastic friends. During the very first days of World War I he shot two German soldiers from his window and was killed as a sniper. His house, including several of his MSS, was burnt down. His masterpieces, the operas *Guercoeur* and *Berenice*, owe something in their structure to the example of Wagner, but also reveal an individual visionary lyricism.

Works include operas *Yolande*, (1891), (destroyed), *Guercœur* (partly destroyed 1900; performed 1931) and *Bérénice*; four symphonies, (1890, 1893, 1896, 1913), *Suite dans le style ancien*, *Chant funèbre*, overture *Hymne à la Justice* and *Hymne à Vénus* for orchestra (1904); string quartet (1903), piano trio, piano and wind quintet; violin and piano sonata, cello and piano sonata; piano pieces; songs.

Magnetton German = 'magnet tone'; an electrophonic instrument invented by Stelzhammer of Vienna in 1933, producing its notes by means of electromagnets and capable of imitating various instruments.

Magnificat the song of the Blessed Virgin, regularly sung as a Vesper canticle in the Roman Catholic Church and as part of the evening service in the Anglican Church; also, more rarely, in a form better suited to concert performance e.g. Bach, Vaughan Williams, etc.

Mahillon, Victor (b Brussels, 10 Mar 1841; d Saint-Jean, Cap Ferrat, 17 Jun 1924), Belgian music scholar. Son of the instrument maker Charles Mahillon (1813–87). Studied at the Brussels Conservatory, where he became curator of the museum of musical instruments. He wrote on acoustics and instruments.

Mahler, Fritz (b Vienna, 16 Jul 1901; d Winston-Salem, NC, 17 Jun 1973), Austrian conductor and composer. Second cousin of Gustav Mahler, he studied composition with Berg and Schoenberg and musicology with Guido Adler (1920–24) at Vienna Universlty. After conducting at the Vienna Volksoper he was in charge of the Radio Orchestra in Copenhagen 1930–35, emigrating to the USA in 1936. He taught at the Juilliard Summer School from 1947 to 1953, when he became conductor of the Hartford SO.

Mahler, Gustav (b Kalište, Bohemia, 7 Jul 1860; d Vienna, 18 May 1911), Austrian composer and conductor. Son of a distillery manager.

Mahler *The composer and conductor Gustav Mahler (1860–1911) in 1907. One of the greatest conductors of his time, Mahler's commitments allowed him time for composition only during the summer months. An intimate knowledge of all the instruments resulted in his supremely orchestrated symphonies.*

He showed great talent as a pianist in his childhood, and in 1875 his family, who had moved to Jihlava (Iglau) soon after his birth, succeeded in entering him at the Vienna Conservatory. His piano professor, Julius Epstein, seeing his real gifts, advised him to study composition and conducting. After leaving the Conservatory in 1878 he wrote the first version of his cantata *Das klagende Lied*. His conducting career began in the summer of 1880 in Hall, Upper Austria. Posts followed at theatres in Ljubljana (1881) and Olmütz (1882). While in Kassel (1883–85) he wrote the *Lieder eines fahrenden Gesellen* and began the thematically related first symphony. In 1885 he was conductor at the Prague Opera, where he gave performances of the operas by Mozart and Wagner which were to form the basis of his repertory; his conducting was already noted for its precision of ensemble, pronounced rubato and individuality in choice of tempi. At Leipzig (1886–88) he was second conductor to Nikisch; his completion of Weber's sketches for *Die drei Pintos* was premiered in 1888. While at Budapest (1888–89) he led the unsuccessful fp of his first symphony.

From 1891–97 he was chief conductor of the Hamburg Opera, where he furthered his reputation for inspiring high standards of theatrical, as well as musical, performance; in 1892 he took the company to London, for the first Covent Garden performances of the *Ring*. In Dec 1895 he led the Berlin fp of his *Resurrection* symphony, achieving his first success as a composer; in the same year his brother committed suicide, one of several family tragedies. In 1897 Mahler's timely baptism into the Catholic church led to his appointment as director of the Vienna Court Opera. In the next ten years he established a magnificent company of singing actors and, most notably with the help of the stage designer Alfred Roller, mounted influential productions which sought to harmonize all aspects of stage and

Mahler
A biographical note

Although he achieved his lasting success as a symphonist, Mahler spent most of his life as a director of opera. His first major appointment was in Prague in 1885. It was there that he led his first productions of Wagner and established his uncompromising working methods. While at Leipzig (1886–88) he was subordinate to Nikisch, but completed the unfinished score of Weber's *Die drei Pintos*. As well as providing him with his first real income from a publisher, it also gave him the creative impetus to proceed with his first two symphonies. As director at Hamburg he took over *Eugene Onegin* from an 'indisposed' Tchaikovsky, and earned the Russian's admiration for his talent. In 1892 he also led the Hamburg company in its only excursion to London, conducting the house premiere of the *Ring* at Covent Garden. One of his most successful singers at Hamburg, and also his mistress, was Anna Mildenburg; she followed him to Vienna after he became director of the Court Opera there in 1897. For ten years Mahler had to combat the virulent anti-semitism of the Viennese, but he established a regime in which he controlled all aspects of stage presentation as well as musical direction. An important collaborator was the stage designer Alfred Roller; associated with Gustav Klimt in the Vienna Secession, he brought a painter's eye for colour and light to stagings of *Tristan, Don Giovanni* and the first two *Ring* operas.

musical experience. He succeeded Richter as conductor of the Vienna PO in 1898 but largely as a result of his autocratic methods he departed in 1901. Various intrigues at the Opera led to his resignation in 1907. During his years in Vienna Mahler wrote his symphonies nos. 4–8 near a villa on the Wörthersee in Carinthia. In the trilogy of purely instrumental symphonies (nos. 5, 6 and 7), nos. 5 and 7 suggest a progression from doubt and darkness to an optimistic conclusion; no. 6 is classically proportioned and ends with three enormous hammer blows, the last of which fells the creator. The massive choral 8th symphony ends with a Goethe setting in which human suffering is transformed in a universal acclamation. In 1902 he had married Alma Schindler; through her teacher, Alexander Zemlinsky, he met Schoenberg. Their friendship is reflected in the complex polyphony and extreme chromaticism of Mahler's later music. The *Kindertotenlieder* of 1904 is the first of several works which integrate vocal music of emotional intensity with sympathetic woodwind accompaniments. This style finds its culmination in *Das Lied von der Erde*, which was begun in the year which saw the death of his daughter Maria, aged 4. On 1 Jan 1908 he made his debut as principal conductor of the NY Met; due to artistic and personal differences his tenure there and with the NY Philharmonic Society was brief. In 1910 he led the triumphant Munich fp of his eighth symphony, and the following year returned to Europe for the last time, mortally ill with a bacterial infection of the blood. Mahler's music took many years to gain acceptance – four of the symphonies were not heard in Britain until after 1945 – but he is now established as a founder of 20th-c. music.

Works include ten symphonies; all except last two premiered by Mahler: no. 1 in D (1883–88, fp Budapest, 20 Nov 1889); no. 2 in C minor with soprano, mezzo and chorus in finale, *Resurrection* (text by composer and Klopstock); 1887–94, fp Berlin, 13 Dec 1895); no. 3 in D minor with alto, women and boys' voices (texts from Nietzsche and *Des Knaben Wunderhorn*; 1893–96, fp Krefeld, 9 Jun 1902); no. 4 in G with soprano in the finale (1899–1901, fp Munich, 25 Nov 1901); no. 5 in C♭ minor (1901–02, fp Cologne, 18 Oct 1904); no. 6 in A minor (1903–06, fp Essen, 27 Apr 1906); no. 7 in E minor (1904–06, fp Prague, 19 Sept 1908); no. 8 in E♭ '*Symphony of a Thousand*', with soloists, adult and boys' choruses (text 9th-c. hymn *Veni creator spiritus* in first movement and from Goethe's *Faust* part II in second;

1906, fp Munich, 12 Sept 1910); no. 9 in D (1908–09, fp Vienna, 26 Jun 1912, conductor Walter); no. 10 in F♭ minor was incomplete at Mahler's death: a performing version by Deryck Cooke was given in London on 13 Aug 1964.

Cantata *Das klagende Lied* (1878–80); song-cycles *Lieder eines fahrenden Gesellen* (1884), *Kindertotenlieder* (1901–04), three books of early songs, five songs to words by Rückert, many other songs, including settings from *Des Knaben Wunderhorn, Das Lied von der Erde*, symphony for mezzo and tenor solo and orchestra (1907–09). (separate entries for vocal works.)

Maichelbeck, Franz Anton (b Reichenau near Constance, 6 Jul 1702; d Freiburg i/B, 14 Jun 1750), German organist and composer. Studied music in Rome, 1725–27, and on his return to Freiburg i/B became organist at the Minster (1728) and professor of Italian at the university (1730). Wrote chiefly keyboard music.

Maid of Orleans, The, *Orleanskaya Dieva*, opera by Tchaikovsky (libretto by composer, based on V A Zhukovsky's translation of Schiller's drama), produced St Petersburg, 25 Feb 1881. Joan of Arc leads the French to miraculous victories over the English, but her father Thibault denounces her as a sorceress. She runs away and is captured by the English, who burn her at the stake.

Maikl, Georg (b Zell, 4 Apr 1872; d Vienna, 1951), Austrian tenor. Debut Mannheim 1899, as Tamino. He was a leading member of the Vienna Opera 1904–44, in operas by Mozart and Wagner, and in the 1916 fp of the revised version of *Ariadne auf Naxos*. Salzburg 1906 and 1910, as Ottavio; 1937 as Aegisthus and in *Die Meistersinger*.

Mainardi, Enrico (b Milan, 19 May 1897; d Munich, 10 Apr 1976), Italian cellist. Studied cello and composition) at Milan Conservatory until 1920 and then cello with H Becker in Berlin. In 1933 he was appointed professor of cello at the Academy of St Cecilia in Rome. Recorded *Don Quixote* under Strauss.

Works include four cello concertos, suite for cello and piano and some chamber music.

Maine, Basil (b Norwich, 4 Mar 1894; d Sheringham, Norfolk, 13 Oct 1972), English critic, novelist and biographer. Studied at Cambridge, and after school-mastering and acting became music critic to the *Daily Telegraph* in London, 1921, and the *Morning Post*, 1926. In 1939 he took orders in the Church of England. His music books include a large biography of Elgar (1933).

We probably derive all our basic rhymes and themes from Nature, which offers them to us, pregnant with meaning in every animal noise.

Gustav Mahler, quoted in Bauer-Lechner, *Recollections of Gustav Mahler*, 1980

Mainzer Umzug work by Hindemith for soloists, chorus and orchestra; composed 1962, fp Mainz, 23 Jun 1962, conductor Hindemith.

Maisky, Mischa (b Riga, 10 Jan 1948), Latvian cellist. Studied at the Moscow Conservatory with Rostropovitch and made his debut with the Leningrad PO, 1965. Emigrated to Israel 1973 and studied further with Piatigorsky in California. US debut 1973, with the Pittsburgh SO, London 1976. Recitalist with Radu Lupu and Boris Belkin; Beethoven, Stravinsky and Shostakovich with Martha Argerich at the 1994 Edinburgh Festival. Played Hindemith's Concerto at the Barbican Hall, London, 1995.

Maison, René (b Frameries, 24 Nov 1895; d Mont d'Or, 11 Jul 1962), Belgian tenor. Debut Geneva 1920, as Rodolfo. He sang in Paris from 1925 and made his US debut at Chicago, in 1928; NY Met. 1935–43, debut as Walther. At Buenos Aires, 1934–37, he was heard in the Italian and French repertory. He taught in NY and Boston after his retirement; Roman Vinay was among his pupils.

maître de chapelle French = ◊maestro di cappella.

maîtrise French = 'mastership'; the former French name for the whole establishment of the choir at cathedrals and collegiate churches, including not only all that appertained to their performance in church, but also to their accommodation and maintenance. The maîtrises were actually schools of music.

Majo, Gian Grancesco di (b Naples, 24 Mar 1732; d Naples, 17 Nov 1770), Italian composer. Pupil of his father, Giuseppe di Majo (1697–1771), *maestro di cappella* at the court at Naples, and later of Padre Martini in Bologna. Appointed Second organist at court in 1750, but lived chiefly as an opera composer.

Works include 20 operas, e.g. *Ricimero, rè dei Goti* (1758), *Astrea Placata* (1760), *Cajo Fabricio*, *Ifigenia in Tauride* (1764), *Eumene* (unfinished at his death, completed by Errichelli and Insanguine), etc.; eight oratorios including *La passione di Gesù Cristo* (1780); five Masses and other church music; cantatas.

major one of the two predominant scales (the other being minor) of the tonal system, characterized by the presence of a major third between the 1st and 3rd degrees. ◊scale. A major key is one based on the major scale. ◊major interval.

major interval seconds, thirds, sixths and sevenths can be major intervals. If the upper note of the major interval is flattened (or the lower note is sharpened) it becomes a minor interval. If the upper note of a major interval is sharpened (or the lower note is flattened) it

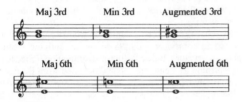

Major, minor, and augmented thirds and sixths.

becomes an augmented interval. If the upper note of a minor seventh is flattened (or the lower note is sharpened) it becomes a diminished seventh.

Makropoulos Case, The, *Věc Makropoulos*, opera by Janáček (libretto based on Karel Čapek's play), produced Brno, 18 Dec 1926. Elena searches with the help and hindrance of lawyers Kolenatý and Prus for the magic document that has prolonged her life for 300 years. She longs for death and young Kristina burns the paper after it is found.

Maksymiuk, Jerzy (b Grodno, 9 Apr 1936), Polish conductor and composer. He studied at the Warsaw Conservatory and after working with the Polish Radio orchestra founded the Polish Chamber Orchestra, 1972. Principal conductor BBC Scottish Orchestra 1983–93. Salzburg Festival debut 1985, with the Polish Chamber Orchestra. Conducted the fps of Macmillan's *The Confession of Isobel Gowdie* (1990) and Robin Holloway's violin concerto (1992). A ballet, *Capriccio*, and a string trio are among his compositions.

Malagueña a Spanish (Andalusian) song whose place of origin is Málaga. It also appears often as an instrumental piece. It begins and ends on the dominant of its key. The second movement of Ravel's *Rapsodie espagnole* (1907) is titled Malagueña.

Malanotte, Adelaide (b Verona, 1785; d Salo, 31 Dec 1832), Italian contralto. Debut Verona 1806. In 1813, at the Teatro Fenice, Venice,

Maisky *The cellist Mischa Maisky. He has made many award-winning recordings, including the six solo cello Suites by Bach. He is known for his consistently intense playing and his eccentric dress sense: during his recitals he often changes into different-coloured shirts for each piece.*

she created Rossini's Tancredi. Said by Hérold to share Susanna's secret.

Malbecque, Guillermus (b *c* 1400; d Soignies, 29 Aug 1465), French composer, member of the papal chapel, 1431–38, and a canon of Soignies from 1440 until his death. Composed three-part *chansons*.

Malcolm, George (b London, 28 Feb 1917), English pianist, harpsichordist and conductor. He studied at the RCM; 1947–59 master of music Westminster Cathedral. Has conducted most major orchestras in Britain. Artistic director Philomusica, London, 1962–66, and has been heard as a pianist in chamber ensembles. CBE 1965.

Malcuzyński, Witold (b Warsaw, 10 Aug 1914; d Palma, 17 Jul 1977), Polish pianist. Studied at Warsaw Conservatory with Turczyski, and then with Paderewski in Switzerland. In 1939 he married the pianist Colette Gaveau and moved to Paris. He played in all parts of the world and was especially well known as an interpreter of Chopin and Liszt.

Maldere, Pierre van (b Brussels, 16 Oct 1729; d Brussels, 1 Nov 1768), Belgian violinist and composer. Travelled as a virtuoso, 1752–58, visiting Dublin, Paris and Vienna, and on his return to Brussels

---

Mischa Maisky – cellist

1   Bach: Cello Suites (Pablo Casals)
    If music was my religion, then my Bible would be Bach's solo cello suites. It's now 35 years since I started playing this music. Casals introduced them into the repertoire, and his recording was very influential on me.

2   Elgar: Cello Concerto
    This piece is very important to me. I first heard it in

Moscow in 1967 played by Jacqueline du Pré. It was one of the most unforgettable concerts of my life. I think du Pré's playing of the piece is the best cello playing I have ever heard.

3   Strauss: *Don Quixote*
    Rostropovich told me that every cellist believes this piece is his. I feel the same way. I have always adored it.

Jerzy Maksymiuk – conductor

1   James MacMillan: *The Confession of Isobel Gowdie*
I like it when a composer can write a long line with only one, strongly developed, idea. This is very unusual in contemporary music. Usually it is one idea, stop! Then another, stop! But building on one idea for three minutes is very complicated. MacMillan is good at it. He is augmenting, unleashing, allowing you to breathe for a long time in the presence of great beauty.

2   Stravinsky: *Petrushka*
Stravinsky is a very personal composer and a perfectionist. There is an intellectual pleasure in the score alone, as well as a special pleasure in performance. When everything is done right, it sounds very beautiful. I love *Petrushka*. It is like a suite of dances, which explodes in the finale. Sometimes it is so complicated I feel it should have two conductors. Where other composers used their imagination to write melody, Stravinsky wrote rhythm. It is a style that cannot be imitated.

3   Zbigniew Penherski: *Signals*
I worked on this composition by one of my fellow countrymen a couple of years ago. The piece is only about five minutes long, and builds throughout up to a climax. Every composition must come to a climax. Penherski's very careful construction builds this climax from a three-note shape. The music becomes thicker and thicker, like water flowing.

---

entered the service of the Duke of Lorraine. Director of the Brussels Opera, 1763–66.
   Works include operas *Le Déguisement pastoral* (1756), *Les Précautions inutiles* (1760), *La Bagarre* (1763), etc.; symphonies; concertos; sonatas.

male alto an artificial extension of the highest male-voice register, produced by falsetto, used in Anglican church choirs and in male-voice quartets and choral societies, particularly in glees and part-songs.

Maler, Wilhelm (b Heidelberg, 21 Jun 1902; d Hamburg, 29 Apr 1976), German composer. Studied with various masters, including Jarnach, and was influenced by Hindemith. He was appointed professor of composition at Cologne Conservatory in 1925 and later also taught at Bonn University.
   Works include oratorio *Der ewige Strom* (1934) and cantata on poems by Stefan George.

Malfitano, Catherine (b New York, 18 Apr 1948), American soprano. She studied in NY and made her debut in 1972. After appearances at Sante Fe, Houston and NY she sang with success in Europe: 1984 Mimi and Manon in Florence and Paris, 1985 Fiorilla in Geneva and Lulu in a new production of Berg's opera by Jean-Pierre Ponnelle at Munich. Also sings Juliette and Poppea. Sang in the fp of Bolcolm's *McTeague* (1992).

Malgoire, Jean-Claude (b Avignon, 25 Nov 1940), French conductor, oboist and musicologist. He studied at the Paris Conservatory and in 1966 founded the ensemble La Grande Écurie et La Chambre du Roy, for performances of Baroque music with an empirical approach towards instrumentation and performing practice: best known for performances and recordings of operas by M-A Charpentier, Lully and Rameau. Many tours in Europe and USA with this ensemble and Florilegium Musicum de Paris (medieval and Renaissance music). In 1986 he conducted a revival of Campra's *Tancrède*, at Aix-en-Provence. Season 1992 with Lully's *Alceste* in Paris and *Montezuma*, his Vivaldi pastiche, at Monte Carlo.

Malheurs d'Orphée, Les, *The Miseries of Orpheus*, opera by Milhaud (libretto by A Lunel), produced Brussels, Théâtre de La Monnaie, 7 May 1926. Peasant Orphée cannot cure the illness of gypsy Euridice and is killed by her sisters.

Malibran (born *Garcia*), Maria (Felicità) (b Paris, 24 Mar 1808; d Manchester, 23 Sept 1836), Spanish soprano. Studied under her father, Manuel Garcia. After much travelling in Italy, etc., and appearing in a child's part in Paer's *Agnese* at Naples in 1814, she made her first concert appearance in Paris in 1824, and on the stage in London in 1825 as Rosina, and Felicia in Meyerbeer's *Il Crociato in Egitto*. NY Park Theatre, 1825–26 in Rossini's *Tancredi*, *Otello* and *Il Turco in Italia*; Paris 1828 in *Semiramide*. She created the title roles in Balfe's *The Maid of Artois* and Donizetti's *Maria Stuarda*. In 1826 she married Malibran, an elderly Frenchman, but left him when he went bankrupt in 1827, and in 1830 she formed an attachment with Bériot, whom she married shortly before her sudden death, after a riding accident.

Malipiero, (Gian) Francesco (b Venice, 18 Mar 1882; d Treviso, 1 Aug 1973), Italian composer. In 1898 he began studying violin at the Vienna Conservatory, but on failing an examination turned to composition, returning to Venice in 1899. Graduated from Bologna Liceo Musicale in 1904. In 1913 he went to Paris, where he attended the fp of *The Rite of Spring*; Debussy was to be a more lasting influence, however. From 1921 to 1923 he was professor of composition at Parma University and from 1939 to 1953 was director of the Liceo Musicale Benedetto Marcello in Venice. He was the editor of the complete edition of Monteverdi's works.
   Works include operatic trilogy *L'Orfeide* (*La morte delle maschere*, *Sette canzoni*, *Orfeo* (first complete performance 1925), operas *Tre Commedie goldoniane* (Goldoni's plays *La bottega da caffè*, *Sior Todero Brontolon*, *Le baruffe chiozzotte* (1926), *Filomela e l'infatuato* (1928), *Merlino mastro d'organi*, *Il mistero di Venezia* (*Le aquile Aquileia*, *Il finto Arlecchino*, *I corvi di San Marco*, 1932), *Torneo notturno* (1931), *La favola del figlio cambiato* (libretto by Pirandello, 1934), *Giulio Cesare* and *Antonio e Cleopatra* (both after Shakespeare, 1936, 1938), *Ecuba*, *I capricci di Callot* (after E T A Hoffmann, 1941), *La vita è sogno* (1943), *L'allegra brigata* (1950), *Il figliuol prodigo* (1957), *Donna Urraca* (1954), *Il capitan spavento* (1963), *Don Giovanni* (1963), *Don Tartufo* (1970), *Uno dei dieci* (1971); ballets *La mascherata della principesse prigioniere* (1924), *Pantea*.

   CHORAL AND ORCHESTRAL: *Virgilli Aeneis* for solo voices, chorus and orchestra (1944; produced 1958), *Li sette peccati mortali* (seven sonnets by Fazio degli Uberti) for chorus and orchestra (1946); for orchestra: *Sinfonia del mare* (1906), *Sinfonia del silenzio e della morte* (1908), *Ditirambo tragico*, *Impressioni dal vero* (three sets, 1913), *Per una favola cavalleresca*, *Pause del silenzio* (1917–26), *Concerti*, *Inni*, *Invenzioni*, *Sinfonia in quattro tempi come le quattro stagioni* (1933), *Sinfonia elegiaca*, *Sinfonie delle campane* and eight others (1946–69); six piano concertos (1934–58), *Variazioni senza tema* for piano and orchestra, two violin concertos, cello concerto.

   CHAMBER AND SOLO VOCAL: *Il commiato* (Leopardi) for baritone and orchestra; oratorios *San Francesco d'Assisi*, *La cena*, *La passione* (1935), *Missa pro mortuis* (1938); eight string quartets (1920–64); including *Rispetti e strambotti*, *Stornelli e ballate* and *Canzoni alla madrigalesca*; *Sonata a tre* for violin, cello and piano, *Sonata a cinque* for flute, harp, violin viola and cello, *Ricercari* and *Ritrovari* for 11 instruments, *Le sette allegrezze d'amore* for voice and 14 instruments (1945) and other chamber music; many piano works: *Preludi autunnali*, *Poemi asolani*, *Barlumi*, *Maschere che passano*, etc.; songs *Tree poesi di Angelo Poliziano*, *Quattro sonetti del Burchiello*, *Due sonetti del Berni*, *Le stagioni italiche*.

Malipiero, Riccardo (b Milan, 24 Jul 1914), Italian composer, nephew of Francesco ◊Malipiero. Studied at Milan and Turin and with his uncle in Venice. Early compositions are neo-classical in spirit; he turned to serialism in 1945.

Works include operas *Minnie la Candida* (1942), *La Donna è mobile* (1957) and *Battano alla Porta* (1962); three piano concertos (1937–61), two cello concertos (1938, 1957); three symphonies (1949–59), *Cadencias* for orchestra (1964), *Mirages* for orchestra (1966); *Ombre* for orchestra (1986); Requiem (1975); three string quartets (1941, 1954, 1960), piano quintet (1957), *Cassazione* for string sextet (1967); piano music.

Maliponte, Adriana (b Brescia, 26 Dec 1938), Italian soprano. She studied at Mulhouse; debut Milan 1958, as Mimi. Paris, Opéra, 1962, as Micaela. US debut Philadelphia 1963; NY Met. from 1971 as Pamina, Juliette, Luisa Miller and Eurydice. La Scala 1970, Manon; CG 1976, Nedda. In 1985 she sang Alice Ford at the Met. Sang Luisa Miller at Trieste, 1990.

Maliszewski, Witold (b Mohylev, Podolia, 20 Jul 1873; d Warsaw, 18 Jul 1939), Polish violinist, pianist and composer. Pupil of Rimsky-Korsakov at St Petersburg Conservatory and 1908–21 was director of the Odessa school of music. He then left for Warsaw, where he taught at the Conservatory and the Chopin School of Music. In 1933 he founded the Chopin Institute in Warsaw.

Malko, Nikolai (Andreievich) (b Brailov, 4 May 1883; d Roseville, Sydney, 23 Jun 1961), Russian conductor. He studied at St Petersburg with Rimsky-Korsakov, Glazunov and N Tcherepnin, and at Karlsruhe with Mottl. After teaching in Moscow and Leningrad he became conductor of the Leningrad PO in 1926 and gave the fps of Shostakovich's first and second symphonies, but left Russia in 1928 for Denmark and USA. He was conductor of the Yorkshire SO 1954–56 and was appointed conductor of the Sydney SO in 1957.

Mallarmé, Stéphane (1842–1898), French poet. ◊Boulez (*Pli selon pli*); ◊Debussy (three poems); ◊Herodiade (Hindemith); ◊Improvisations sur Stéphane Mallarmé (Boulez); ◊Prélude à l'Après-midi d'un faune (Debussy); ◊Ravel (three poems).

Mallinger (born *Lichtenegger*), Mathilde (b Zagreb, 17 Feb 1847; d Berlin, 19 Apr 1920), German-Croatian soprano. Studied first with her father, then at the Prague Conservatory and in Vienna; made her first stage appearance at Munich in 1866 as Norma and created the part of Eva in Wagner's *Meistersinger* in 1868. Berlin 1869–82, debut as Elsa. Other roles included Leonore, Agathe, Pamina, Donna Anna and Sieglinde. Lotte Lehmann was among her pupils.

Malten (actually *Müller*), Therese (b Insterburg, 21 Jun 1855; d Neu-Zschieren, near Dresden, 2 Jan 1930), German soprano. Studied with Gustav Engel in Berlin and made her debut at Dresden in 1873, as Pamina, remaining attached to the Court Opera there. She sang Kundry at Bayreuth in 1882. Other roles included Leonore (London, 1882), Isolde, Brünnhilde, Eva and Armide. Sang in *Ring* cycles presented by Angelo Neumann in Russia in 1889.

Malvezzi, Cristoforo (b Lucca, 28 Jun 1547; d Florence, 22 Jan 1599), Italian composer. Wrote music for the Florentine stage performances of 1589 and 1591.

Mälzel, Johann Nepomuk (b Regensburg, 15 Aug 1772; d at sea, 21 Jul 1838), German inventor. Settled in Vienna in 1792 and invented various mechanical instruments, including, in 1815, the metronome. Later he lived in Paris and from 1826 in USA. Beethoven's *Battle of Victoria* was originally written for Mälzel's 'Panharmonicon' and the second movement of the eighth symphony imitates the ticking of the metronome.

Mamelles de Tirésias, Les, *The Breasts of Tiresias*, opéra bouffe in two acts by Poulenc (libretto by G Apollinaire), produced Paris, Opéra-Comique, 3 Jun 1947. Thérèse. tired of her monotonous life as a wife, becomes a man, Tirésias. Meanwhile her husband takes on the duty of producing children — over 40,000 in one day.

Ma Mère l'Oye, *Mother Goose*, suite by Ravel, written for piano duet in 1908 and pub. 1910, scored for orchestra and produced as a ballet, Paris, Opéra, 11 Mar 1915, scenario by Louis Laloy, choreography by L Staats. The movements are based on tales by Perrault: 1. *Pavan of the Sleeping Beauty*; 2. *Hop-o'-my-Thumb*; 3. *Little Ugly, Empress of the Pagodas*; 4. *Colloquy between the Beauty and the Beast*; 5. *The Fairy Garden*.

Manara, Francesco, Italian 16th-c. composer. In 1555 he was in the service of Alfonso II of Ferrara. Wrote madrigals and some church music.

Manchicourt, Pierre de (b Béthune, *c* 1510; d Madrid, 5 Oct 1564), Flemish composer. He worked at Tournai, 1539–45, Arras, *c* 1555 and Antwerp from 1557. In 1561 he took charge of the Flemish choir of Philip II in Madrid.

Works include Masses, motets; *chansons*.

Mancinelli, Luigi (b Orvieto, 5 Feb 1848; d Rome, 2 Feb 1921), Italian conductor and composer. Studied at Florence, including the cello, and joined the orchestra at the Teatro della Pergola there. In 1874 he went to the Teatro Apollo in Rome, where he deputized for a conductor so successfully that he made operatic conducting his future career. In 1876 he appeared as composer of incidental music and in 1884 produced his first opera. From 1881 to 1886 he was director of the Liceo Musicale at Bologna, as well as *maestro di cappella* at San Petronio and conductor of the Teatro Comunale there, and he organized orchestral and chamber music. Later he appeared as a conductor in London, Madrid and NY. From 1906 to 1912 he was principal conductor at the Teatro Colón in Buenos Aires.

Works include operas *Isora di Provenza* (1884), *Ero e Leandro* (1896), *Paolo e Francesca* (after Dante, 1907), *Tizianello, Sogno di una notte d'estate* (after Shakespeare, 1915–17); incidental music to Pietro Cossa's *Messalina* and *Cleopatra*; oratorio *Isaias* (1887), cantata *St Agnes* (1905); two Masses.

Mancini, Francesco (b Naples, 16 Jan 1672; d Naples, 22 Sept 1737), Italian composer. Pupil of Provenzale and Ursino at the Conservatorio della Pietà dei Turchini in Naples, entered the service of the court and rose to become *maestro di cappella* (1707) and from 1725 till his death. Director of the Conservatorio S Maria di Loreto from 1720.

Works include operas *L'Idaspe fedele* (original title *Gli Amanti generosi*, 1705), *Trajano* (1723) and 19 others; six oratorios; cantatas; violin sonatas; keyboard music.

Mancinus (real name *Mencken*), Thomas (b Schwerin, 1550; d Schwerin, *c* 1612), German composer. Cantor at the cathedral school of Schwerin, 1572–76, tenor at court in Berlin, 1579–81, and then in the service of the Duke of Brunswick at Wolfenbüttel.

Works include Passions according to St Matthew and St John, Latin and German motets and madrigals, secular German songs for several voices.

The pleasant whining of a mandoline.
                              T S Eliot, *The Waste Land*, 1922

---

mandolin(e) a string instrument related to the lute, but with a more rounded back and metal strings, which are played with a plectrum. The fingerboard is fretted to facilitate fingering and intonation.

mandore a small string instrument of the lute family.

Mandragola, La, *The Mandrake*, opera by Castelnuovo-Tedesco (libretto based on Machiavelli's comedy), produced Venice, Teatro La Fenice, 4 May 1926. Callimaco sleeps with the beautiful Lucrezia after Ligurio arranges a supposed magic potion to cure her infertility.

Mandyczewski, Eusebius (b Czernowitz [Cernauti], 18 Aug 1857; d Vienna, 13 Jul 1929), Romanian-born musicologist. Studied at the Vienna Conservatory. In 1887 he became keeper of the archives of the Vienna Philharmonic Society and in 1897 professor at the Conservatory. Co-editor of the complete Schubert and Brahms editions and of that of Haydn's works (later abandoned).

Manelli, Francesco (b Tivoli, c 1595; d Parma, Jul 1667), Italian bass and composer. Singer at Tivoli Cathedral, 1605–24, and *maestro di cappella* there, 1627–29. He then went to Rome, married a singer, and about 1636 settled at Venice, where his wife edited his collected non-operatic works. From about 1645 he was in the service of the Duke of Parma, Ranuccio II. The S Cassiano theatre (the first public theatre in Venice) opened with his first opera.

Works include operas *L'Andromeda* (1637), *La maga fulminata* (1638), *L'Alcate* (1642), *La Licaste* (1664) and others; cantatas, *canzonets, chaconnes.*

Manfred incidental music for Byron's drama by Schumann, op. 115, composed 1849; first concert performance of the overture, Leipzig, Gewandhaus, Mar 1852. The whole produced with Byron's play, Weimar, 13 Jun 1852.

Symphony by Tchaikovsky, op. 58, based on the same play 1885, fp Moscow 6 Apr 1886.

Manfredini, Francesco Onofrio (b Pistoia, bap. 22 Jun 1684; d Pistoia, 6 Oct 1762), Italian composer. He studied with Torelli and Perti in Bologna and held appointments in Ferrara and Monaco before returning to Pistoia by 1727, as *maestro di cappella* at St Philip's Cathedral. His 43 pub. instrumental works including a set of 12 'Concertini', chamber sonatas (1704), 12 *Sinfonie da chiesa* (1709) and six sonatas pub. in London 1764. Four oratorios date from his return to Pistoia.

Manfredini, Vincenzo (b Pistoia, 22 Oct 1737; d St Petersburg, 16 Aug 1799), Italian theorist and composer, son of Francesco ◊Manfredini. After study with his father he went to Moscow in 1758. He became *maestro* at the court of St Petersburg's Italian opera co. in 1762; until he was superseded by Galuppi he wrote operas for Catherine II. After his return to Italy in 1769 he became a teacher and writer on music, notably *Regole armoniche, o sieno Precetti ragionati* (1775). His compositions include settings of Metastasio's *Semiramide* (1760), *Olimpiade* (1762) and *Artaserse* (1772); six symphonies and six string quartets.

Mangold, Karl Ludwig Amand (b Darmstadt, 8 Oct 1813; d Oberstdorf, Allgäu, 4 Aug 1889), German conductor and composer. Studied with his father and brother, and later at the Paris Conservatory. Court music director at Darmstadt from 1848.

Works include opera *Tanhauser* (1846) and others; cantatas; orchestral pieces; male voice choruses.

Mann, Robert (b Portland, OR, 19 Jul 1920), American violinist, composer and conductor. Studied at Juilliard and made debut recital in New York, 1941. Joined faculty of Juilliard after war service and founded the Juilliard Quartet 1948; many concerts worldwide, with fps of works by Schumann, Babbitt, Piston, Sessions, Copland and Foss. Often heard in Schoenberg's quartets and has repertory of 600 works. Resident artist, with members of Juilliard Quartet, at Library of Congress from 1962; Michigan State University from 1977.

Mann, William (Somervell) (b Madras, 14 Feb 1924; d Bath, 5 Sept 1989), English critic and writer on music, educated at Winchester and Cambridge. He studied composition with Seiber and piano with Ilona Kabós, and in 1948 joined the music staff of *The Times*; retired as chief music critic 1980. He pub. a short introduction to Bach (1950), contributed to the Britten symposium (1952) and to the fifth and sixth editions of Grove's *Dictionary* (1954, 1980). He also wrote books on R Strauss's and Mozart's operas and a translation of Wagner's *Ring*.

Männergesangverein German = lit. 'men's singing-association'; a male-voice choral society.

Manners, Charles (actually Southcote Mansergh) (b London, 27 Dec 1857; d Dundrum, Co. Dublin, 3 May 1935), Irish singer and impresario. Studied in Dublin and the RAM in London; later in Italy. After joining an opera chorus he made his first solo stage appearance in 1882, creating Private Willis in *Iolanthe*. Having married Fanny Moody in 1890 he established the Moody-Manners Opera Co. in 1897 and encouraged the performance of British operas.

Mannheim School a group of composers associated with the Electoral court at Mannheim in the mid-18th c. Under the leadership of Johann Stamitz (1717–57) the court orchestra became the most famous of the time, establishing a completely new style of playing, and placing particular emphasis on dynamic contrasts, *crescendo* and *diminuendo*, etc. The Mannheim composers, e.g. (in addition to Stamitz) F X Richter, Holzbauer, Beck and Cannabich, made notable contributions to the early development of the symphony, and also influenced later composers such as Mozart and Beethoven.

Manning, Jane (b Norwich, 20 Sept 1938), English soprano. She studied at the RAM and in Switzerland. Many performances of works by Cage, Schoenberg and Dallapiccola; fps of music by Davies, Birtwistle and Wood. She is married to the composer Anthony Payne.

Manns, August (Friedrich) (b Stolzenberg, near Stettin, 12 Mar 1825; d London, 1 Mar 1907), German-born conductor. At first cellist and violinist in various bands and orchestras in Germany; later bandmaster. Went to London as sub-conductor at Crystal Palace, 1854, becoming full conductor in 1855, when he enlarged the orchestra. Began popular Saturday concerts in 1856, giving early London performances of music by Schubert, Schumann, Wagner and Berlioz, and conducting the Handel Festival, 1883–1900. Knighted 1903.

Manon opera by Massenet (libretto by H Meilhac and P Gille, based on Prévost's novel *Manon Lescaut*), produced Paris, Opéra-Comique, 19 Jan 1884. Manon and Des Grieux fall in love and elope. The distraught Des Brétigny persuades Manon to go with him instead. The distraught Des Grieux plans to become a priest, but Manon returns and they are reunited. She is arrested, accused of prostitution, and sentenced to transportation. She dies in Des Grieux' arms.

Manon Lescaut ballet by Halévy (scenario by Scribe, based on Prévost's novel, choreography by Jean-Pierre Aumer), produced Paris, Opéra, 3 May 1830.

Opera by Auber (libretto by Scribe, based on Prévost's novel), produced Paris, Opéra-Comique, 23 Feb 1856.

Opera by Puccini (libretto, in Italian, by M Praga, D Oliva and L Illica, based on Prévost's novel), produced Turin, Teatro Regio, 1 Feb 1893. Manon and Des Grieux elope, thwarting the schemes of Geronte, who wants her for himself. Later Manon lives with Geronte, but on seeing Des Grieux returns to him. In revenge, Geronte has her arrested. She is deported to America, where she dies in Des Grieux' arms.

Manowarda, Josef von (b Kraków, 3 Jul 1890; d Berlin, 24 Dec 1942), Polish-born Austrian bass. Vienna Staatsoper 1919–42; Salzburg from 1922, as Alfonso and Barak. Bayreuth 1931–42 as Gurnemanz, Marke, Hagen, Pogner and Daland. Berlin Staatsoper 1934–42; roles there included Osmin and Philip II.

Manru opera by Paderewski (libretto by A Nossig after J I Kraszew-

———— **THE OPERA** ————

Manon

A five-act opera by Jules Massenet, based on Antoine Prévost's novel *Manon Lescaut* – the title of Puccini's opera on the same theme. It is set in 18th-century France, where it was first produced in 1884.

I. Manon (soprano) stops at an inn with her brother Lescaut (baritone). She is on the way to a convent, but the Chevalier Des Grieux (tenor) falls in love with her.

II. The lovers are established in a Parisian apartment, but Des Grieux is abducted to leave the way clear for De Bretigny (baritone), a rich friend of Lescaut.

III. Despite the objections of his father, the Comte Des Grieux (bass), Des Grieux is determined to enter the priesthood. But as soon as Manon returns, his resolve disappears.

IV. Manon and Des Grieux run into trouble at an illegal gambling room, and they are arrested for cheating.

V. Although Des Grieux has been freed, Manon is to be deported as a prostitute. Lescaut bribes Manon's guards so that Des Grieux can be alone with her, but she dies in his arms.

ski's novel *The Cabin behind the Wood*, 1843; composed 1892–1901, produced Dresden, 29 May 1901. Ulana marries young gypsy Manru, but loses him to Asa when he returns to his people.

Mansouri, Lofti (b Teheran, 15 Jun 1929), Iranian-born American administrator and stage director. Studied with Herbert Graf and Lotte Lehmann. Debut as producer with *Tosca* at Los Angeles, 1959. Staff director at Zurich 1960–65, Geneva 1965–75 (*Rosenkavalier* and *Die Entführung*). General director Canadian Opera Company 1976–88, presiding over stagings of *Wozzeck*, *Otello* and *Tristan*. Production of Massenet's *Esclarmonde* (for Joan Sutherland) seen at the NY Met. 1976, CG, 1983. General director of the San Francisco Opera from 1988 (produced *Tannhäuser* there, 1994).

Mantelli, Eugenia (b c 1860; d Lisbon, 3 Mar 1926), Italian mezzo. Debut Lisbon, 1883, as Urbain. She toured with Julián Gayarre and appeared with Tamagno in Moscow. CG 1896, as Brünnhilde. At the NY Met. she was heard 1894–1903 as Dalila, Amneris and Ortrud. Retired 1910 and taught in Lisbon.

Mantra work by Stockhausen for two amplified pianos; composed 1969–70, fp Donaueschingen, 18 Oct 1970. Pianists also play woodblock and bells, while they contemplate the Indian word *mantra*, or mystical repetition.

manual, from Latin *manus*, = 'hand'; a keyboard played by the hand, especially the keyboards of the organ as distinct from the pedals.

Manuel Venegas unfinished opera by H Wolf (libretto by M Hoernes, based on Alarcón's *El niño de la bola*), begun 1897. Fragments performed Munich, 1 Mar 1903.

Manzoni, Giacomo (b Milan, 26 Sept 1932), Italian composer. Studied at the Milan Conservatory and taught there 1962–69; Bologna Conservatory 1964–74, before returning to Milan. Published a book on Schoenberg in 1975. His music has featured in festivals at Berlin, Osaka, Prague and Warsaw.

Works include operas *La Sentenza* (1960), *Atemtod* (1965; given by Abbado in the 1965 Salzburg Festival), *Per Massimiliano Robespierre* (1975) and *Doktor Faustus*, after Thomas Mann (1985); *Masse: Omaggio a Edgard Varèse* for piano and orchestra (1977), *Il deserto cresce*, after Nietzsche, for chorus and orchestra (1992); *Ten Poems of Emily Dickinson* for soprano, string quartet, strings and harp (1988); string quartet (1971).

Manzoni Requiem the name sometimes given to Verdi's Requiem, composed 1873 for the anniversary of the death of Alessandro Manzoni, on which it was first performed at Milan, church of San Marco, 22 May 1874; repeated at La Scala on 25 May. The 'Libera me' is adapted from that contributed by Verdi to the collective Requiem he suggested should be written by various Italian composers on the death of Rossini in 1868, a plan which did not materialize. That the 'Libera me' was not merely taken over as it stood is proved by the fact that it contains allusions to material occurring earlier in the Manzoni Requiem. The 'Lachrymosa' is derived from the prison scene in the first version of *Don Carlos* (1867).

Manzuoli, Giovanni (b Florence, c 1720; d Florence, c 1780), Italian castrato soprano. Made his Italian debut in Florence (1731). Later visited Madrid, London and Vienna. In 1763 he sang in the fp of Gluck's *Trionfo di Clelia* (Bologna) and in 1765 was in London, to create the title role in J C Bach's *Adriano in Siria*. He retired in 1771, after creating Ascanio in Mozart's serenata *Ascanio in Alba*.

Maometto Secondo, *Mahomet II*, opera by Rossini (libretto by C della Valle, Duke of Ventignano), produced Naples, Teatro San Carlo, 3 Dec 1820. A French version entitled *Le Siège de Corinthe*, was produced Paris, 9 Oct 1826. Muslim warrior Maometto falls for Anna, but she prefers Calbo, and dies in his defence.

Mara (born *Schmeling*), Gertrud Elisabeth (b Kassel, 23 Feb 1749; d Reval, 20 Jan 1833), German soprano. Taken on tour by her father, a poor musician, as a child prodigy violinist. Her talent as a singer was discovered in 1759 in London, where she had lessons from Paradisi. Sang under Hiller in Leipzig, and made her operatic debut in Dresden in 1767. She married the cellist Mara in 1771 and entered the service of Frederick the Great in Berlin, but left in 1780 and appeared with great success in Vienna and Paris; London 1784–1802, as Handel's Cleopatra and Nasolini's Andromaca.

maraca a percussion instrument used mainly in jazz and swing bands, a rattle made of the dried gourd containing beads, dried seeds or shot.

The empire of the viol was founded and powerfully established by 'le Père Marais'.
Hubert le Blanc, *Défense de la Basse de Viole*, 1740

Marais, Marin (b Paris, 31 May 1656; d Paris, 15 Aug 1728), French bass violist and composer. Pupil of Chaperon at the Sainte-Chapelle and of viol masters; later member of the royal band and the orchestra at the Opéra, where he studied composition under Lully. In 1725 he retired to devote himself to gardening, but continued to teach. He added a seventh string to the bass viol.

Works include operas *Idylle dramatique*, *Alcide* (1693) and *Pantomime des pages* (both with Lully's son Louis), *Ariane et Bacchus* (1696), *Alcyone* (1706), *Séméle* (1709); Te Deum; concertos for violin and bass; trios for flute, violin and bass; pieces for one and two viols; *La Gamme* pieces for violin, viol and harpsichord.

Marais, Roland (b c 1680; d c 1750), French viola da gamba player and composer, son of Marin ♭Marais. Succeeded his father as solo gamba in the royal band, pub. a *Nouvelle méthode de musique* (1711) and two books of pieces for viol.

Mařák, Otakar (b Ostrihom, Hungary, 5 Jan 1872; d Prague, 2 Jul 1939), Czech tenor. Debut Brno 1899, Faust. He sang in Prague from 1900 and was engaged by Mahler for the Vienna Hofoper in 1903. At Berlin in 1911 he created Gennaro in Wolf-Ferrari's *I Gioielli della Madonna*; sang in London from 1908 as Canio, Don José and Turiddu, and in 1913 was the first local Bacchus, under Beecham. At Chicago he was heard as Parsifal (1914) and sang in Prague until 1934. Highly regarded as a lyric tenor.

Maratona ballet by Henze (scenario by Luchino Visconti); composed 1956, produced Berlin, 24 Sept 1957.

Marazzoli (or *Marazzuoli*), Marco (b Parma, c 1605; d Rome, 26 Jan 1662), Italian singer, harpist and composer. Sang in the Papal Chapel in Rome in the 1630s and was in the service of Christina of Sweden there.

Works include operas *Chi soffre speri* (with V Mazzocchi, 1637), *Dal male il bene* (with Abbatini, 1653), *La vita umana* (1656) and others; oratorios, cantatas; songs.

Marbeck (or *Merbecke*), John (b ? Windsor, c 1505; d Windsor, c 1585), English singer, organist and composer. He was lay clerk and organist at St George's Chapel, Windsor, from 1541. In 1543 he was

---

────────── **THE OPERA** ──────────

Manon Lescaut

Giacomo Puccini's four-act version of the Manon story, also made into an opera by Massenet. It is set in France in the second half of the 18th century, and was first performed in Turin in 1893.

I. The Chevalier Des Grieux (tenor) falls in love with Manon (soprano) while she stops at an inn on the way to a convent. They leave in the stolen carriage of Geronte de Ravoir (bass).

II. With the connivance of her brother Lescaut (baritone), Manon is now enjoying life as the mistress of Geronte. Des Grieux makes money gambling, and Manon decides to leave with him. She picks up Geronte's jewels on the way out and he has her arrested for theft and prostitution.

III. At Le Havre, Des Grieux is unable to obtain Manon's release from deportation and begs to be allowed to sail with her to the United States.

IV. The lovers are alone in the Louisiana desert, weak from exhaustion after further escapades. Des Grieux goes to fetch water, but Manon dies in his arms when he returns.

────────── **THE OPERA** ──────────

arrested and in 1544 tried and condemned for heresy as a Calvinist, but he was pardoned and allowed to retain his office.

Works include Mass and two motets (probably early); carol *A Virgine and Mother*; *The Booke of Common Praier noted*, 1550 (i.e. set to notes), being the first musical setting of Anglican prayer book (first version authorized by Edward VI).

Marcabru the earliest troubadour of importance (early 12th c.). The most famous of his four surviving songs with tunes is the semi-religious 'Pax in nomine Domini'.

marcato Italian = 'marked, accentuated'; a direction indicating that a piece or movement is to be played in a decided, energetic manner, to that a part is to be brought out strongly above the accompaniment or surrounding parts in a passage.

Marcel, Lucille (b New York, 1877; d Vienna, 22 Jun 1921), American soprano. She studied in Paris with Jean de Reszke; sang Elektra at Vienna in 1909. She married the director of the Hofoper, Felix Weingartner, in 1911 and with him appeared at Boston in 1913 as Bizet's Djamileh. Also sang in Paris, Hamburg and Darmstadt as Tosca, Aida, Desdemona and Eva.

For the finale of his opera he should write a magnificent scene with elaborate effects, so that the audience will not walk out before the work is half over.

Benedetto Marcello on the art of the librettist, in *Il Teatro alla moda*, 1720

Marcello, Benedetto (b Venice, 2 Aug 1686; d Brescia, 25 Jul 1739), Italian violinist, composer and author. A pupil of Gasparini and Lotti, he combined his musical interests with a career in, law and the civil service. As well as composing, he wrote the libretto for Ruggeri's opera *Arato in Sparta*, and in 1720 pub. the important satire on contemporary opera *Il teatro alla moda*.

Works include operas and serenatas *La fede riconosciuta*, *Arianna*, etc.; oratorios *Il pianto e il riso delle quattro stagioni* (1731), *Giuditta*, *Gioaz* (1726), *Il trionfo della poesia e della musica* (1733); Masses, Misereres and other church music; *Estro poetico-armonico*, settings of 50 psalm-paraphrases by G A Giustiniani; concertos, sonatas, for various instruments. His brother **Alessandro** (b Venice, 24 Aug 1669; d Padua, 19 Jun 1747), wrote cantatas and concertos.

march a piece of music in strongly emphasized regular metre, usually in 4–4 or 2–4 time, but sometimes in 6–8, primarily intended for use at military parades to keep marching soldiers in step, but also the music most often used for processions of various kinds, including those occurring on the stage in operas and other theatre pieces. Funeral marches also have primarily a processional purpose, and they are considerably slower in pace. Marches of all kinds, however, may occur in sonatas, symphonies or suites and are often labelled *alla marcia* or *alla marcia funebre*.

Marchal, André (b Paris, 6 Feb 1894; d St Jean-de-Luz, 27 Aug 1980), French organist, blind from birth. Studied at the Paris Conservatory and from 1915 to 1945 was organist in Paris at St Germain-des-Prés and from 1945 at St Eustache. He was especially well known for his improvisations at the organ.

Marchand, Louis (b Lyon, 2 Feb 1669; d Paris, 17 Feb 1732), French harpsichordist, organist and composer. A child prodigy, he was organist of Nevers Cathedral at the age of 14 and later of Auxerre Cathedral, before settling in Paris, *c* 1689. Organist of various churches there and of the Royal Chapel, 1708–14, he then toured Germany, visiting Dresden in 1717 and there declining to compete with Bach on the organ. On his return to Paris he lived mainly by teaching.

Works include organ music, two books of harpsichord pieces.

Marchand de Venise, Le, *The Merchant of Venice*, opera by Hahn (libretto by M Zamaçoïs, after Shakespeare), produced Paris, Opéra, 25 Mar 1935.

Marchesi (de Castrone) Italian family of singers:

1. Salvatore Marchesi (b Palermo, 15 Jan 1822; d Paris, 20 Feb 1908), baritone and teacher. He came from a noble family, succeeding later to the title of Marchese della Raiata. Studying law and philosophy at Palermo, he took singing and composition lessons from Raimondi and later studied at Milan under Lamperti and others. Having fled to America as a political refugee from the 1848 revolutions, he made his first stage appearance in NY as Carlo in *Ernani*. On his return to Europe he settled in London for a time and appeared there as Leporello and Méphistophélès. He married Mathilde Graumann in 1852. Wrote books on singing, vocal exercises, a number of songs and made Italian translations of various opera libretti, including several by Wagner.

2. Mathilde Marchesi (born Graumann) (b Frankfurt, 24 Mar 1821; d London, 17 Nov 1913), mezzo and teacher, wife of 1. Began to study singing when her father, a wealthy merchant, lost his fortune in 1843. In 1845 she went to Paris to continue her studies with García, whose pupils she took over when he was incapacitated by an accident. Settled in London in 1849, she sang much at concerts. Soon after her marriage to Marchesi she became professor of singing at the Vienna Conservatory, 1854–61; later taught mainly in Paris. Her only stage role was Rosina.

3. Blanche Marchesi (b Paris, 4 Apr 1863; d London, 15 Dec 1940), soprano and teacher, daughter of 2. Studying the violin at first, she took to singing in 1881, appeared in Berlin and Brussels in 1895, in London in 1896, and settled there as teacher and concert singer. She sang Brünnhilde in Prague in 1900; CG 1902 as Elisabeth, Elsa and Isolde.

Marchesi, Luigi (Lodovico) (b Milan, 8 Aug 1754; d Inzago, 14 Jul 1829), Italian castrato soprano. Pupil of Fioroni in the choir of Milan Cathedral, made his operatic debut in Rome in 1773 in Anfossi's *L'incognita perseguitata*. Later travelled widely, visiting London, 1788–1790. Also sang in operas by Bianchi, Sarti and Mayr.

Marchettus (b Padua), Italian 13th-14th c. theorist. Lived at Cesena and Verona at some time and was in the service of Rainier, Prince of Monaco. He wrote a treatise on the division of the scale and two more on notation, which aroused much opposition.

Marching Song opera by Benjamin Frankel (libretto by H Keller, after John Whiting's play); composed 1972–73 and left in short score at Frankel's death. Fp, in edition by Buxton Orr, BBC 3 Oct 1983.

marcia Italian = 'march'.

Marcolini, Marietta (b Florence, *c* 1780), Italian mezzo. She sang in Venice from 1800 and later appeared in Naples, Rome and Milan. She attracted the attention of Rossini and created leading roles in *Ciro in Babilonia*, *La Pietra del Paragone* and *L'italiana in Algeri*. Retired 1820.

Maréchal, Adolphe (b Liège, 26 Sept 1867; d Brussels, 1 Feb 1935), Belgian tenor. Debut Dijon, 1891. At the Paris Opéra-Comique he created Julien in *Louise* (1900) and Alain in Massenet's *Grisélidis*; Jean in *Le jongleur de Notre Dame*, Monte Carlo (1902). At CG in 1902 he was heard as Faust, Don José and Des Grieux. Guest in Brussels, Nice and Moscow.

Marenzio, Luca (b Coccaglio, near Brescia, *c* 1553; d Rome, 22 Aug 1599), Italian singer and composer. Studied with Giovanni Contini, organist at Brescia Cathedral, pub. his first work in 1581, went to Rome soon afterwards where he became *maestro di cappella* to Cardinal d'Este, leaving in 1586. In 1588 he entered the service of Ferdinando de' Medici and in 1589 contributed two *intermedi* for wedding festivities in Florence. He was in Warsaw 1596–98, at the court of Sigismondo III of Poland. His madrigals were introduced into England through Yonge's *Musica transalpina* in 1588 and he was in correspondence with Dowland in 1595. He is best known for his madrigals, which cover a wide range of mood and situation.

Works include Mass, motets, *Sacri concenti*; 500 madrigals (nine vols.), *Villanelle ed arie alla napolitana* (five vols.)

Margherita d'Anjou opera by Meyerbeer (libretto in Italian, by F Romani, based on a play by R C G de Pixérécourt), produced Milan, La Scala, 14 Nov 1820.

Margot-la-Rouge opera in one act by Delius (libretto by B Gaston-

Danville); composed 1901–02, vocal score by Ravel 1902. Unperformed in Delius' lifetime but part of score was used in the *Idyll* of 1930. Given in orchestration by Eric Fenby, BBC 21 Feb 1982; the Delius orchestration was then discovered and given at stage fp, St Louis 17 Jun 1983. Old flame Thibault is accidentally killed by Margot's new lover when he lunges at her during an argument. Margot then kills her lover and is arrested.

Maria di Rohan opera by Donizetti (libretto by S Cammarano), produced Vienna, Kärntnertor-theater, 5 Jun 1843. The Count of Chalais fights a duel to avenge an insult to Maria, wife of the Duc de Chevreuse. Chalais, Maria's former lover, writes her a passionate letter, which is intercepted and delivered to Chevreuse. Chalais kills himself.

Maria di Rudenz opera by Donizetti (libretto by S Cammarano), produced Venice, Teatro La Fenice, 30 Jan 1838. Maria elopes with Corrado, but he prefers her heiress sister, Matilde. Maria stabs Matilde and, unable to move Corrado, dies of wounds previously inflicted by him.

Mariani, Angelo (b Ravenna, 11 Oct 1821; d Genoa, 13 Jun 1873), Italian conductor and composer. Studied at home at Rimini and under Rossini at the Liceo Filarmonico of Bologna; debut as violinist-conductor at Messina in 1844 and was conductor of the court theatre at Copenhagen, 1847–48. After fighting in the revolutionary army in 1848, he went to the sultan's court at Constantinople, 1849–52, and then became conductor at the Teatro Carlo Felice at Genoa. He appeared in many places in Italy and abroad as guest conductor and gave the first Italian performance of Wagner's *Lohengrin* and *Tannhäuser* at Bologna in 1871 and 1872. Also conducted operas by Verdi and Meyerbeer.

Works include Requiem; hymn for the Sultan of Turkey, cantatas *La fidanzata del guerriero* and *Gli esuli*; orchestral music; songs.

Mariani, Luciano (b Cremona, 1801; d Piacenza, 10 Jun 1859), Italian bass. He created Rodolfo in *Sonnambula* (1831) and Alfonso in *Lucrezia Borgia* (1833). With his sister Rosa (b Cremona, 1799) as Arsace he sang Oroe in the fp of *Semiramide* (1823).

Maria Stuarda opera in two acts by Donizetti (libretto by G Bardari, after A Maffei's translation of Schiller's *Maria Stuart*), produced Milan, La Scala, 30 Dec 1835. While in rehearsal at Naples the opera was banned by the King; Donizetti used much of the music in a different work, *Buondelmonte*, which was premiered in Naples on 18 Oct 1834. *Maria Stuarda* was not staged in London until 1966 and in New York, 1972. Leicester intercedes on behalf of the imprisoned Mary, but Elizabeth is jealous of the two and signs Mary's death warrant.

Maria Theresa Symphony name given to Haydn's symphony no. 48 in C major, supposedly composed for a visit of the Empress Maria Theresa to Eszterháza in 1773.

Maria Tudor opera by Gomes (libretto by M Praga, based on Victor Hugo's tragedy), produced Milan, La Scala, 27 Mar 1879. Giovanna, fiancée of Gilberto, is seduced by the disguised Count Fabiano, who is Queen Mary's lover. In a jealous rage Mary arrests both Gilberto and Fabiano. Calling for Fabiano's execution, she intends secretly to substitute Gilberto in his place, but Don Gilberto allows his rival to die instead.

Mariazell Mass the familiar name of Haydn's C-major Mass originally entitled *Missa Cellensis*. Composed 1782 for Anton Liebe von Kreutzner, who on his ennoblement wished to make a votive offering at the Marian shrine at Mariazell.

Marienleben, Das, *The Life of Mary*, cycle of 15 songs for soprano and piano by Hindemith (texts by R M Rilke); composed 1922–23, fp Frankfurt, 15 Oct 1923. Revised 1936–48 and performed Hanover, 3 Nov 1948. Six of the songs were arranged for soprano and orchestra, 1938–48.

Mariés de la Tour Eiffel, Les, *The Wedded Pair of the Eiffel Tower*, ballet by five of 'Les Six': Auric, Honegger, Milhaud, Poulenc and Tailleferre (scenario by Jean Cocteau), produced Paris, Théâtre des Champs-Élysées, 18 Jun 1921.

Mariette, Auguste Edouard (Mariette Bey) (1821–1881), French

Egyptologist. Founder of the museum at Cairo. He outlined the libretto for Verdi's *Aida*, drafted in French by C du Locle and written in Italian by Ghislanzoni.

marimba a Mexican percussion instrument of African origin, made of wood, similar to the xylophone, but larger and with resonance-boxes to each note.

marimba gongs a percussion instrument similar to the marimba, but with metal plates instead of wooden strips to produce the notes.

Marin, Ion (b Bucharest, 8 Jul 1960), Romanian conductor. Studied in Bucharest, at the Salzburg Mozarteum and in Siena. Appeared widely in Eastern Europe, Greece, Italy and France from 1981. Conductor at the Vienna Staatsoper 1987–91, with repertoire from Mozart to Berg. London debut with the LSO 1991; US debut with *L'Elisir d'amore* at Dallas, 1991; *Il Barbiere di Siviglia* at San Francisco, 1992. Conducted Polanski's production of *Hoffmann* at the Opéra Bastille, Paris, (1992) and *Semiramide* at the NY Met. Concerts with the CBSO, Philadelphia Orchestra, Rotterdam PO and Montreal SO (1993). Recordings include *Lucia di Lammermoor*, with Studer and Domingo, and *Semiramide*.

Marin, José (b ? Madrid, 1619; d Madrid, Mar 1699), Spanish tenor and composer. He sang in the Encarnación convent at Madrid in his younger years, became a highwayman and a priest, fled to Rome after committing murder, was imprisoned, but at the end of his life had a great reputation as a musician.

Works include songs with continuo, songs with guitar accompaniment.

Marin (Marie-Martin), Marcel de, Viscount (b Saint-Jean-de-Luz, 8 Sept 1769; d Toulouse, after 1861), French harpist, violinist and composer (?) of Italian descent. In 1783 he became a member of the Arcadian Academy in Rome and during the French Revolution settled in London; later in Toulouse.

Works include chamber music, harp sonatas and pieces, violin sonatas.

Marini, Biagio (b Brescia, *c* 1587; d Venice, 1663), Italian composer and violinist. He was employed successively as violinist at Venice, as music director at the church of Sant' Eufemia at Brescia, at the courts of Parma and Munich, at Düsseldorf, Ferrara and Milan.

Works include psalms, vespers and other church music; symphonies; sonatas, dances, etc., for string instruments, vocal and instrumental chamber music, madrigals, *canzonets*, etc., for several voices; sacred songs for several voices.

Marini, Ignazio (b Bergamo, 28 Nov 1811; d Milan, 29 Apr 1873), Italian bass. He sang at La Scala from 1832 and in London and NY 1850–52; appeared in the fps of *Attila* and *Oberto* and was heard at St Petersburg 1856–63. Other roles included Silva, Mosè and Oroveso.

Marino Faliero opera by Donizetti (libretto by E Bidera, based on Byron's drama), produced Paris, Théâtre Italien, 12 Mar 1835. Doge of Venice, Faliero, is first betrayed by his unfaithful wife Elena, then executed after engaging in a political conspiracy.

Marinuzzi, Gino (b Palermo, 24 Mar 1882; d Milan, 17 Aug 1945), Italian composer and conductor. Studied at Palermo Conservatory; first appeared as conductor at Catania, later worked at Palermo, Madrid, Trieste, Buenos Aires and Chicago. On his return to Italy he conducted opera in all the large cities and was director of the Liceo Musicale at Bologna, 1915–19. He gave the fp of Puccini's *Rondine* (Monte Carlo, 1917), and first European performance of *Il Trittico* (Rome 1919).

Works include operas *Barberina* (1918), *Jacquerie Palla de' Mozzi* (1932); suites *Siciliana* and *Romana*, symphonic poem *Sicania*, *Elegia*, *Rito nuziale* for orchestra; *Andantino all' antica* for flute, strings and harp.

Mario, Giovanni Matteo (Cavaliere di Candia) (b Cagliari, 17 Oct 1810; d Rome, 11 Dec 1883), Italian tenor. First appearance, Paris, 1838 as Robert le Diable; first visit to London the following year as Gennaro in *Lucrezia Borgia*. He was Ernesto in the fp of *Don Pasquale* (Paris, 1843). Other roles included Duke of Mantua, Roméo, and Rossini's Otello, Lindoro and Ramiro. Companion to Giulia Grisi.

Mariotte, Antoine (b Avignon, 22 Dec 1875; d Izieux, Loire, 30 Nov 1944), French composer. A naval officer at first, he left the Navy in 1897 and became a student at the Schola Cantorum in Paris as a pupil of d'Indy. He conducted at Saint-Étienne and then at Lyon, and became director of the Orléans Conservatory in 1920. In 1935–39 he was director of the Opéra-Comique in Paris. He was accused of having plagiarized R Strauss in his *Salomé*, though his work was written before Strauss's was produced.

Works include operas *Salomé* (Oscar Wilde, 1908), *Le Vieux Roi* (1911), *Esther: Princesse d'Israël (1925)*, *Léontine Sœurs*, *Nele Dooryn*, *Gargantua* (after Rabelais); *Avril*, *Pâques françaises* and *Toujours* for unaccompanied chorus; *Impressions urbaines* and *Kakemonos* for piano and orchestra; *En montagne* for three wind or string instruments with string quintet or piano; piano music and songs.

Mark, Peter (b New York, 31 Oct 1940), American conductor and violist. Studied at Columbia and Juilliard. Performed widely as orchestral violist and chamber musician (Chicago Lyric Opera 1960–68, Los Angeles PO 1968–69). Gave fp of concerto by his wife, Thea Musgrave, at Manchester in 1975 and the same year became artistic director of the Virginia Opera Association. Conducted at Covent Garden 1982 and has led opera in New York, Los Angeles, Orlando and Mexico City; gave local fps of *Porgy and Bess* in Brazil, 1992. Recordings include Musgrave's *Mary, Queen of Scots* and *A Christmas Carol*.

Markevich, Igor (b Kiev, 27 Jul 1912; d Antibes, 7 Mar 1983), Russian-born conductor and composer. His parents emigrated and lived in Switzerland, but he went to Paris at the age of 15 as a pupil of Nadia Boulanger. Early in his career he was a protégé of Diaghilev, and was one of his lovers. Became an Italian citizen during war years. He was conductor of the Lamoureux Orchestra, Paris, 1958–61. Monte Carlo Orchestra from 1967.

Works include ballets *Rébus* (1931) and *L'Envoi d'Icare* (1932); cantata on Milton's *Paradise Lost* (performed London, 1935) and others, *Cantique d'Amour*, *Nouvel Age*, cantata for soprano and male-voice chorus (Jean Cocteau); *Hymnes*, concerto grosso and sinfonietta for orchestra; concerto and partita for piano and orchestra; *Galop* for small orchestra; psalm for soprano and orchestra; serenade for violin, clarinet and bassoon.

Marmontel, Jean François (b Bort, Limousin, 11 Jul 1723; d Abloville, Eure, 31 Dec 1799), French author. Librettist for Rameau, Grétry, Piccinni, Cherubini and others; defender of Piccinni against Gluck and author of an *Essai sur les révolutions de la musique en France* (1777).

◊Acante et Céphise (Rameau); ◊Antigone (Zingarelli); ◊Atys (Piccinni); ◊Céphale et Procris (Grétry); ◊Clari (Bishop, from *Laurette*); ◊Démophoon (Cherubini); ◊Didon (Piccinni); ◊Guirlande (Rameau); ◊Rameau (*Lysis et Délie*; *Les Sybarites*); ◊Zémire et Azor (Grétry); ◊Zemire und Azor (Spohr).

Mârouf, savetier du Caire, *Mârouf, the Cobbler of Cairo*, opera by Rabaud (libretto by L Népoty, based on a story in the *Arabian Nights*), produced Paris, Opéra-Comique, 15 May 1914. Mârouf escapes wife, marries Sultan's daughter, and steals his treasure.

Marpurg, Friedrich Wilhelm (b Sechof, near Seehausen, Brandenburg, 21 Nov 1718; d Berlin, 22 May 1795), German theorist and writer on music. In Paris as secretary to General Bodenburg (?) in 1746 he met, among others, Voltaire and Rameau, and was influenced by the latter's theories. From 1749 he lived mainly in Berlin, where he began a music weekly, *Der critische Musicus an der Spree*. This was followed by numerous other critical and theoretical writings, including a notable preface to the second edition of Bach's *Kunst der Fuge*, treatises on fugue, thorough-bass, keyboard playing, etc. He also composed some songs and keyboard music.

Marriage of Figaro (Mozart.) ◊Nozze di Figaro.

Marriage, The, *Zhenitba*, unfinished opera by Mussorgsky (libretto taken from Gogol's comedy), composed 1864; never performed in Mussorgsky's lifetime; produced with piano accompaniment, St Petersburg, 1 Apr 1909; with orchestra, Petrograd, 26 Oct 1917,

with Mussorgsky's *Sorotchintsy Fair*. Podkolesin hires a marriage-broker in pursuit of Agafya.

Comic opera by Martinů (libretto by composer, after Gogol); composed 1952, fp NBC TV, NY, 7 Feb 1953.

Marriner, Neville (b Lincoln, 15 Apr 1924), English conductor and violinist. He studied at the RCM and the Paris Conservatory. His early experience was in the performance of Baroque music; from 1952–68 played the violin in the Philharmonia, then the LSO. Founded Academy of St Martin-in-the-Fields 1958; director until 1978. Minnesota Orchestra 1979–86. Salzburg debut 1982. Conductor of the Stuttgart Radio SO 1983–89. His many recordings include the symphonies of Mozart, *Messiah*, *Die Zauberflöte* and *Don Giovanni*. CBE 1979. Knighted 1985.

Marsalis, Wynton (b New Orleans, 18 Oct 1961), American trumpeter. Played with the New Orleans PO from age 14, and studied at Juilliard. Has performed with jazz ensembles from 1980 and given concerts with the New York and Los Angeles POs, Cleveland Orchestra and LSO. Has received Grammy Awards for his recordings of concertos by Haydn, Hummel and Leopold Mozart.

Marschner, Heinrich (August) (b Zittau, 16 Aug 1795; d Hanover, 14 Dec 1861), German composer. As a boy he played the piano, sang soprano and composed tentatively without much instruction. In 1813 he was sent to Leipzig to study law, but met Rochlitz, who induced him to take music. In 1816 he went to Vienna and Pressburg with a Hungarian, Count de Varkony, and settled in the latter place, composing several operas, until 1823, when he became assistant conductor to Weber and Morlacchi at Dresden. In 1827 he became conductor of the Leipzig theatre and from 1831 to 1859 court conductor at Hanover. He married four times. He is regarded as the most important German opera composer between Weber and Wagner.

Works include operas *Saidar, Heinrich IV und Aubigné* (1820), *Der Kyffhäuserberg* (1822), *Der Holzdieb* (1825), *Lucretia*, *Der Vampyr* (1828), *Der Templer und die Jüdin* (after Scott's *Ivanhoe*, 1829), *Des Falkners Braut* (1832), *Hans Heiling* (1833), *Der Bäbu* (1838), *Das Schloss am Aetna*, *Kaiser Adolf von Nassau* (1845), *Austin, Sangeskönig Hiarne* (1863); incidental music to Kleist's *Prinz Friedrich von Homburg* and other plays; overture on 'God Save the King' and other orchestral works; male-voice choruses; sonatas; songs.

Marschner, Wolfgang (b Dresden, 23 May 1926), German violinist. Studied at the Dresden Conservatory and the Salzburg Mozarteum; professor at Freiburg i/B from 1963. Has appeared at the Edinburgh Festival and with the Berlin and Royal POs. A noted exponent of the Schoenberg concerto, which he premiered in London (1960) and Vienna. Has founded several violin competitions.

Marsh, John (b Dorking, 1752; d Chichester, 1828), English amateur composer. Practised as a lawyer until 1783, when a legacy enabled him to retire and devote his time to music, in which he was largely self-taught. Conducted concerts in Chichester and elsewhere, and composed some notable symphonies, also concertos, chamber music, keyboard music.

Marsh, Roger (b Bournemouth, 10 Dec 1949), English composer. Studied at York University with Bernard Rands and has been lecturer there from 1988.

Works include music theatre pieces *Cass* (1970) and *Calypso* (1974); *Not a Soul but Ourselves*, for four amplified voices (1977), *Point to Point* for ensemble (1981); *Samson*, music theatre (1984); *The Song of Abigail* for soprano and orchestra (1985); *Dying for it*, for ensemble (1987); *The Big Bang* (1989); and *Love on the Rocks*, music theatre (1989); *Stepping Out* for orchestra (1990).

Marshall, Margaret (b Stirling, 4 Jan 1949), Scottish soprano. She studied in Glasgow and with Hans Hotter; won the Munich International Competition in 1974. London debut 1975. Florence 1979 as Eurydice; she returned in 1979 as Mozart's Countess and sang the same role at CG in 1980. US debut 1980, with Boston SO; later NY PO. Fiordiligi at La Scala and Salzburg in 1982. Season 1991/92 as Violetta at Frankfurt, and Mozart's Fiordiligi and Vitellia at Salzburg.

Marson, George (b Worcester, *c* 1573; d Canterbury, 3 Feb 1632),

English organist and composer. He became organist and choirmaster at Canterbury Cathedral *c* 1598.

Works include services, anthem, psalms and other church music; madrigal contribution to *The Triumphes of Oriana*.

Marteau sans maître, Le, *The hammer without a master*, work by Boulez for mezzo, flute, guitar, vibraphone, xylorimba, viola and percussion; composed 1952–54, revised 1957, fp Baden-Baden, 18 Jun 1955, conductor Rosbaud.

martelé, French, *martellato* Italian, lit. 'hammered', detached, strongly accentuated playing or singing, used especially with regard to music for piano and on string instruments for a harsh stroke of the bow producing such an effect.

Martelli, Henri (b Bastia, Corsica, 25 Feb 1895; d Paris, 15 Jul 1980), French composer. Studied at the Paris Conservatory, Widor being among his masters.

Works include opera *La Chanson de Roland* (1921–23; performed 1967) incidental music; three symphonies (1953–57), symphonic poem *Sur la vie de Jeanne d'Arc*, *Bas-reliefs assyriens* and concerto for orchestra; piano concerto; two string quartets; string quintet; piano pieces; songs.

Martenot, Maurice (b Paris, 14 Oct 1898; d Paris, 10 Oct 1980), French scientist and musician. Studied piano and cello at the Paris Conservatory and composition with Gédalge. After various appointments as conductor and teacher he opened the École d'Art Martenot at Neuilly. Inventor of the radio-electrical instrument Ondes Musicales, a development of Theremin's, which he produced in 1928 and is generally known as the Ondes Martenot. In France a number of composers, Honegger, Milhaud, Koechlin and especially Messiaen (whose sister-in-law Jeanne Loriod is the instrument's foremost living exponent), have written for it.

Martha, oder Der Markt von Richmond, *Martha, or The Market at Richmond*, comic opera by Flotow (libretto by F W Riese, pseudonym 'W Friedrich', based on a ballet-pantomime, *Lady Henriette, ou La Servante de Greenwich*, by J H V de Saint-Georges, produced Paris, 21 Feb 1844, with music by F Burgmüller and Deldevez), produced Vienna, Kärntnertortheater, 25 Nov 1847. Lady Harriet and maid Nancy disguise themselves and meet two young farmers, Plumkett and Lyonel, at a country fair. They fall in love, and complications of differing social class are resolved when Lyonel turns out to be of noble blood.

martin the French name of a type of baritone voice of exceptional range, derived from Jean Blaise Martin (1768–1837); he specialized in comic roles in operas by Dalaryac, Boieldieu and Méhul.

Martin, Frank (b Geneva, 15 Sept 1890; d Naarden, Holland, 21 Nov 1974), Swiss composer and pianist. Studied with Joseph Lauber at Geneva and in 1928 became professor at the Institut Jaques-Dalcroze there. Wrote in generally conservative idiom.

Works include operas *The Tempest* (Shakespeare, 1956), *Monsieur Pourceaugnac* (1963); *Six Monologues from 'Jedermann'* (after Hofmannsthal, 1943), ballet *Die blaue Blume*; incidental music for Sophocles' *Oedipus Coloneus* and *Oedipus Rex* and Shakespeare's *Romeo and Juliet*.

Mass for double chorus, oratorios *In terra pax* (1945), *Golgotha* (1948); *Le Mystère de la Nativité* (1957–59); symphonic suite *Rhythmes*, *Esquisse*, symphony for orchestra; *Petite Symphonie concertante* for harp, harpsichord, piano and strings (1945); piano concerto, violin concerto (1951), cello concerto (1966); *Cornet* (Rilke) for contralto and orchestra. Piano quintet, rhapsody for string quintet, string quartet, string trio, piano trio on Irish tunes; *Le Vin herbé* for 12 voices, strings and piano (on the subject of Tristram and Yseult, from Joseph Bédier, 1938–41); two violin and piano sonatas.

Martin, Janis (b Sacramento, 16 Aug 1939), American soprano, originally mezzo. Debut San Francisco 1960; sang at the NY Met. from 1962 and in Europe from 1965. Her first soprano role was Donna Elvira, in 1970, and at Bayreuth she sang Eva, Sieglinde and Kundry. In London, Milan, Berlin and Vienna she has been admired as Brangaene, Tosca, Marina, Elektra and Octavian.

Martinelli, Giovanni (b Montagnana, 22 Oct 1885; d New York, 2 Feb

1969), Italian tenor. After he played the clarinet in an army band his voice was discovered and he studied singing in Milan, making his debut in 1910 as Ernani. He sang at CG 1912–14, 1919 and 1937, as Cavaradossi, Otello and Calaf. The greater part of his career was spent at the NY Met., from 1913 to 1946, as Manrico, Radames, Don Carlos, Faust and Don José. He became one of the most famous tenors of the century, renowned for the controlled power of his performances.

Martinez, Marianne (b Vienna, 4 May 1744; d Vienna, 13 Dec 1812), Austrian composer and keyboard player of Spanish descent. Daughter of the master of ceremonies to the Pope's nuncio in Vienna; pupil of Metastasio, Porpora and Haydn.

Works include oratorios *Isacco* (1782) and *Santa Elena al Calvario*, psalms translated by Metastasio, Mass, motets, cantatas; symphonies; overtures; concertos; sonatas.

Martinez, Odaline de la (b Matanzas, 31 Oct 1949), Cuban-born American conductor and composer. Emigrated to USA 1961 and studied at Tulane University, 1968–72; RAM, London, 1972–76, and with Reginald Smith-Brindle at Surrey University. Founded Lontano 1976, for the performance of contemporary music. Conducted the premiere of Goldschmidt's opera *Beatrice Cenci* (concert) in 1988 and the following year a series of Latin American music at South Bank, London. An advocate of music by women composers, she conducted *The Wreckers* by Ethel Smyth at the 1994 Prom Concerts. Her own music includes the opera *Sister Amiée* (1978–83).

If one plays good music people don't listen, and if one plays bad music people don't talk.
Oscar Wilde, *Portrait of Dorian Gray*, 1891

Martini, Giovanni Battista (or Giambattista, known as Padre Martini) (b Bologna, 24 Apr 1706; d Bologna, 3 Aug 1784), Italian priest, theorist, teacher and composer. Received a thorough education from his father and others in violin, harpsichord, singing and composition. Entered the Franciscan Order in 1721 (priest 1729), and was appointed *maestro di cappella* of San Francesco in Bologna in 1725, after which he rarely left his home town. As the most famous teacher and theorist of his time he attracted many distinguished pupils, including Mozart, and corresponded with musicians throughout Europe. His most important works are the unfinished history of music (three vols, 1757–81) and a treatise on counterpoint (1773–75).

Works include *c* 1,500 works, with *c* 1,000 canons; oratorios *L'assunzione di Salomone* (1734), *San Pietro*, *Il sacrificio d'Abramo*; *c* 32 Masses, motets, psalm settings and other church music; stage works; keyboard works.

Martini (real name *Johann Paul Aegidius Schwartzendorf*), Jean Paul Egide (b Freistadt, Upper Palatinate, 31 Aug 1741; d Paris, 10 Feb 1816), German organist and composer, adopted the name of Martini on settling in Nancy as a music teacher in 1760. In the service of the Duke of Lorraine (the former King Stanislaus of Poland) at Lunéville, 1761–64, he then went to Paris, where he wrote military music and produced his first opera in 1771. After three years' absence during the Revolution, he returned to Paris in 1794 to become one of the inspectors of the Conservatory (1795) and professor of composition (1800). At the Restoration in 1814 he was appointed superintendent of the court music.

Works include operas *L'Amoureux de quinze ans* (1771), *Le Fermier cru sourd* (1772), *Le Rendezvous nocturne* (1773), *Henry IV* (1774), *Le Droit du Seigneur*, *L'Amant sylphe* (1783), *Sapho*, *Annette et Lubin* (1789), *Ziméo* and others; two Masses, two Requiems, Te Deum, psalm settings and other church music, cantata for the marriage of Napoleon and Marie-Louise; chamber music; marches, etc., for military band; songs including 'Plaisir d'amour'.

Martino, Donald (b Plainfield, NJ, 16 May 1931), American composer. Studied with Bacon, Babbitt and Sessions in USA, with Dallapiccola in Florence. Professor of composition New England Conservatory of Music 1970–80; Harvard from 1983. Works often feature his own

Martinů *The composer Bohuslav Martinů (1890–1959) wrote extensively and very quickly in a variety of styles and genres. He used Baroque contrapuntal forms and was influenced by his native Czech folk melodies, impressionism, jazz, and neo-classicism.*

instrument, the clarinet: quartet for clarinet and strings (1957); concerto for wind quintet (1964); B,A,B,B,I,T,T for clarinet (1966); cello concerto (1972); *Paradiso Choruses*, oratorio after Dante (1974); Triple Concerto for three clarinets and orchestra (1977); string quartet (1983).

Martinon, Jean (b Lyon, 10 Jan 1910; d Paris, 1 Mar 1976), French conductor and composer. Studied violin at the Lyon Conservatory and composition under Roussel at the Paris Conservatory. He began to produce works shortly before World War II, during which he was imprisoned in Germany, where he wrote several works. After the war he appeared with success as a conductor in Europe and America (Chicago SO 1963–69); often heard in Roussel, Bartók and Prokofiev.

Works include opera *Hécube* (libretto by S Moreaux after Euripides, 1949–54); Psalm 136 for solo voices, reciter, chorus and orchestra, *Absolve Domine* for men's chorus and orchestra; four symphonies (1936–65), *Symphoniette*.

Martinpelto, Hillevi (b Alvalden, 9 Jan 1958), Swedish soprano. Studied in Stockholm and made her debut there with the Folksopera as Pamina (also seen at Edinburgh). Royal Opera Stockholm debut 1987, as Butterfly; Gluck's two Iphigenias at Drottningholm, 1989–90. Has sung Fiordiligi in Brussels and Hamburg, Wagner's Eva with the Deutsche Oper Berlin in Tokyo and Freia in *Das Rheingold* at Chicago (1993). Mozart's Elettra (*Idomeneo*) and Countess (*Figaro*) under John Eliot Gardiner (also recorded), and Donna Anna at the 1994 Glyndebourne Festival.

Martinů, Bohuslav (b Policka, 8 Dec 1890; d Liestal, Switzerland, 28 Aug 1959), Czech composer. Studied violin at the Prague Conservatory 1906–13 while playing in the Prague Philharmonic Orchestra. In 1922 he took composition lessons with Suk at Prague Conservatory and from 1923 to 1924 studied with Roussel in Paris, and wrote works influenced by jazz and neo-classicism. Operas with Czech subjects followed during the 1930s, and after arriving in the USA as a refugee

in 1941 he confined himself largely to instrumental music. He remained in America until 1946, when he became professor of composition at Prague Conservatory, returning to USA in 1948, where he taught at Princeton and the Berkshire Music Center. From 1957 he lived in Switzerland. His music is often neo-classical in style, with an emphasis on rhythm and counterpoint.

Works include OPERAS: *The Soldier and the Dancer* (after Plautus, 1928), *Les Larmes du couteau* (1928; produced 1968), *Les Vicissitudes de la vie* (1929; produced 1971), *Journée de bonté*, *The Miracles of Our Lady* (1935), *The Suburban Theatre* (1936), *Alexandre bis*, *Julietta* (1938); *Mirandolina*, *Ariadne* (1961), *The Greek Passion* (1961); radio operas *The Voice of the Forest* (1935), *Comedy on a Bridge*; television opera *The Marriage* (1953); ballets *Istar* (1924), *Who is the Most Powerful in the World?* (1925), *Revolt* (1928), *On tourne*, *La Revue de cuisine*, *Échec au roi*, *The Butterfly that Stamped* (1926), *Špalíček*, *Le Jugement de Paris*.

CHORAL: *Czech Rhapsody*, *Bouquet of Flowers*, *Field Mass* for solo voices, chorus and orchestra; madrigals for six voices, *The Epic of Gilgamesh*, oratorio (1955).

FOR ORCHESTRA: six symphonies (1942–53); sinfonia for two orchestras, symphonic poem *Vanishing Midnight*, tone-poem *The Frescoes of Piero della Francesca* (1955), pieces *Half-time*, *La Bagarre*, *La Rapsodie*, overture for the Sokol Festival, *Memorial to Lidice* (1943), Inventions for grand orchestra, concerto grosso, *Tre Ricercari*, *Les Sérénades* and *Les Rondes* for chamber orchestra, partita for string orchestra; five piano concertos (1934–57) and concertino, concerto for two pianos; violin concerto, two cello concertos, harpsichord concerto and various other works for instruments and orchestra.

CHAMBER: String quartet and piano trio with orchestra; seven string quartets (1918–47), string quintet, wind quintet, piano quartet, two piano quintets (1933, 1944) and other chamber music, three violin and piano sonatas, three cello and piano sonatas; various instrumental pieces; *Film en miniature*, *Trois Danses tchèques*, *Préludes*, *Esquisses de danse*, *Ritournelles*, *Train-Fantôme*, etc. for piano; two preludes for harpsichord.

Martín y Soler, Vicente (b Valencia, 2 May 1754; d St Petersburg, 11 Feb 1806), Spanish composer. Chorister at Valencia, made his debut as an opera composer in Madrid in 1776, then went to Italy, where he probably studied with Padre Martini, and produced operas success-fully in Naples, Turin, Venice, etc. In Vienna, 1785–88, he composed three operas on libretti by da Ponte, the most successful of which, *Una cosa rara* (1786), for a time eclipsed Mozart's *Figaro*; Mozart quotes from it in the supper scene in *Don Giovanni*. Apart from a visit to London, 1794–95, he lived from 1788 in St Petersburg, in the service of the Russian court.

Works include operas *Ifigenia in Aulide* (1779), *Ipermestra*, *Andromaca* (1780), *Astartea*, *Partenope*, *L'amor geloso* (1782), *In amor si vuol destrezza (L'accorta cameriera*, 1782), *Vologeso*, *Le burle per amore* (1784), *La vedova spiritosa*, *Il burbero di buon cuore* (1786), *Una cosa rara, o Bellezza ed onestà* (1786), *L'arbore di Diana* (1787), *Gore Bogatyr Kosometovich* (1789), *Melomania* (Russian), *Fedul and his Children* (Russian; libretti of these three by Catherine II), *Il castello d'Atlante* (1791), *La scuola de' maritati* (1795), *L'isola del piacere* (1795), *Le nozze de contadini spagnuoli*, *La festa del villaggio* (1798); prologue *La Dora festeggiante* for *Vologeso*; several ballets; church music; cantatas *La deità benefica* and *Il sogno*; canzonets; canons.

Martland, Steve (b Liverpool, 1958), English composer. Studied with Louis Andriessen at the Hague and with Gunther Schuller at Tangle-wood (1984). His music eschews classical principles and aspires to 'street cred'. *Babi Yar* for orchestra (1983) had a joint fp with the RLPO and the St Louis SO. Other works include *Lotta continua* for orchestra and jazz band (1981); *Orc* for horn and chamber orchestra (1984); *Crossing the Border* for strings (1991); *Remembering Lennon* for seven players (1981); *American Invention* for 13 players (1985); *Patrol* for string quartet (1991); *Terra Firma* for five voices and video (1989); *The Perfect Act* for amplified ensemble and voice (1991); piano pieces and tape items.

Marton, Eva (b Budapest, 18 Jun 1943), Hungarian soprano. She studied at the Liszt Academy, Budapest, and made her debut in 1968 as The Queen of Shemaka, in *Le Coq d'Or*. She has since sung with Frankfurt Opera, 1972–77, and in Hamburg; also heard in Salzburg, San Francisco, New York and at Bayreuth. Chicago 1980, as Gior-dano's Maddalena. Other roles include Tosca, Desdemona, Donna Anna, Eva, Elsa, Elisabeth de Valois and Korngold's Violanta. CG debut 1987, Turandot. Sang the Dyer's Wife at Salzburg, 1992.

Martucci, Giuseppe (b Capua, 6 Jan 1856; d Naples, 1 Jun 1909), Italian pianist, conductor and composer. Was first taught by his father, a bandmaster, and appeared as pianist in his childhood. He then studied at the Naples Conservatory, 1867–72, and became professor there in 1874. He travelled widely as pianist, founded the Quartetto Napoletano for the cultivation of chamber music and became an orchestral conductor. In 1886 he was appointed director of the Liceo Musicale at Bologna and there produced the first Italian performance of Wagner's *Tristan* in 1888. In 1902 he returned to Naples as director of the Conservatory.

Works include oratorio *Samuele*; two symphonies, *4 piccoli pezzi* for orchestra; piano concertos in D minor, B♭ minor (1878, 1885); piano quintet, two piano trios; cello and piano sonata; various instru-mental pieces; variations and fantasy for two pianos; songs, *Pagine sparse*, *Due sogni* and others.

Beauty in music is too often confused with something that lets the ears lie back in an easy chair.
Charles Ives, quoted in Machlis, *Introduction to Contemporary Music*, 1963

Martyrdom of St Magnus, The chamber opera in nine scenes by Peter Maxwell Davies (libretto by composer, from 'Magnus' by George Mackay Brown), produced Kirkwall, Orkney, 18 Jun 1977. Orkney's patron saint murdered by Hakon, Earl of Orkney.

Martyre de Saint Sébastien, Le, *The Martyrdom of St Sebastian*, incidental music by Debussy for the mystery play, written in French, by G d'Annunzio, composed for solo voices, chorus and orchestra in 1911, fp Paris, Théâtre du Châtelet, 22 May 1911, in five acts.

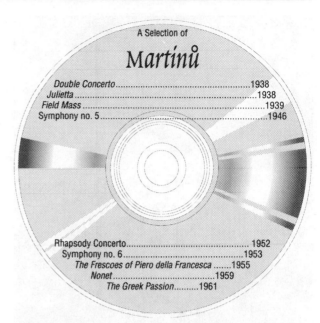

A Selection of

Martinů

Double Concerto 1938
Julietta 1938
Field Mass 1939
Symphony no. 5 1946

Rhapsody Concerto 1952
Symphony no. 6 1953
The Frescoes of Piero della Francesca 1955
Nonet 1959
The Greek Passion.......... 1961

Martyrs, Les opera by Donizetti (libretto by Scribe, based on Cor-neille's *Polyeucte*), produced Paris, Opéra, 10 Apr 1840. ◊Poliuto.

Martzy, Johanna (b Temesvár, 26 Oct 1924; d Glarius, Switzerland, 13 Aug 1979), Hungarian violinist. Studied at Budapest Academy from 1932 to 1942, winning the Reményi Prize at 16, and first prize at the Concours International d'Exécution in Geneva in 1947, in which year she began her true concert career. British debut 1953, US 1957. Well known in Schubert and Bartók.

Maruzin (*Marusin*), Yuri (b Perm, 8 Dec 1947), Russian tenor. Studied in Leningrad and made debut at the Maly Theatre there 1972. Joined the Kirov Opera 1978 and appeared with the company at CG 1987, as Lensky in *Eugene Onegin*. La Scala 1988 in Rimsky-Korsakov's *The Tale of Tsar Saltan*, Vienna Staatsoper as Mussorgsky's Galitsin and San Francisco Opera as Anatol Kuragin in *War and Peace*. Sang Andrei Khovansky at Edinburgh (1991) and Hermann in *The Queen of Spades* at Glyndebourne, 1992.

Marx, Adolph Bernard (b Halle, 28 Nov 1795; d Berlin, 17 May 1866), German musicologist and composer. Studied law, but gave it up for music, to which he devoted himself in Berlin, where in 1824 he founded the *Berliner allgemeine musikalische Zeitung*. In 1830 he became professor of music and in 1850 founded a music school with Kullak and Stern (later Stern Conservatory). He wrote books on the history of music, teaching, on Gluck, Handel, Beethoven, compo-sition, tone-painting, etc.

Works include opera *Jery und Bätely* (Goethe, 1824); melodrama *Die Rache wartet*; oratorios *Johannes der Täufer*, *Moses* (1841), *Nahid und Omar*; instrumental works.

Marx, Joseph (b Graz, 11 May 1882; d Graz, 3 Sept 1964), Austrian composer. Studied in Vienna and in 1922 became director of the Academy of Music there in succession to Ferdinand Löwe. From 1947 he was professor at Graz University

Works include *Autumn Symphony* (1921); *Symphonic Night Music*, *Spring Music* for orchestra; romantic concerto for piano and orchestra; several choral pieces; three string quartets, piano quartet, fantasy for piano trio; violin and piano sonata, cello and piano sonata; *c* 120 songs.

Marx, Karl (b Munich, 12 Nov 1897; d Stuttgart, 8 May 1985), German composer. Studied natural science at first, but met Carl Orff during World War I and later studied music with him. Appointed professor of the Munich Academy in 1924 and conductor of the Bach Society there in 1928. From 1939 to 1945 he taught at Graz Conservatory, becom-ing professor in 1944, and in 1946 he became professor at the

Mascagni *The Italian composer Pietro Mascagni (1863–1945) as depicted in a caricature by Caran d'Ache. Principally an operatic composer, he was a successful exponent of the verismo style, although the early success of* Cavalleria Rusticana *made it difficult for him to progress stylistically beyond that work.*

Hochschule für Musik in Stuttgart. He was much occupied with school music.

Works include passacaglia for orchestra (1932); concertos for piano, violin, two violins, viola and flute; various choral works, some to words by Rilke; divertimento for wind instruments (1934), string quartet and other chamber music; songs, some to words by Rilke.

Märzendorfer, Ernst (b Salzburg, 26 May 1921), Austrian conductor. Studied at the Salzburg Mozarteum and conducted opera in Salzburg from 1940; Graz Opera 1945–51, Deutsche Oper Berlin from 1958, Vienna Staatsoper from 1961 (premiere of Henze's ballet *Tancredi*, 1966). Toured the USA with the Mozarteum Orchestra (1956) and recorded all the Haydn symphonies with the Vienna Chamber Orchestra (1967–71). Premiered his completion of Bruckner's 9th symphony at Graz, 1969.

marziale Italian = 'martial, warlike'.

Masagniello furioso, oder Die neapolitanische Fischer-Empörung, *Masagniello enraged, or The Neapolitan Fisherman's Revolt*, opera by Keiser (libretto by Barthold Feind), produced Hamburg, Theater beim Gänsemarkt, Jun 1706. Masagniello leads his people against unfair taxes, but goes mad and is killed.

Masaniello (Auber.) ◊Muette de Portici.

Mascagni, Pietro (b Livorno, 7 Dec 1863; d Rome, 2 Aug 1945), Italian composer. His father, a baker, wished him to study law, but he managed to take lessons in secret at the Istituto Cherubini. On being discovered, he was adopted by an uncle, and soon reconciled with his father by having two works performed at the Istituto. Later, Count Florestano de Larderel paid for his further musical education at the Milan Conservatory, where Ponchielli was among his masters. But he deserted, not wishing to apply himself to solid study, and joined a travelling opera co. After many wanderings and a marriage that forced him to settle at Cerignola near Foggia to make a precarious

living by teaching, he won the first prize in an operatic competition with *Cavalleria rusticana* in 1889, and after its production in Rome, 17 May 1890, he began to accumulate a great fortune, though his many later operas never repeated its success.

Works include operas *Cavalleria rusticana* (1890), *L'amico Fritz* (1891), *I Rantzau* (both based on Erckmann-Chatrian), *Guglielmo Ratcliff* (after Heine, 1895), *Silvano, Zanetto* (1896), *Iris, Le maschere, Amica* (1905), *Isabeau* (1911), *Parisina* (d'Annunzio), *Lodoletta* (1917), *Il piccolo Marat* (1921), *Pinotta, Nerone* (1935); operetta *Sì*; incidental music for Hall Caine's *The Eternal City*; *Kyrie*, Requiem in memory of King Humbert; cantata for Leopardi centenary (1898), setting of Italian translation of Schiller's *Ode to Joy* for chorus and orchestra, cantata *In Filanda*; symphony in C minor, symphonic poem for a film *Rapsodia satanica* (1917).

What a pity! What a pity! He is a young man, whose feeling for music exceeds his knowledge of it.

Giuseppe Verdi on Pietro Mascagni,
quoted in Monaldi, *Verdi*.

Maschera, Fiorenzo (b ? Brescia, *c* 1540; d Brescia, *c* 1584), Italian composer. Succeeded Merulo as organist at Brescia Cathedral in 1557. Wrote instrumental *canzone*.

mascherata Italian = 'masquerade'; a type of 16th-c. *villanella* to be sung at masked balls or during fancy-dress processions.

Maschere, Le opera by Mascagni (libretto by L Illica), produced Genoa, Milan, Rome, Turin, Venice and Verona, 17 Jan 1901. Rosaura wishes to marry Florindo but her father Pantalone lines up Captain Spaventa for her.

Mascheroni, Edoardo (b Milan, 4 Sept 1859; d Ghirla, 4 Mar 1941), Italian conductor and composer. He began to study music as an adult under Boucheron at Milan. In 1883 he secured an engagement at the Teatro Goldini at Livorno. Not long after he moved to the Teatro Apollo in Rome, and in 1893 he was chosen by Verdi to conduct the production of his *Falstaff* at Milan. Also conducted Puccini, Wagner and Catalani (fp *La Wally*, 1892).

Works include operas *Lorenza* (1901) and *La Perugina* (1909); two Requiems, for solo voices, chorus and orchestra and for voices alone (both on the death of Victor Emmanuel I); chamber music; album of piano pieces.

Maschinist Hopkins opera by Max Brand (libretto by composer), produced Duisburg, 13 Apr 1929. The opera pre-figures several dramatic themes in Berg's *Lulu* and was widely performed in Europe before the rise of the Nazis. First complete post-war performance BBC, London, 9 Feb 1986. Hopkins saves his factory from closure by Bill, who has murdered his wife's first husband. Hopkins blackmails Bill, who seeks to destroy his enemy's shop, but he falls into the machinery and is killed.

masculine cadence a cadence, or full close, the final note or chord of which falls on a strong accented beat of a bar.

Masini, Angelo (b Terra del Sole, near Forlì, 28 Nov 1844; d Forlì 28 Sept 1926), Italian tenor. His early studies were hindered by poverty. He appeared in opera for the first time in 1867, at Modena, as Pollione, and thereafter acquired a wide reputation, particularly in Verdi's operas, as Radames, Don Alvaro and in the Requiem. Also sang in Cairo, Paris and Russia; roles included Faust, Lohengrin and Vasco da Gama.

Masini, Galliano (b Livorno, 1896; d Livorno, 15 Feb 1986), Italian tenor. Debut Livorno 1923, Cavaradossi. He sang in Rome 1930–50 (debut as Pinkerton) and at La Scala was heard as Turiddu and Falla's Paco. In Chicago he sang Edgardo, Rodolfo and Enzo, 1937–38; NY Met. 1939, as Radames. Guest in Vienna and Buenos Aires; retired 1957.

mask ◊masque.

Maskarade opera by Nielsen (libretto by V Andersen after a play by Holberg); composed 1904–06, fp Copenhagen, 11 Nov 1906. Leander meets future wife at masked ball.

Mask of Orpheus, The opera by Birtwistle (libretto by P Zinovieff), composed 1973–84, produced London, Coliseum, 21 May 1986. Main characters in legend seen from three different viewpoints: person, hero, myth.

Mask of Time, The oratorio by Tippett in two parts for soloists, chorus and orchestra; composed 1981–83, fp Boston, 5 Apr 1984, conductor C Davis.

Masnadieri, I, *The Brigands,* opera by Verdi (libretto by A Maffei, based on Schiller's drama *Die Räuber*), produced London, Her Majesty's Theatre, 22 Jul 1847. The only opera commissioned by London from Verdi. Jenny Lind and Lablache appeared in it. Carlo joins band of robbers after betrayal by his brother, Francesco, and disinheritance by his father, Massimiliano. Carlo seeks revenge against Francesco and in the process kills the orphan Amalia.

Mason, Benedict (b Budleigh Salterton, 19 Mar 1954), English composer. Studied with Peter Maxwell Davies, and with Pousseur in Liège. Has won several international prizes, including the Siemens Stiftungpreis, 1992. His *Playing Away* (Munich 1994) was alleged to be the first opera to be based on football. His highly eclectic and allusive music also includes *Lighthouses of England and Wales* for orchestra (1987) and *Concerto for the Viola Section* (1990); *The Hinterstoisser Traverse* for 12 players (1986), *Nodding Trilliums and Curved Line Angles* for four solo percussion and 15 players (1990); *Chaplin Operas* for mezzo, baritone and 22 players (1988), *Seven Self-Referential Songs and Realistic Virelais* for soprano and 16 players (1990); electronic pieces *Six Rilke Songs* (1991), *Animals and the Origins of the Dance* (1992) and *Colour and Information* (1993); *Oil and Petrol Marks on a Wet Road are sometimes held to be spots where a rainbow stood,* for 16 voices (1987); two string quartets (1987, 1993); six Etudes for piano (1988).

Mason, Colin (b Northampton, 26 Jan 1924; d London, 6 Feb 1971), English critic. Studied at the TCM in London, 1944–45, and in Budapest 1947–49, where he learnt Hungarian. He was music critic to the *Manchester Guardian* 1951–59 and later editor of *Tempo.*

Mason, Daniel Gregory (b Brookline, MA, 20 Nov 1873; d Greenwich, CT, 4 Dec 1953), American composer and writer on music, grandson of Lowell Mason and son of a member of the firm of piano makers Mason & Hamlin. Graduated from Harvard and studied music in NY, later with d'Indy in France. He wrote a number of books on music.

Works include three symphonies (1916, 1930, 1937); prelude and fugue for piano and orchestra; chamber music and songs.

Mason, Lowell (b Medfield, MA, 8 Jan 1792; d Orange, NJ, 11 Aug 1872), American hymnologist, grandfather of Daniel ◊Mason. Self-taught in music and a bank clerk at Savannah from 1812. He practised any instrument he could lay hands on and with F L Abel adapted Gardiner's *Sacred Melodies,* mainly themes from the classics, to the psalms, with the result that in 1827 he was called to Boston to supervise church music there. A more important service was his introduction of music teaching into schools.

masque a stage entertainment cultivated in England in the 17th c. and laying great stress on spectacular presentation, but also including songs and dances. It closely resembled the French *ballet de cour,* except that it retained spoken dialogue, which was replaced by recitative in France. The subjects, mainly based on Italian models, were mythological, heroic or allegorical.

Masques et bergamasques music by Fauré, op. 112, for an entertainment by René Fauchois produced Monte Carlo, 10 Apr 1919; Paris, Opéra-Comique, 4 Mar 1920, with a Watteau setting. It included an overture and three dances, newly composed, as well as the Pavane, op. 50, of 1887 and an orchestral version of the Verlaine song *Clair de Lune,* op. 46 no. 2, of the same year, in which the words 'masques et bergamasques' occur.

Mass the chief ritual of the Roman Catholic church service, i.e. the celebration of the Eucharist. Only High Mass is concerned with music, Low Mass being spoken, not sung. The Mass is still sung to plainsong melodies, but from the 14th c. onwards it has also been treated as a form of musical composition, as a rule primarily for the purpose of religious service, but sometimes more elaborately for

concert use. Masses originally written, especially in the 18th and 19th c., for church use with orchestral accompaniment, can now generally be performed only in the concert hall, Pius X's *Motu proprio* of 1903 having forbidden orchestras in church.

The Ordinary of the Mass falls into five main sections: Kyrie, Gloria, Credo, Sanctus with Hosanna and Benedictus, and Agnus Dei with Dona nobis pacem; these remain invariable throughout the year and are usually all that is set to music by composers. The Proper of the Mass consists of additional matter (Introit, Gradual, Alleluia or Tract, Offertory and Communion), and these are less commonly found as parts of a Mass composition. The medieval practice of writing the movements of a Mass on plainsong melodies, sung by the tenor, was soon extended to the employment of secular tunes. *L'Homme armé* on the Continent and *The Western Wind* in England, for example, were especially favoured for this purpose. In the course of the 16th c., however, more and more composers wrote wholly original Masses, though the practice of borrowing material from motets or *chansons* was also common. Even in later times the treatment of the Mass remained essentially polyphonic, though not necessarily throughout. Certain portions, e.g. 'Et vitam venturi saeculi' at the end of the Credo, were almost invariably set as fugues. ◊Requiem.

Massaini, Tiburtio (b Cremona, before 1550; d probably Lodi or Piacenza, after 1609), Italian composer. He served as *maestro di cappella* in Salò, Prague, Salzburg, Cremona (from 1595), Piacenza and Lodi successively. Composed church music and eight books of madrigals, nine of motets, four of Masses and two of psalms.

Massart, Joseph (Lambert) (b Liège, 19 Jul 1811; d Paris, 13 Feb 1892), Belgian violinist and teacher. Studied under Auguste Kreutzer (1778–1832) in Paris and in 1843 became violin professor at the Conservatory there.

Massé, Victor (actually Félix Marie) (b Lorient, 7 Mar 1822; d Paris, 5 Jul 1884), French composer. Studied at the Paris Conservatory, where Halévy was his composition master, and gained the Prix de Rome in 1844. He travelled in Italy and Germany after his stay in Rome; in 1860 became chorus-master at the Paris Opéra and in 1866 professor of composition at the Conservatory.

Works include operas and operettas *La Chambre gothique* (1849), *La Chanteuse violée* (1850), *Galathée* (1852), *Les Noces de Jeannette* (1853), *La Reine Topaze* (1856), *Le Cousin de Marivaux* (1857), *La Fiancée du Diable, Miss Fauvette, Les Saisons, La Fée Carabosse, Mariette la promise* (1862), *La Mule de Pedro* (1863), *Fior d'Aliza* (after Lamartine, 1866), *Le Fils du brigadier* (1867), *Paul et Virginie* (after Saint-Pierre), *La favorita e la schiava, Les Chaises à porteurs, Le Prix de famille, Une Loi somptuaire, Les Enfants de Perrette, La Petite Sœur d'Achille, La Trouvaille* (composed 1873), *Une Nuit de Cléopâtre* (1885); *Messe solennelle*; cantata *Le Rénégat*; songs.

Massenet, Jules (Émile Frédéric) (b Montaud, near Saint-Étienne, 12 May 1842; d Paris, 13 Aug 1912), French composer. Entered the Paris Conservatory at the age of 11, studying composition with A Thomas and gaining the Prix de Rome in 1863. On his return from Rome in 1866 he married a piano pupil and his his first opera, *La Grand'tante,* produced at the Opéra-Comique the next year. He achieved his first major success with the opera *Le Roi de Lahore* (1877), indulging a current taste for the exotic and oriental. Similar success came with *Hérodiade* (Brussels, 1881) but lasting fame came with *Manon* (Paris, 1884), in which Massenet indulged to the full the life-long sympathy he felt for his central female characters. In *Werther* (Vienna, 1892) the lyrical impulse is balanced with a strong dramatic flair. Later operas such as *Cendrillon, Grisélidis, Chérubin* and *Don Quichotte* have found recognition as a result of recent revivals. Professor of composition at the Conservatory, 1878–96.

Works include operas *Don César de Bazan* (1872), *Le Roi de Lahore* (1877), *Hérodiade* (1881), *Manon* (after Prévost, 1884), *Le Cid* (after Corneille, 1885), *Esclarmonde* (1889), *Le Mage, Werther* (after Goethe, 1892), *Le Portrait de Manon, La Navarraise* (1894), *Sapho* (after Daudet), *Cendrillon* (1899), *Grisélidis* (1901), *Le Jongleur de Notre-Dame* (1902), *Thaïs* (1894), (both after A France), *Chérubin* (1905), *Ariane* (1906), *Thérèse* (1907), *Bacchus, Don*

A Selection of

Massenet

Le Roi de Lahore	1877
Manon	1884
Le Cid	1885
Esclarmonde	1888
Werther	1892
Thaïs	1894
Cendrillon	1899
Chérubin	1905
Don Quichotte	1910
Cléopâtre	1911–12

Quichotte (after Cervantes, 1910), *Roma*, *Panurge* (after Rabelais), *Cléopâtre* (1914), *Amadis* (composed 1895; produced 1922); ballets *Le Carillon*, *La Cigale*, *Espada*; incidental music to Leconte de Lisle's *Les Erynnies*, Racine's *Phèdre* and other plays.

Oratorios *Marie-Magdeleine* (1873), *Ève* (1875), *La Vierge*, *La Terre promise* (1900); cantatas *David Rizzio*, *Narcisse*, *Biblis*. 13 orchestral works including *Scènes pittoresques* (1874), *Scènes napolitaines* (1876), and three other similar suites, symphonic poem *Visions*; piano concerto, fantasy for cello and orchestra; *c* 200 songs; duets; choruses.

Massenet feels it as a Frenchman, with powder and minuets: I shall feel it as an Italian, with desperate passion.

Giacomo Puccini on Jules Màssenet's *Manon*, quoted in Carner, *Puccini*, 1974

---

mässig German = 'moderate'.

Massimilla Doni opera by Schoeck (libretto by A Rüeger, based on Balzac's novel), produced Dresden, 2 Mar 1937. Massimilla falls for Emilio in Venetian fable, set at La Fenice opera house. Sub-plot balances the artistic virtues of technique versus passion.

Mass in B minor (Bach.) ◊B minor Mass.

Mass of Life, A setting of words from Nietzsche's *Also sprach Zarathustra* for solo voices, chorus and orchestra by Delius, composed 1904–05, produced (second part only in German) Munich Music Festival, 1908; first complete performance (in English), London, 7 June 1909, conductor Beecham.

Massol, Jean-Etienne August (b Lodève, 23 Aug 1802; d Paris, 30 Oct 1887), French baritone. Debut Paris, Opéra, 1825, in *La Vestale*. He sang as a tenor in the fps of *Guillaume Tell*, Cherubini's *Ali Baba* and *Les Huguenots*; 1840 as baritone in the fp of Donizetti's *Les Martyrs*, 1843 in *Dom Sébastien*. He sang in London 1846–51 in operas by Auber, Meyerbeer and Donizetti (*La favorite*); returned to Paris until 1858.

Masson, Diego (b Tossa, Spain, 21 Jun 1935), French conductor. Studied at the Paris Conservatory with Leibowitz, Maderna and Boulez; worked with Domaine Musical and founded ensemble *Musique Vivante* 1966; early performances of works by Stockhausen, Boulez (*Domaines*), Globokar and Berio. He has directed opera and ballet at Marseille and Angers from 1968. ENO debut 1980, with

La Damnation de Faust. Conducted the fps of Harper's *Hedda Gabler* (1985) and Robert Saxton's *Caritas* (1991).

Master Peter's Puppet Show (Falla.) ◊Retablo de Maese Pedro.

Master-Singers ◊Meistersinger.

Mastersingers of Nuremberg, The (Wagner.) ◊Meistersinger von Nürnberg.

Masterson, Valerie (b Birkenhead, 3 Jun 1937), English soprano. She sang with D'Oyly Carte 1966–70. London, Coliseum, from 1971 as Constanze, Adèle, Oscar, Manon and Sophie; CG from 1974. At the Aix Festival she has sung Rossini's Elisabetta, Fiordiligi and Mozart's Countess. US debut San Francisco, 1980, as Violetta. Her Handel roles have included Morgana (*Alcina*), Cleopatra, Semele (CG 1982) and Romilda in *Xerxes* (ENO 1985). Sang the Marschallin at Liège, 1993.

Mastilovič, Danica (b Negotin, 7 Nov 1933), Yugoslav soprano, later mezzo. She sang in Belgrade 1955–59; Frankfurt from 1959, debut as Tosca. At Hamburg she was heard as Turandot (1964) and during the 1970s sang in Europe and North America as Abigaille, Kundry, Brünnhilde and the Dyer's Wife. CG and NY Met. debuts as Elektra (1973, 1975). Zurich 1973, as Ortrud. Sang Clytemnestra at the Salzburg Landestheater, 1987.

Masur, Kurt (b Brieg, Silesia, 18 Jul 1927), German conductor. He studied in Breslau and Leipzig. After minor engagements at Erfurt and Leipzig conducted Dresden PO 1955–58 (returned 1964–67). Music director, Komische Oper, Berlin, 1960–64; Leipzig Gewandhaus Orchestra from 1970. London debut 1973, with the New Philharmonia. Widely admired in interpretations of Bruckner and Beethoven. US debut 1974, Cleveland Orchestra; principal conductor of the NY PO from 1990. Conducted the Gewandhaus Orchestra at the 1993 London Proms.

Mata, Eduardo (b Mexico City, 5 Sept 1942; d Cuernavaca, Mexico, 4 Jan 1995), Mexican conductor and composer. Studied with Rodolfo Halffter (1954–60) and Carlos Chavez (1960–65); conducting with Erich Leinsdorf and Gunther Schuller. Conducted the Guadalajara SO 1964–66, the PO of the National University of Mexico, 1966–76. Principal conductor of the Phoenix SO 1972–78, Dallas SO 1977–93. Guest conductor in London, elsewhere in Europe and the USA. Compositions include three symphonies (1962, 1963, 1967). Has recorded the complete works for orchestra of Revueltas, with the Philharmonia, and music by Falla with the LSO. He died while piloting his light aircraft.

Matačič, Lovro von (b Sušak, 14 Feb 1899; d Zagreb, 4 Jan 1985), Yugoslav conductor, producer and composer. As a boy he sang with the Wiener Sängerknaben (Vienna Boys' Choir), later studying organ and piano with Dietrich, theory with Walker and composition and conducting with Herbst and O Nebdal, making his debut as conductor in Cologne in 1919. After appointments in Ljubljana and Zagreb he became director of the Belgrade Opera in 1938. From 1956 to 1958 he was music director of the Dresden Opera and in 1961 succeeded Solti at Frankfurt; worked there until 1966. Monte Carlo from 1974. He also wrote a quantity of orchestral and incidental music.

Materna, Amalie (b St Georgen, Styria, 10 Jul 1844; d Vienna, 18 Jan 1918), Austrian soprano. First appeared on the stage at Graz in 1865, then married the German actor Karl Friedrich, with whom she was engaged at one of the minor theatres in Vienna. In 1869 she first sang at the Imperial Opera as Selika; remained until 1894 as Amneris, Elisabeth and Goldmark's Queen of Sheba. She was Wagner's first Brünnhilde and Kundry at Bayreuth in 1876 and 1882. NY Met, 1885, as Rachel, Valentine and Brünnhilde.

Matheus de Sancto Johanne (Mayhuet de Joan) French 14th–15th-c. composer. He served in the chapel of the antipopes at Avignon, 1382–86, and is almost certainly the 'Mayshuet' of the Old Hall MS. Wrote *chansons* and motets.

Mathias, William (b Whitland, Carmarthenshire, 1 Nov 1934; d Menai Bridge, Anglesey, 29 Jun 1992), Welsh composer and pianist. He studied at the RAM with Lennox Berkeley and Peter Katin. Lecturer, University College North Wales, 1959–68; professor from 1970.

Works include opera *The Servants* (1980); *Divertimento* for strings

Colin Matthews – composer

1 Schoenberg: *Gurrelieder*
I've loved this music for as long as I can remember: its depth of feeling was something that Schoenberg never recaptured. Hearing it for the first time turned me into a composer.

2 Mahler: Symphony no. 6 in A minor
Such a powerful work that, for many years now, I have felt that I couldn't listen to it in safety, although it remains as firmly locked in my memory as ever.

3 Berg: *Altenberglieder*
I can't conceive how Berg arrived at this mastery and subtlety almost out of the blue.

4 Skriabin: Sonata no. 6
A work of fierce concentration and endlessly rewarding harmonic complexity. Skriabin is a greatly underrated and misunderstood composer.

5 Stravinsky: *The Rite of Spring*
The cornerstone of the 20th century. Where would we be without it?

6 Ravel: *Daphnis et Chloé*
If I've learned anything about how to write for the orchestra it's from this masterwork of colour and luxury. Ravel's refinement and attention to every detail are phenomenal.

7 Strauss: *Four Last Songs*
I keep returning to the works of Strauss's Indian summer; they seem to me both perfect and timeless.

(1958), Concerto for Orchestra (1966), three symphonies (1966, 1983, 1991), *Dance Variations* for orchestra (1977); concertos for piano (1955, 1961, 1968), harp (1970), clarinet (1975), horn (1982); *In Arcadia* for orchestra (1992); *This Worldes Joie* for soloists, chorus and orchestra (1974); *Lux Eterna* for soloists, chorus, organ and orchestra (1982), *Let us now praise famous men* for chorus and orchestra (1984); two violin sonatas, wind quintet, two piano sonatas (1964, 1979), two string quartets (1968, 1982).

Mathis, Edith (b Lucerne, 11 Feb 1938), Swiss soprano. After her Lucerne debut (1959) she sang at Cologne until 1963; Berlin, Deutsche Oper from 1963. From 1960 she has been heard at Salzburg as Nannetta and Sophie. Glyndebourne 1962–63, as Cherubino. NY Met. and CG debuts 1970, as Pamina and Susanna. She took part in the fp of Henze's *Der junge Lord* (Berlin 1965). Debut at Bern as the Marschallin at Bern, 1990.

Mathis der Maler, *Matthew the Painter*, opera by Hindemith (libretto by composer), produced Zurich, 28 May 1938. The painter is Matthias Grünewald (15th–16th c.). Symphony in three movements performed Berlin, 12 Mar 1934, conductor Furtwängler: *Engelkonzert* (*Concert of Angels*), *Grablegung* (*Entombment*), *Versuchung des heiligen Antonius* (*The Temptation of St Anthony*). Grunewald at first sides with the peasants against the Church authorities, but retreats into his art after witnessing the cruel reality of life.

Matilde di Shabran, ossia Bellezza e cuor di ferro, . . ., *or Beauty and Heart of Iron*, opera by Rossini (libretto by J Ferretti), produced Rome, Teatro Apollo, 24 Feb 1821. Corradino orders poet Isidoro to murder Matilde for supposedly allowing his enemy Edoardo to escape from the dungeon. When Matilde's innocence is proved, Corradino resolves to commit suicide, but is prevented by Edoardo and his father Raimondo.

Matin, Le, Le Midi, Le Soir et la Tempête, *Morning, Noon, Evening and Storm*, the original titles of Haydn's symphonies Nos. 6 in D major, 7 in C major and 8 in G major, composed 1761.

Matrimonio segreto, Il, *The Clandestine Marriage*, opera by Cimarosa (libretto by G Bertati, based on G Colman and D Garrick's play of that name), produced Vienna, Burgtheater, 7 Feb 1792. Geronimo wants to marry his daughter Elisetta to Count Robinson, but the Count prefers her sister, Caroline, who is already secretly married to Paolino. The marriage is revealed and the Count settles for Elisetta.

Mattei, Filippo, called Pippo, the supposed composer of the first act of the opera *Muzio Scevola* (often attributed to Ariosti), the others being by Bononcini and Handel, is probably no other than Filippo Amadei.

Mattei, Stanislao (b Bologna, 10 Feb 1750; d Bologna, 12 May 1825), Italian priest, theorist and composer. Pupil of Padre Martini, whom he succeeded as *maestro di cappella* at the church of San Francesco in Bologna, and later at San Petronio. From 1804 professor at the newly founded Liceo Filarmonico, his pupils included Rossini and Donizetti. He wrote a treatise on playing from figured bass.

Works include eight Masses and other church music; a Passion; intermezzo *La bottega del libraio*, etc.

Matteis, Nicola (b Naples; d London, *c* 1710), Italian violinist. Went to England about 1672; pub. three collections of violin music, one of songs and a treatise, *The False Consonances of Musick*.

Matthay, Tobias (b London, 19 Feb 1858; d Haslemere, Surrey, 15 Dec 1945), English pianist, teacher and composer. Studied at the RAM in London, where he became sub-professor in 1876 and full professor of piano in 1880, remaining until 1925, although he had opened his own school of piano playing in 1900. He wrote several books on his own method of piano playing and composed much piano music, mainly of educational value.

Mattheson, Johann (b Hamburg, 28 Sept 1681; d Hamburg, 17 Apr 1764), German writer on music, organist and composer. From the age of nine sang at the Hamburg Opera, and there produced his first opera in 1699. Became friendly with Handel in 1703 and went with him to Lübeck as a candidate to succeed Buxtehude; but both declined on learning that marriage to Buxtehude's daughter was a condition of the post. After some years as tutor, then secretary to the English Legation, he was appointed minor canon and music director at Hamburg Cathedral in 1715, but had to resign in 1728 because of deafness. Among his many writings on music the most important are *Der vollkommene Capellmeister* (1739), *Grundlage einer Ehrenpforte* (1740) and a treatise on thorough-bass.

Works include operas *Die Pleiades* (1699); *Die unglückselige Cleopatra* (1704), *Henrico IV*, *Boris Goudenow* (1710) and *Nero* (1723); 24 oratorios and cantatas; trio sonatas; etc.; keyboard music.

Matthews, Colin (b London, 13 Feb 1946), English composer. He studied at Nottingham University and taught at Sussex University 1972–77. Worked with Deryck Cooke on the performing version of Mahler's tenth symphony and was assistant to Britten 1974–76; edited and issued several early 'bottom drawer' pieces by Britten.

Works include two *Sonatas* for orchestra (1975, 1980), cello concerto (1984), *Night's Mask* for soprano and chamber orchestra (1984); *Ceres* for nine players (1972), *Rainbow Studies* for piano and four wind (1978), three string quartets (1979, 1982, 1993), oboe quartet (1981); *Five Sonnets: to Orpheus* (texts by Rilke) for tenor and harp (1976), *Shadows in the Water* for tenor and piano (1978); *A Rose at Christmas* for unaccompanied voices (1992).

Matthews, David (b London, 9 Mar 1943), English composer, brother of Colin ⃥Matthews, with whom he collaborated, with Deryck Cooke, on performing version of Mahler's tenth symphony. Graduated in Classics from Nottingham University. Worked as an assistant to Britten 1966–69. Pub. biography of Tippett 1980.

David Matthews – composer

1   Tallis: *Spem in alium*
    Tallis's 40-part motet is simply the most beautiful sound in music.

2   Monteverdi: *Vespers* (1610)
    I love the way the choral music dances, and the ending of the Magnificat is the most joyful music I know.

3   Bach: *Nun ist der Heil* (Cantata no. 50)
    Bach's D major choruses are, I find, guaranteed to cure any depression. This cantata fragment, an amazing display of contrapuntal virtuosity, is especially exhilarating.

4   Beethoven: String Quartet in C sharp minor
    Beethoven's greatest single work, the most comprehensive music ever written.

5   Wagner: *Tristan und Isolde* (Flagstad/Suthaus/Philharmonia/ Furtwängler)
    I became addicted to Wagner in my teens and there is no cure. Flagstad's Isolde is incomparable.

6   Bruckner: Symphony no. 8 (Vienna PO/Furtwängler)
    No one else has matched Furtwängler's understanding of

Bruckner's noblest work, the finest symphony since Beethoven.

7   Mahler: Symphony no. 3
    Hearing a broadcast of this symphony in 1960 (by the Philharmonia Orchestra under Berthold Goldschmidt) converted me to Mahler, who became the most important composer for me as I was learning to compose. The Third remains my favourite Mahler symphony.

8   Sibelius: *Tapiola* (Boston SO/Davis)
    The most mysterious and at times the most hair-raising music ever written. Colin Davis gets right to the heart of it.

9   Stravinsky: *Symphony in Three Movements*
    The opening of the first movement rivals Beethoven in its display of physical energy. It remains for me the most exciting of all Stravinsky's works.

10 Tippett: String Quartet no. 3
    This and the Second Symphony are my favourite Tippett pieces. I particularly admire the fugues in the Third quartet, the only 20th-century ones I know that really work.

Works include four symphonies (1975, 1979, 1985, 1990); three songs for soprano and orchestra (1971); six string quartets (1970–90); *Songs and Dances of Mourning* for cello (1976); *September Music* for small orchestra (1979); *Serenade* for chamber orchestra (1982); violin concerto (1982); clarinet quartet (1984); *In The Dark Time* for orchestra (1985); Variations for Strings (1986); *Chaconne* for orchestra (1987); *Cantiga* for soprano and ensemble (1988); *The Music of Dawn* for orchestra (1990); oboe concerto (1992); *A Vision and a Journey* for orchestra (1993).

Matthews, Denis (b Coventry, 27 Feb 1919; d Birmingham, 24 Dec 1988), English pianist and writer on music. Studied with H Craxton and W Alwyn at the RAM, making his debut in 1939. He travelled widely and was especially noted for his playing of Mozart. Professor of Music, Newcastle upon Tyne, 1971–84. Pub. *Beethoven* in Master Musicians series, 1985. CBE 1975.

Matthisson, Friedrich von (1761–1831), German poet. Remembered chiefly by Beethoven's setting of his 'Adelaide'; Schubert set 26 of his poems. C ◊Schröter (songs).

Matthus, Siegfried (b Mallenuppen, 13 Apr 1934), German composer. Studied in East Berlin during the 1950s, with Wagner-Régeny and Hanns Eisler. Composer-in-residence at the Komische Oper Berlin, from 1964. His music is in a conservative idiom and includes the operas *Der letzte Schuss* (1967), *Noch ein Löffel Gift, Liebling?* (1972), *Omphale* (1976), *Judith* (1984), *Die Weise von Liebe des Cornets Christoph Rilke* (1984), *Graf Mirabeau* (1988) and *Desdemona und ihrer Schwestern* (1992). Other music includes three symphonies (1969, 1976, 1993), concerto for orchestra (1963), concertos for violin (1968), piano (1970), cello (1975), flute (1978), oboe (1985) and triangle (1985); Vocal Symphony for soprano, baritone, two choruses and orchestra (1967), *Holofernes Portrait* for baritone and orchestra (1981), *Wem ich zu gefallen suche* for tenor, baritone and piano (1987); two octets (1970, 1989), string quartet (1972).

Mattila, Karita (b Somero, 5 Sept 1960), Finnish soprano. Studied in Helsinki and won 1983 Cardiff Singer of the World Competition. Opera debut as Donna Anna at Savonlinna, 1981; Finnish National Opera debut 1983, as Mozart's Countess. US debut Washington DC 1983, as Donna Elvira; CG debut 1986 as Fiordiligi, returning as Pamina and Agathe. NY Met. from 1990, as Elvira and Eva. Other

roles include Mozart's Ilia (San Francisco, 1989) and Verdi's Amelia Boccanegra (Geneva 1991). Many concert appearances.

Matzenauer, Margarete (b Temesvar, 1 Jun 1881; d Van Nuys, CA, 19 May 1963), Hungarian mezzo and soprano. She made her debut in Strasbourg and sang in Munich 1904–11. NY Met. 1911–30, debut as Amneris. A versatile artist, she also sang Azucena, Eboli, Aida, Kundry and Brünnhilde, and was the first US Kostelnička, in *Jenůfa* (Met. 1924). Carnegie Hall 1938.

Mauceri, John (b New York, 12 Sept 1945), American conductor. Studied at Yale and Tanglewood. Gave European premiere of Bernstein's Mass (Vienna 1973) and made UK opera debut with *Don Carlos* for WNO (1974). NY Met. debut 1976, *Fidelio*; ENO and Royal Opera (at Manchester) debuts 1983, with *La forza del destino* and *Butterfly*. NY City Opera 1977–82, American SO 1984–87. Music director of Scottish Opera 1987–93, including final version of Bernstein's *Candide* (1988), the UK fp of Weill's *Street Scene* (1989) and his own revision of Blitzstein's *Regina* (1991). Also led *Les Troyens* in Glasgow and at CG. Recordings include *Candide*, *On Your Toes* and *My Fair Lady*.

Mauduit, Jacques (b Paris, 16 Sept 1557; d Paris, 21 Aug 1627), French lutenist and composer. He was, like his father before him, registrar to the courts of justice in Paris, but became famous as a musician. In 1581 he gained the first prize at the annual Puy de Musique at Évreux, and he was associated with Baïf in his experiments with *musique mesurée*, though after Baïf's death in 1590 he relaxed the rigid subordination of music to verbal rhythm in his settings of verse. In 1588 he saved the MSS of the Huguenot Le Jeune from destruction by Catholic soldiers, though he was himself a Catholic.

Works include Requiem on the death of Ronsard (1585), motets, chansons, *Chansonnettes mesurées* for four voices, etc.

Maugars, André (b *c* 1580; d *c* 1645), French violist, politician and translator. He lived in England for four years *c* 1620, on his return entered the service of Cardinal Richelieu, became interpreter of English to Louis XIII and translated Bacon's *Advancement of Learning*. In 1639 he visited Rome and wrote a pamphlet on Italian music. He wrote viol music (lost).

Maunder, John Henry (b London, 21 Feb 1858; d Brighton, 25 Jan 1920), English composer and organist. He studied at the RAM and later played the organ in various London churches. He first wrote operettas, including *The Superior Sex*, and *Daisy Dingle* (1885) but then turned to sacred music. His oratorio *The Martyrs* was performed in Oxford in 1894 and his church cantata *From Olivet to Calvary* (1904) was popular for many years.

Maurel, Victor (b Marseille, 17 Jun 1848; d New York, 22 Oct 1923), French baritone. Went to the school of music at Marseille, after studying architecture, and later to the Paris Conservatory. Made his first appearances in 1868, at the Paris Opéra, as Luna, Nelusko and Alfonso XI, in *La Favorite*, but was later devoted more to Italian opera. He was the first Iago in Verdi's *Otello* and the first Falstaff; he also sang Boccanegra in the fp of the revised version (1881). London, CG, 1873–1904 as Telramund, Wolfram and the Dutchman. NY Met. debut 1894, as Iago.

Má Vlast, *My Country*, cycle of six symphonic poems by Smetana, composed 1874–79 and containing programme works on various aspects of Czech history and geography: 1. *Vyšehrad/The citadel of Prague)*; 2. *Vltava/The river*; 3. *Šarka/The Czech Amazon*; 4. *From Bohemia's Woods and Fields*; 5. *Tabor/The city*; 6.*Blaník/The mountain*.

Mavra opera in one act by Stravinsky (libretto in Russian, by B Koshno, based on Pushkin's *The Little House at Kolomna*), produced in French translation by J Larmanjat, Paris, Opéra, 3 Jun 1922. 'Mavra' is Parasha's lover Vasilly, a hussar disguised as a cook in her mother's house. However, Mavra is discovered shaving, and her true identity is revealed.

Maw, Nicholas (b Grantham, 5 Nov 1935), English composer. Studied with L Berkeley at the RAM 1955–58 and with Nadia Boulanger in Paris 1958–59. Has taught at Cambridge (1966–70) and Yale. Music is largely traditional in character.

Works include Requiem for soprano and contralto soloists, women's chorus, string trio and string orchestra; comic operas *One Man Show* (1964) and *The Rising of the Moon* (1970); *Nocturne* for mezzo-soprano and orchestra (1958); *Scenes and Arias* for solo voices and orchestra (1962); Sonata for strings and two horns (1967); *La Vita Nuova* for soprano and chamber ensemble (1979); *Morning Music* for orchestra (1982); *Spring Music* for orchestra (1983); *Sonata Notturno* for cello and strings (1985); *Odyssey* for orchestra (1972–85); *The World in the Evening* for orchestra (1988), *Little concert* for oboe, two horns and strings (1988), *Shahnama* for orchestra (1992); *Life Studies* for 15 solo strings (1973–76); Chamber Music for flute, clarinet, horn, bassoon and piano (1962); two string quartets (1965, 1982); *Music of Memory* for guitar (1989).

Maximilien opera by Milhaud (libretto by A Lunel, translated from a German libretto by R S Hoffmann, based on Franz Werfel's play, *Juarez und Maximilian*), produced Paris, Opéra, 4 Jan 1932. Misfortunes of Habsburg monarch in Mexican war.

Maxwell, Donald (b Perth, 12 Dec 1948), Scottish baritone. Made debut with Scottish Opera in Musgrave's *Mary, Queen of Scots* (1977), and has sung with the company as Rossini's Figaro, Zurga and Janáček's Forester. WNO as Iago, Renato, Rigoletto and Don Carlo in *Ernani*. CG debut in Sallinen's *The King Goes Forth to France* (1987), returning as Gunther (1990). Falstaff on tour with WNO to Paris, Tokyo and Milan. Sang the Dutchman and Scarpia with Opera North (1989) and Wozzeck for ENO (1990). He is a versatile singing actor.

Maxwell Davies, Peter, Peter Maxwell ◊Davies.

Mayer, Robert (b Mannheim, 5 Jun 1879; d London, 9 Jan 1985), German-English patron of music, a businessman resident in London from 1896. His importance in British musical life was as the founder of the RM Concerts for children and Youth and Music, and other ways of encouraging youthful love of music. Knighted 1939.

Maynard, John (b St Julians, nr St Albans, bap. 5 Jan 1577; d after 1614), English lutenist and composer. He was connected with the school of St Julian in Herts., and at some time in the service of Lady Joan Thynne at Cause Castle in Shropshire.

Works include pavans and galliards for the lute; an organ piece; lessons for lute and bass viol and for lyra-viol; 12 songs *The XII*

Mauceri *The conductor John Mauceri. Principally an operatic conductor, Mauceri began his career with the Yale Symphony while he studied at the University. He is a passionate director, well-suited to the operas of Verdi and Puccini.*

Wonders of the World, describing various characters, for voice, lute and viola da gamba.

May Night, *Maïskaya Notch*, opera by Rimsky-Korsakov (libretto by composer), based on a story by Gogol), produced St Petersburg, 21 Jan 1880. Levko's wedding to Hanna made possible by help from water sprites.

Mayone, Ascanio (b Naples, *c* 1565; d Naples, 9 Mar 1627), Italian composer Pupil of Jean de Macque in Naples; was organist at Saints Annunziata from 1593, *maestro di cappella* from 1621.

Works include madrigals, and solo and chamber instrumental music. His two vols. of keyboard music, *Capricci per sonar* (1603, 1609) contain canzonas and toccatas in an advanced idiom.

Mayr, Johann Simon (b Mendorf, Bavaria, 14 Jun 1763; d Bergamo, 2 Dec 1845), German-Italian composer. Educated at the Jesuit Seminary at Ingolstadt, he later studied with Lenzi in Bergamo and Bertoni in Venice where he settled, at first writing oratorios and church music until 1794, when on the success of his opera *Saffo* he turned to the stage. From 1802 to his death he was *maestro di cappella* at Santa Maria Maggiore, and from 1805 taught at the newly founded Institute of Music there, Donizetti being among his pupils. His opera *L'amor coniugale* is on the same subject and premiered in the same year as Beethoven's *Fidelio*.

Works include over 60 operas, e.g. *Lodoiska* (1796), *Che originali* (1798), *Adelaide di Guesclino* (1799), *Il carretto del venditore d'aceto* (1800), *Ginevra di Scozia* (1801), *I misteri eleusini* (1802), *Alonso e Cora, Elisa* (1801), *L'amor coniugale* (1805), *Adelasia e Aleramo, La rosa rossa e la rosa bianca, Medea in Corinto* (1813); oratorios *Jacob a Labano fugiens, Sisara, Tobiae matrimonium, Davide* (1795), *Il sacrifizio di Jefte* and others; Passion; Masses, motets and other church music.

Mayr, Richard (b Henndorf, near Salzburg, 18 Nov 1877; d Vienna, 1 Dec 1935), Austrian bass-baritone. Studied medicine at Vienna University, but left it for the Conservatory and made his debut at Bayreuth in 1902, as Hagen; sang there until 1924 as Pogner and Gurnemanz. Vienna 1902–35 as Wotan, Sarastro, Figaro and Barak in the fp of *Die Frau ohne Schatten* (1919). London, CG, 1924–31; debut as Ochs, NY Met. 1927–30. Salzburg, 1921–34. In 1910 he sang in the fp of Mahler's eighth symphony (Munich).

Mayrhofer, Johann (1787–1836), Austrian poet. ◊Freunde von Salamanka (Schubert).

47 of his poems were set by Schubert.

Mayseder, Joseph (b Vienna, 26 Oct 1789; d Vienna, 21 Nov 1863), Austrian violinist and composer. First appeared in Vienna, 1800, and later held several important appointments, including that of chamber musician to the emperor.

Works include Mass; three violin concertos; eight string quartets; five string quintets; piano trios and other chamber music, violin duets; piano pieces and studies for violin.

Mazas, Jacques (Féréol) (b Béziers, 23 Sept 1782; d Bordeaux, 26 Aug 1849), French violinist and composer. Studied under Baillot at the Paris Conservatory, appeared with a violin concerto written for him by Auber, travelled widely, lived in Paris 1829–37 and was director of the music school at Cambrai, 1837–41.

Works include opera *Le Kiosque* (1842); two violin concertos; string quartets; violin duets; many violin pieces.

A great fondness for music is a mark of great weakness, great vacuity of mind; not of vice, not of downright folly; but of a want of capacity, or inclination, for sober thought.
William Cobbett, *Advice to Young Men*, 1829

Mazeppa opera by Tchaikovsky (libretto by composer and V P Burenin, based on Pushkin's *Poltava*), produced Moscow, Bolshoi Theatre, 15 Feb 1884. Mazeppa demands Judge Kochubey's daughter Maria as a wife. Kochubey denounces Mazeppa as a separatist but the Tsar does not believe him. Mazeppa has Kochubey executed and Maria goes insane.

Symphonic poem by Liszt, composed in 1854 on Victor Hugo's poem and on the basis of one of the *Grandes Études pour le piano* of *c* 1838 and their new version, the *Études d'exécution transcendante* of 1851, fp Weimar, 16 Apr 1854.

Mazura, Franz (b Salzburg, 21 Apr 1924), Austrian bass-baritone. Debut Kassel 1949. He sang in Mainz and Mannheim and became a member of the Deutsche Oper Berlin in 1963; successful as Pizarro, Scarpia and Schoenberg's Moses. From 1974 he has appeared at Bayreuth; at first as Alberich and Klingsor, then Gunther in the Solti-Hall *Ring*. In 1985 he sang Berg's Doctor at the NY Met., returning as Klingsor 1992.

mazurka a Polish national dance dating at least as far back as the 16th c. and originating in Mazowsze (Mazovia). It was at first accompanied with vocal music. The dance-figures are complicated and subject to much variation, not excluding improvisation. The music is in moderate 3–4 time originally in two sections of eight bars each, both repeated; there is a tendency to accentuate the second or the third beat. Its treatment by composers (e.g. Chopin) often extends and develops it.

Mazurok, Yuri (b Krasnik, Poland, 18 Jul 1931), Russian baritone. He studied in Lwów and Moscow; debut 1964 at the Bolshoi as Eugene Onegin. He later sang Andrei in *War and Peace* in Moscow. CG, 1975, as Renato. US debut 1977, San Francisco. In 1979 he sang Escamillo at the Vienna Staatsoper. Other roles include Rossini's Figaro and Verdi's Posa and Germont. Sang Scarpia at the Met. 1993.

Mazzaferrata, Giovanni Battista (b Como or Pavia; d Ferrara, 26 Feb 1691), Italian composer. *Maestro di cappella* at the Accademia della Morte at Ferrara, 1670–1680. His oratorio was performed at Siena in 1684.

Works include oratorio *Il David* and cantatas; *Salmi concertati* for three–four voices; madrigals and canzonets; cantatas for solo voices; 12 sonatas for two violins and bass.

Mazzinghi, Joseph (b London, 25 Dec 1765; d Downside, near Bath, 15 Jan 1844), English pianist, of Italian descent. Pupil of J C Bach. At the age of ten he succeeded his father as organist of the Portuguese Chapel in London. He then studied further with Bertoni, Sacchini and Anfossi during their stays in England and in 1784 became conductor and composer to the King's Theatre. He taught much and was music master to the Princess of Wales (later Queen Caroline).

Works include operas *La bella Arsena* (1795) and *Il tesoro* (1796); plays with music *A Day in Turkey* (1791), *Paul and Virginia* (with Reeve, after Saint-Pierre, 1800), *The Wife of Two Husbands*, *The Exile*, *The Free Knights* and others; several ballets; Mass for three voices; six hymns; many keyboard sonatas; glees, arias, songs.

Mazzocchi, Domenico (b Veia, near Civita Castellana, bap. 8 Nov 1592; d Rome, 21 Jan 1665), Italian composer. Was in the service of the Aldobrandini Borghese family for 20 years. His music has some of the earliest printed dynamics, e.g. 'crescendo' and 'diminuendo'.

Works include opera *La catena d'Adone* (1626); oratorios *Querimonia di S Maria Maddalena*, *Il martirio dei Saints Abbundia ed Abbundanzio* (1641); *Musiche sacre*; madrigals, *Dialoghi e sonetti*.

Mazzocchi, Virgilio (b Veia, 22 Jul 1597; d Veia, 3 Oct 1646), Italian composer, brother of Domenico ◊Mazzocchi. *Maestro di cappella* at St John Lateran in Rome, 1628–29, and then at St Peter's until his death.

Works include operas *Chi soffre speri* (with Marazzoli, 1637) and *L'innocenza difesa* (1641); psalms for double chorus; *Sacri flores* for two–four voices.

Mazzoleni, Ester (b Sebenico, 12 Mar 1883; d Palermo, 17 May 1982), Italian soprano. Debut Rome 1906, as the *Trovatore* Leonora; La Scala 1908–17, as Giulia in *La Vestale* and Médée. In 1913 she sang Aida at Verona, opposite Zenatello. Appeared as guest in Lisbon, Barcelona and Cairo and sang widely in Italy as Norma, Lucrezia Borgia, Elisabeth de Valois and Meyerbeer's Valentine.

Mc (for names with this prefix ◊Mac ...).

McBride, Robert (b Tucson, AZ, 20 Feb 1911), American composer. Studied and took the Mus.B. at Arizona University and obtained the Guggenheim Fellowship in 1937. Later he joined the faculty of Bennington College.

Works include ballet *Show Piece*; *Mexican Rhapsody* (1934) and *Prelude to a Tragedy* for orchestra; fugato for 25 instruments, *Workout* for 15 instruments (1936); prelude and fugue for string quartet; sonata *Depression* for violin and piano, *Workout* for oboe and piano, *Swing Music* for clarinet and piano (1938); dance suite for piano, *Lament for the Parking Problem* for trumpet, horn and trombone (1968).

McCabe, John (b Huyton, 21 Apr 1939), English composer and pianist. He studied at the RMCM and in Munich. Often heard as pianist in the sonatas of Haydn. Director of the London College of Music, 1983–90. CBE 1985.

Works include operas *The Play of Mother Courage* (1974) and *The Lion, the Witch and the Wardrobe* (1969); ballets *Mary, Queen of Scots* (1976) and *Don Juan* (1973); three symphonies (1965, 1971, 1978), *Variations on a theme of Hartmann* (1964), *The Chagall Windows* (1974), *The Shadow of Light* (1979); Concerto for Orchestra (1982), three piano concertos (1966, 1970, 1976), two violin concertos (1959, 1980); *Notturni ed Alba* for soprano and orchestra (1970), *Stabat Mater* for soprano, chorus and orchestra (1976); three string quartets (1960, 1972, 1979); piano and organ music, songs.

McCormack, John (Count) (b Athlone, 14 Jun 1884; d Dublin, 16 Sept 1945), Irish tenor. Began as chorister in Dublin Roman Catholic Cathedral. Without previous training won the gold medal at the Irish Festival, Dublin, 1902. In 1905 went to Italy to study with Sabbatini at Milan. Made his first concert appearance in London in 1907 and was engaged for opera by CG in the autumn as Turiddu, Ottavio and the Duke of Mantua. Later roles (until 1914) included Faust, Gounod's Roméo, Gerald and Pinkerton. He soon sang in Italy, USA, etc. and made a great reputation, but in later years made popularity rather than serious musical interest his chief concern. His title was a papal one.

McCracken, James (b Gary, IN, 16 Dec 1926; d New York, 29 Apr 1988), American tenor. Made his debut at the NY Met. in 1953; he sang only small roles and left for Europe in 1957. He frequently sang in Europe and was best known for his Otello which he sang first in Washington, 1960. Other roles included Florestan, Don José, Bacchus and Samson.

John McCabe – composer / pianist

It is impossible to réduce this to ten works/performances! I've taken the view that the performances are as important as the music in selecting this list – a comparable selection of ten works most influential upon me as a composer would be considerably different.

In alphabetical order:

1   Brahms: Symphony no. 3 in F (LSO/Boult)
    A powerful performance of this great (and difficult) masterpiece by one of the greatest of all Brahms conductors.

2   Byrd: Mass for three voices (Tallis Scholars/Phillips)
    Extraordinary richness from only three parts – music to ease the soul.

3   Elgar: *Falstaff* (Halle Orch./Barbirolli)
    My favourite Elgar work, interpreted with supreme insight into all its diverse aspects and immense structural grasp.

4   Haydn: Piano Sonata in G minor (Sviatoslav Richter)
    An exquisite performance (by my greatest pianistic hero) of perhaps Haydn's loveliest sonata.

5   Nielsen: Symphony no. 5 (NYPO/Bernstein)
    A white-hot performance of a disturbing but ultimately reinvigorating symphony of astonishing complexity.

6   Ravel: *Miroirs* (Gieseking)
    One of the most significant 20th-century piano works (and underestimated as such), played with marvellous subtlety and sensitivity.

7   Rawsthorne: Piano Concerto no. 1 (Lympany/Philharmonia/ Menges)
    This remains for me one of the freshest and most delightful concerti, with a particularly haunting slow movement – the performance is enchanting, a classic.

8   Schubert: Symphony no. 9 in C (*Great*) (Berlin PO/ Furtwängler)
    A glorious performance of a perennial favourite, bringing back vivid childhood memories of these performers in this music.

9   Sibelius: Symphony no. 5 in E flat (Hallé Orch./Barbirolli)
    Barbirolli was one of the finest of all Sibelians, and understood every facet of this fascinating and cumulatively powerful work.

10 Vaughan Williams: Symphony no. 6 in E minor (BBC SO/Andrew Davis)
    Vaughan Williams' unflinching, profound, and moving statement, interpreted with stunning power and imaginative response.

McDonald, Harl (b near Boulder, CO, 27 Jul 1899; d Princeton, NJ, 30 Mar 1955), American pianist, scientist and composer. Studied at home, at California University, and the Leipzig Conservatory. He toured as a pianist in Europe and USA, settled in Philadelphia as teacher and conductor and in 1930–33 studied physics in relation to acoustic problems with a Rockefeller grant and wrote a book on *New Methods of Measuring Sound*.
    Works include Psalm 84 and *Missa ad Patrem* for chorus and orchestra; four symphonies (1934–38: no. 1 *The Santa Fé Trail*, no. 2 *Rhumba*), two suites and three Poems on Aramaic Themes for orchestra; two piano concertos; string quartet on African-American themes (1932), piano trio; piano works; songs.

McFadden, Clàron (b Rochester, NY, 1961), American soprano. Studied at the Eastman School and made opera debut 1985, in Hasse's *L'Eroe Cinese*, under Ton Koopman. Has sung with William Christie and Les Arts Florissants in Rameau's *Anacréon* and *Les Indes Galantes*; Purcell's *Fairy Queen* in London, 1992. Netherlands Opera 1989, as Zerbinetta, Salzburg 1991 in Mozart's *Impresario. Acis and Galatea* with the King's Consort. Sang Philidel in Purcell's *King Arthur* at CG, 1995. Also sings modern repertory with the Schoenberg Ensemble.

McGegan, Nicholas (b Sawbridgeworth, Herts., 14 Jan 1950), English conductor and keyboard player. Studied piano and baroque flute at TCL and was professor at RAM 1973–79; director of early music 1976–80. Artist-in-residence at Washington University, St Louis, 1979–84. Music director of the Philharmonia Baroque Orchestra at San Francisco from 1985. Conducted Handel's *Teseo* at Boston (1985). *Ariodante* at Santa Fe (1986) and for ENO (1993), *Giustino* at San Francisco 1989 and *L'Allegro* at the Brooklyn Academy 1990. US premiere of Landi's *Il Sant Alessio* at Los Angeles (1988); Monteverdi's *Poppea* for Washington Opera and *Ulisse* for Long Beach Opera. Music director of the Göttingen Handel Festival from 1991; *Agrippina* at Washington 1992. Scottish Opera 1991, *La Clemenza di Tito*. Recordings include a 'pick 'n' mix' *Messiah*, with all Handel's alternative arias.

McGuire, Edward (b Glasgow, 15 Feb 1948), Scottish composer. Studied at the RAM 1966–70 and in Stockholm. Has played flute with folk group The Whistlebinkies from 1973. Music performed at Edinburgh Festival and London Proms.
    Works include operas *The Loving of Etain* (1990) and *Cullercoats* (1993); ballets *Peter Pan* (1989) and *The Spirit of Flight* (1991); orchestral music *Calgacus* (1977), guitar concerto (1989), *A Glasgow Symphony* (1990), *Scottish Dances* (1990), trombone concerto (1991) and *Symphonies of Scots Songs* (1992); *Symphonies of Trains* (1992), *Sidesteps* (1992) and *Zephyr* (1993) for ensemble; *Loonscapes* (1983) and *The Web* (1989) for soprano and ensemble; *Elegy* for piano trio (1990), *Eastern Echoes* (1991) and *Fountain of Tears* (1992) for flute and guitar, *Remembrance* for oboe trio (1993); piano music.

McLaughlin, Marie (b Hamilton, 2 Nov 1954), Scottish soprano. Studied in Glasgow and at the London Opera Centre, from 1977. Debut as Tatiana at Aldeburgh, 1978. ENO from 1978 in *The Consul*, and *Rigoletto*; CG debut as Barbarina, 1981, as Susanna, Zerlina, Iris (*Semele*), Nannetta and Britten's Tytania. Glyndebourne 1985 and 1987, as Micaela and Violetta. Sang Marzelline in *Fidelio* at the NY Met 1986 and Susanna under James Levine at Salzburg, 1987. Other roles include Despina (Geneva 1992), Jenny in *Mahogonny* and Ilia in *Idomeneo* (Rome 1982, and Barcelona 1993).

McIntyre, Donald (b Auckland, New Zealand, 22 Oct 1934), English bass-baritone. He studied at the GSM and sang Zaccaria with the WNO in 1959. SW, London, 1960–66 as Attila and the Dutchman. CG debut 1967, as Pizarro; other roles there included Orestes, Kurwenal, Klingsor and Barak in the first production of *Die Frau ohne Schatten* by a British company. In 1967 he sang Telramund at Bayreuth and returned as Wotan in 1973 (1976 in the Boulez-Chéreau centenary production of the *Ring*). Also sang Wotan at CG and the NY Met. in 1975. Sang Prospero in the UK fp of Berio's *Un re in ascolto* (1989), and returned 1993 as Hans Sachs. Other roles include Amfortas (at Bayreuth), Balstrode (at CG) and Golaud in *Pelléas et Mélisande*. Knighted 1992.

McNair, Sylvia (b Mansfield, OH, 23 Jun 1956), American soprano.

McNair *The soprano Sylvia McNair. She has divided her career between the concert hall, making recordings with Haitink and Rattle, and the theatre, performing in works by Rossini and Mozart. She has an attractive stage presence.*

Studied at Indiana University and made debut in Messiah 1980. Sang Sandrina in Haydn's *L'infedeltà delusa* at New York (1982) and created the title role in Kelterborn's *Ophelia* at Schwetzingen 1984. Has sung Pamina at Santa Fe, the Deutsche Oper Berlin and the Vienna Staatsoper; Morgana in *Alcina* at St Louis. Glyndebourne debut 1989, as Anne Trulove. Salzburg debut 1990 (as Ilia), returning 1993 as Poppea. CG debut 1990 (Ilia); NY Met 1991, as Marzelline in *Fidelio*. Many concerts with Gardiner, Rattle and Harnoncourt.

McPhee, Colin (b Montreal, 15 Mar 1901; d Los Angeles, 7 Jan 1964), Canadian-American composer. Studied at Peabody Conservatory, Baltimore, with Strube and graduated in 1921. Studied piano with Friedheim at the Canadian Academy of Music, where he played a piano concerto of his own in 1924. Then studied composition in Paris with Paul le Flem and piano with I Philipp. Meetings with Varèse from 1926 much influenced his own music. From 1934 to 1939 he spent much time in Bali and Mexico.

Works include three symphonies (1955, 1957, 1962); concerto for piano and eight wind instruments (1928), *Tabuh-Tabuhan* for two pianos and orchestra (1936); *Balinese Ceremonial Music* for two pianos (1942), and other piano music; four *Iroquois Dances* for orchestra. Also a number of books on Bali and its music.

Me the name of the mediant note in any key in Tonic Sol-fa, so pronounced, but in notation represented by the symbol m.

Meale, Richard (b Sydney, 24 Aug 1932), Australian composer. Studied as pianist at NSW Conservatory. Later music has been influenced by Boulez, Messiaen and Indonesian music.

Works include operas *Voss* (1979–86) and *Mer de Glace* (1986–91); *Images* for orchestra (1966), *Clouds Now and Then* for orchestra (1969); *Viridian* for strings (1979); Symphony (1994); flute sonata (1960), wind quintet (1970), two string quartets (1974, 1980).

meantone in tuning, the meantone system was a common technique used for keyboard instruments before ◊equal temperament came into general use. It provided for the pure intonation of the key of C major and those lying near it at the expense of the more extreme sharp and flat keys; which is the reason why remote keys were rarely used in keyboard works, before the adoption of equal temperament. There was, for example, a pure F♯ and B♭, but these notes were out of tune when used as G♭ or A♯.

Meares, Richard (1) (d London, c 1722), English instrument maker. Made lutes, viols, etc. in London in the second half of the 17th c.

Meares, Richard (2) (b London; d London, c 1743), English instrument maker and music publisher, son of Richard ◊Meares (1). He succeeded to his father's business, but enlarged it by selling not only instruments, but music books and cutlery, and he began to pub. music c 1714, including several operas by Handel, e.g. *Radamisto* (1720).

measure, American, = 'bar'.

In English (poetical) a 'measure' is a regularly rhythmic piece of music, especially a dance.

Medea play with music (melodrama) by G Benda (text by F W Gotter), produced Leipzig, 1 May 1775. For plot synopsis, ◊Medea in Corinto.

Medea in Corinto opera (*melodramma tragico*) by Mayr (libretto by F Romani); produced Naples, Teatro San Carlo, 28 Nov 1813. Medea takes revenge on treacherous husband Jason by killing their children and his lover, Creusa.

Médecin malgré lui, Le, *Doctor against his Will*, opera by Gounod (libretto, a small alteration of Molière's comedy by composer, J Barbier and M Carré), produced Paris, Théâtre Lyrique, 15 Jan 1858. Doctor Sganarelle helps Lucinde escape the attentions of a rich suitor and elope with lover Léandre.

Médée opera by Marc-Antoine Charpentier (libretto by T Corneille), produced Paris, Opéra, 4 Dec 1693.

Opera by Cherubini (libretto by F B Hoffmann), produced Paris, Théâtre Feydeau, 13 Mar 1797. Abandoned by Jason, Medea poisons his new wife and kills their two sons. Opera by Milhaud (libretto by Madeleine Milhaud, the composer's wife), produced in Flemish translation, Antwerp, 7 Oct 1939.

Meder, Johann Valentin (b Wasungen o/ Werra, bap. 3 May 1649; d Riga, Jul 1719), German singer and composer. After various appointments he became cantor at Reval in 1674 and at Danzig in 1687, later music director at Königsberg and Riga Cathedral.

Works include operas *Nero* (1695, indebted to Strungk) and others: oratorio, motets; trios; organ music.

Mederitsch, Johann Georg Anton Gallus (also known as Johann Gallus) (b Vienna, 26 Dec 1752; d Lwów, 18 Dec 1835), Bohemian composer and conductor. He was a theatre conductor at Olomouc and Pest, and later for many years a private music teacher in Vienna, Grillparzer being among his pupils.

Works include operas *Babylons Pyramiden* (with Winter, 1797), *Orkatastor und Illiane* (1779), *Der reditche Verwalter* (1779) and others; incidental music for Shakespeare's *Macbeth*; Masses; chamber music.

medesimo tempo Italian = 'same time'; a direction indicating that a change of metre does not imply a change of pace. The more usual term is *l'istesso tempo* (formerly *lo stesso tempo*).

mediant the third degree of the major or minor scale, so called because it stands half way between Tonic and Dominant. The names of the degrees of the entire scale are Tonic, Supertonic, Mediant, Subdominant, Dominant, Submediant and Leading-note.

Medium, The opera in two acts by Menotti (libretto by the composer, produced Columbia University, NY, 8 May 1946. Fraudulent medium Baba accidentally kills her mute assistant Toby, believing him to be a genuine ghost.

Medlam, Charles (b Port-au-Prince, Trinidad, 10 Sept 1949), English conductor and cellist. Studied with Maurice Gendron in Paris and with Harnoncourt in Salzburg. Founded the London Baroque with Ingrid Seiffert, 1978; premiere of Scarlatti's opera *Una villa di Tuscolo* and a revival of *Gli Equivoci Sembiante*. Has directed *Dido and Aeneas* and works by Blow and Lully in Paris, Handel's *Aci, Galatea e Polifemo* on tour in Europe and Rameau contatas with Emma Kirkby. Salzburg Festival debut 1991, with music by Mozart. Also conducts Charpentier, Bach and Monteverdi.

Medtner (or *Metner*), Nikolai Karlovich (b Moscow, 5 Jan 1880; d London, 13 Nov 1951), Russian composer. Studied piano under Safonov at the Moscow Conservatory, gained the Rubinstein Prize there and toured Europe as pianist in 1901–02, becoming professor at the Conservatory for a year on his return, but then retiring to devote himself to composition. After the Revolution he taught at a school in Moscow and in 1921 went on another tour in the West, but found himself unable to return. He settled in Paris for a time and later in London, which he left temporarily for Warwickshire in 1940.

     Works include three piano concertos (1914–43); piano quintet; three sonatas and three nocturnes for violin and piano; 12 piano sonatas and a great number of pieces for piano including *Fairy Tales* op. 8, 9, 14, 20, 26, 34, 35, 42, 48, 51, *Forgotten Melodies* op. 38–40, *Dithyrambs*, *Novels*, *Lyric Fragments*, *Improvisations*, *Hymns in Praise of Toil*, etc.; *Russian Dance* and *Knight-Errant* for two pianos; sonata-vocalise for voice and piano; 17 op. nos. of songs to words by Pushkin, Tiutchev, Goethe, Heine, Nietzsche and others.

Meeresstille und Glückliche Fahrt, *Calm Sea and Prosperous Voyage*, two poems by Goethe, set by Beethoven as a cantata for chorus and orchestra in 1815, op. 112, and dedicated to the poet; and used by Mendelssohn as the subject for a concert overture, op. 27, in 1828. Elgar quotes from the latter in the romance of the 'Enigma' Variations.

Mefistofele opera by Boito (libretto by composer, based on Goethe's *Faust*), produced Milan, La Scala, 5 Mar 1868. Faust gains moment of happiness but loses Margherita after accidentally poisoning her mother. Faust repents and eludes Mephistopheles.

Mehta, Zubin (b Bombay, 29 Apr 1936), Indian conductor, son of the violinist Mehli Mehta. Received first training from his father and in 1954 went to Vienna, where he studied conducting with Swarowsky. In 1958 he won the competition for young conductors in Liverpool and in 1959 was guest conductor with the Vienna PO. He has since conducted throughout Europe, and in 1962 became director of the LA PO; left in 1977 to become music director NY PO. Israel PO and CG, London, from 1977. Guest conductor Vienna PO. Salzburg Opera and NY Met. debuts 1965, *Die Entführung* and *Aida*; CG 1977, *Otello*. Conducted live *Tosca* at Rome 1992, with worldwide TV transmission.

Méhul, Étienne Nicolas (b Givet, near Mézières, Ardennes, 22 Jun 1763; d Paris, 18 Oct 1817), French composer. Organist in his home town at the age of ten, he went to Paris in 1778, where Gluck's operas and the encouragement of the composer himself gave him the ambition to write for the stage. He took piano lessons from Edelmann, and supported himself by teaching until *Euphrosine* (1790) established him as an opera composer, after which he became one of the most notable composers of the Revolution, his greatest success being *Joseph* (1807). On the foundation of the Conservatory in 1795 he became one of its inspectors. His overture *Le Jeune Henri* and operas *Uthal* and *Joseph* are notable for their novel instrumental effects.

     Works include operas *Euphrosine et Coradin, ou Le Tyran corrigé* (1790), *Cora, Stratonice* (1792), *Le Jeune Sage et le vieux fou* (1793), *Horatius Coclès, Mélidore et Phrosine* (1794), *La Caverne, Doria, Le Jeune Henri* (1797), *Le Pont de Lodi* (1797), *Adrien, Ariodant* (1799), *Épicure* (with Cherubini), *Bion, L'irato, ou L'Emporté* (1801), *Une Folie, Le Trésor supposé* (1802), *Joanna, Héléna* (1803), *Le Baiser et la quittance* (with Kreutzer, Boieldieu and Isouard, 1803), *L'Heureux malgré lui*, *Les Deux Aveugles de Tolède* (1806), *Uthal* (without violins), *Gabrielle d'Estrés, Joseph* (1807), *Les Amazones, Le Prince Troubadour* (1813), *L'Oriflamme* (with Paer, Berton and Kreutzer, 1814), *La Journée aux aventures* (1816), *Valentine de Milan* (unfinished, completed by his nephew Louis Joseph Daussoigne-Méhul (1790–1875).

     Ballets: *Le Jugement de Paris* (with additions from Haydn and Pleyel), *La Dansomanie* (1800), *Daphnis et Pandrose* (1803), *Persée et Andromède* (1810); incidental music to Joseph Chénier's *Timoléon*; Mass for the coronation of Napoleon I (not performed); cantatas *Chanson de Roland, Chant lyrique* (for the unveiling of Napoleon's statue at the Institut); patriotic songs *Chant national du 14 juillet*,

---

THE OPERA

Mefistofele

A four-act opera with Prologue and Epilogue, by Arrigo Boito, who also wrote the text based on Goethe's *Faust*. It was first produced in 1868.

Prologue. The devil, Mefistofele (bass), wagers God that he can win the soul of Faust.

I. Disguised as a mysterious greyfriar, Mefistofele rejuvenates the elderly scholar Faust (tenor) and signs him up for one moment of happiness.

II. Faust woos Margherita (soprano) and gives her a drug to keep her mother quiet. At the Walpurgis Night celebrations, Mefistofele shows Faust a vision of Margherita in chains.

III. A distraught Margherita, in prison for poisoning her mother and killing her child by Faust, refuses Mefistofele's offer of help. She affirms her Christian faith before dying.

IV. Taken to Greece by Mefistofele, Faust woos Helen, who has a vision of the burning of Troy.

Epilogue. A repentant Faust longs for death; pitied by God, he dies redeemed, his soul released from the charge of Mefistofele.

THE OPERA

Chant du départ, Chant de retour; symphony; two piano sonatas.

Mel, Girolamo (b Florence, 27 May 1519; d Florence, Jul 1594), Italian theorist. His four surviving works include the *Discorso sopra la musica antica e moderna*, pub. Venice, 1602.

Meier, Johanna (b Chicago, 13 Feb 1938), American soprano. Studied at the Manhattan School of Music and made debut at NY City Opera 1969, as the Countess in *Capriccio*; further appearances as Donna Anna, Senta, Louise and Tosca. NY Met from 1975, as Marguerite, the Marschallin, Brünnhilde (*Die Walküre*) and Strauss's Empress. Sang Isolde with WNO 1980 and at Bayreuth 1981. Vienna Staatsoper from 1983, as Leonore and Senta. Pittsburgh 1989, as Chrysothemis.

Meier, Waltraud (b Wurzburg, 9 Jan 1956), German mezzo-soprano. After study in Cologne sang at Wurzburg from 1976, as Cherubino, Dorabella and Nicklausse. Sang at Mannheim from 1978, Dortmund from 1980, as Carmen, Fricka, Octavian and Eboli. She is widely admired as Wagner's Kundry, which she has sung at Bayreuth (1983), CG (1988) and the NY Met. Other Bayreuth roles have been Brangaena, Waltraute (1988) and Isolde (1993). CG debut 1984 (Eboli), Met 1987 (Fricka in the *Ring*). Has also sung Azucena, Venus, the Composer, Tchaikovsky's Maid of Orleans (Munich 1990) and Sieglinde (Vienna 1993).

Meiland, Jacob (b Senftenberg, Saxony, 1542; d Hechingen, 31 Dec 1577), German composer. He learnt music as a choirboy in the Saxon court chapel at Dresden, studied at Leipzig University, travelled, and was appointed *Kapellmeister* to the Margrave of Ansbach, whose chapel was dissolved in 1574. Meiland was *Kapellmeister* to the Hohenzollem court at Heichingen from 1577.

     Works include Latin and German motets; *Cantiones sacrae* for five–six voices; German songs for four–five voices.

Meistersinger German = 'master-singers'; 14th–16th-c. guilds of poets and musicians who cultivated poetry and singing in various German towns, probably founded at Mainz in 1311 by Heinrich von Meissen (Frauenlob). The members passed through various stages from apprenticeship to mastery, and they were middle-class burghers, merchants, tradesmen and artisans, not nobles like the Minnesinger.

Meistersinger von Nürnberg, Die, *The Mastersingers of Nuremberg*, music drama by Wagner (libretto by composer), produced Munich, Court Theatre, 21 Jun 1868. Walter wins Eva in a song contest, but only after tempering his passion with the wisdom of Hans Sachs.

Mel, Rinaldo del (b Malines, *c* 1554; d *c* 1598), Flemish composer. He went to Rome in 1580 after serving at the Portuguese court, entered the service of Cardinal Gabriele Paleotto and (?) studied under

━━ THE OPERA ━━

Die Meistersinger von Nürnberg

Richard Wagner's three-act opera about the poet and cobbler Hans Sachs is set in Nuremberg in the mid-16th century. It was first performed in Munich in 1868.

I. Walther von Stolzing (tenor) falls in love with Eva (soprano), but her father Veit Pogner (bass) declares that she will become the bride of whomever wins the singing contest, to be held the following day by the Guild of Mastersingers. After Walther has the rules explained to him by the apprentice David (tenor), he sings a trial song in an attempt to join the Mastersingers, but he is rejected by the pedantic marking of town clerk Sixtus Beckmesser (baritone). Only the cobbler Hans Sachs can discern merit in Walther's song.

II. Outside Sachs' shop on midsummer's eve, Eva questions the cobbler about the competition, teasing Sachs that he might take an interest himself. When Beckmesser arrives to serenade Eva, Sachs marks all his mistakes with hammer blows. In the ensuing confusion, Eva and Walther are prevented from escaping, and Beckmesser takes a sound beating from the disturbed populace.

III. After Sachs muses on the world's folly, Walther narrates a song which has come to him in a dream; Sachs writes down the words. When they leave, Beckmesser discovers the manuscript and, when Sachs returns, the clerk is allowed to sing the song at the contest if he is able. A reunion with Eva leads to the festive meadow. Beckmesser is laughed at by all when he attempts Walther's song, but Walther himself triumphs when he takes it up. He at first refuses membership of the Mastersingers, but Sachs reminds him of the duties imposed by German art.

━━ THE OPERA ━━

Palestrina. 1587–91 he was at Liège in the household of Ernst, Duke of Bavaria, but he rejoined Paleotto at Bologna, who appointed him *maestro di cappella* to Magliano Cathedral.

Works include motets, *Sacrae cantiones*, a Litany; 12 vols. of *madrigaletti* and spiritual madrigals.

Melani, Jacopo (b Pistoia, 6 Jul 1623; d Pistoia, 19 Aug 1676), Italian composer. His father was a sexton at Pistoia and had seven other musical sons. He was *maestro di cappella* of Pistoia Cathedral, 1657–67, and wrote a number of comic operas for Florence.

Works include operas *Il potestà di Colognole* (1657), *Il girello*, *Il pazzo per forza* (1658), *Il vecchio burlato* (1659), *Enea in Italia*, *Ercole in Tebe* (1661), *Il ritorno d'Ulisse* (1669).

His brother Alessandro (1639–1703), was *maestro di cappella* at Bologna, Pistoia and Rome, and composed five operas, motets, oratorios, cantatas, etc.

Melartin, Erkki (b Käkisalmi, 7 Feb 1875; d Pukinmäki, 14 Feb 1937), Finnish composer. Studied at the Helsinki Conservatory, Wegelius being his composition master; later in Germany. He became professor of composition at the Conservatory in 1901, and conductor at Viipuri 1908–10. He was director of the Conservatory 1911–22.

Works include opera *Aino* (1907); ballet *Sininen helmi*; eight symphonies (1902–24), five orchestral suites, symphonic poems; violin concerto; four string quartets; violin and piano sonatas; piano sonata and *c* 400 pieces; *c* 300 songs.

Madame Melba has the voice of a lark and, so far as her acting is evidence, the soul of one also.

The New York Times on Nellie Melba as Manon, quoted in Wechsberg, *The Opera*, 1972

Melba, Nellie (actually Helen Mitchell) (b Burnley, near Melbourne, 19 May 1861; d Sydney, 23 Feb 1931), Australian soprano. Studied singing at an early age, but was not allowed to take it up professionally until her marriage to Captain Charles Armstrong in 1882 enabled her to do so. She appeared in London in 1886, went to Paris for further study with Mathilde Marchesi and made her debut at the Théâtre de la Monnaie in Brussels, 1887, as Gilda; CG, London, in 1888 as Lucia. She first visited Paris in 1889, when she sang Juliette, Russia in 1891, Italy in 1892 and North America in 1893; NY Met. until 1911. London until 1924 as Rosina, Violetta, Mimi, Desdemona, Aida and Elsa. She was highly regarded as a coloratura soprano, particularly successful in roles requiring ornamentation. DBE 1918.

Melchert, Helmut (b Kiel, 24 Sept 1910), German tenor. After study at Hamburg made stage debut at Wuppertal, 1939. Hamburg Opera 1943–77, in Wagner roles and the 1960 fp of Henze's *Prinz fon Homburg*. Sang Oedipus Rex at Edinburgh (1956) and Aron in the stage fp of *Moses und Aron* (Zurich, 1957). Created Tiresias in Henze's *The Bassarids* (Salzburg, 1966) and sang character roles in operas by Strauss.

Melchior, Lauritz (b Copenhagen, 20 Mar 1890; d Santa Monica, 18 Mar 1973), Danish-American tenor. Studied in Copenhagen, making his debut as a baritone in 1913. In 1918, after further studies, he made a second debut as a tenor, singing at CG and Bayreuth in 1924; Bayreuth until 1931 as Siegmund, Parsifal, Siegfried and Tristan. NY Met. 1926–1950; debut as Tannhäuser. He was one of the finest Wagner singers of his time.

Melis, Carmen (b Cagliari, 16 Aug 1885; d Longone al Segrino, near Como, 19 Dec 1967), Italian soprano. She studied with Jean de Reszke in Paris. Debut Novara 1905, as Thaïs; Naples 1906, as Mascagni's Iris. Manhattan Opera House 1909, as Tosca; she sang Leoncavallo's Zazà at Chicago in 1916. Paris Opéra 1913, as Minnie, with Caruso and Tita Ruffo. CG 1913 and 1929 as Tosca, Nedda and Musetta. Other roles included Manon Lescaut, Fedora and the Marschallin.

melisma (plural *melismata*), from Greek, = 'song'; an ornament: in plainsong a group of notes sung to a single syllable; in modern music any short passage of a decorative nature.

Melkus, Eduard (b Baden-bei-Wien, 1 Sept 1928), Austrian violinist. He studied in Vienna and has taught at the Hochschule there from 1958. He played in several Swiss orchestras and in 1965 founded the Vienna Capella Academica; many performances and recordings of 17th- and 18th-c. instrumental music.

Mell, Davis (b Wilton, near Salisbury, 15 Nov 1604; d London, 4 Apr 1662), English violinist and composer. Became a member of the

A Selection of

Mendelssohn

A Midsummer Night's Dream	1826
String Quartet op. 13	1827
Symphony no. 5	1830
String Octet	1830
Fingal's Cave (Hebrides) Overture	1830
Symphony no. 4	1833
Piano Trio op. 49	1839
Symphony no. 3	1842
Violin Concerto	1844
Elijah	1846

King's Band at the Restoration (1660) and joint master. Wrote viol music, etc.

Mellers, Wilfrid (Howard) (b Leamington, 26 Apr 1914), English critic and composer. Studied at Cambridge and began to write criticism in the review *Scrutiny*, of which he became music assistant editor. Professor of music at York University 1964–81. OBE 1982. He has written books on Couperin, American music, Bach and Beethoven.

Works include opera *Christopher Marlowe* (1950–52), *Ricercare* for orchestra, ditto (no. 2) for chamber orchestra, ditto (no. 3) for string orchestra; *Concerto grosso* for chamber orchestra; string quartet, piano quartet, *Eclogue* for string trio; string trio (1945); choral music; songs.

Mellon, Agnes (b Épinay-sur-Seine, 17 Jan 1958), French soprano. Studied in Paris and sang in the standard repertoire before turning to Baroque opera; Tibrino in Cesti's *Orontea* at Innsbruck (1986), Eryxene in Hasse's *Cleofide* and Telaire in *Castor et Pollux* (Aix 1991). Sang the title role in Rossi's *Orfeo* with Les Arts Florissants, London 1990. Recordings include *Orfeo*, Cavalli's *Xerxes* and Lully's *Atys*.

melodic minor scale a minor scale in which the sixth and seventh are raised a semitone when ascending and returned to their natural position when descending.

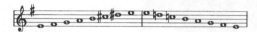

The melodic minor scale on E.

mélodie French = lit. 'a melody or tune'; now generally current in French as an exact equivalent of the English 'song' or the German 'Lied'.

melodrama a spoken play or spoken passages in an opera accompaniment by a musical background. Rousseau's *Pygmalion* and Benda's *Ariadne* and *Medea* are early instances of the former, and the first version of Humperdinck's *Königskinder* and works by Fibich are later ones; familiar examples of the latter occur in Beethoven's *Fidelio* and Weber's *Freischütz*.

melodramma Italian = 'music drama'; a term for 'opera' current in Italy from the end of the 18th c. onwards. ◊melodrama.

melody an intelligible succession of notes defined by pitch and rhythm.

In western music it is unusual to find melodies which do not at least imply harmony.

Melos Ensemble English chamber music group formed 1950 by Cecil Aronowitz (viola), Gervase de Peyer (clarinet), Richard Adeney (flute) and Terence Weil (cello). Further players, up to a total of 12, have been added to give frequent performances and recordings of major chamber works. Also active in modern music, including fp of Britten's *War Requiem*, 1962.

Melos Quartet of Stuttgart German string quartet founded 1965; many concert appearances since winning competitions in Geneva and Rio de Janiero. Members are Wilhelm Melcher (b Hamburg, 1940), Gerhard Ernst (b Burscheid, 1939), Hermann Voss (b Brünen, 1934) and Peter Buck (b Stuttgart, 1937).

Melusine overture (Mendelssohn). ◊Schöne Melusine.

Mendelssohn, Arnold (Ludwig) (b Ratibor, 26 Dec 1855; d Darmstadt, 19 Feb 1933), German composer, son of a cousin of Felix Mendelssohn-Bartholdy. Studied law at Tübingen and music in Berlin, and held teaching and conducting appointments at Bonn, Bielefeld, Cologne, Darmstadt and Frankfurt, where Hindemith was his pupil.

Works include operas *Elsi, die seltsame Magd* (after Jeremias Gotthelf, 1896), *Der Bärenbäuter* (1900) and *Die Minneburg*; cantatas; madrigals to words from Goethe's *Werther*; much church music, symphony in E♭ major; violin concerto; two string quartets; sonatas for violin and piano, cello and piano and piano; songs, part-songs.

Mendelssohn (Bartholdy), Fanny (Cäcile) (b Hamburg, 14 Nov 1805; d Berlin, 14 May 1847), German pianist and composer, sister of Felix Mendelssohn. She studied with Marie Bigot in Paris and C F Zelter in Berlin. She was encouraged in composition by her family but published very few of her 500 works, most of them Lieder and piano pieces. She was the focal point of her Berlin Salon in the 1830s and played her brother's first piano concerto in public in 1838; always close, he survived her death by only five months. Her songs have enjoyed a modest revival and her D minor piano trio of 1846 does not suffer from comparison with the early works of her brother.

Mendelssohn (-Bartholdy, Jakob Ludwig) Felix (b Hamburg, 3 Feb 1809; d Leipzig, 4 Nov 1847), German composer. Son of the banker Abraham Mendelssohn and grandson of the Jewish philosopher Moses Mendelssohn. Mendelssohn's branch of the family embraced Christianity and moved to Berlin in 1812. At six he had piano lessons from his mother and at seven from Marie Bigot in Paris. In 1817, back in Berlin, he learnt composition form Zelter, whose friend Goethe he visited at Weimar in 1821. Before that, in 1818, aged nine, he appeared at a public chamber concert, and before he was 13 he had written many works, including the piano quartet op. 1. His father was wealthy enough to enable him to conduct a private orchestra, and he wrote his first symphony at 15, after writing 13 symphonies for strings. By 1825 he had ready the short opera *Camacho's Wedding*, produced at the family's expense in 1827. Also in 1825 he wrote his first masterpiece, the Octet for strings, often considered the finest work by any teenaged composer. At 17 he had written the overture to Shakespeare's *Midsummer Night's Dream* (the rest of the incidental music followed in 1842). In 1829 he conducted Bach's forgotten *St Matthew Passion* at the Vocal Academy and paid the first of his ten visits to England, conducting the Philharmonic Society in London and taking a holiday in Scotland, where he gathered impressions for the *Hebrides* overture and the 'Scottish' symphony, at which he worked in Italy 1830–31. The 'Italian' symphony he finished in 1833, the year he conducted the Lower Rhine Festival at Düsseldorf, where he was engaged to stay as general music director. He left, however, for Leipzig, where he was appointed 'official' conductor of the Gewandhaus concerts in 1835.

During a visit to Frankfurt he met Cécile Jeanrenaud, descendant of

---

Mendelssohn   *A biographical note*

Mendelssohn received his first musical instruction from his mother, and by the age of nine he was playing the piano in public. His musical education was soon afterwards entrusted to Carl Zelter, the director of the Berlin Singakademie. In 1821 Zelter decided to take the 12-year-old Mendelssohn to visit Goethe at Weimar; before he left, the boy was instructed by his father in the appropriate manners and behaviour in the presence of the 72-year-old poet. A large company had gathered in Goethe's music room to hear the prodigy. After Zelter's introduction, Mendelssohn began to play. 'Whatever you feel is not too difficult for you', Goethe commanded. At first he played a fantasia and then a fugue by Bach, one of Goethe's favourite composers. Increasingly impressed with the boy's gifts, Goethe requested that he play a minuet; Mendelssohn duly obliged with the minuet from *Don Giovanni*. Mendelssohn was just as obliging in later life, and several times while on visits to England accompanied Queen Victoria in his own songs. On one occasion he asked as a reward to be shown all the domestic arrangements of the royal children. The delighted Queen was thus able to conduct the composer through all the scaled-down paraphernalia of the 19th-century nursery, including what seem to modern eyes the morbid casts of infant feet and hands.

Mendelssohn *The composer Felix Mendelssohn-Bartholdy (1809–1847) pictured at the age of 12. He was precociously gifted, composing his first symphony at 15 and his most famous work, the overture to Shakespeare's* A Midsummer Night's Dream, *at 17. Although a Romantic, many of his musical ideals were Classical.*

a French Huguenot family, whom he married on 28 Mar 1837. In Sept of the same year he conducted *St Paul* at the Birmingham Festival. In 1841 he left for Berlin, having been appointed director of the music section of the Academy of Arts, and there furnished incidental music for several classical plays, Greek, English and French. He returned to Leipzig late in 1842 and founded the Conservatory there in Nov, opening it in Apr 1843. He was still living in Berlin, however, but resumed his conductorship at Leipzig in 1845, conducting the premiere of his most popular work, the violin concerto. But he was in poor health, and his visit to England to conduct *Elijah* at the Birmingham Festival on 26 Aug 1846 was his last but one. The death of his sister Fanny Hensel in the spring of 1847 greatly depressed him, and he went to Switzerland too ill to do any work, returning to Leipzig in Sept completely exhausted. Mendelssohn's music is most highly valued for its fusion of a Romantic, lyrical impulse with a sure sense of form. Much of his best music, including the octet, the first five string quartets, *St Paul* and the 'Italian' symphony were written while he was in his teens or twenties; exhaustion through frail health and overwork conspired to prevent him from meeting his full potential, although such late works as the violin concerto and *Elijah* find Mendelssohn returning to his finest vein of inspiration.

Works include OPERAS: *Die Hochzeit des Camacho* (1827), *Die Heimkehr aus der Fremde/Son and Stranger*, 1829) and *Loreley* (unfinished); incidental music to Sophocles' *Antigone* and *Oedipus at Colonos*, Shakespeare's *Midsummer Night's Dream* (1843), Racine's *Athalie*.

ORATORIOS: *St Paul* (1836) and *Elijah* (1846); many choral settings of psalms and other sacred vocal works, *Lobgesang* (*Hymn of Praise*; the second symphony followed by a short cantata), cantata *Lauda Sion*, Goethe's *Erste Walpurgisnacht* for solo voices, chorus and orchestra.

ORCHESTRAL: 13 symphonies for strings (1821–23), five symphonies, in C minor (1824), B♭ 'Lobesgesang' (1840), A minor 'Scottish' (1842), A 'Italian' (1833), D 'Reformation' (1832); four concert overtures, *A Midsummer Night's Dream* (1826), *Fingal's Cave* (1830), *The Fair Melusine* (1833), *Ruy Blas* (1839), and some misc.

orchestral works; two concertos and three shorter works for piano and orchestra; violin concerto in E minor.

CHAMBER MUSIC: including six string quartets, op. 12 in E♭ (1829), op. 13 in A minor (1827), op. 44 nos 1–3, in D, E minor and E♭ (1837–38), op. 80 in F minor (1847), three piano quartets, two string quintets, string octet in E♭ op. 20 (1825), Four Pieces for string quartet, op. 81 (1847, 1847, 1843, 1827); *Variations Concertantes* for cello and piano (1829); two cello sonatas in B♭ op. 45 (1838) and D op. 58 (1843); two piano trios, in D minor op. 49 (1839) and C minor op. 66 (1845), sextet in D op. 110 (1824).

KEYBOARD AND SONGS: a large amount of piano music including 48 *Lieder ohne Worte/Songs without words* three sonatas, fantasies, characteristic pieces, capriccios, variations, preludes and fugues, studies, etc.; six sonatas, three preludes and fugues and other pieces for organ, over 80 songs; 12 sets of vocal duets and part-songs.

I have grown accustomed to composing in our garden ... today or tomorrow I am going to dream there the Midsummer Night's Dream.
Felix Mendelssohn, in a letter to Fanny Mendelssohn, 1826

Mendès, Catulle (1841–1909), French writer, poet and dramatist. He wrote libretti for several composers, including Chabrier, Messager, Pierné, Pessard, Massenet and Debussy. Debussy's work, *Rodrigue et Chimène*, was never finished. Married Judith Gautier (1850–1917), with whom he visited Wagner at Triebschen in Switzerland, 1869; she had an affair with Wagner seven years later at Bayreuth, during the first production of the *Ring*.

◊Bruneau (*Chansons à danser* and *Lieds de France*), **Gwendoline** (Chabrier), ***d'Indy*** (*Médée*), **Leroux** (*Reine Fiammette*).

Meneses, Antonio (b Recife, 23 Aug 1957), Brazilian cellist. Studied with Antonio Janigro. Many tours worldwide since winning 1977 Munich International Competition; appearances with the Berlin PO under Karajan and with the LSO in London and the USA. Recordings include the Brahms Double Concerto and Strauss's *Don Quixote*, conducted by Karajan.

Ménestrandise, French, in 17th- and 18th-c. Paris a corporation of *Ménestriers* protected by an official privilege against the encroachment of other musicians on their exclusive right to play for dancing. Couperin wrote a satirical harpsichord suite on it entitled *Les Fastes de la Grande Mxnxstrxndxsx*.

Mengelberg, Willem (b Utrecht, 28 Mar 1871; d Zuort, Switzerland, 22 Mar 1951), Dutch conductor. Studied at Cologne, became conductor at Lucerne in 1891 and in 1895 was appointed conductor of the Concertgebouw Orchestra in Amsterdam. He made this one of the finest orchestras in Europe, giving early performances of works by Strauss and Mahler, including the first complete cycle of Mahler's symphonies at Amsterdam in 1920, but fell under a cloud when he openly declared his sympathy with the Nazi rule during World War II, and went into exile in Switzerland. In 1933 he had been made Professor of Music at Utrecht University.

Menges, Isolde (b Hove, 16 May 1893; d Richmond, Surrey, 13 Jan 1976), British violinist of German parentage, sister of the conductor Herbert Menges (1902–72). Studied Leipzig and St Petersburg. London debut 1913, US tour 1916. Recorded Beethoven Concerto 1922. Founded Menges Quartet 1931.

Mengozzi, Bernardo (b Florence, 1758; d Paris, Mar 1800), Italian tenor and composer. Studied at Florence and Venice, visited London in 1786 and settled in Paris soon after, becoming professor of singing on the establishment of the Conservatory in 1795. Wrote opera *Pourceaugnac* (after Molière) and *c* 15 others, operettas.

Mennin, Peter (b Erie, PA, 17 May 1923; d New York, 17 Jun 1983), American composer. He studied at the Eastman School and taught composition at Juilliard 1947–58; president there from 1962.

Works include nine symphonies (1942–81), *Sinfonia* for chamber orchestra (1947), *Fantasia* for strings (1948), violin concerto (1950),

Concertato, *Moby Dick* (1952), cello concerto (fp NY, 1956, with Leonard Rose), piano concerto (1958), *Cantata de Virtute*, based on *The Pied Piper* of *Hamelin* (1969), Symphonic Movements (1971) *Reflections of Emily*, to texts by E Dickinson (1979), flute concerto (1982); two string quartets (1941, 1951), piano sonata (1963).

meno mosso Italian = 'less moved'; a direction indicating that a slower pace is to be adopted.

Menotti, Gian Carlo (b Cadegliano, 7 Jul 1911), Italian-born American composer, librettist and conductor. Studied composition with Scalero at the Curtis Institute, Philadelphia. Has written libretti of his own operas and of Barber's *Vanessa*. He founded Festival of Two Worlds at Spoleto, Italy, in 1958. In his operas he has attempted to introduce some popular elements, including values derived from the Broadway musical.

Works include operas *Amelia goes to the Ball* (1937), *The Telephone*, *The Medium* (1946), *The Consul* (1950), *Amahl and the Night Visitors* (1951), *The Saint of Bleecker Street* (1954), *Maria Golovin* (1958), *Le dernier Sauvage* (1963), *Martin's Lie* (1964), *Help, Help the Globoniks!* (1968), *The Hero* (1976), *The Most Important Man* (1971), *Tamu-Tamu* (1973), *La loca* (1979), *A Bride from Pluto* (1982), *Goya* (1986), *The Wedding* (1988); radio opera *The Old Maid and the Thief* (1939).

Symphonic poem *Apocalypse* (1951); *Pastorale* for piano and string orchestra, two piano concertos, violin concerto (1952); four pieces for string quartet, *Trio for a House-warming Party* for flute, cello and piano; *Poemetti*, piano pieces for children; pieces for carillon, etc.; symphony *The Halcyon* (1976).

mensurable music measured or measurable music which can be grouped according to regular successions of beats, as distinct from plainsong, which has no measured rhythmic pulse.

mensural notation the musical notation which, as distinct from ◊modal notation, came into use during the 13th c. and for the first time began to indicate the exact value of notes and rests by its symbols.

Menter, Sophie (b Munich, 29 Jul 1848; d Stockdorf, near Munich, 23 Feb 1918), German pianist and teacher. Studied at the Munich Conservatory, toured first at the age of 15, resumed studies with Tausig and Liszt, married Popper in 1872 and became piano professor at St Petersburg, 1883. Work for piano and orchestra, *Hungarische Zigeunerweisen*, was orchestrated by Tchaikovsky and conducted by him at its fp in 1893. This has recently been advertised as Liszt's 'third piano concerto', although the former attribution was to Menter herself.

Mentzner, Susanne (b Philadelphia, 21 Jan 1957), American mezzo-soprano. Studied at Juilliard and made debut at Houston in *La donna del lago* (1981). Appearances with Dallas Opera, Washington Opera (as Cherubino) and the NY City Opera, as Rosina. Sang with Cologne Opera from 1983, as Cherubino and Cendrillon. CG debut 1985, as Rosina, returning as Jane Seymour (*Anna Bolena*, 1988) and Dorabella (1989). NY Met from 1989, as Cherubino, Idamante, the Composer (*Ariadne*) and Octavian. Other roles include Adalgisa (Monte Carlo) and Annius in *La Clemenza di Tito* (La Scala and Chicago).

menuet French = 'minuet'; the word is a diminutive of *menu* = 'small'.

Menuetto, German-Italian, German composers of the 18th c. often labelled their minuets thus under the impression that they were using an Italian term. The correct Italian is *minuetto*, the German *Menuett*.

Menuhin, Hephzibah (b San Francisco, 20 May 1920; d London, 1 Jan 1981), American pianist. She studied in San Francisco and made her debut there in 1928. Frequent recitals with her brother Yehudi and was often heard in the Mozart concertos.

Menuhin, Yehudi (Lord Menuhin of Stoke d'Abernon) (b New York, 22 Apr 1916), American-born British violinist and conductor. Began studying the violin aged four, first with S Anker and then with L Persinger. Aged seven he played the Mendelssohn violin concerto publicly in San Francisco, then went to Europe for further study with A Busch and Enescu. He made his London debut in 1929 with the Brahms concerto and in 1932 recorded the Elgar concerto with the composer. By 1934 he had completed the first of many world tours;

Menuhin *The violinist and conductor Yehudi Menuhin in 1991. At the age of 16 he played Elgar's Violin Concerto with the 75-year-old composer as conductor, and since then has inspired several composers to write for him. During recent years he has turned increasingly to conducting.*

often performing with his sister, Hephzibah. He quickly became recognized as one of the world's outstanding musicians and virtuosi and in 1944 gave the fp of Bartók's sonata for solo violin. Recently he has devoted less time to solo performance, and concentrated more on conducting (e.g. at the Bath Festival, 1959–69), in which sphere he has also attained eminence. Salzburg conducting debut 1986 (Chamber Orchestra of Europe). Founded Menuhin School of Music at Stoke d'Abernon in Surrey, 1963. He now lives in London. Honorary KBE 1965; British citizen 1985; OM 1987; Life Peer 1993.

The Russian audience can also surprise: once in Odessa ... the well-wishers gathered in the artists' room after the recital offered few compliments on my playing, few comments on my interpretation, but to a man, demanded to know how I fingered this or that passage.

Yehudi Menuhin, *Unfinished Journey*, 1976

Merbecke, John, ◊Marbeck.

Mercadante, (Giuseppe) Saverio (Raffaele) (b Altamura near Bari, bap. 17 Sept 1795; d Naples, 17 Dec 1870), Italian composer. Studied at the Collegio di San Sebastiano at Naples and, having learnt the flute and violin, became leader of the orchestra there. On being dismissed he began to earn his living as a stage composer. After several successes in Italy he won favour in Vienna, visited Spain 1827–29, and in 1833 became *maestro di cappella* at Novara Cathedral in succession to Generali and in 1840 director of the Naples Conservatory. While at Novara he lost an eye and in 1862 he became totally blind. His most successful operas, including *Il giuramento* and *La Vestale*, have a strong dramatic purpose and seriousness of style that influenced Verdi.

Messiaen *The composer Olivier Messiaen (1908–1992) in 1967. One of the most original composers of the 20th century, Messiaen rejected the dominant trends of serialism and neo-classicism, turning instead to Greek and Indian rhythmic sources and birdsong for inspiration. He invented his own system of modes.*

Works include *c* 60 operas, e.g. *Violenza e costanza* (1820), *Elisa e Claudio* (1821), *Caritea, regina di Spagna* (1826), *Gabriella di Vergy* (1828), *I Normanni a Parigi, I briganti, Il giuramento* (1837), *I due illustri rivali* (1838), *Elena da Feltre, Il bravo* (1839), *La Vestale* (1840), *Leonora, Gli Orazi ed i Curiazi* (1846), *Virginia*; 20 Masses, motets, psalms, etc.; cantata *L'apoteosi d'Ercole* and others; instrumental pieces; songs.

Mercury nickname of Haydn's symphony no. 43, in E♭ major, composed *c* 1771.

Méreaux, Nicolas Jean (Le Froid de) (b Paris, 1745; d Paris, 1797), French organist and composer. Organist at the Paris churches of Saint-Sauveur and Petits Augustins and of the royal chapel.
Works include operas *Le Retour de tendresse, Le Duel comique, Laurette, Alexandre aux Indes, Oedipe à Thèbes*, etc.; oratorio *Samson*; motets.

Méric-Lalande, Henriette-Clémentine (b Dunkirk, 4 Nov 1799; d Chantilly, 7 Sept 1867), French soprano. As the daughter of a provincial opera manager she acquired enough experience to appear on the stage at Naples in 1814, but after a good deal of success she decided in 1822 to take lessons from García and appeared in 1823 at the Opéra-Comique in Paris, marrying the horn player Méric there. She studied further in Italy, sang there and first appeared in London in 1830, as Bellini's Imogene; she took part in the fp of Meyerbeer's *Il crociato in Egitto* (Venice, 1824) and created roles in Bellini's *Bianca e Gernando, Il Pirata* and *La Straniera*. In 1833 she created Donizetti's Lucrezia Borgia.

Merikanto, Aarre (b Helsinki, 29 Jun 1893; d Helsinki, 29 Sept 1958), Finnish composer. Studied with Reger and others at Leipzig and with Vassilenko at Moscow. Later became professor at the Helsinki Conservatory. His opera *Juha* has been successfully revived, suggesting an individual style that recalls Janáček.
Works include opera *Juha* (1922, staged 1963); ballet *The Abduction of Kylliki* (on a subject from the *Kalevala*); three symphonies (1916, 1918, 1953), variations and fugue and several suites for orchestra; four violin concertos (1916–54), three piano concertos, two cello concertos, concerto for violin, clarinet, horn and strings; partita for woodwind and harp; choral works; folksong arrangements.

Merkel, Gustav (Adolf) (b Oberoderwitz, Saxony, 12 Nov 1827; d Dresden, 30 Oct 1885), German organist and composer. Studied at

Dresden and became organist at the orphanage church there in 1858, the Kreuzkirche in 1860 and court organist in 1864. He also conducted the Vocal Academy and was professor at the Conservatory.
Works include nine sonatas, preludes and fugues, fantasies, studies, etc., for organ; instrumental pieces with organ; piano works; songs.

Merker German = lit. 'marker' = judge, adjudicator, umpire; one of the masters among the German ◊Meistersinger, who was elected to judge the competitions for mastership and prizes. Beckmesser is the Merker in Wagner's *Meistersinger*.

Mer, La, *The Sea*, three symphonic sketches by Debussy, *De l'aube à midi sur la mer, Jeux de vagues* and *Dialogue du vent et de la mer*, composed 1903–05, fp Paris, 15 Oct 1905.

Merli, Francesco (b Milan, 27 Jan 1887; d Milan, 12 Dec 1976), Italian tenor. Debut Milan 1914, in *Mosè*. Alvaro in Spontini's *Fernando Cortez* at La Scala 1916; sang there until 1946, often under Toscanini. In London and Rome he was the first local Calaf; created Respighi's Belfagor, Rome 1923. Other roles included Otello, Walther, Don José and Samson.

Merlo, Alessandro (called Alessandro Romano or Alessandro della Viola) (b Rome, *c* 1530; d ? Rome, after 1594), Italian tenor-bass, violist and composer. Pupil of Willaert and Rore. Singer in the Papal Chapel in Rome.
Works include motets; madrigals, *Canzoni alla Napolitana, villanelle*.

Merope opera by Gasparini (libretto by A Zeno), produced Venice, Teatro San Cassiano, 26 Dec 1711. Polyphontes overthrows King Cresphontes, executing him and two of his three sons. Aepytus escapes and, after growing up, kills Polyphontus and becomes the rightful king.
Also settings by Jommelli (1741), Terradellas (1743), and Graun (1756).

Merrem-Nikisch, Grete (b Duren, 7 Jul 1887; d Kiel, 12 Mar 1970), German soprano. Debut Leipzig, 1910. She sang at the Berlin Hofoper 1913–30, in lyric roles and as Sophie and Eva, and at the Dresden Staatsoper took part in the fps of *Die toten Augen* (1916), *Intermezzo* (1924) and *Cardillac* (1926). She married Arthur Nikisch's eldest son in 1914 and from 1918 was successful in Lieder recitals.

Merrick, Frank (b Clifton, Bristol, 30 Apr 1886; d London, 19 Feb 1981), English pianist and composer. Studied first with his parents and then with Leschetizky in Vienna, making his London debut in

A Selection of

Messiaen

Quatuor pour la fin du temps	1940
Visions de l'amen	1943
Vingt regards sur l'Enfant Jésus	1944
Trois petites liturgies	1944
Turangalîla-Symphonie	1946–8
Catalogue d'oiseaux	1953
Chronochromie	1960
La Transfiguration de Notre Seigneur	1969
St François d'Assise	1983
Le Livre du Saint Sacrement	1986

1903. In 1910 he won a Rubinstein Prize in St Petersburg and from 1911 to 1929 taught at the RMCM, after which he became professor at the RCM. In 1928 he won a prize offered by the Columbia Graphophone Co., for completing Schubert's 'Unfinished' symphony.

Merrill, Robert (b Brooklyn, 4 Jun 1917), American baritone. Studied first with his mother and then with S Margolis in NY, making his debut in 1944 and joining the NY Met. in 1945, as Germont, followed by Rigoletto, Iago, Scarpia and Figaro. Other roles included Posa, Amonasro and Renato. London, CG, 1967, as Germont.

When in doubt, sing loud.
Robert Merrill, *Saturday Evening Post*, 1957

Merriman, Nan (b Pittsburgh, 28 Apr 1920), American mezzo. Studied in LA with Alexia Bassian, making her debut in Cincinnati in 1942 as La Cieca, but her real career began with Toscanini's patronage, and she recorded roles in *Falstaff*, *Rigoletto* and *Otello* with him. Sang Baba the Turk in *The Rake's Progress* at Edinburgh, 1953.

Merritt, Chris (b Oklahoma City, 27 Sept 1952), American tenor. Studied in the USA and made debut at the Salzburg Landestheater 1978, as Lindoro. Augsburg 1981–84, as Idomeneo, Rodolfo, Julien and Rossini's Otello; other Rossini roles have included Pyrrhus in *Ermione*, Erisso (*Maometto II*) and James in *La donna del lago* (CG debut 1985). Returned to London 1986, as Idreno in *Semiramide* (concert) and Arnold in *Guillaume Tell* (1990). Sang Count Libenskoff in *Il viaggio a Reims* in Vienna and Pesaro, Amenophis in *Moïse et Pharaon* at the Paris Opéra. Opened the 1990 season at Chicago as Gluck's Admète and he is noted for his powerful interpretations of Aeneas in *Les Troyens* and the title role in *Robert le Diable* (Carnegie Hall).

Merry Widow (Lehár.) ◊Lustige Witwe.

Merry Wives of Windsor ◊Falstaff, ◊Lustigen Weiber, ◊Sir John in Love.

Mersenne, Marin (b La Soultière, Maine, France, 8 Sept 1588; d Paris, 1 Sept 1648), French monk, mathematician, philosopher and music theorist. Educated at Le Mans and La Flèche, he became a Minorite friar, being ordained in 1612. He taught philosophy at Nevers and then studied mathematics and music in Paris, Descartes and the elder Pascal being among his colleagues. He corresponded with scholars in England, Holland and Italy, the last of which he visited three times. His treatises include *Harmonie universelle*, two vols., pub. Paris, 1636–37, with a section on instruments, *Questions harmoniques*, *De la nature des sons*.

Merula, Tarquinio (b Cremona, *c* 1594; d Cremona, 10 Dec 1665), Italian composer and organist. Held appointments alternately at Bergamo and Cremona, and was court and church organist at Warsaw in 1624. From 1628 to 1639 he was at Cremona as *maestro di cappella* at the cathedral, and returned to this post in 1652 after an interval at Bergamo.

Works include Masses, motets, psalms, *Concerti spirituali* and other church music; madrigals, *canzoni* for voices and/or instruments; church sonatas.

Merulo (also called *Claudio da Correggio*; real name *Merlotti*), Claudio (b Correggio, 8 Apr 1533; d Parma, 5 May 1604), Italian organist, teacher and composer. Appointed organist at Brescia in 1556 and second organist at St Mark's, Venice, in 1557, advancing to first organist in 1564. In 1584 he left Venice, visited the court of Mantua and became organist to the ducal chapel at Parma. Best known for his keyboard music.

Works include intermezzi for Dolce's *Le Troiane* (1566) and Cornelio Frangipani's *La tragedia* (1574); Masses, motets, *Sacrae cantiones*, Litanies; madrigals; toccatas and *ricercari* for organ.

messa di voce Italian = 'setting or placing of the voice'; sustained singing of notes or phrase; but *messa* may also mean a *crescendo* followed by a *diminuendo* on a single breath.

Messager, André (Charles Prosper) (b Montluçon, 30 Dec 1853; d Paris, 24 Feb 1929), French composer and conductor. Studied at

---

Messiaen   *A biographical note*

While other composers sought to isolate themselves from the fact of war, Messiaen was forced by circumstances to participate. Confined in a Silesian *Stalag* by the Germans, he resisted the cold and hunger by composing and then performing in the *Quatuor pour la fin du temps*. Written for a broken piano and a plangent cello with violin and clarinet, the score is prefaced with the declaration from the Revelation of St John, 'There shall be time no longer.' Similar religious certainties influenced much of Messiaen's subsequent music, including the massive oratorio-like *La Transfiguration de Notre Seigneur Jesus Christ* (1969) and culminating in the four-hour opera *St François d'Assise* (1983). With their affinity for bird life of every description, St Francis and Messiaen were kindred spirits, the composer painstakingly notating bird song on his travels and reproducing it in the *Catalogue d'oiseaux* for piano (1958) and the orchestral *Oiseaux exotiques* (1956). Religious fervour and love of nature were complemented by the human passions in such works as the song cycle *Harawi*, 'A song of love and death' (1945), and the huge *Turangalîla Symphonie*, premiered under Bernstein in 1949. In this work, the great static blocks of Messiaenic affirmations are supported (or undermined, according to taste) by the swooping, unearthly sound of the Ondes Martenot. In later years such overt sensationalism was refined in the nature worship of the orchestral *Chronochromie* (1960) and *Des Canyons aux Étoiles* 1974). A final vision of the divine spirit which is present in all creation was vouchsafed in 1991 with *Éclairs sur L'Au-Delà* (Illuminations of the Beyond).

Niedermeyer's school in Paris and later under Saint-Saëns. In 1876 he won prizes for a symphony and a cantata and in 1883 he produced a completion of an operetta *François les Bas-bleus* left unfinished by Firmin Bernicat. He became conductor of the Opéra-Comique and in 1898 its general director; from 1901 to 1906 he was artistic director at CG, London, and from 1901 to 1913 joint director of the Opéra. He was also a concert conductor. His wife was the Irish composer Hope Temple (Dotie Davies, 1859–1938), who had been a pupil of his. He conducted the fp of Debussy's *Pelléas et Mélisande* in 1902.

Works include operas and operettas *La Fauvette du Temple* (1885), *La Béarnaise*, *Le Bourgeois de Calais* (1887), *Isoline* (1888), *Le Mari de la reine* (1889), *La Basoche* (1890), *Madame Chrysanthème* (after Pierre Loti's novel, 1893), *Miss Dollar*, *Mirette*, *Le Chevalier d'Harmental* (1896), *Les P'tites Michu* (1897), *Véronique* (1898), *Les Dragons de l'impératrice* (1905), *Fortunio*, *Béatrice* (1914), *Monsieur Beaucaire*, (in English, 1919), *La Petite Fonctionnaire* (1921), *L'Amour masqué*, *Passionnement* (1926), *Coup de roulis*; ballets *Les Deux Pigeons* (1886), *Scaramouche* (1891), *Le Chevalier aux fleurs* (1897), *Une Aventure de la Guimard* (1900) and others; instrumental pieces; piano duets; songs.

Messchaert, Johannes (Martinus) (b Hoorn, 22 Aug 1857; d Zurich, 9 Sept 1922), Dutch bass-baritone. Studied with J Stockhausen. He sang much in Holland, Germany and elsewhere and toured as interpreter of songs with Julius Röntgen as pianist.

Messe French and German = 'Mass'.

Messe solennelle ◊Missa solemnis.

Messiaen, Olivier (Eugène Prosper Charles) (b Avignon, 10 Dec 1908; d Clichy, Haute-de-Seine, 27 Apr 1992), French composer and organist, son of the poet Cécile Sauvage. Studied organ under Marcel Dupré, theory under Maurice Emmanuel and composition under Dukas at the Paris Conservatory. Appointed organist of the Trinité in Paris, 1931, and professor at the École Normale de Musique and the Schola Cantorum. With Baudrier, Jolivet and Lesur he formed the group 'La Jeune France'. In 1940 he was taken prisoner by the

Germans but repatriated later and appointed professor of harmony at the Conservatory in 1942 and professor of music and rhythmic analysis in 1947. He married (1) Claire Delbos, (2) Yvonne Loriod. His music makes use of Indian and Greek rhythms, a variety of modes, and in later works a free trancsription of bird-song. His strong Catholic faith also informs most of his music, in particular the vocal works from *O sacrum convivium* (1937) to his masterpiece, the opera *St François d'Assise* (1983). His influence as a teacher was considerable, with Boulez, Xenakis, Stockhausen, Goehr and George Benjamin among his pupils.

Works include opera *St François d'Assise* (1983); *O sacrum convivium* (1937) and *Cinq rechants* (1949) for chorus; *Trois petites liturgies de la Présence Divine* for women's chorus, celesta, vibraphone, Ondes Martenot, piano, percussion and strings (1944), *La Transfiguration* for tenor, baritone, chorus and orchestra (1969).

ORCHESTRAL: *Les Offrandes oubliées* (1930), *Hymne au Saint Sacrement, Turangalîla-Symphonie* (1946–48), *Chronochromie* for orchestra (1960) *Couleurs de la cité céleste* (1963); *Et expecto resurrectionem mortuorum* for woodwind, brass and percussion (1964), *Réveil des oiseaux* for piano and orchestra (1953), *Oiseaux exotiques* for piano and wind instruments, *Sept Haïkai* for piano and wind instruments (1963), *Des canyons aux étoiles* for piano, horn and orchestra (1970–74), *Un vitrail et des oiseaux* (1986), *La ville d'en haut* (1987), *Éclairs sur l'au-delà* (1988–91), *Un sourire* (1989), Concert à quatre for piano, oboe, flute, cello and orchestra (1992; completed by Yvonne Loriod).

INSTRUMENTAL: *Quatuor pour la fin du temps* for clarinet, violin, cello and piano (1940); theme and variations for violin and piano.

ORGAN: *Diptyque, Le Banquet céleste, L'Ascension* (1934), *La Nativité du Seigneur* (1935), *Apparition de l'église éternelle, Les Corps glorieux* (1939), *Messe de la Pentecôte* (1950), *Le Livre d'orgue, Livre du Saint-Sacrement*, in 18 movements (1985).

PIANO: eight *Préludes* (1929), *Fantaisie burlesque* (1931), *Vingt regards sur l'Enfant Jésus* (1944), *Île de feu, Catalogue des oiseaux* (1956–58), *Cantéyodajayâ* (1948); *Visions de l'amen* for two pianos (1943).

SOLO VOCAL: *Poèmes pour Mi* (1936) and *La mort du nombre* for voice and orchestra; *Chants de terre et de ciel* and *Harawi* (1945) for voice and piano.

Among the artistic hierarchy, the birds are probably the greatest musicians to inhabit our planet.

Olivier Messiaen, quoted in Johnson, *Messiaen*, 1975

Messiah, not *The Messiah*, oratorio by Handel (words selected from the Bible by Charles Jennens), performed Dublin, Music Hall in Fishamble Street, 13 Apr 1742; first performance in England, CG, London, 23 Mar 1743.

Messidor opera by Bruneau (libretto by E Zola), produced Paris, Opéra, 19 Feb 1897. Bruneau had already written operas on subjects from Zola's works (*L'Attaque du moulin* and *Le Rêve*), but this was the first for which Zola himself wrote the libretto.

Messner, Joseph (b Schwaz, Tyrol, 27 Feb 1893; d Salzburg, 23 Feb 1969), Austrian organist, conductor and composer. Studied in Munich and was appointed organist to Salzburg Cathedral in 1922. He also conducted there, including the music in the cathedral during the Salzburg Festival.

Works include operas *Hadassa* (1925), *Das letzte Recht* (1932), *Ines, Agnes Bernauer* (1935); 11 Masses, Te Deum and other church music; oratorios *Das Leben* and *Die vier letzten Dinge*; three symphonies, *Symphonische Festmusik* for orchestra; *Sinfonietta* for piano and orchestra.

mesto Italian = 'sad, gloomy'.

Metamorphosen study in C minor for 23 solo strings by Strauss; composed 1945, in response to the wartime devastation of Europe, in particular the destruction of the opera houses, in which his works were performed throughout World War II. Dedicated to Paul Sacher and the Collegium Musicum; fp Zurich, 25 Jan 1946.

Metamorphoses after Ovid, Six, *Pan, Phaeton, Niobe, Bacchus, Narcissus, Arethusa*, work for solo oboe by Britten; composed 1951, fp Thorpeness, 14 Jun 1951.

metamorphosis the transformation of theme or motif, especially rhythmically while the same notes are retained, as for example the *idée fixe* of Berlioz, the themes in Liszt's symphonic poems, etc. and the *Leitmotive* in Wagner's operas.

metaphor aria ◊parable aria.

Metastasio (real name **Trapassi**), Pietro (b Rome, 3 Jan 1698; d Vienna, 12 Apr 1782), Italian poet and librettist. His first original libretto, *Didone*, was produced in 1724 (music by Sarro). The rigid musical and dramatic conventions imposed by his verse dominated opera until Gluck's reforms of 1762. Operas on his libretti ◊*Achille in Sciro, Adriano in Siria, Alessandro nell' Indie, Antigono, Artaserse, Catone in Utica, Cinesi, Clemenza di Tito, Cleofide, Contesa dei numi, Demetrio, Demofoonte, Démophoön, Didone abbandonata, Eroe cinese, Ezio, Galatea, Innocenza giustificata, Ipermestra, Isola disabitata, Lucio Silla, Olimpiade, Partenope, Rè pastore, Ruggiero, Semiramide riconosciuta, Siface, Siroe, Sogno di Scipione, Tito Vespasiano, Trionfo di Clelia*.

◊Hasse, Jommelli and ◊Paisiello.

Metner, Nikolai Karlovich, ◊Medtner.

metre the rhythmic patterns produced in music by notes of varying length combined with strong and weak beats (*arsis* and *thesis*), similar to the different 'feet' (spondees, dactyls, anapaests, trochees, iambics, etc.) in poetry. Metre in music is represented numerically in the time signature at the beginning of a work.

metronome an instrument patented by Mälzel in 1815 and designed to determine and prescribe the pace of any musical composition by the beats of a pendulum. The tempo is indicated by the composer, who prescribes how many time-units of a certain note-value are to occupy one minute: e.g. ♩ = 60 shows that there are to be 60 crotchets to the minute.

Metropolitan Opera House America's leading opera house, founded 1883 in New York. From its earliest days the main emphasis has been on quality of singing, rather than total musical/production values. Early managers included Anton Seidl, Walter Damrosch, Heinrich Conried and Giulio Gatti-Casazza (1908–35). Singers before World War I included C Nilsson, Sembrich, Caruso, the De Reszkes, Melba and Destinn. Edward Johnson became manager in 1935; famous

A Selection of
Meyerbeer

Il crociato in Egitto................................1824
Robert le Diable.....................................1831
Les Huguenots.......................................1836

Le Prophète..............................1849
Le Pardon de Ploërmel (Dinorah) 1859
L'Africaine.....................1865

singers of the inter-war years were Flagstad, Gigli, Leider, Melchior and Tibbett. Under Rudolf Bing's management (1950–72) some attempt was made to improve theatrical standards. In 1966 the co. moved to the Lincoln Center for the Performing Arts, NY. Recent managers include Anthony Bliss (1975–85); Bruce Crawford 1986–89, Hugh Southern 1989–90, Joseph Volpe from 1990. James Levine music director from 1975, artistic director from 1986. The Met. once had a reputation for musical conservatism, but recent years have seen the premieres of Corigliano's *The Ghosts of Versailles* (1991) and *The Voyage* by Philip Glass (1992).

Metternich, Josef (b Hermuhlheim, near Cologne, 2 Jun 1915), German baritone. Debut Berlin, Städtische Oper, 1945, as Tonio. Sang at the NY Met. and was guest in London, Milan and Vienna, as Jochanaan, the Dutchman, Scarpia and Don Carlo. He joined the Munich Opera in 1954 and was Johannes Kepler in the 1957 fp of Hindemith's *Die Harmonie der Welt*.

Metzger-Lattermann, Ottilie (b Frankfurt, 15 Jul 1878; d Auschwitz, Feb 1943), German contralto. She sang at Halle and Cologne 1899–1903 and was engaged at Hamburg 1903–15; guest in Berlin, Vienna and St Petersburg. In Dec 1910 she was Herodias in the first London performance of *Salome*, at CG, under Beecham. Bayreuth 1901–12, as Erda and Waltraute. She sang in Dresden 1915–21 and in 1923 was Magdalena in the first US performance of *Der Evangelimann*, at Chicago. Arrested by the Nazis and died in Auschwitz.

Mewton-Wood, Noel (b Melbourne, 20 Nov 1922; d London, 5 Dec 1953), Australian pianist, studied at the Melbourne Conservatory, the RAM in London and under Schnabel. He first appeared in London in 1940 and made a great impression; gave works by Bliss, Britten, Tippett and Busoni. He died after taking prussic acid.

Meyer, Ernst Hermann (b Berlin, 8 Dec 1905; d Berlin, 8 Oct 1988), German musicologist and composer. Studied in Berlin and Heidelberg. Lived in London from 1933 to 1948, when he was appointed professor of music sociology at the Humbolt University, Berlin. His books include studies of 17th-c. instrumental music and English chamber music from the Middle Ages to Purcell.

Works include opera *Reiter der Nacht* (1973); film and chamber music, etc.

Meyer, Gregor (b Basel, Nov 1576), Swiss organist and composer. He was organist at Solothurn Cathedral and supplied Glareanus with compositions exemplifying the correct use of modes. Works include motets, Kyries, Antiphons.

Meyer, Kerstin (b Stockholm, 3 Apr 1928), Swedish mezzo. Debut Stockholm, 1952 as Azucena. NY Met. debut 1960, Carmen. Glyndebourne since 1961; roles there included Monteverdi's Ottavia and Debussy's Geneviève. Also sang in the first British performance of *Elegy for Young Lovers* and *The Visit of the Old Lady* (von Einem). London, CG, from 1960 as Berlioz's Dido, Octavian and Clytemnestra. Bayreuth 1962–64, as Brangaene. She has sung in the fps of works by Goehr and Searle in Hamburg, and in 1966 created Agave in Henze's *The Bassarids* (Salzburg). Has often returned to Stockholm, and in 1978 created Spermando in Ligeti's *Le Grand Macabre*.

Meyer, Leonard B(unce) (b New York, 12 Jan 1918), American theorist and aesthetician. Studied at Columbia University and the University of Chicago; taught at the University of Chicago (1961) and the University of Pennsylvania (1975). His books include *Emotion and Meaning in Music* (1956) and (with Grosvenor Cooper) *The Rhythmic Structure of Music* (1960).

Meyerbeer, Giacomo (actually Jakob Liebmann Beer) (b Berlin, 5 Sept 1791; d Paris, 2 May 1864), German composer and pianist. His father Herz Beer, a banker, gave him every facility to develop his precocious gifts. He was at first trained as a pianist and had some lessons from Clementi during the latter's stay in Berlin. He played in public at the age of seven, but afterwards studied theory and composition under Zelter, B A Weber and Vogler, to whose house at Darmstadt he moved in 1810, being a fellow-student with C M von Weber there. His first opera was produced at Munich in 1812 and the second at Stuttgart in 1813. He then went to Vienna and, hearing Hummel play, he retired for further piano studies, after which he appeared again as a virtuoso.

Meyerbeer *The composer Giacomo Meyerbeer (1791–1864). German by birth, he settled in Paris and became the greatest composer of Grand Opera. Although today he is famous for Wagner's criticism of his works, Meyerbeer's style was, in fact, the model for Wagner's* Rienzi.

On Salieri's advice he went to Italy to study vocal writing in 1815, and produced his first Italian opera at Padua in 1817. In 1823 he tried his luck in Berlin, but without much success, and having produced *Il crociato* at Venice in 1824, went to Paris for its fp there in 1826. He settled and spent much time there for the rest of his life. He wrote no new work between 1824 and 1831, among the reasons being his father's death, his marriage and the loss of two children. In 1831 *Robert le Diable* made him sensationally fashionable in Paris. This opera, followed by *Les Huguenots* and *Le Prophète* established Meyerbeer as a master of the French grand opera, with ingredients including strong local colour, a sure sense of history, novel instrumental effects and extended ballets. In 1842 the King of Prussia appointed him General Music Director in Berlin. He visited Vienna and London in 1847 and the latter again in 1862, when he represented German music at the International Exhibition. His health began to fail about 1850, and one of his most evocative operas, *L'Africaine*, was left uncompleted at his death.

Works include operas *Jephthas Gelübde* (1812), *Alimelek, oder Die beiden Kalifen, Romilda e Costanza* (1817), *Semiramide riconosciuta* (1819), *Emma di Resburgo* (1819), *Margherita d'Anjou* (1820), *L'esule di Granata, Das Brandenburger Tor, Il crociato in Egitto* (1824), *Robert le Diable* (1831), *Les Huguenots* (1836), *Ein Feldlager in Schlesin* (1844), *Le Prophète* (1849), *L'Étoile du Nord* (1854), *Le Pardon de Ploërmel* (*Dinorah*), *L'Africaine* (1865), *Judith* (unfinished).

Monodrama *Thevelindens Liebe*; incidental music to Michael Beer's (his brother's) drama *Struensee*, Blaze de Bury's *Jeunesse de Goethe* and Aeschylus' *Eumenides*; masque *Das Hoffest von Ferrara*; ballet *Der Fischer und das Milchmädchen* (1810); oratorio *Gott und die Natur* (1811); *Stabat Mater*, Te Deum, psalms and other church music; several cantatas, including two for the Schiller centen-

---- **THE OPERA** ----

The Midsummer Marriage

A three-act opera by Michael Tippett set in England, at the present time, on Midsummer Day. It was first produced in 1955.

I. The businessman King Fisher (bass) wishes to prevent the marriage of his daughter Jenifer (soprano) to Mark (tenor). Before the marriage, they must discover their true selves; Jenifer experiences spiritual purity in her quest, while Mark enjoys bodily abandon in his. They conclude by deciding to return and reverse their experiences.

II. In a parallel with Mozart's *Magic Flute*, the exalted couple are matched by a down-to-earth pair, Jack (tenor), a mechanic, and Bella (soprano), a secretary to King Fisher. They sing of their future happiness and three Ritual Dances follow, in which Mark's alter ego, Strephon, is pursued by a transformed female dancer: The Earth in Autumn, The Waters in Winter, The Air in Spring.

III. A clairvoyant, Madame Sosostris (contralto), has a vision of a happily united Mark and Jenifer. When King Fisher unveils Sosostris, he discovers the couple, protected by a huge lotus flower bud. He is powerless to prevent their union, and dies. Strephon and his followers perform their fourth dance, Fire in Summer, and a transfigured Mark and Jenifer emerge to the sunlight.

---- **THE OPERA** ----

ary, 1859, seven sacred cantatas (Klopstock) for unaccompanied chorus; March for ditto, three Torch Dances, Coronation March, *Overture in the Form of a March* for the London Exhibition; piano works; songs.

Meyerowitz, Jan (b Breslau, 23 Apr 1913), German-born American composer. Studied in Berlin with Zemlinsky and Rome with Respighi. Moved to USA 1946, citizen from 1951.

Works include operas *The Barrier* (1950), *Eastward in Eden* (1951), *Esther* (1957), *Godfather Death* (1961), *Winterballade* (1967); *Silesian Symphony* (1957), oboe concerto (1963), six pieces for orchestra (1967); Cantatas on texts by E Dickinson, Cummings and Herrick; chamber music.

Meyers, Anne Akiko (b San Diego, 1970), American violinist. Studied with Josef Gingold and at Juilliard. Debut as concert soloist aged seven, later playing with the Los Angeles and New York Philharmonics. Far Eastern tours with local orchestras and concerts with the Moscow PO, St Louis SO, Orchestre de Paris and Boston SO. Recordings include concertos by Barber and Bruch, with the Royal Philharmonic.

Meyer von Schauensee, Franz (Joseph Leonti) (b Lucerne, 10 Aug 1720; d Lucerne, 2 Jan 1789), Swiss organist and composer. Studied in Lucerne and Milan, and after a period of military service, 1742–44, returned to Lucerne as a civil servant and musician. Ordained priest in 1752, he became organist of the collegiate church, and in 1762 choirmaster. He founded the Lucerne college of music in 1760.

Works include *Singspiele Hans Hüttenstock* and others; Masses and other church music; arias; instrumental music.

Meyrowitz, Selmar (b Bartenstein, E Prussia, 18 Apr 1875; d Toulouse, 24 Mar 1941), German conductor. Studied at the Leipzig Conservatory and with Bruch in Berlin. His appointments as opera conductor included Karlsruhe, NY, Prague and Berlin, and later he was a concert conductor in Berlin, Hamburg, Vienna, Rome, etc. In 1933 he emigrated to Paris.

mezza Italian fem. = *half*, as in *mezza voce* = half-voice, a special way of producing the voice as if under the breath, resulting not only in a soft tone, but in a quality different from that of the full voice.

mezzo Italian masc. = 'half', as in *mezzo-soprano*, a voice half-way between soprano and contralto in range.

mf (abbr.) = *mezzo forte* 'half-loud'.

M'Gibbon, William (b Edinburgh, *c* 1690; d Edinburgh, 3 Oct 1756), Scottish violinist and composer. Pupil of his father, the oboist Matthew M'Gibbon, and of Corbett in London, on his return to Edinburgh he became leader of the orchestra in the Gentlemen's Concerts. Composed overtures, violin concertos, violin sonatas etc., and pub. three vols of Scottish tunes.

M'Guckin, Barton (b Dublin, 28 Jul 1852; d Stoke Poges, Bucks., 17 Apr 1913), Irish tenor. Choirboy at Armagh Cathedral, became a singer at St Patrick's Cathedral, Dublin, and made his first concert appearance there in 1874. The next year he sang in London, then studied briefly at Milan, and afterwards took to opera. In 1887–88 he appeared in the USA. Sang with Carl Rosa Co. 1878–96. His roles included Des Grieux, Don José and Wilhelm Meister.

Mi the old name for the note E (♭solmization), still used in Latin countries, and in Tonic Sol-fa the Mediant note in any key, represented by the symbol m, pronounced Me.

Miaskovsky, Nikolai Yakovlevich (b Novogeorgievsk near Warsaw, 20 Apr 1881; d Moscow, 9 Aug 1950), Russian composer. Son of a Russian military engineer stationed in Poland, whence the family moved successively to Orenburg, Kazan and Nizhny-Novgorod, where Miaskovsky joined the cadet corps. Intended to follow his father's career, he did not finally take to music until 1907, when he resigned his commission, though he had composed many piano preludes, studied with Glière and Krizhanovsky and entered the St Petersburg Conservatory in 1906, where he studied with Rimsky-Korsakov, Liadov and Wihtol. In 1914–17 he fought on the Austrian front and was badly wounded; in 1921 he became composition professor at the Moscow Conservatory. Although he was denounced in 1948 with Prokofiev and others for 'formalism', his music is in a tonal, conservative idiom.

Works include oratorio *Kirov is with us*; 27 symphonies (1908–50), two sinfoniettas, symphonic poems *Silence* (after Poe) and *Alastor* (after Shelley), serenade and *Lyric Concertino* for small orchestra; violin concerto (1938); cello concertino (1945); *Salutatory Overture* on Stalin's 60th birthday (1939); 13 string quartets (1913–49); two cello and piano sonatas; nine piano sonatas and other piano pieces; 13 op. nos. of songs.

Mica, František Václav (b Třebíč, Moravian, 5 Sept 1694; d Jaroměřice, 15 Feb 1744), Moravian tenor and composer. Probably studied in Vienna, and in 1711 entered the service of Count Questenberg in Jaroměřice, becoming *Kapellmeister* in 1722 and there producing five operas of his own and many by other composers, two symphonies sometimes attributed to him, though clearly too modern in style, are the work of his nephew, Jan Adam František Mica (1746–1811).

Works include operas; cantatas; Passion oratorios.

Theatre music must make its point and communicate its emotion at the same moment the action develops: It cannot wait to be understood until after the curtain comes down.

Gian Carlo Menotti, quoted in Ewen,
American Composers, 1982

Michael, Roger (Rogier) (b Mons, *c* 1550; d Dresden, *c* 1619), Flemish tenor and composer. Studied under his father, Simon Michael, a musician to the Emperor Ferdinand I. He became a tenor in the electoral chapel at Dresden, 1575 and *Kapellmeister* 1587, being succeeded in the latter post by Schütz in 1619.

Works include introits in the motet style, settings of hymn-tunes in four parts and other sacred music, including *Christmas Story*.

Michael, Tobias (b Dresden, 13 Jun 1592; d Leipzig, 26 Jun 1657), German composer, son of Roger ♭Michael. Studied as a boy chorister under his father in the Dresden court chapel and became music director at Sondershausen in 1619. In 1631 he succeeded Schein as cantor of St Thomas's Church at Leipzig.

Works include *Musikalische Seelenlust* containing sacred

madrigals for voices and sacred concertos for voices and instruments (1634–37), other church music.

Michaels-Moore, Anthony (b Essex, 8 Apr 1957), English baritone. Studied with David Matthews and at the Royal Scottish Academy. Has sung at CG from 1987, in *Jenůfa*, *Boris Godunov* and *Rigoletto*. ENO from 1987, as Zurga, Marcello and Mozart's Count (1991). US debut at Philadelphia in 1989, as Guglielmo; Missa Solemnis at Los Angeles. For Opera North has sung Escamillo, Figaro, and Verdi's Posa (1993). Sang Don Ferdinand in the stage premiere of Gerhard's *The Duenna* (Madrid 1992) and opened the season at La Scala in 1993 with Licinius in *La Vestale*.

Micheau, Janine (b Toulouse, 17 Apr 1914; d Paris, 18 Oct 1976), French soprano. Debut Paris, Opéra-Comique, 1933, as Cherubino; sang there until 1956 as Mireille, Olympia and the first local Zerbinetta and Anne Trulove. At the Opéra she took part in the fp of Milhaud's *Bolivar* (1950) and was well known as Sophie, Gilda and Pamina. CG 1937, Micaela. US debut 1938 San Francisco, as Mélisande. At Aix she was heard in Rameau's *Platée* (1955).

Michelangeli, Arturo Benedetti (b Brescia, 5 Jun 1920; d Lugano, 12 Jun 1995), Italian pianist. Studied at the Instituto Musicale Venturi in Brescia and at Milan Conservatory. In 1939 he won the international piano competition in Geneva. Though he was among the foremost pianists of his day, his concert appearances were infrequent and much of his time was taken up with teaching. London debut 1946, US 1948. Gave Beethoven and Chopin recitals at the Barbican, London, 1990.

Micheletti, Gaston (b Tavaco, Corsica, 5 Jan 1892; d Ajaccio, 21 May 1959), French tenor. Debut Rheims 1922, as Faust. He joined the Paris Opéra-Comique in 1925 and was successful there for 20 years as Werther, Don José and Des Grieux. He appeared as guest in Brussels and Monte Carlo.

Micheli, Romano (b Rome, *c* 1575; d Rome, *c* 1660), Italian composer. Studied under Soriano, travelled widely in Italy, became a priest, held appointments at Modena and Aquileia, and returned to Rome in 1625 as *maestro di cappella* of the church of San Luigi de' Francesi.

Works include Masses, motets, psalms; madrigals, canons.

Mi contra Fa a medieval designation of the tritone (the forbidden interval of the augmented fourth), the Mi being the mediant of the hard hexachord beginning on G.

microphone the receiver which transmits and amplifies the sounds of a broadcast performance. It can also be used for other than radio or television purposes, e.g. in theatres and public halls for the relaying of speech, song and taped sound to amplifiers placed at various points of the building.

microtones any interval smaller than a semitone; the small fractional notes into which the musical scale was divided by the Mexican composer Julián Carrillo, who invented special instruments for the purpose; earlier, though unsystematic, use of microtones was made by Ives and Bartók. Alois Hába employed quarter-tones from 1920; later fifth and sixth-tones. With the advent of electronic music and the growing interest in reviving earlier scale temperaments, virtually all pitches have become part of the composer's potential vocabulary.

middle C the note C in the middle of the keyboard, variously represented in notation according to the clef used.

Middle C in bass, tenor, alto, and treble clefs.

Midgley, Walter (b Bramley, 1914; d Ramstead, Surrey, 18 Sept 1980), English tenor. He sang with the Carl Rosa chorus before World War II and from 1945 was heard at SW as Rodolfo, Turiddu and Almaviva. In 1947 he had much success at CG as Calaf; remained until 1953 as Alfredo, Manrico and Cavaradossi. Edinburgh 1947, as Macduff, with the Glyndebourne Co.

Midori, (Goto Mi Dori) (b Osaka, 25 Oct 1971), Japanese violinist. Studied at Juilliard and played with the New York Philharmonic 1982. Many appearances with the Berlin Philharmonic, Boston and

—— THE OPERA ——

A Midsummer Night's Dream

A three-act opera by Benjamin Britten, with text by Peter Pears and the composer based closely on Shakespeare's play of the same name. It was first performed at Aldeburgh in 1960. It takes place in a wood near ancient Athens.

I. Oberon (counter-tenor) quarrels with his Queen Tytania (soprano) over her boy attendant and, in revenge, orders Puck (spoken) to fetch a magic herbal juice. A quartet of Athenians enter: first Hermia (mezzo-soprano) and her lover Lysander (tenor), then Helena (soprano) and Hermia's intended, Demetrius (baritone). After a group of rustics have rehearsed their play for the Duke of Athens, Puck squeezes the juice into the sleeping Lysander's eyes; when he awakes he declares his love for Helena. Next Tytania's eyes are sprinkled by Puck.

II. Tytania wakes to fall in love with the rustic Bottom (bass-baritone), wearing an ass's head. Demetrius now gets Puck's treatment and becomes a rival with Lysandra for Helena, to the fury of Hermia. Oberon commands Puck to restore order.

III. With Tytania's boy restored to him, Oberon releases Tytania and Bottom from their spells. The lovers are reconciled and, at the court of Duke Theseus, the rustics perform their play (in opera, a parody of bel canto convention; at the original production Peter Pears imitated Joan Sutherland as Lucia di Lamermoor).

—— THE OPERA ——

Chicago SOs, London SO, Orchestre de Paris and Philadelphia Orchestra. Played the Tchaikovsky Concerto on debut at the London Proms, 1993. Recordings include the Paganini Caprices and both Bartók Concertos.

Midsummer Marriage, The opera by Tippett (libretto by composer), produced London, CG, 27 Jan 1955. Spiritually-minded Mark and Jenifer are matched by more down-to-earth Jack and Bella in magical initiation ceremonies.

Midsummer Night's Dream, A ◊Songe d'une nuit d'été.

Incidental music by Mendelssohn to Shakespeare's play. Overture composed summer 1826 fp Stettin in Feb 1827; the rest of the music composed in 1842 and used for a stage production at Potsdam on 14 Oct 1843.

Opera by Britten (libretto from Shakespeare), produced Aldeburgh, Jubilee Hall, 11 Jun 1960. Lovers, fairies and rustics intermingle in enchanted forest.

Migenes, Julia (b New York, 13 Mar 1945), American soprano. Studied in New York and appeared on Broadway before NY City Opera debut, 1965. Sang at the Vienna Volksoper 1973–78, as Blondchen, Susanna, Schmidt's Esmerelda, and Olympia. NY Met from 1979, as Jenny in *Mahagonny* and Lulu (also in Vienna); Geneva Opéra 1983, as Salome, and sang Carmen in Francesco Rossi's 1984 film. CG debut 1987 (Manon) and sang Tosca at Earl's Court, 1991. Admired for her spirited performances.

Mighty Handful, The ◊Kutchka.

Mignon opera by A Thomas (libretto by J Barbier and M Carré, based on Goethe's *Wilhelm Meister*), produced Paris, Opéra-Comique, 17 Nov 1866. Gypsy girl Mignon falls for Wilhelm Meister, who seems more interested in the actress Philine. After later nursing Mignon, who is injured in a fire, Wilhelm affirms his love. Mignon turns out to be the long-lost Spirata, daughter of the Lord in whose house she recuperates.

Mignone, Francisco (b São Paulo, 3 Sept 1897; d Rio de Janeiro, 18 Feb 1986), Brazilian composer. Studied at São Paulo Conservatory and later in Milan, in 1929 becoming professor at the National Conservatory in Rio de Janeiro.

Works include operas *O contratador dos diamantes* (1924), *El jayon* (= *L'innocente*, 1927); ballet *Maracatú de Chico-Rei* (1933); clarinet and bassoon concertos; orchestral music; and songs, etc.

Migot, Georges (Elbert) (b Paris, 27 Feb 1891; d Levallois, near Paris, 5 Jan 1976), French composer. Studied with various masters, including Widor, and made a speciality of medieval music. In 1917 he made himself known in Paris by giving a concert of his own, and, holding no official post, he relied on his own efforts to keep before the public.

Works include opera *Le Rossignol en amour* (1926); ballets *La Fête de la bergère* (1924), *Le Paravent de laque*, *Les Aveux et les promesses*; Psalm 19 for chorus and orchestra, *The Sermon on the Mount* for solo voices, chorus, organ and strings; 13 symphonies (1919–67), *Les Agrestides*, *Trois Guirlandes sonores* for strings; *La Jungle* for organ and orchestra; *Le Livre des danseries* for violin, flute and piano and other chamber music; songs.

Mihalovich, Odön (Péter Jozsef de) (b Fericsancze, 13 Sept 1842; d Budapest, 22 Apr 1929), Hungarian composer. Studied with Mosonyi at Budapest, Hauptmann at Leipzig, Cornelius and Bülow in Munich. In 1887 he succeeded Liszt as director of the Music Academy at Budapest, and remained there until 1919.

Works include operas *Hagbarth und Signe* (1882) and *Wieland der Schmied* (Wagner's libretto, both in German), *Toldi Szerelme* (*Toldi's Love*) and *Eliána* (after Tennyson's *Idylls of the King*, produced 1908), (both in Hungarian); four symphonies (1879–1902), *Faust* overture (after Goethe), four Ballads for orchestra.

Mihalovici, Marcel (b Bucharest, 22 Oct 1898; d Paris, 12 Aug 1985), Romanian composer. Studied with d'Indy in Paris and joined a group of advanced French and Russian composers there after the 1914–18 war. He was married to the pianist Monique Haas.

Works include *L'Intransigeant Pluton* (1928); ballets *Karagueuz* (1926), *Divertissement* and others; *Cortège des divinités infernales* (from the opera), *Introduction au mouvement*, *Notturno* and fantasy for orchestra; three string quartets (1923, 1931, 1946); string trio; violin and piano sonata, sonatina for oboe and piano.

Mikado, The, or The Town of Titipu, operetta by Sullivan (libretto by W S Gilbert), produced London, Savoy Theatre, 14 Mar 1885. Nanki-Poo loves Yum-Yum, against the Mikado's wishes. However, she must marry Ko-Ko, the Lord High Executioner. The lovers marry and escape decapitation.

Mikhailova, Maria (b Kharkov, 3 Jun 1866; d Leningrad, 4 Nov 1921), Russian soprano. Debut St Petersburg 1892, as Marguerite de Valois; in 1895 she was Electra there, in the fp of Taneiev's *Oresteia* trilogy, and until 1912 she was heard as Lakmé, Juliette, Ludmila and Amina. She made many early recordings and was guest in Prague, Moscow and Tokyo.

Mikrokosmos, *Microcosm*, a set of 153 small piano pieces by Bartók, arranged in progressive order of technical difficulty and pub. in six vols., setting the player various problems of modern technique, each piece being written on a particular principle or system (special rhythms, time-signatures, chords, intervals, atonal or bitonal combinations, etc.), composed 1926–37, pub. 1940.

Milán, Luis (b Valencia, *c* 1500; d Valencia, after 1561), Spanish vihuelist and composer. He was the son of a nobleman, Don Luis de Milán, played the vihuela, visited Italy and Portugal. One of the first composers to write tempo indications.

Works, all pub. in *El Maestro* (1536), the earliest surviving vihuela collection, include fantasies and pavans for vihuela, Spanish and Portuguese *villancicos*, Spanish ballads and Italian sonnets for voice and vihuela.

Milanese Chant ◊ Ambrosian Chant.

Milano, Francesco da (b Monza, ? 18 Aug 1497; d 15 Apr 1543), Italian lutenist. He served successively at the Gonzaga Court (Mantua), with Cardinal Ippolito de' Medici and at the Papal court of Paul II. Well known as lute virtuoso and wrote three vols. of pieces.

Milanov (originally Kunc), Zinka (b Zagreb, 17 May 1906; d New York, 30 May 1989), Yugoslav soprano. Studied first in Zagreb and then with Ternina, and Carpi in Prague, making her debut in Ljubljana in 1927 as the *Trovatore* Leonora. From 1928 to 1935 she sang in Zagreb and from 1937 her career centred on the NY Met.; roles there until 1966 included Norma, Donna Anna, Tosca and Gioconda. She was especially known for her Verdi singing.

Milanova, Stoika (b Plovdiv, 5 Aug 1945), Bulgarian violinist. Studied with David Oistrakh in Moscow and has had international career since London debut in 1970; US and Canadian debuts 1976, tours of Eastern Europe 1985–86. Duo recitals with Radu Lupu and recordings of the Prokofiev Concertos.

Milder-Hauptmann, (Pauline) Anna (b Constantinople, 13 Dec 1785; d Berlin, 29 Aug 1838), Austrian soprano. The daughter of a courier in the Austrian diplomatic service, she was taken to Vienna as a child and on the recommendation of Schikaneder studied singing under Tomaselli and Salieri, making her first stage appearance in 1803. Beethoven wrote the part of Leonore in *Fidelio* for her and she early became interested in Schubert's songs; she sang in the fp of Schubert's last work, *Der Hirt auf dem Felsen*. In 1810 she married the jeweller Hauptmann. She sang in Mendelssohn's revival of Bach's *St Matthew Passion* in 1829. Famous in Gluck's *Iphigénie en Tauride* and also sang in operas by Süssmayr, Weigl and Cherubini.

Mildmay, Audrey (b Hurstmonceaux, 19 Dec 1900; d London, 31 May 1953), English soprano. Originally a member of the Carl Rosa Opera co., she married John Christie in 1931 and with him founded the Glyndebourne Festival, which opened on 28 May 1934. She sang at the Festival 1934–39 as Susanna, Zerlina and Norina. In 1947 she and Rudolf Bing began the Edinburgh Festival.

Milford, Robin (Humphrey) (b Oxford, 22 Jan 1903; d Lyme Regis, 29 Dec 1959), English composer. Educated at Rugby and studied music at the RCM, where his masters were Holst, Vaughan Williams and R O Morris.

Works include oratorio *A Prophet in the Land*; cantata *Wind, Rain and Sunshine*, *Bemerton Cantatas*, *Five Songs of Escape* for unaccompanied chorus; symphony, concerto grosso, double fugue for orchestra; violin concerto, *The Dark Thrush* (on Hardy's poem) for violin and small orchestra; *Two Easter Meditations* for organ; piano works; songs; part-songs.

The indifference of the public is what's depressing. Enthusiasm, or vehement protest, shows that your work really lives.

Darius Milhaud, quoted in Harding, *The Ox on the Roof*, 1972

Milhaud, Darius (b Aix-en-Provence, 4 Sept 1892; d Geneva, 22 Jun 1974), French composer. Studied violin and composition at the Paris Conservatory from 1909, under Gédalge, Widor and d'Indy. His teachers also included Dukas. In 1917–19 he was attaché to the French Legation at Rio de Janeiro, where he met Paul Claudel, who collaborated frequently with him as librettist. About 1920 he became a member of 'Les Six', and in 1922 he was represented for the first time at the festival of the ISCM. He emigrated to USA in 1940, but returned to Paris in 1947, where he taught at the Conservatory. His music drew on a wide range of influences, including jazz (*La Création du monde*), Brazilian music (*L'homme et son désir*) and polytonality (the simultaneous use of three or more different keys).

Works include STAGE: operas *La Brebis égarée* (1923), *Les Malheurs d'Orphée* (1926), *Esther de Carpentras* (1938), *Le Pauvre Matelot* (1927), *Christophe Colomb* (1930), *Maximilien*, *Bolivar* (1950), minute-operas *L'Enlèvement d'Europe* (1927), *L'Abandon d'Ariane*, *La Délivrance de Thésée* (1928), *La Mère Coupable* (1966); ballets *L'Homme et son désir* (1918), *Le Bœuf sur le toit* (1919), *Les Mariés de la Tour Eiffel* (with others, 1921), *La Création du monde* (1923), *Salade*, *Le Train bleu* (1924), *La Bien-aimée* (after Schubert and Liszt, 1928), *Jeux de printemps* (1944); incidental music for works by Claudel: *Protée*, *L'Annonce faite à Marie* and *Oreste* translated from Aeschylus (*Agamemnon*, *Les Choëphores* and *Les Euménides*, 1917–22), and for Rolland's *14 Juillet* (with six others).

ORCHESTRAL: works include 12 symphonies for large orchestra (1940–62), two symphonic suites, *Suite provençale* (1937), *Séré-*

nade, Suite française, Jeux de printemps, Saudades do Brazil; six symphonies for small orchestra (1917–22); five études, *Ballade, Le Carnaval d'Aix* (1926) and five concertos for piano and orchestra; concerto and *Concertino de printemps* for violin and orchestra (1934), viola, cello and clarinet concertos and concerto for percussion and small orchestra.

CHAMBER: 18 string quartets (1912–62), wind quintet *La Cheminée du Roi René* (1939); two violin and piano sonatas, two sonatas for viola and piano, sonata for two violins and piano; sonata for piano, flute, oboe and clarinet; sonatinas for flute and piano and clarinet and piano; some smaller instrumental pieces; sonatina for organ; six piano works including suite, sonata, *Printemps* (two vols.), *Saudades do Brazil* (two vols, 1920–21), *Three Rag Caprices*; suite *Scaramouche* (1939) and *Bal martiniquais* for two pianos.

SOLO VOCAL AND CHORAL: 14 books of songs including *Poèmes de Léo Latil, Poèmes de Paul Claudel, Poèmes juifs, Poèmes de Cocteau, Les Soirées de Pétrograde*; *Machines agricoles* for voice and seven instruments, *Catalogue des fleurs* for voice and chamber orchestra (1920); two psalms for baritone and orchestra; Psalm 121 for male voices; cantata *Cain and Abel*; four *Poèmes* for voice and violin, *Pacem in Terris* for chorus and orchestra (1963).

military band a wind band attached to military regiments and used by them for their ceremonial occasions, but also often engaged to play for the entertainment of the general public in parks, at the seaside, etc. It includes woodwind, brass and percussion.

'Military' Symphony Haydn's symphony no. 100 in G major (no. 8 of the 'Salomon' symphonies), composed for London in 1794; so called because of the trumpet call and percussion effects found in the second movement.

Mill, Arnold van (b Schiedam, 26 Mar 1921), Dutch bass. Debut Brussels, 1946. He sang in a revival of Spontini's *Agnes von Hohenstaufen* at Florence, in 1953, and in the same year joined the Hamburg Opera. Bayreuth 1951–60, as Hunding, Daland and Fafner; recorded Marke under Solti. He appeared as guest at Berlin, Edinburgh and Rio, as Zaccaria, Osmin and Abul Hassan in Cornelius' *Barbier von Bagdad*.

Miller, Jonathan (b London, 21 Jul 1934), English producer. He studied at Cambridge and qualified as doctor of medicine. Produced plays for Old Vic and National Theatre Companies. First opera production Goehr's *Arden Must Die*, for New Opera Co. at SW, 1974. In 1975 he produced *The Cunning Little Vixen* at Glyndebourne and *Così fan tutte* for Kent Opera. ENO since 1978: *Figaro, Arabella, Otello* and *Don Giovanni* (1985). His Mafia-style *Rigoletto* (1982) provoked some local opposition when the ENO visited NY in 1984. By modern standards, Miller's work is faithful to the composers' intentions; his *Mikado* (ENO, 1986) made a successful transition from Japan to 1920s England. Staged *Káta Kabanova* at the NY Met., 1991, and *Der Rosenkavalier* for ENO, 1993; CG debut *Così fan tutte*, 1995.

Millico, Giuseppe (b Terlizzi near Modena, 19 Jan 1737; d Naples, 2 Oct 1802), Italian castrato soprano and composer. He was discovered by Gluck, in whose *Le feste d'Apollo* he sang at Parma in 1769. Engaged by the imperial opera in Vienna, he sang the following year in the fp of Gluck's *Paride ed Elena*. Later visited London, Paris and Berlin, and from 1780 lived in Naples.

Works include operas *La pietà d'amore* (pub. 1782), *La Zelinda, Ipermestra, Le Cinesi* (1780); cantata *Angelica e Medoro* (with Cimarosa).

Millo, Aprile (b New York, 14 Apr 1958), American soprano. After study in Hollywood she sang Aida in Utah in 1980. Her Giselda in a NY concert performance of *I Lombardi* was much applauded, and she made her Met. debut in 1985, as Amelia Boccanegra. At La Scala she has appeared as Elvira (*Ernani*). Season 1991/92 as Marguerite at Chicago (debut), Elisabeth de Valois at the Met. and Verona, and Aida at the Festival of Caracalla.

Millöcker, Karl (b Vienna, 29 Apr 1842; d Baden near Vienna, 31 Dec 1899), Austrian composer and conductor. Studied at the Vienna Conservatory and became conductor at Graz in 1864 and at the Harmonietheater in Vienna, 1866. In 1869 he was appointed conduc-

tor at the Theater an der Wien there and produced operettas for it.

Works include operettas *Der tote Gast* (1865), *Die beiden Binder, Diana* (1867), *Die Fraueninsel, Ein Abenteuer in Wien* (1873), *Das verwunschene Schloss* (1878), *Gräfin Dubarry* (1879), *Apajune der Wassermann, Der Bettelstudent* (1882), *Der Feldprediger* (1884), *Der Vice-Admiral, Die sieben Schwaben* (1887), *Der arme Jonathan* (1890), *Das Sonntagskind* (1892), *Gasparone* and many others; numerous piano pieces.

Mills, Charles (b Asheville, NC, 8 Jan 1914; d New York, 7 Mar 1982), American composer. Studied with a six-year scholarship under Copland, Sessions and Roy Harris, two years with each, and later devoted himself entirely to composition.

Works include music for solo dance *John Brown*; five symphonies (1940–80), slow movement for string orchestra; concertino for flute and orchestra, prelude for flute and strings; Festival Overture for chorus and orchestra; *Ars poetica* for unaccompanied chorus (1940); chamber symphony for 11 instruments (1939), chamber concerto for ten instruments, chamber concertino for woodwind quintet, five string quartets (1939–59), piano trio in D minor, sonatas for cello, violin and piano.

Milner, Anthony (b Bristol, 13 May 1925), English composer. Studied piano with H Fryer and composition with R O Morris and later with Seiber (1944–47). From 1947 to 1962 he taught at Morley College, when he was appointed to the RCM and then lecturer at King's College, London University, in 1965.

Works include three symphonies (1972, 1978, 1986), *Sinfonia Pasquale* for string orchestra, *April Prologue* for orchestra; chamber symphony (1968), concerto for symphonic wind band (1979), concerto for strings (1982); *The Song of Akhenaten* for soprano and chamber orchestra (1954); cantatas *Salutatio Angelica* (1948), *The City of Desolation* (1955), *St Francis, The Water and the Fire* (1961), *Emmanuel Cantata* (1975); Mass for *a cappella* chorus (1951); string quartet (1975), oboe quartet and wind quintet; songs; piano sonata (1989).

Milnes, Sherrill (b Downers Grove, IL, 10 Jan 1935), American baritone. He joined Boris Goldovsky's touring co. in 1960, and studied with Ponselle in Baltimore. In 1964 he sang Rossini's Figaro at Milan and made his NY, City Opera, debut as Valentin; repeated the role the next year at the Met. London, CG, from 1971 as Renato, Luna, Macbeth and Boccanegra. In 1977 he sang Don Giovanni at Salzburg; Michonnet in *Adriana Lecouvreur* at the Met., 1994. Other roles included Scarpia, Iago, Don Carlo, Thomas' Hamlet and Scindia in Massenet's *Le Roi de Lahore*.

Milstein, Nathan (b Odessa, 31 Dec 1904; d London, 21 Dec 1992), Russian-born American violinist. Studied first at Odessa School of Music and then in St Petersburg with Auer at the Conservatory. At first he appeared publicly with the pianist Horowitz, then moved to Europe in 1925 where he built up his reputation. US debut 1929, with Philadelphia Orchestra. Was one of the most musicianly among modern virtuosi.

Milton opera by Spontini (libretto by V J E de Jouy and M Dieulafoy), produced Paris, Opéra-Comique, 27 Nov 1804. A second Milton was planned by Spontini in 1838, when he visited England in the summer to study the environment. It was to be entitled *Miltons Tod und Busse für den Königsmord/Milton's Death and Expiation for the King's Murder*) (libretto by E Raupach), but turned into *Das verlorene Paradies/Paradise Lost*); it remained unfinished.

Milton, John (b Stanton St John near Oxford, *c* 1563; d London, buried 15 Mar 1647), English composer, father of John Milton the poet. Educated at Christ Church, Oxford. He is said to have received a gold medal from a Polish prince for an In Nomine in 40 parts, was cast out by his father as a Protestant, went to London and in 1600 became a member of the Scriveners' Co., marrying Sarah Jeffrey about that time. Having made a fair fortune as a scribe, he retired to Horton (Bucks.) in 1632, but after his wife's death moved to Reading, *c* 1640 and back to London in 1643, where he lived with his son John.

Works include various sacred pieces for several voices; madrigal contribution to *The Triumphes of Oriana*, four vocal pieces contributed to Leighton's *Teares or Lamentacions*; two tunes for Ravenscroft's Psalter; five fancies for viols.

Mines of Sulphur, The opera by R R Bennett (libretto by Beverley Cross), produced London, SW, 24 Feb 1965, conductor C Davis. Plague-carrying actors punish Boconnion, deserter and murderer.

Minghetti, Angelo (b Bologna, 6 Dec 1889; d Milan, 10 Feb 1957), Italian tenor. He sang in Italy from 1911 and had an international career from 1921; appearances at Rio, Chicago and Buenos Aires. La Scala debut 1923 as Rodolfo; returned until 1932. At CG he was successful 1926–34. At Rome he created Donello in the fp of Respighi's *La Fiamma* (1934).

Mingotti (born *Valentini*), Regina (b Naples, 16 Feb 1722; d Neuburg o/Danube, 1 Oct 1808), Austro-Italian soprano, who became an orphan as a child, was sent to a convent by an uncle at Graz, but had to leave on his death and married the Italian musician Pietro Mingotti (attached to the Dresden Opera), who had her taught singing by Porpora. She made her debut at Hamburg in 1743. She appeared in Italy, Spain, England and France in operas by Porpora, Hasse and Jommelli. Her brothers Pietro and Angelo were opera impresarios, active in Dresden, Graz, Prague and Hamburg.

minim in modern notation the white note with a tail on it, with the value of half a semibreve or two crotchets: ♩; originally the shortest note-value (Latin *minima*).

Minimalism a musical style initiated in the 1960s and represented chiefly by the work of composers such as Terry Riley, Steve Reich and Philip Glass. The simplest possible material is repeated many times, with small changes introduced gradually or with the addition of other comparably simple repetitive material that eventually changes in its synchronisation. The style is admirably suited to an age dominated by machines, and has been termed by the Belgian writer Wim Merten as Repetitive Music.

Minkowski, Marc (b Paris, 4 Oct 1962), French conductor. Studied at the Hague Conservatory and formed Les Musiciens du Louvre 1984: many performances of Baroque opera throughout Europe. For the English Bach Festival he has conducted Handel's *Riccardo Primo* and Gluck's *Iphigénie en Tauride* at CG. Purcell's *Dido* and Handel's *Teseo* in Paris, Monteverdi's *Orfeo* in Valencia and Lully's *Phaeton* at the Lyon Opéra. Further French repertory includes *Alcyone* by Marais, Mouret's *Les Amours de Ragonde* and *Titon et l'Aurore* by Mondonville (all also recorded).

Minnesinger or Minnesänger, German plur., the singers in 12th- and 13th-c. Germany who cultivated minstrelsy on the lines of that of the Troubadours in France, and preceded the Meistersinger, but unlike them were aristocrats, not middle-class merchants and artisans.

minor one of the two predominant scales (the other being major) of the tonal system. There are three forms of the minor scale: the harmonic, the melodic, and the less commonly used natural minor. ◊harmonic minor, ◊melodic minor.

minore Italian = 'minor'; in older music the word is often used as a warning in the course of a composition which is predominantly in a major key.

minor intervals seconds, thirds, sixths and sevenths which are a semitone smaller than the corresponding major intervals.

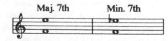

Minor and major seconds and sevenths.

Minotaur, The ballet in one act by Elliott Carter; composed 1947, produced NY, 26 Mar 1947.

minstrel originally the English equivalent of the French *Jongleur* and

the German *fahrender Sänger*, but in a wider sense any travelling musician.

Minter, Drew (b Washington DC, 11 Jan 1955), American countertenor. Studied with Rita Streich and Erik Werba. Stage debut in Handel's *Orlando* at St Louis, 1983; other Handel roles have been Arsace in *Partenope* (Omaha 1988), Ptolomeo in *Giulio Cesare*, directed by Peter Sellars, and Ottone (Göttingen 1992). Santa Fe 1989, in Weir's *A Night at the Chinese Opera* and as Endimione in *La Calisto*. Recordings include Ottone in Handel's *Agrippina* and the title role in *Floridante*.

Minton, Yvonne (b Sydney, 4 Dec 1938), Australian mezzo. She studied in Sydney and moved to Europe in 1960. London, CG, from 1965 as Marina, Dorabella, Brangaene, Waltraute, Orpheus, Sextus and Thea in the 1970 fp of Tippett's *The Knot Garden*. She sang Octavian at Chicago in 1970 and at the NY Met. in 1973. She appeared at Bayreuth in the 1976 centenary production of the *Ring* (as Fricka and Waltraute). In 1979, at the Paris Opéra, she was Countess Geschwitz, in the fp of completed three-act version of Berg's *Lulu*. Season 1993/94 as Berlioz's Marguerite at Wellington and Mme Larina in *Eugene Onegin* at Glyndebourne. CBE 1980.

minuet a dance of French origin (*menuet*, from *menu* — small) first appearing in artistic music about the time of Lully. It is in moderate 3–4 time and in its later developments always has a contrasting trio section, after which the first section is repeated. It was not a regular feature of the suite, but appeared in many of its examples; on the other hand it was the only dance form normally retained in sonatas, quartets, symphonies, etc.

minuetto, Italian, this, not 'menuetto', is the correct Italian name for the minuet.

'Minute Waltz' the nickname sometimes given to Chopin's Waltz in D♭ major, op. 64 no. 1.

Miracle in the Gorbals ballet by Bliss (scenario by M Benthall, choreography by Robert Helpmann), produced London, Prince's Theatre, 26 Oct 1944.

Miracles of our Lady cycle of four one-act operas by Martinů: *The Wise and Foolish Virgins* (libretto by V Nezval after 12th-c. French text); *Little Mariken of Nijmegen* (libretto by H Gheon after 15th-c. Flemish legend); *The Nativity* (libretto by composer after Moravian folk texts); *The Legend of Sister Pasqualina* (libretto by composer after poem by J Zeyer and folk texts). Composed 1933–34, fp Brno, 23 Feb 1935.

Miracle, The nickname of Haydn's symphony no. 96, in D major (no. 4 of the 'Salomon' symphonies), written for London in 1791. The name is due to the story that a chandelier fell from the ceiling at the fp, when the audience miraculously escaped injury; but in fact the accident occurred at the fp of symphony no. 102 in B♭ major (1794–95).

Miraculous Mandarin, The, *A csodálatos mandarin*, pantomime in one act by Bartók (scenario by M Lengyel); 1918–19, produced Cologne, 27 Nov 1926.

Orchestral Suite performed Budapest, 15 Oct 1928, conductor Ernö Dohnányi. The Mandarin of the title is mugged by a prostitute and her gang, but he cannot die until he is sexually united with the woman who has attempted to murder him.

Mireille opera by Gounod (libretto by M Carré, based on the poem *Mirèio* by F Mistral), produced Paris, Théâtre Lyrique, 19 Mar 1864. Vincent and Mireille love each other, but they are opposed by her father, who favours the advances of bull-tamer Ourrais. Ourrais injures Vincent and is drowned by water spirits. Mireille undertakes a pilgrimage to see Vincent and dies of exhaustion in his arms.

Miricioiu, Nelly (b Adjud, 31 Mar 1952), Romanian soprano. Sang the Queen of Night at Iasi (1974) and appeared with Braşov Opera 1975–78. Scottish Opera 1981 as Tosca and Violetta; CG from 1982, as Nedda, Musetta, Marguerite and Antonia. US engagements at San Francisco and Philadelphia (Violetta 1992). Rossini's Armida at Amsterdam (1988) and Ameaide in *Tancredi* at the 1992 Salzburg Festival (concert).

mirliton, French, a toy instrument similar to the eunuch flute. Was also known as kazoo in England.

Miroirs set of five piano pieces by Ravel; composed 1905, fp Paris, 6 Jan 1906: *Noctuelles*, *Oiseaux tristes*, *Une barque sur l'océan* (orchestral version, fp Paris, 3 Feb 1907), *Alborada del gracioso* (orchestral version fp Paris, 17 May 1919), *La Vallée des Cloches*.

mirror canon *or* mirror fugue a canon or fugue in which two or more voices are so inverted that the intervals appear simultaneously upside down as well as right side up, looking on paper like a reflection in water.

Miserly Knight, The, *Skupoy ritsar'*, opera in three scenes by Rakhmaninov (libretto by composer, after Pushkin); 1903–05, produced Moscow, Bolshoi, 24 Jan 1906. Poor son and penny-pinching father have money problems.

Misón, Luis (b Barcelona, ?; d Madrid, 13 Feb 1766), Spanish woodwind player and composer. He entered the royal orchestra at Madrid in 1748 as flautist and oboist, became conductor there in 1756 and produced his first *tonadilla* in 1757.

Works include numerous *tonadillas*, three operas *La festa cinese*, *El tutor enamorado* and *El amor a todos vence*; six sonatas for flute and bass.

Missa Latin = 'Mass'.

Missa parodia Latin = lit. 'parody Mass'; a term arising from a mistaken conjunction of the words *Missa* and *parodia* which occur separately on the title-page of a Mass by the 16th-c. composer Jacques Paix. His Mass is described as 'Parodia mottetae Domine da nobis auxilium', i.e. it is based on material from the motet cited. Neither in this work nor in any other are the words *Missa* and *parodia* joined together. Many 15th- and 16th-c. Mass cycles were based on material from a motet or polyphonic song, usually named in the title.

Missa pro defunctis Latin = 'Mass for the dead'. ◊Requiem.

Missa solemnis (or *solennis*) Latin = 'solemn Mass', a title sometimes used by composers for a Mass of a particularly festive or elaborate kind, e.g. Beethoven's op. 123. Schubert also used it, and it occurs in French as *Messe solennelle* (e.g. Gounod). The title is now used particularly for Beethoven's work, composed 1818–23; fp St Petersburg, 7 Apr 1824. Three sections were given in Vienna on 7 May 1824, in the concert with the fp of the Choral Symphony.

Miss Julie opera by Ned Rorem (libretto by K Elmslie after Strindberg), produced NY, 5 Nov 1965. Daughter of the house seduces servant.

Opera by William Alwyn (libretto by composer, after Strindberg); composed 1961–76, fp BBC 16 Jul 1977.

misura Italian = 'measure, time'; thus *senza misura* = 'without time, not strictly in time'. Also the Italian term for 'bar'.

Mitchell, Donald (Charles Peter) (b London, 6 Feb 1925), English music critic, publisher and author. Largely self-taught in music, though he studied for a year at Durham University (1949–50). He has specialized in late 19th- and 20th-c. music, especially Mahler (three vols. of a projected four pub. 1958–84), Reger and Britten. Chairman, Faber Music, 1977–86.

Mitchell, Leona (b Enid, OK, 13 Oct 1948), American soprano. Debut San Francisco 1973, Micaela; NY Met. debut 1975, same role, and has since sung Pamina, Musetta and the *Forza* Leonora. At Sydney in 1985 she sang her first *Trovatore* Leonora. Other roles include Elvira (*Ernani*), Amelia and Butterfly.

Mitchinson, John (b Blackrod, Lancs., 31 Mar 1932), English tenor. Studied at the RMCM and sang in concert before stage debut as Jupiter in *Semele* with the Handel Opera Society. Notable roles with WNO (1978–82) have been Tristan (under Goodall), Opera North and at the Buxton Festival (Max, 1983). Concerts include Mahler's 8th symphony and *Das Lied von der Erde*, the Glagolitic Mass and *The Dream of Gerontius*.

Mitridate, Rè di Ponto (*Mithridates, King of Pontus*), opera by Mozart (libretto by V A Cigna-Santi, based on a tragedy by Racine), produced Milan, Teatro Regio Ducal, 26 Dec 1770. Brothers Sifare and Farnace love Aspasia, the fiancée of Mithridates. Mithridates is reported killed in battle, but returns and learns of the infidelity. Mortally wounded, however, he gives his blessing to Sifare's and Aspasia's union.

Mitridate Eupatore, Il, *Mithridates Eupator*, opera by A Scarlatti

(libretto by G F Roberti), produced Venice, Teatro San Giovanni Grisostomo, Carnival 1707. Mitridate gains revenge after his mother, Stratonica, murders his father, Pontos.

Mitropoulos, Dimitri (b Athens, 1 Mar 1896; d Milan, 2 Nov 1960), Greek conductor, pianist and composer. He studied piano and composition at the Athens Conservatory and subsequently with Gilson in Brussels and Busoni in Berlin. He conducted the Athens Conservatory Orchestra 1929–37, Minneapolis SO 1937–49, New York PO 1950–58; gave early performances in the USA of works by Berg, Krenek and Schoenberg and the fp of Barber's *Vanessa* (NY Met, 1958). He was an early champion of Mahler and died while conducting a rehearsal of the 3rd symphony.

Works include opera *Sœur Béatrice*; concerto grosso for orchestra; string quartet, violin sonata; piano music; songs, etc.

Mixolydian Mode the scale beginning on G on the white notes of the piano keyboard.

mixtures organ stops controlling a range of pipes with more than one note to each key, sounding some of the keys' harmonics with or without the fundamental note.

Mizler (von Kolof), Lorenz Christoph (b Heidenheim, Württemberg, 25 Jul 1711; d Warsaw, Mar 1778), German music writer and editor. One of Bach's pupils at St Thomas's School, Leipzig; founded the Association for Musical Science there in 1738 and edited a periodical, *Neu eröffnete musikalische Bibliothek*, 1736–54.

Mlada opera-ballet commissioned from Borodin, Cui, Mussorgsky and Rimsky-Korsakov by the Russian Imperial Theatres in 1782, but never completed (libretto by V A Krilov).

Opera by Rimsky-Korsakov (libretto as above), produced St Petersburg, 1 Nov 1892. Voyslava has poisoned rival Mlada, the bride of Prince Yaromir. Using magic to try to seduce him, Voyslava is foiled by Mlada's ghost. Yaromir dreams of the murder and kills Voyslava, before joining Mlada's heavenly spirit.

Mládí, *Youth*, suite for wind sextet in four movements by Janáček, fp Brno, 21 Oct 1924, by professors of the Brno Conservatory.

Mlynarski, Emil (b Kibarty, 18 Jul 1870; d Warsaw, 5 Apr 1935), Polish violinist, conductor and composer. Studied at St Petersburg. Conductor of the Warsaw PO 1901–05 and director of the Conservatory there 1904–09. Conductor of the Scottish Orchestra, 1910–15. Resumed his posts in Warsaw in 1919. From 1929 to 1931 taught at the Curtis Institute, Philadelphia.

Works include opera *A Summer Night* (1914); *Polonia* symphony (1910); violin concerto in D minor (1897).

mock trumpet an early English name for the ◊clarinet.

The public doesn't want new music: the main thing that it demands of a composer is that he is dead.
Arthur Honegger, *I am a Composer*, 1951

---

modal notation a form of notation in use for vocal music in the 12th and early 13th c., where the rhythm was determined not by the shapes of individual notes but by the various types of ligature in which they were combined according to one or other of the rhythmic modes.

moderato Italian = 'moderate'; a direction used either singly or in combination with words meaning fast or slow.

Moderne, Jacques (b c 1495 Pinguente, Istria; d Lyon, c 1562), French 16th-c. musician and publisher, (?) of Italian descent. He became *maître de chapelle* at the church of Notre-Dame du Confort at Lyon and about 1530 established a printing-press there, pub. books of Masses, motets and *chansons* between 1532 and 1567, with contributions by various composers, including himself.

modes the scales which became established in the Middle Ages and were still accepted, at least in theory, in the 16th c. They are easily identified by reference to the white notes of the piano keyboard. Originally known by the Greek words for first, second, third and fourth:

1. *Protus:* D-D   3. *Tritus:* F-F
2. *Deuterus:* E-E   4. *Tetrardus:* G-G

A distinction was made between the authentic modes, with the compass given above, and the four plagal modes which had the same final notes but a different range:

1. A-A (with final D)
2. B-B (with final E)
3. C-C (with final F)
4. D-D (with final G)

The whole series was later renumbered and Greek names were attached, in the belief that the modes corresponded to ancient Greek modes. In each mode a 'reciting note' (now often called 'dominant') was established. In the Authentic modes this note is normally a fifth above the final, and in the Plagal modes a third below the note in the Authentic mode; but where it would logically be B, the note C is substituted. The complete scheme is as follows (*F.* = final, *D.* = dominant):

No.	Name	Range	F.	D.
I	Dorian	D-D	D	A
II	Hypodorian	A-A	D	F
III	Phrygian	E-E	E	C
IV	Hypophrygian	B-B	E	A
V	Lydian	F-F	F	C
VI	Hypolydian	C-C	F	A
VII	Mixolydian	G-G	G	D
VIII	Hypomixolydian	D-D	G	C

The frequent introduction of B♭ in medieval music tended to change the character of some of the modes. Thus mode I with B♭ was simply a transposed form of a mode with a final on A, and mode V with B♭ was identical with a scale of C major transposed to F. Hence Glareanus in the 16th c. proposed that two further modes with their plagal forms, should be recognized, as follows:

No.	Name	Range	F.	D.
IX	Æolian	A-A	A	E
X	Hypoæolian	E-E	A	C
XI	Ionian	C-C	C	G
XII	Hypoionian	G-G	C	E

modes, rhythmic the rhythms of medieval music were classified in six patterns (corresponding to poetic rhythms).

modulation the art of changing from one key to another in the course of a composition by means of logical harmonic progressions.

Moeran, E(rnest) J(ohn) (b Heston, Middlesex, 31 Dec 1894; d Kenmare, Co. Kerry, Ireland, 1 Dec 1950), English composer of Irish descent. He lived in Norfolk in his childhood, his father, a clergyman, holding a living there. Educated at Uppingham School and later studied music at the RCM in London. After serving in the 1914–18 war, he continued his studies with Ireland. In 1923 he came before the public with a concert of his works given in London, but after some years spent there he retired to Herefordshire. His music belongs to the English pastoral tradition, Delius being among his major influences.

Works include Magnificat and Nunc Dimittis, Te Deum and Jubilate, two anthems; *Nocturne* for baritone, chorus and orchestra (1934), *Songs of Springtime* and suite *Phyllida and Corydon* for unaccompanied chorus (1934), *Blue-eyed Spring* for baritone and chorus, madrigals, part-songs and folksong arrangements, Sinfonietta, two rhapsodies, symphonic impression *In the Mountain Country* for orchestra (1921), two pieces for small orchestra *Whythorne's Shadow* (1931) and *Lonely Waters* (1932), symphony in G minor (1934–37); concertos for piano, violin and cello (1942–45); string quartet in A minor, string trio in G major, piano trio in D major, sonata for two violins, violin and piano sonata in E minor; song cycle *Ludlow Town* (texts by Housman) for baritone and piano (1920); seven *Poems of James Joyce* for baritone and piano (1929), etc.

Moeschinger, Albert (b Basel, 10 Jan 1897; d Thun, 25 Sept 1985), Swiss composer. Studied at Bern, Leipzig and Munich, in the latter place under Courvoisier. In 1927 he settled at Bern as professor, but in 1943 he retired to Saas Fee, Ct Valais, and later to Ascona.

Works include motet *Gottes Pfad*, cantata *Angelus Silesius*, *Das Posthorn* for male chorus and orchestra, cantata *Tag unseres Volks*, Mass for chorus and organ (1943), part-songs and other choral works; five symphonies, including *Symphonie à la gloire de . . .* and suite for orchestra, variations on a theme by Purcell for strings and percussion, divertimento for strings, *Fantasia 1944* for chamber orchestra; five piano concertos, violin concerto; six string quartets, piano quintet, six wind trios, etc.

Moffat, Alfred (b Edinburgh, 4 Dec 1866; d London, 9 Jun 1950),

Rhythmic modes as represented by poetic stresses (left), medieval notation (middle), and modern notation (right).

Mödl, Martha (b Nuremberg, 22 Mar 1912), German soprano. Studied in Nuremberg and made her debut in 1942. Sang at Bayreuth 1951–67 as Kundry, Gutrune, Sieglinde, Isolde and Brünnhilde and specialized in dramatic roles, especially Wagner. Hamburg from 1949, London 1950–72. Sang in the fps of Reimann's *Melusine* (1971), Fortner's *Elisabeth Tudor* (1972) and Cerha's *Baal* (1980). Other roles included Leonore, Carmen and Clytemnestra.

Scottish composer and editor. Studied in Berlin and worked there for a time. Settled in London in the 1890s and edited a large collection of early string music, including many English and French works, also several vols of Scottish, Welsh and Irish folksongs.

Moffo, Anna (b Wayne, PA, 27 Jun 1932), American soprano. Studied at Curtis Institute, Philadelphia, in NY and in Rome, making her debut on Italian television in 1956 as Butterfly. NY Met. from 1959 as

Violetta, Pamina, Gilda, Manon, Mélisande and Marguerite. Sang Adrianna Lecouvreur at Parma, 1978.

Mohaupt, Richard (b Breslau, 14 Sept 1904; d Reichenau, Austria, 3 Jul 1957), German conductor and composer. Studied at Breslau University. He conducted opera at several German towns and later toured as conductor in Russia. His ballet was produced in Berlin in 1936, but soon afterwards his works were forbidden by the Nazi régime because he did not subscribe to its ideology and refused to divorce his Jewish wife. In USA, 1939–55.

Works include operas *Die Wirtin von Pinsk* (1937) and *Boleslav der Schamhafte*, comic opera for children; ballets *Die Gaunerstreiche der Courasche* (after Grimmelshausen, 1936) and *Lysistrata* (after Aristophanes, 1941), ballet for children; symphony, concerto, *Drei Episoden* and *Stadtpfeifermusik* (on Dürer's mural *Nürnberger Stadtpfeifer*, for orchestra (1939); piano concerto, 1938), violin concerto (1945).

Moïse, *Moses*, opera by Rossini, French version of *Mosè in Egitto* (libretto by G L Balochi and V J E de Jouy), produced Paris, Opéra, 26 Mar 1827. ◊Mosè for plot synopsis.

Moiseiwitsch, Benno (b Odessa, 22 Mar 1890; d London, 9 Apr 1963), Russian-born English pianist. He studied at the Imperial Music Academy, Odessa, winning the Rubinstein Prize at the age of nine, and from 1904 to 1908 with Leschetizky in Vienna. He first appeared as a soloist in 1908 in London, where he subsequently settled, becoming a British subject in 1937. After World War I he embarked on a series of tours which took him to every continent in the world. US debut NY, 1919. Best known in Russian music.

Moke (or *Mocke* or *Mooke*), Marie (Félicité Denise) (b Paris, 4 Jul 1811; d Saint-Josse-ten-Noode, near Brussels, 30 Mar 1875)), French pianist. Studied under Herz, Moscheles and Kalkbrenner, and toured very successfully. Berlioz fell in love with her before he went to Rome in 1830 and she became engaged to him, but married Camille Pleyel, as whose wife she made an international reputation. Piano professor at the Brussels Conservatory, for 24 years until 1872.

Moldenhauer, Hans (b Mainz, 13 Dec 1906; d Spokane, WA, 19 Oct 1987), American musicologist. Studied with Rosbaud in Mainz and was active as a *répétiteur* and conductor in different European cities. In 1939 he went to the USA, where after further studies he became director and then president of the Spokane (Washington) Conservatory and lecturer at the University of Washington. Moldenhauer's most important contribution to scholarship was his recovery of a large number of Webern MSS and documents, including some previously unknown works, and their publication. Books on Webern include *The Death of Anton Webern, A Drama in Documents* (1961), *Anton Webern: Chronicle of his Life and Work* (1978). Became blind in 1980.

Moldoveanu, Vasile (b Consantine, 6 Oct 1935), Romanian tenor. Debut Bucharest 1966; guest in Brussels, Dresden and Barcelona. Member of Stuttgart Opera from 1973. NY Met. debut 1977, Rodolfo; CG 1979, Don Carlos. At Munich and Vienna he has been heard as Alfredo, the Duke of Mantua and Edgardo. Also sings Ottavio, Tamino and Pedrillo.

Molière, Jean-Baptiste Poquelin (1622–1673), French dramatist. ◊Ariadne auf Naxos (*Bourgeois Gentilhomme*, R Strauss); ◊Bourgeois Gentilhomme (R Strauss); M-A ◊Charpentier (*Comtesse d'Escarbagnas* and *Malade imaginaire*); ◊Festes de l'Amour (Lully); ◊Galuppi (*Vertuouse ridicole*); ◊Grétry (*Amphitryon*); ◊Liebermann (*School for Wives*); ◊Lully (*Mariage forcé*; *Amour médicin, Princesse d'Elide, Sicilien, George Dandin, M de Pourceaugnac, Amants magnifiques* and *Bourgeois Gentilhomme*); ◊Médecin malgré lui (Gounod); ◊Mortari (*Scuola delle mogli*); ◊Purcell (*Female Virtuosos*); J B ◊Quinault (*Bourgeois Gentilhomme* and *Princesse d'Elide*); E ◊Schulhoff (*Bourgeois Gentilhomme*); ◊Shaporin (*Tartuffe*); ◊Signor di Pourceaugnac (Franchetti); ◊Szymanowski (*Bourgeois Gentilhomme*); ◊Wagner-Régeny (*Sganarelle*); ◊Wolf-Ferrari (*Amor medico*).

Molinari-Pradelli, Francesco (b Bologna, 4 Jul 1911; d Aug 1996), Italian conductor. Studied in Bologna and Rome, making his debut in 1938, rapidly becoming known as one of the leading conductors of Italian opera; London, CG, 1955 and 1960 (*Tosca* and *Macbeth*), San Francisco 1957–66, NY Met. 1966–73; debut with *Un ballo in maschera*, and returning with *Romé et Juliette* and operas by Puccini. Several recordings with Tebaldi.

Molinaro, Simone (b Genoa, *c* 1565; d Genoa, *c* 1615), Italian lutenist, editor and composer. Pupil of Gostena, his uncle, whom he succeeded as *maestro di cappella* of Genoa Cathedral in 1599. In 1613 he edited the madrigals of Gesualdo.

Works include Masses, motets, Magnificats, sacred concertos; madrigals, canzonets; lute pieces.

Molique, (Wilhelm) Bernhard (b Nuremberg, 7 Oct 1802; d Cannstadt near Stuttgart, 10 May 1869), German violinist and composer. Pupil of Spohr and of Rovelli at Munich, succeeding him in 1820 as leader of the orchestra; after some time in the orchestra of the Theater an der Wien in Vienna, he toured widely, became leader in the royal orchestra at Stuttgart in 1826, settled in London in 1849 and returned to Germany in 1866.

Works include two Masses; oratorio *Abraham* (1861); symphony; six violin concertos (1827–46); eight string quartets (1841–53), two piano trios, duets for violins and flute and violin; violin studies and pieces.

moll German, from Latin *mollis* = 'soft'; the German word for minor.

Moll, Kurt (b Buir, near Cologne, 11 Apr 1938), German bass. Debut Aachen 1961. He has sung Marke and Pogner at Bayreuth since 1968; joined the Hamburg Opera in 1970. In 1972 he sang Osmin at La Scala and Gurnemanz at the Paris Opéra. Salzburg from 1973. CG debut 1977, as Kaspar; NY Met. 1978, as the Landgrave. Returned 1990 and 1992, as the Commendatore and Gurnemanz. Also heard in sacred music by Bach and Beethoven.

Molteni, Benedetta Emilia (b Modena, 1722; d Berlin, 1780), Italian soprano. Appointed to the court of Frederick II of Prussia in Berlin, 1742–74, where she married J F Agricola in 1751. She sang in the fp of Graun's *Tod Jesu* (1755).

Molter, Johann Melchoir (b Tiefenort, near Eisenach, 10 Feb 1696; d Karlsruhe, 12 Jan 1765), German composer. He was *Kapellmeister* at the court of Baden, where he was responsible for opera production, 1722–33. Director of church music at Eisenach and returned to Baden in 1743. He made several visits to Italy and is known today for having written 170 symphonies (strictly, sinfonias). Also wrote 66 concertos, including six for clarinet, and a Passion.

molto Italian = 'much, very'.

There never was a more imbecile notion than the twentieth-century cult of Pure Music.

W H Mellers, *The Textual Criticism of Music*, 1939

Mombelli, Ester (b Naples, *c* 1794), Italian contralto. She sang throughout Italy and was successful in operas by Rossini and Donizetti: created leading roles in Donizetti's *Zoraida di Granata* (Rome 1822) and *L'aio nell'imbarazzo* (Rome, 1824). Her father **Domenico** (1751–1835) was a tenor and composer who sang in Rossini's early operas.

Moments musicals the title, which in correct French should be *Moments musicaux*, of Schubert's six piano pieces op. 94, written 1823–28.

Mompou, Federico (b Barcelona, 16 Apr 1893; d Barcelona, 30 Jun 1987), Spanish pianist and composer. Studied at the Barcelona Conservatory and later in Paris, where I Philipp was his piano master and Samuel Rousseau taught him composition. He lived at Barcelona again 1914–21, then settled in Paris, returning to Barcelona 1941.

Works include piano pieces *6 Impresiones intimas* (1911–14), *Scènes d'enfants* (1915–18), *Suburgis*, three *Pessebres* (1914–17), *Cançò i dansa*, *Cants magics*, *Fêtes lointaines*, *Six Charmes* (1920–21), *Dialogues*, *Three Variations* (1921), *Dix Préludes* (1927–51); songs *L'hora grisa*, *Cançoneta incerta*, *Quatre Mélodies*, *Le Nuage*, *Trois Comptines*.

Mond, Der, *The Moon*, opera by Orff (libretto by composer after Grimm), produced Munich, 5 Feb 1939. Four boys steal the Moon and hang it on a lamp. When they grow old and die, its light wakes the dead, before the Moon is returned to the sky.

Mondo della luna, Il, *The World of the Moon*, opera by Galuppi (libretto by Goldoni), produced Venice, Teatro San Moisè, 29 Jan 1750.

Opera by Haydn (libretto ditto), produced Eszterháza, 3 Aug 1777. Old Bonafede refuses to allow the marriage of his daughters Clarice and Flaminia to Ecclitico and Ernesto, but is duped into consent in his moonscape garden.

Mondonville, Jean Joseph (Cassanea) de (b Narbonne, bap. 25 Dec 1711; d Belleville near Paris, 8 Oct 1772), French violinist and composer. His parents were aristocrats in reduced circumstances, but he succeeded in studying the violin. He settled in Paris in 1733, made his name as a violinist and composer, and appeared at the Concert Spirituel in 1737, for which he wrote motets until 1770. In 1744 he became superintendent of the royal chapel and was director of the Concert Spirituel 1755–62. During the *guerre des bouffons* in 1752 he was chosen as the representative of the French National school opposing the Italians under the patronage of Mme de Pompadour.

Works include operas and opera-ballets *Isbé* (1742), *Le Carnaval du Parnasse* (1749), *Titon et l'Aurore* (1753), *Daphnis et Alcimaduro* (in Provençal, 1754), *Les Fêtes de Paphos* (1758), *Thésée*, *Psyché* (1762), *Érigone*, *Vénus et Adonis*, *Les Projets de l'Amour*; oratorios *Les Israélites au Mont Oreb* (1758), *Les Fureurs de Saül* (1758), *Les Titans*; the *Privilège du Roi* set as a cantata; trio sonatas for two violins or flutes and bass; sonatas including *Les Sons harmoniques* for violin and bass; sonatas and pieces for harpsichord with violin or voice; harpsichord works including *Pièces de clavecin en sonates*; organ pieces.

Moniuszko, Stanislaw (b Ubiel, Lithuania, 5 May 1819; d Warsaw, 4 Jun 1872), Polish composer. After studying at home, he went to Berlin as a pupil of Rungenhagen, 1837–39, and on his return settled down at Wilno as music teacher and organist, produced the opera *Halka* there 1848 (revised version produced 1858). In 1858 he became conductor at the Opera in Warsaw and later professor at the Conservatory.

Works include opera *Halka* (performed 1848, revised 1857), *Flis*, *Hrabina/The Countess*, 1860), *Verbum nobile* (1860), *Straszny Dwór/The Haunted Mansion*, 1865), *Paria*, *Beata* (1872); incidental music for Shakespeare's *Hamlet* and *Merry Wives of Windsor* and other plays; cantatas *Spectres*, *Crimean Sonnets*, etc.; seven Masses (1850–74), Litanies and other church music; overture *Bajka* (*Fairy Tale*); 270 songs, including ballads by Adam Mickiewicz.

Monk, Meredith (Jane) (b Lima, 20 Nov 1942), Peruvian-born American composer and singer. Studied at Sarah Lawrence College and has appeared worldwide from 1978 with her vocal group Appearances. Her compositions are closely related to her work as an avant-garde performance artist. Her opera *Atlas* was given at Houston in 1991, and other works include *A Raw Recital* for voice and electric organ (1970); *Quarry*, opera for 38 voices and ensemble (1976); *Engine Steps* for tape collage (1983); *Book of Days* for 25 voices, synthesizer and piano (1985); *Cat Song* for voice (1988); *Waltz* for two pianos (1988).

Monn, Matthias Georg (b Vienna, 9 Apr 1717; d Vienna, 3 Oct 1750), Austrian composer and organist. Chorister at Klosterneuburg near Vienna, he was from *c* 1738 organist of the Karlskirche in Vienna. His symphony in D major of 1740 is the earliest dated symphony to have four movements with minuet in third place.

Works include 21 symphonies; ten partitas for string orchestra; six string quartets; seven harpsichord concertos, including one arranged by Schoenberg for cello and orchestra (1933); keyboard music; church music.

Monna Vanna opera by Février (libretto Maeterlinck's play with alterations), produced Paris, Opéra, 13 Jan 1909. Opera by Rakhmaninov (libretto ditto); composed (one act) 1907, fp (concert) Saratoga, NY, 11 Aug 1984. Monna Vanna's husband Guido, com-

mander of besieged Pisa, is suspicious of the help given to relieve the town.

monochord an early instrument, not for playing, but for measuring the vibration of strings. It has a single string (hence its name) stretched over a long, narrow box. it is at least as old as the 6th c. BC, when it was used by Pythagoras, and it is mentioned by Euclid *c* 300 BC, but it still occupied scientists in the Middle Ages. It was found that if the string was stopped exactly in the centre, it gave out the higher octave on each side, and other intervals were found to sound at proportional points.

monocorde French, *monocordo* Italian = 'single string'; a direction used in violin music where the composer wishes a passage to be played on one string.

monodrama a musical stage work for a single singer, an opera with a cast of one, as for example Meyerbeer's *Tevelindens Liebe*, Gomis's *Sensibilidad y prudencia* or Schoenberg's *Erwartung*. ◊*Lélio* (Berlioz).

monody, from Greek for 'single song', a term used to describe music making its effect with a single melodic part, accompanied or not, instead of a collaboration of various parts as in ◊polyphony.

monophonic music in a single melodic part, without harmony, as distinct from homophonic, which is melodic music accompanied by harmony or polyphonic, which is music in a number of melodic parts moving simultaneously.

monothematic an adj. used for a work based throughout, especially in the course of more than one movement, on a single dominating theme. Haydn more than once wrote monothematic movements, e.g. the finale of symphony no. 103 in E♭ major and the first movement of symphony no. 104 in D major.

Monro (or **Monroe**), George (d London, ? 1731), English organist and composer. He was organist at St Peter's Cornhill, in London and played harpsichord at the theatre in Goodman's Fields.

Works include incidental music to Fielding's *The Temple Beau*; a great number of songs, including 'My lovely Celia'.

Monsigny, Pierre Alexandre (b Fauquembergue, near St Omer, 17 Oct 1729; d Paris, 14 Jan 1817), French composer. He studied the violin in his youth, but after the death of his father took an official position in Paris in order to support his family. A performance of *La serva padrona* in 1754 re-awakened his musical interests, and he took composition lessons from the double-bass player Gianotti. His first opera was produced 1759, and his association with Sedaine as librettist soon consolidated his success. After *Félix* (1777), at the height of his fame, he wrote no more. He lost his fortune during the Revolution, but was given an annuity by the Opéra-Comique.

Works include operas and *opéras-comiques Les Aveux indiscrets* (1759), *Le Maître en droit* (1760), *Le Cadi dupé* (1761), *On ne s'avise jamais de tout*, *Le Roi et le fermier* (1762), *Rose et Colas* (1764), *Aline, reine de Golconde* (1766), *L'Isle sonnante* (after Rabelais), *Le Déserteur* (1769), *Le Faucon* (1771), *La Belle Arsène* (1775), *Félix, ou L'Enfant trouvé* (1777), etc.

The metronome has no value ... for I myself have never believed that my blood and a mechanical instrument go well together.

Johannes Brahms, in a letter to
George Henschel, 1880

Montag aus Licht, Monday from 'Light', opera in three acts by Stockhausen (libretto by composer), produced Milan, La Scala, 7 May 1988. The inaugural opera of Stockhausen's *Licht* cycle, but the third to be composed, it celebrates 'Eve's Day'; the three acts are titled *Eve's First Birth*, *Eve's Second Birth* and *Eve's Magic*.

Montagnana, Antonio (b Venice, *c* 1700), Italian bass. Sang in several of Handel's operas in London, 1731–38, including the fps of *Ezio*, *Sosarme* and *Orlando*. Also sang in operas by Porpora and Hasse.

Montagnana, Domenico (b ? *c* 1690; d Venice, 7 Mar 1750), Italian violin-maker. Possibly a pupil of Antonio Stradivari, he worked first at Cremona, and set up a workshop in Venice in 1721.

Montague, Diana (b Winchester, 8 Apr 1953), English mezzo-soprano. Studied at the RNCM and made opera debut in 1977, with GTO as Zerlina. Sang at CG 1978–83, as Annius, Nicklausse and Cherubino. Bayreuth debut 1983, in the *Ring* Chicago 1984 (*Missa Solemnis*). Salzburg Festival debut 1986 (Cherubino), NY Met from 1987, as Sextus, Dorabella and Nicklausse. Glyndebourne debut 1989, as Orpheus. Other roles include Janáček's Fox (CG 1990), Idamante (Salzburg 1990) and Gluck's Taurean Iphigenia (WNO 1992). Many concert engagements.

Montague, Stephen (b Syracuse, NY, 10 Mar 1943), American composer. Studied at Florida State and Ohio State Universities. Resident in London from 1975 and has toured widely with Philip Mead from 1985 in a piano duo. Co-founder of the Electro-Acoustic Music Association of Great Britain. Music has been featured at Warsaw, Paris and Edinburgh Festivals and at the John Cage Festival, London. Works include ballets *Median* (1984) and *The Montague Stomp* (1984); *At the White Edge of Phrygia* for chamber orchestra (1983), *Prologue* for orchestra (1984), piano concerto (1988); *Varshavjan Spring* for chorus and chamber orchestra (1973–80), *Sotto Voce* for chorus and electronics (1976), *Boom-box Virelai* for four male voices (1993); two string quartets (1989, 1992); keyboard music and electronic pieces.

Montarsolo, Paolo (b Portici, near Naples, 16 Mar 1925), Italian bass. From 1954 he sang at La Scala in operas by Rossini, Donizetti and Mozart. Glyndebourne 1957, Mustafa; 1967–71, as Leporello, Osmin, Alfonso and Rossini's Selim. He has sung at the NY Met. and in Paris and Moscow. CG from 1990, as Donizetti's Don Pasquale and Dulcaman.

Monte, Philippe de (b Malines, 1521; d Prague, 4 Jul 1603), Flemish composer. He lived in Naples, 1542–54, and then in the Netherlands. He was in England 1554–55 as a member of the choir of Philip II of Spain, when he met the Byrd family. In 1558 or before he returned to Italy. In 1568 he went to Vienna as *Kapellmeister* to the Emperor Maximilian II, after whose death in 1576 he followed the next emperor, Rudolph II, to Prague. He was made a canon of Cambrai Cathedral, but did not reside there. Among the most important of late Renaissance polyphonists.

Works include 38 Masses, motets; over 30 books of madrigals, including 1,073 secular and 144 spiritual works. His motet *Super flumina Babylonis* was sent to Byrd in 1583, to which the latter responded with *Quomodo cantabimus* in 1584.

Montéclair, Michel (Pinolet) de (b Andelot, Haute-Marne, 4 Dec 1667; d Saint-Denis, 22 Sept 1737), French composer, theorist and teacher. Studied music as a chorister at Langres Cathedral, later sang in other churches and went to Italy in the service of the Prince de Vaudémont. After 1702 he settled in Paris and he was double-bass player at the Opéra 1707–37.

Works include operas and opera-ballets, e.g. *Les Festes de l'été* (1716) and *Jephté* (1732), ballet music for C F Pollaroli's opera *Ascanio*; chamber music, cantatas and sacred music.

Montemezzi, Italo (b Vigasio, 4 Aug 1875; d Vigasio, 15 May 1952), Italian composer. Learnt the piano as a child, then went to Milan to be trained for engineering, but wished to take up music. He entered the Conservatory with some difficulty, but obtained a diploma there in 1900. After the production of his first opera in 1905 he was able to give all his time to composition. From 1939 to 1949 he was in the USA, after which he returned to Italy.

Works include operas *Giovanni Gallurese* (1905), *Hellera* (1909), *L'amore dei tre re* (1913), *La Nave* (d'Annunzio, 1918), *La notte di Zoraima* (1931), *La principessa lontana* (after Rostand's *Princesse lointaine*, 1931); *The Song of Songs* for chorus or orchestra; symphonic poem *Paolo e Virginia* (after Saint-Pierre); elegy for cello and piano.

Monteux, Pierre (b Paris, 4 Apr 1875; d Hancock, ME, 1 Jul 1964), French conductor. Studied violin and composition at Paris Conservatory, winning first prize for violin in 1896. Then played viola in Colonne Orchestra and in 1911 began conducting for Diaghilev, giving fps of, among other works, Stravinsky's *Petrushka*, *The Rite of Spring*, *The Nightingale*, Ravel's *Daphnis et Chloé*, Debussy's *Jeux*. He was conductor of the Boston SO 1919–24, San Francisco SO 1936–52, LSO 1961–64. Monteux conducted all over the world and was recognized as equally fine in both the French and German repertories.

My brother says that he does not compose his works at haphazard because, in this kind of music, it has been his intention to make the words the mistress of the harmony and not the servant.

G C Monteverdi, in the foreword to Claudio Monteverdi's fifth book of madrigals, 1607 edition

---

Monteverdi, Claudio (Zuan Antonio) (b Cremona, 15 May 1567; d Venice, 29 Nov 1643), Italian composer. Son of a doctor; was a choirboy at Cremona Cathedral and a pupil of Ingegneri; became an organist and violist and at 16 pub. sacred madrigals, 1583. Entered the service of the Duke of Mantua, Vincenzo Gonzaga, as violist and singer, and there married the harpist Claudia Cataneo. He was in Gonzaga's retinue in the war against the Turks on the Danube and again in Flanders in 1599. He probably heard Peri's *Euridice* at Florence in 1600, and in 1602 was made music master to the court of Mantua. His wife died after a long illness on 10 Sept 1607, the year Monteverdi finished his first opera, *Orfeo*; this remains the earliest opera to be regularly performed today. The next opera, *Arianna*, made him widely famous; only the *Lamento d'Arianna* survives. In 1610 he dedicated his collection of church music, the *Vespers*, to Pope Paul V; from the opening chorus, based on the Toccata of *Orfeo*, and through to the concluding Magnificat, it is evident that the art of music is moving away for the first time from private use and into the public domain. When Francesco Gonzaga succeeded his brother to the dukedom in 1612, he quarrelled with Monteverdi, who left for his native Cremona to wait for a new appointment, which came from Venice in 1613, where he was made master of music to the republic and worked at St Mark's. He had by this time written much church music and numerous madrigals. His church music makes supremely effective use of the particular architecture of St Mark's, deploying separate groups of instruments and singers in order to exploit antiphonal effects. The nine books of madrigal develop from the small-scale

A Selection of
Monteverdi

Madrigals Book IV 1603
Madrigals Book V 1605
Orfeo 1607
Il Ballo delle ingrate 1608

Vespers 1610
Il combattimento di Tancredi e Clorinda 1624
Selva morale e spirituale 1640
Il ritorno d'Ulisse in patria 1640
L'incoronazione di Poppea 1642
Mass of Thanksgiving

Monteverdi *The composer Claudio Monteverdi (1567–1643). One of the most important figures in the history of music, Monteverdi was instrumental in the evolution from Renaissance to early Baroque styles. He was largely responsible for the establishment and success of opera with* Orfeo *and* l'Arianna.

pieces of 1587 to the hugely extended forms in Book 8 of 1638. In 1630 he took holy orders after escaping the plague at Venice. In 1639 the second public opera theatre in Venice, the Teatro dei SS Giovanni e Paolo, was opened with Monteverdi's *Adone*, and *Arianna* was revived the same year when the Teatro di San Moisè was inaugurated. His last opera was *L'Incoronazione di Poppea*, widely performed today in an increasing variety of editions. Monteverdi's work in this genre was highly important and influential in establishing opera during this early period. More broadly, Monteverdi was a key figure in providing the impetus for change in which secular music and music for the general public became increasingly important.

Works include operas *Orfeo* (1607), *Arianna* (lost except the *Lament*, 1608), *Il combattimento di Tancredi e Clorinda* (after Tasso, 1624), *Il ritorno d'Ulisse in patria* (1640), *L'incoronazione di Poppea* (1642), and about a dozen lost stage works; ballets *Ballo delle ingrate* (1608) and *Tirsi e Clori* (1619); Masses, Magnificats and psalms; *Vespers* (1610), *Sancta Maria* for voice and eight instruments; 40 sacred madrigals; 21 *canzonette* for three voices; nine books of secular madrigals containing 250, including book VIII, *Madrigali guerrieri e amorosi* (Madrigals of love and war); 26 madrigals published in various collections; 25 *Scherzi musicali* for one–three voices (1607).

Montezuma opera by Roger Sessions (libretto by G A Borgese); composed 1941–63, produced West Berlin, 19 Apr 1964.

Montgomery, Kenneth (b Belfast, 28 Oct 1943), Irish conductor. Studied at the RCM and made debut at Glyndebourne 1967, with *L'elisir d'amore*. Conductor at SW 1967–70, Bournemouth Sinfonietta 1973–75. Music director of GTO 1975–76. Gave *Oberon* at Wexford 1972, *Figaro* on CG debut, 1975. Netherlands Opera from 1972, with *Ariadne, Capriccio* and *Hänsel and Gretel*. Conducted *Tosca* and *Die Zauberflöte* for Opera Northern Ireland (1990) and *Alcina* at Vancouver, 1991.

Monti, Laura (b ? Rome, after 1704; d Naples, 1760), Italian soprano. From 1726 to 1735 she sang in comic opera in Rome and in 1733 created Serpina in Pergolesi's intermezzo *La serva padrona*. She sang in the fp of Auletta's *La locandiera* (Naples, 1738) and created a demand for further performances of comic operas in Naples. Also sang in operas by Hasse and Leo. Her cousin Marianna (b Naples 1730; d Naples 1814) was popular in Naples for 20 years in operas by Jommelli, Traetta, Paisiello, Cimarosa and Sacchini. Retired 1780.

Monticelli, Angelo Maria (b Milan, *c* 1710; d Dresden, 1764), Italian castrato soprano. Made his debut in Rome in 1730, sang in London, 1741–46 (in Gluck's two operas for London, *La caduta dei giganti* and *Artamene*), later in Naples, Vienna and, from 1756, in Dresden under Hasse.

Montpellier Manuscript a large MS (400 folios) in eight gatherings, representing about 100 years of music history (1200–1300). It is the largest source of 13th-c. motets and was written down between *c* 1280 and *c* 1310. It is in the library of the Faculté de Médecine, Montpellier, MS. 196.

Montsalvatge (Bassols), Xavier (b Gerona, 11 Mar 1912), Catalan composer. Studied with Morera and Pahissa at Barcelona Conservatory, winning the Pedrell Prize in 1936.

Works include opera *El gato con botas* (1947); four ballets; *Sinfonia mediterranea* (1949); *Concerto breve* for piano and orchestra (1956), *Poema concertante* for violin and orchestra; orchestral suite *Calidoscopo*; string quartet (1952); songs.

Monumentum pro Gesualdo di Venosa ad CD annum three madrigals recomposed in 1960 by Stravinsky for 12 wind instruments and strings to celebrate the 400th anniversary of Gesualdo's birth. Fp Venice, 27 Sept 1960. The madrigals are *Asciugate i belli occhi, Ma tu, cagion di quella, Belta poi che t'assenti*.

mood, Latin *modus*, the relationship between the long (<) and the breve (▮) in mensural notation.

Moodie, Alma (b Brisbane, 12 Sept 1900; d Frankfurt, 7 Mar 1943), Australian violinist. Studied with César Thomson at Brussels and travelled widely, making her reputation especially in Germany, where she married a lawyer at Cologne. Pfitzner wrote his violin concerto for her.

Moody, Fanny (b Redruth, Cornwall, 23 Nov 1866; d Dundrum, Co. Dublin, 21 Jul 1945), English soprano. Studied with Charlotte Sainton-Dolby and made her first stage appearance at Liverpool in 1887. In 1890 she married Charles Manners and in 1897 became his partner in the Moody-Manners Opera Co. She sang Tatyana in the first British performance of *Eugene Onegin* (1892).

I look forward to the first rehearsal with as much appreciation as I do the concert, for here the personality and the musical potential of each artist is assessed by the other.

Gerald Moore, *Am I Too Loud?*, 1962

Moog, Robert, ◊synthesizer.

Moonlight Sonata the nickname of Beethoven's piano sonata in C♯ minor, op. 27 no. 2, probably due to a description of the first movement by Rellstab.

Moór, Emanuel (b Kecskemét, 19 Feb 1863; d Chardonne, 20 Oct 1931), Hungarian pianist, composer and inventor. Studied at Budapest and Vienna, and toured in Europe and America as pianist and conductor. Inventor of the Duplex-Coupler piano. Married the English pianist Winifred Christie.

Works include operas *La Pompadour* (after Musset, 1902), *Andreas Hofer* (1902), *Hochzeitsglocken* (1908); eight symphonies (1893–1910); four violin concertos (1905–07); chamber music; piano works.

Moore, Douglas (Stuart) (b Cutchogue, NY, 10 Aug 1893; d Greenport, Long Island, 25 Jul 1969), American composer. Studied at Yale University and with Horatio Parker, Bloch, d'Indy, Tournemire and

Nadia Boulanger. He served in the US Navy in the 1914–18 war, was organist and lecturer at Cleveland, 1921–25, and became associate professor of music at Columbia University in NY in 1926 and later professor.

Works include operas *The Devil and Daniel Webster* (1939), *The Ballad of Baby Doe* (1956) and *Carrie Nation* (1966), operetta *The Headless Horseman* (1936), chamber opera *White Wings* (1935); motet *Dedication* for six voices, *Simon Legree* for male chorus, *Perhaps to dream* for female chorus; *A Symphony of Autumn*, Overture on an American Tune, *Pageant of P T Barnum* (1924), *Moby Dick* (after Herman Melville), *In Memoriam*, symphony in A for orchestra (1945); string quartet; sonata and *Down East* suite for violin and piano; wind quintet, clarinet quintet.

Moore, Gerald (b Watford, 30 Jul 1899; d Penn, Bucks., 13 Mar 1987), English pianist. Studied in Canada and after a short career as a concert performer became an accompanist, in which profession he quickly rose to fame as the most distinguished of his time, playing for most of the great instrumentalists and singers and raising his art to a level with that of his partner. Among the singers he worked with were Gerhardt, Schumann, Hotter, Fischer-Dieskau and Schwarzkopf. He wrote some valuable books, including *The Unashamed Accompanist*, *Singer and Accompanist* and *Am I too Loud?*

Moore, Grace (b Nough, TN, 5 Dec 1898; d Copenhagen, 26 Jan 1947), American soprano. She appeared in musical comedy 1921–26 and after study in France sang Mimi at the NY Met. in 1928; continued there until 1946 as Manon, Lauretta, Tosca and Louise. London, CG, 1935, as Mimi. Also popular in concerts and films. She was killed in an air crash.

Moore, Jerrold Northrop (b Paterson, NJ, 1934), American musicologist. Studied at Yale and was curator of sound recordings there, 1961–70. Resident in England from 1970 and has become an authority on Elgar. Joint editor of the *Elgar Complete Edition* and has published *Elgar: a Life in Photographs* (1974), *Spirit of England: Edward Elgar in his World* (1984) and *Edward Elgar: A Creative Life* (1984). Also editions of Elgar's letters.

Moore, Thomas (1779–1852), Irish poet. From about 1802 he began to pub. songs with words and occasionally music by himself, and between 1807 and 1834 he produced collections of Irish tunes with new words of his own. He also produced, in 1811, an opera *M P, or The Blue Stocking* with music by himself and C E Horn. He wrote the tune as well as the words of 'The Last Rose of Summer', used by Flotow in *Martha*. For works used by composers W S ◊Bennet) (*Paradise and the Peri*); ◊Clay (*Lalla Rookh*); (Fél.) ◊David (ditto); ◊Feramors (A Rubinstein); ◊Paradise and the Peri (Schumann); ◊Spontini (*Nurmahal* and *Lalla Rookh*); J ◊Stevenson (Irish songs edition); Veiled Prophet (Stanford).

Moorehead, John (b Ireland, *c* 1760; d near Deal, Mar 1804), Irish violinist and composer. Studied in Ireland, went to England as a youth and played at various provincial theatres, viola at Sadler's Wells Theatre in London from 1796, and violin at CG from 1798. He had already produced his first stage work in 1796 and wrote several more for CG. In 1802 he became insane and was confined, entered the Navy on being released, but hanged himself in a fit of madness.

Works include stage pieces *Birds of a Feather* (1796), *Harlequin's Tour* (with Attwood), *Perouse* (with Davy), *The Cabinet* (with Braham, Davy and others), *Family Quarrels* (with Braham and Reeve, 1802), *The Naval Pillar* (1799), Morton's *Speed the Plough* and others; pantomimes.

Morales, Cristóbal (b Seville, *c* 1500; d ? Marchena, Autumn 1553), Spanish composer. Studied at Seville under the cathedral *maestro de capilla* Fernández de Castilleja. Was *maestro de capilla* at Avila, 1526–30, and some time later went to Rome, where he was ordained a priest and became cantor in the Pontifical Chapel, 1535. In 1545 he was given leave to visit Spain, but did not return, living at Toledo, Málaga and Marchena, appointed *maestro de capilla* at the former two places and serving in the household of the Duke of Arcos at the last. Palestrina based a mass on his motet *O sacrum convivium*.

Works include 21 Masses, 16 Magnificats, 91 motets, Lamenta-

tions and other church music; cantatas for the peace conference at Nice (1538) and for Ippolito d'Este; madrigals.

Moralt, Rudolf (b Munich, 26 Feb 1902; d Vienna, 16 Dec 1958), German conductor. Studied at the Munich Music Academy with W Courvoisier and Schmid-Lindner, and in 1919 became a *répétiteur* at the Munich Staatsoper. After a number of posts in various German opera houses he became first conductor at the Vienna Staatsoper in 1940. Made Salzburg concert debut 1939, opera 1952 (*Figaro*). Well known in Mozart and Strauss.

'This must *be the music', said he, 'of the* spears, *for I'm curst if each note of it doesn't run through one!'*
Thomas Moore, *The Fudge Family*, 1818

Moran, Robert (b Denver, 8 Jan 1937), American composer. Studied in Vienna, and with Berio and Milhaud at Mills College. Has performed throughout the USA and Europe as pianist, and has lectured widely. Resident in Philadelphia from 1985. His music has embraced random choice techniques, minimalism and multiple synthesizers; directed the West Coast Music Ensemble and taught at the San Francisco Conservatory. His *Smell Piece for Mills College* (1967) was intended to burn down his alma mater and was followed by the chamber opera *Let's Build a Nut House* (1969). His environment piece *Hitler: Geschichten aus der Zukunft* (1981) was too much for the Germans who commissioned it, and was promptly banned; the succeeding *Erlöser*, music drama in two acts, depicts the rantings of a dying Wagner. A collaboration with Philip Glass on the opera *The Juniper Tree* (1985) prompted a conversion to synthesizer-inspired Romanticism: *Desert of Roses* (1992) is based on the *Beauty and the Beast* story, while *From the Towers of the Moon* (1992) is prompted by an ancient Japanese legend. *The Dracula Diary* (1994) suggested a return to anarchism.

Moravia, Hieronymus de, 13th-c. theorist, probably a Dominican friar living in Paris. His *Tractatus de Musica* is a comprehensive compilation dealing mainly with plainsong, with an extensive tonary attached.

mordent an ornament over a note, indicated by the sign: ✸. ◊Pralltriller.

The notation for mordents on D and F, and the approximate execution of each.

Mörder, Hoffnung der Frauen, (*Murderer, the Hope of Women*), opera in one act by Hindemith (libretto by Oskar Kokoschka); composed 1919, fp Stuttgart, 4 Jun 1921, conductor Fritz Busch. Sado-erotic meeting of a Man and a Woman.

Mordkovitch, Lydia (b Saratov, 1950), Russian-born violinist. Studied with David Oistrakh at the Moscow Conservatory and emigrated to Israel 1974, later moving to London; British debut 1979, with the Hallé Orchestra. US debut with the Chicago SO under Solti, later playing Brahms Concerto with the Philadelphia Orchestra under Muti. London Proms debut 1985. Recordings include the solo violin works of Ysaÿe and Bach, and concertos by Moeran, Prokofiev and Bruch.

Moreau, Jean-Baptiste (b Angers, 1656; d Paris, 24 Aug 1733), French composer. He learnt music as a boy chorister at Angers Cathedral and composed motets as a youth. Appointed choirmaster at the cathedral of Langres, where he married, and later that of Dijon, and went to Paris during the 1680s. He found his way into the court, for which he began to write stage pieces, and in 1688 he was commissioned to write music for Racine's *Esther* for performance at the young ladies' academy of Saint-Cyr. This earned him a pension for life and an appointment at Saint-Cyr jointly with the organist Nivers and later with Clérambault. He remained under the patronage of the king and Mme de Maintenon. He taught both singing and composition, among his pupils for the former being his daughter Claude-Marie Moreau and for the latter Clérambault, Dandrieu and Montéclair.

Works include Requiem, motet *In exitu Israel* (1691), *Cantiques spirituels* (Racine), Te Deum for the king's recovery (1687) and other church music; stage divertissements including *Les Bergers de Marly*; chorus for Racine's *Athalie* (1691); *Idylle sur la naissance de Notre Seigneur*; drinking-songs.

Morena, Berta (b Mannheim, 27 Jan 1878; d Rottach-Egern, 7 Oct 1952), German soprano. Debut Munich 1898, as Agathe; remained until 1924 as Elsa, Eva and Isolde; NY Met. debut 1908, as Sieglinde; sang there until 1912 and returned 1925 for Brünnhilde. CG 1914. Retired 1927.

morendo Italian = 'dying'; a direction used where a phrase is intended to die away. It may mean a decrease not only in tone but in pace as well.

Moresca a Moorish dance of remote antiquity, first introduced by the Moors into Spain and popular all over Europe by the 15th–16th c. Allied to the English Morris Dance, 'morys' being an English variant of 'Moorish'; at any rate one of the latter's features – bells or jingles tied to the legs – belonged to the moresca also.

Morhange, Charles Henri Valentin, ◊Alkan.

Mori, Nicholas (b London, 24 Jan 1796 or 1797; d London, 14 Jun 1839), English violinist and publisher of Italian descent. Pupil of Barthélemon, at whose concerts he played at the age of eight, and later of Viotti. He appeared as soloist at the Philharmonic Society's concerts and became leader of its orchestra. In 1819 he married the widow of the music publisher Lavenu and became a partner with her son.

Moriani, Napoleone (b Florence, 10 Mar 1808; d Florence, 4 Mar 1878), Italian tenor. Made his first appearance at Pavia in 1833; in Pacini's *Gli Arabi nelle Gallie*, and sang in many European cities during the next 14 years. Much admired in operas by Donizetti, Vaccai, Mercadante and Federico Ricci.

Mörike, Eduard (Friedrich) (1804–75), German poet. ◊Schoeck (songs); ◊Sutermeister (*Jorinde*; ◊Trapp (*Letzte König von Orplid*).

Two songs by Brahms, three by Schumann, 57 (including four early) by H Wolf.

Morison, Elsie (b Ballarat, Victoria, 15 Aug 1924), Australian soprano. After study in Melbourne she moved to England in 1946. London, SW, 1948–54. She was the first British Anne Trulove, Edinburgh 1953, and in the same year made her CG debut; remained until 1962 as Mimi, Susanna, Pamina, Micaela and Blanche in *The Carmelites*. Glyndebourne 1954–59 as Anne Trulove, Zerlina and Marzelline.

Mork, Truls (b Bergen, 25 Apr 1961), Norwegian cellist. Studied in Stockholm and with Heinrich Schiff in Austria. Prizewinner at the 1982 Tchaikovsky Competition, Moscow. New York recital debut 1986, London 1988. Founder of the International Chamber Music Festival in Stavanger. Played the Lutosławski Concerto under the composer and has recorded concertos by Shostakovich, Elgar and Haydn.

Morlacchi, Francesco (b Perugia, 14 Jun 1784; d Innsbruck, 28 Oct 1841), Italian composer and conductor. Studied with her father, then at Perugia Cathedral, later with Zingarelli at Loreto and finally with Mattei at Bologna. In 1810 he was appointed music director of the Italian opera at Dresden, where he remained to the end of his life.

Works include operas *Il ritratto* (1807), *Enone e Paride* (1808), *Oreste, Le Daniadi* (1810), *Raoul de Créqui* (1811), *La capricciosa pentita*, *Il barbiere di Siviglia* (after Beaumarchais, 1816), *Boadicea*, *Gianni di Parigi* (1818), *Il Simoncino*, *Donna Aurora*, *Tebaldo ed Isolina* (1820), *La gioventù di Enrico V* (1823), *Il Colombo*, *Francesca da Rimini* (after Dante, unfinished, 1836), and *c* ten others.

13 Masses, Requiem for the King of Saxony (1827), Miserere for 16 voices, unaccompanied Mass for the Greek service and other

church music; oratorios *Gli angeli al sepolcro* (1803), *La morte di Abele* (1821) and *Il sacrifizio d'Abramo*, Passion oratorio (words by Metastasio, 1811); cantatas for the coronation of Napoleon as king of Italy (1805) and for the taking of Paris (1814); Narration of Ugolino from Dante's *Inferno* for baritone and piano.

Morlaye, Guillaume (b ? Paris, *c* 1515; d after 1560), French amateur composer and lutenist, a merchant by profession. He is said to have been in the slave trade and was definitely a publisher; pub. several books of music for lute and for guitar.

If therefore you will compose in this kind, you must possess yourself of an amorous humour ... so that you must in your music be wavering like the wind, sometimes wanton, sometimes drooping, sometimes grave and staid, otherwise effeminate.

Thomas Morley, *A Plain and Easy Introduction to Practical Music*, 1597

Morley, Thomas (b Norwich 1557 or 1558; d London, Oct 1602), English composer. Although a Roman Catholic he was *magister puerorum* at Norwich Cathedral, 1583–87. A pupil of Byrd, he took his B.Mus. degree at Oxford in 1588 and about that time became organist of St Giles's Church, Cripplegate, in London. Soon afterwards he was organist of St Paul's Cathedral and in 1592 became a Gentleman of the Chapel Royal. In 1598 both Morley and Shakespeare, who were probably acquainted, appealed against the assessment for taxes, and in 1599 Morley probably contributed the setting of 'It was a lover and his lass', if not more music, to the production of *As You Like It*. Morley obtained a patent for the printing of music and music paper in 1598, but he had already pub. his treatise, *A Plaine and Easie Introduction to Practicall Musick*, in 1597. Published and edited the madrigal collection *The Triumphes of Oriana* in 1601. He resigned from the Chapel Royal in 1602, (?) owing to ill health.

Works include services, anthems and responses, ten Latin motets; madrigals (including two in *The Triumphes of Oriana*), canzonets and ballets for voices; four tunes contributed to *The Whole Booke of Psalmes*; fancies for viols; virginal pieces.

Morning Heroes symphony for orator, chorus and orchestra by Bliss (words by Homer, Li-Tai-Po, Whitman, Robert Nichols and Wilfred Owen), fp Norwich Festival, 6 Oct 1930.

Moross, Jerome (b Brooklyn, 1 Aug 1913; d Miami, 25 Jul 1983), American composer. Studied at Juilliard and worked in Hollywood from 1940. Best known for ballets and ballet-operas: *Paul Bunyan* (1934), *American Patterns* (1937), *Susannah and the Elders* (1940), *The Eccentricities of Davy Crockett* (1946), *The Golden Apple* (1952), *Sorry, Wrong Number* (composed 1983).

Morris, James (b Baltimore, 10 Jan 1947), American bass-baritone. He studied with Rosa Ponselle. Debut Baltimore 1967, as Crespel; NY Met. 1972, Ramfis. Glyndebourne 1972, as Banquo. He sang the Dutchman at Houston (1984) and in 1985 was Wotan at San Francisco. Salzburg 1985, as Guglielmo; sang in the *Ring* at Munich (1987), Berlin, NY Met. (1989) and CG (1989–91). Recordings of the *Ring* conducted by Levine and Haitink. Other roles include Méphistophélès, Claggart and Donizetti's Henry VIII.

Morris, R(eginald) O(wen) (b York, 3 Mar 1886; d London, 14 Dec 1948), English teacher and composer. Educated at Harrow, New College, Oxford, and the RCM in London, where later he became professor of counterpoint and composition. In 1926 he was appointed to a similar post at the Curtis Institute at Philadelphia, but soon returned to England. His books include *Contrapuntal Technique in the 16th Century*, *Foundations of Practical Harmony and Counterpoint*, *The Structure of Music*.

Works include symphony in D major; violin concerto in G minor, *Concerto piccolo* for two violins and strings; fantasy for string quartet, Motets for string quartet; songs with quartet accompaniment.

Morris Dance an old English folk dance, deriving its name from the

Moorish *Moresca* (old English 'morys' = 'Moorish'), introduced into England about the 15th c. It partook of a pageant in character and was danced in various kinds of fancy dress, with jingles tied to the dancers' legs. In some districts elements of the Sword Dance were introduced into it. The music, a great variety of tunes, was played by a pipe and tabor, or more rarely by a bagpipe or violin.

Mors et Vita, *Death and [New] Life*, oratorio by Gounod, a sequel to *The Redemption*, produced Birmingham Festival, 26 Aug 1885.

Mortari, Virgilio (b Passirana di Lainate, near Milan, 6 Dec 1902; d Rome, 5 Sept 1993), Italian composer. Pupil of Pizzetti. Professor of composition at the S Cecilia Conservatory in Rome from 1940. Director of the Teatro La Fenice, Venice, from 1955 to 1959.

Works include operas (1927), *La scuola delle mogli* (after Molière, 1930); rhapsody for orchestra; concerto for quartet and orchestra, piano concerto; chamber music; partita for violin; songs.

Morton (*Mourton* in France), Robert (b *c* 1430; d *c* 1476), English singer and composer. He was employed at the court of Burgundy 1457–76 under Philip the Good and Charles the Bold. He composed French *chansons*, of which two were among the most popular of their day.

Moscheles, Ignaz (b Prague, 23 May 1794; d Leipzig, 10 Mar 1870), Bohemian pianist and composer. Studied under Dionys Weber at the Prague Conservatory, played a concerto in public at the age of 14, was sent to Vienna and there took lessons in counterpoint from Albrechtsberger and composition from Salieri. He made Beethoven's acquaintance when he arranged the vocal score of *Fidelio* in 1814. He then began to travel widely, and in 1821 appeared in Holland, Paris and London. In 1824 he taught Mendelssohn in Berlin; in 1826 he married Charlotte Embden at Hamburg and settled permanently in London. In 1832 he conducted the fp there of Beethoven's *Missa solemnis*. In 1846 he went to Leipzig at Mendelssohn's invitation to become first piano professor at the new Conservatory.

Works include symphony in C (1829); eight piano concertos (1819–38), e.g. G minor and *Concerto pathétique*; a great number of piano works including *Sonate mélancolique*, *Characteristic Studies*, *Allegro di bravura* and numerous sonatas, variations, fantasies, studies, etc.; *Hommage à Händel* for two pianos.

Moscona, Nicola (b Athens, 23 Sept 1907; d Phildelphia, 17 Sept 1975), Greek bass. Debut Athens 1929. He sang in Florence and Milan during the 1930s. NY Met. debut 1937, as Ramfis; remained until 1962 as leading bass. He recorded the Verdi Requiem, under Toscanini, and roles in *Bohème*, *Mefistofele* and *Rigoletto*.

Mosè in Egitto, *Moses in Egypt*, ◊Moïse.

Opera by Rossini (libretto by A L Tottola), produced Naples, Teatro San Carlo, 5 Mar 1818. Moses frees the Israelites in Egypt and parts the Red Sea on the way home.

Moser, Edda (b Berlin, 27 Oct 1938), German soprano. Debut Berlin 1962, in *Butterfly*. She sang under Henze in London (1967) and appeared with Karajan in the *Ring* at the 1968 Salzburg Easter Festival. NY Met. 1970, the Queen of Night. Salzburg 1971 as Aspasia in Mozart's *Mitridate*. Other roles include Constanze, Leonore and Lucia. She sang Donna Anna in the Lorin Maazel–Joseph Losey film version of *Don Giovanni*. In Jan 1971 she took part in the fp of Henze's *The Raft of the Medusa*, at Vienna.

Moser, Hans Joachim (b Berlin, 25 May 1889; d Berlin, 14 Aug 1967), German singer, musicologist and composer. Studied with his father — Andreas Moser (1859–1925) violinist and writer on music, biography of Joachim — and later at Berlin, Marburg and Leipzig. Became professor of musicology at Halle, Heidelberg and later Berlin. His literary works include a history of German music, studies of medieval string music, Luther's songs, German song, etc., biographies of Hofhaimer, Schütz and Bach, etc.

Moser, Thomas (b Richmond, VA, 27 May 1945), American tenor. Studied at Curtis Institute and in California with Lotte Lehmann. Sang at Graz from 1975 and appeared as Belmonte at Munich, 1976. Vienna Staatsoper from 1977, as Mozart's Ottavio, Tamino, Idomeneo and Titus, Strauss's Flamand and Gluck's Achilles. NY City Opera debut 1979, Salzburg 1983 (*La finta semplice*; fp of Berio's *Un*

──────────── **THE OPERA** ────────────

Moses und Aron

A two-act opera (a third act is incomplete) by Arnold Schoenberg, with text by the composer based on the Book of Exodus. It is set in the Near East in biblical times. The opera was first performed in Zurich in 1957, six years after Schoenberg's death.

I. Moses (spoken) receives the word of God from the Burning Bush (chorus): the Israelites must be freed to the promised land. Moses' brother Aron (tenor) speaks for him to the Israelites in terms of an invisible God. When the people are sceptical, Aron demonstrates the power and reality of God with three miracles: Moses' staff (the Law) is transformed into a snake, his hand is turned leprous then whole again, and a pitcher of water is turned into blood. Moses continues to despair that he cannot communicate God's grandeur in his own, abstract, terms.

II. Aron is told that the people can wait no longer for Moses to return from the Mount of Revelation. Aron gives way for the demand to return to the old gods, and a Golden Calf is built. A long orgy follows, culminating in the sacrifice of four Naked Virgins. An angry Moses descends, carrying with him the tablets of the Commandments. He smashes them when Aron tells him that they too are an image. As the Israelites follow the fiery pillars, Moses collapses, still inarticulate.

──────────── **THE OPERA** ────────────

re in ascolto, 1984). Sang Schubert's Fierabras at Vienna 1988, Florestan at La Scala 1990 and Strauss's Emperor at the 1992 Salzburg Festival. Concert performances in Bach, Beethoven and Britten (*War Requiem*).

Moses und Aron, *Moses and Aaron*, opera in two acts by Schoenberg (projected third act never composed; libretto by composer), fp (concert), Hamburg, 12 Mar 1954; produced Zurich, 6 Jun 1957. (The music was composed 1930–32). Moses and his brother Aaron bring God's message to the people, but the Israelites cannot understand Moses' abstract ideas. Aaron leads an orgy around the Golden Calf, but Moses interrupts with the Tablets of the Law.

Moshinsky, Elijah (b Shanghai, 8 Jan 1946), Chinese-born Australian stage director. Studied at Melbourne and Oxford Universities. Has produced Shakespeare for the BBC and staged classics for the National Theatre. CG debut 1975 (*Peter Grimes*), followed by *Lohengrin* (1977), *The Rake's Progress*, *Samson et Dalila*, Handel's *Samson*, *Otello*, *Attila*, *Simon Boccanegra* and *Aida* (1994). NY Met. debut 1980, *Un ballo in maschera*. Staged the UK premiere of Ligeti's *Le grand macabre* for ENO (1982), followed by *The Mastersingers* and *The Bartered Bride*. His directorial style is indicated by the title of his recent article: *Verdi: A Pox on post-modernism*.

Mosonyi, Mihály (originally Michael Brand) (b Frauenkirchen, Wieselburg, 4 Sept 1815; d Pest, 31 Oct 1870), Hungarian composer. Studied at Pozsony (Pressburg) and was music master to a noble family 1835–42, when he settled at Budapest. He changed his German name of Brand in 1859, when he began to aim at writing Hungarian national music.

Works include operas *Kaiser Max auf der Martinswand* (composed 1857), *The Fair Ilonka* (1861) and *Almos*, 1862; both in Hungarian; three Masses; symphonies, symphonic poems *Mourning for Széchényi* and *Festival Music* and other orchestral works; 20 piano pieces in the Hungarian manner; 25 Hungarian folksong arrangements.

mosso Italian = 'moving, in motion, animated'.

Mossolov, Alexander Vassilievich (b Kiev, 10 Aug 1900; d Moscow, 12 Jul 1973), Russian pianist and composer. His family, which cultivated various branches of art, moved to Moscow in 1904 and in 1921 he entered the Conservatory there, studying under Glière until 1925. He travelled much as a pianist and to study folk music in central Asia.

Works include operas *The Dam*, *The Hero* (1928), *The Signal* (1941); cantatas *Sphinx* (Oscar Wilde) and *Kirghiz Rhapsody*; six symphonies (1929–50), ballet *The Factory* (1927) with realistic sound effects, including a shaken metal sheet, also performed as a concert item with the title *The Iron Foundry* (*Music of Machines*); *Turcomanian Suite* and *Uzbek Dance* for orchestra; two piano concertos (1927, 1935), violin concerto, harp concerto, two cello concertos; string quartet, *Dance Suite* for piano trio; viola and piano sonata; songs to words by Pushkin, Lermontov and Blok; massed choruses, battle songs.

Mosto, Giovanni Battista (b Udine, before 1550; d after 1590), Italian 16th-c. composer. Pupil of Merulo, *maestro di cappella* of Padua Cathedral, 1580–89, and then in the service of Prince Bathori of Transylvania.
Works include church music; madrigals.

Moszkowski, Moritz (b Breslau, 23 Aug 1854; d Paris, 4 Mar 1925), Polish-German pianist and composer. Studied at Dresden and Berlin, where he became professor at Kullak's academy later on. After a successful career as pianist and composer he retired to Paris in 1897. He died in poverty.
Works include opera *Boabdil* (1892); ballet *Laurin* (1896); symphony *Jeanne d'Arc*, two suites, *Phantastischer Zug* and other pieces for orchestra; piano concerto in E major, two concert pieces for piano and orchestra, violin concerto; chamber music; piano pieces.

[Telemann] could write a motet for eight voices more quickly than one could write a letter.

George Frideric Handel, quoted in
Young, *Handel*, 1946

---

motet, Latin *motetus*, a diminutive of French *mot* = 'word', a form of sacred vocal composed for several voices arising out of the rhythmical *clausulae* of ◊organum in the 13th c. It was at first an elaboration of a given plainsong melody by the contrapuntal addition of other melodies with different words (in Latin, French or both). The earliest motets were most frequently for three voices, *triplum*, *motetus* – hence the name of the species – and *tenor*, which was the lowest part. In the 15th c. it became more independent, and gradually developed into an elaborate form of polyphonic sacred composition set to any Latin words not included in the Mass. In the 16th c. it was not uncommon to use the musical material of a motet as the basis for the composition of a Mass.

Mother Goose (Ravel.) ◊Ma Mère l'Oye.

Mother of Us All, The opera by Virgil Thomson (libretto by G Stein), produced NY Brander Matthews Theatre, Columbia University, 7 May 1947.

motion the succession of notes of different pitch. The word is used only with some adjectival qualification or other:
   conjunct motion: a single part moving by steps of adjoining notes.
   contrary motion: two or more parts moving together in different directions.
   disjunct motion: a single part moving by larger than stepwise intervals.
   oblique motion: one part moving when another stands still.
   similar motion: two or more parts moving together in the same direction.

Motiv, German, *motive* English, a brief melodic or rhythmic figure, too short to be called a theme, sometimes used as a purely abstract subject, sometimes in programme music or opera in association with a character, object or idea, in which case it becomes a leading motive like the *idée fixe* of Berlioz or the *Leitmotiv* of Wagner.

moto perpetuo Italian = 'perpetual motion'; a piece exploiting rapid figuration of a uniform and uninterrupted pattern; also called by the Latin name of *perpetuum mobile*.

Mottl, Felix (Josef) (b Unter-St-Veit near Vienna, 24 Aug 1856; d Munich, 2 Jul 1911), Austrian conductor and composer. Studied at a choir school and at the Conservatory in Vienna, became conductor of

the Wagner Society there and in 1876 was engaged by Wagner to conduct the music on the stage in the production of the *Ring*; gave *Tristan* and *Parsifal* at Bayreuth in 1886. In 1881–1903 he was conductor at the ducal court of Karlsruhe, where he directed the symphonic concerts and the opera, producing many unfamiliar works including the fp of all five acts of *Les Troyens* (1890). From 1903 he was conductor in Munich. He collapsed while conducting *Tristan* and died shortly after.
Works include operas *Agnes Bernauer* (after Hebbel), *Rama* and *Fürst und Sänger*; festival play *Eberstein*; music for O J Bierbaum's play *Pan im Busch*; string quartet (1904); songs.

motto in music, a short and well-defined theme usually occurring at the opening of a composition and used again during its course, in its first form or altered, in the manner of a quotation or an allusion to some definite idea. The opening themes in Tchaikovsky's fourth and fifth symphonies are familiar examples.

motu proprio Latin = lit. 'of one's own motion'; a decree issued by the Pope personally, especially that issued by Pius X in 1903 setting down the principles of, and introducing reforms into, the singing of Roman Catholic church music.

Moulu, Pierre (b ? Flanders, c 1485; d c 1550), Franco-Flemish 16th-c. composer. Pupil of Josquin Desprez. Wrote Masses, motets and *chansons*.

Mount-Edgcumbe, Earl of (Richard Edgcumbe) (b Plymouth, 13 Sept 1764; d Richmond, Surrey, 26 Sept 1839), English music amateur and composer. Known chiefly by his *Musical Reminiscences*, pub. privately in 1823, mainly of operatic singing in London 1773–1823.
Works include opera *Zenobia*.

Mount of Olives, The (Beethoven.) ◊Christus am Oelberge.

Mouret, Jean Joseph (b Avignon, 11 Apr 1682; d Charenton, 22 Dec 1738), French composer. He entered the service of the Duchess of Maine in Paris about 1707 and in 1714 began to write for the stage. He was director of the Concert Spirituel 1728–34, also for a time conductor of the Comédie-Italienne. In 1736 he became insane and was taken to the lunatic asylum of Charenton.
Works include operas and opera-ballets *Les Festes de Thalie*, *Ragonde*, *Ariane* (1717), *Les Amours des dieux* (1727), *Le Triomphe des sens* (1732), etc.; Mass, two books of motets; cantatas *Cantatilles*; two *Suites de Symphonies*, 47 divertissements for orchestra; two books of *Concerts de chambre*; fanfares.

Mourning Symphony (Haydn.) ◊Trauer-Sinfonie.

Moussorgsky ◊Mussorgsky.

Mouton, Charles (1626–after 1700), French lutenist and composer. Lived in Turin in the 1670s, twice visited Paris, and eventually settled there. Wrote lute pieces, etc.

Mouton, Jean (b Haut-Wignes, c 1459; d St Quentin, 30 Oct 1522), French composer. Pupil of Josquin des Prés. He was in the service of Louis XII and François I, became canon of Thérouanne, which he left probably on its being taken by the English in 1513, and afterwards of the collegiate church of Saint-Quentin.
Works include 14 Masses, 110 motets, psalms, *Alleluia* and *In illo tempore* for Easter, *Noe, noe, psallite* for Christmas, etc.

mouvement French = 'tempo, pace'; also a movement of a sonata, symphony.

Mouvements de cœur seven songs for bass and piano in memory of Chopin (poems by Louise de Vilmorin): 1. *Prélude*; Henri Sauguet; 2. *Mazurka*: Francis Poulenc; 3. *Valse*: Georges Auric; 4. *Scherzo Impromptu*: Jean Françaix; 5. *Étude*: Léo Preger; 6. *Ballade* (*Nocturne*): Darius Milhaud; 7. *Postlude*: Polonaise: Sauguet.

movable doh the ◊tonic or keynote in the Tonic Sol-fa system which shifts the tonal centre at each modulation into another key instead of prescribing accidentals.

movement an independent section of a large-scale work such as a symphony or sonata. The term is used even when there is a link with the section that follows, e.g., in Mendelssohn's 'Scottish' symphony.

Movements work for piano and orchestra by Stravinsky; composed 1958–59, fp NY, 10 Jan 1960, with Margit Weber, who commissioned the score.

Mozarabic Chant one of the important branches of early Latin chant, also called Visigothic, and used in central and S Spain during the Middle Ages. Liturgically it is associated with the Gallican and Ambrosian rites, pre-dating that of Rome and showing similarities with Eastern liturgies. Its music is found in MSS of the 8th–11th c., but mostly in undecipherable neumes. Only a few melodies survive in readable form. Roman chant and rite were imposed everywhere by 1076 except in Toledo, and in spite of the attempted revival under Cardinal Francisco de Cisneros (*c* 1500), little of the musical tradition has been preserved.

Mozart, (Franz Xaver) Wolfgang Amadeus (b Vienna, 26 Jul 1791; d Karlsbad, 29 Jul 1844), Austrian pianist and composer, son of W A ◊Mozart. Pupil of Hummel, Salieri and Vogler. He settled as music master at Lwów in 1808, but toured in Austria and Germany 1819–22. He settled in Vienna in 1838.

Works include orchestral and chamber music.

The good delivery of a composition in the present taste is not as simple as those people believe who think they are doing very well if, following their own ideas, they ornament and contort a piece in a truly idiotic fashion.

Leopold Mozart, *Versuch einer gründlichen Violinschule*, 1756

Mozart, (Johann Georg) Leopold (b Augsburg, 14 Nov 1719; d Salzburg, 28 May 1787), Austrian violinist and composer. Educated at the Jesuit college in Augsburg and at Salzburg University, he turned entirely to music in 1739, and first held a post with Count Thurn-Valsassina und Taxis. In 1743 he entered the service of the Archbishop of Salzburg, later rising to become court composer (1757) and vice-*Kapellmeister* (1763). Married in 1747 Anna Maria Pertl; of their seven children the only two to survive were Maria Anna and Wolfgang Amadeus. His important violin tutor, *Versuch einer gründlichen Violinschule*, was pub. in 1756.

Works include church music; symphonies; divertimenti and descriptive pieces for orchestra (including 'Musical sleigh-ride', 'Toy Symphony', etc.); concertos for various instruments; chamber music, sonatas for violin.

Mozart, Maria Anna (Nannerl) (b Salzburg, 30 Jul 1751; d Salzburg,

A Selection of

Mozart

Piano Concerto K271 1777
Sinfonia Concertante K364 1779
Die Entführung aus dem Serail 1782
Piano Concerto K482 1785

Le nozze di Figaro 1786
String Quintet K515 1785
Don Giovanni 1787
Symphony no. 41 K551 1788
Così fan tutte 1790
Die Zauberflöte 1791

Mozart *The composer Wolfgang Amadeus Mozart (1756–1791) pictured on the frontispiece of an obituary, 1793. He began composing at the age of five and performed for royalty at six. Before the end of his short life Mozart's genius had transformed or refined every musical genre.*

29 Oct 1829), Austrian pianist and teacher, daughter of Leopold ◊Mozart. Like her brother Wolfgang Amadeus she developed very early as a keyboard player, though not as a composer, and was taken on tour with him by Leopold. Later she taught at Salzburg, in 1784 married Baron von Berchtold zu Sonnenberg, a court councillor at Salzburg and warden of St Gilgen, where she lived. She returned to Salzburg as teacher on his death in 1810 and in 1820 became blind.

Mozart, Wolfgang Amadeus (Johannes Chrysostomus Wolfgangus Theophilus) (b Salzburg, 27 Jan 1756; d Vienna, 5 Dec 1791), Austrian composer, son of Leopold ◊Mozart. He showed early signs of talent, learnt the harpsichord from the age of three or four, and began to compose under his father's supervision when he was five. With his sister (then 11) he was taken to Munich in 1762, then to Vienna, where they played at court. Encouraged by their success, Leopold Mozart set out with the children the following year on a longer tour, which took them first through S Germany to Brussels and Paris (arrival 18 Nov 1763). They appeared at court at Versailles, and four sonatas for violin and harpsichord by Mozart were pub. in Paris. Moving on to London in Apr 1764, they played before the royal family and made a sensation in public concerts. In London Mozart was befriended by J C Bach, three of whose sonatas he arranged as piano concertos, and who also influenced the symphonies, etc., he wrote at the time. They left for Holland on 24 Jul 1765, and after several stops on the journey through France and Switzerland returned to Salzburg in Nov 1766. The next months were spent in study and composition, but on 11 Sept 1767 the whole family went to Vienna. There Mozart composed his first Mass (C minor, K139) and produced the *Singspiel*, *Bastien und Bastienne*, though intrigues thwarted the performance of the opera *La finta simplice*. Returning to Salzburg on 5 Jan 1769, Mozart had barely a year at home before setting out with his father on an extended tour of Italy; in Rome he wrote down Allegri's *Miserere* from memory, in Bologna took lessons from Padre Martini and gained election to the Philharmonic Society with a

Mozart
A biographical note

Mozart was accustomed throughout his life to working in strange circumstances; part of his D minor string quartet was written while his wife was having their first child in the next room. He was particularly fond of billiards and skittles, often composing during the progress of a game. It was shortly after writing the *Kegelstatt* (skittles) trio in 1787 that Mozart travelled to Prague for the premiere of *Don Giovanni*. Despite some straitened circumstances – the parts of Masetto and the Commendatore had to be taken by the same singer – rehearsals went well until a problem was met with a too demure Zerlina. Required to scream offstage in response to the Don's advances, Mozart was dissatisfied with her efforts. Some improvement was made when he crept up behind the singer on the dimly lit stage and pinched her hard on the arm. Mozart had to improvise further when the day of the premiere approached and the overture had still not been written. On the eve of the performance he stayed up all night with his wife while he wrote the overture; he was fortified with glasses of punch and kept awake with Constanze's repetition of familiar fairy stories, and the score was delivered to the copyists by seven in the morning.

contrapuntal exercise, in Milan produced the opera *Mitridate* with great success on 26 Dec 1770. Two further visits to Italy followed, both to Milan, for the performance of the serenata *Ascanio in Alba* (17 Oct 1771) and the opera *Lucio Silla* (26 Dec 1772); at the performance of *Ascanio*, Johann ◊ Hasse is alleged to have said 'This boy will cause us all to be forgotten'. Apart from short visits to Vienna (1773) and Munich (for the production of *La finta giardiniera*, 1775), most of the next five years was spent in Salzburg, his longest period at home since infancy. In Sept 1777, in company with his mother, he embarked on a lengthy journey which took them *via* Mannheim to Paris, where his mother died on 3 Jul 1778. The main object of this trip was to find suitable employment, but being unsuccessful Mozart returned in Jan 1779 to the uncongenial post of court organist at Salzburg. One of the finest of all his instrumental works, the *Sinfonia concertante* K364 was written later that year.

His opera seria *Idomeneo* was produced in Munich on 29 Jan 1781, but later the same year, on a visit to Vienna with the household of the Archbishop of Salzburg, he gave up his post to settle in Vienna as a freelance, living by teaching and playing in concerts. His German opera *Die Entführung aus dem Serail* was produced on 15 Jul 1782, and the next month he married Constanze Weber, whose sister Aloysia, a notable singer, he had courted unsuccessfully in Mannheim four years before. At the height of his fame as a pianist, 1782–86, he composed many concertos for his own use, but thereafter was increasingly plagued by financial worries, which his appointment in 1787 as court composer on the death of Gluck did little to ease. The first of three operas on libretti by da Ponte, *Le nozze di Figaro*, was produced 1786, followed by *Don Giovanni* (for Prague, 1787) and *Così fan tutte* (1790). In these works Mozart brought opera to new heights of musical ingenuity, dramatic truth and brilliance of expression. For almost the first time opera characters are recognizable human beings, rather than stock types. In 1788 he wrote his last three symphonies, the summation of the classical symphonic style. Assimilating all he had learned from Haydn and others, he took standard forms and gave them new meaning. A visit to Berlin with Prince Lichnowsky in 1789 took him through Leipzig, where he discussed Bach's music with Doles, Bach's successor, and in 1790 he made a fruitless journey to Frankfurt, hoping to earn money as a pianist. After several lean years 1791 was one of overwork, which must have contributed to his early death; in addition to the last piano concerto (K595), the clarinet concerto (K622) and several smaller works, he composed the operas *La clemenza di Tito* (for the coronation of the

Emperor Leopold II, produced Prague, 6 Sept) and *Die Zauberflöte* (produced Vienna, 30 Sept). The Requiem, commissioned anonymously by a mysterious stranger who was the steward of a nobleman wishing to pass the work off as his own, remained unfinished at Mozart's death, and was completed later by his pupil Süssmayr. While Mozart was not a great innovator in the manner of Haydn and Beethoven, he set creative standards in a wide variety of forms to which later composers could only aspire.

Works include OPERAS: *Apollo et Hyacinthus* (1767), *Bastien und Bastienne* (1768), *La finta semplice* (1769), *Mitridate, Rè di Ponto* (1770), *Ascanio in Alba* (1771), *Il sogno di Scipione* (1772), *Lucio Silla* (1772), *La finta giardiniera* (1775), *Il Rè Pastore* (1775), *Zaide* (1780), *Idomeneo, Rè di Creta* (1781), *Die Entführung aus dem Serail* (1782), *L'Oca del Cairo* (1783), *Lo Sposo deluso* (1783), *Der Schauspieldirektor* (1786), *Le nozze di Figaro* (1786), *Don Giovanni* (1787), *Così fan tutte* (1790), *Die Zauberflöte* (1791), *La Clemenza di Tito* (1791). Ballet *Les petits riens* (1778).

CHURCH MUSIC: including Motet, *Exsultate, jubilate* for soprano, organ and orchestra, (K165, 1773), *Litaniae Laurentenae*, K195, 1774), *Litaniae de venerabili altaris Sacramento* (K243, 1776), *Vesperae de Domenica* (K321, 1779), *Kyrie* in D minor (K341, 1781), Mass in C, *Coronation* (K317, 1779), Mass in C, *Missa Solemnis* (K337, 1780), *Vesperae solennes de confessore* (K339, 1780), Mass in C minor, unfinished (K427, 1783), Motet, *Ave verum corpus* (K618, 1791), Requiem Mass in D minor, unfinished (K626, 1791).

CHORUS AND ORCHESTRAL: *Die Schuldigkeit des ersten Gebotes*, first part of sacred drama written for Salzburg in 1767; *Grabmusik*, Passion cantata (K42, 1767); *La Betulia Liberata*, oratorio (K118, 1771); *Davidde Penitente*, cantata based on C minor Mass (K469, 1785); concert arias for insertion in Mozart's own operas and operas by Anfossi and Paisiello.

SYMPHONIES: (41; nos. 1–24 composed 1764–73), no. 25 in G minor (K183, 1773), no. 26 in E♭ (K184, 1773), no. 27 in G (K199, 1773), no. 28 in C (K200, 1773), no. 29 in A (K201, 1774), no. 30 in D (K202, 1774), no. 31 in D. *Paris* (K297, 1778), no. 32 in G (K318, 1779), no. 33 in B♭ (K319, 1779), no. 34 in C (K338, 1780), no. 35 in D, *Haffner* (K385, 1782), no. 36 in C, *Linz* (K425, 1783), no. 37 in G is a slow introduction to a symphony by M Haydn (K444, 1783 or 4), no. 38 in D, *Prague* (K504, 1786), no. 39 in E♭ (K543, 1788), no. 40 in G minor (K550, 1788), no. 41 in C, *Jupiter* (K551, 1788). Other music for orchestra includes sets of Country Dances and German Dances, also Cassation in B♭ (K99, 1769); Divertimenti in E♭ (K113, 1771), in D (K131, 1772), in D (K136, 1772), in B♭ (K137, 1772), in F (K138, 1772), in D (K205, 1773), in F (K247, 1776), in D (K251, 1776), in B♭ (K287, 1777), in D (K334, 1779–80); Serenades in D (K203, 1774), in D (K204, 1775), in D (K239, 1776, *Serenata Notturna*), in D (K250, 1776, *Haffner*), in D, for four orchestras (K286, 1777), in D (K320, 1779, *Posthorn*), in B♭ for 13 wind instruments (K361, 1781), in E♭ for eight wind instruments (K375, 1781), in C minor for eight wind instruments (K388, 1782 or 3), in G for strings (K525, 1787, *Eine kleine Nachtmusik*); *Mauerische Trauermusik/Masonic Funeral Music* (K477, 1785).

CONCERTOS: 27 for piano. Nos. 1–4 arranged in 1767 from sonata movements by Raupach, Honauer, and Schobert. No. 5 in D (K175, 1773), no. 6 in B♭ (K238, 1776), no. 7 in F for three pianos (K242, 1776), no. 8 in C (K246, 1776), no. 9 in E♭ (K271, 1777), no. 10 in E♭ for two pianos (K365, 1770), no. 11 in F (K413, 1783), no. 12 in A (K414, 1782), no. 13 in C (K415, 1783), no. 14 in E♭ (K449, 1784), no. 15 in B♭ (K450, 1784), no. 16 in D (K451, 1784), no. 17 in G (K453, 1784), no. 18 in B♭ (K456, 1784), no. 19 in F (K459, 1784), no. 20 in D minor (K466, 1785), no. 21 in C (K467, 1785), no. 22 in E♭ (K482, 1785), no. 23 in A (K488, 1786), no. 24 in C minor (K491, 1786), no. 25 in C (K503, 1786), no. 26 in D, *Coronation* (K537, 1788), no. 27 in B♭ (K595, 1791); five for violin: no. 1 in B♭ (K207, 1775), no. 2 in D (K211, 1775), no. 3 in G (K216, 1775), no. 4 in D (K218, 1775), no. 5 in A (K219, 1775); Concertone in C for two violins (K190, 1774); Sinfonia Concertante for violin, viola and orchestra (K364, 1779); for bassoon in B♭ (K191, 1774); for flute, in G

(K313, 1778), for oboe in C (K314, 1778); for flute and harp in C (K299, 1778); for clarinet in A (K622, 1791), Sinfonia Concertante in E♭ for oboe, clarinet, horn and bassoon (K297b, 1778, judged as spurious by some scholars); four for horn: no. 1 in D (K412, 1782), no. 2 in E♭ (K417, 1783), no. 3 in E♭ (K447, ?1784–87), no. 4 in E♭ (K495, 1786).

CHAMBER MUSIC: 23 string quartets, nos. 1–13 (1770–73), nos. 14–19 dedicated to Haydn (1782–85): in G (K387), in D minor (K421), in E♭ (K428), in B♭ (K458, *The Hunt*), in A (K464), in C (K465, *Dissonance*), no. 20 in D (K499, 1786, *Hoffmeister*), nos. 21–23 dedicated to King of Prussia (1789–90): in D (K575), in B♭ (K589), in F (K590); six string quintets: no. 1 in B♭ (K174, 1773), no. 2 in C minor (K406, 1788; arrangement of serenade K388), no. 3 in C (K515, 1787), no. 4 in G minor (K516, 1787), no. 5 in D (K593, 1790), no. 6 in B♭ (K614, 1791); string trio in B♭, Divertimento (K563, 1788); five piano trios: in B♭ (K254, 1776), in G (K496, 1786), in B♭ (K502, 1786), in E (K542, 1788), in C (K548, 1788); two piano quartets: in G minor (K478, 1785), in B♭ (K493, 1786); oboe quartet (K370, 1781); horn quintet (K407, 1782); quintet for piano and wind (K452, 1784); clarinet quintet (K581, 1789); clarinet trio in E♭ (K498, 1786). 17 piano sonatas, including no. 8 in A minor (K310, 1778), no. 9 in D (K311, 1777), nos. 10–13 in C, A and F (K330–333, 1781–84), no. 14 in C minor (K457, 1784), no. 15 in C (K545, 1788), no. 16 in B♭ (K570, 1789), no. 17 in D (K576, 1789); sonata in D for two pianos (K448, 1781); 35 sonatas for violin and piano: nos. 1–16 composed 1762–66, no. 17 in C (K296, 1778), nos. 18–23, in G, E♭, C, E minor, A and D (K301–306, 1778), no. 24 in F (K376, 1781), no. 25 in F (K377, 1781), no. 26 in B♭ (K378, 1779 or 81), no. 27 in G (K379, 1781), no. 28 in E♭ (K380, 1781), no. 29 in A (K402, 1782), no. 30 in C (K403, 1782), no. 31 in C (K404, 1782 or 88), no. 32 in B♭ (K454, 1784), no. 33 in E♭ (K481, 1785), no. 34 in A (K526, 1787), no. 35 in F (K547, 1788). Variations for piano, Fantasia in D minor (K397, 1782 or 1786–87), Fantasia in C minor (K475, 1785), Rondo in A minor (K511, 1787), Adagio in B minor (K540, 1788), Gigue in G (K574, 1789).

SOLO SONGS AND LIEDER including *Die Zufriedenheit* (K349), *Oiseaux, si tous les ans* (K307), *Das Veilchen* (K472), *Das Veilchen* (K476), *Als Luise* (K520), *Abendempfindung* (K523), *Das Traumbild* (K530), *Sehnsucht nach dem Frühlinge/Longing for Spring* (K596); theme also used in finale of the last piano concerto).

If I have time I shall rearrange some of my violin concertos and shorten them: In Germany we rather like length but after all it is better to be short and good.

Wolfgang Amadeus Mozart in a letter, 1778

Mozart and Salieri opera by Rimsky-Korsakov (libretto Pushkin's dramatic poem, set as it stands), produced Moscow, 7 Dec 1898. Now discredited story (though still believed by some) that Salieri poisoned Mozart.

Mozartiana Tchaikovsky's fourth suite for orchestra, op. 61, composed in 1887. It consists of four works by Mozart scored for orchestra by Tchaikovsky: jig and minuet for piano, K475 and 355; motet *Ave, verum corpus*, K618 and variations on a theme from *La rencontre imprévue* by Gluck for piano, K455. Fp Moscow, 26 Nov 1887.

mp, abbr., = *mezzo piano* = 'half soft'.

Mravina, Evgeniya (b St Petersburg, 16 Feb 1864; d Yalta, 25 Oct 1914), Russian soprano. She was as highly regarded for her dramatic as for her vocal ability; St Petersburg 1886–97 as Antonida, Tatyana, Elsa and Marguerite de Valois.

Mravinsky, Evgeny (b St Petersburg, 4 Jun 1903; d Leningrad, 20 Jan 1988), Russian conductor. He studied at the Leningrad Conservatory and was conductor of the Leningrad PO from 1938. Active on behalf of Soviet music, he gave fps of Shostakovich's symphonies nos. 5, 6,

8, 9 and 10. Conducted the fp of Prokofiev's sixth symphony, Leningrad, 1947. Often heard in the stage works of Tchaikovsky, and conducted orchestral music by Bartók and Stravinsky.

Muck, Carl (b Darmstadt, 22 Oct 1859; d Stuttgart, 3 Mar 1940), German conductor. Studied at Heidelberg University and at the Leipzig University and Conservatory. In 1880 he began a pianist's career, but became conductor at Salzburg, Brno and Graz in succession, at Prague in 1886, and finally in Berlin, at the Royal Opera, in 1892. He gave the first Russian performance of the *Ring* (1889); conducted Wagner in London and from 1901 at Bayreuth (*Parsifal* until 1930), also the Philharmonic concerts in Vienna. From 1906 to 1918, with an interruption, he conducted the Boston SO. He was arrested as an enemy alien in 1918. He returned to Europe after the war and conducted in Hamburg from 1922 to 1933. He was well known in the symphonies of Bruckner.

Mudarra, Alonso de (b Palencia diocese *c* 1508; d Seville, 1 Apr 1580), Spanish vihuelist and composer. He became a canon of Seville Cathedral in 1546, and in the same year pub. a book of vihuela pieces and songs with vihuela includes variations and dances.

Mudd, John (b London, 1555; d Peterborough, buried 16 Dec 1631), English organist and composer. Organist at Peterborough Cathedral from 1583 to 1631. Wrote services, anthems, etc.

Mudd, Thomas (b London, *c* 1560; d after 1619), English composer. He went to St Paul's School in London and in 1578 to Cambridge as a sizar for the sons of London mercers.

Works include services, anthems; dances for three viols.

Muette de Portici, La, *The Dumb Girl of Portici*, opera by Auber (libretto by Scribe and Delavigne), produced Paris, Opéra, 29 Feb 1828. Carafa's *Masaniello*, on the same subject, had been produced at the Opéra-Comique two months earlier. Auber's work is often called *Masaniello*. The seduction of his sister Fenella inspires Masaniello to lead a peasants' revolt against the Spanish viceroy and his son Alphonse. Horrified by the waste of life, however, Masaniello shows mercy to the nobles and as a result is poisoned by his compatriots.

Muffat, Georg (b Mégève, Savoy, bap. 1 Jun 1653; d Passau, 23 Feb 1704), Austrian organist and composer. Studied in Paris, with Lully or members of his school. In 1678 he was appointed organist to the Archbishop of Salzburg, and after visiting Vienna and Rome went to Passau to become organist to the bishop in 1690.

Works include chamber sonatas *Armonico tributo* (1682), *Auserlesene mit Ernst und Lust gemengte Instrumental-Musik*, *Apparatus musico-organisticus* for organ (12 toccatas, chaconne and passacaglia, 1690), *Suaviores harmoniae* (1695), two vols. for harpsichord.

Muffat, Gottlieb (Theophil) (b Passau, bap. 25 Apr 1690; d Vienna, 9 Dec 1770), German organist and composer, son of Georg ◊Muffat. Pupil of Fux in Vienna from 1704, he entered the service of the court in 1717 and became first organist in 1741. Among his pupils were Wagenseil and the Empress Maria Theresa.

Works include 72 fugues and 12 toccatas for organ, *Componimenti musicali* for harpsichord.

Mugnone, Leopoldo (b Naples, 29 Sept 1858; d Naples, 22 Dec 1941), Italian conductor and composer, studied at Naples and at the age of 12 wrote a comic opera; a second was produced in public in 1875. He also began to conduct very young, at 16, but afterwards gained more experience as chorus master and accompanist. In 1890 he was engaged to conduct the production of *Cavalleria rusticana* in Rome, and after that he made a brilliant career as operatic and concert conductor; active on behalf of Giordano, Wagner and Charpentier in Europe and South America. He wrote several more comic operas.

Mühlfeld, Richard (b Salzungen, 28 Feb 1856; d Meiningen, 1 Jun 1907), German clarinettist. In the grand-ducal orchestra at Meiningen from 1873. First clarinettist at Bayreuth, 1884–96. Brahms wrote the four late chamber works with clarinet parts, opp. 114, 115, 120 (i and ii) for him.

Muldowney, Dominic (b Southampton, 19 Jul 1952), English composer. He studied with Jonathan Harvey at Southampton and with

Birtwistle in London. Composer in residence, National Theatre, London, since 1976.

Works include *An Heavyweight Dirge* for soloists and chamber ensemble (1971); *Driftwood to the Flow* for 18 strings (1972); *Klavier-Hammer* for one or more pianos (1973); *Music at Chartres* for 16 instruments (1973); two string quartets (1973 and 1980), *Love music for Bathsheba Evergreen and Gabriel Oak* for chamber ensemble (1974); *Double Helix* for eight players (1977), *Macbeth*, ballet music (1979); five *Theatre Poems*, after Brecht (1981); *The Duration of Exile* for mezzo and chamber ensemble (1982); a realization of *The Beggar's Opera* (1982); piano concerto (1983), saxophone concerto (1984); *The Duration of Exile* for mezzo and ensemble (1983), Sinfonietta (1986), *Ars subtilior* for tape and ensemble (1987), violin concerto (1989); *The Ginger Tree* for piano (1989), concertos for percussion (1991), oboe (1991) and trumpet (1993) .

In directing the measure or beat, one should for the most part follow the Italians, who are accustomed to proceed much more slowly than we do at the directions Adagio, Grave, Largo *etc, so slowly sometimes that one can scarcely wait for them.*

Georg Muffat, *Instrumental Music*, 1701

Mulè, Giuseppe b Termini, Sicily, 28 Jun 1855; d Rome, 10 Sept 1951), Italian cellist and composer. Studied at the Palermo Conservatory, of which he was director 1922–25, when he became director of the Santa Cecilia Conservatory in Rome. He also became secretary to the Fascist syndicate of musicians. He studied Sicilian folksong and found that its roots went back to Greek music; wrote much incidental music for the performance of Greek plays at Syracuse.

Works include operas *La Baronessa di Carini* (1912), *Al lupo*, *La monacella della fontana* (1923), *Dafni* (1928), *Liolà* (on Pirandello's play, 1935), *Taormina*; music for Greek plays; Aeschylus' *Choephori*, *Seven against Thebes*, Euripides' *Bacchae*, *Medea*, *The Cyclops*, *Hippolytus*, *Iphigenia in Aulis*, *Iphigenia in Taruis*, Sophocles' *Antigone*; incidental music for Corradini's *Giulio Cesare*; oratorio *Il cieco di Gerico* (1910); symphonic poems *Sicilia canora* and *Vendemmia*; *Tre canti siciliani* for voice and orchestra; string quartet; violin and cello pieces.

Müller, August Eberhard (b Northeim, Hanover, 13 Dec 1767; d Weimar, 3 Dec 1817), German organist and composer. Held appointments at Magdeburg and Leipzig, where he became cantor of St Thomas's Church in 1804. Appointed court *Kapellmeister* at Weimar in 1810.

Works include Singspiel *Der Polterabend* (1813), two operettas; three cantatas; two piano concertos, 11 flute concertos; piano trio; two violin and piano sonatas; piano sonatas, variations, etc.; sonata, suites, chorale variations, etc., for organ; flute duets and pieces.

Müller, Maria (b Teresienstadt, 29 Jan 1898; d Bayreuth, 13 Mar 1958), Austrian soprano. Debut Linz 1919, as Elsa. NY Met. 1925–35, debut as Sieglinde; in 1932 she was the first US Maria Boccanegra. Bayreuth 1930–44 as Elisabeth, Eva, Gutrune, Elsa and Senta. Berlin 1926–52. London, CG, 1934 and 1937. Other roles included Jenůfa, Strauss's Helen and Donna Elvira.

Müller, Wenzel (b Trnava, Moravian, 26 Sept 1767; d Baden, near Vienna, 3 Aug 1835), Austrian composer and conductor. Pupil of Dittersdorf, became conductor at the Brno theatre in 1783, aged 16 and in 1786 at the Leopoldstadt Theatre in Vienna, where he settled until 1808, and again in 1813, being director at the Prague Opera during those years, when his daughter Therese ◊Grünbaum was engaged there. On his return to Vienna he became again conductor of the Leopoldstadt Theatre.

Works include nearly 200 operas and musical plays, e.g. *Das Sonnenfest der Braminen* (1790), *Die Zauberzither, oder Kaspar der Fagottist* (1791), *Das Neusonntagskind* (1793), *Die Schwestern von Prag* (1794), *Die Teufelsmühle auf dem Wienerberge* (1799), *Die*

travestierte Zauberflöte (a parody of Mozart's *Magic Flute*, 1818); Masses; symphonies.

Müller, Wilhelm (1794–1827), German poet. ◊Schöne Müllerin (Schubert); ◊Winterreise (ditto).

Müller-Hartmann, Robert (b Hamburg, 11 Oct 1884; d Dorking, Surrey, 15 Dec 1950), German critic and composer. He was lecturer in music theory at Hamburg University in 1923–33 and settled in London in 1937.

Works include incidental music to Büchner's *Leonce und Lena* and other plays; variations on a Pastoral Theme and other works for orchestra; chamber music; songs, etc.

Mulliner Book, The a large MS collection of English keyboard music dating from *c* 1550–75, apparently copied by Thomas Mulliner. It contains both organ and virginal pieces, including transcriptions of viol and vocal music with the names of Blitheman, Shepherd, Redford and Tallis predominating. There are 123 pieces, and 11 more for cittern.

Mullings, Frank (b Walsall, 10 May 1881; d Manchester, 19 May 1953), English tenor, studied at the Birmingham and Midland School of Music, appeared at Coventry in *Faust* in 1907 and at a concert in London in 1911. He then specialized in heroic tenor parts in opera, joined the Denhof co. in 1913 and was engaged by Beecham in 1919, singing Wagnerian parts with great intensity and being especially impressive as Verdi's Otello. Other roles included Parsifal, Siegfried, Tristan and Radames.

Mullova, Viktoria (b Moscow, 27 Nov 1959), Russian violinist. She made her debut aged 12 and studied with Kogan at the Moscow Conservatory. After winning the 1982 Tchaikovsky Competition, she left Russia to pursue a career in the West; concerts with the Boston SO, Pittsburgh SO, Philadelphia Orchestra, LSO and the Berlin PO. Her virtuosity has been admired in the concertos of Sibelius, Shostakovich, Tchaikovsky and Paganini.

Mumma, Gordon (b Framingham, MA, 30 Mar 1935), American composer. In 1957 co-founded Space Theatre, giving performances with computerized electronics. Worked at electronic studio, Ann Arbour, from 1958; Merce Cunningham Dance Co. from 1968. Works involve use of computer techniques, called cybersonics; *Sinfonia* for 12 instruments (1960), *Le Corbusier* (1965), *Mesa* (1966), *Ambivex* (1972).

Munch, Charles (b Strasbourg, 26 Sept 1891; d Richmond, PA, 6 Nov 1968), French conductor. Studied at Strasbourg Conservatory and then went to Paris for further violin studies with Capet and Berlin with Flesch. From 1919 to 1925 he taught the violin at Strasbourg Conservatory and led the city orchestra, becoming leader of the Leipzig Gewandhaus Orchestra in 1926. He made his debut as conductor in 1932 in Paris and after various teaching and conducting posts he was conductor of the Boston SO 1949–62 and in 1951 director of the Berkshire Music Center in Tanglewood. Helped found L'Orchestre de Paris, in 1967.

Münchinger, Karl (b Stuttgart, 29 May 1915; d Stuttgart, 13 Mar 1990), German conductor. Studied in Leipzig with H Abendroth and in 1945 founded the Stuttgart Chamber Orchestra, which soon became known as one of the finest ensembles of its kind. Frequent performances of Bach in world tours. US debut San Francisco 1953.

Mundy, John (b *c* 1555; d Windsor, 29 Jun 1630), English organist and composer. Studied under his father, William Mundy, became a Gentleman of the Chapel Royal in London and succeeded Marbeck as one of the organists of St George's Chapel, Windsor, about 1585.

Works include anthems; *Songs and Psalmes* for three–five voices; madrigals (one in *The Triumphes of Oriana*); virginal pieces including the 'Weather' fantasia.

Mundy, William (b *c* 1529; d London, *c* 1591), English singer and composer, father of John ◊Mundy. He was a vicar-choral at St Paul's Cathedral in London and became a Gentleman of the Chapel Royal in 1564.

Works include services, anthems, Latin motets, etc.

Munrow, David (b Birmingham, 12 Aug 1942; d Chesham Bois, 15 May 1976), English early music specialist and performer of wind instruments. He founded the Early Music Consort in 1967 and taught at Leicester University and the RAM. Often heard in medieval and Renaissance music and a frequent broadcaster. Published *Instruments of the Middle Ages and Renaissance*, 1976. He died by suicide.

Murail, Tristan (b Le Havre, 1947), French composer. Studied with Messiaen at the Paris Conservatory. Co-founded the Groupe de L'Itinéraire, to promote performances of music which combine electronic and traditional instruments. Teacher of computer music at IRCAM and the Paris Conservatory.

Works include *Couleur de mer* for ensemble (1969); *Altitude 8000* for orchestra (1970); *Cosmos privé* for orchestra (1973); *Les nuages de Magellan* for ondes Martenot and ensemble (1973); *Sables* for orchestra (1974); *Memoire/Erosion* for horn and nine players (1976); *Désintégrations* for 17 players and tape (1983); *Sillages* for orchestra (1985); *Vues aeriennes* for horn, violin, cello and piano (1988); *Les sept paroles du Christ en Croix* for orchestra (1986–89); *Le fou à pattes bleues* for flute and piano (1990).

Muratore, Lucien (b Marseilles, 29 Aug, 1876; d Paris, 16 Jul 1954), French tenor. Debut Paris, Opéra-Comique, in the 1902 fp of Hahn's *La Carmélite*. At the Opéra he sang in the fps of Massenet's *Ariane* (1906) and *Bacchus* (1909). At Monte Carlo he was Ulysses in the fp of Fauré's *Pénélope* (1913). At Chicago and Buenos Aires he was Prinzivalle in the local fps of Février's *Monna Vanna*. Other roles included Faust and Reyer's Sigurd.

Murino, Aegidius de, 14th-c. theorist and composer of uncertain nationality. He may possibly be the 'Egidius Anglicus' of the MS Chantilly 1047. His treatise *Tractatus de diversis figuris* is about note-forms and motet composition. Two motets and one *chanson* also survive.

Muris, Johannes de (b Lisieux, *c* 1300; d *c* 1350), French mathematician, astronomer and music theorist. He lived for some time in Paris and worked there as mathematician and astronomer. The chief among the music treatises attributed to him is the *Ars novae musicae*, 1319.

murky bass an 18th-c. term of unknown origin for a bass played in broken octaves on keyboard instruments.

Murphy, Suzanne (b Limerick, 15 Aug 1941), Irish soprano. Studied in Dublin and sang with WNO from 1976, as Constanze, Elisabeth de Valois, the *Trovatore* Leonora, Norma, Violetta and Elvira in *Ernani* and *I Puritani*; sang Alice Ford in *Falstaff* with the company in New York and Milan, 1989. For ENO has sung Donna Anna and Tosca (1992), Mozart's Elettra at the Vienna Staatsoper (1987) and Norma at the NY City Opera.

Murray, Ann (b Dublin, 27 Aug 1949), Irish-born mezzo. She studied at the RMCM. Opera debut as Alceste, with Scottish Opera; CG since 1976 as Cherubino, Dorabella and the Composer. She sang Nicklausse at the 1981 Salzburg Festival and returned in 1985 for Minerva in the Henze realization of Monteverdi's *Ulisse*: she had sung the same role in the Leppard version of the work at Glyndebourne in 1979. ENO 1985, Xerxes. NY Met. 1984–85 as Sextus, Annius and Dorabella. Season 1992/93 as Ruggiero in *Alcina* at CG and Mozart's Cecilio at Salzburg. Title role in *Giulio Cesare* at Munich, 1994. Highly regarded as a concert singer.

Murrill, Herbert (Henry John) (b London, 11 May 1909; d London, 25 Jul 1952), English composer. Studied at the RAM in London and at Worcester College, Oxford. After holding various organist's posts from 1926, he became professor of composition at the RAM in 1933, joined the music staff of the BBC in 1936 and became Head of Music in 1950.

Works include opera *Man in Cage* (1930); three hornpipes for orchestra; two concertos and three pieces for cello and orchestra; string quartet and other chamber music.

Murschhauser, Franz Xaver Anton (b Zabern, bap. 1 Jul 1663; d Munich, 6 Jan 1738), Alsatian composer. Pupil of Kerl at Munich, where he became *Kapellmeister* at the church of Our Lady. In 1721, by a remark made in his treatise on composition, *Academia musicopoetica*, he came into conflict with Mattheson.

Works include *Vespertinus latriae* for four voices and strings (1700); organ books *Octitonium novum organum*, *Prototypon longo-*

breve organicum, *Opus organicum tripartitum* (1696).

Murska, Ilma di, ◊Di Murska.

Muset, Colin, French 12th-c. trouvère and jongleur. The poems of 15 and the music of eight of his songs are extant.

musette, French, (1) a form of bagpipe popular in France in the 17th and 18th c.

(2) A piece on a drone bass imitating more or less faithfully the music of a bagpipe. It often took the place of a trio section alternating with a gavotte in classical suites.

Musgrave, Thea (b Barnton, Midlothian, 27 May 1928), Scottish composer and pianist. Studied at Edinburgh University and with N Boulanger in Paris. Lectured at London University 1959–65; University of California from 1970. Her music has employed serial and improvisatory techniques.

Works include operas *The Abbot of Drimock* (1955), *The Decision* (1967), *The Voice of Ariadne* (1974), *Mary, Queen of Scots* (1977), *A Christmas Carol* (1979), *An Occurrence at Owl Creek Bridge* (1981), *Harriet, the Woman Called Moses* (1985), and *Simon Bolivar* (1995); *Scottish Dance Suite* for orchestra, *Divertimento* for string orchestra, *Perspectives* for small orchestra; three chamber concertos for various instruments, Concerto for Orchestra (1967), *Peripateia* for orchestra (1981), *The Seasons* (1988) and *Rainbow* (1990) for orchestra; *Triptych* for tenor and orchestra; *The Five Ages of Man* for chorus and orchestra; string quartet (1958); two piano sonatas; songs.

musica ficta Latin = 'false music'; in common parlance, unwritten accidentals added to editions of medieval and Renaissance music because they would have been incorporated automatically by musicians of the time. Most often they are added to correct augmented or diminished intervals (whether vertical or horizontal) as well as to raise the leading note (or lower the second degree) at a cadence. Editorially, they are normally placed above the stave or in small print to distinguish them from original MS accidentals. But originally the term meant any note that is not on the gamut (see ◊*musica recta*) and therefore include written accidentals as well as unwritten ones. The modern meaning dates perhaps from the 15th c. though it seems to have been normal to operate *musica recta* before *musica ficta*.

musica figurata Latin and Italian = 'figured or decorated music'; the ornamenting of plainsong by auxiliary notes or the addition of a descant sung against a fundamental melody.

musical box a toy instrument made in various shapes of fancy boxes and containing a cylinder with pins which, turning round by clockwork, twangs the teeth of a metal comb producing the notes of a musical scale. The pins are so arranged as to make the pattern of a piece of music, and several sets of pins can be set in the barrel, only one touching the teeth at a time, a choice of more than one piece being thus producible by the simple device of shifting the barrel slightly sideways. The musical box industry is centred mainly in Switzerland.

'The Rite of Spring' is an exciting piece of music, but I don't believe that it has any future as a Broadway musical.

    George Abbot, *Dramatists' Guild Quarterly*, 1974

---

musical comedy, *or* 'musical', a light 20th-c. musical entertainment similar to operetta. As a non-specific term it appears as early as 1765 in a title of a Covent Garden pasticcio, *The Summer's Tale*.

Musical Offering (Bach.) ◊Musikalische Opfer.

musical snuffbox a kind of musical box made especially in the 18th c., with a double bottom concealing a mechanical music apparatus beneath its normal contents.

musica recta Latin = 'orthodox music'; a term used in the 14th and 15th c. to mean the notes of the gamut as projected by the three kinds of hexachord, that is, the white-note scale from G to e" but including B♭ as well as B♮ (or, with a key-signature of one flat, including E♭ as well as E♮, and so on). Since this was the normal scale, the note B could be sung either flat or natural without special indications. This concept is important for editorial accidentals and *musica ficta*: where there is an alternative, *musica recta* should be operated before *musica ficta*.

musica reservata Latin = 'reserved music'; a 16th-c. term applied to music intended for connoisseurs and private occasions, particularly vocal music which faithfully interpreted the words.

Musica Transalpina the title of a collection of Italian (transalpine) madrigals with English words pub. in London by Nicholas Yonge in 1588, containing 75 pieces, including two by Byrd, *La verginella*, set to a translation of two stanzas from Ariosto. The Italian contributors include Palestrina and Marenzio, and there are also Italian madrigals by Flemish composers including Lassus, de Vert and Verdonck. A second volume followed in 1597, containing 24 works, this time all by Italian composers.

music drama an alternative term for 'opera' used by composers, notably Wagner, who felt that the older term implies methods and forms for which they had no use.

Music Makers, The ode for contralto solo, chorus and orchestra by Elgar, op. 69 (poem by Arthur O'Shaughnessy), fp Birmingham Festival, 1 Oct 1912. The work contains a number of quotations from earlier works by Elgar.

A musicologist is a man who can read music but can't hear it.

Thomas Beecham, quoted in Proctor-Gregg, *Beecham Remembered*, 1976

---

musicology the scientific and scholarly study of any aspect of music; hence musicologist, one who pursues such a study.

Musikalische Opfer, Das, *The Musical Offering*, a late work by Bach (BWV 1079) containing two *ricercari*, a fugue in canon, nine canons and a sonata for flute, violin and continuo, all based on a theme given to Bach by Frederick II of Prussia during the composer's visit to Potsdam in 1747.

Musikalischer Spass, Ein, *A Musical Joke*, a work in four movements for two horns and strings by Mozart, K522 (composed Jun 1787), sometimes also known by such names as 'The Village Band'. But the joke is not at the expense of rustic performers; the work is a parody of a symphony by an incompetent composer.

musique concrète music composed by recording live sounds and subjecting them to electronic modification or modification on tape. The term was invented by Pierre Schaeffer in the late 1940s. See also Pierre ◊Henry.

A Selection of

Mussorgsky

Salammbô...1863–6
Night on the Bare Mountain 1867
The Marriage...1868
Boris Godunov...1869

Pictures at an Exhibition..........................1874
Songs and Dances of Death......1875–7
Khovanshchina..............1886

Mussorgsky *The composer Modest Petrovich Mussorgsky (1839–1881). He rejected the Romantic notion of art for art's sake, believing the primary purpose of music to be communication with people. His writing for voice is closely related to the natural inflections of speech.*

musique mesurée French = 'measured music'; a special method of setting words to music cultivated in 16th-c. France by Baïf, Le Jeune, Mauduit and others. The metrical rhythm of the words was based on classical scansion and the musical rhythm followed this exactly, long syllables being set to long notes, and short syllables to short notes.

Mussorgsky, Modest Petrovich (b Karevo, Government of Pskov, 21 Mar 1839; d St Petersburg, 28 Mar 1881), Russian composer. The son of well-to-do landowners, he was sent to St Petersburg at the age of ten to prepare for a military school, which he entered in 1852. He joined a regiment in 1856 and he did not seriously think of a music career until he met Dargomizhsky and Balakirev in 1857 and began to study under the latter. He resigned his commission in 1858, but never studied systematically. His family's fortune waned after the liberation of the serfs in 1861, but he was in sympathy with that movement and content to live on the small pay he obtained for a government employment. His interest in the common people led him to write realistic songs following the inflections of their speech, and he endeavoured to do the same with his operatic characters. He finished *Boris Godunov* in its first form in 1869, but it was rejected by the Imperial Opera and he recast it 1871–72, this second version being produced 1874. It gained wide popularity in an orchestration by Rimsky-Korsakov, but Mussorgsky's original is now more often preferred. He sank more and more into poverty and ruined his health with drink, but between 1872 and 1880 managed to complete most of his historical opera, *Khovanshchina*. He died in hospital from a spinal disease. Mussorgsky was the most original and imaginative of the 'Mighty Handful' of composers.

Works include operas *Salammbô* (after Flaubert, unfinished, 1863–66), *The Marriage* (Gogol, unfinished, 1868, produced 1909), *Boris Godunov* (after Pushkin, 1869 revised 1872), *Khovanshchina* (1886), *Sorochintsy Fair* (after Gogol, unfinished, 1874–80); an act for a collective opera, *Mlada* (with Borodin, Cui and Rimsky-Korsakov, afterwards used for other works); incidental music for Ozerov's *Oedipus Rex*; *The Destruction of Sennacherib* (after Byron, 1867), and *Jesus Navin* for chorus and orchestra.

Mustonen *The Finnish pianist and composer Olli Mustonen. A brilliant and versatile musician, his first major recording featured Alkan's quirky 25 Préludes dans les tons majeurs et mineur. A prolific composer, his Nonet for two string quartets and double bass was premiered at the Wigmore Hall in 1995.*

Four Russian folksongs for male chorus; *Night on the Bare Mountain* for orchestra (later used in *Mlada* [with chorus] and further revised) and three small orchestral pieces; suite *Pictures at an Exhibition* (1874) and 12 small pieces for piano; over 60 songs including cycles *The Nursery* (1870), *Sunless* and *Songs and Dances of Death* (1875–77).

Mussorgsky's greatest misfortune was that he came into the world half a century too early. The technique he would have required in order to achieve his ends had not yet come into being.

              Igor Gliebof, *Boris Godunov articles and studies*, 1930

Mustafà, Domenico (b Sterpara near Foligno, 14 Apr 1829; d Montefalco near Perugia, 18 Mar 1912), Italian castrato and composer. He was the last male soprano of the Sistine Chapel, which he entered in 1848. He was later *maestro di cappella* there until 1902, when he was succeeded by Lorenzo Perosi.

    Works include Miserere, *Tu es Petrus*, *Dies irae* for seven voices, *Laudate* and other church music.

Mustel organ an instrument invented by Victor Mustel (1815–90) of Paris. It is of the harmonium type, but contains some improvements, including a device by which the top and bottom halves of the keyboard can be separately controlled for dynamic expression.

Mustonen, Olli (b Helsinki, 7 Jun 1967), Finnish pianist and composer. Studied in Helsinki and has appeared with leading orchestras in Europe and the USA from 1984; US debut 1986 at the Newport Festival, returning with the Los Angeles PO at the Hollywood Bowl. London debut 1987, with the LPO. Regular chamber concerts with Heinrich Schiff, Sabine Meyer, Steven Isserlis and Dimitri Sitkovetsky. He is also a soloist in his own two piano concertos.

muta Italian = 'change'; a direction used in scores where a change is to be made between instruments (e.g. A and B♭ clarinet or different horn crooks) or in tunings (e.g. kettledrums, strings of instruments of the violin family temporarily tuned to abnormal notes), etc. The plural is *mutano*.

mutation stops a range of organ stops sounding notes a 12th, 17th, 19th or flat 21st above those of the key pressed down. They are not played alone, but only with other stops which sound their own proper notes,

and they fulfil, together with those normal keys, a function similar to mixture stops.

mute the name of various devices of different kinds but all serving to damp the tone of an instrument. Mutes of string instruments are a kind of fork whose prongs are made to grip the bridge and lessen its vibration, and with it the vibration of the strings. Brass wind instruments have cone-shaped mutes inserted into the bell. Drums can be muted without any special mechanical device, merely by a cloth spread over the head.

Müthel, Johann Gottfried (b Mölln, Lauenburg, 17 Jan 1728; d Bienenhof near Riga, 14 Jul 1788), German organist, harpsichordist and composer. Pupil of Kunzen in Lübeck, appointed court organist to the Duke of Mecklenburg-Schwerin in 1747. On leave of absence to study in 1750 he visited Bach in Leipzig just before Bach's death, also Altnikol in Naumburg, C P E Bach in Berlin and Telemann in Hamburg. From 1755 organist in Riga.

    Works include concertos, sonatas and misc. pieces for harpsichord.

Muti, Riccardo (b Naples, 28 Jul 1941), Italian conductor. He studied in Naples and won the 1967 Cantelli International Competition. Principal conductor Florence Maggio Musicale from 1969; has led *Guillaume Tell*, *L'Africaine* and operas by Spontini and Verdi there. US debut 1972, Philadelphia Orchestra; principal conductor from 1981. Chief conductor Philharmonia Orchestra, London, 1973–82; CG debut 1977, *Aida*. From 1971 has often been heard in Salzburg and Vienna, most successfully in Italian music. Musical director, La Scala, from 1986. Conducted *Cosi fan tutte* at La Scala, 1990, *Parsifal* and *La Donna del Lago* in season 1992/93. Conducted Spontini's *Vestale* in his own edition including much ballet music, La Scala, Dec 1993.

Mutter, Anne-Sophie (b Rheinfelden, 29 Jun 1963), German violinist. She attracted the attention of Karajan at the 1976 Lucerne Festival and appeared with him at Salzburg the following year. British debut 1977, with the LSO under Barenboim; later appeared in London with Rostropovich and at the 1985 Aldeburgh Festival. US debut Washington 1980, Moscow Mar 1985. Her youthful virtuosity is admired in the standard concertos, and in Jan 1986 she gave the fp of Lutosławski's *Chain II* for violin and orchestra.

Muzen Siciliens, Die, *The Muses of Sicily*, concerto by Henze for chorus, two pianos, wind and percussion (text from Virgil's *Eclogues*), fp Berlin, 20 Sept 1966.

Muzio, Claudia (b Pavia, 7 Feb 1889; d Rome, 24 May 1936), Italian soprano. Studied piano and harp at first, but her teachers discovered

Muti *The conductor Riccardo Muti in concert. Prominent in both the concert and operatic repertory, he prefers his recordings to be made live in order to capture the most emotion. His strict disciplinary methods are balanced by a sense of humour.*

Mutter *The violinist Anne-Sophie Mutter came to prominence in the mid 1970s when Karajan discovered her. A leading violinist of her generation, she possesses a brilliant technique which she applies with passion to the standard repertory. She has inspired several composers to write for her.*

great vocal gifts, and she made her first stage appearance at Arezzo in 1910 as Manon. Soon afterwards she first visited London and sang Desdemona, Tosca and Mimi. NY Met. 1916–34; roles included Giorgetta, Tatyana and Catalani's Loreley.

Muzio Scevola, Il, *Mucius Scaevola*, opera by Filippo Mattei (or Amadei), Giovanni Bononcini and Handel (libretto by P A Rolli), produced London King's Theatre, Haymarket, 15 Apr 1721.

Myaskovsky, Nikolay, ◊Miaskovsky.

My Country (Smetana.) ◊Má Vlast.

Myers, Rollo H(ugh) (b Chislehurst, 23 Jan 1892; d Chichester, 1 Jan 1985), English critic and writer on music. Educated privately and at Oxford, and had a year at the RCM in London. Music correspondent to *The Times* and *Daily Telegraph* in Paris 1919–34 and on BBC staff in London, 1935–44, Music Officer for British Council in Paris, 1945–46. Edited *Chesterian* from 1947 and *Music To-day* from 1949. Pub. books *Modern Music*, *Music in the Modern World*, *Erik Satie*, *Debussy*; composed songs.

If any of us were to die and then wake hearing it we should know at once that (after all) we had got to the right place.

Neville Cardus, on the beginning of Mozart's
Piano Concerto no. 23 in A Major, in
The Manchester Guardian 1938

Mysliveček, Josef (b near Prague, 9 Mar 1737; d Rome, 4 Feb 1781), Bohemian composer. Studied organ and composition in Prague, and pub. there in 1760 a set of symphonies named after the first six months of the year. Went to study with Pescetti in Venice in 1763, and a year later produced his first opera in Parma. Between 1767 and 1780 followed *c* 30 further operas, most to texts by Metastasio, for the principal theatres in Italy. He also visited Munich, where Mozart, who had already met him in 1772, saw him in 1777 and expressed admiration for his oratorio *Abrame ed Isacco*.

Works include operas *Medea* (1764), *Il Bellerofonte* (1767), *Farnace*, *Demofoonte* (1769), *Ezio*, *Il Demetrio* (1773), etc.; oratorio *Abramo ed Isacco* (1776) and three others; symphonies; concertos; chamber music; church music.

Mystic Trumpeter, The scena for soprano and orchestra by Holst (text by Whitman); 1904, fp London, 29 Jun 1905. Revised 1912 and performed London, 25 Jan 1913.

N

Nabokov, Nikolai (b Lubtcha, 17 Apr 1903; d New York, 6 Apr 1978), Russian-born American composer. Studied in Berlin and Stuttgart. He became attached to Diaghilev's Russian Ballet in the 1920s, and later settled in the USA.

Works include operas *The Holy Devil* (1958) and *Love's Labour Lost* (1973); ballets *Ode on seeing the Aurora Borealis* (1928), *Union Pacific* (1934) and *Don Quixote* (1965); incidental music to a dramatic version of Milton's *Samson Agonistes*; symphonies, *Sinfonia biblica* for orchestra; piano concerto (1932); three symphonies (1930–68); cantata *Collectionneur d'échos* for soprano, bass, chorus and percussion, 6 Poems of Anna Akhmatova for soprano and orchestra (1966).

Nabucco, *Nebuchadnezzar*, opera by Verdi (libretto by T Solera), produced Milan, La Scala, 9 Mar 1842. Nabucco's supposed daughter, Abigaille (actually an adopted slave) attempts to seize power.

Nachbaur, Franz (b Giessen, near Friedrichshafen, 25 Mar 1835; d Munich, 21 Mar 1902), German tenor. Studied with Lamperti at Milan and others, sang at various German opera houses and became attached to the Munich Court opera in 1866, creating the part of Walther in Wagner's *Meistersinger* there in 1868; also created Froh in *Das Rheingold* (1869). London, Drury Lane, 1882 as Adolar. Other roles included Faust, Rienzi, Radames and Roméo.

Nachtanz German = lit. 'after-dance'; a quicker dance following a slower one, often with the same music in different rhythm in the 15th–16th c., especially the galliard following the pavan.

Nacht in Venedig, Eine, *A Night in Venice*, operetta by J Strauss, junior (libretto by F Zell and R Genée), produced Berlin, Städtisches Theater, 3 Oct 1883. Written for the opening of that theatre; first Vienna performance, Theater an der Wien, 9 Oct 1883. Elderly Delaqua wants to marry his ward, but has double competition.

Nachtlager von Granada, Das, *The Night-Camp at Granada*, opera by C Kreutzer (libretto by K J B von Braunthal, based on a play by Friedrich Kind), produced Vienna, Josefstadt Theatre, 13 Jan 1834. Crown Prince of Spain helps Gabriela unite with Gomez.

Nachtmusik German = lit. 'night piece' = ◊nocturne.

Nachtstücke und Arien, *Nocturnes and Arias*, work by Henze for soprano and orchestra (text by I Bachmann), fp Donaueschingen, 20 Oct 1957, conductor Rosbaud.

Naderman, François Joseph (b Paris, 1781; d Paris, 3 Apr 1835), French harpist and composer. Son of a harp maker, he became harpist at the Paris Opéra and in the royal chapel, also harp professor at the Conservatory from 1825.

Works include two harp concertos; chamber music with harp parts; harp solos; also with Duport, nocturnes for cello and harp.

Nagano, Kent (George) (b Morro Bay, CA, 22 Nov 1951), American conductor of Japanese descent. Studied in California and was music director of the Berkeley SO from 1978, giving the US concert premiere of Pfitzner's *Palestrina* in 1982. Assistant conductor of the Boston SO from 1984, and conductor of the Lyon Opera from 1989: productions include *The Love for Three Oranges* and the French

version of Strauss's *Salome*. He led the London concert premiere of Messiaen's *St François d'Assise*, 1988, and the fp of *The Death of Klinghoffer* by John Adams (Brussels 1992). Music director of the Hallé Orchestra from 1992.

Nägeli, Hans Georg (b Wetzikon, near Zurich, 26 May 1773; d Zurich, 26 Dec 1836), Swiss composer, teacher, author and publisher. Studied at Zurich and Bern and began to pub. music at Zurich in 1792. In 1803 he began a series entitled *Répertoire des clavecinistes* and included in it Beethoven's sonatas op. 31 Nos. 1 and 2, adding four bars to the former, much to the composer's annoyance. He established the *Schweizerbund* choral society which soon formed branches, and reformed music teaching in schools on the lines of Pestalozzi's education system. He also wrote on music education and lectured on music in Switzerland and Germany.

Works include church and school music; toccatas and other piano pieces; 15 books of popular songs, including 'Freut euch des Lebens' and 'Lied vom Rhein'.

Naich, Hubert (b ? Liège, *c* 1513; d ? Liège after 1546), Flemish composer. Lived in Rome, where he was a member of the Accademia degli Amici and pub. a book of madrigals there *c* 1540.

nail violin an 18th-c. instrument also called nail fiddle or nail harmonica, invented by German violinist Johann Wilde, living at St Petersburg. It was a semi-circular sound-board studded with nails along the rounded edge, which were scraped with a bow.

THE OPERA

Nabucco

A four-act opera by Giuseppe Verdi about Nebuchadnezzar (Nabucodonosor in Italian). It is set in Jerusalem and Babylon in 586 BC, and was first produced in 1842.

I. The Hebrew High Priest Zaccaria (bass) has taken hostage Fenena (soprano), daughter of Nabucco (baritone), who is attacking Jerusalem with his Assyrian hordes. Ismaele (tenor) is in love with Fenena, but she has competition from her supposed sister, Abigaille (soprano). When Nabucco rides into the temple, Zaccaria threatens to kill Fenena, but Ismaele saves her and is reviled by her people.

II. With the Jews captive in Babylon, Fenena acts as regent in the absence of her father. When Abigaille discovers she is merely Nabucco's adopted slave, she plans to kill Fenena and assume power. Nabucco intervenes and seizes the crown for himself, but he is felled by a thunderbolt and driven mad.

III. As regent, Abigaille plans to kill the Hebrew slaves. By the banks of the River Euphrates, they sing of their homeland.

IV. Released from prison, Nabucco is able to save Fenena from execution. As the people say a thankful prayer, Abigaille appears, having taken poison; she dies begging for forgiveness.

THE OPERA

Naïs pastoral-héroïque by Rameau (libretto by L de Cahusac); composed for the peace of Aix-la-Chapelle, produced Paris, Opéra, 22 Apr 1749. The suitors of Naïs are overwhelmed by Neptune.

Naissance de la Lyre, La, *The Birth of the Lyre,* lyric opera in one act by Roussel (libretto by T Reinach, after Sophocles), produced Paris, Opéra, 1 Jul 1925, with choreography by Nijinska. Symphonic fragments in six movements performed Paris, 13 Nov 1927, conductor Paray.

nakers (from Arabic through old French *nacaires*), an old English name for the Kettledrums, which were then much smaller and therefore higher in pitch, and could not have their tuning altered. In cavalry regiments they were played on horseback, hung on each side of the horse's neck.

Naldi, Giuseppe (b Bologna, 2 Feb 1770; d Paris, 14 Dec 1820), Italian baritone. Studied law at Bologna and Pavia Universities, but turned to music and made his first stage appearance at Milan at an early age. He sang in London each year in 1806–19 in operas by Guglielmi, Mayr, Paer, Paisiello and Piccinni. He was the first London Don Alfonso (1811), Papageno (1811), Figaro (1812) and Leporello (1817). He was killed by an exploding kettle.

Namensfeier, *Name[-Day] Celebration,* concert overture by Beethoven, op. 115, in C major, composed 1814, Vienna, Redoutensaal, 25 Dec 1815, conducted by the composer. The name-day was that of the Austrian emperor, which happened to coincide with the completion of the work; it was not composed specially for that occasion.

Namouna ballet by Lalo (scenario by Charles Nuitter; choreographed by Marius Petipa), produced Paris, Opéra, 6 Mar 1882.

Nancarrow, Conlon (b Texarcana, AK, 27 Oct 1912), American-born Mexican composer. Studied at the Cincinnati College-Conservatory 1929–32 and later with Slonimsky and Sessions in Boston. After involvement in the Spanish Civil War he was resident in Mexico until 1981. His music is notated by perforating piano player rolls, although it has been played by other means: fp of the string quartet no. 3 in 1988 by the Arditti Quartet.

Works include *Blues and Prelude* for piano (1935), *Toccata* for violin and piano (1935), Septet (1940), Sonatina for piano (1940), trio for clarinet, bassoon and piano (1943), Suite for orchestra (1943), three string quartets.

Nanino, Giovanni Bernardino (b Vallerano, *c* 1560; d Rome, 1623), Italian composer. Studied under his brother, went to Rome, and from 1591 to 1608 was *maestro di cappella* at the church of San Luigi de' Francesi there, later at that of San Lorenzo in Damaso. He made early use of the basso continuo.

Works include motets, psalms and other church music some with organ accompaniment; five-part madrigals.

Nanino, Giovanni Maria (b Tivoli, *c* 1545; d Rome, 11 Mar 1607), Italian tenor and composer, brother of Giovanni Bernadino ◊Nanino. After learning music as a choirboy at Vallerano, he went to Rome as a pupil of Mel, became a singer at the church of Santa Maria Maggiore, *maestro di cappella* at the church of San Luigi de' Francesi in 1575, singer in the Papal Chapel, 1577, and *maestro di cappella* at Santa Maria Maggiore, 1579. He opened a music school in 1580 with the assistance of his brother and Palestrina, supplied music to the Sistine Chapel and became *maestro di cappella* there in 1604.

Works include motets (e.g. two for Christmas, *Hodie nobis caelorum rex* and *Hodie Christus natus est*), psalms and other church music; madrigals, canzonets, etc.

Nantier-Didiée, Constance (Betsy Rosabella) (b Saint-Denis, Île de Bourbon [Réunion], 16 Nov 1831; d Madrid, 4 Dec 1867), French mezzo. Studied with Duprez at the Paris Conservatory and made her first stage appearance at Turin, in Mercadante's *La Vestale* (1850), and sang in Paris in 1851. Married a singer named Didiée and first visited London in 1853; returned until 1864 as Ascanio, Siebel and Ulrica. She created Preziosilla in St Petersburg on 10 Nov 1862.

Napolitana a light song for several voices, allied to the *villanella* and cultivated at Naples especially in the 16th and 17th c.

Nápravník, Eduard Franzevich (b Byšt, near Hradec-Králove, 24 Aug 1839; d Petrograd, 23 Nov 1916), Czech (naturalized Russian) composer and conductor. Studied music precariously as a child, being the son of a poor teacher, and was left an orphan and destitute in 1853, but succeeded in entering the Organ School in Prague, where he studied with Kittel and others, and became an assistant teacher. In 1861 he went to St Petersburg as conductor of Prince Yussipov's private orchestra, became organist and assistant conductor at the Imperial theatres in 1863, second conductor in 1867 and chief conductor, succeeding Liadov, in 1869, holding the post until his death; he gave the fps of *Boris Godunov*, five operas by Tchaikovsky, including *The Maid of Orleans*, *Mazepa*, and *The Queen of Spades*, and five by Rimsky-Korsakov, including *May Night*, *The Snow Maiden*, and *Christmas Eve*. He also conducted concerts of the Russian Music Society.

Works include operas *The Nizhni-Novgorodians* (1868), *Harold* (1886), *Dubrovsky* (1895) and *Francesca da Rimini* (on Stephen Phillips's play, 1902); incidental music for Alexei Tolstoy's *Don Juan* (1892); ballads for voices and orchestra *The Voyevode*, *The Cossack* and *Tamara* (after Lermontov); four symphonies (1860–79), no. 3 *The Demon* (after Lermontov), suite, *Solemn Overture*, marches and national dances for orchestra; concerto and fantasy on Russian themes for piano and orchestra, fantasy and suite for violin and orchestra; three string quartets (1873–78), string quintet (1897), two piano trios, piano quartet; violin and piano sonata, two suites for cello and piano; string instrument and piano pieces.

Narciso, *Narcissus,* opera by D Scarlatti (libretto by C S Capece), produced Rome, private theatre of Queen Maria Casimira of Poland, 20 Jan 1714, under the title of *Amor d'un' ombra*. Performed in London, 31 May 1720, with additional music by T Roseingrave, under the new title.

Nardini, Pietro (b Livorno, 12 Apr 1722; d Florence, 7 May 1793), Italian violinist and composer. Studied at Livorno and later with Tartini at Padua. Solo violinist at the ducal court of Württemberg at Stuttgart, 1762–65, then settled at Livorno and in 1769 at Florence as music director to the ducal court of Tuscany.

Works include six violin concertos (pub. in Amsterdam *c* 1765 as op. 1); six string quartets; sonatas for violin, two violins, solo and duets for violins; trios for flute, violin, and bass.

Nares, James (b Stanwell, Mdx., bap. 19 Apr 1715; d London, 10 Feb 1783), English organist and composer. Studied with Gates, Croft and Pepusch as a chorister at the Chapel Royal in London, became deputy organist at St George's Chapel, Windsor, and in 1734 was appointed organist of York Minster. Mus.D., Cambridge, 1756, in which year he returned to the Chapel Royal as organist and composer, becoming Master of the Children in succession to Gates, 1757. He pub. treatises on singing and on harpsichord and organ playing.

Works include services and anthems; dramatic ode *The Royal Pastoral* (*c* 1769); catches, glees and canons; harpsichord lessons; organ fugues.

Narváez, Luis de (b Granada, *c* 1500; d after 1550), Spanish vihuelist and composer. His collection of Vihuela music *Los seys libros* (1538), contains early examples of variation writing.

Nasco, Jean (b *c* 1510; d Treviso, 1561), Flemish composer. He was a master of a music academy at Verona in the 1540s and *maestro di cappella* at Treviso Cathedral from 1559. Composed two Passions, Lamentations, madrigals, *canzoni*, etc.

Nash, Heddle (b London, 14 Jun 1896; d London, 14 Aug 1961), English tenor. He studied in London and after World War I in Milan, where he appeared in Rossini's *Il barbiere di Siviglia*. He appeared in England for the first time at the Old Vic in 1925. He subsequently sang with the BNOC and at Glyndebourne (1934–38 as Ferrando, Don Basilio and Pedrillo). Other roles included Don Ottavio, David and Des Grieux. Sang in oratorio at the Three Choirs Festival and elsewhere. His last appearance in opera was Benjamin's *A Tale of Two Cities* in 1957.

Nasolini, Sebastiano (b Piacenza, *c* 1768; d Venice, 1798, or Naples, 1816), Italian composer. Pupil of Bertoni in Venice, in 1787 appointed *maestro al cembalo* at the opera in Trieste, and 1788–90 maestro di cappella of the cathedral there. From 1790 he devoted himself to opera composition.

Works include operas *Nitteti* (1788), *Andromaca* (1790), *La morte di Cleopatra* (1791), *Eugenia* (1792), *Le feste d'Iside* (1794), *Merope, La morte di Mitridate* (1796), *Il medico di Lucca* (1797), *Gli umori contrari* (1798), *Il ritorno di Serse* (1816).

Nathan, Isaac (b Canterbury, 1792; d Sydney, 15 Jan 1864), English singer and composer. Studied Hebrew, etc., at Cambridge, being intended for a Jewish religious career, but turned to music, studying with D Corri in London and appearing as a singer at CG. In 1841 he went to Australia, settling at Sydney as a singing-master. Sir Charles Mackerras is a descendant.

Works include stage pieces with music, *Sweethearts and Wives* (1823), *The Alcaid* (1824), *The Illustrious Stranger* (1827), *Merry Freaks in Troublous Times* (composed 1843), *Hebrew Melodies* and other songs to words by Byron.

Please, no national music! To the devil with all this 'folksiness'!

Felix Mendelssohn, in a letter to Zelter, 1829

---

nationalism in music nationalism manifests itself through the endeavour of individual composers or schools to find some sort of musical idiom that may be said to express their countries' characteristics, either idiomatically or spiritually. Idiomatic expression of this kind is most usually and easily attained through the adoption, imitation or adaptation of folksong and national dances, which however may become more or less strongly coloured by each composer's individuality and will certainly be much elaborated in the process of sustained composition (e.g. Smetana in Czechoslovakia, Grieg in Norway, Balakirev in Russia, Falla in Spain, Bartók in Hungary, etc.). The reflection of a country's spirit in music is less definite, more subtle and not so easily perceptible, but there is no doubt that certain composers have achieved this without consciously resorting to folk music, and those who sometimes do so may remain just as strongly national when they happen to refrain (e.g. Tchaikovsky and Mussorgsky in Russia [in different ways], Elgar in England, Fauré and Ravel in France), Sibelius in Finland, etc.).

Nattiez, Jean-Jacques (b Amiens, 30 Dec 1945), Canadian musicologist. As director of the Groupe de Recherches en Semiologie Musicale at the University of Montreal (1974) he is important for developing the use of semiotics in musical analysis, as first expounded in his book *Fondements d'une sémiologie musicale* (1975).

natural the sign ♮, which restores to its normal position a note previously raised by a ♯ or lowered by a ♭.

naturale Italian = 'natural'; a direction indicating that a voice or instrument, after performing a passage in some unusual way (*mezza voce*, muted, etc.), is to return to its normal manner.

Naudin, Emilio (b Parma, 23 Mar 1823; d Bologna, 5 May 1890), Italian-born French tenor. Debut Cremona, 1843. He sang in London from 1858, and at CG in 1867 was the first local Don Carlos. Created Meyerbeer's Vasco da Gama at the Paris Opéra (1865) and was successful as Tannhäuser, Lohengrin and Masaniello.

Naumann, Johann Gottlieb (b Blasewitz, near Dresden, 17 Apr 1741; d Dresden, 23 Oct 1801), German composer. At the age of 16 he accompanied the Swedish violinist Wesström to Hamburg, then to Italy, where he studied with Tartini, Hasse and Padre Martini. Produced his first opera in Venice in 1763, and the following year was appointed to the court at Dresden as second composer of church music. Revisited Italy to produce operas 1765–68 and 1772–74, and in 1776 became *Kapellmeister* in Dresden, where, apart from visits to Stockholm, Copenhagen and Berlin, he remained till his death. His opera *Gustav Vasa* was revived in Stockholm, 1991.

Works include operas *Achille in Sciro* (1767), *La clemenza di Tito* (1769), *Solimano, Armida* (1773), *Ipermestra, Amphion* (1778), *Cora och Alonzo* (1782), *Gustaf Vasa*, 1786; all three in Swedish, *Orpheus*

og Euridice (in Danish, 1786), *Protesilao* (with Reichardt), *La dama soldato* (1790), *Aci e Galatea* (1801) and others; 21 Masses and other church music, 13 oratorios.

Navarini, Francesco (b Cittadella, near Rome, 1853; d Milan, 23 Feb 1923), Italian bass. Debut Ferrara 1876, in *Lucrezia Borgia*. La Scala 1883–1900; created Lodovico in *Otello*, 1887. He appeared widely in Russia and Europe; toured USA 1902 with Mascagni's co. Highly regarded as Verdi's Silva, Wagner's Pogner, Hunding and Hagen.

Navarra, André (b Biarritz, 13 Oct 1911; d Paris 31 Jul 1988), French cellist. Studied at Toulouse and Paris Conservatory and in 1949 became professor at the Paris Conservatory. He gave the fps of concertos by Jolivet (1962) and Tomasi (1970).

Navarraise, La, *The Girl of Navarre*, opera by Massenet (libretto by J Claretie and H Cain, based on the former's story *La Cigarette*), produced London, CG, 20 Jun 1894. Anita's attempts to win dowry by assassinating military leader.

Navarro, Garcia (b Chiva, Spain, 30 Apr 1941), Spanish conductor. Studied in Vienna with Swarowsky and was music director of the Valencia SO 1970–74. Portuguese Radio SO 1976–78. Music director Lisbon National Theatre 1980–82, Stuttgart State Opera from 1987; Guest conductor of the Vienna Staatsoper 1987–91, and also guest with the Tokyo Philharmonic and the Deutsche Oper Berlin. Artistic director of the Barcelona SO 1991–93. CG debut 1979 (*La Bohème*), *Carmen* in Paris (1982), *Cav and Pag* and *Tosca* at the Met. (1986–87). Has conducted *Falstaff* and *Andrea Chénier* in Vienna.

Navarro, Juan (b Seville, *c* 1530; d Palencia, 25 Sept 1580), Spanish composer. After the death of Morales in 1553 he competed unsuccessfully for the post of *maestro de capilla* at Málaga Cathedral, but he later obtained a similar post in Salamanca. He (?) visited Rome in 1590, where his nephew Fernando Navarro Salazar arranged for the pub. of some of his church music. After his death Passions and Lamentations in plainsong were pub. in Mexico by his brother, but he probably never lived there himself. He was highly regarded as a polyphonist.

Works include psalms, hymns, Magnificats and other church music, madrigals, etc.

Naylor, Bernard (b Cambridge, 22 Nov 1907; d Keswick, 19 May 1986), English composer, conductor and organist. He studied at the RCM with Vaughan Williams and Holst; conducted in Winnipeg and Montreal from 1932, settled in Canada 1959.

Works include 12 motets in two sets (1949, 1952), *The Annunciation according to St Luke* for soloists, chorus and orchestra (1949); *Variations* for orchestra (1960); string trio (1960); *Stabat Mater* (1961); *The Nymph and the Faun* for mezzo and ensemble (text by Marvell, 1965); *Three Sacred Pieces* for chorus and orchestra (1971).

Naylor, Edward (Woodall) (b Scarborough, 9 Feb 1867; d Cambridge, 7 May 1934), English organist, musicologist and composer. Studied at Cambridge and the RCM in London, and after two organist's appointments there he returned to Cambridge in 1897 to become organist at Emmanuel College, taking the Mus.D. degree at the university. He lectured and wrote on music, pub. a book on *Shakespeare and Music*.

Works include opera *The Angelus* (produced CG 1909); cantata *Arthur the King* (1902); part-songs; piano trio in D major.

Neaman, Yfrah (b Sidon, 13 Feb 1923), Lebanese-born violinist. Studied at the Paris Conservatoire and with Carl Flesch. Debut with the LSO, 1944. Concerts and master classes throughout Europe and the USA. Head of Strings at the GSMD, London. Recordings include concertos by Gerhard, Fricker and Don Banks. OBE 1983.

Neapolitan sixth a chord consisting of a minor third and a minor sixth on the subdominant of the key, which came into vogue in the 17th c. It occurs most often in a cadential progression in a minor key.

Neapolitan Songs, Five, *Fünf neapolitanische Lieder*, work by Henze for baritone and orchestra (anon. 17th-c. text), fp Frankfurt, 26 May 1956, with Fischer-Dieskau.

Neate, Charles (b London, 28 Mar 1784; d Brighton, 30 Mar 1877), English pianist and cellist. He became a pupil of Field, who learnt the cello with him under William Sharp, and made his debut at CG in

The neapolitan sixth in an A minor cadence.

1800. He also studied composition with Woelflute In 1815 he spent eight months in Vienna and made friends with Beethoven, and then five months at Munich studying counterpoint with Winter. He taught and performed for many years in London with much success and wrote music mainly for piano.

Neblett, Carol (b Modesto, CA, 1 Feb 1946), American soprano. Studied at UCLA and made stage debut with NY City Opera 1969, as Musetta. Chicago and Vienna Staatsoper debuts 1975 and 1976, as Chrysothemis and Minnie; CG 1977. NY Met. from 1979, as Senta, Tosca, Amelia (*Ballo*) Manon Lescaut and Alice Ford. Other roles include Norma (Miami Opera), Aida (Cincinnati) and Mozart's Vitelia, in a filmed version of *La Clemenza di Tito*.

Nebra, José de (b Calatayud, bap. 6 Jan 1702; d Madrid, 11 Jul 1768), Spanish organist and composer. He became organist at the Convent of the Descalzas Reales in Madrid and second organist at the royal chapel in 1724. After the destruction of the library there in the fire of 24 Dec 1734, he and Literes were commissioned to replace the lost church music and to restore what had survived. In 1751 he was made vice-*maestro de capilla* under Corselli, who neglected his duties for the composition of Italian operas, and by 1757 he had completely reorganized the court music. In 1758 he composed a Requiem for eight voices, flute and strings for the funeral of Queen Barbara of Braganza, who had been D Scarlatti's patroness.

Works include *c* 20 operas: Requiem, Miserere, psalms and other church music; *villancico* for four voices.

Nedbal, Oskar (b Tábor, 26 Mar 1874; d Zagreb, 24 Dec 1930), Czech conductor, viola player and composer. Pupil of Dvořák, member of the Bohemian String Quartet and from 1896 conductor of the Czech Philharmonic Society in Prague. From 1906 he conducted concerts and opera mainly in Vienna. He composed light opera *Polenblut* (1913) and others; ballets *Pohádka o Honzovi* (1902), *Princezna Hyacinta* (1911), *Des Teufels Grossmutter* (1912).

Neefe, Christian Gottlob (b Chemnitz, 5 Feb 1748; d Dessau, 26 Jan 1798), German conductor and composer. Studied in Leipzig under Hiller, whom he succeeded as conductor of a touring opera co. in 1776. He settled in Bonn in 1779, where he was appointed court organist three years later. Beethoven was his pupil from the age of 11. The French occupation of Bonn in 1794 cost him his post, and from 1796 he was music director of the Bossann theatre co. in Dessau.

Works include operas *Die Apotheke* (1771), *Adelheid von Veltheim*, *Amors Guckkasten* (1772), *Die Einsprüche* (1772), *Heinrich und Lyda* (1776), *Sophonisbe*, *Zemire und Azor* (1776) and others; incidental music for Shakespeare's *Macbeth*; church music; chamber music.

Neel, Boyd (b Blackheath, 19 Jul 1905; d Toronto, 30 Sept 1981), English conductor. Founded Boyd Neel String Orchestra 1933 (fp Britten's *Variations on theme of Frank Bridge*, Salzburg 1937); Orchestra renamed Philomusica of London, 1957. Dean, Toronto Conservatory 1953–70.

Negri, Vittorio (b Milan, 16 Oct 1923), Italian conductor. Studied at the Milan Conservatory and was assistant at the Salzburg Mozarteum from 1952. Appearances at Salzburg, Montreux and Orange Festivals, guest with the Boston SO, the Dresden Staatskapelle and at La Scala. Recordings include the oratorios *Judith Triumphans* by Vivaldi and Mozart's *Betulia Liberata*.

Neidhart von Reuental (b Bavaria, *c* 1180; d *c* 1240), German Minnesinger. Went on a crusade in 1217–19 and settled in Austria on his return. Several songs of his are preserved; many others are attributed to him. A younger contemporary of Walther von der Vogelweide, his music survived in print during the Renaissance.

Neidlinger, Gustav (b Mainz, 21 Mar 1912; d Bad Ems, 26 Dec 1991), German bass-baritone. He made his debut in Mainz and was in Hamburg 1936–50. Stuttgart from 1950; visited Edinburgh 1958 with co., as Lysiart and Kurwenal. His best role was Wagner's Alberich, which he sang at Bayreuth 1952–75, CG from 1963 and in the first studio recording of the *Ring*. Other roles included Pizarro, Klingsor, Sachs and Telramund.

Neikrug, Marc (b New York, 24 Sept 1946), American composer and pianist. Studied in Detmold and with Schuller at Tanglewood. Duo partnership with Pinchas Zukerman and Salzburg debut with him 1978. Opera *Los Alamos* premiered at the Deutsche Oper Berlin 1988. Other works include concertos for piano (1966), clarinet (1970), viola (1974), violin (1985) and flute (1989); two string quartets (1969, 1972); concertino for ensemble (1977); *Eternity's Sunrise* for orchestra (1980).

Nelson, John (b San José, Costa Rica, 6 Dec 1941), American conductor. Studied at Juilliard and led concert performances of *Les Troyens* in New York, 1972; Met. premiere of the opera 1973, followed by *Cav and Pag* and *Jenůfa*. NY City Opera from 1972, with *Carmen* and *Poppea*. Music director Indianapolis SO 1977–88, Opera Theatre of St Louis, 1985–92. Conducted *Benvenuto Cellini* for Lyon Opera 1989, *Béatrice et Bénédict* for WNO 1993.

Nelson, Judith (b Chicago, 10 Sept 1939), American soprano. Studied singing in Santa Barbara and made opera debut as Roberto in A Scarlatti's *Griselda* at Berkeley, 1976. Other roles include Drusilla in *Poppea* (Brussels 1979) and Landi's *Sant 'Alessio* (Innsbruck 1987). Many concerts in the USA. Recordings include Handel's *Alceste* and *Resurrezione*, *Serse* by Cavalli and *Dido and Aeneas* (as Belinda).

Nelson Mass the name given to Haydn's Mass in D minor, composed 1798. It is sometimes said that the fanfares in the Benedictus commemorate Nelson's victory in the battle of the Nile; in fact Haydn cannot have heard the news of the battle until after the Mass was finished. His own title was *Missa in angustiis*. Performed Eisenstadt, 23 Sept 1798.

Nelsova, Zara (b Winnipeg, 23 Dec 1918), Canadian cellist. She studied in London and made her debut there in 1931 with the LSO. Principal cellist with Toronto SO 1940–43. NY debut 1942 and studied further with Casals and Piatigorsky; US citizen 1953. Has taught at Juilliard from 1962. In 1969 she gave the fp of Hugh Wood's concerto.

Nelsson, Woldemar (b Kiev, 4 Apr 1938), Russian conductor. Studied at the Novosibirsk Conservatory and was assistant to Kondrashin at the Moscow PO from 1971. Emigrated to West Germany 1977 and led Stuttgart fp of Henze's ballet *Orpheus* in 1979. Bayreuth Festival 1980–85, *Lohengrin* and *Der fliegende Holländer*; music director at Kassel 1980–87. Washington DC and NY Met with *Orpheus*. Conducted fp of Penderecki's *Die schwarze Maske* at Salzburg (1986) and *Lady Macbeth of Mtsensk* at Copenhagen, 1991.

Németh, Mária (b Körmend, 13 Mar 1897; d Vienna, 28 Dec 1967), Hungarian soprano. She studied in Budapest and made her debut there in 1923. Vienna 1925–46 as Tosca, Santuzza, Aida, Queen of Night and Constanze. London, CG, 1931, as Turandot. Also heard at Salzburg and La Scala, Milan.

Nenna, Pomponio (b Bari, near Naples, *c* 1550; d Rome before 1613), Italian composer. Lived mainly at Naples and was the teacher of Gesualdo, Prince of Venosa, 1594–99; moved to Rome about 1608.

Works include two books of responsories and nine books of madrigals.

Nentwig, Franz Ferdinand (b Duisburg, 23 Aug 1929), German bass-baritone. Made debut at Bielefeld 1962, as Ottokar in *Der Freischütz*. Has sung widely in Germany and appeared as Amfortas at Venice in 1983. Other Wagner roles include Telramund (NY Met. 1984), Hans Sachs on tour to Japan (1987), and Wotan in the first Polish production of the *Ring* (1989). CG debut 1985 as the Music Master in *Ariadne auf Naxos*. Salzburg Festival (1987), as Schoenberg's Moses. Other roles include Rigoletto, Mozart's Count and Dr Schön in *Lulu*.

neo-Bechstein piano an electrophonic piano invented by Vierling of Berlin 1928–33 and further developed by Franco and Nernst, producing its notes by the conversion of electrical waves into audible sounds.

neo-classicism term used to designate modern music which rejected Romantic expressiveness as exemplified by the music of Wagner, using instead models from the 17th and 18th c. as a starting point; traditional formal and harmonic structures are clearly present beneath the composer's often witty or unexpected musical statements. The movement was foreshadowed by Busoni (*Fantasia contrappuntistica*, after The Art of Fugue (1910–12) and six Sonatinas for piano, 1910–20). Prokofiev's *Classical Symphony* of 1916 was composed in emulation of Haydn, and Stravinsky's *Pulcinella* ballet (after Pergolesi, 1920) rejects the huge orchestra and extended forms of *The Firebird*. Hindemith's ◊*Kammermusik* series of seven chamber works (1921–27) emulates the instrumental style of Bach, while his one-act opera *Das Nusch-Nuschi* contains satirical allusions to Wagner's *Tristan* which shocked contemporary audiences. Later neoclassical works were Stravinsky's opera-oratorio *Oedipus Rex* (after Sophocles, 1927) and the ballet *Apollo* (1928). Schoenberg satirized Neo-Classicism in the last of his three pieces for chorus, op. 28 (1925): *Der neue Klassizismus* contains a reference to 'Modernsky' — i.e. Stravinsky. However, Schoenberg himself employed classical forms for his twelve-tone works; the Suite for piano op. 25 (1921–23) is a series of Baroque dance movements and the third string quartet (1927) is a dodecaphonic re-creation of classical four-movement form.

The twelve-tone school tried to revive the spirit of the old forms, while neo-classicism presented replicas of their facades with interesting cracks added.
Ernst Křenek, *Horizons Circled*, 1974

---

neo-modal modern music using new derivations from the modes, harmonized, transposed or otherwise altered.

Neri, Filippo (St Philip Neri) (b Florence, 21 Jul 1515; d Rome, 26 May 1595), Italian saint. Of importance to music for his foundation of the Society of Oratorians in 1564, which cultivated music at the oratory of San Girolamo in Rome, for which among others Animuccia and Palestrina worked in his lifetime and which in 1600 produced Cavalieri's *Rappresentazione di anima e di corpo*. It was from this society that the oratorio received its name as a musical form.

Neri, Giulio (b Turrite di Siena, 21 May 1909; d Rome, 21 Apr 1958), Italian bass. He sang in Rome from 1928 and was a leading bass there from 1938; also appeared at Milan, Florence and Venice. CG 1953, as Oroveso and Ramfis. Later sang at Barcelona and Buenos Aires; Verona 1951–57. Well known as Mefistofele, Alvise and the Grand Inquisitor.

Nero ◊Nerone.
Opera by Rubinstein (libretto, in French [*Néron*], by J Barbier), produced, in German, Hamburg, Municipal Theatre, 1 Nov 1879.

Nerone, *Nero*, opera by Boito (libretto by composer), begun 1879, but left unfinished at Boito's death in 1918. Produced, edited by Tommasini and A Toscanini, Milan, La Scala, 1 May 1924. Corrupt Romans and spiritual Christians in conflict as the city burns.

Neruda, Wilma (Wilhelmina) (Norman-Neruda; Lady Hallé) (b Brno, 21 Mar 1839; d Berlin, 15 Apr 1911), Moravian violinist. Studied under her father, Josef Neruda (1807–75) and with Jansa, and made her first appearance in Vienna with her sister Amalie, a pianist, in 1846. She then went on tour in Germany and appeared in London in

1849. Afterwards she appeared all over Europe, often with her brother, the cellist Franz Neruda (1843–1915). In 1864 she played in Paris and married the Swedish composer Ludvig Norman. In 1888 she became the second wife of Charles Hallé and settled at Manchester. Given title Violinist to the Queen by Queen Alexandra, in 1901.

Nesbet(t), J (d ? 1468), English composer. Wrote a five-part Magnificat (Carver and Eton choirbooks, incomplete in the latter) and a three-part *Benedicamus* (Pepys MS., Magdalene College, Cambridge).

Neschling, John (b Rio de Janeiro, 1945), Brazilian-born conductor. Studied with Swarowsky in Vienna and with Bernstein in the USA. Has guested with the London and Vienna SOs, New York and Israel Philharmonics and at the Vienna Staatsoper (*Figaro*, *Trovatore*, *Butterfly* and *Lucia*). Further opera in Berlin, Hamburg and Stockholm. Principal conductor of the San Carlo Opera at Lisbon, 1981–88, then music director at St Gallen, Switzerland (*Die Zauberflöte*, 1989).

Nessler, Viktor (Ernst) (b Baldenheim, Alsace, 28 Jan 1841; d Strasbourg, 28 May 1890), German composer. Studied theology at Strasbourg, but took to music and produced a French opera there in 1864. He went to Leipzig, became choral and afterwards operatic conductor. He was well known for his opera *Der Trompeter von Säckingen*, often conducted by Mahler.

Works include operas *Fleurette* (1864), *Die Hochzeitreise, Dornröschens Brautfahrt* (1867), *Nachtwächter und Student, Am Alexandertag, Irmingard* (1876), *Der Rattenfänger von Hameln* (1879), *Der wilde Jäger* (1881), *Der Trompeter von Säckingen* (after Scheffel's poem, 1884), *Otto der Schütz* (1886), *Die Rose von Strassburg* (1890); part-songs.

Nesterenko, Evgeny (b Moscow, 8 Jan 1938), Russian bass. Debut Leningrad, 1963, as Gremin. Moscow, Bolshoi, from 1971; sang Boris with the Co. in Milan 1973 and at the NY Met. in 1975. He returned to La Scala in 1978 for Verdi's Philip II and also sang the role on his CG debut the same year. Other roles include Ruslan, Méphistophélès and Don Basilio. Often heard in Shostakovich's 14th symphony.

Neues vom Tage, *News of the Day*, opera by Hindemith (libretto by M Schiffer), produced Berlin, Kroll Opera, 8 Jun 1929, conductor Klemperer. The opera was condemned by Goebbels in 1934: 'in their eagerness to make a sensation atonal musicians exhibit naked women in the bathtub on stage in the most obscene situations'. (Exactly 50 years later Peter Hall's wife, Maria Ewing, took a nude bath in the Glyndebourne production of *Poppea*).

Neuhold, Günter (b Graz, 2 Nov 1947), Austrian conductor. Studied in Rome and Vienna and was first conductor at Hanover and Dortmund from 1980. Guest with the Vienna PO and music director of the Teatro Regio in Parma from 1981. Principal guest with the Dresden Staatskapelle and music director of Royal PO of Flanders from 1986 (tours of Japan and Britain), Director of the Karlsruhe Opera from 1989 (*Tristan*, *Arabella*, *Die Frau ohne Schatten* and *Meistersinger*). Recordings include symphonies by Mahler and Bruckner, the Berlioz *Faust* and *The Rite of Spring*.

Neukomm, Sigismund von (b Salzburg, 10 Jul 1778; d Paris, 3 Apr 1858), Austrian composer. As a chorister at Salzburg Cathedral he was a pupil of M Haydn, who in 1798 sent him to J Haydn in Vienna. In 1806 he went to Sweden and Russia, becoming conductor at the Tsar's German theatre in St Petersburg. He returned to Vienna in 1809 and went to live in Paris soon after, succeeding Dussek in 1812 as pianist to Talleyrand. From 1816 to 1821 he was *maestro de capilla* to Pedro I of Brazil, with whom he returned to Lisbon, after the revolution, afterwards travelling with Talleyrand. In 1829 he visited London, meeting Mendelssohn, and lived there and alternately in Paris for the rest of his life.

Works include opera *Alexander in Indien* (1804), *Niobé* (1809) and others; 48 Masses and Requiem for Louis XVI; oratorios *Mount Sinai, David* and six others; incidental music for Schiller's *Braut von Messina* (1805); songs.

Neumann, Angelo (b Vienna, 18 Aug 1838; d Prague, 20 Dec 1910), Austrian tenor and opera impresario. He made his debut in Berlin, 1859, and sang in Vienna 1862–76. He then worked in Leipzig as an opera manager until 1882 and formed a touring company which gave performances of Wagner's operas all over Europe; the royalties were important to the survival of the Bayreuth Festival. From 1882 he worked in Bremen, then Prague; pub. a volume of reminiscences of Wagner in 1907.

Neumann, František (b Přerov, Moravia, 16 Jun 1874; d Brno, 25 Feb 1929), Czech composer and conductor. Started in commercial and military career but went to study music at the Leipzig Conservatory. After filling various chorus-master's and conductor's posts at German and Czech theatres, he went to Brno as chief conductor at the National Theatre. He conducted the fps of Janáček's *Káta Kabanovà*, *The Cunning Little Vixen*, *Šárka* and *The Makropoulos Case*.

Works include operas *Idalka*, *Die Brautwerbung* (1901), *Liebelei* (on Schnitzler's play, 1910), *Herbststurm* (1919), *Beatrice Caracci* (1922); melodrama *Pan*; ballets *In Pleasant Pastures*, *The Peri*, *Pierrot*; Masses and motets; symphonic poem *Infernal Dance*, suite *The Sunken Bell*, *Moravian Rhapsody*, overtures, etc. for orchestra; octet, piano trio; choruses, songs.

Neumann, Václav (b Prague, 29 Oct 1920; d Vienna, 2 Sept 1995), Czech conductor. He studied at the Prague Conservatory and was a violist with the Czech PO; deputy conducted 1948, principal conductor from 1968. He worked at the Komische Oper, Berlin, 1956–64 and conducted there the Felsenstein production of *The Cunning Little Vixen*. He gave the fp of Cikker's *Play of Love and Death* (Munich, 1969) and was music director of Stuttgart Opera 1969–72.

Neumann, Wolfgang (b Waiern, 20 Jun 1945), Austrian tenor. Made debut in Bielefeld 1973, as Weber's Max. Sang at Augsburg from 1978; Mannheim from 1980. Has sung Tannhäuser at Florence (1983) and Schoenberg's Aron at Barcelona. NY Met. debut 1988, as Siegfried under James Levine. Tenor 1989–90 as the Cardinal in *Mathis der Maler* at Munich and Wagner's Rienzi at Buenos Aires. Concert repertory includes *Das Lied von der Erde* and the *Gurrelieder* by Schoenberg.

Neumark, Georg (b Langensalza, 7 Mar 1621; d Weimar, 8 Jul 1681), German poet and musician. He pub. a collection of sacred and secular songs, *Musikalische-poetischer Lustwald* in 1657, some set to music by himself, including the hymn 'Wer nur den lieben Gott lässt walten'.

neumes the signs in Eastern chant and Western plainsong (and in some medieval song-books) indicating the single notes or groups of notes to which each syllable was to be sung. Originally not set on staves, but merely marked above the words and showing neither precise length nor exact pitch, they served as reminders of tunes already known to the singers.

Neusidler, Hans (b Poszony [Pressburg], *c* 1509; d Nuremberg, 2 Feb 1563), Hungarian lutenist. Settled at Nuremberg, where he pub. books of pieces arranged for lute in tablature in 1536, 1540 and 1544.

Neusidler, Melchior (b Nuremberg, 1531; d Augsburg, 1590), German lutenist, son of Hans ◊Neusidler. He settled in Augsburg in 1552. He visited Italy and pub. two books of lute music at Venice in 1566. In 1574 he pub. at Strasbourg a book of music (*Teutsch Lautenbuch*) by Josquin, Lassus, Arcadelt, Rore and others arranged for the lute. Pub. lute arrangements of six motets by Josquin in 1584.

Nevada (actually *Wixom*), Emma (b Alpha, near Nevada City, CA, 7 Feb 1859; d Liverpool, 20 Jun 1940), American soprano. Studied with Mathilde Marchesi in Vienna and made her debut in London in 1880 as Amina, later singing in Italy, Paris, etc. Her daughter Mignon (1886–1971) sang at CG, London, until 1922 as Ophelia, Olympia, Desdemona and Zerlina.

Neveu, Ginnete (b Paris, 11 Aug 1919; d San Miguel, Azores, 28 Oct 1949), French violinist. Appeared with the Colonne Orchestra at the age of seven. Studied at the Paris Conservatory and with Flesch, and won the highest reputation for virtuosity and passionate musicality. She was killed in an air accident.

Newark, William (b ? Newark-on-Trent, *c* 1450; d Greenwich, 11 Nov 1509), English composer. Became a Gentleman of the Chapel Royal in London, 1477 and, after various other appointments, Master of the Children there in 1493. Composed part-songs.

New England Holidays unnumbered symphony by Ives, composed 1904–13: 1. *Washington's birthday* 2. *Decoration Day* 3. *The Fourth of July* 4. *Thanksgiving*. Fp New York, 10 Jan 1931, conductor Slonimsky.

Newlin, Dika (b Portland, OR, 22 Nov 1923), American musicologist and composer. Studied privately with Sessions and Schoenberg and then taught at Western Maryland College and Syracuse University In 1952 she established a music department at Drew University, NJ. Her writings include studies of Bruckner, Mahler and Schoenberg, translations, particularly of Schoenberg's writings: *Schoenberg Remembered: Diaries and Recollections, 1938–76* (1980). She has also composed for various media, especially chamber music.

I sometimes wonder which would be nicer – an opera without an interval, or an interval without an opera.
Ernest Newman, *Berlioz, Romantic and Classic*, 1972

Newman, Ernest (actually William Roberts) (b Liverpool, 30 Nov 1868; d Tadworth, 7 Jul 1959), English critic and writer on music. Educated at Liverpool. Became critic of the *Manchester Guardian*, 1905, the *Birmingham Post*, 1906, the *Observer*, 1919, and the *Sunday Times*, 1920. Books include *Gluck and the Opera*, *Hugo Wolf*, *A Musical Critic's Holiday* and several works on Wagner, including the largest modern biography (1933–47).

Newman, John Henry (1801–1890), English cardinal and poet. ◊Dream of Gerontius (Elgar).

Newmarch (born *Jeaffreson*), Rosa (Harriet) (b Leamington, 18 Dec 1857; d Worthing, 9 Apr 1940), English writer on music. Wrote programme notes for London Queen's Hall concerts, 1908–27. Her books include *The Russian Opera* and *The Music of Czechoslovakia*; she brought Janáček to London in 1926 and he dedicated his *Sinfonietta* to her.

Newstone, Harry (b Winnipeg, 21 Jun 1921), Canadian-born English conductor. Studied with Herbert Howells at the GSM (1945–49) and in Rome. Formed Haydn Orchestra, giving debut concert 19 May 1949 at the Conway Hall, London. Guest appearances with leading orchestras in Britain and the continent. Music director of the Sacramento SO 1965–78, professor at the GSMD 1979–87. Has recorded works by Bach and Haydn and issued a new edition of Haydn's London symphonies.

Newton, Ivor (b London, 15 Dec 1892; d Bromley, 21 Apr 1981), English pianist and accompanist. Studied in London, Amsterdam and Berlin and then concentrated mainly on accompaniment, playing for many great artists.

'New World' Symphony Dvořák's ninth symphony in E minor, op. 95, with the subtitle *From the New World*, because it was written in USA. Composed 1893, fp NY Philharmonic Society, 16 Dec 1893.

New Year opera in three acts by Tippett (libretto by composer), produced Houston, 5 Oct 1989. Neurotic psychologist Jo Ann finds time-traveller Pelegrin and true love. He teaches her how to be independent before leaving again for the future.

New York City Opera opera company founded 1943 under title City Center Opera Company and opened at West 55th Street 1944 with *Tosca*. Julius Rudel was music director 1957–79, presiding over move to NY State Theater at Lincoln Center in 1966 (Ginastera's *Don Rodrigo*, with Domingo in NY debut role, as opening production). Beverly Sills was director 1979–88, Christopher Keene music director 1983–95, leading local stage premieres of Busoni's *Doktor Faust*, *From the House of the Dead*, and *Moses und Aron*.

New York Philharmonic Orchestra US orchestra founded 1842. Early conductors included Theodore Thomas, Anton Seidl and the Damrosch brothers; Mahler 1909–11; Mengelberg 1921–29; Toscanini 1928–36; Barbirolli 1936–42; Rodzinski 1943–47; Walter 1941–49; Mitropoulos 1949–58; Bernstein, 1958–69; Boulez 1971–77; Mehta 1978–91; Kurt Masur from 1991. Merged with NY SO 1928.

Ney, Elly (b Düsseldorf, 27 Sept 1882; d Tutzing, 31 Mar 1968), German pianist. Studied with Böttcher and Seiss at Cologne Conservatory and then with Leschetitsky and Sauer in Vienna. After winning the Mendelssohn and Ibach Prizes she taught at the Cologne Conservatory in 1906 and began a very successful concert career, becoming especially well known as a Beethoven interpreter; recorded the C minor sonata op. 111 in 1936 and 1958.

Nezhdanova, Antonina (b Krivaya Balka, near Odessa, 16 Jun 1873; d Moscow, 26 Jun 1950), Russian soprano. She studied in Moscow and sang at the Bolshoi 1902–36 as Ludmilla, Antonida, Tatyana, the Snow Maiden and Lakmé. She was a regular guest in the Russian provinces and sang Gilda in Paris in 1912. Taught in Moscow from 1936.

Nibelung Saga, *Nibelungenlied*, ancient Teutonic epic in the Middle High German dialect. ◊Dorn (*Nibelungen*); ◊Draeseke (*Gudrun*); ◊Ring des Nibelungen (Wagner); ◊Sigurd (Reyer).

Nibelung's Ring, The (Wagner.) ◊Ring des Nibelungen.

Niccolini, Giuseppe (b Piacenza, 29 Jan 1762; d Piacenza, 18 Dec 1842), Italian composer. Studied at the Conservatorio di Sant' Onofrio, Naples, under Insanguine. Was at first very successful in opera, but was eventually driven from the stage by Rossini. *Maestro di cappella* at Piacenza Cathedral from 1819.

Works include operas *I baccanti di Roma* (1801), *Traiano in Dacia* (1807), *Coriolano* (1808) and *c* 40 others; Masses and other church music, etc.

Nichelmann, Christoph (b Treuenbrietzen, Brandenburg, 13 Aug 1717; d Berlin, 20 Jul 1762), German harpsichordist and composer. Pupil of Bach at St Thomas's School, Leipzig; lived at Hamburg and Berlin, being appointed second harpsichordist to Frederick the Great in 1744.

Works include opera (serenata) *Il sogno di Scipione*; harpsichord concertos; harpsichord sonatas.

Nicholls, Agnes (b Cheltenham, 14 Jul 1877; d London, 21 Sept 1959), English soprano. Studied RCM; debut London 1895, as Purcell's Dido. CG 1901–10, as Sieglinde and the *Siegfried* Brünnhilde, under Richter, and as Elsa. She married Hamilton Harty in 1904 and toured with him in North America. Often heard in concert and as guest with Beecham, BNOC and Carl Rosa Co. Other roles included Nannetta and Donna Elvira.

Nicholson, George (b Durham, 24 Sept 1949), English composer who studied with Bernard Rands and David Blake. His music is largely for chamber groups. Overture, seven winds (1976), *Recycle*, 11 instruments (1976), *The Arrival of the Poet in the City*, melodrama for actor and seven instruments (1983), Chamber concerto (1980), Brass quintet (1977), *Aubade* for soprano and five instruments (1981), *Movements* for seven instruments (1983), *Stilleven* for five instruments (1985), *Blisworth Tunnel Blues* for soprano and ensemble (1986), *Sea-Change* for 14 strings (1988), cello concerto (1990), flute concerto (1993).

Nicholson, Richard (d Oxford, 1639), English organist and composer. Became choirmaster and organist at Magdalen College, Oxford, in 1595, took the B.Mus. there, 1596, and became the first Professor of Music there in 1627.

Works include anthems, madrigals (one in *The Triumphes of Oriana*), music for viols, 'dialogue' (or song-cycle) for three voices 'Joane, quoth John'.

Nicholson, Sydney H(ugo) (b London, 9 Feb 1875; d Ashford, Kent, 30 May 1947), English organist and church educationist. Studied at the RCM in London and under Knorr at Frankfurt. Organist of Manchester Cathedral, 1908–18, and Westminster Abbey, 1918–27, when he founded the School of English Church Music at Chislehurst, later transferred to Addington. Knighted 1938. His works includes church music, a comic opera, *The Mermaid* (libretto by George Birmingham, 1928) and an opera for boys' voices, *The Children of the Chapel* (1934).

Nicodé, Jean Louis (b Jerczig, near Poznan, 12 Aug 1853; d Langebrück, near Dresden, 5 Oct 1919), German–Polish conductor and composer. The family having moved to Berlin in 1856, Nicodé studied there, first under his father and from 1869 at the Neue Akademie der Tonkunst. Afterwards he taught there and arranged concerts at which he appeared as pianist, toured in the Balkans with Désirée Artot and in 1878 became professor at the Dresden Conservatory. From 1885 he devoted himself to conducting and composition.

Works include symphonic ode *Das Meer* for solo voices, male chorus, orchestra and organ (1889); symphonic poems *Maria Stuart* (after Schiller, 1880), *Die Jagd nach dem Glück*, *Gloria*, symphonic variations, etc., for orchestra; romance for violin and orchestra; cello and piano sonata; sonata and numerous pieces for piano; songs, including cycle *Dem Andenken an Amarantha* (1886); male-voice choruses.

Nicolai, (Carl) Otto (Ehrenfried) (b Königsberg, 9 Jun 1810; d Berlin, 11 May 1849), German composer and conductor. Studied the piano as a child, but was so unhappy at home that in 1826 he ran away and was sent to Berlin by a patron the following year for study under Zelter and Klein. In 1833 another patron sent him to Rome as organist in the Prussian Embassy chapel, and there he studied under Baini. He returned there after a year at the Kärntnertortheater in Vienna, 1837–38. He became court *Kapellmeister* in Vienna in 1841 and founded the Philharmonic concerts there in 1842. In 1847 he became director of the cathedral choir and the Court Opera in Berlin, where he died of a stroke, two months after the production of his *Merry Wives of Windsor*; after initial rejection, this soon became his most popular opera, and is still often heard in Germany.

Works include operas *Enrico II* (later *Rosmonda d'Inghilterra*, 1839), *Il templario* (1840), *Odoardo e Gildippe*, *Il proscritto* (later *Die Heimkehr des Verbannten*, 1841), *Die lustigen Weiber von Windsor* (after Shakespeare, 1849); Mass for Frederick William IV of Prussia, Requiem, Te Deum; Symphonic Festival Overture on 'Ein' feste Burg' for the jubilee of Königsberg University.

Nicolai, Elena (b Sofia, 26 Sept 1905), Bulgarian mezzo. Debut (as E Stolanka) in Malta as Verdi's Maddalena. She sang at Naples from 1938 and at Verona was successful from 1946 as Amneris, Laura and Ortrud; sang in the fp of Pizzetti's *La Figlia di Jorio* (1954) and as guest in Paris, Buenos Aires and Cairo. At Florence she was heard as Handel's Cornelia and as Satire in Spontini's *Olympie*.

Nicolai, Philipp (b Mengeringhausen, 10 Aug 1556; d Hamburg, 26 Oct 1608), German pastor, poet and amateur musician. In 1599 he pub. a hymnbook, *Freudenspiegel des ewigen Lebens*, containing the tunes of 'Wachet auf' and 'Wie schön leuchtet der Morgenstern'.

Nicolaus de Cracovia 16th-c. Polish organist and composer in the service of the royal court. Organ music by him is included in two MSS: that of Jan of Lublin (1537–48) and the Kraków Tablature (1548).

Nicolescu, Marianna (b Gavjani, 28 Nov 1948), Romanian soprano. Studied in Rome and with Elisabeth Schwarzkopf. Sang Violetta at Florence 1976, Gilda and Nedda at the NY Met 1978. La Scala, Milan, debut in Berio's *La vera storia* (1982) and *Un re in ascolto*, as Donna Elvira, and in Rossi's *Orfeo* and Jommelli's *Fetonte*. Salzburg Festival 1990, as Mozart's Elettra. Donizetti roles include Maria di Rohan and Elizabeth I (Monte Carlo, 1992).

Nicolet, Aurèle (b Neuchâtel, 22 Jan 1926), Swiss flautist. Studied in Zurich and Paris and was principal of the Berlin PO 1950–59. Salzburg Festival debut 1958 (Mozart's concerto K314). Soloist with leading orchestras and chamber musician in works by Bach and other Baroque composers. Has premiered works by Denisov, C Halffter (concerto, 1983), Holliger, Klaus Huber and Ligeti (Double concerto, 1972).

Nicolini, Ernest (b St Malo, 23 Feb 1834; d Pau, 19 Jan 1898), French tenor. Debut Paris, Opéra-Comique, 1857, in Halévy's *Les mousquetaires*. He sang at La Scala from 1859, as Alfredo and Rossini's Rodrigo, and at CG and Drury Lane from 1866; the first London Lohengrin and Radames (1875, 1876). Also successful as Edgardo, Faust and Roméo. He first sang with Patti in 1866; married her 1886, after tours with her in Europe and USA.

Nicolini, Nicola Grimaldi (b Naples, bap. 5 Apr 1673; d Naples, 1 Jan 1732), Italian castrato. First appearance in Rome, about 1694; sang in

A Selection of

Nielsen

Symphony no. 1	1892
Saul og David	1902
Symphony no. 2	1902
Maskarade	1906

Symphony no. 3	1911
Violin Concerto	1911
Symphony no. 4	1916
Aladdin	1918–19
Symphony no. 5	1922
Clarinet Concerto	1928

Naples 1697–1724, often in operas by A Scarlatti. First went to England in 1708 and sang the title role in Handel's *Rinaldo* in 1711; created Amadigi in 1715. He returned to Italy in 1718.

Niedermeyer, (Abraham) Louis (b Nyon, Vaud, 27 Apr 1802; d Paris, 14 Mar 1861), Swiss composer and educationist. Studied in Vienna, Rome and Naples, settled as music teacher at Geneva and went to Paris in 1823, settling there after a brief teaching period at Brussels. In Paris he took over Choron's school of music and called it École de Musique Religieuse Classique.

Works include operas *Il reo per amore* (1820), *La casa nel bosco* (1828), *Stradella* (1837), *Marie Stuart* (after Schiller, 1844), *La Fronde* (1853); numerous Masses, motets and anthems; songs to words by Lamartine (e.g. *Le Lac*), Hugo and Deschamps.

Nielsen, Alice (b Nashville, 7 Jun 1876; d New York, 8 Mar 1943), American soprano. Sang in operetta at St Paul and San Francisco from 1893; Shaftesbury Theatre, London, from 1901. Opera debut Naples 1903, as Marguerite. CG 1904, Zerlina. She sang Norina in NY, 1905, and was popular in Boston and at the NY Met. 1909–13 (debut as Mimi). Reverted to operetta 1917.

I think through the instruments themselves, almost as if I had crept inside them.

Carl Nielsen, *Politiken*, 1925

Nielsen, Carl (August) (b Nørre-Lyndelse, near Odense, 9 Jun 1865; d Copenhagen, 3 Oct 1931), Danish composer and conductor. Being poor as a youth, he joined a military band at the age of 14, but at 18 succeeded in entering the Copenhagen Conservatory as a pupil of Gade. In 1891 he entered the royal orchestra and was its conductor 1908–14. He also became conductor of the Music Society and director of the Conservatory. One of the most remarkable late Romantic symphonists, combining traditional forms with a new and original approach to tonality; the first symphony is an example of progressive tonality, ending in a different key to the initial one. Later symphonies developed a complex, rhythmically driven polyphony. The third symphony, *Espansiva*, is the first of these great works in which thematic transformation is achieved within closely-controlled forms. In the fifth symphony, chaos is threatened by a side drummer who is instructed to obliterate the rest of the orchestra; order is restored in a triumphant conclusion.

Works include operas *Saul og David* (1902), *Maskarade* (after

Holberg, 1906); incidental music for Oehlenschäger's *Aladdin* and many other plays; *Hymnus Amoris* for chorus and orchestra (1897); *Springtime on Fyn* for soloists, chorus and orchestra (1922); *Hymn to Art* for vocal soloists and wind instruments (1929); three motets for unaccompanied chorus.

Six symphonies 1. in G minor (1892), 2. *The Four Temperaments* (1902), 3. *Espansiva* (1911), 4. *The Inextinguishable* (1916), 5. (1922), 6. *Sinfonia semplice* (1925), *Saga-Dream*, symphonic rhapsody for orchestra; violin concerto (1911), flute concerto (1926), *An Imaginary Journey to the Faroes*, rhapsody (1927), clarinet concerto (1928). Four string quartets (1887–1919), two string quintets, wind quintet (1922) and other chamber music; two violin and piano sonatas; *Commotio* for organ (1931); suites and other piano works; songs.

Nielsen, Hans (b ? Roskilde, *c* 1580; d ? Copenhagen, *c* 1626), Danish lutenist and composer. After learning music as choirboy in the royal chapel at Copenhagen, he studied with G Gabrieli at Venice between 1599 and 1606, and 1606–08 with the English lutenist Richard Howett at Wolfenbüttel. After that he was lutenist at the Danish court until 1611, when he was dismissed and went to Heidelberg University. In 1623 he was appointed vice-director of the royal chapel in succession to Pedersøln.

Nielsen, Inge (b Holboeke, Seeland, 2 Jun 1946), Danish soprano. Studied in Vienna and sang widely in Switzerland and Germany, following her debut at Gelsenkirchen, 1973; roles included Blondchen, Norina and Zerlina. NY City Opera 1980, as Nannetta and Adele in *Die Fledermaus*. Created Minette in Henze's *The English Cat* at Schwetzingen (1983) and sang Amenaide in *Tancredi* at the 1986 Wexford Festival. CG debut 1987, as Constanze, and sang Aspasia in Mozart's *Mitridate* at Munich, 1990. Gilda at Oslo, 1992.

Nielsen, Ludolf (b Nørre Tvede, 29 Jan 1876; d Copenhagen, 16 Oct, 1939), Danish conductor and composer. Studied at the Copenhagen Conservatory, became conductor at the Tivoli and the Palace until 1909.

Works include operas, *Isabella* (1915), *The Clock*, *Lola* (after Victor Hugo, 1920); ballet *Lakschmi*; three symphonies (1903–13), three symphonic poems, two suites and concert overture for orchestra; three string quartets; piano pieces; songs.

Nielsen, Riccardo (b Bologna, 3 Mar 1908; d Ferrara, 30 Jan 1982), Italian composer of Scandinavian descent. Studied at the Liceo Musicale of Bologna and at Salzburg, and was influenced by Casella.

Works include monodrama *L'Incubo* (1948), radio opera *La via di Colombo* (1953); incidental music for *Maria ed il Nazzareno*; Psalms for male voices and orchestra (1941); concerto for orchestra (1936), two symphonies (1933, 1935); capriccio and *Sinfonia concertante* for piano and orchestra, violin concerto (1932); divertimento for bassoon, trumpet, violin, viola and cello, trio for oboe, bassoon and horn (1934), Adagio and Allegro for cello and 11 instruments; sonatas for violin and piano and cello and piano; *Musica* for two pianos (1939), sonata and *ricercare*, chorale and toccata on BACH for piano; *Laude di Jacopone da Todi* and *Tre satire di Giusti* for voice and piano.

Niemann, Albert (b Erxleben, Magdeburg, 15 Jan 1831; d Berlin, 13 Jan 1917), German tenor. After a precarious beginning on the stage at Dessau, he was discovered by F Schneider, the court music director, and given some lessons, and was also taught by a singer. He gradually obtained better engagements and was sent to Paris by the King of Hanover to study under Duprez. In 1866–88 he was court opera singer in Berlin and in 1876 Wagner chose him to create the part of Siegmund in the *Ring* at Bayreuth; he had sung the title role in the Paris production of *Tannhäuser*, 1861. NY Met. 1886–88, as the first US Siegfried and Tristan.

niente Italian = 'nothing'; the word is generally used in connection with *quasi* (so to speak, almost) when extreme softness of tone is required.

Nietzsche, Friedrich (1844–1900), German philosopher and author. He met Wagner in 1868 and celebrated the ideals of Wagnerian music-drama in *Das Geburt des Tragödie aus dem Geiste der Musik* (1871). However, personal differences culminated in the essay *Der Fall*

Wagner/The Case of Wagner, 1988, in which Nietzsche rejects principal foundations of Romantic music, and specifically Wagner's, turning instead to Bizet as an example to be followed. In later years Nietzsche suffered a nervous collapse brought on by syphilis.

◊Also sprach Zaŧathustra (R Strauss); ◊Mass of Life (Delius); ◊Mahler (third symphony); ◊Medtner (songs); ◊Reznicek (*Ruhm und Ewigkeit*); ◊Rihm (third symphony).

Nigg, Serge (b Paris, 6 Jun 1924), French composer. Studied under Messiaen at the Paris Conservatory, but in 1946 adopted the 12-note technique under the influence of Leibowitz, with which he in turn came to disagree two years later.

Works include melodrama *Perséphone* (1942); symphonic movement for orchestra *Timour* (1944), *La Mort d'Arthus* for voice and orchestra; piano concerto, *Concertino* for piano, wind and percussion; *Jérôme Bosch-Symphonie* (1960); variations for piano and ten instruments; two piano concertos (1954, 1971); sonata and *Fantaisie* for piano, etc.

Night at the Chinese Opera, A opera in three acts by Judith Weir (libretto by composer, based in part on Chi-Chun-Hsiang's *The Chao Family Orphan*), produced Cheltenham, Everyman Theatre, 8 Jul 1987. Chao Liu is in exile after the invasion by Kublai Khan, but after an earthquake interrupts a play which runs parallel to the course of his life, he is arrested. Although the play ends happily Chao is executed.

Nightingale, The, *Soloveg*, opera by Stravinsky (libretto by composer and S N Mitusov, from Hans Andersen's fairy-tale), produced Paris, Opéra, 26 May 1914; revived in the form of a ballet (choreography by Leonid Massin), Paris, Opéra, 2 Feb 1920. Dying Emperor is revived by the sound of the nightingale.

Night on the Bare Mountain a work in various forms by Mussorgsky, more properly called *St John's Night on the Bare Mountain*, based on the incident of the witches' sabbath in Gogol's story *St John's Eve*; composed as a symphonic poem for orchestra 1866–67; later used in a version for chorus and orchestra and called *Night on Mount Triglav* in 1872 as part of the opera *Mlada* commissioned from Mussorgsky, Borodin, Cui and Rimsky-Korsakov, but never completed; revised version of this used as introduction to Act III of the unfinished opera *Sorotchinsty Fair*, began in 1875; this last version revised and arranged as an orchestral piece by Rimsky-Korsakov after Mussorgsky's death.

Nights in the Gardens of Spain (Falla.) ◊*Noches en los jardines de España.*

Nikisch, Arthur (b Lébényi Szant Miklos, 12 Oct 1855; d Leipzig, 23 Jan 1922), Hungarian-German conductor. Studied in Vienna and played the violin in the court orchestra 1874–77. He was conductor at the Leipzig Opera 1878–89. Subsequent posts included the Boston SO, 1889–93, Budapest Opera, 1893–95, Leipzig Gewandhaus, from 1895, and the Berlin PO. He conducted the fp of Bruckner's seventh symphony (1884) and in 1913 gave Wagner's *Ring* at CG, London.

Nikkanen, Kurt (b Hartford, CT, Dec 1965), American violinist. Studied at Juilliard with Dorothy DeLay and made Carnegie Hall debut 1978; Paganini's 1st Concerto with the New York PO 1980. European debut with recital tour of Finland, 1981. UK debut 1988 with the Elgar Concerto at Liverpool; London debut with the Glazunov Concerto, 1991.

Nikolayeva, Tatiana (b Bezhiza, 4 May 1924; d San Francisco, 22 Nov 1993), Russian pianist and composer. Studied in Moscow and taught at the Conservatory from 1959. First prize at 1950 Leipzig Bach Festival and following year premiered the 24 Preludes and Fugues by Shostakovich. UK debut Leeds 1984, London 1986 (later played Bach's Goldberg Variations and Art of Fugue there). Compositions include two piano concertos and a piano quintet.

Nilsson, Birgit (b Karup, 17 May 1918), Swedish soprano. Studied in Stockholm, making her debut in 1946 and becoming a member of the Swedish Royal Opera in 1947. Sang in operas by Wagner, Strauss and Verdi, British debut Glyndebourne, 1951, as Electra in *Idomeneo*; CG from 1957 as Brünnhilde, Isolde, Turandot and Elektra. Bayreuth 1954–70. NY Met. debut 1959, as Isolde. Other roles include Amelia,

Aida, Salome and the Dyer's Wife. Last stage appointment 1982. The leading post-war Wagnerian soprano.

Nilsson, Bo (b Skellefteå, 1 May 1937), Swedish composer. Largely self-taught, he has belonged to the younger generation of avant-garde composers.

Works include *Songs on the Death of Children* for soprano and small orchestra; *Moments of Time* for ten wind instruments; *Frequencies* for chamber ensemble; *A Prodigal Son* for contralto, alto flute and chamber ensemble; *Reactions* for percussion quartet (1960); *Audiograms* for electronic generators; *Quantities* for piano *Attraktionen* for string quartet (1968), *Madonna* for mezzo and ensemble (1977); Piano Quintet (1979); *Wendepunkt* for brass and electronics (1981); *Autumn Song* for baritone and orchestra (1985); *Vagues pour Madame Curie* for soprano and orchestra (1993).

Nilsson, Kristina (Christine) (b Sjöabol, near Vexiö, 20 Aug 1843; d Stockholm, 22 Nov 1921), Swedish soprano. Studied at Stockholm and Paris, and after several appearances in Sweden she made her debut in Paris in 1864 as Violetta, and first went to London the same year where she married Auguste Rouzeaud in 1872. In 1877 she married Count Casa Miranda. She created Thomas' Ophelia (1868) and sang Marguerite at the opening of the NY Met. (1883). Other roles included Lucia (CG 1869), Mignon and Laura.

Nilsson, Sven (b Gavle, 11 May 1898; d Stockholm, 1 Mar 1970), Swedish bass. Studied with Ivar Andrésen and sang at the Dresden Staatsoper 1930–44; created Peneios in Strauss's *Daphne* (1938) and was a distinguished Ochs, Sarastro and Osmin. He sang Pogner and other Wagner roles at Zoppot, 1934–42. CG 1936–37. NY Met. debut 1950, as Daland. At the Royal Opera, Stockholm, from 1946 until his death, just after a performance of *Les Contes d'Hoffmann*.

Nimsgern, Siegmund (b St Wendel, 14 Jan 1940), German bass-baritone. Studied at Saarbrucken and was a member of the Staatstheater there 1971–74; Deutsche Oper, Düsseldorf, from 1975. He was Mephistopheles in a concert performance of the Berlioz *Faust*, London 1972, and sang Amfortas at CG in 1973; returned as Dapertutto in a new production of *Les Contes d'Hoffmann*. He has sung in North America from 1973; NY Met. debut 1978, Pizarro. Well known in the sacred music of Bach, Haydn, Pergolesi and Telemann. His Wotan in the 1983 Solti–Hall *Ring*, at Bayreuth, was much discussed. Sang Telramund at Frankfurt, 1991.

Nin (y Castellanos), Joaquín (b Havana, 29 Sept 1878; d Havana, 24 Oct 1949), Spanish pianist, musicologist and composer. Studied at Barcelona and in Paris, where in 1906 he became piano professor at the Schola Cantorum. After short periods in Berlin and Cuba, he settled in Brussels and later in Paris again. He edited much old Spanish music and wrote three books.

Works include mimodrama *L'Autre*, ballet *L'Écharpe bleue*; violin pieces; piano works; songs.

Nina, o sia La pazza per amore, *Nina, or the Lunatic from Love*, opera by Paisiello (libretto by G Carpani, with additions by G B Lorenzi, based on the French libretto by B J Marsollier), produced Naples, Caserta Palace, for the visit of Queen Maria Carolina of Sicily, 25 Jun 1789; first public performance Naples, Teatro Fiorentino, 1790. Nina is engaged to Lindoro but her father cancels the wedding plans when a rich suitor arrives. Lindoro fights a duel with him and is shot. Nina goes mad, but recovers her sanity when he revives.

Nin-Culmell, Joaquin (Maria) (b Berlin, 5 Sept 1908), American composer and pianist of Cuban descent. Studied in Paris with Dukas and Falla and was concert pianist 1930–50; conductor from 1940. Resident in USA from 1938, teacher at Berkeley 1950–74.

Works include opera *Celestina* (1965–80), Mass (1970), cello concertos for cello and piano, *El Burlador de Sevilla* and *La Rêve de Cyrano* (ballets), incidental music for Shakespeare's *Cymbeline*, 48 *Tonadas* for piano.

ninth the interval a whole tone larger than an octave (major ninth) or a semitòne larger (minor ninth).

Ninth Symphony (Beethoven.) ◊'Choral' Symphony.

Nissen, Georg Nikolaus (b Haderslev, 22 Jan 1761; d Salzburg, 24 Mar

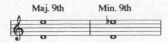

Major and minor ninths.

1826), Danish diplomat and author. He married Mozart's widow in 1809. His important biography of Mozart, incorporating many of Mozart's letters, was pub. posthumously in 1828.

Nissen, Hans Hermann (b Zippnow, near Danzig, 20 May 1893; d Munich, 28 Mar 1980), German bass-baritone. Debut Berlin 1924, as the Caliph in *Der Barbier von Bagdad*. Munich 1925–67 as Almaviva, Renato, Barak and Iago. London, CG, 1928 and 1934 as Sachs and Wotan. NY Met. debut 1938, as Wotan. He sang Sachs under Toscanini at Salzburg in 1936 and recorded Act III of *Die Meistersinger* under Böhm the following year.

Nivers, Guillaume (Gabriel) (b Melun, *c* 1631; d Paris, 30 Dec 1714), French organist, harpsichordist, theorist and composer. Pupil of Chambonnières in Paris and organist of the church of Saint-Sulpice in 1654, also appointed organist to the king in 1678 and music master to the queen. He wrote a treatise on singing, and others.

Works include motets and other church music.

Nixon, Marni (b Altadena, CA, 22 Feb 1930), American soprano. Studied at UCLA and the Berkshire Music Center. Worked in Hollywood and provided the singing voices for the leads in *The King and I*, *West Side Story* and *My Fair Lady*. Opera appearances in Los Angeles, San Francisco and Seattle as Blondchen, Constanze, Zerbinetta and Violetta. Recordings include the complete vocal works of Webern, conducted by Robert Craft.

Nixon in China opera in two acts by John Adams (libretto by Alice Goodman), produced Houston, Grand Opera, 22 Oct 1987. Media-conscious Dick and wife Pat are impressed by Chairman Mao. Nixon is portrayed as a superficial character, in contrast to the revolutionary Mao.

Nobilissima Visione dance legend (ballet) in six scenes by Hindemith (choreography by composer and Massine on story of St Francis), produced Drury Lane, London, 21 Jul 1938. Orchestral-Suite in three movements performed Venice, 13 Sept 1938.

Noble, Dennis (b Bristol, 23 Sept 1899; d Jávea, Spain, 14 Mar 1966), English baritone. Educated as a chorister at Bristol Cathedral, he became a member of Covent Garden Opera in 1938. He sang the solo at the fp of Walton's *Belshazzar's Feast* (Leeds, 1931). Often heard in Verdi, Puccini and Bizet.

Noble, (Thomas) Tertius (b Bath, 5 May 1867; d Rockport, MA, 4 May 1953), English organist and composer. In 1881 he went to Colchester, where he received his education from the rector of All Saints Church, who also made him organist there. In 1886 he entered the RCM in London, styding under Parratt, Bridge and Stanford, and later he joined the staff. After two smaller appointments he became organist at Ely Cathedral in 1892 and at York Minister in 1898, but went to NY in 1912 as organist and conductor; St Thomas's Church until 1947.

Works include incidental music for Aristophanes' *Wasps*; services and other church music, *The Sound of War*, *Gloria Domini* and other choral works; orchestral works; chamber music.

Noces, Les (Stravinsky.) ◊Wedding.

Noches en los jardines de España, *Nights in the Gardens of Spain*, symphonic impressions for piano and orchestra by Falla, begun 1909, finished 1915. Fp Madrid, 9 Apr 1916. There are three movements: 1. *En el Generalife*; 2 *Danza lejana/Dance in the distance*); 3. *En los jardines de la Sierra de Córdoba.*

Nöcker, Hans Gunter (b Hagen, 22 Jan 1927), German bass-baritone. Studied in Munich and made debut in Munster 1953 as Alfio. Has sung widely in Germany, notably in the fps of Egk's *Die Verlobung in San Domingo* (Munich 1963), Fortner's *Elizabeth Tudor* (Berlin 1972) and Reimann's *Gespenstersonate* (Berlin 1984). Guest in London, Florence, Venice (Klingsor, 1983) and Schwetzingen (in Gluck's *Armide*).

Nocturne song cycle for tenor, seven obbligato instruments and strings by Britten (texts, all about night, by Shelley, Tennyson, Coleridge, Middleton, Wordsworth, Owen, Keats and Shakespeare), fp Leeds, 16 Oct 1958, with Pears.

nocturne, French, a 'night piece' or instrumental serenade, generally of a quiet, lyrical character, but sometimes (as in Chopin) with a more agitated middle section. As a piano piece it originated with Field, but the name (*notturno*) was used already in 18th-c. Italy to designate a piece of music similar to the serenade or divertimento in several movements. The nocturne in the modern sense is not necessarily slow, soft and sentimental. *Fêtes* in Debussy's work is a very animated piece; in Vaughan Williams's *London Symphony* the scherzo is a nocturne, i.e. a piece suggesting London's life by night.

Nocturnes three orchestral pieces by Debussy, *Nuages*, *Fêtes* and *Sirènes*, the last with female chorus, composed 1893–99, fp Paris, 9 Dec 1900 (nos. 1 and 2); 27 Oct 1901 (complete).

node from Latin *nodus* = 'knot'; the point in a vibrating string at which the vibration becomes cut into segments.

Nola, Domenico da (Joan Domenico del Giovane) (b Nola, Naples, *c* 1510; d Naples, 5 May 1592), Italian composer. *Maestro di cappella* of the church of the Annunciation at Naples, 1563–88. Composed motets, madrigals, *villanelle*, etc.

nonet a composition for nine instruments, usually in several movements.

Non nobis Domine a canon for voices, ? by Byrd, often sung in England for 'grace' after public dinners. It is a riddle canon capable of being sung with the entries in various positions, also in inversion.

Nono, Luigi (b Venice, 29 Jan 1924; d Venice, 8 May 1990), Italian composer, whose work was initially performed principally in Germany. He studied with Scherchen, who conducted his *Polifonia-monodiaritmica* at Darmstadt in 1951. He married a daughter of Schoenberg, whose music had a strong influence on him.

Works include opera-oratorio *Intolleranza* (1961); *Variazioni canoniche* on a theme of Schoenberg's (from *Ode to Napoleon*), *Due espressioni* and *Diario polacco '58* for orchestra; *Canti* for 13 instruments, *Incontri* for 24 instruments, *Il canto sospeso* (1956) and other choral works include *La Victoire de Guernica*, *Epitaph I for F Garcia Lorca*, *Cori di Didone*.

Cantata *Sul ponte di Hiroshima* for soprano and tenor and orchestra (1962); *La Fabbrica illuminata* for mezzo and electronic tape; *Epitaphs II & III for F Garcia Lorca* (II for flute, strings and percussion, III for speaker, speaking chorus and orchestra); opera *Al gran sole carico d'amore* (1974), electronic music including *Omaggio a Emilio Vedova*, (1960), *Sofferte onde serene* (1976); *Quando stanno morendo* for voices and ensemble (1982).

Noonday Witch, The, Czech *Polednice*, symphonic poem by Dvořák, op. 108; composed 1896, fp London, 21 Nov 1896.

Noordt, Anthony van (d Amsterdam, buried 23 Mar 1675), Dutch organist and composer. Organist of the Nieuwe Kerk at Amsterdam in 1659, when he pub. a book of organ works in tablature, including variations on French psalm tunes and fugal fantasies.

Norberg-Schulz, Elisabeth (b Oslo, Jan 1959), Norwegian soprano. After study in Rome and Zurich sang *Les Illuminations* at Aldeburgh, 1981. Sang Musetta in Japan with company of La Scala (1988), Barbarina at the Rome Opera (1989) and Mozart's Ilia at Florence. Salzburg Mozartwoche 1991, as Pamina; CG debut 1994, as Liú in *Turandot.*

Norcome, Daniel (b Windsor, 1576; d Windsor, before 1626), English singer and composer. He went to the Danish court in his early 20s, but fled from Copenhagen to Germany, Hungary and Venice *c* 1600. Later he became a lay-clerk at St George's Chapel, Windsor, but lost that post on turning Roman Catholic and went to Brussels as an instrumental player to the viceregal chapel.

Works include viol pieces; madrigal contributed to *The Triumphes of Oriana.*

Nordgren, Pehr Henrik (b Saltvik, 19 Jan 1944), Finnish composer. Studied at Helsinki and Tokyo Universities (traditional Japanese music). Works include chamber opera *The Black Monk* (1981); orchestral series *Euphone I-IV* (1967–81); three violin concertos

(1969, 1977, 1981), three viola concertos (1970, 1979, 1986), two symphonies (1974, 1989), two cello concertos (1980, 1983), five string quartets (1967–86), piano quintet (1978), piano trio (1983).

Nordheim, Arne (b Larvik, 20 Jun 1931), Norwegian composer. Studied in Oslo and with Holmboe in Copenhagen. Active as performer and composer of electronic music from 1968.

Works include ballets *Ariadne* (1977), *The Tempest* (1979) and *The End of Time* (1981); *Favola*, musical play for TV (1965), *Colorazione* (1968), *Pace* (1970) and *Osaka-Music* (1970) for electronic instruments; *Be Not Afeared*, for soprano, baritone and ensemble (1978); *Tenebrae* for cello and orchestra (1982), *Varder* for trumpet and orchestra (1986), *Rendezvous* for strings (1987); chamber and choral music.

Nordica, Lilian (actually Lillian Norton) (b Farmington, ME, 12 May 1857; d Batavia, Java, 10 May 1914), American soprano. Studied at Boston and, after successful concert appearances in USA and England, made her first stage appearance at Milan in 1879 as Donna Elvira. US debut Boston 1885; NY Met. debut 1895 as Valentine. London, CG and Drury Lane, 1887–1902 as Lucia, Aida, Donna Anna, Isolde and Brünnhilde.

Nordin, Lena (b Malmø, 18 Feb 1956), Swedish soprano. Studied in Stockholm and sang Rameau's Aricie at the Swedish Baroque Festival, 1984. Royal Opera Stockholm from 1986, as Luisa Miller, Cleopatra, Donna Anna and Maria Stuarda (1990). Wexford Festival and London 1988–89 in Mercadante's *Elisa e Claudio* and Mozart's *Mitridate*. Stockholm 1991, in the modern premiere of Naumann's *Gustav Wase*. Many concert appearances.

Norena, Eidé (b Horten, near Oslo, 26 Apr 1884; d Lausanne, 19 Nov 1968), Norwegian soprano. She studied with Gulbranson and made her stage debut in Oslo as Amor (1907); sang in Stockholm until 1924, then gave Gilda at La Scala, under Toscanini. CG 1924–37, as Desdemona, Violetta and Olympia. At Chicago in 1926 she sang in the fp of Cadman's *A Witch of Salem*. NY Met. 1933–38, debut as Mimi. At the Paris Opéra, 1925–37, she was successful in operas by Meyerbeer, Rimsky-Korsakov and Rossini.

Norgård, Per (b Gentofte, 13 Jul 1932), Danish composer. Studied with Holmboe and Boulanger; has taught at Aarhus from 1965. An early influence was Sibelius, later turned to 'infinite' serialism, pointillism and graphic notation.

Works include operas *The Labyrinth* (1967), *Gilgamesh* (1973), *Siddharta* (1983), *The Divine Tivoli* (1983); four symphonies (1954–81); *Illuminationi* for orchestra (1984); cello concerto (1985), *Helle Nacht* violin concerto (1987); *Pastorale* for strings (1988); *Spaces of Time* for piano and ensemble (1991); *Scintillation* for instruments (1993); seven string quartets (1958–93).

Norma

A two-act tragic opera by Vincenzo Bellini, written in 1831. The action is set in Gaul, during the Roman occupation of the country.
I. The Druid high priestess, Norma (soprano), is in love with the Roman proconsul, Pollione (tenor), and has secretly had two sons by him. Pollione meanwhile has fallen for the acolyte Adalgisa (soprano), and wishes to take her back to Rome with him. Norma's father Oroveso (bass), together with other druids and Gauls, wishes for war against the Romans, but Norma counsels peace. She has protected Pollione, but now learns of his true intention.
II. While Norma debates over killing her sons, Adalgisa fails to persuade Pollione to return to the priestess. Norma incites rebellion against the Romans, and Pollione is sentenced to death after he is captured near the forbidden Druids' temple. Having entrusted her children to Oroveso, Norma offers herself as a replacement for Pollione. They are finally both consigned to the flames of a funeral pyre.

Norman *The soprano Jessye Norman in 1992. Since her debut as Elisabeth (*Tannhäuser*) in 1969, she has applied her beautiful, flexible voice to a variety of works ranging from Mozart to Verdi and Wagner. She has also pursued a highly successful concert career.*

Norma opera by Bellini (libretto by F Romani, based on L A Soumet's tragedy), produced Milan, La Scala, 26 Dec 1831. Druid priestess Norma still loves Roman consul Pollione after he abandons her for another priestess, Adalgisa. Jealousy and rivalry result in the deaths of both Norma and Pollione.

Norman, (Fredrik Vilhelm) Ludvig (b Stockholm, 28 Aug 1831; d Stockholm, 28 Mar 1885), Swedish pianist, conductor and composer. Pub. a book of songs at the age of 11, was left a poor orphan, but enabled by patrons, including Jenny Lind, to study at the Leipzig Conservatory. In 1851 his first piano work was pub. at Schumann's instigation. Returning to Stockholm in 1861, he became conductor of the royal opera, which he conducted until 1879, and was conductor of the symphonic concerts to his death. In 1864 he married the violinist Wilma Neruda.

Works include incidental music to Shakespeare's *Antony and Cleopatra*; three symphonies (1858, 1874, 1885), four overtures; chamber music, including six string quartets; instrumental sonatas; piano works; songs.

Norman, Jessye (b Augusta, 15 Sept 1945), American soprano. She studied at the University of Michigan and made her stage debut in Berlin in 1969 as Elisabeth. She sang Aida at La Scala in 1972 and Cassandre in *Les Troyens* at CG the same year, the latter being also the role of her NY Met. debut in 1983. She returned to CG in 1985, as Ariadne. Well known in performances of Lieder and in concerts, she has sung Berg's aria *Der Wein* and the Berlioz song cycle *Les Nuits d'été*.

Norman, John, English 15th–16th-c. organist and composer. He was master of the choristers, St David's Cathedral, 1509–22; he was at Eton, 1534–45.

Works include Masses, e.g. Mass in five parts, on an Easter plainsong, motets, etc.

Norman-Neruda, Wilma, ◊Neruda.

Norrington, Roger (b Oxford, 16 Mar 1934), English conductor. He studied at the RCM with Boult and performed as a tenor 1962–70.

David Owen Norris – pianist

1 Dunstable: *O rosa bella* (song for unaccompanied voices)
   Haydn to Dufay's Mozart, Dunstable was at the centre of
   Continental attention. The English were throwing their
   weight around in France in other ways too, burning Joan of
   Arc at the stake.

2 Purcell: *A New Scotch Tune* (from *Music's Handmaid* for
   harpsichord)
   I don't know whether this is a folk melody, but the endlessly
   subtle harmonization could only be Purcell's.

3 Haydn: Fantasia in C major for piano
   This witty piece plays with all the listener's expectations,
   and arranges triple rhythms in as many ways as you could
   imagine. Haydn told his publisher that he wasn't sure if the
   public would like it, but he jolly well did.

4 Fauré: Piano Quartet no. 1 in C minor for piano and strings
   A youthful work which unites force and grace in wonderful
   tunes and harmony. When you've got used to the style, the
   Second Quartet's even better.

5 Ives: Sonata no. 2 (*Concord*) for piano
   Ives was working on this during World War I, but the 20th
   century hasn't caught up with him yet. He was so
   straightforward in his thought that he seems eccentric to the
   twisted majority. Someone once asked him how this Sonata
   'should go', and he answered 'If you've been digging
   potatoes, play like you've been digging potatoes.'

6 Walton: *Belshazzar's Feast* for chorus, brass bands and
   orchestra
   I first heard this, sad to say, in my late thirties, and I couldn't
   believe what I'd been missing. Try to hear it live at a
   concert.

Founded the Schütz Choir 1962, succeeded by the Schütz Choir of London. Music director Kent Opera 1968–84; has given Monteverdi's three principal operas in his own editions. US debut Oakland 1974. In 1985 he conducted at the RCM the first stage performance in Britain of Rameau's tragédie-lyrique *Les Boréades*. From 1985 he has given London weekend 'experiences' devoted to single composers: Mozart, Beethoven, Haydn, Berlioz and Purcell.

Norris, David Owen (b Northampton, England, 16 Jun 1953), English pianist and broadcaster. Studied at Oxford and Paris. Professor, RAM 1978–; artistic director, Cardiff Festival, 1992–; Chairman of Faculty, Steans Institute for Singers, Chicago, 1992–; Gresham Professor of Music 1993–. Television appearances across Europe and North America, and performances at the Promenade concerts. First-ever Gilmore Artist, 1991.

Norris, William (b *c* 1669; d ? Lincoln, Jul 1710), English singer and composer. Choirboy in the Chapel Royal in London, later a singer there and choirmaster at Lincoln Cathedral from 1690.
     Works include services and anthems; Ode for St Cecilia's Day.

North, Nigel (b London, 1954), English lutenist and guitarist. Studied at the GSMD (1964–70) and RCM (1971–4). Performances from 1973 with the Academy of Ancient Music (Hogwood), Schütz Choir (Norrington), Kent Opera, English Concert (Pinnock) and The Sixteen (Harry Christophers). Solo debut at Wigmore Hall 1977; all Bach lute works for first time in London, 1985. Bach recitals in USA and throughout Europe. Summer Academies with the Lute Society of America, 1980–88; master-classes in New York and San Francisco.

Many persons come to hear that single voice, who care not for all the rest, especially if it be a fair Lady.
Roger North, *The Musicall Gramarian*, c. 1728

North, Roger (Hon.) (b Tostock, Suffolk, 3 Sept 1653; d Rougham, 1 Mar 1734), English lawyer and amateur musician, brother of Francis North, Lord Guilford (1637–85), who was also a musician and published *A Philosophical Essay on Musick* in 1677. Roger North wrote *Memoires of Musick* including the treatise *The Musicall Gramarian*.

North Country Sketches work for orchestra in four movements by Delius; composed 1913–14, fp London, 10 May 1915, conductor Beecham.

Norup, Bent (b Hobro, 7 Dec 1936), Danish baritone. Studied in Munich and New York. Debut at Copenhagen 1970, as Kurwenal, sang in Denmark until 1973 then widely in Germany (Bayreuth 1983,

as the Wanderer in *Siegfried and Gunther*. Has sung in the USA and throughout Europe as Amfortas, Klingsor, Sachs, Iago and Scarpia. Venice 1990 and Barcelona 1992, as Telramund.

Norwich Festival a triennial music festival established at Norwich in 1824, but preceded by festivals held at irregular intervals between 1770 and 1817.

Nose, The opera by Shostakovich (libretto by A Preis, A Zamyatin, G Yonin and composer, after Gogol); 1927–28, fp Leningrad, Maly Theatre, 12 Jan 1930. Story concerns disappearance of nose belonging to government official; described by contemporary Russian critics as an example of bourgeois decadence. Barber Ivan discovers a nose in his morning bread; Major Kovalyov wakes up missing his nose. The nose later appears running aound in human size and treating everyone with contempt, as the Police Inspector chases it. Eventually it is caught and returned to Kovalyov.

nota cambiata Italian = 'changed note'; a term used in two senses in the analysis of 16th-c. polyphony: (1) a dissonant passing-note on the beat (in Palestrina only on the weak beats); (2) a curling figure (also called 'changing note group') in which a dissonant passing-note (not on the beat) leads to a note a third lower, which then rises one step.

(1)

(2)

A nota cambiata as a simple passing note (1) and as a changing note group (2).

notation the act of writing down music by means of special symbols, as by specially devised letters in Greek music, by neumes in the early Middle Ages, in tablature for old lute and organ music, in notes according to the present system, or in the special syllable form of the

Tonic Sol-fa system. Standard musical notation today follows a system that was more or less established in the 16th c., though at that time different note-values were preferred, commonly using breves and semibreves in a manner analgous to the way composers have since used minims, crotchets, or quavers (which is why modern editions of such music often have their note-values halved or quartered). As late as the 17th c. there are occasional examples of the earlier ternary-based notational systems which operated according to a complicated set of rules, in which the standard metres were ternary rather than binary. Many details and ambiguities in current musical notation can be understood only in the light of its historical development; and even the notation of standard 19th-c. works involves many ambiguities and conventions that are rarely observed today. The musicological discipline of performance practice seeks to solve these problems in the light of evidence found in composers' letters, reports of concerts, other secondary sources, and in evidence revealed by a careful study of the music itself.

Noté, Jean (b Tournai, 6 May 1859; d Brussels, 1 Apr 1922), Belgian baritone. Debut Ghent 1883; sang in Brussels, Lyons and Marseille before his debut at the Paris Opéra in 1893. He remained until his death, as Rigoletto, Thomas' Hamlet, Nelusko, Wolfram and Beckmesser. NY Met. debut 1908, as Escamillo.

note-row ◊serialism and ◊twelve-note music.

Notker Balbulus, = 'The Stammerer' (b St Gall, c 840; d St Gall, 6 Apr 912), Swiss monk and musician at the monastery of St Gall. He wrote on musical notation, the organ and the performance of plainsong, and as a composer contributed to the development of the ◊sequence.

Notker Labeo (950–St Gall, 29 Jun 1022), also known as Teutonicus, German monk at St Gall. He wrote on music and other subjects, including a short treatise in Old High German on the measurement of organ pipes.

Notot, Joseph (b Arras, 12 Feb 1751; d Paris, 24 Aug 1840), French organist and composer. Was sent to Paris as a child for his education, but was discovered as a wonderful extempore player on the organ by Leclerc, the organist of the church of Saint-Germain-des-Prés, who undertook to teach him. Later he became organist at Arras, but the Revolution drove him to England and he gave up music.

Works include four symphonies; three piano concertos; piano sonatas.

Notre Dame opera by Franz Schmidt (libretto by composer and L Wilk, after Hugo) composed 1902–04, produced Vienna, 1 Apr 1914. The well-known *Intermezzo* was performed Vienna, 6 Dec 1903.

Nottebohm, (Martin) Gustav (b Lüdenscheid, Westphalia, 12 Nov 1817; d Graz, 29 Oct 1882), German writer on music. Friend of Mendelssohn and Schumann at Leipzig; settled in Vienna, 1846. He compiled thematic catalogues of Beethoven's and Schubert's works; wrote a book on the former's sketches.

notturno Italian = 'night piece'; the 18th-c. forerunner of the nocturne, not then a single lyrical instrumental piece, but a composition in several movements similar to the serenade or divertimento. In the 19th c. it became simply the Italian equivalent of the nocturne, as for example in Mendelssohn's *Midsummer Night's Dream* music.

Nouguès, Jean (b Bordeaux, 25 Apr 1875; d Auteuil, 28 Aug 1932), French composer. Worked and produced operas at Bordeaux at first, later in Paris.

Works include operas *Le Roy du Papagey* (1890), *Thamyris* (1904), *La Mort de Tintagiles* (after Maeterlinck, 1905), *Chiquito, Quo vadis?* (after Sienkiewicz, 1909), *L'Auberge rouge* (from Balzac's *Nouveaux Contes philosophiques*), *La Vendetta* (1911), *L'Aiglon* (1912), *L'Éclaircie, Dante, Jeanne de France, Le Scarabée bleu* (1931), *Une Aventure de Villon*; ballets *La Danseuse de Pompéi* and *Narcisse*; incidental music for Rostand's *Cyrano de Bergerac*; film music, etc.

Nourrit, Adolphe (b Montpellier, 3 Mar 1802; d Naples, 8 Mar 1839), French tenor. Made his first appearance at the Paris Opéra 1821, remaining attached to that theatre for 16 years. He created roles there in Rossini's *Le siège de Corinthe* (1826), *Moïse* (1827), *Comte Ory*

(1828) and *Guillaume Tell* (1829) and in Meyerbeer's *Robert le diable* and *Les Huguenots*.

Nováček, Ottokar (b Fehertemplom, 13 May 1866; d New York, 3 Feb 1900), Hungarian violinist and composer. Studied with his father, later in Vienna and Leipzig. In the latter city he joined the string quartet of his teacher, Brodsky, as second violin and then as viola. In 1892 he went to NY and became viola leader in Damrosch's orchestra. In 1899 he retired for reasons of health and took to composition.

Works include piano concerto, *Perpetuum mobile* for violin and orchestra; three string quartets; eight caprices and other works for violin and piano; piano music; six songs to words by Tolstoy.

Novae de Infinito Laudes, New Praises of the Infinite, cantata by Henze for soloists, chorus and orchestra (text by Giordano Bruno, 1548–1600, Italian astronomer burnt at the stake by the Inquisition); composed 1962, fp Venice, 24 Apr 1963, with Söderström, Meyer, Pears and Fischer-Dieskau.

Novak, Jan (b Nova Rise na Morave, 8 Apr 1921; d Ulm, 17 Nov 1984), Czech composer. Studied at the Brno Conservatory (1940–46) and at the Prague Academy. Influenced at first by the neo-classicism of Martinů, with whom he studied in New York, but then turned to jazz and serialism.

Works include concerto for two pianos (1955), *Philharmonic Dances* for orchestra (1956), *Variations on a theme of Martinů* for orchestra (1959), *Dodo*, oratorio (1967), *Orpheus et Eurydice* for soprano, viola d'amore and piano (1971), *Ludi Concertantes* for 18 instruments (1981), *Symphonia bipartita* (1983).

Notation, the writing out of compositions, is primarily an ingenious expedient for catching an inspiration, with the purpose of exploiting it later.

Ferruccio Busoni,
Sketch of a New Aesthetic of Music, 1911

Novák, Vítězslav (b Kamenice, 5 Dec 1870; d Skuteč, 18 Jul 1949), Czech composer. He was the son of a doctor, but lost his father early and had to support the family by teaching. While studying law at Prague University he attended the Conservatory, studying piano with Jiránek and composition with Dvořák, who persuaded him to devote himself wholly to music. His first works were pub. with the help of Brahms. He soon made a career as a distinguished teacher of composition and in 1909 was appointed professor at the Conservatory. After the 1914–18 war, which restored his country's independence, he became professor of the 'Master School' and was its director 1919–22.

Works include operas *The Imp of Zvikov* (1915), *A Night at Karlstein* (1916), *The Lantern* (1923), *The Grandfather's Will* (1926), *The Wood Nymph*; ballets *Signorina Gioventù* and *Nikotina*; cantatas *The Storm, The Spectre's Bride* and choral ballads; symphony (1945), dedicated to Stalin after the liberation of Prague, symphonic poems *In the Tatra, Eternal Longing, Toman and the Wood Nymph, De profundis* (1941), overtures *The Corsair* (after Byron), *Maryša, Lady Godiva*, serenade for small orchestra; piano concerto (1895).

Two string quartets, two piano trios, piano quartet, piano quintet; *Sonata eroica, Manfred* (ballad after Byron), *Songs of Winter Nights, Pan, Exoticon*, six sonatinas, *Youth* (children's pieces), etc., for piano; song cycles *Gypsy Songs, Melancholy, In the Valley of a New Kingdom, Melancholy Songs of Love, Nocturnes, Eroticon*, and other songs; part-songs.

Novelletten German = lit. 'short stories'; a category title used by Schumann for his eight piano pieces op. 21, composed 1838, also for no. 9 of the *Bunte Blätter* for piano, op. 99.

Novello, Clara (Anastasia) (b London, 10 Jun 1818; d Rome, 12 Mar 1908), English soprano. Studied at the Paris Conservatory and first appeared at Worcester in 1833. Lived in London but had many successes abroad, especially in Italy and Germany. She sang in the first London performance of Beethoven's *Missa Solemnis*, 1832, and

Nucci The baritone Leo Nucci. He has a wide repertory and is a favourite of Georg Solti, recording both Iago and Germont père with him. His excellent technique and talent for acting are best-suited to the works of Verdi.

sang Semiramide in Bologna (1841). Married Count Gigliucci in 1843.

Novello, Vincent (b London, 6 Sept 1781; d Nice, 9 Aug 1861), English composer, organist, editor and publisher, father of Clara ◊Novello. Founder of the music pub. firm of Novello & Co. in London, 1811. Edited valuable collections of music including Masses by Haydn and Mozart, and composed church music, cantatas, etc.

November Woods a symphonic poem by Bax, composed 1917, fp Manchester, Hallé Orchestra, 18 Nov 1920.

Novotná, Jarmila (b Prague, 23 Sept 1907; d New York, 9 Feb 1994), Czech soprano. She studied with Emmy Destinn and made her debut in Prague in 1926 as Violetta. She joined the Berlin Staatsoper in 1928 and sang in Vienna 1933–38; created Lehár's Giuditta there in 1934. Salzburg 1935–37 as Octavian, Eurydice and Pamina. NY Met. debut 1939, as Mimi; remained until 1940 as Elvira, Butterfly and Mélisande.

Novotný, Jaroslav (b Jičin, 28 Mar 1886; d Miass, Ural, 1 Jun 1918), Czech composer. Studied in Prague, joined the Austrian army during World War I, was a prisoner in Russia, where he wrote much in camp; he was released and was killed near the end of the war fighting on the other side with the Czech legion.

Works include string quartet; choruses; piano sonata; song cycles *The Eternal Wedding* and *Ballads of the Soul*.

Nowak, Grzegorz (b Poznań, 1951), Polish conductor. Studied in Poznań and in the USA at the Eastman School and Tanglewood. Music director of the Slupsk SO 1976–80, then the Biel SO in Switzerland. Guest with the LSO, Orchestra National de France, Montreal SO and orchestras of Rome, Stockholm, Tokyo, Baltimore and Cincinnati. Recordings include Ravel's *Daphnis et Chloë*, with the LSO.

Nowak, Leopold (b Vienna, 17 Aug 1904; d Vienna, 27 May 1991), Austrian musicologist. He studied in Vienna and was professor at the University there 1932–73. Director of the music division at the Vienna National Library, 1946–69. Wrote books on Haydn (1951) and Bruckner (1947, 1973); in 1945 succeeded Robert ◊Haas as editor of the complete works of Bruckner.

Nowowiejski, Feliks (b Wartenburg, E Prussia, 7 Feb 1877; d Poznań, 23 Jan 1946), Polish composer and conductor. Studied in Berlin and church music at Regensburg, afterwards in France, Belgium and Italy. In 1909 he returned to Poland, conducted the Kraków Music Society until 1914 and in 1919 became professor of organ at the Poznań Conservatory and conducted orchestral concerts there.

Works include operas *Baltic Legend* (1924), *The Mountain*

Goblin; opera-ballet *Leluja*; ballets *Tatra*, *Polish Wedding*; Masses, motets and psalms; oratorios *Quo vadis?* (1907), *Beatum scelus*, *Missa pro pace*, etc.; cantata *Upper Silesian Folk Scene*; symphonic poems *Beatrix*, *Nina*, overture *Polish Wooing*, *The Prodigal Son*, *Jerusalem*; nine symphonies.

Noyes Fludde opera in one act by Britten (text from the Chester Miracle Play), produced Orford, 18 Jun 1958. Based on the biblical story of Noah's flood; setting makes much use of children's voices.

Nozzari, Andrea (b Vertova, near Bergamo, 1775; d Naples, 12 Dec 1832), Italian tenor. He studied in Bergamo and sang in Rome, Milan and Paris before joining the San Carlo Theatre, Naples; took part in the fps of nine Rossini operas, including *Elisabetta*, *Otello*, *Armida*, *La donna del lago*, *Maometto II* and *Zelmira*.

Nozze d'Ercole e d'Ebe, Le, *The Nuptials of Hercules and Hebe*, opera by Gluck, produced Pillnitz, near Dresden, at the double wedding of Max Joseph, Elector of Bavaria, and Maria Anna, Princess of Saxony, and Frederick Christian, Prince of Saxony, and Maria Antonia Walpurgis, Princess of Bavaria, 29 Jun 1747.

Opera by Porpora (libretto as above), produced Venice, 18 Feb 1744.

Nozze di Figaro, Le, *The Marriage of Figaro*, opera by Mozart (libretto by L da Ponte, based on Beaumarchais's comedy, *La Folle Journée, ou Le Mariage de Figaro*), produced Vienna, Burgtheater, 1 May 1786. Figaro and Susanna are to married, but first Figaro is pursued by the elderly Marcellina (who turns out to be his mother), Susanna must evade the eager Count Almaviva, and all the characters must disentangle themselves from a web of mistaken identities.

Nozze di Teti e di Peleo, Le, *The Nuptials of Thetis and Peleus*, opera by Cavalli (libretto by O Persiani), produced Venice, Teatro San Cassiano, probably 24 Jan 1639. Thetis and Peleus are to marry, but Aeolus (Peleus' father) opposes the match because he believes Jupiter has seduced Thetis. Pluto sends Discord to interrupt the lovers before the marriage proceeds.

Nucci, Leo (b Castiglione dei Pepoli, Bologna, 16 Apr 1942), Italian

——— **THE OPERA** ———

Le Nozze di Figaro

One of Mozart's best-known works, this four-act comic opera was first produced in 1786. It is set in Count Almaviva's castle near Seville in the mid-18th century.

I. While Count Almaviva's servants Figaro (baritone) and Susanna (soprano) prepare for their wedding, Marcellina (mezzo-soprano) wishes to use an unpaid loan as forfeit for marrying Figaro herself. The count (baritone) arrives to pay court to Susanna, and Cherubino (mezzo-soprano) is forced to hide, having just expressed his love for the countess. When Cherubino is exposed he is sent off to the army.

II. The countess (soprano), Figaro and Susanna plan to trap the count by dressing up Cherubino in Susanna's clothes and arranging a rendezvous with the count. When a suspicious count enters later he forces open the dressing room door, expecting to find Cherubino. When Susanna emerges, he has to apologize. Figaro covers up for Cherubino's commission, which has been found by a gardener, but is set back by Marcellina and Dr Bartolo (baritone) entering with the legal claim on him.

III. A birthmark on Figaro's arm identifies him after all as Marcellina's long-lost son, with Bartolo as his father. Susanna misunderstands when she enters as Figaro is embracing Marcellina.

IV. At night in the garden, Susanna and the countess exchange clothes and at first Figaro is suspicious of Susanna's intentions. The count pays court to his wife under the impression that she is Susanna, and he has to apologize once more when the countess herself appears. All ends happily on a 'mad day'.

baritone. Made his debut at Spoleto in 1967, as Rossini's Figaro (repeated at La Scala 1976). London, CG, from 1978, as Verdi's Miller, returning 1994 as Germont. NY Met from 1980 as Renato, Onegin, Posa, Amonasro and Rigoletto. Salzburg Festival 1989–90 as Renato (*Ballo in maschero*). Sang Iago in concert performances of *Otello* in Chicago and New York (1991); also made recordings.

Nucius (or *Nux* or *Nucis*), Joannes (b Görlitz, *c* 1556; d Himmelwitz, Silesia, 25 Mar 1620), German monk and composer. Entered the Cistercian abbey of Rauden, Upper Silesia, and in 1591 became abbot of its offshoot at Himmelwitz. Composed Masses, motets, etc.

Nuits d'été, Les, Summer Nights, six songs by Berlioz (poems by T Gautier), composed 1840–41 for mezzo or tenor and piano; revised for voice and orchestra 1843 (no. 4) and 1856. 1. *Villanelle*, 2. *Le spectre de la rose*, 3. *Sur les lagunes*, 4. *Absence*, 5. *Au cimetière*, 6. *L'île inconnue*.

Nuitter (actually *Truinet*), Charles (Louis Étienne) (b Paris, 24 Apr 1828; d Paris, 24 Feb 1899), French librettist and writer on music. A lawyer at first, he later devoted himself to the writing and translation of libretti and of books on opera. In 1865 he became archivist of the Paris Opéra.

Nunc dimittis Latin = 'Now lettest thou [thy servant] depart [in peace]'; part of the Evening Service of the Anglican Church and of Compline in the Roman Catholic Church. Often set by composers as a second part following the Magnificat.

Nursery Suite orchestral suite in seven movements by Elgar. Dedicated to the then Duchess of York and her daughters Princess Elizabeth and Princess Margaret Rose; fp (concert) London, Queen's Hall, 20 Aug 1931. Movements are 1. Aubade; 2. The Serious Doll; 3. Busy-ness; 4. The Sad Doll; 5. The Waggon (passes); 6. The Mercy Doll; 7. Dreaming; 8. Envoi.

Nursery, The song cycle by Mussorgsky (words by composer), composed 1868–72: 1. *With Nurse*; 2. *In the Corner*; 3. *The Cockchafer*; 4. *With the Doll*; 5. *Going to sleep*; 6. *On the Hobby-Horse*; 7. *The Cat 'Sailor'*.

Nusch-Nuschi, Das opera in one act for Burmese marionettes by Hindemith (libretto by F Blei; composed 1920, produced Stuttgart, 4 Jun 1921; conductor by Fritz Busch, who claimed to be shocked by satirical references to Wagner's *Tristan*. (The castration of an Oriental philanderer is accompanied by a quotation from King Marke's music: '*Mir-dies?*' ('This – to me?').

nut the area at the heel of a violin or other bow at which the hairs are attached and can be stretched by the turn of a screw; also the strip, usually of ebony, at the end of the fingerboard of a string instrument near the pegs, serving to raise the strings clear of the board.

Nutcracker, *Casse-Noisette*, ballet by Tchaikovsky (choreography by Lev Ivanovich Ivanov, based on a tale by E T A Hoffmann), produced St Petersburg, Maryinsky Theatre, 18 Dec 1892.

Nyman, Michael (b London, 23 Mar 1944), English composer. Studied at the RAM (with Alan Bush) and King's College London (Thurston Dart). Published *Experimental Music – Cage and Beyond* (1974) but his music has followed more populist paths, drawing on a wide range of influences, including post-minimalism, rock and roll, Stravinsky, and a certain indebtedness to Mozart: *I'll Stake my Cremona to a Jew's Trump* (1983), and *Letters, Riddles and Writs*, TV opera for the 1991 bicentenary. Widely known through his Peter Greenaway film scores: *The Draughtsman's Contract* (1982), *The Cook, the Thief, his Wife and her Lover* (1989), and *Prospero's Books* (1991). Also wrote music for *The Piano* (1993) and the opera *The Man who Mistook his Wife for a Hat* (1987). Formed the Michael Nyman Band for the

Nyman *The composer Michael Nyman has written especially for film, ballet and the opera. He composes in an accessible style described as a mixture of 'Stravinsky and rock and roll'. As a critic he coined the term 'minimalism'.*

performance of an eclectic range of pieces (*Piano Concerto*, 1993).

Nystedt, Knut (b Oslo, 3 Sept 1915), Norwegian composer. After study at the Oslo Conservatory and with Copland in the USA, worked as church organist (from 1938) and conductor (Oslo PO 1945). Founded the Norwegian Soloists Choir 1950 and conducted it 1951–90; many performances of modern works.

Works include *Christmas opera With Crown and Star* (1971); *Song of Solomon* church opera (1989); *Lucis Creator Optime* for soloists, chorus and orchestra (1968); *Four Grieg Romances* for chorus a capella (1992); *Sinfonia del Mare* (1983); five string quartets (1938–88).

Nystroem, Gösta (b Österhaninge, near Stockholm, 13 Oct 1890; d Göteborg, 10 Aug 1966), Swedish composer and painter. Son of a headmaster who taught him music and painting, which he afterwards studied at Stockholm, Copenhagen and Paris, where he lived for 12 years and where d'Indy and Sabaneiev were among his masters for composition and he came under the influence of Picasso, Braque, Chirico and other modern painters. After some further studies in Italy and Spain he settled at Göteborg and in 1933 became music critic of the *Göteborgs Handelstidning*.

Works include ballet-pantomime *Maskerade*; incidental music to various plays includes Shakespeare's *Merchant of Venice* and *The Tempest*; four symphonies (*Sinfonia breve, Sinfonia espressiva, Sinfonia del mare, Sinfonia Shakespeariana*), symphonic poems *The Arctic Sea, The Tower of Babel*, Lyric Suite and Festival Overture for orchestra, *Concerto grosso* for string orchestra; violin concerto, viola concerto, *Sinfonia concertante* for cello and orchestra; piano suites and pieces; songs.

O

Oakeley, Herbert (Stanley) (b London, 22 Jul 1830; d Eastbourne, 26 Oct 1903), English organist, educationist and composer. Educated at Rugby and Oxford, studied music in London, Dresden and Leipzig. He became Professor of Music at Edinburgh University in 1865 and Mus.D. (Cantuar.) in 1871. Knighted 1876.

Works include services and anthems; Jubilee Cantata (1887) and other choral works, part-songs; Festal and Funeral Marches for orchestra; organ and piano music; songs.

obbligato Italian = 'obligatory, compulsory'; instrumental part in a work that is 'essential' in the sense that it performs an important soloistic function. The term has also been used to denote the opposite meaning: that an instrumental part may be omitted if necessary.

Oberlin, Russell (b Akron, OH, 11 Oct 1925), American counter-tenor. He studied at Juilliard and was a co-founder with Noah Greenberg of the NY Pro Musica Antiqua; many performances of medieval and Renaissance music. He sang Oberon in *A Midsummer Night's Dream* at CG, in 1961. Well known as a concert singer, he has also recorded *Messiah*.

Oberon, König der Elfen, *Oberon, King of the Fairies*, opera by Wranitzky (libretto by K L Gieseke, based on Wieland's poem and F S Seyler's libretto *Hüon und Amande*), produced Vienna, Theater auf der Wieden, 7 Nov 1789.

Oberon, or The Elf King's Oath opera by Weber (libretto by J R Planché, based on Wieland's poem and further back on the medieval French romance *Huon de Bordeaux*), produced London, CG, 12 Apr 1826. Oberon, King of the Elves, and his queen, Titania, resolve to stay apart until they find a human couple who stay faithful in the face of adversity. Sir Huon and Rieza face a series of tests, restoring the elves' faith in love.

An ill wind that nobody blows good.

Trad., on the oboe

---

obertas a Polish dance performed in figures by couples following a leader. The music is in 3–4 time, not unlike that of the mazurka, but wilder in character.

Oberthür, Charles (b Munich, 4 Mar 1819; d London, 8 Nov 1895), German harpist and composer. After various orchestral engagements in Germany and Switzerland he settled in London in 1844 as a performer and teacher.

Works include opera *Floris von Namur* (1840); Mass *St Philip Neri*; cantatas *The Pilgrim Queen*, *The Red Cross Knight*, *Lady Jane Grey* (1881–86), overture *Rübezahl*, overture for Shakespeare's *Macbeth* (1852) and others; *Loreley* and concertino for harp and orchestra; trios for harp, violin and cello, quartets for harps; many harp solos.

Oberto, Conte di San Bonifacio opera by Verdi (libretto by A Piazza, altered by B Merelli and T Solera), produced Milan, La Scala, 17 Nov 1839, Verdi's first opera. Count Ricardo is to marry Cuniza, but after learning of his earlier affair with Leonora, Cuniza demands that he marry Leonora instead. Oberto, Leonora's father, is killed in a duel with Ricardo, who, stricken with guilt, leaves the country, while Leonora enters a convent.

oboe a woodwind instrument formerly called hautboy, held vertically and played with a double reed. It descended from the shawm and was in full use by the 17th c., though it was not properly developed until the 18th and not wholly perfected until the 19th. Two oboes, together with two horns, were the most constant instruments in the orchestra, apart from the strings, in the 18th c. The oboe has a compass of about 2½ octaves:

The compass of the oboe.

oboe da caccia Italian = 'hunting oboe'; an oboe tuned a fifth lower and transposing a fifth down. Its parts in early music are now generally played on the English horn, whose pitch is the same.

oboe d'amore Italian = 'love oboe'; an oboe tuned a minor third lower and transposing a minor third down.

Oborin, Lev (Nikolayevich) (b Moscow, 11 Sept 1907; d Moscow, 5 Jan 1974), Russian pianist. Studied at Moscow Conservatory with Igumnov, graduating in 1926. Taught at the Moscow Conservatory from 1928, becoming professor in 1935. Although he had much success as a concert performer, he devoted much of his time to teaching. Formed a trio with D Oistrakh and Knushevitsky.

Obraztsova, Elena (b Leningrad, 7 July 1937), Russian mezzo. She studied in Leningrad and made her debut at the Bolshoi, Moscow, as Marina in 1963; sang same role at NY Met. in 1975. Debut with Met. Co. 1976, in *Adriana Lecouvreur*. She has appeared widely in Europe as Carmen, Dalila, Amneris, Eboli and Helen in *War and Peace*. Her Azucena at CG in 1985 had a mixed response.

Obrecht (or *Hobrecht*), Jacob (or Jacobus Obertus) (b Ghent, 1457–58; d Ferrara, 1505), Netherlands composer. Directed the singers at Utrecht (1476), Bergen-op-Zoom (1479), Cambrai (1484), Bruges (1486) and elsewhere in the Low Countries. A short visit to Ferrara in 1487 was followed by his return there as head of Ercole d'Este's choir from 1504 until his death from plague a year later.

Works include 27 Masses, e.g. *Fortuna desperata*, *Maria zart* and *Sub tuum praesidium*; motets, *chansons*.

Obukhov, Nikolai (b Kursk, 22 Apr 1892; d Paris, 13 Jun 1954), Russian composer. Pupil of N Tcherepnin and Steinberg at the St Petersburg Conservatory. He settled in Paris in 1918 and made further studies with Ravel and others. He experimented with a 12-note system.

Works include mystery *Le Livre de la vie, Poèmes liturgiques.*

Oca del Cairo, L', *The Goose of Cario*, unfinished opera by Mozart (libretto by G B Varesco). Produced in a version completed with other Mozartian fragments (libretto by V Wilder), Paris, Fantaisies-Parisiennes, 6 Jun 1867; new version by Virgilio Mortari (libretto by L Cavicchioli), Salzburg, 22 Aug 1936; another by Hans Redlich, London, SW, 30 May 1940.

ocarina an early instrument of the flute type with finger-holes, roughly pear-shaped, with a mouthpiece protruding like a fish's fin, and usually made of terracotta.

Occasional Oratorio oratorio by Handel (libretto from Milton's Psalms completed by ? Morell), composed to celebrate the suppression of the Jacobite rebellion, produced London, CG, 14 Feb 1746.

Occasione fa il ladro, L', *Opportunity makes a Thief*, opera by Rossini (libretto by L Prividali), produced Venice, Teatro San Moisè, 24 Nov 1812.

Oceanides, The, *Allottaret*, symphonic poem by Sibelius, op. 73; composed 1914, fp Norfolk, CT, 4 Jun 1914, conductor Sibelius.

Ochmann, Wieslaw (b Warsaw, 6 Feb 1937), Polish tenor. Sang Donizetti's Edgardo at Bytom in 1959 and appeared with Warsaw Opera from 1964 as Lensky, Cavaradossi and Verdi's Arrigo. Guest at CG (London) and in Berlin, Paris and Prague. Glyndebourne 1968–70, as Tamino and Don Ottavio. NY Met from 1975, as Dmitri (*Boris*), Lensky, and Golitsin in *Khovanshchina*; San Francisco 1987 and 1989 as Hermann and Idomeneo. Other roles include Fritz in Schreker's *Der ferne Klang* (Brussels 1988) and the Shepherd in Szymanowski's *King Roger* (London 1990).

Ochs, Siegfried (b Frankfurt, 19 Apr 1858; d Berlin, 5 Feb 1929), German conductor and composer. After a general education at Darmstadt and at Heidelberg University, he studied music in Berlin and founded a choral society in 1882, which in association with the Philharmonic Orchestra became the Philharmonische Chor in 1888. In the 1920s he became professor at the Hochschule für Musik and conducted the oratorios and other choral concerts there. Gave frequent performances of Bach and Schütz.

Works include opera *Im Namen des Gesetzes*; songs; etc.

Ochsenkuhn, Sebastian (b Nuremberg, 6 Feb 1521; d Heidelberg, 20 Aug 1574), German lutenist. In the service of Otto Heinrich, Elector Palatine of the Rhine, and his successors, 1534–71. He pub. in 1558 a book of arrangements of motets and French and German songs in lute tablature.

Offenbach's music is wicked. It is abandoned stuff: every accent is a snap of the fingers in the face of moral responsibility.

George Bernard Shaw, quoted in Faris, *Jacques Offenbach*, 1980

Ockeghem, Johannes (or Ockenheim, Okeghem, Hoquegan) (b c 1420; d Tours, 6 Feb 1497), Flemish composer. Pupil (?) of Binchois, chorister at Antwerp Cathedral until 1444, in the service of Charles, Duke of Bourbon, at Moulins in 1446–48, and in the service of the French court from c 1452, where he became first *maître de chapelle.* Louis XI appointed him treasurer of Saint-Martin at Tours, where he lived during the latter part of his life, though he visited Spain in 1469. He is regarded as the most ingenious contrapuntalist of his time.

Works include ten Masses, e.g. *Ecce ancilla Domini, L'homme armé* and *Mi-mi*; motets; French *chansons.*

Octandre work by Varèse for small orchestra; composed 1923, fp NY, 13 Jan 1924.

octave an interval embracing eight notes of a diatonic scale. The upper note having exactly twice the number of vibrations of the lower, the phenomenon results that the two appear to be the same, although different in pitch.

octet a composition for eight instruments, usually in several movements. Mendelssohn's Octet for strings, op. 20 and Schubert's for wind and strings, op. 166, are familiar examples.

octo basse, French, *octobass* English, a three-stringed double bass of huge size invented in 1849 by J B Vuillaume in Paris, which never became widely used. It was capable of playing extremely low notes. It

The opening strings of the octobass.

was very unwieldy and its strings were so thick and heavy that they had to be stopped by means of levers and pedals.

Ode a composition, usually vocal, of a dedicatory character; the form of such works varies considerably, reflecting the poetry, but they may appear in several sections with alternating solos and choruses.

Work for orchestra by Stravinsky; composed 1943, fp. Boston, 8 Oct 1943, conductor Koussevitzky.

Ode for St Cecilia's Day setting by Handel of Dryden's poem, produced London, Theatre in Lincoln's Inn Fields, 22 Nov 1739.

Odes for St Cecilia's Day by Purcell; 1. *Laudate Ceciliam* (1683); 2. *Welcome to all the pleasures* (Fishburn; 1683); 3. *Hail, bright Cecilia* (Brady; 1692); 4. *Raise, raise the voice.*

Ode to Napoleon Buonaparte work by Schoenberg for string quartet, piano and reciter (text by Byron); composed 1942. Version with string orchestra performed NY, 24 Nov 1944, conductor Rodzinski.

Ode to the West Wind work for cello and orchestra after Shelley by Henze; composed 1953, fp Bielefeld, 30 Apr 1954.

Odington, Walter de (or Walter of Evesham) (b ? Oddington, Gloucestershire; d Evesham), English 13th-c. monk, musician and astronomer. He entered the Benedictine monastery at Evesham and wrote a treatise *De speculatione musicae.*

Odnoposoff, Ricardo (b Buenos Aires, 24 Feb 1914), Argentine violinist. A child prodigy, he first appeared in public aged five. Studied first in Buenos Aires and then in Berlin with Flesch, winning prizes in Vienna and Brussels (1932 and 1937). Brustad, Berger and Francisco Mignone wrote works for him.

Odo (879–Tours, 18 Nov 942), French monk and musician. Educated at the court of Guillaume, Duke of Aquitaine, took holy orders, joined the monastery of Saint-Martin at Tours, and after studying dialectics and music in Paris, returned there, then entered the Benedictine monastery of Beaume, near Besançon, became abbot of that of Cluny, near Macon, 927–42, but returned to Tours to die. He composed hymns and antiphons and wrote treatises on music.

odzmek a Slovak dance in quick 2–4 time with a more moderately paced middle section. The ninth of Dvořák's *Slavonic Dances* for piano duet is an *odzmek.*

Œdipe à Colone, *Oedipus Coloneus*, opera by Sacchini (libretto by Nicolas François Guillard, after Sophocles), produced Versailles, at court, 4 Jan 1786; first Paris performance Opéra, 1 Feb 1787. Polynices engages Theseus to help drive his brother Eteocles from the usurped throne of Thebes, but he feels guilty about having driven his father Oedipus away in earlier years. Polynices seeks reconciliation with his father even at the price of relinquishing his claim to the throne.

Oedipus auf Kolonos incidental music by Mendelssohn for Sophocles' tragedy, op. 93, for male chorus and orchestra, produced Potsdam, 1 Nov 1845.

Oedipus der Tyrann musical play after Sophocles by Orff, produced Stuttgart, 11 Dec 1959.

Oedipus Rex stage oratorio by Stravinsky (libretto in Latin, by J Daniélou, translated from French by Jean Cocteau, after Sophocles), produced Paris, Théâtre Sarah Bernhardt, 30 May 1927. The parts are sung in costume but without action, and the words are in Latin in order not to distract the ordinary listener by verbal associations. First stage

──── THE OPERA ────
Oedipus Rex

A two-act opera-oratorio by Igor Stravinsky, with text by Jean Cocteau based on the tragedy by Sophocles. First performed as an oratorio in 1927 and as a stage production the following year, the tragic story is set in Thebes in mythological times.

I. The Theban people beg King Oedipus (tenor) to rescue them from the plague. A message from the Oracle declares that the murderer of the former King Laius is hiding in Thebes. The blind seer Tiresias says further that the murderer of Laius is another king. Oedipus angrily rejects the announcements as his wife Jocasta (mezzo-soprano) appears.

II. Jocasta is the former wife of Laius, and she insists that the Oracle must be false because it had said that Laius would be killed by his son, whereas in fact he was killed at a crossroads by thieves. Oedipus declares that he once killed an old man at a crossroads. A further messenger reveals that Oedipus was a foundling, brought up by a shepherd. First Jocasta then Oedipus realize the truth: he is the son of Jocasta and Laius, abandoned as a child. Oedipus has murdered his father and married his mother. Messenger and chorus narrate the death of Jocasta and describe how Oedipus blinds himself with her golden brooch. Oedipus is expelled from Thebes.

──── THE OPERA ────

performance Vienna, Staatsoper, 23 Feb 1928. Oedipus unknowingly kills his father, King Laius, and marries his mother, Jocasta. When the truth is revealed to him, he blinds himself in remorse.

Oedipus Tyrannus incidental music by Mendelssohn for Sophocles' tragedy, never performed and now lost.

Incidental music for ditto by Stanford, produced Cambridge, 22–26 Nov 1887.

Oedipus und die Sphinx unfinished opera by Varèse (text by Hofmannsthal); composed 1909–13. The MS is lost.

Oelze, Christiane (b Cologne, 1965), German soprano. Studied in Cologne 1984–89 and has sung widely in concert (Salzburg recitals 1993 and US debut 1994, with the Atlanta SO). Opera debut as Despina, Ottawa 1990. Sang Mozart's Constanze at Salzburg (1991) and Anne Trulove at the 1991 Glyndebourne Festival. London from 1993, Haydn's *Jahreszeiten*. Recordings include Mozart's Pamina, under Gardiner.

Oestvig, Karl (b Christiania 17 May 1889; d Oslo, 21 Jul 1968), Norwegian tenor. He studied in Cologne and sang in Stuttgart 1914–19. Vienna 1919–27; created the Emperor in *Die Frau ohne Schatten*, 1919. Berlin 1927–30 as Bacchus, Don José, Lohengrin, Walther and Parsifal. Retired to Oslo 1932 and produced opera there during the Nazi occupation.

Offenbach, Jacques, actually Jakob Levy Eberst (b Cologne, 20 Jun 1819; d Paris, 5 Oct 1880), German-French composer. His father was cantor at the synagogue of Cologne, but he was sent to Paris early in his youth, studying at the Conservatory 1833–37, perfecting himself in cello playing and then playing in the orchestra of the Opéra-Comique even before he left the Conservatory. In 1850 he became conductor at the Théâtre Français. In 1853 he produced his first operettas and during a quarter of a century he turned out nearly 100 light stage pieces. In 1855 he took over the management of the Théâtre Comte and renamed it the Bouffes-Parisiens. This lasted until 1861, after which he had no theatre of his own until 1873, when he managed the Théâtre de la Gaîté until 1875. In 1876–77 he was in the USA, but returned to Paris, where he had some of his greatest successes. He was also popular abroad, and such works as *La Belle Hélène*, *La Vie Parisienne*, and *La Périchole* helped establish musical comedy as a significant form, leading to Johann Strauss, Sullivan and the great Broadway musicals. His only large-scale opera, *Les Contes d'Hoffmann*, occupied him for many years, but he left it not quite

finished at his death, and it was revised and partly scored by Guiraud.

Works include opera *Les Contes d'Hoffmann* (1881), 89 operettas including *Barbebleue* (1866), *Ba-ta-clan* (1855), *La Belle Hélène* (1864), *Chanson de Fortunio*, *Le Docteur Ox* (after Jules Verne), *La Fille du tambour-major* (1879), *La Foire de Saint-Laurent*, *Geneviève de Brabant* (1859), *La Grande-Duchesse de Gérolstein* (1867), *L'Île de Tulipatan*, *La Jolie Parfumeuse*, *Madame Favart*, *Orphée aux enfers* (1858), *La Périchole* (1874), *Princesse de Trébizonde*, *Robinson Crusoe* (after Defoe, 1867), *Vert-Vert*, *La Vie Parisienne* (1866), *Voyage dans la lune* (after Verne), *Whittington and his Cat* (1874); ballet *Le Papillon*; incidental music for Barrière's *Le Gascon* and Sardou's *La Haine*; cello concerto. A second opera, *The Goldsmith of Toledo* (after a tale by E T A Hoffmann) is a pasticcio from various operettas, especially *Le Corsaire noir*, produced Mannheim, 1919.

Offertory, Latin *Offertorium*, the third or fourth item of the Proper of the Roman Mass, following the gospel or the *Credo*. It was originally an antiphonal chant, sung with a complete psalm and accompanying the offering of bread and wine. In the 10th c. it became an elaborate responsorial chant provided with complex verses sung by soloists. The verses were later dropped, but the style of what remains is still closer to the Gradual than to the Introit or Communion. In the Anglican church it survived as a spoken biblical sentence, occasionally set to music. The offertory was frequently set by 16th-c. composers, and with instrumental accompaniment by Michael Haydn, Mozart, Schubert, and others.

Offrandes work by Varèse for soprano and chamber ensemble (texts by V Huidobro and J J Tablada); composed 1921, fp NY, 23 Apr 1922.

Offrandes oubliées, Les, *The Forgotten Offerings*, work for orchestra in three parts by Messiaen; composed 1930, fp Paris, 19 Feb 1931.

Ogawa, Noriko (b Kawasaki, 28 Jan 1962), Japanese pianist. Studied in Tokyo and at Juilliard (1981–85). New York debut recital 1982. Third prize Leeds International Competition 1987 and formed duo with clarinettist Michael Collins 1988; Wigmore Hall debut 1988 (Schumann's Fantasy and Liszt's Sonata). Has recorded the Tchaikovsky B♭ minor and Prokofiev 3rd Concertos, with Rozhdestvensky.

Ogdon, John (Andrew H) (b Manchester, 27 Jan 1937; d London, 1 Aug, 1989), English pianist and composer. Studied at Royal Manchester College of Music; London debut 1958, in the Busoni concerto. In 1962 won the Tchaikovsky Competition in Moscow. He was equally at home in both the classical and modern repertory, and also pub. a number of compositions, including a piano concerto. For some years he was afflicted with mental illness, and left hospital to perform.

Ogiński Polish noble family of amateur musicians:

1. Prince Michal Kazimierz Ogiński (b Warsaw, 1728; d Warsaw, 31 May 1800). Studied the violin with Viotti and also played the harp. He kept a small opera co. and orchestra on his estate.

Works include a comic opera, incidental music for two plays, and polonaises for violin and piano.

2. Prince Michal Kleofas Ogiński (b Gozuw, near Warsaw, 25 Sept 1765; d Florence, 15 Oct 1833), nephew of 1. Was taught the piano by Kozlowski and violin by Viotti and others. After the third partition of Poland he emigrated, first to Turkey, then to Hamburg, Paris (1823) and finally Florence. opera *Zélis et Valeur, ou Bonapart au Caire* (1799); military marches; polonaises and mazurkas for piano.

Öglin, Erhard (b Reutlingen), German 15th–16th-c. music publisher. He worked in Augsburg, where he pub. an important collection of four-part songs in 1512.

Ohana, Maurice (b Casablanca, 12 Jun 1914; d Paris, 13 Nov 1992), English composer of Moroccan descent. Studied in Barcelona, Rome and at the Schola Cantorum in Paris. His music belongs to the *avant-garde* school of his time.

Works include operas *Chanson de Toile* (1969) and *La Celestine* (1987), opera for marionettes *Autodafé* (1972); ballets *Prométhée* (1956) and *Paso*; *Les Représentations de Tanit* and *Suite pour un Mimodrame* for small orchestra; guitar concerto; concertino for trumpet; piano concerto (1981); *Études, Choréographiques* for percussion; piano music; choral music, film music.

O'Hara, Ronan (b Manchester, 9 Jan 1964), English pianist. Studied at the RNCM and has appeared throughout Europe and Britain as recitalist and concert performer (all major British orchestras, Zurich Tonhalle, Florida PO and Indianapolis SO). With Stephen Hough has recorded Britten's music for two pianos.

Ohlsson, Garrick (b Bronxville, 3 Apr 1948), American pianist. Studied at Juilliard (1961–71) and won the 1970 Chopin International Competition, Warsaw. Regular concerts in Europe and with the Cleveland, Chicago, San Francisco and Philadelphia Orchestras. Recordings include concertos by Brahms, Liszt and Skriabin.

Ohms, Elisabeth (b Arnhem, 17 May 1888; d Marquartstein, 16 Oct 1974), Dutch soprano. Debut Mainz 1921; Munich from 1923 as Brünnhilde, Isolde, Turandot and Strauss's Helen. She sang Fidelio and Kundry under Toscanini at Milan, 1927–28. London, CG, 1928–35 as Venus, Ortrud and the Marschallin. NY Met. debut 1930, as Brünnhilde.

Oiseau de feu, L' ◊Firebird.

Oiseaux exotiques, *Exotic birds*, work for orchestra by Messiaen for two clarinets, xylophone, glockenspiel, percussion and wind; composed 1955–56, fp Paris, 10 Mar 1956.

Oistrakh, David (Fedorovich) (b Odessa, 30 Sept 1908; d Amsterdam, 24 Oct 1974), Russian violinist. Began his studies aged five, entered the Odessa Conservatory and graduated in 1926, winning a number of prizes, including the Brussels Competition in 1937, which gave him international fame. From 1934 he taught at the Moscow Conservatory, and also appeared widely as a soloist. He gave the fps of violin concertos by Miaskovsky, Khachaturian and Shostakovich; collaborated with Prokofiev in an arrangement of the flute sonata for violin and piano.

Oistrakh, Igor (b Odessa, 27 Apr 1931), Russian violinist, son of David ◊Oistrakh. Studied with his father at the Moscow Conservatory, graduating in 1955 after winning prizes in Budapest (1949) and Poznań (1952). Has taught at Moscow Conservatory from 1958. 60th birthday concert in London 1991, concertos by Mendelssohn and Mozart.

Okeland, Robert, 16th-c. English composer. He was a member of Eton College, 1532–34, and of the Chapel Royal, 1547–48. Music of his is preserved in the 'Gyffard' part-books, c 1555.

Olav Trygvason unfinished opera by Grieg (libretto by Bjørnson), three scenes only, performed in concert form, Christiania, 19 Oct 1889; never staged in Grieg's lifetime, but produced Christiania, 8 Oct 1908.

Olczewska, Maria (b Ludwigsschwaige, near Donauwörth, 12 Aug 1892; d Klagenfurt, 17 May 1969), German mezzo. She studied in Munich and was engaged in Hamburg, Vienna and Munich 1917–25 as Fricka, Ortrud, Carmen and Amneris. London, CG, 1924–33 as Octavian and Orlofsky. NY Met. debut 1933, as Brangaene. Taught in Vienna from 1947.

Old Hall Manuscript a collection of English church music, copied c 1420–30 and named after the college in Ware which housed it until it was purchased by the British Library in 1973.

Oldham, Arthur (William) (b London, 6 Sept 1926), English composer. Studied composition with Howells and piano with Kathleen Long at the RCM in London, also privately with Britten. He was for a time music director at the Mercury Theatre and to the Ballet Rambert, but later devoted himself wholly to composition.

Works include four ballets including *Bonne-Bouche* (1952), incidental music for Ronald Duncan's *This Way to the Tomb*; six anthems; orchestral music, including Sinfonietta for wind band (1974); violin and piano sonata; songs.

Oleg, Raphael (b Paris, 8 Sept 1958), French violinist. Studied at the Paris Conservatoire from 1972 and won the 1986 Tchaikovsky International Competition, Moscow. UK debut with the LSO 1987, playing the Brahms Concerto. Concerts with the Orchestre National de France, the Philadelphia Orchestra and the Concertgebouw Orchestra. Tokyo debut 1989.

Olimpiade, L', *The Olympiad*, Olympie, libretto by Metastasio. Megacles, who loves Aristaea, is to compete in the Olympics under the

Offenbach *The German-born composer Jacques Offenbach (1819–1880), from a chromolithograph of 1912. After moving to Paris as a teenager, he later became a leading composer of opéras-comiques. Wagner, never renowned for his humour, did not appreciate being parodied in* Le Carnaval des revues.

name of his friend, Lycidas. He then learns that Aristaea is to be the prize for the winner. Torn between duty and love, Megacles chooses duty, but after a few twists all ends happily.

Opera by Caldara, produced Vienna, 28 Aug 1733; other settings by Vivaldi (Venice, 1734); Pergolesi (Rome, 1735); Galuppi (Milan, 1747); Hasse (Dresden, 1756); Traetta (Verona, 1758); Jommelli (Stuttgart, 1761); Sacchini (Padua, 1763); and Cimarosa (Vicenza, 1784). There are at least 30 other settings of this libretto *Olimpiade* is probably the most frequently composed work by Metastasio or by any other librettist.

Olimpia vendicata, *Olympia revenged*, opera by A Scarlatti (libretto by A Aureli), produced Naples, Palazzo Reale, 23 Dec 1685.

oliphant from old English 'olifaunt' = 'elephant'; a bugle-like horn made of an elephant's tusk, used for signalling and hunting in old times, often beautifully carved.

Oliver, Stephen (b Liverpool, 10 Mar 1950; d London, 29 Apr 1992), English composer. He studied at Oxford; electronic music with Robert Sherlaw Johnson. The best known of his many operas and theatre pieces is *Tom Jones*, after Fielding, produced Snape, Newcastle and London 1976. Other pieces include *Perseverance* (1974), *Bad Times* (1975), *The Great McPorridge Disaster* (1976), *The Duchess of Malfi* (1971–77), *The Dreaming of the Bones* (1979), *Nicholas Nickelby* (1980), *Blondel* (1983), *Britannia Preserv'd* (1984) and *Timon of Athens* (1991). He was a popular teacher and broadcaster.

Olivero, Magda (b Saluzzo, near Turin, 25 Mar 1912), Italian soprano. Debut Turin 1933, as Lauretta. Sang in Italy until 1941 as Manon,

Elsa, Lucia and Adriana Lecouvreur. Retired on marriage 1941 but returned 1951 as Minnie, Fedora and Iris. London debut 1952 as Mimi. US debut Dallas 1967, as Medea; NY Met. 1975, Tosca.

Oliveros, Pauline (b Houston, 30 May 1932), American composer. Worked at the San Francisco Tape Music Center 1961–67 and has taught electronic music at San Diego from 1967. Her works employ live electronics and scenic effects, often guided by meditation: *To Valerie Solonis and Marilyn Monroe in recognition of their desperation* (1970); *Phantom Fathom*, mixed-media event (1972); *1,000 Acres* for string quartet (1972); *Crow Two*, ceremonial opera (1974); *The Yellow River Map*, meditation (1977); *King Kong Sings Along* for chorus (1977); *Gone with the Wind* for ensembles (1980); *The Wheel of Times* for string quartet and electronics (1982); *The New Sound Meditation* for voices (1989); *Portraits* for brass quintet (1989); *Listening for Life*, electronic (1991); *Midnight Operas*, for chorus (1992); *Nzinga, the Queen King*, music theatre (1993).

Olivieri-Sangiacomo, Elsa, ◊Respighi.

Ollone, Max (properly Maximilien-Paul-Marie-Félix) d' (b Besançon, 13 Jun 1875; d Paris, 15 May 1959), French conductor and composer. Studied under Massenet and Lenepveu at the Paris Conservatory and gained the Prix de Rome in 1897. After conducting at Angers, Geneva and Paris (Opéra-Comique, concerts, etc.), and touring as conductor he became professor at the Conservatory in 1939.

Works include operas *Le Retour*, *Les Amants de Rimini* (after Dante, 1912), *Les Uns et les autres* (on a comedy by Verlaine, 1922), *L'Arlequin*, *Georges Dandin* (after Molière, 1930), and *La Samaritaine* (after Rostand, 1937); ballet *Le Peuple abandonné*; pantomime *Bacchus et Silène*; oratorio *François d'Assise*, cantatas *Frédégonde* (1897), *Jeanne d'Arc à Domrémy*; fantasy for piano and orchestra, *Le Ménétrier* for violin and orchestra, string quartet, piano trio; songs.

Olmi, Paolo (b Ravenna, 23 May 1954), Italian conductor. After study with Franco Ferrara he appeared with leading orchestras from 1979, opera debut 1986, Bologna. Conducted Rossini's *Mosè* in Rome 1988, *Guillaume Tell* in Paris 1990. British debut with the RPO, in a concert performance of *Nabucco*; CG 1994, *Mosè*. Deutsche Oper Berlin 1992, *La forza del destino*. Recordings include Bellini's *Zaira* and the first modern edition of Rossini's *La Siège de Corinthe*.

Whenever I go to an opera, I leave my sense and reason at the door with my half-guinea, and deliver myself up to my eyes and my ears.
Lord Chesterfield in a letter, 1752

Olsen, Keith (b Denver, 1957), American tenor. Studied in San Francisco and at Juilliard; debut in *The Merry Widow* with the NY City Opera, 1982. European debut Karlsruhe 1987, as Rodolfo (also at Hamburg), Frankfurt and the Verona Arena. Has also sung Alfredo at Barcelona, Radames in Rome and Manrico in Berlin, London. CG 1991–94, as Rodolfo, Pinkerton, and Boris in *Káta Kabanová*.

Olsen, Ole (b Hammerfest, 4 Jul 1850; d Oslo, 9 Nov 1927), Norwegian organist, conductor and composer. Studied engineering at Trondhjem, but took to music, taking any appointment as organist and travelling theatre conductor he could secure. In 1870–74 he consolidated his studies at the Leipzig Conservatory and then settled at Christiania where he taught conducting and wrote criticism.

Works include operas *Stig Hvide* (1876), *Lajla*, *Klippeøerne* (1910), and *Stallo*; incidental music to Nordahl Rolfsen's *Svein Uræd* (1890); oratorio *Nidaros*, cantatas *Ludwig Holberg* (1884), *Griffenfelt* (1897), *Broderbud*, *Tourist Cantata*; symphony in G major, symphonic poems *Aasgaardsreien*, *Elfdans*.

Olthoff, Statius (b Osnabrück, 1555; d Rostock, 28 Feb 1629), German composer. Became cantor at St Mary's Church at Rostock in 1579 and there composed four-part settings of George Buchanan's Latin verse paraphrase of the psalms.

Olympians, The opera by Bliss (libretto by J B Priestley), produced London, CG, 29 Sept 1949. Rich Lavatte has arranged for his daughter Madeleine to marry an old nobleman, but she falls in love with young poet Hector. After the appearance of Greek gods, Lavatte is foiled and the lovers are united.

Olympie opera by Spontini (libretto by M Dieulafoy and C Brifaut, based on Voltaire's tragedy), produced Paris, Opéra, 22 Dec 1819.

O'Mara, Joseph (b Limerick, 16 Jul 1861; d Dublin, 5 Aug 1927), Irish tenor. Studied at Milan and made his first appearance in London, 1891, as Sullivan's Ivanhoe. He sang with the Moody-Manners co. 1902–08 and formed his own Grand Opera co. in 1912.

Ombra di Don Giovanni, L', *Don Juan's Shade*, opera by Alfano (libretto by E Moschino), produced Milan, La Scala, 2 Apr 1914; revised as *Don Giovanni de Mañara*, Florence, 28 May 1941.

Oncina, Juan (b Barcelona, 15 Apr 1925), Spanish tenor. Debut Barcelona 1946, as Massenet's Des Grieux; later that year sang Almaviva, opposite Tito Gobbi, at Bologna. Glyndebourne 1952–61, as Don Ramiro, Ferrando, Comte Ory, Busoni's Scaramuccio, Fenton, Don Ottavio and Lindoro. At Florence he was heard in operas by Cherubini and Lully. Attempted Verdi and Puccini roles from 1963. Sang at Hamburg, 1971–74.

Ondes Martenot an electrophonic instrument invented by Maurice Martenot of Paris in 1929, producing notes from the air graded according to the chromatic scale by a special device, not indeterminate in pitch like those of the aetherophone or Theremin. Often used by Messiaen (e.g. *Turangalîla Symphony*).

Ondříček, František (b Prague, 29 Apr 1857; d Milan, 12 Apr 1922), Czech violinist. Pupil of his father and at the Prague and Paris Conservatotries. First appeared in London in 1882 and then went on tour; gave the fp of Dvořàk's Concerto (Prague 1883) and formed a quartet which took part in the Haydn centenary celebrations (Vienna, 1809). Director of the New Vienna Conservatory, 1912–19, and then at that of Prague.

Onegin (born *Hoffmann*), Sigrid (b Stockholm, 1 Jun 1889; d Magliaso, Switzerland, 16 Jun 1943), Swedish contralto of German/French parentage. Studied in Sweden and Germany and appeared frequently in both countries, also in England; debut Stuttgart 1912, as Carmen. Munich 1919–22, Berlin 1926–31. Roles include Amneris, Eboli, Fides and Orpheus. Bayreuth 1933–34 as Fricka, Erda and Waltraute. Her first husband was a great-nephew of Lvov.

O'Neill, Dennis (b Pontardulais, 25 Feb 1948), Welsh tenor. Studied at the RNCM and made debut at Wexford Festival 1973, in *Ivan Susannin*. Sang with State Opera of South Australia 1974–76, Scottish Opera and WNO from 1979 (debut as Alfredo). CG from 1979 as Flavio (*Norma*), Rodolfo, the Duke of Mantua, Edgardo, Foresto (*Attila*), and Radames (1994) US debut Dallas 1983 (Edgardo); NY Met 1987 (Rodolfo).

O'Neill, Norman (b London, 14 Mar 1875; d London, 3 Mar 1934), Anglo-Irish composer and conductor. Great-grandson of Callcott. Studied with Somervell in London and with Knorr at the Hoch Conservatory at Frankfurt. In 1899 he married the French pianist Adine Rückert and in 1908 became conductor at the Haymarket Theatre, for which he wrote much incidental music. In 1919 he became treasurer of the Royal Philharmonic Society and in 1924 professor at the RAM.

Works include incidental music for Shakespeare's *Hamlet* (1904), *Henry V*, *Julius Caesar* (1920), *King Lear* (1909), *Macbeth*, *Measure for Measure* and *The Merchant of Venice* (1922), Maeterlinck's *Blue Bird*, Barrie's *Mary Rose* and *A Kiss for Cinderella*, Ibsen's *Pretenders* (1913), Stephen Phillips's *The Lost Heir*: dramatic adaptations of Dickens' *Pickwick* and Scott's *Bride of Lammermoor*, etc.; *Swinburne Ballet* and *Punch and Judy* ballet; concert overtures, variations, *Miniatures* and other works for orchestra; choral works; piano quintet, two piano trios (1895, 1900); Variations and Fugue on an Irish Air for two pianos; piano pieces; many songs.

On Hearing the First Cuckoo in Spring one of two pieces for small orchestra by Delius (the other being *Summer Night on the River*), composed 1912 and 1911 respectively; fp Leipzig Gewandhaus, 2 Oct 1913. The cuckoo call is heard unobtrusively on the clarinet and the main theme is a Norwegian folksong, *In Ole Dale*, previously used by Grieg, arranged for piano in *Norske Folkeviser*, op. 66 (no. 14).

Onslow, (André) George (or Georges) (Louis) (b Clermont-Ferrand, 27 Jul 1784; d Clermont-Ferrand, 3 Oct 1853), French composer of English descent. Grandson of the first Lord Onslow. He studied piano with Hüllmandel, Dussek and Cramer while living in London for some years as a young man, but settled at Clermont-Ferrand as a country squire, held regular chamber music practices there, studied the cello and went for two years to Vienna to study composition. In the 1820s, wishing to write operas, he made further studies with Reicha in Paris, where he lived alternatively.

    Works include operas *L'alcade de la Vega* (1824), *Le Colporteur* (1827) and *Le Duc de Guise* (1837); four symphonies; three string quartets, 34 string quintets, two piano sextets, piano septet, nonet for strings and wind, six piano trios; violin and piano and cello and piano sonatas; sonatas for piano duet; piano pieces.

On Wenlock Edge song cycle for tenor, piano and string quartet by Vaughan Williams (text by A E Housman), fp London, 15 Nov 1909. Version with string orchestra performed London, 24 Jan 1924.

op, abbr. = *opus*, Latin = 'work', a prefix used for the enumeration of a composer's works. It was at first a publisher's rather than a composer's device and in the early 18th c. (e.g. Handel) was used only for instrumental composers. Later in that century it began to become more general, being used for Haydn but not for Mozart, and from Beethoven onward it began to be used regularly, though the number of an opus is not necessarily a guide to the date of its composition.

open organ pipes of which the upper end is left open and which, unlike the stopped pipes, produce notes corresponding to their full length.

open notes on wind instruments the notes produced naturally as harmonics as distinct from stopped notes produced by valves, keys or other mechanical means, or by the hand in horn playing.

open strings the strings of string instruments as played without being stopped by the left hand on the fingerboard.

opera Italian = 'work': the same as the Latin *opus* and originally used in the same sense; a musical work for the stage of varying types, originating in the last years of the 16th c, in Italy. Its dramatic foundation is a libretto, which is set to music in various ways that may be divided into three main types: (1) recitative carrying on the action and set musical numbers such as arias, concerted pieces for several voices, choruses, etc., forming musical climaxes; (2) similar musical numbers, but with the action carried on in spoken dialogue instead of recitative; (3) the text set continuously throughout, but often with traces of separate musical numbers still apparent. The instrumental share in an opera is almost always orchestral.

    ◊action musicale; ◊azione teatrale; ◊ballad opera; ◊burlesque; ◊burletta; ◊comédie lyrique; ◊commedia per musica; ◊dramma giocoso; ◊dramma per musica; ◊extravaganza; ◊favola per musica; ◊festa teatrale; ◊intermezzo; ◊melodrama; ◊melodramma; ◊music drama; ◊musical comedy; ◊opera-ballet; ◊opéra-bouffe; ◊opera buffa; ◊opéra comique; ◊opera seria; ◊operetta; ◊pastorale; ◊Singspiel; ◊tragédie lyrique; ◊vaudeville.

opera-ballet a combination of opera and ballet originating in 17th-c. France and there called *opéra-ballet* from the beginning.

opéra bouffe, French = 'comic opera', derived from Italian *opera buffa*, a type of French comic opera, or rather operetta, lighter in tone and sometimes flimsier in musical workmanship than an *opéra comique*

opera buffa Italian = 'comic opera'; a light type of opera with a comedy libretto, particulary of the 18th c. in Italy, with dialogue in recitative (accompanied by the harpsichord) and musical numbers: arias, duets, etc., and (more rarely) choruses.

opéra comique French = lit. 'comic opera'; an exclusively French type of opera, not always comic and often by no means light, but originally always with spoken dialogue.

opera seria Italian = 'serious opera'; a type of 18th-c. opera, especially that cultivated by the librettists Zeno and Metastasio, treating mythological or heroic-historical subjects. The musical treatment is mainly by recitative and arias, more rarely duets and other concerted numbers or choruses.

operetta Italian = 'little opera'; a light opera or musical comedy, normally with spoken dialogue.

Opernball, Der, *The Ball at the Opera House*, operetta by Heuberger (libretto by V Léon and H von Waldberg), produced Vienna, Theater an der Wien, 5 Jan 1898. Mistaken identity at the ball, as Angèle and Marguerite test the fidelity of husbands Paul and Georges.

ophicleide, lit. = 'keyed snake' from Greek *ophis*, 'snake', and *kleis*, 'key', a bass brass instrument similar to the key bugle, played with a cup-shaped mouthpiece and having holes covered with keys in the side. It was patented by Halary (i.e. Jean-Hilaire Asté) in Paris, 1821. It had a compass of about three octaves. It was gradually superseded by the bass tuba.

Opie, Alan (b Redruth, 22 Mar 1945), English baritone. Studied at the London Opera Centre and made debut for SW in 1969 as Papageno; has returned to the Coliseum as Oblonsky in the fp of Hamilton's *Anna Karenina* (1981), Beckmesser (1984), Germont, Busoni's Faust, and Melitone. CG debut 1971, in *Il Barbiere di Siviglia*; Traveller in *Death in Venice* 1992. Sang title role in Kodály's *Háry János* at Buxton (1982) and Beckmesser at the 1982 Bayreuth Festival. Glyndebourne from 1990, as Britten's Sid (*Albert Herring*) and Balstrode.

Opieński, Henryk (b Kraków, 13 Jan 1870; d Morges, near Lausanne, 21 Jan 1942), Polish musicologist, composer and conductor. Studied piano with Paderewski, composition with d'Indy at the Schola Cantorum in Paris and conducting and musicology with Nikisch and Riemann at Leipzig. He formed a vocal society at Lausanne in 1918 and lived in Switzerland until his death, except when he was director of the Poznań Conservatory 1920–26. He edited Chopin's letters and wrote on him, Paderewski, and Polish music in general.

    Works include operas *Maria* (Malczewski, 1904), and *Jacob the Lutenist* (1918); incidental music for Calderón's *El principe constante*; oratorio *The Prodigal Son*; cantata *Mickiewicz*; symphonic poems *Zymunt August i Barbara* and *Lilla Weneda*; string quartet; instrumental pieces; songs.

What else is opéra comique, in fact, but sung vaudeville?

Jacques Offenbach, quoted in *Le Ménestrel*, 1856

Opitiis, Benedictus de, 16th-c. Franco-Flemish composer. He wrote two motets for the entry of the future emperor Charles V into Antwerp in 1515; he was the organist at the church of Our Lady in Antwerp, *c* 1514–16, and stayed in England, 1516–18 at Henry VIII's court. He disappears from records after 1522.

opus Latin = 'work'; its abbr., ◊*op.*, is used as a prefix to enumerations of a composer's works.

oratorio a vocal work, usually for solo voices and chorus with some kind of instrumental accompaniment and generally set to sacred works, often direct from the Bible or paraphrased from it, and at any rate nearly always treating a subject of a sacred character (such notable exceptions as Handel's *Hercules* and Haydn's *Seasons* are not strictly speaking oratorios). It originated in the congregation of the Oratorians founded by St Philip Neri in the 16th c., where scenes from scripture were enacted with music. In the 17th c. the oratorio developed side by side with opera and was indistinguishable from it in some of its features, except that greater prominence was nearly always given to the chorus. Settings of one of the Evangelists' narratives of the Passion developed a special type of oratorio, especially in Germany. The form was developed by Mendelssohn, Dvořák and Elgar. Modern examples include Schoenberg's *Die Jakobsleiter* (1917–22), Stravinsky's *Oedipus Rex* (1927) and Tippett's *A Child of our Time* (1939–41).

Orazi ed i Curiazi, Gli, *The Horatii and the Curiatii*, opera by Cimarosa (libretto by A S Sografi), produced Venice, Teatro La Fenice, 26 Dec 1796. The Horatius family of Rome and the Curiatius family of Alba are traditional enemies, but Curiatius' betrothal to Horatia brings the families together. However, Rome and Alba go to

--------- **THE OPERA** ---------

Orfeo ed Euridice

A three-act musical drama by Christoph Gluck. Written in 1762, it is set in Greece in mythological times.

I. Orfeo (contralto), together with a chorus of nymphs and shepherds, mourn the death of Euridice. Orfeo determines to descend to Hades to recover Euridice. Amor (soprano) encourages him in his mission, but once he has found Euridice he must not look back at her until they have departed from Hades.

II. Dancing Furies block Orfeo's way and they call on the three-headed dog Cerberus. Orfeo calms them with his singing and passes through to the Elysian fields, where he finds Euridice (soprano).

III. Orfeo cannot explain to Euridice why he must not look back and eventually she claims that he no longer loves her. At last he turns to look at her and she falls dead. Orfeo is so eloquent in his grief that Amor takes pity and allows Euridice to be reunited with him.

--------- **THE OPERA** ---------

battle and Curiatius is killed by Horatia's brother, Marcus, who then kills Horatia for not rejoicing with him.

Opera by Mercadante (libretto by S Cammarano), produced Naples, Teatro San Carlo, 10 Nov 1846.

orchestra Greek = 'dancing-place'; originally the space in the Greek theatre equivalent to that now occupied by the orchestra in an opera-house; now the name for the assembly of instrumental players itself. The modern orchestra originated in the ballets and operas of the early 17th c. At that time various groups, e.g. strings, brass, were used separately and it was only gradually that they were combined. In the course of the 17th c. trumpets and timpani, originally ceremonial and military instruments, were introduced into the orchestra for festal or heroic music. By the early 18th c. flutes, oboes and bassoons were normal members of the orchestra, though recorders often appeared as alternatives to the flutes, and horns came to be used for music of a jovial character. Throughout this time keyboard instruments were used to support and enrich the ensemble. In the course of the 18th c. clarinets were added, though they only gradually became a normal part of the orchestra, and the keyboard continuo disappeared, except in church music. Up to this time trombones were used only in church music and in solemn operatic scenes; Beethoven incorporated them in ordinary orchestral music. The 19th c. saw the gradual establishment of the piccolo, English horn, bass clarinet, double bassoon, tuba and harp as normal members of the orchestra and the replacement of the older horns and trumpets by valve instruments. Until the end of the 18th c., and sometimes later, the conductor sat at the harpsichord or played first violin. Throughout the 19th c. the orchestra increased steadily in size, reaching its largest numbers in Mahler's Symphony of a Thousand (1910, with chorus). Later composers, such as Schoenberg and Stravinsky (*Pulcinella*, 1919, and later works) have preferred smaller groupings. A notable feature of the post-World War II orchestra is the significantly greater diversity of instruments in the percussion section.

If you want to know how to orchestrate, then don't study Wagner's scores, study the score of Carmen.
Richard Strauss, quoted in *The Gramophone*, 1971

---

orchestration (or *scoring*) the art of setting out a composition for the instruments of an orchestra. Methods of orchestration have changed considerably. Monteverdi in *Orfeo* (1607) used his instruments mainly in groups; Bach chose a particular combination of instruments and retained it throughout a movement or even throughout a work;

Haydn, Mozart and Beethoven developed a new art of combining, doubling and contrasting instruments. Modern orchestration developed mainly from the works of Berlioz, Wagner, Strauss and Debussy, all of whom exploited the characteristic colours of the instruments and their combinations.

Ordonez, Carlo d' (or Ordoñez) (b Vienna, 19 Apr 1734; d Vienna, 6 Sept 1786), Austrian composer and violinist, a major influence in the developing instrumental style of the years 1750–75. He was for most of his life a government administrator in Vienna.

Works include two operas, over 70 symphonies, over 30 string quartets and other chamber music.

Ordoñez, Pedro (b Plasencia *c* 1510; d Palencia 5 May 1585), Spanish singer and composer. In 1539 he went to Rome as a singer in the Pontifical chapel and remained there to his death, attending the Council of Trent in 1545 and again in 1547, when it had moved to Bologna.

ordre, French, the old French name for the ◊suite.

Orefice, Giacomo (b Vicenza, 27 Aug 1865; d Milan, 22 Dec 1922), Italian composer. Studied at the Bologna Liceo Musicale, Mancinelli being among his masters. In 1909 became professor of composition at Milan Conservatory.

Works include operas *Consuelo* (after George Sand, 1895), *Chopin* (on music by Chopin, 1901), *Cecilia* (1902), *Mosè* (1905), *Pane altrui*, *Radda*, *Il castello del sogno* and others; symphony in D minor, *Sinfonia del bosco*, *Anacreontiche* for orchestra (1917); suite for cello and orchestra; *Riflessioni ed ombre* for quintet, piano trio; two violin and piano sonatas, cello and piano sonata; *Preludi del mare*, *Quadri di Böcklin*, *Crepuscoli*, *Miraggi*, etc. for piano.

Orel, Alfred (b Vienna, 3 Jul 1889; d Vienna, 11 Apr 1967), Austrian musicologist. A lawyer and civil servant at first, he studied music with Adler when nearly 30. Later appointed professor at Vienna University and head of the music department of the municipal library. Author of works on Bruckner and co-editor with Robert Haas of the edition of the original versions of Bruckner's works.

Oresteia trilogy of short operas by Taneiev (libretto by A A Venkstern, after Aeschylus), produced St Petersburg, 29 Oct 1895. Scenes depict Greek myths, *Agamemnon*, *Choephorae/The Libation Bearers*, *Eumenides/The Furies*.

Orestes ◊Leben des Orest.

Opera by Weingartner (libretto by composer, after Aeschylus), produced Leipzig, 15 Feb 1902.

Orfeide, L' cycle of operas by Malipiero (libretto by composer), produced complete, in German translation, Düsseldorf, 30 Oct 1925.

I. *La morte delle maschere/The Death of the Maskers*. II. *Sette canzoni/Seven Songs*, produced in French translation, Paris, Opéra, 10 Jul 1920. III. *L'Orfeo, ossia l'ottava canzone/Orpheus, or the Eighth Song*.

Orfeo (Monteverdi.) ◊Favola d'Orfeo.

Orfeo ed Euridice, *Orpheus and Eurydice*, opera by Bertoni (libretto by R da Calzabigi, written for Gluck), produced Venice, Teatro San Benedetto, 3 Jan 1776.

Opera by Gluck (libretto ditto), produced Vienna, Burgtheater, 5 Oct 1762. (For French version ◊Orphée et Eurydice). Orpheus descends into Hades to bring back his deceased Eurydice.

Orfeo, L', *Orpheus*, opera by Luigi Rossi (libretto by F Buti), produced Paris, Palais Royal, 2 Mar 1647.

Orff, Carl (b Munich, 10 Jul 1895; d Munich, 29 Mar 1982), German composer and teacher. Studied at Munich and became professor of composition at the Günther School there. He was also a conductor and editor of early music, notably the operas of Monteverdi. His early success with *Carmina Burana*, founded on rhythmic ostinati and appealing vocal melody, was not repeated in later works.

Works include mainly 11 operas and musical plays, including *Carmina Burana* (settings of medieval poetry, 1937), *Die Kluge* (1943), *Catulli Carmina*, *Antigonae* and *Oedipus der Tyrann* (both Hölderlin, after Sophocles, 1949, 1959), *Trionfo di Afrodite* (1953), *Prometheus* (1966), *De temporum fine comoedia* (1973), cantata *Des Turmes Auferstehung* (Franz Werfel); ballet *Der Feuerfarbene*;

Schulwerk for combinations of popular instruments and similar compositions intended for use by amateurs. Incidental music for Shakespeare's *Midsummer Night's Dream*, 1939–62; first version composed to replace Mendelssohn's music, banned by the Nazis.

organ keyboard instrument in which sound is produced when a depressed key opens a valve, allowing compressed air to pass through a single pipe or a series of pipes; the number of pipes in total may vary, according to the size of the instrument. Its origin lies in remote antiquity, e.g. the syrinx or pan-pipe. Later the wind was no longer supplied by the player's breath, but by bellows; the pipes were opened and closed by an action of keys, and a keyboard of pedals, played by the feet, was added to control the largest bass pipes. The number of pipes, ranging from 32 ft down to a fraction of an inch, was enormously increased, and they were made in a growing variety of shapes from different materials, and with different speaking-mechanisms, each range being controlled by stops which could bring it into action or shut it off at the player's will. The number of manuals (hand keyboards) increased to three or more, which meant that a greater number of stops drawn before the performance could be controlled and varied. From the late 19th c. the bellows, formerly blown by hand, were operated mechanically and devices by which whole ranges of stops could be brought into action in various combinations were invented, still further increasing the resources already enlarged by the couplers, but which the registration controlled by two manuals or by a manual and the pedals could be mechanically united. Expression was added by swell pedals producing *crescendo* and *diminuendo*, but beyond that the player's hands and feet have no power to vary the tone either in strength or in quality. In the 20th c. electricity has been used in organs in a variety of ways: to generate air pressure, to open the valves, even to replace the pipes themselves with synthesized sound through loudspeakers (though this last application arguably disqualifies the instrument as a true organ).

organo pieno Italian; or *[pro] organo pleno* (Latin) = 'full organ'; a direction indicating that an organ passage is to be played with the use of the full extent of the instrument's power, or in earlier music with a substantial body of tone.

organ-point, from German *Orgelpunkt*, another term, used mainly in America for ◊pedal-point.

organ stops ◊diapason, ◊dulciana, ◊gedackt, ◊principal, ◊quint, ◊sesquialtera, ◊tremulant, ◊tromba, ◊voix celeste.

organum Latin = lit. 'instrument', also 'organ'; a term (originally a nickname) for early medieval music in parts, either moving wholly or mainly in parallel lines (9th c.) or independently (11th c.) or with florid melodies above a slow-moving plainsong (12th c.).

In all my work, my final concern is not with musical but with spiritual exposition.
Carl Orff, quoted in Liess, *Carl Orff*, 1968

Orgeni, actually Görger St Jörgen (*Anna Maria*) Aglaia (b Rima Szombat, 17 Dec 1841; d Vienna, 15 Mar 1926), Austrian soprano. Pupil of Pauline Viardot-Garcia. Made her debut in Berlin, 1865, as Amina. London, CG, 1866 as Lucia and Violetta. Vienna and Munich from 1872 as Agathe, Marguerite, the *Trovatore* Leonora and Valentine. Taught at Dresden Conservatory 1886–1914.

Orione, o sia Diana vendicata, *Orion, or Diana Avenged*, opera by J C Bach (libretto by G G Bottarelli), produced London, King's Theatre, 19 Feb 1763. J C Bach's first opera for London.

Orlandi, Santi (b Florence, ?; d Mantua, Jul 1619), Italian composer. He was *maestro di cappella* to Ferdinando Gonzaga at Florence and succeeded Monteverdi as *maestro di cappella* to the Gonzaga family at Mantua in 1612.

Works include opera *Gli amori di Aci e Galatea* (performed Mantua, Mar 1617); five books of madrigals, etc.

Orlandini, Giuseppe Maria (b Florence, 19 Mar 1675; d Florence, 24 Oct 1760), Italian composer. *Maestro di cappella* to the Duke of

organ *Prince Albert playing an organ for Queen Victoria and Felix Mendelssohn, engraved by H Hannal. English organs of this period were at last constructed with pedals (due largely to foreign influence), and they were designed according to the needs of church music in the Victorian religious revival.*

Tuscany at Florence, and appointed to the same post at the cathedral there in 1732.

Works include *c* 50 operas, e.g. *Amore e maestà* (1715), *Antigona* (1718), *Il marito giocatore*, *Nerone* (1720), etc.; oratorios; cantatas.

Orlando, *Roland*, opera by Handel (libretto by G Braccioli, based on Ariosto's *Orlando furioso*), produced London, King's Theatre, Haymarket, 27 Jan 1733. The knight Orlando falls in love with Angelica, but she does not return his feelings because she already loves Medoro. When Orlando discovers this he goes mad, until the magician Zoroastra (or Astolfo in the Vivaldi version) restores his reason. Orlando then blesses Angelica and Medoro's union.

Orlando Furioso opera by Vivaldi (libretto by G B Braccioli), produced Venice, Teatro Sant' Angelo, autumn 1727.

Orlando Paladino opera (*dramma eroicomico*) by Haydn (libretto by C F Badini and N Porta), produced Eszterháza, 6 Dec 1779. Similar to ◊*Orlando*, but here Orlando is already mad when the curtain goes up; Alcina is the sorceress who restores Orlando's senses; the additional character Rodomonte appears, who is also in love with Angelica.

Ormandy (actually *Blau*), Eugene (b Budapest, 18 Nov 1899; d Philadelphia, 12 Mar 1985), Hungarian-born American conductor. Studied violin first with his father and then entered the Budapest RAM for further studies with Hubay. He graduated in 1917, becoming leader of the Blüthner Orchestra in Berlin. In 1921 he went to the USA, taking various posts both as performer and conductor; US citizen 1927. In 1931 he was appointed permanent conductor of the Minneapolis SO, and in 1938 of the Philadelphia SO; gave the fps of Rakhmaninov's Symphonic Dances (1941) and Bartók's third piano concerto (1946). He was awarded the French *Légion d'honneur* in 1952. Was often heard leading works by Shostakovich and Mahler.

Ormindo opera by Cavalli (libretto by G Faustini), produced Venice, Teatro San Cassiano, 1644. Revived in new version by Raymond Leppard, Glyndebourne, 16 Jun 1967. In North Africa, Ormindo has fallen in love with Erisbe, who is married to King Hariadeno (Ormindo's long-lost father). When Hariadeno learns of the couple's planned escape he captures them and is about to execute them, before relenting and allowing Erisbe to join Ormindo.

ornaments throughout musical history until at least the early 19th c. there are many repertories in which it was expected that the performer would add ornamental details, ranging from the smallest trills, appoggiaturas and portamentos through to elaborate cadential embellishments. Shorthand signs to denote the simpler ornaments are found at least from the early 16th c. (though there are traces of them much earlier in the chant repertory); but they began to be codified in elaborate systems described in detailed tables of ornaments from the 17th c. and had their heyday in the first half of the 18th c. Since the early 19th c., performers have tended not to add their own improvised ornaments, relying instead on only explicitly notated embellishments written by the composer.

◊acciaccatura, ◊appogiatura, ◊arpeggio, ◊cadenza, ◊mordent, ◊plica, ◊shake, ◊turn, ◊tremolo, ◊vibrato.

Ornithoparcus (actually *Vogelgesang* or *Vogelsang*), Andreas (b Meiningen, *c* 1490), German music scholar. Studied ? at Tübingen University, travelled in many countries and held some posts at Wittenberg University. Author of the Latin treatise *Musicae activae micrologus* (1517), which was trans. into English by J Dowland (1609).

Ornstein, Leo (b Krementchug, 11 Dec 1892), Russian-born American pianist and composer. Studied at the St Petersburg Conservatory, where he appeared as a child prodigy, settled in NY in 1907, studying further at the Institute of Musical Art, and made his first concert appearance there in 1911. Taught in Philadelphia and retired 1953.

Works include pantomime *Lima Beans*, pantomime ballet; incidental music to Aristophanes' *Lysistrata* (1930); symphony, two Nocturnes, *Nocturne and Dance of the Fates*, symphonic poem *The Fog* for orchestra (1915); piano concerto (1923), three string quartets, piano quintet; two violin and piano sonatas, sonata for cello and piano; choral works; piano music including 20 Waltzes (1955–68) and *Biography in Sonata Form* (1974).

Orologio, Alessandro (b Italy, *c* 1550; d ? Vienna, 1633), Italian composer and instrumentalist. His career took him to Prague, Kassel, Dresden and Wolfenbüttel; became choirmaster at the Austrian monastery of Garsten at the end of his career. He pub. several books of madrigals and canzonets, and a collection of Intradas 'for all kinds of instruments'.

If I had the power I would insist on all oratorios being sung in the costume of the period – with a possible exception in the case of The Creation.
Ernest Newman, *New York Post*, 1924

Orontea opera by Cesti (libretto by G A Ciognini), produced Venice, Teatro dei Apostoli, 1649; revised by G F Apolloni, produced Innsbruck, Teatro di Sala, 19 Feb 1656. Cesti's first opera; successfully revived in modern editions. Orontea, Queen of Egypt, falls in love with lowly painter Alidoro. There is stiff opposition to her wedding plans, but all is resolved when it turns out Alidoro is of noble birth.

Orozco, Rafael (b Cordoba, 24 Jan 1946; d 25 April 1996), Spanish pianist. He studied at the Madrid Conservatory and in 1966 won the Leeds International Competition. Was often heard in Europe and the USA in the Romantic repertory.

orpharion an early instrument of the ◊cittern type. It had six or seven pairs of strings played with a plectrum.

Orphée aux enfers, *Orpheus in the Underworld*, operetta by Offenbach (libretto by H Crémieux and L Halévy), produced Paris, Bouffes-Parisiens, 21 Oct 1858. A spoof on the original *Orpheus*: Orpheus is delighted at the prospect of freedom when Eurydice dies, and arrives in Hades to reclaim her only because Public Opinion forces him to.

Orphée et Eurydice opera by Gluck (libretto by P L Moline, translated from Calzabigi's *Orfeo ed Euridice*, of Gluck's first setting of which it is a revised version), produced Paris, 3 Aug 1774. ◊*Orfeo ed Euridice* for plot synopsis.

Orphéon, French, a French male-voice choral society similar to the German *Liedertafel*.

Orpheus ◊Favola d'Orfeo; ◊Malheurs d'Orphée; ◊Orfeide; ◊Orfeo; ◊Orfeo ed Euridice; ◊Orphée; ◊Orphée aux enfers; ◊Orpheus; ◊Orpheus og Euridice; ◊Orpheus und Eurydike.

Ballet by Stravinsky (choreographed by George Balanchine) produced NY, 29 Apr 1948. Opera by Keiser (libretto by F C Bressand), produced Brunswick (Part I: *Die sterbende Eurydice*) 1699. Hamburg (Part II: *Die verwandelte Leyer des Orpheus*), 1709.

Symphonic poem by Liszt, composed 1853–54, fp as an introduction to Gluck's *Orfeo*, Weimar, 16 Feb 1854, with closing music on the same themes after the opera.

Orpheus ballet in two acts by Henze (scenario by Edward Bond), produced Stuttgart 17 Mar 1979; Suite for ballet, *Apollo triofante*, performed Gelsenkirchen, 1 Sept 1980; *Arias of Orpheus* for guitar, harp, harpsichord and strings performed Chicago, 25 Nov 1981; *Dramatic Scenes from Orpheus* for large orchestra performed in two parts: no. 2 Zurich, 6 Jan 1981, no. 1 Frankfurt, 12 Sept 1982; Concert version of the ballet performed Cologne, 4 Mar 1983.

Orpheus Britannicus a collection of vocal music by Purcell begun soon after Purcell's death by Henry Playford, who pub. a first volume in 1698 and a second in 1702; also a collection of Purcell's songs pub. by John Walsh in 1735.

Orpheus og Euridice opera by Naumann (libretto by C D Biehl, based on Calzabigi), produced Copenhagen, 21 Jan 1786. The first grand opera on a Danish libretto. ◊*Orfeo ed Euridice* for plot synopsis.

Orpheus und Eurydike opera by Krenek (libretto by Oskar Kokoschka), produced Kassel, 27 Nov 1926. A psychoanalytical rendering of the Greek myth.

Orr, Buxton (Daeblitz) (b Glasgow, 18 Apr 1924), Scottish composer and conductor. Studied with Benjamin Frankel 1952–55 and wrote film and theatre music until 1961. Conducted the London Jazz Composers' Orchestra 1970–80 and the Guildhall New Music Ensemble 1975–91. Completed Frankel's opera *Marching Song* for posthumous fp in 1983.

Works include opera *The Wager* (1962), *A Celtic Suite* for strings (1968), trombone concerto, with brass band (1971), *Ring in the New*, music theatre (1986), *Sinfonia Ricercante* (1988) *Refrains VI* for chamber orchestra (1992).

Orr, C(harles) W(ilfred) (b Cheltenham, 31 Jul 1893; d Stroud, 24 Feb 1976), English composer. Educated at Cheltenham College. He suffered much from ill-health in his youth and did not begin to study music at the GSM in London until 1917. He lived most of his life quietly at Painswick, Gloucestershire, and never held any official musical posts; but he did war work in London during World War II.

Works include *A Cotswold Hill Tune* for string orchestra; numerous songs, especially settings of A E Housman, also D G Rossetti, James Joyce, etc.

Orr, Robin (b Brechin, 2 Jun 1909), Scottish composer. Studied at the RCM in London and with E J Dent at Cambridge, also with Casella at Siena and Nadia Boulanger in Paris. From 1938 to 1956 he was organist and director of studies at St John's College, Cambridge. Professor of music at Glasgow University 1956–64, and at Cambridge 1964–76. Chairman, Scottish Opera, 1962–76; Director, WNO, 1971–83.

Works include operas *Full Circle* (1968), *Hermiston* (1975) and *On the Razzle* (1988); three symphonies (1965, 1971, 1978), *Sinfonietta Helvetia* (1990); divertimento for chamber orchestra; three Latin psalms for voice and string quartet; string quintet (1971); sonatina for violin and piano, violin sonata, viola sonata; piano pieces; songs, etc.

Ortiz, Christina (b Bahia, 17 Apr 1950), Brazilian pianist. Studied in Paris with Magda Tagliafero and after winning the 1969 Van Cliburn Competition studied further with Rudolf Serkin at Curtis. New York recital debut 1971, London 1973 (settled there the same year). Salzburg debut 1983, with Mozart's Concerto K453. Concerts with the Vienna, Berlin and New York Philharmonics, Chicago SO and Concertgebouw and Philharmonia Orchestras.

Ortiz, Diego (b Toledo, *c* 1510; d Naples, *c* 1570), Spanish composer. He went to Naples in 1555 to become *maestro de capilla* to the viceroy, the Duke of Alva, where he worked with many other Spanish musicians, including Salinas. He wrote an important treatise on ornamentation in viol music, the *Trattado de Glosas*, pub. in two editions (Spanish and Italian) in Rome, 1553.

Works include motets; variations for bass viol.

Orto, Marbriano de (b *c* 1460; d Nivelles, Feb 1529), Flemish singer and composer. His name may have been Dujardin, the Italian form being taken when he went to Rome, where he was a singer in the Papal chapel in 1484–94, with Josquin Desprez. Early in the 16th c. he became chaplain and singer at the court of Philip the Fair of Burgundy.

Works include Masses, motets and other church music; *chansons*.

Osborne, George Alexander (b Limerick, 24 Sept 1806; d London, 16 Nov 1893), Irish pianist. Studied in Belgium and afterwards taught piano in Brussels. In 1826 he went to Paris, making further studies with Pixis and Kalkbrenner and becoming a friend of Chopin, Berlioz and Rossini. He settled in London in 1843, where he taught and championed Chopin's work.

Osborne, Nigel (b Manchester, 23 Jun 1948), English composer. He studied at Oxford with Wellesz and Leighton and in Poland with Witold Rodziński. Lecturer at Nottingham University from 1978. He is best known for his vivid and iconoclastic stage works.

Works include *Byzantine Epigrams* for chorus (1969); *Seven Words*, cantata (1971); *Charivari* for orchestra (1973); *Chansonnier* for chamber ensemble (1975); *I am Goya* for baritone and instruments (1977); *Concert Piece* for cello and orchestra (1977); *In Camera* for 13 instruments (1979); *Gnostic Passion* for 36 voices (1980); Flute concerto (1980); *The Cage* for tenor and ensemble (1981); *Sinfonia* for orchestra (1982); *Alba* for mezzo, instruments and tape (1984); *Zansa* for ensemble (1985); *Pornography* for mezzo and ensemble (1985), *The Electrification of the Soviet Union*, opera, (1986); *Esquisse* I and II for strings (1987–88), violin concerto (1990), *The Sun of Venice* for orchestra (1991); operas *Terrible Mouth* (1992) and *Sarajevo* (1994).

Osiander, Lucas (b Nuremberg, 16 Dec 1534; d Stuttgart, 17 Sept 1604), German theologian and composer, son of the reformer Andreas Osiander. He composed sacred songs and psalms in four parts with German words.

ossia Italian from *o sia* = 'or be it, or else'; a word shown with an alternative passage, usually easier (but sometimes more difficult) which may be performed at the musician's discretion instead of that originally written down by the composer. Such passages are usually shown in smaller notes above or below the stave. The word may also be used for alternatives where a composer clearly wrote a passage of piano music for a short keyboard and where it is clear that he would have written it otherwise for a modern piano. It also occurs, like the older *ovvero*, in second alternative titles of operas (e.g. *Così fan tutte, ossia La scuola degli amanti*, etc.).

Ossian semi-mythical Gaelic bard whose works, allegedly translated by James Macpherson (1736–96), influenced the early Romantic movement. Ossian's works were in fact by Macpherson, drawing on ancient sources. Schubert set nine Ossian songs (1815–17).

Osten, Eva von der (b Insel, Heligoland, 19 Aug 1881; d Dresden, 5 May 1936), German soprano. She studied in Dresden and made her debut there in 1902; remained until 1927, creating Octavian and appearing also as Ariadne, the Dyer's Wife, Kundry, Tatyana and Brünnhilde. London 1913–14 in Wagner and Strauss roles. Other roles included Louise, Tosca and Zazà.

ostinato Italian = 'obstinate'; a persistently repeated figure in a composition. If it is in the bass, it is called *basso ostinato*. A rhythm also can be called ostinato, and so can some instrumental device, like Tchaikovsky's *pizzicato ostinato* in the fourth symphony.

Ostman, Arnold (b Malmo, 24 Dec 1939), Swedish conductor. After study in Paris and Stockholm he was director of the Vadstena Academy 1969–79, conducting operas by Provenzale, Leo, Monteverdi, Purcell, and Stradella. Music director of the Court theatre at Drottningholm 1979–91, giving period-style performances of eight operas by Mozart, Kraus's *Proserpin* and *Iphigénie en Aulide*. London debut 1983, *Il Matrimonio Segreto* at SW; CG 1984, *Don Giovanni*. Conducted Rossini's *Tancredi* at the Wexford Festival (1986) and Mozart's *Lucio Silla* at the Vienna Staatsoper in 1990. Returned to Drottningholm 1992 for *Orfeo ed Euridice*.

Ostrčil, Otakar (b Smichov, near Prague, 25 Feb 1879; d Prague, 20 Aug 1935), Czech conductor and composer. Studied at Prague University and became professor of modern languages at the Commercial Academy there. He had already studied music especially with Fibich, and in 1909 he became conductor of an amateur orchestra and in 1914 at the Vinohrady Theatre. He succeeded Kovařovic as conductor of the National Theatre in 1920, when he gave the fp of Janáček's *The Excursions of Mr Brouček*.

Works include operas *The Death of Vlasta, Kunala's Eyes* (1908), *The Bud, Legend of Erin* (1921), and *John's Kingdom* (1934); incidental music for Jaroslav Kvapil's play *The Orphan*; *The Legend of St Zita* for tenor, chorus, orchestra and organ (1913) and other choral works; symphony in A major, sinfonietta (1921), two suites, symphonic poem *The Tale of Semik, Rustic Festival* and *Impromptu* for orchestra; *Ballad of the Dead Cobbler* and *Czech Ballad* for declamation and orchestra; string quartet in B major (1899), sonatina for violin, viola and piano; songs.

Ostrovsky, Alexander Nikolaievich (1823–1886), Russian dramatist. ◊Arensky (*Dream on the Volga*); ◊Dzerzhinsky (*Storm*); ◊Kashperov (ditto); Janáček (◊Káta Kabanová); ◊Serov (*Power of Evil*); Rimsky-Korsakov (◊Snow Maiden); ◊Tchaikovsky (*Snegurotchka*); N ◊Tcherepnin (*Poverty no Crime*); Tchaikovsky (◊Voyevoda).

Osud, *Fate*, opera in three scenes by Janáček (libretto by composer and F Bartosova); composed 1903–04, fp Brno Radio 18 Sept 1934; produced Brno, 25 Oct 1958. Produced London, Coliseum, 8 Sept 1984. Composer Živný is reunited with his former mistress Míla but she and her insane mother are killed in a fall.

Oswald von Wolkenstein ◊Wolkenstein.

Otaka, Tadaaki (b Kamakura, 8 Nov 1947), Japanese conductor. Studied at the Toho School of Music and the Vienna Hochschule.

Tadaaki Otaka – conductor

1   Bruckner: Symphony no. 9
    The late Romantics are all my favourites, but Bruckner is special; he is closest to God.

2   Elgar: Symphonies nos. 1 and 2
    I love Elgar very much. The slow movements of both symphonies are from the bottom of the heart; they have the same feeling as the slow movements of Bruckner's Seventh, Eighth, and Ninth. I went to Malvern in 1992 and the year before I went to Sankt Florian, where Bruckner grew up. The landscapes are very similar, with gentle hills, and I thought that the same landscapes had made two great composers.

3   Mozart: Violin Sonata no. 21 in E minor (Grumiaux/Haskil)
    This is a piece I would pick, especially the Clara Haskil recording. I studied the piano, because it is very important for a conductor, and I tried to play this piece, but I couldn't. Simple music is the most difficult.

4   Benny Goodman
    Finally I would pick the music of Benny Goodman. I have to practise a lot so as to be natural at concerts, and when I am 60 or 70 I would like to be as natural as Benny Goodman. He is a great musician.

THE OPERA

Otello

A four-act opera of 1887 by Giuseppe Verdi – not to be confused with a three-act opera of the same name by Gioachino Rossini (1816). It is set in Cyprus in the 15th century.

I. In the middle of a storm, the people of Cyprus await the arrival of their Venetian governor, Otello (tenor). As soon as Otello lands, his ensign Iago (baritone) plots against him. Iago has been passed over for promotion in favour of Cassio (tenor), whose dismissal Iago now engineers by getting him drunk. Under the starlight, Otello and Desdemona (soprano) pledge their love.

II. Prompted by Iago into thinking there is an affair between Cassio and Desdemona, Otello refuses to reinstate his captain. Iago further uses Desdemona's handkerchief, given to her by Otello but seen in Cassio's possession, to further provoke Otello's jealousy.

III. Otello is further convinced of Desdemona's guilt when he hears Cassio talking to Iago about his mistress. Ambassadors from Venice arrive to replace Otello as governor with Cassio. The furious Otello flings his wife to the ground before himself collapsing in a fit.

IV. Desdemona sings a Willow Song, learned from her mother's maid, and Ave Maria as she prepares for bed. Otello enters and, despite Desdemona's pleas, he strangles her. Emilia (mezzo-soprano), wife of Iago, raises the alarm and after the truth has been revealed, Otello stabs himself before the assembled company.

THE OPERA

Principal conductor of the Tokyo PO 1974–81, Sapporo SO 1981–86; BBC Welsh SO from 1987, leading it at the 1991 London Proms in music by Tippett (Piano Concerto) and Strauss (*Heldenleben*).

Otello opera by Verdi (libretto by Boito, after Shakespeare), produced Milan, La Scala, 5 Feb 1887. Otello, driven by the evil Iago, murders his wife Desdemona in a jealous rage, and commits suicide.

Otello, ossia Il Moro di Venezia, *Othello, or The Moor of Venice*, opera by Rossini, libretto by F B Salsa, after Shakespeare, produced Naples, Teatro Fondo, 4 Dec 1816.

Othello ◊Otello.

Concert overture by Dvořák, op. 93, referring to Shakespeare's tragedy, composed 1892 and forming, with *Amid Nature* and *Carnival*, a cycle with thematic connections originally called *Nature, Life and Love*.

Othmayr, Kaspar (b Amberg, 12 Mar 1515; d Nuremberg, 4 Feb 1553), German clergyman and musician. Studied at Heidelberg University and was a pupil of Lemlin for music there. He held church appointments at Heilsbronn and Ansbach, but *c* 1550 retired to Nuremberg on account of religious controversies, himself being a Lutheran. He took part in the development of German polyphonic song.

Works include Latin motets, German hymns and other sacred music; an Epitaph on Luther's death; 26 secular songs contributed to George Foster's collection, etc.

Ott, Hans (b Rain am Lech, near Donauwöth, *c* 1500; d Nuremberg, 1546), German music editor. His collections, all pub. at Nuremberg, including 121 songs (1534) and an important collection of 13 Masses (1539).

ottavino Italian from *ottava* = 'octave'; the current Italian name of the octave flute elsewhere called piccolo (from *flauto piccolo* = 'little flute').

Otter, Anne Sofie von (b Stockholm, 9 May 1955), Swedish mezzo. Studied at the GSM and has sung in London from 1982. Basel Opera 1983–85, debut as Alcina in Haydn's *Orlando Paladino*. Her US debut was in 1985, with the Chicago SO, and she has appeared widely in Europe; CG debut 1985, as Cherubino, returning in 1992 as Bellini's Romeo. NY Met. debut 1988 (Cherubino), Salzburg Festival 1989, as Berlioz's Marguerite. Other roles include Orpheus, Octavian, and Mozart's Sextus and Dorabella.

Otterloo, (Jan) Willem van (b Winterswijk, 27 Dec 1907; d Melbourne, 28 Jul 1978), Dutch conductor and composer. Studied at the Amsterdam Conservatory under Dresden and others. Appointed second conductor of the Utrecht Municipal Orchestra in 1933 and first in 1937; until 1973, when he became music director at Düsseldorf.

Works include symphony, three suites and passacaglia for orchestra; chamber music, piano and organ works.

Otto, Lisa (b Dresden, 14 Nov 1919), German soprano. Studied piano and singing at the Dresden Hochschule für Musik 1938–40, making her debut as a singer in 1941, as Sophie. From 1945 to 1950 she sang at the Dresden Opera and in 1952 became a member of the Berlin Staatsoper. She was best known in lighter soubrette roles, e.g. Blonde, Despina and Marzelline.

Otto, Stephan (b Freiberg, Saxony, bap. 28 Mar 1603; d Schandau, 2 Oct 1656), German composer. Studied at Freiberg under Christoph Demantius, and after an appointment at Augsburg he became cantor at his home town in 1632 and at Schandau in 1639. Hammerschmidt was among his pupils.

Works include *Kronen-Krönlein*, a collection of sacred vocal pieces in a mixed motet and madrigal style, for three–eight voices, setting of Luther's hymn 'Ein' feste Burg' for 19 voices.

Ottone, rè di Germania, *Otho, King of Germany*, opera by Handel (libretto by N F Haym), produced London, King's Theatre, Haymarket, 12 Jan 1723. Otto defeats attempted revolt by Adalberto and is united with his promised bride, Teofane.

Oudin, Eugène (Espérance) (b New York, 24 Feb 1858; d London, 4 Nov 1894), American baritone of French descent. Studied law at Yale University and practised it for a time, but during a holiday in London in 1886 decided to turn to music. He made his debut in NY that year, with Louise Parker, who became his wife on 4 Dec. In 1891 he first appeared in opera in London as the Templar in Sullivan's *Ivanhoe*; he was the first Eugene Onegin in London (1892); St Petersburg 1893–94 as Wolfram and Telramund.

Otter *The mezzo Anne Sofie von Otter. Since her engagement at Basel in 1983 she has sung several male operatic roles (including Cherubino and Octavian), for which her consistent, rich voice is well-suited. She has pursued a successful concert career.*

Our Hunting Fathers song cycle for high voice and orchestra by Britten (text by W H Auden), fp Norwich, 25 Sept 1936, conductor Britten.

Ours, L', *The Bear*, nickname of Haydn's symphony no. 82 in C major, composed for Paris in 1786.

Ouseley, Frederick (Arthur) Gore (b London, 12 Aug 1825; d Hereford, 6 Apr 1889), English organist, composer and clergyman. Studied at Oxford, where he took the Mus.D. in 1854 and was appointed Professor of Music in 1855. Founder of St Michael's College, Tenbury. He succeeded to his father's baronetcy in 1844. He edited early music and wrote books on technique.

Works include 11 services, *c* 70 anthems; oratorios, *The Martyrdom of St Polycarp* and *Hagar*; over 30 preludes and fugues, two sonatas and other works for organ; two string quartets; part-songs, glees; songs.

Ousset, Cécile (b Tarbes, 23 Jan 1936), French pianist. Studied at Paris Conservatory, graduated 1950. Many appearances with leading orchestras. British debut Edinburgh Festival, 1980. US debut with the LA PO, 1984.

Ovchinikov, Vladimir (b Belebey, 2 Jan 1958), Russian pianist. Studied in Moscow and was joint Silver Medal winner at the 1982 Moscow International Competition. Winner of the 1987 Leeds International and made London recital debut same year. Formed piano trio with Alexander Vinnitsky and Alex Rudin in 1989 (recordings of works by Rakhmaninov and Shostakovich). Teacher at the RNCM, Manchester, from 1994.

overblowing the playing of wind instruments in such a way that the upper harmonics are produced instead of the fundamental notes. Brass instruments produce a greater number of harmonics than woodwind. Overblowing may occur by accident in organ pipes by too great a pressure of wind, but safety-valve devices have been invented to prevent this.

overspun the lower strings of instruments of the violin family and also those of the piano, which consist of a central wire around which another wire is spun.

overstrung the bass strings of modern pianos, which cross diagonally over the strings of higher-pitched notes, in order to secure greater length in the strings, thereby improving tone quality.

overtones ◊harmonics *and* ◊partials.

overture from French *ouverture* = 'opening'; an instrumental introductory composition preceding some other large work, especially an opera or oratorio; also sometimes an independent composition for concert use, e.g. Mendelssohn's *Hebrides* and Brahms's *Tragic* Overtures. From the time of Lully to that of Handel the overture in its French form had a slow introduction and a fugal *allegro*, often followed by a return to the slow section or by a new slow portion, and in some cases by one or more independent pieces in dance form, in which case it resembled the ◊suite; hence Bach's overtures are in fact suites with first movements in French overture form. The Italian overture form differed from the French in the late 17th and 18th c. by being in several movements approximating more to the early symphony, to which in fact it gave birth.

In opera the music for the overture had no special relevance to the work itself up to the time of Rameau, and sometimes not afterwards (e.g. Rossini, except his overture to *Guillaume Tell*). Gluck's mature overtures foreshadow the character and atmosphere of the operas to which they belong, and from his time on the actual musical material of the overture was more often than not drawn from the opera itself to a greater or smaller extent.

ovvero Italian = 'or rather, or else'; an earlier word for *ossia*; also found in front of second, alternative titles of musical works.

Owens, Anne Marie (b Tyne and Wear, 15 Aug 1955), English mezzo-soprano. Studied at the GSMD and made debut as Mistress Quickly with GTO. With ENO has sung Charlotte, Rosina, Preziosilla and Solokha in the UK premiere of Rimsky-Korsakov's *Christmas Eve* (1988). CG from 1989, in *Zauberflöte*, *Walküre*, *Hoffmann* and *Boris* (Hostess). Has sung Stravinsky's Jocasta and Dukas' Ariane for Opera North (1990). Other roles include Arnalta in *Poppea* (Glyndebourne), Baba the Turk (Brussels) and Maddalena. US debut with *Messiah* at Detroit.

Owen Wingrave opera in two acts by Britten (libretto by M Piper after Henry James), fp BBC TV 16 May 1971; produced CG, London, 10 May 1973. Pacifist Owen Wingrave drops out of Spencer Coyle's military school. His family is disgusted. Fellow student Lechmere drives Owen to spend the night in a haunted room; a family prophecy comes true and Owen is found dead.

Oxford Elegy, An work by Vaughan Williams for speaker, small chorus and orchestra (text from Matthew Arnold, *The Scholar Gipsy* and *Thyrsis*), fp (private) Dorking, 20 Nov 1949; first public performance Queen's College, Oxford, 19 Jun 1952.

Oxford Symphony the name given to Haydn's symphony no. 92 in G major, composed 1788. It was not written for Oxford, but received its title after it was performed there in Jul 1791 when Haydn was given the honorary degree of Mus.D.

Ox Minuet, *Die Ochsenmenuette*, a *Singspiel* by Seyfried, produced in Vienna, 1823, with music arranged from compositions by Haydn. It was based on two earlier French works, *Le Menuet de bœuf, ou Une Leçon de Haydn* (1805) and *Haydn, ou le Menuet du bœuf* (1812). The title is sometimes mistakenly thought to be the nickname of one of Haydn's minuets.

Ozawa, Seiji (b Hoten, Manchuria, 1 Sept 1935), Japanese conductor. He studied in Tokyo and with Karajan in Berlin. Assistant to Bernstein at the NY PO 1961–65 (debut with orchestra, Carnegie Hall 1961). London debut 1965, with LSO. Toronto SO 1965–69; He has conducted *Così fan tutte* at Salzburg and in 1983 led the fp of Messiaen's *St François d'Assise*, at the Paris Opéra. Boston SO from 1973; worldwide tours, and has conducted Mahler's eighth symphony and Schoenberg's *Gurrelieder* (also recorded).

Ozim, Igor (b Ljubljana, 9 May 1931), Slovenian violinist. Studied in Ljubljana and made debut there 1947. Many concert appearances in Europe, the Americas, Australia and the Far East. Has premiered many modern works, and edited the Mozart concertos for the Neue Mozart Ausgabe.

Ozolin, Arthur (Marcelo) (b Lübeck, 7 Feb 1946), German pianist. Studied at the University of Toronto and the Mannes College of Music. Made his debut with the Toronto SO in 1961 and has since toured frequently in Russia, Europe and the USA; solo recitals in New York, London and St Petersburg. Repertoire includes Tippett's *Handel Fantasy* and concertos by Prokofiev and Mozart, in addition to 19th-c. works.

Ozawa *The conductor Seiji Ozawa. During his long-standing position as Music Director of the Boston Symphony Orchestra he has made many recordings, excelling at works by 20th-century composers. He led the premiere of Messiaen's* St François d'Assise *in 1983.*

P

p, abbr., used in music for *piano* = 'soft', in this form: *p*; sometimes also for the pedal in piano music in this: *P*. In the latter case, however, it is more often *Ped*.

Pabst German family of musicians:

    1. August Pabst (b Elberfeld, 30 May 1811; d Riga, 21 Jul 1885), organist and composer. He became organist at Königsberg and later director of the Music School at Riga. Wrote operas, etc.

    2. Louis Pabst (b Königsberg, 18 Jul 1846; d Moscow, after 1903), pianist and composer, son of 1. Studied under his father, made his first appearance as pianist in 1862, lived at Liverpool, Riga, Melbourne, founding music schools in the latter two places, and finally held a professorship in Moscow. Wrote melodramas, piano works, songs.

    3. Paul Pabst (b Königsberg, 27 May 1854; d Moscow, 9 Jun 1897), pianist and composer, brother of 2. Studied under his father and brother, later under Liszt. Settled in Moscow as professor at the Conservatory. Wrote piano music, operatic paraphrases, etc.

Pacchiarotti, Gasparo (b Fabriano, near Ancona, bap. 21 May 1740; d Padua, 28 Oct 1821), Italian castrato soprano. Chorister at Forli Cathedral, then at St Mark's Venice, under Bertoni, he made his operatic debut 1766 and became *primo musico* at the Teatro San Benedetto in Venice. Later sang in Palermo, London, Naples, etc., and retired to Padua in 1792. He was admired in Bertoni's *Olimpiade*, *Artaserse*, *Quinto Fabio* and *Armida*.

Pacchioni, Antonio (Maria) (b Modena, bap. 5 Jul 1654; d Modena, 15 Jul 1738), Italian priest and composer. Studied at Modena Cathedral, where he became chaplain at the ducal court and later assistant choirmaster. In 1733 he and Pitoni settled a dispute between Marhini and Redi about the solution of a canon by Animuccia.

    Works include Masses and other church music, oratorios.

Pace (also called *Pacius*), Pietro (b Loreto, 1559; d Loreto, 15 Apr 1622), Italian composer. Was organist at Pesaro in 1597 and of the Santa Casa at Loreto, 1591–92, and again, 1611–22.

    Works include music for Ignazio Bracci's *L'ilarocosmo, ovvero Il mondo lieto* (performed Urbino, 29 Apr 1621); Magnificats, motets (with accompaniment) and other church music; *Arie spirituali* and madrigals with and without accompaniment.

Pacelli, Asprilio (b Vasciano near Narni, Umbria, 1570; d Warsaw, 4 May 1623), Italian composer. Choirmaster of the German College (1592–1602), and later at the Vatican basilica in Rome until 1602, when he went to the court of Sigismund III of Poland at Warsaw, succeeding Marenzio.

    Works include motets, psalms, *Sacrae cantiones*; madrigals.

Pachelbel, Johann (b Nuremberg, bap. 1 Sept 1653; d Nuremberg, buried 3 Mar 1706), German organist and composer. Studied under Heinrich Schwemmer at home and after holding brief appointments at Altdorf and Regensburg, went to Vienna, c 1671–72. Between 1677 and 1695 he was organist successively at Eisenach, Erfurt, Stuttgart and Gotha, and in 1695 was appointed organist at St Sebaldus's Church at Nuremberg. He was one of Bach's most important predecessors.

    Works include vocal music, arias, motets, sacred concertos (i.e. cantatas) and 11 Magnificat settings. 94 organ fugues on the Magnificat, organ variations and preludes on chorales; suites for two violins, Canon and Gigue for 3 violins, *Musikalisches Ergötzen*; six sets of variations for harpsichord *Hexachordum Apollinis* (1699).

Pachelbel, Wilhelm Hieronymus (b Erfurt, bap. 29 Aug 1686; d Nuremberg, 1764), German organist and composer, son and pupil of Johann ◊Pachelbel. Organist at St Sebaldus's Church, Nuremberg, from 1719. Wrote organ and harpsichord music.

At the piano bobbed this grubby little fat man playing divine Chopin divinely well, at the same time rising and falling in his seat, turning a beaming countenance first to the right and then to the left, and crying 'Valse, Valse'.

        Barbellion on Vladimir de Pachmann,
        in *Journal of a Disappointed Man*, 1919

Pachmann, Vladimir de (b Odessa, 27 Jul 1848; d Rome, 7 Jan 1933), Russian pianist of Austrian descent. Studied first under his father, a university professor, and later in Vienna, and made his first concert appearance in Russia, 1869. In 1882 he first visited London. He became a famous but somewhat eccentric exponent of Chopin.

Pachelbel *The title page of* Hexachordum Apollinis *by Johann Pachelbel (1653–1706), published by W M Endter in Nürnberg, 1699. This work, consisting of six sets of variations for organ or harpsichord, was Pachelbel's only publication during the last decade of his life.*

Pacific 231 symphonic movement by Honegger, named after a railway engine and depicting its start and progress, not merely realistically, but, the composer claims, 'lyrically'. Fp Paris, at a Koussevitsky concert, 8 May 1924.

Pacini, Giovanni (b Catania, 17 Feb 1796; d Pescia, 6 Dec 1867), Italian composer. Studied first under his father, a famous tenor, and later at Bologna and Venice. At the age of 17 he produced his first opera at Venice. He became *maestro di cappella* to Napoleon's widow, the Empress Marie Louise, and in 1834 settled at Viareggio, where he opened a music school, later transferred to Lucca. For this he wrote some theoretical treatises.

Works include operas *Annetta e Lucindo* (1813), *La sacerdotessa d'Irminsul* (1820), *La schiava in Bagdad* (1820), *La Gioventù di Enrico V* (after Shakespeare's *Henry IV*, 1820), *L'ultimo giorno di Pompei* (not based on Bulwer-Lytton, 1825), *Gli Arabi nelle Gallie* (1827), *Saffo* (1840), *Medea* (1843), *Lorenzino de' Medici* (1845), *La regina di Cipro*, *Il saltimbanco*, *Ivanhoe* (after Scott, 1832) and over 60 others; incidental music for Sophocles' *Oedipus Rex*; Masses, oratorios, cantata for Dante anniversary and others; six string quartets (c 1860).

Paciotti, Pietro Paulo (b Tivoli, c 1550; d ? Rome, after 1614), Italian composer. Choirmaster of the Seminario Romano in Rome, 1591. Wrote Masses, motets, madrigals.

Pacius, Fredrik (b Hamburg, 19 Mar 1809; d Helsinki, 9 Jan 1891), German-born Finnish violinist and composer. Pupil of Spohr and Hauptmann at Kassel, violinist in the court orchestra at Stockholm, 1828–34, when he became music teacher at Helsinki University. He remained in the Finnish capital, established orchestral concerts there in 1845 and became professor of music at the university in 1860.

Works include operas *Kung Karls Jakt* (1852) and *Loreley* (1887); incidental music for Topelius's *Princess of Cyprus* (1860); violin concerto; cantatas; songs including *Suomis Saang* and *Vaart Land*, both adapted as Finnish national anthems.

Packe, Thomas, English 15th–16th-c. composer. He was a knight and probably held no official musical post.

Works include Masses, *Rex summe* and *Gaudete in Domino*, motets and a Te Deum.

If I don't practise for one day, I know it; if I don't practise for two days, the critics know it; if I don't practise for three days, the audience knows it.
Jan Paderewski, quoted in Shapiro, *An Encyclopaedia of Quotations about Music*, 1978

Paderewski, Ignacy (Jan) (b Kurylówka, Podolia, 18 Nov 1860; d New York, 29 Jun 1941), Polish pianist, composer and statesman. Studied at the Warsaw Conservatory and went on his first concert tour in 1877. After teaching 1878–81 at the Conservatory he went to Berlin for further study, finishing with Leschetizky in Vienna, reappearing there and in Paris in 1887. He soon became established as one of the leading virtuosi of the day. In 1890 he paid his first visit to England and in 1891 to the USA. His opera *Manru* was premiered at Dresden in 1901 and given at the Met. the following year. During World War I he collected large sums for the Polish relief fund and in 1919 became the first president of the Polish Republic. He supervised a complete edition of Chopin's music, 1936–38.

Works include opera *Manru* (1901); symphony in B minor (1903–09); concerto in A minor (1888) and Polish Fantasy for piano and orchestra; violin and piano sonata; sonata in E♭ minor and many other piano works; songs.

Padlock, The opera by Dibdin (libretto by I Bickerstaffe, based on a story by Cervantes, *El celoso extremeño*), produced London, Drury Lane Theatre, 3 Oct 1768. Old Don Diego, hoping to marry young Leonora, locks her in the house. Young Leander, however, climbs the wall and woos her.

Padmâvatî opera-ballet by Roussel (libretto in French, by L Laloy), produced Paris, Opéra, 1 Jun 1923. The Sultan Aladdin encircles Chitor with his army and sues for peace, but when he sees Queen Padmâvatî and is struck by her beauty, he demands her in return for not destroying the city. King Ratan-Sen offers her, so Padmâvatî stabs him before joining him on the funeral pyre.

Padua, Bartolino da, Italian 14th–15th-c. composer. Wrote madrigals and *ballate* in the Italian *Ars nova* style.

Paer, Ferdinando (b Parma, 1 Jun 1771; d Paris, 3 May 1839), Italian composer. Studied with Gasparo Ghiretti at Parma, and at the age of 20 became a conductor at Venice. Having married the singer Riccardi, he was invited to Vienna in 1798, where she was engaged at the court opera, and produced *Camilla* there. In 1803 he went to Dresden, remaining as opera conductor until 1806, and there produced *Leonora*, a setting of an Italian version of Gaveaux's opera on which Beethoven's *Fidelio* was also based later. In 1807, after accompanying Napoleon to Warsaw and Posen, he was appointed his *maître de chapelle* and settled in Paris.

Works include *Circe* (1792), *Il tempo fa giustizia a tutti* (1792), *Il nuovo Figaro* (after Beaumarchais' *Mariage de Figaro*, 1794), *Il matrimonio improvviso*, *Idomeneo* (1794), *Eroe e Leandro* (1794), *L'intrigo amoroso*, *Il principe di Taranto*, *Camilla, o Il sotterraneo* (1799), *La sonnambula* (1800), *Achille*, *Leonora, o L'amore conjugale* (1804), *Sofonisba*, *Numa Pompilio* (1808), *Agnese di Fitz-Henry* (1809), *Didone abbandonata* (1810), *Le Maître de chapelle* (1821), *La Marquise de Brinvilliers* (with Auber, Batton, Berton, Blangini, Boieldieu, Carafa, Cherubini and Hérold, 1831) and over 20 others; oratorios *Il santo sepolcro* and *La passione*, Masses and motets; c 12 cantatas (Italian, French and German); Bacchanalian symphony for orchestra, Bridal March for the wedding of Napoleon and Joséphine.

Paganini, Niccolò (b Genoa, 27 Oct 1782; d Nice, 27 May 1840), Italian violinist and composer. Learnt guitar and violin from his father, afterwards with the theatre violinist Servetto and the cathedral *maestro di cappella* Giocomo Costa. At the age of 11 he made his first appearance as a violinist. As a composer he profited by the advice of Gnecco, and in 1795 his father sent him to the violinist Alessandro Rolla at Parma. While there he also studied composition with Gasparo Ghiretti, and in 1797 made his first professional tour, winning early acclaim for his technical virtuosity and flamboyant platform person-

Paderewski *The pianist, composer and politician Ignacy Paderewski (1860–1941). In concert he relied on his expression and individual interpretation rather than flashy technique to win over his audiences. During World War I he toured in support of Poland's liberation and after the war became its prime minister.*

Paganini *The violinist Niccolò Paganini (1782–1840) was one of the foremost virtuosos of the 19th century. He exploited the use of novel effects, such as pizzicatos and harmonics, which were adopted more commonly by his successors. His influence on later artists, including Chopin, Liszt and Schumann, was considerable.*

ality. After that the became increasingly famous, travelled widely, beginning with Vienna and Paris 1828–1831, and in the latter year went to England for the first time. In 1834 he invited Berlioz in Paris to write a concert work for viola *Harold en Italie* was the result, but he never played it.

Works include six violin concertos (1815–30; op. 7 with the *Rondo alla campanella*), variations (e.g. on 'God save the King') and concert pieces for violin and orchestra, three string quartets with a guitar part; 12 sonatas for violin and guitar; 24 *Capricci* (studies) for violin solo.

When the Italian goes away, violin-playing goes with him, unless some disciple of his should arise among us ... as it is, the most masterly performers, hitherto so accounted, must consent to begin again, and be as little boys in his school.

Leigh Hunt on Niccolo Paganini,
in *Leigh Hunt's Dramatic Criticism*, 1949

Paganini Rhapsody a work by Rakhmaninov for piano and orchestra entitled *Rhapsody on a Theme by Paganini*; actually a set of variations, without opus number, composed 1934, fp Baltimore, 7 Nov 1934. The theme, in A minor, from Paganini's *Capricci* for unaccompanied violin, is the same as that used by Brahms for his ◊Paganini Variations.

Paganini Studies a set of six studies for piano by Liszt, transcribed from Paganini's violin *Capricci* (except no. 3 which is another version of *La Campanella*), dedicated to Clara Schumann. There is an original version, *Études d'exécution transcendante d'après Paganini*, written in 1838, and a revised one, *Grandes Études de Paganini*, written in 1851.

Two sets of studies for piano (six each) by Schumann on themes

from Paganini's violin *Capricci*: op. 3, written in 1832, and op. 10, written in 1833.

Paganini Variations two sets of studies for piano in variation form by Brahms, op. 35, composed in 1866, on a theme in A minor from Paganini's violin *Capricci*.

Page, Christopher (Howard) (b London, 8 Apr 1952), English choral director. Studied at Oxford and York Universities; lecturer in Medieval English at Cambridge University. As director of the ensemble Gothic Voices has led many concerts and recordings of works by Hildegard of Bingen (Sequences and Hymns), Guillaume de Machaut and Caccini; collections include *The Mirror of Narcissus*, *The Garden of Zephirus*, *The Castle of Fair Welcome* and *The Service of Venus and Mars*. Publications include *Voices and Instruments of the Middle Ages*.

Pagliacci, *Players*, opera by Leoncavallo (libretto by composer), produced Milan, Teatro dal Verme, 21 May 1892. In a group of actors, Tonio reveals Nedda's lover (Silvio) to her husband Canio. During a play which reflects their real-life situation, Canio stabs his wife and then Silvio.

Pagliardi, Giovanni Maria (b Genoa, 1637; d Florence, 3 Dec 1702), Italian composer. *Maestro di cappella* to the Duke of Tuscany at Florence and in the 1660s at two churches in Rome.

Works include operas *Caligula delirante* (1672), *Lisimaco* (1673), *Numa Pompilio* (1674), *Attilio Regolo*, *Il pazzo per forza* (1687) and *Il tiranno di Colco*; motets, sacred songs; vocal duets, etc.

Pagliughi, Lina (b Brooklyn, 27 May 1907; d Rubicone, 2 Oct 1980), American soprano of Italian parentage. Debut Milan 1927, Gilda; La Scala from 1930, sang Rossini's Sinaida there 1937 and Lucia 1947. CG 1938, as Gilda. Sang widely in Italy and on Italian radio as the Queen of Night, Amina, Rosina and Stravinsky's Nightingale.

Pahissa, Jaime (b Barcelona, 7 Oct 1880; d Buenos Aires, 27 Oct 1969), Spanish composer. Pupil of Morera.

Works include operas *La presó de Lleida* (1906), *Canigó*, *Gala Placidia* (1913), *La Morisca*, *Marianela*, *La Princesa Margarida* (1928); orchestral works; piano pieces.

Paik, Kun-Woo (b Seoul, 10 May 1946), Korean pianist. Debut 1946 playing the Grieg Concerto in Seoul. Studied at Juilliard with Lhevinne and with Kempff in Italy. New York debut at Carnegie Hall 1972; London recital debut 1974, at the Wigmore Hall. Concerts with leading orchestras in Europe and the USA, recordings of solo works by Ravel, Mussorgsky and Schubert.

Paik, Nam June (b Seoul, 20 Jul 1932), Korean composer. Studied in Tokyo and with Wolfgang Fortner in Munich. After further study with Stockhausen in Cologne moved to New York 1964, then Los

---

Paganini   *A biographical note*

After playing in the court orchestra at Lucca until 1809, Paganini adopted the life of a travelling virtuoso, one of the first performers to do so. His bravura style, carefully rehearsed showmanship and brilliant technique cast a spell over audiences hungry for musical sensation. The portrait of Paganini by Delacroix conveys with haunting effect his mesmeric concert presence. The diabolism with which he was sometimes credited is suggested by the pale, sunken cheeks (he had all his teeth extracted) and a faint aura of ill health (he contracted syphilis from a prostitute). The English writer Leigh Hunt spoke tellingly of Paganini's 'long face and haggard features' and a mask-like face 'with a fastidious, dreary expression'. His personal and artistic example had a profound influence on his contemporaries. At Paganini's instigation, Berlioz wrote the symphony of Byron's *Childe Harold*, *Harold en Italie*. By the time Paganini first came to hear the work he was suffering from throat cancer; his gratitude to Berlioz had to be conveyed through his son Achilles.

Angeles 1970. Teacher of media studies at the California Institute of Arts. Performance of music involves such activities as topless cellist Charlotte Moorman using Paik's spine as a finger-board; in *Variations on a Theme of Saint-Saëns* the pianist plays The Swan while the cellist immerses herself in an oil drum. In *Hommage à John Cage* (1959) two pianos are totally destroyed, while in *Performable Music* (1965) the performer is directed to cut his forearm with a razor. Other works include *Symphony for Twenty Rooms* (1961), *Opera Sextronique* (1967) and *Young Penis Symphony* (1970). The *Earthquake Symphony* of 1971 concludes with an appropriate finale.

Paillard, Jean-François (b Vitry-le-François, 28 Apr 1928), French conductor and musicologist. Studied at the Paris Conservatory and with Igor Markevitch at Salzburg. Founded the Jean-Marie Leclair Instrumental Ensemble 1953, becoming the Jean-François-Paillard Chamber Orchestra 1959; many tours of Europe, the USA and the Far East in French Baroque music. Publications include *La Musique Française Classique* (1960) and has recorded Bach's *Brandenburg Concertos*, *Les Indes Galantes* by Rameau, sacred music by Charpentier and *Alexander's Feast* by Handel.

Paine, John Knowles (b Portland, ME, 9 Jan 1839; d Cambridge, MA, 25 Apr 1906), American organist, composer and teacher. Studied at home and at the Hochschule für Musik in Berlin, gave organ recitals in Germany and returned to USA in 1861. He became instructor of music at Harvard University in 1862, assistant professor in 1872 and full professor in 1875. Hon. D. Music of Yale, 1890.

Works include opera *Azara* (produced Leipzig, 1901); incidental music for Sophocles' *Oedipus Tyrannus* and Aristophanes' *Birds*; Mass in D (1867); oratorio *St Peter* (1872); cantatas *A Song of Promise* (1888), *Phoebus arise* (William Drummond), *The Realm of Fancy* (Keats, 1882), *The Nativity* (Milton); symphony in C minor (1875) and A major (*Spring*, 1880), symphonic poems *An Island Fantasy* and *The Tempest* (after Shakespeare), overture for Shakespeare's *As You Like It*; string quartet, piano trio; violin and piano sonata; instrumental pieces.

paintings, drawings, etc, music associated with artists includes:

DAVIES, P MAXWELL, *Vesalii Icones* for dancer, cello and ensemble (Vesalius).

DEBUSSY, *L'Île Joyeuse* for piano (Watteau).

GRANADOS, *Goyescas* for piano, and opera (Goya).

FELDMAN, *De Kooning* for piano, cello, violin, horn and percussion.

——, *The Rothko Chapel* for viola, chorus and percussion.

FERNEYHOUGH, *Carceri d'Invenzione* (etchings by Piranesi).

HENZE, *Los Caprichos* for orchestra (Goya).

——, *Das Floss der Medusa*, oratorio (Géricault).

HINDEMITH, *Mathis der Maler*, opera (Grünewald).

HONEGGER, *Danse des morts* (Holbein).

LISZT, *Hunnenschlact/The Battle of the Huns*, symphonic poem (Kaulbach).

——, *Il sposalizio* (Raphael) in *Années de pèlerinage* for piano.

——, *Totentanz* for piano and orchestra (Orcagna).

McCABE, *The Chagall Windows* for orchestra.

MARTINU, *The Frescoes of Piero della Francesca* for orchestra.

MENOTTI, *Goya*, opera.

MUSSORGSKY, *Pictures at an Exhibition* for piano (Victor Hartmann).

POTTER, *The Enigma* (variations in the style of five painters).

RAKHMANINOV, *The Isle of the Dead*, symphonic poem (Böcklin).

RAUTAVAARA, *Vincent*, (opera on the life of Van Gogh).

REGER, Böcklin suite for orchestra (four pictures).

RESPIGHI, *Trittico Botticelliano* for orchestra.

SCHILLINGS, *Mona Lisa*, opera.

SCHUBERT, song *Liebeslauschen* (Schlechta's poem on a picture by Schnorr).

SCHULLER, *Seven Studies on Themes of Paul Klee* for orchestra.

STRAUSS R, *Friedenstag*, opera (Velásquez).

STRAVINSKY, *The Rake's Progress*, opera (Hogarth).

VAUGHAN WILLIAMS, *Job*, masque for dancing (based on Blake's illustrations for the Book of Job).

WALTON, *Portsmouth Point* and *Dr Syntax* overtures (Rowlandson).

——— THE OPERA ———
Pagliacci

A two-act (originally one-act) opera with Prologue by Ruggero Leoncavallo, first performed in 1892. The tragic action takes place in Montalto, Calabria, on 15 August 1865.

Prologue. Tonio (baritone) assures the audience that they are about to see a true story with real people.

I. Canio (tenor), the leader of a troupe of travelling players, invites the villagers to the play. His jealousy is aroused by a comment made about his attractive wife Nedda (soprano); left alone, she turns away advances made by the deformed Tonio. Overhearing Nedda making plans with her lover Silvio (baritone), Tonio departs to find Canio. Nedda refuses to reveal her lover's name and Canio puts on his clown's costume with a heavy heart.

II. The ensuing play features Canio as the clown Pagliaccio, Nedda as Colombine, and Beppe (tenor) as Harlequin. Canio's own situation is mirrored so closely that he cannot restrain himself from stabbing first Nedda, and then Silvio when he comes to her aid.

——— THE OPERA ———

Paisible (or *Peasable*), James (b ? France, c 1650; d London, Aug 1721), English musician, ? of French extraction. Member of the King's Band in London.

Works include incidental music for Shakespeare's *Henry IV* (*The Humours of Sir John Falstaff*, 1699), Southerne's adaptation of Aphra Behn's *Oroonoko* (1695), Bancroft's *King Edward III* (1690), Cibber's *She wou'd and she wou'd not* and *Love's Last Shift* (1695) and Mme La Roche Guilhen's *Rare en tout*; duets, sonatas and pieces for flute.

Paisiello, Giovanni (b Taranto, 9 May 1740; d Naples, 5 Jun 1816), Italian composer. Pupil of Durante, later of Cotumacci and Abos at the Conservatorio Sant' Onofrio in Naples 1754–63, where he first wrote some oratorios and church music. But with *Il ciarlone* (Bologna, 1764) he began his successful career as a composer of *opera buffa*, and over the next 20 years produced many works in Modena, Naples, Venice, etc. In the service of the Russian court at St Petersburg 1776–84, he there wrote, among others, his most famous opera, *Il barbiere di Siviglia* (after Beaumarchais' *Le Barbier de Séville*, 1782), which held the stage until Rossini's setting of the same story (1816). Back in Naples, he was appointed *maestro di cappella* and court composer to Ferdinand IV. Summoned to Paris as music director of Napoleon's household in 1802, he remained only a year, and returned to his old post in Naples. Modern revivals of such operas as *Il barbiere di Siviglia, Nina*, and *Il Ré Teodoro in Venezia* reveal a composer of real charm and vivacity.

Works include c 100 operas, e.g. *Il ciarlone* (after Goldoni's *La pupilla*, 1764), *I Francesi brillanti, Demetrio* (1765), *Le finte Contesse* (1760), *L'idolo cinese, Socrate immaginario* (1775), *La serva padrona, Il barbiere di Siviglia* (after Beaumarchais, 1782), *Il mondo della luna* (1782), *Il Rè Teodoro in Venezia* (1784), *L'Antigono* (1785), *Nina, ossia La pazza per amore, La molinara* (1789), *Proserpine* (1803), etc.; oratorios *La Passione di Gesù Cristo, Christus* (1783), etc.; cantatas; Masses, two Requiems, *Miserere* and other church music; symphonies; concertos, etc.; six string quartets, 12 piano quartets; keyboard music.

Paix, Jakob (b Augsburg, 1556; d ? Ailtpolstein, after 1623), German composer, organist at Lauingen in Swabia 1576–1601; 1601–17 court organist at Neuburg an der Donau. He wrote German songs and Latin church music, but his chief work was his collection of keyboard music (pub. 1583), including original compositions as well as highly ornamented arrangements of songs and motets.

Paladilhe, Émile (b Montpellier, 3 Jun 1844; d Paris, 8 Jan 1926), French composer. Studied at the Paris Conservatory and gained the Prix de Rome in 1860.

Works include operas *Le Passant* (libretto by F Coppée, 1872), *L'Amour africain* (1875), *Suzanne* (1878), *Diana*, *Patrie* (after Sardou, 1886); oratorio *Saintes Maries de la mer*; two Masses; symphonies and *Fragments symphoniques* for orchestra; songs.

Palester, Roman (b Sniatyn, 28 Dec 1907; d Paris, 25 Aug 1989), Polish composer. Studied at Lwów and under Kasimierz Sikorski in Warsaw. For some years he lived in Paris, later settled in Warsaw. During the 1939–45 war he was imprisoned by the Germans.

Works include opera *The Living Stones* (1941); ballets *Song of the Earth* (1937) and *The End of the World*; incidental and film music; Requiem (1948) and Psalm v for solo voices, chorus and orchestra; five symphonies (1935–72), symphonic suite, *Symphonic Music* (1931), *Wedding Celebration*, *Musique polonaise*, variations (overture) and other orchestral works, *Concertino* for saxophone, piano concerto; *Divertimento* for six instruments, three string quartets (1932–43), sonatinas for three clarinets and for violin and cello, sonata for two violins and piano.

Palestrina opera by Pfitzner (libretto by composer), produced Munich, 12 Jun 1917. Plot concerns the composition of Palestrina's *Missa Papae Marcelli*, which the composer undertakes only after long deliberation. In the end the Mass is performed and the Pope is greatly moved.

This severe ascetic music, calm, and horizontal as the line of the ocean, monotonous by virtue of its serenity, anti-sensuous, and yet so intense in its contemplativeness that it verges sometimes on ecstasy.

Charles Gounod on Palestrina, quoted in Harding, *Gounod*, 1973

Palestrina, Giovanni Pierluigi da (b Palestrina, 9 May 1525; d Rome, 2 Feb 1594), Italian composer. Son of Sante Pierluigi, a well-to-do citizen. Became a choirboy at the cathedral of St Agapit in his native town. When the Bishop of Palestrina went to the church of Santa Maria Maggiore in Rome in 1534, he took Palestrina with him, and he remained there until he was 14, when his voice broke. After a stay at home he returned to Rome in 1540 and (?) became a pupil of Firmin Le Bel. At 19 he was appointed organist and singing-master at St Agapit's at his home. On 12 Jun 1547 he married Lucrezia Gori, who inherited money and property from her father.

Palestrina was appointed *maestro di cappella* of the Julian choir in Rome, 1551, and pub. a madrigal and a first book of Masses in 1554. Pope Julius III made him a member of the Pontifical Choir in 1555, in spite of the resentment of members of his having been elected without examination. Pope Marcellus II, who succeeded that year, to whom Palestrina dedicated the *Missa Papae Marcelli*, intended to reform the church music with Palestrina's help, but died, and under his successor, Paul IV, Palestrina retired from the choir with a pension, becoming *maestro di cappella* at the church of San Giovanni, in the Lateran. When under Pius IV in 1560 that church wished to make economies, Palestrina resigned and was appointed the next year *maestro di cappella* at Santa Maria Maggiore. Before the accession of Pius V in 1566, Palestrina was made director of the new Roman seminary in 1565. The Council of Trent having already laid down some reforms in church music in 1563, the new pope, Gregory XIII, in 1577 directed Palestrina and Zoilo to revise the Gradual. Palestrina's wife having died in Jul 1580, he applied for admission to the priesthood, but having been made a canon, he renounced his vows and was married again on 28 Mar 1581 to Virginia Dormuli, the widow of a prosperous furrier, in whose business he now took a considerable interest. After the accession of the next pope, Sixtus V, there was a scheme to appoint Palestrina *maestro di cappella* of the Pontifical Choir, but it was defeated, 1585. Much of Palestrina's music was pub., particularly in the last ten years of his life, including four vols of motets and six of Masses; the seventh of the latter was sent to press in Jan 1594 when Palestrina was seized with the illness from which he died. Palestrina's achievement lay in creating a tonal blend and expressive beauty of sound at a time when church music was severely limited by Papal decree.

Works include 104 Masses, 41 for four voices, 37 for five voices, 22 for six voices, four for eight voices, one Mass movement for 12 voices; 373 motets, etc., one for three voices, 127 for four voices, 128 for five voices, 40 for six voices, two for seven voices, 62 for eight voices, two for nine voices, 11 for 12 voices; Lamentations, five sets; 11 litanies; 35 Magnificats; 68 Offertories for five voices; 94 secular madrigals; 49 sacred madrigals for five voices.

Paliashvili, Zakharia Petrovich (b Kutais, 16 Aug 1871; d Tiflis, 6 Oct 1933), Russian (Georgian) composer. Studied at the Moscow Conservatory under Taneiev, later taught at Tiflis, conducted the orchestra and made excursions into eastern Georgia to study its folk music on which his work is based.

Works include operas *Abessalom and Eteri* (1919), *Twilight* (1923) and *Latavra*; choral works; folksong arrangements.

palindrome lit. a word or poem reading the same backwards as forwards. In music a piece constructed in the same way, more or less loosely, as e.g. the prelude and postlude in Hindemith's *Ludus tonalis*, his one-act opera *Hin und zurück*, Act III of Berg's *Lulu* or Bartók's fifth string quartet. The procedure is that of *recte et retro* or *rovescio* on a larger scale.

Pallavicini, Carlo (b Salò, *c* 1630; d Dresden, 29 Jan 1688), Italian composer. Lived at Salò, married Giulia Rossi at Padua and settled there, producing operas between 1666 and 1687 at Venice, where he also lived for a time. In 1667–73 he was at the Saxon court at Dresden; first as assistant and later as first music director. In 1674 he was back at Venice, but was recalled to Dresden in 1685 to reorganize the Italian opera.

Works include *Demetrio* (1666), *Diocletiano* (1674), *Enea in Italia* (1675), *Vespasiano* (1678), *Nerone*, *Le amazoni nell' isole fortunate* (1779), *Messalina* (1679), *Bassiano, overro Il maggior impossible* (1682), *Penelope la casta* (1685), *Massimo Puppieno*, *Didone delirante* (1686), *L'amazone corsara*, *La Gerusalemme liberata* (after Tasso, 1687), *Antiope* (finished by Strungk, 1689), and nine others; a Mass and an oratorio; arias and *canzoni* with instruments; string fantasies.

Pallavicini, Vincenzo (b Brescia; d after 1756), Italian composer. *Maestro di cappella* at the Conservatorio degl' Incurabili at Venice.

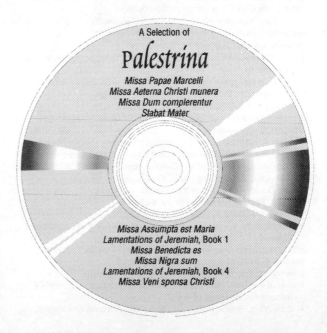

A Selection of

Palestrina

Missa Papae Marcelli
Missa Aeterna Christi munera
Missa Dum complerentur
Stabat Mater

Missa Assumpta est Maria
Lamentations of Jeremiah, Book 1
Missa Benedicta es
Missa Nigra sum
Lamentations of Jeremiah, Book 4
Missa Veni sponsa Christi

Works include opera *Lo speziale* (with Fischietti, libretto by Goldoni, 1754).

Pallavicino, Benedetto (b Cremona, 1551; d Mantua, 26 Nov 1601), Italian composer. He was in the service of the Duke of Mantua from 1582, succeeded de Wert as *maestro di cappella* there in 1596, but was in turn succeeded in 1601, when he retired to the monastery of Camaldoli in Tuscany.

Works include Masses, psalms and other church music; ten vols. of madrigals.

Palm, Siegfried (b Wuppertal, 25 Apr 1927), German cellist. He studied with his father and with Enrico Mainardi; played in various N German orchestras and with the Hamann quartet, 1950–62. From 1962 he has been soloist with leading orchestras and a professor at the Cologne Hochschule für Musik. Intendant, Deutsche Oper, Berlin, 1977–81. A pioneer in *avant-garde* techniques, he has given the fps of works by Penderecki (*Capriccio per S P*), Blacher, Feldman, Ligeti, Xenakis, B A Zimmermann and Fortner.

Palma, Silvestro (b Ischia, 15 Mar 1754; d Naples, 8 Aug 1834), Italian composer. Studied at Naples and was a pupil of Paisiello.

Works include operas *La pietra simpatica* (1795), *I vampiri* (1812), and *c* 15 others; church music.

Palmer, Felicity (b Cheltenham, 6 Apr 1944), English soprano. She studied at the GSM and in Munich. Appeared in various choirs, concert debut 1970. Opera debut 1971, Dido with Kent Opera; then sang Pamina and Elvira with ENO. US debut 1973, as Mozart's Countess in Dallas. Successful in a wide repertory, she has sung Gluck's Armide and works by Messiaen and Shostakovich in concert. Glyndebourne debut 1985, in *Albert Herring*, returning 1992 as the Countess in *The Queen of Spades*. La Scala debut 1987, in the premiere of Testi's *Riccardo III*; Salzburg Festival 1988, *Messiah*. Sang the title role in the stage fp of Gerhard's *The Duenna*, Madrid, 1992.

Palmer, Robert (b Syracuse, New York, 2 Jun 1915), American composer. Studied at the Eastman School of Music at Rochester, NY, where he took degrees in 1938–39, also privately with Roy Harris. In 1943 he became assistant professor of music at Cornell University, Ithaca, NY; retired 1980.

Works include ballet *Irish Legend* with chamber orchestra; symphony, elegy *K. 19* (1945) and concerto for orchestra; concerto for chamber orchestra (1940), piano concerto (1970); *Abraham Lincoln Walks at Midnight* (V Lindsay) for chorus and orchestra (1948); four string quartets (1939–60), two piano quartets (1947, 1974), two string trios; concerto for flute, violin, clarinet, English horn and bassoon; viola and piano sonata; sonata for two pianos; sonata and three preludes for piano.

Palmgren, Selim (b Björneborg, 16 Feb 1878; d Helsinki, 13 Dec 1951), Finnish pianist, composer and conductor. Studied at the Helsinki Conservatory, where Wegelius was among his masters, and later with Ansorge in Germany and Busoni in Italy. On his return he became conductor of the Finnish Students' Choral Society and later of the Music Society at Turku. He also frequently appeared as pianist. Married the singer Maikki Järnefelt, toured Europe and USA with her and from 1923 to 1926 was professor of composition at the Eastman School of Music at Rochester, NY.

Works include operas *Daniel Hjort* (1910) and *Peter Schlemihl* (after Chamisso); incidental music to Kyösti's *Tukhimo* (*Cinderella*); choral works; five piano concertos (II. *The River*; III. *Metamorphoses*; IV. *April*); numerous piano pieces.

Palotta, Matteo (b Palermo, *c* 1688; d Vienna, 28 Mar 1758), Italian composer, priest and music scholar. Studied at Naples, returned to Sicily after being ordained, but was appointed one of the court composers in Vienna in 1733. He wrote treatises on solmization and the modes and composed Masses, motets and other church music.

Paminger, Leonhard (b Aschau, Upper Austria, 25 Mar 1495; d Passau, 3 May 1567), Austrian composer. Educated at the monastery of St Nicholas at Passau, studied in Vienna afterwards, but returned to Passau in 1513 to become a teacher and later secretary at the monas-tery. He became a Lutheran and pub. religious pamphlets and a series of motets for the Lutheran year.

Works include Latin motets, German hymns, psalms, etc.

Pammelia the first part of a collection of canons, rounds and catches pub. by Ravenscroft in 1609, the second being *Deuteromelia*.

Pandolfini, Angelica (b Spoleto, 21 Aug 1871; d Lenno, 15 Jul 1959), Italian soprano. She studied in Paris and made her debut in Modena, 1894, as Marguerite. The following season she was in Malta but returned to Italy and sang in Milan 1897–1908: in 1902 created Adriana Lecouvreur and in 1906 sang in the fp of Franchetti's *La Figlia di Jorio*.

pandoura, from Greek; also from Arabic *tanbur*, 'tamboura', a string instrument of the lute type with a long neck and a small body, surviving in various forms only in the Balkans, Turkey, Egypt and the East.

Pane, Domenico del (Rome–Rome, 10 Dec 1694), Italian singer and composer. Pupil of Abbatini in Rome, went to Vienna in 1650 as a singer in the Imperial Chapel, but returned to Rome to join the Papal Chapel in 1654 and became choirmaster there in 1669.

Works include Masses on motets by Palestrina, motets of his own; sacred concertos; madrigals.

Panerai, Rolando (b Campi Bizenzio, near Florence, 17 Oct 1924), Italian baritone. He studied in Florence and Milan. Debut Naples 1947 as Faraone in *Mosè*. La Scala from 1951 and Salzburg from 1957 as Luna, Germont, Ford, Guglielmo and Rossini's Figaro. At Venice in 1955 he took part in the stage fp of Prokofiev's *The Fiery Angel*. CG debut 1960; returned 1985 and 1990, as Dulcamara.

Panizza, Ettore (b Buenos Aires, 12 Aug 1875; d Milan, 27 Nov 1967), Argentine conductor and composer of Italian descent. Studied at the Milan Conservatory and first appeared as conductor in Rome, 1899, first visiting London (CG) in 1907; he gave there operas by Erlanger, Zandonai and Massenet. La Scala, Milan, 1916–48. NY Met. 1934–42.

Works include operas *Il fidanzato del mare* (1897), *Medio evo latino*, *Aurora* (1908), *Bisanzio*, etc.

Panny, Joseph (b Kolmitzberg, 23 Oct 1794; d Mainz, 7 Sept 1838), Austrian violinist and composer. Studied at home and with Eybler in Vienna, made friends with Paganini during his visits there, appeared in Germany, Norway, Paris and London, founded a school of music at Weisserling in Alsace and another at Mainz.

Works include three Masses, Requiem; three string quartets; piano trios; *Scène dramatique* for the violin G string (for Paganini) and other solos; choruses; songs.

Panofka, Heinrich (b Breslau, 3 Oct 1807; d Florence, 18 Nov 1887), German violinist, singing-teacher and composer. Studied at home and with Mayseder in Vienna, where he first appeared in public in 1827. After living in Munich and Berlin, he settled by turns in Paris, London and Florence, teaching singing and pub. treatises on the subject. Wrote works for violin with piano and with orchestra.

Pan Pipe (or *pandean pipe*) an early wind instrument, also called syrinx, consisting of a bundle of reeds of graded lengths made into pipes giving out a scale of different notes.

Panseron, Auguste (Matthieu) (b Paris, 26 Apr 1795; d Paris, 29 Jul 1859), French composer and singing-teacher. Studied at the Paris Conservatory and took the Prix de Rome in 1813, making further studies in Italy under Mattei. As accompanist at the Opéra-Comique in Paris, he gained much experience in singing and he became professor at the Conservatory in 1826, writing treatises on solfège and singing.

Works include operas *La Grille du parc* (1820), *Le Mariage difficile* (1823) and *L'École de Rome* (1826); two Masses for treble voices, motets and canticles *Mois de Marie*; numerous songs.

pantaleon an instrument of the dulcimer type invented by Pantaleon Hebenstreit in the 18th c. and called pantaleon after him by Louis XIV.

Pantaleoni, Romilda (b Udine, 1847; d Millan, 20 May 1917), Italian soprano. She studied in Milan and made her debut there 1868. Among the roles she created were Desdemona (1887), Tigrana in Puccini's

Edgar (1889) and Ponchielli's Marion Delorme (1885). Also heard as Boito's Margherita and as Santuzza.

pantomime from Greek = 'all-imitating'; properly a play in dumb-show, but in England since the 18th c. a popular stage entertainment with music, deriving from the Italian *commedia dell'arte*. It is still based, even if remotely, on fairy-tales, but it has lost the Harlequinade which used to be an indispensable supplement and has become a spectacular extravaganza, often introducing songs popular at the time. Also term used in 20th c. for mimed episode in ballet (Ravel, *Daphnis et Chloe*), or ballet as a whole (Bartók, *Miraculous Mandarin*).

pantonality a term used by R Réti to describe development in tonality in late 19th and early 20th c. whereby music shifts from one key centre to another, without becoming atonal. Such music is heard first in Wagner (*Tristan*) and is found later in Debussy, Bartók and Hindemith.

Panufnik, Andrzei (b Warsaw, 24 Sept 1914; d London, 27 Oct 1991), Polish composer. Studied with Sikorski at the Warsaw Conservatory and received a diploma in 1936. Some of his music was destroyed in the bombardment of Warsaw. He settled in England in 1954 and from 1957 to 1959 was conductor of the Birmingham SO. KBE 1991.

Works include ballet, *Miss Julie* (produced Stuttgart, 1970), film music; Psalm cxlv for chorus and orchestra, nine symphonies e.g. *Rustica* (1948), *Elegaica* (1957), *Sacra* (1963), *Sfere* (1975), *Mistica* (1977), *Votiva* (1981), no. 9, *Sinfonia di Speranza* (1986), no. 10 (1988, revised 1990), symphonic variations, symphonic studies, Tragic Overture, Heroic Overture; trumpet concerto, piano concerto (1972), bassoon concerto (1985), *Harmony* for chamber orchestra (1989).

Piano trio and other chamber music, five Polish folksongs for treble voices, two flutes, two clarinets and bass clarinet; preludes, mazurkas and other works for piano, two string quartets (1976, 1980).

Pan Voyevoda opera by Rimsky-Korsakov (libretto by I F Tiumenev), produced St Petersburg, 16 Oct 1904. A rarely performed story of love and revenge, set in 17th-c. Poland.

Panzéra, Charles (b Geneva, 16 Feb 1896; d Paris, 6 Jun 1976), Swiss baritone. He studied at the Paris Conservatory and sang Massenet's Albert at the Opéra-Comique in 1919. He was well known as Pelléas, but his career was largely as a concert singer. He gave the fp of Fauré's *L'horizon chimérique* in 1922 and was heard in Europe and the USA in songs by Debussy, Ravel and Duparc. He taught at the Juilliard School, NY, and from 1949 was professor at the Paris Conservatory.

Papandopulo, Boris (b Honnef o/Rhine, 25 Feb 1906; d Zagreb, 17 Oct 1991), Croatian composer and conductor. Studied at Zagreb and Vienna, and became choral and orchestral conductor at Zagreb, returning there after teaching at the Music School of Split 1935–38. Later active as an opera conductor.

Works include operas *The Sun Flower* (1942), *Amphitryon* (1940) and *Rona*; ballet *Gold* (1930); oratorio for unaccompanied chorus *The Torments of Our Lord Jesus Christ* (1935), *Laudamus* for solo voices, chorus and orchestra, *Croatian Mass* for soloists and chorus; two symphonies (1933, 1945), symphonic picture *The Overflowing*; two piano concertos; five string quartets (1927–70), and other chamber music, piano music; songs, etc.

Pape, René (b Dresden, 4 Sept 1964), German bass-baritone. Member of the Dresden Kreuzchor 1974–81 and studied at the Musikhoschule from 1981. From 1987 has sung at the Berlin Staatsoper as the Speaker in *Die Zauberflöte*, in the fp of *Graf Mirabeau* by Matthus and as Prince Gremin. In Vienna, Berlin and elsewhere in Germany has sung Mozart's Figaro and Alfonso, Verdi's Banquo and Procida, and Galitzky in *Prince Igor*. Concerts include Mozart's *Requiem* for the bicentenary (1991).

Papillons, *Butterflies*, a set of short piano pieces by Schumann, op. 2, with a finale suggesting the end of a ball in the early morning, with a clock striking six and a quotation of the *Grossvatertanz* or *Kehraus*, which also appears in *Carnaval*, for which this smaller work might almost be a kind of preliminary sketch. There is a further connection between the two, the opening of *Papillons* being quoted in the

Florestan piece in *Carnaval*. The first part of op. 2 was composed (before op. 1) in 1829, the end in 1831.

parable aria, especially German *Gleichnisarie*, or metaphor aria, a type of mainly operatic aria cultivated in the early 18th c., especially by Zeno and Metastasio in their libretti, where certain abstract conceptions are illustrated by concrete ideas resembling them, e.g. fidelity by a rock in a stormy sea, love by cooing turtle-doves, etc. 'As when the dove' in Handel's *Acis and Galatea* is a parable aria and 'Come scoglio/Like a rock') in Mozart's *Così fan tutte* is both verbally and musically a parody of the type. The music of a parable aria was usually illustrative of the image chosen by the librettist.

Parabosco, Girolamo (b Piacenza, 1520 or 1524; d Venice, 21 Apr 1557), Italian composer and organist. He became a pupil of Willaert in Venice, and pub. two pieces in the misc. collection of instrumental music *Musica Nova* (1540). He succeeded J Buus as first organist at St Mark's, Venice in 1551, a post which he held until his death. Well known for improvisations on the organ.

Parade ballet in one act by Satie (scenario by Cocteau), produced Paris, Théâtre de Châtelet, 18 May 1917, with Diaghilev's Ballets Russes: curtain, décor and costumes by Picasso, conductor Ansermet. Suite for piano four hands in six movements from ballet pub. 1917.

Paradies, Domenico, ◊Paradisi.

Paradis, Maria Theresia von (b Vienna, 15 May 1759; d Vienna, 1 Feb 1824), Austrian pianist, organist, singer and composer. She was blind from childhood, but had a great success, which she extended to Paris and London. Mozart wrote the piano concerto in B♭ major (K456) for her.

Works include operas *Der Schulcandidat* (1792), *Rinaldo und Alcina* (1797); melodrama *Ariadne und Bacchus* (1791); cantata *Deutsches Monument* (on the death of Louis XVI); piano trios; sonatas and variations for piano; songs including a setting of Burger's *Lenore*.

Paradise and the Peri, *Das Paradies und die Peri*, a setting for solo voices, chorus and orchestra of one of the poems in Thomas Moore's *Lalla Rookh*, translated into German with alterations, by Schumann, op. 50; composition first contemplated in 1841, begun Feb 1843; fp Leipzig, 4 Dec 1843.

Paradise Lost opera, '*sacra rappresentazione*' by Penderecki (libretto by C Fry after Milton), produced Chicago, Lyric Opera, 29 Nov 1978.

Paradisi (or *Paradies*), (Pietro) Domenico (b Naples, 1707; d Venice, 25 Aug 1791), Italian harpsichordist and composer. Pupil of Porpora, lived for many years in London as a teacher.

Works include operas *Alessandro in Persia*, (1738), *Il decreto del fato*, *Fetonte* (1747), *La forza d'amore* (1751); cantata *Le Muse in gara*; harpsichord sonatas, toccatas.

parallel motion two or more parts in counterpoint moving up or down, in which the interval between each part does not change.

Paray, Paul (Charles) (b Tréport, 24 May 1886; d Monte Carlo, 10 Oct 1979), French conductor and composer. Studied with Leroux and others at the Paris Conservatory and took the Prix de Rome in 1911. Returning to Paris from imprisonment during the 1914–18 war he became assistant and later successor to Chevillard, whose concerts he continued to conduct until 1933, when he succeeded Pierné as conductor of the Colonne Orchestra. In 1952 he became conductor of the Detroit SO, remained until 1963.

Works include oratorio *Jeanne d'Arc* (1931); ballet *Artémis troublée* (1922); Mass for the 500th anniversary of the death of Joan of Arc (revised of oratorio, 1956); symphony in C major; fantasy for piano and orchestra; string quartet; violin and piano sonata.

Pardon de Ploërmel, Le opera by Meyerbeer (libretto by J Barbier and M Carré), produced Paris, Opéra-Comique, 4 Apr 1859. The work is also known as *Dinorah*. Dinorah has gone mad after losing her husband Hoël during a storm on their wedding day. A year later Hoël returns, seeking a buried treasure, but does not recognize her. After saving her from drowning, Hoël realizes who she is and Dinorah recovers.

Parepa-Rosa, Euphrosyne (b Edinburgh, 7 May 1836; d London, 21 Jan 1874), Scottish soprano of Wallachian descent. She was taught by her mother, the singer Elizabeth Seguin, and by several famous masters, and made her debut at Malta at the age of 16, as Amina, and in London in 1857, as Elvira in *I Puritani*. Married Carl Rosa in 1867 and was the leading soprano of his opera company. US tours 1863–72. Other roles included Donna Anna, Norma and Elsa.

Paride ed Elena, *Paris and Helen*, opera by Gluck (libretto by R Calzabigi), produced Vienna, Burgtheater, 3 Nov 1770. Paris finds Helen more beautiful than the gods and takes her back to Troy, but Athena warns that their joy will not last.

Parikian, Manoug (b Mersin, Turkey, 15 Sept 1920; d London, 24 Dec 1987), British violinist. He studied at the TCL and was leader of the Liverpool PO (1947–48) and the Philharmonia Orchestra (1949–57). Solo career from 1957, and gave the fps of concertos by Crosse, Goehr and Wood; also works by Seiber, Skalkottas and Musgrave. He taught at the RCM 1954–56, RAM from 1959. Director of the Manchester Camerata 1980–84.

Pâris, Alain (b Paris, 2 Nov 1947), French conductor and lexicographer. Studied at the École Normale in Paris and with Paul Paray. Made debut in 1969 and has guested with leading French orchestras, the Dresden PO, Orchestra de la Suisse Romance and the Philharmonia Hungarica. Assistant with the Orchestre Capitole de Toulouse from 1976, conductor 1987; Opéra du Rhin at Strasbourg from 1987. Editor of *Dictionnaire des Interprètes* (fourth edition 1995) and translator of the *New Oxford Companion to Music* and *Baker's Biographical* (1994).

Parisina opera by Donizetti (libretto by F Romani, based on Byron's poem) produced Florence, Teatro della Pergola, 17 Mar 1833. Parisina, wife of Duke Azzo, falls in love with Ugo. Azzo forces her confession when she murmurs Ugo's name in her sleep, then executes Ugo, despite the revelation that Ugo is his long-lost son.

Opera by Mascagni (libretto by G d'Annunzio), produced Milan, La Scala, 15 Dec 1913.

Paris Opéra ◊Académie de Musique.

Paris Symphonies a set of six symphonies by Haydn commissioned by the Concert de la Loge Olympique in Paris: no. 82 in C major (*L'Ours*), composed 1786; no. 83 in G minor (*La Poule*), 1785; no. 84 in E♭ major, 1786; no. 85 in B♭ major (*La Reine*), 1785–6; no. 86 in D major, 1786; no. 87 in A major, 1785.

'Paris' Symphony Mozart's symphony in D, K297, written in Paris for performance at the Concert Spirituel in 1778. After the fp Mozart replaced the slow movement by another.

Paris: The Song of a Great City nocturne for orchestra by Delius; composed 1898 and dedicated to Hans Haym, who gave the fp, Elberfeld 1902. Given by Busoni in Berlin on 15 Nov 1902; first British performance Liverpool, 11 Jan 1908, conductor Beecham.

Parker, Horatio (William) (b Auburndale, MA, 15 Sept 1863; d Cedarhurst, New York, 18 Dec 1919), American organist and composer. Studied at Boston and Munich, where he was a pupil of Rheinberger. In 1884 he returned to NY and became an organist and choirmaster, and taught at the National Conservatory, directed by Dvořák. Later he became organist at Trinity Church, Boston, and in 1894 professor of music at Yale University. He visited England several times for performances of his works at the festivals and to receive the Mus.D. from Cambridge in 1902.

Works include operas *Mona* (1912) and *Fairyland* (1915); oratorios *Hora novissima* (1893), *The Legend of St Christopher* (1897), *Morven and the Grail* (1915); *The Holy Child* (1893), *The Dream of Mary* (1918) and other cantatas, choral ballads and songs; church services; symphony in C major (1885), overtures and other orchestral works; organ concerto; string quartet in F major (1885); organ sonata; piano pieces; songs.

Parker, Jon Kimura (b Vancouver, 25 Dec 1959), Canadian pianist. Studied at Juilliard and won Leeds International Competition 1984; New York and London debuts same year. Concerts with all Canadian orchestras, LPO and LSO, Cleveland Orchestra and Los Angeles PO. A notable exponent of the Brahms D minor Concerto, and has recorded concertos by Tchaikovsky and Prokofiev.

parlando or parlante Italian = 'speaking'; a direction indicating, in

instrumental music, that a passage is to be performed in a 'speaking' manner, expressively but not sustained or 'sung'; in vocal music, that the tone is to be reduced to something approximating to speech.

Parmeggiani, Ettore (b Rimini, 15 Aug 1895; d Milan, 28 Jan 1960), Italian tenor. Debut Milan 1922, Cavaradossi; La Scala 1927–37, debut as Max. Sang Siegmund, Lohengrin and Parsifal and appeared in the fps of Mascagni's *Nerone* (1935) and Respighi's *Lucrezia* (1937). At Genoa in 1936 he took part in the fp of Malipiero's *Giulio Cesare*. After his retirement he taught in Milan, then led the claque at La Scala.

parody Mass ◊Missa parodia.

Paroles tissées, *Woven Words*, work for tenor, strings, harp, piano and percussion by Lutoslawski (text by J F Chabrun); commissioned by Peter Pears, who gave the fp at the Aldeburgh Festival on 20 Jun 1965.

Parrott, Andrew (b Walsall, 10 Mar 1947), English conductor. He studied at Oxford and researched early performance practice. Founded the Taverner Choir 1973, later the Taverner Consort and Players; he has since been guest conductor with the English Chamber Orchestra and the London Bach Orchestra. In 1977 he conducted Monteverdi's *Vespers* at the Promenade Concerts and in later seasons gave Bach's B minor Mass and the *St Matthew Passion* in editions with authentic instruments and small choruses. Conducted the Monteverdi *Vespers* at the 1987 Salzburg Festival and the fp of Judith Weir's *A Night at the Chinese Opera*, 1987. CG debut 1993, *Die Zauberflöte*.

Parrott, Ian (b London, 5 Mar 1916), English composer and writer on music. Studied at the RCM and with B Dale. After various appointments he was Professor of Music at University College of Wales, Aberystwyth, 1950–83.

Works include operas *The Sergeant-Major's Daughter* (1943), *The Black Ram* (1957), ballet *Maid in Birmingham* (1951); instrumental music and songs.

I cannot stand Parry's orchestration: it's dead and is never more than an organ part arranged.
    Edward Elgar on Hubert Parry, quoted in
    Elgar Newsletter, 1978

Parry, (Charles) Hubert (Hastings) (b Bournemouth, 27 Feb 1848; d Rustington, 7 Oct 1918), English composer and writer on music. Studied at Oxford and with Macfarren and Sterndale Bennett. He did not make his mark in public until his piano concerto was played by Dannreuther at the Crystal Palace in 1880 and his choral scenes from Shelley's *Prometheus Unbound* appeared at the Gloucester Festival the same year. Hon. Mus. D., Cambridge 1883, Mus.D., Oxford 1884 and Dublin 1891. After examining for London University and teaching at the RCM, he was appointed director of the latter in succession to Grove in 1894, remaining until his death. Knighted in 1898 and appointed Professor of Music at Oxford in 1900, a post he resigned in 1908. He wrote several books on music, including a study of Bach and a volume of the *Oxford History of Music*.

Works include STAGE: opera Guinevere (1885–86); incidental music to Aristophanes' *The Birds*, *The Frogs* (1891), *The Clouds* (1905), and *The Acharnians* (1914), Aeschylus' *Agamemnon* (1900), Ogilvy's *Hypatia*, P M T Craigie's *A Repentance* and Keats's *Proserpine*.

VOCAL: Oratorios *Judith, Job, King Saul*; six motets, four *Songs of Farewell* and two other motets for chorus; scenes from Shelley's *Prometheus Unbound* (1880), ode *The Glories of our Blood and State* (Shirley, 1883), ode *Blest Pair of Sirens* (Milton, 1887), *Ode on St Cecilia's Day* (Pope), *L'Allegro ed il penseroso* (Milton), ode *Eton* (Swinburne, 1891), choric song from Tennyson's *Lotus Eaters* (1892), *Jerusalem* (Blake) for chorus.

ORCHESTRAL: five symphonies (1878–1912), three concert overtures, symphonic poem *From Death to Life* and *Suite Moderne* for orchestra, *Lady Radnor's Suite* (1894) and *An English Suite* for string orchestra (1921); piano concerto in F♯ minor (1879).

"PARSIFAL" AT COVENT GARDEN.

Parsifal Lauritz Melchior pictured as Parsifal and Göta Ljunberg as Kundry in the 1927 Covent Garden production of Wagner's Parsifal. *A stylized representation was established at Bayreuth in 1882 and continued through the inter-war years.*

CHAMBER AND SONGS: String quintet, three string quartets (1867–80), piano quartet, nonet for wind instruments, four piano trios; sonatas for violin and piano and cello and piano, two suites and many smaller pieces for violin and piano; organ and piano music; over 100 songs including 74 in 12 books of *English Lyrics* (1885–1920).

Parry, John (b Bryn Cynan *c* 1710; d Ruabon, 7 Oct 1782), Welsh harpist. Appeared at Dublin in 1736 and in London and Cambridge in 1746. Handel admired him and Gray wrote his poem *The Bard* on him. He pub. collections of Welsh and other British national melodies.

Parry, John (b Denbigh, 18 Feb 1776; d London, 8 Apr 1851), Welsh clarinettist, bandmaster and composer. Settled in London in 1807 and in 1809 was engaged to write songs for Vauxhall Gardens. Later he became a theatre composer and music critic to the *Morning Post* 1834–48. In the 1820s he conducted Welsh festivals at Wrexham and Brecon.

Works include stage pieces Harlequin Hoax (libretto by T Dibdin, 1814), *Oberon's Oath* (1816), *Ivanhoe* (1820), *The Sham Prince* (1836), etc.; songs and ballads; arrangements of Welsh songs.

Parry, John Orlando (b London, 3 Jan 1810; d East Molesey, 20 Feb 1879), Welsh harpist, pianist, singer and composer, son of John ◊Parry. Studied with his father and later in Italy under Lablache. In 1836 he began a career in London as stage singer, music entertainer and mimic of singers. He wrote and arranged comic songs, glees.

Parsifal music drama (*Bühnenweihfestspiel*, 'sacred festival drama') by Wagner (libretto by composer), produced Bayreuth, Wagner Festival Theatre, 26 Jul 1882. Parsifal recovers the sacred spear from evil magician Klingsor and returns to the Kingdom of the Grail to heal the wounded Amfortas; the 'wild woman' Kundry, whom Parsifal had met earlier, is also redeemed but then dies.

Parsley, Osbert (1511–Norwich, 1585), English singer and composer. Attached to Norwich Cathedral for 50 years. Composed services, motets, Latin psalm settings, a set of Lamentations and *Persli's Clock*.

Parsons, Geoffrey (Penwill) (b Sydney, 15 Jun 1929; d London, 26 Jan 1995), Australian pianist and accompanist. Studied at the Sydney Conservatorium and made first tour of Australia in 1948. Settled in England 1950, at first as accompanist to baritone Peter Dawson, then with Schwarzkopf, Baker, Norman, Los Angeles and Thomas Hampson on tour to Europe and the USA; 25th tour of Australia 1983. Salzburg recital with Hermann Prey, 1977. Geoffrey Parsons and Friends recital series at the Barbican Hall, London, 1982–84, OBE 1977.

Parsons, John (b *c* 1575; d London, buried 3 Aug 1623), English composer. Became parish clerk and organist at St Margaret's Church, Westminster, in 1616, and in 1621 organist and choirmaster of Westminster Abbey. He wrote a Burial Service, which Purcell used in 1685 for the funeral of Charles II.

Parsons, Robert (b Exeter, *c* 1530; d Newark-on-Trent, 25 Jan 1570), English composer, (?) father of John ◊Parsons. He became a Gentleman of the Chapel Royal in London, 1563. He was drowned in the Trent.

Works include services, anthems, motets; madrigals; in nomines for viols or virginal; song *Pandolpho* for a stage play.

part the musical performance by any single singer or player in a work for a number of performers; a single strand of melody in a polyphonic or other composition in a number of voices, whether performed by several people or by a single player on a keyboard instrument; also the copy of the music from which a single singer or player performs in a work for a number of people.

Pärt, Arvo (b Paide, 11 Sept 1935), Estonian composer. He graduated from the Tallinn Conservatory in 1963 and settled in West Berlin 1982. He adopted serial techniques early in his career, later shifted to aleatorism, and finally settled for minimalism and sacred music. His *Nekrolog* for orchestra of 1960 was dedicated to the victims of the Holocaust.

Works include *Stride of the World*, oratorio (1960); three symphonies (1964, 1966, 1971); *Pro et Contra* for cello and orchestra (1964); *Cantus in Memory of Britten* for strings and glockenspiel (1977); *Arbos* for seven instruments (1977); *Wenn Bach Bienen gezüchtet hätte/If Bach had been a bee-keeper*, two versions for harpsichord and ensemble (1978, 1980); *St John Passion* (1981); cello concerto (1981); concerto for violin, cello and chamber orchestra (performed London 1981); Te Deum (1985), *Seven Magnificat Antiphons* (1988), *Magnificat* (1989); *Oedipus*, music drama (1952); *Beatus Petronius* for two choruses and two organs (1990), *The Beatitudes* for chorus and organ (1990), *Berlin Mass* (1991).

partbooks books containing printed or MS music to be sung or played by one or two performers in a work written for a larger number.

The evening becomes tedious rather sooner than usual.

Neville Cardus on *Parsifal* in the
Manchester Guardian, 1939

Partch, Harry (b Oakland, CA, 24 Jun 1901; d San Diego, 3 Sept 1974), American composer. Largely self-taught, he experimented with microtonal scales and new instrumental designs.

Works include *Eight Hitch-hiker Inscriptions from a California Highway Railing* and *US Highball, a Musical Account of a Transcontinental Hobo Trip* for chorus and instruments (1944); *The Letter, a Depression Message from a Hobo Friend*, for voices and instruments (1944); *Oedipus*, music drama (1952); *The Bewitched*, a dance satire (1957); *Revelation in the Courthouse Park*, a music tragedy; *Water, Water*, an American ritual (1962).

Part du diable, La, *The Devil's Share*, opera by Auber (libretto by Scribe), produced Paris, Opéra-Comique, 16 Jan 1843. The work is sometimes called *Carlo Broschi*, the real name of Farinelli, who is the chief character, sung by a soprano.

Partenope opera by Handel (libretto by S Stampiglia), produced London, King's Theatre, Haymarket, 24 Feb 1730. Couples Partenope and Armindo, and Rosmira and Arsace are united after complications of betrayal, jealousy and false identity.

Opera by Hasse (libretto by Metastasio), produced Vienna, Burgtheater, 9 Sept 1767.

Parthenia the title of the first collection of virginal music to be printed in England, pub. 1612–13 and containing 21 pieces by Byrd, Bull and O Gibbons.

Parthenia inviolata a companion volume to ◊*Parthenia*, containing 20 pieces for virginals and bass viol.

Parthia a variant spelling of the German *Partie*, used by Haydn and Beethoven among others. ◊partita.

partials ◊harmonics.

partita Italian = lit. 'set' [as in tennis]; in the 17th and early 18th c. a variation used in the plural (*partite diverse*) to mean a set of Variations, e.g. by Bach in some of his organ works based on chorales. It also acquired the meaning ◊suite (German *Partie*) and was so used also by Bach, e.g. in his six partitas for harpsichord and his three partitas for solo violin. The term has been revived by 20th-c. composers, e.g. Casella, Dallapiccola, Vaughan Williams and Walton.

Partos, Ödön (b Budapest, 1 Oct 1907; d Tel Aviv, 6 Jul 1977), Hungarian-Israeli composer. Studied violin with Hubay and composition with Kodály. Led various orchestras in Lucerne, Berlin and Budapest between 1925 and 1936, and from 1938 played viola with the Israel PO.

Works include *Yis Kor* (*In Memoriam*) for viola and string orchestra (1947); *Song of Praise* for viola and orchestra (1949); symphonic fantasy *En Gev* (1952); *Phantasy on Yement Themes* for chorus and orchestra; *Images* for orchestra (1960); *Fuses* for viola and chamber orchestra (1970); *Arabesque* for oboe and chamber orchestra (1975); two string quartets (1932, 1960).

part-song a composition for several voices (mixed, female or male) usually less polyphonic than a madrigal.

part-writing in composition, the way of managing the satisfactory progress of each single part or voice in texture of any number of parts.

Pasatieri, Thomas (b New York, 20 Oct 1945), American composer. He studied at Juilliard and with Milhaud in Aspen. Pasatieri has avoided the *avant-garde* and remained faithful to a bel canto style.

Among his operas are *The Widow* (Aspen, 1965); *La Divina* (NY, 1966); *Padrevia* (Brooklyn, 1967); *Calvary* (Seattle, 1971); *The Trial of Mary Lincoln* (Boston, 1972); *Black Widow* (Seattle, 1972); *The Seagull* (Houston, 1974); *Signor Deluso* (Greenway, VA, 1974); *The Penitentes* (Aspen, 1974); *Ines de Castro* (Baltimore, 1976); *Washington Square* (Detroit, 1976); *Maria Elena* (Tuscon, 1983); *Three Sisters* (Columbus, OH, 1986).

Pasdeloup, Jules (Étienne) (b Paris, 15 Sept 1819; d Fontainebleau, 13 Aug 1887), French conductor. Studied at the Paris Conservatory. Founder of the Société des Jeunes Artistes du Conservatoire, 1851, and the Concerts Pasdeloup, 1861, at which he produced many works previously unknown in France, including music by Wagner and Schumann. Founded Société des Oratories in 1868; joined Théâtre Lyrique the same year.

Pasero, Tancredi (b Turin, 11 Jan 1893; d Milan, 17 Feb 1983), Italian bass. He studied in Turin and sang in the Italian provinces from 1918. In 1926 he sang Philip II under Toscanini at La Scala, Milan; remained until 1951. NY Met. 1928–33 (debut as Alvise). He sang at the Florence Festival 1933–48 and created roles in operas by Mascagni, Pizzetti and Ghedini. Other roles included Wotan, Gurnemanz, Boris and Sarastro.

Pashchenko, Andrey Filipovich (b Rostov-on-Don, 15 Aug 1883; d Moscow, 16 Nov 1972), Russian composer. Entered the St Petersburg Conservatory in 1914, after receiving private musical instruction, and studied composition under Steinberg and Wihtol. He was active as teacher and music organizer, but devoted most of his time to

--- **THE OPERA** ---

Parsifal

A 'sacred festival drama' in three acts by Richard Wagner. First produced in Bayreuth in 1882, the first scenes of Acts 1 and 3 are set in a forest near the Grail castle at Montsalvat.

I. Amfortas (baritone), son of Titurel (bass), bathes his wounds at a nearby lake. Kundry (soprano) enters with balsam for Amfortas, who is the guardian of the Holy Grail, the sacred cup which received Christ's blood on the Cross. Gurnemanz (bass) explains to two esquires that when Amfortas entered Klingsor's magic garden he was seduced by Kundry and wounded by Klingsor, who also gained control of the sacred spear which was used to pierce Christ on the Cross. Only the touch of the spear can heal the wound of Amfortas, and only a 'pure fool made wise through pity' can regain the spear. A young hunter, Parsifal (tenor), is brought in after shooting a swan. Although unaware of his origins, Gurnemanz takes him to observe the ceremony of the Grail. Parsifal looks on in ignorance, however.

II. Klingsor (bass) watches Parsifal approach his castle and impels the reluctant Kundry to seduce him. Parsifal resists Kundry's Flower Maidens, and Kundry's kiss gives him an awareness of Amfortas's suffering. Klingsor aims the spear at Parsifal but it hangs in the air and, as the youth makes the sign of the Cross, Klingsor's kingdom is destroyed.

III. After many years Parsifal returns to Montsalvat, where he is ritually bathed by Kundry and anointed as the King of the Grail by Gurnemanz. At the temple of the Grail, Amfortas is urged by his knights to celebrate the ritual, but his wounds prevent him. Parsifal enters and heals him with a touch of the spear. Kundry falls lifeless as the Grail is unveiled and Parsifal raises it for all to see.

--- **THE OPERA** ---

composition. During World War II he remained at Leningrad throughout the siege.

Works include operas *The Revolt of the Eagles* (1925), *Emperor Maximilian* (1927), *The Black Cliff* (1931), *The Pompadours* (after Saltikov-Shtchedrin's story, 1939), *The Stubborn Bride* (1956), *Radda and Loyko* (after Gorki's story *Makar Tchudra*, 1957); film music; oratorios *The Liberation of Prometheus* and *Lenin*, Requiem in memory of the heroes of the great war; 15 symphonies (1915–70), *Solemn Polonaise* and *Festive Overture*, symphonic poems *The Giants* and *The Bacchantes*, scherzo *Harlequin and Columbine*, Suite in the Classical Style, *Legend* for orchestra; three pieces for a band of folk instruments; nine string quartets; songs.

Pashkevich, Vassily Alexeievich (b *c* 1742; d St Petersburg, 9 Mar 1797), Russian violinist and composer. Entered the service of Catherine II in 1763 and became conductor and court composer.

Works include operas *The Carriage Accident* (1779), *Fevey*, *The Miser, Fedul and his Children* (with Martín y Soler), 1791), *The Early Reign of Oleg* (with Sarti and Canobbio, 1790), *The Pasha of Tunis*.

Pasino, called Ghizzolo Stefano (b Brescia; d ? Salò), Italian 17th-c. composer. Became town organist at Lonato 1635 and *maestro di cappella* at Salò in 1651.

Works include Masses and motets; sonatas for two–four instruments, instrumental *ricercari*.

Paskalis, Kostas (b Livadia, 1 Sept 1929), Greek baritone. He studied in Athens and made his debut there in 1951 as Rigoletto. Wider recognition came with his Renato at the Vienna Staatsoper in 1958 and in 1964 he sang Macbeth at Glyndebourne; London, CG, 1969–72, as Iago and Scarpia. NY Met. debut 1965, as the *Forza* Carlos, and the following year he created Pentheus in *The Bassarids*, at Salzburg. Sang Don Giovanni with New Jersey Opera 1988, and became director of the National Opera of Greece the same year.

Pasquali, Francesco (b Cosenza; d Rome, in or after 1635), Italian

16th–17th-c. composer. Studied and worked in Rome.
Works include sacred and secular songs, madrigals.

Pasquali, Niccolò (b *c* 1718; d Edinburgh, 13 Oct 1757), Italian violinist and composer. Settled at Edinburgh *c* 1740, lived at Dublin in 1748–51, but returned to Edinburgh, visiting London in 1752. Wrote treatises on thorough-bass and harpsichord playing.

Works include opera *The Enraged Musician* (1753), Masque *The Triumph of Hibernia*; dirge in Shakespeare's *Romeo and Juliet*; oratorios *Noah* and *David*; 12 overtures for (or with) horns; sonatas for violin or two violins and bass; songs contributed to various collections.

Pasquier, Regis (b Fontainebleau, 10 Oct 1945), French violinist. Studied at the Paris Conservatory and with Isaac Stern. Concert tours of Europe from 1958, New York recital debut 1960. Soloist with the Orchestre National de France 1977–86; repertoire has included works by Xenakis and Amy, in addition to the standard repertory. With Bruno Pasquier (viola) and Roland Pidoux (cello) he formed the New Pasquier Trio in 1970. Professor of violin at the Paris Conservatory from 1985.

Pasquini, Bernardo (b Massa Valdinievole, Tuscany, 7 Dec 1637; d Rome, 21 Nov 1710), Italian harpsichordist, organist and composer. Studied with Loreto Vittori and Cesti. As a young man he settled in Rome and became organist of the church of Santa Maria Maggiore. His *Accademia per musica* was performed at the Roman palace of Queen Christina of Sweden in 1687 to celebrate the accession of James II, Corelli leading a string orchestra of 150 players.

Works include operas *La donna ancora è fedele* (1676), *Dov' è amore e pietà* (1679), *La forza d'amore* and 11 others; 13 sonatas and other works for harpsichord.

passacaglia, probably from Spanish *pasar calle* = 'to walk the street', originally an Italian or Spanish dance, but now an instrumental composition based on a ground, i.e. a tune usually found in the bass, which is continually repeated. The best-known example is Bach's for organ. The finale of Brahms's fourth symphony, although not so entitled, is also in this form. A modern example is the Passacaglia by Webern, op. 1 (1908).

passage any melodic or decorative feature in a composition, of indeterminate length, usually on the order of a few beats or a few bars; used often to denote a conspicuous or technically difficult part of a composition.

passaggio, Italian, similar to the term ◊passage, but used in more specialized senses for modulations (i.e. passing from key to key) and for florid vocal or instrumental decorations.

passamezzo, Italian, probably a corruption of *passo e mezzo* = 'pace and a half', a brisk dance of the late 16th and early 17th c., popular not only in Italy but throughout Europe. Its name is probably due to the fact that it was a more lively form of the pavane. It consisted basically of variations on a ground bass. The *passamezzo antico* (Shakespeare's 'passy measures pavyn') was in the minor key, the *passamezzo moderno* in the major. ◊romanesca.

passepied French = lit. 'pass-foot'; a French (probably Breton) dance at least as old as the 16th c. The music is in 3–4 or 3–8 time taken at a moderately running pace. It sometimes occurs in suites, but is not an obligatory part of them.

Passereau (b *fl.* 1533–55), French 16th-c. composer. His *chansons*, some humorous, some obscene, were pub. by Attaignant and others at various times between 1529 and 1572. The best known of them, 'Il est bel et bon', was arranged for organ by Girolamo Cavazzoni.

passing notes incidental notes in one or more parts of a composition which create a temporary dissonance with the prevailing harmony during a scalar passage between two notes consonant with the harmony.

Passione, La, *The Passion*, name given to Haydn's symphony no. 49 in F minor, composed 1768.

Passion music the medieval recitation of the gospel story of Christ's Passion was sung, as it still is, by three singers with different vocal ranges. The singer representing the Evangelist had a medium range, Christus a low range, and the singer responsible for the other characters and the crowd (*turba*) a high range. By the 15th c. the *turba* began to be entrusted to a vocal ensemble, and in the course of the 16th c. the whole text was sung in a polyphonic setting. In the 17th c. Lutheran composers introduced recitative, chorales and instrumental accompaniment. In the early 18th c. the inclusion of arias set to non-Biblical words turned the Lutheran Passion into an oratorio, indistinguishable in form from opera. Bach's two surviving Passions belong to this new category.

Pasta (born *Negri*), Giuditta (b Saronno near Milan, 28 Oct 1797; d Blavio near Como, 1 Apr 1865), Italian soprano. Studied at home, at the Milan Conservatory and in Paris, made her first appearance in 1815 and went to London in 1817, as Telemachus in Cimarosa's *Penelope*. In Paris she was first heard at the Théâtre Italien in 1821 as Rossini's Desdemona. She created Bellini's Norma, Amina and Beatrice di Tenda and Donizetti's Anna Bolena. Also sang in operas by Mayr, Pacini, Mercadante and Paer.

Pasterwiz, Georg (b Bierhütten near Passau, 7 Jun 1730; d Kremsmünster, 26 Jan 1803), Austrian monk, organist and composer. Studied at Kremsmünster Abbey, where he was ordained priest in 1755, and with Eberlin at Salzburg. In 1767–82 he was choirmaster at the abbey, but later lived chiefly in Vienna.

Works include opera *Samson* (1775); 14 Masses, Requiem; numerous fugues and other pieces for keyboard instruments.

pasticcio Italian = lit. 'pie' or 'pasty'; a stage entertainment with music drawn from existing works by one or more composers and words written to fit the music. It was particularly popular in the 18th c.

pastoral a light-hearted English madrigal with words of a pastoral character. ◊pastorale.

Pastoral an anthology by Bliss for mezzo, chorus, flute, drums and strings (words by Theocritus, Poliziano, Ben Jonson, John Fletcher and Robert Nichols), fp London, 8 May 1929.

pastorale, French and Italian, a type of 17th-c. opera, or opera-ballet, with recitatives, airs and choruses, often produced on festive occasions and treating pastoral subjects in a courtly and artificial manner, often allegorically. Its origin was the pastoral drama of the 16th c. In later times the term pastorale has been often used as a title for all kinds of compositions of a pastoral character.

Pastorale, La, called *La Pastorale d'Issy*, opera by Cambert (libretto by Pierre Perrin), produced at Issy near Paris, Apr 1659. Long regarded as the first French opera.

'Pastoral' Sonata Beethoven's piano sonata in D major, op. 28, composed 1801 and dedicated to Joseph, Edler von Sonnenfels. The nickname was not Beethoven's own, but was invented later by the Hamburg publisher Cranz. It suits only the finale.

'Pastoral' Symphony Beethoven's sixth symphony, in F major, op. 68, composed 1807–08, fp Vienna, 22 Dec 1808. The title-page bears Beethoven's own heading of *Symphonie pastorale*, and on the first violin part is the inscription, 'Pastoral-Sinfonie oder Erinnerung an das Landleben (mehr Ausdruck der Empfindung als Mahlerey/Pastoral Symphony or Recollection of Country Life [Expression of Emotion rather than Painting]'.)

Pastoral Symphony, A the third symphony by Vaughan Williams, for

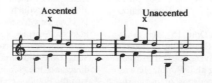

Accented and unaccented passing notes.

orchestra with a soprano voice (without words), composed 1920, fp London, Queen's Hall, 26 Jan 1922, conductor Boult.

Pastor fido, Il, *The Faithful Shepherd*, opera by Handel (libretto by G Rossi after Guarini's pastoral play), produced London, Queen's Theatre, Haymarket, 22 Nov 1712.

pastourelle, French, a medieval pastoral song.

Patanè, Giuseppe (b Naples, 1 Jan 1932; d Munich, 30 May 1989), Italian conductor. Studied at Naples and conducted *La Traviata* there in 1951. Worked at the Deutsche Oper, Berlin, 1962–68 and conducted *Rigoletto* at La Scala, 1969. CG debut 1973, *La forza del destino*. Widely known as orchestral conductor in Europe and USA (American SO, NY, 1982–84).

Pathétique Sonata, Grande sonate pathétique, Beethoven's piano sonata in C minor, op. 13, composed *c* 1798 and dedicated to Prince Carl von Lichnowsky. The title (in French) is, exceptionally, Beethoven's own.

Pathétique Symphony Tchaikovsky's sixth symphony, in B minor, op. 74, composed 1893 and first performed under the composer, St Petersburg, 28 Oct 1893. The title 'Tragic' Symphony was suggested by the composer's brother Modest, but rejected by Tchaikovsky, who afterwards agreed to the adjective 'Pathétique'.

Patience, or Bunthorne's Bride operetta by Sullivan (libretto by W S Gilbert), produced London, Opéra-Comique, 25 Apr 1881. Poets Bunthorne and Grosvenor are rivals for Patience, the milkmaid.

Patiño, Carlos (b Galicia, ?; d Madrid, 5 Sept 1675), Spanish composer. Was in the service of John IV of Portugal early in the 17th c. and in 1633 became choirmaster in the royal chapel at Madrid.

Works include Masses, Benedictus for the funeral of Philip II (1599) and other church music; incidental music for plays; *villancicos*.

Paton, Mary Ann (b Edinburgh, Oct 1802; d Chapelthorpe, Yorkshire, 21 Jul 1864), Scottish soprano. Appeared as a child playing the harp, piano and violin and made her first stage appearance in London in 1822 as Susanna. Married Lord William Pitt Lennox in 1824, but they separated later. She was the first Reiza in Weber's *Oberon* in 1826. Other roles included Agathe, Meyerbeer's Alice and Mandane in Arne's *Artaxerxes*.

Patrie overture by Bizet (not for Sardou's play of that name), composed 1873, fp Paris, 15 Feb 1874.

Patterson, Paul (b Chesterfield, 15 Jun 1947), English composer. He studied with R R Bennett and at the RAM: director of electronic studies since 1975.

Works include wind quintet (1967); trumpet concerto (1969); Concertante (1969); *Piccola Sinfonia* (1971); horn concerto (1971); *Fiesta Sinfonica* (1972); Requiem for chorus and orchestra (1975); concerto for clarinet and strings (1976); *Cracovian Counterpoints* for 14 instruments (1977); Concerto for Orchestra (1981); *Canterbury Psalms* for chorus and orchestra (1981); *Sinfonia* for strings (1982); *Mass of the Sea* for soloists, chorus and orchestra (1984).

patter song a type of song, usually comic, the effect of which depends on a rapid, syllabic delivery of the words to quick music. Many familiar examples occur in Sullivan's operettas.

I asked her why she had never sung any of Wagner's roles. She looked at me with her beautiful eyes, and simply asked me, 'Have I ever done you any harm?'
Sir Felix Semon on Adeline Patti,
in *Autobiography*, 1926

Patti, Adelina (Adela Juana Maria) (b Madrid, 19 Feb 1843; d Craig-y-Nos, Wales, 27 Sept 1919), Italian soprano. Made her first appearance in NY at the age of seven, and after a brief period of study reappeared there in 1859, as Lucia. She went to London in 1861 and sang at CG, as Amina, and in Paris in 1862; appeared at CG until 1894 as Aida, Violetta, Rosina, Juliette and Zerlina. She sang for the last time in 1914.

Patti, Carlotta (b Florence, 30 Oct 1835; d Paris, 27 Jun 1889), Italian soprano, sister of Adelina ◊Patti. Studied piano with Herz in Paris, but turned to singing and made her first appearance in NY in 1861.

Pattiera, Tino (b Cavtat, near Ragusa, 27 Jun 1890; d Cavtat, 24 Apr 1966), Italian tenor. He studied in Vienna and sang at Dresden 1915–41; took part in the Verdi renaissance and was successful as Andrea Chénier, Tannhäuser, Hermann and Bacchus. Berlin Staatsoper 1924–29; Chicago 1922–23.

Patzak, Julius (b Vienna, 9 Apr 1898; d Rottach-Egern, 26 Jan 1974), Austrian tenor. Studied at Vienna University and School of Music, making his debut in Liberec in 1926, as Radames. Brno 1927–28; Munich 1928–45; Vienna 1945–60. His fine lyrical voice and great musical intelligence made him one of the great singers of the century. Well known as Florestan, Palestrina, Tamino and Lohengrin and often heard in concert (*Das Lied von der Erde* and Schmidt's *Das Buch mit sieben Siegeln*).

Pauk, György (b Budapest, 26 Oct 1936), Hungarian-born British violinist. Studied at the Liszt Academy, Budapest, and after winning important competitions in Genoa, Munich and Paris settled in London in 1961. Often plays Bartók; piano trio with Peter ◊Frankl and Ralph ◊Kirshbaum. Professor at the RAM, London, from 1987. Director of the Mozart Bicentenary Festival, London, 1991.

Pauke German; plur. *Pauken* = ◊kettledrum.

Paukenmesse, German, 'Kettledrum Mass', the name given to Haydn's Mass in C major, composed 1796; performed Vienna, 26 Dec 1796. The reason for the unusually prominent timpani, especially in the *Agnus Dei*, is suggested by Haydn's own title, *Missa in tempore belli/Mass in time of war*.

Paukenschlag, Sinfonie mit dem, (Haydn) ◊Surprise Symphony.

Paukenwirbel, Sinfonie mit dem, (Haydn) ◊Drum-Roll Symphony.

Paul Bunyan choral operetta by Britten (libretto by W H Auden), produced Columbia University, NY, 5 May 1941; revised 1974 and given on BBC 1 Feb 1976: this version produced Aldeburgh, 14 Jun 1976.

Paulus the German title of Mendelssohn's oratorio *St Paul*.

Paulus, Stephen (Harrison) (b Summit, NJ, 24 Aug 1949), American composer. Studied at the University of Minnesota with Dominick Argento and founded the Minnesota Composer's Forum 1973. Composer-in-residence with the Minnesota Orchestra 1983–87, Atlanta SO 1987–91. He is best known for his operas, all premiered in St Louis: *The Village Singer* (1979), *The Postman Always Rings Twice* (1981), *The Woodlanders* (1985), and *Harmoonia* (1991). Other works include *Concerto for Orchestra* (1983), *Symphony in Three Movements* (1985), violin concerto (1987), *Symphony for Strings* (1989); *So Hallow'd is the Time* for soloists, chorus and orchestra; two string quartets.

Pauly, Rosa (b Eperjes, 15 Mar 1894; d Tel Aviv, 14 Dec 1975), Hungarian soprano. She studied in Vienna and made her debut in Hamburg as Aida, 1918. In 1922 she joined Otto Klemperer at Cologne and sang there Rachel, Salome and the first Kátya Kabanová in Germany. She moved with Klemperer to the Kroll Opera, Berlin, and sang Leonore, Donna Anna and Carmen, and in Křenek's *Der Diktator*. Vienna 1922–38; London, CG, and NY Met. 1938–40 as Elektra, Venus and Ortrud. Banned by the Nazis in Europe, she sang in North and South America during World War II. Other roles included Gutrune and Strauss's Helen and Dyer's Wife.

Paumann, Conrad (b Nuremberg, *c* 1410; d Munich, 24 Jan 1473), German organist, lutenist and composer. He was blind from birth, and was educated by the Grundherr family of Nuremberg, learnt the organ and composition, and became organist at St Sebald's Church in 1440. In 1451 he was appointed organist to Duke Albrecht III at Munich. He travelled as organist and also played other instruments.

Works include a *Fundamentum organisandi* (1452), or 'Principles of Composition', laid out in keyboard tablature, which exists in several versions; organ arrangement of monophonic and polyphonic pieces; and a German song, 'Wiplich figur'.

Paumgartner, Bernhard (b Vienna, 14 Nov 1887; d Salzburg, 27 Jul 1971), Austrian musicologist and composer. Studied first with his

Pavarotti *The tenor Luciano Pavarotti. The greatest lyric tenor of his generation, Pavarotti has built upon his fame earned in the opera house by giving frequent recitals to mass audiences at outdoor arenas and other venues, and by recording 'Nessun Dorma' for the 1990 World Cup.*

parents, the critic Hans Paumgartner and the singer Rosa Paumgartner, (born Papier), and afterwards with Bruno Walter. He was director of the Mozarteum at Salzburg, 1917–38, and was one of the organizers of the Salzburg festivals; his editions of *Idomeneo* and Cavalieri's *Rappresentazione* were produced there 1956 and 1968. He wrote mainly on Mozart.

Works include operas *Das heisse Eisen* (after Hans Sachs), *Die Höhle von Salamanca* (after Cervantes, 1923), *Rossini in Neapel* (1935), *Aus dem Leben eines Taugenichts* (after Eichendorff's novel); ballet *Pagoden*; incidental music to Shakespeare's *King Lear* and *Twelfth Night* (on old English tunes), Goethe's *Faust*, Gozzi's *Turandot*, music for chorus and for orchestra; songs.

pause the prolongation of a note, chord or rest beyond its normal value, indicated by the fermata sign ⌒. In the 18th-c. concerto it is regularly placed over the ⁶/₄ chord which precedes the cadenza. In a *da capo* it marks the point at which the piece ends after repetition of the first section. In the German chorale or in works based on it, it marks the end of each line and is to be ignored in performance.

Pause German = 'restoration'.

Pause del silenzio, *Pauses of Silence*, seven symphonic expressions by Malipiero, produced Rome, Augusteo, 27 Jan 1918.

Pauvre Matelot, Le, *The Poor Sailor*, opera by Milhaud (libretto by Cocteau), produced Paris, Opéra-Comique, 16 Dec 1927. A sailor returns home to his wife, but passes himself off as a friend of her husband. He tells her that the sailor is a prisoner; when he spends the night in her house the wife kills him (still not realizing his true identity) in order to take his money and free her husband.

pavan, English, *pavane* French, an old dance, probably of Italian origin, since one of its Italian names is padovana ('from Padua'), dating back to at least the 16th c. But the name may also come from Latin *pavo* (peacock), and the real origin of the dance may be Spanish. It was normally in common time and moved at a stately pace. The pavane was often followed by a galliard based on the same thematic material.

Pavane pour une infante défunte, *Pavan for a dead Infanta*, a piano piece by Ravel (1899); fp Paris, 5 Apr 1902. Orchestral version 1910, fp Paris, 25 Dec 1910, conductor Casella.

Pavarotti, Luciano (b Modena, 12 Oct 1935), Italian tenor. After his debut in Reggio Emilia, 1961, he sang Rodolfo at CG in 1963; has returned for Elvino, Alfredo, Cavaradossi, Riccardo and Tonio. La Scala, Milan, from 1965. NY Met. debut 1968, Rodolfo. Other roles include Edgardo, Nemorino, Enzo, Idamante (Glyndebourne), Idomeneo (Met., 1982) and Arturo. The outstanding lyric tenor of his generation. In recent years he has turned increasingly to concerts of popular arias, but sang Otello in concert at NY and Chicago, 1991. NY Met. 1994, as Arvino in *I Lombardi*.

Pavesi, Stefano (b Vaprio, near Crema, 22 Jan 1779; d Crema, 28 Jul 1850), Italian composer. Studied at the Conservatorio dei Turchini, Naples, 1795–99, and became very popular as an opera composer, e.g. *La festa della rosa* (1808), *Fenella* (1831), *Ser Marcantonio*.

Payne, Anthony (b London, 2 Aug 1936), English composer and critic. He studied at Durham University 1958–61; critic with *Daily Telegraph* from 1965. He has written on Schoenberg and British composers.

Works include *Phoenix Mass* for chorus and brass (1965–72); *Sonatas and Ricercars* for wind quintet (1971); Concerto for Orchestra (1975); *First Sight of her and After*, song cycle for 16 voices (texts by Hardy, 1975); *The World's Winter* for soprano and eight instruments (text by Tennyson, 1976); string quartet (1978); *Spring's Shining Wake* for chamber orchestra (1981); *Songs and Dances* for strings (1984); *Half Heard in the Stillness* for orchestra (1987); *Sea-Change* septet (1988); *Time's Arrow* for orchestra (1990); *Symphonies of Wind and Rain* for ensemble (1993).

Paz, Juan Carlos (b Buenos Aires, 5 Aug 1901; d Buenos Aires, 25 Aug 1972), Argentinian composer. Studied in Buenos Aires and was one of the founders of the Group Renovación of progressive composers in 1929, also founded a society for the performance of new music.

Works include incidental music for Ibsen's *Julian the Emperor*; *Canto de Navidad*, *Movimiento sinfónico*, Polytonal Variations, chamber and instrumental music.

Peacock, Lucy (b Jacksonville, FL, 21 Jun 1947), American soprano. Studied in Berlin and has appeared at the Deutsche Oper there from 1969, as Mozart's Pamina, Countess and Servilia, Calisto, Rosina and Micaela. Bayreuth from 1985, as Freia and Eva. Created title role in *Desdemona und ihrer Schwestern* by Siegfried Matthus, Schwetzingen 1992. Guest in Vienna, Geneva, Paris and London.

Peacock Variations variations on a Hungarian Folk-Song, by Kodály; composed 1938–39 to celebrate the 50th anniversary of the Concertgebouw Orchestra, fp Amsterdam, 23 Nov 1939, conductor Mengelberg.

Pears, Peter (b Farnham, 22 June 1910; d Orford, 3 Apr 1986), English tenor. Studied at RCM in London and later with Elena Gerhardt. He sang with the BBC and Glyndebourne choruses (1938) and made his stage debut in London in 1942. From 1943 to 1946 he was a member of SW, but much of his artistic career was associated with Britten's music; he created Peter Grimes (1945) and Albert Herring (1947), and was the first Captain Vere (*Billy Budd*), Essex (*Gloriana*), Quint (*The*

A pavane in A minor by Byrd.

Turn of the Screw), Flute (*A Midsummer Night's Dream*), Sir Philip Wingrave, and Aschenbach in *Death in Venice*. He also created roles in the fps of all three church parables. Other composers were not neglected and he created Pandarus in Walton's *Troilus and Cressida* (1954), and sang in the fps of Henze's *Novae de Infinito Laudes* (1963) and Lutosławski's *Paroles tissées* (1965). His intelligence and musicianship made him one of the great Lieder-singers of his day. Knighted 1978.

Pearsall, Robert (Lucas) (b Clifton, Bristol, 14 Mar 1795; d Wartensee, 5 Aug 1856), English composer. Studied law and was called to the Bar in 1821, but had already composed. In 1825 he settled at Mainz and studied with Panny there, devoting himself entirely to music. Another year in England, 1829–30, was his last, except for visits; he settled in Germany for good, although he inherited a property at Willsbridge, Gloucestershire, in 1836. He sold this and bought Wartensee Castle on Lake Constance.

Works include church music (Anglican and Roman Catholic), Requiem (1853–56); overture and chorus for Shakespeare's *Macbeth*; madrigals, part-songs.

Peasant a Rogue, The, *Selma Sedlák*, comic opera by Dvořák (libretto by J O Veselý), produced Prague, Czech Theatre, 27 Jan 1878. Similar to *Le Nozze di Figaro*, a Prince wants to seduce Bětuška, who already loves Jeník; the Princess helps to stop her husband's attempted exploits by dressing up as Bětuška.

Peasant Cantata, *Mer hahn en neue Oberkeet*, 'We have a new magistracy', a secular cantata by Bach for solo voices, chorus and orchestra, composed in 1742, to words in Saxon dialect. The music is noticeably rustic and comes as near to the manner of folksong as anything Bach ever wrote.

Pêcheurs de perles, Les, *The Pearl Fishers*, opera by Bizet (libretto by E Cormon and M Carré), produced Paris, Théâtre Lyrique, 30 Sept 1863. Leila, once the love of both Zurga and Nadir, returns to the men's village as a priestess of Brahma. She provokes Zurga's jealousy by seeing Nadir; Zurga orders them both to be put to death, but allows them to escape at the last moment.

ped. an abbr. used in the notation of piano music to indicate the use of the sustaining pedal. (The use of the soft pedal is indicated by the words *una corda*) [one string], or sometimes its abbr. *u.c.*) The abbr. also occurs in organ music written on two staves, to indicate which notes or passages are to be played on the pedals.

pedal (1) a sustained note in a polyphonic composition, generally but not invariably in the bass. It often occurs at the climax of a fugue, above which the harmony changes in order to create tension.

(2) ◊pedals.

pedal board the keyboard of pedals.

Pedalflügel German = 'pedal (grand) piano'; ◊pedal piano.

pedal harp the ordinary harp in current use, as distinct from the chromatic harp.

pedal notes the fundamental notes of trombones and other brass wind instruments, the normal compass of which consists of the upper harmonics.

pedal piano a piano specially constructed with a keyboard of pedals and used mainly for organ practice at home. Very little music was written expressly for it except by Schumann.

pedal-point another name for the ◊pedal as applied to composition.

pedals mechanical devices in certain instruments which require manipulation by the feet. Pedals may actually produce notes, as in the organ; they may be means of obtaining certain effects of tone, as in the sustaining and soft piano pedals; or they may be used to alter the length, and thus the tuning, of strings, as in the harp.

Pederson, Mogens (b c 1585; d Copenhagen, c 1623), Danish singer and composer. Pupil of Melchior Borgrevinck in the royal chapel of Christian IV. After a visit to Venice, 1599–1600, he became a singer in the chapel. In 1605–09 he was at Venice again studying with G Gabrieli. In 1611–14 he was in England, but returned to Denmark and became vice-director of the chapel in 1618.

Works include 31 madrigals for five voices, *Pratum spirituale* for voices; a book of Masses and motets, etc.

THE OPERA

Les Pêcheurs de perles

A three-act opera by Georges Bizet set, unusually, in ancient Ceylon. It was first performed in Paris in 1863.

I. Zurga (baritone) is elected chief of the fishermen. He and Nadir (tenor) are reconciled after the rivalry caused by their love for the same priestess, Leila (soprano). When a new priestess arrives, the still-infatuated Nadir recognizes Leila.

II. Leila tells the high priest, Nourabad (bass), how she received a golden chain for helping an unknown fugitive. But when she and Nadir renew their love, they are condemned for sacrilege by Nourabad and Zurga.

III. Leila gives Zurga her gold chain, to be sent to her mother after her death. The lovers are about to be burned to death when Zurga rushes in, having recognized the chain as that which he gave the priestess after he was rescued. He releases the couple and they make good their escape.

THE OPERA

Pederson, Monte (b Sunnyside, WA, 1959), American bass-baritone. Studied with Hans Hotte in Munich and made debut at San Francisco 1986, in *The Medium*. European career from 1987, including Szymanowski's King Roger at Bremen and Wagner's Dutchman at the Bregenz Festival. Sang Pizarro in *Fidelio* at CG (1990) and Amfortas at La Scala and Houston 1991–92. Salzburg Festival 1992, in *From the House of the Dead*. Sang the *Walküre* Wotan to open the season at La Scala, 1990.

Pedrell, Carlos (b Minas, 16 Oct 1878; d Montrouge near Paris, 9 Mar 1941), Uruguayan composer of Spanish descent. Studied at Montevideo, with his uncle Felipe Pedrell at Barcelona 1898–1900 and then with d'Indy and Bréville at the Schola Cantorum in Paris. In 1906 he went to Buenos Aires, where he held various official music posts and founded the Sociedad Nacional de Música in 1915. In 1921 he settled in Paris.

Works include operas *Ardid de amor* (1917) and *Cuento de abril*; ballet *Alleluia* (1936); *Une Nuit de Schéhérazade* (1908), *Danza y canción de Aixa* (1910), *En el estrado de Beatriz, Fantasia Argentina* and *Ouverture catalane* for orchestra; choruses; songs with orchestra and with piano.

Pedrell, Felipe (b Tortosa, 19 Feb 1841; d Barcelona, 19 Aug 1922), Spanish composer and musicologist, uncle of Carlos ◊Pedrell. He began to pub. works in 1871 and produced his first opera in 1874, at Barcelona. From that time he taught music history and aesthetics at the Madrid Conservatory, but settled at Barcelona in 1894, where he worked for the revival of old and the spread of new Spanish music, editing the complete works of Victoria and a collection of early Spanish church music, also early stage and organ music, etc.

Works include operas *El último Abencerraje* (after Chateaubriand, 1868), *Quasimodo* (on Victor Hugo's *Notre-Dame de Paris*, 1875), *Cleopatra* (1881), *Los Pirineos* (1902), *La Celestina, El Conde Arnau* (1904), *Visión de Randa* and four early light operas; incidental music for Shakespeare's *King Lear*; Mass, Requiem and Te Deum; Symphonic poems; string quartet; piano music; songs.

Pedrollo, Arrigo (b Montebello Vicentino, 5 Dec 1878; d Vicenza, 23 Dec 1964), Italian conductor and composer. Studied under his father and at the Milan Conservatory.

Works include operas *Juana* (1914), *La veglia* (after Synge's *The Shadow of the Glen*, 1920), *L'uomo che ride* (after Victor Hugo, 1920), *Delitto e castigo* (after Dostoievsky's *Crime and Punishment*, 1926), *L'amante in trappola* (1936) and five others, three mimodramas; two *Poemetti* for chorus and orchestra; symphony in D minor (1900); chamber music.

Pedrotti, Carlo (b Verona, 12 Nov 1817; d Verona, 16 Oct 1893), Italian composer and conductor. Studied under Domenico Foroni at

THE OPERA

Pelléas et Mélisande

A lyrical drama with five acts and 12 tableaux by Claude Debussy, first staged in 1902. The action takes place in the Kingdom of Allemonde.

I. Golaud (baritone) and Pelléas (tenor) are the sons by different marriages of Geneviève (mezzo-soprano). She is the daughter of Arkel, King of Allemonde. Golaud finds Mélisande (soprano) alone and weeping in a forest. Geneviève reads aloud Golaud's letter to Pelléas telling him of his marriage to Mélisande.

II. At the same moment that Mélisande loses her wedding ring in a fountain, Golaud is thrown from his horse. From his sick bed he orders Mélisande back to the fountain in a mysterious grotto, taking Pelléas with her.

III. Mélisande combs her hair at the window, enveloping the admiring Pelléas below. In a vault under the castle, Golaud gives a thinly veiled warning to Pelléas. Later Golaud holds up his son Yniold (soprano) to spy on the couple.

IV. Golaud bursts in on a meeting between Pelléas and Mélisande, and drags her round the room by her hair. The couple meet for the last time at the fountain and confess their love. Lurking nearby, Golaud kills Pelléas.

V. A dying Mélisande has given birth to a daughter, and is questioned closely by Golaud; she dies quietly with his anxieties unanswered.

THE OPERA

Verona and produced his first opera there in 1840. From that time until 1845 he was conductor at the Italian Opera of Amsterdam, and in 1845–68 he directed the Nuovo and Filarmonico theatres at Verona. In the latter year he settled at Turin, where he became director of the Liceo Musicale, conducting at the Teatro Regio where he gave *Carmen* and *Lohengrin*, and operas by Massenet, Gounod and Goldmark. Founded popular orchestral concerts for classical music. He committed suicide.

Works include operas *Lina* (1840), *Matilde, La figlia dell' arciere* (1844), *Romea di Montfort* (1846), *Fiorina* (1851), *Il parrucchiere della reggenza* (1852), *Gelmina, Genoveffa del Brabante* (1854), *Tutti in maschera* (1856), *Isabella d'Aragona, Mazeppa* (1861), *Guerra in quattro, Marion Delorme* (after Hugo, 1865), *Il favorito, Olema la schiava* (1872).

Peerce, Jan (actually Jacob Pincus Perelmuth) (b New York, 3 Jun 1904; d New York, 17 Dec 1984), American tenor. After beginning his career as a dance-band violinist and singer he was engaged by Radio City Music Hall in 1933 and made his operatic debut in Phildelphia in 1938 as the Duke of Mantua. Sang largely at the NY Met. (1941–66), as Cavaradossi, Rodolfo and, Faust; sang Florestan, Riccardo and Alfredo under Toscanini. The first US singer to appear with the Bolshoi co., Moscow (Alfredo, 1956).

Peer Gynt incidental music for Ibsen's drama by Grieg, produced Christiania, 24 Feb 1876. Grieg afterwards arranged two orchestral suites from it, opp. 46 and 55.

Opera by Egk (libretto by composer), produced Berlin 24 Nov 1938; admired by Hitler.

Peerson, Martin (b March near Ely, c 1572; d London, buried 15 Jan 1651), English organist and composer. He took the B.Mus. at Oxford in 1613 and was soon afterwards appointed organist and choirmaster at St Paul's Cathedral in London.

Works include church music, airs and dialogues for voices, *Mottects or Grave Chamber Musique* for voices and instruments on sonnets from Fulke Greville's *Caelica* (1630), fancies and almains for viols, virginal pieces, *Private Musick* (1620), and contributed to Leighton's *Teares* and Ravenscroft's psalter.

Peeters, Flor (b Tielen, 4 Jul 1903; d Antwerp, 4 Jul 1986), Belgian organist and composer. He studied at Mechlin and at Paris (under Dupré and Tournemire). In 1925 he was appointed organist of

Mechlin Cathedral. He held teaching posts at the Lemmens Institute, Mechlin, Ghent Conservatory, Tilburg Conservatory (Holland) and Antwerp Conservatory, of which he was appointed director in 1952; remained until 1968. Made a baron by King Baudouin in 1971. He also toured widely as a recitalist and edited several collections of early organ music.

Works include eight Masses, Te Deum; organ concerto, piano concerto, concerto for organ and piano; about 200 organ works; chamber music, piano works; songs.

Peinemann, Edith (b Mainz, 3 Mar 1937), German violinist. Has toured widely from 1956 in broad repertory. US debut 1962. Duos with Jörg Demus. New York debut 1965, with Cleveland Orchestra; Salzburg 1977, Mozart's concerto K218. Professor at the Frankfurt Hochschule from 1976.

Pèlerins de le Mecque (Gluck.) ◊Rencontre imprévue.

Pélissier, Marie (1707–Paris, 21 Mar 1749), French singer. She made her debut at the Paris Opéra in 1722 and in the next ten years had much success there and at the Académie Royale. In 1733 she created Rameau's Aricia but the following year was obliged to leave Paris after a public scandal. She returned in 1735 and created leading roles in Rameau's *Indes Galantes, Castor et Pollux, Les fêtes d'Hébé* and *Dardanus*.

Pell, William (b Baltimore, 1946), American tenor. Studied at the Manhattan School of Music and sang first as a baritone: Don Giovanni, Mozart's Figaro (at Toronto) and Germont (San Francisco). Tenor roles from 1975, debut as Rodolfo; Deutsche Oper Berlin from 1982, in the 1987 fp of Rihm's *Oedipus* and as Siegfried. Sang Berg's Alwa at Hanover in 1988 and appeared at Bayreuth 1989–91 as Parsifal. Other roles include Bacchus, Gounod's Roméo, and Jimmy in *Mahagonny* (Frankfurt, 1990).

Pelléas et Mélisande incidental music for Maurice Maeterlinck's play by Fauré, produced London, Prince of Wales Theatre, 21 Jun 1898.

Opera by Debussy (libretto Maeterlinck's play, slightly altered), produced Paris, Opéra-Comique, 30 Apr 1902. Married to Golaud, Mélisande falls in love with Pelléas. Golaud soon becomes jealous, and the lovers realize the futility of their situation. After their last meeting, Pelléas is killed by Golaud, and later Mélisande dies, having borne Golaud a child.

Symphonic poem after Maeterlinck by Schoenberg, op. 5, composed 1902, fp. Vienna, 26 Jan 1905.

Incidental music, orchestral suite in nine movements, by Sibelius, op. 46, composed 1905, produced Helsinki, 17 Mar 1905.

Pellegrini, Vincenzo (b Pesaro; d Milan, 23 Aug 1640), Italian 16th–17th-c. cleric and composer. He was a canon at Pesaro from 1594 and *maestro di cappella* at Milan Cathedral 1611–31.

Works include Masses and other church music; organ canzonets; instrumental pieces in three–four parts; secular canzonets for voices.

Peñalosa, Francisco (b Talavera de la Reina, c 1470; d Seville, 1 Apr 1528), Spanish composer. He was choirmaster to Ferdinand the Catholic 1512–16 and singer in the Julian Chapel in Rome under Leo X, 1517–21.

Works include seven masses and other church music; secular songs for several voices.

Penderecki, Krzysztof (b Debica, 23 Nov 1933), Polish composer. Studied composition with Malawaki and Wiechowicz in Kraków, graduating in 1958. His music has made frequent use of aleatory techniques and microtonal clusters, belonging at one time to the *avant-garde*; recent works have shown an awareness of traditional values and techniques.

Works include operas, *The Devils of Loudun* (1969), *Paradise Lost* (1978), *Die schwarze Maske* (1986) and *Ubu Rex* (1991); *St Luke Passion* for speaker, two soloists, chorus and orchestra (1963–66); *Stabat Mater* and *Psalms of David* for chorus and orchestra (1963, 1958); *Emanations* for two string orchestras (1958); *Anaclasis* for strings and percussion (1960); *Threnody for the Victims of Hiroshima* for 52 strings (1960); *Fluorescences* for chamber ensemble (1961), *De natura sonoris* for orchestra (1966); *Dies Irae*, for soloists, chorus and orchestra (1967); *Utrenja* for soloists, chorus and orchestra

(1969–71); two cello concertos (1972, 1982); two symphonies (1973, 1980); *Canticum canticorum* (1972); *Magnificat* (1974), violin concerto (1977); Te Deum (1979); Viola concerto (1983); *Polish Requiem* (1983); songs of *Cherubim* and *Veni Creator* for chorus (1986–87), *Der Unterbrochene Gedanke* for string quartet (1988); *Passacaglia* (1988) and Adagio (1989) for orchestra; two string quartets (1960, 1968).

Penelope ◊Circe for Keiser's opera.

Opera by Galuppi (libretto by P A Rolli), produced London, King's Theatre, Haymarket, 12 Dec 1741.

Pénélope opera by Fauré (libretto by R Fauchois), produced Monte Carlo, 4 Mar 1913; first Paris performance, Théâtre des Champs-Élysées, 10 May 1913. Other operas on Penelope myth by Monteverdi (*Il ritorno di Ulisse*, 1641), A Scarlatti (1696), Piccinni (1785), Cimarosa (1795) and Liebermann (1954).

penillion an old form of Welsh song to the harp which was improvised (often the words as well as the music) as a counterpoint or descant to the harp part. It is still cultivated, but now tends to rely on tradition rather than improvisation.

Penna, Lorenzo (b Bologna, 1613; d Bologna 31 Oct 1693), Italian monk and composer. Entered the Carmelite order at Bologna (1630) and in 1672 became *maestro di cappella* at the Carmelite church of Parma, also a professor of theology. He wrote treatises on counterpoint and figured bass, including *Primi albori musicali*.

Works include Masses and other church music; *correnti francesi* for four instruments.

Pennario, Leonard (b Buffalo, NY, 9 Jul 1924), American pianist. Made concert debut with the Grieg Concerto at Dallas, 1936. Soloist with the Los Angeles PO 1939 and after war service played the Liszt E♭ Concerto with the New York PO, 1943. First tour of Europe 1952 and gave chamber concerts at Los Angeles with Heifetz and Piatigorsky.

Penny for a Song opera by Richard Rodney Bennett (libretto by C Graham from John Whiting's play), produced London, SW, 31 Oct 1967. In 19th-c. England, Sir Timothy Bellboys is concerned that his country is vulnerable to invasion. Comedy about the local militia that is mistaken for an for an assault force.

penny whistle a small and rudimentary pipe of the fife or recorder type, also known as 'tin whistle', played vertically and having a small range of treble notes controlled by six finger-holes.

pentatone from Greek = 'five notes'; another name for the ◊pentatonic scale.

A Selection of

Penderecki

Threnody for the Victims of Hiroshima 1960
String Quartet no. 1 1960
St Luke Passion 1963–6
De natura sonoris...1966

The Devils of Loudun..1969
Utrenja 1969–71
Violin concerto...1977
Cello Concerto no. 2...1982
Viola Concerto 1983
Polish Requiem............1983

Pepusch   *A biographical note*

The collaboration between Pepusch and Gay in *The Beggar's Opera* was established at a critical time for opera in London. Ever since Handel had achieved a sensational success with *Rinaldo* in 1711, the conventions of Italian opera seria held the stage. It was not long however before the Handelian opera became ridiculed, giving rise to Dr Johnson's definition of opera as 'an exotic and irrational entertainment'. London audiences grew tired of opera sung in a language they could not understand and performed in some cases by singers who had submitted to the mutilation of castration. The ballad opera created by Gay and Pepusch turned conventional opera upside down by alternating spoken dialogue with familiar tunes; these were popular folk ballads or well-known songs by recent composers. *The Beggar's Opera* was an immediate success when premiered in 1728, and its popularity contributed to the bankruptcy of Handel's Royal Academy of Music in the same year. Not everyone was impressed, and Johnson said of the tale of whores and thieves in Newgate Prison, 'such a labefaction of all principles must be injurious to morality'.

pentatonic scale a scale of five notes; actually any 'gapped' scale that omits two of the normal seven notes of the ordinary diatonic scales, but more particularly that represented by the black notes of the piano.

Penthesilea opera by Schoeck (libretto by composer, based on Kleist's drama), produced Dresden, 8 Jan 1927. Achilles falls in love with Amazon Queen Penthesilea, whom he has defeated in combat. When she recovers from her wounds she becomes deranged and kills Achilles. After coming to her senses she commits suicide.

Symphonic poem on ditto by H Wolf, composed 1883–85.

Pentland, Barbara (b Winnipeg, 2 Jan 1912), Canadian composer. Studied in Paris, at Juilliard, and with Copland at Tanglewood. Teacher at the University of British Columbia, 1949–63. Works include four symphonies (1945–59); piano and organ concertos, five string quartets (1945–85), *Variations Concertantes* (1970), *Res Musica* for string orchestra (1975), *Disasters of the Sun* for mezzo, instruments and tape (1976), *Horizons* for piano (1985), *Ice Age* for soprano and piano (1986), *Intrade and Canzona* for recorder quartet (1988).

Pepita Jiménez opera by I Albéniz (libretto, in English, by F B Money-Coutts, based on a story by Juan Valera), produced in Spanish, Barcelona, Liceo, 5 Jan 1896. Rich young widow Pepita has many suitors, but she falls in love only with Don Luis. The priest warns her against this, but despite adversity the two are eventually brought together.

Pepping, Ernst (b Duisburg, 12 Sept 1901; d Berlin, 1 Feb 1981), German composer. Studied at the Hochschule für Musik in Berlin and devoted himself chiefly to the cultivation of Protestant church music, being appointed professor at the Kirchenmusikschule at Spandau in 1947.

Works include setting of the 90th Psalm, unaccompanied motets, Te Deum, *Spandauer Chorbuch* containing vocal pieces for two–six voices for the whole ecclesiastical year in 20 vols., 1934–38; three symphonies (1939–44), piano concerto (1951), two organ concertos; four piano sonatas; chamber music; songs.

Pepusch, Johann Christoph (John Christopher) (b Berlin, 1667; d London, 20 Jul 1752), German composer and theorist. Appointed to the Prussian court at the age of 14; emigrated first to Holland and went to England about 1700, where he settled in London for the rest of his life. Married Margherita de l'Épine in 1718. He arranged the music of *The Beggar's Opera* for John Gay in 1728.

Works include recitatives and songs for a pasticcio opera *Thomyris* (1707) and probably others; incidental music for Colley Cibber's *Myrtillo* (1715); music for masques *Apollo and Daphne* (1716), *The Death of Dido* (1716), *The Union of the Sister Arts*, *Venus and Adonis*

Pepusch *The composer and theorist Johann Christoph Pepusch (1667–1752). A near contemporary of Handel, Pepusch emigrated from his native Germany to London, where his successful arrangement of* The Beggar's Opera *overshadowed his own works. His last 20 years were devoted to musicological studies.*

(1715); dramatic ode for the Peace of Utrecht; overture for *The Beggar's Opera* and arrangements for it and its sequel, *Polly*, and another ballad opera, *The Wedding* (1729); services, anthems and Latin motets; cantatas to words by John Hughes (including *Alexis*) and others; odes, concertos, sonatas.

Pepys, Samuel (b London, 23 Feb 1633; d London, 26 May 1703), English official, diarist and amateur musician. Educated at Huntingdon, St Paul's School in London and Cambridge University He held several government posts and was last secretary to the Admiralty. He kept his diary from Jan 1660 to May 1669. It testifies to his interest in musical performances of all kinds and to his cultivation of music in his home. In 1665 he made a setting of the song 'Beauty retire' from Davenant's *Siege of Rhodes*, produced 1656 with music by H Lawes, Locke and others.

Perabo, Ernst (b Wiesbaden, 14 Nov 1845; d Boston, MA, 29 Nov 1920), German pianist and composer. A very gifted pianist as a child, he was taken to NY in 1852, studied there and from 1848 in Germany, finishing at the Leipzig Conservatory. He returned to the USA in 1865 and soon afterwards settled in Boston.

Works include studies and pieces for piano, e.g. *Pensées* containing an impression of the soliloqies in *Hamlet*, ten transcriptions from Sullivan's *Iolanthe*, concert fantasies on Beethoven's *Fidelio*, etc.

Perahia, Murray (b New York, 19 Apr 1947), American pianist and conductor. He studied at Mannes College and with Horszowski and Balsam. Carnegie Hall debut 1968. He won the Leeds International Competition 1972; London debut 1973. From 1982 to 1989 he was been artistic co-director of the Aldeburgh Festival. Formerly conducted from the keyboard and has recorded all the Mozart concertos. Salzburg Festival debut 1989, Mozart's Concerto K467.

per arsin et thesin Latin = 'by rise and fall'; imitation by contrary motion. One part goes up where the other goes down.

percussion a term used in harmony for the actual incident of a discord, after its ◊preparation and before its ◊resolution.

percussion instruments all instruments played by being struck are called percussion instruments, including all varieties of drums, bells, cymbals, triangles, gongs, etc., also some in which the percussion is produced by the intermediary of a keyboard, such as the celesta. These last instruments, as also bells, xylophone and kettledrums, produce notes of definite pitch; others produce sound without pitch. The piano is classed as a percussion instrument, particularly when used in the orchestra (e.g. by Stravinsky).

perdendosi Italian = 'losing itself'; a direction indicating that the sound of a note or passage is to become gradually weaker until it fades away.

Peress, Maurice (b New York, 18 Mar 1930), American conductor and trumpeter. Studied at Mannes College, NY, and was assistant to Leonard Bernstein from 1961; conducted revivals of *Candide* in Los Angeles 1966 and *West Side Story* in New York, 1968. Music director of the Corpus Christi SO 1962–75, Austin SO 1970–73 and Kansas PO 1974–80. Guest conductor in Vienna, Jerusalem and Mexico City. Led the fp of Bernstein's *Mass* at the opening of Kennedy Center, Washington DC, 1971, and at the Vienna Staatsoper 1981. Orchestrations and performances of music by Duke Ellington and Gershwin *Rhapsody in Blue* at New York, 1984. Teacher at Queen's College, NY.

Perez, Davide (b Naples, 1711; d Lisbon, 30 Oct 1778), Spanish composer. Studied at the Conservatorio di Santa Maria di Loreto at Naples and produced his first opera, *La nemica amante*, in 1735. He became *maestro di cappella* to Prince Naselli at Palermo and in 1752 went to Lisbon, where he became attached to the royal chapel and the new Opera opened in 1755.

Works include operas *Siroe* (1740), *I travestimenti amorosi* (1740), *L'eroismo di Scipione* (1741), *Astartea* (1743), *Medea*

An example from Bach's Art of Fuge *in which the second voice enters by inversion,* per arsin et thesin.

(1744), *L'isola incantata*, *La clemenza di Tito* (1749), *Semiramide* (1750), *Alessandro nell' Indie* (1755), *Demetrio* (1766), *Demofoonte*, *Soimano* (1757), *Il ritorno di Ulisse in Itaca* (1774) and others, many to libretti by Metastasio; *Mattutino de' morti*, Masses and other church music; oratorio *Il martirio di San Bartolomeo*, etc.

Perfall, Karl von (b Munich, 29 Jan 1824; d Munich, 14 Jan 1907), German composer and administrator. Studied at Leipzig with Moritz Hauptmann, returned to Munich in 1850 and founded an oratorio society in 1854. Became Intendant of the court music in 1864 and also of the court theatres in 1867, and had personal differences with Wagner but mounted 700 performances of the operas in 25 years.

Works include operas *Sakuntala* (after Kalidasa, 1853), *Das Konterfei* (1863), *Raimondin* (*Melusine*, 1881) and *Junker Heinz* (1886); incidental music for Shakespeare's *Pericles*; fairy tales for solo voices, chorus and orchestra; *Dornröschen*, *Undine* (after Fouqué) and *Rübezahl*; choruses, songs.

perfect cadence a ◊cadence which conclusively leads to the common chord of the tonic, either by a step from the dominant to the tonic in the bass (authentic cadence) or from the sub-dominant to the tonic (plagal cadence). In England the term is generally confined to the former.

Perfect Fool, The opera by Holst (libretto by composer), produced London, CG, 14 May 1923. A mother (with help from the Wizard) tries to marry her son, the Fool, to the Princess, who falls in love with him after other suitors fail to attract her. A comic wedding.

perfect intervals those intervals which do not possess alternative major and minor forms, but become augmented or diminished by being enlarged or reduced by a semitone, viz. fourths, fifths and octaves, also their repetitions beyond the octave, i.e. 11ths, etc.

performing practice the study of how music is or was performed, normally with the emphasis on how a particular notation is to be realized in sound taking account of the history of instruments and how they were played, the available ensembles, notational practice, improvisation, articulation, temperament and tempo. While originally musicologists were concerned with music of the Baroque period and earlier, the study of performance practice applies to later music as well, including that of the 20th c.

No sooner was heard upon the theatre of Paris the natural yet elegant style of the Serva padrona, *rich with airs so expressive and duets so pleasing, than the far greater part of the French ... became zealous advocates on behalf of the Italian music.*

Francesco Algarotti on Pergolesi's *La serva padrona*, in *Saggio sopra l'opera in musica*, 1755

Pergolesi, Giovanni Battista (b Jesi, near Ancona, 4 Jan 1710; d Pozzuoli near Naples, 16 Mar 1736), Italian composer. Studied in Jesi and from 1725 under Greco, Vinci and Durante at the Conservatorio dei Poveri di Gesù Cristo in Naples. His earliest works were sacred pieces, but he made his debut as a composer for the stage in 1731, and two years later produced the comic intermezzo *La serva padrona* (performed between the acts of his serious opera *Il prigionier superbo*), which was to be decisive in the history of *opera buffa*. *Maestro di cappella* to the Prince of Stigliano from 1732, he entered the service of the Duke of Maddaloni *c* 1734, but returned to Naples the next year, becoming organist to the court. In Feb 1736 he retired on grounds of ill health to the Capuchin monastery in Pozzuoli, where he completed his last work, the *Stabat Mater*, just before his death. His music is most often heard today through the pieces which Stravinsky selected for *Pulcinella*; recent revivals of the operas at La Scala and elsewhere reveal a resourceful and engaging composer.

Works include operas *Salustia* (1732), *Il prigionier superbo* (1733), *Adriano in Siria* (1734), *L'Olimpiade* (1735), *Lo frate 'nnamorato* (1732), *Flaminio* (1735); intermezzi *La serva padrona*, *Livietta e Tracollo* (1737); oratorios *La morte di S Giuseppe* (1731), *La Conversione di S Guglielmo d'Acquitania* (1731), *La morte d'Abel*,

Perahia *The pianist Murray Perahia concentrates on the 18th- and 19th-century repertory. His performances are well-balanced and controlled, and he has conducted the Mozart concertos from the keyboard, a common practice in the 18th century.*

etc.; Masses, *Stabat Mater* for soprano and alto soloists and strings (1736), settings of *Salve Regina* (1736), and other church music; chamber music; keyboard music etc. There are also many other works attributed to Pergolesi which are of doubtful authenticity.

Peri, Jacopo (b Rome, 20 Aug 1561; d Florence, 12 Aug 1633), Italian singer and composer. Pupil of Cristoforo Malvezzi, a canon at the church of San Lorenzo at Florence and *maestro di cappella* to the Medici family. Peri himself became attached to their court from about 1588, later as *maestro di cappella* and chamberlain. He became a member of the progressive artists grouped round Count Giovanni Bardi with Caccini, Corsi, V Galilei and the poet Ottavio Rinuccini. In their endeavour to revive Greek drama with the kind of music they imagined to be genuine Greek they stumbled on the invention of opera. His *Dafne*, begun 1595, is considered to be the earliest opera.

Works include operas *Dafne* (1598), *Euridice* (1600), *Tetide* (composed 1608), *Adone* (composed 1611), tournament with music *La precedenza delle dame* (1625); parts of operas (with others) *La guerra d'amore* and *Flora* (with Gagliano); several ballets; *Lamento d'Iole* for soprano and instruments, madrigals, sonnets and arias in *Songbook* of 1609.

Périchole, La operetta by Offenbach (libretto by H Meilhac and L Halévy, based on Mérimée's *Le Carrosse du Saint-Sacrement*), produced Paris, Théâtre des Variétés, 6 Oct 1868. The Viceroy of Peru, Don Andrès, takes on poor Périchole as chambermaid. Her lover Piguillo agrees unwittingly to marry her. Much confusion when they recognize each other, but happy ending.

Perick, Christof (b Hamburg, 23 Oct 1946), German conductor. Studied in Hamburg and was assistant at the Staatsoper there until 1970. Conductor of the Trier Opera 1970–72, Darmstadt 1972–74, Saarbrücken 1974–77 and Karlsruhe 1977–84. Deutsche Oper Berlin from 1977, including the fp of Rihm's *Oedipus*, 1987. Led *Così fan tutte* at Los Angeles 1988 and appointed director of the Chamber Orchestra there 1992. Conducted *Fidelio* and *Tannhäuser* at the NY Met. 1992. Music director of the city of Hanover, from 1994.

périgourdine a French country dance from the region of Périgord, known to musicians from at least the 18th c. Its music is in 6–8 time.

Pergolesi *The composer Giovanni Battista Pergolesi (1710–1736).
Although he did not achieve much fame during his short life,
Pergolesi's posthumous reputation lies in his development of Italian
opera buffa in an age in which the French style was already well-
established.*

Péri, La (ballet *poème dansé*) by Dukas, produced Paris, Théâtre du
Châtelet, 22 Apr 1912.

Perkowski, Piotr (b Oweczacze, 17 Mar 1901; d Otwock, near Warsaw,
Aug 1990), Polish composer. Studied with Statkowski and Szymanowski at the Warsaw Conservatory and later with Roussel in Paris,
where in 1927 he founded a society of young Polish composers with
Czapski, Labuński and Wiechowicz. He returned to Poland and in
1935 became director of the Torum Conservatory.
   Works include ballets *Swantewid*, *Klementyna*; two symphonies
(1925, 1963), sinfonietta for small orchestra; piano concerto, two
violin concertos (1938, 1960); string quartet; songs.

Perle, George (b Bayonne, NJ, 6 May 1915), American composer and
theorist. Krenek was among his teachers; taught at Queens College,
NY, from 1961; retired 1984. His studies have centred on the Second
Viennese School; books include *Twelve-tone tonality* (1977).
   Works include *Three Movements* for orchestra (1960), cello concerto (1966), *A Short Symphony* (fp 1980); three wind quintets
(1956–67), eight string quartets (1938–88); piano concerto (1990).

Perlea, Jonel (b Orgrada, 13 Dec 1900; d New York, 29 Jul 1970),
Romanian conductor. Studied in Munich and Leipzig, making his
debut in 1923. From 1934 to 1944 he was music director of the
Bucharest Opera and conducted in leading opera houses both in
Europe and America; in 1949–50 he conducted *Tristan*, *Carmen* and
Rigoletto at the NY Met.

Perlemuter, Vlado (b Kaunas, Lithuania, 26 May 1904), French pianist
of Polish parentage. He studied at the Paris Conservatory with Cortot;
professor of composition there from 1950. He studied Ravel's piano
music with the composer in the 1920s; has also specialized in Chopin.
Professor at the Paris Conservatory 1950–77.

Perlman, Itzhak (b Tel Aviv, 31 Aug 1945), Israeli violinist. Afflicted
with polio from infancy but studied at the Tel Aviv Conservatory and
moved to NY (Juilliard School) in 1958. Carnegie Hall debut 1963;
winner, Leventritt Competition 1964. London debut 1968. Has
appeared with all leading orchestras and in chamber music with

Barenboim and Zukerman. Brooklyn College, NY, from 1975. Has
recorded concertos by Elgar, Bartók, Berg and Stravinsky, in addition
to the standard repertory.

Pernerstorfer, Alois (b Vienna, 3 Jun 1912; d Vienna, 12 May 1978),
Austrian bass-baritone. Debut Graz 1936, as Biterolf. He appeared at
the Vienna Volksoper during the war and at the Staatsoper from 1945.
Salzburg from 1948, Zurich 1947–51. Glyndebourne 1951, as Lepo-
rello and Mozart's Figaro. At La Scala he sang Alberich under
Furtwängler (also recorded). Other roles included Pogner, Marke and
Ochs.

Perosi, Lorenzo (b Tortona, 20 Dec 1872; d Rome, 12 Dec 1956), Italian
priest and composer. Studied at Milan and Ratisbon, and among other
appointments became choirmaster at St Mark's, Venice, 1894, and
music director of the Sistine Chapel in Rome, 1898. In 1905 he was
nominated perpetual master of the Pontifical Chapel.
   Works include 33 Masses, four Requiems, *Stabat Mater*, a Te
Deum and much other church music; oratorios *The Transfiguration*
(1898), *The Raising of Lazarus* (1898), *The Resurrection*, *Moses*, *Leo
the Great*, *The Last Judgment* (1904) and *Il sogno interpretato;
Florence, Rome, Venice* and *Bologna* from ten planned symphonies
on the names of Italian cities; organ works.

Perotinus Magnus, now sometimes called Pérotin (b *c* 1160;
d *c* 1205), French composer and scholar. *Maître de chapelle* of the
church of the Blessed Virgin Mary (later Notre-Dame Cathedral). He
is said to have revised the *liber organi de graduali* of Leoninus, and
composed *Organa* in as many as four parts. His best known *organa*
are on the Christmas and St Stephen's Day Graduals, (1198, 1199).

Perotti, Giovanni Agostino (b Vercelli, 12 Apr 1769; d Venice, 28 Jun
1855), Italian composer. Studied under his brother G D Perotti and
Mattei, visited Vienna in 1795 and London in 1798, settled in Venice
c 1800, became second *maestro di cappella* at St Mark's, 1812, and
first in succession to Furlanetto, 1817.
   Works include operas, e.g. *La contadina nobile* (1795), ballets;
church music, oratorios, e.g. Metastasio's *Abele* (1794); piano
sonatas.

Perotti, Giovanni Domenico (b Vercelli, 20 Jan 1761; d Vercelli, 24
Mar 1825), Italian composer, brother of Giovanni Agostino ◊Perotti.
Pupil of G B Martini and *maestro di cappella* of Vercelli Cathedral
from 1779. Composed operas, e.g. *Agesilao re di Sparta* (1789) and
Zemira e Gandarte (1787).

perpetual canon a canon in which each part begins again as soon as it is
finished, the other parts being at that moment at other stages of their
progress. Since even a perpetual canon must finish sooner or later,
however, it is broken off at a point agreed to by the performers.

perpetuum mobile Latin = 'perpetually in motion'; ◊moto perpetuo.

Perrin, Pierre (b Lyons, *c* 1620; d Paris, buried 26 Apr 1675), French
author, who in 1669–72 preceded Lully in holding the patent for the
management of the Académie de Musique (Opéra) in Paris. Librettist
for Cambert and others. J-B ◊Boësset (*Mort d'Adonis*); ◊Pomone
(Cambert).

Perron, Karl (b Frankenthal, 3 Jun 1858; d Dresden, 15 Jul 1928),
German bass-baritone. He studied in Berlin and made his debut in
Leipzig, as Wolfram. During his career at Dresden (1892–1924) he
created Strauss's Jochanaan, Orestes and Ochs. At Bayreuth (1889–
1904) he sang Amfortas, Wotan and Gunther.

Perry, Eugene (b New York, 1955), American baritone. Made debut in
Thomson's *Four Saints in Three Acts*, New York, 1986. Sang Tarj in
the fp of *Under the Double Moon* by Anthony Davis, St Louis 1989,
and the title role in the Peter Sellars production of *Don Giovanni*.
European debut as Alidoro in *Cenerentola*, Nice 1989. New York
City Opera from 1989, in the local fps of *From the House of the Dead*
and *Die Soldaten*, and as Xerxes in the premiere of *Esther* by Weisgall
(1993). Created Mamoud in *The Death of Klinghoffer* by John
Adams, Brussels 1991; repeated in New York and San Francisco.
Recordings include video of *Don Giovanni*.

Perry, George Frederick (b Norwich, 1793; d London, 4 Mar 1862),
English violinist, organist, conductor and composer. Learnt music as
a choirboy at Norwich Cathedral and later became violinist at the

theatre there. Settled in London as conductor of the Haymarket Theatre, 1822, was organist at Quebec Chapel and became leader and later conductor of the Sacred Harmonic Society.

Perry, Janet (b Minneapolis, 27 Dec 1947), American soprano. After study at Curtis made debut in Linz 1969, as Zerlina. Has sung in Munich and Cologne as Donizetti's Norina and Adina, Blondchen, Zerbinetta and Olympia. Glyndebourne 1977, as Aminta in *Die schweigsame Frau*, Halle Festival 1992, as Handel's Cleopatra. Particularly admired for her soubrette roles; recordings include Papagena, conducted by Karajan.

Persée, *Perseus*, opera by Lully (libretto by Quinault), produced Paris, Opéra, 18 Apr 1682. Perseus and Andromeda are in love, but she must marry Phineas. Perseus proves his love in a series of tests and battles.

Perséphone melodrama for the stage or concert-room by Stravinsky (libretto by André Gide), produced Paris, Opéra, 30 Apr 1934. Three scenes about mythical Persephone, who is raped by Pluto; Stravinsky introduces the idea of self-sacrifice into the plot, so that the myth becomes similar to a Christian parable.

Persiani (born *Tacchinardi*), Fanny (b Rome, 4 Oct 1812; d Neuilly, near Paris, 3 May 1867), Italian soprano. Studied under her father, Niccolò Tacchinardi, and appeared at his private pupils' theatre near Florence at the age of 11. Married the composer Giuseppe Persiani in 1830 and made her debut at Livorno 1832; created Donizetti's Lucia in 1835. She first went to Paris in 1837 and to London in 1838, debut as Amina; returned until 1849. Vienna 1837–44 in operas by Donizetti and Verdi.

Persiani, Giuseppe (b Recanati, 11 Nov 1799; d Paris, 14 Aug 1869), Italian composer, husband of Fanny ◊Persiani. He settled as singing-master in Paris.

    Works include operas *Inez di Castro* (1835, a vehicle for Malibran), *Eufemio di Messina*, *Il fantasma* (1843), *L'orfana savoiarda* (1846).

Persichetti, Vincent (b Philadelphia, 6 Jun 1915; d Philadelphia, 14 Aug 1987), American composer. Studied piano with A Jonás and O Samaroff, composition with P Nordoff and Roy Harris, conducting with Fritz Reiner. From 1942 to 1948 he taught composition at the Philadelphia Conservatory, and then at Juilliard, NY. His *Lincoln Address* of 1973 was scheduled for fp at Nixon's inauguration in Washington; the performance was postponed owing to an allusion to the Vietnam War.

    Works include operas *Parable XX* (1976) and *Sibyl* (1984); nine symphonies (1942–71); ballet *King Lear*; 14 serenades for different instrumental groups; *The Hollow Men* for trumpet and string orchestra; piano concerto; two piano quintets, four string quartets (1939–72); 12 piano sonatas, six piano sonatinas; vocal music.

Persuis, Louis (Luc Loiseau) de (b Metz, 4 Jul 1769; d Paris, 20 Dec 1819), French violinist and composer. Studied under his father, member of the music staff at Metz Cathedral, became a violinist in the theatre orchestra and went to Avignon following an actress with whom he had fallen in love. There he studied further, went to Paris, appeared at the Concert Spirituel in 1787, again became a theatre violinist, in 1793 at the Opéra. In 1795–1802 he was violin professor at the Conservatory, in 1810–15 court conductor to Napoleon, inspector of music in 1814 and manager of the Opéra in 1817.

    Works include operas *La Nuit espagnole* (1791), *Estelle* (1794), *Phanor et Angéla* (1798), *Fanny Morna*, *Le Triomphe de Trajan* (with Lesueur, 1807), *Jérusalem délivrée* (after Tasso), *Les Dieux rivaux* (with Berton, R Kreutzer and Spontini, 1816), and others; ballets *Nina, ou La Folle par amour* (1813) and five others (some with R Kreutzer); church music; cantatas *Chant de victoire*, *Chant français* and others.

Persymfans, abbr. of *pervyi symfonitchesky ansamble* = Russian 'first symphonic ensemble', a conductorless orchestra organized in Moscow and making its first appearance there on 13 Feb 1922. It was later discontinued, not from any lack of success, but because it was found that its principle involved an enormous amount of discussion and rehearsing.

Perti, Giacomo (Antonio) (b near Bologna, 6 Jun 1661; d Bologna,

10 Apr 1756), Italian composer. Studied with his uncle Lorenzo Perti, a priest at San Petronio at Bologna, and later with Petronio Franceschini. After visits to Venice and Modena in the 1680s, he became *maestro di cappella* at San Pietro at Bologna in 1690 and of San Petronio in 1696.

    Works include operas *Oreste* (1685), *Marzio Coriolano*, *L'incoronazione di Dario* (1686), *Teodora*, *Il furio Camillo* (1692), *Pompeo*, *Nerone fatto Cesare* (1710), *Penelope la casta* (1696), *Fausta*, *Rodelinda* (1710), *Lucio Vero* (1717) and 17 others; *Missa solemnis* for solo voices, chorus and orchestra, other Masses, motets, etc.; oratorio *Abramo* (1683), four Passion oratorios and several others.

Pertile, Aureliano (b Montagnana near Padua, 9 Nov 1885; d Milan, 11 Jan 1952), Italian tenor. Studied with Orefice, making his debut in Vincenza in 1911. After further study he sang at the NY Met. 1921–22, at La Scala, Milan, 1921–37 as Lohengrin, Chénier, Radames, Riccardo and Manrico; he took part in the fps of *Nerone* by Boito (1924) and Mascagni (1935). CG, London, from 1927 to 1931. On his retirement he taught at the Milan Conservatory.

I shall consider myself to have done enough, having cleared the road for others who, by their merit, may go in my footsteps to that glory which it has not been granted me to reach.

Jacopo Perl, in the foreword to *Euridice*, 1601

---

pes Latin = 'foot'; in medieval English music, the lowest part of a vocal composition in several parts, particularly one that consists of a recurrent figure, as in 'Sumer is icumen in'.

pesante Italian = 'heavy, weighty'; a direction indicating that a passage is to be played very firmly. In the 19th c. and later, often implying a slight ◊ritenuto.

Pescatrici, Le, *The Fisher Girls*, opera by Bertoni (libretto by Goldoni), produced Venice, Teatro San Samuele, 26 Dec 1751.

    opera by Haydn (libretto ditto), produced Eszterháza, Sept 1770. Prince Lindoro must discover who the heiress of Benvento is. Both Nerina and Lesbina claim to be the princess, but their lovers Burlotto and Frisellino foil their plans. Eurilda is revealed as the true heiress.

Pescetti, Giovanni Battista (b Venice, c 1704; d Venice, 20 Mar 1766), Italian composer. A pupil of Lotti, he produced his first opera, *Nerone detronato*, in Venice in 1725. From 1737 to 1745 he lived in London, and was for a time music director of the CG and King's theatres. Appointed second organist at St Mark's, Venice, in 1762.

    Works include operas *Gli odi delusi del sangue* (1728), *Dorinda* (1729, both with Galuppi), *Demetrio* (1732), *Diana ed Endimione* (1739), *La conquista del vello d'oro*, *Tamerlano* (with Cocchi, 1754) and c 20 others; oratorio *Gionata*; church music; harpsichord sonatas.

Pešek, Libor (b Prague, 22 Jun 1933), Czech conductor. Studied in Prague and founded the Prague Chamber Harmony 1959, Sebastian Orchestra 1965. Musical director State Chamber Orchestra of Czechoslovakia 1969–77, Frysk Orkest, Netherlands, 1969–75. Conductor-in-residence with the Czech Philharmonic from 1982, principal of the Royal Liverpool Philharmonic 1987–95. Guest with the Philharmonia, London, and widely in Europe, Russia and the USA. Recordings include the symphonies of Dvořák, *Don Giovanni*, Martinů's *Greek Passion* and Haydn's 'Paris' symphonies.

Pesenti, Michele (b Verona, c 1475; d after 1524), Italian priest and composer. Wrote *frottole*, canzonettas, madrigals, etc.

Peskó, Zoltá (b Budapest, 15 Feb 1937), Hungarian conductor. After study in Budapest and Rome was assistant to Lorin Maazel at the Deutsche Oper Berlin, 1966–69. Conducted at the Berlin Staatsoper 1969–73, Teatro Communale Bologna 1974–76. Conducted Wagner's *Ring* at Turin, 1986–89, and the premiere of Corghi's *Blimunde* at Milan, 1990; other fps of works by Bussotti, Donatoni, Rihm (*Dies*, 1985) and Schnebel (*5 Geistliche Lieder*, 1985). Led Ligeti's *Le grand macabre* at Zurich, 1992, *Norma* at Naples, 1993.

----------- **THE OPERA** -----------

Peter Grimes

A dramatic opera in three acts with Prologue by Benjamin Britten, first performed in 1945 and now the most successful modern English opera. The action takes place in The Borough, a Suffolk fishing village, in about 1830.

Prologue. A verdict of accidental death is reached at the inquest into the death at sea of an apprentice employed by Peter Grimes.

I. At The Boar Inn, Grimes (tenor) is criticized for his conduct. Only schoolmistress Ellen Orford (soprano) defends him and she goes off to fetch another apprentice. Grimes takes him home through the gathering storm.

II. Ellen and Grimes quarrel over his treatment of the boy, who is not allowed Sunday as a day of rest. A deputation from the village approaches Grimes's hut, and he pushes the boy through a back entrance. He stumbles on the cliff edge behind and falls to his death.

III. Grimes and the boy have not been seen for several days when Ellen sees washed up on the beach the pullover which she knitted for the boy. A manhunt for Grimes sets out and when he enters, distraught and demented, he is told to take his boat out to sea and sink it. The village returns to normal life.

----------- **THE OPERA** -----------

Peter and the Wolf symphonic tale for narrator and orchestra by Prokofiev (text by composer), op. 67; composed 1936, fp Moscow, 2 May 1936.

Peter Grimes opera by Britten (libretto by M Slater, based on part of Crabbe's poem *The Borough*), produced London, SW, 7 Jun 1945. Fisherman Peter Grimes is accused of murder when his apprentices keep dying. Only Ellen Orford has faith in him, but that is not enough to stop the villagers from hounding him until he drowns himself.

Peters, C F, a music-publishing firm founded at Leipzig in 1814 by Carl Friedrich Peters (1779–1827), who bought the Bureau de Musique founded by F A Hoffmeister and A Kühnel in 1800. London branch established 1938; NY branch 1948. In 1950 the firm was re-established in Frankfurt.

Peters, Reinhard (b Magdeburg, 2 Apr 1926), German conductor. Studied in Berlin, and in Paris with Cortot and Thibaud. Conducted in Berlin (Städtische Oper and Philharmonic) from 1952; permanent guest of the Deutsche Oper from 1970. Conductor of the Münster Opera 1961–70, Philharmonia Hungarica 1975–79. Led *Don Giovanni* and *Die Zauberflöte* at Glyndebourne, 1969–70; premieres of operas by Blacher, Sutermeister (*Madame Bovary*, 1967) and Reimann (*Melusine*, 1970).

Peters, Roberta (b New York, 4 May 1930), American soprano. Studied in NY with W Hermann, making her debut at the NY Met. in 1950 as Zerlina. She remained as one of America's leading coloratura singers for almost 30 years; other roles included Gilda, Queen of Night, Violetta, Manon and Lucia.

Peter Schmoll und seine Nachbarn, *Peter Schmoll and his Neighbours*, opera by Weber (libretto by J Turk, based on a novel by Carl Gottlob Cramer), produced Augsburg, Mar 1803.

Peterson-Berger, Wilhelm (b Ullånger, 27 Feb 1867; d Östersund, 3 Dec 1942), Swedish composer. Studied at the Stockholm Conservatory, 1886–89, and in Dresden with Kretzschmar. Wrote music criticism 1896–1930 and was stage manager of the Stockholm Opera 1908–10; translated *Tristan und Isolde* and was influenced by Wagner in his own stage works: *Arnljot* (1910) is a national opera which has frequently been revived. Other works include five symphonies (1889–1933), violin concerto (1928) and 100 piano pieces, including *Frösöblomster* (1896); song collection *Svensk lyrik*.

Petite messe solennelle, *Little Solemn Mass*, Mass setting by Rossini for soloists, chorus, two pianos and harmonium; composed 1863,

fp Paris 14 Mar 1864. Arranged with full orchestra, 1867, fp Paris, 24 Feb 1869.

Petites Liturgies de la Presence Divine, Trois ◊Trois Petites Liturgies.

Petite Symphonie Concertante work by Frank Martin for harp, harpsichord, piano and double string orchestra; composed 1944–45, fp Zurich, 17 May 1946. Version with full orchestra in place of solo instruments, Symphonie Concertante, 1946.

Petits Riens, Les, *The Little Nothings*, ballet by Mozart, K299b (choreographed by Jean Noverre), written in Paris and produced there, Opéra, 11 Jun 1778.

Petkov, Dimiter (b Sofia, 5 Mar 1938), Bulgarian bass. Studied in Sofia and sang Ramfis and Zaccaria there 1964. Glyndebourne Festival 1968 and 1970, as Osmin and Gremin. Sang Philip II at the Verona Arena 1969 and has appeared at the Vienna Staatsoper from 1972, as Philip, Boris, Ivan Khovansky, and Mephistopheles. Guest in Paris, Berlin, Milan, Washington DC, Florence and Dallas with all the Verdi bass roles and in operas by Rossini, Bellini and Donizetti. Sang Rimsky-Korsakov's Salieri with the LSO at Daytona Beach, Florida, 1993.

Petrarch, Francesco Petrarca (1304–1374), Italian poet. There are three sonnets set as songs by Schubert in translation by A W Schlegel and three *Sonetti di Petrarca* in Liszt's *Années de Pèlerinage* for piano, arranged 1846 from earlier settings of the poems for voice and piano. Many settings by Italian 16th–17th-c. madrigalists.

Petrassi, Goffredo (b Zagarolo near Palestrina 16 Jul 1904), Italian composer. Learnt music as a child in the singing-school of the church of San Salvatore in Lauro at Rome, but did not study systematically until the age of 21, when he entered the Conservatorio di Santa Cecilia, gaining composition and organ prizes there. He also had advice from Casella, and in 1933 he made his composition debut with a performance of his orchestral Partita at the Augusteo, which was later given at the ISCM festival in Amsterdam. His music makes individual use of 12-note methods.

Works include operas *Il Cordovano* (1949) and *La morte dell'aria* (1950); ballet *Il ritratto di Don Chisciotte* (after Cervantes, 1947); incidental music for A Aniante's play *Carmen*; Psalm ix for chorus and orchestra; *Il coro dei morti* and *Noche oscura* for chorus (1940); Magnificat for voice and orchestra (1940).

Partita, Passacaglia, concertos and concert overture for orchestra (1933–72); *Tre Cori* for chamber orchestra; piano concerto; *Lamento d'Arianna* (Rinuccini) for voice and chamber orchestra (1936), *Introduzione ed Allegro* for violin and 11 instruments (1933). *Sinfonia, Siciliana e Fuga* for string quartet; *Preludio, Aria e Finale* for cello and piano; toccata for piano, *Siciliana e Marcetta* for piano duet; song cycle *Colori del tempo* and other songs.

Petrella, Enrico (b Palermo, 10 Dec 1813; d Genoa, 7 Apr 1877), Italian composer. Studied at Naples with Zingarelli and others and produced his first opera, *Il diavolo color di rosa*, there in 1829.

Works include operas *Le precauzioni* (1851), *Elena di Tolosa* (1852), *La contessa d'Amalfi* (on Feuillet's *Dalila*), *Ione* (1858), *Marco Visconti*, *Giovanna II di Napoli* (1869), *I promessi sposi* (after Manzoni, 1869), *Bianca Orsini* (1874) and many others.

Petri, Egon (b Hanover, 23 Mar 1881; d Berkeley, CA, 27 May 1962), American pianist of Dutch origin, son of the violinist Henri Wilhelm Petri (1856–1914). He studied both the violin and the piano (the latter with Busoni). From 1899 to 1901 he was a violinist in the Dresden Opera orchestra. He first appeared as a solo pianist in 1902. He taught at the RMCM, 1905–11, and subsequently in Berlin, Poland and Basel. He lived in Poland 1926–39. In 1939 he settled in the USA, teaching at Cornell University 1940–47 and at Mills College, Oakland, 1947–57. He excelled as an interpreter of piano music of Liszt and Busoni.

Petri, Michaela (b Copenhagen, 7 Jul 1958), Danish recorder player. Studied in Hanover and made debut on Danish Radio, 1964. Concert debut at the Tivoli Gardens, Copenhagen, 1969. Has played contemporary works by Berio and others and given concerts throughout Europe, the USA (from 1982) and the Far East.

Petrić, Ivo (b Ljubljana, 16 Jan 1931), Slovenian composer. Studied at Ljubljana Academy. Early music was neo-classical in inspiration, later employed aleatory techniques and tone clusters.

Works include three symphonies (1954, 1957, 1960), Concerto Grosso (1955), Concertante music (1962), *Dialogues Concertantes* for cello and orchestra (1972), *Three Images* for violin and orchestra (1973), *Fresque Symphonique* (1973); three wind quintets, chamber concerto (1966), *Quatuor 69* for string quartet.

Petridis, Petro (b Nigdé, Asia Minor, 23 Jul 1892; d Athens, 17 Aug 1977), Greek composer. Studied at Constantinople and in Paris.

Works include opera *Zemfyra* (1923–25); ballet; five symphonies (1928–51), dramatic symphony *Digenis Afrikas*, Greek and Ionian Suites, Elegiac Overture, *Prelude, Aria and Fugue* for orchestra; two piano concertos, cello concerto, concerto grosso for wind instruments, violin concerto (1977); piano trio; two *Modal Suites* for piano; songs.

Petrov, Nikolai (b Moscow, 14 Apr 1943), Russian pianist. Graduated from the Moscow Conservatory 1967 and gave concerts with the Moscow PO from 1968. Many tours of Europe and the USA (New York debut 1986). Most often heard in Tchaikovsky and Rakhmaninov, and has premiered works by Khrennikov and Khachaturian.

Petrov, Ossip Afanassievich (b Elisavetgrad, 15 Nov 1806; d St Petersburg, 11 Mar 1878), Russian bass. Discovered singing in the market at Kursk in 1830, he was taken to St Petersburg and made his first stage appearance there that year, as Sarastro. In 1836 he created the part of Ivan Sussanin in Glinka's *Life for the Tsar*, also created Ruslan (1842) and Varlaam in *Boris Godunov* (1874).

Petrucci, Ottaviano dei (b Fossombrone, near Ancona, 18 Jun 1466; d Venice, 7 May 1539), Italian music printer. He established himself at Venice *c* 1491 and held a patent for the publication of music in tablature and notes 1498–1511, when he returned to Fossombrone to continue business there. He issued many famous collections of Masses, motets, *frottole*, etc.

Petrus de Cruce (b ? Amiens, *c* 1250), 13th-c. composer, possibly from Amiens. His mensural theory is expounded in the works of Robert de Handlo and J Hanboys. Two motets from the Montpellier MS can be assigned to him on the authority of the *Speculum Musicum* by Jacobus of Liège.

Petrushka ballet by Stravinsky (scenario by composer and A Benois; choreography by Fokin), produced Paris, Théâtre du Châtelet, 13 Jun 1911. New version in four parts with 15 movements written 1946; three dances for piano 1921, dedicated to Arthur Rubinstein; *Russian Dance, In Petrushka's's Cell, The Shrove-tide Fair*.

Petrželka, Vilém (b Královo Pole, 10 Sept 1889; d Brno, 10 Jan 1967), Czech composer. He studied with Novák in Prague and Janáček at Brno, became a conductor at Pardubice and in 1919 went to Brno as professor at the Conservatory.

Works include symphonic drama *Sailor Nicholas* (1928); *Hymn to the Sun* for chorus and orchestra; Symphony (1956), *Eternal Return*, two suites, Dramatic Overture for orchestra; five string quartets (1909–15), fantasy and suite for string quartet; sonata and *Intimate Hours* for violin and piano; piano pieces; songs; part-songs; etc.

Pettersson, Gustaf Allan (b Västra Ryd, 19 Sept 1911; d Stockholm, 20 Jun 1980), Swedish composer. Studied at Stockholm Academy and after playing viola in local orchestra 1940–51 studied further, in Paris, with Honegger and Leibowitz. Best known for 16 symphonies (1950–80), influenced by Mahler. Also wrote three concertos for string orchestra (1949–57), violin concerto (1977); *Vox humana*, 18 songs for vocal soloists, chorus and strings (texts by American Indians, 1974); seven sonatas for two violins (1952).

petto Italian = 'chest'; hence *voce di petto*, 'chest voice'.

Petyrek, Felix (b Brno, 14 May 1892; d Vienna, 1 Dec 1951), Czech pianist and composer. Studied with his father, an organist and conductor, and with Adler in Vienna for theory, with Godowsky and Sauer for piano and with Schreker for composition. Later he taught at Salzburg, Berlin, Athens and Stuttgart.

Works include operas *Die arme Mutter und der Tod* (1923), *Der Garten des Paradieses* (1942); pantomime *Comedy*; incidental music

A Selection of

Pfitzner

Palestrina	1917
Piano Concerto	1921
Von deutscher Seele	1922
Violin Concerto	1923

Das dunkle Reich	1930
Cello Concerto no. 1	1935
Kleine Symphonie	1939

for Hans Reinhart's *Der Schatten*; *Das Heilige Abendmahl, Litanei* and other cantatas, three sacred madrigals; sextet (1922); *Kammerlieder* for voice and chamber music; violin and piano sonata; studies, rhapsodies and folksongs for piano.

Pevernage, André (b Harlebeke, near Courtrai, 1543; d Antwerp, 30 Jul 1591), Flemish composer. After holding an appointment at Courtrai, 1565–85, he moved to Antwerp *c* 1587 and became choirmaster at the cathedral, holding the post until his early death. Apart from cultivating church music he held weekly concerts at his house.

Works include *Cantiones sacrae* and other church music; madrigals and five vols. of *chansons*; ode to St Cecilia.

Peyer, Gervase de (b London, 11 Apr 1926), English clarinettist and conductor. Studied with Frederick Thurston at the RCM. Played the Mozart Concerto on BBC Radio while at school and founded the Melos Ensemble 1950. Principal of the LSO 1955–71 and director of the LSO wind ensemble (Salzburg Festival 1973). Guest conductor with the ECO, LSO and Melos Sinfonia; associate of the Haydn Orchestra. Recitals with the Chamber Music Society of Lincoln Center, NY, 1969–89, and toured the USA 1988 with Messiaen's *Quatuor pour la fin du Temps*. Premieres of works by Musgrave, Arnold Cooke and Hoddinott.

pezzo Italian, plur. *pezzi* = piece of music.

Pfitzner, Hans (b Moscow, 5 May 1869; d Salzburg, 22 May 1949), German composer and conductor. His family moved to Frankfurt, where Pfitzner's father, a violinist, became music director of the municipal theatre. He studied piano with Kwast and composition with Knorr at the Conservatory there. In 1893 he gave a first concert of his own works in Berlin, and after some teaching and conducting appointments he became professor at the Stern Conservatory there in 1897, first conductor at the Theater des Westens in 1903. He also conducted the Kaim orchestra at Munich and the Opera at Strasbourg. After the success of his *Palestrina* in 1917 he devoted himself mainly to composition, but wrote many essays and pamphlets attacking modern music, especially Busoni, and defending Romantic and Germanic ideals. He was also a political conservative and wrote *Krakauer Begrüssung* in honour of Hans Frank, Nazi governor of Poland.

Works include operas *Der arme Heinrich* (1895), *Die Rose vom Liebesgarten* (1901); *Christelflein* (1906), *Palestrina* (1917); *Das Herz* (1931); incidental music to Ibsen's *Feast at Solhaug* (1890) and Kleist's *Käthchen von Heilbronn* (1905); cantatas *Von deutscher Seele* (Eichendorff, 1922), *Das dunkle Reich* (1930) and others.

Three symphonies, scherzo for orchestra; piano concerto (1921), violin concerto (1923), two cello concertos (1935–44); ballads and songs for voice, and orchestra; four string quartets (1886–1942), piano quintet, piano trio; violin and piano sonata, cello and piano sonata, sextet (1945); 106 Lieder (1884–1931).

Phaedra dramatic cantata for mezzo and orchestra by Britten (text by R Lowell, after Racine's *Phèdre*); composed 1975, fp Aldeburgh, 16 Jun 1976, with Janet Baker.

Phaëton opera by Lully (libretto by Quinault), produced Versailles, 9 Jan and first performed Paris, 27 Apr 1683. Phaëton abandons his love Théone and wants Princess Libya. He rides recklessly around the sky in a chariot until Jupiter strikes him down with a thunderbolt.

Symphonic poem by Saint-Saëns, fp Paris, 7 Dec 1873.

phagotus, = Italian *fagotto* = 'faggot, bundle', an early instrument developed from the Serbian bagpipe by Afranio Albonese of Pavia early in the 16th c. It consisted of two pipes like those of an organ, supplied with wind from hand bellows, but their pitch was variable by their being fingered on holes.

Phalèse Flemish family of music printers:

1. Pierre Phalèse (b Louvain, *c* 1510; d Louvain, 1573 or 74), began to pub. music at Louvain, in 1545.

2. Pierre Phalèse (b Louvain, *c* 1550; d Antwerp, 13 Mar 1629), son of 1, who moved to Antwerp to join his father's partner, Jean Bellère, there. Pub. many madrigal books, including works by Frescobaldi, Croce, Monteverdi, Marenzio and Vecchi.

3. Madeleine Phalèse (b Antwerp, bap. 25 Jul 1586; d Antwerp, 30 May 1652), daughter of 2, who continued her father's business in partnership with her sister (4).

4. Marie Phalèse (b Antwerp, 1589; d Antwerp, *c* 1674), sister of 3, with whom she continued in partnership and after her death ran the business under her married name of de Meyer.

Phantasy ◊Fantasy.

Philadelphia Orchestra American orchestra founded 1900 by Fritz Scheel. Stokowski was principal conductor 1912–38; Eugene Ormandy 1938–80, Riccardo Muti 1981–92, Wolfgang Sawallisch from 1993.

Philémon et Baucis opera by Gounod (libretto by J Barbier and M Carré, after Ovid), produced Paris, Théâtre Lyrique, 18 Feb 1860. Elderly Philemon and Baucis are rewarded by Jupiter: he restores their youth. But the god falls in love with Baucis, and she requests old age again to dampen his amorous enthusiasm.

Philemon und Baucis, oder Jupiters Reise auf der Erde, *Philemon and Baucis, or Jupiter's journey to Earth*, marionette opera by Haydn (libretto by G K Pfeffel), produced Eszterháza, 2 Sept 1773. Jupiter restores life to Narcissa and her lover Aret, the dead son of Philemon and Baucis, after the god finds shelter in the parents' home. He transforms the hut into a temple and Philemon and Baucis into priests.

Philharmonia Orchestra London-based orchestra founded 1945 by Walter Legge. Many important concerts and recordings with Toscanini, Furtwängler, Karajan and Giulini. Otto Klemperer gave his first concert with the orchestra in 1951 and became its principal conductor 1959. Legge attempted to disband the orchestra in 1964 but it immediately re-formed under the title New Philharmonia, with Klemperer as conductor for life. Principal conductors since Klemperer's death in 1973 have been Riccardo Muti (until 1982) and Giuseppe Sinopoli 1984–94. Original title, Philharmonia, re-adopted in 1977.

Philharmonic Society, London, ◊Royal Philharmonic Society; Vienna, ◊Gesellschaft der Musikfreunde.

Philidor French family of musicians:

1. Jean Philidor (b *c* 1620; d Paris, 8 Sept 1679), fifer, oboist, crumhorn and tromba marina player, brother of Michel Danican, which was the original family name (for reasons of the change of name ◊Danican). He entered the service of Louis XIII about the time of his brother's death, *c* 1659. Wrote dance music.

2. André Philidor (b Versailles, *c* 1647; d Dreux, 11 Aug 1730), bassoonist, oboist, etc., and composer, son of 1. Entered the royal service as a boy, played all sorts of instruments there, competed with

Lully in writing fanfares, marches, etc., and was soon commissioned to provide dances and stage diversions. In 1684 he became librarian of the king's music library and made a huge MS collection of court and church music.

Works include divertissements *Le Carnaval de Versailles* (1687), *Le Mariage de la Couture avec la grosse Cathos*, *La Princesse de Crète* (1688), *La Mascarade du vaisseau marchand* (1700), *Le Jeu d'échecs*.

3. Jacques Philidor (b Paris, 5 May 1657; d Versailles, 27 May 1708), oboist, bassoonist, etc., and composer, brother of 2. Entered court service in 1668, the royal chapel in 1683 and the chamber music as bassoonist in 1690. Composed marches, airs for oboe, dance music.

4. Anne Danican Philidor (b Paris, 11 Apr 1681; d Paris, 8 Oct 1728), oboist and composer, son of 2 by his first wife, Marguerite Monginot. Entered court service as oboist in the chamber music and the royal chapel, founded the Concert Spirituel in Paris, 1725, and later in life superintended the Duchesse de Maine's and the Prince de Conti's private concerts. pastorals *L'Amour vainqueur* (1697), *Diane et Endymion* (1698), *Danaé*, (1701) etc.

5. François Philidor (b Versailles, 17 Mar 1689; d ? Versailles, 1717–18), oboe, crumhorn, tromba marina and bass viol player and composer. In court service, composed flute pieces, etc.

6. François André (Danican) Philidor (b Dreux, 7 Sept 1726; d London, 31 Aug 1795), composer and chess-player, half-brother of 5, being the son of 2 by his second wife. As a page at court he studied music under Campra, and also showed a remarkable precocity for chess, which took him on a tour of Holland, Germany and England in 1745. Further travels followed, and in 1749 he pub. in London his *Analyse du jeu des échecs*. He returned to Paris in 1754, and there produced his first *opéra comique* in 1759, the beginning of a long series of spectacular successes. He continued to visit England as a chess-player, and in 1792 took refuge from the French Revolution in London, where he remained till his death.

Works include: operas *Blaise le savetier* (1759), *L'Huître et les plaideurs*, *Le Quiproquo* (1760), *Le Soldat magicien*, *Le Jardinier et son seigneur* (after La Fontaine, 1760), *Le Maréchal ferrant*, *Sancho Pança dans son île* (after Cervantes, 1762), *Le Bûcheron* (1763), *Les Fêtes de la paix*, *Le Sorcier*, *Tom Jones* (after Fielding, 1765), *Le Jardinier de Sidon* (1768), *L'Amant déguisé* (1769), *La Nouvelle école des femmes* (1770), *Mélide, ou Le Navigateur*, *Le Bon Fils* (1773), *Les Femmes vengées* (1775), *Ernelinde, Persée* (after Lully's old libretto, 1780), *Thémistocle* (1785), *L'Amitié au village*, *La Belle Esclave, ou Valcour et Zeïla* (1787), *Bélisaire* (1796) and others; Requiem for Rameau (1764), motet *Lauda Jerusalem* (1754) and others; settings of Horace's *Carmen saeculare* and Congreve's *Ode on St Cecilia's Day* (1754).

Philips, Peter (b ? London, 1561; d Brussels, 1628), English organist and composer. He left England in 1582, probably because he was a Roman Catholic, visited Italy and Spain, settled at Antwerp in 1590 and became a canon at the collegiate church of Soignies and in 1611 was appointed organist at the royal chapel in Brussels. In 1621 he became chaplain of the church of Saint-Germain at Tirlemont and *c* 1623 canon of Béthune, but may not have resided at either place. He was famous as an organist throughout the Netherlands.

Works include Masses, 106 motets pub. in *Paradisus sacris cantionibus* (Antwerp, 1628), hymns, *Sacrae cantiones*; madrigals; fantasies, pavans and galliards for various instruments; organ and virginal pieces, etc.

Phillipps, Adelaide (b Stratford-on-Avon, 26 Oct 1833; d Carlsbad, 3 Oct 1882), English contralto. The family settled in USA in 1840, where she first appeared as a dancer. On the recommendation of Jenny Lind she turned to music and studied singing with Garcia in London. In 1854 made her debut at Milan, as Rosina. Later she sang chiefly in USA; debut NY, 1856, as Azucena.

Phillips, Henry (b Bristol, 13 Aug 1801; d London, 8 Nov 1876), English baritone. Appeared on the stage as a boy, sang in the chorus at Drury Lane Theatre in London and gradually worked his way up as a concert singer. He also sang in opera, e.g. as Weber's Kaspar, and produced table entertainments from 1843. Gave farewell concert 1863, then taught in Birmingham.

Phillips, Peter (b Southampton, 15 Oct 1953), English choral director. After study at St John's College, Oxford, founded the Tallis Scholars in 1978; many concerts in Britain, Australia (Byrd's five-part Mass at the Sydney Opera House) and the USA (from 1988). London Proms debut 1988, with Victoria's Requiem, and tour of the Far East 1991. With the Tallis Scholars has won renown for recordings of such works as Gesualdo's *Tenebrae Responsories*, *Missa Pastores* by Clemens non Papa, Byrd's *Great Service* and three Masses, the English anthems of Tallis and the masses of Josquin and Palestrina. Author of *English Sacred Music, 1549–1649*, 1991.

Philosopher, The nickname of Haydn's symphony, no. 22 in E♭ major, composed 1764 and containing, exceptionally, parts for two cors anglais.

Philtre, Le, *The Love Potion*, opera by Auber (libretto by Scribe), produced Paris, Opéra, 20 Apr 1831. ◊Elisir d'amore, L'.

Phinot (or *Finot*), Dominique (b *c* 1510; d *c* 1555), French composer. He was associated with the courts of Urbino and Pesaro and wrote many motets and *chansons*.

Phoebus and Pan (Bach) ◊Streit zwischen Phöbus und Pan.

phrase a small group of notes forming a definite melodic or thematic feature in a composition.

Phrygian cadence a cadence which owes its name to the fact that in the Phrygian Mode (E–E) the sixth degree of the scale (D) was not sharpened by *musica ficta*, since this would have resulted in an augmented sixth with the note F, and altering F to F♯ would have destroyed the character of the mode.

A Phrygian cadence on E.

This cadence was so firmly established that it survived the disappearance of the modes and acquired the flavour of a kind of imperfect cadence on the dominant of A minor. Transposed into any key that was required, it was widely used in the late 17th and early 18th c., particularly to mark a transition from one movement to another. This transition was not always harmonically obvious; it was common practice to use it at the end of a slow middle movement in a minor key in order to lead into a final movement in a major key. In Bach's third Brandenburg Concerto it is used by itself without any middle movement at all.

Phrygian Mode the third ecclesiastical mode, represented on the piano by the scale beginning with the note E played on the white notes.

physharmonica a small reed organ invented by Anton Hackel of Vienna in 1818; a forerunner of the harmonium.

Pia de'Tolomei opera by Donizetti (libretto by S Cammarano), produced Venice, Teatro Apollo, 18 Feb 1837. Ghino is infatuated by his sister-in-law Pia, but denounces her as unfaithful when she does not succumb. Her husband Nello imprisons her and poisons her after mistaking her brother Rodrigo for a lover. Ghino confesses, but it is too late.

pianissimo Italian = 'very soft'; a direction rarely written out in full, but indicated by the sign *pp* or a multiplication thereof.

piano Italian = 'soft'; as a rule represented by the symbol *p*. The comparable 'softer' for a dynamic direction between *p* and *pp*, etc., has no symbol, but is expressed by the words *più piano* (or *più p*).

piano the current abbr. name of the ◊pianoforte.

pianoforte Italian = lit. 'soft-loud'; a keyboard instrument originally similar to the harpsichord in appearance, but producing its sound by striking the strings with hammers (a principle derived from the medieval dulcimer) instead of plucking them with quills or leather

pianoforte *Mendelssohn playing before Queen Victoria and Prince Albert, by C Röhling. The illustration depicts an instrument of the mid-19th century. By this time the English design, which produced a rich, sonorous tone, had almost universally superseded the Viennese design.*

tongues. Its beginnings go back to Italy at the end of the 16th c., but the first inventor who probably consolidated it in its present form was Bartolomeo Cristofori of Padua, who settled in Florence about the first decade of the 18th c. The table-shaped square piano came later in the c. and the upright piano followed last in the 19th c. The hammer action was improved by very gradual processes, and English makers contributed the invention of the iron frame, which was capable of supporting a much greater tension of strings, resulting in more powerful tone.

It is possible to make sounds on a piano that are more orchestral than those of an orchestra.
Olivier Messiaen, quoted in Nichols, *Messiaen*, 1975

---

pianola a mechanical device attached to an ordinary piano whereby the hammers are made to touch the strings not by action of the hand on the keyboard but by air-pressure. This is regulated by a roll of perforated paper running over a series of slits corresponding with the musical scale and releasing the air only where the holes momentarily pass over the slits. The mechanism is set in motion by pedals like those of a harmonium. Dynamics were at first controlled by action of the player's hands, more or less roughly according to his skill, but they were later reproduced mechanically exactly as played by the recording artist. This, however, left the manipulator with nothing of any interest to do, and no doubt for that reason the pianola, after enjoying a great vogue in the early 20th c., later fell into neglect.

In 1986 the Viennese firm Bösendorfer produced an instrument which, it is claimed, can reproduce every nuance of a performance.

Optical sensors scan the keys, hammers and pedals 800 times a second and the registered information is fed into a computer. It is stored on tape or floppy disc and can be relayed back to the piano for 'performance'.

piano-organ, or handle-piano, a mechanical instrument similar to the barrel organ in the shape of an upright piano, producing its notes in the same way by a studded cylinder, but from strings struck by hammers instead of pipes. It was widely used by street musicians in the larger English cities in the late 19th and early 20th c., especially in London, of which it was long part of the atmosphere. It was often wrongly called 'barrel organ' and even more incorrectly 'hurdy-gurdy'.

piano quartet quartet for piano, violin, viola and cello. The earliest examples played today are those by Mozart (K478 and K493). The quartet of Beethoven (op. 16) and three quartets of Brahms (op. 25, op. 26, op. 60) are worthy successors.

piano quintet usually a quintet for piano and string quartet (e.g. Brahms, Schumann and Elgar), but Schubert's 'Trout' Quintet is for piano, violin, viola, cello and double bass.

piano trio a trio for piano, violin and cello.

Piatigorsky, Gregor (b Ekaterinoslav, 17 Apr 1903; d Los Angeles, 6 Aug 1976), Russian-born cellist. First studied the violin with his father and then the cello with von Glehn, subsequently playing with various Moscow orchestras. He left Russia in 1921 and went to Berlin, where he studied with J Klengel and became first cello with the Berlin PO. US debut, with NY PO, 1929. Later became known as one of the leading solo performers of his day. In 1930 formed a trio with Horowitz and Milstein; 1949 with Heifetz and Rubinstein. He gave the fps of the concertos by Hindemith (1941) and Walton (1957).

Piatti, Alfredo (Carlo) (b Bergamo, 8 Jan 1822; d Crocetta di Mozzo, 18 Jul 1901), Italian cellist. Studied music under his father, a violinist, and cello under his great-uncle Zanetti. He soon entered a theatre orchestra, came under the notice of Mayr and was sent to study at the Milan Conservatory, making his first public appearance in 1837. He travelled widely later and lived much of his life in London, where he became associated with Joachim and played frequently at the Popular Concerts at St James's Hall. He made his London debut in 1844 and in 1866 gave the fp of Sullivan's Concerto. He wrote two concertos and a number of pieces and studies for cello.

Piave, Francesco Maria (b Murano, 18 May 1810; d Milan, 5 Mar 1876), Italian librettist. He studied briefly for the priesthood and for a time earned subsistence from a publisher. A collaboration with Verdi began in 1844 with *Ernani*. Other libretti for Verdi were *I due Foscari*, *Macbeth*, *Il corsaro*, *Stiffelio*, *Rigoletto*, *La Traviata*, *Simon Boccanegra*, *Aroldo* and *La Forza del Destino*. An abandoned project, *Allan Cameron*, was taken up with Pacini and produced in Venice, 1848. In the same year Piave's libretto for Mercadante's (*La schiava Saracena/The Saracen Slave-Girl* was produced in Milan. Piave did not write libretti for Ponchielli, as has been stated elsewhere.

Picander ◊Henrici.

Piccaver, Alfred (b Long Sutton, Lincs., 25 Feb 1884; d Vienna, 23 Sept 1958), English tenor. He worked as an electrical engineer in NY, where he was brought up, and also sang in student performance at the Met. Opera School. On a visit to Europe in 1907 he applied for an audition and made his debut at the Prague Opera in the same year, as Roméo. After a period of further study he joined the Vienna Opera in 1910 and remained there until 1937. Among his roles were Radames, Lohengrin, Walther, Faust and Florestan. Retired 1937 and settled in London. He returned to Vienna in 1955 and was active as a teacher.

Picchi, Mirto (b S Mauro, Florence, 15 Mar 1915; d Florence, 25 Sept 1980), Italian tenor. Debut Milan 1946, as Radames. At the Cambridge Theatre, London, he sang Rodolfo, Cavaradossi and the Duke of Mantua (1947–48) and visited Edinburgh, with the Glyndebourne co., as Verdi's Riccardo, in 1949. At Florence he appeared in Rossini's *L'Assedio di Corinto* (1949) and in 1957 was heard in *Lucrezia Borgia*, at La Scala. Britten's Billy Budd and Peter Grimes were among his modern roles. Retired 1975.

Piccinni, Niccolò (b Bari, 16 Jan 1728; d Passy near Paris, 7 May 1800),

Italian composer. Studied at the Conservatorio di Sant' Onofrio at Naples, Leo and Durante being among his masters. He produced his first opera at Naples in 1754. In spite of Logroscino's exclusive success, it was well received and soon followed by other operas, both comic and serious. In 1756 he married the singer Vincenza Sibilia, his pupil. In 1760 he made an enormous success in Rome with *La buona figliuola*. After some years of success there he was ousted by Anfossi and returned to Naples in 1773. In 1776 he was invited to Paris, where he was at first in great difficulties, but was helped by Marmontel, who taught him French and wrote the libretto of his first French opera, *Roland*, for him, which was produced in Jan 1778. By this time he had been artifically made into an opponent to Gluck by those who were determined to organize a partisan feud, though neither he nor Gluck had any desire to take a share in this and liked and respected each other. The quarrel of their adherents was heightened by their being both given an *Iphigénie en Tauride* to set to music. At the Revolution he left for Italy, visited Venice and then returned home to Naples, where, however, he was placed under close surveillance and lived in great poverty. In 1798 he at last succeeded in returning to Paris. After a period of comparative affluence, he again fell into poverty, was relieved by a gift from Bonaparte and an inspector's post at the Conservatory, but became paralysed and finally died in distress. His son Luigi (1766–1827) and his natural grandson Louis-Alexandre (1779–1850) were both composers. The former wrote operas for Paris and Stockholm, the latter ballets, melodramas, etc., for the Paris theatres.

Works include *c* 120 operas, e.g. *Le donne dispettose* (1754), *Le Gelosie*, *Zenobia* (1756), *Alessandro nell' Indie* (two versions), *Madama Arrighetta* (1758), *La buona figliuola*, *La buona figliuola maritata* (both after Richardson's *Pamela*, 1760, 1761), *Il cavaliere per amore* (1762), *Le contadine bizarre*, *Gli stravaganti* (1764), *L'Olimpiade* (1761), *I viaggiatori* (1775), *La pescatrice* (1766), *Le finte gemelle*, *Vittorina* (Goldoni), *Roland*, *Atys*, *Iphigénie en Tauride*, (1781), *Didon* (1783), *Le Faux Lord* (1783), *Pénélope*, *Endymion* (1784); oratorio *Jonathan* and three others; Mass, psalms and other church music.

Piccola musica notturna, *Little night Music*, work for orchestra by Dallapiccola, fp Hanover, 7 Jun 1954; arranged for eight instruments, 1961.

piccolo Italian, abbr. for *flauto piccolo* = 'little flute'; the small octave flute, more usually called *ottavino* in Italy, similar in shape and technique to the ordinary flute, but smaller in size and standing an octave higher in pitch. Its music is written an octave below the actual sound.

Piccolo Marat, II opera by Mascagni (libretto by G Forzano and G Targioni-Tozzetti), produced Rome, Teatro Costanzi, 2 May 1921. Story deals with the aftermath of the assassination of Marat, when Paris was scourged by revolutionary fanatics: at the end of the World War II Mascagni was in disgrace for having supported Mussolini. The Prince of Fleury joins the revolutionary movement to save his mother from the guillotine. After freeing her he escapes with his revolutionary lover Mariella.

Picco pipe a woodwind instrument of the recorder or flageolet type which became fashionable in England on being introduced to London in 1856 by a Sardinian player named Picco.

Pichl, Wenzel (b Bechyně near Tábor, 25 Sept 1741; d Vienna, 23 Jan 1805), Bohemian violinist and composer. Studied in Prague and in 1765 became violinist and vice-director of music (under Dittersdorf) to the Bishop of Grosswardein. In 1769 he moved to Vienna and thence to Milan in the service of the Archduke Ferdinand, remaining in Italy until his return to Vienna in 1796. He was admired by Cherubini and Gyrowetz; his quartets were performed at Eszterháza by Haydn.

According to Pichl's own catalogue, works include 12 operas, e.g. four Latin operas (1765–76), four opere buffe, *Der Krieg* (1776) and Italian arrangements of French operas; over 30 Masses; 89 symphonies; *c* 30 concertos; 172 quartets, 21 quintets, etc.; 148 pieces for baryton, etc.

Pickett, Philip (b London, 17 Nov 1950), English director and performer of early wind instruments. Studied with Anthony Baines and David Munrow, gaining experience on the recorder, shawm, rackett and crumhorn. Professor of recorder at the GSMD from 1972 and soloist with leading chamber ensembles. Director of the New London Consort at festivals throughout Europe, Russia and Latin America; *Medieval Christmas Extravaganza* on London's South Bank and *Bonfire of the Vanities* (Medici Wedding Celebrations of 1539) at the 1991 Prom Concerts. Recordings include Monteverdi's *Vespers* and *Orfeo*, *Medieval Pilgrimage to Santiago, Medieval Carmina Burana*, and *The Delights of Posilipo* (Neapolitan Dances).

Pick-Mangiagalli, Riccardo (b Strakonice, 10 Jul 1882; d Milan, 8 Jul 1949), Czech-Italian composer. Studied in Prague, Vienna and Milan. In 1936 he succeeded Pizzetti as director of the Milan Conservatory.

Works include operas *Basi e Bote* (1927), *L'ospite inatteso* and *Notturno romantico* (1936); ballets *Salice d'oro*, *Il carillon magico*, *Casanova a Venezia* (1929), *La Berceuse* and *Variazioni coreografiche*; mime dramas *Sumitra* (1917) and *Mahit* (1923); *Sortileggi* for piano and orchestra; string quartet; violin and piano sonata; piano works, etc.

Pictures at an Exhibition a suite of piano pieces by Mussorgsky, composed in 1874 in memory of the painter and architect Victor Alexandrovich Hartmann (d 1873) and illustrating pictures and designs by him shown at a memorial exhibition, organized by V V Stassov. Orchestral versions of the work have been made by Henry J Wood, Ravel, Stokowski, and Walter Goehr; brass band arrangement by Elgar Howarth. Fp of Ravel orchestration, Paris, Opéra, 19 Oct 1922, conductor Koussevitzky.

pieno Italian = 'full'; a direction used especially in organ music in combination, *organo pieno*, meaning either that a figured bass is to be filled with ample harmony or that the instrument is to be played with full registration.

Pierné, (Henri Constant) Gabriel (b Metz, 16 Aug 1863; d Ploujean, Côtes du Nord, 17 Jul 1937), French conductor and composer. Studied at the Paris Conservatory and gained the Prix de Rome in 1882. In 1890 he succeeded Franck as organist of the church of Sainte-Clotilde, became second conductor of Colonne's orchestra in 1903 and at Colonne's death in 1910 succeeded him as chief conductor. He gave many important fps, including Debussy's *Khamma* (1924) and *La Boîte à joujoux* (1923).

Works include operas *Les Elfes*, *Pandore*, *La Coupe enchantée* (after La Fontaine, 1905), *La Nuit de Noël*, *Vendée*, *La Fille de Tabarin*, *On ne badine pas avec l'amour* (after Musset, 1910), *Fragonard*, *Sophie Arnould* (1927); ballets, pantomimes and incidental music; oratorios, suites for orchestra; piano quintet, piano trio; songs.

Pierrot lunaire Schoenberg's song-cycle with chamber ensemble, op. 21, consisting of 21 poems by Albert Giraud translated into German by Otto Erich Hartleben; composed 1912, fp Berlin, 16 Oct 1912. The treatment of the voice-part is one of the outstanding examples of the use of 'Speechsong' (*Sprechgesang*). The 21 poems are arranged in three sections: 1: *Mondestrunken, Colombine, Der Dandy, Eine blasse Wäscherin, Valse de Chopin, Madonna, Der Kranke Mond*. 2: *Die Nacht, Gebet an Pierrot, Raub, Rote Messe, Galgenlied, Enthauptung, Die Kreuze*. 3: *Heimweh, Gemeinheit, Parodie, Der Mondfleck, Serenade, Heimfahrt, O alter Duft*. The work was commissioned by Albertine Zehme; it was soon admired by composers as different as Puccini and Stravinsky but wider public success did not come until a performance in Berlin on 5 Jan 1924, with Marie Gutheil-Schoder and Gregor Piatigorsky (cello), Artur Schnabel (piano) and Fritz Stiedry (conductor).

Pierson (originally *Pearson*), Henry Hugh (or Heinrich Hugo) (b Oxford, 12 Apr 1815; d Leipzig, 28 Jan 1873), English-born German composer. Educated at Harrow and Cambridge, studied music with Attwood and Corfe, and interrupted a medical course to continue music studies at Leipzig, where he met Mendelssohn, Schumann and

Pickett *Philip Pickett performs on a variety of early wind instruments, including recorder, crumhorn, shawm and rackett. He has appeared as a soloist with several leading orchestras and is director of the New London Consort.*

others. He became Reid Professor of Music at Edinburgh in 1844 in succession to Bishop, but soon resigned and returned to Germany, where he remained, married Caroline Leonhardt and changed the spelling of his name.

Works include operas *Der Elfensieg* (1845), *Leila* (1848) and *Contarini* (composed 1853, produced 1872), *Fenice* (1883); incidental music to Goethe's *Faust* (Part II); oratorio *Jerusalem* (1852); *Macbeth* symphony (1859), overtures to Shakespeare's *Twelfth Night, Julius Caesar* and *Romeo and Juliet* (1874), funeral march for *Hamlet* (1859); numerous songs; part-songs, etc.

Piéton, Loyset (b Bernay, Normandy; d after 1545), French composer, often confused with Compère, both being usually called only by their Christian names. Wrote Masses, motets, psalms and *chansons*. His work was pub. in Lyon and Venice.

pietoso Italian from *pietà* = 'pity'; pityingly, compassionately.

Pietra del paragone, La, *The Touchstone*, opera by Rossini (libretto by I Romanelli), produced Milan, La Scala, 26 Sept 1812. Count Asdrubale and Marchesina Clarice meet at a party; their affections grow. Each tests the other's sincerity with the help of disguises and they are united.

piffaro Italian = 'fife'; a small flute-like pipe, also a shepherd's pipe akin to the oboe or bagpipe. It was often played in Italian cities, especially Rome and Naples, at Christmas time, by pipers from the hills, who seem to have played tunes of the Siciliana type akin to that of the *Pastoral Symphony* in Handel's *Messiah*, which bears the word 'pifa' in the MS, evidently in reference to the piffaro.

Pigheaded Peasants, The, *Tvrdé Palice*, opera by Dvořák (libretto J Stolba), produced Prague, Czech Theatre, 2 Oct 1881. Widower Vávra and widow Ríhová decide their children, Toník and Lenka, should marry, and, knowing their children to be stubborn, use reverse psychology to coax them together.

Pijper, Willem (b Zeist, 8 Sept 1894; d Leidschendam, 18 Mar 1947), Dutch composer. Studied with Wagenaar and was appointed professor of composition) at the Amsterdam Conservatory in 1925; director of the Rotterdam Conservatory in 1930.

Works include opera *Halewijn* (1933); incidental music for

Pinnock *The harpsichordist and conductor Trevor Pinnock. Beginning his career at the keyboard, Pinnock has long advocated the 'authentic' performance of early music. Founder and musical director of The English Concert, he has also conducted since 1980.*

Euripides' *The Cyclops* and *The Bacchantes* (1924), Sophocles' *Antigone* and Shakespeare's *Tempest* (1930); three symphonies, six symphonic Epigrams for orchestra, piano concerto (1927), violin concerto, cello concerto; five string quartets (1914–46), two piano trios, sextet for wind and piano; violin and piano sonatas; piano music; choruses; songs.

Pilarczyk, Helga (b Schöningen, 12 Mar 1925), German soprano. Studied in Brunswick and Hamburg, making her debut at the Brunswick State Theatre, 1951. From 1954 she was a member of the Hamburg State Opera. She was best known for her singing of modern music; Schoenberg's *Erwartung* and *Pierrot lunaire*. The first Lulu in Britain (SW theatre, London, 1962) and sang Berg's Marie on her NY Met. debut in 1965.

Pilgrim's Progress, The opera by Vaughan Williams (libretto by the composer after Bunyan), produced London, CG, 26 Apr 1951. It incorporates most of the composer's one-act opera *The Shepherds of the Delectable Mountains* (produced London, RCM, 11 Jul 1922). The Pilgrim faces many trials on his way to the Celestial City.

Pilkington, Francis (b *c* 1570; d Chester, 1638), English composer. Took the B.Mus. at Oxford in 1595 and was soon after appointed as singer at Chester Cathedral where he remained to his death, becoming a minor canon in 1612.

Works include anthems (one in Leighton's *Teares or Lamentacions*); madrigals and pastorals for three–six voices; lute pieces; songs to the lute.

Pimmalione, *Pygmalion*, opera by Cherubini (libretto by S Vestris), produced Paris, Tuileries, at Napoleon's private theatre, for which it was written, 30 Nov 1809.

Pimpinone three intermezzos by Albinoni (libretto by P Pariati), produced with the opera *Astarto* Venice, 1708. As with Pergolesi's *La serva padrona*, the intermezzo is now better known than the *opera seria* for which it was intended to provide light relief. Vespetta persuades elderly Pimpinone to employ her as a servant. She then makes him promise to marry her, after which she seeks pleasure elsewhere.

Intermezzo by Telemann, produced Hamburg, 1725.

Pincherle, Marc (b Constantine, Algeria, 13 Jun 1888; d Paris, 20 Jun 1974), French musicologist. Professor at the École Normale de Musique in Paris and edited successively of *Le Monde musical* and *Musique*. His works include studies of Corelli, Vivaldi, the violin and violin music.

Pinelli, Ettore (b Rome, 18 Oct 1843; d Rome, 17 Sept 1915), Italian violinist and conductor. Studied in Rome and with Joachim at Hanover, organized chamber concerts in Rome and with Sgambati founded the Liceo Musicale there, became violin professor and conducted orchestral and choral concerts. Composed an overture, a string quartet, etc.

Pinello di Gherardi, Giovanni Battista (b Genoa, *c* 1544; d Prague, 15 Jun 1587), Italian composer. After an appointment at Vicenza Cathedral he went to Innsbruck in the 1570s as musician to the archduke, to the Imperial chapel in Prague soon afterwards and to the Saxon court at Dresden in 1580 in succession to Scandello, but was dismissed because of differences with other musicians, and returned to Prague.

Works include motets, German Magnificats and other church music; madrigals and *canzone napoletane*; part-songs.

Pini-Corsi, Antonio (b Zara, Jun 1858; d Milan, 22 Apr 1918), Italian baritone. Made his first appearance at the age of 20 at Cremona, as Dandini and became one of the leading interpreters of comic parts, Verdi choosing him for Ford in his *Falstaff* in 1893. CG debut 1894, as Puccini's Lescaut; NY Met. 1899, as Masetto. Other roles included Schaunard (creation, 1896), Pasquale and Leporello.

Pinkham, Daniel (b Lynn, MA, 5 Jun 1923), American composer, organist and conductor. Studied with Piston at Harvard and with Boulanger in Paris. Music director of King's Chapel at Boston from 1958.

Works include chamber opera *The Garden of Artemis*, arrangement of *The Beggar's Opera* (1956), four symphonies, two violin concertos, *Wedding* and *Christmas Cantatas*, Requiem and *St Mark Passion* (1965), *Daniel in the Lion's Den* (1972), *The Passion of Judas* (1976), *A Curse, a Lament and a Vision* for chorus and piano (1984), *Getting to Heaven* for soprano and chorus (1987), concerto piccolo (1989).

Pinnock, Trevor (b Canterbury, 16 Dec 1946), English harpsichordist and conductor. Studied RCM; solo debut London 1971. He played with the Galliard Harpsichord Trio 1966–72 and often appeared with the Academy of St Martin-in-the-Fields. Founded the English Concert 1973; 'authentic' performances of early music. He has conducted from 1980; gave Handel's *Solomon* at the 1986 Promenade Concerts, London. NY Met. debut 1988, *Giulio Cesare*; Salzburg 1988, *Messiah*. Principal conductor of the Arts Centre Orchestra at Ottawa, from 1991. CBE 1991. Recordings include Purcell's *King Arthur* and the complete Mozart symphonies.

Pinsuti, Ciro (b Sinalunga, Siena, 9 May 1829; d Florence, 10 Mar 1888), Italian pianist, singing-teacher and composer. Studied with his father and played the piano in public as a child, was taken to England, studying composition with Potter, returning to Italy 1845 and becoming a pupil of Rossini at Bologna. From 1848 he was in England again, teaching singing for many years in London and Newcastle-upon-Tyne and becoming professor at the RAM in 1856.

Works include operas *Il mercante di Venezia* (after Shakespeare, 1873), *Mattia Corvino* (1877) and *Margherita* (1882); Te Deum for the annexation of Tuscany to Italy (1859); hymn for the International Exhibition in London (1871); 30 piano pieces; 230 songs; many vocal duets and trios; part-songs.

Pinto, George Frederic (b London, 25 Sept 1786; d London, 23 Mar 1806), English violinist and composer. His real name was Sanders, but he adopted that of his maternal grandfather. Studied with Salomon and others and appeared at Salomon's concerts from 1796. He then toured in England and Scotland and visited Paris. His early death was allegedly the result of dissipation.

Works include violin and piano sonatas, violin duets, piano sonatas, canzonets.

Pinto, Thomas (b England 1714; d ? Edinburgh 1783), English violinist of Italian descent, grandfather of George ◊Pinto through his first wife. In 1766 he married the singer Charlotte Brent as his second wife. He played in London at an early age, later at the Three Choirs Festival, etc., failed in a speculation with Arnold to run Marylebone Gardens and last lived in Scotland and Ireland.

Pinza, Ezio (Fortunato) (b Rome, 18 May 1892; d Stamford, CT, 9 May 1957), Italian bass. He studied at the Bologna Conservatory and first appeared at Soncino (near Milan) in *Norma*, 1914. After World War I he sang in Rome and other Italy cities as Marke, Pogner and Colline. He joined the Met. Opera, NY, in 1926 and sang Fiesco, Figaro, Don Giovanni and Boris. London, CG, 1930–39. Salzburg, 1934–37, under Walter. In 1948 he left the Met. to devote himself to operetta, films and television.

Piozzi, Gabriel(e) (Mario) (b Brescia, 8 Jun 1740; d Dymerchion, Denbighshire, 26 Mar 1809), Italian, later English, music teacher and composer. Settled in England *c* 1776, and won a good reputatation as a singing-teacher and pianist. In 1784 he married Mrs Hester Thrale, to the displeasure of her friend Dr Johnson.

Works include string quartets, piano quartets, violin sonatas, canzonets.

pipe and tabor a combination of two early instruments, a small pipe of the recorder type, but held with one hand only while the other beats the tabor, a small drum without snares hung round the player's shoulder or strapped to his waist. The instruments have been revived for folk-dancing.

Pipelare, Matthaeus, Flemish 15th–16th-c. composer. In 1498 he became master of the choristers at 's-Hertogenbosch. He wrote Masses, motets, and secular works to French and Dutch texts. His motet *Memorare mater Christi* commemorates the seven sorrows of the Virgin.

Pique-Dame the German title of Tchaikovsky's opera *The Queen of Spades/Pikovaya Dama*.

Pirame et Thisbé, *Pyramus and Thisbe*, opera by Rebel and Francœur (libretto by J L I de La Serre), produced Paris, Opéra, 17 Oct 1726. Pyramus and Thisbe decide to run away together. Thisbe arrives at the rendezvous first but runs away when she sees a wounded lion. Pyramus arrives and, seeing the blood, believes Thisbe has been eaten. He stabs himself; she returns to find him and does likewise.

Pirata, Il, *The Pirate*, opera by Bellini (libretto by F Romani), produced Milan, La Scala, 27 Oct 1827. Ernesto has forces Imogene to marry him despite her love for Gualtiero, who in desperation turns to piracy. Gualtiero is shipwrecked near Ernesto's castle. The lovers meet, but their joy is short-lived: Gualtiero kills Ernesto and is sentenced to death.

Pirates of Penzance, The, or The Slave of Duty operetta by Sullivan (libretto by W S Gilbert), produced Paignton, Bijou Theatre, 30 Dec 1879); pirated performance, NY, Fifth Avenue Theatre, 31 Dec 1879; first London performance, Opéra-Comique, 3 Apr 1880. Frederic, mistakenly apprenticed to some pirates, intends to turn in the outlaws when he comes of age. However, he discovers he was born on 29 Feb in a leap year, and is consequently not yet 21: he must remain an apprentice.

Pires, Maria João (b Lisbon, 23 Jul 1944), Portuguese pianist. Played Mozart Concerto aged seven, then studied at the Lisbon Academy 1953–60 and in Munich. Performed widely in Europe after winning 1970 Beethoven Competition at Brussels but career interrupted by illness. Played Mozart's concerto K449 at Salzburg in 1984 and made London and US debuts 1986. Tour of America 1988, with the New York PO and Houston SO. Famed for her sensitive performances of Mozart, Chopin and Schumann.

Pirro, André (b Saint-Dizier, 12 Feb 1869; d Paris, 11 Nov 1943), French musicologist. Studied law and literature in Paris and at the same time picked up as much musical education as he could, attending the organ classes of Franck and Widor. In 1896 he became professor and a director of the newly opened Schola Cantorum. In 1904 he began to lecture at the École des Hautes Études Sociales and in 1912 succeeded Rolland as professor of music history at the Sorbonne. His books include studies of Schütz, Buxtehude, Bach (general and organ works), the French clavecinists, Descartes and music, early German church and secular music, etc.

Pirro e Demetrio, *Pyrrhus and Demetrius*, opera by A Scarlatti

Pires *The Portuguese pianist Maria João Pires recovered from illness in the late 1970s to make belated British and US debuts and has since assumed the mantle of the legendary Clara Haskil. She is admired for the profound musicianship of her performances.*

(libretto by A Morselli), produced Naples, Teatro San Bartolommeo, probably 28 Jan 1694.

Pirrotta, Nino (b Palermo, 13 Jun 1908), Italian musicologist. He studied at the Conservatories of Palermo and Florence; librarian of the S Cecilia Conservatory, Rome, 1948–56, Professor at Harvard (1956–72) and at Rome (1972–83). His major studies have been of 14th c. Italian music, including the *ars nova*, and 17th-c. Italian opera.

Pisador, Diego (b Salamanca, *c* 1508; d after 1557), Spanish vihuelist. Son of a notary attached to the household of the Archbishop of Santiago. He took holy orders but did not enter the church. In 1552 he pub. a book of transcriptions of old Spanish songs, portions of Masses by Josquin Desprez, motets by Morales and others, etc. for vihuela.

Pisari, Pasquale (b Rome *c* 1725; d Rome, 27 Mar 1778), Italian singer and composer, pupil of Gasparini and Biordi. From 1752 he was a singer in the Papal Chapel in Rome, and wrote church music in the old *a cappella* style.

Works include Masses, motets, etc. His elaborate church music was admired by Martini and Burney.

Pisaroni, Benedetta (Rosamunda) (b Piacenza, 16 May 1793; d Piacenza, 6 Aug 1872), Italian contralto. Studied under Marchesi and others and made her first appearance at Bergamo in 1811, as a soprano, but changed to contralto on Rossini's advice in 1813. She sang in the fps of Rossini's *Ricciardo e Zoriade* (1818), *Erminio* (1819) and *La donna del lago* (1819). Paris from 1827 as Arsace, Tancredi and Isabella.

Pischek (or *Pišek*), Johann Baptist (b Melnik, 13 Oct 1814; d Stuttgart, 16 Feb 1873), Czech baritone. Made his first stage appearance at the age of 21 and in 1844 was appointed court singer to the King of Württemberg. Paid his first visit to England 1845, returned until 1853 in oratorio and in operas by Mozart, Gluck, Spohr and Kreutzer.

Pisendel, Johann Georg (b Cadolzburg, Bavaria, 26 Dec 1687; d Dresden, 25 Nov 1755), German violinist and composer. Studied the violin under Torelli while he was a choirboy at the chapel of the Margrave of Ansbach and theory under Pistocchi. After studying at Leipzig University He went to Dresden to enter the service of the king of Poland there in 1712, travelled widely with the king, became concert master in 1728 on the death of Volumier and led the opera orchestra under Hasse. Wrote concertos and pieces for the violin.

Pisk, Paul A(madeus) (b Vienna, 16 May 1893; d Los Angeles, 12 Jan 1990), Austrian-born American musicologist and composer. Studied under Adler at Vienna University and composition with Schreker and Schoenberg. After conducting at various German theatres, he returned to Vienna, conducting and broadcasting, and became director of the music department of the Volkshochschule, but left for USA 1936 and became professor of musicology at the University of Texas. In 1963 he joined the staff of Washington University, St Louis; retired 1973 and moved to Los Angeles. He edited early music including Masses by Jacobus Gallus, and wrote on modern music and the Second Viennese School.

Works include monodrama *Schattenseite* (1931); ballet *Der grosse Regenmacher* (1927); cantata *Die neue Stadt* (1926); Requiem for baritone and orchestra; Partita for orchestra, suite for small orchestra; *Bucolic Suite* for strings and other orchestral works; string quartet and other chamber music; piano music; songs with organ.

Pistocchi, Francesco (Antonio Mamiliano) (b Palermo, 1659; d Bologna, 13 May 1726), Italian singer and composer. The family moved to Bologna in 1661, where he began to compose at a very early age, entered San Petronio as a choirboy in 1670 and in 1675 began to appear in opera. In 1679 his first opera, for puppets, *Il Leandro* (*Gli amori fatali*), was produced at Venice. In 1687–94 he was a singer at the ducal court of Parma, and he then became music director to the Margrave of Ansbach, returning to Bologna in 1701, founding a singing-school there.

Works include operas *Il girello*, *Narciso* (1697), *Le pazzie d'amore* (1699), *Le risa di Democrito* (1700), and *Il Leandro* (1692); oratorios *Il martirio di Sant' Adriano* (1698), *Maria Vergine addolorata* (1698), *La fuga di Santa Teresa*; church music; vocal duets and trios; airs *Scherzi musicali*, etc.

Piston, Walter (b Rockland, ME, 20 Jan 1894; d Belmont, MA, 12 Nov 1976), American composer. Studied at the École Normale de Musique in Paris and at Harvard University, also with Nadia Boulanger and others. Appointed assistant professor at Harvard in 1926 and professor 1944–60. His music follows European neo-classical models, often favouring contrapuntal textures; several premieres by the Boston SO under Koussevitsky.

Works include ballet *The Incredible Flutist* (1938); eight symphonies (1937–65), suite, concerto, Symphonic Piece, Prelude and Fugue for orchestra; concertino for piano and chamber orchestra (1937), clarinet concertino, two violin concertos (1939, 1960); *Carnival Song* for male chorus and brass instruments; five string quartets (1933–62), piano trio, three pieces for flute, clarinet and bassoon; violin and piano sonata, flute and piano sonata, suite for oboe and piano, partita for violin, viola and organ.

Pistor, Gotthelf (b Berlin, 17 Oct 1887; d Cologne, 4 Apr 1947), German tenor. After his 1923 Nuremberg debut he sang in Würzburg, Darmstadt and Magdeburg; Cologne from 1929. Widely known in Wagner, he appeared at Bayreuth 1925–31, as Froh, Siegmund, Siegfried and Parsifal. Zoppot 1930–38.

In my own case I 'find' G major by singing the signature tune of 'The Archers'.

Antony Hopkins on pitch,
in *Downbeat Music Guide*, 1977

---

pitch the sound produced by a string or other body that vibrates at a certain frequency; also the standard by which notes, with the A above middle C as a starting-point, are to be tuned, a standard which determines at how many vibrations to the second that A is to be taken, as well as every other note in relation to it. Pitch varied at different times and in different countries. Early in the 19th c. it was gradually raised, especially by makers of wind instruments, to secure more brilliant effect, but with results dangerous to singers, and in England

two pitches were in use, the higher for orchestral performances and the lower Classical or French pitch for church and purely vocal music; two systems of pitch were also used during the Baroque period. The pitch with A at 440 cycles per second is now in general use, even by military bands, which until 1927 used the old Philharmonic pitch, which was slightly higher. ◊A.

Pitoni, Giuseppe Ottavio (b Rieti, 18 Mar 1657; d Rome, 1 Feb 1743), Italian composer. Studied with Pompeo Natale from an early age, and became a chorister at the churches of S Giovanni dei Fiorentini and Saints Apostoli in Rome, where he was a pupil of Foggia. After church posts in Monterotondo and Assisi he became *maestro di cappella* at Rieti in 1676, and from the next year to his death at the Collegio San Marco in Rome, later also at the Lateran and St Peter's.

Works include over 250 Masses, 780 psalm settings (including a 16-part *Dixit Dominus* still sung at St Peter's in Holy Week), Magnificats, motets, Litanies, two Passions.

Pitt, Percy (b London, 4 Jan 1869; d London, 23 Nov 1932), English conductor and composer. Educated in France and studied music there and at Leipzig with Reinecke and Jadassohn, and at Munich with Rheinberger. In 1896 he became organist at Queen's Hall in London and in 1902 adviser and conductor at CG; he gave *Ivanhoe*, *Khovanshchina* and *Pelléas* during Beecham's seasons. Later director of the Grand Opera Syndicate at CG, of the BNOC and in 1922 music director of the BBC. In Jan 1923 he conducted *Hänsel und Gretel* at CG; the broadcast was claimed as the world's first of an opera.

Pittore parigino, Il, *The Parisian Painter*, opera by Cimarosa (libretto by G Petrosellini), produced Rome, Teatro Valle, 4 Jan 1781. Eurilla must marry Baron Cricca if she is to receive her inheritance, but she falls in love with Crotignac, a painter. After first choosing money, Eurilla changes her mind and decides on Crotignac.

Pittsburgh Symphony Orchestra US orchestra founded 1895. Elgar and Strauss were early guest conductors but the orchestra was disbanded in 1910; re-formed 1926 and conducted by Antonio Modarelli (1930–37). Principal conductors since 1938: Fritz Reiner (until 1948), William Steinberg (1952–76), André Previn (1976–86); Lorin Maazel from 1986. Resident in Heinz Hall for Performing Arts from 1971. Appeared at the Salzburg Festival in 1985.

più Italian = 'more'; used for various musical directions in combinations such as *più allegro* (faster), *più lento* (slower), *più mosso* (more animated), *un poco più* (a little more [of whatever has been happening before]), etc.

piuttosto Italian = 'somewhat, rather'; a word used with directions where the composer wishes to make sure that an indication of tempo or expression is obeyed in moderation.

Pixérécourt, René Charles Guilbert de (b 1773–1844), French dramatist and librettist, biographer of Dalayrac, author of melodramas with music. ◊*Margherita d'Anjou* (Meyerbeer).

Pixis, Johann Peter (b Mannheim, 10 Feb 1788; d Baden-Baden, 22 Dec 1874), German pianist and composer. Studied with his father, Friedrich Wilhelm Pixis (c 1760–c1810), and began to appear as pianist with his brother Friedrich Wilhelm Pixis (1786–1842), a violinist. Settled in Munich in 1809 and in Paris in 1825, where he became a noted piano teacher. In 1845 he bought a villa at Baden-Baden and continued to train pupils there. He adopted and trained the singer Franzilla Göhringer (1816–?); she created Pacini's Saffo in 1840.

Works include operas *Almazinde* (1820), *Bibiana* (1829) and *Die Sprache des Herzens* (1836); piano concertos; sonatas and pieces for piano, etc.

Pizarro, Artur (b Lisbon, 17 Aug 1968), Portuguese pianist. Studied in Lisbon and at the University of Kansas. Played the Rakhmaninov 3rd Concerto on London debut, 1989, and as winning item in 1990 Leeds International Competition; Ravel's Concerto at the 1991 London Proms. Recitals in Britain, Australia, Japan and the USA.

Pizzetti, Ildebrando (b Parma, 20 Sept 1880; d Rome, 13 Feb 1968), Italian composer. Son of a piano teacher. Studied at Parma Conservatory 1895–1901. In 1908 he was appointed professor of harmony and counterpoint at the Istituto Musicale at Florence, of which he became director 1917. Appointed director of the Conservatory Giuseppe

Verdi, Milan, 1924 and in 1936 he succeeded Respighi as professor of advanced composition at the Accademia di Santa Cecilia in Rome.

Works include STAGE: operas *Fedra* (1915), *Debora e Jaele* (1922), *Lo straniero*, *Fra Gherardo* (1928), *Orséolo* (1935), *L'oro, Cagliostro* (1952), *La figlia d'Jorio*, *Assassinio nella cattedrale* (after T S Eliot, 1958), *Clitennestra* (1965); incidental music for *La Nave* and *La Pisanella* (both by d'Annunzio), Feo Belcari's *Sacra rappresentazione di Abraam ed Isacco* (1917), Sophocles' *Trachiniae* (1933); Corrado d'Errico's *Rappresentazione di Santa Uliva* (1933), *Le feste delle Panatence*, Shakespeare's *As You Like It*.

ORCHESTRAL WORKS: symphony in A major (1940); dances for Tasso's *Aminta*, three symphonic preludes for Sophocles' *Oedipus Rex* and *Coloneus* (1903), *Ouverture per una farsa tragica* (1911), *Concerto dell' estate* (1928), *Rondo veneziano* (1929); piano concerto (1930); cello concerto (1934); violin concerto (1944), harp concerto (1960).

CHORUS AND ORCHESTRA: *L'ultima caccia di Sant' Uberto* (1930), introduction to Aeschylus's *Agamemnon* and *Epithalamium* (1931); film music; *Sinfonia del fuoco* (1914) for d'Annunzio's *Cabirio* and orchestral and choral music for *Scipione l'Africano*; *Missa di Requiem* (1922) and *De profundis* for unaccompanied chorus (1937), also some smaller sacred and secular works.

CHAMBER: two string quartets (1906, 1933), piano trio; sonatas for violin and piano and for cello and piano; sonata, *Foglio d'album* and suite *Da un autunno già lontano* for piano; two songs for baritone and piano quartet, three with string quartet and 21 with piano.

Pizzi, Pier Luigi (b Milan, 15 Jun 1930), Italian stage director and designer. Studied at the Milan Polytechnic and designed *Don Giovanni* at Genoa, 1952. Has designed and produced Handel's *Orlando* (Florence 1959) and *Rinaldo* (Madrid and Lisbon); Rameau's *Hippolyte et Aricie* and *Castor et Pollux* (Aix, 1983 and 1991), with Gluck's *Alceste* for La Scala (1987). Bellini's *Capuleti e i Montecchi* at CG (1984) and *Les Troyens* for the opening of the Opéra Bastille, Paris, 1990. Rossini productions at Pesaro include *Tancredi* (1991). First modern revival of Traetta's *Buova d'Antona*, Venice 1993. He is valued for the artistic and historical truth of his designs and productions.

pizzicato Italian = 'pinched'; a direction indicating that the strings on instruments of the violin family are to be played, not with the bow, but by being plucked with a finger of the right hand, or occasionally with fingers of the left hand between bowed notes.

pizzicato tremolando Italian = 'pinched and trembling'; an effect first used by Elgar in the cadenza of his violin concerto, where the orchestra strings play chords by thrumming the strings both ways across with the fingers of the right hand.

Plaichinger, Thila (b Vienna, 13 Mar 1868; d Vienna, 19 Mar 1939), Austrian soprano. Debut Hamburg 1893; Strasbourg 1894–1901. She sang Isolde at the Berlin Hofoper in 1901 and remained until 1914 as Elektra and Brünnhilde. CG 1904 as Ortrud, Isolde and Venus. Guest in Vienna, Munich and Dresden.

One ought not to sing in churches anything except plainsong in unison.
Gabriel Fauré, *Le monde musicale*, 1904

---

plainchant or plainsong the medieval church music still surviving in some services of the Roman Catholic Church, properly sung in unison, without harmony and with no definitely measured rhythms. Its groupings of notes have, however, a strongly rhythmic character, but it resembles the free rhythm of prose, whereas that of measured music is comparable to the rhythm of verse. The old notation on a stave of four lines, with square or diamond-shaped notes and ligatures, is still used for plainsong.

plainte French = 'complaint'; a lament or memorial piece, whether vocal or instrumental.

Plamenac, Dragan (b Zagreb, 8 Feb 1895; d Ede, Holland, 15 Mar 1983), American musicologist of Croatian origin. Studied law at the

University of Zagreb, then composition with Schreker, musicology with Adler in Vienna and with Pirro in Paris, taking his doctorate in 1925. In 1939 he went to the USA, becoming Professor of Musicology at the University of Illinois in 1955. He pub. a number of studies of pre-classical music and edited the works of Ockeghem.

Planché, James Robinson (b London, 27 Feb 1796; d London, 30 May 1880), English dramatist, librettist and critic of French descent. Lived in London and wrote a number of libretti including *Maid Marian* for Bishop, *Oberon* for Weber and *The Surrender of Calais*, intended for Mendelssohn and later offered to H Smart, who left it unfinished.

Plançon, Pol (Henri) (b Fumay, Ardennes, 12 Jun 1851; d Paris, 11 Aug 1914), French bass. Studied with Duprez and Sbriglia in Paris, made his debut at Lyon in 1877, as St Bris in *Les Huguenots*. Méphistophélès, NY Met, 1893–1908; debut as Jupiter in Gounod's *Philémon et Baucis*. He sang in Paris from 1880 (fps of Massenet's *Le Cid* and Saint-Saëns' *Ascanio*) and first visited London in 1891.

Planets, The suite by Holst for orchestra with organ and (in final section) female chorus. 1. *Mars, the Bringer of War*; 2. *Venus, the Bringer of Peace*; 3. *Mercury, the Winged Messenger*; 4. *Jupiter, the Bringer of Jollity*; 5. *Saturn, the Bringer of Old Age*; 6. *Uranus, the Magician*; 7. *Neptune, the Mystic*. First (private) performance, London, Queen's Hall, 29 Sept 1918; first public performance, London, 15 Nov 1920. The idea of writing music on the planets was not new: Buxtehude wrote a harpsichord suite on them; but Holst dealt with them from the astrological aspect.

Planquette, (Jean) Robert (b Paris, 31 Jul 1848; d Paris, 28 Jan 1903), French composer. Studied briefly at the Paris Conservatory and then wrote songs performed at café-concerts. From this he passed on to operettas, the fourth of which, *Les Cloches de Corneville*, was immensely successful in 1877.

Works include operettas *Valet de cœur*, *Le Serment de Mme Grégoire*, *Paille d'avoine* (1874), *Les Cloches de Corneville* (1877), *Le Chevalier Gaston* (1879), *Les Voltigeurs de la 32me* (*The Old Guard*), *La Cantinière*, *Rip van Winkle* (after Washington Irving, 1882), *Nell Gwynne* (1884), *La Cremaillère*, *Surcouf* (*Paul Jones*), *Capitaine Thérèse*, *La Cocarce tricolore*, *Le Talisman*, *Panurge* (after Rabelais, 1895), *Mam'zelle Quat' Sous* (1897), *Le Paradis de Mahomed* (produced 1906).

Plantade, Charles Henri (b Pontoise, 14 Oct 1764; d Paris, 18 Dec 1839), French pianist, harpist, cellist and composer. Learnt singing and cello as one of the royal pages and later studied composition with Langlé, piano with Hüllmandel and harp with Petrini. Having set up as a teacher of singing and harp, he began to write duets and they gained him access to the stage. He taught singing to Queen Hortense, became *maître de chapelle* at court and professor at the Conservatory, and held other posts and distinctions.

Works include operas *Palma, ou Le Voyage en Grèce* (1797), *Zoé, ou La Pauvre Petite* (1800), *Le Mari de circonstance* (1813) and many others; Masses, Requiem, Te Deum, motets, etc.; romances and nocturnes for two voices.

Plaschke, Friedrich (b Jaroměr, 7 Jan 1875; d Prague, 4 Feb 1952), Czech bass-baritone. Debut Dresden, 1900; remained until 1937 and sang in the fps of Strauss's *Feuersnot*, *Salome*, *Ägyptische Helena*, *Arabella* and *Die schweigsame Frau*. London, CG, 1914 as Amfortas in the British premiere of *Parsifal*. Other roles included Barak, Pogner, Sachs and Gérard.

Plasson, Michel (b Paris, 2 Oct 1933), French conductor. Studied at the Paris Conservatoire and in the USA with Stokowski and Leinsdorf. Music director at Metz 1966–68, Orchestre and Théâtre du Capitole at Toulouse, 1968–83: *Aida*, *Parsifal*, *Meistersinger*, and the premiere of *Montsegur* by Landowski (1985). CG debut 1979, *Werther*; returned for *Guillaume Tell* and *Tosca*, 1990–92. At the Palais Omnisport in Paris has conducted the Verdi *Requiem*, *Aida* and *Nabucco* (1984–87). Principal guest with the Zurich Tonhalle Orchestra from 1987. Recordings include Roussel's *Padmâvatî* and Magnard's *Guercoeur*.

Platée, *Plataea*, comédie-ballet by Rameau (libretto by J Autreau and A J V d'Orville), produced Versailles, at court, 31 Mar 1745; first

Paris performance, Opéra, 4 Feb 1749. Jupiter decides to cure Juno's constant jealousy: he woos the ugly but vain marsh-nymph Plataea, knowing that when Juno discovers Jupiter's new lover is ugly, she will realize how groundless her jealousy is. Juno appears just in time to stop the wedding, to Plataea's rage.

Platel, Nicolas Joseph (b Versailles, 1777; d Brussels, 25 Aug 1835), French cellist. As the son of a royal chamber musician he was educated as a page at court, learning the cello from Duport. After some orchestral appointments in Paris and Lyon, he toured in Belgium and England, settled at Antwerp and then at Brussels, where he became professor at the Conservatory in 1831. Wrote five cello concertos; duets for violin and cello.

Plato (b c 428–c348 BC), Greek philosopher. He outlined a system of 'harmony', as understood by the Greeks, in *Timaeus* and discussed the nature of the modes, from their supposed moral aspect, in *The Republic*. ◊Socrate (Satie).

Platt, Norman (b Bury, 29 Aug 1920), English opera director and baritone. Studied singing with Elena Gerhardt and appeared with SW and the English Opera Group, 1945–48. Member of the Deller Consort 1948–64 and founded Kent Opera 1969; artistic director and principal producer until it was disbanded by the Arts Council in 1989. Productions included *Figaro*, *The Return of Ulysses*, *Agrippina* and *Peter Grimes*. Refounded Kent Opera in 1994.

Platti, Giovanni (b Padua, 9 Jul 1697; d Würzburg, 11 Jan 1763), Italian harpsichordist and composer. Little is known of his life, but he was from 1722 in the service of the archiepiscopal court in Würzburg. He made important contributions towards the development of a modern style of keyboard music.

Works include six Masses and other church music; oratorios, cantatas, etc.; sonatas for flute, cello, etc.; concertos and sonatas for harpsichord and other keyboard music.

Playford, Henry (b London, 5 May 1657; d London, c 1709), English bookseller and publisher. Succeeded to his father's business in 1684; established regular concerts, held three times a week at a London coffee-house from 1699, and another series at Oxford in 1701.

Playford (1), John (b Norwich, 1623; d London, ? Dec 1686), English bookseller and publisher, father of Henry ◊Playford. Established in London about 1648. His first music publication, *The English Dancing Master*, appeared in 1650, dated 1651.

Playford (2), John (b Stanmore Magna, c 1655; d London, 20 Apr 1685), English printer, nephew of John ◊Playford (1). Was apprenticed to the printer William Godbid in London and in 1679 went into partnership with his widow, Anne Godbid. He printed the musical works issued by his cousin Henry.

Pleasants, Henry (b Wayne, PA, 12 May 1910), American writer and broadcaster. Studied Philadelphia Musical Academy and Curtis Institute of Music. Music critic *Philadelphia Evening Bulletin* 1930–42, *New York Times* 1945–55, *International Herald Tribune* (Paris) 1967–. Lecturer and broadcaster USA, UK and Europe. Publications include *The Agony of Music* 1955 and *Opera in Crisis* 1989; contributions to major US and UK music magazines, *Encyclopedia Britannica* and *New Grove Dictionary of Music and Musicians*.

plectrum, Latin, a hard spike of quill or metal with which the strings of certain instruments are made to sound. In the virginals, spinet and harpsichord, the plectrum is attached to the jack, and when used for instruments of the lute type, such as the cittern and the mandolin, it projects from a metal ring placed on the thumb.

Pleeth, William (b London, 12 Jan 1916), English cellist. He studied with Julius Klengel in Leipzig and made his debut there in 1932. London debut 1933. Many appearances as soloist but best known as chamber music player: Blech quartet 1936–41, Allegri quartet 1952–67; often heard in Schubert's string quintet, with the Amadeus quartet. Professor, GSM, 1948–78. OBE 1989.

plein jeu French = 'full play'; the French equivalent of *organo pleno* (or *pieno*).

Pletnev, Mikhail (b Moscow, 14 Apr 1957), Russian pianist and conductor. Studied in Moscow and has had international career as concert pianist and recitalist. Founded the Russian National Orchestra in 1990 and has toured with it as conductor to Japan, the Americas and Europe; guest with the Philharmonia Orchestra, the LSO and the Deutsche Kammerphilharmonie. Recordings include music by Haydn, Rakmaninov and Beethoven as pianist; Tchaikovsky's 6th Symphony as conductor.

Pleyel, Camille (b Strasbourg, 18 Dec 1788; d Montmorency near Paris, 4 May 1855), French piano maker, publisher and pianist, husband of Marie Moke. He succeeded to his father's business in 1824 and associated himself with Kalkbrenner. Studied music with his father and Dussek and pub. some piano pieces.

Pleyel, Ignaz Joseph (b Ruppertsthal, Lower Austria, 18 Jun 1757; d Paris, 14 Nov 1831), Austrian pianist, piano maker and composer, father of Camille ◊Pleyel. Pupil of Wanhal and Haydn, in 1777 became *Kapellmeister* to Count Erdödy, who gave him leave for

---

Henry Pleasants – writer on music

1 Debussy: *Nuages et Fête* (Leopold Stokowski/Philadelphia Orch.)
No other conductor has equalled Stokowski as a symphonic colourist, and no other orchestra has provided a conductor with such colour.

2 Verdi: *Aida* – Nile Scene (Rethberg/ Giuseppe De Luca/ Lauri-Volpi/Metropolitan Opera performance with Tullio Serafin conducting)
One of Verdi's most insired passages, rarely, if ever, so inspiringly sung.

3 Mascagni: *L'amico Fritz* – Cherry Duet (sung by Tito Schipa and Mafalda Favero)
Possibly the loveliest of all operatic duets, never given a lovelier performance.

4 Tchaikovsky: *Eugene Onegin* – Lenski's aria (sung by Ivan Koslovski)
Listen to this, and you will never want to hear Lenski singing in anything but Russian.

5 Wagner: *Lohengrin* – 'Im fernen Land' (sung by Aureliano Pertile)
Sung in Italian, and I am confident that Wagner would have loved it.

6 Weber: *Der Freischütz* – Agathe's Prayer (sung by Tiana Lemnitz)
A memorable blending of vocal virtuosity and communicative artistry as Lemnitz re-lives Agathe's thoughts and moods as she awaits and finally welcomes her returning lover.

7 Dr Arthur Colahan: 'Galway Bay' (sung by Margaret Sheridan)
No singer has loved her native land as Sheridan loved Ireland, and none has declared that love more eloquently.

further study in Rome. In 1783 he moved to Strasbourg as vice-*Kapellmeister*, succeeding Richter as *Kapellmeister* in 1789. Three years later he visited London as conductor of a rival series of concerts to those given by Salomon and Haydn. Settled in Paris 1795, and in 1807 founded his piano factory.

Works include two operas, *Die Fee Urgele* (produced Eszterháza, 1776) and *Ifigenia en Aulide* (produced Naples, 1785); 29 symphonies and five *sinfonie concertanti*; concertos; 45 string quartets and much other chamber music.

plica, Latin, for *plicare* = 'to fold', an ornamental passing note indicated in medieval notation by a vertical stroke at the side of the note. Its length was determined by the length of the stroke, its pitch by the context.

written *neuma*, by confusion with the word for a ǫneume.

Pocahontas ballet by Elliott Carter; composed 1936–39, produced NY, 24 May 1939. Pocahontas (1595–1617) was an American Indian princess who befriended the early settlers in America.

poco Italian = 'little'; often used as a qualifying direction where any indication of tempo or expression is to be applied in moderation; e.g. *poco più mosso*, 'a little faster'; *poco rallentando*, 'slowing down a little'; *poco forte*, 'fairly loud'.

Poème de l'amour et de la mer, *Poem of love and of the sea*, work for mezzo and orchestra by Chausson (text by M Bouchor), composed 1882–90, revised 1893. The work's three sections are *La fleur des eaux, Interlude* and *La mort de l'amour* (closing section *Le temps de lilas*).

Various plicas (left) with literal and modern equivalents (right).

According to theorists it should be sung with a kind of quavering in the throat, but its convenience as an abbr. led to its frequent employment as a substitute for a written note.

Pli selon pli 'Portrait de Mallarmé' for soprano and orchestra in five parts by Boulez. Fp Donaueschingen, 20 Oct 1962.

Plishka, Paul (b Old Forge, PA, 28 Aug 1941), American bass. He studied in New Jersey and Baltimore. NY Met. since 1967 as Leporello, Marke, Procida, Varlaam and Banquo (in Peter Hall's production of *Macbeth*). At San Francisco in 1984 he was admired as Verdi's Silva. Other roles included Henry VIII, Méphistophélès and Orovesco. Season 1991/92 as the Pope in *Benvenuto Cellini* at Geneva and Verdi's Zaccaria at Montreal.

Plowright, Rosalind (b Worksop, 21 May 1949), English soprano. She studied at the RMCM; debut there, 1968, in J C Bach's *Temistocle*. She sang Donna Elvira with the Glyndebourne Touring co. in 1977. ENO, London, debut 1979, as Britten's Miss Jessel; later sang Desdemona, Donizetti's Elisabeth and Verdi's Elena there. US opera debut 1982, in *Il Corsaro*. Her first major role at CG was Donna Anna (1983); returned for Aida in 1984. She has appeared in Paris, Milan, Bern and Munich as Strauss's Ariadne and Danae, Amelia, Suor Angelica and Alceste. Returned to CG in 1986 for Senta, and the *Trovatore* Leonora. Season 1992/93 as Elisabeth de Valois for ENO and Gioconda for Opera North.

Plummer, John (b *c* 1410; d Windsor, *c* 1484), English composer. He was a clerk of the Chapel Royal by 1441 and in 1444 became the first official master of its children. In *c* 1458 he became verger at St George's Chapel, Windsor, while continuing as a member of the Chapel Royal; the Windsor post he held until 1484. His surviving works consist of four antiphons for two and four voices, a Mass, *Omnipotens Pater*, and a Mass fragment.

pneuma Greek = 'breath'; a vocal ornament in plainsong, inserting long cadential phrases on the syllables of certain words, notably 'Alleluia'. The pneuma were also called by the Latin name of *jubili*, and they developed later into tropes and sequences. Sometimes

Poèmes pour Mi, *Poems for Mi*, cycle of nine songs for soprano and piano by Messiaen (texts by composer), fp Paris, 28 Apr 1937; orchestral version 1937, performed Paris 1946, conductor Désormière. (Mi was the composer's name for his first wife.)

Poem of Ecstasy, *Poema ekstasa*, work for orchestra by Scriabin; composed 1905–08, fp NY, 10 Dec 1908; first Russian performance St Petersburg, 1 Feb 1909.

Poet's Echo, The cycle of six songs for high voice and piano by Britten (texts by Pushkin), fp Moscow, 2 Dec 1965, with Vishnevskaya and Rostropovich.

Poglietti, Alessandro (b ?Tuscany; d Vienna, Jul 1683), Austrian organist and composer. His early career is unknown; he became organist of the Imperial chapel in Vienna, 1661, and was killed during the Turkish siege of the Austrian capital.

Works include opera, *Endimione festeggiante* (1677); sacred vocal compositions with instrumental accompaniment; *ricercari*, toccatas and other works for organ; harpsichord suites including *Rossignolo, Sopra la ribellione di Ungheria*, another containing a capriccio on the cries of cocks and hens.

Pogorelich, Ivo (b Belgrade, 20 Oct 1958), Serbian pianist. At the Moscow Conservatory he studied with Aliza Kezeradze (b *c* 1935); they were married in 1980. He won first prize in Montreal International Competition 1980, but when he was eliminated before the final rounds of the Chopin International competition the same year, one of the jury members, Martha Argerich resigned; his success thereafter was assured. Noted for the technical brilliance and control, rather than the profundity, of his interpretations. NY and London debuts 1981; settled in England 1982.

Pohjola's Daughter symphonic poem by Sibelius, op. 49, composed 1906 and based on an incident in the *Kalevala*; fp St Petersburg, Siloti concerts (conducted by composer), 29 Dec 1906.

Pohl, Carl Ferdinand (b Darmstadt, 6 Sept 1819; d Vienna, 28 Apr 1887), German organist, bibliographer and writer on music. Studied with Sechter in Vienna, was organist at the Protestant church in the

Pogorelich *The pianist Ivo Pogorelich achieved instant fame when he was eliminated in the preliminary rounds of the 1980 Chopin Competition and Martha Argerich resigned from the jury. He possesses an awesome technique, notable for its precision and clarity, which contrasts with his famously underplayed stage manner.*

Gumpendorf suburb, 1849–55, lived in London, 1863–66, and in the latter year became librarian to the Philharmonic Society in Vienna. He wrote on this, on Haydn and Mozart in London and the standard biography of Haydn (finished by Botstiber).

Pohl, Richard (b Leipzig, 12 Sept 1826; d Baden-Baden, 17 Dec 1896), German critic and author. Studied at Göttingen and Leipzig, and was for a time editor of the *Neue Zeitschrift für Musik*. Wrote mainly on Wagner, also on Berlioz, Liszt, etc., and composed songs. He claimed that the chromaticism in *Tristan* was derived from Liszt.

Pohlenz, (Christian) August (b Sallgast, Lusatia, 3 Jul 1790; d Leipzig, 10 Mar 1843), German organist, teacher and conductor. Studied at Leipzig, where he became organist at St Thomas's Church and conductor of the Gewandhaus concerts before Mendelssohn.

poi Italian = 'then'; used in directions where some music section is to follow another in a way not made immediately obvious by the notation: e.g. after a repeat of an earlier section, *poi la coda* or *e poi la coda.*

pointing the distribution of the syllables of the Psalms in Anglican chant according to the verbal rhythm.

Poise, (Jean Alexandre) Ferdinand (b Nîmes, 3 Jun 1828; d Paris, 13 May 1892), French composer. Studied with Adam and others at the Paris Conservatory and in 1853 produced his first opera.

Works include operas *Bonsoir Voisin* (1853), *Les Charmeurs* (1855); *Polichinelle* (1856), *Le Roi Don Pèdre, Le Jardinier galant* (1861), *Les Absents, Corricolo* (1868), *Les Trois Souhaits* (1861), *La Surprise de l'amour* (after Marivaux), *L'Amour médecin* (*after Molière, 1880*), *Les Deux Billets, Joli Gilles, Carmosine* (after Musset, produced 1928); oratorio *Cécile* (1888).

Poisoned Kiss, The, or *The Empress and the Necromancer*, opera by Vaughan Williams (libretto by Evelyn Sharp), produced Cambridge Arts Theatre, 12 May 1936. Much of the score is a satire on various musical styles. Long ago the magician Dipsacus was abandoned by one-time love Persicaria. He plans revenge: to kill her son Amaryllus with a poisoned kiss from his daughter Tormentilla. But Amaryllus has the antidote and they all live happily ever after.

Poissl, Johann Nepomuk von (b Haukenzell, Bavaria, 15 Feb 1783; d Munich, 17 Aug 1865), German composer. Studied with Danzi at Munich and became Intendant of the royal orchestra and director of the royal opera there.

Works include operas *Athalia* (after Racine, 1814), *Der Wettkampf zu Olympia* and *Nittetis* (translations of Metastasio's *Olimpiade* and *Nitteti*, 1815 and 1817), *Zayde* (1843) and about ten others; Mass, *Stabat Mater*, Psalm xcv; oratorio *Der Erntetag* (1835).

polacca Italian = 'polonaise'; although polacca is the exact Italian equivalent of the polonaise, the word is often more loosely used for pieces in polonaise rhythm, but not necessarily in polonaise form, in which case they are actually, as indeed they are often designated, *alla polacca.*

Polaroli another form of the surname of Antonio and Carlo Francesco ◊Pollarolo.

Polaski, Deborah (b Richmond Center, WI, 26 Sept 1949), American soprano. Studied at the Ohio Conservatory and in Graz. Sang widely in Germany from 1976, notably as Leonore, Isolde, Sieglinde, and Marie in *Wozzeck*; Waiblingen Festival 1983 in a revival of Keiser's *Croesus*. Has sung Elektra at Oslo (1986), Stuttgart (1989) and Spoleto (1990). After singing a not well-received Brünnhilde at Bayreuth under Barenboim in 1988 she decided to retire, but returned 1991 and sang the *Walküre* Brünnhilde also at CG, 1994. Also admired as the Dyer's Wife in *Die Frau ohne Schatten* (Amsterdam, 1992).

Poldini, Ede (b Budapest, 13 Jun 1869; d Vevey, 28 Jun 1957), Hungarian composer. Studied at Budapest and with Mandyczewski in Vienna.

Works include operas *The Vagabond and the Princess* (1903), *Wedding in Carnival-Time* (*Love Adrift*, 1924), *Himfy* (1938); ballet *Night's Magic*; *Marionettes* for orchestra (originally piano); numerous piano suites and pieces including *Arlequinades, Morceaux pittoresques, Épisodes à la Cour, Images, Moments musicaux, Poupée valsante.*

Polidori, John William (1795–1821), English novelist, Byron's secretary and physician. ◊Vampyr (Lindpaintner and Marschner).

poliphant a string instrument, also called polyphone, of the lute or cittern type but with anything from 25 to 40 strings, invented *c* 1600 by Daniel Farrant and played by Queen Elizabeth I.

'Polish' Symphony Tchaikovsky's third symphony, in D major, op. 29, finished Aug 1875 and produced Moscow, 19 Nov 1875. The finale is in polonaise rhythm.

Poliuto, later *Martyrs* and *I martiri*, opera by Donizetti (libretto devised by A Nourrit and written by S Cammarano, based on Corneille's tragedy *Polyeucte*), finished 1838 for production at Naples, but forbidden by censor; produced in French (translation by Scribe), Paris, Opéra, 1 Apr 1840. In 3rd-c. Armenia, Poliuto is converted to Christianity, but is captured by Callistene, the high priest of Jupiter. His wife Paolina cannot convince him to renounce his faith, and joins him in death.

polka a dance dating from *c* 1830 and probably originating in Bohemia, though the story of its being invented there by a servant-girl, the tune being written down by a musician named Neruda, is not authenticated. It is danced in couples and the music is in 2–4 time and divided into regular two-bar patterns grouped into periods of eight bars.

Pollak, Anna (b Manchester, 1 May 1912), English mezzo. She sang with the SW co. 1945–61 and appeared at Glyndebourne 1952–53 as Dorabella. She created Bianca in *The Rape of Lucreyia* (1946), Ruth in the opera by Berkeley (1956) and Lady Nelson in his *Nelson* (1954). Sang with SW until 1968.

Pollak, Egon (b Prague, 3 May 1879; d Prague, 14 Jun, 1933), Austrian conductor. He studied at the Prague Conservatory and worked at opera houses in Bremen, Leipzig and Frankfurt. He conducted Wagner in Paris (1914) and gave *Ring* cycles at the Chicago Lyric Opera 1915–17; returned 1929–32. Hamburg 1917–31. He took the Vienna Staatsoper Co. to Egypt in 1933 and in the same year collapsed and died during a performace of *Fidelio* in Prague.

Pollarolo, Antonio (b Brescia, bap. 12 Nov 1676; d Venice, 30 May 1746), Italian composer. Pupil of his father, became assistant *maestro di cappella* at St Mark's in Venice, 1723, and *maestro di cappella* in 1740.

Works include operas *Aristeo*, *Leucippo e Teonoe*, *Cosroe*, *I tre voti* and ten others; church music.

Pollarolo, Carlo Francesco (b Brescia, 1653; d Venice, 7 Feb 1723), Italian organist and composer, father of Antonio ◊Pollarolo. Pupil of Legrenzi at Venice, became a singer at St Mark's there in 1665, second organist in 1690 and assistant *maestro di cappella* in 1692. Later taught music at the Conservatorio degli Incurabili.

Works include operas *Roderico* (1686), *La forza dela virtù* (1693), *Ottone* (1694), *Faramondo*, *Semiramide* (1713), *Marsia deluso*, *Ariodante* (1716), *Le pazzie degli amanti*, *Gl'inganni felici*, *Santa Genuinda* (with Violone and A Scarlatti, 1694) and *c* 65 others, most lost; 12 oratorios; organ music.

Polledro, Giovanni Battista (b Piovà, near Turin, 10 Jun 1781; d Piovà, 15 Aug 1853), Italian violinist and composer. Pupil of Pugnani. Made his first appearance at Turin in 1797 and, after touring widely, was leader of the orchestra at Dresden, 1814–24, and court *maestro di cappella* at Turin 1824–44.

Works include two violin concertos, chamber music, symphony, Mass.

Pollet, Françoise (b Boulogne Billancourt, near Paris, 10 Sept 1949), French soprano. After study at the Versailles Conservatory and in Munich made her debut at Lübeck 1983, as the Marschallin; remained at Lübeck until 1986, as Fiordiligi, Donna, Anna and Arabella. Sang Mozart's Vitellia at the Paris Opéra-Comique and Dukas' Ariane at the Théâtre du Châtelet. Appearances at the Montpellier Festival as Reiza (*Oberon*), Elisabeth in *Tannhäuser* and Magnard's Berenice. Sang Valentine in *Les Huguenots* at CG (1991) and Cassandre in *Les Troyens* at Brussels; recordings include Didon in *Les Troyens*, under Charles Dutoit (1994).

Pollini, Francesco (Giuseppe) (b Ljubljana, 25 Mar 1762; d Milan, 17 Sept 1846), Italian pianist and composer. Pupil of Mozart in Vienna and later of Zingarelli at Milan, where he was appointed piano professor at the Conservatory in 1809.

Works include *Stabat Mater*; music for the stage; many piano studies and pieces.

Pollini, Maurizio (b Milan, 5 Jan 1942), Italian pianist and conductor. He studied at the Milan Conservatory and in 1960 won the Chopin International Competition, Warsaw. Many appearances in recital and as soloist in Europe and the USA (debut, Carnegie Hall, NY, 1968). He plays Boulez, Nono and Schoenberg in addition to the standard repertory, and has conducted from the keyboard. In 1981 he conducted Rossini's *La donna del lago* at Pesaro.

Polly ballad opera, sequel to *The Beggar's Opera* (words by John Gay), pub. 1729, but not allowed to be performed. Produced London, with the music arranged by Arnold, Little Haymarket Theatre, 19 Jun 1777. Modern version by F Austin, produced London, Kingsway Theatre, 30 Dec 1922. Polly Peachum and Macheath are exiled in the West Indies, where they meet plantation hands, pirates and Indians.

polonaise a Polish dance of a stately, processional character, dating back to at least the 16th c. The music is in 3–4 time and is characterized by feminine cadences at the end of each section, also often by dotted rhythms. The more primitive examples were in binary form: two sections, each repeated; but later (e.g. Chopin) a trio section developed, after which the main section is repeated.

Polonia symphonic prelude for orchestra by Elgar, op. 76, written for a concert given for the Polish Relief Fund, London, 6 July 1915, and dedicated to Paderewski, a quotation from whose *Polish Fantasy* it contains as well as one from Chopin and the Polish National Anthem.

Polyeucte ◊Poliuto.

Opera by Gounod (libretto by J Barbier and M Carré, based on Corneille's drama), produced Paris, Opéra, 7 Oct 1878.

polyphone ◊poliphant.

polyphony music which combines two or more independent melodic lines.

polyrhythm the combination of different rhythmic formations.

polytonality the simultaneous combination of two or more different keys.

Pommier, Jean-Bernard (b Béziers, 17 Aug 1944), French pianist and

Pollini *The pianist Maurizio Pollini won the 1960 Chopin Competition at the age of 18 and was pigeon-holed for many years afterwards as a Chopin specialist. He has since diversified, showing a particular interest in the works of 20th-century composers.*

conductor. After study at the Paris Conservatoire has had worldwide career from 1962, first launched as a prize winner of the Tchaikovsky Competition that year; Salzburg debut under Karajan 1971. Berlin SO. Has appeared as conductor and soloist with the Northern Sinfonia, Hallé Orchestra and Royal Liverpool PO. Chamber music with the Vermeer and Guarneri Quartets.

Pomo d'oro, Il, *The Golden Apple*, opera by Cesti (libretto by F Sbarra), produced Vienna, Carnival 1667, for the wedding of the Emperor Leopold I and the Infanta Margherita of Spain (reputed to be the most expensive opera production ever mounted). Discord throws a golden apple, inscribed 'to the most beautiful', to Juno, Athena and Venus. Paris judges Venus the most beautiful after she offers him Helen. Disarray amongst the goddesses until Jupiter puts and end to the bickering.

Pomone opera by Cambert (libretto by P Perrin), produced Paris, Opéra, 3 Mar 1671.

Pomp and Circumstance five military marches by Elgar, originally intended as a set of 6, op. 39. 1–4 composed 1901–07, 5 in 1930. The first contains, as a trio, the tune afterwards used in the *Coronation Ode* to the words 'Land of hope and glory'. The title of the set comes from *Othello*, III iii: 'pride, pomp and circumstance of glorious war'. Nos. 1 & 2 fp Liverpool, 19 Oct 1901; no. 3 fp London, 8 Mar 1905; no. 4 fp London, 24 Aug 1907; no. 5 fp London, 20 Sept 1930.

pomposo Italian = 'pompous, stately'; a direction used for music of a sumptuous character.

Ponce, Manuel (b Fresnillo, 8 Dec 1882; d Mexico City, 24 Apr 1948), Mexican composer. Learnt music from his sister at first, became cathedral organist at Aguas Calientes and at 14 composed a gavotte which was later made famous by the dancer Argentina. He entered the National Conservatory at Mexico City and in 1905 went to Europe for further study with Bossi at Bologna and Martin Krause in Berlin. In 1906 he returned home and became professor at the National Conservatory. In 1915–18 he lived at Havana and at the age of 43 went to Paris to take a composition course with Dukas. He is best known for his guitar music, performed by Segovia and others.

Works include symphonic triptych *Chapultepec* (1929), *Canto y danza de los antiguos Mexicanos* (1933), *Poema elegiaco*, *Ferial* for orchestra (1940); piano concerto, violin concerto (1943), concerto for guitar and chamber orchestra (1941); three Tagore songs with orchestra; *Sonata en duo* for violin and viola; two Mexican Rhapsodies and many other piano works; numerous songs.

Ponchielli, Amilcare (b Paderno Fasolaro, near Cremona, 31 Aug 1834; d Milan, 17 Jan 1886), Italian composer. Studied at the Milan Conservatory and produced his first opera, on Manzoni's *Promessi sposi*, at Cremona in 1856. In 1881 he was appointed *maestro di cappella* at Bergamo Cathedral. His masterpiece, *La Gioconda*, was produced at La Scala in 1876; its inspired melody and strong dramatic characterization established him as a worthy successor to Verdi. He died before he could consolidate his promise, however.

Works include operas *I promessi sposi* (1856); *La Savoiarda* (1861), *Roderico* (1863), *Bertrand de Born, Il parlatore eterno* (1873), *I Lituani (Aldona), Gioconda* (after Hugo's *Angelo*, 1876), *Il figliuol prodigo* (1880), *Marion Delorme* (on Hugo's play, 1885), *I Mori di Valenza*, unfinished; produced Monte Carlo, 1914; ballets *Le due gemelle* and *Clarina*; cantatas for the reception of the remains of Donizetti and Mayr at Bergamo and in memory of Garibaldi.

Poniatowski, Józef Michal Xawery Franciszek Jan, Prince of Monte Rotondo (b Rome, 20 Feb 1816; d Chislehurst, 3 Jul 1873), Polish composer and tenor. Studied at the Liceo musicale at Florence and under Ceccherini. He sang at the Teatro della Pergola there and produced his first opera there in 1839, singing the title-part. After the 1848 Revolution he settled in Paris, but after the Franco-Prussian war he followed Napoleon III to England, 1871.

Works include operas *Giovanni da Procida* (1838), *Don Desiderio* (1840), *Ruy Blas* (after Hugo), *Bonifazio de' Geremei (I Lambertazzi*, 1843), *Malek Adel* (1846), *Esmeralda* (after Hugo's *Notre-Dame de Paris*, 1847), *La sposa d'Abido* (after Byron's *Bride of Abydos*), *Pierre de Médicis* (1860), *Gelmina* (1872) and others; Mass in F major.

Ponnelle, Jean-Pierre (b Paris, 19 Feb 1932; d Munich, 11 Aug 1988), French opera designer and producer. He designed the premiere production of Henze's *Boulevard Solitude* (1952), and *König Hirsch* (1956). His first opera production was *Tristan* in Düsseldorf, 1962, and he later produced and designed operas by Mozart in Salzburg and Cologne and a Monteverdi cycle in Zurich. His *Don Pasquale* has been seen at CG, London, and his *Cenerentola* at the NY Met. Noted for his stylish productions and his attention to detail.

Pons, José (b Gerona, Catalonia, 1768; d Valencia, 2 Aug 1818), Spanish composer. Studied at Córdoba, became *maestro de capilla* at Gerona and later at Valencia.

Works include Misereres and other church music; *villancicos* for Christmas with orchestra or organ.

Pons, Juan (b Ciutadella, Menorca, 1946), Spanish baritone. Studied in Barcelona and sang Alfio (*Cavalleria Rusticana*) at CG in 1979; Paris Opéra 1983, as Tonio in *Pagliacci*. Verdi roles include Falstaff (Munich, San Francisco and Rome), Amonasro (Verona Arena 1984), Germont (Chicago 1988) and Renato. NY Met debut 1986 as Scarpia, retrning 1993 as Rigoletto.

Pons, Lily (Alice Joséphine Pons) (b Draguignan, 16 Apr 1898; d Dallas, 13 Jan 1976), French-born American coloratura soprano. Studied piano, aged 13, at the Paris Conservatory, and then singing with Alberti de Gorostiaga, making her debut at Mulhouse in 1928 as Lakmé. From 1931 to 1959 she sang at the NY Met. as Lucia, Amina, Gilda and Olympia.

Ponselle (actually *Ponzillo*), Rosa (b Meridan, CT, 22 Jan 1897; d Green Spring Valley, MD, 25 May 1981), American soprano of Italian parentage. Studied in NY with W. Thorner and Romani, making her debut at the Met. Opera in 1918, as the *Forza* Leonora. She sang there from 1918 to 1937 as Reiza, Laura, Mathilde, Donna Anna, Santuzza and Elisabeth de Valois. At CG 1929–31 as Norma and Violetta. One of the great singers of the century, she retired at the height of her powers to teach.

Ponte, Lorenzo da (actually Emmanuele Conegliano) (b Ceneda near Venice, 10 Mar 1749; d New York, 17 Aug 1838), Italian poet and librettist. Of Jewish parentage, he took the name da Ponte at his baptism. Educated at the theological seminary in Portogruaro, he was ordained in 1773, but led the life of an adventurer, being banished from Venice because of scandal in 1779. Appointed poet to the Court Opera in Vienna in 1784, he moved to London in 1792, and thence, to escape his creditors, to NY in 1804. He pub. his memoirs 1823–27. Wrote the libretti of *Le nozze di Figaro, Don Giovanni* and *Così fan tutte* for Mozart, others for Bianchi, Martín y Soler, Winter, etc. ◊Burbero di buon cuore (Martín y Soler); ◊Ratto di Proserpina (Winter); Scuola de' maritati (Martín y Soler); ◊Tarare (Salieri); ◊Una cosa rara (Martín y Soler).

ponticello Italian = 'little bridge'; the bridge of string instruments over which the strings are stretched to keep clear of the body of the instrument. The direction *sul ponticello* 'on the bridge' indicates that the bow is to be drawn close to the bridge, which results in a peculiar nasal tone.

pont-neuf, French = lit. 'new bridge', a satirical song of the 18th c. similar to the Vaudeville, sung in public mainly on the Pont-neuf in Paris.

Poole, Elizabeth (b London, 5 Apr 1820; d Langley, Bucks., 14 Jan 1906), English soprano and actress. Appeared as a child actress at the Olympic Theatre and made her first appearance in opera at Drury Lane in 1834.

His left hand knoweth not what his right hand doeth.
Nicola Porpora on a church organist, quoted in Hogarth, *Musical History*, 1838

Poole, Geoffrey (b Ipswich, 1949), English composer. Studied at Southampton University with Jonathan Harvey and with Goehr at Leeds. Senior lecturer at Manchester University from 1989. Commissions from the Hallé Orchestra and London Sinfonietta.

Works include *Fragments* for strings (1974); *Visions* for orchestra (1975); *Crow Tyrannosaurus* for soprano and ensemble (1975); *Chamber Concerto* (1979); *Machaut-Layers* for voice and ensemble (1980); *Biggs v Stomp does it again and again ...* music theatre (1981); *The Net and Aphrodite*, symphonic poem (1982); *Cummings Choruses* (1985); *Sailing with Archangels* for wind band (1990); two string quartets (1983, 1990); *In Beauty May I Walk*, vocal duo with strings (1990); *The Magnification of the Virgin*, for female consort and 12 instruments (1992); *Blackbird*, oratorio (1993).

Poot, Marcel (b Vilvoorde near Brussels, 7 May 1901; d Brussels, 12 Jan 1988), Belgian composer. Studied at the Brussels Conservatory. He early became interested in film, radio and jazz music. In 1935 he founded the group known as Les Synthétistes and in 1930 gained the Rubens Prize and went to Paris to study with Dukas. On his return he held several teaching posts, including at the Brussels Conservatory, of which he became director in 1949.

Works include operas *Het Ingebeeld Eiland* (1925), *Het Vrouwtje van Stavoren* (1928), and *Moretus* (1944); ballets *Paris in verlegengheid* (1925), and *Pygmalion* (1951); oratorios *Le Dit du routier* and *Icaros*; six symphonies (1929–78) and other orchestral works; chamber music, etc.

Pope, Alexander (1688–1744), English poet. ◊Acis and Galatea, ◊Jephtha, ◊Semele.

Popp, Lucia (b Uhorska Ves, 12 Nov 1939; d Munich, 16 Nov 1993), Austrian soprano of Czech birth. She studied in Bratislava; appeared at the Vienna Staatsoper and at Salzburg 1963. CG, London debut 1966, as Oscar; returned for Gilda, Despina, Sophie, Eva and Arabella (1986). NY Met, debut 1967, as the Queen of Night, a role which she recorded with Klemperer. Other roles included Pamina, Ilia, Zerlina and the Marschallin. Much admired for her charming stage presence, she was also in demand as a concert singer, e.g. in Orff, Strauss and Mahler.

Popper, David (b Prague, 16 Jun 1843; d Baden near Vienna, 7 Aug 1913), German-Czech cellist and composer. Studied music in general at the Prague Conservatory and the cello under Goltermann at Frankfurt, and made his first concert tour in Germany 1863. In 1868 he became first cellist at the Court Opera in Vienna, in 1872 he married Sophie Menter, but the marriage was dissolved 1886. In 1896 he became cello professor at the Budapest Conservatory.

Works include four cello concertos, *Requiem* for three cellos (performed London, 1891), numerous pieces for cello, etc.

Porgy and Bess opera in three acts by Gershwin (libretto by D B Heyward and I Gershwin, after the play *Porgy* by D B and D Heyward), produced Boston, 30 Sept 1935. Not produced by British co. until 1986 (Glyndebourne). Crippled Porgy takes in abandoned beautiful Bess and falls in love with her. Crown seduces her but Porgy forgives; Porgy later kills Crown, and Bess leaves when she believes he will never return after being arrested as a witness.

Poro, rè dell' Indie, *Porus, King of the Indies*, opera by Handel (libretto by ?, altered from Metastasio's *Alessandro nell' Indie*), produced London, King's Theatre, Haymarket, 2 Feb 1731. Porus faces defeat at the hands of Alexander the Great, fearing especially that he will lose his love, Cleophis, to the invader. A story of jealousy and passion before Alexander realizes the depth of feeling between Porus and Cleophis, and blesses their union.

Porpora, Nicola Antonio (b Naples, 17 Aug 1686; d Naples, 3 Mar 1768), Italian composer and singing teacher. Pupil of Greco and Campanile at the Conservatorio dei Poveri in Naples, where his first opera, *Agrippina*, was produced in 1708. At first *maestro di cappella* to the Imperial Commandant in Naples, Prince Philip of Hesse-Darmstadt, he was appointed singing teacher at the Conservatorio di S Onofrio there in 1715, and ten years later became *maestro* at the Conservatorio degli Incurabili in Venice. Among his pupils were Farinelli and Caffarelli, and, briefly, Hasse. Travelling as an opera conductor, he rivalled Handel in London (1733–36) and Hasse in Dresden (1748–52). In Vienna Haydn was his pupil-valet. Porpora finally settled in Naples in 1760, remaining there till his death.

Works include operas *Basilio* (1713), *Berenice* (1718), *Flavio Anicio Olibrio*, *Faramondo* (1719), *Eumene*, *Amare per regnare* (1723), *Semiramide* (1724), *Semiramide riconosciuta*, *L'Imeneo* (1726), *Adelaide*, *Siface*, *Mitridate* (1730), *Annibale* (1731), *Il trionfo di Camilla*, *Arianna* (1733), *Temistocle* (1743), *Filandro* and *c* 20 others; oratorios *Il martirio di Santa Eugenia* (1721) and eight others; Masses, motets, duets on the Passion and other church music; cantatas; violin sonatas; keyboard music.

Porsile, Giuseppe (b Naples, 5 May 1680; d Vienna, 29 May 1750), Italian composer. He was vice-*maestro de capilla* to the Spanish court in Barcelona from 1695 (*maestro* 1697), and from 1720 court *Kapellmeister* in Vienna.

Works include *c* 12 operas, e.g. *Il ritorno di Ulisse* (1707), *Alceste* (1718), *Meride e Selinunte* (1721), *Spartaco* (1726); 12 oratorios; serenades, cantatas, canzonets.

Porta, Costanzo (b Cremona, *c* 1529; d Padua, 19 May 1601), Italian monk and composer. Pupil of Willaert at Venice. He took orders and became choirmaster at Osimo near Ancona, 1552–64, when he went to Padua to take up a similar post at the Cappella Antoniana, the church of the Minorite order to which he belonged, which he left for a time to work at Ravenna (1567–74), then Loreto (1574–80). Returned to Ravenna 1580–89.

Works include 15 Masses, 200 motets, psalms, hymns, introits and other church music, five books of madrigals, 1555–86.

Porta, Ercole (b Bologna, 10 Sept 1585; d Carpi, 30 Apr 1630), Italian organist and composer. Organist at the college of San Giovanni in Persiceto in 1609. His *Sacro Convito* of 1620 includes a Mass with trombones in the orchestral accompaniment.

Works include sacred vocal concertos; secular works; vocal music.

Porta, Francesco della (b Monza, *c* 1600; d Milan, Jan 1666), Italian organist and composer. Studied with the organist Ripalta at Monza and became organist and *maestro di cappella* of three churches at Milan.

Works include motets, psalms; instrumental *ricercari*; *villanelle* for one–three voices with instruments, etc.

THE OPERA
Porgy and Bess

The first full-length American opera to acknowledge the influence of jazz and blues, this dramatic three-act work by George Gershwin dates from 1935. It is set in Catfish Row, Charleston, in the 1920s.
I. The stevedore Crown (bass) kills his friend Robbins (tenor) while gambling. Before going on the run he leaves his girl, Bess (soprano), in the care of her long-term admirer Porgy (bass-baritone).
II. Although set up with Porgy, Bess meets Crown again and returns to him. The new arrangement does not last long, and Bess decides she prefers Porgy after all. With his friends Jake and Clara out in a hurricane, Crown goes to rescue them.
III. Crown arrives at Porgy's house in search of Bess but Porgy stabs him dead. Bess is not alone for long before the gambler Sportin' Life (tenor) persuades her to go with him to New York. Released by the police for lack of evidence, Porgy follows them.

THE OPERA

Porta, Giovanni (b Venice, *c* 1690; d Munich, 21 Jun 1755), Italian composer. Worked in Rome 1706–16 in the service of Cardinal Ottoboni, then at the Conservatorio della pietà in Venice, and also visited London, where his opera *Numitore* was produced 1720. From 1736 to his death he was *Kapellmeister* to the court in Munich.

Works include over 30 operas, e.g. *Arianna* (1723), *Antigono* (1724), *Ulisse* (1725) and *Semiramide* (1733); oratorios; cantatas; 19 Masses and other church music, etc.

portamento moving from one note to another with some element of slide or glide, particularly on the voice or stringed instruments. In many musical repertories, stylish performance involves considerable use of portamento with a special emphasis on variety of approaches. Sometimes used, incorrectly, to denote *portato* on keyboard instruments.

portative organ a small organ with a single keyboard and one range of pipes, which could be carried, placed on a table or suspended from the shoulder by a strap. Representations are frequent in medieval and Renaissance paintings.

portato, Italian, a semi-detached manner of delivering a musical phrase.

Porter, Andrew (b Cape Town, 26 Aug 1928), English music critic and scholar. He studied at Oxford University and worked for various newspapers and journals from 1949 (edited *Musical Times* 1960–67). He is noted for his research on Verdi and has prepared for performance much material for *Don Carlos* which Verdi discarded at the first production in 1867; several translations of Verdi libretti. His translation of the *Ring* was heard at the Coliseum, London, in 1973 and his version of the *Parsifal* libretto was given there in 1986. Critic, *New Yorker*, 1972–92, the *Observer* from 1992; five vols. of criticism were pub. 1974–91.

My sole inspiration is a telephone call from a producer.
                    Cole Porter in a press interview, 1955

Porter, Cole (b Peru, IN, 9 Jun 1893; d Santa Monica, CA, 15 Oct 1964), American composer. Studied at Yale and at Harvard Law School and School of Music. While still a student he became well known for his football songs. In 1916 he joined the Foreign Legion and after the war studied at the Schola Cantorum in Paris. His output consists entirely of musicals, of which the best known are *Kiss me, Kate*, *Can-Can* and *Silk Stockings*. Individual songs include *Night and Day*, *I get a kick out of you*, and *Let's do it*.

Porter, Walter (b *c* 1588; d London, buried 30 Nov 1659), English composer. He became a Gentleman of the Chapel Royal in London in

1617. At some time, probably earlier, he was a pupil of Monteverdi. In 1639 he became choirmaster at Westminster Abbey and when the choral service was suppressed in 1644 came under the patronage of Sir Edward Spencer.

Works include motets for two voices and instruments, psalms (George Sandys' paraphrases) for two voices and organ; madrigals and airs for voices and instruments (pub. 1632).

Porter, (William) Quincy (b New Haven, CT, 7 Feb 1897; d Bethany, CT, 12 Nov 1966), American composer. Studied at Yale University and School of Music with H Parker and D S Smith, later with Bloch and with d'Indy in Paris. He taught at the Cleveland Institute of Music for two periods during 1922–32, at Vassar College, Poughkeepsie, 1932–38, and at the New England Conservatory at Boston from 1938. He also played viola in various string quartets.

Works include incidental music for Shakespeare's *Antony and Cleopatra* (1934) and T S Eliot's *Sweeney Agonistes* (1933); symphony, *Poem and Dance* for orchestra; *Ukrainian Suite* for strings (1925); *Dance in Three Time* for chamber orchestra (1937); viola concerto, harpsichord concerto (1959), concerto for two pianos; three Greek Mimes for voices, string quartet and percussion; nine string quartets (1923–58); two violin and piano sonatas, suite for viola solo.

Portinaro, Francesco (b Padua, *c* 1520; d ? Padua, after 1578), Italian composer. He was associated with the *Accademia degli Elevati* in Padua (1557), and later with the d'Este family at Ferrara and Tivoli. His three books of motets and six of madrigals were pub. at Venice.

Portman, Richard (d ? London, *c* 1655), English organist and composer. Pupil of O Gibbons, succeeded Thomas Day as organist of Westminster Abbey in London, 1633. Like W Porter, who was choirmaster, he lost this post in 1644 and became a music teacher.

Works include services, anthems; *Dialogue of the Prodigal Son* for two voices and chorus, meditation; *The Soules Life, exercising itself in the sweet fields of divine meditation*; harpsichord music, etc.

Portsmouth Point concert overture by Walton, inspired by Rowlandson's drawing, fp ISCM Festival, Zurich, 22 Jun 1926.

Portugal, Marcus Antonio da Fonseca (called Portogallo in Italian) (b Lisbon, 24 Mar 1762; d Rio de Janeiro, 7 Feb 1830), Portuguese composer. Educated at the Patriarchal Seminary at Lisbon, where later he became cantor and organist, and learnt music from Joño de Sousa Carvalho. He was also a theatre conductor and in 1785 produced his first stage work. In 1792 he went to Naples and began to write Italian operas in great numbers. In 1800 he returned to Lisbon to become director of the San Carlos Theatre, where he continued to write for the stage. In 1807 the French invasion drove the court to Brazil, and he followed it in 1810, but was unable to return with it in 1821, being incapacitated by a stroke.

Works include *Licença pastoril*, *A Castanheira* and 20 other Portuguese operas; *La confusione nata della somiglianza* (1793), *Demofoonte* (1794), *Lo spazzacamino principe*, *La donna di genio volubile* (1796), *Fernando nel Messico* (1799), *Alceste*, *La morte di Semiramide* (1801), *Non irritare le donne*, *L'oro non compra amore* (1804), *Il trionfo di Clelia* (1802), *Il diavolo a quattro*, *La pazza*

giornata (on Beaumarchais' *La Folle Journée* [*Figaro*, 1799]) and *c* 25 other Italian operas; church music; cantata *La speranza*; songs.

Posaune German = ◊trombone.

positif French = 'choir organ'.

positions (1) the points at which the left hand is placed in order to stop the strings on a string instrument. Since only four fingers are available, the hand has to change from one position to another in order to reach higher notes e.g. on the violin.

(2) The points at which the slide of the ◊trombone is arrested, e.g. on the B♭ tenor trombone. Each position offers a complete series of harmonics and hence provides the instrument with a chromatic compass.

positive organ a small chamber organ.

posthorn brass instrument akin to the bugle rather than the horn, used by postillions in the 18th and early 19th c. It had no valves and could therefore produce only the natural harmonics, which were coarse and penetrating in tone. It was hardly ever used in serious music, but Bach imitated it in his Capriccio on his brother's departure for harpsichord and Mozart scored parts for two in his German Dances, K605 and in his Posthorn Serenade, K320.

Postillon de Lonjumeau, Le, *The Coachman of Lonjumeau*, opera by Adam (libretto by A de Leuven and L L Brunswick), produced Paris, Opéra-Comique, 13 Oct 1836. The coachman Chapelou abandons his bride, Madeleine, to join the Paris Opéra. Meeting her ten years later, he does not recognize her, and asks her to marry him; she reveals her identity.

postlude, or postludium, the opposite of prelude or praeludium: a final piece, especially an organ piece played after service.

Postnikova, Viktoria (b Moscow, 12 Jan 1944), Russian pianist. She studied at the Moscow Conservatory and in 1966 was second to Rafael Orozco at the Leeds International Competition. London debut, 1967. Many concerts with leading conductors, also with her husband, Gennady Rozhdestvensky. Played in the fp of Schnittke's concerto for piano duet and orchestra, 1990.

Poston, Elizabeth (b Highfield, Herts., 24 Oct 1905; d Stevenage, 18 Mar 1987), English composer. Studied at the RCM in London and piano with Harold Samuel. In 1925 she pub. seven songs and in 1927 a prize-work, a violin and piano sonata was broadcast. From 1940 to 1945 she was director of music in the foreign service of the BBC.

Works include music for radio productions; choral music, songs.

pot-pourri French = lit. 'rotten pot'; a medley of preserves, identical with the Spanish *olla podrida*, the name of which is applied to selections of themes from various musical works, especially operas or operettas.

Potter (Philip) Cipriani (Hambley) (b London, 3 Oct 1792; d London, 26 Sept 1871), English pianist and composer. Studied under Attwood, Callcott and Crotch, and had finishing piano lessons from Woelfl 1805–10. He became an associate of the Philharmonic Society on its foundation in 1813 and a member when he reached majority, and in 1816 wrote an overture for it, also playing the piano there that year in a sextet of his own. In 1817 he went to Vienna, studied with

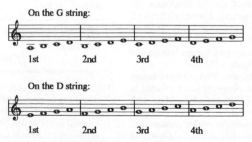

On the G string:

1st   2nd   3rd   4th

On the D string:

1st   2nd   3rd   4th

Various positions on a string instrument (above) and on the trombone (below).

1st 2nd 3rd 4th 5th 6th 7th

Aloys Förster and met Beethoven. After visiting Germany and Italy he returned to London in 1821, became professor of piano at the RAM the next year and principal in succession to Crotch in 1832, but resigned in 1859. In 1855 Wagner conducted one of his symphonies with the Philharmonic Society.

Works include cantata *Medora e Corrado*, Ode to Harmony; nine symphonies (1819–34), four overtures for orchestra; three piano concertos (1832–35), Concertante for cello and orchestra; three piano trios, sextet for piano and strings; horn and piano sonata, duo for violin and piano; two sonatas, *The Enigma* ('Variations in the style of five eminent artists', 1825) and other music for piano; songs.

Pougin, (François Auguste) Arthur (Eugène Paroisse-) (b Châteauroux, 6 Aug 1834; d Paris, 8 Aug 1921), French musicologist. He had little general education, but studied violin with Alard and theory with Réber at the Paris Conservatory. After working at various theatres as violinist and conductor, he began to write biographical articles on 18th-c. French musicians and gradually made his way by writing for papers, contributing to dictionaries and writing music criticism. He wrote biographies of Verdi, Campra, Meyerbeer, V Wallace, Bellini, Rossini, Auber, Adam, Méhul, etc., and studies of French music history.

Pouishnov, Lev (b Odessa, 11 Oct 1891; d London, 28 May 1959), Russian-born British pianist. He first appeared in public when five years old. From 1907 to 1910 he studied at the St Petersburg Conservatory and then toured Europe as a soloist, subsequently playing also in USA, Australia and the Far East. He left Russia in 1920 and settled in England, becoming naturalized in 1931.

Poule, La, *The Hen*, the nickname of a symphony by Haydn, no. 83, in G minor (no. 2 of the 'Paris' symphonies), composed 1786.

Poulenard, Isabelle (b Paris, 5 Jul 1961), French soprano. After study in Paris sang under Jean-Claude Malgoire at Tourcoing in operas by Vivaldi, Scarlatti and Monteverdi. Sang in Rameau's *Hippolyte et Aricie* under William Christie at the Paris Opéra-Comique and in Cesti's *Orontea* at Innsbruck under René Jacobs. Spitalfields Festival, London, as Gluck's Iphigénie (en Aulide). Has sung in Paisiello's *Re Teodoro in Venezia*, Handel's *Alessandro* and Conti's *Don Chisciotte* (Innsbruck, 1992). Recordings include *Les Indes Galantes*, Lully's *Armide* and Monteverdi's *Combattimento*.

On the radio a lady has been caterwauling for a quarter of an hour some songs which may very well have been mine!

Francis Poulenc, *Diary of My Songs*, 1985

Poulenc, Francis (b Paris, 7 Jan 1899; d Paris, 30 Jan 1963), French composer. Received a classical education, but was able to take piano lessons from Ricardo Viñes and to pick up technical knowledge in various ways. When he was called up for war service in 1918 he had already written one or two works under the influence of Satie, and on being demobilized he joined the group of 'Les Six' with Auric, Durey, Honegger, Milhaud and Tailleferre, and thus came for a time under the influence of Jean Cocteau, notably with his three songs *Cocardes* (1919). A commission from Diaghilev led to the ballet score *Les Biches* (1923), influenced by the neo-classical brilliance of Stravinsky but also containing Poulenc's characteristic wit, charm and melancholy. Similar traits are found in his great series of songs (1919–60), settings of poems by Apollinaire, Ronsard, Éluard, Colette and Vilmorin.

Works include STAGE: opera *Dialogues des Carmélites* (1957); comic opera *Les Mamelles de Tirésias* (libretto by G Apollinaire, 1947), monodrama *La voix humaine* (1959); ballets *Les Biches/The House-Party*, 1942), and *Les Animaux modèles* (after La Fontaine, 1942).

CHORAL: Mass in G minor (1937) and cantata *Figure humaine* (P Éluard), *Sécheresses* for chorus and orchestra; choruses (unaccompanied), *Sept Chansons* (Éluard and Apollinaire, 1945), *Poésie et Vérité*; *Stabat Mater* (1950), *Gloria* (1959).

ORCHESTRAL: *Deux Marches et un Intermède* for orchestra; *Concert champêtre* for harpsichord and orchestra (1928), *Marches militaires* for piano and orchestra, concerto in D minor for two pianos and orchestra (1932), organ concerto (1938); *Aubade* for piano and 18 instruments (1929); piano concerto (1949).

CHAMBER: *Rapsodie nègre* for flute, clarinet and string quartet, trio for oboe, horn and piano (1926); sonatas for two clarinets, for clarinet and bassoon (1922) and for horn, trumpet and trombone (1922); violin and piano and cello and piano sonatas (1943, 1948).

SONG CYCLES WITH CHAMBER INSTRUMENTS: *Le Bestiaire* (G Apollinaire, 1919), *Bal Masqué* (M Jacob, 1932) and *Cocardes* (Cocteau, 1919).

PIANO: *Mouvements perpétuels* (1918), *Suite*, *Impromptus* (1920), *Feuillets d'album*, *Nocturnes* (1929–38), *Suite française* (1935), *Villageoises*, etc. for piano; sonata for piano duet (1918).

SONGS: *Cinq Poèmes de Ronsard* (1924–25), *Chansons gaillardes* (1926), *Huit Chansons polonaises* (1934), *Tel jour, telle nuit* (1937), *Fiançailles pour rire* (1939), *Chansons villageoises* (1942, also with chamber orchestra) and other songs.

Pountney, David (b Oxford, 10 Sept 1947), English stage director. Studied at Cambridge and produced Scarlatti's *Trionfo dell'Onore* there 1967; Wexford Festival 1972, *Káta Kabanová*. Director of productions Scottish Opera 1975–80, with *Meistersinger*, *Onegin*, *Jenůfa* and *Don Giovanni*. Staged the premiere of *Satyagraha* by Glass for Netherlands Opera (1980) and was principal producer at ENO 1982–93, with *Rusalka*, *Lady Macbeth of Mtsensk*, *Macbeth*, UK stage premieres of *Osud* and Busoni's *Faust* (1986), *Wozzeck*, the fp of Harvey's *Inquest of Love*, and *The Excursions of Mr Brouček* (also at Munich, 1994). US debut with *Macbeth* at Houston (1973), returning there 1976 for the fp of *Bilby's Doll* by Floyd and staging *The Voyage* by Glass at the NY Met in 1992. Noted for his technical resourcefulness and imaginative visual style.

poussé French = 'pushed'; the upstroke of the bow in the playing of string instruments, the opposite of *tiré* (= drawn).

Pousseur, Henri (b Malmédy, 23 Jun 1929), Belgian composer. Studied at Brussels Conservatory and took private composition lessons from André Souris and Pierre Boulez. In 1958 he founded a studio for electronic music in Brussels; works investigate computer and aleatory techniques, influenced by Berio and Stockhausen. Has lectured at Darmstadt (1957–67), Cologne and State University of NY, Buffalo (1966–69). Professor of composition, Liège Conservatory from 1971.

Works include operas *Votre Faust* (1969), *Die Erprobung des*

A Selection of

Poulenc

Concert champêtre	1928
Concerto for 2 pianos	1932
Les soirées de Nazelles	1936
Mass in G minor	1937
Organ Concerto	1938
Les Biches Suite	1942
Piano Concerto	1949
Dialogues des Carmelites	1957
La voix humaine	1959
Gloria	1959

Praetorius *The title page to the fourth part of the monumental* Musae Sionae *by Michael Praetorius, published by Jacob Lucius in Helmstedt, 1607. In all, the* Musae Sioniae *comprise nine volumes consisting of mostly vocal compositions for between two and twelve parts. Some organ works are also included.*

Petrus Hebraïcus (1974); *Trois Chants sacrés* for soprano and string trio; *Symphonies* for 15 solo instruments; *Modes* for string quartet; quintet to the memory of Webern (1955); *Seismographs* for magnetic tape; *Scambi* for tape (1957); *Rimes pour différentes sources sonores* for orchestra and tape (1959); *Répons* for seven musicians (1960); *Mobile* for two pianos, *Portrait de Votre Faust* for soloists, instruments and tape (1966); *Couleurs croisées* for orchestra (1967); *L'effacement du Prince Igor* for orchestra (1971); *Système des paraboles*, seven tape studies (1972); *Schoenbergs Gegenwart* for actors, singers and instruments (1974); *Chronique illustrée* for baritone and orchestra (1976); *Agonie* for voices and electronics (1981); *Nuits des Nuits* for orchestra (1985); *Déclarations d'Orage* for soloists, tape and orchestra (1989); *Leçons d'enfer*, chamber opera (1991).

Powell, Claire (b Tavistock, 1954), English mezzo. Studied at the RAM and London Opera Centre. Wigmore Hall recital 1979 and Glyndebourne 1979–80, as Juno in *Ulisse* and Meg Page in *Falstaff*, London, CG, from 1980 in *Hoffmann, Midsummer Night's Dream, Lulu* and *Don Carlos* (Eboli, 1989). US debut San Francisco 1990, as Maddalena. Appearances with WNO, ENO, Scottish Opera and Opera North as Carmen, the Berlioz Marguerite, Gluck's Alceste and Orfeo, and Handel's Cornelia, and Cherubino; sang Eboli with Opera North, 1993. Many concert appearances, including *Das Lied von der Erde* for the Royal Ballet at CG.

Powell, Mel (b New York, 12 Feb 1923), American composer. Played piano in dance bands, later studied with Wagenaar, Toch and Hindemith. Founded electronic music studio at Yale, 1960. Dean of Music, California Institute of Arts, 1969–75.

Works include *Stanzas* for orchestra (1957); *Filigree Setting* for string quartet (1959); *Setting* for cello and orchestra; *Immobiles* 1–5 for tape and orchestra (1967–69); string quartet (1982); *Computer*

Prelude (1988); *Duplicates* concerto for two pianos and orchestra (1990).

Power, Leonel (b *c* 1375; d Canterbury, 5 Jun 1445), English composer and theorist. He wrote a treatise on the singing of descant and composed Masses, including *Alma redemptoris*, motets and other church music.

Powers, Anthony (b London, 1953), English composer. Studied at Oxford University, in Paris with Boulanger and at York University with David Blake. Has taught at Dartington College of Arts and Exeter University, both S Devon.

Works include *Souvenirs de voyage* for soprano and piano (1979), *Another Part of the Island* for ensemble (1980); opera *The Search for the Simorgh* (1981); music theatre *A Sussex Carol* (1982); *The Winter Festival*, for mezzo and nine instruments (1985); *Chamber Concerto* (1984); *Music for Strings* (1984); *Vespers* for 21 solo strings (1986); two piano sonatas (1983, 1986); string quartet (1987); *Stone, Water, Stars* for orchestra (1987); Horn concerto (1989); Cello concerto (1990); 2nd string quartet (1991).

pp abbr. = *pianissimo*, Italian = 'softest'. Although the sign indicates a superlative, it can be further multiplied to demand even greater softness of tone.

Praeger, Ferdinand (Christian Wilhelm) (b Leipzig, 22 Jan 1815; d London, 2 Sept 1891), German pianist and composer. Studied under his father and settled in London in 1834; wrote an unreliable book *Wagner as I knew him* in 1885 and composed a symphonic prelude to Byron's *Manfred*, an overture *Abellino*, a piano trio, piano pieces, etc.

praeludium ◊prelude.

Praetorius (real name Schulz, Schulze, Schultz or Schultze) German 16th–17th-c. musicians not of the same family, except 3 and 5:

1. Godescalcus Praetorius (b Salzwedel, 28 Mar 1524; d Wittenburg, 8 Jul 1573), scholar. Professor of philosophy at Wittenberg University. Published in 1557 a volume *Melodiae scholasticae* in which he was assisted by M Agricola.

2. Bartholomaeus Praetorius (b Marienburg, *c* 1590; d Stockholm, buried 3 Aug 1623), composer. Published pavans and galliards in five parts in 1616.

3. Hieronymus Praetorius (b Hamburg, 10 Aug 1560; d Hamburg, 27 Jan 1629), organist and composer. Pupil of his father, Jacob Praetorius (or Schultz), organist at St James's Church, Hamburg, whom he succeeded in 1582. He wrote in the Venetian antiphonal choral style. His collected church music, *Opus Musicum* (1616–22), contains more than 100 motets.

Works include Masses, motets, Magnificats, *Cantiones sacrae*, hymn-tunes; Latin and German songs in 5–20 parts.

4. Michael Praetorius (b Kreuzberg, Thuringia, 15 Feb 1571; d Wolfenbüttel, 15 Feb 1621), organist, composer and author. He was music director at Lüneburg until 1603, when he was appointed organist to the Duke of Brunswick, who later made him his music director. He wrote the voluminous treatise on music and instruments entitled *Syntagma musicum* (1619) and composed a number of vols. of Latin and German sacred and secular songs for several voices. His nine-volume *Musae Sioniae* (1605–10) contains 1,244 chorale settings. He is best known today for the dance collection *Terpsichore* (1612) although the *Lutheran Mass for Christmas*, with characteristic multiple choir effects, has also enjoyed a recent revival.

5. Jacob Praetorius (b Hamburg, 8 Feb 1586; d Hamburg, 21 Oct 1651), organist and composer, son of 3. Pupil of Sweelinck at Amsterdam; appointed organist of St Peter's Church, Hamburg, 1603. Wrote motets, etc.

'Prague' Symphony Mozart's symphony in D major, K504, composed in Vienna, Dec 1786 and performed in Prague, 19 Jan 1787, during a visit for the production there of *Le nozze di Figaro*.

Pralltriller, German, the rapid repetition of a note, with a note a degree higher in between, indicated by the sign ᮝ.

Pratella, Francesco (Balilla) (b Lugo, Romagna, 1 Feb 1880; d Ravenna, 17 May 1955), Italian composer. Studied at the Liceo Musicale of Pesaro, where Mascagni was among his masters. He settled at Milan, where in 1910 he began to make propaganda for

The notation for pralltrillers on F and G, and the approximate notation of each.

futurist music, on which he lectured and wrote in the more progressive periodicals.

Works include operas *Il regno lontano* (1905), *La Sing d'Vargöun* (1909), *L'aviatore Dro* (1920), *Il dona primaverile, Fabiano* (1923), children's opera *La ninna nanna della bambola* (1923); incidental music to plays; symphonic poems on Carducci's ode *La chiesa di Polenta*, five symphonic poems (*Romagna*, 1903–4), *Inno alla vita* (musica futuristica, 1912), three dances *La guerra*, etc. for orchestra; piano trio; violin, organ and piano pieces; songs.

Prati, Alessio (b Ferrara, 19 Jul 1750; d Ferrara, 17 Jan 1788), Italian composer. Pupil of Piccinni at the Conservatorio di Loreto in Naples, went to Paris 1779, then to St Petersburg (1781) and Warsaw (1782). Travelling by way of Vienna (1783) he returned to Ferrara 1784.

Works include *c* 12 operas, e.g. *L'École de la jeunesse* (1779), *Ifigenia in Aulide* (1784) *Olimpia* (1786), *Demofoonte* (1786), etc.; Masses and other church music, arias and misc. other vocal pieces; symphonies and *sinfonia concertante*; concertos; violin sonatas.

Prausnitz, Frederik (b Cologne, 26 Aug 1920), German-born American conductor. Studied at Juilliard and taught there 1947–61. Music director Syracuse SO (NY) 1971–74 Peabody Conservatory, Baltimore, 1976–80. Director of conducting programs from 1980. Often heard in Europe and USA in music by Carter, Varèse, Stockhausen, Schoenberg and Sessions.

Pré aux clercs, Le, *The Scholars' Meadow*, opera by Hérold (libretto by F A E de Planard), produced Paris, Opéra-Comique, 15 Dec 1832. King Henry of Navarre wants Isabelle, a friend of Queen Marguerite, to marry Comminge even though she loves Mergy. Marguerite arranges for the couple's escape and attends their wedding, then Mergy kills Comminge in a duel.

precentor a dignitary in an Anglican cathedral, originally the leading singer in the choir, but also in charge of the vocal church music and superior to the organist. His seat is opposite that of the dean (who takes the Decani side) on the Cantoris side of the chancel.

Preciosa play with music by Weber (libretto by P A Wolff, based on Cervantes's story *La Gilanella*), produced Berlin, Opera House, 15 Mar 1821.

precipitando Italian = 'precipitately'; a direction indicating that an *accelerando* is to be made to increase in pace very rapidly.

Predieri, Luc' Antonio (b Bologna, 13 Sept 1688; d Bologna, 1767), Italian composer. *Maestro di cappella* of the cathedral at Bologna; went to the court chapel in Vienna, 1738, and became chief *Kapellmeister* there in 1746; but returned to Italy 1751.

Works include operas *Il sogno di Scipione* (1735), *Perseo* (1738), *Armida* (1750) and others, serenades and festival plays for the stage oratorios.

Prégardien, Christoph (b Limburg, 18 Jan 1956), German tenor. Studied in Frankfurt and sang there and elsewhere in Germany as Tamino, Fenton and Don Ottavio among others. Many concerts with early music specialists such as Leonhardt, Koopman, Norrington and Brueggen; *Towards Bach and Haydn* series on South Bank, London, 1989; Wigmore Hall debut recital, 1993. Recordings include Bach's *St John* and *Matthew Passions*, under Leonhardt, Buxtehude Cantatas with Koopman and Bach's Lutheran Masses conducted by Herreweghe.

Preindl, Joseph (b Marbach, Lower Austria, 30 Jan 1756; d Vienna, 26 Oct 1823), Austrian church musician and composer, pupil of Albrechtsberger. Appointed *Kapellmeister* at St Peter's, Vienna in 1793, he held the same post at St Stephen's from 1809. Pub. treatises on singing and on composition.

Works include at least 13 Masses, two Requiems, Offertories, motets and other church music; keyboard music.

prelude, from Latin *praeludium*, an introductory piece played, for example, before a church service or a music performance, or forming the first movement of a suite or other sectional work; also one paired with a fugue, to which it forms an introduction; from the 19th c. onwards sometimes a separate concert work, especially for piano (Chopin, etc.) or orchestra; and from Wagner onwards the orchestral introduction to an opera where it does not take the form of a detached overture and leads straight into the first act.

Prélude à l'Après-midi d'un faune, *Prelude to 'The Afternoon of a Faun'*, an orchestral piece by Debussy intended as a musical introduction to Stéphane Mallarmé's poem of that name, composed 1892–94 and first performed Paris, Société Nationale, 23 Dec 1894.

Ballet on this work (choreographed by Vaslav Nizhinsky), produced Paris, Théâtre du Châtelet, 29 May 1912.

Préludes two sets of piano pieces, 12 in each, by Debussy, composed 1910–13. Their contents are: I. 1. *Danseuses de Delphes/Dancing Women of Delphi*; 2. *Voiles/Sails*; 3. *Le Vent dans la plaine/The wind in the plain*; 4. *Les Sons et les parfums tournent dans l'air du soir/Sounds and scents whirl in the evening air*: a quotation from Baudelaire; 5. *Les Collines d'Anacapri/The hills of Anacapri*; 6. *Des Pas sur la neige/Footprints in the snow*; 7. *Ce qu'a vu le vent d'Ouest/What the West Wind saw*; 8. *La Fille aux cheveux de lin/The Flaxen-haired Girl*: based on a Scottish song by Leconte de Lisle; 9. *La Sérénade interrompue/The interrupted serenade*; 10. *La Cathédrale engloutie/The Submerged Cathedral*: on the old Breton tale of the sunken city of Ys); 11. *La Danse de Puck/Puck's Dance*, after Shakespeare's *Midsummer Night's Dream*); 12. *Minstrels* (= music-hall artists, not troubadours). II. 1. *Brouillards/Mists*; 2. *Feuilles mortes/Dead Leaves*; 3. *La Puerta del Vino* (a gate at Granada); 4. *Les Fées sont d'exquises danseuses/The Fairies are exquisite Dancers*; 5. *Bruyères/Heather*; 6. *General Lavine-eccentric* (a music-hall character); 7. *La Terrasse des audiences du clair de lune/The Terrace of the Moonlight Audiences*; a reference to an account of George V's Durbar in 1912; the piece contains a quotation of the folksong 'Au clair de la lune'); 8. *Ondine* (Water-spirit maiden of 19th-c. story); 9. *Hommage à S Pickwick Esq., P.P.M.P.C.* (after Dickens; the piece quotes 'God save the King' in the bass); 10. *Canope* (a Canopic jar holding the ashes of a dead lover); 11. *Les Tierces alternées/Alternating Thirds*); 12. *Feux d'artifice/Fireworks*; quoting a few notes of the *Marseillaise* at the end).

Préludes, Les symphonic poem by Liszt, composed 1848, revised early 1850s, fp Weimar, 28 Feb 1854. The title is taken from a poem by Lamartine, with which in fact the music has no connection.

preparation a term used in harmony for a chord, one note of which will create a dissonance in the chord that follows.

In this example the top voice (C) is prepared for dissonance and resolution.

prestissimo Italian = 'extremely fast'.

presto Italian = 'quick, fast', the direction most commonly used to indicate the fastest speeds in music. *Presto* is quicker than *allegro*.

Preston, Simon (b Bournemouth, 4 Aug 1938), English organist, harpsichordist and conductor. He studied at the RAM and Cambridge; debut London 1962, as organist. Sub-organist Westminster Abbey 1962–67; organist from 1981. Christ Church, Oxford, 1970–81.

Previn The conductor and pianist André Previn. He has had a long-lasting relationship with the London Symphony Orchestra, currently holding the position of Conductor Laureate. His many recordings include persuasive accounts of English music.

Organist and master of the choristers at Westminster Abbey, 1981–87. He has been heard in Europe and the USA in the organ works of Handel, Liszt and Messiaen and has recorded Masses by Haydn with the Christ Church choir.

Preston, Thomas (d ? Windsor, c 1563), English composer. He was (?) organist and master of the choristers, Magdalen College, Oxford, and is recorded as having played at Windsor Chapel in 1558 and 1559. He wrote a large amount of organ music for the Latin rite, including the Proper of the Mass for Easter Day (incomplete).

Prêtre, Georges (b Waziers, 14 Aug 1924), French conductor. Studied at Douai and in Paris, making his debut in 1946 at the Paris Opéra-Comique; music director there 1956–59. London debut 1961, NY Met. 1964. Frequent performances and recordings with Callas. In 1959 conducted the fp of Poulenc's *La voix humaine*.

Preussisches Märchen, *Prussian Tales*, ballet-opera by Blacher (libretto by H von Cramer); composed 1949, produced Berlin, 23 Sept 1952.

Previn, André (born Andreas Ludwig Priwin) (b Berlin, 6 Apr 1929), German-born American conductor, pianist and composer. He studied in Berlin and Paris and worked in Hollywood from 1940 (US citizen 1943). He studied further, with Ernst Toch and Pierre Monteux, and was active as a concert pianist before debut as conductor with St Louis SO in 1962; Houston SO 1967–69, Pittsburgh SO 1976–86. He was chief conductor of the LSO 1968–79 and gave many performances of English music, notably Walton and Vaughan Williams. Music director, RPO 1985–87, LA PO 1986–90. Recordings include symphonies and concertos by Prokofiev, *Carmina Burana* and *Die Fledermaus* with the Vienna PO.

Previtali, Fernando (b Adria, 16 Feb 1907; d Rome, 1 Aug 1985), Italian conductor and composer. Studied composition, organ, piano and cello at Turin Conservatory. From 1928 to 1936 he conducted in Florence (Maggio Musicale Fiorentino), from 1936 to 1953 with the Rome Radio Orchestra, and in 1953 became conductor of the Santa Cecilia Orchestra. US debut Cleveland orchestra, 1955; opera debut

Dallas, 1975, *Anna Bolena*. Principal conductor San Carlo, Naples, from 1972.

Works include ballet *Alluzinazione* (1945); cantata for chorus and orchestra; string quartet, string trio; songs.

Prévost (d'Exiles), Antoine François (1697–1763), French novelist. For works based on *Manon Lescaut* see ◊Henze (*Boulevard Solitude*); Massenet (◊*Manon*); Halévy, Auber and Puccini (◊*Manon Lescaut*).

Prévost, Eugène (Prosper) (b Paris, 23 Apr 1809; d New Orleans, 19 Aug 1872), French composer and singing-teacher. Studied at the Paris Conservatory with Lesueur and others and gained the Prix de Rome in 1831. After producing works in Paris, he became conductor at the theatre of Le Havre for a time, but left for New Orleans in 1838, where he conducted at the French theatre and taught singing. In 1862 he returned to Paris, but went again to New Orleans in 1867.

Works include operas *L'Hôtel de Princes* (1831), *Le Grenadier de Wagram* (1831), *Cosimo* (1835), *Le Bon Garçon, Esmeralda* (after Hugo's *Notre-Dame de Paris*), *L'Illustre Gaspard* (1863); Mass with orchestra; cantata *Bianca Capello*, etc.

Prey, Claude (b Fleury-sur-Andelle, 30 May 1925), French composer. Studied with Milhaud and Messiaen at the Paris Conservatoire. He wrote the chamber opera *Le coeur Révélateur*, after Poe's *The Tell-Tale Heart* (Paris, 1962) and is best known for the operas *Les Liaisons Dangereuses* (Strasbourg, 1974) and *Le Rouge et le Noir* (Aix, 1989). Other stage works include *La Grand Mère Française* (Avignon, 1976), *Lunedi Bleue* (Paris, 1982), *Pauline* (Tourcoing, 1983) and *Sommaire Soleil* (1990).

Prey, Hermann (b Berlin, 11 Jul 1929), German baritone. Studied at the Berlin Hochschule für Musik with Jaro Prohaska. From 1952 to 1953 he sang at Wiesbaden and then became a member of the Hamburg Staatsoper where he created Meton in Krenek's *Pallas Athene weint* (1955). Has sung frequently in Berlin at the Städtische Oper and at the Vienna Staatsoper. NY Met. debut 1960, as Wolfram; London, CG, 1973, as Rossini's Figaro. Other roles included Papageno, Guglielmo and Storch in the first British performance of Strauss's *Intermezzo* (Edinburgh, 1965). He is also well known as a Lieder singer. Pub. autobiography 1986.

Pribyl, Vilem (b Nachod, 10 Apr 1925; d Prague, 13 June 1990), Czech tenor. He sang as an amateur during the 1950s; professional debut Ustí nad Labem 1961, as Lukas in Smetana's *The Kiss*. He joined the Janáček Opera, Brno, the same year and was heard as Smetana's Dalibor and Janáček's Laca, in operas by Prokofiev and Shostakovich and as Radames, Otello and Lohengrin; often appeared with the Prague National Opera and sang Dalibor with the co. when it visited Edinburgh in 1964 (British premiere of the opera). Florestan at CG.

Price, Curtis (Alexander) (b Springfield, NC, 7 Sept 1945), American musicologist. Studied at Harvard 1968–74 and taught at Washington University, St Louis, 1974–81. Professor at King's College, London, from 1988. Principal, RAM 1995. Early English stage music has been at the centre of his studies, and he has published *Henry Purcell and the London Stage* (1984) and edited *Dido and Aeneas*, 1986. Other titles include *Italian Opera and Arson in Late 18th-Century London* (1989) and *The Early Baroque Era* (editor) 1993.

Price, Leontyne (b Laurel, MS, 10 Feb 1927), American soprano. Studied at Central State College, OH, and at Juilliard in NY (1949–52), achieving her first success in *Porgy and Bess*; also sang Bess on her London debut, in 1952; CG debut 1958, as Aida. From 1957 to 1959 she sang with the San Francisco Opera co., notably in the US fp of Poulenc's *Les Dialogues des Carmelites*, and in 1959 became a lyric soprano with the Chicago Opera. Salzburg operatic debut, Donna Anna, 1960, conducted by Karajan. She made her debut at the NY Met. in 1961 as the *Trovatore* Leonora and sang at La Scala, Milan, in 1962, as Aida. In 1966 she created Cleopatra in Barber's *Antony and Cleopatra*, at the opening of the new Met. house. Retired after singing Aida at the Met., 1985.

Price, Margaret (b Blackwood, Mon., 13 Apr 1941), Welsh soprano. She sang Cherubino with WNO in 1962 and at CG in 1963; later London roles have been Pamina, Fiordiligi and Donna Anna. Glyndebourne 1968, as Constanze. Pamina in San Francisco in 1969 and sang with the Paris Opéra on its 1976 tour of the USA. Salzburg debut 1975, as Mozart's Constanze; NY Met., 1985 as Desdemona. She has been successful in Germany, notably Cologne and Munich, and has given many recitals with James Lockhart. Has avoided Wagner on stage but recorded Isolde in 1983. Season 1992/93 as Adriana Lecouvreur and Giovanna d'Arco, in concert performances at the Concertgebouw and Salzburg. CBE 1982. DBE 1992.

Prick, Christof, ◊Perick.

prick-song from the 15th to the 18th c. 'to prick' was used to mean 'to write notes'. Hence prick-song meant written, as opposed to improvised, music.

Prigione di Edimburgo, La, *Edinburgh Gaol*, opera by F Ricci (libretto by G Rossi, based on Scribe and Planard's *Prison d'Édimbourg* and further back on Scott's *Heart of Midlothian*), produced Trieste, 13 Mar 1838.

Prigioniero, Il, *The Prisoner*, opera (prologue and one act) by Dallapiccola (libretto by composer after V de L'Isle Adam and C de Coster); composed 1944–48, fp Turin Radio, 4 Dec 1949. Produced Florence, 20 May 1950. During the era of the Inquisition in Spain, the Prisoner finds hope in a comforting Gaoler. One day the cell is left open and he finds his way to freedom, only to be caught by the Grand Inquisitor.

prima donna Italian = 'first lady'; the singer of the leading soprano part in a particular opera or the leading soprano in an opera co.

People applaud a prima donna as they do the feats of the strong man at a fair: the sensations are painfully disagreeable, hard to endure, but one is so glad when it is all over that one cannot help rejoicing.
Jean-Jacques Rousseau, *La Nouvelle Héloïse*, 1761

Primavera, Giovanni Leonardo (b Barletta, Naples, *c* 1540; d after 1585), Italian composer. *Maestro di cappella* to the Spanish governor of Milan in 1573. Palestrina used his madrigal 'Nasce la gioia mia' as a *cantus firmus* for a Mass, called by that name.

Works include madrigals *Canzoni napoletane* for three voices, *villotte* for three voices, etc.; most works pub. Venice, 1565–84.

prima volta Italian = 'first time'; a direction sometimes given where a repeated portion of a composition takes a new turn after the repetition. The join leading to the repeat is then called *prima volta*, while the different one taking the music on to its continuation is marked *seconda volta*. The figures 1 and 2 are commonly used as abbrs. for these terms.

primo Italian = 'first'; *primo* is often written over the top part in piano duets, the bottom one being *secondo*; the word also appears in orchestral scores where the composer wishes to make sure that a passage is played by only the first of a pair or groups of similar instruments.

primo uomo Italian = 'first man'; the singer of the leading male soprano part in an opera or the leading male soprano in an opera company in the 18th c.

Primrose, William (b Glasgow, 23 Aug 1903; d Provo, UT, 1 May 1982), Scottish viola player. After studying in Glasgow and at the GSM in London, he studied with Ysaÿe in Belgium from 1925 to 1927, and on his advice took up the viola. From 1930 to 1935 he played with the London String Quartet, and in 1937 was selected by Toscanini to become first viola of the NBC SO, with which he remained until 1942. In 1939 he founded his own string quartet. He also commissioned a viola concerto from Bartók, of which he gave the fp in 1949. He taught in Tokyo from 1972.

Prince Igor, *Kniaz Igor*, opera by Borodin (libretto by composer, based on a sketch by Stassov), composed between 1871 and 1887 and left unfinished at Borodin's death in the latter year. Completed and scored by Rimsky-Korsakov and Glazunov. Produced St Petersburg, 4 Nov 1890. Prince Igor and son Vladimir are taken prisoner by the Polovtsi. Khan Konchak treats his prisoners well, blessing the union of his daughter Konchakovna with Vladimir. Igor escapes and is welcomed home.

———— THE OPERA ————

Prince Igor

A four-act opera with Prologue by Alexander Borodin. The music was completed by Glazunov and Rimsky-Korsakov after Borodin's death in 1887, although it was not produced until 1890. The action takes place in Polovtsia in 1185.

Prologue. Prince Igor (baritone) and his son Vladimir (tenor) set out for war despite the misgivings of Igor's wife Yaroslavna (soprano).

I. Boyars inform Yaroslavna of Igor's defeat and capture.

II. At the camp of Khan Konchak (bass), the captive Vladimir falls for the Khan's daughter, Konchakovna (mezzo-soprano). Khan tries to dispel Igor's gloom by commanding his oriental slaves to dance and sing.

III. Igor decides to escape when he hears of an attack on his homeland, although the reluctant Vladimir is captured. A generous Khan reunites him with Konchakovna.

IV. Yaroslavna is distressed at the destruction of her town, but her mood changes to joy when Igor returns safely to her.

———— THE OPERA ————

Prince of the Pagodas, The ballet by Britten (choreography by John Cranko), produced London, CG, Jan 1 1957.

Princesse de Navarre, La comédie-ballet by Rameau (libretto by Voltaire), produced Versailles, 23 Feb 1745, to celebrate the wedding of the Dauphin with Maria Teresa of Spain. Princess Constance escapes from the King of Castille and hides with Don Morillo, evading the amorous pursuit of the Duke of Foix.

Princesse jaune, La, *The Yellow Princess*, opera by Saint-Saëns (libretto by L Gallet), produced Paris, Opéra-Comique, 12 Jun 1872. Kornélis loves everything Japanese. He imagines he is in Japan, but then realizes he loves his Dutch girlfriend Léna more than his fantasy.

Princess Ida, or Castle Adamant, operetta by Sullivan (libretto by W S Gilbert, a parody of Tennyson's *Princess*), produced London, Savoy Theatre, 5 Jan 1884. Prince Hiarion's marriage to Princess Ida was arranged a long time ago, but she has since spurned all men and founded a university for women. But then she falls in love with him.

principal an open diapason organ stop; the term is derived from the German *Prinzipal* to denote a neutral stop, in contrast with the variety of other, more colourful, diapason stops. Also, in early music, the lowest trumpet part, in which high and florid notes were not demanded. In modern terminology a principal is the leading player of any group of orchestral instruments.

Pring, Katherine (b Brighton, 4 Jun 1940), English mezzo. She studied at the RCM; SW/ENO from 1968 as Eboli, Azucena, Waltraute and Agave in the British stage premiere of *The Bassarids* (1974). Other roles include Poppea, Dorabella, Fricka, Tippett's Thea and Stravinsky's Jocasta.

Printemps symphonic suite for chorus and orchestra by Debussy; composed 1887, published 1904 in a reduction for piano four hands. Re-orchestrated by Henri Busser and performed Paris, Salle Gaveau, 18 Apr 1913.

Prinz von Homburg, Der opera by Henze (libretto by I Bachmann, after Kleist), produced Hamburg, Staatsoper, 22 May 1960. The Prince is lost in a fantasy world with his beloved Princess at its centre. As a result, he ignores battle orders and is condemned to death. Offered his freedom after Princess Natalie intervenes, he still prefers an honourable death, but the Elector shows mercy in the end.

Prioris, Johannes, Franco-Netherlands 15th–16th-c. organist and composer. Organist at St Peter's in Rome in 1490 and *maître de chapelle* to Louis XII in 1507. Wrote Masses, motets, Magnificats, Requiem, *chansons* etc.

Prise de Troie, La (Berlioz.) ◊Troyens.

Prisoner in the Caucasus, The, *Kavkasky Plennik*, opera by Cui

Prokofiev
A biographical note

The resilience of Prokofiev in the face of adversity is a testament to the artistic spirit. His music frequently met with hostility and misunderstanding, yet he maintained a high level of creative output throughout his career. His dissonant, one-movement First Piano Concerto, given in Moscow in 1912, was a worthy precursor of Stravinsky's *The Rite of Spring*, premiered the following year. By the time of his *Scythian Suite* of 1916, his reputation as an iconoclast was such that the critic Sabaneiev harshly 'reviewed' a performance which did not actually take place; something similar happened with the critic of the New York Tribune two years later. Seeking calmer waters in the West, Prokofiev settled briefly in France before trying his luck in the United States. His Haydn pastiche the *Classical symphony* had already been dubbed an 'orgy of discordant sounds' by Musical America and his Gozzi fable *The Love for Three Oranges* fared little better in Chicago in 1921. Returning to Europe, Prokofiev had plans for his opera *The Fiery Angel*, but Bruno Walter at the Berlin Städtische Oper feared that the Russian's calculated shock tactics would not go down well with the local bourgeoisie. The tale of spiritual annihilation caused by diabolic possession was judged to be much too close to home for Stalin and his Bolsheviks, and the opera was not performed in Russia until 1983. Even the patriotic *War and Peace*, written after Prokofiev's return home in 1936, did not escape the Party line and, like the earlier ballet *Romeo and Juliet*, it had to be premiered abroad.

(libretto by V A Krilov, based on Pushkin's poem), produced St Petersburg, 16 Feb 1883.

Pritchard, John (b London, 5 Feb 1921; d Daly City, CA, 5 Dec 1989), English conductor. He studied in Italy and went to Glyndebourne in 1947; gave three Mozart operas there in 1951: music director 1969–77. He conducted the fps of Britten's *Gloriana* and Tippett's *Midsummer Marriage* at CG; *King Priam* with the co. at Coventry, 1962. US debut 1953, Pittsburgh SO; NY Met. 1971. Music director LPO 1962–66; BBC SO from 1981. Principal conductor Cologne Opera from 1978. Knighted 1983.

Priuli, Giovanni (b Venice, *c* 1575; d Vienna, 1629), Italian composer. *Kapellmeister* to the Archduke Ferdinand of Austria at Graz early in the 17th c.; remained in his service when he became the Emperor Ferdinand II. He studied with G Gabrieli; his instrumental canzonas contain echo effects.

Works include motets, psalms and other church music; madrigals, *Musiche concertate*, *Delicie musicali* for several voices, etc.

Prix de Rome, French = 'Prize of Rome'; officially Grand Prix de Rome, a prize instituted in 1803 and offered annually in Paris by the Académie des Beaux-Arts, a branch of the Institut de France, to various artists. The prize for music composition was given to the successful competitor at the Conservatory and entitled the holder to three years' study at the French Academy housed in the Villa Medici in Rome. The work required was formerly a dramatic cantata, but was later a one-act opera. Among winners were Berlioz (after three attempts), Gounod, Bizet, Massenet and Debussy. The competition ceased in 1968.

Pro Arte Quartet Belgian string quartet, founded 1912 with members Alphonse Onnou and Laurent Halleux (violins), Germain Prévost (viola) and Robert Maas (cello). Many performances of modern works (Salzburg, 1923, US tour 1926). First visit to Britain 1925; recorded many Haydn quartets 1931–38 (reissued 1985). Moved to USA in 1940; Rudolf Kolisch leader from 1944. Title adopted by quartet of University of Wisconsin at Madison. In 1973 an Austrian string quartet with the same name was founded.

Prodaná Nevěsta (Smetana.) ◊Bartered Bride.

Prod'homme, J(acques) G(abriel) (b Paris, 28 Nov 1871; d Paris, 18 Jun 1956), French musicologist. Studied in Germany and lived at Munich from 1897–1900, where he founded a periodical. After his return to Paris he founded the French section of the Société internationale de musicologie, became its secretary and performed various other music administrative functions, succeeding Bouvert in 1931 as librarian and archivist at the Opéra, and Expert in 1934 as Conservatory librarian. He wrote several works both on Beethoven and on Berlioz, also on Mozart, Schubert, Wagner, etc.

Prodigal Son, The church parable by Britten (libretto by W Plomer), produced Orford, 10 Jun 1968, conductor Britten. In the country, the father of two sons gives his younger son an inheritance, which is squandered during a moral decline in the city. The son repents and is reconciled with his family on his return home.

Ballet by Prokofiev (*L'Enfant prodigue*); composed 1928, fp Paris, 21 May 1929 (Ballets Russes; scenario by B Kokno, choreography Balanchine, décor Georges Roualt; conductor Prokofiev). ◊Enfant prodigue (Debussy).

The programme or title must in itself contain a germ of feeling of movement, but never a crude description of concrete events.

Carl Nielsen on programme music, quoted in Simpson, *Carl Nielsen*, 1952

---

programme music any kind of instrumental music, especially orchestral, based on a literary, pictorial, historical, autobiographical, descriptive or other extra-musical subject and not intended to appeal only as music pure and simple.

programme notes analyses in concert programmes, especially in Britain, describing music performed. Early examples in England were those by ◊Grove for the Crystal Palace concerts.

progression the logical movement of two or more chords in succession, either harmonically with all the notes moving simultaneously or polyphonically with each one being part of a continuously moving horizontal melodic line.

Prohaska, Carl (b Mödling, near Vienna, 25 Apr 1869; d Vienna, 28 Mar 1927), Austrian composer. Studied piano with d'Albert and composition with Mandyczewski and Herzogenberg, being also befriended by Brahms. He taught at the Strasbourg Conservatory 1894–95 and conducted the Warsaw PO 1901–05. In 1908 he became professor at the Conservatory of the Vienna Philharmonic Society.

A Selection of
Prokofiev

Piano Concerto no. 1	1912
Symphony no. 1	1917
Violin Concerto no. 1	1917
The Love for Three Oranges	1921

Piano Concerto no. 3	1921
The Fiery Angel	1919–27
Romeo and Juliet	1938
Alexander Nevsky	1939
War and Peace	1941–42
Symphony no. 5	1944

Prokofiev *The composer Sergey Prokofiev (1891–1953) photographed with his op. 1 piano sonata and the veterinary surgeon Morolev, to whom it is dedicated. A fine pianist, Prokofiev premiered several of his sonatas himself. Others were dedicated to and premiered by Sviatoslav Richter.*

Works include opera *Madeleine Guimara* (1930); oratorio *Frühlingsfeier* (1913), motet *Aus dem Buch Hiob, Lebensmesse, Der Feind, Infanterie* and other choral works; variations on a theme from Rousseau's *Devin du village*, symphonic prelude to Anzengruber's *Das vierte Gebot*, symphonic fantasy, serenade, passacaglia and fugue for orchestra; string quartet, string quintet, piano trio; sonata and *Allegro con spirito* for violin and piano; songs, duets.

Prohaska, Jaro (b Vienna, 24 Jan 1891; d Munich, 28 Sept 1965), Austrian bass-baritone. He was a choirboy and organist before his stage debut in 1922 at Lübeck. He was soon engaged at Nuremberg and sang at Bayreuth 1933–44 as Wotan, Sachs, Amfortas, Telramund and the Dutchman. He sang in the 1935 fp of Graener's *Prinz von Homburg*, in Berlin, and taught there from 1949; Hermann Prey was among his pupils.

Prokina, Elena (b Odessa, 16 Jan 1964), Russian soprano. Studied first as an actress then sang with the Kirov Opera from 1988, as Emma in Khovanshchina, Marguerite and Natasha (also on BBC TV). Sang Káta Kabanová at CG 1994, returning as Desdemona 1995. Further appearances at Los Angeles (Lina in *Stiffelio*) and the Bregenz Festival. Valued for the musical and theatrical truth of her performances.

Prokofiev, Sergey Sergeyevich (b Sontsovka, Ekaterinoslav, 27 Apr 1891; d Moscow, 5 Mar 1953), Russian composer. Began to compose almost before he could write and tried his hand at an opera at the age of nine. He was sent to Glière for lessons, wrote 12 piano pieces in 1902 as well as a symphony for piano duet, and at 12 set Pushkin's play *A Feast in Time of Plague* as an opera. At the St Petersburg Conserva-

tory, which he left in 1914, he studied piano with Anna Essipova, composition with Rimsky-Korsakov and Liadov, and conducting with N Tcherepnin. By that time he had written many works, including the first piano concerto, and he then set to work on a ballet commission for Diaghilev that became the *Scythian Suite* for orchestra. During World War I he lived in London for a time and at its close he went to the USA by way of Japan. The opera *The Love for Three Oranges* was produced at Chicago in 1921, and the next year he went to live in Paris and became connected with Diaghilev's Russian Ballet, which produced several of his works. The visionary opera *The Fiery Angel* was completed in 1923 but not staged until 1955. Limited opportunities in the West impelled him to return to Russia. In 1933 he settled in Moscow and was induced by the Soviet government to simplify and popularize his style, a tendency which is very noticeable in such works as *Peter and the Wolf* and the quantities of film music he wrote there. The cantata derived from the film music for *Alexander Nevsky* is one of his most powerful scores however. Two years later he began his great patriotic opera *War and Peace*, and the victory in the war against Hitler was celebrated with one of his finest scores, the exuberant and expansive 5th symphony. After years of subjection to Stalinist oppression, he died ironically on the same day as Stalin.

Works include OPERAS: *Maddalena* (1911–13, fp 1979), *The Gambler* (after Dostoievsky, 1929), *The Love for Three Oranges* (after Gozzi, 1921), *The Fiery Angel* (1919–27, produced 1955), *War and Peace* (after Tolstoy, 1941–52, produced 1953), *Betrothal in a Monastery* (after Sheridan's *Duenna*, 1940–41), *Semyon Kotko* (1940), *The Story of a Real Man* (1948).

BALLETS: *The Buffoon* (1921), *Le Pas d'acier* (1927), *L'Enfant prodigue*, *Sur le Borysthène* (1932), *Romeo and Juliet* (after Shakespeare, 1938), *Cinderella* (1945).

ORCHESTRAL: includes *Classical symphony* (1921) and six other symphonies (1924–52), *Sinfonietta*, *Scythian Suite* (1914), *Symphonic Song*, Russian Overture *Toast to Stalin* and *Ode to the End of the War*; incidental music for *Egyptian Nights* (after Pushkin, Shakespeare and Shaw, 1934), *Boris Godunov* and *Eugene Onegin* (both Pushkin); film music for *Lieutenant Kijé* (1934), *The Queen of Spades* (after Pushkin), *Ivan the Terrible*, etc.; five piano concertos (1911–32), two violin concertos (1917, 1935), two cello concertos.

CHAMBER: *Overture on Hebrew Themes* for clarinet, string quartet and piano (1919); two string quartets (1930, 1941), quintet for wind and piano, sonata for two violins, sonatas in D major and F minor for violin and piano (1944, 1946), Ballade for cello and piano.

PIANO AND SONGS: nine piano sonatas, *c* 25 other op. nos. of piano pieces, including three studies, toccata, *Sarcasms*, *Visions fugitives*, *Contes de la vieille grand'mère* and two sonatinas; eight sets of songs (one without words, one to words by Pushkin).

CHORAL: *Seven, they are Seven*, for tenor, chorus and orchestra (1918), *Alexander Nevsky* (1939), and some other choral works; cantata for the 30th anniversary of the October Revolution (words by Stalin, Lenin and Marx) for orchestra, military band, accordion band, percussion and double chorus (1947).

I have to hear the Russian language echoing in my ear, I have to speak to people so that they give me back what I lack here; their songs, my songs.
Sergey Prokofiev, quoted in Wolfgang Stahr, *Notes on Piano Concertos*, 1993

---

prolation the division of the semibreve into minims in old notation, where according to the time-signature a semibreve could be equal to two minims (minor Prolation) or to three (major Prolation).

Promenade Concerts a type of popular orchestral concert, cultivated especially at the London Queen's Hall from 1895 until its destruction in 1941, under the direction of Sir Henry Wood, and continued at the Albert Hall. Malcolm Sargent was chief conductor at the London Proms 1948–67. The programmes gradually improved, until they contained most of the best orchestral music and modern novelties. A special feature is that the floor of the hall is left bare for people to stand, not to walk about, for which they have neither room nor inclination. In recent years operas and chamber music have been included in the programmes; William Glock, from 1959, then Robert Ponsonby, further improved the content of the programmes; John Drummond responsible from 1987–95. Promenade concerts were not new to London in 1895; they were started by Musard at Drury Lane in 1840 and by Jullien at CG about the same time.

Promessi sposi, I, *The Betrothed*, opera by Ponchielli (libretto by E Praga based on Manzoni's novel), produced Cremona, 30 Aug 1856. Renzo and Lucia are to marry but the wedding is interrupted by Don Rodrigo. Having sought refuge in a convent, Lucia is kidnapped by L'Innominato; she escapes, and takes holy orders. When at last she meets Renzo again her vows are dissolved and the wedding takes place.

Prométhée, *Prometheus*, open-air spectacle by Fauré (libretto by J Lorrain and A F Hérold, based on Aeschylus), produced Béziers, Arènes, 27 Aug 1900; first Paris performance Hippodrome, 5 Dec 1907.

Prometheus (Beethoven.) ◊Geschöpfe des Prometheus.

Symphonic poem by Liszt, composed 1850 as an overture to the choruses from Herder's *Prometheus*, performed Weimar, 28 Aug 1850; revised 1855, fp Brunswick, 18 Oct 1855. Opera by Orff (libretto by composer after Aeschylus) produced Stuttgart, 24 Mar 1968.

Prometheus, the Poem of Fire symphonic work for piano and orchestra by Skriabin, fp Moscow, 15 Mar 1911. The score contains a part for an instrument projecting coloured lights, called *Tastiera per luce*, which was however never perfected.

Prometheus Unbound setting of Shelley's poem for solo voices, chorus and orchestra by Parry, performed Gloucester Festival, 1880.

Prometheus Variations (Beethoven.) ◊'Eroica' Variations.

Prophète, Le opera by Meyerbeer (libretto by Scribe), produced Paris, Opéra, 16 Apr 1849. John's wedding to Berthe is thwarted by Count Oberthal, when he kidnaps John's mother, Fidès. Later John is hailed as a prophet king, and Berthe, horrified, stabs herself. Imperial troops enter John's palace and he detonates himself along with the forces of order.

Prophetess, The, or The History of Dioclesian, music by Purcell for the play adapted from Beaumont and Fletcher by Thomas Betterton, produced London, Dorset Gardens Theatre, spring 1690. Pepusch wrote new music for its revival, London, Lincoln's Inn Fields Theatre, 28 Nov 1724.

proportion the mathematical relationship between the numbers of vibrations of different notes, which are exactly in tune with each other when the ratios between these vibrations are mathematically correct, e.g. a perfect fifth stands in the relation of 2:3 in the number of vibrations of its two notes. The term proportion was also used in early music to designate the rhythmic relationships between one time-signature and another.

prose another name, chiefly French, for the sequence (in the medieval sense of an ornamental interpolation into the music of the Mass). After the 9th c. words began to be added to the sequences, and this is the reason for their being called proses, since the texts were not originally in verse.

Proserpine opera by Lully (libretto by Quinault), produced Saint-Germain, 3 Feb 1680; first Paris performance, 15 Nov 1680. Attis and Proserpina are in love, but jealous Cyane arranges for Pluto to abduct Proserpine. Attis commits suicide and Cyane confesses her plot. Mercury and Jupiter restore the couple.

Opera by Paisiello (libretto by Quinault, revised by N F Guillard), produced Paris, Opéra, 29 Mar 1803. Paisiello's only French opera.

Proske, Karl (b Gröbnig, Silesia, 11 Feb 1794; d Regensburg, 20 Dec 1861), German priest and editor. Studied medicine and practised for a time, but was ordained priest in 1826 and became attached in a musical capacity to Regensburg Cathedral. There and in Italy he made his great collection of church music entitled *Musica Divina*, four vols. pub. 1853–64.

Protschka, Josef (b Prague, 5 Feb 1946), Czech-born German tenor. After study in Cologne sang at Giessen then Saarbrücken, from 1977. Cologne Opera from 1980, notably the tenor leads in Ponnelle's Mozart cycle and as Tom Rakewell, Faust, Max and Lensky. Salzburg debut 1985, as Pisandro in the Henze/Monteverdi *Ulisse*; Vienna 1988, as Schubert's Fierrabras. London, CG, debut 1990, as Florestan; US debut in *Das Lied von der Erde* at Houston, 1991. Recordings include the Mozart and Mendelssohn Lieder (complete), *Die Schöpfung* and *Die schöne Müllerin*.

Prout, Ebenezer (b Oundle, 1 Mar 1835; d London, 5 Dec 1909), English theorist and composer. Studied piano and organ and began to make a career as organist, piano teacher, music editor and critic. In 1876 he became professor at the National Training-School for Music in London and three years later at the RAM. He wrote a number of books on harmony, counterpoint, form, orchestration, etc. and composed cantatas, symphonies, organ concertos, chamber music.

Provenzale, Francesco (b Naples, ? 1627; d Naples, 6 Sept 1704), Italian composer. Studied (?) at Naples and in 1663–74 taught at the Conservatorio Santa Maria di Loreto there. He was also *maestro di cappella* at the church of San Gennaro and in the royal chapel.

Works include operas *Il Ciro* (1653), *Xerse* (1655), *Artemisa* (1657), *Il Theseo* (1658), *Lo schiavo di sua moglie* (1671), *Difendere l'offensore* (1674); church music; nine cantatas, etc.

Prozess, Der, *The Trial*, opera by Einem (libretto by Blacher and H von Cramer, after Kafka), produced Salzburg, 17 Aug 1953. Joseph K is charged with an unspecified crime; the plot documents his feelings of helplessness and paranoia before being taken to execution.

Prudent, Émile (Racine Gauthier) (b Angoulême, 3 Feb 1817; d Paris, 14 May 1863), French pianist and composer. Having no parents, he was adopted by a piano tuner, entered the Paris Conservatory at the age of ten and afterwards had a hard struggle to make a living, but eventually made his way successfully.

Works include concerto-symphony *Les Trois Rêves* and concerto in B♭ major for piano and orchestra; piano trio; *Étude de genre* and many pieces, fantasies and transcriptions for piano.

Prunières, Henry (b Paris, 24 May 1886; d Nanterre, 11 Apr 1942), French musicologist and editor. Studied with Rolland at the Sorbonne, founded the *Revue musicale* in 1920 and was appointed editor of the complete edition of Lully's works. He wrote books on Lully, on Monteverdi, Cavalli, French and Italian opera and ballet, etc., also a history of music (unfinished).

Pruslin, Stephen (Lawrence) (b New York, 16 Apr 1940), American pianist and librettist. Studied at Princeton until 1963; studied piano with Eduard Steuermann. Moved to London 1964 and gave debut recital at the Purcell Room 1970. Librettist for Birtwistle's *Monodrama* (1967) and *Punch and Judy* (1968). Co-founded Fires of London 1970, premiered the Maxwell Davies piano sonata and collaborated with him on music for *The Devils*. Concert appearances with the London Sinfonietta, BBC SO and Royal Philharmonic.

'Prussian' Quartets a set of three string quartets by Mozart, composed 1789–90 and dedicated to the cello-playing King Frederick William II of Prussia. The quartets K575 in D, K589 in B♭, K590 in F are the first three of an intended set of six. All have prominent cello parts.

Psalms the psalms form part of the offices of the Roman Catholic Church and of the Anglican morning and evening services; in the former they are chanted in plainsong, in the latter to Chants. Psalms have also been set by composers as motets and also as concert works for solo voices, chorus and orchestra.

Psalmus Hungaricus work by Kodály for tenor, chorus and orchestra, based on the Psalm lv, fp Budapest, 19 Nov 1923.

psaltery an instrument of the dulcimer type, triangular in shape and with strings stretched across its frame harp-wise, which were played with the bare fingers or with a plectrum. It became extinct during the 17th c.

Pskovitianka, *The Maid of Pskov*, also known as *Ivan the Terrible*, opera by Rimsky-Korsakov (libretto by composer based on a play by L A Mey), produced St Petersburg, 13 Jan 1873. Revived with a new prologue-opera, *Boyarina Vera Sheloga*, Moscow, 27 Dec 1898. Ivan

Puccini *The composer Giacomo Puccini (1858–1924). One of the last great Romantic composers, Puccini also introduced 20th-century elements of realism (verismo) into his operas. Although his music was successful with the public, many critics have not been able to recognize his genius.*

the Terrible destroys Novgorod but spares nearby Pskov when he discovers his daughter Olga is there. Tucha, who has not heard of the cease-fire, leads a force against Ivan and Olga is killed in the crossfire.

Psyche opera by Locke (libretto by Shadwell), produced London, Dorset Gardens Theatre, 27 Feb 1675. Princess Psyche suffers the evil plots of her sisters Cidippe and Aglaura, who are jealous of her beauty. Venus, also jealous, arranges with Apollo for Psyche to marry a serpent, but Cupid saves her.

Psyché opera by Lully (libretto by T Corneille and B de Fontenelle), produced Paris, Opéra, 19 Apr 1678. ◊Psyche for plot synopsis.

Suite by Franck for orchestra with choral interpolations, composed 1887–88, fp Paris, Société National, 10 Mar 1888.

Puccini Italian family of musicians and opera composers of Lucca:
1. Giacomo Puccini (1712–81).
2. Antonio Puccini (1747–1832), son of 1.
3. Domenico Puccini (1771–1815), son of 2.
4. Michele Puccini (1813–64), son of 3.

Puccini, Giacomo Antonio Domenico Michele Secondo Maria (b Lucca, 23 Dec 1858; d Brussels, 29 Nov 1924), Italian composer, son of Michele ◊Puccini. Although his father died early, he was given a musical education and at the age of 19 was organist and choirmaster at the church of San Martino and had written a motet. In 1880 his mother managed with the aid of a grant from the queen to send him to the Milan Conservatory, where he studied composition first under Bazzini and later under Ponchielli. Here he wrote a *Capriccio sinfonico* for orchestra. Ponchielli urged him to take part in a competition for a one-act opera advertised by the music publisher Sonzogno, and he wrote *Le Villi*; but the prize was won by Mascagni's *Cavalleria rusticana*. *Le Villi*, however, was produced at Milan in 1884, as a result of which Ricordi commissioned him to write a second opera, *Edgar*, produced 1889. It failed but Puccini had his first great success with *Manon Lescaut* at Turin in 1893. The same city brought out *La Bohème* in 1896. His first *Verismo* opera, *Tosca* (Rome, 1900) confirmed his stature: the combination of natural melody, a sure dramatic sense, and unerring aptness of orchestral colouring has made it his most enduring piece. His successes now made him immensely

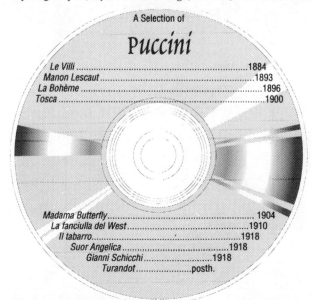

A Selection of

Puccini

Le Villi	1884
Manon Lescaut	1893
La Bohème	1896
Tosca	1900
Madama Butterfly	1904
La fanciulla del West	1910
Il tabarro	1918
Suor Angelica	1918
Gianni Schicchi	1918
Turandot	posth.

wealthy and he bought an estate at Torre del Lago near Lucca, where he lived with Elvira Bonturi, who had left her husband for him, but whom he was unable to marry until much later, when she became a widow. Their life together was marked by scandal in 1909 when their servant girl committed suicide after being accused by Elvira of a sexual relationship with Puccini. The following year *La Fanciulla del West* was produced at the Met. If this opera, and *La Rondine* (1917) represent a decline in Puccini's career, his final work, *Turandot*, unites some of the elements that most fired his imagination: physical passion, cruelty, strong sentiment and oriental flavour. In the last years of his life he suffered from cancer of the throat and died after an operation undergone at Brussels.

Works include operas *Le Villi* (1884), *Edgar* (1889), *Manon Lescaut* (1893), *La Bohème* (1896), *Tosca* (1900), *Madama Butterfly* (1904), *La fanciulla del West* (1910), *La rondine* (1917), *Trittico*; *Il tabarro*, *Suor Angelica* and *Gianni Schicchi* (1918), *Turandot* (unfinished, completed by Alfano, 1926), *Scherzo sinfonico* for orchestra (later used in *La Bohème*); cantata *Juno*; two minuets for strings; a Mass and a motet: *Inno a Roma* for chorus.

While La Bohème *is all poetry and no plot,* Tosca *is all plot and no poetry.*
Giuseppe Giacosa in a letter to Ricordi, 1896

Pugnani, Gaetano (b Turin, 27 Nov 1731; d Turin, 15 Jul 1798), Italian violinist and composer. Pupil of Somis and possibly, later, Tartini, worked for most of his life at the Turin court, and became leader of the orchestra in 1770. But he also travelled widely, visiting Paris (1754) and London (1767–70), where his first opera, *Nanetta e Lubino*, was produced in 1769. His pupils included Viotti, Bruni and Conforti.

Works include operas *Nanetta e Lubino* (1769), *Issea* (1771), *Tamas Kouli-Kan nell' India* (1772), *Aurora*, *Adone e Venere* (1784), *Achille in Scior*, *Demofoonte* (1787), *Demetrio a Rodi* (1789), etc.; oratorio *La Betulia liberata*; orchestral suite on Goethe's *Werther*; concertos, sonatas, etc. for violin and other instrumental music.

Pugno, (Stéphanie) Raoul (b Paris, 23 Jun 1852; d Moscow, 3 Jan 1914), French pianist and composer. Studied at the Paris Conservatory, where after some organist's and choirmaster's posts he became professor of harmony 1892 and of piano in 1896. He first appeared in London in 1894.

Works include operas *Ninetta* (1883), *La Sosie* (1887), *La Valet de cœur* (1888), *Le Retour d'Ulysse* (1889), *La Vocation de Marius* (1890), *La Petite Poucette* (1891), etc.; ballets *Les Papillons* (1884), *Viviane*, *Le Chevalier aux fleurs* (with Messager, 1897); fairy-plays, pantomimes and mimodrama; incidental music for d'Annunzio's *Città morte* (with Nadia Boulanger); oratorio *La Resurrection de Lazare* (1879); sonata and *Les Nuits* for piano; songs.

Pujol, Juan (b Barcelona, *c* 1573; d Barcelona, May 1626), Spanish priest and composer. He was *maestro de capilla* at Tarragona, 1593–95, Saragossa Cathedral, 1595–1612, and Barcelona, 1612–26.

Works include 13 Masses, 74 psalms, nine motets, nine Passions and other church music; secular songs, etc.

Pulcinella ballet by Stravinsky with music adapted from Pergolesi and others (choreography by Massin), produced Paris, Opéra, 15 May 1920. The settings were designed by Picasso. (Orchestral Suite performed Boston, 22 Dec 1922.)

Pullois, Jean (b ? Antwerp, *c* 1420; d 23 Aug 1478), Flemish composer. Choirmaster at Antwerp, 1444–47; failed an audition to join the Burgundian court chapel, 1446; singer at the papal chapel, 1447–68. He is important as one of the few named composers active during Dufay's middle years. Composed mainly songs but some sacred music. His single Mass cycle may really be the work of an English composer.

Punch and Judy opera in one act by Birtwistle (libretto by S Pruslin), produced Aldeburgh, 8 Jun 1968, conductor Atherton. Revised version produced London, 3 Mar 1970. Murderous Punch stabs Judy and sets out on a quest for Pretty Polly, eventually winning her favour after hanging Jack Ketch.

punto ◊stich.

Puppo, Giuseppe (b Lucca, 12 Jun 1749; d Florence, 19 Apr 1827), Italian violinist. Studied at the Naples Conservatory and made a great success as a youth; visited Paris in 1775, then Spain and England. Wrote violin concertos, studies, duets, etc.

Purcell, Daniel (b ? London, *c* 1663; d London, buried 26 Nov 1717), English organist and composer, brother of the following. He was a choirboy in the Chapel Royal and was organist at Magdalen College, Oxford, 1688–95, when he came to London and added music to his dead brother Henry's *Indian Queen*. After a busy career writing music for plays, he became organist of St Andrew's Church, Holborn, in 1713.

Works include music for *Brutus of Alba* (1696), Cibber's *Love's Last Shift* and *Love makes a Man* (1700), Durfey's *Cynthia and Endymion* (1696), Lacy's *Sawny the Scot* (based on Shakespeare's *Taming of the Shrew*, 1698), Steele's *Funeral and Tender Husband* (1705), Farquhar's *The Beaux' Stratagem* (1707), *The Inconstant* and (with Leveridge) *The Constant Couple* (1699), Vanbrugh's *The Relapse* and (with Finger) *The Pilgrim* (1701), an adaptation of Shakespeare's *Macbeth* (1704), and many others; odes for St Cecilia's Day; music for Congreve's *Judgment of Paris* (third prize in competition with Eccles, Finger and Weldon, 1700); odes; church music; sonatas for violin and bass, and for flute and bass; sonatas for trumpet and strings; cantatas for one voice.

Purcell, Henry (b London, 1659; d London, 21 Nov 1695), English composer, brother of Daniel ◊Purcell. Probably son of Thomas Purcell, musician attached to the court after the Restoration of 1660. He showed genius in early childhood and became a choirboy at the Chapel Royal (?) in 1669 under Cooke, from 1672 under Humfrey. Left in 1673 and became assistant to the keeper of the king's instruments and the following year, on Humfrey's death, pupil of Blow; tuned the organ and copied parts for Westminster Abbey; appointed Composer in Ordinary for the Violins, Sept 1677. Songs of his were pub. from the age of 16. In 1679 he succeeded Blow as organist of Westminster Abbey; the next year he wrote string fantasies in the old polyphonic style and his first theatre music for Lee's *Theodosius*. Married in (?) 1681 and became a very successful church and theatre composer; also in 1683, pub. his first instrumental sonatas. Made a speciality of welcome-songs for royalty and odes for official occasions. Wrote a coronation anthem for James II, 1685, and played

A Selection of

Purcell

Dido and Aeneas	1689
King Arthur	1691
Odes for St Cecilia's Day	1692
The Fairy Queen	1692
The Indian Queen	1695
Funeral Sentences	1695
Sonatas in four parts	*c* 1695

Songs from *Orpheus Britannicus*
Anthems and services
Chamber music

at that of William and Mary, 1689. Produced the operas *Dido and Aeneas* at a girls' school in Chelsea, 1689, and collaborated with Dryden in *King Arthur*, produced 1691. Edited the 12th edition of Playford's *Introduction to the Skill of Music* (with substantial additions), 1694. Anthem for the funeral service of Queen Mary composed 1695, the year of his own death. The huge variety, enormous quantity, and unfailing high quality of Purcell's music establish him as one of the major masters of his time and, with Elgar, the greatest of all English composers. The tercentenary of his death was marked 1995 with London productions of *The Fairy Queen* by ENO and *King Arthur* at CG.

Works include OPERAS AND QUASI-OPERAS: *Dido and Aeneas* (1689), *The Fairy Queen* (adapted from Shakespeare's *Midsummer Night's Dream*, 1692), *King Arthur* (1691), *The Prophetess*. ◊Tempest (Weldon), formerly attributed to Purcell.

INCIDENTAL MUSIC AND SONGS FOR PLAYS: Bancroft *Henry II* (1692), Beaumont and Fletcher, *Bonduca*, *The Double Marriage* (*c* 1684), Behn, *Abdelazer* (1695), Congreve, *The Double Dealer* (1693), *The Old Bachelor* (1693), Crowne, *The Married Beau*, *Regulus*, Charles Davenant, *Circe* (1690), Dryden, *Amphitryon* (1690), *Aureng-Zebe*, *Cleomenes* (1692), *Love Triumphant*, *The Spanish Friar*, *Tyrannic Love* (1694), Dryden and Howard, *The Indian Queen* (1695), Dryden and Lee, *Oedipus* (1692), Durfey, *Don Quixote* (1695), *A Fool's Preferment* (adapted from Fletcher), *The Marriage-Hater Matched* (1692), *The Richmond Heiress* (1693), *Sir Barnaby Whigg*, *The Virtuous Wife* (1694), Fletcher, *Rule a Wife and Have a Wife* (1693), Gould, *The Rival Sisters*, Lee, *The Massacre of Paris* (1690), *Sophonisba* (1685), *Theodosius*, Molière (adapted Wright), *The Female Virtuosos* (*Les Femmes savantes*), Norton, *Pausanias*, Ravenscroft, *The Canterbury Guests* (1694), Thomas Scott, *The Mock Marriage*, Settle, *Distressed Innocence*, Shadwell, *Epsom Wells* (1693), *The Libertine* (1692), Shakespeare (adapted Tate), *King Richard II*, (adapted Shadwell), *Timon of Athens* (1694), Southerne, *The Fatal Marriage* (1694), *The Maid's Last Prayer*, *Oroonoko* (adapted from Behn, 1695), *Sir Anthony Love*, *The Wives' Excuse* (1691), *The Gordian Knot Untied*.

Purcell *The composer Henry Purcell (1659–1695) as painted by John Closterman in 1695. One of the greatest of all English composers since Byrd and before Elgar, Purcell contributed to all genres, sacred and secular. He was influenced by both the French and Italian styles.*

CHORAL AND SONGS: 15 odes for voices and orchestra including *Ode for St Cecilia's Day* (1692) and *Come, ye sons of art away*, for birthday of Mary II (1694); nine welcome-songs for voices and orchestra; *Yorkshire Feast Song* for voices and orchestra; nine secular cantatas; 66 anthems; three services; 26 hymns, psalms, chants and sacred canons; 22 sacred songs; 53 catches; four three-part songs; 42 vocal duets; over 100 songs (not counting *c* 150 in the plays).

INSTRUMENTAL: 13 fantasies and four other works for strings; 22 sonatas for two violins and bass and some other misc. chamber works; eight suites (lessons) and *c* 30 other pieces for harpsichord; three or four voluntaries for organ.

Musick and poetry have ever been acknowledged Sisters, which walking hand in hand, support each other.

Henry Purcell, dedication to *Dioclesian*, 1690

Puritani di Scozia, I, *The Puritans of Scotland*, opera by Bellini (libretto by C Pepoli, based on a play by J Ancelot and X B Saintine, *Têtes rondes et cavaliers*, and farther back on Scott's *Old Mortality*), produced Paris, Théâtre Italien, 25 Jan 1835.

Pusar, Ana (b Celje, Yugoslavia, 1954), Slovenian soprano. Studied in Ljubljana and sang there from 1976, as Rosina, Desdemona, Poppea and Manon. Sang at the Berlin Komische 1979–85 and appeared as the Marschallin at the opening of the Semperoper, Dresden, 1985. Vienna Staatsoper from 1986, as Donna Anna, Arabella and Agathe. Sang Strauss's Daphne at Munich and Sieglinde at Bonn 1992. Returned to Ljubljana 1993, as Elisabeth de Valois.

Puschmann, Adam Zacharias (b Görlitz, 1532; d Breslau, 4 Apr 1600), German master-singer. Pupil of Hans Sachs at Nuremberg. He pub. in 1574 a treatise on master-singing, containing songs of his own as well as by Sachs, Behaim and others.

Purcell   *A biographical note*

Nationwide recognition of Purcell's tercentenary celebrations in 1995 came with a televised concert from Westminster Abbey on 5 March. The Abbey's organist Martin Neary conducted his Choir and the New London Consort in a programme which included the *Funeral Music for Queen Mary*, given 300 years to the day after the first performance. In 1695 the music was performed again at the Abbey only eight months later, this time at Purcell's own funeral. Although he was only 36 at his death, he had reached a respectable age for his time, having lived through both the Great Plague of 1665 and the fire of the following year. At the time of his death, Purcell had his music in no fewer than 11 stage productions in London, although he soon fell into posthumous neglect. His music enjoyed a modest revival in the 1930s and 1940s, thanks to such musician as Michael Tippett and Walter Goehr, but it was not until the recent rise of period instrument performance that Purcell has enjoyed a real restoration of fortune. Conductors such as Robert King, Christopher Hogwood and Harry Christophers have brought crisp standards of direction, aided by such singers as Emma Kirby, Catherine Bott and Michael Chance. Not normally showing themselves aware of early music, London's opera houses stirred themselves for the tercentenary. At Covent Garden, *King Arthur* was given in a spectacular production by Graham Vick, with William Christie and his Arts Florissants, even if the whole show had to be imported from Paris.

——— THE OPERA ———

I Puritani di Scozia

A three-act opera by Vincenzo Bellini based ultimately on Scott's novel *Old Mortality* about the Cavaliers and Roundheads during the English Civil War. It was first staged in 1835, and is set in Plymouth, Devon.

I. Puritan Lord Walton (bass) is warden at the fortress where Queen Henrietta (mezzo-soprano), widow of Charles I, is held prisoner. Walton's daughter Elvira (soprano) has permission to marry the Cavalier Arturo (Lord Arthur Talbot, tenor) although she is also loved by the Puritan Riccardo (Sir Richard Forth, baritone). Arturo helps Henrietta escape by dressing her in Elvira's bridal veil. Elvira is driven mad with grief at her betrayal.

II. Arturo has been condemned by Parliament but, for Elvira's sake, Riccardo agrees to save him, as long as he does not join the Royalist ranks.

III. Arturo rejoins Elvira but the sound of their reunion attracts Riccardo and his companions. The mention of the word 'death' in the sentence passed on Arturo brings Elvira to her senses. The couple are united, but the Puritan soldiers demand an execution. News arrives of the defeat of the Stuarts in the Civil War, and a general pardon is issued by Cromwell.

——— THE OPERA ———

Pushkin, Aleksandr (1790–1837), Russian poet, dramatist and novelist. Two contrasting pieces by Pushkin are great works of literature in themselves and also form the basis of the two finest Russian compositions of the 19th c.: *Eugene Onegin* and *Boris Godunov*. Dating from 1825, *Boris* is a huge historical drama, which drew an appropriate response from Mussorgsky in 1869. If the wide political panorama of Pushkin's *Boris*, within the context of a gradually unfolding personal drama, suggests the influence of Shakespeare, then the presence of Byron in the verse novel *Eugene Onegin* (1828) is even more strongly felt. The figure of the sardonic outsider attracted Tchaikovsky for his opera of 1879, and he was drawn to the vulnerable Tatiana, setting her great letter-writing scene first of all. Here, as in other works of Pushkin, a composer was inspired by the poet's fluent naturalness of language and vivid imagery (once again the comparison with Shakespeare is inevitable). Pushkin's huge range encompassed nationalist fairy tale, and his *Ruslan and Ludmilla* of 1820 was the inspiration for Glinka's opera of 1842. Rimsky-Korsakov was also attracted by Pushkin's fantasy, setting *The Tale of Tsar Saltan* (1831) in 1900 and *The Golden Cockerel* (1834) in 1909. Other major settings of Pushkin include Dargomizhsky's *Stone Guest* of 1872 (the poet's version of the Don Juan legend) and Tchaikovsky's *The Queen of Spades*, setting Pushkin's *Conte* of 1830 in 1890. The continued theme in his work of exile from society was personally familiar to Pushkin, and he was banished from Moscow for six years for political dissent. In 1837, one of the most poignant images in all his work, the duel scene in *Eugene Onegin*, was re-enacted in his own life: he was shot dead after challenging a man he suspected of infidelity with his wife.

Putnam, Ashley (b New York, 10 Aug 1952), American soprano. Debut Norfolk, VA, 1976, as Lucia; returned 1977 as Mary in Musgrave's *Mary, Queen of Scots*. NY City Opera from 1978 as Violetta, Maria Stuarda, Ophelia and Bellini's Elvira. Glyndebourne 1978, Musetta; Arabella 1984. In 1986 her Fiordiligi was seen on BBC TV, and she sang Jenůfa at CG. Other roles include Gilda, Donna Anna and Strauss's Danae.

puy, French, a competitive festival held in France in the Middle Ages by literary and music guilds, including the troubadours of the 12th c. Puys continued to the 16th c. and the most famous was that of Évreux, held annually on St Cecilia's Day (22 Nov), 1570–1614. Prizes were given and the laureate was called *roy de puy*.

Puyana, Rafael (b Bogotà, 14 Oct 1931), Colombian harpsichordist. Studied at New England Conservatory, Boston, and with Wanda Landowska. NY debut 1957; London 1966. He performs in a wide range of Baroque music and is often heard in modern works.

Pyamour, John (b before 4 Jul 1431), English composer. He was a member of the Chapel Royal, 1420–21, and of the chapel of the Duke of Bedford in 1427. Wrote church music.

Pycard French composer, represented in the Old Hall MS. His music is remarkable for its extensive use of canon. He served in John of Gaunt's household, in the 1390s.

Pygmalion acte de ballet by Rameau (libretto by B de Savot, after A H de La Motte), produced Paris, Opéra, 27 Aug 1748. Sculptor Pygmalion falls in love with his statue. After it comes to life he must teach it how to move gracefully.

Pygott, Richard (b c 1485; d ? Greenwich, 1552), English composer. He was in Wolsey's private chapel in 1517 as master of the children and in 1533 became a Gentleman of the Chapel Royal. Later he was given a corrody at Coggeshall monastery in Essex and a canonry at Tamworth, but lost some of the benefits at the dissolution of the monasteries; Henry VIII, however, and after him Edward VI, retained his services.

Works include Masses, motets, *Salve Regina*; carols, etc.

A certain Gaudentius writing of music, says that Pythagorus found its beginning in the sound of hammers and the striking of stretched strings.

Cassiodorus, *Institutiones*, AD 550–62

Pythagoras Greek 6th-c. BC philosopher. He contributed to the science of music by working out by mathematics the intervals of the scale according to the number of vibrations to each note and by helping to systematize the tetrachords.

Q

quadrille a dance originating from the figured displays of mounted squadrons at tournaments, introduced into the ballet in the 18th c., where dancers performed similar figures, and in the 19th c. passing into the ballroom for the performance of country dances, five in number and each calling for different figures and different music. Its music, like that of the Lancers, which evidently had a military origin, soon ceased to use the original country-dance tunes and was made up of arrangements of popular songs or more especially fashionable operatic tunes.

quadruple counterpoint counterpoint in which four parts are reversible. ◊triple counterpoint.

quadruplets groups of four notes occurring abnormally in music written in a time in which the regular units are divisible by three.

Quagliati, Paolo (b Chioggia, c 1555; d Rome, 16 Nov 1628), Italian composer. He was organist at the church of Santa Maria Maggiore in Rome from 1601. For the wedding of Gesualdo's daughter, Isabella, in 1623 he wrote a collection of instrumental pieces, *La sfera armoniosa*.

Works include dramatic cantata *Carro di fedeltà d'amore* (1806); motets; spiritual and secular madrigals and canzonets; organ and harpsichord works.

quail a toy instrument. ◊Toy Symphony.

If it were possible for all musicians to sing or play with the same ability and in the same taste, as a result of this lack of an agreeable variety the greater part of our enjoyment in music would be lost.
J J Quantz, *Versuch einer Anweisung die Flöte*, 1752

Quantz, Johann Joachim (b Oberscheden near Göttingen, 30 Jan 1697; d Potsdam, 12 Jul 1773), German flautist and composer. As a boy he learned several instruments, and studied composition with Zelenka in Vienna in 1717. The following year he was appointed oboist to the court of August II in Dresden and Warsaw, but later turned to the flute, studying under Buffardin. After travels in Italy, France and England he returned to Dresden, becoming first flautist to the court, until in 1741 he entered the service of Frederick II of Prussia. He was the king's flute teacher and wrote for him over 500 works for flute. His important treatise, *Versuch einer Anweisung die Flöte traversiere zu spielen*, was pub. 1752.

Works include c 300 concertos and c 200 other works for flute; hymns on poems by Gellert.

quartal harmony a harmonic theory, expounded by Yasser and others, which bases the harmonic system on the intervals of the fourth, instead of the third which decisively determines major or minor tonalities.

quarter note American = crotchet.

quarter-tones intervals half-way between a semitone. They were known to the Greeks and were apparently used in early plainsong but soon came to be abandoned and were not revived in western music until the 20th c. The chief exponent of quarter-tone music is Alois Hába; others, e.g. Bartók and Bloch, have used the device, but not systematically.

The difficult resolution, An effort of inspiration. Must it be? It must be!
Ludwig van Beethoven in a note at the start of the last movement of his Quartet in F, op. 135

---

quartet any work or musical number in a work written for four vocal or instrumental parts; more particularly a chamber work for two violins, viola and cello (string quartet) or violin, viola, cello and piano (piano quartet). The use of the word quartet without further specification usually suggests a ◊string quartet.

Quartetto Italiano Italian string quartet active 1945–86. Members were Paolo Borciani and Elisa Pegreffi (violins), Piero Farulli (viola) and Franco Rossi (cello). Played wide repertory from memory.

Quartettsatz German = 'quartet movement'; the name given to the first movement of Schubert's unfinished string quartet in C minor, composed Dec 1820 (D703) and not performed until 1 Mar 1867, in Vienna. The work was clearly intended to be completed, for Schubert wrote 41 bars of a slow movement in A♭ major

quasi Italian = 'as it were, so to speak'; a qualifying word used in directions suggesting an approximate manner of performance (e.g. *quasi allegro*) or an apparent contradiction of a time signature by the music's actual effect (e.g. *andante quasi allegro*, meaning that although the beats are moderately slow, the figuration is rapid and will give an effect of quickness). *Quasi* is also used for titles of compositions approximating to some particular style, e.g. 'quasi scherzo', Beethoven's sonatas 'quasi una fantasia' (op. 27), etc.

Quatorze Juillet, Le, *The Fourteenth of July*, play by Romain Rolland, forming part of the trilogy *Le Théâtre de la Révolution* with *Danton* and *Les Loups*, pub. and performed c 1900–02, collectively pub. 1909. It was produced in the open air, Paris, Arènes de Lutèce, 14 Jul 1936, with music by Auric, Honegger, Ibert, Koechlin, Lazarus, Milhaud and Roussel.

Quattro pezzi sacri, *Four Sacred Pieces*, four works for chorus and orchestra by Verdi: Ave Maria, Lauda alla Vergine Maria, Te Deum and Stabat Mater, composed 1888–97. The last three pieces were performed Paris, 7 Apr 1898.

Quattro rusteghi, I, *The Four Boors*, opera by Wolf-Ferrari (libretto by G Pizzolato, based on Goldoni's comedy), produced in Germany, Munich, 19 Mar 1906; in England as *The School for Fathers*, London, SW, 7 Jun 1946. Lunardo and Maurizio decide their children, Lucieta and Filipeto, should marry. Having forbidden the couple to meet before the wedding, the parents are foiled when Filipeto manages to meet Lucieta in disguise and they immediately fall in love.

quatuor French = ◊quartet.

THE OPERA

The Queen of Spades

A three-act dramatic opera by Pyotr Tchaikovsky about a compulsive gambler and his downfall. It was first staged in 1890 in St Petersburg, where the action takes place a century earlier.
I. The young officer Hermann (tenor) loves Lisa (soprano), but only from a distance because she is engaged to another. Lisa's grandmother, the countess (mezzo-soprano), is a former gambler known as the Queen of Spades. Hermann's friend Tomsky (baritone) describes how the countess came by a secret of winning at cards. Hermann goes to the countess's house, where Lisa yields to his advances.
II. At a masked ball Lisa gives Hermann a key, and he uses it to gain access to the countess's bedroom. He draws a pistol to persuade her to reveal her secret and she dies of fright. A disillusioned Lisa then sends Hermann away.
III. Alone in his room, Hermann is given the secret of the cards by the ghost of the countess: 'three . . . seven . . . ace'. Hermann is now obsessed with winning, and a distraught Lisa drowns herself. At the gambling house, Hermann plays for high stakes with Prince Eletsky, Lisa's original fiancé. Hermann wins on the first two cards but what he thinks will be the final ace turns up as the Queen of Spades. The ghost appears again as a demented Hermann goes out and drowns himself.

THE OPERA

Quatuor pour la fin du temps, *Quartet for the end of time*, work by Messiaen for piano, clarinet, violin and cello; composed 1940 in a Silesian prisoner-of-war camp. Fp 15 Jan 1941.

quaver the black note (♪) of half the time-value of a crochet or an eighth of a semibreve, symbolized by the figure 8 in time- signatures, e.g. 3–8 indicates barlengths of three quavers.

Queen Mary's Funeral Music music by Purcell for the Westminster Abbey funeral in 1695 of Mary, wife of William III; sequence includes music written three years earlier for Shadwell's play *The Libertine*. Other sections were given at Purcell's own funeral in Nov 1695.

Queen of Cornwall, The opera by Boughton (libretto Thomas Hardy's play, with alterations), produced Glastonbury, 21 Aug 1924. The subject is Tristram and Iseult.

Queen of Golconda, The, *Drottningen av Golconda*, opera by Berwald (libretto by composer after J B C Vial and E G F de Favieres); composed 1864, fp Stockholm, 3 Apr 1968. Aline, widowed Queen of Golconda, and Saint Phar meet after years of separation. Revolutionary disturbances delay only temporarily the couple's union.

Queen of Sheba ◊Königin von Saba; ◊Reine de Saba.

Queen of Spades, The, *Pikovaya Dama*, opera by Tchaikovsky (libretto by M I Tchaikovsky, Tchaikovsky's brother, based on Pushkin's story), produced St Petersburg, 19 Dec 1890. Hermann tries to find the secret of playing cards through the old Countess. She dies but her ghost reveals the winning combination to him. After rejecting Lisa, the Countess' grand-daughter, Hermann loses everything at the gambling table when his necessary ace turns out to be the queen of spades instead.

Queffélec, Anne (b Paris, 17 Jan 1948), French pianist. Studied in Paris and Vienna with Alfred Brendel and Paul Badura-Skoda. Won the Munich International Competition 1968 and has performed in concert with leading orchestras in England, Europe and the USA. Duettist with Imogen Cooper, and chamber concerts with Pierre Amoyal (violin), Augustin Dumay and the Chilingirian Quartet. Recordings include the complete solo works of Satie and Ravel.

Queler, Eve (b New York, 1 Jan 1936), American conductor. She studied at Mannes College and with Walter Susskind. Debut NY, 1967, with *Cavalleria Rusticana*. She was assistant to Julius Rudel at the NY City Opera for five years and from 1971 gave concert performances in NY of rarely heard operas, e.g. Respighi's *Belfagor*, Zandonai's *Francesca da Rimini* and Donizetti's *Parisina d'Este*. In 1977 she conducted the first US performance of Puccini's *Edgar*. Concerts with the Philadelphia Orchestra and the Montreal SO. Recorded Strauss's *Guntram*, 1985.

Querflöte German = transverse ◊flute.

Quest, The ballet by Walton (choreography by Frederick Ashton, based on Spenser's *Faery Queen*), produced London, Sadler's Wells Ballet, 1943.

Quilico, Gino (b New York, 29 Apr 1955), Canadian baritone, son of Louis ◊Quilico. After study at the University of Toronto sang in Canada from 1978; guest in Dallas, and Toronto (as Gershwin's Porgy). Paris Opéra from 1980, in operas by Gluck, Gounod and Massenet. UK debut as Puccini's Lescaut, with Scottish Opera at the 1982 Edinburgh Festival; CG from 1983, as Valentin, Marcello, Belcore, Escamillo and Posa (1989). NY Met debut 1987, as Massenet's Lescaut; Salzburg 1988, as Dandini in *Cenerentola* (also on video). Sang Don Giovanni at Buenos Aires, 1993. Recordings include Choerubus in *Les Troyens*, conducted by Charles Dutoit.

Quilico, Louis (b Montreal, 14 Jan 1929), Canadian baritone, father of Gino ◊Quilico. Studied in Rome and NY; debut City Opera, 1953. Met. 1972. European debut Spoleto, 1959, in Donizetti's *Il Duca d'Alba*; CG 1961, as Rigoletto. In 1966 he sang in the fp of Milhaud's *La mère coupable*, at Geneva.

Quilter, Roger (b Brighton, 1 Nov 1877; d London, 21 Sep 1953), English composer. Educated at Eton and studied music with Knorr at Frankfurt.

Works include opera *Julia* (produced CG, 1936), radio opera *The Blue Boar*; incidental music for Shakespeare's *As You Like It* (1922) and the children's fairy-play *Where the Rainbow ends* (1911); *Children's Overture* on nursery tunes, serenade, *Three English Dances*, for orchestra (1910); song-cycle *To Julia* (Herrick, 1906), songs to words by Shakespeare, Tennyson and others, etc.

Quinault, Jean-Baptiste (Maurice) (b Verdun, 9 Sep 1687; d Gien, 30 Aug 1745), French singer, actor and composer. Sang at the Théâtre Français in Paris 1712–18, and worked as an actor there from 1718. His compositions were almost all written for the Comédie Française. In 1733 he retired to Gien.

Works include ballet *Les Amours des déesses* (1729) and others; stage divertissements; incidental music for Molière's *Bourgeois Gentilhomme* (1716) and *La Princesse d'Élide* (1722), etc.

Quinault, Philippe (b Paris, bap. 5 Jun 1635; d Paris, 26 Nov 1688), French poet and librettist. ◊Alceste (Lully); ◊Amadis (Lully); Amadis de Gaule (J C Bach); ◊Armida (Mysliveček); ◊Armide (Gluck and Lully); ◊Atys (Lully and Piccinni); ◊Cadmus et Hermoine (Lully); ◊Festes de l'Amour (Lully); ◊Floquet (*Nouvelle Omphale* and *Alceste*); ◊Isis (Lully); ◊Lully (*Églogue de Versailles*); ◊Persée (Lully); ◊Phaéton (Lully); ◊Proserpine (Lully and Paisiello); ◊Roland (Lully and Piccinni); ◊Thésée (Lully).

Quinet, Fernand (b Charleroi, 29 Jan 1898; d Liège, 24 Oct 1971), Belgian cellist, conductor and composer. Studied at the Brussels Conservatory, where he was awarded the Belgian Prix de Rome in 1921. Later became director of the Charleroi Conservatory, and of the Liège Conservatory in 1938.

Works include *Esquisses symphoniques*, *Mouvements symphoniques* (1931) for orchestra; suite *L'École buissonière* and fantasy for string quartet, *Charade* for piano trio, suite for two clarinets and bass clarinet (1930); *Moralités non légendaires* for voice and 18 instruments (1930); viola and piano sonata; song-cycle *La Bonne Aventure* and other songs.

quint a 5⅓-ft organ stop transposing a fifth upwards; also called great quint.

quinta falsa Latin = 'false fifth'; another name for the tritone when it appears as a diminished fifth, not an augmented fourth.

quinte, French, the word is now used for the interval of the fifth, but was formerly also the name of a string instrument of the viol family, the tenor viol with five strings; but also later of the viola, another French name of which was taille.

quintet any work or musical number in a work written in five vocal or instrumental parts; more particularly a chamber work of five instruments, e.g. piano and string quartet (piano quintet) or five string instruments. ◊string quintet.

quinton, French, a 19th-c. name for a hybrid string instrument, half viol and half violin.

quintuple time music with five beats to the bar, the time-signature of which is 5–4, 5–8, etc., is said to be in quintuple time.

quintuplets groups of five notes occupying a beat or the space of a note of normal duration.

quintus Latin = 'the fifth'; the fifth part in a composition for five or more voices in early music. It was so called because its range was always equal to that of one of the other parts, so that it could not be described as *cantus*, *altus*, *tenor* or *bassus*.

quire the old English spelling of choir.

quiterne French and old English = ◊cittern.

quodlibet Latin *quod libet* = 'as it pleases'; a composition made up of a medley of tunes, usually familiar songs, in polyphonic combinations. Obrecht's *Missa diversorum tenorum* is an elaborate quodlibet, introducing the melodies of *chansons* by 15th-c. composers. A more familiar example is the quodlibet at the end of Bach's Goldberg Variations. The Spanish term for a quodlibet was *ensalada*.

quotations short passages in musical works taken from other music (*a*) by the same composer (*b*) by another, e.g.,

(*a*) Brahms, *Regenlied* in finale of G major violin sonata;

Elgar, a number of themes from earlier works in *The Music Makers*; demons' chorus from *The Dream of Gerontius* in *The Fourth of August* (as a theme for the enemy);

Mozart, 'Non più andrai' from *Figaro* in second-act finale of *Don Giovanni*;

Prokofiev, March from *The Love for Three Oranges* in ballet *Cinderella*;

Puccini, 'Mimi' theme from *La Bohème* in *Il tabarro*;

Rimsky-Korsakov, theme from *Pskovitianka* (*Ivan the Terrible*) in *The Tsar's Bride* (referring to Ivan);

Saint-Saëns, theme from *Danse macabre* in *Fossils* section of *Le Carnaval des animaux*;

Schumann, opening of *Papillons*, op. 1, in *Florestan* piece in *Carnaval*, op. 9;

Shostakovich, themes from tenth symphony and first cello concerto in eighth string quartet (1960);

Smetana, theme associated with the Vyšehrad citadel of Prague in the first symphonic poem of *Má Vlast* and referring to in the later one entitled *Vltava*;

Strauss, theme from *Guntram* in 'Childhood' section of *Tod und Verklärung*; a number of themes from earlier works in the 'Hero's Works' section of *Heldenleben* and in the dinner music in the *Bourgeois Gentilhomme* incidental music; *Ariadne auf Naxos* in *Capriccio*; transfiguration theme from *Tod und Verklärung* in *Im Abendrot* ('Last Songs');

Vaughan Williams, theme from *Hugh the Drover* in violin concerto;

Wagner, two themes from *Tristan* in *Meistersinger*, III. i; swan motive from *Lohengrin* in *Parsifal*, I; themes from *Siegfried* in *Siegfried Idyll* (some going back to a projected string quartet);

Wolf, song, 'In dem Schatten meiner Locken' from *Spanish Song-Book* in opera *Der Corregidor*, I.

(*b*) Bartók, Nazi march theme from Shostakovich's seventh symphony in *Concerto for Orchestra*; Beethoven's 'Song of Thanksgiving' in the third piano concerto (both composers had just recovered from illness);

Bax, theme from Wagner's *Tristan* in symphonic poem *Tintagel*; passage from Elgar's violin concerto, in G major string quartet dedicated to Elgar;

Beethoven, 'Notte e giorno faticar' from Mozart's *Don Giovanni* in Variations on a theme by Diabelli, op. 120;

Berg, themes from Wagner's *Tristan* and Zemlinsky's *Lyric Symphony* in Lyric Suite for string quartet; Bach chorale *Es ist genug* in

violin concerto;

Berio, scherzo from Mahler's second symphony and other items in *Sinfonia*;

Brahms, 'Batti, batti' from Mozart's *Don Giovanni* in song *Liebe und Frühling*, op. 3 no. 2; Bréville, 'Tarnhelm' motive from Wagner's *Ring* in *Portraits de Maîtres* for piano, indicating a transformation between the pieces imitating various composers;

Britten, theme from Wagner's *Tristan* in *Albert Herring*;

Charpentier, theme from Wagner's *Ring* in *Louise*, II;

Chopin, air from Rossini's *Gazza ladra* in Polonaise in B minor dedicated to Kolberg (1826);

Debussy, theme from Wagner's *Tristan* in *Golliwogg's Cake-Walk* (*Children's Corner*);

Elgar, theme from Mendelssohn's overture *Calm Sea and Prosperous Voyage* in 'Enigma' Variations (*Romance*); Chopin's G minor nocturne and Paderewski's *Polish Fantasy* for piano and orchestra in symphonic prelude *Polonia*;

Falla, opening motive from Beethoven's fifth symphony ('Fate knocking at the door') in ballet *The Three-cornered Hat*;

Fibich, various themes from Mozart's *Don Giovanni* in opera *Hedy* (based on Byron's *Don Juan*);

Křenek, Mendelssohn's *Spring Song* in incidental music for Goethe's *Triumph der Empfindsamkeit*;

Mahler, theme from Charpentier's *Louise* and Hunding's motive from Wagner's *Ring* in the first movement of the ninth symphony; prelude to scene 3 of *Boris Godunov* in *Der Einsame im Herbst* (*Das Lied von der Erde*);

Mozart, tunes from Martín y Soler's *Una cosa rara* and Sarti's *Fra due litiganti* in second act finale of *Don Giovanni*;

Mussorgsky, Handel's 'See the conquering hero' and themes by Famitsin and from Serov's opera *Rogenda* in satirical song *The Peep-Show*; sea motive from Rimsky-Korsakov's *Sadko* in song *The Classicist*;

Offenbach, 'Notte e giorno faticar' from Mozart's *Don Giovanni* in *Tales of Hoffmann*, prologue; 'Che farò' from Gluck's *Orfeo* in *Orphée aux enfers*;

Rimsky-Korsakov, themes from Mozart's Requiem in opera *Mozart and Salieri*;

Saint-Saëns, themes from overture to Offenbach's *Orphée aux enfers* in *Tortoises* section of *Le Carnaval des animaux* (because Orpheus's lute was made of tortoise-shell), also Berlioz's *Dans des Sylphes* in *Elephants* and a phrase from Rossini's *Barber of Seville* in *Fossils* in the same work;

Schumann, theme from Beethoven's *An die ferne Geliebte* in *Carnaval*, op. 9 (written while Schumann was separated from Clara Wieck); aria from Marschner's *Der Templer und die Jüdin* in finale of *Études symphoniques*, op. 13;

Shostakovich, overture from Rossini's *William Tell* and the fate motif from Wagner's *Ring*, in the 15th symphony;

Strauss, Denza's song *Funiculi, funiculá* in symphony *Aus Italien* (under the impression that it was an Italian folksong); giants' motive in Wagner's *Ring* in *Feuersnot*; Wagner's Rhinemaidens' theme in dinner music (salmon) of Strauss's *Bourgeois gentilhomme* (*Ariadne*, first version); themes by Bull, Legrenzi, Monteverdi and Peerson in *Die schweigsame Frau*; fragment from funeral march in Beethoven's 'Eroica' symphony in *Metamorphosen* for strings;

Stravinsky, waltz by Lanner (played on a barrel-organ) in ballet *Petrushka*; themes from Tchaikovsky's piano music and songs in ballet *The Fairy's Kiss/Le Baiser de la fée*;

Tchaikovsky, song from Grétry's *Richard, Cœur de Lion* in *The Queen of Spades*;

Vaughan Williams, opening theme from Debussy's *L'Après-midi d'un faune* in incidental music for Aristophanes' *Wasps*;

Wagner, *Di tanti palpiti*, from Rossini's *Tancredi*, parodied in the tailor's episode in *Meistersinger*, III.

Also numerous examples of quotations from earlier works in the music of contemporary composers, e.g. Kagel, Holloway and Stockhausen (*Beethausen, opus 1970, von Stockhoven*).

R

r the supertonic note in any key in Tonic Sol-fa notation, pronounced Ray.

Raaff, Anton (b Gelsdorf near Bonn, bap. 6 May 1714; d Munich, 28 May 1797), German tenor. Studied in Munich in Bologna, sang much in Italy as well as in Germany and Austria. From 1770 in the service of the Elector Palatine. The first Idomeneo in Mozart's opera of that name.

Rabaud, Henri (Benjamin) (b Paris, 10 Nov 1873; d Paris, 11 Sept 1949), French composer. Studied under his father, the cellist Hippolyte Rabaud (1839–1900), and with Gédalge and Massenet at the Paris Conservatory, where he gained the Prix de Rome in 1894. After his stay in Rome he visited Vienna and travelled elsewhere, and after his return to Paris he became harmony professor at the Conservatory and conductor at the Opéra. In 1920 he succeeded Fauré as director of the Conservatory, and was in turn succeeded in that post by Delvincourt in 1941.

Works include operas *La Fille de Roland* (1904), *Le Premier Glaive* (1907), *Mârouf, savetier du Caire* (1914), *L'Appel de la mer* (after Synge's *Riders to the Sea*, 1924), *Rolande et les mauvais garçons* (1934); incidental music for Shakespeare's *Merchant of Venice* and *Antony and Cleopatra* (1917); music for films *Joueurs d'échecs* and *Le Miracle des loups*; Psalm 4 for chorus; two symphonies, symphonic poem *Andromède*, *La Procession nocturne* (after Lenau's *Faust* (1899), *Le Sacrifice d'Isaac*, *La Flûte de Pan*, *Divertissement grec*, *Divertissement sur des airs russes*, *Poème sur le livre de Job*, etc., for orchestra; string quartet; songs.

Rabin, Shira (b Tel-Aviv, 1 Apr 1970), Israeli violinist. Studied at Juilliard with Dorothy DeLay. Debut concert with the Israel PO 1979 and has since toured widely with the orchestra in Europe, Israel and Canada; appearances with Henryk Szeryng and Isaac Stern in Israel and New York. US debut with the Philadelphia Orchestra under Muti, 1992; Pittsburgh Orchestra under Maazel.

Rachmaninoff ◊Rakhmaninov.

Racine, Jean (1639–1699), French poet and dramatist. ◊Andromaque (Grétry); ◊Athalie (Mendelssohn and others); ◊Boieldieu (*Athalie*); ◊Esther (Handel); ◊Fauré (*Cantique*); ◊Ifigenia in Aulide (Graun); ◊Iphigénie en Aulide (Gluck); ◊Lully (*Idylle sur la paix*); ◊Massenet (*Phèdre* incidental music); ◊Mitridate (Mozart); ◊Moreau (*Cantiques spiritueles*, *Esther* and *Athalie*); ◊Roseingrave (2) (*Phaedra and Hippolytus*); ◊Rossini (*Ermione*); ◊Saint-Saëns (*Andromaque*); ◊Vogler (*Athalie*).

rackett a double-reed instrument, also called racket, ranket or sausage bassoon. Its long tube was folded many times, so that the actual size of the instrument seemed small.

Radamisto opera by Handel (libretto by N F Haym, after Tacitus), produced London, King's Theatre, Haymarket, 27 Apr 1720. Tyrant King Tiridate lusts after Zenobia, wife of Prince Radamisto, sending armies to conquer his rival. When Zenobia opts to die with her husband rather than yield to Tiridate, news arrives of a revolt in the tyrant's army and the married couple are saved.

Radcliffe, Philip (FitzHugh) (b Godalming, 27 Apr 1905; d near Dunkirk, 2 Sept 1986), English scholar, author and composer. Educated at Charterhouse and King's College, Cambridge. University lecturer in music at Cambridge, 1947–72. His compositions include chamber music, part-songs and songs. Also wrote a book on Mendelssohn, and contributed chapters on the Scarlattis, Corelli and Vivaldi to *The Heritage of Music*.

Radford, Robert (b Nottingham, 13 May 1874; d London, 3 Mar 1933), English bass. Studied at the RAM in London and first appeared at the Norwich Festival in 1899 and in opera at CG in 1904, as the Commendatore. He sang in the *Ring* under Richter (1908) and was the first British Boris.

Radicati, Felice Alessandro (b Turin, 1775; d Bologna, 19 Mar 1820), Italian violinist and composer. Pupil of Pugnani, he toured as a violin virtuoso in Italy, France and England, then settled in Bologna in 1815 as leader of the municipal orchestra, *maestro di cappella* at San Petronio and violin professor at the Liceo Filarmonico.

Works include operas *Riccardo Cuor di Leone*, *Fedra*, *Coriolano*, *Castore e Polluce* and some others; violin concertos; violin pieces; aria.

Radino, Giovanni Maria, Italian 16th-c. organist and composer. He was organist at the church of San Giovanni di Verdara at Padua, 1592–98.

Works include madrigals for four voices; dances for harpsichord or lute.

Radnai, Miklós (b Budapest, 1 Jan 1892; d Budapest, 4 Nov 1935), Hungarian composer. Studied at Budapest and Munich, became a professor at the Budapest Conservatory, 1919–25, and then director of the Opera there.

Works include opera *The Former Lovers*; ballet *The Infanta's Birthday* (after Wilde, 1918); Hungarian Symphony, *Mosaic* suite, five poems, *Fairy Tale*, *Orcan the Hero*, for orchestra; piano trio; instrumental sonatas; piano works; songs.

Raff, (Joseph) Joachim (b Lachen, Canton Zurich, 27 May 1822; d Frankfurt, 24 Jun 1882), Swiss composer. Studied to become a schoolmaster, but took to music and in 1843 had some works pub. on Mendelssohn's recommendation. He met Liszt, and at Cologne in 1846 Mendelssohn, who invited him to become his pupil at Leipzig but died before this was done. He then wrote criticism at Cologne, studied further at Stuttgart and in 1850 settled at Weimar to be near Liszt. In 1856 he went to Wiesbaden, where he wrote incidental music for a drama by Wilhelm Genast and married his daughter Doris, an actress. In 1877 he became director of the Hoch Conservatory at Frankfurt. He is best known for such programme symphonies as *Im Walde* and *Frühlingsklänge/Voices of Spring*, suggesting Alpine imagery tinged by German Romanticism.

Works include operas *König Alfred* (1851), *Dame Kobold* (on Calderón's *Dama duende*, 1870) and others; incidental music for Genast's *Bernhard von Weimar* and other plays; oratorio *Weltende* and other choral works; 11 symphonies, including programme symphony *An das Vaterland*, *Im Walde*, *Lenore* (on Bürger's ballad),

Gelebt, gestrebt ..., In den Alpen, Frühlingsklange, Im Sommer, Zur Herbstzeit, Der Winter (unfinished), two suites, three overtures for orchestra; sinfonietta for wind instruments; concerto, suite and *Ode au printemps* for piano and orchestra, two violin concertos, cello concerto; eight string quartets, string sextets, string octet, four piano trios, two piano quartets, piano quintet; five violin and piano sonatas; numerous piano works; violin pieces.

Ragin, Derek Lee (b West Point, NY, 17 Jun 1958), American countertenor. Studied at the Oberlin Conservatory, Ohio, and made his operatic debut in Cesti's *Tito* at the 1983 Innsbruck Festival; NY Met. debut 1988, as Nirenus in *Giulio Cesare*. Salzburg Festival 1990, as Gluck's Orfeo, Britten's Oberon in St Louis 1992. Often appears in recital (Aldeburgh 1984) and has recorded Handel's Tamerlano, Flavio, Tolomeo (*Giulio Cesare*) and Saul; also Vivaldi's cantatas and Hasse's *Cleofide*.

You know, I never did find out what ragtime was.
Irving Berlin, quoted in Palmer,
All You Need is Love, 1976

---

ragtime an American form of syncopated dance music of African-American origin and coming into fashion *c* 1910, the forerunner of jazz and swing. Also title of work by Stravinsky for 11 instruments; composed 1918, fp London, 27 Apr 1920, conductor Bliss.

Raimann, Rezsö (b Veszprém, 7 May 1861; d Vienna, 26 Sept 1913), Hungarian composer, music director to Prince Esterházy at Totis Castle.
Works include operas *Enoch Arden* (after Tennyson, 1894), *Imre Kiraly* and others, operettas; incidental music to plays; piano pieces; songs.

Raimondi, Gianni (b Bologna, 13 Apr 1923), Italian tenor. He sang Ernesto at Bologna in 1948 and in 1953 Alfredo at the Stoll Theatre, London; returned in 1958 for Lord Percy in *Anna Bolena*. US debut, San Francisco, 1957; NY Met, 1965, as Edgardo, La Scala, Milan, from 1955. Other roles include Pollione, Gabriele Adorno and Pinkerton. Sang at the Hamburg Staatsoper 1969–77.

Raimondi, Ignazio (b Naples, *c* 1737; d London, 14 Jan 1813), Italian violinist and composer. After playing violin in the San Carlo opera orchestra in Naples he went to Amsterdam, where he was director of the subscription concerts *c* 1762–80, after which he settled in London.
Works include opera *La Muette* (produced Paris); programme symphony *The Adventures of Telemachus* (1777) and *The Battle* (1785); *sinfonie concertanti*; string quartets and other chamber music.

Raimondi, Pietro (b Rome, 20 Dec 1786; d Rome, 30 Oct 1853), Italian composer. Studied at the Conservatorio di Pietà de' Turchini at Naples and wandered all over Italy in great poverty until he succeeded in producing an opera at Genoa in 1807. Produced operas at Rome, Milan, Naples and in Sicily until 1824, became director of the royal theatres there until 1832, when he became professor of composition at the Palermo Conservatory. In 1852 he was appointed *maestro di cappella* at St Peter's in Rome in succession to Basili.
Works include operas *Le bizzarrie d'amore* (1807), *Il ventaglio* and 60 others including a serious and a comic one which could be performed together; 21 ballets; eight oratorios including trilogy *Giuseppe* (including *Putifar*, *Farao* and *Giacobbe* performable separately or simultaneously), Masses, Requiems, psalms and other church music, much of it in very numerous parts; vocal fugues, one in 64 parts and including others in four parts, four of which could be sung together in 16 parts.

Raimondi, Ruggero (b Bologna, 3 Oct 1941), Italian bass. He studied in Rome and made his debut at Spoleto in 1964 as Colline; sang Procida in Rome the same year and in 1965 appeared as Méphistophélès in Venice. In 1969 he sang Don Giovanni at Glyndebourne, and has become identified with this role; cinema version of the opera under Lorin Maazel. NY Met. debut 1970, as Silva. CG from 1972 (debut as Fiesco); title role in Rossini's *Mosè in Egitto*, 1994. Other roles

include Attila, Boris Godunov, Mosè and Philip II. Season 1992 as Massenet's Don Quichotte at Florence and Scarpia in a televised *Tosca* from Rome.

Raindrop Prelude Chopin's piano prelude in D♭ major, op. 28 no. 15, written at Valdemosa, Majorca, in 1838 and said to have been suggested by the dripping of raindrops from the roof; hence the continuously repeated A♭ = G♯, which is the dominant both of the main key and of the C♯ minor middle section.

Rainforth, Elizabeth (b ? 23 Nov 1814; d Bristol, 22 Sept 1877), English soprano. Studied under George Perry and T Cooke and made her first stage appearance in London in 1836, in Arne's *Artaxerxes*, and in oratorio the following year. She appeared at CG until 1843 as Susanna, the Countess and Cherubini's Lodoïska.

Rainier, Priaulx (b Howick, Natal, 3 Feb 1903; d Besse-en-Chandesse, Auvergne, 10 Oct 1986), South African composer. She studied at Cape Town and after 1920 at the RAM in London; lastly with Nadia Boulanger in Paris. In 1942 she was appointed professor at the RAM.
Works include *Archaic Songs* for chorus; ballet suite for orchestra (1950), *Sinfonia da camera* for strings (1947); *Incantation* for clarinet and orchestra; cello concerto (1964); *Aequora Lunae* for orchestra (1967); *Ploërmel* for winds and percussion (1973); violin concerto (1977), Concertante for oboe, clarinet and orchestra (1981); string quartet (1939); viola and piano sonata; piano works; songs.

Raisa, Rosa (b Bialystok, 23 May 1893; d Los Angeles, 28 Sept 1963), Polish soprano. She studied in Naples and made her debut in Parma in 1913, as Leonora in *Oberto*. Chicago, 1913–36, in operas by Mascagni and Respighi. She was admired by Toscanini, and under him at La Scala, Milan, sang Asteria in the fp of Boito's *Nerone* (1924) and the title role in the fp of *Turandot* (1926). London, CG, 1914 and 1933. Other roles included Mimi, Norma, Tosca and Wolf-Ferrari's Maliella. Opened a singing school in Chicago, 1937.

Raison, André (b before 1650; d Paris, 1719), French organist. Held posts at the Sainte-Geneviève and Jacobin churches in Paris. Composed organ music.

Raitio, Väinö (b Sortavala, 15 Apr 1891; d Helsinki, 10 Sept 1945), Finnish composer. Studied the piano with his mother, later composition with Melartin and Furuhjelm and 1916–17 with Ilyinsky in Moscow. Taught composition at Viipuri 1932–38, but settled at Helsinki and devoted himself entirely to composition.
Works include operas *Jephtha's Daughter* (1931), *Princess Cecilia* (1936) and three others; ballet *Waterspout* (1929); symphonies, ten symphonic poems; piano concerto, concerto for violin and cello (1936), Poem for cello and orchestra (1915); string quartet, piano quintet; violin and piano sonata; songs.

Rajna, Thomas (b Budapest, 21 Dec 1928), Hungarian-born British pianist and composer. Studied with Kodály at the Liszt Academy and with Howells at the RCM after moving to London in 1947. Taught at the GSMD 1963–67, senior lecturer at University of Cape Town from 1970; associate professor 1989. Has appeared widely in Europe and South Africa in Stravinsky, and works by Liszt, Skriabin and Messiaen; also soloist in his own two piano concertos (1962, 1984). Recordings include complete piano works of Stravinsky and Granados.

Rakastava, *The Lover*, three songs for male chorus a capella by Sibelius, op. 14; composed 1893, fp Helsinki, 28 Apr 1894. Version for male chorus and strings, 1894. Rewritten for strings, triangle and timpani, 1911: *The Lover, The Path of the Beloved, Good night*.

Rake's Progress, The opera by Stravinsky (libretto by W H Auden and C Kallman, based on Hogarth), produced Venice, 11 Sept 1951. Tom Rakewell inherits a fortune and leaves sweetheart Anne. Nick Shadow corrupts and ruins him, finally demanding his soul. Tom evades Nick, but loses his reason before dying.

Rakhmaninov, Sergey Vassilievich (b Oneg, Novgorod, 1 Apr 1873; d Beverly Hills, CA, 28 Mar 1943), Russian pianist and composer. Son of a captain in the Imperial Guards and descendant of a wealthy and noble family. The family fortune was gravely impaired during his childhood and his parents separated in 1882, Rakhmaninov living with his mother in St Petersburg. There he continued music lessons in

THE OPERA

The Rake's Progress

A three-act opera with Epilogue by Igor Stravinsky, based on Hogarth's eight engravings of the same name. It was first performed in Venice in 1951 with the composer conducting. It is set in England in the 18th century.

I. Tom Rakewell (tenor) loves Anne Trulove (soprano), but is lazily reluctant to accept the city job offered by her father (bass). Nick Shadow (baritone) appears with the news that Tom has inherited a fortune. Shadow agrees to be Tom's servant for a year and a day; they depart for London where Tom betrays Ann at the brothel of Mother Goose.

II. Tiring of London life, Tom agrees to marry the bearded lady, Baba the Turk (mezzo-soprano). He then goes bankrupt after investing in Shadow's fake machine for turning stones into bread. His goods are sold at auction by Sellem (tenor).

III. Shadow must now be paid for his service; revealing himself as the Devil, he claims Tom's soul. Tom defeats Shadow at cards but is condemned to insanity. At the Bedlam madhouse, he imagines he is Adonis. His Venus, Anne, arrives with her father but they can do nothing for Tom and they depart in sorrow.

THE OPERA

Rakhmaninov *The composer and pianist Sergey Rakhmaninov (1873–1943) pictured with a passage from his Second Piano Concerto. One of the greatest virtuosos of his time, he was essentially a composer for piano, taking Romantic music for the instrument to unparalleled heights.*

a desultory way until Siloti, who was his cousin, advised his mother to send him to Moscow to study under Nikolai Sverev. He went to the Moscow Conservatory and lived in Sverev's house for four years. Later he went to live with his aunt, whose daughter, Natalia Satin, was later to become his wife. He wrote the one-act opera *Aleko* while still a student, and the piano pieces op. 3, containing the popular C♯ minor prelude, at the age of 19. In 1895 he wrote his first symphony and in 1898 he was invited by the Philharmonic Society in London to appear as pianist and to conduct his orchestral fantasy *The Rock*. In 1905–06 he became conductor of the Imperial Grand Opera at Moscow and in 1909 he visited the USA for the first time, writing the third piano concerto for the occasion and playing it himself. He had by this time developed into one of the finest pianists of the time and he remained pre-eminent in that respect throughout his life.

He lived in Moscow again 1910–17 and conducted the Philhar-

monic concerts there, 1911–13. During the war of 1914–18 he played much for charity, and at the death of Skriabin, who had been his fellow-pupil under Arensky, he decided to make a tour playing that composer's works only. It was from that time on that he became a much-travelled pianist, and finding himself out of sympathy with the Revolution in Russia, he took the opportunity of a concert journey to Scandinavia in 1917 to leave his country for ever. He lived in Paris for a time and then spent most of the rest of his life in America, touring there each year from Jan to Apr and visiting Europe as pianist in Oct and Nov, spending some of the summer months at a small property he had acquired in Switzerland on the lake of Lucerne.

Rakhmaninov's reputation with the public has always been secure although until recently his frequently dark and emotional music has had a hard time with critics: the exceptionally tall Rakhmaninov was summed up by the diminutive Stravinsky as 'six and-a-half feet of sheer misery'.

Works include operas *Aleko* (1893), *The Miserly Knight* (1906), *Francesca da Rimini* (1906), and *Monna Vanna* (1907; performed Philadelphia, 1985); choral symphony, *The Bells* (Poe), for solo voices, chorus and orchestra (1913); cantata *The Spring*; *Liturgy of St John Chrysostom* (1910) and Vesper Mass; three Russian folksongs and chorus.

Four piano concertos (1890–1926) and *Rhapsody on a Theme by Paganini* for piano and orchestra (1934); three symphonies (1895, 1907, 1936), fantasy *The Rock*, *Caprice bohémien* and symphonic poem *The Isle of the Dead* (after Böcklin's picture) for orchestra (1909); *Symphonic Dances* (1940).

A Selection of

Rakhmaninov

Symphony no. 1	1895
Piano Concerto no. 2	1901
Piano Preludes	1903
Symphony no. 2	1907

Piano Concerto no. 3	1909
The Isle of the Dead	1909
The Bells	1913
Rhapsody on a Theme by Paganini	1934
Symphony no. 3	1936
Symphonic Dances	1940

Rakhmaninov   *A biographical note*

More perhaps than with many composers, Rakhmaninov's music has always required sympathetic performance to make its full effect. He suffered an early setback in this respect when his First Symphony was premiered at St Petersburg in 1897. The performance was conducted by a drunk and disorderly Alexander Glazunov, and was such a disaster as to prompt fellow composer Cesar Cui to declare that Rakhmaninov's music evoked the seven plagues of Egypt. (The first British performance of the symphony did not take place until 1964, and it soon gained some fame when the opening of the finale was used as a BBC TV signature tune.) Rakhmaninov's response to his setback was to write the Second Piano Concerto, in which he established himself as a popular concert favourite. His mastery of line and legato as a pianist was in evidence at the 1901 Moscow premiere and again eight years later in New York, when he premiered the Third Concerto. The performance was led by Walter Damrosch, and soon conductors as important as Mahler (also in New York) and Mengelberg (London) took up the work. The seal on Rakhmaninov's career as a composer and pianist was set in 1934 when he performed the refulgent Paganini *Rhapsody* at Philadelphia and New York in performances conducted by Eugene Ormandy and Bruno Walter.

Elegiac Trio for violin, cello and piano (1893), string quintet and piano trio (unpub); cello and piano sonata, two pieces for violin and piano and two for cello and piano; a dozen works for piano solo, including two sonatas, variations on themes by Chopin (1903) and Corelli (1931) and 57 smaller pieces (preludes, *Études-Tableaux*, etc.); four works for two pianos; 77 songs.

As a result of the statistical survey conducted by the Parliamentary Secretary to the Ministry of Information of Great Britain ... it is announced in London that the playing of music by Chopin and Rakhmaninov produces an increase of the munitions output from 6 to 12 per cent.
Nicolas Slonimsky, *Music Since 1900*, 1971

Rakoczy March a Hungarian national tune named after Prince Ferencz Rákócki, the leader of the revolt against Austria 1703–11. The origin of the tune is unknown. The Hungarian March in Berlioz's *Damnation of Faust* is an orchestral arrangement of it and Liszt's 15th Hungarian Rhapsody for piano is based on it. Liszt also made a symphonic arrangement for orchestra and himself transcribed this for piano duet.

Ralf, Torsten (b Malmö, 2 Jan 1901; d Stockholm, 27 Apr 1954), Swedish tenor. He studied in Berlin and made his debut in Stettin as Cavaradossi, 1930. Dresden, 1933–44; he created Apollo in Strauss's *Daphne* (1938) and sang in the 1942 fp of Sutermeister's *Die Zauberinsel* (after *The Tempest*). London, CG, 1935–39, 1948, as Lohengrin, Parsifal, Walther, Bacchus and Radames. NY Met., 1945–47. Lived in Sweden from 1948 and retired 1952.

rallentando Italian = 'slowing down'; the same direction is also expressed by *ritardando*, 'retarding'.

RAM, abbr., = Royal Academy of Music (London).

Rameau, Jean Philippe (b Dijon, bap. 25 Sept 1683; d Paris, 12 Sept 1764), French composer and theorist. A pupil of his father, who sent him to study in Italy in 1701, he worked first as an organist in Avignon (1702), Clermont-Ferrand (1702–05), Paris (1705–08), Dijon (succeeding his father as cathedral organist in 1709), Lyon (1714) and from 1715 again in Clermont-Ferrand, where he wrote his important

Rameau *The composer and theorist Jean Philippe Rameau (1683–1764) as painted by Jacques Aved. Rameau's principal compositional accomplishments lie in the fields of keyboard music and opera. His treatise on harmony, a milestone during the period, held influence long after many of its principles were outdated.*

treatise, *Traité de l'Harmonie* (pub. 1722). In the latter year he settled in Paris, where he received support from the wealthy patron La Pouplinière. He had previously pub. some harpsichord pieces, but with *Hippolyte et Aricie* (1733) he began at the age of 50 a second career as an opera composer. Though at first opposed by the adherents of Lully's operas, he quickly established himself as the leading French composer for the stage, and during the Guerre des Bouffons was the champion of French music against the Italian party. Although none of his operas has yet been staged by a major company in Britain or the USA, Rameau's reputation remains. Fringe performances and, above all, recordings reveal a composer of immense variety and resource. From the human drama of *Hippolyte et Aricie* and *Castor et Pollux* through the exotic fancy of *Les Indes Galantes* to the final haunting imagery of *Les Boréades*, Rameau's inventiveness, orchestral colour and forthright dramatic declamation are never failing. On a smaller scale, similar qualities are found in his cantatas and sacred works, chamber music (*Cinq Pièces de clavecin concert*) and 56 harpsichord pieces published in three vols. of suites (1706, 1724, 1728), including *La Vénétienne, Le Rappel des oiseaux, La Villageoise, Les Tendres Plaintes, Les Soupirs, L'Entretien des Muses, Les Cyclopes, La Triomphante, Les Tricotets* (suggesting the clicking of knitting needles wielded by the Paris mob as they gather at the guillotine), *La Poule, Les Sauvages, L'Egyptienne* and *La Dauphine*.

Works include operas and opera-ballets *Hippolyte et Aricie* (1733), *Les Indes galantes* (1735), *Castor et Pollux* (1737, revised 1754), *Les Fêtes d'Hébé* (1739), *Dardanus* (1739), *Les Fêtes de Polyhymnie* (1745), *Le Temple de la gloire, Zaïs* (1748), *Pygmalion, Les Fêtes de l'Hymen et de l'Amour* (1747), *Platée* (1751), *Naïs, Zoroastre* (1749), *Acante et Céphise* (1751), *Les Surprises de l'amour, Les Paladins, Lysis et Délie* (lost), *Daphnis et Églé, Les Sybarites, La Naissance d'Osiris* (1754), *La Princesse de Navarre* (libretto by Voltaire, 1745),

A Selection of

Rameau

Hippolyte et Aricie	1733
Les Indes galantes	1735
Castor et Pollux	1737
Dardanus	1739
Zaïs	1748
Pygmalion	1748
Naïs	1749
Zoroastre	1749
Platée	1751
Les Boréades	1764

La Guirlande (1751), *Zephire* (1757), *La créon* (1757), *Les Sybarites* (1760), *Les Paladins* (1760) and *Les Boréades* (1764, not staged until 1982).

Incidental music for *L'Endriague* and four other plays by Prion; cantatas including *Thétis* (1718), *Aquilon et Orinthie* (1719), *Orphée* (1721), *Le Berger Fidèle* (1728); *Pièces en concert* for violin or flute and harpsichord; three vols. of harpsichord pieces, some adapted from the operas.

While composing music is not the time to recall the rules which might hold our genius in bondage.
Jean-Philippe Rameau, *Le Nouveau système de musique théoretique*, 1726

Ramey, Samuel (b Colby, KS, 28 Mar 1942), American bass-baritone. Debut 1973, Zuniga with NY City Opera; other roles there have been Méphistophélès, Don Giovanni, Leporello, Donizetti's Henry VIII and Attila. Glyndebourne from 1976, as Mozart's Figaro and Nick Shadow. He has taken part in the revival of interest in Rossini's serious operas: Mosè at the Paris Opéra (1983) and Assur in a 1986 concert performance of *Semiramide* at CG. He recorded the title role in *Maometto II*. NY Met. 1984, *Rinaldo*.

Ramirez, Alejandro (b Bogota, 2 Sept 1946), Colombian tenor. Studied in Germany with Annelies Kupper and Gunther Reich. Sang widely in Germany from 1975 (Frankfurt from 1982) and made CG debut 1984, as Nemorino. Vienna Staatsoper 1985, as Alfredo, and sang in the Henze/Monteverdi *Ulisse* at the 1985 Salzburg Festival. Other roles include Don Ottavio (at Munich), Henry Morosus (La Scala), Tamino and Rodolfo (Bonn 1992).

Ramis de Pareja, Bartolome (b Baeza, c 1440; d ? Rome, after 1491), Spanish theorist and composer. He lectured at Salamanca, went to Italy, living at Bologna 1480–82 and later in Rome. He wrote a theoretical work in which he devised a way of tuning the ◊monochord and wrote church music.

Ramler, Karl Wilhelm (1725–98), German poet. J C F ◊Bach (*Tod Jesu*); K H ◊Graun (ditto); ◊Kreusser (ditto); ◊Telemann (*Tod Jesu* and *Auferstehung Christi*); ◊Veichtner (*Cephalus und Procris*); ◊Vogler (*Ino*).

Ramondon, Lewis (d ? London, c 1720), English singer and composer. He sang in opera in London until c 1711 and then made a success as a composer of songs, some pub. in *Pills to Purge Melancholy* (1714). Also contributed to various plays.

Rampal, Jean-Pierre (b Marseille, 7 Jan 1922), French flautist. He studied in Marseilles and Paris. He founded the French Wind Quintet in 1945 and the Paris Baroque ensemble in 1953. Many concert tours as soloist from 1947. He has specialized in 18th-c. music. In 1958 he pub. *Ancient Music for the Flute*.

Ramsey, Robert (b *fl*. Cambridge, c 1612; d 44), English organist and composer. He took the Mus.B. at Cambridge in 1616 and became organist and master of the children at Trinity College there, 1628–44.

Works include services, anthems, motets; madrigals, canons; dialogue between Saul and the Witch of Endor; songs, etc.

Ranczak, Hildegard (b Witkowitz in Mahren, 20 Dec 1895; d Vienna, Feb 1987), Bohemian soprano. After study in Vienna made her debut at Dusseldorf in 1919, as Pamina. Sang in Cologne and Stuttgart before becoming a member of the Munich Staatsoper in 1929; created Clairon in *Capriccio* (1942) and also sang Strauss's Zdenka, Octavian, Dyer's Wife and Aithra (*Die ägyptische Helena*). Sang in Vienna from 1931 and appeared as Salome at CG in 1937. Sang Carmen at Munich in 1950 before retiring.

Randall, John (b 26 Feb 1717; d Cambridge, 18 Mar 1799), English organist, scholar and composer. He was a choirboy under Gates at the Chapel Royal in London; organist of King's College, Cambridge, from 1743 and professor of music there in succession to Greene from 1755, taking the Mus.D. the same year; also organist of Trinity College later.

Works include church music, hymn tunes, setting of Gray's ode for the installation of the Duke of Grafton as Chancellor of the University.

Randegger, Alberto (b Trieste, 13 Apr 1832; d London, 18 Dec 1911), Italian-born conductor, singing-master and composer. Studied at Trieste with L Ricci, became known locally as a composer for the church and stage, and in the 1850s settled in London, where he became professor of singing at the RAM in 1868. He also conducted opera, orchestral and choral concerts and in 1881–1905 the triennial Norwich Festival.

Works include operas *Il lazzarone* (1852), *Bianca Capello* (1854), *The Rival Beauties* (1864); Masses and other church music; cantata *Fridolin* (1873), 150th Psalm, Funeral Anthem for the Prince Consort and other choral works; scena for tenor *The Prayer of Nature*; songs with orchestra and with piano.

Randhartinger, Benedikt (b Ruprechtshofen, Lower Austria, 27 Jul 1802; d Vienna, 22 Dec 1893), Austrian tenor, conductor and composer. Fellow-pupil of Schubert's at the Seminary in Vienna; sang in the court chapel from 1832 and in 1862 became second conductor there.

Works include opera *König Enzio*; c 20 Masses, c 600 motets; choruses; chamber music; c 400 songs.

Randle, Thomas (b Hollywood, 21 Dec 1958), American tenor. After study at UCLA sang in concert throughout Europe and the USA; Tippett *Songs of Dov* in Los Angeles and Bach's *Christmas Oratorio* in Leipzig. Opera debut as Tamino for ENO in 1988; returned as Pelléas (1990) and as Dionysus in the fp of Buller's *Bakxai* (1992). Sang in *The Fairy Queen* at Aix (1989) and appeared at Valencia as Monteverdi's Orfeo. European tour with the Peter Brook version of *Pelléas* and appeared with Netherlands Opera 1994, in the fp of Peter Schaat's *Symposion*, on the life of Tchiakovsky. Opera North and CG, 1993–94, as Robert Devereux in *Gloriana*.

Randová, Eva (b Kolin, 31 Dec 1936), Czech mezzo. She made her debut at Ostrava (1962) and joined the National Theatre, Prague, in 1968. Stuttgart from 1971, as Amneris, Eboli, Santuzza and Azucena. CG debut 1977, as Ortrud; returned for Marina and Venus. Bayreuth from 1973, as Fricka in the Chéreau *Ring*, and Kundry. Salzburg debut 1975, as Eboli under Karajan. NY Met. 1981, Fricka. Janáček's Kostelnička is one of her best roles (CG, 1986); returned to London 1994, as Kabanicha in *Kata Kabanová*; Barbican Hall 1995 in Hindemith's *Sancta Susanna*.

Rands, Bernard (b Sheffield, 2 Mar 1935), English composer. Studied at University College, Bangor, and then in Italy with Roman Vlad and Dallapiccola. He was a lecturer at Bangor (1961–70), and at York University, (1970–76). Since 1976 he has worked in the USA (Universities of California and Boston). Experienced in electronic techniques.

Works include *Refractions* for 24 performers; *Actions for Six* for flute, viola, cello, harp and two percussion players (1963), *Quartet Music* for piano quartet; *Four Compositions* for violin and piano; *Espressione IV* for two pianos; *Three Aspects* for piano; *Formants* for harp (1965); *Agenda* for orchestra (1970); *As All Get Out* for chamber ensemble (1972); *Canti del Sole* for tenor and orchestra (won 1984 Pulitzer Prize); *Ceremonial I* and *II* for orchestra (1985–86), *Serenata 85*; *Hiraeth* for cello and orchestra (1987) *Body and Shadow* for orchestra (1988), ... *in the receding mist* ... for ensemble (1988).

Rangström, Türe (b Stockholm, 30 Nov 1884; d Stockholm, 11 May 1947), Swedish conductor, critic and composer. Studied with Lindegren at Stockholm and Pfitzner at Munich, also in Berlin. He settled in Stockholm as critic in 1907 and 1922–25 conducted the Göteborg SO.

Works include *Kronbruden* (after Strindberg) and *Medeltida* (after Drachman, 1918); incidental music to Ibsen's *Brand* and Strindberg's *Till Damaskus*; four symphonies (1914–36), *August Strindberg in memoriam, Mitt land, Sang under stjärnorna*, symphonic poems *Dityramb, Ett midsommarnattstycke*, symphonic poems *Dityramb, Ett midsommarnattstycke, En höstsang, Havet sjunger*; chamber music; songs, etc.

Ranki, Dezso (b Budapest, 8 Sept 1951), Hungarian pianist. Studied in Budapest from 1964 and won the Liszt Prize 1973. Many concert performances in Europe and Russia, including Bernstein's *Age of Anxiety* Symphony at the 1975 Carinthian Festival; Salzburg debut 1984, Mozart's Concerto K450.

Rankin, Nell (b Montgomery, AL, 3 Jan 1926), American mezzo. Studied with Karin Branzell in New York and made debut at Zurich in 1949. Sang in the Verdi Requiem at La Scala (1951) and appeared at the NY Met. from 1951, as Amneris, Gutrune, Ulrica, Azucena and Marina. Sang Carmen on her CG and San Francisco debuts (1953, 1955), Cassandre in *Les Troyens* at La Scala, 1960.

Rankl, Karl (b Gaaden, 1 Oct 1898; d St Gilgen, 6 Sept 1968), Austrian conductor and composer. He studied composition privately with Schoenberg and Webern. He was an opera conductor at Beichenberg (1925–27), Königsberg (1927–28), at the Berlin Staatsoper (1928–31), Wiesbaden (1931–33), Graz (1933–37), at the German Theatre, Prague, (1937–38), where he conducted the fp of Krenek's *Karl V*), and at CG, London, (1946–51). He did much to re-establish opera in London after World War II. From 1952 to 1957 he was conductor of the Scottish National Orchestra, and in 1957 was appointed conductor of the Elizabethan Trust Opera Co. in Australia.

Works include opera *Deirdre of the Sorrows* (based on Synge's play, 1951); eight symphonies; string quartet; choruses; songs.

Ranz des Vaches a Swiss cowherds' song or alphorn signal by which the cattle are called in June from the valleys to the mountain pastures. There are many different tunes, varying according to the cantons or even districts. They are metrically very irregular and use only the natural notes of the alphorn. Versions are heard in the *William Tell* overture, the *Pastoral* symphony (link between last two movements), and the *Scène aux champs* in the *Symphonie Fantastique*.

Rape of Lucretia, The opera by Britten libretto by R Duncan, based on Livy, Shakespeare and Obey's *Viol de Lucrèce*), produced Glyndebourne, 12 Jul 1946. In ancient Rome Lucretia is reckoned to be the only chaste woman. Prince Tarquinius sets out to test this, arriving at her house and asking for a bed for the night. While Lucretia sleeps, Tarquinius appears in her bedroom and kisses her. At first Lucretia responds, believing it to be her husband, but soon she realizes the awful truth. The next morning she is overcome by shame and stabs herself.

Raphael, Günther (b Berlin, 30 Apr 1903; d Herford, 19 Oct 1960), German composer. Studied under his father, a church organist, and later with Trapp, R Kahn and others at the Berlin Hochschule für

Musik. In his early 20s he succeeded in having works pub., played by the Busch quartet, conducted by Wilhelm Furtwängler and others. Professor at the Leipzig Conservatory 1926–34, at Duisburg Conservatory 1949–53, and from 1957 at the Cologne Musikhochschule.

Works include Requiem (1928), Te Deum (1930), cantata *Vater unser* (1945); 16 motets, Psalm civ and other unaccompanied sacred choral works; five symphonies (1926–53), sinfonietta, *Theme, Variations and Rondo*, divertimento, *Smetana Suite* for orchestra; two violin concertos (1921, 1960), organ concerto (1936); chamber concerto for cello with wind and strings, much other chamber music; organ and piano works.

Rapimento di Cefalo, Il, *The Abduction of Cephalus*, opera by Caccini (libretto by G Chiabrera), produced Florence, Palazzo Vecchio, 9 Oct 1600. Aurora (Dawn) seduces Cephalus, and as a result of her preoccupation, Night remains over the world. Jupiter has Cupid find Dawn and bring her back to illuminate the Earth.

Rappresentazione di anima e di corpo, *Representation of Soul and Body*), a dramatic allegory, words by Manni, music by Emilio de' Cavalieri, produced Rome, oratory of St Philip Neri, Feb 1600.

Rapsodie espagnole, *Spanish Rhapsody*, an orchestral work by Ravel in a Spanish manner as cultivated by a typically French composer with a strong taste for and leanings towards Spanish music; composed 1907, fp Paris, 15 Mar 1908.

Raselius (originally *Rasel*), Andreas (b Hahnbach, near Amberg, Upper Palatinate, *c* 1563; d Heidelberg, 6 Jan 1602), German clergyman, theorist and composer. Studied at the Lutheran University of Heidelberg, became cantor at Regensburg, 1584–1600, and then music director to the Elector Palatine at Heidelberg. Wrote a treatise on the hexachord, set hymn and psalm tunes in five parts and composed German motets.

Rasi, Francesco (b Arezzo, 4 May 1574; d after 1620), Italian singer, poet and composer. He came of a noble family and was a pupil of Caccini at Florence. Musician at the court of Mantua, 1598–1620. He sang in the fps of Peri's *Euridice* and Caccini's *Il rapimento di Cefalo* and is believed to have created Monteverdi's Orfeo.

Works include *Musica di camera e di chiesa*; madrigals (*Dialoghi*, 1620) and opera *Ati e Cefale* (Mantua, 1617).

Raskin, Judith (b New York, 21 Jun 1928; d New York, 21 Dec 1984), American soprano. Studied in NY and in 1956 created the title role in Douglas Moore's *The Ballad of Baby Doe* (Central City, CO). Appeared with NBC TV in operas by Poulenc and Mozart and in 1959 sang Despina at the NY City Opera; Met. debut 1962, as Susanna. She sang Pamina at Glyndebourne in 1963 and in the same year appeared in the fp of Menotti's *The Labyrinth*. Well known as a recitalist and was heard in music by Monteverdi, Rameau, Purcell and Pergolesi.

Rasumovsky Quartets Beethoven's three string quartets, op. 59 in F major, E minor and C major, composed 1806 and dedicated to the Russian ambassador to Vienna, Count (later Prince) Andrey Kyrillovich Rasumovsky (1752–1836), by whose domestic quartet, led by Schuppanizigh, they were first performed. The first two quartets contain Russian themes.

rataplan French onomatopoeic = English 'rub-a-dub'; a word imitating the sound of the side-drum and used for music pieces, especially in opera, of a military-march character.

Ratcliff opera by Andreae (libretto taken from Heine's tragedy *William Ratcliff*), produced Duisburg, 25 May 1914.

Rathaus, Karol (b Tarnopol, Galacia, 16 Sept 1895; d New York, 21 Nov 1954), Polish-born American composer. Studied with Schreker in Vienna and followed him to Berlin when Schreker became director of the Hochschule für Musik, where Rathaus taught 1925–33. In 1934 he took refuge from the Nazi regime in London and later settled in USA, becoming a US citizen 1946.

Works include opera *Strange Soil* (1930); ballets *The Last Pierrot* (1927), and *Lion amoureux* (1937); incidental music to Shakespeare's *Merchant of Venice*, Gutzkow's *Uriel Acosta*, Hebbel's *Herodes und Mariamne*, etc.; choral works; three symphonies (1921–43), overture, serenade, suites, *Four Dance Pieces, Kontrapunktisches Triptychon* (1934), *Jacob's Dream, Polonaise symphonique*

Rattle *The conductor Simon Rattle. He has worked closely with the City of Birmingham Symphony Orchestra since 1980 and is renowned for his eclectic programmes, which favour music of the 20th century. In recent years his repertory has widened and he has performed 19th-century classics in his distinctive energetic style.*

for orchestra; concertino for piano and orchestra, suite for violin and orchestra, *Little Prelude* for trumpet and strings; five string quartets, two trios for violin, clarinet and piano; film music, including *The Brothers Karamazov* (1931) and *The Dictator* (1934).

Ratswahlkantate cantata by Bach (BWV 71), *Gott ist mein König*, written for the election of the town council of Mühlhausen on 4 Feb 1708, and performed on that day in St Mary's Church. Bach was at the time organist of St Blasius'.

rattle a noise-producing toy, a ratchet, occasionally used as a percussion instrument in the modern orchestra.

Rattle, Simon (b Liverpool, 19 Jan 1955), English conductor. He studied at the RAM and held various posts in Liverpool before assistant conductor with Bournemouth SO and Sinfonietta in 1975. London debut 1975, and in the following year made his US debut, with the LSO. In 1977 he conducted *The Cunning Little Vixen* at Glyndebourne (*Porgy and Bess*, 1986) and in 1983 gave the first public performance of Janáček's *Osud* in Britain; *Kátá Kabanová* at the London Coliseum, 1985. He worked with the BBC Scottish SO and RLPO 1977–80 and in 1980 became principal conductor CBSO, forging an unusually close relationship with the orchestra, and sometimes giving adventurous programmes which he would be denied in London. Principal guest conductor LA PO from 1981. US opera debut Los Angeles 1988, *Wozzeck* CG debut 1993, *The Cunning Little Vixen*. Led the CBSO at the 1993 Salzburg Festival. Season 1993/94 with Vienna PO and Philadelphia Orchestra debuts. Glyndebourne 1994, Don Giovanni. He is blessed with a telegenic personality; CBE 1987. KBE 1994.

Ratto di Proserpina, Il, *The Rape of Proserpine*, opera by Winter (libretto by L da Ponte), produced London, King's Theatre, Haymarket, 3 May 1804.

Rauchfangkehrer, Der, *The Chimney-Sweep*, Singspiel by Salieri (libretto by L von Auenbrugger), produced Vienna, Burgtheater,

30 Apr 1781. Volpino, the chimney-sweep, tricks Herr von Bär and von Wölf into giving him a dowry for fiancée Lisel. Bär and Wölf become engaged to the mother and daughter of the house.

Raupach, Christoph (b Tondern, Slesvig, 5 Jul 1686; d Stralsund, 1744), German organist and writer on music. Lived at Hamburg for a time and in 1703 became organist at Stralsund.

Raupach, Hermann Friedrich (b Stralsund, 21 Dec 1728; d St Petersburg, Dec 1788), German harpsichordist and composer, son and pupil of Christoph ◊Raupach. He was in the service of the Russian court at St Petersburg from 1755. In Paris in 1766 he met Mozart, who arranged some movements from sonatas by Raupach for piano and string orchestra.

Works include operas *Alceste* (1758) and *Good Soldiers* (performed 1780) and *Siroe* (Italian); *c* 15 ballets; violin sonatas.

Rautavaara, Einojuhani (b Helsinki, 9 Oct 1938), Finnish composer. Studied at the Sibelius Academy, at Juilliard, and with Sessions and Copland at Tanglewood. Professor at the Sibelius Academy 1976–90. His music embraces a wide variety of idioms, including neoclassicism, serialism and jazz.

Works include *The Mine* (1963), *Apollo and Marsyas* (1973), *Marjatta the Lowly Maiden* (1977), *Thomas* (1985) and *Vincent*, after the life of Van Gogh (1990). Other works include seven symphonies and concertos for cello, piano and violin.

Rautawaara, Aulikki (b Vaasa, 2 May 1906; d Helsinki, 29 Dec 1990), Finnish soprano. She studied in Helsinki and Berlin, making her debut in 1932. Sang Mozart's Countess in the inaugural production at Glyndebourne (1934) and returned until 1938 in *Figaro* and as Pamina. Appeared as the Countess at Salzburg in 1937 and sang songs by Sibelius at the 1949 Edinburgh Festival.

Rautio, Nina (b Bryamsk, 21 Sept 1957), Russian soprano. Studied in Leningrad and sang at the State Theatre there 1981–87. Bolshoi, Moscow from 1987, appearing with the company at Edinburgh and the NY Met. 1991, as Tatiana and as Oksana in *Christmas Eve* by Rimsky-Korsakov. Sang Manon Lescaut and Elisabeth de Valois at La Scala in 1992, Aida and Amelia Boccanegra at CG, 1994–95. Other roles include Lisa in *The Queen of Spades* (Opéra Bastille), Desdemona (Orange Festival), the *Forza* Leonora (Berlin Staatsoper) and Mathilde in *Guillaume Tell*.

Rauzzini, Matteo (b Camerino, 1754; d Dublin, 1791), Italian composer and singing-master. Brought out his first opera at Munich in 1772, went to England and then to Ireland, settling in Dublin as singing-master.

A Selection of

Ravel

String Quartet 1903
Shéhérazade 1903
Gaspard de la nuit 1908
Rapsodie espagnole 1908

Ma Mère L'Oye for orchestra 1912
Daphnis et Chloé 1912
Piano Trio 1914
L'Enfant et les sortilèges 1925
Piano Concerto in G 1929–31
Concerto for piano left hand 1930

Works include operas *I finti gemelli*, *L'opera nuova*, *Il rè pastore*.

Rauzzini, Venanzio (b Camerino, bap. 19 Dec 1746; d Bath, 8 Apr 1810), Italian castrato soprano and composer, brother of Matteo ◊Rauzzini. Made his operatic debut in Rome in 1765, and two years later entered the service of the court in Munich. In 1772 sang the leading role in Mozart's *Lucio Silla* in Milan, where Mozart also wrote for him the motet *Exsultate, jubilate*. In 1774 he settled in England, appearing both as a singer and opera composer. From 1778 he lived increasingly in Bath, where he taught singing and was director of the Assembly Room concerts. Among his pupils were Nancy Storace, John Braham, Mara and Michael Kelly.

Works include operas *Piramo e Tisbe* (1769), *L'ali d'amore* (1776), *L'Eroe Cinese* (1771), *Astarto*, *Creusa in Delfo* (1783), *La Regina di Golconda* (1784), *La Vestale* (1787); Requiem (1801); cantatas; Italian arias, duets, etc.; 12 string quartets and other chamber music; harpsichord sonatas.

Raval, Sebastián (b Diocese of Cartagena, Murcia, *c* 1550; d Palermo, 25 Oct 1604), Spanish composer. He went to Italy early in his career and served various patrons at (?) Naples, Urbino, Rome and Palermo. In Rome in 1593 he was challenged through his boastfulness to a contest with Nanini and Soriano, and defeated by them. His last post was that of *maestro de capilla* to the Spanish Duke of Maqueda at Palermo.

Works include motets, Lamentations; madrigals, canzonets for four voices.

There is a definite limit to the length of time a composer can go on writing in one dance rhythm. This limit is obviously reached by Ravel toward the end of La Valse *and toward the beginning of* Boléro.
Constant Lambert, *Music Ho!*, 1934

Ravel, Joseph Maurice (b Ciboure, Basses-Pyrénées, 7 Mar 1875; d Paris, 28 Dec 1937), French composer. His father was of Swiss and his mother of Basque descent. They moved to Paris the year of his birth and after some preliminary teaching he entered the Conservatory 1889, studying piano with Anthiome and later with Bériot, also theory under Pessard from 1891. He composed a good deal and in 1897 passed to Fauré's class for composition and to that of Gédalge for counterpoint. In 1899 he had an overture *Schéhérazade* (unconnected with the later song-cycle) and the *Pavane pour une infante*

Ravel *The composer Maurice Ravel (1875–1937). Along with Debussy he was the leading impressionist composer. His works are often intricately crafted; Stravinsky compared him to a Swiss watchmaker. He was an innovator of pianistic and orchestral techniques, especially when evoking exotic musical ideas.*

défunte in the original piano version performed by the Société Nationale. In 1905 his rejection by the Paris Conservatory of his Prix de Rome submission provoked a scandal which led to the resignation of the director. Two of his finest works the string quartet (1903) and *Miroirs* (1905) for piano date from the same period. In these pieces, as in others, Ravel's indebtedness to the Impressionist movement as well as a concentration on minute detail may be seen. In 1908 he set a new standard of piano writing with *Gaspard de la Nuit*.

During the next ten years he wrote some of his best works, but his first great public success came in 1911, when the Opéra-Comique brought out *L'Heure espagnole*, and the second in 1912, when Diaghilev's Russian Ballet produced *Daphnis et Chloé*, in which Ravel displays his mastery of colourful orchestration, combining instruments in a subtle, ever-changing palette.

During World War I he served in an ambulance corps at the front, but was demobilized owing to ill-health in 1917. Although physically weakened, he produced such successful post-war works as *La Valse*, depicting a Viennese ballroom at the disintegration of an era, the neo-classical *Tombeau de Couperin* and the childhood opera *L'Enfant et les sortilèges*. He was scornful of *Boléro* ('There's not a note of music in it'), but was grateful for its popular success. The last large-scale works were the piano concerto in G and concerto for piano left hand. In the 1920s he visited London more than once with great success and in 1928 he was made an Hon. D. Mus. of Oxford University. In 1933, after a car accident, he began to suffer from a kind of mental paralysis, and he died after a brain operation.

Works include opera *L'Heure espagnole* (1911); opera-ballet *L'Enfant et les sortilèges* (1925), ballet *Daphnis et Chloé* (1912) and two others arranged from piano works: *Ma Mère l'Oye* (1912) and *Adélaïde, ou Le Langage des fleurs = Valses nobles et sentimentales* (1912), also *La Valse* (composed 1919–20; fp as ballet, 1928) and two from orchestral works: *Rapsodie espagnole* for orchestra (1908), *Boléro* (1928); concerto for piano and orchestra (1929–31); piano concerto for the left hand with orchestra (1930).

CHAMBER: String quartet (1903) *Introduction et Allegro* for harp,

---

Ravel
A biographical note

Ravel was a chameleon composer who reinvented himself several times. Declaring that every composer should seek 'influences', he made sure that few national or individual trends were left untouched by his talent. An early acquaintance with Debussy, evident in *Jeux d'eau* and the string quartet, may have led to his neglect by Conservatoire authority. He later quarrelled with Debussy over which of them had priority use of Hispanic material. Ravel could at least claim a closer personal connection with Spain, and his *Rapsodie Espagnole* was an effective rejoinder to Debussy's *Ibéria*. A similar difference arose with Stravinsky over the initiator of neo-Classicism. Ravel won the argument here with *Le Tombeau de Couperin* (1917), which appeared three years before *Pulcinella*. Classical Greece had been visited five years earlier still in *Daphnis et Chloé*. The instrumental virtuosity of which the ballet was such a startling showcase was to find an outlet in many other works, from the Lisztian panáche of *Gaspard de la nuit*, through the Paganini-inspired exhibitionism of *Tzigane*, to the beguiling fusion of Gershwin and Mozart in the G major concerto.

flute, clarinet and string quartet, (1905), piano trio in A minor (1914); sonata for violin and cello (1922), sonata and *Tzigane* for violin and piano.

PIANO: 15 piano works including *Menuet antique*, *Pavane pour une infante défunte* (1899), *Jeux d'eau* (1901), five *Miroirs* (1905), *Sonatine*, (1905), *Gaspard de la nuit* (three pieces after Louis Bertrand's prose poems, 1908), suite *Le Tombeau de Couperin* (1917); suite *Ma Mère l'Oye* for piano duet.

SONGS: 29 songs including cycles *Shéhérazade* (1903), *Cinq Mélodies populaires grecques* (1906), *Histoires naturelles* (1906); *Trois Poèmes de Mallarmé* for voice, two flutes, two clarinets, string quartet and piano (1913); *Chansons madécasses* for voice, flute, cello and piano (1926); *Don Quichotte à Dulcinée* (after Cervantes) for baritone and small orchestra (1933); three part-songs.

I hope I may be forgiven, that I have not made my opera unnatural, like those in vogue, for I have no recitative.

John Gay, preface to *The Beggar's Opera*, 1728

Ravenscroft, Thomas (b *c* 1582; d ? London, *c* 1633), English composer. He was a chorister at St Paul's Cathedral under Edward Pearce, took the Mus.B. at Cambridge in 1607 and in 1618–22 was music master at Christ's Hospital.

Works include anthems, 48 hymn-tune settings in his Psalter containing 100; madrigals, some of the four-part songs *The Pleasures of five usuall Recreations* in his treatise on notation *A Briefe Discourse* (1614) are by himself; some of the rounds and catches in the collections *Pammelia* (1609), *Deuteromelia* (1609) and *Melismata* (16.1) are probably of his own composing.

Rawnsley, John (b Colne, 14 Dec 1949), English baritone. Studied at the RNCM and made debut in *Der Freischültz* with GTO 1975; Masetto at Glyndebourne, 1977, returning as Marcello and Rossini's Figaro. Sang Mozart's Figaro with WNO 1977 and has appeared with ENO from 1982 as Amonasro, and Rigoletto in Jonathan Miller's production of the opera. La Scala 1987, as Tonio; other roles include Macbeth, Papageno, Boccanegra and Don Alfonso.

Rawsthorne, Alan (b Haslingden, Lancs., 2 May 1905; d Cambridge, 24 Jul 1971), English composer. He studied dentistry at first but turned to music at the age of 20 and in 1926–29 studied at the RMCM. In 1932–34 he taught at Dartington Hall, Totnes; but settled in London in 1935 and married the violinist Jessie Hinchliffe. In 1938–39 he had works performed at the ISCM festivals in London and Warsaw.

Works include ORCHESTRAL: ballet *Mme Chrysanthème* (after Loti, 1955); incidental music for Shakespeare's *King Lear*; film music for *Burma Victory*, *The Captive Heart* and Army films; three symphonies (1950, 1959, 1964), *Symphonic Studies*, overture *Street Corner* and fantasy-overture *Cortèges* for orchestra; two piano concertos, two violin concertos (1948, 1956), concerto for clarinet and strings, cello concerto (1965).

CHAMBER AND VOCAL: two string quartets (1954, 1964), Theme and Variations for string quartet (1939), piano quintet; viola and piano sonata, Theme and Variations for two violins; four Bagatelles for piano; *The Creel* suite for piano duet based on Izaak Walton's *Compleat Angler*; songs *The Enemy Speaks* (C Day Lewis), *Away Delights* and *God Lyaeus* (John Fletcher), *Three French Nursery Songs*.

Ray the name for the Supertonic note in any key in Tonic Sol-fa, so pronounced, but in notation represented by the symbol *r*.

Rayam, Curtis (b Belleville, FL, 4 Feb 1951), American tenor. Studied in Miami and made debut there 1971, in *Manon Lescaut*. European debut at Wexford 1976, in *Giovanna d'Arco*, returning as Wilhelm Meister in *Mignon* by Thomas. Boston 1979, as Olympion in the US fp of *The Ice Break*, La Scala 1985 and 1988, in *Alcina* and Jommelli's *Fetonte*. Sang Arnalta in *Poppea* at the 1993 Schwetzingen Festival.

Raybould, Clarence (b Birmingham, 28 Jun 1886; d Bideford, 27 Mar 1972), English conductor. After study at Birmingham University he assisted Boughton at the early Glastonbury Festivals and later worked for the Beecham Opera Company and BNOC. Conducted the BBC SO from 1936, leading the UK fps (concert) of Hindemith's *Cardillac* (1936) and *Mathis der Maler* (1939). Conducted the National Youth Orchestra of Wales, 1945–66.

Raymonda ballet by Glazunov (choreography by Marius Petipa), produced St Petersburg, Maryinsky Theatre, 19 Jan 1898.

Raymond ou Le Secret de la Reine, *Raymmond, or The Queen's Secret*, opera by A Thomas (libretto by A de Leuven and J B Rosier), produced Paris, Opéra-Comique, 5 Jun 1851.

'Razor' Quartet, *Rasiermesser*, nickname of Haydn's string quartet in F minor, op. 55, no. 2, composed 1788, so called because Haydn is said to have offered the publisher Bland his best quartet in return for a good razor.

RCM, abbr., = Royal College of Music (London).

Re the old name for the note D in Solmization, still used in Latin countries, and in Tonic Sol-fa notation the Supertonic in any key, represented by the symbol *r*, pronounced Ray.

Read, Gardner (b Evanston, IL, 2 Jan 1913), American composer. Studied at the Eastman School, with Pizzetti in Italy and Copland at Tanglewood. Professor at Boston University School for the Arts, 1948–78. Works include opera *Villon* (1967), four symphonies, cello concerto (1945), piano concerto (1977), piano quintet (1945), and other chamber music; organ and piano pieces.

realism (1) strictly realistic representation in music is not easily attainable. Examples are the anvils in Wagner's *Rheingold*, the sheep and wind machine in R Strauss's *Don Quixote* and the nightingale (gramophone record of the bird's song) in Respighi's *Pini di Roma*. Imitations of bells, birds, etc. are very frequent, but usually the more musical they are the less they approach realism.

(2) More generally, a realistic style of Italian opera is known as *Verismo*, in which plots draw away from elaborate traditional mythological or historical subjects, favouring simpler contemporary themes instead.

realization the writing out or playing at sight of the harmony from a ◊thorough-bass; may also involve the preparation for performance of uncompleted or sparsely written score, e.g. Friedrich Cerha's version of Act 3 of Berg's *Lulu*, or Raymond Leppard's popular and imaginative versions of Venetian opera.

In the music of the 18th c. and earlier continuo lines were written in a shorthand that needs realization, often taking account of extremely refined skills cultivated in the Baroque era. Up to the end of the 18th c. many works were written in the expectation that the soloists would improvise and embellish, often quite elaborately. Before about 1700 composers often do not specify the ensembles to be used, and it can be a complex business devising an ensemble appropriate to the style and techniques of the music. Beyond that, there could be a good argument for believing that an historically accurate reconstruction would be insufficient for present-day audiences; and there is a considerable history – going back to the early 19th c. – of recasting earlier works to make them more acceptable to later conditions.

rebab or rebec(k) an early string instrument of violin type of Arab origin, the ancestor of the violin family, though its shape was more like that of the mandolin, which is probably one of its descendants. It had three gut strings and was played with a bow. In France it survived until the 18th c., but only as a street instrument.

Rebel French family of musicians:

1. Jean-Féry Rebel (b Paris, bap. 18 Apr 1666; d Paris, 2 Jan 1747), violinist and composer. Pupil of Lully, entered the Opéra orchestra as a violinist *c* 1700 and produced his first opera there in 1703. It failed, but a violin solo, *Le Caprice*, was so successful that it was long afterwards used as a test piece for ballet dancers. He then wrote similar pieces for a number of ballets, became one of the 24 violins at court in 1717 and chamber musician to the king in 1720.

Works include opera *Ulysse* (1703); ballet pieces for violin; violin sonatas.

2. **Anne-Renée Rebel** (b Paris, bap. 6 Dec 1663; d Versailles, 5 May 1722), singer, sister of 1. Appeared in stage pieces at court from the age of 11, became one of the best singers there and married Lalande in 1684.

François Rebel R. (b Paris, 19 Jun 1701; d Paris, 7 Nov 1775), violinist and composer, son of 1. A pupil of his father, he entered the Opéra orchestra at the age of 13, where he met Francœur, with whom he was to collaborate extensively. Three years later he became a member of the 24 Violons du Roi. In 1723 he went with Francœur to Prague for the coronation of Charles VI. They were joint leaders of the Opéra 1733–43, and directors 1757–67, when they were succeeded by Berton and Trial.

Pyrame et Thisbé (1726), *Tarsis et Zélie, Scanderbeg* (1755), *Les Augustales* (1744), *Le Retour du roi, Zélindor* (1745), *Le Trophée, Ismène* (1747), *Les Génies tutélaires, Le Prince de Noisy* (1749), *Ballet de la Paix* (all with Francœur), *Pastorale héroïque* (1730); Te Deum, De Profundis, cantatas.

Rebelo (or *Rebello*), João Soares (or João Lourenço) (b Caminha, 1609; d S Amaro, near Lisbon, 16 Nov 1661), Portuguese composer. A fellow-student of King John IV, who promoted him on his accession.

Works include psalms, Magnificat, Lamentations, Miserere, St Matthew Passion, Requiem etc.

Reber, Napoléon-Henri (b Mulhouse, 21 Oct 1807; d Paris, 24 Nov 1880), French composer. Studied at the Paris Conservatory with Lesueur and others. He was appointed professor of harmony there in 1851 and of composition in 1862 in succession to Halévy.

Works include operas *La Nuit de Noël* (1848), *Le Père Gaillard* (1852), *Les Papillotes de M Benoît* (1853), *Les Dames capitaines* (1857); second act of ballet *Le Diable amoureux*; cantata *Roland* (1887); four symphonies (1858), overtures to unpublished operas *Le Ménétrier à la cour* and *Naïm*; three string quartets, string quintet, piano quartet, seven piano trios; duets for violin and piano; piano pieces and duets.

Rebhuhn, Paul (b Waidhofen, c 1500; d Ölsnitz, after 10 May 1546), German poet and composer. Wrote dramas, *Susanna* (1536) and others, for which he wrote his own incidental music.

Rebikov, Vladimir Ivanovich (b Krasnoiarsk, 31 May 1866; d Yalta, 4 Aug 1920), Russian composer. Studied at Moscow and Berlin and later settled in the south of Russia and founded music societies at Odessa and Kishinev.

Works include operas and dramatic scenes *The Storm* (1894), *The Christmas Tree* (1903), *Thea, The Woman with the Dagger* (based on Schnitzler's play, 1911), *Alpha and Omega* (1911), *The Abyss* (after Andreiev), *Narcissus* (after Ovid's *Metamorphoses*, 1913), *Fables* (after Krilov); ballet *Snow-White*; suites for orchestra and string orchestra; numerous sets of piano pieces including *Rêveries d'automne* (1897), *Mélomimiques, Aspirer et attendre, Chansons blanches* (on the white keys).

recapitulation ◊sonata.

Re Cervo, Il, *The Stag King*, revision made in 1962 by Henze of his 1955 opera ◊*König Hirsch*; fp Kassel, 10 Mar 1963.

recherché French = 'searched out'; the French equivalent of *ricercato*, from which the ricercare is derived, Beethoven still used this old term, as meaning strict fugal writing, in his *Great Fugue* for string quartet, op. 133, which he called a fugue 'tantôt libre, tantôt recherchée'.

récit, French, in the 17th c. a term for an accompanying solo, such as a vocal aria, an organ piece with a solo stop, etc. Also = swell organ.

recital a musical performance, usually with a misc. programme, given by a single performer or by one singing or playing an instrument with a piano accompanist.

recitative declamation in singing, with fixed notes but without definite metre or time, except where this is imposed by an orchestral accomp. Although the time is free, recitative is generally written by convention in 4–4 time, with bar-lines. There are, broadly speaking, two kinds of recitative:

recitativo accompagnato or *stromentato*, a type of recitative accompanied by the orchestra *Recitativo accompagnato* served to modulate to or near the key of the set musical number, usually an aria,

that followed it, and also to give the singer an opportunity for dramatic declamation, aided and abetted by the orchestra.

recitativo secco, a 19th-c. term for a type of recitative accompanied by a keyboard instrument, played from figured bass. Its chief function was to advance the action and to facilitate dialogue. It also served to modulate from the key of one set musical number to the next.

recitativo stromentato Italian = 'instrumentated recitative'; another term for *recitativo accompagnato*, though a distinction was sometimes made between *recitativo accompagnato*, with a plain orchestral accompaniment, and *recitativo stromentato* with a more independent instrumental participation. ◊recitative.

It is as easy as lying: govern these ventages with your finger and thumb, give it breath with your mouth, and it will discourse most eloquent music.
William Shakespeare, on playing the recorder, in *Hamlet*, Act 3, Scene 2, line 379

---

recorder a woodwind instrument, also known formerly as the English flute. Unlike the flute it is held vertically and blown into through a mouthpiece in which the air is diverted by an obstructive block called the 'fipple' and produces a milder tone than that of the flute. Recorders are made in five different sizes from high treble (sopranino) to bass. In modern times the recorder has been revived, mainly for amateur performances, especially in England and Germany; but it has also engaged the attention of professionals, and modern works have been written for it. In the early 18th c. *flauto* by itself always means recorder.

recte et retro Latin = 'right way and backwards'; a form of canon, also called, in Italian, *al rovescio*, in which a second entry brings in the tune sung or played backwards. Recte et retro is similar to ◊cancrizans.

Redemption, The English oratorio by Gounod (words compiled by the composer), produced Birmingham Festival, 1882.

Redford, John (d London, Nov 1547), English organist, composer and playwright. He was a vicar-choral at St Paul's Cathedral in 1534, when he signed an acknowledgement of Henry VIII's supremacy, and probably succeeded Thomas Hickman as Almoner and Master of the Choristers there in the same year. His duties certainly included the playing of the organ, although the post of organist was not officially recognized at that date. He also supervised the production of choirboy plays with music.

He wrote a large amount of organ music for the liturgy, a few Latin vocal works, and a play, *Wyt and Science*.

Redi, Tommaso (b Siena, c 1675; d Montelupone near Loreto, 20 Jul 1738), Italian composer. Appointed *maestro di cappella* of the church of the Santa Casa at Loreto in 1731. In 1733 he had a dispute with Martini of Bologna about the solution of a canon by Animuccia, which was settled by Pacchioni and Pitoni in Martini's favour.

Works include Requiem (1713), Masses and other church music.

Redlich, Hans (Ferdinand) (b Vienna, 11 Feb 1903; d Manchester, 27 Nov 1968), Austrian-born British musicologist. Studied at the Universities of Vienna, Munich and Frankfurt. In 1925–29 he was opera conductor at Mainz, but in 1939 he took refuge in England. From 1955 to 1962 he was lecturer at Edinburgh University and in 1962 was appointed professor at Manchester University. He specialized in Monteverdi, several of whose works he edited, including the *Vespers* of 1610 and *L'Incoronazione di Poppea*, and on whom he wrote two books (1932 and 1949, English edition 1952). He also wrote on modern music including a book on Alban Berg. Also composed.

redoute, French, used also in German, and derived from Italian *ridotto*, a kind of public ball, particularly in the 18th c., but carried on into the 19th in Austria and Germany where dancers gathered haphazardly from all classes of society, usually at assembly halls called *Redoutensäle* in Germany. Composers of note, especially in Vienna, often wrote dances for redoutes.

réduction, French, an arrangement, especially from a complex to a simpler score, e.g. an opera 'reduced' to a vocal score or an orchestral work arranged for piano.

Reece, Arley (b Yoakum, TX, 27 Aug 1945), American tenor. Studied at the Manhattan School of Music and sang in *Die Königin von Saba* at Carnegie Hall, 1970. Appeared with regional companies in the USA and made European debut at Wexford in 1973, in *The Gambler* by Prokofiev. New York City Opera debut 1974, as Bacchus. Has sung throughout Europe in operas by Berg, Weber, Wagner and Janáček; Warsaw 1989–90, in cycles of the *Ring*. Other roles include Lohengrin, Calaf, Otello and Manrico.

Elgar loved his rivers ... one could almost label the movements in the Violin Concerto, The Severn, The Thames and The Wye, for they seem to flow through all his music.

W H Reed, *The Listener*, 1937

Reed, W(illiam) H(enry) (b Frome, Somerset, 29 Jul 1876; d Dumfries, 2 Jul 1942), English violinist and composer. Studied violin with Sauret and composition with F Corder and Prout at the RAM in London. He joined the LSO on its foundation, 1904 and became its leader 1912; also violin professor at the RCM. He took part in the fps of Elgar's violin sonata, string quartet and piano quintet and wrote two books on Elgar.

Works include symphonic poems *The Lincoln Imp* and *Aesop's Fables*, two *Somerset Idylls* for small orchestra, symphony and variations for string orchestra; concerto in A minor and rhapsody for violin and orchestra; chamber music.

reeds the tongues attached to one end of a tube which, when vibrating, produce the tone of certain woodwind instruments and of organ pipes (in the latter case made of brass); reeds are dependent on air passing across the tip of the tongue in order to initiate vibration. These instruments use so-called 'beating reeds', single for clarinets, saxophones and organ pipes and double for oboes, bassoons and bagpipes. There are also 'free reeds', used in harmoniums and instruments of the concertina and mouth- organ type.

reel a Scottish, Irish and Scandinavian dance, either of Celtic or Scandinavian origin. It is performed with the dancers standing face to face and the music is in quick 2–4 or 4–4, occasionally 6–8, time and divided into regular eight-bar phrases. A musical characteristic of many reels is a drop into the triad of the subdominant unprepared by modulation.

Reese, Gustave (b New York, 29 Nov 1899; d Berkeley, CA 7 Sept 1977), American musicologist. Studied at NY University and became lecturer in music there in 1927 and professor in 1955. He was associate editor of *The Music Quarterly* and its editor on the death of Carl Engel in 1944, but resigned in 1945. His work includes books on *Music in the Middle Ages* and *Music in the Renaissance*.

Reeve, William (b London, 1757; d London, 22 Jun 1815), English composer. Studied with Richardson, the organist at St James's Church, Westminster, and was organist at Totnes, Devon, 1781–83. After various engagements at London theatres, he joined the Covent Garden chorus, and there was asked to complete the ballet-pantomime *Oscar and Malvina* (after Ossian) left unfinished by Shield in 1791 on account of differences with the management. He then became composer at CG and in 1802 part-owner of Sadler's Wells Theatre. In one of his more popular pieces, *The Caravan* (1803), a child was rescued from a tank of water by a well-trained dog; the music of his theatre pieces failed to gain as much attention.

Works include pieces for the stage, *The Apparition* (1794), *Merry Sherwood* (1795), *Harlequin and Oberon* (1796), *Harlequin and Quixote* (after Cervantes), *Joan of Arc* (1798), *Paul and Virginia* (with Mazzinghi, based on Saint-Pierre, 1800), *Rokeby Castle* (1813) and many others (some with Braham, Davy, Mazzinghi or Moorehead); music for Sadler's Wells pantomimes.

Reeves, (John) Sims (b Woolwich, 26 Sept 1818; d Worthing, 25 Oct 1900), English tenor. Learnt music from his father, a musician in the Royal Artillery, studied singing and made his first stage appearance at Newcastle-upon-Tyne, as a baritone. After further study, including Paris and Milan, he made his debut there as Edgardo and first London appearance, 1847. He sang Faust in the oratorio by Berlioz and in the opera by Gounod. Well known in *Messiah* and *St Matthew Passion*.

Refice, Licinio (b Patrica, Rome, 12 Feb 1883; d Rio de Janeiro, 11 Sept 1954), Italian composer. He became professor of church music at the Scuola Pontifica in Rome in 1910 and in 1911 conductor at the church of Santa Maria Maggiore. His two operas combined religious sentiments with post-*verismo* Romantic expression and were promoted by the Vatican.

Works include operas *Cecilia* (1934) and *Margherita da Cortona* (1938); 40 Masses, motets, Requiem, *Stabat Mater* and other church music, two oratorios, three sacred cantatas, three choral symphonies, poems.

'Reformation' Symphony Mendelssohn's fifth symphony, op. 107, in D minor, composed 1830 for the tercentenary of the Augsburg Conference. It was not performed there owing to Roman Catholic opposition, but produced Berlin, Nov 1832.

refrain, from French, a recurrent strain in a song, returning with the same words at the beginning, middle or end of each verse with music which may or may not be derived from the first strain.

regal a small portable reed organ said to have been invented about 1460 by Heinrich Traxdorff of Nuremberg.

Reger, Max (Johann Baptist Joseph Maximilian) (b Brand, Bavaria, 19 Mar 1873; d Leipzig, 11 May 1916), German composer, organist and pianist. First learnt music from his mother and was so precocious that at the age of 13 he became organist at the Catholic church of Weiden in Bavaria, where his parents had moved in 1874. After three years there Reimann was consulted about his gifts and invited him to become his pupil at Sondershausen. Reger went there in 1890 and the next year followed his master to Wiesbaden, where he soon became a teacher at the Conservatory. A period divided between hard work and dissipation led to a serious breakdown, and he lived with his parents at Weiden again 1899–1901, writing vast quantities of music, including many more pieces for organ. In 1901 he went to Munich in the hope of making his way as a composer, but posing as a progressive while being in reality a conservative, he made enemies all round and had some success only with his piano playing. The *Sinfonietta* for orchestra was a failure at its Berlin premiere although it is now recognized as one of his most attractive works. He began to tour Germany and

A Selection of

Reger

Variations and Fugue on a Theme of Beethoven 1904
Variations and Fugue on a Theme of J.A. Hiller...............1907
Piano Concerto...1910
Romantic Suite..1912

Ballet Suite...1913
Böcklin Tone Poems...1913
Introduction, Passacaglia and Fugue for organ 1913
Variations and Fugue on a Theme of Telemann 1914
Variations and Fugue on a Theme of Mozart...1914
Requiem...1915

also visited Prague and Vienna, and gradually he made his work known; he also made a reputation as a remarkable composition teacher. In 1907 he settled at Leipzig as music director to the University and professor at the Conservatory, soon resigning the former post as uncongenial, but retaining the latter for the rest of his life. In 1911 he became conductor of the ducal orchestra at Meiningen, with which he went on tour, but this came to an end in 1914, when he went to live at Jena, travelling to Leipzig each week to carry out his duties at the Conservatory.

Reger was a master of counterpoint, integrating 19th-c. chromatic developments into his works. A master of the fugue, with the ability to control tightly the form and harmonic direction of his compositions, Reger is sometimes regarded as the greatest composer for organ since J S Bach.

Works include CHORAL AND ORCHESTRAL: *Gesang der Verklärten* (1903) and Psalm c (1909) for chorus and orchestra; sinfonietta (1905), serenade (1906), variations on themes by J A Hiller (1907) and by Mozart (1914), Symphonic Prologue to a Tragedy (1908), Comedy Overture, Concerto in the Old Style (1912), Romantic Suite (1912), four tone-poems on pictures by Böcklin for orchestra (1913); piano concerto (1910), violin concerto (1908), two romances for violin and orchestra.

CHAMBER: five string quartets (1900–11), string sextet (1910), clarinet quintet, two piano quartets, string trio, two piano trios, piano quintet; seven violin and piano sonatas, four cello and piano sonatas, three clarinet and piano sonatas.

ORGAN: two sonatas, two suites, Fantasy and Fugue on B.A.C.H., Variations and Fugue on original theme, chorale preludes, preludes and fugues, Introduction, Passacaglia and Fugue, Symphonic Fantasy and Fugue, etc. for organ.

PIANO AND SONGS: Introduction, Passacaglia and Fugue for two pianos (1906); two sonatas, Variations and Fugue on theme by Bach (1904) and numerous smaller works for piano, piano duets; many songs including) *Schlichte Weisen*; part-songs.

Reggio, Pietro (b Genoa, bap. ? 6 Jul 1632; d London, 23 Jul 1685), Italian singer, composer and lutenist. In the service of Queen Christina of Sweden in Rome; later settled at Oxford, where he pub. *A Treatise to sing well any Song whatsoever*, 1677. Wrote motets, song for Shadwell's adaptation of Shakespeare's *Tempest* (1674), songs, duets.

Regino of Prüm (b ? Altrip, near Ludwigshafen, c 842; d Trier, 915),

Benedictine monk and music theorist. He was abbot of Prüm, 892–99. He was (?) the first to arrange antiphons and responsories according to their mode in a *tonarius*.

Regis, Jean (b c 1430; d Soignies, c 1495), Flemish composer. He was choirmaster at Antwerp Cathedral and was Dufay's secretary at Cambrai in the 1440s. He went c 1451 to Soignies, where he remained.

Wrote two Masses, including one on *L'Homme armé*, songs in parts, eight motets, etc.

register a certain set of pipes brought into action in organ playing to produce a particular kind of tone and dynamics; also the different parts of the range of the human voice according to the manner, or supposed manner, of its production as 'head register' or 'chest register'.

Your reed-man is a dab at stirring ye.
Thomas Hardy, *Under the Greenwood Tree*, 1872

---

registration the use of the organ stops by means of which the qualities and power of the instrument, over which the manuals and pedals have no dynamic control, can be altered according to the composer's prescription or the performer's skill and taste.

Regnart, François (b Douai, c 1540; d c 1600), Flemish composer. Learnt music at Tournai Cathedral and studied at Douai University.

Works include motets; *chansons*; *Poésies de Ronsard et autres* for four–five voices.

Regnart, Jacques (b Douai, c 1539; d Prague, 16 Oct 1599), Flemish composer, brother of François ◊Regnart. Went to Vienna and Prague as a pupil of the Imperial chapel at an early age, became a tenor there in the 1560s, and in the 1570s choirmaster and vice-*Kapellmeister*. In 1585–96 he was in the service of the Archduke Ferdinand at Innsbruck, but lived in Prague for the last five years of his life.

Works include 37 Masses, 195 motets; *canzone italiane* and German songs for five voices, etc.

There were two other brothers, Charles and Paschasius, who contributed motets to a collection in which François and Jacques also appeared, edited by a fifth brother, Augustin, a canon at Lille.

Rehfuss, Heinz (Julius) (b Frankfurt, 25 May 1917; d Rochester, NY, 27 Jun 1988), Swiss bass-baritone. Sang at the Zurich Opera 1940–52. From 1952 he was heard widely as Don Giovanni, Boris, Golaud and Dr Schön. He took part in the Venice 1961 fp of Nono's *Intolleranza 60*.

Reich, Günter (b Liegnitz, Silesia, 22 Nov 1921; d Heidelberg, 15 Jan 1991), German-born Israeli bass-baritone. Debut 1961, Iago. Later sang at the Deutsche Oper, Berlin, Munich and Salzburg. Best known in modern music; sang in the fps of Blacher's *200,000 Taler* (1969) and Penderecki's *Die schwarze Maske* (1986) and recorded Schoenberg's Moses with Boulez and Gielen. Other roles included Dallapiccola's Ulisse, Busoni's Faust, Satan in *Paradise Lost* by Penderecki and Morone in *Palestrina*. Sang Dr Schön in the UK fp of the three-act version of *Lulu* (CG 1981).

Reich, Steve (b New York, 3 Oct 1936), American composer. He studied at Juilliard and with Berio and Milhaud. In 1966 founded ensemble Steve Reich and Musicians, and began study of African, Balinese and Hebrew music; became a leading light of the minimalist school of composers, abandoning orthodox notions of harmony and counterpoint in favour of repeated phrases which typically evolve only gradually over time.

His works have had much success in Europe and the USA: *Pitch Charts* for instrumental ensemble (1963); *Music for Piano and Tapes* (1964); *It's Gonna Rain* for tape (1965); *My Name Is*, with audience participation (1967); *Pulse Music* (1969); *Drumming* for eight small tuned drums, three marimbas, three glockenspiels, two female voices and piccolo (1971); *Clapping Music* (1972); *Music for Pieces of Wood* (1973); *Music for 18 Musicians* (1975); Octet (1979); *Tehillim*, Hebrew psalms (1981); *Vermont Counterpoint* for 11 flutes (1982); *The Desert Music* for 24 amplified voices and orchestra (1984); *Sextet*

Reich   *A biographical note*

Few classically trained musicians achieve artistic status when they attempt 'crossover'. Gershwin with his fusion of jazz and symphonic music in *Rhapsody in Blue* was a successful exponent, as was perhaps Bernstein in his post-Broadway scores. Reich numbered Bergsma, Berio and Milhaud among his teachers, but his first music was for the underground films *The Plastic Haircut* and *Oh Dem Watermelons* (1963). Forming his own ensemble, Steve Reich and Musicians, in 1966, he evolved his highly popular brand of minimalism, spellbinding like-minded audiences with music which only gradually changed its ostinato patterns over long time spans. A visit to Ghana in 1970 resulted in *Drumming*, 90 minutes of insistent drum patterns, slowly relieved by voices, marimbas and glockenspiel. Seriously popular status was attained with the enormously successful record *Music for 18 Musicians* (1975). Reich returned to his Jewish roots in *Tehillim* (Psalms) in 1981. In 1988 he revisited his disrupted youth with *Different Trains* for string quartet. By the 1990s he attained international stardom, touring worldwide with the music theatre piece *The Cave* (1994). In *City Life* (1995), pile drivers, air brakes, boat horns and even a protest meeting held outside New York City Hall were all grist to the minimalist mill.

(1985); *New York Counterpoint* for clarinet and tape (1985); *Impact*, dance (1985); *Three Movements* (1986) and *The Four Sections* (1987) for orchestra; *Different Trains* for string quartet and tape (1988); *The Cave*, music theatre (1989–93); *City Life* (1995).

Reich, Willi (b Vienna, 27 May 1898; d Zurich, 1 May 1980), Austrian music author and editor. Studied at Vienna University and music with Berg and Webern. He founded and edited the review *23* in 1932, but in 1938 went to Switzerland, settling at Basel. He pub. a study of Berg's *Wozzeck* and worked with Krenek and Theodor Wiesengrund-Adorno on a biography of the same composer, and later produced independent works on Schoenberg and Berg.

Reicha, Antonín (b Prague, 26 Feb 1770; d Paris, 28 May 1836), Bohemian-born French theorist, teacher and composer. Studied at Wallerstein, Bavaria, under his uncle Joseph Reicha (1746–95), from whose wife he learnt French. In 1785 he went to Bonn with his uncle, who became music director there and worked at the electoral court, where he made friends with Beethoven. From 1794 to 1799 he was a music teacher in Hamburg. In 1799–1802 he had some success as a composer in Paris, but went to Vienna, where he remained until 1808 and was patronized by the empress. He then settled in Paris for the rest of his life and became professor at the Conservatory 1818.

Works include operas *Godefroid de Montfort* (1796), *Ouboualdi, ou Les Français en Égypte* (1798), *Cagliostro* (with Dourlen, 1810), *Natalie* (1816), *Sapho*; 16 symphonies, *Scènes italiennes* for orchestra; 20 string quartets, six string quintets, Diecetto and Octet for strings and wind, 24 wind quintets, six string trios, duets for violins and for flutes; 12 violin and piano sonatas; piano sonatas and pieces.

For everyone, surely, who can enjoy the good things of life, especially for the artist, perhaps quite especially for the musical artist, Vienna is the richest, happiest, and most agreeable residence in Europe.

J F Reichardt, *Briefe geschrieben auf eine Reise nach Wien* (Letters written on a journey to Vienna), 1810

Reichardt, Johann Friedrich (b Königsberg, 25 Nov 1752; d Giebichenstein near Halle, 27 Jun 1814), German composer. Studied at Königsberg University and picked up a rather haphazard musical education. He travelled widely in 1771–74 and pub. his experiences in *Vertraute Breife*. After working as a civil servant at Königsberg, he obtained the post of music director at the Prussian court in 1776, lived at Berlin and Potsdam, produced operas and in 1783 founded a Concert spirituel. He also pub. collections of music and wrote criticism. After the death of Frederick II he made himself disliked more and more and in 1793 he was dismissed, ostensibly for his sympathy with the French Revolution. He retired to Giebichenstein in 1794, only briefly holding a post at the court of Jérême Bonaparte at Kassel in 1808. He wrote several books on music, was a forerunner of Schubert in song composition, married Juliane Benda (1752–83), a singer, pianist and composer, daughter of F Benda, and had a daughter, Louise (1780–1826), who became a singer and also wrote songs. His work is notable for a wide range of literary influences, including Goethe, Shakespeare, Sophocles, Schiller, Milton and even Metastasio.

Works include operas and plays with music *Hänschen und Gretchen* (1772), *Amors Guekkasten* (1773), *Cephalus und Procris* (1777), *Le feste galanti, Claudine von Villa Bella* (Goethe, 1789), *Erwin und Elmire* (Goethe, 1793), *L'Olimpiade* (Metastasio, 1791), *Tamerlan* (in French), *Jery und Bätely* (Goethe), *Der Taucher* (after Schiller's ballad, 1811), *Brenno, Die Geisterinsel* (after Shakespeare's *Tempest*, 1798) and *c* 12 others; incidental music to Shakespeare's *Macbeth* (1795), several plays by Goethe and Kotzebue's *Die Kreuzfahrer*; cantatas *Ariadne auf Naxos, Ino* (1779), *Morning Hymn* (Milton, translated by Herder) and others; instrumental works; about 1,500 songs.

Reichenau, Berno of (d 1048), German Benedictine monk and music theorist. He was first a monk at Prüm, and abbot of Reichenau from 1008. He compiled a *tonale*, dealing with the organization of the church chants into modes.

Reicher-Kindermann, Hedwig (b Munich, 15 Jul 1853; d Trieste, 2 Jun 1883), German mezzo-soprano, daughter of the baritone August Kindermann (1817–91). Studied with her father, and made various small stage appearances in her youth, first appeared as a concert singer at Leipzig in 1871 and on the stage in Berlin in 1874 as Pamina and Agathe. She appeared at Bayreuth in 1876 and from 1880 sang with Angelo Neumann's co. as Fricka, Brünnhilde, Ortrud and Isolde.

Reichert, Manfred (b Karlsruhe, 5 May 1942), German conductor. After study in Karlsruhe founded the chamber group Ensemble 13 in 1973. Director of music festivals at Karlsruhe from 1980, including the Festival of European Culture, 1983–87. Conducted the fps of Jurgen von Böse's *Variations for Strings* (1981), and *Chiffre- Zyklus* (1988) and *Gejagte Form* (1989) by Wolfgang Rihm.

Reichmann, Theodor (b Rostock, 15 Mar 1849; d Marbach, Lake of Constance, 22 May 1903), German bass. Studied in Germany and with Lamperti at Milan and made his first appearance at Magdeburg in 1869. He created Amfortas in *Parsifal* (1882) and also sang Sachs and Wolfram at Bayreuth. In 1892 he sang Wotan under Mahler at CG.

Reigen German = roundelay.

Reimann, Aribert (b Berlin, 4 Mar 1936), German composer and pianist. Studied with Blacher in Berlin; his early music uses serial technique, but he renounced this kind of composition in 1967, turning to literary sources for a musical starting point, including Shakespeare, Strindberg, Kafka (*Das Schloss*), Euripides (*Troades*), Günther Grass, Byron, Edgar Allan Poe and even Sylvia Plath. He is best known for his opera *Lear* (1978), after Shakespeare's *King Lear*. Frequent recitals and recordings with Dietrich Fischer-Dieskau until his retirement in 1992.

Other works include operas *Traumspiel* (after Strindberg's *Dream Play*, 1965), *Melusine* (1971), *Gespenstersonate* (after Strindberg's *Ghost Sonata*, 1984) *Troades* (1986) and *Das Schloss* (1991); the ballet *Stoffreste*, (1957, revised as *Die Vogelscheuchen*, The Scarecrows, 1970); two piano concertos (1961, 1972), cello concerto (1959); *Totentanze* for baritone and orchestra (1960), *Hölderlin-Fragmente* for soprano and orchestra (1963); *Inane*, monologue for soprano and orchestra (1969), *Lines* for soprano and 14 instruments after Shelley (1973), *Wolkenloses Christfest* (Cloudless Christmas), Requiem for baritone, cello and orchestra (1974), *Lear*, symphony for baritone and orchestra (1980), *Unrevealed* for baritone and string quartet (1980), *Chacun sa Chimère* for soprano, mezzo, baritone and orchestra (1982); Trio for violin, viola and cello (1987); *Apocalyptic Fragment* for mezzo, piano and orchestra (1987); *I Fragmente* for orchestra (1988); Concerto for violin, cello and orchestra (1989); *Shine and Dark* for baritone and piano (1990); nine pieces for orchestra (1994).

Reinach, Théodore (b Saint-Germain-en-Laye, 3 Jul 1860; d Paris, 30 Oct 1928), French archaeologist and historian. Author of several works on Greek music and of the libretti of Maurice Emmanuel's *Salamine* (after Aeschylus' *Persae*) and Roussel's *La Naissance de la lyre*.

Reina Codex an important source of Italian and French 14th–15th-c. music now in the Bibliothèque Nationale at Paris (n.a. fr. 6771). It also includes two keyboard arrangements, one of them incomplete, of vocal works by Landini.

Re in ascolto, Un, *A Listening King*, opera by Berio (libretto by I Calvin produced Salzburg, 7 Aug 1984, conductor Maazel; producer Götz Friedrich, with Theo Adam. Ageing Prospero holds auditions for a new theatre production, but is dissatisfied until he hears the female protagonist.

Reinecke, Carl (Heinrich Carsten) (b Altona, 23 Jun 1824; d Leipzig, 10 Mar 1910), German pianist, composer and conductor. Settled in Leipzig from 1843. Appointed pianist to the Danish court, 1846–48 and several times visited Copenhagen. Conductor of the Gewandhaus concerts and professor of composition at the Leipzig Conservatory from 1860.

Works include STAGE AND CHORAL: operas *König Manfred* (after Byron, 1867), *Der vierjährige Posten* (after Körner, 1855), *Ein Abenteuer Händels* (1874), *Auf hohen Befehl* (1886), *Der Gouverneur von Tours* (1891); incidental music for Schiller's *Wilhelm Tell*; oratorio *Belsazar* (1865), two Masses; cantatas *Haakon Jarl*, *Die Flucht nach Aegypten*, fairy-tale cantatas for female voices *Schneewittchen*, *Dornröschen*, *Aschenbrödel* and others.

ORCHESTRAL AND INSTRUMENTAL: three symphonies 1870–95), overtures *Dame Kobold* (Calderón's *Dama duende*), *Aladdin*, *Friedensfeier*, *Zenobia* and other orchestral works; four piano concertos (1879–1900), concertos for violin and for cello; five string quartets, wind octet, seven piano trios and other chamber music; three piano sonatas and many pieces; songs.

Reine de Saba, La, *The Queen of Sheba*, opera by Gounod (libretto by J Barbier and M Carré), produced Paris, Opéra, 28 Feb 1862. King Solomon wants to marry Balkis, Queen of Sheba, but she loves the King's architect Adoniram. They plan to elope but Adoniram is killed as they escape.

Reine (de France), La, *The Queen of France*, nickname of Haydn's symphony No. 85 in B♭ major, composed for Paris 1785–86.

Reiner, Fritz (b Budapest, 19 Dec 1888; d New York, 15 Nov 1963), Hungarian-born American conductor. He studied in Budapest and at Jura University. He held a number of conducting posts in Europe, including Budapest and Dresden, where he gave *Parsifal* and *Die Frau ohne Schatten*, before succeeding Ysaÿe as conductor of the Cincinnati SO in 1922. From 1938 to 1948 he was conductor of the Pittsburgh SO, from 1948 at the Met. and from 1953 conductor of the Chicago SO. He returned to Europe from time to time as a guest conductor and in 1936 conducted *Tristan* at CG; 1955 *Die Meistersinger* for the reopening of the Vienna Opera.

Reiner, Jacob (b Altdorf, Württemberg, c 1560; d Weingarten, 12 Aug 1606), German singer and composer. Learnt music at the monastery of Weingarten and from 1574–75 studied with Lassus at Munich. He returned to Weingarten about 1585 and remained there as singer and choirmaster to his death.

Works include Masses, motets, Magnificats, three Passions; German songs for three–five voices.

Reinhardt, Delia (b Elberfeld, 27 Apr 1892; d Arlesheim, 3 Oct 1974), German soprano. She made her debut in Breslau and from 1916 to 1923 sang in Munich, often with Bruno Walter as conductor Berlin Staatsoper 1923–38, in operas by Strauss, Schreker and Wagner. London, CG, 1924–29 as Octavian, Cherubino and Mimi. NY Met. debut 1923, as Sieglinde. Other roles included Christine, the Empress, Desdemona, Elsa and Eva.

Reinhold, Henry Theodore (d London, 14 May 1751), German-born English bass. He sang small roles in a wide variety of theatre pieces in London during the 1730s. Took part in the fps of Handel's last two operas, *Imeneo* and *Deidamia*, and many parts in the oratorios were written for him: *Samson*, *Semele*, *Belshazzar* and *Saul*.

Reining, Maria (b Vienna, 7 Aug 1903; d Vienna, 11 Mar 1991), Austrian soprano. She sang at the Vienna Staatsoper in the early 1930s as a soubrette and returned 1937 as a dramatic soprano; sang there until 1956. In 1937 she also sang Eva at Salzburg, under Toscanini, and returned as Arabella and the Marschallin; she repeated the latter role at the NY City Opera in 1949. Professor of singing at the Mozarteum, Salzburg, from 1962.

Reinken (or *Reincken*), Johann Adam (Jan Adams) (b Wilshausen, Alsace, 27 Apr 1623; d Hamburg, 24 Nov 1722), German organist and composer. Pupil of Heinrich Scheidemann. Appointed organist of the church of St Catherine at Hamburg, 1663, where he remained to his death. Bach walked from Lüneburg as a youth and later came from Cöthen to hear him play.

Works include chorale preludes, toccatas, fugues, etc. for organ; *Hortus musicus* for two violins, viola da gamba and bass (pub. Hamburg, 1687); keyboard pieces.

Reinmar, Hans (b Vienna, 11 Apr 1895; d Berlin, 7 Feb 1961), Austrian

baritone. He studied in Vienna and Milan. After a 1919 debut in Olomouc he sang in Nuremberg, Zurich and Hamburg. Sang in various Berlin houses, 1928 to 1961; in the 1930s took part in the German revival of Verdi's operas (his roles included Macbeth, Boccanegra and Posa). During World War II he appeared at Bayreuth and Salzburg as Gunther, Amfortas and Mandryka. Munich, 1945–57. Other roles included Boris and Iago.

Reinthaler, Karl (Martin) (b Erfurt, 13 Oct 1822; d Bremen, 13 Feb 1896), German composer and conductor. After some early music training he went to Berlin to study theology, but turned to music, studying under A B Marx. With a grant from Frederick William IV he then studied further in Paris and Italy; in 1825 he joined the staff of the Cologne Conservatory and in 1858 became cathedral organist and choral conductor at Bremen. He conducted the fp of Brahms's German Requiem, in 1868.

Works include operas *Edda* (1875), *Das Käthchen von Heilbronn* (after Kleist, 1881); oratorio *Jephtha* (1856), cantata *In der Wüste*; hymns and other church music; symphonies; part-songs.

Reiss, Albert (b Berlin, 22 Feb 1870; d Nice, 19 Jun 1940), German tenor. After study in Berlin made his debut at Königsberg in 1897 in *Zar und Zimmermann*. He sang at the NY Met. 1901–19 in the fps of *La Fanciulla del West* and *Königskinder* (both 1910) and as the first Met. Alfred (*Fledermaus*), Vašek (*Bartered Bride*) and Valzacchi (*Rosenkavalier*). His best role was David in *Die Meistersinger* which he sang at the Met. and CG (1902–05, 1924–29; also Mime). Returned to Germany (1919) and sang at the Berlin Volksoper then Städtische Oper before retiring 1938.

There's threesome reels, there's foursome reels,/ There's hornpipes and strathspeys, man,/But ae the best dance e'er cam to the land/Was, the de'il's awa wi' th' Exciseman.

Robert Burns (1759–96), *The de'il's awa wi' th' Exciseman*

Reissiger, Karl (Gottlieb) (b Belzig near Wittenberg, 31 Jan 1798; d Dresden, 7 Nov 1859), German composer and conductor. Studied under his father, the cantor and composer Christian Gottlieb Reissiger, and with Schicht at St Thomas's School, Leipzig. Later he studied in Vienna and with Winter at Munich, toured in Holland, France and Italy in 1824, and in 1826 succeeded Weber as conductor of the Dresden opera. In 1842 he conducted the fp of Wagner's first major success, *Rienzi*, and in the following year Wagner became his deputy conductor. He was a respected teacher; Clara Schumann was among his pupils.

Works include operas *Dido* (1824), *Libella* (1829), *Turandot* (after Gozzi, 1835), *Die Felsenmühle zu Estalières* (1831) and others; melodrama *Yelva*; oratorio *David*; nine Masses, motets and other church music; piano concerto; piano trios and other chamber music; piano pieces including *Danses brillantes* (with that known as *Webers letzter Gedanke*).

Reiter, Josef (b Braunau, Upper Austria, 19 Jan 1862; d Vienna, 2 Jun 1939), Austrian composer. Studied with his father, an organist. Taught and conducted in Vienna, 1886–1907, was director of the Mozarteum at Salzburg, 1908–11, and conductor at the Hofburgtheater in Vienna, 1917–18. He dedicated his *Goethe Symphony* to Hitler in 1931 and wrote a cantata to celebrate the *Anschluss*.

Works include operas *Klopstock in Zurich* (1894), *Der Bundschuh* (1894), *Totentanz* (1908) and *Der Tell*; incidental music for Raimund's *Bauer als Millionär*; Masses and Requiem; choral works; six string quartets, two string quintets and other chamber music; part-songs; c 120 songs.

Reizen, Mark (b Zaytsevo, near Lugansk, 3 Jul 1895; d Moscow, 25 Nov 1992), Russian bass. He studied in Kharkov and made his debut there in 1921 as Pimen. He sang in Leningrad, 1925–30 and at the Boshoi, Moscow, 1930–54; returned in 1985 to celebrate his 90th birthday, as Gremin in *Eugene Onegin*. Foreign engagements included Boito's Mefistofele at Monte Carlo, 1930. Other roles included Boris, Dosifey, Don Basilio, Ivan Susanin and Philip II.

Reizenstein, Franz (b Nuremberg, 7 Jun 1911; d London, 15 Oct 1968), German-born English pianist and composer. He was very precocious and studied at the State Academy for Music in Berlin 1930–34, Hindemith being among his masters. The Nazi régime drove him to England in 1934 and he studied with Vaughan Williams at the RCM in London, also piano with Solomon. From 1958 he taught the piano at the RAM.

Works include radio opera *Anna Kraus* (1952); film music; oratorio *Genesis* (1958), cantata *Voices of Night* (1957); orchestral music, cello, piano (2) and violin concertos; chamber music; piano works.

Creation must be completely free: Every fetter one imposes on oneself by taking into account playability or public taste leads to disaster.
Max Reger, in a letter to Kerndl, 1900

---

réjouissance French = 'enjoyment'; a sprightly movement sometimes found as one of the accessory pieces in old suites.

relative the connection between major and minor keys with the same key-signature is said to be relative. The note representing the tonic key of the relative major is always five semitones higher than that of the relative minor. Thus E♭ major is the relative major of C minor (three ♭s), B minor the relative minor of D major (two ♯s), etc.

Re Lear, *King Lear*, opera by Alberto Ghislanzoni (libretto by composer based on Shakespeare), produced Rome, Teatro Reale, 24 Jun 1937.

For Verdi and plot synopsis ◊King Lear.

Reliquie German, from Latin = 'the relic'; a nickname sometimes given to Schubert's unfinished C major piano sonata begun in 1825, of which only the first and slow movements were completed. The fragmentary minuet and finale have been completed by Ludwig Stark, by Ernst Křenek and by Willi Rehberg.

Rellstab, (Heinrich Friedrich) Ludwig (b Berlin, 13 Apr 1799; d Berlin, 27 Nov 1860), German critic, novelist and poet, son of the pub. and critic Johann Karl Friedrich Rellstab (1759–1813). He studied with Ludwig Berger and Bernhard Klein, and followed his father as music critic of the *Vossische Zeitung* and edited the periodical *Iris im Gebiete der Tonkunst* in 1830–1842. He was imprisoned for satirizing Henriette Sontag's devotion to Rossini's operas and attacking Spontini. His books include various musical studies and several novels on musical themes. Schubert set ten of his poems to music, including *Ständchen*. ◊Schwanengesang.

Remedios, Alberto (b Liverpool, 27 Feb 1935), English tenor. He studied at the RCM. SW, London, from 1957; first major role Alfredo, 1960. CG debut 1965, as Dmitri; other roles have been Mark, Bacchus and Siegfried; he sang Siegfried in the Coliseum *Ring* of 1973 and other Wagner roles have been Lohengrin, Walther and Siegmund. Has also sung Otello and Berlioz's Faust and Aeneas. US debut San Francisco, 1973; NY Met. 1976, as Bacchus. Sang the Second Armed Man in *Die Zauberflöte* at CG (1991) and Svetopluk Cech in *The Excursions of Mr Brouček* for ENO, 1992.

Reményi (actually *Hoffmann*), Eduard (b Miskolc, 17 Jan 1828; d San Francisco, 15 May 1898), Hungarian violinist. Studied at the Vienna Conservatory with Joseph Böhm and others. He took part in the 1848 Revolution, toured with Brahms 1852–53 and introduced Hungarian gypsy music to him, made friends with Liszt at Weimar and afterwards toured widely in Europe and USA.

Remigius of Auxerre (b c 841; d c 908), Benedictine monk and music theorist. He was at the monastery of St Germain in Auxerre from 861. His music theory takes the form of a commentary on Martianus Capella.

Remoortel, Edouard van (b Brussels, 30 May 1926; d Paris, 16 May 1977), Belgian conductor. Studied at Brussels Conservatory, at Geneva Conservatory, and then privately with Joseph Krips. In 1951 he became chief conductor of the Belgian National Orchestra, and in 1958 permanent conductor of the St Louis SO in the USA. He left in 1962 and worked in Monte Carlo from 1964.

Renard burlesque by Stravinsky; composed 1915–16, fp Paris, 18 May 1922. A vixen cajoles a cock out of a tree, but it is saved by the cat; during a second attempt the vixen is killed by the cat and a ram.

Renaud, Maurice (Arnold) (b Bordeaux, 24 Jul 1861; d Paris, 16 Oct 1933), French baritone. Studied at the Conservatories of Paris and Brussels, and in 1883 made his first stage appearance at the Théâtre de la Monnaie there; he sang in the fps of Reyer's *Sigurd* and *Salammbô*. In 1890 he first sang in opera in Paris and in 1897 in London, returned until 1904 as Don Giovanni, Escamillo and Rigoletto. US debut 1893, New Orleans; NY Met. 1910–12.

Rencontre imprévue, La, *The Unforeseen Meeting*, later known as *Les Pèlerins de le Mecque/The Pilgrims to Mecca*, opera by Gluck (libretto by L H Dancourt, based on a vaudeville by Lesage and d'Orneval), produced Vienna, Burgtheater, 7 Jan 1764. Ali seeks his bride, the Princess Rezia, kidnapped by pirates and desired by an amorous sultan. ◊*L'Incontro Improvviso* (Haydn).

Rendall, David (b London, 11 Oct 1948), English tenor. After study at the RAM and the Salzburg Mozarteum sang Ferrando with GTO in 1975 (at the Festival in 1976). CG from 1975, in *Der Rosenkavalier* and as Matteo, Almaviva (Rossini), Rodolfo, Rodrigo (*La Donna del lago* and the Duke of Mantua. Has sung with ENO from 1976, as Leicester in *Maria Stuarda*, Alfredo, Tamino, Pinkerton and Cavaradossi. New York City and San Francisco debuts 1978, as Rodolfo and Don Ottavio. Appearances with the NY Met. from 1980, as Ernesto, Belmonte, Idomeneo and Lensky. Sang Don Antonio in the stage premiere of Gerhard's *The Duenna*, Madrid 1992.

Rendano, Alfonso (b Carolei near Cosenza, 5 Apr 1853; d Rome, 10 Sept 1931), Italian pianist and composer. Studied at Naples and Leipzig, also with Thalberg. Appeared at the Leipzig Gewandhaus in 1872, then in Paris and London, where he remained some time, afterwards becoming piano professor at the Naples Conservatory.

Works include opera *Consuelo* (after George Sand, 1902); piano concerto; piano music, etc.

Rennert, Günther (b Essen, 1 Apr 1911; d Salzburg, 31 Jul 1978), German producer and Intendant. He studied in Germany and Argentina; before World War II he worked in Wuppertal, Frankfurt and Mainz. He worked at Hamburg 1946–56 and staged operas by Britten, Berg and Hindemith. Head of production Glyndebourne 1960–67 (Monteverdi's *Poppea* 1962). NY Met. from 1960; Munich 1967–76. With his meticulous standards, and respect for the composer's intentions, he set a standard which many of his younger colleagues have unfortunately not chosen to emulate.

Rennert, Wolfgang (b Cologne, 1 Apr 1922), German conductor. Studied at the Salzburg Mozarteum 1940–47 and made his debut at Dusseldorf in 1948, *Un ballo in maschera*. Conducted in Dusseldorf until 1950, then Frankfurt Opera 1953–67; Theater am Gärtnerplatz, Munich 1967–72. Music director of the Mannheim Opera 1980–85 and has led *Die Zauberflöte* in Dallas, *Die Walküre* at the Staatsoper Berlin (1990) and *Arabella* at the Semperoper Dresden (1992). Conducted *Tannhäuser* at the National Theatre, Lisbon, 1993.

Renvoysy, Richard de (b Nancy, c 1520; d Dijon, 6 Mar 1586), French cleric, lutenist and composer. Canon and choirmaster at the Sainte Chapelle of Dijon. He was condemned to death by fire for committing sodomy with his choirboys.

Works include psalms; Anacreontic odes for four voices, etc.

Reomensis, Aurelianus (Aurelian of Réomé), French 9th-c. Benedictine monk and musician. His theoretical works describe the modal significance of melodic formulae and the correspondence between the rhythm of text and melody.

Re pastore, Il, *The Shepherd King*, opera by Bonno (libretto by Metastasio), produced Vienna, Schönbrunn Palace, 13 May 1751. Shepherd Amyntas is revealed to be the heir of Sidon, but he is willing to give up the throne to marry Elisa. King Alexander of Macedonia allows him both a crown and a wedding.

Opera by Gluck (libretto ditto), produced Vienna, Burgtheater, 8 Dec 1756.

Opera by Mozart (libretto ditto), produced Salzburg, 23 Apr 1775.

repeat the restatement of a section of a composition, not written out a second time, but indicated by repeat signs.

Repeat signs.

In music of the 18th c. the expositions of movements in sonata form are nearly always marked for repetition, and more rarely the working-out and recapitulation also, with or without the coda.

répétiteur French = 'coach'; the musician at an opera-house whose function it is to teach the singers their parts before they gather for rehearsal with the conductor.

Répons work by Boulez for chamber orchestra and six solo instruments and computer; composed 1981, fp Donaueschingen, 18 Oct 1981. Revised London, 18 Jun 1982.

Reppel, Carmen (b Gummersbach, 27 Apr 1941), German soprano. After study with Erna Berger, she made her debut at Flensburg, 1968, as Elisabeth de Valois. Has sung widely in Germany, notably at Bayreuth 1977–80, as Freia and Gutrune; Munich 1986, in the fp of *Troades* by Reimann. US debut San Francisco 1983, in *Ariadne auf Naxos*. La Scala 1987, in the fp of Testi's *Riccardo III* and Sieglinde at Bologna, 1988. Other roles include Salome (Torre del Lago, 1989), Chrysothemis (Vienna 1985) and Donna Anna. Sang Strauss's Empress at Marseille, 1992.

reprise French = lit. 're-taking' = 'repetition'; although the French meaning is that of repeat, in English the word is sometimes used in a special sense, indicating the reappearance of the first subject in a sonata-form movement at the point where the recapitulation begins.

His Requiem is patiently borne only by the corpse.
George Bernard Shaw on Brahms's Requiem,
The Star, 1892

Requiem the Mass for the Dead in the Roman Catholic church service, used generally on All Souls' Day (2 Nov) and specifically at funeral services at any time. It may be sung to plainsong or in more or less elaborate musical settings. Some of the greatest settings, although originally written to order (Mozart) or intended for a special religious occasion (Berlioz, Verdi), are now fit mainly or solely for concert use, and some were actally written for that purpose (e.g. Dvořák). Britten's *War Requiem* combines the liturgical text with settings of poems by Wilfrid Owen.

Requiem (Brahms) ◊German Requiem.

Requiem (Verdi) ◊Manzoni Requiem.

Requiem Canticles work by Stravinsky for mezzo, bass, chorus and orchestra; composed 1965–66, fp Princeton, 8 Oct 1966. Stravinsky's last major work.

Requiem for Rossini a Mass for the Dead planned by Verdi for performance in memory of Rossini's death in 1868, his suggestion being that each portion should be written by a different Italian composer of eminence. He himself composed the 'Libera me' in 1869, and the other contributors were Bazzini, Cagnoni, Coccia, Mabellini, Pedrotti, Petrella and Ricci. Mercadante was also invited, but was unable to comply on account of blindness and infirmity. The work was never performed and the composers all withdrew their contributions. Verdi's was later used, with some alterations, for the Manzoni Requiem of 1873–74.

Rescigno, Nicola (b New York, 28 May 1916), American conductor. After study in Rome conducted in New York from 1943. Co-founder and artistic director of the Chicago Lyric Opera, 1954–46 (conducted US debut of Maria Callas, as Norma, 1954). Co-founder and artistic director of the Dallas Opera, 1957–92, presiding over the US debuts of Placido Domingo, Joan Sutherland and Montserrat Caballé; led

the US major house premieres of Monteverdi's *Poppea* and Handel's *Alcina, Giulio Cesare* and *Samson*. Guest in San Francisco, Washington DC and Houston. NY Met., with *Traviata* and *L'elisir d'amore*. Led the fp of Argento's *Aspern papers* (Dallas, 1988) and *Werther* and *Aida* at Rome (1990).

rescue opera a type of French opera, the libretto of which is based on plots, often taken from true happenings (the words *fait historique* sometimes appear in the subtitle), in which the hero or heroine are saved after fearful trials and tribulations. The taste for such works arose during the Revolution. The most familiar examples are Cherubini's *Les Deux Journées* and Beethoven's *Fidelio*, both with libretti by Bouilly, the latter a German translation of *Léonore* written for Gaveaux.

resin ◊rosin

Resnik, Regina (b New York, 30 Aug 1922), American mezzo, originally soprano. Studied in New York, making her debut in Brooklyn, 1942. In 1943 she sang in Mexico, and at the NY Met. in 1944 as the *Trovatore* Leonora; other roles there have been Ellen Orford, Leonore, Donna Anna and Elvira. She also sang in Europe (Bayreuth, 1953). London, CG, from 1957 as Carmen, Marina and Clytemnestra. Sang the Countess in *The Queen of Spades* at San Francisco, 1982.

resolution a term used in harmony for the process by which a discord is made to pass into a concord. ◊preparation.

Reson, Johannes, early 15th-c. French composer. He wrote *chansons* and a few sacred works, including a Mass cycle.

Respighi (born *Olivieri-Sangiacomo*), Elsa (b Rome, 24 Mar 1894; d Rome, 17 March 1996), Italian singer and composer. Pupil of Ottorino Respighi at the Accademia di Santa Cecilia in Rome and later (1919) his wife. She finished the orchestration of his opera *Lucrezia* and wrote three of her own, also choral works, a symphonic poem, a dance suite for orchestra, songs from the *Rubáiyát* of Omar Khayyám and many others.

Respighi, Ottorino (b Bologna, 9 Jul 1879; d Rome, 18 Apr 1936), Italian composer. He entered the Liceo Musicale of Bologna as a violin student in 1891 and in 1898 he began to study composition under Luigi Torchi and later under Martucci. In 1900 he became first viola in the Opera orchestra at St Petersburg and the next year studied composition and orchestration with Rimsky-Korsakov, who remained the most important influence of Respighi's orchestral technique. In 1902 he took an additional composition course with Bruch in Berlin, but returned home in 1903 to join the Mugellini quintet, of which he remained a member until 1908, when Bologna produced his

A Selection of

Respighi

Semirama	1910
Il Tramonto	1914
Fontana di Roma	1916
Ancient Airs and Dances	1917
Concerto gregoriano	1921
Pini di Roma	1924
Vetrate di chiesa	1925
Trittico Botticelliano	1927
Feste romane	1928
La fiamma	1934

first opera. In 1913 he was appointed professor of composition at the Accademia di Santa Cecilia in Rome and toured Italy as conductor of his own works. The first of his colourful and highly successful symphonic suites, *The Fountains of Rome* was premiered in 1917. *The Pines of Rome* (1924) caused a stir by including a gramophone recording of a nightingale. In 1919 he married his pupil Elsa Olivieri-Sangiacomo, a composer and singer, and from about that time he began to take a keen interest in early Italian music and the church modes. Appointed director of the Accademia in 1923, but resigned in 1925, though retaining the composition professorship.

Works include STAGE: operas *Re Enzo* (1905), *Semirama* (1910), *Belfagor*, *Marie Victoire*, *La campana sommersa* (after Gerhart Hauptmann, 1927), *La bella addormentata nel bosco* (marionette version 1922, child mime version 1934), *Maria Egiziaca*, (1932), *La fiamma* (1934), *Lucrezia* (orchestration finished by his wife), also a transcription of Monteverdi's *Orfeo* (1935); ballets *Scherzo veneziano*, *La Boutique fantasque* (music adapted from Rossini, 1919), *Belkis, regina di Saba*, *Il ponticello dei sospiri* and *Gli uccelli* (adapted from the orchestral suite to form a trilogy with *Maria Egiziaca* and *Lucrezia*).

ORCHESTRAL: including *Sinfonia drammatica* (1914), the suites *Fontane di Roma* (1916), *Pini di Roma* (1924), *Vetrate di chiesa/Church Windows* (1925), *Trittico Botticelliano* (1927), *Gli uccelli* (bird pieces by old masters, 1927), *Feste romane* (1928) and *Sinfonia drammatica*, two sets of old lute airs and dance arrangements, concerto in the Mixolydian mode, also arrangements of three works by Bach; fantasy and toccata for piano and orchestra, concerto in the old style and *Concerto gregoriano* for violin and orchestra (1921), Adagio with variations for cello and orchestra (1920), concerto for oboe, trumpet, violin, double bass, piano and strings (1933).

CHAMBER AND VOCAL: two string quartets (second in the Dorian mode), piano quintet; sonata in B minor and five pieces for violin and piano; three Preludes on a Gregorian melody for piano; *Aretusa* for mezzo and orchestra (1910); *La primavera*, for solo voices, chorus and orchestra (1919); editions of Monteverdi's *Lamento d'Arianna* and Marcello's *Didone* for voice and orchestra; *Il tramonto* (1914) and *La sensitiva* (1914) for voice and string quartet; 52 songs.

respond ◊responsory.

Responses in Anglican church music, the choral and congregational cadences answering the versicles read or chanted in monotone by the priest, e.g. the 'Amen' or 'Have mercy upon us ... ' in the Litany.

Responsorial Psalmody an ancient method of singing the psalms (borrowed from the Jews), in which a soloist is answered by a chorus.

Responsory, Latin *responsorium*, a chant involving the response by a choir to a verse sung by soloists, also called Respond. Originally this would have taken the form of a response by the congregation to the leader or *cantor*. In the 9th c. it became an elaborate musical form demanding trained soloists and choir. The Gradual, Alleluia and (for a time) the Offertory of the Mass were responsorial chants. In the Offices the most important were the *responsoria prolixa*, sung at Matins. Like those of the Mass, they became a vehicle for polyphonic settings, the polyphony being reserved for the soloists' portions of the chant. When from the mid-15th c. choral polyphony became the norm the procedure was frequently, though not invariably, reversed. Late 16th-c. settings, such as those by Victoria for Holy Week, assign the entire text to the polyphonic choir.

rest all organized music consists not only of notes, but also of rests which, like the notes, take part of the measured scheme of a composition and thus have definite time-values in the same way as the notes. Dots can be added to rests as they are to notes.

Resta, Natale (b Milan), Italian 18th-c. composer.

Works include opera *Gli tre cicisbei ridicoli*, 1748 (containing the song 'Tre giorni son che Nina', formerly ascribed to Pergolesi and later said to be by Ciampi, under whose direction Resta's opera was produced in London, 1749, but more probably a popular Neapolitan air).

Resurrection (Alfano.) ◊Risurrezione.

Resurrection Symphony Mahler's second symphony in C minor for soprano, mezzo, chorus and orchestra; composed 1888–94, revised 1910. The finale is a setting of Klopstock's chorale *Aufersteh'n/Resurrection*. Fp Berlin, 13 Dec 1895, conductor Mahler.

Reszke, Edouard de, E ◊De Reszke.

Reszke, Jean de, J ◊De Reszke.

Retablo de Maese Pedro, El, *Master Peter's Puppet Show*, marionette opera by Falla (libretto by composer based on a chapter from Cervantes' *Don Quixote*), produced Seville, 23 Mar 1923, in concert form; first stage performance Paris, 25 Jun 1923. With the bumbling help of Don Quixote, the knight Gayferos rescues his wife Melisendra from the Moors.

retardation a term sometimes used for a suspension which resolves upwards.

In this example the top voice (note B) undergoes retardation, resolved on note C.

Re Teodoro in Venezia, Il, *Theodore at Venice*, opera by Paisiello (libretto by G B Casti), produced Vienna, Burgtheater, 23 Aug 1784. Deposed King Teodoro hides from creditors in Venice. He falls in love with Lisetta, but she is united with Sandrino and Teodoro ends up in debtors' prison.

Rethberg, Elisabeth (b Schwarzenberg, 22 Sept 1894; d Yorktown Heights, NY, 6 Jun 1976), German soprano. She studied in Dresden and sang there 1915–22 as Octavian, Sophie, Constanze and Mimi. NY Met. 1922–42, as Aida, Amelia Boccanegra, Elsa, Eva and in operas by Mozart, Respighi and Meyerbeer. She was a regular visitor to Salzburg, where she sang Leonore, Donna Anna and the Marschallin, and in 1928 returned to Dresden to create the title role in Strauss's *Die Ägyptische Helena*.

Réti, Rudolf (b Užice, Serbia, 27 Nov 1885; d Montclair, NJ, 7 Feb 1957), Austrian composer, pianist, critic and musical analyst. Studied at Vienna Conservatory. A champion of new music from the first, he gave the fp of Schoenberg's op. 11 piano pieces and was one of the founders of the ISCM in 1922. In 1938 he emigrated to the USA. Books include *The Thematic Process in Music* and *Tonality, Atonality and Pantonality*.

Works include opera *Ivan and the Drum* (after Tolstoy), opera-ballet *David and Goliath*; *The Dead Mourn the Living, Three Allegories* for orchestra (1953); two pf concertos; *The Greatest of All* for chorus and orchestra; string quartet; piano pieces; songs.

retrograde motion ◊cancrizans and ◊recte et retro.

Reubke, Julius (b Hausneindorf, near Quedlinburg, 23 Mar 1834; d Pillnitz, 3 Jun 1858), German composer and pianist. Son of the

Breve	Semibreve	Minim	Crotchet	Quaver	Semiquaver	Demisemiquaver

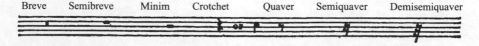

The symbols for various rests. For the crotchet, modern notation favours the left-hand one of the two alternatives.

organ builder Adolf Reubke (1805–75). Pupil of Liszt at Weimar. His early death cut short a very promising career.

Works include organ sonata *The 94th Psalm* (1857); sonata (1857) and pieces for piano; songs; etc.

Reusner (1), Esajas, German 17th-c. lutenist. Pub. a book of sacred songs arranged for the lute in 1645.

Reusner (2), Esajas (b Löwenberg, Silesia, 29 Apr 1636; d Berlin, 1 May 1679), German lutenist and composer, son of Esajas ◊Reusner (1). Studied with a French lutenist at the court of the Polish Princess Radziwill, became lutenist at the court of Leignitz-Brieg in 1655 and at that of Brandenburg in 1674.

Works include four books of lute suites, lute arrangements of 100 sacred tunes.

Reuss, August (b Liliendorf near Znaim, Moravia, 6 Mar 1871; d Munich, 18 Jun 1935), German-Moravian composer. Pupil of Thuille at Munich, where he became professor at the Academy of Music in 1929.

Works include opera *Herzog Philipps Brautfahrt* (1909); two pantomimes; orchestral prologue to Hofmannsthal's *Der Tor und der Tod* (1901); *Johannisnacht* (1903), *Judith*, *Sommer Idylle* (1920), ballet suite for orchestra; piano concerto, serenade for violin and orchestra; two string quartets, piano quintet, string trio; instrumental sonatas; choruses; songs and duets.

Reuter, Rolf (b Leipzig, 7 Oct 1927), German conductor. After appointments at Eisenach and Meinigen was music director at the Leipzig Opera 1961–73. Conducted the *Ring* at the Paris Opéra (1978) and has been music director of the Komische Oper Berlin from 1981, visiting CG with the company 1989, in *The Bartered Bride*. Conducted *Figaro* with the New Israel Opera, 1992. His premieres include *Guayana Johnny* by Alan Bush (1966) and *Judith* by Siegfried Matthus (1985).

Reutter (1), Georg (senior) (b Vienna, bap. 3 Nov 1656; d Vienna, 29 Aug 1738), Austrian organist and composer. In the service of the Viennese court as theorbo player (1697–1703) and organist (from 1700). Appointed organist at St Stephen's Cathedral in 1686, he rose to succeed Fux as second *Kapellmeister*, 1712, and became first *Kapellmeister* in 1715. Wrote principally church music.

Reutter (2), (Johann Adam Karl) Georg (junior) (b Vienna, bap. 6 Apr 1708; d Vienna, 11 Mar 1772), Austrian organist and composer, son of Georg ◊Reutter (1). Pupil of his father and of Caldara, was appointed court composer in Vienna in 1731, and in 1738 succeeded his father as chief *Kapellmeister* of St Stephen's Cathedral, where Haydn was his pupil as a chorister. Second court *Kapellmeister* 1747, first 1751, he held these posts, in plurality with that at St Stephen's to the detriment of the younger generation of composers, including Gluck and Haydn. Music at the cathedral also suffered during this period, but this was at least partly due to budget cuts at the time. He was ennobled 1740.

Works include *c* 40 operas, e.g. *Archidamia* (1727), *La forza dell' amicizia* (with Caldara, 1728), *Alessandro il Grande* (1732), *Dafne* (1734) and *Il sacrifizio in Aulide* (1735); oratorios *Abel*, *La Betulia liberata* (1734), *Gioas* etc.; 81 Masses; six Requiems; 126 motets, and much other church music; symphonies; serenades; chamber music; keyboard music.

Reutter, Hermann (b Stuttgart, 17 Jun 1900; d Heidenheim an der Brenz, 1 Jan 1985), German composer. Studied under Courvoisier and others at Munich. In 1932 he became professor at the Musikhochschule of Stuttgart and later became director of the State Hochschule at Frankfurt. In 1956 he became director of the Stuttgart State Conservatory.

Works include operas *Saul* (1928), *Der verlorene Sohn* (Gide, translated by Rilke, 1929), *Doktor Johannes Faust* (on the old German puppet play, 1936), *Odysseus*, *Die Witwe von Ephesus* (1954), *Die Brücke von San Luis Rey* (1954), *Hamlet* (1980); ballets *Die Kirmes von Delft* (1937), and *Topsy* (1950); oratorios *Volks-Seele* and *Der grosse Kalender*, cantata *Gesang des Deutschen*; four piano concertos (1925–44), violin concerto; chamber music, piano works; song cycle *Weise von Liebe und Tod* (Rilke).

Reveil des oiseaux, *Awakening of the birds*, works by Messiaen for piano and orchestra, fp Donaueschingen, 11 Oct 1953, conductor Rosbaud.

Revelation and Fall work for soprano and 16 instruments by Maxwell Davies (text by Georg Trakl; composed 1965, fp London, 26 Feb 1968, conductor Davies.

Revisor, Der opera in five acts by Egk (libretto by composer after Gogol's story *The Government Inspector*), produced Schwetzingen, 9 May 1957. Minor civil servant Chlestakov is mistaken for government inspector by corrupt town officials and takes advantage of the situation to woo the mayor's daughter.

Revolutionary Study the nickname of Chopin's study in C minor, op. 10 No. 12, for piano, written at Stuttgart in Sept 1831, where, on his way to Paris, he heard of the taking of Warsaw by the Russians.

Revueltas, Silvestre (b Santiago Papasquiaro, 31 Dec 1899; d Mexico City, 5 Oct 1940), Mexican violinist and composer. Studied at Mexico City and at St Edward's College, Austin, TX, also composition with Felix Borowski at Chicago. Appointed at Mexico as violinist 1920, but continued to study the instrument in 1922 under Kochansky and Ševčik. Later he gave recitals of modern music with Chávez as pianist, whom after some theatre appointments he went as conductor to the Orquesta Sinfónica at Mexico City where he also became professor at the Conservatory. His songs and orchestral music are notable for their lively display of local colour.

Works include music for numerous films: *Cuauhnahuac*, *Esquinas* (1930), *Ventanas*, *Alcancías* (1932), *Colorines*, *Planos* (1934), *Caminos*, *Janitzio*, *homenaje á García Lorca*, *El renacuajo paseador*, *Sensemayá*, etc. for orchestra; toccata for violin and small orchestra; two string quartets (1930, 1931), *Feria* for string quartet; pieces for violin and piano; *Siete canciones* and other songs.

Rey, Jean-Baptiste (b Lauzerte, 18 Dec 1734; d Paris, 15 Jul 1810), French conductor and composer. A chorister at the Abbey of St Sernin, he was appointed at the age of 17 *maître de chapelle* at the cathedral in Auch, but left to become opera conductor in Toulouse. Later conducted at various provincial theatres until 1776, when he settled in Paris, becoming chief conductor at the Opéra in 1781; he gave there operas by Gluck and Piccinni. He was a professor at the Conservatory 1799–1802.

Works include operas, Masses, motets, *solfèges*

The composer who stumbles in taking a step forward is worth more attention than the composer who shows us how easily he can step backwards.

Ernest Reyer, quoted in Dean, *Bizet*, 1975

Reyer, Ernest (actually Louis Étienne Rey) (b Marseilles, 1 Dec 1823; d Le Lavandou, Hyères, 15 Jan 1909), French composer. Learnt music at the Free School of Music at Marseille, but showed no exceptional promise. At the age of 16 he was sent to live with an uncle at Algiers and there began to compose songs, etc., and in 1847 succeeded in having a Mass performed at the cathedral. In 1848 he went to Paris and studied with his aunt, the composer Louise Farrenc. He met Flaubert, Gautier and others, with whom he shared an interest in oriental subjects, and they provided him with subjects for his works. He became a critic in the 1850s and in 1871 succeeded d'Ortigue as music critic to the *Journal des Débats*, becoming a champion of Wagner and the new French school; his operas *Sigurd* and *Salammbô* show inevitable indebtedness to Wagner but also reveal a native Gallic charm and vitality.

Works include operas *Maître Wolfram* (1854), *La Statue* (1861), *Érostrate*, *Sigurd* (on the Nibelung Saga, 1884), *Salammbô* (after Flaubert, 1890); ballet-pantomime *Sacountala* (after Malidasa, 1858); symphonic ode *Le Sélam* (words by Gautier), dramatic cantata *Victoire*; *L'Hymne du Rhin* for soprano, chorus and orchestra (1865), hymn *L'Union des Arts*; *Ave Maria*, *Salve Regina* and *O Salutaris*; *La Madeleine au désert* for baritone and orchestra (1874); male-voice choruses; piano pieces; songs.

Reynolds, Anna (b Canterbury, 4 Oct 1928), English mezzo. Her early operatic career, from 1958, was confined largely to Italy; she sang Tancredi, Donizetti's Elizabeth I and Charlotte in Rome, Venice and Milan. She was successful in Wagner roles and sang at Bayreuth 1970–76 and in Karajan's *Ring* cycles at Salzburg and the NY Met. as Fricka and Waltraute. As a concert singer she appeared with Giulini, Barbirolli and Abbado; many recordings of Bach's cantatas. Now a teacher of singing.

Reynolds, Roger (b Detroit, 18 July 1934), American composer. He studied at the University of Michigan, founded avant-garde festivals there and was director of the Center for Music Experiment at San Diego, 1971–77. His music makes use of electronics, synthesized sounds and graphic notation. He won the 1989 Pulitzer Prize for *Whispers out of Time*.

Works include the stage pieces *The Emperor of Ice Cream* (1962), *A Ritual for 23 Performers* (1971) and incidental music for *The Tempest* (1980); *Graffiti* (1964) and *Threshold* (1967) for orchestra; *Between* for chamber orchestra and electronics (1968); *Archipelago* for chamber orchestra and computer (1982); *Whispers out of Time* for string orchestra (1988); chamber and vocal music.

Rezniček, E(mil) N(ikolaus) von (b Vienna, 4 May 1860; d Berlin, 2 Aug 1945), Austrian composer and conductor. Studied law at Graz, but at 22, when he was already married to Milka Thurn, a kinswoman of Weingartner's, he went to the Leipzig Conservatory to study with Reinecke and Jadassohn. He gained stage experience as theatre conductor in various towns and finally became military conductor at Prague, where his most successful work, the opera *Donna Diana* was premiered in 1894. From 1896 to 1899 he was successively court conductor at Weimar and Mannheim. In 1906 he was appointed professor at the Klindworth-Scharwenka Conservatory in Berlin, where he founded a chamber orchestra, and later he conducted the Warsaw Opera (1907–08) and the Komische Oper in Berlin (1908–11). He taught at the Hochschule für Musik in Berlin 1920–26.

Works include operas *Die Jungfrau von Orleans* (after Schiller, 1887), *Satanella*, *Emmerich Fortunat* (1889), *Donna Diana* (after Moreto, 1894), *Till Eulenspiegel* (1902), *Ritter Blaubart*, *Holofernes* (after Hebbel's *Judith*, 1923), *Satuala*, *Spiel oder Ernst* (1930), *Der Gondoliere des Dogen* (1931); incidental music for Strindberg's *Dream Play*; Mass in F major, Requiem in D minor, *Vater unser* for chorus (1919); four symphonies (including *Schlemihl* [after Chamisso], 'Tragic' and 'Ironic'), two symphonic suites, Comedy and Idyllic Overtures, fugue in C♯ minor for orchestra; serenata for strings; violin concerto (1925), Introduction and Valse-Caprice for violin and orchestra; *Ruhm und Ewigkeit* (Nietzsche) for tenor and orchestra; three string quartets (1921–32).

rfz an abbr. used in musical notation for ◊*rinforzando*.

Rhapsodie, so-called 'Alto Rhapsody', a setting of a fragment from Goethe's *Harzreise im Winter* for contralto solo, male chorus and orchestra by Brahms, op. 53, composed 1869, fp Jena, 3 Mar 1870.

Rhapsodies ... are not a very difficult formula, if one can think up enough tunes.
Virgil Thomson, *Modern Music*, 1935

---

rhapsody from Greek *rhapsōidia* = 'epic poem' = lit. 'songs stitched together'; in French *rapsodie*

In the 18th c. a poem set to music of an improvisatory character. Hence an instrumental piece showing similar freedom. In the 19th c. and later the term was applied to large-scale compositions in which different elements, sometimes derived from folksong, were strung together, e.g. Liszt's *Hungarian Rhapsodies*. Brahms's rhapsodies for piano, on the other hand, are self-contained pieces which might equally well be called capriccio or intermezzo.

Rhapsody in Blue work for piano and orchestra by Gershwin, composed Jan 1924 and orchestrated by Grofé. Fp New York 12 Feb 1924, with Gershwin and Paul Whiteman band. Version for symphony

---

THE OPERA

Das Rheingold

A one-act musical drama by Richard Wagner, the first of the *Ring* cycle. It was first performed in Munich in 1869.

In the depths of the Rhine, the Nibelung dwarf Alberich (bass-baritone) pursues the three Rhine-maidens (Flosshilde, Wellgunde and Woglinde). Attracted by the gold they are guarding, Alberich learns that he may possess it only by renouncing love. Realizing that a ring fashioned from the gold will make him master of the world, Alberich robs the Rhine-maidens. The ruler of the gods Wotan (bass-baritone) is made to pledge Freia, the goddess of love (soprano), to the giants Fasolt and Fafner as payment for building Valhalla. Descending to Nibelheim, Wotan and the fire god Loge (tenor) capture Alberich and hold him to ransom; he releases the gold but curses the ring before handing it over. When the giants return with Freia, they demand the ring as well as the gold and the Tarnhelm, a magic helmet. Wotan refuses to part with the ring, but as the giants start to drag Freia away, the earth goddess Erda (contralto) appears and warns Wotan. Fafner kills Fasolt in a quarrel over the booty and takes it all away with him. Wotan, his wife Fricka (mezzo-soprano), and the other gods enter Valhalla while Loge comments cynically and the Rhine-maidens lament below.

THE OPERA

orchestra 1942; one of the earliest orchestral works to integrate jazz elements to a large extent.

Rhau (or *Rhaw*), Georg (b Eisfeld, Franconia, 1488; d Wittenberg, 6 Aug 1548), German composer and publisher. Cantor at St Thomas's School, Leipzig, until 1520, then schoolmaster at Eisleben and printer at Wittenberg, where he pub. various Lutheran music collections including works of his own. Wrote vocal works including hymn-tunes.

Rheinberger, Joseph (Gabriel) (b Vaduz, Liechtenstein, 17 Mar 1839; d Munich, 25 Nov 1901), German organist, teacher and composer. He was so precociously gifted that he was appointed organist at the parish church of his native place at the age of seven. After some lessons at Feldkirch, he went to the Munich Conservatory 1850, continued to study with F Lachner on leaving in 1854, supported himself by teaching and in 1859 became piano professor at the Conservatory. He also worked for a time at the Court Opera, and became a church organist and choral conductor. When the Conservatory was reorganized by Bülow in 1867 he was appointed organ and composition professor. In 1877 he became director of the court church music in succession to Wüllner. Although successful in his lifetime in a wide variety of genres he is largely known today through his demanding organ works.

Works include operas *Die sieben Raben* (1869), *Der Tümers Töchterlein* (1873) and *Das Zauberwort*; incidental music for Calderón's *Mágico prodigioso*; numerous Masses, three Requiems, *Stabat Mater*, motets; cantatas and choral ballads; symphony *Wallenstein* (after Schiller) and 'Florentine', overtures to Shakespeare's *Taming of the Shrew* and Schiller's *Demetrius*, *Academic (fugal) Overture* for orchestra; two organ concertos, piano concerto.

Three string quartets, two piano trios, piano quintet, piano quartet, string quintet; sonatas for violin and piano, cello and piano, horn and piano; 20 organ sonatas and many other organ works, including 22 trios, 12 *Meditations* and 24 fughettes; numerous piano works; songs, part-songs; numerous piano works; songs, part-songs.

Rheingold, Das, *The Rhinegold*, (Wagner) ◊Ring des Nibelungen. The dwarf Alberich steals the magic Rheingold from the Rhinemaidens and forges the all-powerful ring. Wotan, chief of the gods, steals Alberich's hoard, including the ring, in order to pay the giants Fasolt and Fafner for building the gods' palace Valhalla.

'Rhenish' Symphony the name of Schumann's third symphony, in E♭

Rheingold *In Scene 2 of* Das Rheingold *the giants Fasolt and Fafner take the goddess Freia hostage until Wotan returns with the Rheingold as payment for the newly built Valhalla, fortress of the gods.*

major, op. 97, begun after a Rhine excursion in Sept 1850. The fourth of the five movements is an impression of Cologne Cathedral. Fp Düsseldorf, 6 Feb 1851.

Rhys, Philip ap, 16th-c. English or Welsh organist and composer. He was organist at St Mary-at-Hill, London, until 1547, when he took over Redford's duties as organist at St Paul's. He was still organist there in 1559, although Sebastian Westcott had become almoner (Redford's official post) in 1551. He wrote organ music for the liturgy, including a setting of the Ordinary of the Mass (without the *Credo*).

Of all the elements united in the performance of music, rhythm is the one most natural to us, as it is equally natural to all animals.
Jean-Philippe Rameau, *Le Nouveau système de musique théoretique*, 1726

---

rhythm in its largest sense the word is concerned in music with all matters dependent on time, such as the metre, the proper division of the music into bars, the distribution and balance of phrases, etc. Rhythm, however, is not synonymous with metre and may be independent of bar-lines. It also implies the proper performance of music in a natural, living and breathing way, as distinct from a merely mechanical accuracy. What is often called rhythm in modern dance music which is rigidly accurate in time, is therefore not rhythm but merely a strict application of time. ◊harmonic rhythm.

Riadis (actually *Khu*), Emilios (b Salonika, 1 May 1886; d Salonika, 17 Jul 1935), Greek composer. Studied with Mottl and others at Munich and with Ravel in Paris. Assistant director of the Salonika Conservatory from 1918.

Works include operas *Le Chant sur le fleuve*, *Galatea* (1913) and *La Route verte* (1914); incidental music for Euripides' *Hecuba* (1927) and Wilde's *Salome* (1922); Byzantine Mass; *Sunset on Salonika* and other orchestral works; chamber music; piano pieces; etc.

RIAM, abbr., = Royal Irish Academy of Music.

Riccardo I, rè d'Inghilterra, *Richard I, King of England*, opera by Handel (libretto by P A Rolli), produced London, King's Theatre, Haymarket, 11 Nov 1727. King Richard I conquers Cyprus and marries Costanza after defeating jealous Isaac Comnenus, governor of the island.

Ricci, Federico (b Naples, 22 Oct 1809; d Conegliano, 10 Dec 1877), Italian composer. Studied with Bellini and Zingarelli at the Naples Conservatory. In 1835 he produced his first opera with his brother Luigi Ricci at Naples and the first of his own at Venice and after several stage successes he was music director at the Imperial theatres in St Petersburg 1853–69.

Works include operas *Monsieur de Chalumeaux* (1835), *La prigione d'Edimburgo* (on Scott's *Heart of Midlothian*, 1838), *Un duello sotto Richelieu* (1839), *Luigi Rolla e Michelangelo* (1841), *Corrado d'Altamura*, *Vallombra*, *Isabella de' Medici* (1845), *Estella di Murcia* (1846), *Griselda*, *I due ritratti*, *Il marito e l'amante* (1852), *Il paniere d'amore*, *Una Folie à Rome*, *Le Docteur rose* and four others in collaboration with Luigi Ricci; two Masses; cantata for the marriage of Victor Emmanuel; songs.

Ricci, Luigi (b Naples, 8 Jul 1805; d Prague, 31 Dec 1859), Italian composer, brother of Federico ◊Ricci. Studied under Zingarelli at the Naples Conservatory, where he and Bellini became sub-professors in 1819. His first opera was produced there 1823. In 1835, after a number of successful productions, he became conductor of the Opera and music director of the cathedral at Trieste. His attempt at a setting of *Le nozze di Figaro* (Milan, 1838) was a failure, and he moved with his twin-sister mistresses, Francesca and Ludmilla Stolz, to Odessa. He married Ludmilla in 1849 and wrote an opera for the sisters but was confined in an asylum in 1859, having become hopelessly insane.

Works include opera *L'impresario in angustie* (1823), *Il diavolo condannato* (1826), *Il Colombo*, *L'orfanella di Ginevra* (1829), *Chiara di Rosemberg Il nuovo Figaro* (1832), *Un avventura di Scaramuccia* (1834), *Gli esposti* (*Eran due ed or son tre*), *Chi dura vince*, *Chiara di Montalbano* (1835), *La Serva e l'ussaro*, *Le nozze di Figaro* (after Beaumarchais, 1838), *Il birraio di Preston* (1847), *La festa di Piedigrotta*, *Il diavolo a quattro* (1859), and 14 others including four in collaboration with Federico Ricci; church music, song-books *Mes Loisirs* and *Les Inspirations du thé*, etc.

Operas written jointly by the two brothers: *Il colonello* (1835), *Il disertore per amore* (1836), *L'amante di richiamo* (1846) and *Crispino e la comare* (1850).

Ricci, Ruggiero (b San Francisco, 24 Jul 1918), American violinist. Studied with Persinger, making his first public appearance aged 8. In 1932–4 he undertook his first European tour and in 1957 a world tour. He gave the fps of the concertos by Ginastera (1963) and von Einem (1970). Often heard in Paganini, whose rediscovered fourth Concerto he performed 1971. Teacher at Juilliard from 1975, Salzburg chamber concert 1990.

Ricciardo e Zoraide opera by Rossini (libretto by M F B di Salsa), produced Naples, Teatro San Carlo, 3 Dec 1818. Zoraide, daughter of Prince Ircano, falls in love with Christian Knight Ricciardo, but the tyrant Agorante also has designs on her. The couple are captured by Agorante but are saved following a revolt.

Ricciarelli, Katia (b Rovigo, 16 Jan 1946), Italian soprano. She studied in Venice and made her debut in Venice as Mimi, in 1969. US debut Chicago, 1972, as Lucrezia in *I due Foscari*; NY Met, 1975, as Mimi. At CG she has sung Amelia (*Ballo in Maschera*), Aida, Giulietta and Elisabeth de Valois. Other roles include Lucrezia Borgia, Imogene and Giovanna d'Arco. She sang Desdemona in Zeffirelli's 1986 film version of *Otello*, Ninetta in *La Gazza ladra* at Pesaro 1988, and Amenaide in *Tancredi* at Geneva, 1990.

Riccio, (Antonio) Teodoro (b Brescia, *c* 1540; d Ansbach, after 1599), Italian composer. Choirmaster at a church at Brescia, appointed music director by the Margrave of Brandenburg-Ansbach, settled there and followed the margrave to Königsberg in 1579, having become a Lutheran, and returned to Ansbach with his patron in 1586. Eccard served under him there from 1581 and succeeded him at his death.

Works include motets and other church music; madrigals, *Canzoni alla napoletana*; some of his canzonas are based on themes by Gabrieli.

ricercare Italian = 'to search out'; a fugal composition, also called *ricercar* or *ricercata*, the instrumental counterpart of the motet or madrigal in the 17th c., played on keyboard instruments or by a consort of string or wind instruments.

Richafort, Jean (b Hainault, *c* 1480; d ? Bruges, *c* 1547), Flemish composer. Pupil of Josquin Desprez. He was choirmaster at the church of Saint-Gilles at Bruges in the 1540s. Wrote Masses, motets, *chansons*, etc. Palestrina wrote a parody Mass on his four-part motet *Quem dicunt homines*.

Richard Cœur-de-Lion opera by Grétry (libretto by J M Sedaine), produced Paris, Comédie-Italienne, 21 Oct 1784. Beethoven wrote piano variations on the song 'Une fièvre brûlante' from it (WoO 72, 1795). Blondel, squire to King Richard, discovers that his master is held prisoner in Linz castle. He captures the castle governor Florestan and rescues Richard, reuniting him with his love Marguerita.

Richard I, Cœur de Lion (b Oxford, Sept 1157; d Limoges, 11 Apr 1199), King of England and French trouvère. He was the son of Henry II and his mother was Eleanor of Aquitaine. She introduced the art of the Troubadours to the north of France and thus established the school of the Trouvères to which Richard belonged both as poet and as musician.

According to legend another trouvère, Blondel de Nesle, discovered his place of imprisonment in Austria in 1192, when he is said to have sung outside the castle of Dürenstein and to have been answered by Richard in song from within, a fanciful story which furnished the plot for Grétry's opera *Richard Cœur-de-Lion*.

Richards, (Henry) Brinley (b Carmarthen, 13 Nov 1817; d London, 2 May 1885), Welsh pianist and composer. Studied at the RAM in London and with Chopin in Paris. Settled in London, where he taught the piano and lectured on Welsh music.

Works include overture in F minor; additional songs for Auber's *Diamants de la couronne*; piano pieces; songs, including 'God bless the Prince of Wales'; part-songs.

Richardson (real name *Heybourne*), Ferdinand(o) (b *c* 1558; d Tottenham, 4 Jun 1618), English composer. Pupil of Tallis. Groom of the Privy Chamber, 1587–1611. Composed virginal pieces, etc.

Richardson, Marilyn (b Sydney, 10 Jun 1936), Australian soprano. Studied in Sydney and made debut there 1958, in Schoenberg's *Pierrot Lunaire*. Opera debut at Basel 1972, as Lulu. From 1975 has sung with Australian Opera as Salome, Aida, the Marschallin, Desdemona, Eva, Leonore, Isolde (1990) and Tosca (1992). Appearances with regional Australian companies as Fiordiligi, Violetta, Butterfly, Senta, Alcina and Cleopatra. Has premiered about 400 works by Australian composers.

Richardson, Vaughan (b London, *c* 1670; d London, Jun 1729), English organist and composer. Chorister in the Chapel Royal. Appointed organist of Winchester Cathedral in 1692.

Works include services, anthems *O Lord God of my salvation*, *O how amiable* and others; *Song in Praise of St Cecilia* (1700); *Entertainment for the Peace of Ryswick* (1697); songs for one–three voices with instruments.

Richter, Ferdinand (Tobias) (b Würzburg, 22 Jul 1651; d Vienna, 3 Nov 1711), German organist and composer. Appointed court organist in Vienna, succeeding Poglietti, in 1683, and music teacher to the Imperial children.

Works include serenatas *L'istro ossequioso* (1694) and *Le promesse degli dei* (1697); sacred dramas for the Jesuit College; sonata for seven instruments and others in eight parts, *balletti* in four and five

parts; organ toccatas and other works; suites for harpsichord.

Richter, Franz Xaver (b Holešov, Moravian, 1 Dec 1709; d Strasbourg, 12 Sept 1789), Moravian bass, violinist and composer. Appointed vice *Kapellmeister* at the Abbey of Kempten in 1740, he entered the service of the Mannheim court *c* 1747, first as a singer and violinist, later becoming court composer. From 1769 he was music director of Strasbourg Cathedral. His work at Mannheim made him a prominent member of that school of symphonists.

Works include 39 Masses; two Requiems; two Passions; numerous motets, and other church music; almost 70 symphonies; concertos; string quartet and other chamber music.

Richter, Hans (b Györ, Hungary, 4 Apr 1843; d Bayreuth, 5 Dec 1916), Austro-Hungarian conductor. Studied in Vienna, where he played horn at the Kärntnertortheater, 1862–66. Assistant to Wagner, opera conductor at Budapest and Vienna; he organized and played the trumpet in the private premiere of the *Siegfried Idyll* at Triebschen (1870) and was the first to conduct Wagner's *Ring* at Bayreuth, 1876. Conducted at the Birmingham Festival 1885–1909, including the 1900 fp of *The Dream of Gerontius*, and conducted much in London between 1877 and 1910, notably the first *Ring* cycles in English, at CG in 1908; at Drury Lane gave the British premieres of *Tristan* and *Meistersinger* (1882). Conductor of the Hallé Orchestra, Manchester, 1900–11. He gave the fps of Brahms' second and third symphonies, Bruckner's first, third, fourth and eighth symphonies and Elgar's *Enigma Variations* and first symphony. By his unfailing industry over a long period, Richter set new standards for career conductors to follow.

Dear Richter's trumpet blazed out the Siegfried theme splendidly, and he had learned the trumpet especially to do it.

Cosima Wagner on the *Siegfried Idyll*, in *Diaries*, Dec 1870

Richter, Karl (b Plauen, 15 Oct 1926; d Munich, 15 Feb 1981), German organist and conductor. He studied in Dresden and Leipzig; organist Thomaskirche, Leipzig, from 1947. He moved to Munich in 1951 and founded the Munich Bach Orchestra and Choir. Many recordings and tours in the Baroque repertory; US debut Carnegie Hall, NY, 1965. He recorded Bach's B minor Mass and *St Matthew Passion* and was often heard in the keyboard music of Bach.

Richter, Sviatoslav (Teofilovich) (b Zhitomir, 20 Mar 1915), Russian pianist. Entered Moscow Conservatory 1937, where he studied with H Neuhaus, graduating in 1942. He won a national competition in 1945 and was awarded the Stalin Prize in 1949. A magnificent technique and fine musicianship place him in the front rank of modern pianists; US debut 1960, London 1961. He gave the fps of Prokofiev's sixth, seventh and ninth piano sonatas. He is also heard in works of Bach, Beethoven, Liszt and Debussy, as a chamber musician with the Borodin Quartet and as accompanist to leading singers (*Winterreise* with Fischer-Dieskau). Complete recordings issued on CD 1994.

Richter-Haaser, Hans (b Dresden, 6 Jan 1912; d Brunswick, 16 Dec 1980), German pianist. He studied in Dresden and made his debut there in 1928. International recognition did not come until 1953 and he was then heard widely in Europe and North and South America, often playing Schumann and Beethoven. He played in the USA, 1959–74. Also active as a conductor and composer.

Rickards, Steven (b Pottstown, PA, 19 Sept 1955), American countertenor. Sang with the Waverley Consort of New York and other ensembles in the USA and Europe (tour of France with *Messiah*, 1982). Carnegie Hall debut 1987. Boston Early Music Festival in the US fp of Handel's *Teseo* (1985) and Santa Fe 1985, as Ariel in the premiere of Eaton's *The Tempest*. Has sung in recent revivals of Handel's *Siroe* in New York, Locke's *Psyche* in London and Hasse's *L'Olimpiade* in Dresden.

Rickenbacher, Karl Anton (b Basel, 20 May 1940), Swiss conductor. After study at the Berlin Conservatory 1962–66 he was assistant at the

Zurich Opera 1966–69, and principal of the Freiburg Opera, 1969–74. BBC Scottish SO 1977–80, debut with the Deutsche Oper Berlin and Berlin PO 1983. Conducted the Royal Philharmonic Orchestra and Philharmonia from 1987. US debut 1988.

ricochet French = 'rebound'; a special kind of *staccato* in violin music, produced by letting the bow bounce on the strings, whereas in ordinary *staccato* it remains on the string and is moved in rapid jerks.

Ricordi, Giovanni (b Milan, 1785; d Milan, 15 Mar 1853), Italian publisher. Founded the pub. house at Milan *c* 1808.

Ricordi, Giulio (b Milan, 19 Dec 1840; d Milan, 6 Jun 1912), Italian publisher, grandson of Giovanni ◊Ricordi. Became head of the Milan firm on his father's death in 1888. He was also a composer under his own name and that of J Burgmein.

Ricordi, Tito (b Milan, 29 Oct 1811; d Milan, 7 Sept 1888), Italian publisher, father of Giulio ◊Ricordi. Succeeded his father, Giovanni, in 1853. Published many operas by Verdi.

Ridderbusch, Karl (b Recklinghausen, 29 May 1932), German bass. He studied in Essen and from 1961 sang in Munster, Essen and Düsseldorf. Further opportunities came in 1967, when he made his Bayreuth and NY Met. debuts. He first appeared at the Vienna Staatsoper in 1968 and in 1971 made his London, CG, debut as Hunding and Hagen. He sang Sachs under Karajan at Salzburg and appeared as Podestà in Schreker's *Die Gezeichneten* at the 1989 Vienna Festival. Often heard in sacred music by Bach, Schubert and Bruckner.

riddle canon a form of canon written in a single part with no indication where the subsequent entries of the parts are to occur, the performer being left to guess how the music fits by solving a riddle.

Riders to the Sea opera by Vaughan Williams (libretto Synge's play), produced London, RCM, 1 Dec 1937; first public performance Cambridge, Arts Theatre, 22 Feb 1938. The opera opens as the body of Maurya's drowned son Michael is identified. Later, her remaining son Bartley also dies at sea.

Ridout, Alan (b West Wikham, Kent, 9 Dec 1934), English composer. Studied with Gordon Jacob and Herbert Howells at the RCM; professor there 1961–84.

Works include the church operas *The Boy from the Catacombs* (1965), *The Children's Crusade* (1968), *Creation* (1973), *Wenceslas* (1978) and *The White Doe* (1987); opera *The Pardoner's Tale* (1971), *Christmas Oratorio*, eight Cantatas, eight symphonies and 13 concertinos with strings (1975–79).

Riedel, Carl (b Kronenberg near Elberfeld, 6 Oct 1827; d Leipzig, 3 Jun 1888), German choral conductor. Studied at the Leipzig Conservatory after starting life in commerce and founded a choral society there. He gave performances of then-neglected works by Schütz.

Rieder, Ambrosius (b Döbling near Vienna, 10 Oct 1771; d Perchtoldsdorf near Vienna, 19 Nov 1855), Austrian composer. Pupil of Albrechtsberger in Vienna, where he became a choirmaster later on.

Works include Masses and other church music; chamber music; organ works.

Riegel, Kenneth (b Womelsdorf, PA, 19 Apr 1938), American tenor. Studied at the Manhattan School of Music and made debut at Santa Fe 1965, in the US fp of Henze's *König Hirsch*. Sang with NY City Opera 1969–74 and the Met. from 1973, as Iopas in *Les Troyens*, David, Hoffmann and Tamino. At the Paris Opéra sang the Painter in the fp of the three-act version of *Lulu* (1979) and created the Leper in Messiaen's *St François d'Assise* (1983). CG from 1985 in the title role of Zemlinsky's *Der Zwerg*, and as Loge (1991) and Herod (1992). Other roles include Dionysus in *The Bassarids* (Stuttgart, 1989), Busoni's Mephistopheles, and Don Ottavio (in the Joseph Losey film version of *Don Giovanni*).

Riegger, Wallingford (b Albany, GA, 29 Apr 1885; d New York, 2 Apr 1961), American composer. Studied in NY and Berlin, with Goetschius, Stillman-Kelley and others. After conducting in Germany, he returned to USA, where he held various teaching appointments. Wrote several ballet scores in the 1930s but later composed in an atonal idiom.

Works include *American Polonaise–Triple Jazz* (1922),

Rhapsody, Fantasy and Fugue (1955), Lyric Suite, two Dance Suites, Canon and Fugue, etc. for orchestra, various works for dancers; *La Belle Dame sans merci* (Keats) for four voices and chamber orchestra (1924); four symphonies (1943–57); *Dichotomy* and *Scherzo* for chamber orchestra; *Study in Sonority* for ten violins; two string quartets (1939, 1948), piano trio, *Divertissement* for harp, flute, and cello, three Canons for woodwind and other chamber music; Suite for solo flute.

Riemann, (Karl Wilhelm Julius) Hugo (b Grossmehlra near Sondershausen, 18 Jul 1849; d Leipzig, 10 Jul 1919), German musicologist. Studied law at Berlin and Tübingen, music at the Leipzig Conservatory and later became lecturer at the university there, 1878–80, and again, after various appointments elsewhere, in 1895–1901, when he became professor. Among his many publications are a *Musiklexikon* (1882), *Handbuch der Musikgeschichte* (1904), *Opernhandbuch* (1887), works on notation, harmony, phrasing, history, etc. He edited many standard works and also composed mainly teaching pieces for piano.

Rienzi, der Letzte der Tribunen, *Rienzi, the Last of the Tribunes*, (first called *Cola Rienzi*)

Opera in five acts by Wagner (libretto by composer based on Bulwer-Lytton's novel and, further back, on Mary Russell Mitford's play), produced Dresden, 20 Oct 1842. Rienzi, proclaimed tribune of Rome, faces assassination plots from the nobleman led by Orsini and Colonna, whose son Adriano loves Rienzi's sister Irene. After his opponents are killed Rienzi is excommunicated by papal allies of Colonna. He is abandoned by all except Irene, who remains loyal to the end. As the siblings are stoned by the people, Adriano tries to rescue Irene but all three are killed as the burning building collapses.

Ries, Ferdinand (b Godesberg, bap. 28 Nov 1784; d Frankfurt, 13 Jan 1838), German pianist, violinist and composer. He was taught piano and violin by his father, Franz Anton Ries, who also taught Beethoven, and studied cello with B Romberg. After a short course in composition with Winter at Munich in 1801, he went to Vienna that year, and studied piano with Beethoven and composition with Albrechtsberger, and became pianist to Counts Browne and Lichnowsky. Later he lived by turns in Paris, Vienna, Kassel, Stockholm and St Petersburg. In 1813–24 he lived in London, where he married an Englishwoman and played, taught and composed. He bought a property at Godesberg, near Bonn, but in 1826 went to live at Frankfurt, where he returned again after two years as conductor at Aachen, 1834–36. He conducted several of the Lower Rhine Festivals.

Works include operas *Die Räuberbraut* (1828), *Liska* (*The Sorceress*, 1831) and *Eine Nacht auf dem Libanon* (1834); oratorios *Der Sieg des Glaubens* and *Die Könige Israels*; eight symphonies, four overtures; eight piano concertos; 26 string quartets; eight string quintets, three piano quartets, five piano trios, octet, septet and other chamber music; 20 duets for violin and piano; ten sonatas and many other works for piano.

Rieti, Vittorio (b Alexandria, 28 Jan 1898; d New York, 19 Feb 1994), Italian-born American composer. Studied with Frugatta at Milan and Respighi in Rome, but destroyed all his works written up to 1920. In 1939 he became an American citizen.

Works include opera *Teresa nel bosco* (1934); ballets *Noah's Art* (1922), *Barabau* (1925), *Waltz Academy*, *The Sleep-walker*, *Robinson and Friday* (after Defoe, 1924) and *David's Triumph* (1937); incidental music for Pierre Corneille's *L'Illusion comique* and Giraudoux's *Électre*; seven symphonies (1929–77); *Notturno* for strings; concerto for wind instruments and orchestra, violin concerto, harpsichord concerto, three piano concertos (1926, 1937, 1955), two cello concertos; *Madrigal* for 12 instruments (1927), partita for flute, oboe, string quartet and harpsichord; sonata for flute, oboe, bassoon and piano; *Second Avenue Waltzes* for two pianos, piano pieces.

Rietz, Julius (b Berlin, 28 Dec 1812; d Dresden, 12 Sept 1877), German composer and conductor. Studied under his father, cello under B Romberg and others and composition under Zelter. In 1835 he succeeded Mendelssohn as conductor of the opera at Düsseldorf, and the next year became town music director and conducted the orchestral and choral concerts. In 1847–60 he was conductor of the Vocal Academy and the Gewandhaus orchestra at Leipzig and taught composition at the Conservatory. In 1860 he was appointed conductor of the Royal Opera, director of the church chapel and of the Conservatory at Dresden. He edited works by Bach, Beethoven, Mendelssohn and Mozart.

Works include operas *Der Corsär, Das Mädchen aus der Fremde* and *Georg Neumark*, operetta *Jery und Bätely* (Goethe); incidental music for Shakespeare's *Hamlet* and *As You Like It*, Holtei's *Lorbeerbaum und Bettelstab* and plays by Goethe, Calderón, Immermann, etc.; two symphonies and three overtures; *Dithyrambe* for male chorus and orchestra.

Rifkin, Joshua (b New York, 22 Apr 1944), American musicologist, conductor and pianist. He studied at Juilliard and Princeton and with Stockhausen at Darmstadt. He has researched Renaissance and Baroque music; authentic performances, including a recording of the B minor Mass without full-scale chorus. Conducted Bach's *St Matthew Passion* at the 1994 Prom Concerts, London.

Rigacci, Bruno (b Florence, 1921), Italian conductor. Founded the Chamber Orchestra of Florence and conducted at the Royal Opera, Stockholm. Musical director of the Philadelphia Music Theatre from 1974 and principal conductor of San Diego Opera 1980–84; later led Thomas' *Hamlet* there. Has returned to Italy to conduct opera at Lugo (from 1987) and at the Barga Festival; *La Bohème* and *Lucia di Lammermoor* at Florence, Rossi's *Orfeo* at La Scala. Has also conducted *Semiramide* at the Bilbao Festival. Recordings include rare repertory by Donizetti.

rigadoon, English, *rigaudon* French, a French dance, probably from the south (Provence or Languedoc), dating back to the 17th c. at the latest. It is in lively common or 2–4 time and consists of three or four parts, each repeated, the third being the shortest.

Rigby, Jean (b Fleetwood, 22 Dec 1954), English mezzo. Studied at the RAM and from 1982 has sung with ENO as Mercédès in *Carmen*, Britten's Lucretia, Eurydice in the premiere of Birtwistle's *The Mask of Orpheus* (1986), Penelope in Monteverdi's *Return of Ulysses* (1989), and Maddalena in *Rigoletto*. CG debut 1983, returning 1993 as Nicklausse. Glyndebourne debut 1985; sang Cornelia in *Giulio Cesare* at Zurich, 1986.

Righetti-Giorgi, Geltrude (not Maria Brighenti), ◊Giorgi-Righetti.

Righini, Vincenzo (b Bologna, 22 Jan 1756; d Bologna, 19 Aug 1812), Italian composer and singer. A chorister at San Petronio in Bologna and pupil of Padre Martini, he made his stage debut in Parma and went as a singer to Prague, where his *Don Giovanni* was produced 1776, 11 years before Mozart's opera on the same subject. Appointed director of the *opera buffa* in Vienna in 1780, he was in the service of the court at Mainz 1787–92, and from 1793 court *Kapellmeister* in Berlin.

Works include operas *Il convitato di pietra* (*Don Giovanni*), *La vedova scaltra* (1778), *Demogorgone* (1786), *Alcide al bivio* (1790), *Enea nel Lazio, Il trionfo d'Arianna* (1793), *Ariadne, Tigrane* (1800), *La selva incantata* and *Gerusalemme liberata* (both after Tasso, 1803, 1799) and others; oratorio *Der Tod Jesu*; cantatas, etc.; *Missa solemnis*, Requiem, Te Deum and other church music; chamber music; keyboard music; songs.

Rignold, Hugo (Henry) (b Kingston-on-Thames, 15 May 1905; d London, 30 May 1976), English conductor. Taken to Canada as a child, but returned to study at the RAM, violin with H Wessely, oboe with L Goossens and viola with L Tertis. After some years as a freelance violinist in London he became conductor of the Palestine SO, 1944, and in 1945–47, of the Cairo SO. After a year at Covent Garden, where later he gave the fp in Britain of Stravinsky's *Agon*, he became conductor of the Liverpool PO (1948–54), music director of the Royal Ballet, 1957–60, and from 1960 to 1969 conductor of the CBSO.

Rigoletto opera by Verdi (libretto by F M Piave, based on Victor Hugo's play *Le Roi s'amuse*), produced Venice, Teatro la Fenice, 11 Mar 1851. Rigoletto's daughter Gilda is abducted by the Duke of Mantua, who has designs on her. Rigoletto rescues her, but by now

―――――――THE OPERA―――――――

Rigoletto

A three-act opera by Giuseppe Verdi, first produced in 1851 and set in the north Italian city of Mantua in the 16th century.

I. The courtiers of the licentious Duke of Mantua (tenor) decide to teach a lesson to the hunchbacked court jester Rigoletto (baritone); they will abduct the girl they believe to be his mistress. Rigoletto mocks Count Monterone (baritone), whose daughter has been seduced by the duke, and Monterone curses him. On his way home, Rigoletto meets a hired assassin, Sparafucile (bass), who offers his services. Rigoletto warns his daughter Gilda (soprano), but she keeps quiet about meeting a handsome student (the duke in disguise). A despairing Rigoletto is tricked by the courtiers into helping in Gilda's abduction.

II. The duke entertains Gilda in his palace, and Rigoletto learns of her fate when she runs to him. He weeps at her shame, and when Monterone enters on his way to imprisonment, the jester tells him he will be avenged.

III. The duke sings of women's waywardness. Rigoletto has arranged for the duke's murder at Sparafucile's tavern. His sister Maddalena (mezzo-soprano) arranges with him that any stranger appearing before midnight shall be murdered in place of the duke. Overhearing them, Gilda decides to sacrifice her life. Rigoletto duly receives a corpse-filled sack but he is about to dispose of it when the duke's song is heard again. When Rigoletto opens the sack, Gilda only has time to ask her father's forgiveness before she dies.

―――――――THE OPERA―――――――

she loves the Duke. Rigoletto arranges his murder, but Gilda substitutes herself instead.

Rihm, Wolfgang (b Karlsruhe, 13 Mar 1952), German composer. He studied in Karlsruhe and with Stockhausen and Fortner.

Works include operas *Faust and Yorick* (1976), *Harlekin* (1977), *Jacob Lenz* (1979), *Die Hamletmaschine* (1986), *Oedipus* (1987) and *Die Eroberung von Mexico* (1992); three symphonies (1966–77, no. 3 to texts by Nietzsche and Rimbaud); *Ein Imaginäres Requiem* for soloists, chorus and orchestra (1976); *Dis-kontur* and *Sub-kontur* for orchestra (1974–75); *Konzertarie* for soprano and orchestra based on telegram sent by Ludwig II to Wagner (1976); *Cuts and Dissolves*, concerto for 29 players (1976); *Abgesangsszene* nos. 1–5 for voice and orchestra (1979–81); *Lenz-Fragmente* and five songs for soprano and orchestra (1980); *Tutuguri*, series of seven works for various instrumental combinations inspired by Paul Claudel (1981); *Monodram* for cello and orchestra (1983), *Dies* for soloists, chorus and orchestra (1984); *Anderer Schatten* (ditto, 1985); *Kein firmament*, 14 players, *Fusées* for orchestra (1984); *Dämmerung* for orchestra (1985); *Dunkles Spiel* for chamber orchestra (1990), *Umfassung* for orchestra in two groups (1990); *'Mein Tod, Requiem in memoriam Jane S'*, for soprano and orchestra (1989), *Frau/Stimme* for soprano and orchestra (1989), *Départ* for chorus, narrator and 22 players (1988); *Geheimer Block* for voice and orchestra (1989); *Engel* for two male voices and 20 instruments (1989); *Cantus firmus* for 14 players (1990); *Ricercare* for ensemble (1990); *Etude pour Séraphin*, for eight brass instruments and six percussion players (1992); eight string quartets (1968–88); *Deploration* for flute, cello and percussion (1973); *Erscheinung*, sketch after Schubert for nine strings (1978), *Nature Morte* for 13 strings (1980); *Fremde Szene* for piano trio (1983); solo songs and music for piano and for organ.

Riisager, Knudåge (b Port Kunda, Estonia, 6 Mar 1897; d Copenhagen, 26 Dec 1974), Danish composer. Studied political economy at Copenhagen University, but later turned to music, studying composition with Peder Gram and Otto Malling, later with Roussel and Le Flem in Paris and finally with Hermann Grabner at Leipzig.

Works include opera *Susanne* (1950); ballets *Benzin* (1930), *Cock-*

A Selection of

Rimsky-Korsakov

Mlada 1872
The Snow Maiden 1882
Spanish Capriccio.....................................1887
Sheherazade 1888

Sadko 1898
Mozart and Salieri 1898
The Tsar's Bride.......................................1899
The Legend of Tsar Saltan........................1900
Kashtchey the Immortal.............................1902
The Legend of the Invisible City of Kitezh 1907

Works include Masses and *Cantiones sacrae*; madrigals and *villancicos*, etc.

Rimsky-Korsakov, Andrey Nikolaievich (b St Petersburg, 17 Oct 1878; d Leningrad, 23 May 1940), Russian critic and music historian. Studied at the Universities of St Petersburg, Strasbourg and Heidelberg, and did not turn to music until 1913, after his father's death. In 1915 he founded the monthly journal *Muzikalny Sovremennik/The Musical Contemporary*) and in 1922 he became editor of *Muzikalnayu Lietopis/Musical Chronicle*). He edited his father's and Glinka's memoirs, Mussorgsky's letters and documents, Cui's critical writings, his father's correspondence with Tchaikovsky; wrote on Mussorgsky's *Boris Godunov*, the music MSS in the Leningrad Public Library, of which he was curator, etc. He married the composer Julia Lazarevna Weissberg (1878–1942).

Rimsky was ... deeply and unshowingly generous, and unkind only to admirers of Tchaikovsky.
Igor Stravinsky on Rimsky-Korsakov,
Memories and Commentaries, 1960

Rimsky-Korsakov, Nikolay Andreievich (b Tikhvin, Government Novgorod, 18 Mar 1844; d St Petersburg, 21 Jun 1908), Russian composer, father of Andrey ◊Rimsky-Korsakov. He came of a naval family and his ambition was to become a sailor, though he showed great interest in the Russian folksongs and church music he heard in his childhood, as well as in the operas he knew from piano selections. In 1856 he was sent to the Naval College at St Petersburg, where he remained until 1862. He had more piano lessons during that time and learnt a little theory, but was not taught anything systematic even when in 1861 he met Balakirev and his circle, and came under their influence. He began a symphony in E♭ minor, but in 1862 was ordered on a three-year cruise. He wrote the slow movement of the symphony off Gravesend and heard opera in London and NY, but did not take up music again until his return to St Petersburg in 1865, when he worked more seriously under Balakirev, who conducted the symphony. The first important works were the symphonic poem *Sadko* (1867) and the programme symphony *Antar* (1868). In 1868 he also began his first opera, *Pskovitianka/The Maid of Pskov*, finished in 1872. Meanwhile he had been appointed professor of composition at the Conservatory, though in theoretical knowledge he was always little more than one lesson ahead of his pupils. In 1872 he married the pianist Nadezhda Purgold.

Appointed inspector of naval bands in 1873 and director of the Free School of Music in 1874, in succession to Balakirev, until 1881, when he became the latter's assistant in the direction of the Imperial Chapel. He became rather pedantically scholastic during those years, in reaction against his earlier amateurism, but this tendency was counteracted by his interest in Russian folk music and by the influence of Wagner.

His editorship of 100 Russian Folk-Songs (1877) inspired a new phase in his output, leading to the operas *May Night* and *Snegurochka/The Snow Maiden*. During the 1880's he was largely occupied with orchestrations and revisions for Mussorgsky's *Khovanshchina* and Borodin's *Prince Igor*. Although some of the instrumental effects in these operas verged on the excessive, the experience he gained led Rimsky-Korsakov to his most popular work, the orchestral fantasy *Sheherazade* of 1888. It was followed by the operas *Christmas Eve* (after Gogol), *Sadko* (a vivid celebration of Tsarist Russia) and *Mozart and Salieri*; a powerful setting of Pushkin.

In 1892–93 he had a serious nervous breakdown and temporarily gave up composition, but his interest revived. In 1905, when he had sided with the 'wrong' party during political disturbances, he was dismissed from the Conservatory, but there was such a storm of protest that he was reinstated later.

In 1907 Rimsky-Korsakov produced his masterpiece, the opera *The Legend of the Invisible City of Kitezh*. A prophetic depiction of the resilience of the Russian spirit, it tells of the miraculous emerg-

tail Party and *Slaraffenland* (*Land of Cockaigne*, 1942); incidental music to Johannes Jensen's fairy play *Darduse*; chorus works; five symphonies (1925–50), variations *Poème mécanique*, *Jabiru T—DOXC* and overture to Holberg's *Erasmus Montanus* for orchestra; concerto for trumpet and strings; six string quartets (1918–43), sonata for flute, clarinet, violin and cello, serenade for flute, violin and cello; violin and piano sonata; sonata and various pieces for piano; songs.

Riley, Terry (b Colfax, CA, 24 Jun 1935), American composer and saxophonist. He studied at Berkeley and since 1970 has been influenced by Indian music; works involve repeated patterns and series, and contain freedom for improvisation. Belongs to the Minimalist school of composers.

Works include *Spectra* for six instruments (1959); String trio (1965); *Keyboard Studies* (1965); *Poppy Nogood and the Phantom Band* for saxophone, tape and electronics (1968); *Rainbow in Curved Air* (1970); *Genesis '70*, ballet; *Sunrise of the Planetary Dream Collector* and *The Medicine Wheel*, both for string quartet (1981, 1983), works which reflect his interest in astrology. Five of his nine string quartets form the cycle *Salome Dances for Peace* (1988).

Rilke, Rainer Maria (1875–1926), German poet. ◊Beck (*Lyric Cantata*); ◊Burkhard (*song cycle*); L ◊Foss (*Parable of Death*); Martin F Kleneau (*Cornet*); ◊Marienleben (Hindemith); K ◊Marx (choruses and songs); H ◊Reutter (*Weise von Liebe und Tod* and opera translated from Gide); ◊Webern (songs); ◊Weill (songs with orchestra).

Rilling, Helmuth (b Stuttgart, 29 May 1933), German conductor. Studied at the Stuttgart Hochschule and with Fernando Germani and Bernstein. Founded the Gächinger Kantorei 1954, giving worldwide performances of German Baroque music. Founded the Bach-Collegium of Stuttgart 1965, giving US tour 1968 and appearing at English Bach Festival, London 1972. Recordings include cycle of Bach cantatas from 1972, with the Frankfurter Kantorei, Gächinger Kantorei and Figuralchor of Stuttgart.

Rimbault, Edward F(rancis) (b London, 13 Jun 1816; d London, 26 Sept 1876), English music historian and antiquarian. Wrote books on early English music and pub. editions.

Rimonte (or *Ruimonte*), Pedro (b Saragossa, *c* 1570; d after 1618), Spanish composer. The Infanta Isabella took him to the Netherlands on her marriage to the Archduke Albert, governor of the Netherlands, at whose court at Brussels he became chamber musician in 1603. He returned to Spain in 1614, but was in Brussels again four years later.

ence of Kitezh after it has been seemingly destroyed by enemy hordes. Recently, the Kirov Opera has revived most of Rimsky-Korsakov's operas, notably bringing *Kitezh* to acclaimed performances in Paris and London in 1994.

His last opera, based on Pushkin's *Golden Cockerel* (composed 1906–07), was a satire on official stupidity and its performance was forbidden. He conducted a festival of Russian music in Paris at Diaghilev's invitation in 1907. In 1908 he suffered from angina and died four days after the marriage of his daughter Nadia to his pupil M Steinberg. Stravinsky was his most important pupil.

Works include OPERAS: *Pskovitianka* (*Ivan the Terrible*, 1873), *May Night* (1880), *Snegurotchka/The Snow Maiden* (1882), *Mlada* (based on the collective opera commissioned earlier from him, Borodin, Cui and Mussorgsky, composed 1872), *Christmas Eve* (1895), *Sadko* (1898), *Mozart and Salieri* (1898), *Boyarina Vera Sheloga* (prologue to *Pskovitianka*, 1898), *The Tsar's Bride* (1899), *The Legend of Tsar Saltan* (1900), *Servilia* (1902), *Kashchei the Immortal* (1902), *Pan Voievoda*, *The Legend of the Invisible City of Kitezh* (1907), *The Golden Cockerel* (1909).

ORCHESTRAL: three symphonies (second *Antar*); symphonic poem *Sadko* (1867), concert overtures on Russian themes and *Russian Easter*, fantasy on Serbian themes, sinfonietta on Russian themes (1884), symphonic suite *Sheherazade* (1888), *Spanish Capriccio*, *Fairy-Tale*, *On the Tomb* (Belaiev's) and *Dubinushka* for orchestra; piano concerto and fantasy for violin and orchestra (both on Russian themes).

CHAMBER AND SONGS: two string quartets (1875, 1897) and three movements for string quartet contributed to collective sets by various composers, string sextet, quintet for piano and wind instruments (1876); four cantatas; piano pieces; many part-songs, songs, vocal duets, two collections of Russian folksongs.

Rinaldo cantata for tenor solo, male chorus and orchestra by Brahms, op. 50, on a ballad by Goethe, performed Vienna, 28 Feb 1869.

Opera by Handel (libretto by G Rossi, from a sketch based on Tasso by Aaron Hill), produced London, Queen's Theatre, Haymarket, 24 Feb 1711. Handel's first London opera. As knight Rinaldo prepares for victory over Saracen king Argante, the heathen temporarily avoids defeat by enlisting the help of sorceress Armida in abducting Almirena, Rinaldo's love. But Rinaldo saves her; Argante and Armida flee.

Rinaldo di Capua (b Capua or Naples, *c* 1705; d Rome, *c* 1780), Italian composer, according to Burney the illegitimate son of a Neapolitan nobleman. Of more than 30 operas most were produced in Rome, the first in 1737. But some appeared in Florence and Venice, and in 1752–53 the *Bouffons* in Paris performed his *La donna superba* and *La zingara*. His last *opera seria* was written in 1758, after which he devoted himself to comic opera. Burney found him living in poor circumstances in Rome in 1770, after which nothing is known. Only fragments of his music survive.

Works include operas *Ciro riconosciuto* (1737), *Vologeso, rè de' Parti* (1739), *Mario in Numidia* (1749), *Adriano in Siria* (1758), etc.; intermezzi, etc. *Il bravo burlato*, *La donna superba* (1738), *La zingara*, *Le donne ridicole* (1759), *I finti pazzi per amore* (1770), etc.; *Cantata per la natività della Beata Vergine* (1755), etc.

Rinck, (Johann) Christian Heinrich (b Elgersburg, Saxe-Gotha, 18 Feb 1770; d Darmstadt, 7 Aug 1846), German organist, composer and teacher. Studied at Erfurt under the Bach pupil Kittel. In 1805 he settled at Darmstadt, where he became professor, court organist and ducal chamber musician.

Works include *Practical Organ School* and many other works for organ; motets and *Pater noster* for voices and organ; sonatas for piano, violin and piano, cello and piano; piano duets.

rinforzando Italian = 'reinforcing'; a sudden *crescendo* made on a short phrase, similar to the *sforzando*, which is made on a single note or chord.

Ring des Nibelungen, Der, *The Nibelung's Ring*, trilogy of music dramas, with a prologue, by Wagner (libretto by composer, based on the Nibelung Saga); see individual operas for plot synopses:

Das Rheingold/The Rhinegold, produced Munich, Court Opera, 22 Sept 1869.

Die Walküre/The Valkyrie, produced Munich, Court Opera, 26 Jun 1870.

Siegfried, produced Bayreuth, Wagner Festival Theatre, 16 Jun 1876.

Götterdämmerung/The Twilight of the Gods, produced Bayreuth, Wagner Festival Theatre, 17 Aug 1876.

The whole cycle produced Bayreuth, Wagner Festival Theatre, 13–17 Aug 1876.

We've been rehearsing for two hours – and we're still playing the same bloody tune.
Thomas Beecham on rehearsing *Götterdämmerung*, quoted in Reid, *Thomas Beecham*, 1961

Rinuccini, Ottavio (b Florence, 20 Jan 1562; d Florence, 28 Mar 1621), Italian poet and librettist. ◊Arianna (Monteverdi); ◊Bonini (*Lamento d'Arianna*); ◊Dafne (Gagliano, Peri and Schütz); ◊Euridice (Caccini and Peri); ◊Petrassi (*Lamento d'Arianna*).

Rios, Alvaro de los (b *c* 1580; d Madrid, 1623), Spanish composer. Appointed chamber musician to the queen, Margaret of Austria, in 1607.

Works include incidental music to Tirso de Molina's play *El vergonzoso en palacio*, etc.

Riotte, Philipp Jacob (b St Wendel, Saar, 16 Aug 1776; d Vienna, 20 Aug 1856), German composer and conductor. Studied with André at Offenbach, became theatre conductor at Gotha and in 1809 went to Vienna, where he settled, being appointed conductor at the Theater an der Wien in 1818.

Works include operas and operettas *Mozarts Zauberflöte*, *Nureddin*, *Der Sturm* (on Shakespeare's *Tempest*) and many others; ballets; incidental music; cantata *Der Kreuzzug*; symphony; three clarinet concertos; six violin and piano sonatas; nine piano sonatas, piano piece *The Battle of Leipzig*.

ripieno, Italian adj. = 'full'; noun = 'filling, stuffing', an instrument or voice subordinate to a soloist or the leader of a section. In the 18th-c. *concerto grosso* the string players other than the soloists are *ripieni*. Similarly in the brass band a ripieno cornet is one that comes second to the solo cornet.

Rippe, Albert de (b Mantua, *c* 1500; d Paris, 1551), Italian composer, lutenist at the French court from 1529, after service with the Cardinal of Mantua. Most of his lute music was pub. in Paris after his death.

Rippon, Michael (George) (b Coventry, 10 Dec 1938), English bass-baritone. After study at the RAM made his debut in 1963 with the Handel Opera Society as Nireno in *Giulio Cesare*. Sang with WNO 1969–74 (notably as Leporello) and Glyndebourne 1970–73, Mozart's Speaker and Bartolo. Modern repertory includes Henze's *Cimarron*, and Merlin in the fp of Hamilton's *Lancelot* (1985); also sang in the fps of Maxwell Davies' *The Martyrdom of St Magnus* (1977) and *The Lighthouse* (1980).

ripresa Italian = 're-taking, repetition'; a refrain, especially in the 14th-c. Italian *ballata*.

Riquier, Guiraut (b Narbonne, *c* 1230; d *c* 1300), French troubadour. He was the last great exponent of this art. 48 tunes of his songs are extant.

Rising of the Moon, The opera by Maw (libretto by B Cross and composer), produced Glyndebourne, 19 Jul 1970. Cornet Beaumont, new officer of the 31st Lancers, undergoes a series of initiation tests that results in his regiment's withdrawal from Ireland and leaves admirer Cathleen without Beaumont.

rispetto a type of old Italian improvised folk poem of six to ten (usually eight) interrhyming lines, sung to popular tunes.

Rist, Johann (b Ottensen near Hamburg, 8 Mar 1607; d Wedel on Elbe, 31 Aug 1667), German clergyman, poet and musician. He founded a song school at Hamburg and wrote words for a great number of songs and hymns, some of which he composed himself.

Ristori, Giovanni Alberto (b ? Bologna, 1692; d Dresden, 7 Feb 1753),

Italian composer. His first opera was produced in Venice in 1713, but two years later he moved to Dresden with his father, director of an Italian theatrical co. whose music director he became in 1717. Appointed director of the Polish chapel in Dresden in 1718, he became vice-*Kapellmeister* to the court, under Hasse, in 1750.

Works include *c* 20 operas, e.g. *Calandro* (1726), *Don Chisciotte* (1727), *Le fate* (1736), *Didone* (produced CG, 1737), *Temistocle* (1738), *I lamenti di Orfeo* (1749), etc.; three oratorios; 15 cantatas; 15 Masses, three Requiems, motets and other church music.

Risurrezione, *Resurrection*, opera by Alfano (libretto by C Hanau, based on Tolstoy's novel), produced Turin, Teatro Vittorio Emanuele, 30 Nov 1914. Katiusha and Dmitri become lovers and she becomes pregnant. He abandons her and she is sent to Siberia, convicted as a prostitute. Dmitri follows her but she rejects him, favouring another prisoner, Simouson, instead.

Rita opera in one act by Donizetti (libretto by G Vaez); composed 1841, fp (posthumous) Paris, Opéra-Comique, 7 May 1860. Rita dominates weak husband Peppe until ex-husband Gaspar arrives and shows Peppe how to stand up to her.

ritardando Italian = 'retarding'; the same direction is also expressed by *rallentando*, 'slowing down'.

ritenuto, Italian, an indication for the performer to play a passage at a slightly slower tempo than that previously indicated; the original tempo is notated again with *a tempo*. It does not denote a continuous slowing down, unlike *ritardando* or *rallentando*.

Rite of Spring, The ballet by Stravinsky (scenario by composer and Nikolay Roerich, choreographed by Nizhinsky), produced as *Le Sacre du printemps*, Paris, Théâtre des Champs-Élysées, 29 May 1913. There was a riot between partisans and opponents on the first night.

ritmo di ... battute Italian = 'rhythm of ... beats'; an indication that the metrical scheme of a piece or movement is to be accented in groups of as many bars as may be shown in this direction between the second and third word, e.g. in the scherzo of Beethoven's ninth symphony, where the metre changes between *ritmo di tre battute* and *ritmo di quattro battute*.

ritornello Italian = lit. 'little return'; originally 'a refrain and thence', in the early 17th c., a recurrent instrumental piece played in the course of a musical stage work; later the instrumental passages between vocal portions of an anthem or aria, from which in turn is derived the meaning of the word ritornello as applied to the orchestral *tutti* in concertos, especially in rondos where the same theme returns several times.

Ritorno d'Ulisse in patria, Il, *Ulysses' Return to his Country*, opera by Monteverdi (libretto by G Badoaro), produced Venice, Teatro San Cassiano, Feb 1641. Realizations by d'Indy (produced 1925), Dallapiccola (1942), Křenek (1959), Leppard (1972), Harnoncourt, and Henze (1985). With the help of the goddess Minerva, Ulysses finds his way back home to Penelope his wife. Dressed as a beggar, he slays her suitors. Juno and Jupiter restore his identity and Ulysses wins back Penelope.

Ritter, Alexander (b Narva, Russia, 7 Jun 1833; d Munich, 12 Apr 1896), German violinist, conductor and composer. Studied violin with Franz Schubert of Dresden and later went to the Leipzig Conservatory. He married Wagner's niece, Franziska Wagner, in 1854, became an ardent Wagnerian, conductor at Stettin in 1856, settled at Würzburg in 1863, ran a music shop there 1875–82 and then joined the ducal orchestra at Meiningen under Bülow, whose retirement caused him to move to Munich in 1886. He was a close friend of Richard Strauss.

Works include operas *Der faule Hans* (1885), and *Wem die Krone?* (1890); symphonic poems, etc.

Ritter, Christian (b *c* 1650; d after 1717), German organist and composer. Worked at Halle, Dresden, Stockholm and Hamburg.

Works include 22 motets, Te Deum for double chorus; cantatas including *O amantissime sponse Jesu* for soprano and strings; instrumental works.

Ritter, Peter (b Mannheim, 2 Jul 1763; d Mannheim, 1 Aug 1846),

German cellist and composer. Studied cello with Danzi, composition with Vogler, succeeded Danzi in the Mannheim orchestra in 1784 and became conductor in 1803.

Works include operas *Der Eremit auf Formentara* (Kotzebue, 1788), *Die lustigen Weiber* (after Shakespeare's *Merry Wives*, 1794), and *c* 20 others; plays with music; church music, oratorio *Das verlorene Paradies* (after Milton, 1819); cello concertos; chamber music; cello and piano sonatas.

Ritual Dances four dances for chorus and orchestra in Tippett's opera *The Midsummer Marriage*: *The Earth in Autumn*, *The Waters in Winter*, *The Air in Spring*, *Fire in Summer*. Often heard as concert work; fp Basel, 13 Feb 1953 – two years before first production of opera, at CG.

Rituel in memoriam Bruno Maderna work for orchestra by Boulez, fp London, 2 Apr 1975, conductor Boulez.

Rizzi, Carlo (b Milan, 19 Jul 1960), Italian conductor. Studied in Milan and made his debut at the Angelicum there in 1982, with Donizetti's *L'ajo nell'imbarrazzo*. Conducted *Falstaff* at Parma in 1985 and has appeared throughout Italy with *Don Giovanni*, *Tancredi* and *Beatrice di Tenda*. British debut at the 1988 Buxton Festival, Donizetti's *Torquato Tasso*. Has given *Lucrezia Borgia* with Australian Opera and *Tosca* with Opera North. CG, London from 1990, *Cenerentola* and *Il viaggio a Reims*. Music director WNO from 1992 (*Elektra*, *Le Comte Ory* and *Rigoletto*). NY Met. debut 1993, *Il barbiere di Siviglia*. Large concert repertory.

Rizzio, Davidde (b *c* 1525; d Edinburgh, 9 Mar 1566), Italian bass and diplomat. In service at the court of Savoy, he visited Scotland in 1561 in the ambassador's suite and remained in the service of Queen Mary with his brother Giuseppe. He arranged masques at court and became her foreign secretary in 1564, but her favour aroused jealousies and he was stabbed to death in Holyrood Palace. Erroneously alleged to have written several tunes now regarded as traditional Scottish.

RMCM, abbr., = Royal Manchester College of Music.

RNCM, abbr., = Royal Northern College of Music (Manchester).

Roar, Leif (b Copenhagen, 31 Aug 1931), Danish baritone. Sang in Kiel and Düsseldorf from 1967, Munich from 1971 as Wotan and Jochanaan. Sang Wagner's Donner and Kurwenal at the Salzburg Easter Festival under Karajan (1973–74); Bayreuth from 1976, as Telramund and Klingsor. NY Met. debut 1982, as Pizarro in *Fidelio*, Wotan at Arhus, Denmark 1987. Other roles include Hans Sachs (at Stockholm), Don Giovanni, Hindemith's Mathis, and Scarpia.

Robbins, Julien (b Harrisburg, PA, 14 Nov 1950), American bass. Studied with Nicola Moscona in New York and made debut at Philadelphia in 1976, *Un ballo in Maschera*. Sang in Miami, Washington and Chicago, and from 1979 at the NY Met., as Ramfis, Gremin and Masetto; premiere of *The Voyage* by Philip Glass, 1992. Deutsche Oper Berlin from 1992, as Don Giovanni, Escamillo and Timur; has also sung Rossini's Basilio at the Staatsoper.

Roberday, François (b Paris, bap. 21 Mar 1624; d Auffargis, 13 Oct 1680), French organist and composer. He held appointments as a goldsmith under the Queens Anne of Austria and Marie-Thérèse, and was one of Lully's teachers.

Works include *Fugues et Caprices* for organ.

Robert le Diable, *Robert the Devil*, opera by Meyerbeer (libretto by Scribe), produced Paris, Opéra, 21 Nov 1831. Bertram, the Duke Robert's father, is a demon and must repossess his son's soul by midnight. Robert is searching for his love Isabelle, and Bertram tries to lead him astray with offers of help. Alice, Robert's foster sister, saves his soul and helps reunite him with Isabelle, as Bertram returns to Hell.

Roberto Devereux, Conte d'Essex opera by Donizetti (libretto by S Cammarano, based on Jacques Ancelot's tragedy *Élisabeth d'Angleterre*), produced Naples, Teatro San Carlo, 2 Oct 1837. Robert Devereux wears Queen Elizabeth's ring, which guarantees him protection. But he tears it off for love of Sarah, wife of the Duke of Nottingham.

Opera by Mercadante (libretto by F Romani, based on Corneille's *Comte d'Essex*), produced Milan, La Scala, 10 Mar 1833.

Marisa Robles – harpist

1 Mozart: Concerto for Flute, Harp and Orchestra in C
If music could be a religion, Mozart would be my God. For harpists, this is perhaps *the* masterpiece. It continues to change my life every time I play it: the music is fresh, always a challenge. Forty years of playing it – and every time it is as if I am hearing it for the first time.

2 Chopin: Piano works
When I hear Chopin's piano music, it speaks to me like a message of peace; he asks us to be kinder, more gentle. The very architecture of his melodies speaks of suffering and acceptance.

3 Rakhmaninov: Piano Concerto no.2 (Lympany/Philharmonia/Malko)
When I was 20, an Englishman came to one of my concerts and became very fond of me. I was young and really not interested. But one day he sent me a tape of this piano concerto by Rakhmaninov, played by Moura Lympany. Strangely, it moved me so much that I began to welcome his attentions. In the end, I married him! So this piece is the key to a great adventure of love: we had a son together, and although we separated some years later, we still speak about Rakhmaninov.

4 Mozart: Requiem
In May 1990 I went to hospital to have a small lump removed from my breast. It was very early days, but it was cancer. I was very lucky – I'm fine now. But that summer, I cancelled everything. Each evening I spent in the garden, and as the sun went down I put on Mozart's Requiem. That piece gave me a new lease of life; it gave me the strength and serenity to accept those first few months of depressing radiotherapy, to accept it all with love, the love that Mozart put into that piece, even though he knew he was dying.

Roberts, Susan (b NY, 25 Aug 1952), American soprano. Has sung widely in Germany and is best known as Mozart's Blondchen, which she has sung in productions of *Die Entführung* by Ruth Berghaus, Giorgio Strehler and Jean-Pierre Ponnelle. Created roles in Henze's *The English Cat* (1983) and Ohana's *La Celestina* (Paris Opéra 1988) and sang Zan in the new edition of Blitzstein's *Regina* for Scottish Opera (1991). Sang Handel's Agrippina at the 1992 Buxton Festival.

Robertsbridge Manuscript the earliest known source of keyboard music consisting of two leaves bound in with an old Robertsbridge Abbey register (British Museum Additional 28,550). It contains three *estampies* (the first incomplete) showing Italian influence, and three Latin motets (the third incomplete), of which the first two are arrangements of motets included in the French *Roman de Fauvel*. No convincing arguments have been put forward against an English origin for the MS. The date is *c* 1325.

Robertson, Alec (b Southsea, 3 Jun 1892; d Midhurst, 18 Jan 1982), English musicologist. Studied at the RAM in London and became an organist and choirmaster in 1913. After serving in World War I he lectured at LCC evening institutes and in 1920 became lecturer and later head of the Gramophone co.'s education department. Lived in Rome for four years to study plainsong and in 1940 joined the BBC in charge of the music talks in the Home Service. His books include *The Interpretation of Plainchant*, *Art and Religion*, *Dvořák* and *Requiem: Music of Mourning and Consolation*.

Robertson, James (b Liverpool, 17 Jun 1912; d Ruabon, N. Wales, 18 May 1991), English conductor. Studied at the Leipzig Conservatory and the RCM, becoming a coach at Glyndebourne 1937–39. Co-director and conductor at SW, London, 1946–54 leading *Werther*, *Don Pasquale* and the UK fp of Wolf-Ferrari's *Quattro Rusteghi*. Conducted in New Zealand 1954–81, with guest performance at SW 1958–63. Director of the London Opera Centre 1964–77. CBE 1969.

Robeson, Paul (b Princeton, NJ, 9 Apr 1898; d Philadelphia, 23 Jan 1976), American bass. After studying law at Rutgers and Columbia Universities he began a career as an actor, becoming especially well known as Othello. In 1925 he first appeared as a singer, with a recital of African-American spirituals, and soon attained world fame, but his career was impeded by his Communist sympathies. In 1952 he was awarded the Stalin Peace Prize.

Robin et Marion, Le Jeu de, *The Play of Robin and Marion*, a pastoral play with monophonic music by Adam de la Halle, written in Naples between 1283 and his death in 1286 or 1287.

Robinson, Anastasia (b Italy, *c* 1692; d Southampton, Apr 1755), English soprano. A pupil of Croft, she made her stage debut in 1714 and during the next ten years sang in many of Handel's operas, creating roles in *Amadigi*, *Radamisto*, *Ottone*, *Flavio* and *Giulio Cesare*. Having married the Earl of Peterborough, she retired in 1724.

Robinson, Faye (b Houston, 2 Nov 1943), American soprano. After study in New York sang with the City Opera there from 1972 as Micaela, The Queen of Shemakha (*Golden Cockerel*), Violetta and Liù. European debut at Aix 1975, in *Der Schauspieldirektor* and *La serva padrona*; Paris Opéra 1982, as Gounod's Juliette. Sang in the 1984 Boston fp of Tippett's *The Mask of Time*; Constanze at Cologne in 1988.

Robinson, Forbes (b Macclesfield, 21 May 1926; d London, 13 May 1987), English bass. After study at La Scala, he sang at CG from 1954; created the title role in *King Priam* (Coventry, 1962) and was Moses in the British fp of *Moses und Aron* (1965). Also sang Boris, Claggart and Don Giovanni, and in oratorios by Handel and Walton.

Robinson, John (b ? London, 1682; d London, 30 Apr 1762), English organist and composer. Chorister in the Chapel Royal, became organist of St Lawrence, Jewry, and St Magnus, London Bridge, and in 1727 succeeded Croft as organist of Westminster Abbey. In 1716 he married William Turner's daughter Ann (d London, 5 Jan 1741), a singer at the Italian Opera.

Works include Double Chant in E♭ major.

Robinson, Stanford (b Leeds, 5 Jul 1904; d Brighton, 25 Oct 1984), English conductor. He studied at the RAM and worked with the BBC, 1924–66, as chorus master and orchestra conductor; many studio performances of operas. He was at CG, London, in the Coronation season of 1937. Appeared widely in Europe after World War II.

Robinson Crusoé operetta by Offenbach (libretto by E Cormon and H Crémieux, based distantly on Defoe's novel), produced Paris, Opéra-Comique, 23 Nov 1867. Robinson meets Vendredi (Man Friday) and his friends in a farcical plot on the desert island.

Robledo, Melchior (b *c* 1520; d Saragossa, 1587), Spanish composer. Spent some time in Rome, but returned to Spain in 1569 and became *maestro de capilla* at the old cathedral of Saragossa, where, as at the new one, his work alone was sung with that of Morales, Victoria and Palestrina.

Works include Masses, motets.

Robles, Marisa (b Madrid, 4 May 1937), Spanish harpist. She studied at the Madrid Conservatory and made her debut in 1954. Settled in England 1959, teaching at RCM from 1971. Well known in concert and recital.

Robson, Christopher (b Falkirk, 9 Dec 1953), Scottish countertenor. After study at the TCL and with Paul Esswood made London concert debut 1976, in Handel's *Samson*; opera debut Birmingham 1979, as Argones in *Sosarme*. Member of the Monteverdi Choir 1974–84 and

Christopher Robson – singer

1   Tallis: Lamentations of Jeremiah (Hilliard Ensemble)
A truly great and faithful recording of a masterpiece by one of England's finest Church composers, and sung by true artists.

2   Vivaldi: *The Four Seasons* (Standage/English Concert/Pinnock)
From the day this recording was released, no other has been as satisfying, rich or virtuosic, and the recorded sound is breathtaking.

3   Handel: *Jephtha*
A personally biased choice for the heartsearching performance by my brother Nigel in the title role. The risks taken in 'Waft her, Angels' prove that a live performance can be equally moving and exciting with every hearing.

4   Bach: *Goldberg Variations* (Glenn Gould, 2nd recording)
Apart from being one of the most challenging keyboard pieces to play, it is also a challenge to sit through. The first time I truly sat down and listened was when someone played me this recording in 1984, leading me into a whole new world of Bach and, of course, Glenn Gould!

5   Mozart: *Così fan tutte* (English Baroque Soloists/Gardiner)
The famous trio sets up the dreadful tragedy of this very modern work. To go from such poignancy to an ending of true ambiguity can only be the work of a great composer and an equally great librettist.

6   Schumann: *Dichterliebe* (Britten/Pears)
A difficult journey for any artist to undertake. 'Wenn ich in Deine Augen seh' reveals a bitterness and sadness hard for a singer to come to terms with when performing this pinnacle of the German lieder repertoire. Britten's playing surpasses all other interpretations in its intensity and artistic accomplishment.

7   Berlioz: *Symphonie fantastique* (London Classical Players/Norrington)
To hear the colours of an 'authentic' band playing one of the 19th century's most exciting orchestral adventures takes the listener into the pioneering mind of a great Romantic. The lyricism of the woodwinds contrast with the raw edge of the narrow-bored brass, the purity of the strings with the almost apocalyptic timpani.

8   Wagner: *Siegfried's Funeral March* (Bayreuth Festival/Boulez)
I have never been to Bayreuth, and would have given an arm and a leg to be in the theatre on the first night of the Boulez cycle. I saw it on TV, and what happened in these few minutes said everything. A personal memory of the greatest moment (for me, anyway) in probably the best acted *Ring* ever staged.

9   Birtwistle: *The Mask of Orpheus* (no recording)
1986 was a historic year in opera, with an English National Opera overwhelmed by the magnitude of its undertaking. One day it will be heard and seen again, but the memory of those few performances will never die. A unique achievement by all concerned, and possibly the greatest opera of the 20th century.

10   Cage: *Royanji*
Again, a personal choice, having performed it in front of the man himself during his last visit to Zurich. A piece inspired by the beauty and serenity of a Japanese garden. Timeless, peaceful, always moving.

---

created Glass's Akhnaten at Houston and New York, 1984. Other Handel roles include Ptolemy in *Giulio Cesare* (Scottish Opera), Arsamenes in *Xerxes* and Polinesso in *Ariodante* (ENO) and Tamerlane for Opera North. Many concert performances in music by Handel, Monteverdi and Purcell.

Rocca, Lodovico (b Turin, 29 Nov 1895; d Turin, 25 Jun 1986), Italian composer. Pupil of Orefice. Appointed director of the Turin Conservatory in 1940.
     Works include operas *La morte di Frine*, *La corona del rè Gaulo*, *Il Dibuk* (1934), *In terra di leggenda* (1933), *Monte Ivnor* (1939) and *L'uragano* (1952); symphonic poems *Contrasti*, *Aurora di morte*, *L'alba del malato* (1922), and *La foresta delle Samodive* (1921), also *La cella azzurra*, *Chiaroscuri* and *Interludio epico* for orchestra; chamber music.

Rochberg, George (b Paterson, NJ, 5 Jul 1918), American composer. He wrote in a serial idiom until 1964, when a family tragedy inspired a change of heart. Such works as the *Sacred Song of Reconciliation* (1970) and the *Transcendental Varieties* for strings (1975) have embraced tonality once more. Studied composition with Szell and L Mannes (1939–41) in NY, and then at the Curtis Institute, Philadelphia, with Scalero and Menotti. In 1950 he was awarded a Fulbright Fellowship and in 1956 a Guggenheim Fellowship. From 1948 to 1954 he taught at the Curtis Institute. Professor of music at Pennsylvania University 1968–83.
     Works include opera *The Confidence Man* (after Melville, 1982),

symphonic poem *Night Music*, six symphonies (1958–87), *Time-Span* (1960), *Waltz Serenade*, *Sinfonia Fantasia* for orchestra; *Cantio Sacra* for chamber orchestra; seven string quartets (1952–79); *Imago Mundé* for orchestra (1975), violin concerto (1974), oboe concerto (1983); clarinet sonata; fantasia for violin and piano; two piano sonatas.

Roche, Jerome (b Cairo, 22 May 1942; d Durham, 2 Jun 1994), English musicologist. Studied at Cambridge University 1959–67, and was lecturer at Durham from 1967. Early Italian music was at the centre of his research and he published books on Palestrina (1971), the Italian madrigal (1972) and Lassus (1982). With wife Elizabeth edited *Dictionary of Early Music, from the Troubadours to Monteverdi* (1981). Also *North Italian Church Music in the Age of Monteverdi* (1984) and *The Flower of Italian Madigrals* (1988).

Rochlitz, Johann Friedrich (b Leipzig, 12 Feb 1769; d Leipzig, 16 Dec 1842), German music critic and poet. Studied under Doles at the St Thomas's School, Leipzig, later theology at the university. In 1798 he founded the *Allgemeine musikalische Zeitung*, which he edited until 1818. He also composed, wrote libretti and poems, three of which were set by Schubert; others were set by Weber and Spohr.

Rodde, Anne Marie (b Clermont-Ferrand, 21 Nov 1946), French soprano. After study in Paris made debut at Aix in 1971, as Amor in *Orfeo ed Euridice*. With the English Bach Festival in London, has appeared in *Hippolyte et Aricie* and *Les Boréades*, by Rameau. Has sung at the Paris Opéra and in Stockholm, Rome and Montreal in the

George Rochberg – composer

1   Handel: 12 concerti grossi, op. 6 (Academy of St Martin-in-the-Fields/Brown)
I see these as one work possessed of seriousness and irrepressible energy of mind and soul unmatched in the baroque.

2   Bach: *Goldberg Variations*
The only way to 'know' this music is to play it yourself – which I try to do, especially when I need to contact spiritual purity.

3   Schubert: Piano sonata in B flat major, D960 (Etsko Tazaki)
Schubert's nobility of heart is different from Beethoven's, more touching.

4   Liszt: Piano sonata in B minor (Etsko Tazaki)
Perfect example of Liszt's fantasy and fire with some of the tenderest moments he ever wrote.

5   Mozart: Piano concerto no. 20 in D minor (Perahia/English Chamber Orch.)
One of Mozart's most passionate in the D minor of *Don Giovanni*.

6   Beethoven: Piano Sonata no. 29 in B flat (*Hammerklavier*) (Beveridge Webster)
Beethoven brings 'news of the universe' in this incredible music with a heartbreakingly sad slow movement in F sharp minor (the same key as Mozart's most painful piano concerto slow movement and the same Neapolitan 6th cadence).

---

standard repertory. Has recorded *Les Boréades* and Rameau's *Les Indes Galantes*, Handel's *Xerxes* and Lully's *La Triomphe d'Alcide*.

Rode, (Jacques) Pierre (Joseph) (b Bordeaux, 16 Feb 1774; d Château de Bourbon, near Damazon, 25 Nov 1830), French violinist and composer. After making great progress as a child, he was sent to Paris in 1787 and became a pupil of Viotti, making his first public appearance in 1790; subsequently gave many performances of Viotti's concertos. He joined the orchestra at the Théâtre Feydeau and in 1794 began to tour abroad, visiting Holland, Germany and England. On his return to Paris he became professor at the new Conservatory and leader at the Opéra. In 1799 he visited Spain, where he met Boccherini. In 1800 he became violinist to Napoleon and in 1803 went to St Petersburg with Boieldieu, remaining until 1808. In 1811–13 he travelled in Germany again, going to Vienna in the latter year, where Beethoven finished the sonata op. 96 for him. In 1814 he settled in Berlin, where he married, but soon afterwards went to live in retirement near Bordeaux.

Works include 13 violin concertos; many string quartets; violin duets; 24 caprices, variations, etc., for violin.

Rodelinda opera by Handel (libretto by A Salvi, adapted by N F Haym), produced London, King's Theatre, Haymarket, 13 Feb 1725. Rodelinda, wife of usurped King Bertarido, agrees to marry Grimoaldo to save her son Flavio. Bertarido returns to see Rodelinda and is captured. Unolfo rescues him, and Bertarido kills the rebel Garibaldo before assuming the role of king again.

Rodelinda, regina de' Longobardi opera by Graun (libretto by G G Bottarelli, altered from A Salvi), produced Berlin, at court, 13 Dec 1741. The plot is similar to that of ◊*Rodelinda*.

Rodgers, Joan (b Whitehaven, 4 Nov 1956), English soprano. After study at the RNCM made debut at Aix in 1982, as Pamina. CG debut 1983 as the Princess in Ravel's *L'Enfant*, returning as Zerlina and Servilia (1988–89). Glyndebourne debut 1989, as Susanna in an 'authentic' *Figaro*; Salzburg debut 1991, in a Mozart concert. Season 1991–92 as Mozart's Countess for ENO, Handel's Cleopatra for Scottish Opera and Tchaikovsky's Iolanta for Opera North. Her charm and vitality are also admired on the concert platform.

Rodgers, Richard (b New York 28 Jun 1902; d New York, 30 Dec 1979), American composer. Studied at Columbia University (1919–21) and at the Institute of Musical Art, NY (1921–23). For 18 years he worked with the librettist Hart, producing very successful musical comedies, including *The Girl Friend* (1926), *On Your Toes* (1936), and *The Boys from Syracuse* (1938) and *Pal Joey* (1940). After Hart's death he worked with Oscar Hammerstein II, producing *Oklahoma* (1943), which was awarded a Pulitzer Prize in 1944; also *Carousel*, *South Pacific* (1948, Pulitzer Prize 1950), *The King and I* (1951), *The Flower Drum Song* (1955) and *The Sound of Music* (1959). Among

the best-known songs from his shows are *The Lady is a Tramp*, *My Funny Valentine*, *Oh What a Beautiful Morning*, *Nothing like a Dame*, *Some Enchanted Evening* and *Bewitched, Bothered and Bewildered*.

Rodio, Rocco (b Bari, *c* 1535; d Naples, shortly after 1615), Italian composer. He wrote church music (including ten Masses), madrigals and instrumental music and a treatise, *Regole di Musica*, pub. Naples, 1600, but known only from its second and third editions (1609, 1626), edited by his pupil Olifante.

Rodolphe, Jean Joseph (originally Johann Joseph Rudolph) (b Strasbourg, 14 Oct 1730; d Paris, 18 Aug 1812), French horn and violin player and composer. Studied horn and violin with his father, and from 1746 violin with Leclair in Paris. In 1754 he went to Parma, in 1761 to Stuttgart and in 1767 back to Paris. He studied composition under Traetta and Jommelli. In later years he taught, from 1798 at the Conservatory.

Works include operas *Le Mariage par capitulation* (1764), *L'Aveugle de Palmyre* (1767) and *Isménor* (1773); ballets; horn concertos; violin duets; horn pieces.

Rodrigo opera in three acts by Handel (libretto after F Silvani's *Il duello d'Amore e di Vendetta*), produced Florence, Teatro del Cocomero, autumn 1707. Rodrigo gains the throne of Aragon by murder but eventually abdicates. Revived with recently discovered Act 3 material by Handel Opera Society, 1985.

Rodrigo, Joaquín (b Sagunto, Prov. Valencia, 22 Nov 1901), Spanish composer and critic. He was blind from the age of three, but persevered in studying music and in 1927 he went to Paris as a pupil of Dukas. He returned to Spain 1933 and again, after travels in Europe, in 1936, settling in Madrid 1939. He is well known for his accessible concertos, which incorporate the local flavour of Spain. Written for such virtuosi as Segovia, James Galway and Julian Lloyd Webber.

Works include *Ausencias de Dulcinea* for bass, four sopranos and orchestra; Heroic concerto and other works for orchestra; 'Aranjuez' concerto for guitar (1939), 'Summer' concerto for violin (1944), *Concierto en modo galante* for cello (1949), *Concierto Serenada* for harp (1954), *Fantasia para un gentil hombre* for guitar and orchestra (1954), *Concierto andaluz* for four guitars and orchestra (1967), *Concierto Pastoral*, for flute (1978), *Concierto como um divertimento* for cello (1981), *Concierto para una fiesta*, for guitar (1982). Also pieces for solo guitar, and songs.

Rodríguez de Hita, Antonio (b *c* 1724; d Madrid, 21 Feb 1787), Spanish composer. He was *maestro de capilla* of Palencia Cathedral, and from 1757 of the Convent of the Incarnation in Madrid. In collaboration with the poet Ramón de la Cruz he made important contributions to Spanish opera.

Works include operas *Briseida* (1768), *Las segadoras de Vallecas*

Rogé The pianist Pascal Rogé. He has excelled as an interpreter of the Romantic repertory and has won several prizes for his recordings. His playing is characterized by its subtle nuances of shading and well-sculpted phrasing.

(1768), *Las labradoras de Murcia* (1769); hymns for four and eight voices.

Rodzinski, Artur (b Spalato, Dalmatia, 1 Jan 1892; d Boston, 27 Nov 1958), Yugoslav, later American conductor. Studied law at the University of Vienna, and then music at the Vienna Academy, with E Sauer, F Schalk and Schreker. He made his debut as a conductor in Lwów in 1920, then took up posts in Warsaw. In 1926 he became assistant to Stokowski and in 1929 permanent conductor of the LA PO and of the Cleveland Orchestra in 1933. Conducted the US fp of *Lady Macbeth of the Mtsensk District*, Cleveland 1935. In 1937 he organized the NBC SO for Toscanini and conducted many of its concerts. From 1942 to 1947 he was permanent conductor of the NY PO and from 1948 of the Chicago SO. In 1953 in Florence he conducted the fp (stage) of Prokofiev's *War and Peace*.

Rogé, Pascal (b Paris, 6 Apr 1951), French pianist. Studied at Paris Conservatory. London and Paris debuts, 1969. Won Long-Thibaud Competition, 1971. Often heard in Ravel and Liszt.

Rogel, José (b Orihuela, Alicante, 24 Dec 1829; d Cartagena, 25 Feb 1901), Spanish composer and conductor. Studied under the cathedral organist at Alicante, but was sent to Valencia to study law. There he pursued further studies under Pascual Pérez, and after taking his degree in law, became a theatre conductor. He wrote or collaborated in over 80 stage works, some with Barbieri.

    Works include operas and *zarzuelas*: *Loa a la libertad* (1854), *El joven Telémaco, Revista de un muerte* (1865), *Un viaje de mil demonios, El General Bumbum*, etc.

Roger-Ducasse, Jean Jules Aimable Roger Ducasse (b Bordeaux, 18 Apr 1873; d Taillan near Bordeaux, 20 Jul 1954), French composer. Studied at the Paris Conservatory, where he was a composition pupil of Fauré. Appointed inspector of singing in the Paris city schools in 1909, and in 1935 succeeded Dukas as composition professor at the Conservatory.

    Works include opera *Cantegril* (1931), mimed drama *Orphée* (1914); *Au Jardin de Marguerite* (1905) and *Ulysse et les Sirènes* for

voices and orchestra; motets and secular vocal works including *Sur quelques vers de Virgile, Madrigal sur des vers de Molière; Suite française* (1909), *Le Joli Jeu de furet, Prélude d'un ballet, Nocturne de printemps* (1920), *Épithalame, Poème symphonique sur le nom de Fauré* for orchestra; *Variations plaisantes* for harp and orchestra; piano works; instrumental pieces; songs.

Rogers, Benjamin (b Windsor, May 1614; d Oxford, Jun 1698), English organist and composer. Learnt music from his father, Peter Rogers, a lay-clerk at St George's Chapel, Windsor, and from the organist, Giles. He became himself a lay-clerk, but in 1639 went to Dublin as organist of Christ Church Cathedral. He returned to Windsor in 1641, but in 1644 the choir was disbanded and he taught music privately. Mus. B., Cambridge, 1658, and in 1669 Mus.D., Oxford, where he had become organist and choirmaster at Magdalen College, in 1664, being dismissed for musical and other irregularities in 1685, but given a pension.

    Works include services and anthems, *Hymnus Eucharisticus* (sung at Magdalen tower at 5 a.m. on 1 May each year); instrumental pieces; organ works.

Rogers, Bernard (b New York, 4 Feb 1893; d Rochester, New York, 24 May 1968), American composer. Studied at the NY Institute of Musical Art and with Bloch at Cleveland. He gained several prizes and distinctions and for a time did music journalism. In 1938 he became professor of composition at the Eastman School of Music at Rochester, NY.

    Works include operas *The Marriage of Aude* (1931), *The Warrior* (1947), *The Veil* and *The Nightingale* (1940); cantatas *The Raising of Lazarus* and *The Exodus, Passion* with organ accompaniment; five symphonies (1926–59), overture *The Faithful, Three Eastern Dances, Two Amer, Frescoes, Four Fairy Tales, The Supper at Emmaeus* (1937), *The Colours of War, The Dance of Salome* (1940), *The Song of the Nightingale, The Plains, The Sailors of Toulon, Invasion* and *Characters from Hans Andersen* for orchestra; soliloquies for flute and strings and bassoon and strings, fantasy for flute, viola and orchestra; *Pastorale* for 11 instruments, string quartet; *Music for an Industrial Film* for two pianos; songs.

Rogers, Nigel (b Wellington, 21 Mar 1935), English tenor. He studied at Cambridge and with Gerhard Hüsch in Munich. Has been heard in Lieder and in modern music, e.g. Goehr's *Arden must Die* (London, 1974), but is best known in Baroque opera: frequent performances of Monteverdi under Nikolaus Harnoncourt and Gustav Leonhardt (*Ulisse* in Vienna, *Orfeo* and *Poppea* in Amsterdam). Recordings include the Monteverdi *Vespers*, Florentine *Intermedi, Dido and Aeneas* and *Hippolyte et Aricie*.

Rogg, Lionel (b Geneva, 21 Apr 1936), Swiss organist and harpsichordist. He studied in Geneva and made his debut there 1961. Has recorded all the organ works of Buxtehude and J S Bach and is particularly admired in *The Art of Fugue*. Also gifted as an improvisor.

Rogier, Philippe (b Namur *c* 1560; d Madrid, 29 Feb 1596), French composer. He must have been sent to Spain as a child, being a choirboy at Madrid in 1572; member of the royal chapel from 1586, *maestro de capilla* from 1588, working for Philip II.

    Works include Masses, motets, etc.

Rogowski, Ludomir (Michal) (b Lublin, 3 Oct 1881; d Dubrovnik, 14 Mar 1954), Polish composer. Studied at the Warsaw Conservatory and with Reimann and Nikisch at Leipzig. On his return to Poland he founded a symphony orchestra at Wilno, lived in Paris 1914–21 and withdrew to a monastery in Yugoslavia, 1926.

    Works include opera *Tamara* (after Lermontov, 1918) and *Prince Marco* (1930); film opera *Un Grand Chagrin de la Petite Ondine* (1920), ballets *St John's Eve* and *Fairy Tale* (1923); seven symphonies (1926–51), suites *Pictures of my Daughter, The Seasons, Les Sourires, Villafranca, Phantasmagoria* (1920), *Sporting Scene, Fantasy Pictures* for orchestra; quartet for four cellos, suites for six and nine instruments and other chamber music; instrumental pieces; piano works; choral songs with and without accompaniment.

Roi Arthus, Le, *King Arthur*, opera by Chausson (libretto by composer); written 1886–95, under the influence of Wagner's *Tristan*, produced Brussels, Théâtre de la Monnaie, 30 Nov 1903. Mordred betrays Lancelot's affair with Guinevere to King Arthur. Arthur battles his knight, killing him, and Guinevere strangles herself.

Roi David, Le dramatic Psalm by Honegger (libretto by R Morax), produced Mézières, Switzerland, open-air Théâtre du Jorat, 11 Jun 1921.

Roi de Lahore, Le, *The King of Lahore*, opera by Massenet (libretto by L Gallet), produced Paris, Opéra, 27 Apr 1877. Hindu priestess Sitâ is loved by both King and evil Scindia in exotic setting.

Roi des Violons, French, = 'King of the Violins'; the title of the head of the guild of violin players, the Ménétriers, founded in Paris 1321. It was not abolished until 1773.

Roi d'Ys, Le opera by Lalo (libretto by E Blau), produced Paris, Opéra-Comique, 7 May 1888. Ys is the submerged city of Debussy's piano prelude *La Cathédrale engloutie*. Margared, daughter of the King of Ys, breaks off her engagement to Karnac when she sees childhood love Mylio. But he now loves her sister Rozenn. Margared joins forces with Kernac for revenge; she sacrifices herself as she opens the sluices, flooding the city.

Roi l'a dit, Le, *The King has said it*, opera by Delibes (libretto by E Gondinet), produced Paris, Opéra-Comique, 24 May 1873. The Marquis di Moncontour presents young Benoit to the King as his own son; Benoit feigns death during a duel to prevent the true identify from being revealed.

Roi malgré lui, Le, *King against his Will*, opera by Chabrier (libretto by E de Najac and P Burani, based on a comedy by Ancelot), produced Paris, Opéra-Comique, 18 May 1887. King Henri of Poland faces a conspiracy to remove him from the throne, led by Count Laski. At Laski's ball the King attends in disguise, escaping detection. King Henri returns to the throne after the plot fails.

Roland for plot synopsis ◊Orlando.

Opera by Lully (libretto by Quinault), produced Versailles, at court, 8 Jan 1685; first Paris performance, 8 Mar 1685.

Rolandi, Gianna (b New York, 16 Aug 1952), American soprano. Studied in New York and made her debut at the City Opera in 1975, as Olympia; NY Met. from 1979, as Sophie, Olympia, Stravinsky's Nightingale and Zerbinetta. Glyndebourne Festival from 1981, as Zerbinetta, Zdenka, Susanna, and Despina (1991). Sang Handel's Cleopatra for ENO 1983, Lucia at San Francisco 1986. Rome 1989, in Cimarosa's *Gli Orazi e i Curazi*.

Roland-Manuel (actually *Lévy*), Alexis (b Paris, 22 Mar 1891; d Paris, 2 Nov 1966), French composer and critic. Pupil of Roussel at the Schola Cantorum in Paris and of Ravel. In 1947 he became a professor at the Paris Conservatory. He wrote much criticism and books on Ravel and Falla.

Works include operas *Isabelle et Pantalon* (1920), *Le Diable amoureux* (1932); ballets *Le Tournoi singulier*, *L'Écran des jeunes filles*, *Elvire* (on music by D Scarlatti) (1936); film music *L'Ami Fritz* (after Erckmann-Chatrian) *La Bandéra* and others; oratorio *Jeanne d'Arc*; symphonic poems *Le Harem du vice-roi*, *Tempo di ballo* (1924), suite *Pena de Francia* for orchestra; suite in the Spanish style for harpsichord, oboe, bassoon and trumpet, string trio; part-songs; songs.

Rolfe Johnson, Anthony (b Tackley, Oxfordshire, 5 Nov 1940), English tenor. Debut 1973, with EOG, in *Iolanthe*. Glyndebourne 1974–76, as Storch, Lensky and Fenton. From 1977 he has toured widely in Europe as opera and concert singer. Season 1993/93 as Monteverdi's Ulisse and Orfeo for ENO, Lucio Silla at Salzburg and Oronte in *Alcina* at CG. Peter Grimes at Glyndebourne, 1994, Britten's Aschenbach at the NY Met. Other roles include Ottavio, Ferrando and Handel's Acis. He has recorded operas by Haydn and oratorios by Handel (*Jephtha, Alexander's Feast*).

roll a very rapid succession of notes on drums produced by quick alternating strokes of the two sticks.

Roll, Michael (b Leeds, 17 Jul 1946), English pianist. Studied with Fanny Waterman and made London debut with the Schumann Concerto at the Festival Hall, 1958. Won the 1963 Leeds International

Competition and has since appeared with leading orchestras in Britain, Europe and Russia, US debut with the Boston SO, 1974; New York recital debut 1992.

Rolla, Alessandro (b Pavia, 6 Apr 1757; d Milan, 15 Sept 1841), Italian violinist (later especially viola player) and composer. Studied with Renzi and Conti, was in the service of the court at Parma 1782–1802, where Paganini was his pupil in 1795. In 1803 he was appointed orchestra director at the Scala in Milan, in 1805 professor at the Conservatory there.

Works include ballets; two symphonies; violin and viola concertos; string quintets, six quartets, and other chamber music; violin duets, studies.

The object of art is to fill up what is missing in the artist's experience.

Romain Rolland, quoted in Orledge,
Gabriel Fauré, 1979

Rolland, Romain (b Clamency, Nièvre, 29 Jan 1866; d Vézelay, Yvonne, 30 Dec 1944), French musicologist and author. He had a first-rate general education, but devoted himself to music and other artistic studies. In 1901 he became president of the music section of the École des Hautes Études Sociales and lectured on music first at the École Normale Supérieure and from 1903 at the Sorbonne. He also contributed essays on music to various periodicals and wrote plays and other literary works. From 1913 he lived in Switzerland, having retired owing to bad health. He returned to France 1938 in order not to evade the war, was interned in a concentration camp by the Germans and released only when he was mortally ill. His works include books on Handel and Beethoven, on early opera, *Musiciens d'autrefois*, *Musiciens d'aujourd'hui*, *Voyage musical au pays du passé*, the novel *Jean- Christophe* (ten vols.) with a musician as hero, etc.

Rolland, Sophie (b Montreal, 18 Jul 1963), Canadian cellist. Studied with Pierre Fournier in Geneva and William Pleeth in London. Debut with the Montreal SO 1982, under Charles Dutoit. Regular concerto appearances throughout Europe and the USA; Beethoven Sonata series at the Carnegie Hall and at London's Wigmore Hall (1993), with pianist Marc-André Hamelin. Frequent chamber music concerts.

Rolle, Johann Heinrich (b Quedlinburg, 23 Dec 1716; d Magdeburg, 29 Dec 1785), German organist and composer. Pupil of his father, Christian Friedrich Rolle (1681–1751). He was appointed organist of St Peter's, Magdeburg, at the age of 17. After legal studies in Leipzig he entered the service of Frederick II of Prussia 1741, but returned to Magdeburg 1746 as organist of St John's, and became municipal music director 1752, succeeding his father.

Works include over 20 dramatic oratorios, e.g. *David und Jonathan* (1766), *Der Tod Abels Saul* (1770), etc.; Passion oratorios; cantatas and numerous other church works; instrumental music; songs.

Roller, Alfred (b Vienna, 2 Oct 1864; d Vienna, 12 June 1935), Austrian stage designer and painter. In the 1890s he was associated with Klimt and Egon Schiele in Vienna. From 1903 he worked with Mahler at the Vienna Hofoper, and with his designs for *Tristan*, *Fidelio*, *Don Giovanni* and *Die Walküre* helped to provide settings in which colour and light were integral parts of the dramatic conception. He provided the sets for the first productions of Strauss's *Elektra* and *Rosenkavalier*, in Dresden, and returned to Vienna for *Die Frau ohne Schatten* (1919). Continued to work in Vienna and in Salzburg until 1934.

Rolón, José (b Ciudad Guzmán, Jalisco, 22 Jun 1883; d Mexico City, 3 Feb 1945), Mexican composer. Studied with his father and later with Moszkowski in Paris, where however he came under the influence of the modern school. He returned to Mexico 1907 and founded a music school at Guadalajara, but at the age of 44 he returned to Paris to study with Dukas and Nadia Boulanger.

Works include symphony, ballet, *El festin de los enanos* (1925), *Scherzo sinfónico*, *Baile Michoacana*, *Zapotlán*, *Cuauhtémoc* for orchestra; piano concerto (1935).

Roma orchestral suite by Bizet, composed 1866–68, fp Paris, 1869.

Roman, Johan Helmich (b Stockholm, 26 Oct 1694; d Haraldsmåla near Kalmar, 20 Nov 1758), Swedish composer. Pupil of his father, leader of the court orchestra in Stockholm, he entered the royal service in 1611. In England from 1714, he studied with Ariosti and Pepusch and was in the service of the Duke of Newcastle. Returning to Stockholm he became vice-*Kapellmeister* (1721), then *Kapellmeister* (1729). Toured England, France and Italy 1735–37, became a member of the Swedish Academy in 1740 and retired in 1745.

Works include Mass, motets, psalms, festival cantatas; 21 symphonies, six overtures; concertos; over 20 violin sonatas, 12 sonatas for flute, viola da gamba and harpsichord, *Assaggio* for solo violin, etc.

Roman, Stella (b Cluj, 23 Aug 1904; d New York, 12 Feb 1992), Romanian soprano. Studied in Rome and after appearing there from 1932 sang Strauss's Empress at La Scala in 1940. New York Met. 1941–50, as Aida (debut), Desdemona, Amelia (*Ballo in maschera*), Gioconda, Santuzza, Tosca and the *Trovatore* Leonora; sang at San Francisco during the 1940s as the Marschallin, Mimi and Donna Anna.

romance, English and French, a piece or song of a 'romantic' nature, usually moderate in tempo and emotional in style. There is no prescribed form, but it is as a rule fairly short and in the character of a song.

romance, French, as above, but more often and more specifically a song. In France single-voice songs were called *romances* from about the end of the 18th c. onward until recently, and the term is still in use, though the more general one now is *mélodie*.

romanesca originally the melody of a 16th-c. Spanish song with a simple bass, used as a theme for variations.

A simple form of the romanesca starting on C.

Romani, Felice (b Genoa, 31 Jan 1788; d Moneglia, 28 Jan 1865), Italian librettist and poet. His first libretti were for Simone Mayr, (*Medea in Corinto*, 1813). He soon began a collaboration with Rossini and wrote *Aureliano in Palmira* and *Il Turco in Italia*. For Donizetti he wrote *L'Elisir d'amore* (1832) and *Anna Bolena* (1835). His most important work was for Bellini: *Il Pirata* (1827), *I Capuleti* (1830), *La Sonnambula* and *Norma* (1831) and *Beatrice di Tenda* (1833). His only libretto for Verdi was *Un Giorno di Regno* (1840).

Romanticism a term subject to as vague an application as are Classicism and Modernism. Applied to a period it defines with fair accuracy the greater part of music of the 19th c., from late Beethoven and Schubert to Brahms and Wagner, as well as a good deal of the music of the early 20th c. As a definition of mood and outlook it may be said to describe music which is consciously an expression of the composer's state of mind, a mood of place, season or time of day, in some cases the feeling or content of some other work of art (e.g. a poem or a picture), etc.

It's the kind of music you go into the theatre whistling.

George Gershwin on Siegmund Romberg, attr.

Romantic Symphony Bruckner's fourth symphony, in E♭. First version composed 1874, fp Linz, 20 Sept 1875; version with new scherzo and revised finale performed Vienna, 20 Feb 1881, conductor Richter.

Romanze German = 'romance'; ◊romance (English and French).

Romberg, Andreas (Jakob) (b Vechta near Münster, 27 Apr 1767; d Gotha, 10 Nov 1821), German violinist and composer. Pupil of his father, Gerhard Heinrich Romberg (1745–1819). He appeared in string duets with his cousin Bernhard Romberg at the age of seven and at 17 played at the Concert Spirituel in Paris. In 1790 he joined the electoral orchestra at Bonn and in 1793–96 he was in Italy, Spain and Portugal with Bernhard, whom he joined again in Paris in 1800 after visits to Vienna and Hamburg. He returned to the latter place, married and remained for 15 years, after which he became court music director at Gotha.

Works include operas *Don Mendoce, ou Le Tuteur portugais* (with Bernhard Romberg), *Das blaue Ungeheuer* (composed 1793), *Der Rabe* (1794), *Die Ruinen zu Paluzzi* (1811), *Die Grossmut des Scipio* (1816) and others; Te Deum, Magnificat, psalms and other church music; setting of Schiller's *Lied von der Glocke* for solo voices, chorus and orchestra, and other cantatas *The Transient and the Eternal*, *The Harmony of the Spheres*, *The Power of Song*, etc.; six symphonies and Toy Symphony; string quartets and quintets.

Romberg, Bernhard (b Dinklage, Oldenburg, 12 Nov 1767; d Hamburg, 13 Aug 1841), German cellist and composer, cousin of Andreas ◊Romberg. Pupil of his father Anton Romberg; appeared at the age of seven with his cousin and in Paris at 14. In 1790–93 he was in the electoral orchestra at Bonn, together with Andreas, also Beethoven, Reicha and F A Ries; then, until 1796, he was in Italy, Spain and Portugal with Andreas. After visits to Vienna and Hamburg he taught the cello at the Paris Conservatory, 1801–03, and 1804–06 he was cellist in the royal orchestra in Berlin, where he was court music director 1815–19, after a tour in Russia, retiring to Hamburg 1819. In the meantime he had visited London, Paris, Vienna, St Petersburg and Moscow.

Works include operas *Don Mendoce, ou le tuteur portugais* (with Andreas Romberg), *Die wiedergefundene Statue* (after Gozzi, composed 1792, *Der Schiffbruch*, *Alma*, *Ulysses und Circe* (1807), *Rittertreue*; ten cello concertos, concerto for two cellos; funeral symphony for Queen Louise of Prussia; 11 string quartets, piano quartets and other chamber music, cello pieces.

Romberg, Siegmund (b Szeged, 29 Jul 1887; d New York, 9 Nov 1951), Hungarian-born American composer. Studied at University of Bucharest and then in Vienna with Heuberger. In 1909 he went to the USA as an engineer, but later began composing with great success.

Works include operettas *Blossom Time* (after music by Schubert, 1921), *The Rose of Stamboul*, *The Student Prince* (1924), *The Desert Song* (1926).

Romeo and Juliet ◊Giulietta e Romeo, ◊Capuleti e Montecchi.

Fantasy overture by Tchaikovsky, based on Shakespeare's tragedy; fp Moscow, 16 Mar, 1870; revised Oct 1870.

Ballet by Prokofiev, fp Brno 30 Dec 1938.

Roméo et Juliette opera by Gounod (libretto by J Barbier and M Carré, after Shakespeare), produced Paris, Théâtre Lyrique, 27 Apr 1867. After Shakespeare: lovers Romeo and Juliet cannot escape the feud between their families, the Montagues and the Capulets, and die for their love.

Symphony by Berlioz, op. 17, for solo voices, chorus and orchestra, based on Shakespeare's tragedy, composed 1839, fp Paris Conservatory, 24 Nov 1839.

Romeo und Julia opera by Sutermeister (libretto by composer, after Shakespeare), produced Dresden, 13 Apr 1940. ◊*Roméo et Juliette* for plot synopsis.

Opera by Blacher (libretto ditto); composed 1943, produced Salzburg, 9 Aug 1950.

Romeo und Julia auf dem Dorfe ◊Village Romeo and Juliet.

Romeo und Julie opera by G Benda (libretto by F W Gotter), produced Gotha, at court, 25 Sept 1776. The first opera to be based on Shakespeare's tragedy. ◊*Roméo et Juliette* for plot synopsis.

Romero, Mateo (known as Maestro Capitán) (b Liège, *c* 1575; d Madrid, 10 May 1647), Spanish singer, composer and priest. He joined the royal chapel at Madrid in 1594. He was a pupil of Rogier and belonged to the Flemish section of the choir. In 1598 he succeeded Rogier as *maestro de capilla*. He was ordained priest in 1609 and retired with a pension in 1633, but was sent on a musical mission to Portugal in 1638.

Works include motets and other church music; secular song for three and four voices, including settings of poems by Lope de Vega, etc.

Ronald, Landon (b London, 7 Jun 1873; d London, 14 Aug 1938), English conductor, pianist and composer, illegitimate son of Henry Russell. Studied at the RCM, made his first public appearance as pianist in Wormser's *L'Enfant prodigue* and gained experience as assistant conductor to Mancinelli at Covent Garden (debut with *Faust*, 1896) and accompanist to Melba. Later he conducted symphonic concerts and visited the Continent as conductor (guest with the Berlin PO). Principal of the GSMD, London, 1910–38. Often conducted Elgar; *Falstaff* was dedicated to him. Recorded Beethoven's violin concerto with Isolde Menges the same year. Knighted 1922.

Works include incidental music to dramatic version of Robert Hichen's *Garden of Allah*; *Birthday Overture* for orchestra; *Adonais* (Shelley) for voice and orchestra; piano pieces; songs.

Ronconi, Giorgio (b Milan, 6 Aug 1810; d Madrid, 8 Jan 1890), Italian baritone. Pupil of his father, Domenico Ronconi (1772–1839). Made his first appearance at Pavia in 1831 in *La Straniera*. He sang in the fps of Donizetti's *Torquato Tasso*, *Il campanello di notte*, *Pia de 'Tolomei*, *Maria Padilla* and *Maria di Rohan*. Travelled all over Italy and first visited London in 1842. Married the singer Elguerra Giannoni and visited many European countries as well as the USA. In 1874 he became professor of singing at the Madrid Conservatory.

Ronconi, Luca (b Susah, 8 Mar 1933), Tunisian-born stage director. After study in Rome produced Busoni's *Arlecchino* at Turin, 1967. At La Scala has produced operas by Jommelli (*Fetonte*), Berio, Stockhausen (fp of *Donnerstag aus Licht*, 1981), Rossi (*Orfeo*, 1985) and Cherubini (*Lodoiska*, 1990). Other work has included *Così fan tutte* at Venice (1983), Piccinni's *Iphigénie en Tauride* at Bari (also in Paris and Rome), Rimsky-Korsakov's *The Tsar's Bride*, and *Don Giovanni* (Bologna, 1990). Rossini's *Ricciardo e Zoraide* at the 1990 Pesaro Festival.

rondeau, French, a medieval song with a refrain. Also, by analogy, in the 17th and 18th c. and instrumental piece in which one section recurs. ◊rondo.

rondeña a Spanish folksong type of Andalusia, resembling the fandango, with words in stanzas of four lines of eight syllables.

Rondine, La, *The Swallow*, operetta by Puccini (libretto by G Adami, translated from the German of A M Willner and H Reichert), produced Monte Carlo, 27 Mar 1917. Originally intended to be set to the German words for the Carl Theater in Vienna, but Italy being at war with Austria, this fell through. Prunier, a poet, convinces Magda of the power of love. She meets Ruggero, who falls in love with her; but she abandons him to return to Rambaldo, leaving him devastated.

rondo an instrumental piece or movement in which a theme heard at the beginning recurs between contrasting episodes and at the end. In the late 18th and early 19th c. the form was combined with sonata form, i.e. the first episode, in a related key, was repeated in the tonic key before the last appearance of the rondo theme. Thus a simple rondo might be in the following form: *ABACADA*, and a sonata rondo: *ABACAB'A*, where *C* has the character of a development. Variants of the latter scheme are not uncommon. The final movements of sonatas, symphonies, etc. in the period mentioned are often rondos.

Röntgen, Engelbert (b Deventer, 30 Sept 1829; d Leipzig, 12 Dec 1897), Dutch violinist. Studied at the Leipzig Conservatory and became a member of the opera and Gewandhaus orchestras there, and in 1869 violin professor at the Conservatory. In 1873 he succeeded David as leader at the Gewandhaus. He married a daughter of a former leader, Moritz Klengel.

Röntgen, Julius (b Leipzig, 9 May 1855; d Utrecht, 13 Sept 1932), German pianist, composer and conductor of Dutch descent, son of Engelbert ◊Röntgen. Studied at the Leipzig Conservatory, but reverted to Holland, living at Amsterdam 1878–1924 as teacher and conductor, becoming director of the Conservatory 1914. He was a great friend of Grieg, of whom he wrote a biography; other influences in his creative life were Brahms, Schumann and, later in his career, Reger.

Works include operas *Agnete*, *The Laughing Cavalier* (on Frans Hals' painting), *Samûm* (on Strindberg's play); film music; 21 symphonies; seven piano concertos; chamber music; arrangements of old Dutch songs and dances.

Ronzi de Begnis, Giuseppina (b Milan, 11 Jan 1800; d Florence, 7 Jun 1853), Italian soprano. She made her debut in Bologna, 1816, and much of her early career, in Italy, London and Paris was devoted to Rossini: well known as Ninetta and Rosina and in *Il Turco in Italia*, *La donna del lago* and *Matilde di Shabran*. From 1831 she sang in the fps of five operas by Donizetti, including *Fausta*, *Maria Stuarda*, *Gemma di Vergy* and *Roberto Devereux*. Her husband Giuseppe (1793–1849) was the first Dandini, in *Cenerentola*.

Roocroft, Amanda (b Coppull, Lancs., 9 Feb 1966), English soprano. Studied at the RNCM, appearing as Alcina and Fiordiligi there. Sang Strauss's Sophie with WNO 1990 and continued to sing in concert. Sang Pamina with GTO 1990 and on 1991 CG debut; Glyndebourne 1991 as Fiordiligi, returning 1994 as Donna Elvira. ENO 1993, as Ginevra in *Ariodante*; sang Fiordiligi at CG, 1995. She is admired for the dramatic committment of her performances.

Rooley, Anthony (b Leeds, 10 Jun 1944), English director and lutenist. Studied guitar at the RAM, London and co-founded the Consort of Musicke in 1969; often gives concerts with a Renaissance theme, and music theatre includes a staging of *Le Veglie di Siena* (music by Vecchi) in Copenhagen and London. London Prom concert 1988, with setting of Tasso. Further concerts in Scandinavia and the USA. Recordings include complete lute music of Dowland and Italian madrigals and other vocal items with soprano Emma Kirkby.

root according to 19th-c. theory, the lowest note of a major or minor triad, or of chords in which one or more thirds are superimposed on such triads (sevenths, ninths, 11ths, 13ths).

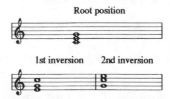

A chord in root position on C. The second diagram shows first and second inversions. According to this theory, which takes no account of the different functions of chords, a four-note chord has three possible inversions, and so on.

Rootering, Jan-Hendrik (b Munich, 18 Mar 1950), German bass. Studied in Hamburg and sang there and at Munich from 1982; Frankfurt 1983, as Marke in *Tristan*. Season 1987 as Orestes in Geneva, Sarastro at CG and Marcel in *Les Huguenots* at the Deutsche Oper, Berlin. New York Met. from 1987, as the Landgrave, Claggart (*Billy Budd*), Sparafucile, and Pogner (1993). Other roles include Baron Ochs (at Munich), Fasolt and Falstaff.

Rootham, C(yril) B(radley) (b Bristol, 5 Oct 1875; d Cambridge, 18 Mar 1938), English organist, educationist and composer. Studied under his father, the singer, organist and conductor Daniel Rootham (1837–1922), later at St John's College, Cambridge, and the RCM in London. In 1901 he went back to Cambridge as organist and music director at St John's College and took the Mus. D. in 1910.

Works include opera *The Two Sisters* (1922); choral and orchestral works *Andromeda Coronach*, *For the Fallen* (Binyon), *Brown Earth*, *Ode on the Morning of Christ's Nativity* (Milton), *City in the West*, Psalm ciii: two symphonies (second with choral finale); instrumental music and songs.

Rooy, Anton(ius Maria Josephus) van (b Rotterdam, 1 Jan 1870; d Munich, 28 Nov 1932), Dutch bass-baritone. Originally engaged in commerce, he went to Frankfurt to study singing with Stockhausen, sang at concerts in Germany and obtained his first stage engagement at Bayreuth 1897; sang there until 1902 as Wotan, Sachs and the Dutchman: banned after 1903 for singing Amfortas in the 'pirate' NY performance of *Parsifal*. He visited London as a Wagner singer at Covent Garden 1898–1913.

Ned Rorem – composer

These works, being French with a vengeance, speak to my condition (as we American Quakers say), and run counter to the teutonic pressures of most music nowadays.

My three favourite pieces are:

1 Satie: *Socrate*
   Because it is the only musical work that captures the essence of Plato, yet is stylistically unidentifiable (is it Gregorian? Greek? ancient? modern?), and does not seek to draw attention, like other Satie works, to its author.

2 Ravel: *L'Enfant et les sortilèges*
   Because it contains the most beautiful tunes I know – and tunes are the pith of all music.

3 Debussy: *Pelléas et Mélisande*
   Because it is wholly and purely an opera, yet without resorting to the conceits of acrobatic performance found in most 19th-century opera. It is about music, not about the interpretation of music.

Rore, Cipriano de (Cyprien de) (b Mechelen, *c* 1516; d Parma, Sept 1565), Flemish composer. Studied under his fellow-countryman Willaert at Venice, where he was a singer at St Mark's, and began to pub. madrigals in 1542. He left Venice *c* 1550 to enter the service of Ercole II, Duke of Ferrara. In 1558 he visited his parents at Antwerp and the court of Margaret of Austria in the Netherlands, into the service of whose husband, Ottavio Farnese, Duke of Parma, he passed. He succeeded Willaert as *maestro di cappella* of St Mark's, Venice, in 1563, but returned to Parma in Jul 1564.

Works include five Masses, 65 motets, one Passion and other church music; 125 madrigals; instrumental fantasies and *ricercari*, etc.

> *The current state of music presents a variety of solutions in search of a problem, the problem being to find somebody left to listen.*
> **Ned Rorem**, *Music From Inside Out*, 1967

Rorem, Ned (b Richmond, IN, 23 Oct 1923), American composer. He studied at the Curtis Institute and Juilliard. Has held academic posts at Universities of Buffalo and Utah, and the Curtis Institute (from 1980).

Works include operas *A Childhood Miracle* (1955), *The Robbers* (1958), *Miss Julie* (1965), and *Hearing* (1976); three symphonies (1950, 1956, 1958), three piano concertos (1950, 1969, 1992); *The Poet's Requiem* for soprano, chorus and orchestra (1957); *Eagles* for orchestra (1958); Double concerto for violin, cello and orchestra (1979); *Sunday Morning*, symphonic suite (1981); *Whitman Cantata* (1983); *An American Oratorio* (1984); *String Symphony* (1985); organ concerto (1985); violin concerto (1985); Septet: *Scenes from Childhood* (1985); *Homer* for chorus and eight instruments (1986); *Diversions*, brass quintet (1989); cor anglais concerto (1993); church music; keyboard pieces and songs; song cycles *Flight for Heaven*, *King Midas*, *Poems of Love and the Rain*, *War Scenes*, *Women's Voices* and *After Long Silence*.

Rosa (originally *Rose*), Carl (August Nikolaus) (b Hamburg, 22 Mar 1842; d Paris, 30 Apr 1889), German violinist and conductor. Studied at the Leipzig and Paris Conservatories, became orchestra leader at Hamburg and visited England in 1866 and afterwards the USA, where he met and in 1867 married Euphrosyne Parape (1836–74), with whom he formed an opera co., which included Santley and G Ronconi. This he took to England and carried on as the Carl Rosa Opera Company; many performances of English operas, and foreign works in translation.

Rosalia the usual name for the Real Sequence repeating a phrase higher or lower, not within the scale of the same key, as in the tonal sequence, but by so changing the key that its steps retain exactly the same succession of whole tones and semitones.

The name derives from an Italian popular song, 'Rosalia, mia cara', in which this device occurs. ◊Schusterfleck.

Rosamond opera by Arne (libretto by J Addison), produced London, Theatre in Lincoln's Inn Fields, 7 Mar 1733.

Opera by Clayton (libretto ditto), produced London, Drury Lane Theatre, 4 Mar 1707. Queen Eleanor, wife of King Henry, discovers his mistress Rosamond and forces her to drink a bowl of poison. When Henry repents, she reveals the liquid was not lethal, and that Rosamond has become a nun.

Rosamunde incidental music by Schubert for a play by Helmina von Chézy, *Rosamunde, Prinzessin von Cypern*, produced Vienna, Theater an der Wien, 20 Dec 1823. The music consists of three entr'actes, two ballet tunes, a romance for contralto, a chorus of spirits, a shepherd's melody and shepherds' chorus, and a hunting-chorus. No overture was specially written for the piece. At the fp, that to the opera *Alfonso und Estrella* was used; later that to the melodrama *Die Zauberharfe* was pub. as *Rosamunde* overture and is still so played.

Rosbaud, Hans (b Graz, 22 Jul 1895; d Lugano, 29 Dec 1962), Austrian conductor. He studied at the Frankfurt Conservatory and began his career as a conductor at Mainz, 1921. His numerous other appointments included the Radio Orchestra at Baden-Baden, from 1948, the Zurich Opera, 1950–58, and the festivals at Aix-en-Provence and Donaueschingen. He had a unique reputation as an interpreter of contemporary music; gave the concert and stage fps of Schoenberg's *Moses und Aron* (1954, 1957). His Boulez fps included *Le marteau sans maître* and *Improvisation sur Mallarmé*.

Roscoe, Martin (b Halton, 3 Aug 1952), English pianist. Studied at the RMCM and won the 1981 Sydney International Competition. Many concerto performances in Britain, South America, the Middle East and Australia; repertoire includes works by Berwald, Liszt and Beethoven. Partnership with violinist Tasmin Little, notably in the Kreutzer Sonata, and works by Delius.

rose, *or* knot, the ornamental fretwork soundhole of many flat-bellied string instruments of the lute and guitar type, also of dulcimers, harpsichords, etc., sometimes serving as the makers' trade-mark.

Rosé, Arnold (Josef) (b Jassy, Rumania, 24 Oct 1863; d London,

A rosalia in which the first two bars are repeated a whole tone higher.

———— THE OPERA ————

Der Rosenkavalier

A three-act opera by Richard Strauss about clandestine love affairs in high places. It was first produced in 1911 and is set in Vienna during the reign of Maria Theresa.

I. The Marschallin (soprano) and her young lover Octavian (soprano or mezzo-soprano) are interrupted by the entry of Baron Ochs (bass), the Marschallin's ill-mannered cousin. He seeks a nomination for the Knight of the Rose, who will make a presentation to his intended bride, Sophie (soprano). Disguised as a maid, Mariandel, Octavian is pursued by Ochs and, when he reappears as himself, tries to reassure a fatalistic Marschallin. Octavian rushes off and the Marschallin has to send his Knight's Rose after him.

II. The nouveau riche merchant Faninal (baritone) and his daughter await Octavian's arrival. At the presentation of the Silver Rose he and Sophie are instantly attracted. Ochs enters and behaves coarsely, at which Octavian wounds him lightly in a duel. As he recovers Ochs receives a note of assignation from 'Mariandel'.

III. Ochs meets the coy Mariandel at an inn; they are interrupted by apparitions designed to frighten Ochs, culminating in his disgruntled employee Annina (soprano) appearing as a deserted wife with crying children in tow. Ochs calls the police and they are followed by the Marschallin, who dismisses everyone except the young couple. While they sing of their love, the Marschallin accepts the situation with good grace.

———— THE OPERA ————

25 Aug 1946), Austro-Hungarian violinist. He was leader of the opera orchestra in Vienna from 1881 to 1938 and founded the Rosé quartet in 1882; gave the fps of Schoenberg's first two quartets (1907, 1908), also *Verklärte Nacht* (1902). He married a sister of Mahler.

Rose, Jürgen (b Bernburg, 25 Aug 1937), German stage designer. Studied in Berlin and designed for the Stuttgart Ballet, 1962–73. Collaborated with director Otto Schenk for *Don Carlos* and *Meistersinger*, in Vienna, *Simon Boccanegra,* and *Rosenkavalier* at Munich and *Così fan Tutte* in Berlin; Bayreuth 1972 and 1990, *Tannhäuser* and *Der fliegende Holländer*, in productions by Götz Friedrich and Dieter Dorn. Designs for *Lucia* and *Lohengrin* at Hamburg, *Die Zauberflöte* in Munich (also seen at CG and on video); designed *Un ballo in maschera* for CG 1975, seen at Los Angeles 1993.

Rose, Leonard (b Washington DC, 27 Jun 1918; d White Plains, NY, 16 Nov 1984), American cellist. Studied at Curtis Institute, Philadelphia, with F Salmond and then played in the NBC Orchestra under Toscanini and later as first cello in the NY PO. From 1951 he taught at the Juilliard and the Curtis Institute, and also pursued a distinguished career as a soloist.

Roseingrave, English, family of musicians;

1. Daniel Roseingrave (c 1650; d Dublin, May 1727), organist and composer. Educated in music as a chorister in the Chapel Royal in London. From 1679 to 1698 he was successively organist of Gloucester, Winchester and Salisbury Cathedrals, and was then appointed to St Patrick's and Christ Church Cathedrals, Dublin.

Works include services, anthems, etc.

2. Thomas Roseingrave (b Winchester, 1688; d Dunleary, near Dublin, 23 Jun 1766), English organist and composer, son of 1. Pupil of his father at Dublin, where he was educated at Trinity College. In 1710 he went to Italy where he met A and D Scarlatti, making great friends with the latter and travelling with him. He went to London before 1720, when he produced D Scarlatti's opera *Narcisco* with interpolations of his own. In 1725 he was appointed organist of St George's Church, Hanover Square. He retired in 1741 and moved to Dublin, living probably with his nephew William Roseingrave.

WORKS: opera *Phaedra and Hippolytus* (on Edmund Smith's play based on Racine, 1753); services and anthems; organ voluntaries and fugues; suites for harpsichord and an introductory piece for his edition of Scarlatti's sonatas; 12 solos for flute and harpsichord; 12 Italian cantatas (1735).

3. Ralph Roseingrave (b Salisbury, c 1695; d Dublin, 1747), English organist and composer, brother of 2. Studied with his father, who petitioned for him to succeed him as organist of St Patrick's Cathedral, Dublin, in 1719; but he was appointed vicar-choral and not organist till 1726. He also became organist of Christ Church Cathedral on his father's death.

Works include services, anthems, etc.

Rosen, Albert (b Vienna, 14 Feb, 1924), Austrian-born conductor. Studied in Prague and Vienna and made opera debut at Pilsen. Principal conductor of the Smetana Theatre, Prague, from 1964; RTE SO in Dublin from 1969. At the Wexford Festival (from 1972) has led important revivals of *Káta Kabanová*, *The Gambler*, *Hans Heiling*, *La cena delle beffe* (Giordano), *The Devil and Kate*, *Der Templer und die Judin* (Marschner) and *Il Piccolo Marat* (Mascagni, 1992). US debut San Francisco 1980, *Jenůfa*. For ENO has led the UK fp of Rimsky-Korsakov's *Christmas Eve* (1988) and *Káta Kabanová*. Music director of Irish National Opera at Dublin from 1993.

Rosen, Charles (b New York, 5 May 1927), American pianist and musicologist. He studied at Princeton (MA 1949). Debut as pianist, NY, 1951; well known for his thoughtful interpretations of Bach, Beethoven and modern music, including Carter, Schoenberg and Boulez. He has taught in NY and at Berkeley, California. Books include *The Classical Style* (1971), *Schoenberg* (1975) and *Sonata Forms* (1980).

Rosenberg, Hilding (Constantin) (b Bosjökloster, 21 Jun 1892; d Stockholm, 19 May 1985), Swedish composer and conductor. Studied at the Stockholm Conservatory, and at Dresden, Berlin, Vienna and Paris. On his return to Sweden he was conductor of the Stockholm Opera 1932–34.

Works include operas *Journey to America* (including *Railway Fugue*), *The Marionettes* (on Benavente's *Los intereses creados*, 1939), *The Isle of Felicity* (1945) and *The Two Princesses* (1940); choreographic pantomime *The Last Judgment*; ballet *Orpheus in the City* (1938), incidental music for Sophocles' *Oedipus Tyrannus*, Euripides' *Medea* and plays by Calderón, Goethe, Musset, O'Neill, Masefield, and Obey; film music.

Eight symphonies (1917–15) including no. 2 *Sinfonia grave*, no. 3 *The Four Ages of Man*, no. 4 *The Revelation of St John*), *Due Sinfonie da chiesa*, *Adagio non troppo*, *Three Fantasy Pieces* for orchestra; chamber symphony, concerto and suite on Swedish folk tunes for strings, violin concerto, two cello concertos.

Twelve string quartets (1920–57), trios for flute, violin and viola, and for oboe, clarinet and bassoon; sonata and suite for violin and piano, sonatina for flute and piano, sonata for unaccompanied violin; piano suite.

Rosenhain, Jacob (b Mannheim, 2 Dec 1813; d Baden-Baden, 21 Mar 1894), German pianist and composer. Studied with Kalliwoda, Schnyder von Wartensee and others, and made his first appearance as a pianist at Frankfurt in 1832. He visited London in 1837 and then settled in Paris, where he played and taught.

Works include operas *Der Besuch im Irrenhause*, *Liswenna* (*Le Démon de la Nuit* 1851), *Volage et jaloux*; three symphonies; piano concerto; three string quartets, four piano trios; two cello and piano sonatas; sonata, studies and pieces for piano; songs.

Rosenkavalier, Der, *The Rose Cavalier*, opera by R Strauss (libretto by Hugo von Hofmannsthal), produced Dresden, Royal Opera, 26 Jan 1911. Octavian, young lover of the Marschallin, bears a silver rose to Sophie, the proposed betrothed of loutish Ochs. When he meets her Octavian falls in love and conspires to end the arranged marriage, exposing Ochs as a philanderer. The Marschallin, although unhappy, gives Octavian and Sophie her blessing.

Rosenmüller, Johann (b Ölsnitz, Saxony, c 1619; d Wolfenbüttel, buried 12 Sept 1684), German composer. Studied at Leipzig Univer-

Der Rosenkavalier *Yvonne Minton as Octavian and Jules Bastin as Ochs in the 1974 production of* Der Rosenkavalier *at Covent Garden.*

sity and in 1642 became assistant master at St Thomas's School there, studying music with the cantor, Tobias Michael, and acting as his deputy when he became infirm. He was marked out for the succession and in 1651 became organist of St Nicholas's Church; but in 1655 he was imprisoned for homosexual offences with his choirboys, escaping to Hamburg and later fleeing to Venice, where he settled and was influenced as a composer by the local style. There J P Krieger became his pupil. In 1674 he was recalled to Germany by an appointment to the court of Duke Anton Ulrich of Brunswick, at Wolfenbüttel.

Works include Masses, motets, vesper psalms and Lamentations, Latin and German motets *Kernsprüche* for three–seven voices and instruments, German motets and cantatas, hymns, hymn by Albinus 'Straf mich nicht'; *Sonata da camera* for five instruments, sonatas for two–five instruments, suites of instrumental dances.

Rosenshein, Neil (b New York, 27 Nov 1947), American tenor. After study in New York made debut in 1972 with Florida Opera, as Almaviva. Has sung widely in the USA, including Alfredo at Chicago (1988) and in the 1988 fp of *The Aspern Papers* by Argento, at Dallas. CG debut 1986, as Lensky; Berlioz Festival Lyon 1989, as Bevenuto Cellini. At the New York Met. has sung Werther, Faust, Alfredo, and Léon in the 1991 fp of Corigliano's *The Ghosts of Versailles*. Season 1992 with the Berlioz Faust at Turin and Peter Grimes with the Australian Opera.

Rosenstock, Joseph (b Kraków, 27 Jan 1895; d New York, 17 Oct 1985), Polish-born American conductor. Studied at Kraków Conservatory and with Schreker in Vienna. Held opera appointments at Darmstadt, Wiesbaden and Mannheim (1922–33). NY Met. debut 1929 (*Meistersinger*). Tokyo 1936–41. Music director NY City

Opera 1948–55; Cologne Opera 1958–61; returned to conduct in USA 1961.

Rosenthal, Harold (b London, 30 Sept 1917; d London, 19 Mar 1987), English critic and writer on opera. He was archivist at CG, London, 1950–56 and in 1953 became editor of *Opera Magazine* (retired 1986). He broadcast and lectured in USA and Britain. Books include *Two Centuries of Opera at Covent Garden* (1958), *Concise Oxford Dictionary of Opera* (co-editor with John Warrack, 1964, revised 1979), autobiography *My Mad World of Opera* (1983). Contributed many entries on singers to the *New Grove Dictionary* and revised the Loewenberg *Annals of Opera*, 1978.

Rosenthal, Manuel (originally Emmanuel) (b Paris, 18 Jun 1904), French composer and conductor. Studied at the Paris Conservatory, with Ravel and others. He became leader of various orchestras. From 1935 to 1939 and from 1944 to 1946 he conducted the French National Radio Orchestra and from 1949 to 1951 the Seattle SO. Conducted *Carmina Burana* and *Oedipus Rex* at the New York City Opera 1977; Met. from 1981, including *Manon* and *Dialogues des Carmelites. Der Ring des Nibelungen* at Seattle, 1986.

Works include operas *Rayon des soieries* (1928) and *Hop Signor!* (1961); operettas *Les Bootleggers* and *La Poule noire*; ballet *Un Baiser pour rien*; oratorio *Saint François d'Assise* (1944); suite *Jeanne d'Arc, Fête du vin, Les Petits Métiers*, serenade for orchestra; sonatina for two violins and piano; piano pieces; songs.

Rosenthal, Moriz (b Lwów, 18 Dec 1862; d New York, 3 Sept 1946), Polish pianist, son of a professor at the Academy of Lwów. He began to learn the piano at the age of eight and in 1872 entered the Lwów Conservatory, where he studied under the director Carl Mikuli. In

1875 the family moved to Vienna, where he continued his studies under Joseffy. He gave his first recital there in 1876 and then began to tour, finishing his studies with Liszt and also qualifying in philosophy. In 1895 he first appeared in England.

Rosetti, Francesco Antonio, ◊Rösler.

Rose vom Liebesgarten, Die opera by Pfitzner (libretto by J Grun); composed 1897–1900, produced Elberfeld, 9 Nov 1901. During the celebration of spring, Fairy queen Minneleide is abducted by the Night Sorceror. Siegnot, who loves her, is killed while rescuing her but is restored to life.

rosin, *or* resin, a preparation made of gum of turpentine, applied to the hair of the bows of string instruments to produce the required friction on the strings.

Rosina ballad opera by Shield (libretto by F Brooke, based on an episode in Thomson's *Seasons* and Favart's *Les Moissonneurs* with Duni's music, produced London, CG, 31 Dec 1782. Rosina is the object of both Mr Belville's and Captain Belville's attentions. After the Captain tries to abduct her, Mr Belville realizes she loves him and he proposes marriage.

Rosinda opera by Cavalli (libretto by G Faustini), produced Venice, Teatro San Apollinaire, 1651.

I wrote the overture to La Gazza Ladra *on the day of the first performance in the theatre itself, where I was imprisoned by the director and watched over by four stage-hands, who had instructions to throw my manuscript out of the window page by page to the copyists who were waiting to transcribe it below. In the absence of pages they were to throw me.*

Gioachino Rossini, in a letter

Roslavets, Nikolai Andreievich (b Surai, Government of Tchernigov, 5 Jan 1881; d Moscow, 23 Aug 1944), Russian composer. He came from a peasant family, but studied music at the Moscow Conservatory and attracted adverse attention by his advanced tendencies. Some of his music has been revived, including the violin concerto of 1925, but did not quite live up to its avant-garde reputation.

Works include cantata *Heaven and Earth* (after Byron, 1912); symphony, violin concerto (1925), two symphonic poems; five string quartets (no. 3 12-tone); quintet for oboe, two violins, cello and harp, two piano trios; five violin and piano sonatas, two cello and piano sonatas; many piano pieces; songs.

Rösler, Franz Anton (b Litoměřice, *c* 1750; d Ludwigslust, Mecklenburg-Schwerin, 30 Jun 1792), Bohemian composer. Destined for the priesthood, he attended the Jesuit College of Olomouc, but in 1773 entered the service of the Prince of Ottingen as double bass player and later became conductor. He left for Ludwigslust in 1789 and was court music director there to his death. He wrote under the name of Francesco Antonio Rosetti.

Works include opera *Das Winterfest der Hirten* (1789); oratorios *Der sterbende Jesus* (1786) and *Jesus in Gethsemane*; Requiem for Mozart (1791); 34 symphonies; concertos for piano, violin, flute, oboe, clarinet and horn; chamber music, violin sonatas.

Ros Marba, Antoni (b Barcelona, 2 Apr 1937), Spanish conductor. Studied in Barcelona and made debut there in 1962. Principal conductor of the City of Barcelona Orchestra (1967–77), Spanish National Orchestra (1978–81) and Netherlands Chamber Orchestra (1979–86). Music director of the National Theatre at Madrid from 1989, leading the 1992 stage premiere of Gerhard's *The Duenna*. Concerts throughout Europe, the Americas and the Far East.

Rosmene, La, ovvero L'Infedeltà fedele, *Rosmene, or Faithful Faithlessness*, opera by A Scarlatti (libretto by G D de Totis), produced Naples, Palazzo Reale, Carnival 1688.

Rosselini, Renzo (b Rome, 2 Feb 1908; d Monte Carlo, 14 May 1982), Italian composer. Pupil of Sallustio, Setacioli and Molinari. His brother was the film director Roberto Rosselini.

Works include operas *Alcassino e Nicoletta* (1930), *La guerra* (1956), *Uno squàrdo dal ponte* (after A Miller, 1961) and *La Reine Morte* (1973); ballet *La danza di Dassine* (1935), (music adapted from *Hoggar* suite); two oratorios; film music, rhapsodic suite *Hoggar*, *Preludio all' Aminta del Tasso*, *Canti di marzo* and *Ditirambo a Dioniso* for orchestra; piano trio.

Rosseter, Philip (b *c* 1568; d London, 5 May 1623), English lutenist and composer. Worked in London and was associated with R Jones, Kingham and Reeve in the training of the children for the queen's revels; from 1610 he was licensed with Jones to mount plays at the Whitefriars theatre. With Campion pub. a book of songs to the lute, some if not all of the words by Campion and half of the music by Rosseter.

Works include *A Booke of Ayres* with lute, orpheoreon and bass viol; *Lessons for the Consort* for six instruments by various composers.

Rossetto, Stefano (b Nice), Italian 16th-c. organist and composer. He lived at Florence in the 1560s as musician to Cardinal de' Medici, was court organist at Munich in 1579–80 and later (?) organist at Novara.

Works include motets in five–six parts for voice and instruments in different combinations; madrigal cycle *Il lamento di Olimpia* (1566), other madrigals for four–six voices.

Rossi, Giovanni Gaetano (b Borgo San Donnino, near Parma, 5 Aug 1828; d Genoa 31 Mar 1886), Italian composer and conductor. Studied at the Milan Conservatory. Appointed leader of the theatre orchestra and organist at the court chapel of Parma; director of the Conservatory there 1864–73; conductor of the Teatro Carlo Felice at Genoa, 1873–79.

Works include operas *Elena di Taranto* (1852), *Giovanni Giscala* (1855), *Nicolò de' Lapi* (1865), *La Contessa d'Altemberg*; three Masses, Requiem; oratorio; symphony *Saul*.

Rossi, Lauro (b Macerata, 19 Feb 1810; d Cremona, 5 May 1885), Italian composer. Studied at Naples with Zingarelli and others, and began to produce operas at the age of 18. He had much success in Italian cities until 1835, when he left for Mexico in disgust after a failure. He later travelled to India, but returned to Europe in 1843 and again produced many operas. In 1870 he succeeded Mercadante as director of the Naples Conservatory.

Works include operas *La contesse villane* (1829), *Il casino di campagna*, *Costanza ed Oringaldo*, *La casa disabitata* (1834), *Amelia*, *Leocadia*, *Cellini a Parigi* (1845), *Azema di Granata* (1846), *Il borgomastro di Schiedam*, *Il domino nero* (1849), *Bianca Contarini*,

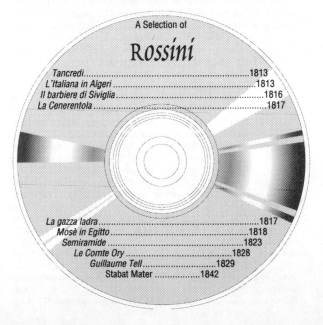

A Selection of

Rossini

Tancredi	1813
L'Italiana in Algeri	1813
Il barbiere di Siviglia	1816
La Cenerentola	1817
La gazza ladra	1817
Mosè in Egitto	1818
Semiramide	1823
Le Comte Ory	1828
Guillaume Tell	1829
Stabat Mater	1842

La Contessa di Mons (1874), *La figlia di Figaro* (1846), *Biorn* (after Shakespeare's *Macbeth*) and 15 others; oratorio *Saul*; Mass; six fugues for strings; elegies on the deaths of Bellini and Mercadante.

Rossi, Luigi (b Torremaggiore *c* 1598; d Rome, 20 Feb 1653), Italian singer and composer. He was in the service of Cardinal Barberini in Rome 1641–46. In 1646 he was called to Paris at the instigation of Mazarin and produced his *Orfeo* in 1647 as one of the first Italian operas to be given there. It was lavishly produced at court, the expense provoking anti-monarchist feeling in the Parisian populace. Composed in an elaborate style, and developing the innovations of Monteverdi, *Orfeo* has been successfully revived in Bloomington and London (1988, 1990).

Works include operas *Il palagio d'Atlante* (or *Il palazzo incantato*), *L'Orfeo* (1647); oratorio *Giuseppe, figlio di Giacobbe*, cantatas, etc.

Rossi, Mario (b Rome, 29 March 1902; d Rome, 29 Jun 1992), Italian conductor. Studied in Rome and was deputy at the Opera there 1926–36. Conducted at the Maggio Musicale, Florence, 1937–44, leading the 1938 fp of Malipiero's *Antonio e Cleopatra* and *Iris* by Mascagni in 1937. Salzburg Festival debut 1952 (*Otello*) and conductor of the Turin Radio Orchestra 1946–69; many performances of contemporary works.

Rossi, Michel Angelo (b Genoa *c* 1600; d Rome, buried 7 Jul 1656), Italian organist and composer, pupil of Frescobaldi. His opera *Erminia sul Giordano*, to a libretto by Giulio Rospigliosi, later Pope Clement IX, was given in Rome in 1633.

Works include operas *Erminia sul Giordano* (after Tasso) and *Andromeda* (1638); toccatas and *correnti* for organ or harpsichord.

Rossi, Salomone (b ?Mantua, 19 Aug 1570; d ?, Mantua, *c* 1630), Italian composer. He worked at the court of Mantua (1587–1628) and enjoyed the privilege of dispensing with the wearing of the yellow badge that stigmatized the Jews in Italy.

Works include music for Guarini's *Idropica* and oratorio *Maddalena* (both with Monteverdi and others, 1608, 1617); 28 Hebrew psalms for four–eight voices; madrigals and canzonets; instrumental works *Sinfonie e gagliarde* and *Sonate*.

Rossignol, Le (Stravinsky) ◊Nightingale.

Rossi-Lemeni, Nicola (b Istanbul, 6 Nov 1920; d Bloomington, 12 Mar 1991), Italian bass. After study in Verona made his debut at La Fenice, Venice, in 1946, as Varlaam. Sang at La Scala 1947–60, notably as Mephistopheles (in *Faust* and *Mefistofele*), Philip II and Boris. Also sang Boris in San Francisco (1951) and CG (1952) debuts and the Gounod Mephistophélès at the NY Met. in 1953. Sang Britten's Claggart at Florence in 1965, and Tommaso in the 1958 fp at La Scala of Pizzetti's *L'Assassinio nella cattedrale*.

Rossini, Gioachino (Antonio) (b Pesaro, 29 Feb 1792; d Passy near Paris, 13 Nov 1868), Italian composer. He was the most successful

Rossini *The composer Gioachino Rossini (1792–1868) in a cartoon by André Gill (1867). Most famous for the filigree of his comic operas, Rossini retired as a composer for the stage at the age of 37,* Guillaume Tell *being his last and one of his most successful operas.*

opera composer of his time and helped create the *bel canto* style. His father was a horn and trumpet player, his mother a singer in a small way. He learnt piano, singing and harmony early and sang in churches and theatres; at 13 he was employed as an accompanist at the theatre; at 14, when he had already tried his hand at an opera and other works, he entered the Bologna Liceo Musicale, studying counterpoint and cello. In 1808 he won a prize with a cantata and in 1810 had his first comic opera, *La cambiale di matrimonio*, produced at Venice. From that time he went from success to success, the first great one being *Tancredi* at Venice in 1813, but *Il barbiere di Siviglia* was at first a failure in Rome in 1816. The two sides of Rossini's creative genius were now well established: the wit, effervescence and florid vocal writing of his comic operas and the considerable dramatic power of his serious works, each in its own distinctive musical 'colour'. His huge popular following was consolidated by *Otello* in 1816 (only distantly related to Shakespeare), *La Cenerentola* in 1817 and *Mosè in Egitto* in 1818 (later revised for Paris). *Mosè* was premiered in Naples and was one of six remarkable serious operas produced there in only five years, the others being *Armida*, *Ermione*, *La donna del lago*, *Maometto II* and *Zelmira*; each of these works has only recently become widely known, through revivals and recordings.

His first great foreign success came during a visit to Vienna in 1822; he met Beethoven and saw his operas achieve a greater success with the Viennese than any Austrian work. Also in 1822 he married Isabella Colbran. She had already created leading roles in *Elisabetta*, *Otello*, *Mosè* and *Armida*. In 1823 she sang the title role in *Semiramide*, produced at Venice and his last opera written for the Italian

---

Rossini
A biographical note

Rossini was little influenced by his greatest musical contemporaries. His comic operas were hugely popular in Vienna, and in 1822 the time seemed right to try his fortune there with the tragedy *Zelmira*, premiered earlier that year in Naples. Taking the opportunity to visit Beethoven with the poet Carpani, he found the German in his temporary lodgings living in his customary squalor and disorder. Rossini was particularly struck by the cracks in the ceiling (Beethoven usually collected leaking rain water in his chamber pot). Beethoven had just completed his mighty *Missa solemnis*, but was not in the mood for any seriousness from Rossini. He complimented him on *The Barber of Seville*, and advised him never to attempt anything but comic opera. The tactless advice was not taken to heart by Rossini; the following year his great tragedy *Semiramide* was produced in Venice, and his operatic career culminated two years after Beethoven's death with *Guillaume Tell*.

stage: he and his wife went to Paris and to London that year, remaining in England until Jul 1824, being well received at court. He wrote a lament on the death of Byron for eight voices.

On returning to Paris he was appointed director of the Théâtre Italian, where he produced a new and two revised works, followed by a French comic opera, *Le Comte Ory*, and finally *Guillaume Tell* (1829) at the Opéra. The strain of composing *Tell*, a huge summation of his life's work, brought on a prolonged period of ill-health and after that, although only 37, he gave up opera and lived alternately at Bologna and Paris. In the early 1830s he met Olympe Pélissier, a *demi-mondaine*, and entered into a liaison with her; his separation from Isabella was legalized in 1837, she died in 1845, and he married Olympe on 21 Aug 1846. Serious illness afflicted him during this period, but he completed the *Stabat Mater* (1832–42). In 1839 he was commissioned to reform the Liceo Musicale at Bologna, where he had once been a pupil, and he worked there at intervals until 1848, when he left for Florence, to remain until 1855, leaving Italy for the last time for Paris that year. In his retirement he wrote many small pieces for the entertainment of his friends and in 1863 the *Petite Messe solennelle*; his musical soirées were much sought after by fashionable society and contemporary musicians.

For many years Rossini's comic operas have overshadowed his serious works, but recent productions have helped to produce a more balanced view of his output: *La donna del lago*, *Guillaume Tell* and *Mosè in Egitto* at Covent Garden, *Semiramide* (perhaps his finest work) at the New York Met., and *Ermione* at Glyndebourne in 1995.

Works include OPERAS: *Demetrio e Polibio* (1806), *La cambiale di matrimonio* (1810), *L'equivoco stravagante* (1811), *L'inganno felice* (1812), *Ciro in Babilonia* (1812), *La scala di seta* (1812), *La pietra del paragone* (1812), *L'occasione fa il ladro* (1812), *Il signor Bruschino* (1813), *Tancredi* (1813), *L'Italiana in Algeri* (1813), *Aureliano in Palmira* (1813), *Il Turco in Italia* (1814), *Sigismondo* (1814), *Elisabetta, regina d'Inghilterra* (1815), *Torvaldo e Dorliska* (1815), *Il barbiere di Siviglia* (after Beaumarchais, 1816), *La gazzetta* (1816), *Otello* (last act after Shakespeare, 1816), *La Cenerentola* (1817), *La gazza ladra* (1817), *Armida* (1818), *Adelaide di Borgogna* (1817), *Mosè in Egitto* (1818), *Adina* (1818), *Ricciardo e Zoraide* (1818), *Ermione* (on Racine's *Andromaque*, 1819), *Eduardo e Cristina* (1819), *La donna del lago* (after Scott, 1819) *Bianca e Falliero* (1819), *Maometto secondo* (1820), *Matilde di Shabran* (1821), *Zelmira* (1822), *Semiramide* (1823), *Il viaggio a Reims* (1825), *Le Siège de Corinthe* (French revised version of *Maometto secondo*, 1826), *Moïse* (French revised version of *Mosè in Egitto*, 1827), *Le Comte Ory* (1828), *Guillaume Tell* (after Schiller, 1829).

Messa di Gloria (1820), *Stabat Mater* (1842), *La Foi, l'Espérance, la Charité*, *Petite Messe solennelle* and some shorter sacred pieces; *Soirées musicales* (songs and duets); *Péchés de vieillesse* (small piano pieces, songs, etc.); a number of works written in his youth included the opera *Demetrio e Polibio* (1812), a Mass for male voices, duets for horns, four overtures and six string quartets. Pasticcios with music from his works were produced in his lifetime, and a modern one is the ballet *La Boutique fantasque*, arranged by Respighi from *Péchés de vieillesse*.

Rössler, Franz Anton, ◊Rösler.

Rostal, Max (b Teschen, 7 Aug 1905; d Bern, 6 Aug 1991), Austrian-born British violinist. Studied with Rosé and Flesch, and in 1927 became leader of the Oslo PO. From 1930 to 1933 was professor at the Berlin Hochschule für Musik. From 1934 he lived in England and from 1944 to 1958 was professor at the GSM. Among his many pupils were members of the Amadeus Quartet. Although much of his time was spent teaching, his technical excellence and musicianship made him one of the leading violinists of his day. Professor at the Cologne State Academy from 1957 and the Bern Conservatory from 1958. CBE 1977.

Rostropovich, Mstislav (Leopoldovich) (b Baku, 27 Mar 1927), Russian cellist, pianist and conductor. Studied at the Moscow Conservatory, where he became a professor in 1957. He rapidly acquired a worldwide reputation as a soloist. He is also an accomplished pianist,

and often accompanies his wife, Galina Vishnevskaya. They were obliged to leave Russia in 1974, but returned following the collapse of Communism, taking an active part in politics. Debut as conductor Moscow, Bolshoi, 1968; London 1974. Prokofiev and Shostakovich wrote concertos for him, Britten the three suites for solo cello and cello symphony. As a conductor has premiered works by Schnittke (*Life with an Idiot* and *Gesualdo*), Penderecki (*Polish Requiem*) and Gubaidulina (opera-oratorio *The Age of Aquarius*). Hon. KBE 1987.

Roswaenge, Helge (b Copenhagen, 29 Aug 1897; d Munich, 19 Jun 1972), Danish tenor. Debut Neustrelitz 1921, as Don José. He sang at the Berlin Staatsoper 1929–49 and in Vienna 1936–60, as the Duke of Mantua, Calaf and Manrico. Bayreuth 1934–36, as Parsifal. He was admired by Toscanini and sang at Salzburg as Huon, Tamino and Florestan.

Rota, Andrea (b Bologna, *c* 1553; d Bologna, Jun 1597), Italian composer. He became choirmaster at San Petronio at Bologna in 1583.

Works include Masses, motets, *Agnus Dei* (with double canon), *Dixit Dominus* for eight voices and other church music; madrigals.

Rota, Nino (b Milan, 3 Dec 1911; d Rome, 10 Apr 1979), Italian composer. Studied with Pizzetti, Casella and in USA. On his return to Milan he obtained a degree with a treatise on Zarlino and Italian Renaissance music. Appointed director of the Bari Conservatory 1950.

Works include operas *Il principe porcaro* (after Hans Andersen, composed 1925), *Ariodante* (1942), *Il capello di paglia di Firenze/The Italian straw hat* 1955); oratorio *L'infanzia di San Giovanni Battista*; two Masses; three symphonies (1936–39), serenade and concerto for orchestra; *Invenzioni* for string quartet, quintet for flute, oboe, viola, cello and harp; *Il presepio* for voice, string quartet and piano; sonatas for violin and piano, viola and piano and flute and harp; songs *Liriche di Tagore*, *Tre liriche infantili*; film music.

rote an instrument of the lyre type, also called rota or rotte, and similar to the crwth. It was in use up to medieval times.

Rothenberger, Anneliese (b Mannheim, 19 Jun 1924), German soprano. Studied at Mannheim Musikhochschule and made her debut in Koblenz in 1943. She sang in Hamburg 1946–74, as Lulu, Sophie, Cherubino and Hindemith's Regina (role of British debut, Edinburgh, 1952). In 1956 she became a member of the Deutsche Oper am Rhein, and in 1958 of the Vienna Staatsoper. Glyndebourne debut 1959, as Sophie. She was equally at home in the classical and modern repertory and was one of the most successful singers on the German stage. NY Met. debut 1960, as Zdenka. Created Sutermeister's Madame Bovary, Zurich 1967.

Rothmüller, Marko (b Trnjani, 31 Dec 1908; d Bloomington, 20 Jan 1993), Yugoslav baritone. He sang Rigoletto on his Hamburg debut, 1932, and from 1935 to 1947 appeared at Zurich, notably as Truchsess in the fp of Hindemith's *Mathis der Maler* (1938). In 1947 he sang Jochanaan at CG and returned until 1955 as Scarpia, and Wozzeck in the 1952 British first stage performance of Berg's opera. Glyndebourne 1949–55, as Guglielmo, the Count, Don Carlo, Macbeth and Nick Shadow. Sang with the New York City Opera and CG, 1948–52; NY Met. debut 1959, as Kothner; returned until 1964.

Rouget de Lisle, Claude Joseph (b Lonsle-Saulnier, 10 May 1760; d Choisy-le-Roi, 26–7 Jun 1836), French soldier, author and musician. Having embarked on a military career, he was stationed at Strasbourg in 1791 and made a name as poet, violinist and singer. He wrote the *Hymne à la liberté*, set by I Pleyel, that year and words and music of the *Marseillaise* in 1792. Similar later pieces of the kind were *Hymne dithyrambique*, *Le Chant des vengeances*, *Le Chant des combats*, *Hymne à la Raison*, *Hymne du neuf Thermidor* and *Les Héros du Vengeur*. He also wrote libretti, including *Bayard dans Bresse* for Champein and *Macbeth* (based on Shakespeare) for Chelard.

Rouleau, Joseph (b Matane, Quebec, 28 Feb 1929), Canadian bass. Studied in Montreal and made debut there in 1951, with *Un ballo in maschera*; Verdi's Philip II 1955. Sang at CG from 1957, as Colline, in *Les Troyens*, *Aida*, and *Don Giovanni* (Commendatore) and as Philip in the local fp of the French-language *Don Carlos* (1983), Paris

Opéra 1960 and 1974, as Raimondo and Gurnemanz. Returned later to Canada and sang Mozart's Bartolo with Vancouver Opera, 1992.

round a kind of canon best defined by saying that its successive entries consist of complete melodies rather than mere phrases. The entries are thus apt to lie farther apart. Unlike canons, rounds are always sung with the theme in its original position or in the octave, never at other intervals. An older name for the round was rota: *Sumer is icumen in*, known as the 'Reading Rota', is a typical early round. A familiar later example is in the second-act finale of Mozart's *Così fan tutte*.

rounds round dances, i.e. dances performed in circles, and hence tunes intended for such dances.

I deduce that the French have no music and cannot have any music – and if they ever have, more's the pity for them.

Jean-Jacques Rousseau,
Lettre sur la musique française, 1753

Rousseau, Jean-Jacques (b Geneva, 28 Jun 1712; d Ermenonville near Paris, 2 Jul 1778), Swiss-French philosopher, author and composer. He was a chorister at Annecy Cathedral but had little formal training in music. Went to Paris in 1741, where he presented a paper to the Académie des Sciences advocating a new system of notation (pub. in 1743 as *Dissertation sur la musique moderne*) and later contributed music articles to Diderot's *Encyclopédie*, which were severely criticized by Rameau for their inaccuracy. As secretary to the French ambassador in Venice 1743–44, he became acquainted with Italian music, and during the Guerre des Bouffons sided with the Italian party, decrying French music in his controversial essay, *Lettre sur la musique française* (1753). His most important composition, the one-act *intermède Le Devin du village*, though in French, was supposedly written in tuneful Italian style. In 1767 he pub. his valuable *Dictionnaire de musique*. The 'monodrama' *Pygmalion* (1770), only two pieces of which were by Rousseau, attempted to found a new form, and in its combination of spoken words and music was the ancestor of the later melodrama. Among his other writings are two essays in support of Gluck.

Works include operas *Iphis et Anaxerète* (1740), *La Découverte du nouveau monde* (1741), *Le Devin du village* (1752), *Daphnis et Chloé* (unfinished); opera-ballet *Les Muses galantes* (1745); monodrama *Pygmalion* (1770). *c* 100 songs, etc., pub. as *Consolations des misères de ma vie*.

Roussel, Albert (b Tourcoing, 5 Apr 1869; d Royan, 23 Aug 1937), French composer. Educated in Paris for the Navy, but took piano lessons at the same time. Wrote his first compositions while engaged in naval service and voyaging to the East, but he resigned in 1893 to devote himself to music, studying with Gigout and d'Indy. In 1902 he became professor at the Schola Cantorum, where he had studied. In 1912 he wrote one of his most popular works, *Le festin de l'araignée/ The Spider's Banquet*, in which the hungry arachnid is depicted with appropriate, delicate scoring. Following this work, Roussel moved away from an impressionistic palette. In World War I he served with the Red Cross and later with the transport service, in 1918 retired, broken in health, to Perros-Guirec in Brittany and in 1920 to a villa near Varengeville.

His service in Indo-China had a lasting impression on Roussel, colouring his finest work, the opéra-ballet *Padmâvatî* with Indian melodic patterns. Ballet and choral singing are found also in *La naissance de la lyre*, an evocation of ancient Greece. Other characteristics of Roussel's varying style appear in his third symphony, which includes polytonality and vital rhythmic patterns.

Works include STAGE: opera *Padmâvatî* (1923); operetta *Le Testament de Tante Caroline* (1936); ballets *Le Festin de l'araignée* (1913), *Bacchus et Ariane* (1931), *Énée*, *Les Enchantements d'Alcine* (after Ariosto) and contributed to *L'Éventail de Jeanne*; incidental music to Jean-Aubry's *Le Marchand de sable qui passe* (1908), *La*

naissance de la Lyre (1925), prelude to Act II of Roland's *14 Juillet* (with six others).

VOCAL AND ORCHESTRAL: Psalm 80 for tenor, chorus and orchestra (in English); four symphonies, 1908–34; (no. 1 *Le Poème de la forêt*), *Trois Évocations* (third with chorus), *Pour une fête de printemps*, *Suite en Fa* (1927), *Concert*, *Petite Suite* (1929), *Rapsodie flamande* for orchestra (1936); sinfonietta for strings; *A Glorious Day* for military band; piano concerto (1927), concertino for cello and orchestra (1936).

CHAMBER AND SONGS: string quartet (1932), *Divertissement* for wind and piano (1906), serenade for flute, violin, viola, cello and harp (1925), string trio, trios for violin clarinet and piano and flute, violin and clarinet; two violin and piano sonatas, *Joueurs de flûte* for flute and piano; Impromptu for harp; *Segovia* for guitar; suite *Des heures passent*, *Rustiques*, suite, sonatina, prelude and fugue (*Hommage à Bach*), etc., for piano; songs *Six Odes anacréontiques* (1926), *Deux Poèmes chinois* (1927), eight poems by Henri de Régnier, two poems by Ronsard, *A Flower given to my Daughter* (James Joyce).

Rousselière, Charles (b St Nazir, 17 Jan 1875; d Joue-les-Tours, 11 May 1950), French tenor. He studied in Paris and made his debut there in 1900 as Samson. He sang in operas by Mascagni and Saint-Saëns in Monte Carlo. In 1913 he created Charpentier's Julien and took part in the fp of Fauré's *Pénélope*. Met. debut 1906, as Gounod's Roméo. Other roles included Siegmund, Parsifal, Loge, Max and Manrico.

rovescio Ɖal rovescio.

Rovetta, Giovanni (b Venice, *c* 1595; d Venice, 23 Oct 1668), Italian priest and composer. Learnt music as a choirboy at St Mark's in Venice and in 1623 was appointed a bass there. He was ordained priest, became vice-*maestro di cappella* at St Mark's in 1627 and first *maestro di cappella* in succession to Monteverdi in 1644.

Works include Masses, motets, psalms, operas, *Ercole in Lidia* (1645) and *Argiope* (1649); madrigals.

Rowe, Walter (d Berlin, 1647), English 16th–17th-c. violinist and composer. He was at Hamburg before 1614, when he was appointed violist at the court chapel in Berlin. His son (d Berlin, Apr 1671) had the same name and occupation.

Works include music for viola da gamba.

Rowicki, Witold (b Taganrog, 27 Feb 1914; d Warsaw, 1 Oct 1989), Russian-born Polish conductor. Studied at Kraków Conservatory. Music director Katowice Radio SO 1945–50, Warsaw PO 1958–77. Director, Warsaw Theatre Opera Centre 1965–70. Often heard in Penderecki and Lutoslawski.

Roxburgh, Edwin (b Liverpool, 6 Nov 1937), English composer, teacher and conductor. Studied at RCM and with Nono and Dalla-piccola. Professor of composition at RCM from 1967. Active as oboist and conductor on behalf of modern music.

Works include Variations for orchestra (1963), *The Tower*, ballet (1964), *A Mosaic for Cummings* for two narrators and orchestra (1973), wind quintet (1974), *The Rock*, oratorio (1979).

Roxelane, La authentic name of Haydn's symphony no. 63 in C major, composed *c* 1777–80, so called apparently after an old French melody used for variations in the slow movement.

Roy, Bartolomeo (b Burgundy, *c* 1530; d Naples, 2 Feb 1599), composer of French origin who lived for a time in Rome, and from 1583 until his death as *maestro di cappella* at the royal palace at Naples. Composed madrigals and church music.

Royal Academy of Music founded in London in 1822 and opened in Mar 1823 with Crotch as principal, who was followed by Potter (1832), Charles Lucas (1859), Sterndale Bennett (1866), Macfarren (1875), Mackenzie (1888), McEwen (1924), Stanley Marchant (1936), Reginald Thatcher (1949), Thomas Armstrong (1955), Anthony Lewis (1968), David Lumsden (1982), Lynn Harrell (1993) and Curtis Price (1995).

Royal College of Music founded in London in 1882 and opened on 7 May 1883 with Grove as director, who was followed by Parry (1894), Hugh Allen (1918), George Dyson (1937), Ernest Bullock (1953), Keith Falkner (1960), David Willcocks (1974), M Gough Matthews (1985) and Janet Ritterman (1993).

Royal Liverpool Philharmonic Orchestra British orchestra founded 1840 with John Russell as conductor. Julius Benedict was conductor 1867–79, Max Bruch 1880–83 and Charles Hallé 1883–95. Recent conductors have been Malcolm Sargent (1942–48), Hugo Rignold (1948–54), John Pritchard (1955–63), Charles Groves (1963–77) and Walter Weller (1977–80). David Atherton was chief conductor 1980–83, succeeded by Marek Janowski (1983–86). Libor Pešek 1987–95.

Royal Manchester College of Music founded in 1893. First principal was Sir Charles Hallé, followed by A Brodsky (1895), J R Forbes (1929), F R Cox (1953) and J Wray (1970–72). In 1972 the RMCM merged with the Northern School of Music to form the Royal Northern College of Music (principal J Manduell).

Royal Musical Association a society formed to promote the investigation of all aspects of music. It was founded in London in 1874 as The Musical Association and became 'Royal' in 1944. Apart from regular meetings and conferences, the Association publishes the *Proceedings of the RMA* (from 1987, *Journal of the RMA*), *RMA Research Chronicle* (founded 1961), *RMA Monographs* (founded 1985) and initiated *Musica Britannica* (1951).

Royal Northern College of Music ◊Royal Manchester College of Music.

Royal Opera House. ◊Covent Garden.

Royal Philharmonic Orchestra London-based orchestra founded in 1946 by Beecham; he remained principal conductor until his death in 1961. Rudolf Kempe was chief conductor 1961–63, conductor for life from 1970. Later conductors have been Antal Dorati (1975–78), Walter Weller (1980–85) and André Previn (1985–86). Vladimir Ashkenazy musical director 1987–94, Daniel Gatti from 1995. The RPO was house orchestra at the Glyndebourne Festival 1947–63.

Royal Philharmonic Society a society formed in London for the cultivation of good orchestral music in 1813 by J B Cramer, P A Corri and W Dance. The first concert was given at the Argyll Rooms, 8 Mar 1813, conducted by Clementi (at the piano) and led by J P Salomon. Among the first members were Attwood, Ayrton, Bishop, Horsley, Knyvett, V Novello, Potter, Shield, G Smart, Viotti and Webbe, junior. It has continued uninterruptedly until the present day. Among later conductors were Weber, Mendelssohn, Spohr, Wagner, Sullivan, Mackenzie, H J Wood, Nikisch, Chevillard, Elgar, Safonov, Bruno Walter, Beecham, Mengelberg, Stanford, Hamilton Harty, Furtwängler, Weingartner and Monteux. Beethoven figured in the programmes from the first and when he was on his deathbed the Society sent him the sum of £100. (His Ninth symphony had been commissioned by the Society but the fp was given at Vienna in 1824).

Royal Scottish National Orchestra symphony orchestra founded 1891 as Scottish Orchestra, with George Henschel as conductor (until 1894). Principal conductors since 1933–36 (Barbirolli) have been George Szell (1936–39), Warwick Braithwaite (1940–46), Walter Susskind (1946–52), Hans Swarowsky (1957–59), Alexander Gibson (1959–84), Neeme Järvi (1984–88), Bryden Thomson (1988–90), Walter Weller from 1991. The orchestra was reorganized 1950 under the title Scottish National Orchestra. A new Glasgow Concert Hall, the Royal International Hall, was opened 1990. Present title granted 1990.

Royal Winter Music two sonatas on Shakespearean characters for guitar by Henze: no. 1 1975–76, fp Berlin, 20 Sept 1976, with Julian Bream; no. 2 1979, fp Brussels, 25 Nov 1980.

Rozario, Patricia (b Bombay, 1959), Indian-born soprano. Studied with Vera Rosza and has sung with the Songmakers' Almanac, notably on tour to the USA. Frequent concerts in Bach, Handel and Mozart (*Il re Pastore* on London's South Bank). Opera roles include Gluck's Euridice for Opera North, Mozart's Bastienne and Pamina with Kent Opera, Florinda in Handel's *Rodrigo* at Innsbruck, Ilia with GTO, and Nero in *Poppea*. Created Miriam in Casken's *Golem* (1989) and the title role in Taverner's *Mary of Egypt* (1992).

Rozhdestvensky, Gennady (b Moscow, 4 May 1931), Russian conductor. He studied at the Moscow Conservatory and worked at the Bolshoi 1951–70, giving operas by Prokofiev and Britten as well as

the usual ballets. His London debut was in 1956 and in 1970 he conducted *Boris Godunov* at CG. Chief conductor BBC SO 1978–81, Vienna SO from 1981. He is experienced in a much wider range of modern works than his limited programmes in London would suggest, although in 1991 he gave the fp there of *Jacob's Ladder* by Smirnov.

Rozkošný, Josef Richard (b Prague, 21 Sept 1833; d Prague, 3 Jun 1913), Czech pianist and composer. Studied in Prague and toured widely as pianist. Later had a great success as a popular opera composer.

Works include operas *Nicholas* (1870), *The Rapids of St John* (1871), *Cinderella* (1885), *Stoja, Zavis of Falkenstein* (1877), *Krakonos* (1889), *The Poacher, Satanella, The Black Lake* (1906); piano pieces; songs.

Rózsa, Miklós (b Budapest, 18 Apr 1907; d Los Angeles, 27 July 1995), Hungarian-born American composer. Studied piano and composition in Leipzig, and in 1932 settled in Paris, achieving success as a composer. In 1935 he moved to London, where he worked in the film industry and in 1940 settled in Hollywood, writing music for such films as *The Jungle Book*, *Spellbound* (1945) and *Ben Hur* (1959).

Works include *Ballet Hungarica*; symphony (1930), *Scherzo, Theme, Variations and Finale* for orchestra (1933); concert overture, serenade for chamber orchestra; concerto for string orchestra; two violin concertos, viola concerto (1984); string quartet; piano quintet, trio for violin, viola and clarinet; film music etc.

Różycki, Ludomir (b Warsaw, 6 Nov 1883; d Katowice, 1 Jan 1953), Polish conductor and composer. Studied with Noskowski at the Warsaw Conservatory and with Humperdinck in Berlin. In 1912 he became conductor at Lwów, and later lived by turns in Warsaw and Berlin.

Works include operas *Bolesław the Bold* (1908), *Medusa* (1911), *Eros and Psyche* (1916), *Casanova, Beatrice Cenci* (1926), *The Devil's Mill* (1930); ballet *Pan Twardowski*; symphonic poems *Bolesław the Bold, Anhelli* and others, prelude *Mona Lisa Giaconda* and ballad for orchestra; piano concerto in G minor; string quartet (1916), piano quintet (1913), piano music, songs.

rubato Italian = lit. 'robbed'; a manner of performing music without adhering strictly to time. Various rules have been established at different times, e.g. that what is taken away by hurrying from the time properly occupied by a composition as written, must be given back elsewhere by slackening, or that in some piano music, in which the right hand only may play rubato while the left keeps strict time; but rubato should be subject, not to rules, but to feeling, and it cannot easily be taught to those who have either no musical sense or an exaggerated notion of it.

Rubbra, Edmund (b Northampton, 23 May 1901; d Gerrards Cross, 14 Feb 1986), English composer. Studied at Reading University and the RCM in London, Holst, and Vaughan Williams being among his masters. Lecturer at Oxford University 1947–68. His music is solidly made, and broadly in the spirit of his teachers.

Works include STAGE AND CHORAL: *Bee-Bee-Bei* (1933), incidental music for Shakespeare's *Macbeth*; Canterbury Mass, (1945), *Missa in honorem Sancti Dominici* (1948), Festival Te Deum; *La Belle Dame sans merci* (Keats) and *The Morning Watch* (Henry Vaughan) for chorus and orchestra; Masses, motets, madrigals and other choral works.

ORCHESTRAL: 11 symphonies (1935–79), Double and Triple Fugues, *Improvisations on Virginal Pieces by Farnaby* (1939) and Festival Overture for orchestra; *Sinfonia concertante* for piano and orchestra, rhapsody for violin and orchestra, viola concerto (1953), piano concerto (1956), *Soliloquy* for cello and small orchestra; works for voice and orchestra.

CHAMBER: four string quartets (1934–77), trio for violin, cello and piano and other chamber music; five sonnets by Spenser for voice and string quartet (1935); three sonatas and sonatina for violin and piano, cello and piano sonata; piano and organ music; songs.

Rubinelli, Giovanni Battista (b Brescia, 1753; d Brescia, 1829), Italian castrato alto. Made his debut in 1771 in Stuttgart, where he was in the service of the Duke of Württemberg, but from 1774 sang in the leading Italian opera houses. Visited London, 1786, singing in revivals of operas by Handel. He retired 1800.

Rubini, Giovanni Battista (b Romano near Bergamo, 7 Apr 1794; d Romano, 3 Mar 1854), Italian tenor. He began with small engagements, but made his way to Venice, Naples and Rome, where his successes in opera increased steadily. In 1819 he married the French singer Chomel at Naples, visited Paris for the first time in 1825 and sang in Rossini's *Cenerentola*, *Otello* and *Donna del lago*. He created leading roles in Bellini's *Bianca e Gernando*, *Il pirata*, *La sonnambula* and *I Puritani*. London, 1831–43. In 1843 he toured Holland and Germany with Liszt, and went on alone to St Petersburg.

Rubinstein, Anton Grigorievich (b Vykhvatinets, Volhynia, 28 Nov 1829; d Peterhof, 20 Nov 1894), Russian pianist and composer of German-Polish descent. Learnt the piano from his mother and from a teacher named Villoing at Moscow. He appeared in public at the age of nine and in 1840 went on tour with his teacher, who took him to Paris and placed him under Liszt for further instruction. He afterwards toured in Europe and from 1844 to 1846 studied composition with Dehn in Berlin. After teaching in Vienna and Pressburg he returned to Russia in 1848, becoming chamber virtuoso to the Grand Duchess Helena Pavlovna. From 1854 onward he again travelled widely as a pianist and in 1858 he was appointed imperial music director at St Petersburg, founding the Conservatory in 1862. Rubinstein is best remembered as a great and influential pianist; his many compositions are still little known although *The Demon* was successfully revived at Wexford in 1991.

Works include OPERAS AND STAGE ORATORIOS: *Dimitry Donskoy* (1852), *The Siberian Hunters* (1854), *Children of the Heath* (1858), *Feramors* (from Moore's *Lalla Rookh*, 1863), *The Tower of Babel* (1870), *The Demon* (after Lermontov, 1875), *The Maccabees* (after Otto Ludwig, 1875) *Paradise Lost* (after Milton, 1875), *Nero* (1879), *The Merchant of Moscow* (1880), *The Shulamite*, *Moses* (1892), *Christus* and others.

VOCAL AND ORCHESTRAL: Songs and Requiem for Mignon from Goethe's *Wilhelm Meister* for solo voices, chorus and piano; six symphonies, 1850–86: (2. *Ocean*, 4. *Dramatic*), four concert overtures (one on Shakespeare's *Antony and Cleopatra*), musical portraits *Faust* (after Goethe), *Ivan the Terrible*, *Don Quixote* (after Cervantes), suite in Eb major for orchestra (1894); five concertos and *Conzertstück* for piano and orchestra (1850–89); violin concerto, two cello concertos.

CHAMBER: ten string quartets (1855–81), string quintet and sextet, octet for piano, strings and wind, five piano trios, piano and wind quintet, piano quintet and quartet; three violin and piano sonatas; instrumental pieces; four sonatas, Theme and Variations and many other works for piano; songs.

The old romanticism is dead; long live the new!
Arnold Schoenberg, quoted in Machlis, *Introduction to Contemporary Music*, 1963

Rubinstein, Arthur (b Łódź, 28 Jan 1886; d Geneva, 20 Dec 1982), Polish-born American pianist. After early studies in Poland he was sent to Berlin, studying piano with H Barth and R M Breithaupt, composition with R Kahn and with Bruch. He made his debut aged 12 in a concert conducted by Joachim. He then studied with Paderewski in Switzerland, and toured the USA in 1906. Made his London debut in 1912, then settled in Paris and continued to tour the USA. His family was decimated in the Holocaust and he refused to play in Germany after the war. In 1946 he became an American citizen. He was best known for his playing of Chopin, to which he brought great virtuosity combined with elegance and poetry. Also successful in chamber music, notably with violinists Henryk Szeryng and Jascha Heifetz, and the Guarneri Quartet.

Rubinstein, Nikolai Grigorievich (b Moscow, 14 Jun 1835; d Paris, 23 Mar 1881), Russian pianist and composer of German-Polish

descent, brother of Anton ◊Rubinstein. Studied under Kullak and Dehn in Berlin and after his return to Russia settled at Moscow, where he founded the Russian Music Society in 1859 and the Conservatory in 1864, to which he invited Tchaikovsky as professor.

Rubsamen, Walter H(oward) (b New York, 21 Jul 1911; d Los Angeles, 19 Jun 1973), American musicologist. Studied at Columbia University, NY, and at Munich University, later joined the music department of his college and in 1938 became lecturer and in 1955 professor at the University of California at LA. His works included studies of Pierre de La Rue, early Italian secular music, etc.

Ruckers Flemish family of harpsichord and virginal makers at Antwerp, active 1579–1667 and producing instruments which provided contrast in register and tone; about 100 instruments survive, in both single and two-manual versions. The firm was founded by Hans Ruckers (c. 1530–98), succeeded by his sons Joannes (1578–1642) and Andries (1579– c. 1645).

Rückert, Friedrich (1788–1866), German poet. ◊Kindertotenlieder (Mahler), also five other songs by Mahler for voice and orchestra (*Ich atmet' einen linden Duft*, *Liebst du um Schönheit*, *Blicke mir nicht in die Lieder*, *Ich bin der Welt abhanden gekommen*, *Um Mitternacht*, 1901–03), five songs by Schubert, 18 by Schumann, two by Brahms.

Rückpositiv German = 'back positive'; small organ at organist's back, to the front of the gallery. From 15th–17th c. the second main manual of most organs, providing colouristic and contrasting functions.

Ruddigore, or The Witch's Curse, operetta by Sullivan (libretto by W S Gilbert), produced London, Savoy Theatre, 22 Jan 1887. Robin, the villainous Sir Ruthven and bad baronet of Ruddigore, is condemned by a family curse to commit a crime a day.

Ruders, Poul (b Ringstead, 27 Mar 1949), Danish composer and organist. Studied at the Copenhagen Conservatory; commissions from London Sinfonietta and Ensemble Intercontemporain.

Works include *Wind-Drumming* for wind quintet and four percussion (1979); two violin concertos (1981, 1991); two string quartets (1971, 1979); *Manhattan Abstractions* (for the New York PO, 1982); *Thus Saw Saint Joan*, for orchestra (1984); *Break Dance* for piano and ensemble (1984); clarinet concerto (1985); *Dramaphonia* for piano and orchestra (1987); *Nightshade* for ensemble (1987); *Tycho*, opera (after the Danish astronomer who was obliged to replace his nose with a proboscis made of copper, 1986); Symphony, *Himmelhoch Jauchzend-zum Tode betrubt* (1989); *The City in the Sea* for contralto and orchestra (1990), *Trapeze* (1992) and *Zenith* (1993) for orchestra; *The Bells* for soprano and chamber ensemble (1993); *Anima*, cello concerto (1993).

Rudersdorff, Hermine (b Ivanovsky, Ukraine, 12 Dec 1822; d Boston, 26 Feb 1882), German soprano. Learnt music from her father, the violinist Joseph Rudersdorff, and singing in Paris, Milan and London. She made her first appearance in Germany at the age of 18, sang in the production of Mendelssohn's *Hymn of Praise* at Leipzig in 1840 and then appeared in opera at Karlsruhe and Frankfurt. In 1854 she first visited London, where she remained for a number of years, but settled in Boston in the 1870s.

Rudhyar, Dane (actually Daniel Chennevière) (b Paris, 23 Mar 1895; d San Francisco, 13 Sept 1985), French-American composer. Studied in Paris and settled in USA in 1916, receiving a composition prize in 1920.

Works include ballet *Dance Poem*; symphonic poem *Surge of Fire* (1920), six 'syntonies' for orchestra (1920–59), *Cosmic Cycle* for orchestra (1981); piano music and songs.

Rudolf, Max (b Frankfurt, 15 Jun 1902; d Philadelphia, 28 Feb 1995), German-born American conductor. Studied in Frankfurt and conducted at the Hesse State Opera 1923–29, German Opera Prague 1929–35 and in Sweden 1935–39. Conducted at the New York Met. from 1946, after emigrating to the USA, and led *Rosenkavalier* on debut; returned 1975, in Mozart and Strauss. Music director of the Cincinnati SO 1958–70 and conducted the Dallas SO 1973–74, and the Detroit SO, from 1983. Head of opera at Curtis from 1981.

Rudolph (Johann Joseph Rainer) von Österreich (of Austria), Archduke (b Florence, 8 Jan 1788; d Baden near Vienna, 24 Jul 1831),

Austrian amateur musician. Pupil of Anton Teyber (music instructor of the Imperial children), and later of Beethoven, who wrote the *Missa solemnis* for his installation as Archbishop of Olomouc (1820), though he finished it two years too late. Beethoven also dedicated, among others, the fourth and fifth piano concertos, Archduke trio and 'Hammerklavier' sonata to him.

Works include sonata for clarinet and piano; variations for piano on themes by Beethoven and Rossini.

Rudorff, Ernst (Friedrich Karl) (b Berlin, 18 Jan 1840; d Berlin, 31 Dec 1916), German pianist, teacher and composer. Pupil of Bargiel, Clara Schumann and others, later studied at the Leipzig University and Conservatory. In 1865 he became professor at the Cologne Conservatory and 1869–1910 at the Hochschule für Musik in Berlin. He also conducted Stern's Vocal Academy 1880–90.

Works include *Der Aufzug der Romanze* (Tieck) for solo voices, chorus and orchestra, *Gesang an die Sterne* (Rückert) for chorus and orchestra; three symphonies, two sets of variations, ballad, serenade, three overtures for orchestra; romance for cello and orchestra; string sextet; variations for two pianos; pieces for piano solo and duet; songs, part-songs.

Rudy, Mikhail (b Tashkent, 3 Apr 1953), Russian pianist. Studied at the Moscow Conservatory and won Bach International Competition Leipzig 1971. Made European debut at Paris in 1977, with Beethoven's Triple Concerto. US debut 1981, with the Cleveland Orchestra. Salzburg 1987, under Karajan. Chamber concerts with the Amadeus Quartet (until 1987), Guarneri Quartet and Vienna Philharmonic Wind Ensemble. London debut 1988, with the LSO, and returned to Russia, 1990, for concerts with the St Petersburg PO.

Rue, Pierre de la, ◊La Rue.

Rufer, Josef (b Vienna, 18 Dec 1893; d Berlin, 7 Nov 1985), Austrian writer on music. Studied with Zemlinsky and Schoenberg, becoming Schoenberg's assistant in Berlin 1925–33. In 1945, with H H Stuckenschmidt, he founded the periodical *Stimmen*, and from 1956 taught at the Free University in Berlin. His books on music include *Composition with 12 notes related only to one another* (a study of Schoenberg's methods) and the valuable catalogue *The Works of Arnold Schoenberg* (1959).

Ruffo, Titta (b Pisa, 9 Jun 1877; d Florence, 6 Jul 1953), Italian baritone. He studied in Rome and made his debut there in 1898. Wider recognition came in 1903, with appearances in London and Milan, and until 1931 he was heard in Europe and North and South America as Hamlet, Luna, Renato, Nelusko and Barnaba. US debut Philadelphia 1912, as Rigoletto; NY Met. 1922–28 (debut as Rossini's Figaro).

Ruffo, Vincenzo (b Verona, *c* 1510; d Sacile near Udine, 9 Feb 1587), Italian male soprano and composer. Appointed *maestro di cappella* at Verona Cathedral in 1554 and from 1563 to 1572 at that of Milan. He occupied a similar post at Pistoia in 1574–79, but then returned to Milan. His sacred music shows the influence of Tridentine reforms, which insisted on verbal clarity.

Works include Masses, motets, Magnificat, psalms and other church music; madrigals.

Rugby Honegger's second symphonic movement for orchestra, following *Pacific 231* and succeeded by *Mouvement symphonique No. 3*. It is an impression of a game of rugby football. Fp Paris, Orchestre Symphonique, 19 Oct 1928.

ruggiero a simple bass line, first found in the 16th c., which was widely used for variations. A typical form is illustrated below. It may originally have been a dance, though it is found also in vocal settings. ◊romanesca.

Ruggiero, o vero L'eroica gratitudine, *Ruggiero, or Heroic Gratitude*, opera by Hasse (libretto by Metastasio), produced Milan, Teatro Regio Ducal, 16 Oct 1771. Hasse's last opera. Rogerus, imprisoned by the Greeks after a battle, is rescued by Leone, who is now betrothed to Bradamante, Rogerus' beloved. Rogerus reluctantly accepts the situation, preferring suicide to a fight against Leone. But all resolves happily: Rogerus and Bradamante are reunited.

Ruggles, Carl (b Marion, MA, 11 Mar 1876; d Bennington, VT, 24 Oct 1971), American composer and painter. Studied at Harvard University, with John Knowles Paine. Afterwards he conducted the Symphony Orchestra at Winona, MN, for a time. From 1917 lived in New York, where his music was given in concerts organized by Varèse; also associated with Ives and was an early American exponent of atonalism.

Works include opera *The Sunken Bell* (composed 1912–23), *Men and Angels* (1920), *Men* destroyed, *Angels* for four trumpets and three trombones (revised 1938), *Men and Mountains* for small orchestra (1924), *Portals* for 13 strings (1925, revised 1929, 1941 and 1953), *Sun Treader* (1932), *Evocations* for orchestra (1971); concertino for piano and orchestra; *Vox clamans in deserto* for voice and chamber orchestra; *Polyphonic Compositions* for three pianos, *Evocations* and other works for piano.

Ruins of Athens, The incidental music by Beethoven, op. 113, for a play by Kotzebue written for the opening of the German theatre at Pest, 9 Feb 1812. It comprises an overture and eight numbers, including the *Turkish March*, already composed by Beethoven for his piano variations, op. 76, in 1809.

Rule, Britannia a patriotic song by Arne, now almost a second British national anthem, originally part of the masque *Alfred*, produced 1 Aug 1740, at Cliefden (now Cliveden) House near Maidenhead, the residence of Frederick, Prince of Wales.

rule of the octave an 18th-c. procedure in the treatment of thoroughbass, especially in Italy (*regola dell' ottava*), providing a series of simple chords of the tonic, dominant and subdominant for the elementary harmonization of a bass formed by a rising diatonic scale.

Rung, Frederick (b Copenhagen, 14 Jun 1854; d Copenhagen, 22 Jan 1914), Danish composer and conductor. Pupil of his father Henrik Rung (1807–1871), of Gade and others. He went to the Royal Opera, as coach, became assistant conductor 1884 and succeeded Svendsen as first conductor 1911; gave early Danish performances of Wagner and Puccini. He also taught at the Conservatory and Horneman's music school and conducted choral societies, including a madrigal choir founded by him.

Works include two operas, two ballets, symphony in D minor, two string quartets.

Runge, Peter-Christoph (b Lübeck, 12 Apr 1933), German baritone. After study in Hamburg made debut at Flensburg in 1958, as Guglielmo. Wuppertal Opera 1959–64, Dusseldorf from 1964. Sang at Glyndebourne between 1966 and 1983, as Papageno, Pelléas, Amindo in *L'Ormindo* and Pantaloon in *The Love of Three Oranges*. Sang Stolzius in the UK fp of Zimmermann's *Die Soldaten* (Edinburgh, 1972) and in the premieres of Goehr's *Behold the Sun* (Duisburg, 1985) and Reimann's *Das Schloss* (Berlin 1992). Other roles include Wozzeck and Beckmesser (Nice Opera, 1986).

Rungenhagen, Carl Friedrich (b Berlin, 27 Sept 1778; d Berlin, 21 Dec 1851), German composer and conductor. Worked in Berlin, where he became assistant conductor to Zelter of the Vocal Academy in 1815 and succeeded to the post of first conductor in 1833.

Works include four operas, three oratorios; Mass, *Stabat Mater* for

A typical ruggiero in G major.

female voices and other church music; orchestral works; chamber music; songs.

Runnicles, Donald (b Edinburgh, 16 Nov 1954), Scottish conductor. After study in Edinburgh and London made opera debut at Mannheim in 1980 (*Hoffmann*); chief conductor 1984–87. Conducted *Lulu* at the NY Met. 1988 and the *Ring* at San Francisco in 1990, the year in which he became music director there. Led *Prince Igor* at the Vienna Staatsoper 1990, *Don Giovanni* at Glyndebourne 1991 and *Tannhäuser* at Bayreuth 1993. Music director of Freiburg Opera from 1989.

Runswick, Daryl (b Leicester, 12 Oct 1946), English composer. After study at Cambridge played double bass with the London Sinfonietta, 1970–82. Tenor singer with Electric Phoenix from 1983 and musical director of the Green Light Theatre Company from 1990.

Works include rock opera *Taking the Air* (1989), *Lady Lazarus* for amplified female voice (1985), *Patents: Pending* for six solo voices (1988), *Needs Must when the Devil Drives* for voices and electronics (1990), *Main-lineing*, clarinet quintet (1991). Orchestration of *Aida* for 24 players (WNO 1983). Recordings of Berio and Cage with Electric Phoenix.

Ruslan and Ludmila opera by Glinka (libretto by V A Shirkov and C A Bakhturin, based on Pushkin's poem), produced St Petersburg, 9 Dec 1842. During her wedding to the knight Ruslan, Ludmilla is abducted by the evil dwarf sorceror Chernomor. Ruslan overcomes his magic and saves his bride.

Russalka, *The Water-Sprite*, opera by Dargomizhsky (libretto by composer, from Pushkin's dramatic poem), produced St Petersburg, 16 May 1856. Natasha, abandoned by a prince, drowns herself and becomes Queen of the river nymphs who lure men into the water. Her father, the Miller, laments her loss and goes mad, throwing the Prince into the river, where he joins Natasha.

Opera by Dvořák (libretto by J Kvapil), produced Prague, Czech Theatre, 31 Mar 1901.

Russell, Henry (b Sheerness, 24 Dec 1812; d London, 8 Dec 1900), English singer, organist and composer. Studied at Bologna and with Rossini at Naples, appeared as singer in London in 1828, lived in Canada and USA (organist at Rochester, NY) 1833–41 and then gave entertainments in London with Charles Mackay for which he wrote many popular songs. Landon ◊Ronald was his illegitimate son.

Works include songs 'Cheer, boys, cheer', 'There's a good time coming', 'A life on the ocean wave' (march of the Royal Marines), etc.

Russian bassoon a serpent made in the shape of a bassoon.

'Russian' Quartets one of the nicknames of Haydn's six string quartets, op. 33, composed 1781 and dedicated to the Grand Duke of Russia. Also known as *Gli scherzi* or *Jungfernquartette*.

Russo, William (b Chicago, 25 Jun 1928), American composer. After study in Chicago worked with the Stan Kenton Orchestra 1950–54, as trombonist and composer- arranger. Directed his own orchestra in New York, 1958–61 and the London Jazz Orchestra 1962–65. Teacher at Columbia University, NY, from 1979.

Works include operas *Land of Milk and Honey* and *Antigone* (both Chicago, 1967), *A Cabaret Opera* (New York 1970), *Aesop's Fables* (1971), *The Shepherds' Christmas* (1979), *Isabella's Fortune, The Pay-Off* (1984) and *Talking to the Sun* (Chicago 1989); ballets *The World of Alcina* (1954) and *The Golden Bird* (1984); two symphonies (1957–58); music for jazz bands, and rock cantatas; sonata for violin and piano (1986).

Russolo, Luigi (b Portogruoro, 30 Apr 1885; d Cerro, 6 Feb 1947), Italian composer. In 1909 he joined the Futurist movement of Marinetti and formulated a music based on noise, about which he pub. a book in 1916, *L'arte dei rumori*. His Futurist manifesto of 1913 expanded the orchestra to include explosions, clashes, shrieks, screams and groans. He also invented the Russolophone, which could produce seven different noises in 12 different gradations.

Works include *Meeting of the Automobiles and the Aeroplanes*, *Awakening of a City*.

Rust, Friedrich Wilhelm (b Wörlitz near Dessau, 6 Jul 1739; d Dessau,

28 Feb 1796), German violinist and composer. Pupil of W F Bach in Halle, where he studied law, then of F Benda and C P E Bach in Berlin, later of G Benda, Pugnani and Tartini in Italy, 1765–66. He returned to Dessau in 1766, taught at Basedow's *Philanthropin* from its foundation in 1774, and a year later became municipal music director.

Works include monodramas and duodramas *Inkle und Yariko* (1777), *Colma* (1780), etc.; cantatas; odes and songs; piano sonatas and other keyboard music.

Rust, Wilhelm (b Dessau, 15 Aug 1822; d Leipzig, 2 May 1892), German pianist, violinist and composer, grandson of Friedrich Wilhelm ◊Rust. Studied with his uncle W K Rust and F Schneider and settled in Berlin as pianist, organist and teacher. In 1870 he became professor at the Stern Conservatory there and in 1878 organist and two years later cantor at St Thomas's Church, Leipzig. He edited his grandfather's piano sonatas, much modernizing them, on the strength of which edition d'Indy declared F W Rust to be a prophetic forerunner of Beethoven.

Works include piano and vocal music.

Rust, Wilhelm Karl (b Dessau, 29 Apr 1787; d Dessau, 18 Apr 1855), German pianist and teacher, uncle of Wilhelm ◊Rust and son of F W Rust. Pupil of his father and of Türk at Halle. In 1807 he went to Vienna, where he met Beethoven, and remained there as teacher until 1827, when he returned to Dessau.

Rustic Wedding, *Ländliche Hochzeit*, symphonic poem by Goldmark, fp Vienna, 5 Mar 1876. Usually described today as a symphony.

Rutini, Fernando (b Modena, 1767; d Terracina, 13 Nov 1827), Italian composer, son and pupil of Giovanni Maria Rutini, later *maestro di cappella* at Macerata and Terracina.

Works include 36 operas; cantatas; sonatas.

Rutini, Giovanni Maria (also called G Marco and G Placido) (b Florence, 25 Apr 1723; d Florence, 22 Dec 1797), Italian composer, father of Fernando ◊Rutini. Pupil of Leo and Fago at the Conservatorio della Pietà dei Turchini in Naples, he went to Prague in 1748, where his first opera was produced 1753. Visited Dresden and Berlin, and went to St Petersburg 1758. Returning to Italy 1762, he was *maestro di cappella* to the Crown Prince of Modena 1765–70, and lived mostly in Florence.

Works include *c* 20 operas, e.g. *Semiramide* (1753), *Il matrimonio in maschera* (1763), *L'Olandese in Italia* (1765), etc.; cantatas; violin sonatas; numerous harpsichord sonatas.

Rutter, John (b London, 24 Sept 1945), English composer and choral director. Studied at Cambridge and founded the Cambridge Singers 1981, making US debut in 1990. Has written carols, anthems and other choral music (mostly sacred) for use by non-professional choirs. He edited and recorded the original version of Fauré's Requiem in 1984 and composed his own Requiem the following year.

Ruy Blas opera by William Howard Glover (1819–1875) (libretto by composer, based on Victor Hugo's drama), produced London, Covent Garden Theatre, 24 Oct 1861. Seeking revenge against the Queen of Spain, Don Sallustio sends his servant Ruy Blas to her court disguised as a nobleman. He rises through the ranks and is exposed later by the Don as a plebeian, thus dishonouring the Queen. But Ruy Blas earns his honour by killing the vengeful villain and drinking poison.

Opera by Marchetti (libretto in Italian, by Carlo d'Ormeville, based on Hugo), produced Milan, La Scala, 3 Apr 1869.

Overture and chorus for Hugo's drama by Mendelssohn, op. 95 and op. 77 no. 3, composed for a production at Leipzig, 9 Mar 1839.

Ruyneman, Daniel (b Amsterdam, 8 Aug 1886; d Amsterdam, 25 Jul 1963), Dutch composer. He was trained for commerce and self-taught in music. He made many experiments with composition and instruments and invented cup-bells with a rich and long- sustained sonority, which he used in several of his works.

Works include opera *The Brothers Karamazov* (1928), psycho-symbolic play with vocal and instrumental orchestra *The Clown* (1915); scena for tenor and orchestra from Kafka's *Der Prozess*; two symphonies, partita for strings, *Hieroglyphs* for chamber orchestra; string quartet (1946); sonata in G major and *Klaaglied van een Slaaf* for violin and piano; nine sonatas, three *Pathemologies* and sonatina for piano; two Sacred Songs (Tagore) and several other sets.

RV in catalogues of Vivaldi's works, refers to ♭Ryom.

Rydl, Kurt (b Vienna, 8 Oct 1947), Austrian bass. After study in Vienna made his debut at Stuttgart in 1973, as Daland. Vienna Staatsoper from 1976, as Rocco, Zaccaria, Procida (*Vêpres siciliennes*), Philip II, King Marke and the Landgrave (*Tannhäuser*). Salzburg 1985, in the Henze/Monteverdi *Ulisse*, and Baron Ochs in Turin and Florence. Sang Hagen in the Vienna Staatsoper's *Götterdämmerung*, 1993.

Ryelandt, Joseph (b Bruges, 7 Apr 1870; d Bruges, 29 Jun 1965), Belgian composer. Pupil of Tinel.

Works include opera *Sainte Cécile*; oratorios *La Parabole des vierges* (1894), *Purgatorium* (1904), *De Komst des Heeren* (1907), *Maria, Agnus Dei* and *Christus Rex* (1922), cantatas *Le Bon Pasteur* and *L'Idylle mystique*; five symphonies (1897–1934), symphonic poem *Gethsémani*, two overtures for orchestra; chamber music; 11 piano sonatas; numerous songs.

Ryom, Peter (b Copenhagen, 31 May 1937), Danish musicologist. He catalogued Vivaldi's works in *Verzeichnis der Werke Antonio Vivaldis* (Leipzig, 1974; second edition 1979).

Rysanek, Leonie (b Vienna, 12 Nov 1926), Austrian soprano. Studied in Vienna with Jerger, and later with R Grossmann, whom she married. She made her debut in Innsbruck in 1949 as Agathe, Bayreuth from 1951 as Sieglinde, Elsa, Senta and Elisabeth. From 1950 to 1952 she sang at the Saarbrucken Opera as Tosca and Arabella, and in 1954 became a member of the Vienna Opera. Much of her success has been at the New York Met. from 1959, as Lady Macbeth, Tosca, Leonore, Aida, Elisabeth de Valois, and the Kostelnička in Jenůfa (1992). Admired in Strauss, notably as Salome, the title role in the CG fp of *Die Liebe der Danae* (1953), Chrysothemis, the Marschallin and Helena; sang Clytemnestra at the New York Met. 1992. Also admired as Kundry, Ortrud and Cherubini's Médée.

Rytel, Piotr (b Wilno, 20 Sept 1884; d Warsaw, 2 Jan 1970), Polish composer. Studied at the Warsaw Conservatory, and taught there 1911–52. He was rector of the Zoppot Conservatory 1952–62. For many years he was active as a critic.

Works include opera *Ijola* (1828); ballet *Faun and Psyche* (1931); four symphonies, symphonic poems *The Corsair* (Byron), 1911, *Grazyna* (Mickiewicz), *Dante's Dream, The Holy Grove, The Legend of St George* (1918), *An Introduction to a Drama*; piano concerto, violin concerto (1950); chamber music; piano works; songs.

Rzewski, Frederic (Anthony) (b Westfield, MA, 13 Apr 1938), American composer and pianist. Studied at Harvard with Randall Thompson and with Dallapiccola. Pianist from 1960 and taught at the Cologne Hochschule in the 1960s. Co-founder of electronic music studio at Rome (1966) and professor at the Liège Conservatory (with Henri Pousseur) from 1977; visiting professor at Yale from 1984.

Works include *Zoologischer Garten* (1965); *Spacecraft* (1967); *Impersonation*, audiodrama (1966); *Requiem* (1968); *Symphony for Several performers* (1968); *Coming Together* for speaker and instruments (1972); *Satyrica* for jazz band (1983); *Machine* for two pianos (1984).

S

s the dominant note in any key in Tonic sol-fa notation, pronounced Soh.

Saariaho, Kaija (b Helsinki, 14 Oct 1952), Finnish composer. Studied at the Helsinki Conservatory 1976–81, and with Brian Ferneyhough and Klaus Huber at Freiburg. She has composed orchestral and instrumental music employing computers and electronics.

    Works include theatre and multimedia pieces *Study for life* (1980); *Kollisionen* (1984); *Earth*, ballet (1991); *Verblendungen* for orchestra (1984), *Graal Théâtre* for violin and orchestra (1994); ensemble pieces *Nymphea* (1987), *For the Moon* (1990), *Aer* (1991), *Gates* (1991); *Amers* (1992); *Nocturne* for violin (1994); vocal music *The Bride*, song cycle (1977), *No and Not*, three songs for four female voices and choir (1979), *From the Grammar of Dreams* for two sopranos (1989), *Nuits, Adieux*, for four voices and live electronics (1991); *La dame à la licorne*, sound installation, with tape (1993), *Trois rivières* for percussion quartet and electronics (1993); *Graal Théâtre* for violin and orchestra (1995).

Sabaneiev, Leonid Leonidovich (b Moscow, 1 Oct 1881; d Antibes, 3 May 1968), Russian critic and composer. Studied with Taneiev at the Moscow Conservatory and at the university there. He left Russia in 1929 and settled eventually in France. He wrote on Skriabin, Debussy and Taneiev; also wrote an attack on Prokofiev's *Scythian Suite* at a concert that did not take place.

    Works include ballet *L'Aviatrice*; symphonic poem *Flots d'azur*; chamber music; songs; piano music.

Sabata, Victor de, ◊De Sabata.

Sabbatini, Galeazzo (b ? Pesaro, 1597; d Pesaro, 6 Dec 1662), Italian composer. He was *maestro di cappella* at Pesaro in the 1620s and director of chamber music to the Duke of Mirandola in the 1630s. He was also at Bergamo some time. In 1628 he pub. a treatise on thorough-bass.

    Works include Masses, motets, two books of *Sacrae faudes* (1637, 1641) and other church music; madrigals.

Sabbatini, Giuseppe (b Rome, 11 May 1957), Italian tenor. Played the double bass with orchestras in Rome and Verona; opera debut at Spoleto in 1987, as Edgardo (*Lucia*). Has sung such roles as Werther, Alfredo, the Duke of Mantua and Rodolfo in Vienna, Paris, Chicago and Hamburg. CG debut, London, 1991 as the Duke of Mantua, then Arturo (*I Puritani*) and Lensky.

Sabbatini, Luigi Antonio (b Albano Laziale near Rome, 24 Oct 1732; d Padua, 29 Jan 1809), Italian composer. A pupil of Padre Martini and Vallotti, he was *maestro di cappella* of Mariono Cathedral 1766, at the Church of the Holy Apostles in Rome 1772, finally from 1786 at S Antonio in Padua. He pub. a number of treatises on counterpoint, fugue, etc. Composed chiefly church music.

    Works include Masses, motets, psalms.

Sabbatini, Pietro Paolo (b Rome, *c* 1600; d ? Rome, after 1657), Italian composer. He was *maestro di cappella* in Rome, from 1630 of the church of San Luigi de' Francesci, and professor of music from 1650, when he pub. a treatise on thorough-bass.

Works include psalms, spiritual songs; *villanelle* and *canzonette* for one–three voices, etc.

Sabino, Ippolito (b Lanciano, Chieto, 1550; d Lanciano, 25 Aug 1593), Italian composer. In 1587 he was employed as a musician in the cathedral of his native town. He pub. many collections of church music and madrigals; two of the latter contain madrigals by his brother (?) Giovanni Francesco.

Sacchini, Antonio Maria Gaspare (b Florence, 14 Jun 1730; d Paris, 6 Oct 1786), Italian composer. Pupil of Durante at the Conservatorio Santa Maria di Loreto at Naples, where his intermezzo *Fra Donato* was produced in 1756. He worked first at the Conservatory, but produced his first serious opera, *Andromaca*, in 1761, and three years later gave up teaching to devote himself to composition. After a time in Rome he went to Venice in 1769, where he became director of the Ospedaletto. Visited Germany, and in 1772 went to London, remaining there ten years and producing many operas. Settling in Paris in 1782, he had the support of Marie Antoinette, and there wrote two operas which show the influence of Gluck. But (like Gluck before him) he became unwillingly involved in rivalry with Piccinni and had little success.

    Works include *c* 60 operas, e.g. *Alessandro nell' Indie* (1763), *Semiramide* (1764), *Isola d'amore*, *Il Cidde* (after Corneille), *Armida* (1772), *Tamerlano*, *Perseo* (1774), *Nitetti*, *Montezuma* (1775), *Rosina*, *Dardanus*, *Oedipe à Colone* (1786), etc.; Masses, motets and other church music; two symphonies; string quartets, trio sonatas and other chamber music; violin sonatas.

Sacco, Peter (b Albion, NY, 25 Oct 1928), American composer. Studied at the Eastman School with Hanson and Rogers, 1953–58. Teacher at San Francisco State University 1959–80.

    Works include chamber opera *Mr Vinegar* (1967), oratorios *Jesu* (1956), *Midsummer Night Dream Night* (1961) and *Solomon* (1978); three symphonies (1955, 1965–76 and 1968); piano and chamber music, songs.

Sacher, Paul (b Basel, 28 Apr 1906), Swiss conductor. Studied with Nef and Weingartner, and in 1926 founded the Basel Chamber Orchestra, for which he commissioned works from many distinguished composers including Bartók (Divertimento), Fortner, Henze, Hindemith, Honegger, Ibert, Křenek, Martin, Martinů, Malipiero, Roussel, Strauss, Stravinsky and Tippett; composers of the Second Viennese School were not favoured. In 1933 he also founded the distinguished chamber ensemble Schola Cantorum Basiliensis.

Sachs, Curt (b Berlin, 29 Jun 1881; d New York, 5 Feb 1959), German musicologist. First studied history of art at Berlin University, graduating in 1904. After some years as an art critic he studied music with Kretzschmar and J Wolf, specializing in the history of musical instruments. In 1919 he became director of the Berlin Museum of Musical Instruments, and also professor at Berlin University. From 1933 to 1937 he lived in Paris, then moved to NY, where he became professor at the university. From 1953 he was also professor at Columbia University, in NY. His many writings extend not only over the field of musical instruments, but also over many others.

Sachs, Hans (1494–1576), German cobbler, master-singer and poet. He wrote more than 4,000 poems and features in Wagner's *Die Meistersinger* (the longest role in all opera).

Sack, Erna (b Berlin, 6 Feb 1898; d Wiesbaden, 2 Mar 1972), German soprano. She sang in Berlin from 1925 and joined the Dresden Opera 1935; created Isotta in *Die schweigsame Frau*. She visited CG with the Dresden co. in 1936, as Zerbinetta, and Chicago in 1937, as Rosina and Lucia. Worldwide concert tours either side of the war. Her unusually wide vocal range earned her the nickname 'the German nightingale'.

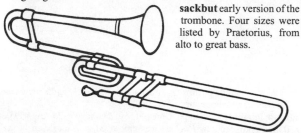

sackbut early version of the trombone. Four sizes were listed by Praetorius, from alto to great bass.

Sackman, Nicholas (b London, 1950), English composer. Studied with Goehr at Leeds University. Lecturer at Nottingham University from 1990.

Works include two string quartets (1979, 1991); *Ensembles and Cadenzas*, for cello and five players (1972); *A Pair of Wings* for three sopranos and ensemble (1973); *Doubles* for two instrumental groups (1978); *And the World – A Wonder Waking*, for mezzo and eight instruments (1981); *Time-Piece*, brass quintet (1983); *Corronach* for seven players (1985); flute concerto (1989); *Hawthorn* for orchestra (premiered at the 1993 London Proms).

Sadie, Stanley (John) (b Wembley, 30 Oct 1930), English critic, writer and editor. He studied at Cambridge with Thurston Dart and Charles Cudworth; MA 1957, PhD 1958. Music critic with *The Times* 1964–81, editor *The Musical Times* 1967–87. He has written books on Handel, Mozart and Beethoven, and in 1970 became editor of *The New Grove Dictionary of Music and Musicians*; ten years and 2,326 contributors later the 20 vols. were published. Many offshoots have since appeared under Sadie's direction, e.g. the *New Grove Dictionary of Musical Instruments* (1984) and, with H Wiley Hitchcock, the *NG Dictionary of American Music* (1986). *Grove Concise Dictionary of Music* (1988), *New Grove Dictionary of Opera* (1992). The newest *Grove* (in 24 volumes) is promised for 1999. General editor of *Master Musicians* series since 1976. CBE 1982.

His wife Julie Anne (b Eugene, OR, 1948) trained as a viola da gambist and edited the *Companion to Baroque Music* (1991). Co-editor *The New Grove Dictionary of Women Composers*

It is possible to be as much of a musician as Saint-Saëns, it is impossible to be more of one!

Franz Liszt, quoted in Williams, *Portrait of Liszt*, 1990

Sadko opera by Rimsky-Korsakov (libretto by composer and V I Bielsky), produced Moscow, 7 Jan 1898. The music is partly based on Rimsky-Korsakov's symphonic poem of the same name, op. 5; composed 1867, produced St Petersburg, 21 Dec 1867; revised 1869 and 1892. Cast adrift as a sacrifice to the sea gods, minstrel Sadko weds nymph Volkova before returning to his wife.

Sadler's Wells Opera ◊English National Opera.

Sádlo, Miloš (b Prague, 13 Apr 1912), Czech cellist. Studied at the Prague Conservatory and with Casals (1955). Was cellist of the Czech Trio 1940–56, Suk Trio 1957–60, and the Prague Trio 1968–73. Soloist with the Czech PO from 1949, notably in Dvořák's early A major concerto, which he edited, and the concerto in C by Haydn (discovered 1962).

Saedén, Erik (b Vänersborg, Stockholm, 3 Sept 1924), Swedish bass-baritone. Debut Stockholm 1952; well known there as Figaro, Pogner, Wozzeck and Wolfram, and took part in the fps of Blomdahl's *Aniara* (1959), Berwald's *Queen of Golconda* (1968) and Ligeti's *Le Grand Macabre* (1978). Bayreuth 1958, Kurwenal; visited Edinburgh in 1959 and 1974. In 1968 he created Dallapiccola's Ulisse, at the Deutsche Oper, Berlin.

saeta, Spanish, an unaccompanied Andalusian folksong sung during a halt in a religious procession.

Sæverud, Harald (b Bergen, 17 Apr 1897; d Siljustol, 27 Mar 1992), Norwegian composer and conductor. Studied at Bergen and Berlin, conducting under Clemens Krauss. He returned to Bergen as conductor and received a state pension for composition in 1933.

Works include *Minnesota Symphony*; nine symphonies (1916–66); concertos for oboe, cello, violin and piano; incidental music for Shakespeare's *Rape of Lucretia* (1935) and Ibsen's *Peer Gynt*; 50 variations for chamber orchestra; three string quartets (1969, 1975, 1979), piano pieces, etc.

Saffo, *Sappho*, opera by Pacini (libretto by S Cammarano), produced Naples, Teatro San Carlo, 29 Nov 1840. Alcander (bass), angered by Sappho's song, convinces her husband Phaon that she has another lover. Phaon abandons her; she later finds him about to marry Clymene, and overturns the altar. Penitent, she leaps to her death from the Leucadian rock.

Safonov, Vassily Illich (b Itsiursk, Terek, 6 Feb 1852; d Kislovodsk, Caucasus, 27 Feb 1918), Russian conductor and pianist. Studied at St Petersburg; professor at the Conservatory there, 1881, and at Moscow, 1885. Became director of Moscow Conservatory, 1889. Established popular concerts there and was conductor of the Moscow branch of the Russian Musical Society, 1890–1905. Appeared frequently in London and NY; guest conductor NY PO from 1904.

Saga, En symphonic poem by Sibelius, op. 9, composed 1891, fp Helsinki, 16 Feb 1893, revised 1901. It depicts no particular incident, but has a distinctly narrative, ballad-like tone.

Sagittarius the Latin form of the name of Schütz, sometimes used on his title-pages. Like his German name it means 'archer'.

Saint-Foix, (Marie Olivier) Georges (du Parc Poullain) de, Count (b Paris, 2 Mar 1874; d Aix-en-Provence, 26 May 1954), French musicologist. Studied law, and music at the Schola Cantorum in Paris. He wrote on various subjects, including Beethoven and Boccherini, but mainly on the classification and analysis of Mozart's works in a large five-volume work, the first two vols. in collaboration with Théodore de Wyzewa.

Saint François d'Assise opera in eight tableaux by Messiaen (libretto by composer); 1975–83. fp Paris, Opéra, 28 Nov 1983. St Francis heals leper, preaches to birds and receives stigmata before his death and resurrection.

Saint-Huberty (actually *Clavel*), Antoinette (Cécile) (b Strasbourg, 15 Dec 1756; d London, 21 Jul 1812), French soprano. Studied with the conductor Lemoyne at Warsaw and made her first appearance there, then sang in Berlin and Strasbourg, and first appeared in Paris 1777 as Melissa in the fp of Gluck's *Armide*; later took part in the fps of Piccinni's *Didon*, Salieri's *Les Danaïdes* and Sacchini's *Chimène*. In 1790 she married the Comte d'Entraigues, a royalist, with whom she escaped to Lausanne. In 1797 she rescued her husband from prison at Milan. They went first to St Petersburg and then to London, where they settled and were murdered by a servant.

Saint-Lambert, (? Michel) de, French 17th–18th-c. harpsichord player, teacher and author. He lived and taught in Paris, and wrote two books, *Les Principes du clavecin* (1702) and *Nouveau Traité de l'accompagnement* (1707).

Sainton, Prosper (Philippe Cathérine) (b Toulouse, 5 Jun 1813; d London, 17 Oct 1890), French violinist and composer, husband of Charlotte ◊Sainton-Dolby. Studied violin under Habeneck at the Paris Conservatory, played at the Société des Concerts and the Opéra there, then travelled widely in Europe and in 1840 became professor at the Toulouse Conservatory. In 1844 he visited London and played under Mendelssohn, returning in 1845 to settle down as member of the Beethoven Quartet Society, orchestra leader and teacher.

Works include two violin concertos and other solos with orchestra; variations, romances, operatic fantasies, etc. for violin and piano, etc.

Sainton-Dolby (born *Dolby*), Charlotte (Helen) (b London, 17 May 1821; d London, 18 Feb 1885), English contralto and composer. Studied at the RAM in London and made her first appearance at a Philharmonic concert there in 1842. In 1845 Mendelssohn invited her to sing with Jenny Lind at Leipzig, and later she had success in France and Holland In 1860 she married Prosper Sainton.

Works include cantatas *The Legend of St Dorothea* and *The Story of a Faithful Soul*, cantata for female voices *Florimel*.

Saint-Saëns, (Charles) Camille (b Paris, 9 Oct 1835; d Algiers, 16 Dec 1921), French composer. He began to compose at the age of five and played the piano well at that age. Gave a public recital in 1846 and entered the Conservatory as an organ scholar in 1848, gaining a first prize in 1851, when he entered Halévy's class for composition. Appointed organist at the church of Saint-Merry in Paris, 1853, the Madeleine, 1857, and piano professor at the École Niedermeyer in 1861; his virtuosity at the organ was admired by Liszt, and he promoted performances of the Hungarian's symphonic poems. His first two symphonies were performed in 1853 and 1859, he played his second piano concerto in 1868 and founded the Société Nationale de Musique with Romain Bussine in 1871; his own symphonic poems, *Le Rouet d'Omphale* and *Phaëton*, date from this time. He played in England several times from 1871 and toured Spain and Portugal in 1880. One of his most frequently performed works, the 1st cello concerto in A minor, had been composed in 1872; it displays the composer's familiar and conservative French Romantic style together with melodic inventiveness. The biblical opera *Samson et Dalila*, begun in 1868 and prohibited on the French stage on account of its subject, was conducted by Liszt at Weimar in 1877; it was allowed in Paris from 1892, the year he received the honorary Mus.D. at Cambridge. The massively proportioned 3rd symphony, with organ obbligato, dates from 1886, and his appealing 3rd violin concerto in B minor followed in 1890. Also in 1886 he wrote his most popular, although uncharacteristic piece, *The Carnival of the Animals*. Saint-Saëns recognized that its success with the public would lead to neglect of his more important compositions and banned performance of the *Carnival* during his lifetime. In 1906 he visited the USA, and again in 1916, together with South America.

Works include STAGE: *La Princesse jaune* (1872), *Le Timbre d'argent* (1877), *Étienne Marcel* (1879), *Samson et Dalila* (1877),

Saint-Saëns *The composer Camille Saint-Saëns (1835–1921) seated with Lloyd, Brewer and Elgar behind him (left to right) at the Gloucester Music Festival of 1913. The 'Mozartian Romantic' Saint-Saëns was horrified by Stravinsky's primeval* Rite of Spring, *premiered in the year this photograph was taken.*

Henri VIII (1883), *Proserpine*, *Ascanio* (1890), *Phryné* (1893), *Les Barbares* (1901), *Hélène* (1904), *L'Ancêtre* (1906), *Déjanire* (1911); ballet *Javotte*; incidental music for Sophocles' *Antigone*, Racine's *Andromaque* and six other plays.

ORCHESTRAL: three symphonies (1853, 1859, 1886, the third with organ and piano duet), symphonic poems *Le Rouet d'Omphale* (1872), *Phaëton*, *Danse macabre* (originally a song), *La Jeunesse d'Hercule* (1877), suite and *Suite algérienne* for orchestra, other orchestral pieces including *Une Nuit à Lisbonne*, *Jota aragonesa* (1880), *Ouverture de fête*; five piano concertos (1858–96), *Allegro appassionato*, *Rapsodie d'Auvergne* and *Africa* for piano and orchestra, three violin concertos (1858, 1859, 1890) and *Introduction et Rondo capriccioso* (1863), *Romance*, *Morceau de concert* and *Caprice andalou* for violin and orchestra, two cello concertos (1872, 1902), various pieces for wind instruments and orchestra.

CHAMBER: *Le Carnaval des animaux* for chamber ensemble (1886); two string quartets (1899, 1918), piano quintet and quartet (1865, 1875), two piano trios, septet for piano, strings and trumpet (1881); two violin and piano sonatas, two cello and piano sonatas (1872, 1905), suite for cello and piano, sonatas for oboe, clarinet and bassoon and piano; fantasies for harp and for violin and harp; many smaller instrumental pieces with piano.

PIANO AND VOCAL: 24 op. nos. of piano music, six op. nos. for piano duet, five op. nos. for two pianos including variations on a theme by Beethoven (1874); seven organ works; Mass (1855), Requiem (1878), two Psalms and other church music for chorus and orchestra (some with solo voices); *Ode à Sainte Cécile* and *La Fiancée du timbalier* for voice and orchestra; oratorio *Le Déluge*; several cantatas; many songs.

Sala, Nicola (b Tocco-Caudio near Benevento, 7 Apr 1713; d Naples, 31 Aug 1801), Italian composer and theorist. Studied with Fago and Leo at the Conservatorio de' Turchini at Naples and later became a master

A Selection of

Saint-Saëns

there, principal in 1787, succeeding Cafaro. In 1794 he pub. *Regole del contrappunto prattico* in three vols.

Works include operas *Vologeso* (1737), *Zenobia* (1761), *Merope* (1769) and *Demetrio* (1762); oratorio *Giuditta*; Mass, Litany and other church music; Prologues for the birth of kings of Naples.

Salammbô opera by Reyer (libretto by C duLocle, based on Flaubert's novel), produced Brussels, Théâtre de la Monnaie, 10 Feb 1890.

Unfinished opera by Mussorgsky (libretto by composer, based on Flaubert), partly composed in the 1860s. A concert performance of the available fragments was given in Milan on 10 Nov 1980.

The two operas have similar plots initially: Carthaginian princess Salammbô seduces Libyan warrior Mathô, to regain the sacred veil which he has stolen. After this, in Reyer's version, Salammbô commits suicide when ordered to kill Mathô, and he follows her. In Mussorgsky's version, Mathô is imprisoned and brutally killed; Salammbô is horror-stricken and dies.

Salazar, Adolfo (b Madrid, 6 Mar 1890; d Mexico City, 27 Sept 1958), Spanish musicologist and composer. Pupil of Pérez Casas and Falla. He edited the *Revista Musical Hispano-Americano* in 1914–18 and from 1918 to 1936 was music critic to *El Sol* in Madrid. He emigrated to Buenos Aires after the Spanish Civil War and lived in Mexico after 1939. His books include studies of modern music, Spanish music, symphonies and ballet, etc.

Works include symphonic poem *Don Juan en los infiernos*, *Paisajes* and *Tres preludios* for orchestra; string quartet, *Arabia* for piano quintet; violin and piano sonata; piano pieces; *Romancilla* for guitar.

Salazar, Manuel (b San José, 3 Jan 1887; d San José, 6 Aug 1950), Costa Rican tenor. Studied in Italy and NY. After his 1913 debut in Vicenza, as Edgardo, he had a wide success in Italy; sang with Titta Ruffo in Havana, 1917. NY Met. 1921–23, as Alvaro, Canio, Radames and Andrea Chénier.

Sales, Pietro Pompeo (b Brescia, *c* 1729; d Hanau, 21 Nov 1797), Italian composer. Appointed *Kapellmeister* to the Prince- Bishop of Augsburg in 1756, he served the Electoral Court in Koblenz in the same capacity from 1770. Also travelled in England and Italy (1776), appearing as a virtuoso gamba-player.

Works include operas *Le nozze di Amore e di Norizia* (1765), *L'Antigono* (1769), *Achille in Sciro*, *Il rè pastore*, etc.; oratorios *Giefte* (1762), *Giuseppe ricognosciuto*, *La Betulia liberata*, etc.; church music; two symphonies; concertos; arias.

Saléza, Albert (b Bruges, Basses-Pyrénées, 28 Oct 1867; d Paris, 26 Nov 1916), French tenor. Debut Paris 1888, in *Le Roi d'Ys*; the same year he was the first local Otello, at the Opéra. Sang in Monte Carlo and Nice and in the 1898 first London performance of Mancinelli's *Ero e Leandro*. NY Met. 1899–1905; debut as Faust and also successful as Rodolfo and Don José.

Salieri, Antonio (b Legnago near Verona, 18 Aug 1750; d Vienna, May 1825), Italian composer, conductor and teacher. Studied with his brother Francesco Salieri, a pupil of Tartini. Orphaned at 15; his education at the school of San Marco in Venice was cared for by the Mocenigo family. There he met Gassmann, who in 1766 took him to Vienna, saw to his further education and introduced him at court. On Gassmann's death in 1774 he became court composer and conductor of the Italian opera. Visited Italy 1778–80, where his opera *Europa riconosciuta* was produced at the opening of La Scala, Milan, and Paris (1774 and 1786–87); his *Tarare* of 1787 had sufficient dramatic strength to be ascribed initially to Gluck. From 1788, when he succeeded Bonno as court *Kapellmeister*, he lived mostly in Vienna. His intrigues against Mozart were exaggerated into the story that he had poisoned Mozart. He was conductor of the Tonkünstler Society until 1818, and played the continuo in the fp of Haydn's *Creation* in 1798. Among his pupils were Beethoven, Schubert, Hummel and Liszt. Recent revivals of operas such as *Les Danaïdes*, *La grotta di Trofonio* and *Falstaff* show Salieri to be a more resourceful and entertaining composer than his reputation suggests.

Works include *c* 40 operas, e.g. *Armida* (1771), *La fiera di Venezia* (1772), *La locandiera* (1773), *Europa riconosciuta* (1778), *La scuola*

Salieri *The composer and teacher Antonio Salieri (1750–1825). Although his music was belittled in the film* Amadeus, *he was admired and respected by his contemporaries, especially in the field of opera. Salieri's longest-lasting influence was as a teacher of Beethoven, Schubert and Liszt.*

de gelosi (1778), *La dama pastorella*, *Der Rauchfangkehrer* (1781), *Les Danaïdes* (1784), *Tarare*, *Les Horaces* (the last three for Paris), *La grotta di Trofonio* (1785), *Il talismano*, *Palmira, regina di Persia* (1795), *Falstaff* (after Shakespeare, 1799), *Cesare in Farmacusa*, *Angiolina* (1800).

Incidental music to Kotzebue's *Die Hussiten vor Naumburg*; Passion oratorio and others; seven Masses, Requiem, Litanies and other church music; cantatas including *La riconoscenza* for the 25th anniversary of the Tonkünstler-Societät (1796); three symphonies and *sinfonia concertante*; concertos; serenades, etc.; arias, duets, canons and misc. other small vocal pieces.

Salignac, Thomas (b Generac, near Nîmes, 19 Mar 1867; d Paris, 1945), French tenor. He sang at the Paris Opéra-Comique from 1893 and made his NY Met. debut in 1896, as Don José. CG 1897–1904. In Paris he sang in the fps of operas by Widor, Leroux, Laparra and Milhaud (*La Brebis égarée*, 1923; first private performance of Falla's *El retablo de Maese Pedro*, the same year). He later worked as opera director, teacher and administrator.

Salimbeni, Felice (b Milan, *c* 1712; d Ljubljana, Aug 1751), Italian soprano castrato. Pupil of Porpora, made his first appearance in Rome in 1731 and afterwards sang in Italy, Vienna, Berlin and Dresden, and was one of Hasse's chief interpreters.

Salinas, Francisco de (b Burgos, 1 Mar 1513; d Salamanca, 13 Jan 1590), Spanish organist, theorist and folksong investigator. He was the son of an official in the treasury of Charles V and became blind at the age of ten, whereupon his parents decided to let him study music. He was taken to Rome in 1538, where he met the lutenist Francesco da Milano and became a great admirer of Lassus. In 1558 he became organist to the Duke of Alba, viceroy of Naples, under Ortiz. In 1561 he returned to Spain, became organist at León in 1563 and professor of music at Salamanca University, 1567. There he made friends with the poet Luis de León, who wrote a poem on his organ playing. In his

───────── **THE OPERA** ─────────

Salome

A one-act opera by Richard Strauss, based on Oscar Wilde's tragedy of the same name, whose gory action takes place in Herod's palace in Jerusalem in AD 30. It was first performed in 1905.

The captain of the guard, Narraboth (tenor), praises the beauty of the 16-year-old Salome (soprano). While her stepfather Herod (tenor) banquets, Salome listens to the imprisoned Jochanaan (John the Baptist, baritone) as from below he denounces Herodias (mezzo-soprano) for having married her husband's brother. Salome orders Jochanaan to be brought to her and, as she expresses her longing for him, Narraboth commits suicide. Jochanaan repels Salome's advances and tells her to seek comfort in the coming of the Messiah. After Jochanaan has been returned to his prison, Herod enters and asks Salome to dance for him; she agrees on condition that he grant her whatever she desires. Following her Dance of the Seven Veils, Salome demands the head of Jochanaan, brought to her on a silver platter. Herod does all he can to dissuade her but eventually the executioner is dispatched. A revolted Herod can hardly watch as Salome lustfully addresses the severed head; when she kisses Jochanaan on the lips, Herod orders his soldiers to kill her and she is crushed beneath their shields.

───────── **THE OPERA** ─────────

treatise *De musica libri septem* (1579) he quotes the tunes of many Spanish folksongs.

Sallinen, Aulis (b Salmi, 9 Apr 1935), Finnish composer. He studied at the Sibelius Academy, Helsinki, and taught there 1963–76. Manager Finnish Radio SO 1960–70. He is best known for the strong characterization and sustained dramatic intensity of his operas.

Works include operas *The Horseman* (1975), *The Red Line* (1978), *The King goes forth to France* (1984) and *Kullervo* (1992); ballet *Variations sur Mallarmé* (1968); six symphonies (1971–90), *Mauermusik*, for a German killed at Berlin Wall (1962), *Metamorphoses* for piano and chamber orchestra (1964), violin concerto (1968), cello concerto (1978); *Chorali* for wind, percussion, harp and celesta (1970), *Dies Irae* for soprano, bass, male chorus and orchestra (1978); five string quartets (1958–82).

Salmhofer, Franz (b Vienna, 22 Jan 1900; d Vienna, 22 Sept 1975), Austrian composer and conductor. Having learnt music as a choirboy, he studied at the Vienna Acad, under Schreker and others, later taught at Horak's music school and in 1929–39 was conductor at the Burgtheater, for which he wrote incidental music to over 300 plays. From 1955 he was director of the Vienna Volksoper.

Works include operas *Dame im Traum* (1935), *Iwan Sergejewitsch Tarassenko* (1938), *Das Werbekleid* (1946) and several others; ballets *Das lockende Phantom* (1927), *Der Taugenichts in Wien, Weihnachtsmärchen* (1933), *Österreichische Bauernhochzeit*; incidental music for Shakespeare's *The Tempest, King Lear, Romeo and Juliet, Othello, The Merry Wives of Windsor*, Goethe's *Faust* (pts. I and II), etc.; overture to Maeterlinck's *L'Intruse* and others, *Der geheimnisvolle Trompeter, Fairy-Tale* for orchestra; suite for chamber orchestra; concertos for cello, violin and cello and trumpet; six string quartets, piano quartet in F minor, serenade for string trio, etc.

Salminen, Matti (b Turku, 7 Jul 1945), Finnish bass. Studied in Helsinki and made debut there 1969, as Philip II. Sang Glinka's Ivan Susanin at the 1973 Wexford Festival, Fasolt at CG 1974. Principal roles at Cologne, Zurich and Berlin from 1972; Savonlinna Festival from 1975, as Sallinen's Horseman, Sarastro and Daland. Bayreuth Festival from 1976 as Hunding, King Mark and others; NY Met. from 1981, as Rocco, Osmin, Hunding and Hagen. Widely admired as Boris and has also sung Prince Khovansky (San Francisco 1984).

salmo Italian, plur. *salmi* = psalm.

Salmon (born *Munday*), Eliza (b Oxford 1787; d London, 5 Jun 1849),

English soprano. Studied with John Ashley and made her first appearance at a Lenten concert at CG in 1803. She married James Salmon in 1806 and they settled at Liverpool, but she continued to sing in London and at the festivals until she lost her voice in 1825. She died in poverty, after earning £5,000 in 1823.

Salmon, Jacques (b Picardy), 16th-c. French composer. He was in the royal service from 1575 and contributed to the *Ballet comique de la Royne* (1581). A few *chansons* have also survived.

Salmon, Thomas (b London, 24 Jun 1648; d Mepsal, Bedfordshire, buried 16 Aug 1706), English clergyman and writer on music. Wrote on notation and temperament. His *Essay on the Advancement of Musick* in 1672 involved him in a controversy with Locke.

Salmond, Felix (b London, 19 Nov 1888; d New York, 19 Feb 1952), English cellist. Studied at the RAM in London, later in Brussels, and made his debut in London in 1909. In 1919 he played in the fps of Elgar's string quartet, piano quintet and cello concerto. He settled in USA in 1922 and in 1942 became cello professor at the Juilliard School in NY. He toured extensively.

Salomé opera by Mariotte (libretto Oscar Wilde's original in French), produced Lyon, 30 Oct 1908. Composed earlier than R Strauss's opera, although produced later.

Salome opera by R Strauss (libretto H Lachmann's German translation of Oscar Wilde's play, written in French), produced Dresden, Royal Opera, 9 Dec 1905. Spurned by John the Baptist, Salome demands his severed head after performing a seven-veil striptease for lecherous Herod.

Ballet in two acts by Peter Maxwell Davies (choreographed by Flemming Flindt), produced Stockholm, 10 Nov 1978. Concert suite performed London, 6 Mar 1979.

◊Tragédie de Salome.

Salomon, Johann Peter (b Bonn, bap. 20 Feb 1745; d London, 28 Nov 1815), German violinist, conductor, manager and composer. Studied at Bonn and joined the electoral orchestra in 1758. After a tour in 1765 he became court musician at Rheinsberg to Prince Henry of Prussia, who, however, dissolved his orchestra *c* 1780, when Salomon went to Paris and thence to London, 1781, where he settled as concert violinist, quartet player and conductor. He gave subscription concerts at the Hanover Square Rooms and invited Haydn to London in 1790 and again in 1794, later arranging for smaller forces some of the symphonies which Haydn wrote for London. He wrote four French operas and an English one, *Windsor Castle*, for the marriage of the Prince of Wales in 1795, an oratorio *Hiskias*, violin sonatas.

Salomon Symphonies the 12 symphonies written by Haydn 1791–95 for the concerts given by Johann Peter Salomon in London during Haydn's two visits to England, 1791–92 and 1794–95. They are nos. 93–104.

Salonen, Esa-Pekka (b Helsinki, 30 Jun 1958), Finnish conductor. After early career as a horn player made London debut 1983, with the Philharmonia in Mahler's 3rd Symphony. Chief conductor of the Swedish Radio SO from 1985, music director of the Los Angeles PO from 1992. Principal guest of the Philharmonia and the Oslo Philharmonic. Led the premiere of Saxton's *Circles of Light* (1986) and Messiaen's *St François d'Assise* at the 1992 Salzburg Festival. Conducted *Mathis der Maler* at CG, 1995. Recordings include Messiaen's *Turangalîla-Symphonie* and Lutosławski's Third.

saltando Italian = 'springing, bounding'; a special way of playing the violin and other string instruments in such a manner that the bow is made to rebound from the strings.

saltarello an Italian dance, including jumps (*salti*) and in the 16th c. a kind of after-dance in common time, also called by the Latin name of *proportio* and the German one of *Proporz*, the name being due to its using the same music as the first dance (Passamezzo), but with the 'proportions' (i.e. time) altered; later a Roman dance in animated 3–4 or 6–8 time, not unlike the Neapolitan tarantella, but using jerky instead of even musical figuration. In performance by dancers it gradually increased its pace towards the end. The best known saltarello is the finale of Mendelssohn's Italian symphony.

Salter, Lionel (b London, 8 Sept 1914), English harpsichordist, pianist,

Esa-Pekka Salonen - conductor / composer

1 Bruckner: Symphony no. 4
When I was about ten I heard this on the radio. I switched it on in the middle of the Scherzo and I was completely hooked by the enormous mass that was moving, bathing me in E flat major. My mother bought me a record of it and I played it until it practically disintegrated. That started a lifelong love for Bruckner.

2 Messiaen: *Turangalîla-Symphony*
The discovery that musical form can be built in many different ways led me to Messiaen, in the early '70s. I sat at home listening to the radio and realized, 'Music can also

sound like *this*'; the mixture of the sugar-sweet, heavenly harmonies and the more austere Indian rhythms completely overwhelmed me.

3 Ligeti: *Atmosphères*
When I heard this I realized that the possibilities for music were infinite. Ligeti impressed me with his sheer beauty, clarity of thought; his ability to create a completely different kind of reality. *Atmosphères* is short, but things happen to you during that piece that might take years otherwise. You are sucked into a different planetary system. *Nothing* in my education prepared me for this.

conductor and writer. He studied at Cambridge and with Constant Lambert and Arthur Benjamin at the RCM. He started work at the BBC before the war in music on TV and held various administrative posts until 1974; head of TV opera 1963, assistant Controller of Music 1967–74. He is well known as a critic and writer and has translated operas; several editions of Scarlatti, Cavalli and Lully. Contributor to *Grove Opera* (1992).

Saltzmann-Stevens, Minnie (b Bloomington, 17 Mar 1874; d Milan, 25 Jan 1950), American soprano. She studied with Jean de Reszke in Paris and sang Brünnhilde and Isolde at CG 1909–13. Bayreuth 1911–13, as Sieglinde and Kundry. Chicago 1914–16. After illness sang only in concert.

Salve Regina, Latin *Hail, Queen*, one of four antiphons to the Virgin Mary. Earliest MS source is from 11th c., probably by Adhemar of Pui. Many settings by 15th-c. English composers; also set by La Rue, Josquin, Obrecht and Ockeghem. Six settings by Schubert (1812–24).

Salvini-Donatelli, Fanny (b Florence, *c* 1815; d Milan, Jun 1891), Italian soprano. Debut Venice 1839, as Rosina. She sang Abigaille at Vienna in 1842; other Verdi roles were Lady Macbeth, Elvira and Gulnara. She created Violetta (Venice, 1853) but as a supposed consumptive did not create a convincing impression, owing to her corpulence. London, Drury Lane, 1858.

Salzburg Festivals summer festivals of music and drama begun at Salzburg in 1921, mainly at the instigation of the poet Hugo von Hofmannsthal, the producer Max Reinhardt, the conductor Franz Schalk and the composer Richard Strauss (eight Mozart festivals had been held, 1877–1910). The music performed includes opera, church music, orchestral concerts, chamber music and serenades, a festival opera-house being built 1926 and opened 1927. A new Festspielhaus was opened in 1960, with the largest stage in the world. As Mozart's birthplace, Salzburg gave prominence to his works, but cultivated a wide range of music. The Festivals were interrupted in 1944 when Strauss's *Die Liebe der Danae* reached dress rehearsal stage, but resumed in 1946. The fps of operas by Strauss, Orff, Henze, Cerha, Berio and Penderecki have been given there. Herbert von Karajan artistic director 1964–89; Easter Festival from 1967, with Karajan mounting productions of Verdi and Wagner. Solti was artistic director 1990–92, succeeded by Claudio Abbado.

Salzedo, Carlos (b Arcachon, Gironde, 6 Apr 1885; d Waterville, ME, 17 Aug 1961), French-American harpist and composer. Studied piano and harp at the Paris Conservatory and went to NY at Toscanini's invitation to become first harp at the Met. Opera. Much interested in modern music, he founded the International Composers' Guild with Varèse, edited *Eolus* and conducted many concerts. Professor of harp at the Juilliard School in NY and the Curtis Institute at Philadelphia.

Works include *The Enchanted Isle* for harp and orchestra, concerto for harp and seven wind instruments, *Préambule et Jeux* for harp and chamber orchestra; sonata for harp and piano, many pieces and arrangements for harp.

Salzman, Eric (b New York, 8 Sept 1933), American composer and

musicologist. Studied with Beeson and Babbitt. Music critic in NY, founded Quog Music Theater 1970. Edited *Music Quarterly* from 1984. Often writes for electronic forces, and calls for improvisation in his works.

Works include *Larynx Music* (1968), *Civilization and its Discontents, opera* (1977).

Samara, Spiro (b Corfu, 29 Nov 1863; d Athens, 7 Apr 1917), Greek composer. Studied at Athens, later with Delibes and others at the Paris Conservatory. The Italian publisher Sonzogno procured him his first operatic production at Milan. He subsequently produced other works at Rome, Naples, Florence, Milan and Genoa, with no more than ephemeral success, and the last appeared at Athens in 1914.

Works include operas *Flora mirabilis* (1886), *Medgé*, *Lionella* (1891), *La martire*, *La furia domata* (after Shakespeare's *Taming of the Shrew*, 1895), *Storia d'amore* (1903), *Mademoiselle de Bella-Isle*, *Rhea*, *La guerra in tempo di guerra*, *The Princess of Saxony* (in Greek); suite for piano duet, piano pieces; songs.

Samazeuilh, Gustave (Marie Victor Fernand) (b Bordeaux, 2 Jun 1877; d Paris 4 Aug 1967), French composer and critic. Pupil of Chausson and after his master's death of d'Indy and Dukas at the Schola Cantorum. His writings include studies of Rameau and Dukas, translations of Wagner's *Tristan* and Schumann's *Genoveva*, songs by Wagner and Liszt, etc. He also made piano arrangements of modern French music.

Works include *Étude symphonique pour 'La Nef'* (Élemire Bourges), *Nuit*, *Naïades au soir*, *Le Sommeil de Canope* for orchestra; the last also for voice and orchestra; string quartet; etc.

Saminsky, Lazare (b near Odessa, 8 Nov 1882; d Port Chester, NY, 30 Jun 1959), Russian-American composer, conductor and writer on music. Pupil of Liadov and Rimsky-Korsakov at St Petersburg Conservatory. Conductor at Tiflis 1915–18 and then director of the People's Conservatory there. After a period in London, he went to the USA, where he became naturalized. He was one of the founders of the League of Composers in 1924, became music director of the Jewish Temple of Emanu-El, and conducted widely in Europe and America. Author of *Music of Our Day* and *Music of the Ghetto*.

Works include opera-ballets *The Vision of Ariel*, *Lament of Rachel* (1913) and *The Daughter of Jephtha* (1929), chamber opera *Gagliarda of the Merry Plague*; Requiem; five symphonies (1917–30), three symphonic poems.

Sammarco, Mario (b Palermo, 13 Dec 1868; d Milan, 24 Jan 1930), Italian baritone. Pupil of Antonio Cantelli; made his first appearance at Milan as Hamlet and first visited London in 1904, when he sang Scarpia; appeared in London until 1914 and the USA 1907–13. He created Gérard in *Andrea Chénier* (1896) and sang in operas by Leoncavallo, Donizetti and Wolf-Ferrari. He was a director of La Scala, Milan, from 1918.

Sammartini (or *San Martini*), Giovanni Battista (b Milan, *c* 1700; d Milan, 15 Jan 1775), Italian composer. He spent his whole life in Milan as a church musician, from 1730 *maestro di cappella* at the convent of Santa Maria Maddelena. Gluck was his pupil 1737–41 and borrowed material from Sammartini's symphonies for two of his operas. He was the most important Italian symphonist of his time, and contributed much towards the founding of a modern style of instrumental music.

Works include two operas including *L'Agrippina, moglie di Tiberio* (1743); two oratorios; three Masses and other church music; over 80 symphonies; *c* 15 concertos; six *concerti grossi*; six string quintets, *c* 20 quartets, almost 200 trios, and other chamber music.

Sammartini (or *San Martini*), Giuseppe (b Milan, 6 Jan 1695; d London, Nov 1750), Italian oboist and composer, brother of Giovanni Battista ◊Sammartini. Settled in England *c* 1727, became oboist at the opera, and 1732–44 was director of the Hickford's Room concerts with Arrigoni, then was appointed director of chamber music to the Prince of Wales.

Works include setting of Congreve's masque *The Judgment of Paris* (1740); *Concerti grossi*; concertos for harpsichord and for violin; sonatas for two flutes, two violins, etc. with bass, flute solos (? all flute works intended also for oboe).

Sammons, Albert (b London, 23 Feb 1886; d Southdean, Sussex, 24 Aug 1957), English violinist. Taught by his father, an amateur, John Saunders and F Weist-Hill, he first played at a London hotel, where Beecham heard him in 1908 and engaged him as leader of his orchestra. Sammons later led the London String quartet and gradually emerged as a splendid soloist; he gave the fp of the Delius Concerto (1919) and made the first recording of the Elgar (1929). He excelled both in virtuosity and in musicianship.

Samson oratorio by Handel (libretto by N Hamilton, based on Milton's *Samson Agonistes*, *Hymn on the Nativity* and *At a Solemn Musick*), produced London, CG, 18 Feb 1743.

Samson et Dalila opera (originally oratorio) by Saint-Saëns (libretto by F Lemaire), produced Weimar, German, 2 Dec 1877; not performed in Paris until 31 Oct 1890, and at the Opéra, 23 Nov 1892, having been at first forbidden on account of its biblical subject. Delilah seduces Samson and betrays the secret of his strength. Later, blinded, he prays for strength and brings down the temple on himself and his Philistine enemies.

Samstag aus Licht, *Saturday from Light*, opera by Stockhausen, second of his cycle *Licht*. The four scenes are *Lucifer's Dream*, *Kathinka's Song*, *Lucifer's Dance* and *Lucifer's Farewell*. Fp Milan, 25 May 1984.

Samuel, Harold (b London, 23 May 1879; d London, 15 Jan 1937), English pianist. Studied under Dannreuther and Stanford at the RCM in London, where he became piano professor later. He made a speciality of Bach's keyboard works, but he also excelled as a chamber music player.

San Carlo, Teatro di, Naples, Italian opera house opened 1737. Works by Pergolesi, Piccinni, Cimarosa and Rossini (*Elisabetta*) produced there until house destroyed by fire in 1816; rebuilt same year. Later Rossini fps included *Armida* (1817), *Mosè* (1818) and *La donna del lago* (1819). Donizetti's *Lucia di Lammermoor* (1835) and Verdi's *Luisa Miller* (1849) also first performed there.

Sances, Giovanni Felice (b Rome, *c* 1600; d Vienna, buried 12 Nov 1679), Italian tenor and composer. He went to Vienna as a singer in the Imperial Chapel 1637, became vice-music director 1649 and first music director 1669.

Works include operas *Apollo deluso* (with the Emperor Leopold I), *Aristomene Messenio* and others; oratorios; cantatas for solo voice, *Capricci poetici*, *Trattenimenti musicali per camera*.

Sánchez de Fuentes y Peláez, Eduardo (b Havana, 3 Apr 1874; d Havana, 7 Sept 1944), Cuban composer and music historian. He wrote several books on the history of Cuban folk music.

Works include operas *Dolorosa* (1910), *Doreya* (1918) and three others, operettas and *zarzuelas*; oratorio *Novidad*; suite *Bocetos cubanos*, symphonic prelude *Temas del Patio* for orchestra; vocal *habañera Tú espera*.

Sancho Pança dans son île, *Sancho Panza on his Island*, opera by Philidor (libretto by A A H Poinsinet, based on Cervantes's *Don*

THE OPERA
Samson et Dalila

A three-act opera by Camile Saint-Saëns based on the Bible story in Judges 14–16. It is set in Israel in 1150 BC. The opera was first performed (in German) in Weimar in 1877. The first French production took place in Rouen in 1890.

I. The Hebrews lament their treatment under the Philistines. The warrior Samson (tenor) assures them that God speaks through him, and he inspires a revolt against the Philistines. The High Priest of Dagon (baritone) is powerless but the priestess Dalila (mezzo-soprano) dances provocatively in front of Samson and persuades him to visit her at her dwelling.

II. The high priest tells Dalila she must discover the secret of Samson's strength. At first Samson will not surrender to Dalila, but he finally enters her house and the Philistine soldiers follow.

III. His hair shorn and his eyes put out, Samson is imprisoned at Gaza. He is led to the temple of Dagon, where a celebration is in progress and he is mocked by Dagon and Dalila. Praying for his strength to return he pulls down the temple, crushing himself and the Philistines.

THE OPERA

Quixote), produced Paris, Comédie-Italienne, 8 Jul 1762.

Sancio Panza, governatore dell' isola Barattaria, *Sancho Panza, Governor of the Isle of Barataria*, opera by Caldara (libretto by G C Pasquini, based on Cervantes' *Don Quixote*), produced Vienna, Burgtheater, 27 Jan 1733.

Sancta Civitas, *The Holy City*, oratorio by Vaughan Williams (words from the Bible, etc.) for solo voices, chorus and orchestra, fp Oxford, 7 May 1926.

Sancta Susanna opera in one act by Hindemith (libretto by A Stramm); composed 1921, produced Frankfurt, 26 Mar 1922. Story concerns a sex-obsessed nun who tears the loincloth from a statue of Christ.

Sanctus the fourth chant of the Ordinary of the Roman Mass. Its text is founded on Isaiah vi. 3 and Matthew xxi. 9, and it was incorporated into the Latin liturgy at least as early as the 6th c. in Gaul. The earliest known melody is that of Mass XVIII (Vatican edition). It is basically syllabic; it forms a natural continuation from the music of the Preface which precedes it; it is psalmodic in structure; and its last phrase echoes the *Per omnia saecula saeculorum* formula which occurs three times during the Preface and Canon of the Mass. Later settings are more complex: a total of 231 melodies were catalogued in 1962. The Sanctus was set in polyphony from the 13th c., and became an integral part of all settings of the Ordinary of the Mass.

Sandberger, Adolf (b Würzburg, 19 Dec 1864; d Munich, 14 Jan 1943), German musicologist and composer. Studied in a number of European centres and in 1894 became lecturer in music at Munich University and was professor 1900–29, being at the same time curator of the music department of the State Library. He was chief editor of the incomplete edition of Lassus and the *Denkmäler der Tonkunst in Bayern*, and his books include studies of the Bavarian court chapel under Lassus, of Cornelius, etc.

Works include operas *Ludwig der Springer* and *Der Tod des Kaisers*; symphonic poem *Viola* (on Shakespeare's *Twelfth Night*), symphonic prologue *Riccio*; chamber music; piano works; songs.

Sanderling, Kurt (b Arys, 9 Sept 1912), German conductor. He worked at the Berlin Staatsoper from 1931 but left Germany at the rise of the Nazis. He became conductor of the Moscow Radio SO 1937 and joined the Leningrad PO 1941. Returned to Berlin 1960 and was conductor East Berlin SO until 1964; then worked in Dresden with the Staatskapelle and at the opera house; Salzburg Festival debut 1965; London debut 1970, with Leipzig Gewandhaus Orchestra. Well known in late Romantic music, conducted Shostakovich's 8th Symphony with the Los Angeles PO at Birmingham (1991).

Sanderson (or *Saunderson*), James (b Washington, Durham, Apr

1769; d London, *c* 1841), English violinist and composer. He was self-taught and in 1783 obtained an engagement as violinist at the Sunderland theatre. Later he taught at Shields, became leader at the Newcastle-upon-Tyne theatre, 1787, and at Astley's Amphitheatre in London, 1788. He began to write stage pieces and in 1793 went as music director and composer to the Royal Circus (Surrey Theatre).

Works include stage pieces and pantomimes *Harlequin in Ireland*, *Blackbeard*, *Cora*, *Sir Francis Drake*, *The Magic Pipe*, *Hallowe'en* and many others; instrumental interludes for Collin's *Ode to the Passions*; violin pieces; many popular songs.

Sanderson, Sibyl (b Sacramento, CA, 7 Dec, 1865; d Paris, 15 May 1903), American soprano. Studied at the Paris Conservatory and made her debut at The Hague in 1888, in Massenet's *Manon*. She was later Massenet's mistress, and created the title roles in *Esclarmonde* and *Thaïs*.

Sándor, György (b Budapest, 21 Sept 1912), Hungarian pianist. Studied Budapest with Bartók and Kodály. Moved to US 1939 and in 1946 gave the fp of Bartók's third concerto, at Philadelphia. Recorded all the piano music of Bartók and Kodály.

Sandrin, Pierre Regnault (d after 1561), French composer. He was a member of the royal chapel, 1543–60, during which time he also travelled to Italy. He composed only *chansons*, of which the majority were pub. by Attaingnant. Lassus based a Mass on the *chanson* 'Doulce memoire'.

San Francisco Opera Company founded 1923 by Gaetano Merola. He was succeeded as director by Kurt Herbert Adler (1953–82), Terence A Metwen (1982–88) and Lofti Mansouri (from 1988). Opening production at War Memorial Opera House in 1934 was *Tosca*. John Pritchard was music director 1986–89, Donald Runnicles from 1992. Venue of US fps of operas by Orff (*Carmina Burana*, 1958), Poulenc (*Carmélites*, 1957), Strauss (*Die Frau ohne Schatten*, 1959), Shostakovich (*Katerina Izmailova*, 1964) and Tippett (*The Midsummer Marriage*, 1983).

San Francisco Symphony Orchestra American orchestra founded 1911. Pierre Monteux was conductor 1935–52. Recent conductors have been Seiji Ozawa (1970–76), Edo de Waart (1977–85), Herbert Blomstedt (1985–95), Michael Tilson Thomas from 1995.

Sanguine Fan, The ballet by Elgar, op. 81 (scenario by Ina Lowther); composed 1917, produced Chelsea, 20 Mar 1917, conductor Elgar; not heard again complete until recording of 1973.

Santa Cruz (or *Wilson*), Domingo (b La Cruz, 5 Jul, 1899; d Santiago, 7 Jan 1987), Chilean composer, teacher and critic. Studied at Santiago de Chile and Madrid. In 1918 he founded a Bach Society at Santiago and in 1932 became dean of the Fine Arts Dept. at the University of Chile and rector of the university from 1948 to 1951.

Works include four symphonies (1948–69); five *Piezas brevas* for string orchestra; three string quartets; three violin and piano pieces; piano works; songs.

Santa Fe Opera opera company in New Mexico founded 1957 by John ◊Crosby. Theatre burned down in 1967 but rebuilt following year. World premieres there have included Berio's *Opera* (1970), Rochberg's *The Confidence Man* (1982) and Eaton's *The Tempest* (1985). Season consists of two-month summer festival, with US fps of works by Cavalli (*Egisto*), Hindemith (*Cardillac* and *Neues vom Tage*), Henze (*Bassarids* and *We Come to the River*), Strauss (*Daphne*), Schoenberg (*Von Heute auf Morgen*) and Massenet (*Chérubin*).

Sant'Alessio, Il opera in prologue and three acts by Landi (libretto by Rospigliosi), produced Rome, Paluz Barberini, 21 Feb 1632. Alessio returns home from the Holy Land, resists worldly temptation and continues his life of renunciation.

Santa Maria, Tomás de (b Madrid *c* 1515; d Valladolid, 1570), Spanish monk and organist. He joined a Dominican monastery and in 1565 pub. a treatise on playing polyphonic fantasies on keyboard instruments and lutes.

Santi, Nello (b Adria, 22 Sep 1931), Italian conductor. He studied in Padua and made his debut there in 1951, with *Rigoletto*. Has conducted at the Zurich Opera from 1960 (principal there 1985–96) and at the Met. from 1962 (debut with *Un ballo in maschera*) and regular

appearances from 1976 (*Rigoletto*, 1992). CG 1960 with *La Traviata*, returning 1983 for *La Fanciulla del West*. Conducted London's first 'arena' opera (*Aida*, 1988) but is more accustomed to Verona, leading *Tosca*, *Trovatore* and *Aida* there. Conducted *Turandot* at the Met., 1995.

Santini, Fortunato (b Rome, 5 Jan 1778; d Rome, 14 Sept 1861), Italian priest, music scholar and composer. He studied music with Jannaconi and after being ordained in 1801 began to make an immense collection of early music, scoring it from parts in various music libraries. He made friends with Mendelssohn and through him introduced many works by Bach into Italy, as well as other German sacred music.

Works include Requiem for eight voices, Masses and other church music.

Santley, Charles (b Liverpool, 28 Feb 1834; d London, 22 Sept 1922), English bass-baritone. Learnt music as a choirboy and at first appeared as an amateur singer, but went to Milan in 1855 to study with Gaetano Nava, made a stage appearance at Pavia and in 1857 returned to England, continuing his studies with Manuel García in London, where he first appeared on 16 Nov, as Adam in *Die Schöpfung*. He soon sang in opera, oratorio and at the great festivals with enormous success, notably in operas by Balfe, Wallace and Benedict; sang Valentine in the first British performance of *Faust* (1865) and was the first London Daland (1870). He toured the USA in 1871 and Australia in 1890. In 1907 he celebrated his 50th anniversary as a singer and was knighted.

Santoliquido, Francesco (b San Giorgio a Cremano, Naples, 6 Aug 1883; d Anacapri, 26 Aug 1971), Italian composer. Studied at the Liceo di Santa Cecilia in Rome, conducting his student work, *Crepuscolo sul mare*, at Nuremberg in 1909 and producing his first opera at Milan in 1910. He then went to live in Tunisia, in the small Arab village in Hammamek, where he studied the local music.

Works include operas *La favola di Helga* (1910), *Ferhuda* (1918), *L'ignota* and *La porta verde* (1953), mimed drama *La baiadera della maschera gialla* (1917); symphony in F major.

Sanzogno, Nino (b Venice, 13 Apr 1911; d Milan, 4 May 1983), Italian conductor, composer and violinist. Studied with Malipiero and Scherchen, and then played violin in the Guarnieri quartet, later becoming conductor at La Fenice opera house in Venice and at La Scala, Milan. He conducted the first production of Prokofiev's *The Fiery Angel* (1955) and Poulenc's *Carmélites*; also gave operas by Berg (Italian fp of *Lulu*, 1949), Shostakovich and Britten (*A Midsummer Night's Dream*, 1961).

Works include symphonic poems *The Four Horsemen of the Apocalypse*, *Vanitas*; concertos for viola, cello; songs.

Sapho opera by Gounod (libretto by Émile Augier), produced Paris, Opéra, 16 Apr 1851. Gounod's first opera. For plot synopsis ◊Saffo.

Opera by Massenet (libretto by H Cain and A Bernède, based on Daudet's novel), produced Paris, Opéra-Comique, 27 Nov 1897. The heroine is not the Greek poet Sappho but artist's model Fanny Legrand who poses as Sappho. She runs away with Jean Gaussin, but he abandons her after hearing of her sordid past. Later he returns to her but she rejects him.

saraband, English, *sarabande* French, a dance, possibly originating in Spain in the 16th c. Its name was formerly supposed to be derived from a dancer called Zarabanda, but it is very likely of more remote eastern origin. It was introduced to the French court in 1588 and in 17th-c. England became a country dance. The music is in slow 3–2 time with, as a rule, a peculiar rhythm of a minim, dotted minim and crotchet in the first bar. The sarabande was one of the four regular movements in the 17th- and 18th-c. suite, together with the allemande, courante and gigue (jig).

Sarabande and Cortège two studies for orchestra by Busoni for his opera *Doktor Faust*; composed 1918–19, fp Zurich, 31 Mar 1919.

Sarasate (y Navascuéz), Pablo (Martín Melitón) (b Pamplona, 10 Mar 1844; d Biarritz, 20 Sept 1908), Spanish violinist and composer. Pupil of Alard at the Paris Conservatory. He soon began to make a remarkable career as a virtuoso, at first in France and Spain, later all over Europe and America. He first appeared in London in 1861. Bruch,

The sarabande from Bach's English Suite, No. 6

Saint-Saëns, Lalo and Wieniawski dedicated concertos to him.

Works include romances, fantasies, four books of Spanish Dances, etc. for violin.

Saraste, Jukka-Pekka (b Heinola, 22 Apr 1956), Finnish conductor. Studied in Helsinki and made debut there with the Philharmonic in 1980; toured the USA with the Orchestra in 1983. London debut with the LSO, 1984. Principal conductor of the Finnish Radio SO from 1987, Scottish Chamber Orchestra 1987–94; Toronto SO from 1994. Guest in Vienna, Minnesota, Munich and Rotterdam. Recordings include Sibelius' Symphonies, Debussy's *Images* and Mahler's 5th.

Sarbu, Eugen (b Bucharest, 1949), Romanian violinist. Made solo debut aged six and after study in Paris joined Ivan Galamian at Curtis and studied further at Juilliard and with Nathan Milstein in Zurich. Regular concerts throughout Britain, including London Proms debut 1982, Europe, the Americas and the Far East. Recordings include Vivaldi's *Four Seasons*, and concertos by Sibelius and Mozart.

sardana a Spanish dance of Catalonia revived in the middle of the 19th c. and performed to pipe and drum.

Sarema opera by Zemlinsky (libretto by composer, after R von Gottschall's play *Die Rose vom Kaukasus*), composed 1895, produced Munich, Hofoper, 10 Oct 1897. Zemlinsky's first opera. Circassian heroine torn between love for Russian officer and her own country.

Sargent, (Harold) Malcolm (Watts) (b Stamford, Lincs., 29 Apr 1895; d London, 3 Oct 1967), English conductor. Studied at the Royal College of Organists, winning the Sawyer Prize in 1910. From 1911 to 1914 he was assistant organist at Peterborough Cathedral; served in World War I and in 1919 took his D. Mus. at Durham. He made his debut as a conductor at a Promenade Concert in a work of his own in 1921. Later he taught at the RCM and conducted in many parts of the world, including a period with the Diaghilev ballet co. 1927–30. In 1928 he became chief conductor of the Royal Choral Society and from 1950 to 1957 chief conductor of the BBC SO, and of the Promenade Concerts until his death. He gave the fps of *Belshazzar's Feast* (1931), *Troilus and Cressida* (1954) and Vaughan Williams's ninth symphony (1958). Knighted 1947.

Šárka, Smetana, ◊Má Vlast.

Opera by Fibich (libretto by A Schulzová), produced Prague, Czech Theatre, 28 Dec 1897. Bohemian Šárka leads women against the oppressive Duke Přemysl and his men; but she falls in love with warrior Ctirad, eventually betraying her cause to save him. Guilty, she commits suicide.

Opera by Janáček (libretto by J Zeyer); composed 1887–88, revised 1918 and 1925, scoring completed by O Chlubna, produced Brno, 11 Nov 1925. UK fp at Edinburgh, 1993 (concert).

sarod Indian plucked or bowed lute with up to six melody strings and addditional ◊sympathetic strings for added resonance. It is smaller than the ◊sitar and has two resonating chambers.

Sarro (or *Sarri*), Domenico (b Trani, Naples, 24 Dec 1679; d Naples,

25 Jan 1744), Italian composer. Pupil of Durante at the Conservatorio S Onofrio in Naples, he became vice-*maestro di cappella* to the court in 1703. He lost his post in 1707 but returned 1725, succeeding Mancini as *maestro di cappella* in 1737.

Works include *c* 50 operas, e.g. *Didone abbandonata* (the first setting by any composer of a libretto by Metastasio, produced Naples, 1724); four oratorios; cantatas, etc.; much church music; instrumental music.

sarrusophone a brass wind instrument with a double-reed mouthpiece invented in 1856 by Sarrus, a bandmaster in the French Army, intended to be made in various sizes to cover a whole range of tone, replacing oboes and bassoons in military bands. In the orchestra only the contrabass has been used, mainly by French composers.

Sarti, Giuseppe (b Faenza, bap. 1 Dec 1729; d Berlin, 28 Jul 1802), Italian composer and conductor. Pupil of Vallotti in Padua and of Padre Martini in Bologna, he was organist of Faenza Cathedral 1748–51, then music director of the theatre there in 1752 and produced his first opera the same year. In 1753 he went to Copenhagen as conductor of the Mingotti opera co., and two years later was appointed *Kapellmeister* to the Danish court, staying there, except for three years in Italy 1765–68, until 1775. Director of the Ospedaletto Conservatory in Venice 1775–79, he was then *maestro di cappella* of Milan Cathedral, where Cherubini was his pupil.

Appointed music director to the Russian court in 1784, he travelled to St Petersburg *via* Vienna, there meeting Mozart, who quoted the aria 'Come un agnello' from his opera *Fra due litiganti* in the supper scene in *Don Giovanni*. He produced a number of operas in Russia, including *Oleg* on a libretto by the empress, and stayed there until 1802, founding a music school in the Ukraine and becoming director of the Conservatory in St Petersburg in 1793. He then intended to retire in Italy, but died in Berlin on the way.

Works include operas (libretti in Italian, Danish, French and Russian), e.g. *Pompeo in Armenia* (1752), *Il rè pastore* (1753), *La giardiniera brillante* (1768), *Farnace*, *Le gelosie villane*, *Fra due litiganti* (1782), *Medonte* (1777), *Giulio Sabino*, *I finti eredi*, *Armida e Rinaldo* (1786), *Oleg* (Russian, with Pashkevich and Canobbio), etc.; two Russian oratorios; Requiem for Louis XVI (1793); Masses, Te Deum and other church music; keyboard music.

Sartorio, Antonio (b Venice, *c* 1630; d Venice, 30 Dec 1680), Italian composer. He was music director at the Court of Brunswick 1666–75 and then vice-*maestro di cappella* at St Mark's, Venice, preceding Legrenzi. His gifts are well displayed in the opera *Orfeo* of 1672, with opportunities for choral and solo laments.

Works include operas *Seleuco* (1666), *La prosperità di Elio Seiano* (1667), *La caduta di Elio Seiano*, *Adelaide*, *Orfeo* (1672) and ten others; psalms and motets; cantatas for chorus and for solo voices; canzonets.

Sartorius (or *Schneider*), Paul (b Nuremberg, 16 Nov 1569; d Innsbruck, 28 Feb 1609), German organist and composer. He was organist to the Archduke Maximilian of Austria in 1599 and lived at Nuremberg.

Works include Masses, *Sonetti spirituali* for six voices (1601), motets, madrigals, *Neue teutsche Liedlein*.

Sarum Use the liturgy in use at Salisbury before the Reformation, differing in some respects from that of Rome and widely spread through medieval England until it was abolished in 1547, though revived from 1553–59.

Sás Orchassal, André (b Paris, 6 Apr 1900; d Lima, 25 Jul 1967), Peruvian composer, of French-Belgian parentage. Studied in Brussels and went to Peru in 1924 as violin teacher at the National Academy of Music at Lima. He married the Peruvian pianist Lily Rosay and with her founded a private music school in 1929. He made extensive research into Peruvian folklore and frequently used folktunes in his works.

Works include *Himno al sol*, *Himno y danza* and *Poema Indio* for orchestra; *Rapsodia peruana* for violin and orchestra; *Quenas* for voice, flute and harp; *Sonatina india* for flute and piano; works for violin and piano; piano pieces; songs.

Sass (or *Saxe*), Marie (Constance) (b Ghent, 26 Jan 1838; d Auteuil near Paris, 8 Nov 1907), Belgian soprano. Pupil of Delphine Ugalde, had her debut in Paris in 1859 and went to the Opéra in 1860, where the following year she sang Elisabeth in the French version of Wagner's *Tannhäuser*; created Sélika (1865) and Elisabeth de Valois (1867). Died impoverished.

Sass, Sylvia (b Budapest, 12 Jul 1951), Hungarian soprano. She studied in Budapest and made her debut there in 1971. She sang Desdemona with Scottish Opera in 1975 and in 1976 was Giselda in the first CG production of Verdi's *I Lombardi*. Sang Violetta at Aix in the same year and Tosca on her NY Met. debut in 1977. She has been heard in Vienna, Hamburg and Paris as Donna Anna, Fiordiligi and Bartók's Judith. Sang Adriana Lecouvreur at Budapest, 1993.

For Erik Satie, the sweet medieval musician who has strayed into this century for the joy of his very friendly Claude Debussy.

Claude Debussy, dedication in a copy of
Cinq Poèmes de Baudelaire

Satie, Erik (Alfred Leslie) (b Honfleur, 17 May 1866; d Paris, 1 Jul 1925), French composer. He was brought up in a musical home, his father being a composer and music pub. in Paris and his mother, of Scottish origin, a minor composer of piano pieces under the name of Eugénie Satie-Barnetsche. He spent only a year at the Paris Conservatory and later made a precarious living by playing at cafés, writing music for the Montmartre song-writer Hypsa and the music-hall singer Paulette Darty. Through his friendship with Debussy, *c* 1890, he came into contact with intellectual circles. He also studied at the Schola Cantorum under d'Indy and Roussel at the age of 40. He continued to pub. small piano works under eccentric titles. A commission from Diaghilev led to the ballet *Parade*, with instrumentation for siren, typewriter and steam-ship whistle. In later years he came into touch with Jean Cocteau and established a school at Arcueil where he exercised some influence on younger composers, in particular leading them away from the late Romantic style influenced by German composers, especially Wagner, towards a terser, more concise and epigrammatic style. Satie's inclination towards the simplistic has been at times attributed to a lack of technique.

Works include STAGE AND CHORAL: symphonic drama *Socrate* (1920); incidental music for Péladan's *Le Fils des étoiles*; ballets *Parade* (1917), *Relâche* (1924) and *Mercure*, 1924; operettas *Geneviève de Brabant* (for marionettes, 1899), *Pousse-l'Amour* and *Le Piège de Méduse*; pantomime *Jack in the Box* (orchestrated by Milhaud); *Messe des pauvres* for voices and organ (1895).

PIANO: piano pieces *Ogives*, *Trois Sarabandes*, *Trois Gymnopédies* (1888), *Trois Gnossiennes* (1890), *Danses gothiques* (1893), *Sonner-*

ies de la Rose-Croix, *Pièces froides* (1897), *Prélude en tapisserie*, *Trois Véritables Préludes flasques (pour un chien)*, three Descriptions automatiques (1913), *Trois Embryons desséchés* (1913), *Trois Croquis et agaceries d'un gros bonhomme en bois* (1913), *Trois Chapitres tournés en tous sens* (1913), *Trois Vieux Sequins et vieilles cuirasses* (1913), *Heures séculaires et instantanées* (1914), *Trois Valses du précieux dégoûté*, *Avant-dernières pensées*, etc.; *Trois Morceaux en forme de poire* (1903), *Aperçus désagréables* and *En habit de cheval* for piano duet; four sets of songs.

Satyagraha opera by Philip Glass (libretto by C DeJong), based on the life of Gandhi, produced Rotterdam, 5 Sept 1980. Title is based on Gandhi's slogan, the two Hindi words *saty*, 'truth' and *agraha*, 'firmness'. The opera is sung in Sanskrit. Gandhi's early struggles in South Africa are balanced with portraits of Tolstoy, Tagore and Martin Luther King.

Sauer, Emil (George Konrad) (b Hamburg, 8 Oct 1862; d Vienna, 27 Apr 1942), German pianist and composer. Studied with N Rubinstein at the Moscow Conservatory and later with Liszt. Began to tour Europe 1882 and first visited England 1894. From 1901, with certain intervals, he directed a master class at the Vienna Conservatory.

Works include two piano concertos; two sonatas, 24 concert studies, *Suite moderne* and many pieces for piano.

Sauguet, Henri (b Bordeaux, 18 May 1901; d Paris, 22 Jun 1989), French composer and critic. Studied piano and organ at Bordeaux, then became a pupil of J. Canteloube at Montauban and in 1922 of Koechlin in Paris. Introduced by Milhaud to Satie, he joined the latter's school at Arcueil. In 1936 he succeeded Milhaud as music critic to *Le Jour-Écho de Paris*, and his major work, the opera *La Chartreuse de Parme*, followed in 1939. Other works include the operas *La Gageure imprévue* (Sedaine, 1944) and *Les caprices de Marianne* (1954); operettas *Le Plumet du colonel* (1924) and *La Contrebasse* (1932); ballets *La Charte*, *David*, *La Nuit*, *Fastes* and *Les Forains*; incidental music for Molierè's *Le Sicilien*, Roger Ferdinand's *Irma*, Pierre Emmanuel's *Les Lépreux* and other plays.

Four symphonies including *Symphonie expiatoire* (in memory of war victims); three piano concertos; *La Voyante* for soprano and chamber orchestra; two string quartets (1926, 1948); sonatina for flute and piano; sonata in D major and other works for piano; songs to poems by Tagore; film music.

Saul oratorio by Handel (libretto by C Jennens), produced London, King's Theatre, 16 Jan 1739.

Saul og David opera in four acts by Nielsen (libretto by E Christiansen); composed 1898–1901, produced Copenhagen, Royal Theatre, 28 Nov 1902, conductor Nielsen. When David defeats Goliath, Saul becomes jealous and outlaws him. David runs away with Michal, Saul's daughter. Saul commits suicide after losing a battle against the Philistines, and David becomes king.

Saunders, Arlene (b Cleveland, 5 Oct 1935), American soprano. Debut NY 1958, as Rosalinde. She sang in Italy from 1960 and was a member of the Hamburg Opera from 1963; sang in the 1965 fp of Klebe's *Jacobowsky und der Oberst* and well known as Agathe, Arabella, the Marschallin and Mozart's Countess. Glyndebourne 1966, Pamina. At Washington in 1971 she was heard in the fp of Ginastera's *Beatrix Cenci*. NY Met. debut 1976, as Eva. Retired from stage after singing the Marschallin at Buenos Aires, 1985.

Sauret, Émile (b Dun-le-Roi, 22 May 1852; d London, 12 Feb 1920), French violinist and composer. Pupil of Bériot. He began to travel at an early age, first visited London in 1862, played much at the French court in the last years of the second Empire, visited the USA twice 1872–76, studied composition with Jadassohn at Leipzig and appeared with Liszt. In 1872 he married Teresa Carreño, but they were divorced before long. In 1891 he succeeded Sainton as violin professor at the RAM in London and in 1903 he took up a similar post at Chicago.

Works include two concertos, *Ballade*, *Légende*; serenade for violin and orchestra; many violin pieces, studies and arrangements.

sausage bassoon ◊racket.

sautillé French = 'springing, bounding'; a special way of playing the violin and other string instruments in such a manner that the bow is made to rebound from the strings.

Sauzay, Charles Eugène (b Paris, 14 Jul 1809; d Paris, 24 Jan 1901), French violinist and composer. Studied at the Paris Conservatory, Baillot and Reicha being among his masters. He joined Baillot's quartet and married his daughter, became court violinist in 1840 and professor at the Conservatory in 1860.

Works include incidental music for Molière's *George Dandin* and *Le Sicilien*; string trio, piano trio; violin and piano pieces; *Études harmoniques* for solo violin; songs, etc.

Savile, Jeremy, English 17th-c. composer. Contributed songs to *Select Musicall Ayres and Dialogues* in 1653. Compositions include part-song *The Waits*, song 'Here's a health unto His Majesty'.

Sāvitri opera by Holst (libretto by composer, based on an episode in the *Mahabharata*), produced London, Wellington Hall, 5 Dec 1916; first public performance London, Lyric Theatre, Hammersmith, 23 Jun 1921. Death comes to claim woodman Satyavān, but he is restored when his wife Sāvitri outwits the grim reaper.

Sawallisch, Wolfgang (b Munich, 26 Aug 1923), German conductor and pianist. Studied at the Munich Hochschule für Musik with J Haas, making his debut in Augsburg 1947, where he remained until 1953, when he became music director at the opera in Aachen. From 1957 to 1959 he conducted at the Wiesbaden opera and from 1959 to 1963 in Cologne. Bayreuth 1957–62 (*Tristan*, *Der fliegende Holländer* and *Tannhäuser*). Salzburg opera debut 1964 (*Macbeth*); US debut 1964, with the Vienna SO. Music director Bavarian Opera, Munich 1971–93; chief conductor of the Philadelphia Orchestra from 1992. Suisse Romande Orchestra 1970–80. Well known as piano accompanist to leading singers. Recordings include *Die Frau ohne Schatten* and the *Ring*, on video.

Sawyer, David (b Stockport, 14 Sep 1961), English composer. Studied at York University and with Kagel in Cologne; directed premieres of works by Kagel at the 1983 Huddersfield Festival and was piano soloist in his *Phonophonie* in London, 1987. Works have been played by the London Sinfonietta and the BBC SO (London Proms 1992) and at the Almeida Festival: chamber opera *The Panic* (1992); *Etudes* for actors and ensemble (1984); *Cat's Eye* (1986), *Take Off* (1987) and *Rhetoric* (1989) for ensemble; *Songs of Love and War* for 24 voices, two harpsichords and percussion (1990); *The Melancholy of Departure* for piano (1990); *Byrnan Wood* for orchestra (1992); *The Memory of Water* (1993).

Sax Belgian family of instrument makers:
1. Charles Joseph Sax (b Dinant, 1 Feb 1791; d Paris, 26 Apr 1865). He set up in business at Brussels, made wind instruments and produced several inventions, especially in connection with horns and other brass instruments.
2. Adolphe (actually Antoine Joseph) Sax (b Dinant, 6 Nov 1814; d Paris, 4 Feb 1894), son of 1. Studied flute and clarinet at the Brussels Conservatory and worked with his father, made several improvements in wind instruments and established himself in Paris in 1842. His chief inventions are the saxhorn and the saxophone.
3. Alphonse Sax (b Brussels, 9 May 1822; d Paris, 26 Jun 1874), brother of 2. He made some inventions in connection with the valves of brass instruments and established himself independently in Paris, but did not succeed.

Saxe, Marie, ◊Sass.

and contrabass in B♭. They are rarely used in the orchestra, but are regular constituents of military and brass bands.

saxophone a wind instrument made of brass, but with woodwind characteristics, invented by Adolphe Sax *c* 1840 and patented by him in 1846. It is played through a mouthpiece with a single reed of the clarinet type and the notes are controlled by keys. It is made in five or six pitches: sopranino in E♭ (rare), soprano in B♭, alto in E♭, tenor in B♭ (these two the most common), baritone in E♭ and bass in B♭.

Saxton, Robert (b London, 8 Oct 1953), English composer. He studied with Elisabeth Lutyens, Robin Holloway, Robert Sherlaw Johnson and Berio. Head of composition at GSMD, London, from 1990.

Works include *La Promenade d'Automne* for soprano and ensemble (1972), *What does the song hope for?* for soprano and ensemble (1974), *Reflections on Narziss and Goldmund* for two chamber groups, harp and piano (1975), *Canzona* for chamber ensemble (1978), *Choruses to Apollo* for orchestra (1980), *Traumstadt* for orchestra (1980), *Processions and Dances* for 11 instruments (1981), *Piccola Musica per Luigi Dallapiccola* for chamber ensemble (1981), *Eloge* for soprano and ensemble (1981), *Ring of Eternity* for orchestra (1983), Concerto for Orchestra (1984), *Circles of Light* for chamber orchestra (1985), viola concerto (1986), *In the Beginning* for orchestra (1987), *Elijah's Violin* for orchestra (1988), concertos for violin (1989) and cello (1993), *Psalm: a Song of Ascents* for trumpet and ensemble (1992), Piano Quintet (1994), Symphony for soprano, baritone and orchestra (1993).

Sayão, Bidú (Balduina de Oliveria Sayão) (b Niteroi, Rio de Janiero, 11 May 1902), Brazilian soprano. After study with Jean de Reszke she sang Rosina in Rome (1926). Appeared widely in Italy and South America and gave Lakmé at Washington in 1936. NY Met. debut 1937, as Manon. Other NY roles were Juliette, Mélisande, Norina, Zerlina and Susanna. Sang in concert from 1952; retired 1957.

Scacchi, Marco (b Rome, *c* 1602; d Gallese near Rome, *c* 1685), Italian composer and writer on music, pupil of G F Anerio. In 1628 he was appointed director of music to the court at Warsaw, whence he returned to Italy in 1648. He introduced Italian opera to Warsaw, Danzig and Vilna. He wrote some theoretical tracts.

Works include operas *Il ratto di Helena*, *Narciso transformato*, *Armida abbandonata*, *Enea*, *Le nozze d'Amore e di Psiche* and *Circe delusa*; Masses; oratorio *S Cecilia*; madrigals.

Scalabrini, Paolo (b ? Bologna or Lucca, *c* 1713; d Lucca, 28 Feb 1806), Italian composer. Went to Copenhagen in 1747 as conductor of the Mingotti opera co., and stayed there as music director to the Danish court 1748–53 and again 1775–81, when he retired to Italy. He was among the first to write an opera to Danish words.

Works include Danish operas *Love rewarded, or The Faithful Lovers* (1756), *The Oracle* (1776), *Love without Stockings*, and *c* 20 Italian operas; oratorio *Giuseppe riconosciuto*; symphonies.

Scala di seta, La, *The Silken Ladder*, opera by Rossini (libretto by G Rossi, based on Planard's libretto *L'Échelle de soie* set by Gaveaux), produced Venice, Teatro San Moisè, 9 May 1812. Dorvil makes nightly ascent to Giulia, whom he has secretly married against the wishes of her guardian, Dormont. All is resolved when Dormont's choice, Blansac, falls in love with Lucilla.

scala enigmatica *or enimmatica*, Italian = 'enigmatic scale'; Verdi's term for the curious scale on which he constructed his *Ave Maria* for four voices composed *c* 1889.

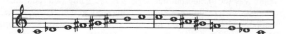

The scala enigmatica on C.

saxhorn a brass wind instrument allied to the bugle, but with valves, invented by Adolphe Sax and patented by him in 1845. It is played with a cup mouthpiece and made in seven different pitches, covering between them a range of some five octaves: soprano in E♭, alto in B♭ (both also called flügelhorns), tenor in E♭, baritone in B♭ (both also called althorns), bass in B♭ (euphonium), bass tuba in E♭ (bombardon)

Scala Theatre (*Teatro alla Scala*) the great opera-house at Milan, built, after the destruction by fire of the Teatro Regio Ducal in 1776, on the site of the church of Santa Maria alla Scala, and opened 3 Aug 1778 with Salieri's *Europa riconosciuta*. Operas by Rossini, Donizetti, Bellini (*Norma*), Verdi (*Falstaff* and *Otello*) and Puccini (*Madama Butterfly*) later received their premieres there. Toscanini was conductor at various times between 1899 and 1929, giving many performances of Wagner and fps of Italian works. Victor De Sabata was director 1931–57, Claudio Abbado 1968–86; Riccardo Muti from 1986.

Scalchi, Sofia (b Turin, 29 Nov 1850; d Rome, 22 Aug 1922), Italian contralto. Studied with Boccabadati and made her debut at Mantua in 1866, as Ulrica. She first visited England in 1868 and sang regularly in London until 1890; roles there included Amneris, Fides, Ortrud and Leonore in *La Favorite*. Also travelled widely in Europe and first went to USA in 1882, when she sang Arsaces; Siebel on the opening night of the Met. (1883).

The formation of scales and the web of harmony is a product of artistic invention, and is in no way given by the natural structure or by the natural behaviour of our hearing.
Hermann von Helmholtz, *Theory of Sound*, 1862

---

scale, from Latin and Italian *scala* = 'ladder', succession of adjoining notes whether proceeding in ascent or descent. ◊scala enigmatica.

Pentatonic

Major

Minor (melodic)

Minor (harmonic)

Whole-tone

Pentatonic, major, minor, and whole-tone scales on C.

Scandello (or *Scandellus*), Antonio (b Bergamo, 17 Jan 1517; d Dresden, 18 Jan 1580), Italian composer. He is first heard of as a cornettist in Bergamo (1541) and was a member of the Saxon court chapel at Dresden in 1553, but he often returned to Brescia for visits, as in 1567, when he and his family took refuge there during the plague at Dresden. Among the court musicians was his brother Angelo Scandello, and also employed at the court was the Italian painter Benedetto Tola, whose daughter Agnese became Scandello's second wife in 1568. In the same year he was appointed *Kapellmeister* in place of Matthieu Le Maistre, whose assistant *Kapellmeister* he had been for two years. He became involved in quarrels with the German court musicians and the Flemish singers because the Italians received higher pay.

Works include Masses, motets, setting for voices of the Passion and Resurrection narrative according to St John (1561), hymn tunes for several voices and other church music; madrigals, epithalamia, *canzoni napoletane* for four voices, sacred and secular German songs for several voices and instruments; lute music.

Scapino comedy-overture by Walton; fp Chicago, 3 Apr 1941, conductor Stock.

Scaria, Emil (b Graz, 18 Sept 1838; d Blasewitz near Dresden, 22 Jul 1886), Austrian bass. Studied at the Vienna Conservatory and made his first stage appearance at Budapest in 1860 as St Bris in *Les Huguenots*. In 1862 he visited London to study under Manuel García and sang at the Crystal Palace. In 1882 he sang Gurnemanz in the fp of Wagner's *Parsifal* at Bayreuth. He sang Wotan with Angelo Neumann's touring co. (Berlin 1881, London 1882).

Scarlatti Italian family of musicians:

1. (Pietro) Alessandro (Gaspare) Scarlatti (b Palermo, 2 May 1660; d Naples, 22 Oct 1725), composer. At the age of 12 he moved with his parents to Rome, where the success of his first opera, *Gli equivoci nel sembiante* (1679), won him the appointment of *maestro di cappella* to Queen Christina of Sweden (1680–83). He also held a similar post at the church of San Gerolamo della Carità before moving to Naples as conductor of the San Bartolomeo opera house (1683–84) and *maestro di cappella* to the court (1684), remaining there for almost 20 years. In Florence 1702–03 he found a patron in Ferdinand (III) de' Medici, for whom he continued to write operas later, but 1703–08 lived mostly in Rome, working first as assistant (1703) then as chief *maestro di cappella* (1707) at the church of Santa Maria Maggiore, and receiving support from Cardinal Ottoboni, who made him his private *maestro di cappella*. In Rome he was restricted by ecclesiastical opposition to opera, but, in addition to operas for Florence, composed numerous oratorios, serenatas, cantatas, etc. After a brief visit to Venice in 1707 he was recalled to his old post in Naples at the end of the following year, and was knighted in 1715. He again lived chiefly in Rome 1717–22, but then returned finally to Naples. Among his pupils were his son Domenico ◊Scarlatti, Geminiani and Hasse.

Recent revivals of such operas as *La Griselda, Mitridate Eupatore* and *Gli equivoci nel sembiante* reveal a composer who could maintain a consistently high level of invention with such technical innovations as the use of an orchestral ritornello (*Teodora*, 1692), the Italian overture (*Dal male il bene*, revival of 1696) and accompanied recitative (*L'Olimpia vendicata*, 1685).

Works include 115 operas, including *Gli equivoci nel sembiante* (1679), *L'honestà negli amori, Il Pompeo* (1683), *Olimpia vendicata, La Rosmene* (1686), *La Statira* (1690), *Gli equivoci in amore, Pirro e Demetrio* (1694), *La caduta de' decemviri* (1697), *Il prigioniero fortunato* (1698), *L'Eraclea*, *Il Mitridate Eupatore* (1707), *Il Tigrane* (1715), *Il trionfo dell' onore*, *Marco Attilio Regolo* (1719), *La Griselda* (1721), etc.; oratorios *La Maddalena pentita*, *Giuditta*, *San Filippo Neri*; Passion; 16 extant Masses, including five with orchestra; *Salve Regina*, *Stabat Mater*, motets and other church music; over 600 cantatas; 12 *Sinfonie da concerto grosso*; concertos; chamber music; keyboard music.

2. Francesco Scarlatti (b Palermo, 5 Dec 1666; d ? Dublin, *c* 1741), violinist and composer, brother of 1. He became violinist to the court at Naples on Alessandro Scarlatti's appointment as *maestro di cappella* in 1684, and later worked in Palermo. In Vienna in 1715 Fux unsuccessfully recommended him for appointment at court. He was in London 1619–24, and later probably went to Dublin.

Works include operas; church music; cantatas, arias.

3. (Giuseppe) Domenico Scarlatti (b Naples, 26 Oct 1685; d Madrid, 23 Jul 1757), harpsichordist and composer, nephew of 2. Pupil of his father, in 1701 he was appointed organist and composer to the court at Naples, where his operas *L'Ottavia restituita al trono* and *Il Giustino* were produced 1703. Sent by his father to Venice in 1705, he travelled by way to Florence, where he presented himself to Alessandro's patron, Ferdinando de' Medici. In Venice he met Gasparini, and probably studied with him. Moving to Rome, he is said to have engaged with Handel in a contest in harpsichord and organ playing, arranged by Cardinal Ottoboni. He was *maestro di cappella* to Queen Maria Casimira of Poland in Rome 1709–14, and of the Cappella Giulia 1714–19, but the next year went to the Portuguese court in Lisbon. Back in Italy 1724–29, he then went to Seville (later Madrid) in the service of the Spanish court, where he remained until his death.

Works include operas *La silvia* (1710), *Tolomeo ed Alessandro* (1711), *L'Orlando* (1711), *Tetide in Sciro*, *Ifigenia in Aulide* (1713), *Ifigenia in Tauride* (1713), *Amor d'un' ombra*, *Ambleto*, etc.; oratorios; church music; cantatas, etc.; *c* 600 harpsichord pieces (30 of them pub. in his lifetime under the title *Essercizi*), now commonly called sonatas.

4. Giuseppe Scarlatti (b Naples, *c* 1718; d Vienna, 17 Aug 1777), composer, cousin (?) of 3. Wrote operas for the Italian stage, possibly spent some time in Spain, and settled in Vienna in 1757.

Works include operas *Merope* (1740), *Dario* (1741), *I portentosi effetti della Madre Natura* (libretto by Goldoni, 1752), *L'isola disabitata* (1757), *L'amor geloso*, etc.; arias; cantatas; keyboard music.

Scelsi, Giacinto (b La Spezia, 8 Jan 1905; d Rome, 9 Aug 1988), Italian composer. After study in Geneva and Vienna became an early exponent of 12-note techniques (from 1936). Under influence of visit to Tibet, developed an early form of Minimalism (*Four pieces, each*

Scarlatti *The composer Alessandro Scarlatti (1660–1725) established Naples as an important centre of opera during the late 17th century. He was greatly admired by his patrons for the profundity of his works, but his public audience was not always able to appreciate this.*

one on a single note, for small orchestra 1961); *Aion* for orchestra (composed 1961, fp 1985), further evokes virtual stillness. Other works include *Pfhat* and *Konx-Om-Pax* for orchestra (1986), 11 piano suites, five string quartets. Reclusive by nature as well as inspiration, he threatened to kill intrusive photographers.

scena Italian = 'stage, scene', i.e. the subdivision of an act in a dramatic piece; a technical term for operatic solo numbers on a large scale, usually a recitative followed by one or more aria-like sections; also similar pieces designed for concert performance.

scenario, Italian, the sketch or rough draft for the plot of an opera libretto or for the story of a ballet, etc.

Scenes from Goethe's 'Faust' (Schumann) ◊Szenen aus Goethe's 'Faust'.

Scènes Historiques two suites for orchestra by Sibelius: no. 1 in three movements, 1899, revised 1911; no. 2 in three movements, 1912.

This son of mine is an eagle whose wings are grown; he ought not to stay idle in the nest and I ought not to hinder his flight.

Alessandro Scarlatti on Domenico Scarlatti, to
Ferdinand de Medici, 1705

Schaaf, Johannes (b Bad Cannstadt, 7 Apr 1933), German stage director. Produced classical plays at the Stuttgart Schauspielhaus and from 1967 made series of TV films about leading musicians. Has staged *Les Contes d'Hoffmann* at the Vienna Volksoper, *Idomeneo* at the Staatsoper and *Capriccio* at Salzburg (1985). Work at Geneva Opera includes *Eugene Onegin*, *Fidelio* (1989) and *Die Frau ohne Schatten* (1992). From 1987 staged Mozart's Da Ponte operas at Covent Garden in productions which stressed the theatrical conflicts between characters.

Scarlatti

A biographical note

Domenico Scarlatti is perhaps the earliest of many composers who have suffered from the well-meaning attentions of their protective fathers. Scarlatti was born in the same year as Bach and Handel. His father had earned wide fame as a composer of opera, gaining the patronage of ex-Queen Christina of Sweden, who presided over her academy in Rome until 1689. At the age of 20, Scarlatti was sent to study in Venice; there he became friends with Handel. For ten years from 1707, Scarlatti was obliged to work under his father's wing in Rome, composing routine sacred and operatic music. He gained his legal independence at the age of 32, and in 1719 travelled to Lisbon to assist King John V of Portugal in establishing a major centre of Portuguese church music. Scarlatti's artistic freedom was celebrated with the highly original harpsichord sonatas he wrote for the king's daughter Maria. He followed Maria to Seville in 1729, when she married the Spanish crown prince, and in 1733 to Madrid. He now had the opportunity to further develop the expressive possibilities of keyboard technique, adding Moorish and flamenco rhythms to his repertoire.

Schachbrett, (or *Schachtbrett*), German, probably an early form of harpsichord. It is mentioned in Cersne von Minden's *Minneregeln* of 1404. The name derives from an old Germanic word *Schacht*, meaning spring or quill (*cf.* English 'jack').

Schack (originally *Žák*), Benedict (b Mirotice, 7 Feb 1758; d Munich, 10 Dec 1826), Bohemian tenor and composer. A member of Schikaneder's opera co., he was the first Tamino in Mozart's *Magic Flute*. Mozart wrote piano variations on a song probably by him, 'Ein Weib ist das herrlichste Ding' (K613).

Works include *Singspiele* (some with Gerl and others), *Der dumme Gärtner* (1789), *Der Stein der Weisen* (1790), *Der Fall ist noch weit seltner* (sequel to Martín y Soler's *Una cosa rara*, 1790), etc.; also church music.

Schadaeus, Abraham (b Senftenberg, 1566; d Finsterwalde, 10 Oct 1626), German composer. He became *Rektor* of the *Lateinschule* in Speyer in 1603. His *Promptuarium musicum*, a collection of motets, was pub. in Strasbourg in three parts, in 1611, 1612 and 1613. A *bassus generalis* was added to his friend Caspar Vincentius. (A fourth part, 1617, was entirely by Vincentius.)

Schaeffer, Pierre (b Nancy, 14 Aug 1910; d Aix, 19 Aug 1995), French composer, acoustician and novelist. Worked in Paris radio studio from 1942 and in 1948 broadcast a programme of pieces assembled from random noises, made into montage with the use of tape; coined the term 'musique concrète' to define such activity.

Works include (some in collaboration with Pierre Henry), *Étude aux chemins de fer*, *Concerts de bruits* (1948), *Symphonie pour un homme seul* (1950) and *Orphée* (1953). Later turned to writing novels.

Schaeffner, André (b Paris, 7 Feb 1895; d Paris, 11 Aug 1980), French musicologist. Studied at the Schola Cantorum in Paris and after 1920 became music critic to various periodicals. His books include studies of Stravinsky and of the origin of musical instruments. In 1929 he became director of the ethnomusicological section of the Musée de l'Homme in Paris.

Schafer, R Murray (b Sarnia, Ontario, 18 Jul 1933), Canadian composer and teacher. He studied in Toronto and Vienna and worked in England as a journalist. Works employ electronics and involve transformation and motivic distortion: opera *Loving/Toi* (staged Toronto, 1978), *Minnelieder* for mezzo and wind quintet (1956), *St Jean de Brebeuf* for baritone and orchestra (1961), *Requiems for the Party Girl* for soprano and nine instruments (1966), *From the Tibetan Book of the Dead* for soprano, chorus and ensemble (1968), *The Son of Heldenleben* (after a work by Strauss, 1968), *Sappho* for mezzo and ensemble (1970), four string quartets (1970, 1976, 1989, 1988), *In Search of Zoroaster* for male voice, chorus and percussion (1971), *Adieu, Robert Schumann* for mezzo and orchestra (after Clara Schumann's diaries detailing her husband's madness, 1976), *Apocalypsis* for soloist, chorus and orchestra (after St John the Divine, 1980); flute concerto (1985); series of multimedia theatre pieces, including *The Black Theatre of Hermes* (1989) and *The Crown of Ariadne* (1992).

Schäffer, Bogusław (b Lwów, 6 Jun 1929), Polish composer. Studied in Kraków with A Malawski and musicology in Warsaw with Jachimecki. For some of his works he has used graphic notation.

Works include theatre pieces *Miniopera* (1988) and *Liebesblicke* (1989); *Scultura* for orchestra; *Monosonata* for 24 string instruments; *Topofonica* for 40 instruments; *Equivalenze sonore* for percussion instruments; concerto for harpsichord, percussion and orchestra; *Four Movements* for piano and orchestra; *Tertium datum* for clavichord and chamber orchestra; ten symphonies (1960–79); three piano concertos (1957, 1967, 1988); two harpsichord concertos (1958, 1961); violin concerto (1963); *Kesukaan* for strings (1978); concertos for guitar (1984), organ and violin (1984), flute and harp (1986), saxophone (1986) and for violin and three oboes (1987); six string quartets (1954–73).

Schaffrath, Christoph (b Hohenstein near Dresden, 1709; d Berlin, 17 Feb 1763), German harpsichordist, organist and composer. In 1733, when in the service of a Polish prince, he competed unsuccessfully with W F Bach for the post of organist at St Sophia's Church at Dresden, but in 1736 he became chamber musician to the crown prince of Prussia and remained with him when he acceded as Frederick II.

Works include 13 symphonies and overtures for orchestra; harpsichord and violin concertos; chamber music.

Schale, Christian Friedrich (b Brandenburg, 10 Mar 1713; d Berlin, 2 Mar 1800), German organist and composer. Pupil of C F Rolle in Magdeburg, he entered the service of Frederick II of Prussia 1741 and became organist of Berlin Cathedral in 1763. Composed mostly keyboard music.

Schalk, Franz (b Vienna, 27 May 1863; d Edlach, 2 Sept 1931), Austrian conductor. Pupil of Bruckner and, after various engagements, chief conductor at the Vienna Court Opera in succession to Ferdinand Löwe, and director (partly with R Strauss) 1918–29. He first visited England 1898. He was responsible for a spurious revision of Bruckner's symphonies. He conducted Wagner in NY and London (1898–1911) and gave the fp of *Die Frau ohne Schatten* (Vienna, 1919).

Scharwenka, (Franz) Xaver (b Szamotuly, Poznań, 6 Jan 1850; d Berlin, 8 Dec 1924), German-Polish pianist, composer and teacher, brother of Philipp ◊Scharwenka. Studied at Kullak's school of music in Berlin, where the family had settled in 1865, and made his first appearance as a pianist there in 1869. Later he travelled widely, paying his first visit to England in 1879. In 1881 he opened a Conservatory of his own in Berlin, which in 1893 became amalgamated with Klindworth's. In 1891–98 he lived mainly in NY, where he had opened a branch of his school.

Works include opera *Mataswintha* (on Felix Dahn's novel *Ein Kampf um Rom*, 1896); symphony in C minor; four piano concertos (pub. 1876–1908); piano quartet, two piano trios; two cello and piano sonatas; Theme and Variations, Polish dances and numerous other works for piano.

Scharwenka, (Ludwig) Philipp (b Szamotuły, Poznań, 16 Feb 1847; d Bad Nauheim, 16 Jul 1917), German-Polish composer and teacher. On the family's removal to Berlin he studied music at Kullak's school there and remained as teacher until 1881, when he joined his brother's newly opened Conservatory, which he directed in 1891 on the latter's departure for America, together with Hugo Goldschmidt. In 1880 he married the violinist Marianne Stresow (1856–1918).

Works include two symphonies, serenade, Festival Overture, *Liebesnacht*, *Arcadian Suite*, symphonic poems *Frühlingswogen* and *Traum und Wirklichkeit*; violin concerto (1895); *Herbstfeier* and *Sakuntala* (after Kalidasa) for solo voices, chorus and orchestra; piano trio in C♯ minor; three concert pieces for violin and piano, violin and cello studies; *Album polonais*, three sonatas and many other works for piano.

Schat, Peter (b Utrecht, 5 Jun 1935), Dutch composer. Studied in Utrecht and The Hague, and then with Seiber and Boulez. Became well known as an experimental composer, although he later came under the influence of minimalism.

Works include *Mosaics* for orchestra; *Cryptogamen* for baritone and orchestra *Signalement* for six percussion instruments and three double basses; *Improvisations and Symphonies* for wind quintet; *Labyrinth*, work for 'musical theatre' with 'happenings' (produced Amsterdam, 1966); *Houdini*, circus opera (1976); opera *Symposium* (1994) on the life of Tchaikovsky.

Schauspieldirektor, Der, *The Impresario*, play with music by Mozart (libretto by G Stephanie, junior), produced Vienna, Schönbrunn Palace, at court, 7 Feb 1786; first Vienna performance, Kärntnertortheater, 18 Feb 1786. Rivalry between prima donnas Mme Silberklang and Mme Herz as Frank and Puf audition singers.

Schech, Marianne (b Geitbau, 18 Jan 1914), German soprano. She made her debut as Marta in *Tiefland* at Coblenz in 1937; sang widely in Germany and was a member of the Bavarian State Opera 1945–70, notably as Pamina, Chrysothemis, the Marschallin and Sieglinde. NY Met. and CG debuts 1956, both as Venus in *Tannhäuser*. San Francisco 1959, as the Dyer's Wife in the US fp of *Die Frau ohne Schatten*. She recorded Wagner's Senta and Venus, under Franz Konwitschny.

Schechner, Anna (Nanette) (b Munich, 1806; d 29 Apr 1860), German soprano. Pupil of Weber and studied in Italy; first appeared in Munich and in 1826 in Vienna; sang there until 1835 as Leonore, Donna Anna, Euryanthe, and in operas by Gluck and Spontini. She married the painter Karl Waagen 1832.

Scheff, Fritzi (b Vienna, 30 Aug 1879; d New York, 8 Apr 1954), Austrian soprano. Debut Munich 1897, as Donizetti's Marie. CG 1897–1900, as Nedda, Zerlina and Martha. NY Met. 1900–04; debut as Marzelline and also heard as Elsa, Cherubino and Juliette, and in the 1902 local fp of Paderewski's *Manru*. Operetta from 1904.

Scheherazade (Ravel and Rimsky-Korsakov.) ◊Shéhérazade and ◊Shahrazad.

Scheibe, Johann Adolph (b Leipzig, 5 May 1708; d Copenhagen, 22 Apr 1776), German writer on music, critic and composer. Studied law at Leipzig University and in 1736 settled in Hamburg, where he edited the periodical *Der critische Musikus* (1737–40), in which he attacked Bach. He was *Kapellmeister* to the Margrave of Brandenburg-Culmbach 1739–44, and conductor of the court opera in Copenhagen 1744–48.

Works include one opera (*Thusnelde*, 1749); cantatas; Masses and other church music; instrumental music; songs.

Wagner did not like the saxophone: he said it sounds like the word Reckankreuzungsklankwerkzeuge.

Nicolas Slonimsky,
A Thing or Two About Music, 1948

Scheidemann German family of organists and composers.

1. David Scheidemann (b Hamburg; d Hamburg), organist in Wöhrden and subsequently at St Catherine's Church, Hamburg. Pub. a hymn-book with H and J Praetorius and Joachim Decker in 1604, with the tunes in the soprano part, not, as earlier, in the tenor.

2. Heinrich Scheidemann (b Wöhrden, c 1596; d Hamburg, 1663), son of 1. Pupil of his father and later of Sweelinck at Amsterdam. In 1625 he succeeded his father as organist at St Catherine's Church, Hamburg, where on his death he was himself succeeded by Reinken, who was his pupil, as were Fabricius and Weckmann. He contributed to Part V of Rist's hymn-book *Neue himmlische Lieder* (1651).

Works include church music and organ pieces.

Scheidemantel, Karl (b Weimar, 21 Jan 1859; d Weimar, 26 Jun 1923), German baritone. Studied with Bodo Borchers and made his first stage appearance at Weimar in 1878. After further study with Stockhausen he became famous, mainly as a Wagner singer. He first visited London in 1884, when he sang Pizarro, Telramund and Kurwenal, and was first engaged at the Bayreuth Wagner theatre in 1886; sang there until 1892 as Klingsor, Sachs, Amfortas and Wolfram. From 1920 to 1922 he was director of the Dresden Landesoper. He wrote two books on singing.

Scheidl, Theodor (b Vienna, 3 Aug 1880; d Tübingen, 22 Apr 1959), Austrian baritone. Debut Vienna 1910, in *Lohengrin*; Stuttgart 1913–21. Bayreuth 1914–30, as Klingsor, Amfortas and Kurwenal. Also admired as Wagner singer at the Berlin Staatsoper, 1921–32, and at Prague from 1932.

Scheidt, Robert vom (b Bremen, 16 Apr 1879; d Frankfurt, 10 Apr 1964), German baritone. He sang at Cologne 1897–1903 and Hamburg 1903–12. Frankfurt 1912–40, in the fps of Schreker's *Die Gezeichneten* (1918) and *Der Schatzgräber* (1920), and Egk's *Die Zaubergeige* (1935). Bayreuth 1904, as Donner and Klingsor.

Scheidt, Samuel (b Halle, bap. 3 Nov 1587; d Halle, 24 Mar 1654), German organist and composer. Organist at St Maurice's Church, Halle, 1603. Pupil of Sweelinck at Amsterdam. He returned to Halle in 1609, and became court organist to the Margrave of Brandenburg, in his capacity as Protestant administrator of the archbishopric of Magdeburg, and *Kapellmeister* in 1619. He lost his appointment in 1625 as a result of the 30 Years War. His influential *Tabulatura nova* for the organ (1624) was printed in score, not in the old German tablature.

Works include *Cantiones sacrae* for eight voices; sacred concertos for 2–12 voices with instruments; pavans and galliards for four–five voices; *Liebliche Krafft-Blümlein* for two voices and instruments; organ accompaniments for or transcriptions of 100 hymns and psalms; *Tabulatura nova* containing a great variety of organ pieces in three vols.

Schein, Johann Hermann (b Grünhain, Saxony, 20 Jan 1586; d Leipzig, 19 Nov 1630), German composer. After the death of his father, a Lutheran pastor, he went to Dresden as a choirboy in the court chapel in 1599, to the grammar-school at Schulpforta in 1603 and to Leipzig University in 1607. In 1615 he was appointed *Kapellmeister* at the court of Weimar and in 1616 became cantor at St Thomas's School, Leipzig, on the death of Calvisius, remaining there until his death. His music is influenced by Lutheran chorales and by the latest expressive techniques of the early Italian madrigalists.

Works include *Cantiones sacrae* for 5–12 voices; two vols. of sacred concertos for three–five voices with instruments; *Fontana d'Israel* containing biblical words set for four–five voices and instruments; *Cantional* hymn-book with c 80 tunes of his own; songs for five voices, *Venus-Kränzlein*, *Studenten-Schmaus* and *Diletti pastorali*; instrumental dances *Banchetto musicale*; songs with instruments *Musica boscareccia*; wedding and funeral cantatas.

Schelble, Johann Nepomuk (b Hüfingen, Black Forest, 16 May 1789; d Frankfurt, 7 Aug 1837), German singer, teacher and conductor. Studied with Vogler and others, lived and sang in Vienna in 1813–16 and then settled at Frankfurt, where he taught and founded the Caecilian Society in 1818.

Schelle, Johann (b Geissing near Meissen, 6 Sept 1648; d Leipzig, 10 Mar 1710), German organist and composer. He was a choirboy at Dresden, Wolfenbüttel and Leipzig. Studied at Leipzig, became cantor at Eilenburg and in 1677 cantor at St Thomas's Church, Leipzig.

Works include cantatas, songs.

Schelling, Ernest Henry (b Belvidere, NJ, 26 July 1876; d New York, 8 Dec 1939), American pianist and composer. After his debut as a child prodigy at Philadelphia at the age of four, he studied at the Paris Conservatory, also in Vienna with Leschetizky for piano and Bruckner for composition, as well as elsewhere with Paderewski, Moszkowski and others. He toured widely, joined the American army 1918 and later lectured on the orchestra to children in his New York PO Children's concerts (1924–39).

Works include symphony in C minor, *Symphonic Legend* (1904), fantasy *A Victory Ball* and *Morocco* for orchestra; *Fantastic Suite* and *Impressions from an Artist's Life* for piano and orchestra.

Schelomo Hebrew rhapsody for cello and orchestra by Bloch, based on Book of Ecclesiastes; composed 1916, fp NY 3 May 1917, conductor Bloch.

Schemelli, Georg Christian (b Herzberg, c 1678; d Zeitz, 5 Mar 1762), German musician and music editor. Pupil at St Thomas's School, Leipzig, cantor at the palace of Zeitz. His *Musicalisches Gesang-Buch*, edited by Bach, was pub. 1736. On some of the hymns in it Bach wrote chorale preludes.

Schenck, Johan(n) (b Amsterdam, bap. 3 Jun 1660; d c 1712), German or Dutch viola da gamba player and composer. He worked at the electoral court at Düsseldorf and in Amsterdam.

Works include opera *Ceres en Bacchus*; chamber sonatas for two violins, viola da gamba and bass, viola da gamba sonatas and suites.

Schenk, Johann Baptist (b Wiener Neustadt, 30 Nov 1753; d Vienna, 29 Dec 1836), Austrian composer. Pupil of Wagenseil 1774–77, he made his public debut as an opera composer 1785. Beethoven was his pupil in 1793, and he was also a friend of Mozart and Schubert.

Works include *Singspiele: Die Weinlese* (1785), *Die Weihnacht auf dem Lande* (1786), *Achmet und Almanzine*, *Der Dorfbarbier* (1796), *Die Jagd*, *Der Fassbinder* (1802), etc.; Masses and other church music; cantatas *Die Huldigung* and *Der Mai*; ten symphonies; four harp concertos; five string quartets and trios; songs.

Schenk, Manfred (b Stuttgart, 23 Jan 1930), German bass. After study in Stuttgart was a member of the Frankfurt Opera, 1967–90. Sang

Sarastro at Glyndebourne 1973, Hunding at the NY Met. 1977 and Pogner at Bayreuth 1981; has returned as Fasolt, and as Gurnemanz (1992). CG debut 1981, as King Henry in *Lohengrin*. Salzburg Festival 1985, as Nettuno in the Henze/Monteverdi *Ulisse*; other roles include Sachs, Wotan, the Grand Inquisitor and Rocco.

Schenk, Otto (b Vienna, 12 Jun 1930), Austrian producer. Produced *Die Zauberflöte* at Salzburg (Landestheater) 1957. *Lulu* (1962) and *Jenůfa* (1964) at Vienna Staatsoper; later staged *Der Rosenkavalier* (1969) and *Der Freischütz* (1972). *Fidelio* at NY Met. 1970; began *Ring* production with *Die Walküre* in 1986. Completed with *Götterdämmerung* in 1991. Admired by audiences for a naturalistic approach and reluctance to polemicize. Produced an austere *Ballo in maschera* at CG in 1975.

Schenker, Heinrich (b Wisniowczyki, 19 Jun 1868; d Vienna, 13 Jan 1935), Polish-Austrian theorist. Studied with Bruckner at the Vienna Conservatory and on Brahms's recommendation published some early compositions. He taught a number of pupils privately and in his literary works, including *Neue musikalische Theorien und Phantasien* and *Das Meisterwerk in der Musik*, laid down his detailed analytical methods.

Scherchen, Hermann (b Berlin, 21 Jun 1891; d Florence, 12 Jun 1966), German conductor. Self-taught in music, he played the viola in the Blüthner Orchestra 1907–10, also playing with the Berlin PO. He made his debut as a conductor in 1912 with Schoenberg's *Pierrot lunaire*, and in 1914 became conductor of the Riga SO, being interned in Russia during World War I. After the war he founded the Neue Musikgesellschaft and edited the periodical *Melos* (1920–1). From 1928 to 1933 he was conductor of the Königsberg Radio Orchestra. He was especially well known as a conductor of new music, the cause of which he championed throughout his life; he gave the fps of Dallapiccola's *Il prigioniero* (1950) and Henze's *König Hirsch* (1956) and the first German production of *Moses und Aron* (Berlin, 1959).

Scherchen-Hsiao, Tona (b Neuchatel, 12 Mar 1938), Swiss-born French composer, daughter of Hermann ◊Scherchen. Studied with her parents, with Henze at Salzburg, with Messiaen in Paris (1963–65) and with Ligeti in Vienna.

Works include *Shen* for six percussion (1968); *Khouang* for orchestra (1968); *Tao*, for contralto and orchestra (1971); *Vague T'ao* for orchestra (1975); *L'Invitation au voyage* for chamber orchestra (1977); *Ziguidor*, wind quintet (1977); *Tzing* for brass quintet (1979); *L'illegitime* for orchestra and tape (1986); electronic and mixed-media pieces *Un cadre univers ouvert* (1985), *Between*, son et lumière for trombone and tape (1986), *Spaceflight* for tape (1987) and *Fuite* for low voice and ensemble (1987).

Scherer, Sebastian Anton (b Ulm, Oct 1631; d Ulm, 26 Aug 1712), German organist and composer. He rose through various posts to that of organist of Ulm Cathedral in 1671.

Works include Masses, motets and psalms; sonatas for two violins and bass; organ pieces; suites for flute.

Schering, Arnold (b Breslau, 2 Apr 1877; d Berlin, 7 Mar 1941), German musicologist. Studied at Leipzig University, where in 1907 he became lecturer and later professor of music. From 1909 he also lectured at the Conservatory. In 1920 he became professor at Halle University and in 1928 at Berlin University. His books include studies of the early violin concerto, the development of the oratorio and sonata, the performance of early music, early organ and chamber music and a series of attempts to prove that Beethoven's sonatas and quartets are based on Shakespeare's plays and other dramatic works.

scherzando Italian = 'playful, humorous, skittish'; a direction written by composers over passages intended to be performed in that manner. It may also be used as an adj. in tempo directions, e.g. *allegretto scherzando*.

Scherzi, Gli, *The Jokes*, one of the nicknames of Haydn's six string quartets, op. 33, composed 1781. Also known as the *Russian* quartets or *Jungfernquartette*.

Scherz, List und Rache, *Jest, Cunning and Revenge*, operetta by Bruch (libretto by Goethe, altered by L Bischoff), produced Cologne, 14 Jan 1858.

For other settings ◊Goethe.

scherzo one of the two middle movements, more usually the third, of a four-movement symphony, sonata or other sonata-form work, where it displaced the minuet. It does not occur regularly before the early 19th c., being established mainly by Beethoven and Schubert; but the term scherzo dates back to the 17th c., when Italian canzonets were often called 'scherzi musicali' and instrumental pieces were also sometimes pub. under that title. (For an early use of the name Haydn's *Gli Scherzi*) The scherzo, having arisen from the minuet, is normally in fast triple time, generally 3–4 with one beat in a bar, and it has as a rule a contrasting trio section. But examples in duple or quadruple time occur, e.g. in Beethoven's E♭ major piano sonata, op. 31 no. 3, in Mendelssohn and in Schumann. Sometimes the trio occurs twice, e.g. in Beethoven's seventh symphony, or there may be, especially in Schumann, two different trios. A coda may be based on elements derived from the trio. There are very successful scherzos which do not conform to the classical pattern, e.g. Chopin's. In the twentieth century Scherzo movements have often assumed sharper, more sarcastic dimensions: Mahler's 9th symphony and Shostakovich's 10th.

Schiavetto, Giulio, Italian composer, active in Dalmatia during the second half of the 16th c. His madrigals and motets, pub. in Venice in 1563 and 1565 respectively, were dedicated to Gerolamo Savorgnano, bishop of Šibenik.

Schibler, Armin (b Kreuzlingen, Lake Constance, 20 Nov 1920; d Zurich, 7 Sept 1986), Swiss composer. Studied music while at school at Aarau and then at the Zurich Conservatory. In 1942 he became a pupil of Burkhard and later in England with Rubbra and Tippett. He had local success in a variety of musical forms.

Works include oratorio *Media in vita*; operas *Der spanische Rosenstock* (1950), *The Devil in the Winter Palace* (1953), *The Feet in the Fire*; three chamber ballets; cantatas *Marignano*, *Vision des Mittelalters*, *Die Hochzeit* (Gotthelf) and *Cantata domestica*; three symphonies (1946–57), symphonic variations, toccata and fugue for string orchestra; violin concerto, piano concerto, horn concerto (1956), trombone concerto (1957), percussion concerto, fantasy for violin and orchestra; concerto for violin, cello and strings; toccata, interlude and fugue for wind instruments; piano quartet; five string quartets (1945–75), violin and piano sonata; toccata for organ; *Circulus Fugae* for piano; songs.

Schicht, Johann Gottfried (b Reichenau near Zittau, 29 Sept 1753; d Leipzig, 16 Feb 1823), German harpsichordist and composer. Studied law at Leipzig University but turned to music and was engaged as harpsichordist by J A Hiller for his concerts, later succeeding him as their conductor In 1810 he was appointed cantor at St Thomas's Church.

Works include three oratorios, church music, chamber works.

Schick (born *Hamel*), Margarete Luise (b Mainz, 26 Apr 1773; d Berlin, 29 Apr 1809), German soprano. Studied at Würzburg and with Righini at Mainz, where she made her debut in 1788. In 1791 she married Ernst Schick and in 1793 they were both engaged by Frederick William II of Prussia and went to Berlin. She became successful in operas by Mozart and was best known in the title role of Gluck's *Iphigénie en Tauride*.

Schicksalslied, *Song of Destiny*, a setting by Brahms for chorus and orchestra of a poem in Hölderlin's *Hyperion*, op. 54, composed in 1871; fp Karlsruhe, 18 Oct 1871.

Schiedermair, Ludwig (b Regensburg, 7 Dec 1876; d Bensberg near Cologne, 30 Apr 1957), German music scholar. Studied with Sandberger and Beer-Walbrunn at Munich, where he took a degree in 1901. After further studies with Riemann and Kretzschmar in Berlin he became lecturer at Marburg and in 1914 professor of music at Bonn University. There he became director of the Beethoven Archives, and among his books are bibliographical works on Beethoven and an edition of Mozart's letters with an iconographical volume.

Schiff, Andras (b Budapest, 21 Dec 1953), Hungarian pianist. He studied at the Liszt Academy, Budapest and with George Malcolm in

London. He made his debut in Budapest and won prizes at the Tchaikovsky Competion, Moscow, in 1974 and the Leeds International in 1975. New York concerto debut 1978, recital 1989; Salzburg debut 1982. He has a wide repertory but is best known for his interpretations of Bach notably in the Goldberg Variations, Well-Tempered Clavier and English Suites.

Schiff, Heinrich (b Gmunden, 18 Nov 1951), Austrian cellist and conductor. He studied in Vienna and with André Navarra in Detmold. He has won prizes in competitions in Warsaw, Geneva and Vienna, and has appeared as soloist with orchestras in Vienna, London, Stockholm and Tokyo. Also plays in recital and made US debut in 1982. Debut as conductor with the Vienna SO in 1984; artistic director of the Northern Sinfonia from 1990. Henze wrote the *Liebeslieder* (1986) for cello and orchestra for him.

Schikaneder, (Johann Josef) Emanuel (b Straubing, 1 Sept 1751; d Vienna, 21 Sept 1812), German actor, singer, playwright and theatre manager. Settled in Vienna in 1784. Author or part-author with Ludwig Gieseke of the libretto of Mozart's *Magic Flute*, which he produced with himself as Papageno. He also wrote libretti for Schack, Gerl, Süssmayr, Woelfl, Seyfried, Winter and others.

Schiller, (Johann Christoph) Friedrich von (1759–1805), German poet and dramatist. ◊Bride of Messina (Fibich); ◊Briganti (Mercadante); ◊Bruch (*Lied von der Glocke* and *Macht des Gesanges*); ◊'Choral' Symphony (Beethoven); ◊Costa (*Don Carlos*); ◊Don Carlos (Verdi); ◊Giovanna d'Arco (Verdi); ◊Guillaume Tell (Rossini); ◊Ideale (Liszt); ◊Luisa Miller (Verdi); ◊Maid of Orleans (Tchaikovsky); ◊Mascagni (*Ode to Joy*); ◊Masnadieri (Verdi); ◊Seyfried (*Räuber* and *Jungfrau von Orleans*); ◊Smetana (*Wallenstein's Camp*); ◊Turandot (Weber); ◊Vaccai (*Giovanna d'Arco* and *Sposa di Messina*); ◊Zumsteeg (*Räuber*; *Wallensteins Lager* and *Ritter Toggenburg*).

42 songs by Schubert.

Schillinger, Joseph (b Kharkov, 31 Aug 1895; d New York, 23 Mar 1943), Russian, later American, composer and theoretician. Studied at St Petersburg Conservatory with Tcherepnin, among others, and then taught at Kharkov Music Academy 1918–22, and 1926–28 in Leningrad. In 1929 he settled in the USA, teaching a mathematical method of his own; among his many pupils was Gershwin. He pub. his system in a number of books, and also some compositions, including *March of the Orient*; *First Airphonic Suite* for theremin, orchestra and piano; piano pieces.

The oldest, truest, most beautiful organ of music, the origin to which alone our music owes its being, is the human voice.

Richard Wagner, quoted in *Opera and Drama*, 1851

Schillings, Max von (b Düren, Rhineland, 19 Apr 1868; d Berlin, 24 Jul 1933), German conductor and composer. Studied at Bonn and Munich, where he settled, taking part in the Wagner performances at Bayreuth. In 1908 he went to Stuttgart, where he gradually rose to the post of general music director of the Court Opera. In 1919 he went to Berlin as director of the Staatsoper. His best known work is the opera *Mona Lisa* in which his wife, the soprano Barbara Kemp, sang the lead.

Works include operas *Ingwelde* (1894), *Der Pfeifertag* (1899), *Moloch* (after Hebbel, 1906) and *Mona Lisa* (1915); incidental music for Aeschylus's *Orestes* and Goethe's *Faust*; symphonic fantasies *Meergruss* and , symphonic prologue, *Oedipus* (after Sophocles) for orchestra; recitations with orchestra including Wildenbruch's *Hexenlied*; violin concerto (1910), *Zweigespräch* for violin, cello and small orchestra (1896); *Hochzeitslied* for solo voices, chorus and orchestra (1910); *Dem Verklärten* (Schiller) and *Glockenlieder* for solo voice and orchestra; string quartet in E minor, string quintet in E♭ major; improvisation for violin and piano.

Schindler, Anton (b Meedl near Neustadt, Moravia, 13 Jun 1795; d Bockenheim near Frankfurt, 16 Jan 1864), Austrian violinist and writer on music. Studied in Vienna, met Beethoven in 1814, played at his concerts and later became his factotum and cared for him on an almost daily basis in the 1820s. He was an early biographer of Beethoven but he was guilty of forging some entries in the composer's conversation books (used by him as a means of communication after total deafness had set in). He was successively leader of the orchestra at the Josephstadt Theatre and the Kärntnertortheater, and later music director at Münster and Aachen.

Schiøtz, Aksel (b Roskilde, 1 Sept 1906; d Copenhagen, 19 Apr 1975), Danish tenor. He studied in Copenhagen and made his debut there in 1939, as Ferrando. He gave his first Lieder recital in 1942 and was later widely admired in Schubert and Schumann. In 1946 he sang the Male Chorus in the first production of Britten's *Rape of Lucretia*, at Glyndebourne. After a brain tumour operation in 1950 he was heard occasionally as a baritone, and taught in Canada and the USA. Returned to Denmark in 1968.

Schipa, Tito (actually Raffaele Attilio Amadeo) (b Lecce, 2 Jan 1889; d New York, 16 Dec 1965), Italian tenor. First studied composition, producing some songs and piano pieces. Then studied singing, making his debut in Vercelli in 1910 as Alfredo. From 1919 to 1932 he was a member of the Chicago Civic Opera and from 1932 to 1935 sang at the NY Met. as Don Ottavio and in operas by Thomas, Mascagni and Massenet, becoming admired for his ease and elegance of delivery. He lived in the USA until 1941, when he returned to Italy and sang there until 1952; concert tour of Russia 1957.

Works include operetta *La Principessa Liana*; a Mass; a Hosanna.

Schippers, Thomas (b Kalamazoo, MI, 9 Mar 1930; d New York, 16 Dec 1977), American conductor. First appeared in public aged six, at the piano, and became a church organist aged 14. From 1944 to 1945 he studied at the Curtis Institute in Philadelphia and 1946–47 privately with O Samaroff. He also studied at Yale University and the Juilliard; made his debut as a conductor with the Lemonade Opera Co. in 1948; started an association with the operas of Menotti in 1950. After appearances with the NY City Opera Co. and the NY PO, he appeared at the NY Met; led the production of Barber's *Antony and Cleopatra* which opened the new house at Lincoln Center. Bayreuth 1963, *Die Meistersinger*; London, CG, 1968, *Elektra*.

Schira, Francesco (b Malta, 21 Aug 1809; d London, 15 Oct 1883), Italian composer and conductor. Studied at the Conservatory of Milan and produced his first opera there in 1832, on the strength of which he was engaged as conductor and composer for the Opera at Lisbon, where he also taught at the Conservatory. In 1842 he left for Paris in the hope of obtaining a French librettist, but met the manager of the Princess's Theatre in London, who engaged him as conductor. In 1844 he went to Drury Lane as Benedict's successor and in 1848 to CG. He remained in London to his death. In 1873 the Birmingham Festival commissioned a cantata from him.

Works include operas *Elena e Malvina* (1832), *I cavalieri di Valenza* (1837), *Il fanatico per la musica*, *Kenilworth* (in English, after Scott), *Mina* (1849), *Theresa, the Orphan of Geneva* (1850), *Niccolo de' Lapi*, *Selvaggia* (1875), *Lia*, operetta *The Ear-Ring*; cantata *The Lord of Burleigh* (after Tennyson); vocal trios and duets; songs.

Schirmer, G, Inc., firm of US music publishers founded jointly in NY (1861) by Gustav Schirmer and Bernard Beer; Schirmer in full control from 1966. Composers published by the firm include Schoenberg, Harris, Barber, Schuman and Menotti.

Schläger German = lit. 'beaters'; sometimes used in scores, etc. as an abbr. for percussion. Also in the singular, a popular song.

Schlaginstrumente German = lit. 'beaten instruments' = percussion instruments.

Schlagobers, *Whipped Cream* in Viennese dialect, ballet by R Strauss (choreography by H Kröller), produced Vienna, Opera, 9 May 1924.

Schlagzither German = lit. 'striking-zither'; a zither played by striking the strings with hammers, i.e. a ◊dulcimer rather than a zither.

Schlegel, August Wilhelm von (1767–1845), German poet, critic and translator. ◊Fierrabras (Schubert).

Seven poems by Schlegel set as songs by Schubert.

schleppen German = 'to drag'; sometimes used by German composers as a negative imperative, *nicht schleppen*, 'do not drag'.

Schlick, Arnolt (b Heidelberg, before 1460; d Heidelberg, after 1521), German organist, composer and theorist. His early life was spent in Heidelberg, but he subsequently travelled widely: to Frankfurt in 1486, where he played the organ during the festivities for the coronation of Maximilian I; to Holland in 1490; to Strasbourg (many times); to Worms in 1495, where he met Sebastian Virdung; and subsequently to Speyer, Hagenau and elsewhere. During these journeys he gained an enormous reputation for testing new organs. He was blind, probably from infancy.

In 1511 he pub. his *Spiegel der Orgelmacher und Organisten*, a treatise on organ building and playing. The *Tabulaturen etlicher Lobgesang und Lidlein* (Mainz, 1512) followed; it was the first printed book of keyboard music to appear in Germany, and contained liturgical organ music, lute pieces and songs with lute. He also wrote music for the coronation of Charles V in Aachen, 1520.

Schlick, Barbara (b Würzburg, 21 Jul 1943), German soprano. Sang widely in concert from 1966, notably with Adolf Scherbaum's Baroque Ensemble; other concerts with the chamber orchestra Paul Kuentz (tour of USA 1972) and the Monteverdi Choir under Jürgen Jürgens. Sang in C P Bach's *Die letzten Leiden* at the 1988 York Festival and has appeared in a Haydn series at the South Bank, London, and in Mozart's Requiem under Ton Koopman. Also admired in Passions and cantatas by J S Bach, Vivaldi's Gloria, and *Messiah*. Recordings include Handel's Cleopatra, conducted by René Jacobs, and Rodelinda, under Michael Schneider.

Schlick, Johann Konrad (b ? Münster, 1748; d Gotha, 12 Jul 1818), German cellist and composer. He worked in the episcopal chapel at Münster, and in 1777 entered the service of the court in Gotha. He married the violinist Regina Strinasacchi in 1785.

Works include concertos; string quintets and quartets; piano trios; cello sonatas; guitar pieces.

Schlosser, Karl (b Amberg, 17 Oct 1835; d Utting am Ammersee, 2 Sept 1916), German tenor. His early career was in Switzerland; sang at Munich 1868–1904 and created David in *Die Meistersinger*. Created Mime in *Siegfried* (Bayreuth 1876) and sang the role with Neumann's co. in London 1882. Other roles included Max, Almaviva and Beckmesser.

Schlusnus, Heinrich (b Braubach, 6 Aug 1888; d Frankfurt, 19 Jun 1952), German baritone. Studied with Bachner in Berlin and made his debut in Frankfurt in 1912 as a concert singer, and as an opera singer in Hamburg in 1915. From 1915 to 1917 he was a member of the Nuremberg Opera, and from 1917 to 1945 of the Berlin Staatsoper. His last role was Rigoletto (Frankfurt 1948). He took part in the pre-World War II Verdi revival and sang Amfortas at Bayreuth in 1933.

Schlüssel German = lit. 'key' = clef.

Schlüter, Erna (b Oldenburg, 5 Feb 1904; d Hamburg, 1 Dec 1969), German soprano. Debut Oldenburg 1922; Mannheim from 1925, Düsseldorf 1930–40. She appeared at Hamburg 1940–56 and was the first Ellen Orford there (1947). NY Met. 1946–47, as Brünnhilde and Isolde. Salzburg 1948, Leonore. Sang as guest at CG, Vienna and Brussels. Well known as Elektra.

Schmedes, Erik (b Gjentofte near Copenhagen, 27 Aug 1866; d Vienna, 23 Mar 1931), Danish tenor. Studied in Germany and Austria and with Padilla in Paris; made his first stage appearance at Wiesbaden in 1891. From 1898 to 1924 he sang at the Vienna Court Opera, at first under Mahler, and in 1899 he was first engaged for the Wagner theatre at Bayreuth; sang there until 1906 as Siegfried and Parsifal. Other roles included Cavaradossi, Palestrina and Florestan.

Schmeltzl, Wolfgang (b Kemnat, Upper Palatinate, *c* 1500; d *c* 1560), German composer. He became cantor at Amberg and married there, but later became a Catholic priest and left his family. He was a schoolmaster in Vienna in 1540.

Works include a book of songs, quodlibets and folksong settings for four–five voices.

Schmelzer, (Johann) Heinrich (b Scheibs, Lower Austria, *c* 1623;

d Prague, Mar 1680), Austrian composer, father of Andreas ◊Schmelzer. He was chamber musician at the Austrian court in Vienna from 1649, assistant conductor from 1671 and first conductor from 1679.

Works include ballet music for *c* 40 operas by ◊Draghi and others; *Missa nuptialis* and other church music; instrumental sonatas including the *Sonatae unarum fidium* (1664) for violin and coninuo, the earliest of their kind; trumpet fanfares.

schmetternd German = 'brassy, brazen, clanging'; the term is prescribed, like the French *cuivré*, when that kind of tone is required of brass instruments, especially horns.

Schmid(t), Bernhard the Elder (b ? Strasbourg, 1535; d Strasbourg, 1592), German composer and poet. He pub. a collection of music arranged for organ in two parts: the first contained motets, the second secular songs and dances (Strasbourg, 1577).

Schmid(t), Bernhard the Younger (b Strasbourg, bap. 1 Apr 1567; d Strasbourg, 1625), German composer, son of Bernhard ◊Schmidt the Elder. His own collection of organ arrangements, highly ornamented, was pub. at Strasbourg 1607.

Schmid, Erich (b Balsthal, 1 Jan 1907), Swiss conductor. Studied in Frankfurt 1927–30, and with Schoenberg in Berlin. Music director at Glarus 1934–39 and conductor of the Zurich Tonhalle Orchestra 1949–57, giving works by Schibler, Huber, Kelterborn and Conrad Beck. Beromunster Radio SO 1959–72, and guest with all the BBC orchestras in Britain, 1978–82. Brahms festival in San Diego.

Schmidt, Andreas (b Dusseldorf, 1959), German baritone. Studied with Fischer-Dieskau in Berlin and made his debut at the Deutsche Oper there in 1984, as Malatesta; returned to Berlin 1987, as Oedipus in the fp of Rihm's opera and as Ryuji in the premiere of Henze's *Das verratene Meer*. CG, London from 1986, as Valentin and Guglielmo. Concerts include Mephistopheles in the Berlioz *Faust* at the London Barbican and Papageno at the Proms. Salzburg opera debut 1990, as Olivier in *Capriccio*; sang Lysiart in *Euryanthe* at the 1993 Aix-en-Provence Festival.

Schmidt, Bernhard, Bernard ◊Smith.

Schmidt, Franz (b Pressburg, 22 Dec 1874; d Perchtoldsdorf, 11 Feb 1939), Austrian cellist, pianist and composer. Studied at the Vienna Conservatory and in 1896 became cellist in the Hofoper orchestra, under Mahler from 1897. He left in 1910 to become piano professor at the Vienna Music Academy, of which he became director in 1925. He also appeared as concert pianist. As a composer he was largely unaffected by the innovations of his contemporaries; his success in Austria has been based on his kinship with Bruckner; the Intermezzo from *Notre Dame*, the 4th symphony and the biblical oratorio *Das Buch mit sieben Siegeln* are his most representative pieces.

Works include operas *Notre-Dame* (after Hugo, 1914) and *Fredigundis* (1922); oratorio *Das Buch mit sieben Siegeln* (1938); four symphonies (1899, 1913, 1928, 1933) chaconne and *Variations on a Hussar's Song* for orchestra; variations on a theme by Beethoven for piano and orchestra; string quartet (1925), piano quintet, two clarinet quintets (1932, 1938); seven organ works.

Schmidt, Gustav (b Weimar, 1 Sept 1816; d Darmstadt, 11 Sept 1882), German composer and conductor. Studied with Hummel and others at Weimar and with Mendelssohn at Leipzig. He began as opera conductor at Brno and then served in the same capacity in several German towns, last at Darmstadt.

Works include operas *Prinz Eugen der edle Ritter*, *Weibertreue*, *La Réole*, *Alibi*; incidental music for a play based on Dickens's *Christmas Carol*; male-voice choruses; songs.

Schmidt, Johann Christoph, senior and junior, John Christopher ◊Smith.

Schmidt, Joseph (b Davidende, 4 Mar 1904; d Girenbad, 16 Nov 1942), Romanian-born German tenor. He sang in the synagogue at Czernowitz and studied at Vienna. In 1928 he was heard on Berlin radio in *Idomeneo*. His diminutive stature prevented a stage career but he gained a huge following through records, concerts and films: the 1932 film *Ein Lied geht um die Welt* further increased his popularity. With the rise of the Nazis he was obliged to tour Europe and America. He escaped to Switzerland but died in an internment camp, near Zurich.

Schmidt, Ole (b Copenhagen, 14 Jul 1928), Danish conductor and composer. Studied in Copenhagen and conducted the Royal Ballet and Opera there 1959–65. Chief conductor of the Danish Radio SO from 1971, Arhus SO 1979–85. London debut with the BBC SO 1977, returning with all the regional orchestras. LSO concert 1980, in Havergal Brian's *Gothic* Symphony. US debut with the Oakland SO, 1980. Guested with the RNCM 1986–89 and led the first Czech-language performance in England of *From the House of the Dead* (1989). Has composed two symphonies and five string quartets.

Schmidt, Trudelise (b Saarbrücken, 7 Nov 1943), German mezzo. Debut Saarbrücken; sang at Düsseldorf from 1969, Hamburg and Munich from 1971. Bayreuth debut 1975, in *The Ring*. Glyndebourne 1976, Dorabella. Guest appearances at Salzburg and Milan (Fatima in *Oberon* 1989). Among her best roles are Strauss's Composer and Octavian, Mozart's Cherubino and Idamante, and Janáček's Vixen. *Iphigénie en Tauride* and *Mathis der Maler* are among her recordings.

Schmidt, Wolfgang (b Kassel, 1954), German tenor. Sang first with the Pocket Opera of Nuremberg, then at the Court Theatre, Bayreuth. Has sung at Dortmund from 1986, notably as Otello and Siegfried, and at Bregenz in 1989, as Wagner's Erik. Salzburg Festival 1991 in *Die Zauberflöte*; Bayreuth 1992–94, as Tannhäuser and as Siegfried in a new production of the *Ring* conducted by James Levine.

Schmidt-Isserstedt, Hans (b Berlin, 5 May 1900; d Hamburg, 28 May 1973), German conductor. Studied with Schreker and also at the University of Cologne, graduating in 1923. He began his career at the Wuppertal opera and then 1928–31 conducted at Rostock, 1931–33 at Darmstadt, and 1935–42 was principal conductor at the Hamburg Staatsoper. He was director of the Deutsche Oper in Berlin 1942–45 and then chief conductor of the North German Radio SO. He gave *Figaro* at Glyndebourne in 1958 and *Tristan* at CG, London, in 1962.

Schmieder, Wolfgang (b Bromberg, 29 May 1901; d Fürstenfeldbruck, 8 Nov 1990), German musicologist. After study at Heidelberg he was archivist at Breitkopf and Härtel in Leipzig, 1933–42. Head of the music division at Frankfurt State Library, 1946–63. In 1950 published thematic catalogue of J S Bach's music (the Bach-Werke-Verzeichnis) which provides standard numbering for the composer's works (preceded by initials BWV).

Schmiege, Marilyn (b Milwaukee, 1954), American mezzo. Studied at Boston University and the Zurich Opera School. Debut as Dorabella at Wuppertal, 1978. Sang at the Theater am Gärtnerplatz, Munich, 1978–82, as Rosina, Cherubino, and Hänsel. Sang Rossi's Orfeo at La Scala in 1983 and has appeared as Octavian and the Composer at the Vienna Staatsoper. Concert repertory includes *Das Lied von der Erde* (Aldeburgh 1985). Marguerite in the Berlioz *Faust* and cantatas by Haydn. Sang Waltraute in *Götterdämmerung* at the Théâtre du Châtelet, Paris, 1994.

Schmitt, Florent (b Blamont, 28 Sept 1870; d Neuilly-sur-Seine, 17 Aug 1958), French composer. Studied music at Nancy from 1887 and in 1889 was sent to the Paris Conservatory, where he was first a pupil of Dubois and Lavignac and afterwards of Massenet and Fauré for composition. Won the Prix de Rome in 1900 and wrote his first mature works during his three years in Rome. His most successful work is the ballet *La Tragédie de Salome* (revised as a symphonic poem 1910). Taking Strauss's recent example as a starting point Schmitt also admits the influence of such colourful contemporaries as Debussy and Massenet. Director, Lyon Conservatory 1922–24.

Works include ballets *La Tragédie de Salomé* (1907), *Le Petit Elfe Ferme-l'œil* (1924), *Reflets, Ourvasi* and *Oriane et le Prince d'Amour* (1938), incidental music for Shakespeare's *Antony and Cleopatra* (translated by Gide); film music for an adaptation of Flaubert's *Salammbô* (1925); Psalm 46 for soprano solo, chorus, organ and orchestra.

Symphonic study *Le Palais hanté* (after Poe), symphony (1958), *Trois Rapsodies, Ronde burlesque, Çancunik, Kermesse-Valse, Symphonie concertante* and *Suite sans esprit de suite* for orchestra; *Légende* for saxophone and orchestra (1918), *Final* for cello and orchestra; piano quintet, *Lied et Scherzo* for double wind quintet, *Andante et Scherzo for chromatic harp and string quartet, Suite en Rocaille* for strings, flute and harp, *Sonatine en trio* for flute, clarinet and harpsichord (or piano), string quartet (1949), string trio; *Sonate libre* for violin and piano; piano pieces.

Schmitt, (Georg) Aloys (b Hanover, 2 Feb 1827; d Dresden, 15 Oct 1902), German conductor, pianist and composer. Pupil of his father, the pianist and composer Aloys Schmitt (1788–1866). He toured widely in Europe as pianist and after various conductor's posts settled at Dresden in 1893 as director of the Mozart Society. He married the singer Cornelia Czany (1851–1906) and completed and edited Mozart's unfinished C minor Mass.

Works include opera *Trilby* (adapted from Nodier by Scribe), *Das Wunderwasser* and *Maienzauber*; incidental music for plays; overtures and other orchestral works; concert piece for oboe and orchestra; string quartets, piano trios; piano pieces; songs.

Schmittbauer, Joseph Aloys (b Bamberg, 8 Nov 1718; d Karlsruhe, 24 Oct 1809), German composer. Pupil of Jommelli, he was *Kapellmeister* of Cologne Cathedral 1775–77, and at the court at Karlsruhe from 1777 to his retirement in 1804.

Works include operas *L'isola disabitata* (1762), *Lindor und Ismene* (1771), *Herkules auf dem Oeta* (1772), *Betrug aus Liebe*, etc.; much church music; cantatas; symphonies; concertos; chamber music.

Schmitt-Walter, Karl (b Gernesheim am Rhein, 29 Dec 1900; d Kreuth, Oberbayern, 14 Jan 1985), German baritone. Studied in Nuremberg and made his debut there in 1921. After singing in Wiesbaden 1929–34 he was engaged in Berlin until 1950. Munich 1950–61; appeared at CG, London, 1953 with the Co. as the Count in the British premiere of *Capriccio*. He sang Papageno at Salzburg and from 1956–61 was Beckmesser at Bayreuth.

I know two kinds of audience only – one coughing and one not coughing.
Artur Schnabel, *My Life and Music*, 1961

Schnabel, Artur (b Lipnik, Austria, 17 Apr 1882; d Axenstein, Switzerland, 15 Aug 1951), Austrian pianist and composer. Studied piano with Essipova and Leschetizky, music in general with Mandyczewski in Vienna. He married the singer Therese Behr in 1905, travelled extensively and made a great reputation for himself as a thoughtful interpreter, particularly of Beethoven, Schubert and Brahms. He taught in Berlin, but was forced by the Nazi rule to leave in 1933; settled in USA in 1939, but later returned to Europe. Frequent recitals with his wife and in various ensembles with Casals, Hindemith, Fournier and Szigeti.

Works include symphonies and other orchestral music; piano concerto; string quartet and other chamber music; piano pieces and atonal cadenzas for Mozart's piano concertos.

Schnabelflöte German = lit. 'beak flute', from French *flûte à bec* = recorder.

Schnadahüpfeln, Austrian dialect, folk dances, often sung with words, of the *Ländler* or slow waltz type as a rule, belonging to the Tyrol or other Austrian mountain regions.

Schnaut, Gabriele (b Mannheim, 1951), German soprano. Studied in Frankfurt and Berlin, singing first in Darmstadt (1978–80). Bayreuth Festival from 1977, as Waltraute, Venus and Sieglinde. US debut Chicago as Fricka in a concert of *Das Rheingold*. Sang Ophelia in the fp of Rihm's *Die Hamletmaschine* (1987) and appeared at CG from 1988, as Ortrud and Sieglinde. US stage debut at San Francisco 1991, as Isolde. Sang Brünnhilde at Cologne 1990 and Théâtre du Châtelet, Paris, 1994.

Schnebel, Dieter (b Lahr, Baden, 14 Mar 1930), German composer and theologian. Has taught religious studies from 1953. Influenced by Kagel and Stockhausen, has produced such 'non-music' items as music for reading (*mo- no*, 1969), and for conductor only (*Nostalgie*, 1969). His orchestral pieces include *Webern- Variationen* (1972), *Wagner-Idyll* (1980), *Beethoven-Sinfonie* (1985), *Mahler- Momente* (1985) and *Sinfonie X* (1987–92).

Schnéevoigt, Georg (Lennart) (b Viipuri, 8 Nov 1872; d Malmö, 28 Nov 1947), Finnish conductor. Studied in Helsinki, Leipzig, Dresden and Vienna, became cellist in the Helsinki orchestra and in 1901 decided to make conducting his whole career. He held several appointments abroad and toured extensively. From 1930 to 1947 he conducted the Malmö SO, and from 1932 to 1941 was permanent conductor of the Finnish National Orchestra in succession to Kajanus.

Schneider, (Johann Christian) Friedrich (b Alt-Waltersdorf near Zittau, 3 Jan 1786; d Dessau, 23 Nov 1853), German composer, teacher and conductor. Studied at Zittau and at Leipzig while a student at the University. He advanced through several posts there to that of organist at St Thomas's Church and conductor at the municipal theatre. In Dec 1810 at Leipzig he gave the first known performance of Beethoven's Emperor Concerto. In 1821 he moved to Dessau, where he was appointed *Kapellmeister* to the ducal court. There he founded a vocal academy and a music school.

Works include seven operas; oratorios *Die Höllenfahrt des Messias*, *Das Weltgericht*, *Die Sündflut*, *Das verlorene Paradies* (after Milton), *Das befreite Jerusalem*, *Gethsemane und Golgotha* and several others; 14 Masses and other church music; 25 cantatas; 23 symphonies, overture on 'God save the King'; six concertos; 60 sonatas; 400 male-voice part-songs; 200 songs.

Schneider, Alexander (b Vilna, 21 Oct 1908; d New York, 2 Feb 1993), Russian-born American violinist and conductor. He studied in Frankfurt and worked in Germany before joining the Budapest Quartet as second violin (1932–44, 1955–64). Emigrated to US 1939 and became active in chamber music and as teacher. Co-founded Prades Festival 1950, with Casals. Founded Brandenburg Players 1972 and at the end of his career often led the Chamber Orchestra of Europe (London Concerts 1991).

Schneider, Johann Gottlob (b Alt-Gersdorf, 28 Oct 1789; d Dresden, 13 Apr 1864), German organist and composer, brother of Friedrich ◊Schneider. Studied at Leipzig and became organist to the University there, remaining until 1825, when he became court organist at Dresden. His fame was enormous and he had many distinguished pupils, including Mendelssohn, Schumann and Liszt.

Works include fantasy and fugue in D minor, and others for organ.

The Idiot's name is Vova, diminutive of Vladimir, Lenin's first name . . . and he sets about destroying the lives of those he has invaded.

Gerard McBurney on Schnittke's opera *Life with an Idiot* in *Opera*, 1995

Schneider, Peter (b Vienna, 26 Mar 1939), Austrian conductor. After study with Swarowsky in Vienna conducted *Giulio Cesare* at the Salzburg Landestheater in 1959. Conducted at Heidelberg from 1961 and Dusseldorf from 1968, notably a complete cycle of Janáček's operas. Bayreuth Festival from 1981, with *Der fliegende Holländer*, *Lohengrin* and the *Ring* (1987). In 1986 led *Die Zauberflöte* at CG and *Rosenkavalier* in Tokyo, with the company of the Vienna Staatsoper. Music director of the Bayerische Staatsoper at Munich from 1993 (*Die Frau ohne Schatten* in first year).

Schneiderhan, Wolfgang (Eduard) (b Vienna, 28 May 1915), Austrian violinist and conductor. Studied with Ševčik in Písek, in Prague and with Winkler in Vienna. In 1932 he became leader of the Vienna SO and in 1936 joined the Vienna Staatsoper Orchestra, becoming professor at the State Academy and leader of the Vienna PO. From 1938 to 1951 he led his string quartet, and from 1949 to 1960 a piano trio; from the 1970s he has also conducted (Schmidt's *Notre Dame* at the Vienna Volksoper in 1975). In 1948 he married the soprano Irmgard Seefried; gave with her the fp of Henze's *Ariosi* (1963).

Schneider-Siemssen, Günther (b Augsburg, 7 Jun 1926), German designer. He studied in Munich and worked in Bremen 1954–62. He designed the Peter Brook production of *Erwartung* at CG, 1961 and returned 1962–64 for the *Ring*. He has worked at Salzburg since 1965,

A Selection of

Schnittke

Symphony no. 1	1969–72
Concerto Grosso no. 1	1972
Symphony no. 2	1979
Seid nüchtern und wachet	1983

String Quartet no. 3	1984
Viola Concerto	1985
Cello Concerto no. 1	1985–6
Quasi una Sonata	1987
Concerto Grosso no. 5	1990–1
Life with an Idiot	1990–1

both summer and Easter Festivals; notable collaborations with Karajan include *Boris Godunov*, *The Ring*, *Tristan* and *Die Frau ohne Schatten*. Also designed premiere production of Berio's *Un Re in Ascolto*, Salzburg 1984. Designs for Otto Schenk's *Ring* production at the NY Met. 1986–91 (also on video). Noted for subtle use of colour and light; influenced by ideas of Alfred ◊Roller.

Schnittke (or *Schnitke*, or *Shnitke*), Alfred (b Engels, 24 Nov 1934), Russian composer. He studied in Vienna and at the Moscow Conservatory; taught there 1961–72. He has been influenced by serialism and the advanced techniques of Ligeti and Stockhausen, but has more recently accepted the social-realist principles of Shostakovich. His music often plays on the dichotomy between reality and illusion. For example, his cadenza of the Beethoven violin concerto strikes a sensitive balance between an orderly traditional formula and atonal disintegration. He has adopted the term 'polystylism', to describe music which is many-layered and highly allusive. The operas *Historia von Dr Johann Fausten* and *Gesualdo* were premiered at Hamburg and Vienna respectively, 1995.

Works include operas *Life with an Idiot* (1992), *Historia von Dr Johann Fausten* (1995) and *Gesualdo* (1995); eight symphonies: no. 1 (1969–72), no. 2 *St Florian* for small chorus and orchestra (1979), no. 3 (1981), no. 4 for SATB soloists and chamber orchestra (1984), no. 5 (*Concerto Grosso*, no. 4 (1988), no. 6 (1992), no. 7 (1993), no. 8 (1994); four violin concertos (1957–82), piano concerto (1960), concerto for piano and strings, five concerti grossi (1977, 1982, 1985, 1988, 1991), two cello concertos (1986, 1990), (*Ein Sommernachtstraum* for orchestra (1985), *Epilogue, Peer Gynt* for orchestra and tape (1987), Trio-Sonata (orchestration of string trio, 1987); two oratorios, *Nagasaki* (1958) and *Songs of War and Peace* (1959); *Der gelbe Klang* for nine instruments, tape, chorus and light projection, after Kandinsky; *Requiem* (1975), *Minnesang* (Lovesong) for 48 voices a cappella (1981), *Seid nüchtern und wachet* ... based on the Faust legend of 1587, for chorus (1983); two violin sonatas (1963, 1968), three string quartets (1966, 1981, 1984); cello sonata (1978), *Moz-art* for two violins; *Stille Musik* for violin and cello (1979), Septet for flute, two clarinets and string quartet (1982), string trio (1985), piano quartet (1988); *Moz-art à la Mozart* for eight flutes and harpsichord (1990).

Schnorr von Carolsfeld, Ludwig (b Munich, 2 Jul 1836; d Dresden, 21 Jul 1865), German tenor. Studied at Dresden, Leipzig and Karlsruhe, where he sang at the Opera and married the soprano Malwina Garrigues (1825–1904). In 1860 they were engaged by the Dresden

Schoenberg

A biographical note

Schoenberg was famously indifferent to worldly success and the demands of his colleagues. He had admired Hollywood films while living in Europe, but by the time he moved to California he had grown out of his infatuation. Several emigrés nevertheless had successful careers writing for films, and Schoenberg might have joined them when Irving Thalberg, production boss at MGM, heard *Verklärte Nacht* on the radio and sent an assistant to Schoenberg to make him an offer. Pearl Buck's novel *The Good Earth* was about to get the Hollywood treatment: 'In the midst of a terrific storm the earth starts to shake and Oo-Lan gives ecstatic birth' was the set-up described to Schoenberg. 'So what do you need my music for?' was the composer's dry reply. At a later meeting with Thalberg himself Schoenberg demanded an impossible $50,000 for his services, and was promptly shown the door. Jascha Heifetz was another failed prospect: 'Herr Schoenberg, to play your concerto I need six fingers on my left hand', the violinist protested. 'Don't worry, maestro, I can wait', came the response.

Court Opera and sang in operas by Wagner and Meyerbeer. He was Wagner's first Tristan at the Munich production in 1865, but died six weeks later.

Schnorr von Carolsfeld, Malwina, ◊Garrigues.

Schoberlechner, Franz (b Vienna, 21 Jul 1797; d Berlin, 7 Jan 1843), Austrian pianist and composer. He played a piano concerto by Hummel, composed for him, at the age of ten and was sent to Vienna by Prince Esterházy to study with Förster. In 1814 he went to Italy and in 1823 to Russia, marrying the singer Sophie dall' Occa there in 1824. After four years in St Petersburg they retired to a villa near Florence in 1831.

Works include operas *I virtuosi teatrali* (1817), *Il Barone di Dolzheim* (1827) and *Rossane* (1839); two piano concertos; chamber music; sonatas and other works for piano.

Schoberlechner (born *dall' Occa*), Sophie (b St Petersburg, 1807; d St Petersburg, Jan 1864), Russian singer of Italian descent, daughter of a singing-master, with whom she studied. She married Schoberlechner in 1824, sang at concerts at first, but in 1827 was engaged by the Imperial Opera in St Petersburg. She retired with her husband in 1831, but returned to Russia later to teach singing.

Schobert, Johann (Jean) (b ? Silesia or Nuremberg, c 1720; d Paris, 28 Aug 1767), German harpsichordist and composer. He lived in Paris, in the service of the Prince of Conti from c 1720, but died young, with his wife and child, as a result of fungus poisoning. Mozart arranged one of his sonata movements as the second movement of the concerto K39.

Works include *opéra comique Le Garde-Chasse et le braconnier*; six harpsichord concertos; six *Sinfonies* for harpsichord, violin and two horns; piano quartets (with two violins); piano trios; sonatas for piano and violin; sonatas for harpsichord.

Schock, Rudolf (b Duisburg, 4 Sept 1915; d Gürzenich, 14 Nov 1986), German tenor. Debut Brunswick 1937; sang in Berlin after World War II, Hamburg 1947–56 (visited Edinburgh with the co. 1952. Salzburg from 1948, as Idomeneo and in the 1954 fp of Liebermann's *Penelope*). He sang Walther at Bayreuth in 1959 and recorded the role with Kempe. Other roles included Florestan, Tamino and Bacchus; also popular in operetta.

Schoeck, Othmar (b Brunnen, 1 Sept 1886; d Zurich, 8 Mar 1957), Swiss composer. He was at first undecided whether to follow his father as a painter, but at 17 went to the Zurich Conservatory to study with Niggli and others, finishing with Reger at the Leipzig Conservatory. In 1907–17 he conducted choral societies at Zurich and remained there when appointed conductor of the St Gall symphony concerts that year. The university conferred an honorary doctor's

degree on him in 1928. His music is undemanding and lyrical in character and was successfully performed in Germany during the Nazi era.

Works include OPERAS *Don Ranudo* (after Holberg, 1919), *Venus* (after Mérimée, 1922), *Penthesilea* (after Kleist, 1927), *Vom Fischer und syner Fru* (after Grimm, 1930), *Massimilla Doni* (after Balzac, 1937), *Das Schloss Dürande* (after Eichendorff, 1943), operetta *Erwin und Elmire* (Goethe), *scena* and pantomime *Das Wandbild*.

CHORAL: *Der Postillon* (Lenau) for tenor solo, chorus and orchestra (1909), *Dithyrambe* (Goethe) for double chorus and orchestra (1911); *Trommelschläge* (Whitman's *Drum Taps*) for chorus and orchestra, *Für ein Gesangfest im Frühling* (Keller) for male voices and orchestra (1942).

ORCHESTRAL: Serenade for small orchestra, praeludium for orchestra, pastoral intermezzo *Sommernacht* (after Keller) for strings (1945), suite for strings; *Lebendig begraben* (Keller), song-cycle for baritone and orchestra; violin concerto, cello concerto (1947), horn concerto (1951).

CHAMBER AND SOLO VOCAL: two string quartets (1913, 1923); two violin and piano sonatas, sonata for bass clarinet and piano; song-cycles *Elegie* with chamber orchestra (1923), *Gaselen* (Keller) with six instruments, *Wandersprüche* (Eichendorff) with four instruments, *Notturno* with string quartet (1933); piano pieces; song-cycles and numerous sets of songs.

Schoeffler, Paul (b Dresden, 15 Sept 1897; d Amersham, Bucks., 21 Nov 1977), German, later Austrian, baritone. Studied in Dresden, Berlin and Milan, making his debut in Dresden in 1925, where he remained until 1937, when he was engaged by the Vienna Staatsoper. He also sang at CG, 1934–39 and 1949–53, as Scarpia, Gunther, Figaro, Don Giovanni and Wotan. NY Met. 1949–56. He was especially well known in the role of Hans Sachs, which he sang at Bayreuth during the war. He created Von Einem's Danton (1947) and Strauss's Jupiter (1952), both at Salzburg.

Schoelcher, Victor (b Paris, 21 Jul 1804; d Houilles, 24 Dec 1893), French politician and writer on music. He lived in exile in London during the reign of Napoleon III and worked on Handel research, part of the result of which he published in an English biography in 1857. He also made a collection of music which he presented to the Paris Conservatory.

Pierrot lunaire is one of those unfortunate masterpieces destined to be more often – and more heatedly – discussed than actually listened to.

R D Darrell, notes on Arnold Schoenberg's *Pierrot lunaire*, 1969

Schoenberg, Arnold (b Vienna, 13 Sept 1874; d LA, 13 Jul 1951), Austrian composer. He sought to extend the dominance of German music beyond the range of Wagner and Brahms, but his own works resonate with their influence. He played violin as a boy and cello as a youth, and at 16 decided to become a musician, studying counterpoint with Zemlinsky, but being otherwise self-taught. About the turn of the century he earned his living by scoring operettas, but his own works of that period were the string sextet *Verklärte Nacht* and the *Gurre-lieder*, which still owe considerably to Wagner's influence. He married Mathilde von Zemlinsky, his teacher-friend's sister, and in 1901 became conductor of the *Überbrettl* cabaret in Berlin and a little later teacher at the Stern Conservatory there. Back in Vienna in 1903, he gradually changed his style, and his *Chamber Symphony* op. 9 created a riot in 1907, but Mahler defended him. 1907 also saw the premiere of his 1st string quartet, in D minor, a huge and lyrical celebration of cyclic form. The second string quartet, with soprano solo, and parts of *Das Buch der hängenden Gärten*, is the first work in which he moved decisively away from tonality; the fp in 1908 of the quartet was the occasion of further disturbances; particular objection was made to the use of the folk melody *Ach, du Lieber Augustin*. By 1911 he had returned to Berlin and had taken to painting in an

Schoenberg *The composer Arnold Schoenberg (1874–1951) in his role as teacher at UCLA. After escaping the Nazis in 1933 he settled in the USA as a lecturer, eloquently preaching the laws of harmony despite his serialist compositional philosophy.*

expressionist manner; the highly influential *Pierrot lunaire* was given in Berlin in 1912; the *Five Orchestral Pieces* were performed in London the same year. Neither work was an immediate success with the public, which preferred the more traditional *Gurrelieder* (premiered in 1913 but composed over ten years earlier).

After World War I, during which he did garrison duty, Schoenberg settled at Mödling, near Vienna. At the end of 1918 he founded with his pupils Berg, Webern and Steuermann the Society for Private Musical Performances; the Society presented new progressive works in carefully rehearsed concerts from which unsympathetic elements were excluded. From this time dates one of Schoenberg's most compelling works, the unfinished oratorio *Die Jakobsleiter*. The scoring was completed by Winfried Zillig and the work was premiered under Kubelik at Vienna in 1961. In 1920 he taught at Amsterdam, where he had begun to attract attention. In 1921 he began to write his first work wholly in the 12-note method, the *Suite* op. 25 for piano. Further renewed creative vigour resulted in the *Serenade*, the wind quintet, third string quartet and the comic opera *Von Heute auf Morgen*, in all of which dodecaphony was further explored. His wife died in 1923 and in 1926 he was recalled to Berlin, to teach at the Prussian Academy of Arts; Zemlinsky had given the premiere of his monodrama *Erwartung* at Prague (1924) and in 1928 Furtwängler conducted the Berlin fp of the *Variations for Orchestra* op. 28. The *Variations* were not favourably received, at least partly due to Furtwängler's lack of empathy with it. He remained at Berlin until 1933 and married a sister of the violinist Rudolf Kolisch. His masterpiece, the opera *Moses und Aron*, was composed 1930–32 but not performed until three years after his death; the work's powerful and expressive drama has done more than any other to establish the artistic validity of twelve-note music.

The Nazi regime drove Schoenberg from Germany and he settled in the USA, teaching in Boston and NY, 1933–34, and later in LA, where he was appointed professor at the University of California in 1936, retiring in 1944. In 1947 he was elected a member of the American Academy of Arts and Letters; a translation of his *Harmonielehre* (1911) was pub. the same year. Through this and other writings Schoenberg's influence as a teacher remained considerable; Berg and Webern were the best-known pupils of his pre-war years.

In his last major instrumental work, the string trio of 1946, Schoenberg attempted to recreate the near death experience he had recently undergone in hospital. The following year *A Survivor from Warsaw* vividly evoked the experience of his fellow Jews in the Holocaust. A wide acceptance of Schoenberg's music did not begin until after his death, with premieres of *Moses und Aron* at Hamburg (concert, 1954) and Zurich (staged, 1957).

Works include OPERAS: *Erwartung*, monodrama, op. 17 (1909; produced Prague, 1924, conductor Zemlinsky), *Die glückliche Hand*, one-act drama, (1910–13; produced Vienna, 1924, conductor Stiedry), *Von Heute auf Morgen*, one-act comedy (1929, produced Frankfurt, 1930, conductor Steinberg), *Moses und Aron* (1930–32; fp Hamburg, concert, 1954; stage, Zurich, 1957, conductor Rosbaud).

ORCHESTRAL: *Frühlingstod*, symphonic poem (1899; fp Berlin, 1983, conductor R Chailly), *Pelleas und Melisande*, symphonic poem after Maeterlinck (1902–03), Chamber Symphony no. 1 for 15 instruments op. 9 (1906; arranged for orchestra 1922), *Five Orchestral Pieces* (1909; fp London, 1912, conductor Wood), *Three Little Pieces* for chamber orchestra (1911; fp Berlin, 1957), *Variations* op. 31 (1926–28; fp Berlin, 1928, conductor Furtwängler), *Begleitungsmusik zu einer Lichtspielszene*, op. 34 (1929–30; fp Berlin, 1930, conductor Klemperer), Suite in G for strings (1934; fp Los Angeles, 1935, conductor Klemperer), violin concerto, op. 36 (1934–36; fp Philadelphia, 1940, with Krasner, conductor Stokowski), Chamber Symphony no. 2 (1906–16, revised 1939; fp NY, 1940, conductor Stiedry), piano concerto op. 42 (1942; fp NY, 1944, with Steuermann, conductor Stokowski), theme and variations for wind op. 43a, arranged for orchestra op. 43b. Also: string sextet *Verklärte Nacht* arranged for strings (1917), cello concerto after Georg Monn (1933), concerto for string quartet and orchestra, after Handel (1933) and version for orchestra of Brahms G minor piano quartet op. 25 (1937; fp Los Angeles, 1938, conductor Klemperer).

VOCAL AND CHORAL: *Friede auf Erden* for unaccompanied chorus (1907), *Gurrelieder* for soloists, chorus and orchestra (1900–11), Six Songs with Orchestra (1904), *Das Buch der hängenden Gärten* (S George) for soprano and piano (1909), *Herzgewächse* for soprano, celesta, harmonium and harp (1911), *Pierrot lunaire* for speaker and chamber ensemble op. 21 (1912), *Four Songs* with orchestra (1916), *Die Jakobsleiter*, oratorio (1917–22), *Three Satires* for chorus (1925), *Kol Nidre* for rabbi, chorus and orchestra (1938), *Ode to Napoleon Buonaparte* for reciter, string quartet and piano (1942), *A Survivor from Warsaw* for speaker, male chorus and orchestra (1947),

A Selection of

Schoenberg

String Quartet no. 1 1897
Gurrelieder 1900–11
String Quartet no. 2 1905
Erwartung 1909

Pierrot lunaire 1912
Variations for orchestra 1926–8
String Quartet no. 4 1927
Moses und Aron 1930–2
Violin Concerto 1934–6
String Trio 1946

Modern Psalms for chorus, speaker and orchestra (1950).

CHAMBER: five string quartets (1897, 1905, 1908, 1927, 1936), *Verklärte Nacht* for string sextet, op. 4 (1899), Serenade op. 24 for seven instruments with baritone in fourth movement (1923), wind quintet op. 26 (1924), *Suite* for three clarinets and piano quintet op. 29 (1926), string trio op. 45 (1946), *Phantasy* for violin and piano (1947).

PIANO: *Three Pieces* op. 11 (1909), *Six Little Pieces* (1911), *Five Pieces* op. 23 (1923), Suite op. 25 (1921), *Two Pieces* op. 33 (1931).

Arrangements for orchestra of Bach organ music and Johann Strauss; Theme and variations for wind band op. 43 (1943); cabaret pieces; seven sets of Lieder composed 1897–1903, three Lieder op. 48 (1933) and songs for Ernst von Wolzogen's *Überbrettl*.

Scholes, Percy A(lfred) (b Leeds, 24 Jul 1877; d Vevey, Switzerland, 31 Jul 1958), English critic, music author and editor. He became music critic to the *Evening Standard* and the *Observer* in London, founded and edited the *Music Student* and *Music and Youth*, in 1923 became music critic to the BBC, but later settled in Switzerland, where he lived until the outbreak of World War II and twice after it. He was a D.Litt. of Lausanne and Oxford Universities and an honorary Mus.D. of Oxford. He wrote many books to further the popularity and appreciation of music and compiled the dictionaries *The Oxford Companion to Music* (1938) and *The Concise Oxford Dictionary of Music* (1952).

Schönberg, Arnold, ◊Schoenberg.

Schonberg, Harold (b New York, 29 Nov 1915), American critic and writer on music. Studied in New York and was critic with the NY *Sun* 1946–50, *Times* from 1950 (senior critic 1960–80); Pulitzer Prize for criticism, 1971. Has published *Great Pianists* (1963, revised 1987), *Great Conductors* (1967), *Lives of Great Composers* (1970, 1981), *Classical Music's Legendary Performers* (1985) and *Horowitz, his Life and Music* (1992).

Schöne, Lotte (b Vienna, 15 Dec 1891; d Paris, 22 Dec 1977), Austrian soprano. She studied in Vienna and made her debut there in 1915. She sang in Vienna until 1926 and then appeared at the Städtische Oper Berlin until 1933; her roles included Cherubino, Susanna, Zerlina, Norina and Zerbinetta. Also much admired in operas by Puccini, and sang Liù at CG in 1927. Salzburg 1922–35. She was obliged by the Nazis to leave Germany but returned to Berlin in 1948 and sang there until her retirement in 1953.

Schöne, Wolfgang (b Bad Gandersheim, 9 Feb 1941), German bass-baritone. After study in Hamburg appeared in concert throughout Europe and in the USA. Opera career from 1970 at the State Operas of Hamburg, Vienna and Stuttgart, notably as Guglielmo, Wolfram and Germont. Created Tom in Henze's *The English Cat*, Schwetzingen 1983. Sang Don Giovanni at Stuttgart in 1984, Alidoro in *Cenerentola* and the Count in *Capriccio* at Salzburg (1988, 1990). Admired as Dr Schön in *Lulu* at the Paris Châtelet (1992) and Amfortas at Amsterdam, 1993.

Schöne Melusine, Die, *The Fair Melusina*, concert overture by Mendelssohn, op. 32, composed 1833 after a performance in Berlin of K Kreutzer's opera *Melusina*, with a libretto by Grillparzer originally written for Beethoven.

Schöne Müllerin, Die, *The Fair Maid of the Mill*, song cycle by Schubert (poems by Wilhelm Müller), composed 1823, D795. The 17 songs are 1. *Das Wandern* 2. *Wohin?* 3. *Halt; Danksagung an den Bach* 4. *Am Feierabend* 5. *Der Neugierige* 6. *Ungeduld* 7. *Morgengrüss* 8. *Des Müllers Blumen* 9. *Tränenregen* 10. *Pause; Mit dem grünen Lautenbande* 11. *Der Jäger* 12. *Eifersucht und Stolz* 13. *Die liebe Farbe* 14. *Die böse Farbe* 15. *Trockne Blumen* 16. *Der Müller und der Bach* 17. *Des Baches Wiegenlied*.

Schønwandt, Michael (b Copenhagen, 10 Sep 1953), Danish conductor. Studied at Copenhagen University and at the RAM, London (1975–77). Concert debut at Copenhagen 1977, Royal Danish Opera 1978. Led *I Capuleti e i Montecchi* at CG in 1984 and the French version of *Don Carlos* at San Francisco, 1992. Principal guest at the Monnaie, Brussels, 1984–87; Danish Radio SO from 1989.

Recordings include Kuhlau's *Lulu*, the symphonies of Gade and the Berlioz Requiem.

Schönzeler, Hans-Hubert (b Leipzig, 22 Jun 1925), German conductor and musicologist (British citizen from 1947). After study at the New South Wales Conservatorium conducted the 20th-Century Ensemble in London, 1951–61. Led the Western Australia SO at Perth from 1967. An advocate of Bruckner, he has written a book on the composer (1970), recorded the Requiem and gave the fp of the original version of the 8th symphony (1973, BBC). Many concerts with the regional BBC orchestras.

School for Fathers, The (Wolf-Ferrari.) ◊Quattro rusteghi.

Schoolmaster, The nickname of Haydn's symphony no. 55 in E♭ major, composed 1774.

Schöpfungsmesse, Creation Mass, the nickname of Haydn's Mass in B♭ major of 1801, where a theme from *The Creation* is used in the 'Qui tollis'.

Schorr, Friedrich (b Nagyvárad, 2 Sept 1888; d Farmington, CT, 14 Aug 1953), Austro-Hungarian baritone. Studied in Vienna and made his debut at Graz in 1910, as Wotan, a part he made peculiarly his own. Sang in Cologne 1918–23, under Klemperer; Berlin, Staatsoper, 1923–30 as Barak, Nelusko and Doktor Faust. The outstanding Wagnerian baritone of his time. He first appeared in London and NY in 1924 and from 1925 until 1931 was Wotan in the Bayreuth Wagner performances.

Schott, Anton (b Castle Staufeneck, Swabia, 24 Jun 1846; d Stuttgart, 6 Jan 1913), German tenor. Pupil of Pischek and Agnes Schebest, made his debut at Frankfurt in 1870; sang with Angelo Neumann's touring co. from 1882 (Rienzi, Lohengrin, Tannhäuser) and in US from 1884 (first Met. Siegmund).

Schott, B and Sons, German music publishers. The company was founded by Bernhard Schott in 1780 at Mainz and continued by his sons from 1817. The London branch was opened in 1835, and others were established in Paris, Leipzig, Rotterdam and New York. The firm published late works of Beethoven and among other composers pub. are Haydn, Hindemith, Henze, Tippett, Davies and Goehr. Owner of Eulenberg Editions since 1957.

Schottisch German = 'Scottish'; a ballroom dance fashionable in the 19th c. introduced to England 1848, not identical with the *Écossaise*. In England it is usually called by its plural, *Schottische*. The music is in 2–4 time, much like that of the polka, but played rather slower.

Schrade, Leo (b Allenstein, 13 Dec 1903; d Spéracédès, 21 Sept 1964), German musicologist. He studied at several German universities and taught at Königsberg University 1929–32 and at Bonn University from 1932 to 1937, when he left Germany and settled in USA. He taught at Yale University 1938–58, becoming professor in 1948. From 1958 he was professor at Basel University His studies ranged widely over medieval, Renaissance and Baroque music and included a book on Monteverdi and editions of the works of Philippe de Vitry, Machaut, Landini and other 14th-c. composers.

Schramm, Hermann (b Berlin, 7 Feb 1871; d Frankfurt, 14 Dec 1951), German tenor. Debut Breslau 1895, in Kreutzer's *Die Nachtlager von Granada*. Cologne 1896–1900, Frankfurt 1900–33; sang in the 1920 fp of Schreker's *Der Schatzgräber* and was the best-known Mime and David of his time. CG 1899, also guest in Paris and Brussels. His son *Friedrich* (1900–81) produced *Fidelio* and operas by Wagner at CG 1947–51.

Schreier, Peter (b Meissen, 29 Jul 1935), German tenor and conductor. He sang as a choirboy in Dresden during the war and made his adult debut there in 1959. He has sung at the Berlin Staatsoper since 1963 and in 1966 made his London debut, as Ferrando. In 1967 he made his first appearances at the NY Met., Salzburg and the Vienna Opera; among his roles have been Tamino, Sextus, Loge, Don Ottavio and Belmonte. He has been widely admired in Lieder and in the Bach Passions. Active as a conductor since 1969. *See illustration on page 592.*

Schreker, Franz (b Monaco, 23 Mar 1878; d Berlin, 21 Mar 1934), Austrian composer, conductor and teacher. Studied under Fuchs in Vienna, founded the Philharmonic Choir there in 1911 and conducted

Schreier *The tenor and conductor Peter Schreier. His singing has been admired for its smooth legato and phrasing, which aims towards simplicity rather than floridity. Since 1970 he has been successful as a conductor, notably in Mozart's Requiem and* Idomeneo.

the fp of Schoenberg's *Gurrelieder* in 1913. Taught at the Imperial Academy of Music until his appointment as director of the Academy of Music in Berlin in 1920; forced by the Nazis to resign in 1933. His operas were late Romantic in expression and popular in the 1920s; fps were conducted by Otto Klemperer (Cologne) and Bruno Walter (Munich).

Works include OPERAS: *Flammen* (1902), *Der ferne Klang* (1912), *Das Spielwerk und die Prinzessin* (1913; revised as a mystery play, *Das Spielwerk*, 1920), *Die Gezeichneten* (1918), *Der Schatzgräber* (1920), *Irrelohe* (1924), *Der singende Teufel* (1928), *Christophorus* (1924–29; produced 1978), *Der Schmied von Gent* (1932); pantomime *Der Geburtstag der Infantin*, after Wilde, 1908; reworked as *Spanisches Fest*, 1927).

ORCHESTRAL: symphony (1899), *Intermezzo* for strings (1900), *Romantic Suite* (1902), Chamber symphony for 23 solo instruments (1917; also in version for full orchestra, as Sinfonietta), *Kleine Suite* for small orchestra (1931).

VOCAL: Psalm 116 for female chorus and orchestra (1900), *Schwanengesang* for chorus and orchestra (1902), *Zwei lyrische Gesänge* for voice and orchestra to poems by Whitman, 1929); 43 Lieder to texts by Heyse, Tolstoy, and Scherenberg (1895–1916).

Schröder-Devrient, Willhelmine (b Hamburg, 6 Dec 1804; d Coburg, 26 Jan 1860), German soprano. She learnt much from her parents, the baritone Friedrich Schröder-Devrient (1744–1816) and the actress Antoinette Sophie Bürger, and when still in her teens appeared as a classical actress at the Burgtheater in Vienna, where she made her first operatic appearance in 1821 as Pamina. In 1822 she greatly pleased Beethoven as Leonore in the revival of *Fidelio*. In 1823 she was engaged by the Dresden Court Opera and soon afterwards married the actor Karl Devrient, from whom she separated in 1828; her roles included Donna Anna, Norma, Euryanthe and Reiza. In 1830 she first sang in Paris and in 1832 in London. She worked long enough to create Wagner's Adriano (1842), Senta (1843) and Venus (1845).

Schröder-Feinen, Ursula (b Gelsenkirchen, 21 Jan 1936), German soprano. She sang in Gelsenkirchen during the 1960s as Aida, Alceste, Oscar, Turandot and Salome. NY Met. debut 1970 as Chrysothemis. She has sung Brünnhilde at Bayreuth (debut 1971) and in Paris and NY. In London she has been heard as Ortrud and Kundry and at the 1975 Edinburgh Festival she sang Salome.

Schroeter, Christoph Gottlieb (b Hohnstein, Saxony, 10 Aug 1699; d Nordhausen, 20 May 1782), German musician. He was educated in theology as well as music and in 1721 invented a hammer action to apply to the harpsichord, but was anticipated in the actual invention of the piano by Cristofori.

Schroeter, Leonhard (b Torgau, *c* 1540; d Magdeburg, *c* 1595), German composer. Succeeded Gallus Dressler as cantor of Magdeburg Cathedral in 1564.

Works include German Te Deum for double choir (1584), *Hymni sacri* for four–five voices, *Weihnachts-Liedlein* for several voices (1587).

Schröter, Corona (Elisabeth Willhelmine) (b Guben, 14 Jan 1751; d Ilmenau, 23 Aug 1802), German singer, actress and composer. She learnt music from her father, the oboist Johann Friedrich Schröter, lived in Warsaw and Leipzig as a child, appeared in the latter town at the age of 14. Between 1772 and 1774 she was in London with her family, but Goethe invited her to the court of Weimar in 1776, where she appeared in his plays and wrote the music for his play *Die Fischerin*, which included a setting of *Erlkönig* by her. She retired in 1786 to teach, paint and compose.

Works include play with music *Die Fischerin*; songs, including settings of Goethe's *Der neue Amadis* and *Erlkönig*, Schiller's *Der Taucher* and *Würde der Frauen*, poems by Herder, Klopstock, Matthisson.

Schröter, Johann Samuel (b Warsaw, *c* 1752; d London, 2 Nov 1788), German pianist and composer. Pupil of his father, he made his debut as a pianist in Leipzig in 1767, and in 1772 went on tour with his father and sister to Holland and England, where he appeared at one of the Bach-Abel concerts. Settling in England, he succeeded J C Bach as music master to the queen in 1782. It was his widow with whom Haydn had an autumnal affair during his first visit to London; Haydn made copies of her letters to him.

Works include keyboard concertos, sonatas, etc.; piano quintets and trios.

Schuback, Thomas (b Stockholm, 1943), Swedish conductor. Studied in Stockholm and has conducted at the Royal Opera there from 1971; productions at Drottningholm include *Poppea*, and *L'arbore di Diana* by Martín y Soler. Gluck's *Paride ed Elena* and Haeffner's *Electra*: visited the Barbican, London, with the company in 1993. Musical director of the Lyric Opera of Queensland from 1982; guest in San Diego, Sydney and Copenhagen. Many concert appearances and has been recital accompanist to Barbara Bonney and Hakon Hagegard.

Schubart, Christian Friedrich Daniel (b Obersontheim, Swabia, 24 Mar 1739; d Stuttgart, 10 Oct 1791), German author, editor and musician. Lived as organist and teacher in Geislingen and Ludwigsburg, later in Augsburg, where he edited the *Deutsche Chronik* (from 1774), and Ulm (1777–87), held as a political prisoner at Hohen-

---

Schubert

A biographical note

Schubert's song *Death and the Maiden* was written in 1817, a relatively untroubled time in the composer's life when he had just met the singer Johann Vogl, later to become one of his strongest supporters. With no assured income, Schubert often had to rely on the generosity of his friends; his disordered personal life was a strain on his health and he fell seriously ill when he contracted syphilis during 1822–23. He composed part of the song cycle *Die schöne Müllerin* while in hospital, and by the time he turned again to *Death and the Maiden*, the song had assumed a sad significance for him. The string quartet which bears its name opens with a five-note phrase in D minor which immediately establishes the work's tragic stature. The song itself is the theme for the slow movement's variations, sombre and relentless in character, totally at variance with the equivalent movement in the *Trout* quintet. The quartet concludes with a tarantella movement which has been described as a Dance of Death. Schubert's death four years later was caused by typhoid; syphilis has been given as the cause but the final stages of the disease are always accompanied by mental degeneration, and the String Quintet of 1828 is hardly evidence of that.

asperg. From 1787 was poet to the court and theatre in Stuttgart. He was the author of *Die Forelle*, *An den Tod* and *Grablied auf einen Soldaten*, all set to music by Schubert. His autobiography was pub. 1791–93. Also wrote keyboard music and songs.

Schubaur, Johann Lukas (b Lechfeld, Swabia, bap. 23 Dec 1749; d Munich, 15 Nov 1815), German composer. Had a distinguished career as a doctor, but was also a successful *Singspiel* composer (from 1783).

Works include *Singspiele Die Dorfdeputierten, Das Lustlager, Die treuen Köhler*.

Though I have worked very hard at the Winterreise *the last five years, every time I come back I am amazed not only by the extraordinary mastery of it ... but by the renewal of the magic; the mystery remains.*
Benjamin Britten on Franz Schubert's *Winterreise*, in *On Receiving the First Aspen Award*, 1964

Schubert, Franz (Peter) (b Vienna, 31 Jan 1797; d Vienna, 19 Nov 1828), Austrian composer. Son of a schoolmaster who cultivated music in his household. Began to learn piano and violin early and received lessons from Michael Holzer at the age of nine, learning also organ and counterpoint. Admitted to the Seminary for choristers in the Imperial Chapel in 1808, played violin in the orchestra there and sometimes conducted as deputy. At 13 he wrote a fantasy for piano duet and sketched other works, and in 1811 composed his first song. Played viola in the string quartet at home. His mother died in 1812 and his father married again in 1813, when Schubert wrote the first symphony and left the Seminary, continuing studies under Salieri. At 17 he became assistant teacher in his father's school, but disliked teaching; composed the G major Mass, the second and third symphonies and several dramatic pieces. In 1814 he allegedly sold his overcoat in order to buy a ticket for the revival of *Fidelio*; his own first opera, *Des Teufels Lustschloss*, was written in the same year. Like all his stage works, it was unsuccessful, but he also composed at this time his first great song, *Gretchen am Spinnrade*. The following year he wrote almost 150 songs. In 1816 he left the school and joined his friend Schober in rooms, gathering a circle of literary and artistic rather than musical friends round him and in 1817 meeting the singer Michael Vogl, who took a great interest in his songs and succeeded in getting his play with music *Die Zwillingsbrüder/The Twin Brothers* produced Jun 1820.

A Selection of

Schubert

Schubert *The composer Franz Schubert (1797–1828), after the portrait by Rieder. Schubert is best-known for his melodic gift, which was put to good use in more than 600 Lieder. His harmonic language and often-cyclic conception of works foreshadow later developments of the 19th century.*

By this time he had written some of his finest instrumental works, including the 4th and 5th symphonies, the sonatinas for violin and piano and the *Trout Quintet*. His reputation grew beyond his own circle, but publishers failed to recognize him until his friends had 20 songs pub. at their own expense in 1821. (Most of his large-scale works were unpublished during his lifetime, however.) His mastery of various instrumental genres is demonstrated in the 'Unfinished' symphony and 'Wanderer' Fantasy for piano of 1822; the last three string quartets, in A minor, D minor, 'Death and the Maiden', and G, followed in 1824 and 1826. His 9th symphony of 1825 is one of the most carefully crafted and consistently inspired work of its kind ever written.

He lived in Vienna all his life, except for some summer excursions and two visits to Hungary as domestic musician to the Esterházy family on their country estate at Zséliz, 1818 and 1824. He never held an official appointment and failed to stabilize his financial position, but earned enough casually to lead a modest if improvident and Bohemian existence. His industry was phenomenal. His death was due to typhoid, his condition having been weakened by syphilis.

OPERAS AND SINGSPIELE (some incomplete): *Der Spiegelritter* (1811–12, fp Swiss Radio 1949), *Des Teufels Lustschloss* (1813–15; fp Vienna, 1879), *Adrast* (1817–19, fp Vienna, 1868), *Der vierjährige Posten* (1815, fp Dresden, 1896), *Fernando* (1815, fp Vienna, 1905), *Claudine von Villa Bella* (1815, fp Vienna, 1913), *Die Freunde von Salamanka* (1815, fp Halle, 1928), *Die Burgschaft* (1816, fp Vienna, 1908), *Die Zwillingsbrüder* (1819, fp Vienna, 1820), *Alfonso und Estrella* (1821–22, fp Weimar, 1854), *Die Verschworenen* (1823, fp Vienna, 1861), *Fierrabras* (1823, fp Karlsruhe, 1897); also melodrama *Die Zauberharfe* (1820, fp Vienna, 1820) and incidental music *Rosamunde, Fürstin von Zypern* (1823, fp Vienna, 1823).

VOCAL WITH ORCHESTRA: church music including five Masses, in F, G, C, A♭ and E♭ (1814–28), *Deutsche Messe* (1827), *Lazarus*, unfinished oratorio (1820), six settings of the *Salve regina* (1812–24). Works for voices, with and without accompaniment, including *Frühlingsgesang* (1822), *Gesang der Geister über den Wassern* (1817; second version with orchestra 1821), *Gondelfahrer* (1824), *Miriams Sieges-gesang* (1828) and *Ständchen* (1827).

ORCHESTRAL: nine symphonies: no. 1 in D (1813), no. 2 in B♭ (1815), no. 3 in D (1815), no. 4 in C minor (1816), no. 5 in B♭ (1816), no. 6 in C (1818), no. 7 in E (1821; sketches, unscored), no. 8 in B minor ('Unfinished', 1822), no. 9 in C ('Great', 1825); two overtures in the Italian style (1817, 1819), five German Dances (1813; also in scoring by Webern), Rondo in A for violin and orchestra (1816).

CHAMBER: 15 string quartets, nos. 1–7 composed 1812–14, no. 8 in B♭ (1814, D112), no. 9 in G minor (1815, D173), no. 10 in E♭ (1813, D87), no. 11 in E (1816, D353), no. 12 in C minor (*Quartettsatz*, 1820, D703), no. 13 in A minor (1824, D804), no. 14 in D minor (*Der Tod und das Mädchen*, 1824, D810), no. 15 in G (1826, D887); Octet in F for string quartet, double bass, clarinet, bassoon and horn (1824, D803), string quintet in C (1828, D956), piano quintet in A (*Die Forelle*, 1819, D667), piano trios in B♭ (1827, D898) and E♭ (1827, D929); for piano and violin: sonata in A (1817, D574), three sonatinas, in D, A minor and G minor (1816, D384, D385 and D408), *Rondo brillant* in B minor (1826, D895), Fantasia in C, based on song *Sei mir gegrüsst* (1827, D934).

WORKS FOR PIANO: including *Divertissement à la hongroise* (D818), Fantasia in F minor (D940), sonata in B♭ (D617) and sonata in C, Grand Duo (D813), all for four hands; 21 piano sonatas: nos. 1–12 composed 1815–19, some unfinished, no. 13 in A (D664), no. 14 in A minor (D784), no. 15 in C (D840), no. 16 in A minor (D845), no. 17 in D (D850), no. 18 in G (D894), no. 19 in C minor (D958), no. 20 in A (D959), no. 21 in B♭ (D960); Fantasia in C, based on the song *Der Wanderer* (D760), eight impromptus in two sets: in C minor, E♭, G♭ and A♭ (D899), in F minor, A♭, B♭, F minor (D935), three Kalvierstücke, in E♭ minor, E♭ and C (D946), six *Moments Musicaux*, in C, A♭, F minor, C♯ minor, F minor and A♭ (1823–8, D780); two sets of waltzes, D145 and D365.

SONGS: three cycles, *Die schöne Müllerin* (1823), *Winterreise* (1827) and *Schwanengesang* (1828). Some of the best known of more than 600 Lieder are *Abendstern* (Mayrhofer, 1824), *Die Allmacht* (Pyrker, 1825), *Am Bach im Frühling* (Schober, 1816, *An den Mond* (Goethe, 1815), *An die Entfernte* (Goethe, 1822), *An die Musik* (Schober, 1817), *An Schwager Kronos* (Goethe, 1816), *An Sylvia* (Shakespeare, 1826), *Auf dem Wasser zu singen* (Stolberg, 1823), *Auf der Donau* (Mayrhofer, 1817), *Auflösung* (Mayrhofer, 1824), *Ave Maria* (Scott, trans. Storck, 1825), *Bei dir allein* (Seidl, 1826), *Delphine* (Schütz, 1825), *Du bist die Ruh* (Rückert, 1823), *Der Einsame* (Lappe, 1825), *Erlkönig* (Goethe, 1815), *Der Fischer* (Goethe, 1815), *Fischerweise* (Schlechta, 1826), *Die Forelle* (Schubart, 1817), *Frühlingsglaube* (Uhland, 1820), *Ganymed* (Goethe, 1817), *Die Götter Griechenlands* (Schiller, 1819), *Gretchen am Spinnrade* (Goethe, 1814), *Gruppe aus dem Tartarus* (1817), *3 Harfenspieler Lieder* (Goethe, 1816), *Heidenröslein* (Goethe, 1815), *Der Hirt auf dem Felsen*, with clarinet obbligato (Müller, 1828), *Horch, horch die Lerch* (Shakespeare, 1826), *Im Frühling* (Schulze, 1826), *Die junge Nonne* (Craigher, 1825), *Lachen und Weinen* (Rückert, 1823, *Liebhaber in aller Gestalten* (Goethe, 1817), *Der Musensohn* (Goethe, 1822), *Nacht und Träume* (Collin, 1822), *Nur wer die Sehnsucht kennt* (Goethe, five versions), *Prometheus* (Goethe, 1819), *Sei mir gegrüsst* (Rückert, 1822), *Die Sterne* (Leitner, 1828), *Der Tod und das Mädchen* (Claudius, 1817), *Dem Unendlichen* (Klopstock, 1815), *Der Wanderer* (Lübeck, 1816), *Wanderers Nachtlied* (Goethe, 1822), *Der Zwerg* (Collin, 1822).

Schubert, Richard (b Dessau, 15 Dec 1885; d Oberstaufen, Allgau, 12 Oct 1959), German tenor. Debut Strasbourg 1909, as baritone. Studied further in Milan and Dresden, sang as tenor at Nuremberg 1911–13 and Wiesbaden 1913–17. Hamburg 1917–35, in Wagner and as Paul in the 1920 fp of Korngold's *Die tote Stadt*. Vienna 1920–29. Chicago 1921–2, as Tristan and Tannhäuser.

Schuch, Ernst von (b Graz, 23 Nov 1846; d Dresden, 10 May 1914), Austrian conductor. Studied at Graz and Vienna, had his first conducting engagement at Breslau, and after several others went to

Dresden in 1872 and was made court music director the next year; while in Dresden he gave the fps of Strauss's *Feuersnot*, *Elektra*, *Salome* and *Rosenkavalier*. He also conducted the symphonic concerts of the Royal (later State) Orchestra.

Schuch, Willi (b Basel, 12 Nov 1900; d Zurich, 4 Oct 1986), Swiss musicologist. Studied under Courvoisier and Sandberger at Munich and Ernst Kurth at Bern, where he took a doctor's degree in 1927. He became a critic at Zurich. From 1930 to 1944 he taught at the Zurich Conservatory. His works include studies of Schütz, Swiss folk and early music, Schoeck, etc. In 1976 he pub. the first volume in the authorized biography of Richard Strauss.

Schuch-Proska, Clementine (b Vienna, 12 Feb 1850; d Kötzschenbroda near Dresden, 8 Jun 1932), Austrian soprano, wife of Ernst von ◊Schuch. Pupil of Mathilde Marchesi at the Vienna Conservatory, was engaged by the Dresden Court Opera 1873 and married Schuch there 1875; she sang in Dresden until 1904.

Schuhplattler, German, a Bavarian country dance with music in moderate 3–4 time similar to that of the Ländler. The dancers are men only and they strike their palms on their knees and soles.

Schulhoff, Erwin (b Prague, 8 Jun 1894; d Wülzburg, Germany, 18 Aug 1942), Czech pianist and composer. Studied at the conservatories of Prague, Vienna, Leipzig and Cologne. As a communist in Nazi- ruled Czechoslovakia, he sought refuge in Soviet citizenship; after the 1941 invasion of Russia he was arrested. He died in a concentration camp. Recent performances of the opera *Flammen/Flames* (1928) suggests a powerful assimilation of a wide range of contemporary influences, including jazz and micro tonality.

Works include opera *Flames*; ballets *Ogelala* and *Moonstruck*; incidental music to Molière's *Bourgeois gentilhomme*; two symphonies; piano concerto; chamber music; piano works.

Schuller, Gunther (b New York, 22 Nov 1925), American composer and horn player. After playing horn in the Cincinnati SO he joined the NY Met. Orchestra (1945–59). Professor of composition at the New England Conservatory, Boston, MA 1966–77. Joint artistic director of the Berkshire Music Center, 1970–85. Has written on and been influenced by jazz.

Works include operas *The Visitation*, after Kafka (1966), *The Fisherman and his Wife* (1970) and *A Question of Taste* (1989); *Seven Studies on Themes of Paul Klee* (1959), *Three Studies in Texture* for orchestra; ballet *Variants*; symphonies; concertos for cello, horn, piano; violin concerto (1976), double-bassoon concerto (1978), saxophone concerto (1983), *Concerto quaternio* (1984); *Concerto festivo* for brass quintet and orchestra (1984); Concertos for bassoon (1985), Viola (1985), string quartet (1988), flute (1989) and piano three hands (1989); *Fantasia concertante* for three trombones and piano; quartet for four double basses; five pieces for five horns.

Schuloper German = 'school opera'; a German work of a special type of the 20th c. with a didactic purpose; the same as a *Lehrstück*, but invariably intended for the stage.

Schultheiss, Benedict (b Nuremberg, 20 Sept 1653; d Nuremberg, 1 Mar 1693), German organist and composer. Pupil of his father, Hieronymus Schultheiss (1600–69). He was appointed organist of the church of St Giles at Nuremberg.

Works include hymn tunes; harpsichord pieces.

Schultz, or Schulz, probably the German form of the name of the musicians calling themselves Praetorius.

Schulz, Johann Abraham Peter (b Lüneburg, 31 Mar 1747; d Schwedt, 10 Jun 1800), German composer, conductor and musicologist. A pupil of Kirnberger, he travelled in Austria, Italy and France in 1768, and after holding a post in Poland returned in 1773 to Berlin, where he collaborated in Kirnberger and Sulzer's encyclopaedia. Conductor at the French theatre in Berlin 1776–78, he was court composer to Prince Heinrich of Prussia at Rheinsberg 1780–87, then at the Danish court in Copenhagen until his return to Germany in 1795. Wrote a number of theoretical works, including (with Kirnberger) a treatise on harmony.

Works include operas (French) *Clarisse*, *La Fée Urgèle* (after Voltaire, 1782), *Le Barbier de Séville* (after Beaumarchais, 1786) and

Aline, reine de Golconde (Danish 1787), *The Harvest Home* (1790), *The Entry* (1793) and *Peter's Wedding*; German melodrama *Minona*; incidental music for Racine's *Athalie* and other plays; *Christi Tod, Maria und Johannes* and other sacred works; chamber music, *Lieder im Volkston* and many other songs.

Schulz-Beuthen, Heinrich (b Beuthen, Silesia, 19 Jun 1838; d Dresden, 12 Mar 1915), German composer. Studied at the Leipzig Conservatory, taught at Zurich 1866–80, at Dresden 1880–93, in Vienna 1893–95, and at the Dresden Conservatory from 1895.

Works include operas *Aschenbrödel* (1879; text by Mathilde Wesendonk), *Die Verschollene* and three others; Christmas play *Die Blume Wunderhold*; Requiem, six Psalms and other choral works; eight symphonies (no. 6 on Shakespeare's *King Lear*), symphonic poems on Schiller's *Wilhelm Tell*, on Böcklin's picture 'The Isle of the Dead', on Grillparzer's *Des Meeres und der Liebe Wellen* and others, two suites, two scenes from Goethe's *Faust*, serenade and other works for orchestra; piano concerto; wind octet, string quintet and trio; two sonatas and pieces for piano; numerous songs.

Schuman, William H(oward) (b New York, 4 Aug 1910; d New York, 15 Feb 1992), American composer. Studied at Columbia University and at the Mozarteum, Salzburg. In 1936 he was appointed teacher at the Columbia University summer school and in 1938 at the Sarah Lawrence College in NY. Studied later with Roy Harris and had his first major success when the 3rd symphony was premiered under Stokowski in 1933. In 1945 he succeeded Carl Engel as director of music publications in the house of Schirmer in NY and Ernest Hutcheson as president of the Juilliard School of Music. Director of the Lincoln Center, NY 1961–69. His ten symphonies are at the heart of his output, embracing typical new world virtues of energy, high spirits and solid craftsmanship.

Works include baseball opera *The Mighty Casey* (1953); ballets *Choreographic Poem*, *Undertone*, *Night Journey*; incidental music for Shakespeare's *Henry VIII*; film music for *Steeltown*; two secular cantatas for chorus and orchestra; ten symphonies (1936–76), *American Festival* and *William Billings* overtures, *Prayer in Time of War* (1943) and *Side-Show* for orchestra; symphony for string orchestra (1943); *Judith* (choreographic poem); *Newsreel* for military band; piano concerto, violin concerto (1947); four *Canonic Choruses*, *Pioneers*, *Requiescat* (without words), etc., for unaccompanied chorus; four string quartets (1936–50), canon and fugue for piano trio; quartettino for four bassoons; *Three-Score Set* for piano.

Schumann (born *Wieck*), Clara (Josephine) (b Leipzig, 13 Sept 1819; d Frankfurt, 20 May 1896), German pianist and composer. Pupil of her father, Friedrich Wieck, made her first public appearance at the age of nine in 1828 and gave her own first concert at the Leipzig Gewandhaus on 8 Nov 1830. In 1837 she was in Vienna for some time. Her engagement to Schumann was violently opposed by her father, but they married after many difficulties on 12 Sept 1840. She appeared in public less frequently during her married life, but after Schumann's death in 1856 she was obliged to do so continuously and to teach. She went to live in Berlin with her mother, who had married Bargiel, but in 1863 she settled at Baden-Baden and in 1878 became chief piano professor at the Hoch Conservatory at Frankfurt.

Works include piano concerto in A minor; piano trio in G minor; variations on a theme by Robert Schumann and *c* 12 other op. nos. for piano; several sets of songs.

Schumann, Elisabeth (b Merseburg, 13 Jun 1888; d New York, 23 Apr 1952), German soprano. Studied at Dresden, Berlin and Hamburg; at the last she made her stage debut in 1909 and remained attached to the Opera until she joined the Vienna Opera in 1919; NY Met. debut 1914, as Sophie. She toured the USA in 1921 with Strauss and first appeared at CG in 1924; sang there until 1931 in Strauss and Mozart. Her Susanna, Zerlina and Sophie set new standards in lyrical singing. In 1938 she settled in USA and taught at the Curtis Institute in Philadelphia, becoming an American citizen 1944.

Schumann, Patricia (b Los Angeles, 4 Feb 1954), American soprano. After study at Santa Cruz University sang first with San Francisco Opera. Later appearances with the New York City Opera and in Paris

Schumann *The composer Robert Schumann (1810–1856). After permanently damaging a finger as a result of over-practising, he gave up his career as a pianist to devote himself full-time to composition. His wife Clara was a fine pianist in her own right.*

and Venice. Toured with the Peter Brook version of *Carmen* and sang in Brussels from 1983, as Dorabella and Zerlina. St Louis 1986, in the US fp of *Il Viaggio a Reims*, and Poppea at the Paris Châtelet in 1989. NY Met. and CG debuts as Donna Elvira, 1990 and 1992.

Schumann, Robert (Alexander) (b Zwickau, Saxony, 8 Jun 1810; d Endenich near Bonn, 29 Jul 1856), German composer. Son of a bookseller and publisher. Began to learn the piano from a schoolmaster and organist at the age of eight and played well by the time he was 11, besides studying all the music found at his father's shop, where he also developed a literary taste. He played at school concerts and private houses and made such progress in improvisation and composition that in 1825 Weber was approached to teach him, but could not, being busy preparing *Oberon* for London and expecting to go there. Schumann's father died in 1826, and in 1828 he was sent to Leipzig University to study law. There he met Wieck, from whom he took piano lessons, and first met his daughter Clara, neglecting his legal studies, as he did again when in 1829 he moved to Heidelberg University, where he came under the influence of Thibaut. Back at Leipzig in 1830, he lodged at Wieck's house, wrote his first pub. works (op. 1 and 7) and the next year went to the St Thomas cantor, Weinlig, for instruction, but left him for the younger Dorn. In 1832 he permanently injured his hand with a mechanical contrivance he had invented for finger-development and thus had to give up a pianist's career for that of a composer.

With a circle of young intellectuals he founded the *Neue Zeitschrift für Musik* in 1833, and the circle calling itself the 'Davids-bündler'. He fell in love with Ernestine von Fricken in 1834, but the engagement was broken off next year during which he wrote his first great keyboard work, *Carnaval*. In 1836 Wieck's daughter Clara, already a remarkable pianist, was 17 and she and Schumann fell seriously in love. Some of his feelings were expressed in the C major Fantasy for piano, which also quotes from Beethoven's *An die ferne Geliebte/To the Distant Beloved*. Clara's father violently opposed a match and in 1839 they took legal proceedings against him; he failed to yield, but they married on 12 Sept 1840, the day before she came of age.

Now followed the most prolific period of Schumann's creative life:

A Selection of

Schumann

Carnaval	1835
Fantasie op. 17	1836
Dichterliebe	1840
Liederkreis op. 39	1840

Symphony no. 1	1841
Piano Concerto	1841–5
Piano Quintet	1842
String Quartet op. 41 no. 3	1842
Symphony no. 2	1846
Symphony no. 3	1850

the 'Spring' symphony of 1841 seems to symbolize artistic as well as natural growth and the same fervent, vital impulse informs the song cycles *Dichterliebe* and *Liederkreis* (op. 24, op. 39), the string quartets op 41 and the Piano Quintet, all of this same period; the first, rhapsodic movement of the Piano Concerto also dates from this time (1841–42); the last two movements were added 1845. In 1843 Schumann suffered a crisis of mental exhaustion and he had a more serious breakdown after a tour in Russia with Clara in 1844, at the end of which year they settled at Dresden.

Although his nervous complaint grew more marked after periods of recovery, he accepted the conductorship at Düsseldorf, including subscription concerts, choral practices and church music, in 1850, a post for which he proved quite unfit.

In spite of his personal problems Schumann completed in 1850 the most exuberant and accomplished of all his orchestral works, the 3rd symphony in E♭, which celebrates the Rhineland, the flowing of the Rhine itself and Cologne cathedral. The committee at Düsseldorf tactfully suggested his resignation in 1852, but with Clara's injudicious support he obstinately refused to withdraw. Signs of a mental collapse grew more and more alarming and his creative work progressively less convincing, and in Feb 1854 he threw himself into the Rhine. On being rescued he was sent at his own request to a private asylum at Endenich, where he died more than two years later.

Schumann's works of all genres tend towards the lyrical qualities found most obviously in his songs; although the spontaneity and melodic naturalness of his piano music and Lieder have rightly been praised his chamber and orchestral music shows similar qualities, although on a larger scale. One of Schumann's most attractive features is the essentially private nature of his genius. The quintessential Romantic, his personal experiences, and in particular his love for Clara, found expression in his music. His inward-looking personality is reflected in the musical cryptograms of many of his works.

Works include opera *Genoveva* (1850); incidental music to Byron's *Manfred* (1852); 15 works for chorus and orchestra with or without solo voices, including *Das Paradies und die Peri* (1843), *Vom Pagen und der Königstochter* (Geibel); *Das Glück von Edenhall* (Uhland); *Requiem für Mignon* and scenes from Goethe's *Faust* (1844–53).

ORCHESTRAL: four symphonies (1841, 1846, 1850, 1841; revised 1851); *Overture, Scherzo and Finale*; five concert overtures; concertos for piano, violin and cello (1841–45, 1853, 1850), two short

works for piano and orchestra, fantasy for violin and orchestra and *Concertstück* for four horns and orchestra (1849).

CHAMBER: three string quartets, op. 41 nos. 1–3 (1842), three piano trios, piano quartet (1842), piano quartet, *Fantasiestücke* and *Märchenerzählungen* for piano trio (the latter with clarinet and viola); two violin and piano sonatas; sets of pieces for horn, clarinet, oboe, viola and cello with piano.

PIANO: 36 op. nos. of piano music including *Papillons* (1831), *Six Intermezzi, Davidsbündlertänze* (1837), *Carnaval* (1835), three sonatas, *Fantasiestücke* (two sets), *Études symphoniques* (1837), *Kinderscenen* (1838), *Kreisleriana* (1838), *Humoreske, Nachtstücke, Faschingsschwank aus Wien* (1840), three romances, *Album für die Jugend, Waldscenen, Bunte Blätter, Albumblätter*; four works for piano duet (33 pieces); *Andante and Variations* for two pianos; Studies and Sketches for pedal piano; six organ fugues.

SONGS: 35 op. nos. of songs (some containing numerous pieces), including *Kerner Lieder* op. 35 and the cycles *Frauenliebe und Leben* (1840) and *Dichterliebe* (1840), also *Liederkreise* (Heine and Eichendorff, 1840) and *Myrthen*; three pieces for declamation and piano; four op. nos. of vocal duets, one of vocal trios, four of vocal quartets; 14 op. nos. of part-songs.

Lose no opportunity of practising on the organ; there is no instrument which takes a swifter revenge on anything unclear or sloppy in composition and playing.

Robert Schumann, *Aphorisms, c.* 1833

Schumann-Heink (born *Rössler*), Ernestine (b Lieben near Prague, 15 Jun 1861; d Hollywood, CA, 16 Nov 1936), German, later American, contralto. Studied with Marietta Leclair at Graz and made her first stage appearance at Dresden in 1878; in 1909 she created Clytemnestra there. In 1892 she paid her first visit to London and sang under Mahler in the first CG performance of the *Ring*. In 1896 made her first appearance at the Wagner theatre at Bayreuth, where she remained until 1906. She settled in USA after 1898, though continuing to appear in Europe, and was naturalized in 1908.

Schumann   *A biographical note*

Schumann was a student of law at Leipzig University from 1828, but soon abandoned his studies, gaining his mother's permission to become a live-in student of Frederick Wieck. Among Wieck's children, who enjoyed acting out ghost stories with Schumann, was the nine-year-old Clara. A hand injury prevented a career as a pianist, and Schumann sought an outlet in composition, several of his early piano pieces reflecting his current infatuations: *Carnaval* is based on the notes A flat minor, E flat, C and B, corresponding to the German notes ASCH, the home town of Ernestine von Fricken. By the late 1830s, Schumann was in bitter conflict with Wieck over Clara; although she and Schumann had fallen in love, her father thought the unstable and unrecognized young composer a poor prospect. Wieck's misgivings were to some extent fulfilled, after Schumann had married Clara and they had both established successful careers. A total absorption in literature and music drove Schumann to increasing isolation; the duality which he had established for himself in the imaginary literary character of Florestan (lively) and Eusebius (dreamy) later became manifest in extreme mental disturbance. A manic-depressive condition caused Schumann severe aural hallucinations and in February 1854 he threw himself into the Rhine, but was rescued. Confined to an asylum where Clara was not allowed to visit him, he died there in 1856.

Schunk, Robert (b Neu-Isenburg, 1948), German tenor. After study in Frankfurt sang with the Karlsruhe Opera, 1973–75. Bayreuth Festival from 1977, as Siegmund, and Erik and others. Sang Strauss's Emperor at Hamburg in 1981, Weber's Max at the 1983 Bregenz Festival. NY Met. 1986–87, as Siegmund and Florestan. Munich Opera 1989, as the Emperor, and Vladimir in *Prince Igor*.

Schuppanzigh, Ignaz (b Vienna, 20 Nov 1776; d Vienna, 2 Mar 1830), Austrian violinist. Worked in Vienna; director of the Augarten concerts, founder of a quartet of his own and that of Prince Rasumovsky. He was the first to lead quartets by Beethoven and Schubert.

Schuricht, Carl (b Danzig, 3 Jul 1880; d Corseaux-sur-Vevey, 7 Jan 1967), German conductor. He studied with Humperdinck and Reger. Wiesbaden 1911–44; many early performances of Debussy, Schoenberg and Stravinsky. From 1944 he was guest conductor with leading orchestras and in London was heard in the standard repertory with the LSO. Toured the USA with the Vienna PO in 1956 and in 1957 appeared with the Chicago SO and the Boston SO.

Schürmann, Georg Caspar (b Idensen, Hanover, *c* 1672; d Wolfenbüttel, 25 Feb 1751), German singer and composer. He was first engaged at the Hamburg opera 1693–97, then at Wolfenbüttel, entered the service of the Duke of Brunswick, who sent him to Italy for further study and gave him leave 1702–07 to enter the service of the Duke of Meiningen, after which he remained at Wolfenbüttel.

Works include operas *Télémaque* (after Fénelon), *Heinrich der Vogler* (in two parts, 1718 and 1721), *Die getreue Alceste* (after Euripides, 1719), *Ludovicus Pius* (1726) and *c* 16 others; New Year cantata.

Schurmann, Gerard (b Kertosono, Indonesia, 19 Jan 1928), British composer of Dutch parentage. He went to England in 1941 and studied at the RCM; largely self-taught.

Works include Wind quintet (1963, revised 1976), two string quartets, flute sonatina (1968), *Variants* for orchestra (1970), *Six Studies of Francis Bacon* for orchestra (1968), piano concerto (1973), *Contrasts* for piano (1973), *The Double Heart*, cantata (1976), violin concerto (1978), *Piers Plowman* for soloists, chorus and orchestra (1980), piano quartet (fp Cheltenham, 1986).

Schusterfleck German = 'cobbler's patch'; a playful German description of a technical device, especially the rosalia, used as an easy subterfuge in composition. Beethoven called Diabelli's waltz, on which he wrote the variations op. 120, a Schusterfleck.

Schütz, Hans (b Vienna, 16 Dec 1862; d Wiesbaden, 12 Jan 1917), Austrian baritone. Debut Linz 1891. After engagements in Zurich and Düsseldorf sang at Leipzig 1898–1908, often in Wagner. Bayreuth 1899–1902, as Amfortas, Klingsor and Donner. CG 1902–04. Wiesbaden from 1908.

Schütz, Heinrich (b Köstritz, Saxony, bap. 9 Oct 1585; d Dresden, 6 Nov 1672), German composer. Learnt music as a choirboy in the chapel of the Landgrave of Hesse-Kassel, studied law at Marburg University and music under G Gabrieli at Venice, 1609–12. He returned to Kassel as court organist, but left for Dresden in 1614, with an appointment as music director to the Elector Johann Georg of Saxony. He did much there to establish the fashion for Italian music and musicians, but although he had written Italian madrigals at Venice, he set his own works to German or Latin words, notably the 26 *Psalmen Davids* of 1619. In 1627 he wrote the first German opera, *Dafne*, on a translation of Rinuccini's libretto by Martin Opitz, for the marriage of the elector's daughter to the Landgrave of Hesse-Darmstadt. After the death of his wife in 1628, he again went to Italy in 1629 where he learned about the newly established form of opera from Monteverdi. In 1633, the 30 Years' War having disorganized the Dresden court chapel, he obtained leave to go to Copenhagen, and he spent the years until 1641 there and at other courts. Returning to Dresden, he did not succeed in reorganizing the court music satisfactorily until the later 1640s. In the 1650s he became much dissatisfied with the new tendencies among the Italian court musicians and had many quarrels with Bontempi, but did not succeed in obtaining his release, and after some improvements later on he remained at the Saxon court for the rest of his life. Schütz was the most important of

Schütz *The composer Heinrich Schütz (1585–1672). In his works, which are almost all sacred, a wide range of influences is felt, from his native Germany as well as Italy and the Netherlands. Throughout his long career he became musically more conservative.*

Bach's German predecessors, uniting the lyric and dramatic elements of Venetian vocal style with German polyphony.

Works include operas *Dafne* (1627, lost) and *Orpheus und Euridice* (1638, lost); motets, *Cantiones sacrae*, psalms, *Symphoniae Sacrae* (1629, 1647, 1650) and concertos for voices and instruments (*Geistliche Concerte* (1636, 1639) and other church music; Christmas (1664), Passion and Resurrection oratorios, *The Seven Words of Christ*; Italian madrigals; *Exequien* (funeral pieces) for six–eight voices, Elegy on the death of the electress of Saxony.

Schützendorf, Gustav (b Cologne, 1883; d Berlin, 27 Apr 1937), German baritone. He studied in Milan; debut Düsseldorf 1905, as Don Giovanni. NY Met. 1922–35, in operas by Strauss, Janáček, Stravinsky and Weinberger.

Schützendorf, Leo (b Cologne, 7 May 1886; d Berlin, 18 Dec 1931), German baritone, brother of Gustav ◊Schützendorf. After singing in Düsseldorf, Vienna and Wiesbaden he joined the Berlin Staatsoper in 1920, where he created the role of Wozzeck in 1925; sang in Berlin until 1929 as Ochs, Boris and Beckmesser. His brothers Guido and Alfons were also successful singers.

Schuyt, Cornelis (b Leyden, 1557; d Leyden, buried 12 Jun 1616), Flemish composer. He travelled to Italy to study music, returning in 1581. He held a succession of organ appointments in the Netherlands. He pub. several books of madrigals and a book of instrumental pieces.

Schwanda (Švanda) the Bagpiper ◊Švanda Dudák.

Schwanenberg (or *Schwanenberger*), Johann Gottfried (b Wolfenbüttel, 28 Dec 1740; d Brunswick, 5 Apr 1804), German composer.

Pupil of Hasse. He was appointed court conductor at Brunswick in 1762.

Works include operas *Romeo e Giulia* (1776), (after Shakespeare), *Adriano in Siria* (1762), *Solimano* (1762), *Zenobia* and *c* ten others; symphonies; piano concertos; piano sonatas.

Schwanendreher, Der, *The Swan-Turner*, concerto after German folksongs for viola and small orchestra by Hindemith; composed 1935, fp Amsterdam, 14 Nov 1935 conductor Mengelberg. The title alludes to the cooking of swans by turning them on a spit.

Schwanengesang, *Swan Song*, song cycle by Schubert, containing the last songs written by him in 1828, including seven settings of Rellstab, six of Heine (his only settings of that poet) and Seidl's *Pigeon Post/Die Taubenpost*. The idea of a cycle was not Schubert's, but that of the pub., as was the title, which was invented as an allusion to Schubert's death; the inclusion of Seidl's song was also the publisher's afterthought. The songs are *Liebesbotschaft*, *Kriegers Ahnung*, *Frühlingssehnsucht*, *Ständchen*, *Aufenthalt*, *In der Ferne*, *Abschied*, *Der Atlas*, *Ihr Bild*, *Das Fischermädchen*, *Die Stadt*, *Am Meer*, *Der Doppelgänger* and *Die Taubenpost*.

Schwarz, Boris (b St Petersburg, 26 Mar 1906; d New York, 31 Dec 1983), American musicologist, violinist and conductor. He studied with Flesch and Thibaud in Berlin and Paris; after a 1920 debut he performed widely in Europe, settling in the USA in 1936. He held various academic posts in NY from 1941 and made a special study of Soviet music.

Schwarz, Gerard (b Weehawken, NJ, 19 Aug 1947), American conductor and trumpeter. Played trumpet in American Brass Quintet, 1965–73, and studied at Juilliard 1969–72. Musical director of the Waterloo Festival at Stanhope, NJ, from 1975; principal conductor from 1986. Directed the New York Chamber Symphony 1977–86, Los Angeles Chamber Orchestra 1978–86. Music director of the Seattle SO from 1986; conducted *Fidelio* for Seattle Opera in 1991.

Schwarz, Hanna (b Hamburg, 15 Aug 1943), German mezzo. Studied Hamburg and Essen; debut Hanover 1970. From 1973 she has been a member of the Hamburg Opera; many guest appearances in Europe and North America. Sang under Boulez in the 1976 Bayreuth *Ring* (Erda) and in the 1979 Paris fp of the complete *Lulu*. Other roles include Fricka, Jocasta and Brangaene.

Schwarz, Joseph (b Riga, 10 Oct 1880; d Berlin, 10 Nov 1926), German baritone. He was a member of the Vienna Volksoper and later of the Berlin Court (afterwards State) Opera; also sang in London and NY; he sang Rigoletto at CG in 1924.

Schwarz, Paul (b Vienna, 30 Jun 1887; d Hamburg, 24 Dec 1980), Austrian tenor. He sang at Bielitz and Vienna 1909–12; appeared in many roles at Hamburg, 1912–33: Manrico, Turiddu, David and Pedrillo. Glyndebourne 1936, Monostatos. Lived in USA during the war. Retired 1949.

Schwarz, Rudolf (b Vienna, 29 Apr 1905; d London, 30 Jan 1994), Austrian, later English, conductor. Studied piano and violin, playing viola in the Vienna PO. In 1923 he became an assistant conductor at the Düsseldorf Opera and from 1927 to 1933 conductor at the Karlsruhe Opera, after which he became music director of the Jewish Cultural Union in Berlin until 1941, when he was sent to Belsen concentration camp. He survived and went to Sweden in 1945 and then England, where he became conductor of Bournemouth SO (1947–51), CBSO (1951–57), BBC SO (1957–62) and Northern Sinfonia Orchestra (1964–73).

Schwarz, Vera (b Agram, 10 Jul 1888; d Vienna, 4 Dec 1964), Yugoslav soprano. She sang in Vienna from 1912, Hamburg from 1914. In Berlin she was popular in the operettas of Lehár, and sang in the 1927 fp of *Der Zarewitsch*, opposite Tauber. Salzburg 1929, Octavian; Glyndebourne 1938, Lady Macbeth, in the first local production of *Macbeth*. Appeared widely in USA during World War II.

Schwarze Maske, Die, *The Black Mask*, opera by Penderecki (libretto by composer after G Hauptmann), produced Salzburg, 15 Aug 1986. Hysterical Benigna suspects that masked party-crasher is former seducer Johnson, an escaped African-American slave.

Schwarzkopf, Elisabeth (b Jarotschin, near Poznań, 9 Dec 1915), German soprano. Studied in Berlin with M Ivogün, making her debut at the Berlin Staatsoper in 1938 as a Flowermaiden in *Parsifal*. Salzburg and CG, London, debuts, 1947 as Susanna and Donna Elvira; La Scala, 1948 as Mozart's Countess. She was especially well known for her singing of Mozart and R Strauss, and also created the role of Anne Trulove in Stravinsky's *The Rake's Progress* (Venice, 1951); other roles included the Marschallin (CG 1959, Met. 1964), Elvira, Alice Ford and Leonore. She was equally famous as a Liedersinger, although some felt that the dividing line between art and artifice was drawn too narrowly. DBE 1992.

Schweigsame Frau, Die, *The Silent Woman*, opera by R Strauss (libretto by Stefan Zweig, based on Ben Jonson's *Epicoene*), produced Dresden, 24 Jun 1935. Henry returns home to his uncle, Sir Morosus, who hates music and noise. Henry hopes to receive an inheritance, but is instead disowned because he has joined a band of singers. He gets revenge, tricking Morosus into marriage with 'Timida', the noisy Aminta in disguise.

Staying in Venice as the guest of old friends, I learned that the long unchanged theory of composing melodies had set aside the ancient rhythms to tickle the ears of today with fresh devices.

Heinrich Schütz, dedication to *Symphoniae Sacrae*, 1629

Schweitzer, Albert (b Kaysersberg, Upper Alsace, 14 Jan 1875; d Lambaréné, 4 Sept 1965), Alsatian theologian, medical missionary, organist and music scholar. Studied organ at Strasbourg and with Widor in Paris. He was lecturer in theology at Strasbourg University 1902–12 and later undertook medical missions in Central Africa, where he spent most of his life, visiting Europe periodically and giving organ recitals of Bach's works. Author of a work on Bach pub. in France 1905 and in an enlarged German edition 1908. He was awarded the Nobel Peace Prize in 1952.

Schweitzer, Anton (b Coburg, bap. 6 Jun 1735; d Gotha, 23 Nov 1787), German composer and conductor. Studied with Kleinknecht in Bayreuth and in Italy 1764–66, and was appointed to the court in Hildburghausen in 1766. Conductor of the Seyler opera troupe 1769, he was at Weimar 1772–74 and Gotha from 1774 to his death, succeeding G Benda as court conductor there in 1780.

Works include *Singspiele* and operas *Walmir und Gertraud* (1769), *Die Dorfgala* (1772), *Alceste* (libretto by Wieland, 1773), *Rosamunde* (ditto), etc.; monodramas *Pygmalion* (after Rousseau, 1772), *Polyxena*; dramatic prologues *Elysium*, *Apollo unter den Hirten*, etc.; incidental music to Goethe's *Clavigo* (1776), Molière's *Le Bourgeois Gentilhomme* (1771), etc.; ballets; cantatas; symphonies.

Schwemmer, Heinrich (b Gumbertshausen, Franconia, 28 Mar 1621; d Nuremberg, 26 May 1696), German composer. Studied with Kindermann at Nuremberg, where he became a master at a school in 1650 and in 1656 choirmaster at the church of Our Lady. Among his pupils were J Krieger and Pachelbel.

Works include wedding and funeral anthems, motets, hymn tunes and other church music.

Schwenke, Christian Friedrich Gottlieb (b Wachenhausen, Harz, 30 Aug 1767; d Hamburg, 27 Oct 1822), German organist, composer, conductor and editor. Pupil of his father, Johann Gottlieb Schwenke (1744–1823) and of Kirnberger and Marpurg in Berlin, he succeeded C P E Bach as municipal music director in Hamburg in 1789. His sons Johann Friedrich (1792–1852) and Karl (1789–after 1870), as well as the former's son, Friedrich Gottlieb (1823–96), were also musicians.

Works include music for the stage; two oratorios; cantatas; church music settings of odes by Klopstock; oboe concerto; six organ fugues; piano sonatas, etc. Also edited Bach's '48', Mozart's Requiem, and works by Hasse, Handel and Spohr.

Schwertsik, Kurt (b Vienna, 25 Jan 1935), Austrian composer. Studied at the Vienna Academy (1949–57), and with Friedrich Cerha founded the ensemble *Die Reihe* (1958), for the performance of new music. Has reacted against the contemporary avant-garde; teacher at the Vienna Conservatory from 1978.

Works include operas *Der lange Weg Zur grossen Mauer* (1975) and *Das Märchen von Fanferlieschen Schönefusschen* (1982); ballets *Walzerträume* (1976) and *Macbeth* (1988); *Draculas Haus und Hofmusik*, for strings (1968); *Symphonie in MoB-Stil* (1971; association with H K Gruber); Violin concerto (1977); *Starker Tobak* for soprano and seven instruments (1983); *Verwandlungsmusik* for orchestra (1983); concerto for trombone (1988); Double bass concerto (1989).

Schwindel, Friedrich (b Amsterdam, 3 May 1737; d Karlsruhe, 7 Aug 1786), Dutch or German violinist, flautist, harpsichordist and composer. He was at The Hague when Burney stayed there in 1770, later at Geneva and Mulhouse, and finally at Karlsruhe as music director to the Margrave of Baden. As a symphonist he belonged to the Mannheim school.

Works include operas *Das Liebesgrab* and *Die drei Pächter*; Mass in E♭; 28 symphonies; quartets, trios.

Schytte, Ludvig Theodor (b Aarhus, Jutland, 28 Apr 1848; d Berlin, 10 Nov 1909), Danish pianist and composer. He was in business as a chemist, but took to music in 1870, studying with Gade and others in Copenhagen and later with Taubert in Berlin and Liszt at Weimar. In 1887 he settled in Vienna as concert pianist and teacher.

Works include monodrama *Hero*, operettas *Der Mameluk* and *Der Student von Salamanca*; piano concerto; piano music.

Sciarrino, Salvatore (b Palermo, 4 Apr 1947), Italian composer. Studied electronic music at Rome (1969) and has taught at the Milan Conservatory from 1974. He is best known for his operas, which take an irreverent view of the conventions of the genre, filtering familiar myths through a surreal sensibility: *Amore e Psyche* (1973), *Aspern* (1978), *Vanitas* (1981), *Lohengrin* 'azione invisible' (1983), *Perseo e Andromeda* (1991). Other works include *Sonata da camera* for orchestra (1971), variations for cello and orchestra (1974), *Clair de Lune* for piano and orchestra (1975), *Kindertotenlied* for soprano, tenor and chamber orchestra (1978), two string quintets (1976, 1977), violin concerto (1985), two piano trios (1975, 1986).

Scimone, Claudio (b Padua, 23 Dec 1934), Italian conductor and musicologist. After study with Franco Ferrara founded the ensemble I Solisti Veneti; has toured throughout Europe and the USA performing 18th-c. repertory and modern Italian works. Teacher of the Verona Conservatory 1967–74, director at Padua from 1983. Has issued an edition of Rossini's works and recorded the opera *Zelmira* (1990). Other discs of Vivaldi's *Orlando Furioso* and *La Cetra* by Marcello. Conducted *Il barbiere di Siviglia* at Caracalla, 1992.

Scio, Julie-Angélique (b Lille, 1768; d Paris, 14 Jul 1807), French soprano. Sang in the provinces from 1786, Paris from 1792. She created Cherubini's Médée, Théâtre Feydeau 1797, and sang there in

Scipio releases the couple after being impressed by the depth of Berenice's love.

Scipione Affricano opera by Cavalli (libretto by Minato), produced Venice, Teatro SS Giovanni e Paolo, 9 Feb 1664. Plot is similar to *Scipio*, with the addition of a sub-plot involving the efforts of King Syphax to rescue his abducted wife, Sophonisba.

Sciutti, Graziella (b Turin, 17 Apr 1927), Italian soprano. Studied in Rome, making her debut at Aix-en-Provence in 1951; roles there were Despina, Susanna and Zerlina. She was especially well known in soubrette roles. Glyndebourne debut 1954 (Rosina); CG from 1956 as Oscar, Nannetta and Despina. In recent years she has turned to operatic production (*La Voix Humaine*, Glyndebourne, *L'elisir d'amore* at CG).

Scontrino, Antonio (b Trapani, Sicily, 17 May 1850; d Florence, 7 Jan 1922), Italian double bass player and composer. Although the son of a poor carpenter, he was brought up in a musical atmosphere, his father running a primitive but enthusiastic amateur orchestra in which he played double bass parts on an adapted cello. In 1861 he went to the Palermo Conservatory and in 1870 began to tour as a double bass virtuoso. In 1876 he produced his first opera, having studied for another two years at Munich. In 1891 he became professor at the Palermo Conservatory, and in 1892 at the Reale Istituto Musicale at Florence.

Works include operas *Matelda* (1879), *Il progettista* (1882), *Il sortilegio* (1882), *Gringoire* (after Banville's play) and *La cortigiana* (1896); incidental music for d'Annunzio's *Francesca da Rimini*; motet *Tota pulchra*, *O Salutaris*, *Salve Regina* and other church music; *Sinfonia marinesca* and *Sinfonia romantica* for orchestra; three string quartets and prelude and fugue for string quartet; songs.

scordatura Italian = 'mistuning'; tuning of the violin or other string instruments temporarily to other intervals than the normal perfect fifths, etc., for the purpose of facilitating the playing of chords with certain intervals or altering the instrument's tone-quality. The music is still written as for the normal tuning (and fingering), so that the instrument becomes to that extent a transposing instrument.

score the copy of any music written in several parts on separate staves, with the simultaneously played notes appearing vertically over each other. Complete orchestral or choral scores showing all the parts are given the name of full score; arrangements of operas, oratorios, etc., for voices and piano are vocal scores; arrangements for piano only are piano scores; composers' sketches reduced to a few staves, to be elaborated and fully written out later, are known as short scores. The usual lay-out of orchestral scores is in groups of various types of instruments, with the treble instruments of each group at the top and the bass instruments at the bottom. The order is as a rule woodwind at the top, brass in the middle and strings at the bottom. Harps, percussion and any other extras are placed between brass and strings.

scoring ♭orchestration.

Scotch snap the technical name for rhythmic figures inverting the order of dotted notes, the short note coming first instead of last.

The Scotch snap in the upper voice of a passage from Handel's Alcina.

the 1800 fp of *Les Deux Journées*. Also appeared in works by Berton and Dalayrac.

Scipione, *Scipio*, opera by Handel (libretto by P A Rolli, based on Zeno's *Scipione nelle Spagne*), produced London, King's Theatre, Haymarket, 12 Mar 1726. Roman pro-consul Scipio successfully besieges New Carthage and falls in love with Berenice, a Spanish captive. But she loves Luceius, who is captured trying to rescue her.

Its name in England, which is also Scots catch, is no doubt due to the fact that the Scotch snap is a feature in the Scottish Strathspey. It was popular in Italy in the 17th and 18th c. and was called by German writers the 'Lombardy rhythm'.

Scott, Cyril (Meir) (b Oxton, Cheshire, 27 Sept 1879; d Eastbourne, 31 Dec 1970), English composer and poet. He played the piano and began to compose as a child. Studied in Frankfurt as a child and from

1895 to 1898. In 1898 he settled at Liverpool as pianist and gave some lessons, and soon after the turn of the century he began to become known as a composer in London, having some works performed and a number of songs and piano pieces published. In 1913 Alma Mahler, the composer's widow, invited him to Vienna, where he gave some performances. During World War I some works were produced in England and in 1925 the opera *The Alchemist* was given, in German, at Essen.

Works include opera *The Alchemist* (1917); ballet *The Incompetent Apothecary* (1923); *La Belle Dame sans merci* (Keats), *Nativity Hymn* (Milton), *Let us now praise famous men* for chorus and orchestra (1935); two symphonies, piano concerto, violin concerto; three string quartets; piano music, songs.

Scott, Marion M(argaret) (b London, 16 Jul 1877; d London, 24 Dec 1953), English musicologist. Studied at the RCM in London, 1896–1904, with which she afterwards remained associated as secretary of the RCM Union and editor of the *RCM Magazine*. She wrote criticism for various periodicals and many articles, notably on Haydn, in whose work she specialized and on whom she was engaged in writing a large work. She also contributed a volume on Beethoven to the Master Musicians Series (1934).

Scott, Walter (1771–1832), Scottish poet and novelist. Celtic romance, a popular subject in the 19th c., was celebrated by Scott in his narrative poems, which were successful in translation throughout Europe. Turning later to the novel, often based on English history, he met with similar success. On a visit to Paris in 1826 Scott attended a pastiche of his *Ivanhoe* (1820) with music by Rossini; more faithful versions of the story were composed by Marschner (*Der Templer und die Jüdin*, 1829) and Sullivan (1891). The first major Italian setting of Scott was Rossini's *La donna del lago* (1819) based on the poem of 1810, *The Lady of the Lake*. This was followed by Donizetti's *Elisabetta al castelio di Kenilworth* (1829) and the most successful setting of Scott, *Lucia di Lammermoor* (1835) based on *The Bride of Lammermoor* (1819). Notable French music derived from Scott includes the *Waverley* and *Rob Roy* overtures of Berlioz (1828, 1832) and Bizet's unjustly neglected opera *La Jolie fille de Perth* (1867), after Scott's *The Fair Maid of Perth*, 1828.

Scotti, Antonio (b Naples, 25 Jan 1866; d Naples, 26 Feb 1936), Italian baritone. Pupil of Ester Trifani-Paganini. Made his first appearance at Malta in 1889 and first visited London, after successful tours in Italy, Spain and South America, in 1899, as Don Giovanni. NY Met. 1899–1933 as Scarpia, Rigoletto and Falstaff.

Scottish Fantasy work for violin and orchestra in four movements by Bruch, based on Scottish folksongs. Composed 1879–80 and dedicated to Sarasate, who gave the fp in Hamburg, 1880.

Scottish National Orchestra ◊Royal Scottish National Opera.

Scottish Opera opera co. founded 1962 by Alexander Gibson. Based in Glasgow but tours widely and has visited London (*Pelléas and Tristan*, 1973). *Les Troyens* was mounted in 1969 and *The Ring* 1966–71. The company moved to a renovated Theatre Royal in 1975. An enterprising approach to modern opera (Janáček series with WNO) and some interesting new productions (*Orlando* and *Oberon*, 1985). John Mauceri music director 1987–93, Richard Armstrong from 1993. Richard Jarman administrator from 1991.

'Scottish' Symphony Mendelssohn's third symphony, op. 56, in A minor and major, begun in Italy in 1831 and finished in Berlin, 20 Jan 1842; fp Leipzig, Gewandhaus, 3 Mar 1842.

Scotto, Renata (b Savona, 24 Feb 1933), Italian soprano. Studied in Milan, making her debut at the Milan National Theatre in 1953. In 1957 she sang Violetta and Donna Elvira in London, and replaced Callas as Amina in *La sonnambula* at the Edinburgh Festival. CG from 1962, Met. from 1965. Other roles included Adina, Lucia, Norma and Lady Macbeth.

Scriabin ◊Skriabin.

Scribe, Eugène (b Paris, 25 Dec 1791; d Paris, 21 Feb 1861), French playwright and librettist. He supplied many of the libretti for the most successful French operas of the 19th c., in particular the Parisian grand operas of Meyerbeer.

◊Adriana Lecouvreur (Cilea); ◊Africaine (Meyerbeer), A N ◊Alexandrov (*Adrienne Lecouvreur*); ◊Ali Baba (Cherubini); ◊Ballo in maschera (Verdi); ◊Châlet (*Adam*); ◊Cheval de bronze (Auber); ◊Comte Ory (Rossini); ◊Dame blanche (Boieldieu); ◊Diamants de la Couronne (Auber); ◊Domino noir (Auber); ◊Dom Sébastien (Donizetti); ◊Elisir d'amore (ditto); ◊Étoile du Nord (Meyerbeer); ◊Favorite (Donizetti); ◊Fra Diavolo (Auber); ◊Gustave III (ditto); ◊Huguenots (Meyerbeer); ◊Juive (Halévy); ◊Leicester (Auber); ◊Lortzing (*Yelva*); ◊Maçon (Auber); ◊Manon Lescaut (Auber); ◊Marquise de Brinvilliers (eight composers); ◊Martyrs (Donizetti); ◊Muette de Portici (Auber); ◊Philtre (Auber); ◊Prophète (Meyerbeer); ◊Robert le Diable (Meyerbeer); A ◊Schmitt (*Trilby*); ◊Setaccioli (*Adrienne Lecouvreur*); ◊Shebalin (*Glass of Water*); ◊Vêpres siciliennes (Verdi).

Sculthorpe, Peter (b Launceston, Tasmania, 29 Apr 1929), Australian composer. Studied at Melbourne University Conservatory and Oxford. Lecturer at Sydney University.

Works include opera *Rites of Passage* (1971–73) and theatre music *Tatea* (1988); *Sun Music I* for orchestra; *Irkanda IV* for strings and percussion; *Sun Music II* for chorus and percussion (1969); *Mangrove* for orchestra (1979); piano concerto (1983); two sonatas for strings (1983, 1988); twelve string quartets (1947–88), string trio, piano trio; sonata for viola and percussion; piano sonatina.

Scylla et Glaucus opera by Leclair (libretto by d'Albaret), produced Paris, Opéra, 4 Oct 1746; revived London (concert) 1979. In pursuit of the nymph Scylla, Glaucus asks Circe for help but the jealous sorceress turns Scylla into the rock which accompanies the whirlpool Charybdis.

Sea Drift setting of a poem by Walt Whitman for baritone solo, chorus and orchestra by Delius, composed 1903; in German, Essen Music Festival, 24 May 1906; in English, Sheffield Festival, 7 Oct 1908.

Sea Interludes (Britten.) ◊Four Sea Interludes.

Seal Woman, The opera by Bantock (libretto by Marjorie Kennedy Fraser), produced Birmingham, Repertory Theatre, 27 Sept 1924. A Celtic folk opera containing many traditional Hebridean tunes.

Seaman, Christopher (b Faversham, 7 Mar 1942), English conductor. Studied at the GSMD, London, and was assistant conductor of the BBC Scottish SO 1968–70 (principal 1971–77). Northern Sinfonia 1973–79 and chief guest with the Utrecht SO 1979–83. Has been chief conductor of the Robert Mayer children's concerts, London, and conductor-in-residence of the Baltimore SO from 1987.

Sea Pictures song cycle for contralto and orchestra by Elgar, op. 37: 1. *Sea Slumber Song* (Roden Noel); 2. *In Haven* (Alice Elgar); 3. *Sabbath Morning at Sea* (Elizabeth Barrett Browning); 4. *Where Corals lie* (Richard Garnett); 5. *The Swimmer* (A L Gordon); fp Norwich Festival, 5 Oct 1899, with Clara Butt.

Searle, Humphrey (b Oxford, 26 Aug 1915; d London, 12 May 1982), English composer and writer on music. Educated at Winchester College and Oxford, he studied music with Ireland at the RCM in London and in Vienna with Webern, later employed 12-note methods extensively in his own music. In 1938 he joined the BBC and in 1947 became Hon. Sec. to the ISCM. He served in the army 1940–46. Professor, RCM 1965–77.

Works include operas *The Diary of a Madman* (after Gogol, 1958), *The Photo of the Colonel* (after Ionesco, 1964), *Hamlet* (Shakespeare, 1968); ballets *The Great Peacock, Dualities*; *Gold Coast Customs* and *The Shadow of Cain* (Edith Sitwell) and *The Riverrun* (James Joyce) for speakers, chorus and orchestra; *Jerusalem* for speaker, tenor, chorus and orchestra (1970).

Five symphonies (1953–64), two suites and *Highland Reel* for orchestra; two nocturnes and two suites for chamber orchestra; piano concerto; *Intermezzo* for chamber ensemble, quintet for horn and strings; quartet for violin, viola, clarinet and bassoon; sonata, *Vigil* and *Ballad* for piano; two Housman songs.

Seasons, The ballet by Glazunov (choreography by Petipa), produced St Petersburg, Maryinsky Theatre, 20 Feb 1900.

Oratorio (*Die Jahreszeiten*) by Haydn (German words by Gottfried van Swieten, based on Thomson's poem), composed 1798–1801; produced Vienna, Schwarzenberg Palace, 24 Apr 1801.

Sea Symphony, A the first symphony by Vaughan Williams, for solo voices, chorus and orchestra (words by Walt Whitman), performed Leeds Festival, 12 Oct 1910.

Sébastian, Georges (b Budapest, 17 Aug 1903; d Paris, 12 Apr 1989), Hungarian-born French conductor. Studied with Bartók and Kodály at the Budapest Academy; worked as opera coach in Munich and NY, conducted Leipzig Gewandhaus orchestra and Berlin Städtische Oper 1927–31, notably in *Bluebeard's Castle* and *Jonny Spielt auf*. Conducted Moscow PO in the 1930s; worked in North and South America during World War II. From 1947 was heard at the Paris Opéra (debut with *Rigoletto*), and with the Orchestre National (Brahms, Strauss and Verdi). Conducted *Ariadne auf Naxos* at Aix in 1966 and recorded *Mignon* and *Thaïs*.

Sebastiani, Claudius (b *fl.* 1557; d 1565), German music theorist. Organist at Fribourg and Metz, but famous particularly for his treatise *Bellum Musicale* (Strasbourg, 1563).

Sebastiani, Johann (b Weimar, 30 Sept 1622; d Königsberg, spring 1683), German composer. Studied probably in Italy. Went to Königsberg *c* 1650, where he became cantor in 1661 and music director at the electoral church in 1663, retiring 1679.

Works include a Passion for voices and strings, with chorales included in a Passion setting for the first time; sacred concertos for voices and instruments and other church music; wedding and funeral cantatas; sacred and secular songs *Parnass-Blumen*.

sec French = 'dry'; a term used by some French composers, especially Debussy, where a note or chord is to be struck and released again abruptly without any richness of tone.

secco Italian = 'dry'; ◊recitativo secco, for which it sometimes serves as an abbr.

Sechter, Simon (b Friedberg, Bohemia, 11 Oct 1788; d Vienna, 10 Sept 1867), Bohemian-Austrian theorist, organist and composer. Settled in Vienna in 1804 and continued studies there, wrote piano accompaniments for Dragonetti's double bass concertos in 1809, while the Italian player took refuge in Vienna, and in 1812 became teacher of piano and singing at the Institute for the Blind. In 1825 he succeeded Voříšek as court organist. In 1850 he became professor at the Conservatory. He wrote several theoretical works.

Works include opera *Ali Hitsch-Hatsch* (1844); Masses, Requiem and other church music; oratorios and cantatas; choruses from Schiller's *Braut von Messina*; chorale preludes, fugues, etc. for organ; variations, fugues and other works for piano.

second the interval between two adjacent notes on the stave.

Major, minor, and augmented seconds.

secondo Italian = 'second'; the part of the second player in a piano duet, that of the first being called primo. Also as an adj., applied to the second player of a pair or a group, e.g. *clarinetto secondo*.

second subject ◊sonata.

Secret, The, *Tajemstvi*, opera by Smetana (libretto by E Krásnohorská), produced Prague, Czech Theatre, 18 Sept 1878. Kalina and Róza are finally united when Kalina discovers a secret passage leading to his beloved's house. In subplot, Blaženka and Vít make public their secret love.

Secunde, Nadine (b Independence, OH, 21 Dec 1953), American soprano. After study with Margaret Harshaw sang at Wiesbaden from 1980 as Agathe, Ariadne and Káta Kabanova. Cologne from 1985, debut as Káta. Bayreuth Festival 1987–88, as Elsa and Sieglinde, London, CG, and Chicago debuts 1988, as Elsa and Elisabeth; sang Cassandre in *Les Troyens* at Los Angeles, 1991. One of her best roles is Strauss's Chrysothemis, which she has sung at San Francisco and Chicago, 1991 and 1992.

Sedaine, Michel Jean (b Paris, 4 Jul 1719; d Paris, 17 May 1797), French playwright and librettist. Aline, Reine de Golconde (Berton and Monsigny); ◊Aucassin et Nicolette (Grétry); ◊Grétry (*Raoul Barbe-bleue*); ◊Guillaume Tell (Grétry); J A Hiller ◊Jagd; ◊Richard Cœur de Lion (Grétry).

Sedie, Enrico delle, ◊Delle Sedie.

Seefried, Irmgard (b Königfried, Bavaria, 9 Oct 1919; d Vienna, 24 Nov 1988), German soprano. After her first engagement at Aachen (1939–43) joined the Vienna Staatsoper; sang with the co. at CG in 1947 as Fiordiligi and Susanna. Other roles included Eva, Ariadne, Judith and Marie. She was especially well known as a Mozart singer, and also in Lieder. In 1948 she married the violinist Wolfgang Schneiderhan. Last stage appearance Vienna, 1976, as Káta Kabanová.

Seeger, Charles (Louis) (b Mexico City, 14 Dec 1886; d Bridgewater, CT, 7 Feb 1979), American conductor, teacher and composer. Studied at Harvard University. After conducting at the Cologne Opera in 1910, he was Professor of Music at California University, 1912–19, where from 1958 he was engaged in research. Author of books on theory and ethnomusicology.

Works include masques *Derdra* and *The Queen's Masque*; overture *Shadowy Waters* for orchestra; chamber music; violin and piano sonata; numerous songs.

Seegr, Joseph (Ferdinand Norbert) (b Repin, near Mělník, 21 Mar 1716; d Prague, 22 Apr 1782), Bohemian organist and composer. Studied in Prague and became singer, violinist and organist at several churches there. On hearing him play, Joseph II offered him a court appointment in Vienna, but he died before he could take it up.

Works include Masses, psalms, litanies and other church music; toccatas and fugues for organ.

Segal, Uri (b Jerusalem, 7 Mar 1944), Israeli conductor. Studied in Jerusalem and at the GSM. He won the 1969 Mitropoulos Competition and in the same year made his debut, in Copenhagen. He was assistant to Bernstein with the NY PO 1969–70 and in 1972 made his US debut, with the Chicago SO; opera debut at Santa Fe 1973, *Der fliegende Holländer*. He has lived in London since 1970 and was principal conductor of Bournemouth SO 1980–82. Has recorded Mozart piano concertos with Radu Lupu.

Segerstam, Leif (b Vasa, 2 Mar 1944), Finnish conductor and composer. Studied at the Sibelius Academy, Helsinki, and the Juilliard School, NY. He was conductor of the Finnish National Opera, then Stockholm Royal Opera, 1965–72, and the Deutsche Oper, Berlin, 1971–73. Salzburg Festival debut 1971 (*Die Entführung*). Principal conductor Austrian Radio Orchestra 1975–82. Finnish Radio SO 1977–87. Danish Radio SO from 1989.

Works include Divertimento for strings (1963), *Concerto Serioso* for violin and orchestra (1967), two piano concertos (1978, 1981), 16 symphonies (1977–90), six cello concertos, eight violin concertos, many works for orchestra under title *Orchestral Diary Sheets*; *Song of Experience* after Blake and Auden for soprano and orchestra (1971); 26 string quartets (1962–82), two piano trios (1976–77), three string trios (1977–78), 22 Episodes for various instrumental combinations (1978–81).

Segni, Giulio (Giulio da Modena) (b Modena, 1498; d Rome, 24 Jul 1561), Italian composer. After a short period as organist of St Mark's, Venice (1530–33), he entered the service of Pope Clement VII. Composed three *ricercari à 4* (pub. in *Musica Nova*, 1540) and other instrumental works.

Segovia, Andrés (b Linares, 17 Feb 1893; d Madrid, 3 Jun 1987), Spanish guitarist. Self-taught, he first appeared in public aged 14. From his first concert in Paris in 1924 he was regarded as foremost among modern guitarists, and Falla, Ponce, Rodrigo, Turina and Villa-Lobos wrote works especially for him. Last London concert Jun 1986.

Segreto di Susanna, Il, *Susanna's Secret*, opera by Wolf-Ferrari (libretto by E Golisciani), produced Munich, Court Opera, in German translation by Max Kalbeck, 4 Dec 1909. Susanna is a secret smoker and her jealous husband Count Gil suspects she has been harbouring a lover because of her mysterious disappearances (to the tobacconist's).

segue Italian = 'follows'; an indication, like *attacca*, that a piece, number or section is to be played or sung immediately after another one. In manuscripts the word is sometimes used instead of *VS* (*volti subito*) where a blank space is left at the bottom of a page to avoid turning over during the performance of what follows on the next.

seguidilla a Spanish dance dating back to at least the 16th c. and first heard of in La Mancha, though possibly of earlier Moorish origin. The original form was the seguidilla manchega, but when the dance spread over Spain others developed: the seguidilla bolero – slow and stately; the seguidilla gitana – slow and sentimental. The seguidilla is usually played on guitars, often with castanet accompaniment and sometimes with violin or flute. Frequently popular verses are sung to the seguidilla consisting of *coplas*, 'couplets' of four lines followed by *estribillos* 'refrains' of three lines.

Seguin, Arthur (Edward Shelden) (b London, 7 Apr 1809; d New York, 9 Dec 1852), English bass. Studied at the RAM in London and made his first appearance at the Exeter Festival in 1829 and at CG and Drury Lane, London, in 1833 in operas by Handel and Cimarosa. Visited USA in 1838, settling later in NY. He married the soprano Ann Childe (1814–88).

Electric guitars are an abomination, whoever heard of an electric violin? An electric cello? Or for that matter an electric singer?

Andres Segovia,
The Beatles, Words Without Music, 1968

Seiber, Mátyás (b Budapest, 4 May 1905; d Kruger National Park, South Africa, 24 Sept 1960), Hungarian composer, conductor and cellist. Studied with Kodály at the Budapest Academy of Music. Travelled abroad, including North and South America; from 1928 to 1933 taught in the newly established jazz class at the Hoch Conservatorium in Frankfurt, also cellist in a string quartet there and conductor at a theatre and of a workers' chorus. In 1935 he settled in London, as choral conductor and film composer, and joined the teaching staff at Morley College. Influences in his music range from Bartók and Schoenberg to jazz.

Works include opera *Eva plays with Dolls* (1934); two operettas; incidental music for plays; film and radio music; *Missa brevis* for unaccompanied chorus; cantata *Ulysses* (chapter from James Joyce, 1947); two Besardo Suites (from 16th-c. lute tablatures), *Transylvanian Rhapsody* for orchestra; *Pastorale* and *concertante* for violin and strings (1944), *Notturno* for horn and strings; concertino for clarinet and strings; four Greek songs for voice and strings.

Three string quartets (1924, 1935, 1951), wind sextet, quintet for clarinet and strings, duo for violin and cello; fantasy for cello and piano, violin pieces; piano works; songs, choruses, folksong arrangements.

Seidl, Anton (b Pest, 7 May 1850; d New York, 28 Mar 1898), Hungarian-born German conductor. Studied at the Leipzig Conservatory from 1870 and two years later went to Bayreuth as Wagner's assistant. Conductor at the Leipzig Opera, 1879–82, afterwards toured and conducted German opera at the Met. Opera House in NY from 1885 to his death; conducted the first US performances of *Tristan*, *Meistersinger* and *The Ring* and the fp of Dvořák's 'New World' symphony (1893).

Seidl-Kraus, Auguste (b Vienna, 28 Aug 1853; d Kingston, NY, 17 Jul 1939), Austrian soprano, wife of Anton ◊Seidl. She sang in Vienna from 1877; married Seidl 1884 and they made their NY Met. debuts together, the following year, in *Lohengrin*. She was the first US Eva (1886) and Gutrune (1888) and the first Met. Sieglinde.

Seiffert, Peter (b Dusseldorf, 4 Jan 1954), German tenor. Studied in Dusseldorf and sang first with the Deutsche Oper there. Berlin (Deutsche Oper) from 1982, as Lensky, Huon (*Oberon*) and Faust. Munich Opera from 1983, notably as Lohengrin, and La Scala and

Vienna Staatsoper debuts 1984; CG debut 1988, as Parsifal. Sang Strauss's Emperor with the Bayerische Staatsoper at the opening of Japan's first opera house (Nagoya 1992). Florestan with the Glyndebourne Opera at the Festival Hall, London, 1995.

Seinemeyer, Meta (b Berlin, 5 Sept 1895; d Dresden, 19 Aug 1929), German soprano. Debut Berlin 1918, as Eurydice; also sang Elisabeth and Agathe. Dresden from 1925, as Marguerite, the *Forza* Leonora and Manon Lescaut. At CG in 1929 she sang Sieglinde, Elsa and Eva, shortly before her early death.

Seixas, (José Antonio) Carlos de (b Coimbra, 11 Jun 1704; d Lisbon, 25 aug 1742), Portuguese organist and composer. Pupil of his father, whom he succeeded as organist at Coimbra Cathedral in 1718, he was organist to the court in Lisbon from 1720 to his death, at first serving under D Scarlatti.

Works include church music; symphony and overture; toccatas, sonatas, etc. for organ and harpsichord.

Séjan, Nicolas (b Paris, 19 Mar 1745; d Paris, 16 Mar 1819), French organist and composer. Pupil of his uncle, N-G Forqueray, he was organist of various Paris churches from 1760, succeeding Daquin at Notre Dame in 1772 and Armand-Louis Couperin at the chapel royal in 1789. At the Revolution he lost his post, but returned to it in 1814, having been meanwhile professor at the Conservatory and organist at the Invalides.

Works include three piano trios; six violin and piano sonatas; keyboard music.

Sekles, Bernhard (b Frankfurt, 20 Mar 1872; d Frankfurt, 15 Dec 1934), German composer. Studied at the Hoch Conservatory at Frankfurt, under Knorr and others, conducted for a time at Heidelberg and Mainz and then joined the teaching staff at his former school.

Works include operas *Schahrazade* (after the *Arabian Nights*, 1917), and *Die zehn Küsse* (1926), burlesque *Die Hochzeit des Faun*, dance play *Der Zwerg und die Infantin* (after Wilde); symphonic poem *Aus den Gärten der Semiramis, Kleine Suite, Die Temperamente* for orchestra; passacaglia and fugue for organ and orchestra; chamber and piano music, songs; serenade for 11 instruments; passacaglia and fugue for string quartet; cello and piano sonata; piano pieces; songs.

Sellars, Peter (b Pittsburgh, 27 Sep 1957), American stage director. Studied at Harvard and produced Handel's *Orlando* at Cambridge, MA, in season 1981–82. Director of the Boston Shakespeare Company 1983, staging the US fp of *The Lighthouse* by Maxwell Davies. At Purchase, NY, produced Mozart's Da Ponte operas in contemporary settings: *Così fan tutte* (1986) in Despina's Diner, *Don Giovanni* (1987) with the lead singer main-lining on drugs and *Figaro* (1988) set at Trump Tower, Manhattan. Premieres of Adam's *Nixon in China* at Houston (1987) and *The Death of Klinghoffer* at Brussels (1991). Premiere of Osborne's *The Electrification of the Soviet Union* for GTO (1987) and at Glyndebourne 1990 staged *Die Zauberflöte* without dialogue but with skateboards; Messiaen's *St François d'Assise* at Salzburg, 1992 (the composer had died earlier that year).

Selle, Thomas (b Zörbig, Saxony, 23 Mar 1599; d Hamburg, 2 Jul 1663), German composer. Was rector and cantor at various places, finally at the Johanneum in Hamburg from 1641.

Works include Passion music including St John Passion (1641), the first Passion to include instrumental interludes, motets, sacred concertos; madrigals; sacred and secular songs.

Selneccer, Nikolaus (b Hersbruck near Nuremberg, 6 Dec 1528; d Leipzig, 12 May 1592), German theologian and organist. Court preacher at Dresden, 1557–61, later held various posts at Jena, Leipzig and Wolfenbüttel. Wrote words and music of many chorales, of which he pub. an important book, containing the work of others and his own, in 1587.

Sembach, Johannes (b Berlin, 9 Mar 1881; d Bremerhaven, 20 Jun 1944), German tenor. He studied in Vienna, and with Jean de Reszke. Dresden 1905–13; created Aegisthus in *Elektra* (1909) and was admired as Lensky and in Wagner. NY Met. 1914–22, as Siegmund and Siegfried. Guest appearances in London and Paris.

Sembrich, Marcella (actually Praxede Marcelline Kochanska)

(b Wisniewczyk, Galicia, 15 Feb 1858; d New York, 11 Jan 1935), Polish soprano. Pupil of her father, Kasimir Kochanski (Sembrich being her mother's name), and appeared at the age of 12 as pianist and violinist. In 1875 she began to study singing with Rokitansky in Vienna and then with Lamperti at Milan and Richard Lewy in Germany In 1877 she made her debut at Athens as Elvira (*I Puritani*). In 1880 she first visited London (CG, Lucia). Later sang mainly at the Met.; until 1917 as Lucia, Rosina, Queen of Night, Elsa, Eva and Mimi.

Semele opera-oratorio by Handel (libretto by Congreve with anonymous alterations), performed London, CG, 10 Feb 1744. Congreve's libretto was originally intended for an opera. Revived CG 1982. After Semele aspires to immortality, jealous Juno tricks her into being consumed by the fire of her lover Jupiter.

semibreve the largest note-value now in current use, called 'whole note' in America. It is half the value of the old breve, and is represented by the symbol o.

semi-chorus a group of singers detached from a chorus for the purpose of obtaining antiphonal effects or changes of tone-colour. It does not often literally consist of half the voices, but is more usually a much smaller contingent.

semicroma Italian = semiquaver.

semiquaver the note-value of half a quaver, and $^1/_{16}$ of a semibreve, represented by the symbol ♪.

Semiramide, *Semiramis*, opera by Rossini (libretto by Giacomo Rossi, based on Voltaire's tragedy), produced Venice, Teatro La Fenice, 3 Feb 1823. Queen of Babylon, Semiramide, murders her husband but dies at the hand of Arsace, her long-lost and unrecognized son.

Semiramide riconosciuta, *Semiramis Recognized*, opera by Gluck (lib. by Metastasio), produced Vienna, Burgtheater, 14 May 1748. Also settings by Vinci (Rome, 1729) and Hasse (Venice, 1744). Semiramide rules Assyria disguised as a man, and eventually marries her former lover Scitalce after complications involving princess Tamiri and her suitors.

semiseria Italian fem. = 'half-serious'; the term for a hybrid between *opera seria* and *opera buffa*.

semitone the smallest interval normally used in Western music. Except for adjustments of leading-notes (◊musica ficta) only two semitone intervals occur in any of the modes and in the diatonic scales, the others being whole tones; in the chromatic scales all the intervals are semitones. ◊scale.

Semkow, Jerzy (b Radomsko, 12 Oct 1928), Polish conductor. He studied in Kraków and in 1950 was assistant to Mravinsky at the Leningrad PO. He worked at the Bolshoi Theatre and had further study with Kleiber, Walter and Serafin. Principal conductor Warsaw Opera 1959–62, Copenhagen 1966–76. US debut 1968, with the Boston SO, and has returned with all the leading orchestras there. His London debut was in 1968, and in 1970 he conducted *Don Giovanni* at CG. Music director of the St Louis SO 1976–79, principal conductor of the Rochester, NY, PO 1985–89. Well known in Romantic and modern repertory. Recordings include *Boris Godunov* and *Prince Igor*.

semplice Italian = 'simple'; a direction indicating that a passage or whole work is to be performed in an unaffected or not over- expressive manner.

Senallié (or *Senaillé*), Jean Baptiste (b Paris, 23 Nov 1687; d Paris, 8 or 15 Oct 1730), French violinist and composer. Studied under his father, Jean Senallié, a member of the royal orchestra, and with the latter's colleague there, Queversin; later with Corelli's pupil Anet and with Vitali at Modena, where he was appointed to the ducal court. He returned to Paris in 1720 and received an appointment at court under the regent, the Duke of Orleans, later confirmed under Louis XV.

Works include sonatas for unaccompanied violin; violin sonatas with bass; pieces for violin and harpsichord.

Sénéchal, Michel (b Tavery, 11 Feb 1927), French tenor. He studied at the Paris Conservatory and in 1952 won the Geneva International Competition. He sang at Salzburg in 1953 and in 1956 was heard as Rameau's Platée at Aix. In 1966 he sang Ravel's Gonzalve at Glyndebourne. Much admired in Europe in operas by Britten, Masse-

net and Mozart. From 1980 directed opera school at the Paris Opéra. NY Met debut 1982, in *Les Contes d'Hoffmann*. Paris Opéra 1985, as Pope Leo X in the premiere of Boehmer's *Docteur Faustus*.

Senesino, actually Francesco Bernardi (b Siena, *c* 1680; d Siena, *c* 1758), Italian male soprano. Studied with Bernacchi at Bologna. Attached to the court opera at Dresden in 1717 and there invited by Handel to London, where he first appeared in 1720; sang in the fps of *Floridante, Ottone, Giulio Cesare, Admeto, Sosarme* and *Orlando*. He was admired for a wide range of vocal skills but left Handel's company in 1733 and returned to Italy in 1736, singing in Porpora's *Il trionfo di Camilla* (Naples, 1740).

Senfl, Ludwig (b Basel, *c* 1490; d Munich, *c* 1543), Swiss composer. Pupil of Isaac in Vienna and his successor as *Kapellmeister* to Maximilian I, which post he held until the emperor's death in 1519. In 1520 he went to Augsburg and in 1523 to Munich, where he settled as first musician at the ducal court. In 1530 he was in correspondence with Luther. He is regarded as the most important German-speaking composer of the motet and song during the Reformation.

Works include seven Masses, Magnificats, motets and other church music; odes by Horace for voices; *c* 250 German songs.

Senilov, Vladimir Alexeievich (b Viatka, 8 Aug 1875; d Petrograd, 18 Sept 1918), Russian composer. Studied law at first, but went to Leipzig for musical studies under Riemann and later worked under Glazunov and Rimsky-Korsakov at the St Petersburg Conservatory.

Works include operas *Vassily Buslaiev* and *Hippolytus* (after Euripides), music action *George the Bold*; symphony in D major, overture *In Autumn*, symphonic poems *The Wild Geese* (after Maupassant), *The Mtsyrs* (after Lermontov), *Pan*, *The Scythians* and *Variations on a Chant of the Old Believers* for orchestra; *Chole forsaken* for voice and orchestra; cantata *John of Damascus*; three string quartets; poems for cello and piano, scherzo for flute and piano.

Senn, Marta (b Geneva, 1958), Swiss-born mezzo. Studied in the USA and sang Carmen for Washington Opera in 1982; sang further with the New York City Opera, Houston Grand Opera and Lyric Opera of Chicago. La Scala 1984, as Rosina and in the title role of Rossi's *Orfeo*. Has sung Massenet's Dulcinée at Barcelona and Annius (*La Clemenza di Tito*) and Angelina (*Cenerentola*) at the 1988 Salzburg Festival. Best known as Carmen, she has sung the role at Munich, Stuttgart and Paris (Opéra Bastille, 1994). Other roles include Charlotte, Salud in *La Vida Breve* and Rossini's Isabella.

sennet a word found in stage-directions of English plays of the Elizabethan period where the author asks for music to be played on or off the stage. It is probably either a variant of 'signet' = 'sign' or a corruption of *sonata*.

sensible French noun, or *note sensible* = leading-note.

senza Italian = without.

Seow, Yitkin (b Singapore, 28 Mar 1955), Malaysian pianist. Studied at the Menuhin School 1967–72 and the RCM, London, 1972–75. Made Wigmore Hall debut 1968 and appeared with the RPO in concert 1975. Appearances throughout Europe and with the regional BBC orchestras (tour of Russia 1985). Recordings include works by Debussy, Satie and Janáček; also the co-operative Chinese *Yellow River* Concerto.

septet any work, or part of a work, written in seven parts for voices or instruments.

Sept Haï-kaï work by Messiaen for piano, 13 wind instruments, xylophone, marimba, four percussion instruments and eight violins; composed 1962, fp Paris, 30 Oct 1963.

septimole or septuplet a group of seven notes to be fitted into a beat or other time-unit in which its number is irregular.

sequence (1) a development of the long vocalizations at the end of the Alleluia in the Mass. In the late 9th or early 10th c. words were fitted to these melodies on the principle of one syllable to a note. Since the melodies were in no regular rhythm the texts were not in verse and were in fact known as *prosae*. The sequence was so called because it followed (Latin *sequor*, 'I follow') the Alleluia, which in turn followed the Gradual. In the course of time new melodies were written and rhyming verse came to be adopted for the texts. At the

An example of a sequence from Handel's Acis and Galatea.

Council of Trent in the 16th c. all but four sequences were abolished: *Victimae paschali* (Easter), *Veni, sancte spiritus* (Whitsun), *Lauda Sion* (Corpus Christi) and *Dies irae* (Requiem Mass). *Stabat mater* (Seven Dolours) (13th c.), not originally liturgical, was admitted as a sequence in the 18th c.

(2) The repetition of a melodic figure at a higher or lower degree of the scale.

Serafin, Tullio (b Rottanova di Cavarzere near Venice, 8 Dec 1878; d Rome, 2 Feb 1968), Italian conductor. Studied at the Milan Conservatory, making his debut 1900 in Ferrara, in 1909 becoming conductor at La Scala, Milan giving the Italian premieres of *Der Rosenkavalier* and *Oberon*. He conducted *La Bohème, Carmen* and *La Gioconda* at Covent Garden in 1907, returning 1931 for *Falstaff, Fedra, La forza del destino* and *La Traviata*. From 1924 he was one of the chief conductors at the NY Met. and gave there the fps of operas by Deems Taylor, Louis Gruenberg and Howard Hanson with the US fps of *Turandot* and *Simon Boccanegra*. Returned to Italy in 1935, where he conducted mostly in Milan and Rome; gave there operas by Pizzetti, Alfano, Berg and Britten. He also appeared in London and Paris (CG 1959, *Lucia*).

Serban, Andrei (b Bucharest, 21 Jun 1943), Romanian stage director. Worked first with Peter Brook on theatre productions in Paris and New York. Stagings with WNO from 1980 of *Eugene Onegin, Rodelinda, The Merry Widow* and *Norma; Aida* in a reduced version (1983). A vivid *Turandot* for CG and Los Angeles was shown in 1984; other London productions include a controversial *Fidelio* and successful *Prince Igor; Alcina* for New York City Opera 1983, fp of *The Juniper Tree* by Glass at Baltimore, 1985. Artistic director of the National Theatre at Bucharest from 1990.

Serebrier, José (b Montevideo, 3 Dec 1938), Uruguayan conductor and composer. He moved to the USA in 1956; studied at the Curtis Institute and with Copland at Tanglewood. Early experience as conductor with Monteux and Dorati (Minneapolis SO, 1958–60). Music director Cleveland PO, 1968–71; guest conductor in Europe and Australia. His compositions use mixed-media devices and include *Colores Mágicos* for orchestra (1971) in which sounds are converted by 'synchorama' into visual patterns and a violin concerto (1992). He is married to the soprano Carole Farley.

serenade evening song or evening music, whether for one or more voices or for instruments. In the 18th c. it often took the form of a suite.

Serenade work for violin, percussion and strings by Bernstein, after Plato's *Symposium*, fp Venice, 12 Sept 1954, with Isaac Stern.

Serenade for Tenor, Horn and Strings song cycle by Britten (texts by Cotton, Tennyson, Blake, Jonson and Keats, all on the theme of night), fp London, 15 Oct 1943, with Dennis Brain and Peter Pears.

Serenaden, Die cantata by Hindemith for soprano, oboe, viola and cello (texts by A Licht, J L W Gleim, L Tieck, J von Eichendorff, J W Meinhold and S A Mahlmann), fp Winterthur, 15 Apr 1925.

Serenade to Music work by Vaughan Williams for 16 solo voices and orchestra (text from *The Merchant of Venice*); composed 1938 for the jubilee of Henry Wood and conducted by him London, 5 Oct 1938. Version for orchestra performed London 10 Feb 1940, conductor Wood.

serenata, Italian, actually the Italian word for serenade, but used in English with a specific meaning for 18th-c. works, often of an occasional or congratulatory type, either produced on the stage as small topical and allegorical operas or at concerts (and even then sometimes in costume) in the manner of a secular cantata.

Sereni, Mario (b Perugia, 25 Mar 1928), Italian baritone. Debut Florence 1953. He sang Wolfram at Palermo in 1955; Buenos Aires 1956. NY Met. debut 1957, Gérard. La Scala from 1963, Vienna from 1965. Other roles included Germont, Rigoletto and Posa.

seria Italian fem. = 'serious'; ◊opera seria.

serialism composition that uses as a prime structural basis a fixed sequence of musical elements. Most commonly this sequence is a series of twelve pitches embracing the entire chromatic octave, ◊twelve-note music; but shorter and longer sets are also encountered. This series can characteristically be presented in any transposition as well as inverted or retrograde, or any combination of those. In the years after World War II certain composers expanded this system, known as integral serialism, to include the serialization of note-lengths, of tempo, of dynamics and even of tone-colour.

> *The twelve-toners behave as if music should be seen and not heard.*
>
> **Ned Rorem**, *Paris Diary*, 1966

series ◊tone-row.

Serkin, Peter (b New York, 24 Jul 1947), American pianist. He studied with his father Rudolf and at the Curtis Institute. He has given regular chamber and orchestral concerts since 1959. He has a wide repertory and favours Bach, Schoenberg and Messiaen; formed the chamber group Taschi in 1973 and has been heard as an improviser and in jazz music. Has premiered works by Henze, Berio, Goehr, Takemitsu and Knussen.

Serkin, Rudolf (b Eger, Bohemia, 28 Mar 1903; d Guilford, Vt., 8 May 1991), American pianist of Russian parentage, father of Peter ◊Serkin. He studied in Vienna, piano with R Robert. Although he made his debut aged 12, it was not until 1920 that he began his true concert career. He appeared frequently with the violinist A Busch and married Busch's daughter. US solo debut 1936, with the NY PO; from 1939 he taught at the Curtis Institute in Philadelphia; director, 1968–76. He excelled in the Viennese classics, particularly intellectually rigorous works such as Beethoven's late sonatas and *Diabelli Variations*.

Serly, Tibor (b Losonc, 25 Nov 1901; d London, 6 Oct 1978), Hungarian-born American composer. He arrived in the USA 1905, becoming a citizen 1911; studied with Bartók and Kodály in Budapest and played the violin with the Philadelphia Orchestra on return to the USA (1928–35). Played with the NBC SO under Toscanini and befriended Bartók in New York when he arrived as a refugee. Completed the last bars of Bartók's 3rd piano concerto and in 1945 made a version of Bartók's viola concerto, from the surviving sketches.

Sermisy, Claudin de (b c 1490; d Paris, 13 Oct 1562), French composer (usually known as Claudin). In 1508–14 he was attached to the Sainte-Chapelle in Paris and in 1515 became a singer in Louis XII's royal chapel, just before that king's death, and later he succeeded Antoine de Longueval as master of the choirboys. In 1533 he was made a canon of the Sainte-Chapelle, with a living and a substantial salary attached to it; but his duties there were light and he remained in the royal chapel, with which, under François I, he visited Bologna, where his choir competed with the Papal choir before Leo X, in 1515. In 1520, with the same king, he met Henry VIII at the Field of the Cloth of Gold, a similar meeting following in 1532 at Boulogne; and on both occasions the French and English choirs sang together.

Works include 11 Masses, motets; over 200 *chansons* for several voices.

Serocki, Kazimierz (b Toruń, 3 Mar 1922; d Warsaw, 9 Jan 1981), Polish composer. Studied at Łódź and later with N Boulanger (1947–48). From 1950 to 1952 he appeared in Europe as a pianist, but later devoted himself to composition in a modernist idiom, including aleatory devices.

Works include two symphonies (1952, 1953; second for soprano, baritone, chorus and orchestra), *Triptych* for orchestra; piano concerto, trombone concerto; choral music; *Episodes* for strings and three percussion groups, *Segmenti* for chamber ensemble and percussion (1960); *Symphonic Frescoes* (1963); *Dramatic Story* for orchestra (1971); *Ad Libitum*, five pieces for orchestra (1976); *Pianophonie* for piano and electronics (1978); chamber music.

Serov, Alexander Nikolaievich (b St Petersburg, 23 Jan 1820; d St Petersburg, 1 Feb 1871), Russian composer and critic. Studied law, but found time to cultivate music, which eventually, after a career as a civil servant, he took up professionally. He studied cello and theory from *c* 1840 and began an opera on Shakespeare's *Merry Wives* in 1843, but was reduced to taking a correspondence course of musical instruction when transferred to Simferopol. He became a music critic and in 1858, when he returned from a visit to Germany as an ardent admirer of Wagner, he began to attack the Russian nationalist school of composers, but found a powerful opponent in Stassov. He was over 40 when he began his first opera. He married the composer Valentina Semionovna Bergman (1846–1927), who wrote some operas of her own, including *Uriel Acosta* (based on Gutzkow's play). When he died from heart disease, he had just begun a fourth opera on Gogol's *Christmas Eve Revels*.

Works include operas *Judith* (1863), *Rogneda* (1865), *The Power of Evil* (after Ostrovsky's play; orchestration finished by Soloviev, 1871); incidental music to Nikolai Pavlovich Zhandr's tragedy *Nero*; *Stabat Mater* and *Ave Maria*; *Gopak, Dance of the Zaporogue Cossacks* and other orchestral works.

serpent early wind instrument, formerly the bass of the cornett family, with a long winding wooden tube covered with leather and played with a cup-shaped mouthpiece. It probably originated in France late in the 16th c. and was used both in bands and in churches, but fell out of use in the 19th c.

Serra, Luciana (b Genoa, 4 Nov 1946), Italian soprano. Debut Budapest 1966, in Cimarosa's *Il convito*. Teheran Opera 1969–76. From 1974 she has sung widely in Italy as Gilda, Rosina, Ophelia, and Bellini's Elvira and Giulietta. CG debut 1980, as Olympia; her coloratura has been admired as Norina, Amina and the Queen of Night. Chicago, Lyric Opera, 1983. Season 1992 as Zerlina in *Fra Diavolo* at La Scala and Pamira in *Le Siège de Corinthe* at Genoa.

Serrano y Ruiz, Emilio (b Victoria, Alava, 15 Mar 1850; d Madrid, 9 Apr 1939), Spanish pianist and composer. He became court pianist to the Infanta Isabella, director of the Royal Opera in Madrid and professor at the Conservatory.

Works include operas *Mitridate* (1882), *Giovanna la pazza, Irene de Otranto* (1891), *Gonzalo de Córdoba* (1898) and *La maja de Rumba* (1910); symphonic poem *La primera salide de Don Quijote* (after Cervantes).

Serrao, Paolo (b Filadelfia, Catanzaro, 1830; d Naples, 17 Mar 1907), Italian composer. Studied at the Naples Conservatory and became a professor there in 1863.

Works include operas *Pergolesi* (1857), *La duchessa di Guisa* (1865), *Il figliuol prodigo* (1868), *L'impostore, Leonora de' Bardi*; oratorio *Gli Ortonesi in Scio* (1869), Passion *Le tre ore d'agonia*; Mass, Requiem and other church music; funeral symphony for Mercadante (1871); overture for orchestra; piano pieces.

Serse, *Xerxes*, (◊Xerse), opera by Handel (libretto by N Minato, altered), produced London, King's Theatre, Haymarket, 15 Apr 1738. It contains the famous so-called *Largo*, 'Ombra mai fù'. The original libretto was that for Cavalli's *Xerse* (1654). King Xerxes of Persia falls in love with Romilda, who is in love with Arsamene. After complications, the lovers are allowed to marry when Amastre, who was earlier jilted by Xerxes, arrives to reclaim him.

Servais, (Adrien) François (b Hal near Brussels, 6 Jun 1807; d Hal, 26 Nov 1866), Belgian cellist and composer. Studied with Platel at the Brussels Conservatory, visited Paris and London, later toured all over Europe and in 1848 became professor at the Conservatory.

serpent *The serpent combines the mouth technique of brass instruments and the finger technique of woodwind. It originated in the late 16th century as an auxiliary instrument for choirs and was used in bands until the 19th century, when brass instruments replaced it.*

Works include three cello concertos and 16 fantasies for cello and orchestra; duets for violin and cello; many cello studies and pieces.

Servais, Joseph (b Hal near Brussels, 28 Nov 1850; d Brussels, 29 Aug 1885), Belgian cellist, son of François ◊Servais. Pupil of his father, with whom he travelled afterwards. In 1868–70 he was at the court of Weimar, in 1875 made his first appearance in Paris, and eventually settled at Brussels.

Serva padrona, La, *The Maid as Mistress*, intermezzo by Paisiello (libretto by G A Federico), produced St Petersburg, Hermitage, at court, 10 Sept 1781. Serpina tricks her master Uberto into marriage, when she threatens to run away with a soldier, in fact servant Vespone in disguise.

Intermezzo by Pergolesi (libretto ditto), produced Naples, Teatro San Bartolommeo, between the acts of Pergolesi's serious opera *Il prigionier superbo*, 28 Aug 1733.

service as a musical term the word implies the setting of those parts of the services of the Anglican Church which lend themselves to musical treatment, i.e. Morning Prayer, Evening Prayer (Magnificat and Nunc dimittis) and Communion.

Servilia opera in five acts by Rimsky-Korsakov (libretto by composer, based on a play by L A Mey), produced St Petersburg, 14 Oct 1902. Daughter of Neronian senator converts to Christianity and provides an example for many noble Romans.

sesquialtera, Latin, short for *pars sesquialtera* = 'a quantity 1 ½ times as much'; in mensural notation the proportion 3:2. ◊proportion.

Sessions, Roger (b Brooklyn, NY, 28 Dec 1896; d Princeton, NJ, 16 Mar 1985), American composer. Studied at Harvard University and later at Yale University with H Parker, also with Bloch in NY and

Cleveland. In 1917–21 he taught at Smith College, Northampton, MA and 1921–25 was head of the theoretical department of the Cleveland Institute of Music. He lived in Italy and Germany 1925–33, then taught for two years at Boston University and afterwards at Princeton and Berkeley. He was professor at Princeton University 1953–65; taught at Juilliard 1965–85. His music accommodated a wide range of contemporary continental influences.

Works include operas *Lancelot and Elaine* (after Tennyson), *The Trial of Lucullus* (1947) and *Montezuma* (1964); incidental music for Andreiev's *The Black Maskers* (1923) and Gozzi's *Turandot* (translated by Vollmöller); *Turn O Libertad* (Whitman) for chorus and piano duet.

ORCHESTRAL AND CHAMBER: nine symphonies (1927–80), three dirges for orchestra; music for four trombones and tuba; violin concerto (1940), piano concerto, Concerto for Orchestra (1981); two string quartets (1935, 1951), piano trio, duo for violin and piano; sonata and three chorale preludes for organ; two sonatas and pieces for piano; songs to words by James Joyce and others.

set an old English name for the suite. Also a series, normally of pitches but also of rhythms or other musical parameters, used in the composition of a piece. ◊serialism and ◊twelve-note music.

Setaccioli, Giacomo (b Corneto Tarquinia, 8 Dec 1868; d Siena, 5 Dec 1925), Italian composer. Studied at the Accademia di Santa Cecilia in Rome and became a professor there in 1922, but moved to Florence in 1925 on being appointed director of the Cherubini Conservatory there.

Works include operas *La sorella di Mark* (1896), *L'ultimo degli Abenceragi* (after Chateaubriand, 1893), *Il mantellaccio* (produced 1954) and *Adrienne Lecouvreur* (after Scribe); Requiem for Humbert I, *Cantica* for solo voices, chorus and orchestra, motets, *Quadro sinfonico* for chorus, organ and orchestra; symphony in A major, symphonic poems, chamber music, songs.

Sette canzoni, *Seven Songs*, opera by Malipiero (libretto by composer), produced, in French version by Henry Prunières, Paris, Opéra, 10 Jul 1920. Part II of the operatic cycle *L'Orfeide*; a series of contrasting moral and emotional principles, drawn from the composer's own life.

Settle, Elkanah (1648–1724), English poet and dramatist. J ◊Clarke (*World in the Moon*, with D Purcell); ◊*Fairy Queen* (Purcell); ◊Finger (*Virgin Prophetess*); ◊Purcell (*Distressed Innocence*).

Sevčík, Otakar (b Horaždovice, 22 Mar 1852; d Pisek, 18 Jan 1934), Czech violinist and teacher. Studied at the Prague Conservatory and became leader at the Mozarteum at Salzburg and gave concerts in Prague. In 1873 he settled in Vienna, was professor at the Music School at Kiev 1875–92 and then became chief violin professor at the Prague Conservatory. He wrote a violin method in four vols. and in 1903 formed a string quartet.

seventh the interval of 10 semitones (minor seventh), or of 11 semitones (major seventh).

Major, minor, and diminished sevenths.

Seven, They are Seven Akkadian Incantation for tenor, chorus and orchestra by Prokofiev, op. 30 (text by K Balmont), composed 1917–18, fp Paris, 29 May 1924, conductor Koussevitzky.

Seven Words of the Saviour on the Cross, The, or *The Seven Last Words*, 1. orchestral work by Haydn consisting of seven slow movements, commissioned by Cádiz Cathedral in 1785 as musical meditations for a three-hour service on Good Friday. Later arranged by Haydn for string quartet (op. 51, 1787) and as a choral work (1796).

2. Oratorio by Schütz (*The Seven Words of Christ*) (words from the four Gospels plus two verses of a chorale), composed 1645.

Séverac, (Joseph Marie) Déodat de (b Saint-Félix de Caraman, Lauragais, 20 Jul 1873; d Céret, Pyrénées Orientales, 24 Mar 1921), French composer. Studied at the Toulouse Conservatory and the Schola

Shaham *American violinist Gil Shaham has been closely associated with André Previn, notably in recordings of the Prokofiev Concertos, and has given many performances of Vivaldi's* Four Seasons *with the conductorless Orpheus Chamber Orchestra.*

Cantorum in Paris, with Magnard and d'Indy. He returned to the south of France and devoted himself entirely to composition, neither his health nor his taste permitting him to hold any official position.

Works include opera *Le Cœur du moulin* (1909); ballet *La Fête des vendanges*; incidental music for Sicard's *Héliogabale* and for Verhaeren's *Hélène de Sparte*; *Ave, verum corpus* and other church music; *Chant de vacances* for chorus; string quintet; 19 songs to poems by Ronsard, Verlaine, Maeterlinck and Poe.

sevillana, Spanish, an Andalusian folksong type similar to the seguidilla and originally confined to Seville.

sextet any work, or part of a work, written in six parts for voices or instruments. ◊string sextet.

sextolet a group of six notes, or double triplet, when used in a composition or movement whose time-unit is normally divisible into two, four or eight note-values.

sextus in old vocal music the sixth part in a composition for six or more voices, always equal in compass to one of the voices in a four-part composition: soprano, alto, tenor or bass.

Seyfried, Ignaz Xaver von (b Vienna, 15 Aug 1776; d Vienna, 27 Aug 1841), Austrian composer, teacher and conductor. Originally intended for a legal career, he turned to music, and was a pupil of Mozart and Kozeluch for piano, Albrechtsberger and Winter for composition. From 1797 to 1828 he was conductor and composer to Schikaneder's theatre (from 1801 known as the Theater an der Wien; in 1806 he conducted the first revival of *Fidelio*). After his retirement he composed almost exclusively church music. He was known for the quantity, rather than the quality, of his output.

Works include over 100 operas and *Singspiele*, e.g. *Der Löwenbrunnen*, *Der Wundermann am Rheinfall* (1799), *Die Ochsenmenuette* (pasticcio arranged from Haydn's works, 1823), *Ahasverus* (arranged from piano works of Mozart); biblical dramas; incidental music to Schiller's *Die Räuber* and *Die Jungfrau von Orleans*, etc.; about 20 Masses, Requiem, motets and other church music; *Libera me* for Beethoven's funeral, etc. Also edited Albrechtsberger's theoretical works and pub. an account of Beethoven's studies in figured bass, counterpoint and composition (1832).

Sf., abbr., = *sforzando*.

sfogato Italian = 'airy'; sometimes used as a direction by composers, e.g. Chopin, to indicate a delicate and ethereal performance of certain passages; also as an adj., especially *soprano sfogato*, 'light soprano'.

sforzando or sforzato Italian = 'forced, reinforced'; a direction indicating that a note or chord is to be strongly emphasized by an accent.

Sfz. abbr. = *sforzando*.

Sgambati, Giovanni (b Rome, 28 May 1841; d Rome, 14 Dec 1914), Italian pianist and composer. Studied at Trevi in Umbria and in Rome and was a pupil of Liszt; later established important orchestral and chamber concerts for the cultivation of serious music in the Italian capital; conducted Liszt's *Dante Symphony* and *Christus*. In 1869 he visited Germany and first heard works by Wagner, whom he met in Rome in 1876 and who induced his publisher, Schott, to bring out some of Sgambati's works. In 1882 he first revisited England.

Works include Requiem; symphony in D and E♭ major, *Epitalamio*

Played with the Israel PO in 1982, under Mehta, and has since appeared with the LSO at the London Barbican, the Bavarian Radio SO in Munich and with the Philadelphia Orchestra on tour to South America, 1988. Season 1989 with the Berlin PO and Orchestre de Paris. His gifts are best displayed in such Romantic repertory as the concertos by Bruch and Sibelius.

Shahrazad, *Sheherazade*, symphonic suite by Rimsky-Korsakov on the subject of the story-teller in the *Arabian Nights* and of some of the tales, op. 35, finished summer 1888 and produced St Petersburg, 3 Nov 1888. Ballet based on it (choreographed by Mikhail Fokin, settings by Leon Bakst), produced Paris, Opéra, 4 Jun 1910. ◊Shéhérazade.

shake a musical ornament consisting of the rapid alternation of the note written down with that a whole tone or semitone above, according to the key in which the piece is written, or according to the composer's notation. See also ◊mordent, ◊pralltriller.

In general A, B, C and F denote a short shake, or a pralltriller, while D and E denote a more extended trill.

Various shakes and their approximate realizations.

sinfonico, overture *Cola di Rienzi* and Festival Overture for orchestra; piano concerto in G minor; string quartet, two piano quintets; piano music.

Shacklock, Constance (b Sherwood, 16 Apr 1913), English mezzo. Studied at the RAM. Sang in the first production of the Covent Garden Opera Company (Purcell's *Fairy Queen*, 1946) and continued until 1956 as Octavian, Carmen, Azucena, Marina, Ortrud, Fricka and Amneris. She sang Brangaene in Amsterdam and Berlin, under Kleiber. Well known in *Messiah* and *The Dream of Gerontius*. OBE 1971.

Shade, Ellen (b New York, 17 Feb 1944), American soprano. Studied at Juilliard and made debut at Frankfurt in 1972, as *Liù*. US debut Pittsburgh 1972, as Micaela; Chicago Lyric Opera 1976–78, as Emma in *Khovanshchina* and Eve in the fp of Penderecki's *Paradise Lost*. Sang Wagner's Eva at the NY Met. 1976, Donna Elvira at the City Opera in 1981. Season 1988 as Florinda in Schubert's *Fierrabras* in Vienna and Káta Kabanova at Geneva. Further roles as Sieglinde in the *Ring* at the Met. and the Empress in *Die Frau ohne Schatten* at the 1992 Salzburg Festival.

Shaham, Gil (b Illinois, 1971), American violinist. He studied at the Rubin Academy, Jerusalem, and with Dorothy DeLay at Juilliard.

Shakespeare, William (1564–1616), English poet and dramatist. Among works based on his plays are:

ANTONY AND CLEOPATRA: ◊Barber (opera, 1966); ◊R Kreutzer (ballet, *Amours d'Antoine et de Cléopâtre*, 1808); ◊Malipiero (opera, 1938); Prokofiev (Symphonic Suite, *Egyptian Nights*, 1934).

AS YOU LIKE IT: ◊Veracini (opera, *Rosalinda*, 1744).

COMEDY OF ERRORS, THE: ◊Storace (opera, *Gli equivoci*, 1786).

CORIOLANUS: ◊Cikker (opera, 1974).

CYMBELINE: ◊Schubert (*Hark, hark, the lark*, 1826); ◊Zemlinsky (incidental music, 1914).

HAMLET: ◊Berlioz (*La Mort d'Ophélie* and *Marche funèbre* from *Tristia*, 1848); ◊Blacher (ballet, 1950); ◊Bridge (*There is a willow* for orchestra, 1928); ◊Faccio (opera, 1865); ◊Liszt (symphonic poem, 1858); ◊Mercadante (opera, 1822); ◊Searle (opera, 1967); ◊Shostakovich (incidental music, 1931, and suite, 1932); ◊Szokolay (opera, 1969); ◊Tchaikovsky (Fantasy overture, 1888); A ◊Thomas (opera, 1868); ◊Walton (film music, 1947).

HENRY IV, parts 1 and 2: ◊Elgar (*Falstaff*, symphonic study, 1913); ◊Holst (opera, *At the Boar's Head*, 1925); ◊Mercadante (opera, *La gioventù di Enrico V*, 1834); ◊Pacini (opera, ditto, 1820).

HENRY V: ◊Vaughan Williams (*Thanksgiving for Victory*, 1945); ◊Walton (film music, 1944).

JULIUS CAESAR: ◊Klebe (opera, *Die Ermordrung Cäsars*, 1959); ◊Malipiero (opera, 1936); ◊Schumann (overture, 1851).

KING LEAR: ◊Berlioz (overture, 1831); Frazzi (opera, *Re Lear*, 1939); ◊Ghislanzoni (opera, ditto, 1937); ◊Reimann (opera, *Lear*, 1978); ◊Shostakovich (incidental music, 1940).

LOVE'S LABOURS LOST: ◊Nabokov (opera, 1973).

MACBETH: ◊Bloch (opera, 1910); ◊Collingwood (opera, 1934); ◊Strauss (tone poem, 1890); ◊Verdi (opera, 1847).

MEASURE FOR MEASURE: ◊Wagner (opera, *Das Liebesverbot*, 1836).

MERCHANT OF VENICE, THE: ◊Castelnuovo-Tedesco (opera, *Il mercante di Venezia*, 1961); ◊J B Foerster (opera, *Jessika*, 1905); ◊Vaughan Williams (*Serenade to Music*, 1938).

MERRY WIVES OF WINDSOR, THE: ◊A Adam (opera, *Falstaff*, 1856); ◊Balfe (opera, ditto, 1838); ◊Dittersdorf (opera, *Die lustigen Weiber von Windsor und der dicke Hans*, 1796); ◊Nicolai (opera, *Die lustigen Weiber von Windsor*, 1849); ◊Salieri (opera, *Falstaff osia le tre burle*, 1799); ◊Vaughan Williams (opera, *Sir John in Love*, 1929); ◊Verdi (opera, *Falstaff*, 1893).

MIDSUMMER NIGHT'S DREAM, A: ◊Britten (opera, 1960); ◊Mendelssohn (incidental music, 1842; overture written 1826); ◊Orff (incidental music, 1939; commissioned under the Nazi régime to replace Mendelssohn's music); ◊Purcell (*The Fairy Queen*, 1692); ◊Siegmeister (opera, *Night of the Moonspell*, 1976).

MUCH ADO ABOUT NOTHING: ◊Berlioz (opera, *Béatrice et Bénédict*, 1862); ◊Stanford (opera, 1901).

OTHELLO: ◊Blacher (ballet, *Der Mohr von Venedig*, 1955); ◊Dvořák (overture, 1892); ◊Rossini (opera – last act only after Shakespeare – 1816); ◊Verdi (opera, 1887).

RICHARD III: ◊Smetana (symphonic poem, 1856); ◊Walton (film music, 1954).

ROMEO AND JULIET: ◊Bellini (opera, *I Capuleti e i Montecchi*, based on Shakespeare's sources, 1830); ◊Berlioz (dramatic symphony, 1839); ◊Blacher (scenic oratorio, 1947; revised as opera, 1950); ◊Gounod (opera, 1867); ◊Malipiero (opera, 1950); ◊Prokofiev (ballet, 1938); ◊Sutermeister (opera, 1940); ◊Tchaikovsky (Fantasy overture, 1869, revised 1870 and 1880); ◊Vaccai (opera, 1825); ◊Zandonai (opera, 1922); ◊Zingarelli (opera, 1796).

TAMING OF THE SHREW, THE: ◊Goetz (opera, *Der Widerspänstigen Zähmung*, 1874); ◊Wolf-Ferrari (opera, *Sly*, 1927).

TEMPEST, THE: ◊Arne (incidental music, 1740); ◊Eaton (opera, 1985); ◊Halévy (opera, *La Tempestà*, 1850); ◊Martin (opera, *Der Sturm*, 1956); ◊Sibelius (incidental music, 1924); ◊Sutermeister (opera, *Die Zauberinsel*, 1942); ◊Tchaikovsky (Symphonic fantasy, 1873); ◊John Weldon (incidental music, 1712; formerly attributed to Purcell), ◊Winter (opera, *Der Sturm*, 1798), ◊Zumsteeg (opera, *Die Geisterinsel*, 1798).

TIMON OF ATHENS: ◊Antonio Draghi (1634–1700) (opera, *Timone misantropo*, 1696); ◊Oliver (opera, 1991).

TROILUS AND CRESSIDA: ◊Zillig (opera, 1951).

TWELFTH NIGHT: ◊Smetana (opera, *Viola*, 1874–84, unfinished; produced 1924).

TWO GENTLEMEN OF VERONA, THE: ◊Schubert (*An Sylvia*, 1826).

WINTER'S TALE, THE: ◊Bruch (opera, *Hermione*, 1872), ◊Goldmark (opera, *Ein Wintermärchen*, 1908).

Shakespeare, William (b Croydon, 16 Jun 1849; d London, 1 Nov 1931), English tenor, teacher and composer. Studied under Molique in London and later at the RAM with Sterndale Bennett, afterwards with Reinecke at the Leipzig Conservatory, where he produced his symphony. Later he studied singing with Lamperti at Milan. In 1875 he returned to London and made his name as a concert singer, and in 1878 became professor of singing at the RAM; Perceval ◊Allen was among his pupils. He wrote several books on singing.

Works include symphony in C minor, two overtures for orchestra; concerto and *Capriccio* for piano and orchestra; two string quartets, piano trio; piano pieces; songs, etc.

Shalyapin, Feodor Ivanovich (b Kazan, 13 Feb 1873; d Paris, 12 Apr 1938), Russian bass-baritone. After a childhood spent in poverty, he joined a provincial opera co. and in 1892 studied singing at Tiflis. In 1894 he made his first appearance at St Petersburg and began to become famous when he was engaged for Mamontov's Private Opera at Moscow in 1896; Bolshoi 1899–1914. He sang at Milan 1901–33 as Mefistofele, Don Basilio, Ivan the Terrible and Boris and was engaged for Paris and London by Diaghilev in 1913. He left Russia 1920 and from 1921 to 1925 sang at the Met.; appeared at Drury Lane, London, 1913–14 as Dosifey and Konchak. Monte Carlo 1905–37 as the Demon, Philip II and Don Quichotte. He was famous both for his voice and for his unrivalled stage presence.

Shankar, Ravi (b Varanasi, Uttar Pradesh, 7 Apr 1920), Indian sitar-player and composer. Worked first with group of musicians and dancers led by his brother, Uday Shankar. Founded the National Orchestra of All-India Radio and was founder-director of the Kinnara School of Music at Bombay, 1962. Many tours of Europe and the USA as sitar-player, attracting the attention of Yehudi Menuhin and other like-minded Western musicians. Compositions include the opera-ballet *Ghanashyam/A Broken Branch*, premiered by the City of Birmingham Touring Opera, 1989; two concertos for sitar and orchestra (1971, 1976); film and TV music, including the film *Ghandi*.

Shapero, Harold (Samuel) (b Lynn, MA, 29 Apr 1920), American composer and pianist. Studied with Nicolas Slonimsky at Boston (1936–38) and with Křenek and Piston at Harvard. Professor of music at Brandeis University from 1952 and has founded an electronic music studio there. His music also admits elements of jazz and serialism: *Symphony for Classical Orchestra* (1947); *On Green Mountain* for jazz ensemble (1957; version for orchestra 1981); *Studies* for piano and synthesizer (1969); *Hebrew Cantata* (1954); piano music and songs.

Shapey, Ralph (b Philadelphia, 12 Mar 1921), American composer and conductor. Studied with Stefan Wolpe and conducted a youth orchestra in Philadelphia, 1938–47. Founder and musical director of Contemporary Chamber Players, Chicago University 1954; professor of music there from 1964. Works include *Invocation*, violin concerto (1959), double concerto for violin, cello and orchestra (1983), *Symphonie Concertante* (1985), Concerto for piano, cello and strings (1986); seven string quartets (1946–72); Trio for violin, cello and piano (1992); *Constellations*, for Bang on Can All-stars (1993) and other instrumental pieces.

Shaporin, Yuri Alexandrovich (b Glukhov, 8 Nov 1887; d Moscow, 9 Dec 1966), Russian composer. Educated at St Petersburg, where he graduated in law at the university. In 1913 he entered the Conservatory there, studying under Sokolov, Steinberg and N Tcherepnin. On leaving he became interested in stage music and founded the Great Dramatic Theatre with Gorky and Blok. In 1937 he moved to Moscow.

Works include opera *The Decembrists* (libretto by A N Tolstoy, 1953); incidental music for Shakespeare's *King Lear* and *Comedy of Errors*, Schiller's *Robbers*, Molière's *Tartuffe*, Pushkin's *Boris Godunov*, Beaumarchais' *Marriage of Figaro*, Turgenev's *The Nest of Gentlefolk* (*Liza*), Labiche's *The Italian Straw Hat*, etc.; film music including *General Suvarov*; symphonic cantata *On the Kulikov Field* (1939); symphony in E minor, suite *The Flea* for orchestra, two suites for piano; song cycles to words by Pushkin and Tiutchev, and other songs.

sharp the sign ♯, which raises a note by a semitone; also an adj. describing out-of-tune intonation on the sharp side.

Sharp, Cecil (James) (b London, 22 Nov 1859; d London, 28 Jun 1924), English folksong collector. Educated at Uppingham and Clare College, Cambridge. After living in Australia 1889–92, he returned to London and in 1896 became principal of the Hampstead Conservatory. In 1899 he began to collect folksongs and dances, later he joined the Folksong Society and in 1911 founded the English Folk-Dance Society. In 1916–18 he visited the USA to collect songs in the Appalachian mountains, where many English songs were still preserved in the early form by descendants of 17th-c. emigrants.

Shaw, George Bernard (b Dublin, 26 Jul 1856; d Ayot St Lawrence, Herts., 2 Nov 1950), Irish critic, dramatist, novelist and political author. Settled in London early in his career and wrote music criticism for the *Star* and the *World*, 1890–94. He was an early and articulate champion of Wagner and Elgar but could see little merit in Brahms and Dvořák. ◊corno di bassetto.

> *The true critic … is the man who becomes your*
> *personal enemy on the sole provocation of a bad*
> *performance, and will only be appeased by good*
> *performances.*
> **George Bernard Shaw**,
> *Music in London 1890–94*, 1932

Shaw (born *Postans*; called *Mrs Alfred Shaw*), Mary (b Lea, Kent, 1814; d Hadleigh Hall, Suffolk, 9 Sept 1876), English contralto. Student at the RAM in London and then pupil of G Smart. She made her first appearance in 1834 and the following year married the painter Alfred Shaw. In 1838 she sang at the Gewandhaus, Leipzig, under Mendelssohn, and the next year at La Scala, Milan, as Cuniza in the fp of *Oberto*. London from 1842, in Rossini's *Semiramide* and *La donna del lago*.

Shaw, Robert (b Red Bluff, CA, 30 Apr 1916), American conductor. He founded the Collegiate Chorale, NY, in 1941 and with them gave the 1946 fp of Hindemith's Walt Whitman *Requiem*; debut as orchestra conductor the same year, with the NBC SO. He worked at Juilliard and Tanglewood and in 1948 founded the Robert Shaw Chorale; many performances in the USA and abroad in works by Bartók, Britten and Copland, in addition to the standard repertory. He worked with George Szell and the Cleveland Orchestras 1956–67; Atlanta SO 1967–88. He was an early US advocate of performances of Bach and Handel using small forces.

Shawe-Taylor, Desmond (b Dublin, 29 May 1907; d Wimborne, Dorset, 1 Nov 1995), Irish critic. He was educated at Shrewsbury and Oxford, became a literary critic at first, but in 1945 became music critic to the *New Statesman and Nation* and in 1959 to the *Sunday Times*, in succession to Ernest Newman; retired as regular critic in 1983. He was especially interested in singing and the gramophone. His books are *Covent Garden* ('World of Music' series, 1948) and, with Edward Sackville-West, *The Record Guide* (1951) and *The Record Year* (1952).

shawm (or **shalm**) an early woodwind instrument, the forerunner of the oboe, with a double-reed mouthpiece and a wide bell. The largest types had bent tubes to their mouthpieces and thus approximated more to the bassoon.

Shchedrin, Rodion (b Moscow, 16 Dec 1932), Russian composer. Studied at Moscow Conservatory with Shaporin, graduating 1955.

Works include opera *Not for Love Alone* (1961), *Dead Souls* (1976), *Lolita* (1994); ballet *The Little Hump-backed Horse* (1955), *Carmen Suite* (1968) and *Anna Karenina* (1972); two symphonies (1958, 1964); Musical Offering for organ and ensemble (1982); three piano concertos; oratorio *Poetoria* for poet, woman's voice, chorus and orchestra (1968), cantata *Lenin Lives* (1972), piano quintet, two string quartets, 24 Preludes and Fugue for piano (1963–70); songs.

Shcherbachev, Vladimir Vassilievich (b Warsaw, 24 Jan 1889; d Leningrad, 5 Mar 1952), Russian composer. Studied with Steinberg, Liadov and Wintol at the St Petersburg Conservatory, and later became professor at the Leningrad Conservatory.

Works include opera *Anna Kolossova* (1939); film music, *The Tempest*; five symphonies (1913–50, no. 4 choral), suite and other orchestral works; nonet for voice and instruments and other chamber music; two piano sonatas and other piano works.

Shebalin, Vissarion Yakovlevich (b Omsk, 11 Jun 1902; d Moscow, 28 May 1963), Russian composer. Son of a teacher; received his first musical training at the Omsk School of Music, entered the Moscow Conservatory as a pupil of Miaskovsky in 1923 and stayed there as a professor in 1928, as well as teaching at the Gnessin School of Music.

Director of the Moscow Conservatory 1942–58, but sacked after being denounced by Stalinists, as a formalist (along with other leading contemporary composers in the Soviet Union).

Works include operas *The Taming of the Shrew* (1957), *Sun over the Steppes* (1958), comic opera *The Embassy Bridegroom* (1942); incidental music for Schiller's *Robbers* and *Mary Stuart*, Pushkin's *Mozart and Salieri* and *The Stone Guest* (Don Juan), Lermontov's *Masquerade*, Scribe's *A Glass of Water*, etc.; film music; symphonic cantata *Lenin* for solo voices, chorus and orchestra; five symphonies (1925–62), two suites and two overtures for orchestra; violin concerto, concertinos for violin and strings and for harp and small orchestra; nine string quartets (1923–63), string trio; sonatina for violin and viola, suite for solo violin; two piano sonatas and three sonatinas; songs (Pushkin, Heine, etc.), popular choruses and war songs.

Shéhérazade song-cycle with orchestra by Ravel (poems by Tristan Klingsor), composed 1903 on the basis of an unpublished overture of the same name of 1898. There are three songs: *Asie*, *La Flûte enchantée* and *L'indifférent*. Fp Paris, 17 May 1904.

Sheherazade, Rimsky-Korsakov, ◊Shahrazad.

Shekhter, Boris Semionovich (b Odessa, 20 Jan 1900; d Moscow, 16 Dec 1961), Russian composer. Pupil of Miaskovsky at the Moscow Conservatory. Later he made a close study of Turcomanian folk music, and based some of his works on it.

Works include operas *The Year 1905* (with Davidenko, 1935) and *The Son of the People*; suite *Turkmenia* for orchestra, five symphonies (1929–51, including symphony *Dithyramb* for the 20th anniversary of the Russian revolution; piano concerto; song cycles.

Shelbye, William, English composer and organist. He was organist at Canterbury Cathedral, 1547–53. A *Felix namque* and *Miserere* are in the Mulliner Book.

Shelley, Howard (b London, 9 Mar 1950), English pianist and conductor. Studied at the RCM with Harold Craxton, Lamar Crowson and Ilona Kabos. Made Wigmore Hall debut 1971 and has performed widely, playing Mozart (concertos conducted from the keyboard) and the Romantic repertory (first complete series of Rakhmaninov piano music, London 1983). Piano duets with wife, Hilary Macnamara, and further recitals with Jane Manning (soprano) and Malcolm Messiter (oboe). Conducting debut with the LSO 1985; principal guest of the London Mozart Players, 1992.

Shelton, Lucy (b Pomona, CA, 22 Feb 1954), American soprano. Studied at the New England Conservatory and has sung in Europe and the USA from 1980; sang Jenifer in London TV production of *The Midsummer Marriage* (1989) and has appeared as Gluck's Euridice, Falla's Salud and the Woman in *Erwartung*. Concert repertoire ranges from Monteverdi to Boulez; works written for her by Stephen Albert, Oliver Knussen and Nicholas Maw.

Shenshin, Alexander Alexeievich (b Moscow, 18 Nov 1890; d Moscow, 18 Feb 1944), Russian composer. Studied philology in Moscow and became a teacher of history and Latin. Only then did he begin to study music with Gretchaninov and Glière, and in 1912 he pub. his first work.

Works include opera *O'Tao* (1925) and other works for the stage; song cycles *From Japanese Anthologies* and other songs.

Shepherd, Arthur (b Paris, ID, 19 Feb 1880; d Cleveland, 12 Jan 1958), American composer and conductor. After a period of teaching at Salt Lake City he was professor at the New England Conservatory, Boston, 1908–17, when he joined the army. From 1920 to 1926 he was assistant conductor of the Cleveland SO, and from 1927 to 1950 at Western Reserve University.

Works include two symphonies including *Horizons*, *Choreographic Suite* for orchestra (1927); fantasy for piano and orchestra; violin concerto; three string quartets (1935, 1936, 1944); *Triptych* (from Tagore's *Gitanjali*) for voice and string quartet; violin and piano sonata; two piano sonatas and pieces; songs.

Shepherds of the Delectable Mountains, The opera by Vaughan Williams (libretto by composer, based on Bunyan's *Pilgrim's Progress*), produced London, RCM, 11 Jul 1922. Pilgrim on way to

Celestial City is summoned by heavenly messenger and is duly anointed by three Shepherds, who assist his journey on the River of Death. ♭Pilgrim's Progress.

shepherd's pipe a rustic wind instrument akin to the oboe, the French musette, played with a double reed, like the chanter of a bagpipe, but usually used separately.

Sheppard, John (b ? London, *c* 1515; d *c* 1563), English composer. Learnt music as a choirboy at St Paul's Cathedral in London under Thomas Mulliner. In 1542 he became organist and choirmaster at Magdalen College, Oxford, and later was in Queen Mary's Chapel Royal.

Works include Masses *The Western Wynde*, *The French Masse*, *Be not afraide* and *Playn Song Mass for a Mene*, 21 Office responds, 18 hymns, motets, two Te Deums, two Magnificats, anthems, etc.

Sherrington, Hellen, ♭Lemmens-Sherrington.

Shicoff, Neil (b New York, 2 Jun 1949), American tenor. Studied at Juilliard and sang there in the fp of Virgil Thomson's *Lord Byron* (1972). First major role as Ernani at Cincinnati (1979), NY Met. from 1976, as Rinuccio, Lensky, the Duke of Mantua, Werther, Hoffmann, Faust and Don Carlos. European career from 1976, with Cilea's Maurizio at Munich and Pinkerton at CG (1978, returning in 1993). Further appearances in Chicago and San Francisco.

Shield, William (b Swalwell, Co. Durham, 5 Mar 1748; d London, 25 Jan 1829), English violinist and composer. Orphaned at the age of nine, he was apprenticed to a shipbuilder, but studied music with Avison in Newcastle, where he also appeared as a solo violinist and led the subscription concerts from 1763. After engagements in Scarborough and Stockton-on-Tees he went to London as second violin in the Opera orchestra in 1772, becoming principal viola the following year. After the success of his first opera, *The Flitch of Bacon* (1778), he was appointed composer to Covent Garden Theatre (1778–91 and again 1792–1807). In 1791 he met Haydn in London, and visited France and Italy. Two treatises, on harmony and thorough-bass, were pub. 1800 and 1817, in which year he was appointed Master of the King's Music.

Works include over 50 works for the stage, e.g. *The Flitch of Bacon* (1778), *Rosina* (1782), *Robin Hood* (1784), *Richard Cœur de Lion* (1786), *The Marriage of Figaro* (after Beaumarchais, 1797), *Aladdin*, *The Woodman* (1791), *The Travellers in Switzerland* (1794), *Netley Abbey*, *The Italian Villagers*, etc.; string quartets and trios; violin duets; songs.

Shifrin, Seymour J (b Brooklyn, 28 Feb 1926; d Boston, 26 Sept 1979), American composer. Studied with Otto Luening and William Schuman. Taught at Brandeis University, MA, from 1966. Music is known for chromatic intensity: Chamber Symphony (1953), three pieces for orchestra (1958), *Five Last Songs* (1979); five string quartets (1949–72), piano trio (1974), *A Renaissance Garland* (1975), *The Nick of Time* for ensemble (1978).

Shimell, William (b Ilford, 23 Sep 1952), English baritone. Studied at the GSMD and the London Opera Centre; has sung with ENO from 1980, as Schaunard, Mercutio (Gounod's *Romeo*), Papageno and Don Giovanni. Has sung in *Egisto* for Scottish Opera, Figaro and *The Rake's Progress* for Opera North and as Guglielmo at CG 1988; US debut as Nick Shadow at San Francisco, 1988. Best known as Mozart's Figaro, which he has sung at Geneva, the Vienna Staatsoper and La Scala; Don Giovanni at Zurich, 1993.

Shirley, George (b Indianapolis, 18 Apr 1934), American tenor. After private study he sang Rodolfo in Milan in 1960. NY Met. debut 1961, as Ferrando. Sang at Santa Fe 1963–65 in the US fps of *Lulu* (as Alwa), *Daphne* (Apollo) as *König Hirsch* (Leand). Glyndebourne 1966–74, as Tamino, Lord Percy and Idomeneo; CG from 1967 as Don Ottavio, Pelléas, Loge and David; also sang in *Die Meistersinger* at Berlin, 1984.

Shirley-Quirk, John (b Liverpool, 28 Aug 1931), English bassbaritone. Studied with Roy Henderson. Early in his career he was identified with Britten's operas: created roles in the church parables, *Death in Venice* and *Owen Wingrave* (CG 1973). With Scottish Opera he has been heard as Golaud, Almaviva and Henze's Mittenhofer;

returned to CG in 1977 to create Lev in Tippett's *The Ice Break*. Widely admired as a concert singer, in Lieder, and in oratorios by Bach, Elgar, Berlioz and Tippett.

Shnitke, Alfred, ♭Schnittke.

Shore English family of musicians:

1. Mathias Shore (d London, 1700), trumpeter. In the service of the court of James II and William and Mary in the post of Sergeant Trumpeter.

2. William Shore (b London, *c* 1665; d London, Dec 1707), trumpeter, son of 1. Succeeded his father in his post.

3. John Shore (b London, *c* 1662; d London, 20 Nov 1752), trumpeter and lutenist, son of 1. Succeeded in his brother's post in 1707. Often heard in works by Purcell, e.g. the ode *Come, ye Sons of Art* (1694).

4. Catherine Shore (b London, *c* 1668; d London, *c* 1730), singer and harpsichordist, daughter of 1. Pupil of Purcell; married Colley Cibber in 1693.

short octave on old keyboard instruments the notes governed by the extreme bottom keys were sometimes not tuned to the ordinary scale,

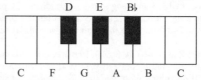

An example of the possible appearance and tuning of a short octave.

but to a selection of lower notes more likely to be frequently required. The bottom octave so tuned was called the short octave.

short score ♭score.

Shostakovich, Dmitri (b St Petersburg, 25 Sept 1906; d Moscow, 9 Aug 1975), Russian composer. Entered the Petrograd Conservatory in 1919 and studied with Nikolaiev, Steinberg and Glazunov. He left in 1925, having already written a great many works. The first symphony, which dates from that year, was performed in 1926 and subsequently throughout Europe, quickly establishing his reputation internationally. He came into conflict with Soviet authority in 1930, when his opera, *The Nose*, based on a story by Gogol, was denounced as bourgeois and decadent. The next, *Lady Macbeth of Mtsensk*, produced 1934, was even more violently attacked in 1936 and had to be withdrawn; his fourth symphony was also withdrawn. It has been

A Selection of

Shostakovich

Symphony no. 1	1925
Lady Macbeth of Mtsensk	1934
Symphony no. 5	1937
Symphony no. 7	1941
Symphony no. 8	1943
Symphony no. 10	1953
Cello Concerto no. 1	1959
String Quartet no. 8	1960
Violin Concerto no. 1	1967
Symphony no. 14	1969

claimed that Stalin himself dictated the *Pravda* article entitled 'Chaos instead of Music' in which the composer was denounced for 'petty-bourgeois sensationalism': Stalin had been seated very near the orchestra at a performance of the opera, and had caught the full blast of the brass as they depicted the violent love-making of Sergei and Katerina. Already of a nervous disposition, Shostakovich was shattered by official denunciation. His popular 5th symphony, labelled by a party hack (not the composer himself) as 'A Soviet artist's practical creative reply to just criticism' helped to restore him in official favour although the deliberately empty bombast of the finale may betray the composer's true feelings. Similar subterfuge is found in the first movement of the 7th Symphony, arising from the siege of Leningrad: the banal march theme suggests Stalinist oppression as much as it does invading Nazis.

In his later years he largely suited his manner to the government's requirements, which in turn became somewhat modified, and established himself as the leading composer of the day, gaining the Stalin Prize with his piano quintet in 1941. With other leading composers he was again denounced in 1948 and did not resume significant composition until 1953, when he wrote his mighty 10th symphony in which the recently deceased Stalin is depicted in a sarcastic scherzo. He is sometimes regarded as the greatest symphonist of the 20th century.

Works include operas *The Nose* and *Lady Macbeth of Mtsensk*; ballets *The Golden Age*, *The Bolt*, and *The Limpid Stream*; incidental music to several plays including Shakespeare's *Hamlet*, *King Lear* and *Othello*, Piotrovsky's *Rule*, *Britannia* and an adaptation from Balzac's *Human Comedy*; cantata *The Execution of Stefan Razin*; music to *c* 14 films.

ORCHESTRAL: 15 symphonies, no. 1 in F minor (1925), no. 2 in B (*October*, with chorus, 1927), no. 3 in E♭ (*First of May*, with chorus, 1929), no. 4 in C minor (1936; not performed until 1961), no. 5 in D minor (1937; sub-titled *A Soviet Artist's Practical Creative Reply to Just Criticism*), no. 6 in B minor (1939), no. 7 in C (*Leningrad*, 1941), no. 8 in C minor (1943), no. 9 in E♭ (1945), no. 10 in E minor (1953), no. 11 in G minor (*The Year 1905*, 1957), no. 12 in D minor (1917, 1961), no. 13 in B♭ minor *Babi Yar*, with bass, bass chorus and orchestra, 1962), no. 14 for soprano, bass, strings and percussion (1969; 11 poems on the theme of death by Lorca, Apollinaire, Küchelbecker and Rilke), no. 15 in A (1971); two piano concertos (1933, 1957), two violin concertos (1948, 1967), two cello concertos (1959, 1966).

CHAMBER: 15 string quartets, no. 1 in C (1938), no. 2 in A (1944), no. 3 in F (1946), no. 4 in D (1949), no. 5 in B♭ (1953), no. 6 in G (1956), no. 7 in F♯ minor (1960), no. 8 in C minor (1960), no. 9 in E♭ (1964), no. 10 in A♭ (1964), no. 11 in F minor (1966), no. 12 in D♭ (1968),

Shostakovich *The composer Dmitri Shostakovich (1906–1975) in 1960. One of the foremost symphonists of the 20th century, his first work in the genre was written when he was only 19, and it established his international reputation. He was able to compose under any conditions, even with the radio playing by him.*

no. 13 in B♭ minor (1970), no. 14 in F♯ major (1973), no. 15 in E♭ minor (1974); two piano trios (1923, 1944), piano quintet (1940), sonata for cello and piano (1934), sonata for violin and piano (1968), sonata for viola and piano (1975).

VOCAL AND PIANO: Songs to texts by Pushkin, Shakespeare, Lermontov, Blok, Michelangelo and Dostoievsky; two piano sonatas (1926, 1942), 24 Preludes for piano (1933), 24 Preludes and Fugues for piano (1951).

Orchestrations of Mussorgsky's *Boris Godunov* (1940, performed 1959) and *Khovanshchina* (1959), re-orchestration of Schumann's cello concerto, for Rostropovich (1963).

Shostakovich
A biographical note

In his memoirs Shostakovich described as the most memorable day of his life the occasion in January 1936 when he was denounced in *Pravda*. Bearing all the signs of coming from Stalin himself, the article condemned Shostakovich's opera *Lady Macbeth of Mtsensk*, premiered two years earlier. Some of the abuse handed out by the dictator has entered the language of invective. Headed 'Chaos instead of Music', the article declared that 'the listener is from the outset confused by a stream of deliberately discordant sounds ... singing is replaced by screaming. The composer ... escapes into the jungle of musical confusion, with grunts, quacks and growls'. Stalin was not quite correct in saying that the opera had enjoyed great success with bourgeois audiences abroad. He had been anticipated in his condemnation by the critic of the *New York Sun*: 'The composer has written music which for realism and brutal animalism surpasses anything else in the world ... Shostakovich is without doubt the foremost composer of pornographic music in the history of art.'

One paper made the following announcement of my concert: 'Today there is a concert by enemy of the people Shostakovitch.'

Dmitri Shostakovitch, *Testimony*, 1979

Shostakovich, Maxim (b Leningrad, 10 May 1938), Russian conductor and pianist. Son of Dmitri Shostakovich. Studied at the Leningrad Conservatory (conducting with Rozhdestvensky) and was assistant with the Moscow SO 1953–65; USSR State Orchestra 1966–71, principal conductor 1971–81. Made London debut with the LPO 1968 and conducted *The Nose* there in 1979. Gave the fp of his father's 15th symphony (1972) and settled in the USA 1981; principal conductor of the New Orleans SO 1986–91. Conducted *Lady Macbeth of the Mtsensk District* at Juilliard 1984 and Hamburg 1990.

Shuard, Amy (b London, 19 Jul 1924; d London, 18 Apr 1975), English soprano. Studied at the TCM in London, making her debut in Johannesburg in 1949. Appeared in London, SW, 1949–55 as Káta Kabanová, Carmen, Eboli and Tosca. She was well known as a dramatic singer, especially in Wagner. From 1954 she sang at CG; roles there included Aida, Turandot, Brünnhilde, Kundry, Elektra and Jenůfa.

She sang Isolde at Geneva in 1972 and appeared in North and South America.

Shudi, Burkat (Burkhardt Tschudi) (b Schwanden, Glarus, 13 Mar 1702; d London, 19 Aug 1773), Swiss (anglicized) harpsichord maker. He settled in London as a cabinet maker in 1718, joined the harpsichord maker Tabel and set up on his own account in the 1730s. ◊Broadwood.

Shumsky, Oscar (b Philadelphia, 23 Mar 1917), American violinist and conductor. Debut 1925 with Philadelphia Orchestra, under Stokowski; studied with Auer and Zimbalist and joined the NBC orchestra, under Toscanini, in 1938. After a brief career as a soloist he played with and conducted various chamber groups in Canada and the USA; Juilliard School from 1953. His career as a virtuoso was resumed in the 1980s, to wide acclaim.

Sibelius, Jean (Johan Julius Christian) (b Tavastehus, 8 Dec 1865; d Järvenpää near Helsinki, 20 Sept 1957), Finnish composer. Son of a surgeon. Having been given a classical education, he intended originally to pursue a career in law, and entered Helsinki University. He learned piano and violin as a child and tried composing long before he had any instruction. While studying law he managed to take a special course under Wegelius at the Conservatory and in 1885 went there altogether, giving up the university. He left in 1889 and had a string quartet and a suite for string orchestra performed in public. With a government grant he went to study counterpoint with A Becker in Berlin and later orchestration with Fuchs in Vienna, where he also consulted Goldmark. When he returned home he became a passionate nationalist, studying the *Kalevala* and other Finnish literature for subjects for his works, the first being *Kullervo*, performed at Helsinki on 28 Apr 1892. Sibelius had a great success with the work, capturing a popular feeling of protest against foreign, particularly Russian,

A Selection of

Sibelius

Karelia Suite	1893
King Christian II Suite	1898
Symphony no. 1	1899
Symphony no. 2	1902

Violin Concerto	1903
Symphony no. 3	1904–7
Symphony no. 4	1911
Symphony no. 5	1915
Symphony no. 7	1924
Tapiola	1926

oppression. Further nationalist sentiments were aroused with the tone-poem *Finlandia* in 1899, becoming an unofficial national anthem.

An annual grant was voted to Sibelius by the government in 1897 and increased in 1926, and he was thus enabled to devote himself entirely to composition without having to fill any official or administrative post.

The First Symphony, influenced by Tchaikovsky, was premiered 1899. The Second Symphony followed in 1902 and is a wholly individual work, building massive paragraphs of sound from short phrases, and moving inevitably towards a triumphant finale. He gradually made his way abroad, but not in every country. Much of his work was pub. in Germany, but not widely performed there. In England he became much better known after the performance of the fourth symphony at the Birmingham Festival in 1912; composed the previous year, it seems to exemplify the view expressed by Sibelius to Mahler in 1907 that a symphony's justification is the 'profound logic creating a connection between all the motifs'. The heavily revised 5th Symphony of 1915–19 further develops this ideal.

Sibelius conducted the fp of *The Oceanides* at Norfolk, CT in 1914, when Yale University conferred a doctor's degree on him. During the Russian Revolution after World War I there was much unrest in Finland, and Sibelius's country home at Järvenpää was invaded; but he spent most of his life there quietly, devoted wholly to composition. The 7th symphony of 1924 is a summation of the composer's career beyond which it was difficult to develop. The conventional four movements are linked thematically into a single unit, creating an awe-inspiring structure as each idea unfolds and develops over a huge span.

Works include opera, *The Maiden in the Tower* (*Jungfrun i Tornet*, 1896); *incidental music to Adolf Paul's King Christian* (1898), Arvid Järnefelt's *Kuolema* (including *Valse triste*, 1903), Maeterlinck's *Pelléas and Mélisande* (1905), Hjalmar Procopé's *Belshazzar's Feast* (1906), Strindberg's *Svanevit*, Paul Knudsen's *Scaramouche*, Hofmannsthal's version of *Everyman*, Shakespeare's *Tempest*.

ORCHESTRAL: seven symphonies, no. 1 in E minor (1899), no. 2 in D (1902), no. 3 in C (1904–7), no. 4 in A minor (1911), no. 5 in E♭ (1915), no. 6 in D minor (1923), no. 7 in C (1924); *Kullervo*, with solo voices and chorus (1892), symphonic poem *En Saga* (1892), *Karelia* overture and suite (1893), *Rakastava* for strings and timpani, *Spring Song*, Four Legends (*Lemminkäinen and the Maidens of Saari*, *The Swan of Tuonela*, *Lemminkäinen in Tuonela*, *Lemminkäinen's Return*

Sibelius *The composer Jean Sibelius (1865–1957). Most of his works date from after 1897, when the Finnish government voted to give him an annual grant to enable him to compose full-time. He was an ardent nationalist, transferring his passion for Finland into his music.*

Sibelius   *A biographical note*

The reputation of Sibelius was established in Finland at the turn of the century with performances of the *Karelia Suite*, the *Lemminkäinen* legends (including *The Swan of Tuonela*), and *Finlandia*. He soon found champions in England through such conductors as Henry Wood, who gave the *King Christian II Suite* in 1901, the First Symphony in 1903 and the Violin Concerto in 1907, all at Promenade Concerts. The sublime Second Symphony was conducted by Hans Richter in Manchester in 1905. Sibelius visited Birmingham in 1912 to conduct the English premiere of his Fourth Symphony, but the American premiere of the work in 1913, under Walter Damrosch in New York, was not a success. *Musical America* opined 'the music looks and sounds like the awkward efforts of amateur composers with little or no training.' A later performance in Boston evoked a similar response to a sparsely beautiful work in which the symphonic apparatus is pared to its essentials, 'the bare bones of music,' as it has been described. Sibelius's first success in the United States came in 1914, when he conducted the premiere of *The Oceanides* at Norfolk, Connecticut. He returned to England in 1921 and 1925, giving well-received performances of the Fifth and Sixth symphonies.

(1895), two suites of *Scènes historiques* (1899), tone-poem *Finlandia* (1899), two pieces *The Dryads* and *Dance Intermezzo*, violin concerto (1903), symphonic fantasy *Pohjola's Daughter* (1906), dance intermezzo *Pan and Echo*, tone-poem *Night-Ride and Sunrise* (1907), funeral march *In Memoriam*, tone-poems *The Bard* (1913); symphonic poems *The Oceanides* (1914) and *Tapiola* (1926), a number of smaller orchestral pieces;

CHAMBER: String quartet *Voces intimae* (1909), sonatina and many smaller pieces for violin and piano; *Malinconia* (1901) and two *Serious Pieces* for cello and piano; 18 op. nos. of piano works including sonata in F major, *Pensées lyriques* (1914), *Kyllikki*, three sonatinas; two organ pieces.

VOCAL: Choral works with orchestra (with or without solo voices): *Impromptu* (female chorus), *The Origin of Fire*, *The Ferryman's Bride*, *The Captive Queen*; *Luonnotar* for soprano and orchestra (1910–13); a number of part-songs; 85 songs; Rydberg's *Skogsrået* and Runeberg's *Nights of Jealousy* for recitation and instrumental accompaniment.

Sibelius justified the austerity of his old age by saying that while other composers were engaged in manufacturing cocktails he offered the public pure cold water.

Neville Cardus, *Manchester Guardian*, 1958

Siberia opera by Giordano (libretto by L Illica), produced Milan, La Scala, 19 Dec 1903; revised 1921, produced Milan, 5 Dec 1927. Vassili is exiled to Siberia for wounding rival Prince Alexis in a duel and is joined there by Stephana; they are both killed trying to escape.

Siboni, Erik (Anton Valdemar) (b Copenhagen, 26 Aug 1828; d Frederiksberg, 11 Feb 1892), Danish pianist, organist and composer of Italian origin. Studied at Copenhagen, J P E Hartmann being among his masters, and with Moscheles and Hauptmann at Leipzig. He fought on the Danish side in the war of Slesvig-Holstein in 1848. In 1851–53 he continued his studies with Sechter in Vienna. After his return to Copenhagen he settled as a music teacher, among his pupils being Princess Alexandra. In 1864–83 he was professor of the Royal Academy at Soroł.

Works include operas *Loreley* (1859) and *Carl den Andens Flugt* (1861); Psalm 111, *Stabat Mater*, cantatas *The Battle of Murten* and

The Assault of Copenhagen for solo voices, chorus and orchestra; two symphonies and other orchestral works; piano concerto (1864); string quartets, piano quartet, piano trio; violin and piano and cello, and piano sonatas; duet for two pianos; piano pieces; songs.

Siboni, Giuseppe (b Forlì 27 Jan 1780; d Copenhagen, 29 Mar 1839), Italian tenor, father of Erik ◊Siboni. He made his first appearance at Florence in 1797, and having appeared elsewhere in Italy, went to Prague, London (from 1806), Vienna and St Petersburg, settling at Copenhagen in 1819, where he became director of the Royal Opera and the Conservatory. He was well known in operas by Paer, Portugal, Paisiello and Nasolini.

Sicher, Fridolin (b Bischofszell, Switzerland, 6 Mar 1490; d Bischofszell, 13 Jun 1546), Swiss organist, priest and arranger. He compiled an MS (St Gall, MS 530) including works by himself and arrangements of vocal works by others.

siciliana or **siciliano**, Italian, a piece or song in dotted 6–8 rhythm derived from a Sicilian dance. It is rather slow, and indeed may form the slow movement of a sonata or suite. Arias in siciliano rhythm were common in the 18th c.

Sicilian Vespers (Verdi.) ◊Vêpres siciliennes.

sicilienne French = siciliana, siciliano.

side drum the military drum, which is the smallest drum used in the orchestra, covered with a skin at either end and having a snare of catgut string stretched over the lower one, to produce a rattling sound when the upper one is struck by a pair of hard wooden drumsticks. Single strokes on the side drum are ineffective: it is usually made to produce small patterns of repeated notes or more or less prolonged rolls. Its tone is bright and hard, without definite pitch. It can be muted by relaxing the tension of the snare.

Sieben Todsünden der Kleinbürger, Die, *The Seven Deadly Sins of the Petit-Bourgeois*, ballet with songs by Weill (libretto by Brecht), produced Paris, 7 Jun 1933; choreographed by Balanchine.

Sieden, Cynthia (b Glendale, CA, 10 Sept 1954), American soprano. Studied with Elisabeth Schwarzkopf and has sung widely in Europe from 1984: Xenia in *Boris Godunov*, under Abbado (1984), Helena in the fp of *Troades* by Reimann (Munich 1986), Cunegone in *Candide* for NY City Opera (1989) and Sifare in Mozart's *Mitridate* at the 1989 Wexford Festival. Other roles include the Queen of Night (Opéra Bastille), Gluck's Amor (Salzburg Festival, under Gardiner), Zerbinetta (Vienna Staatsoper) and Blondchen in *Die Entführung* (Paris Châtelet); Sophie in *Der Rosenkavalier* there 1993.

Siefert, Paul (b Danzig, 28 Jun 1586; d Danzig, 6 May 1666), German organist and composer. Pupil of Sweelinck at Amsterdam. After serving in the royal chapel of Sigismund III at Warsaw, he became organist at St Mary's Church, Danzig, *c* 1620.

Works include Te Deum, psalms for four–eight voices and other church music; organ pieces.

Siège de Corinthe (Rossini.) ◊Maometto Secondo.

Siegel, Jeffrey (b Chicago, 18 Nov 1942), American pianist. Studied at Juilliard and made solo debut with the Chicago SO in 1958. Has appeared with the leading orchestras of the USA, including the New York and Los Angeles POs and the Boston SO; London engagements with the LSO, LPO and Philharmonia Orchestra. Has recorded works by Gershwin and Rakhmaninov.

Siege of Rhodes, The opera by Locke, H Lawes, H Cooke, Coleman and Hudson (libretto by W Davenant), produced London, Rutland House, Sept 1656. The first English opera. Music now lost.

Siegfried (Wagner.) also ◊Ring des Nibelungen; fp 16 Aug 1876. Siegfried, having been brought up by the dwarf Mime, slays the dragon Fafner and acquires the ring. He confronts the god Wotan, shattering his spear; the end of the gods is near. Although fearless in the face of battle, Siegfried awakens Brünnhilde and is frightened by the prospect of love, before being overcome by its power.

Siegfried Idyll a symphonic piece for small orchestra by Wagner, composed at Triebschen on the Lake of Lucerne in Nov 1870 and performed on Cosima Wagner's birthday, 25 Dec, on the staircase of the villa. It was therefore at first entitled *Triebschener Idyll* and called 'Treppenmusik' in the family circle. The thematic material is taken

THE OPERA

Siegfried

A three-act music drama by Richard Wagner, the third of the *Ring* cycle. It was first performed in Bayreuth in 1876.

I. At his dwelling in the forest, the dwarf Mime (tenor) hopes to forge the fragments of the sword Nothung. Siegfried (tenor) enters and learns that he was entrusted as a baby to Mime by his mother Sieglinde, who also gave the dwarf the sword fragments. When Siegfried has left, Wotan, disguised as the wanderer, tells Mime that the sword can only be forged by a hero. Siegfried returns and succeeds in forging the sword. Together with Mime, he goes in search of the dragon Fafner.

II. In the depths of the forest, Fafner (bass) guards the Nibelung treasure and is unimpressed when Alberich (bass-baritone) warns him of the approach of a hero. Siegfried's horn calls attract Fafner; in the ensuing fight the dragon is killed and Siegfried takes the ring and Tarnhelm. The dragon's blood burns Siegfried's finger; sucking it, he understands the language of a woodbird (soprano) who warns that Mime wishes to kill him, and tells him of the sleeping Brünnhilde. Siegfried kills Mime and follows the bird to the Valkyries' rock.

III. The wanderer wakes Erda (contralto) and foretells the end of her wisdom; his will must prevail and the gods will be destroyed. The wanderer tries to bar the path to the rock but Siegfried smashes his spear with Nothung, climbs through the encircling fire, and claims Brünnhilde as his bride.

THE OPERA

from *Siegfried*, except the German cradle song 'Schlaf, Kindlein, schlaf', but some of it, even though included in *Siegfried*, dates back to a string quartet of 1864. The musicians had to rehearse in secret, to maintain the element of surprise for Cosima; Hans Richter (six years later to premiere the *Ring* at Bayreuth) practised his trumpet part from a rowing boat in the middle of Lake Lucerne.

Siegl, Otto (b Graz, 6 Oct 1896; d Vienna, 9 Nov 1978), Austrian composer, conductor and violinist. Studied violin with E Kornauth and composition with Mojsisovics in Vienna. Joined the Vienna SO as a violinist, worked at the Graz Opera and then went to Germany, becoming music director at Paderborn, at the same time conducting and teaching at Bielefeld and Essen. In 1933 he became composition professor at the Cologne Conservatory, returning to Vienna 1948.

Works include fairy opera *Der Wassermann*; music for two puppet plays; oratorios *Das Grosse Halleluja* (Claudius), *Eines Menschen Lied* (1931), *Klingendes Jahr* (1933), *Trostkantate*, *Mutter Deutschland*; *Missa Mysterium Magnum*; *Verliebte alle Reime* for chorus; three symphonies, sinfonietta, *Lyrische Tanzmusik*, *Festliche Ouvertüre*, *Pastoralouvertüre* (1939), *Concerto grosso antico* (1936), *Galante Abendmusik*, *Festmusik und Trauermusik* for orchestra; piano concerto (1963), violin concerto, concerto for string quartet and string orchestra; five string quartets; songs.

Siegmeister, Elie (b New York, 15 Jan 1909; d Manhasset, NY, 10 Mar 1991), American composer. Studied Columbia University, Paris and Juilliard. Organized ensemble American Ballad Singers, 1939.

Works include operas *Dublin Song* (1963) and *Night of the Moonspell* based on *A Midsummer Night's Dream* (1976); six symphonies (1947–85), piano concerto (1976, revised 1982); choral and chamber music including *Cantata for FDR*, for baritone, chorus and wind ensemble (1981).

Siehr, Gustav (b Arnsberg, 17 Sept 1837; d Munich, 18 May 1896), German bass. Debut Neustrelitz 1863. He sang in Prague, Wiesbaden and Munich, 1865–96; created Hagen at Bayreuth (1876) and from 1882 to 1889 was successful there as Gurnemanz and Marke.

Siems, Margarethe (b Breslau, 30 Dec 1879; d Dresden, 13 Apr 1952), German soprano. Debut Prague 1902, as Marguerite de Valois. Her career was centred in Dresden, where she appeared 1908–25; created

there Strauss's Chrysothemis (1909) and the Marschallin (1911). She also created Zerbinetta (Stuttgart, 1912) and was heard in a wide repertory, including Norma, Lucia, Aida, Venus and Isolde.

Siepi, Cesare (b Milan, 10 Feb 1923), Italian bass. Studied at Milan Conservatory, making his debut 1941. From 1946 he sang at La Scala, Milan, and from 1950 was a leading member of the NY Met.; roles there included Philip II, Boris, Gurnemanz and Figaro. He sang Don Giovanni at Salzburg under Furtwängler in 1953 (also filmed) and at CG in 1962. Sang Roger in Verdi's *Jerusalem* at Parma in 1985.

Siface, (Giovanni Francesco Grossi) (b Uzzanese Chiesina, near Pescia, 12 Feb 1653; d near Ferrara, 29 May 1697), Italian male soprano. Became singer at the Papal Chapel in Rome, 1675, and went to England about 1679. Sang at the court of James II, but soon returned to Italy. Purcell wrote a harpsichord piece, *Sefauchi's Farewell*, on his departure. He was murdered on the orders of a jealous rival.

signature ♭key signature; ♭time signature.

Signor Bruschino, Il, ossia Il figlio per azzardo, *Mr Bruschino, or The Son by Accident*), opera by Rossini (libretto by G M Foppa), produced Venice, Teatro San Moisè, Jan 1813. Sofia must marry Bruschino's son, but her lover Florville, disguised as the proposed groom, wins her hand.

Sigtenhorst Meyer, Bernhard van den (b Amsterdam, 17 Jun 1888; d The Hague, 17 Jul 1953), Dutch musicologist and composer. Studied with Zweers, D de Lange and others and later in Paris, afterwards travelling to Java and the Far East. He returned to Amsterdam, but moved to The Hague, where he lived for many years. Editor of works by Sweelinck and author of books on him.

Works include incidental music to Tagore's play *The King's Letter*; oratorio *The Temptation of Buddha*, *Stabat Mater*, *Hymn to the Sun* (St Francis of Assisi); two string quartets; songs.

Sigurd opera by Reyer (libretto by C du Locle and A Blau, based on the Nibelung Saga), produced Brussels, Théâtre de la Monnaie, 7 Jan 1884. Similar to the plot of *Götterdämmerung*. Sigurd rescues Brunehild under the influence of Hilda's love potion and gives her to King Gunther. However, evil Hagen convinces Gunther that Sigurd and Brunehild are lovers, and Gunther then kills Sigurd. Brunehild throws herself on his funeral pyre.

Siklós, Albert (b Budapest, 26 Jun 1878; d Budapest, 3 Apr 1942), Hungarian cellist, musicologist and composer. Studied at the Hungarian Music School in Budapest and appeared as cellist in 1891, as lecturer in 1895 and began to compose seriously in 1896, when he finished a cello concerto, a symphony and an opera. He held distinguished teaching posts in Budapest and was appointed professor 1913.

Works include three operas, two ballets, choral and a vast number of orchestral works, concertos, chamber and much piano music, etc., also ten books of songs.

Sikorski, Kazimierz (b Zurich, 28 Jun 1895; d Warsaw, 5 Jul 1985), Polish composer. Studied at the Chopin High School in Warsaw and later in Paris. In 1927 he became professor at the Warsaw Conservatory. In 1936 he was one of the founders of the Society for the Publication of Polish Music.

Works include Psalm 7 for chorus and orchestra; four symphonies (1918–71) and symphonic poem for orchestra; three string quartets, string sextet; songs; part-songs. His son *Tomasz* (b Warsaw, 19 May 1939) is a pianist and composer who has written instrumental music in various advanced idioms; noted as an early Polish minimalist.

Silbermann German family of organ builders and harpsichord makers.

1. Andreas Silbermann (b Kleinbobritzsch near Frauenstein, Saxony, 16 May 1678; d Strasbourg, 16 Mar 1734), son of the carpenter Michael Silbermann. Worked with Casparini in Görlitz 1797–*c* 99. Settled in Strasbourg in 1721 and built the cathedral organ there 1713–16.

2. Gottfried Silbermann (b Kleinbobritzsch, 14 Jan 1683; d Dresden, 4 Aug 1753), brother of 1. At first apprenticed to a bookbinder, he joined his brother Andreas in Strasbourg in 1702, staying there till 1710. He then settled in Freiberg, where he built the cathedral organ (1711–14), and died while at work on a new organ for the Dresden

court. This organ, for the Katholische Hofkirch in Dresden, was largely destroyed by the RAF in 1945. He also built harpsichords and clavichords (one of them commemorated by a piece by C P E Bach entitled 'Farewell to my Silbermann Clavichord'), and was the first German to make pianos, including a grand which may have been used by J S Bach.

3. Johann Andreas Silbermann (b Strasbourg, 26 May 1712; d Strasbourg, 11 Feb 1783), son of 1. He built 54 organs including two at Strasbourg and another at Arlesheim Cathedral.

4. Johann Daniel Silbermann (b Strasbourg, 31 Mar 1717; d Leipzig, 9 May 1766), brother of 3. Worked with his uncle, 2, whose organ at Dresden he finished.

5. Johann Heinrich Silbermann (b Strasbourg, 24 Sept 1727; d Strasbourg, 15 Jan 1799), brother of 4. He made harpsichords and pianos, some with pedal boards.

Silbersee, Der opera by Weill (libretto by G Kaiser), produced Leipzig, Erfurt and Magdeburg, 18 Feb 1933. Wounded by Olim, Severin joins him in house by Silver Lake; when they enter suicide pact the water freezes over and they escape across the surface to a new life.

Silcher, Friedrich (b Schnaith near Schorndorf, Württemberg, 27 Jun 1789; d Tübingen, 26 Aug 1860), German composer and conductor. Pupil of his father and others. He became a schoolmaster, but in 1815 went to Stuttgart as conductor and in 1817 to the University of Tübingen in the same capacity. Some of his songs have become folksongs in Germany.

Works include two hymn-books (three and four voices), collections of songs, some arranged, some composed by himself, including *Aennchen von Tharau, Loreley* (Heine), *Morgen muss ich fort, Zu Strassburg auf der Schanz.*

Silent Woman (R Strauss.) ◊Schweigsame Frau.

Silja, Anja (b Berlin, 17 Apr 1935), German soprano. She sang Rosina at Brunswick aged 19; formed a close personal and artistic relationship with Wieland Wagner and sang many times at Bayreuth and Stuttgart until his death in 1966. In London she has been heard since 1963 as Leonore, Marie, and Cassandre. US debut Chicago 1968, as Senta; NY Met. 1972, Leonore. Other roles have included Lulu, Salome, Isolde and The Woman in *Erwartung*. With her husband Christoph von Dohnányi she is often heard in concert. Highly regarded for her acting in opera, e.g. as Elena Makropoulos at Glyndebourne, 1995.

Silk, Dorothy (b Alvechurch, Worcs., 4 May 1884; d Alvechurch, 30 Jul 1942), English soprano. Studied at Birmingham and in Vienna, giving her first recital in London in 1920. She specialized in Bach and earlier composers, but also studied modern works; she sang in Boughton's *Bethlehem* and in the fp of Holst's *Sāvitri* (1921).

Sills, Beverly (b Brooklyn, NY, 25 May 1929), American soprano. She performed on radio from the age of three and soon acquired the nickname Bubbles. Opera debut Philadelphia, 1947; NY City Opera from 1955 (debut as Rosalinde). Wider fame came with her Cleopatra, in a 1966 adaptation of Handel's *Giulio Cesare*; also successful as Manon and Violetta and in Donizetti's three Tudor operas. She sang Lucia at CG in 1970, and Pamira in Rossini's *Le siège de Corinthe* was the role of her belated NY Met. debut. In 1979 she became director of the NY City Opera (until 1989). Chair of the Lincoln Center for Performing Arts, 1994.

Siloti, Alexander (Ilyich) (b near Kharkov, 9 Oct 1863; d New York, 8 Dec 1945), Russian pianist and conductor. Studied at the Moscow Conservatory under Tchaikovsky, N Rubinstein and others, later with Liszt. He first appeared at Moscow in 1880 and later travelled widely. He left Russia 1919 and lived in USA at the end of his life. From 1925 to 1942 he taught at the Juilliard School in NY.

Silva, Andreas de (Silvanus or Sylvanus), Spanish 15th–16th-c. singer and composer. Sang in the Papal Chapel in Rome early in the 16th c. and was in the service of the Duke of Mantua from 1522. One of his motets was used as the basis of a Mass by Palestrina.

Works include Masses, motets; madrigals.

Silva Leite, António Joaquim da (b Oporto, 23 May 1759; d Oporto, 10 Jan 1833), Portuguese composer. Pupil of the Italian Girolamo Sartori (?), he was *mestre de capela* at Oporto Cathedral from 1814.

Works include Italian operas *Puntigli per equivoco* and *Le astuzie delle donne*; *Tantum ergo* with orchestra; sonatas and studies for guitar. A projected anthology of organ music was never finished.

Silvana opera by Weber (libretto by F K Hiemer, altered from Steinsberg's *Waldmädchen*), produced Frankfurt, 16 Sept 1810. Weber's second version of *Das Waldmädchen* of 1800. Struck dumb after being kidnapped, Silvana eventually revives when discovered in the forest by Count Rudolf.

Silvani, Giuseppe Antonio (b Bologna, 21 Jan 1672; d Bologna, before 1727), Italian composer and publisher. *Maestro di cappella* at the church of San Stefano at Bologna, 1702–25. He inherited the music publishing business of his father, Marino Silvani.

Works include Masses, motets, Lamentations, *Stabat Mater*, Litanies, sacred cantatas and other church music for voices with string or organ accompaniment.

Silveri, Paolo (b Ofena, near Aquila, 28 Dec 1913), Italian baritone. Made his debut in Rome in 1944 as Germont and sang at Covent Garden 1947–49, as Rigoletto, Escamillo and Boris, and at the NY Met. 1950–53. After a brief period as a tenor in 1959 (Otello in Dublin) he reverted to baritone in 1960. Other roles have included Marcello, Don Giovanni and Renato.

Silverstein, Joseph (b Detroit, 21 Mar 1932), American violinist and conductor. Studied with Zimbalist at the Curtis Inst. Played in various orchestras before joining Boston SO in 1955; leader 1962, assistant conductor 1971–83. Guest conductor with most major American orchestras. Music director Utah SO from 1983. Has taught at Yale and Boston Universities. A leading interpreter of modern music.

Silvestri, Constantin (b Bucharest, 13 May 1913; d London, 23 Feb 1969), Romanian conductor, composer and pianist. Studied at the Bucharest Conservatory, making his debut as a pianist in 1924 and as a conductor in 1930. He became conductor at the Bucharest Opera in 1935 and of the Bucharest PO in 1945. British debut 1957 (LPO); from 1961 he conducted the Bournemouth SO. CG debut 1963 (*Khovanshchina*).

Works include *Music for Strings, Three Pieces for String Orchestra*; two string quartets; two sonatas for violin and piano; sonatas for harp, flute, clarinet, bassoon.

simile Italian = 'like'; an abbr. often used to indicate that certain passages are to be performed in the same way as similar passages occurring before.

Simionato, Giulietta (b Forlì 15 Dec 1910), Italian mezzo. Studied in Florence, winning a prize at a competition there in 1933. Her early roles included Rosina, Cherubino and Mignon. La Scala 1946–66 as Charlotte, Carmen and Cinderella. CG 1953 as Adalgisa and Amneris. NY Met. debut 1959, Azucena. Retired 1966, after singing Servilia in *La Clemenza di Tito* at the Piccola Scala, Milan.

Simmes (or *Simes* or *Sims*), William, English 16th–17th-c. composer. Works include anthems; fantasies for viols.

Simon, Antoine (Antony Yulievich) (b Paris, 5 Aug 1850; d St Petersburg, 1 Feb 1916), French composer and conductor. Studied at the Paris Conservatory and in 1871 settled at Moscow, where he became conductor of the Théâtre-Bouffe. In the 1890s he became piano professor at the Philharmonic Music School and superintendent of the orchestra of the Imperial theatres.

Works include opeas *Rolla* (1892), *The Song of Love Triumphant* (after Turgenev, 1897), *The Fishers* (after Hugo, 1899); mimed drama *Esmeralda* (after Hugo's *Notre-Dame*, 1902); ballets *The Stars* and *Living Flowers*; incidental music for Shakespeare's *Merchant of Venice*; Mass; concertos for piano and for clarinet; string quartets; songs.

Simon, Geoffrey (b Adelaide, 3 Jul 1946), Australian conductor. Studied at Melbourne University and Juilliard. Guest with orchestras in Europe, the USA and Australia from 1974. Music director of Albany SO, NY, 1987–89; artistic advisor of the Sacramento SO from 1993. Guest with the CBSO, London Philharmonia and ECO and Tokyo Metropolitan Orchestra. Recordings include rare repertoire by Respighi, Tchaikovsky and Paul Patterson (*Mass of the Sea*).

Simon, Simon (b Vaux-de-Cernay near Rambouillet, *c* 1730; d ?

THE OPERA

Simon Boccanegra

A three-act dramatic opera with Prologue by Guiseppe Verdi, first performed in Venice in 1857. The action takes place in 14th-century Genoa.

Prologue. Simon Boccanegra (baritone) awaits his election as Doge. He hopes to marry Maria Fiesco, by whom he has had a daughter, but she is kept in her father's palace. Jacopo Fiesco himself (bass) announces the death of Maria and rejects Boccanegra; his baby daughter has disappeared. As Boccanegra discovers Maria's body, the crowd celebrates his election.

I. Boccanegra's daughter Amelia (soprano) has been brought up unknown to him by his enemies; among these are her guardian Fiesco (living as Andrea) and Gabriele Adorno (tenor) who loves Amelia. Boccanegra recognizes Amelia and forbids Paolo, one of his courtiers, to marry her. Paolo decides on abduction. At the Doge's Council a riot erupts when Gabriele breaks in and accuses Boccanegra of having abducted Amelia; Amelia then rushes in and as she intervenes Boccanegra calls for peace between plebeians and patricians.

II. Paolo administers a slow poison to Boccanegra and Gabriele agrees to kill the Doge on being told that Amelia is his mistress. Amelia again intervenes for her father and Gabriele is made to realize their true relationship.

III. Defeated in battle, Paolo is led to execution. Boccanegra recognizes Fiesco once more and before he dies names Gabriele as his successor.

THE OPERA

Versailles, after 1780), French harpsichordist and composer. Pupil of Dauvergne. He was appointed harpsichord master to the queen and the royal children at Versailles.

Works include three books of harpsichord pieces, pieces and sonatas for harpsichord with violin.

Simon Boccanegra opera by Verdi (libretto by F M Piave, based on a Spanish drama by A G Gutiérrez), produced Venice, Teatro La Fenice, 12 Mar 1857; revised version, with the libretto altered by Boito, produced Milan, La Scala, 24 Mar .1881. Doge of Venice Boccanegra discovers long-lost illegitimate daughter, Amelia. She loves his enemy, Gabriele Adorno, and he and Boccanegra are reconciled. Finally Boccanegra dies, poisoned by his jealous courtier, Paolo.

Simoneau, Léopold (b Quebec, 3 May 1918), Canadian tenor. He studied in NY and made his debut in Montreal in 1941. He moved to Europe in 1949 and was heard at the Paris Opéra-Comique in operas by Gounod and Stravinsky. Glyndebourne 1951–54 as Don Ottavio and Idamante. He was heard in Aix, London, Vienna and Chicago during the 1950s. NY Met. debut 1963, as Ottavio. He taught singing in San Francisco from 1973.

Simonetti, Achille (b Turin, 12 Jun 1857; d London, 19 Nov 1928), Italian violinist and composer. Pupil of Pedrotti for composition and later of Sivori at Genoa for violin. Having appeared as a concert artist, he went to Paris for further study with Dancla and Massenet. Later he settled in London as performer, teacher and member of the London Trio. Toured throughout Europe as a soloist; well known in the Brahms concerto.

Works include two string quartets; two violin and piano sonatas, violin pieces.

Simonov, Yuri (b Saratov, 4 Mar 1941), Russian conductor. Studied at Leningrad Conservatory; conducted Kislovodsk PO 1967–69. Bolshoi Theatre, Moscow, from 1969, debut with *Aida* and was chief conductor 1970–78. Led the Bolshoi at the NY Met. in 1975, *War and Peace*. CG debut 1982, *Eugene Onegin*, and has guested with many British orchestras. Led the fp of Shchedrin's ballet *Anna Karenina* in 1972.

simple intervals any intervals not larger than an octave, those exceeding that width being called compound interval.

simple time any musical metre in which the beats can be subdivided into two, e.g. 2–4, 3–4, 4–4. *Cf* ◊compound time.

Simpson, Christopher (b Yorkshire, *c* 1605; d London, summer 1669), English viola da gamba player, theorist and composer. He joined the royalist army under the Duke of Newcastle in 1643 and endured much hardship, but later came under the patronage of Sir Robert Bolles, at whose residences at Scampton and in London he lived in comfort, teaching the children of the family and taking charge of the domestic music-making. He wrote an instruction book for the viola da gamba, *The Division Violist*. He bought a house and farm at Pickering, Yorkshire, but died at one of Sir John Bolles's houses. He wrote another treatise, *The Principles of Practicle Musick* and annotations to Campion's *Art of Descant*.

Works include *Months and Seasons* for a treble and two bass viols, fancies and consorts for viols, suite in three parts for viols, divisions (variations) and pieces for viola da gamba.

Simpson, Robert (Wilfred Levick) (b Leamington, 2 Mar 1921), English composer and music critic. Studied privately with Howells and took D.Mus. at Durham in 1952. He was active in the BBC and is a writer on music, especially that of Bruckner, Nielsen and Sibelius; his own music displays tonal stability and an emphasis on organic unity, influenced by Beethoven and Bruckner.

Works include 11 symphonies (1951–90), *Nielsen Variations* (1986), concertos for violin (1959), piano (1967), flute (1989) and cello (*Variations and Fugue on a theme of Bach* for strings (1991); fantasia for strings; 15 string quartets (1952–91); piano music.

Simpson, Thomas (b Milton, near Sittingbourne, bap. 1 Apr 1582; d after 1630), English violist and composer. Settled in Germany early in the 17th c., was in the service of the Elector Palatine in 1610, in that of the Prince of Holstein-Schaumburg in 1617–21, and afterwards at the Danish court in Copenhagen (1622–25).

Works include pavans, galliards and other dances for viols; songs with instruments.

Sinclair, Jeanette (b London, 1928), English soprano. Studied with Joan Cross and made debut at SW 1954, as Cherubino; Glyndebourne debut 1955, as Barbarina. CG, London, from 1954, as Constance in the UK fp of Poulenc's *Carmelites* (1958) and as Micaela, Bella (*The Midsummer Marriage*), Susanna and Zerlina. Sang Mimi with WNO in 1964 and made many concert appearances.

Sinclair, John (b near Edinburgh, 9 Dec 1791; d Margate, 23 Sept 1857), Scottish tenor. Studied at Aberdeen and first appeared in London in 1810; at CG he was heard in operas by Linley and Bishop. In 1819 he visited Paris, studied in Italy and sang there with success until 1823. He often sang in operas by Rossini and appeared in the fp of *Semiramide* (Venice 1823).

Sinclair, Monica (b Evercreech, Somerset, 1925), English mezzo. Studied RAM and RCM. She sang Suzuki with the Carl Rosa co. in 1948; CG from 1949, appeared in the fp of *Pilgrim's Progress*, 1951. Glyndebourne 1954–60, in operas by Mozart, Strauss and Rossini. At Bordeaux in 1955 she sang Lully's Armide. Married a CG horn player and had six children.

Sinding, Christian (b Kongsberg, 11 Jan 1856; d Oslo, 3 Dec 1941), Norwegian pianist and composer. Studied at Liepzig, Berlin and Munich. He settled at Oslo as pianist and composer.

Works include opera *The Holy Mountain* (1912); four symphonies and *Rondo infinito* for orchestra, piano concerto in D♭ major, three violin concertos (1898, 1901, 1917); string quartet (1904), piano quintet, piano trio; sonatas and suite for violin and piano; variations for two pianos; suite, studies and numerous pieces for piano, including the well-known *Frühlingsrauschen/Rustle of Spring*; songs.

Sinfonia, Italian, symphony. In the early 18th c. the sinfonia was simply an instrumental piece in an opera or other vocal work, especially the overture; it is in fact out of the latter that the symphony developed.

Title of work by Berio (1968) which uses collage techniques: scherzo of Mahler's second symphony is quoted.

Sinfonia Antartica symphony by Vaughan Williams (his seventh) for soprano, women's chorus and orchestra; composed 1949–52 and based on his music for the film *Scott of the Antarctic*, 1947–48; fp Manchester, 14 Jan 1953, conductor Barbirolli.

I want you to sound like 22 women having babies without *chloroform*.
Sir John Barbirolli, to the chorus at a rehearsal of *Sinfonia Antartica*, quoted in Kennedy, *Barbirolli, Conductor Laureate*, 1971

Sinfonia concertante a work in symphonic form with one or more solo instruments, similar to a concerto. Familiar examples are Mozart's K364 for violin, viola and orchestra of 1779 and Haydn's Op. 84 in B♭ for violin, cello, oboe, and bassoon (1792).

Sinfonia da Requiem work for orchestra in three movements by Britten; commissioned to celebrate the 2,600th anniversary of the Imperial Japanese dynasty. The work was rejected for its allusions to the Catholic liturgy and the fp was in NY on 29 Mar 1941, conductor Barbirolli; eight months before Pearl Harbor.

Sinfonia domestica (R Strauss.) ◊Symphonia domestica.

Sinfonia Espansiva symphony no. 3 (with wordless soprano and baritone voices) by Nielsen, op. 27; composed 1910–11, fp Copenhagen, 30 Apr 1912, conductor Nielsen. Not performed in public in Britain until London, 7 May 1962, conductor B Fairfax.

Sinfonia Semplice sub-title of Nielsen's sixth and last symphony; composed 1924–25, fp Copenhagen, 11 Dec 1925, conductor Nielsen.

sinfonietta Italian = 'little symphony'; a work in symphonic form, but of smaller dimensions and usually lightly scored. Examples are by Janáček, Prokofiev, Poulenc, Britten and Roussel.

Singakademie German = lit. 'singing-academy' = vocal academy; the special name of certain choral societies in Germany and Austria.

Singspiel German = 'song play'; originally a translation of the Italian *dramma per musica*, i.e. opera. In the course of the 18th c. the term was restricted to comic opera with spoken dialogue, e.g. Mozart's *Die Entführung*.

Sinigaglia, Leone (b Turin, 14 Aug 1868; d Turin, 16 May 1944), Italian composer. Studied at the Turin Conservatory and with Mandyczewski in Vienna. After his return home he settled down to composition and folksong collecting.

Works include suite *Piemonte*, overture to Goldoni's *Le baruffe chiozzote*, *Danze piemontesi* for orchestra (1903); concerto, *Rapsodia piemontese* and romance for violin and orchestra; string quartet in D major concert study and variations on a theme by Brahms for string quartet; sonatas for cello and violin, folksongs.

sino Italian = 'until', or abbr. *sin'* when followed by a vowel; a word used in such directions as that indicating a repeat *sin' al fine* (until the end) or *sin' al segno*... (to the sign...), etc.

Sinopoli, Giuseppe (b Venice, 2 Nov 1946), Italian conductor and composer. He studied medicine in Padua, then conducting in Vienna, with Swarowsky. Founded the Bruno Maderna ensemble in 1975, for performances of modern music, and appeared with the Berlin PO from 1979. Opera debut at Venice 1978, *Aida*. In 1983 he made his US debut with the NY PO, and led *Manon Lescaut* at CG, London. Bayreuth debut *Tannhäuser*, 1985 and led *Tosca* at the NY Met. in the same year. Principal conductor Philharmonia Orchestra 1984–94. Music director of the Deutsche Oper Berlin 1990, Dresden 1993. Popular with audiences, although not some critics, for certain 'creative' fluctuations in tempo.

Works include opera *Lou Salomé* (1981), *Sunyata* for string quintet (1970), *Opus daleth* for orchestra (1971), *Symphonie imaginaire* for solo voices and chorus (1973), piano concerto (1974), *Requiem Hashshirim* for unaccompanied chorus (1976), string quartet (1977).

Sirius work by Stockhausen for soprano, baritone and ensemble, dedicated to American pioneers and astronauts. Fp Washington DC, 18 Jul 1976.

Sir John in Love opera by Vaughan Williams (libretto selected by

Sinopoli *The conductor Giuseppe Sinopoli achieved rapidly growing success in the early 1980s in both his concert and operatic careers. He is also a composer, and founded in 1972 the Bruno Maderna Ensemble for the performance of new music.*

composer from Shakespeare's *Merry Wives of Windsor*), produced London, RCM, 21 Mar 1929.

Sirmen (born *Lombardini*), Maddalena (b Venice, ? 1735; d after 1785), Italian violinist, singer and composer. Studied at the Conservatorio dei Mendicanti at Venice and violin with Tartini at Padua. In 1760 she began to tour in Italy and at Bergamo she met Ludovico Sirmen, a violinist and conductor at the church of Santa Maria Maddalena there, and married him. They visited Paris in 1768 and in 1771 she first appeared in London, where she also played the harpsichord.

Works include six violin concertos; six string quartets, six trios for two violins and cello; six duets and six sonatas for two violins.

Siroe, rè di Persia, *Siroes, King of Persia*, libretto by Metastasio.

Opera by Handel, produced London, King's Theatre, Haymarket, 17 Feb 1728. Also settings by Vinci (Venice, 1726), Hasse (Bologna, 1733) and Pérez (Naples, 1740). Passed over by his father Cosroe for succession to throne, Siroe is accused of treachery but survives the plots of Laodice and brother Medarse to gain crown.

Širola, Božidar (b Žakanj, 20 Dec 1889; d Zagreb, 10 Apr 1956), Yugoslav composer. Studied at Zagreb and in Vienna, where he took a doctor's degree. Later director of the Music Academy at Zagreb.

Works include operas *Stanac* (1915), *The Wandering Scholar* and four others; ballet *Shadows*; incidental music to plays; three oratorios; symphony, suite and overtures for orchestra; 13 string quartets (1920–55), three piano trios; songs.

sistrum an ancient instrument, probably originating in Egypt, played like a rattle. It had a metal frame fitted to a handle and metal bars or loops were loosely hung on the frame and made to strike against it by shaking the instrument.

sitar Indian stringed instrument, of the lute family. It has a pear-shaped body and long neck supported by an addditional gourd resonator. A principal solo instrument, it has three to seven strings extending over movable frets, two concealed strings that provide a continuous drone, and nine to thirteen ♭sympathetic strings. It is played with a plectrum, producing a luminous and subtle melody responsive to nuances of pressure. Since the 1960s the sitar has become more widely known in the West, largely due to the work of Ravi ♭Shankar.

Sitkovetsky, Dmitry (b Baku, 27 Sep 1954), Ukrainian-born American violinist. Studied in Moscow between 1961 and 1977 and at Juilliard with Ivan Galamian. Won 1979 Kreisler Competition in Vienna and made debut with the Berlin PO in 1980. US debut with the Chicago SO 1983, returning with the New York PO 1988. London Proms 1986, returning 1990–91, with the Elgar and Brahms Concertos. Frequent guest with the Edinburgh, Salzburg, Mostly Mozart (New York) and Vienna festivals. Has recorded Bach's *Goldberg Variations*, in his own version for string trio, the Schubert Piano Trios, with Gerhard Oppitz and David Geringas, and the Mozart Concertos.

Sitsky, Larry (b Tientsin, China, 10 Sep 1934), Australian composer of Russian descent. Studied at the New South Wales Conservatorium, 1951–55 and with Egon Petri, former pupil of Busoni, in San Francisco. Active as a pianist in the music of Busoni and other major moderns; head of keyboard studies at the Canberra School of Music 1966–78, composition from 1981.

Works include operas *Fall of the House of Usher* (1965); *Lenz* (1972) and *Golem* (composed 1980, premiered 1993); three violin concertos (1971–87), concertos for clarinet (1981), trombone (1982), guitar (1984) and piano (1991); three string quartets (no. 3 1993) and piano pieces with accompanying electronic effects.

Sitt, Hans (b Prague, 21 Sept 1850; d Leipzig, 10 Mar 1922), Czech-German violinist, teacher and editor. Studied at the Prague Conservatory, became leader at Breslau, 1867, and conducted at Breslau and Prague, 1870–73, Chemnitz, 1873–80, and Nice. He returned to Leipzig, where he joined Brodsky's quartet as violist. He was professor of violin at the Leipzig Conservatory, 1883–1921. He edited much violin music.

Works include three violin concertos, viola concerto, two cello concertos, chamber music, violin studies and pieces, songs.

I was once a Chopinist, then a Wagnerist, now I am only a Scriabinist.

Alexander Skriabin in 1903, quoted in Bowers, *Scriabin*, 1969

Sivori, (Ernesto) Camillo (b Genoa, 25 Oct 1815; d Genoa, 19 Feb 1894), Italian violinist and composer. Pupil of Paganini, who wrote his works for quartet with guitar for him and, going on tour, sent him to another master, Giacomo Costa, and later to Dellepiane, with whom he went on tour, making his debut at Turin, 1827. They went on to France and London, but in 1829 Sivori returned to Genoa to study composition with Giovanni Serra. He then travelled widely in Europe and North and South America until 1870. Although he lacked the power of Paganini, Sivori's technique was flawless despite small hands.

Works include two concertos, *Tarantelle napolitaine*, etc. for violin and orchestra; duet for violin and double bass (with Bottesini); two *Duos concertants* for violin and piano; *Andante spianato* and numerous other pieces and fantasies on operatic airs for violin and piano; violin studies.

Six, Les a group of French composers who in their youth gathered together, under the leadership of Satie and Jean Cocteau, for the furtherance of their interests and to some extent those of modern music in general. It was formed in Paris in 1917 and its active composing members were Auric, Durey, Honegger, Milhaud, Poulenc and Tailleferre; the chief performers were the singer Jane Bathori and the pianist Andrée Vaurabourg, the latter becoming Honegger's wife. The group gradually lost its solidarity during the 1920s.

sixth the interval between two notes lying eight semitones (minor sixth) or nine semitones (major sixth) apart.

The so-called 'chord of the sixth' – or 6–3 chord – (major or minor) consists of a third with a fourth above it.

Major, minor, and augmented sixths; major and minor 6–3 and 6–4 chords.

The '6–4' chord (the second inversion of a chord) consists of a fourth with a third above it.

Chords of the augmented sixth are known in three forms, French sixth, German sixth and Italian sixth. ♭augmented sixth chords.

Sjögren, (Johan Gustaf) Emil (b Stockholm, 16 Jun 1853; d Stockholm, 1 Mar 1918), Swedish composer. Studied at the Stockholm Conservatory and later in Berlin, also came under the influence of Lange-Müller during a stay of six months at Meran. In 1891 he became organist at St John's Church, Stockholm, but devoted most of his time to teaching and composition.

Works include five violin and piano sonatas; organ works; two piano sonatas, *Erotikon*, *Novellettes* and numerous other works for piano; songs.

Skalkottas, Nicos (b Chalkis, Euboea, 21 Mar 1904; d Athens, 19 Sept 1949), Greek composer. Studied at the Athens Conservatory and with Economidis, later in Germany with Schoenberg, Weill and Jarnach, living there for 12 years. From 1933 he lived in Athens. Until 1938 his compositions were influenced by the 12-note method of Schoenberg. Much of his music was not performed until after his death, notably in Hamburg and London.

Works include two ballets *The Maid and Death* (1938) and *The Sea* (1949), 36 Greek Dances (1931–6), *Sinfonietta*, overture *The Return of Ulysses* and two suites for orchestra; concerto and symphony for wind instruments, three piano concertos (1931, 1938, 1939), violin concerto (1938), cello concerto (1938), concerto for violin and viola (1940), concerto for two violins; four string quartets (1928–40), Octet for woodwind quartet and string quartet (1931), four sonatinas for violin and piano (1929–35).

Škerjanc, Lucijan Marija (b Graz, 17 Dec 1900; d Ljubljana, 27 Feb 1973), Yugoslav pianist, composer and conductor. Studied in Prague, Vienna (J Marx), Basel and Paris (d'Indy), taught and conducted at Ljubljana, but later retired to devote himself to composition.

Works include cantatas, five symphonies (1931–43) and other orchestral works, violin and piano concertos, five string quartets (1917–45).

Skilton, Charles Sanford (b Northampton, MA, 16 Aug 1868; d Lawrence, KS, 12 Mar 1941), American composer. Studied at Yale University and in Germany. In 1903 he was appointed Professor of Music at Kansas University and there made a study of native American tunes.

Works include operas *Kalopin* (composed 1927), *The Sun Bride* (1930), *The Day of Gayomair* (composed 1936); incidental music for Sophocles' *Electra* and Barrie's *Mary Rose*; oratorio *The Guardian Angel* and cantatas; *Primeval Suite* and other suites and overtures for orchestra; *Two Indian Dances* for string quartet; violin and piano sonata; organ and piano works.

skočná a Czech dance in quick 2–4 time in which three-bar phrases are a feature. The fifth, seventh and 11th of Dvořák's *Slavonic Dances* for piano duet are *skočnás*.

Skram, Knut (b Saebo, 18 Dec 1937), Norwegian baritone. Debut Oslo 1964, as Amonasro. Well known in concerts and Lieder recitals.

Glyndebourne 1969–76, as Guglielmo, Papageno and Mozart's Figaro. US debut with Kentucky Opera in 1979, as Papageno. Has recently turned to Wagnerian repertory: Amfortas and Kurwenal in Borlini, Hans Sachs in Nice (1992).

Skriabin, Alexander Nikolaievich (b Moscow, 6 Jan 1872; d Moscow, 27 Apr 1915), Russian composer and pianist. Giving up a military career, he studied piano with Safonov and composition with Taneiev at the Moscow Conservatory, where he became professor of piano in 1898 after touring successfully in western Europe. He gave up that post in 1904 to devote himself entirely to composition and occasional appearances as pianist. Apart from the piano concerto of 1897, his early works were for solo piano (preludes, mazurkas and nocturnes) and were much indebted to Chopin, but by 1903 his harmonic language had become more chromatic and made fragmentary use of modes including the so-called 'mystic' chord.

Influenced by the theosophy of Madame Blavatsky, he regarded his art as an 'ecstatic mystery', expressed in music of complex chromaticism. *The Poem of Ecstasy* was premièred in Paris 1908 and given again in St Petersburg the following year. Skriabin himself was the soloist in *Prometheus: a Poem of Fire* at Moscow in 1911. He had meanwhile gained vital support from the publisher and conductor Serge Koussevitsky, whose firm Editions Russes guaranteed the composer an annual contract of 5,000 roubles.

He visited England on several occasions, notably in 1913 and 1914 when his *Prometheus* was performed under Wood, who avoided the composer's request for a keyboard which projected various colours on to a screen, changing according to the 'appropriate' harmonics (Skriabin believed that each harmony was correlated with a distinct colour, anticipating Messiaen 50 years later). *Prometheus* was nevertheless a success as was the symphony no. 3 'The Divine Poem' which had been premiered at Paris under Nikisch in 1905. Skriabin's compositional style may be summed up by a marking on the score of *The Poem of Ecstasy*: 'With ever-increasing intoxication'.

Works include three symphonies (1899–1904; no. 3 *The Divine Poem*), *Rêverie* and *Poem of Ecstasy* for orchestra; piano concerto in F♯ minor (1896), *Prometheus: a Poem of Fire* for orchestra, piano and organ (and a projected colour organ, 1910); ten piano sonatas (1892–1913) and 58 op. nos. of other piano works, including preludes, impromptus, studies, mazurkas, nocturnes, *Tragic Poem*, *Satanic Poem*, *Vers la flamme*, prelude and nocturne for the left hand.

Škroup, František Jan (b Osice near Pardubice, 3 Jun 1801; d Rotterdam, 7 Feb 1862), Bohemian composer. Studied law, but was from

A Selection of

Skriabin

Piano Concerto 1896
Symphony no. 1 1900
Symphony no. 2 1901
Symphony no. 3 1904

Poem of Ecstasy 1908
Prometheus: A Poem of Fire 1910
Piano Sonata no. 7 (*White Mass*) 1911
Piano Sonata no. 11 (*Black Mass*) 1913

1827 second and in 1837–57 first conductor at the National Theatre in Prague; from 1860 conducted at the Opera of Rotterdam. Composed the first Czech opera and the national anthem.

Works include operas *Drátenik* (*The Tinker*, 1826), *The Marriage of Libuša* (1835), *Oldřich and Božena* (1828), *Drahomira* (1848) and some other Czech and German operas; incidental music to Tyl's *Fidlovačka*; three string quartets and other chamber music; songs.

Skrowaczewski, Stanislaw (b Lwów, 3 Oct 1923), Polish-born American conductor. He studied in Poland, and with Boulanger in Paris. After an early career as a pianist he held various conducting posts in Poland, 1946–59. US debut Cleveland, 1958; music director Minneapolis SO 1960–79. Principal conductor Hallé Orchestra 1984–91. Also composes, including four symphonies (1936–54) and four string quartets.

Skuherský, František Zdeněk (b Opočno, 31 Jul 1830; d Budejovice, 19 Aug 1892), Bohemian composer and teacher. He gave up medical studies for music, which he studied under Kittl and Pitsch, the directors of the Prague Conservatory and Organ School respectively. In 1854–65 he was conductor at Innsbruck, but returned to Prague as director of the Organ School in the latter year. He was also active as pianist and as lecturer at the Czech University, and he took part in the reform of church music after studying it in Rome and Regensburg. He wrote several theoretical treatises.

Works include operas *Samo* (composed 1854), *Vladimir: God's Chosen* (1863), *Lora* (1861), *Rector and General* (1873) and *The Love Ring*; symphonic poem *May* and three fugues for orchestra; string quartet (1871), piano quintet, piano trio.

Skyscrapers ballet by Carpenter (choreography by Heinrich Kröller), produced Monte Carlo, Russian Ballet, 1925; first US performance NY Met. 19 Feb 1926.

Slatkin, Leonard (b Los Angeles, 1 Sept 1944), American conductor. He studied with Castelnuovo-Tedesco in LA and at the Juilliard School. He has been guest conductor with most leading orchestras in the USA and with the LSO and Concertgebouw Orchestra Principal conductor St Louis SO from 1979. Many performances of contemporary music.

Sleeping Beauty, The, *Spyashchaya krasavitsa*, ballet by Tchaikovsky (choreography by Petipa), produced St Petersburg, Maryinsky Theatre, 15 Jan 1890; new version, with additional orchestration by Stravinsky and additions to the choreography by Bronislava Nizhinska, London, Alhambra Theatre, 2 Nov 1921.

slentando Italian = 'gradually decreasing in pace'.

Slezak, Leo (b Šumperk, 18 Aug 1873; d Egern, Bavaria, 1 Jun 1946), Moravian tenor. He studied engineering, but had his voice trained at the same time and in 1896 made his debut at Brno as Lohengrin. He was a member of the Vienna Staatsoper from 1901 to 1926 as Tannhäuser, Lohengrin and Radames. NY Met. 1908–13 as Otello, Walther and Manrico. After retiring from the stage he made a successful career as a film actor. He pub. several autobiographical works.

slide the device of passing from one note to another on string instruments by moving the finger along the string instead of lifting it to make way for another finger; also the movable part of the tube of the trombone by which the positions, and therefore the notes, are altered, as well as mechanisms on other wind instruments by which the pitch can be adjusted by a change in the length of the tube.

Slobodskaya, Oda (b Vilna, 10 Dec 1888; d London, 29 Jul 1970), Russian soprano. Debut St Petersburg, 1919, as Lisa; much admired in operas by Rimsky-Korsakov and Glinka and as Sieglinde and Elisabeth de Valois. She created Parasha in Stravinsky's *Mavra*, Paris 1922, and at CG in 1935 she was Palmyra in the first British performance of Delius' *Koanga*, under Beecham. In Milan and Buenos Aires she was heard in operas by Tchaikovsky and Mussorgsky. She settled in London and taught at the GSM.

Slonimsky, Nicolas (originally Nikolai) (b St Petersburg, 27 Apr 1894; d Los Angeles, 25 Dec 1995), Russian musical author, conductor and composer. Studied at the St Petersburg Conservatory and in 1923 settled in USA, becoming a naturalized American in 1931. He compiled a survey, *Music since 1900* (1937, revised 1971; supplements 1986 and 1995); edited *Baker's Biographical Dictionary of Musicians*, editions 5, 6, 7 and 8 (1958, 1978, 1985, 1992; editions 7 and 8 with Dennis McIntire). As a conductor he gave early performances of works by Varèse, Ruggles, Cowell and Ives.

Works include *Fragment from Orestes* (Euripides) for orchestra (in quarter-tones); *Studies in Black and White* for piano The opera *Mary Stuart* by his nephew *Sergei* (b 1932) was produced at the 1986 Edinburgh Festival.

slur an arching stroke in musical notation drawn over a group of notes and indicating that they are to be played *legato*. It is also used in vocal music where two or more notes are to be sung to the same syllable.

Sly, i.e. Christopher Sly, opera by Wolf-Ferrari (libretto by G Forzano, based on the prologue of Shakespeare's *Taming of the Shrew*), produced Milan, La Scala, 29 Dec 1927. Sly suffers a practical joke: he is made to believe he is an aristocrat suffering from amnesia rather than a poor poet. Dolly, mistress of the Duke of Westmoreland, falls for him, but she cannot save him from a lowly death in the dungeon.

Smallens, Alexander (b St Petersburg, 1 Jan 1889; d Tucson 24 Nov 1972), Russian-born American conductor. He studied in NY and at the Paris Conservatory; became a US citizen in 1919 and conducted the Chicago Opera 1919–23 (fp Prokofiev *The Love for Three Oranges*). He worked in Philadelphia 1924–36 and gave there the first US performances of Strauss's *Feuersnot* and *Ariadne auf Naxos*, Rimsky-Korsakov's *Invisible City of Kitezh* and Gluck's *Iphigénie en Aulide*. He conducted the fp of *Porgy and Bess*, Boston 1935, and gave its British premiere in London in 1952. Retired 1958.

Smalley, Roger (b Swinton, Manchester, 26 Jul 1943), English composer and pianist. He studied at the RCM with Fricker; study with Stockhausen in Cologne was a formative influence. From 1969 to 1976 active with group Intermodulation; electronic and aleatory effects also present in his music. Teacher at University of Western Australia from 1976.

Works include septet for soprano and ensemble (text by cummings, 1963), *Gloria tibi Trinitas* for orchestra (1965), *Missa Parodia* for ensemble (1967), *The Song of the Highest Tower* for soprano, baritone, chorus and orchestra (texts by Blake and Rimbaud, 1968), *Pulses* for five × four players (1969), *Beat Music* for four electronic instruments and orchestra (1971), *Zeitebenen* for four players and tape (1973), *William Derrincourt* for baritone, chorus and ensemble (1977), string quartet (1979), *Konzertstück* for violin and orchestra (1980), Symphony in one movement (1981), *The Narrow Road to the Deep North*, music theatre (1983), piano concerto (1985), *Ceremony I* for percussion quartet (1987), *Strung Out* for 13 solo strings (1988).

By the grace of God and with his help I shall one day be a Liszt in technique and a Mozart in composition.

Bedřich Smetana, *Diary*, 1845

Smareglia, Antonio (b Pola, Istria, 5 May 1854; d Grado, near Trieste, 15 Apr 1929), Italian composer. He was sent to Vienna to study engineering, but on hearing works by the great masters there he left for Milan in 1872 and studied composition under Faccio at the Conservatory. He produced his first opera there in 1879, but he never had any real success, in spite of the good quality of his work, and in 1900 he went blind.

Works include operas *Preziosa* (1879), *Bianca da Cervia* (1882), *Rè Nala* (1887), *Der Vasall von Szigeth* (1889), *Cornelius Schutt* (1893), *Nozze istriane*, *La Falena* (1897), *Oceàna* (1903), *L'Abisso*; symphonic poem *Leonore*, songs.

Smart, George (Thomas) (b London, 10 May 1776; d London, 23 Feb 1867), English organist, composer and conductor. He was sent by his father, George Smart, a music pub., to become a choirboy at the Chapel Royal under Ayrton, and later became a composition pupil of Arnold. He became an organist, teacher and conductor, was one of the original members of the Philharmonic Society in 1813 and succeeded

Smetana *The composer Bedřich Smetana (1824–1884). Although Bohemian by birth, Smetana was educated in Germany and did not speak Czech like a native. He nevertheless wrote music in a Czech nationalist style, for example* Má vlast/My homeland *and* Dalibor.

Charles Knyvett as organist of the Chapel Royal in 1822. In 1825 he gave the fp in Britain of Beethoven's ninth symphony and went to Dresden with Charles Kemble to engage Weber to write *Oberon* for Covent Garden. It was at his house that Weber stayed during the production in 1826 and died in the night of 4–5 Jun. Smart was knighted in 1811, and became a favourite festival conductor, giving the English fps of Beethoven's *Christ at the Mount of Olives* in 1814 and Mendelssohn's St Paul in 1936.

Works include anthems, chants and other church music; canons and glees.

Smart, Henry (Thomas) (b London, 26 Oct 1813; d London, 6 Jul 1879), English organist and composer, nephew of George Smart. Learnt music from his father, the violinist Henry Smart (1778–1823), and later under W H Kearns, but was largely self-taught. After an organist's appointment at Blackburn in 1831–36 he returned to London and was successively organist at several churches until he became blind in 1864.

Works include operas *Berta, or The Gnome of the Hartzberg* (1855), *Undine* and *The Surrender of Calais* (last two unfinished); cantatas *The Bride of Dunkerron*, *King René's Daughter* (after Herz, 1871), *The Fishermaidens* (1871) and *Jacob* (1873); festival anthems *Sing to the Lord* and *Lord, thou hast been our refuge*; organ works; part-songs.

Smert, Richard (b ? Devon), English 15th-c. composer. Carols of his for two voices and three-part chorus, some written with John Truelove, are preserved. He was a vicar choral of Exeter Cathedral, 1428–c 1465 and rector at Plymtree, Devon, 1435–77.

Smetáček, Václav (b Brno, 30 Sept 1906; d Prague, 18 Feb 1986), Czech conductor and oboist. He studied at the Prague Conservatory; played in Prague Wind Quintet 1928–55. Conducted Prague Radio

A Selection of

Smetana

Piano Trio	1855
The Brandenburgers in Bohemia	1866
The Bartered Bride	1866
Dalibor	1868
My Country	1872–94
Two Widows	1874
String Quartet no. 1	1876
The Secret	1878
Libuše	1881
String Quartet no. 2	1883

orchestra 1934–43 and was often heard with the Czech PO. British debut 1938. On record and in tours of Europe and South America he conducted operas by Smetana, Janáček, Mussorgsky and Shostakovich.

Smetana, Bedřich (b Litomyšl, Bohemia, 2 Mar 1824; d Prague, 12 May 1884), Czech composer. Son of a brewer. He played piano and violin at a very early age and was soon able to play in the domestic string quartet. He was educated in Germany and all his life, in spite of his musical nationalism, spoke and wrote Czech like a foreigner. He was sent to school first in Prague and then at Pilsen. His father opposed a musical career, but he was in the end allowed to study music in Prague, though with a very small allowance. In 1844 he obtained the post of music master in Count Thun's family, which helped to support him until 1847. In 1848 he took part in the revolution against Austria, married the pianist Kateřina Kolařová, established a school of music for which Liszt supplied funds, and was recommended by the latter to the Leipzig pub. Kistner.

In 1856 he went to Göteborg in Sweden, where at first he taught but later became conductor of the new Philharmonic Society and gave piano and chamber music recitals. He returned to Prague in 1859 because the northern climate did not suit his wife, who died at Dresden on the way back, 19 Apr. He married Bettina Ferdinandová in Jul 1860 and returned to Sweden in the autumn, but finally returned to Prague in the spring of 1861. After a long tour in Germany, Holland and Sweden to collect funds, he settled in the Czech capital in 1863 and opened another school of music, this time with distinctly national tendencies, and became conductor of the choral society Hlahol. His work too was now becoming thoroughly Czech in character, and he began to produce Czech operas in the national theatre established in 1864, of which he became conductor in Sept 1866.

The nationalist opera *The Brandenburgers in Bohemia* was a success in Jan 1866 although *The Bartered Bride*, with which he was to be most closely identified, was a failure in May. In 1872 he began composing his great cycle of symphonic poems, *Má Vlast/My Country* which is often performed in the Czech Republic at times of national celebrations, notably after the recent release from Communist rule. In 1874 he suddenly became totally deaf, as the result of a syphilitic infection, but still composed operas as well as the string quartet *From my Life*, with its strong autobiographical theme, depicting his love for his wife and children (all of whom had died by 1859) and at the beginning of the last movement the onset of his deafness, portrayed by a piercing high note on the violin. In 1881 he had his last

major success, when his great patriotic festival opera *Libuše*, was premiered in Prague. In 1883 he became insane and in May 1884 he had to be taken to an asylum, where he died.

Works include OPERAS: *The Brandenburgers in Bohemia* (1866), *The Bartered Bride* (1866), *Dalibor* (1868), *Libuše* (1881), *Two Widows* (1874), *The Kiss*, *The Secret* (1878), *The Devil's Wall* (1882), *Viola* (based on Shakespeare's *Twelfth Night*, unfinished).

ORCHESTRAL: three concert overtures; symphonic poems *Richard III* (after Shakespeare, 1858), *Wallenstein's Camp* (after Schiller), *Haakon Jarl* (1861); cycle of symphonic poems *My Country* containing *Vyšehrad*, *Vltava*, *Šárka*, *In the Bohemian Woods and Fields*, *Tábor*, *Blanik* (1872–79); Festival March.

CHAMBER AND PIANO: piano trio in G minor (1855), two string quartets (1876, 1883; first *From my Life*); 8 op. nos. of piano works and many misc. piano pieces including *Wedding Scenes*, *Scenes from Macbeth*, Czech dances, etc.; a cantata and a number of part-songs; three books of songs.

Smirnov, Dmitri (b Minsk, 2 Nov 1948), Russian composer. Studied at the Moscow Conservatory 1967–72, with Edison Denisov. He belongs to the group of Russian composers who emigrated to the West after the collapse of Communism; with his wife Elena Firsova joint composer-in-residence at Keele University, UK, from 1992. His music draws on eclectic stylistic sources and is often concerned with refinement of instrumental texture. Includes settings of Blake, Pushkin, Coleridge and Alexander Blok: three string quartets (1973, 1985, 1993), two violin sonatas (1969, 1979), piano quintet (1993); operas *Triel* (1983) and *The Lamentations of Thel* (1986); Symphony no. 1 (*The Seasons*) (1980), two piano concertos (1971, 1978), concerto for violin and 13 strings (1990), cello concerto (1992), *Mozart-Variations* for orchestra (1987); *Jacob's Ladder* for 16 players (1990; premiered under Rozhdestvensky in London, 1991).

Smirnov, Dmitry (b Moscow, 7 Nov 1881; d Riga, 27 Apr 1944), Russian tenor. Sang at Bolshoi 1904–10, St Petersburg until 1917. Appeared in the Diaghilev seasons, Paris. NY Met. debut 1910, Duke of Mantua. Sang in Rimsky-Korsakov's *May Night* at Drury Lane, London, 1914. Other roles included Lensky, Luigi and Lohengrin.

Smit, Leo (b Philadelphia, 12 Jan 1921), American composer. Studied at Curtis (1930–32) and composition with Nabokov. Pianist with Balanchine's American Ballet Company, 1936–37; teacher at UCLA 1957–63 and director of Monday Evening concerts there.

Works include operas *The Alchemy of Love* (1969; libretto by astronomer Fred Hoyle) and *Magic Water* (1978); three symphonies (1956, 1965, 1981); piano concerto (1968); *Symphony of Dances and Songs* (1981); sonata for solo cello (1982); string quartet (1984).

Smith, Bernard (Bernhard Schmidt) (b Germany, 1629; d London, Feb 1708), German organ builder. Settled in England from 1660. His first English organ was at the Chapel Royal in London. Appointed organist at St Margaret's Church, Westminster, after building the organ there. He also built organs at Durham Cathedral and St Paul's Cathedral, London. Known as Father Smith.

Smith, Carleton Sprague (b New York, 8 Aug 1905), American critic, musicologist and flautist. Studied at Harvard University and in Vienna. After a year as critic to the *Boston Transcript*, he became chief librarian of the music section of the NY Public Library and lecturer in history of music at Columbia University. In 1938 he was president of the American Musicological Society.

Smith, Cyril (James) (b Middlesbrough, 11 Aug 1909; d London, 2 Aug 1974), English pianist. Studied at RCM; debut Birmingham. Well known in Brahms and Rakhmaninov. Married Phyllis Sellick and formed piano duet with her from 1941. Suffered stroke 1956, paralysing left arm; thereafter played music for three hands with his wife. OBE 1971.

Smith, David Stanley (b Toledo, OH, 6 Jul 1877; d New Haven, CT, 17 Dec 1949), American composer, conductor and teacher. Studied with H Parker at Yale University and later in London, Munich and Paris. In 1903 he became instructor and later professor of music at Yale.

Works include *The Fallen Star* for chorus and orchestra (1904), *Rhapsody of St Bernard* for solo voices, chorus and orchestra (1915),

The Vision of Isaiah for chorus (1926); anthems; part-songs; four symphonies (1905–37); ten string quartets; songs.

Smith, Jennifer (b Lisbon, 13 Jul 1945), British soprano. Made her debut in *Don Carlos* at Lisbon in 1968, then studied further with Pierre Bernac in London. Sang Mozart's Countess with WNO (1979) and Alphise in the stage fp of Rameau's *Les Boréades* (Aix, 1982); Amintas in *Il re Pastore* at Lisbon (1987) and Cybele in the US fp of Lully's *Atys* (New York 1988, with Les Arts Florissants). Sang the Queen of Night in Roger Norrington's Mozart Experience, London 1989, and the title role in *Iphigénie en Tauride* with the English Bach Festival at CG, 1992. Much admired for her recordings of operas by Rameau, Purcell, Mondonville (*Titon et L'aurore*) and Marais (*Alcyone*).

Smith, John Christopher (b Ansbach, 1712; d Bath, 3 Oct 1795), German (anglicized) organist and composer, son of Johann Christoph Schmidt of Ansbach, who went to London as Handel's treasurer and copyist. Smith became a pupil of Handel, and later of Pepusch and T Roseingrave. In 1746–48 he travelled on the Continent and in 1754 became organist of the Foundling Hospital. He acted as Handel's amanuensis during the composer's blindness. Between 1759 and 1768 he conducted annual performances of *Messiah* at the Foundling Hospital.

Works include operas *Teraminta*, *Ulysses* (1733), *Issipile* (1743), *Ciro riconosciuto* (1745), *Dario* (1746), *The Fairies* (from Shakespeare's *Midsummer Night's Dream*, 1755), *The Tempest* (after Shakespeare, 1756); *Rosalinda* (1740), *The Enchanter, or Love and Magic* (Garrick, 1760); oratorios *David's Lamentation over Saul and Jonathan* (1738), *Paradise Lost* (after Milton, 1758), *Rebecca, Judith* (1758), *Jehoshaphat* (1764), *The Redemption* (1774); Burial Service; instrumental works.

He had suddenly remembered I was a girl, to take whom seriously, was beneath a man's dignity, and the quality of the work, which had I been an obscure male he would have upheld against anyone, simply passed from his mind.

Ethel Smyth on Brahms,
in *Impressions That Remained*, 1919

Smith, John Stafford (b Gloucester, 30 Mar 1750; d London, 21 Sept 1836), English organist, tenor and composer. Pupil of his father, Martin Smith, organist at Gloucester Cathedral, and later of Boyce and Nares in London, where he was a chorister in the Chapel Royal. He became a Gentleman of the Chapel Royal in 1784, organist of Gloucester Cathedral in 1790 and in 1802 of the Chapel Royal in succession to Arnold, succeeding Ayrton as Master of the Children in 1805. He assisted Hawkins in his *History of Music*.

Works include anthems, glees, catches, canons, madrigals, part-songs; songs including *Anacreon in Heaven* (now *The Star-spangled Banner*).

Smith, Robert (b c 1648; d ? London, 22 Nov 1675), English composer. Chorister at the Chapel Royal in London under Cooke; became Musician in Ordinary to the King on the death of Humfrey in 1674. Works include incidental music for numerous plays (some with Staggins and others); music for strings; harpsichord pieces; songs, duets.

Smith, Ronald (b London, 3 Jan 1922), English pianist and writer on music. He studied at the RCM and made his debut in London at a 1942 Promenade concert; he has given many performances of the huge piano works of Alkan: his books on the composer include *Alkan, The Man and His Music* (1975), *Alkan The Enigma* (1976) and *Alkan in Miniature* (1978).

Smith Brindle, Reginald (b Bamber Bridge, 5 Jan 1917), English composer, teacher and writer on music. He studied in Italy with Pizzetti and Dallapiccola and worked for RAI, Italian radio, 1956–61. Professor, University of Surrey, 1970–85. His music is influenced by Berio and Stockhausen, and employs electronic techniques. His writings include *Serial Composition* (1966) and *The New Music* (1975).

Works include chamber opera *Antigone* (1969), Symphony (1954), *Variations on theme of Dallapiccola* for orchestra (1955), *Extremum carmen* for voices and orchestra (1956), *String quartet Music* (1958), *Creation Epic* for orchestra (1964), *Worlds without End* for speaker, voices, orchestra and tapes (1973), *The Walls of Jericho* for tuba and tape (1974), *Guitar Cosmos* (1976), *Journey towards Infinity* for orchestra (1987).

Smithers, Don (Le Roy) (b New York, 17 Feb 1933), American music historian and trumpeter. Studied at Columbia University, NY, and Oxford (PhD 1967 on the Baroque trumpet). Has taught at Syracuse University, NY, 1966–75 and at the Hague, Netherlands. Active as trumpeter and cornet player in various early music groups, including New York Pro Musica, the Leonhardt Consort, Concentus Musicus Wien and the Early Music Consort of London. Books include *The Music and History of the Baroque Trumpet Before 1721*, 1973.

smorzando Italian = 'extinguishing, dimming, toning down'; a direction indicating that a passage is to be performed with an effect of calming down or fading away, with a diminuendo and to an extent also ritardando.

Smyth, Ethel (Mary) (b London, 22 Apr 1858; d Woking, 9 May 1944), English composer. Studied at the Leipzig Conservatory and then privately there with Herzogenberg. She had some works performed there and after her return to England one or two appeared in London, including the Mass in 1893. She was encouraged by the conductor Hermann Levi (who had premiered *Parsifal* in 1882) to write an opera. *Fantasio* was given at Weimar in 1898 and was taken up three years later by Felix Mottl in Karlsruhe. *Der Wald/The Forest* was premiered at the Royal Opera Berlin in 1902 and was given at Covent Garden three months later; the following year it became the first opera by a woman to be shown at the NY Met. *The Wreckers* was completed 1904 and premiered at Leipzig 1906; its 1909 performance in London under Beecham almost caused the conductor to alter his unflattering opinion of women composers. She lived much abroad, but in 1910 received the honorary D.Mus. degree from Durham University and about that time joined actively in the movement for women's suffrage.

In 1911 when jailed at Holloway she led her fellow suffragettes in her song *March of the Women*, conducting them with a Government-issue toothbrush. She continued to be fierce in the promotion of her music and in 1916 her most successful opera *The Boatswain's Mate* was premiered in London. After the war she turned increasingly to writing, producing ten entertaining volumes of memoirs. In her later years she lived at Woking in Surrey and, regarding herself as neglected on account of her sex, composed less and less. She received the honour of a DBE in 1922. During her last years she suffered much from deafness and distorted hearing.

Works include operas *Fantasio*, after Musset (Weimar, 1898), *The Forest* (Berlin, 1902), *The Wreckers* (Leipzig, 1906), *The Boatswain's Mate* (after W W Jacobs, 1916), *Fête galante* (1923), *Entente cordiale* (1925); Mass in D major; *The Prison*, for solo voices, chorus and orchestra; overture to Shakespeare's *Antony and Cleopatra*, serenade for orchestra (1890); concerto for violin, horn and orchestra; three Anacreontic Odes for voice and orchestra; string quintet, string quartet; sonatas, songs.

Smythe, William (b c 1550; d Durham, c 1600), English composer. He was a minor canon and later master of the choristers (1594–98) at Durham Cathedral. He wrote a number of works for the Anglican church, not to be confused with those by his later namesake, 'William Smith of Durham'.

snare drum, or side drum, a double-headed drum used in military bands and orchestras, with skins at both the upper and lower ends of the instrument. Cords or wires lying against the underside skin rattle when the upper skin is played, adding definition to each new attack.

snares gut strings stretched over one of the heads of some types of drum, especially the side drum, adding brilliance to their tone by vibrating against the skin as the drum is struck. If that effect is not required, the snares can be temporarily slackened.

Snow, Valentine (b ? London; d London, Dec 1770), English trumpeter. Son of (?) Moses Snow, a Gentleman of the Chapel Royal in London and lay-vicar at Westminster Abbey. In 1753 he succeeded John Shore as Sergeant Trumpeter to the King. Handel wrote the trumpet obbligato parts in his oratorios for him.

Snow Maiden, The, *Snegurotchka*, opera by Rimsky-Korsakov (libretto by composer, based on a play by A N Ostrovsky), produced St Petersburg, 10 Feb 1882. The Snow Maiden lives amongst humans but cannot love. She falls for Mizgir and, granted the ability to love by Spring, melts in the sunlight.

Sobinov, Leonid (b Yaroslavl, 7 Jun 1872; d Riga, 14 Oct 1934), Russian tenor. He sang minor roles in Moscow from 1893; Bolshoi from 1897. In Russia and at La Scala, Monte Carlo and Berlin he was successful as Roméo, Lohengrin and Werther, and in such native roles as Lensky, Dubrovsky and Vladimir in *Prince Igor*. Noted for his elegance of manner and voice.

Sobolewski, (Friedrich) Eduard (b Königsberg, 1 Oct 1808; d St Louis, 17 May 1872), German-Polish composer and conductor. He was conductor at the Königsberg Theatre in succession to Dorn, 1830–36. Later he lived at Weimar and in 1859 emigrated to USA, where he became conductor to the St Louis Philharmonic Society.

Works include operas *Komala* (after Ossian, produced by Liszt at Weimar, 1858), *Imogene* (after Shakespeare's *Cymbeline*, 1833), *Velleda* (1836), *Salvator Rosa* and *Mohega* (1859); oratorio *The Saviour*; symphonies, symphonic poems.

Society for Private Musical Performances, Verein für Musikalische Privataufführengen, society founded in Vienna on 23 Nov 1918 by Schoenberg, with his pupils Berg, Webern and Steuermann as leaders of events. Aim was to provide carefully rehearsed performances of recent and contemporary music; subscribers only were admitted and critics excluded: Schoenberg and his pupils had suffered from the hostile public reception of their music in Vienna. The first concert on 29 Dec 1918 included Mahler's 7th symphony arranged by Webern for piano four hands; Schoenberg later arranged *Das Lied von der Erde* for chamber ensemble. Other composers featured were Debussy, Bartók, Stravinsky, Skriabin, Ravel, and Johann Strauss (in further arrangements by Schoenberg). Society disbanded 1922.

Socrate, *Socrates*, symphonic drama by Satie (libretto taken from Victor Cousin's French translation of Plato's *Dialogues*), produced Paris, 14 Feb 1920, and performed Prague, festival of the ISCM, May 1925. Philosophical musings end in suicide.

Söderman, (Johan) August (b Stockholm, 17 Jul 1832; d Stockholm, 10 Feb 1876), Swedish composer. Learnt music from his father, a theatre conductor, at 18 went to Finland as director of music to a Swedish company of musicians, and in 1856 producing his first operetta at Helsinki. After a period of study at Leipzig he was appointed chorus master at the Royal Opera at Stockholm 1860 and second conductor 1862.

Works include operetta *The Devil's First Lesson* (1856) and others; incidental music to Schiller's *Maid of Orleans*, Topelius's *Regina* and other plays; Mass for solo voices, chorus and orchestra; *Swedish Wedding* for female voices, cantatas and part-songs; vocal settings of Bellman's rhapsodies; *Circassian Dance* and concert overture for orchestra; sacred songs and hymns with organ; ballads and songs for voice and piano.

Söderström, Elisabeth (b Stockholm, 7 May 1927), Swedish soprano. Studied in Stockholm, making her debut there in 1947 as Bastienne. Glyndebourne from 1957 as the Composer, Octavian, Christine and Leonore. London, CG, from 1960 as the Countess, Fiordiligi and Mélisande. NY Met. 1959–64 (debut as Susanna). Janáček roles included Jenůfa and Emilia Marty. She was noted for her warmth of voice and appealing stage presence. Sang in the fp of Argento's *The Aspern Papers* (Dallas 1988) and became the artistic director of the Drottningholm Court Theatre in 1993.

Soffel, Doris (b Hechningen, 12 May 1948), German mezzo. Studied with Marianne Schech in Munich and sang in *Das Liebesverbot* at the

1972 Bayreuth Youth Festival. Sang with the Stuttgart Opera from 1973 and appeared as Waltraute at the 1976 Bayreuth Festival. CG debut 1983, as Sextus in *La Clemenza di Tito*, and returned as Orlofsky. Munich Opera 1986 and 1991, in the premieres of *Troades* by Reimann and Penderecki's *Ubu Rex*. Concert repertory includes *Das Lied von der Erde* and the Missa Solemnis.

Sofonisba, La opera by Caldara (libretto by Francesco Silvani), produced Venice, Teatro S Giovanni Crisostomo, Dec 1708. Siface, King of Numidia, is captured by the Romans. Wife Sophonisba joins him, but commits suicide rather than face the humiliation of her chains.

Opera by Gluck (libretto ditto, with airs from different libretti by Metastasio), produced Milan, Teatro Regio Ducal, 18 Jan 1744.

soft pedal the popular name for the damping pedal of the piano.

soggetto Italian = 'subject', in the musical sense, especially the subject of a fugue.

soggetto cavato Italian = 'extracted subject'; in the 15th c. and thereabouts a vocal theme sung to a melody formed from the vowels of a sentence converted by the composer into musical notes of the hexachord: a = fa or la, e = re, i = mi, o = do, u = ut.

Sogno di Scipione, Il, *Scipio's Dream*, dramatic serenade by Mozart (libretto by Metastasio), produced Salzburg, at the installation of the new archbishop, Hieronymus von Colloredo, 1 May 1772. Faced with two goddesses in a dream, Scipio chooses Constancy rather than Fortune.

Soh the name for the dominant note in any key in tonic sol-fa, so pronounced, but in notation represented by the letter s.

Sohal, Naresh (b Harsipind, Punjab, 18 Sep 1939), Indian composer. Studied with Jeremy Dale Roberts and Alexander Goehr in England. First came to attention with his *Asht Prahar* of 1965, performed by the LPO in 1970; *The Wanderer* for baritone, chorus and orchestra was given at the 1982 Prom Concerts, London, and *From Gitanjali* by the New York PO under Mehta in 1985. Other works include *Indra-Dhanush* for orchestra (1973), *Inscape* for chorus, flute and percussion (1979), two brass quintets (1983, 1984), *Undulation* for cello (1984) and *Tandova Nritya* for orchestra (1984).

Thaw ev'ry breast/Melt ev'ry eye with woe/Here's dissolution/By the hand of death!/To dirt; to water turned/The fairest Snow/O the King's Trumpeter/Has lost his Breath.

Epitaph for Valentine Snow, d. 1770

Sohier, Mathieu (b Noyon; d c 1560), French composer. He was master of the choristers at Notre-Dame, Paris, from 1533, and later canon of St Denis-du-Pas. Composed Masses, motets and *chansons*.

Sol the old name for the note G (♭solmization), still used in Latin countries, and in tonic sol-fa notation the dominant note in any key represented by the symbol *s*, pronounced Soh.

Solage late 14th-c. French composer. Wrote several *chansons*, found in the Chantilly MS.

Soldaten, Die, *The Soldiers*, opera in four acts by Bernd Alois Zimmermann (libretto by composer, after the play by Jakob Lenz, 1776); composed 1958–60, revised 1963–64, fp Cologne, 15 Feb 1965, conductor Gielen. Vocal Symphony for five soloists and orchestra derived from the opera in 1958; use is made of ballet, mime, *sprechstimme*, electronics and film. The composer committed suicide in 1970, two years before the first British performance, in Edinburgh. The moral degradation of Marie: she is at first engaged to Stolzius and then seduced by Baron Desportes and Major Mary. Stolzius poisons himself and Deziortes; Marie becomes a beggar.

Soleil des eaux, Le, *The Sun of the Waters*, music by Boulez for radio play by René Char, 1948; revised as cantata for soprano, tenor, baritone and chamber orchestra; fp Paris, 18 Jul 1950; revised with addition of chorus and performed Darmstadt, 9 Sept 1958; further revised for soprano and chorus and given in Berlin 1965.

Soler, Antonio (b Olot, Catalonia, bap. 3 Dec 1729; d El Escorial,

20 Dec 1783), Spanish friar, organist and composer. A chorister at Montserrat, he was *maestro de capilla* at Lérida Cathedral and entered the Escorial monastery in 1752, becoming organist and choirmaster there the following year. He was probably a pupil of D Scarlatti 1752–57. His treatise *Llave de la Modulación* was pub. in 1762.

Works include incidental music for plays by Calderón and others; nine Masses, motets and other church music; 132 *villancicos*; quintets for organ and strings; organ concertos; 120 harpsichord sonatas.

Solerti, Angelo (b Savona, 20 Sept 1865; d Massa Carrara, 10 Feb 1907), Italian musicologist. He wrote several works on the origins of dramatic music in the early 17th c..

sol-fa ◊solmization and ◊tonic sol-fa.

solfège, French, *solfeggio* Italian, an elementary method of teaching sight-reading and of ear-training, practised mainly in France and Italy. The names of the notes ('Do, re, mi', etc.) are pronounced while the notes are sung unaccompanied and the intervals have thus to be learnt by ear.

soli, Italian, a group of solo performers as distinct from the whole vocal or orchestral body employed in a work.

Solié (originally *Soulier*), Jean-Pierre (b Nîmes, 1755; d Paris, 6 Aug 1812), French singer, cellist and composer. A chorister at Nîmes Cathedral, he learnt the cello from his father and played in local theatres. He made his debut as a singer in 1778 and from 1787 was at the Opéra-Comique in Paris, rising to become leading baritone. Many of Méhul's roles were written for him. From *c* 1790 he also had success as an opera composer.

Works include 33 *opéras-comiques*, e.g. *Jean et Geneviève* (1792), *Le Jockey* (1796), *Le Secret*, *Le Chapitre second* (1799), *Mademoiselle de Guise*, *Le Diable à quatre* (1809), *Les Ménestrels* (1811).

solmization, from Latin *solmisatio*, the designation of the musical scales by means of syllables. The notes of the Greek Tetrachords were already designated by syllables, but Guido d'Arezzo in the 11th c. replaced them by the hexachords and used the Latin syllables Ut, Re, Mi, Fa, Sol, La for their six notes, Si being added later for the seventh and Ut being replaced by Do in Italy and elsewhere, though still largely retained in France. These syllables, as in modern Tonic Sol-fa with movable Doh, were not immutably fixed to C, D, E, F, G, A, but could be transferred by mutation to other degrees of the scale, so long as the semitone always occurred between Mi and Fa. The so-called 'natural hexachord' beginning on C could thus be changed to the 'hard hexachord' beginning on G, in which case Mi- Fa corresponded with B–C, or to the 'soft hexachord' beginning on F (◊hexachord). The syllables were derived from a hymn of the year 770 for the festival of St John the Baptist, the lines of the plainsong of which began on the successive notes of the hexachord.

UT queant laxis
REsonare fibris
MIra gestorum
FAmuli tuorum
SOLve polluti
LAbii reatum
Sancte Ioannes.

The seventh syllable, Si, was derived from the initial letters of the last line.

solo Italian = 'alone'; as a noun, a piece or part of a composition sung or played by a single performer, with or without accompaniment. The word is also used adjectivally in directions given in Italian, e.g. *violino solo*, 'to be played by one violin alone', *voce sola*, 'voice unaccompanied', etc.

> *Poor Accompanists are admittedly numerous enough, but there are very few good ones, for today everyone wants to be the soloist.*
> **Leopold Mozart**, *Versuch einer gründlichen Violinschule*, 1756

Solomon oratorio by Handel (libretto ? by Newburgh Hamilton), performed London, CG, 17 Mar 1749.

Solomon, actually Solomon Cutner (b London, 9 Aug 1902; d London, 2 Feb 1988), English pianist. Debut at Queen's Hall aged eight, in Tchaikovsky's first piano concerto, and then studied in Paris, beginning his true career in 1923. His brilliant technique and musicianship made him outstanding among modern pianists; widely admired in Mozart, Chopin and Brahms. Paralysed from 1955.

Solomon, Yonty (b Cape Town, 6 May 1938), South African-born British pianist. Studied with Myra Hess in London and made debut there in 1963. Has given concerto performances in Europe, North America and South Africa, with fps of solo works by Sorabji; other large scale repertory includes Bach's *Goldberg Variations* and the *Concord Sonata* of Ives. Duos with Sylvia Rosenberg (violin) and Radu Adulescu (cello). Professor at the RCM.

Soloviev, Nikolai Feopemptovich (b Petrozavodsk, 9 May 1846; d Petrograd, 27 Dec 1916), Russian composer. Began by studying medicine, but turned to music and entered the St Petersburg Conservatory, Zaremba being among his masters. He became professor there in 1874. In 1871 Serov, when dying, charged him with the orchestration of his opera *The Power of Evil*. He was also a critic and collector of folksongs; he was highly critical of Tchaikovsky as well as the nationalist composers Stasov and Cui. His opera *Vakula the Smith* lost to Tchaikovsky in a competition of 1875, but some members of the jury apparently preferred Soloviev's work.

Works include operas *Cordelia* (after Sardou's *La Haine*, 1885), *Vakula the Smith* (on Gogol's *Christmas Eve*, 1875) and *The Cottage of Kolomua*; cantata for the bicentenary of Peter the Great; symphonic poem *Russians and Mongols* and Fantasy on a Folksong for orchestra; piano pieces; songs.

Soltesz, Stefan (b Nyiregyhaza, 6 Jan 1949), Hungarian conductor. After study in Vienna with Swarowsky (1963–72) conducted at the Theater an der Wien, Vienna, 1971–73; Salzburg Festivals from 1978 and Graz Opera 1979–81. Conductor of the Hamburg Opera 1983–85 and at the Deutsche Oper Berlin from 1985. Music director at Brunswick 1989–93. Principal guest of the Leipzig Opera from 1992 and has given concerts throughout Europe. US opera debut with *Otello* at Washington, DC, 1992.

Solti, Georg (b Budapest, 21 Oct 1912), Hungarian-born conductor and pianist, British citizen from 1972. Studied at the Budapest Conservatory, piano with Dohnányi and composition with Kodály and Bartók. From 1930 to 1939 he conducted at the Budapest Opera and then went to Switzerland, where he was active both as a pianist and conductor,

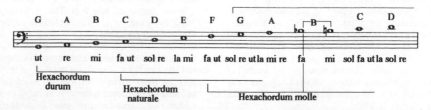

Solmization of the gamut, with different possible readings according to the particular hexachord.

Solti *The conductor and pianist Georg Solti. During his long and distinguished career as conductor, Solti has galvanized performances in all genres, especially 19th-century music. He gave the first complete studio recording of the* Ring *cycle and his sets of symphonies convey all the excitement of the concert hall.*

winning first prize for piano at the Concours International at Geneva in 1942. In 1946 he became conductor at the Munich Staatsoper and 1952–61 director of the Frankfurt Opera. US debut San Francisco 1953 (*Elektra*). In 1959 he made his debut at Covent Garden in *Der Rosenkavalier* and was director 1961–71; his decade was noted for productions of the *Ring*, *Arabella*, *Moses und Aron* and *Die Frau ohne Schatten*. Chicago SO 1969–91, LPO 1979–83. In spite of an international career he has not neglected British music: often heard in Tippett and Elgar, giving at Chicago the fps of Tippett's 4th symphony (1977) and *Byzantium* (1991). Re-appeared as concert soloist 1986 (Mozart's D minor concerto). He has also made many highly successful recordings, among them the complete *Ring* (1958–64), and is the first conductor to record all of Wagner's major operas. He conducted the *Ring* at Bayreuth in 1983 and was artistic director of the Salzburg Easter Festival 1990–92. Although noted earlier for the brilliance and energy of his performances, Solti has mellowed, favouring a more reflective style, as in his performances of *Otello* at CG, 1992. Honorary knighthood 1971.

A young conductor has to compromise. He will put more energy in and get less back.
Georg Solti, interviewed in *Classic CD*, 1995

Soltys, Adam (b Lwów, 4 Jul 1890; d Lwów, 6 Jul 1968), Polish composer and conductor. Studied at Lwów Conservatory, the Berlin Hochschule für Musik and the Kunstakademie, and Berlin University. Professor at Lwów Conservatory from 1921 (director, 1930–39) and conductor of the symphony orchestra.

Works include two symphonies, symphonic poem *Slowianie/The Slavs*; chamber music; variations for piano; songs.

Soltys, Mieczyslaw (b Lwów, 7 Feb 1863; d Lwów, 12 Nov 1929), Polish composer and conductor, father of Adam ◊Soltys. Studied in Vienna and Paris, where he was a pupil of Saint-Saëns. He returned to Lwów in 1891 and became director of the Conservatory and conductor of the Music Association.

Works include operas *The Republic of Babin* (1905), *Maria* (on Antoni Malczewski's poem), *Panie Kochanku* (1924) and others; oratorios; symphony, symphonic poem *The Fugitive*.

Somary, Johannes (b Zurich, 7 Apr 1935), Swiss-born American conductor. Studied at Yale and made debut in New York, 1960. Has conducted orchestras and choral societies in New York; guest with the ECO in London (1968–79), the Royal Philharmonic and the Brno State PO. Has recorded *Messiah*, *St Matthew Passion*, the *Four Seasons* and a series of Handel operas (*Sosarme*, 1994).

Sombrero de tres picos, El, *The Three-cornered Hat*, ballet by Falla (scenario by Martínez Sierra, based on Alarcón's story; choreographed by Massin), produced London, Alhambra Theatre, 22 Jul 1919. The setting and costumes were designed by Picasso.

Somervell, Arthur (b Windermere, 5 Jun 1863; d London, 2 May 1937), English composer and educationist. Educated at Uppingham School and King's College, Cambridge, where he studied composition with Stanford, going later to Kiel and Berlin, to the RCM in London in 1885 and to Parry as a private pupil in 1887. In 1894 he became professor at the RCM. Knighted 1929.

Works include Masses in C minor (1891) and D minor (the latter for male voices, 1907), anthem *Let all the world*, oratorio *The Passion of Christ*, cantatas *A Song of Praise*, *The Power of Sound*, *The Forsaken Merman* (Matthew Arnold), *Ode to the Sea* and others; symphony in D minor, *Thalassa* (1912), concerto in G minor and *Concertstück* for violin and orchestra; clarinet quintet; violin and piano sonata; Variations on an Original Theme for two pianos; violin pieces; piano pieces; song cycles *Maud* (Tennyson), *A Shropshire Lad* (A E Housman, 1904).

Somfai, László (b Jaszladany, 15 Aug 1934), Hungarian musicologist. Studied at the Franz Liszt Academy, Budapest, and has been professor of musicology there from 1980. Has published several works on Haydn: as opera director (1960), his life on contemporary pictures (1966) and on the piano sonatas (1979). Also studies of Liszt, Stravinsky, Webern and Bartók.

Somigli, Franca (originally Marion Bruce Clark) (b Chicago, 1901; d Trieste, 14 May 1974), American soprano. Debut Rovigo 1926, as Mimi; Pavia 1927, as the *Trovatore* Leonora. Rome and La Scala 1933–44; 1935 in the fp of Pizzetti's *Orséleo*, and as Arabella, the Marschallin, Kundry and Sieglinde. At Salzburg she sang Alice Ford, under Toscanini. NY Met. 1937, Butterfly. At the Berlin Staatsoper in 1944 she was Salome, under De Sabata.

Somis, Giovanni Battista (b Turin, 25 Dec 1686; d Turin, 14 Aug 1763), Italian violinist and composer. Pupil of Corelli in Rome and (?) Vivaldi at Venice. Returning to Turin, he was appointed violinist to the King of Piedmont and leader of the royal orchestra. About 1733 he lived in Paris for a time. He taught many famous pupils, including Leclair, Giardini and Pugnani.

Works include violin concertos; sonatas.

Somis, Lorenzo (b Turin, 11 Nov 1688; d Turin, 29 Nov 1775), Italian violinist and composer, brother of Giovanni Battista ◊Somis. Lived in Turin as violinist in the royal orchestra. Composed violin sonatas, etc.

Sommeils, French, plur. of *sommeil* = 'sleep', quiet airs in old French operas, supposed to induce sleep.

Sommer, Hans (actually Hans Friedrich August Zincken, sometimes anagram 'Neckniz') (b Brunswick, 20 Jul 1837; d Brunswick, 28 Apr 1922), German composer. Studied at Göttingen University and became professor of physics there. In 1875 he became director of the Technical High School at Brunswick, settled in Berlin in 1885, at Weimar in 1888, and in 1898 returned to Brunswick. He had been composing as an amateur since before 1865, when he produced his first opera.

Works include operas *Der Nachtwächter* (1865), *Loreley* (1891), *Saint-Foix*, *Der Meermann*, *Augustin*, *Münchhausen*, *Rübezahl* (1904), *Riquet mit dem Schopf* (1907) and *Der Waldschratt* (1912); song cycles from Julius Wolff's *Der wilde Jäger* (*Mädchenlieder*), *Hunold Singuf* and *Tannhäuser*, from Carmen Sylva's *Sappho* and many other songs.

Son and Stranger (Mendelssohn.) ◊Heimkehr aus der Fremde.

sonata, Italian and English, a term designating both a type of composition and a musical form. The classical sonata is normally a composition in three or four movements, the first of which is with few exceptions in sonata form, and often the last movement as well, though that is at least as frequently a rondo. The word is derived from *suonare* or *sonare* = 'to sound': a sonata is thus originally simply 'a thing sounded', i.e. played, as distinct from a cantata (from *cantare*), 'a thing sung'. But in the 17th c. the sonata developed into the two types described here, the sonata da camera and the sonata da chiesa. In the 18th c. the one-movement sonatas of D Scarlatti began to approximate to the modern first-movement form, while other works of the kind, especially in Germany, still approximated to the suite, from which indeed the mature sonata borrowed the minuet (later developed into the scherzo), but often dropped it in favour of a three-movement composition: first movement in sonata form, slow movement, and finale in sonata or rondo form.

The modern first-movement form, developed through C P E Bach and some of his contemporaries, reached full maturity in the hands of Haydn, Mozart and others, and was greatly stretched by the innovations of Beethoven, e.g. in his type of ◊*sonata quasi una fantasia* and late works, which admitted fugal developments and variations.

After Beethoven the sonata was treated according to two divergent philosophies. In the hands of Chopin and Brahms, for example, the classical structure was retained while increasingly expressive harmonies were introduced; at the other extreme, the traditional form itself disintegrated in order to give the composer additional freedom, as in the B minor sonata of Liszt, which substitutes a continuous thematic transformation as the chief cohesive technique, rather than the traditionally clearly delineated sections.

The sonata form in its fully matured but not sophisticated manifestations shows the following main outlines: a single movement in two or three principal sections, the first called the exposition, ending in another key than that of the tonic. Two main thematic groups make up its material, with room for subsidiary themes and connecting bridge passages. These groups are traditionally described as First and Second Subjects. The first is in the tonic key, the second in a related key (e.g. the dominant in a movement in a major key and the relative major in one in a minor key). The second section begins with a development, which, as its name suggests, develops some of the foregoing material in new ways, but may also partly or even exclusively introduce new matter (e.g. as in Mozart). This development leads to the recapitulation which is usually classified as a separate third section in works of the later 18th c. and onward, where the opening of the movement, i.e. the first subject, returns as before, though possibly with varied treatment; the second subject also appears in the tonic key, major or minor, and in the latter case it is often in minor even if in the first section it appeared in major. All this necessitates a new modulatory transition between first and second subjects. The movement may end in the tonic exactly as the first section ended in another key; but there may be a coda added, either a very brief tail-piece of a merely ceremonial nature or a more developed section which may further work upon the foregoing material, as often in the case of Beethoven. Not only works so called are sonatas, but also chamber music of the normal classical type and symphonies.

sonata da camera Italian = 'chamber sonata'; an instrumental work of the late 17th and early 18th c. of the suite or partita type in several movements, mainly in dance forms, but always for more than one instrument, most usually two violins with continuo for bass viol or cello with a keyboard instrument, generally harpsichord. Unlike the sonata da chiesa, the sonata da camera usually had a quick first movement.

sonata da chiesa Italian = 'church sonata'; an instrument work of the late 17th and early 18th c., frequently, though not invariably, in four movements (slow introduction, fugal *allegro*, slow *cantabile* movement and quick finale), written for more than one instrument, most usually two violins with continuo for bass viol or cello with a keyboard instrument, which if played in church must have been generally the organ.

sonata quasi una fantasia Italian = 'sonata, as it were a fantasy'; a term invented by Beethoven for some of his sonatas in which he began to modify the form freely, the two works of op. 27 for piano being the first of the kind.

sonatina Italian dim. of sonata = 'little sonata'; a work of the sonata type in a condensed form or easy to play. The first movement of a sonatina usually contains the normal first and second subjects, though as a rule they are less extended, but it may have only a rudimentary working-out section and coda or none at all. The key-scheme for the reappearance of the two subjects in the second section, however, will be similar to that in a sonata. Sonatinas have often been written for teaching purposes, especially for the piano.

The sonata was said by a German critic to be intended by the earliest writers to show in the first movement what they could do, in the second what they could feel, and in the last how glad they were to have finished.

Philip H Goepp,
Symphonies and their Meaning, 1897

Sondheim, Stephen (Joshua) (b New York, 22 Mar 1930), American composer and lyricist. Studied at Williams College, MA, and with Milton Babbitt. Wrote the lyrics for Bernstein's *West Side Story* (1957) and Styne's *Gypsy* (1959); words and music for such shows as *A Little Night Music* (1972), *Pacific Overtures* (1976), *Sweeney Todd* (1979), *Sunday in the Park with George* (1984), *Into the Woods* (1987), *Assassins* (1990) and *Passion* (1994). He is alleged to have brought new levels of profundity to the musical theatre.

song strictly speaking any poem set to music for a single voice, with or without an accompaniment, is a song, but the species is distinct from other forms of vocal composition such as the aria, the ballad, the couplet, etc. A song may either be set to a repetition of the same tune ('strophic'), or be set continuously ('through-composed'), the music developing throughout in a manner calculated to illustrate the progress of the words.

song cycle a series of songs set as a rule to a number of poems with a connected narrative or some other unifying feature. Schubert's *Die schöne Müllerin* and *Winterreise*, for example, are thus song cycles properly speaking, while his *Schwanengesang* is not. An earlier example is Beethoven's *An die ferne Geliebte*: later ones are Schumann's *Dichterliebe* and *Frauenliebe und -leben*, Fauré's *La Bonne Chanson*, Debussy's *Chansons de Bilitis* and Vaughan Williams's *On Wenlock Edge*.

Songe d'une nuit d'été, Le, *The Dream of a Midsummer Night*, opera by A Thomas (libretto by J B Rosier and A de Leuven, not based on Shakespeare's play), produced Paris, Opéra-Comique, 20 Apr 1850. Shakespeare, Queen Elizabeth and Falstaff appear in it as characters.

Songmakers' Almanac, The. English ensemble founded 1976 by artistic director and pianist Graham Johnson. Many tours throughout Britain, the USA and Australia, giving song and recital programmes devoted to literary and other themes. Singers with the ensemble have included Sarah Walker, Ann Murray, Felicity Lott, Richard Jackson, and Anthony Rolfe Johnson.

Song of Destiny (Brahms.) ◊Schicksalslied.

Song of the Earth (Mahler.) ◊Lied von der Erde.

Song of the High Hills, The work by Delius for wordless chorus and orchestra; composed 1911, fp London, 26 Feb 1920, conductor Albert Coates.

Song of Triumph (Brahms.) ◊Triumphlied.

Songs and Dances of Death song cycle by Mussorgsky (poems by A A Golenishtchev-Kutuzov), composed 1875–77: 1. *The Peasant's Lullaby*; 2. *Serenade*; 3. *Trepak*; 4. *The Field Marshal*. Orchestrated by Shostakovich, 1962.

Songs of Farewell work by Delius for chorus and orchestra (text by Walt Whitman); composed 1930, fp London, 21 Mar 1932, conductor Sargent.

Songs of Sunset work by Delius for mezzo, baritone, chorus and orchestra (text by Ernest Dowson); composed 1906–08, fp London, 16 Jun 1911, conductor Beecham.

Songs of Travel nine songs for voice and piano by Vaughan Williams (texts by Robert Louis Stevenson), fp of nos. 1–8 London, 2 Dec 1904, with Hamilton Harty at the piano; first complete performance BBC, 21 May 1960.

Songs without Words (Mendelssohn.) ◊Lieder ohne Worte.

Sonnambula, La, *The Sleepwalker*, opera by Bellini (libretto by F Romani), produced Milan, Teatro Carcano, 6 Mar 1831. Amina is found at night in the bedroom of Count Rodolfo, to the dismay of her betrothed Elvino; he is only placated when Amina's sonambulistic tendencies are revealed.

sonore French = 'sonorous'; an indication that a passage is to be played or sung with full tone. The Italian term is *sonoro*.

Sons, Maurice (b Amsterdam, 13 Sept 1857; d London, 28 Sept 1942), Dutch violinist. Studied at the Brussels Conservatory with Wieniawski and others, and with Rappoldi at Dresden. After an appointment in Switzerland he settled in Scotland as leader of the Scottish Orchestra and in 1904 became leader of the Queen's Hall Orchestra in London, where he remained until 1927. He was violin professor at the RCM 1903–37.

Sontag, Henriette (Gertrud Walpurgis) (b Koblenz, 3 Jan 1806; d Mexico City, 17 Jun 1854), German soprano. The daughter of actors, she appeared on the stage as a child, but in 1815 entered the Prague Conservatory as a singing-student, and in 1821 made a very successful stage appearance as an understudy in Boieldieu's *Jean de Paris*. She was then taken to Vienna for further study and at once appeared there in Italian and German opera, Weber choosing her to sing the title-part in *Euryanthe* in 1823. The following year in Vienna she took part in the fp of the Choral Symphony. She first visited Paris in 1826 and London in 1828 (both debuts as Rosina). She married Count Rossi, a diplomat of the Sardinian court, and retired, living with him at various courts in Holland, Germany and Russia, but after the 1848 revolutions she reappeared on the stage, especially in England and USA. Other roles included Donna Anna, Semiramide and Carolina in *Il matrimonio segreto*.

Let a man try the very uttermost to speak what he means, before singing is had recourse to.
Thomas Carlyle, *Journal*, 1843

Soomer, Walter (b Liegnitz, Silesia, 12 Mar 1878; d Leipzig, Aug 1955), German bass-baritone. He studied in Berlin. Debut Kolmar, 1902. Leipzig 1906–27, Dresden 1911–15. He had an important career at Bayreuth: 1906–25 as Kurwenal, Wotan, Amfortas, Sachs, Hagen and Gurnemanz. NY Met. 1908–11.

Soot, Fritz (b Neunkirchen, 20 Aug 1878; d Berlin, 9 Jun 1965), German tenor. Stage debut Dresden 1908, as Tonio; remained until 1918 and created the Italian Singer in *Der Rosenkavalier*. Stuttgart 1918–22. At the Berlin Staatsoper he created the Drum Major in *Wozzeck* (1925) and was the first local Lača and Mephistopheles (Busoni); also sang in the fps of Schreker's *Der singende Teufel* (1928) and Pfitzner's *Das Herz* (1931). At Zoppot and CG (1924–5) he was heard as Siegfried, Tristan and Walther. He was well known as Waldemar, in Schoenberg's *Gurrelieder*.

Sophocles (b 497 or 495; d 405BC), Greek dramatist. ◊Antigonae (Orff); ◊Antigone (incidental music, Mendelssohn; operas, Honegger, Zingarelli); ◊Bantock (*Electra*); ◊Elektra (R Strauss); ◊Enescu (*Œdipe*); A ◊Hüttenbrenner (*Odipus auf Kolonos*); ◊Oedipus auf Kolonos (Mendelssohn); ◊Oedipus Rex (Stravinsky); ◊Oedipus der Tyrann (Orff); ◊Oedipus und die Sphinx (Varèse); ◊Pizzetti (*Trachiniae, Oedipus Rex* and *Coloneus*); ◊Saint-Saëns (*Antigone*); ◊Zingarelli (*Edipo a Colono*).

sopra Italian = 'above'; the word is used in piano music to indicate in passages for crossed hands whether the right is to go above the left or *vice versa*. ◊come sopra.

sopranino as an adj. indicates the highest member of a family of wind instruments, e.g. sopranino recorder, sopranino saxophone.

soprano the highest female voice. Up to the end of the 18th c. there were also artifical male sopranos, produced by castration. Boy sopranos are

The soprano range has approximately the compass shown, but often extended further in florid operatic arias requiring dexterity.

more often described as trebles. Some instruments made in various ranges use the word soprano as a prefix for those types which roughly equal the compass of the soprano voice (e.g. soprano saxophone).

soprano clef the C clef so used as to indicate that middle C stands on the bottom line of the stave:

The soprano clef.

Sor (or *Sors*), Fernando (b Barcelona, 13 Feb 1778; d Paris, 10 Jul 1839), Spanish guitarist and composer. Educated at the Escolanía at Montserrat, produced his first opera at the age of 19, went to Paris and c 1815 to London, where he played and taught the guitar, returning to Paris in 1823.

Works include operas *Telemaco nell' isola di Calipso* (1797); six ballets including *Cendrillon* (1822), successful in London, Paris and Moscow; guitar pieces and studies. His guitar tutor was pub. in 1830.

Sorabji, Kaikhosru Shapurji (originally Leon Dudley) (b Chingford, Essex, 14 Aug 1892; d Wareham, 14 Oct 1988), English Parsee pianist and composer. His mother was Spanish. Lived in England all his life. Except for the piano, he was mainly self-taught, but was fortunate to be able to give all his time to musical studies. He appeared as pianist in his own works in London, Paris and Vienna, and also wrote criticism, including a book, *Around Music*. His piano works are in a complex, late Romantic style and test the endurance of performers and audiences: *Opus clavicembalistium* lasts for almost three hours and concludes with a passacaglia of 81 variations. Sorabji premiered the *Opus* at Glasgow in 1930 but forbade further performances of all his music from 1936 to 1976. Yonty *Solomon* premiered the 3rd Sonata, and the *Opus* was given at Chicago in 1983.

Works include two symphonies for orchestra, piano, organ and chorus (1922, 1951); *Chaleur and Opusculum* for orchestra; eight piano concertos (1915–22), symphonic variations for piano and orchestra; two symphonies for organ; two piano quintets (1920, 1953); five sonatas, *Opus clavicembalisticum, Fantasia Hispanica*, three toccatas, symphony, variations on *Dies irae* for piano; *Trois Poèmes* (Verlaine and Baudelaire), *Fêtes galantes* (Verlaine) for voice and piano.

Sorcerer's Apprentice, The (Dukas.) ◊Apprenti sorcier.

Sorcerer, The operetta by Sullivan (libretto by W S Gilbert), produced London, Opera Comique, 17 Nov 1877. Plot similar to Donizetti's *L'elisir d'amore*, with characters Alexis and Aline, sorcerer John Wellington Wells, and parents Sir Marmaduke and Lady Sangazure.

Soriano, Francesco (b Soriano sul Cimino, c 1549; d Rome, 19 Jul 1621), Italian composer. Became a choirboy at St John Lateran in Rome and studied with various masters including) G B Nanini and Palestrina. After a first appointment he went to the court of Mantua, 1583–86, and then became *maestro di cappella* in Rome, by turns at Santa Maria Maggiore, St John Lateran and in 1603 St Peter's.

Works include Masses, an arrangement of Palestrina's *Missa*

Papae Marcelli for eight voices, motets, psalms, Magnificat, a Passion and other church music; madrigals.

Sorochintsy Fair, *Sorochinskaya Yarmarka*, unfinished opera by Mussorgsky (libretto by composer, based on Gogol's *Evenings on a Farm near Dakanka*), composition begun 1875; revised by Liadov for concert performance, 1904; performed in original form, St Petersburg, Comedia Theatre, 30 Dec 1911; a version by Sakhnovsky produced Moscow, Free Theatre, 3 Nov 1913; version by Cui with music of his own added produced St Petersburg, Musical Drama Theatre, 26 Oct 1917; version by N Tcherepnin produced Monte Carlo, 17 Mar 1923 (in French); another version made by Shebalin in 1931 was produced Leningrad, Little Opera Theatre, 21 Dec 1931. Parasya meets lover Gritzke at the Fair but her mother objects to their marriage.

sortita, Italian from *sortire* = 'to come out', the aria sung by a principal character in an 18th-c. opera at his of her first entry on the stage.

Sosarme, rè di Media, *Sosarmes, King of the Medes*, opera by Handel (libretto based on Matteo Noris's *Alfonso primo*), produced London, King's Theatre, Haymarket, 15 Feb 1732. Haliate besieges the city controlled by his rebellious son Argone; Melo is announced as Haliate's successor instead of Argone. Sosarme reconciles the rival claimants to throne and weds Elmira.

sostenuto Italian = 'sustained'; a direction which may mean either that a note or notes are to be held to their full value (as with *tenuto*) or that a passage is to be played broadly, though not exactly slowed down (as with *ritenuto*).

Sotin, Hans (b Dortmund, 10 Sept 1939), German bass. He made his Hamburg debut in 1964 and sang there in the 1966 fp of Blacher's *Incidents at a Forced Landing* and the 1969 fp of Penderecki's *The Devils of Loudun*. Sarastro was the role of his Glyndebourne (1970) and NY Met. (1972) debuts. Bayreuth since 1972 as the Landgrave, Marke, Pogner and Gurnemanz. He sang Hunding at CG (1974) and returned 1977, in a new production of *Der Freischütz*. Sang Gurnemanz and Daland at Bayreuth, 1992.

> *Folk music is the ungarbled and ingenuous*
> *expression of the human mind and on that account it*
> *must reflect the essential and basic qualities of the*
> *human mind.*
>
> **Cecil Sharp**, *English Folk Song*, 1907

Soto de Langa, Francisco (b Langa near Osma, 1534; d Rome, 25 Sept 1619), Spanish priest, male soprano and arranger. He entered the Papal choir in Rome in 1562, joined the Oratory of St Philip Neri and continued to sing to the end of his long life. He adapted five books of *laudi spirituali* for three and four voices (pub. Rome, 1577–88), using Italian folksongs and various Italian and Spanish compositions.

sotto voce Italian = 'under the voice'; a direction indicating that a passage is to be performed in an undertone. As the term indicates, it was originally applied to vocal music, but it became current for instrumental music also.

soubrette, French from Provençal *soubret* = 'coy', a stock figure in opera given to a singer with a light soprano voice and impersonating characters of the type of servants, young confidantes, girls usually connected with the sub-plot, etc. (e.g. Despina in Mozart's *Così fan tutte*, Aennchen in Weber's *Freischütz*). Occasionally the soubrette may assume a principal part (e.g. Serpina in Pergolesi's *La Serva padrona*, Susanna in Mozart's *Figaro*, etc.).

Souez, Ina (b Windsor, CO, 3 Jun 1908; d Santa Monica, 9 Dec 1992), American soprano. She studied in Denver and Florence and in 1929 sang Liù at CG. After marrying an Englishman she settled in England and sang every season at Glyndebourne 1934–39 as Fiordiligi and Donna Anna in the first production there of *Così fan tutte* and *Don Giovanni*. She returned to the USA in 1939 and after World War II sang in a jazz band.

Souliotis, Elena (b Athens, 28 May 1943), Greek soprano. She studied in Milan; debut Naples, 1964, as Santuzza. Wider fame in 1966, with

Abigaille at La Scala and Boito's Elena at the Lyric Opera, Chicago. NY Met. and CG debuts 1969, as Lady Macbeth. An apparent attempt to model herself on Callas led to an early vocal decline, although she has appeared from 1986 at Florence and Catania in operas by Prokofiev (*The Gambler*), Puccini (*Suor Angelica*) and Mascagni (*Guglielmo Ratcliff*).

sound-board a resonant wooden part of various instruments, including organ, piano, dulcimer, cimbalom, etc. which adds to the volume of tone by vibrating with the notes.

sound-holes the holes in the tables of string instruments, also in the sound-boards of harpsichords, etc. In instruments of the violin family they take the shape of *f* holes or something approximating to them; in keyboard instruments as well as lutes, guitars, etc., usually the shape of a 'rose'.

sound-post the piece of pine wood standing upright between the table and the back of string instruments, inserted partly to support the pressure of the strings on the bridge, but mainly to act as the chief distributor of the vibrations.

sourdine, French from *sourd* = 'deaf', an instrument of the bassoon type, which derived its name from the fact that its tone was muffled. It was known as *Sordun* in Germany and *sordone* in Italy.

Šourek, Otakar (b Prague, 10 Oct 1883; d Prague, 15 Feb 1956), Czech music critic. Although an engineer by profession, he became critic to two Prague newspapers and pub. important works, mainly on Dvořák, including a thematic catalogue and a large two-volume life and study of the works. Also showed interest in Janáček.

Souris, André (b Marchienne-au-Pont, 10 Jul 1899; d Paris, 12 Feb 1970), Belgian composer. He worked under the influence of French impressionism at first, but from 1926 endeavoured to produce in music some equivalent to the surrealist painters.

Works include incidental music for *Le Dessous des cartes; Musique* for orchestra (1928); fanfare *Hommage à Babeuf* (1934); *Petite Suite* for four brass instruments; *Quelques airs de Clarisse Juranville* for contralto and piano.

Sousa, John Philip (b Washington, 6 Nov 1854; d Reading, PA, 6 Mar 1932), American bandmaster and composer. After some years' experience as an orchestra violinist he became master of the US Marine Corps band in 1880 and in 1892 formed a band of his own. In his compositions he became the leading exponent of the military march, with such inspiring numbers as *The Washington Post* (1889), *The Stars and Stripes Forever* (1896) and *Hands Across the Sea* (1899). Also wrote the operettas *The Queen of Hearts* (1885) and *El Capitán* (1895).

sousaphone a brass instrument of the Tuba type made for Sousa's band in 1899 with a bell opening towards the audience.

sousedská a Bohemian country dance in slow triple time. The third, fourth and 16th of Dvořák's *Slavonic Dances* for piano duet are sousedskás.

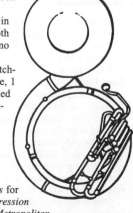

Souster, Tim(othy) Andrew James (b Bletchley, Bucks., 29 Jan 1943; d Cambridge, 1 Mar 1994), English composer. He studied at Oxford and Darmstadt and was assistant to Stockhausen in Cologne, 1971–73. Co-founder with Roger Smalley of group Intermodulation, to explore electronic and aleatory techniques. He worked at King's College, Cambridge, and Keele University.

Works include *Songs of the Seasons* for soprano and viola (1965), *Poem in Depression* for soprano and ensemble (1965), *Metropolitan Games* for piano duet (1967), *Titus Groan Music* for wind quintet, tape and electronics (1969), *Chinese Whispers* for percussion and synthesizers (1970), *Waste Land Music*, for saxophone, piano and organ (1970), *Triple Music* for three orchestras (1970), *Song of an Average City* for small orchestra and tape (1974),

Afghan Amplitudes for keyboards and synthesizers (1976), *Arcane Artefact*, trio (1977), *Driftwood Cortège*, tape (1978), *Sonata* for cello and ensemble (1979), *Equalisation*, brass quintet (1980), *The Transistor Radio of St Narcissus* (1983), *Curtain of Light* for percussion (1984), *Hambledon Hill*, for amplified string quartet (1985), trumpet concerto (1986).

Soustrot, Marc (b Lyon, 15 Apr 1949), French conductor. Studied conducting with Manuel Rosenthal at the Paris Conservatory, 1969–76. Won the Rupert Foundation Competition (London 1974) and the Besançon International (1975). Assisted André Previn at the LSO 1974–76; deputy then director of the Loire PO 1976–86. Artistic director of Nantes Opera 1986–90; led *Tristan und Isolde* and *Manon* there (1989–90); *Hoffmann* at the Geneva Opera (1990) and *Carmen* at the Bregenz Festival.

souter liedekens Dutch = 'little psalter songs'; metrical psalms sung in Holland to popular tunes, translated and provided with appropriate melodies by (probably) Willem van Zuylen van Nyevelt. The first complete collection, printed by Symon Cock at Antwerp in 1540, contained 159 texts: Psalm 119 was in four sections, and the Te Deum and five canticles were included. Clemens non Papa later arranged the whole collection for three voices, pub. in Antwerp as the fourth–seventh of Susato's *Musyck Boexken* (little music books) in 1556–57. Ten settings are by Susato himself, perhaps because of Clemens's premature death. The eighth–eleventh books contained another complete setting, the work of Gerhard Mes.

Souzay, Gérard (Marcel) (b Angers, 8 Dec 1918), French baritone. Studied with Pierre Bernac. Paris debut 1945, NY 1950. Well known in Lieder and French song; took part in 1956 fp of Stravinsky's *Canticum Sacrum*. NY Met. and Glyndebourne, 1965, as Mozart's Count.

Soviero, Diana (b St Paul, 1952), American soprano. Sang Lauretta and Manon at St Paul, from 1974, and joined the New York City Opera 1976. Sang further at Miami, San Francisco and Chicago and made NY Met. debut in 1986, as Gounod's Juliette. Geneva 1988, as Gretchen in Busoni's *Faust*; Philadelphia and San Diego 1988, as Margherita in *Mefistofele* and Marguerite in *Faust*. CG debut 1989, as Nedda; sang Puccini's *Trittico* heroines at Dallas in 1992.

Sowerby, Leo (b Grand Rapids, MI, 1 May 1895; d Fort Clinton, OH, 7 Jul 1968), American composer and pianist. Studied at the American Conservatory of Chicago, where he taught later. He served as band-master in Europe during World War I and in 1922 won the American Prix de Rome. He appeared as pianist in USA, England, Italy and Austria. He was organist of St James's Episcopal Cathedral in Chicago 1927–62.

Works include oratorio *Christ Reborn*, cantata *Great is the Lord* and Te Deum for mixed chorus and organ; five symphonies (1921, 1928, 1940, 1947, 1964), suite *From the Northland*, overture *Comes Autumn Time*, *Irish Washerwoman*, *Money Musk*, *Set of Four*, symphonic poem *Prairie*, *Theme in Yellow* for orchestra; sinfonietta for strings; rhapsody for chamber orchestra; *Sinconata* for jazz orchestra; two piano concertos (1912, 1932), organ concerto, two cello concertos (1917, 1934), violin concerto, ballad *King Estmere* for two pianos and orchestra, *Medieval Poem* for organ and orchestra.

Two string quartets (1924, 1935), wind quintet, serenade for string quartet; sonata and suite for violin and piano; symphony, sonata and suite for organ; *Florida Suite* and other piano works; songs.

Soyer, Roger (b Paris, 1 Sept 1939), French bass. He studied at the Paris Conservatory and has appeared at the Opéra since 1962 as Arkel, Procida and Méphistophélès. Aix Festival since 1965 in operas by Monteverdi, Mozart and Rossini. He was particularly identified with the role of Don Giovanni and sang it on his NY Met. (1972) and Edinburgh (1973) debuts. Sang in *L'Heure Espagnole* at Turin, 1992.

Spagna, la a 15th-c. *basse danse* tune originating in Castile.

Spagnoletti, Paolo (real surname ? Diana) (b Cremona, 1768; d London, 23 Sept 1834), Italian violinist. Studied at Naples and settled in London in 1802 as orchestra leader, teacher and soloist and worked mainly as leader of the orchestra of the Philharmonic Society. He wrote some violin pieces and songs.

Spalding, Albert (b Chicago, 15 Aug 1888; d New York, 26 May 1953), American violinist and composer. Studied at Bologna and Paris and made his first appearance at the latter in 1905. After touring widely in Europe he first appeared in NY in 1908. Wrote a fanciful biography of Tartini, *A Fiddle, a Sword and a Lady* (1953).

Works include suite for orchestra; two violin concertos; string quartet in E minor; sonata and suite for violin and piano, *Etchings* and other works for violin and piano; piano pieces; songs.

Spanisches Liederbuch, *Spanish Song Book*, H Wolf's settings of Spanish poems in German translation by Emanuel Geibel and Paul Heyse, composed Oct 1889–Apr 1890. There are ten sacred and 34 secular poems in his set.

Spanish Lady, The unfinished opera by Elgar (libretto by B Jackson, based on Ben Jonson's play *The Devil is an Ass*). Begun 1932–33; only a number of sketches are left; arrangements by Percy Young pub. 1955–56. A performing version of the sketches was made by Dr Young and premiered at Cambridge (University Opera) 24 Nov, 1994.

Špasirka a Czech dance in alternating slow and quick 4–8 time. The 13th of Dvořák's *Slavonic Dances* for piano duet is a Špasírka.

Spataro, Giovanni (b Bologna, ? 1458; d Bologna, 17 Jan 1541), Italian composer and theorist. He was a pupil of Ramos de Pareia and corresponded with Pietro Aron; *maestro di cappella* at San Petronio, Bologna, from 1512. He was involved in a protracted controversy with Gafurius, against whom two of his printed treatises are directed. He composed a number of sacred works; six motets and one *laude* are extant.

speaker keys extra keys fitted to reed wind instruments to facilitate the production of harmonic notes: e.g. two on the oboe produce octaves (also known as octave keys) and one on the clarinet produces 12ths.

speaking-length that portion of an organ pipe in which the air vibrates to produce the note.

Specht, Richard (b Vienna, 7 Dec 1870; d Vienna, 18 Mar 1932), Austrian writer on music. Studied architecture, but encouraged by Brahms and others took up music criticism, joined the staff of *Die Zeit* and in 1909 founded *Der Merker* with Bittner and Richard Batka. His books include studies of Brahms, J Strauss, R Strauss, Mahler (1913), Puccini, Bittner, Beethoven, Furtwängler (1922), the Vienna Opera, etc.

species the various types of counterpoint taught in academic contrapuntal instruction.

specification the detailed list of the pipes, stops, keyboards and mechanisms of an organ given to the builder or used to describe the instrument.

Spectre's Bride, The, actually *The Wedding-Shift*, dramatic cantata by Dvořák, op. 69 (Czech words by K J Erben), composed 1884, performed in England, Birmingham Festival, Aug 1885.

speech-song ◊Sprechgesang.

Spelman, Timothy Mather (b Brooklyn, NY, 21 Jan 1891; d Florence, 21 Aug 1970), American composer. Studied in NY, at Harvard University and with Courvoisier at the Munich Conservatory.

Works include operas *La Magnifica* (1920), *The Sea Rovers* (1928), *Babakan* and *The Sunken City* (1930); pantomimes *The Romance of the Rose* and *Snowdrop; Litany of the Middle Ages* for soprano, women's chorus and orchestra (1928), *Pervigilium Veneris* for soprano, baritone, chorus and orchestra (1929); symphony in G minor, symphonic poem *Christ and the Blind Man* (1918); instrumental music.

Speziale, Lo, *The Apothecary*, opera by Haydn (libretto by Goldoni), produced Eszterháza, autumn 1768. Elderly apothecary Sempronio has designs on Griletta but she weds young Mengone, his assistant.

spianato Italian = 'smoothed, level'.

spiccato Italian = 'articulated'; a direction indicating a special kind of bowing on instruments of the violin family, possible only in rapid passages of notes of equal duration, which are played with the middle of the bow and a loose wrist, allowing the bow to rebound off the strings after each note.

Spiegel von Arkadien, Der, *The Mirror of Arcadia*, opera by Süssmayr (libretto by Schikaneder), produced Vienna, Theater auf der Wieden, 14 Nov 1794. Noble pair Ballamo and Philanie, with comic duo (the viper-catchers Metallio and Giganie) in *Zauberflöte* sequel. See also ◊Magic Opera.

Spieloper German = 'play-opera'; a type of light German opera of the 19th c. the subject of which is a comedy and the musical numbers of which are interspersed with dialogue.

Spielwerk und die Prinzessin, Das, *The Musical Box and the Princess*, opera by Schreker (libretto by composer); 1909–12, produced Frankfurt and Vienna, 15 Mar 1913; revised in one act as a mystery play, *Das Spielwerk*, and produced Munich, 30 Oct 1920, conductor Walter. Sound from Meister Florian's musical box intoxicates Princess but she is redeemed by a flute-playing wayfarer.

Spies, Claudio (b Santiago, 26 Mar 1925), Chilean-born American composer. Moved to USA 1942 and studied at New England Conservatory and with Fine and Piston at Harvard. Appointed Professor of Music, Princeton, 1970. Has written extensively on Stravinsky and conducted the fp of an early version of *The Wedding*.

Works include *Music for a Ballet* for orchestra (1955), *Il Cantico del frate Sole* for baritone and orchestra (1958), *Tempi* for 14 instruments (1962), seven *Enzensberglieder* for baritone and ensemble (1972).

Spies, Hermine (b Löhneberger Hütte, near Weilburg, Nassau, 25 Feb 1857; d Wiesbaden, 26 Feb 1893), German contralto. Studied at the Wiesbaden Conservatory, in Berlin and with Stockhausen at Frankfurt. She sang while a student at the Mannheim Festival in 1880, made her debut at Wiesbaden in 1882, later travelled widely and visited London in 1889. She married a lawyer at Wiesbaden in 1892. Brahms was one of her warmest admirers; often heard in his Lieder.

Spiess, Ludovic (b Cluj, 13 May 1938), Romanian tenor. He studied in Bucharest and Milan and sang in operetta before singing Dmitri in *Boris Godunov* at the 1967 Salzburg Festival, under Karajan; the following year he was heard as Radames in Zurich and as Dalibor in Vienna. NY Met. debut 1971; CG 1973 as Radames. In Europe and South America he has sung Calaf, Don José, Florestan and Lohengrin.

Spinaccino, Francesco (b Fossombrone; d Venice, after 1507), Italian 15th–16th-c. lutenist. Pub. two books of arrangements of songs, *ricercari* and dances in lute tablature (pub. 1507).

Spinelli, Nicola (b Turin, 29 Jul 1865; d Rome, 17 Oct 1909), Italian pianist, conductor and composer. Studied at Florence, Rome and Naples, pupil of Mancinelli and Sgambati. His second opera, *Labilia*, came second to Mascagni's *Cavalleria rusticana* in the competition for the Sonzogno Prize in 1889. He suffered from a mental complaint during his last years.

Works include operas *Labilia* (1890), *A basso porto* (1894), etc.

spinet a small harpsichord, pentagonal in shape and with a single manual. Its name may derive from the Italian *spina* = thorn, referring to the plectra with which the strings were plucked.

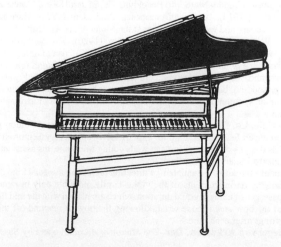

Spink, Ian (b London, 29 Mar 1932), English writer on music and teacher. Studied at the TCL and was senior lecturer at University of Sydney, 1962–68; head of music department at Royal Holloway College, London University from 1969. Has edited Volumes 17–19 of *English Lute Songs* (1961, 1963, 1966); *English Song, Dowland to Purcell* (1974, revised 1986); editions of music by Arne and Purcell and published *The Seventeenth Century* in 1992.

Spinner, Leopold (b Lwów, 26 Apr 1906; d London, 12 Aug 1980), Polish-born Austrian composer. Settled in England 1938. His works are influenced by Webern, with whom he studied 1935–38.

Works include symphony (1934), Passacaglia for chamber orchestra (1936), Concerto for Orchestra (1957); two string quartets (1941, 1952), piano trio (1950), sonatina for cello and piano (1973).

Spirit of England, The three cantatas for soprano solo, chorus and orchestra by Elgar, op. 80, *The Fourth of August*, *To Women* and *For the Fallen* (poems by Laurence Binyon); composed 1916–17; nos. 1 and 2 performed London, 7 May 1916; complete performance London, 24 Nov 1917.

spiritoso Italian = 'spirited'; a direction indicating that a composition, movement or passage is to be performed briskly and energetically.

spiritual an African-American song of the southern states of USA, with religious words and folksong tunes. One of the chief influences from which jazz and swing have sprung. It has influenced many serious American composers as well as some European ones; Tippett's oratorio *A Child of our Time* (1939–41) uses spirituals.

Spitta, (Julius August) Philipp (b Wechold, Hanover, 27 Dec 1841; d Berlin, 13 Apr 1894), German musicologist. Studied at Göttingen University and in 1875 became professor of music history at Berlin University. He also taught the subject at the Hochschule für Musik, of which he became director in 1882. He was joint editor with Adler and Chrysander of the *Vierteljahrsschrift für Musikwissenschaft*, and edited the complete works of Schütz and the organ works of Buxtehude. His chief literary work is his book on Bach in two vols. (1873–80).

Spivakov, Vladimir (b Oufa, 12 Sep 1944), Russian violinist and conductor. Studied in Moscow and gave concerts in Eastern Europe and the USA from 1975; Tchiakovsky's Concerto in London, 1977. Founded and conducted the Moscow Virtuosi Orchestra, giving the *Four Seasons* at the 1990 London Proms. Artistic director of the Colmar International Festival, France.

Spivakovsky, Tossy (b Odessa, 4 Feb 1907), Russian-born American violinist. Studied in Berlin and made debut there aged ten. Toured Europe and Australia between the wars, then settled in USA. Has displayed novel bowing techniques in the solo works of Bach.

Spofforth, Reginald (b Southwell, 1768 or 1770; d London, 8 Sept 1827), English composer. Pupil of his uncle Thomas Spofforth, organist of Southwell Minster, and of B Cooke in London, where he settled. He gained several of the Glee Club's prizes.

Works include farce with music *The Witch of the Wood, or The Nutting Girls* (1796), additions to Salomon's *Windsor Castle* (1795); many glees, including 'Hail, smiling morn'.

There was a composer named Spohr/Whose works were a hundred or mohr./His great work Jessonda/ *Long time was a wonda/But now his successes are o'hr.*

Anon, *Musical Herald*, 1888

Spohr, Louis (b Brunswick, 5 Apr 1784; d Kassel, 22 Oct 1859), German composer and violinist. He first learnt music from his parents, who were both musical, although his father was a physician. They lived at Seesen in his childhood, and he was afterwards taught by two amateurs, but sent to school and for further studies to Brunswick. He played a violin concerto of his own at a school concert and at 14 went to Hamburg trying to gain a hearing. He failed and on his return petitioned the duke for assistance and was sent to Franz Eck for lessons. They went to Russia in 1802, where he met Clementi and

spinet *The spinet refers to a small kind of harpsichord in which, as the illustration shows, the strings are perpendicular to the keys instead of parallel. It was similar or identical to the virginal and almost invariably had only one manual.*

Field. He performed and composed much at that time, returned to Brunswick in 1803, heard Rode there and entered the ducal orchestra. In 1804 he visited Berlin and played there with Meyerbeer, aged 13. In 1805 he became leader in the Duke of Gotha's orchestra and married the harpist Dorette Scheidler, with whom he toured widely. After producing his third opera at Hamburg in 1811, he visited Vienna in 1812, becoming leader at the Theater an der Wien and staying until 1815.

In 1813 and 1814 he wrote two of his most popular pieces, the nonet and octet; after producing *Faust* in Prague, he travelled in Italy 1816–17 and then became conductor at the Frankfurt opera 1817–19. In 1820 he first visited London and Paris, meeting Cherubini, R Kreutzer, Viotti and others.

After a visit to Dresden he became court music director at Kassel on 1 Jan 1822, having accepted the post declined by Weber, who had recommended him in his place. He remained there for the rest of his life, but continued to travel. In 1831 he finished his *Violin School*, in 1834 his wife died, and in 1836 he married the pianist Marianne Pfeiffer. In 1839 he revisited England for the performance of *Cavalry* at the Norwich Festival, and was commissioned to write an English oratorio, *The Fall of Babylon*, for the next festival of 1842, in which year he conducted Wagner's *Flying Dutchman* at Kassel. He was not allowed leave to go to England for the oratorio, but went during his summer vacation in 1843, when he appeared before Queen Victoria and Prince Albert and toured England and Wales. During the 1848 revolutions he showed liberal leanings and so annoyed the elector that he was refused leave of absence, and having taken his vacation without leave, he became involved in a long law-suit, which he lost after four years. In 1852 he adapted *Faust* without recitatives for a production in Italian in London and in 1853 he produced Wagner's *Tannhäuser* at Kassel. He was pensioned off against his will in 1857. Spohr's music was widely performed during the 19th c., and he was particular popular in Victorian England. Today he is known largely through the 8th violin concerto and a few tuneful chamber works.

Works include operas *Die Prüfung* (1806), *Alruna* (1808), *Der Zweikampf mit der Geliebten* (1811), *Faust* (1816, revised 1852), *Zemire und Azor* (1819), *Jessonda* (1823), *Der Berggeist* (1825), *Pietro von Albano* (1827), *Der Alchymist* (1830), *Die Kreuzfahrer* (1845); oratorios *Das jüngste Gericht*, *Die letzten Dinge* (both *The Last Judgment*), *Des Heilands letzte Stunden* (*Calvary*, 1835), *The Fall of Babylon* (1842); Mass, psalms, hymn *St Cecilia*, cantata *Vater unser* (Klopstock).

ORCHESTRAL: nine symphonies (4. *Die Weihe der Töne*, 1832, 6. Historic Symphony, 1839, 9. *The Seasons*, 1850), five overtures (including one on Shakespeare's *Macbeth*); 15 violin concertos (8. *In modo d'una scena cantante*, 1816) and concertinos, concert pieces for violin and orchestra; four clarinet concertos (1812–28).

CHAMBER: 33 string quartets (1807–57), four double string quartets, eight string quintets, two string sextets, septet for piano, strings and wind, octet for strings and wind (1814), nonet for ditto (1813), five piano trios; pieces, variations, pot pourris, etc. for violin; violin duets; sonatas for violin and harp; harp pieces; songs; part-songs.

> *The older composers had a magnificent style of their own, of which the moderns – not excepting Spontini, boiling over in luxurious abundance – have no idea.*
> **E T A Hoffmann**,
> *The Poet and the Composer*, 1819–21

Spontini, Gaspare (Luigi Pacifico) (b Maiolati near Jesi, 14 Nov 1774; d Maiolati, 24 Jan 1851), Italian composer and conductor. His parents, who were poor peasants, and an uncle destined him for the priesthood, but he ran away to Monte San Vito, where another uncle allowed him to study music, and when he had advanced sufficiently, he returned home and was allowed to study at the Conservatorio de' Turchini at Naples from 1791, Sala and Tritto being among his masters. In 1795 he became a pupil-teacher. In 1796 he produced his first opera in Rome, having run away from the Conservatory, but he was readmitted at the intercession of Piccinni, from whom he learnt much. He now produced one opera after another, and in 1798 went to Palermo with the Neapolitan court, which took refuge there and appointed him music director in the place of Cimarosa, who refused to leave Naples. In 1803 he left for Paris, where he taught singing and tried his hand at French comic opera, but made his first real success with the serious opera *La Vestale* in 1807. He was appointed composer to the Empress Joséphine and in 1810 became director of the Italian opera at the Théâtre de l'Impératrice, giving the first local performance of *Don Giovanni*. In 1812 he was dismissed, but the Bourbon restoration in 1814 reinstated him. He soon sold his post to Angelica Catalani, however.

In 1820 he was summoned to the court of Frederick William III in Berlin as general music director to the Prussian court. He was not on good terms with the intendant, Count Brühl, though he succeeded in introducing excellent reforms at the court opera; but his success was obscured in 1821 by that of Weber's *Freischütz*, which aroused an appetite for German opera, as distinct from foreign opera set to German words. In 1822–23 he visited Dresden, where he met Weber, also Vienna and Paris. In 1838 he spent the summer in England to study English history and local colour for a new opera on the subject of Milton, differing from his early one, which however was never finished; neither was an earlier work, *Les Athéniennes*. On the king's death in 1840 his position became more and more difficult, partly through his own fault, for he quarrelled with the new intendant, Count Redern, and became involved in a law-suit, and after much trouble and threatened imprisonment he left Berlin in Jul 1842. He went to live in Paris, visited Dresden in 1844 to conduct a performance of *La Vestale* rehearsed for him by Wagner, became deaf in 1848 and returned to his birthplace, founding a music school at Jesi.

In recent years Spontini's operas have enjoyed a limited revival, with performances on the continent of *Fernand Cortez*, *Agnese di Hohenstaufen* and *Olympie*. In 1993 Riccardo Muti opened the season at La Scala with a performance of *La Vestale* including much ballet music heard for the first time since the composer's lifetime.

Works include operas *I puntigli delle donne* (1796), *Adelina Senese* (1798), *L'eroismo ridicolo*, *Il finto pittore*, *La finta filosofa*, *La fuga in maschera* and eight other Italian operas, *La Petite Maison* (1804), *Julie, ou Le Pot de fleurs* (1805), *Milton* (in French), *La Vestale* (1807), *Fernand Cortez* (1809), *Olympie* (French, revised on German as *Olympia*, 1819), *Pélage, ou Le Roi de la paix*, (1814), *Nurmahal* (German, after Moore's *Lalla Rookh*, 1821), *Alcidor*, *Agnes von Hohenstaufen* (1829), *Les Dieux rivaux* (with Berton, R Kreutzer and Persuis); festival play with music on Moore's *Lalla Rookh* (original version of the opera); ballet for Salieri's *Les Danaïdes*; *Domine salvum fac* and other church music; cantata *L'eccelsa gara* for the victory of Austerlitz, coronation cantata for Nicholas I of Russia; vocal duets and trios; songs with piano or harp; *Sensations douces*.

Spontone, Bartolommeo (b Bologna, bap. 22 Aug 1530; d Treviso, 1592), Italian composer. Pupil of Nicola Mantovano and Morales, singer and in 1577–83 *maestro di cappella* at San Petronio at Bologna, and in 1584–86 at Santa Maria Maggiore, Bergamo. Composed Masses, madrigals.

Sporer, Thomas (b *c* 1490; d Strasbourg, 1534), German composer. Wrote songs with accompaniment, then rare, but cultivated by Isaac, Hofhaimer, Senfl and others beside Sporer.

Sprechgesang German = 'speech-song'; a term for a kind of singing that approximates to speech and touches the notes, indicated by special signs, without intoning them clearly at the proper pitch. It is used especially by Schoenberg (e.g. in *Pierrot lunaire*) and his disciples (e.g. Berg in *Wozzeck* and *Lulu*).

'Spring' Sonata the familiar nickname given to Beethoven's violin and piano sonata in F major, op. 24, composed 1801.

'Spring' Symphony Schumann's original name for his first symphony, in B♭ major, op. 38, finished Feb 1841 and first performed at Leipzig by Mendelssohn, 31 Mar 1841. Also the title of a choral work by Britten, fp Amsterdam, 9 Jul 1949.

sprung rhythm a term invented by Gerard Manley Hopkins for displacements of metrical stresses in poetry, not new to his verse, but exploited by him consciously and with great persistence and variety; and transferred to musical terminology by Michael Tippett in the prefatory notes to his second string quartet, where sprung rhythm is used with a deliberation similar to Hopkins's in the finale. It is no new thing to music, where it may be said to include such devices as syncopation, transference of stresses to weak beats or by trying notes over bar-lines or beats, the omission of rhythmic units by rests or the addition of them by triplets, etc.

Squarcialupi, Antonio (b Florence, 27 Mar 1416; d Florence, 6 Jul 1480), Italian composer and organist. He was organist at Florence Cathedral from 1432 until his death, and was a friend of Dufay. No compositions have survived. He was the owner of a MS now in the Laurentian Library at Florence (Med. Pal. 87), containing a large repertory of Italian 14th- and 15th-c. music. It has been edited by Johannes Wolf (Lippstadt, 1955).

Squire, W(illiam) Barclay (b London, 16 Oct 1855; d London, 13 Jan 1927), English musicologist. Educated at Frankfurt and Pembroke College, Cambridge. In 1885 he took charge of the department of printed music in the British Museum. He was also a critic and the author of the libretto of Standford's opera *The Veiled Prophet*, honorary secretary of the Purcell Society and one of the honorary secretaries of the International Musical Society. He pub. catalogues for the British Museum and the RCM, edited Purcell's harpsichord music and other works, and with Fuller-Maitland the *Fitzwilliam Virginal Book*.

St ◊Saint for names combined with it.

Stabat Mater a medieval Latin sacred poem, probably by Jacopone da Todi, not originally liturgical, but increasingly used for devotional purposes until it was admitted as a Sequence to the Roman missal in 1727.

Stabile, Annibale (b Naples, *c* 1535; d Rome, Apr 1595), Italian

composer. Pupil of Palestrina in Rome, where he became *maestro di cappella* at the Lateran. From 1579 to 1590 he held a similar post at the Collegio Germanico there, in 1591 at the church of Santa Maria Maggiore.

Works include motets, Litanies and other church music; madrigals.

Stabile, Mariano (b Palermo, 12 May 1888; d Milan, 11 Jan 1968), Italian baritone. Studied in Rome and made his first appearance on the stage at Palermo in 1909, as Amonasro. His international reputation dated from his performance in the title role of Verdi's *Falstaff* at La Scala, Milan, in Dec 1921. He appeared several times in opera at Covent Garden (1926–31), Glyndebourne (1936–39, as Figaro, Malatesta and Alfonso) and Salzburg (1935–39). Other roles included Don Giovanni, Hamlet, Iago and Scarpia.

staccato Italian = 'detached'; a special manner of performing musical phrases without slurring the notes together, articulating each separately. The staccato actually shortens the value of each note as written by the insertion of a minute pause, so that for example crotchets marked staccato become something like quavers followed by a quaver rest. The notation of staccato is a dot placed over each note or chord to be so performed.

Stade, Frederica von (b Somerville, NJ, 1 Jun 1945), American mezzo. She studied in NY and made her Met. debut in 1970; repertory there has included Zerlina, Adalgisa, Idamante and Octavian. She sang Cherubino on her Glyndebourne (1973) and Salzburg (1974) debuts, and returned to Glyndebourne in 1979 for Monteverdi's Penelope. CG, 1965, as Rosina; 1985 as Elena in *La donna del lago*. Other roles include Cenerentola, Sextus, Dorabella, Nina in Pasatieri's *The Seagull* (fp, Houston, 1974) and Tina in Argento's *The Aspern Papers* (fp Dallas, 1988). Sang Rosina at the Met in 1992.

Staden, Johann (b Nuremberg, bap. 2 Jul 1581; d Nuremberg, buried 15 Nov 1634), German organist and composer. He was in the service of the Margrave of Kulmbach and Bayreuth 1603–16, after which he became organist of St Lorenz's Church at Nuremberg and soon afterwards of St Sebald's Church.

Works include motets for voices alone, motets with instrumental thorough-bass, sacred concertos for voices and instruments; *Hausmusik* for voices and instruments with German words (1628); sacred and secular songs with continuo for organ or lute; secular songs for four–five voices; instrumental pavans, galliards, *canzoni*.

Staden, Sigmund Gottlieb (or Theophilus) (b Kulmbach, bap. 6 Nov 1607; d Nuremberg, 30 Jul 1655), German organist, violist and composer, son of Johann ◊Staden. Pupil of his father, then of Jacob Baumann at Augsburg, 1620, and for *viola bastarda* of Walter Rowe in Berlin, 1626. In 1627 he became town musician at Nuremberg and in 1634 organist of St Lorenz's Church, whose organist, Valentin Dretzel, succeeded his father at St Sebald's. In 1636 he pub. a book on singing.

Works include opera (1644); hymn tunes for four voices; containing hymn-tunes for four voices with thorough-bass for domestic use (1644–48); songs with figured bass.

Stader, Maria (b Budapest, 5 Nov 1911), Swiss soprano. Studied at Karlsruhe with H Keller, I Darigo at Zurich and Lombardi in Milan, in 1939 winning first prize at an international singing competition in Geneva. She was well known as an opera and concert singer, especially of Mozart and Bach, and taught at the Zurich Academy of Music. Retired 1969.

Stadlen, Peter (b Vienna, 14 Jul 1910; d London, 20 Jan 1996), Austrian-born British pianist and critic. Studied at the Vienna Hochschule and gave concerts from 1934 (fp of Webern's Variations op. 27 in 1937). Moved to England 1939 and taught at Darmstadt 1947–51, giving also the local fp of Schoenberg's Piano Concerto (1948). Music critic with the *Daily Telegraph* from 1960; chief critic 1977–86. Wrote articles including *Serialism Reconsidered*, *Beethoven and the Metronome* (1967), and *Berg's Cryptography*.

Stadler, Anton (b Bruck an der Leitha, 28 Jun 1753; d Vienna, 15 Jun 1812), Austrian clarinettist. Lived in Vienna and there became acquainted with Mozart, who wrote for him, e.g. the quintet K452, trio (K498), quintet (K581) and concerto (K622). He also played the basset-horn and took part in the fp of *La Clemenza di Tito*.

Stadler, Maximilian (b Melk, 4 Aug 1748; d Vienna, 8 Nov 1833), Austrian priest, organist and composer. Pupil of Albrechtsberger, he entered the Benedictine monastery of Melk in 1766 (priest 1772), became prior there in 1784, abbot of Lilienfeld (1786) and of Kremsmünster (1789). In 1796 he settled in Vienna, and after working as a parish priest 1803–15 returned there to devote himself entirely to music. A friend of Mozart, he completed some of the latter's unfinished works, and wrote in defence of the authenticity of the Requiem (pub. Vienna, 1825).

Works include Masses, two Requiems, Te Deum, three Magnificat settings and other church music; oratorio *Die Befreyung von Jerusalem* (1811); music for Collin's tragedy *Polyxena* (1811); cantatas *Frühlingsfeyer* (Klopstock, 1813), etc.; organ sonatas and fugues; piano music.

Stadlmayr, Johann (b ? Freising, Bavaria, c 1575; d Innsbruck, 12 Jul 1648), German composer. He was in the service of the Archbishop of Salzburg from 1603, and *Kapellmeister* of the Archdukes Maximilian and Leopold in 1610 and 1625 and of the Archduchess Claudia in 1636, at Innsbruck.

Works include Masses, Magnificats, Marian canticles, introits, hymns, psalms and other sacred music, some with instruments.

Staempfli, Edward (b Bern, 1 Feb 1908), Swiss composer. Studied medicine at first but gave it up for music, which he studied with Jarnach at Cologne and with Dukas in Paris.

Works include ballets *Das Märchen von den zwei Flöten* and *Le Pendu* (1942); cantata *Filles de Sion* for solo voices, chorus and orchestra; three symphonies (1938, 1942, 1945), four *Sinfonie concertanti* and other orchestral works; four piano concertos (1932–63), two violin concertos, concerto for two pianos and strings; music for 11 instruments, concerto for piano and eight instruments, six string quartets (1926–62), quintet for wind, quartet for flute and strings, piano trio, string trio and other chamber music; piano pieces; songs.

staff notation the ordinary musical notation, so called to distinguish it from the notation used for tonic sol-fa.

Staggins, Nicholas (b ? London, 1645; d Windsor, 13 Jun 1700), English composer. Pupil of his father, Isaac Staggins (d 1684). Charles II appointed him Master of the King's Band in 1674. He took the Mus.D. degree at Cambridge in 1682, becoming professor of music there in 1684. He advanced to the post of Master of the King's Music, but was succeeded in it by Eccles in 1698.

Works include masque *Calisto, or The Chaste Nimph* (Crowne); incidental music for Etheredge's *The Man of Mode*, Lee's *Gloriana*, Dryden's *Conquest of Granada* and *Marriage à la Mode* and Shadwell's *Epsom Wells* (last two with Robert Smith); odes for the birthday of William III; songs.

stagione Italian = 'season'; the term is used especially for an opera season.

Stahlman, Sylvia (b Nashville, 5 Mar 1929), American soprano. Studied at Juilliard and sang at the Monnaie, Brussels, from 1951 (debut as Elvira in *I Puritani*). Sang further as Lucia and Meyerbeer's Dinorah; member of the Frankfurt Opera 1954–72. New York City Opera 1956 (as Blondchen), Glyndebourne 1959, as Mozart's Ilia. Sang in the US fp of Strauss's *Daphne* at Santa Fe (1964) and appeared at Aix-en-Provence 1967.

Stahlspiel German = lit. 'steel-play'; a percussion instrument with tuned steel plates or bars which are played with hammers. It is known in English military bands as lyra, being made for them in the shape of a lyre. The modern glockenspiel, being also made of steel bars, and no longer of actual bells, is now to all intents and purposes the same instrument.

Stainer, Jacob (b Absam near Hall, 14 Jul 1621; d Absam, 1683), Austrian violin maker. He learnt his craft at Innsbruck and (?) with one of the Amati family at Cremona or (?) with Vimercati at Venice. He began to work on his own account at Absam c 1640. He died insane, after being accused of Lutheran tendencies.

Stainer, John (b London, 6 Jun 1840; d Verona, 31 Mar 1901), English organist and composer. He became a choirboy at St Paul's Cathedral at the age of seven and before long was able to deputize at the organ. After working under various masters and receiving an organist's appointment in the City of London, he was appointed by Ouseley organist of St Michael's College, Tenbury, in 1856. In 1860 he went to Oxford as an undergraduate at St Edmund Hall and organist to Magdalen College, then became organist to the University in succession to Elvey and in 1865 took the Mus.D. degree. In 1872 he returned to London as organist at St Paul's Cathedral. In 1888, having resigned from St Paul's through failing eyesight, he was knighted and in 1889 became Professor of Music at Oxford. He wrote on music in the Bible, and edited *Early Bodleian Music*, *Dufay and his Contemporaries*, etc. His enduring success is the oratorio *The Crucifixion* favoured by many amateur performers.

Works include oratorios *Gideon* (1865) and *The Crucifixion* (1887); *Sevenfold Amen*, services and anthems; cantatas *The Daughter of Jairus* (1878) and *St Mary Magdalen* (1887).

Stamitz climbed gradually – following a dramatic plan not drawn by every capellmeister – from the ears into the heart, as though from Allegros into Adagios.
                                   Jean Paul, *The Hesperus*, 1795

Stamitz Bohemian family of musicians:

1. Johann Wenzel Anton Stamitz (b Německý Brod, 19 Jun 1717; d Mannheim, 27 Mar 1757), violinist and composer. He entered the service of the Electoral court at Mannheim in 1741, became principal violinist in 1743 and later music director. Under him the orchestra became the most famous in Europe, called by Burney 'an army of generals'. He was the founder and most important member of the Mannheim school of symphonists, which had a profound influence on Mozart's instrumental style.

Works include 74 symphonies (58 extant); concertos for violin, harpsichord, flute, oboe, clarinet; trio sonatas and other chamber music, violin sonatas.

2. Carl Stamitz (b Mannheim, bap. 8 May 1745; d Jena, 9 Nov 1801), violinist and composer, son of 1. Pupil of his father, entered the Mannheim orchestra as second violin in 1762, then went to Strasbourg (1770), Paris and London, appearing as a virtuoso on the violin and viola d'amore. He continued to travel widely, visiting Prague in 1787 and Russia in 1790, until in 1794 he settled in Jena as music director to the university.

Works include operas *Der verliebte Vormund* (1787) and *Dardanus* (1800); c 80 symphonies and *sinfonies concertantes*; concertos; chamber music.

3. Johann Anton Stamitz (b Německý Brod, 27 Nov 1750; d Paris, before 1809), violinist and composer, brother of 2. Pupil of his father and of Cannabich, in 1770 he went with his brother Carl to Paris, where he settled as violinist in the court orchestra. Kreutzer was his pupil.

Works include 12 symphonies; concertos for violin, viola, flute, oboe, etc.; chamber music.

Standage, Simon (b High Wycombe, 8 Nov 1941), English violinist. He studied at Cambridge and in NY; joined the LSO 1969 and became sub-leader of the English Chamber Orchestra. From 1973 he has led the English Concert, under Trevor Pinnock, and the City of London Sinfonia, under Richard Hickox. Founded the Salomon String Quartet 1981; performs with authentic instruments. Teacher of baroque violin at the RAM since 1983 and founded the Collegium Musicum PO in 1990.

Ständchen German = serenade.

Standford, Patric (actually John Patric Standford Gledhill) (b Barnsley, 5 Feb 1939), English composer and teacher. Studied with Rubbra at GSM and Lutoslawski at Dartington. Professor of composition at the GSMD, London, 1967–80; director of music at Bretton Hall College, University of Leeds, 1980–93.

Works include opera *Villon* (1972–84); five symphonies: no. 1 for orchestra (1972), no. 2 *Christus-Requiem* for soloists, chorus and orchestra (1972), no. 3 *Towards Paradise* for chorus and orchestra (1973), no. 4 *Taikyoku* for two pianos and six percussion (1976), no. 5 for orchestra (1984); cello concerto (1974), violin concerto (1975), piano concerto (1979), *Rage* for orchestra (1993); Mass for brass and chorus (1980), *Mass of our Lady St Rochas* (1988), *A Messiah Reborn* for soloists, chorus and orchestra (1992); three string quartets (1964, 1973, 1992).

Standfuss, J C (d ? Hamburg, *c* 1759), German violinist and composer. At one time a member of Koch's opera troupe in Leipzig, he was the first to produce a German *Singspiel*, in adapting Coffey's *The Devil to Pay* as *Der Teufel ist los* (1752). Coffey's sequel *The Merry Cobbler* was similarly arranged as *Der lustige Schuster* in 1759. His third *Singspiel* was *Der stolze Bauer Jochem Tröbs* (1759).

Stanford, Charles Villiers (b Dublin, 30 Sept 1852; d London, 29 Mar 1924), Irish composer. In 1870 he became choral scholar at Queens' College, Cambridge, and in 1873 organist of Trinity College, where he took classical honours the next year; also conductor of the Cambridge University Musical Society. In 1874–76 he studied with Reinecke at Leipzig and with Kiel in Berlin, and in the latter year Tennyson suggested him as composer of incidental music for his *Queen Mary*. Mus.D. at Oxford 1883 and Mus.D. at Cambridge 1888, where he had succeeded Macfarren as Professor of Music in 1887. He was also conductor of the Bach Choir in London and professor of composition at the RCM, where he conducted the orchestral and opera classes. Knighted 1901.

Stanford's operas enjoyed some success at the turn of the century, with *Savonarola* and *Much Ado about Nothing* premiered at CG, but only the Brahms-influenced orchestral music is revived today.

Works include operas *The Veiled Prophet of Khorassan* (1881), *Savonarola* (1884), *The Canterbury Pilgrims* (after Chaucer, 1884), *Shamus O'Brien* (after Le Fanu), *Much Ado About Nothing* (on Shakespeare, 1901), *The Critic* (on Sheridan, 1916), *The Travelling Companion* (produced 1926); incidental music for Tennyson's *Queen Mary* and *Becket*, Aeschylus' *Eumenides*, Sophocles' *Oedipus Tyrannus*, Binyon's *Attila* and Louis N Parker's *Drake*.

ORCHESTRAL: seven symphonies (1876–1911); five Irish Rhapsodies (1901–14), three concert overtures, serenade and Irish dances for orchestra; three piano concertos (1896–1919), two violin concertos, cello concerto (1919), clarinet concerto, suite for violin and orchestra, Variations on an English Theme for piano and orchestra.

CHAMBER: eight string quartets (1891–1919), two string quintets, two piano trios, two piano quartets, piano quintet, serenade for nine instruments; two sonatas for violin and piano, two sonatas for cello and piano, clarinet and piano sonata, some smaller instrumental pieces with piano; piano works including suite, toccata, sonata, three *Dante Rhapsodies*; 11 organ works including five sonatas; oratorios *The Three Holy Children*, *Eden* (1891); Mass (1892), Requiem, Te Deum, *Stabat Mater*, Magnificat; two psalms, six services, three anthems; choral ballads and 20 op. nos. of songs.

Stanley, John (b London, 17 Jan 1712; d London, 19 May 1786), English composer and organist. He was blind from the age of two, but became a pupil of Greene and held various organist's appointments in London later. In 1759 he joined John Christopher Smith to continue Handel's oratorio concerts, and when Smith retired in 1774, he continued with T Linley. In 1779 he succeeded Boyce as Master of the King's Music.

Works include opera *Teraminta*; dramatic cantata *The Choice of Hercules*; music for Lloyd's *Arcadia, or The Shepherd's Wedding* (1761) and *Tears and Triumphs of Parnassus* and Southerne's *Oroonoko* (1759); oratorios *Jephtha* (1752), *Zimri* (1760) and *The Fall of Egypt* (1774); 12 cantatas to words by John Hawkins; six concertos for strings; solos for flute or violin; cantatas and songs for voice and instruments.

'St Anne' Fugue the fugue in E♭ major at the end of Part III of Bach's *Clavierübung*, so named in England because its subject is identical with the opening of Croft's (?) hymn-tune *St Anne*.

'St Anthony' Variations (Brahms.) ◊'Haydn' Variations.

Stapp, Olivia (b New York, 31 Mar 1940), American mezzo. Studied in Italy and New York and made debut at Spoleto 1960, in *L'amico Fritz*. Sang in Vienna, Berlin and elsewhere in Europe. New York City Opera from 1972, notably as Norma and Carmen; NY Met. from 1982, Lady Macbeth and Tosca. Returned to Europe and sang Turandot and Mozart's Electra at La Scala (1983–84), Verdi's Hélène at Geneva (1985) and the title role in *Katerina Ismailova* at Hamburg (1990).

Stappen, Crispinus van (b *c* 1470; d Cambrai, 10 Mar 1532), Flemish composer. He became a singer at the Ste Chapelle, Paris, in 1492, and shortly afterwards, until 1507, at the Papal Chapel in Rome. In 1524–25 he was *maestro di cappella* at the Casa Santa, Loreto. He held a canonry at Cambrai from 1504. He wrote sacred and secular works, including a *strambotto* in praise of Padua.

Starek, Jiří (b Mocovice, 25 Mar 1928), Czech conductor. Studied in Prague, and was chief conductor of the Radio Orchestra there, 1953–68. Music director of the Collegium Musicum Pragense, 1963–68. Has also led the RIAS Sinfonietta in Berlin (1976–80), the Trondheim SO (1981–84) and the Pfalztheater in Germany (1989–92). Guest with the San Francisco chamber orchestra, Munich and Stuttgart POs and BBC Scottish SO. Returned to conduct in Prague 1990 (Dvořák's *New World* symphony) after a politically-enforced absence.

Starer, Robert (b Vienna, 8 Jan 1924), Austrian-born American composer. Studied in Vienna, then moved to Jerusalem at the Anschluss. Moved to USA 1947, studying at Juilliard; has taught at Brooklyn College from 1963.

Works include operas *The Intruder* (1956), *Pantagleize* (1973), *The Last Lover* (1975) and *Apollonia* (1979); ballets *The Dybbuk* (1960), *Samson Agonistes* (1961), *Phaedra* (1962), *The Lady of the House of Sleep* (1968), *Holy Jungle* (1974); three symphonies (1950–69); three piano concertos (1947, 1953, 1972), concertos for viola (1959), violin and cello (1968), violin (1981) and cello (1988); *Voice at Brooklyn* (in seven parts) for soloists, chorus and orchestra (1980–84); string quartet (1947), two piano sonatas; cantatas on biblical subjects.

Starker, János (b Budapest, 5 Jul 1924), Hungarian-born American cellist. Studied at Budapest Academy of Music, becoming first cello in the Budapest Opera orchestra. In 1946 he settled in the USA, playing with the Dallas SO, the orchestra of the NY Met. (1949–53) and the Chicago SO (1953–58). In 1958 he became professor at Indiana University, Bloomington. As a soloist he has toured widely in both Europe and America; well known in the solo suites of Bach.

Starlight Express, The incidental music by Elgar for a play by V Pearn, after Algernon Blackwood's *A Prisoner from Fairyland*; composed 1915. Suite in nine movements, with soprano and bass soloists, performed Kingsway Theatre, London, 29 Dec 1915; very popular as escapist entertainment during the worst days of World War I, but forgotten until recent recording.

Staryk, Steven (b Toronto, 28 Apr 1932), Canadian violinist and teacher. Studied at the Royal Conservatory, Toronto, and in 1956 became leader of the RPO, under Beecham. Led the Concertgebouw Orchestra 1960 and the Chicago SO 1963–67. Has been heard as soloist and has taught at Amsterdam Conservatory, in the USA, Toronto and Ottawa. Head of the string division at the University of Washington, Seattle, from 1987.

Starzer, Josef (b Vienna, 1726; d Vienna, 22 Apr 1787), Austrian composer and violinist. Violinist at the French theatre in Vienna from 1752, he was court composer and leader of the orchestra in St Petersburg 1758–70. Back in Vienna he wrote music for Noverre's ballets, and was active in the Tonkünstler-Society, for whose concerts he re-orchestrated Handel's *Judas Maccabeus* in 1779. From 1783 increasing corpulence enforced his retirement.

Works include *Singspiele Die drei Pächter* and *Die Wildschützen*; ballets *Roger et Bradamante* (1771), *Adèle de Ponthieu* (1773), *Gli Orazi ed i Curiazi* (all with Noverre) and many others; oratorio *La Passione di Gesù Cristo*; symphonies, divertimenti, etc. for orchestra; violin concerto; chamber music.

Stassov, Vladimir Vassilievich (b St Petersburg, 14 Jan 1824; d St

Petersburg, 23 Oct 1906), Russian scholar and art critic. Educated at the School of Jurisprudence and joined the Imperial Public Library in 1845. He studied in Italy from 1851 to 1854, after which he returned to the Library and in 1872 became director of the department of fine arts there. He was the first champion of the Russian nationalist school of composers, writing on Cui, Glinka, Borodin and Mussorgsky and coining the phrase 'Mighty Handful'.

Statkowski, Roman (b Szczypiórno near Kalisz, 5 Jan 1860; d Warsaw, 12 Nov 1925), Polish composer. Studied with Zeleński at Warsaw and with Soloviev at St Petersburg. On the death of Noskowski in 1909 he was appointed professor of composition at the Warsaw Conservatory.

Works include operas *Philaenis* (1904) and *Maria* (after Malczewski, 1906); fantasy, polonaise and other works for orchestra; five string quartets (1896–1929); violin and piano pieces; *Krakowiak* and other works for piano; songs.

Staudigl, Joseph (b Wöllersdorf, 14 Apr 1807; d Döbling near Vienna, 28 Mar 1861), Austrian bass. Learnt music as a novice at the monastery of Melk, but ran away to Vienna in 1827 and entered the chorus of the Kärntnertortheater, where he soon rose through small parts to a position of eminence. He first visited England in 1841, when he sang Sarastro and Lysiart at Drury Lane; later sang at CG and Her Majesty's in *Les Huguenots, Norma* and *Robert le diable*. In 1846 he created the title part in Mendelssohn's *Elijah* at the Birmingham Festival. He died insane.

Staudigl, Joseph (b Vienna, 18 Mar 1850; d Karlsruhe, Apr 1916), Austrian baritone, son of Joseph ◊Staudigl. He studied at the Vienna Conservatory and sang in Karlsruhe 1875–83. He appeared at the NY Met. 1884–86 and was Pogner in the first US performance of *Die Meistersinger*. In 1886 he also sang Don Giovanni at Salzburg under Richter. His wife Gisela (born Koppmayer) sang in Vienna, Hamburg and Karlsruhe from 1879. She sang Adriano and the Queen of Sheba with the Met. co. on tour, in 1886, and Brangaene and Magdalene at Bayreuth, 1886–92.

Let us not forget that the greatest composers were also the greatest thieves. They stole from everyone and everywhere.

Pablo Casals, *Song of the Birds*, 1980

Steber, Eleanor (b Wheeling, W VA, 17 Jul 1916; d Langhorne, PA, 3 Oct 1990), American soprano. Studied in NY. After winning a NY Met. radio competition in 1940, she made her debut there in the same year, as Sophie; sang there until 1966 as Donna Anna, Pamina, the Countess, Desdemona, Tosca, Eva, Elsa and Marie. She created the title role in Barber's *Vanessa* (1958).

Stefan, Paul (b Brno, 25 Nov 1879; d New York, 12 Nov 1943), Austrian writer on music. Studied at Brno, at Vienna University and with Graedener and Schoenberg. Settled in Vienna as music critic and correspondent and in 1921 founded the *Musikblätter des Anbruch*. In 1938 he left Austria owing to the Nazi régime and went to Switzerland, later to USA. He wrote books on music in Vienna, on Schubert, Dvořák, Mahler, Schoenberg, Toscanini, Bruno Walter, etc.

Steffani, Agostino (b Castelfranco, 25 Jul 1654; d Frankfurt, 12 Feb 1728), Italian diplomat and composer. Learnt music as a choirboy at Padua and was taken to Munich, where he studied music under Kerl at the expense of the Elector Ferdinand Maria. After further studies in Rome, 1673–74, he returned to Munich and became court organist in 1675; having also studied mathematics, philosophy and theology he was ordained priest in 1680. He was made director of the court chamber music, but in 1688 the younger Bernabei was appointed general music director on the death of his father, and Steffani, disappointed of the post, left Munich. After a visit to Venice he went to the court of Hanover, where the post of music director was offered him, and there he also filled other posts, including diplomatic ones. The philosopher Leibniz, who was also at the court, sent him on a diplomatic mission to various German courts in 1696; in 1698 he was

ambassador to Brussels, and on the death of the Elector Ernest Augustus transferred his services to the Elector Palatine at Düsseldorf. In 1706 he was made a nominal bishop. In 1708–09 he was on a diplomatic mission in Italy, where he met Handel, who went into service at the Hanoverian court at his suggestion. His best known opera, *Tassilone*, dates from this time; it unites the Italian and German musical influences which were paramount in Steffani's life. In 1722–25 he lived at Padua and in 1727 he was elected honorary president of the London Academy of Vocal Music. In 1727 he went to Italy for the last time. He died at Frankfurt during a diplomatic visit.

Works include operas *Marco Aurelio* (1680), *Solone* (1685), *Servio Tullio, Alarico il Baltha* (1687), *Niobe* (1688), *Enrico Leone, La lotta d'Hercole con Achelao* (1689), *La superbia d'Alessandro* (1690), *Orlando generoso* (1691), *Le rivali concordi, La libertà contenta* (1693), *I trionfi del fato* (1695), *Baccanali, Briseide, Arminio, Enea* and *Tassilone* (1709); music for a tournament *Audacia e rispetto*; motets, vesper psalms for eight voices, *Stabat Mater* for six voices, strings and organ (1727), *Confitebor* for three voices and strings and other church music; madrigals; vocal chamber duets with bass; chamber sonatas for two violins, viola and bass.

Steffek, Hanny (b Biala, 12 Dec 1927), Polish-born Austrian soprano. Studied at the Salzburg Mozarteum and appeared in *Die Zauberflöte* at the Festival in 1950. Sang with the Munich Staatsoper 1958–72, notably as Christine in *Intermezzo* when the company visited the Edinburgh Festival in 1965. CG debut 1959, as Sophie in *Der Rosenkavalier* and appeared at the Vienna Staatsoper 1964–73. Other roles included Mozart's Ilia, Blondchen and Papagena (Salzburg, 1950–55).

Steffkins Family of lutenists and violists of German origin, settled in London in the 17th c.:

1. Dietrich (or Theodore) Steffkins (d *c* 1674), teacher of the lute and viola da gamba and member of Charles I's band. He lived in Hamburg during the Commonwealth, returning in 1660 to serve under Charles II. He was much admired by John Jenkins.

2. Frederick William Steffkins (b London; d ? London), son of 1. Violist in the royal service after the Restoration.

3. Christian Steffkins (b London; d London), brother of 2. Violist in the royal service.

Stehle, Sophie (b Hohenzollern-Sigmaringen, 15 May 1838; d Schloss Harterode, near Hanover, 4 Oct 1921), German soprano. Debut Munich 1860, in Weigl's *Die Schweizerfamilie*; created Fricka in *Das Rheingold* (1869) and Brünnhilde in *Die Walküre* (1870). Other roles included Elisabeth, Elsa, Eva, Senta and Marguerite.

Stehle-Garbin, Adelina (b Graz, 1860; d Milan, 24 Dec 1945), Austrian soprano. After her 1881 debut in Broni, as Amina, she sang widely in Italy; created Nedda (1892) and Nannetta (1893) and sang in the fps of operas by Gomez, Catalani and Mascagni. She appeared elsewhere in Europe with her husband, Edoardo Garbin, as Mimi, Manon, Adriana Lecouvreur and Fedora.

Steibelt, Daniel (b Berlin, 22 Oct 1765; d St Petersburg, 2 Oct 1823), German composer and pianist. He learnt much about keyboard instruments in his childhood, being the son of a harpsichord and piano maker, and studied music with Kirnberger. After serving in the army, he made his first appearance as pianist and composition in Paris during the late 1780s. At the end of 1796 he visited London, where he remained until 1799 and married an Englishwoman. He visited Hamburg, Dresden, Prague, Berlin and Vienna, where he had an encounter with Beethoven at the piano, and in Aug 1800 again settled in Paris, but spent as much of his time in London. In 1808 he left for the court at St Petersburg, where he became director of the French Opera on the departure of Boieldieu in 1810. His setting of *Romeo and Juliet* was his most successful work after initial rejection and was admired by Berlioz, who may have been influenced by it in his own dramatic symphony.

Works include operas *Roméo et Juliette* (after Shakespeare, 1793), *La Princesse de Babylone, Cendrillon* (1810), *Sargines* and *Le Jugement de Midas* (unfinished); ballets *Le Retour de Zéphyr* (1802), *Le Jugement du berger Paris* (1804), *La Belle Laitière, La Fête de l'empereur* (1809); intermezzo *La Fête de Mars* for the victory at Austerlitz; incidental music; eight piano concertos (1796–1820); 50 studies and numerous pieces and transcriptions for piano.

Steiger, Anna (b Los Angeles, 13 Feb 1960), American soprano. After study at the GSMD (1977–83) sang Dorabella with Opera 80 in 1984. Micaela with ESTO 1985, returning for the 1987 fp of Osborne's *The Electrification of the Soviet Union*; Poppea at the Glyndebourne Festival 1986. CG and ENO debuts 1987–88, Weill's Jenny at Los Angeles in 1989; Ravel's Concepcion with the New York City Opera 1990. Other roles include Mozart's Despina (at Stuttgart) and Donna Elvira (for Netherlands Opera). She is the daughter of the actor Rod Steiger.

Steigleder, Hans Ulrich (b Schwäbisch-Hall, 22 Mar 1593; d Stuttgart, 10 Oct 1635), German organist and composer. After an appointment as organist at Lindau on Lake Constance, he became organist at a monastery at Stuttgart in 1617 and musician to the court of Württemberg.

Works include *ricercari* and variations on a Lord's Prayer hymn-tune for organ.

Stein German family of piano makers:

1. Johann Andreas Stein (b Heidelsheim, 6 May 1728; d Augsburg, 29 Feb 1792), organ builder and piano maker. Learnt his craft from his father, Johann Georg Stein (1697–1754), worked with J A Silbermann in Strasbourg and settled in Augsburg in 1751. Mozart preferred his pianos above all others.

2. Maria Anna (Nanette) Stein (b Augsburg, 2 Jan 1769; Vienna, 16 Jan 1833), pianist and piano maker, daughter of 1. She played to Mozart as a child during his visit to Augsburg in 1777, and on her father's death in 1792 carried on the business with her brother, 3, but married Andreas Streicher in 1794 and moved with him to Vienna, where they established a new firm, jointly with 3. Later she and her husband became friends of Beethoven.

3. Matthäus Andreas Stein (b Augsburg, 12 Dec 1776; d Vienna, 6 May 1842), piano maker, brother of 2. He accompanied his sister and her husband to Vienna in 1793 and joined their firm, but established himself independently in 1802.

4. Andreas Friedrich Stein (b Augsburg, 26 May 1784; d Vienna, 5 May 1809), pianist and composer, brother of 3. Went to Vienna as a child with his sister and brother, and studied piano playing, also composition with Albrechtsberger. He appeared in public frequently, especially with Mozart's concertos.

Works include three operettas; pantomime *Die Fee Radiante*; violin concerto; piano trio; piano sonata; songs.

5. Karl Andreas Stein (b Vienna, 4 Sept 1797; d Vienna, 28 Aug 1863), composer and piano maker, nephew of 4, son of 3. Pupil of Förster. He first devoted himself to composition, but later mainly to his father's factory, to which he succeeded.

Works include comic opera *Die goldene Gans*; two overtures; two piano concertos, etc.

Stein, Erwin (b Vienna, 7 Nov 1885; d London, 19 Jul 1958), Austrian musicologist. Pupil of Schoenberg. After conducting at various places, he joined the Universal Edition in Vienna, but settled in London after the Anschluss. He wrote much on Schoenberg.

Stein, Horst (b Elberfeld, 2 May 1928), German conductor. He studied in Cologne; from 1951 he has held major posts at opera houses in Hamburg, Berlin (Staatsoper, 1955–61), Mannheim (1963–70) and Vienna (Staatsoper) from 1970. He is a sound, if unspectacular, conductor of Mozart, Bruckner, Schoenberg and Wagner (*Parsifal* and the *Ring* at Bayreuth from 1969.) Conducted *Capriccio* at the 1985 Salzburg Festival and returned for *Fidelio*, 1990.

Stein, Peter (b Berlin, 1 Oct 1937), German stage director. Directed plays by Goethe and Schiller in Munich and co-founded the Berlin Schaubühne 1970 (artistic director until 1985). Opera debut with *Das Rheingold* in Paris (1976). For WNO has staged *Otello* (1986), *Falstaff* (1988) and *Pelléas et Mélisande* (1992), showing a strong sense of theatrical values. Director of drama at the Salzburg Festival from 1992.

Steinbach, Emil (b Lengenrieden, Baden, 14 Nov 1849; d Mainz, 6 Dec

1919), German conductor and composer. Studied at the Leipzig Conservatory and became conductor and theatre director at Mainz. Composed orchestral works, chamber music, songs, etc. He gave the first public performance of the *Siegfried Idyll* (1877) and conducted *Tristan* and *Siegfried* at CG in 1893.

Steinbach, Fritz (b Grünsfeld, Baden, 17 Jun 1855; d Munich, 13 Aug 1916), German conductor and composer, brother of Emil ◊Steinbach. Studied with his brother and at the Leipzig Conservatory. After working as second conductor at Mainz 1880–86, he went to the court of Meiningen, with whose orchestra he visited London in 1902, when he succeeded Wüllner as municipal conductor and director of the Conservatory at Cologne. His works include a septet and a cello sonata.

Steinberg, Maximilian Osseievich (b Wilno, 4 Jul 1883; d Leningrad, 6 Dec 1946), Russian composer. Studied at St Petersburg University and Conservatory. Pupil (and later son-in-law) of Rimsky-Korsakov, also of Liadov and Glazunov. He became professor at the Leningrad Conservatory. Stravinsky's *Fireworks* was given its fp at his wedding (1908).

Works include ballets *Midas* (after Ovid) and *Till Eulenspiegel*; incidental music; oratorio *Heaven and Earth* (after Byron); four symphonies (1907, 1909, 1929, 1933), dramatic fantasy on Ibsen's *Brand*, overture to Maeterlinck's *La Princesse Maleine* and other orchestral works; violin concerto (1946); two string quartets; songs including two Tagore cycles, folksong arrangements.

Steinberg, Pinchas (b New York, 12 Feb 1945), American conductor. Studied at Tanglewood and made debut there in 1964. Associate at the Chicago Lyric Opera from 1967, debut with *Don Giovanni*. Has conducted symphony orchestras in Europe from 1972; Frankfurt Opera from 1979, and has led opera in Hamburg, Berlin and at CG. Music director at Bremen 1985–89, chief conductor at the Verona Arena 1989. Conducted *La Wally* at the 1990 Bregenz Festival and Rossini's *Tancredi* (concert) at the 1992 Salzburg Festival.

Steinberg, William (b Cologne, 1 Aug 1899; d New York, 16 May 1978), German-born American conductor. After an early start in composition he studied at Cologne Conservatory, graduating 1920 and becoming assistant to Klemperer at the Cologne Opera and in 1924 its principal conductor. In 1925 he went to the German Theatre in Prague and in 1929 became music director of the Frankfurt Opera; gave there an early performance of *Wozzeck* and the fp of Schoenberg's *Von Heute auf Morgen* (1930). In 1933 he was removed from this post by the Nazis and became connected with the Jewish Cultural Society; from 1936 to 1938 conducted the Palestine SO and in 1938 the NBC SO in America. From 1945 he conducted the Buffalo PO and from 1952 the Pittsburgh SO (retired 1976). He worked with the LPO 1958–60 and conducted the Berlin PO at the 1962 Salzburg Festival.

Steinitz, (Charles) Paul (Joseph) (b Chichester, 25 Aug 1909; d Oxted, 22 Apr 1988), English organist and conductor. He studied at the RCM and was church organist in Ashford 1933–42. Founded South London Bach Society 1947 (later known as London Bach Society). With the Steinitz Bach Players (founded 1969) he gave annual performances in London of the *St Matthew Passion*. Professor, RAM, from 1945.

Steinway, originally Steinweg, a firm of piano makers in New York, founded 1849 by Heinrich Engelhard Steinweg (1797–1871) at Brunswick, who emigrated with five sons and established himself in 1853. Branches of the firm were later set up in London, Hamburg and Berlin.

St Elizabeth (Liszt.) ◊Legende von der heiligen Elisabeth.

Stella, Antonietta (b Perugia, 15 Mar 1929), Italian soprano. Debut Spoleto 1950, as the *Trovatore* Leonora. She sang in Germany from 1951; La Scala 1953–63, as Tosca. Violetta and Elisabeth de Valois. CG and Verona 1955, as Aida and the *Forza* Leonora. NY Met. 1956–60. Also successful as Amelia Boccanegra, Mimi and Linda di Chamounix. Sang in the premiere of *Maria Stuarda* by De Bellis at Naples, 1974.

stem the stroke attached to the heads of all notes of smaller value than a semibreve.

Stendhal, actually Henri Beyle (1783–1842), French critic and novelist. Wrote a biography of Rossini, letters on Haydn (partly plagiarized from Carpani), etc. ◊Chartreuse de Parme (Sauguet).

Stenhammar, (Karl) Wilhelm (Eugen) (b Stockholm, 7 Feb 1871; d Stockholm, 20 Nov 1927), Swedish composer, conductor and pianist. Pupil of his father, the composer Per Ulrik Stenhammar (1829–75), and later of Sjögren and others; also studied in Berlin. He became conductor of the royal orchestra at Stockholm and also conductor at Göteborg.

Works include operas *The Feast of Solhaug* (based on Ibsen, 1899), and *Tirfing* (1898); incidental music to Shakespeare's *Twelfth Night*, *Hamlet* and *Romeo and Juliet*, Strindberg's *Ett drömspel*, Gozzi's *Turandot*, Tagore's *Chitra* and other plays; cantatas *The Princess and the Page*, *Snöfrid* (1891), *Hemmarschen* and *Sangen*.

ORCHESTRAL AND CHAMBER: two symphonies (1903, 1915), symphonic overture *Excelsior*, *Prelude and Bourrée*, serenade in F major for orchestra; two piano concertos (1893–1907), two *Sentimental Romances* for violin and orchestra; six string quartets (1894–1909), piano quartet; violin and piano sonata; four sonatas and fantasy for piano; part-songs including *Sverige*; songs.

Stenka Razin symphonic poem by Glazunov, op. 13, composed 1884, fp St Petersburg, 1885. It contains the tune of the Volga boatmen's song *Ey ukhnem*.

stentando Italian = 'toiling, labouring'; a direction indicating a dragging delivery of a passage.

Stenz, Marcus (b Bad Neuenahr, 28 Feb 1965), German conductor. Studied at the Cologne Conservatoire, where he was noticed by Hans Werner Henze; conducted Henze's *Elegy* in Venice (1988), *The English Cat* in Berlin (1989) and the fp of *Das verratene Meer* (1990). Musical director of the Montepulciano Festival (1989–92) and director of the Bremen Opera from 1993. Conducted *Figaro* in Los Angeles (1993) and *Don Giovanni* for ENO in 1994; guest with the BBC PO, BBC Scottish SO and the Bavarian Radio SO. Principal of the London Sinfonietta from 1993, leading it at the at the 1993 Proms in music by Ives, Kurtág and Xenakis; music by Schnittke and Henze's *Requiem* for chamber orchestra also feature in his programmes.

Štěpán, Vaclav (b Pečky, 12 Dec 1889; d Prague, 24 Nov 1944), Czech pianist, critic and composer. Studied with Novák and others and became professor of musical aesthetics at the Prague Conservatory. His literary works include a study of *Musical Symbolism of Programme Music* and his compositions a poem *Life's Halcyon Days* for cello and piano.

Stepanian, Aro (b Elisabetopol, 24 Apr 1897; d Erevan, 9 Jan 1966), Russian composer. He began to teach music in the Armenian school of his native town and later of Alexandropol before he was 20; then studied at the Moscow School of Music under Glière and Gnessin and at the Leningrad Conservatory under Shcherbatchev. Settled as professor of music at Erevan in Russian Armenia, where he studied the local folksongs.

Works include operas *Nazar the Brave* (1935), *David Sassunsky* (1937) and *The Dawn* (1938); three symphonies (1944–53); symphonic poem *To the Memory of Twenty-six Commissars*; chamber music, instrumental pieces; songs.

Stephan, Rudi (b Worms, 29 Jul 1887; d Gorlice, Galicia, 29 Sept 1915), German composer. Studied at Worms, with Sekles at Frankfurt and at Munich. His music was influenced by such major contemporaries as Strauss, Debussy, and Reger. He died in battle near Gorlice.

Works include opera *Die ersten Menschen* (produced 1920); ballad *Liebeszauber* (Hebbel) for baritone and orchestra; *Music for Orchestra* (1912); *Music for Fiddle and Orchestra*; *Music for Seven Stringed Instruments* (including piano and harp, 1912), piano pieces; songs.

Stephens, Catherine (b London, 18 Sept 1794; d London, 22 Feb 1882), English soprano. First appeared in Italian opera in 1812 in London, and at CG in 1813, as Mandane in Arne's *Artaxerxes*; later sang Polly in *The Beggar's Opera* and Susanna and Zerlina in the first English versions of *Figaro* and *Don Giovanni*. Weber wrote his last composition for her (1826).

Steptoe, Roger (b Winchester, 25 Jan 1953), English composer, pianist and teacher. Studied at the RAM 1974–77 and was administrator of

International Composer Festivals there, 1986–93. Debut as pianist at the Wigmore Hall, 1982. Works include opera *The King of Macedon* (1979); symphony (1988), *Sinfonia Concertante* for string trio and strings (1981), concertos for oboe (1982), tuba (1983), clarinet (1989), organ (1990), and cello (1991); *Winter's Cold Embraces Dye*, for soloists, chorus and orchestra (1985), *Life's Unquiet Dream* for baritone, chorus and chamber orchestra (1992); two string quartets (1976, 1985) and other chamber music; choral music and pieces for brass.

Sterkel, Johann Franz Xaver (b Würzburg, 3 Dec 1750; d Würzburg, 12 Oct 1817), German composer and pianist. Educated at Würzburg University, he was ordained priest in 1774, and in 1778 became chaplain and musician at the court in Mainz. After a visit to Italy in 1782, where he met Padre Martini, he returned to Mainz, becoming music director to the court in 1793. Lived in Regensburg 1802–10, then in Aschaffenburg, and finally retired to Würzburg in 1815.

Works include opera *Farnace* (1782); 24 symphonies, two overtures for orchestra; six piano concertos; string quintet, piano quartet, six string trios; sonatas for piano solo and duet, piano pieces, variations, etc.; German songs, Italian canzonets; vocal duets.

Sterling, Antoinette (b Sterlingville, NY, 23 Jan 1850; d London, 9 Jan 1904), American contralto. Studied in NY and made her first appearance in England in 1868. After a visit to Germany and further studies with Pauline Viardot-García and Manuel García, she sang in USA and London, where she settled and married John MacKinlay. Often heard in Sullivan. Mother of the folk singer Jean Sterling MacKinlay and the baritone Sterling MacKinlay.

Learning music by reading about it is like making love by mail.

Isaac Stern, quoted in Ayre, *The Wit of Music*, 1966

Stern, Isaac (b Kemenetz, 21 Jul 1920), American violinist of Russian origin. Brought to San Francisco as a child, he received his first musical training at home, later studying the violin with N Blinder and L Persinger and making his debut in San Francisco, aged 11. He has toured widely and is one of the most musical and successful of modern virtuosi; formed a trio with Leonard Rose and Eugene Istomin in 1961. He has given the fps of concertos by Schuman, Bernstein (*Serenade*, 1954) and Peter Maxwell Davies (1986).

Stern, Julius (b Breslau, 8 Aug 1820; d Berlin, 27 Feb 1883), German conductor and educationist. Studied in Berlin, Dresden and Paris, and after a career as choral conductor, opened a Conservatory in Berlin with Kullak and Marx, who later withdrew from it.

Stern, Leo(pold Lawrence) (b Brighton, 5 Apr 1862; d London, 10 Sept 1904), English cellist. After beginning a career as a chemist, he studied at the RAM in London and with J Klengel and Davidov at Leipzig, making his debut in London in 1886; he returned in 1896 to premiere Dvořák's Cello Concerto, with the London Philharmonic Society, conducted by the composer. Stern later played the work in Berlin, Prague and Leipzig; he toured widely in North America at the turn of the century. Toured USA 1897–98.

Sterndale Bennett William Sterndale ◊Bennett.

Sternklang, *Starsound*, 'park music' for five electronic groups by Stockhausen. Fp Berlin, 5 Jun 1971.

stesso tempo, lo Italian, more frequently *l'istesso tempo* = 'the same pace'; a direction given where a change is indicated in the time-signature, but the composer wishes the music to continue at the same pace or beat.

Steuermann, Eduard (b Sambor near Lwów, 18 Jun 1892; d New York 11 Nov 1964), Polish, later American, pianist. Studied piano with Busoni and composition with Schoenberg (1911–14). Later taught at the Paderewski School in Lwów and 1932–36 at the Jewish Conservatory in Kraków. In 1937 he settled in the USA. He dedicated himself to the cause of modern music, especially that of Schoenberg, from whose operas and orchestral works he made piano scores; he took part in the fps of *Pierrot lunaire* (1912), Schoenberg's Suite op. 29 (1927) and the piano concerto (1944).

Steuermann, Jean Louis (b Rio de Janeiro, 16 Mar 1949), Brazilian-born pianist. Made his debut in 1963 at Rio de Janeiro and has appeared worldwide with major orchestras; UK debut 1976, returning 1985 for the London Proms and 1989 with the Hallé Orchestra (Schumann's Concerto). At San Francisco and elsewhere he has given recitals of keyboard music by Bach, most of which he has recorded.

Stevens, Bernard (b London, 2 Mar 1916; d Gt Maplestead, Essex, 2 Jan 1983), English composer. Studied at Cambridge with E J Dent and Rootham and at the RCM in London with R O Morris. He gained the Leverhulme Scholarship and Parry Prize for composition. In 1940–46 he served in the army. Appointed professor of composition at the RCM, 1948.

Works include film music; cantata *The Harvest of Peace* (1952) and other choral works; symphony, *Symphony of Liberation* (1946) and Fugal Overture for orchestra, *Ricercar* and *Sinfonietta* for strings, overture *East and West* for wind band; violin concerto (1946), cello concerto (1952); string quartet, piano trio, theme and variations for string quartet (1949), *Fantasia* for two violins and piano; violin and piano sonata; piano music; songs.

Stevens, Denis (William) (b High Wycombe, 2 Mar 1922), English musicologist and conductor. He studied at Oxford 1940–42 and 1946–49, and after playing in orchestras was a member of the BBC music department in London 1950–54. He has edited the Mulliner Book in *Musica Britannica* and Monteverdi's *Vespers* and *Orfeo*; has pub. books on Tomkins and Tudor church music. Professor at Columbia University, NY, 1964–74. He conducted Monteverdi at Salzburg and the London Proms (both 1967); editions of the *Vespers* (1961, revised 1993) and *Orfeo* (1967). He was co-founder of the Ambrosian Singers. CBE 1984.

Stevens, Halsey (b Scott, NY, 3 Dec 1908; d Long Beach, CA, 20 Jan 1989), American composer, teacher and writer on music. Studied at Syracuse University and with Bloch at Berkeley, 1944. Chairman of the music department at UCLA, 1948–76. Best known for his *Life and Music of Béla Bartók* (1953, revised 1964); also wrote three symphonies (1945–46), three string quartets, three piano sonatas (1933–48), *The Ballad of William Sycamore* for chorus and orchestra (1955), and *Te Deum* for chorus, brass septet and organ (1967).

Stevens, John (Edgar) (b London, 8 Oct 1921), English literary historian and musicologist. Lecturer in English at Cambridge University, 1952; Professor of Medieval and Renaissance English there 1978. In addition to his important editions of early English music he is particularly influential for his books *Music and Poetry in the Early Tudor Court* (1961) and *Words and Music in the Middle Ages* (1986). CBE 1980.

Stevens, Richard (John Samuel) (b London, 27 Mar 1757; d London, 23 Sept 1837), English organist and composer. Learnt music as a choir-boy at St Paul's Cathedral and became organist of the Temple Church 1786, also at the Charterhouse 1796, and was appointed Gresham Professor of Music 1801.

Works include harpsichord sonatas; glees; songs.

Stevens, Risë (b New York, 11 Jun 1913), American mezzo. Studied in NY at Juilliard and with Gutheil- Schoder in Vienna, making her debut in Prague in 1936; sang Orpheus and Octavian there. She sang at the NY Met. (1938–61) and also in Europe; Glyndebourne 1939 and 1955, as Cherubino and Dorabella. Among her most distinguished roles was that of Carmen. Taught at Juilliard School from 1975 and was president of Mannes College, NY, 1975–78.

Stevenson, John (Andrew) (b Dublin, Nov 1761; d Kells, Co. Meath, 14 Sept 1833), Irish organist and composer. Learnt music as a chorister at Christ Church and St Patrick's Cathedrals at Dublin and later became vicar choral at both. In 1814 he was appointed organist and music director at the Castle Chapel. Knighted in 1803.

Works include operas *The Contract* (with Cogan, 1782) and *Love in a Blaze* (1799); music for O'Keeffe's farces *The Son-in-Law*, *The Dead Alive* (1781) and *The Agreeable Surprise* (1782), music for

other stage pieces; oratorio *Thanksgiving*; services and anthems; glees, canzonets and duets; songs; accompaniments for Irish songs edited with words by Thomas Moore.

Stevenson, Robert M(urrell) (b Melrose, NM, 3 Jul 1916), American musicologist. Studied at Juilliard, Yale, Harvard and Oxford (with Westrup). Professor at University of California (LA) from 1949; faculty research lecturer from 1981. His chief areas of study have been Latin American colonial music and Spanish music; books include *La Musica en las Catedrales de España durante el siglo do oro* (1992). Many articles for *The New Grove Dictionary* (1980).

Stevenson, Ronald (b Blackburn, 6 Mar 1928), English composer, pianist and writer on music. He studied at the RMCM and in Italy, and has taught at Edinburgh University Has made a special study of Busoni: first piano concerto (*Triptych*) 1960, is based on themes from *Doktor Faust*. Other works include *Passacaglia on DSCH*, an 80-minute work for piano (fp Cape Town, 1963), and *Peter Grimes Fantasia* for piano (1971). Piano concerto no. 2 (*The Continents*, 1972), *Ben Dorain*, choral symphony (1973), violin concerto (The Gypsy, 1973), *Corroboree for Grainger* for piano and wind ensemble (1987), *St Mary's May Songs* for soprano and strings (1988).

Stewart, Thomas (b San Saba, TX, 29 Aug 1926), American baritone. He sang La Roche while still a student in NY, and in 1957 appeared as Ashton opposite the Lucia of Callas, in Chicago. He soon moved to Europe and from 1960–78 was heard at CG as Gunther, Don Giovanni and Golaud. Bayreuth 1960–72 as Wotan, Amfortas and the Dutchman. Met. debut 1966, as Ford; sang in San Francisco from 1971 and in 1981 was heard there in the title role of Reimann's *Lear*; frequent performances with his wife, Evelyn Lear. Other roles included Onegin, Sachs, Luna, Iago and Escamillo. Returned to the Met 1995, as Balstrode.

St Gall Swiss monastery famous for its MSS of Gregorian chant, the earliest of which date back to the 10th c.

Stiastný, Jan (b Prague, 1764; d Mannheim, after 1826), Czech composer and cellist. Studied at Prague, together with his brother, Bernard Wenzel (1760–1835), also a cellist, later lived by turns at Frankfurt, Nuremberg and Mannheim, and became known both in London and in Paris.

Works include concertino and Andante for cello with flute and strings; trio for cello with viola and second cello; duets for two cellos; cello pieces and studies.

sticcado-pastrole a glass dulcimer popular in England in the 18th c.

Stich, Johann Wenzel (called Punto) (b Žehušice, near Časlav, 28 Oct 1746; d Prague, 16 Feb 1803), Bohemian horn player and composer. Studied in Prague, Munich and Dresden, held posts in various court orchestras, and made a great reputation as a travelling virtuoso under the name of Punto. Beethoven's horn sonata, op. 17, was written for him.

Stich-Randall, Teresa (b W Hartford, CT, 24 Dec 1927), American soprano. Studied at Hartford School of Music, making her debut aged 15 as Aida; sang in *Falstaff* and *Aida* under Toscanini. In 1951 she won a singing competition at Lausanne and in 1952 joined the Vienna Staatsoper. NY Met. debut 1961, as Fiordiligi. She was especially well known as a Mozart singer. Retired 1971.

Stiedry, Fritz (b Vienna, 11 Oct 1883; d Zurich, 8 Aug 1968), Austrian-born American conductor. Studied law at Vienna University and music theory at the Vienna Conservatory. From 1907 to 1908 he was assistant to E von Schuch in Dresden and from 1914 to 1923 was principal conductor at the Berlin Staatsoper. From 1923 to 1925 he conducted in Vienna at the Volksoper, where he gave the 1924 fp of Schoenberg's *Die glückliche Hand*, and from 1928 to 1933 at the Berlin Städtische Oper; associated with the Verdi revival and gave *Macbeth* and *Boccanegra* there. Forced to leave Germany by the Nazis, he conducted in Leningrad 1933–37 and in 1938 settled in the USA. From 1946 to 1958 conducted at the NY Met. He was especially distinguished as a Wagner conductor, and also in modern music, giving the 1940 fp of Schoenberg's 2nd chamber symphony. CG, 1953–54 (*The Ring* and *Fidelio*).

Stiehl, Heinrich (Franz Daniel) (b Lübeck, 5 Aug 1829; d Reval, 1 May

1886), German organist, composer and conductor. Studied with his father, Johann Dietrich Stiehl (1800–72), organist at Lübeck, and at Weimar and Leipzig. He lived by turns in Russia, Austria, Italy, England, Ireland, and England and Russia again, working as organist, conductor and teacher. His brother Karl Johann Christian (1826–1911) was an organist and conductor.

Works include operas *Der Schatzgräber* and *Jery und Bätely* (Goethe); *The Vision* and other orchestral pieces; string quartets, three piano trios; cello and piano sonata; *Sonata quasi fantasia* and other piano works.

Stierhorn German = 'bull horn'; a primitive wind instrument, made of a bull or cow horn, sounding a single note of rough quality. Wagner used it for the watchman in *The Mastersingers*.

Stiffelio opera by Verdi (libretto by F M Piave), produced Trieste, 16 Nov 1850. Revised as *Aroldo* (1856–57). Priest Stiffelio forgives adulterous wife Lina after her father Stankar has killed her lover, Raffaele.

Stignani, Ebe (b Naples, 10 Jul 1904; d Imola, 5 Oct 1974), Italian mezzo. She studied in Naples and made her debut there in 1925, as Amneris. A favourite of Toscanini, she appeared at La Scala, Milan, from 1926 as Eboli, Azucena, Ortrud, Brangaene and Orpheus. London, CG, 1937–57 as Adalgisa and Amneris. She appeared in San Francisco before and after World War II.

stile rappresentativo Italian = 'representative style'; a term used by Italian musicians of the new monodic school in the early years of the 17th c. to describe the new vocal style of declamatory, recitative-like dramatic music which tried to imitate human speech as closely as possible and thus endeavoured to 'represent' dramatic action in a naturalistic way.

Still, William Grant (b Woodville, MS, 11 May 1895; d Los Angeles, 3 Dec 1978), American composer. Educated at Wilberforce University and studied music at Oberlin Conservatory, later with Chadwick at Boston and with Varèse. He made arrangements for the Paul Whiteman band and his own music employs American elements, blues melodies and American folksongs. *The Afro-American Symphony* of 1930 was the first by a black American composer to be performed by a major orchestra and the opera *Troubled Island* has a similar distinction, becoming in 1949 the first premiere given by the newly-formed City Center Opera Company of New York.

Works include operas *Blue Steel* (1934), *Troubled Island* (1949), *A Bayou Legend* (1941, fp 1974), *Highway no. 1* (1942–63), *Costaso* (1949, fp 1992), and *Minette Fontaine* (1958, fp 1985); ballets *La Guiablesse* (1927) and *Sahdji* (1930), *Lenox Avenue* for radio announcer, chorus and orchestra (1937); five symphonies, including *Afro-American Symphony* (no. 1, 1930), *Africa*, *Poem*, *Phantom Chapel* for strings and other orchestral works; *Kaintuck* for piano and orchestra (1935); *From the Black Belt* and *Log Cabin Ballads* for chamber orchestra.

Stilwell, Richard (b St Louis, 6 May 1942), American baritone. Debut NY City Opera 1970, as Pelléas; also role of CG debut, 1974. Glyndebourne from 1973 as Ulisse, Olivier, Onegin and Ford. At Houston in Mar 1974 he sang in the fp of Pasatieri's *The Seagull*; Baltimore 1976 in the same composer's *Ines de Castro*. NY Met. debut 1975, as Guglielmo. Dallas Opera from 1988, in the fp of Argento's *The Aspern Papers* and as Malatesta and Mozart's Count (1992).

Stimme German = 'voice and part'; not only the human voice, but also any part, vocal or instrumental, in a composition, especially a polyphonic one; also the copy of an orchestral, vocal or chamber music part used for performance.

Stimmführung German = part-writing.

Stimmung, *Mood*, work by Stockhausen for six amplified voices. Fp Paris, 9 Dec 1968.

sting an old term describing the effect of vibrato in lute playing.

Stivori, Francesco (b Venice *c* 1550; d Graz, 1605), Italian organist and composer. Pupil of Merulo. He became town organist at Montagnana in 1579 and was later in the service of the Archduke Ferdinand of Austria until 1605.

Works include Masses, Magnificat, *Sacrae cantiones* (1595); madrigals; instrumental *ricercari*.

St James's Hall a concert hall in London, between Regent Street and Piccadilly (the site of the present Piccadilly Hotel), opening on 25 Mar 1858 and sold for demolition in 1905, when the last concert took place on 11 Feb. It was large enough for an orchestra, but used also for chamber music, particularly the Monday Popular Concerts ('Monday Pops'), at which artists of international fame appeared.

St John Passion Bach's setting of the Passion narrative as told in St John's Gospel, with interpolated texts after Brockes and chorales, for soloists, chorus and orchestra, first performed in St Nicholas', Leipzig, on 7 Apr 1724; a second version was given in St Thomas's, Leipzig, on 30 Mar 1725.

St Louis Symphony Orchestra. American orchestra founded in March 1881 (originally as the St Louis Choral Society) and given present title in 1907. Max Zach was conductor 1907–21, followed by Rudolph Ganz, then Vladimir Golschmann 1931–58. Edouard van Remoortel 1958–62; concerts in Powell Symphony Hall from 1968. Walter Susskind director 1968–75, Jerzy Semkov 1976–79 and Leonard Slatkin 1979–95.

St Ludmilla oratorio by Dvořák, op. 71 (Czech words by J Vrchlický), composed 1886 and performed 15 Oct at the Leeds Festival, in an English translation.

St Luke Passion work by Penderecki for narrator, soloists, choruses and orchestra; fp Münster, 30 Mar 1966, conductor Czyz.

St Martial the Benedictine abbey at Limoges. The important MSS of 12th- c. tropes, sequences, *versus* and early polyphony known as the St-Martial repertory are now known to come from many parts of Aquitaine and the repertory is better described as Aquitanian. Concentrated mainly in the early 12th c., it is the main coherent repertory before that of Notre-Dame.

He is a very fine man I am sure and interested in many things – but not, I think, in music.
Jean Sibelius on Leopold Stokowski, quoted in Gattey, *Peacocks on the Podium*, 1982

St Matthew Passion Bach's setting of the Passion narrative as told in St Matthew's Gospel, with interpolated texts by Picander and chorales, for soloists, chorus and orchestra, and performed in St Thomas's, Leipzig, probably on 11 Apr 1727 and certainly on 15 Apr 1729.

Stobaeus, Johann (b Graudenz, West Prussia, 6 Jul 1580; d Königsberg, 11 Sept 1646), German composer and bass. While attending the University at Königsberg, he studied music with Eccard, and after holding various minor appointments there became *Kapellmeister* to the Elector of Brandenburg in 1626.

Works include *Cantiones sacrae* for five–ten voices (pub. 1624), Magnificats for five–six voices, five-part settings of hymn-tunes; Prussian Festival Songs for five–eight voices (with Eccard; two vols, pub. 1624 and 1644); sacred and secular occasional compositions.

Stock, Frederick (Friedrich August) (b Jülich, 11 Nov 1872; d Chicago, 20 Oct 1942), German, later American, violinist and conductor. Studied with his father, a bandmaster, and at the Cologne Conservatory, later with Humperdinck, Jensen and Wüllner. He joined the Cologne orchestra as a violinist in 1890, but settled at Chicago in 1895 in the same capacity, becoming assistant conductor to Theodore Thomas and succeeding him in 1905, as conductor of the orchestra to become the Chicago SO; remained until his death and gave early performances of works by Mahler, Schoenberg, Hindemith and Prokofiev. Also composed.

stock-and-horn an early Scottish instrument, similar to the pibgorn, made of wood or bone fitted with a cow horn. It was played like the chanter of a bagpipe, with a single reed. A different instrument from the stockhorn, which was a forester's horn.

Stockhausen, Julius (b Paris, 22 Jul 1826; d Frankfurt, 22 Sept 1906), German baritone. Pupil of his mother and later of Manuel García in Paris for singing and Hallé and Stamaty for piano. He made his first important concert appearance at Basel, 1848, visited England the next year and then divided his attention between French opera and German song. In May 1856 he gave the first public performance of Schubert's *Die schöne Müllerin* (Vienna). From 1862 to 1869 he was director of the Philharmonic Concerts in Hamburg. In 1869 he became chamber singer to the King of Württemberg, but left Stuttgart in 1874, teaching by turns at Berlin and Frankfurt. Well known in the Lieder of Brahms; the *Magelone Lieder* were written for him.

What is modern today will be tradition tomorrow.
Karlheinz Stockhausen, *Notes on Telemusik*, 1966

Stockhausen, Karlheinz (b Mödrath, near Cologne, 22 Aug 1928), German composer. He studied at the Cologne Musikhochschule and in Paris with Messiaen and Milhaud. He has also learned from the example of Webern, whose tightly controlled brand of serialism inspired Stockhausen's brief venture into 'integral' serialism (in which all elements of sound – pitch, duration, dynamics, etc – are controlled according to pre-determined formulae). Webern's orchestrational technique also influenced Stockhausen's 'group' compositions of the 1950s. Since 1953 he has worked intensively at the studio for electronic music of the West German Radio at Cologne, influencing contemporaries such as Berio and Boulez and younger composers such as Tim Souster and Brian Ferneyhough. He is one of the most enterprising of the composers creating electronic music but has also written music for traditional media.

Stockhausen's creative process begins with the premise that all elements of composition can be vigorously controlled, with the progress of a work determined by pre-set acoustic and scientific formulae. In spite of this the performer has often allowed a multitude of choices in terms of how he 'reads' a score and how he deploys the equipment at his disposal (the influence of John Cage is evident here). He has lectured in the USA and Britain, building up a specialist audience for his music. Professor of composition, Hochschule für Musik, Cologne, from 1971. Members of his family take part in performances of his works, notably his son Markus, who played the trumpet in the premiere of *Donnerstag aus Licht* (Milan, 1981). In the purely instrumental second act of the opera the archangel Michael is represented by a solo trumpeter who plays from inside a rotating globe, appearing at intervals to perform above the members of the orchestra grouped below. Stockhausen has so far completed four of the projected seven operas, one for each day of the week.

Works include *Kreuzspiel*, for oboe, clarinet, piano and three percussion (1951), *Formel* for 29 instruments (1951), *Punkte* for orchestra (1952), *Kontra-Punkte* for ensemble (1952), *Klavierstücke I–XI* (1952–56), *Zeitmasze* for wind quintet (1956), *Gruppen* for three orchestras (1957), *Gesang der Jünglinge* for voice and tapes (1956), *Zyklus* for percussion (1959), *Carré* for four choruses and four orchestras (1960), *Refrain* for ensemble (1959), *Kontakte* for piano, percussion and four-track tape (1960), *Momente* for soprano, four choruses and ensemble (1961–64), *Mikrophonie* I and II for electronics (1964–65), *Mixtur* for five orchestras, sine wave generators and four ring modulators (1964–67), *Stop* for instrumental ensemble (1969–73), *Telemusik* for four-track tape (1966), *Hymnen* for four-track tape (1967), *Stimmung* for voices and ensemble (1968), *Kurzwellen* (*Short Waves*) for electronics and four short-wave radios (1968).

Aus den sieben Tagen, 15 pieces for various instrumental groups (1968), *Spiral* for soloist and short-wave receiver (1969), *Mantra* for two pianos, woodblock and two ring modulators (1970), *Sternklang*, park music for five groups (1971), *Trans* for orchestra and tape (1971), '*Am Himmel wandre ich ...*' for soprano and baritone (1972), *Intervall* for piano duo (1972), *Inori* for one/two soloists and orchestra (1974), *Atmen gibt das Leben* for chorus (1974), *Herbstmusik* for four players (1974), *Musik im Bauch/Music in the Belly*, for six percussion, 1975), *Sirius* for soprano, baritone and ensemble (1977), *Jubiläum* for orchestra (1977).

Stockhausen *Karlheinz Stockhausen has been one of the most influential composers since World War II. Seated here behind a mixing panel, he has pioneered the course of electronic music, and with Boulez led the world in developments of integral serialism and chance procedures.*

Operas in *Licht* cycle: *Donnerstag* (1981), *Samstag* (1984), *Montag* (1988), *Dienstag* (1992); scenes from *Licht* have been given as concert pieces: no. 1 *Der Jahreslauf* for dancers and orchestra (1977), no. 2 *Michaels Reise um die Erde* for trumpet and ensemble (1978), no. 3 *Michaels Jugend* for soprano, tenor, brass instruments, piano, dancers and tape (1979), no. 4 *Michaels Heimkehr* for soloists, chorus and orchestra (1979); also *Lucifer's Dream* from *Samstag* (1983).

Beethausen, opus 1970, von Stockhoven was compiled for the Beethoven bicentenary and includes fragments of music in quotation and a reading of the Heiligenstadt Testament (developed from *Kurzwellen*).

Stockhausen (born *Schmuck*), Margarete (b Gebweiler, 1803; d Colmar, 6 Oct 1877), German soprano, mother of Julius Stockhausen and wife of the harpist and composer Franz Stockhausen (1792–1868). Studied with Catrufo in Paris and first toured with her husband in 1825.

Stodart a firm of English 18th–19th-c. harpsichord and piano makers, founded *c* 1776 by Robert Stodart, carried on by his son William Stodart, whose employee William Allen invented the metal frame for the piano, and later by his grandson Malcolm Stodart.

Stoessel, Albert (Frederic) (b St Louis, 11 Oct 1894; d New York, 12 May 1943), American violinist, composer and conductor. Studied at home and later at the Hochschule für Musik in Berlin. On his return to America he appeared as solo violinist, served as a bandmaster during the 1914–18 war and in 1922 succeeded W Damrosch as conductor of the Oratorio Society of NY and director of music at the Chautauqua Institution. In 1930 he became director of the opera and orchestra at the Juilliard Graduate School there. Conducted the New York fp of *Ariadne auf Naxos*.

Works include opera *Garrick* (1937); suites *Hispania* (1921) and *Early Americana* (1935), *Suite antique*, symphonic portrait *Cyrano de Bergerac* (after Rostand), Concerto grosso, etc. for orchestra; *Suite antique* arranged for two violins and piano (1922), violin and piano sonata and pieces.

Stojowski, Zygmunt (Denis Antoni) (b Strzelce, 14 May 1869; d New York, 6 Nov 1946), Polish composer and pianist. Studied with

A Selection of
Stockhausen

Formel	1951
Kreuzspiel	1951
Punkte	1952
Kontakte	1960
Momente	1961–4
Stimmung	1968
Aus den sieben Tagen	1968
Mantra	1970
Donnerstag aus Licht	1981
Samstag aus Licht	1984

Zeleński at Kraków, then with Diémer, Dubois, Delibes and Massenet in Paris, and finally, on his return, with Gorski and Paderewski. After touring Europe as a pianist he settled in NY in 1905 and became head of the piano department at the Institute of Musical Art in 1911.

Works include *A Prayer for Poland* for chorus, organ and orchestra (1915), cantata; symphony in D minor; two piano concertos, *Symphonic Rhapsody* for piano and orchestra, Concerto and Romanza for violin and orchestra, cello concerto; chamber music; instrumental sonatas; piano pieces; songs.

Stokem, Johannes (also Stokhem, etc.) (b *c* 1440; d *c* 1500), Flemish composer. He was probably born and spent his early life near Liège. He was in the service of Beatrice of Hungary in the early 1480s and a singer in the Papal Choir, 1487–89. He was a friend of Tinctoris, who sent him portions of his 12th treatise (all that survives) with a letter. A few sacred and secular works survive, including four *chansons* printed in Petrucci's *Odhecaton A* (1501).

Stoker, Richard (b Castleford, Yorkshire, 8 Nov 1938), English composer. He studied in Huddersfield and at the RAM with Lennox Berkeley; professor 1963–87.

Works include operas *Johnson Preserv'd* (1967) and *Thérèse Raquin* (after Zola, 1975), *Petite Suite* (1962) and *Little Symphony* (1969) for orchestra; three string quartets (1960–69), Wind quintet (1963), violin sonata (1964), Sextet (1965), piano trio (1965), Oboe quartet (1970).

Stokowski, Leopold (Antonin Stanislaw Boleslawowicz) (b London, 18 Apr 1882; d Nether Wallop, Hants., 13 Sept 1977), American conductor, the son of a Polish father and an Irish mother. Studied at the RCM and took the B.Mus. at Oxford. In 1900 he became organist at St James's Church, Piccadilly, and later studied in Paris and Munich. From 1905 to 1908 he was organist in NY, and in 1908 conductor in London, in 1909 becoming conductor of the Cincinnati SO and of the Philadelphia SO in 1912, where he introduced much modern music; he gave the 1926 fp of *Amériques*, by Varèse, and in 1931 conducted the American premiere of Berg's *Wozzeck*; also gave first US performances of Mahler's eighth symphony, *The Rite of Spring* and the *Gurrelieder*. He was a champion of Rakhmaninov, and led the fps of the 3rd symphony, 4th piano concerto and *Rhapsody on a Theme of Paganini*. From 1942 to 1944 conducted the NBC SO with Toscanini; he conducted with the orchestra the 1944 fp of Schoenberg's piano concerto: NBC terminated his contract after the concert. In 1945 he became music director of the Hollywood Bowl and

1949–50 of the NY PO, taking over the Houston SO in 1955. In 1962 he formed the American SO, in NY, and gave the 1965 fp of Ives' fourth symphony with the orchestra. In 1940 he won wider fame when he appeared in the cartoon film *Fantasia*, arranging *The Rite of Spring* to the mystification of the composer. He was thrice married, acted in films, made many arrangements of music and was one of the most colourful and gifted executants of the century.

Stollen German = 'props'; the songs of the German Minnesinger and Meistersinger usually had stanzas divided into three sections: two stollen of equal length often sung to the same and always to very similar music (called *Aufgesang*, fore-song) followed by an *Abgesang* (after-song) forming a concluding section of unspecified length and with different music. The whole song was called a *Bar*.

Stoltz, Rosine (actually Victorine Noël) (b Paris, 13 Feb 1815; d Paris, 28 Jul 1903), French mezzo. Studied at Choron's school, became a chorus singer after the 1830 Revolution, made a first appearance as a soloist at Brussels in 1832 and from 1837 to 1847 sang at the Paris Opéra. She created Ascanio in *Benvenuto Cellini* (1838) and sang in the fps of operas by Donizetti and Halévy. Her success was as much due to her amatory as to her musical talent; she became the mistress of the Emperor of Brazil and made several highly rewarded tours.

Stoltzer, Thomas (b Schweidnitz, Silesia, *c* 1486; d Ofen, 1526), German composer. Became *Kapellmeister* to King Louis of Bohemia and Hungary at Buda, but left after the battle of Mohács in 1526 and took up a post in the service of Duke Albert of Prussia at Königsberg. He drowned in the river Taja.

Works include Latin motets and psalms, Latin hymns for four–five voices, Psalm 37 in Luther's German translation for three–seven voices in motet form and four others; German sacred and secular songs.

Stoltzman, Richard (b Omaha, 12 Jul 1942), American clarinettist. Studied Yale University and the Marlboro Music School. Teacher at the California Institute of the Arts, 1970–75. Carnegie Hall debut 1976, and played with the Amadeus Quartet at the 1978 Aldeburgh Festival; other chamber concerts with the Cleveland, Vermeer and Guarneri Quartets. London Proms debut 1989, with the Mozart Concerto. Has recorded the concertos of Copland and Corigliano.

Stolz, Robert (Elisabeth) (b Graz, 25 Aug 1880; d Berlin, 27 Jun 1975), Austrian composer and conductor. Early career was as pianist; conductor at the Theater an der Wien from 1907. First of about 60 operettas and musicals was *Die lustigen Weiber von Wien* (produced Munich, 1909). Worked in Berlin in 1920s, writing for early film musicals. Moved to Hollywood 1940 and after returning to Vienna in 1946 wrote music for ice revues. Conducted while in his 90s.

Works include *Der Favorit* (1916), *Der Tans ins Glück* (1921), *Mädi* (1923), *Wenn die kleinen Veilchen blühen* (1932), *Venus in Seide* (1932), *Der verlorene Walzer* (1933), *Frühling in Prater* (1949), *Trauminsel* (1962); *c* 100 film scores, many individual songs, waltzes, and a funeral march for Hitler, written in anticipation of his death.

Stolz (originally *Stolzová*), Teres(in)a (b Kostelec nad Labem, 2 Jun 1834; d Milan, 22–23 Aug 1902), Bohemian-Italian soprano. Studied under Lamperti at Milan and made her first stage appearance in 1860. She was Verdi's first Aida at Milan and the soprano in the fp of his Requiem. Other roles included Elisabeth de Valois and Leonora (*Forza*). Her elder twin sisters, **Francesca** and **Ludmilla** (b Kostelec, 13 Feb 1826), were also singers and together were the mistresses of the composer Federico Ricci.

Stolze, Gerhard (b Dessau, 1 Oct 1926; d Garmisch-Partenkirchen, 11 Mar 1979), German tenor. Studied in Dresden and made his debut there in 1949. From 1951 he sang at Bayreuth and from 1957 at the Vienna Staatsoper; London, CG, 1960–63 as Mime. He was a highly dramatic character singer, specializing in more modern roles. He created Orff's Oedipus (Stuttgart 1959).

Stölzel, Gottfried Heinrich (b Grünstädtel, Saxony, 13 Jan 1690; d Gotha, 27 Nov 1749), German composer. Studied at Leipzig University, taught in Breslau 1710–12, and visited Italy 1713–14,

Richard Stoltzman – clarinettist

1 Debussy: *L'apres-midi d'un faune*
I first heard this when I was 14, lonely and disorientated. I didn't know if I'd continue with the clarinet. With the encouragement of a high-school teacher, I listened to *L'apres-midi d'un faune*. I had never heard anything like it; I'd never even gone to a symphony concert. I felt that this music was speaking to me in ways that I couldn't explain. It transformed my mundane emotions into something pure and gave me a new world to go to, as though it had made a secret bond of friendship.

2 Gershwin/Gil Evans: *Porgy and Bess* (Miles Davis)
I've always been attracted to American music, with its strong jazz influence. When I was 15 I heard a recording of Miles Davis playing his muted trumpet in Gil Evans's arrangement of *Porgy and Bess*. I was taken by the unique, plaintive and compelling sound that Davis produced. It's rare when any instrumentalist can find so truly personal an expression.

3 Alban Berg: *Lyric Suite*
When I was attending university, a friend dragged me to a concert to hear the Juilliard Quartet play this piece by Berg. I'd only heard a string quartet once or twice; I was overwhelmed by the intensity of the four players as they interacted. I couldn't understand Berg's musical language,
but was tremendously intrigued to learn more about it. I grew to appreciate fully the powerful way he combines complete compositional control of the highest intellectual order with raw extremes of musical passion.

4 Messiaen: *Quatour pour le fin de temps*
I've played this frequently, and it is one of my most intense musical experiences. Messiaen wrote it in 1940, while a prisoner in a German-run camp in Silesia. The work is deeply religious and overtly symbolic. The third movement, 'Abîme des Oiseaux', written for solo clarinet, begins supremely slowly. At one point, a long-held note develops from the softest possible sound to the loudest. Messiaen conceived this as a cry of longing, as if to transcend the limits imposed by time.

5 Brahms: Clarinet Quintet
This is the piece that has had the greatest single impact upon me. I first heard it when I was 22. Until then, although I'd liked playing the clarinet, I hadn't felt a total commitment to it. While listening to that performance, something inside me changed. I realized how poignant and profound the voice of the clarinet could be and how eloquently it could interrelate with the other instruments. I understood that clarinet playing could be a means of expressing infinite shades of colour and feeling. In that forty minutes I found my 'calling'.

---

meeting Gasparini, Vivaldi and others. Lived in Prague, Bayreuth and Gera, and from 1719 was *Kapellmeister* to the court at Gotha.

Works include 22 operas, e.g. *Narcissus* (1711), *Orion* (1712), *Venus und Adonis* (1714), etc.; 14 oratorios; Masses, motets, etc.; Passions; *concerti grossi*; trio sonatas.

Stonard, William (d Oxford, 1630), English organist and composer. In 1608 he took a degree at Oxford and became organist of Christ Church Cathedral there, retaining the post until his death.

Works include services, anthems; catch 'Ding dong bell'.

Stone, Robert (b Alphington, Devon, 1516; d London, 2 Jul 1613), English composer. He learnt music as a chorister at Exeter Cathedral, but *c* 1543 went to London to enter the Chapel Royal, of which he became a Gentleman. Wrote a setting of the Lord's Prayer, part of his Morning Service.

Stone, William (b Golsboro, NC, 1944), American baritone. Sang first in concert and made opera debut at Youngstown 1975, as Germont. Sang Adam in the fp of Penderecki's *Paradise Lost* at Chicago in 1978, repeated at La Scala 1979. Florence 1979 and 1981, as Wozzeck and Gluck's Orestes. Appeared in the US fp of Schoenberg's *Von Heute auf Morgen* (Santa Fe 1980) and as Mozart's Count at the New York City Opera in 1990; title role in Busoni's *Faust*, 1992. Other roles include Marschner's Templar (Wexford, 1989), Rossini's Figaro and Verdi's Posa.

Stone Flower, The, *Kamenny Tsvetok*, ballet in three acts by Prokofiev (scenario by L Lavrovsky and M Mendelson-Prokofieva after a story by P Bazhov); composed 1948–53, produced Moscow, Bolshoi, 12 Feb 1954.

Stone Guest, The, *Kamenny Gost*, opera by Dargomizhsky (libretto Pushkin's drama, set unaltered), not performed in the composer's lifetime; produced St Petersburg, 28 Feb 1872. Don Juan dallies with Laura and Donna Anna on way to Hell.

Stone to Thorn, From work by Peter Maxwell Davies for mezzo and ensemble, fp Oxford, 30 Jun 1971, conductor Davies.

Stonings (or *Stoninge*), Henry, English composer of the second half of the 16th c. Wrote (?) a Latin Magnificat; also *In nomines* and other works for strings. His first name is known only from a statement by
Hawkins, and it is possible that the Magnificat, at least, may be by Oliver Stonyng .

Stonyng, Oliver, English 16th-c. composer. He was a fellow of Eton College, 1530–47, and precentor, 1533–35. He composed (?) a Latin Magnificat (British Museum Add. MSS 1782–85).

stopped notes on wind instruments the notes not produced naturally as harmonics, but by valves, keys or other mechanical means, or sometimes by the hand in horn playing. On string instruments any notes not produced on open strings.

stopping the placing of the left-hand fingers on the strings of string instruments to change the pitch of the notes of the open strings. The playing of two notes in this way simultaneously is called double stopping, but the term is also used loosely for the playing of chords with more than two notes. Stopping is also a device in horn playing: the placing of the hand in the bell to produce a special quality of sound and formerly, before the invention of the valves, to change the pitch of some notes.

stops the devices by which the registration of the organ can be regulated and altered. The larger kinds of harpsichords also have stops, producing different qualities of tone and different pitches.

Storace, (Ann Selina) Nancy (b London, 27 Oct 1765; d London, 24 Aug 1817), English soprano. Pupil of Rauzzini in London and of Sacchini in Italy, sang leading roles in Florence, Milan and Venice. In 1784 was engaged as *prima donna* at the Vienna opera, where she was the first Susanna in Mozart's *Nozze di Figaro* (1786). She returned to London in 1787. Retired 1808.

Storace, Stephen (b London, 4 Apr 1762; d London, 19 Mar 1796), English composer, brother of Ann ◊Storace. Studied at the Conservatorio di Sant' Onofrio in Naples, in *c* 1784 went to Vienna, where he produced two operas and became friendly with Mozart, and returned to London with his sister in 1787, becoming composer to Sheridan's co. at the Drury Lane Theatre. His Mozart-influenced Shakespearean opera, *Gli equivoci*, has been successfully revived in London 1974 and at Wexford 1992.

Works include operas *Gli sposi malcontenti* (1785), *Gli equivoci* (after Shakespeare's *Comedy of Errors*, 1786), *La cameriera astuta*

(1788), *The Haunted Tower, No Song, No Supper* (1790), *The Siege of Belgrade* (1791), *The Pirates, Dido: Queen of Carthage* (1792), *The Cherokee* (1794), *The Iron Chest* (Colman), *Mahmoud, or The Prince of Persia* (unfinished, completed by Kelly and Ann Storace, produced 1796) and others; ballet *Venus and Adonis*.

Storchio, Rosina (b Venice, 19 May 1876; d Milan, 24 Jul 1945), Italian soprano. Debut Milan 1892, as Micaela; La Scala from 1895; created Madama Butterfly, 1904. Other creations were Leoncavallo's Musetta (1897) and Zazà (1900), Giordano's Stefana (*Siberia*, 1903) and Mascagni's Lodoletta (1917). At Buenos Aires (1904–14) and in NY she was admired as Norina, Violetta, Manon and Linda di Chamounix.

Story of a Real Man, The, *Povest' o nastoyashchem cheloveke*, opera in four acts by Prokofiev (libretto by composer and M Mendelson-Prokofieva); composed 1947–48. Prokofiev sought to gain official favour with story of heroic legless Soviet aviator, but after private performance in Leningrad, 3 Dec 1948, it was not staged until 8 Oct 1960, at the Bolshoi, Moscow.

Stott, Kathryn (b Nelson, 10 Dec 1958), English pianist. She studied at the Menuhin School and the RCM; debut at the Purcell Room, London, 1978. Concerts throughout Britain and in Holland and Germany. Has recorded Fauré's piano works and also plays Mozart and Schumann with spirit and perception.

St Paul oratorio by Mendelssohn, op. 36, performed Düsseldorf, Lower Rhine Festival, 22 May 1836; in England, Liverpool, 7 Oct 1836.

St Paul's Suite work for string orchestra in four movements by Holst. Composed for St Paul's Girls' school and performed there 1913.

St Petersburg Philharmonic Orchestra. founded in 1921 as Leningrad PO, from members of the Tsarist Court Orchestra. Principal conductors have included Emil Cooper (1921–22), Nikolai Malko (1926–29), Fritz Stiedry (1934–37), and Evgeny Mravinsky (1938–88; under him premiered the Shostakovich symphonies nos. 5, 6, 8, 9 and 10, the first violin concerto and the first cello concerto). Yuri Temirkanov principal from 1988; changed name to St Petersburg PO 1991.

Strada, Anna Maria (also known by her married name of Strada del Pò), Italian soprano. Brought to London by Handel in 1729, she sang in several of his operas, remaining in England till 1738. She created leading roles in *Partenope, Ezio, Sosarme, Orlando, Ariodante, Alcina* and *Berenice*.

Stradella, Alessandro (b Rome, 1 Oct 1644; d Genoa, 25 Feb 1682), Italian composer, singer and violinist. Of noble birth, he never held any official posts, and most of what is known of his career seems to be based on legend rather than fact, notably in the opera *Alessandro Stradella* by Floton (1844) in which composer avoids being murdered by a pair of bandits by singing to them of kindness and mercy. He wrote operas and oratorios for Rome, Modena and Genoa. He (?) entered the service of the Duchess of Savoy and regent of Piedmont, Marie de Nemours, at Turin. He had numerous love affairs, the last of which led to his assassination.

Works include operas *La forza dell' amor paterno* (1678), *Doriclea, Il trespolo tutore balordo* (1679), *Il Floridoro*; motets and other church music; oratorio *San Giovanni Battista* (1675) and others; sacred and secular cantatas; serenade *Qual prodigio che io miri* and others; madrigals; concerto for strings.

Stradella, Flotow, ◊Alessandro Stradella.

Stradivari, Latinized Stradivarius, Italian family of violin makers:
1. Antonio Stradivari (b Cremona, 1644; d Cremona, 18 Dec 1737), founder of the workshop at Cremona in the 1660s, after serving an apprenticeship to Nicolo Amati. He continually modified the design of his instruments, achieving by 1690 the 'Long Strad'. His finest instruments, including cellos and violas, were produced in the first two decades of the 18th c. About 600 of his instruments survive and have achieved the status (and sale-room prices) of works of art.
2. Francesco Stradivari (b Cremona, 1 Feb 1671; d Cremona, 11 May 1743), son of 1. He carried on his father's craft with

3. Omobono Stradivari (b Cremona, 14 Nov 1679; d Cremona, 8 Jun 1742), brother of 2.

Straeten, Edmond van der (b Oudenarde, 3 Dec 1826; d Oudenarde, 25 Nov 1895), Belgian musicologist. Studied law at Alost and Ghent, but on returning home cultivated music history. He became secretary to Fétis for the purpose of studying with him and contributed to his Dictionary. He also acted as critic and wrote books on Flemish music, including *La Musique aux Pays-bas* in eight vols. He also composed incidental music and a Te Deum.

strambotto, Italian, a form of verse used by the composers of *frottole* in the 15th-16th c. It had eight lines (*ottava rima*), the first six rhyming alternately and the last two consecutively. In the *strambotto siciliano* all eight lines rhyme alternately.

Straniera, La, *The Stranger*, opera by Bellini (libretto by F Romani), produced Milan, La Scala, 14 Feb 1829. Arturo, betrothed to Isoletta, becomes infatuated with the veiled stranger, Agnese disguised as Alaide. Arturo seems to kill Agnesi's brother Vableburgo, believing him to be a lover; in fact he is only wounded. When it is revealed that Agnese is the Queen of France, Arturo kills himself.

Stransky, Josef (b Humpolec, 9 Sept 1872; d New York, 6 Mar 1936), Czech conductor and composer. Studied medicine at first, but turned to music, studying under Fibich and Dvořák in Prague and Fuchs and Bruckner in Vienna. He became conductor of the German Opera in Prague, then of the Hamburg Opera, 1909, and in 1911–22 conducted the NY Philharmonic Society, following Mahler. In 1922 gave the fp of Schoenberg's transcriptions of Bach chorale preludes. Figures in Strauss's *Intermezzo* as Stroh.

Works include opera *Beatrice and Benedick* (after Shakespeare's *Much Ado*), operetta *The General* (produced Hamburg); symphony; chamber music; songs.

strascinando Italian = 'dragging, slurring'.

Stratas, Teresa (b Toronto, 26 May 1938), Canadian soprano. She studied in Toronto and made her debut there in 1958 as Mimi. NY Met. from 1959 as Lisa, Nedda, Zerlina and Cherubino. In 1962 she took part in the posthumous fp of Falla's *Atlántida*. She has sung Susanna at CG, London, and Salzburg. In 1979 she sang the title role in the first complete performance of Berg's *Lulu* (Paris, under Boulez); she also created Marie Antoinette in Corigliano's *The Ghosts of Versailles*, NY Met. 1991. Other roles include Micaela, Giovanna d'Arco, Mélisande (Chicago, 1992) and Violetta.

Strathspey a Scottish folk dance in quick common time, similar to the reel, but with dotted rhythms. The name derives from the strath (valley) of Spey and is first heard of in 1780, though dances of the kind are much older.

Straube, (Montgomery Rufus) Karl (Siegfried) (b Berlin, 6 Jan 1873; d Leipzig, 27 Apr 1950), German organist and conductor, son of a German father and an English mother. Studied with his father, an organist and harmonium maker, and with Heinrich Reimann among others. He was appointed organist of Wesel Cathedral in 1897 and of St Thomas's, Leipzig, in 1902. There he became conductor of the Bach Society in 1903, professor of organ at the Conservatory in 1907, and cantor of St Thomas's in 1918. He travelled all over Europe with the choir of St Thomas's. He pub. many editions of organ and choral music of the past. He was made an honorary Ph.D. of Leipzig University in 1923.

Straus, Ludwig (b Pressburg, 28 Mar 1835; d Cambridge, 23 Oct 1899), Austrian violinist. Studied at the Vienna Conservatory and made his debut there in 1850. In 1855 he made a tour including Italy and in 1857 another in Germany and Sweden, with Piatti. In 1860 he first visited England and in 1864 settled in Manchester as leader of the Hallé Orchestra, and in 1888 in London.

Straus, Oscar (b Vienna, 6 Mar 1870; d Ischl, 11 Jan 1954), Austrian composer and conductor. Studied with Graedener and Bruch in Berlin and became theatre conductor at various towns, including Bratislava, where he premiered his first operetta, *Der Weise von Cordoba*, in 1895. His first major success came in 1907 and 1908, with *Ein Walzertraum* and *Der tapfere Soldat* (given also in New York and London as *The Chocolate Soldier*). He then settled in Berlin and in

Strauss *The composer Johann Strauss the Younger (1825–1899). His father Johann Strauss the Elder, who established the Viennese waltz tradition, forbade him to learn music, but he mastered the art in secret and later superseded his father as a composer of waltzes.*

1927 in Vienna and subsequently in Paris. In 1940 he emigrated to the USA, returning to Europe in 1948.

Works include operas *Die Waise von Cordova* and *Das Tal der Liebe* (1909), operettas *Ein Walzertraum* (*A Waltz Dream*, 1907), *Der tapfere Soldat* (*The Chocolate Soldier*, after Shaw's *Arms and the Man*, 1908), *Love and Laughter* (1913), *The Last Waltz, Riquette* and others; overture to Grillparzer's *Der Traum ein Leben*, serenade for string orchestra.

Strauss Austrian family of musicians:

1. Johann (Baptist) Strauss (b Vienna, 14 Mar 1804; d Vienna, 25 Sept 1849), composer, conductor and violinist. His parents were innkeepers and apprenticed him to a bookbinder, but he learnt the violin and viola and was eventually allowed to study with Seyfried. He played viola in private string quartets, at 15 managed to join Pamer's orchestra at the Sperl, a place of entertainment, music and dancing, then Lanner's band, in which he became deputy conductor. In 1825 he and Lanner parted and he began a rival band, for which he wrote dances, especially waltzes, which had by that time become fashionable. He was invited to return to the Sperl, which had enlarged the orchestra, and in 1833 began travelling abroad with a visit to Pest. By 1837 he had been to Germany, Holland, Belgium, France and Britain. He added the quadrille to the music of the Viennese ballrooms, having picked it up in Paris, and made a great hit with the *Radetzky Marsch*. He toured again and was then made conductor of the court balls.

Works include 150 waltzes (*Täuberl, Kettenbrücken, Donaulieder Walzer*, etc.), 35 quadrilles, 28 galops, 19 marches, 14 polkas.

2. Johann Strauss (b Vienna, 25 Oct 1825; d Vienna, 3 Jun 1899), composer, conductor and violinist, son of 1. He was not allowed to follow his father's profession, but learnt the violin and studied secretly with Drechsler and others. In 1844 he appeared as conductor at Dommayer's hall in the Heitzing suburb, and his father capitulated. After the latter's death he amalgamated his orchestra with his own, toured in Austria, Poland and Germany and in 1855–65 visited St Petersburg in the summer. In 1863 he became conductor of the court balls, and directed them until 1872. The previous year his first operetta had been produced at the Theater am der Wien and in 1874 he had his most enduring stage success with *Die Fledermaus*. His greatest popularity was achieved with such waltzes as *Tales from the Vienna Woods* (1868), *The Blue Danube* (1867), *Wiener Blut* (1870), *Roses from the South* (1880), *Frühlingsstimmen* (1883) and the *Emperor Waltz* (1885).

Works include operettas *Indigo und die vierzig Räuber* (1871), *Der Karneval in Rom* (1873), *Die Fledermaus* (1874), *Cagliostro in Wien* (1875), *Prinz Methusalem, Blindekuh, Das Spitzentuch der Königin* (1880), *Der lustige Krieg* (1881), *Eine Nacht in Venedig, Der Zigeunerbaron* (1885), *Simplizius* (1887), *Ritter Pázmán, Fürstin Ninetta* (1893), *Jabuka, Waldmeister* (1895), *Die Göttin der Vernunft* (1897); ballet *Aschenbrödel; Traumbilder* for orchestra; polkas, galops and other dances.

It was quite a pleasure to see Strauss conduct his dance music – the nimble little man with the small magic violin in his hand; he hopped, nodded, fiddled, and moved to and fro in gladsome excitement to the time of the intoxicating tones.

Karoline Bauer on Johann Strauss I,
in *Memoirs*, 1885

---

3. Josef Strauss (b Vienna, 22 Aug 1827; d Vienna, 21 Jul 1870), composer and conductor, brother of 2. He became an architect at his father's wish, but secretly studied music and during an illness of Johann Strauss conducted his band with success. He then formed his own band and wrote 283 dances for it. He died after a visit to Warsaw, where he injured his hand in a fall on the platform at his last concert.

Strauss, Richard   *A biographical note*

Thomas Beecham was a tireless champion of Strauss in the early years of the century, but he ran into trouble when he wished to conduct *Salome* at Covent Garden. The office of the censor, presided over by the Lord Chamberlain, refused to license the performance on the grounds that it featured a Biblical character, St John the Baptist. On pointing out that *Samson et Dalila* had been performed under a similar disadvantage, Beecham was told that Saint-Saëns had had the foresight to feature Old Testament characters, rather than New Testament ones. The opera could be performed only if Beecham agreed to certain alterations in the text, so that John became simply the Prophet and all Salome's expressions of sexual longing for him had to be rendered as requests for spiritual guidance. The necessary changes were made to the German text, to the bewilderment of the imported cast, and all seemed set when it occurred to the censor that, in the last scene of the opera, St John's head is delivered to Salome on a silver platter. An arm or a leg might have been allowed, but not his head; the offending object must remain completely covered by a cloth. All seemed at last to be going well during the premiere, when Beecham noticed with horror that the singers were reverting to the original text, ending with Salome's desire to kiss the lips of the severed head. The Lord Chamberlain was completely satisfied, however: 'It has been wonderful; we are delighted.'

4. Eduard Strauss (b Vienna, 15 Mar 1835; d Vienna, 28 Dec 1916), composer and conductor, brother of 3. Studied harp and composition and appeared as conductor in 1862. After 1865 he took Johann Strauss' place at the summer concerts in St Petersburg and in 1870 became conductor of the court balls. He toured much, appearing at the Inventions Exhibition in London in 1885. His works include over 300 dances.

Strauss, Christoph (b Vienna, *c* 1580; d Vienna, Jun 1631), Austrian organist and composer. He entered the service of the court in 1594 and in 1601 became organist at the church of St Michael. In 1617–19 he was court conductor and afterwards *Kapellmeister* at St Stephen's Cathedral.

Works include Masses, Requiems, motets for voices and instruments.

Strauss, Richard (Georg) (b Munich, 11 Jun 1864; d Garmisch-Partenkirchen, 8 Sept 1949), German composer and conductor. His father, Franz Strauss (1822–1905), was horn player at the Court Opera in Munich, but had married into the wealthy brewers' family of Pschorr. Strauss began to compose at the age of six and at ten wrote his first two pub. works, the *Festival March* and the serenade for wind instruments. In 1880 he finished a symphony in D minor and the next year his A major string quartet was performed in public. He entered Munich University in 1882, but left it in 1883, went to Berlin for a short period of study, but became assistant conductor to Bülow at Meiningen very soon after. A member of the orchestra, Alexander Ritter, turned his classical leanings into admiration for Berlioz, Wagner and Liszt. In 1885 Bülow resigned and Strauss became first conductor at Meiningen; his first truly characteristic piece, the first horn concerto, had been premiered under Bülow in March. In spring 1886 he visited Italy and afterwards wrote the symphony *Aus Italien*, produced at Munich in spring 1887, when he became sub-conductor at the Opera there. *Macbeth*, his first symphonic poem, was composed that year. In 1889 he became assistant conductor to Lassen at the Weimar Court Opera and gained his first major success with the tone poem *Don Juan*; the famous exuberant opening of the work seems to announce the young composer in all his confidence and technical assurance. In 1891 Cosima Wagner invited him to conduct *Tannhäuser* at Bayreuth.

Under Wagner's influence he wrote his first opera, *Guntram*, most of it during a tour in the Mediterranean undertaken to counteract threatening lung trouble. It was produced at Weimar on 10 May 1894. The heroine was sung by Pauline de Ahna, whom he married in June, and he was that year appointed conductor of the Berlin PO in

Strauss *The composer and conductor Richard Strauss (1864–1949). His life may be divided compositionally into two phases: the early orchestral works (including the tone poems) and the operas, which were written from the turn of the century and later. He is no relation of either Johann Strauss.*

succession to Bülow. Although *Guntram* was not a success, in the next five years he composed some of his most popular and enduring tone poems, each one superbly orchestrated and with its own distinctive character: *Till Eulenspiegel, Also sprach Zarathustra, Don Quixote*, and *Ein Heldenleben*. In 1905 his opera *Salome* was premiered at Dresden; in Vienna, London and New York it was to have trouble with the censors for its lurid treatment of a Biblical subject. Strauss further collaborated with librettist Hugo von Hofmannstahl in a setting of Sophocles' *Elektra*, in which he was considered wild and dissonant. More general favour was found with *Der Rosenkavalier* (1911), a tumescent view of 18th-c. Vienna, with anachronistic waltzes. Strauss had been conductor of the Berlin Royal Opera from 1898 but resigned in 1918 and the following year his masterpiece, *Die Frau ohne Schatten*, was produced in Vienna; the rich allusiveness and symphonic amplitude of the score was a fitting farewell to a world which had all but disappeared in the Great War.

Strauss had bought a country house at Garmisch in the Bavarian highlands, and all his later works were written there. After Hofmannsthal's death in 1929 Strauss, who had already written a libretto of his own for the autobiographical *Intermezzo*, produced at Dresden, 1924, worked with Stefan Zweig on *Die schweigsame Frau* (based on Ben Jonson's *Epicoene*). It was produced at Dresden in 1935 but quickly withdrawn on a trumped-up excuse because Zweig, as a Jew, had to be boycotted by the Nazi party. Strauss thereupon resigned his appointment as president of the Reichs-Musikkammer and was himself under a cloud for a time, but had long been too important a figure in German musical life to be ignored. He wrote music for the 1936 Berlin Olympic Games and composed four further operas during the Nazi regime. The best known of these is *Capriccio*, although some of Strauss's most attractive music is in the trilogy of operas based on Greek mythology. The *Four Last Songs* were premiered posthumously.

Works include OPERAS *Guntram* (1894), *Feuersnot* (1901), *Salome*

A Selection of

Richard Strauss

Don Juan	1889
Don Quixote	1898
Ein Heldenleben	1899
Salome	1905
Elektra	1909
Der Rosenkavalier	1911
Ariadne auf Naxos	1912
Die Frau ohne Schatten	1919
Arabella	1933
Vier letzte Lieder	1948

(1905), *Elektra*, *Der Rosenkavalier* (1911), *Ariadne auf Naxos* (1912), *Die Frau ohne Schatten* (1919), *Intermezzo*, *Die ägyptische Helena* (1928), *Arabella* (1933), *Die schweigsame Frau* (1935), *Friedenstag* (1938), *Daphne* (1938), *Die Liebe der Danae* (produced 1944), *Capriccio* (1942); ballets *Josephs-Legende*, *Schlagobers*; incidental music to Molière's *Le Bourgeois Gentilhomme* (originally connected with *Ariadne auf Naxos*, 1912).

ORCHESTRAL: two symphonies: F minor and *Aus Italien* (1884, 1887); symphonic poems *Macbeth* (1887), *Don Juan* (1889), *Tod und Verklärung* (1890), *Till Eulenspiegels lustige Streiche* (1895), *Also sprach Zarathustra* (1896), *Don Quixote* (1898), *Ein Heldenleben* (1899), *Symphonia domestica* (1904), *Eine Alpensinfonie* (1915); other orchestral works: *Festival March*, two serenades for wind instruments (1881–84), two military marches, *Festliches Praeludium*; violin concerto (1883), two horn concertos (1885, 1942), *Burleske* for piano and orchestra (1886), *Parergon zur Symphonia domestica* for piano left hand and orchestra (1925), *Japanische Festmusik* (1940), Divertimento on pieces by Couperin (1942), oboe concerto (1945); two sonatinas for wind instruments (1943, 1945), *Metamorphosen* for 23 solo string instruments (1946).

CHAMBER: string quartet in A major (1880), piano quartet in C minor; sonatas for violin and piano and cello and piano (1883, 1887).

VOCAL: 11 songs with orchestra including three Hymns by Hölderlin, *Vier letzte Lieder* (1948); 26 op. nos. of songs (*c* 150) including cycles *Schlichte Weisen* (Felix Dahn), *Mädchenblumen*, *Krämerspiegel* and six songs by Shakespeare and Goethe; piano sonata, nine piano pieces; Tennyson's *Enoch Arden* (1890) and Uhland's *Das Schloss am Meer* for recitation and piano (1899).

stravaganza Italian = 'extravagance'; a word sometimes used for a composition of a freakish nature.

Stravinsky, Fyodor Ignat'vevich (b Rechitskiy, Minsk Province, 20 Jun 1843; d St Petersburg, 4 Dec 1902), Russian bass, father of Igor ◊Stravinsky. He studied in St Petersburg and made his debut at Kiev in 1873, as Rodolfo in *La Sonnambula*. Sang at the Mariinsky Theatre 1876–1902, notably in the fps of Tchaikovsky's *Vakula the Smith* (1876), *The Maid of Orleans* (1881) and *The Enchantress* (1887).

I may not be a first-rate composer, but I am a first-rate second-rate composer!

Richard Strauss, quoted in Del Mar, *Richard Strauss*, 1962

Also created Grandfather Frost in Rimsky-Korsakov's *The Snow Maiden* (1882) and was successful as Mussorgsky's Rangoni and Varlaam, Panas in *Christmas Eve* and Farlaf in *Ruslan and Ludmilla*. The Mephistopheles of Gounod and Boito were his best known non-Russian roles.

Stravinsky, Igor (Fyodorovich) (b Oranienbaum, near St Petersburg, 17 Jun 1882; d New York, 6 Apr 1971), Russian composer (American citizen from 1945). His father, Fyodor ◊Stravinsky, was the leading bass at the Imperial Opera. Along with Schoenberg, Stravinsky was the most important composer of the early 20th c. who determined more than any others the course of music for the following 50 years. His creative output can be divided into three distinct phases, beginning with Russian nationalism and continuing through neo-classicism to twelve-note technique. In 1903 Stravinsky met Rimsky-Korsakov at Heidelberg and played him his early compositions, but did not become his pupil until 1907, by which time he had finished a piano sonata, begun a symphony and married his second cousin, Nadezhda Sulima, on 11 Jan 1906. In 1908 he had the symphony performed and wrote *Fireworks* for orchestra for the marriage of Nadia Rimsky-Korsakov and M Steinberg, and a *Funeral Chant* on Rimsky-Korsakov's death. The performance of the *Fantastic Scherzo* in 1909 drew Diaghilev's attention to Stravinsky, who was commissioned to write *The Firebird* for the Russian Ballet. It was produced in Paris in 1910, and Stravinsky began to become known in western Europe. *Petrushka* followed in 1911 and *The Rite of Spring* in

Stravinsky *The composer Igor Stravinsky (1882–1971), painted by J E Blanche. Along with Schoenberg he was the most important figure of the early 20th century. He did not embrace serial technique until late in his career, his earlier works favouring first a rhythmically vital dissonant style and then neo-classicism.*

1913, both produced in Paris, where the latter provoked a riot of protest and fanatical partisanship. In spite of the public protest at its premiere, *The Rite of Spring* was soon successfully performed all over Europe, Russia and the USA, establishing Stravinsky, with Schoenberg, as the leading avant-garde composer of his time. In 1914 he settled in Switzerland, on the Lake of Geneva and in Paris the same year Diaghilev produced the fairy tale opera-ballet *The Nightingale*. From 1914 he became as well known in London as in Paris, and in 1925 he first made a tour in USA. In the inter-war years many of his works were written in the spirit of neo-classicism, beginning most clearly with the ballet *Pulcinella* (1922), based on pieces attributed to Pergolesi, and continuing with the concerto for piano with wind instruments (1925). *Oedipus Rex*, an opera-oratorio (after Sophocles), was premiered in 1927, followed by the classically-inspired ballet *Apollon Musagète* (1928), the ballet (after Tchaikovsky) *The Fairy's Kiss*, *Capriccio* for piano and orchestra, and the *Symphony of Psalms*, premiered under Ansermet in 1930.

Stravinsky became a French citizen in 1934 and in 1937 his ballet *Jeu de Cartes* was produced by Balanchine at the New York Met. The American connection was strengthened when he settled in Hollywood in 1939, and the following year he conducted the Chicago SO in his symphony in C. The powerful *Symphony in Three Movements* was premiered by the New York PO in 1946 and in 1948 Balanchine staged the ballet *Orpheus*. A meeting with W H Auden led to the summation of Stravinsky's neo-classical music, the Hogarth-inspired opera *The Rake's Progress*, premiered at Venice in 1951. Stravinsky had meanwhile met the conductor Robert Craft and under his influence turned towards the serial music of the Second Viennese School.

Stravinsky   *A biographical note*

Stravinsky did not have an easy time when his music was premiered in England. Only six weeks after it was given in Paris, in May 1913, Pierre Monteux visited London to conduct the Ballets Russes in *The Rite of Spring*. That august journal *The Musical Times* was not impressed: 'The music baffles verbal description. To say that much of it is hideous as sound is a mild description ... practically it has no relation to music at all, as most of us understand the word.' In 1921 Koussevitsky conducted the premiere of the austerely beautiful *Symphonies of Wind Instruments*. Ernest Newman, the leading critic of the day, was scarcely equal to the occasion: '[The work] was written in memory of Debussy ... I had no idea Stravinsky disliked Debussy as much as this. If my own memories of a friend were as painful as Stravinsky's of Debussy seem to be, I would try to forget him.' Newman's opinion of the Russian had improved by 1953, and he was able to say of *The Rake's Progress*, 'Stravinsky is as clever as 50 cats.' The brilliant stage work *Les Noces* was given its London premiere in 1926, with Francis Poulenc among the pianists. *The Musical Times* was consistent in its opinion: 'The music flouts western civilization ... it is a first class curiosity, one of the documents of our hapless age.'

This marks the beginning of the composer's third great period. Interestingly, Stravinsky began fully to explore this kind of music only when its chief proponent, Schoenberg, had died. Although the two men lived only a short distance away from each other in Los Angeles, they never met, exisitng in their own entirely separate musical and social circles. The ballet *Agon* and the religious vocal works *Canticum Sacrum* (1955) and *Threni* combine rigorous methods with Stravinsky's familiar creative generosity. Later music was increasingly sparse, however. His *Requiem Canticles* of 1966 was performed at his funeral in Venice, a city which he regarded as his spiritual home.

Works include STAGE: *The Firebird* (ballet, 1910), *Petrushka* (ballet, 1911), *The Rite of Spring* (ballet, 1913), *The Nightingale* (opera after Andersen, 1914), *Renard* (*The Fox*, burlesque, chamber opera; composed 1916, fp 1922), *The Soldier's Tale* (dance scene, 1918), *Pulcinella* (ballet with song, 1920), *Mavra* (opera buffa, 1922), *Les Noces* (*The Wedding*, Russian choreographic scenes; composed 1914–17 and 1921–23, fp 1923), *Oedipus Rex* (opera-oratorio, 1927), *Apollon Musagète* (ballet, 1928), *The Fairy's Kiss* (ballet after Tchaikovsky, 1928), *Perséphone* (melodrama, 1934), *Jeu de Cartes/The Card Game*, ballet, (1937), *Scènes de ballet* (1944), *Orpheus* (ballet, 1948), *The Rake's Progress* (opera, 1951), *Agon* (ballet, 1957), *The Flood* (musical play, 1962).

CHORAL: *The King of the Stars* (cantata, 1912), *Symphony of Psalms* (1930), *Babel* (cantata, 1944), *Mass*, with double wind quintet (1944–48), *Cantata* (1952), *Canticum Sacrum* (1955), *Threni* (1958), *A Sermon, A Narrative and A Prayer* (cantata, 1961), *Anthem, The Dove Descending* (text by T S Eliot, 1962), *Requiem Canticles* (1966).

ORCHESTRAL: Symphony in E♭ (1907), *Scherzo fantastique* (1908), *Fireworks* (1908), Suite from *The Firebird* (1911; revised 1919 and 1945), *Rag-time* for 11 instruments (1918), *Symphonies of Wind Instruments* (1920), *The Song of the Nightingale*, symphonic poem from *The Nightingale* (1917; staged 1920), Suite from *Pulcinella* (1922), Concerto for piano and wind (1924), *Capriccio* for piano and orchestra (1929), Violin concerto in D (1931), Divertimento from *The Fairy's Kiss* (1934), Concerto, *Dumbarton Oaks* (1938), *Symphony in C* (1940), *Danses concertantes* (1942), *Ode, elegiacal chant* (1943), *Symphony in three movements* (1945), *Ebony concerto* for clarinet and jazz band (1945), Concerto in D for strings (1946), *Movements* for piano and orchestra (1959), *Variations* (1964).

CHAMBER AND INSTRUMENTAL: three Pieces for string quartet (1914), Suite from *The Soldier's Tale* (1918), Concertino for string quartet (1920), Octet (1923), Suite from *Pulcinella* for violin and piano (1925); *Suite Italienne* for cello and piano (1934), *Duo Concertant* for violin and piano (1932), Septet (1952). For piano: two sonatas (1904 and 1924), three Movements from *Petrushka* (1921), Serenade in A (1925), Concerto for two pianos (1935), Sonata for two pianos (1944).

SOLO VOCAL including *Faun and Shepherdess* for mezzo and orchestra (1906), *Two Poems of Paul Verlaine* (1910), *Two Poems of Balmont* (1911), *Three Japanese Lyrics* for soprano and ensemble (1913), *Pribaoutki* for male voice and ensemble (1914), *Four Russian Songs* (1919), *Three Songs from Shakespeare* for mezzo, flute, clarinet and viola (1953), *In memoriam Dylan Thomas* for tenor, string quartet and four trombones (1954), *Abraham and Isaac*, sacred ballad for baritone and chamber orchestra (1963), *Elegy for J F K* for baritone and three clarinets (1964).

Stravinsky, Soulima (b Lausanne, 23 Sept 1910; d Sarasota, FL, 28 Nov 1994), Russian pianist and composer, son of Igor ◊Stravinsky. Studied at the Paris Conservatoire with Boulanger and Cortot before making his debut at Barcelona 1933, in his father's *Capriccio*; premiered the Concerto for two pianos in Paris, 1935. Remained in France with his father but continued to perform his music and was also admired in Debussy's *Préludes*. His compositions include three string quartets and a piano trio.

Street Scene opera in two acts by Kurt Weill (libretto by Elmer Rice), produced Philadelphia, Shubert Theatre, 16 Dec 1946. Also produced New York 1947 and London 1987 (Camden Festival). Slice of New York tenement life, as Anne Maurrant is murdered by her jealous husband Frank, and Sam Kaplan fails to make out with Anne's daughter Rose.

Strehler, Giorgio (b Barcola, Trieste, 14 Aug 1921), Italian stage director. Studied in Milan and founded Piccolo Teatro there, 1947. Debut as opera producer with *La Traviata*, 1947; later staged the Italian fps of *Lulu, The Love for Three Oranges* and Weill's *Mahagonny*. An *Entführung* shown in silhouettes was staged at Salzburg in 1965 and a memorably beautiful *Simon Boccanegra* was seen at La Scala 1971 and at CG 1976. Other Scala stagings include *Macbeth* (1975), and *Don Giovanni* (1988). *Le nozze di Figaro* was given at Versailles in 1973 and *Die Zauberflöte* at Salzburg, 1974.

Streich, Rita (b Barnaul, Siberia, 18 Dec 1920; d Munich, 20 Mar 1987), German soprano. Studied first in Augsburg and then with Maria Ivogün and Erna Berger in Berlin and later with Domgraf-

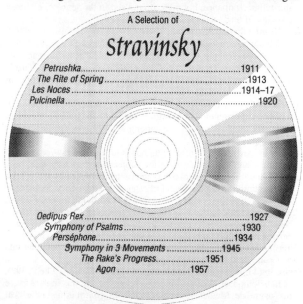

A Selection of

Stravinsky

Petrushka	1911
The Rite of Spring	1913
Les Noces	1914–17
Pulcinella	1920
Oedipus Rex	1927
Symphony of Psalms	1930
Perséphone	1934
Symphony in 3 Movements	1945
The Rake's Progress	1951
Agon	1957

Fassbänder, making her debut in 1943. From 1946 to 1950 she sang at the Berlin Staatsoper and from 1950 at the Berlin Städtische Oper. In 1953 she joined the Vienna Staatsoper and made her debut in London in 1954. US debut San Francisco, 1957, as Sophie. Glyndebourne 1958, Zerbinetta. She was best known for her singing of Mozart and R Strauss and coloratura roles, e.g. Queen of Night, Constanze and Olympia.

Streicher German plur. = 'strings', as in English, for string instruments.

Streicher German family of piano makers:

1. Johann Andreas Streicher (b Stuttgart, 13 Dec 1761; d Vienna, 25 May 1833), music teacher in Vienna and founder there of a piano manufacture after 1794, when he married

2. Maria Anna (Nanette) Streicher (born Stein) (b Augsburg, 2 Jan 1769; d Vienna, 16 Jan 1833). ◊Stein, family, 2.

3. Johann Baptist Streicher (b Vienna, 3 Jan 1796; d Vienna, 28 Mar 1871), son of 2. He succeeded his parents in business, and from him it descended to his son Emil.

Streicher, Theodor (b Vienna, 7 Jun 1874; d Wetzelsdorf near Graz, 28 May 1940), Austrian composer, great-grandson of J A and M A Streicher. Studied in Vienna, Dresden and Bayreuth.

Works include *Mignons Exequien* (after Goethe's *Wilhelm Meister*) for chorus, children's chorus and orchestra (1907), *Die Schlacht bei Murten* for chorus and orchestra; *Kleiner Vogel Kolibri* for chamber orchestra; *Um Inez weinten* for soprano and orchestra; *Die Monologe des Faust* (after Goethe) for string sextet (1912); many songs, including 36 settings from *Des Knaben Wunderhorn*.

Streichinstrumente German = string instruments.

Streichzither German lit. = 'stroke-zither'; a variety of ◊zither played with a violin bow instead of being plucked with the fingers or with a plectrum.

Streit, Kurt (b Itazuke, 1959), Japanese-born American tenor. Studied at the University of New Mexico and appeared in opera at Santa Fe and Dallas before singing with the Hamburg Opera, in works by Rossini, Donizetti and Mozart. Sang at Aix and Salzburg Festival 1989 and Tamino at Glyndebourne 1990, returning as Ferrando 1992. CG debut 1992, as Ferrando, and has sung in concert with the St Petersburg PO, the Orchestre National de France and the LSO.

Streit zwischen Phöbus und Pan, Der, *The Dispute between Phoebus and Pan*, secular cantata by Bach, written in 1731 and satirizing Johann Adolf Scheibe, editor of *Der critische Musikus*, in the part of Midas.

strepitoso Italian = 'noisy'; a direction suggesting a forceful and spirited performance, but more often used in the sense of a climax growing in force and speed.

Strepponi, Giuseppina (b Lodi, 8 Sept 1815; d Busseto, 14 Nov 1897), Italian soprano, daughter of the composer Feliciano Strepponi (1797–1832). Studied at the Milan Conservatory and made her first appearance in 1835, at Trieste in Rossini's *Mathilde di Shabran*. Verdi's second wife, previously his mistress; she created Abigaille in *Nabucco* (Milan 1842).

stretta Italian = lit. 'pressure, tightening, squeezing'; a passage, usually at the end of a composition, especially an operatic finale, in which the tempo is accelerated either gradually or by sections and so makes a climax.

stretto Italian = lit. 'narrow, tightened, squeezed'; a device in fugal writing whereby the entries of the subject are drawn more closely together in time. Instead of following each other voice by voice, each waiting until the last has been fully stated, in stretto they are made to overlap, the second coming in before the end of the first, and so on.

stretto maestrale Italian = lit. 'masterly stretto'; a stretto in which the fugal subject not only appears in close, overlapping entries, but is carried through from beginning to end at each entry.

strict counterpoint the traditional name for counterpoint written according to the rules of the species.

Striggio (1), Alessandro (b Mantua, *c* 1535; d Mantua, 29 Feb 1592), Italian composer, organist, lutenist and violist. He was in the service of Cosimo de' Medici at Florence, 1560–74, contributing to the local

intermedi, and subsequently visited several European courts. He returned to Mantua, to the court of Duke Guglielmo Gonzaga.

Works include Masses, motet in 40 parts for voices and instruments; madrigal comedy *Il cicalamento delle donne al bucato* (1567); intermezzi for performance between the acts of plays; madrigals; various works for voices and instruments in many parts.

Striggio (2), Alessandro (b Mantua, 1573; d Venice, 6 Jun 1630), Italian librettist, son of Alessandro ◊Striggio (1). He was secretary to the Duke of Mantua and string player at court until 1628. Author of the text of Monteverdi's *Orfeo* and *Tirsi e Clori*.

Strinasacchi, Regina (b Ostiglia near Mantua, 1764; d Dresden, 1839), Italian violinist and guitar player. Studied at the Conservatorio della Pietà in Venice, toured Italy 1780–83, and in 1784 visited Vienna, where Mozart wrote for her the violin sonata in B♭ major, K454. She married the cellist J C Schlick in 1785.

string quartet a chamber combination consisting of two violins, viola and cello. The form was devised early in the 18th c. and developed by Haydn and Mozart. Some of the most profound music of Beethoven and Schubert employs the medium; later 19th-c. composers wrote important quartets, e.g. Mendelssohn, Schumann, Brahms, Smetana and Dvořák. In the 20th c. the most highly regarded string quartets are by Bartók (6), Schoenberg (4) and Janáček (2). Other composers include Shostakovich (15), Britten (4) and Elliott Carter (5).

Music is far closer to mathematics than to literature – not perhaps to mathematics itself, but certainly to something like mathematical thinking and mathematical relationships.

Igor Stravinsky, *Conversations*, 1958

string quintet Boccherini wrote many works for two violins, viola and two cellos. The same form was adopted by Schubert for the greatest of his chamber works (1828). Two violins, two violas and cello were favoured by Mozart – in four of his finest instrumental pieces – and by Beethoven, Brahms and Nielsen. Dvořák's string quintet op. 77 uses a double bass instead of second viola.

strings the cords, usually of gut (violin family, harps, etc.) or wire (lute, violin and guitar families, pianos, etc.), by means of which the notes are produced on such instruments. The term strings is also used to designate string instruments collectively, especially those of the violin family in the orchestra.

string sextet the combination of two violins, two violas and two cellos, e.g. Dvořák's op. 48, Brahms's op. 18 and op. 36 and Schoenberg's *Verklärte Nacht/Transfigured Night*, 1899). The prologue to Strauss's *Capriccio* (1940–41) is a string sextet.

string trio after humble beginnings with Haydn and Boccherini the combination of violin, viola and cello is found in one of Mozart's finest works, the Divertimento K563. Beethoven emulated Mozart's example in his trio op. 3 and further developed the form's potential in his set of three trios op. 9. After comparative neglect during the Romantic period, notable trios of the 20th c. including those of Roussel, Hindemith, Dohnányi and Webern. Schoenberg's string trio of 1945 depicts the composer's feelings as he lay ill after an operation.

stromentato Italian = 'instrumented, orchestrated, scored'; the word is associated mainly with recitative (*recitativo stromentato*), where it implies a more or less independent orchestral accompaniment.

Strong, G(eorge) Templeton (b New York, 26 May 1856; d Geneva, 27 Jun 1948), American composer. Studied at the Leipzig Conservatory, became a member of the Liszt circle, was in close touch with MacDowell while living at Wiesbaden 1886–89, and after teaching at Boston in 1891–92 settled in Switzerland on the Lake of Geneva, living first at Vevey and later in Geneva.

Works include *Knights and Dryads* for solo voices, chorus and orchestra; two cantatas for solo voices, male chorus and orchestra; three symphonies: *Sintram* (after Fouqué, 1888), *In the Mountains* (1886) and *By the Sea*, symphonic poem *Undine* (after Fouqué); two

American Sketches for violin and orchestra; trio for two violins and viola *A Village Music-Director* and other chamber music.

Strong, Susan (b Brooklyn, 3 Aug 1870; d London, 11 Mar 1946), American soprano. Studied RCM; debut London 1895, with Hedmont co., as Sieglinde. CG 1895–1902, as Brünnhilde, Donna Anna and Venus. Mapelson co. in NY 1896, as Elsa and Marguerite. Vienna Hofoper 1901, under Mahler.

strophic bass an instrumental bass part used without change throughout a series of verses of a song or chorus the upper parts of which vary at each occurrence; or a similar device in instrumental music.

strophic song the simplest form of song, structurally considered, in which each verse of a poem is set to the same music.

Strozzi, Barbara (b Venice, 6 Aug 1619; d (?) Venice, *c* 1664), Italian singer and composer. Adopted daughter of the poet Giulio Strozzi; studied with Cavalli, singing in several of his operas. Also sang at Accademic degli Unisoni, established by Giulio Strozzi in 1637. Composed madrigals, cantatas, sacred songs with continuo, duets, ariettas, etc.

Strozzi, Gregorio (b San Severino, *c* 1615; d Naples, *c* 1690), Italian priest, organist and composer. Studied with Sabino in Naples, and succeeded him as organist of the Church of the Madonna there.

Works include responsories, Lamentations, psalms, motets, etc.; *Capricci da sonare Cembali et Organi.*

Strungk (or *Strunck*), Delphin (b *c* 1601; d Brunswick, buried 12 Oct 1694), German organist and composer. He was, after 1630, successively organist at Wolfenbüttel, Celle and Brunswick.

Works include music for the Duke of Brunswick in five vocal and eight instrumental parts; various vocal works with instruments; chorale preludes and other works for organ.

Strungk, Nikolaus Adam (b Brunswick, bap. 15 Nov 1640; d Dresden, 23 Sept 1700), German composer, violinist and organist, son of Delphin ◊Strungk. Pupil of his father, for whom he deputized at the organ at Brunswick from the age of 12. While at Helmstedt University he learnt the violin at Lübeck during vacations. In 1660 he joined the court orchestra at Wolfenbüttel, then at Celle, and in 1665 went to the court of Hanover. After a period at Hamburg from 1678, two visits to Vienna and one to Italy, he returned to Hanover, 1682–86, but in 1688 he went to Dresden as chamber organist and second *Kapellmeister* to the Saxon court in succession to Ritter, and succeeded Bernhard as first *Kapellmeister* in 1692. In 1693 he opened an opera-house at Leipzig, where he produced his later stage works and where his daughters Philippine and Elisabeth sang.

Works include operas *Der glückseligsteigende Sejanus, Der unglücklichfallende Sejanus* (1678), *Esther, Doris* (1680), *Semiramis, Nero, Agrippina* (1699) and others, completion of Pallavicini's *L'Antiope*; oratorio *Die Auferstehung Jesu* (1688); *ricercare* on the death of his mother; sonatas and chaconnes for violin or viola da gamba; sonatas for two violins and viola and for six strings; airs and dances for recorders.

Strunk (William) Oliver (b Ithaca, NY, 22 Mar 1901; d Grottaferrata, near Rome, 24 Feb 1980), American musicologist. He studied at Cornell University and in Berlin; worked at the Library of Congress from 1928 and taught at Princeton 1937–66. His *Source Readings in Music History* (1950) remains a classic. He was among the most influential musicological teachers of his generation, but his most important pubs. concerned Byzantine chant.

Strunz, Jacob (b Pappenheim, 1783; d Munich, 23 May 1852), German composer. Pupil of Winter at Munich. He travelled all over Europe in 1798–1845 and also visited Egypt; then settled at Munich for the rest of his life. He was a friend of Meyerbeer, Berlioz and Balzac, who dedicated his story *Massimilla Doni* to him.

Works include operas *Le Maître de chapelle* and *Les Courses de Newmarket*; several ballets; incidental music (the first) for Hugo's *Ruy Blas*; three string quartets; songs.

Stuck, Jean Baptiste (usually called Batistin) (b Florence, *c* 1680; d Paris, 8 Dec 1755), French cellist and composer of German origin. He went to France at an early age and was the first cellist in the Paris Opéra orchestra, also court musician to the Duke of Orleans.

Works include operas *Rodrigo in Algieri* (with Albinoni), *Méléagre* (1709), *Mantho la fée* (1711) and *Polidore* (1720); many court ballets; cantatas; airs.

Stucken, Frank (Valentin) van der (b Fredericksburg, TX, 15 Oct 1858; d Hamburg, 16 Aug 1929), American conductor and composer. Studied in Europe with Benoît, Reinecke, Grieg and others. In 1884–95 he conducted a male-voice choir in NY, where he also conducted orchestral concerts. In 1895–1903 he was director of the Cincinnati College of Music and from the same year to 1907 he conducted the Symphony Orchestra there, giving the US fp of Mahler's 5th symphony on 24 Mar 1905; this was only the second performance of a Mahler symphony anywhere in America. After 1908 he lived much in Europe.

Works include opera *Vlasda*; incidental music to Shakespeare's *Tempest*; choral works.

Stuckenschmidt, Hans Heinz (b Strasbourg, 1 Nov 1901; d Berlin, 15 Aug 1988), German musicologist. Studied piano, violin and composition in Berlin; and also analysis with Schoenberg. He held many posts as music critic and from 1948 taught at the Technical University in Berlin; Professor Emeritus 1967. Especially well known as a writer on 20th-c. music, including Schoenberg and the Viennese School; pub. biographies of Schoenberg in 1951 and 1978.

Stückgold, Grethe (b London, 6 Jul 1895; d Falls Village, CT, 15 Sept 1977), German soprano. After singing in concert made her stage debut, Nuremberg 1917. Berlin from 1922; sang in the 1929 fp of Hindemith's *Neues vom Tage*, under Klemperer, at the Kroll Opera. NY Met. 1927–40; debut as Eva. Also sang in San Francisco, Philadelphia and Chicago.

Studer, Cheryl (b Midland, MI, 24 Oct 1955), American soprano. Studied with Hans Hotter in Vienna and appeared at the Staatsoper in Munich from 1980, as Daphne, Sieglinde, the Empress and Euryanthe. US debut Chicago 1984, as Micaela; NY Met. from 1990, as Mozart's Donna Anna and Electra. Bayreuth Festival 1984 and 1985 as Eva and Elisabeth. Sang Chrysothemis at Salzburg in 1988, returning as the Empress in *Die Frau ohne Schatten*, 1992. A versatile artist, she has also given strongly characterized performances of Rossini's Mathilde (at La Scala, 1988) and Aida (CG, 1994).

Studer *The soprano Cheryl Studer. She has concentrated on roles by Mozart, Wagner, Strauss and Verdi – an extraordinary endeavour considering the divergent demands of each composer. Her beautiful and flexible voice is also well-displayed in lighter roles.*

study an instrumental piece, usually for a single instrument, written mainly for the purpose of technical exercise and display, but not necessarily devoid of expression and high artistic quality. The French word *étude* is more often used for it.

stump a string instrument of the cittern type invented *c* 1600 by Daniel Farrant. The MS of the only surviving piece written for it, 'To the Stump by F P', is in Christ Church, Oxford (MUS.532). From it have been inferred various details such as length of strings, no. of courses and compass.

Stumpf, Carl (b Wiesentheid, 21 Apr 1848; d Berlin, 25 Dec 1936), German music scientist and psychologist. Studied at Göttingen University and held professorships at Würzburg, Prague, Halle, Munich and, from 1893, in Berlin. He collaborated with Hornbostel in editing the *Beiträge zur Akustik und Musikwissenschaft* and wrote much on the psychological aspects of acoustical phenomena.

Stuntz, Joseph (Hartmann) (b Arlesheim near Basel, ? 23 Jul 1793; d Munich, 18 Jun 1859), Swiss composer and conductor. Studied with Winter at Munich and Salieri in Vienna. He spent three years in Italy and in 1825 succeeded Winter as first conductor of the Royal Opera at Munich.

Works include operas *La rappresaglia* (1820), *Costantino, Argene e Dalmiro, Elvira e Lucindo, Heinrich IV zu Givry* (after Voltaire's *Charlot*, 1820) and *Maria Rosa*; ballets; church music; cantatas and part-songs, symphony in D minor and concert overtures; songs.

Sturgeon, Nicholas (b *c* 1390; d London, 31 May 1454), English composer. He was a scholar of Winchester College, 1399, aged 8–12. He may have visited France with Henry V in 1416. In 1442, after serving as a clerk of the Chapel Royal, he became a canon of Windsor and precentor of St Paul's Cathedral. He contributed to the Old Hall MS during the second phase of its existence, when it was in use at the Chapel Royal. Five known works by him survive.

Sturm, Der, *The Tempest*, operas based on Shakespeare's play with this title by Peter Winter (Munich, 1798) and Frank Martin (Vienna, 17 Jun 1956): work for chorus and orchestra by Haydn (not based on Shakespeare) composed 1798 and performed at his concerts in London.

Also commonly used as title to Beethoven's piano sonata Op. 31 no. 2 in D minor.

Sturton, Edmund, English 15th–16th-c. composer. He was (?) clerk and instructor of the choristers at Magdalen College, Oxford, 1509–10. He wrote an *Ave Maria* and *Gaude virgo mater*, the latter in the Eton Choirbook.

Sturzenegger, Richard (b Zurich, 18 Dec 1905; d Bern, 24 Oct 1976), Swiss composer and cellist. He studied at the Zurich Conservatory and with Alexanian, Casals and Nadia Boulanger in Paris. Later he joined the Dresden Opera orchestra and studied further with Feuermann for cello and Toch for composition. He settled as cello professor in Bern.

Works include cantatas and other choral works; theatre music; four cello concertos (1933–72); chamber music.

St Victor, Adam of (d 1177 or 1192), French monk. In *c* 1130 he joined the abbey of St Victor near Paris. He wrote sequences composed in pairs of metrically regular three-line stanzas, and was the first important exponent of this type. He apparently composed the melodies of his sequences.

subdiapente ◊diapente; from Latin and Greek 'a fifth lower'. The term is used especially for canons at the fifth.

subdiatessaron, from Latin and Greek, 'a fourth lower'.

subdominant the fourth degree of the major or minor scale. For the subdominant chord see ◊cadence.

subject a theme used as a principal feature in a composition, especially in a fugue, where it is brought in a number of times, voice by voice, or in a rondo, where it is a recurrent main theme returning after a series of episodes. In sonata form first and second subjects are the main structural features, but there they are thematic groups more often than single themes.

submediant the sixth degree of the major or minor scale, so called because it is the opposite of the mediant, i.e. it is a third below instead of above the tonic. The submediant of a major scale is the tonic of its relative minor.

Subotnick, Morton (b Los Angeles, 14 Apr 1933), American composer. Studied at Mills College with Milhaud. Director of electronic music at California Institute of Arts, LA, from 1969. His works often employ synthesizers. He is married to Joan ◊La Barbara.

Works include *Concert*, for wind quintet and electronics; *Music for 12 Elevators*; *Silver Apples of the Moon* (1967); *Before the Butterfly* for orchestra (1975); *The Double Life of Amphibians*, music drama; *Angels* for string quartet and electronics (fp 1984); *The Key to Songs* for chamber orchestra and synthesizer (1985), *In Two Worlds* saxophone concerto (1988), *And the Butterflies Began to Sing* (1988), *All my Hummingbirds have Alibis*, for flute, cello, midi piano, mallets and computer (1991; available on CD Rom); incidental music for plays by Brecht and Beckett.

subsemitonium Latin = 'under-semitone'; the old name for the leading-note, especially when used in the modes by sharpening the seventh of the scale.

subtonium Latin = 'under-[whole] tone'; the old name for the seventh degree of the Modes, except the Lydian (and later the Ionian), so called because it was a whole tone below the final, though it was often sharpened in performance according to the principle of *musica ficta*.

Sucher, Josef (b Döbör, Hungary, 23 Nov 1843; d Berlin, 4 Apr 1908), Austro-Hungarian conductor and composer. Learnt music as choirboy of the Austrian court chapel at the Löwenburg seminary in Vienna and later studied with Sechter. After various conducting appointments at Viennese theatres, including the Court Opera, he went to Leipzig as conductor of the municipal theatre in 1876; in 1878 he gave the first local *Ring* cycle. In 1877 he married the singer Rosa Hasselbeck. He was conductor of the court opera in Berlin from 1888 to 1899; gave there a complete cycle of Wagner's operas, from *Rienzi*.

Works include opera *Ilse*; Masses and cantatas, overtures for orchestra; song cycle *Ruheort*.

> *His three oratorios, his cantatas, and his admirable orchestral compositions, will live long after his lighter works have gone out of fashion.*
>
> **Emil Naumann** on Sir Arthur Sullivan, in *The History of Music*, 1886

Sucher (born *Hasselbeck*), Rosa (b Velburg, Bavaria, 23 Feb 1849; d Eschweiler near Aachen, 16 Apr 1927), German soprano, wife of Josef ◊Sucher. She made her first appearance at Trier and advanced rapidly to more important opera houses, going with her husband to Hamburg in 1879, where he became conductor of the Opera. They visited England in 1882 and at Drury Lane, under Richter, she was the first London Isolde and Eva; CG 1892 as Brünnhilde and Isolde, under Mahler. In 1886 she sang Isolde at Bayreuth; remained until 1894. NY Met. debut 1895, as Isolde.

Suchoň, Eugen (b Pezinok, 25 Sept 1908; d Bratislava, 5 Aug 1993), Slovak composer. Studied at Bratislava Conservatory 1927–31, and then in Prague with Novák 1931–33. From 1933 to 1941 he taught at the Bratislava Academy of Music and was professor at the State Conservatory 1941–47. From 1947 to 1953 he was professor at the Slovak University and from 1953 at the Pedagogic High School in Bratislava.

Works include operas *The Whirlpool* (1949) and *Svätopluk* (1960); serenades for strings, for wind quintet (1932–33); choral music; piano quartet, piano pieces.

Suggia, Guilhermina (b Oporto, 27 Jun 1888; d Oporto, 31 Jul 1950), Portuguese cellist. She played in the Oporto orchestra and a string quartet before she was 13, in 1904 was sent to Leipzig to study with Klengel, appeared there under Nikisch and lastly studied with Casals, with whom she lived 1906–12, in Spain. She lived in London for many years, but returned to Portugal some years before her death. Her portrait was painted by Augustus John in 1923.

suite a form of instrumental music consisting of a number of move-ents, originally dances, but now any pieces the composer desires, including chosen numbers from operas, ballets, etc. In the late 17th c. a tradition was established of including four regular dance movements: allemande, courante, sarabande and gigue (to give the French names as the most frequently used). These were almost invariably in the same key, probably because suites were often written for lutes, which had to be newly tuned for each key. Other dances could be added at will, such as the gavotte, minuet, bourrée, rigaudon, hornpipe, etc., and the whole could be preceded by a prelude (e.g. Purcell, Bach's English Suites, etc.). There could also be fancy pieces with a variety of titles, as in Bach's Partitas (*partita* being another name for suite) and more especially in the suites by French composers, e.g. those by Couperin. The chief features inherited from the suite by early sonata form were the binary form of the dances, which became the exposition (first half), and working-out and recapitulation (second half) of the sonata form, and the minuet, which was retained particularly in symphonies and in the 19th c. turned into the scherzo. The form was revived in the 20th c. by Schoenberg (Suite for piano op. 25, 1921, and Suite op. 29 for three clarinets and piano quintet, 1924–26).

Suitner, Otmar (b Innsbruck, 16 May 1922), Austrian conductor. Studied with Clemens Krauss. In 1960 became chief conductor of the Dresden Staatsoper and Staatskapelle. Music director Deutsche Staatsoper, Berlin, 1964; gave there the fps of Dessau's *Puntila* (1966) and *Einstein* (1974) and *Leonce und Lena* (1979). He has conducted at the San Francisco Opera from 1969. Bayreuth 1964–69, *Der fliegende Holländer*, *Tannhäuser* and the *Ring*. *Der Freischütz* at Munich, 1990.

suivez French = 'follow'; a direction used in two senses: (1) to indicate that one movement of a composition is to follow the preceding one immediately (equivalent to Italian *attacca*); (2) to indicate that accompanying parts are to follow a vocal or other solo part moving independently of the prescribed rhythm or tempo (equivalent to Italian *colla parte*).

Suk, Josef (b Křečovice, 4 Jan 1874; d Benešov near Prague, 29 May 1935), Czech composer, violinist and violist. Studied with Dvořák in Prague and in 1898 became his son-in-law. In 1892 he formed the Bohemian String quartet with Karel Hofmann, Oscar Nedbal and Otto Berger, playing second violin He began to compose early and in 1922 became professor of composition at the Prague Conservatory, of which he was director 1924–26. Much of his music was influenced by personal experiences, especially the death of his wife in 1905, e.g. the piano pieces *About Mother* written for his infant son, and by that of Dvořák, e.g. the *Asrael* symphony, which refers to those two deaths.

Works include Mass in B♭ major; incidental music for Julius Zeyer's *Radúz and Mahulena* (1898); *Epilogue* for baritone solo, women's chorus and orchestra; symphony in E major (1899) and *Asrael* (1906), symphonic poems *Prague*, *A Summer Tale* and *Maturity*, Dramatic Overture and overture to Shakespeare's *Winter's Tale* (1894), *A Tale* and *Under the Appletrees* for orchestra; serenade (1892) and meditation on a chorale for string orchestra; fantasy for violin and orchestra (1902); two string quartets (1896, 1911), piano quartet, piano trio, elegy for violin and cello with string quartet, harmonium and harp; *Ballade and Serenade* for cello and piano; sets of piano pieces; part songs.

Suk, Joseph (b Prague, 8 Aug 1929), Czech violinist. Grandson of Josef ◊Suk and great-grandson of Dvořák. Studied at Prague Conservatory with J Kocian, graduating in 1950. Founded Suk Trio 1952. US debut 1964, with Cleveland Orchestra; British debut at the 1964 Promenade concerts. Founded the Suk Chamber Orchestra 1974; played at the 1991 Bath Festival. Named National Artist of Czechoslovakia, 1977.

Suk, Váša (b Kladno, 1 Nov 1861; d Moscow, 12 Jan 1933), Czech violinist, conductor and composer. Studied at the Prague Conservatory and became violinist and conductor successively at Warsaw, Kiev and Moscow.

Works include opera *The Forest King*; symphonic poem *Jan Hus*; serenade for string orchestra, etc.

Sullivan, Arthur (Seymour) (b London, 13 May 1842; d London, 22 Nov 1900), English composer. Son of a bandmaster and professor at

Sullivan *The composer Arthur Sullivan (1842–1900). After teaming up with W S Gilbert he was highly successful in a long stream of operettas. His music is peculiarly British in its character, humour and reserve, and it adapts well to the varying thematic demands of the libretti.*

the Royal Military School of Music, entered the Chapel Royal in 1854 and was taught by Helmore. In 1856 he gained the Mendelssohn scholarship at the RAM, where he studied under Sterndale Bennett, Goss and O'Leary. The scholarship entitled him to a course of study at the Leipzig Conservatory, where he studied composition, conducting and piano, returning in 1861 to London, where he became organist at St Michael's Church, Chester Square. He first made his mark as a composer with incidental music to Shakespeare's *Tempest* when it was given at the Crystal Palace under August Manns in 1862; the Irish Symphony followed in 1864. His first collaboration with W S Gilbert, the operetta *Thespis*, was produced in London 26 Dec 1871. It was followed by *Trial by Jury* in 1875. After that he and Gilbert repeated their joint triumphs until 1889, when they reached their climax in *The Gondoliers*.

He was knighted in 1883 by Queen Victoria who suggested he wrote a grand opera. The outcome was *Ivanhoe* (1891) which ran for 161 performances but had little lasting success. Sullivan taught and conducted intermittently; he had been appointed professor of composition at the RAM in 1866. The following year he and Grove went to Vienna and discovered a pile of forgotten MSS of Schubert's works including the 'Great' C major symphony.

Works include opera *Ivanhoe*; operettas (with Gilbert as librettist) *Thespis, or The Gods Grown Old* (1871), *Trial by Jury* (1875), *The Sorcerer* (1871), *HMS Pinafore* (1878), *The Pirates of Penzance* (1879), *Patience* (1881), *Iolanthe* (1882), *Princess Ida* (1883), *The Mikado* (1885), *Ruddigore* (1886), *The Yeomen of the Guard* (1888), *The Gondoliers* (1886), *Utopia Limited* (1893), *The Grand Duke* (1896); other operettas: *The Sapphire Necklace, Cox and Box* (1867), *The Contrabandista* (1867), *The Zoo* (1875), *Haddon Hall, The Chieftain* (adapted from *The Contrabandista*, 1894), *The Beauty Stone* (1898), *The Rose of Persia, The Emerald Isle* (unfinished, completed by German, 1901); ballets *L'Île enchantée* and *Victoria and Merrie England*; incidental music to Shakespeare's *Tempest, Merchant of Venice, Merry Wives of Windsor, Henry VIII* and *Macbeth*, Tennyson's *The Foresters* and Comyns Carr's *King Arthur*.

CHORAL: *Kenilworth* (after Scott), *The Prodigal Son*, *On Shore and*

Sea, The Light of the World (1873), *The Martyr of Antioch, The Golden Legend* (1886; revived in performance conducted by Charles Mackerras, Leeds, 15 Mar 1986).

ORCHESTRAL: symphony in E major; overtures *In Memoriam, Di ballo*, to Shakespeare's *Timon of Athens* and *Marmion* (after Scott); *Procession March, Princess of Wales March, Imperial March*; cello concerto (1866; score was destroyed but reconstructed by Charles Mackerras and performed 1985).

CHAMBER: romance for string quartet; various piano pieces; song cycle *The Window* (Tennyson), a number of songs including 'Orpheus with his lute', *The Lost Chord* and Kipling's *The Absent-minded Beggar*.

sul ponticello Italian = 'on the bridge'; a direction in music for bowed string instruments to play a passage very near (not actually on) the bridge to produce a peculiar nasal and rustling sound.

sul tasto, Italian, a direction indicating that a passage of string music is to be played with the bow over the finger-board.

Sulzer, Salomon (b Hohenems, Vorarlberg, 30 Mar 1804; d Vienna, 17 Jan 1890), Austrian baritone, Jewish cantor and editor. He was placed in charge of the music at the new Vienna synagogue in 1825 and studied with Seyfried. He edited a collection of Jewish hymns and commissioned various composers to contribute to it. Schubert's setting of Psalm 92 in Moses Mendelssohn's translation for baritone and male chorus originated in this way. In 1844–47 Sulzer was professor of singing at the Vienna Conservatory.

Sumer is icumen in, *Summer has come*, an English song in parts, dating from *c* 1270 and known as the Reading Rota (round). It is a canon for four voices and there are two additional bass voices adding a pes or ground-bass, also in canon. In the MS the tune is also provided with Latin words, beginning *Perspice, Christicola*, but the accompanying voices (or pes) merely have 'Sing cuccu nu' in both versions, though the music they sing is actually part of an Easter antiphon.

Summers, Jonathan (b Melbourne, 2 Oct 1946), Australian baritone. Studied with Otakar Kraus in London (1974–80) and made debut with Kent Opera in 1975, as Rigoletto; Falstaff with GTO, 1976. CG from 1976, as Papageno, Malatesta, Balstrode, Mozart's Figaro and Ford in *Falstaff*. With Scottish Opera has sung Mozart's Count and Don Giovanni; Nabucco and Onegin with Opera North. Sang Germont with Australian Opera in 1981 and made NY Met. debut 1988, as Marcello; Chicago 1990, as Enrico in *Lucia*. Season 1992 as Verdi's Rodrigo and Don Carlo (*Forza*) for ENO. Also in demand at La Scala, the Paris Opéra and in Florence and Geneva.

Sundine, Stephanie (b Illinois, 1954), American soprano. Studied in New York and sang at the City Opera 1981–84, as Santuzza, Ariadne and Margherita. Sang the title roles in the US fps of Prokofiev's *Maddalena* (St Louis 1982) and *Judith* by Matthus (Santa Fe, 1990). She is best known as Strauss's Salome, which she sang on her CG and NY Met. debuts (1988, 1990). Sang Isolde at Nantes in 1989 and Fusako in the premiere production of Henze's *Das verratene Meer* (Berlin, 1990). Also sings Tosca, Gioconda and Emilia Marty.

Sunless song cycle by Mussorgsky (words by A A Golenishchev-Kutuzov), composed 1874: 1. *Between four walls*; 2. *Thou didst not know me in the crowd*; 3. *The idle, noisy day is ended*; 4. *Boredom*; 5. *Elegy*; 6. *On the River*.

Sunnegardh, Thomas (b Stockholm, 11 Jul 1949), Swedish tenor. Studied at the Vadstena Academy and appeared in operetta with the Swedish National Touring Opera. Royal Opera Stockholm from 1982, as Ferrando, Albert Herring, Tamino and Taverner. He is widely admired as Lohengrin, which he has sung at Moscow, Stuttgart and Barcelona (1992) and has also sung Wagner's Walther, Parsifal and Erik (CG debut 1991, returning 1992 as Florestan). Has appeared further at the Deutsche Oper Berlin and in Tokyo, Munich and Brussels. He created the title role in Norgard's *Siddharta*, Stockholm, 1983.

'Sun' Quartets the nickname of the six string quartets op. 20 by Haydn, composed 1772.

Suor Angelica (Puccini.) ◊Trittico.

supertonic the second degree of the major or minor scale, so called because it stands above the tonic.

Supervia, Conchita (b Barcelona, 9 Dec 1899; d London, 30 Mar 1936), Spanish mezzo. She made her debut in Buenos Aires (1910) and the following year sang Octavian in Rome. She first appeared in London in the 1920s as a concert singer, excelling in Spanish songs as well as in arias from the parts written by Rossini for his wife, Isabella Colbran; later she appeared in some of these parts, as well as in *Carmen*, at Covent Garden, 1934–35. Other roles included Isabella, Rosina and Cenerentola. She became English by marriage.

Suppé, Franz von (actually Francesco Ezechiele Ermenegildo Suppe Demelli) (b Spalato [Split], 18 Apr 1819; d Vienna, 21 May 1895), Austrian composer and conductor of Belgian descent. He showed a talent for composition early, producing a Mass and a comic opera *Der Apfel* at Zara in 1834; but he was sent to Padua University by his father to study medicine. On his father's death, however, he settled in Vienna with his mother, studied with Seyfried and conducted at various Viennese and provincial theatres, including the Josephstadt, Wieden and Leopoldstadt Theatres in Vienna from 1841 to his death. *Das Pensionat* (1860) was the first successful Viennese operetta in response to the French model. His later works are largely known today outside German-speaking countries through their tuneful overtures.

Works include operettas *Das Mädchen vom Lande* (1847), *Das Pensionat* (1860), *Paragraph 3, Zehn Mädchen und kein Mann* (1862), *Pique Dame/Die Kartenschlägerin*, (1862) *Flotte Bursche* (with an overture on students' songs, 1863), *Die schöne Galatee* (1865), *Leichte Kavallerie* (*Light Cavalry* 1866), *Fatinitza, Boccaccio* (1879), *Donna Juanita* (1880), *Die Afrikareise* and several others; farces; ballets; incidental music to Elmar's *Dichter und Bauer* (*Poet and Peasant*, 1846), Shakespeare's *Midsummer Night's Dream*, Schiller's *Wallensteins Lager* and others (more than 200 stage works); Mass, Requiem (*L'estremo giudizia*, 1855; first British performance 1984, BBC).

Surinach, Carlos (b Barcelona, 4 Mar 1915), Spanish-born American composer. After study in Germany conducted Barcelona PO from 1944. Settled in USA 1951, citizen 1959.

Works include ballets *Monte Carlo* (1945) and David and Bathsheba (1960); three symphonies (1945–57), *Sinfonietta flamenca* (1954), *Melorhythmic Dramas* for orchestra (1966); chamber music, songs.

'Surprise' Symphony Haydn's symphony no. 94 in G major, composed for London in 1791, so called after the sudden loud interruption after 16 quiet bars at the beginning of the slow movement. Known in Germany as 'Symphonie mit dem Paukenschlag/Symphony with the Drum-beat'.

Survivor from Warsaw, A work by Schoenberg for narrator, men's chorus and orchestra, op. 46 (text by composer), fp Albuquerque, 4 Nov 1948.

Surzyński, Józef (b Szrem near Poznań, 15 Mar 1851; d Kościan, 5 Mar 1919), Polish priest and composer. Studied at Regensburg and Leipzig, later taking holy orders in Rome. In 1882 he became director of the cathedral choir at Poznań and in 1894 provost at Kościan. He edited the *Monumenta Musices Sacrae in Polonia* and *Musica Ecclesiastica*.

Works include numerous Masses, hymns and other church music, *Polish Songs of the Catholic Church*.

Susa, Conrad (b Springfield, PA, 26 Apr 1935), American composer. He studied at Juilliard and from 1988 has taught at the San Francisco Conservatory of Music. Dramaturg of the Eugene O'Neill Center in Conneticut from 1986. Has composed a symphony, *A Sonnet Voyage* (1963), and choral works including *Dawn Greeting* (1986) and *Earth Song* (1988) but is best known for his operas: *Transformations* (Minnesota, 1973) is a re-telling of Grimm's *Fairy Tales* and has been widely performed. *Black River: A Wisconsin Idyll* (1975) tells of rural angst in 19th-c. America, and *The Love of Don Perlimplin* (1984) draws on 18th-c. musical sources.

Susanna oratorio by Handel (libretto anon.), performed London, CG, 10 Feb 1749.

Susanna's Secret (Wolf-Ferrari.) ◊Segreto di Susanna.

Susato, Tielman (b Cologne, *c* 1500; d ? Antwerp, between 1561 and 1564), Flemish composer, publisher and editor. He worked in Antwerp from 1529 and was the outstanding Dutch music pub. of his time; established his business 1543, and in 1547 built his own premises 'At the Sign of the Crumhorn'. His 11 *Musyck Boexken* ('little music books', 1551) contained Dutch songs, dance music and the *Souter Liedekens* of Clemens non Papa and Gerhard Mes. He also published vols. of Masses, motets and *chansons* by the leading composers of his day. Many of these include works by himself.

suspension, English, the sustaining of a note which forms part of a consonant chord so that it creates a dissonance with one or more of the notes of the next chord: the dissonant note then descends ('resolves' is the technical term) to the next note below so as to turn the dissonance into a consonance.

In this example the top voice (note C) is suspended before resolution on note B.

In normal 16th-c. practice the suspended note is first heard on a weak beat, the dissonance occurs on a strong beat, and the resolution follows on a weak beat: this practice was largely followed by later composers, who extended the idea by resolving the dissonant note upwards (also known as retardation) as well as downwards. Suspensions can occur simultaneously in more than one part, and the effect is the same if the note which is to create the dissonance is repeated instead of being tied over.

Susskind, Walter (b Prague, 1 May 1913; d Berkeley, CA, 25 Mar 1980), English conductor and pianist of Czech origin. Studied composition with J Suk and A Hába, conducting with Szell, making his debut at the German Opera House in Prague in 1932. From 1942 to 1945 he conducted with the Carl Rosa Opera Co. and then at SW in 1946. From 1946 to 1952 he was also conductor of the Scottish National Orchestra, and from 1954 to 1956 he conducted in Australia, becoming conductor of the Toronto SO from 1956 to 1965. In 1968 he took over the St Louis SO and conducted it until 1975, when he became principal guest conductor Cincinnati SO. In England he was heard as a piano soloist, and in 1977 gave the fp in Britain of Zemlinsky's *Lyric Symphony*.

Süssmayr, Franz (Xaver) (b Schwanenstadt, Upper Austria, 1766; d Vienna, 17 Sept 1803), Austrian composer. Educated at the monastery of Kremsmünster and pupil of Salieri and Mozart in Vienna. He assisted Mozart with *La clemenza di Tito* (probably the recitatives) and completed his unfinished Requiem. In 1792 he became conductor of the Kärntnertortheater. His completion of Mozart's Requiem has been reviled in recent years by scholars but it remains the most satisfactory solution to a remaining musical problem.

Works include operas *Moses* (1792), *L'incanto superato* (1793), *Der Spiegel von Arkadien* (1794), *Il Turco in Italia* (1794), *Idris und Zenide* (1795), *Die edle Rache, Die Freiwilligen, Der Wildfang* (after Kotzebue), *Der Marktschreier* (1799), *Soliman II* (after Favart, 1799), *Gulnare* (1800), *Phasma* and others; two ballets; Masses and other church music; cantatas *Der Retter in Gefahr* (1796), and *Der Kampf für den Frieden* (1800); clarinet concerto; serenades for flute, viola and horn and for violin, guitar and English horn; instrumental pieces.

sustaining pedal the so-called 'loud' pedal of the piano, not used to produce greater volume of tone, but to sustain any notes struck after it has been depressed by raising all the dampers from the strings, even after the fingers have left the keys, until it is released again.

Sutermeister, Heinrich (b Feuerthalen, Canton Schaffhausen, 12 Aug 1910; d Vaux-sur-Morges, 16 Mar 1995), Swiss composer. Studied philology at Paris and Basel, where he entered the Conservatory, later studying with Courvoisier, Pfitzner and others at Munich. In 1934 he settled at Bern, at first as operatic coach at the municipal theatre. In 1963 appointed professor of composition at the Hochschule für Musik in Hanover. He wrote in a consistently conservative idiom.

Works include operas *Romeo und Julia* (1940) and *Die Zauberinsel* (*The Tempest*, 1942) (both based on Shakespeare), *Niobe, Raskolnikov* (on Dostoievsky's *Crime and Punishment*, 1948), *Madame Bovary* (after Flaubert, 1967), *Das Flaschenteufel* (TV, 1971), *Le roi Bérenger* (1985), radio opera *Die schwarze Spinne* (after Jeremias Gotthelf, 1936; produced 1949); ballet *Das Dorf unter dem Gletscher*; Christmas radio play *Die drei Geister* (after Dickens); incidental, film and radio music; chamber oratorio *Jorinde und Jorindel* (after Mörike); *Baroque Songs* for tenor, women's chorus and instruments, songs for chorus; *Cantata 1944* for contralto, small chorus and piano; Requiem (1952) and seven other cantatas; *Sieben Liebesbriefe* for tenor and orchestra; divertimento for string orchestra; three piano concertos (1943, 1953, 1962), two cello concertos; three string quartets, string trio and other chamber music; piano and organ pieces; songs.

Suthaus, Ludwig (b Cologne, 12 Dec 1906; d Berlin, 7 Sept 1971), German tenor. He made his debut in Aachen (Walther, 1928) and sang in Berlin 1941–65. Bayreuth 1943–57 as Loge, Siegmund and Walther. After the war he sang in North and South America as Tristan, Steva and the Emperor. At the Vienna Staatsoper, 1948–70, he was heard as Florestan, Otello and Bacchus. He was a favourite of Furtwängler and recorded Tristan and Siegmund with him. Other roles included Rienzi, Samson and Sadko.

Sutherland, Joan (b Sydney, 7 Nov 1926), Australian soprano. Studied first in Australia and then at the RCM in London with C Carey. She made her London debut at CG in 1952 as the First Lady in *Die Zauberflöte* and in 1959 obtained international acclaim in *Lucia di Lammermoor* at that opera house. She then established herself as one of the leading coloratura sopranos of the day. Her early repertory included Jenifer in the fp of Tippett's *The Midsummer Marriage* (CG 1955) and roles in operas by Poulenc, Mozart and Handel. Wider fame came in the operas of Massenet, Donizetti,

Sutherland *The soprano Joan Sutherland. Her highly flexible voice is well-suited to a variety of roles, but her greatest success was in Italian bel canto opera of the 18th and 19th centuries. She has a huge range and was one of the foremost coloratura sopranos of the century.*

Bellini and Rossini, under the guidance of her husband, the conductor Richard Bonynge (b Sydney, 1930). US debut at Dallas in 1960, as Alcina; NY Met. debut 1961, as Lucia. From 1964 re-visited her native Australia and retired after singing Marguerite de Valois in *Les Huguenots* with Australian Opera, 1990. DBE 1978; OM 1991.

Sutor, Wilhelm (b Edelstetten, Bavaria, *c* 1774; d Linden near Hanover, 7 Sept 1828), German composer and tenor. Studied singing with Valesi and others, settled at Stuttgart in 1800 and from 1818 was music director at the court of Hanover.

Works include opera *Apollos Wettgesang* and four others; incidental music to Shakespeare's *Macbeth*; oratorio and cantatas; part-songs; songs.

Sutton, John, English 15th-c. composer. He was a fellow of Magdalen College, Oxford, 1476, and of Eton, 1477–*c* 1479. He (?) obtained the Mus.B. at Cambridge, 1489. A *Salve regina* for seven voices is in the Eton Choir-book.

Švanda Dudák, *Shvanda the Bagpiper*, Opera by Weinberger (libretto by Miloš Kareš), produced Prague, Czech Theatre, 27 Apr 1927. Shvanda beguiles Queen Ice Heart with his piping, but finding him already married she orders his execution, and he has to be saved by Babinsky.

Svanholm, Set (b Västerås, 2 Sept 1904; d Saltsvoe-Duvnaes, 4 Oct 1964), Swedish tenor. Studied at Stockholm Conservatory with Forsell, making his debut in Stockholm in 1930 as a baritone. After further study he developed a tenor voice, making a second debut in 1936. In 1942 he first sang at Bayreuth and 1946–56 at the NY Met.; debut as Siegfried, last performance as Parsifal. London, CG, 1948–57, often with Flagstad. Other roles included Tristan, Radames, Otello and Siegmund. After retiring became intendant of the Stockholm Opera House until 1963. He was best known as a heroic tenor, especially in the works of Wagner.

Svenden, Birgitta (b Porjus, 20 Mar 1950), Swedish mezzo. Sang first with the Stockholm Opera, as Dorabella and Cherubino; Queen Christina in the fp of the opera by Hans Gefors (1986). Bayreuth Festival from 1983 (Erda and First Norn in James Levine's *Ring*, 1994). NY Met. and CG debuts 1988 and 1990, as Erda (London 1995 in a new production of *Siegfried*). She is also a successful concert artist, notably in Mahler's 3rd Symphony.

Svendsen, Johan (Severin) (b Christiania, 30 Sept 1840; d Copenhagen, 14 Jun 1911), Norwegian composer. Learnt music from his father, a bandmaster, and at first adopted that profession himself. But, playing several instruments, he joined the orchestra at the Christiania theatre, began extensive travels in Sweden and Germany in 1861 and studied at the Leipzig Conservatory 1863–67. After travelling in Scandinavia and Scotland in 1867, he settled in Paris in 1868. In 1870–71 he was in Germany again, mainly at Leipzig and Weimar, and in 1872–77 he taught and conducted at Christiania. After visits to Munich, Rome, London, and Paris, he became court conductor at Copenhagen, 1883–1908.

Works include incidental music to Coppée's *Le Passant* (1869), two symphonies, overture to Bjøłnson's *Sigurd Slembe*, *Carnaval à Paris*, *Carnaval des artistes norvégiens*, four Norwegian Rhapsodies, legend *Zorahayda*, overture to Shakespeare's *Romeo and Juliet*, etc. for orchestra; violin concerto (1870) and romance, cello concerto (1870); string quartet (1865), string quintet, string octet; Marriage Cantata; songs.

Svetlanov, Evgeny (b Moscow, 6 Sept 1928), Russian conductor and composer. He studied at the Moscow Conservatory and was conductor with the Bolshoi theatre 1954–65 notably in Borodin, Tchaikovsky, Rimsky-Korsakov, Bartók's *Bluebeard's Castle* and works by Soviet composers; took the Bolshoi to La Scala, Milan, in 1964. Principal conductor USSR State SO from 1965: many performances of Soviet works and tours to Europe, Japan and the USA. Principal guest conductor LSO from 1979.

Works include piano concerto (1951), *Siberian Fantasy* for orchestra (1953), Symphony (1956), chamber music.

Svoboda, Josef (b Časlav, 10 May 1920), Czech stage designer and director. He worked in Prague from 1945; influenced by Appia and Roller, he developed a style which used novel lighting techniques, including film projections and laser beams, in order to create an integrated stage picture. His designs for *Les vêpres siciliennes* were first seen in Hamburg (1969) and did the rounds of the major houses before appearing at the London Coliseum in 1984. Also on view in London, at CG, have been *Die Frau ohne Schatten* (1967), *Pelléas et Mélisande* (1969), *Nabucco* (1972) and *The Ring* (1974–76). Designed the Czech premiere of Martinů's *Ariadne* at Prague in 1987; produced and designed *La Sonnambula* at the 1992 Macerata Festival.

Swain, Freda (b Portsmouth, 31 Oct 1902; d Chinnor, Oxfordshire, 29 Jan 1985), English composer and pianist. Studied at the Tobias Matthay Piano School in London and at the RCM, composition with Stanford and piano with Arthur Alexander, to whom she was married in 1921. In 1924 she became professor at the RCM.

Works include *Pastoral Fantasy* for orchestra; piano concerto (*Airmail*), *The Harp of Aengus* (after Yeats) for violin and orchestra; string quartet *Norfolk*; violin and piano sonatas in C minor and *The River*, cello and piano sonata, duets for two violins; songs to texts by Burns, Bridges and Housman.

Swan Lake, *Lebedinoye ozero*, ballet by Tchaikovsky (choreography by Marius Petipa and L I Ivanov), produced Moscow, Bolshoi Theatre, 4 Mar 1877.

Swan of Tuonela, The symphonic legend by Sibelius, op. 22, one of four on subjects from the *Kalevala*; composed 1893–95, fp Helsinki, 1895.

Swan Song (Schubert.) ◊Schwanengesang.

Swarowsky, Hans (b Budapest, 16 Sept 1899; d Salzburg, 10 Sept 1975), Austrian conductor and teacher. Studied with Schoenberg, Webern and R Strauss, and then devoted himself mainly to conducting, being active at opera houses in Stuttgart, Hamburg, Berlin and Zurich. From 1944 to 1945 he conducted the Kraków PO, the Vienna SO 1947–50, and was director of the Graz Opera 1947–50. Worked at the Vienna Opera from 1965. Often gave performances of the Mahler and the Second Viennese School. An influential teacher; among his pupils were Zubin Mehta and Claudio Abbado.

Swarthout, Gladys (b Deepwater, MO, 25 Dec 1900; d Florence, 7 Jul 1969), American contralto. Debut Ravinia, near Chicago, 1925, as Carmen. NY Met. 1929–45; debut as La Cieca and popular as Mignon, Siebel, Adalgisa and Carmen. She sang in the 1934 fp of Hanson's *Merry Mount*. From 1940 widely known as concert singer; retired 1954.

Swayne, Giles (b Stevenage, 30 Jun 1946), English composer. He studied at Cambridge and the RAM, and with Messiaen from 1976. Has worked as an opera répétiteur and at Bryanston School. St Paul's Girls' School 1976. Visited the Gambia and Senegal in the early 1980s to study the music of the Jola people.

Works include two string quartets (1971, 1977), *The Good Morrow*, for mezzo and piano, to texts by Donne (1971), *Synthesis* for two pianos (1974), *Orlando's Music* for orchestra (1974), *Pentecost-Music* for orchestra (1977), string quartets nos. 1 and 2 (1971, 1977), *Cry* for 28 amplified solo voices, in which the creation of the world is depicted (1979), *A World Within*, ballet with tape, on the life of the Brontës (1978), *Count-Down* for 16-part chorus and two percussion (1981), *Song for Hadi* for drums and instruments (1983), symphony for small orchestra (1984), opera *Le Nozze di Cherubino* (1984), *Missa Tiburtina* (1985), *Into the Light* for seven players (1986), *Tonos* for five players (1987), *Songlines* for flute and guitar (1987), *Harmonies of Hell*, melodrama (1988), *The Song of Leviathan* for chamber orchestra (1988), *A Memory of Sky*, brass quintet (1989), *Circle of Silence*, for six voices (1991), *The Song of the Tortoise*, children's drama (1992), *The Owl and the Pussycat*, for narrator and seven instruments (1993), string quartet no. 3 (1993).

Sweelinck, Jan Pieterszoon (b Deventer, May 1562; d Amsterdam, 16 Oct 1621), Dutch composer, organist and harpsichordist. Studied under his father, Pieter Sweelinck, who became organist at the Old Church at Amsterdam in 1566, and others. His father died in 1573 and he succeeded to his post between 1577 and 1580, holding it to his death. He had many famous pupils, some from foreign countries, and his organ playing was celebrated; he was also a highly skilled harpsichordist. His music was influenced by the English virginalists and the Venetian organists. The poet Vondel wrote an epitaph on his death.

Works include four books of psalms of four–eight voices, including three books of *Psalms of David* (1604–14), *Cantiones sacrae* for several voices; organ fantasias, toccatas and chorale variations; harpsichord pieces; *chansons* for five voices, *Rimes françoises et italiennes*.

Sweet, Sharon (b New York, 16 Aug 1951), American soprano. Studied at Curtis and made opera debut at Munich in 1985, as Aida. With the Deutsche Oper Berlin sang Wagner's Elisabeth in Japan; Elisabeth de Valois in Paris and Hamburg, 1987. US debut as Aida at San Francisco (1988) and appeared in the house fp of Verdi's *Stiffelio* at the NY Met., 1994. CG debut 1994, as Turandot. Admired for her powerful projection of dramatic roles, she has also sung Norma (Brussels 1988) and the *Trovatore* Leonora (Orange Festival, 1992).

swell a device on the harpsichord and the organ for the artificial production of *crescendo* and *diminuendo*, which these instruments are incapable of producing by touch. It took various forms, the most successful being a contrivance in the form of a slatted blind (hence the name Venetian swell), which, opening and shutting by means of a pedal, increased or reduced the volume of tone.

Swieten, Gottfried (Bernhard) van (b Leyden, 29 Oct 1733; d Vienna, 29 Mar 1803), Austrian diplomat and amateur musician of Dutch descent. Came to Vienna with his family in 1745 and in 1755 entered the diplomatic service. He held posts in Brussels, Paris and Warsaw, and visited England in 1769, but spent much of his time on music and wrote two *opéras comiques* and some symphonies. As ambassador in Berlin 1770–77 he became acquainted with the works of the Bach family and of Handel, and on his return to Vienna did much to promote interest in their music. He commissioned six symphonies from C P E Bach, and Mozart's arrangements of Handel oratorios were made for the concerts he organized; in 1791 he made the preparations for Mozart's hasty funeral. He was librettist of Haydn's *Creation* and *Seasons*, and a patron of the young Beethoven, who dedicated his first symphony to him.

Swingle, Ward (Lamar) (b Mobile, AL, 21 Sep 1927), American conductor and arranger. Studied at the Cincinnati Conservatory (1947–51) and conducted the Ballets de Paris (1955–59). Founded the Swingle Singers 1962 and until 1991 gave many concerts worldwide, notably in arrangements of Bach and in complex modern scores, such as Berio's *Sinfonia*.

Syberg, Franz (Adolf) (b Kerteminde near Odense, 5 Jul 1904; d Kerteminde, 11 Dec 1955), Danish composer and organist. His father, the painter Fritz Syberg, sent him to study at the Leipzig Conservatory, and later he became a private pupil of Karg-Elert. In 1930 he returned to Denmark to study organ with Peder Thomsen in Copenhagen, and in 1933 he became organist at Kerteminde.

Works include incidental music to Büchner's *Leonce and Lena* (1931) and the marionette comedy *Uffe hin Spage* (1929); symphonies; concertino for oboe and strings; string quartet (1931), string trio, quintet for flute, clarinet, violin, viola and cello; suite for organ.

Sygar, John, English 15th-c. composer. He was a singer and chaplain at King's College, Cambridge, in 1499–1501 and 1508–15, and contributed a Magnificat (now incomplete) to the Eton Choirbook.

Sylphides, Les ballet with music adapted from Chopin (choreography by Fokin), produced Paris, Théâtre du Châtelet, 2 Jun 1909.

Sylvester, Michael (b Indiana, 1955), American tenor. After study at Bloomington he sang at Stuttgart in 1987, as Radames and Pinkerton. Cincinnati Opera 1987, as Sam in Floyd's *Susannah*; New York City Opera debut 1987, as Rodolfo. Season 1990 as Pollione at the Paris Opéra. Don José at Hamburg and Cavaradossi at the Vienna Staatsoper. Sang Samson at CG 1990, returning as Gabriele Adorno 1991. NY Met. 1991–92, as Rodolfo in *Luisa Miller* and Don Carlo under James Levine (also recorded).

Sylvia, ou La Nymphe de Diane ballet by Delibes (scenario by Jules Barbier and Baron de Reinach, choreography by Louis Mérante), produced Paris, Opéra, 14 Jun 1876.

sympathetic resonance an acoustical phenomenon observed in resonant bodies, such as a string, a glass, a tuning-fork, etc., which will vibrate and give forth a faint sound without being touched, if their fundamental note is sung or played on an instrument near them.

sympathetic strings a set of strings in certain types of pianos and string instruments vibrating in sympathetic resonance with those actually played.

symphonia Latin lit. = symphony, especially in the earlier sense of any piece of music in which instruments play together in consort; also an early instrument, possibly a kind of bagpipe and, in a later sense, a clavichord. ◊sinfonia (the Italian term).

Symphonia domestica, *Domestic Symphony*, a symphony by R Strauss, op. 53, composed 1903, fp NY, 31 Mar 1904. Like *Heldenleben* the work is autobiographical, but describes the composer's private life, including love-making and bathing the baby, while the earlier work showed him as a public figure.

Symphonic Metamorphosis on Themes by Carl Maria von Weber work for orchestra by Hindemith; composed 1940–43, fp NY, 20 Jan 1944, conductor Rodzinski. The four movements use material from Weber's piano music and the incidental music for a Stuttgart production of Gozzi's *Turandot* in Schiller's translation, 1809.

symphonic poem a type of orchestral work coming under the category of programme music, i.e. descriptive of literary subjects, actual events in history or contemporary life, landscapes and natural phenomena, paintings, etc. The term symphonic poem was the invention of Liszt, who wrote 13 works of the kind.

symphonic study a term invented by Elgar for his *Falstaff*, probably because it is intended to be as much an outline of Falstaff's character as a description of the events surrounding him. Schumann's *Études Symphoniques* (Symphonic Studies) of 1835 consists of a theme and variations for piano solo.

symphonie concertante, French, ◊sinfonia concertante.

Symphonie fantastique symphony by Berlioz, op. 14, composed 1830, revised in Italy and first performed Paris, 5 Dec 1830, and with its sequel, *Lélio*, Paris, 9 Dec 1832. Berlioz gave it a programme arising out of his disappointed love for Harriet Smithson and representing the crazy dreams of a poet crossed in love who has taken poison. The five movements are: 1. *Rêveries-passions*; 2. *Un bal*; 3. *Scène aux champs*; 4. *Marche au supplice*; 5. *Songe d'une nuit de Sabbat*.

Symphonie funèbre et triomphale symphony by Berlioz, op. 15, for military band, strings and chorus, composed 1840 by order of the French government and performed at the tenth anniversary of the 1830 Revolution, Paris, 28 Jul 1840.

Symphonie liturgique Honegger's third symphony, composed 1945–46 and dedicated to Charles Munch, who gave the fp in Zurich on 17 Aug 1946.

Symphonies of Wind Instruments work by Stravinsky, dedicated to the memory of Debussy; composed 1920, revised 1945–47, fp London, 10 Jun 1921, conductor Koussevitzky.

After the symphonies of Beethoven, it was certain that the poetry that lies too deep for words does not lie too deep for music.
George Bernard Shaw, *The Perfect Wagnerite*, 1898

symphony originally a piece of music for several performers, e.g. Schütz's *Symphoniae sacrae* (1629–50), which are for voices and instruments. In 17th-c. Italy a symphony (*sinfonia*) was an instrumental movement, particularly the overture, in an opera or similar work. The term was still used in this sense in the early part of the 18th c., e.g. in Bach's cantatas. The development of the opera overture into a work in three movements in the time of A Scarlatti led to the composition of similar works independent of the theatre. Symphonies of this kind were written in the 18th c. not only in Italy but also in Vienna and particularly in Mannheim. The German and Austrian symphony came to incorporate elements of the suite (minuet) and the divertimento. The originality of Haydn's symphonies is owed perhaps to his isolation from the world at Eszterháza. Mozart, more cosmopolitan, was influenced as a boy by the elegance of J C Bach's symphonies but rapidly developed a style of his own. Dramatic elements are to be found in the symphonies of C P E Bach, Haydn and Beethoven, and programmatic features in those of Spohr, Berlioz and Liszt. The problem of integrating symphonic structure and Romantic expression was solved most successfully by Brahms. The scherzo came to replace the minuet in the symphonies of Beethoven, whose use of voices in his ninth symphony was followed by Mendelssohn (*Lobgesang*), Mahler and others. The linking of movements into a continuous whole, practised by Schumann and Mendelssohn, was followed by a number of later composers, e.g. Sibelius. Thematic relationships between movements occur in the symphonies of Franck, Tchaikovsky and Elgar among others. A symphony is not necessarily a heavily serious or weighty composition: Prokofiev's *Classical Symphony* and Shostakovich's ninth symphony are both light-hearted works. Shostakovich's six other post-war symphonies are major landmarks, and the symphony has achieved renewed vigour through such composers as Lutosławski (4), Maxwell Davies (5), Tippett (4), Henze (8) and William Schuman (10).

Symphony in Three Movements work for orchestra by Stravinsky; composed 1942–45, fp NY, 24 Jan 1946. The outer movements were inspired by Stravinsky's experiences of the war, as viewed from the USA. The central slow movement derives from music for a planned film on St Bernadette.

Symphony of a Thousand name sometimes given to Mahler's eighth symphony, in E♭, composed 1906–07. Forces required include eight vocal soloists, double chorus, boys' chorus, and orchestra with 20 woodwind, 17 brass instruments, celesta, piano, harmonium and mandolin. The first movement is a setting on the hymn *Veni creator spiritus* and the second the closing scene from Goethe's *Faust*. The fp, in Munich on 12 Sept 1910, was conducted by Mahler and was the greatest public success of his career. First US performance Philadelphia, 2 Mar 1916, conductor Stokowski. Not performed in Britain until 15 Apr 1930 (London, conductor Wood).

Symphony of Psalms work by Stravinsky for mixed chorus and orchestra; written 1930, to celebrate the 50th anniversary of the Boston SO, but the fp was in Brussels on 13 Dec 1930, conductor Ansermet.

syncopation a displacement of the musical accent to weak beats or off-beats in the bar, where they are normally expected to lie on the first

Syriac. In addition to the cantillation of the lessons and the singing of psalms, common to all liturgies, a repertory of hymns emerged, anticipating in some cases the forms of Byzantine chant. The *memrâ* was a poetical homily, sung to a recitative formula. The *madrâshâ* was a strophic hymn sung by a soloist, with a refrain sung by the choir (*cf.* Byzantine *kontakion*). The *sogîthâ* was a poem of dramatic character. Lesser forms, inserted between the verses of psalms, are comparable to the *troparion* and *sticheron* of the Byzantine liturgy. The outstanding poet was St Ephraem (306–73). Apart from some indecipherable cantillation formulae the music of the early Syrian church has not survived; and it is impossible to say how closely what is sung today resembles it.

syrinx ◊Pan pipe.

system in England a system is a number of music staves required for the scoring of a composition, e.g. two for a piano work, one + two for a song, four for a quartet, etc., up to any number needed for an orchestral full score. Such a system is connected on the left-hand side of the page by various kinds of braces or brackets; an open space between these shows that the next system begins lower down on the same page.

Szabelski, Boleslaw (b Radoryz, 3 Dec 1896; d Katowice, 27 Aug 1979), Polish composer. Studied with Szymanowski and Statkowski at the Warsaw Conservatory, and from 1945 taught composition and organ at the Katowice Conservatory. Embraced ideals of the Polish avant-garde from the late 1950s.

Works include five symphonies (1926–68), sinfonietta, *Concerto grosso* for orchestra; concertino and concerto for piano and orchestra; two string quartets; Magnificat for soprano, chorus and orchestra; piano and organ music.

Szábo, Ferenc (b Budapest, 27 Dec 1902; d Budapest, 4 Nov 1969), Hungarian composer. Pupil of Bartók and Kodály at the Budapest Conservatory. A convinced Communist, he settled in Russia 1932, returning to Hungary after World War II and becoming director of the Budapest High School for Music 1957.

Works include opera *Be Faithful unto Death* (posthumously produced Budapest 1975); *Song Symphony*, symphonic poems *Class Struggle* and *November seventh*, suite *The Collective Farm*; two string quartets, three piano trios; mass songs including *A Song of Voroshilov*; songs.

Szalowski, Antoni (b Warsaw, 21 Apr 1907; d Paris, 21 Mar 1973), Polish composer. Studied with his father, a violin professor at the Warsaw Conservatory, also piano with two masters and composition with Sikorski; later with Nadia Boulanger in Paris, where he settled and produced works in which local French influences predominated.

Works include symphonies, symphonic variations; capriccio and

Syncopation in a passage from Handel's Water Music. *The second note of bars 2–5 is syncopated.*

beat and, less pronounced, on the other main divisions of the bar. The effect is that of a syncope (i.e. missing a heart-beat): hence the name.

Syncopations are no indication of light or trashy music, and to shy bricks at 'hateful ragtime' no longer passes for musical culture.
Scott Joplin, *The School of Ragtime*, 1908

---

synthesizer an electronic machine produced commercially since 1965 by Robert Moog, used for the generation and modification of sounds, often connected to a computer and employed in the composition of electronic music. Predecessors of the synthesizer include the *Theremin* and *Ondes Martenot*.

Syrian Chant the earliest of the independent branches of Christian chant. Its language was the Eastern Aramaic dialect, also called

overture for string orchestra; piano concerto (1930); three songs with orchestra; four string quartets (1928–56); trio for oboe, clarinet and bassoon; suite for violin and piano, sonatina for clarinet and piano; violin and piano pieces; partita for solo cello; sonata, two sonatinas and other works for piano.

Szamotulczyk, Waclaw (Waclaw of Szamotuly) (b Szamotuly, near Poznań, *c* 1525; d ? Pińczów on the Nida, 1560), Polish composer. He studied at Poznań and at Kraków University, and in 1547 became composer to the king; from 1555 *Kapellmeister* to Prince Michael Radziwill. He wrote much *a cappella* church music, some of it pub. by Berg and Neuber of Nuremberg.

Szántó, Tivadar (or Theodor) (b Vienna, 3 Jun 1877; d Budapest, 7 Jan 1934), Hungarian composer and pianist. Studied in Vienna and Budapest, and with Busoni in Berlin. Lived in Paris 1905–14, in Switzerland in 1914–21 and then settled at Budapest. He revised Delius's C minor piano concerto, which is dedicated to him.

Works include opera *Typhoon* (after Lengyel's play, 1924); symphony *Land and Sea*, *Japan Suite* (1926) and other suites, symphonic rhapsody for orchestra; violin and piano sonata; Variations on a Hungarian Folksong, *Essays in Japanese Harmony* and other works for piano.

Székely, Mihály (b Jászberény, 8 May 1901; d Budapest, 6 Mar 1963), Hungarian bass. Debut Budapest 1920, as Ferrando in *Trovatore*; soon graduated to Marke and Méphistophélès. NY Met. 1946–50 (debut as Hunding). Glyndebourne 1957–61, as Sarastro, Osmin, Mozart's Bartolo and Rocco. At Paris and the Holland Festival he was admired as Bartók's Bluebeard.

Székely, Zoltán (b Kocs, 8 Dec 1903), Hungarian violinist and composer. Studied violin with Hubay and composition with Kodály at Budapest. After touring as soloist he formed the Hungarian String quartet in 1935, giving many performances of Bartók. In 1939 he gave the fp of Bartók's second concerto (Amsterdam).

Works include string quartet; sonata for unaccompanied violin, duet for violin and cello, etc.

Szeligowski, Tadeusz (b Lwów, 13 Sept 1896; d Poznań, 10 Feb 1963), Polish composer. Studied at Lwów and Kraków, later with Nadia Boulanger in Paris. He taught at Poznań, Lublin, Wilno and Warsaw. He made special studies of folksong and early church music and was also influenced in his compositions by French neo-classicism.

Works include incidental music for plays, e.g. Maeterlinck's *Blue Bird*; two psalms for solo voices, chorus and orchestra; concerto, *Phantaisie rapsodique*, suite *St Casimir Fair* for orchestra; clarinet concerto, piano concerto; two string quartets (1929, 1934); *Lithuanian Song* for violin and piano; *Children's Album* for piano; *Green Songs*, *Flower Allegories* and other songs.

Conductors must give unmistakeable and suggestive signals to the orchestra – not choreography to the audience.

George Szell, *Newsweek*, 1963

Szell, Georg (b Budapest, 7 Jun 1897; d Cleveland, 29 Jul 1970), Hungarian-born conductor and pianist. A child prodigy, he studied with R Robert in Vienna, playing a work of his own with the Vienna SO aged 11. He studied composition with J B Foerster, Mandyczewski and Reger, and then, through the influence of R Strauss, he obtained a conducting post in Strasbourg, which he held 1917–18, having already made his debut in Berlin in 1914. After further posts in Prague, Darmstadt and Düsseldorf he became first conductor at the Berlin Staatsoper 1924–30, also teaching at the Berlin Hochschule für Musik 1927–30. From 1930 to 1936 he again conducted in Prague, taking over the Scottish National Orchestra 1937–39, when he went to the USA. There he was guest conductor with the NBC SO 1941–42, conductor at the NY Met.; much admired in Wagner. From 1942 to 1945, and from 1943 to 1956, frequent guest conductor with the NY PO. In 1946 he became permanent conductor of the Cleveland PO. Conducted *Der Rosenkavalier* at Salzburg 1949, returning for the fps of Liebermann's *Penelope* (1954) and Egk's *Irische Legend* (1955). Bartók and Janáček were among the few modern composers in his programmes. Szell was one of the last of a generation of composers who dominated orchestras with iron discipline and sarcastic humour.

Szenen aus Goethes 'Faust' a setting of a number of scenes from Goethe's drama for solo voices, chorus and orchestra by Schumann; composition begun with a setting of the final chorus, Aug 1844, resumed 1849, completed without the overture, 1850, overture added 1853.

Szeryng, Henryk (b Warsaw, 22 Nov 1918; d Kassel, 3 Mar 1988), Polish, later Mexican, violinist. Studied with W Hess and with Flesch in Berlin, and made his debut at Warsaw in 1933, with the Brahms Concerto. From 1948 he taught as professor in Mexico City. Toured Europe and US in 1983, to mark the 50th anniversary of his career. He

was an international virtuoso who always maintained strong musical values.

Szigeti, Joseph (b Budapest, 5 Sept 1892; d Lucerne, 19 Feb 1973), Hungarian, later American, violinist. Studied in Budapest with Hubay, and received advice from Joachim and Busoni, making his debut in 1905. From 1917 to 1925 he was professor at the Geneva Conservatory, settling in the USA 1926. He gave the fps of violin concertos by Busoni and Bloch, and did much for the cause of modern music; often played works by Bartók and Prokofiev.

Szirmay, Marta (b Kaposvar, 1939), Hungarian mezzo. Sang at the Hungarian State Opera from 1964, as Amneris, Brangaena and Orpheus. CG, London, from 1977 as Clytemnestra, Erda and Mistress Quickly. Sang Ericles in the Henze/Monteverdi *Ulisse* at Salzburg (1985) and has appeared at Cologne (from 1976), Vienna, Hamburg and Berlin. Turin 1992, in *Blimunda* by Corghi.

Szmytka, Elzbieta (b Prochowice, 1956), Polish soprano. Studied in Krakow (1975–82) and first appeared in the West as Mozart's Blondchen, Despina and Serpina (*Finta giardiniera*). Sang Nannetta in *Falstaff* at Brussels and Aix (1987–88), and Papagena at the Vienna Staatsoper in 1988. Glyndebourne 1991, as Ilia and Servilio (*La clemenza di Tito*). Salzburg Festival 1992, in *From the House of the Dead*, and Mozartwoche there 1993, as Cinna in *Lucio Silla*.

Szokolay, Sándor (b Kúnágota, 30 Mar 1931), Hungarian composer. He studied at the Budapest Academy; teacher there since 1966. He has been influenced by Hungarian national music and by Stravinsky and Orff.

Works include violin concerto (1957), *Urban and the Devil*, ballet (1958), piano concerto (1958), *Fiery March*, oratorio (1958), *The Ballad of Horror*, ballet (1960), *Ishtar's Descent into Hell*, oratorio (1960), *Blood Wedding*, opera after Lorca (1964), *Déploration*, Requiem for Poulenc for piano, chorus and chamber orchestra (1964), trumpet concerto (1968), *Hamlet*, opera (1968), *Apocalypse*, oratorio after Dürer (1971), *Samson*, opera (1974), *Deluded Peter*, radio opera (1978), Passion-opera *Ecce Homo* (1987).

Szulc, Józef (Zygmunt) (b Warsaw, 4 Apr 1875; d Paris, 10 Apr 1956), Polish composer and pianist. Studied with Noskowski at the Warsaw Conservatory and later with Moszkowski in Paris. On the advice of Paderewski he began a career as concert pianist, but later devoted himself to composition. He settled in Paris.

Works include French operettas *Une Nuit d'Ispahan*, *Flup!* (1913), *Divin Mensonge*, *Flossie*, *Le Garçon de chez Prunier*, *Le Coffre-fort vivant* and others; overture for orchestra; violin and piano sonata; songs.

A Selection of

Szymanowski

Violin Sonata	1904
Symphony no. 1	1909
Symphony no. 2	1910
Symphony no. 3	1916
Violin Concerto no. 1	1916
King Roger	1926
Stabat Mater	1926
String Quartet no. 2	1927
Symphonia concertante	1932
Violin Concerto no. 2	1933

Szymanowski , Karol (Maciej) (b Timashovka, Ukraine, 6 Oct 1882; d Lausanne, 29 Mar 1937), Polish composer regarded as the founder of 20th-c. Polish music. Learnt music privately as a child and composed a set of piano preludes, op. 1, in 1900. In 1903 he entered the Warsaw Conservatory, studying with Noskowski, and at the Lwów Chopin Festival won a first prize with a C minor piano sonata in 1905. Lived in Berlin for a time from 1906 and worked on behalf of Polish music. He was initially influenced by Debussy and Strauss but also created his own lyrical late-Romantic vision, particularly in the 3rd symphony *Song of the Night*, the violin concerto, the *Stabat Mater* and the opera *King Roger*. His more abstract works such as his piano sonatas and mazurkas embrace more modern techniques within traditional forms, and his masques seems almost improvisatory. As an aristocrat he lost his property in World War I and was imprisoned in Russia, but escaped to Warsaw, where in 1922 he became professor of composition and director of the State Conservatory. His masterpiece *King Roger* was premiered in 1926 and one of his most successful pieces, the *Stabat Mater*, followed in 1929. His last years were marred by tuberculosis and he had to go to a sanatorium in Switzerland, where he died.

Works include operas *Hagith* (1922) and *King Roger* (1926); ballets *Mandragora* (also incidental music to Molière's *Le Bourgeois Gentilhomme*) and *Harnasie* (1935); incidental music to Miciński's *Prince Potemkin*.

ORCHESTRAL: four symphonies no. 1 in F minor (1907), no. 2 in B♭ minor (1910, reorchestrated 1936), no. 3 for tenor or soprano, male chorus and orchestra (*Song of the Night*, 1916), *Sinfonia concertante* for piano and orchestra (1932); two violin concertos (1916, 1933); *Penthesilea* (Wyspiański) for soprano and orchestra; *Hafiz Love Songs* for voice and orchestra; *Stabat Mater* (1926), *Veni Creator* (1929) and *Litany* for solo voices, chorus and orchestra.

CHAMBER: two string quartets (1917, 1927); piano trio; numerous violin and piano pieces; three sonatas and many other works for piano; many songs including cycles *Songs of the Infatuated Muezzin* (J Iwaszkiewicz), *Stopiewnie* (Julian Tuwim), *Children's Rhymes* (J Illakowicz) and settings of poems by Kasprowicz, Miciński, James Joyce, Tagore and others.

T

t the leading-note in Tonic sol-fa notation, pronounced Te.

Tabachnik, Michel (b Geneva, 10 Nov 1942), Swiss conductor and composer. Studied at the Geneva Conservatory and was assistant to Boulez, 1967–71. Conducted BBC orchestras from 1966 and the Orchestre National de Paris from 1971. Conductor of the Gulbenkian Orchestra at Lisbon, 1973–75, artistic director of the Ensemble Intercontemporain at Paris, 1976–77. Guest with the Berlin Philharmonic and the Suisse Romande and Concertgebouw Orchestras. Conductor of the Lorraine PO, 1975–81. His own orchestral works include *Mondes* (1972) and *Cosmogonie pour une rose* (1981).

Tabarro, Il (Puccini) ◊Trittico.

tabla a pair of Indian tuned drums, one cylindrical, one bowl-shaped, played with the fingers and used to accompany other instruments, such as the ◊sitar. They produce a clear, rich sound and are responsible for maintaining the music's *tala* (rhythmic identity).

tablature various old systems of writing down music, especially for organ (for the left hand only or for both hands) and for lute, without notes, but by means of letters or numbers. The only modern instruments for which a tablature notation is now normally in use are the ukelele and similar guitar types. (For the old German Mastersingers' tablature ◊Tabulatur.)

table, French, (1) the belly of a string instrument. (2) The sounding-board of the harp. *Près de la table* is an instruction to play near the sounding-board, producing a metallic sound. (3) *Musique de table*. ◊Tafel-Musik.

Tableau parlant, Le, *The Speaking Picture*, opera by Grétry (libretto by L Anseaume), produced Paris, Comédie-Italienne, 20 Sept 1769. Isabelle's tutor Cassandre has designs on her after her lover Léandre has been missing for two years, but he returns in time to marry her.

table entertainment an 18th-c. English entertainment, only partly musical in character, given by a single performer sitting at a table and telling stories and jokes, giving displays of mimicry, singing songs, etc. The first table entertainments on record are those of George Alexander Steevens at Dublin in 1752. Dibdin began a series in London in 1789 and continued for 20 years, introducing most of his songs in this way.

tabor a small drum with a high, narrow body and small drum-heads made of animal skin, sounding an indefinite pitch and struck with drumsticks. It was rarely used alone, but accompanied a pipe of a fife or recorder type, similar to the modern tin whistle. It is occasionally used in the modern orchestra to produce a dry, dull, percussive sound, and has been revived for folk-dancing.

Tabor (Smetana.) ◊Mà Vlast.

Tabulatur German = 'tablature'; in one sense the German word differs from the English, meaning the table of rules for the instruction and guidance of the Mastersingers.

Tacchinardi, Nicola (b Livorno, 3 Sept 1772; d Florence, 14 Mar 1859), Italian tenor. He studied literature and art at first, but learnt the violin, joined the orchestra at the Florence Opera 1789, and in 1794 began to appear as a singer. He soon sang in the principal theatres of Italy, in operas by Paer, Morlacchi and Zingarelli, and in 1811–14 visited Paris, where he sang Don Giovanni (transposed) and in operas by Paisiello, Pucitta and Cimarosa. He then settled at Florence in the service of the Grand Duke of Tuscany. Later in his career he often appeared in operas by Rossini.

tacet Latin = 'is silent'; an indication in old vocal part-books and later in orchestral parts to show that a voice or instrument has finished its part in a work, although the work itself is still continuing. In that case the wording is usually *tacet al fine*, 'tacet to the end'. But the word tacet alone may also stand below a certain number or section of a work to show that the voice or instrument in question does not perform during that portion of the music, though it will come in again later.

Tacitus, Cornelius (b c 55–120), Roman historian. ◊Incoronazione di Poppea (Monteverdi); ◊Radamisto (Handel).

Taddei, Giuseppe (b Genoa, 26 Jun 1916), Italian baritone. Made his debut in Rome in 1936, as the Herald in *Lohengrin*. He was especially well known as a dramatic Verdi singer, and also in *buffo* roles: Scarpia, Falstaff, Dulcamara. Also sang Pizarro, Rigoletto, Sachs and the Dutchman. CG, London, from 1960. Sang Falstaff at the New York Met. 1985, Stuttgart 1990.

Tadolini, Giovanni (b Bologna, 18 Oct ?1789; d Bologna, 29 Nov 1872), Italian singer and composer. Studied composition with Mattei and singing with Babini, and in 1811 was engaged by Spontini as accompanist and chorus master at the Théâtre des Italiens in Paris, leaving in 1814, but going there again 1830–39, after living in Italy and composing operas in between. He married the soprano, *Eugenia Savonari* (1809–after 1848); she created Donizetti's Linda di Chamounix (1842) and Maria di Rohan (1843) and Verdi's Alzira (1845).

Works include operas *Le bestie in uomini* (1815), *La principessa di Navarra* (1816), *Il credulo deluso* (*Il finto molinaro* (1817), *Tamerlano* (1818), *Moctar, Mitridate* (1826), *Almanzor* (1827); canzonets, including *Eco di Scozia* with horn obbligato, etc.

Tafel-Musik German = 'table music'; music performed at or after dinner (French *musique de table*).

Tag, Christian Gotthilf (b Beierfeld, Saxony, 2 Apr 1735; d Niederzwönitz near Zwönitz, 19 Jul 1811), German composer. Pupil of Homilius at Dresden. In 1755 he became cantor at Hohenstein-Ernstthal, Saxony.

Works include 11 Masses, motets; 103 cantatas; symphony for organ and orchestra, songs.

Tag des Gerichts, Der, *The Day of Judgement*, oratorio by Telemann (text by C W Alers), composed 1762.

Tageszeiten, Die, *The times of the day*, song cycle for male chorus and orchestra by R Strauss (text by Eichendorff); composed 1927, fp Vienna, 21 Jul 1928. The movements are 'Der Morgen', 'Mittagsruh', 'Der Abend' and 'Die Nacht'.

Cantata by Telemann.

Tageweisen German = 'day tunes': songs formerly used in Germany to announce the break of day from church towers or by nightwatchmen in the streets. They were often folksongs and some have passed into currency as hymns for the Lutheran church.

Taglia, Pietro, Italian 16th-c. composer, active at Milan. Wrote three books of madrigals (1555, 1557, 1564).

Tagliapietra, Gino (b Ljubljana, 30 May 1887; d Venice, 8 Aug 1954), Italian composer and pianist. Studied with Julius Epstein in Vienna and with Busoni in Berlin. In 1906 he was appointed professor of piano at the Liceo Musicale at Venice. He pub. an anthology of keyboard music in 18 vols.

Works include ballet *La bella addormentata nel bosco* (1926); Requiem and other choral works; piano concerto; piano pieces and studies.

Tagliavini, Ferruccio (b Reggio Emilia, 14 Aug 1913; d Reggio Emilia, 29 Jan 1995), Italian tenor. Studied at Parma Conservatory and won first prize in a singing competition in Florence in 1938, which enabled him to study in that city with A Bassi, where he made his debut in 1938 as Rodolfo. He soon established himself as a leading *bel canto* singer, appearing at the NY Met. 1947–54 and CG 1950–56. Other roles included Edgardo, Werther, Cavaradossi and Mascagni's Fritz.

Täglichsbeck, Thomas (b Ansbach, 31 Dec 1799; d Baden-Baden, 5 Oct 1867), German violinist and composer. Studied in Munich and became deputy conductor to Lindpaintner there in 1820. From 1827 he was music director to the Prince of Hohenzollern-Hechingen until the 1848 Revolution. He toured frequently during this period as soloist and as conductor.

Works include operas *Webers Bild* (1823), *König Enzio* (1843); Mass; two symphonies; two violin concertinos; piano trio; part-songs.

Taglietti, Giulio (b Brescia, c 1660; d Brescia, 1718), Italian composer. *Maestro di cappella* of the Jesuit Collegio dei Nobili at Brescia. Composed numerous works for two violins and bass with organ or harpsichord, violin sonatas with bass, etc.

Tailer, John (b (also Taylor, etc.); d ? London, after 1569), English composer. From 1561 to 1569 he was master of the choristers at Westminster Abbey. A *Christus resurgens* (Christ Church, Oxford, MSS 948–8) may be by him, or by Thomas Taylor, who obtained the B.Mus. at Oxford, 1531.

taille French = 'cut, edge'; the tenor part in a vocal and instrumental ensemble, applied particularly in the 17th and 18th c. to the viola and the *oboe da caccia*.

Tailleferre, Germaine (b Parc Saint-Maur, near Paris, 19 Apr 1892; d Paris, 7 Nov 1983), French composer. Studied in Paris and joined the group of 'Les Six', first appearing as a composer in public in 1920. She lived in the USA 1942–46.

Works include opera *Il était un petit navire* (1951); ballet *Le Marchand d'oiseaux* (1923); *Pastorale* for small orchestra; piano concerto (1919) and ballade for piano and orchestra; string quartet (1918); two violin and piano sonatas (1921, 1951); *Jeux de plein air* for two pianos (1918); songs.

Tajo, Italo (b Pinerolo, Piedmont, 25 Apr 1915; d Cincinnati, 29 Mar 1993), Italian bass. Debut Turin, 1935, as Fafner in *Das Rheingold*. Sang Figaro and Banquo at the 1947 Edinburgh Festival with the Glyndebourne co. In London he was heard as Donizetti's Don Pasquale and Dulcamara (1947–50). In the USA he sang at Chicago, San Francisco and the NY Met. during the 1940s; taught at the Cincinnati Conservatory from 1966. Other roles included Leporello, Don Magnifico and Berg's Doctor.

Takemitsu, Tōru (b Tokyo, 8 Oct 1930; d Tokyo, 20 Feb 1996), Japanese composer. He studied privately and in 1951 co-founded an experimental laboratory in Tokyo, to examine oriental music and the best in Western techniques; used tape and was influenced by serialism, Messiaen and *musique concrète*.

Works include *Requiem* for strings (1957), *Music of Trees* for orchestra (1961), *Textures* for piano and orchestra (1964), *The Dorian Horizon* for 17 strings (1966), *November Steps* for biwa, shakuhachi and orchestra (1967), *Asterism* for piano and orchestra (1968), *Corona* for 22 strings (1971), *Cassiopea* for percussion and orchestra (1971), *Gemeaux* for oboe, trombone and two orchestras (1972),

Bouquet of Songs for marimba and orchestra (1975), *A Flock Descends into the Pentagonal Garden* for orchestra (1977), *Dream Time* for orchestra (1981; ballet version 1983), *Rain Coming* for chamber orchestra (1982), *To the Edge of Dream* for guitar and orchestra (1983), *Star Isle* for orchestra (1984); *Orion and Pleiades* for cello and orchestra (1984), *Riverrun* for piano and orchestra (1984); *I hear the water dreaming* for flute and orchestra (1987); *Tree Line* for chamber orchestra (1988); *A String Around Autumn* for viola and orchestra (1989); *Visions* for orchestra (1990); *My Way of Life* for baritone, chorus and orchestra (1990); *From me flows what you call time* for five percussion and orchestra (1990); chamber music including string quartet *A Way Alone* (1981), series of works for instruments with title *Stanza*, *Entre- temps* for oboe and string quartet (1986); *All in Twilight* for guitar (1987); *Itinerant* for flute (1989). Works for tape alone, etc.

Tal, Josef (b Pinne, near Poznań, 18 Sept 1910), Israeli composer. Studied in Berlin with Tiessen and Trapp, settling in Palestine 1934. In 1937 he became professor of composition and piano at the Jerusalem Conservatory and in 1950 lecturer at the Hebrew University there, also being director of the Conservatory 1948–55.

Works include operas *Saul at Ein Dor* (1957), *Amnon and Tamar* (1961), *Ashmedai* (1971), *Massada 967* (1973), *Die Versuchung* (1976), *Der Turm* (1987), *Der Garten* (1988), and *Josef* (1993); *The Death of Moses*, requiem oratorio for soloists, chorus and tape (1967); two symphonies; *Exodus*, choreographed poem for orchestra; *Visions* for string orchestra; six piano concertos (1944–70), viola concerto; symphonic cantata *A Mother Rejoices*; sonatas for violin, oboe; piano pieces; songs; electronic music.

tala a term used to describe the cyclically repeated patterns which form the rhythmic basis of much Indian music, especially as played by a percussion instrument.

Talbot, Michael (Owen) (b 4 Jan 1943), English musicologist. Studied at Cambridge and the RCM and has been professor of music at Liverpool University from 1986. An authority on Venetian music of the 18th c., he has published studies of Vivaldi (Master Musicians series) and Albinoni (*The Venetian Composer and his World*, 1994).

talea Latin = 'a cutting'; the name given to the repeated rhythmic pattern used in isorhythmic motets. ◊isorhythmic.

Tales of Hoffmann (Offenbach.) ◊Contes d'Hoffmann.

Talich, Václav (b Kroměříž, 28 May 1883; d Beroun near Prague, 16 Mar 1961), Czech conductor. He studied with his father and was a pupil of Ševčík for the violin at the Prague Conservatory. He held various posts as violinist, conductor and teacher 1904–19, when he was appointed conductor of the Czech PO. He retained this post till 1941 and was also director of the National Opera at Prague 1935–45. Post-war conditions made his position in Prague impossible and he moved to Bratislava. His merits were finally recognized by the government in the last years of his life. Well known performer of Smetana, Dvořák and Janáček.

Enterred here doth ly a worthy wyght/who for long Tyme in Musick bore the bell:/His Name to shew was Thomas Tallys hyght,/In honest vertuous Lyff he did excel.

From a tombstone from c. 1585 in Greenwich old church, destroyed c. 1720.

Tallis, Thomas (b c 1505; d Greenwich, 23 Nov 1585), English composer and organist. He was organist at the Benedictine Priory, Dover, in 1532, and held a post at Waltham Abbey before its dissolution in 1540. He became a Gentleman of the Chapel Royal c 1543. He was one of the earliest composers to write for the Anglican liturgy (1547–53) but some of his most ornate music, including the Mass *Puer natus est nobis* dates from the brief Catholic reign of Mary Tudor (1553–58). In 1557 Queen Mary granted him, jointly with Richard

A Selection of

Tallis

Mass *Puer natus est nobis*
Psalm Tunes for Archbishop Parker's Psalter
Lamentations of Jeremiah

Spem in alium
Gaude gloriosa Dei mater
Missa Salve intemerata virgo
Mass for four voices
Magnificat and nunc dimittis

Bowyer, Master of the Children in the Chapel Royal, a lease of the manor of Minster, Thanet, and at her death he passed into the service of Elizabeth, who in 1575 granted him, jointly with Byrd, a patent for the sole right to print music and music paper in English; but two years later, not finding this immediately profitable, they petitioned for an annual grant, which was sanctioned. The two masters were then joint organists at the Chapel Royal. A tune written for Archbishop Parker's Psalter of 1567 was used by Vaughan Williams in his celebrated *Fantasia*. Tallis has become best known for the elaborate and ingenious 40-part motet *Spem in alium* (1573). In his last years he and his wife Joan, whom he had married *c* 1552, lived at their own house at Greenwich.

Works include three Masses, including *Puer natus est nobis* (1554), two Latin Magnificats, two sets of Lamentations for voices, *c* 40 Latin motets etc., including *Spem in alium* in 40 parts; services, psalms, Litanies, *c* 30 anthems and other English church music; secular vocal pieces; two In Nomines for strings; organ and virginal pieces.

Tallis Scholars see ◊Phillips, Peter.

talon, French, the heel (or nut) of the bow of a string instrument.

Talvela, Martti (Olavi) (b Hiitola, Karelia, 4 Feb 1935; d Juva, 22 Jun 1989), Finnish bass. Debut Stockholm, 1961, Commendatore. Bayreuth, 1962–70, as Hunding, Hagen, Daland and Marke. NY Met. debut 1968, as the Grand Inquisitor; returned in 1974 as Boris Godunov, in the original version of Mussorgsky's opera. At CG he was admired in the early 1970s as Hagen, Dosifey and Gurnemanz. From 1972 he was artistic director of the summer Savonlinna Festival, Finland, and took part in the fps of works by Kokkonen and Sallinen there. Other roles included Sarastro and King Henry.

Tamagno, Francesco (b Turin, 28 Dec 1850; d Varese, 31 Aug 1905), Italian tenor. At first a baker's apprentice and locksmith, he studied at the Turin Conservatory, sang in the opera chorus there, studied further with Pedrotti at Palermo and made his first appearance there in 1873. He sang at La Scala 1877–87, the NY Met. 1891–95 and CG 1895 and 1901. Among his best roles were Ernani, Don Carlos, Manrico, Radames, Faust and Samson. He was celebrated for the dramatic conviction of his performances and was Verdi's first Otello (1887). Retired 1904.

Tamara symphonic poem by Balakirev, based on a poem by Lermontov (sometimes called *Thamar* in English), begun 1866, finished 1882; fp St Petersburg, Free School of Music, 1882. Ballet on this work (choreographed by M Fokine, setting by L Bakst), produced Paris, Théâtre du Châtelet, 20 May 1912.

Tamberlik, Enrico (b Rome, 16 Mar 1820; d Paris, 13 Mar 1889), Italian tenor. At first intended to become a lawyer, he made his debut at Naples in 1841 as Tybalt in Bellini's *I Capuleti*; sang in Portugal and Spain. In 1850 first appeared in London, as Auber's Masaniello; sang there until 1877 as Manrico, Cellini and Rossini's Otello. At St Petersburg in 1862 he created Alvaro in *La forza del destino*.

tambourin French = tabor; the *tambourin du Béarn* was a zither with strings sounding only tonic and dominant and struck by a stick. Hence tambourin was used to mean a dance with a drone bass.

tambourine a small, shallow drum with a single skin stretched over the edge of one side of its rim, into which jingles are loosely set to add their noise when the skin is struck or rubbed by the hand or to resound separately when the instrument is shaken.

tambura an Indian plucked drone instrument with four strings, tuned by a movable bridge, which provides accompaniment, often for the ◊sitar. The south Indian version, the *mayuri*, can also be played with a bow.

Tamburini, Antonio (b Faenza, 28 Mar 1800; d Nice, 8 Nov 1876), Italian baritone. Was at first taught the horn, but appeared in opera at the age of 18 at Bologna, in Generali's *La Contessa*. He first sang in London in 1832, his roles over the next 20 years there included Donizetti's Alfonso, Earl of Nottingham and Enrico. At the Paris Théâtre-Italien he created Riccardo in *I Puritani* (1835) and

tambourine *Originating in the Middle East, the tambourine found its way to Europe in the 13th century as a result of the Crusades. It was popular throughout the Middle Ages and Mozart was one of the first composers to use it in an orchestral setting.*

Melvyn Tan – pianist

1   Richard Strauss: *Der Rosenkavalier* (Schwarzkopf/Ludwig/Karajan)
This must remain one of the classic interpretations of the opera.

2   Ravel: Piano concertos (Perlemuter)
A sentimental journey. Having been a pupil of Perlemuter's I remember his stories of Ravel and when I hear his performances it somehow brings me as close to Ravel as is physically possible!

3   Stravinsky: *The Rite of Spring*
It's difficult to believe that such a masterpiece could have caused such a stir and rumpus during the first night. That said, the barbarism and wildness in the music still sound as convincing and wonderful today as they did then.

4   Mozart: *Così fan tutte*
There have been many great interpretations of this work and every time I listen to this opera I discover something new as though I were listening to it for the first time. Mozart certainly knew how to write for all his singers!

5   Chopin: Études (Arrau)
I constantly listen to these and refer to them for the sheer pianism and artistry in the performances. Arrau brings a lucidity which makes the listener feel that it really cannot be any other way.

6   Ravel: *Daphis et Chloé*
A pianist always thinks of 'colours' in the instrument that he or she is playing. In orchestration these colours are much more readily apparent and one can wallow in the textures of this piece and simply imagine!

Malatesta in *Don Pasquale* (1843). Sang in Russia for ten years.

tamburo Italian = 'drum'; the term is used in scores, with various adjectival qualifications, for any kind of drum except the ◊kettle-drums, which are called *timpani* in Italian.

Tamerlano, Tamburlane, opera by Handel (libretto by A Piovene, adapted by N F Haym), produced London, King's Theatre, Haymarket, 31 Oct 1724. Tamerlano offers his betrothed, Irene, to ally Andronicus in return for his beloved Asteria, daughter of the captured emperor Bajazet. After feigning cooperation Asteria refuses and is imprisoned; her father takes poison before the original relationships are restored.

Taming of the Shrew, The ◊Sly; ◊Widerspänstigen Zähmung.

tampur a three-stringed Caucasian instrument of the lute type, but played with a bow.

tam-tam onomatopoeic = ◊gong.

Tan, Melvyn (b Singapore, 13 Oct 1956), Malaysian-born English keyboard player. Studied at the Menuhin School, notably with Vlado Perlemuter, and at the RCM (performing practice). Played the piano until 1980 then gave concerts on the harpsichord and fortepiano with such ensembles as the Academy of Ancient Music, ECO and London Classical Players (Beethoven Concerto series in London, 1987, and the Beethoven Experience in Purchase, NY). Has played with and directed the New Mozart Ensemble and plays music by Schumann, Weber and Chopin, in addition to earlier repertory.

Tancrède tragédie-lyrique by Campra (libretto by A Danchet after Tasso), produced Paris, Opéra, 7 Nov 1702. Revived Aix-en-Provence, 1986. Saracen Clorinde saves her crusader lover Tancrèdi from death, but must return to her people. Later Tancrèdi despairs when he kills her in battle, believing that she was the Saracen leader Argante.

Tancredi, *Tancred*, opera by Rossini (libretto by G Rossi, based on Tasso's *Gerusalemme liberata* and Voltaire's tragedy *Tancrède*), produced Venice, Teatro La Fenice, 6 Feb 1813. Rossini's first serious opera. Revived Wexford, 1986. Amenaide, daughter of Argirio, refuses to marry her family's enemy, Orbazzano; she is later accused of aiding the Saracens when her letter to lover Tancredi is found. He champions her, kills Orbazzano, and leads the Syracusans against the Saracens.

Taneiev, Alexander Sergeievich (b St Petersburg, 17 Jan 1850; d Petrograd, 7 Feb 1918), Russian composer. Entered state service after studies at St Petersburg University, but also studied music there and at Dresden, and came under the influence of the Balakirev circle.

Works include operas *Cupid's Revenge* (1899) and *The Snow-storm*; three symphonies (1890, 1903, 1908), symphonic poem *Alesha Popovich*, overture to Shakespeare's *Hamlet*, two suites for orchestra; three string quartets; pieces for violin and piano and for piano; songs, part-songs.

Taneiev, Sergey Ivanovich (b Government of Vladimir, 25 Nov 1856; d Djudkowa, 19 Jun 1915), Russian composer and pianist. Studied at the Moscow Conservatory, intending at first to become a pianist, but also studying composition with Tchaikovsky; gave the Moscow fp of Tchaikovsky's 1st Piano Concerto, 1875, and completed the original, vocal version of *Romeo and Juliet*. In 1876 he toured Russia, in 1877–78 visited Paris, and after playing in the Baltic Provinces became professor of orchestration at the Moscow Conservatory, in 1881 chief professor of piano on N Rubinstein's death and in 1885 director, succeeding Hubert. He was followed by Safonov in 1889 and concentrated on teaching counterpoint and fugue. He achieved a major success with his last work, the cantata *At the Reading of a Psalm* (1915).

Works include operatic trilogy *Oresteia* (based on Aeschylus, 1895); cantata *John of Damascus* for solo voices, chorus and orchestra (1884); four symphonies, Overture on Russian Themes for orchestra; concert suite for violin and orchestra; 11 string quartets, two string trios, piano trio; prelude and fugue for two pianos; *c* 40 songs to words by Tiutchev and others; part- songs.

tañer Spanish = 'to touch'; a 16th-c. lute prelude with which the strings were 'touched', or tried; equivalent to a toccata.

tangents the screwdriver-shaped pins striking the wire strings in the ◊clavichord. The strings continue to sound while the tangents touch them, and their tone can thus approximate a violin's *vibrato* by altering the pressure of the finger on the depressed key (◊Bebung).

tango a Latin American dance whose origins, sometimes said to be African, are obscure. Clearly related to the Cuban habanera etc., it was indigenous to Argentina in the 19th c. before becoming popular with dancers and jazz bands in Europe in the first 15 years of the 20th c. It is in 2–4 time, like the habanera, but faster in pace, and is accompanied with a rhythm of four quavers, the first of which is dotted.

Tango, Egisto (b Rome, 13 Nov 1873; d Copenhagen, 5 Oct 1951), Italian conductor. Debut Venice, 1893; La Scala from 1895. Rome 1911, in the first Italian performance of *Rosenkavalier*. At Budapest he gave the fps of Bartók's *Wooden Prince* (1917) and *Bluebeard's Castle* (1918). Copenhagen from 1927.

Tannhäuser und der Sängerkrieg auf der Wartburg, *Tannhäuser and the Singers' Contest at the Wartburg*, opera by Wagner (libretto by composer), produced Dresden, 19 Oct 1845; revised for Paris, with bacchanale in first act, and produced at the Opéra, 13 Mar 1861. Torn between conflicting demands of carnal Venus and virginal Elisabeth, Tannhäuser expires before absolution arrives from Rome.

Tansman, Alexandre (b Łódz, 12 Jun 1897; d Paris, 15 Nov 1986), Polish-born French composer. Studied at home and then at Warsaw, and in 1919 took two prizes for composition. He settled in Paris, but travelled extensively as pianist and conductor. Married the French pianist Colette Cras.

Works include operas *La Nuit Kurde* (1927), *La Toison d'or, Le Serment* (1955) and *Sabbataï Lévi, le faux Messie* (1961); ballets *Sextuor* (1924) and *La Grande Ville* (1932); seven symphonies (1925–44), *Sinfonietta* (1925), symphonic overture, *Toccata, Sonatine transatlantique, Quatre Danses polonaises, Triptyque, Partita, Deux Pièces, Études symphoniques*, serenade, *Rapsodie polonaise* and suites for orchestra; variations on a theme by Frescobaldi for strings; two concertos (1925–26) and concertino for piano and orchestra.

CHAMBER: eight string quartets (1917–56), mazurka for nine instruments, *Divertimento* for oboe, clarinet, trumpet, cello and piano, *Danse de la sorcière* for five wind instruments and piano; *Sonata quasi una fantasia* for violin and piano; five sonatas and other piano works; songs.

Tapiola symphonic poem by Sibelius, op. 112, composed in 1926 for the Symphonic Society in NY. The title is the old mythological name of Finland, derived from the forest god Tapio, who appears in the *Kalevala*. Fp NY, 26 Dec 1926.

Tapissier, Johannes (Jean de Noyers) (b *c* 1370; d before Aug 1410), French composer. Though at the Burgundian court from 1391 to the end of his life, he seems to have been active mainly in Paris. Two Mass movements and an isorhythmic motet survive, though records indicate that he was a prominent and prolific composer.

Tappert, Wilhelm (b Ober-Thomaswaldau, Silesia, 19 Feb 1830; d Berlin, 27 Oct 1907), German music scholar. Studied with Dehn and Kullak in Berlin and after eight years as teacher and critic at Glogau settled in Berlin in 1866, where he taught at Tausig's piano school and wrote numerous musico-literary works, including a *Wagner-Lexikon* (a collection of anti-Wagner reviews) and other works on Wagner, studies of notation, old lute music, the settings of Goethe's *Erlkönig* (54), etc. He also wrote piano pieces, including 50 studies for the left hand, songs, etc.

tarantella an Italian dance deriving its name from Taranto, formerly sometimes sung, but now purely instrumental. It is in quick 6–8 time, increasing its speed progressively towards the end, and consists of alternating major and minor sections. It was danced by a couple, or in couples, who often accompanied the music with timbrels. Two superstitions were connected with it: (1) that the bite of the tarantula caused a kind of madness which made people dance it; (2) that the dance was a remedy against such madness.

Tarare opera by Salieri (libretto by Beaumarchais), produced Paris, Opéra, 8 Jun 1787. It became known later under the title of *Axur, re d'Ormus* (Italian version by Da Ponte, produced Vienna, Burgtheater, 8 Jan 1788). Captain Tarare rescues abducted wife Astasie from King Atar and stages successful rebellion.

Taras Bulba rhapsody for orchestra by Janáček, after Gogol; composed 1915–18, fp Brno, 9 Oct 1924, conductor F Neumann. The three movements are 'Death of Andrea', 'Death of Ostap' and 'Capture and Death of Taras Bulba'.

Tarchi, Angelo (b Naples, *c* 1760; d Paris, 19 Aug 1814), Italian composer. Studied at the Pietà dei Turchini Conservatory at Naples with Fago and Sala. For La Scala, Milan, he wrote *Ademira* (1783), *Ariarte* (1786), *Il Conte di Saldagna* (1787), *Adrasto* (1792) and *Le Danaidi* (1794). He attempted to re-write the last two acts of Mozart's *Marriage of Figaro*. He visited London in 1789 and wrote the operas *Il disertore* and *La generosità d'Alessandro* for the King's Theatre. Later he lived in Paris.

Works include over 40 Italian and seven French operas.

tardando Italian = 'delaying'; a direction indicating that a passage is to be played in a lingering manner.

Tarditi, Orazio (b Rome, 1602; d Forli, 18 Jan 1677), Italian composer, monk and organist. He was organist at various Italian towns and from 1647 to 1670 *maestro di cappella* at Faenza Cathedral.

——— THE OPERA ———

Tannhäuser

A three-act Romantic opera by Richard Wagner, who also wrote the text. It is set at the Wartburg, Thuringia, early in the 13th century, and was first performed, with Wagner conducting, in 1845. A revised version (in French) received only three inadequate performances in Paris in 1861 before being withdrawn by the composer.

I. Within the Venusberg, Tannhäuser (tenor) is replete with the pleasures which Venus (mezzo-soprano) has to offer. He invokes the name of the Virgin and as the Venusberg disappears he finds himself at the foot of the Wartburg. Tannhäuser prays as pilgrims pass by, and he is greeted by his friend Wolfram (baritone) and the Landgrave Hermann (bass) who tells of the sadness of his niece since Tannhäuser's departure.

II. At the hall in Wartburg Castle, Elisabeth (soprano) is reunited with Tannhäuser. Knights and lady guests gather for a song contest on the theme of love. While Wolfram sings of an idealized love, Tannhäuser returns to praise of Venus. He is condemned by the company but saved by Elisabeth. He must now seek absolution with the pilgrims on their way to Rome.

III. In the valley of the Wartburg, Elisabeth prays to the Virgin and Wolfram asks for the evening star to protect and guide her. Tannhäuser at last returns and says the Pope has denied him absolution. The funeral procession of a grief-stricken Elisabeth passes by and Tannhäuser expires over her body. The pilgrims now enter with the Pope's staff, miraculously covered in leaves. God has shown his forgiveness and the pilgrims chorus their hallelujahs.

——— THE OPERA ———

Works include Masses, motets, madrigals, canzonets.

Tarr, Edward H(ankins) (b Norwich, CT, 15 Jun 1936), American trumpeter and musicologist. Studied in Boston, Chicago and Basel (with Schrade). Founded Edward Tarr Brass Ensemble (1967) for performances of Renaissance and Baroque music; edited complete trumpet works of Torelli. Also plays works by Kagel, Berio and Stockhausen (e.g. *Michaels Reise um die Erde*).

Tartaglino, Hippolito (b ? Modena, ? 1539; d Naples, 1582), Italian composer. He was successively *maestro di cappella* at Santa Maria Maggiore in Rome and organist at the Church of the Annunciation, Naples. Works said to include Masses and motets for three and four choruses (now lost).

Tartini, Giuseppe (b Pirano, Istria, 8 Apr 1692; d Padua, 26 Feb 1770), Italian composer and violinist. Intended for the Church, he went to Padua University, but was forced to flee after his runaway marriage with Elisabetta Premazore in 1710, and supported himself as an orchestral violinist. Taking refuge at the Franciscan Monastery at Assisi, he was a violin pupil of Černohorský, but a meeting with Veracini in Venice in 1716 convinced him of his technical inadequacy, and he went to Ancona for further study. In 1721 he was appointed principal violinist at the Basilica of Sant' Antonio, where apart from a period in the service of Count Kinsky in Prague (1723–26) and occasional travels elsewhere, he remained till his death. He was successful as a virtuoso, and his compositions were noted for their elegance and brilliance of style. In 1728 he established a school of violin playing in Padua, where his pupils included Nardini and Pugnani. He claimed to have discovered *combination tones* and he commended their use to his pupils as a guide to true intonation. From 1750 he increasingly withdrew from composition to devote himself to theoretical study, and pub. a number of treatises, including *Trattato di musica* (1754).

Works include *Miserere* (said to have been composed for Pope Clement XII) and other church music; over 100 violin concertos;

100 violin sonatas, including *Il Trillo del diavolo/The Devil's Trill*, trio sonatas.

Taruskin, Richard (Filler) (b New York, 2 Apr 1945), American musicologist. Took his PhD at Columbia University 1975 and taught there 1973–87; professor at Berkeley from 1987. He has published *Opera and Drama in Russia* (1981) and wrote the articles on Russian composers and operas in *Opera Grove* (four volumes, 1992). Also writes for the *New York Times* and is a critic of the early music movement.

Taskin, Émile Alexandre (b Paris, 18 Mar 1853; d Paris, 5 Oct 1897), French baritone. Studied at the Paris Conservatory and was a member of the Opéra-Comique 1879–94; saved many lives with his calm demeanour when the opera house caught fire in May 1887 during a performance of Thomas' *Mignon*.

Tasso, Torquato (1544–95), Italian poet. ◊Armida and ◊Armide (11 operas on *Gerusalemme liberata*), (*Aminta*); F ◊Caccini, (*Rinaldo innamorato*); ◊Combattimento di Tancredi e Clorinda (Monteverdi); ◊Madrigal Comedy (*Aminta*); ◊Pizzetti (*Aminta*); ◊Righini (*Gerusalemme liberata*); ◊Rinaldo (Handel); M A ◊Rossi (*Erminia sul Giordano*); ◊Tancrède (Campra); ◊Tancredi (Rossini); ◊Torquato Tasso (Donizetti).

Tasso, lamento e trionfo, *Tasso's Lament and Triumph*, symphonic poem by Liszt, based on a poem by Byron; composed 1849. Fp Weimar, 28 Aug 1849, as an overture to Goethe's drama *Torquato Tasso*; revised 1850–51 with a new middle section and performed Weimar, 19 Apr 1854.

tastar Italian, from *tastare* = 'to touch'; a 16th-c. lute prelude with which the strings were 'touched', or tried; equivalent to a toccata.

tastiera per luce Italian = 'keyboard for light'; an instrument appearing in the score of Skriabin's *Prometheus*, designed to throw differently coloured lights. It was never perfected for practical use.

tasto Italian = key (of keyboard instruments); also fingerboard (of string instruments).

tasto solo Italian = 'key alone'; a direction indicating that in a composition with a thorough-bass the bass notes are for the moment to be played alone on the keyboard instrument used, without any harmony above them.

Tate, Jeffrey (b Salisbury, 28 Apr 1943), English conductor. Overcoming the handicap of spina bifida, he was to become répétiteur at CG, 1971–77; assistant to Boulez at Bayreuth and Paris, 1976–80. Opera debut Göteborg, 1978, *Carmen*. At the NY Met. he gave the three-act version of *Lulu* (1980) and has returned for *Rosenkavalier*, *Wozzeck* and *Lohengrin*. CG debut 1982, *La Clemenza di Tito*; *Ariadne auf Naxos*, 1985. At the 1985 Salzburg Festival he conducted the fp of Henze's realization of Monteverdi's *Ulisse*. Regular concerts with English Chamber Orchestra from 1982. Principal conductor CG 1986–91; Rotterdam PO 1991. Conducted the fp of Liebermann's *La Forêt* (Geneva 1987) and the *Ring* at the Théâtre du Châtelet, Paris, 1994.

Tate, Phyllis (Margaret) (b Gerrards Cross, 6 Apr 1911; d London, 27 May 1987), English composer. Studied composition with Harry Farjeon at the RAM in London, 1928–32. Several of her works were performed when she was still a student, and in 1933 her cello concerto was her first work heard at a public concert. Her works were generally small scale, and carefully crafted.

Works include operas *The Lodger* (1960), *Dark Pilgrimage* (1963) and *Twice in a Blue Moon* (1968); operetta *The Policeman's Serenade* (A P Herbert); *Secular Requiem* for chorus and orchestra (1967), *Serenade to Christmas* for mezzo, chorus and orchestra (1972), *All the World's a Stage* for chorus and orchestra (1977); symphony and suite for orchestra, *Valse lointaine* and prelude, interlude and postlude for chamber orchestra (1941); cello and saxophone concertos (1933, 1944), *Panorama* for string orchestra (1977).

Divertimento for string quartet, sonata for clarinet and cello (1947), *Nocturne* (S Keyes) for four voices, string quintet, celesta and bass clarinet; *London Waits* for two pianos; *Songs of Sundry Natures* on Elizabethan poems for voice and piano, songs to words by Blake, W H Davies, Hardy, Hood, Tennyson and others, *The Phoenix and the Turtle* for tenor and instrumental ensemble.

Tatrai, Vilmos (b Kispest, 7 Oct 1912), Hungarian violinist. After study at the Budapest Conservatory played in the Municipal Orchestra

---

Jeffrey Tate – conductor

1 Schubert: *Die Winterreise* (Fischer-Dieskau/Moore)
For me to draw a dividing line between the many wonderful pieces of music that I grew to love and the effect made upon me by inspiring performances would be difficult. My first really profound concert-going experience was hearing Dietrich Fischer-Dieskau sing Schubert's song cycle *Die Winterreise* when I was 13. The moment he began to sing, the hall seemed to shrink into a tiny room that contained only him and me. I had acquainted myself with the text, but I never imagined that lieder could develop such cumulative force of expression, such extraordinary dramatic tension. That evening was my introduction to the real power of Schubert. In his art, fatalism and consolation stand side by side.

2 Britten: *War Requiem* (Vishnevskaya/Pears/Fischer-Dieskau/LSO & Chorus/Britten)
When I was 19, I first heard a performance of Britten's *War Requiem*, conducted by the composer himself. His way of juxtaposing the Latin text with the immensely powerful Wilfred Owen poems had a direct, emotional impact; the work speaks timelessly about war and aggression. The concluding passage – the conversation between the German and English soldiers – is unbelievably moving. I felt I had the privilege of hearing a masterpiece of our century.

3 Beethoven: String Quartet in B flat (Busch Quartet or Quartetto Italiano)
A friend played me a recording of this work while I was at Cambridge. It came as a revelation. I felt that I had crossed a threshold – that I had entered an inner world of enormous expression and complexity, a world that no other composer explores so thoroughly as Beethoven. This was the beginning of a life-long love of his quartets and of chamber music.

4 Beethoven: *Missa solemnis* (Soloists/New Philharmonia Orch. & Chorus/Klemperer)
The *Missa solemnis* is the most life-affirming music I know. I view it not as a religious work but as a humanistic one, a tribute to the energy of man. For me – and this is a very personal view – the work achieves the summit of choral and instrumental writing. Yes, I rank it above Bach's Passions, the Mass in B minor, or even Beethoven's Ninth Symphony.

5 Wagner: *Die Meistersinger von Nürnberg*
My first absolutely transcendental operatic experience came when I was about 25 with *Die Meistersinger*, conducted by Reginald Goodall at Sadler's Wells Theatre, London. From the moment the curtain went up, I was caught like a fish on a hook. In Goodall's hands, every phrase was of ineffable beauty. It was my first experience of *Die Meistersinger*, and it will probably remain my best.

there, 1933–36. Leader of the Hungarian State SO, 1940–78, and founded the Tatrai Quartet 1946, giving many tours of Europe and the Far East from 1955 with appearances at the Salzburg, Edinburgh and Vienna Festivals. (Quartet's repertory of 360 compositions has included more than 100 premieres; has recorded complete cycles of the Haydn, Beethoven and Bartók quartets). Founder and leader of the Hungarian Chamber Orchestra 1957, professor at the Franz Liszt Academy from 1965.

Tattermuschová, Helena (b Prague, 28 Jun 1933), Czech soprano. She sang Musetta at Ostrava in 1955 and joined the Prague National Theatre in 1959; many tours with the co., including Edinburgh 1970, in the first British performance of Janáček's *The Excursions of Mr Brouček*. Sang Smetana, Mozart and Strauss; best known as Janáček's Vixen.

Tauber, Richard (b Linz, 16 May 1892; d London, 8 Jan 1948), Austrian, later British, tenor. Studied at Freiburg and made his debut at Chemnitz in 1913 as Tamino. Dresden 1913–26, after which he took largely to operetta; Vienna 1926–38. In 1931 he had first appeared in England, where he settled in 1940. Sang in the USA 1931–47. Other roles included Ottavio, Calaf, Rodolfo and parts in the operettas of Lehár.

Taubert, (Karl Gottfried) Wilhelm (b Berlin, 23 Mar 1811; d Berlin, 7 Jan 1891), German composer, conductor and pianist. Pupil of Ludwig Berger for piano and of Klein for composition, and student at Berlin University. He became Prussian court pianist, in 1841 conductor of the Royal Opera and in 1845 court music director.

Works include operas *Die Kirmess* (1832), *Der Zigeuner* (1834), *Marquis und Dieb* (1842), *Joggeli*, *Macbeth* (after Shakespeare) and *Cesario* (on Shakespeare's *Twelfth Night*, 1874); incidental music to *Medea* (Euripides), *The Tempest* (Shakespeare) and other plays; three Psalms and other church music; four cantatas; four symphonies; three string quartets; c 300 songs including *Kinderlieder*; duets, part-songs.

Taucher, Curt (b Nuremberg, 25 Oct 1885; d Munich, 7 Aug 1954), German tenor. Debut Augsburg, 1908, as Faust. After engagements in Chemnitz and Hanover he sang at the Dresden Staatsoper, 1920–34; created there Menelaos in *Ägyptische Helena* (1928) and the title role in Weill's *Der Protagonist* (1926). NY Met. 1923–27, as Siegmund and Siegfried. London, CG, 1932, and sang in Barcelona, Berlin and Munich. Retired 1935. Well known in Wagner roles and as Strauss's Emperor.

Tausch, Julius (b Dessau, 15 Apr 1827; d Bonn, 11 Nov 1895), German composer and conductor. Pupil of Schneider at Dessau and at the Leipzig Conservatory. He became conductor of the Künstlerliedertafel at Düsseldorf in 1847, and succeeded Schumann as conductor of the Music Society in 1855.

Works include incidental music to Shakespeare's *Twelfth Night* (1863); Festival Overture for orchestra; piano pieces; songs.

Tausig, Carl (b Warsaw, 4 Nov 1841; d Lepizig, 17 Jul 1871), Polish pianist and composer of Bohemian origin. Pupil of his father, the pianist Aloys Tausig (1820–85), and of Liszt at Weimar. In 1858 he made his debut, at a concert conducted by Bülow in Berlin, then toured, settled at Dresden and in 1862 in Vienna, where he gave concerts with programmes of modern music. In 1865 he married, settled in Berlin and opened a school of advanced piano playing.

Works include symphonic poems; piano concerto; concert studies, exercises, bravura pieces and numerous transcriptions for piano.

Tausky, Vilem (b Perov, 20 Jul 1910), Czech-born English conductor and composer. Studied in Brno and was director of the National Opera there, 1929–39. Emigrated to England and was music director of the Carl Rosa Opera, 1945–49; guest with the BBC, SW and CG from early 1950s. Director of opera at the GSMD, London, from 1966. Led the UK fps of Janáček's *Osud* (1972) and Suppé's *Requiem* (1984). Conducted Smetana's *The Brandenburgers in Bohemia* with Chelsea Opera Group, 1994. Recordings include William Alwyn's Strindberg opera *Miss Julie*, and has published *Leos Janáček: Leaves from his Life*.

Tavener, John (Kenneth) (b London, 28 Jan 1944), English composer. He studied at the RAM with Lennox Berkeley and David Lumsdaine.

His music shows a wide range of influences, and he is often drawn towards religious subjects (he is a member of the Greek Orthodox Church). Once admired for its variety and complexity, his music has recently gained popularity by more simple means.

Works include three *Holy Sonnets* for baritone and orchestra (texts by Donne, 1962), piano concerto (1963), *The Cappemakers*, dramatic cantata (1965), *Cain and Abel*, dramatic cantata (1965), *Little Concerto* (1965), *The Whale*, cantata (1966), *Grandma's Footsteps* for ensemble (1968), *Introit for the Feast of St John Damascene* for soloists, chorus and orchestra (1968), *Concerto for Orchestra* (1968), *In alium* for soprano, orchestra and tape (1968), *Celtic Requiem* (1969), *Ultimos Ritos* for soloists, speakers, chorus and orchestra (1969–72), *Coplas* for soloist, chorus and tape (1970), *Ma fin est mon commencement* for tenor, chorus, brass and percussion (1972), *Little Requiem for Father Malachy Lynch* (1972), *Requiem for Father Malachy* (1973).

Thérèse, opera (1973–76; produced 1979), *Kyklike kinesis* for soprano, chorus, cello and orchestra (1977), *Palintropos* for piano and orchestra (1977), *Liturgy of St John Chrysostom* for unaccompanied chorus (1978), *Akhmatova: rekviem* (1980), *Sappho: Lyrical Fragments* for two sopranos and strings (1980), *Risen!* for chorus, piano, organ and orchestra (1980), *Funeral Ikos* for chorus (1981), *Trisagion* for brass quintet (1981), *Ikon of Light* for chorus and string trio (1984), *Eis Thanaton*, dramatic cantata (1987).

The Protecting Veil for cello and strings (1987), *Akathist of Thanksgiving* (1987), *Ikon of St Seraphini* (1988), *Resurrection* for soloists, actors, chorus and orchestra (1989), *The Repentant Thief*, for clarinet and ensemble (1990), *Mary of Egypt*, music theatre (1991), *We Shall See Him as he is* for soloists, chorus and ensemble (1992), *Eternal Memory* for cello and ensemble (1992), *Hymns of Paradise* for bass, chorus and strings (1993), *The Apocalypse* for soloists, chorus and orchestra (1994).

Taverner opera by Maxwell Davies (libretto by composer); composed 1962–70, produced London, CG, 12 Jul 1972. Plot is based on now discredited story that John Taverner was an agent of Thomas Cromwell dedicated to the persecution of the Catholic Church.

Taverner, John (b South Lincs., c 1490; d Boston, Lincs., 18 Oct 1545), English composer and organist. In 1526 he was appointed master of the choristers at Wolsey's new college (Cardinal College, later Christ Church) at Oxford and organist at St Frideswide's Church (later Cathedral) attached to it. In 1528 he was involved in heresy at the college, and in 1530, following Wolsey's eclipse, he left, probably to

A Selection of

Taverner

The Western Wind Masses
Missa Corona spinea Missa Gloria tibi Trinitas
Missa Mater Christi

Missa O Michael
Missa Sancti Wilhelmi
Motets
in nomine for 4 viols

John Tavener – composer

1 'Today He who hung the earth upon the waters is hung upon the Cross' (Antiphon Fifteen. Mode II Plagal, from the Patriarchal Church of the Ecumenical Patriarchate, Constantinople)
This ancient Troparion is sung by the Priest as he carries the great cross from the sanctuary round the church and places it in the centre. For me this is the most moving moment of the whole year, both musically and spiritually, because I cannot separate what is 'musical' and what is 'spiritual'.

2 Mozart: *Die Zauberflöte/The Magic Flute* (Vienna PO/ Böhm or Ingmar Bergman's film *The Magic Flute*)
This opera can be understood by a six year old, and a sixty year old. When I first heard it at Glyndebourne when I was twelve, I was enchanted by it. It is the western opera that I can take seriously, because Mozart abandons the secular humanistic 18th-century landscape for one of archetypes – fools, wise men, rituals – and prototypes.

3 'Thy Bridal Chamber, I see adorned ...' (from the Russian Orthodox 'Bridegroom Services' of Holy Week)
The music has a quality of simplicity and transparency. I hear it every year, sung by Arch Priest Michael Fortounatto in the Russian Orthodox Cathedral. The chant is medieval, and both the music and the text are so perfectly 'married', that one could not exist without the other.

4 Stravinsky: *Canticum Sacrum*
I first heard this music when I was twelve. It was broadcast from Venice. It was this music that made me want to become a composer. I have never heard a satisfactory performance of it, however, and I would like to conduct it myself!

5 Tchaikovsky: *Casse Noisette/Nutcracker*
This music, like *The Magic Flute*, can be understood by a six year old and a sixty year old. For me, Tchaikovsky can never put a note wrong, consequently I love every note that he wrote.

---

return to his native Lincolnshire. There is no foundation in the allegations that he gave up music to devote himself to the persecution of Catholics as an agent of Thomas Cromwell. In 1537 he was elected a member of the Guild of Corpus Christi in Boston. His music shows some influence of Josquin and his fluently developed Mass settings made him the leading English composer of his time. The instrumental In Nomine tradition originated from a passage at those words in his Mass *Gloria tibi Trinitas*.

Works include eight Masses (including *The Western Wind*, *Gloria tibi Trinitas*), 25 Latin motets, three Magnificats and other church music.

Taylor, (Joseph) Deems (b New York, 22 Dec 1885; d New York, 3 Jul 1966), American composer and critic. Studied at the Ethical Culture School and the University in NY, received piano lessons, but was self-taught in other musical subjects. He became music critic to the *New York World* in 1921, but from 1925 devoted himself to composition.

Works include operas *The King's Henchman* (1927), *Peter Ibbetson* (after G du Maurier, 1931), and *Ramuntcho* (after Loti, 1942); incidental music for T Wilder's *Lucrece* and for other plays; symphonic poems *The Siren Song* and *Jurgen* (after J B Cabell), suites *Through the Looking-Glass* (after L Carroll) and *Circus Day* (1925), *Lucrece* suite for string quartet; choral works.

Tchaikovsky, Pyotr Il'yich (b Kamsko Votkinsk, 7 May 1840; d St Petersburg, 6 Nov 1893), Russian composer. He successfully united Western European influences with native Russian fervour and emotion. His father, an inspector of mines, allowed him to have music lessons from the age of four, and at six he played well. The family moved to St Petersburg in 1848; he received more systematic teaching there and in 1850 was sent to the School of Jurisprudence, which he left in 1859 to become a clerk in the Ministry of Justice. He approached music as an amateur, but in 1862 entered the newly opened Conservatory, having already studied with Zaremba, and had lessons in orchestration from A Rubinstein. N Rubinstein, having opened a similar Conservatory at Moscow, engaged him as professor of harmony in 1865, and there he began to compose seriously and professionally. In 1868 he met Balakirev and his circle of nationalist composers in St Petersburg, but remained aloof. In the same year his First symphony *Winter Daydreams* was successfully performed in Moscow; it remains in some ways the freshest and most spontaneous music in this form. His first opera *The Voyevoda* was premiered at the Bolshoi 1869 and *Romeo and Julliet* in 1870.

The second symphony, a distinctly nationalist work, was per-

formed 1873, and the B♭ minor piano concerto, though at first rejected by N Rubinstein, was given at Boston by Bülow in 1875 and given its first Moscow performance later that year by Taneiev. In 1876 he began a correspondence with Nadezhda von Meck, the widow of a wealthy engineer, who greatly admired his work and made him an allowance to free him from financial anxiety, but never met him face to face. His first important opera *Vakula the Smith* was premiered 1876 and the following year the first of his great ballets, *Swan Lake*, was premiered at the Bolshoi, 1877. The hero's name (Siegfried) is probably derived from Wagner's *Ring*, which he had just seen at Bayreuth. Also in 1877 he married Antonina Milyukova; but he was an undeclared homosexual and left her less than a month after the wedding, on the verge of mental collapse. After some months in

Tchaikovsky
A biographical note

Tchaikovsky was deeply troubled by his homosexuality – his preference was for rough trade encountered in the streets – and lived in fear that his secret would become public knowledge. An answer to his problem seemed to come when he was working on his Fourth Symphony. Receiving a love letter from an unknown woman named Antonina Milyukova, he was at first non-committal, but then agreed to meet her when she threatened suicide. Shortly before their meeting he had read Pushkin's *Eugene Onegin*, and was struck by the scene in which Tatiana writes an impulsive love letter to Onegin. Perhaps not wishing to emulate Onegin's cold rejection of his admirer, Tchaikovsky agreed to marry Antonina – with the proviso that their relationship should remain platonic. Antonina imagined herself to be irresistible to men and no doubt thought she could mend Tchaikovsky's ways. By the time of his marriage on 18 July, Tchaikovsky had sketched two-thirds of his opera *Eugene Onegin*, beginning with the letter scene. His wedding night was not a success. He took the train with Antonina to travel from Moscow to St Petersburg, but reported later to his brother Anatoly: 'As soon as the train started I was ready to scream out loud; I was wracked with choking sobs but I had to make conversation with my wife until at last it was dark and I was able to lie down in my armchair.' The marriage soon ended in separation, and after bearing several illegitimate children Antonina died in a mental institution.

Switzerland and Italy, he resigned the post at the Moscow Conservatory and lived in the country, wholly devoted to composition. The first of his universally popular symphonies, the 4th in F minor, was premiered in 1878; its insistent 'Fate' motive heralds a trilogy of works in which the tension between life affirmation and self-annhilation, is dominant. In *Eugene Onegin* of 1879 are mirrored some of the recent circumstances of Tchaikovsky's own life; Tatiana writes an optimistic love letter to the reluctant Onegin just as Antonina had done to Tchaikovsky. His most brilliant and least introverted orchestral work, the Violin Concerto in D, was given at Vienna in 1881 and seven years later he composed the most powerful and fully-integrated of the symphonies, the 5th in E minor.

In 1888 he made a first international tour as conductor of his own works, which became known in many countries, and the following year he completed the finest of his three ballets, *The Sleeping Beauty*. In 1890 he had a misunderstanding with Mme von Meck which brought their friendship by correspondence to an end; but he was by that time quite able to earn his own living.

He visited the USA in 1892 and London in the summer of 1893, when the Mus.D. degree was conferred on him by Cambridge University. On his return to Russia, he completed the sixth symphony ('Pathétique'), which was fp at St Petersburg on 28 Oct. Nine days later Tchaikovsky was dead; the cause of death is usually given as cholera, although it has recently been suggested that he took poison at the decree of a secret court of honour instituted to avert a scandal following allegations of a liaison between him and an aristocrat's nephew.

Works include operas *The Opritchnik* (1874), *Vakula the Smith* (afterwards *Tcherevichki or Oxana's Caprices*, 1876), *Eugene Onegin* (1879), *Maid of Orleans* (1881), *Mazeppa* (1884), *The Sorceress*, *The Queen of Spades* (1890), *Iolanta* (1892) and three partly lost early works; incidental music to Ostrovsky's *Snegurochka* and Shakespeare's *Hamlet*; ballets *Swan Lake* (1877), *The Sleeping Beauty* (1890) and *The Nutcracker* (1892).

ORCHESTRAL: seven symphonies, no. 1 in G minor (*Winter Daydreams*, 1866, revised 1874), no. 2 in C minor (*Little Russian*, 1872, revised 1880), no. 3 in D (*Polish*, 1875), no. 4 in F minor (1878), no. 5 in E minor (1888), no. 6 in B minor (*Pathétique*, 1893), no. 7 in E♭ (unfinished, 1892); four suites: no. 1 in D (1879), no. 2 in C (1883), no. 3 in G (1884), no. 4 (*Mozartiana*, 1887); *Manfred* symphony, after Byron (1885); fantasy-overture *Romeo and Juliet* (1869), symphonic fantasies *The Tempest* (1873) and *Francesca da Rimini* (1876),

Tchaikovsky *The composer Pyotr Tchaikovsky (1840–1893) in a drawing by W I Bruckman. Although he distanced himself from Balakirev's circle of nationalist composers, Tchaikovsky's love of his country and its folk song ensured that a Russian flavour remained.*

Capriccio italien, Serenade for string orchestra (1880), overture *The Year 1812* (1880), fantasy-overture *Hamlet* (1888), symphonic ballad *The Voyevoda* (1891); three piano concertos, no. 1 in B♭ minor (1875), no. 2 in G (1880), no. 3 in E♭ (unfinished, 1893), violin concerto (1878), *Variations on a Rococo Theme* for cello and orchestra (1876) and some smaller pieces for solo instruments and orchestra.

CHAMBER: string sextet *Souvenir de Florence* (1887), three string quartets (1871, 1874, 1876), piano trio (1882); 17 op. nos. of piano compositions including six pieces on one theme, sonata in G major, *The Seasons*; 50 Russian folksongs for vocal duet; 13 op. nos. of songs (nearly 100); six vocal duets; three cantatas; some church music; part-songs.

Tchaikowsky, André (b Warsaw, 1 Nov 1935; d Oxford, 26 Jun 1982), Polish-born British pianist and composer. He escaped from the Warsaw ghetto and was brought up in Paris. Returning to Poland, he studied with Stefan Askenase. Lived in London from 1957 and was well known as a concert pianist; he was by no means reluctant to embellish Mozart's piano concertos. He bequeathed his skull to the Royal Shakespeare Company for use in its performances of *Hamlet*. The skull was duly placed in a stock cupboard, with two others, and appeared on stage in 1984.

Works include clarinet sonata (1959), two string quartets, (1967, 1970), piano concerto (1971), *Trio notturno* (1973). An opera *The Merchant of Venice*, was almost complete at his death.

Tcherepnin, Alexander (Nikolaievich) (b St Petersburg, 21 Jan 1899; d Paris, 29 Sept 1977), Russian composer. Studied under his father, Nikolai Tcherepnin, Sokolov and others, learning the piano from

A Selection of

Tchaikovsky

Symphony no. 1	1866
Romeo and Juliet	1869
Piano Concerto no. 1	1875
Swan Lake	1877
Violin Concerto	1878
Eugene Onegin	1879
Symphony no. 5	1888
Sleeping Beauty	1890
The Nutcracker	1892
Symphony no. 6	1893

Anna Essipova. He appeared as a boy pianist and began to pub. his works, but in 1921 settled in Paris with his father, studying composition with Gédalge and piano with Philipp at the Conservatory. From 1925 and 1938 he taught in Paris, and from 1949 at De Paul University in Chicago.

Works include operas 01–01 (after Andreiev, 1928) and *Die Hochzeit der Sobeide* (after Hofmannsthal, 1933); ballets including *The Frescoes of Ajanta* (1923) and (with Honegger and Harsányi) *Shota Roustaveli*; incidental music for Wilde's *Salome*, Rolland's *L'Esprit triomphant* and Hauptmann's *Hannele*; cantata *Le Jeu de la Nativité*.

Four symphonies (1927–58), three pieces for chamber orchestra, six piano concertos (1923–72), *Rapsodie géorgienne* for cello and piano, *Concerto da camera* for flute, violin and small orchestra; two string quartets (1922, 1926), piano trio; violin and piano sonata, three cello and piano sonatas; sonata, studies and pieces for piano.

Tcherepnin, Nikolai (Nikolaievich) (b St Petersburg, 15 May 1873; d Issy-les-Moulineaux, near Paris, 26 Jun 1945), Russian composer and conductor, father of Alexander ◊Tcherepnin. He gave up a legal career at the age of 22 and studied at the St Petersburg Conservatory with Rimsky-Korsakov and others. Having appeared as pianist, he became conductor of the Belaiev concerts in 1901, and then became conductor of opera at the Maryinsky Theatre. In 1908 he joined Diaghilev and conducted Russian opera and ballet in Paris and elsewhere, remaining with the company until 1914, when he returned to Petrograd, to become director of the Conservatory at Tiflis in 1918. In 1921 he settled in Paris.

Works include operas *Vanka the Chancellor* (after Sologub, 1935), and *Poverty no Crime* (after Ostrovsky); ballets *Armida's Pavilion* (1907), *Narcissus* (1911), *A Russian Fairy-Tale*, *The Romance of a Mummy* (after Gautier), *The Masque of the Red Death* (after Poe, 1916), *The Tale of the Princess Ulyba*, *Dionysius*.

Symphony, sinfonietta, symphonic poems *Narciss and Echo* and *The Enchanted Kingdom*, witches' scene from *Macbeth*, suite *The Enchanted Garden* (1904), overture to Rostand's *La Princesse lointaine* (1903), six pieces on Pushkin's *The Golden Fish* for orchestra; piano concerto in C♯ minor (1907), lyric poem for violin and orchestra; string quartet in A minor; piano pieces on Benois' picture-book *The Russian Alphabet* and other piano works; songs.

Te the name for the leading-note in any key in tonic sol-fa, so pronounced, but in notation represented by the symbol *t*.

Tear, Robert (b Barry, 8 Mar 1939), Welsh tenor. He studied at Cambridge and sang with the EOG 1963–71; created roles in Britten's church parables *The Burning Fiery Furnace* and *The Prodigal Son*. He created Dov in *The Knot Garden* at CG in 1970; other London roles have been Grimes, Lensky and Paris in *King Priam*. Loge was the role of his Paris, Opéra, debut (1976) and he returned in 1979 to sing the Painter in the first complete performance of Berg's *Lulu*. Salzburg Festival 1985, as Eumeo in the Henze/Monteverdi *Ulisse*. Created the title role in Penderecki's *Ubu Rex* (Munich 1991), and was Mephisto in Prokofiev's *Fiery Angel* at CG, 1992. Well known in oratorio and recitals.

Teares and Lamentacions of a Sorrowfull Soul, The ◊Leighton, William.

Tebaldi, Renata (b Pesaro, 1 Feb 1922), Italian soprano. Studied at Parma Conservatory, and then with Carmen Melis from 1939 to 1942,

Te Kanawa *The soprano Kiri Te Kanawa. She left her native New Zealand and made her debut at Covent Garden in 1971 as Mozart's Countess Almaviva. Her warm voice is matched by a magnetic stage presence.*

making her debut in Rovigo in 1944 as Boito's Elena. She sang at the re-opening of La Scala, Milan, in 1946 under Toscanini and at CG in 1950, with the Scala co. US debut San Francisco, 1950, as Aida; NY Met. debut 1955, as Desdemona. Returned to NY until 1973 and toured Russia, 1976. Other roles included Violetta, Tosca, Mimi, Adriana Lecouvreur and Eva. She was known as one of the best Verdi and Puccini singers of her day.

tedesca *or* tedesco Italian = 'German'. The term *alla tedesca* means 'in the German manner', but more particularly indicates a piece or movement in rather slow waltz time, in the character of the *Deutscher* or *Ländler*.

Te Deum laudamus, *We praise thee, O God*, Latin hymn or psalm in 'rhythmical prose', possibly by Nicetas of Remesiana (*c* 400). It is in three sections: a hymn to the Trinity, a hymn to Christ, and a series of prayers. The first part is set to a psalmodic formula ending on G, and the second to a similar formula ending on E, but concluding with a more extended melody in the same mode to the words 'Aeterna fac'. The third part makes further use of these last two melodies.

The Te Deum was set in polyphony during the Middle Ages, especially in England, for voices or organ in alternation with the plainsong. It became a normal part of the Anglican 'Morning Service' and it has also been set in English for occasions of rejoicing (e.g. by Handel, Walton). The Latin text has often been set with orchestral accompaniment, e.g. by Haydn (2), Berlioz, Bruckner and Kodály.

Te Kanawa, Kiri (b Gisborne, Auckland, 6 Mar 1944), New Zealand-

---

Robert Tear – singer / conductor

1	Tallis: Lamentations of Jeremiah A work of timeless sincerity and honour.	4	Mendelssohn: Symphony no. 4 in A (*Italian*) Dear love observable in every bar.
2	Handel: Concerto grosso op. 6 no. 2 Intellect and imagination in perfect balance.		
3	Mozart: Symphony no. 41 in C (*Jupiter*) The last movement is an outrageous exhibition of talent.	5	Stravinsky: *Symphony of Psalms* An archetype. Music that could be understood by a 6th-century listener.

Telemann   *A biographical note*

Immensely prolific as a musician, Telemann was also pro-
ductive in his personal life. His first wife, daughter of the
composer Daniel Eberlin, died in childbirth, but by his second,
whom he married three years later, he had ten children. Sadly,
all but two died in infancy and, wearied by her labours and
disappointments, his wife deserted him for a Swedish officer.
She left huge debts behind, and Telemann was reduced to
soliciting his friends for funds with a satirical poem on the
subject of feminine extravagance. He had recently met with his
widowed mother's opposition to a musical career, but a meeting with Handel at Halle on the way to law school at Leipzig
was crucial in deciding his vocation. At Leipzig University he
founded the Collegium Musicum, becoming one of the first
composers to make serious money through teaching music. In
appointments in Frankfurt and then Hamburg, he wrote many
of his 1700 church cantatas; his rejection of the less lucrative
post at the St Thomas Choir School at Leipzig fortuitously
allowed Bach to take up the most important position of his
career.

born British soprano. She sang Elena in Rossini's *La donna del lago* at
the 1969 Camden Festival, London. Came to wider attention with
Mozart's Countess at CG, in 1970, and since then has sung Marguerite, Micaela, Fiordiligi, Arabella and the Marschallin in London. US
debut 1972, San Francisco, as the Countess; NY Met. 1974, Desdemona. Sang the Countess in Capriccio at CG 1990, Amelia Boccanegra 1991. She is admired for the lyric beauty of her voice and her
attractive stage presence. In recent years she has broadened her
appeal, and has sung at weddings and on television. DBE 1982.

Telemaco, Il, ossia L'isola di Circe, *Telemachus, or Circe's Island*,
opera by Gluck (libretto by M Coltellini), produced Vienna, Burgtheater, 30 Jan 1765. Sorceress Circe loves prisoner Ulysses on her
enchanted island. His son Telemachus, also shipwrecked, falls in love
with Asteria, Circe's maid (later revealed to be his intended wife).
They escape while Circe swears revenge.

---

*I have always aimed at facility. Music ought not to be
an effort.*
Georg Philipp Telemann, quoted in Headington, *The
Bodley Head History of Western Music*, 1974

Telemann, Georg Philipp (b Magdeburg, 14 Mar 1681; d Hamburg, 25
Jun 1767), German composer. Educated at Magdeburg and Hildes-
heim, and at Leipzig University, where he read law, he seems to have
been largely self-taught in music. In Leipzig he founded a student
Collegium musicum and was appointed organist of the New Church
(St Matthew's) in 1704, but the same year moved to Sorau as
Kapellmeister to Count Promnitz. In the service of the court at
Eisenach 1708–12 (*Kapellmeister* from 1709) he made the acquaintance of Bach in nearby Weimar, then worked in Frankfurt until his
appointment in 1721 as Cantor of the Johanneum and municipal
music director in Hamburg, where he stayed for the rest of his life. In
1722 he declined the post of Cantor of St Thomas's, Leipzig, and
Bach was appointed. He travelled a good deal, several times visiting
Berlin, and in 1737 made a successful visit to Paris. He is famed for his
huge output, although some of his instrumental music can sound
routine and written to order; his most attractive music is often in the
vocal works, notably the operas, oratorios and cantatas. He was the
best-known German composer of his time with a contemporary
reputation much greater than Bach's.

Works include *c* 45 operas (few survive complete), e.g. *Der
geduldige Socrates* (1721), *Der neumodische Liebhaber Damon*

(1724), *Miriways* (1728), *Pimpinone* (1725), *Emma und Eginhard*
(1728); oratorios *Die Tageszeiten, Die Auferstehung und Himmelfahrt Christi* (1760), *Der Tag des Gerichts* (1762), etc.; Passion
oratorios (Brockes and Ramler); 46 liturgical Passions; 12 sets of
cantatas for the church's year; motets, psalms, etc.; large quantities of
instrumental music, including collection called *Musique de table*
(Hamburg, 1733); concertos, orchestral suites, trio sonatas and other
chamber music, keyboard music.

Tellefsen, Arve (b Trondheim, 1948), Norwegian violinist. Studied
with Ivan Galamian in New York from 1960 and won Harriet Cohen
Award 1962. Professor at the Oslo Academy from 1973 and has
appeared widely as soloist (tour of Norway 1985, with the RPO);
British engagements with Okko Kamu and Kurt Sanderling. Founded
the Oslo Chamber Music Festival 1989 and has recorded concertos by
Berwald, Nielsen, Shostakovich and Sibelius.

Telmányi, Emil (b Arad, 22 Jun 1892; d Holte, Denmark, 12 Jun 1988),
Hungarian violinist and conductor. Studied at the Budapest Con-
servatory and appeared with the Berlin PO 1911, with the first
continental performance of the Elgar Concerto. He married Carl
Nielsen's daughter in 1918 and appeared with the composer in
London, 1923. Conducted concerts throughout Europe and opera at
Budapest. In 1956 formed string quintet with second wife and her
three children. Teacher at the Arhus Conservatory 1940–69 and
responsible for development of 'Vega' bow, for the performance of
Baroque music, especially by Bach.

Temirkanov, Yuri (b Nalchik, 10 Dec 1938), Russian conductor. Made
debut with the Leningrad Opera, after graduating in 1965. Conducted
the Leningrad SO 1968–76 and made Salzburg debut (with Vienna
PO) 1971. Conductor of the Kirov Opera and Ballet 1977. London
debut with the RPO 1977, becoming principal conductor 1992. Took
the Kirov to CG 1986 with *Boris Godunov, Eugene Onegin*, and *The
Queen of Spades*. Succeeded Mravinsky as chief conductor of the
Leningrad (later St Petersburg PO) 1988; Tchaikovsky cycles in
Japan and Europe, 1992/93.

Telemann *The composer Georg Philipp Telemann (1681–1767)
showing off an unidentified manuscript. He was acknowledged as the
most eminent German composer during his lifetime, unlike Bach who
was restored to greatness only in the 19th century. His works are more
accessible and light-hearted than Bach's.*

A Selection of

Telemann

Pimpinone...1725
Tafelmusik...1733
Overture-Suites 1730s

Don Quichotte...1730s
Paris Quartets...1738–39
Cantatas...1730s
Violin Concertos...1730s
Der Tag des Gerichts.................1762

Temistocle, *Themistocles*, opera by Porpora (libretto by A Zeno), produced Vienna, 1 Oct 1718.

Opera by J C Bach (libretto M Verazi, after Metastasio) produced Mannheim, Hoftheater, 5 Nov 1772. Driven away by the people of Athens, Themistocles seeks refuge in the land of his enemy, Xerxes, King of Persia. Themistocles finds his daughter Aspacia there suffering the advances of Xerxes. When Aspacia would choose suicide rather than marriage to him and when Themistocles would do likewise rather than renounce Greece, Xerxes is impressed by their virtue and makes a happy ending.

temperament a term used to designate the tuning of the musical scale in such a way as to produce satisfying intonation in some way not according to the natural harmonics. ◊equal temperament.

Temperley, Nicholas (b Beaconsfield, 7 Aug 1932), English-born musicologist (American citizen 1977). Studied at Cambridge 1954–59 and was assistant lecturer there 1961–66; professor at University of Illinois 1972, chairman of musicology division 1992. Has published editions of Loder's *Raymond and Agnes* (produced Cambridge 1966) and the *Symphonie Fantastique* in the New Berlioz edition, 1972. *English Songs, 1800–60* (1979), *The Music of the English Parish Church* (two volumes, 1979), *London Pianoforte School* (20 volumes 1984–87). Completion of Mozart's *L'oca del Cairo* produced Illinois, 1991.

Tempestà, La opera by Halévy (libretto by Scribe, originally written in French for Mendelssohn, based on Shakespeare's *Tempest* and translated into Italian), produced London, Her Majesty's Theatre, 8 Jun 1850.

Tempest, The incidental music by Sibelius, op. 109, composed for Shakespeare's play at the Theatre Royal, Copenhagen, 1926.

Opera by Fibich (libretto by J Vrchlický, based on Shakespeare), produced Prague, Czech Theatre, 1 Mar 1895.

Prospero, Miranda and Ferdinand shipwrecked on an island with Ariel and Caliban.

Symphonic fantasy by Tchaikovsky, after Shakespeare, suggested by Stassov, begun Aug 1873, fp Moscow, 19 Dec 1873.

Tempest, The, or The Enchanted Island opera adapted from Shakespeare by T Shadwell, with music by (?) Locke, Humfrey, Reggio, James Hart, G B Draghi and Banister, produced London, Dorset Gardens Theatre, 30 Apr 1674.

Opera adapted from Shakespeare by Shadwell, with music by Weldon, formerly attributed to H Purcell, composed *c* 1712.

Templario, Il, *The Templar*, opera by Nicolai (libretto by G M Marini, based on Scott's *Ivanhoe*), produced Turin, Teatro Regio, 11 Feb 1840.

Templer und die Jüdin, Die, *The Templar and the Jewess*, opera by Marschner (libretto by W A Wohlbrück, based on Scott's *Ivanhoe*), produced Leipzig, 22 Dec 1829. Saxon Rowena and Jewish Rebecca compete for the attention of knight Ivanhoe. Ivanhoe champions Rebecca after she is accused of witchcraft.

Templeton, John (b Riccarton, Kilmarnock, 30 Jul 1802; d New Hampton, 2 Jul 1886), Scottish tenor. Appeared as a child singer at Edinburgh, studied there and in London, and made his debut at Worthing in 1828. In 1831 he became known in London and in 1833 Malibran engaged him as her partner. He was well known as Ottavio and Tamino and sang in operas by Auber, Hérold and Rossini.

Any musical composition must necessarily possess its unique tempo ... A piece of mine can survive almost anything but wrong or uncertain tempo.

Igor Stravinsky, *Conversations*, 1958

---

tempo Italian = lit. 'time' = 'pace', the speed of any musical composition, determined, not by the note-values, which are relative, but by the directions set above the stave at the opening of a piece or section (e.g. *allegro*, *andante*, *adagio*, etc.). The exact pace can be established only by means of metronome marks (e.g. ♩ = 96, i.e. 96 crotchets to the minute, etc.). In Italian *tempo* also means a movement of a sonata, symphony, etc.

tempo giusto Italian = 'strict time', also the right speed.

tempo ordinario Italian = 'common time, ordinary pace'; either (1) moderate speed or (2) four beats in a bar (C), as opposed to *Alla breve* (¢), where there are two beats in a bar.

tempo primo Italian = lit. 'first time' = 'first tempo'; after a change of tempo the direction *tempo primo* means that the pace first indicated is to be resumed.

Tenaglia, Antonio Francesco (b Florence, *c* 1610–20; d Rome, after 1661), Italian composer. Studied and lived in Rome, where he was organist for a time at St John Lateran.

Works include two operas (lost); many cantatas for soprano and *continuo*.

Tender Land, The opera by Copland (libretto by H Everett), produced NY, 1 Apr 1954, conductor Schippers. Orchestral suite 1956. High-school graduate Laurie comes of age when young Martin fails to show up after agreeing to elope with her.

Tenducci, Giusto Ferdinando (b Siena, *c* 1735; d Genoa, 1790), Italian castrato soprano and composer. Made his debut in Naples, then went to London in 1758, remaining there, apart from visits to Ireland (1765–68) and Scotland (1768–69), until 1791, when he returned to Italy. Popular in England as a singer of Handel, he was also heard in his own adaptation of Gluck's *Orfeo*. He pub. a treatise on singing, composed songs, harpsichord sonatas, etc., and compiled song collections, etc. He was thrice married: his nickname 'Triorchis' (triple-testicled) indicates that his condition as a castrato did not hinder his off-stage activities.

Tennstedt, Klaus (b Merseburg, 6 Jun 1926), German conductor. He studied at the Leipzig Conservatory and worked in Halle until 1958. After posts at the Dresden Opera and with the Schwerin State Orchestra, 1958–61, he worked in Göteborg and Stockholm. Music director Kiel Opera, then US debut, with Boston SO, in 1974; NY Met. debut 1983, with *Fidelio*. 1979–83 principal guest conductor Minnesota Orchestra and North German Radio SO; Hamburg. LPO 1983–87, notably in symphonies of Bruckner and Mahler. In recent years his concert appearances have been limited by illness.

tenor the highest male voice produced naturally, i.e. not in falsetto, like the male alto. It is so called (from Latin *teneo* = 'I hold') because it 'held' the plainsong theme in early polyphonic compositions using a *Cantus firmus*.

The word tenor was formerly also used for the viola.

The approximate range of the tenor voice.

tenor clef the C clef is used as to indicate that middle C stands on the fourth line of the stave.

The tenor clef.

It was formerly used for the tenor voice but is now used only for the tenor trombone and the higher reaches of the bassoon, cello and double bass.

tenor cor a military-band brass instrument invented *c* 1860 to provide a better substitute for the horn than had been found in the saxhorn. It is in the circular form of a horn, though half the length, and has valves. It is made in F, with an extra slide to change it to E♭.

tenor drum a drum with two skins stretched over either end, similar in shape to the side drum and bass drum, but of intermediate size. It produces a duller sound than that of the side drum, having no snares, but gives out clearer notes, though of indefinite pitch, than the bass drum.

tenore robusto Italian = 'robust tenor'; one of the categories of operatic voices: a tenor capable of sustaining parts of a heroic type; equivalent to the German *Heldentenor*.

tenor horn a brass valve wind instrument of the saxhorn type, made in various tunings and compasses.

tenoroon an early instrument of the bassoon type, smaller and tuned higher than the bassoon.

tenor tuba another name for the ♭euphonium.

tenor violin early name for the viola. A small cello, tuned a fifth or a fourth above the normal cello, was sometimes known as a tenor violin.

Tenors get women by the score.
James Joyce, *Ulysses*, 1922

---

tenson a troubadour, trouvère or Minnesinger song, the words of which took the form of a dispute.

tenuto Italian = 'held'; a direction usually marked *ten*, indicating that the note or notes to which it applies are to be sustained to their full value, or even an almost imperceptible fraction beyond, but not so much so as to give the different effect of *ritenuto*: the meaning is 'held', not 'held back'.

Terfel, Bryn (b Pantglas, 9 Nov 1965), Welsh bass-baritone. Studied at the GSM, London and won the Lieder prize as the 1990 Cardiff Singer of the World Competition. Debut as Guglielmo with WNO, 1990; US (Santa Fe) and ENO debuts 1991, as Mozart's Figaro; Masetto at CG, 1992. Sang Jochanaan at Salzburg 1992, returning in the Brahms Requiem 1993 and as Leporello (1994). Vienna Staatsoper 1993, as Mozart's Count, Figaro at the Met. in 1994. Recordings include Schubert's *Schwanengesang*, and Figaro in the John Eliot Gardiner version of the opera. Regarded as one of the most promising baritones of his generation.

ternary a vocal or instrumental piece in three distinct sections, the third of which is a repetition of the first, is said to be in ternary form. The middle section is usually a contrast, sometimes based on similar but more often on different thematic material, but always relevant in style if not in mood. In vocal music *da capo* arias and in instrumental music minuets or scherzos with trios are outstanding examples of ternary form.

Ternina, Milka (b Doljnji, Moslavina, 19 Dec 1863; d Zagreb, 18 May 1941), Croatian soprano. Studied at home from the age of 12 and in

Terfel *The baritone Bryn Terfel. He made his debut with the Welsh National Opera in 1990 as Guglielmo and has since begun an international career. His warm, large voice is complemented by his talent as an actor.*

1880–82 in Vienna. She appeared as Amelia at Zagreb when still a student, then sang light parts at Leipzig, rising gradually through greater parts at Graz and Bremen to the Court Opera at Munich, to which she was attached 1890–99. Created the title role in Zemlinsky's first opera, *Sarema* (Munich 1897). In 1895 she first sang in London, making her first appearance at CG in 1898 as Isolde, and the next year, having become one of the great Wagner singers, she was engaged for Bayreuth. She sang there until 1903, when she was banned for having sung Kundry in the 'pirate' NY Met. performance of *Parsifal*. US debut Boston, 1896, as Elsa. Retired 1916.

Terpander (b *fl. c* 675BC), Greek poet and musician. He won a prize at the music festival in Sparta between 676 and 672BC. His contributions to music are uncertain, but are said to have included the composition of drinking-songs, the increasing of the lyre strings from four to seven and the introduction of new metres into poetry and consequently into music.

Terradellas, Domingo Miguel Bernabe (b Barcelona, bap. 13 Feb 1713; d Rome, 20 May 1751), Spanish composer. Pupil of Durante at the Conservatorio dei Poveri di Gesù at Naples 1732–38, he there composed two oratorios. Produced his first opera in 1739 in Rome, where he was *maestro di cappella* at the Spanish church 1743–45. He visited London (1746–47), producing three operas there and in Paris, then returned to Rome.

Works include operas *Astarto* (1739), *Gli intrighi delle cantarine, Cerere, Merope* (1743), *Artaserse, Semiramide riconosciuta, Mitridate* (1746), *Bellerofonte* (1747), *Imeneo in Atene, Didone, Sesostri, rè d'Egitto*; oratorios, *Giuseppe riconosciuto* (1736) and *Ermenegildo martire*; Masses, motets and other church music.

Terrasse, Claude (Antoine) (b Grand-Lemps, near Grenoble, 27 Jan 1867; d Paris, 30 Jun 1923), French composer and organist. He studied at the Lyon Conservatory and then at Niedermeyer's school in Paris, afterwards privately with Gigout. After living obscurely as an organist at Auteuil and a piano teacher at Arcachon, he began to compose and settled in Paris in 1895 as organist of the Trinité.

Works include opera *Pantagruel* (after Rabelais), operettas *La Fiancée du scaphandrier*, *Choncette*, *Le Sire de Vergy* (1903), *Monsieur de la Palisse* (1904), *L'Ingénu libertin*, *Le Coq d'Inde*, *Le Mariage de Télémaque* (1910), *Les Transatlantiques* (1911), *La Petite Femme de Loth* (T Bernard), *Les Travaux d'Hercule* (1901), *Cartouche* (1912), *Le Cochon qui sommeille*, *Faust en ménage*, *Le Manoir enchanté* and several others; incidental music for various comedies; music for T Gautier's and T de Banville's *Matinées poétiques*; *Trio bouffe* for strings, *Sérénade bouffe* for piano and strings; songs.

Terry, Charles Sanford (b Newport Pagnell, Bucks., 24 Oct 1864; d Westerton of Pitfodels near Aberdeen, 5 Nov 1936), English music historian. He was appointed professor of history at Aberdeen University in 1903. He also did invaluable work for music by writing an authoritative biography of J S Bach (1928) as well as numerous detailed studies of various aspects of his work, and a biography of J C Bach (1929, revised 1967 by H C R Landon).

At Ranelagh I heard the famous Tenducci, a thing from Italy: it looks for all the world like a man, though they say it is not.
Tobias Smollett, *Humphrey Clinker*, 1771

Tertis, Lionel (b W Hartlepool, 29 Dec 1876; d London, 22 Feb 1975), English viola player. First studied violin at Leipzig Conservatory and the RAM, and then took up the viola at the suggestion of Alexander Mackenzie, playing with various string quartets. This, and his appearances as a soloist, made him one of the most famous violists of his time. In 1925 he was soloist in the fp of Vaughan Williams's *Flos campi*. He also introduced a new, large viola called the 'Tertis Model'. He retired from the concert platform in 1936, but re-emerged during World War II and performed in public until he was 87. CBE 1950.

terzet, English, *or* terzetto, Italian, a composition for three voices or for instruments in three parts.

Teschemacher, Margarete (b Cologne, 3 Mar 1903; d Bad Wiessee, 19 May 1959), German soprano. After her 1922 Cologne debut she sang widely in Germany; Dresden 1934–45, where she created Strauss's Daphne (1938) and Sutermeister's Miranda in his opera based on *The Tempest* (*Die Zauberinsel*, 1942). London, CG, 1931 and 1936 as Pamina, Elsa and Elvira. In Buenos Aires she was the first local Arabella. Other roles included Senta, Jenůfa, Minnie and Francesca da Rimini.

Teseo, *Theseus*, opera by Handel (libretto by N F Haym), produced London, Queen's Theatre, Haymarket, 10 Jan 1713. Teseo, prince of Athens, marries Algilea in spite of interference from the enchantress Medea.

Tesi (or *Tramontini*), Vittoria (b Florence, 13 Feb 1700; d Vienna, 9 May 1775), Italian contralto. Made her first appearance at a very early age. In 1719 she was at Dresden, from 1749 in Vienna. It is one of the well-known and purely fictitious Handel stories that he fell in love with her at Florence when his *Rodrigo* was produced there 1707: the date of her birth refutes it effectively. From 1716 she was successful in Italy, Dresden and Vienna in operas by Lotti, Gluck and Jomelli.

Tessarini, Carlo (b Rimini, *c* 1690; d Amsterdam, after 15 Dec 1766), Italian composer and violinist. He worked as a violinist in Venice at St Mark's (from 1720) and Saints Giovanni e Paolo, obtained a post at Urbino Cathedral in 1733 but left the same year to enter the service of Cardinal Schrattenbach in Brno, returning to Urbino in 1738. He visited Holland in 1747 and 1762, and probably also Paris.

Works include *Concerti grossi*; violin concertos; *sinfonie*; violin sonatas and duets; trio sonatas, etc. Also wrote a treatise on violin playing (1741).

Tessier, Charles (b *fl. c* 1600), French lutenist and composer. He was a *musicien de la chambre du roy* to Henri IV and visited England for some time in the 1590s, dedicating a book of *chansons* to Lady Penelope Rich (Sidney's Stella).

Works include *chansons* for four–five voices (1597), *Airs et villanelles* for three–five voices (1604), setting of the eighth song in Sidney's *Astrophel and Stella*.

tessitura Italian = lit. 'texture'; the prevailing range of a voice part in a composition. It may be high, low or normal for the voice required.

Testament de la Tante Caroline, Le opéra-bouffe by Roussel (libretto by Nino), produced Olomouc, 14 Nov 1936. Aunt Caroline leaves fortune to first of three nieces to produce a male child; spinster niece obliges.

testudo Latin = 'tortoise'; a Latin name for the Greek lyre, which was often made of tortoiseshell; transferred to the lute in 16th- c. Latin.

tetrachord from Greek = 'having four strings'; a scale of four notes embracing the interval of a perfect fourth; a basis for melodic construction in ancient Greek music theory and 20th-c. serial technique.

Tetrazzini, Luisa (b Florence, 29 Jun 1871; d Milan, 28 Apr 1940), Italian soprano. Studied with Ceccherini at the Florence Liceo Musicale and with her sister Eva (1862–1938), the wife of the conductor Cleofante Campanini. She made her first appearance at Florence in 1890, as Meyerbeer's Ines, then toured, first in Italy and later in Europe, Mexico and South America. In 1907 she first appeared in London; returned (1908–12) as Violetta and Lucia. She sang the same roles in NY (1908–11) becoming famed for her brilliant coloratura, but soon retired from the stage. Active as concert singer until 1934.

Teufels Lustschloss, Des, *The Devil's Pleasure Palace*, opera by Schubert (libretto by A von Kotzebue), composed 1814 but not performed until 1879. Knight Oswald, wife Luitgarde and squire Robert endure series of trials at haunted castle of Luitgarde's uncle.

Teutsche, German, ◊Deutsche Tänze.

texture the vertical density of a musical composition. While the nature of the texture is often one of the main distinguishing features of a work, particularly in 20th-c. music, variety of texture is an important component of a work's progression and life in virtually all music.

Teyber, Anton (b Vienna, bap. 8 Sept 1754; d Vienna, 18 Nov 1822), Austrian composer. Appointed court composer to the Imperial Chapel in 1793 and music teacher to the royal family.

Works include melodrama *Zermes und Mirabella* (1779); oratorio *Joas* (1786); Passion, Masses and other church music; symphonies; chamber music.

Teyber, Franz (b Vienna, bap. 25 Aug 1758; d Vienna, 21 or 22 Oct 1810), Austrian composer, conductor and organist, brother of Anton ◊Teyber. Conductor of Schikaneder's company and late in his life appointed court organist.

Works include operas, e.g. *Laura Rosetti* (1785), *Adelheid von Veltheim* (1788), *Die Schlaftrunk* (1801) *Die Dorfdeputierten* (1785), *Alexander* (1801); oratorio; church music; songs.

Teyte (originally *Tate*), Maggie (b Wolverhampton, 17 Apr 1888; d London, 26 May 1976), English soprano. Studied at the RCM and then in Paris with Jean de Reszke (1903–07), making her debut in Monte Carlo in 1907. She appeared with Debussy in song recitals and was selected by him to succeed Mary Garden as Mélisande (1908). London, CG, 1910–38; in 1923 she created the Princess in Holst's *The Perfect Fool* there. Chicago 1911–14, Boston 1915–17. Other roles included Butterfly, Cherubino and Purcell's Belinda (London, 1951). DBE 1958.

Thaïs opera by Massenet (libretto by L Gallet, based on the novel by A France), produced Paris, Opéra, 16 Mar 1894. It contains the popular *Méditation* as an orchestral interlude. Young monk Athanaël persuades courtesan Thaïs to enter a convent but falls in love with her before she dies.

Thalben-Ball, George (Thomas) (b Sydney, 18 Jun 1896; d London, 18 Jan 1987), Australian-born British organist. Studied at RCM and worked in London and Birmingham before and after World War II; associated with BBC 1939–70. Famed for a subjective approach to interpretation. Knighted 1982.

Thalberg, Sigismond (Fortuné François) (b Geneva, 8 Jan 1812;

d Posillipo near Naples, 27 Apr 1871), Austrian pianist and composer. Said to be illegitimate son of Count Moritz Dietrichstein and Baroness von Wetzlar. When he was ten his father sent him to school in Vienna, where he later studied piano with Hummel and theory with Sechter. He soon played at private parties, appeared at Prince Metternich's house in 1826 and in 1830 made his first tour, in Germany, having by this time begun to publish his compositions. In 1835 he made further studies with Pixis and Kalkbrenner in Paris, and in 1836 first appeared in London. By the 1850s he was pursuing an international career, rivalled only by Liszt as a virtuoso performer.

Works include operas *Florinda* (1851) and *Cristina di Suezia* (1855); piano concerto; piano sonata, studies, nocturnes, romances and numerous other pieces for piano, operatic fantasies on works by Rossini, Weber and Verdi, and other transcriptions for piano; over 50 German songs.

Thamos, König in Aegypten, *Thamos, King of Egypt*, incidental music by Mozart (K345) to T P von Gebler's play, composed 1779 (two choruses already 1773), not produced in Mozart's lifetime except in an adaptation to another play, Plümicke's *Lanassa*.

Thayer, Alexander Wheelock (b S Natick, MA, 22 Oct 1817; d Trieste, 15 Jul 1897), American biographer. Studied law at Harvard University and in 1849 went to Germany, living at Bonn and Berlin, also to Prague and Vienna, collecting material for a Beethoven biography. After some journalistic activities in NY and Boston, he again went to Europe 1854–56 and for a third time in 1858, eventually becoming US consul at Trieste. His Beethoven biography reached only the year 1816, and the unfinished fourth volume, covering the composer's last decade of life, was completed by Hermann Deiters in a German edition of the work. An English edition was pub. 1921 by Krehbiel and a revision of this by Elliot Forbes in 1964.

Thebom, Blanche (b Monessen, PA, 19 Sept 1918), American mezzo of Swedish parentage. She sang at the NY Met. 1944–67 as Fricka, Carmen, Azucena and Ortrud. Glyndebourne 1950, as Dorabella; CG 1957 as Dido in the fp of *Les Troyens* in a single evening. She recorded Brangaene with Furtwängler and was well known as Baba the Turk, Amneris and Laura. Taught at San Francisco State University from 1980.

Theile, Johann (b Naumburg, 29 Jul 1646; d Naumburg, buried 24 Jun 1724), German composer. Learnt music as a youth at Magdeburg and Halle, and later studied at Leipzig University, where he took part in the students' performances as singer and viola da gamba player. He then became a pupil of Schütz at Weissenfels and taught music at Stettin and Lübeck. In 1673–75 he was *Kapellmeister* to the Duke of Holstein at Gottorp, but fled to Hamburg during the Danish invasion. In 1676 he competed unsuccessfully for the post of cantor at St Thomas's Church, Leipzig. He was the first composer to contribute to the repertory of the newly opened opera at Hamburg in 1678. In 1685 he succeeded Rosenmüller as music director at Wolfenbüttel and in 1689 he was appointed to a similar post at Merseburg. In his last years he lived in retirement at his birthplace.

Works include operas *Adam und Eva* (1678; lost) and *Orontes* (1678; seven arias extant); ten Masses, seven Psalms; Passion according to St Matthew, church cantatas.

Theinred of Dover 12th-c. English music theorist and monk of Dover Priory. His treatise, a study of intervals and proportions, is known only from an early 15th-c. copy (Oxford, Bodleian Library, MS Bodley 842). It includes a diagram of the different forms of alphabetical notation, and a section on the measurement of organ pipes.

theme a musical idea, generally melodic, sufficiently striking to be memorable and capable of being developed or varied in the course of a composition. A theme is generally complete in itself, whereas a motive is a figure which contributes something to a larger conception; but a precise distinction between the two is often impossible in practice.

Theodora oratorio by Handel (libretto by T Morell), produced London, CG, 16 Mar 1750.

theorbo a bass lute of large size with a double neck on which only the upper strings are stretched over a fingerboard, the bass strings being at the side of it and capable only of producing single notes, except by returning. The number of strings varied from 14 to 17. It was used mainly to accompany singers.

Theremin, ♭aetherophone, an electrophonic instrument invented by Léon Theremin (1896–1993) of Leningrad in 1920. It was incapable of detaching notes, so that all intervals were linked together by a wailing *portamento*, like that of a siren; but later on Theremin invented another instrument shaped like a cello on which notes could be produced detached from each other by means of a cello fingerboard.

Thérèse opera by Massenet (libretto by J Claretie), produced Monte Carlo, 7 Feb 1907. Torn between her husband André and former love Armand, Thérèse decides to run away with Armand until André is captured by revolutionaries. She decides to join him at the guillotine.

Opera by John Tavener (libretto by G McLarnon); composed 1973–76, produced CG, 1 Oct 1979, conductor Downes. Poet Rimbaud guides spiritual growth of St Thérèse of Lisieux, as she experiences various 20th-c. horrors.

Theresienmesse, *Theresa Mass*, Haydn's Mass in B♭ no. 12, composed 1799. Despite its name, it seems to have no connection with Maria Theresa, wife of the Emperor Franz II.

Thésée, *Theseus*, opera by Lully (libretto by Quinault), produced Saint-Germain, 12 Jan 1675; first Paris performance, Apr 1675. Jealous Medea tries to prevent union of Theseus and Aegle. She fails when King Aegeus recognizes Theseus as his long-lost son.

Thespis, or The Gods Grown Old operetta by Sullivan (libretto by W S Gilbert), produced London, Gaiety Theatre, 26 Dec 1871. Sullivan's first work written in association with Gilbert.

Thibaud, Jacques (b Bordeaux, 27 Sept 1880; d Mont Cemet near Barcelonette, 1 Sept 1953), French violinist. Studied at the Paris Conservatory and took a first prize in 1896, but was at first obliged to play in a café. Colonne heard him and engaged him for his orchestra and by 1898–99 he was established as a concert artist. He travelled widely, excelled in Mozart and gave much time to chamber music, forming a trio with Casals and Cortot. He was killed in a plane crash.

Thibaudet, Jean-Yves (b Lyon, 7 Sept 1961), French pianist. Studied at the Lyon Conservatoire from age five and at the Paris Conservatory 1974–81. Has given recitals and concerts throughout Europe and the USA; appearances with the Boston SO, Cleveland Orchestra, Chicago SO and Los Angeles PO (Hollywood Bowl, 1989). London

Thibaudet *The pianist Jean-Yves Thibaudet. His repertory centres on works by Romantic and Impressionist composers including Chopin, Liszt and Ravel. He has recorded the complete works for piano solo by Ravel and has worked on more than one occasion with violinist Joshua Bell.*

Proms 1994 in music by Ravel. Has recorded chamber music with Joshua Bell, and the *Turangalîla-Symphonie* with the Concertgebouw Orchestra.

Thibaut IV (b Troyes, 30 May 1201; d Pamplona, 7 Jul 1253), King of Navarre and a trouvère, more than 45 of whose songs are still extant.

Thill, Georges (b Paris, 14 Dec 1897; d Paris, 17 Oct 1984), French tenor. He studied in Paris and sang with the Opéra 1924–40 and with the Opéra-Comique until 1953; appeared in the fps of works by Canteloube and Rabaud and was successful as Calaf, Julien, Don José, Tannhäuser and Parsifal. NY Met. 1930–32 as Roméo, Faust and Radames. He sang in a Wagner concert as late as 1956 and made several films, including *Louise*, with Grace Moore.

Thillon (born *Hunt*), Sophie Anne (b Calcutta or London, 1819; d Torquay, 5 May 1903), English soprano. She was taken to France for study at the age of 14 and married one of her masters, the Le Havre conductor Claude Thomas Thillon. After appearing in the provinces she came out in opera in Paris, 1838, studied with Auber and sang with great success in his own and other composers' operas: she created roles in Auber's *La Neige* and *Les Diamants de la Couronne*. In 1844 she made her stage debut in London and sang much there during the next ten years in operas by Balfe; also at Brussels and in USA.

third the interval between two notes lying two degrees of a scale apart.

| Maj. | Min. | Diminished |

Major, minor, and diminished thirds.

Thomas, Arthur Goring (b Ratton Park, Sussex, 20 Nov 1850; d London, 20 Mar 1892), English composer. Educated for the civil service, but studied music after he came of age, with Émile Durand in Paris and with Sullivan and Prout at the RAM in London. Later went to Bruch in Berlin for orchestration. He began to work on an opera to a libretto by his brother, *Don Braggadocio*, and although he did not finish it, he persevered and eventually received a commission from the Carl Rosa Opera Company. He became insane in 1891. His music reflects the comfortable, undemanding French style of his time.

Works include operas *The Light of the Harem* (after Thomas Moore), *Esmeralda* (after Hugo's *Notre-Dame de Paris*), *Nadeshda* and *The Golden Web*; anthem *Out of the Deep* for soprano, chorus and orchestra; cantatas *The Sun Worshippers* and *The Swan and the Skylark*; *Suite de Ballet* for orchestra; songs, duets.

Thomas, (Charles Louis) Ambroise (b Metz, 5 Aug 1811; d Paris, 12 Feb 1896), French composer. Learnt music from his father as a child and in 1828 entered the Paris Conservatory, where he gained the Prix de Rome in 1832. He also studied piano privately with Kalkbrenner and composition with Lesueur. Soon after his return from Rome he began to win operatic successes in Paris. In 1852 he became professor at the Conservatory and in 1871 director in succession to Auber. His operas were written to please contemporary bourgeois Parisian taste; his most successful works *Mignon*, and *Hamlet* were written in emulation of Gounod.

Works include operas *La Double Échelle* (1837), *Le Perruquier de la Régence* (1838), *Le Panier fleuri* (1839), *Carline* (1840), *Le Comte de Carmagnola, Le Guerillero* (1842), *Angélique et Médor* (1843), *Mina, Le Caïd, Le Songe d'une nuit d'été* (not Shakespeare, 1850), *Raymond* (1851), *La Tonelli, La Cour de Célimène* (1855), *Psyché* (1857), *Le Carnaval de Venise, Le Roman d'Elvire* (1860), *Mignon* (after Goethe's *Wilhelm Meister*, 1866), *Gille et Gillotin, Hamlet* (after Shakespeare, 1868), *Françoise de Rimini* (after Dante, 1882); ballets *La Gipsy* (1839), *Betty* and *La Tempête* (1889); *Messe solennelle* (1857), *Messe de Requiem*, motets; cantata *Hermann et Ketty*, cantatas for the unveiling of a Lesueur statue and for the Boieldieu centenary; fantasy for piano and orchestra; string quartet, string quintet, piano trio; piano pieces; six Italian songs; part-songs, etc.

Thomas, David (b Orpington, 26 Feb 1943), English bass-baritone. Sang with the St Paul's Cathedral Choir and studied at Cambridge.

Sang in concert with such groups as the Academy of Ancient Music and the consort of Musicke. Opera debut 1981 with Kent Opera as Pluto in *Il ballo dell' ingrate*. Concert repertory includes *Messiah* (US debut at Hollywood Bowl, 1984), Bach's Passions and B minor Mass, *Winterreise* (Cornell University, 1993), Handel's *Theodora* and *Susanna* (in San Francisco) and Haydn's *Creation*. Sang the Devil in the US fp of Landi's *Sant' Alessio* (Los Angeles, 1988).

Thomas, Jess (Floyd) (b Hot Springs, SD, 4 Aug 1927; d San Francisco, 11 Oct 1993), American tenor. He studied at Stanford University and appeared in Europe from 1958 (debut Karlsruhe, as Lohengrin); sang Bacchus at Munich in 1960 and returned in 1963 for the Emperor. Bayreuth 1961–69 as Parsifal and Siegfried. NY Met. debut 1962, as Walther; created Caesar in the 1966 production of Barber's *Antony and Cleopatra*, which opened the Met.'s house at Lincoln Center. CG 1969–71 as Walther and Tristan. Sang Siegfried in the centenary *Ring* at Bayreuth, 1976. Other roles included Radames, Lensky and Tannhäuser.

Thomas, Michael Tilson (b Hollywood, 21 Dec 1944), American conductor. After study in California he conducted at the Ojai Festival, initially as assistant to Boulez, and at Tanglewood. Music director Buffalo PO from 1971, principal guest conductor Boston SO from 1972. London debut 1970, with LSO (principal conductor 1988–95). LA PO from 1981. He conducts many works outside the standard repertory. In 1979 at Santa Fe he conducted the first US performance of the three-act version of Berg's *Lulu*. He has recorded Stravinsky as conductor and pianist. Principal conductor of the San Francisco SO from 1995.

Thomas, Theodore (Christian Friedrich) (b Esens, E Friesland, 11 Oct 1835; d Chicago, 4 Jan 1905), German, later American, conductor. He was taken to the USA in 1845 and became a professional violinist; appeared in NY, with an orchestra formed by himself, in 1862; organized the Cincinnati Music Festival in 1873 and became conductor of the NY Philharmonic Society in 1877 and of the Chicago SO in 1891. He did much to introduce new music to the USA, and to bring orchestral music to artistic backwaters.

Thomas and Sally, or The Sailor's Return, opera by Arne (libretto by I Bickerstaffe), produced London, CG, 28 Nov 1760. Thomas returns from sea in time to scupper Squire's attempts to woo Sally.

Thomé, Francis (actually Joseph François Luc) (b Port Louis, Mauritius, 18 Oct 1850; d Paris, 16 Nov 1909), French composer. Studied

Thomas *The conductor Michael Tilson Thomas. Born in Hollywood, he has earned the name 'Tinsel' as a substitute for 'Tilson', but he nevertheless deserves more credit in his choice of repertory, which includes many 20th-century works.*

at the Paris Conservatory. He afterwards settled down as a private teacher of music.

Works include operas *Martin et Frontin* (1877), *Le Caprice de la reine* (1892), operettas *Vieil Air, jeune chanson* (1894), *Le Château de Koenigsberg* (1896), *Le Chaperon rouge* (1900); ballets including *Endymion et Phœbé, La Bulle d'amour* (1898), *La Folie parisienne* (1900); incidental music to plays, including Shakespeare's *Romeo and Juliet*, and mystery *l'Enfant Jésus*; *Hymne à la nuit* for chorus; *Simple Aveu* for piano with many arrangements.

Thompson, Oscar (b Crawfordsville, IN, 10 Oct 1887; d New York, 3 Jul 1945), American music critic. In 1937 he succeeded W J Henderson as music critic of the *New York Sun*. He was the author of several books on music and the editor of the *International Cyclopedia of Music and Musicians* (1939).

Thompson, Randall (b New York, 21 Apr 1899; d Boston, 9 Jul 1984), American composer. He studied at Harvard University and among his teachers was Bloch. He lived in Rome in 1922–25, was assistant professor of music at Wellesley College and was later appointed to study musical conditions at the American colleges. Professor of music at University of California in 1937, director of the Curtis Institute at Philadelphia in 1939, professor at Harvard University from 1948.

Works include opera *Solomon and Balkis* (after Kipling's *Just So Stories*, 1942); incidental music for Labiche's *The Italian Straw Hat*; three symphonies (1930–49), *Pierrot and Cothurnus* (1923) and *The Piper at the Gates of Dawn* (1924), for orchestra; *Jazz Poem* for piano and orchestra (1928); *Passion according to St Luke*, cantata *The Testament of Freedom, Odes of Horace* for unaccompanied chorus, *Rosemary* for women's chorus, *Americana* for mixed chorus and piano; two string quartets (1941, 1967), *The Wind in the Willows* for string quartet; sonata and suite for piano; songs.

Thomson, Bryden (b Ayr, 16 Jul 1928; d Dublin, 14 Nov 1991), Scottish conductor. Studied at the Royal Scottish Academy and with Hans Schmidt-Isserstedt in Hamburg. Assistant at the BBC Scottish SO 1958–62. Principal of the BBC Northern SO 1968–73, music director of the Ulster Orchestra 1977–85. Principal of the BBC Welsh SO 1978–82; RTE SO, Dublin, 1984–87. Conducted the Scottish National Orchestra from 1988 and recorded music by Elgar, Bax (complete symphonies), Schumann and Vaughan Williams.

Thomson, César (b Liège, 17 or 18 Mar 1857; d Bissone near Lugano, 21 Aug 1931), Belgian violinist. Studied at the Liège Conservatory from the age of seven, and in 1882 he became violin professor there, after a career as virtuoso that took him to Italy, Germany, etc. In 1897 succeeded Ysaÿe at the Brussels Conservatory. He taught in NY from 1924 to 1927, when he returned to Europe.

Thomson, George (b Limekilns, Fife, 4 Mar 1757; d Leith, 18 Feb 1851), Scottish official and music collector. Pub. collections of national Scottish, Welsh and Irish airs arranged by Haydn (187), Beethoven (126), Koželuch, Weber, Bishop and others.

The way to write American music is simple: all you have to do is be an American and then write any kind of music you wish.

Virgil Thomson, quoted in Machlis, *Introduction to Contemporary Music*, 1963

Thomson, Virgil (b Kansas City, 25 Nov 1896; d New York, 30 Sept 1989), American composer. Studied at Harvard University and composition with Rosario Scalero and Nadia Boulanger. He was assistant music instructor at Harvard 1920–25 and organist at King's Chapel in Boston 1923–24, then lived in Paris until 1932, when he became critic to several papers and periodicals in the USA, becoming famed for his perceptive views. The most important influences on his music were Satie and the neo-classical Stravinsky.

Works include operas *Four Saints in Three Acts* (1934), *The Mother of us all* (1947) (libretti by G Stein), *Byron* (1972); ballet *The Filling-Station*; incidental music for Euripides' *Medea*, Shake-

speare's *Hamlet* and other plays, film music; two symphonies, suite *The Plough that Broke the Plains* (1936), two *Sentimental Tangoes*, *Portraits, Symphony on a Hymn- Tune* (1948), *Sonata da Chiesa* for orchestra.

Oraison funèbre (Bossuet) for tenor and orchestra; *2 Missae breves*, three Psalms for women's voices, *Capital Capitals* (G Stein) for men's chorus and piano; two string quartets (1922, 1932), *5 Portraits* for four clarinets; *Stabat Mater* for soprano and string quartet, *Five Phrases from the Song of Solomon* for soprano and percussion; *50 Portraits* for violin and piano, sonata for violin and piano; piano music, songs.

Thorborg, Kerstin (b Venjan, 19 May 1896; d Dalarna, 12 Apr 1970), Swedish mezzo. She studied in Stockholm and sang there 1924–30 as Ortrud and Amneris. Salzburg and Vienna from 1935. CG 1936–39 as Kundry, Brangaene and Fricka. NY Met. 1936–50 as Orpheus, Marina, Dalila and Clytemnestra. She recorded *Das Lied von der Erde* with Walter (Vienna, 1936). Considered to be the foremost Wagnerian mezzo of her day.

Thorne, John (d York, 7 Dec 1573), English organist, composer and poet. He was appointed organist of York Minster in 1542, and worked there in various capacities until two years before his death. A motet, *Stella coeli*, was copied by John Baldwin, and another, *Exsultabant sancti*, is extant, in organ score. A four-part in nomine also survives, and there are three poems by him in the same MS as Redford's *Play of Wit and Science* (British Library Additional MS 15233) and in the *Paradyse of Daintie Devices* (1576).

thorough-bass a system of shorthand notation for keyboard instruments that came into use during the early part of the 17th c. and persisted until about the middle of the 18th (and in church music later still). Instead of writing out the full harmony they required for an accompaniment, composers provided only a single bass-line, under or over which they wrote figures or accidentals indicating what the harmony above that bass was to be, but not how it was to be spaced or distributed. Thorough-basses were not always completely figured, and sometimes not at all. The Italian term is *basso continuo*. ◊continuo.

Thrane, Waldemar (b Christiania (now Oslo), 8 Oct 1790; d Christiania, 30 Dec 1828), Norwegian composer. Learnt music at home, his parents being keen amateurs at whose house many musicians met. Although intended for commerce, he continually exercised himself in music and in 1825 wrote the first Norwegian opera, which however was not staged until 1850. He also studied Norwegian folk music.

Works include opera *Fjeldeventyret* (*The Mountain Adventure*, 1825); overtures for orchestra; choral works, etc.

Three Choirs Festival a music festival, founded *c* 1715, centred on the combined cathedral choirs of Gloucester, Worcester and Hereford, and held annually at each town in turn in late summer. The programmes are predominantly choral, but orchestral and chamber music concerts are also given. New works by English composers, eg. Elgar (*Froissart*), Vaughan Williams (*Tallis Fantasia* and *Hodie*), Holst (*Choral Fantasia*) and Bliss, have been a traditional feature of the festival. In recent years works by Jonathan Harvey, Maxwell Davies and William Matthias have been performed.

Three-Cornered Hat ◊Sombrero de tres picos; *also* ◊Corregidor.

Three Places in New England work for orchestra by Ives, also known as *Orchestral Set no. 1*; composed 1903–14, fp NY, 10 Jan 1931, conductor Slonimsky. The three movements are: 1. 'The "St Gaudens" in Boston Common: Colonel Shaw and his Colored Regiment'; 2. 'Putnam's Camp, Redding, Connecticut'; 3. 'The Housatonic at Stockbridge'.

Threni, id est Lamentationes Jeremiae Prophetae, work by Stravinsky for soprano, mezzo, two tenors, two basses, chorus and orchestra; composed 1957–58, fp Venice, 23 Sept 1958, conductor Stravinsky. ◊Lamentations.

Threnody for the Victims of Hiroshima work by Penderecki for 52 solo strings; composed 1959–60; fp Warsaw, 31 May 1961.

Thuille, Ludwig (b Bozen, 30 Nov 1861; d Munich, 5 Feb 1907), Austrian composer. Learnt music from his father, an amateur, on

(a)

Er kommt, er kommt der Braut-gam kommt! Ihr Toch-ter
Zi-ons, kommt her-aus sein Aus-gang ei-let aus der Ho-he in
eu - er Mut - ter Haus

Bach, *Cantata 140*

The figured bass symbols from Bach's Cantata 140 *(a) and a possible realization* (b).

whose death he was sent as a choirboy to the monastery of Krems-münster. At the age of 15 he began to study with Joseph Pembaur in Innsbruck, and in 1879 he went to the Music School at Munich, where Rheinberger was among his masters. In 1883 he became professor at the Munich school, and there was influenced by R Strauss and Alexander Ritter, who wrote the libretto for his first opera, the two later ones being by Otto Julius Bierbaum. Apart from teaching and composition, he also conducted the male-voice choir Liederhort.

Works include operas *Theuerdank* (1897), *Lobetanz* (1898) and *Gugeline* (1901); *Romantic Overture* (originally for *Theuerdank*) for orchestra; *Weihnaht im Walde* for male chorus, *Traumsommernacht* and *Rosenlied* for female chorus; piano quintet, sextet for wind and piano; cello and piano sonata; piano pieces; songs.

thump Old English = plucking of strings (*pizzicato*); also a piece employing *pizz*.

Thus spake Zarathustra (R Strauss.) ◊Also sprach Zarathustra.

Tibbett, Lawrence (b Bakersfield, CA, 16 Nov 1896; d New York, 15 Jul 1960), American baritone. He studied singing after serving in the Navy in World War I and first appeared at the NY Met. in 1923; sang until 1950 as Boccanegra, Wolfram, Telramund, Scarpia, Iago and Rigoletto. He took part in the fps of Taylor's *The King's Henchman* (1927) and *Peter Ibbetson* (1931) and Gruenberg's *Emperor Jones* (1933). In addition to a successful career in opera he became popular as a film actor.

Tiburtino, Giuliano (b c 1510; d Rome, 16 Dec 1569), Italian composer and violinist. In 1545 he was in the service of Pope Paul III. Twelve *ricercari* and one fantasia for instrumental ensemble were included in a pub. of 1549 which also includes works by Willaert and Rore.

Tichatschek (or *Ticháček*), Joseph (Aloys) (b Ober-Weckelsdorf, Bohemia, 11 Jul 1807; d Blasewitz near Dresden, 18 Jan 1886), Bohemian tenor. Studied medicine at first, but learnt singing and in 1830 joined the chorus at the Kärntnertortheater in Vienna, then sang small parts, and made his debut at Graz. He was a member of the Dresden opera from 1838 until he retired in 1870, and was Wagner's first Rienzi and Tannhäuser. London, Drury Lane, 1841, as Adolar, Robert le diable and Tamino.

tie an arching stroke used to connect two notes of the same pitch (or a group of such notes in chords), indicating that the notes are to be sounded as one note having the duration of their combined value.

You by the help of tune and time,/Can make that song that was but rhyme.

Edmund Waller (1606–87) to Henry Lawes.

Tiefland, *The Lowland*, opera by d'Albert (libretto by R Lothar, based on a Catalan play, *Terra baixa*, by A Guimerá), produced Prague, German Theatre, 15 Nov 1903. Sebastiano marries off his mistress Marta to simple shepherd Pedro, who does not realize that he has been dishonoured by marrying her. Later, Pedro learns the truth and strangles Sebastiano when he again stakes a claim on Marta.

tiento, Spanish, a 16th-c. type of organ piece similar to the ◊ricercare.

tierce an early term for the interval of the third, major or minor. It survives, however, as the technical term for one of the tones of a church bell, a minor third above the note of the bell.

tierce de Picardie French = 'Picardy third'; the major third introduced into the final chord of a composition in a minor key. The major third corresponds to a natural harmonic, the ⇨tierce but the minor third does not: it was therefore for a long time considered, if not an actual dissonance, at any rate not a finally satisfactory ingredient in a concluding chord, for which reason the tierce de Picardie was often substituted. The origin of the name is not known.

Tierney, Vivian (b London, 26 Nov 1957), English soprano. Sang at first with the D'Oyly Carte company and sang elsewhere in operetta before appearing with ENO, from 1987: Offenbach's Euridice, Regan in the UK fp of Reimann's *Lear* (1989), Clarissa in the fp of Holloway's Opera (1990) and Mimi. Engaged with Freiburg Opera as Shostakovich's Lady Macbeth; Marie in *Wozzeck* at the Almeida Festival and for Opera North (1993). Glyndebourne 1992, as Ellen Orford. Other roles include the Gypsy Princess (Los Angeles), Renata in *The Fiery Angel*, and the Marschallin.

Tietjen, Heinz (b Tangier, 24 Jun 1881; d Baden-Baden, 30 Nov 1967), German conductor and producer. After working in Trier, Saarbrücken and Breslau he was engaged at the Berlin Städtische Oper 1925–30 and again 1948–54. He was Generalintendant of all Prussian State theatres 1930–45 and came into conflict with Otto Klemperer over the closing of the Kroll Opera, Berlin, in 1931. He was artistic director at Bayreuth 1931–44 and conducted there the *Ring*, *Meistersinger* and *Lohengrin*. He produced operas by Wagner at CG in 1950 and 1951 and worked in Hamburg 1954–59; returned to Bayreuth 1959 (*Lohengrin*).

Tietjens, Therese (Carolina Johanna Alexandra) (b Hamburg, 17 Jul 1831; d London, 3 Oct 1877), Hungarian soprano of Belgian descent. Made her first appearance at Hamburg in 1849; paid her first visit to England in 1858, remaining there for good except for her appearances abroad. Her London roles included Verdi's Hélène, Amelia and Leonora (*Forza*), Marguerite, Norma, Donna Anna and Lucrezia Borgia; she was renowned for her convincing portrayal of dramatic roles.

Tigers, The opera by Havergal Brian (libretto by composer); 1916–19, orchestrated 1928–29. The score was lost, but rediscovered in 1977 and given by the BBC on 3 May 1983. Comical adventures of World War I Home Guard.

Tigrane, Il, *Tigranes*, opera by Gluck (libretto by F Silvani, altered by Goldoni), produced Crema, 26 Sept 1743. Also operas by A Scarlatti (Naples, 1715) and Hasse (Naples, 1729). As a child Tigranes was kidnapped by the Emperor Cyrus from his mother Thonyris. Later he is torn between love for his betrothed, Meroe, and duty. Eventually, all is resolved when Tigranes' true identity is revealed.

Tigrini, Orazio (b ? Arezzo, *c* 1535; d Arezzo, 15 Oct 1591), Italian composer. He appears to have spent his entire mature life in Arezzo, and was *maestro di canto* first at Santa Maria della Pieve and then at the cathedral where, after a period at Orvieto, he was *maestro di canto* and *di cappella* till his death. He pub. two books of madrigals and a treatise, *Il Compendio della Musica* (1588).

Till Eulenspiegels lustige Streiche, *Till Eulenspiegel's Merry Pranks*, symphonic poem by R Strauss, op. 28, based on the old Low German folk-tale, composed 1894–95, fp Cologne, 5 Nov 1895.

Tilney, Colin (b London, 31 Oct 1932), English harpsichordist. He studied at Cambridge and with Gustav Leonhardt. Widely heard since 1964 as recitalist and soloist with leading ensembles; plays on historical instruments and replicas. Often heard in Bach, Purcell and the English virginalists. US debut 1971.

timbre French = lit. 'chime-bell'; in music the word is used, in English as well as French, for tone-colour.

time the physical conditions in which all the arts have their existence, so far as they become communicable to the human senses, are either space (painting, sculpture, etc.) or time, or both (drama and in a sense all literature). Music exists in time, and has therefore to be written down in symbols representing certain divisions of time in which it is to be made audible. Time must not be confused with tempo or pace, which determines the speed at which a composition should go; the time of a composition is its division into units of notes or rests, and their subdivisions. A piece in 3–4 time, for example, has three crotchets to a bar and normally a metrical stress on the first beat after the bar-line; and it makes no difference to this fundamental time whether two crotchets are replaced by a minim, or whether one is displaced by a rest or divided into smaller fractions in any pattern of notes. The time of a piece or movement remains fixed until the composer changes the time signature. Time is called 'simple' when the beats are divisible by two, e.g. 2–4, 3–4, 4–4, 'compound' when they are divisible by three, e.g. 6–8, 9–8, 12–8. Where there are five beats in the bar the listener, and often the composer, tends to regard them as 2 + 3 or 3 + 2: bars with 7, 11 or 13 beats will divide in a similar way.

time signature the sign at the beginning of a composition indicating the time-divisions governing the metre of the piece. The time signature is shown in the shape of a fraction, but does not represent a mathematical fraction: it is a symbol showing in the lower figure the unit of the note-values into which each bar is divided and in the upper the number of such note-values contained in a bar: e.g. $\frac{3}{4}$ means that there are three crotchets to the bar, with either three beats or (in fast time) one beat to the bar; $\frac{6}{8}$ is six quavers to the bar, with two basic beats; $\frac{2}{2}$ is two minims to the bar, etc. There are also two conventional abbrs., which are signs surviving from the old notation, where the time signatures were a full circle for perfect time (*tempus perfectum*) and a broken circle resembling letter C for imperfect time (*tempus imperfectum*). The broken circle has survived as indicating $\frac{4}{4}$ time and as ¢ indicating *alla breve* time, i.e. $\frac{4}{4}$ taken at up to double speed and beaten in 2s.

timpan, or timpe, from Latin *tympanum*, a kind of psaltery used in the British Isles in medieval times. It had wire strings stretched on a frame and they were plucked by the fingers or a plectrum, later struck with a rod.

timpani Italian = kettle-drums.

The English are popularly said to shout while the French sing.
Johannes Tinctoris, *Proportionale Musices*, c. 1476

Tinctoris, Johannes (b Braine l'Alleud, near Nivelles, *c* 1435; d ? 1511), Flemish theorist and composer. Studied both law and theology, was ordained priest and became a canon of Poperinghe. He went to Italy and in 1476 was in the service of the King of Naples, Ferdinand of Aragon. He founded a school of music and between 1484 and 1500 was in the Papal Chapel in Rome. He wrote a number of important theoretical works and composed Masses, motets and *chansons*. His dictionary of musical terms, *Terminorum musicae diffinitorium* (1495) was the first of its kind.

Tinney, Hugh (b Dublin, 28 Nov 1958), Irish pianist. Studied with Louis Kentner and made debut at Purcell Room, London, 1983. Many concerts in Europe and the USA, including Washington, DC, and Newport; London Proms debut 1993. Often heard in Liszt and other Romantic composers.

Tinsley, Pauline (b Wigan, 27 Mar 1928), English soprano. She studied in London and Manchester; sang professionally from 1951. WNO from 1962 as Lady Macbeth, Elsa, Susanna and Aida. Since 1963 she has appeared with SW, later ENO, in London as Mozart's Countess and Fiordiligi, Queen Elizabeth in *Maria Stuarda* and Verdi's Elvira. US debut Santa Fe, 1969, as Anna Bolena; has since appeared in Houston, New Orleans and at the NY City Opera. Other roles include Elektra, Turandot and the Kostelnička. CG 1989, as Lady Billows in *Albert Herring*.

tin whistle a small and rudimentary pipe of the fife or recorder type, also called 'penny whistle', played vertically and having a small range of high notes controlled by six finger-holes.

Tippett, Michael (Kemp) (b London, 2 Jan 1905), English composer. Studied with C Wood and R O Morris at the RCM in London. He became conductor of educational organizations under the London County Council and music director at Morley College, a post formerly held by Holst. During the war he was a conscientious objector

Tippett *The composer Michael Tippett in 1964. He has left his mark on every genre, and despite the absorption of a wide range of influences, his eclectic style is characterized by a common force of rhythm, as in the Second Symphony.*

and was imprisoned for refusing to help the war effort by working on the land. His oratorio *A Child of our Time* was written in response to the persecution of the Jews. With Britten, he became the foremost English composer of his generation. His first major success was with the Concerto for Double String Orchestra (1939); it was followed by the equally fertile *Fantasia Concertante on a theme of Corelli* (1953). Tippett's early lyrical exuberance reached its zenith in the opera *The Midsummer Marriage* (1955) and the associated piano concerto (1953–55). A sparer sound was achieved with the opera *King Priam* (1962) and 2nd piano sonata, although by the time of *The Knot Garden* (1970) some reconciliation between his two earlier styles was achieved. In this context, his most significant later works are the Triple Concerto, the oratorio *The Mask of Time* and the 5th string quartet. *The Rose Lake* for orchestra (1994) was announced as his last major work. Amidst many contemporaries whose music could be described as static, one gains above all from Tippett's music a sense of movement. KBE 1966. OM 1988.

Works include OPERAS: *The Midsummer Marriage* (1955), *King Priam* (1962), *The Knot Garden* (1970), *The Ice Break* (1977), *New Year* (1989).

CHORAL: oratorios *A Child of our Time* for soloists, chorus and orchestra (1939–41), *The Vision of St Augustine* for baritone, chorus and orchestra (1963–65) and *The Mask of Time* for soloists, chorus and orchestra (1981–84); *A Song of Liberty* (from Blake's *Marriage of Heaven and Hell*) for chorus and orchestra; anthem *Plebs angelica* for double chorus, motet *The Weeping Babe* (E Sitwell) for soprano and chorus.

ORCHESTRAL: four symphonies (1944, 1957, 1972, 1976), concerto for double string orchestra (1939), concerto for orchestra, *Fantasia concertante* on a theme by Corelli (1953); fantasy on a theme by Handel for piano and orchestra (1941), piano concerto (1953–55), concerto for string trio and orchestra (1979), *The Rose Lake* (fp 1995).

CHAMBER AND SOLO VOCAL: five string quartets (1935, 1943, 1946, 1979, 1991); four piano sonatas (1938, 1962, 1973, 1979); cantata *Boyhood's End* for tenor and piano (from W H Hudson's *Far Away and Long Ago*, 1943); part-songs *The Source* and *The Windhover* (Hopkins).

I like to think of composing as a physical business. I compose at the piano and like to feel involved in my work with my hands.

Michael Tippett, quoted in Schafer, *British Composers in Interview*, 1963

tirade French = 'pulling' or 'dragging'; an ornamental scale passage between two notes of a melody or two chords.

tirana a Spanish dance of Andalusia in 6–8 time, usually danced to guitar music and accomp. by words in four-lined *coplas*.

tiré French = 'drawn'; the downstroke of the bow in the playing of string instruments, the opposite of *poussé*, 'pushed'.

Tirimo, Martino (b Larnaca, 19 Dec 1942), Greek-Cypriot pianist and conductor. Studied at the RAM, London, and the Vienna Academy.

A Selection of

Tippett

Concerto for Double String Orchestra 1939
A Child of our Time 1939–41
Fantasia concertante 1953

Piano Concerto 1953–5
The Midsummer Marriage 1955
King Priam 1962
Symphony no. 3 1972
The Ice Break 1977
The Mask of Time ... 1981–4

Cyprus recital debut 1949, London 1965; gave complete series of Schubert sonatas in 1975 and 1985. Plays the concertos of Brahms and Tippett, and has directed the Beethoven concertos from the keyboard (Dresden and London, 1985–86).

Tischenko, Boris (b Leningrad, 23 Mar 1939), Russian composer. Studied with Shostakovich at the Leningrad Conservatory, 1962–65; has taught there from 1965, professor from 1986. Works include operas *The Stolen Sun* (1968), ballets *The Twelve* (1963), *Fly-bee* (1968), and *The Eclipse* (1974; six symphonies (1961–68), piano concerto (1962), two cello concertos, two violin concertos, five string quartets (1957–84), nine piano sonatas (1957–92); Akhmatova Requiem (1966); *Garden of Music*, cantata (1987); film music.

Titelouze, Jean (b Saint-Omer, c 1563; d Rouen, 24 Oct 1633), French composer, priest and organist. He became a canon at Rouen Cathedral in the 1580s; often visited Paris to inaugurate new organs, including that at Notre-Dame in 1610.

Works include three Masses; Magnificats and hymns for organ.

Tito Manlio opera by Vivaldi (libretto by M Noris), produced Mantua, Teatro Arciducale, carnival 1720. Titus Manlius, the Roman Consul, must condemn his son Manlius to death for disobeying orders; but later the two are reconciled.

Titov, Alexey Nikolaievich (b St Petersburg, 24 Jun 1769; d St Petersburg, 20 Nov 1827), Russian musician. He managed the Imperial Opera for some time before the death of Catherine the Great in 1796 and became a major-general in the cavalry guards. Wrote around 20 operas, vaudevilles, melodramas and other stage works.

Tito Vespasiano, ovvero La clemenza di Tito, *Titus Vespasian, or The Clemency of Titus*, opera by Caldara (libretto by Metastasio, partly based on Corneille's *Cinna*), produced Vienna, 1734.

Opera by Hasse (libretto ditto), produced Pesaro, Teatro Pubblico, 24 Sept 1735.

Titus, Alan (b New York, 28 Oct 1945), American baritone. Studied with Aksel Schiotz and at Juilliard; sang Marcello at Washington DC, and the Celebrant in the fp of Bernstein's *Mass* (1971). Sang *Pelléas* on his European debut (Amsterdam, 1973) and Papageno at San Francisco 1975; NY Met. debut 1976, as Strauss's Harlekin and sang Storch in *Intermezzo* at Santa Fe (1985). Other roles include Creonte in Haydn's *Orfeo* (Salzburg 1990), Mandryka (at La Scala) and Donizetti's Duc d'Alba (Spoleto). Sang title role in a new production of Hindemith's *Mathis der Maler*, CG 1995.

toccata from Italian *toccare* = lit. 'to touch, figuratively to play'; originally, in the 17th c., simply 'a thing to play', as distinct from

cantata, 'a thing to sing'. But it soon acquired a sense of touching an instrument for the purpose of trying or testing it, which meant that it usually contained scales, trills and other brilliant figuration, often interspersed with slow chordal passages. 19th- and 20th-c. toccatas usually lay stress on brilliance and rapid execution alone, and are often more or less uniform in figuration throughout.

Toch, Ernst (b Vienna, 7 Dec 1887; d Los Angeles, 1 Oct 1964), Austrian-born American composer and pianist. Studied medicine and philosophy at first and was self-taught in music, but in 1909 was awarded the Frankfurt Mozart prize and studied there under Willy Rehberg, being appointed piano professor at the Mannheim Hochschule für Musik in 1913. He served in World War I, and settled in Berlin in 1929, but emigrated in 1932, visiting the USA, then London for a time, to settle permanently in the USA in 1934, first teaching in NY for two years and then moving to Hollywood as film composer and teacher. After an early modernist phase most of his music was neo-classical in spirit.

Works include operas *Wegwende* (1925), *Die Prinzessin auf der Erbse* (1927), *Egon und Emilie* (1928), *Der Fächer* (1930); incidental music for Euripides' *Bacchantes*, Shakespeare's *As You Like It*, Zweig's *Die Heilige aus USA* and other plays; music for radio play *The Garden of Jade* and others; film music for *Catherine the Great*, *The Private Life of Don Juan*, etc.

Passover Service (1938); cantata *Das Wasser* (1930); *Der Tierkreis* for unaccompanied chorus; seven symphonies (1949–64), *Bunte Suite*, *Kleine Theater Suite*, *Big Ben*, *Pinocchio* overture (after Collodi's story) for orchestra; *Spiel* for wind band; concerto (1926) and symphony for piano and orchestra; *Poems to Martha* for baritone and strings; 13 string quartets (1902–53), piano quintet, string trio, divertimento for violin and viola; two violin and piano sonatas; sonata, 50 studies and c 12 op. nos. of piano pieces.

Toczyska, Stefania (b Gdansk, 11 Aug 1943), Polish mezzo. Made debut at Gdansk 1973, as Carmen, and appeared elsewhere in Poland as Dalila and Leonore in *La favorita*. Vienna Staatsoper from 1977, as Ulrica, Azucena and Eboli. Has sung Lara and Amneris at San Francisco; Anna Bolena at Chicago (1986) and Adalgisa at Houston

(1987). CG 1983–84, as Azucena and Amneris. Sang Wagner's Venus at Hamburg, 1990.

Todi (born *d'Aguiar*), Luiza Rosa (b Setubal, 9 Jan 1753; d Lisbon, 1 Oct 1833), Portuguese mezzo. A pupil of Perez, she made her debut as an actress in 1768 and as a singer two years later in Scolari's *Il viaggiatore ridicolo*. Was at the Italian opera in London in 1777, then went to Madrid, where she had her first big success in Paisiello's *Olimpiade* in 1777. She visited Paris, Berlin and Turin, sang at the opera in St Petersburg 1784–87, at the court of Catherine the Great in operas by Sarti, and subsequently in Prague and in several Italian cities. She retired to Lisbon 1803.

Tod und das Mädchen, Der, *Death and the Maiden*, song, D531, by Schubert on words by M Claudius, composed 1817. The latter part was adapted as a theme for variations in the second movement of his D minor quartet (1824, D810), which is for that reason commonly known by the same name.

Tod und Verklärung, *Death and Transfiguration*, symphonic poem by R Strauss, op. 24, composed 1888–89, fp Eisenach, 21 Jun 1890.

Toeschi, Carl Joseph (b Ludwigsburg, bap. 11 Nov 1731; d Munich, 12 Apr 1788), Italian composer and violinist. Attached to the Mannheim school of early symphonists, and its only Italian member. He became violinist in the court orchestra there in 1752 and leader in 1759; later he followed the court to Munich.

Works include ballet music for various operas by other composers; symphonies; chamber music.

Tofts, Catherine (b *c* 1685; d Venice, 1756), English soprano. She was one of the first English singers to appear in Italian opera in London in 1704; her maid threw oranges at her great rival L'Epine on stage at Drury Lane. She went mad in 1709; at least temporarily recovered, she married Joseph Smith, and accompanied him on his appointment as English consul in Venice.

Togni, Camillo (b Gussago, Brescia, 18 Oct 1922), Italian composer and pianist. Studied composition with Casella in Rome 1939–43 and piano with Michelangeli. He also graduated in philosophy from Pavia University in 1948. He has composed in an advanced serial idiom, one of the first Italians to do so after the previous vogue of neo-classicism.

Works include Variations for piano and orchestra (1946); *Psalmus 127* for voices, violin, viola and cello (1950); *Choruses after T S Eliot* for chorus and orchestra; *Fantasia concertante* for flute and string orchestra (1958); *Tre Studi per 'Morts sans sépulture' di J P Sartre* and *Helian di Trakl* for soprano and piano; *Ricerca* for baritone and five instruments (1953); flute sonata.

Tolomeo, Rè di Egitto, *Ptolemy, King of Egypt*, opera by Handel (libretto by N F Haym), produced London, King's Theatre, Haymarket, 30 Apr 1728. Cleopatra favours younger son Alessandro for succession and exiles Tolomeo to Cyprus, where is is joined by his wife Seleuce; Tolomeo is eventually crowned King of Egypt.

Tomášek (or *Tomaschek*), Václav Jan Křtitel Wenzel Johann (b Skuteč, 17 Apr 1774; d Prague, 3 Apr 1850), Bohemian composer, organist and pianist. His father having been reduced to poverty, he was educated at the expense of two elder brothers. He became a choirboy at the monastery of Jihlava, which he left in 1790 to study law and philosophy in Prague. He also studied the great theoretical treatises on music assiduously, as well as any music he could lay hands on, and established a reputation as teacher and composer before the end of the century; his early symphonies followed classical models. Count Bucquoi von Longueval offered him a well-paid post in his household, to which he remained attached even after his marriage to Wilhelmine Ebert in 1823. He often visited Vienna, and met Beethoven in 1814, and he played his settings of Goethe's poems to the poet at Eger. He pub. his autobiography in instalments 1845–50.

Works include opera *Seraphine* (1811) and two not produced; three Masses, including Coronation Mass (1836), two Requiems and other church music; vocal scenes from Goethe's *Faust* and Schiller's *Wallenstein*, *Maria Stuart* and *Die Braut von Messina*; three symphonies (1801, 1805, 1807), two piano concertos (1805–06); three string quartets (1792–93), piano trio; five piano sonatas, *Elegie auf eine Rose* (after Hölty), seven sets of *Eclogues* and two of *Dithyrambs* and

many other works for piano; numerous songs to words by Goethe, Schiller and others.

Tomasi, Henri (b Marseilles, 17 Aug 1901; d Avignon, 13 Jan 1971), French composer and conductor. Studied at the Paris Conservatory and in 1927 gained the Prix de Rome. On his return from Rome in 1930 became conductor of the national Radio-Paris. Conducted Monte Carlo Opera, 1946–50. His music has typical French qualities of wit, sophistication and virtuosic orchestration.

Works include operas *Don Juan de Mañara* (1956) and *Sampiero Corso* (1956); ballets *La Grisi* (1935), *La Rosière du village* (1936) and *Les Santons* (1938); symphony, *Scènes municipales* (1933), *Chants laotiens* (1934), *Petite Suite médiévale*, *Deux Danses cambodgiennes*, *Danses brésiliennes* for orchestra; capriccio for violin and orchestra; flute concerto (1947), trumpet concerto (1949), viola concerto, saxophone concerto (1951), horn concerto (1955); *Ajax* and *Chants de Cyrnos* for chorus and orchestra.

> *Tonality is a natural force, like gravity.*
> **Paul Hindemith**, *The Craft of Musical Composition*, 1937

Tomasini Italian and Austrian family of musicians:

1. Luigi Tomasini (b Pesaro, 22 Jun 1741; d Eisenstadt, 25 Apr 1808), violinist and composer. Member of the orchestra at Eisenstadt, from 1757, and later at Eszterháza, where he became leader in 1761; Haydn's violin concertos were written for him. Wrote violin concertos, string quartets, divertimenti for baryton, violin and cello, etc.

2. Anton (Edmund) Tomasini (b Eisenstadt, 17 Feb 1775; d Eisenstadt, 12 Jun 1824), violist, son of 1. He played in Esterházy's orchestra as an amateur from 1791 and became a regular member in 1796.

3. Alois (Basil Nikolaus) Tomasini (b Eszterháza 10 Jul 1779; d Neustrelitz, 19 Feb 1858). violinist, brother of 2. Travelled as a virtuoso, became a member of the Esterházy orchestra in 1796, and in 1808 entered the service of the court of Neustrelitz, becoming *Konzertmeister* in 1725.

tombeau French = 'tomb[stone]'; a commemorative composition, especially in 17th-c. French music.

Tombeau de Couperin, Le, *Couperin's Tomb*, a suite for piano by Ravel in the form of a suite such as Couperin might have written, but resembling his music in spirit rather than in style, Ravel's idiom being as modern here as in any of his works. It was written 1914–17 and consists of six movements: *Prélude, Fugue, Forlane, Menuet, Rigaudon* and *Toccata*. Ravel orchestrated it in 1919, without the fugue and toccata; fp of that version, Paris, 8 Nov 1920.

Tom Jones opera by Philidor (libretto by A A H Poinsinet, based on Fielding's novel), produced Paris, Comédie-Italienne, 27 Feb 1765.

Tomkins English family of musicians:

1. Thomas Tomkins (b St Davids, Pembrokeshire, 1572; d Martin Hussingtree, near Worcester, buried 9 Jun 1656), organist and composer. Pupil of Byrd, appointed organist of Worcester Cathedral 1596. He married a widow, Alice Patrick (born Hassard) and in 1607 took the B.Mus. at Oxford. Although remaining at Worcester until the second siege of 1646, he became one of the organists in the Chapel Royal in 1621 and in 1625 wrote music for Charles I's coronation. His last ten years were spent at Martin Hussingtree, where the manor house was the property of the wife of his son Nathaniel (5). He was one of the most important English composers of his time, the last English virginalist and writer of madrigals; most of his church music was pub. after his death (*Musica Deo sacra*, 1668).

Works include seven services, *c* 100 anthems (including the well-known *When David heard that Absalom was slain*); madrigals and balletts for three–six voices; music for viols; pieces for virginals.

2. John Tomkins (b St Davids, *c* 1586; d London, 27 Sept 1638), organist and composer, half-brother of 1. Educated at King's College, Cambridge, where he became organist in 1606. In 1619 he went to London as organist of St Paul's Cathedral, and in 1625 he became a

Gentleman Extraordinary of the Chapel Royal, with a reversion of the next vacant organist's post. Works include eight anthems; variations on *John come kiss me now* for virginals.

3. Giles Tomkins (b St Davids, after 1587; d Salisbury, before 30 Nov 1668), organist and virginalist, brother of 2. In 1624 he succeeded Matthew Barton in his brother's former post as organist of King's Chapel, Cambridge, but in 1629 went to Salisbury Cathedral as organist and choirmaster, and in 1630, though remaining at Salisbury, he succeeded Dering as Musician for the Virginals to Charles I.

4. Robert Tomkins, composer, brother of 3. He became a musician to Charles I in 1633 and remained in the royal household until 1641 or later. Wrote anthems and other church music.

5. Nathaniel Tomkins (b Worcester, 1599; d Martin Hussingtree, 20 Oct 1681), amateur musician, son of 1. He joined the choir of Worcester Cathedral in 1629 and saw his father's *Musica Deo sacra* through the press in 1668.

Tomlinson, John (b Oswaldwistle, Lancs., 22 Sept 1946), English bass. Studied at the RMCM and sang in opera from 1972; Colline with GTO and Leporello with Kent Opera. ENO debut 1974 (Monk in *Don Carlos*) appearing later as Bluebeard (Bartók), Wagner's Pogner in the *Ring* at Bayreuth from 1988 and at CG 1994–95 (also as the Green Knight in the fp of Birtwistle's *Gawain*, 1991). Has sung Gurnemanz at the Berlin Staatsoper and for Opera North sang the title role and directed Verdi's *Oberto* (1994). He is valued for his huge voice and commanding stage presence.

Tommasini, Vincenzo (b Rome, 17 Sept 1878; d Rome, 23 Dec 1950), Italian composer. Studied at the Liceo di Santa Cecilia in Rome and became an associate of the Accademia di Santa Cecilia. He travelled much before 1910 and then settled down to compose; his best known piece is his ballet after Scarlatti, *The Good- Humoured Ladies*.

Works include operas *Medea* (1906) and *Uguale Fortuna* (1913); ballet *The Good-humoured Ladies* (on music by D Scarlatti, 1917); *Il Carnevale di Venezia* for orchestra (1929), violin concerto (1932); choral works on Dante, Petrarch and others; overture to Calderón's *Life is a Dream*, *Poema erotico*, prelude to Baudelaire's *Hymne à la beauté*, suite, *Chiari di luna*, *Il beato regno*, *Paesaggi toscani* for orchestra; three string quartets; violin and piano sonata.

Tomowa-Sintow, Anna (b Stara Zagora, 22 Sept 1941), Bulgarian soprano. Debut Stara Zagora, 1965, as Tatyana. Leipzig from 1967; Butterfly at the Berlin Staatsoper, 1969. She was 'discovered' by Karajan and in 1973 sang in the fp of Orff's *De temporum fine comedia*, at Salzburg; has returned there as Elsa, Mozart's Countess and the Marschallin. CG debut 1975 (sang Yaroslavna in *Prince Igor* there, 1990); NY Met. debut 1978, as Donna Anna. Paris Opéra 1984, as Wagner's Elisabeth.

Ton German = lit. 'tone, sound'; in its early sense the word was used by the German Minnesinger for the words and melody of their songs, and by the Meistersinger for the melody alone. The latter used all kinds of adjectives, sometimes of extreme oddity, to differentiate the numerous tunes. Specimens of such names appear in Wagner's *Meistersinger*, where a *Ton* is also called a *Weis* (*Weise* = 'tune').

tonada, Spanish, a type of Castilian ballad at least as old as the 16th c.

tonadilla, Spanish, from 'tonada', a stage interlude for a few singers, introduced in the 18th c.

tonale or tonarium, Latin, medieval theoretical work dealing with the arrangement of chants according to their mode, and especially of the antiphons and the choice of psalm-tone to go with them. The earliest known is by Regino of Prüm (*c* 900).

tonality synonymous with key, but also meaning, more specifically, the feeling of a definite key suggested by a composition or passage. In modern musical terminology various antithetical derivatives of the word have appeared. ◊atonality, ◊polytonality, ◊bitonality, ◊pantonality.

Tondichtung German = tone-poem, symphonic poem.

tone in England the term is used for pure musical notes not charged with harmonics, each harmonic being itself a tone; also for the quality of a musical sound, especially with reference to performance. In America

tone is synonymous with 'note', and 'note' is normally reserved for the written symbol.

(2) The interval between the first and second degrees of the major scale, also between the second and third, fourth and fifth, fifth and sixth, and sixth and seventh.

(3) A melodic formula to which a psalm is sung in plainsong.

Tone is light in another shape ... In music instruments perform the functions of the colours employed in painting.

Honoré de Balzac, *Gambara*, 1839

---

tone-colour or timbre, is a convenient term for the sound of an instrument or voice as regards the peculiar quality produced by it; also for combinations of such sounds.

Tonelli (actually *De' Pietri*), Antonio (b Carpi, 19 Aug 1686; d Carpi, 25 Dec 1765), Italian composer and cellist. Learnt music from his parents, who were both good amateurs, then studied with the choirmaster of Carpi Cathedral and at Bologna and Parma, where the duke became his patron. He spent three years at the Danish court, returned to his home town and became choirmaster at the cathedral in 1730, but resigned in the 1740s and spent some of his time in other towns and on tour, returning to his post in 1757. He was active to an advanced age and expressed his affections to marry a pupil more than 60 years his junior.

Works include operas *L'enigma disciolto* and *Lucio Vero*; intermezzi *Canoppo e Lisetta*; oratorio *Il trionfo dell' umiltà di S Filippo Neri* and others; church music; cantatas; a *Canzonieri* against nuns.

tone-poem ◊symphonic poem.

tone-row a translation of the German *Tonreihe*, to designate the 'rows' of 12 notes on which compositions in twelve-note music are based. Also known in England as 'series'.

tonic the keynote: the note on which the scale begins and ends which determines the key of a piece of music in major or minor or defines the mode. F, for example, is the tonic of a piece in the Lydian mode or in F major or minor. A Lydian piece, whether harmonized or not, will end on the note F, which is therefore also called the final; one in F major or minor will usually end on the major or minor common chord of its tonic, F.

tonic sol-fa a system of musical notation without staves and notes, invented by John Curwen in the middle of the 19th c. on a basis of the principles of Solmization and Solfeggio, and once widely used in Britain and the dominions by choral singers, for whom it simplifies the sight-reading of music.

Tonic sol-fa notation is based on the old syllabic system of Do (Ut), Re, Mi, etc. and takes the following from: *d, r, m, f, s, l, t*, the names of the notes being Doh, Ray, Me, Fah, Soh, Lah, Te. The substitution of 'Te' for the old 'Si' was made to avoid the duplication of the letter 's' in the abbrs. The range of voices being limited, upper and lower octaves can be sufficiently indicated by a simple stroke placed behind the letters in a higher or lower position, thus: *d*− represents the note an octave above *d*, which in turn is an octave above *d'*. Accidentals are indicated by the addition of a letter 'a' (ra, ma, etc., or exceptionally 'u' for du) for flats and 'e' (de, re, etc., or exceptionally 'y' for my) for sharps. But accidentals appear comparatively rarely now that the system of the 'movable Doh' has been adopted. This is a system of transposition according to which everything is except, for some very short incidental modulations, sung from a notation that looks as though the music were always in C major or A minor.

The actual key is indicated at the beginning of a piece, so that singers know at once, for example, if the composition is in A major, that their *d* is to be read as A, their *r* as B, etc. If the piece modulates to another key, a change is indicated, so that temporarily *d* may become any other note of the scale, etc.; but in major keys it will always remain the tonic, in whatever key the music moves, *s* always the dominant, *f* always the sub-dominant, etc., while in minor keys *l* will be the tonic, *m* the dominant, *r* the sub- dominant, etc. (A special syllable, 'ba', is used for the sharp sixth in the melodic minor scale.) The time divisions are indicated by short bar lines, and there are subdivisions between these. The way in which the notes fill these spaces determines their time-values, though there are special signs for dotted notes, triplets, etc. A blank space means a rest, dashes after a note mean that it is to be held beyond the space it occupies over one or more of the following time-divisions.

The merits of tonic sol-fa have always been subject to controversy, no doubt because there is much to be said on either side. Its great defect is that it is insufficient for any general study of music as an art and that it is apt to keep choral singers from expanding their musical experience. Its advantages to instrumental players, even where it might be applicable, as in the case of non-harmonic instruments, are very slight, since it is not so much easier to learn than staff notation, nor so flexible in picturing the composer's intentions. For choral singers it has not only the merit of simplicity, but the greater one of teaching them a sense of relative pitch as well as removing all difficulties connected with transposition.

Tonkünstler-Societät, 'Musicians' Society', a musicians' benevolent society in Vienna, founded in 1771, which gave charity performances twice yearly, in Lent and Advent. These were the first truly public concerts in Vienna. Haydn's oratorio *Il ritorno di Tobia* and Mozart's cantata *Davidde Penitente* (adapted from the C minor Mass) were written for the society, though both composers were refused membership.

tonos, Spanish, short vocal pieces for several voices sung at the opening of plays in 17th-c. Spain.

Tonreihe ◊tone-row.

tonus lascivus Latin = 'playful, frolicsome, wanton tone'; the medieval name for what later became the Ionian mode and the major scale, not recognized as a church mode at the time, but often used for

Works include *Concerti grossi* (op. 8, 1709); violin concertos; *sinfonie* (concertos) for trumpet and orchestra.

Torke, Michael (b Milwaukee, 22 Sept 1961), American composer. Studied at the Eastman School and with Jacob Druckman at Yale (1984–85). His music is highly eclectic, with some popular modern idioms.

Works include opera *The Directions* (1986) and ballet *Black and White* (1988); *Ceremony of Innocence* (1983) and *The Yellow Pages* (1984), both for flute and ensemble; *Vanada* (1984), *Bright Blue Music* (1985), *Ecstatic Orange* (1986) and *Green* (1986), all for orchestra; *Adjustable Wrench* for chamber ensemble (1987); *Purple* for orchestra (1987); *Copper* for brass quintet and orchestra (1987); *Rust* for piano and winds (1989); *Mass* for baritone, chorus and ensemble (1990); *Bronze* for orchestra (1990); piano concerto (1991); *Chalk* for string quartet (1992); *Run* for orchestra (1992); *Four Proverbs* for female voice and ensemble (1993).

tornada, Spanish, the refrain which is a feature of many old Catalan songs.

Törne, Bengt (Axel) (b Helsinki, 22 Nov 1891; d Turku, 4 May 1967), Finnish composer. Studied with Furuhjelm at the Helsinki Conservatory and later privately with Sibelius, on whom he wrote a book. Kajanus allowed him to try out his orchestral works with the Finnish State Orchestra.

Works include six symphonies (1935–66), three sinfoniettas; six symphonic poems; violin concerto, piano concerto; chamber music; piano pieces.

Torquato Tasso opera by Donizetti (libretto by J Ferretti), produced Rome, Teatro Valle, 9 Sept 1833. Poet Tasso is in love with Eleonore but her brother, Duke Alfonso, sends him to an asylum for seven years; on his return Eleonore has died and Tasso must seek refuge in his poetry.

In   ex-i-tu Is-ra-el de Ae-gy-pto   do-mus Ja-cob de po-pu-lo bar-ba-ro

The two bars of the example are centred on different notes, illustrating the essential quality of tonus peregrinus.

secular songs by minstrels and not unknown in plainsong melodies.

tonus peregrinus Latin = 'foreign tone'; a plainsong chant which, unlike the eight regular psalm tones, had two reciting notes, one in the first half of the chant and another in the second. For this reason it was described as 'foreign' and was reserved for the psalm 'In exitu Israel/When Israel came out of Egypt'. So far as its tonality is concerned it is in Mode I with flattened B. The melody was also sung in the Lutheran church: Bach uses it in his Magnificat and also in the cantata *Meine Seel' erhebt den Herren* (a setting of the German Magnificat).

Tooley, John, ◊Covent Garden.

Toovey, Andrew (b London, 1962), English composer. Studied with Jonathan Harvey, and with Morton Feldman at Dartington. Director of Ixion from 1987, giving performances of music by Xenakis, Cage and Ferneyhough.

Works include *Winter Solstice* for voice and seven players; *Untitled String Quartet* (1985); *Ate* for chamber ensemble (1986); *Shining* for violin and cello (1987); *String Quartet Music* (1987); *Shimmer Bright* for string trio (1988); *Black Light* for chamber ensemble (1989); music theatre pieces *The Spurt of Blood* (1990), *Ubu* (1992) and *The Juniper Tree* (1993); *Mozart for strings* (1991); piano music *Artaud* (1986), *Out Jumps Jack Death* (1989), *Down there by the Sea* (1989) and *Embrace* (two pianos, 1990).

Torelli, Giuseppe (b Verona, 22 Apr 1658; d Bologna, 8 Feb 1709), Italian composer and violinist. Probably a pupil of Perti in Bologna, he played in the orchestra of San Petronio there 1686–96, then went to Vienna, and was *Konzertmeister* at the court of the Margrave of Brandenburg 1697–99. He returned to Bologna 1701. With Corelli he was one of the most important composers in the history of the early concerto.

Torri, Pietro (b Peschiera, Lake Garda, *c* 1650; d Munich, 6 Jul 1737), Italian composer. Pupil of Steffani. He became court organist at Bayreuth in 1667 and at Munich in 1689, visiting *Kapellmeister* at Hanover in 1696, and returned to Munich in 1703 as director of the chamber music, becoming music director in 1715. Like Abaco, he followed the Elector Max Emanuel into exile at Brussels.

Works include operas *Merope*, *Lucio Vero* (1720), *Griselda* (1723) and around 20 others; oratorio *Les Vanités du monde*; chamber concerto; chamber duets.

Tortelier, Paul (b Paris, 21 Mar 1914; d Villarceaux, 18 Dec 1990), French cellist and composer. Solo debut in 1931; played in the Monte Carlo and the Boston SOs before World War II. In 1947 he was the soloist in Strauss's *Don Quixote*, under Beecham, in London; US debut 1955, with the Boston SO. He was noted for a subjective approach to interpretation, and was famous for his masterclasses. He composed cello music and an *Israel Symphony* (1956). His daughter **Maria de la Pau** is a pianist.

Tortelier, Yan Pascal (b Paris, 19 Apr 1947), French conductor, son of Paul ◊Tortelier. Studied with Boulanger at the Paris Conservatoire. Debut 1962, as violinist in London performance of the Brahms Double Concerto, with his father. Studied conducting with Franco Ferrara and was associate with the Orchestre du Capitole, Toulouse, 1974–83. Led the RPO in London concert 1978 and the Seattle SO 1985. Principal of the Ulster Orchestra 1988–92, BBC Philharmonic from 1992. Orchestration of the Ravel Piano Trio performed 1993. Led the London fp of Hindemith's opera *Sancta Susanna*, 1995.

Torvaldo e Dorliska opera by Rossini (libretto by C Sterbini), produced Rome, Teatro Valle, 26 Dec 1815. Defeated Torvaldo returns in disguise to castle of Duke of Ordow to rescue Dorliska, but both are imprisoned until the Duke's servants rescue them.

Torke *American composer Michael Torke joins respectable modern composers such as Skriabin, Messiaen and Schoenberg who have been inspired by colour.* Verdant Music *of 1986 became* Green *by its appearance at the 1995 London Proms, and evokes the pastures of the composer's native Wisconsin.*

Tosca, La opera by Puccini (libretto by G Giacosa and L Illica, based on Sardou's drama), produced Rome, Teatro Costanzi, 14 Jan 1900. Tosca commits suicide when she unsuccessfully bargains with lecherous Baron Scarpia for the life of her lover Cavaradossi, who is executed for treason and harbouring the convict Angelotti.

'Mr Gershwin wanted it this way', I had explained.
'Thata poor boy ... he was asick', said Toscanini.
Oscar Levant, *Memoirs of an Amnesiac*, 1960

Toscanini, Arturo (b Parma, 25 Mar 1867; d New York, 16 Jan 1957), Italian conductor. Studied at the Conservatories of Parma and Milan and began his career as a cellist. At a performance of *Aida* in Rio de Janeiro, when the conductor was taken ill, he conducted the work from memory at a moment's notice. Engagements followed in Italy where he conducted the fps of *Pagliacci* (1892) and *La Bohème* (1896). Such was his success that he was appointed chief conductor in 1898 at La Scala and in 1907 at the NY Met.; remained until 1915, giving the 1910 fp of *La fanciulla del West* and early US performances of operas by Mussorgsky, Giordano, Dukas and Gluck. He returned to La Scala 1921–29 and in 1930–31 gave *Tristan* and *Parsifal* at Bayreuth, but in 1933 he refused to conduct there on account of his anti-fascist convictions. At Salzburg (1934–37) he was heard in *Falstaff*, *Fidelio* and *Meistersinger*. He gave his first NY concert in 1913 and from 1940 conducted the NBC SO, gaining a reputation for intense and highly disciplined music making; recorded several Verdi operas and conducted works by Strauss, Ravel, Prokofiev and Debussy, in addition to the standard repertory. Toscanini had a reputation for fidelity to the printed score, but some of his later recordings leave an impression of relentlessly hard-driven performances. He was one of the last of a generation of conductors which dominated (and terrorized) orchestras by sheer strength of personality and power over hiring and firing of musicians.

Tosi, Giuseppe Felice (b Bologna; *fl.* 1677–93), Italian composer. Organist at San Petronio at Bologna, and later *maestro di cappella* at San Giovanni in Monte and the cathedral of Monte di Ferrara.

Works include operas; *salmi concertati* and other church music; chamber cantatas.

Tosi, Pier Francesco (b Cesena, *c* 1653; d Faenza, 1732), Italian castrato, teacher and composer, son of Giuseppe ◊Tosi. He learnt music from his father and travelled much until 1682, when he settled as singing-master in London. From 1705 to 1711 he was composer at the Imperial court in Vienna. After a further visit to London he finally returned to Italy and was ordained in 1730. He pub. a book on florid singing (1723), and wrote an oratorio, and cantatas for voice and harpsichord.

Tosti, (Francesco) Paolo (b Ortona sul Mare, Abruzzi, 9 Apr 1846; d Rome, 2 Dec 1916), Italian singing-master and composer. Studied at Naples under Mercadante and others from 1858 and was appointed a student-teacher, remaining until 1869. During a long illness at home he wrote his first songs. He then went to Rome, where Sgambati helped him to give a concert and Princess Margherita of Savoy (afterwards queen of Italy) appointed him her singing-master. In 1875 he first visited London, returning each year until 1880, where he remained as singing-master to the royal family. His songs were highly popular in his day. Knighted 1908.

Works include Italian, English and French songs, e.g. *Non m'ama più*, *Lamento d'amore*, *Aprile*, *Vorrei morire*, *Forever*, *Good-bye*, *Mother*, *At Vespers*, *That Day*, *Mattinata*, *Serenata*; *Canti popolari abruzzesi* for vocal duet, etc.

Tost Quartets 12 string quartets written by Haydn 1788–90 for the Viennese merchant and violinist Johannes Tost: op. 54 nos. 1–3, op. 55 nos. 1–3, op. 64 nos. 1–6, Tost also commissioned works from Mozart, including the D major string quintet K593.

Toten Augen, Die, *The Dead Eyes*, opera by d'Albert (libretto originally French by M Henry, German translation by H H Ewers), produced Dresden, 5 Mar 1916. Blind Myrtocle is granted her sight by Jesus but when she looks upon ugliness of her husband Arcesius decides she would rather remain blind, by staring at the sun.

Totenberg, Roman (b Łódz, 1 Jan 1911), Polish-born American violin-

---

THE OPERA

Tosca

A three-act opera by Giacomo Puccini which tells of love, murder and suicide. It is based in Rome in 1800, and was first produced there a century later.

I. An escaped political prisoner, Angelotti (bass), seeks refuge in the Attavanti Chapel. His friend, the painter and republican Cavaradossi (tenor), gives him the keys to his villa. When Cavaradossi's lover – the singer Floria Tosca (soprano) – arrives, she is jealous that the portrait of Mary Magdalene has been modelled on the Marchesa Attavanti. Cavaradossi has to leave with Angelotti for his villa, and the cruel chief of police Scarpia (baritone) tries to get information from Tosca by arousing her jealousy; he has her followed when she leaves.

II. Dining alone at the Palazzo Farnese, Scarpia expresses his violent desire for Tosca. She is brought in while Cavaradossi is tortured in the next room. Unable to bear her lover's cries, Tosca reveals Angelotti's hiding place. She realizes that she can only save Cavaradossi by giving herself to Scarpia. He rises from the desk at which he has been writing a safe-conduct, and Tosca grabs a knife and stabs him.

III. As Cavaradossi awaits execution, Tosca tells him that it is only a sham but he must feign death. Cavaradossi falls as the squad fires, but when Tosca goes to him she finds that he is indeed dead; Scarpia has cheated her. As soldiers rush in to arrest her, she throws herself from the parapet.

THE OPERA

ist and teacher. Studied with Carl Flesch in Berlin and Enescu in Paris. Debut 1922, and gave European recitals with Szymanowski, 1935–36. US citizen from 1943, head of violin at the Aspen School of Music, 1950–60. Professor of Music at Boston University, 1961–78, Director of the Longy School of Music at Cambridge, MA, 1978–85. Recordings include Bach's solo works and the Bloch Concerto (1992).

Tote Stadt, Die, *The Dead City*, opera by Korngold (libretto by P Schott, based on G Rodenbach's play *Bruges-la-morte*), produced Hamburg and Cologne, 4 Dec 1920. Paul exorcizes memory of dead wife Marie when he meets Mariette, who bears a striking resemblance to her. But he strangles his new lover when she insults his faith.

'To the Memory of an Angel', *Dem Andenken eines Engels*, Berg's dedication for his violin concerto, composed 1935 in memory of Manon Gropius, the daughter of Walter Gropius and Mahler's widow, Alma. The work begins with a musical portrait of Manon and ends with an adagio based on the Bach chorale *Es ist genug*. Fp Barcelona, 19 Apr 1936, with Louis Krasner, conductor Scherchen. First London performance 1 May 1936, conductor Webern.

touch (modern), the way of approaching the keys in piano playing to produce the tone required. Scientists deny the possibility of varying the quality of tone by anything but weight, since it is obviously impossible to transmit to the hammers and strings anything but degrees of strength by the intermediary of the action, which (unlike the clavichord's) is not susceptible to any but a mechanical response to the player's hand. However, different physical approaches to the piano can indeed result in different responses from the instrument (especially when regarding passages in which the texture invites contrast between simultaneously played notes), because different 'touches' can subtly but directly influence the player's attack and release of each key, thereby causing minute variations of articulation and dynamics which the conscious mind alone would be challenged to achieve. It is these infinitesimal inequalities and inaccuracies which account for subtleties of touch, and although they too are in the last resort mechanical, they do express the player's interpretative intentions and translate themselves into aesthetic values.

touch (old), as a verb the word, up to *c* the early 17th c., meant simply to 'sound' an instrument, exactly as *toccare* does in Italian; as a noun ('touch' or 'touche') it was equivalent to ◊toccata. ◊tucket.

Tourel (actually *Davidovich*), Jennie (b Vitebsk, 22 Jun 1900; d New York, 23 Nov 1973), Russian-born French-Canadian mezzo. Studied in Paris with Anna El-Tour, whose name she adopted in anagram form. Debut at the Paris Opéra-Comique in 1933 as Carmen; NY Met. debut 1937, as Mignon. Other roles included Cherubino, Adalgisa, Rosina and Charlotte. Often heard in concert, in particular with Leonard Bernstein. She created the role of Baba the Turk in Stravinsky's *Rake's Progress* (Venice, 1951).

Tournai Mass an early 14th-c. polyphonic setting of the Ordinary of the Mass, including *Ite missa est*. It is not the work of a single composer, nor is it necessarily from Tournai, where the MS now is, but may have been written at least in part in the South of France.

Tournemire, Charles (Arnould) (b Bordeaux, 22 Jan 1870; d Arcachon, 4 Nov 1939), French composer and organist. Studied at the Paris Conservatory and later with d'Indy. In 1898 he was appointed to Franck's former organist's post at the church of Sainte-Clotilde. Later he became professor of chamber music at the Conservatory and travelled much as organ recitalist on the Continent.

Works include operas *Les Dieux sont morts* (1924) and *Nittetis* (1905–07); *Le Sang de la Sirène* for solo voices, chorus and orchestra; eight symphonies; piano quartet, piano trio and other chamber music; *Pièces symphoniques*, *Triple Choral*, *l'Orgue mystique*, *Petites Fleurs musicales* and other organ works; piano pieces; songs.

Tourte, François (b Paris, 1747; d Paris, 26 Apr 1835), French bowmaker. He learnt his craft from his father and set up in business with his elder brother Xavier, but they quarrelled and set up each for himself. He made great improvements in the violin bow, especially after 1775.

Tovey, Donald (Francis) (b Eton, 17 Jul 1875; d Edinburgh, 10 Jul 1940), English music scholar, pianist and composer. He was privately educated and learnt the piano early, playing it astonishingly as a child and memorizing Bach and other classics. At 13 he was a pupil of Parry. He went to Balliol College, Oxford, in 1894, after giving a concert with Joachim at Windsor, and there he distinguished himself by brilliant scholarship and by taking a leading part in the university's musical life. In 1900–01 he gave piano recitals at St James's Hall in London, and 1901–02 in Berlin and Vienna. In 1914 he was appointed Reid Professor of Music at Edinburgh University, a post he held to his death, and also conducted the Reid orchestral concerts there. He wrote several books, including six vols. of *Essays in Musical Analysis*. Knighted 1935.

Works include opera *The Bride of Dionysus* (1929); incidental music for Maeterlinck's *Aglavaine et Sélysette*; symphony in D major; suite for wind band; piano concerto (1903), cello concerto (1935); two string quartets; conjectural completion of Bach's *Art of Fugue* (1931).

I was compelled to leave at the end of the first movement, which seemed to last as long as my first term at school.

Constant Lambert on Tovey's Cello Concerto, *The Sunday Referee*, 1937

Tower, Joan (b New Rochelle, NY, 6 Sept 1938), American composer. Studied at Columbia University with Otto Luening and founded the Da Capo Chamber Players 1969. She taught at Bard College, New York from 1972, returning 1988. Her music has moved from serial influences to a more impressionistic style.

Works include percussion quartet (1963); *Breakfast Rhythms* for clarinet and five instruments (1975); *Amazon II* and *Sequoia* for orchestra (1979, 1981); *Petroushskates* for ensemble (1980); *Amazon III* for chamber orchestra (1983); *Music* for cello and orchestra (1984); Piano concerto (1985); clarinet and flute concertos (1988, 1989); Concerto for Orchestra (1991); violin concerto (1992); *Stepping Stones: A Ballet*, for orchestra (1993).

Toy Symphony piece by Leopold Mozart (formerly attributed to Haydn) with parts for toy instruments (cuckoo, quail, nightingale, etc.). Similar works have been written by Mendelssohn, A Romberg and others, most recently Malcolm Arnold.

Tozzi, Giorgio (b Chicago, 8 Jan 1923), American bass. He studied in Milan and appeared on Broadway in 1948 (Britten's *Rape of Lucretia*). He sang widely in Europe 1950–54 as Philip II, Don Giovanni and Pogner. NY Met. debut 1955, as Alvise; later roles were Figaro, Marke, Sachs and Boris. Sang with the Boston Opera 1977, in the US fp of *Ruslan and Ludmilla*. Also appeared in musicals and films.

Trabaci, Giovanni Maria (b Monte Pelusio [now Irsina], *c* 1575; d Naples, 31 Dec 1647), Italian composer and organist. He was appointed organist in the royal chapel at Naples in 1603 and *maestro di cappella* in 1614.

Works include Masses, four Passions, motets, psalms; madrigals; toccatas, *ricercari* and other organ pieces.

Traci Amanti, I, *The Amorous Turks*, opera by Cimarosa (libretto by G Palomba), produced Naples, Teatro Nuovo, 19 Jun 1793.

tract a chant with penitential words, sung after the Gradual in the Mass in Lent (in place of the Alleluia). Tracts are the only surviving examples in the regular chants of the Mass of 'direct psalmody', sung without antiphon or respond. They occur only in modes two and eight, and it is possible that those of mode two were originally Graduals. Their structure is that of a highly elaborated psalm-tone. The number of verses ranges from two to 14.

Traetta, Tommaso (Michele Francesco Saverio) (b Bitonto, near Bari, 30 Mar 1727; d Venice, 6 Apr 1779), Italian composer. Pupil of Porpora and Durante at the Conservatorio di Santa Maria di Loreto in Naples 1738–48, he first worked as a composer of church music, but after the success of *Farnace* (1751) soon established himself as an opera composer. He was much influenced by recent innovations of

French opera, in particular the *tragédies lyriques* of Rameau, but also continued the Metastasian tradition of *opera Seria. Maestro di cappella* and singing teacher at the court of the Infante Felipe of Spain in Parma 1758–65, he was director of the Conservatorio dell' Ospedaletto in Venice 1765–68, then went to St Petersburg as music director at the court of Catherine II of Russia. He returned to Italy 1775, visited London 1777, and finally lived in Venice. The early comic opera *Buovo d'Antona* (1758) and later serious works have been successfully revived in recent years.

Works include over 40 operas, e.g. *Farnace* (1751), *Didone abbandonata* (1757), *Ippolito ed Aricia* (1759), *I Tindaridi* (1760), *Le serve rivali* (1766), *Amore in trappola, Antigona* (1772), *Merope* (1776), *Germondo* (1776), *Il cavaliere errante*, etc.; oratorio *Rex Salomone*; Passion; *Stabat Mater* and other church music; divertimenti for four orchestras *Le Quattro stagioni e il dodici mesi dell'anno; sinfonie, etc.*

Tragédie de Salomé, La ballet by Florent Schmitt (choreography by Guerra), produced Paris, Théâtre des Arts, 9 Nov 1907.

tragédie lyrique, French, a 17th–18th-c. term for French opera of a serious character, e.g. Rameau's *Les Boréades* (1764).

Tragic Overture, *Tragische Ouvertüre*, an overture by Brahms, op. 81, composed 1880 as a companion-piece to the *Academic Festival Overture*, written as an acknowledgment of the honorary degree of doctor of philosophy conferred on him by Breslau University in 1879. Fp Vienna, 26 Dec 1880.

'Tragic' Symphony Schubert's fourth symphony, in C minor, composed 1816, first public performance Leipzig, 19 Nov 1849. The title was added to the score by the composer.

Tragoedia work for wind quintet, harp and string quartet by Birtwistle, composed 1965.

Trampler, Walter (b Munich, 25 Aug 1915), German-born American violist and teacher. Played in German Radio SO then emigrated to USA in 1939 (naturalized 1944). Played in New Music String Quartet 1947–55; extra viola for Budapest and Juilliard Quartets. Taught at Juilliard from 1962, Boston University from 1972. Gave fp of the concerto by Simon Bainbridge (1978).

tranquillo Italian = 'quiet, calm, tranquil'; the adverb, more rarely used as a direction, is *tranquillamente*.

Transfiguration de Notre Seigneur Jésus-Christ, La work in 14 movements for soloists, chorus and orchestra by Messiaen (texts from the Bible, the Missal and St Thomas Aquinas); composed 1965–69, fp Lisbon, 7 Jun 1969, conductor Baudo.

transitions passages in a composition between two salient thematic features, more often than not modulating from one key to another. In a movement in sonata form an important feature often lies in the transition between first and second subjects and in the different turn it takes in the exposition and recapitulation.

transposing instruments many wind instruments are built in fundamental tunings in which the major scale without key signature, written as C major, actually sounds higher or lower. A clarinet in B♭, for example, will automatically play the scale of that key when the music is written in C major; or, conversely stated, if it is to play a piece in F major, the music must be written in G major, and so on. A horn in F will transpose a fifth down, a trumpet in F a fourth up, and both will play, for example, in E♭ if their music is written in B♭, but the former an octave lower than the latter. Among the most common orchestral instruments English horns, clarinets, horns and trumpets are transposing instruments; flutes, oboes, bassoons and trombones are not. In brass bands all the instruments except the bass trombone are transposing instruments.

transposing keyboards contrivances of various sorts to shift the manuals of keyboard instruments so that the music played becomes automatically higher or lower, saving the players from learning to transpose at sight. Such keyboards appeared on some organs as early as the 16th c. and later on Ruckers harpsichords. Several inventions of the kind were made for the piano late in the 18th and throughout the 19th c.

transposition the process, in either composition or performance, of turning a piece or passage from one key into another in such a way that the music remains exactly the same except for the change in pitch. It follows that all accidentals arising incidentally in the course of the music (i.e. not contained in the key signature) still remain accidentals. In a piece transposed from E major up to F major, for example, an incidental A♯ will become B♮, incidental F♯ will become G♮, and so on. Accompanists are often required to transpose at sight when a song is too high or low for a singer's voice, and occasionally the instrumental

This passage from Bach's St John Passion *is transposed from E major to F major.*

Trans work by Stockhausen for string orchestra, wind, and percussion with tape and light projection. Fp Donaueschingen, 16 Oct 1971.

transcription an arrangement of a composition for some other medium than that intended by the composer. Strictly speaking, a transcription differs from an arrangement by not merely reproducing the original as closely as possible, but by introducing more or less imaginative changes which may be supposed to conform to the composer's own procedure if he had written for the different medium.

parts of a whole orchestra have to be transposed in the same way for similar reasons. Horn players, using today an F-B♭ horn, have to transpose at sight older horn parts written for horns in C, D, E♭, etc.

transverse flute the modern flute held horizontally, as distinct from the flutes of the recorder type, which are held vertically.

Trapp, Max (b Berlin, 1 Nov 1887; d Berlin, 29 May 1971), German composer. Studied composition with Juon and piano with Dohnányi at the Berlin Hochschule für Musik, became piano professor there

1920 and professor of advanced composition 1924. He also taught at Dortmund. The fp of his second *Concerto for Orchestra* (1935) was conducted by Furtwängler.

Works include marionette play *Der letzte König von Orplid* (after Mörike); incidental music to Shakespeare's *Timon of Athens*; seven symphonies, two concertos, two divertimenti, symphonic suite, *Notturno* for orchestra; piano concerto, violin concerto (1926), cello concerto (1937); two string quartets, piano quintet, three piano quartets; variations for two pianos; sonatina for piano.

traquenard French = lit. 'trap, snare; also racking-pace' [of horses]; a 17th-c. dance, the dotted rhythm of which refers to the second sense of the word.

Traubel, Helen (b St Louis, 20 Jun 1899; d Santa Monica, 28 Jul 1972), American soprano. Studied in St Louis and made her debut there in 1925. In 1937 she began a long career at the NY Met., which lasted until 1953; roles included Elisabeth, Brünnhilde, Isolde, Kundry and the Marschallin. She also appeared in night clubs, which led to her resignation from the Met. after a frank exchange of views with Rudolf Bing. She pub. some successful detective novels, including *The Metropolitan Opera Murders*.

Trauermarsch German = funeral march.

Trauermusik work for viola and strings in four movements by Hindemith; composed 21 Jan 1936 in response to the death of George V and performed the next day in London with Hindemith as soloist, conductor Boult.

Trauer-Ode, *Funeral Ode*, Bach's cantata no. 198, written on the death of the Electress Christiane Eberhardine of Saxony and performed at the memorial ceremony at Leipzig, 17 Oct 1727.

Trauer-Sinfonie, *Mourning Symphony*, the nickname of a symphony by Haydn, no. 44, in E minor, composed *c* 1771.

Trauerwalzer, *Mourning Waltz*, the title given by the pub. to Schubert's waltz for piano, op. 9 no. 2, in 1821, a piece later wrongly attributed to Beethoven. Schubert, who wrote it in 1816, disapproved of the title. The attribution to Beethoven occurred in 1826, when Schott of Mainz brought out a *Sehnsuchtswalzer* (also called *Le Désir*) under his name, although it was a compound of Schubert's piece and Himmel's *Favoritwalzer*.

--------------- **THE OPERA** ---------------

La Traviata

A dramatic three-act opera by Giuseppe Verdi. It was first performed in 1853 and is set in Paris at about the same time.

I. The consumptive courtesan Violetta (soprano) is courted by Alfredo Germont (tenor), who urges her to abandon her way of life. Violetta is intrigued by her suitor but decides on a life of freedom.

II. Alfred and Violetta have been living together for three months at a country house near Paris. Alfredo's father, Giorgio Germont (baritone), calls and pleads with Violetta to give up her relationship; the scandal threatens the marriage prospects of his daughter. Violetta reluctantly writes Alfredo a letter ending their affair, and leaves before he can dissuade her. At the house of her friend Flora, Violetta is partying with Baron Duphol (baritone), her former protector who has now returned. When Alfredo arrives, Violetta urges him to leave but, announcing to the guests that he is paying her for past services, he flings down the money he has won at cards. Alfredo's father arrives and everyone comments on his insult.

III. Lying sick in her bedroom, Violetta reads a letter from Germont saying that he has told his son of her sacrifice. Alfredo begs her forgiveness when he arrives, and they briefly look forward to the future. Violetta collapses suddenly, but before she dies expresses the hope that Alfredo will find a wife more worthy of him.

--------------- **THE OPERA** ---------------

Traumgörge, Der, *Dreaming George*, opera by Zemlinsky (libretto by L Feld); composed 1904–06 and accepted for production at the Vienna Hofoper by Mahler. Not performed until 11 Oct 1980, at Nuremberg. Idealist Görge abandons fiancée Grete and takes up with Gertraud, through whom his dreams are eventually realized.

trautonium an electrophonic instrument invented by Friedrich Trautwein of Berlin in 1930, producing notes from the air graded according to the chromatic scale by means of a special device, not indeterminate in pitch like those of the aetherophone or Theremin. Hindemith wrote a Konzertstück for trautonium and strings.

Travers, John (b *c* 1703; d London, Jun 1758), English organist and composer. Learnt music as a choirboy at St George's Chapel, Windsor, and later studied with Greene and Pepusch in London, where in his early 20s he became organist at St Paul's Church, Covent Garden, and later at Fulham church. In 1737 he succeeded Jonathan Martin as organist in the Chapel Royal.

Works include services, anthems, Te Deum; *The Whole Book of Psalms* for one–five voices with continuo; 18 canzonets for two–three voices to words by M Prior and others; organ voluntaries; harpsichord pieces.

traversa Italian = 'transverse'; an abbr. sometimes used in old scores for the *flauto traverso*, the modern flute played sideways, as distinct from flutes of the recorder type, which are held vertically.

traversière French = 'transverse'; the *flûte traversière* was the French name for the *flauto traverso*, or transverse ◊flute.

Traviata, La, *The Lady Gone Astray*, opera by Verdi (libretto by F M Piave, based on the younger Dumas' *La Dame aux camélias*), produced Venice, Teatro La Fenice, 6 Mar 1853. Consumptive courtesan persuaded by Alfredo's father to renounce love for the sake of his family's honour. She has an affair with Baron Douphol before Alfredo learns the truth about her actions; the lovers are reconciled before she dies.

Travis, Roy (b New York, 24 Jun 1922), American composer. Studied at Juilliard and Columbia University (1947–51) and with Milhaud at the Paris Conservatoire. Taught first in New York then at UCLA (professor from 1968).

Works include operas *The Passion of Oedipus* (1968) and *The Black Bacchantes* (1982); string quartet (1958); *Duo Concertante* for violin and piano (1967); *Barma*, septet (1968), *Collage* for orchestra (1968); Piano concerto (1969); electronic music pieces (studio at UCLA from 1969).

Traxel, Josef (b Mainz, 29 Sept 1916; d Stuttgart, 8 Oct 1975), German tenor. Debut Mainz, 1942, as Don Ottavio; later sang at Nuremberg, then Stuttgart. In 1952 created Mercury in Strauss's *Die Liebe der Danaë* at Salzburg. Bayreuth 1953, Walther. Also sang Evangelist in Bach's Passions.

Discord oft in musick makes the sweeter lay.
Edmund Spenser, *The Faerie Queen*, 1590

Trebelli (real name *Gillebert*), Zélia (b Paris; 1838; d Etretat, 18 Aug 1892), French mezzo. She began serious music studies, including piano, at the age of six, and at 16 was allowed to take a course in singing. She made her first stage appearances at Madrid in 1859, as Rosina, Azucena and Arsaces. Travelled in Germany 1860–61 with Merelli's Italian co. and first visited London in 1862; returned until 1888 as Siebel, Preziosilla, and Cherubino. NY Met. from 1883 as Boito's Elena and as Carmen.

treble the highest voice in a vocal composition in several parts, derived from the Latin *triplum*, which was the top part of the earliest three-part motets. It is the normal term for a boy's voice.

treble clef the G clef, designating the G above middle C (being a modification of the letter G and indicating the position of the note G on the stave), the higher of the two clefs used for piano music, also replacing the former different C clefs used for soprano, alto and tenor voices. If used for the tenor, it is understood that the voice sounds an octave lower.

The treble clef (a), and the treble clef transposed an octave lower (b).

treble viol the smallest of the normal members of the viol family.

Open strings of the treble viol.

trecento, Italian = lit. '300' but normally a shorthand reference to 'the 1300s', the Italian musical repertory of the 14th c., or more specifically, in terms of what survives, the years *c* 1340 to 1420. The music is notated with the techniques first described by Marchettus of Padua and tends to be extremely florid. The main composers were Jacopo da Bologna and Francesco Landini.

tre corde Italian = 'three strings'; a direction in piano music indicating that after the use of the left pedal (*una corda*) normal playing is to be resumed.

Tree, Ann Maria (b London, Aug 1801; d London, 17 Feb 1862), English mezzo and actress. Studied singing with Lanza and T Cooke, joined the chorus at Drury Lane Theatre and made her first important stage appearances at Bath in 1818 and in London in 1819. Later she became a good Shakespearian actress as well as a stage singer.

Tregian, Francis (1574–London, 1619), English amateur musician. He was the eldest of a large, highly cultivated Cornish Roman Catholic family, and travelled extensively abroad, returning finally in 1605. He was imprisoned for recusancy in 1609 in the Fleet, where he died. He copied (probably for the most part in prison) two collections of vocal works (the Sambrooke MS in New York, and British Library, Egerton MS 3665) and the Fitzwilliam Virginal Book. The latter two contain a few of his own compositions.

Treigle, Norman (b New Orleans, 6 Mar 1927; d New Orleans, 16 Feb 1975), American bass. He studied in LA and sang at the NY City Opera for almost 20 years from 1953; among his roles were Handel's Caesar, Boris, Don Giovanni and the villains in *Les Contes d'Hoffmann*. In NY and New Orleans he took part in the fps of operas by Carlisle Floyd. He sang Gounod's Méphistophélès at CG in 1974 and committed suicide the following year.

Treleaven, John (b Cornwall, 1949), English tenor. Studied in London and Naples. Appearances with WNO as Tamino, Alfredo, Pinkerton and Tippett's Mark; ENO as Don José, Cavaradossi, the Berlioz Faust, Hoffmann and Don Carlos. Has sung Tamino and Peter Grimes at CG; Florestan, Werther and Radames with Scottish Opera. Other roles include Gluck's Pylades (Paris Opéra), Prince Golitsin in *Khovanshchina* (San Francisco, 1990) and Siegmund (Mainz, 1993). Concerts from 1981, including the Verdi Requiem and *The Dream of Gerontius*.

tremolando Italian = 'trembling'; a direction sometimes used instead of the conventional notation for string tremolo, or for a passage to be sung in a tremulous voice.

tremolo, Italian = 'quivering', (1) the rapid repetition of a single note. In 17th-c. Italy the vocal tremolo was called *trillo*.

(2) The rapid alternation of two or more notes, produced on wind instruments, the organ, the piano and bowed string instruments by the fingers.

The notation of a tremolo on a single note, and between two notes.

tremulant a mechanical device on the organ, operated by a draw stop, for producing *vibrato*.

trenchmore an English country dance 'longways for as many as will', known in the 16th and 17th c. and introduced into the court and noble houses as a kind of democratic dance in which masters and servants could take part together, temporarily relaxing strict class distinctions.

Trent Codices seven MSS (Trent, 87–93) of 15th-c. music, compiled 1440–80 and including works by Power, Dufay, Dunstable, Ockeghem and Binchois. The first six were bought by the Austrian Government in 1891, and a selection appeared in six vols. of the series *Denkmäler der Tonkunst in Österreich*. They became the property of Italy after World War I, and in 1920 the seventh MS was found.

Trento, Vittorio (b Venice, 1761; d ? Lisbon, 1833), Italian composer. Pupil of Bertoni. In the last decade of the 18th c. he visited London as conductor at the King's Theatre and in 1806 became impresario at Amsterdam, going to Lisbon in the same capacity soon after. After a further visit to London he returned to Venice before his death.

Works include operas *La finta ammalata*, *Quanti casi in un giorno* (1801), *Teresa vedova*, *Ifigenia in Aulide*, *Climene* (1812) and *c* 35 others; ballet *Mastino della Scala* and more than 50 others; oratorios *The Deluge*, *The Maccabees* and others.

trepak a Russian dance of Cossack origin in animated 2–4 time.

Treptow, Günther (b Berlin, 22 Oct 1907; d Berlin, 28 Mar 1981), German tenor. He studied in Berlin (debut 1936) and sang there until 1942, when he moved to Munich; roles included Adolar, Parsifal, Walther, Otello and Florestan. NY Met. debut 1951, as Siegmund. CG 1953, as Siegfried. He sang in Vienna 1947–55; appointed Kammersänger 1971.

Treu, Daniel Gottlob (b Stuttgart, 1695; d Breslau, Aug 1749), German violinist and composer. Pupil of Cousser and from 1716 of Vivaldi in Venice, where he was called, by the literal translation of his name, Fedele. In 1725 he went to Breslau as conductor of an Italian opera co., in 1727 to Prague as music director and in 1740 into the service of Count Schaffgotsch at Hirschberg.

Works include operas *Astarto* (1725), *Ulisse* (1726), *Don Chisciotte* (1727) and others; cantatas; orchestral music.

triad a chord composed of two superimposed thirds.

Major, minor, augmented, and diminished triads.

trial a French term for a special type of operatic tenor voice of a high, thin, rather nasal quality suited to comic parts, derived from Antoine ◊Trial.

Trial French family of musicians:

1. Jean-Claude Trial (b Avignon, 13 Dec 1732; d Paris, 23 Jun 1771), composer. Studied violin with Garnier at Montpellier, settled in Paris, where he became a friend of Rameau, was appointed conductor at the Opéra and later of the private orchestra of the Prince de Conti, whose influence procured him the joint directorship of the Opéra with Berton.

Works include operas *Ésope à Cythère* (with Vachon, 1766), *La Fête de Flore* (1770), *Silvie* (with Berton), *Théonis* (ditto) and *Renaud d'Ast* (with Vachon, 1765); cantatas; overture and divertissements for orchestra.

2. Antoine Trial (b Avignon, 1737; d Paris, 5 Feb 1795), tenor and actor, brother of 1. He was educated as a church singer, but went on the stage, toured in the provinces and in 1764 appeared for the first time in Paris. He took part in the Revolution, lost his reason and poisoned himself.

3. Armand-Emmanuel Trial (b Paris, 1 Mar 1771; d Paris, 9 Sept 1803), pianist and composer, son of 2. He began to compose at an early age, married Jeanne Méon, an actress at the Théâtre Favart, and died from the effects of a wild life.

Works include operas *Julien et Colette* (1788), *Adélaïde et Mirval*

(1791), *Les Deux Petits Aveugles* (1792); revolutionary pieces *La Cause et les effets*, *Le Congrès des rois* (with other composers) and *Le Siège de Lille*.

Trial by Jury one-act opera by Sullivan (libretto by W S Gilbert), produced London, Royalty Theatre, 25 Mar 1875. When Angelina takes Edwin to court for breach of promise, the judge proposes to her himself.

triangle a percussion instrument consisting of a simple steel bar in three-cornered form with an open end, hooked so that it can be suspended to hang freely. It is struck with a short steel rod and produces a bright tinkling sound of no definite pitch.

Tridentine Council ◊Council of Trent.

trihoris an old French dance of Lower Brittany, also called trihory, triori or triory, allied to the branle.

Trillo del diavolo, Il, *The Devil's Trill*, Tartini's violin sonata written at Assisi *c* 1745 and said to have been inspired by a dream in which he bargained with the devil for his soul in return for musical inspiration, the devil playing the violin to him. He related that on waking he immediately wrote down what he had heard, but that the music as written fell far short of the dream devil's performance. The work is in four movements, written for violin and continuo; the famous trill is in the finale. An opera on the story of the sonata was written by Falchi.

Trinity College of Music a school of music in London incorporated in 1875.

trio (1) a composition or movement for three vocal or instrumental parts: more particularly a chamber work for three instruments, especially violin, cello and piano (piano trio) or violin, viola and cello (string trio).

(2) The alternative section in a minuet, scherzo, march or similar movement, so called because such sections were originally written for two oboes and bassoon.

Trionfi del fato, I, ovvero Le glorie d'Enea, *The Triumphs of Fate, or The Glories of Aeneas*, opera by Steffani (libretto by O Mauro), produced Hanover, Court Opera, Dec 1695.

Trionfo dell' onore, Il, *The Triumph of Honour*, opera by A Scarlatti (libretto by F A Tullio), produced Naples, Teatro dei Fiorentini, autumn 1718. Honour wins out as Flaminio is united with Cornelia and Riccardo with Leonora.

Trionfo di Afrodite, *Aphrodite's Triumph*, concerto scenico by Orff, second of three works called collectively *Trionfi* (text by composer, after Catullus, Sappho and Euripides), produced Milan, La Scala, 14 Feb 1953, conductor Karajan. Songs and games in honour of bridal couple.

Trionfo di Clelia, Il, *Clelia's Triumph*, opera by Gluck (libretto by Metastasio), produced Bologna, Teatro Comunale, 14 May 1763. Also settings by Hasse (Vienna, 1762) and Jommelli (Lisbon, 1774). Roman noblewoman Clelia is captured by Etruscan king but saves her city with her courage and nobility.

Opera by Jommelli (libretto ditto), produced Lisbon, Teatro d'Ajuda, 6 Jun 1774.

Trionfo di Dori, Il, *The Triumph of Doris*, collection of Italian madrigals pub. by Gardano of Venice in 1592. It contains 29 six-part madrigals on various poems all ending with the line 'Viva la bella Dori', which suggested the similar uniform final line in the English collection modelled on this, *The Triumphes of Oriana*. The composers, all represented by one piece each, include Anerio, Asola, Baccusi, Croce, G Gabrieli, Gastoldi, Marenzio, Palestrina, Striggio and Vecchi.

trio sonata the medium predominantly used for chamber music with a keyboard continuo part in the later 17th and early 18th c. Trio sonatas were most usually written for two violins and bass viol or cello, with background supplied by a harpsichord or other keyboard instrument played from the figured bass part.

tripla an old term for triple time in old mensurable music, but also the figure three shown in the time-signature and later, when the device of the triplet came into use, the figure 3 set over a group of notes. Also a dance in quick triple time.

Triple Concerto a concerto with three solo parts, for example Beethoven's concerto for violin, cello and piano and orchestra, or Tippett's concerto for string trio and orchestra.

triple counterpoint counterpoint in which three parts are reversible, each being capable of appearing at the top, in the middle or at the bottom.

triplet a group of three notes performed in the time of two and indicated by the figure 3.

Rests instead of notes may form part of triplets.

Example of a triplet (bar 2).

triple time three beats in a bar, e.g. 3–4.

triplum Latin = 'the third'; the highest of the original three voices in the motet, and thus the origin of the English word treble.

Tristan work by Henze for piano, tape and orchestra; composed 1973, fp London, 20 Oct 1974, conductor C Davis.

Tristan chord ◊augmented sixth chords.

Tristan und Isolde music-drama by Wagner (libretto by composer, based on the Tristram and Iseult legend), produced Munich, Court Opera, 10 Jun 1865. Tristan and Isolde fall under spell of a love potion during a journey prior to her marriage with King Mark of Cornwall; Mark's servant Melot mortally wounds Tristan and Isolde sings the famous Liebestod over his corpse.

Tristitiae remedium, *The Remedy for Sadness*, a MS collection of motets, anthems and madrigals by English and Italian composers (Byrd, Croce, Milton, Peerson, Tallis, Tye, etc.) made by the clergyman Thomas Myriell of Barnet in 1616.

tritone the interval of the augmented fourth (e.g. F–B, progressing upwards). ◊Diabolus in Musica.

THE OPERA

Tristan und Isolde

A legendary tale of love and death in three acts by Richard Wagner, who also wrote the text of the opera. The action begins on Tristan's ship crossing between Ireland and Cornwall, in legendary times. The opera received its first performance in 1865.

I. Isolde (soprano) is to be the unwilling bride of King Mark of Cornwall, taken to him by the warrior Tristan (tenor). Custom and honour forbid Tristan from seeing Isolde, but his squire Kurwenal (baritone) acts as an intermediary. Isolde tells her attendant Brangaene (mezzo-soprano) how Tristan slew her fiancé Morold, and at the same time was wounded himself. Isolde had the chance to kill Tristan but healed him instead. Isolde orders Brangaene to prepare a death drink for them, but a love potion is substituted. As the ship nears shore, Tristan and Isolde fall into each other's arms.

II. While her husband Mark (bass) and Melot (tenor) are out hunting, Isolde meets Tristan and they express their passion. Oblivious to the distant warnings of Brangaene, they reject the false realities of day and seek instead another, eternal world of night. Mark and his followers burst in and the king expresses his sorrow at Tristan's betrayal. Tristan allows himself to be wounded by Melot.

III. At his castle in Brittany, the sick Tristan is attended by Kurwenal as he awaits Isolde's ship. Tristan wakes to a sad tune played on a shepherd's pipe. He curses the love potion and has a vision of Isolde before a joyful piping heralds her arrival. Tristan tears off his bandages and dies in Isolde's arms. Mark and Melot arrive in a second ship and Kurwenal dies killing Melot. In a final transfiguration, Isolde embraces the death in which she will be united with Tristan.

THE OPERA

Tritonius, Petrus (actually Peter Treybenreif) (b Bozen (now Bolzano), *c* 1465; d ? Hall, Tyrol, ? 1525), Austrian composer and scholar. Studied at Vienna and Ingolstadt Universities and later became teacher of Latin and music at the cathedral school of Brixen. After study at Padua University, he was invited to settle in Vienna by Conradus Celtis, a professor there whom he had met in Italy, and joined the literary and humanist society founded by that scholar, making his setting of Horatian odes for it. Senfl later took the tenor parts of these as *cantus firmi* for his own settings, and Hofhaimer imitated Tritonius's settings. On the death of Celtis in 1508 Tritonius returned to the Tyrol and became director of the Latin school at Bozen; in 1513 he was in Hall, and in 1521 he retired to Schwaz am Inn.

Works include hymns in four parts; odes by Horace and other Latin poems set in four parts, etc.

Trittico, *Triptych*, cycle of three one-act operas by Puccini, produced NY Met., 14 Dec 1918:

I. *Il Tabarro/The Cloak* (libretto by G Adami, based on D Gold's *Houppelande*). Michele kills wife Giorgetta's lover and hides the body under a cloak. II. *Suor Angelica/Sister Angelica* (libretto by G Forzano). As convent dweller Angelica is told of death of her illegitimate son she takes poison and is granted a vision of the Virgin with her child. III. *Gianni Schicchi* (libretto by ditto, based on the story of a rogue who is mentioned in Dante's *Divina commedia*). Gianni Schicchi assumes the identity of the rich, recently-deceased Bicose Donati and dictates a will favourable to himself.

Tritto, Giacomo (b Altamura, near Bari, 2 Apr 1733; d Naples, 16 or 17 Sept 1824), Italian composer. Pupil of Cafaro at the Conservatorio dei Turchini in Naples, he later taught there and in 1806 became co-director (with Paisiello and Fenarolo). From *c* 1760 he wrote over 50 operas. He also wrote treatises on thorough-bass and counterpoint.

Works include operas *La fedeltà in amore* (1764), *Il convitato di pietra* (on the Don Giovanni story), *Arminio*, *La canterina*, *Gli Americani* (1802), *Marco Albinio* (1810), etc.; Masses and other church music.

Triumphes of Oriana, The an English collection of madrigals written in honour of Queen Elizabeth I, edited by Morley and published 1601. It was modelled on the Italian collection of *Il Trionfo di Dori* of 1592 and contains a similar series of different poems all ending with the same line, 'Long live fair Oriana'. There are 25 pieces by 23 English composers: Bennet, Carlton, Cavendish, Cobbold, Este, Farmer, E Gibbons (2), Hilton, Holmes, Hunt, E Johnson, R Jones, Kirby, Lisley, Marson, Milton, Morley (2), Mundy, Nicolson, Norcome, T Tomkins, Weelkes, Wilbye. A madrigal by Bateson intended for the collection arrived too late and was included in his own *First Set of English Madrigals* (1604).

Triumphlied, *Song of Triumph*, a setting by Brahms of words from the Revelation of St John for eight-part chorus, orchestra and organ *ad lib.*, op. 55, composed in spring 1871 to celebrate the German victory in the Franco-Prussian war; fp Karlsruhe, 5 Jun 1872.

Triumph of Neptune, The ballet by Lord Berners (scenario by S Sitwell, choreographed by Balanchine), produced London, Lyceum Theatre, 3 Dec 1926. The settings were based on B Pollock's 'penny plain, two-pence coloured' toy theatre designs.

Triumph of Peace, The masque by James Shirley with music by W Lawes and Simon Ive, produced at the Banqueting House in Whitehall, 3 Feb (Candlemas) 1634.

Troades opera by Reimann (libretto based on Werfel's version of Euripides' *The Trojan Women*), produced Munich, 7 Jul 1986.

Troilus and Cressida opera in three acts by Walton (libretto by C Hassall, after Chaucer), produced Covent Garden, 3 Dec 1954. Revived with Cressida's role altered to mezzo (Janet Baker), London, CG, 12 Nov 1976. Trojan Troilus follows Cressida when she accompanies her father Calchas to the Greek camp; although they love each other, she agrees to marry Diomede after she believes Troilus has abandoned her. But all is revealed before Calchas stabs Troilus in a fight and Cressida commits suicide.

Trois Petites Liturgies de la Présence Divine, *Three Little Liturgies of the Divine Presence*, work by Messiaen for 18 sopranos, piano, ondes Martenot, celesta, vibraphone, three percussion and strings (text by composer), fp Paris, 21 Apr 1945, conductor Désormière.

tromba Italian = 'trumpet', also one of the names for the trumpet organ stop (8 ft). ¢clarino.

tromba da tirarsi Italian = lit. 'trumpet to draw itself [out]'; the slide trumpet, an instrument of the trumpet type. It was used in Germany in the 18th c. and had the advantage before the invention of valves of being capable of producing more notes than the fundamental harmonics by the temporary changes in the length of the tube, as in the trombone. It never attained a wide currency.

Trombetti, Ascanio (b Bologna, bap. 27 Nov 1544; d Bologna, 20 or 21 Sept 1590), Italian composer. In the service of the Signoria of Bologna.

Works include motets in 5–12 parts for voices and instruments; madrigals for four–five voices, *napolitane* for three voices.

Tromboncino, Bartolomeo (b ? Verona, *c* 1470; d ? Venice, after 1534), Italian composer. At the ducal court of Mantua, 1487–95, then at Venice, Vicenza, Casale, at Mantua again in 1501–13, and then at Ferrara.

He enjoyed brief fame for having murdered his adulterous wife (1499) and was later in the service of the notorious poisoner, Lucrezia Borgia.

Works include Lamentations, one motet and 17 *laude*; over 170 *frottole* for four voices.

trombone a brass wind instrument, developed from the sackbut, made in four basic sizes: alto, tenor, bass and contrabass, the first of which is now rarely used, parts written for it being played on the tenor trombone, while the last hardly ever appears in the orchestra, except in Wagner's *Ring*. The instrument's most characteristic feature is the slide, by means of which the tube can be adjusted to different lengths in seven positions, so that all the notes of the chromatic scale can be produced as natural harmonics. The trombone was thus a chromatic instrument long before the horn and trumpet became so by the invention of valves. The intonation, as in string instruments, is not fixed, but depends entirely on the player's ear and skill. Many notes are of course, available in more than one position (as different harmonics), so that the player often has the choice between an easier and a more difficult way of passing from note to note. A strict *legato* between notes in different positions is not possible, as the breath has to be interrupted during the change of the slide to avoid an unpleasant scoop; but this scoop, which

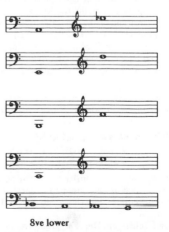

The compass of the alto, tenor, and bass trombones; the compass of the tenor-bass trombone; 'pedal' notes on the trombone.

trombone *The trombone originated in the 15th century and was used in consorts or in choirs because of its compatibility with the human voice. It was a common feature of the orchestra only after 1800. The illustration depicts a bass trombone.*

is usually designated by the term *glissando*, can be used as a special effect.

The compass of the contrabass lies an octave below the tenor's. The tenor-bass, a combined instrument in Bb with a switch lowering the pitch a fourth to F, is widely used at the present day. The length of the slide makes it impossible to play the lowest note (Bb) of the bass trombone on this instrument: the compass therefore starts from C and goes as high in the tenor range as the player can manage.

In the 19th c. valve trombones were invented and gained favour in military and brass bands as being easier to play, though their tone is inferior. The valve trombone never gained a firm footing in the orchestra.

Never look at the trombones. It only encourages them.

> **Richard Strauss**, quoted by Sir Brian Young, BBC radio broadcast, 1983

Trommelbass German = lit. 'drum bass'; a technical term for the notes of a bass part divided up into groups of repeated even quavers, a device used especially in the 18th c. to give a kind of artificial animation to music.

Trompeter von Säckingen, Der, *The Trumpeter of Säckingen*, opera by Nessler (libretto by R Bunge, based on Scheffel's poem), produced Leipzig, 4 May 1884. Trumpeter Werner loves Maria but her parents prefer Damian, who turns out to be a coward and a simpleton. After being banished, Werner returns to save the Baron from an uprising and is allowed to marry Maria. Very popular in its day and often conducted by Mahler.

tronco Italian = 'truncated, cut off, interrupted'; a direction indicating that a note or chord is to cease abruptly.

trope the verb 'to trope' meant to insert ◊tropes into ecclesiastical chanting. The process was also called 'farcing' (i.e. larding).

Tropen German = 'tropes'; the term, which does not refer to the old tropes, was used by Josef Hauer for his own version of the system of twelve-note music. He divided the possible combinations of the 12 notes of the chromatic scale, which run into hundreds of millions, into 44 main groups, and these are what he called *Tropen*, and he further divided each row of 12 notes into two halves of six, which form two fundamental chords, whatever the order in which each six may appear. The *Tropen* for him were equivalent to keys in the diatonic system, and a change from one *Trope* to another is equivalent to modulation.

troper a book or collection containing ◊tropes, e.g. the 11th-c. Winchester Tropers, which contain tropes used at Winchester Cathedral.

tropes interpolations into liturgical chants dating from the 8th or 9th c. and probably of Byzantine origin. They were at first vocalized as purely musical ornamentations or sung on syllables of certain words, especially 'Alleluia', but later they became so important that special words were newly written for them. Sometimes new words came first and demanded new music; thus the sequence, which began merely as a special kind of trope, developed into a poetical form with musical setting.

troppo Italian = 'too much'; the word is often used in the negative in musical directions; *non troppo*, 'not too much', or *ma non troppo*, 'but not too much'.

Trotter, Thomas (b Birkenhead, 4 Apr 1957), English organist. Studied at the RCM and Cambridge University. Debut at the Festival Hall, London (1980) and has made concert tours of Europe, Australia, Japan and the USA. Organist at St Margaret's, Westminster 1982, City of Birmingham 1983. Recordings include works by Reubke, Alain, Soler and Messiaen.

troubadour, French, from Provençal *trobador* [? from Latin *tropus*],

THE OPERA

Il Trovatore

A four-act opera by Giuseppe Verdi, first performed in 1853. The very confusing plot is set in northern Spain in the 15th century.

I. Ferrando (bass) tells how 20 years before, a gypsy was burned at the stake for putting the evil eye on the infant brother of Count Luna (baritone). The gypsy's daughter, Azucena (mezzo-soprano), had kidnapped the infant in revenge, and when his brother Luna grew up he was commanded by their father to search for him. Leonora (soprano) is serenaded at the palace gardens by Manrico (tenor), a mystery troubadour (the *Trovatore* of the title). Leonora's other admirer, Count Luna, intervenes and challenges Manrico.

II. Azucena has brought up Manrico as her son, and tells him how she mistakenly burned her own son in attempting to avenge her mother's death. Believing Manrico dead, Leonora wishes to enter a convent; Luna decides to abduct her, but Manrico gets there before him.

III. Believing that Azucena is Manrico's mother, Luna tortures her; Manrico interrupts his wedding to Leonora to rescue her.

IV. Leonora offers herself to Luna in return for Manrico's freedom, and then takes poison when he accepts. Manrico denounces her until he realizes the sacrifice she has made. As Manrico dies, Azucena tells Luna in triumph that he has killed his own brother, but is later captured by Luna's men.

THE OPERA

a poet-musician of southern France in the 11th–13th c. Troubadours always wrote their own poems and probably the tunes as well: some 280 melodies are still extant. The poems were usually *poésies courtoises* (mainly love-songs, but also included satires, etc.), while story-telling *chansons à personnages*, though also cultivated by them, belonged chiefly to the northern Trouvères. Only the melodies were written down, in a notation which showed the pitch but not, as a rule, the rhythm of the notes, the latter being either committed to memory or else determined by the poetic metre, a question that has never been solved beyond controversy. Neither is it known how the songs were accompanied: probably on instruments of the harp or lute type, either by the troubadours themselves or by attendants, for the troubadours were not poor wandering musicians but gentlemen whose audiences were at courts and noble houses.

'Trout' Quintet a quintet in A major for violin, viola, cello, double bass and piano, D667, by Schubert, composed summer 1819 during an excursion to Upper Austria; so called because the fourth of the five movements is a set of variations on his song *The Trout/Die Forelle*, D550, (1817).

trouvère, French, from old French *trovere* or *troveur*, a poet-musician of northern France in the 12th and 13th c. The trouvères cultivated an art similar to that of the ◊troubadours in southern France. The art was encouraged in the north by Eleanor of Aquitaine, who married Louis VII in 1137: about 1,700 melodies have been preserved. The poems include *chansons à personnages* (narrative songs), *poésies courtoises* (courtly poems, mainly love-songs) and crusaders' songs. The notation and manner of performance of the songs was similar to that of the troubadours.

Trovatore, Il, *The Troubadour* or *The Minstrel*, opera by Verdi (libretto by S Cammarano, based on a Spanish play, *El trovador*, by A G Gutiérrez), produced Rome, Teatro Apollo, 19 Feb 1853. Manrico and Count Luna are rivals for the love of Leonora; when Luna is unsuccessful he orders Manrico's execution. Leonora offers her body to the Count in exchange for Manrico's life, but she takes

——————— THE OPERA ———————

Les Troyens

A dramatic five-act opera by Hector Berlioz. He finished the composition in 1858, but the first performance was of part only in 1863 (as *Les Troyens à Carthage*), followed by the remainder 27 years later (as *La Prise de Troie*). The first complete performance was also given in 1890. The action opens in the abandoned Greek camp outside Troy.

I. Cassandre (soprano) cannot convince the Trojans· of her forebodings about the wooden horse left behind by the Greeks. Her lover Chorèbe (baritone) tries to placate her. The Trojans celebrate their deliverance but are interrupted first by the silent figure of Andromache, Hector's widow, then with news of the mistrustful priest Laocöon, devoured by sea serpents. The Trojan March accompanies the arrival of the wooden horse inside Troy.

II. Inside the palace, Hector's ghost (bass) tells Aeneas (tenor) to escape Troy and found a new city in Italy. In Priam's quarters, Cassandre tells how Chorèbe was killed but Aeneas escaped; she and the other women kill themselves as the Greeks burst in.

III. Dido, Queen of Carthage (mezzo-soprano), celebrates peace with her people. Aeneas enters with the Trojans in disguise, but when invasion is threatened they are ready to defend Carthage.

IV. Dido and Aeneas pause while out hunting; during the Royal Hunt and storm they seek shelter and fulfil their love. Dido is entertained at her gardens by the sea but her reverie with Aeneas is broken by Mercury (baritone), who summons Aeneas to Italy.

V. As the Trojans prepare to leave, the ghosts of dead heroes urge Aeneas on. Dido reproaches him without success, and she mounts a funeral pyre as the Trojans depart.

——————— THE OPERA ———————

Trotter *An organist with an exceptionally wide range, Thomas Trotter's recordings feature the Grand Organ of Birmingham Town Hall. His repertory includes the technically demanding concertos by Antonio Soler, the virtuoso displays of Liszt, and the immensely long religious meditations of Messiaen.*

poison before he is freed and Manrico is subsequently killed. It is revealed that he is the Count's brother.

Trowell, Brian (b Wokingham, 21 Feb 1931), English musicologist. Studied at Cambridge with Thurston Dart and was lecturer at Birmingham University 1957–62. Director of opera at GSMD, London, 1963–67, reader then professor at King's College from 1970. Professor of music at Oxford University from 1988; has edited music by Dunstable (joint editor, complete works); has published *The Early Renaissance* (1963), translations and articles on opera; also *Elgar's Use of Literature*.

Troyanos, Tatiana (b New York, 12 Sept 1938; d New York, 21 Aug 1993), American mezzo. She studied at the Juilliard and sang Britten's Hippolyta at the NY City Opera in 1963. She has sung in Europe since 1965 and in 1969 created Jeanne in the Hamburg fp of Penderecki's *The Devils of Loudun*. CG from 1969 as Octavian, Carmen and the Composer. NY Met. debut 1976, as Octavian; she returned there in 1984 for Bragaene, and Dido in *Les Troyens*. On 11 Aug 1984 she sang the title role in the fp (concert) of Rakhmaninov's opera *Monna Vanna* (Saratoga, NY). Sang Dorabella at the Met. 1990, Mozart's Vitellia at Chicago 1989. Noted for her spirited stage presence.

Troyens, Les, *The Trojans*, opera by Berlioz in two parts (libretto by composer, after Virgil):

I. *La Prise de Troie/The Taking of Troy*, produced Karlsruhe (in German), 6 Dec 1890; Cassandra's warnings are ignored as the departing Greeks leave their wooden horse; warned by the ghost of Hector, Aeneas escapes the massacre of the Trojans. II. *Les Troyens à Carthage*, produced Paris, Théâtre-Lyrique, 4 Nov 1863, and later at Karlsruhe (in German), 7 Dec 1890 (the fp of the complete work). Aeneas and Dido, Queen of Carthage, fall in love but he must depart for Italy to found Rome, and as he leaves Dido mounts her funeral pyre. The fp of the complete work in French was at Brussels, 26 and 27 Dec 1906; fp in French complete on one night, CG, 17 Sept 1969, conductor C Davis.

Truelove (or *Trouluffe*), John (*fl. c* 1470), English composer. He was a canon of St Probus, attached to Exeter Cathedral, 1465–78. He

trumpet *The trumpet has existed for thousands of years in many different cultures. The Western trumpet was introduced into Europe during the Crusades. Initially used primarily for fanfares and the like, it gained a place in the orchestra during the 17th century.*

appears to have been associated with Richard Smert in the composition of four carols in the Ritson MS.

The trumpet's loud clangor/Excites us to arms/With shrill notes of anger/And mortal alarms.
John Dryden, *A Song for St Cecilia's Day*, 1687

trumpet a brass wind instrument of ancient origin. Until the invention of the valves in the 19th c. the trumpet was capable of producing only the natural harmonic notes, for which reason, combined with that of its incisive and carrying tone, it was found useful for fanfares, and for military purposes was often combined with timpani; this practice is clearly reflected in the scores of classical orchestral works up to the early 19th c. In order to make it possible to play in different keys, crooks were used, as with the horn. The valves made the trumpet a chromatic instrument.

A still smaller trumpet in F (with a compass a minor third higher than that of the D trumpet) has been made for the performance of Bach's second Brandenburg concerto, and there is also one in high B♭ (with a compass an octave higher than that of the normal B♭ trumpet). ◊Bach trumpet, ◊bass trumpet, ◊clarino, ◊principal and ◊tromba da tirarsi.

The written compass and actual notes of the B flat trumpet; the actual compass of the trumpet in D.

trumpet marine an early string instrument with a single string and thus allied to the monochord, played with a bow. It was used mainly for popular music-making, especially in Germany, but also in convents, as the German name *Nonnengeige*, 'nun's fiddle' indicates. It was also called *Trummscheit*, 'trumpet [*tromba*] wood' or *Brummscheit*, 'humming wood', and the Italian and English names connecting it with a trumpet were doubtless due to its penetrating tone. The provenance of the adjective 'marine' is unknown. The instrument produced harmonics very easily and, like the old trumpet, often restricted itself to them, its normally produced notes being very poor and coarse in quality.

trumpet voluntary in the late 17th c. a piece, not for trumpet, but an organ voluntary the tune of which was played on the trumpet stop. The example still familiar is that by J Clarke, long wrongly attributed to Purcell, popularized by Henry Wood's orchestral arrangement. This is in fact *The Prince of Denmark's March*, which Clarke pub. in 1700 as a harpsichord piece, but which also occurs in a suite for wind instruments by Clarke.

Tsar and Carpenter (Lortzing) ◊Zar und Zimmermann.

Tsar Saltan (Rimsky-Korsakov) ◊Legend of Tsar Saltan.

Tsar's Bride, The, *Tsarskaya Nevesta*, opera by Rimsky-Korsakov (libretto by I F Tumenev, based on a play by L A Mey), produced Moscow, Imperial Opera, 3 Nov 1899. Marfa is chosen by Ivan the Terrible as his bride, but she loves Lykov and is poisoned by a jealous rival; Lykov is beheaded for the crime as Marfa expires.

Ts'ong, Fou, ◊Fou Ts'ong.

tuba (1) an ancient Roman military trumpet.
(2) The bass instrument of the ◊saxhorn family, used in the orchestra as the bass of the brass instruments.

Military and brass bands also use tubas in E♭ and low B♭. ◊bombardon, ◊euphonium and ◊Wagner tuba.

Tubin, Eduard (b Kallaste, 18 Jun 1905; d Stockholm, 17 Nov 1982), Estonian-born Swedish composer. Conducted in Estonia 1931–44, before settling in Sweden.

Works include operas *Barbara of Tisenhusen* (1969) and *The Priest from Reigi* (1971); ten symphonies (1934–73), two violin concertos (1942, 1945), balalaika concerto (1964); *Requiem for Fallen Soldiers* (1979); two violin sonatas (1936, 1949).

The orchestral tuba is normally in F (non-transposing) with four valves and this compass.

tubular bells metal tubes tuned to the musical scale and used for bell effects in the orchestra, real bells being cumbersome and difficult to play with precision.

Tucci, Gabriella (b Rome, 4 Aug 1929), Italian soprano. She sang in Milan, London and San Francisco from 1959; NY Met. 1960 as *Butterfly*. Other roles include Marguerite, Mimi and Violetta. Teacher at Indiana University from 1983.

Tuček, Vincenc (Tuczek, Vinzenz) (b Prague, 2 Feb 1773; d Pest, in or after 1821), Bohemian tenor, conductor and composer. After working as singer and conductor at theatres in Prague and Vienna, he was *Kapellmeister* to the Duke of Courland in Sagan 1797–99, then music director at the Silesian national theatre in Breslau (1799) and at the Leopoldstädtertheater in Vienna (1806–09). Later he also worked in Budapest.

Works include operas and *Singspiele Dämona, Lanassa, Der Zauberkuss*, etc.; Masses and other church music; cantatas.

Tucker, Norman (b Wembley, 24 Apr 1910; d London, 10 Aug 1978), English administrator and translator. Studied at Oxford and the RCM. Joint director at SW, London 1947–54, sole director 1954–66; translator for the UK fps of Janáček's *Káta Kabanová* and *Cunning Little Vixen* (1951, 1961); also translated *Simon Boccanegra* for its UK fp (1948), and Verdi's *Don Carlos*. Encouraged the careers of such conductors as Charles Mackerras and Colin Davis.

Tucker, Richard (b New York, 28 Apr 1914; d Kalamazoo, MI, 8 Jan 1975), American tenor. Studied in NY with P Althouse, making his debut at the NY Met. in 1945, and remaining as its leading tenor; sang more than 600 performances in French and Italian repertory up to 1975 notably as Rodolfo, Gabriele Adorno, Riccardo, Alfredo, Don Carlos and Samson. European debut Verona, 1947, as Enzo; CG 1958 as Cavaradossi. He began his career in synagogues, and in 1973 sang Eléazar in *La Juive* (New Orleans).

Tucker, William (d London, 28 Feb 1679), English composer. Gentleman of the Chapel Royal in London, and minor canon and precentor of Westminster Abbey from 1660.

Works include services and anthems.

tucket a word found in stage directions of English plays of the Elizabethan period where the author asks for a fanfare to be played on or off the stage ('tucket within'). Another form is 'tuck'. A derivation from Italian *toccata* seems unlikely since tuck and its variants are found in old French and Middle English before the early 17th-c. Italian tradition of trumpet fanfares called toccatas.

For the next three days I produced a series of noises so dreadful and so sordid that a rumour went about in the neighbourhood that we were keeping a live elephant in the bath.

Gerard Hoffnung on playing the tuba, BBC Music Club, 1954

Tuckwell, Barry (Emmanuel) (b Melbourne, 5 Mar 1931), Australian-born British horn player and conductor. He played with the Sydney SO before leaving for Britain in 1950. Principal, LSO, 1955; left in 1968 to pursue career as soloist and chamber music player. He formed his own quintet and has performed with the London Sinfonietta; highly regarded in the standard repertory. Thea Musgrave, Iain Hamilton and Don Banks are among composers who have written works for him. Conducted the Tasmanian SO 1980–83.

Tuder, John (b (*fl* 1466–96)), English composer. Responsories, Lamentations and the hymn *Gloria, laus* are included in the Pepys MS of *c* 1465 (Magdalene College, Cambridge), and there is a carol by him in the Fayrfax Book of *c* 1500.

Tudor, David (b Philadelphia, 20 Jan 1926; d USA, 13 Aug 1996), American pianist and composer. Studied piano and composition with S Wolpe. Best known for his close association with John Cage, much of whose music he performs or helps to realize, played in the fps of

Music of Change, Piano concerto and *Atlas Eclipticalis*. Gave the first US performance of Boulez's second piano sonata (NY, 1950) and was heard in works by Kagel and Bussotti.

Works include for various electronics including *Fluorescent Sound* (1964), *Bandoneon! Reunion, Rainforest* I-V (1968–73) and *Fontana Mix* (in collaboration with Cage).

Tudway, Thomas (b ? Windsor, *c* 1650; d Cambridge, 23 Nov 1726), English composer and organist. Became chorister in the Chapel Royal in London soon after the Restoration (1660) and lay vicar at Windsor in 1664; appointed organist at King's College, Cambridge, 1670, and professor of music in the university there, 1705, in succession to Staggins. In 1714–20 he compiled a large collection of English cathedral music in six vols. He wrote an *Ode for Queen Anne* although he was suspended from his posts at Cambridge for lèse majesté.

Works include services, anthems.

Tůma, František Ignác Antonín (b Kostelec nad Orlicí, 2 Oct 1704; d Vienna, 30 Jan 1774), Bohemian viola da gamba player and composer. Arrived in Vienna by 1729, studied with Fux, was in the service of Count Kinsky 1731 (or earlier) to 1741, and *Kapellmeister* to the Dowager Empress Elisabeth Christina 1741–50. He retired to a monastery 1768.

Works include numerous Masses, motets and other church music; instrumental pieces.

Tumagian, Eduard (b Bucharest, 1944), Romanian baritone. Sang at the Bucharest Opera from 1968, as Alfonso, Mozart's Count and Wolfram. Strasbourg from 1974, as Scarpia, Escamillo and Belcore and Eugene Onegin. Has sung further with WNO and ENO and in the USA (debut 1986 at Pittsburgh as Don Carlo in *Forza*); Carnegie Hall as Nabucco and in *Béatrice et Bénédict*. Other roles include Simon Boccanegra, Verdi's Montfort (at La Scala) and Rigoletto.

Tumanyan, Barseg (b Erevan, 3 Aug 1958), Armenian bass. Studied at La Scala and the Moscow Conservatory. Sang with the Spendiaryan Opera (Armenia) from 1980 and has sung widely in the West from 1988: Basilio at Naples and US debut at Boston 1989, as Ramfis in *Aida*. CG, London, from 1990, as Colline, Attila and Basilio. Sang King Philip in *Don Carlos* at Los Angeles, 1990. Season 1993, as Méphistophélès (*Faust*) and Escamillo at the Opéra Bastille, Paris.

Tunder, Franz (b Bannesdorf near Burg, Fehmarn, 1614; d Lübeck, 5 Nov 1667), German composer and organist. In 1632 he was appointed court organist at Gottorf and in 1641 organist of St Mary's Church at Lübeck, where he preceded Buxtehude, who had to marry his daughter in order to secure the post. He greatly improved the church music and also instituted the *Abendmusiken/Evening Music*, which soon became famous beyond the town, and was further developed by Buxtehude.

Works include church cantatas, sacred arias with strings and organ; chorale variations for organ.

tune another word for melody, more colloquial and therefore often considered vulgar. 'In tune' denotes accurate intonation, 'out of tune' the opposite. 'To tune' is to adjust the intonation of an instrument.

tuning-fork a small and simple instrument in the form of a metal fork with two long prongs, invented by the trumpeter John Shore in 1711. It not only retains pitch accurately, but gives out a pure sound free from harmonic upper partials.

Tuotilo, or Tutilo (d St Gall, 27 Apr 915), ? Swiss monk and musician at the monastery of St Gall. He composed tropes, including (?) the Christmas trope *Hodie cantandus est nobis puer*.

Turandot incidental music for Schiller's Germany version of Gozzi's play by Weber, op. 37, composed 1809 and including the *Overtura cinese/Chinese Overture*), composed on a Chinese theme, 1805.

Opera by Busoni (German libretto by composer, based on Gozzi's play), produced Zurich, 11 May 1917, together with another short opera *Arlecchino*. The music of *Turandot* was elaborated from incidental music for M Reinhardt's production of K Vollmöller's version of Gozzi's play, produced Berlin, Deutsches Theater, 27 Oct 1911.

Opera by Puccini (Italian libretto by G Adami and R Simoni, based on Gozzi's play), left unfinished by Puccini and completed by Alfano; produced Milan, La Scala, 25 May 1926. Calaf saves his head by

THE OPERA

Turandot

A three-act opera by Giacomo Puccini, set in Peking in legendary times. It received its first performance in Milan in 1926.

I. The head is forfeit of any candidate who cannot answer the three riddles of the cruel Princess Turandot (soprano). A crowd gathers to witness the execution of the latest candidate, and the unknown Prince Calaf (tenor) recognizes his father Timur (bass), accompanied by a slave girl, Liù (soprano). When Turandot appears at the palace balcony, Calaf falls in love with her, and he will not be dissuaded by Timur, Liù, or the emperor's three ministers, Ping (baritone), Pang (baritone) and Pong (tenor). He strikes three blows on a gong to signal his intent.

II. The ministers reminisce about the executions they have seen. The Emperor Altoum (tenor) warns Calaf further and when Turandot appears she declares that no man will ever possess her. She is in despair when Calaf answers her three riddles correctly, but he offers her his head if she can discover his name by dawn.

III. No one is allowed to sleep as the people of Peking are impelled to find the stranger's secret. Liù is arrested, but her love for Calaf helps her resist her torturers; she stabs herself as she is led to execution. Left alone with Turandot, Calaf kisses her but she begs him to leave. He finally reveals his name and she is moved by his emotion. Before the emperor and the people Turandot announces that she knows the stranger's name: 'His name is love!'

THE OPERA

answering three riddles of cold-hearted Turandot, and eventually wins her love.

Turangalîla-symphonie work for orchestra in ten movements by Messiaen, with prominent parts for piano solo and the ondes Martenot. Commissioned by Koussevitzky and composed 1946–48; fp. Boston, 2 Dec 1949, conductor Bernstein. The middle of a triptych of works inspired by the Tristan legend; the others are *Harawi* for soprano and piano (1945) and *Cinq Rechants* for unaccompanied chorus. ('Turangalîla' is a compound Sanskrit word: *turanga* = 'time, rhythm', *lîla* = 'divine action'.)

turca Italian = 'Turkish'; the word is used in the combination *alla turca* (in the Turkish manner) by Mozart for the finale of the A major piano sonata, K331, and by Beethoven for the *Marcia alla turca* in *The Ruins of Athens*, which is the theme of the piano variations, op. 76.

Turco in Italia, Il, *The Turk in Italy*, opera by Rossini (libretto by F Romani), produced Milan, La Scala, 14 Aug 1814. Turkish Prince Selim arrives in Naples and after much confusion is reconciled with his former love, Zaida.

Tureck, Rosalyn (b Chicago, 14 Dec 1914), American pianist and conductor. Made her debut aged 11 with the Chicago SO and then studied with O Samaroff at Juilliard, graduating in 1936. From 1943 she taught at the school, also becoming well known for her playing of Bach. Professor at Juilliard from 1972. Founded the Tureck Bach Players, New York, 1981.

Turges, Edmund (b *c* 1450), English composer. In 1469 he was admitted to a guild of parish clerks in London.

Works include a Magnificat (in the Eton Choirbook), *Gaude flore virginali* (two settings); carols.

Turina, Joaquín (b Seville, 9 Dec 1882; d Madrid, 14 Jan 1949), Spanish composer. Studied at Seville and Madrid, later with d'Indy at the Schola Cantorum in Paris. He devoted much time to teaching as well as composition and wrote a small treatise, *Enciclopedia abreviada de música*. His most successful works are those which employ local Spanish colours; *La procesion del Rocio*, *Danzas fantásticas*. However, he adopted conventional European forms more consistently than his contemporaries Albéniz, Granados and Falla.

Works include operas *Margot* (1914) and *Jardin de oriente* (1923) (libretti by G Martínez Sierra); incidental music for Moreto's *La adúltera penitente* (1917), Martínez Sierra's *Navidad* (1916) and other plays; *La procesión del Rocio* (1913), *Danzas fantásticas*, *Sinfonía sevillana* (1920), *Ritmos* and other works for orchestra; string quartet (1911), piano quintet (1907), *Escena andaluza* for viola, piano and string quartet; *Poema de una Sanluquena* for violin and piano; suites *Rincones sevillanos* and *Sevilla* and other works for piano; songs.

I've never had a gramophone; I never had a picture of myself in my life.
Maggie Teyte, BBC broadcast, 1959

Turini, Francesco (b Prague, *c* 1589; d Brescia, 1656), Italian composer. His father Gregorio Turini was cornett player and composer to the Emperor Rudolph II in Prague, but died early, whereupon the emperor sent Turini to Venice and Rome to study music and later made him his chamber organist. He left Prague in 1624 to become cathedral organist at Brescia.

Works include Masses and motets; madrigals, canons.

Türk, Daniel Gottlob (b Claussnitz near Chemnitz, 10 Aug 1750; d Halle, 26 Aug 1813), German theorist and composer. Studied under his father and under Homilius at Dresden. Later he went to Leipzig University, where he became a pupil and friend of J A Hiller, who procured him appointments as violinist at the Opera and the orchestral concerts. In 1776 he became organist at St Ulrich's Church at Halle, in 1779 music director of the university and in 1787 organist at the church of Our Lady. He wrote treatises on organ, and clavier playing, thorough-bass and temperament.

Works include opera *Pyramus und Thisbe* (1784); cantata *Die Hirten bei der Krippe zu Bethlehem* (1782); piano sonatas and pieces.

turn an ornament indicated by the sign ∾. Composers have more

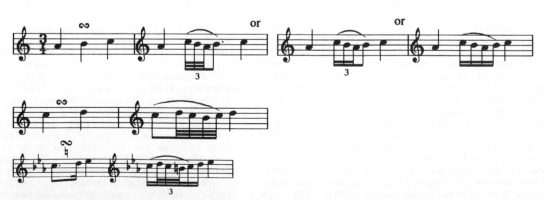

Various turns and their possible executions.

Mark-Anthony Turnage – composer

1 Louis Andriessen: *De Staat* (Schoenberg Ens./Reinhart de Leeuw)
A very significant late-20th-century work, influencing nearly everyone.

2 Britten: Serenade for Tenor, Horn and Strings (Pears/Tuckwell/English Chamber Orch.)
One of my favourite pieces – almost perfect and always deeply moving.

3 Debussy: *Pelléas and Mélisande* (Vienna PO/Abbado)
Couldn't see the point at first but once it clicked for me I was obsessed. One of the most beautiful endings in music.

4 Hans Werner Henze: *Requiem* (Ens. Modern/Metzmacher)
A great achievement. Great playing from the Ensemble Modern.

5 Oliver Knussen: Symphony no. 3 (Philharmonia/Tilson Thomas)
A brilliant orchestral tapestry from my former teacher.

6 Puccini: *La Bohème* (Freni/Pavarotti/Berlin PO/Karajan)
Not a duff tune in the whole work. Pavarotti's final anguished cry is heartbreaking.

7 Sibelius: Symphony no. 4 (CBSO/Rattle)
Dark and sombre. Rattle and the CBSO are superb Sibelius interpreters.

8 Shostakovich: Symphony no. 13 (*Babi Yar*) (Royal Concergebouw Orch./Haitink)
Exhilarating music.

9 Stravinsky: Violin Concerto in D (Perlman/Boston SO/Ozawa)
Ranging from icily precise in the outer movements to a searing lament at its centre. My favourite composer.

10 Tippett: Symphony no. 2 (LSO/Davis)
Keeps you riveted right from those opening pounding Cs.

---

recently applied the turn to denote an ornament which starts on the principal note.

Turnage, Mark Anthony (b Grays, Essex, 10 Jun 1960), English composer. Studied at the RCM with Oliver Knussen (1974–78) and with Henze and Schuller at Tanglewood. Composer-in-association with the CBSO, 1989–93; featured composer at the 1986 Bath Festival and 1987 Glasgow Musica Viva. His music admits a wide range of influences, including popular elements. His major success has been with *Greek*, performed at Munich and Edinburgh, 1988.

Works include *Night Dances* (1982) and *Kind of Blue* (1982) for orchestra; *Let us Sleep Now* for chamber orchestra (1979–82); *After Dark* for wind quintet and string quintet (1983); *Lament for a Hanging Man* for soprano and ensemble (1983); *Ekaya* for orchestra (1984); *On all Fours* for ensemble (1985); *One Hand in Brooklyn Heights*, for 16 mixed voices, *Release* for eight players (1987); *Greek*, opera (1988); *Three Screaming Popes* for orchestra (1989); *Kai* for cello and ensemble (1990); *Momentum* for orchestra (1991); *Are you sure?* for string quartet (1991); *Leaving* for soloists, chorus and ensemble (1991); *Set To* for brass ensemble (1992); *Drowned Out* for orchestra (1993); *Your Rockaby* saxophone concerto (1993); *Blood on the Floor* for ensemble (1994).

Turner, Eva (b Oldham, 10 Mar 1892; d London, 16 June 1990), English soprano, Studied at the RAM and joined the Carl Rosa Opera (1916–24) singing Aida, Tosca and Butterfly. She then sang at La Scala, Milan, with Toscanini; roles included Freia and the *Trovatore* Leonora. She was well known as a dramatic singer in Verdi and Wagner; London, CG, 1920–48 as Sieglinde, Brünnhilde, Isolde and Amelia. One of her most famous roles was that of Puccini's Turandot. DBE 1962.

Turner, W(alter) J(ames) (Redfern) (b Shanghai, 13 Oct 1889; d London, 18 Nov 1946), English poet, novelist and music critic. Studied music with his father, became organist at Melbourne and later studied at Dresden, Munich and Vienna. He pub. books of misc. musical essays, works on Mozart, Beethoven, Berlioz and Wagner, *English Music* for the *Britain in Pictures* series, edited by him.

Turner, William (b Oxford, 1651; d London, 13 Jan 1740), English tenor and composer. Chorister at Christ Church, Oxford, and later in the Chapel Royal in London, where he joined Blow and Humfrey in composing the so-called 'club anthem'. Later became singer successively at Lincoln Cathedral, St Paul's Cathedral and Westminster Abbey. Mus.D., Cambridge, 1696. The singer Ann Turner (d 1741), wife of John Robinson, was his youngest daughter.

Works include services, anthems (one for Queen Anne's coron-

ation); masque *Presumptuous Love*; songs for Durfey's *A Fond Husband* (1677) and *Madam Fickle* (1676), Shadwell's *The Libertine* (1675), Settle's *Pastor fido* (1676) and other plays; catches, songs.

Turnhout, Gérard de (b Turnhout, *c* 1520; d Madrid, 15 Sept 1580), Flemish singer and composer. He became a church singer at Antwerp in 1545 and *maître de chapelle* of the cathedral in 1562. In 1571 he was called into the service of Philip II at Madrid.

Works include Masses and motets; *chansons*.

Turnhout, Jan-Jacob van (or Jean-Jacques de) (b ? Brussels, *c* 1545; d ? Brussels, after 1618), Flemish composer, brother or nephew of Gérard de ◊Turnhout. He became *maître de chant* at St Rombaut, Malines, in 1577, and later at the viceregal court at Brussels. He pub. madrigals and sacred Latin works.

Turn of the Screw, The opera in a prologue and two acts by Britten (libretto by M Piper, after Henry James), produced Venice, 14 Sept 1954, and in London, 6 Oct 1954. The Governess arrives at her new post to find children Flora and Miles in the power of two malevolent ghosts Quint and Jessil. Eventually the evil spirits are banished but Miles dies in the process.

The grand tune is the only thing in music that the great public really understands.

Thomas Beecham, quoted in Atkins and Newman, *Beecham Stories*, 1978

Turnovsky, Martin (b Prague, 29 Sept 1928), Czech conductor. Studied with Zncerl and Szell, before 1952 debut, with the Prague SO. Conducted the Czech Army SO 1955–60, Brno State PO 1960–63, Dresden Staatsoper 1967–68. Music director of Norwegian Opera 1975–80, Bonn Opera 1979–83. Led the Cleveland Orchestra 1968 and has guested elsewhere with the Bournemouth SO, New York PO, Detroit SO and the Stockholm PO. Conducted *Eugene Onegin* with WNO 1988, *Otello* and *Ballo in Maschera* with the Prague State Opera, 1993; music director of the Prague SO, 1992.

Tusch German = 'fanfare'; the word is probably derived from French *touche* and is thus related to the English tucket or tuck.

tut a device in lute-playing: the damping of a note by a finger not used for stopping.

tutti Italian = 'all'; a term used, in the first place, to designate the singing and playing together of all the forces engaged in a musical performance; but it is also used for the purely orchestral passages in a concerto, where the solo instrument is silent, whether the whole orchestra happens to be playing or only part of it. Used as a noun, the word means any passage in an orchestral work in which the whole force is employed, especially when playing at full strength.

Tveitt (or *Tveit*), (Nils) Geirr (b Hardanger, 19 Oct 1908; d Oslo, 1 Feb 1981), Norwegian composer and pianist. After study in Vienna and Paris toured Europe as pianist. In his compositions he made effective use of Norwegian folk melodies.

Works include operas *Dragaredokko*, *Roald Amundsen* and *Jeppe* (1964); three ballets; six piano concertos (1930–60), concerto for string quartet and orchestra (1933), violin concerto (1939), two harp concertos, two concertos for ◊hardanger fiddle four symphonies; two string quartets; 29 piano sonatas.

twelve-note music the system of composition on which the later works of Schoenberg and the music of some of his disciples (e.g. Berg, Křenek, Pisk, Webern) are based, as well as that of many composers in various countries. It abolishes keys and with them the predominance of certain notes in a scale (tonic, dominant, subdominant and mediant), using instead the 12 notes of the chromatic scale, each of which has exactly the same importance as any other. This rules out, in principle, any feeling of tonality, though especially in more recent twelve-note music tonal implications are often created intentionally through the choice of the series (see below) and its application. Although traditional modulation is excluded from 12-note composition, an analogous process may be achieved through manipulation of the row by means of various methods.

his pupils has proved one of the great liberating forces in the history of music.

Among the composers who have made use of the '12-note system' are Berio, Blacher, Boulez, Cage, Castiglioni, Dallapiccola, P M Davies, Fortner, A Goehr, Hartmann, Haubenstock-Ramati, Henze, Kagel, Leibowitz, Ligeti, Lutosławski, Lutyens, Maderna, Martin, Messiaen, Nigg, Nono, Pousseur, Searle, Seiber, Stockhausen, Stravinsky, Xenakis.

Twilight of the Gods, The (Wagner.) ◊Ring des Nibelungen.

Two Widows, *Dvě Vdovy*, opera by Smetana (libretto by E Züngel, based on a French comedy by P J F Mallefille), produced Prague, Czech Theatre, 27 Mar 1874. Anežka falls for landowner Ladislav, but as a widow feels she must instead mourn her dead husband. Widow Karolina feigns a seduction of Ladislav and Anežka finally admits her love.

Tye, Christopher (b *c* 1505; d ? 1572), English composer and poet. He became a lay-clerk at King's College, Cambridge, in 1537. In 1543 he was appointed choir-master at Ely Cathedral and in 1545 he took the Mus.D. at Cambridge. He may have been music master to Edward VI 1544–50, and he was made a Gentleman of the Chapel Royal. In 1561 he resigned his post at Ely and was succeeded by R White. Having been ordained, he accepted the living at Doddington-cum-Marche in the Isle of Ely, and for some time later held two other livings in the neighbourhood; but he had to resign them, on account of carelessness in the matter of payments due. He wrote a good deal of verse in his

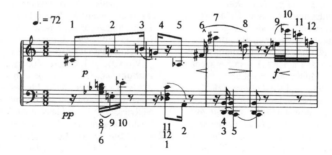

A passage from Schoenberg's 'Waltz' (5 Piano Pieces op. 23*); the numbers represent the particular sequence of notes in the note-row.*

In order to make sure that no note assumes an even temporary predominance, the rule has been established that a 'series' must consist of all the 12 notes of the chromatic scale, and that each note must appear only once in its course (transposition into any octave being allowed); but this does not mean that all melodic patterns of twelve-note music are necessarily of the same length, for they may be given any rhythmic shape the composer desires, and these shapes may be varied throughout a work, though the order of the notes, once determined at his desire, may not. Notes may, however, appear simultaneously as well as successively. Moreover, three ways of achieving melodic and by implication harmonic variety are open to the composer: he may restate his theme (1) inverted (i.e. turned upside down), (2) in reverse (retrograde) or *cancrizans* (i.e. turned backwards) or (3) inverted and reversed at the same time.

In the years since 1945 the '12-note system' has found wide acceptance among composers of the younger generation, and among already established figures Stravinsky was an outstanding convert, his later music being indebted to his study of Webern. Although the techniques of Schoenberg and Webern have to a greater or lesser extent been superseded, their basic concepts are still recognized as one of the most practical and satisfying ways of organizing totally chromatic music. In addition, the sound world introduced by the Viennese composers, free from tonal ties, has resulted in a completely new attitude toward aural experience. The work of Schoenberg and

later years. His music shows some acquaintance with contemporary continental composers.

Works include Masses (e.g. *Euge bone* and *Western Wind*), motets, services, anthems, *The Actes of the Apostles* in English metrical versions set for four voices (1533, dedicated to Edward VI); In Nomines for instruments.

tyrolienne French = 'Tyrolese' a country dance similar to the *Ländler* or slow waltz, supposed to be native of the mountain regions of the Tyrol, but really an artificial growth introduced into ballets and operas and loosely based on melodic figurations imitating various forms of yodel. Tyroliennes also became fashionable in the form of piano pieces and songs, etc.

Tyrrell, John (b Salisbury, Rhodesia, 17 Aug 1942), English musicologist. Studied at Cape Town and Oxford Universities. Lecturer at Nottingham University 1976, reader in opera studies 1989. Editorial staff of *New Grove* (1980) and *Opera Grove* (1992) Dictionaries, with articles on Janáček and his operas. Has published elsewhere *Káta Kabanová* (1982), *Czech Opera* (1988), *Janáček's Operas: A Documentary Account* (1992) and *Intimate Letters: Janáček's Correspondence with Kamila Stösslova* (1994).

Tyrwhitt, Gerald, Lord ◊Berners.

tzigane or *tsigane* , French, a gypsy or musician of the bohemian world of Paris. The title of a rhapsody for violin and piano by Ravel composed 1924; fp London, 26 Apr 1924, with Jelly d'◊Aranyi.

U

Überbrettl, Das E ◊Wolzogen.

Uberti, Antonio (b Verona, 1697; d Berlin, 20 Jan 1783), Italian castrato of German origin. Pupil of Porpora and known as Porporino. He sang Italian opera in Germany and became chamber singer to Frederick II of Prussia. Among his pupils was Mara.

UC an abbr. used for *una corda* (one string), indicating the use of the damping pedal in piano music.

Uccellini, Marco (b *c* 1603; d Forlimpopoli, 10 Sept 1680), Italian composer and violinist. Master of instrumental music at the ducal court of Modena 1641–62 and *maestro di cappella* at Modena Cathedral 1647–65, after which he held that post at the Farnese Court at Parma.

Works include opera *Gli eventi di Filandro ed Edessa* (1675); ballets *La nave d'Enea* (1673) and *Giove di Elide fulminato* (1677); psalms and litanies for voices and instruments; *Composizioni armoniche* and *Sinfonici concerti* for violin and other instruments, *Sinfonie boscareocie* and sonatas for violin and bass.

Uchida, Mitsuko (b Tokyo, 20 Dec 1948), Japanese pianist. She studied in Tokyo and in Vienna, where she won the Beethoven Competition in 1968. Prize-winner in Chopin International, Warsaw, 1969. In 1982 she gave a cycle of the complete Mozart sonatas in London and Tokyo; much success 1985–86 with the English Chamber Orchestra in London as director-soloist in the complete Mozart concertos. Has appeared with the Berlin PO, Boston SO and Chicago SO. Esteemed in Bartók.

Ugarte, Floro M(anuel) (b Buenos Aires, 15 Sept 1884; d Buenos Aires, 11 Jun 1975), Argentine composer. Studied with Fourdrain in Paris and became a private music teacher on his return in 1913 and professor at the National Conservatory at Buenos Aires, 1924. He also became music director of the Teatro Colón, resigning in 1943.

Works include opera *Saika* (1918) and others; symphonic poems and suites for orchestra; instrumental pieces.

Ugolini, Vincenzo (b Perugia, *c* 1580; d Rome, 6 May 1638), Italian composer. Pupil of Bernardino Nassini. *Maestro di cappella* at the church of Santa Maria Maggiore in Rome, 1603–09. He then retired after a severe illness, but in 1610 became *maestro di cappella* at Benevento Cathedral and returned in 1616 to Rome, where after some other appointments he became Soriano's successor in the Julian Chapel in 1620 and *maestro di cappella* of San Luigi dei Francesi in 1631, a post he had held 1616–20.

Works include Masses, motets, psalms and other church music, madrigals.

Ugolino of Orvieto (b ? Orvieto, *c* 1380; d Ferrara, 1457), Italian composer and theorist. His *Declaratio musicae discipline* (1435) is mainly a practical handbook for the performing musician of his day.

Uhde, Hermann (b Bremen, 20 Jul 1914; d Copenhagen, 10 Oct 1965), German bass-baritone. He sang in Bremen and Freiburg before the war and in The Hague and Munich 1940–44. Prisoner-of-war 1944–47, after which he sang in Hamburg, Vienna and again Munich (1951–60). Bayreuth 1951–57 as Gunther, Klingsor, the Dutchman and Wotan. London, CG, 1953, as Mandryka, and 1954–60 in operas by Wagner and Offenbach. NY Met. 1955–64 (debut as Telramund). He collapsed and died during a performance of Niels Bentzon's *Faust III*. Other roles included Wozzeck and Creon in *Antigonae* (fp Salzburg, 1949).

Uhl, Fritz (b Vienna-Matzleinsdorf, 2 Apr 1928), Austrian tenor. He sang first in operetta; opera debut Graz, 1950. Sang widely on the Continent and was a member of the Munich opera from 1957. Bayreuth 1957–64 as Siegmund, Erik and Loge. He sang the title role in Solti's recording of *Tristan* (1960) and Walther at CG in 1962. Professor at the Vienna Conservatory from 1981.

Uhland, Johann Ludwig (1787–1862), German poet. ◊*Black Knight* (Elgar); ◊Humperdinck (*Glück von Edenhall*); ◊Schoeck (songs); ◊Schumann (*Glück von Edenhall*); R ◊Strauss (*Schloss am Meer*).

Uhlig, Theodor (b Wurzen, near Leipzig, 15 Feb 1822; d Dresden, 3 Jan 1853), German violinist, author and composer of theoretical works. Pupil of Schneider at Dessau. He entered the royal orchestra at Dresden in 1841 and became an intimate friend of Wagner there; published articles in Wagner's praise and had an extensive correspondence with him.

Uchida *The pianist Mitsuko Uchida. A Mozart specialist, she played and directed the complete set of Mozart concertos with the English Chamber Orchestra 1985–86; she has also recorded his piano sonatas.*

ukelele, lit. 'jumping flea', a small Hawaian guitar, introduced to the Sandwich Islands by the Portuguese in 1877 and more recently into Europe as a popular instrument. It has four gut strings and can be played from a notation resembling lute tablature.

Ulfung, Ragnar (Sigurd) (b Oslo, 28 Feb 1927), Norwegian tenor. Stage debut Oslo, 1951, in Menotti's *The Consul*. Royal Opera, Stockholm, from 1958; sang in the fp of Blomdahl's *Aniara* and visited CG with the co. in 1960. He created the title role in Maxwell Davies' *Taverner* (1972) and returned to CG as Mime in Friedrich's production of the *Ring*. US debut San Francisco, 1967; NY Met. 1972, as Mime. Other roles included Tom Rakewell, Don Carlos, Alfredo and Cavaradossi. Sang Strauss's Valzacchi at Santa Fe, 1992. Also active in concert and oratorio.

Ulibïshev, Alexander Dimitrievich (b Dresden, 13 Jan 1794; d Lukino near Nizhny-Novgorod, 8 Feb 1858), Russian writer on music and amateur musician. As the son of a nobleman he served in the army and then lived in retirement on his estate. He was a good violinist and quartet player. He made a special study of Mozart and pub. a work in three vols. on him (Moscow, 1843), but disliked the late works of Beethoven and attacked Lenz's book on that composer.

Ulisse opera by Dallapiccola (libretto by composer, after Homer); composed 1959–68, produced Berlin, Deutsche Oper, 29 Sept 1968, conductor Maazel. BBC studio performance, 20 Sept 1969. Ulysses meets Princess Nausicaa and recounts his story. He then spends a year with the enchantress Circe before visiting the Sirens and Hades on the way home to his wife Penelope.

There is delight in singing, tho' none hear beside the singer.

Walter Savage Landor (1775–1864) *To Browning*

Ullmann, Viktor (b Prague, 1 Jan 1898; d Auschwitz, 1944), Sudeten-German composer. Pupil of Schoenberg in Vienna, later theatre conductor at Aussig and music teacher in Prague. In Theresienstadt concentration camp he wrote a one-act opera, *Der Kaiser von Atlantis*, about a tyrannical monarch who outlaws death (fp Amsterdam, 16 Dec 1975). He was transferred to Auschwitz on 16 Oct 1944.

Works include operas *Peer Gynt* (after Ibsen), *Der Sturz des Antichrist* and *Der Kaiser von Atlantis* (1943); variations and double fugue on a theme by Schoenberg for orchestra; octet, two string quartets.

Ultimo giorno di Pompei, L', *The Last Day of Pompeii*, opera by Pacini (libretto by Tottola, not founded on Bulwer- Lytton's novel, which was not then pub.), produced Naples, Teatro San Carlo, 19 Nov 1825. Rejected by Ottavia, wife of Sallustio, Diomede attempts to revenge himself on her, but all are engulfed by Vesuvius.

Ultimos Ritos, *Last Rites*, oratorio by Tavener for soloists, five speakers, chorus and orchestra; composed 1972, fp Haarlem, 22 Jun 1974.

Ulysses ♭Circe and ♭Penelope), opera by Keiser (libretto by F M Lersner), produced (in German) Copenhagen, at court, Nov 1722.

Cantata by Seiber for tenor, chorus and orchestra (text by composer, after Joyce); 1946–47, fp London, 27 May 1949.

Umbreit, Karl Gottlieb (b Rehstadt, near Gotha, 9 Jan 1763; d Rehstadt, 28 Apr 1829), German organist and composer. Pupil of Kittel. He was appointed organist at Sonneborn, Coburg, and became a famous organ teacher.

Works include chorales, chorale preludes, preludes and fugues, etc. for organ.

Umlauf(f), Ignaz (b Vienna, 1746; d Vienna, 8 Jun 1796), Austrian composer. He became a viola player in the orchestra of the court opera in 1772, and on the foundation of the national *Singspiel* theatre by Joseph II in 1778 became its director, the inaugural work being his *Die Bergknappen*. From 1789 he was Salieri's deputy as *Kapellmeister* of the court chapel. He also took part with Mozart in the performance of Handel's oratorios organized by Gottfried van Swieten.

Works include *Singspiele Die Insel der Liebe* (1722), *Die Bergknappen* (1778), *Die Apotheke, Die schöne Schusterin oder die pucegefarbenen Schuhe* (1779), *Das Irrlicht* (1782), *Welches ist die beste Nation?*, *Die glücklichen Jäger* (1786), *Die Ringe der Liebe* (sequel to Grétry's *Zémire et Azor*); incidental music for *Der Oberamtmann und die Soldaten* (after Calderón); church music.

Umlauf(f), Michael (b Vienna, 9 Aug 1781; d Baden near Vienna, 20 Jun 1842), Austrian composer and conductor, son of Ignaz ◊Umlauf. Pupil of his father, became a violinist at the Opera and was conductor of the two court theatres 1810–25 and again from 1840. On and after the revival of *Fidelio* in 1814 he assisted Beethoven, who was then too deaf to hear the orchestra, to conduct some of his major works.

Works include opera *Das Wirtshaus in Granada* (1812), play with music *Der Grenadier* (1812); 12 ballets; church music; piano sonatas.

una corda Italian = 'one string'; a direction used by Beethoven and others in piano music to indicate the use of the damping pedal, which so shifts the hammers that they touch only one or two strings for each note, instead of two or three.

Una cosa rara, o sia Bellezza ed onestà, *A Rare Thing, or Beauty and Honesty*, opera by Martin y Soler (libretto by L da Ponte, based on a story by L V de Guevara), produced Vienna, Burgtheater, 17 Nov 1786. Mozart quotes an air from it in the finale of the second act of *Don Giovanni*. Lilla remains faithful to Lubino in spite of attentions from Don Lisergo, Prince Giovanni and Corrado.

Unanswered Question the first of Two Contemplations for orchestra by Charles Ives (no. 2 *Central Park in the Dark*). Fp New York 11 May 1946 (composed 1906).

Undine opera by E T A Hoffmann (libretto by the composer), produced Berlin, Schauspielhaus, 3 Aug 1816. Water nymph Undine can gain a soul by marrying a mortal. She meets and falls in love with the knight Huldbrand, but when he changes allegiance to Berthalda, Undine kisses him, drowning him.

Opera by Lortzing (libretto by composer, based on Fouqué), produced Magdeburg, 21 Apr 1845. Similar to Hoffmann's version, but Huldebrand is called Hugo von Ringstetten.

Ballet by Henze (choreographed by Ashton); composed 1956–57, produced London, CG, 27 Oct 1958, conductor Henze, with Fonteyn. *Wedding Music* from the ballet arranged for wind orchestra 1957; two orchestral suites 1958; *Undine, Trois pas des Tritons* for orchestra, performed Rome, 10 Jan 1959, conductor Celibidache.

unequal temperament a system of tuning, especially on old keyboard instruments, in which some of the accidentals were treated as sharps according to just intonation and some as flats (e.g. F♯, not G♭; B♭, not A♯). An attempt was thus made to make some of the more frequently used keys come nearer to just intonation than is possible in the tempered scale of the modern piano, but the result was also that the more extreme sharp and flat keys were out of tune. This is one of the chief reasons why these keys were rarely used by early composers.

unequal voices a composition for several voices which do not lie within the same compass is said to be for unequal voices.

Unfinished Symphony Schubert's 'Unfinished' Symphony, in B minor, written Oct/Nov 1822, was planned as a four-movement work, though only the first two movements, and a sketch of the scherzo, survive. Some authorities, however, believe that the finale was used a year later as the basis of the B minor Entr'acte in *Rosamunde*. After the Styrian Music Society, through Josef and Anselm Hüttenbrenner, had awarded Schubert their Diploma of Honour in 1823, he promised to send in return 'one of my symphonies at the earliest opportunity'. Later he handed to Josef the score of the two completed movements. Anselm Hüttenbrenner made an arrangement of the work for piano duet in 1853, but made no attempt to get it performed. Johann Herbeck, who gave the fp in Vienna in Dec 1865, coaxed the score out of Anselm with a promise to perform one of the latter's own works. Schubert was the first composer to associate a tragic tone and intense personal feeling with B minor in a substantial symphonic work; in this the 'Unfinished' looks forward to late Romantic works such as Tchaikovsky's 'Pathetique' Symphony and Dvořák's Cello Concerto. In the original *Gesamtausgabe* it is called no. 8, but is more often referred to simply as the 'Unfinished'.

Unger, Caroline (b Székesfehérvár, Hungary, 28 Oct 1803; d near

Florence, 23 Mar 1877), Austrian contralto. Pupil of Aloysia Lange, Mozart's sister-in-law, and Vogl in Vienna, where she made her debut in 1824. She sang the contralto part, with Sontag as soprano, in the fp of Beethoven's *Choral* symphony (1824); at the end of the performance she turned the composer towards the audience to see the applause he could not hear. Later she sang in Italy and Paris; Donizetti wrote *Parisina* and *Maria di Rudenz* for her. She created the title role in Bellini's *La Straniera* (1829). In 1840 she married François Sabatier. She retired in 1843.

Unger, Georg (b Leipzig, 6 Mar 1837; d Leipzig, 2 Feb 1887), German tenor. Studied theology at first, but took to singing and made his first stage appearance at Leipzig in 1867. He was Wagner's first Siegfried in the production of *The Ring* at Bayreuth in 1876.

Unger, Gerhard (b Bad Salzungen, Thuringia, 26 Nov 1916), German tenor. From 1947 he sang in Weimar and Dresden as Tamino, Alfredo and Pinkerton. Appeared at the Berlin Deutsche Oper from 1952, moved to Stuttgart in 1961; Hamburg 1962–73. He was best known as Pedrillo (recorded under Beecham) and David, which he sang in Kempe's recording of *Meistersinger*. Well known at Bayreuth, Salzburg, Vienna and in North America; much admired as Mime, and at the end of his career in operas by Berg, Britten and Janáček.

Unger, (Gustav) Hermann (b Kamenz, Saxony, 26 Oct 1886; d Cologne, 31 Dec 1958), German composer. Studied in Munich and later with Reger at Meiningen. Taught for more than 30 years in Cologne. He wrote books on Reger and Bruckner and a treatise on harmony (1946).

Works include opera *Richmondis* (1928) and *Der Zauberhandschuh*; incidental music for Shakespeare's *Tempest*, Kleist's *Penthesilea*, Hofmannsthal's *Der Tor und der Tod*, Hauptmann's *Hannele*, Unruh's *Heinrich aus Andernach* and many other plays; *Der Gott und die Bajadere* (Goethe) and *Old German Songs* for chorus and orchestra; two symphonies; chamber music; songs.

Universal Edition Publishing house founded in Vienna, 1901. ◊Hertzka and ◊Kalmus.

un poco Italian = 'a little'; a qualifying direction used where any indication of tempo or expression is to be applied in moderation. Often used in the abbr. form *poco*.

Unterbrochene Opferfest, Das, *The Interrupted Sacrificial Feast*, opera by Winter (libretto by F X Huber), produced Vienna, Kärntnertortheater, 14 Jun 1796. During Inca sacrifice Elvira and Villacumar unsuccessfully attempt to make Murneg, lover of Myrha, the victim.

upbeat an unstressed note or group of notes beginning a composition, or phrase, and standing before the first bar-line, which indicates the first main accent. The word derives from the act of beating time in conducting, where opening notes before the bar-line are indicated by an upward motion.

up bow the motion of the bow in the playing of string instruments in the direction from the point to the heel.

Uppman, Theodore (b Palo Alto, CA, 12 Jan 1920), American baritone. Studied at Curtis Institute and sang Papageno at Stanford University 1946. He created Billy Budd (CG 1951) and sang Pelléas at the NY Met. in 1953 and appeared there until 1977, as Papageno, Masetto and Guglielmo. Also sang in fps of operas by Floyd, Villa-Lobos and Pasatieri; Bernstein's *A Quiet Place* at Houston, 1983, La Scala, 1984 and Vienna, 1986.

Upshaw, Dawn (b Nashville, 17 Jul 1960), American soprano. Sang in the 1983 US fp of Hindemith's *Sancta Susanna*, while at the Manhattan School of Music. New York Met. from 1985, as Echo (*Ariadne*), Despina, Sophie (*Werther*), and Susanna. Salzburg 1987, as Barbarina, returning 1992 as the Angel in *St François d'Assise*. Other roles include Pamina (1990 Proms, London) and Anne Trulove (Aix 1992). Widely known through her recording of Gorecki's 3rd Symphony and also features in Schoenberg's 2nd quartet, with the Arditti (1994).

Urbani, Peter (b Milan, 1749; d Dublin, Dec 1816), Italian singer, publisher and composer. After a period in London he went to Glasgow in 1780 and to Edinburgh in 1784, singing Scottish songs and later pub. them with his own accompaniments, with words by Burns, with

whom he made friends, and others. Towards the end of the c. he became a music-seller and pub., but *c* 1810 he failed and went to Dublin, where he died in poverty.

Works include operas *Il Farnace* (1784), *Il trionfo di Clelia* (1785) and others; Scottish songs with accompaniments.

Urbani, Valentino, ◊Valentini.

Urhan, Chrétien (b Montjoie, near Aix-la-Chapelle, 16 Feb 1790; d Belleville, near Paris, 2 Nov 1845), Belgian violinist, violinist and composer. Learnt the violin from his father, was heard by the Empress Joséphine and sent by her to Paris with a recommendation to Lesueur. He joined the Opéra orchestra in 1814, becoming leader in 1823 and solo violin in 1836. He played much in public, including the viola and viola d'amore, also in chamber music. He gave early French performances of Bach, Schubert and Beethoven.

Works include two string quintets, two quintets for three violas, cello and double bass (with drums *ad lib.*) and other chamber music; violin and piano pieces; piano works, including duets; songs and duets.

Uribe Holguín, Guillermo (b Bogotá, 17 Mar 1880; d Bogotá, 26 Jun 1971), Colombian composer. Studied at home and with d'Indy at the Schola Cantorum in Paris. In 1910 he became director of the National Conservatory at Bogotá, where he founded and conducted symphonic concerts.

Works include Requiem; 11 symphonies (1916–59), *3 Danzas*, *Carnavelesca*, *Marche funèbre*, *Marche de fête*, *Suite tipica*, all for orchestra; concert and *Villanesca* for piano and orchestra, two violin concertos; ten string quartets, piano quartet, two piano quintets; five violin and piano sonatas, two cello and piano sonatas; piano pieces, including 300 folk dances; songs.

Urio, Francesco Antonio (b Milan, *c* 1632; d Milan, 1719 or later), Italian priest and composer. A Franciscan monk, he was *maestro di cappella* at Saints Apostoli in Rome in 1690, seven years later at the Frari church in Venice, and finally from 1715 at S Francesco in Milan.

Works include Te Deum (once attributed to Handel, who borrowed from it for his *Dettingen Te Deum*, *Saul*, *Israel in Egypt* and *L'Allegro*); oratorios; motets and psalms for voices and instruments.

Urlus, Jacques (b Hergenrath, 9 Jan 1867; d Noordwijk-aan-Zee, 6 Jun 1935), Dutch tenor. Studied at the Amsterdam Conservatory and made his debut at Utrecht in 1887. He then studied opera and made his stage debut there in 1894. Becoming a Wagnerian singer, he was soon invited to Bayreuth (1911–12, Siegmund). In 1910 he first visited London (Tristan, under Beecham). Well known as a concert singer, especially in Mahler. He pub. his autobiography in 1930.

Ursuleac, Viorica (b Czernowitz, 26 Mar 1894; d Ehrwald, Tyrol, 22 Oct 1985), Romanian soprano. She studied in Berlin with Lilli Lehmann; debut Zagreb, 1922, as Charlotte. She sang in Frankfurt 1926–30, under her husband, Clemens Krauss. In 1928 she took part in the Wiesbaden fp of Krenek's opera *Der Diktator*. Best known in Strauss, she created Arabella (Dresden, 1933), Maria in *Friedenstag* (Munich, 1938) and the Countess in *Capriccio* (Munich, 1942). In the 1930s she sang at the State Opera houses of Vienna and Berlin; Munich during World War II. London, CG, 1934 as Desdemona. Other roles included Ariadne, the Empress, Sieglinde and Tosca.

Usiglio, Emilio (b Parma, 8 Jan 1841; d Milan, 7 or 8 Jul 1910), Italian composer and conductor. He conducted operas by Boito, Thomas and Bizet, but in 1874 had to abandon a performance of *Aida* when he became too drunk to continue.

Works include operas *Le educande di Sorrento* (1868), *Le donne curiose* (after Goldoni, 1879) and six others; many ballets; chamber music.

Usper, Francesco (real name Spongia, Sponga or Sponza) (b Parenzo, before 1570; d Venice, 1641), Italian priest, organist and composer. In 1614 he became organist at the church of San Salvatore at Venice, in 1621 he deputized for Grillo as organist at St Mark's and in 1627 he became principal of the school of St John the Evangelist.

Works include Masses, motets, psalms, for voices with instruments, vesper psalms for four–eight voices and bass, some for double choir; *La battaglia* for voices and instruments, madrigals; *ricercari* and *arie francesi* in four parts.

Ussachevsky, Vladimir (Alexis) (b Hailar, Manchuria, 3 Nov 1911; d New York, 4 Jan 1990), American composer of Russian parentage. Moved to USA in 1930 and studied with Hanson at the Eastman School. Professor, Columbia University, NY, 1964–80. Collaborated with Luening in pioneering the development of electronic music.

Works include (some with Luening) *Sonic Contours* for tape (1952), *Incantation* for tape (1953), *Rhapsodic Variations* for orchestra and tape (1954), *Creation Prologue* for four chorus and tape (1961), *Missa brevis* for soprano, chorus and brass (1972), *Celebration* for string orchestra and electronic valve instruments (1980).

Ustvolskaya, Galina (b Petrograd, 17 Jun 1919), Russian composer. Studied 1939–50 at the Leningrad Conservatory with Shostakovich; defended by him when she was criticized by Stalinist authorities. Employing the minimum of means, her music has drawn from serialism and from local Russian traditions; but ultimately her style is completely independent: Shostakovich commented that he felt under her influence and not the reverse.

Works include five symphonies: no. 1 for two descant voices and orchestra (1955), no. 2 'True and Eternal Bliss' for boy speaker and orchestra (1979), no. 3 'Jesus, Messiah, Save Us' with boy speaker (1983), no. 4 'Prayer' with trumpet, tam-tam and piano (1987), no. 5 'Amen' with male speaker (1990); Trio for clarinet, violin and piano (1949); Octet (1950); *Composition I-III* (1970–75); six piano sonatas (1947–88).

Ut the old name for the note C, still used in France, but elsewhere replaced by Do. For its origin ♭solmization.

Utendal, Alexander (b *c* 1535; d Innsbruck, 7 May 1581), Flemish composer. Learnt music as a choirboy in the Archduke Ferdinand's chapel in Prague, and in 1566 became a singer in his chapel at Innsbruck. In *c* 1572 he became second *Kapellmeister*. On the death of Scandello at Dresden in 1580 he was offered the post of *Kapellmeister* to the Saxon court, but declined it.

Works include three Masses, motets, *Sacrae cantiones*; secular French and German songs.

Uthal opera by Méhul (libretto by J M B B de Saint-Victor, based on Ossian), produced Paris, Opéra-Comique, 17 May 1806. The work is scored without violins. Malvina's husband Uthal deposes her father Larmor as tribal chief: she is torn between love for them both. Larmor's troops defeat Uthal and Malvina joins him in exile before being pardoned.

Utrecht Te Deum and Jubilate work by Handel, composed for the celebration of the Peace of Utrecht and performed London, St Paul's Cathedral, 7 Jul 1713.

Utrenja, *Morning Service*, work in two parts by Penderecki, for soloists, choruses and orchestra: 1. *The Entombment of Christ* (fp Altenberg Cathedral, 8 Apr 1970); 2. *Resurrection of Christ* (fp Munster Cathedral, 28 May 1971).

Uttini, Francesco Antoni Baldassare (b Bologna, 1723; d Stockholm, 25 Oct 1795), Italian singer and composer. Pupil of Perti and Padre Martini in Bologna, he was elected a member of the Philharmonic Academy there in 1743 and became president in 1751. As conductor of the Mingotti opera troupe he travelled to (?) Madrid and Copenhagen (1753–54), and in 1755 settled in Stockholm, becoming musical director to the court in 1767. He visited London the following year. His *Thetis och Pelée* is claimed to be the first grand opera in Swedish.

Works include 13 Italian (texts by Metastasio) and five French operas, Swedish operas *Thetis och Pelée* (1773) and *Aline* (1776) (all mostly lost); trio sonatas; harpsichord sonatas.

V

Vaccai, Nicola (b Tolentino, 15 Mar 1790; d Pesaro, 5 or 6 Aug 1848), Italian composer. He went to school at Pesaro, then studied law in Rome, but at the age of 17 or 18 gave it up for music and studied counterpoint with Jannaconi. In 1811 he studied with Paisiello at Naples and in 1815 produced his first opera there. He then lived at Venice for seven years, produced two operas there, afterwards taught singing at Trieste and Vienna, in 1824 produced two operas at Parma and Turin and in 1825 had his greatest success, at Milan, with *Giuletta e Romeo*, after Shakespeare. In 1829–31 he lived in Paris and afterwards briefly in London, which he visited again 1833–34. In 1838 he succeeded Basili as director of the Milan Conservatory, retiring to Pesaro in 1844.

Works include operas *I solitari dl Scozia* (1815), *Pietro il grande* (1824), *La pastorella feudataria*, *Giulietta e Romeo* (1825), *Marco Visconti* (1838), *Giovanna Grey* (1836), *Virginia*, *Giovanna d'Arco* (1827), *La sposa di Messina* (both after Schiller) and others; church music; cantata on the death of Malibran and others; *Ariette per camera* for voice and piano.

Vachon, Pierre (b Arles, June 1731; d Berlin 7 Oct 1803), French violinist and composer. Studied in Paris, where he appeared at the Concert Spirituel from 1756. Principal violinist in the orchestra of the Prince of Conti 1761, he visited England in 1772 and *c* 1775, and later settled in Berlin, where he was appointed *Konzertmeister* to the court in 1786.

Works include operas *Les Femmes et le secret* (1767), *Sara, ou La Fermière écossaise* (1773), *Hippomène et Atalante* (1769), *Ésope à Cythère* (1766), *Renaud d'Ast* (both with J C Trial); violin concertos; chamber music, including about 40 string quartets; sonatas for violin and bass.

Vacqueras ◊Vaqueras.

Vaduva, Leontina (b Rosiile, 1 Dec 1960), Romanian soprano. Studied at the Bucharest Conservatory and made debut at Toulouse 1987, as Manon; repeated the role at CG 1988, and has returned as Gilda, Micaela, Antonia, and Juliette (1994). Has sung in Paris as Ninetta in *La Gazza Ladra*, Monteverdi's Drusilla, and Ismene in *Mitridate*. Other roles include Leila and Adina (at Toulouse), Norina in *Don Pasquale*, Susanna and Mimi. She is noted for her beautiful voice and appealing stage presence. Has also sung at Bordeaux, Barcelona and the Vienna Staatsoper.

Vaet, Jacobus (b Courtrai or Harelbeke, 1529; d Vienna, 8 Jan 1567), Flemish composer. He was choirmaster to Maximilian, King of Bohemia, in the 1560s and in 1564 became chief music director in Vienna, a post formerly held by Jachet Buus, when his patron became the Emperor Maximilian II.

Works include Masses, motets, Magnificats, Te Deum for eight voices and other church music; *chansons*.

vagans Latin = 'wandering, vagrant'; the name sometimes given in five-part 15th- and 16th-c. polyphonic music to the fifth part, which duplicates in range one of the basic four voices: treble, alto, tenor and bass. The voice required within one quintus part-book, though usually a second tenor, may vary from piece to piece; whence *vagans*.

vagrant chord a term coined by Schoenberg (as *vagierender Akkord*) to describe chromatic chords which confuse or lead away from any definite key-centre.

Vaisseau-fantôme, Le, *The Phantom Vessel*, opera by Dietsch (libretto by B H Révoil and P H Foucher, founded on Wagner's scenario for *Der fliegende Holländer*, intended for an opera of his own to be produced at the Opéra, which however accepted the libretto only and had it set by Dietsch), produced Paris, Opéra, 9 Nov 1842.

Vakula the Smith, *Vakula Kuznets*, opera by Tchaikovsky (libretto by Y P Polonsky, based on Gogol's *Christmas Eve*), produced St Petersburg, 6 Dec 1876; revised version entitled *Cherevichki/The Little Boots*, produced Moscow, 31 Jan 1887. It is also known as *Oxana's Caprices*. At Oxana's request Vakula flies on the back of the Devil to St Petersburg, to claim from the Tsaritsa a pair of high-heeled leather boots.

Valdengo, Giuseppe (b Turin, 24 May 1914), Italian baritone. Studied in Turin, making his debut in Parma in 1936. He is best known for his recorded performance of Verdi's Iago (1947) and Falstaff (1950) under Toscanini; also recorded Amonasro (1949). Glyndebourne 1955, Don Giovanni and Raimbaud.

Valen, (Olav) Fartein (b Stavanger, 25 Aug 1887; d Haugesund, 14 Dec 1952), Norwegian composer. Studied languages at Oslo University, but later entered the Conservatory, finishing his studies with Reger at the Hochschule für Musik in Berlin. In 1925–35 he was in the music department of the library of Oslo University, but then received a government grant for composition.

Works include three sets of motets and other choral works; five symphonies (1937–51), *Sonetto di Michelangelo*, *To Hope* (after Keats), *Pastorale*, *Epithalamion*, *Le Cimetière marin* (after P Valéry), *La isla en las calmas*, *Ode to Solitude* for orchestra; piano concerto, violin concerto (1940); six works for soprano and orchestra; two string quartets (1928–31), piano trio, serenade for five wind instruments; violin and piano sonata; two sonatas, variations and other works for piano; organ music; songs.

Valente, Antonio (b *fl.* 1565–80), Italian composer, active in Naples. Blind from his youth, he was organist of S Angelo a Nilo from 1565 to 1580. He pub. two collections of keyboard music (1576 and 1580).

Valente, Benita (b Delano, CA, 19 Oct 1934), American soprano. Studied at Curtis 1955–60 with Margaret Harshaw. Sang at first in concert and made opera debut at Freiburg 1962, as Pamina; also role of 1973 NY Met. debut, and has returned as Mozart's Countess and Susanna, Ilia, Nannetta, and Almirena in *Rinaldo* (1985). Further appearances throughout the USA as Mimi, Anne Trulove, Violetta and Mélisande. Sang Ginerva in *Ariodante* at Santa Fe, 1987.

Valentini, Giovanni (b Venice, *c* 1583; d Vienna, 29 or 30 Apr 1649), Italian organist and composer. In 1614 he was organist to the Archduke Ferdinand at Graz, and on his patron's succession to the title of Emperor Ferdinand II in 1619 remained in his service, becoming *Kapellmeister* in 1629 and continuing in this employment under

Ferdinand III. His church music is highly ornate for its time.

Works include Masses, motets and other church music; madrigals, *Musiche a due voci*.

Valentini, Giuseppe (b Florence, c 1680; d ? Paris, after 1759), Italian composer. In the service of the Grand Duke of Tuscany at Florence from c 1735. His most characteristic music is in the florid violin sonatas.

Works include opera *La costanza in amore* (1715); oratorios *Absalone* (1705) and *S Alessio* (1733); Concerti grossi; symphony, *Bizarrie*, 12 fantasies, *Idee per camera* and 12 sonatas for three string instruments and bass; chamber sonatas and *Alletamenti* for violin, cello and bass.

Valentini, Pier Francesco (b Rome, c 1570; d Rome, 1654), Italian composer. Pupil of G M Nanini in Rome. He was best known for music involving elaborate counterpoint (canon for 96 voices).

Works include operas (*favole*) *La mitra* (1620) and *La transformazione di Dafne* (1623); motets, litanies and other church music; *Canzonetti spirituali* and *Musiche spirituali* for the Nativity; madrigals and canons; *canzoni* and arias for one–two voices.

There is no avant-garde: only some people a bit behind.

Edgard Varèse, attr.

Valentini, Valentino Urbani (*fl.* 1690–1719), Italian alto castrato. First went to London in 1707. He sang in pasticcios and in the fps of Handel's *Rinaldo*, *Il pastor fido* and *Teseo*.

Valentini-Terrani, Lucia (b Padua, 28 Aug 1948), Italian mezzo. Debut Brescia, 1969, as Cenerentola. NY Met. debut 1974, as Rossini's Isabella. Guest appearances in Milan, Paris and Vienna. In 1987 she sang Rosina at CG.

Valeriano, Valeriano Pellegrini, Italian countertenor. He sang in Düsseldorf 1705–16, and took part in the fp of Steffani's *Tassilone* there. Sang in the fp of Handel's *Agrippina* (Rome, 1709). He was in England 1712–13 and sang in the fps of Handel's *Il pastor fido* and *Teseo*.

Valesi, Giovanni, real name Johann Evangelist Walleshauser (b Unterhattenhofen, Bavaria, 28 Apr 1735; d Munich, 10 Jan 1816), German tenor. Chamber singer to the Elector of Bavaria from 1756, later studied in Italy and sang there with success. At Munich he sang in the fps of Mozart's *La finta giardiniera* (1775) and *Idomeneo* (1781). Weber was his pupil for a short time in 1798.

Välkki, Anita (b Sääkmäki, 25 Oct 1926), Finnish soprano. Studied in Helsinki and sang at the National Opera there from 1955. Stockholm Opera from 1960, as Aida, Brünnhilde and Santuzza; also sang Brünnhilde at CG and the NY Met., 1961–65. Bayreuth Festival, 1963–64. Sang at Helsinki 1986, in *Juha* by Merikanto. Recordings include *The Horseman* by Sallinen.

Valkyrie, The, *Die Walküre*, (Wagner.) ◊Ring des Nibelungen.

Valledor y la Calle, Jacinto (b Madrid, 1744; d Madrid, c 1809), Spanish composer. Settled in Madrid and wrote *tonadillas* and other works for the stage, including *La decantada vida y muerte del General Mambrú* (1785).

Valletti, Cesare (b Rome, 18 Dec 1922), Italian tenor. He made his debut at Bari in 1947, as Alfredo; wider recognition came in 1950: *Il Turco in Italia* in Rome and Fenton at CG. At La Scala he was heard as Lindoro, Nemorino and Almaviva. US debut San Francisco, 1953, as Werther. NY Met. 1953–62 as Ottavio, Ferrando and Ernesto. Retired 1968.

Vallin, Ninon (b Montalieu-Vercieu, 8 Sept 1886; d Lyons, 22 Nov 1961), French soprano. Studied at Lyon Conservatory. Sang in fp of Debussy's *Le Martyre de Saint Sébastien* (1911). Opéra Comique 1912–16; Buenos Aires 1916–36, as Manon, Thaïs, Mélisande and Alceste. After World War II sang in Paris as Mozart's Countess. Also heard in operas by Falla and Respighi and in the songs of Fauré and Chausson.

Vallotti, Francesco Antonio (b Vercelli, 11 Jun 1697; d Padua, 10 Jan

1780), Italian composer and theorist. He became third organist at the basilica of Sant' Antonio at Padua in 1722 and *maestro* in 1730. He wrote a learned treatise, *Della scienza teorica e pratica della moderna musica*.

Works include motets, Requiem for Tartini and other church music.

Valls, Francisco (b Barcelona, 1665; d Barcelona, 2 Feb 1747), Spanish composer. After posts at Mataró and Gerona he moved to Barcelona in 1696; *maestro di capilla* at the cathedral there from 1709. Retired in 1740 to write a treatise called *Mapa armónico*, in which he defended the use of dissonance in church music as employed by Spanish composers against the more orthodox views of Alessandro Scarlatti. Valls is best known today for his Mass *Scala aretina*.

Works include Masses *Scala aretina* for 11 voices and orchestra (1702), *Regalis* (for the King of Portugal), 1740), ten others; 22 responsories, 16 Magnificats, 12 psalms, two Misereres, c 35 motets, c 120 *villancicos*.

Valse, La choreographic poem for orchestra by Ravel, finished 1920; fp Paris, 12 Dec 1920. It imitates or parodies the style of J Strauss's waltzes and has several times served for ballets, as its description shows that it was intended to do.

Valses nobles et sentimentales a set of waltzes by Ravel, composed 1911 and afterwards scored for orchestra. The title is derived from Schubert, who pub. two sets: *Valses nobles*, D969, and *Valses sentimentales*, D779. Ravel's work was turned into a ballet, *Adélaïde, ou Le Langage des fleurs*, produced Paris, 22 Apr 1912.

valves the keys added to brass wind instruments, invented early in the 19th c. to make it possible for horns, trumpets, cornets, etc. to produce the complete chromatic scale instead of only the natural harmonics. Valves are fitted to all members of the saxhorn family and have also been used on the trombone as a substitute for the slide.

Vampyr, Der, *The Vampire*, opera by Lindpaintner (libretto by C M Heigel, based on J W Polidori's story, pub. in 1819 and thought to be by Byron, and on a French melodrama by C Nodier, P F A Carmouche and A de Jouffroy), produced Stuttgart, 21 Sept 1828.

Opera by Marschner (libretto by W A Wohlbrück, based on the sources above), produced Leipzig, 29 Mar 1828. To postpone Satan's claim on his soul, the newly created vampire Lord Ruthven must sacrifice three girls; Janthe and Emmy fall victim but Malvina escapes the fangs.

Van Allan, Richard (b Nottingham, 28 May 1935), English bass. He studied with David Franklin and appeared at Glyndebourne from 1966: sang in fp of Maw's *The Rising of the Moon*, 1970. ENO, London, since 1969; CG from 1971. He has sung with WNO and at Wexford, the Paris Opéra and in Boston and San Diego. Among his best roles are Leporello, Don Giovanni, Philip II, Boris and Ochs (San Diego, 1976). Director National Opera Studio from 1986. Sang in the fps of Buller's *Bakxai* and Osborne's *Terrible Mouth* (1992); Don Jerome in the stage fp of Gerhard's *The Duenna*, Madrid 1992.

Van Beinum, Eduard, Eduard van ◊Beinum.

Van Dam, José (b Brussels, 25 Aug 1940), Belgian bass. He studied in Brussels and sang in Paris 1961–65. Deutsche Oper, Berlin, from 1967 as Mozart's Figaro and Leporello, Attila and Prince Igor. He is well known at Salzburg and Aix and has often appeared in concert with Karajan. Much admired as Escamillo (CG, 1973). In 1983 he sang the title role in the fp of Messiaen's *St François d'Assise*. Sang Falstaff at Salzburg, 1993.

Vaness, Carol (b San Diego, 27 Jul 1952), American soprano. Debut San Francisco, 1977, as Vitellia; later sang Cleopatra and Donna Anna. NY City Opera from 1979, as Antonia, Violetta and Alcina; Met. 1984 as Armida in *Rinaldo*. Glyndebourne from 1982, as Donna Anna, Mozart's Electra and Fiordiligi and Amelia Boccanegra (1986). CG from 1982, as Mimi, Vitellia, Dalila in Handel's *Samson* and Donna Anna (1992). Sang Desdemona at the Met., Norma at Seattle, 1994.

Vanessa opera by Barber (libretto by Menotti), produced NY Met., 15 Jan 1958. Vanessa marries Anatol, son of her former lover by the same name, in spite of the fact that her niece Erika is pregnant by him.

Vanhal, Johann Baptist (b Nové Nechanice, 12 May 1739; d Vienna, 20 Aug 1813), Bohemian composer. Came to Vienna in 1760 and studied there with Dittersdorf, travelled in Italy 1769–71, and lived on the estate of Count Erdödy in Hungary 1772–80. Back in Vienna, he supported himself as a freelance composer. He wrote about 100 symphonies and 100 quartets; his works were performed by Mozart and Haydn.

Works include two operas (*Demofoonte* and *Il trionfo di Clelia*, both lost); over 50 Masses and much other church music; *c* 70 symphonies; *c* 100 string quartets; many caprices and programmatic works for keyboard.

Van Keulen, Isabelle (b Mijdrecht, 16 Dec 1966), Dutch violinist. Studied with Sandor Vegh and in Amsterdam. Concerts from 1983 with the Berlin PO, Vienna SO, Concertgebouw Orchestra, Detroit and Minnesota SOs. Appearances at the Salzburg Festival and with Gidon Kremer's Lockenhaus Soloists. Repertoire includes concertos by Dutilleux, Strauss, Schnittke, Spohr and Stravinsky. Also plays the viola (quintets with the Orlando and Borodin Quartets).

Vanni-Marcoux (b Turin, 12 Jun 1877; d Paris, 22 Oct 1962), French bass and baritone. Debut Turin, 1894. CG 1905–14, as Rossini's Don Basilio and Arkel. Sang in Paris from 1908, notably as Massenet's Don Quichotte. US debut Chicago, 1913, as Scarpia. Other roles included Don Giovanni, Boris Godunov and Golaud (CG, 1937).

Van Rooy, Anton(ius Maria Josephus), Anton Van ◊Rooy.

Vaqueras, Bertrandus (b *c* 1450; d ? Rome, *c* 1507), Spanish singer and composer. He was in the Papal Chapel 1483–1507. Wrote church music and *chansons*.

Varady, Julia (b Oradea, 1 Sept 1941), Romanian soprano. She studied in Cluj and sang there 1960–70 as Liù, Judith and Santuzza. After two years at Frankfurt sang in Munich from 1972; roles there have included Donna Elvira, Fiordiligi, Elisabeth de Valois, Butterfly and Arabella. British debut Edinburgh, 1974, as Alceste. Season 1992/93 as the *Trovatore* Leonore in Munich and Elisabeth de Valois at the Deutsche Oper Berlin. She is married to Dietrich Fischer-Dieskau.

Varèse, Edgard (Victor Achille Charles) (b Paris, 22 Dec 1883; d New York, 6 Nov 1965), French-born American composer. Pupil of d'Indy and Roussel at the Schola Cantorum in Paris and of Widor at the Conservatory. He conducted choral and orchestral music in Paris, Berlin and Prague until 1914, when he joined the French army to take part in World War I; but he was discharged for reasons of health in 1915 and settled in the USA in 1916. He did much to advance the cultivation of modern music in NY and joined Salzedo in 1921 to found the International Compsosers' Guild. Varèse is an important figure in the field of 20th-c. experimental music, dispensing with thematic development and instead working with different types of 'noise', either purely instrumental (*Arcana*, 1927) or combined with tape-recorded sounds (*Déserts*, 1954), or derived from percussion (*Ionisation*, 1931). His influence on modern European and American music has been considerable.

Works include *Amériques* for orchestra (1918–21, revised 1927), *Offrandes* for soprano and small orchestra (1921), *Hyperprism* for nine wind, six percussion (1922–23), *Octandre* for wind and double bass (1923), *Intégrales* for 11 wind and four percussion (1923), *Arcana* for orchestra (1925–27), *Ionisation* for 13 percussion (1929–31), *Ecuatorial* for eight brass, piano, organ, two ondes Martenot, six percussion and bass soloist (1932–34), *Density 21.5* for solo flute (1936), *Études pour Espace* for chorus, two pianos and percussion (1947), *Déserts* for 14 wind, piano, five percussion and two-track tape (1950–54), *Poème electronique* for three-track tape (1957–58), *Nocturnal* for soprano, chorus and small orchestra (1961, unfinished); opera, *Oedipus und die Sphinx* (1909–13, text by Hofmannsthal; lost).

Varesi, Felice (b Calais, 1813; d Milan, 13 Mar 1889), Italian baritone. Studied at Milan. He sang at the Kärntnertortheater, Vienna, 1842–47, in operas by Donizetti. He was Verdi's first Macbeth in 1847, first Rigoletto in 1851 and first Germont, père, in 1853. He visited London in 1864, when he sang Rigoletto.

Varga, Tibor (b Györ, 4 Jul 1921), Hungarian, later British, violinist. Studied at Budapest Music Academy with Hubay and later with Flesch. From 1939 to 1943 he studied philosophy at Budapest University, and since 1949 he has been professor of violin at the Detmold Music Academy. He was best known for his playing of modern music, e.g. the concertos by Blacher (fp, 1950), Bartók and Schoenberg. Founded his own chamber orchestra, 1954, and conducted it until 1988.

variations varied treatments of a theme, sometimes with a restatement of the theme in its first form at the end (e.g. Bach's 'Goldberg' Variations), sometimes with a more elaborate final section, such as a fugue (e.g. Beethoven's 'Eroica' Variations for piano or Brahms's Handel Variations for piano), or a passacaglia (e.g. Brahms's Haydn Variations for two pianos or orchestra). There is at least one instance (d'Indy's *Istar*) where the theme does not appear in its primitive form until the end. Historically the variation principle goes back as far as instrumental music, but sets of variations first emerge in the course of the 16th c., especially in England and Spain. The English virginal composers wrote sets on popular tunes for their instrument and another favoured medium for variations was the lute. In 17th-c. England variations were called divisions, because they split up the theme into smaller rhythmic patterns, and they could be based on a ground, i.e. an unchanging bass.

The later history of the form continues to show the two different tendencies of (1) varying the tune and (2) maintaining the foundation of the same bass, with greater or lesser incidental changes, while the superstructure can be handled very freely and need not keep to the melodic line of the theme at all. Mozart's variations, for example, are predominantly melodic, and so are Beethoven's earlier sets, but the latter reverts to the 'ground' type by keeping chiefly to the harmonic framework in such a work as the 'Diabelli' Variations and in the 32 Variations for piano he keeps so close to the bass that the work is more like a passacaglia, which is true also of the finale of Brahms' fourth symphony. In Elgar's 'Enigma' Variations for orchestra, each of which represents a portrait of one of the composer's friends, and in R Strauss's *Don Quixote*, the form is complicated by an element of programme music.

No theme but twelve variations on it.
Unnamed critic of Berg's *Twelve Piano Variations*
in 1908, quoted in Reich,
The Life and Work of Alban Berg, 1963

Variations on a Theme by Haydn (Brahms) ◊Haydn Variations.

Variations on a Theme of Frank Bridge work for string orchestra by Britten, composed 1937 for the Boyd Neel Orchestra, performed Salzburg, 27 Aug 1937. The theme is from Bridge's Idyll no. 2 for string quartet.

Varnay, Astrid Ibolyka Maria (b Stockholm, 25 Apr 1918), American soprano of Austro-Hungarian parentage. Both her parents were singers. She studied first with her mother and then with H Weigert, whom she married in 1944. She made her debut at the NY Met. in 1941, as Sieglinde, and remained there as a leading Wagner and Strauss singer until 1956. CG, 1948–68; Bayreuth, 1951–67, as Brünnhilde, Isolde and Kundry. Other roles included Tosca, Lady Macbeth and Orff's Jocasta (1959).

Varviso, Silvio (b Zurich, 26 Feb 1924), Swiss conductor. He studied in Zurich and Vienna. Worked at the Basel Opera, 1950–62 (music director from 1956). At San Francisco in 1960 he conducted the US fp of *A Midsummer Night's Dream*; NY Met. from 1961 (debut in *Lucia*). In 1962 he gave *Figaro* at Glyndebourne and *Rosenkavalier* at CG; has returned to London for operas by Mozart and Puccini. Music director, Stockholm Opera, 1965–72. Stuttgart from 1972 (*Lohengin*, 1990); Bayreuth from 1969 (*Der Fliegende Holländer*, *Meistersinger* and *Lohengrin*). Paris, Opéra, 1981–85. Conducted *Die Frau ohne Schatten* at Florence, 1993.

Varvoglis, Mario (b Brussels, 10 Dec 1885; d Athens, 31 Jul 1967), Greek composer. Studied painting at first, then music in Paris with Leroux and Caussade from 1904 and d'Indy from 1913, having his first successes there. He returned to Greece 1922, became professor at the Athens Conservatory and in 1924 at the Hellenic Conservatory, of which he became director with Evangelatos, 1947.

Works include one-act opera *The Afternoon of Love* (1935, produced 1944); classical Greek plays; *Pastoral Suite* (1912), *Meditation* and incidental music to prelude, chorale and fugue on B.A.C.H. for strings; chamber music; piano works; songs.

Vásáry, Tamás (b Debrecen, 11 Aug 1933), Hungarian-born Swiss pianist and conductor. He studied in Budapest and worked as an accompanist from 1948; encouraged by Kodály. He left Hungary in 1956; Swiss citizen from 1971. London debut 1961, NY 1962. Often heard in Chopin, Liszt, Bach and Mozart. Debut as conductor Menton, 1971; joint conductor Northern Sinfonia, 1979–82. He has also conducted widely in the USA. Principal conductor of Bournemouth Sinfonietta 1989–91, music director of Budapest SO from 1993.

Vasilenko, Sergey Nikiforovich (b Moscow, 30 Mar 1872; d Moscow, 11 Mar 1956), Russian composer, conductor and teacher. After receiving private lessons from Gretchaninov and Konius, and studying law, he entered the Moscow Conservatory in 1895, studying composition with Taneiev and Ippolitov-Ivanov. In 1905 he taught there and was soon appointed full professor. He organized and conducted historical concerts.

Works include operas *The Legend of the Holy City of Kitezh* (1902), *The Son of the Sun* (1929), *Christopher Columbus* (1933), *Suvarov* (1941); ballets *Joseph the Beautiful* (1925), *The Gypsies* (after Pushkin), etc.; five symphonies (1904–47), *Epic Poem*, symphonic poem on Oscar Wilde's *The Garden of Death* and others and suite *In the Sun* and others, *Three Bloody Battles* (after Tolstoy) and other orchestral works; violin concerto (1913); cantata for the 20th anniversary of the Oct Revolution; four string quartets, woodwind quartet, piano trio and other chamber music; viola and piano sonata; songs, folksong arrangements.

Vasquez, Juan, ◊Vázquez.

Vaterländischer Künstlerverein German = 'Patriotic Artists' Association'; the title of Part II of the variations commissioned by Cappi and Diabelli of Vienna to be written by Beethoven and others on a waltz by Diabelli. Beethoven eventually wrote 33 variations instead of one, and they were pub. separately as Part I in 1824, Part II following with contribs. by Czerny, Hummel, Kalkbrenner, C Kreutzer, Liszt (aged 11), Moscheles, Franz Xaver Mozart, the Archduke Rudolph, Schubert, Sechter and *c* 40 others.

After conducting one of his own works Vaughan-Williams, as he left the podium, was heard to mutter, 'If that's modern music – I don't like it.'
Bernard Shore, *The Orchestra Speaks*, 1938

---

vaudeville, French, a term with various meanings and of uncertain origin. Le Roy, in his *Airs de Cour* of 1571, says that such songs were formerly called *voix de ville*, 'town voices'; but the form *vau de Vire* is also known, and may have referred to the valley of Vire in Normandy, the home of Olivier Basselin (*c* 1400–50), a composer of such songs. In 18th-c. France, vaudevilles were at first satirical songs, then songs with words set to popular tunes used in comedies with music (*comédies mêlées de vaudevilles*), as in the English ballad opera (songs specially composed being called *ariettes*). In time vaudevilles in France became songs sung at the end of spoken stage pieces, taken up verse by verse by all the characters and sometimes by the chorus, and this device was sometimes introduced into opera, in France and elsewhere, as for example at the end of Rousseau's *Devin du village* and Mozart's *Entführung aus dem Serail*. The next step from this was to call a whole light music stage entertainment a vaudeville.

Vaughan, Denis (b Melbourne, 6 Jun 1926), Australian conductor and organist. After study in Melbourne and London was assistant to Beecham at the RPO, forming the Beecham Choral Society 1953. Has conducted widely in Europe and was music director of the State Opera of South Australia, 1981–84. US opera debut 1983, with Bellini's

Vaughan Williams *The composer Vaughan Williams (1872–1958). Once labelled a 'cowpat' composer by a heartless serialist, Vaughan Williams is best-loved for his evocative English pastoral style. He did, however, move towards a more dissonant idiom during the 1940s.*

I Capuleti at the Juilliard Opera Center. Has edited and corrected the scores of operas by Puccini and Verdi.

Vaughan, Elizabeth (b Llanfyllin, Montgomeryshire, 12 Mar 1936), Welsh soprano. She studied at the RAM and sang Abigaille with WNO in 1960. CG from 1961 as Mimi, Tytania, Teresa, Gilda, Amelia and Butterfly. NY Met. debut 1972, as Donna Elvira. In recent years she has also sung mezzo roles: Kabanicha in *Kàta Kabanová* with Scottish Opera, 1993.

Vaughan Williams, Ralph (b Down Ampney, Gloucestershire, 12 Oct 1872; d London, 26 Aug 1958), English composer. Son of a clergyman, he was educated at Charterhouse School, 1887–90, and Trinity College, Cambridge, 1892–95, the intervening years being devoted to study at the RCM in London, where he returned for another year after Cambridge. He learnt the piano and organ but was from the first determined to be a composer. On leaving the RCM in 1896 he became organist at South Lambeth Church in London and saved enough money to gain further experience by study abroad, first at the Akademie der Künste in Berlin, under Bruch, and in 1909 with Ravel, who was younger than him, in Paris. In 1901 he took the Mus.D. at Cambridge. In 1904 he joined the Folk-Song Society and began to take an active share in the recovery and study of old country tunes, collecting some in Norfolk. His first public success was with *Toward the Unknown Region* at the Leeds Festival in 1907 and this was followed in 1909 by his first great and charactistic compositions, the *Wasps* overture, song cycle *On Wenlock Edge*, and *A Sea Symphony* (the first to employ a chorus throughout). His editorship of the *English Hymnal* (from 1906) resulted in one of his best-loved works, the *Fantasia on a theme of Thomas Tallis*, for strings, 1910. (The sense of religious wonder evoked by this music was later enhanced in such Biblically-inspired works as the masque *Job* and the opera *The Pilgrim's Progress*). Although Vaughan Williams' compositions are

A Selection of

Vaughan Williams

A Sea Symphony	1903–9
On Wenlock Edge	1909
Fantasia on a Theme by Thomas Tallis	1910
A London Symphony	1912–13
The Lark Ascending	1914
Flos Campi	1925
Symphony no. 4	1937
Serenade to Music	1938
Symphony no. 5	1943
The Pilgrim's Progress	1951

usually classified broadly as pastoral, making use of folk melodies, or at least the lyrical and often model aspects of such melodies, he was conscious of contemporary musical developments and often involved a greater degree of dissonance in his works written after World War I, such as *Sinfonia antartica* (no. 7).

In World War I he first served as a private in Macedonia and France, but later rose to officer's rank, and after the declaration of peace he was appointed professor of composition at the RCM. The English pastoral tradition was revived in Vaughan Williams' 3rd symphony (1921) and the complementary, visionary source of his inspiration was renewed in such sacred works as the Mass in G minor, *Sancta Civitas*, and *Benedicite*. His two best-known symphonies, nos. 4 and 5, were composed between 1934 and 1943; the angularity and fierce accents of the earlier work lead to the repose and serenity of its companion. The last four symphonies continue the composer's spiritual quest, already begun in *The Pilgrim's Progress*.

Works include OPERAS: *Hugh the Drover* (1910–14, produced 1924), *Sir John in Love* (on Shakespeare's *Merry Wives*, 1929), *The Poisoned Kiss* (1929, produced 1936), *Riders to the Sea* (Synge, 1937) and *The Pilgrim's Progress* (after Bunyan, begun 1925, premiered 1951); ballets *Old King Cole* (1923) and *On Christmas Night* (after Dickens, 1926), masque *Job* (on Blake's illustrations, 1931); incidental music for Aristophanes' *Wasps* (1909), film music including *49th Parallel* (1941) and *Scott of the Antarctic* (1948).

CHORAL: three motets, Mass in G minor, Te Deum in G major, Anglican services, Festival Te Deum, hymn tunes; (with orchestra) *Toward the Unknown Region* (Whitman), *Willow Wood* (D G Rossetti), *A Sea Symphony* (no. 1) (Whitman, 1903–09), *Five Mystical Songs* (Herbert, 1911), *Fantasia on Christmas Carols*, *Flos Campi* (Song of Solomon, 1925), *Sancta Civitas* (1925), *Benedicite*, Magnificat, *Dona nobis pacem*, *Five Tudor Portraits* (Skelton, 1935), *The Sons of Light* (U Wood), *Serenade to Music* for 16 solo voices and orchestra (from Shakespeare's *Merchant of Venice*, 1938), *Oxford Elegy* (M Arnold, 1949).

ORCHESTRAL: *Norfolk Rhapsodies*, nos. 1–3 (1905–06), *In the Fen Country*, *Fantasia on a Theme by Thomas Tallis* (strings, 1910), *A London Symphony* (no. 2, 1912–13), *A Pastoral Symphony* (no. 3, 1921), symphonies nos. 4–9 (1937, 1943, 1947, 1952, 1955, 1957), *Five Variants of 'Dives and Lazarus'* (strings and harps, 1939), *Two Hymn-tune Preludes* (small orchestra), *Concerto grosso* (strings, 1950), *English Folk Song Suite* (military band); *The Lark Ascending* (after Meredith) for violin and orchestra (1914), *Concerto*

accademico for violin and strings (1925), piano concerto (later version for two pianos, 1926–31), suite for viola and orchestra (1934), concerto for oboe and strings (1944), *Romance* for mouth organ and orchestra, tuba concerto (1954).

CHAMBER AND SONGS: two string quartets (1909, 1944), Phantasy quintet for strings, *On Wenlock Edge* (Housman) for tenor, string quartet and piano (1909); suite for piano, introduction and fugue for two pianos; three preludes on Welsh hymn-tunes and prelude and fugue for organ; many songs including cycle *The House of Life* (D G Rossetti [including *Silent Noon*]), *Songs of Travel* (Stevenson, 1901–04), *Along the Field* (Housman), for low voice and violin (1927); numerous part-songs; folksong arrangements.

Vautor, Thomas (*fl.* 1600–20), English composer. Educated at Lincoln College, Oxford, where he took the B. Mus. in 1616. He was for many years in the service of Sir George Villiers, father of the later Duke of Buckingham, at Brooksby, and later of his widow at Goadby. Pub. one book of madrigals (1619–20).

Vavrinecz, Mauritius (b Czegléd, 18 Jul 1858; d Budapest, 5 Aug 1913), Hungarian composer. Studied at the Budapest Conservatory and with Volkmann and in 1886 became music director of Budapest Cathedral.

Works include operas *Ratcliff* (after Heine) and *Rosamunde*; five Masses, Requiem, *Stabat Mater*; oratorio *Christus*; symphony, overture to Byron's *Bride of Abydos*, Dithyramb for orchestra.

Vázquez, Juan (b Badajoz, *c* 1510; d ? Seville, *c* 1560), Spanish composer. *Maestro de capilla* at Badajoz Cathedral, 1545–50, and was later in the service of Don Antonio de Zuñiga. He was an important exponent of the *villancico* , and also wrote church music.

Veasey, Josephine (b Peckham, 10 Jul 1930), English mezzo. She studied in London and sang at CG from 1955; roles there included Carmen, Waltraute, Dorabella, Eboli, Dido and Octavian. Often sang under Solti. She sang Cherubino at Glyndebourne in 1958 and returned in 1969 for Charlotte. NY Met. debut 1968, as Fricka, under Karajan. Paris, Opéra, 1973, Kundry. Often heard in concert. Retired from opera 1982 and became vocal coach at ENO, London.

Vecchi, Lorenzo (b Bologna, before 1564; d Bologna, 3 Mar 1628), Italian composer. He was a pupil at San Petronio at Bologna, where he became *maestro di cappella* in 1605. Wrote Masses, Requiem and other church music.

Vecchi, Orazio (Tiberio) (b Modena, bap. 6 Dec 1550; d Modena, 19 Feb 1605), Italian composer and priest. *Maestro di cappella* Salò Cathedral (1581), Modena (1584) and Reggio Emilia (1586), canon (1586) and archdeacon (1591) at Correggio. His madrigal-comedy *L'Amfiparnaso* is regarded as an important forerunner of opera. He returned to Modena as *maestro di cappella* in 1596, and then became *maestro* at the d'Este court in 1598. He became famous, being summoned to the court of the Emperor Rudolph II at one time and invited to compose music for the king of Poland. In 1604 his pupil Geminiano Capi-Lupi intrigued successfully against him and supplanted him in his post.

Works include madrigal comedy *L'Amfiparnaso* (fp 1594); Masses, motets, Lamentations and other church music; madrigals, canzonets.

Vecchi, Orfeo (b ? Milan, *c* 1550; d Milan, before April 1604), Italian composer. *Maestro di cappella* of the church of Santa Maria della Scala at Milan from *c* 1590.

Works include Masses, motets, psalms, Magnificats, *Cantiones sacrae* and other church music; madrigals.

Vegh, Sandor (b Koloszvar, 17 May 1905), Hungarian conductor and violinist. Studied in Budapest with Jeno Hubay and Zoltan Kodály. Played in the Hungarian String Quartet 1935–40, giving the European fp of Bartók's 5th, 1936. Founder and leader of the Vegh Quartet 1940–80, making world tours with works by Bartók and Beethoven. Performed with Casals and others at the Prades Festival, 1953–69, and directed the Sandor Vegh Chamber Orchestra, 1968–71; teacher at Salzburg from 1971 and director of the Camerata there from 1979. Founded the International seminar at Prussia Cove, Cornwall, 1972; conducted the Chamber Orchestra of Europe in London, 1990.

Veichtner, Franz Adam (b Regensburg, 10 Feb 1741; d Klievenhof, Courland, 3 Mar 1822), German violinist and composer. Pupil of F Benda for violin and of Riepel for composition, he was in the service of Count Kaiserling at Königsberg 1763–64, *Konzertmeister* to the Duke of Courland in Mitau 1765–95, then in St Petersburg as chamber musician to the Russian court until his retirement in 1820.

Works include *Singspiele*, e.g. *Cephalus und Prokris* (1779) and *Cyrus und Cassandana* (1784); five symphonies; violin concerto; three string quartets (1802); 24 fantasias on Russian songs for violin and bass; 24 violin sonatas.

Veilchen, Das, *The Violet*, song by Mozart, K476: his only setting of a poem by Goethe, composed 8 Jun 1785.

Vejvanovský, Pavel Josef (b Hukvaldy or Hlučín, c 1655; d Kroměříž, buried 24 Sept 1693), Moravian composer and trumpeter. He studied at Opava and from 1661 worked at Kroměříž, composing and playing the trumpet at the court there; many of his Masses, offertories and motets feature technically fluent parts for trumpets, trombones and cornets. Much of his music shows the influence of J H Schmelzer and other composers at the court of Emperor Leopold I in Vienna.

Vejzovic, Dunja (b Zagreb, 20 Oct 1943), Croatian mezzo. Sang first at Zagreb, then Frankfurt from 1978. She has most often been heard as Wagner's Kundry: Bayreuth 1978, Salzburg Easter Festival (recorded with Karajan), NY Met., and Houston (1992). Also admired for her dramatic conviction as Venus (La Scala), Ortrud (Paris and Vienna), Massenet's Hérodiade and Chimène (*Le Cid*), and Senta.

It may be a good thing to copy reality; but to invent reality is much, much better.
Giuseppe Verdi in a letter to Clarina Maffie, 1876

Velluti, Giovanni Battista (b Montolmo [now Corridonia], near Ancona, 28 Jan 1780; d Sambruson di Dolo, 22 Jan 1861), Italian soprano castrato (one of the last). Made his first stage appearance at Forlì in 1800, and then appeared in Naples, Milan and Venice in operas by Guglielmi, Cimarosa and Mayr. In 1812 he visited Vienna. He created Arsace in Rossini's *Aureliano in Palmira* (Milan, 1813) and Armando in Meyerbeer's *Il crociato in Egitto* (Venice, 1824), and sang the latter role on his first visit to London (1825).

veloce Italian = 'quick, swift, rapid, fluent'; the direction does not so much indicate increased speed, though it may include that meaning, as smoothness of rapid figuration.

Veltri, Michelangelo (b Buenos Aires, 18 Aug 1940), Argentinian conductor. Conducted in South America before moving to Europe, 1970: Stuttgart, Milan and Vienna. Artistic director at Barcelona and Avignon; CG 1986, *Lucia di Lammermoor*; NY Met. 1989, *La Traviata*. Other Verdi repertory includes *Ballo in Maschera*, *Don Carlos* (at Marseille), *Aida* (Orange), *Otello* and *I due Foscari*. *Il Trovatore* at Buenos Aires, 1990.

Vendredis, Les a set of pieces for string quartet by Artsibushev, Blumenfeld, Borodin, Glazunov, Kopylov, Liadov, M d'Osten-Sacken, Rimsky-Korsakov, Sokolov and Wihtol, written for Friday chamber-music reunions in St Peterburg.

Venegas de Henestrosa, Luis (b c 1510; d c 1557 or later), Spanish vihuelist and composer. He pub. a book of variations and transcriptions in a special tablature suitable for keyboard instruments, harp, vihuela or guitar (1557). The notation was later used by Cabezóni and Arauxo.

Vengerov, Maxim (b Novosibirsk, 15 Aug 1974), Russian violinist. Played Schubert's *Rondo Brillant* in Moscow, aged 11. Gave concerts at first in Russia then played with Concertgebouw Orchestra and the BBC PO. Won the 1990 Carl Flesch Competition, London. US debut 1990 with the New York PO; Israel PO in Tel Aviv and on tour to USA. Further concerts with the St Petersburg PO and Berlin PO at the London Proms (Sibelius and Brahms Concertos), LPO under Mehta, Chicago SO under Barenboim and Vienna PO under Menuhin. One of the most promising virtuosi of his generation.

Ventadorn, Bernart de (d 1195), French troubadour. 45 of his poems and 19 of his melodies have been preserved.

Vento, Ivo de (b c 1544; d Munich, 1575), ? Flemish composer. In 1564 he was appointed *Kapellmeister* to Duke William of Bavaria at Landshut and in 1569 he became organist in the ducal chapel at Munich under Lassus.

Works include motets; German sacred and secular songs for several voices.

Vento, Mattia (b Naples, 1735; d London, 22 Nov 1776), Italian composer. Produced operas in Rome and Venice, and settled in London in 1763, staging six Italian operas and several pasticcios there.

Works include operas *La finta semplice* (1759), *La Egiziana* (1763), *Leucippo* (1764), *Demofoonte*, *Sofonisba* (1766), *La conquista del vello d'orco* (1767), *Artaserse* (1771), *Il bacio* (1776), *La Vestale*; cantata *Threnodia augustilia* (Goldsmith) on the death of George III's mother; trio sonatas; violin sonatas; keyboard music; songs.

Venturi del Nibbio, Stefano (b *fl*. 1592–1600), Italian composer. Wrote two choruses in Caccini's *Rapimento di Cefalo* (lost), five books of madrigals, three motets.

Venturini, Francesco (b ? Brussels, c 1675; d Hanover, 18 Apr 1745), German composer and violinist. Pupil of J B Farinelli at Hanover, where he joined the electoral chapel in 1698 and succeeded his master as head of the instrumental music in 1713, later becoming court *Kapellmeister*. He pub. a set of chamber concertos (Amsterdam, c 1714).

Venus and Adonis masque by Blow (librettist unknown), produced London, at court, c 1682; Chelsea, Josiah Priest's boarding school for young gentlewomen, 17 Apr 1684. Venus persuades Adonis to join the hunt but he returns mortally wounded, gored by a boar.

Vêpres siciliennes, Les, *The Sicilian Vespers*, opera by Verdi (libretto by Scribe and C Duveyrier), produced Paris, Opéra, 13 Jun 1855. Verdi's first French opera, the only other set to French words being *Don Carlos*. Produced in Italy, as *Giovanna di Guzman*, Milan, La Scala, 4 Feb 1856, but later called *I vespri siciliani* there. Sicilians Procida, Hélène and Henri engage in a plot to assassinate Montfort, the French Governor of the island. But when Henri learns that Montfort is his father he prevents the murder and Procida and Hélène are arrested, later being released when Henri reluctantly accepts Montfort as his parent. At Henri's and Hélène's wedding the Sicilians rise and kill Montfort.

A Selection of

Verdi

Rigoletto 1851
Il trovatore 1853
La traviata 1853
Simon Boccanegra 1857

Un ballo in maschera 1859
Don Carlos 1867
Aida 1871
Requiem 1874
Otello 1887
Falstaff 1893

Veprik, Alexander Moiseievich (b Balta, 23 Jun 1899; d Moscow, 13 Oct 1958), Russian composer. Studied with Reger at Leipzig, with Kalafati and Zhitomirsky at St Petersburg and with Miaskovsky at Moscow. He also had some lessons from Janáček.

Works include five Episodes for chorus and orchestra; *Songs and Dances of the Ghetto* (1927), *A Song of Mourning* (1932), *A Song of Joy* for orchestra (1935); *Songs of Death* for viola and piano; two piano sonatas.

Veracini, Antonio (b Florence, 17 Jan 1659; d Florence 26 Oct 1733), Italian violinist and composer. Was in the service of the Grand Duchess Vittoria of Tuscany at Florence.

Works include four oratorios (music lost); three volumes of sonatas for one and two violins.

Veracini, Francesco Maria (b Florence, 1 Feb 1690; d Florence, 31 Oct 1768), Italian composer and violinist, nephew of Antonio ◊Veracini. Pupil of his uncle and later of Casini and Gasparini in Rome, possibly also of Corelli, he began touring as a virtuoso in 1711, and visited England in 1714. Returning *via* Germany to Italy, he demonstrated his superiority over Tartini (two years his junior) in a contest in Venice in 1716. The following year he entered the service of the Elector of Saxony in Dresden (where he is said to have attempted suicide in 1722), but left for Prague in 1723, then returned to Italy. In 1735 he went again to London, where he produced his first opera, *Adriano in Siria*, followed by several others (1735–44), but as a violinist was overshadowed by Geminiani. His instrumental music was influenced by Corelli and Vivaldi. He probably lived in Pisa *c* 1750–55, then retired to Florence.

Works include operas *Adriano in Siria* (1753), *La clemenza di Tito* (1737), *Partenio* (1738), *Rosalinda* (after Shakespeare's *As You Like It*, 1744), eight oratorios (music lost); cantatas include *Nice e Tirsi* (1741) and *Parla al ritratto della amata*; violin sonatas; concertos; treatise *Il Erionfo della pratica musicale*.

Vera costanza, La, *True Constancy*, opera by Anfossi (libretto by F Puttini), produced Rome, Teatro delle Dame, 2 Jan 1776.

Opera by Haydn (libretto ditto, altered by P Travaglia), produced Eszterháza, 25 Apr 1779. Secretly married to wayward Count Enrico, fisher maid Rosina faces Baroness Irene, who has arrived to arrange a marriage between Rosina and Villoto. Enrico and Rosina are reconciled when he meets their son; the Baroness marries Ernesto.

Vera Sheloga (Rimsky-Korsakov.) ◊Pskovitianka.

Verdi
A biographical note

Towards the end of 1852, Verdi and his librettist Francesco Maria Piave agreed to write an opera for La Fenice, Venice, based on the play *La Dame aux camélias* by Dumas, given in Paris earlier that year. The tale of a 'kept' woman was a sensitive one for the Venetian censors, and they insisted that the proposed title for the opera be changed to *Amore e morte* (Love and Death); they further rejected Verdi's proposal for a modern dress performance, and the action was distanced by being set in the early 18th century. The subject of the opera (now known as *La Traviata*) had a particular significance for Verdi, because he had been living for several years with the singer Giuseppina Strepponi, so he knew at first hand of the social pressures endured in relationships outside marriage. Verdi's commitment to the opera's topic is signified by his completing the score in record time. The premiere was the one disaster of his maturity, perhaps caused in part by a grossly overweight Violetta failing to suggest the consumptive fragility of the heroine. The historical model for Dumas' courtesan was Alphonsine Duplessis; she quickly became a prostitute after arriving in Paris at the age of 12 in 1836. She later gained many rich admirers, for whom she signified her availability by wearing a white camellia for 25 days of the month.

Verdi *The composer Giuseppe Verdi (1813–1901) in a print published in 1886, the year before his Otello appeared. He was one of the greatest opera composers of all time, but his music was once devalued by scholars for following predictable formulae until, ironically, German critics of the 1920s recognized his genius.*

verbunkos an 18th-c. Hungarian recruiting dance for soldiers, who performed it in full uniform with swords and spurs. Like the later Csárdás, to which it is related, it contained a slow (*lassú*) and quick (*friss*) section. Liszt's Hungarian Rhapsodies make use of the dance.

Verdelot, Philippe (b Verdelot, Les Loges, Seine-et-Marne; d before 1552), French composer and singer. He went to Italy, probably at an early age, and was *maestro di cappella* at Florence Cathedral 1523–27.

Works include two Masses, *c* 50 motets; *c* 100 madrigals, three *chansons*.

Verdi, Giuseppe (Fortunino Francesco) (b Roncole near Busseto, 9 or 10 Oct 1813; d Milan, 27 Jan 1901), Italian composer. Son of an innkeeper and grocer. From the age of only three he was taught by the local organist, in whose place he was appointed at nine. At 11 he was sent to Busseto and went to school there, walking home twice a week to carry on the organist's duties. Barezzi, a friend of Verdi's father at Busseto, took him into his house in 1826, and he learnt much from the cathedral organist Provesi. He had an overture for Rossini's *Il barbiere di Siviglia* performed 1828, and the next year he wrote a symphony and deputized for Provesi. In 1831 he was sent to Milan with a scholarship and some financial help from Barezzi, but was rejected by the Conservatory as over entrance age. He studied with Lavigna, the *maestro al cembalo* at La Scala. When Provesi died in 1833 he tried for the post of cathedral organist, and when it was given to an inferior musician the Philharmonic Society made him an allowance. In 1836 he married Barezzi's daughter, Margherita, with whom he had two children, but both mother and children died between 1837 and 1840. Meanwhile he had composed his first opera, *Oberto*, produced at La Scala, 17 Nov 1839.

A second (comic) opera, *Un giorno di regno*, was a failure, having been composed at the time of his bereavement; but *Nabucco*, produced at La Scala in 1842, had a great success; the chorus of the Hebrew slaves was later to provide a rallying cry for the disaffected Italian people in their quest for freedom. In the cast of *Nabucco* was Giuseppina Strepponi, who lived with Verdi from 1848 and in 1859 became his second wife. He now went from strength to strength as an operatic composer, and his fame spread beyond Milan: *Ernani* was produced at Venice in 1844, *I due Foscari* in Rome, 1844, *Alzira* at Naples, 1845 and *Macbeth* at Florence, 1847. Meanwhile *Ernani* had gone to Paris in 1846 and London commissioned *I masnadieri*, produced there 22 Jul 1847. From 1848 most of Verdi's life was spent at his estate of Sant' Agata near Busseto. *Luisa Miller* (1849) and *Stiffelio* (1850), were the last of his 'galley' operas, in which vigorous drama and strongly expressed emotion are accompanied by some basic orchestration. *Rigoletto*, the first of his great masterpieces, was premiered at Venice in 1851; together with *Il trovatore* and *La traviata* (1853) it marks Verdi's emergence as a supreme melodist. At the same time he shows new refinement of characterization and a radically improved awareness of orchestral timbre. The first version of *Simon Boccanegra* was performed 1857 and two years later *Un ballo in maschera* was premiered in Rome – it was one of several operas which ran into trouble with the censors, Verdi's support for Italian independence from Austrian rule was sometimes detected in his work.

An opera on Shakespeare's *King Lear*, at which he worked intermittently, was never completed; otherwise all his plans materialized once they had taken definite shape. France, Russia and Egypt offered him special commissions and his fame spread all over the world. He represented Italy at the International Exhibition in London in 1862 and wrote a *Hymn of the Nations*; in the same year. *La forza del destino* was produced at St Petersburg on 10 Nov. The potentially sensitive subject of *Don Carlos*, dealing with Spanish oppression of the Netherlands, was performed in Paris, 1867; it is Verdi's most sombre, powerful and richly varied opera. *Aida* was given at Cairo in 1871 and the Requiem followed three years later; it was described by Hans von Bülow as an opera in ecclesiastical garb, and is melodically the most consistently inspired of all Verdi's works. In 1868 he had suggested a Requiem for Rossini, to be written by various Italian composers, but the plan came to nothing. He used his contribution in 1873 for a Requiem of his own, commemorating the death of Manzoni. *Otello* was produced at La Scala on 5 Feb 1887 and with its musical and dramatic unity marked Verdi's greatest public success. After a six-year break from composition, *Falstaff* was given at the same theatre on 9 Feb 1893, when Verdi was in his 80th year; the unique subtlety of this work was at first lost on its audiences. Giuseppina died in 1897 and he was himself growing very weak, but still wrote some sacred pieces for chorus and orchestra in 1895–97.

Works include operas *Oberto, Conte di San Bonifacio* (1839), *Un giorno di regno* (1840), *Nabucco* (1842), *I Lombardi alla prima crociata* (1843), *Ernani* (1844), *I due Foscari* (1844), *Giovanna d'Arco* (1845), *Alzira* (1845), *Attila* (1845–6), *Macbeth* (1847), *I masnadieri* (1846–47), *Jérusalem* (French revised version of *I Lombardi*, 1847), *Il corsaro* (1848), *La battaglia di Legnano* (1849), *Luisa Miller* (1849), *Stiffelio* (1850), *Rigoletto* (1851), *Il trovatore* (1853), *La traviata* (1853), *Les Vêpres siciliennes* (1855), *Simon Boccanegra* (1857, revised 1881), *Aroldo* (revision of *Stiffelio*) (1857), *Un ballo in maschera* (1859), *La forza del destino* (1862), *Don Carlos* (1867, revised 1884), *Aida* (1871), *Otello* (1887), *Falstaff* (1893); choral works *Inno delle nazioni*, Requiem (1874), *Pater noster, Ave Maria, Stabat Mater, Lauda alla Vergine Maria*, Te Deum (1896); *Ave Maria* for soprano and strings; 16 songs; one part-song; string quartet (1871).

Verdi, Giuseppina, ◊Strepponi.

Verdonck, Cornelis (b Turnhout, 1563; d Antwerp, 5 Jul 1625), Flemish singer and composer. In the service of Cornelius Pruenen, treasurer and later sheriff of Antwerp until 1598, when on the death of

his patron he served two of his nephews. He was singer at the royal chapel in Madrid 1584–98.

Works include Magnificat, *Ave gratia plena*, four motets; 21 *chansons*, 42 madrigals.

Verein für musikalische Privataufführungen ◊Society for Private Musical Performances.

Veress, Sándor (b Kolozsvár, Transylvania, 1 Feb 1907; d Bern, 6 Mar 1992), Hungarian pianist and composer. Learnt the piano from his mother and later entered the Budapest Conservatory. He also studied with Bartók and Kodály. In 1929 he studied at the Ethnological Museum and began collecting folksongs. He settled at Budapest as teacher of piano and composition and assistant to Bartók at the Scientific Academy of Folk Music.

Works include ballet *The Miraculous Pipe* (1937, produced Rome 1941); two symphonies (1940, 1953) and divertimento for orchestra; violin concerto (1939); *Hommage à Paul Klee* for orchestra (1952); clarinet concerto (19882); flute concerto (1989); Concerto for two trombones (1989). Cantata and folksong arranged for unaccompanied chorus; two string quartets (1931, 1937), string trio, trio for oboe, clarinet and bassoon; violin and piano sonata, cello and piano sonata; two piano sonatas.

Veretti, Antonio (b Verona, 20 Feb 1900; d Rome 13 Jul 1978), Italian composer. Studied at Bologna and took a diploma, also a newspaper prize in 1927 for the opera *Il medico volante* (after Molière). In 1943 he became director of the Conservatorio della Gioventù Italiana in Rome and in 1950 of the Pesaro Conservatory.

Works include opera *Il favorito del re* (1932); ballets *Il galante tiratore* and *Una favola di Andersen* (1934); film music; oratorio *Il figliuol prodigo* (1942), *Sinfonia sacra* for men's chorus and orchestra; *Sinfonia italiana* (1929), *Sinfonia epica* (1938) and *Ouverture della Campanella* for orchestra.

Vergnet, Edmond (b Montpellier, 4 Jul 1850; d Nice, 25 Feb 1904), French tenor. Debut Paris, Opéra, 1874; also sang there 1875–93. In 1881 sang Radames and Faust at CG and appeared in the fp of Massenet's *Hérodiade*, at Brussels. Other roles included Samson, Florestan and Lohengrin.

Verheyen, Pierre Emmanuel (b Ghent, *c* 1750; d Ghent, 11 Jan 1819), Belgian composer and tenor. Pupil of the organist of St Bavon in Ghent, he abandoned his university career to become a singer in the choir there, and in 1779 was appointed principal tenor at Bruges Cathedral, but soon after joined a travelling opera co. Later he returned to Ghent, where he became composer to the archbishop and (from 1790) music director at the church of St Pharaïlde.

Works include operas *Les Chevaliers, ou Le Prix de l'arc* (1779) and *De Jachtparty van Hendrik IV* (1794), *Arlequin magicien* (1795); Masses, psalms, Requiem for Haydn, Te Deum and other church music; cantata *La Bataille de Waterloo* (1816).

Verhulst, Johannes (Josephus Hermanus) (b The Hague, 19 Mar 1816; d The Hague, 17 Jan 1891), Dutch composer and conductor. Studied at The Hague Royal School of Music and after some work as violinist at the Opera at Cologne went to Leipzig in 1838 and became conductor of the Euterpe concerts at Mendelssohn's invitation; was a friend of Schumann and became a member of the *Davidsbund*. In 1842 he returned to The Hague as court music director and also conducted important music societies at Amsterdam and Rotterdam.

Works include Requiem for male voices and other church music; symphonies, overtures, intermezzo *Greetings from Afar* for orchestra; string quartets; songs; part-songs.

verismo Italian = 'realism'; a term used to classify Italian opera of a supposedly 'realistic' order, including the works of Puccini, Mascagni, Leoncavallo, Giordano, Zandonai, etc.

Verklärte Nacht, *Transfigured Night*, string sextet by Schoenberg, op. 4, composed Sept 1899, fp Vienna, 18 Mar 1902. Arranged for string orchestra *c* 1917, revised 1942; given as ballet, *The Pillar of Fire*, at the NY Met. on 8 Apr 1942. It was inspired by a poem in R Dehmel's *Weib und die Welt*.

Vermeer Quartet American string quartet founded 1969 by leader Shmuel Ashkenazi, with staff members of North Illinois University:

Pierre Menard, Nobuko Imai and Marc Johnson; Richard Young violist from 1985. European tours from 1973.

Vermeulen, Matthijs (b Helmond, 8 Feb 1888; d Laren, 26 Jul 1967), Dutch composer and critic. Studied with Diepenbrock and from 1908 to 1921 was a music critic, when he settled in Paris, where he remained until 1946, after which he returned to Amsterdam.

Works include seven symphonies (1914–56); chamber music; songs.

Vermont, Pierre (d Paris, 1532), French 16th-c. singer and composer. He sang in the Papal chapel in Rome from 1528 to 1530, then in the royal chapel in Paris. Wrote motets, *chansons* for several voices, etc. His (?) brother Pernot Vermont (d 1558) also sang, and wrote a few *chansons*.

Vernizzi, Ottavio (b Bologna, 27 Nov 1569; d Bologna, 28 Sept 1649), Italian organist and composer. Organist at San Petronio at Bologna from 1596 until his death.

Works include motets, *Concerti spirituali*; music (all lost) for *intermedii*.

Vernon, Joseph (b c 1739; d London, 19 Mar 1782), English actor, tenor and composer. He was a choirboy at St Paul's Cathedral in London and first appeared on the stage as a boy soprano in 1751, and as a tenor in 1754. Later he became famous chiefly as a singing actor in Shakespeare and in Sheridan's *Duenna* and *School for Scandal*, where Linley's song was written for him.

Works include pantomime *The Witches*; songs for Shakespeare's *Two Gentlemen of Verona* and *Twelfth Night* and for Garrick's *The Irish Widow* and *Linco's Travels* (1767); ballads.

Music and women I cannot but give way to, whatever my business is.

Samuel Pepys, *Diary*, 9 March 1666

Véronique operetta by Messager (libretto by A Vanloo and G Duval), produced Paris, Bouffes-Parisiens, 10 Dec 1898. Hélène, disguised as shopgirl Véronique, meets the man she has arranged to marry, the Viscount Florestan. He falls in love with 'Véronique' and is shocked to meet her as Hélène at the altar, but nevertheless a happy ending.

Verrett, Shirley (b New Orleans, 31 May 1931), American mezzo, later soprano. She studied in LA and at Juilliard, NY. Opera debut NY City Opera, 1958; sang in Europe from 1959, and in 1962 was heard at Spoleto as Carmen. She later sang the role on her Bolshoy, La Scala and NY Met. (1968) debuts. In 1966 she sang Ulrica at CG; she returned for Eboli, Amneris, Orpheus and Selika in *L'Africaine*. In Oct 1973 she sang both Cassandre and Didon in *Les Troyens* at the Met. Other roles include Judith, Tosca, Azucena and Lady Macbeth. Sang Dido in *Les Troyens* at the opening of the Opéra Bastille, Paris, 1990.

Verschworenen, Die, oder Der häusliche Krieg, *The Conspirators, or Domestic Warfare*, operetta by Schubert (libretto by I F Casteli, based on Aristophanes' *Lysistrata*), never performed in Schubert's lifetime; produced Frankfurt, 29 Aug 1861. Crusaders' wives attempt to convert their husbands to peace by withdrawing sexual favours.

verse anthem ◊anthem.

verset, French, *versetto* Italian, a short organ piece, often but not necessarily fugal and frequently incorporating or containing some reference to a given plainsong tune. The name is derived from the former practice in the Roman Catholic service of replacing every other sung verse of psalms, etc. by interludes on the organ to relieve the supposed monotony of plainsong.

Verstovsky, Alexey Nicolaievich (b Seliver-stavo, Government of Tambov, 1 Mar 1799; d Moscow, 17 Nov 1862), Russian composer. Studied civil engineering at St Petersburg, but picked up musical training at the same time, studying theory, singing, violin and piano, the last with Field and Steibelt. As a rich man's son he remained an amateur, but produced his first operetta at the age of 19. In 1824 he was appointed inspector of the Imperial Opera at Moscow, where in 1828 he produced his first opera, which was influenced by Weber's

Freischütz. His *Askold's Tomb* was the first Russian opera staged in the USA (New York, 1869). In 1842 he married the famous actress Nadezhda Repina.

Works include *Pan Twardowski* (1828), *Vadim* (1832), *Askold's Tomb* (1835), *Homesickness* (1839), *The Valley of Tchurov* (1841) and *Gromoboy* (after Zhukovsky); 22 operettas; cantatas, melodramas and dramatic scenas; 29 songs, including Pushkin's *The Black Shawl*.

vertical an adjective applied to the combination of simultaneous sounds, as seen on the page, in contrast to the horizontal appearance of notes in succession.

Vesalii Icones, *Images of Vesalius*, theatre piece by Maxwell Davies for dancer, solo cello and instrumental ensemble; composed 1969, fp London, 9 Dec 1969. The 14 movements are based on anatomical drawings in a treatise (1543) by the physician Andreas Vesalius depicting Christ's Passion and Resurrection.

Vespers, from Latin *vespera*, 'evening', the service preceding Compline in the Office of the Roman Church. It includes psalms with their antiphons, a hymn and the Magnificat. A number of composers have made elaborate settings for voices and instruments of all or part of the texts, notably Monteverdi and Mozart.

Vespri siciliani, I (Verdi) ◊Vêpres siciliennes.

Vesque von Püttlingen, Johann (pseudonym J Hoven) (b Opole, Poland, 23 Jul 1803; d Vienna, 30 Oct 1883), Austrian composer of Belgian descent. He was born at the residence of Prince Alexander Lubomirsky. The family moved to Vienna in 1815 and he studied music there with Leidesdorf, Moscheles and Voříšek. In 1822 he entered Vienna University and in 1827 the civil service. In 1829 he exercised himself in opera by setting the libretto of Rossini's *Donna del lago* (based on Scott) and in 1833 he studied counterpoint with Sechter.

Works include opera *Turandot* (after Gozzi, 1838), *Jeanne d'Arc* (1840), *Liebeszauber* (after Kleist's *Käthchen von Heilbronn*, 1845), *Ein Abenteuer Carl des Zweiten* (1850), *Der lustige Rath* (1852) and two unfinished; two Masses.

Vestale, La opera by Mercadante (libretto, in Italian, by S Cammarano), produced Naples, Teatro San Carlo, 10 Mar 1840.

Opera by Spontini (libretto, in French, by V J E de Jouy, ? based on Winckelmann's *Monumenti antichi inediti*), produced Paris, Opéra, 16 Jan 1807. Holy fire of vestal virgins becomes extinguished as Julia attempts to elope with former betrothed Lycinius; as she is led to execution lightning rekindles the flame and she is spared.

Vestris (born *Bartolozzi*), Lucia Elizabeth (or Eliza Lucy) (b London, 3 Jan or 2 Mar 1797; d London, 8 Aug 1856), English actress and contralto of Italian descent, daughter of Gaetano Bartolozzi and granddaughter of the engraver Francesco Bartolozzi. Studied singing with Domenico Corri, married the dancer Auguste-Armande Vestris (1788–1825) in 1813 and in 1815 made her debut in London; sang in the local fps of Rossini's *La gazza ladra*, *La donna del lago*, *Mathilde di Shabran*, *Zelmira* and *Semiramide*. She was Fatima in the fp of Weber's *Oberon* in 1826.

Viadana (real name *Grossi da Viadana*), Lodovico (b Viadana, near Parma, c 1560; d Gualtieri, near Parma, 2 May 1627), Italian composer. Pupil of Porta and before 1590 appointed *maestro di cappella* at Mantua Cathedral. In 1596 he joined the Franciscan order, in 1609 became *maestro di cappella* at Concordia, in 1612 at Fano Cathedral; in 1615 went to live at Piacenza, whence he retired to the Franciscan monastery at Gualtieri.

Works include Masses, psalms and other church music; 100 *Concerti ecclesiastici* for one–four voices with organ continuo; madrigals, canzonets.

Viaggio a Reims, Il, ossia L'albergo del giglio d'oro, *The Journey to Rheims, or the Golden Lily Inn*, opera by Rossini (libretto by G L Balochi), produced Paris, Théâtre-Italien, 19 Jun 1825. The opera failed but the music was largely re-used in *Le Comte Ory* (1828). Assorted national types including Lord Sidney, Don Profondo and Belfiore are delayed at the inn of Madame Cortese on way to coronation at Rheims.

Vianna da Motta, José (b São Tomé, 22 Apr 1868; d Lisbon, 31 May 1948), Portuguese pianist and composer. Studied at the Lisbon Conservatory and with the Scharwenka brothers in Berlin, later with Liszt at Weimar and Bülow at Frankfurt. He began to tour Europe and South America in 1902, was appointed Prussian court pianist and taught at Geneva 1915–17. He was director of the Lisbon Conservatory 1919–38.

Works include *Lusiads* (Camões) for chorus and orchestra; symphonies; string quartet; *Portuguese Scenes*, *Portuguese Rhapsodies*, etc. for piano: songs.

Viardot-García, (Michelle Ferdinande) Pauline (b Paris, 18 Jul 1821; d Paris, 17 or 18 May 1910), French mezzo and composer of Spanish descent, daughter of Manuel García and sister of Maria Malibran. Pupil of her father, also studied piano. Made her first appearance as a singer at Brussels in 1837 and first visited London in 1839, as Rossini's Desdemona; in Paris she sang Fides, and Orpheus in an arrangement of Gluck's opera by Berlioz. In 1840 she married the opera manager and critic Louis Viardot (1800–83). After retiring from stage, sang in the fps of Massenet's *Marie-Magdeleine* and Brahms's *Alto Rhapsody* (1870). She wrote operettas *Le Dernier Sorcier*, *L'Ogre* and *Trop de femmes*, to libretti by Turgenev; also wrote songs.

vibraphone an electrophonic instrument, the resonators of which emit vibrato by means of an electric motor connected to a turning fan-like rod that runs the length of the instrument.

Stop shaking all those notes and trembling them, because you're gonna be shaking enough when you get old.

Miles Davis on vibrato, in *Miles*, 1989

---

vibrato Italian = 'vibrating, oscillating'; a special musical effect produced on a single note by means of fluctuation of pitch (or occasionally intensity). Until the 19th c. it was often regarded as an expressive ornament. On the clavichord a vibrato effect is possible by shaking the finger on the key without releasing it (*Bebung*). On string instruments, a warmer and more vibrant tone is produced by shaking the fingers of the left hand on the finger-board while pressing down the string. On the organ a similar effect is made possible by the use of the tremulant. Vibrato on wind instruments is controlled by the breath.

Vicentino, Nicola (b Vicenza, 1511; d Milan, *c* 1576), Italian composer and theorist. Pupil of Willaert at Venice. He entered the service of Ippolito d'Este, cardinal of Ferrara, with whom he went to live in Rome. He sought to revive the Greek modes in his madrigals, invented an instrument he called the archicembalo, which could play various microtones. His treatise *L'antica musica ridotta alla moderna prattica* (1555) involved him in a controversy with Lusitano in which he was defeated. He returned to Ferrara with his patron and became his *maestro di cappella*. He wrote madrigals and motets.

Vick, Graham (b Liverpool, 30 Dec 1953), English stage director. Studied at RNCM and was director of productions, Scottish Opera, 1984–87; City of Birmingham Touring Opera from 1987, notably with the *Ring* Saga (1990) and *Les Boréades* (1993). ENO from 1984, *Madama Butterfly*, *Eugene Onegin* and the fp of Oliver's *Timon of Athens*. CG from 1989: *Un rè in Ascolto*, *Mitridate* and *Die Meistersinger*. *War and Peace* for the Kirov Opera (1991) and *The Queen of Spades* at Glyndebourne, 1992 (director of productions 1994). NY Met debut 1994, *Lady Macbeth of the Mtsensk District*; *King Arthur* at the Paris Châtelet and CG, 1995. His work is noted for its artistic fidelity and tendency toward innovation, achieved with an economy of means.

Vickers, Jon(athan Stewart) (b Prince Albert, Saskatchewan, 29 Oct 1926), Canadian tenor. Studied at the Toronto Conservatory and made his debut at the Stratford Festival, 1956, as Don José. First appeared at CG, 1957, as Riccardo; returned as Aeneas (Berlioz), Radames, Don Carlos, Samson (Saint-Saëns and Handel), Florestan

and Tristan. Bayreuth, 1958 and 1964 (Siegmund and Parsifal). NY Met. 1960, as Canio; later Grimes. He was notable for his Wagner, Verdi and Beethoven, all performed with strong dramatic conviction.

Victoria, Tomás Luis de (b Avila, 1548; d Madrid, 20 Aug 1611), Spanish composer. He knew Palestrina and possibly studied with him. He may have been in touch with St Teresa, also a native of Avila. In 1565 he received a grant from Philip II and went to Rome, where he became a priest and singer at the German College. He was choirmaster there 1573–*c* 1577. From 1578 to 1585 he was a chaplain at San Girolamo della Carità. From 1587 to 1603 he was chaplain to the dowager empress María, Philip II's sister, at the convent of the Descalzas Reales in Madrid, where the empress lived and her daughter, the Infanta Margaret, became a nun. On the death of the empress in 1603 he wrote an *Officium defunctorum* (Requiem Mass) for six voices. He was one of the greatest composers of his time, noted for his expressive settings of the mass (*Ave regina caelorum*, etc.) and other sacred Latin texts.

Works include 20 Masses (including two Requiems), 18 Magnificats, one Nunc dimittis, nine Lamentations, 25 responsories, 13 antiphons, eight polychoral psalms, 52 motets, 36 hymns, one Litany, two Passions, three Sequences.

Victorinus, Georg, German 16th–17th-c. monk and composer. He became music prefect at the Jesuit monastery of St Michael, where a sacred play with music by him was performed in 1597. Other works include three Magnificats, three Litanies, *c* 20 sacred pieces.

Victory opera by R R Bennett (libretto by B Cross, after Conrad), produced CG, 13 Apr 1970. Reclusive Heyst is tempted into a fuller life by chorus girl Lena.

Vida breve, La, *Life is Short*, opera by Falla (libretto in Spanish, by C F Shaw), produced Nice, in French, translated by P Milliet, 1 Apr 1913. Gypsy Salud hopes to marry Paco but is jilted for Carmela. Salud confronts Paco at the wedding and falls dead.

Vidal, Peire (b fl. *c* 1175; d *c* 1210), French troubadour, *c* 50 of whose poems are preserved, 12 with music.

vielle organisée, French = 'organed [not 'organized'] hurdy-gurdy'; Italian *lira organizata*, a hurdy-gurdy (*vielle*) into which are incorporated one or two sets (stops) or organ pipes. These can be made to sound separately or together, or shut off at will. Haydn wrote five concertos for two of these instruments.

Vienna Philharmonic Orchestra Austrian orchestra founded 1842 with Otto Nicolai as conductor. Richter was principal conductor 1875–98; succeeded by Mahler (1898–1901), Weingartner (1907–

A Selection of

Victoria

Missa surge propera
Missa O magnum mysterium
Missa Ave maris stella

Missa O quam gloriosum
Lamentations of Jeremiah 1585
Passions (St John and St Matthew).......... 1585
Officium defunctorum.................. 1605
Responsories for Tenebrae

27), Furtwängler (1927–28, 1933–54). Böhm and Karajan were regular post-war conductors; Abbado from 1971. The orchestra is unsurpassed in a limited and conservative repertory. The orchestra is also conservative in its employment practices: with the exception of the harpist, only men are hired. Also plays at Vienna Staatsoper.

Vienna State Opera Wiener Staatsoper. Operas were staged at the Viennese court from the 1630s and for many years opera continued as a court entertainment. The Burgtheater was opened in 1748 and ten operas by Gluck, including *Orpheus* (1762), were premiered there. Later in the century Mozart's *Figaro*, *Così fan tutte* and *Don Giovanni* were staged there, although operas by Salieri and Cimarosa were more popular successes.

A new house, the Oper am Ring, was opened in 1869. Mahler was director at this Court Opera (Hofoper) 1897–1907, achieving new standards in dramatic and musical integration. Later directors included Felix Weingartner (1907–11), Franz Schalk (1919–24) and Clemens Krauss (1929–34). In 1918 the Court Opera was re-named the State Opera (Staatsoper) and in 1919 Richard Strauss became joint director; among singers who took part in the fps of *Ariadne auf Naxos* (revised version, 1916) and *Die Frau ohne Schatten* (1919) were Maria Jeritza, Selma Kurz, Lotte Lehmann, Lucy Weidt, Richard Mayr and Karl Oestvig.

The opera house was heavily damaged by bombs in 1945 but, after rebuilding according to the original plans, was re-opened in 1955. The opera company performed at the Theater an der Wien and the Volksoper in the immediate post-war years; singers such as Schwarzkopf, Seefried, Jurinac, Gueden, Dermota, Hotter and Schoeffler visited Covent Garden with the company in 1947. Post-war directors have included Karl Böhm (1955–56), Herbert von Karajan (1957–64), Lorin Maazel (1982–84) and Claudio Abbado (1986–91). Few major premieres have been given at the Staatsoper, although Schnittke's *Gesualdo* was staged 1995.

Vie parisienne, La, *Life in Paris*, operetta by Offenbach (libretto by H Meilhac and L Halévy), produced Paris, Théâtre du Palais-Royal, 31 Oct 1866. Bobinet and Gardefeu trick Swedish aristocrats on tour in Paris, posing as guests in the Grand Hôtel. Gardefeu pursues the Baroness while her husband is too preoccupied with other women to notice.

Vierdanck, Johann (b c 1605; d Stralsund, Mar 1646), German organist and composer. Learnt music as a choirboy in the court chapel at Dresden, where he subsequently served as an instrumentalist. From 1635 until his death he was organist at St Mary's Church, Stralsund.

Works include sacred concertos for two–nine voices; dances for two violins, viol and continuo, capriccios, canzonets and sonatas for two–five instruments with and without continuo.

Vier ernste Gesänge, *Four Serious Songs*, settings by Brahms for baritone and piano of words from the Bible, op. 121, composed May 1896. The corresponding passages in English are 'One thing befalleth', 'So I returned', 'O death, how bitter is thy sting', 'Though I speak with the tongues of men and of angels'.

Vierjährige Posten, Der, *The Four Years' Sentry*, comic opera by Schubert (libretto by T Körner), composed 1815, but never performed in Schubert's lifetime. Produced Dresden, Opera, 23 Sept 1896. Abandoned French soldier is in trouble for desertion with returning army, after four-year dalliance with village girl.

Vier letzte Lieder (R Strauss) ◊Four Last Songs.

Vierling, Georg (b Frankenthal, Bavaria, 5 Sept 1820; d Wiesbaden, 1 May 1901), German organist and conductor. Studied under his father, Jacob Vierling (1796–1867), a schoolmaster and organist, later as Darmstadt and Berlin. In 1847 he became organist and choral conductor at Frankfurt an der Oder. Later he went to Mainz for a short time and then settled in Berlin, where he became royal music director in 1859 and professor of the Academy in 1882.

Works include cantatas for chorus and orchestra *Hero and Leander*, *The Rape of the Sabines*, *Alaric's Death* and *Constantine*; symphonies, overtures to Shakespeare's *Tempest*, Schiller's *Maria Stuart* and others; piano trio; *O Roma nobilis* for unaccompanied chorus; part-songs; piano pieces; songs.

Vierling, Johann Gottfried (b Metzels, near Meiningen, 25 Jan 1750; d Schmalkalden, 22 Nov 1813), German organist and composer. Studied at Schmalkalden with the organist J N Tischer (whom he succeeded as church organist there in 1773). In 1770 he studied with Kirnberger in Berlin. He wrote treatises on thorough-bass and on preluding to hymns.

Works include *Singspiel, Empfindung und Empfindelei*; *c* 160 cantatas, other church music; many chorales and chorale preludes for organ; two symphonies; piano quartet; eight piano sonatas.

Vierne, Louis (b Poitiers, 8 Oct 1870; d Paris, 2 Jun 1937), French organist and composer. Pupil of Franck and Widor at the Paris Conservatory. Although blind, he became assistant organist to Widor at the church of Saint-Sulpice and later organist at Notre-Dame, where he died at the console.

Works include *Messe solennelle* for chorus and two organs; symphonies; string quartets; sonatas for violin and piano and cello and piano; six symphonies (1899–1930) 24 *Pièces en style libre*, 24 *Pièces de fantaisie* and other works for organ.

Vieuxtemps, Henry (b Verviers, 17 Feb 1820; d Mustapha, Algeria, 6 Jun 1881), Belgian violinist and composer. Learnt the violin at home and at the age of six was able to play a concerto by Rode. At seven he was taken on tour by his father and heard by Bériot, who offered to teach him at Brussels. In 1828 his master took him to Paris and produced him there. In 1833 he went on tour in Germany and Austria, remaining in Vienna to study counterpoint with Sechter. In 1834 he first visited London, where he met Paganini, and the following year he studied composition with Reicha in Paris. He afterwards travelled long and extensively in Europe and in 1844 went to the USA. He was admired for his virtuosity in his own music, but also played the Beethoven concerto to acclaim. In 1845 he married the Viennese pianist Josephine Eder. In 1846–52 he was violin professor at the St Petersburg Conservatory. In 1871–73 he taught at the Brussels Conservatory; he suffered a stroke in 1873, and finally resigned in 1879.

Works include seven violin concertos, *Fantaisie-Caprice* and *Ballade et Polonaise*, etc. for violin and orchestra; violin and piano sonata; cadenzas for Beethoven's violin concerto.

Vignoles, Roger (b Cheltenham, 12 Jul 1945), English pianist and conductor. Studied at Cambridge and made London debut 1967. Has accompanied such singers as Söderström, Fassbaender, Thomas Allen and Sylvia McNair in recitals throughout Europe and the USA; Salzburg debut 1984, with Heinrich Schiff. Professor at the RCM 1974–81. Conducted Handel's *Agrippina* at the 1992 Buxton Festival.

If I tell the Berliners to step forward, they do it. If I tell the Viennese to step forward, they do it. But then they ask why.

Herbert von Karajan on the Berlin and Vienna Philharmonic Orchestras, *Sunday Times*, 1983

vihuela a Spanish plucked instrument, approximately guitar-shaped but strung like a lute with six paired courses and normally ten frets. Its repertory appears mainly in seven printed anthologies of the 16th c., starting with Luis Milan's *El maestro* (1536), Luis de Narváez's *Delphin de música* (1538) and Alonso Mudarra's *Tres libros* (1546). Some pieces in these vols. appear also in French lute collections, and there is little technical difference between lute and vihuela music except that the vihuela, with its small body and long neck, was able to be played in higher positions than the lute, as exploited particularly in the collections of Valderrábano (1547) and Fuenllana (1554). The name, used for any stringed instrument with a flat back, appears in the 13th c., and as early as the 14th c. there is a distinction between the *vihuela de arco* (bowed vihuela) and the *vihuela de peñola* (plectrum vihuela) which, with the development of finger-plucking, became the *vihuela de mano*. It seems likely that the *vihuela de arco* evolved into the viol at the end of the 15th c.

Vila (or Alberch Vila, Pere), Pedro Alberto (b Vich, near Barcelona,

1517; d Barcelona, 16 Nov 1582), Spanish organist and composer, organist of Barcelona Cathedral from 1538.

Works include madrigals and organ music.

Vilar, José Teodor (b Barcelona, 10 Aug 1836; d Barcelona, 21 Oct 1905), Spanish composer and conductor. Studied with the cathedral organist Ramón Vilanova (1801–70) at Barcelona and in 1859 went to Paris to study piano with Herz and composition with Bazin and Halévy. Returning home in 1863, he became conductor at one of the minor theatres and later at the principal theatre. He also taught.

Works include zarzuelas La romería de Recaseéns (1867), L'ultim rey de Magnolia (1868), Los pescadores de San Pol (1869), Una prometensa (1870), La rambla de las flores (1870), Pot més que pinta (1870), La lluna en un cove, L'esca del pecat (1871), La torre del amore (1871).

Vilback, (Alphonse Charles) Renaud de (b Montpellier, 3 Jun 1829; d Brussels, 19 Mar 1884), French organist, pianist and composer. Studied at the Paris Conservatory, Halévy being among his masters, and gained the Prix de Rome in 1844. He was organist of Ste Eugène, Paris, from 1856 to 1871. After an early success he was unfortunate, made a precarious living by arranging and other editorial hack-work for unscrupulous publishers, became blind and died in poverty.

Works include operas Au Clair de la lune (1857) and Don Almanzor (1858); Messe solennelle; cantata Le Renégat de Tanger (1842); Pompadour Gavotte, Chant cypriote, Marche serbe for orchestra; piano pieces.

Village Romeo and Juliet an opera in prologue and three acts by Delius (libretto by composer, after Keller's Leute von Seldwyla), produced Berlin, Komische Oper, 21 Feb 1907. Sali and Vreli are encouraged by the Dark Fiddler to leave their warring fathers and wander through Paradise Garden to liebestod on river.

A truly creative musician is capable of producing, from his own imagination, melodies that are more authentic than folk-lore itself.

Heitor Villa-Lobos, quoted in Machlis, *Introduction to Contemporary Music*, 1963

Villa-Lobos, Heitor (b Rio de Janeiro, 5 Mar 1887; d Rio de Janeiro, 17 Nov 1959), Brazilian composer. He studied the cello at first, but became a pianist and for some time toured as a concert artist. In 1912 he began to explore his country's folk music and in 1915 gave the first concert devoted to his own works at Rio de Janeiro. A government grant enabled him to live in Paris for a few years from 1923, but on his return he did much useful work as conductor and music educationist, being appointed director of music education for the schools in the capital in 1930. In 1929 he pub. a book on Brazilian folk music, Alma de Brasil. He is best known for the colourful orchestral series of nine works after Bach, Bachianas brasileiras.

Works include operas Izath (1914, concert performance 1940), Yerma (1956, produced 1971); musical comedy Magdalena (1948); ballet Uirapuru; oratorio Vidapura; 14 works entitled Chôros cast in a new form and consisting of four for orchestra, one for piano and orchestra, one for two pianos and orchestra, two for chorus and orchestra and six for various combinations and solo instruments (1920–28); orchestral works including symphonic poem Amazonas, Bachianas Brasileiras (nine suites in the spirit of Bach, 1930–44), 12 symphonies (1916–57); five piano concertos, two cello concertos, harp concerto; nonet for wind, harp, percussion and chorus, quintet for wind instruments (1923); 17 string quartets (1915–58), three piano trios (1911–18); four sonata-fantasies for violin and piano (1912–23); a very large number of piano works; songs.

villancico, Spanish, a type of verse with a refrain and a complex rhyme-scheme; also the music to which such poems were set, at first tunes without harmony, later pieces similar to madrigals; sometimes a composition for solo voices, strings and organ to sacred words, especially connected with the Nativity.

villanella Italian = lit. 'country girl'; an Italian part-song of the middle

16th to the earlier 17th c., set to rustic words and light in character.

Villanella rapita, La, *The Ravished Country Girl*, opera by Bianchi (libretto by G Bertati, based on J M Favart's Le Caprice amoureux), produced Venice, Teatro San Moisè, autumn 1783. Mozart wrote an additional quartet and a trio for the Vienna performance, 25 Nov 1785. Mandina is abducted by the Count before her wedding to Pippo. Her father Biaggio and her betrothed rescue her after questioning her allegiance, and welcome her back to the village.

villanelle, French, in French music a villanelle is not the equivalent of the Italian villanella and the Spanish villancico, but a vocal setting of a poem in villanelle form, which consists of stanzas of three lines, the first and third lines of the opening stanza being repeated alternately as the third line of the succeeding stanzas. Best known example is first song of Berlioz' cycle Les Nuits d'été.

Villi, Le, *The Witches*, opera by Puccini (libretto by F Fontana), produced Milan, Teatro dal Verme, 31 May 1884. Roberto abandons his betrothed, Anna, who dies of grief. When he later returns Anna's ghost haunts him with other ghosts of jilted girls, dancing with him until he dies.

Vinaccesi, Benedetto (b Brescia, ? 1670; d Venice, ? 1719), Italian composer. *Maestro di cappella* to Prince Ferdinand Gonzaga di Castiglione in 1687, he was appointed second organist at St Mark's, Venice, 1704.

Works include two operas (lost); four oratorios (only Susanna (1694) extant); motets and other church music; six Suonate da camera and 12 Sonate da chiesa for two violins and continuo.

Vinay, Ramón (b Chillán, 31 Aug 1912; d Puebla, Mexico, 4 Jan 1996), Chilean baritone, later tenor and baritone. Debut 1931, Mexico City, as Donizetti's Alfonso. Baritone roles until 1943, then sang Don José in Mexico. He was best known as Otello and recorded the role under Toscanini; also sang part at La Scala, CG and Salzburg. NY Met. 1946–61; Bayreuth 1952–57 as Tristan, Tannhäuser, Siegmund and Parsifal; sang Telramund there in 1962. Other baritone roles were Iago, Scarpia and Falstaff.

Vincent, John (b Birmingham, AL, 17 May 1902; d Santa Monica, CA, 21 Jan 1977), American composer and teacher. Studied composition with Chadwick at the New England Conservatory, with Piston at Harvard and Boulanger in Paris. Professor of composition at UCLA, 1946–69 (in succession to Schoenberg). Evolved basically tonal style which he termed paratonality. Works include opera Primeval Voice (Vienna, 1973), ballet Three Jacks (1941); Nude Descending a Staircase, for xylophone and strings (1972); Symphony in D (1954); Symphonic Poem after Descartes (1958); La Jolla Concerto (1959); Consort for piano and strings (1960); Benjamin Franklin Suite for orchestra and glass harmonica (1963); Stabat Mater (1970); Mary at Cavalry for soprano, chorus and organ (1976); two string quartets (1936, 1967); songs and choruses.

Vincent, Thomas (b London, c 1720; d London, ? 10 May 1783), English oboist and composer. Pupil of Sammartini. He entered the king's band as oboist in 1735.

Works include solos for oboe, flute or violin with harpsichord continuo; harpsichord lessons.

Vincentius, Caspar (b St Omer, c 1580; d Würzburg, 1624), Flemish composer and organist. He was a choirboy at the Imperial chapel in Vienna 1595–97, and town organist at Speyer c 1602–04, where he met Schadaeus. He later held appointments at Worms and, from 1618 until his death, Würzburg. He provided a bassus generalis to the three vols of Schadaeus's Promptuarium musicum, and later added a fourth volume of his own (1617). He also wrote a continuo part for Lassus' Magnum opus musicum.

Vinci, Leonardo (b Strongoli, Calabria, c 1690; d Naples, 27 or 28 May 1730), Italian composer. Pupil of Greco at the Conservatorio dei Poveri di Gesù Cristo in Naples, established himself first as a composer of Neapolitan dialect commedie musicali (from 1719) and produced his first opera seria in 1722. Appointed as an acting maestro di cappella at court in 1725, he was from 1728 also maestro at his old Conservatory, where Pergolesi was among his pupils.

Works include commedie musicali: Lo cecato fauzo (1719, lost),

Le zite 'n galera (1722); *opere serie: Silla dittatore* (1723), *L'Astianatte* (1725), *Siroe* (1726), *La caduta dei Decemviri* (1727), *Artaserse* (1730) and 19 others; six cantatas; chamber music.

Vinci, Leonardo da (b Vinci near Empoli, 1452; d Amboise, near Paris, 2 May 1519), Italian painter, scientist, inventor and musician. In this last capacity he excelled as a player of the *lira da braccio*. He investigated acoustics and designed many improved and new instruments.

Vinci, Pietro (b Nicosia, Sicily, *c* 1535; d Nicosia or Piazza Armerina, *c* 1584), Italian composer. He was *maestro di cappella* at the Basilica of Santa Maria Maggiore at Bergamo in 1568–80 and in 1581 took on a similar post at his birthplace.

Works include Masses, motets; madrigals; ricercari.

Viñes, Ricardo (b Lérida, 5 Feb 1875; d Barcelona, 29 Apr 1943), Spanish pianist. Studied and lived in Paris, where he did much useful work for modern French and Spanish music. He gave early performances of music by Falla, Ravel and Debussy, including the fps of *Miroirs*, *Gaspard de la Nuit* and *Images I*.

Vingt-quatre Violons du Roy, *The King's 24 Violins*, the French court string band of the 17th c., used for ballets, court balls, dinners, etc., and included all the instruments of the violin family. A similar string orchestra was founded, on the French model, by Charles II in London after his restoration in 1660.

Vingt regards sur l'Enfant Jésus work for piano in 20 sections by Messiaen; composed 1944, fp Paris, 26 Mar 1945, by Yvonne Loriod.

Vinzing, Ute (b Wuppertal, 9 Sept 1936), German soprano. Studied with Martha Mödl; debut Lübeck 1967, as Marenka. Sang at Wuppertal 1971–76 and throughout Europe as Kundry, Isolde and Leonora. Seattle, 1975–84, as Brünnhilde; NY Met., debut 1984, Elektra. Sang the Dyer's Wife in Sawallisch's recording of *Die Frau ohne Schatten*.

We call 'viols' those instruments with which gentlemen, merchants, and other virtuous people pass their time. The other kind is called the 'violin', which is commonly used for dancing.

Philibert Jambe-de-Fer in 1556, quoted in Mellers, *François Couperin*, 1950

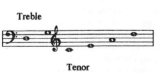

viol the generic name of a family of bowed string instruments. The Italian name was *viola da gamba*, 'leg viol'. Viols first appeared in the 15th c. and were in vogue until near the end of the 17th, disappearing completely, apart from the bass viol, in the 18th. The main representatives were the treble, the tenor and the bass, all of which were tuned on the same plan. The double bass of the family was called *violone*. ◊treble viol, ◊viola da gamba and ◊violone.

Treble

Tenor   or

Bass

The open strings of the treble, tenor, and bass viols.

Viola unfinished opera by Smetana (libretto by E Krasnohorská, on Shakespeare's *Twelfth Night*), begun 1883.

viola the tenor instrument of the violin family. It has four strings, and is the regular middle part in the string section of the orchestra and in the string quartet, etc, and normally reads from an alto clef.

The open strings of the viola.

Viola, Alfonso dalla (b Ferrara, *c* 1508; d Ferrara, *c* 1573), Italian composer and instrumentalist. *Maestro di cappella* at Ferrara Cathedral and in charge of the *musica da camera segreta* at the court of Ercole d'Este (II), Duke of Ferrara, where he wrote madrigals and music (now lost) for plays.

viola alta Italian = 'high viola'; an exceptionally large viola designed by Hermann Ritter and made by Hörlein of Würzburg in the 1870s for use in the orchestra at the Wagner festivals at Bayreuth. In 1898 a fifth string was added, tuned to the E of the highest violin string.

viola bastarda Italian = lit. 'bastard viol'; the Italian name for the lyra viol, called *bastarda* because it was midway in size between the tenor viol and the bass viol.

viola da braccio Italian = 'arm viol'; in the 16th and early 17th c. the generic name for members of the violin family, since the smaller instruments were played on the arm and not, as was the case with the *viola da gamba* family, on or between the legs. Since the cello was the bass of the family it was known, illogically, as *bassa viola da braccio*. The treble instrument came to be known exclusively by the diminutive *violino*, and *viola da braccio* was reserved for the alto or tenor, shortened to *viola* in Italy and corrupted into *Bratsche* in Germany.

viola da gamba Italian = 'leg viol'; the generic name for the members of the viol family, all of which, small or large, are played on or between the legs. Unlike the violin family they have flat backs, sloping shoulders, six strings and frets. The smaller instruments of the family gradually went out of use in the course of the 17th c., but the bass was retained as a solo instrument and for continuo playing. Hence in the 18th c. *viola da gamba* normally means the bass viol. Examples of its use are Bach's three sonatas with harpsichord and the obbligatos in the *St Matthew Passion*. All the members of the family have been successfully revived in modern times. For their tuning ◊viol.

viola d'amore Italian = lit. 'love viol'; (1) in the 17th c. a violin with wire strings. (2) A bowed string instrument of the viol type with seven strings and from seven to 14 sympathetic strings not touched by the bow but vibrating with those actually played. There was no standard tuning.

viola da spalla Italian = 'shoulder viola'; a portable cello used mainly by wandering musicians in the 17th and 18th c., held by a shoulder strap. Also an alternative name for the cello.

viola di bordone Italian = 'drone viol'; an alternative name for the ◊baryton.

viola pomposa a special type of bowed string instrument of the violin

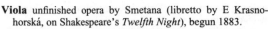

family, very rarely used. It seems to have had five strings, the lower four tuned as on the viola and the fifth tuned to the E of the violin.

violet the English name sometimes given to the viola d'amore.

violetta marina Italian = lit. 'little marine viol'; a special type of viol, allied to the ◊viola d'amore, like which it has sympathetic strings.

violetta piccola Italian = 'small little viol'; an early name for the treble viol and the violin.

violin the principal modern bowed string instrument, to whose family belong also the viola and violoncello. The violin has four strings. It began to displace the viol in the 17th c. and completely superseded it in the 18th. ◊basse-contre, ◊cellone, ◊dessus, ◊double bass, ◊fiddle, ◊hardanger fiddle, ◊haute-contre, ◊kit, ◊quinton, ◊taille, ◊tenor violin, ◊viola, ◊viola alta, ◊viola da braccio, ◊viola da spalla, ◊viola pomposa, ◊violino piccolo, ◊violon d'amour, ◊violoncello, ◊violoncello piccolo, ◊violotta.

The open strings of the violin.

violino piccolo Italian = 'little violin'; a small string instrument of the violin family with four strings. It stands a fourth or a minor third above the violin in pitch.

The open strings of the violino piccolo.

Violins of St Jacques, The opera by Williamson (libretto by W Chappell), produced London, SW, 29 Nov 1966.

violoncello the bass instrument of the violin family. It has four strings. Its upward range is considerable. In the 17th and 18th c. it was also made with five strings, i.e. with an E string a fifth above the A.

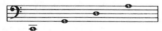

The open strings of the violoncello.

violoncello piccolo a small cello on which the playing of high passage was easier than on the normal cello. A familiar example of its use is the obbligato in Bach's aria 'Mein gläubiges Herze/My heart ever faithful' in the cantata no. 68, *Also hat Gott die Welt geliebt/God so loved the world.*

violon d'amour French = lit. 'love violin'; the member of the modern string family corresponding to the viola d'amore of the viol family,

The open strings of the violon d'amour.

used in the 18th c., but now obsolete. It had five strings and six sympathetic strings, not touched by the bow but vibrating with those actually played.

violone the double bass of the viol family, similar to the bass viol but larger, with six strings similarly tuned an octave lower. The name was also applied to the double bass of the violin family.

violotta a modern string instrument of the violin family, invented by Alfred Stelzner (d 1906) of Dresden. It has four strings tuned so as to stand in pitch between the viola and the cello.

The open strings of the violotta.

violone *According to modern terminology, the name refers specifically to the double bass viol, forerunner of the modern double bass. Originally the term referred to any member of the viol or even violin family.*

Viotti, Giovanni Battista (b Fontanetto da Po, Piedmont, 12 May 1755; d London, 3 Mar 1824), Italian violinist and composer. Pupil of Pugnani, joined the court orchestra at Turin in 1775, but obtained leave of absence in 1780 to go on tour with Pugnani. (A supposed meeting with Voltaire, who died in 1778, is apparently apocryphal.) Visited Switzerland, Dresden, Berlin, Warsaw, St Petersburg and in 1782 arrived in Paris, where he stayed ten years. He played at the Concert spirituel, was solo violinist to Marie Antoinette 1784–86, conducted some concerts of the Loge Olympique (for which Haydn wrote his 'Paris' symphonies), and from 1788 was involved in the foundation of a new opera co. at the Théâtre de Monsieur. In 1792 he went to London, where he played in Salomon's concerts and became acting manager and leader of the orchestra at the King's Theatre opera, but was forced to leave England for political reasons in 1798, and lived near Hamburg, writing an autobiographical sketch. Returning to London in 1801, he withdrew almost completely from music and entered the wine trade, but twice visited Paris (1802 and 1814) and in 1819 became director of the Opera there, finally returning to London in 1823.

Works include 29 violin concertos (1782–*c* 1805); two *Symphonies concertantes* for two violins and orchestra; 15 string quartets (*c* 1783–1817); 21 string trios for two violins and cello; violin duos, sonatas etc.; six piano sonatas.

Viotti, Marcello (b Lausanne, 29 Jun 1954), Swiss conductor. Studied in Geneva and has conducted opera at Turin from 1985; director of Lucerne Opera (1987–92), music director at Bremen Opera. Guest in

Frankfurt (*Andrea Chénier*, 1989), Lucerne (*Zauberflöte* and *Sonnambula*) and with the Suisse Romande Orchestra. Conductor of the Saarland Radio SO, 1991.

Virdung, Sebastian (b Amberg, Upper Palatinate, *c* 1465; d *c* 1511), German cleric and writer on music. Studied at Heidelberg University. He sang and then was *Kapellmeister* at the Palatine court chapel in Heidelberg, and in 1507 became succentor at Konstanz Cathedral. In 1511 he pub. at Basel his book on musical instruments, *Musica getutscht und ausgezogen*, dedicated to the Bishop of Strasbourg.

virelai, French, from *virer*, 'to turn', and *lai*, 'a song', a type of medieval French song with a refrain before and after each verse.

To teach men's sons and daughters on the virginal and viol, it is as harmless a calling as any man can follow.

Solomon Eccles, *A Musick-Lector*, 1667

---

virginal a stringed keyboard instrument of the 16th and 17th c., often called 'virginals' or 'a pair of virginals' in England, where the term was applied to any quilled keyboard instrument well into the 17th c. The virginal is rectangular or polygonal in shape and is distinguished from the harpsichord and spinet by its strings being set at right angles to the keys, rather than parallel with them. The most likely explanation of the name is that the instrument was often played by girls. There are several MS collections of virginal music by English composers, including *The Fitzwilliam Virginal Book*, *My Ladye Nevells Booke*, *Will Forster's Book*, *Benjamin Cosyn's Book* and *Elizabeth Rogers's Book*.

Virsaladze, Eliso (b Tblisi, 14 Sept 1942), Georgian pianist. Studied at the Tbilisi Conservatory and has toured worldwide from 1966; US recital debut 1981, followed by concert with the RPO; tours of Britain with the USSR SO and the Bournemouth SO. Further tours of Japan and the USA.

Visconti (di Modrone), Count Luchino (b Milan, 2 Nov 1906; d Rome, 17 Mar 1976), Italian producer. His first production was at La Scala in 1954 (*La vestale*, with Callas); later Milan productions with Callas included *La sonnambula*, *Anna Bolena* and *Iphigénie en Tauride*. His first production at CG was *Don Carlos* (1958) and he returned for *Il trovatore*, *Traviata*, and *Der Rosenkavalier*. His work on *Macbeth* and *Manon Lescaut* (1972) at Spoleto was admired; his productions were notable for taste, discretion and fidelity to the composer's intentions. As an alleged Marxist, he was notable in not allowing his views to colour his work.

Visée Robert de (b *c* 1660; d *c* 1725), French lutenist, guitarist and composer. He was guitar and theorbo player to the dauphin and chamber musician to the king from near the end of the 17th c. to 1720.

Works include two books of guitar pieces, and one of pieces for lute and theorbo.

Vishnevskaya, Galina (Pavlovna) (b Leningrad, 25 Oct 1926), Russian soprano. Opera debut Leningrad, 1950; Bolshoi, Moscow, from 1952. Her roles included Tatyana, Lisa, Tosca, Cherubino and Natasha. Aida was the role of her NY Met. (1961) and CG (1962) debuts. She has been associated with Britten (*The Poet's Echo*, *War Requiem*) and Shostakovich (sang in fp of the 14th symphony, Leningrad, 1969). She married Mstislav Rostropovich in 1955; they were obliged to leave the Soviet Union in 1975 and three years later they were stripped of their citizenship. Autobiography (*Galina*), 1985.

Vision of St Augustine, The work by Tippett for baritone, chorus and orchestra (text in Latin); composed 1963–65, fp London, 19 Jan 1966, with Fischer-Dieskau.

Visions de l'Amen suite by Messiaen in seven movements for two pianos; composed 1943, fp Paris, 10 May 1943, by Loriod and Messiaen.

Visions Fugitives 20 pieces for piano by Prokofiev; composed 1915–17, fp Petrograd, 15 Apr 1918, by composer. Orchestral version by Rudolf Barschai.

Visse, Dominique (b Lisieux, 30 Aug 1955), French countertenor. Studied singing with Alfred Deller and René Jacobs. Opera debut in *Poppea* at Tourcoing, 1982. Has sung with Les Arts Florissants and other ensembles in Vivaldi's *L'incoronazione di Dario* (1984), Charpentier's *Actéon* (Edinburgh 1985) and as Nirenus in *Giulio Cesare* at the Paris Opéra (1987). Delfa in Cavalli's *Giasone* at Innsbruck and Annio in Gluck's *Clemenza di Tito* at Lausanne, 1991. Has recorded Hasse's *Cleofide*, Rameau's *Anacréon* and Cavalli's *Xerse*.

Vitali, Filippo (b Florence, *c* 1590; d ? Florence, 1653), Italian priest, tenor and composer. He worked at Florence until 1631, when he was called to Rome as singer in the Papal chapel. While there he became attached to the household of Cardinal Francesco Barberini; but in 1642 he returned to Florence to become *maestro di cappella* to the Duke of Tuscany at San Lorenzo. In 1653 he became a canon there.

Works include opera *L'Aretusa* (1620); *intermedii* for J Cicognini's comedy *La finta Mora* (1623); psalms for five voices, hymns, *Sacrae cantiones* (1625) and other church music; madrigals; various works for voices and instruments in several parts.

Vitali, Giovanni Battista (b Bologna, 18 Feb 1632; d Bologna, 12 Oct 1692), Italian violist and composer. Pupil of Maurizio Cazzati, *maestro di cappella* of San Petronio at Bologna, where Vitali himself was a string player and singer from 1658. In 1673 he became *maestro di cappella* of the Santissimo Rosario, and in 1674 he went to Modena as vice-*maestro* of the ducal chapel. His oratorio on Monmouth was produced there in 1686, the year after Monmouth's execution.

Works include psalms for two–five voices and instruments; oratorios *Il Giono* and *L'ambitione debellata overo La Caduta di Monmouth*; ten cantatas; numerous dances for several instruments; sonatas for two violins and continuo and others for various instrumental combinations.

Vitali, Tomaso (Antonio) (b Bologna, 7 Mar 1663; d Modena, 9 May 1745), Italian violinist and composer, son of Giovanni Battista ◊Vitali. Pupil of his father, later member of the court chapel at Modena under him. He taught the violin to distinguished pupils, including Dall' Abaco and Senallié. He was best known for his instrumental music; notably trio sonatas and a celebrated chaconne for violin and keyboard (which has recently come into doubt regarding Vitali's authorship of it).

Works include sonatas for two violins and continuo.

Vitava (Smetana) ◊Má Vlast.

Vitry, Philippe de (b Paris, 31 Oct 1291; d Paris, 9 Jun 1361), French diplomat, priest, music theorist, poet and composer. He was secretary to Charles IV and Philip VI of France, in 1350 arranged a meeting between the king and the pope at Avignon and was created Bishop of Meaux the following year. His poetry, like his music, was much esteemed, Petrarch writing him a letter of appreciation. He wrote a treatise, *Ars nova*, in which he codified a new mensural notation that included the minim and imperfect mensuration. 12 motets by him survive.

Vittadini, Franco (b Pavia, 9 Apr 1884; d Pavia, 30 Nov 1948), Italian composer and conductor. Studied at the Milan Conservatory, became conductor at Varese and later settled at Pavia, where he became director of the Istituto Musicale.

Works include operas *Il mare di Tiberiade* (composed 1914), *Anima allegra* (after the Quintero brothers, 1921), *Nazareth* (after Lagerlöf, 1925), *La Sagredo* (1930) and *Caracciolo* (1938); ballets *Vecchia Milano*, *La dame galanti* and *Fiordisole*; ten Masses and motets; oratorio *Il natale di Gesù* (1931), *Le sette parole di Cristo* for chorus (1933); symphonic poem *Armonie della notte*; organ works.

Vittori, Loreto (b Spoleto, bap. 5 Sept 1600; d Rome, 23 Apr 1670), Italian soprano castrato and composer. Studied with Soto, Nanini and Soriano in Rome and lived for a time at the court of Cosimo II de' Medici at Florence, but returned to Rome and entered the Papal Chapel in 1622. Among his pupils were Queen Christina of Sweden, during her residence in Rome, and Pasquini.

Works include opera *La Galatea* (1639); plays with music *La fiera di Palestrina* and *Le zitelle canterine* (music of both lost); three sacred dramas (music lost); arias.

Vivaldi *The composer Antonio Vivaldi (1678–1741) in an engraving by J Caldwell. He was the most significant Italian composer of his day and helped to develop the concerto as a form, especially through his works for violin, the most famous of which is* The Four Seasons.

Vittoria, Tommaso Lodovico da, Tomás Luis de ◊Victoria.

Vitzthumb, Ignaz (b Baden near Vienna, 20 Jul 1720; d Brussels, 23 Mar 1816), Austrian-born South Netherlands composer and conductor. Studied in Vienna and settled in Brussels in the service of Prince Charles of Lorraine. He conducted at Ghent, Amsterdam and at the Théâtre de la Monnaie in Brussels, but lost his posts and pension during the Revolution and died in poverty.

Works include comic operas *Le Soldat par amour* (1766), *La Foire de village* (1786), etc., Masses, motets and other church music; four symphonies.

vivace Italian = 'lively, animated'.

Vivaldi, Antonio (Lucio) (b Venice, 4 Mar 1678; d Vienna, 28 Jul 1741), Italian composer and violinist. Pupil of his father Giovanni Battista Vivaldi, a violinist at St Mark's, Venice, and possibly also of Legrenzi, he entered the church in 1693 and was ordained priest in 1703 (being commonly known as *il prete rosso*, 'the red [-haired] priest'), but soon afterwards was given dispensations from priestly duties; he nevertheless came into conflict with the church authorities for keeping a mistress. He was associated with the Conservatorio dell' Ospedale della Pietà in Venice 1703–40 (*maestro di violino*, 1711), for which he wrote oratorios and instrumental music, but was frequently absent. His first opera, *Ottone in Villa* was produced in Vicenza in 1713, followed by many others in Venice, Florence, Munich, Parma, Milan, etc. He was in Mantua as *maestro di cappella da camera* to the Margrave Philip of Hesse- Darmstadt 1720–23, wrote *The Four Seasons* in about 1725 and toured Europe 1729–33, but of his extensive travels throughout his career little is known. He returned to Venice in 1739, but his popularity was falling, and two years later he died in poverty in Vienna. One of the most prolific composers of his day, he was particularly influential through his concertos, several of which were transcribed by Bach. In recent years his vocal music has become increasingly admired, in particular the oratorio *Juditha Triumphans*, the settings of the Gloria, and the Serenatas.

Works include OPERAS: *c* 21 extant, including *Ottone in Villa* (1713), *Arsilda* (1716), *Tito Manlio* (1720), *Ercole* (1723), *Giustino* (1724), *Orlando furioso* (1727), *La fida ninfa* (1732), *L'Olimpiade* (1734), *Griselda* (1735); Latin oratorio *Juditha* and others.

SECULAR VOCAL: serenatas *Gloria e Himeneo* (*c* 1725), *La Sena festeggiante* (1729), *Mio cor povero cor*; nine solo cantatas, with instruments, 30 with continuo.

SACRED VOCAL: including Gloria (two settings), *Dixit Dominus* (2), *Laudate pueri* (3), *Nisi Dominus*, *Magnificat* (2), *Salve regina* (3), *Stabat mater*.

INSTRUMENTAL: over 230 violin concertos (including *The Four Seasons*, nos. 1–4 of *Il cimento dell'armonia e dell'inventione*, op. 8), *c* 120 solo concertos (for bassoon, cello, oboe, flute, oboe d'amore, recorder and mandolin), over 40 double concertos (*c* 24 for violins, three for two oboes), over 30 ensemble concertos (instruments included clarinets, horns, theorbos and timpani), nearly 60 string orchestra concertos (without soloists) and over 20 concertos for solo ensemble (without string ripieno); *c* 90 solo and trio sonatas.

> *I heard him undertake to compose a concerto, with all the parts, with greater dispatch than a copyist can copy it.*
>
> **Charles de Brosses** on Antonio Vivaldi, in a letter, 1739

vivo Italian = 'lively, animated', the same as *vivace*, but more rarely used.

Vlad, Roman (b Cernauţi, 29 Dec 1919), Romanian-born Italian composer. Studied at the Cernauţi Conservatory but in 1938 settled in Rome, where he finished studies under Casella. He is the author of books on Dallapiccola and Stravinsky.

Works include radio opera *Il dottore di vetro* (1959), ballets *La strada sul caffè* (1945) and *La dama delle camelie* (after Dumas); film music; *De profundis* for soprano, chorus and orchestra; *Divertimento* for 11 instruments; *Studi dodecafonici* for piano.

Vladigerov, Pancho (b Zurich, 13 Mar 1899; d Sofia, 8 Sept 1978), Bulgarian composer. Studied with Juon and Georg Schumann in Berlin and at the Sofia Conservatory.

Works include opera *Tsar Kaloyan* (1936); incidental music for Strindberg's *A Dream Play*; Bulgarian Rhapsody *Vardar*; two violin concertos (1921, 1968); piano concerto; piano trio; violin and piano sonata; piano pieces; songs.

vocalise, French, *vocalizzo* Italian, any kind of vocal exercise without words, also sometimes in recent years a composition for voice without words for concert performance (the most ambitious being Medtner's *Sonata-Vocalise*); also used as a synonym for solfège and solfeggio.

A Selection of

Vivaldi

Violin Concertos op. 4	*c* 1714
Juditha Triumphans	1716
Violin Concertos op. 8 nos. 1–4	*c* 1725
Violin Concertos op. 9	1727

Cello Concertos
Flute Concertos op. 10
Oboe Concertos
Violin Sonatas
Gloria in D
Salve Regina

Vogel, Charles (Louis Adolphe) (b Lille, 17 May 1808; d Paris, 11 Sept 1892), Franco-Belgian composer of German descent. Studied at the Paris Conservatory.

Works include operas *Le Podestat* (1831), *Le Siège de Leyde* (1847), *La Moissonneuse* (1853), *Rompons!* (1857), *Le Nid de cigognes* (1858), *Gredin et Pigoche* (1866), *La Filleule du roi*; oratorio *Le Jugement dernier*; symphonies; string quartets, string quintets; songs including *Les Trois Couleurs*.

Vogel, Johann Christoph (b Nuremberg, bap. 18 Mar 1756; d Paris, 28 Jun 1788), German composer. Pupil of Riepel at Regensburg, went to Paris in 1776 and there became an enthusiastic supporter of Gluck, to whom he dedicated his first opera, *La Toison d'or* and *Démophon* (1789); symphonies; *symphonies concertantes* for wind instruments and orchestra.

Vogel, (Johannes) Emil (Eduard Bernhard) (b Wriezen an der Oder, 21 Jan 1859; d Nikolassee, near Berlin, 18 Jun 1908), German music scholar. Studied at Berlin University and privately. In 1883 he went to Italy as assistant to F X Haberl on his Palestrina edition. From 1893 to 1901 he was librarian of the Musikbibliothek Peters and editor of the Peters *Jahrbuch*.

Vogel, Wladimir (Rudolfovich) (b Moscow, 29 Feb 1896; d Zurich, 19 Jun 1984), Swiss composer of German and Russian descent. Studied in Russia, later with Tiessen and Busoni in Berlin; settled in Switzerland 1933. From the time of his violin concerto (1937) he wrote serial music, striving to maintain clarity in his writing and to emphasize the less dissonant aspects of his 12-note rows.

Works include cantatas *Wagadu's Untergang* for solo voices, chorus, speaking chorus and five saxophones (1930); *Thyl Claes* (after *Till Eulenspiegel*, 1938–45); *Sinfonia fugata*, four studies, *Devise*, *Tripartita* for orchestra; violin concerto (1937), cello concerto (1955); *Komposition* and *Etude Toccata* for piano.

Vogelhändler, Der, *The Bird Dealer*, operetta by Zeller (libretto by M West and L Held), produced Vienna, Theater an der Wien, 10 Jan 1891. When village postmistress Christel attempts to secure a job for birdseller boyfriend Adam, a case of mistaken identify causes complications eventually resolved with the couple's reconciliation.

Vogelweide, Walther von der (b *c* 1170; d ? Würzburg, *c* 1230), German poet, minnesinger and composer. Pupil of Reinmar von Hagenau in Austria. He was in service at the court of Duke Leopold V in Vienna, then led a wandering life in Germany and after 1220 probably lived at an estate given to him at Würzburg. Only a few of his tunes have survived. He appears as a character in Wagner's *Tannhäuser*.

Vogl, Heinrich (b Au, near Munich, 15 Jan 1845; d Munich, 21 Apr 1900), German tenor and composer. Began his career as a schoolmaster, but learnt singing from F Lachner at Munich and also studied acting. He made his debut there in 1865 as Max. He married the soprano Therese Thoma (1845–1921) in 1868. He appeared in the first two parts of Wagner's *Ring* at Munich 1869–70, as Loge and Siegmund, and in the production of the whole work at Bayreuth in 1876, as Loge. He sang in the first London *Ring* cycle (1882) and at the NY Met. from 1890 (Lohengrin, Tannhäuser and Tristan).

Works include opera *Der Fremdling* and songs.

There were Schubert evenings when wine flowed generously, when the good Vogl sang all those lovely lieder and poor Franz Schubert had to accompany him endlessly so that his short and fat fingers would hardly obey him.

von Bauernfeld, *Einiges von F Schubert*, 1869

Vogl, Johann Michael (b Ennsdorf near Steyr, 10 Aug 1768; d Vienna, 19 Nov 1840), Austrian baritone. Educated at the monastery of Kremsmünster and Vienna University, he was engaged by Süssmayr in 1794 and made his debut as a court opera singer in 1795; well known as Pizarro, Gluck's Orestes and Mozart's Count. He met

---

> # Vivaldi   *A biographical note*
>
> After a ten-year training for the priesthood, Vivaldi was ordained in March 1703. Later the same year he was appointed violin teacher at the Ospedale della Pietà. Nominally a girls' orphanage, most of the residents were the illegitimate daughters of the thousands of prostitutes who flourished in Venice from the 14th century. The position of Venice as a great port led to vigorous trade of all kinds and at one time the Ospedale, together with three sister institutions, was a haven for more than 5,000 girls. They often began life at the Ospedale after being left anonymously by their mothers in a small hole in the wall of the building. Vivaldi's duties included the provision of music for the regular Sunday concerts given by the girls in the nearby church of Pietà, and it was for these that he wrote many of his concertos, including *The Four Seasons*. Vivaldi himself was in full view of the public, his long red hair making a vivid impression, but the girls performed from behind an ornate screen; many were to become nuns and their calling would be compromised if they appeared in public.

Schubert in 1816 and was the first important artist to sing his songs in public. He retired from the stage with a pension in 1821 and devoted himself to song; gave *Erlkönig* in public and many other Schubert songs in private.

Vogl (born *Thoma*), Therese (b Tutzing, 12 Nov 1845; d Munich, 29 Sept 1921), German soprano. Studied at the Munich Conservatory and made her first stage appearance at Karlsruhe in 1865; she created Sieglinde (Munich, 1870) and also sang Ortrud, Isolde and Medea. In 1868 she married Heinrich Vogl.

Vogler, Carl (b Oberrohrdorf, Aargau, 26 Feb 1874; d Zurich, 17 Jun 1951), Swiss composer. Studied at Lucerne, with Hegar and others at Zurich and with Rheinberger and others at Munich. In 1915 he became professor at the Zurich Conservatory and in 1919 joint director with V Andreae.

Works include operas *Rübezahl* (1917) and *Fiedelhänschen* (1924), play with music *Mutter Sybille* (1906); organ works; songs and part- songs.

Vogler, Georg Joseph (known as Abbé Vogler) (b Pleichach near Würzburg, 15 Jun 1749; d Darmstadt, 6 May 1814), German composer, teacher and theorist. Son of an instrument maker and violinist, he studied theology at Würzburg and Bamberg Universities, went to Mannheim in 1771, becoming court chaplain the following year, and in 1773 received a scholarship from the Elector to go to Italy. Studied with Padre Martini in Bologna and Palotti in Padua, and in 1775 returned to Mannheim as vice-*Kapellmeister*. Mozart met him there in 1778 and disliked him. When the electoral court moved to Munich in 1778 Vogler at first remained in Mannheim, but later followed, becoming *Kapellmeister* in 1784. He was *Kapellmeister* to the Swedish court in Stockholm 1786–99, but was able to travel extensively, going as far afield as N Africa and Greece. After leaving Stockholm he lived successively in Copenhagen, Berlin, Prague, Vienna and Munich, until in 1807 he was appointed *Kapellmeister* to the Grand Duke of Hesse-Darmstadt. He was a notable teacher: his pupils included Weber, Meyerbeer and Crusell, and he wrote a number of theoretical works. His opera *Gustav Adolph och Ebba Brahe* has been revived at Drottningholm.

Works include *Singspiele*: *Albert III von Bayern* (1781), *Erwin und Elmire* (1781, Goethe); operas *La Kermesse* (1783), *Castore e Polluce* (1787), *Gustav Adolph och Ebba Brahe* (1788), *Samori* (1804) and others; operetta *Der Kaufmann von Smyrna* (1771); ballet *Jäger-Ballet* (1772); incidental music to Shakespeare's *Hamlet* (1779); choruses for Racine's *Athalie* and Skjöldebrand's *Hermann von Unna*; Masses, seven Requiems, motets, psalms and other church music; cantata *Ino* (Ramler); symphonies; several piano variations for piano and orchestra; piano trios and much other chamber music; piano and violin sonatas; piano sonatas and variations; six sonatas for two pianos.

Vogt, Lars (b Duren, 8 Sept 1970), German pianist. Studied in Hanover and played throughout Germany before winning second prize at the 1990 Leeds International (Schumann Concerto). UK concerts with the CBSO, Northern Sinfonia and the RPO. US debut 1991, with the Los Angeles PO in Beethoven's 4th Concerto; tour with the Salzburg Mozarteum Orchestra, 1993. Noted for a virtuoso technique but the feeling of a musician.

Voice of Ariadne, The opera by Thea Musgrave (libretto by A Elguera, after Henry James's *The Last of the Valerii*); composed 1972–73, fp Aldeburgh, 11 Jun 1974. Count Valerio becomes obsessed with an excavated statue of Ariadne, neglecting his wife, until Countess merges her voice with that of the goddess.

Voices work by Henze for mezzo, tenor and instrumental ensemble (22 settings based on texts by Ho Chi Minh (*Prison Song*), E Fried, Brecht, M Enzensberger and others); composed 1973, fp London, 4 Jan 1974.

voices the parts in a polyphonic composition, even those for instruments.

voicing (1) the production of particular qualities of tone by mechanical means in organ construction, and more particularly the control of the tone of a whole range of pipes governed by a single stop in such a way that the tone-colour is exactly the same throughout. (2) In piano playing the emphasis of one voice over another simultaneously played notes usually in order to create a singing effect.

Voigt, Deborah (b Chicago, 4 Aug 1960), American soprano. Studied in San Francisco and made debut there in Shostakovich's 14th symphony. Sang in the Verdi Requiem at Carnegie Hall (1988) and Rossini's Stabat Mater at Washington, DC. Opera roles include Mozart's Electra (Helsinki 1991) and Verdi's Amelia (*Ballo*), which she has sung in Chicago and at the NY Met. (1991 debut). Sang Chrysothemis in *Elektra* at the 1993 London Proms; CG debut 1995, as Amelia.

voix céleste French = 'heavenly voice'; an 8-ft organ stop with two pipes to each note, one tuned slightly sharper than the other, so that they produce a quivering effect.

Voix Humaine, La, *The Human Voice*, tragédie lyrique (monodrama) by Poulenc (libretto by Cocteau), produced Paris, Opéra-Comique, 6 Feb 1959. Jilted woman in fruitless telephone conversation with her lover strangles herself with the flex.

Volans, Kevin (b Pietermaritzburg, 1949), South African composer. Studied with Kagel and Stockhausen at Cologne. Composer-in-residence at Princeton University, 1992. His music combines avant-garde techniques with native African idioms. The opera *The Man Who Strides the Wind* was given at the 1993 Almeida Festival, London.

Works include *Chevron* (1989) and *One Hundred Frames* (1991) for orchestra; *White Man Sleeps* for two harpsichords, viola, da gamba and percussion (1982), four string quartets: no. 1 *White Man Sleeps* (1986), no. 2 *Hunting: Gathering* (1987), no. 3 *The Songlines* (1988); no. 4 *The Ramanujan Notebook* (1990); *She Who Sleeps with a small blanket* for percussion (1986); *Kneel my Dance* for two pianos (1985, six pianos, 1992); *Cicada* for two pianos (1994); electronic music.

Volbach, Fritz (b Wippelfürth, Rhineland, 17 Dec 1861; d Wiesbaden, 30 Nov 1940), German composer and conductor. Studied at the Cologne Conservatory. He joined the staff of the Royal Institute of Church Music in Berlin, 1886, became music director at Mainz in 1892 and professor of music at Tübingen University in 1907, moving to Münster University in 1919.

Works include opera *Die Kunst zu lieben* (1910); ballads for male voices and orchestra *Der Troubadour*, *Am Siegfrieds-Brunnen*, *König Laurins Rosengarten* (1913); *Raffael* for chorus, orchestra and organ; *Hymne an Maria* (Dante) for chorus, solo instruments and organ (1922); symphony in B minor, symphonic poems *Es waren zwei Königskinder* and *Alt Heidelberg*; *Ostern* for organ and orchestra; piano quintet for wind and piano; song cycle *Vom Pagen und der Königstochter* (Geibel).

Völker, Franz (b Neu-Isenburg, 31 Mar 1899; d Darmstadt, 4 Dec 1965), German tenor. Debut Frankfurt, 1926, as Florestan. He sang at the Vienna Staatsoper 1931–50 and in Berlin from 1935. Salzburg 1931–39, as Ferrando, Max and the Emperor. Bayreuth 1933–42 as Siegmund, Lohengrin, Parsifal and Erik. CG 1934 and 1937 as Florestan and Siegmund. Retired 1952.

Volkert, Franz (Joseph) (b Vienna, 12 Feb 1778; d Vienna, 22 Mar 1845), Austrian organist, composer and conductor. Settled in Vienna as organist by 1801 and was deputy *Kapellmeister* at the Leopoldstadt Theatre *c* 1814–24.

Works include *c* 150 music pieces for the stage (farces, melodramas, pantomimes, etc.); Masses; organ and piano pieces; songs.

Volkmann, (Friedrich) Robert (b Lommatzsch near Dresden, 6 Apr 1815; d Budapest, 29 Oct 1883), German composer. Pupil of his father, a schoolmaster and cantor, and of another local musician for string instruments. In 1836 he went to Leipzig for further study, was a private music tutor in Prague, 1839–41, lived and taught at Budapest 1841–54 and in Vienna 1854–78, when he became professor of composition at the National Music Academy in Budapest.

Works include incidental music for Shakespeare's *Richard III*; two Masses for male voices; two symphonies, three serenades, Festival Overture for orchestra; *Concertstück* for piano and orchestra; cello concerto, six string quartets, two piano trios and other chamber music; two sonatinas for violin and piano, violin and piano pieces, cello and piano pieces; sonata and *c* 20 other op. nos. for piano; several piano duet works; nine op. nos. of songs.

Volkonsky, Andrey Mikhaylovich (b Geneva, 14 Feb 1933), Russian composer. Studied piano with Lipatti and composition with N Boulanger in Paris, and in 1948 went to Moscow to study with Shaporin. He is a modernist among Russian composers, using a form of the 12-note system. Discouraged from composing by the Soviet authorities, he emigrated to Israel in 1973.

Works include cantata *The Image of the World* (1953); *The Laments of Shchaza* for soprano and chamber orchestra; concerto for orchestra (1954); piano quintet (1954); viola sonata.

That instrument of mixed sex ... this hermaphrodite of the orchestra.

Thomas Beecham on the viola,
in *A Mingled Chime*, 1944

Volkslied German = 'folksong'; although Germany possesses a treasury of old folksongs, many of which became hymns for the Lutheran church, the term *Volkslied* no longer exclusively or even principally designates them: what Germans now mean by *Volkslied* is a type of popular song, such as Silcher's *Loreley*, the composers of which are known (which is not the case with genuine folksongs), and which have passed into general currency.

volkstümlich German adj. from *Volkstum* = 'folk matters, folklore'; a word used in Germany to describe popular music that has become or is likely to become part of the nation's musical heritage, without actually belonging to traditional folk music.

Volo di Notte, *Night Flight*, opera in one act by Dallapiccola (libretto by the composer, after St-Exupéry), produced Florence, 18 May 1940. Airfield director Rivière is a pioneer in promoting night flights during the 1930s, but his stubborn insistence is partially responsible for the death of Simona Fabien's pilot husband, whose plane runs out of fuel.

volta Italian = 'time, turn, jump'; the word is used in such musical directions as *prima volta* ('first time'), *seconda volta* ('second time'), *ancora una volta* ('once again'). It is also the name of an old dance including a characteristic jump. ◊lavolta.

Volumier, Jean Baptiste (b ? Spain, *c* 1670; d Dresden, 7 Oct 1728), Flemish violinist, dulcimer player and composer. Educated at the French court and in 1692 transferred to that of Prussia in Berlin, where he became leader of the orchestra and director of the dance music. In

1709 he went to Dresden as music director to the Saxon court; he was acquainted with J S Bach.

Works include ballets, divertissements, dances (all lost).

voluntary an organ piece intended for use in church, but not part of the service. In modern practice it is used only at the beginning and (especially) at the end of a service, in the latter case often serving to play the congregation out.

Vom Fischer un syner Fru, *The Fisherman and his Wife*, dramatic cantata by Schoeck (libretto by composer, after P O Runge, after Grimm); composed 1928–30, produced Dresden, Staatsoper, 3 Oct 1930, conductor Busch. Fisherman catches turbot which turns out to be a prince under a spell; fisher wife expects series of wishes to be fulfilled.

Von deutscher Seele romantic cantata by Pfitzner for soloists, chorus and orchestra (text after Eichendorff); composed 1921, fp Berlin, 27 Jan 1922.

Von Heute auf Morgen, *From Today until Tomorrow*, opera in one act by Schoenberg (libretto by 'Max Blonda' = the composer's wife Gertrud), produced Frankfurt, 1 Feb 1930. Husband and wife quarrel over supposed lovers and are then reconciled, in 12-tone conversation piece.

Vonk, Hans (b Amsterdam, 18 Jun 1942), Dutch conductor. He studied in Amsterdam and with Scherchen. Associate conductor Concertgebouw Orchestra 1969–72; Netherlands Opera from 1971. Dutch Radio Orchestra from 1972, Residentie Orchestra from 1980. He made his British debut with the RPO, 1974; associate conductor from 1977. US debut San Francisco SO, 1974. Often heard in Bruckner.

Vopelius, Gottfried (b Herwigsdorf, near Zittau, 28 Jan 1645; d Leipzig, 3 Feb 1715), German composer. Appointed cantor of St Nicholas's Church, Leipzig, 1677. Compiled a book of chorales (1682) and harmonized many, besides writing tunes for some.

Voříšek (Worzischek), Jan Václav (Johann Hugo) (b Vamberk, 11 May 1791; d Vienna, 19 Nov 1825), Bohemian composer and organist. Pupil of his father, a schoolmaster, and later of Tomášek. He went to Vienna in 1813 and when Hummel left he recommended Voříšek as piano teacher to all his pupils. He became pianist and conductor to the Philharmonic Society and in 1823 court organist. He was an important contemporary and admirer of Beethoven and was a successful composer in a wide variety of genres.

Works include church music, including Mass (1824); symphony; duet for cello and piano; divertissement for two pianos; piano works.

Voyevoda opera by Tchaikovsky (libretto by composer and A N Ostrovsky, based on a play by the latter), produced Moscow, 11 Feb 1869. Elderly Voyevoda (provincial governor) attempts to wed sister of his betrothed but is thwarted by a replacement governor.

Voz (or *Vos*), Laurent de (b Antwerp, 1533; d Cambrai, Jan 1580), Flemish composer. Brother of the painter Martin de Vos. Worked at Antwerp Cathedral and was appointed music director and choirmaster at Cambrai Cathedral by the archbishop Louis de Berlaymont. When the latter's place was usurped by Inchy, Voz composed a motet compiled from words from the Psalms in such a way as to attack Inchy, who had Voz hanged without trial.

Works include motets, *chansons*.

Vrchlický, Jaroslav (1853–1912), Czech poet and playwright. Works based on his writings include Dvořák, opera *Armida*, oratorio *St*

Ludmilla; Fibich, operatic trilogy *Hippodamia* and melodramas *Haakon* and *Queen Emma*; J B Forster, melodramas *The Three Riders* and *The Legend of St Julia*; Janáček, choral work *Amarus*; Novák, opera *A Night at Karlstein*.

Vrieslander, Otto (b Münster, 18 Jul 1880; d Tegna, 16 Dec 1950), German musicologist and composer. Studied at the Cologne Conservatory. Settled at Munich in 1906 and went to live at Locarno in Switzerland in 1920. As a musicologist he was a pupil of Schenker, whose unfinished *Harmonielehre* he completed. He also wrote on C P E Bach and edited some of his works.

Works include songs from *Des Knaben Wunderhorn*, on Giraud's *Pierrot lunaire* (1904) and to words by Goethe, Keller, Theodor Storm.

VS, abbr., = *volti subito* (Italian = 'turn at once'). This is often written at the foot of a right-hand page in MS music as an indication that a quick turn is necessary in order to be ready for what follows on the next page.

Vučković, Vojislav (b Pirot, Serbia, 18 Oct 1910; d Belgrade, 25 Dec 1942), Yugoslav composer, musicologist and conductor. Studied in Prague and became professor and conductor at Belgrade. He was murdered by the Nazi police.

Works include several choral compositions; two symphonies, three symphonic poems; string quartet; two songs for soprano and wind instruments.

Vuillaume, Jean-Baptiste (b Mirecourt, Vosges, 7 Oct 1798; d Paris, 19 Mar 1875), French violin and cello maker. Established independently in Paris, 1828.

Vulpius, Melchior (b Wasungen near Meiningen, *c* 1570; d Weimar, buried 7 Aug 1615), German composer and writer on music. He became cantor at Weimar in 1602 and remained there to his death. He harmonized many hymn tunes not his own and wrote a treatise, *Musicae compendium* (1608).

Works include *Sacrae cantiones* for five–eight voices, canticles, hymns for four–five voices and other sacred music; *St Matthew Passion* (1613).

vuota Italian = 'void, empty'; a direction to string players to play a note or notes on an open string. Also the equivalent of GP = 'general pause'.

Vycpálek, Ladislav (b Vrsovice, near Prague, 23 Feb 1882; d Prague, 9 Jan 1969), Czech composer. Studied philosophy at Prague University, took a doctorate in it, and became secretary to the University library. He also studied composition with Novák at the Conservatory.

Works include cantata *The Last Things of Man*; song-cycles *Quiet Reconcilement* (1909), *Visions*, *In God's Hands*, Moravian ballads and folksongs; piano pieces; chamber music; choruses for mixed and male voices.

Vyšehrad (Smetana.) ◊Má Vlast.

Vyvyan, Jennifer (Brigit) (b Broadstairs, 13 Mar 1925; d London, 5 Apr 1974), English soprano. Studied at the RAM and then with F Carpi in Switzerland, making her debut with the EOG in 1947. She created the roles of Penelope Rich in *Gloriana* (1953), the Governess in *The Turn of the Screw* (1954) and Tytania in *A Midsummer Night's Dream* (1960) all by Britten. Other roles included Mozart's Electra (Glyndebourne, 1953), Donna Anna and Constanze (SW, 1952). She was well known in Bach, Britten, Monteverdi and Handel.

Waart, Edo de (b Amsterdam, 1 Jun 1941), Dutch conductor. He was principal oboe of the Concertgebouw Orchestra in 1963, and after winning the Mitropoulos conducting competition in 1964 became assistant conductor in 1966; US tour 1967. He founded the Netherlands Wind Ensemble and from 1967 was guest conductor with the Rotterdam PO; chief conductor 1973–79. Santa Fe Opera Festival 1971; CG 1976 (*Ariadne*). He appeared with the San Francisco SO 1977–85; music director from 1977.

Wachtel, Theodor (b Hamburg, 10 Mar 1823; d Frankfurt am Main, 14 Nov 1893), German tenor. Debut Hamburg, 1849. CG debut 1862, as Edgardo; London debut 1865, as Vasco da Gama. He sang at Berlin 1862–79 and returned to London until 1877. Among his best roles were Arnold, Manrico, Raoul and Adam's Chapelou. An attempt to sing Wagner (Lohengrin, 1876) was a failure.

Wächterlieder German = 'watchmen's songs'; songs formerly used in Germany by night watchmen in the streets to announce the hours and by fire-watchers on church towers to proclaim festival days, etc. They were often folksongs and some have passed into currency as hymns for the Lutheran Church.

Wadsworth, Stephen (b Mount Kisco, NY, 3 Apr 1953), American stage director, librettist and translator. Directed operas by Monteverdi with Skylight Opera, Milwaukee, from 1982. Wrote libretto for Bernstein's *A Quiet Place* (1983) and directed it in Milan and Vienna. Productions for Seattle Opera include *Jenůfa* and Gluck's *Orphée*; *Fidelio* and *Clemenza di Tito* for Scottish Opera, 1991. San Francisco 1990, *Die Entführung*. CG debut 1992, *Alcina*; has also translated operas by Handel.

Waechter, Eberhard (b Vienna, 9 Jul 1929; d Vienna, 29 Mar 1992), Austrian baritone. Studied in Vienna, making his debut there 1953 as Silvio and a year later became a member of the Vienna Staatsoper. CG 1956–59, as Almaviva, Amfortas and Renato. Bayreuth 1958–63 (debut as Amfortas). NY Met. debut 1961, as Wolfram. He sang the title role in Giulini's recording of *Don Giovanni*. Director of the Vienna Volksoper 1987–92, artistic co-director of the Vienna Staatsoper 1991–92. Also sang Lieder.

Waffenschmied (von Worms), Der, *The Armourer* [*of Worms*], opera by Lortzing (libretto by composer, based on F J W Ziegler's comedy *Liebhaber und Nebenbuhler in einer Person*), produced Vienna, Theater an der Wien, 31 May 1846. Weigl's opera *Il rivale di se stesso/His own Rival*, production Milan 1808, was based on the same play. Marie, daughter of armourer Stadinger, is wooed by Count Liebenau in his own person and, successfully, as an apprentice smith, Conrad. Marie's father Hans Stadinger opposes the match but eventually gives in.

Wagenaar, Bernard (b Arnhem, 18 Jul 1894; d York, ME, 18 May 1971), Dutch-born American composer. Studied with his father, Johan Wagenaar, and at the Utrecht Conservatory and learnt the violin and keyboard instruments. In 1921 he settled in NY, joined the NY PO and from 1927 taught at the Juilliard Graduate School there.

Works include chamber opera *Pieces of Eight* (1944); four symphonies (1926–46), sinfonietta, divertimento, *Feuilleton*, etc. for orchestra; violin concerto, triple concerto for flute, harp and cello (1935); three string quartets (1932–60), concertino for eight instruments; violin and piano sonata, sonatina for cello; three Chinese songs for voice, flute, harp and piano; piano sonata; Eclogue for organ; including settings of Edna St Vincent Millay.

Wagenaar, Johan (b Utrecht, 1 Nov 1862; d The Hague, 17 Jun 1941), Dutch composer, father of Bernard ◊Wagenaar. Studied with Richard Hol and with Herzogenberg in Berlin. Appointed organist at Utrecht Cathedral in 1888 and director of the Conservatory there in 1904, also conductor of a choral society. In 1919 he became director of the Royal Conservatory at The Hague, retiring in 1937 in favour of S Dresden.

Works include operas *The Doge of Venice* (1901), *El Cid* (after Corneille, 1916) and *Jupiter amans* (1925); overtures to Shakespeare's *Taming of the Shrew*, Goldoni's *Philosophical Princess*, Kleist's *Amphitryon*, and Rostand's *Cyrano de Bergerac* (1905), overture *Saul and David* (1906), funeral march and waltz suite for orchestra; fantasy on Dutch folksongs for male chorus and orchestra, female choruses with piano; violin and piano pieces; piano pieces; songs.

Wagenseil, Georg Christoph (b Vienna, 29 Jan 1715; d Vienna, 1 Mar 1777), Austrian composer. Studied in Vienna with Fux and others and in 1735, on recommendation, received a court scholarship, becoming court composer in 1739. In 1741–50 he was also organist to the dowager empress and he was appointed music master to the Empress Maria Theresa and her daughters. Mozart at the age of six played at court a concerto by Wagenseil, who turned pages for him.

Works include operas *Ariodante* (1745), *Le cacciatrici amanti* (1755) and *c* ten others (six on libretti by Metastasio); oratorios *La rendenzione* and *Gioas, rè di Giuda* (both 1735); nearly 20 Masses, Requiem, motets and other church music; symphonies; keyboard concertos; divertimenti for solo keyboard.

Wagenseil, Johann Christoph (b Nuremberg, 26 Nov 1633; d Altdorf, 9 Oct 1708), German historian and librarian. Wrote a treatise on the art of the Meistersinger, pub. in 1697, which served Wagner as a source for *Die Meistersinger*.

Waghalter, Ignaz (b Warsaw, 15 Mar 1882; d New York, 7 Apr 1949), Polish-German composer and conductor. Pupil of Gernsheim. He conducted opera in Berlin and Essen, 1907–23, and in 1925 conducted the State SO in NY, returning to Berlin later and going to Prague in 1933. He settled in NY in 1938.

Works include operas *Der Teufelsweg* (1911), *Mandragola* (after Machiavelli, 1914), *Jugend*, *Der späte Gast* (1922) and *Sataniel* (1923), operettas; violin concerto; string quartet; violin and piano sonata.

Wagner, Johanna (b Seelze near Hanover, 13 Oct 1826; d Würzburg, 16 Oct 1894), German soprano, adopted daughter of Albert Wagner (1799–1874), brother of Richard Wagner, who engaged her for the Royal Opera at Dresden, where she created Elisabeth in his *Tannhäuser* in 1845. In 1847 she went to Paris to study with García; sang at

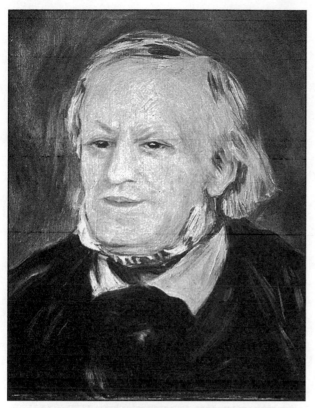

Wagner *The composer Richard Wagner. Probably the most influential composer of the Romantic movement, he conceived of opera as a continuous flow of music, unbounded by conventional form and traditional cadences. His plots were of epic proportion.*

the Court Opera, Berlin 1850–61 (Elisabeth, Ortrud). London, Her Majesty's, 1856 as Tancredi, Lucrecia Borgia and Bellini's Romeo. In 1859 she married an official named Jachmann. Lost her voice in the 1860s but sang in 1872 celebratory performance of the *Choral* symphony at Bayreuth and sang the First Norn in the fp of *Götter-dämmerung*, 1876.

Wagner, Siegfried (Helferich Richard) (b Tribschen, 6 Jun 1869; d Bayreuth, 4 Aug 1930), German composer and conductor, son of Richard ◊Wagner. Although intended to be an architect, he studied music with Humperdinck and Kneise, and gained much experience by assisting at the Wagner festival performances at Bayreuth, some of which he conducted after 1896. When his mother, Cosima, became too old to manage the affairs of the theatre, he took its direction in hand in 1909.

Works include operas *Der Bärenhäuter* (1899), *Herzog Wildfang* (1901), *Der Kobold* (1904), *Bruder Lustig* (1905), *Sternengebot* (1908), *Banadietrich* (1910), *An allem ist Hütchen schuld* (1917), *Schwarzschwanenreich* (1918), *Sonnenflammen* (1918), *Der Schmied von Marienburg* (1923), *Der Friedensengel* (1926), *Der Heidenkönig* (1933) and two others not performed or pub.; symphonic poem *Sehnsucht*; violin concerto, flute concerto.

Wagner, Sieglinde (b Linz, 21 Apr 1921), Austrian soprano. Debut Linz 1942, as Erda in *Das Rheingold* Sang at the Vienna Volksoper 1947–52, Berlin Städtische (later Deutsche) Oper 1952–86. Salzburg from 1949, as Leda in the fp of Strauss' *Romeo und Julia* (1950) and Wagner-Régeny's *Das Bergwerk zu Falun* (1961). Bayreuth 1962–73. Often heard in Bach's sacred music (e.g. *Christmas Oratorio*).

Wagner, Wieland (Adolf Gottfried) (b Bayreuth, 5 Jan 1917; d Munich, 17 Oct 1966), German producer, son of Siegfried ◊Wagner. Studied

painting in Munich, also music and stage production. He designed sets for *Parsifal* at Bayreuth in 1937. His first productions were at Nuremberg 1942–44 (*Walküre* and *Siegfried*). After World War II he sought to evade his own and Bayreuth's Nazi past, and from the reopening of the Bayreuth theatre in 1951 till his death he was in charge of production; his work was noted for its highly stylized values, often achieved with a minimum of props but careful lighting. He was also invited to produce operas in other European cities, notably at Stuttgart (including *Fidelio*, *Salome*, *Wozzeck* and *Lulu*).

Wagner, (Wilhelm) Richard (b Leipzig, 22 May 1813; d Venice, 13 Feb 1883), German composer and author. Son of a clerk to the city police, who died six months after Wagner's birth. His mother moved to Dresden and married the actor and painter Ludwig Geyer in 1815, who in turn died in 1821. Wagner learnt the piano but tried to read vocal scores of operas instead of practising and also acquired knowledge of opera from two elder sisters who were both stage singers. He wrote poems and a tragedy at the age of about 13, and at 14 went to school at Leipzig, where the family had returned. There he heard Beethoven's works and tried to imitate them in compositions of his own. In 1830 Dorn conducted an overture of his (*Columbus*), in the theatre, but it was received with scorn as a very crude work. He then studied harmony and counterpoint with Weinlig at St Thomas's School and entered the university in 1831. At 19 he began an opera, *Die Hochzeit*, but on the advice of his sister abandoned it for *Die Feen*. The libretti of these two works, as in his later works, he wrote himself. *Die Feen* remained unperformed until 1888 although it contains many premonitions of the composer's talent.

He became chorus master at the theatre of Würzburg in 1833 and conductor of a summer theatre at Lauchstädt, the company of which was at Magdeburg in winter, where he went with it. Minna Planer (1809–66) was there as an actress, and he married her on 24 Nov 1836, at Königsberg, where she had a new engagement. The Magdeburg company had been dissolved soon after a disastrous production of Wagner's third opera, *Das Liebesverbot*, on 29 Mar 1836. The opera was much influenced by Bellini and Donizetti and has been success-fully revived in heavily cut versions. The Königsberg theatre also went into liquidation just after Wagner had been appointed conductor, but in the summer of 1837 he became conductor at Riga. In Jan 1839 his post was given to Dorn and he decided to go to Paris by sea. A very stormy voyage took them as far as the coast of Norway and then to England, they did not reach Paris until September. They spent nearly all the time there until Apr 1842 in wretched poverty, but Wagner, in

A Selection of

Richard Wagner

Der fliegende Holländer 1843
Tannhäuser 1845
Lohengrin 1850
Tristan und Isolde 1865

Die Meistersinger von Nürnberg 1868
Das Rheingold 1869
Die Walküre 1870
Siegfried 1876
Götterdämmerung 1876
Parsifal 1882

Wagner   *A biographical note*

Early in 1864, Wagner's financial extravagance caught up with him and he was obliged to leave Vienna or risk imprisonment for debt. Reaching Stuttgart early in May, he was suspicious on hearing that a 'Franz von Pfistermeister, Secretary to the King of Bavaria' wished to see him; doubtless a persistent creditor had adopted this disguise. Eventually agreeing to see the emissary, Wagner was amazed to be handed a ring, portrait and fond message from Ludwig, recently succeeded to the throne of Bavaria. Hastening to the young king's side, Wagner was assured of a passionate artistic devotion and the promise of almost unlimited funds to fulfil his dream of staging his 'unperformable' music dramas; Ludwig had been committed to Wagner ever since hearing *Lohengrin* as a boy. Emotionally, Ludwig remained in a childlike state most of his life, and Wagner undoubtedly exploited him for his own ends. The royal coffers provided Wagner with a rich lifestyle, and *Tristan und Isolde* was duly premiered at Munich in 1865. *Die Meistersinger* followed in 1868, but Wagner's affair with Cosima von Bülow and his deception of the king over the nature of their relationship led to his exile at Tribschen. Ludwig continued to finance the growing *Ring* project, and insisted that the premieres of *Das Rheingold* and *Die Walküre* be given in Munich, although against Wagner's wishes. Wagner gained some independence with the establishment of Bayreuth in 1876, but the eventual success of the festival theatre would not have been possible without the king's further help. He lived to hear privately-arranged performances of *Parsifal* before being labelled insane by his ministers and drowning in Lake Starnberg.

patrons, who saw to it that after the production on 13 Mar 1861 the work should fail disastrously. Wagner next went to Vienna, where he heard *Lohengrin* for the first time, though it had been produced by Liszt at Weimar in 1850.

In 1862 he settled at Biebrich on the Rhine to work on *Die Meistersinger*, but he was in Vienna again by the end of the year, and stayed there until Mar 1864, when he was pursued by his creditors and threatened with imprisonment. At the critical moment he was invited by Ludwig II of Bavaria to join his court at Munich as friend and artistic adviser, and he ensured that Hans von Bülow was appointed conductor. Bülow's wife, Cosima (1837–1930), was Liszt's daughter; she and Wagner soon fell deeply in love. This created a scandal which was fully exploited by his enemies, the courtiers and officials who feared his influence on the youthful and idealistic king, and soon after the production of *Tristan* (10 Jun 1865), Wagner was obliged to go into exile once more. *Tristan* was an immensely influential work, and an enduringly great piece of music in its own right. Wagner extended chromaticism and modulatory devices to new heights in this opera in order to portray the love of his protagonists, a love that transcends all human passion by its awareness of mortality: the belief that fulfilment can be found only in death. *Tristan*'s antithesis is found in *Meistersinger*, a partly autobiographical comedy in which a romantic hero and a profound poet combine to confound their pedant enemies. While composing *Meistersinger* (in 1866) Wagner moved to Tribschen on the lake of Lucerne in Switzerland, where Cosima

---

---

joined him in Mar 1866. Bülow divorced her in 1870 and on 25 Aug she married Wagner, whose first wife had died on 25 Jan 1866.

After the production of *Die Meistersinger* on 21 Jun 1868 at Munich, Wagner quietly continued work on the *Ring* cycle, dropped so many years before, and planned a festival theatre to be erected by subscription at Bayreuth in Bavaria. The family took a house there in 1874; rehearsals began the following year, and the four works were produced 13–17 Aug 1876. (*Das Rheingold* and *Die Walküre* had already been given in Munich, against Wagner's wishes, 1869–70.) Although Wagner was dissatisfied with some aspects of the Bayreuth *Ring*, his genius as a composer and dramatist was triumphantly vindicated. The immensely complex musical and moral strands of the *Ring* are brought together in the final opera, *Götterdämmerung*; drama on a cosmic scale is matched by a constantly allusive orchestral accompaniment through the use of leitmotives. Wagner's creative testament came with *Parsifal* in which his concept of the 'complete art work' was further refined. By the time of his death in 1883 Wagner's influence had already spread throughout the musical world and far beyond; his belief in music drama as a synthesis of all the arts represents the culmination of his Romantic philosophy.

Works include operas *Die Hochzeit* (unfinished), *Die Feen* (composed 1833; produced 1888), *Das Liebesverbot* (1836), *Rienzi* (1842), *Der fliegende Holländer* (1843), *Tannhäuser* (1845), *Lohengrin* (1850), *Tristan und Isolde* (1865), *Die Meistersinger von Nürnberg* (1868), *Der Ring des Nibelungen*, comprising *Das Rheingold* (1869), *Die Walküre* (1870), *Siegfried* (1876) and *Götterdämmerung* (1876), *Parsifal* (1882).

Symphonies, nine concert overtures (two unpublished), including *Eine Faust Ouvertüre* (after Goethe), three marches for orchestra, *Siegfried Idyll* for small orchestra (1870); several choral works; a number of songs, including seven from Goethe's *Faust*, five poems by Mathilde Wesendonck (1857–58) and six settings of French poems; a sonata and some smaller piano works; string quartet (lost).

Wagner, Wolfgang (Manfred Martin) (b Bayreuth, 30 Aug 1919), German producer, brother of Wieland ◊Wagner. Studied production

---

such time as he could spare from hack work, had managed to finish both *Rienzi* and *Der fliegende Holländer*, the former of which had been accepted by Dresden and was produced there on 20 Oct 1842. *Rienzi* finds Wagner attempting the contemporary grand opera of Meyerbeer, a composer he affected to despise. The opera was Wagner's first major success with the public and was followed by *Der fliegende Holländer* two months later. Although less immediately popular it reveals for the first time Wagner's individual voice as a composer; the evocation of stormy seas, and the sense of impending doom are particularly effective. The opera was premiered on 2 Jan 1843, and Wagner was appointed second conductor at the court opera a month later. *Tannhäuser* was finished Apr 1845 and produced 19 Oct. The lifelong theme of the conflict between sacred and profane love is most powerfully projected in this opera. The spiritual side of the issue was portrayed in *Lohengrin*, composed 1845–48.

When the French Revolution of 1848 spread its influence across Europe, Wagner showed sympathy with liberal ideas, and after the revolt at Dresden failed in May 1849 he had to flee when a warrant for his arrest was issued, should he be found in Saxony. Not deeming the rest of Germany safe, he went to Switzerland. There, at Zurich, he worked on the libretti and music for the *Ring des Nibelungen* cycle. The text of the *Ring* had been written by 1853 and Wagner began composing *Das Rheingold*, the prologue in the same year. The music of the first scene, set at the bottom of the Rhine, immediately shows the composer's genius for creating convincing sound worlds. Composition of the *Ring* was interrupted at Act II of *Siegfried* by work on *Tristan und Isolde*, written under the influence of Mathilde Wesendonck, the wife of a friend and benefactor with whom he fell more and more deeply in love. In 1858 Minna confronted Wagner and Mathilde; the latter decided to stay with her husband, Wagner going to Venice and later to Lucerne, where *Tristan* was finished in Aug 1859. In 1860 a revised version of *Tannhäuser*, with a ballet, was commissioned by the Paris Opéra, and Wagner complied so far as his artistic conscience would let him, which was not enough for the at the Berlin Staatsoper, where he produced one of his father's operas in 1944. He was associated with his brother at Bayreuth from 1951 and himself produced operas there from 1953 (artistic director from 1966). He invited Patrice Chéreau (1976) and Peter Hall (1983) to produce *The Ring* there. Lacking the conspicuous talent of his relatives, he has nevertheless exercised considerable influence at Bayreuth. Autobiography, *Acts*, published 1994.

Wagner-Régeny, Rudolf (b Szász-Régen, 28 Aug 1903; d East Berlin, 18 Sept 1969), German composer of Romanian descent. Studied at Leipzig and Berlin. He was a political chameleon, finding success under both Nazi and Communist régimes in Germany.

Works include operas *Moschopulos* (1928), *Sganarelle* (after Molière, 1929), *Der nackte König* (1930), *Esau und Jakob* (1930), *La Sainte Courtisane* (1930), *Günstling* (1935), *Die Bürger von Calais* (after Froissart, 1939) and *Das Bergwerk zu Falun* (after Hoffmannsthal, 1961); ballet *Der zerbrochene Krug* (after Kleist's comedy, 1937); vocal and instrumental pieces.

Wagner tubas brass wind instruments devised by Wagner for his *Ring des Nibelungen*, which exist in three different kinds: two tenor tubas not unlike the euphonium, but with funnel-shaped mouthpieces.

The compass of tenor and bass Wagner tubas.

wait an instrument of the oboe type, similar to the shawm, used in England by the Christmas waits and, in the 13th c., by the keepers of the City of London gates and other town gates for the purpose of signalling 'All's well', etc.

waits originally the keepers of town gates, in the 15th–16th c., salaried bands employed to play at various functions, afterwards amateur singers and players performing outside the houses of the more substantial citizens for rewards in money and refreshment at Christmas.

Wakasugi, Hiroshi (b Tokyo, 31 May 1935), Japanese conductor. Conducted the Kyoto SO 1975–77, Cologne Radio SO 1977–83; music director Deutsche Oper am Rhein, 1982–87. Guest with the Berlin and Munich POs, Montreal and Pittsburgh SOs; US debut with Boston SO 1981. Chief conductor Tonhalle Orchestra, Zurich, from 1985; Tokyo Metropolitan Orchestra 1987–91. Has led the Japanese fps of Schoenberg's *Gurrelieder* and *Pelléas*, operas by Strauss and Wagner.

Wakefield, (Augusta) Mary (b Sedgwick, near Kendal, 19 Aug 1853; d Grange-over-Sands, Lancs., 16 Sept 1910), English amateur contralto, pianist and composer. In 1885 she started the first competitive festival at her home at Sedgwick, which was later transferred to Kendal and became the Westmorland Music Festival.

Walcha, Helmut (b Leipzig, 27 Oct 1907; d Frankfurt, 11 Aug 1991), German organist. He studied at the Leipzig Institute but became blind a year before his debut in 1924. He was assistant organist at the Thomaskirche, Leipzig, from 1926 and from 1929 performed and taught in Frankfurt; retired 1972. Best known in the organ music of Bach, all of which he recorded; he pub. a version of *Die Kunst der Fuge* for organ. Also performed Reger, on whom he wrote a book.

Waldhorn German = 'forest horn'; the German name for the horn without valves, producing only the natural harmonics (Italian *corno da caccia*).

Waldmädchen, Das, *The Woodland Maid*, opera by Weber (libretto by C F von Steinsberg), produced Freiberg, Saxony, 23 Nov 1800. Early version of *Silvana*; only two fragments survive.

Waldmann, Maria (b Vienna, 1844; d Ferrara, 6 Nov 1920), Austrian mezzo. The first Amneris in the Milan production of Verdi's *Aida* and the mezzo in the fp of his Requiem. Sang in Germany, Holland and Moscow as Aennchen, Preziosilla and Zerlina. She married Duke Galeazzo Massari of Ferrara and retired from the stage.

Waldstein, Ferdinand (Ernst Joseph Gabriel), Count (b Duchov, 24 Mar 1762; d Vienna, 29 Aug 1823), Bohemian music amateur. Patron of Beethoven, whom he met in the early days at Bonn and knew later in Vienna.

'Waldstein' Sonata Beethoven's piano sonata in C major, op. 53, composed 1804, so called (not by Beethoven) because it is dedicated to Ferdinand ◊Waldstein.

Waldteufel (actually *Lévy*), (Charles) Émile (b Strasbourg, 9 Dec 1837; d Paris, 12 Feb 1915), French composer and pianist. Studied at the Paris Conservatory. He joined a piano factory and was later appointed pianist to the Empress Eugénie. He had a great success as a composer of waltzes.

Works include many hundreds of waltzes and other dances, including a waltz on Chabrier's *España*.

Walker, Edyth (b Hopewell, NY, 27 Mar 1867; d New York, 19 Feb 1950), American mezzo. She studied in Dresden and Berlin; debut Berlin 1894, as Fides. Sang at the Vienna Hofoper 1895–1903, often under Mahler, but was eventually dismissed by him. CG 1900, as Ortrud, Fricka and Waltraute; returned in 1908 and 1910 for Isolde and Elektra. NY Met. 1903–06 (debut as Amneris). At the 1908 Bayreuth Festival she sang Ortrud and Kundry. Hamburg 1903–12, Munich 1912–17. She taught singing in Fontainebleau and New York during the 1930s.

Walker, Frank (b Gosport, Hants., 10 Jun 1907; d Tring, c 25 Feb 1962), English writer on music. Educated at Portsmouth Grammar School, engaged in an electro-technical career and during World War II was attached to the Royal Corps of Signals in Italy. His researches there resulted in his second book, *The Man Verdi*, the first being a biography of Hugo Wolf. He committed suicide.

Walker, Penelope (b Manchester, 12 Oct 1956), English mezzo. Studied in London and with Brigitte Fassbaender in Munich. Sang in concert from 1976, London opera debut as Pacini's Maria Tudor (Opera Rara, 1983). ENO from 1985, as Tippett's Sosostris and Kate Pinkerton; Fricka in the *Ring* for WNO, 1986, and Anna in *Les Troyens* for Scottish Opera. Member of Zurich Opera from 1991. Many concert appearances, in Handel, Elgar and Wagner.

Walker, Sarah (b Cheltenham, 11 Mar 1943), English mezzo. She studied violin at the RCM. In 1970 she sang Monteverdi's Ottavia with Kent Opera and Cavalli's Diana at Glyndebourne. From 1972 she has sung Dorabella, Fricka and Mary Stuart with ENO; and Gloriana in London (1984) and with the co. at the NY Met. CG debut 1979, as Charlotte; Handel's Micah in 1985. Many recitals in Europe and North America with the pianist Roger Vignoles. In 1976 she sang in the London fp of Henze's *Jephte* (realization of Carissimi). Created roles in *Taverner* (1972) and Buller's *Bakxai* (1992).

Walküre, Die, *The Valkyrie*, (Wagner.) See ◊Ring des Nibelungen. The saga continues as siblings Sieglinde and Siegmund meet and fall in love. Brünnhilde disobeys Wotan by attempting to allow Siegmund to escape death; she helps Sieglinde to escape to bear her child, the future Siegfried. Wotan punishes Brünnhilde by sending her to sleep, surrounded by a ring of fire.

Wallace, John (b Fife, 14 Apr 1949), Scottish trumpeter and music director. Studied at King's College, Cambridge, the RAM and York University. Principal of the Philharmonia from 1976, with regular concerto performances with the orchestra. Further solo appearances throughout the UK, the Far East and the USA. Malcolm Arnold, Tim Souster and Maxwell Davies have written concertos for him; premiered the concertos of Muldowney, Macmillan and Saxton, 1993. Played Birtwistle's *Endless Parade* at Glasgow, 1995. Many concerts of Baroque music with his group the Wallace Collection.

Wallace, William (b Greenock, 3 Jul 1860; d Malmesbury, Wiltshire, 16 Dec 1940), Scottish music author and composer. Educated at Edinburgh and Glasgow Universities and in Vienna as an eye specialist, began to practise in 1888, but gave up his profession for music

Walküre A painting inspired by Wagner's Die Walküre/The Valkyrie, Act III. Brünnhilde begs her father, the god Wotan, not to condemn her to marry a mortal. He is furious with her after she disobeys him by trying to protect the fleeing twins Siegmund and Sieglinde.

THE OPERA

Die Walküre

A three-act music drama by Richard Wagner, part of the *Ring* cycle, first performed in Munich in 1870. To protect Valhalla, Wotan has begotten of Erda nine Valkyrie daughters, the favourite of whom is Brünnhilde. The slain heroes they carry to Valhalla will be revived there and protect the fortress, in order to free the gods of Alberich's curse and return the ring to the Rhine-maidens. Wotan has also begotten two human children, the twins Siegmund and Sieglinde; he hopes that eventually Siegmund will free the ring from Fafner's possession. The twins lead separate lives.

I. Driven by a storm, Siegmund (tenor) enters a forest hut. He is attracted to Sieglinde (soprano) but they are unaware of each other's identities. Sieglinde's husband Hunding (bass) realizes that Siegmund has killed his kinsman and challenges him to fight the following day. Wotan has left the sword Nothung embedded in the hut's supporting oak tree; Siegmund draws it out before escaping with Sieglinde.

II. Wotan is forced by Fricka (mezzo-soprano), the guardian of marriage vows, to side with Hunding in the coming fight. When Siegmund enters with the pregnant Sieglinde, he is supported by the disobedient Brünnhilde. In spite of this Wotan shatters Nothung and allows Hunding to kill Siegmund.

III. After the Ride of the Valkyries, the sword fragments are gathered by Brünnhilde and she gives them to Sieglinde, soon to give birth to Siegfried. Wotan punishes Brünnhilde by removing her immortality; she will be put to sleep on the rock and will now fall prey to any man. In a final plea Brünnhilde begs her father to surround her with a ring of fire; only a hero may then claim her. Wotan kisses her farewell and summons Loge to provide a magic fire.

THE OPERA

(1863), *Estrella* (unfinished), operettas *Gulnare* and *Olga*; cantata *Maypole*; violin concerto; piano music.

Wallat, Hans (b Berlin, 18 Oct 1929), German conductor. Studied at Schwerin and conducted the Opera there 1953–56. Leipzig Opera 1958–61, Stuttgart 1961–64; music director at Bremen 1965–70, Mannheim 1970–80. Guest at the Vienna Staatsoper from 1968, Bayreuth 1970 (*Meistersinger*). NY Met. debut 1971. Music director at Dortmund 1979–85, Deutsche Oper am Rhein 1986 (Schreker's *Die Gezeichneten* at the 1989 Vienna Festival).

Wallberg, Heinz (b Herringen, 16 Mar 1923), German conductor. After study in Dortmund and Cologne conducted various regional orchestras in Germany, 1946–54. Opera debut with *Figaro* at Munster, 1947. Music director at Augsburg, then Bremen (1955–60). CG debut 1963, *Der Rosenkavalier*. Regular at the Vienna Staatsoper and conductor of the Bavarian Radio SO 1975–82, Essen PO 1975–91. Salzburg debut with the fp of Wagner-Régeny's *Das Bergwerk zu Falun*, 1961. US debut with the National SO, Washington, DC, 1991; Conducted *Die Meistersinger* at Wellington, 1990, *Fidelio* with Australian Opera, 1992.

Wallek-Walewski, Bolesław (b Lwów, 23 Jan 1885; d Kraków, 9 Apr 1944), Polish composer and conductor. Studied at his home town, at Kraków with Zeleński and Szopski, and with Riemann at Leipzig. On returning to Lwów he became choral and operatic conductor and director of the Conservatory.

Works include operas *Destiny* and *Jontek's Revenge* (1926; a sequel to Moniuszko's *Halka*); oratorio *Apocalypse*; Masses, Requiem, motets, psalms and other church music; scherzo *Bawel and Gawel* for orchestra; male-voice choruses; folksong arrangements.

Wallenstein three symphonic poems by d'Indy, op. 12, after Schiller's dramatic trilogy, composed 1873–79: 1. *Le Camp de Wallenstein*; 2. *Max et Thécla* (first called *Piccolomini*); 3. *La Mort de Wallenstein*. First complete performance Paris, 26 Feb 1888.

except during World War I. In 1889 he entered the RAM in London for a brief course in composition, and later he became successively secretary and trustee of the Philharmonic Society. His books include *The Threshold of Music* (1908), *The Musical Faculty* (1914), *Richard Wagner as he lived* (1925) and *Liszt, Wagner and the Princess* (1927).

Works include opera *Brassolis*; symphony *Koheleth* for chorus and orchestra; symphony *The Creation*, symphonic poems *The Passing of Beatrice* (after Dante's *Paradiso*, 1892), *Anvil or Hammer* (after Goethe's *Koptisches Lied*), *Sister Helen* (after D G Rossetti), *To the New Country*, *Wallace*, *AD 1305–1905*, *Villon*, suite *The Lady from the Sea* (after Ibsen), symphonic prelude to Aeschylus' *Eumenides*; cantatas, chamber music and songs.

Wallace, (William) Vincent (b Waterford, 11 Mar 1812; d Château de Haget, near Hautes-Pyrénées, 12 Oct 1865), Irish composer. Pupil of his father, a bandmaster and bassoon player, who moved to Dublin, where Wallace played the organ and violin in public as a boy. In 1831 he married Isabella Kelly, but they separated in 1835 (in NY in 1850 he met the pianist Hélène Stoepel, with whom he lived and had two sons). In 1834 he appeared at Dublin with a violin concerto of his own. Between 1835 and 1845 he was in Australia and elsewhere abroad, but he went to London in the latter year and was induced to compose *Maritana*. After a successful operatic career, including a visit to South America in 1849 and 14 years in Germany, a commission from the Paris Opéra (which he was unable to finish owing to failing eyesight) and another visit to South and North America 1850–53, his health broke down and he was ordered to the Pyrenees.

Works include operas *Maritana* (1845), *Matilda of Hungary* (1847), *Lurline* (1860), *The Maid of Zurich* (unpublished), *The Amber Witch* (1861), *Love's Triumph* (1862), *The Desert Flower*

Wallenstein, Alfred (b Chicago, 7 Oct 1898; d New York, 8 Feb 1983), American conductor and cellist of German parentage. He studied medicine at Leipzig University, and also the cello with J Klengel (1920–21). Returned to the USA and was first cello with the Chicago SO (1922–29) and then with the NY PO until 1936. He made his debut as a conductor 1931 and 1943–56 was conductor of the LA PO, in 1952 also becoming music director of the Hollywood Bowl.

Wallfisch, Raphael (b London, 15 Jun 1953), English cellist. Studied with Amaryllis Fleming, Derek Simpson and Piatigorsky. Worldwide career since winning the 1977 Cassado Competition at Florence. London debut in the Schumann Concerto with the ECO, 1974. Frequent chamber recitals (trios with Anthony Goldstone and Ronald Thomas). Has recorded concertos by Bax, Finzi, Moeran, Bliss and Delius. His father Peter Wallfisch (1924–93) was a German-born pianist, often heard as a recitalist.

His wife Elizabeth is violinist with the London Fortepiano Trio (Haydn series 1982) and the Purcell Quartet (debut concert 1984); plays Baroque concertos in period style.

Walliser, Christoph Thomas (b Strasbourg, 17 Apr 1568; d Strasbourg, 26 Apr 1648), German composer. Pupil of Vulpius and others. In 1599 he became a teacher at the Academy and later music director of two churches at Strasbourg.

Works include incidental music for Aristophanes' *The Clouds* and other plays; *Ecclesiodae* containing psalms for four–six voices (1614), *Ecclesiodae novae* including Te Deum, litany, etc., for four–seven voices (1625), German psalms for five voices and other church music.

Wally, La opera by Catalani (libretto by L Illica, based on W von Hillern's novel *Die Geyer-Wally*), produced Milan, La Scala, 20 Jan 1892. Wally is intended for Gellner but she loves Hagenbach, and after complications and reconciliation, they die together in an avalanche. Championed by Toscanini, who named his daughter Wally.

Walmisley, Thomas Attwood (b London, 21 Jan 1814; d Hastings, 17 Jan 1856), English organist and composer. Learnt music from his father, the glee composer and teacher, Thomas Forbes Walmisley (1783–1866), and studied with his godfather, Attwood. After three years as organist at Croydon, he became organist of Trinity and St John's Colleges, Cambridge, in 1833, where he also devoted himself to the study of mathematics and wrote poetry. In 1836 he became professor of music, though he did not take the Mus. D. degree until 1848.

Works include services and anthems; three odes for the installation of university chancellors; madrigal *Sweete Flowers*; duets for oboe and piano; organ works; songs.

Walmsley-Clark, Penelope (b London, 19 Feb 1949), English soprano. Appearances at CG as the Queen of Night, in the UK fps of Berio's *Un rè in Ascolto* (1989), and as Guinevere in the fp of Birtwistle's *Gawain* (1991). Other modern repertory includes *Le Grand Macabre* (in Vienna), Shostakovich's 14th symphony, *Moses und Aron* and Henze's *Elegy for Young Lovers* (in Venice). Has recently sung such mainstream roles as Donna Anna (ENO, 1995).

Walpurga (or *Walpurgis*), Maria Antonia (b Munich, 18 Jul 1724; d Dresden, 23 Apr 1780), German composer. Daughter of the Elector of Bavaria, afterwards Emperor Charles VII. Pupil of Giovanni Ferrandini, Porpora and Hasse; married Frederick Christian, electoral prince of Saxony. She was a member of the Arcadian Academy in Rome under the name of Ermelinda Talèa Pastorella Arcada (pseudonym E.T.P.A.).

Works include operas *Il trionfo della fedeltà* (with additional music by Hasse, 1754) and *Talestri, regina della Amazoni* (1760).

Walsh (1), John (b 1665 or 1666; d London, 13 Mar 1736), English music publisher and instrument maker. Founded his pub. house in London *c* 1690 and in 1692 became instrument maker to the King. Published much of Handel's music.

Walsh (2), John (b London, 23 Dec 1709; d London, 15 Jan 1766), son of John ◊Walsh (1); succeeded his father as music publisher.

Walter, Bruno (actually Bruno Walter Schlesinger) (b Berlin, 15 Sept 1876; d Beverly Hills, CA, 17 Feb 1962), German conductor and pianist. He studied at Stern Conservatory in Berlin and made his first appearance as a conductor at Cologne 1894. After appointments as an opera conductor at Hamburg (under Mahler), Breslau, Pressburg, Riga, Berlin and Vienna (1901–12) he was director of the Munich Opera from 1913 to 1922; conducted the fps of Pfitzner's *Palestrina* (1917) and Schreker's *Das Spielwerk* (1920). From 1925 to 1933 he

---

The end of his baton is like a cradle in which he rocks me.

Lotte Lehmann on Bruno Walter, quoted in Gattey, *Peacocks on the Podium*, 1982

---

was director of the Städtische Oper, Berlin, and from 1929 to 1933 of the Gewandhaus concerts in Leipzig, in succession to Furtwängler. He first appeared in England in 1909 and was the regular conductor of the German seasons at CG 1924–31 (productions included *Figaro* and *Rosenkavalier*). He was also active during this period as conductor at the Salzburg festival. He was compelled to leave Germany in 1933 and was artistic director of the Vienna Opera 1936–38. After the *Anschluss* he emigrated to France 1938 and to the USA 1939, where he lived till his death. From 1941 he conducted frequently at the NY Met. (debut with *Fidelio*; also *Don Giovanni* in first season). From 1946 returned to Europe as guest conductor, he appeared at the 1947 Edinburgh Festival.

He excelled in the works of Mozart and of Romantic composers, especially Mahler, of whose *Lied von der Erde* and ninth symphony he gave the fps (1911, 1912). As a pianist he accompanied many of the famous singers of his time, including Lotte Lehmann and Kathleen Ferrier, and also appeared as soloist in Mozart's concertos. He pub. a study of Mahler, an autobiography (*Theme and Variations*) and three vols of essays.

Walter, Gustav (b Bilin, 11 Feb 1834; d Vienna, 30 Jan 1910), Bohemian-Austrian tenor. Studied at the Prague Conservatory, appeared there and at Brno, and in 1856 made his first appearance in Vienna, where he settled.

Walter, Johann (b Kahla, Thuringia, 1496; d Torgau, 25 Mar 1570), German composer and bass. He sang in the service of the Elector of Saxony and in 1548 organized and directed the singers of the court chapel at Dresden. In 1554 he retired to Torgau with a pension. He was a friend of Luther and in 1524 went to Wittenberg to assist him in framing the German Protestant Mass.

Works include Magnificat, German hymns for four voices, sacred songs, some with words by Luther; instrumental pieces.

Walter, (Johann) Ignaz (b Radonice, Bohemia, 31 Aug 1755; d Regensburg, 22 Feb 1822), Bohemian tenor and composer. A pupil of Starzer in Vienna, he made his debut as a singer there in 1780; later became music director of the Grossman opera co. and (1804) of the opera in Regensburg.

Works include *Singspiele: Doktor Faust* (after Goethe, 1797), *Der Spiegelritter* and others; *Cantata sacra* for the coronation of Emperor Leopold II; memorial music for Schiller.

Walter of Evesham ◊Odington.

Waltershausen, Hermann Wolfgang (Sartorius) Freiherr von (b Göttingen, 12 Oct 1882; d Munich, 13 Aug 1954), German composer and music author. Studied at Strasbourg, lost his right arm and foot in an accident but learnt to play the piano and conduct, with the left hand. He further studied at Munich from 1901 and attended Sandberger's lectures at the university, founded a music school in 1917 and in 1920 became professor at the Munich State Academy of Music, being appointed director in 1922. His books include works on musical style, opera and R Strauss.

Works include operas *Else Klapperzehen* (1909), *Oberst Chabert* (after Balzac, 1912), *Richardis* (1915), *Die Rauensteiner Hochzeit* (1919), *Die Gräfin von Tolosa* (composed 1938); *Apocalyptic Symphony*, *Hero und Leander*, Partita on three Hymn-tunes, comedy overture, *Passions- und Auferstehungsmusik* for orchestra; *Krippenmusik* for harpsichord and chamber orchestra; piano works; songs.

Walther, Johann Gottfried (b Erfurt, 18 Sept 1684; d Weimar, 23 Mar

1748), German composer organist and lexicographer. Pupil of J B Bach at Erfurt, where in 1702 he became organist at St Thomas's Church. In 1707 he was appointed town organist at Weimar, where he was in close touch with J S Bach, to whom he was related. He pub. a _Musicalisches Lexicon_ in 1732.

Works include much organ music, including preludes and fugues and chorale variations; concertos by other composers arranged for solo harpsichord.

Walther, Johann Jakob (b Witterda, near Erfurt, _c_ 1650; d Mainz, 2 Nov 1717), German violinist and composer. In the service of the Elector of Saxony and later that of Mainz. Composed _Scherzi_ for violin and continuo and _Hortulus chelicus_ for solo violin and strings containing pictorial effects.

Walther von der Vogelweide ◊Vogelweide.

Walton, William (Turner) (b Oldham, Lancs., 29 Mar 1902; d Ischia, 8 Mar 1983), English composer. Showed great precocity of talent at home and was sent to Christ Church Cathedral, Oxford, as a choirboy, later becoming an undergraduate at Christ Church. He had some composition lessons from Hugh Allen, but after the age of 16 was self-taught, though he later received some advice from Busoni and others. In 1923 he appeared for the first time at the ISCM festival, at Salzburg, where his spiky first string quartet was performed. He settled in London and was in close touch with the literary family Edith, Osbert and Sacheverell Sitwell; their association led to _Façade_, for reciter and ensemble, whose 1923 premiere provoked an uproar. Hindemith was the soloist in his first widely successful work, the viola concerto (1929), and two years later the aggressively mannered cantata _Belshazzar's Feast_ was premiered at Leeds.

In 1934 his symphony in B♭ minor was performed in London before it was completed (the finale was added the next year). In 1938 he went to the USA to confer with Jascha Heifetz about the solo part of the violin concerto, which is dedicated to him. As in the Viola Concerto and the First Symphony, the best of contemporary continental influences, including Stravinsky, Poulenc and Prokofiev can be discerned here. A more ruminant, quasi-Romantic strain is evident in the post-war works, beginning with the opera for Covent Garden _Troilus and Cressida_ (1948–54) and continuing with the cello concerto for Piatigorsky. The _Hindemith Variations_ is an orchestral tribute to his former friend and colleague, and also a kindred spirit in terms of iconoclast turned conservative.

Works include DRAMATIC: operas _Troilus and Cressida_ (after Chaucer, 1954, revised 1976) and _The Bear_ (after Chekhov, 1967); ballets _The Wise Virgins_ (arrangement of Bach, 1940) and _The Quest_ (after Spenser, 1943); incidental music for Shakespeare's _Macbeth_; film music for _As You Like It, Henry V_ and _Hamlet_ (Shakespeare), _Major Barbara_ (Shaw), _The First of the Few_ (including _Spitfire_ prelude and fugue); radio music for _Christopher Columbus_ (L MacNeice).

VOCAL: _Façade_ for reciter and instrumental ensemble; (E Sitwell, 1922). Cantatas _Belshazzar's Feast_ (Bible, arranged by O Sitwell, 1931) and _In Honour of the City of London_ (Dunbar), Coronation Te Deum (1953), Gloria, all with orchestra; _Where does the uttered music go?_ (Masefield) for unaccompanied chorus; _A Song for the Lord Mayor's Table_ for soprano and orchestra or piano (1962).

ORCHESTRAL: overtures _Portsmouth Point_ (on Rowlandson's drawing) and _Scapino, Siesta_ for small orchestra, two symphonies (1931–35 and 1960), Coronation Marches _Crown Imperial_ and _Orb and Sceptre_ (1937 and 1953), _Johannesburg Festival Overture, Partita; Sinfonia concertante_ for piano and orchestra (1927), viola concerto (1929), violin concerto (1939), cello concerto (1956), _Partita_ (1957), _Variations on a theme of Hindemith_ (1963), _Capriccio Burlesco_ (1968), _Improvisations on an Impromptu of Benjamin Britten_ (1969), Sonata for Strings (from string quartet of 1947, 1971), _Varii Capricci_ (1976), _Prologo e Fantasia_ (1982).

INSTRUMENTAL: two string quartets (1922 and 1947), piano quartet (1918–19, revised 1976); sonata for violin and piano (1949); piano duets for children.

[A] favourite saying of his was that to compose music was far worse for him than to bear children is for a woman, as it took longer than nine months and was much more painful.

Susana Walton on William Walton, _William Walton: Behind the Facade_, 1988

---

waltz, a ballroom dance coming into fashion in the earlier 19th c. and developing from the German dances (_Deutsche_) and the Austrian _Ländler_, Beethoven, Weber and Schubert being among the first composers to cultivate it seriously, and the elder J Strauss and Lanner among the first ballroom composers to develop its vogue in Vienna, whence it rapidly spread all over Europe. It is in 3–4 time, varying in pace at different periods and in different countries, but usually rather leisurely, and its most typical feature is a bass note on the first beat followed by two repeated chords of the upper harmony of that bass on the second and third.

Waltz, Gustavus (_fl._ 1732; d 1759), German bass. He is said, on scanty evidence, to have been for a time Handel's cook in London. In 1732 he appeared as Polyphemus in Handel's _Acis and Galatea_ and then, until 1751, in many operas and oratorios. He sang in the fps of _Arianna, Ariodante, Alcina_ and _Atalanta_.

Waltz Dream (Strauss.) ◊Waltzertraum.

Walzertraum, Ein, _A Waltz Dream_, operetta by Oscar Straus (libretto by F Dörmann and L Jacobson), produced Vienna, Karl Theatre, 2 Mar 1907. Newly married Lieutenant Niki abandons wife Helene to go to a ball on his wedding night. There he falls in love with Franzi, who teaches Helene how to win back Niki's heart.

Wand, Günter (b Elberfeld, 7 Jan 1912), German conductor and composer. After study in Cologne he held posts at Wuppertal and Detmold. He conducted at the Cologne Opera 1939–44 and was musical director there 1945–48. He was responsible for the Gürzenich concerts, Cologne, 1946–74, giving frequent performances of Ligeti, Varèse and Schoenberg. London debut 1951 (with the LSO at CG). He conducted the Bern SO from 1974 and has been principal conductor of the NDR SO (Hamburg) 1982–91. Also heard in operas by Mozart and Verdi.

'Wanderer' Fantasy Schubert's fantasy in C major for piano, D760, composed Nov 1822. It is so called because it contains material from his song _The Wanderer_, written 1816.

Wand of Youth, The two orchestral suites by Elgar, opp. 1a and b, which are based on music he wrote for a play in his childhood, 1869.

A Selection of

Walton

Façade 1922
Viola Concerto 1929
Belshazzar's Feast 1931
Symphony no. 1 1931–5

Violin Concerto 1939
String Quartet no. 2 1947
Symphony no. 2............................... 1960
Variations on a Theme by Hindemith 1963
The Bear.................................... 1967

Revised and scored in the present form in 1907; fp London, 14 Dec 1907, conductor Wood.

Wannenmacher, Johannes (b ? Neuenburg am Rhein *c* 1485; d Bern, 1551), Swiss priest and composer. He was appointed cantor of the collegiate foundation of St Vincent at Bern in 1510, but left in 1514 after a dispute and went to Germany as canon and cantor at Freiburg, Baden. After a brief return to Switzerland, in 1519, when he went to Sion (Valais), he went back to Freiburg, but having come under the influence of the Swiss reformer Zwingli, he embraced Protestantism in 1530, was tortured and banished, returned to Bern and, finding no employment there, became town clerk at Interlaken.

Works include Psalm cxxxvii for three–six voices, motets; German sacred and secular songs.

War and Peace, *Voyna i mir*, opera by Prokofiev (libretto by M Mendelson, based on Tolstoy's novel), performed in concert, Moscow, 17 Oct 1944; produced Leningrad, 12 Jun 1946 (first eight of 13 scenes only). Revised 1941–52, in 11 scenes, and produced Florence, 26 May 1953, conductor Rodzinski. First seven scenes concern Peace, with the love of Andrei and Natasha, and the last six War, with Napoleon's capture of Moscow.

Ward, David (b Dumbarton, 3 Jul 1922; d Dunedin, NZ, 16 Jul 1983), Scottish bass. Studied at the RCM with C Carey and then with H Hotter. After singing with the chorus (1952) he made his debut as soloist in 1953. London, CG, from 1960 as Pogner, Wotan, Arkel, Rocco and Morosus in the first British performance of *Die schweigsame Frau* (1961). He appeared in minor roles at Bayreuth and as Wotan in Buenos Aires (1967).

Ward, John (b Canterbury, bap. 8 Sept 1571; d before 31 Aug 1638), English composer. He was in the service of Sir Henry Fanshawe, Remembrancer of the Exchequer, at Ware Park, Herts., and in London.

Works include services and 22 verse anthems; madrigals; fantasies for viols.

Ward, Robert (b Cleveland, OH, 13 Sept 1917), American composer and conductor. Studied at the Eastman School and Juilliard; teacher there 1946–56. Professor at Duke University, NC, from 1979. Best known for his opera *The Crucible* (after Arthur Miller) produced by the New York City Opera 1961. Other works include four operas, (*Abelard and Heloise*, 1982); five symphonies (1941–76, no. 5 *Canticles of America*, based on Whitman and Longfellow); saxophone concerto (1984); *Raleigh Divertimento* for wind quintet (1986).

Warfield, William (b West Helena, AL, 22 Jan 1920), American bass. After study at the Eastman School sang on Broadway, in the 1949 fp of Blitzstein's *Regina*. Recital debut at New York Town Hall, 1950. Toured Europe 1952–53, as Gershwin's Porgy with his then wife Leontyne Price as Bess; also appeared in *Showboat* at the Vienna Volksoper. Concerts included *Messiah*, and Mozart's *Requiem*, under Bruno Walter.

He who has heard the cry of a curlew on a lone and desolate moor has heard the music of this richly gifted personality.

Eric Fenby on Peter Warlock,
in *Delius as I Knew Him*, 1936

Warlock (real name Philip (Arnold) Heseltine), Peter (b London, 30 Oct 1894; d London, 17 Dec 1930), English composer (as Warlock); musicologist and writer on music (as Heseltine). Educated at Eton, where he studied music in particular and later influenced by Delius and van Dieren. Founded the *Sackbut*, a combative music paper, wrote numerous articles, edited early English music, especially of the lutenist school, and pub. books on the English ayre, Delius and (with Cecil Gray) Gesualdo. His music reflects the extreme mood swings of his personality; he died by suicide.

Works include *Three Dirges by Webster* (1925) and other choral works; *An Old Song* and *Serenade* for string orchestra; *The Curlew* for

tenor, flute, English horn and string quartet (1921), *Corpus Christi* and *Sorrow's Lullaby* (Beddoes) for soprano, baritone and string quartet; *Capriol* suite for full or string orchestra on dances from Arbeau's *Orchésographie* (1926); over 100 songs, many on Elizabethan and Jacobean poems.

Warrack, Guy (Douglas Hamilton) (b Edinburgh, 8 Feb 1900; d Englefield Green, 12 Feb 1986), Scottish conductor and composer. He studied at Oxford and with Boult and Vaughan Williams at the RCM; taught there 1925–35. Debut as conductor, London, 1925; BBC Scottish Orchestra 1936–45, SW Ballet 1948–51. He wrote music for various documentary films, including the official film of the 1953 coronation.

Warrack, John (Hamilton) (b London, 9 Feb 1928), English writer on music and administrator, son of Guy ◊Warrack. After studying oboe at the RCM he was assistant music critic of the *Daily Telegraph* from 1954; *Sunday Telegraph* 1961–72. He has been a member of *Opera* magazine's editorial board from 1953 and a critic for *Gramophone* from 1958. The author of well-received books on Tchaikovsky and Weber, he co-edited with Harold Rosenthal the *Concise Oxford Dictionary of Opera* (1964, revised 1979); further revision: as *Oxford Dictionary of Opera* (1992; Concise version 1995). Artistic director, Leeds Festival, 1977–83. Lecturer, Oxford University 1983–93.

Warren (actually *Warenoff*), Leonard (b New York, 21 Apr 1911; d New York, 4 Mar 1960), American baritone. Studied in NY and Milan, making his debut at the NY Met. in 1939 as Verdi's Paolo. Sang at La Scala, 1953, as Rigoletto and Iago. Other roles included Tonio, Boccanegra and Scarpia. He was especially well known as a Verdi singer; his death occurred during a performance of *La forza del destino* at the Met.

War Requiem choral work by Britten, op. 66 (text of the Requiem Mass, together with poems by W Owen), fp Coventry Cathedral, 30 May 1962.

Wasps, The incidental music for Aristophanes' comedy by Vaughan Williams, fp Cambridge, in Greek, by undergraduates, 26 Nov 1909; orchestral suite performed London, 23 Jul 1912.

Watanabe, Akeo (b Tokyo, 5 Jun 1919; d Tokyo, 22 June 1990), Japanese conductor. He studied in Tokyo and at the Juilliard School from 1950. Conductor, Tokyo PO, 1948–54, Nippon PO 1956–68. Music director, Kyoto SO from 1970. Frequent guest appearances with European and US orchestras.

Watanabe, Yoko (b Fukuoka, 12 Jul 1953), Japanese soprano. Studied in Tokyo and Milan. Debut Treviso 1978, as Nedda; La Scala 1985, as Liu. Most often heard as Butterfly, which she has sung with the Royal Opera at Manchester (1983) and CG (1989), Chicago (1986), and the NY Met. (1987). Other roles include Suor Angelica, Donna Elvira, Micaela and Mimi; Margherita in *Mefistofele* at Zurich, 1988.

Water Music a set of instrumental pieces by Handel, fp London, 1715, on a boat following the royal barge on the Thames. The music is said to have reconciled George I to Handel after the latter's desertion from the court of Hanover, but the story is doubtful.

Watkins, Michael Blake (b Ilford, 4 May 1948), English composer. Studied with Lutyens and Richard Rodney Bennett (1966–75). Former fellow in TV composition with London Weekend.

Works include *Double Concerto* for oboe, guitar and orchestra (1973); *Youth's Dream* and *Time's Truth* for tenor, trumpet, harp and strings (1973); Concertante for 11 players (1973), horn concerto (1974); violin concerto (1977); *The Spirit of the Universe* for soprano and ensemble (1978); string quartet (1979); Sinfonietta (1982); concertos for trumpet (1988) and cello (1992); oboe quartet (1984).

Watkinson, Carolyn (b Preston, 19 Mar 1949), English mezzo. She studied at the RMCM. Many appearances with the Concertgebouw Orchestra and recordings of Handel (*Rinaldo, Serse, Messiah*) and Bach (B minor Mass and *St Matthew Passion*). At Brussels and Spoleto she has sung Poppea, at Salzburg Mozart's Idamantes, and at La Scala Ariodante. Glyndebourne from 1984 as Cherubino and Cenerentola. Sang with the Boston SO at Tanglewood, 1985; Monteverdi's Nero at Innsbruck, 1990.

Watson, Claire (b New York, 3 Feb 1927; d Utting, 16 Jul 1986),

American soprano. She studied with Elisabeth Schumann in NY; debut Graz, 1951, as Desdemona. In 1955 she was engaged by Solti for the Frankfurt Opera and sang Pamina, Elisabeth and Aida. She was well known in operas by Strauss and made her CG (1958) and Glyndebourne (1960) debuts as the Marschallin; other Strauss roles included Arabella, the Countess and Ariadne. Munich from 1958 (Eva in the 1963 production of *Die Meistersinger*, which opened the rebuilt National Theatre). She appeared in the USA from 1969 and retired in 1976.

Watson, Lilian (b London, 4 Dec 1947), English soprano. Studied in London and made her debut at the 1970 Wexford Festival (*Albert Herring*). WNO debut 1971, as Papagena; CG from 1971, as Barbarina, Blondchen, Tytania and Janáček's Vixen (1990). Glyndebourne from 1976, as Sophie, Despina and Susanna; Salzburg 1982, as Beethoven's Marzelline (Blondchen in 1988). Aix-en-Provence 1991–92; Titania. Sang the Fairy Godmother in Massenet's *Cendrillon*, WNO 1993. Further engagements in Paris, Vienna and Munich.

Watson, Thomas (b London, c 1557; d London, buried 26 Sept 1592), English scholar and amateur musician. He pub. in 1590 *The First Sett of Italian Madrigalls Englished*, the successor of N Yonge's *Musica Transalpina* (1588) and with it the foundation of the native English school of madrigalists.

Watts, André (b Nuremberg, 20 Jun 1946), American pianist, of Hungarian and American parentage. He studied in Philadelphia and made his debut there aged nine, in Haydn's D major concerto. Wide success came with his 1963 performance of Liszt's E♭ concerto with the NY PO under Bernstein. European debut 1966, with the LSO; returned to Nuremberg for a solo recital in 1970. Often performs Brahms and Chopin.

Watts, Helen (b Milford Haven, 7 Dec 1927), Welsh contralto. She studied at the RAM and made her concert debut in 1955; sang with the Handel Opera Society from 1958 in *Theodora* and as Ino and Rinaldo. She toured Russia with the EOG in 1964 and made her US debut three years later, in *The Mass of Life* by Delius at New York. She was heard in operas by Verdi, Tippett and Wagner but was best known in Lieder and oratorio; much admired in Mahler, Elgar and Berlioz.

Waverley overture by Berlioz, op. 1b, inspired by Walter Scott, fp Paris, 26 May 1828.

Wayenberg, Daniel (b Paris, 11 Oct 1929), French-born Dutch pianist. Studied with Marguerite Long and was in hiding during World War II, playing in private houses. Public debut Paris 1946; US debut Carnegie Hall 1953, playing Rakhmaninov's 2nd concerto, under Mitropoulos. Many concerts and recordings in 19th-c. repertory, notably works by Beethoven and Tchaikovsky.

Webbe (1), Samuel (1740–London, 25 May 1816), English composer and organist. From 1776 he held posts at various foreign embassies in London. He was awarded a prize by the Catch Club in 1766 and became its secretary in 1794. He was also librarian of the Glee Club from 1787. Wrote principally glees, catches, etc., also church music.

Webbe (2), Samuel (b London, c 1770; d Liverpool, 25 Nov 1843), English pianist, organist and composer, son and pupil of Samuel ◊Webbe (1). He obtained the Catch Club prize in 1794 and others later. He settled at Liverpool in 1798, returning briefly to London in 1817 to teach jointly with Logier and became organist of the Spanish embassy chapel, but he returned to Liverpool, where he held several church organist posts.

Works include operatic farce *The Speechless Wife*; motets, glees, songs.

Weber, Aloysia (b Zell or Mannheim, between 1759 and 1761; d Salzburg, 8 Jun 1839), German soprano, second daughter of Fridolin Weber. Mozart, who eventually married her sister Constanze, fell in love with her in Mannheim in 1778 and later wrote for her the part of Constanze in *Die Entführung*; he also wrote arias for her. She sang Donna Anna in the first Viennese production of *Don Giovanni* (1788). She married the actor Joseph Lange in 1780.

Weber, Ben (b St Louis, 23 Jul 1916; d New York, 9 May 1979), American composer and teacher. He studied at the University of Chicago but was largely self-taught as a composer; adopted the 12-note system in 1938 and was encouraged by Schoenberg. His music retained tonal associations, however. Moved to NY in 1945.

Works include *Symphony on Poems of William Blake* for baritone and orchestra (1952), violin concerto (1954), *Prelude and Passacaglia* for orchestra (1955), *Chamber Fantasy* for small orchestra (1959), piano concerto (1961); two string quartets (1942, 1952), two string trios (1943, 1946), serenade for string quintet (1955); *Sinfonia Clarion* for orchestra (1974).

Weber, Bernhard Anselm (b Mannheim, 18 Apr 1764; d Berlin, 23 Mar 1821), German composer, conductor and pianist. Pupil of Vogler, he was music director of the Grossmann opera troupe in Hanover 1787–90, then toured Scandinavia with his old teacher, and conducted at the court opera in Berlin from 1792 (*Kapellmeister* 1804).

Works include operas and *Singspiele*, e.g. *Mudarra* (1800) and *Die Jungfrau von Orleans* and *Wallenstein* and other plays; two melodramas; songs.

Weber, Bernhard Christian (b Wolferschwenda, Thuringia, 1 Dec 1712; d Tennstedt near Erfurt, 5 Feb 1758), German organist and composer. Appointed organist at Tennstedt in 1732. It was long claimed that he anticipated Bach by writing a set of preludes and fugues for keyboard in all the keys, entitled *Das wohltemperierte Clavier*, but he actually was an imitator, the work, wrongly dated 1689 (23 years before his birth), being in fact written in 1743.

Weber, Carl Maria (Friedrich Ernst) von (b Eutin near Lübeck, ? 18 Nov 1786; d London, 5 Jun 1826), German composer, conductor, pianist and critic. He was taken about the country in his childhood and received a desultory education, but his father, anxious to make a prodigy of him, taught him all the music he knew. When at last they settled down at Salzburg, the boy, aged ten, became a pupil of Michael Haydn. After his mother's death in Mar 1798 he was taken to Vienna and Munich. There he studied under Valesi (Wallishauser) and Kalcher, and at 13 was a good enough pianist to appear at concerts. By

Weber, von *The composer Carl Maria von Weber (1786–1826) as represented on a chromolithograph of 1912. Weber's most notable achievements are in the operatic works and music for clarinet. Although essentially a Classical composer, he is acknowledged as a forerunner of the Romantic style.*

1800 he had written a good deal of juvenile music and learned lithography with Senefelder; but the wandering life was resumed and he was reduced to continuing his studies with the aid of theoretical books.

At Augsburg in 1803 he succeeded in having his opera *Peter Schmoll und seine Nachbarn* produced. In Vienna again in 1803–04, he became Vogler's pupil for a time, and his master recommended him for a conductorship at Breslau, where he went in the autumn of 1804. In 1806 he became domestic musician to Duke Eugen of Württemberg, who, on being obliged to dismiss his musicians, recommended Weber as private secretary to his younger brother Ludwig.

> *What love is to man, music is to the arts and mankind, for it is actually love itself, the purest, most ethereal language of the emotions.*
> **Carl Maria von Weber**, review of Hoffmann's *Undine*, 1817

He settled at Stuttgart in July 1807, where he led a rather dissolute life and incurred the displeasure of the king, his patron's elder brother. In 1810 he was banished from the kingdom on a trumped-up charge and went to Mannheim and later to Darmstadt, where he resumed his studies with Vogler more seriously. His brilliant works for clarinet and orchestra (two concertos and a concertina) date from 1811; the clarinet quintet followed four years later.

After much travelling he secured the conductorship at the German theatre in Prague in 1813. In Dec 1816 he was appointed conductor of the Dresden court opera, where he did much to establish German opera in the face of the strong opposition of Morlacchi and other Italians. On 4 Nov 1817 he married the opera singer Caroline Brandt, who was still at Prague, and he took her to Dresden after a concert tour. On 4 May 1821 his most famous opera, *Der Freischütz*, was produced in Berlin; this opera was immediately recognized throughout Germany as helping to establish a truly national style. *Euryanthe* followed in Vienna on 25 Oct 1823 and marked a major development with the way in which spoken dialogue, traditional in German opera, was replaced by continuously composed music. In 1824 CG commissioned an English opera from him, and he took English lessons to make a success of *Oberon*. He suffered badly from a severe disease of the throat and felt unfit to visit London, but in order to keep his family from want he took the risk in Feb 1826, visiting Paris on the way. He

A Selection of

Carl Weber

Peter Schmoll und seine Nachbarn	1803
Symphony no. 1	1807
Clarinet Concerto no. 1	1811
Clarinet Quintet	1815
Grand duo concertant	1815
Konzertstück	1821
Der Freischütz	1821
Euryanthe	1823
Oberon	1826
Lieder	

arrived in London on 5 Mar, conducted works of his own at a Philharmonic concert and produced *Oberon* on 12 April; in spite of a confused libretto the opera contained too much fine music to justify its neglect. Although he felt increasingly ill with tuberculosis, he still conducted the succeeding performances and appeared at several concerts. Utterly worn out early in June he made preparations for a hasty return home but died during the night at the house of his host, George Smart.

In spite of his early death Weber had already created a body of work which forms an important foundation of 19th-c. German Romanticism. Wagner and Mahler were particularly indebted to him.

Works include STAGE: operas *Die Macht der Liebe und des Weins* (lost), *Das Waldmädchen* (fragment; early version of *Silvana*, 1800), *Peter Schmoll und seine Nachbarn* (1803), *Rübezahl* (fragments only), *Silvana* (1810), *Abu Hassan* (1811), *Der Freischütz* (1821), *Die drei Pintos* (fragment; later finished by Mahler, produced 1888), *Euryanthe* (1823), *Oberon* (1826); 32 other works including incidental music to Schiller's translation of Gozzi's *Turandot* and P A Wolff's *Preciosa* and extra songs, arias and other interpolations for plays.

ORCHESTRAL: two symphonies (1807); 22 works for solo instruments and orchestra, including two piano concertos (1810–12), *Concertstück* for piano and orchestra (1821), concertino for clarinet and orchestra (1811), two clarinet and one bassoon concertos (all 1811); three overtures.

INSTRUMENTAL: quintet for clarinet, two violins, viola and cello (1815), trio for flute, cello and piano (1819); 27 piano works including eight sets of variations, four sonatas (1812–22), *Momento capriccioso*, *Rondo brillante*, *Aufforderung zum Tanz* (*Invitation to the Dance*).

VOCAL: six cantatas, three Masses, two offertories (all with orchestra); accompanied and unaccompanied part-songs, over 80 songs.

Weber, Constanze, ◊Mozart.

Weber, Fridolin (b Zell, Baden, 1733; d Vienna, 23 Oct 1779), German singer and violinist, father of Aloysia, Constanze (Mozart) and Josepha Weber, and uncle of Carl Maria von Weber. In the service of the electoral court at Mannheim, later lived in Vienna.

Weber, (Friedrich) Dionys(us) (b Velichov, 9 Oct 1766; d Prague, 25 Dec 1842), Bohemian teacher and composer. Pupil of Vogler. He was one of the founders and the first director of the Prague Conservatory and wrote several theoretical treatises. He conducted the first

Weber
A biographical note

After Carl Weber's great success with *Der Freischütz* in 1821, he was in demand throughout Europe, travelling to most of the major musical centres. In 1824 he was invited to write an opera, *Oberon*, for London, but by this time he was mortally ill with tuberculosis. Although warned against making the trip, Weber knew that he did not have much time to provide some security for his wife and children. Saying farewell to them in February 1826, Weber made the then physically demanding journey to London. Although so weakened he was scarcely able to stand without support, he took a full part in the rehearsals for the opera at Covent Garden. British stage convention demanded that actors perform along with the singers; Anne Goward, performing the mermaid, could not be heard clearly and the stage manager demanded that her song must go. An agitated Weber called out, 'Wherefore shall it not go!' and immediately took the baton from the conductor to show how the song should sound. The premiere was a great triumph for Weber, and every aria was interrupted several times by applause. Weber's success had secured the financial future for his family, but he died in his sleep the day before he was due to return home.

Webern *The composer Anton Webern (1883–1945). One of the three composers of the Second Viennese School, Webern was artistically the most strict and concise of the group. Although he received very little recognition during his lifetime, he is acknowledged as having had an enormous impact on future composers.*

performance of Wagner's C major symphony in 1832.

Works include operas and military band music.

Weber, (Jacob) Gottfried (b Freinsheim near Mannheim, 1 Mar 1779; d Kreuznach, 21 Sept 1839), German composer and theorist. He pursued a lawyer's profession at Mannheim (1804), Mainz (1812) and Darmstadt (1818). In 1810 his family provided refuge for their namesakes, C M von Weber and his father, after the former's banishment from Stuttgart, and they formed a music and cultural society. Weber wrote a number of theoretical books.

Works include three Masses and other church music; instrumental sonatas and pieces; songs with piano and guitar.

Weber, Ludwig (b Vienna, 29 Jul 1899; d Vienna, 9 Dec 1974), Austrian bass. Debut Vienna, Volksoper, 1920. He sang in Düsseldorf and Cologne and was engaged at the Staatsoper, Munich, 1933–45. CG 1936 as Pogner, Gurnemanz and Hagen; returned with Vienna co. in 1947 and sang Boris in 1950. His Gurnemanz at the 1951 Bayreuth Festival, under Knappertsbusch, set a standard (it was recorded); continued at Bayreuth until 1961 as Daland, Marke and Hagen. Other roles included Ochs, Sarastro, Osmin, Rocco and Wozzeck. Sang in fp of Strauss's *Friedenstag* (1938).

Weber, (Maria) Josepha (b Zell, 1758 or 1759; d Vienna, 29 Dec 1819), German soprano, eldest daughter of Fridolin Weber. Pupil of Righini, she joined Schikaneder's opera co. in Vienna, and was the first Queen of Night in Mozart's *Die Zauberflöte* (1791). Her husband Sebastian Mayer (1773–1835), created Beethoven's Pizarro (1805).

Webern, Anton (Friedrich Wilhelm von) (b Vienna, 3 Dec 1883; d Mittersill, 15 Sept 1945), Austrian composer and conductor. Studied musicology with Adler and took the Ph.D. degree at Vienna University in 1906. He became a pupil of Schoenberg for composition. His first major work was the Passacaglia for orchestra, written with an awareness of the example of Brahms, and it was followed by the Five Movements for string quartet, which exhibit some of Weber's later epigrammatic style. Song settings of Schoenberg's favourite poet,

Stefan George, are Webern's first excursions into atonality. He conducted for a time at German provincial theatres and in Prague. After World War I he settled at Mödling near Vienna and devoted himself to teaching and composition, though he still conducted, especially the modern performances of the Verein für Musikalische Privataufführrungen and the workers' symphony concerts. He also conducted in London and Barcelona, and in all the German-speaking countries. He adopted Schoenberg's 12-note method of composition in the Three Traditional Rhymes of 1925. In succeeding works, such as the string trio, the symphony op. 21 and the concerto op. 24, Webern adopted ever more rigidly controlled methods; he was also influenced there by Heinrich Isaac (b 1450). His death was the result of a tragic misunderstanding (he was shot by an American soldier). Although almost entirely unrecognized during his lifetime, Webern's music has proved very influential in the years since 1945: it introduced new concepts of sound, rhythm and quasi-mathematical organization. It is almost as much through his work as through Schoenberg's that the '12-tone system' came to find so wide an acceptance; Webern's serial technique was stricter than his colleagues Schoenberg and Berg, and later composers have capitalized on its rigour in their development of integral serialism (in which rhythm, dynamics, and even timbre are serialized). Among composers who have been particularly influenced by Webern are Stravinsky (from the early 1950s), Stockhausen and Boulez.

Works include ORCHESTRAL: *Im Sommerwind*, idyll (1904; fp Seattle, 1962, conductor Ormandy), Passacaglia op. 1 (1908), Six Pieces op. 6 (1909, fp 1913, conductor Schoenberg; revised 1928), Five Pieces op. 10 (1911–13, fp 1926), Five Movements arranged for string orchestra from Five Movements for string quartet (1928–29), symphony op. 21 (1928), Variations op. 30 (1940).

VOCAL: *Entflieht auf leichten Kähnen* for unaccompanied chorus op. 2 (1908, fp 1927), two songs for chorus and ensemble op. 19 (texts by Goethe, 1926), *Das Augenlicht* for chorus and orchestra op. 26 (1935), Cantata no. 1 for soprano, chorus and orchestra (1938–9), Cantata no. 2 for soprano, bass, chorus and orchestra (1941–3, fp 1950); two sets of five songs for voice and piano opp. 3 and 4 (texts by George, 1909), two songs for voice and ensemble op. 8 (texts by Rilke, 1910), four songs for voice and piano op. 12 (1915–17), four songs for voice and orchestra op. 13 (1914–18), six songs for voice and instruments (texts by Trakl, 1919–21), *Five Sacred Songs* for voice and instruments op. 15 (1917–22), five canons on Latin texts for voice, clarinet and bass clarinet op. 16 (1923–24, fp NY, 1951), *Three*

A Selection of

Webern

Passacaglia op. 1	1908
Five Movements op. 5	1909
Six Pieces op. 6	1909
Five Pieces op. 10	1911–13
Six Songs op. 14	1919–21
Symphony op. 21	1928
Concerto op. 24	1934
String Quartet op. 28	1938
Variations op. 30	1940
Cantata no. 2	1941–3

Traditional Rhymes for voice and instruments op. 17 (1925, fp NY, 1952), three songs for voice, clarinet and guitar op. 18 (1925, fp LA, 1954), three songs for voice and piano op. 23 (1934), three songs for voice and piano op. 25 (1934).

INSTRUMENTAL: string quartet in one movement (1905, fp Seattle, 1962), piano quintet in one movement (1909), Five Movements for string quartet op. 5 (1909), four pieces for violin and piano op. 7 (1910), six Bagatelles for string quartet op. 9 (1911–13), *Three Little Pieces* for cello and piano op. 11 (1914), string trio op. 20 (1927), quartet for violin, clarinet, tenor saxophone and piano op. 22 (1930), concerto for nine instruments op. 24 (1934), string quartet op. 28 (1938), variations for piano op. 27 (1936).

ARRANGEMENTS: including Schoenberg's first chamber symphony (instrumental ensemble, 1923), Schubert's *Deutsche Tänze* (orchestra, 1931) and the six-part ricercare from Bach's *Musical Offering* (orchestra; fp London, 1935, conductor Webern).

Doomed to a total failure in a deaf world of ignorance and indifference, he inexorably kept on cutting out his diamonds, his dazzling diamonds, the mines of which he knew to perfection.

Igor Stravinsky on Webern, quoted in Kolneder, *Anton Webern*, 1968

Webster, David (Lumsden) (b Dundee, 3 Jul 1903; d London, 11 May 1971), British administrator. He assisted in several opera productions while at Liverpool University. He was general administrator at CG 1945–70 and helped to establish the Royal Opera House as a leading centre of opera and ballet. He encouraged many British artists in international careers. Knighted 1961.

Wecker, Georg Caspar (b Nuremberg, bap. 2 Apr 1632; d Nuremberg, 20 Apr 1695), German organist and composer. Pupil of his father, an instrumental performer, and Erasmus Kindermann. He was organist at various Nuremberg churches from the age of 19 and in 1686 was appointed to the principal one, St Sebald's. J Krieger and Pachelbel were among his pupils.

Works include 18 sacred concertos (church cantatas) for voices and instruments; organ music.

Weckerlin, Jean-Baptiste (Théodore) (b Guebwiller, Alsace, 9 Nov 1821; d Trottberg, near Guebwiller, 20 May 1910), French composer and editor. Studied at the Paris Conservatory. Although unsuccessful, he was determined to make his way as a musician, collected much early French music and in 1863 became archivist of the Société des Compositeurs de Musique, whose library he established. In 1869 Auber invited him to the Conservatory library, of which he became head in 1876. He edited many collections of early French songs and other music.

Works include opera *L'Organiste dans l'embarras* (1953) and five others (some in Alsatian dialect); *Roland* for solo voices, chorus and orchestra; Mass and motets; symphony and suite for orchestra; chamber music; songs.

Weckmann, Matthias (b Niederdorla, Thuringia, *c* 1619; d Hamburg,

and other Hamburg musicians) and during a visit to Dresden competed as an organist with Froberger.

Works include sacred concertos for voices and instruments; organ music.

We Come to the River opera ('actions for music') by Henze (libretto by E Bond); composed 1974–76, produced London, CG, 12 Jul 1976. After a battle, the General sentences the Deserter to be shot; he later finds the condemned man's wife trying to survive amongst the corpses. Realizing the misery he has caused, the General refuses orders and is sent to a mental asylum where the inmates imagine a river carries them to freedom.

Wedding, The ballet by Stravinsky (choreographed by B Nizhinska), produced Paris, Théâtre Lyrique, 13 Jun 1923. The work is scored for chorus (Russian words), four pianos and percussion. It is more generally known as *Les Noces*.

Wedekind, Frank (1864–1918), German dramatist. ◊Ettinger (*Frühlingserwachen*); ◊Lulu (Berg). His sister Erika (1868–1944) sang at Dresden 1894–1909 as Eva, Mimi and Butterfly; Salzburg 1901–04 as Blondchen and Zerlina. Also sang in Vienna (1904), Berlin and Stockholm.

'Wedge' Fugue Bach's E minor organ fugue, BWV 548.ii, so called because of the progressively widening intervals of its subject.

The subject of Bach's 'Wedge' fugue, BWV 548.ii.

24 Feb 1674), German organist and composer. He became a pupil of Schütz as a choirboy in the electoral chapel at Dresden and in 1637 was sent at the elector's expense to study further with J Praetorius at Hamburg. In 1641 he became court organist at Dresden, where he remained until 1655, except for a visit to Nykøbing in the service of the crown prince of Denmark, some time before 1647. He then became organist at St James's Church, Hamburg. He organized a concert society (*Collegium musicum* with Scheidemann, Selle, Schop

Weelkes, Thomas (b *c* 1576; d London, buried 1 Dec 1623), English composer. He was in the service of George Phillpot at Compton near Winchester in his early years and then that of Edward Darcye, Groom of the Privy Chamber. In 1598 he was appointed organist at Winchester College and in 1602 he took the B.Mus. at Oxford. In 1601 or 1602 he became organist and choirmaster at Chichester Cathedral, but increasing drunkenness led to his dismissal in 1617. He died during a visit to London. He was one of the most important madrigalists of his time, contributing *As Vesta was from Latmos Hill descending* to the *Triumphs of Oriana* (1601).

Works include services and numerous anthems; three books of madrigals, *Ayeres or Phantasticke Spirites* for three voices (1608), two vocal pieces contributed to Leighton's *Teares or Lamentacions*; three In Nomines for four–five viols and other pieces for five viols.

Weerbeke, Gaspar van (b Oudenaarde, *c* 1445; d after 1517), Flemish composer, singer and priest. Pupil of the *maîtrise* at Oudenaarde and of Ockeghem. He took holy orders at Tournai and went to Italy in the 1470s, becoming *maestro di cappella* at Milan Cathedral and a singer at the ducal court. He was in Rome as a singer at the Papal Chapel in 1481–89, but in 1488 produced music for allegorical plays given at the marriage of Galeazzo Sforza, Duke of Milan, to Isabella of Aragon. He visited his home town in 1490 and was received with honours.

Works include eight Masses, 28 motets, *Stabat Mater* and other church music.

Weideman(n), Carl Friedrich (Charles Frederick) (d London, 1782), German flautist and composer. Settled in London *c* 1726. He was concerned with Festing in the foundation of the Royal Society of Musicians in 1739 and in 1778 became conductor of the royal orchestra. He wrote concertos, solos, duets, trios and quartets for flute.

Weidemann, Friedrich (b Ratzeburg, 1 Jan 1871; d Vienna, 30 Jan 1919), German baritone. After study at Hamburg and Berlin he sang at Essen, Hamburg and Riga. In 1903 he moved to the Hopfoper, Vienna; he was admired there, until his death, in operas by Mozart and Wagner, at first under Mahler. He was the first Viennese Orestes, Golaud and Faninal, and in London sang Jochanaan and Kurwenal (1910). At the 1906 Salzburg Festival he was heard as Mozart's Count, again under Mahler.

My subject is War, and the pity of War./The Poetry is in the pity./All a poet can do today is warn.
Wilfred Owen (1893–1918), quoted by Benjamin Britten as preface to the *War Requiem*, 1961

Weidinger, Christine (b Springville, NY, 31 Mar 1946), American soprano. Studied in Phoenix and with Margaret Harshaw. Debut as Musetta at Washington, DC, 1972. Sang at the NY Met. from 1974; West Germany and elsewhere in Europe from 1981. Roles have included such dramatic and bel canto repertory as Norma, Donna Anna, Mozart's Electra, Amina, Gilda and *Trovatore*. Sang Constanze at Monte Carlo (1988), Vitellia at La Scala (1990) and Lucia di Lammermoor for Cincinnati Opera, 1991.

Weidt, Lucie (b Troppau, Silesia, *c* 1876; d Vienna, 28 Jul 1940), Austrian soprano. She made her debut in Leipzig, 1900, and in 1902 was engaged by Mahler for the Vienna Hofoper; her debut role was Elisabeth and later she was the first Viennese Lisa, Kundry and Marschallin. In 1919 she created the Nurse in *Die Frau ohne Schatten*. She sang as guest in Paris and Buenos Aires and in 1910 was Brünnhilde at the NY Met.

Weigl, Joseph (b Eisenstadt, 28 Mar 1766; d Vienna, 3 Feb 1846), Austrian composer, son of Joseph Franz ◊Weigl and godson of Haydn. Pupil of Albrechtsberger and Salieri, he was the latter's deputy at the court opera in Vienna from 1790 and succeeded him as conductor and composer in 1792. He visited Italy to produce operas 1807–08 and again in 1815, but shortly afterwards withdrew from opera composition and wrote mainly church music. He became vice-*Kapellmeister* at court in 1827.

Works include over 30 operas, *Der Schureizerfamilie* and Singspiels (1809), e.g. *Die betrogene Arglist* (1783), *Das Waisenhaus* (1808), *Die Schweizerfamilie* (1809); *Der Bergsturz* (1813); 18 ballets; incidental music; 11 Masses and other church music; cantatas, arias, songs.

Weigl, Joseph (Franz) (b Bavaria, 19 May 1740; d Vienna, 25 Jan 1820), German cellist. He joined Prince Esterházy's orchestra at Eisenstadt

under Haydn in 1761, but left in 1769 for the Vienna Court Opera and joined the Imperial Chapel there in 1792.

Weigl, Karl (b Vienna, 6 Feb 1881; d New York, 11 Aug 1949), Austrian composer. Studied musicology at Vienna University, worked as assistant conductor under Mahler at the Vienna Opera, became a teacher at the New Vienna Conservatory in 1918 and later lecturer at the university. He settled in the USA in 1938, becoming an American citizen in 1943 and teaching successively at Hartford, Brooklyn and Boston.

Works include cantata *Weltfeier* for solo voices, chorus, orchestra and organ; six symphonies (1908–47); various concertos; eight string quartets (1903–49); cello and piano sonata; songs with piano and with chamber accompaniment.

Weigl, Thaddäus (b Vienna, 1776; d Vienna, 10 Feb 1844), Austrian composer and publisher, son and pupil of Joseph Weigl. Was for a time conductor at the court theatres, but in 1801 became a music publisher.

Works include opera *Der Jahrmarkt zu Grünewald* and others; ballet *Cyrus und Thomyris* and others.

Weihe des Hauses, Die, *The Consecration of the House*, overture by Beethoven, op. 124, written in 1822 for the opening of the Josefstadt Theatre in Vienna, and performed there 3 Oct.

Weikert, Ralf (b St Florian, 10 Nov 1940), Austrian conductor. Studied with Hans Swarowsky and worked with the Salzburg Landestheater, from 1963. Music director Bonn Opera 1966, guest at Copenhagen with operas by Verdi, Mozart and Stravinsky. Vienna and Hamburg Staatsoper debuts 1974 and 1975. Zurich Opera from 1976, Deutsche Oper Berlin 1978. US debut 1980 with *Giulio Cesare* at the City Opera and in Los Angeles; NY Met. 1987–90, *Elisir d'Amore*, *Barbiere di Siviglia* and *La bohème*. Chamber concerts in the UK and at the Salzburg Festival.

Weikl, Bernd (b Vienna, 29 Jul 1942), Austrian baritone. He studied in Hanover and sang there 1968–70. After an engagement at Düsseldorf he sang in Hamburg from 1973. Salzburg from 1971 and Bayreuth from 1972, as Wolfram, Amfortas, Dutchman and Sachs (1991). CG debut 1975, as Rossini's Figaro; NY Met. 1977, Wolfram (Hans Sachs there in 1993). Other roles include Mandryka and Don Giovanni.

Weil, Bruno (b Hahanstaten, 1949), German conductor. Studied in Vienna and was music director at Augsburg Opera, 1979–89. Concerts with the Berlin PO from 1979, Deutsche Oper from 1980. Vienna Staatsoper debut 1985, *Aida*; *Don Giovanni* at the 1988 Salzburg Festival. US debut with a New York Schubertiade, 1988; *Così fan tutte* at Glyndebourne, 1992.

Weil, Hermann (b Muhlburg, near Karlsruhe, 29 May 1876; d Blue Mountain Lake, NY, 6 Jul 1949), German baritone. After study in Freiburg he made his 1901 debut there, as Wolfram. Stuttgart 1904–33. In 1911 he sang Kurwenal at the NY Met. under Toscanini; he remained with the co. until 1917. Bayreuth 1911–25, as Sachs, Amfortas and Gunther. Vienna 1920–23. He emigrated to NY after the rise of the Nazis.

Weill, Kurt (Julian) (b Dessau, 2 Mar 1900; d New York, 3 Apr 1950), German composer. Studied locally at first, later with Humperdinck and Busoni in Berlin. He had his first stage success at the age of 26 with *Der Protagonist*. His collaboration with Brecht on a modern version of Gay's *Beggar's Opera* (*Die Dreigroschenoper*) made an enormous hit in 1928, but the Nazi regime condemned his works in 1933 as both Jewish and decadent, and he left Germany; official opinion also disapproved of Weill's effective use of jazz in his stage works, and there was further suspicion of the sharp social satire in *Die Dreigroschenoper* (*Mahagonny* satirized American frontier values). He visited London in 1935 for the production of *A Kingdom for a Cow*, an English version of an earlier operetta, but went the same year to settle in USA (naturalized 1943) and wrote works for Broadway, the finest of which is *Street Scene*.

Works include operas and operettas (several on libretti by Brecht) *Der Protagonist* (1926), *Der Silbersee* (1933), *Der Zar lässt sich photographieren* (libretto by G Kaiser), *Royal Palace* (1927), *Die*

Dreigroschenoper (1928), *Happy End* (1929), *Aufstieg und Fall der Stadt Mahagonny* (1930), *Der Jasager* (1930), *Die Bürgschaft*, *A Kingdom for a Cow* (1935), *Johnny Johnson* (1936), *Knickerbocker Holiday* (1938), *The Firebrand of Florence* (1945), *Down in the Valley* (1948), *Street Scene* (1947), *Love Life* (1948), *Lost in the Stars* (1949).

Biblical music drama *The Eternal Road*; ballet *Die sieben Todsünden* (*Anna Anna*, 1933); cantatas *Der neue Orpheus* and *Der Lindberghflug* (1929); two symphonies (1921, 1933), *Fantasia, Passacaglia und Hymnus*, *Divertimento* and *Quodlibet* for orchestra; concerto for violin and wind band (1924); two string quartets (1919, 1923); works for voices and chamber orchestra, songs (Rilke) with orchestra.

Weinberger, Jaromír (b Prague, 8 Jan 1896; d St Petersburg, FL, 8 Aug 1967), Czech composer. Studied with Hoffmeister and Kricka in Prague and with Reger in Germany. Professor of composition at the Conservatory of Ithaca, NY, 1922–26; returned to Europe to conduct and teach. His best-known work, the brilliant folk- opera *Schvanda the Bagpiper* was premiered at Prague, 1927. Settled in USA in 1938; committed suicide.

Works include operas *Shvanda the Bagpiper* (1927), *The Beloved Voice* (1931), *The Outcasts of Poker Flat* (after Bret Harte, 1932) and *Wallenstein* (after Schiller); pantomime *The Abduction of Eveline*; incidental music for Shakespeare's and other plays; variations on the English song, *Under the Spreading Chestnut Tree* for piano and orchestra (1939), *Lincoln Symphony*, *Czech Rhapsody* for orchestra; works for organ, piano, violin.

Wein, Der, *The Wine*, concert aria by Berg (text by Baudelaire, in German translation by S George); composed 1929, fp Königsberg, 4 Jun 1930, conductor Scherchen.

Weiner, Leó (b Budapest, 16 Apr 1885; d Budapest, 13 Sept 1960), Hungarian composer. Studied at the National Academy of Music in Budapest, where he became a professor in 1908.

Works include ballet on and incidental music for Vörösmarty's *Csongor and Tünde* (1916); three divertimentos (1934–49), scherzo, serenade and humoresque *Carnival* for orchestra; *Pastoral, Fantasy and Fugue* for strings; two violin concertos; three string quartets (1906–38), string trio; two violin and piano sonatas; piano works.

Weingartner, (Paul) Felix (b Zara, Dalmatia, 2 Jun 1863; d Winterthur, Switzerland, 7 May 1942), Austrian conductor and composer. Studied at Graz, at the Leipzig Conservatory and under Liszt at Weimar, where he produced his first opera in 1884. He became conductor at Königsberg, Danzig, Hamburg and Mannheim before 1891, when he was appointed conductor of the Court Opera in Berlin and conductor of the symphony concerts. In 1898 he left for Munich to become conductor of the Kaim orchestra and in 1908 he succeeded Mahler as chief conductor at the Vienna Hofoper; resigned 1911 but conducted Vienna PO concerts until 1927. After 1911 he frequently conducted throughout Europe and the USA, notably in the symphonies of Beethoven; at CG he gave *Tannhäuser* and *Parsifal* in 1939. The last years of his life he spent, still actively, in Switzerland, especially at Basel. He was five times married. He wrote books on conducting, on Beethoven's symphonies, etc.

Works include operas *Sakuntala* (after Kalidasa, 1884), *Malawika* (1886), *Genesius*, *Orestes* trilogy (after Aeschylus, 1902), *Kain und Abel* (1914), *Dame Kobold* (after Calderón), *Die Dorfschule, Meister Andrea*, *Der Apostat*; incidental music for Shakespeare's *Tempest* and Goethe's *Faust*; seven symphonies (1899–1937), symphonic poem *King Lear* (after Shakespeare); three string quartets; songs.

Weinlig, Christian Theodor (b Dresden, 25 Jul 1780; d Leipzig, 7 Mar 1842), German theorist and composer. Pupil of his uncle, Christian Ehregott Weinlig (1743–1813), cantor of the Kreuzschule at Dresden. He succeeded Schicht as cantor of St Thomas's School at Leipzig in 1823. Clara Schumann and Wagner were his pupils for a short time. He wrote a treatise on fugue. His compositions include an oratorio, two German Magnificats and church cantatas.

Weir, Gillian (Constance) (b Martinborough, New Zealand, 17 Jan 1941), New Zealand organist and harpsichordist. Studied at the RCM and with Anton Heiller and Marie-Claire Alain. From 1965 has been heard widely in Poulenc, Messiaen, Couperin and Bach. US debut at New York, 1984. William Mathias wrote a concerto for her.

Weir, Judith (b Aberdeen, 11 May 1954), Scottish composer. She studied with John Tavener and worked with computer music, MIT (1973). Later studied with Robin Holloway at Cambridge.

Works include operas *The Black Spider* (1985), *A Night at The Chinese Opera* (1987), *The Vanishing Bridegroom* (1990) and *Blond Eckbert* (1994); orchestral pieces *Wunderhorn* (1979) *The Ride Over Lake Constance* (1984), *Variations on 'Summer is icumen in'* (1987), *Music Untangled* (1992), *Heroic Strokes of the Bow* (1992); *Heaven Ablaze in his Breast* for chorus, two pianos and eight dancers (1989); re-compositions of Mozart's *Il sogno di Scipione* (1991) and Monteverdi's *Il Combattimento di Tancredi e Clorinda* (1992); music for ensemble, chamber music; songs and keyboard pieces.

Weis, Flemming (b Copenhagen, 15 Apr 1898; d Copenhagen, 30 Sept 1981), Danish composer. A member of a musical family, he began to compose as a child. In 1916 he entered the Copenhagen Conservatory and in 1920 finished studies at Leipzig. Active on behalf of contemporary music and also as a music critic.

Works include *The Promised Land* for chorus and orchestra; two symphonies (1942, 1948), symphonic overture and *In temporis vernalis* for orchestra; *Introduction grave* for piano and strings, four string quartets (1922–77) and other chamber music; sonatas for various instruments, suite and sonatina for piano; songs.

Weis, Karel (b Prague, 13 Feb 1862; d Prague, 4 Apr 1944), Czech composer and conductor. Studied at the Prague Conservatory and with Skuherský and Fibich at the Organ School. After various posts as organist, teacher and orchestra player (violin and horn), he became conductor at the National Theatre at Brno in 1886, but from 1888 devoted himself to composition.

Works include operas *Viola* (after Shakespeare's *Twelfth Night*, 1892; revised as *The Twins*, 1917), *The Polish Jew* (after Erckmann-Chatrian), *The Attack on the Mill* (after Zola, 1912), *The Blacksmith of Lesetin* (1920), operettas *The Village Musicians* and *The Revisor* (after Gogol's comedy); choral scene *Triumfator*; symphonic poem *Helios and Selene*; string quartet; violin and piano sonata; piano pieces; folksong arrangements.

I believe that the musical theatre is the highest, the most expressive, and the most imaginative form of theatre.

Kurt Weill, quoted in Ewen, *American Composers*, 1982

Weisgall, Hugo (David) (b Ivaniçice, Czechoslovakia, 13 Oct 1912), Czech-born American composer. His family settled in the USA in 1920. He studied at the Peabody Conservatory, Baltimore, and later with Sessions in NY and R Scalero at the Curtis Institute in Philadelphia. He taught at the Juilliard School 1957–68. His music admits a wide range of influences (including neo-classical and serial) and his operas have been particularly successful.

Works include operas *Night* (1932), *Lillith* (1934), *The Tenor* (1952), *Six Characters in Search of an Author* (after Pirandello, 1959), *Athaliah* (1964), *Nine Rivers from Jordan* (1968), *The 100 Nights* (1976), *The Gardens of Adonis* (1992, composed 1959), *Esther* (1994); ballets *Quest, One Thing is Certain, Outpost*; overture in F major for orchestra; choral music; songs.

Weismann, Julius (b Freiburg, 26 Dec 1879; d Singen, Bodensee, 22 Dec 1950), German composer. Studied at Munich with Herzogenberg in Berlin and again at Munich with Thuille. He gained Nazi favour by accepting a commission to compose music for *A Midsummer Night's Dream* which was intended to replace that of Mendelssohn (who was Jewish); *Die pfiffige Magd* was performed throughout Germany during the war years.

Works include operas *Schwanenweiss* (1923), *Traumspiel* (1925), *Gespenstersonate* (all after Strindberg), *Leonce und Lena*

(G Büchner, 1924), *Landsknechte, Regina del Lago* (1928), *Die pfiffige Magd* (after Holberg, 1939); three symphonies, three pieces for orchestra, three sinfoniettas; four violin concertos, three piano concertos, cello concerto; 11 string quartets (1905–47), three piano trios (1908–21); sonata for violin solo, five violin sonatas, two cello sonatas, variations for oboe and piano; choral works; variations for two pianos; seven op. nos. of piano pieces; 15 op. nos. of songs.

Weiss, Adolph (b Baltimore, 12 Sept 1891; d Van Nuys, CA, 21 Feb 1971), American composer of German parentage. Studied piano, violin and bassoon, and at the age of 16 played first bassoon with the Russian Symphony Orchestra of NY and then in the NY PO under Mahler. He then studied composition at Columbia University with C Rybner and later with Schoenberg in Vienna. Later worked with various California orchestras.

Works include *I Segreti* (1923) and *American Life* (1928) for orchestra; *The Libation Bearers*, choreographed cantata for soloists, chorus and orchestra; theme and variations for orchestra; trumpet concerto; three string quartets (1925–32); music for wind instruments; songs; piano music.

Weiss (actually *Schneeweiss*), Amalie (b Marburg, Styria, 10 May 1839; d Berlin, 3 Feb 1898), Austrian contralto. Made her first stage appearance at Troppau in 1853, was later engaged in Vienna and Hanover, and at the latter place married Joachim in 1863. She then appeared only as a concert singer. They separated in 1884.

Weiss, Franz (b Glatz, Silesia, 18 Jan 1778; d Vienna, 25 Jan 1830), Austrian violist and composer. Settled in Vienna and became the viola player in Prince Rasumovsky's quartet, founded 1808.

Works include symphony for flute, bassoon and trumpet with orchestra, variations for violin and orchestra; string quartet; duets for violins and for flutes; piano sonatas.

Weiss, Sylvius Leopold (b Breslau, 12 Oct 1686; d Dresden, 16 Oct 1750), German lutenist and composer. He was in the service of the Polish Prince Alexander Sobieski, with whom he went to Rome *c* 1708, later at the courts of Hesse-Kassel, Düsseldorf, and from 1718 Dresden, where he worked with Lotti, Hasse, Porpora, Hebenstreit, Pisendel and others; he was sent to Vienna with a visiting Saxon orchestra that year. In 1723 he played in Prague with Quantz and H Graun in Fux's coronation opera *Costanza e fortezza*. Wrote lute music, including over 70 partitas.

Weissenberg, Alexis (Sigismond) (b Sofia, 26 Jul 1929), Bulgarian-born French pianist. Studied at the Juilliard School from 1946, won Leventritt Competition 1948. Retired 1956–66 for study. London debut 1974.

Weissenburg, Hainz, ◊Albicastro.

Weissensee, Friedrich (b Schwerstedt, Thuringia, *c* 1560; d Altenweddingen, 1622), German clergyman and composer. Became rector of the grammar school at Gebessee, *c* 1590, and cantor of the town school of Magdeburg in *c* 1596. About 1602 he became rector at Altenweddingen. His works include motets in the Venetian style.

Weisshan (or *Winsheim*), Abraham, 16th–17th-c. lutenist and composer. In 1568 he went into service at the Saxon court at Dresden, ans was still there in 1611.

Works include a collection of lute preludes, fantasies and dances *Silvae musicalis libri VII*.

welcome-odes, or welcome-songs, cantatas by Purcell for the return to London of Charles II and James II on various occasions. One, of 1682, is addressed to James as Duke of York, before his accession.

Weldon, George (b Chichester, 5 Jun 1906; d Cape Town, 16 Aug 1963), English conductor. Studied at the RCM with Sargent, and conducted various provincial orchestras, in 1943 becoming conductor of the CBSO, a post he held until 1951; later assistant conductor of the Hallé Orchestra under Barbirolli.

Weldon, John (b Chichester, 19 Jan 1676; d London, 7 May 1736), English organist and composer. Educated at Eton, where he studied music under the college organist John Walton, he later became a pupil of Purcell in London. In 1694 he was appointed organist of New College, Oxford, and in 1700 gained the first prize for the setting of Congreve's masque *The Judgement of Paris* against Eccles, Finger

and D Purcell. In 1701 he became a Gentleman of the Chapel Royal and in 1708 organist there on the death of Blow; he also became organist of St Bride's and (1726) St Martin's-in-the-Fields churches.

Works include masque *The Judgment of Paris* (1701); music for *The Tempest* (*c* 1712), songs for Cibber's *She would and she would not* and other plays; anthems; songs.

Welitsch (actually *Velickova*), Ljuba (b Borissovo, 10 Jul 1913), Bulgarian-born Austrian soprano. Played the violin as a child, studied philosophy at Sofia University, and then studied singing in Vienna with Lierhammer, making her debut in Sofia in 1936. Sang at Graz, Hamburg and Munich, then visited CG with Vienna co. as Salome, her most famous role. She returned to CG for Musetta, Aida and Tosca. Met. 1948–52.

Weller, Walter (b Vienna, 30 Nov 1939), Austrian conductor and violinist. He joined the Vienna PO in 1956 and founded the Weller Quartet in 1958; toured with the ensemble in Europe and the USA, and recorded works by Berg and Beethoven. After study with Krips and Szell became a conductor from 1966; British debut 1973, with LSO. Principal conductor RLPO 1977–80, RPO 1980–85. Conducted Prince Igor in Berlin, 1990. Music director of the Royal Scottish National Orchestra from 1992. He has given concerts in Japan and Israel and conducted at Salzburg and Florence. Well known in late Romantic repertory.

Wellesz, Egon (b Vienna, 21 Oct 1885; d Oxford, 9 Nov 1974), Austrian musicologist and composer. Studied with Schoenberg, Bruno Walter and others in Vienna, also musicology with Adler at the university, where he graduated Ph.D. in 1908. In 1913 he became lecturer in music history there and professor 1930–38. He specialized in Byzantine and modern music, edited and wrote on the former and pub. works on Schoenberg, Cavalli and the Venetian opera, modern orchestra, etc. In 1932 he received the honorary Mus.D. from Oxford University and in 1938 he settled there, becoming lecturer 1943 and Reader 1948–56. He was a member of the editorial board of the *New Oxford History of Music* and editor of volume I and one of the editions of *Monumenta Musicae Byzantinae*. His books include *A History of Byzantine Music* and *Eastern Elements in Western Chant*. CBE 1957.

Works include operas *Die Prinzessin Girnara* (J Wassermann, 1921), *Alkestis* (Hofmannsthal, 1924) and *Die Bacchantinnen* (after Euripides, 1931), *Operfung des Gefangenen* (1926), *Scherz, List und Rache* (Goethe's libretto), 1928), *Incognita* (on Congreve's story, 1951); ballets *Das Wunder der Diana* (1924), *Persian ballet* (1920), *Archilles auf Skyros* (1921) and *Die Nächtlichen* (1923).

VOCAL AND ORCHESTRAL: unaccompanied choruses to old English poems: *Gebete der Mädchen zu Maria* for soprano, chorus and orchestra; nine symphonies (1945–71), symphonic poem *Vorfrühling*, symphonic suite *Prosperos Beschwörungen* (after Shakespeare's *Tempest*, 1938), *Festival March* for orchestra; *Amor timido* (Metastasio) and *Lied der Welt* (Hofmannsthal) for soprano and orchestra, *Leben, Traum und Tod* (Hofmannsthal) for contralto and orchestra (1935); dance suite for violin and chamber orchestra; piano concerto; violin concerto; three Masses, motets, cantata *Mitte des Lebens*.

CHAMBER AND INSTRUMENTAL: *The Leaden Echo and the Golden Echo* (G M Hopkins) for soprano, clarinet, viola, cello and piano (1944); nine string quartets (1911–66), string quintet; clarinet quintet; octet; solo sonatas for violin, cello, oboe, clarinet, etc.; piano pieces; songs.

Well-tempered Clavier Das ◊Wohltemperierte Clavier.

Welser-Möst, Franz (b Linz, 16 Aug 1960), Austrian conductor. Studied in Munich and was principal conductor of the Austrian Youth Orchestra, 1979–85 (Bruckner's 5th in the Vienna Musikverein). Salzburg debut 1985; UK 1986, LPO principal conductor (1990–95). Opera debut with Rossini's *Italiana* at the Vienna Staatsoper, 1986. US debut with the St Louis SO, 1989. Conducted the LPO in *Tristan und Isolde* (concert, 1993) and *Peter Grimes* at Glyndebourne, 1994. Music director of Zurich Opera from 1996.

Welsh, Moray (b Haddington, 1 Mar 1947), Scottish cellist. Studied with Rostropovitch and made London debut 1972. Concerts with major orchestras, including the fp of L Berkeley's Concerto (1988). Co-principal of the LSO from 1993. Recordings include concertos by Goehr, Hugh Wood, Boccherini and Vivaldi.

Welsh National Opera opera co. founded 1946. Based in Cardiff and tours widely in Wales and the English provinces. An adventurous repertory including early Verdi (first British performance of *La battaglia di Legnano*, 1960) and a well-received cycle, with Scottish Opera, of Janáček's operas. The WNO production of *The Ring* was brought to London, CG, in 1986 and *Tristan* in 1993. Music directors from 1963 have been Bryan Balkwill (until 1967) James Lockhart (1968–73) and Richard Armstrong (1973–86); Charles Mackerras 1986–92, succeeded by Carlo Rizzi. Singers who have appeared with the co. include Gwyneth Jones, Geraint Evans, Margaret Price and Anne Evans.

Welting, Ruth (b Memphis, 11 May 1949), American soprano. After study in New York made debut at the City Opera there in 1970, as Blondchen. Best known for her coloratura in the role of Zerbinetta, which she sang on her CG (1975), NY Met. (1976) and Salzburg (1982) debuts. Other roles include Lucia de Lammermoor, Rosina, Olympia, and Ophelia in *Hamlet* (Chicago, 1990).

Wendling (born *Spurni*), Dorothea (b Stuttgart, 21 Mar 1736; d Munich, 20 Aug 1811), German soprano. Worked at the court of Mannheim and Munich; wife of Johann Baptist ◊Wendling. She created Ilia in *Idomeneo* (1781).

Music, alas! too long has been/Pressed to obey the Devil.

Charles Wesley (1707–1788),
The True Use of Music, 1749

Wendling, Johann Baptist (b Rappoltsweiler, Alsace, 17 Jun 1723; d Munich, 27 Nov 1797), German flautist, husband of Dorothea ◊Wendling. In the service of the court at Mannheim from c 1751 to 1752, also travelled widely.

Wenkoff, Spas (b Tŏvnovo, 23 Sept 1928), Bulgarian tenor. Studied in Sofia and Dresden, appearing in East Germany from 1965 (Tristan at Dresden, 1975). Member of the Berlin Staatsoper from 1975; Bayreuth 1976–83, as Tristan and Tannhäuser. Sang Tristan on NY Met. debut (1981) and at Cologne 1990. Appeared further in Vienna and Munich.

Wennberg, Siv (b Timrå, 18 Sept 1944), Swedish soprano. Studied in Stockholm and made debut there 1971, as Mozart's Marcellina; soprano debut as Sieglinde, 1972. Stuttgart Opera 1973–76, Frankfurt from 1976. Vienna Staatsoper and Geneva 1972, as Senta, and Elisabeth in *Tannhäuser*. London, CG, 1975 as the Empress in *Die Frau ohne Schatten*. Sang in the fp of *Christina* by Gefors, Stockholm 1986.

Wenzinger, August (b Basel, 14 Nov 1905), Swiss conductor, cellist and gamba-player. Studied first at the Basel Conservatory, until 1927, and then with P Jarnach in Cologne until 1929. Then played cello with various orchestras, and taught at the Schola Cantorum Basiliensis 1934–70. He was especially well known as a conductor of Baroque (and earlier) music, using period instruments.

Werba, Erik (b Baden, near Vienna, 23 May 1918), Austrian composer, piano accompanist and writer on music. Studied with J Marx, Wellesz and Schenk, graduating in 1940. In 1948 he became professor at the Vienna State Academy. He was frequently heard in recital, with Christa Ludwig, Peter Schreier and Nicolai Gedda.

Werckmeister, Andreas (b Benneckenstein, 30 Nov 1645; d Halberstadt, 26 Oct 1706), German organist and theorist. Organist at Hasselfelde, Quedlinburg and Halberstadt in succession. Wrote theoretical works, especially on keyboard tuning.

Werfel, Franz (b Prague, 10 Sept 1890; d Beverly Hills, CA, 26 Aug 1945), Austrian novelist and playwright. Studied at Prague and Leipzig University His works include a novel on Verdi and translations of many of Verdi's operas e.g. *Forza del destino* (1925), *Simon Boccanegra* (1929) and *Don Carlos*. ◊Grosz (*Spiegelmensch*); ◊Max

imilien (Milhaud); ◊Orff (*Turmes Auferstehung*); ◊Troades (Reimann); ◊Zwingburg (Krenek).

Werle, Lars Johann (b Gävle, 23 Jun 1926), Swedish composer. Studied at Uppsala University with Bäck. Teacher at the National School of Music in Stockholm. He is best known for his technically varied output of operas: *Dream about Thérèse* (1964), *The Journey* (1969), *Tintomara* (1973), *A Midsummer Night's Dream* (1985), *Lionardo* (1988), *The Painting: An Afternoon at the Prado* (1990), double- bill *Hercules* and *Väntarna* (1995).

Werner, Gregor Joseph (b Ybbs an der Donau, 28 Jan 1693; d Eisenstadt, Burgenland, 3 Mar 1766), Austrian composer. Appointed music director to the Esterházy family in 1728; predecessor of Haydn there and his superior for five years from 1761. Shortly before his death Werner reported to Prince Nikolaus von Esterházy on Haydn's alleged laziness and ineptitude.

Works include over 20 Masses, three Requiems and other church music; 18 oratorios; symphony; string quartet, six introductions and fugues for string quartet (pub. by Haydn); sonatas, etc., for two violins and bass.

Werrecore (or *Verecore*), Matthias Hermann (d after 1574)), ? Flemish 16th-c. composer. In 1522 he became *maestro di cappella* of Milan Cathedral in succession to Gafori.

Works include motets for five voices, four-part song on the battles of Bicocca and Pavia, in which Francesco Sforza gained the mastery of Milan.

Wert, Giaches (or *Jaches*) de (b ? Weert, 1535; d Mantua, 6 May 1596), Flemish composer. Was sent to Italy as a choirboy and at nine became a member of the choir of the Novellara at Reggio. He began to pub. madrigals towards the end of the 1550s and c 1560 went into service at the ducal court of Mantua under Guglielmo Gonzaga. He was also attached to the church of Santa Barbara, where he succeeded Giovanni Contina as *maestro di cappella* in 1565. In 1566 he accompanied the duke to Augsburg and there declined an offer from the Emperor Maximilian II. In 1567 he visited Venice with the court and later Ferrara under Alfonso (II) d'Este. About that time he suffered much from the intrigues of the Italian musicians, who disliked him as a foreigner, and in 1570 one of them, Agostino Bonvicino, was dismissed for a love-affair with Wert's wife. In 1580 he and his family were given the freedom of the city of Mantua in perpetuity.

Works include motets, 11 books of madrigals for five voices (1558–95), one for four voices, canzonets, *villanelle*.

Werther opera by Massenet (libretto by E Blau, P Milliet and G Hartmann, based on Goethe's novel), produced in German, Vienna, Opera, 16 Feb 1892, conductor Jahn; first Paris performance, Opéra-Comique, 16 Jan 1893. Charlotte promised her dead mother that she would marry Albert, but Werther falls in love with her. Unable to reconcile himself to the situation, Werther shoots himself, dying in her arms.

Wesendonck Lieder five songs for voice and piano by Wagner (texts by Mathilde Wesendonck (1828–1902), with whom the composer was in love); composed Zurich, 1857–58. Usually heard in orchestral arrangement by Felix Mottl. Titles are 1. *Der Engel*; 2. *Stehe still*; 3. *Im Treibhaus*; 4. *Schmerzen*; 5. *Träume*. Nos. 3 and 5 were studies for *Tristan*, also written under the influence of Mathilde Wesendonck. (Her influence on other composers was not strong; a poem about cremation sent to Brahms was swiftly incinerated by him.)

Wesley English family of musicians.

    1. Charles Wesley (b Bristol, 11 Dec 1757; d London, 23 May 1834), English organist and composer. Pupil of Kelway and Boyce in London and later organist at various churches and chapels. He also appeared in public as harpsichordist.

    Works include incidental music for Mason's *Caractacus*; concerto grosso; six organ or harpsichord concertos; six string quartets (1776); anthems, hymns, harpsichord pieces; songs.

    2. Samuel Wesley (b Bristol, 24 Feb 1766; d London, 11 Oct 1837), English organist, composer and conductor, brother of 1 and nephew of John Wesley. Like his brother he showed precocious musical gifts at a very early age. At six he was taught by the organist of the church of

---------- **THE OPERA** ----------

Werther

A four-act opera by Jules Massenet, first performed in 1892.
A tale of unrequited love and an unhappy Christmas, it is set in Wetzlar in the second half of 1772.

I. Werther (tenor) is entranced by Charlotte (mezzo-soprano), who is caring for her widowed father with her sister Sophie (soprano). Charlotte's fiancé Albert arrives as she is looking after the other children of the house. After being introduced, Charlotte and Werther walk arm in arm while he declares his love; she replies that she has made a promise to her dying mother that she will marry Albert (baritone).

II. Charlotte and Albert are now married. Werther regrets the happiness he has lost and, although Charlotte tells him he may return later, he informs Sophie that he is leaving never to return. Charlotte is worried about his intentions.

III. On Christmas Eve Charlotte and Werther are briefly united but she breaks away distressed. Werther asks to borrow Albert's pistols, and Charlotte hurries out in a snow storm in search of him.

IV. Charlotte finds Werther mortally wounded; for the first time she declares her love and they kiss. Werther dies as the children sing 'Noel' outside.

---------- **THE OPERA** ----------

St James, Barton, Bristol, at eight he finished the oratorio *Ruth* and soon after appeared at the organ as a prodigy. In 1784 injured his head in an accident, with the result that he periodically fell into strange behaviour for the rest of his life. He did much to spread a knowledge of Bach in England and edited some of his works. He conducted the Birmingham Festival in 1811, lectured at the Royal Institution and gave frequent organ recitals, but had periodically to retire for several years. Shortly before his death he met Mendelssohn and they played the organ to each other.

Works include oratorios *Ruth* (1774) and *The Death of Abel* (1779); four Masses, numerous Latin and English anthems including *In exitu Israel*, *Exultate Deo*, *Dixit Dominus*, *All go unto one place*, *Behold how good*, *Hear, O thou shepherd* (some with organ), Morning and Evening Service in F major and other church music; Ode on St Cecilia's Day; four symphonies (1784–1802), and five overtures; organ and violin concertos; two string quartets and other chamber music; organ fugues, voluntaries, etc.; numerous piano works; glees, songs and duets.

3. Samuel Sebastian Wesley (b London, 14 Aug 1810; d Gloucester, 19 Apr 1876), English organist and composer, illegitimate son of 2. Pupil of his father and choirboy in the Chapel Royal from 1820. In 1826 he was appointed organist of a London church and by 1830 he held similar posts at two more. In 1832 he became organist of Hereford Cathedral, in 1835 (when he married) of Exeter Cathedral; in 1842–49 he was organist of Leeds Parish Church, in 1849–65 of Winchester Cathedral and then, until his death, of Gloucester Cathedral. He took the Mus.D. at Oxford in 1839 and became organ professor at the RAM in London in 1850. He continued his father's promotion of Bach's music and conducted the St Matthew Passion at Gloucester (Three Choirs Festival) in 1871.

Works include five services. 24 anthems, Psalm c, two settings of *By the waters of Babylon* with soprano and with contralto solo, chants and hymn tunes; organ works; *Ode to Labour* and *The Praise of Music* for chorus; three glees; nine songs (two with cello *ad lib.*); piano pieces.

Wessely, Carl Bernhard (b Berlin, 1 Sept 1768; d Potsdam, 11 Jul 1826), German composer and conductor. Pupil of J A P Schulz. He was conductor at the Berlin National Theatre, 1788–95, and 1796–1802 at Prince Heinrich's private theatre at Rheinsberg. After the prince's death he became a civil servant at Potsdam, where he founded a society for the performance of classical music.

Works include operas *Psyché* (1789), *Louis IX* (1797); *Herbstes* (1789); ballet *Die Wahl des Helden* (1788); incidental music to Shakespeare's *Tempest*, Kotzebue's *Sonnenjungfrau* and other plays; cantatas on the deaths of Moses Mendelssohn and Prince Henry of Prussia (1802); string quartets; songs.

Westrup, Jack (Allan) (b London, 26 Jul 1904; d Headley, 21 Apr 1975), English musicologist, critic, composer and conductor. Educated at Dulwich College and Balliol College, Oxford, where as an undergraduate he edited Monteverdi's *Orfeo* and *Incoronazione di Poppea* for performance by the Oxford University Opera Club. He taught classics at Dulwich College 1928–34, and was an assistant music critic on the *Daily Telegraph* 1934–40. From 1941 to 1944 he was lecturer in music at King's College, Newcastle-upon-Tyne, 1944–46 professor of music at Birmingham University and 1947–71 professor at Oxford. He conducted *Idomeneo* and *Les Troyens*, the fp of Wellesz's *Incognita* and the first British performance of *Hans Heiling* and *L'Enfant et les sortilèges*. He was chairman of the editorial board of the *New Oxford History of Music* and editor of volume VI. Editor of *Music and Letters* from 1959. Other literary work includes a book on Purcell and the fourth and fifth editions of the *Everyman Dictionary of Music* (1962 and 1971). Knighted 1961.

Works include motet *When Israel came out of Egypt* for unaccompanied double chorus; part-song *Weathers*; passacaglia for orchestra; three Shakespeare songs.

Wettergren, Gertrud (b Eslöv, 17 Feb 1897), Swedish contralto. Debut Stockholm, Royal Opera, 1922 as Cherubino; remained with the co. until 1952 as Eboli, Marfa, Kostelnička and in operas by Schreker, Boito and Britten. NY Met. debut 1935, as Amneris; CG 1936–39. Other roles included Carmen, Azucena and Fricka.

Wetzler, Hermann (Hans) (b Frankfurt am Main, 8 Sept 1870; d New York, 29 May 1943), German, later American composer and conductor. Spent his childhood in the USA, but in 1882 went to study at the Hoch Conservatory at Frankfurt under Scholz, Knorr, Humperdinck, Clara Schumann and others. In 1897–1901 he was organist at a NY church. In 1903 he organized symphonic concerts there, but in 1905 returned to Germany and became conductor at various opera houses. About 1930 he retired to Ascona, Switzerland, and in 1940 settled in USA.

Works include opera *The Basque Venus* (after Mérimée, 1928); incidental music to Shakespeare's *As You Like It* (1917); Magnificat for soprano, chorus and organ (1936); *Symphonic Fantasy, Visions, Assisi* for orchestra (1924); *Symphonie concertante* for violin and orchestra (1932); Easter music for wind instruments and organ; variations for oboe, clarinet and strings; *Scottish Songs* and six other op. nos. of songs.

Wexford Festival season of three operas held each autumn at town in Eire, established 1951. A feature of the festival has been the revival of neglected French works (Thomas' *Mignon*, 1986) and the encouragement of young singers (Kathleen Kuhlmann as Rossini's Tancredi, 1986). Elaine Padmore was director 1982–94, presiding over Rubinstein's *Demon* and Wagner's *Das Liebesverbot* in her last season; Luigi Ferrari from 1995.

Weyse, Christoph Ernst Friedrich (b Altona, 5 Mar 1774; d Copenhagen, 8 Oct 1842), German-Danish pianist and composer. Pupil of J A P Schulz at Copenhagen from 1789. He settled there as organist and music teacher. He also collected and edited Danish folksongs.

Works include operas *The Sleeping-Draught* (1804), *Faruk, The Cave of Adullam* (1816), *An Adventure in Rosenborg Gardens* (1827), *Floribella, The Feast at Kenilworth* (after Scott), operettas; seven symphonies; *c* 30 cantatas; organ and piano works; Danish folksongs, etc.

When Lilacs Last in the Dooryard Bloom'd American Requiem for mezzo, baritone, chorus and orchestra by Hindemith (text by W Whitman); fp NY, 14 May 1946, conductor Robert Shaw. Written in memory of Roosevelt and US war dead.

Whettham, Graham (Dudley) (b Swindon, 7 Sept 1927), English composer. Largely self-taught, he writes in a fairly conservative style: more honoured abroad then in his own country, he has pub. his works himself from 1970.

Works include opera *The Chef who Wanted to Rule the World* (1969), ballet *The Masque of the Red Death* (after Poe, 1968); concertos for oboe, clarinet and violin, four symphonies, *Sinfonietta stravagante* (1964), Sinfonia concertante (1966); *Hymnos* for strings (1978); *An English Suite* for orchestra (1984), Ballade for violin and orchestra (1988), two oboe quartets (1960, 1973), three string quartets (1967, 1978, 1980), horn trio (1976), concerto for ten wind (1979); choral music, including *A Mass for Canterbury* (1986), songs; music for brass band and for organ.

Whitaker, John (1776–London, 4 Dec 1847), English composer, organist and publisher. He was organist at the church of St Clement, Eastcheap, in London and a partner in the music pub. firm of Button and Whitaker. He was in request as a composer of music for the Sadler's Wells Theatre pantomimes, including the song 'Hot Codlins' sung by the clown Grimaldi.

Works include stage pieces *The Outside Passenger* (with Corri and Reeves), *A Chip of the Old Block*, *A Friend Indeed*, *Three Miles from Paris*, *A Figure of Fun*, *The Apprentice's Opera*, *The Rake's Progress* and others; songs for a stage adaptation of Scott's *Guy Mannering*; anthems and other sacred music; settings of English translations of Anacreon's Odes and Aesop's Fables; 12 pedal exercises for organ.

Whitbroke, William (*fl*. 1520–1550), English cleric and composer. He was educated at Cardinal College (later Christ Church), Oxford, where he was ordained priest 1529. In 1531 he was appointed sub-dean at St Paul's Cathedral in London and soon afterwards also vicar of All Saints' Church at Stanton, Suffolk, where he may have retired on leaving St Paul's in 1535.

Works include Mass for four voices, Magnificat and other church music.

White, Eric Walter (b Bristol, 10 Sept 1905; d London, 13 Sept 1985), English writer on music. Studied at Balliol College, Oxford. He was active in various non-musical posts, in 1946 becoming a member of the Arts Council for Great Britain. He wrote books on Stravinsky, Britten, Tippett and *A History of English Opera* (1982).

White, Paul (b Bangor, ME, 22 Aug 1859; d Rochester, NY, 31 May 1973), American composer, conductor and violinist. Studied at the New England Conservatory, also composition with Chadwick, violin with E Ysaÿe and conducting with Goossens, whose orchestra at Cincinnati he joined. Later became conductor of the Civic and Eastman School orchestras at Rochester, NY, and in 1938 became a member of the faculty of the Eastman School.

Works include *Voyage of the Mayflower* for chorus and orchestra; symphony in E minor, *Lyric Overture*; string quartet.

White (or *Whyte*), Robert (b *c* 1538; d London, Nov 1574), English composer. He was probably the son of a London organ builder, also named Robert White, and took the Mus.B. degree at Cambridge in 1560. In 1561 he succeeded Tye as choirmaster at Ely Cathedral. He married Tye's daughter Ellen in 1565 and left Ely in 1566 (he was succeeded by John Farrant) to become choirmaster of Chester Cathedral until *c* 1570, when he went to London to take up a similar post at Westminster Abbey. Along with nearly the whole of his family, he succumbed to the plague of 1574.

Works include 19 Latin motets etc.; English anthems; In Nomines for viols; hexachord fantasia for keyboard.

White, Willard (b St Catherine, Jamaica, 10 Oct 1946), Jamaican bass. He studied at the Juilliard School and made his debut at the NY City Opera in 1974, as Colline. After engagements on the Continent he sang Monteverdi's Seneca with ENO in 1976; returned as Hunding, 1983 and as Ivan Khovansky, 1994. Glyndebourne from 1978, as the Speaker, Osmin, the King in *Love for Three Oranges* (1982) and Gershwin's Porgy (1986). Sang Wotan with Scottish Opera (1989, 1991), and Monteverdi's Pluto at the 1990 Salzburg Festival. CBE 1995. He has been heard in concert in works by Shostakovich and Elgar.

Whitehill, Clarence (Eugene) (b Marengo, IA, 5 Nov 1871; d New York, 19 Dec 1932), American bass-baritone. Studied at Chicago and Paris and made his first stage appearance at Brussels in 1898, as Donner. After first singing in NY in 1900 he studied further with Stockhausen at Frankfurt and learnt Wagnerian parts with Cosima Wagner at Bayreuth; sang there 1904–09 as Wolfram, Amfortas and Gunther. He created Delius' Koanga (Elberfeld, 1904) and in 1908 sang Wotan under Richter at CG. NY Met. 1909–32 as Sachs, Amfortas and Golaud.

Whitehouse, W(illiam) E(dward) (b London, 20 May 1859; d London, 12 Jan 1935), English cellist. Studied at the RAM in London, Piatti being among his masters, and joined the teaching-staff there 1882. He travelled with Joachim and became a member of several chamber-music organizations.

Whiteman, Paul (b Denver, 28 Mar 1890; d Doylestown, PA, 29 Dec 1967), American bandleader. Played the viola with the Denver SO and San Francisco SO, then founded first band 1919. With the collaboration of leading jazz musicians developed a style he termed symphonic jazz; commissioned and premiered Gershwin's *Rhapsody in Blue*, 1924. Most orchestrations by Ferde Grofé, the fp of whose *Grand Canyon Suite* Whiteman gave in 1931.

whithorn an early English instrument of the oboe type, also called May-horn, made of willow bark with a double reed of material from the same tree. It was formerly used in Oxfordshire for the Whit-Monday hunt.

Whitlock, Percy (William) (b Chatham, 1 Jun 1903; d Bournemouth, 1 May 1946), English organist and composer. Learnt music as a choirboy at Rochester Cathedral and later studied at the GSM and the RCM in London. Assistant organist at Rochester Cathedral, 1921–30 and organist at Chatham and Borstal; from 1932 borough organist at Bournemouth.

Works include services, anthems, motets and hymn-tunes; music for a Rochester pageant; symphony for organ and orchestra; sonata in C minor, *Plymouth Suite* and other works for organ.

Whitman, Walt(er) (1819–1892), American poet. ◊Brian (*For Valour*); ◊Carpenter (*Sea Drift*); ◊Carter (*Warble for Lilac Time*); ◊Coleridge-Taylor (*Sea Drift*); ◊Converse (*Mystic Trumpeter* and *Night and Day*); R ◊Harris (suite); ◊Harty (*Mystic Trumpeter*); ◊Henze (chamber cantata); ◊Holst (*Ode to Death*); ◊Loeffler (*Beat! Beat! Drums!*); ◊Morning Heroes (Bliss); ◊Mystic Trumpeter (Holst); ◊Schoeck (*Trommelschläge*); ◊Sea Drift (Delius); ◊Sea Symphony (Vaughan Williams); ◊Sessions (*Turn, O Libertad*); ◊Vaughan Williams (*Toward the Unknown Region*); ◊When Lilacs Last in the Dooryard Bloom'd (Hindemith).

Whittaker, W(illiam) G(illies) (b Newcastle upon Tyne, 23 Jul 1876; d Orkney Isles, 5 Jul 1944), English educationist, conductor, editor and composer. Taught and conduced choirs at Armstrong and King's Colleges, Newcastle-upon-Tyne, and founded a Bach Choir there. In 1929 he was appointed professor of music at Glasgow University and principal of the Scottish Academy of Music there. He edited much early music, including Byrd's Great Service (conducting it for the first time in 300 years at Newcastle, Westminster and Oxford, 1924). Published misc. essays and a book on Bach's cantatas.

Works include overture and choruses for Aeschylus' *Choreophorae*, *A Lykewake Dirge* for chorus and orchestra; piano quintet *Among the Northumbrian Hills*; part-songs and folksong arrangements.

Who is Silvia? song by Schubert from Shakespeare's *Two Gentlemen of Verona*, translated by E von Bauernfeld as *An Silvia* and composed 1826.

whole-tone scale a musical scale progressing by steps of nothing but whole tones. Only two such scales are possible, but they can of course begin at any point, there being no feeling of tonality or of any keynote;

The two possible whole-tone scales.

neither is there, consequently, any possibility of modulation, and the possibilities of harmonizing whole-tone music are limited. The accidentals may, of course, be equally well written as sharps or flats.

Whyte, Robert, ◊White.

Whythorne, Thomas (b Ilminster, 1528; d London, c 31 Jul 1596), English composer. He travelled in Italy and elsewhere on the Continent and pub. his first book of music in 1571 and his second in 1590; the second volume contains the earlier printed English instrumental music. His autobiography was pub. 1961.

Works include psalms and secular songs for two–five voices or solo voice with instruments.

Wich, Günther (b Bamberg, 23 May 1928), German conductor. Debut Freiburg, 1952; conducted opera there until 1959, then worked at Graz, Hanover and Duisburg/Düsseldorf (1965–87). Conducted *Die Zauberflöte* at CG, 1968. Often heard in modern music, he gave the British premiere of Zimmermann's *Die Soldaten* (1972) and has been heard in *Moses und Aron* and all three one-act operas by Schoenberg. He has recorded in the Baroque repertory.

Wicks, Dennis (b Ringmer, 6 Oct 1928), English bass. Sang at Glyndebourne from 1950, operas by Mozart (as Antonio), Verdi and Stravinsky. British fp of Rossini's *La Pietra del Parigone* at the Camden Festival, 1963. Member of the Covent Garden co. throughout the 1960s, in operas by Strauss, Wagner, Beethoven and Verdi. WNO 1990, as the Police Commissioner in *Der Rosenkavalier*.

Widdop, Walter (b Norland, near Halifax, 19 Apr 1892; d London, 6 Sept 1949), English tenor. He appeared as a Wagnerian singer with the BNOC in the 1920s and was almost alone among English tenors to fill heroic parts of this kind, appearing with Kirsten Flagstad and Frida Leider; CG 1924–38, as Siegfried, Siegmund and Tristan. He appeared at Barcelona (1927), in Holland and Germany, also sang in oratorio.

Widerspänstigen Zähmung, Der, *The Taming of the Shrew*, opera by Götz (libretto by J V Widmann, after Shakespeare), produced Mannheim, 11 Oct 1874. Before Lucentio and Bianca can wed, Petruchio must tame Katherine.

Widmann, Erasmus (b Schwäbisch Hall, bap. 15 Sept 1572; d Rothenburg ob der Tauber, 31 Oct 1634), German organist and composer. He wrote Latin and sacred works and secular Germany songs, and dance music, *canzone*, etc. for instruments.

Widor, Charles-Marie-(Jean-Albert) (b Lyon, 21 Feb 1844; d Paris, 12 Mar 1937), French organist, teacher and composer. Studied under his father, an organist at Lyon, and later with Lemmens and Fétis in Brussels. In 1870 he became organist of the church of Saint-Sulpice in Paris, and in 1890 succeeded Franck as organ professor at the Conservatory. He became professor of composition in succession to Dubois in 1896.

Works include operas *Maître Ambros* (1886), *Les Pêcheurs de Saint-Jean* (1905), *Nerto* (after Mistral); ballet *La Korrigane*; pantomime *Jeanne d'Arc*; incidental music to *Conte d'Avril* (adaptation of Shakespeare's *Twelfth Night*) and Coppée's *Les Jacobites*; Mass for double chorus and two organs, Psalm cxii for chorus, orchestra and organ.

Two symphonies (1870, 1886), symphonic poem *Une Nuit de Valpurgis*; symphony for organ and orchestra, two concertos for piano (1876 and 1906) and one for cello (1882); piano quintet, piano trio; violin and piano sonata, suite for flute and piano; six duets for piano and organ; ten symphonies (1876–1900) and pieces for organ; piano works; songs.

Wieck, Clara, ◊Schumann.

Wieck, Friedrich (b Pretzsch, near Torgau, 18 Aug 1785; d Dresden, 6 Oct 1873), German pianist and teacher of his instrument, father of Clara Schumann. Taught at Leipzig and Dresden, and had Schumann and Bülow among his pupils. Toured with Clara as soloist. He was violently opposed to her marriage with Schumann.

Wiedemann, Hermann (1879–Berlin, 2 Jul 1944), German baritone. Debut Elberfeld, 1905. His early career was in Brno, Hamburg and Berlin; created Raffaele in Wolf-Ferrari's *The Jewels of the Madonna*, 1911. From 1916 until his death he was a member of the

Vienna Opera and he sang at Salzburg 1922–41 as Guglielmo and Beckmesser (1936, under Toscanini). He appeared at CG in 1933 and 1938, and at Munich and Buenos Aires was heard as Donner and Alberich in the *Ring*.

Wiegenlied German = 'cradle song'; a title often given by German composers to vocal lullabies or to instrumental pieces in their manner.

Wiemann, Ernst (b Stapelberg, 21 Dec 1919; d Hamburg, 17 May 1980), German bass. After study in Hamburg and Munich he made his debut at Kiel in 1938. He sang in Berlin and Nuremberg after the war and in 1957 joined the Hamburg Staatsoper. During the 1960s he was successful at the NY Met. (debut 1961, as King Henry). He was heard widely in Europe and North America in the Wagner bass repertory (Met. 1961–69) and in operas by Mozart and Verdi; sang Gurnemanz at CG (1971) and was much admired as Sachs, Philip II, Osmin, Rocco and Arkel.

Wiener, Otto (b Vienna, 13 Feb 1913), German baritone. He sang first with the Vienna Boys' Choir; concert singer from 1939. He continued in concert after the war and made his stage debut at Graz (Boccanegra, 1953). Düsseldorf 1956–59, Vienna from 1957, Munich from 1960. At Bayreuth, 1957–63, he sang Sachs, Wotan, Gunther and the Dutchman. He appeared as guest in London and Milan and sang in Klemperer's first recording of the *Missa Solemnis*.

Wieniawski, Henryk (b Lublin, 10 Jul 1835; d Moscow, 31 Mar 1880), Polish violinist and composer, father of Poldowski. Was sent to the Paris Conservatory at the age of eight and in 1846 allowed to make his first tour, in Poland and Russia. From 1850 he travelled with his brother Józef and in 1860 was appointed solo violinist to the Tsar, living in St Petersburg most of his time until 1872, when he toured the USA with A Rubinstein. In 1875 he succeeded Vieuxtemps as first violin professor at the Brussels Conservatory. But he travelled again towards the end of his life, in spite of serious ill-health, which caused his sudden death in Russia.

Works include two violin concertos (1853, 1862); *Souvenir de Moscou, Le Carnaval russe, Légende* and numerous other pieces, fantasies and studies for violin.

Wieniawski, Józef (b Lublin, 23 May 1837; d Brussels, 11 Nov 1912), Polish pianist and composer, brother of Henryk ◊Wieniawski. Studied at the Paris Conservatory. He began to tour Europe with his brother, in 1850 and became professor of piano successively at Moscow and Brussels.

Works include chamber music and piano pieces.

Wigglesworth, Mark (b Sussex, 19 Jul 1964), English conductor. Studied at the RAM (1986–89) and made debut with the Dutch Radio PO, 1989. Has led the Bournemouth SO, LPO and English CO. London Proms debut 1991, with the BBC SO (associate conductor 1992). Music director of Opera Factory from 1991, with Mozart's Da Ponte operas and Birtwistle's *Yan Tan Tethera*; Scottish Opera 1991, *Figaro*, US debut with the Philadelphia Orchestra and the Dallas SO, 1993. Concert repertory includes Shostakovich and Mahler (10th Symphony).

Wihan, Hanuš (b Police u Broumova, 5 Jun 1855; d Prague, 1 May 1920), Czech cellist. Studied at the Prague Conservatory and made his first appearance in Berlin, 1876. Solo cellist in the Munich court orchestra, 1880, and professor at Prague Conservatory, 1888. Founded the Czech String quartet in 1892. Dvořák's cello concerto is dedicated to him, although he did not premiere the work. Met Wagner and Liszt. Strauss wrote his cello sonata for him (fp Nuremberg, 8 Dec 1883).

Wihtol, Joseph (b Wolmar, 26 Jul 1863; d Lübeck, 24 Apr 1948), Latvian composer. Studied with Rimsky-Korsakov and others at the St Petersburg Conservatory; in 1886 he returned to Latvia and took an important share in its musical independence as a separate nation, becoming director of the National Opera at Riga and director of the Latvian Conservatory.

Works include music for fairy play *King Brussubard*; symphonies, symphonic poem *The Feast of Ligo*, Latvian overture *Spriditis*, dramatic overture for orchestra; fantasy on Latvian folksongs for cello and orchestra.

Wilbraham, John (b Bournemouth, 15 Apr 1944), English trumpeter. Studied at the RAM (1962–65), and with Maurice André. Trumpeter with the New Philharmonic Orchestra 1966–69, RPO first trumpeter 1969–72; BBC SO from 1972. Recordings include concertos by Telemann, Torelli, Hummel and Haydn.

Wilby, Philip (b Pontefract, 1949), English composer. Studied at Oxford and with Herbert Howells. Lecturer at Leeds University from 1972. Works include *Voyaging*, Symphony 1991; *Laudibus in Sanctis* for wind band (1993); *Trinity Service* for chorus and organ (1992); chamber and keyboard music. Mozart reconstructions include concerto for violin and piano K315f and concerto for string trio and orchestra K320e.

Wilbye, John (b Diss, Norfolk, bap. 7 Mar 1574; d Colchester, c Sept 1638), English composer. His father, a tanner and landowner, seems to have given him a good education. He was patronized by the Cornwallis family at Brome Hall and c 1595 went into the service of their son-in-law, Sir Thomas Kytson, at Hengrave Hall near Bury St Edmunds, and was frequently in London with the family. After the death of his patron he remained in the service of his widow, who died in 1628, whereupon he went to Colchester to join the household of her daughter, Lady Rivers. He never married and was well-to-do, having been granted the lease of a sheep-farm by Kyston and gradually acquiring property at Diss, Bury St Edmunds and elsewhere. Among his most characteristic works are the popular madrigals *Draw on Sweet Night* 1609, and *Sweet honey sucking bees* 1609.

Works include two sacred vocal pieces contributed to Leighton's *Teares or Lamentacions*; two books of 64 madrigals (1598, 1609), madrigal *The Lady Oriana* contributed to *The Triumphes of Oriana*; five sacred works; three fantasies for viols (incomplete), lute lessons (lost).

Wild, Earl (b Pittsburgh, 26 Nov 1915), American pianist. He studied with Egon Petri and appeared with Toscanini and the NBC SO in 1942; soon became widely known in USA in late Romantic repertory and commissioned concertos by Paul Creston and David Levy. London debut 1973.

Wildbrunn, Helene (b Vienna, 8 Apr 1882; d Vienna, 10 Apr 1972), Austrian soprano. She sang at Dortmund as a contralto, 1907–14, as Ortrud, Amneris and Dalila; Stuttgart 1914–18, when her voice changed to soprano. She appeared in Berlin and Vienna 1916–32 and at Buenos Aires from 1922 was heard as Brünnhilde, Isolde and the Marschallin. CG, 1927, as Leonore. Other roles included Kundry (La Scala, 1922), Fricka and Donna Anna.

Wilde, David (b Manchester, 25 Feb 1935), English pianist and conductor. Studied at the RNCM 1948–53 and with Nadia Boulanger. Won the Liszt-Bartók Competition at Budapest (1961) and has been heard throughout Europe and the USA with these composers in addition to Schumann and Beethoven. Guest conductor with the RPO and other British orchestras.

Wilder, Philip van (b ? Flanders, c 1500; d London, 24 Feb 1553), Flemish lutenist and composer. Appointed lutenist to Henry VIII, 1538 and later became gentleman of the privy chamber to Edward VI. Composed motets, *chansons*, etc.

Wildschütz, Der, oder Die Stimme der Natur, *The Poacher, or The Voice of Nature*, opera by Lortzing (libretto by composer, based on a play by Kotzebue), produced Leipzig, 31 Dec 1842. Schoolmaster Baculus shoots a buck on the estate of Count of Eberbach and his betrothed, young Gretchen, offers to intercede for him. But knowing his philandering reputation, the Count's sister (Baroness Freimann) impersonates Gretchen instead. After disguise and confusion, a happy ending.

Wilhelm, Carl (b Schmalkalden, 5 Sept 1815; d Schmalkalden, 26 Aug 1873), German conductor and composer. He conducted a male-voice choral society at Crefeld 1840–65, and in 1854 set the words of Max Schneckenburger's *Die Wacht am Rhein* as a patriotic song, for which Bismark granted him a pension in 1871.

Wilhelmj, August (Emil Daniel Ferdinand Viktor) (b Usingen, Nassau, 21 Sept 1845; d London, 22 Jan 1908), German violinist. Made his first public appearance in 1854 and in 1861 was sent by Liszt to

Willaert *The composer Adrian Willaert (c. 1490–1562). Flemish by birth, he became director of music at St Mark's in Venice. He was one of the leading composers between Josquin and Palestrina, and influenced future generations of musicians as a teacher and as one of the first madrigal composers.*

Leipzig to study with David at the Conservatory. In 1865 he began to travel and in 1866 first visited London, where in 1894 he settled as violin professor at the GSM.

Wilkinson, ? Thomas (*fl.* ? 1579–96), English composer. He may have been a singer at King's College, Cambridge, and he contributed three anthems to Myriell's *Tristitiae remedium* in 1616.

Works include services, 12 verse anthems, three pavans for viols.

Wilkinson, Robert (b c 1450; d ? Eton, 1515 or later), English composer. Composed two settings of *Salve Regina* for five and nine voices, *Credo in Deum/Jesus autem* for 13 voices in canon, four incomplete works (all in Eton Choirbook).

Willaert, Adrian (b ? Bruges, c 1490; d Venice, 17 Dec 1562), Flemish composer and probably the most influential musician of the mid-16th c. Trained in law but studied music with Mouton in Paris. Singer for members of the d'Este family at Rome, Ferrara and Esztergom, 1515–27; then *maestro di cappella* at St Mark's, Venice, where his pupils included Cipriano de Rore, Nicola Vicentino, Andrea Gabrieli, Gioseffe Zarlino and Costanzo Porta. He revisited Flanders in 1542 and 1556–57. He was one of the earliest composers of madrigals but his most important works are his motets.

Works include Masses, hymns, psalms, motets, madrigals, *chansons* and instrumental ensemble pieces. They mark him as the most versatile and one of the most prolific composers of his generation.

Willan, Healey (b London, 12 Oct 1880; d Toronto, 16 Feb 1968), English–Canadian organist and composer. Began his career as church organist in London, but emigrated to Toronto, where he became lecturer at the university in 1914 and music director to the Hart House Players in 1919. He became vice-principal of the Conservatory in 1920 and later professor at the university.

Works include incidental music to plays; church music, war elegy *Why they so softly sleep*, *Apostrophe to the Heavenly Hosts* and *Coronation* Te Deum for chorus and orchestra (1953); two symphonies (1936, 1948); *Marche solennelle* for orchestra; preludes and fugues, *Epilogue, Introduction, Passacaglia and Fugue* and other works for organ; songs to words by Yeats and others.

Willcocks, David (Valentine) (b Newquay, 30 Dec 1919), English conductor, organist and teacher. He studied at the RCM and King's College, Cambridge. Organist at Salisbury then Worcester Cathedrals 1947–57, and of King's College 1957–74; many tours and successful recordings with the chapel choir. He conducted the Bach Choir from 1960 in annual performances of Bach's *St Matthew Passion* and in works by Fricker, Crosse and Hamilton. Director of RCM, 1974–84. Knighted 1977.

Willer, Luise (b Seeshaupt, Bavaria, 1888; d Munich, 27 Apr 1970), German contralto. Debut Munich 1910, as Mozart's Annius; remained with co. until 1955 and took part in the fps of Pfitzner's *Palestrina* (1917) and *Das Herz* (1931). CG 1926 and 1931 as Erda, Waltraute and Brangaene. At Salzburg she was heard as Gluck's Clytemnestra and Strauss's Adelaide. Retired 1955, after singing Erda at Munich.

William Ratcliff opera by Cui (libretto by A N Pleshtcheiev, based on Heine's drama), produced St Petersburg, 26 Feb 1869. Betty's jealous husband MacGregor kills her lover Edward Ratcliffe; Betty dies soon afterwards. Edward's son William is haunted by their ghosts until multiple deaths appease the ghosts. ◊Guglielmo Ratcliff.

Williams, Alberto (b Buenos Aires, 23 Nov 1862; d Buenos Aires, 17 Jun 1952), Argentine pianist, conductor, poet and composer of English and Basque descent. Studied at the Buenos Aires Conservatory and later in Paris, where he studied piano with Chopin's pupil Mathias, harmony with Durand, counterpoint with Guiraud and composition with Franck. In 1889 he returned home, where he gave piano recitals, conducted symphonic concerts and founded the Buenos Aires Conservatory.

Works include nine symphonies (1907–39, no. 2 *La bruja de las montanas*) and other orchestral works; choruses; works for violin and piano and cello and piano; *El rancho abandonado* and other pieces; songs.

If one hears bad music, it is one's duty to drown it by one's conversation.
Oscar Wilde, *The Picture of Dorian Gray*, 1891

Williams, Grace (Mary) (b Barry, Glamorgan, 19 Feb 1906; d Barry, 10 Feb 1977), Welsh composer. Educated at Cardiff University, where she took the B.Mus. in 1926; studied with Vaughan Williams at the RCM 1926–30 and with Wellesz in Vienna, 1930–31.

Works include opera *The Parlour* (1961); *Hymn of Praise* (*Gogonedawg Arglwydd*, from 12th-c. Black Book of Carmarthen) for chorus and orchestra (1939); Welsh overture *Hen Walia*, legend *Rhiannon*, *Fantasy on Welsh Nursery Rhymes*, symphonic impressions *Owen Glendower* (after Shakespeare's *Henry IV*), *Penillion* (1955); violin concerto (1950); two psalms for soprano and orchestra, *The Song of Mary* (Magnificat) for soprano and orchestra; *Sinfonia concertante* for piano and orchestra (1941); elegy and *Sea Sketches* for string orchestra; songs to words by Herrick, Byron, Belloc, D H Lawrence, etc.; arrangements of Welsh folksongs.

Williams, John (b Melbourne, 24 Apr 1942), Australian guitarist. London debut 1955; studied with Segovia from 1957. Professor at RCM, 1960–73. Plays a wide repertory; André Previn has written for him.

Williamson, Malcolm (Benjamin Graham Christopher) (b Sydney, 21 Nov 1931), Australian-born British composer. Studied with Eugene Goossens at the Sydney Conservatory and with Lutyens in London, where he later became an organist. His music draws on a wide range of influences, moving from an awareness of the avant-garde to a more popular style. Master of the Queen's Music from 1975.

Works include operas *English Eccentrics* (1964), *Our Man in Havana* (1965), *The Violins of St Jacques* (1966), *Lucky Peter's Journey* (1969); concerto for organ and orchestra, four piano con-

Williams, J *The guitarist John Williams studied first with his father Leonard Williams and then with the great Segovia. He has collaborated with Julian Bream and has championed new works for guitar in traditional and non-Western idioms, using electronic tape and manipulation of sound as well as acoustic means.*

certos (1957–94), violin concerto (1965), seven symphonies (1957–84); *Santiago de Espada*, overture for orchestra; *Mass of Christ the King*, for soloists, chorus and orchestra (1975–78); *Mass of St Etheldreda* (1990), *A Year of Birds* for soprano and orchestra (1995); chamber music; piano and organ works.

Wilm, (Peter) Nikolai von (b Riga, 4 Mar 1834; d Wiesbaden, 20 Feb 1911), Latvian composer. Studied at the Leipzig Conservatory. In 1857 became second conductor at the Riga municipal theatre and in 1860 went to St Petersburg as professor at the Nikolai Institute. He lived at Dresden 1875–78 and then at Wiesbaden.

Works include motets; string quartet, string sextet; two sonatas and two suites for violin and piano, sonata for cello and piano; numerous piano pieces; songs; part-songs.

Wilson, (James) Steuart (b Bristol, 21 Jul 1889; d Petersfield, 18 Dec 1966), English tenor and administrator. He sang Tamino at Cambridge in 1910 and the following year sang *On Wenlock Edge* by Vaughan Williams, who wrote for him *Four Hymns* (1914), of which Wilson gave the premiere (Cardiff, 1920). He suffered lung damage in the war, but studied with Jean de Reszke and pursued a successful career in concert (oratorios by Bach and Elgar) and in operas by Mozart and Boughton (following successful libel action against a schoolmaster who had questioned his vocal technique, he financed and conducted a production of Boughton's *The Lily Maid* in 1939). After teaching at the Curtis Institute during the war he held appointments with the BBC and the Arts Council and was deputy general administrator at CG, 1949–55. Many Lieder translations. Knighted 1948.

Wilson, John (b Faversham, 5 Apr 1595; d London, 22 Feb 1674), English lutenist, singer and composer. Contributed, (?) with Coperario and Lanier, to *The Maske of Flowers*, performed at Whitehall in 1614. He became one of the king's musicians in 1635. Lived at Oxford during the Civil War and took the Mus.D. there in 1645; soon afterwards was in private service in Oxfordshire, but 1656–61 was professor of music at Oxford University; then returned to London to be at or near the restored court and became a Gentleman of the Chapel Royal in 1662 in succession to H Lawes.

Works include music for Brome's *The Northern Lass* (1629), songs for *The Maske of Flowers*; anthem *Hearken, O God*; *Psalterium Carolinum* for three voices and continuo; elegy on the death of W Lawes; *Cheerful Ayres* for three voices; airs and dialogues with lute; songs including Shakespeare's 'Take, O take those lips away' and 'Lawn as white as driven snow'; catches.

Wilson, Robert (b Waco, TX, 4 Oct 1941), American stage director and designer. Studied at Texas University and in New York. Collaborations with Philip Glass began 1974 (designs for *Einstein on the Beach* at Avignon and the NY Met.); wrote the *Civil Wars* with Glass and Gavin Bryars (1984–87). Designed *Salome* for La Scala (1987) and produced *Die Zauberflöte* at the Opéra Bastille, 1991. Technically innovative work also includes *Alceste* at Chicago (1990) and *Parsifal* for Houston Opera (1992).

Wilson, Thomas (Brendan) (b Trinidad, CO, 10 Oct 1927), American-born Scottish composer. He studied at Glasgow University; lecturer there from 1927), His works have employed serial technique and include the operas *The Charcoal Burners* (1968) and *Confessions of a Justified Sinner* (1976); four symphonies (1956, 1965, 1982, 1988), *Touchstone*, 'portrait for orchestra' (1967), concerto for orchestra (1967), piano concerto (1984), chamber concerto (1986), viola concerto (1987), chamber symphony (1990), violin concerto (1993); four string quartets, piano trio (1966), cello sonata (1973); three Masses, Te Deum and other church music; piano sonata and sonatina.

Wilson-Johnson, David (b Northampton, 16 Nov 1950), English baritone. Studied at the RAM (1973–76) and has appeared at CG from 1976 (debut in the fp of *We Come to the River*). Frequent recitalist in *Winterreise* and is heard also in *Belshazzar's Feast* and the Choral Symphony. Created Arthur in the fp of *The Lighthouse* (Edinburgh 1980) and sang the title role in the UK fp (concert) of *St François d'Assise* (London, 1988). Other modern repertory includes Choregos in *Punch and Judy* (Amsterdam, 1993).

Winbergh, Gösta (b Stockholm, 30 Dec 1943), Swedish tenor. After study in Stockholm made debut in Gothenburg 1971, as Rodolfo. Stockholm Opera 1973–80, Glyndebourne 1980 (Belmonte) and Salzburg 1982 (Jacquino). Sang Mozart's Titus at CG 1982, Don Ottavio at the NY Met. 1983. Other roles include Tamino (La Scala 1985) Ferrando (Houston, 1988) and Nermorino. Has recently sung some heavier roles, with Lohengrin at Zurich (1991) and Walther at CG (1993).

Windgassen, Wolfgang (b Andemasse, 26 Jun 1914; d Stuttgart, 5 Sept 1974), German tenor. Studied with his father and at the Hochschule für Musik in Stuttgart. From 1941 he sang in Pforzheim (debut as Alvaro) and from 1951 was a member of the Stuttgart Opera. Windgassen was the leading heroic tenor of the post- war years, excelling in Wagnerian roles; Bayreuth 1951–71 as Parsifal, Siegmund, Loge, Lohengrin and Walther. CG 1955–66 as Tristan and Siegfried. Other roles included Adolar, the Emperor and Otello.

wind machine (or *aeoliphone*) a stage device used e.g. by R Strauss in *Don Quixote*, Ravel in *Daphnis et Chloé*, Vaughan Williams in *Sinfonia antartica* and Tippett in his fourth symphony. It is a barrel covered with silk, the friction of which on being turned produces a sound like a whistling wind.

Winkelmann, Hermann (b Brunswick, 8 Mar 1849; d Vienna, 18 Jan 1912), German tenor. After his 1875 debut at Sonderhausen, as Manrico, he moved to Hamburg and in 1879 created the title role in Rubinstein's *Nero*. He sang in Vienna from 1881; impressed Richter as Lohengrin, and sang under him at Drury Lane, London, in 1882 as the first London Tristan and Walther. Later the same summer Winkelmann created Parsifal; remained at Bayreuth until 1891 in this role and as Tannhäuser and Walther. He toured the USA in 1884 and was successful at Vienna until 1907 as Tristan, Otello and Kienzl's Evangelist.

Winkler, Herman (b Duisberg, 3 Mar 1924), German tenor. Studied in Hanover and appeared at Bayreuth from 1957 (Parsifal 1977). Frankfurt and Zurich Operas from 1970, as Florestan and Lohengrin and in Mozart roles. Salzburg debut 1976, as Arbace in *Idomeneo*, returning 1981 in the fp of Cerha's *Baal*. US debut Chicago 1980 (Don Ottavio), CG 1984 (the Captain in *Wozzeck*). Other roles include Strauss's Emperor, and Peter Grimes (Zurich 1985, 1989). Also heard in *Das Lied von der Erde*.

Winter, Peter (von) (b Mannheim, bap. 28 Aug 1754; d Munich, 17 Oct 1825), German composer. Played as a boy in the court orchestra at Mannheim, where he was a pupil of Vogler and met Mozart in 1778. Moved with the court to Munich, but went to Vienna 1780–81 and studied with Salieri. On his return to Munich he produced the first of his many operas, *Helena und Paris*, became vice-*Kapellmeister* to the court in 1787 and *Kapellmeister* in 1798, but was periodically absent on tour.

Works include operas etc. *Helena und Paris* (1782), *Der Bettelstudent* (1785), *I fratelli rivali* (1793), *Das unterbrochene Opferfest* (1796), *Das Labyrinth* (sequel to Mozart's *Magic Flute*, 1798), *Maria von Montelban* (1800), *Tamerlan* (1802), *La grotta di Calipso* (1803), *Il trionfo dell' amor fraterno*, *Il ratto di Proserpina* (1804), *Zaira*, *Colmal* (1809), *Maometto II* (1817), *Scherz, List und Rache* and *Jery und Bätely* (both libretti by Goethe) and *c* 20 others; ballets *Heinrich IV* (1779), *Inez de Castro*, *La Mort d'Hector* and six others.

Masses and other church music; oratorios *Der Sterbende Jesus*, *La Betulia liberata* and others; cantata *Timoteo, o Gli effetti della musica* and others; three symphs, *Schlachtsymphonie* and overtures; concerted pieces for various instruments; songs, part-songs.

Winter Journey (Schubert.) ◊Winterreise.

Wintermärchen, Ein, *A Winter's Tale*, opera by Goldmark (libretto by A M Willner, after Shakespeare), produced Vienna, Opera, 2 Jan 1908.

Winterreise, *The Winter Journey*, song cycle by Schubert (poems by Wilhelm Müller), composed, Part i, Feb 1827; Part ii, Oct 1827. The 24 songs are 1. *Gute Nacht*; 2. *Die Wetterfahne*; 3. *Gefrorne Tränen*; 4. *Erstarrung*; 5. *Der Lindenbaum*; 6. *Wasserflut*; 7. *Auf dem Flusse*; 8. *Rückblick*; 9. *Irrlicht*; 10. *Rast*; 11. *Frühlingstraum*; 12. *Einsamkeit*; 13. *Die Post*; 14. *Der greise Kopf*; 15. *Die Krähe*; 16. *Letzte Hoffnung*; 17. *Im Dorfe*; 18. *Der stürmische Morgen*; 19. *Täuschung*; 20. *Der Wegweiser*; 21. *Das Wirtshaus*; 22. *Mut*; 23. *Die Nebensonnen*; 24. *Der Leiermann*.

'Winter Wind' Study the nickname sometimes given to Chopin's piano Study in A minor, op. 25 no. 11.

Winter Words song cycle by Britten to poems by Thomas Hardy for high voice and piano; fp Harewood House, Leeds, 8 Oct 1953, by Peter Pears. The titles of the songs are 1. 'At Day-close in November'; 2. 'Midnight on the Great Western'; 3. 'Wagtail and Baby'; 4. 'The Little Old Table'; 5. 'The Choirmaster's Burial'; 6. 'Proud Songsters'; 7. 'At the Railway Station'; 8. 'Before Life and After'.

Wipo (or *Wigbert*) (b Solothurn, *c* 995; d in the Bavarian Forest, *c* 1050), German poet and priest, who ended his life as a hermit. He is the reputed author (and perhaps adaptor of the music) of the sequence *Victimae paschali*.

Wirén, Dag (Ivar) (b Striberg, Närke, 15 Oct 1905; d Stockholm, 19 Apr 1986), Swedish composer and critic. Studied at the Stockholm Conservatory. In 1932 he received a stage grant and continued his studies with Sabaneiev in Paris. On his return he became a music critic at Stockholm.

Works include five symphonies (1932–64), sinfonietta; serenade for strings; cello concerto, violin concerto, piano concerto; five string quartets (1930–70), two piano trios, two sonatinas for cello and piano; piano pieces; songs.

Wise, Michael (b ? Salisbury, *c* 1647; d Salisbury, 24 Aug 1687), English organist and composer. Choirboy at the Chapel Royal in London in 1660. In 1663 he became a lay-clerk at St George's Chapel, Windsor, and in 1668 organist and choirmaster of Salisbury Cathedral. He was admitted a Gentleman of the Chapel Royal in 1676, but retained his post at Salisbury until 1685. At the time of the coronation of James II he was suspended from the Chapel Royal, probably because of characteristically difficult conduct. In 1687 he became almoner and choirmaster at St Paul's Cathedral in London, but he still visited Salisbury, where his wife had remained. After a dispute with her at night he left the house and was killed in a quarrel with a watchman.

Works include services and anthems (including *The Ways of Zion Mourn*); songs and catches.

Wishart, Peter (b Crowborough, 25 Jun 1921; d Frome, 14 Aug 1984), English composer. He studied with Boulanger and at Birmingham University; lecturer there 1950–59. King's College, London, 1972–77, professor Reading University 1977–84. His music was influenced by Stravinsky and Orff.

Works include operas *Two in the Bush* (1956), *The Captive* (1960), *The Clandestine Marriage* (1971) and *Clytemnestra* (1973); ballets *Beowulf* and *Persephone* (1957); two symphonies (1953, 1973), two violin concertos (1951, 1968), concerto for orchestra (1957); Te Deum (1952) and much other choral music; string quartet (1954); organ sonata.

Witt, Christian Friedrich (b Altenburg, *c* 1660; d Altenburg or Gotha, 13 Apr 1716), German composer. Court music director at Altenburg.

Works include *Psalmodia sacra*, cantatas; French overtures and suites for orchestra; organ and harpsichord works.

Witte, Erich (b Graudenz, 19 Mar 1911), German tenor. After his 1932 debut at Bremen he sang in Wiesbaden and Breslau and in 1938–39 was heard at the NY Met. as Froh and Mime. He sang David at Bayreuth during the war and was admired there and at CG during the 1950s as Loge; produced *Meistersinger* at CG in 1957 and sang Walther. He appeared at the Berlin Staatsoper until 1960 and was producer there from 1964. Other roles included Otello, Florestan and Peter Grimes.

He who does not prefer the first 'Prelude' in the Well-tempered Clavier *played without nuances as the composer wrote it for the instrument, to the same prelude embellished with a passionate melody, does not love music.*

Saint-Saëns, *École buissonière*, 1913

Wittgenstein, Paul (b Vienna, 5 Nov 1887; d Manhasset, NY, 3 Mar 1961), Austrian pianist. He was a pupil of Leschetizky in Vienna and gave his first recital in 1913. He lost his right arm in World War I and devoted the rest of his career to playing works for the left hand only. Among the composers who wrote works for him were Strauss (*Parergon zur Symphonia domestica*), Ravel (concerto in D major), Korngold (concerto in C♯ major), Schmidt (*Variations on a Theme of Beethoven*), and Britten (*Diversions on a Theme*).

Wittich, Marie (b Giessen, 27 May 1868; d Dresden, 4 Aug 1931), German soprano. Debut Magdeburg, 1882, as Azucena. She sang at Dresden 1889–1914 and in 1905 created Salome there. Bayreuth 1901–09, as Sieglinde, Kundry and Isolde. CG 1905–06, as Elsa, Elisabeth and Brünnhilde.

Wixell, Ingvar (b Luleå 7 May 1931), Swedish baritone. He sang Papageno at the Royal Opera, Stockholm, in 1955 and was heard as Ruggiero in *Alcina* when the co. visited CG (1960). Glyndebourne 1962, Guglielmo. At the 1966 Salzburg Festival he sang Mozart's Count and the following year he joined the Deutsche Oper, Berlin. Regular visitor to CG from 1970 where he has sung Boccanegra, Scarpia, Mandryka and Mozart's Count. US debut Chicago, 1967, as Belcore; NY Met. debut Jan 1973, as Rigoletto. Bayreuth from 1971. Sang Scarpia at Earl's Court, London, 1991. Other roles include Pizarro and Don Giovanni.

Wlaschiha, Ekkerhard (b Pirna, 28 May 1938), German bass-baritone. Studied in Weimar and made his debut at Gera 1961, as Don Fernando (*Fidelio*). Dresden and Weimar Operas 1964–70; Leipzig from 1970, as Pizarro, Jochanaan and Scarpia. Sang Kaspar at the re-opening of the Dresden Semperoper (1985), Kurwenal at Bayreuth 1986. Has sung Telramund in Berlin, and is best known as Alberich, which he has sung in *Ring* productions at CG (1990), NY Met., and Chicago (both 1993).

Woelfl, Joseph (b Salzburg, 24 Dec 1773; d London, 21 May 1812), Austrian pianist and composer. Pupil of L Mozart and M Haydn at Salzburg, where he was a choirboy at the cathedral. In 1790 he went to Vienna and *c* 1792 made his first public appearance, at Warsaw. He soon made his name as a virtuoso and after producing some stage

works in Vienna married the actress Therese Klemm in 1798 and went on a long tour in Bohemia and German. He lived 1801–05 in Paris, where he produced two more operas, and then settled in London.

Works include operas *Der Höllenberg* (1795), *Das schöne Milchmädchen* (1797), *Der Kopf ohne Mann* (1798), *Liebe macht kurzen Prozess* (with others), *L'Amour romanesque* (1804), *Fernanda, ou Les Maures* (1805); ballets *La Surprise de Diane* and *Alzire* (on Voltaire's play); symphonies; *Le calme* and other piano concertos; chamber music; *Non plus ultra* and other piano sonatas, various piano works.

Wohltemperierte Clavier, Das, *The Well-tempered Clavier*, two sets of preludes and fugues by Bach for keyboard (not exclusively clavichord, as has sometimes been inferred from a misunderstanding of the title), finished in 1722 and 1744 respectively. Each set consists of a cycle of 24 preludes and fugues in all the major and minor keys in ascending order. The two books together are commonly known in England as 'The 48'. ◊Weber (Bernhard Christian) .

wolf a technical term for a jarring sound produced between certain intervals on keyboard instruments tuned in meantone ◊temperament or on string instruments by defective vibration on a certain note or notes.

Wolf, Ernst Wilhelm (b Grossgehringen, near Gotha, bap. 25 Feb 1735; d Weimar, Nov 1792), German composer. He was leader and from 1768 court conductor at Weimar.

Works include operas *Die Dorfdeputierten* (after Goldoni, 1772), *Das grosse Los* (1774), *Der Zauberirrungen* (after Shakespeare's *Midsummer Night's Dream*), *Erwin und Elmire* (Goethe) and others; monodrama *Polyxena*; cantata *Seraphina* (Wieland, 1775); church music; oratorios, Easter cantatas (Herder); symphonies; string quartets and other chamber music; songs.

Wolf, Hugo (Filipp Jakob) (b Windischgraz [now Slovenj Gradec], 13 Mar 1860; d Vienna, 22 Feb 1903), Austrian composer. His father, a leather merchant, encouraged his early gifts by teaching him piano and violin. After visiting various schools, he was allowed to enter the Vienna Conservatory in 1875, but left it the following year, preferring to pick up his own instruction where he could. From 1877, his father having incurred great losses in business, he was obliged to earn his own living by teaching. He often lived in great poverty, but when his pride would allow, he was befriended by various musical families; Schalk and Mottl took a professional interest in him. In 1881 he was engaged as second conductor at Salzburg under Muck, but was found to be temperamentally so unfitted for the post that the engagement was terminated within three months. From 1884 to 1887 he was music critic for the Vienna *Salonblatt*, but here again he offended many people by his irascibility and intolerance (which saw no fault in Wagner and no good in Brahms). Meanwhile his masterful song settings of Möricke and Eicherdorff won him wide recognition. However, he had contracted syphilis, and in 1897 his mind became unhinged. He was sent to a sanatorium. Discharged as cured in Jan 1898, he had a relapse after becoming involved in a quarrel with Mahler at the Vienna Opera, and was taken to an asylum in a hopeless condition in December, remaining there until his death. His achievement lay in developing the Lied from beyond the essentially lyrical settings of Schubert and Schumann; Wolf sought to enhance the dramatic and emotional potential of the poetry he set by establishing an equal partnership between singer and pianist.

Works include operas *Der Corregidor* (1896) and *Manuel Venegas* (unfinished); incidental music to Ibsen's *The Feast at Solhaug* (1891); 48 early songs, 53 songs to words by Mörike (1888); 20 to words by Eichendorff (1880–88), 51 to words by Goethe (1888–89), *Italienisches Liederbuch* (46 songs, 1890–91), *Spanisches Liederbuch* (44 songs, 1889–90), 31 songs to words by various poets, including six by G Keller and three sonnets by Michelangelo (1897).

Symphonic poem *Penthesilea* (after Kleist, 1883); *Italian Serenade* for string quartet in D minor (1880); *Christnacht* for solo voices, chorus and orchestra, *Elfenlied* from Shakespeare's *Midsummer Night's Dream* for soprano, chorus and orchestra (1890), *Der Feuerreiter* and *Dem Vaterland* for chorus and orchestra; six part-songs.

Wolf, Johannes (b Berlin, 17 Apr 1869; d Munich, 25 May 1947),

German musicologist. Studied with Spitta in Berlin and took a doctor's degree at Leipzig in 1893. In 1908 he became professor of music at Berlin University and in 1915 librarian of the music section of the Prussian State Library, where he succeeded Altmann as director in 1928. He specialized in and wrote on early music, treatises and notations.

Wolff, Albert (Louis) (b Paris, 19 Jan 1884; d Paris, 20 Feb 1970), French conductor and composer. Studied at the Paris Conservatory, became chorus master at the Opéra-Comique in 1908 and conductor in 1911, succeeded Messager as chief conductor in 1922. In 1928–34 he conducted the Lamoureux concerts and later the Pasdeloup concerts. Conductor of the Paris Opéra from 1949. He conducted the fps of Roussel's fourth symphony (1935) and Poulenc's *Les mamelles de Terésias* (1947).

Works include opera *L'Oiseau bleu* (after Maeterlinck; NY Met, 1919).

Wolff, Christian (b Nice, 8 Mar 1934), French-born American composer who came to the USA in 1941. Studied with Cage, and also classical languages at Harvard University, obtaining his Ph.D., and in 1962 becoming a lecturer there in classics. His music makes use of a strictly mathematical basis, particularly as regards rhythms and rests, while also including chance elements.

Works include *Nine* for nine instruments (1951), *For six or seven players*, *Summer* for string quartet, *In Between Pieces* for three players, *For five or ten Players* (1962), *For one, two or three people*, septet for any instruments (1964), *For Pianist*, *For Piano I, II, Duo for Pianists I and II, Duet I* for piano (four hands), *Duet II* for horn and piano, *You Blew It* for chorus (1971).

Wolff, Fritz (b Munich, 28 Oct 1894; d Munich, 18 Jan 1957), German tenor. After study in Würzburg he sang Loge at the 1925 Bayreuth Festival; returned until 1941 in this role and as Parsifal and Walther. He sang at the Berlin Staatsoper from 1928 and took part in the fp of Schreker's *Der Singende Teufel*. He was admired in Wagner at CG (1929–38), and was heard in Chicago and Cleveland 1934–35.

Wolf-Ferrari, Ermanno (b Venice, 12 Jan 1876; d Venice, 21 Jan 1948), German–Italian composer. He was sent to Rome to study art by his German father, a painter, but turned to music and studied with Rheinberger at Munich. In 1899 he sent his oratorio to Venice and succeeded in having it performed, and in 1900 he brought out his first opera, after which his stage successes were frequently repeated. Many of his operas were first produced in Germany, including several that sought to evoke the spirit of 18th-c. Venetian comedy. In 1902–12 he was director of the Liceo Benedetto Marcello at Venice.

Works include operas *Cenerentola* (1900), *Le donne curiose* (1903), *I quattro rusteghi* (1906), *Il segreto di Susanna* (1909), *I gioielli della Madonna* (1911), *Amor medico* (after Molière, 1913), *Gli amanti sposi* (1925), *Das Himmelskleid* (1927), *Sly* (after Shakespeare's *Taming of the Shrew*, 1927), *La vedova scaltra* (1931), *Il campiello* (1936), *La dama boba* (after Lope de Vega, 1939), *Gli dei a Tebe* (1943).

Cantatas *La Sulamita* and *La vita nuova* (after Dante, 1903); violin concerto, chamber symphony for strings, woodwind, piano and horn (1901); piano quintet, piano trio, two violin and piano sonatas; organ pieces; cello pieces; *Rispetti* for soprano and piano.

Wolfram von Eschenbach (b c 1170; d c 1220), German Minnesinger. He took part in a singing contest at Wartburg in 1207. Seven lyric poems survive, without music, though two tunes are ascribed to him. He wrote an epic, *Parzival*, which was the principal source for Wagner's *Parsifal*. He appears as a character in Wagner's earlier opera, *Tannhäuser*.

Wolfrum, Philipp (b Schwarzenbach, Bavaria, 17 Dec 1854; d Samaden, Switzerland, 8 May 1919), German composer and organist. Studied at Munich with Rheinberger and others, later became organist and music director to Heidelberg University, and also conducted choral performances.

Works include oratorio *Weihnachtsmysterium* (1899), *Das grosse Hallelujah* (Klopstock, 1886) for male chorus, hymns *Der evangelische Kirchenchor* for chorus, *Festmusik* for baritone and male

chorus (1903); string quartet, quintet, string trio, cello and piano sonata; three sonatas, 57 preludes, *3 Tondichtungen* for organ; piano pieces; songs.

Wolkenstein, Oswald von (b Schöneck Castle, Tyrol, c 1377; d Meran, 2 Aug 1445), Austrian Minnesinger and politician. Led a very adventurous life; travelled much, even as far as Asia and Africa. From 1415 he was in the service of King (later Emperor) Sigismund and was sent to Spain and Portugal on diplomatic missions. In 1421–27 he involved himself in much strife and was twice imprisoned in his endeavour to extend his land by encroaching on that of his neighbours. Although he sang of courtly love, he enjoyed a long adulterous affair.

Works include songs of love, spring, travel, etc. for one–three voices (to his own words).

Wolpe, Stefan (b Berlin, 25 Aug 1902; d New York, 4 Apr 1972), American composer of Russian and Austrian parentage. Studied with Juon and Schreker in Berlin and in 1933–34 with Webern, after which he went to Palestine and in 1938 settled in the USA.

Works include operas *Schöne Geschichten* and *Zeus und Elida*; ballet *The Man from Midian* (1942); symphonies, symphony for 21 instruments (1956), Passacaglia and two Fugues for orchestra; cantatas *The Passion of Man*, *On the Education of Man*, *About Sport* (1932), *Unnamed Lands*, *Israel and his Land*; chamber music.

I sent him a song five years ago, and asked him to mark a cross in the score wherever he thought it was faulty ... Brahms sent it back unread, saying, 'I don't want to make a cemetery of your composition.'

Hugo Wolf, quoted in Lochner, *Fritz Kreisler*, 1951

Wolstenholme, William (b Blackburn, 24 Feb 1865; d London, 23 Jul 1931), English organist and composer. Precociously gifted, although blind, he was trained in music at the College for the Blind at Worcester, where Elgar taught him the violin. He cultivated the organ and piano especially, became church organist at Blackburn in 1887 and at various churches in London from 1902. In 1908 he toured the USA as a recitalist.

Works include church music; orchestra and military band works; chamber music; c 100 works for organ, including sonatas, fantasy, prelude and fugue; piano pieces.

Wolzogen, Ernst von (b Breslau, 23 Apr 1855; d Munich, 30 Jul 1934), German writer. Studied at the Universities of Strasbourg and Leipzig. With O J Bierbaum and F Wedekind he established the satirical cabaret *Das Überbrettl* in Berlin in 1901, for which Zemlinsky, O Straus and Schoenberg provided some of the music. The cabaret lasted two successful years, before finally closing. He was the author of the libretto of R Strauss's *Feuersnot*.

Wolzogen, Hans (Paul) von (b Potsdam, 13 Nov 1848; d Bayreuth, 2 Jun 1938), German writer on music, half-brother of Ernst von ◊Wolzogen. He was called to Bayreuth by Wagner in 1877 to become editor of the *Bayreuther Blätter*, and wrote several works of analysis and propaganda on Wagner's music dramas.

Wood, Anthony (à) (b Oxford, 17 Dec 1632; d Oxford, 29 Nov 1695), English antiquarian. Educated at Merton College, Oxford, where he took the M.A. in 1655. He wrote several works on the history of Oxford and compiled biographical particulars of musicians. He was expelled from the university 1693 for libelling the Earl of Clarendon.

Wood, Charles (b Armagh, 15 Jun 1866; d Cambridge, 12 Jul 1926), Irish music scholar, teacher and composer. Learnt music from the organist of Armagh Cathedral, where his father was lay vicar, and in 1883–87 studied at the RCM in London, where he became professor in 1888. From 1888 to 1894 he conducted the University Music Society at Cambridge, where he took the Mus.D. in 1894. In 1897 he became music lecturer to the University and in 1924 succeeded Stanford as professor of music.

Works include opera *The Pickwick Papers* (after Dickens, 1922); incidental music to Euripides' *Ion* and *Iphigenia in Tauris*; *Ode to the*

West Wind (1890) and *The Song of the Tempest* for solo voices, chorus and orchestra; *Ode on Music* (Swinburne, 1894), *Ode on Time* (Milton, 1898), *Dirge for Two Veterans* (Whitman), *Ballad of Dundee* for chorus and orchestra; *Passion according to St Mark*; eight string quartets.

Wood, Haydn (b Slaithwaite, Yorkshire, 25 Mar 1882; d London, 11 Mar 1959), English violinist and composer. Having appeared as a child prodigy, he studied violin with Arbós and composition with Stanford at the RCM in London, the former also with Thomson in Brussels.

Works include cantata *Lochinvar* (from Scott's *Marmion*); rhapsodies, overtures, picturesque suites, variations and other works for orchestra; concertos for violin and for piano; fantasy string quartet; instrumental pieces; over 200 songs.

Wood, Henry J(oseph) (b London, 3 Mar 1869; d Hitchin, Herts., 19 Aug 1944), English conductor. He showed precocious gifts, especially as an organist, and gave recitals and held church appointments as a boy. In 1889 he had his first experience as a conductor, in opera, in which he toured for the next few years; he conducted the British premiere of *Eugene Onegin* in 1892. In 1895 he was engaged by Robert Newman to take charge of the Promenade Concerts at the newly built Queen's Hall, and he remained in charge of them for 50 years to the end of his life, celebrating their half-centenary just before his death. He began modestly with popular programmes, but soon included many of the latest foreign and English novelties as they appeared; gave the fp of Schoenberg's Five Orchestral Pieces (1912) and first British performances of Mahler's first, fourth, seventh and eighth symphonies. He conducted further performances of music by Bartók, Strauss, Sibelius and Skriabin. He also conducted many music festivals and gave the fps of works by Delius and Vaughan Williams (*Serenade to Music*, 1938). In 1898 he married the Russian soprano Olga Urussov (who died in 1909) and in 1911 Muriel Greatorex. Knighted 1911.

Wood, Hugh (b Parbold, Lancs., 27 Jun 1932), English composer. Studied composition with A Milner, I Hamilton and Seiber. Taught at Morley College 1959–62, and then at the RAM; Liverpool University 1971–73; Cambridge from 1976.

Works include *Scenes from Comus* for soprano, tenor and orchestra (1965); cello concerto (1969), chamber concerto (1971), violin concerto (1972), symphony (1982), piano concerto (1991); four string quartets (1959–93), quintet for clarinet, horn and piano trio (1967), piano trio (1984), horn trio (1989); songs to texts by Logue, Hughes, Muir and Neruda.

Wooden Prince, The, *A fából faragott királyfi*, ballet in one act by Bartók (scenario by Bela Balazs); composed 1914–16, produced Budapest, 12 May 1917, conductor Tango. Orchestral suite (1931) performed Budapest, 23 Nov 1931, conductor Ernö Dohnányi.

Woods, Michael (*fl.* 1568–73), English organist and composer. Was organist of Chichester Cathedral in the middle of the century, and wrote motets.

Woodson, Leonard (b Winchester, *c* 1565; d ? Eton, ? 1641), English organist, singer and composer. He was in the choir at St George's Chapel, Windsor, early in the 17th c. and became organist of Eton College in 1615.

Works include Te Deum and other church music; music for viols; songs.

Woodson, Thomas, English 16th–17th c. composer. In 1581 he became a member of the Chapel Royal, his place being taken by William West in 1605. Composed 40 canonic settings of the plainsong *Miserere* for keyboard, only 20 of which survive.

Woodward, Richard (b ? 1743; d Dublin, 22 Nov 1777), Irish organist and composer. Learnt music as a choirboy at Christ Church Cathedral, Dublin, where his father, Richard Woodward, was vicar-choral; in 1765 he was appointed organist there. He took the Mus.D. at Trinity College, Dublin, in 1771.

Works include services, anthems, chants and other church music; catches and canons; songs.

Woodward, Roger (b Sydney, 20 Dec 1942), Australian pianist. He studied at the Sydney Conservatory 1952–62 and moved to London 1964 (where he has lived since 1971); studied further in Poland and won the 1968 Chopin Competition, Warsaw. London debut 1967; he took part in the 1972 fp of Stockhausen's *Intervall* for piano duo and has given frequent performances of works by Penderecki, Bussotti, Boulez, Cage and Barraqué. In 1986 he gave the NY fp of *Keqrops*, for piano and orchestra, by Xenakis. OBE 1980.

Wooldridge, H(arry) E(llis) (b Winchester, 28 Mar 1845; d London, 13 Feb 1917), English painter and music scholar. He was Slade Professor of Fine Arts at Oxford from 1895–1904, but made a special study of medieval music. His chief works were the first two vols of the *Oxford History of Music*.

Woolrich, John (b Cirencester, 3 Jan 1954), English composer. Studied with Edward Cowie at Lancaster. Has taught at Durham, the GSM in London, Dartington and Reading. *The Ghost in the Machine* for orchestra was performed at the 1990 Proms, London. Other works include *The Barber's Timepiece* (1986), and *The Theatre Represents a Garden: Night* for orchestra (1991); *It is Midnight, Dr Schweitzer* for strings (1992); *Quick Steps*, wind octet (1990); *The Death of King Renaud*, string quintet (1992); ensemble pieces and songs.

Wozzeck ... marks the summing up of opera, and perhaps Berg has finally written 'finis' to the history of opera.

Pierre Boulez, notes to his production of *Wozzeck*, 1963

Wordsworth, Barry (b Worcester Park, Surrey, 1949), English conductor. Studied at the RCM with Adrian Boult; harpsichord with Gustav Leonhardt in Amsterdam. Debut for the Royal Ballet, playing Martin's Harpsichord concerto, and has since conducted there, for Australian Ballet and the National Ballet of Canada. Music director of the BBC Concert Orchestra 1991 (Last Night of the Proms with the BBC SO, 1993). CG opera debut 1991, *Carmen*.

Wordsworth, William B(rocklesby) (b London, 17 Dec 1908; d Kingussie, Scotland, 10 Mar 1988), English composer, a direct descendant of the poet's brother. He did not begin to study music seriously until he was 20. Became a pupil of Tovey in 1935. During the 1939–45 war he took to farming, but after that devoted himself entirely to composition.

Works include oratorio *Dies Domini* (1944); *The Houseless Dead* (D H Lawrence) for baritone chorus and orchestra, *Hymn of Dedication* (Chesterton) for chorus and orchestra; eight symphonies (1944–86), theme and variations, *Three Pastoral Sketches* for orchestra, *Sinfonia* and *Canzone and Ballade* for strings; piano concerto, cello concerto.

Six string quartets (1941–64); string trio; two sonatas for violin and piano, two sonatas for cello and piano; sonata and suite for piano; three hymn-tune preludes for organ; *Four Sacred Sonnets* (Donne, 1944) and other songs; rounds for several voices.

Worgan, John (b London, 1724; d London, 24 Aug 1790), English organist and composer. Pupil of T Roseingrave. Appointed organist of the church of St Andrew Undershaft *c* 1749 and of Vauxhall Gardens *c* 1751 in succession to his brother James Worgan (*c* 1715–53), to which he was also attached as composer until 1761, and again 1770–74. He took the Mus.D. in 1775. He became famous as an organ recitalist.

Works include oratorios *The Chief of Maon*, *Hannah* (1764), *Manasseh* (1766) and *Gioas* (unfinished); anthem for a victory, psalm-tunes; serenata *The Royal Voyage*, dirge in memory of Frederick, Prince of Wales; ode on the rebellion of 1745; organ pieces; harpsichord lessons; glees; songs.

working-out, or development, the second section of a movement in sonata form, following the exposition, where thematic material is subjected to various developments, and the harmony undergoes more adventurous modulation than in the exposition or recapitulation, generally avoiding the tonic key before its reappearance in the recapitulation. The usual procedure is to develop the first or second subjects or both, but the procedure is by no means fixed and new matter may be introduced at will.

Worldes Blis work for orchestra by Peter Maxwell Davies, fp London, 28 Aug 1968; although not well received by older members of the Promenade audience, the work established Davies with the younger set as a leading composer.

Worshipful Company of Musicians of London, The an association dating back to the Middle Ages, but not formally incorporated by royal charter until 1604, under James I, though minstrels had already been allowed to form themselves into guilds by Edward IV in 1469. Among its present functions is the award of prizes and scholarships.

Wotquenne, Alfred (Camille) (b Lobbes, Hainault, 25 Jan 1867; d Antibes, 25 Sept 1939), Belgian music bibliographer. Studied at the Brussels Conservatory and became its librarian in 1894. He pub. its catalogue, bibliographies of C P E Bach, Galuppi, Gluck and Luigi Rossi.

Woytowicz, Boleslaw (b Dunajowce, Podolia, 5 Dec 1899; d Katowice, 11 Jul 1980), Polish pianist and composer. Began by studying mathematics and philosophy at Kiev University and law at Warsaw University, but coming of a musical family, turned to the piano, which he studied at the Chopin High School at Warsaw, where he later became a teacher. He next took to composition, studying first with Szopski, Maliszewski and others, and in 1930 with Nadia Boulanger in Paris.

Works include concertino, concert suite, *Poème funèbre* on the death of Pilsudski, three symphonies (1926–63), variations in the form of a symphony for orchestra; piano concerto; two string quartets, trio for flute, clarinet and bassoon, *Cradle Song* for soprano; clarinet bassoon and harp (1931); variations and other works for piano.

Wozzeck opera by A Berg (libretto by composer, from G Büchner's drama of 1836), produced Berlin, Opera, 14 Dec 1925. Jealous soldier Wozzeck knifes mistress Marie after she is seduced by the Drum Major and he is taunted by the Captain and Doctor. Insane, he drowns himself.

Opera by M Gurlitt (libretto ditto), produced Bremen, 22 Apr 1926.

Wranitzky, Anton (b Nová Říše, 13 Jun 1761; d Vienna, 6 Aug 1820), Moravian violinist and composer. Pupil of Haydn, Mozart and Albrechtsberger, he was *Kapellmeister* to Prince Lobkowitz from 1797, and from 1814 music director at the Theater an der Wien in Vienna. He was a friend of Beethoven and arranged Haydn's *Creation* for string quartet.

Works include symphonies, concertos, serenades; string quartets, quintets, sextets, and other chamber music.

Wranitzky, Paul (b Nová Říše, 30 Dec 1756; d Vienna, 26 Sept 1808), Moravian violinist and composer, brother of Anton ◊Wranitzky. Pupil of J M Kraus and Haydn in Vienna, in the 1780s he was in the service of Count Esterházy (not Prince Esterházy, Haydn's employer) and from *c* 1790 leader of the court opera orchestra in Vienna.

Works include operas and *Singspiele*, e.g. *Oberon, König der Elfen* (1789), *Das Fest der Lazzaroni* (1794), *Der Schreiner* (1799), etc.; ballet divertissements *Das Waldmädchen* (1796), *Die Weinlese* (1794), *Zemire und Azore, Das Urteil von Paris* (1801); 51 symphonies; *c* 100 string quartets and quintets; piano quartets; violin sonatas and large numbers of other instrumental works; over 200 canons; vocal duets, trios, etc.; church music.

wrest the old English term for a tuning-key, from the verb meaning to twist or wrench. The tuning-pins of the piano are still called wrestpins and the board into which they are inserted is the wrest-plank.

Wright, Brian (b Tonbridge, 4 Aug 1946), English conductor. Studied at the GSM and with Jascha Horenstein. Debut at the RFH, London, 1972 (*Messiah*). Conducted the BBC SO Chorus 1976–84, leading the Berlioz Requiem and Liszt's *Christus*. Guest with major London orchestras in *A Child of our Time*, the Verdi and Dvořák Requiems

——— THE OPERA ———

Wozzeck

A three-act opera by Alban Berg, first performed in 1925. A story of military infidelity, it is set in an Austrian garrison town in about 1820.

I. Private soldier Wozzeck (baritone) shaves his captain (tenor) and receives a lecture from him about morality. While out cutting sticks with his friend Andres (tenor), Wozzeck has a vision of a blazing fire in the sky. Sitting with their child, Wozzeck's mistress Marie (soprano) admires a passing Drum-Major (tenor). Wozzeck tries to earn some money by submitting to crackpot medical experiments by an excitable doctor (bass); Marie takes the Drum-Major into her house.

II. Wozzeck is already suspicious of Marie, and the captain and the doctor taunt him with her infidelity. Wozzeck watches Marie dancing with the Drum-Major at an inn. He cannot sleep when he returns to barracks, and the Drum-Major arrives boasting drunkenly. The men fight and Wozzeck is beaten.

III. Marie reads from a Bible and tries to comfort her child, although she has forebodings. She walks with Wozzeck by a pond and he stabs her. Drinking later at a tavern, blood is seen on Wozzeck's hands and he runs away. He returns to the pond for his knife but drowns as he wades further in. Wozzeck's child is playing with other children and he does not understand them when they tell him his mother is dead.

——— THE OPERA ———

and Tippett's *Mask of Time*. Fps of works by Robert Simpson and Wilfred Josephs.

Wryght, Thomas, English 16th-c. composer. He was a member of the Chapel Royal. 1547–48; his *Nesciens mater* is in the 'Gyffard' part-books.

Wührer, Friedrich (b Vienna, 29 Jun 1900; d Mannheim, 27 Dec 1975), Austrian pianist and teacher. He studied at the Vienna Academy with Franz Schmidt and Löwe, and taught there 1922–32, 1939–45. Other teaching posts at Mannheim, the Salzburg Mozarteum and Munich (1955–68). His concert career began in 1923; toured Europe and USA, usually including works by Bartók, Hindemith, Prokofiev and members of the Second Viennese School.

Wüllner, Franz (b Münster, 28 Jan 1832; d Braunfels, 7 Sept 1902), German conductor, composer and pianist. Studied at home and at Frankfurt, and appeared as pianist at Brussels in 1852–53, where he enlarged his experience by meeting Fétis, Kufferath and other musicians. He then made a tour in Germany, settled at Munich in 1854 and in 1856 became piano professor at the Conservatory. In 1858–64 he was music director at Aachen, where he did much choral and orchestral conducting, but he returned to Munich as court music director, reorganized the court church music and became conductor of the court opera 1869, in succession to Bülow. Against Wagner's wishes he gave the fps of *Das Rheingold* (1869) and *Die Walküre* (1870). In 1877–82 he was court music director at Dresden, succeeding Rietz, and from 1884 director of the conservatory at Cologne in succession to F Hiller and conductor of the Gürzenich concerts; gave there the fps of Strauss's *Till Eulenspiegel* (1895) and *Don Quixote* (1898). Wrote church and chamber music. His son Ludwig (1858–1938) was a tenor and baritone; well known as Elgar's Gerontius and sang *Kindertotenlieder* under Mahler in NY, 1910.

Wunderlich, Fritz (b Kusel, 26 Sept 1930; d Heidelberg, 17 Sept 1966), German tenor. He studied at Freiburg and made his debut at Stuttgart as Tamino in 1955. He moved to Frankfurt in 1959 and later sang at Munich and Vienna; sang Tiresias in the 1959 fp of Orff's *Oedipus der Tyrann* (Stuttgart) and Henry in *Die schweigsame Frau* at Salzburg the same year. His Don Ottavio at CG (1966) will long be remembered. The ease, elegance and expressive power of his voice are well displayed in his recording of *Das Lied von der Erde* with

Klemperer. He sang Tamino at the Edinburgh Festival shortly before his accidental death. Still regarded as a lyric tenor beyond compare. Other roles included Belmonte, Leukippos and Palestrina.

Wuorinen, Charles (b New York, 9 Jun 1938), American composer, conductor and pianist. He studied at Columbia University, and taught there 1964–71. His early works are tonal but he was later influenced by Varèse, Babbitt and serial technique.

Works include masque *The Politics of Harmony* (1967), 'baroque burlesque' *The Whore of Babylon* (1975); three symphonies (1958–59), four chamber concertos (1957–59), *Evolutio transcripta* for orchestra (1961), two piano concertos (1966, 1974), *Contrafactum* for orchestra (1969), concerto for amplified violin and orchestra (1971), *Percussion Symphony* (1976), *Bamboula Squared* for orchestra (1983), Concerto for saxophone quartet and orchestra (1993), *The Mission of Virgil* for orchestra (1993); *Dr Faustus Lights the Light* for narrator and instruments (1957), octet (1962), string trio (1968), chamber concerto (1970), wind quintet (1977), horn trio (1981), three string quartets (1971, 1979, 1987), Saxophone quartet (1992); *Symphonia sacra* for vocal soloists and instrumental ensemble (1961), *The Prayer of Jonah* for voices and string quintet (1962), *The Celestial Sphere*, sacred oratorio for chorus and orchestra (1979); electronic music.

Wyk, Arnold van (b near Calvinia, Cape Province, 26 Apr 1916; d Cape Town, 27 May 1983), South African composer. Began to learn the piano at 12 and, after working in an insurance office at Cape Town, entered Stellenbosch University in 1936. In 1937 he was commissioned to write music for the centenary of the Voortrekkers and in 1938 he went to live in London, having gained the Performing Right Society's scholarship. He studied composition with Theodore Holland and piano with Harold Craxton at the RAM, joined the BBC for a short time and later devoted himself to composition.

Works include two symphonies (1944, 1952), suite for small orchestra on African tunes *Southern Cross* (1943); *Saudade* for violin and orchestra; string quartets, five elegies for string quartet (1941); three improvisations on a Dutch folksong for piano duet.

Wylde, John (*fl. c* 1425–50), English music theorist, precentor of Waltham Abbey, near London. He wrote a summary of Guido d'Arezzo's theoretical work, entitled *Musica Gwydonis monachi*. This stands at the head of a collection compiled by him (British Library, Lansdowne MS. 763) which later belonged to Tallis, whose signature it bears.

Wyner, Yehudi (b Calgary, Canada, 1 Jun 1929), American composer, conductor and pianist. Studied at Juilliard and Yale and at Harvard with Hindemith and Walter Piston. Teacher at Yale University 1963–77, Purchase, NY, 1978–90 (professor of music) and Brandeis (from 1989). His wife **Susan Davenny** (b 1945) has premiered his works and pieces by Del Tredici and Carter (*A Mirror on Which to Dwell*, 1976). New York City Opera debut 1977 (as Poppea); Met. 1982 (Woglinde).

Works include *Da Camera* for piano and orchestra (1967); *Intermedia* for soprano and strings (1974); *On This Most Voluptuous Night* for soprano and seven instruments (1982); Wind quintet (1984); string quartet (1985); *Changing Time* for ensemble (1991); cello concerto (1994).

Wynne, David (b Penderyn, Glamorgan, 2 Jun 1900; d Pencoed, Glamorgan, 23 Mar 1983), Welsh composer. He worked as a coalminer during adolescence but studied at University College, Cardiff, from 1925; was active in the promotion of Welsh music.

Works include operas *Jack and Jill* (1975) and *Night and Cold Peace* (1979); five symphonies (1952–80), two rhapsody concertos, *Octade* for orchestra (1978); five string quartets (1944–80); sextet for piano and orchestra (1977); song cycles and choral music.

Wynslate, Richard (d Winchester, buried 15 Dec 1572), English composer. He was a singer at St Mary-at-Hill, London, 1537–40, and master of the choristers, Winchester Cathedral, 1540–72. An organ piece, *Lucem tuam*, has survived.

Wyzewa (originally *Wyzewski*), Théodore de (b Kalusik, 12 Sept 1862; d Paris, 17 Apr 1917), French musicologist of Polish parentage. He lived in France from 1869. In 1884 he founded the *Revue Wagnérienne* with Édouard Dujardin and in 1901 the Société Mozart with Boschot. He became a political and literary journalist, but his chief work is his study of Mozart, of which he completed two vols. in collaboration with Georges de Saint-Foix. He was a friend of Renoir and Mallarmé.

X

Xenakis, Iannis (b Braîla, 29 May 1922), Greek composer. First studied engineering and worked for some years as an architect with Le Corbusier, at the latter's invitation, in Paris. He also studied music with Honegger, Milhaud and Messiaen, and evolved a method of composition using the mathematics of chance and probability and also employing computers (sometimes referred to as 'stochastic' music). His ideas have exercised considerable influence on other composers.

Works include theatre music *Oresteia* (1966) and *The Bacchae* (1993); *Metastasis* for orchestra (1954), *Pithoprakta* for string orchestra (1956), *Achorripsis* for 21 instruments (1957), *Syrmos* for 18 strings (1959); *Akrata* for 16 wind (1965), *Polytope* for small orchestra (1967), *Synaphaï* for piano and orchestra (1969), *Noomena* for orchestra (1975), *Palimpsest* for piano and ensemble (1982), *Keqrops* for piano and orchestra (1986), *Tracées* for orchestra (1987), *Tuorakemsu* for orchestra (1990).

Electronic compositions include *Diamorphosis* (1958), *Orient-Occident* (1960); *Morsima-Amorsima* (1) for four players (1956–62), (2) for ten players (1962); ballets *Kraanerg* for orchestra and tape (1969) and *Antikhton* (1971); *Oresteia* for chorus and chamber ensemble (1966), *Chants des Soleils* (1983), *Idmen A* for chorus and percussion quartet (1985), *Idmen B* for chorus and percussion sextet (1986), *Knephas* for unaccompanied chorus (1990); chamber works *Atrées* (1962), *Anaktoria* (1969), *Auroura* (1971), *Phlegra* (1975), *Retours-Windungen* (1976), *Tetras* for string quartet (1983), *Thallein* for 14 players (1984), *Jalons* for 15 players (1986), *Akea* piano quarter (1986), *Waarg* for 13 players (1988), *Okho* for three players (1989), *Epicycle* for cello and 12 players (1989), *Dox-Orkh* for violin and 89 players (1991); *Akanthos* for soprano and ensemble (1977).

Xerse, *Xerxes*, ◊*Serse*.

Opera by Cavalli (libretto by N Minato), produced Venice, Teatro dei SS Giovanni e Paolo, 12 Jan 1654.

The purpose of music is to draw toward a total exaltation in which the individual mingles, losing his consciousness in a truth immediate.
      Iannis Xenakis, *New York Times*, 1976

---

xylophone, from Greek *xulon*, 'wood', and *phōnē*, 'sound', a percussion instrument with a series of wooden bars suspended over resonators and tuned in a chromatic scale. It is played with hammers and makes a dry, rattling, but perfectly clear and richly sonorous sound. It is made in various sizes.

xylorimba a percussion instrument, a small marimba made in America.

Xyndas, Spyridon (b Corfu, 8 Jun 1814; d Athens, 25 Nov 1896), Greek composer. His opera *The Parliamentary Candidate* was the first to a Greek libretto.

Works include Italian operas *Anna Winter* (1855), *I due rivali* (1878), *Il Conte Giuliano*, *Il candidato al parlamento* (1867) and others; piano pieces; many songs. and orchestra (1977); song cycles and choral music.

Y

Yakar, Rachel (b Lyon, 3 Mar 1938), French soprano. Studied with Germaine Lubin in Paris. Debut in Strasbourg, 1963. Sang with the Deutsche Oper am Rhein 1964–85. Bayreuth and CG 1976. 1978 (as Freia). Has sung Donna Elvira and the Marschallin at Glyndebourne (1977, 1980), Geneva 1980 (Jenůfa). Widely known in the Baroque repertory: Monteverdi's Poppea at Zurich, Handel's Cleopatra at Amsterdam, Rameau's Aricie and Cecilio in *Lucio Silla*. Recordings include *Les Indes Galantes*, Leclair's *Scylla et Glaucus* and Lully's *Armide*.

Yansons, Arvid (b Leipaja, 24 Oct 1914; d Manchester, 21 Nov 1984), Latvian conductor. Debut Riga Opera, 1944. Leningrad PO from 1952. Chief guest conductor Hallé Orchestra from 1964. His son is Marriss ◊Jansons.

Yan Tan Tethera opera by Harrison Birtwistle; (text by T Harrison). Written 1983–84 for television, fp London, 5 Aug 1986. Shepherd Alan arouses jealousies of Caleb Raven, who causes wife Hannah and twins to be imprisoned; they are released after seven years.

Year 1812, The festival overture by Tchaikovsky, op. 49, written for the commemoration of the 70th anniversary of Napoleon's retreat from Moscow and first performed during the Moscow Arts and Industrial Exhibition, 20 Aug 1882, at the consecration of the Cathedral of the Redeemer in the Kremlin.

Yellow Cake Review, The work by Maxwell Davies for singers and piano (text by composer), which describes threat to Orkneys posed by uranium mining, fp Kirkwall, Orkney, 21 Jun 1980.

Yeoman of the Guard, The, or The Merryman and his Maid, operetta by Sullivan (libretto by W S Gilbert), produced London, Savoy Theatre, 3 Oct 1888.

yodel an elaborate form of song in Switzerland, Tyrol, Styria, etc., usually sung by men in falsetto, with rapid changes to chest voice, very free in rhythm and metre and using as a rule the restricted scale of the natural harmonics of instruments like the alphorn. The yodel is thus very probably derived or copied from the ◊ranz des vaches.

Yonge, Nicholas (b ? Lewes; d London, buried 23 Oct 1619), English singer and music editor. Worked in London and pub. in 1588 a volume of Italian madrigals with English translations, entitled *Musica transalpina*.

Yorkshire Feast Song, The an ode or cantata by Purcell, 'Of old when heroes', for two altos, tenor, two basses, five-part chorus, recorders, oboes, trumpets and strings, words by Thomas Durfey, written in 1690 for the annual reunion of Yorkshiremen in London, intended to be held that year on 14 Feb but postponed to 27 Mar owing to parliamentary elections.

Youll, Henry, English 16th–17th-c. composer. Pub. a book of canzonets and balletts for three voices in 1608.

Young, (Basil) Alexander (b London, 18 Oct 1920), English tenor. Studied in London, Naples and Vienna. After singing in the Glyndebourne chorus and some small parts, he became one of the leading English operatic and concert singers. One of his best-known roles was that of Tom Rakewell in *The Rake's Progress*, which he recorded under the composer's baton. CG, 1955–70 as Vašek, Matteo and Lysander; SW as Count Ory, Almaviva and Belmonte. Other roles included Orpheus (Gluck and Monteverdi) and many in Handel. Teacher at the RNCM, 1973–86.

Young, Cecilia (b London, 1711; d London, 1 Oct 1789), English soprano, daughter of Charles Young, organist of All Hallows, Barking in London, married Arne in 1737.

Young, Douglas (b London, 18 Jun 1947), English composer and pianist. He studied at the RCM with Anthony Milner; several of his compositions are open-ended 'works in progress' influenced by Boulez.

Works include ballets *Pasipae* (1969), *Charlotte Brontë – Portrait* (1973) and *Ludwig, Fragments of a Puzzle* (1986); sinfonietta (1970), *Aubade* for orchestra (1973), piano concertino (1974), *Rain, Steam and Speed* for orchestra (1981), *Lament on the Destruction of Forests* for orchestra (1986); *The Listeners*, cantata-ballet for speaker, voices and orchestra (1967), *Sir Patrick Spens*, ballad for voices and orchestra (1970); *Not Waving but Drowning*, song cycle to poems by Stevie Smith (1970); *Realities* (Yeats) for soprano, tenor and ensemble (1974); sonata for string trio (1968), *Essay* for string quartet (1971), *Chamber Music* (James Joyce) for soprano and guitar (1976–82); *The Hunting of the Snark* for chorus, piano and orchestra (1982); chamber music includes *String Trio* (1985).

Young, La Monte (b Bern, ID, 14 Oct 1935), American composer. Studied at University of California, Los Angeles, 1956–57 and at Berkeley 1957–60. In 1959 he also studied with Stockhausen, and then lectured for a time on guerrilla warfare at the NY School for Social Research: the direction on one of his works is 'urinate'.

Works include *The Tortoise Droning Selected Pitches from the Holy Numbers for the Two Black Tigers, the Green Tiger and the Hermit* (1964); *The Tortoise Recalling the Drone of the Holy Numbers as they were Revealed in the Dreams of the Whirlwind and the Obsidian Gong, Illuminated by the Sawmill, the Green Sawtooth Ocelot and the High-Tension Line Stepdown Transformer* (both works staged with voice, gong and strings, 1964); *Orchestral Dreams* (1984); Piano music including the six-hour *Well-Timed Piano* from 1964).

There exists a common fallacy that all music of the first half of the eighteenth century not written by Bach was written by Handel.

Percy M Young, *Handel*, 1947

Young, Percy M(arshall) (b Northwich, Ches., 17 May 1912), English music educationist, conductor and writer on music. Educated at Christ's Hospital and Cambridge, where he was organ scholar at Selwyn College and took the M.A. and Mus.B. degrees. Mus.D. at Trinity College, Dublin. In 1934 he became director of music at the Teachers' Training College, Belfast, in 1945 director of music studies at Wolverhampton Technical College. Published part-songs and various collections for children, articles in music periodicals and a large number of books: subjects include Elgar, Handel, Sullivan and Vaughan Williams. His realization of Elgar's sketches for the opera *The Spanish Lady* was premiered at Cambridge, 24 Nov 1994.

Young, Polly (or Mary) (b London, 1749; d London, 20 Sept 1799), English singer, niece of Cecilia Young. She appeared in opera in London and married Barthélemon in 1766.

Young, Simone (b Sydney, 1961), Australian conductor. Conducted *The Mikado* for Australian Opera (1985) and assisted Barenboim at Bayreuth. Cologne Opera 1987, Berlin Komische Oper 1992, *La Bohème*; Vienna Volksoper 1992 (*Hoffmann*) and first woman to conduct Vienna PO. London, CG debut 1994 (*Rigoletto*). Has also conducted in Paris (Opéra Bastille), Munich and Florence. NY Met. 1996. Other repertory includes *Tosca*, *Jenůfa*, *Tristan*, *Siegfried*, *Elektra* and *Salome*.

Young, Thomas (b Canterbury, 1809; d London, 12 Aug 1872), English alto. Educated as a choirboy at Canterbury Cathedral where he became an alto in 1831. In 1836 he went to London to join the choir at Westminster Abbey and in 1848 he became first alto at the Temple Church. He also frequently sang at concerts.

Young, William (d Innsbruck, 23 Apr 1662), English violist, violinist, flautist and composer. He was in the service of the Archduke Ferdinand Karl (probably in the Netherlands), but returned to England to join the king's band in 1660. From 1664 he and others were also allowed to play for Killigrew at the theatre. Visited Innsbruck 1655 and played for Queen Christina of Sweden.

Works include 21 sonatas for three–five instruments with appended dances, three-part fantasies for viols, pieces for lyra viol and for viola da gamba; airs for two treble viols and bass.

Young Apollo work by Britten for piano, string quartet and string orchestra (1939, fp Toronto, 27 Aug 1939; withdrawn until 1979).

Yradier, Sebastian (b Sauciego, Álava, 20 Jan 1809; d Vitoria, 6 Dec 1865), Spanish composer. He was in Paris for a time as singing-master to the Empress Eugénie and later lived in Cuba for some years. Wrote popular Spanish songs, including *La Paloma* and the melody which formed the basis of the habañera in Bizet's *Carmen*.

Ysaÿe, Eugène(-Auguste) (b Liège, 16 Jul 1858; d Brussels, 12 May 1931), Belgian violinist, conductor and composer. Studied with his father, Nicolas Ysaÿe, then at the Liège Conservatory and later with Wieniawski and Vieuxtemps. Having already appeared in public in 1865, he played at Pauline Lucca's concerts at Cologne and Aachen, where he met F Hiller and Joachim, and later, at Frankfurt, he came into touch with Raff and Clara Schumann. He was based in Paris 1883–86, becoming close to Debussy, Fauré and Saint-Saëns, formed the Ysaÿe Quartet, 1886 and premiered Debussy's quartet in 1893. In 1886–98 he was violin professor at the Brussels Conservatory, and

founded and conducted orchestral concerts in the Belgian capital. He toured extensively, first visiting England in 1889 and the USA in 1894, playing the Beethoven Concerto with the New York PO. Admired everywhere for his skill and musicianship, he was often heard in the Franck Sonata (dedicated to him) and the Elgar Concerto. Conducted the Cincinnati SO 1918–22.

Works include opera *Piére li Houîeu* (in Walloon dialect, 1931); eight violin concertos; *Poème élégiaque*, mazurkas and other pieces for violin and piano.

Ysaÿe, Théo(phile) (b Verviers, 22 Mar 1865; d Nice, 24 Mar 1918), Belgian pianist and conductor, brother of Eugène ◊Ysaÿe. Studied at the Liège Conservatory, with Kullak in Berlin and with Franck in Paris. He often appeared at concerts with his brother and also gave recitals of his own.

Works include Requiem; symphonies, symphonic poems, fantasy, *Suite wallonne* for orchestra; piano concerto; piano quintet.

Yun, Isang (b Tong-yong, 17 Sept 1917; d Berlin, 3 Nov 1995), Korean-born German composer. He studied in Korea and Japan, and with Blacher and Rufer in Berlin. An espousal of serial techniques led to withdrawal of works written before 1959. In 1967 he was kidnapped from West Berlin by South Korean agents and charged with sedition; after release taught at Hochschule für Musik, Berlin, 1970–85.

Works include operas *Der Traum des Liu-Tung* (Berlin, 1965), *Die Witwe des Schmetterlings* (Berlin, 1967), *Geisterliebe* (Kiel, 1971); *Sim Tjong* (Munich, 1972); *Colloides sonores* for string orchestra (1961), *Dimensionen* for orchestra (1971), cello concerto (1976), flute concerto (1977), five symphonies, I (1983), II (1984), III (1985), IV 'Singing in the Dark' (1986), V for baritone and orchestra (1987); *Om Mani padame hum*, cycle for soprano, baritone, chorus and orchestra (1964), *Der weise Mann*, for baritone, chorus and small orchestra (1977); four string quartets, piano trio (1975), *Pièce concertante* for chamber ensemble (1977), flute quartet (1988).

Yurisich, Gregory (b Mt Lawley, West Australia, 13 Oct 1951), Australian baritone. After study in Perth made debut in Sydney 1976, as Paolo (*Simon Boccanegra*); other roles with Australian Opera have been Germont, Varlaam and Masetto. Sang Britten's Bottom at Frankfurt 1989; ENO as Escamillo and in the fps of Oliver's *Timon of Athens* (1991) and Buller's *Bakxai* (1992). CG from 1990, as William Tell and Bartolo. US debut as Donizetti's Henry VIII in New York (1985); Glyndebourne 1991, Leporello.

Yvain, Maurice (Pierre Paul) (b Paris, 12 Feb 1891; d Paris, 28 Jul 1965), French composer. Studied at the Paris Conservatory. He served in the army during World War I. Resuming his studies later, he devoted his whole attention to the composition of operettas, the first of which, *Ta bouche*, was an immediate success in 1921. It was followed by many others, as well as a ballet, *Vent*.

Z

Zabaleta, Nicanor (b San Sebastián, 7 Jan 1907; d San Juan, 31 Mar 1993), Basque harpist. He studied in Madrid and Paris; debut Paris, 1925. He was among the leading interpreters of 18th-c. harp music. Ginastera, Milhaud, Piston and Joseph Tal wrote concertos for him.

Zacar (b *fl. c* 1400), two or possibly three composers active in Italy, apparently divisible as follows:

1. Antonio Zacara da Teramo (*fl.* 1391–c 1420), active in the Papal chapel and perhaps in the Veneto. Works, found in MSS from many parts of Europe and evidently very influential, including Mass movements and Italian and French songs.

2. Nicola Zacharie of Brindisi (*fl.* 1420–34), documented in Florence. Works: perhaps only one Italian song, one motet and one Mass movement.

Zaccaria, Nicola (Angelo) (b Piraeus, 9 Mar 1923), Greek bass. He sang in Athens from 1949 and appeared at La Scala, Milan, in 1953; remained until 1974. CG 1957 and 1959 as Oroveso and Creon; both roles opposite Callas, with whom he joined in recordings of operas by Verdi, Bellini and Rossini. He took part in the 1958 Scala fp of Pizzetti's *Assassinio nella cattedrale* and was heard at Salzburg from 1967. Other roles included Zaccaria, Silva, Bartolo and Sarastro. Sang King Mark in *Tristan* at Dallas (1976) and Puccini's Colline at Macerata, 1982.

Zacconi, Lodovico (b Pesaro, 11 Jun 1555; d Fiorenzuola di Focara, near Pesaro, 23 Mar 1627), Italian priest and music theorist. He went to live at Venice, joined the monastic order of St Augustine and was *maestro di cappella* at its church. In 1593, at the invitation of the Archduke Charles, he went to Vienna, where he became court music director and remained until 1619, when he returned to Venice. He wrote a large treatise in four vols, *Prattica di musica* (1592–1622).

Zach, Jan (b Čelákovice, near Prague, bap. 13 Nov 1699; d Ellwangen, 24 May 1773), Bohemian organist and composer. Worked as a violinist and organist in Prague, where he came under the influence of Černohorský; later left for Germany and in 1745 was appointed *Kapellmeister* to the Electoral court in Mainz. Dismissed *c* 1757, he spent the rest of his life travelling, without permanent employment.

Works include 33 Masses, three Requiems; *Stabat Mater* and other church music; symphonies and partitas for orchestra; chamber music; organ music.

Zacharias, Christian (b Tamshedpur, India, 27 Apr 1950), German pianist. Studied with Vlado Perlemuter in Paris and has appeared in England from 1976 (LSO, RLPO and other orchestras). US debut 1979, with the Boston SO; later concerts with the Cleveland Orchestra and the New York PO. Salzburg Festival from 1981; chamber concerts with Heinrich Schiff and the Alban Berg Quartet.

Zachau, Friedrich Wilhelm (b Leipzig, bap. 14 Nov 1663; d Halle, 7 Aug 1712), German organist and composer. Pupil of his father, a town musician, under whom he learnt to play all the current instruments. The family moved to Eilenburg in 1676 and in 1684 he was appointed organist at the church of Our Lady of Halle, where Handel in due course became his pupil. Works include church cantatas, organ pieces.

Zadok the Priest, first of four anthems composed 1727 by Handel for coronation of George II; given at all subsequent coronations.

Zadek, Hilde (b Bromberg, 15 Dec 1917), Austrian soprano and teacher. After study in Zurich made debut at the Vienna Opera 1947, as Aida. Salzburg from 1948, as Brangaene in Martin's *Le vin herbé*, Eurydice in the premiere of Orff's *Antigonae* and Vitellia. Glyndebourne 1950–51, as Ariadne and Donna Anna. Sang Aida at CG, 1950 and also appeared in London as Lisa and Tosca. Engagements in the USA (Met. and San Francisco) and throughout Europe. Teacher in Vienna from 1967.

Zádor, Jenö (b Bátaszék, 5 Nov 1894; d Hollywood, 4 Apr 1977), Hungarian composer. Studied with Heuberger in Vienna and Reger at Leipzig, also took a course in musicology and graduated with the Ph.D. in 1921. In 1921 he became professor at the new Vienna Conservatory and in 1934 at the Budapest Academy of Music. In 1939 he settled in the USA and devoted himself largely to the orchestration of film music by other composers.

Works include operas *Diana* (1923), *The Island of the Dead* (1928), *Asra* (1936) and others; romantic symphony, dance symphony, variations on a Hungarian folksong, carnival suite, Hungarian carpiccio, etc.; chamber music; piano works; songs.

Zagrosek, Lothar (b Waging, 13 Nov 1942), German conductor and composer. Studied in Vienna with Swarowsky and with Karajan and Maderna. Appointments in Salzburg, Kiel and Darmstadt 1967–73. From 1978 has often conducted the London Sinfonietta, in music by Ligeti, Messiaen, Weill and Stravinsky; also guest conductor with BBC SO. USA (San Diego and Seattle) from 1984. Music director, Paris Opéra 1986–88, premiere of Höller's *Der Meister und Margarita* 1989. Glyndebourne debut 1987, *Così fan Tutte*; ENO 1989, *The Magic Flute*. Premiered Křenek oratorio *Symeon der Stylit* at Salzburg 1988; music director of the Leipzig Opera from 1990.

Zaide unfinished opera by Mozart (libretto in German, by J A Schachtner), begun 1779, first produced Frankfurt, 27 Jan 1886. Sultan Soliman's favourite Zaide escapes with prisoner Gomatz but they are recaptured.

Zaïs *ballet héroïque* in a prologue and four acts by Rameau (libretto by L de Cahusac), produced Paris, Opéra, 29 Feb 1748. Spirit Zaïs sacrifices magic powers for love of shepherdess Zélide but they are restored by spirit-ruler Oromases.

Zajc, Ivan (also known as Giovanni von Zaytz) (b Rijeka [Fiumel], 3 Aug 1832; d Zagreb, 16 Dec 1914), Croatian composer and conductor. Pupil of his father, a bandmaster in the Austrian army and of Lauro Rossi at the Milan Conservatory. He lived at Fiume and Vienna and was from 1870 conductor at the theatre and director of the Conservatory at Zagreb.

Works include 15 Croatian operas, Italian opera *Amelia* (after Schiller's *Räuber*, 1860) and others, 15 German and Croatian oper-

Francesca Zambello – opera director

1   Wagner: *Der Ring des Nibelungen*
My ambition from an early age was to be a theatre director. Then, during a student vacation, I went to see Patrice Chéreau's production of Wagner's *Ring* at Bayreuth. That was a life-changing experience. It opened the door to opera for me: I realized that it is music which turns on that fluid in your brain that makes you hear with images. Music was the conduit to the whole expressionist theatrical experience I was searching for.

2   Handel: *Julius Caesar*
Here is the most perfect opera by a pure composer. The connections between character, text, music and feeling are honest and uninhibited. This has become the opera I listen to the most. It brings me back to opera characters who are real people singing of true and sincere emotions.

3   Rossini: *Stabat Mater*
Before I heard this, I had found religious works rather chilled. But this was a wonderful fusing of the theatrical and spiritual which moved me beyond belief. The cycle of the mass is very charged and I listen to it when I want to be centred.

4   Glass: *Satyagraha*
I've known and worked with many modern composers over the years, but it wasn't until I heard this piece that I felt that contemporary music could speak to us politically. In it, the great opera tradition and the world today are fused completely, like a spot of ink in the blood which becomes one with it.

5   Berlioz: *The Trojans*
This work has had an enormous impact on me. I always go back to *The Trojans* when I am suffering from hero/heroine anxieties, when I think there are no characters left who are real humans as well as being heroic. Cassandra is an interesting heroine, not a victim, someone leading others, holding on to her dignity. I believe that Berlioz really understood women.

6   Mahler: Symphonies nos. 3 and 8
I discovered Mahler in my twenties. You grow past Beethoven and meet Mahler – the experience was as piquant as discovering espresso after American coffee! I can't choose between his Third and Eighth symphonies for total transcendental experience.

7   Mozart: Piano Concertos nos. 21 and 23
Mozart has been with me my whole life: his music is in our subconscious aural vernacular. I particularly love these piano concertos: they free the mind and allow it to relax, opening the inner eye to revitalizing, regenerating images!

ettas including *Sonnambula* (produced Vienna, 1868); oratorio *The Fall of Man*; church music including 19 Masses and four requiems; songs.

Zajick, Dolores (b Nevada, 1959), American mezzo. Studied at the Manhattan School of Music and made debut at San Francisco 1986, as Azucena. NY Met. from 1988, as Amneris, Eboli and Azucena. Has sung further at Carnegie Hall (as Tchaikovsky's Maid of Orleans), Chicago, Vienna and Verona. CG debut 1994. Concerts include the Verdi Requiem and Prokofiev's *Alexander Nevsky*.

Žak, Benedict, ◊Schack.

Zambello, Francesca (b New York, 24 Aug 1956), American stage director. Studied with Jean-Pierre Ponnelle and was artistic co-director of the Skylight Music Theater at Milwaukee (1985–90). Also worked at the San Francisco Opera (1983–84) and at Wexford (from 1988); has staged *The Devil and Kate*, *Der Templer und die Jüdin* (Maschner), Donizetti's *L'assedio di Corinto* and Tchaikovsky's *Cherevichki*. Seattle Opera 1990 (*War and Peace*), Los Angeles 1991 (*Les Troyens*). First US director at the Bolshoi (*Turandot*, 1991), and staged *Khovanshchina* for ENO, 1994; premiere of Goehr's *Arianna* at CG, 1995. Her work is noted for its historical style and dramatic truth.

Zamboni, Luigi (b Bologna, 1767; d Florence, 28 Feb 1837), Italian bass. Debut Ravenna, 1791, in Cimarosa's *Il fanatico burlato*; was widely known in comic operas by Fioravanti and Paisiello and created Rossini's Figaro (Rome, 1816).

Zamboni, Maria (b Peschiera, 25 Jul 1895; d Verona, 25 Mar 1976), Italian soprano. She studied at Parma and made her debut at Piacenza in 1921, as Marguerite. She sang at La Scala 1924–31 and created Liù there in 1926. In 1930 she took part in the Rome fp of Pizzetti's *Lo straniero*. She was well known in South America and at Buenos Aires, Rio, Sao Paulo and Santiago was admired as Orpheus, Elsa, Eva, Mimi and Manon.

Zampa, ou La Fiancée de marbre, *Zampa, or The Marble Betrothed*, opera by Hérold (libretto by A H J Mélesville), produced Paris, Opéra-Comique, 3 May 1831. The wedding of Camille and Alphonse is interrupted by the pirate Zampa, the older brother of Alphonse. Before Zampa can force Camille to marry him the statue of his former bride Alice kills him.

Zampieri, Mara (b Padua, 24 May 1941), Italian soprano. Studied in Padua and made debut at Pavia 1972, as Nedda. La Scala in 1978 as Élisabeth de Valois, Amalia in *I Masnadieri* and Amelia (*Ballo*) and in subsequent years. Vienna from 1979, as Odabella (*Attila*), Lady Macbeth, and Salome (1991). CG debut 1984. Has sung in San Francisco, and appeared at the Bregenz Festival from 1990, as La Wally, Fedora and Francesca da Rimini.

Zancanaro, Giorgio (b Verona, 9 May 1939), Italian baritone. Debut Milan 1970, as Riccardo in *I Puritani*. Salzburg 1971, Hamburg 1977 (as Luna). La Scala from 1981, as Ford in *Falstaff*, Luna and William Tell. NY Met. debut 1982 (Renato), CG 1985 as Gerard in *Andrea Chénier*. Noted for his forceful interpretations of such roles as Ezio in *Attila* (CG 1990), Macbeth, Nabucco and Posa.

Zandonai, Riccardo (b Sacco, Trentino, 30 May 1883; d Pesaro, 5 Jun 1944), Italian composer. Studied at Roveredo and later at the Liceo Musicale of Pesaro, where Mascagni was director. He left in 1902 and at Milan met Boito, who introduced him to the publisher Ricordi, by whom his first opera was commissioned. His greatest success was with the verismo opera *Francesca da Rimini*, still performed on the Continent and at the NY Met.

Works include operas *Il grillo sul focolare* (after Dickens's *Cricket on the Hearth*, 1908), *Conchita* (after Louÿs's *La Femme et le pantin*, 1911), *Melenis* (1912), *La via della finestra*, *Francesca da Rimini* (on d'Annunzio's play, 1914), *Giulietta e Romeo* (after Shakespeare, 1922), *I cavalieri di Ekebù* (after Selma Lagerlöf, 1925), *Giuliano* (1928), *La farsa amorosa* (1933), *Una partitia*.

Film music for *Princess Tarakanova*; Requiem (1915), *Pater noster* for chorus, organ and orchestra; *Ballata eroica*, *Fra gli alberghi delle Dolomiti*, *Quadri di Segantini* (1931), *Rapsodia trentina*, overture *Colombina* for orchestra; *Concerto romantico* for violin and orchestra (1919); serenade and *Concerto andaluso* for cello and orchestra; string quartet; songs.

Zandt, Marie van (b New York, 8 Oct 1861; d Cannes, 31 Dec 1919), American soprano. Debut Turin, 1879, as Zerlina. She sang Amina at Her Majesty's, London, the same year and from 1880 was successful at the Paris Opéra-Comique, as Mignon, Rosina and Cherubino. She created Lakmé (1883) and repeated the role in London two years later. NY Met. 1891–92 and 1896.

Zanelli, Renato (b Valparaiso, 1 Apr 1892; d Santiago, 25 Mar 1935), Chilean tenor, formerly baritone. Debut Santiago, 1916, as Valentine; sang Amonasro at the NY Met. in 1919 and studied further in Italy, appearing at Naples in the tenor roles of Raoul and Alfredo. His best role was Otello, which he sang at CG in 1928; he was widely known in Italy as Lohengrin, Siegmund and Tristan.

Zannetti, Francesco (b Volterra, 28 Mar 1737; d Perugia, 31 Jan 1788), Italian composer. Pupil of Clari in Pisa, he became *maestro di cappella* at Perugia Cathedral in 1760, remaining there till his death.

Works include seven operas including *L'Antigono* (1765) *La Didone abbandonata* (1766) and *Artaserse* (1782); Masses, Requiems and other church music; string quintets, string trios, trio sonatas.

Zanotti, Camillo (b Cesana, *c* 1545; d Prague, 4 Feb 1591), Italian composer. Worked as vice-*Kapellmeister* at court of Rudolf II in Prague from Aug 1587. Four books of madrigals were pub. 1587–90.

Zanotti, Giovanni (b Bologna, 14 Oct 1738; d Bologna, 1 Nov 1817), Italian composer. He was *maestro di cappella* at San Petronia, Bologna, 1774–89, wrote opera *L'Olimpiade* (1767); his *Dixit* (1770) was admired by Burney.

Zarathustra (R Strauss) ◊Also sprach Zarathustra.

Zareska, Eugenia (b Rava Ruska near Lwów, 9 Nov 1910; d Paris, 5 Oct 1979), Ukrainian, later British, mezzo. She studied with Bahr-Mildenburg; made her stage debut in 1939 and sang Dorabella at La Scala, Milan, 1941, repeating the role at Glyndebourne, 1948. Her London debut was as Rosina (Cambridge Theatre, 1947) and the following year she sang Carmen at CG. She sang Berg's Countess Geschwitz in 1949 at Venice and in 1952 settled in England, appearing as guest on the Continent and returning to CG until 1958. Other roles included Marina and Monteverdi's Ottavia.

Zar lässt sich photographieren, Der, *The Tsar has his photograph taken*, opera in one act by Weill (libretto by Kaiser), produced Leipzig, 18 Feb 1928. Amorous Tsar flirts at Parisian photo studio with would-be assassin.

The opera ... is the only one in existence that might conceivably have been written by God.

Neville Cardus on *Die Zauberflöte*, in the *Manchester Guardian*, 1961

Zarlino, Gioseffe (b Chioggia, 31 Jan 1517; d Venice, 4 Feb 1590), Italian theorist and composer. Studied theology and received minor orders in 1539, but was learned also in philosophy, sciences and languages. He settled in Venice in 1541, became a fellow-student with Rore under Willaert and in 1565 became first *maestro di cappella* at St Mark's. In 1583 he was offered the bishopric of Chioggia, but declined it, preferring to remain at St Mark's. He wrote two large treatises, the three-volume *Istitutioni armoniche* (1558) and *Dimostrationi armoniche* (1571), for which he was attacked by V Galilei, whereupon he issued another volume, *Sopplimenti musicali* (1588), a fourth, non-musical, being added to the complete edition later. He sought to summarize and develop Greek musical theory.

Works include Mass for the foundation of the church of Santa Maria della Salute and other church music; pageant for the victory of Lepanto.

Zar und Zimmermann, oder Die zwei Peter, *Tsar and Carpenter, or the Two Peters*, opera by Lortzing (libretto by composer, based on a French play by A H J Mélesville, J T Merle and E Cantiran de Boirie), produced Leipzig, 22 Dec 1837. Under disguise in a foreign shipyard,

---

— **THE OPERA** —
Die Zauberflöte

A two-act opera by Mozart, set in Ancient Egypt. It was first performed in 1791.

I. Prince Tamino (tenor) is rescued from a serpent by three ladies (attendants of the Queen of Night – soprano), but the birdcatcher Papageno (baritone) boasts that he was responsible. Tamino is shown a portrait of the abducted Pamina (soprano), and falling in love, vows to rescue her. The men are given a magic flute and magic bells, and are led by three boys to Sarastro's palace, where Pamina is held captive. The wicked Moor Monostatos (tenor), in Sarastro's service, assaults Pamina but Papageno intervenes. Tamino meanwhile is told by a priest of the temple that it is not Sarastro who is evil, but the queen. Pamina and Papageno charm Monostatos and his threatening slaves with the magic bells. When Tamino and Pamina meet they fall in love and place themselves under Sarastro's protection.

II. To enter the brotherhood, Tamino and Papageno must first undergo a trial of silence. The queen gives Pamina a dagger with which to stab Sarastro, but he says that the brotherhood knows no thought of revenge. Papageno is deemed unworthy of his ideal Papagena, and Pamina is in despair when she interprets Tamino's silence for desertion. The three boys prevent her suicide and lead her to Tamino and they successfully undergo trials by fire and water; Papageno is united with Papagena and Sarastro's enemies disappear in a clap of thunder. Sarastro himself leads the celebration of light's victory over darkness. The gods Isis and Osiris are praised in a final chorus.

— **THE OPERA** —

Tsar Peter the Great is confused with deserter Peter Ivanov, whom he befriends.

◊Borgomastro di Saardam.

zarzuela, Spanish, a light Spanish musical stage play or comic opera, usually in one act but sometimes in two, generally of a satirical but occasionally tragic nature, and often a skit on a spoken play. The music is as a rule strongly nationalist. The libretti have spoken dialogue and allow improvised interpolations, in which the audience sometimes joins.

Zauberflöte, Die opera by Mozart (libretto by E Schikaneder, ? with the aid of K L Giesecke), produced Vienna, Theater auf der Wieden, 30 Sept 1791. Winter's opera *Das Labyrinth* is a sequel to it. There is also an unfinished libretto by Goethe intended for a sequel. Prince Tamino and Pamina undergo trials of their love while birdcatcher Pagageno finds a mate.

Zauberharfe, Die, *The Magic Harp*, magic play with music by Schubert (libretto by G E von Hofmann), produced Vienna, Theater an der Wien, 19 Aug 1820).

Zauberoper, German, ◊Magic Opera.

Zauberzither, Die, oder Caspar der Fagottist, *The Magic Zither, or Jasper the Bassoonist*, Singspiel by Wenzel Müller, produced Vienna, Leopoldstadt Theatre, 8 Jun 1791. The plot shows close resemblances to that of Schikaneder's libretto for Mozart's *Zauberflöte*, which may have been borrowed from it or based on the same source.

Zazà opera in four acts by Leoncavallo (libretto by composer, after play by Simon and Berton). Produced Milan, Teatro Lirica, 10 Nov 1900. Music hall singer Zazà returns to Cascart after learning that her current lover Milio Dufresne is a married man.

Zdravitsa, *Hail to Stalin*, cantata for chorus and orchestra on folk texts by Prokofiev, op. 85; composed 1939, fp Moscow, 21 Dec 1939. first British performance BBC, 21 Dec 1944, conductor Boult: the performance had been scheduled for a Prom concert in Aug 1944 but was cancelled owing to the threat of flying bombs.

Zeani, Virginia (b Solovastru, 21 Oct 1928), Romanian soprano. She sang Violetta at her Bologna, 1948, debut and repeated the role in

Die Zauberflöte *A scene from the 1980 production of* Die Zauberflöte/The Magic Flute *at Covent Garden. Thomas Allen as Papageno and Stuart Burrows as Tamino with the Three Ladies. Originally produced in Vienna 1791, it was Mozart's last opera.*

London, Paris, NY (Met., 1966) and at the Bolshoi. She sang at La Scala from 1956 as Handel's Cleopatra, Rossini's Desdemona and Blanche in the 1957 fp of Poulenc's *Carmélites*. She was successful as Lucia, Alzira and Maria di Rohan, and later sang Verdi's Desdemona, Leonora (*Forza*) and Aida, as well as Puccini's Manon and Tosca. Indiana University, Bloomington, from 1980.

Zedda, Alberto (b Milan, 2 Jan 1928), Italian conductor and musicologist. Studied with Giulini in Milan and made debut 1956. Conducted at the Deutsche Oper Berlin 1961–63. New York City Opera from 1963; has led revivals of Rossini's *Ermione* and *Maometto II* in Europe and the USA. His editions of *Il barbiere di Siviglia* and *Cenerentola* have been recorded by Abbado. CG debut 1975 (*Barbiere*). Co-editor with Philip Gossett of the Rossini complete edition. Artistic director of La Scala from 1992.

Zednik, Heinz (b Vienna, 21 Feb 1940), Austrian tenor. He has sung at the Vienna Opera since 1965 in such character roles as Pedrillo, Jacquino and Monostatos. Bayreuth debut 1970; Loge and Mime in the 1976 Chéreau-Boulez centennial *Ring*: in the same year he took part in the fp of Einem's *Kabale und Liebe* (Vienna). He has appeared as guest in Paris, Moscow and Montreal. Other roles include Berg's Painter, David and Lortzing's Tsar Peter.

Zeffirelli (actually *Corsi*), Franco (b Florence, 12 Feb 1923), Italian producer and designer. After an early career as an actor he became assistant to Visconti and produced *La Cenerentola* at La Scala (1953) followed by *Il Turco in Italia* and *Don Pasquale*. His productions of *Lucia di Lammermoor*, *Pagliacci* and *Cavalleria rusticana* (CG 1959) revealed a taste for opulent Romantic realism. He returned to London for *Don Giovanni* and *Alcina* (1962) and *Tosca* (1964). His *Falstaff* has been seen at CG and at the Met.; returned to NY for Barber's *Antony and Cleopatra* (1966), in a production which inaug-

urated the Met. co. at Lincoln Center. In an age of austerity, his major work is now confined to film: *La Traviata* (1983) and *Otello* (1986). Produced and designed *Traviata* and *Don Giovanni* at the Met., 1989–90; *Don Carlos* for La Scala, 1992.

In my productions the principals are of the least importance.

Franco Zeffirelli, quoted in Jacobson,
Reverberations, 1975

Zehetmair, Thomas (b Salzburg, 23 Nov 1961), Austrian violinist. Studied at the Salzburg Mozarteum and has appeared in the USA with the Boston SO, Chicago SO and Cleveland Orchestra. Has played throughout Europe and with leading British orchestras; plays concertos by Szymonowski, Berg, Schoenberg and Bartók; Hindemith's Concerto at the Barbican London, 1995.

Zehme, Albertine (b Vienna, 7 Jan 1857; d Naumburg, 11 May 1946), Austrian actress and soprano. After performing in plays by Schiller and Shakespeare at Leipzig she studied with Cosima Wagner at Bayreuth (1891–93); learnt the roles of Venus, Brünnhilde and Kundry and returned to Leipzig, becoming successful in Ibsen's plays and in recitations. In Jan 1912 she commissioned Schoenberg to write a cycle of recitations based on Albert Giraud's poems from *Pierrot lunaire*. After frequent consultations with Schoenberg, Zehme gave the work's fp in Berlin (12 Oct 1912) and toured widely with it in Europe: Munich, Stuttgart, Vienna, Prague. At Leipzig in 1914 she gave the recitation in the first German performance of the *Gurrelieder*.

Zeitlin, Zvi (b Dubrovnia, 21 Feb 1923), Russian-born American violinist. He studied at Juilliard and in Jerusalem; debut there 1940. His US debut was in 1951 and London debut 1961. From 1967 he has been on the faculty of Eastman School, Rochester. An authority on Nardini but is best known for his performances of modern works: the leading exponent of Schoenberg's concerto (recorded with Kubelik, 1971).

Zeitmasze work by Stockhausen for flute, oboe, horn, clarinet and bassoon; composed 1955–56, fp Paris, 15 Dec 1956, conductor Boulez.

Zelenka, Jan Dismas (b Lounovice, 16 Oct 1679; d Dresden, 23 Dec 1745), Bohemian composer. Studied at Prague, was double bass player in the court band at Dresden from 1710 and went to Vienna to study under Fux in 1716; then went to Italy but returned to Dresden to collaborate with Heinichen, whom he succeeded as director of the church music in 1735. He is best known today for his bold and adventurous instrumental music (e.g. *Hippocondrie*, 1723).

Works include Latin *Melodrama de Sancto Wenceslao* (1723); oratorios *I penitenti al sepolcro* (1736), *Il serpente di bronzo* (1730) and *Gesù al Calvario* (1735); 20 Masses, motets, psalms and other church music; Latin cantatas.

Zeleński, Wladysłław (b Grodkowice, 6 Jul 1837; d Kraków, 23 Jan 1921), Polish teacher and composer. Studied at Prague University, also music (with Krejci) there and later in Paris. He became professor at the Warsaw Conservatory 1872 and director of the Kraków Conservatory 1881.

Works include operas *Konrad Wallenrod* (1885), *Goplana* (1896), *Janek* (1900), *Balandina* and *An Old Story* (1907); Masses and motets; cantatas; two symphonies (1871, 1912), *Woodland Echoes*, concert overture *In the Tatra* and other orchestral works; piano concerto; four string quartets, piano quartet, variations for string quartet, sextet for strings and piano, piano trio; violin and piano sonata; piano pieces.

The setting to music of a poem must be an act of love, never a marriage of convenience.

Poulenc, quoted in Bernac, *Francis Poulenc*, 1977

Zeller, Carl (Johann Adam) (b St Peter-in-der-Au, 19 Jun 1842; d Baden, near Vienna, 17 Aug 1898), Austrian composer. He was a choirboy in the Imperial chapel in Vienna and studied law at the university. He also had counterpoint lessons from Sechter. He made his career in the civil service but was continuously active as a composer.

Works include operettas *Der Vogelhändler* (1891), *Der Obersteiger* (1894), *Der Vagabund* (1886) and many others.

Zelmira opera by Rossini (libretto by A L Tottola, based on a French tragedy by P L B de Belloy), produced Naples, Teatro San Carlo, 16 Feb 1822. Zelmira is rescued by returning husband, Ilo, Prince of Troy, after usurper Antenore and Leucippo accuse her of killing her father Polidoro, whom in fact she has kept safe from treacherous Antenore.

Zelter, Carl Friedrich (b Berlin, 11 Dec 1758; d Berlin, 15 May 1832), German conductor, teacher and composer. Having completed his training as a master mason he joined his father's firm, and abandoned the trade completely only in 1815, but meanwhile was active as a musician. Pupil of Schultz and Fasch, he succeeded the latter as conductor of the Berlin Singakademie in 1800, founded the Berliner Liedertafel in 1809, the same year became professor at the academy, and in 1822 founded the Royal Institute of Church Music. Among his pupils were Nicolai, Loewe, Meyerbeer and Mendelssohn, whose plans to revive Bach's *St Matthew Passion* in 1829 he at first opposed but later approved. In the Singakademie he had himself done much to revive interest in Bach's music. He was a personal friend of Goethe, many of whose poems he set; he rejected Schubert's Lieder. Wrote principally songs, also church music, cantatas, instrumental music.

Zémire et Azore opera by Grétry (libretto by Marmontel), produced Fontainbleau, at court, 9 Nov 1771; first Paris performance, Théâtre Italien, 16 Dec 1771. Prince Azor has been transformed into an ugly beast until he is loved by a woman. Zémire offers herself as a sacrifice to him to save her father Sandor. Of course she eventually falls in love and Azor is restored.

Zemire und Azor opera by Spohr (libretto by J J Ihlee, based on that by Marmontel) produced Frankfurt, 4 Apr 1819. The familiar song 'Rose, softly blooming' is in this work. For plot synopsis, ◊Zémire et Azor.

Zemlinsky, Alexander von (b Vienna, 14 Oct 1871; d Larchmont, NY, 15 Mar 1942), Austrian composer and conductor. Studied at the Vienna Conservatory. He became conductor at the Vienna Volksoper 1906 and at the Hofoper 1908, later at Prague, where he conducted the German Opera and the 1924 fp of Schoenberg's monodrama *Erwartung*; finally in 1927–31, he was one of the conductors at the Berlin State Opera and at the Kroll Opera, where he gave the first Berlin performance of *Erwartung*. He returned to Vienna in 1933 and later emigrated to the USA. Schoenberg was among his pupils and married his sister. His personal ties with Schoenberg scarcely influenced his own music; he started composing in a Classical style and later was drawn to the progressive, late-Romantic style of Mahler, Strauss and even Schreker. An uncompleted opera, *Der König Kandaules*, was realized from the sketches and scheduled for performance at Hamburg, 1996.

Works include operas *Sarema* (1897), *Es war einmal* (1900), *Kleider machen Leute* (G Keller, 1908, produced 1922), *Eine florentinische Tragödie*, *Der Zwerg* (both after O Wilde, 1917, 1922), *Der Kreidekreis* (after Klabund, 1933), *Der Traumgörge* (1906, produced 1980), ballet *Das gläserne Herz* (after Hofmannsthal, 1903), incidental music for *Cymbeline* (1914).

Two symphonies (1892, 1897), suite for orchestra (1894), *Die Seejungfrau* for orchestra (1903), sinfonietta (1934), *Lyric Symphony* for soprano, baritone and orchestra (1923), *Symphonische Gesänge* for voice and orchestra (1926).

String quintet (1895), trio for clarinet, cello and piano (1895), four string quartets (1895–1936); Lieder to texts by Heine and Eichendorff.

Zenatello, Giovanni (b Verona, 22 Feb 1876; d New York, 11 Feb

---

Zemlinsky
A biographical note

Struggling throughout his life to escape from the shadow of his great Viennese contemporaries Mahler, Berg and Schoenberg, Zemlinsky's career was nevertheless inseparable from them. At the turn of the century he enjoyed a one-sided relationship with his pupil, the beautiful Alma Schindler, later to become Mahler's wife. Her rejection of him was a blow from which he scarcely recovered; his 1922 opera *Der Zwerg* (The Dwarf) encapsulated his sense of physical inadequacy. His career was given an early boost when Mahler programmed *Es war einmal* (Once upon a Time) at the Vienna Court Opera in 1900, but its successor *Der Traumgörge* was cancelled when Mahler left Vienna. In 1901 his sister Mathilde married Schoenberg, his former pupil. The association developed further in 1914 when Zemlinsky's 2nd quartet 'recomposed' Schoenberg's seminal D minor quartet of 1907, and further still in 1924 when he premiered Schoenberg's *Erwartung* while music director at the German Theatre in Prague. Only two days earlier, Zemlinsky had premiered his own *Lyric Symphony*, modelled on Mahler's *Das Lied von der Erde*. In 1926 Berg was to quote from the Symphony in his *Lyric Suite* for string quartet, using the words *Du bist mein eigen* (You are my only one) in tribute to his putative mistress, Hanna Fuchs-Robettin. Berg's secret was not revealed until many years after his death, when he appeared in a dream to Zemlinsky's widow and commanded her to reveal the truth.

1949), Italian tenor, first appeared as a baritone at Naples, but changed to tenor. He then studied at Milan, appeared in Italy, South America and the USA, and first in London in 1905, as Riccardo. NY 1907–28, as Otello, Don José and Radames. He created the role of Pinkerton in Puccini's *Madama Butterfly*. He married Maria Gay in 1913.

Zender, Hans (b Wiesbaden, 22 Nov 1936), German conductor and composer. He studied at Frankfurt and Freiburg and in Rome under B A Zimmermann, whose works he has frequently conducted. He worked at opera houses in Freiburg, Bonn and Kiel and was music director of Hamburg Opera 1984–87 (Principal conductor from 1977). Conducted *Parsifal* at Bayreuth 1975; conductor of the Netherlands Radio Chamber Orchestra from 1987. Brussels Opera 1989, *Fidelio*.

Works include opera *Stephen Climax* (1986), piano concerto (1956), *Zeitströme* for orchestra (1974), cantata *Der Mann von La Mancha* for voices and Moog synthesizer (1969), *Continuum and Fragments* for chorus, *Cantos I–V* for voices and instruments and electronic works.

Zeno, Apostolo (b Venice, 11 Dec 1668; d Venice, 11 Nov 1750), Italian poet and librettist. For operas on his libretti ◊Ambleto (Gasparini and D Scarlatti); ◊Faramondo (Handel); ◊Ifigenia in Aulide (Caldara); ◊Lucio Papiro (ditto and Hasse); ◊Merope (Gasparini, Jommelli and Terradellas); ◊Scipione (Handel); ◊Temistocle (Porpora and J C Bach).

Zerr, Anna (b Baden-Baden, 26 Jul 1822; d Winterbach, 14 Nov 1881), German soprano. She sang at Karlsruhe 1839–46; joined the Kärntertortheater 1846 and the following year created Flotow's Martha there. She visited London 1851–52, singing the Queen of Night, and Rosa in the fp of the revised version of Spohr's *Faust* (CG, 4 Apr 1852).

Ziani, Marc' Antonio (b Venice, c 1653; d Vienna, 22 Jan 1715), Italian composer. *Maestro di cappella* at the church of Santa Barbara and conductor at the theatre at Mantua, 1686. He went to Vienna, where he became vice-music director 1700 and first music director 1711.

Works include operas *Alessandro magno in Sidone* (1679), *Damira placata* (1680), *Meleagro* (1706), *Chilonida* (1709) and 41 others; Masses, motets and other church music; oratorios, cantatas.

Ziani, Pietro Andrea (b Venice, c 1620; d Naples, 12 Feb 1684), Italian composer, uncle of Marc' Antonio ◊Ziani. He was organist at Venice, then at Santa Maria Maggiore, Bergamo, visited Vienna and Dresden in 1660–67 and became organist at St Mark's, Venice, in succession to Cavalli in 1669. He went to Naples on failing to be appointed *maestro di cappella* in 1676, becoming a teacher at the Conservatorio di Sant' Onofrio and in 1680 royal *maestro di cappella*.

Works include operas *Le fortune di Rodope e di Damira* (1657), *L'Antigona delusa da Alceste* (1660) and 21 others; Masses, psalms, oratorios; instrumental sonatas; organ pieces.

Zich, Otakar (b Králové Městec, 25 Mar 1879; d Oubĕnice near Benešov, 9 Jul 1934), Czech composer. He was at first a secondary schoolmaster, but took a degree at the University of Brno and was appointed professor of aesthetics there. He also collected folksongs.

Works include operas *The Painter's Whim* (1910), *The Sin* (1922) and *Les Précieuses ridicules* (after Molière, 1926); *The ill-fated Marriage* and *Polka Rides* for chorus and orchestra; songs.

Zichy, Géza, Count (b Sztára Castle, 22 Jul 1849; d Budapest, 14 Jan 1924), Hungarian pianist, poet and composer. Pupil of Volkmann and Liszt at Budapest. He lost his right arm at 14 in a hunting accident and wrote much piano music for the left hand. He became president of the Hungarian Academy of Music and the National Conservatory. As Intendant from 1891 of the Budapest Opera, he sacked Mahler.

Works include operas *Castle Story*, *Alár* (1896), *Master Roland* (1899), trilogy *Rákóczi* (*Nemo*, *Rákóczi/Ferenc* and *Rodostó*, 1905–12); ballet *Gemma*; piano concerto for the left hand; sonata, six studies, etc. for the left hand and other piano music.

Židek, Ivo (b Kravaře, 4 Jun 1926), Czech tenor. He sang Werther at Ostrava in 1944 and sang at the National Theatre, Prague, from 1948; appeared as guest at Vienna from 1956 and visited Edinburgh with the Prague co. in 1964 and 1970 (first British performance of Janáček's

Mr Brouček). He was well known as Smetana's Jeník and Janáček's Gregor and also appeared in operas by Verdi, Bizet and Mozart.

Ziegler, Delores (b Atlanta, 4 Sept 1951), American mezzo. Sang Verdi's Maddalena at St Louis, 1979, and appeared in Europe (Bonn and Cologne) from 1981, as Dorabella, Octavian and Cherubino. Glyndebourne 1984, Dorabella; Salzburg 1985, in the Henze/Monteverdi *Ulisse*. La Scala 1984 and San Francisco 1991, as Bellini's Romeo; other 'trouser' roles include Siebel in *Faust* (Met. debut 1990); Cherubino 1991.

Zieleński, Mikołaj (1550–1615), Polish 17th-c. organist and composer. Composed offertories and communions for the service of the whole year. In service of Archbishop of Gniezno 1608–15 and studied with Gabrieli in Italy.

Ziesak, Ruth (b Hofheim, 1963), German soprano. Sang at Heidelberg from 1988, as Gilda, Handel's Sesto, and Despina. Concert tour of Japan 1989, with *Messiah* and Mozart's Requiem. Sang Pamina at Salzburg 1991, Strauss's Sophie at the Deutsche Oper Berlin, 1993. Opéra Bastille, Paris 1994 (Susanna). Recorded roles include Mozart's Servilia and Weber's Aennchen.

Zigeunerbaron, Der, *The Gypsy Baron*, operetta by J Strauss, junior (libretto by I Schnitzer, based on another by M Jókai founded on his own story *Saffi*), produced Vienna, Theater an der Wien, 24 Oct 1885. After returning from exile Sándor Barinkay finds family lands occupied by gypsies but falls for Sáffi, gypsy princess in disguise.

Zilcher, Hermann (b Frankfurt, 18 Aug 1881; d Würzburg, 1 Jan 1948), German composer. Studied at the Hoch Conservatory at Frankfurt, became professor at the Academy of Music at Munich in 1908 and in 1920 director of the Würzburg Conservatory.

Works include opera *Doktor Eisenbart* (1922); incidental music for plays by Shakespeare, Dehmel's children's play *Fitzbutze* (1903) and Hauptmann's *Die goldene Harfe*; oratorio *Liebesmesse*; five symphonies, *Tanzphantasie* and other works for orchestra; pieces for solo instruments and orchestra; chamber music.

The oldest, truest, most beautiful organ of music, the origin to which alone our music owes its being, is the human voice.
Richard Wagner, quoted in *Opera and Drama*, 1851

Ziliani, Alessandro (b Busseto, 3 Jun 1907; d Milan, 18 Feb 1977), Italian tenor. Debut Milan, 1928, as Pinkerton; La Scala 1932–47 (debut as Enzo, took part in the first Italian performance of Respighi's *Maria Egiziaca*, 1934). He also sang in early performances of works by Wolf-Ferrari, Busoni (*Turandot*) and Mascagni (*Pinotta*, written 1880 but not produced until 1932).

Zilli, Emma (b Fagnana, Udine, 11 Nov 1864; d Havana, Jan 1901), Italian soprano. Debut Ferrara, 1887, in Donizetti's *Poliuto*. She appeared widely throughout Europe and in 1893 created Alice Ford in *Falstaff*; repeated the role at CG in May 1894. She was successful in Puccini roles; died of fever while on tour in Central and South America.

Zillig, Winfried (b Würzburg, 1 Apr 1905; d Hamburg, 18 Dec 1963), German composer and conductor. Studied with Schoenberg in Vienna and from 1927 to 1928 was assistant to Kleiber at the Berlin Staatsoper. From 1928 to 1947 he conducted in various German theatres, becoming director of music at the radio station, first in Frankfurt and then in Hamburg. He also made a performing version of Schoenberg's unfinished oratorio *Die Jakobsleiter* (performed Vienna, 1961).

Works include operas *Die Windesbraut* (1941), *Troilus und Cressida* (1951), *Das Opfer*, TV opera *Bauernpassion* (1955), radio opera *Die Verlobung von St Domingo* (1956); violin and cello concertos; four serenades for various instrumental groups; choral music; songs.

Ziloti, Alexander, ◊Siloti.

Zimbalist, Efrem (b Rostov on the Don, 21 Apr 1889; d Reno, NV, 22 Feb 1985), Russian-born American violinist and composer. Studied

Zimerman *The pianist Krystian Zimerman. Since winning the 1975 Chopin Competition he has consolidated his reputation as the foremost pianist of his generation. His performances and recordings, which concentrate on the Romantic repertory, are admired for their depth, intensity and an impressive technique.*

first with his father and then with L Auer at the St Petersburg Conservatory 1901–07, making his debut in Berlin, 1907. In 1911 he emigrated to the USA, where he married the singer Alma Gluck (1914) and in 1941 became director of the Curtis Institute in Philadelphia, which had been founded by his second wife. He gave the 1952 fp of Menotti's concerto (Philadelphia).

Works include opera *Landara* (1956); *American Rhapsody* for orchestra; concerto and three Slavonic Dances for violin and orchestra; string quartet; violin sonata.

Zimerman, Krystian (b Zaorze, 5 Dec 1956), Polish pianist. He studied at Katowice and won the 1975 Chopin Competition, Warsaw. He has had successful engagements in Munich, Paris and London with the late Romantic repertory, and in 1976 appeared with Karajan and the Berlin PO. US debut 1979, with the NY PO. Played Lutosławski's Concerto at the 1989 London Proms.

Our sweetest songs are those that tell of saddest thought.
Percy Bysshe Shelley, 'To a Skylark', 1819

Zimmerman, Franklin B(ershir) (b Wauneta, KS, 20 Jun 1923), American musicologist. He studied in CA and at Oxford, where his teachers included Egon Wellesz and Jack Westrup. He has taught at NY, Dartmouth and the Universities of Kentucky and Pennsylvania; best known for his research on Baroque music and Purcell. His Purcell thematic catalogue (1963) gives the definitive numbering for the composer's works.

Zimmermann, Bernd Alois (b Bliesheim near Cologne, 20 Mar 1918; d Grosskönigsdorf, 10 Aug 1970), German composer. Studied in Cologne with Lemacher and P Jarnach, and also studied linguistics and philosophy at the Universities of Bonn, Cologne and Berlin. From 1950 to 1952 he taught at Cologne University and from 1958 at the Hochschule für Musik in Cologne. He is widely known for his expressionist opera *Die Soldaten*, which employs film, electronics, mime and other avant-garde effects. He committed suicide.

Works include opera *Die Soldaten* (1965); ballets *Kontraste* (1953) and *Alagoana* (1955); cantata *Lob der Torheit* (1948); symphonies; concertos for violin, oboe and cello; concerto for string orchestra (1948): *Photoptosis*, prelude for orchestra (1968), *Stille und Umkehr*, sketches for orchestra (1970); *Die Soldaten*, vocal symphony from opera (1959); *Requiem for a Young Poet* (1969).

Zimmermann, Erich (b Meissen, 29 Nov 1892; d Berlin, 24 Feb 1968), German tenor. After his 1918 Dresden debut he had engagements in Munich, Vienna and Hamburg; retired 1951, as a member of the Berlin Städtische Oper. Bayreuth 1935–44, as David, Mime and Loge. He sang at CG before and after the war as Jacquino and Mime. At Salzburg (1930–32) he was heard in operas by Mozart and Strauss.

Zimmermann, Frank Peter (b Duisburg, 27 Feb 1965), German violinist. Played Mozart's 3rd Concerto at Duisburg aged ten, studying later with Gawrillof and Krebbers. US debut with the Pittsburgh SO 1984. Played Mozart's 4th Concerto at the 1986 Salzburg Festival and has appeared throughout Europe, Australia and the Far East. Recordings include the Tchaikovsky and Sibelius Concertos.

Zimmermann, Tabea (b Lahr, 8 Oct 1968), German violist. Studied with Sandor Vegh and has made many concert appearances, notably in the Mozart Sinfonia Concertante K364 (Salzburg, Prades and other festivals). Has played Penderecki's Concerto under the composer and premiered the viola sonata by Ligeti (Cologne, 1993). Recitals with pianist Hartmut Holl.

Zimmermann, Udo (b Dresden, 6 Oct 1943), German composer. He founded the Studio for New Music, Dresden, in 1974 and has worked in experimental music there. Composer and producer at the Dresden Opera from 1970. Director of the Studio Neue Musik concerts at Dresden from 1976, Intendant of the Leipzig Opera from 1990.

Works include operas *Die Weisse Rose* (1967), *Die zweite Entscheidung* (1970), *Levins Mühle* (1973), *Der Schuhu und die fliegende Prinzessin* (1975), *Die Wundersame Schustersfrau* (1982); *Music for Strings* (1967), *Sieh, meine Augen* for chamber orchestra (1970), *Mutazioni* for orchestra (1972); *Der Mensch*, cantata for soprano and 13 instruments (1969), *Psalm der Nacht* for chorus, percussion and organ (1973), *Pax questousa* for five soloists, three choruses and orchestra (1980); *Choreographieren nach Edgar Degas* for 21 instruments (1974).

Zingara, La, *The Gypsy Girl*, intermezzo by Rinaldo di Gapua, produced Académie Royale de Musique, 19 Jun 1753. Assisted by brother Tagliaborsi, gypsy Nisa tricks rich miser Calcante into marrying her.

Zingarelli, Niccolò Antonio (b Naples, 4 Apr 1752; d Torre del Greco, 5 May 1837), Italian composer. Studied at the Conservatrio S Maria di Loreto in Naples, where his intermezzo *I quattro pazzi* was produced 1768. Leaving the Conservatory 1772 he at first worked as an organist, but with *Montezuma* (Naples, 1781) began his career as an opera composer and 1785–1803 produced works in all the main Italian cities and also in Paris. He was appointed *maestro di cappella* at the cathedral in Milan in 1793, Loreto 1794, and in 1804 succeeded Guglielmi at St Peter's, Rome, from about this time onwards devoting himself chiefly to church music. He became director of the Real Collegio di Musica in Naples in 1813, and *maestro di cappella* of the cathedral there in 1816. Bellini and Mercadante were among his pupils.

Works include 37 operas, e.g. *Montezuma* (1781), *Armida* (1786), *Antigono*, *Ifigenia in Aulide* (1787), *Antigone* (1790), *Il mercato di Monfregoso* (1792), *Artaserse, Quinto Fabio, Gli Orazi e Curazi, Giulietta e Romeo* (after Shakespeare, 1796), *Andromeda, La morte di Mitridate* (1797), *I veri amici* (1798), *Il ratto delle Sabine* (1799), *Edipo a Colono* (after Sophocles, 1802), *Berenice, regina d'Armenia* and *c* 20 others.

Oratorios *La Passione* (1787), *Gerusalemme distrutta* (1812), *La medificazione di Gerusalemme* and others; many cantatas; 23 Masses,

Requiems and other church music, including 55 Magnificats; canon for eight voices; *partimenti* and *solfeggi* for vocal exercise.

zingaresa, zingarese, Italian, words used to describe music in, or supposed to be in, a gypsy manner; e.g. the finale of Brahms's violin concerto. The adj. is used in the form of *alla zingarese*.

Zingari, Gli, *The Gypsies*, opera by Leoncavallo (libretto by E Cavacchioli and G Emanuel, after Pushkin), produced London, Hippodrome, 16 Sept 1912.

Zinman, David (b New York, 9 Jul 1936), American conductor. He studied at Tanglewood and was Pierre Monteux's assistant 1961–64. Music director Netherlands Chamber Orchestra 1956–77; Rotterdam PO 1979–82. Chief conductor Rochester PO from 1974, principal guest conductor Baltimore SO from 1983.

Zipoli, Domenico (b Prato, 16 Oct 1688; d Córdoba, Argentina, 2 Jan 1726), Italian composer. Pupil (?) of A Scarlatti in Naples and Pasquini in Rome, where he became organist of the Jesuit church, he entered the Jesuit Order and in 1717 went to South America as a missionary.

Works include three oratorios (music lost); church music; keyboard music (two vols. of *Sonate d'intavolatura* pub. 1716).

Zitek, Vilém (b Prague, 9 Sept 1890; d Prague, 11 Aug 1956), Czech bass. He sang at Prague 1911–47 as Kečal, Gremin, Boris and Mozart's Figaro. In the 1920s he appeared at La Scala, often under Toscanini, as Hunding, Fafner and the Commendatore. He sang as guest in Paris, Berlin and the USSR; often compared with Shalyapin. Other roles included Don Quichotte, Philip II and parts in operas by Dvořák and Smetana.

zither, German, from Greek *kithara*, a string instrument of the dulcimer type, although etymologically connected with the cittern, which it does not resemble. It has many strings (27–40) stretched over a flat soundbox, and is played with the tips of the finger, the bass strings alone being struck with a plectrum fixed to the thumb by a ring.

Zoghby, Linda (b Mobile, AL, 17 Aug 1949), American soprano. She sang Donna Elvira with Houston Opera in 1975 and the following year Bellini's Giulietta at Dallas. At Glyndebourne she appeared as Mimi (1978) and repeated the role at her 1982 NY Met. debut (Ilia in 1986). She is well known as Pamina, Fiordiligi and Marguerite and has recorded Haydn's *L'isola disabitata* and *L'incontro improvviso*; *La fedeltà premiata* at Glyndebourne, 1980.

Zoilo, Annibale (b Rome, c 1537; d Loreto, 30 Jun 1592), Italian singer and composer. *Maestro di cappella* at the churches of St John Lateran and San Luigi in Rome, singer in the Papal Chapel from 1570 to c 1582, and *maestro di cappella* of the Santa Casa at Loreto in 1584–92. He worked with Palestrina on a revised edition of the *Graduale*.

Works include Masses, madrigals and songs.

Zoilo, Cesare (b Rome, c 1584; d after 1622), Italian composer, (?) son of Annibale ◊Zoilo. Wrote motets, madrigals, etc.

Zöllner, Heinrich (b Leipzig, 4 Jul 1854; d Freiburg, 4 May 1941), German composer, son of the composer Carl Friedrich Zöllner (1800–60). Studied at the Leipzig Conservatory. Apppointed teacher at Dorpat University (Tartu, Estonia) in 1878, conductor at Cologne, lived in USA in 1890–98, became music director of Leipzig University in succession to Kretzschmar until 1906, conducted the Flemish Opera at Antwerp from 1907 and retired to Freiburg in 1914.

Works include operas *Frithjof* (after Tegnér), *Faust* (on part of Goethe's original text, 1887), *Der Überfall* (on a story by Wildenbruch, 1895), *Die versunkene Glocke* (on Hauptmann's play, 1899) and others; festival cantata *The New World* and others; five symphonies (1883–1928), overture *Under the Starry Banner*.

Zopfstil German = lit. 'pigtail style'; derogatory term sometimes applied to the formal courtly style of the later 18th c.

zoppa Italian = 'limp'; a strong accent on a second note off the beat or a long note following a short one, as in the ◊Scotch snap. The motion of a musical piece in such a rhythm is called *alla zoppa*.

Zoraida di Granata opera seria by Donizetti (libretto by B Merelli after F Gonzales), produced Rome, Teatro Argentina, 28 Jan 1822. Almuzir murders king and hopes to marry his daughter Zoraide but is defeated in combat by Knight Abenamet.

Zorian, Olive (b Manchester, 16 Mar 1916; d London, 17 May 1965), English violinist. She studied at the RMCM and the RAM; formed her own string quartet which gave works by Bliss and Bartók; the fps of Tippett's second and third quartets (1943, 1946), of the revised version of his first quartet (1944), and of Britten's second quartet (1945). She was active as a soloist and led the Alan Bush chamber orchestra and the EOG orchestra (1952–57). She was married to the writer and broadcaster John Amis (1948–55).

Zoroastre opera by Rameau (libretto by L de Cahusac) produced Paris Opéra, 5 Dec 1749. Following the death of the Bactrian King, High Priest Abramane seizes power, enlisting the help of Princess Erinice. Zoroastre is banished and his beloved Amélite is dragged away to be tormented by demons. Later, Zoroastre returns to free his people, defeating the evil powers of Abramane and marrying Amélite.

Ah music! What a beautiful art! But what a wretched profession!

George Bizet, attributed, 1867

Zottmayr, Georg (b Munich, 24 Jan 1869; d Dresden, 11 Dec 1941), German bass. He sang first in concert then appeared at the Vienna Hofoper, 1906–09, under Mahler. From 1910 he was popular at Dresden as Gurnemanz, Daland, Sarastro, Pogner and Marke: his father Ludwig had created Marke at Munich in 1865.

Zschau, Marilyn (b Chicago, 9 Feb 1944), American soprano. Studied at Juilliard and sang Korngold's Marietta at the Vienna Volksoper 1967; Staatsoper 1971, as the Composer (*Ariadne*). New York City Opera from 1978, as Butterfly; Minnie, and Odabella (*Attila*). NY Met debut 1985, Musetta; La Scala 1986, the Dyer's Wife. Other roles include Salome, Lady Macbeth, Renata (*The Fiery Angel*) and the Marschallin, Florence 1993, as the Kostelnička in *Jenůfa*.

Zukerman, Pinchas (b Tel-Aviv, 16 Jul 1948), Israeli violinist, violist and conductor. He studied at Juilliard and won the 1967 Leventritt Competition; appeared with the NY PO and at Brighton in 1969. Many performances of chamber music with Stern and Barenboim. Debut as conductor London, 1974; music director St Paul Chamber Orchestra from 1980; guest conductor in New York, Los Angeles and Boston. Well known as soloist in standard repertory and especially Elgar's concerto. Principal guest conductor of the Dallas SO, 1993.

Zukovsky, Paul (b Brooklyn, 22 Oct 1943), American violinist. He studied at Juilliard and in 1969 started a series of concerts, 'Music for the 20th-Century Violin': he performed sonatas by Ives and concertos by Schuman and Sessions; in 1972 at Tanglewood, with the Boston SO, he gave the fp of the concerto for amplified violin and orchestra by Charles Wuorinen. Has recorded works by Cage, Carter (Duo), Penderecki (*Capriccio*), Glass (*Einstein on the Beach*), and Feldman.

Zumpe, Hermann (b Oppach, 9 Apr 1850; d Munich, 4 Sept 1903), German composer and conductor. Educated at a seminary at Bautzen to become a schoolmaster, but he was so taken up with music that he went to Leipzig in 1871, where he taught in a school and studied with A Tottmann. In 1872–76 he assisted Wagner at Bayreuth with the preparation of the *Ring* score and then succeeded in securing one post after another as theatre conductor until in 1891 he became court music director at Stuttgart. In 1895–97 he conducted the Kaim orchestra at Munich; he then became court conductor at Schwerin, from 1901 at Munich. Conducted at CG 1898, *Tristan* and *Die Walküre*.

Works include operas *Anahra* (1881), *Die verwunschene Prinzess*, *Das Gespenst von Horodin* (1910) and *Sawitri* (from the Mahābhārata, unfinished; produced 1907), operettas *Farinelli* (1886), *Karin* (1888) and *Polnische Wirtschaft* (1889).

Zumsteeg, Johann Rudolf (b Schsenflur, Baden, 10 Jan 1760; d Stuttgart, 27 Jan 1802), German composer. Fellow-pupil and friend of Schiller at the Karlschule in Stuttgart, he entered the service of the court there as a cellist in 1781, becoming *Konzertmeister* in 1792. His extended ballads were especially influential, some later being used as models by Schubert.

Works include operas *Das Tartarische Gesetz* (1780), *Le delizie campestri, o Ippolito e Atricia* (1782), *Armida* (1785), *Die Geisterinsel* (after *The Tempest*, 1798), *Das Pfauenfest* and others; melodrama *Tamira*; incidental music to *Hamlet* (1785), *Macbeth*, Schiller's *Räuber* and other plays; cantatas; Masses and other church music; ten cello concertos (1777–92), songs and ballads *Lenore* (Bürger), *Colma* (Ossian), *Die Büssende, Ritter Toggenburg* (Schiller), *Die Entführung*.

Zur Mühlen, Raimund von (b Livonia, 10 Nov 1854; d Steyning, Sussex, 9 Dec 1931), German tenor. Educated in Germany; he began to learn singing at the Hochschule für Musik in Berlin, later went to Stockhausen at Frankfurt and Bussine in Paris. He first visited London in 1882, frequently returned and finally settled in England, where he was much sought after as a teacher of singing.

Zusammenschlag German = 'hit together'; ◊acciaccatura or ◊mordent.

Zweig, Fritz (b Olomouc, 8 Sept 1893; d Los Angeles, 28 Feb 1984), Bohemian-born American conductor. After study with Schoenberg, he worked at opera houses in Mannheim and Elberfeld; moved to Berlin 1923, working with Bruno Walter at the Städtische Oper. At the Kroll Opera, 1927–31, he was Klemperer's assistant and gave there operas by Gounod, Auber and Gluck, and the first German performance of Janáček's *From the House of the Dead*. With the rise of the Nazis Zweig fled from one centre to another: Berlin Staatsoper, German Opera (Prague) and Paris. In 1938 he conducted *Rosenkavalier* at CG; moved to the USA in 1940 and taught at Los Angeles.

Zweig, Stefan (1881–1942), Austrian novelist and dramatist. ◊Schweigsame Frau, Die (R Strauss); ◊Toch (*Heilige aus USA*).

He collaborated with Strauss from 1932; *Die schweigsame Frau* was produced at Dresden (1935) but soon proscribed because of Zweig's Jewish ancestry. Zweig intended to write the libretto for Strauss's *Friedenstag*, suggested to him by Joseph Gregor; but the Nazi régime making his appearance on any German stage impossible after 1935, this was afterwards undertaken by Gregor himself.

Zwerg, Der, *The Dwarf*, opera in one act by Zemlinsky (libretto by G C Klaren, after Wilde's *The Birthday of the Infanta*); 1920–21, fp Cologne, 28 May 1922, conductor Klemperer. At Edinburgh and at CG the work has been given in a production by the Hamburg Opera, under the new title *The Birthday of the Infanta*, with new libretto by A Dresen. The Spanish Infanta is given the Dwarf as a birthday present. She toys with him as he declares his love for her. When the Dwarf sees his reflection in a mirror he is horrified by his ugliness and dies of a broken heart.

Zwilich, Ellen Taaffe (b Miami, 3 Apr 1939), American composer. Studied at Florida State University and with Ivan Galamian in New York. Played violin in the American SO under Stokowski and studied further at Juilliard, and with Sessions and Carter. Her *Symposium* for orchestra was conducted by Boulez in 1974, and her 1st symphony won the 1983 Pulitzer Prize. Her music is basically tonal in idiom, sometimes recalling minimalist or late Romantic precedents. Other works include *Symbolom* for orchestra (1988), Symphony no. 2 'Cello' (1985) and no. 3 (1992, commissioned by the New York PO), concertos for trombone (1988), flute (1990), oboe (1990), bassoon (1992), horn (1993) and trumpet (1994); choral and solo vocal music, chamber pieces including Double Quartet for strings (1984) and Quintet for clarinet and strings (1990).

Zwillingsbrüder, Die, *The Twin Brothers*, play with music by Schubert (libretto by G E von Hofmann), produced Vienna, Kärntnertortheater, 14 Jun 1820. The betrothal of Anton and Lieschen is complicated by prior claim of Franz Spiers and reappearance of his missing twin brother Friedrich.

Zwingburg scenic cantata by Křenek (libretto by F Werfel), composed 1922, fp Berlin, Staatsoper, 21 Oct 1924; Křenek's first work for the stage. Tyrannical overlord is overthrown in coup but new masters establish same regime.

Zwischenspiel German = interlude.

Zwyssig, (Johann) Joseph (Father Alberik) (b Bauen, Uri, 17 Nov 1808; d Mehrerau near Bregenz, 18 Nov 1854), Swiss priest, organist and composer. Educated at the monastery school of Wettingen, ordained priest and became music teacher and cathedral organist and conductor. After the dissolution of the monastery he led a precarious existence, but was in demand as an authority on the organ.

Works include Masses, offertories and other church music; choruses, e.g. the patriotic *Schweizerpsalm* 'Trittst im Morgenrot daher' (1841); songs.

Zyklus work for percussion by Stockhausen, involving random choice and improvisation; fp Darmstadt, 25 Aug 1959.

Zylis-Gara, Teresa (b Landvarov, 23 Jan 1935), Polish soprano. She studied at Łódz and sang Halka at Katowice in 1956. From the early 1960s she appeared in West Germany as Poppea and Butterfly. Glyndebourne 1965 as Octavian; CG 1968 and 1976 as Elvira and Violetta. Elvira was the role of her Salzburg and NY Met. debuts (1968) and she was widely admired as Anna Bolena, Fiordiligi and the Marschallin. Sang Desdemona at Hamburg 1988.

Zywny, Wojciech (b Bohemia, 13 May 1756; d Warsaw, 21 Feb 1842), Polish piano teacher and composer. He studied with Jan Kuchar and worked at the Polish court of Stanisław August during the 1780s. Later moved to Warsaw and was Chopin's piano teacher 1816–22. Works include piano pieces, overtures and songs.

Key signatures

Both the major and minor keys are shown in this diagram. The white note represents the major key and the black note the minor.

Note names and harmonies

The terms 'tonic ... leading note' may describe either a single note or a chord. The diagram lists both scale degrees and chord abbreviations applicable to any key, in addition to providing the specific case of C major. The roman numerals are upper-case if the associated harmony is major and lower-case if minor. The leading note is rarely harmonized and therefore appears in parentheses.

analytical name	scale degree	note in key of C	abbreviation of harmony chord	basic chord in the key of C
tonic	1	C	I	CEG
supertonic	2	D	ii	DFA
mediant	3	E	iii	EGB
subdominant	4	F	IV	FAC
dominant	5	G	V	GBD
submediant	6	A	vi	ACE
leading note	7	B	(vii)	(BDF)

Notes and rests

name		note	rest
semibreve	(whole note)	𝅝	▬
minim	(half note)	𝅗𝅥	▬
crotchet	(quarter note)	♩	𝄽 or 𝄽
quaver	(eighth note)	♪	𝄾
semiquaver	(16th note)	♬	𝄿
demisemiquaver	(32nd note)	𝅘𝅥𝅰	𝅀
hemidemisemi-quaver	(64th note)	𝅘𝅥𝅱	𝅁

Pitch-naming system

Pitches are specified using the system A0 to C8. For example, concert-tuning pitch is A4, in which 'A' is the name of the note and '4' describes the particular register (in this case the fourth octave from the bottom note of the keyboard).

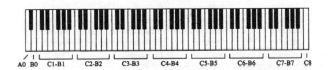

Time signatures

simple time				compound time		
note-value of each beat			number of beats to each bar	note-value of each beat		
𝅗𝅥	♩	♪		𝅗𝅥.	♩.	♪.
²⁄₂ or ₵	²⁄₄	²⁄₈	2	⁶⁄₄	⁶⁄₈	⁶⁄₁₆
³⁄₂	³⁄₄	³⁄₈	3	⁹⁄₄	⁹⁄₈	⁹⁄₁₆
⁴⁄₂	⁴⁄₄ or C	⁴⁄₈	4	¹²⁄₄	¹²⁄₈	¹²⁄₁₆

Role	Voice	Opera	Composer	Role	Voice	Opera	Composer
Abigaille	soprano	Nabucco	Verdi	Armida	soprano	Armida	Rossini
Acis	soprano	Acis and Galatea	Handel	Armide	soprano	Armide	Gluck
Adalgisa	mezzo	Norma	Bellini	Arnold	tenor	Guillaume Tell	Rossini
Adèle	soprano	Le Comte Ory	Rossini	Aron	tenor	Moses and Aron	Schoenberg
Adina	soprano	L'Elisir d'Amore	Donizetti	Arsace/Arsaces	mezzo	Semiramide	Rossini
Admète	tenor	Alceste	Gluck	Arturo	tenor	Lucia di Lammermoor	Donizetti
Adolar	tenor	Euryanthe	Weber	Arturo	tenor	I Puritani	Bellini
Adriana Lecouvreur	soprano	Adriana Lecouvreur	Cilea	Ascanio	mezzo	Benvenuto Cellini	Berlioz
Adriano	mezzo	Rienzi	Wagner	Aschenbach	tenor	Death in Venice	Britten
Aegisthus	tenor	Elektra	R Strauss	Assad	tenor	Die Königin von Saba	Goldmark
Aeneas	baritone	Dido and Aeneas	Purcell	Assur	baritone	Semiramide	Rossini
Aennchen	mezzo	Der Freischütz	Weber	Athanaël	baritone	Thaïs	Massenet
Agathe	soprano	Der Freischütz	Weber	Attila	baritone	Attila	Verdi
Agrippina	soprano	Agrippina	Handel	Azucena	mezzo	Il Trovatore	Verdi
Aida	soprano	Aida	Verdi	Baba the Turk	mezzo	The Rake's Progress	Stravinsky
Alberich	bass-baritone	Rheingold, Siegfried, Götterdämmerung	Wagner	Babinski	tenor	Shvanda the Bagpiper	Weinberger
				Bacchus	tenor	Ariadne auf Naxos	R Strauss
Alceste	soprano	Alceste	Gluck	Balstrode	baritone	Peter Grimes	Britten
Alfonso (see Don Alfonso)				Banquo	bass	Macbeth	Verdi
Alfredo	tenor	La Traviata	Verdi	Barak	baritone	Die Frau ohne Schatten	R Strauss
Alice	soprano	Robert le Diable	Meyerbeer	Bardolf	tenor	Falstaff	Verdi
Alice Ford	soprano	Falstaff	Verdi	Barnaba	baritone	La Gioconda	Ponchielli
Alkmene	soprano	Alkmene	Klebe	Baron Ochs (see Ochs)			
Almaviva	tenor	Il Barbiere di Siviglia	Rossini	Bartolo	bass	Le Nozze di Figaro	Mozart
Almaviva	baritone	Le Nozze di Figaro	Mozart	Bartolo	bass	Il Barbiere di Siviglia	Rossini
Alphonse	baritone	La Favorite	Donizetti	Basilio	tenor	Le Nozze di Figaro	Mozart
Alvaro (see Don Alvaro)				Basilio	baritone	Il Barbiere di Siviglia	Rossini
Alvise	bass	La Gioconda	Ponchielli	Baucis	soprano	Philémon et Baucis	Gounod
Alwa	tenor	Lulu	Berg	Beatrice	soprano	Beatrice di Tenda	Bellini
Amadis	tenor	Amadis	Massenet	Béatrice	soprano	Béatrice et Bénédict	Berlioz
Amelia Boccanegra	soprano	Simon Boccanegra	Verdi	Beckmesser	baritone	Die Meistersinger	Wagner
Amelia	soprano	Un Ballo in Maschera	Verdi	Belcore	baritone	L'Elisir d'Amore	Donizetti
Amfortas	baritone	Parsifal	Wagner	Belfagor	baritone	Belfagor	Respighi
Amina	soprano	La Sonnambula	Bellini	Belinda	soprano	Dido and Aeneas	Purcell
Aminta	soprano	Il Rè Pastore	Mozart	Bella	soprano	The Midsummer Marriage	Tippett
Aminta	soprano	Die schweigsame Frau	R Strauss				
Amneris	mezzo	Aida	Verdi	Benoit	baritone	La Bohème	Puccini
Amonasro	baritone	Aida	Verdi	Benvenuto Cellini	tenor	Benvenuto Cellini	Berlioz
Amor	soprano	Orfeo ed Euridice	Gluck	Beppe	tenor	Pagliacci	Leoncavallo
Andrea Chénier	tenor	Andrea Chénier	Giordano	Billy Budd	baritone	Billy Budd	Britten
Andromaca	soprano	Andromaca	Nasolini	Biterolf	baritone	Tannhäuser	Wagner
Anna Bolena	soprano	Anna Bolena	Donizetti	Blondchen/Blonde	soprano	Die Entführung	Mozart
Anne Trulove	soprano	The Rake's Progress	Stravinsky	Bluebeard	baritone	Duke Bluebeard's Castle	Bartók
Annius	soprano	La Clemenza di Tito	Mozart				
Antigonae	soprano	Antigonae	Orff	Boccanegra	baritone	Simon Boccanegra	Verdi
Antonia	soprano	Les Contes d'Hoffmann	Offenbach	Boris Godunov	bass	Boris Godunov	Mussorgsky
				Borromeo	baritone	Palestrina	Pfitzner
Antonida	soprano	A Life for the Czar	Glinka	Brangaene	mezzo	Tristan und Isolde	Wagner
Antony	bass-baritone	Antony and Cleopatra	Barber	Brunehild	soprano	Sigurd	Reyer
Apollo	tenor	Daphne	R Strauss	Brünnhilde	soprano	Die Walküre, Siegfried, Götterdämmerung	Wagner
Arabella	soprano	Arabella	R Strauss				
Archibaldo	baritone	L'Amore dei Tre Re	Montemezzi				
Ariadne	soprano	Ariadne auf Naxos	R Strauss	Butterfly	soprano	Madama Butterfly	Puccini
Aricie	soprano	Hippolyte et Aricie	Rameau	Caesar (see Giulio Cesare)			
Ariodante	mezzo	Ariodante	Handel				
Arkel	bass	Pelléas et Mélisande	Debussy	Calaf	tenor	Turandot	Puccini

Role	Voice	Opera	Composer
Calisto	soprano	*La Calisto*	Cavalli
Canio	tenor	*Pagliacci*	Leoncavallo
Captain	tenor	*Wozzeck*	Berg
Cardillac	baritone	*Cardillac*	Hindemith
Carmen	soprano	*Carmen*	Bizet
Carolina	soprano	*Il Matrimonio Segreto*	Cimarosa
Cassandre	soprano	*Les Troyens*	Berlioz
Castor	tenor	*Castor et Pollux*	Rameau
Cavaradossi	tenor	*Tosca*	Puccini
Cenerentola (Angelina)	mezzo	*La Cenerentola*	Rossini
Ceres	soprano	*Il Ratto di Proserpina*	Winter
Chapelou	tenor	*Le Postillon de Lonjumeau*	Adam
Charlotte	mezzo	*Werther*	Massenet
Chérubin	soprano	*Chérubin*	Massenet
Cherubino	mezzo	*Le Nozze di Figaro*	Mozart
Child	mezzo	*L'Enfant et les Sortilèges*	Ravel
Christine	soprano	*Intermezzo*	R Strauss
Chrysothemis	soprano	*Elektra*	R Strauss
Cio-Cio-San (*see* Butterfly)			
Claggart	baritone	*Billy Budd*	Britten
Cleopatra	soprano	*Giulio Cesare*	Handel
Clytemnestra	mezzo	*Elektra*	R Strauss
Clytemnestra	soprano	*Iphigénie en Aulide*	Gluck
Colline	bass	*La Bohème*	Puccini
Commendatore	bass	*Don Giovanni*	Mozart
Composer	mezzo	*Ariadne auf Naxos*	R Strauss
Concepcion	soprano	*L'Heure Espagnole*	Ravel
Constanze	soprano	*Die Entführung*	Mozart
Cornelia	mezzo	*Giulio Cesare*	Handel
Cortez	tenor	*Fernand Cortez*	Spontini
Count (Mozart; *see* Almaviva)			
Count Ory	tenor	*Le Comte Ory*	Rossini
Countess	mezzo	*The Queen of Spades*	Tchaikovsky
Countess Almaviva	soprano	*Le Nozze di Figaro*	Mozart
Countess Geschwitz	mezzo	*Lulu*	Berg
Countess Madeleine	soprano	*Capriccio*	R Strauss
Creon	bass	*Médée*	Cherubini
Czar Peter	baritone	*Zar and Zimmermann*	Lortzing
Daland	bass	*Der fliegende Holländer*	Wagner
Dalibor	tenor	*Dalibor*	Smetana
Dalila	mezzo	*Samson et Dalila*	Saint-Saëns
Danae	soprano	*Der Liebe der Danae*	Strauss
Dandini	bass	*La Cenerentola*	Rossini
Danton	baritone	*Dantons Tod*	Einem
Dapertutto	baritone	*Les Contes d'Hoffmann*	Offenbach
Daphne	soprano	*Daphne*	R Strauss
Dardanus	tenor	*Dardanus*	Rameau
David	tenor	*Die Meistersinger*	Wagner
Demetrius	baritone	*A Midsummer Night's Dream*	Britten
Demon	baritone	*The Demon*	Rubinstein
Des Grieux	tenor	*Manon*	Massenet
Des Grieux	tenor	*Manon Lescaut*	Puccini
Desdemona	soprano	*Otello*	Rossini
Desdemona	soprano	*Otello*	Verdi
Despina	soprano	*Così fan Tutte*	Mozart
Diana	mezzo	*La Calisto*	Cavalli
Dick Johnson	tenor	*La Fanciulla del West*	Puccini
Dido	soprano	*Dido and Aeneas*	Purcell
Didon	soprano	*Les Troyens*	Berlioz
Dimitri	tenor	*Boris Godunov*	Mussorgsky
Dinorah	soprano	*Dinorah*	Meyerbeer
Djamileh	mezzo	*Djamileh*	Bizet
Doctor	baritone	*Wozzeck*	Berg
Don Alfonso	baritone	*Così fan Tutte*	Mozart
Don Alvaro	tenor	*La Forza del Destino*	Verdi
Don Carlo	tenor	*Ernani*	Verdi
Don Carlo	baritone	*La Forza del Destino*	Verdi
Don Carlos	tenor	*Don Carlos*	Verdi
Don Fernando	bass	*Fidelio*	Beethoven
Don Giovanni	baritone	*Don Giovanni*	Mozart
Don José	tenor	*Carmen*	Bizet
Don Magnifico	baritone	*La Cenerentola*	Rossini
Don Ottavio	tenor	*Don Giovanni*	Mozart
Don Pasquale	baritone	*Don Pasquale*	Donizetti
Don Quichotte	bass	*Don Quichotte*	Massenet
Don Ramiro	tenor	*La Cenerentola*	Rossini
Don Rodrigo	tenor	*Don Rodrigo*	Ginastera
Donna Anna	soprano	*Don Giovanni*	Mozart
Donna Elvira	soprano	*Don Giovanni*	Mozart
Donner	bass-baritone	*Das Rheingold*	Wagner
Dorabella	mezzo	*Così fan Tutte*	Mozart
Dosifey	bass	*Khovanshchina*	Mussorgsky
Dr Schön	baritone	*Lulu*	Berg
Drum Major	tenor	*Wozzeck*	Berg
Drusilla	soprano	*L'Incoronazione di Poppea*	Monteverdi
Duke of Mantua	tenor	*Rigoletto*	Verdi
Dulcamara	baritone	*L'Elisir d'Amore*	Donizetti
Dutchman	bass-baritone	*Der fliegende Holländer*	Wagner
Dyer's Wife	soprano	*Die Frau ohne Schatten*	R Strauss
Earl of Essex	tenor	*Roberto Devereux*	Donizetti
Eboli	mezzo	*Don Carlos*	Verdi
Edgardo	tenor	*Lucia di Lammermoor*	Donizetti
Eglantine	soprano	*Euryanthe*	Weber
Eisenstein	tenor	*Die Fledermaus*	J Strauss
Electra/Elettra	soprano	*Idomeneo*	Mozart
Elektra	soprano	*Elektra*	R Strauss
Elena	soprano	*Mefistofele*	Boito
Elisabeth	soprano	*Tannhäuser*	Wagner
Elisabeth de Valois	soprano	*Don Carlos*	Verdi
Elisabetta	soprano	*Elisabetta, Regina d'Inghilterra*	Rossini
Elizabeth I	soprano	*Maria Stuarda*	Donizetti
Elizabeth Zimmer	soprano	*Elegy for Young Lovers*	Henze
Ellen Orford	soprano	*Peter Grimes*	Britten
Elsa	soprano	*Lohengrin*	Wagner
Elvino	tenor	*La Sonnambula*	Bellini
Elvira	soprano	*Ernani*	Verdi
Elvira	soprano	*I Puritani*	Bellini
Emilia Marty	soprano	*The Makropoulos Case*	Janáček
Emma	soprano	*Khovanshchina*	Mussorgsky
Emperor	tenor	*Die Frau ohne Schatten*	R Strauss
Empress	soprano	*Die Frau ohne Schatten*	R Strauss
Enée	tenor	*Les Troyens*	Berlioz
Enobarbus	bass	*Antony and Cleopatra*	Barber
Enrico	baritone	*Lucia di Lammermoor*	Donizetti
Enzo	tenor	*La Gioconda*	Ponchielli

Role	Voice	Opera	Composer	Role	Voice	Opera	Composer
Erda	alto	*Das Rheingold, Siegfried*	Wagner	Giulietta	soprano	*I Capuleti e i Montecchi*	Bellini
Erik	tenor	*Der fliegende Holländer*	Wagner	Giulietta	soprano	*Les Contes d'Hoffmann*	Offenbach
Ernani	tenor	*Ernani*	Verdi	Giulio Cesare	alto	*Giulio Cesare*	Handel
Ernesto	tenor	*Don Pasquale*	Donizetti	Gloriana	soprano	*Gloriana*	Britten
Escamillo	tenor	*Carmen*	Bizet	Golaud	baritone	*Pelléas et Mélisande*	Debussy
Eugene Onegin	baritone	*Eugene Onegin*	Tchaikovsky	Golitsin	tenor	*Khovanshchina*	Mussorgsky
Euridice	soprano	*Favola d'Orfeo*	Monteverdi	Grand Inquisitor	bass	*Don Carlos*	Verdi
Euridice	soprano	*Orfeo ed Euridice*	Gluck	Gregor	tenor	*The Makropoulos Case*	Janáček
Euryanthe	soprano	*Euryanthe*	Weber	Gremin	bass	*Eugene Onegin*	Tchaiskovsky
Eva	soprano	*Die Meistersinger*	Wagner	Grigory (*see* Dimitri)			
Fafner	bass	*Das Rheingold, Siegfried*	Wagner	Grisélidis	soprano	*Gresélidis*	Massenet
Falke	baritone	*Die Fledermaus*	J Strauss	Guglielmo	baritone	*Così fan Tutte*	Mozart
Falstaff	baritone	*Falstaff*	Verdi	Guillaume Tell	baritone	*Guillaume Tell*	Rossini
Faninal	baritone	*Der Rosenkavalier*	R Strauss	Gunther	baritone	*Götterdämmerung*	Wagner
Fasolt	bass-baritone	*Das Rheingold*	Wagner	Gurnemanz	bass	*Parsival*	Wagner
Fatima	mezzo	*Oberon*	Weber	Gutrune	soprano	*Götterdämmerung*	Wagner
Faust	baritone	*Doktor Faust*	Busoni	Gwendoline	soprano	*Gwendoline*	Chabrier
Faust	tenor	*Faust*	Gounod	Hagen	bass	*Götterdämmerung*	Wagner
Faust	tenor	*Mefistofele*	Boito	Halka	soprano	*Halka*	Moniusko
Fedora	soprano	*Fedora*	Giordano	Hamlet	baritone	*Hamlet*	Thomas
Female Chorus	mezzo	*The Rape of Lucretia*	Britten	Hans Sachs	bass-baritone	*Die Meistersinger*	Wagner
Fenena	soprano	*Nabucco*	Verdi	Helen	soprano	*Die Agyptische Helena*	R Strauss
Fenton	tenor	*Falstaff*	Verdi	Helen	mezzo	*War and Peace*	Prokofiev
Fenton	tenor	*Die Lustigen Weiber von Windsor*	Nicolai	Helena	soprano	*A Midsummer Night's Dream*	Britten
Fernand	tenor	*La Favorite*	Donizetti	Hélène	soprano	*Les Vêpres Siciliennes*	Verdi
Ferrando	tenor	*Così fan Tutte*	Mozart	Henry Morosus	tenor	*Die schweigsame Frau*	R Strauss
Fides	mezzo	*Le Prophète*	Meyerbeer	Henry VIII	bass	*Anna Bolena*	Donizetti
Fiesco	bass	*Simon Boccanegra*	Verdi	Hermann	tenor	*The Queen of Spades*	Tchaikovsky
Figaro	baritone	*Il Barbiere di Siviglia*	Rossini	Herod	tenor	*Salome*	R Strauss
Figaro	baritone	*Le Nozze di Figaro*	Mozart	Hérodiade	soprano	*Hérodiade*	Massenet
Fiordiligi	soprano	*Così fan Tutte*	Mozart	Herodias	mezzo	*Salome*	R Strauss
Fiorilla	soprano	*Il Turco in Italia*	Rossini	Hoffmann	tenor	*Les Contes d'Hoffmann*	Offenbach
Flamand	tenor	*Capriccio*	R Strauss				
Florestan	tenor	*Fidelio*	Beethoven	Hunding	bass	*Die Walküre*	Wagner
Ford	baritone	*Falstaff*	Verdi	Huon	tenor	*Oberon*	Weber
Forester	baritone	*The Cunning Little Vixen*	Janáček	Iago	tenor	*Otello*	Rossini
				Iago	baritone	*Otello*	Verdi
Francesca da Rimini	soprano	*Francesca da Rimini*	Zandonai	Idamante	soprano	*Idomeneo*	Mozart
Frasquita	soprano	*Carmen*	Bizet	Idomeneo	tenor	*Idomeneo*	Mozart
Frau Fluth	soprano	*Die Lustigen Weiber von Windsor*	Nicolai	Ighino	soprano	*Palestrina*	Pfitzner
				Ilia	soprano	*Idomeneo*	Mozart
Freia	soprano	*Das Rheingold*	Wagner	Imogene	soprano	*Il Pirata*	Bellini
Frère Laurent	bass	*Roméo et Juliette*	Gounod	Ines	mezzo	*L'Africaine*	Meyerbeer
Fricka	mezzo	*Das Rheingold, Die Walküre*	Wagner	Ino	mezzo	*Semele*	Handel
				Iolanta	soprano	*Iolanta*	Tchaikovsky
Fritz	tenor	*L'Amico Fritz*	Mascagni	Iphigénie	soprano	*Iphigénie en Aulide*	Gluck
Froh	tenor	*Das Rheingold*	Wagner	Iphigénie	soprano	*Iphigénie en Tauride*	Gluck
Gabriele Adorno	tenor	*Simon Boccanegra*	Verdi	Iris	soprano	*Iris*	Mascagni
Geneviève	mezzo	*Pelléas et Mélisande*	Debussy	Isabeau	soprano	*Isabeau*	Mascagni
Gennaro	tenor	*Lucrezia Borgia*	Donizetti	Isabella	mezzo	*L'Italiana in Algeri*	Rossini
Genoveva	soprano	*Genoveva*	Schumann	Ismaele	tenor	*Nabucco*	Verdi
Gerald	tenor	*Lakmé*	Delibes	Isolde	soprano	*Tristan und Isolde*	Wagner
Gérard	tenor	*Andrea Chénier*	Giordano	Ivan the Terrible	bass	*Pskovitanka*	Rimsky-Korsakov
Germont	baritone	*LaTraviata*	Verdi				
Gertrude	mezzo	*Hamlet*	Thomas	Ivanhoe	tenor	*Ivanhoe*	Sullivan
Gianetto	tenor	*La Gazza Ladra*	Rossini	Jack	tenor	*The Midsummer Marriage*	Tippett
Gianni Schicchi	baritone	*Gianni Schicchi*	Puccini				
Gilda	soprano	*Rigoletto*	Verdi	Jack Rance	baritone	*La Fanciulla del West*	Puccini
Gioconda	soprano	*La Gioconda*	Ponchielli	Jenifer	soprano	*The Midsummer Marriage*	Tippett
Giovanna d'Arco	soprano	*Giovanna d'Arco*	Verdi				
Giselda	soprano	*I Lombardi*	Verdi	Jeník	tenor	*The Bartered Bride*	Smetana
Giuditta	soprano	*Giuditta*	Léhar	Jenůfa	soprano	*Jenůfa*	Janáček

Role	Voice	Opera	Composer
Jocasta	mezzo	Oedipus der Tyrann	Orff
Jocasta	mezzo	Oedipus Rex	Stravinsky
Jochanaan	baritone	Salome	R Strauss
Judith	mezzo	Duke Bluebeard's Castle	Bartók
Julien	tenor	Julien	Charpentier
Juliette	soprano	Roméo et Juliette	Gounod
Juno	soprano	La Calisto	Cavalli
Jupiter	baritone	Der Liebe der Danae	R Strauss
Katerina Ismailova	soprano	Lady Macbeth of the Mtsensk District	Shostakovich
Katya Kabanová	soprano	Katya Kabanová	Janáček
Kecal	bass	The Bartered Bride	Smetana
Khovansky	bass	Khovanshchina	Mussorgsky
King Fisher	bass	The Midsummer Marriage	Tippett
King Henry	bass	Lohengrin	Wagner
King Marke (see Marke)			
King Priam	bass-baritone	King Priam	Tippett
Klingsor	bass	Parsifal	Wagner
Koanga	baritone	Koanga	Delius
Konchak	bass	Prince Igor	Borodin
Kostelnička	soprano	Jenůfa	Janáček
Kothner	baritone	Die Meistersinger	Wagner
Kundry	soprano	Parsifal	Wagner
Kurwenal	baritone	Tristan und Isole	Wagner
La Cieca	mezzo	La Gioconda	Ponchielli
Lača	tenor	Jenůfa	Janáček
Lady Billows	soprano	Albert Herring	Britten
Lady Macbeth	soprano	Macbeth	Wagner
Lakmé	soprano	Lakmé	Delibes
Landgrave	bass	Tannhäuser	Wagner
Laura	mezzo	La Gioconda	Ponchielli
Lauretta	soprano	Gianni Schicchi	Puccini
Le Cid	tenor	Le Cid	Massenet
Leila	soprano	Les Pêcheurs de Perles	Bizet
Lensky	tenor	Eugene Onegin	Tchaikovsky
Léonor	mezzo	La Favorite	Donizetti
Leonora	soprano	La Forza del Destino	Verdi
Leonora	soprano	Oberto	Verdi
Leonora	soprano	Il Trovatore	Verdi
Leonore	soprano	Fidelio	Beethoven
Leporello	baritone	Don Giovanni	Mozart
Lescaut	baritone	Manon	Massenet
Lescaut	baritone	Manon Lescaut	Puccini
Leukippos	tenor	Daphne	R Strauss
Libuše	soprano	Libuše	Smetana
Linda di Chamounix	soprano	Linda di Chamounix	Donizetti
Lindoro	tenor	L'Italiana in Algeri	Rossini
Lionel	tenor	Martha	Flotow
Lisa	soprano	The Queen of Spades	Tchaikovsky
Liù	soprano	Turandot	Puccini
Lodoïska	soprano	Lodoïska	Cherubini
Lodoletta	soprano	Lodoletta	Mascagni
Loge	tenor	Das Rheingold	Wagner
Lohengrin	tenor	Lohengrin	Wagner
Lola	mezzo	Cavalleria Rusticana	Mascagni
Lord Percy	tenor	Anna Bolena	Donizetti
Loreley	soprano	Loreley	Catalani
Loris	tenor	Fedora	Girodano
Louise	soprano	Louise	Charpentier
Lucia	soprano	Lucia di Lammermoor	Donizetti
Lucio Silla	tenor	Lucio Silla	Mozart
Lucrezia Borgia	soprano	Lucrezia Borgia	Donizetti
Ludmila	soprano	Ruslan and Ludmila	Glinka
Luigi	tenor	Il Tabarro	Puccini
Luisa Miller	soprano	Luisa Miller	Verdi
Lulu	soprano	Lulu	Berg
Luna	baritone	Il Trovatore	Verdi
Lysander	tenor	A Midsummer Night's Dream	Britten
Lysiart	bass	Euryanthe	Weber
Macbeth	baritone	Macbeth	Verdi
Macduff	tenor	Macbeth	Verdi
Maddalena	soprano	Andrea Chénier	Giordano
Maddalena	mezzo	Rigoletto	Verdi
Magdalene	mezzo	Die Meistersinger	Wagner
Malatesta	baritone	Don Pasquale	Donizetti
Malcolm	mezzo	La Donna del Lago	Rossini
Maliella	soprano	I Gioelli della Madonna	Wolf-Ferrari
Mandryka	baritone	Arabella	R Strauss
Manon	soprano	Manon	Massenet
Manon Lescaut	soprano	Manon Lescaut	Puccini
Manrico	tenor	Il Trovatore	Verdi
Marcellina	mezzo	Le Nozze di Figaro	Mozart
Marcello	baritone	La Bohème	Puccini
Mařenka	soprano	The Bartered Bride	Smetana
Marfa	mezzo	Khovanshchina	Mussorgsky
Margherita	soprano	Mefistofele	Boito
Marguerite	soprano	Faust	Gounod
Marguerite de Valois	soprano	Les Huguenots	Meyerbeer
Maria Stuarda	soprano	Maria Suarda	Donizetti
Marie	soprano	La Fille du Régiment	Donizetti
Marie	soprano	Wozzeck	Berg
Marietta	soprano	Die Tote Stadt	Korngold
Marina	mezzo	Boris Godunov	Mussorgsky
Mark	tenor	The Midsummer Marriage	Tippett
Marke	bass	Tristan und Isolde	Wagner
Mârouf	tenor	Mârouf	Rabaud
Marschallin	soprano	Der Rosenkavalier	R Strauss
Martha	soprano	Martha	Flotow
Marzelline	soprano	Fidelio	Beethoven
Masaniello	tenor	La Muette di Portici	Auber
Masetto	baritone	Don Giovanni	Mozart
Mathilde	soprano	Guillaume Tell	Rossini
Mathis	baritone	Mathis der Maler	Hindemith
Mazeppa	baritone	Mazeppa	Tchaikovsky
Medea/Médée	soprano	Médée	Cherubini
Mefistofele	bass	Mefistofele	Boito
Meg Page	mezzo	Falstaff	Verdi
Mélisande	soprano	Pelléas et Mélisande	Debussy
Melitone	baritone	La Forza del Destino	Verdi
Menelaos	tenor	Die Ägyptische Helena	R Strauss
Méphistophélès	bass	Faust	Gounod
Mercédès	soprano	Carmen	Bizet
Micaela	soprano	Carmen	Bizet
Micah	mezzo	Samson	Handel
Michele	baritone	Il Tabarro	Puccini
Mignon	soprano	Mignon	Thomas
Milada	soprano	Dalibor	Smetana
Miller	baritone	Luisa Miller	Verdi
Miller	bass	Russalka	Dargomizhsky
Mime	tenor	Das Rheingold, Siegfried	Wagner
Mimi	soprano	La Bohème	Puccini
Minnie	soprano	La Fanciulla del West	Puccini
Mireille	soprano	Mireille	Gounod
Miss Jessel	soprano	The Turn of the Screw	Britten

Role	Voice	Opera	Composer	Role	Voice	Opera	Composer
Miss Wingrave	soprano	Owen Wingrave	Britten	Palestrina	tenor	Palestrina	Pfitzner
Mistress Quickly	mezzo	Falstaff	Verdi	Pamina	soprano	Die Zauberflöte	Mozart
Mittenhofer	baritone	Elegy for Young Lovers	Henze	Papagena	soprano	Die Zauberflöte	Mozart
				Papageno	baritone	Die Zauberflöte	Mozart
Monostatos	tenor	Die Zauberflöte	Mozart	Paolo	bass	Simon Boccanegra	Verdi
Montfort	baritone	Les Vêpres Siciliennes	Verdi	Paris	tenor	Paride ed Elena	Gluck
Mosè	bass	Mosè in Egitto	Rossini	Parsifal	tenor	Parsifal	Wagner
Moses	spoken	Moses und Aron	Schoenberg	Paul	tenor	Die Tote Stadt	Korngold
Mrs Grose	soprano	The Turn of the Screw	Britten	Pedrillo	tenor	Die Entführung	Mozart
Musetta	soprano	La Bohème	Puccini	Peer Gynt	baritone	Peer Gynt	Egk
Mustafà	bass	L'Italiana in ALgeri	Rossini	Pelléas	baritone	Pelléas et Mélisande	Debussy
Nabucco	baritone	Nabucco	Verdi	Penelope	mezzo	Il Ritorno d'Ulisse	Monteverdi
Nadir	tenor	Les Pêcheurs de Perles	Bizet	Pénélope	soprano	Pénélope	Fauré
Nannetta	soprano	Falstaff	Verdi	Peter Grimes	tenor	Peter Grimes	Britten
Natasha	soprano	War and Peace	Prokofiev	Phébé	soprano	Castor et Pollux	Rameau
Nedda	soprano	Pagliacci	Leoncavallo	Philip II	bass	Don Carlos	Verdi
Nelusko	baritone	L'Africaine	Meyerbeer	Pimen	bass	Boris Godunov	Mussorgsky
Nemorino	tenor	L'Elisir d'Amore	Donizetti	Pinkerton	tenor	Madama Butterfly	Puccini
Neptune	bass	Il Ritorno d'Ulisse	Monteverdi	Pistol	bass	Falstaff	Verdi
Nero	soprano or tenor	L'Incoronazione di Poppea	Monteverdi	Pizarro	bass-baritone	Fidelio	Beethoven
				Platée	tenor	Platée	Rameau
Nerone	tenor	Nerone	Boito	Plunkett	bass	Martha	Flotow
Nerone	tenor	Nerone	Mascagni	Pluto	bass	Orfeo ed Euridice	Haydn
Nevers	baritone	Les Huguenots	Meyerbeer	Pogner	bass	Die Meistersinger	Wagner
Nick Shadow	baritone	The Rake's Progress	Stravinsky	Pollione	tenor	Norma	Bellini
Nicklausse	mezzo	Les Contes d'Hoffmann	Offenbach	Polly Peachum	soprano	The Beggar's Opera	Gay/Pepush
Nightingale	soprano	The Nightingale	Stravinsky	Poppea	soprano	L'Incoronazione di Poppea	Monteverdi
Ninetta	soprano	La Gazza Ladra	Rossini				
Norina	soprano	L'Elisir d'Amore	Donizetti	Porgy	bass-baritone	Porgy and Bess	Gershwin
Norma	soprano	Norma	Bellini	Posa	baritone	Don Carlos	Verdi
Nurse	mezzo	Die Frau ohne Schatten	R Strauss	Preziosilla	mezzo	La Forza del Destino	Verdi
Oberon	countertenor	A Midsummer Night's Dream	Britten	Prince Igor	baritone	Prince Igor	Borodin
				Princesse de Bouillon	mezzo	Adriana Lecouvreur	Cilea
Oberson	tenor	Oberon	Weber	Procida	bass	Les Vêpres Siciliennes	Verdi
Ochs	bass	Der Rosenkavalier	R Strauss				
Octavian	mezzo	Der Rosenkavalier	R Strauss	Proserpine	soprano	Il Ratto di Proserpina	Winter
Odabella	soprano	Attlia	Verdi	Puck	mezzo	Oberon	Weber
Oedipus	tenor	Oedipus der Tyrann	Orff	Pylades	tenor	Iphigénie en Tauride	Gluck
Oedipus	tenor	Oedipus Rex	Stravinsky	Queen of Night	soprano	Die Zauberflöte	Mozart
Olivier	baritone	Capriccio	R Strauss	Queen of Sheba	soprano	Die Königin von Saba	Goldmark
Olympia	soprano	Les Contes d'Hoffmann	Offenbach	Queen of Sheba	soprano	La Reine de Saba	Gounod
				Queen of Shemakha	soprano	The Golden Cockerel	Rimsky-Korsakov
Ophelia	soprano	Hamlet	Thomas	Rachel	soprano	La Juive	Halévy
Orestes	baritone	Elektra	R Strauss	Radames	tenor	Aida	Verdi
Orestes	baritone	Iphigénie en Tauride	Gluck	Radamisto	soprano	Radamisto	Handel
Orfeo	tenor	Favola d'Orfeo	Monteverdi	Raimbaud	baritone	Le Comte Ory	Rossini
Orfeo	mezzo	Orfeo ed Euridice	Gluck	Raimondo	bass	Lucia di Lammermoor	Donizetti
Orlofsky	mezzo/tenor	Die Fledermaus	J Strauss	Ramfis	bass	Aida	Verdi
Orontea	soprano	Orontea	Cesti	Ramiro	tenor	La Cenerentola	Rossini
Oroveso	baritone	Norma	Bellini	Raoul	tenor	Les Huguenots	Meyerbeer
Ortrud	mezzo	Lohengrin	Wagner	Reiza	soprano	Oberon	Weber
Oscar	soprano	Un Ballo in Maschera	Verdi	Renata	soprano	The Fiery Angel	Prokofiev
Osmin	bass	Die Entführung	Mozart	Renato	baritone	Un Ballo in Maschera	Verdi
Otello	tenor	Otello	Rossini	Riccardo	tenor	Un Ballo in Maschera	Verdi
Otello	tenor	Otello	Verdi	Riccardo	bass	I Puritani	Bellini
Ottavia	soprano	L'Incoronazione di Poppea	Monteverdi	Rienzi	tenor	Rienzi	Wagner
				Rigoletto	baritone	Rigoletto	Verdi
Ottone	countertenor	L'Incoronazione di Poppea	Monteverdi	Rinaldo	mezzo	Rinaldo	Handel
				Robert	tenor	Robert le Diable	Meyerbeer
Ottavio (see Don Ottavio)				Rocco	bass	Fidelio	Beethoven
				Rodelinda	soprano	Rodelinda	Handel
Owen Wingrave	tenor	Owen Wingrave	Britten	Rodolfo	tenor	La Bohème	Puccini
Padmâvatî	soprano	Padmâvatî	Roussel	Rodolfo	tenor	Luisa Miller	Verdi
Painter	tenor	Lulu	Berg	Rodolfo	bass	La Sonnambula	Bellini

Role	Voice	Opera	Composer
Romeo	mezzo	*I Capuleti e i Montecchi*	Bellini
Romeo	tenor	*Giulietta e Romeo*	Zandonai
Roméo	tenor	*Roméo at Juliette*	Gounod
Rosalinde	soprano	*Die Fledermaus*	J Strauss
Rosina	soprano	*Il Barbiere di Siviglia*	Rossini
Ruslan	baritone	*Ruslan and Ludmila*	Glinka
Russalka	soprano	*Russalka*	Dvořák
Sachs (*see* Hans Sachs)			
Sadko	tenor	*Sadko*	Rimsky-Korsakov
Saffo	soprano	*Saffo*	Pacini
Salammbô	soprano	*Salammbô*	Reyer
Salomé	soprano	*Hérodiade*	Massenet
Salome	soprano	*Salome*	R Strauss
Samson	tenor	*Samson et Dalila*	Saint-Saëns
Sancho Panza	baritone	*Don Quichotte*	Massenet
Santuzza	soprano	*Cavalleria Rusticana*	Mascagni
Sapho	soprano	*Sapho*	Massenet
Sarastro	bass	*Die Zauberflöte*	Mozart
Saul	bass-baritone	*Saul and David*	Nielsen
Scaramucchio	tenor	*Ariadne auf Naxos*	R Strauss
Scarpia	baritone	*Tosca*	Puccini
Schaunard	baritone	*La Bohème*	Puccini
Schigolch	bass	*Lulu*	Berg
Scipione	alto	*Scipione*	Handel
Selika	soprano	*L'Africaine*	Meyerbeer
Selim	bass	*Il Turco in Italia*	Rossini
Sellem	tenor	*The Rake's Progress*	Stravinsky
Semele	soprano	*Semele*	Handel
Semiramide	soprano	*Semiramide*	Rossini
Seneca	bass	*L'Incoronazione di Poppea*	Monteverdi
Senta	soprano	*Der fliegende Holländer*	Wagner
Sergei	tenor	*Lady Macbeth of the Mtensk District*	Shostakovich
Servilia	soprano	*La Clemenza di Tito*	Mozart
Sextus	mezzo	*La Clemenza di Tito*	Mozart
Sharpless	baritone	*Madama Butterfly*	Puccini
Shuisky	tenor	*Boris Godunov*	Mussorgsky
Shvanda	baritone	*Shvanda the Bagpiper*	Weinberger
Siebel	soprano	*Faust*	Gounod
Sieglinde	soprano	*Die Walküre*	Wagner
Siegmund	tenor	*Die Walküre*	Wagner
Silva	bass	*Ernani*	Verdi
Silvio	baritone	*Pagliacci*	Leoncavallo
Sinaide	soprano	*Mosè in Egitto*	Rossini
Snow Maiden	soprano	*The Snow Maiden*	Rimsky-Korsakov
Sobinin	tenor	*A Life for the Tsar*	Glinka
Sophie	soprano	*Der Rosenkavalier*	R Strauss
Sophie	soprano	*Werther*	Massenet
Sparafucile	bass	*Rigoletto*	Verdi
Speaker	bass-baritone	*Die Zauberflöte*	Mozart
Steva	tenor	*Jenůfa*	Janáček
Storch	baritone	*Intermezzo*	R Strauss
Suor Angelica	soprano	*Suor Angelica*	Puccini
Susanna	soprano	*Le Nozze di Figaro*	Mozart
Suzuki	mezzo	*Madama Butterfly*	Puccini
Tamerlano	alto/mezzo	*Tamerlano*	Handel
Tamino	tenor	*Die Zauberflöte*	Mozart
Tancredi	mezzo	*Tancredi*	Rossini
Tannhäuser	tenor	*Tannhäuser*	Wagner
Tatyana	soprano	*Eugene Onegin*	Tchaikovsky
Telramund	baritone	*Lohengrin*	Wagner
Teresa	soprano	*Benvenuto Cellini*	Berlioz
Thaïs	soprano	*Thaïs*	Massenet
Thea	soprano	*The Knot Garden*	Tippett
Titania	soprano	*Oberon*	Weber
Titus	tenor	*La Clemenza di Tito*	Mozart
Tom Rakewell	tenor	*The Rake's Progress*	Stravinsky
Tonio	tenor	*La Fille du Régiment*	Donizetti
Tonio	baritone	*Pagliacci*	Leoncavallo
Tosca	soprano	*Tosca*	Puccini
Tristan	tenor	*Tristan und Isolde*	Wagner
Trulove	bass	*The Rake's Progress*	Stravinsky
Turandot	soprano	*Turandot*	Puccini
Turiddu	tenor	*Cavalleria Rusticana*	Mascagni
Tytania	soprano	*A Midsummer Night's Dream*	Britten
Ulisse	baritone	*Il Ritorno d'Ulisse*	Monteverdi
Ulrica	mezzo	*Un Ballo in Maschera*	Verdi
Urbain	soprano	*Les Huguenots*	Meyerbeer
Vakula	tenor	*Vakula the Smith*	Tchaikovsky
Valentin	baritone	*Faust*	Gounod
Valentine	soprano	*Les Huguenots*	Meyerbeer
Varlaam	bass	*Boris Godunov*	Mussorgsky
Vasco da Gama	tenor	*L'Africaine*	Meyerbeer
Venus	mezzo	*Tannhäuser*	Wagner
Violetta	soprano	*La Traviata*	Verdi
Vitellia	soprano	*La Clemenza di Tito*	Mozart
Vixen	soprano	*The Cunning Little Vixen*	Janáček
Vreli	soprano	*A Village Romeo and Juliet*	Delius
Wally	soprano	*La Wally*	Catalani
Walther	tenor	*Die Meistersinger*	Wagner
Waltraute	mezzo	*Götterdämmerung*	Wagner
Wanderer (Wotan)	baritone	*Siegfried*	Wagner
Werther	tenor	*Werther*	Massenet
Wilhelm Meister	tenor	*Mignon*	Thomas
Wolfram	baritone	*Tannhäuser*	Wagner
Wotan	bass-baritone	*Rheingold, Walküre, Siegfried*	Wagner
Wurm	bass	*Luisa Miller*	Verdi
Xerxes	mezzo	*Serse*	Handel
Yniold	soprano	*Pelléas et Mélisande*	Debussy
Zaccaria	bass	*Nabucco*	Verdi
Zaïde	soprano	*Zaïde*	Mozart
Zazà	soprano	*Zazà*	Zandonai
Zdenka	soprano	*Arabella*	R Strauss
Zerbinetta	soprano	*Ariadne auf Naxos*	R Strauss
Zerlina	soprano	*Don Giovanni*	Mozart
Zurga	baritone	*Les Pêcheurs de Perles*	Bizet

1594

2 Feb: Death of Palestrina, Rome
14 Jun: Death of Lassus, Munich
L'Amfiparnaso (Vecchi)

1595

Mass in Five Parts (Byrd)
Canzonets and Ballets (Morley)

1596

Tomkins appointed Master of Choristers at Worcester Cathedral

1597

Peri's opera *La Dafne* produced in Florence, Carnaval

1598

Birth of Luigi Rossi

1599

22 Aug: Death of Luca Marenzio, Rome
8 Nov: Death of Francisco Guerrero, Seville

1600

Feb: *La rappresentazione di anima e di corpo* (Cavalieri)
28 Jul: Death of Claude Le Jeune, Paris
6 Oct: *Euridice* (Peri)
9 Oct: *Il Rapimento di Cefalo* (G Caccini); French version of the
libretto in 1608 (*Le Ravissement de Cefale*) became the first
translation of an opera

1601

Publication in London by Thomas Morley of *The Triumphes of
Oriana* (madrigals in honour of Queen Elizabeth I) Monteverdi
becomes music director at the Gonzaga Court in Mantua

1602

14 Feb: Birth of Francesco Cavalli, Crema
11 Mar: Death of Emilio de' Cavalieri, Rome
Oct: Death of Thomas Morley, London
5 Dec: *L'Euridice* (G Caccini)

1603

4 Jul: Death of Philippe de Monte, Prague
Publication of Monteverdi's Fourth Book of Madrigals

1604

5 May: Death of Claudio Merulo, Parma
Dowland publishes his *Lachrimae or Seaven Teares*, for viols and
lute

1605

19 Feb: Death of Orazio Vecchi, Modena
Publication of Monteverdi's Fifth Book of Madrigals
18 Apr: Birth of Giacomo Carissimi, Rome
Publication of Victoria's Requiem in Madrid
Completion of Byrd's *Gradualia*

1606

2 Feb: Death of Guillaume Costeley, Evreux
Carnaval: *Eumelio* (Agazarri)

1607

24 Feb: *L'Orfeo* (Monteverdi)
Publication of Monteverdi's *Scherzi musicali* in Venice

1609

15 May: Death of Giovanni Croce, Venice
28 May: *L'Arianna* (Monteverdi)
While an inmate of London's Fleet Prison, Francis Tregian begins
his transcription of the *Fitzwilliam Virginal Book*

1610

Completion ad publication of Monteverdi's *Vespers*
Publication of Dowland's *Musicall Banquet*

1611

20 Aug: Death of Tomás Luis de Victoria, Madrid. Publication of
Byrd's *Psalmes, Songs and Sonnets*
Publication in Venice of the first book of madrigals by Schütz
Gesualdo completes his *Responseries*

1612

8 Jun: Death of Hans Leo Hassler, Frankfurt
Publication of the dance collection *Terpsichore*, by Praetorius
Parthenia, or The Maydenhead, England's first collection of
printed keyboard music, published in London

1613

12 Aug: Death of Giovanni Gabrieli, Venice
19 Aug: Monteverdi appointed director of music at St Mark's,
Venice
8 Sept: Death of Carlo Gesualdo, Naples

1614

27 Sept: Death of Felice Anerio, Rome
Publication of Monteverdi's Sixth Book of Madrigals

1615

Posthumous publication of Gabrieli's *Symphoniae Sacrae*, book 2,
and *Canzoni e Sonate*

1616

19 May: Birth of Johann Froberger, Stuttgart
Carnaval: *Il Pianto d'Orfeo* (Belli)

1617

5 Apr: Death of Alonso Lobo, Seville
Publication of Schein's instrumental suites, *Il Banchetto Musicale*

1618

10 Dec: Death of Giulio Caccini, Florence
Publication in Leipzig of Schein's motet collection *Opella nova*

1619

1 Jun: *La Morte d'Orfeo* (Landi)
Publication of Monteverdi's Seventh Book of Madrigals
Completion of the *Fitzwilliam Virginal Book*

1620

8 Feb: *L'Aretusa* (Vitali)
1 Mar: Death of Thomas Campion, London
17 Nov: Grandi becomes deputy to Monteverdi at St Mark's,
Venice

1621

15 Feb: Death of Michael Praetorius, Wolfenbüttel
16 Oct: Death of Jan Sweelinck, Amsterdam

1622

Publication in Hamburg of part one of Scheidt's *Concertum
sacrorum*

1623

4 Jul: Death of William Byrd, Standon Massey, Essex
5 Aug: Birth of Antonio Cesti, Arezzo
30 Nov: Death of Thomas Weelkes, London
Completion of *The Resurrection Story*, by
Schütz

1624

Monteverdi composes *Il combattimento di Tancredi e Clorinda*

1625

2 Feb: *La Liberazione di Ruggiero dall'Isola d'Alcina* (F Caccini)

5 Jun: Death of Orlando Gibbons, Canterbury

1626

20 Feb: Death of John Dowland, London

Publication of part two of Schein's *Opella nova*

1627

23 Apr: *Dafne* (Schütz); the first German opera-music lost

1628

12 Mar: Death of John Bull, Antwerp

5 Jul: Death of Michael Cavendish, London

11 Oct: *La Flora* (Gagliano and J Peri)

1629

Death of Sigismondo D'India, Modena

Publication in Venice of Schütz's first book of *Symphoniae sacrae*

1630

16 Feb: Death of William Brade, Hamburg

22 Mar: Death of Richard Dering, London

12 Jun: Burial of Giovanni Anerio, Graz

19 Nov: Death of Johann Schein, Leipzig

1631

22 Feb: *Chlorinda* (Ben Jonson and Inigo Jones; their last court masque)

1632

21 Feb: *Il Sant'Alessio* (Landi)

28 Feb: Birth of Jean Baptiste Lully, Florence

1633

24 Jan: Death of Nathaniel Giles, Windsor

12 Aug: Death of Jacopo Peri, Florence

1634

29 Sept: *Comus* (Lawes); masque to a text by John Milton

15 Nov: Death of Johann Staden, Nuremburg

1635

Publication in Venice of Frescobaldi's sacred collection, *Fiori musicali*

1636

Musikalische Exequien by Schütz, the first German Requiem

1637

Feb: *L'Andromeda* (Manelli); written for the inauguration of the world's first public opera house, the Teatro San Cassiano in Venice

1638

Publication of Monteverdi's *Madrigali guerrieri et amorosi*

1639

24 Jan: *La Nozze di Teto e di Peleo* (Cavalli); his first opera

1 Jun: Death of Melchior Franck, Coburg

28 Oct: Death of Stefano Landi, Rome

21 Dec: *L'Adone* (Monteverdi); his first opera for a public theatre

1640

25 Nov: Death of Giles Farnaby, London

Il Ritorno d'Ulisse in Patria (Monteverdi)

1641

Carnaval: *La Didone* (Cavalli)

29 Sept: Tunder becomes organist at the Marienkirche in Lubeck, later founding the Abendmusiken

1642

22 Feb: *Il Palazzo incanto d'Atlante* (Luigi Rossi)

1643

L'Incoronazione di Poppea (Monteverdi)

1 Mar: Death of Girolamo Frescobaldi, Rome

29 Nov: Death of Claudio Monteverdi, Venice

1644

12 Aug: Birth of Heinrich Biber, Wartenburg

Seelewig (Staden); the first extant German opera

1 Oct: Birth of Alessandro Stradella, Rome

Messa Concertata (Cavalli)

1645

24 Sept: Death of William Lawes, Chester

The Seven Last Words (Schütz)

1646

24 Sept: Death of Duarte Lobo, Lisbon

Lully enters service with the cousin of Louis XIV, Anne Marie Louise d'Orleans

1647

2 Mar: *L'Orfeo* (Luigi Rossi)

1648

17 Nov: Death of Thomas Ford, London

Geistliche Chor-Musik, motet collection by Schütz

1649

5 Jan: *Giasone* (Cavalli)

20 Jan: *Orontea* (Cesti); his first opera

23 Feb: Birth of John Blow, Newark

25 Oct: Death of Giovanni Rigatti, Venice

1650

20 Jan: *Alessandro Vincitor di se Stesso* (Cavalli)

20 Feb: *L'Orimonte* (Cavalli)

24 Nov: Death of Manuel Cardoso, Lisbon

1651

Publication of Monteverdi's Ninth Book of Madrigals

28 Nov: *Calisto* (Cavalli)

1652

17 Jan: *Eritrea* (Cavalli)

7 Feb: Death of Gregorio Allegri, Rome

1653

17 Feb: Birth of Arcangelo Corelli, Fusignano

18 Feb: Death of Luigi Rossi, Rome

Jun: *Orione* (Cavalli)

1 Sept: Pachelbel baptized, Nuremberg

1654

12 Jan: *Xerse*: (Cavalli)

24 Mar: Death of Samuel Scheidt, Halle

1655

30 Dec: *Erismena* (Cavalli)

1656

31 May: Birth of Marin Marais, Paris

9 Jun: Death of Thomas Tomkins, near Worcester

Sept: *The Siege of Rhodes* (Locke, Lawes, and others)

1657

15 Dec: Birth of Michel Lalande, Paris

L'Oronte (Kerll); written for the inauguration of the Residenz Theater in Munich, the city's first opera house

1658

12 Jun: *Hipermestra* (Cavalli)

1659

Apr: *Pastorale* (Cambert); sometimes claimed as the first French opera

30 Nov: Death of Walter Porter, London

Purcell born, London

1660

2 May: Alessandro Scarlatti born, Palermo

4 Dec: Birth of André Campra, Aix-en-Provence

1661

Carnival: *La Dori* (Cesti)

16 May: Lully becomes superintendent of music to Louis XIV

29 Aug: Death of Louis Couperin, Paris

1662

7 Feb: *Ercole amante* (Cavalli)

1663

8 Jan: *Ballets des Arts* (Lully)

1664

9 Feb: *Scipione affricano* (Cavalli)

1665

Birth of Nicolaus Bruhns, Schwabstadt

St John Passion (Schütz)

1666

13 Feb: *Il Tito* (Cesti)
20 Feb: *Pompeo Magno* (Cavalli)
24 Feb: Death of Nickolas Lanier, Greenwich
St Matthew Passion (Schütz)

1667

May: Death of Johann Froberger, Héricourt

1668

12 July: *Il Pomo d'Oro* (Cesti)
10 Nov: Birth of François Couperin, Paris

1669

13 Feb: *Ballet de Flore* (Lully)
14 Oct: Death of Antonio Cesti, Florence

1670

14 Oct *Le Bourgeois Gentilhomme* (Lully and Molière)

1671

3 Mar: *Pomone* (Cambert); written for the inauguration of
the Académie Royale des Opéra, later to become the Paris
Opéra
8 Jun: Birth of Tommaso Albinoni, Venice

1672

April: Lully becomes director of Académie Royale de
Musique
6 Nov: Death of Heinrich Schütz, Dresden

1673

27 Apr: *Cadmus et Hermione* (Lully)

1674

12 Jan: Birth of Reinhard Keiser, Teuchern
12 Jan: Death of Giacomo Carissimi, Rome
19 Jan: *Alceste* (Lully)

1675

12 Jan: *Thesée* (Lully)
9 Mar: *Psyche* (Locke); sometimes regarded as the first English
opera

1676

14 Jan: Death of Francesco Cavalli, Venice
19 Dec: Birth of Louis Clérambault, Paris

1677

Purcell appointed composer to the King's Violins

1678

4 Mar: Birth of Antonio Vivaldi, Venice
27 Oct: Death of John Jenkins, Kimberley, Norfolk
30 Dec: Birth of William Croft, Warwickshire

1679

Feb: *Gli Equivoci nel Sembiante* (A Scarlatti); his first opera
Purcell becomes organist at Westminster Abbey

1680

3 Feb: *Proserpine* (Lully)

1681

20 Jan: Birth of Francesco Conti, Florence
14 Mar: Birth of Georg-Philipp Telemann, Magdeburg
Publication of Corelli's Trio Sonatas, op. 1
28 Sept: Birth of Johann Mattheson, Hamburg

1682

25 Feb: Death of Alessandro Stradella, assassinated in Genoa
Purcell becomes organist at the Chapel Royal

1683

9 Jan: *Phaeton* (Lully)
25 Sept: Birth of Jean-Philippe Rameau, Dijon
22 Nov: *Ode for St Cecilia's Day* (Purcell)

1684

18 Jan: *Amadis* (Lully)
12 Sept: Death of Johann Rosenmüller, Wolfenbüttel

1685

23 Feb: Birth of Handel, Halle
21 Mar: Birth of J S Bach, Eisenach
26 Oct: Birth of Domenico Scarlatti, Naples
Venus and Adonis (Blow)

1686

15 Feb: *Armide* (Lully)
17 Aug: Birth of Nicola Porpora, Naples

1687

22 Mar: Death of Jean Baptiste Lully, Paris
20 Jun: Death of Carl Abel, London
5 Dec: Birth of Francesco Geminiani, Lucca

1688

San Giovanni Battista, oratorio (Stradella)

1689

Dido and Aeneas (Purcell)

1690

The Prophetess, or The History of Dioclesian
(Purcell)

1691

Early summer: *King Arthur* (Purcell)

1692

8 Apr: Birth of Tartini, Pirano
Apr: *The Fairy Queen* (Purcell)
22 Nov: *Ode for St Cecilia's Day* 'Hail Bright Cecilia'
(Purcell)

1693

4 Dec: *Médée* (Charpentier)

1694

Publication of Albinoni's first set of Trio Sonatas, op. 1

1695

3 Sept: Birth of Pietro Locatelli, Bergamo
21 Nov: Death of Henry Purcell, London

1696

Feb: *Circe* and *Penelope* (Keiser)

1697

29 Mar: Death of Nicolaus Bruhns, Husum
10 May: Birth of Jean-Marie Leclair, Lyons
24 Oct: *L'Europe Galante* (Campra)

1698

Posthumous publication of Purcell collection *Orpheus Brittanicus*

1699

25 Mar: Birth of Johann Hasse, Bergedorf
Publication of Pachelbel's keyboard variations
Hexachordum Apollinis

1700

Cristofori develops the *Gravicembalo col piano e forte*, forerunner
of modern piano

1701

Kuhnau becomes cantor at the Leipzig Thomasschule
Telemann abandons law studies for composition

1702

Mar: Handel becomes organist at Halle cathedral
7 Nov: *Tancrède* (Campra)

1703

Sept: Vivaldi appointed to the Pietà orphanage in Venice and
Bach becomes organist at Arnstadt

1704

24 Feb: Death of M A Charpentier, Paris
3 May: Death of Heinrich Biber, Salzburg
20 Oct: *Cleopatra* (Mattheson); Handel played the harpsichord
and fought a duel with Mattheson

1705

6 Jan: *Almira* (Handel); his first opera

1706

18 Oct: Birth of Baldassare Galuppi, Burano
June: *Masagniello furioso* (Keiser)
Publication of the first volume of Rameau's *Pièces de
clavecin*

1707

9 May: Death of Dietrich Buxtehude, Lübeck
Nov: *Rodrigo* (Handel); his first Italian opera
1 Dec: Death of Jeremiah Clarke, London

1708

8 Apr: *La Resurrezione* (Handel)

1 Oct: Death of John Blow, Westminster

1709

26 Dec: *Agrippina* (Handel)

1710

4 Jan: Birth of Giovanni Battista Pergolesi, Iesi

28 May: Birth of Thomas Arne, London

17 Jun: *Les Fêtes Venitiennes* (Campra)

Handel arrives in London

22 Nov: Birth of W F Bach, Weimar

1711

24 Feb: *Rinaldo* (Handel); his first opera for London

11 Sept: Birth of William Boyce, London

1712

12 Jan: *Idomenée* (Campra)

3 Dec: *Il Pastor Fido* (Handel)

1713

8 Jan: Death of Arcangelo Corelli, Rome

10 Jan: *Teseo* (Handel)

2 Jul: Birth of Christoph Willibald Gluck, Erasbach

1714

8 Mar: Birth of C P E Bach

Weimar Publication of Vivaldi's concertos,
   La Stravaganza

10 Sept: Birth of Niccolò Jommelli, Aversa

1715

5 Jun: *Amadigi* (Handel)

1716

Autumn: *Arsilda* (Vivaldi)

1717

30 Jun: Birth of Johann Stamitz, Havlíčkův

17 Jul: Handel's *Water Music* performed on the Thames

Bach is appointed at the court of Prince Leopold of
   Cöthen

1718

May: *Acis and Galatea* (Handel)

1719

Don Chisciotte in Sierra Morena (Conti)

1720

27 Apr: *Radamisto* (Handel)

1721

Dedication by Bach of his Brandenburg Concertos to the
   Margrave of Brandenburg

1722

First book of Bach's *Well-Tempered Clavier*

1723

12 Jan: *Ottone* (Handel)

Christmas Magnificat (Bach)

1724

20 Feb: Giulio Cesare (Handel)

7 Apr: *St John Passion* (Bach)

1725

13 Feb: *Rodelinda* (Handel)

22 Oct: Death of Alessandro Scarlatti, Rome

14 Dec: Publication of Vivaldi's *Four Seasons*

1726

5 May: *Alessandro* (Handel); first rivalry between sopranos
   Faustina Bordoni and Francesca Cuzzoni

18 Jun: Death of Michel Lalande, Versailles

1727

31 Jan: *Admeto* (Handel)

14 Aug: Death of William Croft, Bath

11 Oct: Handel's *Coronation Anthems* for George II

1728

29 Jan: *The Beggar's Opera* (Gay/Pepusch)

1 Jun: Closure of Handel's Royal Academy

15 Aug: Death of Marin Marais, Paris

1729

15 Apr: *St Matthew Passion* (Bach)

2 Dec: *Lotario* (Handel); first opera of Handel-Heidegger
   company at the King's Theatre

1730

24 Feb: *Partenope* (Handel)

1731

2 Feb: *Poro, re dell'Indie* (Handel)

1732

15 Feb: *Sosarme* (Handel)

23 Feb: *Esther* (Handel); Handel's first English oratorio

31 Mar: Birth of Franz Joseph Haydn, Rohrau

1733

27 Jan: *Orlando* (Handel)

12 Sept: Death of François Couperin, Paris

1 Oct: *Hippolyte et Aricie* (Rameau)

1734

17 Jan: Birth of François Gossec, Vergnies

26 Jan: *Arianna* (Handel)

Christmas Oratorio (Bach)

1735

8 Jan: *Ariodante* (Handel)

12 Jan: Death of John Eccles, Hampton Wick

16 Apr: *Alcina* (Handel)

28 Aug: *Les Indes Galantes* (Rameau)

5 Sept: Birth of J C Bach, Leipzig

1736

19 Feb: *Alexander's Feast* (Handel)

16 Mar: Death of Giovanni Battista Pergolesi,
   Pozzuoli

28 Dec: Death of Antonio Caldara, Vienna

1737

18 May: *Berenice* (Handel)

14 Sept: Birth of Michael Haydn, Rohrau

24 Oct: *Castor et Pollux* (Rameau)

1738

Mass in B minor (Bach)

1739

16 Jan: *Saul* (Handel)

4 Apr: *Israel in Egypt* (Handel)

12 Sept: Death of Reinhard Keiser, Hamburg

2 Nov: Birth of Karl Dittersdorf, Vienna

1740

Haydn becomes a choirboy at the court chapel in Vienna

1741

8 Feb: Birth of André Grétry, Liège

13 Feb: Death of Johann Fux, Vienna

Aug–Sept: Handel composes *Messiah*

26 Dec: *Artaserse* (Gluck); his first opera

1742

13 Apr: *Messiah* (Handel)

Publication of Bach's *Goldberg Variations*

1743

18 Feb: *Samson* (Handel)

19 Feb: Birth of Luigi Boccherini, Lucca

1744

10 Feb: *Semele* (Handel)

29 Jun: Death of André Campra, Versailles

1745

31 Mar: *Platée* (Rameau)

8 May: Birth of Carl Stamitz, Mannheim

1746

4 Oct: *Scylla et Glaucus* (Leclair)

7 Oct: Birth of William Billings, Boston

1747

1 Apr: *Judas Maccabeus* (Handel)

1748

14 May: *Semiramide riconosciuta* (Gluck)

1749
27 Apr: *Music for the Royal Fireworks* (Handel)
26 Oct: Death of Louis Clérambault, Paris
5 Dec: *Zoroastre* (Rameau)
17 Dec: Birth of Domenico Cimarosa, Aversa
The Art of Fugue (Bach)

1750
28 Jul: Death of J S Bach, Leipzig
18 Aug: Birth of Antonio Salieri, Legnano

1751
17 Jan: Death of Tommaso Albinoni, Venice
20 Jan: *Il Ciro riconosciuta* (Hasse); Faustina Bordoni-Hasse's
last public appearance

1752
23 Jan: Birth of Muzio Clementi, Rome
26 Feb: *Jephtha* (Handel)
20 Jul: Death of Johann Pepusch, London

1753
1 Mar: *Le Devin du Village* (Rousseau)

1754
2 May: Birth of Martín y Soler, Valencia
26 Oct: *Il Filosofo di Campagna* (Galuppi)

1755
6 Jan: *Montezuma* (Graun)

1756
27 Jan: Birth of W A Mozart, Salzburg

1757
27 Mar: Death of Johann Stamitz, Mannheim
23 Jul: Death of Domenico Scarlatti, Madrid

1758
3 Oct: *L'Isle de Merlin* (Gluck)

1759
14 Apr: Death of George Frideric Handel, London
8 Aug: Death of Carl Graun, Berlin

1760
6 Feb: *La buona Figliuola* (Piccinni)
12 Feb: Birth of Jan Dussek, Časlav
Sept: Birth of Luigi Cherubini, Florence

1761
Haydn in service with Nicholas Esterházy at Eisenstadt,
writes his symphonies *Le Matin, Le Midi, Le Soir*
(nos. 6–8)

1762
17 Sept: Death of Francesco Geminiani, Dublin
5 Oct: *Orfeo ed Euridice* (Gluck)

1763
19 Feb: *Orione* (J C Bach)
14 Jun: Birth of Johann Mayr, Mendorf
15 Jun: Birth of Franz Danzi, Schwetzingen
22 Jun: Birth of Étienne Méhul, Givet

1764
30 Mar: Death of Pietro Locatelli, Amsterdam
23 Apr: Mozart arrives in London with his family
12 Sept: Death of Jean-Philippe Rameau, Paris
22 Oct: Death of Jean-Marie Leclair, Paris

1765
30 Jan: *Il Telemaco* (Gluck)
27 Feb: *Tom Jones* (Philidor)

1766
3 Mar: Haydn becomes music director at Esterházy

1767
25 Jun: Death of Georg-Philipp Telemann, Hamburg
26 Dec: *Alceste* (Gluck)

1768
5 Aug: *Lo Speziale* (Haydn)
Sept–Oct: *Bastien und Bastienne* (Mozart)

1769
1 May: *La Finta Semplice* (Mozart)

1770
26 Feb: Birth of Antonin Reicha, Prague; death of Giuseppe
Tartini, Padua
Nov: *Paride e Helena* (Gluck)
17 Dec: Beethoven baptized, Bonn
26 Dec: *Mitridate, rè di Ponto* (Mozart)

1771
17 Oct: *Ascanio in Alba* (Mozart)
9 Nov: *Zemire et Azore* (Grétry)

1772
1 May: *Il Sogno di Scipione* (Mozart)
26 Dec: *Lucio Silla* (Mozart)
Haydn composes string quartets op. 20

1773
17 Jan: *Exsultate, jubilate* (Mozart)
26 Jul: *L'Infedeltà delusa* (Haydn)

1774
19 Apr: *Iphigénie en Aulide* (Gluck)
25 Aug: Death of Niccolò Jommelli, Naples
14 Nov: Birth of Gaspare Spontini, Maiolati

1775
13 Jan: *La finta giardiniera* (Mozart)
15 Jan: Death of Giovanni Battista Sammartini, Milan
23 Apr: *Il rè pastore* (Mozart)
15 Oct: Birth of Bernhard Crusell, Turku
16 Dec: Birth of François Boieldieu, Rouen

1776
21 Jul: 'Haffner' Serenade (Mozart)

1777
3 Aug: *Il mondo della luna* (Haydn)
23 Sept: *Armide* (Gluck)

1778
5 Mar: Death of Thomas Arne, London
12 Jun: Paris Symphony (Mozart)
2 Aug: La Scala opens with Salieri's *Europa riconosciuta*

1779
7 Feb: Death of William Boyce, Kensington
6 Apr: Death of Tommaso Traetta, Venice
25 Apr: *La Vera Costanza* (Haydn)
18 May: *Iphigénie en Tauride* (Gluck)
6 Dec: *L'isola disabitata* (Haydn)

1780
Symphony no. 34 K338 (Mozart)

1781
29 Jan: *Idomeneo* (Mozart)
25 Feb: *La fedeltà premiata* (Haydn)
10 Sept: *La Serva Padrona* (Paisiello)

1782
1 Jan: Death of J C Bach, London
16 Jul: *Die Entführung aus dem Serail* (Mozart)
26 Jul: Birth of John Field, Dublin
27 Oct: Birth of Niccolò Paganini, Genoa
6 Dec: *Orlando Paladino* (Haydn)

1783
26 Oct: Mass in C minor (Mozart)
4 Nov: 'Linz' Symphony (Mozart)
16 Dec: Death of Johann Hasse, Venice

1784
26 Feb: *Armida* (Haydn)
5 Apr: Birth of Louis Spohr, Brunswick
1 Jul: Death of W F Bach, Berlin
Mozart's piano concertos K449, K450, K451, K453, K456, K459

1785
3 Jan: Death of Baldassare Galuppi, Venice
Haydn's Paris Symphonies
Mozart's string quartets dedicated to Haydn, K387, K421, K428,
K458, K464, K456
Mozart's piano concertos K466, K467, K482

1786
1 May: *Le nozze di Figaro* (Mozart)
18 Nov: Birth of Carl Maria von Weber, Eutin
Mozart's piano concertos K488, K491, K503
1787
19 Jan: 'Prague' Symphony (Mozart)
26 Mar: *The Last Seven Words* (Haydn, string quartet version)
29 Oct: *Don Giovanni* (Mozart)
15 Nov: Death of Christoph Willibald Gluck, Vienna
1788
26 Jun–10 Aug: Mozart composes last three symphonies
Haydn's string quartets op. 54 and op. 55
14 Dec: Death of C P E Bach, Hamburg
1789
22 Dec: Clarinet quintet (Mozart)
1790
26 Jan: *Così fan Tutte* (Mozart)
Haydn invited to visit London by Johann Peter Solomon
1791
11 Mar: First series of Salomon/Haydn London concerts begins
5 Sept: Birth of Giacomo Meyerbeer, Berlin
6 Sept: *La Clemenza di Tito* (Mozart)
30 Sept: *Die Zauberflöte* (Mozart)
5 Dec: Death of W A Mozart, Vienna
1792
7 Feb: *Il Matrimonio Segreto* (Cimarosa)
29 Feb: Gioachino Rossini born, Pesaro
1793
Beethoven's String Trio, op. 3
1794
10 Feb: Second series of Salomon/Haydn London concerts begins
1795
22 Jan: Death of Michel Corrette, Rouen
29 Mar: Beethoven makes public Vienna debut, with 2nd piano concerto op. 19
4 May: Military Symphony (Haydn)
16 Aug: Birth of Heinrich Marschner, Zittan
17 Sept: Birth of Saverio Mercadante, Altamura
18 Dec: Piano Concerto no. 1 (Beethoven)
1796
23 Jul: Birth of Franz Berwald, Stockholm
Missa in tempore belli/Mass in Time of War (Haydn)
1797
31 Jan: Birth of Franz Schubert, Vienna
29 Nov: Birth of Gaetano Donizetti, Bergamo
Haydn's string quartets op. 76
1798
23 Sept: Lord Nelson Mass, in D minor (Haydn)
1799
19 Mar: *Die Schöpfung*, public premiere (Haydn)
24 Oct: Death of Karl Dittersdorf, Neuhof, Bohemia
1800
2 Apr: Symphony no.1 (Beethoven)
26 Sept: Death of William Billings, Boston
24 Nov: *Das Waldmädchen* (Weber)
1801
11 Jan: Death of Domenico Cimarosa, Venice
29 May: *Die Jahreszeiten*, public premiere (Haydn)
23 Oct: Birth of Albert Lortzing, Berlin
3 Nov: Birth of Vincenzo Bellini, Catania
9 Nov: Death of Carl Stamitz, Jena
1802
3 Mar: Publication of Beethoven's piano sonata op. 27 no. 2 *Moonlight*
6 Oct: Beethoven writes the 'Heiligenstadt Testament'
1803
5 Apr: Symphony no. 2 and Piano Concerto no. 3 (Beethoven)
17 May: 'Kreutzer' Sonata (Beethoven)

11 Dec: Birth of Hector Berlioz, Côte-Saint-André, Isére
1804
1 Jun: Mikhail Glinka born, Novospasskoye
3 Oct: *Leonora* (Paer)
1805
7 Apr *Eroica* Symphony (Beethoven)
20 Nov: *Fidelio* (Beethoven)
28 May: Death of Luigi Boccherini, Madrid
1806
11 Feb: Death of Vicente Martín y Soler, St Petersburg
17 May: *Uthal* (Méhul)
23 Dec: Violin Concerto (Beethoven)
Razumovsky Quartets (Beethoven)
1807
Mar: Symphony no. 4 and Piano Concerto no. 4 (Beethoven)
Sept: Mass in C (Beethoven)
16 Dec: *La Vestale* (Spontini)
1808
22 Dec: Symphonies nos. 5 and 6 (Beethoven)
1809
3 Feb: Birth of Felix Mendelssohn, Hamburg
31 May: Death of Franz Joseph Haydn, Vienna
28 Nov: *Fernand Cortez* Spontini
1810
22 Feb: Birth of Frédéric Chopin, Zelazowa Wola
8 Jun: Birth of Robert Schumann, Zwickau
15 Jun: *Egmont* (Beethoven)
3 Nov: *La cambiale di matrimonio* (Rossini); his first opera to be staged
1811
5 Aug: Birth of Ambroise Thomas, Metz
22 Oct: Birth of Franz Liszt, Raiding
26 Oct: *L'equivico stravagante* (Rossini)
28 Nov: Piano Concerto no. 5 (Beethoven)
'Archduke Trio' (Beethoven)
1812
8 Jan: *L'Inganno Felice* (Rossini)
20 Mar: Death of Jan Dussek, Paris
27 Apr: Birth of Friedrich von Flotow, Teutendorf
9 May: *La Scala di Seta* (Rossini)
26 Sept: *La Pietra del Paragone* (Rossini)
1813
6 Feb: *Tancredi* (Rossini)
Feb: Birth of Alexander Dargomïzhsky, Troitskoye
22 May: Birth of Richard Wagner, Leipzig; *L'Italiana in Algeri* (Rossini)
24 Sept: Death of André Grétry, Paris
9 Oct: Birth of Giuseppe Verdi, Le Roncole
30 Nov: Birth of Charles-Valentin Alkan, Paris
8 Dec: Symphony no. 7 (Beethoven)
1814
27 Feb: Symphony no. 8 (Beethoven)
23 May: *Fidelio*, final version (Beethoven)
14 Aug: *Il turco in Italia* (Rossini)
1815
4 Oct: *Elisabetta Regina d'Inghilterra* (Rossini)
Erlkönig and Symphony no. 3 (Schubert)
1816
20 Feb: *Il Barbiere di Siviglia* (Rossini)
13 Apr: Birth of William Sterndale Bennet, Sheffield
4 Dec: *Otello* (Rossini)
Symphonies nos. 4 and 5 (Schubert)
1817
25 Jan: *La Cenerentola* (Rossini)
22 Feb: Birth of Niels Gade, Copenhagen
18 Oct: Death of Étienne Méhul, Paris
11 Nov: *Armida* (Rossini)

1818
5 Mar: *Mosè in Egitto* (Rossini)
18 Jun: Birth of Charles Gounod, Paris
14 Nov: *Enrico di Borgogna* (Donizetti); his first opera
Symphony no. 6 (Schubert)
1819
20 Jun: Birth of Jacques Offenbach, Cologne
24 Oct: *La Donna del lago* (Rossini)
'Trout' Quintet (Schubert)
1820
14 Jun: *Die Zwillingsbruder* (Schubert); his first stage work to be
performed
19 Aug: *Die Zauberharfe* (Schubert)
3 Dec: *Maometto II* (Rossini)
1821
18 Jun: *Der Freischütz* (Weber)
Piano Sonatas op. 109 and 110 (Beethoven)
1822
16 Feb: *Zelmira* (Rossini)
3 Oct: Overture, *Die Weihe des Hauses* (Beethoven)
10 Dec: Birth of César Franck, Liège
Beethoven begins composition of the Choral Symphony
1823
3 Feb: *Semiramide* (Rossini)
25 Oct: *Euryanthe* (Weber)
20 Dec: *Rosamunde* (Schubert)
Die Schöne Müllerin (Schubert)
'Diabelli Variations' (Beethoven)
Beethoven begins composition of the last five string quartets
1824
2 Mar: Birth of Smetana, Litomysl
7 Mar: *Il Crociato in Egitto* (Meyerbeer)
7 Apr: *Missa Solemnis* (Beethoven)
7 May: 'Choral Symphony' (Beethoven)
4 Sept: Birth of Anton Bruckner, Ansfelden
1825
7 May: Death of Antonio Salieri, Vienna
19 Jun: *Il Viaggio a Reims* (Rossini)
25 Oct: Birth of Johann Strauss the younger, Vienna
1 Dec: *Adelson e Salvini* (Bellini); his first opera
Beethoven string quartets op. 127, 132 and 130
Mendelssohn Octet
1826
12 Apr: *Oberon* (Weber)
13 Apr: Death of Franz Danzi, Karlsruhe
4 Jun: Death of Carl Maria von Weber, London
Beethoven string quartets op. 131 and 135
1827
20 Feb: Concerto in A♭ for two pianos (Mendelssohn)
26 Mar: Death of Ludwig van Beethoven, Vienna
29 Apr: *A Midsummer Night's Dream*, overture (Mendelssohn)
1828
Schubert String Quintet and last three piano sonatas
20 Aug: *Le Comte Ory* (Rossini)
19 Nov: Death of Franz Schubert, Vienna
1829
14 Feb: *La Straniera* (Bellini)
16 Feb: Death of François Gossec, Passy
11 Mar: Mendelssohn revives Bach's *St Matthew Passion*,
Berlin
3 Aug: *Guillaume Tell* (Rossini)
28 Nov: Birth of Anton Rubinstein, Vykhvatinets
22 Dec: *Der Templer und die Jüdin* (Marschner)
1830
28 Jan: *Fra Diavolo* (Auber)
11 Mar: *I Capuleti e i Montecchi* (Bellini)
17 Mar: Piano Concerto no. 2 (Chopin)
11 Oct: Piano Concerto no. 1 (Chopin)

5 Dec: *Symphonie Fantastique* (Berlioz)
26 Dec: *Anna Bolena* (Donizetti)
1831
8 Jan: Death of Franz Krommer, Vienna
6 Mar: *La Sonnambula* (Bellini)
21 Nov: *Robert le Diable* (Meyerbeer)
26 Dec: *Norma* (Bellini)
Publication of Schumann's op. 1, the *Abegg Variations*
1832
10 Mar: Death of Muzio Clementi, Evesham
12 May: *L'Elisir d'Amore* (Donizetti)
24 May: 'Hebrides' Overture (Mendelssohn)
Chopin Études op. 10
1833
16 Mar: *Beatrice di Tenda* (Bellini)
7 May: Birth of Johannes Brahms, Hamburg
12 Nov: Birth of Alexander Borodin, St Petersburg
26 Dec: *Lucrezia Borgia* (Donizetti)
1834
3 Apr: Schumann founds the *Neue Zeitschrift für
Musik*
7 Apr: *Die schöne Melusine*, overture (Mendelssohn)
8 Oct: Death of François Boieldieu, Jarey
23 Nov: *Harold en Italie* (Berlioz)
26 Dec: *Gemma di Vergy* (Donizetti)
1835
24 Jan: *I Puritani* (Bellini)
23 Feb: *La Juive* (Halevy)
23 Sept: Death of Vincenzo Bellini, Paris
26 Sept: *Lucia di Lammermoor* (Donizetti)
9 Oct: Birth of Camille Saint-Saëns, Paris
Études Symphoniques and *Carnaval* (Schumann)
1836
21 Feb: Birth of Léo Delibes, St Germain du Val
29 Feb: *Les Huguenots* (Meyerbeer)
29 Mar: *Das Liebesverbot* (Wagner); his first opera to be
staged
22 May: *St Paul* (Mendelssohn)
28 May: Death of Antonin Reicha, Paris
9 Dec: *A Life for the Tsar* (Glinka)
1837
2 Jan: Birth of Mily Balakirev, Nizhnyr Novgorod
23 Jan: Death of John Field, Moscow
17 Oct: Death of Johann Nepomuk Hummel, Weimar
29 Oct: *Roberto Devereux* (Donizetti)
5 Dec: *Grande Messe des Morts* (Berlioz)
1838
6 Jan: Birth of Max Bruch, Cologne
28 Jul: Death of Bernhard Crusell, Stockholm
10 Sept: *Benvenuto Cellini* (Berlioz)
25 Oct: Birth of Georges Bizet, Paris
1839
21 Mar: Birth of Modest Mussorgsky, Karevo; premiere of
Schubert's Ninth Symphony
17 Nov: *Oberto* (Verdi); his first opera
24 Nov: *Roméo et Juliette* (Berlioz)
1840
11 Feb: *La Fille du Régiment* (Donizetti)
7 May: Pyotr Tchaikovsky born, Kamsko-Votkinsk
27 May: Death of Niccolò Paganini, Nice
25 Jun: Mendelssohn 2nd Symphony, *Lobgesang*
2 Dec: *La Favorite* (Donizetti)
Dichterliebe, Frauenliebe und Leben, Liederkreis op. 24 and
op. 39 (Schumann)
1841
31 Mar: Symphony no. 1 (Schumann)
8 Sept: Birth of Antonin Dvořák, Nelahozeves
26 Dec: *Maria Padilla* (Donizetti)

1842

7 Jan: Stabat Mater (Rossini)
3 Mar: 'Scottish' Symphony (Mendelssohn)
9 Mar: *Nabucco* (Verdi)
20 Oct: *Rienzi* (Wagner)
9 Dec: *Ruslan and Ludmilla* (Glinka)
String quartets op. 41, Piano Quintet, Piano Quartet (Schumann)

1843

2 Jan: *Der fliegende Holländer* (Wagner)
3 Jan: *Don Pasquale* (Donizetti)
11 Feb: *I Lombardi* (Verdi)
15 Jun: Birth of Edvard Grieg, Bergen
14 Oct: *A Midsummer Night's Dream*, incidental music (Mendelssohn)
4 Dec: *Das Paradies und die Peri* (Schumann)

1844

9 Mar: *Ernani* (Verdi)
18 Mar: Birth of Nikolay Rimsky-Korsakov, Tikhvin
3 Nov: *I due Foscari* (Verdi)

1845

15 Feb: *Giovanna d'Arco* (Verdi)
13 Mar: Violin Concerto (Mendelssohn)
12 May: Birth of Gabriel Fauré, Pamiers
12 Aug: *Alzira* (Verdi)
19 Oct: *Tannhäuser* (Wagner)
2 Dec: Death of Johann Mayr, Bergamo

1846

1 Jan: Piano concerto (Schumann)
17 Mar: *Attila* (Verdi)
26 Aug: *Elijah* (Mendelssohn)
5 Nov: Symphony no. 2 (Schumann)
6 Dec: *La Damnation de Faust* (Berlioz)

1847

14 Mar: *Macbeth* (Verdi)
22 Jul: *I Masnadieri* (Verdi)
4 Nov: Death of Felix Mendelssohn, Leipzig
25 Nov: *Martha* (Flotow)

1848

21 Jan: Birth of Henri Duparc, Paris
27 Feb: Birth of Hubert Parry, Bournemouth
8 Apr: Death of Gaetano Donizetti, Bergamo
25 Oct: *Il Corsaro* (Verdi)

1849

27 Jan: *La Battaglia di Legnano* (Verdi)
9 Mar: *Die Lustigen Weiber von Windsor* (Nicolai)
16 Apr: *Le Prophète* (Meyerbeer)
28 Aug: *Tasso* (Liszt)
17 Oct: Death of Frédéric Chopin, Paris
8 Dec: *Luisa Miller* (Verdi)

1850

25 Jun: *Genoveva* (Schumann)
24 Aug: *Orpheus* (Liszt)
28 Aug: *Lohengrin* (Wagner)
16 Nov: *Stiffelio* (Verdi)
21 Dec: Birth of Zdeněk Fibich, Šerbořice

1851

21 Jan: Death of Albert Lortzing, Berlin
24 Jan: Death of Gaspare Spontini, Maiolati
6 Feb: Symphony no. 3, 'Rhenish' (Schumann)
11 Mar: *Rigoletto* (Verdi)

1852

13 Jun: *Manfred* (Schumann)
30 Sept: Birth of Charles Stanford, Dublin
Wagner writes texts of *Das Rheingold* and *Die Walküre*

1853

19 Jan: *Il Trovatore* (Verdi)
6 Mar: *La Traviata* (Verdi)
17 Dec: Brahms Piano Sonata in C, op. 1

1854

16 Feb: *L'Étoile du Nord* (Meyerbeer)
28 Feb: *Les Préludes* (Liszt)
24 Jun: *Alfonso und Estrella* (Schubert)
3 Jul: Birth of Leoš Janáček, Hukvaldy
1 Sept: Birth of Engelbert Humperdinck, Siegburg
10 Dec: *L'Enfance du Christ* (Berlioz)

1855

20 Jan: Birth of Ernest Chausson, Paris
17 Feb: Piano Concerto no. 1 (Liszt)
13 Jun: *Les Vêpres Siciliennes* (Verdi)
27 Nov: Piano Trio no. 1 (Brahms)

1856

9 Apr: *Le Docteur Miracle* (Bizet)
29 Jul: Death of Robert Schumann, Endenich
31 Aug: *Missa solemnis* (Liszt)
25 Nov: Birth of Sergei Taneiev, Vladimir-na-Klyazme

1857

7 Jan: Piano Concerto no. 2 (Liszt)
22 Jan: Piano Sonata in B minor (Liszt)
12 Mar: *Simon Boccanegra* (Verdi)
2 Jun: Birth of Edward Elgar, Broadheath
5 Sept: *A Faust Symphony* (Liszt)
Wagner interrupts composition of *Siegfried* to start work on *Tristan und Isolde*

1858

15 Jan: *Le Médecin malgré lui* (Gounod)
21 Dec: *Orphée aux Enfers* (Offenbach)
23 Dec: Birth of Giacomo Puccini, Lucca

1859

22 Jan: Piano Concerto no. 1 (Brahms)
17 Feb: *Un Ballo in Maschera* (Verdi)
19 Mar: *Faust* (Gounod)
4 Apr: *Le Pardon de Poermel* (Meyerbeer)
2 Oct: *Les Béatitudes* (Franck)
22 Oct: Death of Louis Spohr, Kessel

1860

10 Feb: Serenade no. 2 (Brahms)
18 Feb: *Philémon et Baucis* (Gounod)
13 Mar: Hugo Wolf born, Windischgraz
7 Jul: Gustav Mahler born, Kaliste
3 Oct: Serenade no. 1 (Brahms)
20 Oct: String Sextet no. 1 (Brahms)

1861

13 Mar: *Tannhäuser*, revised version (Wagner)
12 Jul: Birth of Anton Arensky, Novgorod
16 Nov: Piano Quartet no. 1 (Brahms)
7 Dec: Variations and Fugue on a theme by Handel (Brahms)
14 Dec: Death of Heinrich Marschner, Hanover
18 Dec: Birth of Edward MacDowell, New York

1862

29 Jan: Birth of Frederick Delius, Bradford
9 Aug: *Béatrice et Bénédict* (Berlioz)
22 Aug: Birth of Claude Debussy, Saint Germain-en-Laye
10 Nov: *La Forza del Destino* (Verdi)
29 Nov: Piano Quartet no. 2 (Brahms)

1863

30 Sept: *Les Pêcheurs de Perles* (Bizet)
4 Nov: *Les Troyens à Carthage* (Berlioz)
7 Dec: Birth of Pietro Mascagni, Livorno

1864

14 Mar: *Petite messe solennelle* (Rossini)
19 Mar: *Mireille* (Gounod)
2 May: Death of Giacomo Meyerbeer, Paris
11 Jun: Birth of Richard Strauss, Munich
29 Sept: Mass in D minor (Bruckner)
17 Dec: *La Belle Hélène* (Offenbach)

1865
28 Apr: *L'Africaine* (Meyerbeer)
9 Jun: Birth of Carl Nielsen, Odense
10 Jun: *Tristan und Isolde* (Wagner)
1 Oct: Birth of Paul Dukas, Paris
7 Dec: Horn Trio (Brahms)
8 Dec: Birth of Jean Sibelius, Tavastehus
1866
5 Jan: *The Brandenburgers in Bohemia* (Smetana)
1 Apr: Birth of Ferruccio Busoni, Empoli
17 May: Birth of Erik Satie, Honfleur
30 May: *The Bartered Bride* (Smetana)
31 Oct: *La Vie Parisienne* (Offenbach)
17 Nov: *Mignon* (Thomas)
1867
3 Feb: String Sextet no. 2 (Brahms)
11 Mar: *Don Carlos* (Verdi)
27 Apr: *Roméo et Juliette* (Gounod)
27 Jul: Birth of Enrique Granados, Lerinda
27 Nov: Birth of Charles Koechlin, Paris
26 Dec: *La Jolie fille de Perth* (Bizet)
1868
15 Feb: Symphony no. 1 (Tchaikovsky)
5 Mar: *Mefistofele* (Boito)
9 Mar: *Hamlet* (Thomas)
24 Mar: Piano Quintet (Brahms)
9 May: Symphony no. 1 (Bruckner)
16 May *Dalibor* (Smetana)
21 Jun: *Die Meistersinger von Nürnberg* (Wagner)
1869
11 Feb: *Voyevoda* (Tchaikovsky)
18 Feb: *Ein Deutsches Requiem* (Brahms)
8 Mar: Death of Hector Berlioz, Paris
5 Apr: Birth of Albert Roussel, Tourcoing
5 May: Birth of Hans Pfitzner, Moscow
22 Sept: *Das Rheingold* (Wagner)
1870
16 Mar: *Romeo and Juliet*, first version (Tchaikovsky)
25 May: *Coppelia* (Delibes)
26 Jun: *Die Walküre* (Wagner)
17 Dec: Death of Saverio Mercadante, Naples
1871
14 Oct: Birth of Alexander Zemlinsky, Vienna
24 Dec: *Aida* (Verdi)
1872
6 Jan: Birth of Alexander Skriabin, Moscow
22 May: *Djamileh* (Bizet)
12 Oct: Birth of Ralph Vaughan Williams, Down Ampney
10 Nov: *L'Arlésienne* (Bizet)
1873
13 Jan: *The Maid of Pskov* (Rimsky-Korsakov)
7 Feb: Symphony no. 2, *Little Russian* (Tchaikovsky)
18 Oct: String Quartet no. 2, in A minor (Brahms)
26 Oct: Symphony no. 2 (Bruckner)
2 Nov: *Variations on a theme of Haydn* (Brahms)
1 Dec: String Quartet no. 1, in C minor (Brahms)
1874
8 Feb: *Boris Godunov* (Mussorgsky)
29 Mar: Symphony no. 3 (Dvořák)
5 Apr: *Die Fledermaus* (Johann Strauss)
22 May: Requiem (Verdi)
13 Sept: Birth of Arnold Schoenberg, Vienna
20 Oct: Birth of Charles Ives, Danbury
1875
3 Mar: *Carmen* (Bizet)
7 Mar: Birth of Maurice Ravel, Ciboure
3 Jun: Death of Georges Bizet, Paris
25 Oct: Piano Concerto no. 1 (Tchaikovsky)

18 Nov: Piano Quartet no. 3 (Brahms)
19 Nov: Symphony no. 3 (Tchaikovsky)
1876
8 Apr: *La Gioconda* (Ponchielli)
16 Aug: *Siegfried* (Wagner)
17 Aug: *Götterdämmerung* (Wagner)
4 Nov: Symphony no. 1 (Brahms)
23 Nov: Birth of Manuel de Falla, Cadiz
6 Dec: *Vakula the Smith* (Tchaikovsky)
1877
4 Mar: *Swan Lake* (Tchaikovsky)
9 Mar: *Francesca da Rimini* (Tchaikovsky)
27 Apr: *Le Roi de Lahore* (Massenet)
2 Dec: *Samson et Dalila* (Saint-Saëns)
16 Dec: Symphony no. 3 (Bruckner)
30 Dec: Symphony no. 2 (Brahms)
1878
22 Feb: Symphony no. 4 (Tchaikovsky)
23 Mar: Birth of Franz Schreker, Monaco
25 May: *HMS Pinafore* (Sullivan)
18 Sept: *The Secret* (Smetana)
1879
1 Jan: Violin Concerto (Brahms)
25 Mar: Symphony no. 5 (Dvořák)
29 Mar: *Eugene Onegin* (Tchaikovsky)
9 Jul: Birth of Ottorino Respighi, Bologna
29 Nov: Violin Sonata no. 1 (Brahms)
17 Dec: String Quartet op. 51 (Dvořák)
30 Dec: *The Pirates of Penzance* (Sullivan)
1880
17 Jan: Piano Quintet (Franck)
21 Jan: *May Night* (Rimsky-Korsakov)
24 Jul: Birth of Ernest Bloch, Geneva
20 Sept: Birth of Ildebrando Pizzetti, Parma
5 Oct: Death of Jacques Offenbach, Paris
26 Dec: Tragic Overture (Brahms)
1881
10 Feb: *Les Contes d'Hoffmann* (Offenbach)
24 Mar: *Simon Boccanegra*, revised version (Verdi)
25 Mar: Birth of Béla Bartók, Nagyszentmiklós;
     Symphony no. 6 (Dvořák)
9 Nov: Piano Concerto no. 2 (Brahms)
12 Nov: Piano Concerto no. 2 (Tchaikovsky)
1882
10 Feb: *The Snow Maiden* (Rimsky-Korsakov)
17 Jun: Birth of Igor Stravinsky, St Petersburg
26 Jul: *Parsifal* (Wagner)
8 Oct: *Dimitrij* (Dvořák)
16 Dec: Birth of Zoltán Kodaly, Kecskemét
28 Dec: Piano Trio no. 2, String Quartet no. 1 (Brahms)
1883
13 Feb: Death of Richard Wagner, Venice
14 Oct: Violin Concerto (Dvořák)
27 Oct: Piano Trio in F minor (Dvořák)
2 Dec: Symphony no. 3 (Brahms)
3 Dec: Birth of Anton Webern, Vienna
22 Dec: Birth of Edgard Varèse, Paris
1884
10 Jan: *Don Carlos*, Italian version (Verdi)
19 Jan: *Manon* (Massenet)
15 Feb: *Mazeppa* (Tchaikovsky)
12 May: Death of Bedřich Smetana, Prague
31 May: *Le Villi* (Puccini)
30 Dec: Symphony no. 7 (Bruckner)
1885
9 Feb: Birth of Alban Berg, Vienna
4 Mar: Horn Concerto no. 1 (Strauss)
22 Apr: Symphony no. 7 (Dvořák)

24 Oct: *Der Zigeunerbaron* (Johann Strauss)
25 Oct: Symphony no. 4 (Brahms)
30 Nov: *Le Cid* (Massenet)
1886
21 Feb: *Khovanshchina* (Mussorgsky)
23 Mar: *Manfred* Symphony (Tchaikovsky)
1 May: *Romeo and Juliet*, final version (Tchaikovsky)
31 Jul: Death of Franz Liszt, Bayreuth
24 Nov: Cello Sonata no. 2 (Brahms)
2 Dec: Violin Sonata no. 2 (Brahms)
1887
5 Feb: *Otello* (Verdi)
28 Feb: Death of Alexander Borodin, St Petersburg
2 Mar: *Aus Italien* (Strauss)
18 Oct: Double Concerto (Brahms)
1 Nov: *The Enchantress* (Tchaikovsky)
17 Dec: *Capriccio Espagnol* (Rimsky-Korsakov)
1888
29 Jun: *Die Feen* (Wagner); composed 1833
5 Oct: *Caractacus* (Elgar)
3 Nov: *Sheherazade* (Rimsky-Korsakov)
17 Nov: Symphony no. 5 (Tchaikovsky)
24 Nov: *Hamlet* (Tchaikovsky)
22 Dec: Violin Sonata no. 3 (Brahms)
1889
12 Feb: *The Jacobin* (Dvořák)
17 Feb: Symphony in D minor (Franck)
21 Apr: *Edgar* (Puccini)
14 May: *Esclarmonde* (Massenet)
11 Nov: *Don Juan* (Strauss)
20 Nov: Symphony no. 1 (Mahler)
1890
15 Jan: *The Sleeping Beauty* (Tchaikovsky)
2 Feb: Symphony no. 8 (Dvořák)
17 May: *Cavalleria Rusticana* (Mascagni)
21 Jun: *Tod und Verklärung* (Strauss)
4 Nov: *Prince Igor* (Borodin)
19 Dec: *The Queen of Spades* (Tchaikovsky)
1891
16 Jan: Death of Léo Delibes, Paris
31 Jan: *Ivanhoe* (Sullivan)
27 Apr: Birth of Sergey Prokofiev, Ekaterinoslav
9 Oct: Requiem (Dvořák)
31 Oct: *L'Amico Fritz* (Mascagni)
1 Dec: Clarinet Trio and Clarinet Quintet (Brahms)
1892
10 Mar: Birth of Arthur Honegger, Le Havre
28 Apr: *Kullervo Symphony* (Sibelius)
21 May: *Pagliacci* (Leoncavallo)
2 Nov: *Mlada* (Rimsky-Korsakov)
18 Dec: Symphony no. 8 (Bruckner)
18 Dec: *The Nutcracker* (Tchaikovsky)
1893
1 Feb: *Manon Lescaut* (Puccini)
9 Feb: *Falstaff* (Verdi)
28 Oct: *Pathétique Symphony* (Tchaikovsky)
6 Nov: Death of Pyotr Tchaikovsky, St Petersburg
16 Dec: Symphony nó. 9, *From the New World* (Dvořák)
29 Dec: String Quartet (Debussy)
1894
1 Jan: String Quartet in F, *The American* (Dvořák)
10 Feb: *The Beginning of a Novel* (Janáček)
14 Mar: Symphony no. 1 (Nielsen)
16 Mar: *Thaïs* (Massenet)
10 May: *Guntram* (Strauss)
23 Dec: *Prélude à l'après-midi d'un faune* (Debussy)
1895
7 Jan: Clarinet Sonatas (Brahms)

30 Apr: *La Bonne Chanson* (Fauré)
5 Nov: *Till Eulenspiegel* (Strauss)
16 Nov: Birth of Paul Hindemith, Hanau
10 Dec: *Christmas Eve* (Rimsky-Korsakov)
13 Dec: Symphony no. 2 *Resurrection* (Mahler)
1896
1 Feb: *La Bohème* (Puccini)
16 Mar: *Lieder eines fahrenden Gesellen* (Mahler)
19 Mar: Cello Concerto (Dvořák)
28 Mar: *Andrea Chénier* (Giordano)
11 Oct: Death of Anton Bruckner, Vienna
27 Nov: *Also sprach Zarathustra* (Strauss)
1897
15 Mar: Symphony no. 1 (Rakhmaninov)
17 Mar: String Quartet in D (Schoenberg)
3 Apr: Death of Johannes Brahms, Vienna
27 Apr: *Hymnus Amoris* (Nielsen)
10 Oct: *Sarema* (Zemlinsky)
28 Dec: *Šarka* (Fibich)
1898
7 Jan: *Sadko* (Rimsky-Korsakov)
28 Feb: *King Christian II* (Sibelius)
8 Mar: *Don Quixote* (Strauss)
21 Jun: *Pelléas et Mélisande* (Fauré)
26 Sept: Birth of George Gershwin, New York
17 Nov: *Fedora* (Giordano)
1899
3 Mar: *Ein Heldenleben* (Strauss)
26 Apr: Symphony no. 1 (Sibelius)
19 Jun: *Enigma Variations* (Elgar)
5 Oct: *Sea Pictures* (Elgar)
3 Nov: *The Tsar's Bride* (Rimsky-Korsakov)
23 Nov: *The Devil and Kate* (Dvořák)
1900
14 Jan: *Tosca* (Puccini)
2 Mar: Birth of Kurt Weill, Dessau
2 Jul: *Finlandia* (Sibelius)
23 Aug: Birth of Ernst Krenek, Vienna
3 Oct: *The Dream of Gerontius* (Elgar)
14 Nov: Birth of Aaron Copland, Brooklyn
1901
27 Jan: Death of Giuseppe Verdi, Milan
31 Mar: *Rusalka* (Dvořák)
20 Jun: *Cockaigne* Overture (Elgar)
27 Oct: Piano Concerto no. 2 (Rakhmaninov)
21 Nov: *Feuersnot* (Strauss)
24 Nov: Symphony no. 4 (Mahler)
1902
5 Mar: Symphony no. 2 (Sibelius)
18 Mar: *Verklärte Nacht* (Schoenberg)
29 Mar: Birth of William Walton, Oldham
30 Apr: *Pelléas et Mélisande* (Debussy)
9 Jun: Symphony no. 3 (Mahler)
28 Nov: *Saul and David* (Nielsen)
1903
11 Feb: Symphony no. 9 (Bruckner)
22 Feb: Death of Hugo Wolf, Vienna
12 May: Birth of L Berkeley, Oxford
6 Jun: Birth of Aram Khachaturian, Tiblisi
8 Oct: *Helios* overture (Nielsen)
15 Oct: *The Apostles* (Elgar)
1904
21 Jan: *Jenůfa* (Janáček)
8 Feb: Violin Concerto (Sibelius)
17 Feb: *Madama Butterfly* (Puccini)
5 Mar: String Quartet (Ravel)
1 May: Death of Antonin Dvořák, Prague
18 Oct: Symphony no. 5 (Mahler)

1905

2 Jan: Birth of Michael Tippett, London
26 Jan: *Pelleas und Melisande* (Schoenberg)
8 Mar: Introduction and Allegro (Elgar)
29 May: *The Divine Poem* (Skriabin)
9 Sept: *Salome* (Strauss)
15 Oct: *La Mer* (Debussy)

1906

24 May: *Sea Drift* (Delius)
27 May: Symphony no. 6 (Mahler)
25 Sept: Birth of Dmitri Shostakovich, St Petersburg
3 Oct: *The Kingdom* (Elgar)
11 Nov: *Maskarade* (Nielsen)
26 Dec: *Pohjola's Daughter* (Sibelius)

1907

3 Feb: *Miroirs* (Ravel)
5 Feb: String Quartet no. 1, in D minor (Schoenberg)
8 Feb: Chamber Symphony no. 1 (Schoenberg)
20 Feb: *Legend of the Invisible City of Kitezh* (Rimsky-Korsakov)
22 Feb: Introduction and Allegro (Ravel)
26 Sept: Symphony no. 3 (Sibelius)

1908

4 Feb: Symphony in E♭ (Stravinsky)
19 Sept: Symphony no. 7 (Mahler)
3 Dec: Symphony no. 1 (Elgar)
10 Dec: Birth of Olivier Messiaen, Avignon
11 Dec: Birth of Elliott Carter, New York
21 Dec: String Quartet no. 2 (Schoenberg)

1909

9 Jan: *Gaspard de la Nuit* (Ravel)
25 Jan: *Elektra* (Strauss)
7 Jun: *A Mass of Life* (Delius)
7 Oct: *The Golden Cockerel* (Rimsky-Korsakov)
15 Nov: *On Wenlock Edge* (Vaughan Williams)
28 Nov: Piano Concerto no. 3 (Rakhmaninov)

1910

19 Mar: String Quartet no. 1 (Bartók)
25 Jun: *The Firebird* (Stravinsky)
6 Sept: *Fantasia on a Theme of Thomas Tallis* (Vaughan Williams)
12 Sept: Symphony no. 8 (Mahler)
12 Oct: *A Sea Symphony* (Vaughan Williams)
10 Dec: *La fanciulla del West* (Puccini)

1911

26 Jan: *Der Rosenkavalier* (Strauss)
3 Apr: Symphony no. 4 (Sibelius)
18 May: Death of Gustav Mahler, Vienna
24 May: Symphony no. 2 (Elgar)
13 Jun: *Petrushka* (Stravinsky)
20 Nov: *Das Lied von der Erde* (Mahler)

1912

8 Jun: *Daphnis et Chloë* (Ravel)
26 Jun: Symphony no. 9 (Mahler)
7 Aug: Piano concerto no. 1 (Prokofiev)
3 Sept: Five Orchestral Pieces (Schoenberg)
5 Sept: Birth of John Cage, Los Angeles
16 Oct: *Pierrot Lunaire* (Schoenberg)

1913

26 Jan: *Images pour Orchestre* (Debussy)
23 Feb: *Gurrelieder* (Schoenberg)
15 May: *Jeux* (Debussy)
29 May: *The Rite of Spring* (Stravinsky)
2 Oct: *Falstaff* (Elgar)
22 Nov: Birth of Benjamin Britten, Lowestoft

1914

27 Mar: *A London Symphony* (Vaughan Williams)
1 Apr: *Notre Dame* (Schmidt)
26 May: *The Nightingale* (Stravinsky)

4 Jun: *The Oceanides* (Sibelius)
28 Aug: Death of Anatol Liadov, Novgorod
3 Sept: Death of Albéric Magnard, Marne

1915

5 Feb: *Variations and Fugue on a theme of Mozart* (Reger)
15 Apr: *El Amor Brujo* (Falla)
27 Apr: Death of Alexander Skriabin, Moscow
10 May: *North Country Sketches* (Delius)
28 Oct: *Eine Alpensinfonie* (Strauss)
8 Dec: Symphony no. 5 (Sibelius)

1916

28 Jan: *Goyescas* (Granados)
29 Jan: *Scythian Suite* (Prokofiev)
1 Feb: Symphony no. 4, *The Inextinguishable* (Nielsen)
9 Apr: *Nights in the Gardens of Spain* (Falla)
4 Oct: *Ariadne auf Naxos*, revised version (Strauss)
10 Dec: Sonata for flute, viola and harp (Debussy)

1917

20 Jan: Symphony no. 3 *The Song of the Night* (Szymanowski)
5 May: Violin Sonata (Debussy)
11 May: *Arlecchino* and *Turandot* (Busoni)
12 May: *The Wooden Prince* (Bartók)
27 May: *La Rondine* (Puccini)
12 Jun: *Palestrina* (Pfitzner)

1918

25 Mar: Death of Claude Debussy, Paris
21 Apr: Symphony no. 1 *Classical* (Prokofiev)
24 May: *Duke Bluebeard's Castle* (Bartók)
25 Aug: Birth of Leonard Bernstein, Lawrence, MS
29 Sept: *The Planets* (Holst)
14 Dec: *Il Trittico* (Puccini)

1919

10 Apr: *Masques et Bergamasques* (Fauré)
11 Apr: *Le Tombeau de Couperin*, piano (Ravel)
22 Jul: *The Three-Cornered Hat* (Falla)
10 Oct: *Die Frau ohne Schatten* (Strauss)
21 Oct: *Fennimore and Gerda* (Delius)
27 Oct: Cello Concerto (Elgar)

1920

21 Jan: *Der Schatzgräber* (Schreker)
25 Mar: *The Hymn of Jesus* (Holst)
21 Apr: Birth of Bruno Maderna, Venice
23 Apr: *The Excursions of Mr Brouček* (Janáček)
15 May: *Pulcinella* (Stravinsky)
8 Nov: *Le Tombeau de Couperin*, ballet (Ravel)
12 Dec: *La Valse* (Ravel)

1921

18 Apr: *Diary of a Young Man who Disappeared* (Janáček)
10 Jun: *Symphonies of Wind Instruments* (Stravinsky)
14 Jun: *The Lark Ascending* (Vaughan Williams)
23 Nov: *Katya Kabanova* (Janáček)
16 Dec: Piano Concerto no. 3 (Prokofiev)
30 Dec: *The Love for Three Oranges* (Prokofiev)

1922

24 Jan: Symphony no. 5 (Nielsen)
26 Jan: *A Pastoral Symphony* (Vaughan Williams)
26 Mar: *Sancta Susanna* (Hindemith)
13 May: *L'Horizon Chimérique* (Fauré)
18 May: *Renard* (Stravinsky)
19 Oct: *Pictures at an Exhibition* (Mussorgsky/Ravel)

1923

19 Feb: Symphony no. 6 (Sibelius)
4 Mar: *Hyperprism* (Varèse)
1 Jun: *Padmavatî* (Roussel)
12 Jun: *Façade* (Walton)
13 Jun: *The Wedding* (Stravinsky)
18 Oct: Violin Concerto no. 1 (Prokofiev)

1924

24 Mar: Symphony no. 7 (Sibelius)
6 Jun: *Erwartung* (Schoenberg)
9 Oct: *Taras Bulba* (Janáček)
14 Oct: *Die glückliche Hand* (Schoenberg)
6 Nov: *The Cunning Little Vixen* (Janáček)
29 Nov: Death of Giacomo Puccini, Brussels

1925

21 Mar: *L'Enfant et les Sortilèges* (Ravel)
26 Mar: Birth of Pierre Boulez, Montbrison
21 May: *Doktor Faust* (Busoni)
24 Oct: Birth of Luciano Berio, Oneglia
11 Dec: Symphony no. 6 *Semplice* (Nielsen)
14 Dec: *Wozzeck* (Berg)

1926

25 Apr: *Turandot* (Puccini)
12 May: Symphony no. 1 (Shostakovich)
29 Jun: Sinfonietta (Janáček)
1 Jul: Birth of Hans Werner Henze, Gütersloh
27 Nov: *The Miraculous Mandarin* (Bartók)
18 Dec: *The Makropoulos Case* (Janáček)

1927

8 Jan: *Lyric Suite* (Berg)
10 Feb: *Jonny spielt auf* (Krenek)
30 May: Oedipus Rex (Stravinsky)
1 Jul: Piano Concerto no. 1 (Bartók)
19 Sept: String Quartet no. 3 (Schoenberg)
5 Dec: *Glagolitic Mass* (Janáček)

1928

27 Apr: *Apollon Musagetes* (Stravinsky)
6 Jun: *Die Aegyptische Helena* (Strauss)
12 Aug: Death of Janáček, Morava-Ostrava
22 Aug: Birth of Karlheinz Stockhausen, Cologne
31 Aug: *Die Driegroschenoper* (Weill)
11 Sept: String Quartet no. 2 *Intimate Letters* (Janáček)
2 Dec: Variations for Orchestra (Schoenberg)

1929

20 Mar: String Quartet no. 2 (Bartók)
21 Mar: *Sir John in Love* (Vaughan Williams)
29 Apr: *The Gambler* (Prokofiev)
8 Jun: *Neues vom Tage* (Hindemith)
3 Oct: Viola concerto (Walton)
6 Dec: *Capriccio* (Stravinsky)

1930

1 Feb: *Von Heute auf Morgen* (Schoenberg)
9 Mar: *Aufstieg und Fall der Stadt Mahagonny* (Weill)
12 Apr: *From the House of the Dead* (Janáček)
23 Oct: *Job* (Vaughan Williams); concert
13 Dec: *Symphony of Psalms* (Stravinsky)

1931

10 Jan: *Three Places in New England* (Ives)
19 Feb: *Les Offrandes Oubliées* (Messiaen)
3 Oct: Death of Carl Nielsen, Copenhagen
8 Oct: *Belshazzar's Feast* (Walton)
23 Oct: Violin Concerto (Stravinsky)
27 Nov: Concerto for the piano, left hand (Ravel)

1932

14 Jan: Piano Concerto (Ravel)
21 Feb: Four Songs for voice and orchestra (Schoenberg)
10 Mar: *Die Burgschaft* (Weill)
21 Mar: *Songs of Farewell* (Delius)
24 Apr: *The Spinning Room* (Kodály)
28 Oct: *Duo Concertante* (Stravinsky)

1933

18 Feb: *Der Silbersee* (Weill)
23 Feb: Piano Concerto no. 2 (Bartók)
6 Mar: *Ionisation* (Varèse)

23 Mar: *Hymne au Saint-Sacrement* (Messiaen)
1 Jul: *Arabella* (Strauss)
23 Nov: Birth of Krzysztof Penderecki, Debica

1934

22 Jan: *Lady Macbeth of Mtsensk* (Shostakovich)
23 Feb: Death of Edward Elgar, Worcester
15 Jul: Birth of Harrison Birtwistle, Accrington
8 Sept: Birth of Peter Maxwell Davies, Manchester
7 Nov: *Paganini Rhapsody* (Rakhmaninov)
24 Nov: Birth of Alfred Schnittke, Engels

1935

8 Apr: String Quartet no. 5 (Bartók)
10 Apr: Symphony no. 4 (Vaughan Williams)
30 Sept: *Porgy and Bess* (Gershwin)
6 Nov: Symphony no. 1 (Walton)
1 Dec: Violin Concerto no. 2 (Prokofiev)
24 Dec: Death of Alban Berg, Vienna

1936

4 Mar: Birth of Aribert Reimann, Berlin
19 Apr: Violin Concerto (Berg)
25 Sept: *Five Tudor Portraits* (Vaughan Williams); *Our Hunting Fathers* (Britten)
6 Nov: Symphony no. 3 (Rakhmaninov)
11 Dec: *Dances of Galanta* (Kodály)

1937

9 Jan: String Quartet no. 4 (Schoenberg)
21 Jan: *Music for Strings, Percussion and Celesta* (Bartók)
2 Jun: *Lulu*, acts 1 and 2 (Berg)
8 Jun: *Carmina Burana* (Orff)
27 Aug: *Variations on a theme of Frank Bridge* (Britten)
21 Nov: Symphony no. 5 (Shostakovich)

1938

16 Jan: Sonata for two pianos and percussion (Bartók)
28 May: *Mathis der Maler* (Hindemith)
22 Jun: *Karl V* (Krenek)
5 Oct: *Serenade to Music* (Vaughan Williams)
15 Oct: *Daphne* (Strauss)
30 Dec: *Romeo and Juliet* (Prokofiev)

1939

20 Jan: *Concord Sonata* (Ives); composed 1909–15
23 Mar: Violin Concerto no. 2 (Bartók)
17 May: *Alexander Nevsky* (Prokofiev)
24 May: *Billy the Kid* (Copland)
5 Nov: Symphony no. 6 (Shostakovich)
7 Dec: Violin Concerto (Walton)

1940

30 Jan: *Les Illuminations* (Britten)
28 Mar: Violin Concerto (Britten)
21 Apr: Concerto for Double String Orchestra (Tippett)
11 Jun: *Divertimento* (Bartók)
7 Nov: Symphony in C (Stravinsky)
6 Dec: Violin Concerto (Schoenberg)

1941

15 Jan: *Quatuor pour le fin du Temps* (Messiaen)
20 Jan: String Quartet no. 6 (Bartók)
7 Feb: Cello Concerto (Hindemith)
14 Feb: Concerto Grosso (Martinů)
30 Mar: *Sinfonia da Requiem* (Britten)
11 Dec: *Canti di Prigionia* (Dallapiccola)

1942

16 Jan: *Diversions* (Britten)
8 Feb: *Danses Concertantes* (Stravinsky)
5 Mar: Symphony no. 7, *Leningrad* (Shostakovich)
15 Mar: Death of Alexander Zemlinsky, Larchmont, NY
28 Oct: *Capriccio* (Strauss)
5 Dec: *A Ceremony of Carols* (Britten)

1943

28 Mar: Death of Sergey Rakhmaninov, Beverly Hills
10 May: *Visions de l'Amen* (Messiaen)
5 Jun: *Boyhood's End* (Tippett) .
24 Jun: Symphony no. 5 (Vaughan Williams)
15 Oct: *Serenade* (Britten)
4 Nov: Symphony no. 8 (Shostakovich)

1944

20 Jan: *Symphonic Metamorphosis* (Hindemith)
6 Feb: Piano Concerto (Schoenberg)
19 Mar: *A Child of our Time* (Tippett)
16 Aug: *Die Liebe der Danae* (Strauss)
17 Oct: *War and Peace*, concert (Prokofiev)
1 Dec: Concerto for Orchestra (Bartók)

1945

13 Jan: Symphony no. 5 (Prokofiev)
21 Apr: *Trois Petites Liturgies* (Messiaen)
7 Jun: *Peter Grimes* (Britten)
15 Sept: Death of Anton Webern, Mittersill
26 Sept: Death of Béla Bartók, New York
3 Nov: Symphony no. 9 (Shostakovich)

1946

24 Jan: Symphony in Three Movements (Stravinsky)
8 Feb: Piano Concerto no. 3 (Bartók)
26 Feb: Oboe Concerto (Strauss)
5 Apr: Symphony no. 3 (Ives); composed 1901–04
12 Jul: *The Rape of Lucretia* (Britten)
16 Dec: *Street Scene* (Weill)

1947

27 Jan: Concerto for Strings (Stravinsky)
1 May: String Trio (Schoenberg)
7 May: *The Mother of us All* (Thomson)
3 Jun: *Les Mamelles de Tirésias* (Poulenc)
20 Jun: *Albert Herring* (Britten)
11 Oct: Symphony no. 6 (Prokofiev)

1948

6 Apr: Symphony no. 1 (Lutosławski)
21 Apr: Symphony no. 6 (Vaughan Williams)
29 Apr: *Orpheus* (Stravinsky)
24 Oct: Sinfonietta (Poulenc)
27 Oct: Mass (Stravinsky)
4 Nov: *A Survivor from Warsaw* (Schoenberg)

1949

8 Apr: Symphony no. 2, *The Age of Anxiety* (Bernstein)
9 Jul: *Spring Symphony* (Britten)
8 Sept: Death of Richard Strauss, Garmisch
1 Dec: *Il Prigioniero* (Dallapiccola)
2 Dec: *Turangalîla-Symphonie* (Messiaen);
Viola Concerto (Bartók)

1950

3 Apr: Death of Kurt Weill, New York
22 May: *Four Last Songs* (Strauss)
8 Jun: Horn Concerto (Hindemith)
23 Jun: Cantata no. 2 (Webern)
18 Jul: *Le Soleil des Eaux* (Boulez)
31 Dec: Death of Charles Koechlin, Canadal, Var

1951

22 Feb: Symphony no. 2 (Ives); composed 1897–1902
9 Mar: Symphony no. 5, *Tre Re* (Honegger)
26 Apr: *The Pilgrim's Progress* (Vaughan Williams)
13 Jul: Death of Arnold Schoenberg, Los Angeles
11 Sept: *The Rake's Progress* (Stravinsky)
1 Dec: *Billy Budd* (Britten)

1952

18 Feb: Symphonie Concertante (Prokofiev)
24 Jan: Symphony, *Die Harmonie der Welt* (Hindemith)
17 Feb: *Boulevard Solitude* (Henze)
3 May: *Water Music* (Cage)

12 Jun: *Trouble in Tahiti* (Bernstein)
11 Nov: *Cantata* (Stravinsky)

1953

14 Jan: *Sinfonia Antartica* (Vaughan Williams)
24 Jan: *Altenberglieder* (Berg); composed 1912
26 Feb: String Quartet no. 1 (Carter)
5 Mar: Death of Sergey Prokofiev, Moscow
8 Jun: *Gloriana* (Britten)
29 Aug: *Fantasia Concertante* (Tippett)

1954

12 Mar: *Moses und Aron*, concert (Schoenberg); composed 1930-32
19 May: Death of Charles Ives, New York
12 Sept: *Serenade* (Bernstein)
14 Sept: *The Turn of the Screw* (Britten)
26 Nov: Concerto for Orchestra (Lutosławski)
3 Dec: *Troilus and Cressida* (Walton)

1955

27 Jan: *The Midsummer Marriage* (Tippett)
21 Mar: *Le Livre d'Orgue* (Messiaen)
18 Jun: *Le Marteau sans Maître* (Boulez)
29 Sept: *The Fiery Angel*, stage (Prokofiev)
29 Oct: Violin Concerto no. 1 (Shostakovich)
27 Nov: Death of Arthur Honegger, Paris

1956

10 Mar: *Oiseaux Exotiques* (Messiaen)
13 Sept: *Canticum Sacrum* (Stravinsky)
23 Sept: *König Hirsch* (Henze)
29 Oct: *Candide* (Bernstein)
30 Oct: Piano Concerto (Tippett)
15 Dec: *Zeitmasze* (Stockhausen)

1957

25 Jan: Cello Concerto (Walton)
26 Jan: *Dialogues des Carmélites* (Poulenc)
17 Jun: *Agon* (Stravinsky)
11 Aug: *Die Harmonie der Welt* (Hindemith)
20 Sept: Death of Jean Sibelius, Jarvenpaa
30 Oct: Symphony no. 11 (Shostakovich)

1958

5 Feb: Symphony no. 2 (Tippett)
24 Mar: *Gruppen* (Stockhausen)
2 Apr: Symphony no. 9 (Vaughan Williams)
26 Aug: Death of Ralph Vaughan Williams, London
23 Sept: *Threni* (Stravinsky)
16 Oct: *Nocturne* (Britten)

1959

6 Feb: *La Voix Humaine* (Poulenc)
15 Apr: *Catalogue d'Oiseaux* (Messiaen)
25 Aug: *Zyklus* (Stockhausen)
28 Aug: Death of Bohuslav Martinů, Liestal
20 Sept: *Strophes* (Penderecki)
4 Oct: Cello Concerto no. 1 (Shostakovich)

1960

22 May: *Der Prinz von Homburg* (Henze)
11 Jun: *Kontakte* (Stockhausen);
A Midsummer Night's Dream (Britten)
2 Sept: Symphony no. 2 (Walton)
16 Oct: *Chronochromie* (Messiaen)
28 Oct: *Carré* (Stockhausen)

1961

13 Apr: *Intolleranza 1960* (Dallapiccola)
31 May: *Threnody [for the Victims of Hiroshima]* (Penderecki)
9 Jun: *The Greek Passion* (Martinů)
16 Jun: *Die Jakobsleiter* (Schoenberg); composed 1917–22
6 Sept: Double Concerto (Carter)
22 Oct: *Atmosphères* (Ligeti)

1962

21 May: *Momente* (Stockhausen)
29 May: *King Priam* (Tippett)
30 May: *War Requiem* (Britten)
18 Jun: *Atlantida* (Falla); composed 1927-46
20 Oct: *Pli selon Pli* (Boulez)
18 Dec: Symphony no. 13, *Babi Yar* (Shostakovich)

1963

30 Jan: Death of Francis Poulenc, Paris
23 Apr: *Strategie* (Xenakis)
24 Apr: *Novae de infinito Laudes* (Henze)
30 Sept: *Sept Haikai* (Messiaen)
20 Oct: *Punkte* (Stockhausen)
28 Dec: Death of Paul Hindemith, Frankfurt

1964

10 Jan: *Figures-Doubles-Prismes* (Boulez)
12 Mar: Cello Symphony (Britten)
12 Jun: *Curlew River* (Britten)
11 Jul: *Entr'actes and Sappho Fragments* (Birtwistle)
13 Aug: Symphony no. 10 (Mahler); composed 1909–10
17 Oct: *Couleurs de la Cité Céleste* (Messiaen)

1965

15 Feb: *Die Soldaten* (Zimmermann)
26 Apr: Symphony no. 4 (Ives); composed 1910–16
7 May: *Et Expecto Reurrectionem Mortuorum* (Messiaen)
20 Jun: *Paroles Tissées* (Lutosławski)
15 Jul: *Chichester Psalms* (Bernstein)
20 Aug: *Tragoedia* (Birtwistle)

1966

19 Jan: *The Vision of St Augustine* (Tippett)
30 Mar: *St Luke Passion* (Penderecki)
9 Jun: *The Burning Fiery Furnace* (Britten)
6 Aug: *The Bassarids* (Henze)
16 Sept: *Antony and Cleopatra* (Barber)
8 Oct: *Requiem Canticles* (Stravinsky)

1967

6 Jan: Piano Concerto (Carter)
14 Feb: *Chorales for Orchestra* (Birtwistle)
19 Apr: Cello Concerto (Ligeti)
9 Jun: Symphony no. 2 (Lutosławski)
26 Sept: Violin Concerto no. 2 (Shostakovich)
30 Nov: *Hymnen* (Stockhausen)

1968

8 Jun: *Punch and Judy* (Birtwistle)
28 Aug: *Worldes Blis* (Davies)
29 Sept: *Ulisse* (Dallapiccola)
10 Oct: *Sinfonia* (Berio)
9 Dec: *Stimmung* (Stockhausen)
20 Dec: *Domaines* (Boulez)

1969

12 Feb: *Verses for Ensembles* (Birtwistle)
22 Apr: *Eight Songs for a Mad King* (Davies)
8 May: *Down by the Greenwood Side* (Birtwistle)
7 Jun: *La Transfiguration* (Messiaen)
20 Jun: *The Devils of Loudun* (Penderecki)
8 Dec: *Livres pour Cordes I* (Boulez)

1970

5 Feb: Concerto for Orchestra (Carter)
12 Aug: *Opera* (Berio)
25 Sept: *Cummings ist der Dichter* (Boulez)
29 Sept: Symphony no. 14 (Shostakovich)
14 Oct: Cello Concerto (Lutosławski)
2 Dec: *The Knot Garden* (Tippett)

1971

29 Jan: *Das Floss der Medusa* (Henze)
6 Apr: Death of Igor Stravinsky, New York
2 Jun: *An Imaginary Landscape* (Birtwistle)
5 Jun: *Sternklang* (Stockhausen)

30 Jun: *From Stone to Flower* (Davies)
3 Dec: *Drumming* (Reich)

1972

8 Jan: Symphony no. 15 (Shostakovich)
20 Mar: *Meditations sur le mystère de la Sainte-Trinité* (Messiaen)
1 Jun: *The Triumph of Time* (Birtwistle)
22 Jun: Symphony no. 3 (Tippett)
12 Jul: *Taverner* (Davies)
15 Oct: *Polytope* (Xenakis)

1973

5 Jan: ... *'explosante fixe'*... (Boulez)
23 Jan: String Quartet no. 3 (Carter)
16 Mar: *Satyricon* (Maderna)
16 Jun: *Death in Venice* (Britten)
15 Oct: *Clocks and Clouds* (Ligeti)
13 Nov: Death of Bruno Maderna, Darmstadt

1974

9 Feb: Symphony no. 1 (Schnittke)
22 Jun: *Ultimos Ritos* (Tavener)
16 Oct: *Points on a curve to find* (Berio)
20 Oct: *Inori* (Stockhausen);
Tristan (Henze)
20 Nov: *Des Canyons aux Étoiles* (Messiaen)

1975

8 Jan: *San Francisco Polyphony* (Ligeti)
19 Feb: Death of Luigi Dallapiccola, Florence
2 Apr: *Rituel* (Boulez)
4 Apr: *Al gran sole carico d'amore* (Nono)
16 May: *Atem gibt das Leben* (Stockhausen)
9 Aug: Death of Dmitri Shostakovich, Moscow

1976

24 Feb: *A Mirror on which to Dwell* (Carter)
24 Apr: *Music for Eighteen Musicians* (Reich)
18 Jul: *Sirius* (Stockhausen)
25 Jul: *Einstein on the Beach* (Glass)
18 Sept: *Melencolia I* (Birtwistle)
4 Dec: Death of Benjamin Britten, Aldeburgh

1977

17 Feb: *Symphony of Three Orchestras* (Carter)
21 Mar: Concerto Grosso no. 1 (Schnittke)
5 Jul: *Bow Down* (Birtwistle)
7 Jul: *The Ice Break* (Tippett)
6 Oct: Symphony no. 4 (Tippett)
20 Nov: *The Magic Fountain* (Delius); composed 1894–95

1978

24 Jan: *Carmen Arcadiae Mechanicae Perpetuum* (Birtwistle)
2 Feb: Symphony no. 1 (Davies)
10 Feb: *Syringa* (Carter)
12 Mar: *Les Espaces du Sommeil* (Lutosławski)
9 Jul: *Lear* (Reimann)
10 Nov: *Salome* (Davies)

1979

25 Jan: *Ritorno degli snovidenia* (Berio)
29 Jan: Violin Concerto no. 3 (Schnittke)
24 Feb: *Lulu* (Berg); three-act version
17 Mar: *Orpheus* (Henze)
9 Apr: *....agm....* (Birtwistle)
20 May: String Quartet no. 4 (Tippett)

1980

23 Apr: Symphony no. 2 (Schnittke)
22 Aug: Triple Concerto (Tippett)
24 Aug: Double Concerto (Lutosławski)
2 Sept: *The Lighthouse* (Davies)
5 Sept: *Satyagraha* (Glass)
14 Nov: Piano Concerto (Ligeti)

1981
23 Jan: Death of Samuel Barber, New York
26 Feb: Symphony no. 2 (Davies)
3 Apr: *Donnerstag aus Licht* (Stockhausen)
18 Oct: *Répons* (Boulez)
5 Nov: Symphony no. 3 (Schnittke)
21 Nov: *Tehillin* (Reich)
1982
20 Feb: *Grand Pianola Music* (Adams)
21 Feb: *Margot-la-rouge* (Delius); composed 1901–02
9 Mar: *La Vera Storia* (Berio)
15 Apr: *Offertorium* (Gubaidulina)
11 May: *Black Pentecost* (Davies)
1 Oct: *Vermont Counterpoint* (Reich)
1983
23 Apr: *Triple Duo* (Carter)
22 May: *Into the Labyrinth* (Davies)
2 Jun: *The English Cat* (Henze)
19 Jun: *Seid nuchtern und wachet ...* (Schnittke)
29 Sept: Symphony no. 2 (Lutosławski)
28 Nov: *St François d'Assise* (Messiaen)
1984
17 Mar: *The Desert Music* (Reich)
24 Mar: *Akhnaten* (Glass)
5 Apr: *The Mask of Time* (Tippett)
25 May: *Samstag aus Licht* (Stockhausen)
7 Aug: *Un re in Ascolto* (Berio)
13 Dec: Symphony no. 7 (Henze)
1985
18 Feb: Symphony no. 3 (Davies)
1 Mar: *Harriet, the Woman called Moses*
   (Musgrave)
21 Mar: *Harmonielehre* (Adams)
31 Mar: *Esprit rude/Esprit doux* (Carter)
19 Apr: *Behold the Sun* (Goehr)
26 Jul: *Penthode* (Carter)
1986
9 Jan: Viola Concerto (Schnittke)
20 Jan: *New York Counterpoint* (Reich)
14 Mar: *Earth Dances* (Birtwistle)
21 May: *The Mask of Orpheus* (Birtwistle)
5 Aug: *Yan Tan Tethera* (Birtwistle)
15 Aug: *Die schwarze Maske* (Penderecki)
1987
15 Jan: *Formazioni* (Berio)
1 May: *Endless Parade* (Birtwistle)
5 Jul: *Eis Thanaton* (Tavener)
8 Jul: *A Night at the Chinese Opera* (Weir)
5 Nov: *Electric Counterpoint* (Reich)
12 Dec: *Europeras* 1 and 2 (Cage)
1988
7 May: *Montag aus Licht* (Stockhausen)
19 Aug: Piano Concerto (Lutosławski)

21 Sept: Trumpet Concerto (Davies)
29 Oct: *Fearful Symmetries* (Adams)
2 Nov: *Different Trains* (Reich)
10 Nov: Concerto Grosso no. 4 (Schnittke)
1989
8 Apr: *Odyssey* (Maw)
10 Sept: Symphony no. 4 (Davies)
30 Sept: Death of Virgil Thomson, New York
5 Oct: *Three Occasions* for Orchestra (Carter)
21 Oct: String Quartet no. 4 (Schnittke)
27 Oct: *New Year* (Tippett)
1990
2 May: Violin Concerto (Carter)
27 May: Cello Concerto no. 2 (Schnittke)
3 Nov: Violin Concerto (Ligeti)
14 Oct: Death of Leonard Bernstein, New York
17 Oct: *Partita* for violin and orchestra (Lutosławski)
2 Dec: Death of Aaron Copland, Tarrytown, NY
1991
19 Mar: *The Death of Klinghoffer* (Adams)
11 Apr: *Byzantium* (Tippett)
30 May: *Gawain* (Birtwistle)
19 Sept: *The Repentant Thief* (Tavener)
19 Dec: *The Ghosts of Versailles* (Corigliano)
23 Dec: Death of Ernst Krenek, Palm Springs
1992
15 Feb: Death of William Schuman, New York
13 Apr: *Life with an Idiot* (Schnittke)
27 Apr: Death of Olivier Messiaen, Clichy
10 May: *Dienstag aus Licht* (Stockhausen)
12 Aug: Death of John Cage, New York
12 Oct: *The Voyage* (Glass)
1993
17 Jan: Chamber Symphony (Adams)
5 May: *Antiphonies* for piano and orchestra (Birtwistle)
16 May: *The Cave* (Reich)
4 Jun: *Gra* (Carter)
25 Sept: Symphony no. 6 (Schnittke)
8 Oct: *Cassandra* (Firsova)
1994
7 Feb: Death of Witold Lutosławski, Warsaw
17 Feb: *Partita* (Carter)
9 Aug: Symphony no. 5 (Davies)
19 Oct: Triple Concerto (Schnittke)
24 Oct: *The Second Mrs Kong* (Birtwistle)
29 Nov: *Zeitgestalten* (Gubaidulina)
1995
16 Jan: *The Cry of Anubis* (Birtwistle)
7 Mar: *City Life* (Reich)
3 Apr: *The Beltane Fire* (Davies)
26 May: *Gesualdo* (Schnittke)
22 Jun: *Historia von D Johann Fausten* (Schnittke)
15 Sept: *Arianna* (Goehr)

This brief discography gives suggested recordings which are of recognized quality but not necessarily 'definitive' and provide a wide range of performance styles. Local music libraries often contain items which are not immediately available in shops.

Bach
Partita in D minor for solo violin (Grumiaux) Philips
Brandenburg Concerto no. 1 (Harnoncourt) Teldec
Orchestral Suite no. 3 (Koopman) Harmonia Mundi
Magnificat in D (Kirkby/Chance/Ainsley/Hickox) Chandos
St Matthew Passion (English Baroque Soloists/Gardiner) Archiv
Cantata no. 140 (Baird/Minter/Rifkin) L'Oiseau Lyre
Christmas Oratorio (Schlick/Chance/Herreweghe) Virgin
Goldberg Variations (Pinnock) Archiv
Mass in B minor (Janowitz/Ludwig/Karajan) DGG
The Art of Fugue (Walcha) Archiv

Bartók
Duke Bluebeard's Castle (Ramey/Marton/A Fischer) CBS
The Miraculous Mandarin (Philharmonia/Järvi) Chandos
Piano Concerto no. 2 (Pollini/Chicago SO/Abbado) DGG
String Quartet no. 5 (Emerson) DGG
Music for Strings, Percussion and Celesta (Oslo PO/Jansons) EMI
Sonata for 2 pianos and 2 percussion (Solti/Glennie) CBS
Violin Concerto no. 2 (Midori/Berlin PO/Mehta) Sony
Divertimento for strings (Chicago SO/Solti) Decca
Concerto for Orchestra (Chicago SO/Reiner) RCA
Piano Concerto no. 3 (Anda/Fricsay) DGG

Beethoven
Septet (Vienna Octet) Decca
Symphony no. 3 (*Eroica*) (Philharmonia/Klemperer) EMI
Fidelio (Ludwig/Vickers/Klemperer) EMI
Symphony no. 6 (London PO/Tennstedt) EMI
Piano Concerto no. 5 (*Emperor*) (Pollini/Berlin PO/Abbado) DGG
Symphony no. 7 (Vienna PO/C Kleiber) DGG
Symphony no. 9 (*Choral*) (Vienna PO/Furtwängler) EMI
Mass in D (*Missa Solemnis*) (English Baroque Soloists/Gardiner) Archiv
Variations on a Waltz by Diabelli (Kovacevich) Philips
String Quartet in A minor (Vegh) Telefunken

Bellini
Il pirata (Cappuccilli/Caballe/Gavazzeni) EMI
Zaira (Ricciarelli/Olmi) Nuova Era
I Capuleti e i Montecchi (Ricciarelli) Nuova Era
La sonnambula (Callas/Votto) EMI
Norma (Callas/Ludwig) EMI
Beatrice di Tenda (Sutherland/Pavarotti) Decca
I puritani (Callas/Di Stefano/Serafin) EMI
Oboe Concerto (Holliger/Inbal) Philips

Berg
7 Early Songs (Popp/Gage) RCA
String Quartet op. 3 (Kronos) Nonesuch
Altenberglieder (Price/LSO/Abbado) DGG
Three Orchestral Pieces (Berlin PO/Karajan) DGG
Wozzeck (Grundheber/Behrens/Abbado) DGG
Chamber Concerto (Barenboim/Zukerman/Boulez) DGG
Lyric Suite for string quartet (Alban Berg) Teldec
Der Wein (Norman/Boulez) Sony
Lulu (Stratas/Mazura/Riegel/Boulez) DGG
Violin Concerto (Mutter/Chicago SO/Levine) DGG

Berio
Opus Number Zoo (Vienna/Berlin Ens) Sony
Circles (Berberian/Casadesus) Wergo
Wasserklavier (K and M Labèque) Sony
Sequenza V (Lindberg) BIS
Sinfonia (Electric Phoenix/R Chailly) Decca

Laborintus II (Musique Vivante/Berio) Harmonia Mundi
Eindrücke (French National Orch/Boulez) Erato
11 Folk Songs (Vaness/R Chailly) Decca
Coro (Cologne RSO/Berio) DGG
Formazioni (Concertgebouw Orch/R Chailly) Decca

Berlioz
Symphonie fantastique (Orch Revolutionnaire/Gardiner) Philips
Harold en Italie (Imai/LSO/C Davis) Philips
Benvenuto Cellini (Gedda/Soyer/C Davis) Philips
Messe des morts (Domingo/Paris Orch/Barenboim) DGG
Roméo et Juliette (Otter/Morris/Berlin PO/Levine) DGG
Nuits d'été (Crespin/Ansermet) Decca
La damnation du Faust (Gedda/Veasey/Bastin/C Davis) Philips
L'enfance du Christ (Tear/Murray/Allen) EMI
Les Troyens (Vickers/Lindholm/C Davis) Philips
Béatrice et Bénédict (Graham/McNair/Nelson) Erato

Bernstein
Symphony no. 1 (*Jeremiah*) (St Louis SO/Bernstein) RCA
On the Town (Von Stade/Hampson/LSO/Thomas) DGG
Prelude, Fugue and Riffs (Stoltzman/LSO) RCA
Symphony no. 2 (*The Age of Anxiety*) (Kahane/Bournemouth SO) Virgin
Serenade (Kremer/Israel PO/Bernstein) DGG
Candide (Hadley/Anderson/LSO/Bernstein) DGG
West Side Story (Te Kanawa/Carreras/Bernstein) DGG
Chichester Psalms (Israel PO/Bernstein) DGG
Mass (Titus/Bernstein) Sony
Songfest (Dale/Reardon/Gramm) DGG

Birtwistle
Verses for Ensembles (Netherlands Wind Ensemble) Etcetera
Punch and Judy (Roberts/DeGaetani/Atherton) Etcetera
The Triumph of Time (Philharmonia/Howarth) Collins
Melencolia I (Pay/London Sinfonietta/Knussen) NMC
Carmen Arcadiae Mechanicae Perpetuum (London Sinfonietta/Howarth) Etcetera
Secret Theatre (London Sinfonietta/Howarth) Etcetera
Earth Dance (BBC SO/Eötvös) Collins
Endless Parade (BBC PO/Howarth) Philips
Ritual Fragment (London Sinfonietta/Knussen) NMC
Gawain's Journey (Philharmonia/Howarth) Collins

Bizet
Symphony in C major (French Radio Orch/Beecham) EMI
Roma (RPO/Batiz) ASV
Les Pêcheurs de perles (Hendricks/Aler/Plasson) EMI
Jeux d'enfants (Montreal SO/Dutoit) Decca
Djamileh (Munich Radio Orch/Gardelli) Orfeo
L'Arlésienne (Philharmonia/Karajan) EMI
Carmen (Berganza/Domingo/Milnes/Abbado) DGG

Borodin
Symphony no. 1 (Gothenburg SO/Järvi) DGG
String Quartet no. 1 (Borodin) EMI
Symphony no. 2 (Concertgebouw Orch/Kondrashin) Philips
In the Steppes of Central Asia (USSR SO/Svetlanov) Melodiya
String Quartet no. 2 (Emerson) DGG
Petite Suite orch Glazunov (Gothenburg SO/Järvi) DGG
Symphony no. 3 (Toronto SO/A Davis) CBS
Prince Igor (Ghiaurov/Tchakarov) Sony

Boulez
Piano Sonata no. 1 (Helffer) Koch
Le Visage Nuptial (Bryn-Julson/Boulez) Erato

Piano Sonata no. 2 (Pollini) DGG
Le Soleil des eaux (Nendick/BBC SO/Boulez) EMI
Le Marteau sans maître (Deroubaix/Boulez) Ades
Improvisation sur Mallarmé I (A Mihaly) Hungarton
Pli selon pli (Bryn-Julson/Boulez) Erato
Figures-Doubles-Prismes (BBC SO/Boulez) Erato
cummings ist der dichter (Ens Intercontemporain) Erato
Rituel in memoriam Bruno Maderna (Paris Orch/Barenboim) Erato

Brahms
Piano Concerto no. 1 (Kovacevich/LPO/Sawallisch) EMI
String Sextet op. 18 (Academy of St-Martin-in-the-Fields) Chandos
Piano Quintet (Pollini/Quartetto Italiano) DGG
A German Requiem (Terfel/Bavarian Radio SO/C Davis) RCA
Symphony no.1 (Berlin PO/Abbado) DGG
Symphony no. 2 (Boston SO/Haitink) Philips
Violin Concerto (Perlman/Berlin PO/Barenboim) EMI
Piano Concerto no. 2 (Brendel/Berlin PO/Abbado) Philips
Violin Sonata no. 1 (Suk/Katchen) Decca
Symphony no. 4 (Vienna PO/C Kleiber) DGG

Britten
Sinfonia da Requiem (LPO/Slatkin) RCA
Serenade (Pears/Britten) Decca
Peter Grimes (Pears/Watson/CG Orch/Britten) Decca
Billy Budd (Glossop/Pears/Britten) Decca
Gloriana (Barstow/Mackerras) Argo
The Turn of the Screw (Langridge/Lott/Bedford) Collins
A Midsummer Night's Dream (Deller/Pears/Britten) Decca
War Requiem (Harper/Langridge/Hickox) Chandos
Cello Symphony (Rostropovitch/Britten) Decca
Death in Venice (Shirley-Quirk/Bedford) Decca

Bruckner
Mass no. 1 in D minor (Rodgers/K Lewis/Best) Hyperion
Symphony no. 2 (Berlin PO/Karajan) DGG
Symphony no. 3 (Vienna PO/Böhm) Decca
Symphony no. 4 (Philharmonia/Klemperer) EMI
Symphony no. 5 (Vienna PO/Haitink) Philips
String Quintet (Melos Quartet) Harmonia Mundi
Symphony no. 7 (Vienna PO/Abbado) DGG
Symphony no. 8 (Vienna PO/Karajan) DGG
Te Deum (Norman/Ramey/Chicago SO/Barenboim) DGG
Symphony no. 9 (Cleveland Orch/Dohnányi) Decca

Busoni
Violin Sonata no. 1 (Mordkovitch/Postnikova) Chandos
Violin Concerto (Szigeti/Scherman) Sony
Violin Sonata no. 2 (Szigeti/Horsowski) Sony
Piano Concerto (Ohlsson/Cleveland Orch/Dohnányi) Telarc
Fantasia contrappuntistica (Ogdon) Select
Arlecchino (Mentzner/Nagano) Virgin
Turandot (Gessendorf/Nagano) Virgin
Doktor Faust (Fischer-Dieskau/Leitner) DGG
Divertimento (Albrecht) Capriccio
Tanzwalzer (RIAS Orch Berlin/Albrecht) Capriccio

Byrd
The Great Service (Tallis Scholars/Phillips) Gimell
Mass for Three Voices (Winchester Cathedral Choir) Argo
Mass for Four Voices (Oxford Camarata/Summerly) Naxos
Mass for Five Voices (Tallis Scholars/Phillips) Gimell
Gradualia (William Byrd Choir) Hyperion
Motets (New College Choir) CRD
My Lady Nevells Booke (Hogwood) L'Oiseau Lyre
Fantasias (U Duetschler) Claves

Carter
String Quartet no. 1 (Juilliard) Sony
Variations for orchestra (Cincinnati SO/Gielen) New World
String Quartet no. 2 (Arditti) Etcetera
Piano Concerto (Oppens/Gielen) New World
Concerto for Orchestra (London Sinfonietta/Knussen) Virgin
String Quartet no. 3 (Juilliard) Sony
Brass Quintet (Wallace Collection) Collins
String Quartet no. 4 (Arditti) Etcetera

Three Occasions (London Sinfonietta/Knussen) Virgin
Violin Concerto (Bohn/Knussen) Virgin

Charpentier
Le Malade imaginaire (Feldman/Minkowski) Erato
Marian Devotions (Concert des Nations) Astrée Auvidis
Anthems for Advent (Les Arts Florissants) Harmonia Mundi
Port Royal Mass and Magnificat (Capella Ricercar) Ricercar
Actéon (Visse/Mellon/Christie) Harmonia Mundi
Office de Ténèbres (Parlement de Musique) Opus III
David et Jonathas (Les Arts Florissants) Harmonia Mundi
Médée (Les Arts Florissants) Harmonia Mundi

Chopin
Piano Concerto no. 2 (Perahia/Israel PO) Sony
Piano Concerto no. 1 (Pollini/Philharmonia) EMI
Waltzes (Pommier) Erato
Nocturnes (Katin) Olympia
Mazurkas (Ashkenazy) Decca
Ballades (Zimerman) DGG
Études op. 25 (Pollini) DGG
24 *Preludes* op. 28 (Argerich) DGG
Piano Sonata op. 35 (Gavrilov) DGG
Piano Sonata op. 58 (Demidenko) Hyperion

Copland
Piano Concerto (Lin/Hopkins) Chandos
Songs (R Alexander/Vignoles) Etcetera
El Sálon México (LSO/Copland) Sony
Lincoln Portrait (J E Jones/Schwarz) Delos
Rodeo (Detroit SO/Dorati) Decca
Appalachian Spring (LSO/Copland) Sony
Symphony no. 3 (St Louis SO/Slatkin) RCA
Clarinet Concerto (Drucker/Bernstein) DGG
The Tender Land (Brunelle) Virgin
Connotations (New York PO/Bernstein) DGG

Davies
Eight Songs for a Mad King (Fires of London) Unicorn
Stone Litany (D Jones/Davies) Collins
Miss Donnithorne's Maggot (M Thomas/Davies) Unicorn
The Martyrdom of St Magnus (M Rafferty) Unicorn
Solstice of Light (Mackie/S Cleobury) Argo
Black Pentecost (Wilson-Johnson/BBC PO) Collins
An Orkney Wedding with Sunrise (Scottish CO) Unicorn
Trumpet Concerto (Wallace/Davies) Collins
Symphony no. 4 (Scottish CO/Davies) Collins
Strathclyde Concerto no. 5 (Scottish CO/Davies) Collins

Debussy
String Quartet (Ysaÿe) Decca
Prélude à l'après midi d'un faune (Cleveland Orch/Boulez) DGG
Trois Nocturnes (Boston SO/Munch) RCA
Pelléas et Mélisande (Le Roux/Vienna PO/Abbado) DGG
La Mer (NBC SO/Toscanini) RCA
Images for piano (Koscis) Philips
Préludes (Michelangeli) DGG
Images for orchestra (LSO/Abbado) DGG
Jeux (Suisse Romande Orch/Ansermet) Decca
Violin Sonata (Mintz/Bronfman) DGG

Delius
Florida (RPO/Beecham) EMI
Appalachia (Shirley-Quirk/Hickox) Decca
Paris: the Song of a Great City (BBC SO/A Davis) Teldec
A Village Romeo and Juliet (Mackerras) Argo
Sea Drift (Terfel/Hickox) Chandos
A Mass of Life (LPO/Groves) EMI
Brigg Fair (BBC SO/A Davis) Teldec
On Hearing the First Cuckoo in Spring (Mackerras) Argo
Summer Night on the River (Beecham) EMI
Violin Concerto (Little/Mackerras) Argo

Donizetti
Anna Bolena (Callas/Rossi-Lemeni) EMI
L'elisir d'amore (Pavarotti/Sutherland) Decca
Lucrezia Borgia (Caballé/Kraus) RCA
Maria Stuarda (Baker/Plowright) EMI
Lucia di Lammermoor (Studer/Domingo) DGG

La fille du régiment (Sutherland/Pavarotti) Decca
La favorite (Cossotto/Pavarotti) Decca
Maria Padilla (McDonell/D Jones) Opera Rara
Don Pasquale (Bruscantini/Freni) EMI
Poliuto (Ricciarelli/Carreras) CBS

Dvořák
Symphony no. 5 (LSO/Kertesz) Decca
Serenade for Strings (Academy of St-Martin-in-the-Fields) Philips
Symphonic Variations (Concertgebouw Orch/C Davis) Philips
Symphony no. 6 (Cleveland Orch/Dohnányi) Decca
Symphony no. 7 (Oslo PO/Jansons) EMI
Piano Quintet (Curzon/Vienna PO Quartet) Decca
Piano Trio op. 90 (Suk Trio) Denon
Symphony no. 9 (Berlin PO/Kubelik) DGG
String Quartet op. 96 (Quartetto Italiano) Philips
Cello Concerto (Rostropovitch/Talich) Supraphon

Elgar
Enigma Variations (Philharmonia/Barbirolli) EMI
The Dream of Gerontius (Baker/Gedda/Boult) EMI
Cockaigne Overture (LPO/Solti) Decca
Falstaff (Chicago SO/Solti) Decca
In the South (LPO/Slatkin) RCA
Introduction and Allegro (Boston SO/Munch) RCA
Symphony no. 1 (LPO/Boult) EMI
Violin Concerto (Kennedy/LPO) EMI
Symphony no. 2 (BBC SO/A Davis) Teldec
Cello Concerto (Du Pré/LSO) EMI

Falla
La vida breve (LSO/Navarro) DGG
Noches en los jardines de España (de Larrocha/LPO) Decca
7 Canciones populares españolas (Barrientos) EMI
El amor brujo (Nafe/Lausanne CO) Denon
Fantasia Bética (de Larrocha) EMI
El sombrero de tres picos (Los Angeles/Giulini) EMI
El retablo de maese Pedro (Best/Matrix Ens) ASV
Harpsichord Concerto (Falla) EMI
L'Atlántida posth. (Suisse Romande Orch/Ansermet) Cascavelle

Fauré
Cantique de Jean Racine (City of London Sinf/Rutter) Collins
Violin Sonata no. 1 (Grumiaux) Philips
Requiem (English CO/Ledger) EMI
La Bonne Chanson (Walker/Nash Ens) CRD
Piano Quartet no. 1 (Stern/Ma/Ax) Sony
Pelléas et Mélisande (Boston SO/Ozawa) DGG
Chansons (Walker/Martineau) CRD
Pénélope (Monte Carlo PO/Dutoit) Erato
Masques et bergamasques (Mexico City PO/Batiz) ASV
L'Horizon chimérique (Souzay) Philips

Franck
Les Béatitudes (Stuttgart Radio SO/Rilling) Hanssler
Les Éolides (Basle SO/Jordan) Erato
Piano Quintet (Curzon/Vienna PO Quartet) Decca
Le Chasseur maudit (Philadelphia Orch/Muti) DGG
Prélude, Chorale et Fugue (Perahia) Sony
Variations symphoniques (Curzon/LSO/Boult) Decca
Violin Sonata (Perlman/Ashkenazy) Decca
Symphony in D minor (Chicago SO/Monteux) RCA
Psyché (Basle SO/Jordan) Erato
String Quartet (Bartholdy) SGN

Gershwin
Rhapsody in Blue (New York PO/Bernstein) CBS
Piano Concerto (Wild/Boston Pops Orch) RCA
Strike up the Band (Mauceri) Nonesuch
An American in Paris (MacGregor/LSO) Collins
Girl Crazy (Mauceri) Nonesuch
Variations on 'I Got Rhythm' (Wild/Boston Pops Orch) RCA
Porgy and Bess (White/Haymon/Rattle) EMI
Film music (Hollywood Bowl Orch/Mauceri) Philips

Glass
Einstein on the Beach (Philip Glass Ens) CBS
Satyagraha (Keene) CBS
Akhnaten (Stuttgart Opera/D R Davies) CBS

Company for string quartet (Kronos) Nonesuch
Glassworks (Philip Glass Ens) Sony
Metamorphosis for piano (Glass) CBS
Low Symphony (Brooklyn PO/D R Davies) Point Music
Hydrogen Jukebox (Ginsberg) Nonesuch

Gluck
Le Cinesi (Otter/Gardelli) Orfeo
Don Juan (Tafelmusik/Weil) Sony
Orfeo ed Euridice (McNair/Sieden/Gardiner) Philips
La Rencontre imprévue (L Dawson/Gardiner) Erato
Paride ed Elena (R Alexander/M Schneider) Capriccio
Iphigénie en Aulide (L Dawson/Otter/Gardiner) Erato
Orphée et Eurydice (Otter/Hendricks/Gardiner) EMI
Alceste (Gedda/Norman) Orfeo
Iphigénie en Tauride (Montague/Allen/Gardiner) Philips
Écho et Narcisse (Streit/Jacobs) Harmonia Mundi

Gounod
Sapho (Fournellier) Koch
Symphony no. 1 (St Paul CO/Hogwood) Decca
St Cecilia Mass (Te Kanawa/English CO) Philips
Faust (Sutherland/Corelli) Decca
Philémon et Baucis (Scotto/Sanzogno) Foyer
Mireille (Gedda/Cluytens) EMI
Roméo et Juliette (Kraus/Malfitano) EMI
Songs (Lott/Murray/Johnson) Hyperion
Mors et Vita (Hendricks/Aler/Plasson) EMI
Petite Symphonie (Athena Ens) Chandos

Grieg
Piano Concerto (Kovacevich/BBC SO/C Davis) Philips
Sigurd Jorsalfar (Gothenburg SO/Järvi) DGG
Songs (Otter) DGG
Peer Gynt (Royal PO/Beecham) EMI
Holberg Suite (Israel CO/Talmi) Chandos
Violin Sonata no. 3 (Dumay/Pires) DGG
Symphonic Dances (Gothenburg SO/Järvi) DGG
Lyric Suite (English CO/Leppard) Philips
praphon

Handel
Water Music (English Baroque Soloists) Philips
Acis and Galatea (Burrowes/White/Gardiner) Archiv
Giulio Cesare (Larmore/Schlick/Jacobs) Harmonia Mundi
Coronation Anthems (Dawson/The Sixteen/Christophers) Chandos
Alcina (Auger/Kuhlmann/Hickox) EMI
Saul (L Dawson/Ainsley/Gardiner) Philips
Israel in Egypt (Argenta/D Thomas/Parrott) EMI
Messiah (Kirkby/Watkinson/Hogwood) L'Oiseau Lyre
Semele (Battle/Horne/McNair) DGG
Music for the Royal Fireworks (English Concert/Pinnock) Archiv

Haydn
Symphony no. 48 (Hanover Band/Goodman) Hyperion
String Quartet op. 20 no. 5 (Mosaïques) Astrée Audivis
Symphony no. 86 (New York PO/Bernstein) Sony
String Quartet op. 64 no. 5 (Amadeus) DGG
Symphony no. 104 (Brüggen) Philips
Symphony no. 99 (LPO/Solti) Decca
String Quartet, op. 76 no. 2 (Takacs) Decca
Mass in D minor (*Nelson*) (Lott/Watkinson/Pinnock) Archiv
Die Schöpfung (*The Creation*) (Fischer-Dieskau/Wunderlich/Karajan) DGG
Die Jahreszeiten (*The Seasons*) (Bonney/A Schmidt/Gardiner) Arch

Henze
Boulevard Solitude (I Anguelov) Cascavelle
Der junge Lord (Mathis/Grobe/Dohnányi) DGG
The Bassarids (Riegel/K Armstrong) Koch
El Cimarrón (P Yoder) Koch
Voices (G Pelker) CPO
String Quartet no. 5 (Arditti) Wergo
Barcarola (CBSO/Rattle) EMI
Orpheus (Danish Radio Chamber Choir) Chandos
The English Cat (Parnassus Orch/Stenz) Wergo
Symphony no. 7 (CBSO/Rattle) EMI

Hindemith

Kammermusik (Kulka/Harrell/R Chailly) Decca
Cardillac (Fischer-Dieskau/Keilberth) DGG
Concert Music for brass and strings (Bernstein) Sony
Der Schwandendreher (San Francisco SO/Blomstedt) Decca
Mathis der Maler (Fischer-Dieskau/King) EMI
Nobilissima Visione (Philharmonia/Hindemith) EMI
The Four Temperaments (Shelley/Y P Tortelier) Chandos
Cello Concerto (Wallfisch/BBC PO) Chandos
Symphonic Metamorphosis (London SO/Abbado) Decca
Requiem (Atlanta SO/Shaw)

Holst

Beni Mora (LPO/Boult) Lyrita
The Cloud Messenger (LSO/Hickox) Chandos
St Paul's Suite (Academy of St-Martin-in-the-Fields) Collins
The Planets (LPO/Boult) EMI
The Hymn of Jesus (BBC Chorus and SO/Boult) Decca
The Perfect Fool (Mackerras) Virgin
Fugal Overture (English CO/I Holst) Lyrita
Egdon Heath (LPO/Boult) Decca

Honegger

Pastoral d'été (Toulouse Capitole Orch) DGG
Le Roi David (Czech PO/Baudo) Supraphon
Pacific 231 (Oslo PO/Jansons) EMI
Symphony no. 1 (Bavarian Radio SO/Dutoit) Erato
Les Miserables (film music) (Bratislava Radio SO) Marco Polo
Jeanne d'Arc au bûcher (Pollet/Ozawa) DGG
Symphony no. 2 (Berlin PO/Karajan) DGG
Symphony no. 3 (Oslo PO/Jansons) EMI
Symphony no. 4 (*Deliciae Basiliensis*) (Lausanne CO/Lopez-Cobos) Virgin
Symphony no. 5 (*Di Tre Re*) (Boston SO/Munch) RCA

Ives

Symphony no. 1 (Chicago SO/Thomas) Sony
Symphony no. 2 (New York PO/Bernstein) DGG
String Quartet no. 1 (Emerson) DGG
Symphony no. 3 (St Louis SO/ Slatkin) RCA
Three Places in New England (St Louis SO/Slatkin) RCA
New England Holidays (Chicago SO/Thomas) CBS
The Unanswered Question (New York PO/Bernstein) DGG
Symphony no. 4 (LPO/Serebrier) Chandos
Violin Sonata no. 4 (Szigeti/Foldes) Biddulph
Piano Sonata no. 2 (*Concord*) (MacGregor) Collins

Janáček

Jenůfa (Söderström/Mackerras) Decca
Taras Bulba (Cleveland Orch/Dohnányi) Decca
The Excursions of Mr Brouček (Pribyl/Jilek) Supraphon
Káta Kabanová (Söderström/Mackerras) Decca
The Cunning Little Vixen (Popp/Mackerras) Decca
The Makropoulos Case (Söderström/Mackerras) Decca
Sinfonietta (LSO/Thomas) Sony
Glagolitic Mass (CBSO/Rattle) EMI
String Quartet no. 2 (Talich) Supraphon
From the House of the Dead (Zidek/Zitek/Mackerras) Decca

Josquin Desprez

Missa Ave Maris Stella (Taverner Choir/Parrott) EMI
Missa L'Homme armé sexti toni (Tallis Scholars/Phillips) Gimell
Missa Pange Lingua (Tallis Scholars/Phillips) Gimell
Missa Hercule dux Ferrarie (New London Chamber Choir) Hyperion
Motets (Chappelle Royale Choir) Harmonia Mundi
Missa L'Homme armé super voces musicales (Turner) Archiv
Deploration (New London Chamber Choir) Amon Ra
Missa La sol fa re mi (Tallis Scholars/Phillips) Gimell

Kodály

Summer Evening (Budapest PO/Kodály) DGG
Duo for violin and cello (Gingold/Starker) Delon
Sonata for solo cello (Starker) Delon
String Quartet no. 2 (Hagen) DGG
Psalmus Hungaricus (Kosma/Kertesz) Decca
Háry János Suite (Cleveland Orch/Szell) Sony
Marosszék Dances (Phil Hungarica/Dorati) Decca

Dances of Galánta (Chicago SO/Järvi) Chandos
Variations on a Hungarian Folk Song (Budapest PO/Lehel) Hungarot
Concerto for Orchestra (Budapest PO/Kodály) DGG

Lassus

Misa Bell'Amfitrit'altera (Schola Cantorum of Oxford) Naxos
Lagrime di San Pietro (Ens Vocale Européen) Harmonia Mundi
Chansons (Ens Clement Jannequin) Harmonia Mundi
Prophetiae Sibyllarum (Cantus Cölln) Harmonia Mundi
Missa Qual donna attende a gloriosa fama (Darlington) Nimbus
Missa Osculetur me (Tallis Scholars/Phillips) Gimell
Lamentations of Jeremiah à 5 (Herreweghe) Harmonia Mundi
Psalmi Davidis poenitentiales (Turner) Archiv
Missa Pro defunctis – 4vv (M Brown) Hyperion
Missa Pro defunctis – 5vv (Turner) Harmonia Mundi

Ligeti

String Quartet no. 1 (Hagen) DGG
Atmosphères (Sudwestfunk SO/Bour) Wergo
Cello Concerto (Perenyi/Eötvös) Sony
Ten Pieces for Wind Quintet (Sudwestfunk Quintet) Wergo
Ramifications (Saarbrucken CO/Janigro) Wergo
Chamber Concerto (Reihe Ens/Cerha) Wergo
Melodien (London Sinfonietta) Decca
Concerto for flute and oboe (Nicolet/Holliger) Decca
Le Grand Macabre (Howarth) Wergo
Piano Concerto (Wiget/Ens Modern) Sony

Liszt

Piano Concerto no. 2 (Brendel/Haitink) Philips
Tasso: lamento e trionfo (Berlin PO/Karajan) DGG
Les Préludes (New York PO/Bernstein) Sony
Études d'exécution transcendante (Richter) RCA
Piano Sonata (Argerich) DGG
A Faust Symphony (Royal PO/Beecham) EMI
Piano Concerto no. 1 (Zimerman/Ozawa) DGG
A Dante Symphony (Budapest SO/Lehel) Hungaroton
Mephisto Waltz no. 1 (Wild) Etcetera
Année de pèlerinage (Bolet) Decca

Lully

Le Bourgeois Gentilhomme (Leonhardt) Harmonia Mundi
Alceste (Palmer/Malgoire) CBS
Atys (Mellon/Christie) Harmonia Mundi
Te Deum (Paillard) RCA
Phaéton (Minkowski) Erato
Armide (Laurens/Herreweghe) Harmonia Mundi
Harpsichord works (Gilbert) Harmonia Mundi

Lutosławski

Variations on a theme of Paganini (Jablonski/Ashkenazy) Decca
Symphony no. 1 (Warsaw National PO/Stokowski) Preludio
Funeral Music (Cleveland Orch/Dohnanyi) Decca
String Quartet (Hagen) DGG
Livre pour Orchestre (Polish Radio SO/Krenz) Ades
Cello Concerto (Rostropovitch/Lutosławski) EMI
Preludes and Fugues (Polish CO/Lutosławski) Polskie Nagrania
Symphony no. 3 (Los Angeles PO/Salonen) CBS
Chain II for violin and orchestra (Mutter/BBC SO) DGG
Piano Concerto (Zimerman/Lutosławski) DGG

Mahler

Symphony no. 1 (Berlin PO/Abbado) DGG
Symphony no. 2 (Auger/Baker/Rattle) EMI
Symphony no. 3 (Ludwig/Bernstein) DGG
Symphony no. 4 (Upshaw/Dohnányi) Decca
Symphony no. 5 (Berlin PO/Abbado) DGG
Symphony no. 6 (Berlin PO/Karajan) DGG
Symphony no. 8 (Kollo/Popp/Vienna PO/Solti) Decca
Symphony no. 9 (Concertgebouw Orch/Haitink) Philips
Das Lied von der Erde (Ludwig/Wunderlich/Klemperer) EMI
Symphony no. 10 posth. (Bournemouth SO/Rattle) EMI

Martinů

Double Concerto (Brno State PO/Mackerras) Conifer
Julietta (Zidek/Krombholc) Supraphon
Field Mass (Czech PO/Mackerras) Supraphon
Symphony no. 5 (Czech PO/Neumann) Supraphon

Rhapsody Concerto (Golani/Berne SO/Maag) Conifer
Symphony no. 6 (Czech PO/Belohlavek) Chandos
The Frescoes of Piero della Francesca (Ansermet) Cascavelle
Nonet (Vienna–Berlin Ens) DGG
The Greek Passion (Mitchinson/Mackerras) Supraphon

Massenet
Le Roi de Lahore (Sutherland/Milnes) Decca
Manon (Los Angeles/Monteux) EMI
Le Cid (Domingo/Bumbry/Queler) CBS
Esclarmonde (Sutherland/Aragall) Decca
Werther (Carreras/Von Stade/Davis) Philips
Thaïs (Esposito/A Wolff) Chant du Monde
Cendrillon (Von Stade/Gedda/Rudel) CBS
Chérubin (Von Stade/Anderson/Steinberg) RCA
Don Quichotte (Ghiaurov/Bacquier/Kord) Decca
Cléopâtre (Harries/Fourniller) Koch Schwann

Mendelssohn
A Midsummer Night's Dream (Gewandhaus Orch/Masur) Teldec
String Octet (Hausmusik) EMI
String Quartet op. 13 (Carmina) Denon
Symphony no. 5 (LSO/Abbado) DGG
Fingal's Cave (*Hebrides*) Overture (Berlin PO/Karajan) EMI
Symphony no. 4 (Cleveland Orch/Dohnányi) Telarc
Piano Trio op. 49 (Thibaud/Casals/Cortot) EMI
Symphony no. 3 (San Francisco SO/Blomstedt) Decca
Violin Concerto (Mullova/Academy of St-Martin-in-the-Fields) Philips
Elijah (Groop/Ainsley/Herrweghe) Harmonia Mundi

Messiaen
Quatuor pour le fin du temps (De Peyer/Pleeth/Beroff) EMI
Visions de l'amen (Loriod/Messiaen) Ades
Vingt regards sur l'Enfant Jéses (P Hill) Unicorn
Trois petites liturgies de la Présence Divine (London Sinfonietta Chorus) Virgin
Turangalîa-Symphonie (Los Angeles PO/Salonen) CBS
Catalogue d'oiseaux (P Hill) Unicorn
Chronochromie (BBC SO/Dorati) EMI
La Transfiguration de Notre Seigneur Jésus Christ (Washington Nat SO/Dorati) Decca
St François d'Assise (Eda-Pierre/Van Dam/Ozawe) Cybelia
Le Livre du Saint Sacrement (Bate) Unicorn

Meyerbeer
Il crociato in Egitto (Kenny/D. Jones) Opera Rara
Robert le Diable (Anderson/Vanzo/Ramey) HRE
Les Huguenots (Borst/Leech/Ghiuselev) Erato
Le Prophète (Scotto/Horne/McCracken) CBS
Le Pardon de Ploërmel (*Dinorah*) (D Jones/Du Plessis) Opera Rara
L'Africaine (Verrett/Domingo) Pioneer

Monteverdi
Madrigals Book IV (Concerto Italiano) Opus III
Madrigals Book V (Consort of Musicke/Rooley) L'Oiseau Lyre
Orfeo (New London Consort/Pickett) L'Oiseau Lyre
Il Ballo delle ingrate (Tragicomedia/Stubbs) Teldec
Vespers (Taverner Players/Parrott) EMI
Il combattimento di Tancredi e Clorinda (P Holman) Hyperion
Selva morale e spirituale (Kirkby/Parrott) EMI
Il ritorno d'Ulisse in patria (Pregardien/Jacobs) Harmonia Mundi
L'incoronazione di Poppea (McNair/Gardiner) Archiv
Mass of Thanksgiving (Parrott) EMI

Mozart
Piano Concerto K271 (Perahia/English CO) CBS
Sinfonia Concertante K364 (Perlman/Zukerman/Israel PO) DGG
Die Entführung aus dem Serail (Gruberova/Talvela/Solti) Decca
Piano Concerto K482 (Ashkenazy/Philharmonia) Decca
Le nozze di Figaro (Taddei/Schwarzkopf/Giulini) EMI
String Quintet K515 (Salomon Quartet) Hyperion
Don Giovanni (Siepi/Della Casa/Krips) Decca
Symphony no. 41 K551 (English Baroque Soloists) Philips
Così fan tutte (Schwarzkopf/Ludwig/Böhm) EMI
Die Zauberflöte (Bonney/Jo/Streit/Oestmann) L'Oiseau Lyre

Mussorgsky
Salammbô (Shemchuk/Pesko) CBS
The Marriage (Rozhdestvensky) Olympia
Night on the Bare Mountain (Oslo PO/Jansons) EMI
Boris Godunov (Kotchgera/Berlin PO/Abbado) Sony
Pictures at an Exhibition (Bronfman) Sony
Songs and Dances of Death (Hvorostovsky/Gergiev) Philips
Khovanshchina (Haugland/Lipovšek/Abbado) DGG

Nielsen
Symphony no. 1 (San Francisco SO/Blomstedt) Decca
Saul og David (Haugland/Lindroos/Järvi) Chandos
Symphony no. 2 (Gothenburg SO/Chung) BIS
Maskarade (Haugland/Frandsen) Unicorn
Symphony no. 3 (Royal Danish Orch/Berglund) RCA
Violin Concerto (Lin/Salonen) CBS
Symphony no. 4 (San Francisco SO/Blomstedt) Decca
Aladdin (Rozhdestvensky) Chandos
Symphony no. 5 (New York PO/Bernstein) Sony
Clarinet Concerto (Drucker/Bernstein) Sony

Palestrina
Missa Papae Marcelli (Westminster Abbey Choir/Preston) Arch
Missa Aeterna Christi munera (J O'Donnell) Hyperion
Missa Dum complerentur (Darlington) Nimbus
Stabat Mater (King's College Choir/Willcocks) Decca
Missa Assumpta est Maria (Tallis Scholars/Phillips) Gimell
Lamentations of Jeremiah, Book 1 (Oxford Camerata/Summerly) Naxos
Missa Benedicta es (Tallis Scholars/Phillips) Gimell
Missa Nigra sum (Tallis Scholars/Phillips) Gimell
Lamentations of Jeremiah, Book 4 (Turner) Pickwick
Missa Veni sponsa Christi (St John's College Choir) Decca

Penderecki
Threnody for the Victims of Hiroshima (Penderecki) EMI
String Quartet no. 1 (LaSalle) DGG
St Luke Passion (Polish National SO/Penderecki) Argo
De natura sonoris (Penderecki) EMI
The Devils of Loudun (Troyanos/Janowski) Philips
Utrenja (Warsaw National PO) Polskie Nagrania
Violin concerto (Accardo) Nuova Era
Cello Concerto no. 2 (Polish National SO) Polskie Nagrania
Viola Concerto (Zimmermann) Wergo
Polish Requiem (NDR SO/Penderecki) DGG

Pfitzner
Palestrina (Gedda/Fischer-Dieskau/Kubelik) DGG
Von deutscher Seele (Giebel/Wunderlich) DGG
Piano Concerto (Bratislava RSO) Marco Polo
Violin Concerto (Gawriloff/Bamberg SO) CPO
Das dunkle Reich (R Holl) Preiser
Cello Concerto no. 1 (Geringas/Bamberg SO) CPO
Kleine Symphonie (Bamberg SO/W A Albert) CPO

Poulenc
Concert champêtre (Van de Wiele/Prêtre) EMI
Concerto for 2 pianos (K and M Labèque/Boston SO) Philips
Les soirées de Nazelles (Rogé) Decca
Mass in G minor (Trinity College Choir) Conifer
Organ Concerto (Weir/Hickox) Virgin
Les Biches Suite (CBSO/Frémaux) EMI
Piano Concerto (Rogé/Philharmonia/Dutoit) Decca
La voix humaine (Pollet/Casadesus) Harmonia Mundi
Gloria (Hendricks/Prêtre) EMI
Dialogues des Carmélites (Dubosc/Gorr/Nagano) Virgin

Prokofiev
Piano Concerto no. 1 (Ashkenazy/LSO/Previn) Decca
Symphony no. 1 (CO of Europe/Abbado) DGG
Violin Concerto no. 1 (Chung/LSO/Previn) Decca
The Love for Three Oranges (Bacquier/Nagano) Virgin
Piano Concerto no. 3 (Argerich/Berlin PO) DGG
The Fiery Angel (Gothenburg SO/Järvi) DGG
Romeo and Juliet (Cleveland Orch/Maazel) Decca
Alexander Nevsky (Zajick/Rostropovitch) Sony
War and Peace (Gedda/Miller/Vishnevskaya) Erato
Symphony no. 5 (CBSO/Rattle) EMI

Puccini

Le Villi (Scotto/Domingo/Maazel) CBS
Manon Lescaut (Freni/Pavarotti/Levine) Decca
La Bohème (Tebaldi/Bergonzi/Serafin) Decca
Tosca (Callas/Di Stefano) EMI
Madama Butterfly (Scotto/Bergonzi/Barbirolli) EMI
La fanciulla del West (Neblett/Domingo/Mehta) DGG
Il tabarro (Merrill/Tebaldi/Gardelli) Decca
Suor Angelica (Scotto/Horne/Maazel) CBS
Gianni Schicchi (Gobbi/Cotrubas/Maazel) CBS
Turandot (Nilsson/Corelli) EMI

Purcell

Dido and Aeneas (Bott/Ainsley/Hogwood) L'Oiseau Lyre
King Arthur (English Baroque Soloists) Erato
Odes for St Cecilia's Day (King's Consort) Hyperion
The Fairy Queen (Les Arts Florissants/Christie) Harmonia
  Mundi
The Indian Queen (Deller) Harmonia Mundi
Funeral Sentences (Herreweghe) Harmonia Mundi
Sonatas in four parts (Purcell Quartet) Chandos
Songs from *Orpheus Brittanicus* (Mellon) Astrée Auvidis
Anthems and services (King's Consort) Hyperion
Chamber music (London Baroque) Harmonia Mundi

Rakhmaninov

Symphony no. 1 (Royal PO/Litton) Virgin
Piano Concerto no. 2 (Richter/Warsaw National PO) DGG
Piano Preludes (Weissenberg) RCA
Symphony no. 2 (LSO/Rozhdestvensky) Pickwick
Piano Concerto no. 3 (Horowitz/Reiner) RCA
The Isle of the Dead (Philadelphia Orch/Rakhmaninov) Pearl
The Bells (LSO/Previn) EMI
Rhapsody on a Theme by Paganini (Ashkenazy/Concertgebouw
  Orch) Decca
Symphony no. 3 (St Petersburg PO/Jansons) EMI
Symphonic Dances (St Petersburg PO/Jansons) EMI

Rameau

Hippolyte et Aricie (Watkinson/Auger/Malgoire) CBS
Les Indes galantes (Poulenard/Christie) Harmonia Mundi
Castor et Pollux (Mellon/Christie) Harmonia Mundi
Dardanus (Von Stade/Van Dam/Leppard) Erato
Platée (J Smith/de Mey/Minkowski) Erato
Zaïs (Elwes/Egmond/Leonhardt) Stil
Pygmalion (Mellon/Les Arts Florissants) Harmonia Mundi
Naïs (Caley/Caddy/McGegan) Erato
Zoroastre (Elwes/Mellon/Kuijken) Harmonia Mundi
Les Boréades (Smith/Rodde/Gardiner) Erato

Ravel

String Quartet (Melos) DGG
Shéhérazade (Auger/Philharmonia/Dešek) Virgin
Gaspard de la nuit (Perlemuter) Nimbus
Rapsodie espagnole (Chicago SO/Barenboim) Erato
Ma Mère L'Oye for orchestra (Montreal SO/Dutoit) Decca
Daphnis et Chloé (LSO/Monteux) Decca
Piano Trio (Heifetz/Rubinstein) RCA
L'Enfant et les sortilèges (Berbié/Rehfuss/Maazel) DGG
Piano Concerto in G (Michelangeli/Philharmonia) EMI
Concerto for piano left hand (Argerich/Berlin PO/Abbado)
  EMI

Reger

Variations and Fugue on a Theme of Beethoven (LPO/Järvi)
  Chandos
Variations and Fugue on a Theme of J A Hiller (Concertgebouw
  Orch/Järvi) Chandos
Piano Concerto (Oppitz/Bamberg SO) Koch Schwann
Romantic Suite (Berlin Radio SO/Albrecht) Koch Schwann
Ballet Suite (Segerstram) BIS
Böcklin Tone Poems (Dresden PO/Weigle) Capriccio
Introduction, Passacaglia and Fugue for organ (Kee) Chandos
Variations and Fugue on a Theme of Telemann (Bolet) Decca
Variations and Fugue on a Theme of Mozart (Bavarian Radio
  SO/C Davis) Philips
Requiem (NDR Chorus and SO) Koch Schwann

Respighi

Semirama (Marton/Gardelli) Hungaroton
Il Tramonto (Baker/City of London Sinfonia) Collins
Fontana di Roma (Montreal SO/Dutoit) Decca
Ancient Airs and Dances (Orpheus CO) DGG
Concerto gregoriano (Mordkovitch/Downes) Chandos
Pini di Roma (Philadelphia Orch/Ormandy) RCA
Vetrate di chiesa (Cincinnati SO/Lopez-Cobos) Telarc
Trittico Botticelliano (Philharmonia/Simon) Cala
Feste romane (NBC SO/Toscanini) RCA
La fiamma (Takacs/Tokody/Gardelli) Hungaroton

Rimsky-Korsakov

Mlada (Bolshoi/Lazarev) Teldec (video)
The Snow Maiden (Arkhipova/Fedoseyev) Chant du Monde
Spanish Capriccio Espagnol (Berlin PO/Maazel) DGG
Sheherazade (Chicago SO/Reiner) RCA
Sadko (Kirov/Gergiev) Philips (video)
Mozart and Salieri (Nesterenko/Ermler) Olympia
The Tsar's Bride (Bolshoi Orch) Harmonia Mundi
The Legend of Tsar Saltan (I Petrov/Bolshoi) Chant du Monde
Kashtchey the Immortal (Bolshoi Orch) Chant du Monde
The Legend of the Invisible City of Kitezh (Gorchakova/Gergiev)
  Philips

Rossini

Tancredi (Cuberli/Horne) CBS
L'Italiana in Algeri (Horne/Ramey/Battle) Erato
Il barbiere di Siviglia (Bartoli/Burchuladze) Decca
La Cenerentola (Berganza/Alva/Abbado) DGG
La gazza ladra (Ricciarelli/Ramey) Sony
Mosè in Egitto (Anderson/Raimondi) Philips
Semiramide (Sutherland/Horne) Decca
Le Comte Ory (Jo/Montague/Gardiner) Philips
Guillaume Tell (Bacquier/Caballé/Gedda) EMI
Stabat Mater (Lorengar/Pavarotti) Decca

Saint-Saëns

Introduction et Rondo capriccioso (Chung/RPO/Dutoit) Decca
Piano Concerto no. 2 (Rogé/RPO/Dutoit) Decca
Le Rouet d'Omphale (RPO/Beecham) EMI
Cello Concerto no. 1 (Starker/LSO/Dorati) Mercury
Piano Concerto no. 4 (Rogé/Philharmonia) Decca
Samson et Dalila (Domingo/Obraztsova) DGG
Septet (M Bauer) Erato
Le Carnaval des animaux (LSO/members/Wordsworth) Pickwick
Symphony no. 3 (Preston/Berlin PO/Levine) DGG
Violin Concerto no. 3 (Perlman/Paris Orch) DGG

Schnittke

Symphony no. 1 (Stockholm PO/Segerstram) BIS
Concerto Grosso no. 1 (Kremer/CO of Europe) DGG
Symphony no. 2 (Rozhdestvensky) Melodiya
Seid nüchtern und wachet (*Faust Cantata*) (Malmo SO/DePreist)
  BIS
String Quartet no. 3 (Borodin) Virgin
Viola Concerto (Bashmet/LSO/Rostropovitch) RCA
Cello Concerto no. 1 (Gutman/LPO/Masur) EMI
Quasi una Sonata (English CO/Rostropovitch) Sony
Concerto Grosso no. 5 (Vienna PO/Dohnányi) DGG
Life with an Idiot (Duesing/Rostropovitch) Sony

Schoenberg

Verklärte Nacht (Sinfonia Varsovia/Krivine) Denon
String Quartet no. 1 (Schoenberg Quartet) Schwann
Gurrelieder (Fassbaender/Berlin Radio SO/R Chailly) Decca
String Quartet no. 2 (LaSalle/M Price) DGG
Erwartung (Norman/Levine) Philips
Pierrot lunaire (Manning/Nash Ensemble/Rattle) Chandos
Variations for orchestra (Berlin PO/Karajan) DGG
String Quartet no. 4 (LaSalle) DGG
Moses und Aron (Mazura/Langridge/Solti) Decca
Violin Concerto (Zeitlin/Kubelik) DGG
String Trio (Mann/Rhodes/Krosnick) Sony

Schubert

Piano Quintet in A (*The Trout*) (Brendel/Cleveland Quartet)
  Philips

Symphony no. 8 (Vienna PO/C Kleiber) DGG
Die schöne Müllerin (Fischer-Dieskau/Moore) DGG
String Quartet in D minor (Lindsay) ASV
Octet (Vienna Octet) Decca
Symphony no. 9 (Dreden Staatskapelle/Böhm) DGG
Piano Trios (Beaux Arts Trio) Philips
Piano Sonata in B♭ (Brendel) Philips
Winterreise (Schreier/Richter) Philips
String Quintet in C (Rostropovitch/Emerson Quartet) DGG

Schumann
Carnaval (Barenboim) DGG
Fantasie op. 17 (Pollini) DGG
Dichterliebe (Fischer-Dieskau/Eschenbach) DGG
Liederkreis op. 39 (Bär/Parsons) EMI
Symphony no. 1 (LPO/Masur) Teldec
Piano Concerto (Lupu/LSO/Previn) Decca
Piano Quintet (Bernstein/Juilliard Quartet) Sony
String Quartet op. 41 no. 3 (Voces Intimae) BIS
Symphony no. 2 (Bavarian Radio SO/Kubelik) Sony
Symphony no. 3 (Concertgebouw Orch/Bernstein) DGG

Shostakovich
Symphony no. 1 (Concertgebouw Orch/Solti) Decca
Lady Macbeth of Mtsensk (Vishnevskaya/Gedda) EMI
Symphony no. 5 (RPO/Ashkenazy) Decca
Symphony no. 7 (Chicago SO/Bernstein) DGG
Symphony no. 8 (Leningrad PO/Mravinsky) Philips
Symphony no. 10 (Berlin PO/Karajan) DGG
Cello Concerto no. 1 (Rostropovich/Ormandy) CBS
String Quartet no. 8 (Borodin) EMI
Violin Concerto no. 1 (Sitkovetsky/BBC SO/A Davis) Virgin
Symphony no. 14 (Varady/Fischer-Dieskau) Decca

Sibellus
Karelia Suite (Berlin PO/Karajan) EMI
King Christian II Suite (Gothenburg SO/Järvi) BIS
Symphony no. 1 (Vienna PO/Bernstein) DGG
Symphony no. 2 (San Francisco SO/Blomstedt) Decca
Violin Concerto (Little/RLPO) EMI
Symphony no. 3 (Scottish National Orch/Gibson) Chandos
Symphony no. 4 (Philharmonia/Ashkenazy) Decca
Symphony no. 5 (CBSO/Rattle) EMI
Symphony no. 7 (Vienna PO/Maazel) Decca
Tapiola (Berlin PO/Karajan) EMI

Skriabin
Piano Concerto (Ashkenazy/LPO) Decca
Symphony no. 1 (Philadelphia Orch/Muti) EMI
Symphony no. 2 (Stockholm PO/Segerstram) BIS
Symphony no. 3 (*Divine Poem*) (Danish Radio SO/Järvi) Chandos
Poem of Ecstasy (New York PO/Sinopoli) DGG
Prometheus: A Poem of Fire (Ashkenazy/LPO/Maazel) Decca
Piano Sonata no. 7 (*White Mass*) (Ashkenazy) Decca
Piano Sonata no. 11 (*Black Mass*) (Demidenko) Conifer

Smetana
Piano Trio (Beaux Arts Trio) Philips
The Brandenburgers in Bohemia (Prague National Theatre/Tichy) Supraphon
The Bartered Bride (Benačkova/Dvorsky) Supraphon
Dalibor (Pribyl/Smetacek) Supraphon
Ma Vlast/My Country (RLPO/Pešek) Virgin
Two Widows (Prague Radio SO/Krombholc) Praga
String Quartet no. 1 (Alban Berg) Decca
The Secret (Soukupova/Košler) Supraphon
Libuše (Benackova/Zitek/Košler) Supraphon
String Quartet no. 2 (Medici) Nimbus

Stockhausen
Formel (Sudwestfunk SO) Stockhausen
Kreuzspiel (London Sinfonietta) Stockhausen
Punkte (NDR SO) Stockhausen
Kontakte (Stockhausen) Wergo
Momente (G Davy/R Smalley) Stockhausen
Stimmung (Singcircle) Hyperion
Aus den sieben Tagen (Masson/Stockhausen) Harmonia Mundi
Mantra (Mikashoff/Bevan) New Albion

Donnerstag aus Licht (Gambill/Hölle/Eötvös) DGG
Samstag aus Licht (Holle/M Stockhausen) DGG

Strauss
Don Juan (Staatskapelle Dresden/Kempe) EMI
Don Quixote (Tortelier/Beecham) EMI
Ein Heldenleben (Berlin Phil/Karajan) DGG
Salome (Studer/Terfel/Sinopoli) DGG
Elektra (Nilsson/Resnik/Vienna PO/Solti) Decca
Der Rosenkavalier (Ludwig/Jones/Berry/Bernstein) CBS
Ariadne auf Naxos (Janowitz/King/Kempe) EMI
Die Frau ohne Schatten (Varady/Domingo/Solti) Decca
Arabella (Fischer-Dieskau/Varady/Sawallisch) Orfeo
Vier letzte Lieder (Popp/LPO/Tennstedt) EMI

Stravinsky
Petrushka (CBSO/Rattle) EMI
The Rite of Spring (LPO/Haitink) Philips
Les Noces (Argerich/Zimerman) DGG
Pulcinella (Murray/Rolfe Johnson/Boulez) Erato
Oedipus Rex (Pears/Meyer/LPO/Solti) Decca
Symphony of Psalms (CBC SO/Stravinsky) Sony
Perséphone (Rolfe Johnson/LPO/Nagano) Virgin
Symphony in 3 Movements (Berlin Radio SO/Ashkenazy) Decca
The Rake's Progress (Langridge/Ramey/R Chailly) Decca
Agon (Los Angeles SO/Stravinsky) Sony

Szymanowski
Violin Sonata (Mordkovitch) Chandos
Symphony no. 1 (Polish State PO) Marco Polo
Symphony no. 2 (Polish Radio SO/Kaspszyk) EMI
Symphony no. 3 (*Song of the Night*) (CBSO/Rattle) EMI
Violin Concerto no. 1 (Wilkomirska/Rowicki) Polskie Nagrania
King Roger (Warsaw National Opera) Olympia
Stabat Mater (Szmythka/Quivar/Rattle) EMI
String Quartet no. 2 (Carmina) Denon
Symphonia concertante (Zmudzinski/Rowicki) Polskie Nagrania
Violin Concerto no. 2 (Juillet/Montreal SO/Dutoit) Decca

Tallis
Psalm Tunes for Archbishop Parker's Psalter (Tallis Scholars/Phillips) Gimell
Lamentations of Jeremiah (Tallis Scholars/Phillips) Gimell
Spem in alium (Taverner Choir/Parrott) EMI
Gaude gloriosa Dei mater (Tallis Scholars/Phillips) Gimell
Missa Salve intemerata virgo (St John's College Choir) EMI
Mass for four voices (Hilliard Ensemble) ECM
Magnificat and nunc dimittis (New College Choir) CRD
Mass *Puer natus est nobis* (Clerkes of Oxenford) Calliope

Taverner
The Western Wind Mass (New College Choir) CRD
Missa Corona spinea (The Sixteen/Christophers) Hyperion
Missa Gloria tibi Trinitas (Tallis Scholars/Phillips) Gimell
Missa Mater Christi (Christ Church Cathedral Choir) Nimbus
Missa O Michael (The Sixteen/Christophers) Hyperion
Missa Sancti Wilhelmi (The Sixteen/Christophers) Hyperion
Motets (Taverner Choir/Parrott) EMI
in nomine for 4 viols (Fretwork) Hyperion

Tchaikovsky
Symphony no. 1 (Oslo PO/Jansons)
Romeo and Juliet (Chicago SO/Abbado) Sony
Piano Concerto no. 1 (Argerich/RPO/Dutoit) DGG
Swan Lake (LSO/Thomas) Sony
Violin Concerto (Mullova/Boston SO/Ozawa) Philips
Eugene Onegin (Allen/Freni/Levine) DGG
Symphony no. 5 (LSO/Rozhdestvensky) Pickwick
Sleeping Beauty (Kirov/Gergiev) Philips
The Nutcracker (RPO/Temirkanov) RCA
Symphony no. 6 (Vienna PO/Karajan) DGG

Telemann
Pimpinone (Ostendorf/Baird) Newport Classics
Der Tag des Gerichts (R Alexander/Equiluz/Harnoncourt) Teldec
Tafelmusik (Vienna Concentus Musicus) Teldec
Overture-Suites (English Concert/Pinnock) Archiv
Don Quichotte (Schopper/La Stagione/M Schneider) CPO
Paris Quartets (Trio Sonnerie) Virgin

Cantatas (René Jacobs) Capriccio
Violin Concertos (Standage) Chandos

Tippett
Concerto for Double String Orchestra (Marriner) Decca
A Child of our Time (Baker/Norman/BBC SO/C Davis) Philips
Fantasia concertante (Academy of St-Martin-in-the-Fields/
    Marriner) Decca
Piano Concerto (Tirimo/BBC PO) Nimbus
The Midsummer Marriage (Carlyle/Harwood/C Davis)
    Philips
King Priam (Bailey/Harper/Tear/Atherton) Decca
Symphony no. 3 (F Robinson/Hickox) Chandos
The Ice Break (Harper/Clarey/Robson/Atherton) Virgin
The Mask of Time (S Walker/Tear/A Davis) EMI

Vaughan Williams
A Sea Symphony (Lott/Summers/LPO/Haitink) EMI
On Wenlock Edge (Langridge/Shelley/Britten Quartet) EMI
Fantasia on a Theme by Thomas Tallis (LPO/Haitink) EMI
A London Symphony (LPO/Boult) EMI
The Lark Ascending (Little/BBC SO/A Davis) Teldec
Flos Campi (Imai/English CO/Best) Hyperion
Symphony no. 4 (LSO/Previn) RCA
Serenade to Music (Burrowes/Hodgson/Boult) EMI
Symphony no. 5 (Hallé Orch/Barbirolli) EMI
The Pilgrim's Progress (Armstrong/Noble/Boult) EMI

Verdi
Rigoletto (Gobbi/Callas/di Stefano) EMI
Il trovatore (Domingo/Price/Milnes/Mehta) RCA
La traviata (Fabriccini/Alagna/Muti) Sony
Simon Boccanegra (Cappuccilli/Freni/Carreras) DGG
Un ballo in maschera (M Price/Pavarotti/Bruson) Decca
Don Carlos (Domingo/Caballé/Raimondi) EMI
Aida (Caballé/Cossotto/Domingo) EMI
Requiem (Ludwig/Gedda/Ghiaurov/Guilini) EMI
Otello (Pavarotti/Nucci/Te Kanawa/Solti) Decca
Falstaff (Gobbi/Alva/Moffo/Karajan) EMI

Victoria
Missa surge propera (Mixylodian/P Schmidt) Pickwick
Missa O magnum mysterium (Westminster Cathedral Choir)
    Hyperion
Missa Ave maris stella (Westminster Cathedral Choir) Hyperion
Missa O quam gloriosum (Oxford Camerata/Summerly) Naxos
Lamentations of Jeremiah (Trinity College Choir) Conifer
Passions (St John and St Matthew) (Spanish Radio Choir)
    Philips
Officium defunctorum (Tallis Scholars/Phillips) Gimell
Responsories for Tenebrae (Westminster Cathedral Choir)
    Hyperion

Vivaldi
Violin Concertos op. 4 (Huggett/Hogwood) L'Oiseau Lyre
Juditha Triumphans (Nemeth/McGegan) Hungaroton
Violin Concertos op. 8 nos. 1–4 (Carmirelli) Philips

Violin Concertos op. 9 (La Cetra/Standage/Hogwood) L'Oiseau
    Lyre
Cello Concertos (Harnoy/Toronto CO) RCA
Flute Concertos op. 10 (Rampal/Solisti Veneti) CBS
Oboe Concertos (Boyd/CO of Europe) DGG
Violin Sonatas (North/Toll) Harmonia Mundi
Gloria in D (The Sixteen/Christophers) Collins
Salve Regina (Il Seminario Musicale) Virgin

Wagner
Der fliegende Holländer (Hale/Varady/Sawallisch) EMI
Tannhäuser (Kollo/Dernesch/Ludwig/Solti) Decca
Lohengrin (Thomas/Grümmer/Ludwig/Kempe) EMI
Tristan und Isolde (Nilsson/Windgassen/Ludwig/Böhm) DGG
Die Meistersinger von Nürnberg (Heppner/Weikl/Studer/
    Sawallisch) EMI
Das Rheingold (Adam/Neidlinger/Böhm) Philips
Die Walküre (Tomlinson/Evans/Hölle/Barenboim) Teldec
Siegfried (Tomlinson/Jerusalem/Barenboim) Teldec
Götterdämerung (Nilsson/Windgassen/Frick/Solti) Decca
Parsifal (Windgassen/Weber/Knappertsbusch) Decca

Walton
Façade (Sitwell/Pears/Boult) Decca
Symphony no. 1 (CBSO/Rattle) EMI
Viola Concerto (Imai/LPO/Latham–Koenig) Chandos
Belshazzar's Feast (Luxon/LPO/Solti) Decca
Violin Concerto (Kennedy/RPO/Previn) EMI
String Quartet no. 2 (Britten Quartet) Collins·
Symphony no. 2 (RPO/Ashkenazy) Decca
Variations on a Theme by Hindemith (Cleveland Orch/Szell) CBS
The Bear (D Jones/Opie/Hickox) Chandos

Weber, Carl Maria von
Peter Schmoll und seine Nachbarn (Hagen PO) Marco Polo
Symphony no. 1 (Hanover Band/Goodman) Nimbus
Clarinet Concerto no. 1 (Stoltzman/A Schneider) RCA
Clarinet Quintet (Vienna Octet, members) Decca
Grand duo concertant (Johnson/Back) ASV
Konzertstück (Brendel/LSO/Abbado) Philips
Der Freischütz (Schreier/Janowitz/Weikl/C Kleiber) DGG
Euryanthe (Norman/Hunter/Gedda/Janowski) HMV
Oberon (Heppner/Ziegler/Lakes/Conlon) EMI
Lieder (Fischer-Dieskau/Holl) Claves

Webern
Passacaglia op. 1 (Vienna PO/Abbado) DGG
Six Pieces op. 6 (Berlin PO/Karajan) DGG
Five Pieces op. 10 (Vienna PO/Abbado) DGG
Six Songs op. 14 (Harper/Boulez) Sony
Symphony op. 21 (Berlin PO/Karajan) DGG
Five Movements op. 5 (Quartetto Italiano) Philips
Concerto op. 24 (Nash Ens/Rattle) Chandos
String Quartet op. 28 (Arditti) Disques Montaigne
Variations op. 30 (Vienna PO/Abbado) DGG
Cantata no. 2 (Lukomska/LSO/Boulez) Sony